S0-AHI-454

The history of Saul, David, and Solomon, by Andre d'Ypres, c. *1448.*
(© Historical Picture Archive/CORBIS)

NEW CATHOLIC ENCYCLOPEDIA

NEW CATHOLIC ENCYCLOPEDIA

SECOND EDITION

13
Seq–The

Detroit • New York • San Diego • San Francisco • Cleveland • New Haven, Conn. • Waterville, Maine • London • Munich

in association with

THE CATHOLIC UNIVERSITY OF AMERICA • WASHINGTON, D.C.

The New Catholic Encyclopedia, Second Edition

Project Editors
Thomas Carson, Joann Cerrito

Editorial
Erin Bealmear, Jim Craddock, Stephen Cusack, Miranda Ferrara, Kristin Hart, Melissa Hill, Margaret Mazurkiewicz, Carol Schwartz, Christine Tomassini, Michael J. Tyrkus

Permissions
Edna Hedblad, Shalice Shah-Caldwell

Imaging and Multimedia
Randy Bassett, Dean Dauphinais, Robert Duncan, Leitha Etheridge-Sims, Mary K. Grimes, Lezlie Light, Dan Newell, David G. Oblender, Christine O'Bryan, Luke Rademacher, Pamela Reed

Product Design
Michelle DiMercurio

Data Capture
Civie Green

Manufacturing
Rhonda Williams

Indexing
Victoria Agee, Victoria Baker, Sylvia Coates, Francine Cronshaw, Lynne Maday, Do Mi Stauber, Amy Suchowski

For more information, contact
The Gale Group, Inc.
27500 Drake Rd.
Farmington Hills, MI 48331-3535
Or you can visit our Internet site at
http://www.gale.com

LIBRARY OF CONGRESS CATALOGING-IN-PUBLICATION DATA

New Catholic encyclopedia.—2nd ed.
p. cm.
Includes bibliographical references and indexes.
ISBN 0-7876-4004-2
1. Catholic Church—Encyclopedias. I. Catholic University of America.
BX841 .N44 2002
282' .03—dc21
2002000924

ISBN: 0-7876-4004-2 (set)
0-7876-4005-0 (v. 1)
0-7876-4006-9 (v. 2)
0-7876-4007-7 (v. 3)
0-7876-4008-5 (v. 4)
0-7876-4009-3 (v. 5)
0-7876-4010-7 (v. 6)
0-7876-4011-5 (v. 7)
0-7876-4012-3 (v. 8)
0-7876-4013-1 (v. 9)
0-7876-4014-x (v. 10)
0-7876-4015-8 (v. 11)
0-7876-4016-6 (v. 12)
0-7876-4017-4 (v. 13)
0-7876-4018-2 (v. 14)
0-7876-4019-0 (v. 15)

Printed in the United States of America
10 9 8 7 6 5 4 3 2 1

For The Catholic University of America Press

Foreword

This revised edition of the *New Catholic Encyclopedia* represents a third generation in the evolution of the text that traces its lineage back to the *Catholic Encyclopedia* published from 1907 to 1912. In 1967, sixty years after the first volume of the original set appeared, The Catholic University of America and the McGraw-Hill Book Company joined together in organizing a small army of editors and scholars to produce the *New Catholic Encyclopedia.* Although planning for the *NCE* had begun before the Second Vatican Council and most of the 17,000 entries were written before Council ended, Vatican II enhanced the encyclopedia's value and importance. The research and the scholarship that went into the articles witnessed to the continuity and richness of the Catholic Tradition given fresh expression by Council. In order to keep the *NCE* current, supplementary volumes were published in 1972, 1978, 1988, and 1995. Now, at the beginning of the third millennium, The Catholic University of America is proud to join with The Gale Group in presenting a new edition of the *New Catholic Encyclopedia.* It updates and incorporates the many articles from the 1967 edition and its supplements that have stood the test of time and adds hundreds of new entries.

As the president of The Catholic University of America, I cannot but be pleased at the reception the *NCE* has received. It has come to be recognized as an authoritative reference work in the field of religious studies and is praised for its comprehensive coverage of the Church's history and institutions. Although Canon Law no longer requires encyclopedias and reference works of this kind to receive an *imprimatur* before publication, I am confident that this new edition, like the original, reports accurate information about Catholic beliefs and practices. The editorial staff and their consultants were careful to present official Church teachings in a straightforward manner, and in areas where there are legitimate disputes over fact and differences in interpretation of events, they made every effort to insure a fair and balanced presentation of the issues.

The way for this revised edition was prepared by the publication, in 2000, of a Jubilee volume of the *NCE,* heralding the beginning of the new millennium. In my foreword to that volume I quoted Pope John Paul II's encyclical on Faith and Human Reason in which he wrote that history is "the arena where we see what God does for humanity." The *New Catholic Encyclopedia* describes that arena. It reports events, people, and ideas—"the things we know best and can verify most easily, the things of our everyday life, apart from which we cannot understand ourselves" (*Fides et ratio,* 12).

Finally, I want to express appreciation on my own behalf and on the behalf of the readers of these volumes to everyone who helped make this revision a reality. We are all indebted to The Gale Group and the staff of The Catholic University of America Press for their dedication and the alacrity with which they produced it.

Very Reverend David M. O'Connell, C.M., J.C.D.
President
The Catholic University of America

Preface to the Revised Edition

When first published in 1967 the *New Catholic Encyclopedia* was greeted with enthusiasm by librarians, researchers, and general readers interested in Catholicism. In the United States the *NCE* has been recognized as the standard reference work on matters of special interest to Catholics. In an effort to keep the encyclopedia current, supplementary volumes were published in 1972, 1978, 1988, and 1995. However, it became increasingly apparent that further supplements would not be adequate to this task. The publishers subsequently decided to undertake a thorough revision of the *NCE,* beginning with the publication of a Jubilee volume at the start of the new millennium.

Like the biblical scribe who brings from his storeroom of knowledge both the new and the old, this revised edition of the *New Catholic Encyclopedia* incorporates material from the 15-volume original edition and the supplement volumes. Entries that have withstood the test of time have been edited, and some have been amended to include the latest information and research. Hundreds of new entries have been added. For all practical purposes, it is an entirely new edition intended to serve as a comprehensive and authoritative work of reference reporting on the movements and interests that have shaped Christianity in general and Catholicism in particular over two millennia.

SCOPE

The title reflects its outlook and breadth. It is the *New Catholic Encyclopedia,* not merely a new encyclopedia of Catholicism. In addition to providing information on the doctrine, organization, and history of Christianity over the centuries, it includes information about persons, institutions, cultural phenomena, religions, philosophies, and social movements that have affected the Catholic Church from within and without. Accordingly, the *NCE* attends to the history and particular traditions of the Eastern Churches and the Churches of the Protestant Reformation, and other ecclesial communities. Christianity cannot be understood without exploring its roots in ancient Israel and Judaism, nor can the history of the medieval and modern Church be understood apart from its relationship with Islam. Interfaith dialogue requires an appreciation of Buddhism and other world religions, as well as some knowledge of the history of religion in general.

On the assumption that most readers and researchers who use the *NCE* are individuals interested in Catholicism in general and the Church in North America in particular, its editorial content gives priority to the Western Church, while not neglecting the churches in the East; to Roman Catholicism, acknowledging much common history with Protestantism; and to Catholicism in the United States, recognizing that it represents only a small part of the universal Church.

Scripture, Theology, Patrology, Liturgy. The many and varied articles dealing with Sacred Scripture and specific books of the Bible reflect contemporary biblical scholarship and its concerns. The *NCE* highlights official church teachings as expressed by the Church's magisterium. It reports developments in theology, explains issues and introduces ecclesiastical writers from the early Church Fathers to present-day theologians whose works exercise major influence on the development of Christian thought. The *NCE* traces the evolution of the Church's worship with special emphasis on rites and rituals consequent to the liturgical reforms and renewal initiated by the Second Vatican Council.

Church History. From its inception Christianity has been shaped by historical circumstances and itself has become a historical force. The *NCE* presents the Church's history from a number of points of view against the background of general political and cultural history. The revised edition reports in some detail the Church's missionary activity as it grew from a small community in Jerusalem to the worldwide phenomenon it is today. Some entries, such as those dealing with the Middle Ages, the Reformation, and the Enlightenment, focus on major time-periods and movements that cut across geographical boundaries. Other articles describe the history and structure of the Church in specific areas, countries, and regions. There are separate entries for many dioceses and monasteries which by reason of antiquity, size, or influence are of special importance in ecclesiastical history, as there are for religious orders and congregations. The *NCE* rounds out its comprehensive history of the Church with articles on religious movements and biographies of individuals.

Canon and Civil Law. The Church inherited and has safeguarded the precious legacy of ancient Rome, described by Virgil, "to rule people under law, [and] to establish the way of peace." The *NCE* deals with issues of ecclesiastical jurisprudence and outlines the development of legislation governing communal practices and individual obligations, taking care to incorporate and reference the 1983 *Code of Canon Law* throughout and, where appropriate, the *Code of Canons for the Eastern Churches*. It deals with issues of Church-State relations and with civil law as it impacts on the Church and Church's teaching regarding human rights and freedoms.

Philosophy. The Catholic tradition from its earliest years has investigated the relationship between faith and reason. The *NCE* considers at some length the many and varied schools of ancient, medieval, and modern philosophy with emphasis, when appropriate, on their relationship to theological positions. It pays particular attention to the scholastic tradition, particularly Thomism, which is prominent in Catholic intellectual history. Articles on many major and lesser philosophers contribute to a comprehensive survey of philosophy from pre-Christian times to the present.

Biography and Hagiography. The *NCE,* making an exception for the reigning pope, leaves to other reference works biographical information about living persons. This revised edition presents biographical sketches of hundreds of men and women, Christian and non-Christian, saints and sinners, because of their significance for the Church. They include: Old and New Testament figures; the Fathers of the Church and ecclesiastical writers; pagan and Christian emperors; medieval and modern kings; heads of state and other political figures; heretics and champions of orthodoxy; major and minor figures in the Reformation and Counter Reformation; popes, bishops, and priests; founders and members of religious orders and congregations; lay men and lay women; scholars, authors, composers, and artists. The *NCE* includes biographies of most saints whose feasts were once celebrated or are currently celebrated by the universal church. The revised edition relies on Butler's *Lives of the Saints* and similar reference works to give accounts of many saints, but the *NCE* also provides biographical information about recently canonized and beatified individuals who are, for one reason or another, of special interest to the English-speaking world.

Social Sciences. Social sciences came into their own in the twentieth century. Many articles in the *NCE* rely on data drawn from anthropology, economics, psychology and sociology for a better understanding of religious structures and behaviors. Papal encyclicals and pastoral letters of episcopal conferences are the source of principles and norms for Christian attitudes and practice in the field of social action and legislation. The *NCE* draws attention to the Church's organized activities in pursuit of peace and justice, social welfare and human rights. The growth of the role of the laity in the work of the Church also receives thorough coverage.

ARRANGEMENT OF ENTRIES

The articles in the *NCE* are arranged alphabetically by the first substantive word using the word-by-word method of alphabetization; thus "New Zealand" precedes "Newman, John Henry," and "Old Testament Literature" precedes "Oldcastle, Sir John." Monarchs, patriarchs, popes, and others who share a Christian name and are differentiated by a title and numerical designation are alphabetized by their title and then arranged numerically. Thus, entries for Byzantine emperors Leo I through IV precede those for popes of the same name, while "Henry VIII, King of England" precedes "Henry IV, King of France."

Maps, Charts, and Illustrations. The *New Catholic Encyclopedia* contains nearly 3,000 illustrations, including photographs, maps, and tables. Entries focusing on the Church in specific countries contain a map of the country as well as easy-to-read tables giving statistical data and, where helpful, lists of archdioceses and dioceses. Entries on the Church in U.S. states also contain tables listing archdioceses and dioceses where appropriate. The numerous photographs appearing in the *New Catholic Encyclopedia* help to illustrate the history of the Church, its role in modern societies, and the many magnificent works of art it has inspired.

SPECIAL FEATURES

Subject Overview Articles. For the convenience and guidance of the reader, the *New Catholic Encyclopedia* contains several brief articles outlining the scope of major fields: "Theology, Articles on," "Liturgy, Articles on," "Jesus Christ, Articles on," etc.

Cross-References. The cross-reference system in the *NCE* serves to direct the reader to related material in other articles. The appearance of a name or term in small capital letters in text indicates that there is an article of that title elsewhere in the encyclopedia. In some cases, the name of the related article has been inserted at the appropriate point as a *see* reference: (*see* THOMAS AQUINAS, ST.). When a further aspect of the subject is treated under another title, a *see also* reference is placed at the end of the article. In addition to this extensive cross-reference system, the comprehensive index in volume 15 will greatly increase the reader's ability to access the wealth of information contained in the encyclopedia.

Abbreviations List. Following common practice, books and versions of the Bible as well as other standard works by selected authors have been abbreviated throughout the text. A guide to these abbreviations follows this preface.

The Editors

Abbreviations

The system of abbreviations used for the works of Plato, Aristotle, St. Augustine, and St. Thomas Aquinas is as follows: Plato is cited by book and Stephanus number only, e.g., Phaedo 79B; Rep. 480A. Aristotle is cited by book and Bekker number only, e.g., Anal. post. 72b 8–12; Anim. 430a 18. St. Augustine is cited as in the Thesaurus Linguae Latinae, e.g., C. acad. 3.20.45; Conf. 13.38.53, with capitalization of the first word of the title. St. Thomas is cited as in scholarly journals, but using Arabic numerals. In addition, the following abbreviations have been used throughout the encyclopedia for biblical books and versions of the Bible.

Books

Acts	Acts of the Apostles
Am	Amos
Bar	Baruch
1–2 Chr	1 and 2 Chronicles (1 and 2 Paralipomenon in Septuagint and Vulgate)
Col	Colossians
1–2 Cor	1 and 2 Corinthians
Dn	Daniel
Dt	Deuteronomy
Eccl	Ecclesiastes
Eph	Ephesians
Est	Esther
Ex	Exodus
Ez	Ezekiel
Ezr	Ezra (Esdras B in Septuagint; 1 Esdras in Vulgate)
Gal	Galatians
Gn	Genesis
Hb	Habakkuk
Heb	Hebrews
Hg	Haggai
Hos	Hosea
Is	Isaiah
Jas	James
Jb	Job
Jdt	Judith
Jer	Jeremiah
Jgs	Judges
Jl	Joel
Jn	John
1–3 Jn	1, 2, and 3 John
Jon	Jonah
Jos	Joshua
Jude	Jude
1–2 Kgs	1 and 2 Kings (3 and 4 Kings in Septuagint and Vulgate)
Lam	Lamentations
Lk	Luke
Lv	Leviticus
Mal	Malachi (Malachias in Vulgate)
1–2 Mc	1 and 2 Maccabees
Mi	Micah
Mk	Mark
Mt	Matthew
Na	Nahum
Neh	Nehemiah (2 Esdras in Septuagint and Vulgate)
Nm	Numbers
Ob	Obadiah
Phil	Philippians
Phlm	Philemon
Prv	Proverbs
Ps	Psalms
1–2 Pt	1 and 2 Peter
Rom	Romans
Ru	Ruth
Rv	Revelation (Apocalypse in Vulgate)
Sg	Song of Songs
Sir	Sirach (Wisdom of Ben Sira; Ecclesiasticus in Septuagint and Vulgate)
1–2 Sm	1 and 2 Samuel (1 and 2 Kings in Septuagint and Vulgate)
Tb	Tobit
1–2 Thes	1 and 2 Thessalonians
Ti	Titus
1–2 Tm	1 and 2 Timothy
Wis	Wisdom
Zec	Zechariah
Zep	Zephaniah

Versions

Apoc	Apocrypha
ARV	American Standard Revised Version
ARVm	American Standard Revised Version, margin
AT	American Translation
AV	Authorized Version (King James)
CCD	Confraternity of Christian Doctrine
DV	Douay-Challoner Version

ERV	English Revised Version
ERVm	English Revised Version, margin
EV	English Version(s) of the Bible
JB	Jerusalem Bible
LXX	Septuagint
MT	Masoretic Text
NAB	New American Bible
NEB	New English Bible
NIV	New International Version
NJB	New Jerusalem Bible
NRSV	New Revised Standard Version
NT	New Testament
OT	Old Testament
RSV	Revised Standard Version
RV	Revised Version
RVm	Revised Version, margin
Syr	Syriac
Vulg	Vulgate

S

SEQUENCE

In the Roman rite, a musical setting of rhymed poetry with paired lines, occurring after the Alleluia verse and before the Gospel in the Mass for certain solemnities and important feasts. The revision of the Lectionary that was promulgated by Paul VI in 1969 brought about some changes in the use of the Sequence. Prior to the revision, five sequences were used: Easter, *Victimae paschali laudes* (obligatory for the feast and its octave); Pentecost, *Veni, Sancte Spiritus* (obligatory for the feast and its octave); Corpus Christi, *Lauda Sion* (obligatory on the feast, optional during the octave, suppressed since 1960); Requiem Masses, *Dies irae*; Friday after Passion Sunday and September 15, Feast of Our Lady of Sorrows, *Stabat Mater* (obligatory on both days). The Council of Trent had suppressed thousands of sequences in its reform of the liturgy, salvaging only the first four for liturgical use. The fifth, *Stabat Mater* was reinstated by Benedict XIII in 1727.

The General Instruction of the Roman Missal says quite simply: ''Except on Easter Sunday and Pentecost the sequences are optional'' (GIRM 40). This means, in practice, that the Easter Sequence is optional during its octave; the calendar has eliminated the Pentecost octave, leaving the Sequence for the feast alone; the *Lauda Sion* is optional for the feast of Corpus Christi; the calendar revision has eliminated duplicate feasts, leaving the feast of Our Lady of Sorrows to be celebrated only on September 15, with its Sequence also optional; the *Dies irae* has been dropped completely from Masses for the Dead. In the 1969 revision, the Sequence is now placed *before* the Alleluia, since this acclamation properly belongs to the Gospel proclamation.

Musical structure. Musically the Sequence does resemble the hymn in its monophonic, syllabic structure, but it differs from it in structure and liturgical function. Whereas all the strophes of the hymn are constructed according to the same poetic plan and are sung to the same music in all verses, the Sequence displays progressive repetitions consisting of successive paired lines (double versicles), both of which have the same melody, and often includes a single line at the beginning and end. The conventional diagram is: The *x* and *y* represent the optional unpaired introduction and postlude.

The Sequence process consists essentially in underlaying a limited number of well-known tunes with new texts. These texts are freshly created verse lines consisting of words whose succession contains the same or nearly the same number of syllables as there are individual tones in the collective neumes or melismas of the preexistent melody. In the process the shape of the original tune is literally preserved, but its musical identity is transformed. The striking parallel between this process and the *cantus firmus* procedure of medieval polyphony should not be overlooked. Unlike the tradition of classical plainchant, moreover, the lyricism of the new text results from the meaning and the representation of individual syllables, and the syntax and shape of the new text are derived from the slower-moving succession of heightened pitches borrowed from a neumatic or melismatic melody. The new text, derived from a transformed melody, has abdicated its own poetic canons and obeys a new kind of syllabic organization.

Emergence of the sequence. The term ''Sequence'' appeared first in the ninth century, when it signified an extended series of tones. Scholars are uncertain whether the precise etymology of the word is to be viewed as essentially musical (i.e., to describe the quality of a melody as an indifferent succession of tones) or liturgical (to describe the function of a melody to follow a liturgical text). Usage of the term was much less clearly defined then than in later writings; yet in all these ninth-century sources, the series of tones it designated was in some way related to the Alleluia and its verse, as is indicated in an *Antiphonale Missarum* from Mount Blandin, a text from the *De ecclesiasticiis officiis* of AMALARIUS, and a famous dedicatory preface by NOTKER BALBULUS of the Abbey of St. Gall (Sankt Gallen). The *Antiphonale* contains the phrase *cum sequentia* at the end of the text for several Al-

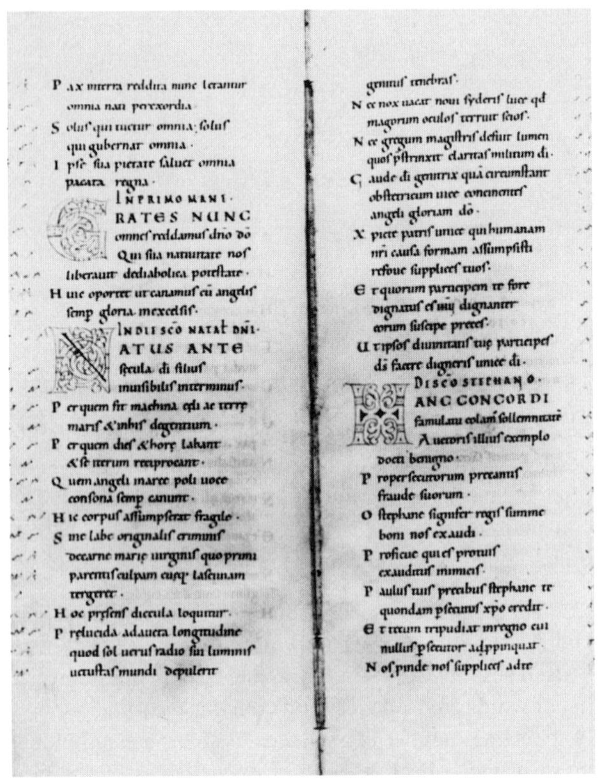

Manuscript folios showing Notker Sequences, "Natus ante saecula," for Christmas feast, "Hane concordi famulatu," for St. Stephen's Day, from the Abbey of St. Emmeran.

leluia verses. Amalarius describes the Alleluia verse as a jubilation that the singers called Sequence (*haec jubilatio quam cantores sequentian vocant*). These early references seem to suggest that at the end of chants whose texts already conveyed a mood of enthusiasm and exaltation, melodies were at times added to extend in temporal quantity the joyful mood of the liturgy. This extension was accomplished by a sonorous repetition of the word *alleluia* by the entire choir. The volume, pace, and character of the responsorial chant were, however, modified by this choral repetition of the Alleluia, as was demanded by the rubrics. This repetition, being collective rather than individual, could not be improvised; yet there was an improvisatory spirit to these added Alleluias—no doubt psychologically engendered by the difference between spontaneous textless jubilations and the set, controlled texts of the other chants.

The dedicatory letter of Notker accompanied a group of these elongated melodies underlaid with texts, which he sent to Bishop Lieutward of Vercelli *c.* 885. In this letter, in which he referred to the melodies as Sequences, he confessed that his creative imagination had been stirred when he first beheld compositions of this type in a Norman antiphonary brought to St. Gall by a refugee from the recently devastated Abbey of JUMIÈGES. Some verses for the long melodies in this antiphonary were written out; and Notker, who explained that as a young man he had had difficulty remembering the very long additions (*melodiae longissimae*) to the Alleluia verses, decided to imitate this practice as a memory aid, reducing groups of wordless melismas to syllabic units he could remember. His first efforts, however, must not have been entirely syllabic melodies, for, as he states, it was his master, Yso, who suggested that he adopt a completely syllabic style and praised the results when he did so. It was a collection of these praiseworthy pieces that Notker wished to share with his episcopal friend. The prevailing tone of his document is more psychological than musical, for in reducing larger rhythmical groups (neumes and melismas) to smaller units (syllables and notes) he recognized a solution to his memory problem.

Notker claimed that he had improved upon an existing technique of text adaptation and also suggested that he was a creator and not a mere imitator. Accordingly, certain historians have mistakenly attributed the invention of the Sequence form to him. The title of his collection, *Liber hymnorum,* does indeed indicate his belief that a new musical as well as liturgical style had been invented, for although the Church's hynm tradition was very old, the hymn as a form was assigned to the Divine Office, not to the Mass. Perhaps Notker was conscious of having contrived a musical form with both popular appeal and liturgical precedent, besides being usable in the Mass, and was intimating to Bishop Lieutward that there was need for just such a form. Whatever artistic refinements Notker and his St. Gall confreres added to the sequence as a liturgical form, most scholars now agree that he did not innovate it. Besides Jumièges, which Norter himself mentions, Saint-Benoît sur Loire, Toul, and Lâon have been cited as possible sources. Southern France, despite the rich resources of the library at Saint-Martial Abbey at Limoges, contributes most to the literature of the Sequence only after the rise of Aquitainian notation (*c.* 1000).

Development. Between Notker's memory aids and the five present-day Sequences with their parallel structure, their regularity in textual strophic construction, and their use of textual rhyme, there intervened a long and complicated development. Musicologists distinguish between early Sequences and later Sequences and also divide the Sequence repertory into two independent but not separate traditions—an Anglo-French and an Italo-German. These same traditions are observed in the trope, which emerged in the same centers at about the same moment, though its life span was much shorter than that of the Sequence. Stylistically the creative periods of Sequence composition have been designated as the early pe-

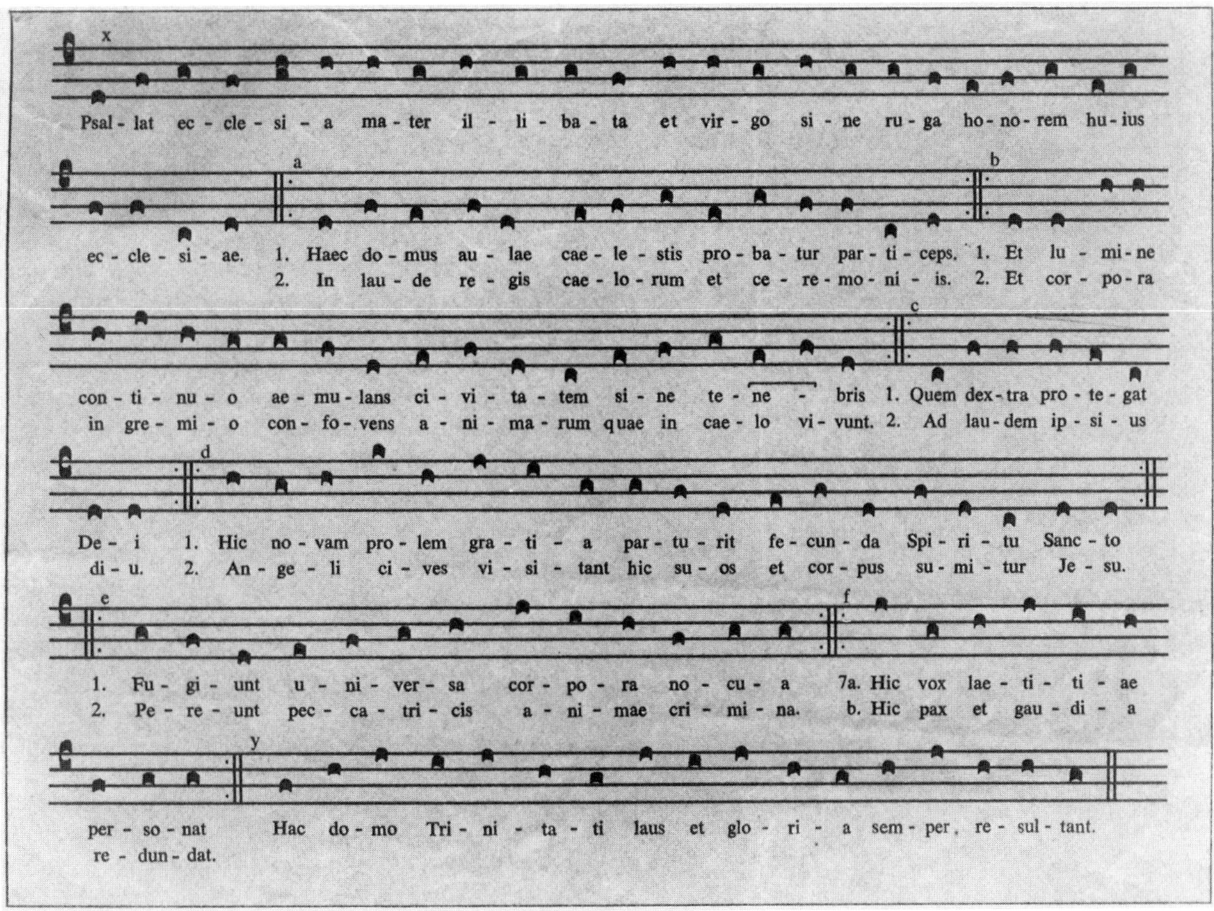

''Psallat ecclesia mater,'' musical sequence by Motker Balbulus.

riod (850–1050), transitional period (1050–1100), and later period (1100–1300). For the early period, there are three extant manuscript sources from the second half of the ninth century: Munich, Bayerische Staatsbibliothek, Clm. 14823; Verona, Biblioteca Capitolare XC; and Paris, Bibliothèque Nationale, fonds Lat. 1154. These contain texts, mostly without neumes, that are scattered among other paraliturgical forms. In the second half of the tenth century appeared the first cycle of Sequences and texts arranged according to the Church year, the *Congregatio prosarum;* and this earliest sequentiary—that is, the section of the manuscript containing this cycle—is bound with a troper as Paris, Bibliothèque Nationale, fonds Lat. 1240. With the exception of these specific items, the sources for early Sequences and tropes are identical.

As for the two traditions posited by scholars, Anglo-French sources consistently apply the word ''Sequence'' for a melismatic extension of an Alleluia melody without text; *prosa* for the text to be underlaid to an extended Alleluia melody, printed with or without the syllabic melody; *sequentia cum prosa* for an extended Alleluia melody whose neumes have been dissolved by syllables or words; and *prosula* for a text set to an extended, similarly dissolved melody of some chant other than the Alleluia. The Gradual, the Alleluia verse, or the Offertory verse of the Proper, or the *Kyrie, Sanctus,* or *Benedicamus Domino* of the Ordinary contained such extended melodies sometimes underlaid with *prosula* texts. Italo-German sources, however, consistently apply the word ''Sequence'' for both text and melody, written together on a single page. The melismatic extension of an Alleluia melody is written in the margin around the text. In this tradition, the term implies the total picture of words and music as they appear on a manuscript page. The practice of referring to both text and tune by the collective term apparently began in the Italo-German tradition shortly after the time of Notker, who, as noted above, called his compositions hymns. English scholars often use the term *sequelae* to describe the extended and wordless melismas of the Alleluia at the end of the Alleluia verse. As a pedagogic device, this usage is sometimes convenient, since it obviates the double meaning for the word ''sequence.'' There

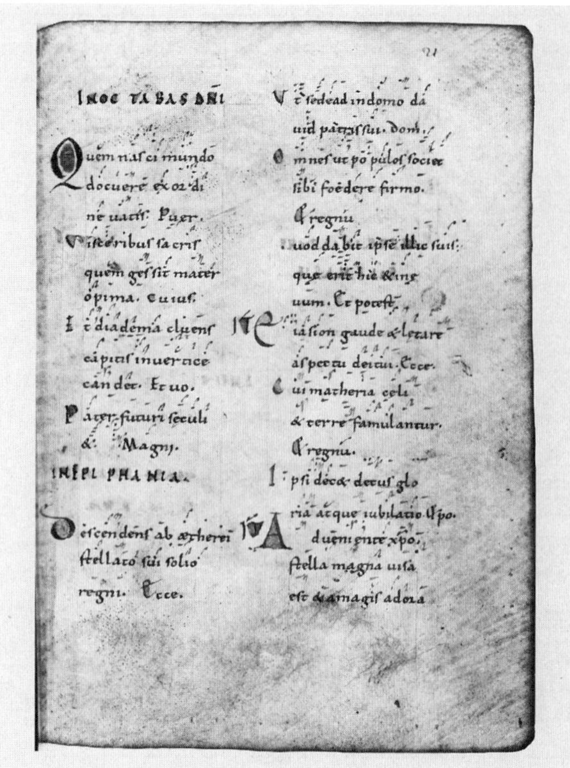

Manuscript folio 21 of "Congregatio Prosarum," sung during Feast of the Holy Innocents, earliest noted sequentiary, late 10th century.

is no evidence that it was ever employed in such official books as the gradual and antiphonary containing canonical texts, or such unofficial books as troper and sequentiary containing paraliturgical texts.

Prosa, Prosula, Sequence. *Prosula* texts, as was indicated above, are intended as an underlay to certain texts of the official repertory, the official texts being set in a musical style that is neumatic, with occasional melismatic extensions. Something of the nature of the new *prosula* may be discovered by comparing it with its liturgical model. Numerous examples have been published, including the *prosula* text *Non vos homines* for the Alleluia verse; *Non vos me elegistis,* in *Analecta hymnica* (Leipzig 1886–1922) 49:252, ed. C. Blume; or the *prosula* text and melody *Mirabilis atque laudabilis* for an Alleluia verse, *Mirabilis Dominus,* cited by P. Evans. The *prosula* text is asymmetrical; it is free rhythmic prose with irregular accents, and assonance seems to be the only poetic device employed. The structural canons of its poetry come to light when compared with the poetry and music of the original. The *prosula* is a melody-orientated verse. Its high points are dictated by the canons of melody, not by those of poetry. The number of syllables corresponds generally to the number of notes occurring in a given melisma between melodic high points. The placing of end assonance is occasioned by the position of certain vowel sounds in the melodic pattern of the official text. The number of individual notes in the neumes and melismas of the original liturgical piece being underlaid determines the length of the new verse. While there is indeed craftsmanship displayed here, it is of a different order from that which characterizes the official chant, for the phraseology and tone groupings of the classical chant have been transformed into the sounds and individual notes of a new musical texture. Volumes 7 and 53 of *Analecta hymnica* contain texts of the earliest Sequences. While these texts display many of the same characteristics as *prosula* texts, assonance is less prevalent in them. Without an official text with given sounds at given pitch levels to be matched by the same sounds in the new text, the *prosa* composer was freer in his choice of syllabic succession than the composer of the *prosula.* Anglo-French texts frequently began with the word "Alleluia." In the subsequent *prosa,* the assonance "a" was prevalent. An "e" assonance, generated from the same introductory Alleluia, characterizes Spanish texts of the same Anglo-French tradition. Italo-German texts, on the other hand, begin directly without the word "alleluia" and display less assonance.

Melodic extension by phrase repetition is freer in the Sequence than in the *prosula* melody. Literal repetition of shorter antiphons to prolong the solemnity of a feast is mentioned in John's life of Odo of Cluny (*Patrologia Latina,* 217 v. [Paris 1878–90] 133:43–68). This may have been the liturgical reason for the repetition by phrase in the longer Sequences. It is usually indicated by letter abbreviations: *d* (duplex, *dupliciter*), *t* (*trahere*), and *s* (*semel*). Musical content of the Sequence extensions permitted greater freedom of invention than corresponding continuations of *prosulae.* The latter extensions returned to the melodic line of the official melody, while the Sequence melody apparently did not. EKKEHARD, in the *Casus Sancti Galli* (*Patrologia Latina,* 217 v. [Paris 1878–90] 131:1003), praises some of Tuotillo's tunes invented on the *rolla* or *psalterium.* Melodies invented to extend the spirit of a liturgical feast and to be participated in by a community of modest musical ability may have displayed corresponding ties with folk idiom, as this liturgical folk style developed.

Whatever their differences in terminology for the early period of Sequence writing, modern scholars agree on the artistic process involved: It was a procedure of text underlay to an already existing melody. Inventing a new text to a familiar tune is not an uncommon practice in any period and seems to have been fairly common in the liturgy during this period. A collection of new texts, apparently for liturgical use, exists in the earliest sequentiary

(Paris, Bibliothèque Nationale, fonds Lat. 1240) under the collective heading *Congregatio prosarum.* Two forms of a melody for some of these texts are included in different parts of the book: one, a syllabic form written over a prose text; the other, a neumatic or a melismatic form written either with the official text if it is neumatic, or as one of a group of Sequences if it is melismatic. This is the ordinary method of notation for books of the Anglo-French tradition.

Transitional period. With the emergence of the cathedral as a parochial entity, the character of the liturgy was modified; this change in liturgical structure occasioned concomitant changes in the forms that were expressions of this structure, the Sequence among them. While retaining an organic relation with the past, the Sequence became a different kind of artistic form.

The *Victimae Paschali laudes,* attributed to Wipo, a diocesan priest of Burgundy, is an example of a Sequence from the transitional period. The text, while retaining elements of the unrhymed and irregular earlier Sequences, presages the regular form of the Sequences of ADAM OF SAINT-VICTOR and the later composers. In its terseness and brevity, it employs at times regular alternation of accented and unaccented syllables, as well as rhyme. The melody, while borrowing its *Incipit* from an Alleluia currently assigned to the fourth Sunday after Easter, continues freely as a melody. It has been called the perfect musical expression of Easter. The clarion melody of the Sequence has a character different from the continuation of the Alleluia melody. Moreover, the dialog form characterizing the second part of the Sequence was a purposeful artistic nuance, not the result of a process of text underlay, and was achieved by a play of motives in different ranges.

Later Sequences. The final period in the development of the Sequence was reached with the Victorine poets, particularly Adam. With them the form as it is known today was defined and fixed, and the musical style became relatively consistent. The musical style in general is logogenic, that is, the tunes follow the words and are musically comparable to those of a popular folk style of the period. In the late period, an irregular folk style discovered in an existing liturgical practice had become a regular folk style with fixed criteria for both its poetry and its music. Some of these later Sequence melodies were at times eminently suited to the musical expression of sentiments already contained in the words of the Sequence texts. As musical expressions in themselves or as expressions of the period of which they were a part, however, they were by no means sophisticated or progressive. Like similar examples in earlier or perhaps even ancient musical tradition, the better examples of this repertory were often merely good renderings in song of a collective sentiment. Hence they were destined by their very nature to be modest and conservative. Their symmetry was predictable, their range limited, and their stress on the individual word. This primitive style was suitable for active participation—appealing to an audience of modest competence and to a performer or group of performers without virtuoso skills.

In the literary purview, even in the refined texts of Adam there are features reminiscent of more primitive early processes. His terraced rhymes, which gain in weight and frequency as the climax approaches, elicit a musical response to the mounting tension. His word play and word coinage are sometimes at the level of the common pun. Limerick-style prosody, as well as poetic effects derived from the canons of music, were features of the Sequence of the early period. Adam's verse was in a metrical mold already popular in the hymn. It consists of a group of rhymed trochaic lines of eight syllables with a caesura after the fourth syllable at the end of a word closing with a seven-syllable line. Each of these three-line stanzas is set to identical music, thus preserving the rhyming and parallel structure.

Bibliography: P. AUBRY and E. MISSET, eds., *Les Proses d'Adam de Saint-Victor* (Paris 1900). C. BLUME et al., eds., *Analecta Hymnica* v. 49. (Leipzig). W. H. FRERE, ed., *The Winchester Troper* (London 1894). H. M. BANNISTER, *Anglo-French Sequelae,* ed. A. HUGHES (London 1934). A. SCHUBIGER, *Die Sängerschule St. Gallens* (Einsiedeln 1858). P. EVANS, "Some Reflections on the Origin of the Trope." *Journal of the American Musicological Society* 14 (1961) 119–130. H. HUSMANN, "Alleluia, Vers und Sequenz," *Annales musicologiques* 4 (1956) 19–53; "Sequenz und Prosa," *ibid.* 2 (1954) 61–91; "Die Alleluia und Sequenz der Mater-Gruppe," *International Musicological Society: Report of the Congress* 5 (1956) 276–284; "Die älteste erreichbare Gestalt des St. Galler Tropariums." *Archiv für Musikwissenschaft* 13 (1956) 25–41; "Die St. Galler Sequenz-tradition bei Notker und Ekkehard," *Acta musicologica* 26 (1954) 6–18. P. DRONKE, "The Beginnings of the Sequence," *Beiträge zur Geschichte der deutschen Sprache und Literatur* 87 (1965) 43–73. R. CROCKER, "Some Ninth-Century Sequences," *Journal of the American Musicological Society* 20 (1967) 367–402; *The Early Medieval Sequence* (Berkeley 1977).

[E. LEAHY/L. DURST, EDS.]

SERAPHIM

Plural noun probably derived from Hebrew transitive verb meaning to burn. It designates celestial beings of the court of Yahweh in the vocational vision of Isaiah (6.2–6), which is the only occurrence of the word in this sense in the Bible. Commonly they are called the burning ones, not to indicate their intransitive flame of charity toward Yahweh, but rather referring to purifying mission of one seraph to Isaiah, preparing him for his prophetic vocation.

Carved sculpture of Seraphim adorning top of wall plaque, Santa Caterina a Formiello Church, Naples, Italy. (©Mimmo Jodice/CORBIS)

Various opinions identify seraphim with winged grifons of Egypt, CHERUBIM, and Akkadian–Canaanite genii associated with divine majesty. But Isaiah clearly presents them as humanlike beings with faces, hands, feet, and equipped with six wings. With one pair of wings they veil their faces lest they see Yahweh (Ex 33.20); with a second pair they ''hovered aloft''; with the third pair they veiled their feet (euphemism for pudenda). They may have been well known in Israelite lore because Isaiah mentions them without preparation or explanation. Unwarrantedly, some have associated seraphim with the saraph (burning) serpents of Nm 21.4–9; Dt 8.15; Is 14.29, 30.6, whose bite caused a burning sensation; or with the Nohestan (bronze serpent) of 2 Kgs 18.4. As to their number, while some say choirs of seraphim are indicated, the text favors the opinion that just two seraphim cry the Trisagion ''one to the other.''

Unliteral acceptance of ''burning'' intransitively as of the flame of love, together with seraphim choirs praising thrice holy Yahweh, have led Christian speculation, piety, and art to place seraphim as the highest and most ardent of the angelic orders.

Bibliography: J. STEINMANN, *Le Prophète Isaïe: sa vie, son oeuvre et son temps* (2d ed. Paris 1955) 36–38. E. LACHEMAN, ''Seraphim of Isaiah 6,'' *Jewish Quarterly Review* 59 (1968) 71–72. J. D. SAVIGNAC, ''Les seraphim,'' *Vetus Testamentum* 22 (1972) 320–325. J. DAY, ''Echoes of Baal's Seven Thunders and Lightnings in Psalm 29 and Habakkuk 3:9 and the Identity of the Seraphim in Isaiah 6,'' *Vetus Testamentum* 29 (1979) 143–151.

[T. L. FALLON/EDS.]

SERAPHINA (FINA), ST.

Virgin; b. San Gimignano, Tuscany, 1238; d. there, March 12, 1253. She led a religious life in her parental home and was an example of piety, charity, mortification, and patience during a long serious illness. She was buried in the village church of San Gimignano.

Feast: Mar. 12.

Bibliography: G. COPPI, *La historica vita e morte di s.F. di S. Gimignano* (Florence 1575). *Acta Sanctorum* March 2:231–238. *Bibliotheca hagiographica latina antiquae et mediae aetatis* (Brussels 1898–1901) 1:2978. J. L. BAUDOT and L. CHAUSSIN, *Vies des saints et des bienheureux selon l'ordre du calendrier avec l'historique des fêtes* (Paris 1935–56) 3:279–280. J. BAUR, *Lexikon für Theologie und Kirche*, ed. J. HOFER and K. RAHNER (Freiburg 1957–65) 4:132.

[K. NOLAN]

SERAPHINA SFORZA, BL.

Abbess; b. Sueva Montefeltro, Urbino, Italy, 1434; d. Pesaro, Sept. 8, 1478. After being orphaned quite young, she was reared in Rome by her uncle, Prince Colonna. She married Alexander Sforza, Duke of Pesaro, at 16. After a short time this marriage was made unhappy, first by her husband's long absence on military campaigns, and then by his involvement with a mistress. When he expelled Sueva from his house in 1457, she was sheltered by the POOR CLARES. She later entered this convent at Pesaro and became abbess in 1475 after her husband's death. Her cult was approved in 1754.

Feast: Sept. 9.

Bibliography: B. FELICIANGELI, *Sulla monacazione di Sueva Montefeltro-Sforza* (Pistoia 1903). F. VAN ORTROY, *Analecta Bollandiana* 24 (1905) 311–313. A. BUTLER, *The Lives of the Saints*, rev. ed. H. THURSTON and D. ATTWATER (New York, 1956) 3:517–518.

[N. G. WOLF]

SERAPHINO, ST.

Capuchin lay brother; b. 1540; d. Ascoli, Oct. 12, 1604. Seraphino (of Montegranaro) spent his early youth as a shepherd, returning to his home upon the death of his parents. He first desired to be a hermit, but hearing of the Capuchins, he applied for admission to the order at Tolentino. After repeated refusals, the provincial finally accepted him. He received the habit at Jesi in 1556 and was professed a year later. He progressed rapidly in the spiritual life, but he was a failure at the ordinary duties of a lay brother, and received many rebukes and complaints about his awkwardness. Because of his fidelity to the Franciscan rule, his miracles, and his practice of charity to all, he won the devotion of the people. He was beatified in 1729, and canonized by Clement XIII in 1767.

Feast: Oct. 12.

Bibliography: *Lexicon Capuccinum* (Rome 1951) 1583–84. *Bullarium O.F.M. Cap.*, v.1–7 (Rome 1740–52), v.8–10 (Innsbruck 1883–84). v.7, 10. D. SVAMPA, *Vita di San Serafino da Montegranaro, laico capuccino* (Bologna 1904).

[E. SCHMIDT]

SERAPION OF THMUIS, ST.

Monk, theologian; consecrated bishop of Thmuis (Lower Egypt) before 339; d. after 362 (feast, March 21; Coptic Church, March 7). Scrapion had been superior of a colony of monks and was an intimate friend of St. ANTHONY OF EGYPT (the Hermit). He received a number of letters from St. ATHANASIUS of Alexandria, among them the four *Concerning the Holy Spirit,* the first formal treatise ever written on this subject. In 356 Athanasius sent Serapion with four other Egyptian bishops to the court of Constantius II to refute the calumnies of the Arians (Sozomen, *Hist. eccl.* 4.9). It was under the same Emperor that Serapion was ousted from his see by the Arian usurper Ptolemaius (359); and Jerome calls him a ''confessor'' (*De vir. ill.* 99). The same source states that Serapion was given the title *scholasticus* on account of his great learning.

Sozomen (*loc. cit.*) calls him ''a prelate distinguished by the wonderful sanctity of his life and the power of his eloquence.'' Jerome mentions among his works ''an excellent treatise *Against the Manicheans,* one on the titles of the Psalms, and useful Epistles to various persons.'' The work on the Psalms is lost, but that against the Manichaeans was published in 1931 by R. Casey who discovered it in a 12th-century manuscript of the Monastery of Vatopedi on Mount Athos. It gives ample evidence of the rhetorical, philosophical, and theological erudition of the author. Serapion does not refute the entire Manichaean system, but limits himself to a criticism of the main points, especially of the dualistic theory of a good and bad principle.

Though there existed at one time a collection of 23 of his letters, only three are extant, two in Greek discovered by Cardinal Mai (the first addressed to Bishop Eudoxius; the second, to monks at Alexandria), and one in Syriac recently published by R. Draguet, addressed to some disciples of St. Anthony the hermit on the occasion of his death. Jerome does not mention the *Euchologion,* discovered by A. Dimitrijewskij (1894) in an 11th-century manuscript of the Laura Monastery of Mount ATHOS. There is no doubt that Serapion is the author of this Sacramentary, which has great importance in the history of the liturgy. It consists of 30 prayers, 18 connected with the Eucharistic liturgy, seven with Baptism and Confirmation, three with Ordination, and two with the blessings of the oils and funerals. It contains the earliest certain evidence for the *Sanctus* in the Mass. Most striking is the prayer for the union of the Church drawn from the DIDACHE and inserted between the words of the Institution for the bread and the cup, and the *EPICLESIS* of the Logos, rather than the Holy Spirit, which seems to be Serapion's contribution. The author is a compiler of traditional material, but shows a bold independence that leads to the creation of new prayers and revisions of early Christian forms.

Bibliography: R. P. CASEY, *Serapion of Thmuis against the Manichees* (Cambridge, Mass. 1931). *Patrologia Graeca,* ed. J. P. MIGNE (Paris 1857–66) 40:923–942. R. DRAGUET, *Muséon* 64 (1951) 1–25, with Fr. tr. A. DIMITRIJEWSKIJ, ed., *Euchologium* (Kiev 1894). G. WOBBERMIN, *Texte und Untersuchungen zur Geschichte der altchristlichen Literatur* N5 2.3b (Berlin 1898). F. E. BRIGHTMAN, *Journal of Theological Studies* 1 (Berlin 1900) 88–113, 247–277. F. X. FUNK, ed., *Didascalia et constitutions apostolorum,* 2 v. (Paderborn 1905) 2:158–195. J. QUASTEN, ed., *Monumenta eucharista et liturgica vetustissima* (Bonn 1935–37) 7.1:48–69. J. WORDSWORTH, tr., *Bishop Serapion's Prayer-Book* (London 1899). G. BARDY, *Dictionnaire de théologie catholique,* ed. A. VACANT et al., (Paris 1903–50; Tables générales 1951–) 14.2:1908–12. H. DÖRRIE, *Paulys Realenzyklopädie der klassischen Altertumswissenschaft,* ed. G. WISSOWA et al. Suppl. 8 (Stuttgart 1956) 1260–67; J. QUASTEN, *Patrology* (Westminster, Md. 1950–) 3:80–85. G. DIX, *The Shape of the Liturgy* (2d ed. London 1945; repr. 1960) 162–172. P. E. RODOPOULOS, *Theologia* 28 (1957) 252–275, 420–439, 578–591; 29 (1958) 45–54, 208–217, Sacramentary. K. FITSCHEN, *Serapion von Thmuis : echte und unechte Schriften sowie die Zeugnisse des Athanasius und anderer* (Berlin; New York 1992). M. E. JOHNSON, *The Prayers of Sarapion of Thmuis: A Literary, Liturgical, and Theological Analysis* (Rome 1995).

[J. QUASTEN]

SERBIA AND MONTENEGRO, THE CATHOLIC CHURCH IN

The joint government of Serbia and Montenegro, formerly part of the self-proclaimed Federal Republic of Yugoslavia, is located in southeastern Europe, on the Balkan Peninsula. The region is bound by Hungary on the north, Romania on the northeast, Bulgaria on the east, Macedonia and Albania on the south, the Adriatic Sea on the southwest, and Bosnia-Herzegovina and Croatia on the west. Encompassing the former Yugoslavian provinces of Vojvodina, Kosovo, Serbia and Montenegro, the region is characterized by fertile plains in the north, rising

Capital: Belgrade (Serbia) and Podgorica (Montenegro).
Size: 39,507 sq. miles.
Population: 10,662,087 in 2000.
Languages: Serbian, Albanian.
Religions: 426,480 Catholics (4%), 6,930,360 Orthodox (65%), 2,025,795 Muslims (19%), 106,672 Protestants (1%), 1,172,780 follow other faiths.
Archdioceses: Belgrade, with suffragans Subotica and Zrenjanin; Kotor, suffragan of Split-Makarska (in Croatia); and Bar, which is immediately subject to the Holy See. In addition, the Serbian Orthodox Church has a patriarchate in Belgrade, as well as numerous eparchies.

to rolling hills and mountains in the south, while the eastern area is predominated by limestone outcroppings and ranges. Petroleum, natural gas, coal, antimony, copper, lead and nickel are among the wealth of natural resources in the area.

As the most populous and most dispersed nationality, ethnic Serbs exerted great influence on the former federated Yugoslavian republic. Although concentrated in Serbia proper, in 1981 they also accounted for substantial portions of the remainder of Yugoslavia, a result of their migration to avoid oppression during the Ottoman occupation. Attempting to limit Serbian domination, Yugoslavia's communist government immediately redrew the region's federal units to achieve political recognition of Macedonian and Montenegrin ethnic individuality and the mixed populations of Vojvodina, Kosovo and Bosnia-Herzegovina. Ethnic rivalries continued to simmer, coming to a head following the break up of Yugoslavia in the early 1990s, and resulting in mass genocide in the region of Kosovo.

Early Church in Serbia. Using the Drina and Zeta rivers as lines of demarcation, in 379 the Roman Empire divided Illyricum in half. Greek Byzantine culture predominated within Eastern Illyricum, which included the region that eventually became modern Serbia and Montenegro, while the Latin rite developed in the west. The eastern region was joined to the Rome Patriarchate until 732, when it became subject to the Patriarchate of CONSTANTINOPLE.

The first Serbian bishopric was established near the Raška River, and by 1020 was a suffragan to the Archdiocese of Ohrid. The founder of the independent medieval Serbian state was Stephen Nemanja, who emancipated it from Byzantine rule in 1183. Stephen abdicated in 1196 and gave to Vlcanus, his eldest son, Dioclia (now Montenegro), and to his younger son Stephen, Raška. Afterward he and his youngest son, St. Sava Nemana, founded the monastery of Chilandar. Stephen ultimately became the ruler of all his father's dominions and requested a royal crown from Honorius III. The pope granted his petition and sent a special legation to Serbia for the coronation *c.* 1220 that won Stephen the surname Prvo-venčani ("first-crowned") and united Serbia with the Holy See and the Catholic Church. However, the union was undermined by Sava, who was negotiating with the patriarch of Constantinople in Nicaea to establish an autocephalous archepiscopate in Serbia. In 1219 the patriarch consecrated Sava as the first archbishop of Serbia. After founding ten dioceses, consecrating their bishops and promoting religious instruction and monastic life, Sava died in 1235.

The Serbian Orthodox Church developed in the Byzantine rite amid a thriving Serbian culture. The most important ruler of medieval Serbia, Dušan the Great (1331–55), convoked an ecclesiastical national synod in 1346 and established the first Serbian Patriarchate, with its seat in Peć. After Dušan's death Serbia was defeated by the Ottoman Turks, who occupied the region in 1389. The Church attempted to preserve Serbian culture during this period, canonizing medieval Serbian kings as fresco painters preserved their images and priests recited a litany of their names at daily masses. Under Turkish domination Orthodox Christians suffered greatly. Particularly onerous was the human tax exacted by the Turks, who carried away the most promising youngsters, educated them as Muslims, and trained them as soldiers in the elite detachment in the Turkish army called janizaries. By chance a janizary of Serbian origin named Mehmed Sokolović (or Sokoli), became grand vizier. Cognizant of his ancestry, he reestablished the Serbian patriarchate in 1557 and appointed his brother first patriarch of this second patriarchate (1557–1766). After the Christians vanquished the Turks at Vienna (1683) and their armies arrived in South Serbia, the Serbs joined in a losing battle against the Turks. Fear of reprisals caused many Serbs to leave their country in 1690 under the leadership of the Partiarch Arsenius III Crnojević and to migrate to Croatia and Hungary. In 1766 the Greeks induced the Turks to suppress the second Serbian patriarchate and subject it to Constantinople.

The independence movement of the 19th century, while sparking further uprisings against the Turks, also saw significant cultural changes, including the creation of a modern Serbian literary language based on ordinary speech. In 1880 the patriarch of Constantinople granted to Serbia the status of autocephalous church; in 1920 the third Serbian Orthodox patriarchate would combine the formerly autonomous Serbian metropolitans of Belgrade, Karlovci, Bosnia and Montenegro, and the Diocese of Dalmatia. Before 1918 a very small number of immigrant Croats and other foreigners represented the Roman Catholic Church in Serbia. In 1924 the Archdiocese of Belgrade was established.

Early Church in Montenegro. Montenegro lies south of Serbia and borders on the Adriatic, the Zeta River serving as its western border. Slavs settled here in the 7th century and later adopted the Byzantine rite. Along the Adriatic coast, however, a small minority belonging to the Latin rite still exists, and belongs to the Archdiocese of BAR. The Montenegrins considered by some as Serbs and by others as a special South Slav nationality, put up heroic resistance to the Turks who occupied Montenegro in 1499. The Turks entrusted some civil responsibilities to the Orthodox metropolitan at Cetinje. After 1697 the metropolitans were elected from the family of Petrović-Njegoš. They also functioned as ethnarchs and as such created and headed the principality of Montenegro. In 1918 the kingdom merged with Yugoslavia, and in 1920 the Orthodox Church of Montenegro merged with the Serbian patriarchate, thus losing its autonomous status.

United Within Yugoslavia. The Kingdom of the Serbs, Croats and Slovenes—later Yugoslavia ("South Slavia")—was constituted on Dec. 1, 1918 and became the Kingdom of Yugoslavia in 1929. During World War II Germany invaded the region and caused it to be divided (April 10, 1941). Germany and Italy occupied Slovenia; Hungary, Bachka (Bačka); Bulgaria, Macedonia; and Italy, Montenegro. Croatia proclaimed its independence, while Serbia remained nominally independent but was actually under German control.

When Serbia and Montenegro united in 1918 as part of Yugoslavia, their merger created a single Eastern Orthodox church; the Macedonian Orthodox Church would later split from the Serbian church, while the Romanian Orthodox Church was a small sect present only in Vojvodina. An estimated 11.5 million Yugoslavs, primarily Serbs, Montenegrins and Macedonians, were Eastern Orthodox by family background. The Serbian political elite of the interwar Kingdom of Yugoslavia was unwilling to share power. The Army officer corps and the civilian bureaucracy were dominated by Serbs, reflecting the hegemony that triggered a backlash during World War II as Croat nationalist fanatics butchered Serbs, Jews and Gypsies with a brutality that appalled even the Nazis.

In the Kingdom of Yugoslavia Serbs had great political and cultural influence, a situation that caused resentments to build among other ethnic groups. While the constitution gave equality to all religions, the Serb-controlled government gave special concessions to the Serbian Orthodox Church, causing many to join that church as a way to social betterment. In 1922 the Yugoslav government began negotiations with the Holy See, and reached agreement in 1935. This concordat would have regularized the Catholic Church's organization to create corresponding diocesan and state borders: Belgrade would be the metropolitan see for Serbia; Ljubljana, for Slovenia; and Split, for Dalmatia. The Roman-Slavonic liturgy was to prevail in all parts of Yugoslavia where Catholics so desired. However, the Yugoslavian Parliament heeded the opposition of the Orthodox Church and refused ratification.

Communists seized power after World War II and established the Federal People's Republic of Yugoslavia under Josip Broz Tito in 1945. Although the Nov. 30, 1946 constitution guaranteed religious liberty, the government demonstrated its opposition to all religions in many ways, even the Orthodox, and persecuted them openly. The Orthodox Metropolitans Barnabas of Sarajevo and Arsenius of Montenegro were condemned to 11 years in prison, sharing the fate of many other religious leaders. Catholic schools were closed, and Church buildings and lands confiscated. It was only after the friction between Tito and Soviet leaders began in 1948 that the Yugoslav government sought a *modus vivendi* with religious groups, hoping it would win them good will among Western powers. In 1956 the Communists inaugurated a policy of limited cooperation, permitting the Holy See to appoint new bishops, freeing imprisoned clergy, opening minor seminaries and permitting Yugoslav Catholic bishops to attend Vatican Council II in 1962. On June 25, 1966 the Vatican and the Yugoslavian government signed an agreement under which Yugoslav bishops could remain subject to the spiritual jurisdiction of Rome through regular contact.

The Serbian, Bulgarian and Greek Orthodox hierarchies recognized no distinct Macedonian nation or independent Macedonian Orthodox Church until 1958, when the Serbian Orthodox hierarchy consecrated a Macedonian bishop. Shortly thereafter the Macedonian Orthodox Church came into official existence, but it remained under the authority of the Serbian Orthodox Church. In 1967 Macedonian clergymen proclaimed their church independent. Aware that a self-governing Macedonian church would enhance the sense of Macedonian nationhood within the Yugoslav federation and help balance Serbian hegemony, political authorities gave the church their full support. The Serbian Church hierarchy refused to recognize the Macedonian Orthodox Church when it was granted autonomous status by the Yugoslav state. Without recognition from the Serbian hierarchy, the Macedonian church remained isolated from the international Orthodox community.

Tensions Rise in Kosovo. In the mid-1980s, a few years after Tito's death, a wave of Serbian nationalism swept through Yugoslavia. Among those fearing the ramifications of this resurgence was Kosovo, an impoverished region located south of Serbia. Between 1948 and 1990, the number of Serbians living in Kosovo had dropped from 23 percent to less than 10 percent, while ethnic Albanians increased, a democratic shift caused by immigration as well as by a postwar Serbian exodus which escalated when the Kosovar government fell under Albanian control in 1966. In an effort to regain control over the region, in 1989 the Serbian government began a resettlement program in Kosovo. As few former Kosovar Serbs desired to return, this program proved unsuccessful.

On April 11, 1992, following declarations of independence from Croatia, Slovenia, Bosnia-Herzegovina and Macedonia, Serbia and Montenegro proclaimed themselves the Federal Republic of Yugoslavia, although several governments, including the United States, refused to recognize them as a continuation of the former communist state. The appointment of nationalist Serbian president Slobodan Milosevic as president of the new federation in July of 1997 sparked protest from Montenegrins, as did the government's radical policies. In 1999 the Serbian government began a program of ''ethnic cleansing'' in Kosovo as a way to eliminate the Albanian majority in the region, a policy it had attempted in Bosnia in 1992 before being repulsed by UN troops. Leaders from Muslim, Catholic and Orthodox faiths joined together in condemning the horrors perpetrated by Serbian forces, and dedicated their efforts to aiding the thousands of refugees who survived the mass killings and fled Kosovo. Pope John Paul II also appealed for peace, asking that ''political and military leaders . . . pursue every possible initiative that might lead to just and lasting peace.'' NATO and Russian peacekeeping forces entered the area following the bombing of Serbia. A U.N. Interim Administration Mission remained in Kosovo into the next decade, dealing with outbreaks of violence that continued to be directed toward Albanians, although on a smaller scale than before.

Into the 21st Century. By 2000 the Catholic Church included 238 parishes tended by 157 secular and 37 religious priests, with seven brothers and over 300 sisters administering schools and attending to medical and humanitarian needs. In contrast, the Serbian Orthodox Church included about 2,000 parishes, over 2,500 religious, numerous monasteries and convents, four seminaries and a school of theology. It also published ten periodicals. Completed in 1985, the Cathedral of St. Sava in Belgrade became the largest Eastern Orthodox Church in the world. Most Roman Catholics were ethnic Hungarians who lived in Vojvodina.

Unlike Montenegro, within the constituent Republic of Serbia, while the constitution provided for freedom of religion, the government did not uphold this right in practice. Although not named as the state religion, the Serbian Orthodox Church had access to state-run television and received other benefits from the government. Despite this, Orthodox leaders remained outspoken in their condemnation of Milosevic and his ethnic policies. Unlike other European nations affected by communist confiscations of property, Serbia had yet to make restitution to any religious group within its borders. While acts of violence were reported against Catholics in Vojvodina during the 1990s, the incidents of such acts had declined by 2000. Following the start of the conflict in Kosovo in the late 1990s, Serbian Orthodox churches in the region became the target of retaliatory violence by Albanians, and 80 churches had been desecrated or destroyed by 2000. Tensions between Montenegrin Orthodox and Serbian Orthodox members were also reported due to efforts taken to undermine or otherwise cancel certain religious services. In 2000 the Pope's private charity, Cor Unum, donated $115,000 to help refugees of Kosovo, and the following year the Vatican supported the formation of an International Tribunal to prosecute violators of humanitarian law.

Bibliography: *Monumenta spectantia historiam Slavorum meridionalium* (Zagreb 1868–) 46 v. to 1951. M. SPINKA, *A History of Christianity in the Balkans* (Chicago, IL 1933). R. RISTELHUEBER, *Histoire des peuples balkaniques* (Paris 1950). P. D. OSTROVÍC, *The Truth about Yugoslavia* (New York 1952). W. MARKERT, *Jugoslawien* (Cologne 1954). F. DVORNIK, *The Slavs: Their Early History and Civilization* (Boston 1956); *The Slavs in European History and Civilization* (New Brunswick, NJ 1962). K. S. LATOURETTE, *Christianity in a Revolutionary Age: A History of Christianity in the Nineteenth and Twentieth Centuries,* 5 v. (New York 1958–62) v.1, 2, 4. F. MACLEAN, *The Heretic: The Life and Times of Josip Broz-Tito* (New York 1957). J. K. JIREČEK, *Istorija Srba* (2d ed. Belgrade 1952). J. MOUSSET, *La Serbie et son Église 1830–1904* (Paris 1939). D. M. SLIJEPČEVIĆ, *Istorija Srpske Pravoslavne crkve,* v.1 (Munich 1962). S. P. RAMET, *Nihil Obstat: Religion, Politics, and Social Change in East-Central Europe and Russia* (Durham, NC 1998). J. MATL, *Lexikon für Theologie und Kirche*[2], eds., J. HOFER and K. RAHNER, 10 v. (2d, new ed. Freiburg 1957–65) 5:1191–94. B. SPULER and H. KOCH, *Die Religion in Geschichte und Gegenwart*[3], 7 v. (3d ed. Tübingen 1957–65) 3:1054–60. *Bilan du Monde,* 2:914–928. *Annuario Pontificio* has annual data on all dioceses and apostolic administrations.

[P. SHELTON]

SERGEANT, JOHN

Secular priest, controversialist, and informer; b. Barrow-upon-Humber, Lincolnshire, 1622; d. London, 1707. He entered St. John's College, Cambridge, in 1639 and graduated in 1642. For a short time he was secretary to Thomas Morton, Bishop of Durham, and he then became converted to Catholicism. He entered the English College, Lisbon, in November 1643, was ordained in 1650, and fulfilled various offices in the college. He returned to England in 1652 and became secretary of the English Secular Clergy Chapter. Sergeant hoped for toleration of Catholics on the basis of the acceptance of the Oath of Allegiance and the banishment of the Jesuits from England. He maintained that the Chapter was the organ of ecclesiastical authority for Catholics in England, and that the only alternative to the Chapter was the appointment of a bishop with ordinary jurisdiction. Sergeant's intransigence led to his resignation as secretary of the Chapter in 1667. In 1673 he was in Paris, where he engaged in controversy with Peter TALBOT, Archbishop of Dublin, who, with the support of John Warner, SJ, had delated some of Sergeant's writings to Rome as being heretical on the subject of the *prolegomena fidei.*

In common with certain other English and Irish priests who supported the Oath of Allegiance, Sergeant was under ''protection'' from the English government from about 1671 onward. At the outbreak of the Titus OATES PLOT, October 1678, a special Privy Council order was made restricting him to his house, but in June 1679 he left England for Flanders. There he came in contact with the apostate Rookwood, who introduced him to the English envoy at The Hague, Henry Sidney, as being willing to make a ''discovery'' concerning the Jesuits and the Plot. In October 1679 Sergeant made his deposition to the Privy Council, which was printed by the Oxford Parliament in March 1681. For this he received a salary from Secret Service funds. In 1681 he wrote to Henry Hyde, Second Earl of Clarendon, offering to act as informer against the Jesuits. In the reign of James II he was secretary to the Duke of Perth, and to the very end of his life he tried to assert his authority over the English Secular Clergy Chapter. His controversial and philosophical writings are voluminous and turgid. Like Kenelm Digby and Thomas WHITE (alias Blacklow), he was one of the few 17th-century English Catholic writers who tried to adapt his epistemology to the new philosophical tendencies of the age. *Method to Science* (1696) is anti-Cartesian; *Solid Philosophy* (1697) is an early critique of Locke—Locke's own annotated copy is in St. John's College, Cambridge.

Bibliography: T. COOPER, *The Dictionary of National Biography from the Earliest Times to 1900,* 63 v. (London 1885–1900; reprinted with corrections, 21 v., 1908–09, 1921–22, 1938; supplement 1901–) 17:1189–91. J. GILLOW, *A Literary and Biographical History or Bibliographical Dictionary of the English Catholics from 1534 to the Present time,* 5 v. (London–New York 1885–1902 repr. New York 1961) 5:491–498. M. V. HAY, *The Jesuits and the Popish Plot* (London 1934). J. WARNER, *The History of the English Persecution of Catholics and the Presbyterian Plot,* tr. J. BLIGH, ed. T. A. BIRREL *(Publications of the Catholic Record Society* 47–48; 1953–55). T. A. BIRRELL, ''English Catholics without a Bishop 1655–72,'' *Recusant History* 4.4 (1957–58) 142–178.

[T. A. BIRRELL]

SERGEANT, RICHARD, BL.

Priest, martyr; *alias* Lee, Lea, or Long[e]; b. in Gloucestershire, England; hanged, drawn, and quartered April 20, 1586 at Tyburn. He was the son of Thomas Sergeant of Stone and his wife Katherine Tyre of Hardwick. After earning his baccalaureate at Oxford (*c.* 1570–71), he entered the English College at Rheims and was ordained priest at Laon (1583). He left for England on September 10, working for several years in the mission prior to his indictment at the Old Bailey on April 17, 1586, as Richard Lea, *alias* Longe. He suffered with Bl. William THOMSON, who was also executed as an unlawful priest. He was beatified by Pope John Paul II on Nov. 22, 1987 with George Haydock and companions.

Feast of the English Martyrs: May 4 (England).

See Also: ENGLAND, SCOTLAND, AND WALES, MARTYRS OF.

Bibliography: Harleian Soc. Publ. xxi (London, 1885), 258. R. CHALLONER, *Memoirs of Missionary Priests,* ed. J. H. POLLEN (rev. ed. London 1924) 1, nos. 32, 33. J. FOSTER, *Alumni Oxonienses* (Oxford 1892). J. H. POLLEN, *Acts of English Martyrs* (London 1891).

[K. I. RABENSTEIN]

SERGIUS, PATRIARCH OF MOSCOW

Patriarch of Moscow; b. Arzamas, Nizhni Novgorod region, Jan. 11, 1867; d. Moscow, May 15, 1944. Ivan Nikolaievich Stragorodsky (later Sergius) became, like his father, a priest in the Russian Orthodox Church after theological studies in Novgorod and St. Petersburg. In 1890 he became a monk and was sent, at his request, as missioner to Japan for three years, until recalled to St. Petersburg to teach the Old Testament. He was rector of the St. Petersburg Theological Academy, and became bishop of Yamburg (1901), archbishop of Finland and Vyborg (1905), member of the HOLY SYNOD (1911), and metropolitan of Novgorod (1917).

When Patriarc TIKHON was imprisoned (1922–23) for denouncing the Soviet antireligious campaign, Sergius supported the ''Living Church,'' which was subservient to the Communists; but he publicly confessed his error after Tikhon's release. During 1925 Tikhon died and Metropolitan Peter of Krutitsky, the patriarchal administrator, went to prison. Sergius, his deputy, went into exile (1925–27). Soon after his release he issued a declaration, as acting head of the Orthodox Church, that all the faithful were duty-bound to support the Soviet regime, and that all the clergy must take this pledge of loyalty or lose their positions.

Despite mounting persecutions, Sergius denied in 1930 the existence of religious persecution in the U.S.S.R. The 1927 declaration by Sergius caused a split in the Russian Orthodox Church outside Russia, up to then loyal to the Moscow patriarchate. When Sergius tried to deprive Metropolitan Eulogy of Paris in 1930 of his western European bishopric, Eulogy placed this section of the Church under the patriarch of Constantinople. In 1934 Sergius became metropolitan of Moscow. During World War II he supported the Soviet government. Stalin rewarded him in 1943 by allowing a synod to convene, which elected him patriarch, contrary to the election regulations approved in 1917. Sergius was also reputed for his writings on theology and the missions

Bibliography: J. S. CURTISS, *The Russian Church and the Soviet State, 1917–1950* (Boston 1953). M. SPINKA, *The Church in Soviet Russia* (New York 1956).

[G. A. MALONEY/EDS.]

SERGIUS I, PATRIARCH OF CONSTANTINOPLE

April 18, 610, to Dec. 9, 638. Of Syrian provenance, Sergius proved one of the most effective and individual personalities ever to head the Patriarchate of CONSTANTINOPLE. He took the patriarchal throne at the very time Emperor HERACLIUS began his rule, and patriarch and emperor maintained the closest of ties throughout their long reigns. On the political level, for example, Heraclius formed a regency of Sergius and a civil official to rule Constantinople while he fought the Persians from 622 to 628. It was in this position that Sergius galvanized Byzantine resistance to beat the AVARS back effectively from the capital in 626. In religious affairs Sergius's all-pervading problem was the reconciliation of the continuing split between orthodox, or Chalcedonian, Christology and the Monophysitic viewpoint (*see* MONOPHYSITISM), which was very strongly represented in the eastern provinces of the BYZANTINE EMPIRE—provinces contemporarily being recovered from the Persians. With the strong support of Cyrus, patriarch of Egypt, Sergius first produced (*c.* 633) a formula that attributed to Christ two natures with but one energy. This was temporarily tolerated by Pope HONORIUS I, but the Orthodox spokesman Sophronius, the recently appointed (634) patriarch of Jerusalem, strongly denounced it. Thus before he died in 638, Sergius was instrumental in formulating a compromise that took cognizance of the objections of Honorius and Sophronius and deemphasized the single Energy, taking the position that Christ had two natures but one will (*see* MONOTHELITISM). This compromise, which was incorporated in Heraclius's Ecthesis, was ineffective: it was rejected completely by the Monophysitic opposition and by the new patriarch of Jerusalem, and was not acceptable to the Roman See. Sergius, together with his successors the Monothelite patriarchs PYRRHUS I and PAUL II, was declared anathema by the Latin Church in 649 and again by both East and West in the General Council of CONSTANTINOPLE III (681). In both the Eastern and Western Churches, Sergius became the symbol of cooperation between Church hierarchy and emperor and also, to an extent, a symbol of the independence of the patriarch of Constantinople vis-à-vis the patriarch of the West.

Bibliography: J. PARGOIRE, *L'église byzantine* (Paris 1905). V. GRUMEL, ''Recherches sur l'histoire de monothélisme,'' *Échos d'Orient* 27 (1928) 6–16, 257–277; 28 (1929) 19–34, 272–282; 29 (1930) 16–28. V. GRUMEL, *Les Regestes des actes du patriarcat de Constantinople*. G. OSTROGORSKY, *History of the Byzantine State*, tr. J. HUSSEY from 2d German ed. (Oxford 1956); American ed. by P. CHARANIS (New Brunswick, N.J. 1957) 90–98. H. G. BECK, *Kirche und theologische Literatur im byzantinischen Reich* (Munich 1959) 292–295.

[D. A. MILLER]

SERGIUS II, PATRIARCH OF CONSTANTINOPLE

Reigned June 1001 to July 1019; d. Constantinople. Sergius belonged to the family of PHOTIUS, and became a monk and *hegoumenos,* or abbot, of the Monastery of Manuel. He received a synodical letter from Pope SERGIUS IV (1009–12) upon the latter's election; according to later tradition, because of the pope's use of the term FILIOQUE, Sergius excommunicated him, removing his name from the diptychs. This action was first cited by Cerularius after 1054, and is repeated thereafter in numerous theological tracts against the Latins.

In asserting the right of the patriarch to decree public honors for a saint, Sergius condemned SYMEON THE NEW THEOLOGIAN to banishment when he attempted to organize public veneration for his deceased master Symeon Eulabes, the Elder. The patriarch had permitted a private cult after reading the justifying reasons, but had forbidden all festivity. Sergius supported the great landowners against Emperor Basil II in the matter of the *allelengyon,* or collective responsibility, for the payment of taxes by the community when, to preserve the peasantry, Basil put the burden of furnishing taxes for the impoverished on the *dynatoi*, the powerful. However, in 1016, he accepted the *charistikion*, whereby monasteries were deeded to lay people or to other monasteries, which was opposed by his predecessor SISINNIUS II. Sergius asserted his right to the title Ecumenical Patriarch. His synodal tome on the profane alienation of monastic property and his canonical decisions on marriage have been preserved.

Bibliography: *Patrologia Graeca* ed. J. P. MIGNE (Paris 1857–66) 119:741. T. NIGGL, *Lexikon für Theologie und Kirche*, ed. J. HOFER and K. RAHNER (Freiberg 1957–65) 9:687. V. LAURENT, *Échos d'Orient* 33 (1934) 301–305; 35 (1936) 73–75. A. MICHEL, *Humbert und Kerullarios* (Paderborn 1924–30) 1:1629; 2:17–24; *Römische Quartalschrift für christliche Altertumsckunde und für Kirchengeschichte* 41 (1933) 133–137; 141–147; *Historisches Jahrbuch der Görres-Gesellschaft* 70 (1951) 53–55. J. DARROUZÈS, *Les Regestes des actes du Patriarcat de Constantinople*, ed. V. GRUMEL, v.1, fasc. II–III (Paris 1989) 815–25. V. GRUMEL, *Revue des études byzantines* 10 (1952) 5–23. H. G. BECK, *Kirche und theologische Literatur im byzantinischen Reich* (Munich 1959) 94, 136, 274, 599. J. KODER, ''Normale Mönche und Enthusiasten: der Fall des Symeon Neos theologos'' in *Religiöse Devianz*, ed. D. SIMON (Frankfurt am Main 1990) 97–119. J. P. THOMAS, *Private Religious Foundations in the Byzantine Empire* (Washington, D.C. 1987) 155, 164–5, 217, 228, 233.

[F. CHIOVARO]

SERGIUS I, POPE, ST.

Pontificate: Dec. 15, 687 to Sept. 7, 701; b. Palermo, Sicily; d. Rome. Sergius, born of a Syrian family from

Antioch living in Palermo, went to Rome under Pope ADEODATUS, was ordained, and under Leo II became titular priest of St. Susanna. After Pope CONON'S death, a triple election of the archdeacon Paschal, the archpriest Theodore, and Sergius, was resolved in Sergius's favor (December of 687). Theodore submitted but Paschal died in prison five years later, unrepentant. The exarch John Platyn demanded the gold promised him by Paschal if elected, and Sergius was forced to pay before Platyn would permit his consecration. Sergius rejected the reforming decrees of the QUINISEXT or Trullan council (692) that opposed Roman practices and laws: canons 3, 13, and 30 sanctioned a married clergy; canon 36 called for the exaltation of Constantinople as had the Councils of Constantinople I and Chalcedon; and canons 52 and 55 differed sharply from western Lenten practices. Papal legates in Constantinople signed the acts, but Sergius disavowed their action. Emperor Justinian II arrested two councilors of the pope and tried to capture the pope himself, but the militias of Ravenna, the Pentapolis, and Rome prevented this. Schismatic Aquileia, alienated by the THREE CHAPTERS controversy, was restored to unity through the Lombard King Cunipert and the pope. Sergius baptized King CAEDWALLA OF WESSEX (689), sent the pallium to Abp. BRITHWALD OF CANTERBURY, ordered WILFRID OF YORK restored to his see, and granted the privileges ALDHELM had requested. He wrote to JARROW ABBEY asking that a learned monk (BEDE?) be sent to aid the curialists in Rome. Sergius was also on good terms with the Frankish kingdom, and it was he who blessed and encouraged WILLIBRORD'S mission to the Frisians. Sergius added the Agnus Dei to the Mass and introduced processions on the four great feasts of Our Lady.

Feast: Sept. 9.

Bibliography: P. JAFFÉ, *Regesta pontificum romanorum ab condita ecclesia ad annum post Christum natum 1198*, ed. P. EWALD (repr. Graz 1956) 1:244–245. *Liber pontificalis*, ed. L. DUCHESNE (Paris 1886–92) 1:371–382. C. J. VON HEFELE, *Histoire des conciles d'après les documents originaux*, tr. H. LECLERCQ (Paris 1907–38) 3.1:560–581. H. K. MANN, *The Lives of the Popes in the Early Middle Ages from 590 to 1304* (London 1902–32) 1.2:77–104. A. FLICHE and V. MARTIN, eds., *Histoire de l'église depuis les origines jusqu'à nos jours* (Paris 1935) 5:316–323, 407–409. G. BARONE ADESI, *Monachesimo ortodosso d'Oriente e Dritto romano nel tardo antico* (Milan 1990). É. AMANN, *Dictionnaire de théologie catholique*, ed. A. VACANT et al. (Paris 1903–50) 14.2:1913–16. O. BERTOLINI, *Roma di fronte a Bisanzio e ai Longobardi* (Bologna 1941); "I papi e le relazioni politiche di Roma con i ducati Longobardi . . . ," *Rivista di storia della Chiesa iri Italia* 8 (1954) 1–22. R. M. CHOLU, *Married Clergy, and Ecclesiastical Continence in Light of the Council in Trullo (691)* (Rome 1986). J. HERRIN, "'Femina byzantina' The Council in Trullo on Women," *Dumbarton Oaks Papers* (1992) 97–105. H. OHME, "Das Concilium Quinisextum. Neue Einsichten zu einem umstrittenen Konzil," *Orientalia Christiana Periodica* 58 (Rome 1992) 367–400. C. G. PITSAKIS, "Le droit matrimonial dans les canons du concile in Trullo," *Annuarium Historiae Conciliorum* 24 (1992) 158–185. M. VAN ESBROECK, *Aux origines de la Dormition de la Viérge. Études historiques sur les traditions orientales* (1995). J. N. D. KELLY, *Oxford Dictionary of Popes* (New York 1986) 82–83.

[C. M. AHERNE]

SERGIUS II, POPE

Pontificate: Jan. 25, 844 to Jan. 27, 847; b. Rome. He was a member of the Roman nobility, who were responsible for his election and who overcame the opposition of the popular antipope John, a deacon, who very briefly held the Lateran palace after the death of GREGORY IV. Sergius was consecrated in St. Peter's (January 844) without informing the Emperor LOTHAIR I as prescribed in the *Constitutio Romana* (*see* EUGENE II). Thereupon the Emperor sent his son LOUIS (II) to call the pope to account; Sergius received Louis on condition that he swear not to attack Rome, and then on June 15, 844, anointed and crowned him king of the Lombards. Thereafter an altercation arose when Louis's adviser, DROGO, Bishop of Metz, insisted that the Romans swear fidelity to Louis, a plan that Sergius rejected; instead he had the Romans swear such an oath to the Emperor Lothair in accord with the *Constitutio.*

Sergius later appointed Drogo his legate to the Franks. EBBO, deposed archbishop of Reims, also received support from Sergius. The pope's intervention in the dispute between the patriarchs of Grado and Aquileia was interrupted by his sudden death. Sergius is accused of failing to provide Rome with adequate protection against the Saracen attack of Aug. 23, 846, despite advance warning. The extensive building program of Sergius's reign was carried out largely by his brother, Benedict. The Marcian aqueduct was restored and the Lateran basilica enlarged "according to Sergius's own design." The fact that the pope suffered from a crippling gout may have been the reason for his brother's prominence and his own allegedly testy disposition.

Bibliography: *Liber pontificalis*, ed. L. DUCHESNE (Paris 1886–92) 2:86–105. P. JAFFÉ, *Regesta pontificum romanorum ab condita ecclesia ad annum post Christum natum 1198*, ed. P. EWALD (repr. Graz 1956)1:327–329. L. DUCHESNE, *The Beginnings of the Temporal Sovereignty of the Popes,* tr. A. H. MATHEW (London 1908). H. K. MANN, *The Lives of the Popes in the Early Middle Ages from 590 to 1304* (London 1902–32) 2:232–257. A. FLICHE and V. MARTIN, eds., *Histoire de l'église depuis les origines jusqu'à nos jours* (Paris 1935) 6:275–281. J. HALLER, *Das Papsttum* (Stuttgart 1950–53) 2.1:27–30. G. SCHWAIGER, *Lexikon des Mittelalters,* 7 (Munich-Zurich 1994–95). D. TRESTIK, *[Die Taufe der tschechischen Fürsten im Jahre 845 und die Christianisierung der Slawen—tschechish]: Český časopis historický 92,* (Praha 1994). J. N. D. KELLY, *Oxford Dictionary of Popes* (New York 1986) 103–104.

[C. M. AHERNE]

SERGIUS III, POPE

Pontificate: Jan. 29, 904 to April 14, 911; b. Rome; d. Rome. A Roman deacon, bishop of Cere, and partisan of Pope STEPHEN VI, he made an abortive attempt to seize the papacy in 897. In 904, however, with the aid of Alberto I of Spoleto, he succeeded. His two immediate predecessors, Pope LEO V and antipope Christopher, were strangled in prison. A Roman synod again invalidated the Orders conferred by Pope FORMOSUS, much to the confusion of the Church. Sergius's decision in favor of the fourth marriage of Emperor LEO VI weakened the prestige of the papacy in the East. In Rome he was supported by the THEOPHYLACTUS family, by one of whose daughters, MAROZIA, he is supposed to have had a son (later Pope JOHN XI). Sergius must be given credit for the restoration of St. John LATERAN, which had been heavily damaged by an earthquake at the time of the Formosus trial. The authors of the narrative sources for Sergius's life are patently subjective. To AUXILIUS OF NAPLES, Sergius is a criminal, whereas the grammarian EUGENIUS VULGARIUS praises him immoderately. LIUTPRAND OF CREMONA's opinion is entirely negative.

Bibliography: P. JAFFÉ, *Regesta pontificum romanorum ab condita ecclesia ad annum post Christum natum 1198*, ed. S. LÖWENFELD (repr. Graz 1956) 1:445–447. *Liber pontificalis*, ed. L. DUCHESNE (Paris 1886–92) v. 2. C. J. VON HEFELE, *Histoire des conciles d'après les documents originaux*, tr. H. LECLERCQ (Paris 1907–38) v. 4. P. F. KEHR, *Regesta Pontificum Romanorum, Italia Pontificia* (Berlin 1928) 1, 2, 3, 5, 6.2, 7.1, 7.2, 8. L. DUCHESNE, "Serge III et Jean XI," *Mélanges d'archéologie et d'histoire* 33 (1913) 25–55. J. BECKER, ed., *Die Werke Liutprands von Cremona, Monumena Germaniae Historica: Scriptores rerum Germanicarum* (Berlin 1826) 38. É. AMANN, *Dictionnaire de théologie catholique*, ed. A. VACANT et al. (Paris 1903–53) 14.2:1918–21. V. BRAGA, *Dizionario biografico delgi italiani* 43 (Rome 1993). G. FASOLI, *I re d'Italia, 888–962* (Florence 1949). F. X. SEPPELT, *Geschichte der Päpste von den Anfängen bis zur Mitte des 20. Jh.* (Munich 1954–59) v. 2. H. K. MANN, *The Lives of the Popes in the Early Middle Ages from 590 to 1304* (London 1902–32) v. 4. C. GNOCCHI, "Ausilio e Vulgario. L'eco della 'Questione formosiana' in area napoletana," *Mélanges de l'École Française di Moyen Âge. Temps Modernes* (Rome 1995) 1, 65–75. R. POKORNY, "Eine Kurzform der Konzilskanones von Trosly (909). Zur Reformgesetzgebung in der ausgehenden Karolingerzeit," *Deutsches Archiv für Erforschung des Mittelalters* 42 (1986) 118–44. A. PRATESI, "Un controverso privilegio di papa Sergio III," *Archivo dell Società Romana di Storia Patria* 108 (1985) 5–36. R. SCHIEFFER, *Lexikon des Mittelalters* 7 (Munich-Zurich 1994–95). J. N. D. KELLY, *Oxford Dictionary of Popes* (New York 1986) 119–120.

[V. GELLHAUS]

SERGIUS IV, POPE

Pontificate: July 31, 1009, to May 12, 1012; b. unknown. d. May 12, 1012. Sergius was the son of Peter the shoemaker of the Ad Pinea district in Rome. He was originally named Peter, but he received the nickname Pig's snout (*Bucca porci*) presumably because of his peculiar appearance. From approximately 1004 to 1009 Sergius served as the bishop of Albano. The following year, he was elected to the papacy but the details of the event are not clear. In all probability, his election was secured through the influence of John II, head of the Crescentii. Contrary to tradition, Sergius was not the first pope to change his name but he is still credited with having made the practice common. Also, the story that Sergius touched off the Eastern Schism by sending Patriarch Sergius of Constantinople the *Synodicon* containing the *filioque* clause is erroneous. Finally, his authorship of a manifesto for a crusade against the Muslim power is almost certainly spurious. The few known details of Sergius's reign are vague. There is some evidence that he exempted several monasteries from episcopal jurisdiction and that he was a friend of the poor during a time of famine. Apparently Sergius also had the trust of some nobles who put their lands under his protection. The fact that Sergius died just six days prior to Cresentius coupled with the violent political upheaval and the rapid election of a Tusculan candidate for the papacy suggests foul play to most historians. Sergius was buried in the Lateran Basilica.

Bibliography: P. JAFFÉ, *Regesta pontificum romanorum ab condita ecclesia ad annum post Christum natum 1198,* ed. S. LÖWENFELD et al., 2 v. (2d ed. Leipzig 1881–88; repr. Graz 1956) 882–1198, ed. S. LÖWENFELD, 1:504–505. L. DUCHESNE, ed., *Liber pontificalis,* v. 1–2 (Paris 1886–92) 2. H. K. MANN, *The Lives of the Popes in the Early Middle Ages from 590 to 1304,* 18 v. (London 1902–32) 5. É. AMANN, *Dictionnaire de théologie catholique,* ed. A. VACANT et al., 15 v. (Paris 1903–50; Tables générales 1951–) 14.2:1921–22. A. FLICHE and V. MARTIN, eds., *Histoire de l'église depuis les origines jusqu'à nos jours* (Paris 1935–) 7. A. GIEYSZTOR, "The Genesis of the Crusades: The Encyclical of Sergius IV (1009–1012)," *Medievalia et humanistica* 5 (1948) 3–23; 6 (1950) 3–34. F. X. SEPPELT, *Geschichte der Päpste von den Anfängen bis zur Mitte des 20. Jh.* v.1, 2, 4, 5 (Leipzig 1931–41) 2. B. SCHIMMELPFENNIG, *The Papacy,* tr. J. SIEVERT (New York 1992) 113, 115–116. J. N. D. KELLY, *Oxford Dictionary of Popes* (Oxford 1986) 139.

[J. A. SHEPPARD]

SERGIUS OF RADONEZH, ST.

Russian monk and ascetical master; b. Rostov, May 3, 1314; d. Radonezh, Sergian monastery of the Trinity (near Moscow), Sept. 25, 1392. Sergius came from a once rich family, and his early years, as recorded by his biographer and disciple, Epiphanius the Wise, were filled with marvelous incidents. As a child he played truant rather than learn to read and write, until one day a mysterious monk changed his life. He then began to read the Bible, the books of the liturgy, and the Fathers, and visited the nearby monasteries. In spite of a desire for solitude, he

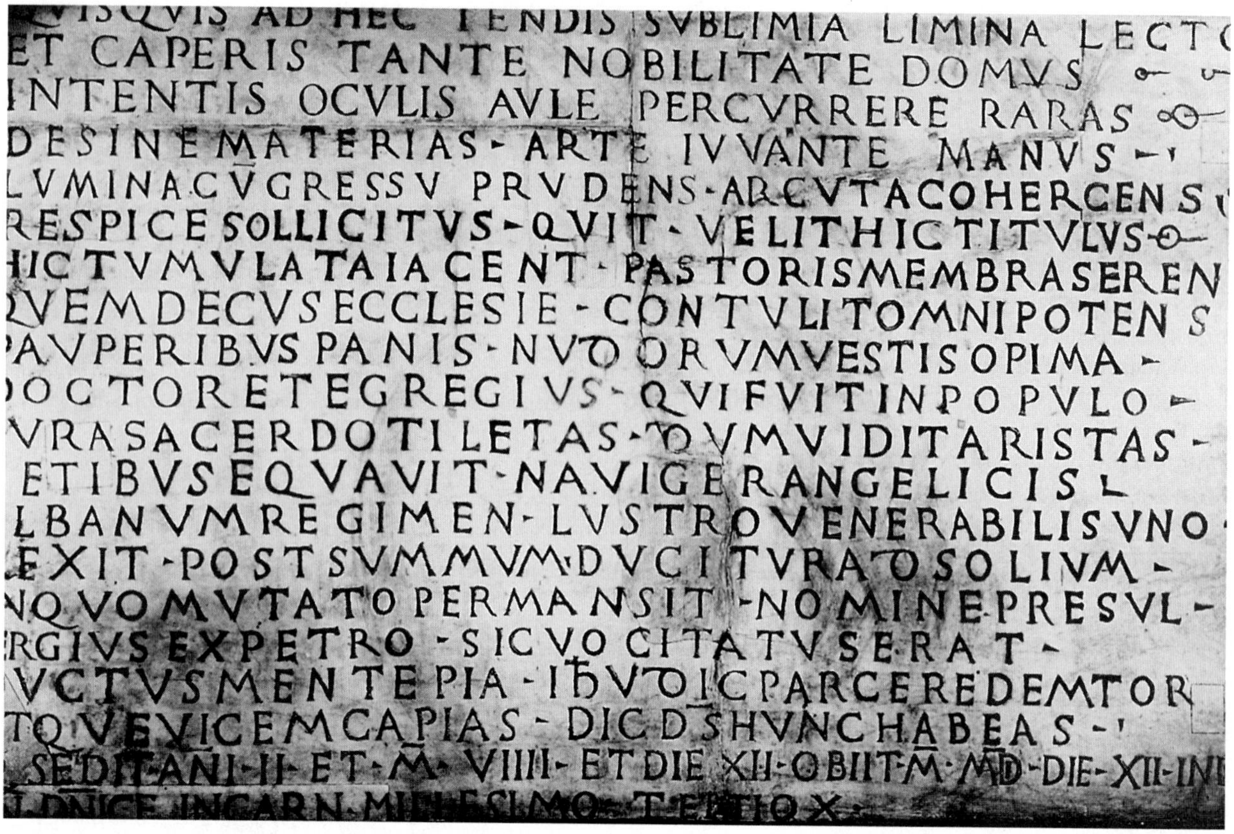

Epitaph for Pope Sergius IV, in St. John Lateran, Rome.

remained with his parents until their death (1334). He retired to the forest of Radonezh (1336), became a priest, and built a chapel in honor of the Trinity that by 1354 became a monastic center (the TROITSKAYA LAURA) at the request of the patriarch of Constantinople. Austere with himself, Sergius showed great humanity toward others, and in humility refused the Patriarchate of Moscow (1378).

His reputation of sanctity based on the miracles and visions with which he was credited caused his monastery of the Trinity to become a center of religious attraction for all Russians. He went on missions of peace to the various Russian princes with the hope of consolidating Russian hegemony under the principality of Moscow against the ravages of the Tatars. On his advice Prince Dimitri resolved to repel the attack of the Mongols in 1380. While Sergius left no literary heritage, his disciples founded many monasteries and spread his teaching in such fashion that his monastery of the Trinity became a principal influence in Russian spirituality.

Feast: Sept. 25.

Bibliography: Life by EPIPHANIUS THE WISE in *Monuments de l'ancienne littérature* 58 (St. Petersburg 1885). N. ZERNOV, *Saint Sergius, Builder of Russia* (Society for Promoting Christian Knowledge; London 1939). P. KOVALEVSKY, *Saint Serge et la spiritualité russe* (Paris 1958). L. MÜLLER, *Die Religion in Geschichte und Gegenwart*, 7 v. (3d ed. Tübingen 1957–65) 5:1712–13. S. STASIEWSKI, *Lexikon für Theologie und Kirche*, ed. J. HOFER and K. RAHNER, 10 v. (2d, new ed. Freiburg 1957–65) 9:689. I. KOLOGRIWOF, *Das andere Russland* (Munich 1958) 93–123. I. SMOLITSCH, *Russisches Mönchtum* (Würzburg 1953). E. BENZ, *Russische Heiligenlegenden* (Zurich 1953) 292–362.

[P. ROCHE]

SERGIUS OF RESAINA

Sixth-century Syrian physician and translator; d. Constantinople, 536. A Christian, in early life probably a Monophysite, Sergius may well be the grammarian Sergius with whom SEVERUS OF ANTIOCH exchanged letters between 515 and 520. He studied in Alexandria, became a physician, and later may have become a monk and priest. Sergius is one of the fathers of Syriac literature. Besides composing several short philosophical treatises of his own in Syriac, he translated more than 20 Greek philosophical, medical, and horticultural works into Syriac; he also translated the treatises of PSEUDO-DIONYSIUS the Areopagite (for the first time) and perhaps, too, the *Gnostic Centuries* of the Origenist EVAGRIUS PONTICUS, with which he was familiar. About 535 he went to Antioch, where he so impressed the patriarch Ephraem that Ephraem sent him to Rome as legate to ask the support of Pope Agapetus against the rising tide of Monophysitism in Constantinople. Sergius accompanied Agapetus on his visit to Constantinople in 536, and died soon after.

Bibliography: A. BAUMSTARK, *Lucubrationes Syro-graecae* (Leipzig 1894) 358–384, 405–470; *Geschichte der syrischen Literatur* (Bonn 1922) 167–169. K. GEORR, ed., *Les Catégories d'Aristote dans leurs versions syro-arabes* (Beirut 1948) 17–23. P. SHERWOOD, *Lexikon für Theologie und Kirche,* ed. J. HOFER and K. RAHNER, 10 v. (2d, new ed. Freiburg 1957–65) 9:687–688; "Sergius of Reshaina and the Syriac Versions of the Pseudo-Denis," *Sacris erudiri* 4 (1952) 174–184; *L'Orient syrien* 5 (1960) 433–437. A. GUILLAUMONT, *Les "Kephalaia gnostica" d'Evagre le Pontique* (Paris 1963) 222–227. I. HAUSHERR, *Orientalia Christiana periodica* 2 (1936) 488. J. M. HORNUS, *Revue d'histoire et die philosophie religieuses* 41 (1961) 35–38.

[D. B. EVANS]

SERIPANDO, GIROLAMO

Theologian and cardinal legate at the Council of TRENT; b. probably at Naples, Oct. 6, 1492; d. Trent, March 17, 1563. Seripando entered the Neopolitan Convent of San Giovanni a Carbonara of the Hermits of St. Augustine in 1507, was named secretary of the order in 1514 by the superior general, and began in 1517 to serve as rector of the order's house of studies at Bologna. In 1524 he returned to Naples as vicar of the Congregation of San Giovanni a Carbonara. In 1530, stimulated by the members of the *Academia Pontaniana,* he composed his 109 *Quaestiones,* in which he espoused a Christian Platonism with Thomistic modifications. In 1538 he was named vicar-general of his order upon the death of the general, G. A. Aprutino; and the following year, upon the request of Paul III, he was elected general during the general chapter held at Naples. During his visitation of the order's houses in Italy, France, Spain, and Portugal, he fought the Lutheranism that had penetrated his order and worked for the reform of his religious. Since 1530 Seripando had been drawn into the quarrel over Italian evangelism; he rejected the spiritualism of Juan Valdés, while his own spirituality and his teaching on justification took on a Biblical-Augustinian character.

At the Council of Trent, Seripando tried to prevent tradition from being put on the same level as Holy Scripture and worked for the study of biblical languages. His ideas about concupiscence, the meaning of faith, and the justice of Christ were not incorporated into the decrees on original sin and justification, although as counselor of the legate, Cardinal M. Cervini, he had had a very influential part in the formulation of those decrees. After the transfer of the Council of Trent to Bologna, he continued to participate in the deliberations, but because of a stroke (1551), he was forced to resign as general of the Augustinians.

Seripando subsequently regained his health. In 1553, after the death of the viceroy, Pedro de Toledo, he accepted the city of Naples's commission to negotiate with the emperor in Brussels for a moderation of certain of the dead viceroy's measures. Elected archbishop of Salerno on March 30, 1554, Seripando convoked a diocesan synod the same year and conducted a visitation of the entire diocese between 1556 and 1558. He tried also to fulfill the Tridentine ideal of a bishop as preacher and pastor. The death of Marcellus II prevented Seripando from collaborating in that pope's plan of Church reform, for Paul IV deprived him of influence. However, Pius IV made him a cardinal on Feb. 26, 1561 and entrusted him with a revision of Paul IV's *Index.*

Having been named legate to the Council of Trent by Pius IV, Seripando directed chiefly the work on the dogmatic decrees during the council's third period. In the spring of 1562, however, he fell into disgrace in Rome, and his recall was considered because of his alleged support of the thesis that a bishop's obligation to reside in his own diocese is of divine law. During the conciliar crisis of the winter of 1562 and 1563, he tried to mediate the conflict between the *Zelanti,* on the one hand, and the French and Spanish party, on the other; he failed, however, because of Cardinal L. Simonetta. Though Seripando died at the height of the crisis, he went down in history as one of the most influential of the council Fathers.

The voluminous collection of Seripando's manuscripts was transferred from the library of the Convent of San Giovanni di Carbonara to the Biblioteca Nazionale in Naples. During his lifetime only his *Oratio in funere Caroli V* was printed (Naples 1559), but after his death many of his works appeared in print: *Commentarius in epist. Pauli ad Galatas* (Antwerp 1567), bound together with a commentary on Romans (Naples 1601); *Doctrina orandi sive expositio orationis Dominicae* (Louvain 1661); *Prediche sopra il simbolo degli apostoli* (Venice 1567); *Diarium de vita sua 1513–62* [ed. D. Guttiérrez, *Analecta Augustiniana* 26 (1963): 5–193]; *Commentarii in Concilium Tridentinum* (*Concilium Tridentinum,* 13 v. [Freiburg 1901–38] 2:397–488); and numerous treatises (*ibid.* 12:483–496, 517–521, 549–553, 613–636, 824–849).

Bibliography: H. JEDIN, *Papal Legate at the Council of Trent: Cardinal Seripando,* tr. F. C. ECKHOFF (St. Louis 1947); "Seelenleitung und Vollkommenheitsstreben bei Kardinal Seripando," *Sanctus Augustinus, vitae spiritualis magister,* 2 v. (Rome 1959) 2:389–410. E. STAKEMEIER, *Der Kampf um Augustin auf dem Tridentinum* (Paderborn 1937). A. BALDUCCI, *Girolamo Seripando ar-*

civescovo di Salerno (Cava 1963). A. FORSTER, *Gesetz und Evangelium bei Seripando* (Paderborn 1964). F. CESAREA, *A Shepherd in Their Midst: The Episcopacy of Girolamo Seripando* (Villanova 1999); ''The Reform of the Diocese of Salerno during the Episcopacy of Girolamo Seripando,'' *Analecta Augustiniana* 61 (1998): 97–124.

[H. D. JEDIN]

SERMISY, CLAUDE DE

Celebrated Renaissance polyphonist, often called Claudin; b. *c.* 1490; d. Paris, 1562. A cleric (1508) and later canon at Sainte Chapelle (1533–62) and Notre Dame de la Ronde, Rouen (to 1524), he sang in the French royal chapel before 1515, and became its *sous maître* in 1532 under Cardinal François de Tournon and its director before 1554. During the Spanish occupation he lent his Paris house to refugee canons from Saint Quentin for deliberations (1559). His admirers included the Duke of Ferrara, recipient of his motet *Esto mihi*, and Certon, who composed a *déploration* for him. He composed 13 Masses, some 80 motets, Lamentations, a Passion, and about 160 chansons, frequently transcribed or quoted in *fricassées*. The principal poet for his texts was Clément Marot. His sacred works portray their texts reverently, in spite of a trace of chanson patterns (e.g. his brief and simple polyphonic Masses). In the realm of the predominantly homorhythmic lyrical chanson, he is unexcelled.

Bibliography: G. G. ALLAIRE, *The Masses of Claudin de Sermisy* (Doctoral diss. microfilm; Boston U. 1960). I. A. CAZEAUX, *The Secular Music of Claudin de Sermisy*, 2 v. (Doctoral diss. microfilm; Columbia U. 1961). J. HAAR, ed., *Chanson and Madrigal, 1480–1530* (Cambridge, Mass. 1964). G. REESE, *Music in the Renaissance* (rev. ed. New York 1959). *Histoire de la musique*, ed. ROLAND-MANUEL (Paris 1960–63) v.1. C. STAINER and M. L. PEREYRA, *Grove's Dictionary of Music and Musicians* ed. E. BLOM, 9 v. (5th ed. London 1954) 7:709–710. G. G. ALLAIRE, ''The Masses of Claudin de Sermisy'' (Ph.D. diss. Boston University, 1960). J.-P. OUVRARD, ''Du narratif dans la polyphonie au 16th siècle, *Martin menoit son pourceau au marché*: Clément Marot, Clément Janequin, Claudin de Sermisy,'' *Analyse Musicale* 9 (1987), 11–16. D. M. RANDEL, ed., *The Harvard Biographical Dictionary of Music* 826 (Cambridge, Massachusetts 1996). N. SLONIMSKY, ed., *Baker's Biographical Dictionary of Musicians*, Eighth Edition 1686 (New York 1992). R. STEVENSON, ''Claudin de Sermisy'' in *The New Grove Dictionary of Music and Musicians*, vol. 17, ed. S. SADIE (New York 1980) 171–177.

[I. A. CAZEAUX]

SERMON

In Catholic usage, a term generally applied to any discourse or address given in connection with an ecclesiastical function. Thus, it is taken to include the homily, a commentary on Sacred Scripture; instruction, given from the pulpit, on matters of faith, morals, liturgical practice, etc.; the panegyric, a talk, generally given on a great feast, on the virtues of a saint; the eulogy, a funeral speech extolling the life and accomplishments of a dead person; the ''occasional'' sermon, an address to honor a special event, such as the dedication of a Church, or the consecration of a bishop. In popular usage, it is often used interchangeably with the term HOMILY.

For further discussion and bibliography, see under: HOMILY.

[P. MULHERN]

SERPENT (AS SYMBOL)

This article considers the symbolism behind the snake that seduced Eve to eat of the forbidden fruit of the TREE OF KNOWLEDGE in the Garden of EDEN.

The Serpent's Actions and Fate. The serpent is introduced at the very opening of Genesis ch. 3, where it is given the epithet in Hebrew of *'ārûm,* variously translated as ''crafty,'' ''sly,'' ''wily,'' ''cunning,'' etc., with an obvious reference back to Gn 2.25, where man and woman live in perfect bliss and are unashamed of being naked (*'ărummîm*). The epithet is also a foreshadowing of Gn 3.7, where the term *'êrûmmîm* describes the naked man and woman, now ashamed of their condition. The serpent is described as a creature (3.1), but the slyest of all the ''wild beasts'' (H. Orlinsky) that God had made. The serpent (who speaks!) may possibly be described as a ''had been'' (pluperfect tense) in the Hebrew verb (3.1), but it is nonetheless shrewd enough to strike up a subversive conversation with the woman rather than with the man; and in the lively narrative style of the YAHWIST, it takes but a moment for the serpent to make the woman see everything in a new light. Soon she has transgressed the very precept that she had explained in an excessively stringent manner to the serpent. The narrator does not allow the serpent to escape when its destructive work is complete. Rather it stays during the arrival of Yahweh and the interrogation scene, and it hears the woman state that ''the serpent deceived me'' (3.14–15).

The sentence pronounced over the serpent is highly significant, reflecting a religious and moral outlook of the greatest importance. Against E. A. Speiser, who, despite the parallel with 3.17, translated *'ārûr* as merely ''banned,'' the serpent is generally understood as being cursed by God and in a way that no other wild animal (literally, beast of the field) is cursed. It must crawl on its belly (with the possible assumption, supported by ancient illustrations, that it once stood erect); it must eat dirt (or dust)—a thing associated with its horizontal and slithering mode of locomotion; it and its ''seed'' (usually indicating progeny, but possibly having the nuance here of ''genus'') are to be at perpetual strife with woman(kind), and while it snaps at her heel, she aims at crushing its head (though the precise sense of the same verb that is translated in one case as ''striking'' and in the other as ''crushing'' is not certain). The serpent is, then, completely humiliated in 3.14, and this may aid in seeing in 3.15 more than a mere struggle to the finish without any references to victory. Although such scholars as S. R. Driver and Speiser see nothing eschatological in this conflict, most Catholic authors (and some of them perhaps excessively) see some kind of victory in the future over the serpent.

Question of the Serpent's Reality. The question of the nature of the serpent and its identity is one of considerable importance. Bound up with this is the equally important question of why it should be a serpent that leads the attack on man and woman. It may be well here to note that later Jewish theology, reflected in Wis 2.24 and the NT (especially in Jn 8.44; Rv 12.9), easily makes the identification of the serpent with the DEVIL or SATAN, and this matter was taken up with further precision by the PONTIFICAL BIBLICAL COMMISSION, which declared (June 30, 1909) that there is question in Genesis of the transgression of a divine precept *diabolo sub serpentis specie suasore* (the devil acting as persuader under the form of a serpent). The decree, however, led to further discussion.

Was the serpent merely a symbol, not real? This question, which apparently betrays a historicizing attitude toward the Yahwist narrative that really spoils much of its unique literary character and fails to grasp the methodology of this most clever writer, was answered more or less affirmatively by so great a scholar as M. J. Lagrange and more or less negatively by A. Bea (though one is hardly justified, especially in the latter case, in saying that this remained the unaltered viewpoint of either author). The view that the serpent is a symbol, i.e., not really a serpent, is the common present-day outlook, but it is usually presented in a way that reflects the whole literary workmanship and genius of the Yahwist. The Yahwist, working in these chapters on matters that are highly illusive and out of all normal historical reach, had little choice but to ''theologize'' along lines that were both in keeping with his genius and, at the same time, suited to a subject so remote from, and yet so close to, him and us. Hence, there is a heavy and most effective use of symbolism: garden, trees, rivers, rib, and a host of others, all of them clearer in the 10th and 9th centuries B.C. than to the present-day reading audience, whether largely or in no wise familiar with the background of those times. The more that is known of the Yahwist, however, and the more the ancient Near Eastern background of Genesis ch. 2–3 is discovered, so much the more does it become apparent that the symbolism of these chapters is loaded with reality. It is not empty symbolism or mere symbolism, but highly effective symbolism.

Pope John Paul II delivers a sermon in Los Angeles, California, 1987. (©Jacques M. Chenet/CORBIS)

Thus one may refer to the serpent as real, but of a special nature. The narrative entails much more than an individual serpent, miraculously endowed with speech, with razor-sharp wit, and with ability to beguile woman both quickly and completely. Behind the serpent lies a whole ideology about serpents and their significance and about man and woman and what has made them as they are today.

Mythological Monster. The notion, therefore, that the serpent was a mythological monster has been invoked; in Is 27.1 reference is made to LEVIATHAN, the fleeting serpent and the twisting serpent, which is mentioned in strikingly similar language in the Ugaritic literature (*see* UGARIT) as Lōtān (see C. H. Gordon, *Ugaritic Manual* [Rome 1955] 2.011); and in both Am 9.3 and Jb 26.13 mention is made of a serpent that presumably dwells in the sea. It may be noted that in Rv 12.9 the serpent is equated with a dragon. Although this equation need not be conclusive and it may be presumed that there

Hezekiah ordering destruction of pagan idols, 17th century, Judah. (©Historical Picture Archive/CORBIS)

were no sea serpents in the Garden of Eden, there could nonetheless be a lurking and partial reference to such a monster in the Yahwist's imagery; so, McKenzie, 563–564. The argument that Lōtān was hostile to man from the beginning but that the serpent in Paradise was at first friendly is entirely gratuitous in the second part. Everything points precisely to his hostility, though, as the narrative runs, it is neither suspected by the woman nor manifested by the serpent as hostility.

Natural Snake Regarded as Having Magical Powers. The notion of the serpent as having magical powers may already be seen in description of the creature in Gn 3.1 as cunning or crafty. Then, too, in the preliminaries to the Exodus from Egypt there is a description of how both Moses and the Egyptian court magicians changed their wands into serpents and again back into wands (Ex 7.8–12). Even the standard Hebrew word for serpent, *nāḥāš,* is used, whether by authentic etymological connection or not, as a verb form *niḥēš* meaning both to practice divination and to seek an omen. The link may be only through folk etymology, but the identity of the nominal and the verbal roots cannot be denied. The phrase in Mt 10.1.6, ''as shrewd as serpents,'' also conveys a notion that must have remained prevalent into the time of Christ. The words of Prv 30.19, though less telling, at least point to the mysterious aspect of the serpent. If the serpent symbolizes magic to some degree, its humiliating sentence in Gn 3.14–15 would, at the same time, be the condemnation of and polemic against magical practices only too prevalent in Israelite history (Ex 22.18; Lv 19.31; 20.6, 27; Dt 18.10–14; 1 Sm 28.3; 2 Kgs 17.17; 21.6; 23.24; Is 8.19; Ez 13.17–23). (*See* MAGIC [IN THE BIBLE].) Such a symbolism attached to the serpent would be in keeping with the therapeutic powers attributed to the bronze serpent (still venerated during Hezekiah's reign: 2 Kgs 18.4) in Nm 21.8–9, but explained as symbolizing God's healing powers in Wis 16.6–8 and as typifying Christ's salvation of mankind through His being raised up on the cross in Jn 3.14–15. One may note in this, as far as the serpent of Genesis ch. 3 is concerned, a probable polyvalent symbolism: magic power, illicit acquisition of knowledge, healing, and hence life itself.

Fertility Symbol. In keeping with this same rich background of the serpent's imagery in the ancient Near East, a number of scholars have stressed the notion of fertility. This is not merely because the serpent shows some affinity to fertility by shedding its skin, thus taking on new life, but also because there is some connection with the sexually oriented fertility rites as practiced, among other places, in Canaan. There is, of course, a danger of making out of Genesis ch. 2–3 little more than a mysterious sex story and passing over other factors of the highest importance. But there is the danger also of missing what was obviously a grave concern of the guardians of pure Yahwism while the Israelites were gradually settling down in Canaan, where the fertility cults were widely practiced. One may note that, at least indirectly, the serpent led the woman toward motherhood in tempting her, for the fruit of the tree of knowledge is obviously linked to an awakening of sexual desire and to the explicit mention of carnal knowledge in Gn 4.1, an act that may have taken place before the expulsion from the garden (as the story goes), since the verb may well be translated as: ''Now the man had known Eve, his wife.'' It is of interest, too, that the Talmud, Philo Judaeus, and Clement of Alexandria all identified the serpent with concupiscence or evil thoughts. Their reasons for this were probably drawn from their own experience with mankind as well as from the texts of the Bible. In an age of archeology and of the discovery of ancient texts, however, there are added reasons for seeing in the serpent, in addition to other things, a symbol of fertility and hence of sex.

Symbol of Life. Closely bound up with these notions is the concept of the serpent as the symbol of life. It should be stressed that these notions often overlap, for the Semites were inclined to universalize, to see things as a whole, rather than to departmentalize or neatly categorize. One may assume from figurines found at such famous Canaanite sites as Megiddo, Thaanack (Taanach), Tell Beit Mirsim, and Gezer, not only that the reproductive function of the human female was greatly stressed, but also that the serpent served either as a phallic symbol (its position with relation to the figurines can hardly be regarded as accidental) or as a symbol of fertility and life. The evidence amassed by Canon Joseph Coppens of Louvain in this regard is highly indicative, although some outstanding Catholic scholars have not been influenced by it; see R. de Vaux; H. Renckens, *Israel's Concept of the Beginning,* tr. C. Napier (New York 1964) 272–282. Nevertheless, even apart from extrabiblical sources, Gn 3.7, 16 and the so-called sexual milieu of the account (placed against the Yahwist's contemporary background) have seemed sufficient to other leading scholars for the admission of an inclusively sexual interpretation of the serpent. The figures in S. H. Langdon's *Semitic Mythology* are extremely interesting in this regard, as are those in J. B. Pritchard, *The Ancient Near East in Pictures Relating to the Old Testament* (Princeton 1954), No. 469–474, 480, and others (*see* SERPENT). In Egypt the serpent called *'nḫ* is pictured with the plant of life in its mouth, thus bringing out the symbolism of both life and wisdom (mouth).

Eve handing Adam the apple while serpent watches. (Popperfoto/Archive Photos)

From what has been said it may be seen that to speak of a ''real serpent'' or to confine one's analysis of the serpent to one phase of symbolism is to fail to exhaust the rich background that such an image plays in the Yahwist's account, which is so cleverly organized and has so many fine nuances of thought. Whatever line of interpretation is followed, one may say, judging from the sacred text and from these few representative artifacts and texts

Bl. Junípero Serra.

from the ancient Near East, that the Yahwist had ample reason to present the tempter under the guise of a serpent.

Bibliography: *Encyclopedic Dictionary of the Bible,* tr. and adap. by L. HARTMAN (New York 1963), from A. VAN DEN BORN, *Bijbels Woordenboek* 2174–79. O. BIEHN et al., *Lexikon für Theologie und Kirche,* ed. J. HOFER and K. RAHNER, 10 v. (2d, new ed. Freiburg 1957–65) 9:408–409. L. F. HARTMAN, "Sin in Paradise," *Catholic Biblical Quarterly* 20 (1958) 26–40, esp. 39–40. J. COPPENS, *La Connaissance du bien et du mal et le péché du Paradis* (Louvain 1948), and the important though partially dissenting review of R. DE VAUX, *Revue biblique* 56 (1949) 300–308. J. L. MCKENZIE, "The Literary Characteristics of Genesis 2–3," *Theological Studies* 15 (1954) 541–572, esp. 563–572. E. A. SPEISER, *Genesis* (Garden City, N.Y. 1964) 21–28.

[I. HUNT]

SERRA, JUNÍPERO, BL.

Founder of Franciscan missions of California; b. Petra de Mallorca, Spain, Nov. 24, 1713; d. Carmel, Calif., Aug. 28, 1784; beatified Sept. 25, 1988, by Pope John Paul II. His parents, Antonio Nadal and Margarita Rosa (Ferrer) Serra, were farmers. José Miguel, as he was baptized, joined the Franciscan Order in Palma de Mallorca, Sept. 14, 1730, taking the name Junípero. Even before his ordination in 1738, he was assigned to teach philosophy in his province. Later he received his doctorate in theology from Lullian University, Palma, and in 1743 was appointed to the Duns Scotus chair of philosophy there. In 1749 he sailed for Mexico to enter the Apostolic College of San Fernando, Mexico City. En route he preached his first American mission at San Juan, Puerto Rico. From 1750 to 1758, he worked successfully in the missions of the Sierra Gorda, built the central mission of Santiago de Jalpan, supervised the mission district for three years as president, and learned the Otomí language. In 1752 he was appointed commissary of the Holy Office of the Inquisition. After returning to Mexico City in 1758, Serra was employed for the next nine years in administrative offices at the Apostolic College and as a missionary in the dioceses of Mexico, Puebla, Oaxaca, Valladolid, and Guadalajara.

In 1767, when the Spanish government exiled the Jesuits, Serra was designated *presidente* (administrator) of the Baja California missions, with headquarters at Loreto. When the conquest of Alta California was undertaken by Spain in 1769, Serra accompanied the military expedition under Don Gaspas de Portolá to San Diego where he founded his first mission in the territory on July 16. In June 1770 he established his permanent headquarters at San Carlos Mission at Monterey-Carmel. Under his administration nine missions were founded in Alta California where Junípero served as *presidente* until his death. These missions were San Diego, San Carlos Borromeo (1770), San Antonio (1771), San Gabriel (1771), San Luis Obispo (1772), San Francisco (1776), San Juan Capistrano (1776), Santa Clara (1777), and San Buenaventura (1782).

In his California foundations, Serra insisted on the full activation of the Spanish mission system, which had been in use for several centuries. Frequent conflicts with the military and civil authorities over their treatment of Native Americans prompted him, in 1773, to present a *Representación* of 32 points for the better conduct of mission affairs to Viceroy Bucareli in Mexico City. Serra visited all the missions a number of times, administering the sacrament of confirmation after 1778. Contrary to legend, he did not travel exclusively by foot. Though he walked thousands of miles during his misson career, he did, at times, travel by packet boat, carriage, or mule, at times accompanied by a military guard or a page.

The writings of Serra, confined almost exclusively to mission affairs, varied from factual reports to commentary that afford insight into his character. Though fundamentally robust, he suffered from an ulcerated leg and foot during his years in Mexico and California. His apostolate was characterized by a devotion to the natives that resulted in over 6,000 baptisms and 5,000 confirmations, and in a marked improvement in their standards of living. Under his administration, agriculture and domestic animals, as well as European trades, were introduced to the indigenous peoples of California.

After his death, Junípero Serra was buried with military and naval honors in the sanctuary of San Carlos Mission, Carmel; his remains were identified in 1943. Since the middle of the 19th century, the literature on Serra has reached great proportions in both Europe and America. Many monuments and memorials have been erected in his honor. The most significant distinction came in 1931 when his statue was placed in the Statuary Hall in the Capitol at Washington, D.C. His cause was opened in 1934 at the request of the bishop of Monterey-Fresno and of the Franciscan provincial of the Province of St. Barbara.

Feast: July 1.

Bibliography: F. WEBER, *A Bicentennial Compendium of Maynard J. Geiger's: The Life and Times of Fr. Junipero Serra* (Santa Barbara 1988). B. FONT OBRADOR, *Fr. Junipero Serra: Mallorca, Mexico, Sierra Gorda, Californias* (Palma 1992). A. XAVIER, *Junipero Serra* (Barcelona 1986). M. MORGADO, *Junipero Serra's Legacy* (Mount Carmel 1987), bibliography. M. GEIGER, *Franciscan Missionaries in Hispanic California 1769–1848: A Biographical Dictionary* (San Marino 1969), 239–45.

[M. GEIGER/T. RUSCIN/F. WEBER]

SERRA INTERNATIONAL

An association of local Serra clubs to foster vocations to the priesthood and religious life. The Serra movement, named after the Spanish Franciscan Junípero SERRA, Apostle of California, began in Seattle, WA, in 1935 and soon gained episcopal approval. On July 2, 1938, five Serra clubs federated and the name Serra International became official. The Serra movement spread rapidly and remained dedicated to the achievement of a better understanding of the nature and the mission of the consecrated priesthood, and the promotion of religious vocations.

At the beginning of the 21st century, there were over 13,000 Serrans in 318 Serra Clubs in 13 regions within the United States. Worldwide, there were about 768 Serra Clubs in 35 countries in the Americas, Europe, Africa and Asia. Individual clubs sponsor programs promoting vocations to the priesthood and religious life, as well as assist local bishops in support of seminary programs. In the U.S., the association publishes a quarterly review, the *Serran*, and maintains its headquarters at Chicago, IL.

[J. J. KORTENDICK/EDS.]

SERTILLANGES, ANTONIN GILBERT

Dominican preacher, apologist, and philosopher; b. Clermont-Ferrand, France, Nov. 16, 1863; d. Sallanches (Haute-Savoy), July 26, 1948. In 1883 Sertillanges entered the order (then exiled from France) in Belmont, Spain, taking the name of Dalmatius. He was ordained in 1888 and in 1890 was assigned to teach theology in Corbara, Corsica. Named secretary of the *Revue Thomiste* in Paris (1890), he taught moral theology at the Catholic Institute from 1900 to 1920. At the same time he gave an important series of conferences that was uninterrupted by the expulsion of religious in 1903. From then on he published books and articles that numbered more than 700 by the time of his death. His principal theological works include *La preuve de l'existence de Dieu et l'éternité du monde* (Fribourg 1898), *Les sources de la croyance en Dieu* (Paris 1903), *S. Thomas d'Aquin* (2 v. Paris 1910), *La philosophie morale de S. Thomas d'Aquin* (Paris 1916), and *L'idée de création et ses retentissements en philosophie* (Paris 1945). In religious sociology he wrote *Le patriotisme et la vie sociale* (Paris 1903), *La politique chrétienne* (Paris 1904), *Socialisme et christianisme* (Paris 1905), and *La famille et l'etat dans l'éducation* (Paris 1907). In Christian aesthetics his works include *Un pélerinage artistique à Florence* (Paris 1895), *Art et apologétique* (Paris 1909), and *Prière et musique* (Paris 1930). One of the most famous and inspirational of all Sertillanges's works, however, was *La vie intellectuelle* (Paris 1921).

World War I increased his preaching activity; the three series of *La vie héroïque* (Paris 1914–18) contain the most important sermons of this period. The political tenor of one sermon in 1917 led to his suspension from the ministry after 1922 and to his successive exiles in Jerusalem in 1923, in Rijckholt (Holland) in 1924, and in Saulchoir (Belgium) from 1928 to 1939, when he was permitted to return to France.

Although he had already published such works as *Jesus* (Paris 1897), moral suffering intensified his output of spiritual books: *Ce que Jésus voyait du haut de la Croix* (Paris 1924); *L'eglise* (2 v. Paris 1926); *Les plus belles pages de S. Thomas* (Paris 1929); and the four volumes *Recueillements, Affinités, Devoirs,* and *Spiritualité* (Paris 1935–38). His open-mindedness and respect for the opinions of others made him an outstanding apologist. This is evident more particularly in *Le catéchisme des incroyants* (Paris 1930) and in *Dieu ou rien* (2 v. Paris 1933). He was elected as a philosopher to the Academy of Moral and Political Sciences in 1918. He made a close study of Henri BERGSON, with whom he was intimately associated, in *Avec Henri Bergson* (Paris 1941); *Henri Bergson et le catholicisme* (Paris 1941); and *Lumière et périls du bergsonisme* (Paris 1943). He studied also Claude Bernard in *La philosophie de Claude Bernard* (Paris 1944), and wrote the synthesis *Le christianisme et la philosophie* (2 v. Paris 1939–41) and *La philosophie des lois* (Paris 1946). His last work, interrupted by his death, was *Le problème du mal* (2 v. Paris 1948).

Bibliography: M. F. MOOS, *Le père sertillanges: maître de vie spirituelle* (Brussels 1958); *Cahiers S. Dominique* 44 (1964) 172–177. The introductions of H. LELONG to A. D. SERTILLANGES, *De la mort* (*Le jas du Revest-Saint Martin;* 1963) 13–56; *De la vie* (*ibid.;* 1964) 13–50.

[M. H. VICAIRE]

SERVANTS OF MARY

This title embraces various congregations of sisters who are members of the Servite Third Order (OSM) and who were known traditionally also as *Mantellate* by reason of the long veil worn by some of these religious (*see* SERVITES). According to their tradition, they were founded in Florence, Italy, in the 13th century by (St.) Juliana FALCONIERI. Juliana received the habit in 1284 from (St.) PHILIP BENIZI, Servite prior general, who also formulated a rule of life for her and the first convent she established in 1287. Detained by the care of her aged mother, Juliana did not live with the community she had founded until after the death of her mother, Ricordata, in 1306. Juliana then entered the convent and was at once elected prioress. One of her first cares was to establish the sisters as members of the Servite Third Order Regular, for although they lived a communal life and wore a monastic habit, they were until then secular tertiaries. Juliana's uncle, Alexis Falconieri, one of the Seven Founders of the Servite Order, helped her effect this transformation.

Documentation concerning the Servite Sisters prior to the approval of the third order rule by Martin V in 1424 is practically nonexistent. Innocent VII had already given this same rule, with slight modifications, to Dominican tertiaries in 1405. New convents of Servite Sisters were founded or aggregated to the order as a result of the work of the Servite Congregation of the Primitive Observance that came into existence early in the 15th century. Very little, however, is known of these sisters, and it is often difficult to distinguish the convents of the sisters of the third order from the monasteries of the nuns of the second order.

By mid-20th century there were 24 congregations and four independent convents of Servite Sisters distributed throughout the world. Of these, 11 were pontifical institutes and 13 were diocesan institutes. Convents were located in Italy, Austria, Germany, Hungary, France, Belgium, Spain, England, Albania, Canada, the U.S., Mexico, and Brazil. Missionary work was carried on in India, Burma, the Republic of South Africa, Swaziland, Chile, and Brazil.

Four congregations of Servite Sisters are represented in the U.S., with motherhouses in Omaha, NE (Official Catholic Directory #3580); Ladysmith, WI (Official Catholic Directory #3590); Plainfield, OR (Official Catholic Directory #3572); and Blue Island, IL (Official Catholic Directory #3570) (*see* MANTELLATE SISTERS).

The sisters of the Omaha motherhouse (Official Catholic Directory #3580) constitute an American province that pertains to the Franco-Anglo-American Servite branch with headquarters in Begbroke, Oxford, England. The first permanent foundation of this province was made by Mother Mary Gertrude in 1893 at Mt. Vernon, IN. The sisters of the Ladysmith congregation (Official Catholic Directory #3590) are a diocesan institute. They were founded in 1912 through the joint efforts of John Sheahan, a Servite priest, and Mother Mary Alphonse, first prioress general. The work of the sisters is in education, healthcare, parish ministry, social outreach and care of the aged and infirm.

[J. M. RYSKA/EDS.]

SERVANTS OF MARY, SISTERS

(SM, Official Catholic Directory #3600); also known as the Handmaids of Mary, or Ministers to the Sick (*Siervas de María, ministras de enfermos*), a religious congregation founded in 1851 in Madrid by (St.) María Soledad TORRES ACOSTA primarily to care for the sick in hospitals and private homes. In its early years the congregation nearly foundered because of the large percentage of defections, the state's unwillingness to recognize the rule composed by the foundress, and the serious slanders against María Soledad, which resulted in her removal as superior general. In 1867 the Holy See issued a *decretum laudis* and gave temporary approval to the constitutions. The first foundation in the U.S. was in New Orleans (1914). The U.S. provincialate is in Kansas City, KS. The generalate is in Rome.

Bibliography: J. A. ZUGASTI, *La madre María Soledad Torres Acosta y el Instituto de las Siervas de María*, 2 v. (Madrid 1916).

[J. F. BRODERICK/EDS.]

SERVANTS OF OUR LADY QUEEN OF THE CLERGY

(SRC, Official Catholic Directory #3650); a diocesan congregation of sisters whose purpose is to assist the clergy by performing domestic work. The congregation was founded on Dec. 8, 1929, at Salmon Lake, Matapédia County, Canada, by the Rev. Alexandre Bouillon (1873–1943) and Mother Mary of St. Joseph of the Eucharist. With the approval of Rome, granted on Jan. 25, 1936, the community was canonically established by George Courchesne, bishop (later archbishop) of Rimouski. The sisters perform kitchen and domestic services and care for sacristies in seminaries and clerical residences. They came to the U.S. in 1936. The motherhouse is in Quebec, Canada.

[M. S. T. ROY/EDS.]

SERVANTS OF THE PARACLETE

(Official Catholic Directory #1230, S.P.); a pontifical congregation of men ministering to priests and religious brothers; founded, Jemez Springs, N. Mex., 1947 by Rev. Gerald Michael Cushing Fitzgerald. The congregation was granted papal approbation on the feast of the Pentecost, June 1, 1952, with Rev. Fitzgerald named the first Servant General. Its original therapeutic program, "Via Coeli," in Jemez Springs, gained a reputation for its ministry to priests troubled by addictions and other problems, being one of the first to offer specialized treatment for the clergy. Dioceses and religious orders from across the country sent priests to the center located at Jemez Springs for treatment of addictions and problems of various kinds, including pedophilia. A number of priests were rehabilitated and returned to the active ministry in their home dioceses; some stayed to work in New Mexico; and some relapsed. It was this last group that created serious problems for the congregation, the archdiocese and the archbishops of Santa Fe. Subsequently, the Servants of the Paraclete closed the therapeutic program at Jemez Springs, concentrating instead on retreats and spiritual renewal. The congregation continues to offer holistic therapeutic programs for priests and religious in Jemez Springs, New Mexico; St. Louis and Dittmer in Missouri; and Stroud, England. A retreat ministry is also offered at Fitzgerald Center in Jemez Springs. The U.K. foundation of the congregation (Our Lady of Victory) was established, 1959, in Brownshill, Stroud, Gloucestershire. The generalate is in Jemez Springs, N. Mex.

[EDS.]

SERVETUS, MICHAEL

Anti-Trinitarian theologian, physician; b. Villanueva, Spain, probably 1511; d. Geneva, October 27, 1553. Servetus was born of a pious family; he studied law at Toulouse. He early developed radical theological ideas that stemmed from a concern for the conversion of Moors and Jews, which had been made difficult by the orthodox doctrine of the Trinity. Servetus decided that parts of that doctrine were erroneous, particularly the dogma of the eternality of the Son. He developed this argument in books, published in 1531 and 1532, which were sharply criticized by orthodox theologians. Their attacks led him to adopt a disguise and begin a second career as a physician and student of science. In this role he was among the first to describe the pulmonary transit of the blood; he also worked on geography and astrology. Servetus returned to the study of theology, however, not only repeating his earlier attacks on the definition of the Trinity, but also rejecting infant Baptism and advancing an extreme view of the immanence of Christ. Publication of these views in 1552 led to his arrest and condemnation as a heretic by an inquisitorial court in Vienne, France. He escaped but was arrested and condemned again, at John Calvin's insistence, by a secular Protestant court in Geneva. He was then burned. His execution provoked an extended controversy over the toleration of religious dissent.

Michael Servetus.

Bibliography: R. H. BAINTON, *Hunted Heretic: The Life and Death of Michael Servetus* (Boston 1953). E. M. WILBUR, *A History of Unitarianism,* 2 v. (Cambridge, Mass. 1945–52); *Bibliography of the Pioneers of the Socinian-Unitarian Movement . . .* (Rome 1950). B. BECKER, ed., *Autour de Michel Servet et de Sébastien Cas-*

Basilica of Our Lady of Sorrows, American motherhouse of the Servite order, Chicago, Illinois.

tellion: Recueil (Haarlem 1953). G. H. WILLIAMS, *The Radical Reformation* (Philadelphia 1962). H. BORNKAMM, *Die Religion in Geschichte und Gegenwart,* 7 v. (3rd ed. Tübingen 1957–65)[3] 5:1714.

[R. M. KINGDON]

SERVITES

The Order of Friar Servants of St. Mary (OSM, Official Catholic Directory #1240) is a religious family that embraces the following forms of membership: friars (priests and brothers), contemplative nuns, religious sisters, a Secular Order and two secular institutes for unmarried women: the Servite Secular Institute founded in England and the Regnum Mariae founded in Italy. Servites lead a monastic life in the tradition of the MENDICANT ORDERS and undertake various apostolic works. The friars' present habit consists of a black tunic, scapular, cowl with hood attached, and a leather belt. Some sisters and nuns have a long veil and for this reason are called *Mantellates;* several monasteries of nuns are discalced.

Foundation, Organization, and Growth. Servites trace their origins to a group of seven companions, cloth merchants of Florence, Italy, who left their native city, their families, and profession to retire outside the gate of Balla in an area known as Cafaggio for a life of poverty and penance. The names of only two of these men is known with certainty, although the Bull of Canonization of Leo XIII provides the following list: Bonfilius, John Bonagiunta, Gerard Sostegni, Bartholomew Amidei, Benedict dell'Antella, Ricoverus Uguccione, and Alexis FALCONIERI. They are known collectively and venerated as the Seven Founders.

There was at first no intention of beginning an order but only an ardent desire to fulfill a common longing for a life in the spirit of the primitive Church. They wore the grey habit of the Brothers of Penance, followed their rule, and also belonged to a Marian society whose members ministered at a hospital at Fonte Viva and called themselves Servants of Mary.

During Advent and Lent (1244 to 1245), (St.) PETER MARTYR, a Dominican, was visiting Florence, and with his help the first steps were taken toward founding an order. The seven withdrew to the heights of Monte Senario, some 12 miles from Florence, taking with them for their exclusive use the name Servants of Mary. Those members of the society who remained behind were then known as the Greater Society of Our Lady. At that time the seven began to wear a habit identical with that of the DOMINICANS, except that it was black, and adopted the Rule of St. Augustine (*see* AUGUSTINE, RULE OF ST.). It was there on the mountain that they drew up their first legislation and received from Ardingus, Bishop of Florence (1231 to 1247), his approval. In 1249 the papal legate in Tuscany, Raynerius Capocci, received the Servites under the protection of the Holy See, and on March 23, 1256, Alexander IV solemnly approved them as an order of friars living in strict corporate poverty.

About 1253 (St.). PHILIP BENIZI entered the order. While superior general (1267 to 1285), he brought together the various tendencies of the nascent years and gave a second legislation that provided a framework for the future. In 1274 the order was suppressed by the Second Council of Lyons, but because of the diplomatic intervention of Philip in the Roman Curia, the fact that the Servites no longer professed their original strict poverty, and their small number, the decree was not carried out. In the definitive approval of the order by Benedict XI in 1304 no mention is made of its strict mendicancy.

Servites have always followed the Roman liturgy, adding their own usages. The first chapter of the earliest constitutions (*c.*1295) prescribes certain reverences in honor of the Mother of God for the choir and Mass. During the generalate of (Blessed) Lothar (1285 to 1300) the number of German priories increased to seven, but in Italy the precarious juridical position caused many to abandon the order. At the close of the 13th century there were three provinces: Tuscany, Umbria, and the Romagna, with a total of about 40 priories and some 350 friars.

The long generalate of Peter of Todi (1314 to 44) brought new vigor and growth. There was a great desire on the part of the prior general and of many in the order for a return to its primitive simplicity and poverty. Peter made many new foundations in the North of Italy and thus moved the order outside its traditional center. To effect his desire for a real poverty he alienated the possessions of various priories and incurred the wrath of the friars in Tuscany who excommunicated both him and his secretary in 1334. The earliest writing on the origins of the Servites comes from Peter of Todi; in it one can discern his ideals. Peter died at the hermitage of St. Ansan, near Bologna, in 1344. During his time numerous men and women attained renown for their sanctity. At Siena there were (Bl.) Joachim (d. 1305) and (Bl.) Francis (d. 1328); at Forlì, (St.) Peregrine Laziosi; at Florence, (St.) Juliana Falconieri; and in Germany, (Bl.) John of Frankfurt (d. 1345).

Studies received little if any attention during the first century of the order because of its eremitical character; they are not mentioned in the earliest constitutions. Toward the close of the 13th century lectures were given at the priory in Bologna on the metaphysics of Avicenna, and students were sent to Paris. The general chapter of 1318 was the first to legislate regarding studies. That same year the order had its own *studium* at Paris, but as theological faculties were opened in Italy, the number of Servites attending Paris lessened considerably. From the priory of Bologna came the two most famous Servite scholastics of the period: Lawrence (d. 1400), called Opimus, who wrote a treatise *Commentarius in quatuor libros sententiarum,* and Urban (d. 1434), called Urbanus Averroista, who wrote *In commenta Averroys super librum physicorum Aristotelis interpretatio.*

Reform Movement. The general chapter of Ferrara in 1404 decreed the revitalization of the eremitical life at Monte Senario and sent (Bl.) Anthony of Siena there as prior with several friars. A novitiate was established in 1412, and the reconstruction of the church was completed in 1418. At the general chapter of Pisa in 1413 the hermitage was withdrawn from the jurisdiction of the Tuscan province and placed under the prior general. The renewal that took place at Monte Senario caused a rebirth in the order, both in Italy and beyond the Alps. Through the energetic support of an outstanding general, Nicholas of Perugia (1427 to 1460), the restored eremitical life at Monte Senario gave rise to the Congregation of the Observance. The year of his election the hermits made three foundations as a starting point for the new reform. Near Bologna they reentered St. Ansan and founded St. Margaret; at Modena they began the hermitage of St. Saviour. In June 1430 Francis of Florence and ten others left the hermitage of St. Margaret for Brescia.

Eugene IV in 1431 delegated Ludovico Barbo, the Abbot of St. Justina, Padua, to grant to the Servites the church and monastery of St. Alexander, which formerly belonged to the Austin Canons (*see* CANONS REGULAR OF ST. AUGUSTINE). In 1435 the sanctuary of St. Mary at Monte Berico, Vicenza, was relinquished by the Order of St. Saviour to the Servites. In 1439 they again replaced the Austin Canons, this time at Cremona in the church and monastery of St. Catald. Eugene IV in June 1440 granted the members of the Observance canonical approval and exemption from the authority of the Servite conventuals (the nonreformed), except that of the prior general, with permission to elect their own vicar. At this time the members of the Observance numbered about 40 friars.

In 1463 the observant friars entered the priory and shrine of St. Peregrine at Forlì, which had formerly belonged to the conventuals. This became one of their chief centers, and the saint became their special patron. There was a gradual breaking away from the hermits of Monte Senario because the observant friars tended to undertake the works of the active ministry. The influence of the DEVOTIO MODERNA is evident in their monastic spirit and apostolate. The fraternal character and simplicity of the Rule of St. Augustine were emphasized, poverty and common life were enforced, and preaching was the principal activity. They were devoted to the Holy Name and the crucified Savior. The observant movement continued its semi-independent existence until May 5, 1570, when Pius V reunited its members to the conventuals.

With the suppression of the observants the need was again felt for a stricter life, and in 1593 Clement VIII reestablished the hermitage of Monte Senario and decreed that the life there was to be according to the primitive observance. Several Servite friars spent a period of time at Camaldoli in order to acquire the eremitical spirit (*see* CAMALDOLESE). Until this time the Servite hermits had followed the constitutions of the order with the addition of their own usages, but in October 1609 Paul V approved constitutions designed specifically for Monte Senario. A new aspect of the life was soon developed when several hermits became recluses. In 1617 an eremitical congregation was formed, and two years later the first general chapter was convoked. The hermits, custodians of the relies of the Seven Founders, propagated this cult throughout the order. In September 1778 Pius VI suppressed the hermitage at Monte Senario and two daughter hermitages for political reasons, at the request of Peter Leopold the Grand Duke of Tuscany and brother of the Emperor JOSEPH II. The two remaining hermitages in the Papal States near Tolfa continued a meager existence for a short while.

Leaders of the Reform. These various reform movements were strengthened by the activity of vigorous priors general: Stephen of Borgo (1410 to 1424), Nicholas of Perugia (1427 to 1460), Christopher of Istria (1461 to 1485), and Anthony of Bologna (1485 to 1495). Some

Servites renowned for holiness were: (Bl.) James Philip of Faenza (d. 1483), (Bl.) Bonaventure of Forlì (d. 1491), (Bl.) John Angelo of Milan (d. 1506), and (Bl.) Elizabeth of Mantua (d. 1486).

In 1503 the constitutions of the order were printed for the first time; this edition was followed by five others in that century. The edition of 1580 was the most important for it not only applied the legislation of Trent, but also served as the juridic norm for many years to come. Two Servite generals distinguished themselves at the Council of Trent: Agostino Bonucci (1542 to 1553) and Lorenzo Mazzochio of Castelfranco (1554 to 1557). Bonucci, the last superior general to be elected for life, is known principally for his vehement opposition to the theory that revelation is contained partly in Scripture and partly in tradition. He promoted studies in the order and adhered to the traditional attachment to the school of Augustine and Scotus (*see* AUGUSTINIANISM). Mazzocchio, a doctor from Paris, is remembered for his intervention on justification and on the Sacraments.

The eremitical spirit of the order was given prominence by Angelus Maria Montursius (1574 to 1600), who withdrew to a cell in his priory as a recluse to recall the friars of his community to a better observance. He occupied himself with the study of the Scriptures and the Fathers and wrote five volumes on the Bible entitled *Elucubrationes,* several volumes of spiritual exercises, and other ascetical works. He is remembered especially for his *Lettera spirituale* of 1596 (an admonition to a more fervent conventual life). After almost nine years of solitude, he was appointed by Clement VIII as vicar-general in May 1597, and a month later, general. After a short but effective government he died in February 1600.

Spain and France. Although the province of Spain was listed as the eighth in numerical order in 1493, there is no mention of the number of friars or priories. Later, the prior general, Giacomo Tavanti, made a concerted effort to spread the order in the Iberian Peninsula. In 1577 a Spanish Servite was sent to the region of Valencia, and another to Aragon. In 1578 an unsuccessful attempt was made to found the order in Portugal. In the 17th century Servite priories were situated mainly in Valencia and Catalonia, where the center of activity was Barcelona. At that time the friars in Spain numbered about 200. Until 1774 Spanish delegates were present at the general chapters. By the end of the 19th century only one Servite foundation remained in Spain, a monastery of nuns. The first priories in France, founded in the late 15th century, constituted the Province of Narbonne in 1533. At that time there were eight houses, all in Provence. The religious wars of the 16th century worked serious harm in the province, but the 17th century witnessed a rebirth from the few remaining foundations near Marseilles. Before the plague of 1720 the province again had eight priories and about 100 friars. In 1740 the order was forbidden by the civil government to receive novices, and several years later half of the foundations were closed, Suppression of the order in France was decreed by Louis XV in 1770.

Central Europe. In May 1611 Anna Katharina Gonzaga, the Archduchess of Austria, requested the assistance of the Servites for the monastery of nuns, St. Mary of the Virgins, which she was building at Innsbruck. Thus began the most important reform in the history of the order, Nikolaus Barchi, a Capuchin and confessor of the Archduchess, was soon clothed as a Servite at Anna Katharina's request. The Archduchess herself was received into the Servites and called Sister Anna Juliana. On the day of her profession, Nov. 21, 1613, she ordered the friars to put aside the habit of the conventuals for that of the new reform movement then taking place among the hermits of Monte Senario. The Servite general, Dionisio Bussotti, approved the Germanic reform in 1634, and Clement IX gave papal approbation in 1668. The priories of the reform in Austria, Germany, and Bohemia were erected into a province in 1657 and were ruled over by a vicar-general appointed by the general of the Servite conventuals. Clement XI approved the constitutions of the reform in 1709. In the years prior to the French Revolution the Germanic observant friars attained their greatest development and numbered about 450 in three provinces. The Revolution and the policies of Emperor Joseph II seriously affected them, for the Bohemian province disappeared completely, and the other provinces were left in a weakened state. The observants continued until 1907, when the new constitutions of the conventuals were made obligatory also in those provinces. The Germanic Servite reform contributed much to both the order and the Church, especially through the many theologians and spiritual writers at the University of Innsbruck. It was the only movement in the history of the order to have developed a school of spirituality.

Marian Devotion. During the 16th century there arose a type of devotion to Our Lady that viewed her isolated under one title and in a sense separated from the great Christological unity of a previous age. In this climate the Servite Order gradually developed its particular cult of her Sorrows. At first this devotion was encouraged by the order for the lay people frequenting its churches. From 1600 on, a rapid literary production propagated this devotion and it gradually became a principal characteristic of the Servites. The general chapter of 1660 decreed that there should be a statue of Our Lady of Sorrows in all churches of the order; the chaplet of the Seven Sorrows was ordered to be worn on the habit in 1674. The

Servites received permission to celebrate the feast of Our Lady of Sorrows in 1668, and that of Passiontide in 1714. Finally, the church of Monte Senario, previously dedicated to the Assumption, was rededicated in 1717 to the Sorrows of Our Lady.

In this period of Servite history the figure of Paolo SARPI, theological advisor to the senate of the Republic of Venice and historian of the Council of Trent, is the most famous. Arcangelo Giani published the *Annales Ordinis Servorum* between 1618 and 1622. This valuable work is the culmination of the industry of Servite historiographers of the 15th and 16th centuries who developed into full narratives the meager and simple elements of the primitive legends of the 14th century. In 1666 a *studium generale* was founded in Rome in the priory of St. Marcellus under the title of HENRY OF GHENT, who was erroneously thought to have been a Servite.

Modern Renewal. In 1839 the order undertook its first mission work. This was at Aden in Arabia and at Mindanao in the Philippine Islands. Unhappily, within ten years both of these promising undertakings were abandoned. Previously, Renaissance chroniclers attributed a grand missionary expansion to Philip Benizi and his successors, along with numerous foundations in Europe, but their accounts are not true. The alleged missionary expansion might be explained by the existence of a priory in Crete in the 14th century.

The modern rebirth began in 1864 when two Italian priests left Florence for London to act as chaplains at the motherhouse of the Servite Sisters. From this developed the present English Province. In 1870 Austin Morini, with three other friars, departed from England for the United States to work in the Diocese of Green Bay, Wisconsin, at St. Charles Church, Doty's Island, near Menasha. Early ministry centered in this area, but in the spring of 1874 Morini was invited by Bishop Thomas Foley of Chicago, Illinois, to make a foundation in that city. The result was the parish of Our Lady of Sorrows, which soon became the center and motherhouse for the order in America. The priories in the United States were under the jurisdiction of a vicar-general until 1901, when they were formed into a commissary province. In March 1909 the first province was erected with its motherhouse in Chicago, and in 1952, the second, with its motherhouse at Denver, Colorado. There are 27 foundations in the United States belonging to these provinces, and some 325 friars.

In 1964 the order counted 1,683 friars in 12 provinces: Tuscan, Roman, Bolognese, Venetian, Piedmontese, Neapolitan, Tyrolese, Hungarian, English, Our Lady of Sorrows (United States), St. Joseph (United States), and Brazilian; two rectorates, Belgium and Spain; and six commissariates, comprising the following—France, Germany, Sicily, Venezuela, central Chile, Bolivia, Uruguay, Argentina, and Mexico. There were also foundations in Switzerland, Ireland, Scotland, and Western Australia and missions in Africa, and in Chile and Brazil.

Following the Second Vatican Council (1962 to 1965), the order undertook a revision of its constitutions, which began with the General Chapter of 1965 under the leadership of the first American Prior General, Joseph Loftus. The new text was drawn up and authorized by the General Chapter of 1968. It was approved by the Congregation for Religious and Secular Institutes in 1987. The liturgical books of the order were also revised; the Proper of Masses in 1971 and the Liturgy of the Hours in 1975.

In 1983 the Order celebrated its 750th anniversary of foundation. The General Chapters of 1983, 1989, and 1995, in the light of diminishing numbers and the aging of the friars, focused their efforts on restructuring the various jurisdictions, some of which were founded in the intervening years between 1964 and 1995. This restructuring involved also the creation of regional conferences: the North American Conference (NAC) embracing Canada, Mexico and the United States; Cono Sur comprising Chile, Bolivia, Peru, Argentina and Brazil; Serviteur involving the province of the Isles (Great Britain and Ireland), France and Belgium; the Federation of Italy, Tyrol and Spain (FITES); the Inter South African Conference (ISAC) which includes Swaziland, Zululand, Mozambique and Uganda, and, finally, the Conference of Australia and Asia (CASA) which is made up of Australia, India and the Philippines. In 2001 there were nine provinces: Brazil, Province of the Isles, Lombardo-Veneto, Romagna-Piemonte, Annunziata (Tuscany, Rome, Naples), Spain, Austria, Mexico and the United States; one vicariate: Chile-Bolivia-Peru; and seven delegations: Argentina, Australia, France-Belgium, India, Philippines, Swaziland, and Zululand. There are also foundations in Hungary, the Czech Republic, and Albania.

The motherhouse of the order is the hermitage of Monte Senario, and the generalate is at St. Marcellus, Rome. The order maintains its own Pontifical theological faculty ''Marianum'' in Rome with an institute for advanced studies in Mariology.

Bibliography: *Monumenta Ord. Servorum S. Mariae,* ed. A. MORINI et al. 20 v. (Brussels-Rome 1897–1930). A. GIANI and A. M. GARBI, *Annales Sacri Ordinis Fratrum Servorum B. Mariae Virginis,* 3 v. (2d ed. Lucca 1719–25). *Studi storici sull'Ordine dei Servi di Maria,* 4 v. (Rome 1933–42). *Bibliotheca Servorum Veneta* (Vicenza 1963–).

[J. M. RYSKA/P. M. GRAFFIUS]

SESTO AL RÉGHENA, ABBEY OF

A former Benedictine monastery in the Diocese of Concordia, in northern Italy. It was founded about mid-8th century by Erfo and Marco (or Anto) about six miles from Concordia, on the banks of the Réghena (Veneto), under the title of *Sancta Maria in Sylvis.* In 775 Charlemagne granted it the privilege of exemption. Destroyed by the barbarian invasions at the end of the 9th century, it was rebuilt under Abbot Adolph (960–965), and castles and farms were built on lands given by benefactors and were granted as fiefs to vassals. At the same time, the monks organized the gradual reclamation of the marshy and unwholesome areas fronting the Tagliamento River. In 967 Otto I presented the monastery to the patriarch of AQUILEIA, to whom it remained subject for two centuries, always disputing with the patriarch questions of revenues and jurisdiction. The 13th century already brought with it a decline, hastened by the molestations and devastations of Ezzelino da Romano, discord with its vassals, disorders and strife among the religious themselves, and finally the practice of COMMENDATION, instituted by EUGENE IV in 1431. At first protected by the Congregation of St. Justina, the monastery was later placed directly under the control of the Republic of Venice. In 1441 Pietro Barbo, later Pope PAUL II, was named commendatory. The previous year, however, the monastery had been abandoned by the BENEDICTINES, who were succeeded in turn by the AUGUSTINIANS, the DOMINICANS, and the FRANCISCANS. In 1612 PAUL V intervened to give it to the VALLOMBROSANS. In 1790 both the monastery and its commendam were suppressed and the holdings were sold at auction. In 1921 the temporary pastor of the church received the honorary title of abbot. Of the buildings of this imposing monastery almost nothing remains; but some of its library holdings are preserved in Udine, Venice, and Portogruaro (see of the bishop of Concordia). The basilica, which still stands as a distinguished monument from the 9th century, preserves the bell tower, formerly a tower of the monastery, an interesting entrance hall, and the crypt, all romanesque, and also several remarkable frescoes of the 11th and 12th centuries and others of the school of Giotto and of the later Renaissance.

Bibliography: L. H. COTTINEAU, *Répertoire topobibliographique des abbayes et prieurés,* 2 v. (Mâcon 1935–39) 2:3020. G. B. PERESSUTTI, *L'Abbazia di Seato al Réghena* (Udine 1937). T. GEROMETTA, *L'Abbazia benedettina di Santa Maria in Sylvis* (Portogruaro, Italy 1957).

[I. DE PICCOLI]

SETON, ELIZABETH ANN BAYLEY, ST.

Convert to Roman Catholicism, foundress of the American Sisters of Charity, a wife, mother, widow, sole parent, educator, social minister, and spiritual leader, b. Aug. 28, 1774, New York City; d. Emmitsburg, Md., Jan. 4, 1821.

Elizabeth Ann Bayley Seton was the first person born in the United States to become a canonized saint (Sept. 14, 1975). Of British and French ancestry, Elizabeth was born into a prominent Anglican family in New York and was the second daughter of Dr. Richard Bayley (1744–1801) and Catherine Charlton (d. 1777). The couple's first child, Mary Magdalene Bayley (1768–1856), married (1790) Dr. Wright Post (1766–1828) of New York. Catherine Bayley (1777–1778), the youngest child, died the year after the untimely death of her mother, which was probably a result of childbirth.

Native of New York. The Bayley and Charlton families were among the earliest colonial settlers of the New York area. Elizabeth's paternal grandparents were William Bayley (*c.*1708–*c.*1758) and Susannah LeConte (LeCompte, b.1727), distinguished French Huguenots of New Rochelle. Her maternal grandparents, Mary Bayeux and Dr. Richard Charlton (d.1777), lived on Staten Island where Dr. Charlton was pastor at Saint Andrew's Episcopal Church.

After the death of his first wife, Dr. Bayley married (1778) Charlotte Amelia Barclay (*c.* 1759–1805), of the Jacobus James Roosevelt lineage of New York, but the marriage ended in separation as a result of marital conflict. The couple had seven children, three daughters and four sons. Among them was Guy Carleton Bayley (1786–1859), whose son, James Roosevelt Bayley (1814–1877), converted to Roman Catholicism and became the first bishop of Newark (1853–1872) and eighth archbishop of Baltimore (1872–1877).

Elizabeth and her sister were rejected by their stepmother. On account of her father's travel abroad for medical studies, the girls lived temporarily in New Rochelle, New York, with their paternal uncle, William Bayley (1745–1811), and his wife, Sarah Pell Bayley. Elizabeth experienced a period of darkness around the time when her stepmother and father separated. Reflecting about this period of depression in later years in her journal entitled *Dear Remembrances*, she expressed her relief at not taking the drug laudanum, a opium derivative: "This wretched reasoning—laudanum—the praise and thanks of excessive joy not to have done the 'horrid deed'—thoughts and promise of eternal gratitude.'' Elizabeth had a natural bent toward contemplation; she loved nature, poetry, and music, especially the piano. She was given to introspection and frequently made entries in her journal expressing her sentiments, religious aspirations, and favorite passages from her reading.

Elizabeth wed William Magee Seton (1768–1803), a son of William Seton, Sr., (1746–1798) and Rebecca Curson Seton (*c.* 1746–*c.* 1775), Jan. 25, 1794, in the Manhattan home of Mary Bayley Post. Samuel Provoost (1742–1815), the first Episcopal bishop of New York, witnessed the wedding vows of the couple.

Socially Prominent. William Magee, a descendant of the Setons of Parbroath, was the oldest of 13 children of his father's two marriages. The elder Seton married (1767) Rebecca Curson (*c.* 1746–1775) and the year after her death he married (1776) his sister-in-law, Anna Maria Curson (d.1792). William Magee, educated in England, along with his father and brother James, was a founding partner in the import-export mercantile firm, the William Seton Company, which became the Seton, Maitland and Company in 1793. He had visited important counting houses in Europe in 1788 and was also a friend of Filippo Filicchi (1763–1816), a renowned merchant of Livorno, Italy.

Socially prominent in New York, the Setons belonged to the fashionable Trinity Episcopal Church. Elizabeth was a devout communicant there under the influence of Rev. John Henry Hobart (1775–1830, later bishop), who was her spiritual director. Elizabeth, along with her sister-in-law Rebecca Mary Seton (1780–1804), her soul-friend and dearest confidant, nursed the sick and dying among family, friends, and needy neighbors. Elizabeth was among the founders and charter members of The Society for the Relief of Poor Widows with Small Children (1797) and also served as treasurer of the organization.

Happily married, Elizabeth and William Magee Seton had five children: Anna Maria (1795–1812), William (1796–1868), Richard Bayley (1798–1823), Catherine Charlton (1800–1891), and Rebecca Mary (1802–1816).

Anna Maria, who had accompanied her parents to Italy in 1803, became afflicted with tuberculosis as an adolescent and made her vows as a Sister of Charity on her deathbed. Rebecca fell on ice sometime before 1812, causing a hip injury which resulted in lameness and early death, also from tuberculosis. Both Anna Maria and Rebecca are buried in the original cemetery of the Sisters of Charity at Emmitsburg, Maryland. After joining the United States Navy (1822), Richard died prematurely off the coast of Liberia on board the ship *Oswego.*

Catherine Charlton (also called Josephine), was beautiful and witty. She distinguished herself by her linguistic and musical talents, developed at Saint Joseph's Academy, Emmitsburg. She was the only Seton present at her mother's death. Catherine later lived with her brother William and his family and traveled to Europe with them several times before entering the Sisters of Mercy in New York City (1846). As Mother Mary Catherine, she devoted herself for more than 40 years to prison ministry in New York. William received a commission as lieutenant in the United States Navy in February 1826 and married (1832) Emily Prime (1804–1854). Seven of their nine children lived to adulthood, including Archbishop Robert Seton (1839–1927) and Helen (1844–1906), another New York Sister of Mercy (Sister Mary Catherine, 1879–1906).

Elizabeth Seton. (Archive Photos)

Change of Tide. After the death (1798) of William Seton, Sr., her father-in-law, responsibility was thrust on Elizabeth's husband for both the Seton, Maitland and Company and the welfare of his younger half-siblings. About six months pregnant with her third child at the time, Elizabeth managed the care of both families in the Seton household. There she enjoyed her initial teaching experience with her first pupils, Charlotte (1786–1853), Henrietta (Harriet) (1787–1809), and Cecilia (1791–1810), her youngest sisters-in-law.

During their monetary crisis Elizabeth tried to assist her husband at night by doing the account books of his firm, but the company went bankrupt (1801), and the Setons lost their possessions and the family home at 61 Stone Street in lower Manhattan. William Magee began to show evidence of tuberculosis as their financial problems escalated.

Faith-filled Journey. Elizabeth, William Magee, and their oldest daughter Anna Maria made a sea voyage (1803) to the warm climate of Italy in a desperate effort to restore her husband's health. Italian authorities at the port of Livorno feared yellow fever then prevalent in New York. As a result the officials quarantined the Setons in a cold, stone lazaretto. The Filicchi family did all they could to advocate for them and to provide some relief during their month of isolation. Two weeks after his discharge, William Magee died in Pisa, December 27, and was buried in the English cemetery in Livorno, leaving Elizabeth a widow at age 29 with five young children.

The experiences in Italy of Elizabeth and her daughter transformed their lives forever. Antonio Filicchi (1764–1847) and his wife, Amabilia Baragazzi Filicchi (1773–1853) provided gracious hospitality to the widow and child until the Setons returned to the United States the next spring. Filippo and his wife, the former Mary Cowper (1760–1821) of Boston, along with Antonio and Amabilia Filicchi, introduced Elizabeth to Roman Catholicism. Elizabeth came upon the text of the *Memorare*, and began to inquire about Catholic practices, first from her lack of familiarity with the religion, then her inquisitiveness arose out of sincere interest. She asked about the Sacred Liturgy, the Real Presence in the Eucharist, and the Church's direct unbroken link with Christ and the apostles. *The Italian Journal*, her long memoir written for her sister-in-law Rebecca Seton, reveals the intimate details of Elizabeth's heart-rending personal journey of inner conflict and conversion (cf., Bechtle and Metz, p. 243). Antonio, who had business interests in America, accompanied the Setons back to America, and instructed Elizabeth about the faith and offered wise counsel during her indecision. Elizabeth felt deeply for Antonio, who provided not only emotional support but also substantial financial resources to her.

Although Elizabeth left the United States a firm Protestant, she returned to New York with the heart of a Roman Catholic in June 1804. Immediately opposition and insecurity threatened her resolve. Elizabeth's religious inclinations incurred the ire of both family and friends. Their hostility coupled with the death of her beloved Rebecca, her sister-in-law and most intimate confidant, caused Elizabeth deep anguish. She was also troubled by her strained financial situation. Her five children were all less than eight years of age. As their sole parent Elizabeth faced many challenges and frequently had to relocate into less expensive housing.

While Elizabeth was discerning God's will for her future, the Virgin Mary became her prism of faith. In her discernment she relied on several advisors among the clergy, especially Rev. John Cheverus (1768–1836), the first bishop of Boston, and his associate Rev. Francis Matignon (1753–1818). After wrestling with doubts and fears in her search for truth, Elizabeth resolved her inner conflict regarding religious conversion and embraced Roman Catholicism.

Rev. Matthew O'Brien (1758–1815) received Elizabeth's profession of the Catholic faith at Saint Peter's Church, Barclay Street in lower Manhattan, March 14, 1805. Elizabeth received her First Communion two weeks later on March 25. Bishop John Carroll (1735–1815, later archbishop), whom she considered her spiritual father, confirmed her the next year on Pentecost Sunday. For her Confirmation name Elizabeth added the name of Mary to her own and thereafter frequently signed herself "MEAS," which was her abbreviation for Mary Elizabeth Ann Seton. Accordingly the three names, Mary, Ann, and Elizabeth, signified the moments of the mysteries of Salvation for her.

Elizabeth's initial years as a Catholic (1805–1808) in New York were marked by disappointments and failures. Rampant anti-Catholic prejudice prevented her from beginning a school, but she secured a teaching position at the school of a Protestant couple, Mr. & Mrs. Patrick White but they failed financially within a short time. Elizabeth's next venture was a boarding house for boys who attended a school directed by Rev. William Harris of Saint Mark's Episcopal Church, but disgruntled parents withdrew their sons. Seton family members also distrusted Elizabeth's influence on younger family members. Their fears were realized when Cecilia converted to Catholicism (1806), then Harriet also made her profession of faith (1809). During Cecilia's struggles as a new convert, Elizabeth wrote an instructive *Spiritual Journal* (1807) for her, offering her wise counsel.

Although Elizabeth was frustrated in establishing herself to provide for the welfare of her children, she remained faith-filled. She was convinced that God would show her the way according to the Divine Plan. In considering her future and examining alternatives, Elizabeth remained a mother first and foremost. She regarded her five "darlings" as her primary obligation over every other commitment.

Maryland Mission. Rev. Louis William Dubourg, S.S., (1766–1833), was visiting New York when Elizabeth met him quite providentially about 1806. Dubourg had desired a congregation of religious women to teach girls in Baltimore since 1797. He, with the concurrence of Bishop John Carroll, invited Elizabeth to Baltimore with the assurance that the French priests belonging to the Society of Saint Sulpice (Sulpicians), who were émigrés in Maryland would assist her in forming a plan of life which would be in the best interests of her children. The Sulpicians wished to form a small school for religious education of children.

After her arrival in Maryland, June 16, 1808, Elizabeth spent one year as a school mistress in Baltimore. The Sulpicians envisioned the development of a sisterhood modeled on the Daughters of Charity of Paris (founded 1633), and they actively recruited candidates for the germinal community. Cecilia Maria O'Conway, (1788–1865), of Philadelphia, was the first to arrive, Dec. 7, 1808. She was followed in 1809 by Mary Ann Butler (1784–1821)of Philadelphia, Susanna Clossey (1785–1823) of New York, Catharine Mullen (1783–1815) of Baltimore, Anna Maria Murphy Burke (*c.* 1787–1812) of Philadelphia, and Rosetta (Rose) Landry White (1784–1841), a widow of Baltimore. Only Elizabeth pronounced vows of chastity and obedience to John Carroll for one year in the lower chapel at Saint Mary's Seminary, Paca Street, March 25, 1809. The archbishop gave her the title "Mother Seton." On June 16, 1809, the group of sisters appeared for the first time dressed alike in a black dress, cape and bonnet patterned after the widows weeds of women in Italy whom Elizabeth had encountered there.

Samuel Sutherland Cooper, (1769–1843), a wealthy seminarian and convert, purchased 269 acres of land for an establishment for the sisterhood near Emmitsburg in the countryside of Frederick County, Maryland. Cooper wished to establish an institution for female education and character formation rooted in Christian values and the Catholic faith, as well as services to the elderly, job skill development, and a small manufactory, which would be beneficial to people oppressed by poverty. Cooper had Elizabeth in mind to direct the educational program.

Emmitsburg Foundation. Their stone farmhouse (*c.*1750) was not yet ready for occupancy when Elizabeth and her first group arrived in Emmitsburg, June, 1809. Rev. John Dubois, S.S., (1764–1842), founder of Mount Saint Mary's College and Seminary (1808), offered his cabin on Saint Mary's Mountain for the women to use until they would be able to move to their property in the nearby valley some six weeks later. According to tradition, Elizabeth named the area Saint Joseph's Valley. There the Sisters of Charity of Saint Joseph's began July 31, 1809 in the Stone House, the former Fleming farmhouse (*c.* 1750). In mid-February, 1810, Elizabeth and her companions moved into Saint Joseph's House (which became known as the White House.) Elizabeth opened Saint Joseph's Free School Feb. 22, 1810. It educated needy girls of the area and was the first free Catholic school for girls staffed by sisters in the country. Saint Joseph's Academy began May 14, 1810, with the addition of boarding pupils who paid tuition which enabled the Sisters of Charity to subsidize their charitable mission. Saint Joseph's Academy and Free School formed the cradle of Catholic education in the United States.

Divine Providence guided Elizabeth and her little community through the poverty and unsettling first years. Numerous women joined the Sisters of Charity. During the period 1809–1820, of the 98 candidates who arrived in Elizabeth's lifetime, 86 of them actually joined the new community; 70 percent remained Sisters of Charity for life. Illness, sorrow, and early death were omnipresent in Elizabeth's life. She buried 18 sisters at Emmitsburg, in addition to her two daughters Annina and Rebecca, and her sisters-in-law Harriet and Cecilia Seton.

The Sulpicians assisted Elizabeth in adapting the 17th-century French *Common Rules of the Daughters of Charity* (1672) for the Sisters of Charity of Saint Joseph's in accord with the needs of the Catholic Church in America. Elizabeth formed her sisters in the Vincentian spirit according to the tradition of Louise de Marillac (1591–1660) and Vincent de Paul (1581–1660). Eighteen Sisters of Charity, including Elizabeth, made private, annual vows of poverty, chastity, obedience, and service of the poor for the first time, July 19, 1813; thereafter they made vows annually on March 25.

Elected by the members of the community to be the first Mother of the Sisters of Charity, Elizabeth was reelected successively and remained at its head until her death. The Sulpicians, who had conceived and founded the community, filled the office of superior general through 1849. Elizabeth worked successively with three Sulpicians in this capacity: Rev. Louis William Dubourg, S.S., Rev. Jean-Baptiste David, S.S., (1761–1841) and Rev. John Dubois, S.S.

The Sisters of Charity intertwined social ministry with education in the faith and religious values in all they undertook in their mission. Elizabeth dispatched sisters to Philadelphia to manage Saint Joseph's Asylum, the first Catholic orphanage in the United States in 1814. The next year she opened a mission at Mount Saint Mary's to oversee the infirmary and domestic services for the college and seminary near Emmitsburg. In 1817 sisters from Saint Joseph's Valley went to New York to begin the New York City Orphan Asylum (later Saint Patrick's Orphan Asylum).

The Seton Legacy. Rev. Simon Gabriel Bruté, S.S., (1779–1839), of Mount Saint Mary's served as the chaplain to the Sisters of Charity and Elizabeth's spiritual director until her death. He was her principle guide along the path to sanctity. He, along with DuBois, actively inculturated the spirit of Vincent de Paul and Louise de Marillac among the Sisters of Charity. Bruté advised Elizabeth to read and translate the lives of Louise and Vincent and some of their spiritual writings.

The work of education and charity lives on in Elizabeth's spiritual daughters around the world. James Gibbons (1834–1921, later cardinal), archbishop of Baltimore, initiated her cause for canonization in 1882. Officially introduced at the Vatican in 1940, it made steady progress. Blessed John XXIII declared Elizabeth venerable Dec. 18, 1959, and also beatified her March 17, 1963. Pope Paul VI canonized Saint Elizabeth Ann Seton Sept. 14 during the Holy Year of 1975 and the International Year of the Woman. The Holy See accepted three miracles through her intercession. These included the cures of Sister Gertrude Korzendorfer, D.C., (1872–1942), of Saint Louis, of cancer; a young child, Ann Theresa O'Neill, (b.1948), of Baltimore, from acute lymphatic leukemia; and the miraculous recovery of Carl Kalin, (1902–1976), of New York, from a rare form of encephalitis.

The extraordinary manner in which Elizabeth lived an ordinary life flowed from the centrality of the Word of God and the Eucharist in her life. These strengthened her enabling her to be a loving person toward God, her family, her neighbor, and all of creation. She undertook works of mercy and justice. Not only did she and her Sisters of Charity care for orphans, widows, and poor families, but they also addressed unmet needs among persons oppressed by multiple forms of poverty. Elizabeth had a special concern for children who lacked educational opportunities, especially for religious instruction in the faith.

Her life-long response to God's will throughout her life led her to sanctity. Her holiness developed from her early religious formation as an Episcopalian. Her longing for Eternity began at a young age. Throughout her earthly journey of 46 years, Elizabeth viewed herself as a pilgrim on the road of life. She faced each day with eyes of faith, looking forward to eternity.

Dominant themes in her life and writings include her pursuit of the Divine Will, nourishment from the Eucharist and the Bible, confidence in Divine Providence, and charitable service to Jesus Christ in poor persons. From her deathbed in Emmitsburg she admonished those gathered about her: ''Be children of the Church, be children of the Church.''

She prayed her way through life's joys and struggles using sacred scripture. This enabled her to live serenely come what may. Psalm 23, which she learned as a child, remained her favorite treasury of consolation throughout her life of suffering and loss. Elizabeth's pathway to inner peace and sanctity flowed from her way of living the Paschal Mystery in her own life.

She moved from devotional reception of Holy Communion as an Episcopalian to awe as a Roman Catholic and often ecstatic adoration of the Real Presence. Her Eucharistic devotion and faith in God's abiding presence nourished her imitation of Jesus Christ, the source and model of all charity. As she established the Sisters of Charity in their mission of charity and education, she adopted *The Regulations for the Sisters of Charity in the United States* (1812). The choice of the Vincentian rule reflects how Elizabeth understood her mission as one of apostolic service honoring Jesus Christ through service to poor persons. Elizabeth's spiritual pathway involved other people—her advisors, friends, collaborators, and those she served. The relational aspects of her spirituality were a natural gift which she used as a religious leader and animator in community.

Seton Writings. Elizabeth was a prolific writer. Extant documents are published in *Elizabeth Bayley Seton Collected Writings* (New York). Also in her hand are some of the primitive documents of the Sisters of Charity of Saint Joseph's and her own last will and testament. In addition to voluminous correspondence, Elizabeth also wrote meditations, instructions, poetry, hymns, notebooks, journals, and diaries. Her journals include both spiritual reflections and chronicle accounts, like *The Italian Journal. Dear Remembrances* is an autobiographical retrospective memoir or life review. Her meditations deal with the liturgical seasons, sacraments, virtue, biblical themes, and the saints, including Vincent de Paul whose rule of life the Sisters of Charity adopted. Among her instructions are those used in preparing children for their First Communion, and formation conferences for the Sisters of Charity on such topics as service, charity, eternity, the Blessed Sacrament, and Mary, the Mother of God.

Elizabeth rendered the prototypical English translation of their first biographies, *The Life of Mademoiselle Le Gras* (Nicolas Gobillon, 1676) and *The Life of the Venerable Servant of God Vincent de Paul* (Louis Abelly, 1664). Elizabeth also translated selections from the *Conferences of Vincent de Paul to Daughters of Charity* and *Notes on the Life of Sister Françoise Bony, D.C.*, (1694–1759). Also included among the Seton translations are excerpts from selected conferences of Francis de Sales, portions of works by Saint Theresa of Avila, meditations by Rev. Louis Du Pont, S.J., and the beginning of the life of Saint Ignatius of Loyola. Elizabeth had a habit of copying meaningful passages from books she was reading and of making marginal notes in her bible. Her copybooks containing notes from *A Commentary on the Book of Psalms* (1792) by George Horne, and notes on sermons of Rev. John Henry Hobart. Bibles containing her jottings and marginal notes are preserved in the Rare Books and Special Collections, Hesburgh Library, University of Notre Dame, Indiana, and in the Simon Bruté Collection of the Old Cathedral Library, Vincennes, Indiana.

The Sisters of Charity as a community grew and blossomed into independent new communities in North America: The Sisters of Charity of Saint Vincent de Paul of New York (1846); the Sisters of Charity of Cincinnati (1852); the Sisters of Charity of Saint Vincent de Paul of Halifax (1856); the Sisters of Charity of Saint Elizabeth, Convent Station, New Jersey (1859); and the Sisters of Charity of Seton Hill, Greensburg, Pennsylvania (1870). As a result of mandates from their General Assembly (1829 and 1845) requiring the Sulpicians to return to their founding charism of the education and formation of priests, the Sulpician superiors arranged for the Sisters of Charity of Saint Joseph's to join (1850) the Daughters of Charity of Saint Vincent de Paul of Paris, France. These communities formed (1947) the *Conference of Mother Seton's Daughters* which developed into *The Sisters of Charity Federation in the Vincentian and Setonian Tradition* (1996) with member congregations from the United States and Canada. All Federation members are rooted in the rule of Vincent de Paul and Louise de Marillac.

Elizabeth left an enduring legacy, which makes Catholic education available for needy pupils. Popular devotion acclaims Saint Elizabeth Ann Seton as a patron of Catholic schools because of her pioneer role in values-based education.

Elizabeth's vision of faith remains relevant for all ages. Her journey of faith presents an outstanding model for all people. In a letter to her lifelong friend Julia Sitgreaves Scott (1765–1842), Elizabeth summarized her way of life: "Faith lifts the staggering soul on one side, hope supports it on the other, experience says it must be and love says let it be" (March 26, 1810). Saint Elizabeth Ann Seton died Jan. 4, 1821, in the White House at Saint Joseph's Valley, near Emmitsburg, Maryland. Her remains repose there in the Basilica of Saint Elizabeth Ann Seton.

Bibliography: Excerpts from Elizabeth Bayley Seton Papers courtesy of Archives Saint Joseph's Provincial House, Daughters of Charity of Saint Vincent de Paul (Emmitsburg, Maryland). *Elizabeth Seton in Dialogue with Her Time and Ours*, papers from *The Seton Legacy* symposium of 1992, *Vincentian Heritage* 14, no. 3 (1993). *Elizabeth Seton: Bridging Centuries Bridging Cultures*, papers from *The Seton Legacy* symposium of 1996/1997, *Vincentian Heritage* 18, no. 2 (1998). J. I. DIRVIN, C.M., *The Soul of Elizabeth Seton—A Spiritual Portrait* (San Francisco 1990). J. I. DIRVIN, C.M., *Mrs. Seton: Foundress of the American Sisters of Charity* (New York 1962). R. BECHTLE, S.C., and J. METZ, S.C., eds., E. M. KELLY, mss.ed., *Elizabeth Bayley Seton Collected Writings*, v. 1 (New York 2000). R. BECHTLE, S.C., and J. METZ, S.C., eds., E. M. KELLY, mss.ed., *Elizabeth Bayley Seton Collected Writings*, v. 2–3 (forthcoming). E. M. KELLY, ed., *Elizabeth Seton's Two Bibles. Her Notes and Markings* (Huntington, Indiana 1977). E. M. KELLY, *Numerous Choirs*, v. 1 (Evansville, Indiana 1981). E. M. KELLY and A. MELVILLE, *Elizabeth Seton Selected Writings* (New York 1987). A. M. MELVILLE, *Elizabeth Bayley Seton. 1774–1821*, (New York 1951). R. M. LAVERTY, S.C., *Loom of Many Threads. The English and French Influences on the Character of Elizabeth Ann Bayley Seton* (New York 1958).

[B. A. MCNEIL]

SETON, ROBERT

Archbishop, author; b. Pisa, Italy, Aug. 28, 1839; d. Convent Station, N.J., March 22, 1927. He was the fourth of William and Emily (Prime) Seton's seven children, the grandson of St. Elizabeth Bayley SETON, and cousin of Abp. James Roosevelt BAYLEY. He spent his childhood at Cragdon, the family estate in Westchester County, N.Y. In 1850 he entered Mt. St. Mary's, Emmitsburg, Md., but two years later accompanied his parents to Pau in southern France where he continued his schooling. After his mother died there in 1854, Seton traveled on the Continent and studied in Spain and Germany. In 1857 he went to Rome and entered the Urban College of the Propaganda to study for the priesthood, transferring in 1859 to the North American College as its first student. In 1861 he was enrolled in the Pontifical College of Noble Ecclesiastics and was ordained under the title of patrimony on April 15, 1865. Seton was named a papal chamberlain by Pius IX in 1886 and a prothonotary apostolic in 1867, the first American to be given these honors. In 1867, after receiving his D.D. degree, he returned to the U.S.

Seton became an assistant at the cathedral in Newark, N.J., for a short time and then, because of his health, was given the chaplaincy of St. Elizabeth's, Convent Station, N.J. He was inordinately proud of his name and his distinguished American and Scottish ancestry and considered his role as chief notary at the Third Plenary Council of Baltimore inadequate American recognition of his merits, although he was also chosen to deliver a paper at the Parliament of Religions in 1893. Seton always upheld the authority of Bp. Winand WIGGER, even though he had little personal sympathy with Wigger, whom he considered too German. Although fond of Europe and traveling, he considered himself thoroughly American and thought the church in the U.S. should, wherever possible, accommodate the customs and educational system of the country. He wanted immigrants to learn English and to be thoroughly Americanized.

Seton's belief that there were deliberate efforts to overlook him in the U.S. led him in 1901 to resign his parish of St. Joseph, Jersey City, where he had been since 1876, and go to Rome. The next year he asked Cardinal James Gibbons, whose seal he had designed, to recommend him for a titular archbishopric. On July 5, 1903, he was consecrated titular archbishop of Heliopolis. Archbishop Seton was active in Roman society, but financial reverses reduced his patrimony, forcing him to leave Rome in 1914 because he could no longer live there in the manner to which he was accustomed and which he thought proper to his name and rank. The next years were spent mainly in Europe until 1921, when he returned to St. Elizabeth's Convent where he had been chaplain.

His published works include *Essays on Various Subjects Chiefly Roman* (1862); *Memoir, Letters and Journal of Elizabeth Seton* (1869); *An Old Family, or the Setons of Scotland and America* (1899); *Memories of Many Years, 1839–1922* (1923). In Rome he acted as correspondent for the *New York Times* under the pen name of Fyvie.

Bibliography: J. B. CODE, *Dictionary of American Biography*, ed. A. JOHNSON and D. MALONE, 20 v. (New York 1928–36; index 1937; 1st suppl. 1944; 2d suppl. 1958), 16:597–598.

[C. D. HINRICHSEN]

SETTIMO, ABBEY OF

Benedictine monastery in the Diocese of Florence in northern Italy. It was founded about the middle of the 10th century by Lothar of Cadolo and was located seven miles outside of Florence (hence the name Settimo, seventh). The Cluniacs were brought in almost immediately and obtained such rich endowments in Tuscany and Emilia that in 1048 the title of count was conferred on the abbot. During this period the monastery was deeply influenced by St. JOHN GUALBERT, but does not appear to have become a VALLOMBROSAN monastery as such. On Feb. 12, 1068, the Vallombrosan monk PETER (IGNEUS) ALDOBRANDINI here sustained the famous ORDEAL by fire. He passed unharmed through a corridor of fire to demonstrate the truth of the accusations of simony made by the monks against the Florentine Bishop Peter of Pavia, called the Mezzabarha (Halfbeard), who was later deposed, but died reconciled to the Church in this same monastery. In 1236 GREGORY IX entrusted the monastery to the Cistercians of SAN GALGANO near Siena, who had the primitive Romanesque church dedicated to Our Lord decorated with frescoes and enlarged the monastery. The monastery achieved its greatest development in the first half of the 14th century, soon followed by decline: for as early as 1435 EUGENE IV had introduced the practice of COMMENDATION. Among the commendatories, who were usually fairly efficient at looking after the well-being of the monastery, was Cardinal Domenico CAPRANICA, founder of the college in Rome that bears his name. In the Renaissance period the monastery buildings were remodeled and enlarged on a grand scale, but spiritually the monastery was of no further substantial importance down to its suppression in 1783. In 1944 the remaining buildings, which had been restored in 1931, suffered severe damage in air raids.

Bibliography: C. C. CALZOLAI, *La storia della Badia a Settimo* (Florence 1958), with bibliog.

[I. DE PICCOLI]

SEVEN LAST WORDS

Of the seven last words of Jesus from the cross, only the cry of dereliction is found substantially in more than one Gospel (Mt 27.46; Mk 5.34); three are reported independently by Luke (23.34, 43, 46); three others by John (19.26–27, 28, 30). These words are listed here in the order in which they usually appear in the harmonies of the Gospels, since the chronological order in which they were spoken cannot be determined with certainty. Each Evangelist, depending on the Passion narrative found in the early catechesis, has selected, arranged, and elaborated on his material according to his specific plan.

First Word. ''Father, forgive them, for they do not know what they are doing'' (Lk 23.34). Though not found in a number of important manuscripts, it is almost certainly an authentic word of Jesus. For, as echoed in Acts 7.59–60, forgiveness is one of the most typically Christian themes in the gospel tradition. According to Lk 23.35–37, both Jewish rulers and Roman soldiers see in the Crucifixion the refutation of Jesus' claim to a divine purpose in life. Our Lord's prayer for forgiveness is motivated by their respective ignorance. Basically, ignorance is applicable only to the Roman soldiers who unwittingly carry out the execution. However, from the aspect of SALVATION HISTORY, both Jew and pagan (Acts 3.17; 13.27; 17.30) were blinded to the supreme revelation of God's omnipotence and wisdom in the cross (1 Cor 1.23–24). Biblically, therefore, their combined ignorance is sinful and incurs guilt. But, the ignorance of both Jew and pagan, which serves as a motive for forgiveness, becomes inexcusable after the Resurrection (Acts 17.30–31).

Second Word. ''Amen I say to thee, this day thou shalt be with me in paradise'' (Lk 23.43). One of the crucified criminals, acknowledging the justice of his condemnation, confesses the innocence of Jesus, thereby eliciting an act of faith in the claim for which Christ dies.

Adopting what is probably the correct reading of Lk 23.42, "Lord, remember me when thou comest in thy kingly power," the penitent malefactor appeals for pardon at judgment when Jesus returns as king to inaugurate His kingdom. To this request, which looks to the future, Jesus opposes His "today," promising that the thief would be with Him in paradise.

In early Hebrew thought, to die meant to descend into SHEOL, where the just and the wicked alike endured a miserable existence. Later, when belief arose in retribution even before the Resurrection, divisions appeared in Sheol; a place called GEHENNA was reserved for the wicked, whereas ABRAHAM'S BOSOM (Lk 16.22) became the abode of the just. Although paradise in Jewish thought at the time is not equivalent to heaven, in this context of Christ coming immediately in His royal power, the penitent is assured of happiness by being with Him.

Third Word. "Woman, behold thy son. . . . Behold thy mother" (Jn 19.26–27). John, who has put meaningful Old Testament words on Jesus' lips or has seen deeper meaning in what Jesus endured (19.24, 28, 36, 37), certainly intended to have Jesus express by these words something more than filial piety. Here, as well as in 2.1–11, Mary is addressed by her Son as "woman." The strangeness of the address is due to John's theological intentions. The word, "woman," aptly portrays Johannine symbolism with regard to Mary's role in giving life to the "Life-giver." As Adam calls his wife "Life" (Ζωή) in Gn 3.20, because she is the "mother of all living," similarily John suppresses Mary's name, calling her simply "woman," in order to present her as the new Eve, the mother of all whom Jesus loves in the person of "the disciple whom he loved." John also never mentions this Disciple's name in order to emphasize his symbolic role. Thus, John proclaims the spiritual motherhood of Mary, the new Eve, with regard to the faithful represented by the beloved disciple.

Fourth Word. "Eli, Eli, lama sabachthani?" In the Greek transliteration of their Semitic form, the words of Jesus, "My God, my God, why hast thou forsaken me" (Mt 27.46; Mk 15.34), appear differently in Matthew (ἠλὶ ἠλὶ λεμὰ σαβαχθάνι) and Mark (ἐλωῒ ἐλωῒ λαμά σαβαχθάνι). Mark's is a more Aramaic rendition of the opening words of Psalm 21(22): *'ēlî 'ēlî lāmâ 'ăzabtānî,* while Matthew's is a mixture of Aramaic and Hebrew. Palestinian tradition would naturally have preserved the saying in Aramaic; but because the bystanders in Mt 27.47 and Mk 15.35 appear to have confused the first words with the Hebrew form of Elia's name (*'ēlîyâ*), it is more likely that Jesus Himself uttered the cry in Hebrew, not Aramaic.

Totally unacceptable are the interpretations that treat the saying as a cry of despair and see in Christ's abandonment a dissolution of the HYPOSTATIC UNION, a withdrawal of grace from His soul, or a cessation of the beatific vision. These views are inconsistent with the love of God and with a proper understanding of the hypostatic union, and they are without foundation in Scripture. Much more acceptable is the view that, in the light of Psalm 21(22) as a whole, sees in the cry a final utterance of unshaken faith in God. Though the Psalmist, perplexed by God's abandoning him to his enemies, begins with a lament (v. 2–22), he does not despair. Rather, anticipating deliverance, he moves to a hymn of thanksgiving, calling upon all that fear God to join in adoration (v. 23–27). Finally, the conclusion (v. 28–32), which has points of contact with Deutero-Isaia, triumphantly proclaims that the suffering and vindication of the just will bring others to acknowledge God's mercy, thereby hastening the establishment of God's kingdom on earth.

That the interpretation of the saying lies in this direction is supported by the inspired witness of the early Church. Jesus Himself probably uttered only the opening words of the Psalm, whereas the Evangelists used the entire Psalm as an OT "testimony" (*see* TESTIMONIA) to line Passion. Thus, the godless who "wag their heads" (v. 8–9) are mentioned in Mk 15.29, their words of mockery being placed in the mouths of the chief priests in Mt 27.43; in Jn 19.24 the dividing of Christ's garments is clearly understood as a fulfillment of Ps 21 (22).19; lastly, in Heb 2.12 the same words of thanksgiving (v. 23) are put on Christ's lips.

Although the allusions to the Psalm correspond to the historical facts, it was used primarily to indicate that all had taken place according to God's will as revealed in Scripture. Consequently, if Christ's lament is recorded at all, it is not meant to describe His collapse, but rather to show that God's eternal counsel of salvation was being fulfilled. This fulfillment far transcends the prophetic outline presented in the Psalm: the conversion of nations follows, not only because of the manifestation of God's justice in the sufferer's deliverance, but in consequence of his suffering. Only in the Suffering Servant (Is 52.13–53.12), i.e., in Jesus Himself, is the full redemptive mission of suffering accomplished (*see* SUFFERING SERVANT, SONGS OF THE); only through Him is God's kingdom definitively established.

Fifth Word. "I thirst" (Jn 19.28). John records Jesus' thirst to bear witness to His humanity against DOCETISM and to show the fulfillment of God's plan. Vinegar or sour wine, the soldiers' ordinary drink, is given Christ. John intends to teach a deeper meaning in this reference to Ps 68(69).22: "In my thirst they gave me vinegar to drink." Since the Psalm describes the just oppressed man, typical of the poor lowly ones whose prayers God hears (v. 33–35), Jesus on the cross fulfills the Father's plan of salvation for His poor by drinking the cup that the Father has given Him (Jn 18.11; cf. Lk 24.25–27, 44–46).

Sixth Word. Having received the bitter wine, ''Jesus said: 'It is consummated,' and, bowing his head, he gave up his spirit'' (Jn 19.30). Instead of the first two Gospels' cry of dereliction, John uses the highly significant word τετέλεσται, whose dominant meaning is ''to bring to completion,'' ''to fulfill.'' The completion of the work entrusted by the Father to Jesus is defined as the disclosure of God's ''name'' and the deliverance of His words to the Disciples (17.3–8). His mission is accomplished by transforming mankind and by opening up to it a truly spiritual or divine life through His death. The completion of His self-oblation (17.19) is the means of man's rebirth into eternal life. In this context, the unusual phrase ''he gave up his spirit,'' emphasizes John's theme that through Jesus' death His Spirit was given to men to take away the sin of the world and to make all those who believe in Him God's sons (1.29–34; 1.12–13).

Seventh Word. ''Father, into thy hands I commend my spirit'' (Lk 23.46). Luke substitutes for the cry of dereliction an expression of trust and faith [Ps 30(31).6]. Jesus' supreme surrender is made not in anguish and desolation, but in the confident submission of the Son of Man to His heavenly Father's plan of redemption. He willingly entrusts His life to His Father, crowning a life of obedience with His sacrifice of supreme love.

Bibliography: H. CONZELMANN, *Theology of St. Luke,* tr. G. BUSWELL (London 1960). C. H. DODD, *The Interpretation of the Fourth Gospel* (Cambridge, England 1953). F. M. BRAUN, *La Mère des fidèles* (Tournai 1953).

[S. MAKAREWICZ]

SEVEN SLEEPERS OF EPHESUS

According to a pious legend, stemming perhaps from the 6th century, seven early Christian Ephesians who were walled up in a cave near their city when taking refuge from the persecution of Decius. Their names, with certain variations, were Maximian, Malchus, Marcion, Denis, John, Serapion, and Constantine. To shield them from the wrath of the emperor, according to the story, God put them to sleep. Some 200 years later the seven Ephesians awakened and found that their city had become Christian. Discovered by the astonished citizenry of Ephesus, the seven sleepers promptly died and were venerated as saints. BARONIUS, in the 16th century, challenged the authenticity of the story, which, as recorded by Jacob of Serugh and GREGORY OF TOURS, had enjoyed great popularity in the East and the West. H. Thurston and D. Attwater describe it as a Christianization of a pagan or Jewish legend closely akin to the tale of Rip Van Winkle.

Bibliography: H. LECLERCQ, *Dictionnaire d'archéologie chrétienne et de liturgie,* ed. F. CABROL, H. LECLERCQ and H. I. MARROU, 15 v. (Paris 1907–53) 15.1:1251–62. A. BUTLER, *The Lives of the Saints,* ed. H. THURSTON and D. ATTWATER, 4 v. (New York 1956) 3:193–196. F. L. CROSS, *The Oxford Dictionary of the Christian Church* (London 1957) 1246.

[E. DAY]

SEVENTH-DAY ADVENTISTS

The Seventh-Day Adventists is the largest of the ADVENTIST groups stemming from the preaching of William MILLER (1782–1849).

Origin. When Miller's predictions of the Second Coming of Christ in 1843 and 1844 failed to materialize, most of his followers returned to their former churches or abandoned religion. A few continued to believe that the end of the world was near. One group restudied the Biblical prophecies regarding time and concluded that they indicated mother event—the beginning of the final judgment—and that the Second Coming was still imminent, but the day and hour unpredictable. Through the persuasion of a Seventh Day Baptist, a group of Adventists in Washington, N.H., became convinced that Saturday, not Sunday, was still the Sabbath commanded by God. This belief was accepted by Joseph Bates, Joshua Himes, Hiram Edson, and James and Ellen White, who formed the nucleus of what is now known as the Seventh–day Adventist Church. James White later served as president of the general conference of Seventh–day Adventists after the denomination was organized at Battle Creek, Mich., in 1863, although the first president was John Byington, a former Methodist minister. Mrs. Ellen G. White (1827–1915) exercized a dominant influence on the sect for many years. Much of the instruction Mrs. White gave the church derived from visions that she experienced while in a state of trance. Such instruction is considered by this church as inspired. She related one such vision in which the commandment to keep holy the Sabbath was surrounded by a halo to indicate its paramount importance; according to her, the change to Sunday was introduced by the anti-Christ or papacy. Under her guidance the tiny band of dispirited Adventists grew into a strong, organized body.

A unique practice that sets Seventh-day Adventists apart from other Christian churches is the observance of the Sabbath from sundown Friday to sundown Saturday. All unnecessary work, including cooking, is avoided as in Jewish households during these hours. Members attend church and Sabbath school on Friday evening and Saturday morning.

Bibliography: L. E. FROOM, *The Prophetic Faith of Our Fathers,* 4 v. (Washington 1946–54). F. D. NICHOL, *The Midnight Cry* (Washington 1944). A. E. LICKEY, *Highways to Truth* (Washington 1952). B. HERNDON, *The Seventh Day* (New York 1960). *Seventh–Day Adventists Answer Questions on Doctrine* (Washington 1957). A. W. SPALDING, *Captains of the Host,* 2 v. (Washington 1949).

[W. J. WHALEN/EDS.]

SEVENTY-FOUR TITLES, COLLECTION OF

A compilation of 315 *capitula* or ordinances distributed unequally under seventy-four titles, the whole entitled *Diversorum patrum sententie.* The important titles are: 1, 2, on the primacy of the Roman Church; 3, 4, on monastic and ecclesiastical privileges; 5–14, clerical immunity, accusation, and trial; 15, unworthy clergy; 16–21, entry to the priesthood and episcopacy; 22, 23, the Roman pontificate; 59–61, prohibition of lay control of church property. Seventy-four Titles is a well-ordered collection down to title 28, chapter 202. One group of manuscripts, known as the Swabian group, contains 15 additional titles (chapters 316–330) on excommunication. The author of this addition was probably BERNOLD OF CONSTANCE (*c.* 1090).

This collection was probably compiled about 1074 at Rome. The unknown author belonged to the circle of reformers influenced by the ideas of Cardinal HUMBERT OF SILVA CANDIDA (d. 1061). The collection had three main influences: (1) it spread the notion of Roman primacy and clerical independence of secular power; (2) it presented a convenient text for papal legates, abbeys, and churches that opposed lay influence or wanted to reform lax clergy; (3) it was a model and main source of many later collections, including those of St. ANSELM II OF LUCCA, St. IVO OF CHARTRES, the unpublished *Collection in Four Books,* the *Polycarpus,* and possibly the *Decretum* of GRATIAN. The Seventy-four Titles exists in some form or other in more than 60 manuscripts: the best text is given in the Namur 5 and Monte Cassino 522.

The majority of the *capitula* come from papal sources or were papal oriented. The FALSE DECRETALS was the formal source of some 259 chapters. This helped to popularize the False Decretals in Italy and elsewhere. Burchard of Worms was not used as a source, although later collections combined the Seventy-four Titles, Burchard, and canons of the councils.

The Seventy-four Titles' influence in the period *c.* 1076–1141 was not merely in canonical collections already listed, but upon ideas and in polemical writings, e.g., BERNOLD OF CONSTANCE and MANEGOLD OF LAUTENBACH. In 1525 Johannes COCHLAEUS printed title 1, and thereafter there were spasmodic references until Theiner (1836), Thaner (1878), and the important article by Fournier (1894). In recent years the work of Anton Michel, especially *Die Sentenzen des Kardinals Humbert: Dos erste Rechtsbuch der päpstlichen Reform* (Leipzig 1943), has created a new interest and controversy about the Seventy-four Titles.

William Miller, founder of the Seventh-Day Adventists. (Archive Photos)

Bibliography: A. M. STICKLER, *Historia iuris canonici latini: Vol. 1, Historia fontium* (Turin 1950) 1:170–172, 187. J. AUTENRIETH, "Bernold von Konstanz und die erweiterte 74-Titelsammlung," *Deutsches Archiv für Enforschung des Mittelalters* 14 (1958) 375–394. J. T. GILCHRIST, "Canon Law Aspects of the Eleventh Century Gregorian Reform Programme," *The Journal of Ecclesiastical History* 13 (1962) 21–38.

[J. T. GILCHRIST]

SEVENTY WEEKS OF YEARS

A term given to the cryptic passage of Dn 9.24–27 in which such a period represents the length of Judah's afflictions. Jeremiah (25.11; 29.10), in God's name, foretold that, after 70 years (to be taken as a round number) of exile, the people of Judah would be restored to prosperity in Palestine. The prophecy was really fulfilled by their repatriation under Cyrus in 538 B.C. (2 Chr 36.20–22; Ez 1.1–2; see also Is 40.2), yet only in an imperfect manner (Zec 1.12). After the return from Exile came trials and, under Antiochus IV Epiphanes, persecution, so that it was felt that a deeper meaning was implied by the prophecy of Jeremiah. In the apocalyptic passage of Dn 9.24–27, composed *c.* 164 B.C., the prophecy is reinterpreted midrashically, but in conformity with a fundamental idea of Hebrew religion (cf. Lv 26.18, 24, 27–28) as meaning, not 70 years, but 70 weeks of years, i.e., 490 years. Three theories that have been proposed to explain the final week of Daniel's apocalyptic vision would place it respectively in the Maccabean, the Roman, or the eschatological age.

Maccabean age. Some scholars understand the final week to refer to the period and persecution of the Syrian King ANTIOCHUS IV Epiphanes (170–164 B.C.). The 70 weeks are divided in Daniel as composed of three distinct periods of 7 + 62 + 1. According to this theory the first period, ''the utterance of the word'' (v. 25), would begin in 587 B.C. when the prophetic word to Jeremiah began to take effect at the beginning of the exile rather than in 605 (Jer 25.11) or 598 (29.10) when Jeremiah uttered the prophecy. The first period (49 years), i.e., the Exile, ends with ''one who is anointed and a leader,'' who could have been CYRUS (cf. Is 45.1), or JOSHUA son of Josedech, or Zerubbabel (Hg 1.1; Zec 3.1), all from *c.* 538 B.C. The second period of 62 weeks (434 years) runs from *c.* 538 to ''the cutting down of an anointed one'' (v. 26), i.e., the treacherous murder of the pious high priest Onias III at Daphne, near Antioch, in 170 B.C. (2 Mc 4.30–38; cf. Dn 11.22). Daniel's 434 years are actually 66 too many. The 62 weeks, like Jeremiah's 70 years, may be a round number, or the author might have been working with some current, though inexact chronology for the Persian period. Even the Jewish historians Demetrius (*c.* 200 B.C.) and Josephus (*Ant.* 20.10.2) err respectively by excess of 70 and 60 years. The final week covers the relations of Antiochus with the Jews (170–164 B.C.) in a manner similar to that of Dn 7.7–8, 23–26; 8.8–25; 11.28–39. In the middle of the week, i.e., in 167 B.C., the Temple was desecrated by the ''horrible abomination'' (Dn 7.25; 11.31).

The Maccabean chronology, then, is that which is indicated by the general context of the book of Daniel and is, in fact, the oldest attested interpretation of his apocalyptic vision, since it is that of 1 Mc 1.54, 59 (*c.* 100 B.C.), of the Septuagint rendering of Dn 9.24–27 [see Fraidl, 4–27; A. Bludau, *Die alex. Uebersetzung des B. Daniel, Biblische Studien* 2 (Freiburg 1897) 104–130], and probably of 1 Enoch ch. 85–90, esp. 89.59; 90.14 (see Fraidl, 11–15). It is the view now almost universally defended.

Roman Age. Another view is that Daniel's apocalyptic vision was fulfilled in the events of the beginning of the Christian Era. Jewish exegesis saw the fulfillment in the Jewish wars of A.D. 67–70 (attested already in Josephus; see Fraidl, 18–23, and cf. Mt 24.15; Mk 13.14) and A.D. 132–135. Traditional Christian exegesis, traceable back only to the end of the 2d Christian century, though varying in details, would take Dn 9.24–27 as a prophecy of the advent, ministry, and death of Christ. This Christological exegesis has affected the PESHITTA and Vulgate renderings of the passage. In general its supporters take 7 + 62 weeks as one period of 483 years, which is made to begin with some Persian decree, e.g., that of Artaxerxes I in 458 B.C. This is exactly 483 years before Christ's ministry, and the prophecy is considered to contain an exact chronology of the life and death of Jesus. The theory, unfortunately, explains Dn 9.24–27 outside the general Maccabean context of the book; it takes 7 + 62 less naturally as one period and views the entire 70 weeks as beginning at a different date from Jeremiah's 70 years. If the vision is an exact prophecy of the date of Christ's ministry, it is surprising that no use was made of it in the NT or in early Christian apologetics. This ''traditional'' exegesis, challenged from the 16th century onward, is now rarely defended; see, however, G. Closen, *Verbum Domini* 18 (1938) 47–56, 115–125.

Eschatological Age. Some would see in the vision a prophecy of the end of the world; cf. 2 Thes 2.4. Though the theory was defended by certain Church Fathers (see Bigot, 76–77), it is now universally abandoned. Some of the images of the passage, can, of course, be taken as types of eschatological events.

Bibliography: Commentaries on Dn 9.24–27. J. A. MONTGOMERY (*International Critical Commentary* 22; 1927) 390–401. S. R. DRIVER (Cambridge, England 1901) 143–150. G. RINALDI (4th ed. Milan 1962) 131–135, bibliog. 33–34. F. FRAIDL, *Die Exegese der siebzig Wochen Daniels in der alten und mittleren Zeit* (Graz 1883). L. BIGOT, *Dictionnaire de théologie catholique,* ed. A. VACANT, 15 v. (Paris 1903–50) 4.1:75–103. M. G. GRUENTHANER, ''The Seventy Weeks,'' *The Catholic Biblical Quarterly* 1 (Washington 1939) 44–54. J. T. NELIS, *Encyclopedic Dictionary of the Bible,* translated and adapted by L. HARTMAN (New York, 1963) 2569–72.

[M. MCNAMARA]

SEVERIAN OF GABALA

Bishop of Gabala, Syria, opponent of St. JOHN CHRYSOSTOM; b. 4th century; d. after 408. Although he was bishop of Gabala, Severian's ambitions demanded more than provincial success. Inspired by the good fortune of Antiochus of Ptolemais at CONSTANTINOPLE, he went to the imperial capital *c.* 401. Well received by Chrysostom,

Severian won popularity with the people and the imperial court by his oratory; and when Chrysostom visited Asia in 401, he left nominal authority with Severian, although he gave real power to Serapion, his archdeacon. Severian reacted angrily to Serapion's report that he had been attempting to undermine Chrysostom. On his return, Chrysostom induced Severian to leave for his own diocese; but the imperial court recalled him to Constantinople, and the Empress Eudoxia forced Chrysostom to receive him, although no genuine reconciliation was effected.

Severian served as accuser and judge of Chrysostom at the Synod of the OAK, charging him with stirring clerical leaders against himself, and he was in part responsible for Chrysostom's first exile. This gained him general unpopularity; and when Chrysostom returned from exile, Severian and his friends fled from the capital.

Severian accused Chrysostom a second time, contending that he had burned his own church, and warned Emperor Arcadius (June 404) that there would be no peace in Constantinople until Chrysostom was removed. Working with Acacius of Beroea, Paul of Heraclea, Antiochus of Ptolemais, and Cyrinus of Chalcedon, he finally effected the second exile of Chrysostom. His last recorded act is his demand that Chrysostom be removed from Cucusus, which he considered too mild as a place of exile (407). Severian left Constantinople probably after 408 and returned to his diocese of Gabala; there is no evidence concerning his subsequent life.

Severian was a productive writer, influenced by the theology of the school of ANTIOCH. Many of his works have survived, ironically, under the name of his enemy, John Chrysostom. While Severian was no great thinker, his writings indicate that he knew the Scriptures well, was an able Biblical exegete, and was a popular speaker of at least moderate talents, although he possessed a slightly rough voice and a pronounced Syrian accent. He is remembered not for the importance of his writings, but for his struggle against Chrysostom.

Severian's homilies have survived in Greek, Syriac, Armenian, Arabic, and Coptic versions. Among the Greek homilies are *Orationes sex in mundi creationem; Hom. in illud Abrahae dictum Gen. 24, 2; Hom. in dictum illud Matth. 21, 23; Hom. de ficu arefacta; Hom. de sigillis librorum; Hom. de pace; In Dei apparitionem; De serpente quem Moyses in cruce suspendit;* and *Contra Judaeos.* In addition, fragments of his commentary on the Epistles of St. Paul have been preserved.

Bibliography: *Patrologia Graeca*, ed J. P. MIGNE (Paris 1857–66) 56:411–564; 59:585–590; 63:531–550. J. QUASTEN, *Patrology* (Westminster, Maryland 1950–) 3:484–486. G. BARDY, *Dictionnaire de théologie catholique*, ed. A. VACANT et al. (Paris 1903–50) 14.2:2000–06. H. D. ALTENDORF, *Untersuchungen zu Severian von Gabala* (Diss. U. of Tübingen 1957). C. BAUR, *John Chrysostom and His Time,* tr. M. GONZAGA, 2 v. (Westminster, Md. 1960) 2:155–164. B. MARX, *Orientalia Christiana periodica* 5 (1939) 281–367, works attributed to Chrysostom.

[W. E. KAEGI, JR.]

SEVERIN, SS.

The name of several saints in the early Church.

Severin, abbot and apostle of Noricum; d. Jan. 8, 482. He was an Oriental monk of Latin origin, who for 30 years evangelized the lands surrounding Comagene and Astura (modern Stockerau and Hainburg on the banks of the Danube and Inn rivers in modern Bavaria). He founded a monastery at Boiotro near Passau and another at Faviana, where he died. When Odoacer repatriated the Romans, the monks transported Severin's body to Luculanum, near Naples (488), and later his relics were placed in the Benedictine monastery of S. Severino in Naples (910). Eugippius wrote his life.

Feast: Jan. 8.

Severin, sixth-century bishop of Septempeda in the Marches of Ancona; d. Ancona, 540. The town of Ancona changed its name to San Severino.

Feast: June 8.

Severin, abbot and confessor; d. Chateau-Landon, near Sens, France, 507. He is the abbot of the Monastery of Agaunum credited with a miraculous cure of CLOVIS I, King of the Franks, and is probably identical with the St. Severin, hermit (feast, Nov. 27), after whom the church in Paris takes its name.

Feast: Feb. 11.

Severin, fifth-century bishop of Treves. He replaced (St.) Amand as bishop of Bordeaux and died there. In 587 Venantius Fortunatus wrote his life.

Feast: Oct. 23.

Severin, venerated as an ancient protector of Cologne. GREGORY OF TOURS praises him for his virtue. Legend made him an opponent of Arianism in Tongres and placed his death in Bordeaux, whence his relics were translated to Cologne.

Feast: October 10.

Bibliography: EUGIPPIUS, *Vita,* ed. P. KNOELL (Corpus scriptorum ecclesiasticorum latinorum 9.2; Vienna 1886). V. FORTUNATO, *Vita,* ed. W. LEVISON (Monumenta Germaniae Historica, Scriptores rerum Merovingicarum 7.1; Berlin 1919) 205–224. G. PELLOSO, A. MERCATI and A. PELZER, *Dizionario ecclesiastico*, 3 v. (Turin 1954–58) 3:833–834. M. HEUWEISER, *Lexikon für Theologie und Kirche*, ed. M. BUCHBERGER, 10 v. (Freiburg 1930–38) 9:506–507.

[A. DANET]

SEVERINUS, POPE

Pontificate: May 28 to Aug. 2, 640; b. unknown; d. August 640. Very little is known about him. He was Roman and the son of a man named Avienus, but there is no other information relating to his early life. Also the short duration of his reign makes his pontificate virtually impossible to assess. It is clear, however, that he was of an advanced age when he was elected to the chair of Peter and that his consecration as pope was hampered by his refusal to sign a Monothelite declaration of faith called the *Ekthesis*.

After the required three days had elapsed following the death of Honorius I, Severinus was elected pope in mid-October 638. Yet he had to wait nearly 20 months for his consecration because Emperor Heraclius demanded that the pope-elect must adhere to the *Ekthesis*. Since Severinus was perhaps better informed than his predecessor was about the eastern objections to monothelitism, he refused to sign the document. Since Isaac, the exarch of Ravenna, refused to allow his consecration, papal envoys were sent to Constantinople, where they began protracted negotiations for Severinus's confirmation.

While the papal envoys were being detained by the emperor, Severinus weathered a series of attacks that may have been intended to force his adherence to the *Ekthesis*. The violence began when Isaac's military registrar, Maurice, incited a mob of angry soldiers to attack the Lateran Palace. Apparently, the soldiers had not been paid for some time and Maurice took advantage of the situation by convincing them that their arrears of pay were held in the papal treasures. The rumor had its effect, and although Severinus himself was not hurt, the disaffected troops besieged the palace for three days. The situation did not improve with the arrival of Isaac. Ostensibly, his presence was meant to alleviate the situation, but upon gaining access to the Lateran Palace, he plundered the papal treasures and divided it among his soldiers, his officials, and Emperor Heraclius.

The papal envoys in Constantinople obtained confirmation for Severinus in June, but it came too late as the aged pope would only live for two more months. It is not at all clear as to whether Severinus found the time to officially condemn the *Ekthesis* and reports that he did so should be viewed cautiously. Apparently, Severinus opposed the pro-monastic policies of Gregory I, and he held the secular clergy in high regard. In the *Liber pontificalis* Severinus is described as, "holy, kind to all men, a lover of the poor, generous, and the mildest of men." Severinus was buried in St. Peter's, the apse of which he is credited with having rebuilt.

Bibliography: *Patrologia latina* ed. P. MIGNE (Paris 1844–1864) 129:583–586. *Liber Pontificalis* ed. L. DUCHESNE (Paris 1957). J. N. D. KELLY, *Oxford Dictionary of Popes* (Oxford 1986). F. X. SEPPELT, *Geschichte der Päpste* 2 (Munich 1955) 56–57.

[J. A. SHEPPARD]

SEVEROLI, ANTONIO GABRIELE

Cardinal, diplomat; b. Faenza, Italy, Feb. 28, 1757; d. Rome, Sept. 8, 1824. The count of Severoli was bishop of Fano (1787–1801), titular archbishop of Petra (1801), and nuncio to Vienna (1801–16), where relations with the Holy See were strained because of persistant JOSEPHINISM at the imperial court. After Severoli made known the papal brief deploring the secularization of ecclesiastical states in Germany and disapproved the monarchy's exercise of jurisdiction in Church affairs, the minister Count Cobenzl, who was particularly opposed to him, sought his removal. Rome refused. His position improved after the fall of Cobenzl and the accession of Metternich as foreign minister (1809). Severoli was one of two nuncios who remained at their posts during the captivity of PIUS VII. He was active in the reorganization of the Church in Germany and strove to prevent excessive Austrian influence in the States of the Church, but a coldness eventually developed between him and Cardinal CONSALVI, secretary of state. Created cardinal in 1816, he directed zealously the see of Viterbo (1817–24), to which he had been appointed in 1808. At the conclave in 1823 Austria vetoed his candidacy when he was only six votes short of being elected pope.

Bibliography: G. MORONI, *Dizionario de erudizone storico-ecclesiastica,* 103 v. in 53 (Venice 1840–61); index, 6 v. (1878–79) 65:48–54. M. PETROCCHI, *La restaurazione: Il cardinale Consalvi e la riforma del 1816* (Florence 1941).

[A. RANDALL]

SEVERUS IBN AL-MUKAFFA'

Arabic-writing Coptic author of the mid-tenth century. After occupying certain public offices, Severus became a monk and was later (in 987) named bishop of Ushmunein in Upper Egypt. With him began, strictly speaking, the second period of Coptic literature, that is, literature written by Copts in Arabic. He composed many theological and polemical works, most of which are still unedited and some now lost. He is especially known for his *History of the Patriarchs*, i.e., the patriarchs of Alexandria from the legendary first patriarch, St. Mark, to the contemporary, Philotheus (976–979). The principal sources used for the early period were the writings of Eusebius of Caesarea, a Sahidic–Coptic history of the patriarchs, and the biographies written by George and by John of Nikiu. Severus's work was continued by other historians, until it formed a sort of official history of the patriarchate of Alexandria, not unlike the Liber pontificalis of the Roman Church. Despite its critical defects, the work of Severus is of much value for its information on the church, not only in Egypt, but also in Nubia and Ethiopia. Some of his writings have been translated into Syriac and Ethiopic.

Severus's *History of the Patriarchs* was published by C. F. Seybold in *Corpus scriptorum christianorum orientalium, Script. Ar. Ser.* 3, v.9 (Paris 1904–10) and by B. Evetts in *Patrologia Orientalis* 1.2–4, 5.1, 10.5; the latter edition was continued by Yassā 'Abd al-Masiḥ, 'Aziz Suryal 'Aṭīya, and O. H. E. Burmester (Cairo 1943–59); a Latin translation of the work by E. Renaudot was published at Paris (1713). Other works of Severus are: *The Book of the Councils*, ed. P. Chébli, *Patrologia Orientalis* 3:121–242; *The Second Book of the Councils* (completed in A.D. 955), ed. L. Leroy, *Patrologia Orientalis* 6.4 (1900), with a study by S. Grebaut of the Ethiopic version (*ibid.* 601–639); *The Book of the Exposition* (14 treatises on the Christian religion), ed. Murkus Girğis (Cairo 1925).

Bibliography: G. GRAF, *Orientalia Christiana periodica* 3 (1937) 49–77; *Geschichte der christlichen arabischen Literatur* 2:300–318. J. ASSFALG, *Lexikon für Theologie und Kirche* [2] 9:703.

[P. BELLET]

SEVERUS OF ANTIOCH

Monophysite theologian, patriarch of Antioch (512–518), honored in the Coptic Church as a saint and martyr; b. Sozopolis in Pisidia, *c.* 465; d. Xoïs, Egypt, 538. Considered the founder of MONOPHYSITISM as a theological system, Severus was of Greek parentage and studied rhetoric in Alexandria and law at Beirut. A companion of Zachary the Rhetor, he was baptized in 488 at Leontinum in Libya. He then devoted himself to a strict life of asceticism, first in a Monophysite monastery near Maiuma, Palestine, then as a solitary, finally founding his own monastery near Gaza. He was ordained by the exiled Bishop Epiphanius of Magydos in Pamphilia.

Originally opposed to the HENOTICON, Severus journeyed to Constantinople in 509 to complain of persecution by the converted Chalcedonian, Nephalius, agent of Patriarch ELIAS OF JERUSALEM, and became a confidant of the Emperor ANASTASIUS I, accepted the Henoticon, and wrote against the EUTYCHES, the Messalians, and Chalcedonians. Rejected by the populace as successor to MACEDONIUS of Constantinople, he was consecrated patriarch of Antioch on Nov. 6, 512, by the metropolitans of Tarsus and Mabbugh (PHILOXENUS) after a council at Laodicea had deposed the Catholic Patriarch Flavian. As a moderate Monophysite, he was repudiated by both the Catholics and the extreme Monophysites; however, by his oratory, writing, and asceticism he achieved a reputation for profound learning and holiness among the clergy and the people of both Syria and Egypt.

Upon the accession of JUSTIN I in 518, he fled to Egypt. There he organized resistance to the imperial policy and served as leader of the Monophysite movement. Secretly supported by Empress Theodora, he returned to Constantinople in 535 and entered into close relations with the Patriarch ANTHIMUS until the latter was deposed by Pope AGAPETUS I in 536. Severus, when his writings were condemned by Justinian (in the Edict of Aug. 6, 536), fled once more to Egypt.

His vast literary output, written in Greek, has been preserved only partially in ancient Syriac. His *Philalethes* (509 or 511) was a commentary on 244 chapters of St. CYRIL OF ALEXANDRIA's Christological doctrine, quoted against Severus by an anonymous Chalcedonian. He wrote a tract, the *Contra impium grammaticum,* against JOHN THE GRAMMARIAN OF CAESAREA (fl. A.D. 500), and the two *Orationes ad Nephalium* directed against the Catholic interpretation of patristic Christology. His four letters to Sergius were anti-Eutychian polemics. In his *Antijulianistica,* he composed four works against the teaching of JULIAN OF HALICARNASSUS on the incorruptibility of Christ's body (Aphthartodocetism).

Of his sermons as patriarch of Antioch, 125 cathedral homilies have been preserved, as well as 4,000 of his letters in Syriac along with liturgical writings, hymns and an *Octoechos,* or collection of prayers, including the Marian oration *Sub tuum praesidium.* He is the first author to mention the writings of PSEUDO-DIONYSIUS. His biography was written by Zachary the Rhetor (early life to 512) and John of Beit-Aphthonia.

A polemicist in all his writings, Severus professed to follow incontestably the doctrine of St. Cyril, and he demonstrates an exceptional knowledge of Scripture and the writings of the early Fathers. His book against John the Grammarian contains an extremely rich florilegia of patristic texts (1,250 citations). Inconsistent in the use of the terms *physis, hypostasis,* and *prosopon* (nature, substance, and person), he admits the two natures in Christ: ''When the hypostatic union which is perfected of the two [natures] is confessed, there is but one Christ without admixture; one person, one hypostasis, one nature, that of the Word Incarnate'' (*Ep. ad Sergium,* in Lebon, 243). But if, on the contrary, in thought, one asserts that Christ is in two natures, one has not only two natures, but also two hypostases and two persons (*Patrologia Graeca,* 161 v. [Paris 1857–66] 86:908). ''There is but one sole complete being, one sole hypostasis composed of two [natures]'' (*Contra imp. gram.* 2.6).

In the final analysis, the thought of Severus on the person of Christ and the COMMUNICATION OF IDIOMS is compatible with that of Pope LEO I and the Council of Chalcedon, although Severus had rejected the Chalcedonian terminology as Nestorian while totally opposing the extreme Monophysitism of the Eutychians.

Bibliography: SEVERUS OF ANTIOCH, *Liber contra impium grammaticum,* ed. J. LEBON, 3 v. in 6 in *Corpus scriptorum Christianorum orientalium* (Paris-Louvain 1903) 93–94, 101–102, 111–112, Scriptores Syri ser. 4.4–6; 1929–38; *Orationes ad Nephalium: Eiusdem, ad Sergii Grammatici epistulae mutuae,* ed. J. LEBON, 2 v. in *ibid.* 119–120, Scriptores Syri ser. 4.7; 1949; *Antifulianistica,* ed. A. SANDA (Beirut 1931). R. DRAGUET, ''Une Pastorale antijulianiste des environs de 530,'' *Muséon* 40 (1927): 75–92. M. A. KUGENER, ''Allocution prononcée par Sévère après son élévation le trône patriarcal d'Antioche,'' *Oriens Christianus* 2 (1902): 265–282. B. ALTANER, *Patrology* (New York 1960) 610–612. G. BARDY, *Dictionnaire de théologie catholique,* 15 v. (Paris 1903–50) 14.2:1988–2000. R. HESPEL, ed., *Le Florilège cyrillien réfuté par Sévère d'Antioche: Étude et édition critique* (Bibliothèque du Muséon 37; Louvain 1955); ed. and tr., *Sévère d'Antioche: Le Philalèthe* in *Corpus scriptorum Christianorum orientalium* (Paris-Louvain 1903) 133–134, Scriptores Syri ser. 68–69; 1952.

[A. PENNA]

SEWAL DE BOVILL

Archbishop, champion of the rights of the English church against the papacy; d. York, May 10, 1258. Having been a contemporary of EDMUND OF ABINGDON at OXFORD where he studied theology and Canon Law, Sewal became chancellor of the university on May 11, 1244, archdeacon of York from 1245 to 1247, and then dean in 1247. He was elected archbishop of YORK in 1255 and consecrated in 1256 after obtaining papal dispensation on account of his illegitimacy. The writings attributed to him by Bishop Bale ''are probably plausible creations of Bale's imagination'' (A.B. Emden), while the synodal statutes attributed to him were probably those of his successor, Abp. Godfrey Ludham. He resisted the pope's intrusion of an Italian as his successor in the deanery of York and suffered papal excommunication. He thereby won the approval of the antipapal, contemporary chronicler, Matthew PARIS, who said that as much as he was cursed by the pope he was blessed by the people. He refused to collate the prebends of his cathedral to foreigners at the pope's will; thus, like Bp. Robert GROSSETESTE, he set himself against what many Englishmen regarded as an abuse of papal authority (*see* PROVISION). His correspondence with the Franciscan, Adam Marsh in 1256 further suggests that he belonged to the party that viewed with disfavor papal taxation and royal support for it.

Bibliography: M. PARIS, *Chronica majora,* ed. H. R. LUARD, 7 v. (Rolls Series 57; 1872–83) v.5. C. L. KINGSFORD, *The Dictionary of National Biography from the Earliest Times to 1900,* 63 v. (London 1885–1900) 17:1217. A.B. EMDEN, *A Biographical Register of the University of Oxford to A.D. 1500,* 3 v. (Oxford 1957–59) 1:233–234. M. GIBBS and J. LANG, *Bishops and Reform, 1215–1272* (London 1934; repr. 1962).

[H. MAYR-HARTING]

SEX

Viewed at the biological level, sex is a differentiation that occurs in animals of the higher types and renders each individual either male or female. The same hormones (in different proportions for male and female) are responsible for both the sex characteristics and the development of the spermatozoa and ova that together generate new life. In some lower animals, known as hermaphrodites, male and female characteristics can be exhibited by one and the same individual. In humans, the differences are determined at the time of fertilization and are recognizable, through life, by distinctive physiological, biochemical, and psychological features.

This article is not concerned primarily with the biology, psychology, or sociology of sex, but rather with its philosophy and theology as these are viewed by Catholics. It explains the sex urge in man, its peculiarly human character, its place in marriage, and its inseparable link to the procreation of the human race.

Sexual Urge. An unprejudiced analysis of the biological phenomenon of sex reveals its radical difference from other instincts. In man it is more an urge than an instinct since, although it arises in man without his conscious will, unlike animals he has the capacity to direct it. This is true of instincts such as hunger, thirst, and the need for sleep but there is a more comprehensive dimension to the sex urge. The fact that every human is either male or female, means that a person's whole being is oriented in a particular way within as well as outward to persons of the opposite sex. The need men and women have for each other shows that the sexual urge does not arise from the attraction of the sexes; rather, masculinity and femininity are for the sake of the sex urge. It is a manifestation of the contingent nature of the human person who can fulfill himself only through encountering another person (Wojtyła, *Love and Responsibility,* 45–49).

The normal sexual urge is always directed to a person of the opposite sex not just to the sexual attribute of the person. It is this personal dimension of the sexual urge, which provides the framework for love. The sexual urge is also supra-personal and has an existential value because it is the vehicle for prolonging the species (Wojtyła, *Love and Responsibility,* 51–53). The love that grows out of the sex urge is not purely biological or even psychological. It is given its defining form by acts of the will, which is the property of the person. Since each human person is *sui iuris,* that is, no one can will for him, it violates the person's nature to treat him simply as an object, especially a sexual object.

The total nature of sexual love is revealed in sexual ecstasy, which goes to the very depth of bodily existence. It has in its overwhelming power something extraordinary, to which terrible bodily pains are alone a counterpart. Apart from its depth, sex possesses an extraordinary intimacy. Every disclosure of sex is the revelation of something intimate and personal; it is the initiation of another into one's secret. In a sense, sex is the secret of each individual; it is for this reason that the domain of sex is also the sphere of SHAME in its most noble sense. This again explains the central position of sex in the human personality. It is a voice from the depths, the utterance of something central and of utmost significance. In and with sex, man in a special sense gives himself.

Complementarity and Conjugal Love. Man and woman have different and complementary parts to play in sexual intercourse. The man takes the initiative in response to the physical attraction of the woman. The woman, aroused by his caresses, surrenders to him, receiving him with his seed into herself. Both give and receive in the sex act. ''Male sexuality is an emphasis on giving in a receiving sort of way, whereas female sexuality is an emphasis on receiving in a giving sort of way'' (May, *Marriage: The Rock on Which the Family Is Built,* 26).

Because of these characteristics, sex is able to become an expression of conjugal LOVE and to constitute an ultimate personal union. It is not only able to do so, but it is meant to become incorporated into this love; it is destined to serve the mutual self-donation to which spousal love aspires. Indeed, to understand the true nature of sex, its meaning, and its value, one must start with the glorious reality of the love between man and woman, the love of which the Vulgate says: ''If a man gave all the substance of his house for love, he would despise it as nothing'' (Sg 8.7).

Just as it is wrong to reduce all types of love to sex, as pansexualist psychologists attempt to do, so it is also erroneous to think that love between man and woman differs from other types of love only through its connection with sex. The specific quality of this love is apparent even before one takes note of the sexual urge.

It is true that spousal love can exist only between men and women. Yet man and woman are not only different biologically or physiologically—the sex hormones affect every cell of the human body—they are also different expressions of human nature. The specific feminine and masculine features of human personality show the same complementary character that is evident in sexual intercourse. Man and woman are spiritually ordered toward each other, being created for each other. They possess not a ''fractional'' complementarity as two halves of a whole but an asymmetrical or ''integral sex complementarity,'' in which ''the whole is always more than the sum of its parts'' (see Allen, ''Integral Sex Complementarity''). Each becomes more him or herself in the encounter with the other.

In this love, the beloved is more thematic than in any other love, becoming in fact the great human theme. Such a theme expresses itself also in the *intentio unionis;* although common to all categories of love, this assumes in man its highest tension and its furthest extension. The lover longs for union with the very being of the beloved; he longs for a common life, and the requital of his love assumes an incomparable importance.

Of this spousal and enamoured love Pope Pius XII said: ''The charm exercised by human love has been for centuries the inspiring theme of admirable works of genius, in literature, in music, in the visual arts; a theme always old and always new, upon which the ages have embroidered, without ever exhausting it, the most elevated and poetic variations'' (Address to newlyweds [Oct. 23, 1954] *Pope Speaks,* 21). Such love, aspiring to bodily union as a specific fulfillment of total union, is a unique, deep, and mutual self-donation. If someone loves another person with this love, he realizes fully the mystery of the bodily union and aspires to it simply because he loves the beloved.

Sex in Marriage. But one must also realize the tremendous commitment implied in this union. It is a self-donation that cannot be separated from marriage, from the will to enter into lasting union with the beloved. The will to be permanently united in marriage results organically from the very nature of spousal love. In sex man gives himself. The conjugal act involves so deep and radical a self-donation that it itself actualizes the indissoluble union to which spousal love aspires. The becoming ''one flesh,'' of the very nature of this reciprocal gift, clearly presupposes not only love, but *consensus,* i.e., the solemn will of the spouses to bind themselves forever.

The role of sex in spousal love extends, however, much farther than the conjugal act. It manifests itself in the entire realm of intimacy granted to the spouses, in a symphony of effusions of tenderness culminating in this act. The fact that sexual desire often arises without being embedded in spousal love, and that sex can also, when isolated, exert a tremendous fascination, is no argument against its intrinsic relation to spousal love and to marriage. As a consequence of ORIGINAL SIN, the sphere of sex can become a pure actualization of CONCUPISCENCE and assume a completely different aspect. Yet the possibility of abuse and perversion of a thing in no way alters its true meaning and essence. For example, it is no proof against the mission, nature, and essence of man's intellect to grasp truth that many are attracted by intellectual activity as a mere display of dexterity or to satisfy pride. Similarly the tendency to isolate sex is no objection against its authentic mission and meaning.

Sex in Isolation. Sex possesses a tender, mysterious, and ineffably uniting quality only when it becomes the expression of something more ultimate, namely, wedded love. As soon as sex is isolated and sought for its own sake, its qualities are reversed. The depth, the seriousness, the mystery disappear, to make room for a fascinating, exciting, and befuddling charm that excludes anything beyond. Wherever sex is encountered in an unlawful form as a temptation, there is heard the siren song of lust, with its honeyed poison. The sublime joy of ultimate surrender—touching, chaste, intimate, and mysterious—that accompanies sex under other circumstances, is then completely absent. Sex is always extraordinary, but its characteristic extraordinariness assumes diametrically opposite forms. At one time, it is awe-inspiring, mysterious, noble, chaste, and free; at another, illegitimate, intoxicating, and befogging.

In sex, there is an element of promise, linked with a vague expectation of happiness. As long as this promise does not tend toward isolated satisfaction but remains in a reverent submission, awaiting its future as embedded in deep, spousal love, it itself is true. As soon as it is detached from such love—as when one expects the delights of paradise from sex as such—the promise becomes a treacherous one. Those who treat sex as the primary reality that can be understood in itself without recurring to spousal love thus fall prey to a fatal error. They are blind both to the nature of love and to the nature of sex. Ironically enough, in trying to reduce everything to sex, they fail to understand the nature of sex itself.

Sex and Revelation. This union, which is the sphere of such a sublime love as well as the conception of a new human person, Christ has raised to the level of a sacrament. The one-flesh union of Adam and Eve has been called the ''primordial sacrament'' because it made visible the destiny of man and woman to participate in divine Trinitarian communion—the mystery hidden from all ages. It was man's body that made visible invisible realities. The body in its masculinity and femininity possesses the nuptial attribute or the capacity for expressing love, which John Paul II calls the ''nuptial meaning of the body.'' Even in his body man in some way images God. Man and woman image God alone but even more they image God as a communion of persons (John Paul II, *The Theology of the Body,* Feb. 20, 1980).

With the Fall, sacramental grace was lost. Separated from God, man became divided within himself and this disorder affected especially the sexual relationship. A tendency toward lust, toward treating the person of the opposite sex as an object of use instead of a ''disinterested'' gift, now distorts relations between men and women. Christ came to restore human nature. He not only called the human heart, where concupiscence arises, to conversion, but through His death and Resurrection He enabled its transformation through grace. The one-flesh union of marriage is once again an image of divine realities, the total self-giving love of Christ for His Church. This is the source and ultimate reason for its indissolubility. As a result of original sin concupiscence can be overcome only through grace and effort but man and woman are called to their original destiny of divine Trinitarian communion. Redemption, which brought this about, also made possible another way of living the nuptial meaning of the body, celibacy for the kingdom. It, too, is a spousal relation and points toward the resurrected state where there will be no marriage. Masculinity and femininity will remain as the basis for a new and perfect realization of interpersonal communion in our glorified bodies deriving from face-to-face communion with God (John Paul II, *The Theology of the Body,* Jan 13, 1982).

Sex and Procreation. To the sublime union of marriage God has confided the coming into being of a new man, a cooperation with His divine creativity. Such deep mystery calls for reverence and awe. It is no accident that God has invested an act of this kind with creative significance. As God's love is the creative principle in the universe, so love is everywhere creation. Thus there is profound significance in the nexus—at once symbol and reality—whereby, from the creative act in which two become one flesh, both from love and in love, a new human being proceeds. This mystery of the profound link between love and procreation sets forth the gravity of artificial birth control in a new light.

The capacity to generate life is intrinsically united to the sexual constitution of the human person. The encyclical *Humanae vitae* speaks of the inseparability of the unitive and procreative dimensions of sexual intercourse (*Humanae vitae,* no. 12). When a couple seek to unite and at the same time withhold their procreative powers during the fertile period, they are not ''reading'' the language of the body in truth. Conjugal love, which Paul VI describes as human, total, faithful, and exclusive, ceases to be total. When a couple, with serious reasons to postpone a pregnancy make use of the infertile times of the cycle for sexual intercourse they are doing nothing to impede the natural consequences of the act. Their love remains total.

Parenthood also rightfully belongs to marriage alone. Only those who have committed themselves totally to each other in marriage have made themselves fit to receive and to nurture life. Since they have given each other the identity of husband and wife, they are able to give the unconditional love necessary for the sustained care of offspring. Those who are not married have failed by their own choices to fit themselves to be parents.

Christian View of Sex. The Christian perceives the true mystery of sex; he perceives its depth, its seriousness, and its intimacy. He understands implicitly its ordination to serve the ultimate union in marriage, and the coming to be of a new human being. He is aware of the high value that it embodies as effecting mutual self-donation in wedded love, and as source of procreation. He clearly perceives the fearful profanation that every abuse of sex represents, the deadly poison defiling the soul and separating it from God; this is what sexual pleasure generates when treated as its own end. He shrinks from any contact with sex as soon as it is thus isolated and rendered poisonous. He possesses a deep reverence for its mystery, remaining at a respectful distance when not called by divine vocation to enter its domain. His is not a Puritanical or Manichean despisal of sex; for him, the conjugal act is neither something lowly, tolerated in marriage for the sake of procreation; nor is it merely a ''normal'' claim of the body finding in marriage its legitimate outlet.

The Christian understands that an ultimate interpenetration of sex and conjugal love takes place in mutual self-donation; sexual experience is thus not something parallel to love, but is absorbed and elevated by this love. Moreover, the Christian understands that sex belongs in a special manner to God, and that he may make such use of it only as explicitly sanctioned by Him. Only with God's express permission may he eat of the fruit of this tree. The awareness of this fact engenders a reverence that pervades his approach to sex even within the marriage bond. This enables him clearly to understand the sinfulness of artificial birth control, with its irreverent severing of the deep link between the ultimate love union and procreation. He understands the tremendous dignity with which the conjugal act is endowed by marriage's being a Sacrament. This implies that his very love calls for being transformed in Christ. He is aware of the fact that only in Christ and through Christ can he live up to the full glory and depth to which this love by its very nature aspires. As Pius XII has stated:

> But what new and unutterable beauty is added to this love of two human hearts, when its song is harmonized with the hymn of two souls vibrating with supernatural life! Here, too, there is a mutual exchange of gifts; and then . . . through natural affection and its impulses, through a spiritual union and its delights, the two beings who love each other identify themselves in all that is most intimate in them, from the unshaken depths of their beliefs to the highest summit of their hopes. [*Ibid.*].

See Also: CHASTITY; CONTINENCE; MODESTY; VIRGINITY

Bibliography: D. VON HILDEBRAND, *In Defense of Purity* (New York 1931; repr. Baltimore 1962). W. E. MAY, *Marriage: The Rock on Which the Family Is Built* (San Francisco 1995). JOHN PAUL II, *The Theology of the Body: Human Love in the Divine Plan* (Boston 1997); *Familiaris Consortio.* PAUL VI, *Humanae Vitae.* P. M. QUAY, *The Christian Meaning of Human Sexuality* (Evanston, Ill. 1985). M. SHIVANANDAN, *Crossing the Threshold of Love: A New Vision of Marriage in the Light of John Paul II's Anthropology* (Washington, D.C. 1999). K. WOJTYŁA, *Love and Responsibility* (San Francisco 1981). P. ALLEN, ''Integral Sex Complementarity and the Theology of Communion,'' *Communio* 17 (Winter 1990) 523–544.

[D. VON HILDEBRAND/M. SHIVANANDAN]

SEX (IN THE BIBLE)

The Apostle Paul and the evangelists, Mark and Matthew, referred to God's creative will in responding to issues regarding human sexual conduct during the second half of the first century A.D. The creation stories to which they alluded appear at the beginning of the Bible in Gn 1–2. Although these stories are the first in the Torah, they were written after Israel's legal tradition had begun to take its form. These etiological narratives include theological reflection on the reality and purpose of human sexuality. At the outset they affirm that the existence of humanity in two genders results from God's creative activity. Jewish monotheism precluded any suggestion that human sexuality was a means by which men or women could enter into communion with the gods. Israel did not abide any form of ritual prostitution nor did it allow the practice of fertility rites.

Traditions lying behind the creation story in Gn 2 appear to be older than those in Gn 1. Gn 2:18–25 is a simple etiological narrative that seeks to ''explain'' human sexuality. Its modestly metaphorical language speaks of sexual intercourse and sexual desire. It proclaims that human sexuality is an integral element of the human condition intended to alleviate loneliness and provide an impetus for lasting companionship. The focus of this early tradition is on the male-female relationship.

The narrative in Gn 1 places the relationship between man and woman in a cosmic perspective. In the widest possible view of things, humans are the crown of God's work of creation. He has created them ''male and female'' (Gn 1:27). In God's cosmic plan of creation, humanity exists in male and female genders. Human fertility results from the divine initiative. Created by God, the two human genders are blessed so that humanity itself may ''be fruitful and multiply'' (Gn 1:27).

The inspired texts of Gn 1–2 provide a vision of gender, procreation, sexual attraction, sexual intercourse, and companionship which offered Paul and the evangelists a perspective on the basis of which to develop responses to particular questions of sexual ethics.

New Testament. Paul's First Letter to the Thessalonians is the oldest Christian text that speaks about human sexuality. In the context of an exhortation on holiness (1 Thes 4:3–8), Paul encouraged the Christians of Thessalonica to shun sexual immorality (*porneia*). He offers further specifics as to what this means reminding them not to act lustfully as Gentiles were wont to do. This negative comparison with the sexual conduct of Gentiles reflects a traditional Jewish bias with regard to the sexual mores of those who did not acknowledge the God of Abraham. The Jewish character of Paul's exhortation on sexuality is also apparent in that he addresses the responsibilities of men. He urges them to be married and to refrain from adultery. The metaphorical and imprecise way in which Paul's exhortation in 1 Thes 4:4–6 has, however, led some interpreters to translate his words as meaning self-control with regard to sex and propriety in business affairs.

The NT's only extended consideration of human sexuality is provided in 1 Cor 5–7. The matter to which Paul initially responds is a concern that some member of the community is having a sexual relationship with his father's wife, i. e., a second wife. Paul expresses his outrage that the community had tolerated this aberration and reminds them that although they cannot avoid some association with non-Christians whose sexual mores are not acceptable, they should shun members of the community who are engaged in sexual misconduct, idolatry, drunkenness, and robbery (1 Cor 5:7–13).

After a digression on Christians' taking other Christians to secular courts, Paul examines a slogan that seems to have bene invoked by some members of the Corinthian community, ''all things are lawful for me'' (1 Cor 6:12). Affirming that not everything which is lawful is beneficial and that the Christian should not be enslaved to anything, Paul offers an anthropological reflection that provides the ground for a Christian understanding of human sexuality. He views the Christian person as one who, in his embodied existence, is a member of the body of Christ in which the Spirit of God dwells. His citation of Gn 2:24 (1 Cor 6:16) indicates that the biblical [Jewish] view of human sexuality is very much part of his reflection. Paul offers the case of a Christian man having sex with a prostitute. His introduction of this topic should not be construed as an indication that Christians' visits to prostitutes were a particular concern. The case is rather that sex with a prostitute was the typical example by Hellenistic moralists reflecting on sexual ethics. Paul's reflections on human sexuality would have been inadequate had he not treated this subject.

A second concern to which Paul responds is a troubling slogan about which some Corinthians had written, ''It is well for a man not to touch a woman'' (1 Cor 7:1). Earlier generations of scholars considered that this slogan was advice that Paul was offering to the Corinthians; subsequent scholarship has concluded that the slogan sums up the problem to which Paul must respond. Paul offers his reaction in a series of five responses. For the married, the normal state for adult Christians, he encourages an active sexual life with mutual responsibility and authority on the part of husband and wife. To the widowed, he proclaims, as did some contemporary moralists, the virtue of remaining faithful to one's deceased spouse but he counsels that the sexual drive must be taken seriously. To those contemplating divorce, whether on the wife's or the husband's initiative, he recalls the forbidding ''word of the Lord.'' To those married to non-Christians he urges fidelity to their spouse for the sake of their own happiness, the holiness of the spouse, and the sake of their children.

Finally, Paul addresses those not yet married (1 Cor 7:25–38). Having reflected that Christians ought not to change their social status, Paul's words addressed to the unmarried reflect his expectation of an imminent Parousia. From this perspective, Paul urges that they remain in their unmarried condition but, he says, if their sexual drive is strong ''let them marry'' (1 Cor 7:36). First Corinthians' extensive consideration of human sexuality is rich in its practicality, its Christian anthropology, its reflection of the Jewish tradition, and the kind of ethical appeal similar to that found in Hellenistic moralists contemporary with Paul.

With these moralists Paul shares the hortatory use of catalogues of vices (1 Cor 5:10, 11; 1 Cor 6:9–10). In the context of First Corinthians, Paul's lists contain several sexual vices, the generic vice of sexual immorality (*porneia*), adultery (*moicheia*), and two terms that are rendered ''male prostitutes and sodomites'' (1 Cor 6:9). The latter term appears to be a term invented by Paul, and not used elsewhere in his correspondence (cf. 1 Tm 1:10), to refer to a practice prohibited by Lv 18:22. The meaning of the Greek word translated ''male prostitutes'' is unclear. The term may refer to people who have a soft life and disdain manual labor.

Paul's only extensive treatment of homosexuality is in Rom 1:24–32. The passage appears in Paul's carefully crafted appeal to Christian Jews in Rome intended to convince them that Gentiles and Jews alike are sinners who need justification by Christ. He appeals to the Jewish bias about the sexual mores of Gentiles by reminding them of their conviction that voluntary homosexual activity (Rom 1:26–27) was an abomination. He shared with his readers the Jewish conviction that homosexuality and other forms of sexual immorality were a consequence of idolatry (cf. 1 Cor 6:9). With this his audience would agree, convinced as they were that the Gentiles were sexually reprobate. Having appealed to this Jewish prejudice to proclaim that Gentiles were sinners, Paul went on to list an additional 21 vices of which Gentiles were ''guilty'' (Rom 1:29–31). Then came his punch line, ''you [Jewish Christians], the judge, are doing the very same things'' (Rom 2:1).

Paul's treatment of homosexuality derives from his Jewish convictions. He and his contemporaries would have known nothing about what is currently called ''sexual orientation.'' With his ancestors, he shared the view that incest, sex with a menstruant, child sacrifice, homosexual activity, and bestiality were symptomatic of Egyptian and Canaanite culture, the mores of people who did not know God (Lv 18:2–5). Ancient peoples were very attentive to distinctions of race, class, and gender. The Bible's penalty of death for homosexual activity (Lv 20:13), its prohibition of cross-dressing (Dt 22:5), and the ban on bestiality (Lv 18:23) are an indication of a desire imbedded in their cultures to maintain categories intact.

The biblical sanction of homosexual activity by death was a departure from the practices of contemporary Near Eastern soldiers. Later, the Greco-Roman world in which Paul lived tolerated and sometimes even encouraged male homosexual activity, particularly between an older man and an adolescent. Paul's rhetoric opposed the sexual toleration of the world in which he lived. His biblical tradition nurtured his attitude on voluntary male homosexual activity but did not directly address homosexual activity among females (cf. Lv 18:22–23; 20:15–16). Paul held that men and women were similarly responsible for their sexual activity (cf. 1 Cor 7). Thus, the diatribal rhetoric of Rom 1 includes a mention of voluntary sexual activity between females (Rom 1:26). With this inclusion, Paul seems to have been the first Hellenistic moralist to censure same-sex sexual activity among women whose nature would normally lead them to sexual activity with males.

Divorce and Adultery. Paul (cf. 1 Cor 6:16; 11:8–9, 11–12) was not alone among early Christian writers in appealing to the biblical stories of creation as warrants for proper sexual relationships. In his reflection on the church, the author of the Epistle to the Ephesians cites the encomium of Gn 2:24 (Eph 5:31) to metaphorically speak of the relationship between Christ and his church. In Matthew and Mk's story of Jesus teaching about divorce, use is made of both the Yahwistic (Gn 2) and Priestly (Gn 1) narratives of creation. Mark's version (Mk 10:1–12), the earlier of the two, offers the story of a group of Pharisees coming to Jesus and asking about the legitimacy of a man divorcing his wife. Rather than respond to their legal question, Jesus answers with a vision of the relationship between man and woman based on Gn 1:27; 2:24. He dismisses the allowance of divorce provided by Dt 24:1 as a result of men's hardheartedness. Jesus' response concludes with a prophetic challenge, ''what God has joined together, let no one separate'' (Mk 10:9).

In Mark's version of this story, Jesus did not respond to the question of law but offered a vision of the man-woman relationship. Hence, the disciples queried him further about the legal matter (Mk 10:10–12). In his version of Jesus' response, Mark has reprised the traditional saying of Jesus on divorce (Mt 5:32; 19:9; Lk 16:18; 1 Cor 7:10–11) with two significant emendations. He presents a man's divorce as an act of adultery against the aggrieved wife and adds that the situation of a woman who divorces her husband is likewise an act of adultery.

Mark's references to women show that his gospel was written for a Hellenistic readership. In the Greco-Roman world it was possible for a woman to divorce her husband, something that was virtually impossible in the Jewish world. Mark's reflection on the creation narratives indicates that an issue regarding the relationship between man and woman must be considered primarily not from a legal perspective but from the perspective of the creative will of God who created them ''male and female.''

Matthew rewrote the Markan story for a Jewish audience. His version of the story (Mt 19:1–12) is tailored for that audience. The question posed by the Pharisees raises the issue not of the legitimacy of divorce in itself, but of the situation that warrants a divorce. Matthew concludes the story of the repartee between Jesus and the Pharisees on a legal note, ''whoever divorces his wife, except for unchastity (*porneia*, a word whose specific meaning in this context is a matter of debate among scholars) and marries another commits adultery'' (Mt 19:9). In Matthew, the disciples are taken aback by the severity of Jesus' response and suggest that it is better not to marry. Not so: only those to whom God gives the gift of celibacy are called not to marry.

Matthew's consideration of human sexuality from the perspective of Jewish law similarly appears in the Sermon on the Mount. In his exposition of precepts of the Decalogue, Matthew teaches that the commandment ''you shall not commit adultery'' requires that the disciples of Christ should shun lusting after a woman, masturbation, and divorce (Mt 5:27–32). The way that Matthew deals with the commandment is similar to the way that rabbis extrapolated halakah, instructions on conduct, from biblical texts. The wording of his teaching on lust and masturbation is similar to a tradition of Jesus' words found in Mk 9:42–48 which speak of the serious moral evil of the sexual abuse of children, masturbation, adultery, and lust.

In the biblical era, the prohibition of adultery (Ex 20:14; Dt 5:18) was sanctioned by death (Lv 20:10; Dt 22:23–24), but it is more likely that adultery was more often punished by divorce and the woman being stripped of the clothing provided by her husband. Adultery was understood to be sexual intercourse between a married woman and a man who was not her husband. The man's own marital status was not an issue. The issues were paternity, inheritance of property, and family ties. The rights of the male Israelite were of paramount importance. The right of an Israelite male to marry and to enjoy sexual intercourse with his wife is expressed in the Deuteronomic stipulation that young husbands be exempt from military service for a year after their marriage (Dt 20:7; 24:5).

An aggrieved husband generally had the right to impose the penalty for adultery on his wife in the Ancient Near East. He was required to mete out the same penalty to her paramour. It was his rights that had been violated by adultery. Israel, however, gradually came to the conviction that sexual practices were not only a private matter; they were also a matter of public concern. The presence of the prohibition of adultery in the Decalogue, a covenantal text, was a sign of public concern and control. Another indication of Israel's developing realization that sexual mores were a matter of public concern is the way in which Ex 22:14–16 and Dt 22:28–29 respectively regulate the seduction of an unmarried virgin. The earlier law required that the seducer offer the bride price (*māhōr*) to the young woman's father. Deuteronomy mandates that the seducer who has paid the bride price and married the woman is forever forbidden to divorce her. The seducer had not followed the proper arrangements in acquiring his wife.

As the biblical tradition on sexuality developed, it was the ethos of Israel that was ultimately at stake in the way in which men and women expressed their sexual identities. Hence, Paul's strong condemnation of a Christian community which tolerated incest (1 Cor 5). A prohibition of incest is found in all cultures although there are varying definitions of what actually constitutes incest. Is, for example, marriage to one's half sister a case of incest? In the Holiness Code, the Book of Leviticus spells out a list of the forbidden sexual relationships in Israel (Lv 18; cf. Lv 20; Dt 27). Surprisingly, none of the biblical lists specifically prohibits a man from having a sexual relationship with his own daughter. Nonetheless, the expectation that a young woman be a virgin at the time of her marriage implies that Israel's ethos precluded a man having sexual intercourse with his daughter. The death penalty was prescribed for the crimes of incest with one's father's wife or one's own mother-in-law or daughter-in-law (Lv 20:11, 12, 14), as it was for homosexual activity among men (Lv 20:13) and copulation with an animal, whether by man or woman (Lv 20:15; cf. Lv 18:23). Rape of a betrothed woman was punishable by death of the perpetrator, ''because this case is like that of someone who attacks and murders a neighbor,'' but the violated woman was considered innocent (Dt 22:25–27). If, however, a woman was raped in the city and did not cry out for help it was presumed that she consented to the adulterous liaison.

Sexual Mores. Concerns for ritual purity entered into Israel's sexual mores. Men were enjoined from sex with a menstruating woman. They could not enter the temple until a day after sexual intercourse or wet dream, perhaps even after three days (cf. Ex 19:15; Lv 22:4–6; 1 Sm 21:4–5). The earnings of a prostitute were not acceptable as a temple offering. Priests were not allowed to marry a prostitute or a divorced woman (Lv 21:7).

In its injunction that a young married man have a year to spend and be happy with his wife before leaving for a military campaign (Dt 24:5), Israel's legal tradition shows its awareness of the role of healthy sexual relationships within marriage. Such awareness would be echoed in later rabbinic pronouncements that spoke of a husband's obligation to pleasure his wife and of her right to have pleasure with her husband. Israel's wisdom tradition treats human sexuality in a matter-of-fact way and in all its practicality. Thus it speaks of the roles of men and woman in a household (e. g., Prv 31:10–31). It speaks of the seductive attraction of the whore (Prv 5:3–4; 7:6–27; Sir 19:2) and warns against a man wasting his money on prostitutes (Prv 29:3; Sir 9:6). Israel's sapiential literature speaks glowingly of the importance of erotic love. The Book of Proverbs describes the intoxication of erotic love (Prv 5:15–20; cf. Sir 36:27). The Song of Songs is an erotic love song whose place in the biblical canon attests to the significance of the physical and emotional aspects of human sexuality in God's creative will and salvific plan. This is true notwithstanding the tendency of some later commentators to see in the eroticism of the canticle merely an allegory of the love between God and Israel or Christ and the church.

Inspired, and normative for the faith of the church, the biblical texts constitute a legacy on the basis of which the church and its members continue to respond to issues in sexual ethics.

Bibliography: W. A. M. BEUKEN, ''The Human Person in the Vision of Gn 1–2'' (LS 24 [1999] 3–20). R. F. COLLINS, ''The Bible and Sexuality,'' *Biblical Theology Bulletin* 7 (Rome 1977) 149–67; 8 (1978) 3–18; *Divorce in the New Testament* (GNS 38; Collegeville: 1992); '''Male and Female He Created Them,''' *Chicago Studies* 32 (1993) 9–18; *Sexual Ethics and the New Testament: Behavior and Belief* (Companions to the New Testament; New York 2000). W. DEMING, *Paul on Marriage and Celibacy: The Hellenistic Background of 1 Cor 7* (SNTSMS 83; Cambridge 1995). T. FRYMER-KENSKY, ''Law and Philosophy: The Case of Sex in the Bible,'' *Semeia* 45 (1989) 89–102. M. SATLOW, *Tasting the Dish: Rabbinic Rhetorics of Sexuality* (BJS 303; Atlanta 1995).

[R. F. COLLINS]

SEXISM

Sexism refers primarily to the belief that persons are superior or inferior to one another on the basis of their sex. It also refers to attitudes, value systems, and social patterns which express or support this belief. It is a contemporarily coined term, rising out of the women's movement, and not ordinarily used neutrally in its application to men or women. Rather, it indicates almost always the belief that it is men who are superior and women who are inferior because of their sex. As an evaluative term it includes the judgement that this belief is false and that the formal and informal social patterns which support it are unjust.

There is dispute regarding the labeling of certain social patterns as sexist. Some argue that what is called sexist is merely the differentiation of social roles for men and women. Others argue that such role-differentiation is always culturally biased and is sexist because such culturally determined gender characteristics involve an inevitable inequity in the assignment of roles to persons on the basis of sex. Whatever the articulated beliefs regarding ''different but equal'' roles for women and men, women's gender-assigned roles have invariably been subordinate, passive, and/or restricted to the private sphere.

Christian Theology. Christian theology has played an important part in both establishing and challenging sexist beliefs and structures. Centuries of Christian theology continued to justify cultural patterns of hierarchy and subordination in relationships between men and women. Though early Christian experience had offered a glimpse of equality between the sexes, the order of inequality was too entrenched to be changed. Primitive Christian insights that ''in Christ there is neither Jew nor Greek, slave nor free, neither male nor female'' (Gal 3.28) were soon obscured by their transposition into the dominant patterns of the time and into theologies of an eschatological future.

Two strains of thought within Christian theology have served to undergird sexism in particularly enduring ways. On the one hand, women have been associated with symbols of evil; on the other hand, the innate inferiority of women has been affirmed, even to the point of denying to them full identity as human images of God. Ancient myths associating woman with chaos, darkness, mystery, matter, and sin found echoes in Christian interpretations of concupiscence, of sexuality as a dangerous source for evil, and thence of woman as temptress, as a symbol of sin. The texts of Justin Martyr, Irenaeus, Tertullian, of Origen, Augustine, Jerome, of Thomas Aquinas, and Bonaventure, of Luther, John Knox, and the Puritans, all bear witness to the fact that woman appears throughout the centuries as a special agent of evil. Instead of losing an identification with pollution and evil through the development of Christian thought, the notion of woman became theoretically intertwined with theologies of original sin and anthropological dualisms of higher and lower nature, mind and body, rationality and desire.

The identification of woman with evil has perhaps been overshadowed as a cause of the practical inequality between the sexes by the refusal of Christian theology to attribute the fullness of the *imago Dei* to women. It is not only in the order of sin but in the order of nature and the order of grace that women have been declared lesser humans. Though all persons were considered to have been created in the image of God, men partook of that image primarily and fully, while women shared in it only derivatively and partially.

Contemporary Theological Evaluation. In the 20th century theology has generally ceased to affirm explicitly the inferiority of women. No longer is it argued that women are intellectually inferior to men or that wholly passive roles should be assigned to women either biologically or theologically. Doctrines of creation that place persons in graded hierarchies according to sex have been challenged and generally revised. The dignity of the human person, which Christian theology has always affirmed, grounds the principle of equality as a fundamental principle of justice. *Gaudium et spes*, Vatican II's pastoral constitution on the Church in the world, states that "every type of discrimination, whether social or cultural, whether based on sex, race, color, social condition, language, or religion, is to be overcome and eradicated as contrary to God's intent" (GS 29). When commenting on how biblical texts are to be interpreted, the Pontifical Biblical Commission writes: "Clearly to be rejected also is every attempt at actualization set in a direction contrary to evangelical justice and charity, such as, for example, the use of the Bible to justify racial segregation, anti-Semitism or sexism whether on the part of men or of women" (*The Interpretation of the Bible in the Church*, 4.A.3). Popes Paul IV and John Paul II also condemn sexism in their writings and homilies (e.g. *Octogesima adveniens* 16, *Christifideles laici*, 49), as have many bishops and episcopal conferences (e.g. *Strengthening the Bonds of Peace: A Pastoral Reflection on Women in the Church and Society*, USCC, 1994).

Despite these magisterial statements condemning sexism, some theologians see a latent form of sexism in those contemporary Christian anthropologies that describe men and women as complementary. Proponents of such theories say that gender-role differentiation does not violate the principle of equity since such differentiation is based on the special nature of the woman's role in bearing children. Those who disagree with theories of gender complementarity point out that traits ascribed to one gender or another vary considerably from one society to another and from one historical era to another; efforts to apply certain traits exclusively to one sex are thus culturally conditioned and subject to many exceptions. They also point out that such schemes often revert to the same dualisms (passive/active, bodily/spiritual, emotional/rational) that have been used in previous eras to justify women's oppression. The relationship between gender roles and physical sexual characteristics, and whether or not their determination is colored by a culture's latent sexism, continues to be a topic of sometimes heated debate at the beginning of the 21st century.

Bibliography: E. K. ABEL and M. L. PEARSON, eds., *Across Cultures: the Spectrum of Women's Lives* (New York 1989). S. BUTLER, ed., *Catholic Theological Society of America, Research Report: Women in Church and Society, 1978* (Bronx, NY 1978). Center for Concern, *Comments on the Second Draft, NCCB Pastoral Letter "One in Christ Jesus: A Pastoral Response to the Concerns of Women for Church and Society"* (Washington, DC 1990). J. CORIDEN, ed., *Sexism and Church Law* (New York 1977). D. H. CURRIE and V. RAOUL, eds., *Anatomy of Gender: Women's Struggle for the Body* (Ottawa 1992). J. ENGLISH, ed., *Sex Equality* (Englewood Cliffs, NJ 1977). M. FARLEY, "Sources of Sexual Inequality in the History of Christian Thought," *Journal of Religion* 56 (1976) 162–176. K. K. FITZGERALD, "Sexism as Sin: Essential Spiritual Considerations," *Orthodox Women Speak* (Geneva 1999) 190–199. A. L. HAGEMAN, ed., *Sexist Religion and Women in the Church* (New York 1974). M. KOLBENSCHLAG, ed., *Women in the Church I* (Washington, DC 1987). M. L. KRIER MICH, *Catholic Social Teaching and Movements* (Mystic, CT 1998). C. E. MCENROY, *Guests in Their Own House: The Women of Vatican II* (New York 1996). R. RUETHER, ed., *Religion and Sexism* (New York 1974); "Gender Equity and Christianity: Premodern Roots, Modern and Postmodern Perspectives," *Faith and Praxis in a Postmodern Age* (London 1998) 60–74.

[M. FARLEY/L. HARRINGTON]

SEXTUS, SENTENCES OF

Greek maxims (451) on moral and spiritual perfection, compiled *c.* 180–230, partly from Neo-Pythagorean aphorisms (*see* NEO-PYTHAGOREANISM) by Sextus, an otherwise unknown author. Origen cited them as Christian, and RUFINUS, ascribing them to Pope St. SIXTUS II, translated them into Latin. They are extant in part in Syriac, Armenian, and Georgian. There is a citation of the Sentences of Sextus in the Rule of St. Benedict (7).

Bibliography: SEXTUS PYTHAGORAEUS, *Sentences,* ed. H. CHADWICK (New York 1959). G. DELLING, "Zur Hellenisierung des Christentums in den 'Sprüchen des Sextus'," *Texte und Untersuchungenzur Geschichte der altchristlichen Literatur* 77 (1961) 208–241.

[H. CHADWICK]

SEYCHELLES, THE CATHOLIC CHURCH IN

The Republic of Seychelles encompasses an archipelago of 92 islands (33 inhabited) located in the Indian Ocean 970 miles east of Kenya. Mahé and the surrounding islands to the northeast are granite, their hilly terrain dropping to narrow lowlands at the coast. The 52 southern islands are coral reefs. A tropical climate predominates, although the region avoids severe storms. Natural resources include copra and fish, while agricultural products consist of coconuts, cinnamon, vanilla, sweet potatoes and bananas.

The region was uninhabited when the British East India Company arrived in 1609, and for over 150 years the islands provided a haven for pirates on the Indian Ocean. The French claimed the region in 1756 as part of the colony of Mauritius and made the first permanent settlement in 1768 to establish spice plantations. In 1814, under the Treaty of Paris, they became a British dependency, and in 1903 a separate colony, along with the widely scattered Amirante, Cosmoledo and Aldabra groups. In 1976 the region became an independent republic. Most Seychellois are descendants of French colonists, Africans brought from Mauritius as slaves or from East

Capital: Victoria, on the island of Mahé.
Size: 156 sq. miles.
Population: 79,325 in 2000.
Languages: English, Creole French.
Religions: 71,395 Catholics (90%), 6,350 Anglicans (8%), 1,580 follow other faiths or are without religious affiliation.
Diocese: Port-Victoria, immediately subject to the Holy See.

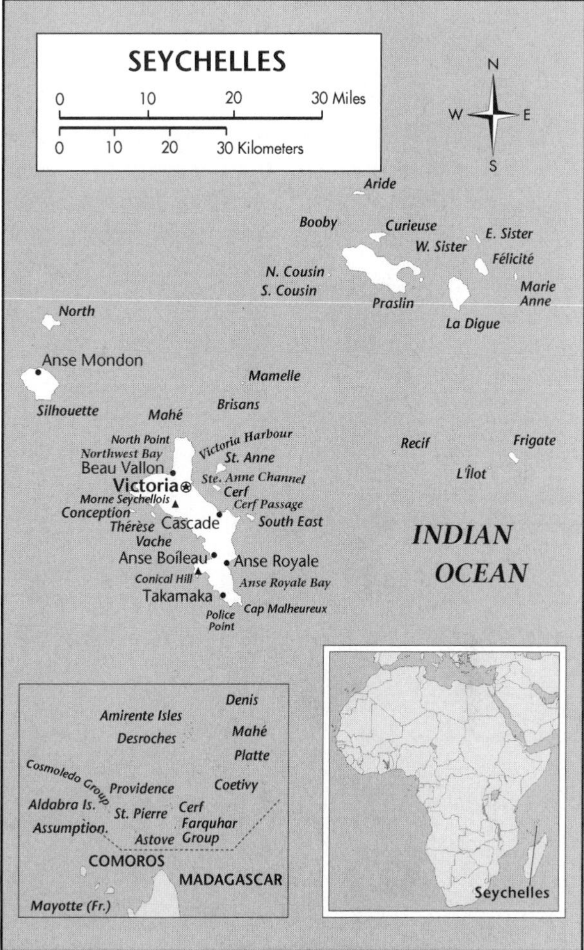

Africa as freed slaves, or are of Indian and Chinese ancestry. The majority of the population lives on the island of Mahé.

Education in the region was entirely in the hands of the Catholic missioners, which included the BROTHERS OF CHRISTIAN INSTRUCTION OF PLOËRMEL and the St. Joseph Sisters of Cluny, until 1954. After that time the government paid and named the teaching personnel, leaving to the mission a right of veto over nominations. In 1958 the region's 50 Catholic schools educated about two-thirds of all schoolchildren. The island gained independence from Great Britain on June 29, 1976, but continued under one-party socialist rule into the early 1990s, when Bishop Felix Paul joined those in favor of instituting a multiparty democracy. Free elections were held in the country in 1993, and a new constitution was promulgated on June 18 of the same year. The region, which relied heavily on the tourism industry during much of the 20th century, sought to diversify its economy into agriculture and small-scale manufacturing. This move was encouraged by the Vatican, which viewed tourism as a threat due to the introduction of crime and consumerism that it fostered.

By 2000 there were 17 parishes tended by 11 diocesan and four religious priests. Other religious included approximately five brothers and 60 sisters, who served in the island's parochial schools. The Church was allowed tax-free status and its services were broadcast weekly on the government-sponsored radio service. It was estimated that close to half the population of the islands regularly attended mass in 2000.

Bibliography: *Bilan du Monde,* 2:788–789. *Annuario Pontificio* (1964) 349. For additional bibliog. *see* AFRICA.

[J. BOUCHAUD/EDS.]

SFONDRATI

A noble Milanese family, originally from Cremona, that flourished in the 16th and 17th centuries. Among its members were many prominent ecclesiastics, including:

Francesco, cardinal; b. Cremona, Oct. 26, 1493; d. there, July 31, 1550. He received his doctorate at Pavia in 1520 and taught at Padua, Bologna, Rome, and Turin. He held public offices under Charles V, who made him Count of Riviera di Lecco on Oct. 23, 1537. After the death of his wife, Anna Visconti (1538), Francesco, a senator of Milan, entered religion; Paul III named him cardinal in 1544. He served in the Curia as a member of the Inquisition. As legate to the Emperor Charles V from Dec. 19, 1544, he dealt with the affairs of England on the death of Henry VIII; he was recalled from Germany June 10, 1548. Francesco governed the Diocese of Capaccio from March 23, 1547, to Nov. 9, 1549, when he was transferred to Cremona. Francesco was the father of Niccolò.

(Niccolò; for his biography, *see* GREGORY XIV, POPE.)

Paolo Camille (also Emilio), cardinal, grandson of Francesco; b. 1561; d. Feb. 14, 1618. He lived in Rome, where he associated closely with (St.) Philip Neri and the Oratorians. He was a man of artistic taste, but had little knowledge of practical affairs. On Dec. 19, 1590, he was named cardinal and secretary of state by his uncle, Gregory XIV. He misused his uncle's confidence, abandoned

Cathedral of the Immaculate Conception in Victoria, Seychelles. (©Nik Wheeler/CORBIS)

his early high ideals, and became interested in wealth. During his uncle's pontificate he was in almost complete control of both religious and civil affairs. Under his direction the body of St. Cecilia was found on Oct. 20, 1599, in his titular church, where he interred her with great solemnity. He ruled the Diocese of Cremona until his death.

Celestino, prince-abbot of St. Gall and cardinal; b. Milan, Jan. 11, 1644; d. Rome, Sept. 4, 1696. On April 26, 1660, he took the Benedictine habit at St. Gall, where he became professor, master of novices, vicar-general, and abbot. From 1679 to 1682 he taught Canon Law at the University of Salzburg; he was appointed bishop of Novara in 1686 by Innocent XI, and then prince-abbot of St. Gall on April 17, 1687. For his learning, piety, and monastic discipline, he was named cardinal of St. Cecilia by Innocent XII on Dec. 12, 1695; he died nine months later and is buried in his titular church. Besides various philosophical and theological works he wrote on the prerogatives of the Holy See. Among the more noted are: *Tractatus regaliae* (St. Gall 1682); *Gallia vindicata* (St. Gall 1688); *Legatio Marchionis Lavardini eiusque cum Innocentio XI dissidium* (St. Gall 1688); *Nodus praedestinationis ex sacris litteris, doctrinaque sanctorum Augustini et Thomae . . . dissolutus* (posthumous, Rome 1697), which accepted the doctrine on predestination as explained by LESSIUS. It was attacked by Bossuet, but defended by Cardinal Giovanni Gabrielli (1654–1711).

Bibliography: H. JEDIN and V. REDLICH, *Lexikon für Theologie und Kirche*, ed. M. BUCHBERGER, 10 v. (Freiburg 1930–38) 9:517. L. PASTOR, *The History of the Popes From the Close of the Middle Ages*, 40 v. (London-St. Louise 1938–61), v.13–40, from 1st German ed. *Geschichte der Päpste seit dem Ausgang des Mittelalters*, 16 v. i 21 (Freiburg 1885–1933; repr. 1955–) v. 22–24, *passim*.

[R. L. FOLEY]

SFORZA

Northern Italian noble family. *Muzio Attendolo,* its founder; b. in the village of Cotignola in the Romagna, 1369; d. 1424, in the river Pescara, attempting to save the life of a page. As a boy he joined a band of mercenaries and later served under the *condottiere* Alberico da Barbiano, who gave him the name of Sforza, adopted by his descendants. As a leader of mercenary troops and a shrewd soldier he acquired wealth and fame. Several of his numerous illegitimate sons founded princely houses. Most famous among them was *Francesco,* first of the Sforza dukes of Milan; b. 1401; d. 1466. A *condottiere* like his father, he married (1441) Bianca Maria Visconti, illegitimate daughter of Filippo Maria, last Visconti duke of Milan (d. 1447). Francesco claimed his state and succeeded him in 1450. An outstanding statesman, he played an important role in Italian politics, concentrating on the maintenance of peace and order in his territories. Humanists at his court included Filelfo and Decembrio.

Among his more than 30 legitimate and illegitimate children, the following were outstanding. *Ascanio Maria,* legitimate; b. 1455; d. Rome, 1505. He became a cardinal in 1484 and held many benefices, including the bishopric of Pavia. A partisan of Cardinal Roderigo Borgia, he supported his election as Pope ALEXANDER VI in 1492 and helped to bring about the marriage of Lucrezia Borgia, the Pope's daughter, with his own nephew *Giovanni Sforza* di Pesaro. A worldly prelate involved in politics, he kept a brilliant court in his Roman palace, *Ippolita Maria,* legitimate; b. 1445; d. 1488. She married Alfonso, Duke of Calabria, in 1465. Educated by humanists, she was famous for her learning and the fine library she collected. *Sforza Secondo,* illegitimate; b. 1435; d. 1491; founded the collateral branch of Sforza di Borgonovo. Francesco's successor as duke of Milan was his oldest legitimate son, *Galeazzo Maria;* b. 1447; who was assassinated by three youths for personal motives in 1476. Galeazzo's children included *Bianca Maria,* legitimate; b. 1472; d. 1510; who was married to the Emperor Maximilian I in 1493. *Caterina,* illegitimate; b. *c.* 1463; d. 1509; was famous for her involvement in politics and military affairs. Descendants of her marriage to Girolamo Riario (1477), the nephew of Pope SIXTUS IV, were the princes Riario-Sforza. Her third husband, Giovanni di Pierfrancesco de'Medici, was the ancestor of the grand dukes of Tuscany. Galeazzo Maria left as his heir his son *Gian Galeazzo;* b. 1469; d. 1494. After a short regency by his mother, Bona of Savoy, and her adviser Cicco Simonetta, the rule of Milan was usurped in 1478 by *Ludovico il Moro;* b. 1452; d. 1508; legitimate son of Francesco, and uncle of the young duke. As regent and, after the death of Gian Galeazzo (1494), as duke of Milan, he kept a brilliant court and was famous as patron of the arts. His appeal to King Charles VIII of France in 1494 led to the French invasion of Italy and to his ultimate defeat. He died in a French prison in Loches. Ludovico's two sons ruled Milan for a brief time. *Massimiliano;* b. 1493; d. 1530; was duke from 1512 to 1515. His brother *Francesco II;* b. 1495; d. 1535; reigned from 1521 until his death under the supervision of the Spanish, to whom Milan fell in 1535.

Other branches of the Sforza family founded by illegitimate sons of Muzio Attendolo were the *Sforza di Santafiora,* descended from Bosio; b. 1411; d. 1476; and the *Sforza di Pesaro,* going back to Alessandro; b. 1409; d. 1473. A third branch, the *Sforza di Caravaggio,* descended from *Giampaolo;* b. 1497; d. 1535; illegitimate son of Ludovico il Moro.

Bibliography: G. B. PICOTTI et al., *Enciclopedia Italiana di scienzi littere ed arti,* 36 v. (Rome 1929–39) 31:5711–577. C. M. ADY, *A History of Milan under the Sforza,* ed. E. ARMSTRONG (London 1907). L. COLLISON-MORLEY, *The Story of the Sforzas* (New York 1934). N. VALERI, *L'Italia nell'età dei principati, dal 1343 al 1516* (Milan 1949). *Storia di Milano* (Milan 1953–) v.7–8, for bibliog. G. PEYRONNET, "Il ducato di Milano sotto Francesco Sforza (1450–1466): Politica interna, vita economica e sociale," *Archivio-storico italiano* 116 (1958) 36–53.

[E. G. GLEASON]

SGAMBATI, ANDREAS

Theologian; b. Naples, about 1735; d. Rome, July 17, 1805. Little is known of his early life. He was awarded a doctorate in theology at the Roman College of St. Bonaventure in 1763. He was assigned to assist in the compilation of the *Bullarium Franciscanum,* and in 1771 was appointed professor of theology and rector of the university college of the Conventual Franciscans in Naples.

"Monument of Cardinal Paolo Sfondrati," sculptural group by Carlo Maderno, in the Church of S. Cecilia, Rome. (Alinari-Art Reference/Art Resource)

His *De theologicis institutis* (14 v., Naples 1775–82; 2d ed. Madrid 1833) became the prescribed text in seminaries of the Conventuals, was adopted by other religious orders, and in 1830 was made the official text in the seminaries of the Spanish Observants. A second work, *De praecipuis locis theologicis,* appeared in Naples (2 v. 1785). In this year Sgambati was appointed professor at the Roman College of St. Bonaventure and named a consultor to the Congregation of Rites. Unlike many of his Conventual contemporaries, he was inspired more by Bonaventure than by Scotus. He made special efforts to eliminate every trace of enlightenment philosophy from his works. This was, perhaps, the chief source of his popularity among the adherents of a more traditional orthodoxy.

Bibliography: D. SPARACIO, *Frammenti bio-bibliografici di scrittori ed autori minori conventuali* (Assisi 1931). H. HURTER, *Nomenclator literarius theologiae catholicae,* 5 vol. (3rd ed. Innsbruck 1903–13) 5.1. A. TEETAERT, *Dictionnaire de théologie*

Ludovico il Moro Sforza, engraving. (©Bettmann/CORBIS)

catholique, ed. A. VACANT et al., 15 vol. (Paris 1903–50) 14.2:2018–19.

[P. D. FEHLNER]

SHABBATAIÏSM

A widespread messianic movement among the Jews of the 17th and 18th centuries, named after one of the principal pseudo-Messiahs of this period, Shabbatai (Sabbatai) Sevi (Zevi). It is known also as Shabbataianism (Sabbataianism) after the Shabbataians (Sabbataians), or followers of this man.

MAIMONIDES (1135–1204) formulated one of the 13 basic principles of Judaism as follows: ''I believe with perfect faith in the coming of the Messiah, and, though He tarry, I will wait daily for His coming.'' Ever since the destruction of Jerusalem, Jewish history records a great number of messianic movements, none of which can compare in importance with Shabbataiïsm. With the expulsion of the Jews, toward the end of the 15th century, first from Spain and then from Portugal, with the great sufferings in the wake of the Thirty Years' War, with the Chmielnicki massacres between 1648 and 1658 in Poland and the Ukraine, in which approximately 100,000 Jews perished and countless refugees sought asylum throughout Europe, messianic expectations among Jews came to a climax. The horrible sufferings seemed to be the *ḥablê šel māšîaḥ,* the birth pangs of the messianic age, as foretold by tradition. Even the Christian world was in expectation, and the main argument put forward by Manasseh ben Israel (1604–57) in his petition for the readmission of Jews in England, submitted to the Parliament in 1650, was that unless the Jews were introduced into the British Isles, the Dispersion would not be complete and thus the messianic deliverance would be unattainable.

Background. The outbreak of Shabbataiïsm must be understood against the background of the resurgence of the cabalistic speculations in Safed, Upper Galilee, in the 16th century. But for the revival of cabalism (*see* CABALA) by Isaac LURIA (1534–72) of Safed, Shabbataiïsm would have been deprived of theological foundation. According to the Lurianic doctrine, Israel's exile is only an aspect of the cosmic fall of the creation and the whole cosmos is in desperate need of salvation. The task of mankind, viz, of its elect portion Israel, consists in taking an active part in the great work of saving the world by a life of sanctity, mystical concentration, and the fulfillment of the divine commandments, which are mystically related to the structure of the cosmos. The restoration (*tiqqûn*) of the divine sparks (*niṣṣûṣîm*) imprisoned in the ''shells'' (*qelîpôt*), i.e., fallen matter and fallen souls, or the repair of the ''broken vessels,'' is the aim of the initiates of Safed. All this religious fervor and asceticism was focused on the coming of the Messiah and the eager expectation of the deliverance.

Climax. This expectancy reached its peak when Shabbatai Sevi, the messiah of Smyrna, arose. Born in 1626 of a family exiled from Spain, young Shabbatai attended the Talmudic school of Rabbi Joseph Escapa, but apparently the casuistical teaching did not appeal to him. His favorite studies were the cabalistic writings, especially the practical cabala, and his way of life was modeled on the ascetic principles of the masters of Safed. G. Scholem, the foremost authority on Jewish mysticism, has shown conclusively that Shabbatai suffered from manic-depressive personality troubles, melancholic depression alternating with ecstatic exaltation. In 1648, a year considered by cabalistic circles as the year of the manifestation of the Messiah, Shabbatai revealed his claim to messiahship to a small group of followers by pronouncing the sacred tetragrammaton (the divine name) in Hebrew. The elders of the Jewish community of Smyrna put him and his followers under ban; Shabbatai himself left his home town and started a wandering life through the Orient, without friends or real disciples and without doing anything for the furtherance of the messianic aspirations that dominated him at periods of exaltation.

The second and definitive awakening of Shabbatai's messianic consciousness was a result of an ecstatic vision of the cabalist Nathan of Gaza (1644–80), who announced in 1665 that the messianic age was to begin in the following year and that Shabbatai was the messiah. It was Nathan who dispelled Shabbatai's doubts and prevailed upon him to proclaim himself the messiah. The declaration was made in the synagogue of Smyrna on Rosh Hashanah (New Year's Day), amidst the blowing of horns and the multitude shouting: "Long live our King, our Messiah!"

"Letters were sent broadcast throughout Europe, Asia, and Africa announcing the good tidings. Everywhere the approaching deliverance was hailed with jubilation. Prayers were offered up in all the synagogues on behalf of 'Our Lord, King and Master, the holy and righteous Shabbatai Sevi, the anointed of the God of Israel.' The frenzy of the masses knew no bounds. Chaste matrons fell into trances and prophesied, in tongues of which they had previously had no knowledge, the marvels that were soon to take place. There was a wave of penance and ascetic exercises. Special liturgies poured from the printing presses. The merchant princes of the community of Amsterdam, men whose signature would have been good for almost any amount on the bourse, prepared a petition to forward to the pretender assuring him of their implicit faith" [C. Roth, *A Short History of the Jewish People* (rev. ed. Oxford 1943) 329].

All the Jewish communities from Persia and Yemen to England and Holland were involved in the tremendous upheaval and even Gentiles expected the return of the Jews to the Holy Land within a short time. Shabbatai Sevi became a figure of legend, seldom attained by a person still living.

When the Sultan judged that things were going too far, Shabbatai was summoned to Constantinople and imprisoned in the fortress of Abydos on the Gallipoli peninsula. There he established a sort of court, receiving delegations and sending out messengers. Relatives and friends were given provinces of his future kingdom. His birthday, the fast of the 9th day of the month of Ab in memory of the destruction of the Temple, was proclaimed a day of rejoicing. The enthusiasm of the Turkish Jews knew no limits, and warnings from some opponents and disbelievers were not heeded. Finally, faced with death or conversion to Islam, Shabbatai made the latter choice and, since he continued to make trouble, was exiled to Dulcigno in Albania, where he died in 1676.

The emotional impact was so deep and the belief in the legitimacy of the messiah struck such firm roots that even the apostasy of their master did not shake the faith of his followers. Nathan of Gaza, who possessed the secret of interpreting ancient texts, succeeded in elaborating a theory justifying Shabbatai's defection: the messianic deliverance requires the liberation of the sparks of holiness out of the reign of the uncleanness; the messiah would save the world from sin through sin; for the sake of redemption, he would accept worse than death, the disgrace of sin—and the worst of sins, apostasy; this, however, was not real, only apparent: the *descensus ad inferos* would he followed by the ascension to heaven.

Aftermath. Even the death of Shabbatai did not change the belief of his followers. They held that the messiah did not really die; he was "carried off." The doctrine of the reincarnation held by the cabalists justified this interpretation. The believers were faced with the alternative, either to follow Shabbatai in his apostasy or to remain, as a heretical underground, within the framework of Judaism. A minority were converted to Islam and formed the group of the *Doenmeh* ("apostate" in Turkish), who even today, after 300 years, are aware of their Jewish descent. The *Doenmeh* constituted a compact group in Salonica that broke up only in 1924, in the wake of the exchange of populations between Greece and Turkey. The Shabbatian underground continued in some circles of European Jewry for over 150 years, disappearing only in the early 19th century.

After Shabbatai's death, a number of pseudo-messiahs claimed to be his successor, having inherited a portion of his messianic soul. The last in this line was Jacob FRANK of Galicia (1726–91), an unscrupulous adventurer, who, with his followers, temporarily entered the Catholic Church.

After the Shabbatian conflagration, rabbinical circles tried to minimize its extent and to suppress the evidence concerning it. It is the merit of the scholars of the Hebrew University of Jerusalem, outstanding among them Professor Gershom Scholem, to have established on the grounds of a thorough study of manuscript material available, the significance of the Shabbatian movement.

Bibliography: G. G. SCHOLEM, *Sabbatai Zvi and the Sabbatean Movement during His Lifetime,* 2 v. (New York 1957); "In Search of Sabbatai Zevi," in *Hadassah* (June 1961), magazine published in NY; *Major Trends in Jewish Mysticism* (3d ed. London 1955), ch. 8; "Die krypto-jüdische Sekte der Dönme (Sabbatianer) in der Türkei," *Numen* 7 (1960) 93–122. I. BEN-ZEVI, *The Exiled and the Redeemed,* tr. I. A. ABBADY (Philadelphia 1957.). J. H. GREENSTONE, *The Messiah Idea in Jewish History* (Philadelphia 1906). A. H. SILVER, *A History of Messianic Speculation in Israel: From the First through the Seventeenth Centuries* (Boston 1959). R. J. Z. WERBLOWSKY, "Crises of Messianism," *Judaism* 7 (1958) 106–120.

[M. J. STIASSNY]

SHADDAI

No fully satisfactory explanation has been found for the divine epithet, Shaddai (*šaddai*), which appears chiefly in the Pentateuch and Job (where it is used in imitation of the ancient style). The Hebrew verb *šādad,* which it resembles, means ''to lay waste or to destroy''; it is unacceptable because Shaddai is invariably associated with a blessing (Gn 17.1–2; 28.3;35.11; etc.). Under the title of Shaddai God revealed Himself to Patriarchs Abraham, Isaac, and Jacob (Ex 6.3) as the God who protected and watched over them. Shaddai also connoted strength to ancient translators. The Septuagint (LXX) translates it as God, or Lord, or the all-powerful; Aquila and Symmachus use ''the sufficient one''; while St. Jerome construes it as ''the Almighty.'' The Akkadian *šadû,* mountain, suggests grandeur and power; other texts describe God as a rock or fortress [Gn 49.24; 2 Sm 22.2; Ps 77(78).35; Ps 90(91).2]. El-Shaddai may have been the ancestral name for God acquired by Abraham's family during its sojourn in Haran, not far from the north Mesopotamian mountains; later Yahweh was associated with Mt. SINAI. Shaddai was not merely a local deity whom the Hebrews made their own; rather, he was a manifestation of the supreme God, EL. The name Shaddai therefore marks a step in God's progressive revelation of Himself (Ex. 6.3).

See Also: ELOHIM; YAHWEH.

Bibliography: B. W. ANDERSON, *Interpreters Dictionary of the Bible,* ed. G. A. BUTTRICK et al. (Nashville 1962) 2:412. R. DE VAUX, *Ancient Israel, Its Life and Institutions* (New York 1961). W. EICHRODT, *Theology of the Old Testament,* tr. J. A. BAKER (London 1961–).

[R. T. A. MURPHY]

SHAHAN, THOMAS JOSEPH

Bishop, historian, educator; b. Manchester, N.H., Sept. 11, 1857; d. Washington, D.C., March 9, 1932. His parents, Maurice Peter and Mary Anne (Carmody) Shahan, were Irish immigrants. He attended the public schools of Millbury, Mass., and the Sulpician College, Montreal, Canada (1872–78). From 1878 to 1882 he studied at the North American College, Rome, where he was ordained on June 3, 1882, having earlier earned a doctorate in theology. After beginning his priestly work at St. John's, New Haven, Conn., he was appointed in 1883 chancellor of the Diocese of Hartford and secretary to Bishop Lawrence McMahon. Serving in this capacity until 1888, he gained experience in organizing the chancery and building the cathedral.

Scholarship and Writing. Monsignor John J. Keane invited him to teach at The CATHOLIC UNIVERSITY OF AMERICA, Washington, D.C.; Shahan prepared for his assignment by graduate study at the University of Berlin (1889–91), under Adolph Harnack, and at the Sorbonne and Institut Catholique, Paris (1891), under Louis Duchesne. In 1891 he joined the faculty of The Catholic University as professor of church history and patrology; he kept this post until 1909. He was an effective teacher of ecclesiastical history and, after 1895, of Roman law, but his primary interest was in research and publication. As a productive scholar, he contributed for more than 40 years to Catholic periodicals on both sides of the Atlantic. His influence on American Catholic thought was perhaps exerted chiefly through the *Catholic University Bulletin,* a journal noted for its scholarly standards during his editorship (1895–1909). Among other achievements was his work as associate editor of the old *Catholic Encyclopedia,* for which he wrote over 200 articles, and rewrote or translated more than 100 others. The prestige of The Catholic University of America was further advanced by Shahan's books: *The Blessed Virgin in the Catacombs* (1892), *Giovanni Baptista de Rossi* (1900), *The Beginnings of Christianity* (1903), *The Middle Ages, Sketches and Fragments* (1904), *St. Patrick in History* (1904), *The House of God* (1905), and a translation of Bardenhewer's *Patrologie* (1908). Shahan's scholarship brought him rare honors. In 1923 the University of Louvain, Belgium, by the unanimous vote of its Faculty of Theology, conferred on him its infrequently bestowed doctorate of theology, while in 1926 he was elected a fellow of the Medieval Academy of America, an honor reserved for the outstanding mediaevalists of America and Europe. Other awards, in 1928, included a doctorate in canon and civil law from Georgetown University, Washington, D.C., and appointment as assistant at the pontifical throne.

Rectorship. In 1909 Shahan was appointed a domestic prelate and rector of The Catholic University of America. Five years later, he was named titular bishop of Germanicopolis and consecrated by Cardinal Gibbons on Nov. 15, 1914, in the Baltimore Cathedral. Shahan's administration as head of The Catholic University was inspired by his conception of the university's mission in the United States. He envisioned a national university that would be the source of leadership for the American Church. Such preeminence, of which critics both within and without the Church were skeptical, could, he believed, be attained only by developing at the highest level, the graduate schools, an institution comparable in learning, faculty, plant, and academic atmosphere to the best American universities. He enlarged the size of the faculty fourfold, gathering eminent scholars and protecting their academic freedom, even in controversial fields. Tenure became secure, the endowment was tripled, and the departments of theology, canon law, and oriental studies were improved. A number of religious communities were induced to establish houses of study near the university, while an earlier recommendation for extensive affiliation of Catholic educational institutions with the university was put into operation (*see* SHIELDS, THOMAS EDWARD). Shahan also inaugurated the first university summer session under Catholic auspices, the beginning of a significant movement in American Catholic education.

Shahan's concern for the intellectual advancement of the university was matched by his appreciation of the need for adequate buildings. Known as the ''rector scholar,'' he may also be called the ''rector builder.'' The John K. Mullen Memorial Library attested his desire to give his faculty all the library facilities needed, and the Martin Maloney Chemical Laboratory reflected his stress on modern methods and sciences. Additional housing and the central power and heating plant were also his achievements. He built Cardinal Gibbons Memorial Hall to house lay students and Graduate Hall, with its university dining hall, to provide for the increasing number of graduate students. To these he added St. Thomas Hall, occupied by the Paulist Fathers before the erection of St. Paul's College, and St. John's Hall, erected by the Catholic War Council for rehabilitation work after World War I. No structure was more central to his thought, however, than the university church, which he conceived as a national shrine to the Mother of God (*see* NATIONAL SHRINE OF THE IMMACULATE CONCEPTION). He was unusually devoted to the Blessed Mother, and he hoped that the Catholic people of the United States would visit Mary's church and become acquainted with the university supported by their annual collection. Shahan had even more ambitious building plans, but the lack of funds, which was a chronic problem during his rectorship, always stood in the way.

Shahan's activities extended beyond the university campus to affect the cultural life of American Catholicism. Archbishop John T. McNicholas called him ''the Apostle of Enlightenment.'' In this role he shared his bibliographical knowledge with fellow scholars and inspired many educational organizations. He was one of the founders of the Catholic Education Association, which he served as president from 1909 to 1928; the National Conference of Charities, of which he was a member from 1910 to 1928; the Catholic Sisters College (1911); the American Catholic Historical Association (1917); the International Federation of Catholic Historical Associations (1917); and the National Shrine of the Immaculate Conception, in whose crypt he is buried. In 1928 he retired from the rectorship and spent his remaining years at Holy Cross Academy, Washington.

Bibliography: P. J. MCCORMICK, ''Bishop Shahan: American Catholic Educator,'' *The Catholic Educational Review* 30 (1932): 257–265.

[R. J. DEFERRARI]

SHAKERS

Popular name of the members of the United Society of Believers in Christ's Second Appearing, also called the Alethians, or the Millennial Church. This most successful of the communistic societies of 19th–century America originated from the conversion of Ann Lee at a Quaker revival under Jane and James Wardley in Manchester, England. Ann Lee was born in Manchester, England, in 1736, converted in 1758, and married in 1762; her unhappy marital experience, coupled with severe illness, brought about a conviction that concupiscence was the basic cause of human depravity and the world's wrongs. Public confession was the key to regenerate life; celibacy, its rule and cross. Under her leadership the meetings of the group in England were characterized by shaking, whirling, shouting, prophesying, dancing, and singing in strange tongues. In 1773 Ann Lee and some of her followers so disturbed the morning services in Christ Church that they were imprisoned; during this time she claimed visions regarding the manifestation of Christ, ''the male principle.'' She called herself ''Ann of the Word,'' or the ''female principle in Christ''; her followers gave her the title of ''Mother Ann.'' In 1774, after release from prison, she immigrated to America with seven of her followers and settled in the woods near Albany, N.Y. After her death (Sept. 8, 1784), she was succeeded by Joseph Meacham and Lucy Wright, under whom a number of Shaker communal societies were founded, of which the one at Mount Lebanon, N. Y. (1787), is considered the mother community. During his 12 years, Meacham gave the Shakers their effective organization. For the next 25 years the leadership again devolved on a woman, a fact of importance in the peculiar development of the group.

In their religious tenets the Shakers deny every specific Christian doctrine; the underlying principle is rather a strange form of dualism. Mother Lee taught that since Adam and Eve as male and female are essentially made in the image of God, God must exist as the Father and Mother. This dualism is extended even to the plant and mineral kingdoms. The Shakers believe the history of the world is divided into four cycles, that of Noah, Moses, Jesus, and the fourth reaching its culmination in Ann Lee who, as the female counterpart of Jesus, the bride of Jesus, and the mother of all spiritual things, is worthy of the same honor as Jesus. The Shakers spread from New

Interior of the Shaker Meetinghouse, designed by Moses Johnson, built in 1794. (©Michael Freeman/CORBIS)

York to New England and with the Second Awakening into Ohio, Kentucky, and Indiana (*see* GREAT AWAKENING). The sect reached its zenith in the middle of the 19th-century with a membership made up of about 6,000 adults, enjoying great prosperity based principally on agriculture. By 1905, however, the membership had dwindled to less than 1,000; in the 1950s there were fewer than 29 members, and by the 1960s the sect was practically extinct.

Bibliography: M. F. MELCHER, *The Shaker Adventure* (Princeton 1941). E. D. ANDREWS, *The People Called Shakers: A Search for the Perfect Society* (Dover; New York 1953; rev. Gloucester, Mass. 1963). R. B. TAYLOR, *Encyclopedia of Religion and Ethics,* ed. J. HASTINGS (Edinburgh 1908–27) 3.781–783. H. C. DESROCHES, *Les Shakers américains* (Paris 1955).

[E. R. VOLLMAR/EDS.]

SHAKESPEARE, WILLIAM

Dramatist, poet, actor; b. Stratford-on-Avon, April 1564; d. there, April 23, 1616. The facts of Shakespeare's life, preserved in authentic records, are considerable. Unfortunately he left no diaries or personal letters nor did he attract the notice of gossips or notetakers, so that all attempts to write an intimate life must rely on guesswork.

The Biographical Record

The records show that he was the son of John Shakespeare, yeoman and glover, a leading citizen of Stratford, and of Mary Arden of Wilmcote, whose family were staunch Catholic gentlefolk. William was baptized April 26, 1564.

According to Nicholas Rowe (1674–1718), who published the first short biography in 1709, Shakespeare was educated at the Stratford grammar school. The masters of the school during and after his boyhood—all grad-

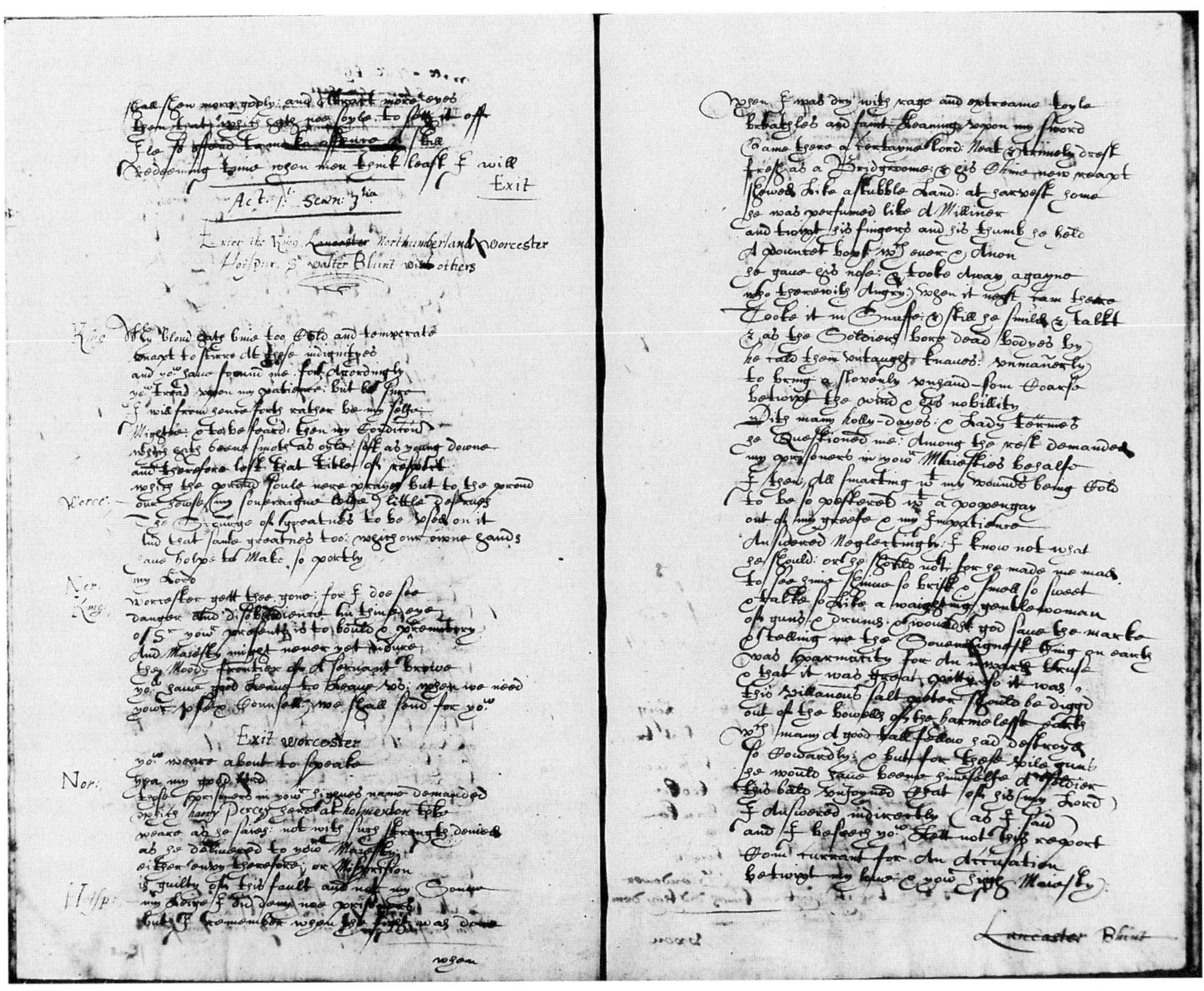

Manuscript pages, "Henry IV," Part 1, II, Act I, Scene 3, by William Shakespeare.

uates of Oxford—were Walter Roche, 1569 to 1571; Simon Hunt, 1571 to 1575 (when he went overseas to Douai and was later admitted into the Society of Jesus in 1578); Thomas Jenkins, 1575 to 1579; John Cottam,1579 to 1581; and Alexander Aspinall, 1581 to 1624. At Elizabethan grammar schools, boys were subjected to an elaborate memory training in Latin (and to a lesser degree in Greek) and read a fair selection of the greater classics. All this fostered in brighter boys a keen interest in language and its use as well as a general knowledge of classical mythology and history.

On Nov. 28, 1582, a license was issued by the Bishop of Worcester to "William Shagspere" to marry "Anne Hathwey" of Stratford after one reading of the banns. According to the inscription on her gravestone, Anne Shakespeare died on Aug. 6, 1623, aged 67 years, and was thus eight years older than her husband. Their three children were baptized in Stratford church—Susanna on May 26, 1583, and Hamnet and Judith (twins) on Feb. 2, 1585. Nothing is certainly known of Shakespeare's early manhood; traditions that he was forced to flee Stratford for stealing deer from Sir Thomas Lucy, the local magnate, and that he was for some time a schoolmaster in the country are disputed and unverifiable but may have some foundation in fact.

Actor and Playwright. From 1592 onward the outline of Shakespeare's life is clear. He had become an actor and playwright in London. On March 3, 1592, Philip Henslowe, owner of the Rose playhouse, noted in his account book the first performance of "harey the vj" (presumably *I Henry VI*), which was the most successful play of the season. Shakespeare was now attracting attention. In August he was venemously attacked by Robert Greene in *A Groatsworth of Wit* (published posthumously). His first poem, *Venus and Adonis,* was entered for printing on April 18, 1593, with a signed dedication to Henry Wriothesley, Earl of Southampton, to whom Shakespeare also dedicated *The Rape of Lucrece* in May

William Shakespeare.

1594. By the end of the year he was a leading sharer in the Lord Chamberlain's company of players, and was mentioned with Richard Burbage and William Kempe as receiving payment for court performances during the Christmas holidays. Shakespeare's son Hamnet was buried Aug. 11, 1596. In October a grant of arms was issued by the College of Heralds to Shakespeare's father, whereby father and son were entitled to call themselves gentlemen. In November, Shakespeare and others were quarrelling with one William Wayte who craved a surety of the peace against them. This record was discovered and published by Leslie Hotson in 1931, but no details of the affair have come to light. On May 4, 1597, Shakespeare was able to purchase for £60 a large house known as New Place in the center of Stratford.

Established Dramatist. By 1598, Shakespeare's reputation as a dramatist was established. Francis Meres in his *Palladis Tamia: Wits' Treasury* (a book of commonplaces entered for printing Sept. 7, 1598) added a ''comparative discourse'' of English poets in which Shakespeare was mentioned more often than any other writer, as poet and writer of comedy and tragedy. Meres also recorded the names of 12 of Shakespeare's plays: *Two Gentlemen of Verona, Comedy of Errors, Love's Labour's Lost, Love's Labour's Won* (apparently lost), *A Midsummer Night's Dream, The Merchant of Venice, Richard II, Richard III, Henry IV, King John, Titus Andronicus, and Romeo and Juliet.* In September 1598, Shakespeare acted a part in Jonson's *Every Man in His Humor.* At the end of the year he, with six other members of the Chamberlain's Company, shared in the expense of erecting the new Globe playhouse on the bankside. On May 1, 1602, he bought 107 acres of arable land in Stratford for £320.

Queen Elizabeth I died on March 24, 1603. Her successor, James I, soon after arriving in London, appointed the Chamberlain's Company to be his own players—The King's Men, as they were henceforward known—and in the license of appointment, Shakespeare's name stands second. Thereafter the King's Men prospered; in the new reign they acted at court four times as often as under the old Queen. About this time Shakespeare was boarding in the house of Christopher Mountjoy, a Huguenot tire-maker, near St. Olave's Church in Cripplegate. Mountjoy's daughter married an apprentice named Stephen Bellot, and Shakespeare aided the negotiations. In 1612, Bellott sued his father-in-law for failing to provide his daughter with the promised portion. Shakespeare was a principal witness in the case. On July 24, 1605, Shakespeare was able to invest £440 in the right to tithes in and about Stratford, which yielded him an income of £60 a year; and in March 1613, he bought for £140 a dwelling house erected over the gatehouse of the old Blackfriars monastery in the city of London.

Final Years. The last years of Shakespeare's life were spent at Stratford, and his name is several times mentioned in local records. On March 25, 1616, he made his will, a lengthy document of three large parchment sheets, now preserved in Somerset House, London. He died on April 23, 1616, and was buried on the 25th in the chancel of the church at Stratford. Soon afterward a tablet with a memorial bust within an ornate arch was erected on the north wall overlooking the grave. A far more important memorial was provided in 1623 when Heminge and Condell, surviving members of the original Chamberlain's Company, sponsored the publication of 36 of Shakespeare's plays in one large volume known as the First Folio. It preserved 22 plays that would otherwise have perished.

These and other similar records show that William Shakespeare was born at Stratford-on-Avon, married at 18, and after a manhood spent no one knows how and where, became a successful dramatist in London; that he prospered and invested his gains; that he died and was buried in his native town (to the great profit of subsequent inhabitants). The lack of heroic or romantic anecdotes has proved so disappointing to some that they have even denied that William Shakespeare of Stratford was indeed the author of his own plays—a doubt which no reputable scholar has ever endorsed.

During Shakespeare's lifetime, 16 of his plays were printed (and reprinted) separately in quarto form; of these some were issued without any author's name. (Those editions in which Shakespeare's name is given on the title page are marked with an asterisk.) *Titus Andronicus,* 1594 (reprinted 1600, 1611); *Richard II,* 1597 (reprinted 1598* twice, 1608*, 1615*); *Richard III,* 1597 (reprinted 1598*, 1602*, 1605*, 1612*); *Romeo and Juliet,* 1597 (a pirated text, 1599—good text, reprinted 1609); *Love's Labour's Lost,* 1598*; *Henry IV,* pt. I, 1598 (reprinted 1599*, 1604*, 1608*, 1613*); *Henry IV,* pt. II, 1600*; *Henry V,* 1600 (corrupt pirated text reprinted 1602); *The Merchant of Venice,* 1600*; *A Midsummer Night's Dream,* 1600*; *Much Ado about Nothing,* 1600*; *The Merry Wives of Windsor,* 1602* (corrupt pirated text); *Hamlet,* 1603* (corrupt pirated text), 1604* (complete text, reprinted 1611*); *King Lear,* 1608*; *Troilus and Cressida,* 1609*; *Pericles,* 1609* (reprinted 1611*), not included in the Folio.

The Plays

Shakespeare came to the theater at just the right time. The Theater—the first playhouse erected in London solely for plays—had been built in 1576; theater-going was increasingly popular; professional actors had gained competence and were prospering; and although the art of drama had not yet fully matured, most of the major problems of play writing had been resolved. Shakespeare's immediate predecessors—especially Marlowe and Kyd—were learning how to construct a plot with a theme, how to create character, and to write effective dramatic speeches and quick, lively dialogue. Moreover, the London theater was just becoming a national institution that, as never before or since, expressed the feelings of a nation. In addition, Shakespeare had to earn his living by writing plays that would please mixed audiences, so that he was not tempted to appeal solely either to the intellectuals or to the groundlings. Ben Jonson quipped that Shakespeare had little Latin and less Greek, but this could be an advantage. When Shakespeare wanted a metaphor or a simile, he was less inclined to borrow from the classics or the commonplace book; instead he used those direct experiences that came to him through his five senses, with the result that his words have a unique and permanent vitality.

Shakespeare's working life falls into four periods of activity, broken by intervals when the playhouses were shut because of outbreaks of the plague in London. These occurred in 1592 to 1594, 1603, and 1609 to 1611. In each period there were notable developments in his dramatic skill and technique.

The First Period—to 1594. To the period before 1594 belong the three parts of *Henry VI,* which begins with the funeral of Henry V and ends with the murder of the saintly but ineffectual Henry VI by Richard of Gloucester. Their general theme is the anarchy that befell England during the Wars of the Roses (1455–85) when the descendants of Edward III fought each other for the throne—a theme very close to Englishmen of the 1590s who feared that the death of Elizabeth I without an acknowledged heir would again lead to a disputed succession and general anarchy. In this period Shakespeare also wrote *The Taming of the Shrew* (a recasting of an old play), *The Comedy of Errors* (another version of Plautus's comedy of mistaken identities, *The Twin Menechmi*), *The Two Gentlemen of Verona* (a romantic story of the treachery of Proteus toward his friend Valentine), and the brilliant society play *Love's Labour's Lost* (which abounds in witty topicalities, most of which are now unintelligible). He also wrote one tragedy, *Titus Andronicus,* an accumulation of horrors—rape, mutilation, murder, and unwitting cannibalism—one of his most popular plays.

In all these early plays Shakespeare showed considerable facility with words and a conscious concern with literary art: alliteration, wordplay, puns, variety of meter, rhetorical devices of every kind, and an excess of elaborate, obvious poetic imagery used more for its own sake than to illumine meaning. At first Shakespeare was the clever amateur showing off his skill in entertaining an audience rather than a serious dramatist.

The Second Period—1594 to 1603. After the plague of 1592 to 1594, the playing companies were reorganized and Shakespeare became a full sharer in the Chamberlain's company. In *Romeo and Juliet,* his first great play (and the finest drama produced in English to that time), he had become a serious professional writer who saw significance behind the story, for the theme of the tragedy is not only the useless deaths of two passionate young lovers but the futility of family hatred. Similarly, in *Richard III,* which concluded the story of the Wars of the Roses with the death of Richard and the establishment of the Tudor dynasty, Shakespeare concentrated on the character of a man morally warped by physical deformity. Evil deeds bring inevitable retribution. In *The Merchant of Venice* he first showed complete mastery of dramatic technique. Shakespeare had considerable understanding of Shylock's wrongs and in the trial scene he touched, though not very deeply, on the fundamental issue of justice versus mercy.

About the same time as *Romeo and Juliet,* Shakespeare had returned to history in *Richard II* to show how the civil wars started; some two or three years later he wrote the two parts of *Henry IV,* which are concerned partly with the education of Prince Hal but even more with the disreputable adventures of Sir John Falstaff, the greatest comic character in English drama. Shakespeare ended the series with *Henry V,* the portrait of a great soldier-king. In these plays Shakespeare revealed deep understanding of the lonely responsibility, everlasting anxiety, and ruthlessness essential to a successful ruler of men. He also stressed the moral that, in dethroning the anointed King Richard II, Henry of Bolingbroke was the direct cause of the long agonies of the Wars of the Roses.

To this second period also belong the three most popular comedies: *Much Ado about Nothing,* which combines the romantic story of the wronging of Hero and the realistic comedy of how Benedick the vowed bachelor and Beatrice the sworn manhater are tricked into love; *As You Like It,* a pastoral romance with a considerable vein of mockery; and *Twelfth Night,* another story of the mistakes caused by twins, but so exquisitely wrought that it is the most frequently acted of all Shakespeare's comedies. *The Merry Wives of Windsor,* though still actable, is not one of the greater comedies; the attempt to show Falstaff in love (by royal command of Queen Elizabeth) was beyond anyone's powers, for Falstaff is essentially a man's man. In 1599, Shakespeare wrote also the Roman tragedy of *Julius Caesar,* a straight, competent dramatization of the story told in Plutarch's *Lives;* Antony's speech delivered at Caesar's funeral showed that Shakespeare had a full understanding of the arts of demagogy. *Hamlet,* the most fascinating and most controverted play ever written, and *Othello,* the best constructed of all the tragedies, were written at the turn of the century, as was *Troilus and Cressida,* a bitter comment on false and romantic notions of love, honor, and war.

The art of drama had advanced very rapidly in the last years of the old queen, and Shakespeare now had rivals, chief among them Jonson, Marston, Chapman, and Dekker. Playgoers had become keen, critical, and sophisticated in their demands. At the accession of James I in March 1603, the prospects of Shakespeare's company improved, especially after the king had made them his own players; but in May the worst outbreak of plague for many years again interrupted playgoing until the end of the year.

The Third Period—1603 to 1616. In the third period, Shakespeare's first play was the "dark comedy" *Measure for Measure;* it reflects the newer moods of the public but is not one of his best. In it he states a stark problem in ethics—whether Claudio's life should be saved at the price of Isabella's chastity—but offers no other solution than darkling assignations, substituted lovers and heads, and a melodramatic happy ending. The play has, however, continued to intrigue modern critics.

The Tragedy of King Lear, the deepest of all the tragedies, was written in 1605–06. In it Shakespeare offers a vision of how the good is powerless against absolute evil, and how, ultimately, man can but "endure his going hence even as his coming hither." *Macbeth* was written about the same time; it dramatizes a story of ambition and murder and the subsequent degeneration of Macbeth and his ruthless wife. There are some signs that the play was written in haste to please King James. In both *Lear* and *Macbeth* the language is difficult because of its excessive concentration of phrase and image; the thought has become too overwhelming for clearly logical expression. *Antony and Cleopatra* followed, continuing the story of Antony to his ruin through his fatal passion for Cleopatra, a play which Shakespeare obviously wrote with zest; it abounds in his finest dramatic verse.

The last of the tragedies was *Coriolanus,* a political play in which the balance of antipathy (rather than of sympathy) is held evenly between the arrogance of a proud patrician and the opportunism of the tribunes of the people; but the major theme is the dominance of Volumnia over the son whom she has so disastrously molded. The last of the series was *Timon of Athens,* probably never finished, in which the misanthropy that had been accumulating in Shakespeare's plays reached its depth. By this time (1609) the taste of playgoers was turning from serious drama to the more facile kind of tragicomedy popularized by the two young dramatists Beaumont (1584–1616) and Fletcher (1579–1625).

Another long interruption occurred between 1609 and 1611. When Shakespeare resumed playwriting, his themes and methods changed. The next four plays were the comedies of the "final period." Shakespeare was only part author of *Pericles; Cymbeline,* a fantastic mingling of a story by Boccaccio of a bet on the chastity of a faithful wife and dubious Romano-British history, was dubbed by Dr. Johnson "unresisting imbecility." In *The Winter's Tale,* a dramatization of a story by Greene, the fatal suspicion of Leontes that his wife Hermione has committed adultery with his friend Polixenes is finally purged when the son of Polixenes is betrothed to Hermione's long-lost daughter Perdita.

The last of the comedies was *The Tempest,* which some regard as the finest and greatest of the poetic dramas. Shakespeare's last surviving play, *Henry VIII* (in which he may have collaborated with Fletcher), was a return to English history. As an oblique comment on the Reformation in England and its causes, the play is enigmatic, for, as the events are shown, the author's sympathies are all with Katherine, Henry's much wronged wife and Queen. To Shakespeare's contemporaries, for whom the Reformation was still a vital issue, the play would have been most remarkable for what it left unsaid.

Shakespeare also wrote two long narrative poems, *Venus and Adonis* and *The Rape of Lucrece,* and *The Sonnets. Venus and Adonis* (1593) tells how the goddess Venus hotly but vainly wooed the love of young Adonis, who was slain by a wild boar. The poem was regarded by contemporaries as lascivious; it was very popular. *The Rape of Lucrece* is a versifying of the sad story of how Lucrece, treacherously outraged by Tarquin, killed herself to redeem her lost honor. *The Sonnets* (published in 1609, but probably written in the 1590s) are mostly written to a beautiful young man. If they are autobiographical, they reveal a story of Shakespeare's relations with a young man of better fortune than himself, of quarrels and rivals, of the theft of the poet's mistress by the young friend, of reconciliation. A small group of the sonnets is addressed to the faithless mistress—the Dark Lady. Various candidates for the post of the young man have been proposed, of whom the two favorites are Henry Wriothesley, Earl of Southampton, and William Herbert, Earl of Pembroke; but for neither is the evidence as yet conclusive.

Shakespeare's Religion

Shakespeare has been claimed by Catholics, Anglicans, Puritans, and agnostics. For the Anglican claim, it can be pointed out that he and his children were all baptized in the Anglican church at Stratford, in which he was also buried. In his plays he echoes the English Bible and the Anglican Book of Common Prayer. But he shows equally a considerable knowledge of Catholic teaching, doctrine, and practice; and there is good evidence that his father, John Shakespeare, was a zealous Catholic, for in 1592 his name appears in a list of 42 who were reported to the Bishop of Worcester as "recusants."

His Father's "Will." More significant is a little-known document called "John Shakespeare's Will." The original, long since destroyed, was found hidden in the tiles of his house in Henley Street at Stratford. A transcript was made by a local antiquary, John Jordan, and published in *The Gentleman's Magazine* in 1783. The document was accepted as genuine by Edmund Malone, who reprinted it in his edition of Shakespeare's works in 1790. The will is a profession of the Catholic faith in the form of a spiritual testament in 14 clauses, each beginning with "I, John Shakespeare." The testator declares that at the time of writing he may die unprepared by any sacrament, and if so he prays that he may be spiritually anointed. This form of spiritual testament was drawn up by St. Charles BORROMEO and was especially designed for times of religious persecution. Versions are known in Spanish, Italian, and the Swiss dialect. It is a sign of John Shakespeare's steadfastness that he hid rather than burnt so dangerous a document, especially after the troubles that befell his wife's family in 1583–84.

The senior member of the Arden family at that time was Edward Arden of Park Hall, who maintained a priest, Hugh Hall, to say Mass. In 1583, when the mission of St. Edmund CAMPION was still disturbing the Privy Council, Edward Arden's son-in-law, John Somerville, oppressed by private and religious troubles, went out of his mind, eluded his family, and made for London where he was heard to utter wild threats against the life of Elizabeth. As a result the whole family was involved in a charge of high treason. Edward Arden was condemned to death and executed by quartering at Smithfield on Dec. 26, 1584. His wife and Hall were also condemned. Mrs. Arden was subsequently pardoned; the priest and Somerville died in prison. Edward Arden was a cousin of Shakespeare's mother. Shakespeare was 20 at this time. In Warwickshire the chief agent in the persecution of the Ardens was that Sir Thomas Lucy who, according to the legends of Shakespeare's early manhood, was the cause of his flight from Stratford. When Shakespeare reemerged from obscurity, he dedicated his *Venus and Adonis* to the young Earl of Southampton, whose family was Catholic.

Catholic Sympathies. It is thus likely that Shakespeare was brought up in a Catholic home, but there is no evidence that he practiced the faith in his maturity. His sympathies in the plays—so far as the plays can be used as evidence—are generally Catholic. His priests, such as Friar Laurence in *Romeo and Juliet,* Friar Francis in *Much Ado,* the priest in *Twelfth Night,* are grave, patient, well-meaning men whom everyone respects. In *Measure for Measure,* the Duke, for worthy motives, disguises himself as a friar, and even hears confessions—an action which no one seemed to question.

The few Protestant ministers who appear in the plays are less admirable. Sir Hugh Evans in *The Merry Wives* is amusing; Sir Nathaniel in *Love's Labour's Lost* is a worthy man and a good bowler though an indifferent actor; in *As You Like It,* Sir Oliver Martext is a poor specimen. It is also relevant that in his version of *King John,* Shakespeare wiped out the hearty anti-Catholic propaganda of the old play he recast. In *Hamlet* there are several instances of Catholic doctrine and sentiment. The Ghost of Hamlet's father, for example, comes back from Purgatory (and not, as was more usual with returned ghosts in Elizabethan dramas, from a classical Hades), whither he was suddenly dispatched "unhouseled, disappointed, unanealed"—without absolution, preparation or Extreme Unction; but to Hamlet, death is a consummation devoutly to be wished only if it leads to the annihilation of a dreamless sleep. Hamlet himself is more interested in man than in God.

While the early plays are sprinkled with Christian sentiments, orthodox and often quite conventional, the later plays, especially the tragedies, seem to indicate that Shakespeare had lapsed into an almost Greek belief in fate. Finally in *The Tempest* where—if ever—Shakespeare speaks out of part through Prospero, he sees the universe dissolving to leave not a rack—a wisp of cloud —behind.

> We are such stuff
> As dreams are made on; and our little life
> Is rounded with a sleep.

Until further evidence is available, the question of Shakespeare's religious convictions and practice must remain unsolved. There is no record that he ever suffered for his faith either in purse or in person; unlike his father or Ben Jonson, he is not known to have been delated as a recusant or fined for failure to attend the services of the state Church. Nevertheless there is the flat statement of Archdeacon Richard Davies (d. 1708), a Warwickshire antiquary, that "he died a papist."

Bibliography: The bibliography of Shakespeare is enormous and increases yearly by more than 200 items. The best general guide is F. W. BATESON, ed., *The Cambridge Bibliography of English Literature,* 5 v. (Cambridge, Eng. 1940–57). New work is recorded annually in *Year's Work in English Studies* (London 1919–), *Shakespeare Survey* (Cambridge, Eng. 1948–), and *Shakespeare Quarterly* (New York 1950–). The following is but a very short selection. General and reference. E. K. CHAMBERS, *William Shakespeare: A Study of Facts and Problems,* 2 v. (Oxford 1930) includes all relevant records and documents concerning Shakespeare. J. BARTLETT, *A New and Complete Concordance . . . to the Dramatic Works of Shakespeare* (London 1894, 1896, 1922, 1927, 1937). C. M. INGLEBY, *The Shakespeare Allusion-Book,* ed. J. J. MUNRO, 2 v. (London 1932). T. W. BALDWIN, *William Shakespere's Small Latine and Lesse Greeke,* 2 v. (Urbana, Ill. 1944) comprehensive account of Elizabethan education. H. GRANVILLE-BARKER and G. B. HARRISON, eds., *A Companion to Shakespeare Studies* (New York 1934). Stage conditions. E. K. CHAMBERS, *The Elizabethan Stage,* 4 v. (Oxford 1923). W. W. GREG, ed., *Henslowe's Diary,* 2 v. (London 1904–08); *Henslowe Papers, idem.* (London 1907). J. C. ADAMS, *The Globe Playhouse* (Cambridge, Mass. 1942). C. W. HODGES, *The Globe Restored* (London 1953). A. HARBAGE, *Shakespeare's Audience* (New York 1941). Sources of the plays. G. BULLOUGH, *ed., Narrative and Dramatic Sources of Shakespeare* (New York 1957–) in progress; 4 v. issued. Study of the text. W. W. GREG, *The Shakespeare First Folio: Its Bibiographical and Textual History* (Oxford 1955). Shakespeare's religion. (Catholic), H. MUTSCHMAN, *Shakespeare and Catholicism* (New York 1952). (Protestant). E. I. FRIPP, *Shakespeare, Man and Artist,* 2 v. (London 1938), very full about Shakespeare's Stratford background. Criticism. The best of the early criticism is included in D. N. SMITH, ed., *Shakespeare Criticism* (London 1916), beginnings to Carlyle. Of the established critics, the most important are: S. T. COLERIDGE, *Coleridge's Shakespearean Criticism,* ed. T. M. RAYSOR, 2 v. (London 1930). W. HAZLITT, *Characters of Shakespeare's Plays* (London 1917). E. DOWDEN, *Shakespeare: A Critical Study of His Mind and Art* (London 1875). A. C. BRADLEY, *Shakespearean Tragedy* (New York 1904). H. GRANVILLE-BARKER, *Prefaces to Shakespeare,* 5 series (London 1923–1947). Representative of modern approaches are G. W. KNIGHT, *The Wheel of Fire* (London 1930). E. E. STOLL, *Shakespeare Studies* (New York 1927). C. F. E. SPURGEON, *Shakespeare's Imagery, and What It Tells Us* (New York 1936). R. B. HEILMAN, *This Great Stage* (Baton Rouge 1948). E. JONES, *Hamlet and Oedipus* (Garden City, N.Y. 1949). W. CLEMEN, *The Development of Shakespeare's Imagery* (Cambridge, Mass. 1951). Annotated texts. S. JOHNSON, *ed. The Plays of William Shakespeare,* 8 v. (London 1765). H. H. FURNESS, ed., *A New Variorum Edition of Shakespeare* (Philadelphia 1871–). U. ELLIS-FERMOR, ed., *The Arden Shakespeare* (new ed. Cambridge, Mass. 1951–). A. QUILLER-COUCH and J. D. WILSON, eds., *The New Shakespeare* (New York 1921–). G. B. HARRISON, ed., *Shakespeare: The Complete Works* (New York 1952). G. M. PINCISS, *Forbidden Matter: Religion in the Drama of Shakespeare and His Contemporaries* (Newark, Del.; London; and Cranbury, N.J., 2000). S. MARX, *Shakespeare and the Bible* (Oxford and New York 2000). H. FISCH, *The Biblical Presence in Shakespeare, Milton, and Blake: A Comparative Study* (Oxford and New York 1999). D. D. WATERS, *Christian Settings in Shakespeare's Tragedies* (Rutherford, N.J.; London; and Cranbury, N.J. 1994). R. W. BATTENHOUSE, ed., *Shakespeare's Christian Dimension: An Anthology of Commentary.* (Bloomington, Ind. 1994). J. DOLLIMORE, *Radical Tragedy: Religion, Ideology, and Power in the Drama of Shakespeare and His Contemporaries* (Durham, N.C. 2nd ed., 1993). R. R. REED, *Crime and God's Judgment in Shakespeare* (Lexington, Ky. 1984).

[G. B. HARRISON]

SHAMAN AND MEDICINE MAN

The Tungus term *shaman,* probably derived from the Sanskrit *śramana* (ascetic) via the Pali *samana* (Buddhist monk) is used by anthropologists for that class of male and female religious practitioners who acquire or purchase supernatural power to be used primarily in causing, diagnosing, or curing disease, but also in DIVINATION, rainmaking, communication with the dead, finding lost objects, and in hunting, war, and fertility MAGIC. Shamans are differentiated by social scientists from priests in that they do not study a specific body of doctrine, but acquire their powers as the result of a "vision quest" or other contact with the spirit world, while others pay to learn these skills through apprenticing themselves to famous practitioners. Also, shamans do not follow prescribed rituals, as priests do, but are free to develop individual "performances" that may involve narcotically induced trances, singing, dancing, drumming, sleight of hand, and such theatrical effects as the "shaking lodge" of the Salteaux or the private "angakok" language of Eskimo shamans. In early reports of travelers, and still in the popular press, shamans are often described as "medicine men," but this term and its synonyms, "conjurer," "witch doctor," "wizard," and "magician," are too imprecise for scholarly use.

Shamanism in its most developed form exists in eastern Siberia and Manchuria among the Tungus, Koryak, Ostyak, Chuckchee, Yakut, and Samoyed, where the shaman maintains his position as spiritual leader by acting as intermediary between the ethnic group and the unseen world of gods, demons, and ancestral spirits. Related magical curing practices extend across northern Asia to the Lapps and Finno-Ugrian communities of Europe, and have been incorporated into popular BUDDHISM in Sri Lanka, Southeast Asia, Tibet, China, Korea, and Japan.

Shamanistic practices vary so widely throughout the New World that some may have resulted from independent invention rather than from diffusion from Asia. For instance, only Eskimo shamans are thought actually to be possessed by their spirit helpers during trances, as in Siberia, while elsewhere in the New World the spirits merely communicate their wishes through the entranced shaman as medium. Because shamans are paid for their services, they often become the richest members of their groups, and because their power is feared, they usually become politically powerful. In at least three areas, the American Southeast, among the Guarani of central South America, and in Sumatra, shamans have exercised effective political control. Thus, although a manifestation of epilepsy, transvestism, crippling disease, or other physical and mental disorder is often interpreted as a call to become a shaman, the evidence suggests that most shamans are fully in touch with their own cultural realities.

Like fetishism, shamanism has sometimes been used as a general category of primitive RELIGION, stressing the role of the magic practitioner in controlling spiritual forces. But such attempts to classify religions systems on the basis of one or more criteria have been superseded principally by studies that show how a religious system is integrated with its social and cultural matrix.

Bibliography: H. N. MICHAEL, ed., *Studies in Siberian Shamanism* (Toronto 1963). M. CZAPLICKA, *Aboriginal Siberia* (Oxford 1914) pt.3. S. M. SHIROKOGOROV, *Psychomental Complex of the Tungus* (London 1935), pt.4. M. ELIADE, *Shamanism: Archaic Techniques of Ecstasy,* tr. W. R. TRASK (Bollingen Series 76; rev. ed. New York 1964).

[D. J. CROWLEY]

SHAME

Shame is the painful feeling of finding oneself exposed, uncovered, and vulnerable. Shame takes different forms and serves different purposes. *Shame anxiety* relates to what is anticipated and is what people experience when they are suddenly exposed and sense the threat of rejection. The state of *being ashamed*, a complex cognitive and affective pattern, is a reaction to something which has already happened. The *sense of shame* serves to restrain a person's behavior and is sometimes referred to as a sense of discretion or modesty.

Female shaman mixes potion in Balinese village, Bali, Indonesia. (©Buddy Mays/CORBIS)

Distinctions between Shame and Guilt. Shame and guilt are closely related and yet are distinct phenomena. Some affect theorists see guilt as part of the shame family of emotions, arguing that guilt is at least shame about action. However, the two terms seem to refer to different experiential worlds. Experiences having to do with shame typically include embarrassment, humiliation, disgrace, ridicule, dishonor, and weakness. Guilt seems to touch on the experience of transgression, injury, debt, obligation, and wrongdoing. Shame involves more of a physiological response than guilt does. From a psychoanalytic perspective, shame is a response to the self's shortcomings or failure whereas guilt is a response to some transgression. Shame has a more global character while guilt typically points to something specific.

Anthropological Perspectives. There is a tendency in contemporary society to minimize, if not deny, the role of shame in adult life. To bolster this position, reference is sometime made to the distinction in anthropology between shame cultures and guilt cultures. According to this distinction, ancient and traditional societies maintain social control through shame because they depend on external sanctions, whereas modern societies that employ internal sanctions depend on guilt. Modern society is seen as having advanced beyond shame. As a result of such a perspective the role of shame in creating and maintaining certain pathologies, as well as the positive contribution shame makes to maintaining a healthy sense of self, is often overlooked.

A more balanced anthropological perspective on shame is willing to acknowledge its positive dimension. By sustaining the human need for privacy, shame functions as a protective covering for the process of self-integration. The sense of shame connects here with awe, that religious feeling elicited in the presence of the holy whose mystery must be respected. An appropriate sense of shame indicates that one has a proper estimation of the mystery of oneself as well as of the surrounding world and knows one's place within it. Shame is like the protective covering over the *tremendum* of which Rudolf Otto spoke in his analysis of the experience of the holy.

The other side of shame, better known by most people, is one's uncomfortable awareness that one falls short of what one should be. It is the feeling that there is a major discrepancy between the ideal and the reality of oneself. In some significant way the self is perceived to be wanting, to be defective. The efforts to block the pain of this type of shame explain a number of behavioral problems and interpersonal difficulties.

Dynamics of Shame as a Painful Affect. Affect theorists see shame as a feeling that functions to increase awareness so that a person is more attuned to whatever activated shame and the varied mental and physical responses that stimulus elicited. Shame as a sense of defectiveness begins in significant interpersonal relationships such as a child has with its parents. One way of thinking about the shame-inducing process is to focus on the interpersonal bridge that exists between a person and significant others in his or her life. Such a bridge is built on expectations that the other will respond in an appropriate way to particular needs that are expressed, such as the need for affirmation. Shame originates when that bridge is severed and the other fails to respond. Basic expectations of that other are suddenly revealed as wrong.

Shame is an alienating affect in which the sharp awareness that the self is in some way deficient as a human being affects how one lives and operates. It is not a trivial experience, for there seems to be no way to change the situation of one's basic deficiency. Shame impacts on the whole self; it is a soul sickness. A process of internalization further insures that a given shame experience has lasting influence through the beliefs and attitudes about the self as defective that come to shape one's sense of identity.

As a painful affect shame invites certain defending strategies. Contempt for others, blaming, rage, or perfectionism are strategies which are designed to help a person cope with shame. However, employing such strategies leads to distorted relationships with others. People can come to disown those parts of themselves which have provoked the shame experience. Addictions can emerge to further mask and hide the shame-producing aspect of the self. Twelve-step programs such as Alcoholics Anonymous seek to address the issue of shame as well as to guide people in forming more adequate images of self.

Shame and Culture. Culture is itself an interpersonal bridge that holds people together. It deems certain activities and behaviors as appropriate, and consequently shields those who engage in such activities and behaviors from the discomfort of shame which they might experience in a different culture. At the same time, culture can subtly dictate the way people are to act and respond, providing them with a cultural ''script'' to be followed in the course of their life. So, for instance, in American society there are proposed scripts which, when ignored, bring shame to those who do not adhere to them. Three such scripts are commonly described as prominent on the American scene. The success script proposes that success through accomplishments is the way to declare one's worth; not to succeed is to reveal one's inadequacy. The independence script suggests that a cause for pride is one's self-sufficiency; a cause for shame is one's neediness. The popularity script underscores the importance of conformity; it is shameful to be different.

In the face of such cultural forces, the Christian theological tradition reminds people of their innate dignity and value as persons made in the image of God. It urges an acceptance and indeed a celebration of human finitude and limitations before a God who is infinite. Finally, the cross, an ancient instrument of shame and now *the* Christian symbol, reminds believers of how Christ has embraced all of human suffering and liberated humanity from all that weighs it down.

Bibliography: R. H. ALBERS, *Shame: A Faith Perspective* (New York 1995). G. KAUFMAN, *Shame: The Power of Caring*, 3d ed., revised and expanded (Rochester, Vt. 1992). D. L. NATHANSON, *Shame and Pride: Affect, Sex, and the Birth of the Self* (New York and London 1992). C. D. SCHNEIDER, *Shame, Exposure, and Privacy* (New York 1977). *The Widening Scope of Shame*, ed. M. R. LANSKY and A. P. MORRISON (Hillsdale, N.J. 1997). L. WURMSER, *The Mask of Shame* (Northvale, N.J. 1981).

[R. STUDZINSKI]

SHARBEL MAKHLOUF, ST.

Maronite hermit (*see* MARONITES); b. in the mountain village of Biqa-Kafra, Lebanon, May 8, 1828; d. Dec. 24, 1898. The youngest of five children born to a poor Maronite family, he was christened Joseph. At the age of 23 he entered the monastery of Our Lady of Mayfouk (north of Byblos). After two years of novitiate, in 1853, he was sent to St. Maron monastery in Annaya where he pronounced the monastic vows and took on the name of an early Eastern martyr, Sharbel. He then studied philosophy and theology in the monastery of Kfifan where his teachers, one of whom was Bl. Neemtallah El Hardini (1808–1858), nurtured within him a deep love for monastic life. After he was ordained to the priesthood in 1859, Sharbel was sent back to the St. Maron monastery where he lived for the next 16 years.

In 1875 Sharbel asked for and was granted permission to take up residence in St. Peter and Paul hermitage, located on a hill near the monastery. He lived there for the last 23 years of his life. Although he did not leave behind any writings, his life and love for God became an open book read by many people, and God granted him the gift of performing miracles even during his lifetime. He suffered a stroke during the Holy Liturgy, Dec. 18, 1898, and died a week later at the age of 70. His tomb in the Monastery of Saint Maron in Annaya, Lebanon, is a place of pilgrimage.

On the evening of St. Sharbel's funeral, his superior wrote, ''Because of what he will do after his death, I need not talk about his behavior.'' A few months after his death a bright light was seen surrounding his tomb. When his superiors opened it, they found his body still intact. Pope Paul VI beatified Sharbel at the closing of the Second Vatican Council, Dec. 5, 1965, and on Oct. 9, 1977 he canonized him.

Feast: Dec. 24.

Bibliography: P. DAHER, *A Miraculous Star in the East, Charbel Makhlouf* (Beirut 1952). J. EID, *The Hermit of Lebanon* (New York 1955). J. P. HADDAD, *Charbel un saint du liban* (ed. Maisonneuve 1978).

[D. ASHKAR]

SHAUGHNESSY, GERALD

Fourth bishop of Seattle, Wash., diocese (now archdiocese); b. Everett, Mass., May 19, 1887; d. Seattle, May 18, 1950. He was the son of Joseph and Margaret (Colwell) Shaughnessy, and attended Boston College on a Cronin scholarship, graduating in 1909. From then until 1916 he taught in Maryland, Montana, and Utah, where he became acquainted with the Society of Mary. He entered their novitiate Sept. 7, 1916, taking perpetual vows May 10, 1918. After theological studies at Marist College in Washington, D.C., he was ordained there June 20, 1920, by Abp. (later Cardinal) John Bonzano, Apostolic Delegate to the U.S. In addition to earning baccalaureate, licentiate, and doctoral degrees in theology at the Catholic University of America, he was a member of the apostolic delegation from 1919 to 1932, professor at Marist College from 1920 to 1923 and 1928 to 1930, member of the original staff of Notre Dame Seminary, New Orleans, La., from 1923 to 1924, and a member of the Marist Mission Band from 1924 to 1928. On completion of his second novitiate at Lyons, France, from 1930 to 1931, he did special literary work in Rome, and the next year became master of the Marist second novitiate in Washington. On July 1, 1933, he was named to the see of Seattle and was consecrated on September 19 by Abp. Amleto G. Cicognani, then Apostolic Delegate, at the National Shrine of the Immaculate Conception, Washington, D.C.

Beginning his episcopate during the Great Depression, he put the precarious finances of the diocese on a firm footing and launched a strenuous program of building and consolidating. In 1938 he convoked the Fifth Diocesan Synod of Seattle. In addition to his fiscal and pastoral activities he was given charge of the Missionary Servants of the Most Holy Trinity and approved the SERRA INTERNATIONAL for priestly vocations. He contributed to the (old) *Catholic Encyclopedia* supplement and to various reviews, and published an often quoted statistical study, *Has the Immigrant Kept the Faith?* (1925). He also adapted from the French two works of Julius Grimal, published under the English titles *To Die with Jesus* (1925) and *With Jesus to the Priesthood* (1932).

Richly endowed intellectually, he was also an energetic worker, spending himself with unstinted devotion until November 1945 when he suffered a serious stroke from which he never completely recovered. On Feb. 28, 1948, the coadjutor he had requested was granted him in the person of Thomas A. Connolly, Auxiliary Bishop of San Francisco, who succeeded him on his death.

Bibliography: Archives of the Society of Mary: General, in Rome; Provincial, in Washington, D.C.

[N. A. WEBER]

SHEA, JOHN DAWSON GILMARY

Historian; b. New York City, July 22, 1824; d. Elizabeth, N.J., Feb. 22, 1892. His father, James Shea, emigrated from Ireland to New York City to become principal of the Columbia College grammar school,

John Dawson Gilmary Shea.

which John attended, and a leader in local Democratic politics. His mother, Mary Ann (Flannigan) Shea, was from an old Boston family and a descendant of Nicholas Upsall, who came to America with Gov. John Winthrop in 1630. Shea early evidenced an interest in Catholic history; he obtained work with a Spanish merchant in order to acquire a knowledge of the language, and at the age of 14 he published a biography of Cardinal Alvarez Carrillo de Arbornóz in the *Young People's Catholic Magazine* (1838). Although he turned to the study of law and was admitted to the New York bar (1846), Shea continued his interest in Catholic history with a number of articles in the *U.S. Catholic Magazine*. He joined the Society of Jesus (1848), taking the name Gilmary; he studied at St. John's College, Fordham, N.Y., and St. Mary's College, Montreal, Canada, until 1852, when he left the Society to resume his historical work. His *Discovery and Exploration of the Mississippi Valley* (1852) brought favorable notice from non-Catholic scholars and launched a career during which he wrote or edited more than 250 titles. His articles appeared in popular Catholic serials, notably the *Catholic World*, the *American Catholic Quarterly Review*, and the *Boston Pilot*, and also in popular encyclopedias.

In 1854 he married Sophie Savage and thereafter engaged in numerous endeavors to support his family. He contracted with publishing firms for such well received school histories as *A General History of Modern Europe* (1854), *An Elementary History of the U.S.* (1855), and *The Catholic Church in the U.S.* (1856). He contributed also to Justin Winsor's noted history, acted as historiographer of the Archdiocese of New York, and served as editor of D. and J. Sadlier's *General Catholic Directory and Almanac* (1859–90), of the *Historical Magazine* (1859–65), and of the *Catholic News* (1889–92). None of this interfered with his labor in American Catholic history. His early interest in Catholic missions among the natives led in 1854 to the *History of the Catholic Missions among the Native American Tribes of the U.S., 1529–1854* and to the 26-volume Cramoisy Series of Jesuit explorations in North America (1857–87). His reputation as an authority on the Native Americans was advanced by his editing of the 15-volume *Library of American Linguistics* (1860–74), a collection of grammars and dictionaries. Shea's great work, however, was his four-volume *History of the Catholic Church in the U.S.* (1886–92), on which he was working at his death.

Shea's research received some support from Georgetown University, Washington, D.C., whose centennial history he wrote in 1891, and from the Plenary Council of Baltimore in 1884. Nevertheless, he failed to win an appointment at The Catholic University of America, Washington, D.C., and there was little market for his works in Catholic schools and colleges. He was a pioneer in his work, arousing interest as cofounder and first president of the U.S. Catholic Historical Society (1884) and laboriously collecting the sources for future historical research. He left a large collection of Americana and a tradition of careful scholarship, reliability, and bibliographical diligence. Recognition of his primary position in American Catholic historiography came from Fordham and Georgetown, which gave him honorary degrees, and from the University of Notre Dame, Ind., which awarded him its Laetare medal (1883).

In addition to the works already mentioned. Shea's best-known books include his *Hierarchy of the Catholic Church in the U.S.* (1886), as well as *Early Voyages up and down the Mississippi* (1861), *The Operations of the French Fleet under Count de Grasse* (1864), a translation of P. F. X. Charlevoix's *History and General Description of New France* 6 v. (1866–72), *The Life of Pius IX* (1877), *The Catholic Churches of N.Y.C.* (1878), *The Catholic Church in Colonial Days* (1883), and *The Story of a Great Nation* (1886).

Bibliography: R. J. PURCELL, *Dictionary of American Biography*, ed. A. JOHNSON and D. MALONE (New York 1928–36) 17:50–51. P. K. GUILDAY, *John Gilmary Shea: Father of American Catholic History, 1824–1892* (New York 1926). J. D. THOMAS, ''A

Century of American Catholic History,'' *U.S. Catholic Historian* 6 (Winter 1987) 25–49.

[J. L. MORRISON]

SHECHEM

Shechem was an important city in ancient Palestine. It was named (Heb. *šᵉkem,* shoulders) because of its position in the valley between the ''shoulders'' of Mt. Ebal to the north and Mt. Gerizim to the south. It has been identified as Tell Balâṭah, east of Nablus and partially covered to the south by the modern Arab village of Balâṭah. Between 1913 and 1934, five expeditions of German archeologists dug at the site; their work was corrected and completed by five American expeditions between 1956 and 1964 under the direction of G. E. Wright. Although the archeological findings, Biblical testimony, and pertinent extra-Biblical texts do not always clearly agree with one another, they have shed sufficient light on each other to afford a substantially reliable history of this Canaanite-Israelite city.

Early History. The site bears scattered evidence of encampments in the Chalcolithic Period (*c.* 4000 B.C.), but the first real building activity dates from the Early Middle Bronze Period (*c.* 1800 B.C.) and was perhaps the work of the AMORRITES, whose great migrations are generally assigned to the latter period. Two Egyptian texts from this time are the earliest extra-Biblical references to Shechem, and they suggest that the city was even then a center of opposition to Egypt.

The Hyksos Period in its earliest phase (1750–1650 B.C.) has revealed a large wall separating the acropolis from the lower city, and also a courtyard structure similar to a Hittite courtyard temple. This apparently sacred area was abandoned for a time (perhaps because of a wave of later Hyksos invaders, known as the Hurrians or Horrites) and, in the Hyksos Period in its later phase (1650–1550 B.C.), was covered with an artificial mound upon which a mighty temple-fortress was built. The city fortifications were expanded to the north, and a new city wall was constructed, with two gates built into it on the northwest and the east; this latter gate was destroyed three times within the 50 years that marked the end of the Shechem of the Hyksos and Middle Bronze Period. This destruction is usually attributed to the Egyptian reconquest of Canaan. The next extra-Biblical witnesses to Shechem picture its king as a vassal of Egypt: in letters found at Tell el-Amarna in Egypt Lab'ayu, King of Shechem, protests to the Pharaoh against the charge that he is in league with the marauding bands of the Habiri (possibly including the HEBREWS) who had been causing great disturbance in Canaan (Late Bronze Period, *c.* 1375 B.C.).

Patriarchal Period. The Israelite traditions of the Patriarchs refer to the Shechem of the Early Middle Bronze Period, but their historical value is very difficult to assess. Several of them give the impression of a peaceful settlement in and around the city. Abraham's first stop in Canaan is at the sanctuary (*māqôm*) of Shechem, by the sacred terebinth, where God appears to him. He builds an altar there and then passes on to build an altar near Bethel (Gn 12.6–8). Jacob also comes to Shechem, where he buys land near the city from the ''sons of Hemor.'' There he erects a memorial pillar (or perhaps an altar). After burying the family idols under the sacred terebinth, he commands that his family perform rites of purification in preparation for the journey to Bethel, where he then constructs an altar to God (Gn 33.18–20; 35.1–5). Later, Jacob sends Joseph to visit his brothers who are pasturing their flocks at Shechem (Gn 37.12–14). There is much in these traditions, however, that seems to reflect later history. The building of a sanctuary by the patriarchs seems to be a later justification for Israelite worship at a formerly Canaanite shrine. The journey from Shechem to Bethel, especially in the Jacob narrative, has the characteristics of a pilgrimage, which may reflect a later transfer of the ark from Shechem to Bethel (note the ''great fear'' in Gn 35.5, like the terror in the ranks of Israel's enemies when the ark was carried into battle). Jacob's renunciation of idolatry may reflect the later covenant ritual performed by Joshua at Shechem (Jos 24.15). Joseph's visit to Shechem, as well as the entire tradition of a peaceful settlement at Shechem, seems to reflect the arrival of the Josephite tribes Ephraim and Manasseh under Joshua, who was able to take possession of Shechem without a notable struggle.

Such an interpretation is further urged by the very ancient pre-Mosaic tradition of a violent capture of Shechem by the tribes of Simeon and Levi (Gn 34.1–31), achieved through a treachery that was later held to be the cause of their dissolution (Gn 49.5–7). This tradition concerning a pact made with Shechem, the son of Hemor (Heb. *ḥāmôr*), as well as the tradition of Jacob's purchase of land from the sons of Hemor (Gn 33.19), may well point to covenants between the Israelites and an Amorrite-Horrite population of Shechem. The Amorrites and Horrites (not always clearly distinguished in the Biblical traditions, and sometimes confused also with the Hevites) are known to have included the slaughter of an ass as part of their covenant ritual. Since *ḥāmôr* is the Hebrew word for ass, the original sense of ''sons of Hemor'' may well be ''sons of the Ass Covenant.'' That Shechem was known as such a covenant center is indicated also by the name of the city's god Baal-berith (Lord of the Covenant: Jgs 9.4). Since the Hurrians formed part of the later Hyksos migration, it seems that these traditions concerning the sons of Hemor have preserved elements from Israel's first contacts with the native population of Shechem. It is impossible to determine historically the origins of the Simeon-Levi tradition, nor can one refer the archeological data to a particular event in the scriptural traditions with any certitude; still, the Simeon-Levi tradition may illumine the historical background of the expanded fortifications at Shechem during the Hyksos Period, and perhaps even the destruction of the city at the end of this period, while others see it as reflecting the later unrest of the Tell el-Amarna Period. In either case, the tradition may partially explain how a previous Israelite occupation of Shechem prepared the way for JOSHUA, SON OF NUN, to gain peaceful control of the city.

Period of Joshua and the Judges. After the Hyksos Period, Shechem went into decline. There was some reconstruction, however. A new temple, with much slighter walls, was built on the site of the former great temple, and a large memorial stone (*maṣṣēbâ*) was set at its entrance. Also, the East Gate was refortified, although the city defenses were now much weaker than before. The layers at the area of the East Gate make it clear that the transition from Late Bronze to Early Iron (*c.* 1200 B.C.) was made peacefully. There is no clear evidence of a destruction of the temple throughout the Iron I Period even into the period of the divided monarchy, although several pits dug into the temple site in the 8th century B.C. contained debris from a great fire.

The Biblical testimony agrees with the archeological in suggesting Joshua's peaceful acquisition of the city. Nowhere is Shechem listed among the cities conquered by Israel. The ancient tradition of the Shechem covenant (Jos 24.1–28) suggests rather that the immigrating Josephite tribes settled peacefully with the former inhabitants of the city (Jos 24.15; Gn 48.22, where memories of past struggles are combined with the peaceful acquisition by the Josephite tribes). Some regard this tradition as the basis for an ancient covenant feast at Shechem. In its present position, it forms a second conclusion to the book of Joshua, and seemingly also a conclusion to a postexilic Deuteronomic edition of the HEXATEUCH. The content of the treaty, as well as the ritual followed, are noticeably absent from the text, but are possibly contained in the code of the BOOK OF THE COVENANT (Ex 20.22–33) and the Sinai ritual of Ex 34.3–8, both the code and the ritual having been transposed to an ancient Sinai context by the DEUTERONOMISTS lest they detract from the later Deuteronomic material. Sometime after the occupation of Shechem by the Josephite tribes, a site there became known as the tomb of Joseph (Jos 24.32). As a shrine, Shechem was now gradually eclipsed by Siloe.

The rise and fall of Abimelech (Jgs 9.1–57) centers around Shechem. He was crowned king at the terebinth (9.6), surely to be linked with the sacred tree in the Abraham, Jacob, and Joshua stories, and perhaps identical with the ''Terebinth of the Diviners'' (where oracles were received) in Jgs 9.37. The Beth-Mello (House of the Filling) of this story (9.6) is most likely the acropolis of the city, which had been filled in with earth and separated by a wall from the lower city. Magdal-Shechem (Fortress of Sichem, 9.48) may be the same area, but is more likely the temple-fortress itself, also called the Temple of Baal-berith (9.46). The debris piled into the pits later dug into the temple area is thought to date from Abimelech's destruction of the temple (9.49), but there is no clear evidence of a destruction of the temple itself in the Early Iron Age. The topography of Shechem in the Abimelech narrative would also correspond well to that of a much earlier date, as would the mention of the ''men of Hemor'' (9.28). Perhaps the Abimelech story has its roots in the turbulent Hyksos Period and only secondarily has been inserted into the lists of the Judges.

Monarchical Period and Final Stages. That Shechem was still relatively important is clear: David could rejoice in possessing it [Ps 59(60).8—an ancient oracle quoted in a postexilic Psalm]; Roboam came here to be crowned (1 Kgs 12.1); after the kingdom was divided, Jeroboam made Shechem his capital for a time (1 Kgs 12.25). As a shrine, however, Shechem was now still further eclipsed by Bethel. It appears to have remained an important administrative center, however, as a Samaria ostracon indicates, and as may be reflected in the construction of a granary upon the former temple site. A clear division between upper and lower class dwellings appears, the former having suffered more serious damage in the Assyrian conquest (*c.* 724 B.C.).

Shechem remained very sparsely inhabited and for a time was totally abandoned until the Hellenistic rebirth of the city in the 4th century B.C. It seems to have been rebuilt by the Samaritans, who were no longer able to settle in thoroughly paganized Samaria, and who then sought refuge in the city beneath their mighty temple on Mt. Garizim. The Jewish high priest John Hyrcanus devastated the city in 127 B.C., though it lingered on for a few years afterward. In the Roman Period, New Testament SICHAR was most likely on this site.

Bibliography: *Encyclopedic Dictionary of the Bible,* tr. and adap. by L. HARTMAN (New York 1963) from A. VAN DEN BORN, *Bijbels Woordenboek* 2204–08. E. F. CAMPBELL, JR. and J. F. ROSS, ''The Excavation of Sichem and the Biblical Tradition,'' *The Biblical Archaeologist* (New Haven 1938–) 26:2–27. J. L'HOUR, ''L'Alliance de Sichem,'' *Revue biblique* (Paris 1892–) 69:5–36, 161–184, 350–368.

[P. J. KEARNEY]

SHEED, FRANCIS JOSEPH

Writer, lecturer, publisher, Catholic activist, and lay theologian; b. Sydney, Australia, March 20, 1897; d. Jersey City, N.J., Nov. 20, 1981. Sheed's mother was Mary (Min) Maloney, a Roman Catholic who emigrated from County Cork by herself at age 14, and his father was John Sheed, a Marxist from a staunch Scotch-Irish Presbyterian family. At age six, for two years, while his father's job took him elsewhere, and under his mother's influence, Sheed practiced Catholicism and was sent, at age eight, to the parish school run by Sacred Heart nuns. After two weeks, his father ordered him to attend public school and for the next six years, the Methodist Church. In *The Church and I* (1974), Sheed details the variety of "brainwashings" in his childhood: "Methodism three times every Sunday, Marxism at breakfast and dinner . . . confession at a local Sacred Heart Fathers' mission one Saturday morning each month, daily Mass and communion during the two weeks of my father's annual vacation."

Sheed earned a law degree from Sydney University after a four-year break during his studies for a trip to England, to which he later returned. In London, he joined the Catholic Evidence Guild, which had been founded in 1918, with the encouragement of Cardinal Bourne, to train lay speakers for outdoor platforms in Hyde Park and at London street corners. Sheed became one of the most able speakers in the guild, ultimately giving 7,000 soapbox speeches during his lifetime. According to the *London Times* (Nov. 24, 1981), "He had a remarkable gift for the lucid exposition of doctrine of which he had a considerably deeper knowledge than is acquired by the average layman, a simple, effective platform style, [and] a sense of humour that won the goodwill of his hecklers." In 1926, he married fellow guild member, Maisie Ward, and together they founded the publishing house of Sheed & Ward (on Pater Noster Row next to Ave Maria Lane), with the purpose of publishing authors of the English Catholic Revival. Hilaire Belloc, G. K. Chesterton, Christopher Dawson, and Edward I. Watkin became advisers and writers for the early company and were soon followed by other English authors: Christopher Hollis, Ronald Knox, "Sheed & Ward's lead Englishman" (W. Sheed, *Frank and Maisie*), Caryll Houslander, and numerous others. Translations of continental authors soon followed: Jacques Maritain, Paul Claudel, François Mauriac, Léon Bloy, Romano Guardini, and Sigrid Undset.

In 1933, Sheed & Ward opened a New York branch with little capital and without "statues, altarpieces, vestments . . . or Catholic textbooks" (*The Church and I*). For 40 years, the aim would be to publish books "just above the middle of the brow." Dorothy DAY and Catherine de HUECK, American Catholic activists, would have works published, as well as would more controversial writers: Henri de LUBAC, Hans Küng, Charles Davis, and Karl ADAM.

Sheed, after commuting across the Atlantic for six years, moved his family (wife Maisie, daughter Rosemary—later a translator for Sheed & Ward— and son Wilfrid—later the novelist and critic) to Jersey City in 1940, but he would continue to travel between the United States, London, and Australia for the rest of his life.

The early works of Sheed, the writer, were translations: Etienne GILSON's *The Philosophy of St. Bonaventure* (1938), *The Confessions of St. Augustine* (1942), Oreste Ferrara's *The Borgia Pope, Alexander the Sixth* (1942), and numerous lives of the saints by Henri Gheon. Sheed's street corner speeches led him to write his own books, beginning with *Nullity of Marriage* (1931), followed by *A Map of Life* (1933), *Ground Plan for Catholic Reading* (1937), in 1938, *Communism and Man* (used in some communist study groups), *Theology and Sanity* (1947), *Society and Sanity* (1953), *To Know Christ Jesus* (1962), *God and the Human Condition* (1966), and *Genesis Regained* (1969). After Vatican II, Sheed wrote *Is It the Same Church?* (1968) and generally concluded that "the Church will re-shape itself, more or less ideally" and "only the innocent would prophesy" (*The Church and I*).

In 1973, Sheed & Ward was sold to the Universal Press Syndicate and the firm name was changed to Andrews & McNeel, with the Sheed & Ward imprint used to reissue "Sheed & Ward classics."

In the years following the sale of Sheed & Ward, Sheed continued his speaking at universities and elsewhere. He was no longer the "flaming radical" who had "dared to poach the clerical preserve and assert the layman's right to think" [Wilfrid Sheed, *Current Biography* (1981) 373]. This self-taught lay theologian, whose humor was noted by all, received "during the . . . postwar [period], an honor that no lay Catholic had ever come close to: a doctorate in sacred theology from Rome itself, entitling him to wear a four-pointed biretta (priests only rate three)" (W. Sheed, *Frank and Maisie*, 202).

Bibliography: *Contemporary Authors*, v. 105 (Detroit) 447. S. G. KENNEDY, *New York Times* (Nov. 21, 1981). *Newsweek* (Nov. 30, 1981) 110. *Publishers Weekly* (Dec. 4, 1981) 16. F. SHEED, *The Church and I* (New York 1974). W. SHEED, *Frank and Maisie: A Memoir with Parents* (New York 1985).

[M. MAHONEY]

SHEEHAN, LUKE FRANCIS

Capuchin missionary, pioneer of the Church in Oregon; b. Feb. 28, 1873, Cork City, Ireland; d. Feb. 11,

1937, Hood River, Oregon. After his ordination in 1896 and teaching philosophy for six years in the Capuchin house of formation in Kilkenny, Sheehan volunteered to work in Aden, the British colony on the Southwestern coast of the Arabian peninsula. Illness forced him to return to Ireland. In 1910 he went to Hermiston, Oregon after Bishop Joseph O'Reilly of the Diocese of Baker City asked the Irish Capuchins to come to the United States. Leaving a confrere to care for Hermiston, Sheehan moved to reconnoiter Crook County, Oregon, and the barely developed town of Bend where there were only one hundred and fifty Catholics scattered over an area of eight thousand square miles. When the railroad came to Bend in 1916, Sheehan began building a new church and, shortly thereafter, a clinic that became what is today St. Charles Medical Center. Twenty years later he succeeded in opening a parish school. In addition to suffering innumerable physical hardships, he endured the bigotry of many of Crook County's residents, especially members of the Ku Klux Klan. In 1935 he courageously challenged the Klan at one of their meetings and was instrumental in their decline in Oregon. Sheehan died twenty-seven years after his arrival in Bend. His Capuchin confreres praised him as ''the greatest missionary of them all whose life bore great fruit, for he was a man of single purpose.''

Bibliography: C. DONOVAN, ''The Irish Capuchins in the United States of America,'' *Capuchin Annual* (1973), 249–289.

[R. J. ARMSTRONG]

SHEEN, FULTON J.

Radio preacher, television personality, bishop; b. El Paso, Illinois, May 8, 1895; d. New York, N.Y., Dec. 9, 1979. He was one of the four sons of Newton Morris and Delia (Fulton) Sheen. Baptized Peter, he took the name of John at confirmation and later adopted his mother's maiden name. While still a small child, he moved with his family to Peoria where he attended Saint Mary's Cathedral School and then went on to Spalding Institute, a Peoria high school then conducted by the Brothers of Mary where he graduated in 1913. It was at Saint Viator College, Bourbonnais, Illinois, that young Sheen's forensic talents as a member of the debating team, which for the first time defeated Notre Dame, foreshadowed his future fame. He was likewise on the editorial staff of *The Viatorian*, the journal of his college that had been founded in 1865 by the Clerics of Saint Viator.

Having received his A.B. in 1917, along with his classmate and fellow diocesan, Charles A. Hart, a future professor of philosophy in the CATHOLIC UNIVERSITY OF AMERICA, the two pursued their theological training in the Saint Paul Seminary, Saint Paul, Minnesota, which ended with ordination to the priesthood on Sept. 20, 1919. After receiving S.T.L. and J.C.B. degrees at The CATHOLIC UNIVERSITY OF AMERICA in 1920 Sheen was sent by Edmund M. Dunne, Bishop of Peoria, himself a Louvain alumnus, to The Catholic University of LOUVAIN where he earned his Ph.D. degree, winning in 1925 for his scholarly volume, *God and Intelligence in Modern Philosophy*, Louvain's coveted *Agrégé en philosophie*, the first American to receive this distinction. Further studies at the Sorbonne and Rome's Collegio Angelico brought the S.T.D. degree, whereupon the young priest returned to Peoria where for a year he served as a curate at Saint Patrick's Church.

Called to the faculty of The Catholic University of America in 1926, Sheen taught theology and the philosophy of religion there until 1950 when he was appointed National Director of the Society for the Propagation of the Faith with residence in New York. By this time he had attained a national reputation for his broadcasts on the Catholic Hour, a reputation that was enhanced by his ''Life Is Worth Living'' telecasts begun in 1951, as well as for his preaching, notably in Saint Patrick's Cathedral, New York. Many of these religious discourses were later published and constituted a majority of the nearly 70 books that appeared under his name. Meanwhile he instructed an uncommon number of converts from those of humble station such as his devoted housekeeper, Fanny Washington, to nationally known figures such as the journalist Heywood Broun, Clare Boothe Luce, et al. As the years passed Fulton Sheen was the recipient of numerous honors in the form of awards and honorary degrees, along with ecclesiastical distinctions from that of papal chamberlain (1934) to the rank of bishop in 1951 and titular archbishop of Newport in 1969. For three less-than-happy years (1966–1969) he served as the sixth bishop of Rochester, N.Y.

Influence. Fulton Sheen's influence was unquestionably widespread: from groups of priests and members of religious orders and congregations to whom he frequently recommended a practice of his own life, namely, a daily hour of prayer, to vast audiences of lay persons, both Catholic and non-Catholic, to whom he brought a religious perspective on life and its meaning, as well as eloquent and forceful addresses on world problems such as the dangers of communism.

The present writer lived with Sheen for three years (1938–41) in his residence on Cathedral Avenue in Washington, where he was a daily observer of the dynamic churchman's notable generosity to those in need, and his unfailing consideration for and courtesy to those around him. It can be said that with the sole exception of a strain of vanity over his prowess as a public speaker it would be difficult to think of any serious defect in the man. And in this regard his extraordinary gift of a beautiful and compelling voice, a marked flair for the dramatic, along with normally well-reasoned content, humanly speaking, the vanity was understandable. The bishop was a man of deep conviction, and when he felt he was in the right he withstood all opposition, for example, in his difference with Cardinal Francis SPELLMAN, Archbishop of New York, over the disposition of the funds of the Society for the PROPAGATION OF THE FAITH.

As he once told me, he consciously abandoned the life of a scholar for that of the preacher, realizing in a realistic way that it was impossible to serve both simultaneously. All things considered, it was a wise decision, for there can be no doubt that Sheen possessed unique gifts for public address, gifts that were employed with telling effect as thousands of his immense audience would bear testimony.

It is owed to the memory of this remarkable churchman to state that in his hey-day almost literally millions called his name blessed for the religious inspiration, the kindling of renewed hope, and the spiritual enrichment that he brought to their lives.

Bibliography: *Treasure in Clay. The Autobiography of Fulton J. Sheen* (Garden City, N.Y. 1980). J. T. ELLIS, *Catholic Bishops: A Memoir* (Wilmington, Del. 1984) 78–84. K. RILEY, *Bishop Fulton J. Sheen: An American Catholic Response to the Twentieth Century* (Ph.D. diss., Notre Dame 1988). M. MASSA, *Catholics and American Culture: Fulton Sheen, Dorothy Day, and the Notre Dame Football Team* (New York 1999).

[J. T. ELLIS]

Fulton J. Sheen. (Archive Photos)

SHEEN CHARTERHOUSE

Or House of Jesus of Bethlehem, former Carthusian priory, founded by King Henry V on a royal manor at Richmond, Surrey, England, in 1414. Endowed with land for the most part from alien priories, Sheen was the object of protests, notably those from SAINT-EVROULT (1416) and Saint-Pierre, Ghent, which were carried to the Council of BASEL. Later, King Henry VI endowed it (1442), as did Edward IV (1461). King James IV of Scotland was reputedly buried there after Flodden Field (1513). Dean Colet lodged and died there. HENRY VIII's Oath of Supremacy (1534) caused a rift in the community; but Prior Henry Man submitted, and the monastery was dissolved (1539). In 1557 it was refounded by Queen Mary Tudor, only to be dissolved again by Queen Elizabeth I (1559). No trace remains.

Bibliography: W. DUGDALE, *Monasticon Anglicanum* (London 1655–73); best ed. by J. CALEY, et al., 6 v. (1817–30) 6:29–34. *The Victoria History of the County of Surrey,* ed. H. E. MALDEN (Westminster, England 1902–) v. 2. E. M. THOMPSON, *The Carthusian Order in England* (New York 1930), *passim.* L. H. COTTINEAU, *Répertoire topobibliographique des abbayes et prieurés,* 2 v. (Mâcon 1935–39) 2:3026.

[V. I. J. FLINT]

SHEERAN, JAMES B.

Confederate chaplain; b. Temple Mehill, County Longford, Ireland, 1819; d. Morristown, N.J., April 3, 1881. He immigrated to Canada at the age of 12 and went to New York City in 1833. From there he moved to McConnellsville, Pennsylvania, then to Monroe, Michigan, where he worked as a tailor and taught at a boys' school conducted by the Redemptorists. He married (*c.* 1842), but became a widower in 1849 and resumed his teaching until 1855, when he entered the Redemptorist Congregation. He was ordained on Sept. 18, 1858, and was sent that year to the Redemptorist church in New Orleans, Louisiana, where he adopted Southern views in the secessionist crisis and volunteered as a chaplain with the Confederate Army. Assigned to the Army of Northern Virginia on Sept. 2, 1861, Sheeran kept a journal of his wartime experiences and observations from August 1862 until his return to New Orleans in 1865. The journal affords insight into the duties of a Civil War chaplain, the attitudes of a Southern patriot, and the life of the Confederate soldier, and contains eyewitness accounts of such major engagements as Antietam and Gettysburg. Sheeran was often critical of Confederate troop commanders and Congressmen. Seized by Gen. P. H. Sheridan's forces in the Shenandoah Valley in September 1864, Sheeran was imprisoned at Winchester, Virginia, and then transferred to Ft. McHenry, Baltimore, Maryland, where he was released on December 5. He returned to New Orleans as the war ended and helped care for the victims of the yellow-fever epidemic in 1867. Soon thereafter, he was released from his vows as a Redemptorist and joined the Diocese of Newark, New Jersey, where he was made pastor of the Church of the Assumption, Morristown. There he built a new church and school, and labored on behalf of Catholic education until his death from a stroke.

Bibliography: J. B. SHEERAN, *Confederate Chaplain: A War Journal,* ed. J. T. DURKIN (Milwaukee 1960).

[J. L. MORRISON]

SHEHAN, LAWRENCE J.

Twelfth archbishop of Baltimore; cardinal; b. Baltimore, Maryland, March 18, 1898; d. there, Aug. 26, 1984. The son of Irish immigrant parents, Thomas P. and Anastasia (Schofield) Shehan, young Lawrence was educated in parochial schools of Baltimore. He attended St. Charles College, Catonsville, Maryland (1911–17), St. Mary's Seminary, Baltimore (1917–20), and North American College, Rome, Italy (1920–23). Ordained in Rome, Dec. 23, 1922, Shehan engaged in pastoral work in the Archdiocese of Baltimore (1923–47), serving as pastor of St. Patrick Church, Washington, D.C. (1941–47). He held several offices in the diocesan curia from notary in 1934 to officialis of the archdiocese of Baltimore and Washington (1938–45). Pope Pius XII named him a papal chamberlain (1939), and a domestic prelate of the papal household (1945).

In 1945 Pius XII appointed him to the Titular See of Lydda, and as auxiliary bishop of Baltimore and Washington. When in 1947 the Archdiocese of Washington was separated from the Archdiocese of Baltimore, Bishop Shehan was named vicar-general of the Archdiocese of Baltimore until he was installed as ordinary of the newly erected See of Bridgeport, Connecticut, in 1953.

Shehan was president of the National Catholic Education Association (1958–59), episcopal moderator of the National Welfare Conference Bureau of Information (1945–49), and episcopal chairman of the Department of Education in the National Catholic Welfare Conference (1959–62). He was named vice president of the International Eucharistic Congresses (1960), and served as a member of the Episcopal Committee on Motion Pictures, Radio and Television. He was also the National Chaplain of the Ancient Order of Hibernians.

Promoted by Pope John XXIII to the Titular Archepiscopal See of Nicopolis ad Nestum, July 10, 1961, he was appointed Coadjutor Archbishop of Baltimore, Maryland, and was installed Sept. 27, 1961. On the death of Archbishop Francis B. Keough he became the 12th archbishop of Baltimore on December 8 of the same year. Pope Paul VI elevated Archbishop Shehan to the cardinalate on Feb. 22, 1965. His titular church was San Clemente in Rome. In March of that year the new cardinal was appointed to the Consistorial Congregation. During the Second Vatican Council Pope Paul appointed Cardinal Shehan to the Body of Presidents of the council on July 9, 1965. Later that month he was made a member of the Congregation for the Doctrine of the Faith.

Cardinal Shehan was an outstanding ecumenist. In 1962 he established the nation's first Commission for Christian Unity. In November 1963 he was named to the Vatican Secretariat for Christian Unity, and a year later became head of the U.S. Bishop's Committee for Ecumenical Affairs. In December 1965 the National Conference of Christians and Jews conferred upon him its highest honor, the National Brotherhood Award, in recognition of his outstanding achievements in the field of ecumenical relations and religious understanding. As the Vatican Council drew to a close, Cardinal Shehan went to Istanbul as the delegate of Paul VI to deliver an historic document to Patriarch Athenagoras, spiritual leader of the Eastern Orthodox Church, revoking the excommunication imposed 900 years before. At precisely the same moment Metropolitan Meliton handed to Paul VI a similar document lifting the excommunication of the papal legate by Constantinople.

In March 1963 Cardinal Shehan issued his famous pastoral letter on ''Racial Justice,'' calling for an end to discrimination of any kind based upon color, strictly forbidding it in the Catholic hospitals, schools, and other institutions of the archdiocese. In succeeding years, as racial tensions mounted and violence flared in many places, the cardinal never relaxed his efforts to assure justice and equal opportunity for blacks and the nation's other minority groups. He defended the right of priests and nuns to march in civil rights demonstrations, and flew to Montgomery, Alabama, to take part in the funeral ceremonies for Dr. Martin Luther King, Jr., after the black leader was assassinated there in April 1968.

Cardinal Shehan died on Aug. 26, 1984, and was interred beneath the sanctuary of the Cathedral.

Bibliography: L. J. SHEHAN, *A Blessing of Years: The Memoirs of Lawrence Cardinal Shehan* (Notre Dame 1982).

[T. A. MURPHY]

SHEIL, BERNARD J.

Known as ''apostle of youth,'' ''labor's bishop,'' ''apostle of the poor,'' and ''apostle of the underdog''; b. Chicago, Feb. 18, 1886; d. Tucson, Arizona, Sept. 13, 1969. At St. Viator College, Bourbonnais, Illinois, ''Benny'' Sheil's athletic prowess was so outstanding that major-league baseball clubs made tantalizing offers, but he chose instead to enter St. Viator Seminary. After his ordination on May 21, 1910, by Archbishop James E. Quigley, he was assigned to St. Mel parish in Chicago, remaining there until World War I when he was transferred to Great Lakes Naval Training Center as chaplain. He left the navy in 1919, and was assigned to Holy Name Cathedral with additional duties as chaplain at Cook County jail. In 1924 he was appointed assistant chancellor and in 1928 chancellor and auxiliary bishop of the Chicago archdiocese. Later that same year he was named vicar general, a post he held until 1939. While vicar general he was appointed pastor of St. Andrew parish (1935–1966). In 1959, Sheil was named titular archbishop by Pope John XXIII.

Following a directive of Cardinal Mundelein, Sheil established the Catholic Youth Organization (CYO) in 1930. Drawing upon his experiences as jail chaplain and his own interests in sports, Sheil drew up a program designed to keep young people out of trouble by offering them recreational activities, free medical and dental services, and theater workshops. Twenty-four years later and after the organization had been established nationally, Sheil resigned as its general director. Also in 1930, Sheil founded the Lewis School of Aeronautics, which is now known as Lewis College.

Although at the beginning boxing and basketball were the chief attractions at the CYO building, other programs were introduced. The Sheil Lecture Forum led to the formation of the CYO Educational Department in 1942 and a year later the Sheil School of Social Studies. The school had no requirements of previous education, race, color, creed, or money and was free and open to all. The subjects taught fell into three main classifications: (1) theology and philosophy, (2) social studies, and (3) liberal studies. Some additional by-products of the CYO programs were: the Pilot Dog Foundation for the blind, the Newman Center at Northwestern University in Evanston, Illinois, the national Legion of Decency, the national scouting program, labor education schools, and the Catholic Salvage Bureau. In 1949, Sheil established radio station WFJL for broadcasting Catholic news; next to the Vatican station this was the most powerful Catholic radio outlet.

In 1939, when labor unions were struggling for recognition, Sheil emerged as ''labor's bishop.'' That year a battle developed between the meat industry and the Congress of Industrial Organizations, which wanted to organize the stockyard laborers. Sheil supported the union, despite threats from the opposition, until it was victorious. That same year he cooperated with Saul Alinsky in forming the Chicago Back-of-the-Yards Neighborhood Council.

Breaking with tradition, Sheil attended many interfaith meetings. He fought discrimination, publicly opposing the anti-Semitism of ''radio priest'' Charles E. COUGHLIN. At a forum on Christian-Jewish relations he was confronted by a woman who after calling him ''rabbi'' concluded her tirade by spitting on him. The bishop replied,''That is what they called our Lord.'' Though an American patriot, he was not an extremist. Speaking before the international educational conference of the United Automotive Workers in Chicago in 1954, he dared to challenge the anticommunism of Senator Joseph McCarthy of Wisconsin. After declaring McCarthyism was no way to combat communism, he condemned the Wisconsin senator and his methods.

Bibliography: Chicago Archdiocesan Archives. *The New World* (Chicago) Sept. 19, 1969. R. L. TREAT, *Bishop Sheil and the CYO* (New York 1951). A. WARD, *Chicago's Tribute to Bishop Sheil on the 25th Anniversary of His Consecration* (1953).

[M. J. MADAJ]

SHEKINAH

A post-biblical Hebrew word meaning Divine Presence, used mostly in the TALMUD as a substitute for the name of YAHWEH. In the Old Testament growing reverence for God's transcendent holiness had already led to a reluctance to refer directly to Him. Thus the introduction of various roundabout expressions: the angel of God (Ex 14.19; cf. 13.21); Yahweh's face (Dt 31.11; ''to appear before'' is literally ''to behold the face of''); Yahweh's spirit (Is 63.14), Yahweh's word [Ps 32(33).6], etc. The rabbis later preferred the word *šᵉkînâ,* whose Hebrew root *šākan,* to pitch a tent, was suggestive of the TENT OF MEETING in the wilderness where God's GLORY abode. Various allusions in the New Testament draw on this notion and connect Jesus with the Shekinah. In Mt 18.20 there seems to be an allusion to a sentence in the MISHNAH: ''If two men are met together and words of the Torah are spoken between them, the Shekinah dwells among them'' (Ob 3.2). Also, Jn 1.14 may be translated ''and the Word was made flesh and pitched his tent among us,'' a clear reference to the Tent of Meeting. Paul seems also to have the Shekinah image in mind in Col 2.9: ''For in him dwells all the fullness of the Godhead bodily.''

Bibliography: W. J. PHYTHIAN-ADAMS, *The People and the Presence* (New York 1942). J. ABELSON, *Immanence of God in Rabbinical Literature* (London 1912). S. TERRIEN, *The Elusive Presence: Toward a New Biblical Theology* (1978, 1984).

[J. T. BURTCHAELL]

SHELLEY, EDWARD, BL.

Lay martyr; b. ca. 1528–38, Warminghurst, Sussex, England; hanged at Tyburn (London), Aug. 30, 1588. Edward was well born. His father, also named Edward, was a master of the king's household and the settlor in ''Shelley's case.'' The future martyr was living in East Smithfield, London, at the time of his arrest in April 1584 for possessing a book entitled *My Lord Leicester's Commonwealth* and assisting an illegal priest, Bl. William DEAN. Thereafter he was imprisoned in the Clink, condemned for his ''crimes'', and executed. He was beatified by Pius XI on Dec. 15, 1929.

Feast of the English Martyrs: May 4 (England).

See Also: ENGLAND, SCOTLAND, AND WALES, MARTYRS OF.

Bibliography: R. CHALLONER, *Memoirs of Missionary Priests,* ed. J. H. POLLEN (rev. ed. London 1924; repr. Farnborough 1969). J. H. POLLEN, *Acts of English Martyrs* (London 1891).

[K. I. RABENSTEIN]

SHEN JIHE, ST.

Lay martyr, servant, member of the Third Order of St. Francis; b. 1851, Ankeo, Hughan Xian, Shanxi Province, China; d. July 9, 1900, Taiyüan, Shanxi Province. Thomas Shen Jihe (sometimes written as Sen or Sen-Ki-Kuo), the son of Peter Shen Buniu and Maria Guo, was raised as a Catholic. He was footman to Paul Zhang and went with him to Dongergou (1875), where he served Fr. Peter Jiang. For the final decade of his life, Thomas was a servant in the household of Bp. Gregorio GRASSI. Thomas was among the innumerable Christians martyred during the Boxer Rebellion and among the several dozen trapped inside the Taiyüan cathedral, arrested, and beheaded several days thereafter. He was beatified by Pope Pius XII (Nov. 24, 1946) and canonized (Oct. 1, 2000) by Pope John Paul II with Augustine Zhao Rong and companions.

Feast: July 4.

Bibliography: L. M. BALCONI, *Le Martiri di Taiyuen* (Milan 1945). *Acta Apostolica Sedis* 47 (1955) 381–388. *Vita del b. A. Crescitelli* (Milan 1950). M. T. DE BLARER, *Les Bse Marie Hermine de Jésus et ses compagnes, franciscaines missionnaires de Marie, massacrées le 9 juillet 1900 à Tai–Yuan–Fou, Chine* (Paris 1947). *Les Vingt–neuf martyrs de Chine, massacrés en 1900, béatifiés par Sa Sainteté Pie XII, le 24 novembre, 1946* (Rome 1946). L. MINER, *China's Book of Martyrs: A Record of Heroic Martyrdoms and Marvelous Deliverances of Chinese Christians during the Summer of 1900* (Ann Arbor 1994). J. SIMON, *Sous le sabre des Boxers* (Lille 1955). C. TESTORE, *Sangue e palme sul fiume giallo. I beati martiri cinesi nella persecuzione della Boxe Celi Sud–Est, 1900* (Rome 1955). *L'Osservatore Romano*, Eng. Ed. 40 (2000): 1–2, 10.

[K. I. RABENSTEIN]

SHENOUTE OF ATRIPE

Shenoute or Schenoudi, second abbot of the famous White Monastery, called also the Deir Auba Chenouda (Monastery of Shenoute) after him; b. *c.* 348; d. 466. He was a strict disciplinarian and had a towering temper. He ruled the monastery for 83 years, from 383 until his death. His pupil and successor Besa says that Shenoute had under his rule 2,200 monks and 1,800 nuns. An outstanding organizer, Shenoute did not hesitate to modify the rule of Pachomius, which Shenoute held in many places to be too lax. Shenoute forced his monks to sign a monastic profession in which they swore to obey the inflexible rule he had drawn up. On one occasion he killed with his own hand a monk guilty of a theft and a small lie. He gave permission to individual monks to withdraw to the desert after a few years of cenobitic life without completely severing their ties with the monastery. Shenoute made numerous lengthy journeys to combat heretics and pagans; notably, he accompanied CYRIL OF ALEXANDRIA to the Council of EPHESUS in 431. His prolonged absences destroyed the continuity of his influence over his monks, and he often complained of their refractoriness and disciplined them severely for it. Though little liked by his monks, he enjoyed great prestige in Egypt, where he was regarded as a saint, though the church has never given him that title.

Shenoute wrote many letters and sermons that have been preserved. The letters, mostly addressed to monks and nuns, deal with monastic questions; some are polemics against pagans and heretics. The sermons are vivid in language and eschatological in character. Several apocalypses and visions are attributed to him. There are presently Ethiopic, Arabic, and Syriac versions of his works, but it has been difficult to distinguish the authentic writings from the spurious.

Bibliography: J. LEIPOLDT and W. E. CRUM, eds., *Sinuthii archimandritae vita et opera omnia,* Lat. tr. H. WIESMANN, 3 v. (*Cor-*

pus scriptorum Christianorum orientalium 41–42, 73, 1906–13; repr. as v. 96, 108, 129; 1951–54), v.1, 4–5 of *Scriptores Coptici,* ser. 2; repr. as v. 8, 12, 16. J. LEIPOLDT, *Schenute von Atripe und die Entstehung des nationalägyptischen Mönchtums* (*Texte und Untersuchungen zur Geschichte der altchristlichen Literatur* 25.1; 1903). L. T. LEFORT, "Athanase, Ambroise et Chenoute: Sur la virginité," *Muséon* 48 (1935) 55–73, use of Athanasius; "La Chasse aux reliques des martyrs en Égypte au IVe siècle," *La Nouvelle Clio* 6 (1954) 225–230. K. H. KUHN, "The Observance of the 'Two Weeks' in Shenoute's Writings," *Studia patristica* v.2 (*Texte und Untersuchungen zur Geschichte der altchristlichen Literatur* 64; 1957) 427–434.

[A. G. GIBSON]

SHEOL

A Hebrew word (*šᵉ'ôl*) that occurs more than 60 times in the Old Testament to signify the nether world. Its etymology is very uncertain, being variously derived from *šā'al,* "ask, inquire," [thus, a place that keeps asking for more (Prv 27.20; 30.15–16) or a place of interrogation of the dead], from *šā'âl,* "be hollow, deep," from *šwl,* "be low," from *šā'â,* "be desolate," plus an archaic suffix *l,* or from various Akkadian roots.

In the Bible it designates the place of complete inertia that one goes down to when one dies whether one be just or wicked, rich or poor.

See Also: AFTERLIFE, 2; GEHENNA; ABRAHAM'S BOSOM.

Bibliography: *Encyclopedic Dictionary of the Bible,* translated and adapted by L. HARTMAN (New York, 1963) 2196.

[H KÖSTER]

SHEPEY, JOHN DE

English canonist, dean of Lincoln Cathedral; d. early 1412. The son of Jordan de Shepey of Coventry, England, Shepey was a doctor of civil law by 1367, when he was still an advocate of the court of Canterbury. In 1368 he was appointed the official of the court of Winchester. From 1363 to 1376 he was chancellor of Lichfield; then canon of York; and from 1378 to his death, dean of Lincoln cathedral. In this sensitive post he served under Bp. John Buckingham (1363–98); the young Bp. Henry BEAUFORT (1398–1404), half brother of King Henry IV and later cardinal; and under Bp. Philip REPINGTON, Lollard-suspect become cardinal. A king's clerk, Shepey was an envoy to the Flemings concerning a treaty in 1372, an envoy to the court of AVIGNON in 1373; to Bruges in 1375; and one of two envoys appointed to treat with the king of Scotland in 1397. RICHARD II summoned him to a council at Oxford (1399) to advise him about future English policy in the WESTERN SCHISM. Shepey's notes for 12 Oxford lectures on the decretals are extant (London, British Museum, Royal MS.9.E.viii). He is buried in Lincoln Cathedral.

Bibliography: J. H. DAHMUS, ed., *The Metropolitan Visitations of William Courteney: Archbishop of Canterbury, 1381–1396* (Urbana, Ill. 1950) 47, 161. K. EDWARDS, *The English Secular Cathedrals in the Middle Ages* (Manchester, Eng. 1949). A. B. EMDEN, *A Biographical Register of the Scholars of the University of Oxford to A.D. 1500,* 3 v. (Oxford 1957–59) 3:1683–84.

[M. J. HAMILTON]

SHEPTYTS'KYĬ, ANDRIĬ

Ukrainian metropolitan and apostle; b. Prylbyči, July 29, 1865; d. Lvov, Nov. 1, 1944. Sheptyts'kyĭ was born of an aristocratic family. After studying in Breslau, he joined the Basilian Order (May 23, 1888), changing his Christian name from Roman Alexander to Andriĭ. He was ordained in 1892; Pope Leo XIII named him bishop of Stanislav (Galicia) on June 17, 1898, and metropolitan of Lvov on Jan. 16, 1901. By visitations of his vast archdiocese and by his charity—manifested in the establishment of orphanages, hospitals, and homes for the aged and poor—as well as by some 150 pastoral letters, he reinvigorated Catholicism in the western Ukraine. He founded minor and major seminaries in both Stanislav and Lvov. By founding an Ecclesiastical Academy (1928) and a theological journal in Lvov, Sheptyts'kyĭ revived the study of theology in the Ukraine. He also restored the order of the monks of St. Basil, and by revising the ancient rule of St. THEODORE THE STUDITE, he revived Oriental monaticism among Catholics. He persuaded the general of the Congregation of the Most Holy Redeemer to establish a Byzantine-Slav branch (approved by the Congregation of the Propaganda Fide on April 27, 1913). Although this Redemptorist vice province, brought to Galicia by Belgians, was suppressed by the U.S.S.R. in 1948, a branch founded in Canada and the U.S. is still flourishing.

As metropolitan, Sheptyts'kyĭ defended his people vigorously against Russian subversion and was imprisoned by the Czar during World War I (1914–17). In his zeal for the protection of the Byzantine-Slavic rite in Russia before the Revolution, he had pursued reunion movements, particularly among the Catholics and Orthodox of the Ukraine, and had visited Moscow in 1907. After the Revolution, he held a provincial synod and suggested the naming of Leonidas Fedorov as Catholic exarch for Russia. He also rebuilt the churches and ecclesiastical institutions destroyed during the war, and opposed both the Communists in Russia and the Latinizing policies of the Polish government in 1938 and 1939.

Sheptyts'kyĭ translated the ascetical works of St. BASIL OF CAESAREA into Ukrainian and published *De Sapientia Dei* (Lvov 1932). He visited the Ukrainian immigrants in North and South America and arranged for their spiritual welfare by persuading the Holy See to erect a hierarchy for them in the U.S. (1907); after his attendance at the Canadian Eucharistic Congress (1910), Canada obtained a Ukrainian hierarchy (1912). For the furtherance of his ecclesiastical policies, he founded a Ukrainian National Museum and gave encouragement to the pursuit of Ukrainian art and scholarship. His cause for beatification has been introduced in the Congregation of Rites.

Bibliography: B. STASIEWSKI, *Lexikon für Theologie und Kirche*, ed. J. HOFER and K. RAHNER (Freiberg 1957–65) 9:1265–66. *Analecta Ordinis S. Basilii Magni,* Ser. 1 (Zhovkva 1924–1935) Ser. 2 (Rome 1949–) 2:268–284. G. PROKOPTSCHUK, *Der Metropolit: Leben und Wirken des . . . Andreas Szeptzckyj* (Munich 1955), *Beatificationis et canonizationis Servi Dei Andreae Szeptikyj* (Rome 1958). A. HERMAN, *De fontibus iuris ecclesiastici Russorum* (Vatican City 1936). M. GORDILLO, *La civilità cattolica* 112.3 (1961) 474–483. PIUS XII, *Orientales omnes Ecclesias* (Letter, Dec. 23, 1945). *Acta Apostolicae Sedis* 38 (1946) 33–63.

[F. X. MURPHY]

SHERBORNE, ABBEY OF

Originally a house of secular canons in Sherborne, Dorset, England. Its establishment is attributed to St. ALDHELM, at the time of the foundation of the See of Sherborne in 705, though it may already have existed in the time of King Cenwalh (643–674). It was rebuilt and converted into a BENEDICTINE monastery *c.* 993, the bishop remaining head of the house until it was raised to the dignity of an abbey in 1122. The abbey was rebuilt after the greater part of it was destroyed by fire in 1436 during a riot between the monks and townspeople over rights in the abbey church. The abbey was dissolved in 1539 under Henry VIII, and in the next year for 100 marks (about £67 of the period) the parishioners purchased the church, which has been the town's parish church ever since.

Bibliography: J. HUTCHINS, *The History and Antiquities of the County of Dorset,* ed. W. SHIPP and J. W. HODSON, 4 v. (3d ed. Westminster, England 1861–74) v.4. D. KNOWLES, *The Monastic Order in England, 943–1216* (2d ed. Cambridge, England 1962). *The Victoria History of the County of Dorset,* ed. W. PAGE (London n.d.) v.2.

[J. L. GRASSI]

SHERIDAN, TERENCE JAMES

Jesuit writer and editor, b. Dublin, Ireland, Sept. 16, 1908; d. Manila, Philippines, Dec. 11, 1970. Educated at Belvedere College, Dublin, Sheridan entered the Jesuit novitiate in 1927. During juniorate and philosophy studies, he began his lifetime career as a writer of plays and topical sketches. Assigned to Hong Kong in 1934, he studied Cantonese at Shiuhing, got his first taste for the Cantonese opera, and wrote for *The Rock*, a Hong Kong literary periodical. From 1935–37, he was on the teaching staff of Wah Yan College, Hong Kong. After studying theology in Dublin, he was ordained to the priesthood in 1940 and stayed to give missions and retreats in Ireland till he returned to Wah Yan in 1946.

He became involved almost immediately in the cultural life of post-war Hong Kong. He began working on his annual series of Cantonese operas in English, witty translation-adaptations of the well-known themes of Cantonese opera. His productions were always alive, exciting, and very colorful; the most famous was *A Lizard Is No Dragon.* In 1951 he launched both a Chinese magazine for young people and *Outlook*, a literary and current affairs magazine. A leading member and producer for the Hong Kong Stage Club, he wrote a number of religious plays, film scripts, and scenarios, as well as pageants for the Marian Year and about the history of Hong Kong and Macao.

In the early 1960s, Sheridan was assigned to Singapore to edit the *Malaysian Catholic News*, which became a lively paper in his hands, and he was quickly involved in radio, drama, and TV in the city. In 1966, after difficulties about his editorship of the newspaper, he resigned from the post and was sent to Manila to work toward an Overseas Program in Radio Veritas. After some months he left that job and joined the staff of the East Asian Pastoral Institute. He lectured in the Philippines and in Chicago (Loyola Institute of Pastoral Studies) on the study, evaluation, and use of film. He was working on the official film record of Pope Paul's visit to Manila when he died suddenly of cardiac failure.

Bibliography: T. J. SHERIDAN, *Letters to Bart* (London 1938); *Seven Chinese Stories* (London 1959); *Four Short Plays* (London 1960). J. HOFINGER and T. J. SHERIDAN, eds., *The Medellín Papers* (Manila 1969).

[T. O'NEILL]

SHERMAN, THOMAS EWING

Missionary, educator; b. San Francisco, Calif, Oct. 12, 1856; d. New Orleans, La., April 29, 1933. He was the son of William Tecumseh Sherman, the famous Civil War general, and Ellen (Ewing) Sherman, a Catholic. After a Catholic upbringing by his mother, he was sent to Georgetown University, Washington, D.C., where he

Coat of Arms at Sherborne Abbey. (©Tom Bean/CORBIS)

graduated with an A.B. in 1874. He continued his education at Yale University (B.S., 1876) and at Washington University, St. Louis, Mo., where he studied law until 1878. At Roehampton, England, he entered the Society of Jesus on June 14, 1878, served his novitiate in England, and then returned (1880) to study philosophy at Woodstock College, Md., until 1883. After spending several years as an instructor in physics and classics at St. Louis University (1883–85) and the University of Detroit, Mich. (1885–87), he took his theology at Woodstock and was ordained in Philadelphia, Pa., by Abp. Patrick J. Ryan on July 7, 1889. He was assigned to St. Louis University (1891), where he soon acquired a reputation as a pulpit orator and a Catholic spokesman. His lecture tours drew large audiences, and after 1895 he was freed from other duties to concentrate on missionary preaching. His Chicago, Ill., Music Hall speech on Feb. 4, 1894, was an outstanding defense of the Church and the Jesuits. His lectures were discontinued in 1896, and he left the mission band to seek complete rest. When the Spanish-American War began (1898), Sherman enlisted as a chaplain with the Fourth Missouri Volunteers and later served as post chaplain at San Juan, Puerto Rico. Returning to the U.S. in 1899, he was assigned as a traveling missionary, with headquarters at Chicago. During the next decade he delivered a memorable plea for the education of Catholic women and directed the activities of the Catholic Truth Society of Chicago, which he founded in 1901. In 1911 Sherman suffered a nervous breakdown and was confined to a private sanitarium near Boston, Mass. Partially recovered by 1915 and jointly supported by his family and his society, he traveled through Europe and America until 1929, when he settled at Santa Barbara, Calif. He became ill again in 1931 and was taken to De Paul Sanitarium, New Orleans, where he died.

Bibliography: J. T. DURKIN, *General Sherman's Son* (New York 1959)

[J. L. MORRISON]

SHERT, JOHN, BL.

Priest, martyr; b. Shert Hall, near Macclesfield, Cheshire, England; d. hanged, drawn, and quartered at Tyburn (London), May 28, 1582. After earning his baccalaureate at Brasenose College, Oxford (1566), John Shert was a schoolmaster in London. At some point he became convicted of the truth of Catholicism and converted. Thereafter he was a servant, perhaps a tutor, in the household of Dr. Thomas Stapleton at Douai. He entered the English College there in 1576, and completed his seminary studies in Rome. Following his ordination in Rome (1576), he returned to Rheims, then England (Aug. 27, 1579). Shert served two years in the missions of Cheshire and London before his arrest and imprisonment in the Tower of London (July 14, 1581). He was condemned on a fictitious charge of conspiring against the king in Rheims and Rome He was beatified by Pope Leo XIII.

Feast of the English Martyrs: May 4 (England).

See Also: ENGLAND, SCOTLAND, AND WALES, MARTYRS OF.

Bibliography: R. CHALLONER, *Memoirs of Missionary Priests,* ed. J. H. POLLEN (rev. ed. London 1924; repr. Farnborough 1969). J. H. POLLEN, *Acts of English Martyrs* (London 1891).

[K. I. RABENSTEIN]

SHERWIN, RALPH, ST.

Priest, martyr; b. Roddesly, Derbyshire, England, *c.* 1550; d. Tyburn, Dec. 1, 1581. In 1568 Sir William Petre, the second founder of Exeter College, Oxford, nominated Sherwin, along with Richard Bristow, one of the translators of the Douay Bible, to a fellowship. Probably Sherwin owed this favor to the influence of John Woodward, his uncle, a Marian priest, formerly rector of Ingatestone and chaplain to the PETRE family. At Oxford he enjoyed much influence and the attention of the queen's favorite, the Earl of Leicester. Reconciled to the Church in 1574, he left the following year for Douai. After ordination there on March 23, 1577, he went to the English College, Rome, where he took a leading part in the dissentions between the English and Welsh students. He was one of the four who petitioned Gregory XIII to place the college under the direction of the Jesuits. On April 18, 1580, he left for England in a company that included (St.) Edmund CAMPION and (St.) Luke KIRBY. They landed in England early in August, and Sherwin was arrested the following November while preaching in the house of Nicholas Roscarrock in London. After a month in chains in the Marshalsea prison, he was sent to the Tower, where on December 15 he was cruelly racked, left to lie in the snow, racked a second time, and deprived of food for five days and nights. It was said that he was offered a bishopric if he would apostatize. After his trial and condemnation with Edmund Campion, (St.) Alexander BRIANT, and others, he wrote to his uncle: ''Innocencie is my only comfort against all the forged villanie which is fathered on my fellow priests and me.'' He is the protomartyr of the English College, Rome, where his portrait, discovered at Darlington in 1962, now hangs. Sherwin was beatified by Leo XIII on Dec. 29, 1886, and canonized by Paul VI on Oct. 25, 1970 as one of the Forty Martyrs of England and Wales.

Feast: Dec. 1; Oct. 25 (Feast of the 40 Martyrs of England and Wales); May 4 (Feast of the English Martyrs in England).

See Also: ENGLAND, SCOTLAND, AND WALES, MARTYRS OF.

Bibliography: B. CAMM, ed., *Lives of the English Martyrs Declared Blessed by Pope Leo XIII in 1886 and 1895,* 2 v. (New York 1904–14) 2:358–396. M. WAUGH, *Blessed Ralph Sherwin* (Postulation Pamphlet; London 1962). R. CHALLONER, *Memoirs of Missionary Priests,* ed. J. H. POLLEN (rev. ed. London 1924; repr. Farnborough 1969).

[G. FITZHERBERT]

SHERWOOD, THOMAS, BL.

Lay martyr; b. London, England, 1551; d. hanged, drawn, and quartered at Tyburn (London), Feb. 7, 1578. After leaving school (1566), Thomas assisted his father, a London wool draper who himself had been imprisoned for the faith. Discerning a vocation to the priesthood, Thomas was arranging to attend the English College at Douai when he was recognized in Chancery Lane and betrayed by George Marten, son of Lady Tregonwell. When questioned about his opinion of the excommunication of the queen, he acknowledged his ignorance of Pius V's bull, but stated that if she were indeed excommunicated, her rule could not be lawful. Thus, he was detained at Westminster for further examination and committed to the Tower of London by the Privy Council (Nov. 17, 1577). He was repeatedly examined, threatened with the horrors of the dungeon, and twice racked to betray other Catholics, but he remained steadfast. Eventually he was cast naked into the fetid dungeon without food and without permission for visitors to supply his needs. He was tried on Feb. 3, 1578, and condemned for denying the Act of Supremacy. He died at the age of 27. He was beatified by Pope Leo XIII on May 13, 1895.

Feast of the English Martyrs: May 4 (England).

See Also: ENGLAND, SCOTLAND, AND WALES, MARTYRS OF.

Bibliography: R. CHALLONER, *Memoirs of Missionary Priests,* ed. J. H. POLLEN (rev. ed. London 1924; repr. Farnborough 1969). J. H. POLLEN, *Acts of English Martyrs* (London 1891).

[K. I. RABENSTEIN]

SHIBBOLETH

Hebrew, *šibbōlet,* ear of grain or flowing stream. The common meaning of shibboleth, "test-word" or "criterion," has its origin in Jgs 12.4–6. In the 11th century B.C., a group of Ephraimites sought to escape a band of Galaadites by attempting to cross the Jordan back into Palestine. The fugitives pretended to be Galaadites when they were halted at the Jordan. However, they betrayed themselves by their inability to pronounce the chosen test-word in the Gileadite manner. The telltale element was the initial sound of the word shibboleth. The accepted theory is that the dialectal peculiarity was with the West-Jordanian Ephraimites who used the Amorrite "s" instead of the Canaanite "sh." E. A. Speiser, however, believes that the dialectal peculiarity was with the Galaadites in whose dialect the initial sound in shibboleth was "th" instead of "sh." Thus, not only the Ephraimites, but Judeans or Galileans, had they been in the same predicament, would have likewise betrayed themselves. Whichever theory is accepted, the result was the same: the Ephraimites failed the phonetic test and execution followed, although the alleged number of victims is probably exaggerated.

Bibliography: E. A. SPEISER, "The Shibboleth Incident (Judges 12:6)," *The Bulletin of the American Schools of Oriental Research* 85 (February 1942) 10–13. R. MARCUS, "The Word *Šibboleth* Again," *ibid.* 87 (October 1942) 39.

[J. MORIARITY]

SHIELDS, THOMAS EDWARD

Educator; b. Mendota, MN, May 9, 1862; d. Washington, DC, Feb. 15, 1921. The son of Irish immigrants, he was somewhat unruly as a child and finished his formal schooling late. He was admitted to St. Francis Seminary, Milwaukee, WI, in 1882, and to St. Thomas Seminary, St. Paul, MN, in 1885. At St. Thomas he published his first book, *Index Omnium* (1888), which was designed to help professional men correlate data gathered from wide reading. After his ordination on March 4, 1891, he studied for his Ph.D. at the Johns Hopkins University, Baltimore, MD. His dissertation, *The Effect of Odors Upon the Blood Flow* (1895), influenced psychological research, and in 1902 he joined the faculty of The Catholic University of America, Washington, DC, as an instructor in psychology.

Shields soon transferred his interest to education. In 1905 he set up a correspondence course, supplemented by diocesan summer institutes, for sisters in the expanding Catholic school system. He established the university's department of education in 1909 and served as its first chairman. The following year he founded the *Catholic Educational Review.* In 1911 he conducted the first Summer Institute for Catholic Sisters at the university, and he founded the Sisters College, of which he was dean. In 1912 he was instrumental in securing the adoption of the University Affiliation Program. To correlate the curriculum of the Catholic school, Shields wrote a series of four widely used texts in religion. He was also the author of *The Education of Our Girls* (1907), a dialogue; *The Making and Unmaking of a Dullard* (1909), a description of his youth; and *The Philosophy of Education* (1917), the first Catholic book of its kind in English. He was perhaps the leading Catholic educator in the U.S. during the first quarter of the 20th century.

Bibliography: J. WARD, *Thomas Edward Shields* (New York 1947).

[J. W. EVANS]

SHĪ'ITES

One of the two main branches of Islam, the other being the SUNNITES.

The initial Arabic phrase *shi'atu 'Ali,* "Partisans of Ali," was used to refer to a number of early Muslims who backed Ali ibn Abi Talib (the cousin of the Prophet MUḤAMMAD to whom his daughter Fatima was married) in the matter of the succession of the Prophet. The Shi'a claim that the Prophet appointed Ali as his successor, an important act which the community ignored by recognizing Abu Bakr as the first caliph (Arabic "khalifah," i.e., "successor"), 'Umar I as the second, and 'Uthman as the third. Upon the murder of 'Uthman, Ali was invited to be the fourth caliph (35–40 A.H., 656–661 A.D.). His appointment only resulted in increased tension between his supporters and his detractors, leading to the first civil war within the Islamic community that ultimately gave rise to the division of Islam into the Shi'a and Sunni branches.

Shi'a Islam is distinguished from Sunni Islam mainly in its interpretation of the role of the IMAM in the Islamic social order. The essential distinction between Shi'a and Sunni Islam is the doctrine of the imamate, which is essential for all Shi'a. The Shi'a believe that the human race needs divinely guided leaders and teachers, who are the imams who continue the mission of the prophets in every respect, except bringing new scriptures. The imams are endowed with *'isma,* i.e., immunity from sin and error

Al Hussein Mosque, Karbala, Iraq. (©Francoise de Mulder/ CORBIS)

in order to fulfill their divine mission. All Shi'a believe that without the imams the world would cease to exist, yet they are divided over the question of the number of the imams, leading to the emergence of different branches within Shi'a Islam.

Twelver Shi'a. The Twelver Shi'a, *Ithna 'Ashariya,* or *Imamiyah*, constitute the largest group within the Shi'a, and believe in the following 12 Imams:

1. 'Ali ibn Abi Talib (d. A.H. 40/661 A.D.)
2. Hasan ibn 'Ali (d. A.H. 49/669 A.D.)
3. Husayn ibn 'Ali (d. A.H. 60/680 A.D.)
4. 'Ali ibn al-Husayn, Zayn al-'Abidin (d. A.H. 95/ 714 A.D.)
5. Muhammad al-Baqir (d. A.H. 115/733 A.D.)
6. Ja'far al-Sadiq (d. A.H. 148/765 A.D.)
7. Musa al-Kazim (d. A.H. 183/799 A.D.)
8. 'Ali al-Rida (d. A.H. 203/818 A.D.)
9. Muḥammad Jawad al-Taqi (d. A.H. 220/835 A.D.)
10. 'Ali al-Naqi (d. A.H. 254/868 A.D.)
11. Al-Hasan al-'Askari (d. A.H. 260/874 A.D.)
12. Muhammad al-Mahdi, al-Qa'im (major occultation in A.H. 329/941 A.D.)

For the Twelvers, the imam possesses a divine light which guides him in interpretation and legislation. The shrines of the imams, especially that of Imam Hussain in Karbala (Iraq), Imam Ali in Najaf (Iraq), and Imam Rida in Mashhad (Iran) are pilgrimage sites. The imams are not only the religious teachers, they also have an eschatological significance, for they can intercede for believers on Judgment Day. Therefore, knowing the imam is necessary for salvation. This point is especially emphasized by the messianic belief in the hidden imam, Muhammad al-Muntazar al-Mahdi, who is alive and in occultation. Beginning in 872 A.D. and during the minor occultation the imam would communicate with his followers through four direct representatives from among them. Since 941, he has been in major occultation and will only reappear when the world is filled with injustice and oppression in order to establish justice and to prepare the second coming of Christ. This messianism within Shi'a doctrine has revealed itself in both political and non-political forms, leading at times to quietism and at others to activism.

While the Twelvers have their own distinct school of law founded by the sixth Imam, Ja'far al-Sadiq (d. A.H 148/765 A.D.) (hence called the Ja'fari school), it is considered as the same sacred law; *shari'ah* with little difference in matters of ritual worship from any of the four major Sunni schools of Islamic jurisprudence. In matters of transactions the difference can be summarized in the Shi'i acceptance of temporary marriage (*mut'a*) as well as an additional tax (*khums*) to the regular religious tax (*zakat*). Also important in Shi'a doctrine are the principles of justice (*'adl*) and intellect (*'aql*). The latter plays a significant role, not only in their attitude towards intellectual sciences, but also in the continuous reinterpretation of the law and the ongoing task of *Ijtihad*, independent analysis, that remains open within Shi'a Islam. In contrast, after the establishment of the four Sunni schools of law a thousand years ago, the gates of *Ijtihad* within the Sunni world were considered closed.

Isma'ilis. It is to Isma'il the son of Ja'far al Sadiq that the Isma'ilis trace their line. As the elder son of the Imam, Isma'il was his designated successor, but he predeceased him. Those who viewed this designation irreversible either denied the death of Isma'il proclaiming his return as the Qaim (this group was later known as 'pure Isma'iliya') or accepted his son Muhammad as the rightful imam after Ja'far (known at the time as Mubarakiyah). The two groups came to hold Muhammad ibn Isma'il as the legitimate Imam in the absence of Isma'il. It was not until the middle of the ninth century that the Isma'iliya appeared as a well organized, secret movement with revolutionary principles and elaborate doctrine. There is little certainty about the early history of the Isma'ilies since the available sources are with few exceptions anti-Isma'ili.

The Isma'ili doctrine can be identified as possessing a gnostic nature with a structure that maintains emphasis on a distinction between the outer, exoteric (*zahir*) or the acessible meaning of the scriptures and the religious law brought by the prophets and the inner, esoteric (*batin*) of religion which are unchangeable truths hidden in all scriptures and can be revealed by *ta'wil*, esoteric interpretation. While the Isma'ili groups from early *da'wa* (Isma'ili missionaries) to the Fatimid dynasty and the Qaramatah movement propagated same aspects of religious doctrine, in political and social matters they cannot be identified with each other. At times appearing as a political movement and at others identifying with mystical elements and coming together with Sufi orders, they were nevertheless, a strong source of activity in arts and sciences. Today, the two branches of Isma'ilis of the Mongol invasion era, the Nizaris and the Musta'lis, continue to live as religious communities in Indo-Pakistani subcontinent, Syria, East Africa, and other regions.

Zaydis. The Zaydis were found mainly in Yemen. Zayd, a grandson of Ali's son Husayn, revolted against UMAYYAD rule at Kufa in 740 A.D. Although the revolt was defeated, his followers kept his memory alive. More than a century later, they established two principalities, one in Tabaristan, which was short-lived, and the other in Yemen, which lasted until the Imam was overthrown in 1962. Among the various Shi'a groups, the Zaydis are the closest to Sunni doctrine and practice, distinguished from the Sunnis by common Shi'i features such as a distinctive call to prayer, the five-fold funerary prayers, and the rejection of certain minor Sunni practices. Unlike the other Shi'a groups, the Zaydis reject temporary marriages, succession by inheritance, child Imams, and hidden Imams.

Bibliography: M. H. TABATABA'I, *Shi'ite Islam*, ed. and trans. S. H. NASR (London 1975); *Ideals and realities of Islam*, 2nd ed. (London 1975); "Ithna 'ashariyya" in *The Encyclopedia of Islam*, new ed. (Leiden 1960). A. A. SACHEDINA, *Islamic Messianism: The Idea of Mahdi in Twelver Shi'ism* (Albany 1981). N. R. KEDDIE, ed., *Religion and Politics in Iran: Shi'ism From Quietism to Revolution* (New Haven 1983). D. M. DONALDSON, *The Shi'ite Religion* (London 1933). W. C. CHITTICK, trans. and ed., *A Shi'ite Anthology* (Albany 1981). S. A. ARJOMAND, *The Shadow of God and the Hidden Imam* (Chicago 1984).

[B. DAVARY]

SHIMAZAKI, TŌSON

Japanese novelist and poet; b. Nagano Prefecture, March 25, 1872; d. Aug. 22, 1943. He achieved stature as one of modern Japan's leading writers chiefly as a master of *shi shōsetsu,* a genre peculiar to Japanese literature, partially paralleled in the West by the *Ich Roman.*

Shimazaki was born in the mountain district of central Japan into a family that traced its ancestry back 200 years, and reared under the sharp discipline of his father, who was a scholar of Chinese and Japanese classics. He first went to Tokyo as a boy of ten; at 16 he entered a Tokyo mission school, Meiji Gakuin, and here first encountered Christianity. In the next year, 1888, he was baptized by Pastor Kumaji Kimura at the Daichō Church. After graduation in 1892, he joined the faculty of Meiji Girls' School, also a mission school, where he came under the influence of his colleague, the Christian critic Tōkōku Kitamura. These two joined several other friends in founding *Bungaku kai* (The World of Literature), the magazine that developed as the fountainhead of the Romantic movement in Japan, and which frequently reflected the impact of Christian thought.

Like many Japanese literatteurs, Shimazaki gradually drifted away from Christianity. Although he lacked any definite consciousness of his apostasy, the severance seems to have been complete by 1893. Nevertheless his work clearly points to the influence of Christianity at considerable depth.

His first book, *Wakana shu* (1897, Young Herbs), was a collection of early poems in colloquial style with minimal use of Chinese characters; the movement is graceful and fluid after the mode of certain hymns to which he was at that time deeply attached. The poem, for example, that begins, "Yūgure shizuka ni . . ." ("Quiet is the evening . . .") is plainly fashioned after a hymn. *Hakai* (1906, The Breach of the Code) launched his career as a novelist. The novel's main theme, in which Christian influence appears, is compassionate indignation over the treatment accorded the *burakumin* ("the outcast-community"). One of his later major works, *Shinsei* (1919, New Life), treats delicately the problem of incest.

Bibliography: Collected works. *Shimazaki Tōson zenshū,* 31 v. (Tokyo 1956–57). K. KAMEI, *Shimazaki Tōson ron* (Tokyo 1956). K. HIRANO, *Shimazaki Tōson* (Tokyo 1957).

[M. HYODO]

SHINTOISM

Shintō denotes the whole complex of religious and ethical ideas that existed in Japan before the introduction of religious elements from the high cultures of China and India. Shintō, like the racial origin of the Japanese people, goes back to many different sources. It is generally acknowledged that the Japanese are of mixed racial com-

Shintō Festival at a Japanese Meiji shrine. (©Bettmann/CORBIS)

position. People were living in Japan at the end of the Paleolithic Age or, at the latest, by the Mesolithic Age. They were hunting tribes from North Asia and food-gathering and hunting people from the tropical forests. Later new peoples came from South China, Southeast Asia, Oceania, and also from East Asia. Sometime between the third and fourth centuries A.D. the last and most powerful tribes of Altaic stock came to Japan by way of the Korean Peninsula, conquered the farming people who had settled in the Japanese islands, and established their dynasty. Shintō assimilated various religious elements from these racial components.

Early History. The religion of ancient Japan was not called Shintō. The term Shintō first appeared in the *Nihonshoki,* or "Chronicles of Japan" (edited in A.D. 720). Shintō means "the way of the Gods" (*shin* is a Chinese character representing the Japanese word *kami,* which means god or deity). Shintō as the way of the gods came into existence when it was necessary to distinguish the old religion of Japan from the newly introduced *Butsudō,* "the way of Buddha." *Kami* is the essential object of Shintō worship. Though there are doubts among scholars concerning the etymology of the word *kami,* many agree that *kami,* "god," is connected with a word of similar form that means "above us." According to this theory, *kami* means "High Being." In ancient Japanese cosmogony, the making of the universe was explained by the ascent of heaven from the earth. Until that moment, heaven and earth were united and mixed in one chaos. In another myth, the god *Izanagi,* representing heaven, married the goddess *Izanami,* the earth. They produced lands, islands, seas, rivers, mountains, trees, animals, etc. The sun, moon, and storms were also the offspring of their marriage. When *Izanami* died of severe burns after giving birth to fire, the parents of the universe had to be separated; *Izanagi,* the sky father, ascended to heaven, while *Izanami,* the earth mother, descended to the Lower World to become its goddess.

Essential Elements. The two essential elements of Shintō are nature worship and ancestor worship, and shamanistic trails are widespread. Vestiges of the worship of the Supreme Being also are found. In its most primitive stage Shintō worship was confined to natural phenomena. Later the idea of spirits and demons entered Shintō. The sun is considered a benefactor who bestows upon the people the special favor of good crops. The sun was also worshiped with special respect as the Emperor's divine ancestress, *Amaterasu.* The role of the sun in ancestor worship is a later development, fostered by political considerations. The Emperor's daughter was selected to be the high priestess to serve the sun-god. The Emperor, apparently, worshiped a sky god, but one not identical to the primitive sun-god. Among the divine animals worshiped in Shintō, the fox has an important role. The fox, at first, was the food god's messenger, although in later periods the fox came to be regarded as a god himself.

Between heaven and earth, spirits and demons live everywhere in mountains, trees, and in all animals. When angry, spirits and demons send unhappiness, sickness, and disasters to plague the people. Therefore, various rites are performed to calm the spirits and demons, and prayers are offered to secure their favors.

The main purposes of the Shintō cult in general are positive ones, to gain good crops or successful fishing. Shintō worship is practiced today at particular shrines. In ancient times, however, people performed the ceremonies not in special buildings, but in the mountains and woods or on the banks of rivers, where spirits and demons were thought to dwell. The woods, especially, were very likely the original sites of these religious rites. Originally, there were no professional priests, and a layman was elected by divination to carry out each ceremony. Women played important roles in worship. At one time the Emperor himself, the ruler of the nation, acted as the chief priest. The phallic aspect of Shintō worship reflects its connection with fertility cults in general.

In the Heian Period (794–1192) Shintō was combined by force with Buddhism (which was introduced in 552), but no genuine union of the two religions was ever realized. Generally speaking, Buddhism expresses belief in the hereafter, whereas Shintō is the religion of the present world and exhibits little concern for the world beyond the grave.

Bibliography: W. T. DE BARY et al., comps., *Sources of Japanese Tradition* (Records of Civilization 54; New York 1958). H. HARDACRE, *Shinto and the state, 1868–1988* (Princeton, N. J. 1989). D. C. HOLTOM, *The National Faith of Japan: A Study of Modern Shinto* (London/New York 1938, 1995). J. BREEN and M. TEEUWEN, eds., *Shinto in History: Ways of the Kami* (Honolulu 2000).

[F. K. NUMAZAWA/EDS.]

SHIPMAN, ANDREW JACKSON

Lawyer, author; b. Springvale, Fairfax County, VA, Oct. 15, 1857; d. New York City, Oct. 17, 1915. He was the son of John James and Priscilla (Carroll) Shipman. After private tutoring he attended Georgetown College (now University), Washington, DC, graduating in 1878. He joined the Catholic Church while he was a student at Georgetown. After moving to Hocking Valley, OH (1880), where he became superintendent of W. P. Rend & Company, a coal mining firm, he displayed unusual interest in the Eastern–rite Catholics, who were numerous among the miners and whose religious needs were inadequately met. In 1884 he became a clerk in the New York Customs House, and two years later he obtained a law degree from the University of the City of New York. After his marriage to Adair Mooney in 1893, he established Blandy, Mooney, & Shipman, a law firm specializing in cases involving Greek–rite Catholics and ecclesiastical law; it handled the St. Stephen's Church cases (1890–1900) and the Hopkins will cases (1902–06).

In addition to his law practice, Shipman was active in civic and charitable affairs. He supported the MARQUETTE LEAGUE for Indian missionaries and promoted the Catholic Theater Movement. He served as delegate to the New York constitutional convention (1915), director of the Sevilla Home for Children and the Mohansic State Hospital, and member of the New York Board of Regents. His principal concern, however, was the welfare of Greek, Slavic, and Ruthenian Catholics. His knowledge of their life and language was intimate; he labored to interest the bishops in their problems, helped to promote their cultural assimilation, and acted as their most effective propagandist, seeking to make Catholics aware of them, explaining their rites, and dispelling Catholic fears about their orthodoxy. He wrote about them in such popular publications as *McClure's Magazine* and in the *Catholic Encyclopedia,* of which he was a director. He also translated their rite into English in *The Holy Mass according to the Greek Rite* (1911), participated actively in their local affairs, helped establish a Ruthenian Catholic Church, organized a Ukrainian choir, and assisted the Syrian Church of St. Joachim. He was an adviser to Bp. Stephen S. Ortynsky, who officiated at a Greek rite funeral service for him in St. Patrick's Cathedral, New York City.

Bibliography: C. B. PALLEN, ed., *A Memorial of Andrew J. Shipman* (New York 1916).

[J. L. MORRISON]

SHIRWOOD, JOHN

Bishop of Durham; b. York, England; d. Rome, Jan. 14, 1493. He received degrees from Cambridge University and a doctorate in theology from Oxford (by 1460). Proficiency in Latin letters helped him win the favor of George Neville, Bishop of Exeter, later Archbishop of York. This association existed in 1460, when Shirwood became chancellor of Exeter cathedral. In 1484 he received the bishopric of DURHAM by papal provision. His preferment to high Church office reflects the favor not only of Neville but also of King Edward IV. Beginning in 1477, he served as king's advocate at the Curia. He enjoyed also the favor of King Richard III. His career suffered from the victory of King Henry VII (1485), but eventually he won the new ruler's confidence, again becoming advocate at Rome in 1492. Shirwood first attracted Neville's attention through his humanistic scholarship (*see* HUMANISM). He was one of the first English humanists to master Greek. His Latin poetry is lost, but his *Liber de ludo arithmomachia,* describing a board game, was printed in 1482. He made an important collection of manuscripts and printed books, emphasizing the Greek and Latin classics.

Bibliography: A. B. EMDEN, *A Biographical Register of the Scholars of the University of Oxford to A.D. 1500,* 3 v. (Oxford 1957–59) 3:1692–93. E. I. CARLYLE, *The Dictionary of National Biography from the Earliest Times to 1900,* 63 v. (London 1885–1900) 18:146. R. WEISS, *Humanism in England during the Fifteenth Century* (2d ed. Oxford 1957). P. S. ALLEN, ''Bishop Shirwood of Durham and His Library,'' *English Historical Review* 25 (1910) 445–456. B. BEHRENS, ''Origins of the Office of English Resident Ambassador in Rome,'' *English Historical Review* 49 (1934) 640–656.

[C. G. NAUERT, JR.]

SHOWBREAD

Term having reference to the Israelite practice of keeping specially prepared bread or cakes constantly ''set before'' Yahweh in His Temple. The antiquity of this custom is attested by 1 Sm 21.1–6: the priest at Nob gave David and his men, all ritually pure, the consecrated or ''holy bread,'' for he had no other bread than the ''bread of the Presence'' (*leḥem happānîm,* literally ''bread of the face''), which had been removed from ''before Yahweh'' and replaced with ''hot'' bread. This passage implies that the bread was called ''bread of the Presence'' because it was always in the presence or sight of Yahweh. (See articles cited in the bibliography for other Hebrew terms for this bread.) Jesus cited the episode at Nob in one of His Sabbath controversies (Mt 12.1–8 and parallels). The legislation in Lv 24.5–9 provides that each Sabbath day 12 freshly baked cakes must be placed in two equal piles on a gold-plated table standing in front of the Holy of Holies and some pure incense placed on each pile. This bread was to serve as a perpetual memorial of Israel's covenant with Yahweh. The 12 cakes may have symbolized the 12 tribes of Israel. One of the duties of the Levites was the weekly renewal of the showbread (1 Chr 9.32; 23. 27–29; 2 Chr 13.11). Only the priests had the right to eat the bread set out the previous Sabbath (Lv 24.9; but cf. 1 Sm 21.1–6: either the law was not yet enacted or it could be nullified by an exceptional circumstance). The ''table of showbread'' is described in Ex 25.23–30; 37.10–16; for its location in the TENT OF MEETING and presumably also in the Temple, see Ex 40.22–23. Ten such tables are mentioned in 2 Chr 4.8, 19, but only one in 29.18. The Arch of Titus (Rome) contains a relief of the table of showbread from Herod's Temple.

Bibliography: A. PELLETIER, *Dictionnaire de la Bible,* suppl. ed. L. PIROT, et al. (Paris 1928–) 6:965–976. *Encyclopedic Dictionary of the Bible,* translated and adapted by L. HARTMAN (New York, 1963) 12202–03.

[D. DIETLEIN]

SHRINES

The term shrine refers to a place, usually the object of pilgrimages, where a relic, miraculous statue or picture, or other holy object receives special veneration; also to a spot designated to foster some Catholic belief or devotion. In Latin *scrinium* meant a box to contain manuscripts. Anglo-Saxon writers used *scrin* for a coffer or ark (*arca* in Latin) in which sacred relics were preserved, by analogy with the Biblical ARK OF THE COVENANT (*'ărôn* in Hebrew), which was a chest of acacia wood overlaid with gold, holding the Tables of the Law, Aaron's rod, and a golden pot of manna (Heb 9.4). The ark was set in the Temple, in the Holy of Holies, a true shrine honored with religious ceremonial (2 Chr 5.6).

The sarcophagi in the Roman CATACOMBS were *arcae* containing the bodies of the dead. The *arcosolium* developed, together with the tomb beneath an arch with a width equal to that of the tomb slab. This slab served as an altar table where Christian martyrs were interred. As in the case of St. POLYCARP, local cult established a solid tradition concerning the burial places of the martyrs and the authenticity of their relics (*Martyrdom of Polycarp* 18.2).

The translation of Christian relics began in the East at the time of Emperor Constantine I. Thus, in 356 relics believed to be those of St. Timothy and in 357 those of Saints Andrew and Luke were placed amid great ceremony in the Basilica of the Apostles in Constantinople. In the West, however, civil law and Christian sentiment forbade removal of relics. For some centuries these remained in marked tombs. Pope Honorius I (625 to 638) reversed a ruling by Pope Gregory I (590 to 604) when he had the head of St. AGNES brought to the greater safety of the Lateran in Rome. The history of the shrines devoted to her indicates clearly what was happening in many other places.

Four types of shrines will be noted, according as they honor objects of Our Lord's Passion, the Blessed Virgin Mary, the saints, or Catholic beliefs and devotions.

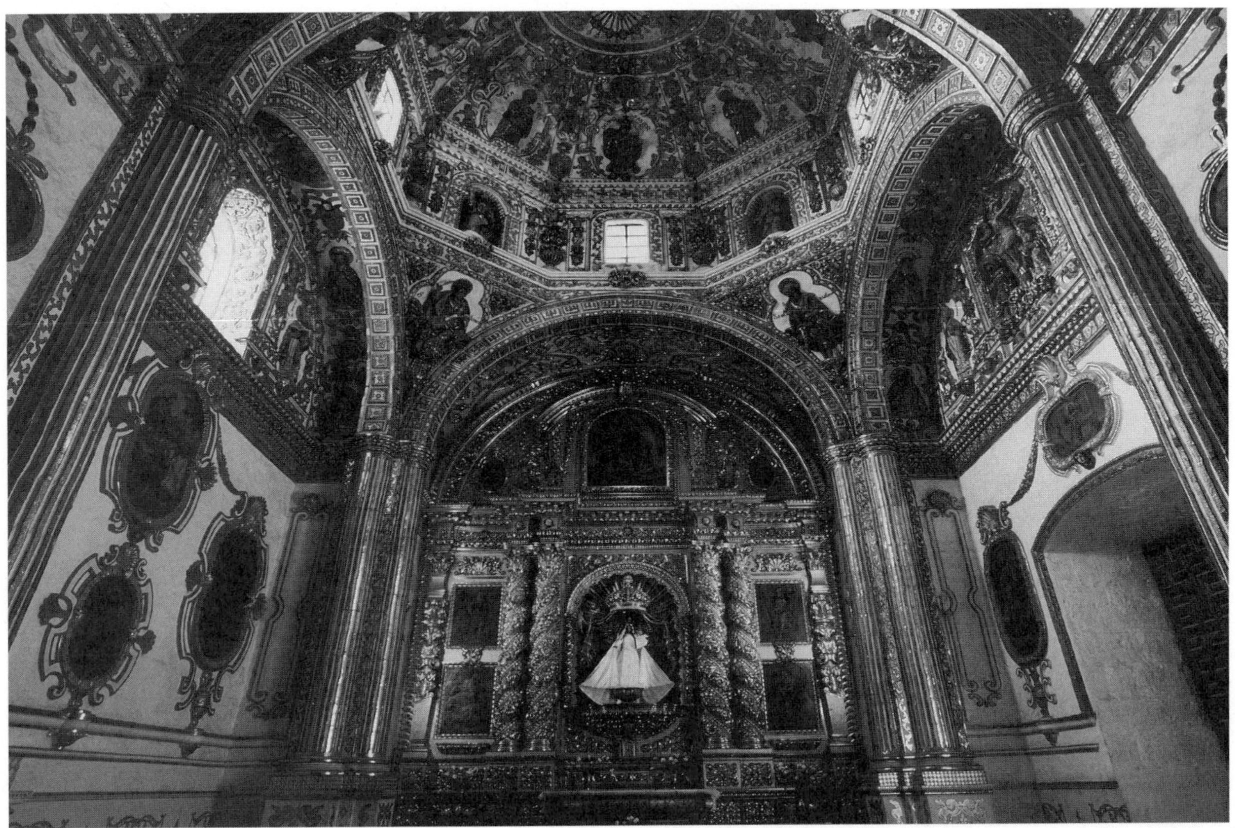

Interior of the Church of Santo Domingo, Oaxaca, Mexico. (©Kelly-Mooney Photography/CORBIS)

Shrines of Relics of the Passion. The instruments of the Passion came to be regarded as symbols of the supreme martyrdom and to be treated as major relics. Constantine I in 327 had the Holy SEPULCHER excavated (Eusebius, *Vita Constantini* 3.28). Eusebius does not mention the finding of the cross; but St. Ambrose states with some authority that the cross, title, and nails were unearthed (*De obit. Theodosii* 46, 57). (*See* CROSS, FINDING OF THE HOLY.) The title would identify the cross. In normal Roman usage, which the Gospels indicate was followed, the title consisted of a wooden board, then called *album,* gouged with the words of indictment and painted black or red. It is feasible that a title of this kind, fixed to a wooden cross which was flung hastily into a disused cistern, could have been preserved more than three centuries. Archeologists have recorded many such survivals.

Dispersal of what was regarded as true relics of the Passion began immediately. Parts of the cross and its title remained in Jerusalem, where they were venerated by Aetheria in 385. St. Cyril of Jerusalem, age seven when the holy sepulcher was located, wrote *c.* 347: ''All the world is full of the particles of the cross'' (*Catecheses* 4). St. HELENA is said to have sent to Constantine I, her son, parts of the cross and title.

The Jerusalem relic of the cross suffered many hazards. Chosroes II (590 to 628) captured it, but Heraclius regained it in 629 and subdivided it into 19 parts, which were distributed to great churches at Antioch, Alexandria, Edessa, and elsewhere. Four parts remained in Jerusalem and were in turn divided many times. During the period of the CRUSADES the crusaders removed portions, which thereby lost their tradition of origin. Some were authentically derived from the main deposit. Many particles consisted of mere splinters. When Rohault de Fleury made a detailed study of all relics of the cross then known, he showed that far less than one-fortieth was accounted for, although he overestimated the size and cubic content of the cross (*Mémoire sur les Instruments de la Passion,* 1870).

Church of Santa Croce in Gerusalemme, Rome. Constantine I sent part of the cross and title to Rome, where it was deposited in a chapel annexed to the Sessorian basilica subsequently dedicated to the holy cross. This remains the most important shrine of relics of the Passion and is the prototype of several later European shrines.

The relics at first were kept in a chamber behind the apse. This is the *memoria,* situated behind the *martyrium* at Golgotha and other Constantinian foundations, but not

The interior of Our Lady of Guadalupe Chapel, a shrine built on the site where Juan Diego claimed to have seen the Virgin Mary in 1531, Guadalupe Hidalgo, Mexico. (©Archive Photos)

elsewhere in Rome, where relics remained beneath altars, not behind them. Other ancient European shrines, such as the one at Saragossa, placed the relics behind the altar. The feretory of St. Edward the Confessor still remains in a distinct chamber behind the high altar of Westminster Abbey, London. The Santa Croce relic of the cross, reduced to three pieces no longer than six inches, are currently encased in a silver reliquary.

It is the relic of the title at Santa Croce that is unique. Confronted by Visigoth attacks, the clergy (*c.* 455) hid the title high above the main arch behind a marble slab inscribed ''Hic est titulus crucis.'' Here it was found in 1492 and enclosed in glass by Innocent VIII. A nail and two thorns from the crown of thorns are also venerated at Santa Croce.

Notre Dame Cathedral, Paris. This shrine claims a relic of the CROWN OF THORNS. The crown was shown to pilgrims in Jerusalem until about 810 and was then removed to the imperial chapel in Constantinople. Previously some of the thorns had been given away, notably to Aachen, Germany. Otto I in turn donated in 937 part of the Aachen relic to Athelstan, King of Wessex. After St. LOUIS IX, King of France, settled the war debts of Baldwin II of Constantinople, he received the sacred crown, a nail, and some of the wood of the cross. These were brought to Paris in an enormous procession, met by the King at Sens, where he bestowed several thorns on princes who were present. One of these is enshrined in the cathedral at Barcelona. Another later was brought to Scotland by Mary, Queen of Scots, and eventually came to Stonyhurst College in Lancashire.

St. Louis IX built the Sainte Chapelle in Paris to house the crown of thorns, translated it there (March 21, 1248), and enshrined it above the baldachino of the high altar. The relic was damaged in the process of concealing it during the French Revolution. In 1806 it was placed in Notre Dame Cathedral. There it is kept, along with the fragment of the cross and the nail, in a gilded bronze ark in resplendent cases. The relics are exposed every Lent and then returned to the cathedral treasury at the end of Holy Week.

Cathedral at Trier, Germany. The ark of relics that tradition claimed were sent to this imperial city by St. Helena remained sealed until 1101, when it was opened and revealed a large relic of the cross, a nail, and a garment, supposedly Christ's and since then called the holy coat of Trier. Argenteuil, near Paris, also claimed to possess the holy tunic, as did other places. The authenticity of the relics has given rise to much controversy. Trier and Argenteuil have been centers of pilgrimage whenever these relics were exposed (*see* TRIER).

Cathedral at Turin, Italy. The holy shroud was brought in 1578 to Turin, where it has since been kept in a silver casket inside an iron chest in a great marble urn in its own chapel in the cathedral. This chapel, approached by 37 steps behind the high altar, is a magnet for daily throngs of pilgrims. The shroud is exposed for veneration every 33 years.

Sancta Sanctorum Chapel, Rome. This is one of the most frequented of all shrines since it possesses what have been claimed to be relics of the cross, Christ's sandals, a portrait of Our Lord ''not painted by mortal hands,'' and the holy stairs (*scala sancta*). These 28 white marble steps, which once led to the praetorium of Pilate at Jerusalem according to tradition, are mounted by pilgrims on their knees.

Other Shrines. The holy thorn given to King Athelstan remained in GLASTONBURY ABBEY until 1539 and is now preserved at STANBROOK ABBEY in England. The cathedral at Ghent enshrines one of the largest fragments of the cross. In Florence the cathedral retains a relic of the nail.

Shrines of Our Lady. The earliest shrines of the Blessed Virgin Mary were in the places related to the life of her son, Nazareth and Bethlehem. By the 4th century there was a church near the *probatica* pool in Jerusalem on the site of her supposed birthplace. At Ain Karim, four miles distant, is the church of the Visitation; and at Mt. Zion, the church of the dormition. (*See* PALESTINE, 9.)

Modern excavations at Ephesus have revealed an important 4th-century chapel on the site of a much older

Catholic priest blessing the congregation during Mass at the Basilica of the National Shrine of the Immaculate Conception, Washington, D.C. 1997, photograph by William Philpott. (AP/Wide World Photos)

building. In 1950 it was restored as a shrine in the belief that Mary lived there with St. John. The nearby ruins of the church of St. Mary, scene of the ecumenical council in 431, ranked as a great Marian shrine. Loreto, Italy, claims the house of the Holy Family, said to have come from Nazareth.

Shrines with Cloth Relics. In the absence of corporeal relics, veneration attached to the Blessed Virgin's cloak, veil, and cincture, which emerged as relics somewhat later than those of the Passion. THEODORE LECTOR mentions that Eudocia sent to Constantinople (*c.* 450) an icon painted by St. Luke and refers to oratories possessing the cincture, cloak, or veil. The dispersal of these relics was gradual.

The cathedral in CHARTRES claims the veil of Mary, long misnamed her tunic, and said to have been given to King Charles the Bald in 876 by Constantine V. The ark, or *châsse,* covered with gold and richly jeweled, remained unopened until 1712. When opened it was found to contain not a tunic but a silken veil 16 feet long. During the French Revolution the reliquary was looted, but the relic was preserved, being cut into pieces and dispersed. These pieces were reassembled (1806 to 1818) and restored to veneration.

AACHEN, Germany, where Pope Leo III consecrated the basilica of St. Mary in 804, is the depository of Marian relics dating from this period. The swaddling clothes of Our Lord and Mary's cloak or veil are encased in a silver *Marienschrein* dating from 1237, and exposed every seven years.

The cincture, *calchopratea,* may have been distributed widely. Tortosa, Spain, claims a portion, said to have arrived miraculously at the altar in 1278. Prato in Tuscany has a relic of the cincture, which was long kept beneath the altar; and in 1320 it was taken to a new chapel designed by Pisano and adorned by Agnolo Gaddi, Bruno Mazzei, and Pisano and was encased in a remarkable reliquary made by Maso di Bartolomeo.

Shrines Possessing Icons. The ICON mentioned by Theodore Lector as painted by St. Luke was almost certainly the one known as *hodegetria,* the guide of the way, enshrined in a monastery rebuilt by Emperor Michael III (842 to 867). This, the prototype of many shrine icons and the palladium of Constantinople, was hacked to pieces when the city fell in 1453. The notion once prevailed that the Evangelist painted these icons. Confusion may have arisen among the uncritical because all these pictures, similar in iconography, were called Lucan and attributed to St. Luke on the strength of Theodore Lector's remark.

Shrines that honor greatly venerated Lucan-type icons include St. Mary Major, Rome, whose "Salus populi romani" icon is kept in the Borghese chapel and has many times been carried through the city in time of plague. Bologna possesses a "Madonna di S. Luca" from Constantinople in the sanctuary of the same name founded in 1193. The cathedral in Bari has an icon, "S. Maria di Costantinopoli." Monte Vergine, near Avellino, honors the "Madonna Schiavona" enshrined in 1310. Poland has a famous shrine honoring Our Lady of CZESTOCHOWA. In the Levant the most important Marian shrine is at Dair as-Sagura, Syria, where Orthodox nuns preserve the "Saidnaia Madonna."

Many other shrines have become famed for icon-type pictures stemming from Byzantine or Greco-Italian sources. Their main theme is the *hodegetria* or a variant of it, such as the *eleousa,* or tender caress. Thus in Rome is found the madonna of "S. Maria in Portico" in the church of S. Maria in Campitelli, transferred there in 1659. The Redemptorist church of S. Alfonso holds the world-famous icon "Our Lady of Perpetual Help," of mid-15th-century Cretan origin. The "Madonna della Strada" in the Jesuit church of the Gesù has always been intimately connected with the history of this order. There is at Genazzano an extremely popular shrine to Our Lady of Good Counsel. In the Eastern rite monastery at Grottaferrata, near Frascati, is the icon "S. Maria di Grottaferrata," dating from the early 11th century. Castel di Leva honors the 14th-century "Madonna del Divino Amore." At Monte Nero in Livorno the shrine has a Greek icon, "Plena Gratia." Montallegro in Rapallo honors the madonna "Stella Maris," dating from 1557, possibly of Dalmation origin. The church of the Consolata in Turin is the shrine of Our Lady of Consolation, dating from 1104. There is an affiliated daughter shrine at West Grinstead, England, crowned in 1893, which possesses an excellent facsimile of the icon. Shrines with icons of the *hodegetria* type tend to locate along those portions of the Mediterranean coast where Greek or Byzantine influence was strong. Eastern rite churches, Catholic or Orthodox, have innumerable shrines, each with its holy icon.

Shrines of Celebrated Images. These images, as distinct from icons, have become distinguished by some phenomenon or prodigy or miracles believed to have been granted at their sanctuaries. They can be found in many lands and have been noted in every century since, perhaps, the 4th. St. Irenaeus records a heretical sect in Alexandria which was honoring images *c.* 160 (*Adv. haer.* 1.25.6). The total number of shrines, as distinct from lady altars, to which pilgrimages are made defies precise enumeration. J. E. B. Drochon has supplied details concerning 1,300 in France alone, 75 of which have been honored with papal crowning, 200 with papal indulgences. Italian shrines are even more numerous. More than 200 of them have been crowned, many by the popes. Their numbers are small only in formerly Catholic countries where iconoclastic Calvinism eliminated them or in regions where Catholicism has not penetrated. In Holland some 60 Marian shrines survive or replace others which have been destroyed. A. E. de Staercke has recounted the essential facts about 250 Belgian shrines. Croatia has more than 50 such sanctuaries.

England had 65 Marian pilgrimage shrines before 1538, when their destruction was ordered by government edict. Some of the more notable historic centers have been revived in the 20th century, namely, those at Aylesford, Caversham, Doncaster, Evesham, Glastonbury, Osmotherley (Mount Grace), Truro (Our Lady of the Portal), Willesden. The shrine of Our Lady of Pewe (Power) is now in Westminster Cathedral. Surpassing all is Walsingham (see below).

Wales also has enjoyed similar revivals. At Penrhys the site of the shrine favored by the ancient Welsh bards was regained in 1939. At Cardigan near the former national pilgrimage center a statue of Our Lady of the Taper was reenshrined (1956).

In the United States 106 pilgrimage shrines of Our Lady have been listed [*The Marian Era* 4 (1963) 140–43]. Some of these are small, but others rank with historic European shrines. Santa Fe cathedral has a shrine honoring Our Lady of the Conquest (La Conquistadora), established in 1625. St. Augustine, Florida, had the shrine of Nuestra Senora de la Leche in 1620. The present statue is a replica. Canada possesses an important sanctuary at Cap-de-la-Madeleine, in a small chapel founded by Jesuits in 1659. The tiny chapel is now surrounded by a large Marian park with a basilica-type church. The statue was crowned in 1904.

In Latin America Bolivia has a shrine to Our Lady of Copacabana built in 1583. In Luján, Argentina, there is a national shrine honoring Our Lady of Luján, patroness of Argentina, Paraguay, and Uruguay. Since 1929 Brazil has placed itself under the patronage of Our Lady, "Aparacida," whose statue dates from the early 17th century. At Quinche, Ecuador, "La Pequeñita" (The Little Loved One) is one of the most beautiful of shrine statues.

Shrines Honoring Apparitions of Mary. In recent times ecclesiastical authorities have been cautious about giving credence to accounts of apparitions of Mary and permitting cult at these spots. In 1830 St. Catherine LABOURÉ received at the Rue de Bac, Paris, the first of her VISIONS, which were substantiated by episcopal inquiry. Since then 186 reports of such phenomena have been investigated, but only the following 10 have received canonical sanction and have become the location of shrines. First was the apparition to Marie Alphonse RATISBONNE in the church of S. Andrea delle Frate, Rome (1842). In 1846 the apparition at LA SALETTE occurred, and in 1858, those at LOURDES; both places have become world-famous sanctuaries. A large shrine was built at Ilaca, Croatia, after the apparitions to a peasant and other persons (1865 to 1867). A basilica was erected in 1871 in Philippsdorf, Bohemia, after the apparition to 30-year-old Magdalena Kade (1866). The vision to four children in a starlit sky at Pontmain, Normandy (Jan. 17, 1871), resulted in the construction of a basilica as a national votive offering since it also marked the start of withdrawal of Prussian invading forces. The shrine of Our Lady at Knock, Ireland, arose after the visions to a number of persons there (Aug. 21, 1879). FATIMA, Portugal, has become a world-renowned shrine since the apparitions there in 1917. Visions to five children at the May-tree in Beauraing, Belgium (1932 to 1933), were subjected to long ecclesiastical inquiries. The spot has become the center of international pilgrimages. After the appearances to a small girl in Banneux, Belgium, in 1933, episcopal recognition was granted in 1949, and a chapel was erected there.

Cult is permitted at the shrine in Pellevoisin, France, where Estelle Faguette, a maidservant, enjoyed an amazing cure and claimed to receive apparitions; but no official pronouncement has been made concerning their authenticity. Neither has there been official approval of the cult at Tre Fontane, near Rome, where Bruno Cornacchiola claimed visions in 1947; but devotional visits are not forbidden.

In earlier centuries apparitions of the Blessed Virgin have been honored with numerous shrines. Among the most famous is the French national shrine at Le Puy, which originated in the 3d century according to tradition and whose church was begun in 493. The sanctuary at Evesham, England, originated after the visions of Eoves, a swineherd, and Bishop Egwin in 700. After its destruction in 1538, a new shrine was erected in 1939 and became the goal of many pilgrimages.

WALSINGHAM, England, became one of the most popular places of pilgrimage in Europe subsequent to a vision in 1061. The shrine was demolished in 1538, but devotion rekindled *c.* 1894 and increased when the English hierarchy in 1934 reestablished the shrine in the 14th-century Slipper Chapel, the sole pilgrim chapel that had remained intact. The new statue was crowned in 1954 in accordance with a brief of Pius XII.

Aylesford, England, now commemorates the disputed apparition of Mary with the scapular to St. SIMON STOCK, which occurred at Cambridge (1251). In 1949 the CARMELITES regained their medieval monastery at Aylesford, home of St. Simon and resting place of some of his relics since 1951. A new pilgrims' church was completed in 1962.

GUADALUPE, near Mexico City, has become one of the most popular shrines in the world since the apparitions in 1531.

France and Italy are the most common locations of shrines resulting from apparitions. French ones, with dates of apparitions, include those at Celles (1686), Garaison (1500), La Vange (1800), Le Laus (1664), and Vinay (1656), which honors "Notre-Dame de l'Osier."

In Italy the following shrines are marked by magnificent sanctuaries and attract numerous pilgrims: Caravaggio (1432); Crema (1490); Genoa (1490), which honors Our Lady "della Guardia" on Monte Figogna; Monte Berico (1426); Monte Nero in Livorno province (1345); Montallegro in Rapallo (1537); and Savona (1536), where the basilica is a national architectural monument.

Shrines of the Saints. So numerous are the shrines that are still centers of cult that they cannot even be listed here. It must suffice to say something about the location of shrines and arrangement of their relics and to mention a few of the more famous sanctuaries.

Arrangement of Shrines and Relics. In the early Church the normal arrangement was to place shrines in vaults beneath altars. This derived from the custom of building churches directly over the tombs of the saints there venerated. Later, when shrines were transferred to churches already erected, the arks were placed beneath altars above ground, and then usually in sealed chests. But in western Europe and England, following a pattern seen in Jerusalem, the relics were commonly translated to chapels directly behind the high altar, raised on catafalque-type structures of costly marbles. Or the relic chests were enclosed in the normal tomb space in the bases of these shrine monuments, with apertures that allowed pilgrims to touch the casket within. The shrine of St. ALBAN, protomartyr of Britain, in the abbey church dedicated to him, was such a structure. It was demolished in 1539, but the pieces have been reassembled and rebuilt *in situ* so that visitors can see what the arrangement was, but without the wealth of adornment that once enriched the shrine. The relics were scattered. Even so, a number of pilgrims, especially among Anglicans, visit the now empty shrine. The abbey church is now the Anglican cathedral of St. Albans.

Later still, under Renaissance influence, it became the practice to dress relics in sacerdotal or episcopal vestments, or religious garb, sometimes with silver or waxen masks, all enclosed within crystal-fronted caskets so that the apparent corpse could be seen. This was done as recently as 1925, when the remains of St. Bernadette SOUBIROUS were translated to the resplendent reliquary in the convent chapel at Nevers. It has also been done at the shrines in Paris of St. VINCENT DE PAUL and St. Catherine Labouré. In the latter case the heart, removed from the body, is enclosed in a separate crystal heart reliquary. This practice exists also outside France. In 1930 the relics of St. John SOUTHWORTH were translated to Westminster Cathedral and covered with crimson Mass vestments and deposited in a bronze casket with crystal sides. Silver masks cover hands and face.

Shrines of the Apostles. The tombs of Saints Peter and Paul, Apostles, in Rome have for centuries received special honor. The venerable sanctuary of St. James, son of Zebedee, at SANTIAGO DE COMPOSTELA in Spain retains its great popularity. At Toulouse, which used to be on the famous pilgrim route to Santiago, the crypt in the basilica of St. Sernin honors supposed relics of eight apostles. Most popular here is the shrine of St. JUDE as patron of lost causes. St. BARTHOLOMEW is honored in the church dedicated to him on the island in the Tiber, Rome, where a porphyry urn contains relics, thought to be his when Otto III removed them from Benevento (983). An elaborate shrine in Amalfi, Italy, contains relics claimed to be those of St. ANDREW. The head was removed to St. Peter's Basilica, Rome (1462), but Pope Paul VI ordered its return to Patras, Greece (1964). St. THOMAS is greatly venerated at Mylapore, India, by Malabar rite Christians, and also at Ortona, Italy, which retained the reliquary intact after the destruction of the cathedral (1943). St. John was honored at Ephesus by a chapel in the 2d century and by a basilica in the 6th, which became a mosque (1330) before its destruction by Tamerlane (1402). Excavations in 1926 made it possible to visit the tomb, now empty, in a vault beneath the altar.

Founders of Religious Orders. Saints who have founded religious orders, particularly the larger ones, are revered in several shrines. That of St. BENEDICT at MONTE CASSINO, Italy, is of immense historic interest. St. DOMINIC is enshrined in the church of San Domenico, Bologna, in a marble *arca,* the head being preserved apart in a silver head reliquary. The relics of St. Francis are the object of immense devotion in the crypt beneath the lower church at Assisi. St. IGNATIUS OF LOYOLA is venerated in the church of the Gesù, Rome, where his remains repose in an urn of gilt bronze beneath an altar of *lapis lazuli,* above which is a statue of the Jesuit founder in solid silver. The shrine of St. Philip NERI in the Chiesa Nuova is very popular with Romans.

Missioners. Shrines honor also saints who have evangelized various countries or effected religious revivals. Thus St. BONIFACE, apostle of Germany, is enshrined at Fulda Abbey in an elaborate tomb. St. CHAD, apostle of Mercia, was honored at the cathedral in Lichfield, England, until the Reformation, when his relics were rescued and hidden. Pugin designed the shrine that now contains them in St. Chad's cathedral, Birmingham. St. WILLIBRORD, apostle of the Frisians, was buried in the abbey of ECHTERNACH in Luxembourg, which soon became a very popular pilgrimage center. Still surviving is the ancient dancing procession each Whit Tuesday, when thousands of pilgrims perform a curious dance step along an established route while reciting centuries-old litanies. This custom of walking along routes (*Bidweggen,* prayer ways) fixed by tradition is found at such Belgian and Dutch shrines as those at Hal, Maastricht, Roermond, and Walcourt. One of the most popular shrines in the United States is that of the NORTH AMERICAN MARTYRS at Auriesville, New York.

The classic example of a famous medieval shrine that continues to function in the 20th century as it did in the 11th is that of St. NICHOLAS OF MYRA, patron of sailors and children and prototype of Santa Claus. His remains are in the crypt of the basilica at Bari, Italy, where the altar, tomb, statue, and lamps are in solid silver and the icon is a rich, 14th-century gift from King Mosario of Serbia.

Sanctuaries of Honor. Desire to honor Catholic beliefs or devotions accounts for another group of sanctuaries. They are called shrines although they do not necessarily contain relics or miraculous images. One of the most celebrated shrines of this type is in the Convent of the Visitation, PARAY-LE-MONIAL (Saone-et-Loire), France, place of the revelations granted to St. Margaret Mary Alacoque, associated with the devotion to the SACRED HEART. In Paris the basilica of Sacré-Coeur on the summit of Montmartre was built by national subscription as a manifestation of contrition and hope after the Franco-Prussian War (1870 to 1871). The NATIONAL SHRINE OF THE IMMACULATE CONCEPTION in Washington, D.C., was given this designation by the hierarchy of the United States and built in honor of the patroness of the United States. Great numbers of parish churches and other sacred edifices, some enjoying more than local fame, are called shrines and serve as stimuli to devotion.

See Also: ICON; IMAGES, VENERATION OF; MARTYRIUM; PILGRIMAGES; RELICS; RELIQUARIES

Bibliography: Treatments of a general kind are lacking, although works on individual shrines or types of shrines abound. F.

PHILIPIN DE RIVIÈRES, *Holy Places: Their Sanctity and Authenticity* (London 1874). J. K. CARTWRIGHT, *The Catholic Shrines of Europe* (New York 1955). P. KINSEL and L. HENRY, *The Catholic Shrines of the Holy Land* (New York 1951). H. M. GILLETT, *The Story of the Relics of the Passion* (Oxford 1935); *Famous Shrines of Our Lady,* 2 v. (London 1949); *Shrines of Our Lady in England and Wales* (London 1957). E. WATERTON, *Pietas Mariana Britannica* (London 1879). Z. ARADI, *Shrines of Our Lady Around the World* (New York 1954). M. J. DORCY, *Shrines of Our Lady* (New York 1956). J. E. B. DROCHON, *Histoire illustrée des pèlerinages français de la très sainte Vierge* (Paris 1890). I. COUTURIER DE CHEFDUBOIS, *Mille pèlerinages de Notre-Dame,* 3 v. (Paris 1954). A. SALVINI, *Santuari Mariani d'Italia* (Rome 1940). A. GABRIELLI, *Saints and Shrines of Italy* (Rome 1950). G. RODRIGUE, *Les Sanctuaires de Marie en Belgique* (Renaix, Belgium 1924), A. E. DE STAERCKE, *Notre-Dame des Belges* (Brussels 1954). J. A. F. KRONENBURG, *Maria's Heerlijkeid in Nederland,* 8 v. (Amsterdam 1904–14). I. ALLARDYCE, *Historic Shrines of Spain* (New York 1912). D. MANFREDI CANO, *Santuarios de la Virgen María en España y América* (Madrid 1954). R. VARGAS UGARTE, *Historia del culto de María en Ibero-américa y de sus imagenes y santuarios más celebrados* (3d ed. Madrid 1956). B. CAMM, *Pilgrim Paths in Latin Lands* (St. Louis 1923); *Forgotten Shrines* (St. Louis 1910). J. C. WALL, *Shrines of British Saints* (London 1905). B. C. BOULTER, *The Pilgrim Shrines of England* (London 1928). C. HOLE, *English Shrines and Sanctuaries* (London 1954). D. D. C. POCHIN MOULD, *Irish Pilgrimage* (New York 1957). F. G. HOLWECK, *A Biographical Dictionary of the Saints* (St. Louis 1924). R. L. and H. F. WOODS, *Pilgrim Places in North America: A Guide to Catholic Shrines* (New York 1939). F. B. THORNTON, *Catholic Shrines in the United States and Canada* (New York 1954). A. M. BOZZONE, A. MERCATI and A. PELZER, *Dizionario ecclesiastico,* 3 v. (Turn 1954–58) 3:714–15.

[H. M. GILLETT]

SHROUD OF TURIN

The Shroud of Turin, an aged, patched and scorched rectangular piece of linen that has been preserved since the late 16th century in the Cathedral of St. John at Turin, is perhaps the best-known artifact in the Christian West. The entire fabric, woven in a fine three-to-one herringbone twill, measures 14.25 feet long by 3.58 feet wide, including a 3.5 inch matching linen strip that at some point was attached to one of the long sides. On one side of this cloth can be seen faint images, sepia-yellow in color, of the front and back of a naked human body, the body of a 5 foot, 11 inch bearded male Caucasian weighing about 170 pounds. Because these images are oriented on the cloth in a head-to-head fashion, the object appears to be a burial shroud. If indeed such, the body would have been placed on one half of the cloth and the other half would have been drawn over the head and upper body of the corpse and then down over the feet to enshroud the dead person completely.

Many wounds and bruises are visible on the body images, some in association with apparent bloodstains. The conformity of this evidence with the gospel accounts

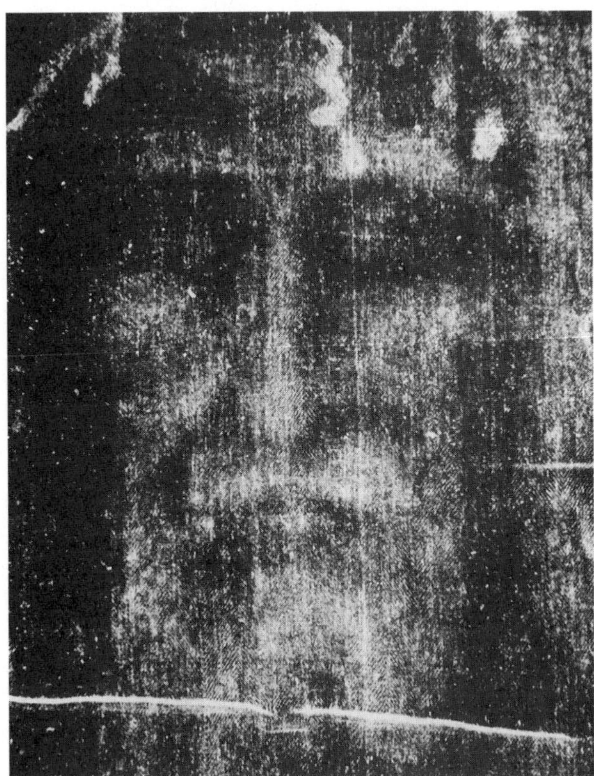

Facial impression, believed to be that of Jesus Christ, from the Shroud of Turin. (©David Lees/CORBIS)

of Jesus' crucifixion is striking. For example, bloodstains flow from the base of the man's left hand—his right wrist, covered by the left hand, is not visible—and from both of his feet. Furthermore, at his rib cage on the right side there is also a wound with a large blood stain around it (see Jn 19.31–37). Visible around the man's head are smaller lesions from which blood has trickled downward, a detail corresponding to Jesus's crowning with thorns (Mt 27.29 and parr.). Also visible are numerous small wounds covering the entire body, front and back, from the shoulders downward, and these accord with the account of Jesus' scourging by Roman soldiers preparatory to his crucifixion (Mt 27.26 and parr.). Given the many points of agreement between the gospel narratives and the evidence of the shroud, scholars agree that this object can only be either Jesus' actual burial shroud or a well-crafted later imitation.

History of the Shroud. The whereabouts of this object is well attested back to the mid-14th century but not earlier. While Ian Wilson and other investigators have proposed various theories about the shroud's history prior to that date, these, because of the lack of hard evidence, have not enjoyed universal scholarly support. There is clear evidence, however, that about 1357 the shroud was exhibited in Lirey, a village near Troyes in northeastern

France. The Musée de Cluny in Paris still preserves a pilgrim's medallion from this exhibition, and this object attests that the shroud was then in possession of Geoffrey de Charny and his wife, Jeanne de Vergy. In 1460 its ownership passed from the de Charnys to the House of Savoy. They at first kept the shroud in a silver reliquary chest in the chapel of their castle at Chambéry, France, where it narrowly escaped destruction in a serious fire that broke out in 1532. Although the reliquary was daringly rescued from the flaming chapel, a drop of melting silver burned right through the shroud's many folds, and the entire cloth, which had also suffered extensively from scorching and water damage, required two years of patching and repair work. Despite all this, the body images on the shroud remained generally intact. In 1578 the Savoy family decided to move the shroud from Chambéry to the Royal Chapel in the Cathedral at Turin, and there it is still preserved. Only in 1983, however, did actual legal title to the shroud pass from the House of Savoy to the Holy See.

Authenticity. Church authorities have been generally reserved, or even quite negative, about the shroud's authenticity. When the de Charny family displayed the shroud at Lirey in 1357, the bishop of Troyes, Henry of Poitiers, objected strongly, claiming that the shroud was a fraudulent invention. In 1389 a later bishop of Troyes, Pierre d'Arcis, wrote a letter to Pope Clement VII at Avignon in which he expressed strong agreement with his predecessor's concerns. Because the shroud, said Bishop D'Arcis, is "a product of human handicraft" (*manufactus*) and "an artificial painting or depiction" (*artificialiter depictus*), the pope should act to put an end to its public display. While the pope in his response chose a more cautious route, he did insist that when the shroud was displayed, there should be no liturgical ceremony or pomp. Furthermore, he ordered that on each occasion a priest was to announce to those present "in a loud and intelligible voice, without any trickery, that the aforesaid representation [the shroud] is not the true burial cloth (*sudarium*) of our Lord Jesus Christ but only a kind of painting or picture made as a form or representation (*in figuram seu representationem*) of the burial cloth." While later Church leaders were more receptive to the shroud—in 1578, for example, Charles Borromeo, then the archbishop of Milan, journeyed on foot to Turin in order to venerate the shroud—they avoided making any affirmation of the shroud's authenticity. Although in 1670 a papal congregation granted an indulgence to those who would come and pray before the Shroud, it carefully specified that those who did so would receive the indulgence "not for venerating the cloth as the true Shroud of Christ but rather for meditating on the Passion," a neat sidestepping of the question of authenticity.

During the whole of the 20th century, and particularly after 1969 when it became possible for scientists and other researchers to study the shroud in greater detail, debate has raged about its authenticity as Jesus' actual burial cloth. While at this point the preponderance of evidence would seem to suggest a medieval date for the origin of this object, there are still scholars who would strenuously argue for its authenticity. The matter is made all the more complicated because there is no agreement whatsoever as to how the body images came to exist on the cloth.

Particularly damaging to any theory of authenticity were the Carbon-14 tests separately conducted in 1988 by laboratories in Tucson, Oxford, and Zurich on small fragments taken from a single portion of the shroud clear of any patching or charring. Although each laboratory utilized its own methods for eliminating possible contaminants from its sample and checked its results against control samples of known origin and date, their results with respect to the shroud accorded closely. The Research Laboratory of the British Museum did a statistical analysis of these results and reported that, within 95 percent confidence limits, the date for the linen of the shroud had to range somewhere between 1260 and 1390 AD, not earlier. These findings have been vigorously contested by the defenders of the shroud's authenticity. They argue, for example, that the fire of 1532 may well have added carbon isotopes to the linen and that the shroud's fibers over time became coated with bacteria and fungi, a factor which also could have added C-14 to the cloth and so have produced an inaccurate later dating. While debate continues about such issues, C-14 dating is hardly a new technology and scientists at this point have extensive familiarity with the problem of contaminants and methods for dealing properly with them in this sort of analysis.

There are other problems as well, particularly with the bloodstains. Questions remain, first of all, as to whether these stains were produced by actual human blood or even by blood at all. The team of scientists who examined the shroud in October 1978 at the close of its public display found albumin, porphyrinic material and iron associated with these stains and concluded that they had to have been produced by genuine human blood rather than by paint or some other substance. W. McCrone and others have questioned these findings. They link the iron discovered to the iron-oxide of artist's paint and raise difficulties about the red color of the stains, very odd for such ancient blood. On the other hand, the scientists involved in the 1978 study found no evidence whatever of brush strokes or other "directional" markings that would indicate that either the blood stains or the body images as a whole had been painted on the cloth.

Whatever is to be said about the medium that caused these bloodstains, there is a further and much more serious difficulty. These stains, clear in outline and unsmudged, show a downward trend in their flow. Such would have been the direction taken by blood flowing from Jesus' various wounds while he hung vertically on the cross but not while his body lay prone in the tomb, if such flows could still have occurred at that point. Assuming the authenticity of the shroud, this state of affairs required that when Jesus' friends drew the nails from his hands and feet, took his body from the cross, carried it for some unknown distance to the tomb, and then laid it on the cloth of the shroud, they did all these things without smearing or disturbing the bloodstains on his body, an impossible supposition. F. Zugibe, who supports the authenticity of the shroud, has argued that Jesus' body was washed before being placed upon his burial shroud and that the shroud preserves a post-mortem oozing of blood from the various wounds. But in saying this, he fails to address the directionality of the blood flows seen on the shroud.

The hand of an artist may also be betrayed by the way in which the body of Jesus appears on the shroud. If Jesus' dead body actually produced the images seen on the shroud, those bodily areas closer to or touching the cloth should be delineated very clearly while those further away should be less distinct. In fact, however, Jesus' hands and face, including even the recessed areas around his eyes, are quite distinct (as one would expect in portrait art) while other areas of his body such as his buttocks and his navel are faintly outlined or even invisible. A pious concern for modesty may well account for this discrepancy. Very likely such a consideration also explains why the right arm and hand of the figure on the shroud are abnormally elongated. This permitted Jesus' genital area to be covered in modest fashion by his hands, an arrangement physically impossible for an ordinary dead body lying relaxed and prone. A further oddity is that no wrinkles or other irregularities distort the shroud's images, an improbability if this cloth had actually covered the irregular form of Jesus' body. Finally, the very fact that the man of the shroud looks just like our typical devotional images of Jesus raises questions since this so familiar iconographic convention can only be traced with certainty back to the Byzantine period. Earlier representations of Jesus in the catacombs of Rome, for example, depict him as beardless, and the canonical Gospels provide no description whatever of Jesus' physical appearance.

In terms of chronology, all efforts to situate this cloth in 1st century Palestine have so far proven inconclusive. Both its three-to-one herringbone weave and the presence of cotton fragments amid its linen threads as easily point to medieval Europe as to the Greco-Roman world. Pollen from Palestinian flora found trapped in the weave could well be contaminants carried by the wind or deposited by other means. Some think that they can discern a coin from the administration of Pontius Pilate covering Jesus' right eye. Yet the photographs of this ''coin'' are very blurred, and the use of coins to cover the eyes of the dead is not attested for 1st century Palestine.

In short, while many unanswered questions still remain, not least that of how the images came to appear on the cloth in the first place, it is most unlikely that this object is the authentic burial shroud of Jesus. Instead, while possibly a forgery deliberately intended to deceive the faithful, it very well could have been produced to serve as a devotional object, a pious reminder of how Jesus gave up even his own life for the salvation of humanity.

Bibliography: N. CALDARARO, ''The Status of Research into the Authenticity of the Shroud,'' *Approfondimento Sindone* 1.1 (1997) 51–66. P. E. DAMON et al., ''Radiocarbon Dating of the Shroud of Turin,'' *Nature* 337, 6208 (1989) 611–15. J. H. HELLER, *Report on the Shroud of Turin* (Boston 1983). J. IANNONE, *The Mystery of the Shroud of Turin: New Scientific Evidence* (New York 1998). R. WILD, S.J., ''The Shroud of Turin—Probably the Work of a 14th-Century Artist or Forger,'' (Biblical Archaeology Review) 10, 2 (March–April 1984) 30–46. I. WILSON, *The Shroud of Turin* (New York 1978); *The Mysterious Shroud* (Garden City, N.Y. 1986); *The Blood and the Shroud* (New York 1998).

[R. A. WILD]

SHROVE TUESDAY

As the last day before Lent, which begins on Ash Wednesday, Shrove Tuesday ended the traditional period set aside for celebrating the Sacrament of Reconciliation and receiving canonical absolution in preparation for the great 40-day fast. The adjective *shrove* is derived from the Old English verb ''to write'' or to *shrive* (related to the German *schreiben* or the Dutch *schrijven*) and denotes the medieval English practice of giving, ''writing down,'' or designating penance. The penance having been prescribed, the penitent was considered shriven, a practice referred to in Abbot Aelfric's translation of Theodolphus' *Ecclesiastical Institutes c.* 1000 A.D.

The term Shrove tide is the old English equivalent of Carnival referring to the final weeks before Lent. Rooted in the Latin phrase *carnem levare*—to withdraw or take away meat—households used this time to prepare rich pastries containing eggs, milk, and sugar, then, frying them in butter or fat and in this manner removing from the home foods forbidden during Lent. Herein lies the origin of ''Fat Tuesday'' or the respective French *Mardi Gras.* Throughout these days the English consume pancakes, Austrians and Germans various forms of *fast-*

nacht cakes, and central Italians *frappe.* Polish Americans share jelly doughnuts, called pączki, or light-pastry ''angel wings,'' called chruściki. Local supermarkets in the Detroit, Michigan, area distribute specialty yeast-raised doughnuts from ethnic bakeries in Hamtramck, a town which holds an annual *Pączki* Day Parade. These dessert delicacies are traditionally made of foods which needed to be used up before the next seven weeks of Lenten abstinence.

Present day Carnival or Mardi Gras celebrations are held across the world, the most famous being in New Orleans, Louisiana, and Venice, Italy, and Rio de Janiero, Brazil. In the United States, the streets of Old New Orleans, particularly Bourbon Street, celebrate a parade organized by social clubs called *Krewes.* The *Krewes* at one time were instruments through which the daughters of New Orleans citizens were introduced to society. A unique *Krewe* begun among the poorer blacks during the days of segregation is the *Krewe* of Zulu, which is famous for tossing almonds or gilded coconuts from their floats. Other *Krewes* throw plastic beads, play jazz music, host dance receptions, with the characteristic ''King Cake'' tradition, where the person who discovers a small baby-like figurine in their cake sponsors next year's party.

The ''city of canals built on the sea,'' Venice, annually hosts a captivating masquerade parade, where costumed residents stroll the enchanting streets and bridges, the final destination being a civic gala held on the Piazza in front of St. Mark's Basilica. Wearing of masks and costumes is common to many cultures during the early spring and autumn (Halloween in North America). It is a traditional manner of ritually ''protecting'' oneself from cosmic crisis or of ''hiding'' from evil spirits, which were once believed to emerge during the tenuous passage from the familiar ''old'' to the unknown ''new'' (New Year's Eve costume balls) or seasonal transitions from the dark, late winter to the ever increasing warmth and light of spring. The Venetian Carnival is characterized by a spectacular display of colorful costumes. Many people dress in elaborate period gowns from the 18th century. Others masquerade as characters of the Venetian theater, the commedia dell'arte of Goldoni et al., still others as forms of nature or cosmic forces. A symbol of death frequently appears in the form of a mimed funeral reminding the frolickers that the sobering days of Lent are near. Each night during the final days before Ash Wednesday celebrations culminate as choral renditions, music, and dancing fill St. Mark's Square, turning the city into a great masked ball.

At times, the carnival season is an occasion for excessive behavior as recently noted in Rio de Janiero. Various forms of erotic behavior in the Brasilian capital has warranted pastoral letters from the local conference of bishops. Across the centuries civil and church authorities have responded to various abuses surfacing during these late winter days. In 1466, the Venetian-born Pope Paul II organized alternative civic pageants and horse races reminiscent of the splendor of the chariots of ancient Rome. These festivities gave the name to the famous *Via Del Corso* (''The Street of the Races''), the former *Via Lata* (Broad Street), connecting the *Piazza Venezia* with *Piazza Del Popolo.* Municipal authorities in Vienna (1654) issued a first-annual edict threatening with fines and possible arrest anyone who participated in indecent behavior or carried dangerous weapons. In an effort to dissuade participation in potentially immoral activity, Pope Benedict XIV in 1747, issued a special constitution, *Super Bachanalibus,* granting a plenary indulgence to all who took part in Eucharistic adoration during the days of Carnival.

Byzantine Churches call the two weeks prior to Lent, respectively, meatfare and cheesefare week. The faithful ''bid farewell'' by consuming it to the end of the first or meatfare week. Dairy products, on the other hand, are eaten until the end of the second or cheesefare week. In the capital of Ukraine, Kiev, the famous *Pecherska Lavra* monastery holds a ceremony of mutual forgiveness, every Cheesefare Sunday. Mirroring the penitential practices of Shrovetide, both the faithful and monks prepare for the 40-day journey to Easter by begging each other for forgiveness. Having reconciled differences, they embrace each other with the kiss of peace and sing the Resurrection verse: ''Today, Christ, our Pasch, is revealed, a sacred Pasch, a new holy, and mystical Pascha, sanctifying all believers . . . . Let us embrace one another in joy and say 'Bretheren and enemies too: we forgive everything on the Resurrection day!'''

Alleluia Tuesday is another name given to this day, as the Roman Catholic Church symbolically ''buries'' the Resurrection outcry, chanting it the for the last time before Easter. Responsorial verses are replaced with a sung alleluia and the mass of the day frequently ends with the solemn Easter dismissal. Understanding the alleluia as a Resurrection chant, and as such, inappropriate to the penitential nature of Lent, may be traced to sixth-century Spain as well as Pope Gregory the Great. Tenth-century pontificals attest to this practice deeming it a ''celestial hymn.'' Two centuries later at Rome, the presider himself breaks the somber silence of forty days by intoning the first alleluia at the Easter Vigil.

Bibliography: J. JUNGMANN, *The Mass of the Roman Rite,* (Westminster, Maryland: Christian Classics Inc., 1986). J. KATRIJ, *A Byzantine Liturgical Year,* (Detroit, Michigan: Basilian Fathers

Publication, 1983). H. THURSTON, *Lent and Holy Week,* (London 1904).

[C. M. KRYSA]

SHUSTER, GEORGE N.

American journalist, author, and educator, b. Lancaster, Wis., 1894, d. South Bend, Ind., 25 Jan. 1977. Editor of *COMMONWEAL* 1928–40, president of Hunter College, assistant to the president of the University of Notre Dame, and director of the Center for the Study of Man in Contemporary Society, Shuster was a towering Catholic figure of the 20th century. In World War I he served as a sergeant in Army intelligence. He was later educated at Notre Dame, the Universities of Poitiers and of Berlin, and at Columbia. He was head of the English department at Notre Dame (1920–24), then taught at Brooklyn Polytechnic Institute and St. Joseph's College for Women (1924–34). When he began his 20–year tenure at Hunter (1940), it was the largest public college for women in the world. He returned to Notre Dame as assistant to the president (1961–71), then as professor emeritus of English. In his early career he was interested in the Catholic influence in English literature, a concern reflected in *Catholic Spirit in Modern English Literature* (1922), *English Literature: a Textbook* (1926), *Catholic Church in America* (1927), and *Catholic Church in Current Literature* (1930). He edited *The World's Great Catholic Literature* (1942; rev. ed. 1964). In the 1930s he became alarmed at the rise of Hitler, as reflected in his *Germans: An Inquiry and an Estimate* (1932), *Strong Man Rules* (1934), *Like a Mighty Army: Hitler versus Established Religion* (1935), and, with Arnold Bergstraesser, *Germany, a Short History* (1944). He was a United States delegate to the United Nations Conference on International Education (1945) and thus helped create UNESCO. His book *Cultural Co-operation and the Peace* (1953) was a sympathetic account of UNESCO's failures and successes. Shuster's chagrin at aspects of the Communist regimes in Eastern Europe is reflected in his *Religion behind the Iron Curtain* (1954) and in his account of the ordeal of Cardinal Mindzenty, *In Silence I Speak* (1956, in collaboration with Tibor Horanyi). Shuster's reflections on a lifetime career in education are found in *Education and Moral Wisdom* (1960) and *The Ground I Walked on; Reflections of a College President* (1961). He wrote numerous topical articles in the confusion following Vatican Council II. Special mention, however, should be made of two works he edited, containing the results of conferences held at Notre Dame: *Freedom and Authority in the West* (1967); and *Evolution in Perspective: Commentaries in Honor of Pierre Lecomte du Noüy* (1968). More controversial was his *Catholic Education in a Changing World* (1967), his reflections on the results of surveys conducted by Notre Dame and the National Opinion Research Center as part of a study of Catholic education. He recommended that elementary schools be abandoned in order to strengthen other parts of the system and that parochial schools be seen as a matter of lay rather than of clerical concern. At about the same time, he was chairman of a group of 37 scholars who conducted the first population-control research done under Catholic auspices. The group gave qualified endorsement to the use of contraceptives and suggested a change in the church's traditional position on the subject.

Bibliography: G. N. SHUSTER, *On the Side of Truth: George N. Shuster, an Evaluation with Readings*, ed. W. P. LANNIE (South Bend, Ind. 1974).

[E. J. DILLON]

SIBERT OF BEKA

Carmelite theologian; b. Beka, Gelderland (lower Rhineland); d. Cologne, Germany, Dec. 29, 1332. He entered the Carmelites at Cologne, *c.* 1280. Instrumental in founding the Carmelite house in Geldern (1300), he was prior there (1312–15) and then at Cologne (1315–17). He became a master in theology at the University of Paris (*c.* 1316–17), where he was regent of theology (1318–20). He served as provincial prior of Germany (1317; 1327–32), and of lower Germany (1318–27). While at the Curia in AVIGNON, he had the bull *Super cathedram* extended to the Carmelites, granting them the privileges of preaching and hearing confessions (1326). He was head of the commission investigating the complaint of the archbishop of Cologne against Meister ECKHART (1327). Active in the struggle between Pope JOHN XXII and Emperor Louis IV the Bavarian, he composed a tract refuting the six errors of the *Defensor pacis* of MARSILIUS OF PADUA (1326–27). Other writings (mostly unedited) included an ordinal (*c.* 1312) adopted by the Carmelite general chapter in 1315 and in use for 200 years, *Considerationes super regulam ordinis Carmelitarum, Summa censurarum novi juris, Bullarium ordinis sine privilegia Carmelitarum,* two *Quodlibeta, Commentarius in sententias,* and *Annotatio capitulorum generalium.* Sibert's thought is, in general, traditional, often following THOMAS AQUINAS's, but more often similar to that of GODFREY OF FONTAINES, whose influence may possibly have been transferred to Sibert through Guy Terrena of Perignan.

Bibliography: SIBERT OF BEKA, Tract against *Defensor* in R. SCHOLZ, *Unbekannte kirchenpolitische Streitschriften aus der Zeit Ludwigs des Bayern, 1327–1354,* 2 v. (Rome 1911–14) 1:3–12; 2:3–15; *Ordinaire de l'ordre de Notre-Dame du Mont Carmel,* ed.

B. ZIMMERMAN (Paris 1910). *Chartularium universitatis Parisiensis*3:661. B. M. XIBERTA Y ROQUETA, ''Duo *quolibet* inedita Siberti de Beka,'' *Analecta Ordinis Carmelitarum Calceatorum* 4 (1922) 305–341; *De scriptoribus scholasticis saeculi XIV ex ordine Carmelitarum* (Louvain 1931) 142–166. P. GLORIEUX, *Répertoire des maîtres en théologie de Paris au XIII*[e] *siècle* 2:344–345.

[D. ANDREINI]

SIBYLLINA BISCOSSI, BL.

Dominican tertiary; b. Pavia, 1287; d. Pavia, March 19, 1367. While still a child, she worked as a servant. At 12, having become blind, she was received into a house of Dominican tertiaries. Three years later she began to live as a recluse in a cell next to the Dominican church. A companion died after three years, and Sibyllina lived alone for the remaining 67 years of her life, practicing severe penances. Many persons consulted her and asked for her prayers; she is said to have had the gifts of prophecy and clairvoyance. Sibyllina's special devotions were to the Eucharist and the Holy Spirit; she regarded Pentecost as the greatest feast. She died in 1367. When her cult was confirmed in 1853, her body was found incorrupt. Plus IX beatified Sibyllina, who is the patron of servant girls in Italy.

Feast: March 23.

Bibliography: *Année Dominicaine,* 23 v. March 2:475–485. M. C. DE GANAY, *Les Bienheureuses dominicaines* (4th ed. Paris 1924) 177–191. A. BUTLER, *The Lives of the Saints*, rev. ed. H. THURSTON and D. ATTWATER (New York, 1956) 1:665–666. *Acta Sanctorum* March 3:67–71. I. TAURISANO, *Hierarchia Ordinis Praedicatorum* (Rome 1916) 31. G. GIERATHS, *Lexikon für Theologie und Kirche*, ed. J. HOFER and K. RAHNER, 10 v. (2d, new ed. Freiburg 1957–65) 9:725.

[M. J. FINNEGAN]

SIBYLLINE ORACLES

A Sibylline oracle is synonymous with a rebus or riddle. The Sibyl, a prophetess, usually preferred, in fact, to give obscure responses or responses with double meanings. According to popular etymology (*see* Varro in Lactantius *Inst.* 1.6.7), the name signified ''one who announces the counsels or plans of the gods'' (ὑθεοβύλη). Proper originally to a Sibyl in Asia Minor, the name passed to a whole class of female seers, the most famous being the Sibyls of Delphi and Cumae, two places in which there was a special worship of Apollo.

Pagan Sibylline Books. The Sibyl of Delphi had a rival in the Pythia. The Cumaean Sibyl, according to Pseudo-Aristotle (*Mirab.* 1188) was identical with the Sibyl of Erythrae. The collection of her oracles was given official recognition at Rome from the period of the monarchy, and was one of the most efficacious instruments in Hellenizing Roman religion. The Sibylline books were lost when the Capitol was destroyed by fire in 83 B.C.

Earlier than these two Sibyls, Cassandra, the daughter of Priam and the beloved of Apollo, had provoked Heraclitus to write: ''With lips inspired, she utters words that were mirthless, without ornament, and without perfume, but through the power of the god her voice reaches down a thousand years.'' (*Frg.* 92, in H. Diels, *Die Fragmente der Vorsokratiker: Griechisch und Deutsch.*) Cassandra foretold the fall of Troy and the death of Agamemnon. In general, on the basis of the later tradition as found, e.g., in Vergil (*Aen.* 6), the Sibyl foretold an end and a new beginning. Interpretations respecting the date of the fatal day exhibited a constant and wide divergence, and on numerous occasions men believed that the end of the world was near.

Judeo-Christian Sibylline Books. The Judeo-Christian collection of *Sibylline Oracles,* which is extant, goes back, in its oldest part (bk. 3) at least, to the end of the Machabeean period (2d half of the 2d century B.C.). The Sibyl ''foretells'' *post factum* the history of the world from its origin to the present. Book 8, which is violently anti-Roman, predicts the fall of the Empire. The author of the great medieval sequence, the *Dies irae,* will place the Sibyl beside David (*Teste David cum Sibylla*), and she will be honored, as numerous sculptures and paintings bear witness, for having foretold not only the Last Judgment, but also the coming of our Savior.

See Also: GOLDEN AGE.

Bibliography: Editions. J. GEFFCKEN, ed., *Oracula sibyllina* (Die Griechischen christlichen Schriftsteller der ersten drei Jahrhunderte 8; Leipzig 1902). A. KURFESS, *Sibyllinische Weissagungen* (Munich 1951). Studies. J. QUASTEN, *Patrology,* 3 v. (Westminster, MD 1950–) 1:168–170. F. L. CROSS, *The Oxford Dictionary of the Christian Church* (London 1957) 1252–53, with good bibliography. H. LECLERCQ, *Dictionnaire d'archéologie chrétienneet de liturgie,* ed. F. CABROL, H. LECLERCQ and H. I. MARROU, 15 v. (Paris 1907–53) 12.2:2220–44. E. BEVAN, *Sibyls and Seers* (London 1928). A. RZACH, *Paulys Realenzyklopädie der klassischen Altertumswissenschaft,* ed. G. WISSOWA, et al. (Stuttgart 1893–) 2.2:2073–2183.

[E. DES PLACES]

SICARDUS OF CREMONA

Bishop, canonist, historian, and liturgist; b. Cremona, *c.* 1150; d. Cremona, June 8, 1215. Having studied in the schools of Bologna, Sicardus went to Paris about 1170 and taught canon law and theology there until about 1180. In that year he was collated to a prebend at Mainz,

''The Tiburtine Sibyl.'' (©Archivo Iconografico, S.A./CORBIS)

where he taught in the cathedral school and fashioned his Paris lectures into a *Summa decretorum.* After his appointment as bishop of Cremona on Aug. 23, 1185, he successfully defended the rights of the city against Brescia and Milan, won independent status for the city from Frederick I Barbarossa, and pushed forward a great scheme of fortifications (1186). From 1202 until 1205 he took part in the papal mission of Cardinal Peter of Capua in Armenia and at Constantinople; in 1212 he welcomed Frederick II to Cremona and obtained from him the confirmation of Barbarossa's privileges.

Writings. The following works represent only a part of the varied output of Sicardus, for certain early treatises of which he himself speaks are no longer extant. *Mitrale* (1200) is one of the most important liturgical treatises of the Middle Ages, and a source of much of the famous *Rationale* of William DURANTI, the Elder, almost a century later. The *Mitrale* consists of nine books (printed in *Patrologia Latina,* 217 v. [Paris 1878–90] 213:13–434): bk. 1, churches and church fittings; bk. 2, sacred orders and vestments; bk. 3, the Mass; bks. 4–8, the liturgical year; bk. 9, *Sanctorale.* (2) *Chronica universalis* (1213). This, the first Italian example of a history from the beginning of time, was completed to 1201 when Sicardus left for the East in 1202, and on his return, continued to 1213 [printed in L. A. Muratori, *Rerum italicarum scriptores, 500–1500,* 25 v. in 28 (2d new ed. Città di Castello 1990—) 7:521–626, whence in *Patrologia Latina* 213:441–540; *Monumenta Germaniae Historica: Scriptores* 31:22–103]. Because it was chiefly valuable for recent or contemporary events, especially those of the Fourth Crusade, it was a prime source of the early part of the Chronicle (*c.* 1283) of SALIMBENE of Parma. (3) *Summa decretorum.* This most important work of Sicardus was put together, or at least completed, in Mainz between 1179 and 1181 (see the ''apology'' attached in many manuscripts: ''Ego vero Sychardus . . .''); it follows the plan of the *Decretum* of GRATIAN (ministers,

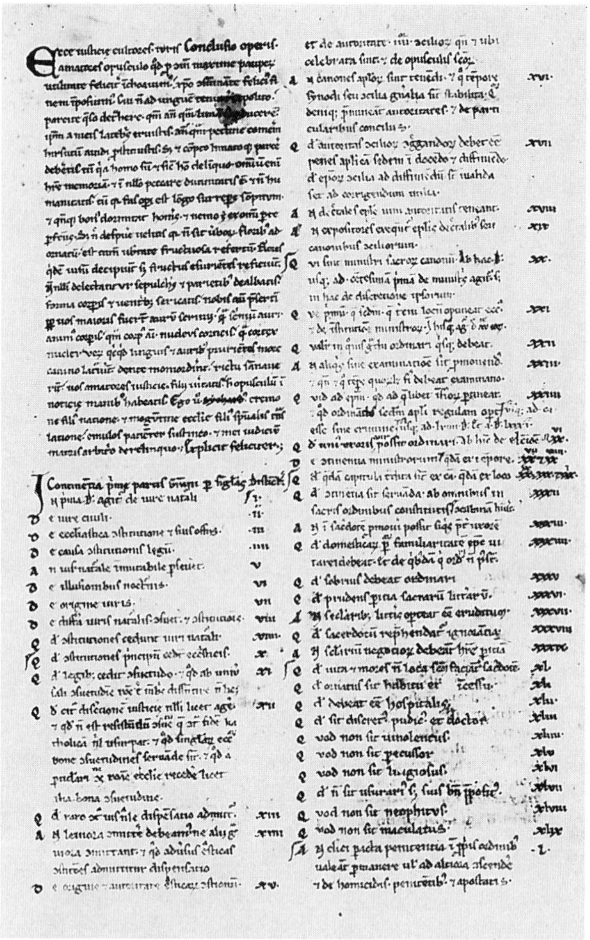

Manuscript folio from "Summa Decretorum," by Sicardus of Cremona, containing the apology "Ego vero Sychardus."

discipline, Sacraments), and owes something to various predecessors of Sicardus, particularly to SIMON OF BISIGNANO and to the French school of DECRETISTS. It has not been printed, but a list of manuscripts, with a view to an edition (now in the hands of P. J. Kessler of Münster, Westphalia), will be found in S. Kuttner, "An interim checklist of manuscripts," *Traditio* 12 (1956): 562; see also *ibid.* 13 (1957): 470 and *ibid.* 15 (1959): 499.

Contribution. Although there is no radical departure from Gratian's sequence of topics, it is the merit of Sicardus that he loosened up the formal divisions of the *Decretum.* There is a marked attempt to be systematic that is enhanced by a use of *distinctiones* (dramatic pauses in order to view a point as a whole—an oral technique originally) and of *quaestiones.* The latter are not the *quaestiones disputatae,* or the classroom exercises of a slightly later period. Originally they were answers to problems that cropped up in the course of teaching, but as employed by glossators as a literary device they became known as *quaestiones decretales* and first made their appearance in the last quarter of the 12th century. Although the *Summa* of Sicardus possibly reflects techniques already in use in Paris, there seems to be no doubt that the *Summa,* with its novel arrangement into *quaestiones principales* (problems occurring as such in the *Decretum*) and *quaestiones incidentales* (problems suggested by a text), promoted the spread of the *quaestio decretalis.*

If Sicardus is thus an early example of an emerging decretist *genre littéraire* that is not narrowly along the lines of Gratian's *Decretum,* he is no less a witness to a breakaway from the canonico-theological tradition of Gratian and his immediate successors. Although trained in that atmosphere at Bologna, Sicardus significantly abandons "to the theologians" a whole group of questions relating to the Eucharist, and he has no discussion whatsoever of Gratian's long *De poenitentia.* Apart from a material dependence on Sicardus of EVERARD OF YPRES (denied by some authors) and a more obvious debt of the anonymous *Summa* "In eadem civitate," some of the specific teaching of Sicardus was adopted toward the end of the century by the *Summa lipsiensis* and the *Summa coloniensis,* while HOSTIENSIS (*Lectura* II, VII, 1, v. *divinae et humanae,* n. 7) subscribed to his view that canon law was of divine origin.

Bibliography: J. F. VON SCHULTE, *Die Geschichte der Quellen und der Literatur des kanonischen Rechts,* 3 v. in 4 pts. (Stuttgart 1875–80; repr. Graz 1956) 1:143–145. O. HOLDER-EGGER, "Einiges zur Quellenkritik der Chronik Sicards," *Neues Archiv der Gesellschaft für ältere deutsche Geschichtskunde* 26 (1900) 471–555; 29 (1903) 177–245. A. FRANZ, *Die Messe im deutschen Mittelalter* (Freiburg 1902) 448–453. J. BRYS, *De dispensatione in iure canonico* (Bruges 1925) 101, 104, 107, 108, 117, 120, 136, 139. J. JUNCKER, "Summen und Glossen: Beiträge zur Literaturgeschichte des kanonischen Rechts im zwölften Jahrhundert," *Zeitschrift der Savigny-Stiftung für Rechtsgeschichte, Kanonistische Abteilung* 14 (1925): 384–474. S. CAVALCABÒ, *La Famiglia del Vescovo Sicardo* (Cremona 1931). S. KUTTNER, *Repertorium der Kanonistik* (Rome 1937) 150–153, 187–190; "Zur Biographie des Sicardus von Cremona," *Zeitschrift der Savigny-Stiftung für Rechtsgeschichte, Kanonistische Abteilung* 25 (1936): 476–478; "Réflexions sur les brocards des glossateurs," *Mélanges Joseph de Ghellinck,* 2 v. (Gembloux 1951) 2:783–788. J. DE GHELLINCK, *Le Mouvement théolgique du XIIe siècle* (2d ed. Bruges 1948) 460–462, 504. E. BROCCHIERI, *Sicardo di Cremona e la sua opera letteraria* (Cremona 1958). C. LEFEBVRE, *Dictionnaire de droit canonique,* ed. R. NAZ, 7 v. (Paris 1935–65) 7:1008–1111.

[L. E. BOYLE]

SICILY

Ancient Tinacria, the largest island in the Mediterranean, to the south and west of Italy, having an area of 9,926 square miles.

History. The physical partition into western and eastern Sicily is reproduced in its history. Greek writers of the 5th century B.C. speak of two nuclei of inhabitants: the Siculi in the east and Sicani in the west. Its position in the Mediterranean basin subjected Sicily to invasion by all the seafaring nations, and it was frequently the object of wars between different peoples. Phoenicians founded their first commercial base in Sicily in the 8th century B.C.; and with the consolidation of the Greek colonies in the 7th century, two zones of interest and cultures formed: Semitic to the west and Greek to the east. The Greek colonies reached an advanced culture; and though not generally given to colonial imperialism, they concentrated on founding autonomous city-states having close ties with the mother country. The rise of vast personal holdings (the Tirraneans) modified this situation. Gelonus, ruler of Syracuse (485 B.C.), held hegemony over Magna Graecia until a democratic revolution by municipal opponents was sustained by demands for liberty on the part of the mercantile classes. With the first Punic War (264–241) Sicily became a Roman colony. It was the theater for the Slave War (135–100), and after the Battle of Actium (31 B.C.) Augustus made it a senatorial province governed by a Proconsul.

William II of Sicily presents a model of his church (the Cathedral) to the Virgin, 12th-century mosaic in the choir, the Cathedral at Monreale, Sicily.

Christianity. No precise evidence exists for the penetration of Christianity into Sicily. St. Paul stopped at Syracuse on his journey to Rome (Acts 28.12); but it was only when the Church possessed a solid organization that it thought of tracing its origins to the Apostles. A late legend suggests evangelization from Antioch, which may explain the Oriental derivation of Sicily's Christianity; this is supported by epigraphic and monumental artifacts. Its links with Rome are indicated in the letter of Pope INNOCENT I to the bishop of Gubbio (*Patrologia Latina,* ed. J. P. Migne 20:552). Several episcopal sees existed in 251, as is signified in a letter of the Roman clergy to St. CYPRIAN (*Corpus scriptorum ecclesiasticorum latinorum* 3.2:553), and the Church of Sicily took an active part in the 4th-century Donatist and Arian disputes and in the 5th- and 6th-century Christological troubles.

It was disturbed by the barbarian movements when the Vandals took control in 455, and the Church was subject to the vexations of their intolerance. In 491 Theodoric the Goth (493–526) conquered the island; it fell into the hands of Belisarius and the Byzantines (535) and remained under their control for three centuries. During this period the Church in Sicily attempted to rebuild and it entered into close relations with Rome, which held vast possessions there: under Gregory I (590–604) there were two papal patrimonies with more than 400 properties. As a result, the cults of St. AGATHA and St. LUCY were extended to Rome, and in the 7th century several popes were Sicilians.

Political Vicissitudes. The ecclesiastical institutions changed under Leo the Isaurian, who desired to break papal resistance by sequestrating the Church's patrimony in 732; he subjected the bishops of Sicily to the Patriarchate of Constantinople. But Greek penetration into Sicily was of long standing. The fall of Syria to the Arabs in 636 and of Egypt in 640 forced many Greeks, particularly monks, to emigrate to the island of Sicily. The Arabs took control after a war that endured from 827 to 902; sad conditions of the Church under Islam were made worse by Byzantine attempts at reconquest.

Despite a wide culture the Arabs did not have deep roots there, and the Normans seized a propitious moment in 1061 to initiate the conquest at Messina, which they completed in 1091 at Noto. In the plan for the reorganization of the island they favored Greco-Italian monasticism, which under the Normans reached its golden age. Roger I obtained the right of apostolic legate for himself and successors from Pope Urban II (July 5, 1098), This privilege caused great conflict between the papal and political powers and was finally abrogated with the bull *Suprema* (Jan. 28, 1864; published Nov. 10, 1867).

With William II (d. 1189) the Norman dynasty was extinguished and the Hohenstaufens took control under Emperor Henry VI. The Hohenstaufens were ousted by Charles I of Anjou (1266). The Sicilian Vespers (1282) began a general anti-Frankish revolt on the island and resulted in a federation of cities under popular control (*Communitas Sicilae*), which eventually offered the crown to Peter III of Aragon.

In 1415 Viceroy governments were introduced by Aragon, then by Spain. Here the story of the island virtually ends; and its destiny forms part of the history of Spain and Italy. There was no lack of uprisings due to the loss of autonomy. To forestall centrifugal tendencies, the absentee sovereigns reserved ecclesiastical offices for their relatives and fellow nationals. Only with Charles V did the Sicilians obtain equality with the Spaniards: for every vacancy in a benefice, a Spaniard and a Sicilian were named alternately. But this system did not last long. In the end Charles III of Bourbon reserved the bishoprics, abbacies, and canonicates for Sicilians (1738).

Sicily passed to Savoy in 1713; to Austria in 1720; and at the end of the War of the Polish Succession (1733–1738) to the Bourbons of Naples, who held it until it was annexed to the Kingdom of Sardinia following the legendary campaign of Garibaldi's One Thousand.

Archeology. Of notable importance are the archeological remains, and particularly the complex of cemeteries, found in Syracuse (pre-Constantinian), Agrigento, Palermo, Selinute, Noto, and Termini Imerese, which stem from at least the 4th and 5th centuries. Inscriptional discoveries abound particularly in Syracuse and Catania and form the most consistent nuclei for Christian epigraphy outside Rome; they are of considerable importance for HAGIOGRAPHY and ecclesiastical history, going back to the 3d century. Ruins of 4th- and 5th-century churches are found in Palermo, Priolo, Palagonia, Catania, Malvagna, and Syracuse.

Bibliography: J. BERARD, *La Colonisation grecque . . . de la Sicile* (Paris 1941). I. SCATURRO, *Storia di Sicilia,* 2 v. (Rome 1950). G. AGNELLO, *Gli studi di archeologia cristiana in Sicília* (Catania 1950). S. L. AGNELLO, *Silloge di iscrizioni paleocristiane della Sicilia* (Rome 1953). A. FERRUA, ''Epigrafia sicula pagana e cristiana,'' (*Revista di archeologica Cristiana*) 18 (1941) 151–243. F. MILONE, *Sicilia: La natura e l'uomo* (Turin 1960). O. GARANA, *Le catacombe sicilane e i loro martiri* (Turin 1963). *Encyclopedia of World Art* (New York 1959–) 8:736–738.

[G. ORLANDI]

SIDONIUS APOLLINARIS, ST.

Fifth-century bishop of Clermont; b. Lyons, France, Nov. 5, 431 or 432; d. Clermont, between 487 and 489. As a son of a well-to-do family, he completed his classical studies and in 452 married Papianilla, daughter of the Emperor Avitus whose panegyric he pronounced before the senate in 456. When Avitus was deposed in favor of Majorian, Sidonius delivered Majorian's panegyric. On his return to Gaul he lived with his wife and three children close to Lyons or at Aydat in Auvergne. In 468 his panegyric honoring the new Emperor Anthemius gained him the prefecture of Rome. On his return to Gaul he was elected bishop of Clermont (471 or 472). He organized the resistance to the Arian Visigoths when they invaded Auvergne in 474 and was exiled to Carcassone by Euric; however, he obtained a pardon and returned to his bishopric where he died. His name, inscribed in the MARTYROLOGY OF ST. JEROME, was retained in the Roman MARTYROLOGY. His cult was active in Aydat until the French Revolution. Provençal legends of Lazarus made Sidonius out to be the man born blind and cured by Christ in the Gospels (Jn 11.1–53). As the author of 24 carmina modeled on Virgil and Claudianus, three panegyrics, and verse letters, he manifests a considerable knowledge of prosody and an authentic poetic sentiment. While bishop he wrote some 147 letters, which though not theological in content contain historical, political, social, and literary information on fifth-century Gaul.

Feast: Aug. 23.

Bibliography: *Opera omnia, Patrologia Latina,* ed. J. P. MIGNE, 217 v. (Paris 1878–90) 58:435–751; ed. P. MOHR (Bibliotheca scriptorum Graecorum et Romanorum Teubneriana; Leipzig 1895); *Poems and Letters,* v.1 ed. and tr. W. B. ANDERSON (Loeb Classical Library; London-New York-Cambridge, Mass. 1936). H. RUTHERFORD, *Sidonius Apollinaris* (Clermont 1938). C. E. STEVENS, *Sidonius Apollinaris and His Age* (Oxford 1933). G. BARDY, *Dictionnaire de théologie catholique,* ed. A. VACANT et al., (Paris 1903–50; Tables générales 1951–) 14.2:2033–35. H. LECLERCQ, *Dictionnaire d'archéologie chrétienne et de liturgie,* ed. F. CABROL, H. LECLERQ, and H. I. MARROU, 15 v. (Paris 1907–53) 15.1: 1423–27. B. ALTANER, *Patrology,* tr. H. GRAEF from 5th German ed. (New York 1960) 598–599.

[L. VEREECKE]

SIEDENBURG, FREDERIC

Pioneer in Catholic social work; b. Cincinnati, Ohio, Jan. 28, 1872; d. Detroit, Mich., Feb. 20, 1939. A graduate of St. Xavier's College (now Xavier University), Cincinnati, Ohio, he entered the Society of Jesus, received his seminary training at St. Louis University (M.A., 1899), and was ordained June 26, 1907. After further work in sociology and economics at the universities of Innsbruck, Berlin, and Vienna (1909–11), he established in 1914 the first American Catholic school of social work at Loyola University, Chicago, and served as dean from 1914 to 1932. He lectured and preached widely to promote understanding of social problems and the application of Catholic social principles. He was a director of the National Catholic Welfare Council, and an influential member of the National Conference of Catholic Charities, the National Conference of Social Work, and the Illinois Board of Public Welfare Commissioners. He was also vice president of the Committee on Cultural Relations with South America, and founder and president of the Illinois Catholic Historical Society. As executive dean of the University of Detroit, he established the College of Dentistry, became chairman of the Detroit Regional Labor Board, and president of the Michigan Conference of Social Service. He visited the Soviet Union. Siedenburg was dedicated to improving conditions for the underprivileged and establishing professional standards in Catholic social work; he worked also to create an appreciation of the constructive mission of the Catholic Church among his fellow citizens.

Bibliography: J. A. RYAN, *Social Doctrine in Action* (New York 1941). M. SHEEHAN, "A Catholic School of Sociology," *Catholic Charities Review* 5 (June 1921) 196–198. A. J. MURPHY, "Father Siedenburg, S.J.," *Catholic Charities Review* 23 (1939) 85–86.

[R. C. HARTNETT]

SIEDLISKA, FRANCISZKA, BL.

Religious name: Mary of Jesus the Good Shepherd; foundress of the Sisters of the Holy Family of Nazareth (Congregatio Sororum Sacrae Familiae de Nazareth [CSFN]); b. Roszkowa Wola, Poland, Nov. 12, 1842; d. Rome, Nov. 21, 1902, Rome. Frances Siedliska was born into a noble family; yet as a child she was gifted with a deep spiritual sensitivity that grew into an intense longing for God. She realized her call to religious life at age 12, but her father was deeply disappointed by her rejection of the family's wealth and social status. She struggled courageously with his disapproval and her own poor health before finally fulfilling her vocation to become a nun at age 30 (1872).

Siedliska's first spiritual advisor, Leander Lendzian, OFMCap, recognized the uniqueness of her vision and discerned that she was called to establish a new religious community. In 1875 she founded the Sisters of the Holy Family of Nazareth in Rome. She discovered within the Holy Family the perfect model for loving surrender to God. Committed to extending the reign of God's love on earth through ministry to families, she and her sisters established 29 foundations across Europe and the United States before her death in 1902.

After authenticating a miracle attributed to her intercession, Pope John Paul II beatified Frances Siedliska on April 23, 1989.

Feast: Nov. 21.

Blessed Mary of Jesus the Good Shepherd (Franciszka Siedliska). (Courtesy of the Sisters of the Holy Family of Nazareth)

Bibliography: F. SIEDLISKA, *Autobiography* (preface by M. T. JASIONOWICZ, trans. M. P. KRASOWSKI) (Pittsburgh 1997). K. BURTON, *Where There is Love: The Life of Mother Mary Frances Siedliska of Jesus the Good Shepherd* (New York 1951). M. MICHAEL GECEWICZ, *Love Finds a Way: The Life of Mother Mary of Jesus the Good Shepherd,* illustrated by M. RITA KOBIEROWSKA (Philadelphia 1986). M. DECHANTAL, *Out of Nazareth: A Centenary of the Sisters of the Holy Family of Nazareth in Service of the Church,* foreword by JOHN CARDINAL KROL (New York 1974). A. RICCIARDI, *His Will Alone: The Life of Mother Mary of Jesus the Good Shepherd,* trans. R. N. BARWIG (Oshkosh, Wisc. 1970). M. I. STRZALKOWSKA, *Blessed Mary of Jesus the Good Shepherd Frances Siedliska,* trans. M. J. BASIEWICZ, M. R. BRADLEY et al. (Rome 1989). M. I. STRZALKOWSKA, *For Me to Live is Christ,* trans. M. P. KRASOWSKI, illustrated by G. DE SILVA (Pittsburgh 1995).

[L. V. MIKOLAJEK]

SIENA

City south of Florence in Tuscany, Italy, known for its late medieval art. Originally an Etruscan colony, it became the Roman *Sena Julia* in 29 B.C. The archdiocese, metropolitan since 1459, had 98,000 Catholics, 119 secular and 70 religious priests, 90 men in 11 religious houses, and 324 women in 37 convents in 1963; it was 367 square miles in area. Its four suffragans, having 373,800 Catholics, 309 priests, and 527 sisters, are Chiusi-Pienza

Niccolò Pisano, the blessed in paradise, marble pulpit in the Cathedral at Siena, 1265–68. (Alinari-Art Reference/Art Resource, NY)

(established in the 4th century), Grosseto (1238), Massa Marittima (first-known bishop in 501), and Sovana-Pitigliano (first-known bishop in 680).

Bishopric and the city. Christianity was introduced by St. Ansano, a young Roman noble martyred at Arbia in 303; he became chief patron of the diocese and his relics were translated to Siena in 1107. The first-known bishop, Eusebius, attended a synod in Rome in 465. Little is known of Roman Siena; but the city, a refuge easily defended, grew during the barbarian invasions. Under the Lombard King Rotharis (636–653) the see became important. Bishops Maurus and Vitalian attended councils in Rome in 649 and 680. Several parishes long in dispute with the bishop of Arezzo were awarded to that see by King Liutprand in 715, but under Louis II (844–875) they were returned to Siena. The Benedictine monastery of S. Eugenio was founded in 730, but the Abbey of S. Salvatore del Monte Amiata, founded *c.* 750, was more important in Siena's history. From *c.* 900 the cathedral chapter had a life in common with the religious school for boys, several masters of which are known. The canons, who to the end of the 14th century elected the bishop, founded a hospital for pilgrims run by laymen.

The Lombard gastaldo, who ruled Siena in the name of the king, was replaced in the city under the FRANKS by the count, who later gave way in the city government to consuls. The political power of the bishops, already evident in the 9th century, slowly increased, as documents show, through the 11th century. Under their tutelage the commune came into being, and, with the consuls, they are mentioned as the chief magistrates of the city. During the dispute between Alexander III and Frederick I, Bishop Ranieri (1129–67), who compiled the obituary calendar of Siena *c.* 1140 and excommunicated the consuls for imprisoning clerics, had to flee Siena until his death in 1170. Through the 11th and 12th centuries the commune fought the powerful nobles of the country, making them build houses in the city and live there part of the year. The podesta, a higher official for military government and criminal judgments, was introduced in 1199. In 1186 Siena had obtained from Emperor Henry VI the right to elect its own consuls, to coin money, and to extend its jurisdiction over the county, reserving cases of final appeal to the judges and *missi* of the emperor. This official recognition of the commune by the emperor was called the Magna Carta of Siena. Thereafter the city had good relations with the empire and regularly followed a Ghibelline course (*see* GUELFS).

Siena Cathedral, Siena, Italy. (©Stephanie Colasanti/CORBIS)

Siena was Ghibelline, moreover, because of the antagonism of her commercial rival and neighbor, rich and powerful FLORENCE, which never missed a chance to obstruct Siena's trade. Siena dominated the main roads to Rome, and a large part of the Via Francigena passed through its territory. Along this road went much of the trade across the Alps; and so Florence, seeking control of the road, waged a 50-year war with Siena, until Siena, aided by Manfred's cavalry, defeated her in the battle of Montaperti in 1260. The preaching against this war by Bishops Bruno (1189–1215) and Buonfiglio (1216–52), who had to deal also with ALBIGENSES, was in vain, as was the activity of the new mendicant orders toward the same end. Siena failed to gain lasting results from the victory, however, and began to decline. When Alexander IV excommunicated all of Siena for its obstinate Ghibelline policy, many debtors of the Siena banking company defaulted in their payments, and the bankers found themselves in serious difficulty. After 1252 Florence coined the florin, a well-struck gold coin of stable value, while Siena kept a coin of silver mixed with baser metal. Siena's trade in cloth also suffered from competition with the better cloth of Florence. Finally, the death of Manfred (1266) and the tragic end of Conrad of Swabia (1268) deprived Siena of imperial protection and led to its defeat in the battle of Colle Val d'Elsa (1269) and to a suit for peace with Florence.

Consequently, Sienese Ghibellinism faded away in favor of the Guelf Monte dei Nove government (1292–1355). Important public works were built, but family feuds developed and a number of catastrophes hastened the decline of the city. In 1304 the Gran Tavola, an important banking firm of the Buonsignori, failed. The Black Death of 1348 cost Siena 65,000 of its population of 80,000. Faced with crisis, Siena replaced the government of the Nine with a new one of 12 citizens from the lesser merchants, assisted on specific occasions by a college of the nobility. But the new government, the result of party rivalries, was worse than the preceding government—arbitrary, partial, and incapable. Companies of adventurers devastated the land, taking so large a tribute in coin that the treasury was depleted. Florence resumed its expansionism, and for protection Siena turned to Gian Galeazzo Visconti, giving him lordship of the city in 1399. When Gian Galeazzo died in 1402, Siena regained its liberty. At this time Sovana and the seaports became swamps.

In 1319 Bl. Bernard Tolomei (1272–1348) founded the Congregation of the Olivetani. In 1321 students from Bologna migrated to the University of Siena, begun before 1200 from the 10th-century cathedral school and made a *studium generale* by Charles IV in 1357. Bishop Donusdeo (1313–50), known for his charity and his firmness with the FRATICELLI, in 1339 blessed work done at the order of the commune on the present Gothic cathedral (begun *c.* 1200, façade by Giovanni Pisano 1284–99). The JESUATI were founded in Siena *c.* 1360. St. CATHERINE (1347–80) sought to make peace in Siena's internal discord and to promote reform in the Church, causing the popes to return to Rome from Avignon. St. Bernardine (1380–1444) preached penance and the reform of morality against a prevailing material comfort. The Church council that moved to Siena from Pavia in 1423 was without result.

In 1459 Siena was made a metropolitan see by Pius II, previously Bp. Enea Silvio Piccolomini of Siena (1450–58). Other PICCOLOMINI prelates of Siena were Antonio (1458–59), Francesco (1460–1501, Pius III), Giovanni (1503–29), Francesco Bandini (1529–88), Ascanius I (1588–97), Ascanius II (1628–71), and Celio (1671–82). Pandolfo Petrucci seized power in Siena in 1487, ruling wisely and favoring arts and letters until his death in 1512. His heirs were expelled in 1524 for incapacity. Protestantism did not affect religious life, except for the isolated case of Bernardino OCHINO, fourth general of the Capuchins, who became a Protestant in 1542. In 1533 Charles V took Siena under imperial protection, putting a Spanish garrison there. Siena rebelled and expelled the Spanish in 1552, but an imperial army besieged the city (1553–55), and after its capitulation Siena passed from an independent state to a small part of a large dominion. Philip II gave it to Cosimo I de' MEDICI in 1557 and it was incorporated in the Grand Duchy of Tuscany, whose fate it shared until in the plebescite of 1860 it joined the kingdom of ITALY. The diocese was hardly touched by JANSENISM.

Illustrious sons of Siena include Pope Alexander III, the jurist Cardinal Riccardo Petroni (*c.* 1250–1313), Pope Paul V, Pope Alexander VII, the poet and theologian Ambrose Caterino (1487–1553), the poet philologist Claudio Tolomei (1480?–1555), the converted Jew and biblical exegete Sixtus (1520–69), and the economist Salustio Bandini (1677–1760). Cardinal M. Bichi (1612–14) founded the seminary, which now has major and minor seminarians. *La Voce del Popolo* is a weekly Catholic newspaper.

Bibliography: G. A. PECCI, *Storia del vescovado della città di Siena* (Lucca 1748). E. G. GARDNER, *The Story of Siena and San Gimignano* (2d ed. London 1904). F. SCHEVILL, *Siena: The History of a Medieval Commune* (New York 1909; pa. 1964). R. L. DOUGLAS, *History of Siena* (London 1902). P. DU COLOMBIÈRE, *Sienne et la peinture siennoise* (Paris 1956). A. GAROSI, *Siena nella storia della medicina, 1240–1555* (Florence 1958). T. BURCKHARDT, *Siena, City of the Virgin,* tr. M. M. BROWN (New York 1960). R. VALENTI, *Storia di Siena* (Siena 1963). *Bulletino Senese di storia patria* (1894–). W. BRANDMÜLLER, *Lexikon für Theologie und Kirche*

(Freiburg 1957–65) 9:742–744. *Annuario Pontificio* (Rome 1964) 418, 1413.

[E. SCOZZAFAVA]

Art. With major buildings from the 13th and 14th centuries demonstrating a living synthesis of northern Gothic and local Romanesque of Lombard origin, Siena outwardly remains a medieval city. The typically Sienese style, manifested throughout most of Tuscany as well as in Siena, found its prototype in the 13th-century Cistercian Abbey of S. Galgano, in the Valle della Merse. The abbey, now in ruins, leaves the cathedral, with its free-standing campanile and baptistery (derived from early Christian tradition), as the best-preserved example of Sienese style. The monastic churches (St. Francis, St. Dominic, St. Augustine) offer less splendid renditions of the same style. During these years some of the most important palaces were built: Palazzo Tolomei (the oldest), the Chigi-Saracini, the Buonsignori, the Salimbeni, the imposing Palazzo Pubblico with its Torre del Mangia, and some of the majestic city gates. In the 15th century, a strong Florentine influence appeared with Bernardo Rossellino (Palazzo delle Papesse) and Giuliano da Maiano (Palazzo Spannocchi). The most famous Sienese architects, Francesco di Giorgio and Peruzzi, distinguished themselves chiefly outside Siena.

The cathedral pulpit, by Niccolò PISANO (*c.* 1205–78), in a lofty epic style derived from antiquity, and the passionately expressive Gothic-like statues by his son Giovanni (*c.* 1250–1320) on the cathedral façade (also by Giovanni) are the first great monuments of Sienese and Italian sculpture. Almost a century later, Jacopo della Quercia (1374–1438) vigorously revived the Pisanesque tradition, as in his Fonte Gaia in the Piazza del Campo. Jacopo's later style was influenced by the Florentines Ghiberti and Donatello, with whom he had worked on the baptismal font of S. Giovanni. His powerfully plastic bas-reliefs in Bologna certainly influenced MICHELANGELO. Antonio Federighi followed Jacopo, and Francesco di Giorgio emulated Donatello. In the 16th century, the aestheticizing classicism of Lorenzo Mariano, called Marina, was anything but Sienese; similarly, the well-known 19th-century sculptor Giovanni Dupré recollects little of his native Sienese tradition.

Siena's glory is its painting, which best embodies the noble and refined soul of this profoundly mystical city. The traditions of Byzantium and of early Sienese illuminations formed the lofty style of the 13th-century *croce dipinta* and the panels by the oldest known Sienese painter, Guido da Siena (fl. *c.* 1250–75). Characterized by rhythmic line and glowing color upon a gold ground, this style reached its perfection in Duccio, whose iconic *Maestà* (1308–11) and scenes from the life of Christ express an intensely contemplated inner vision. Duccio's follower, Simone Martini (1284–1344), influenced by his friend Petrarch, developed a lyrical linear style, disdainful of prosaic feelings. The brothers Pietro and Ambrogio Lorenzetti assimilated the Giottesque influence and created a narrative style best seen in Ambrogio's frescoes showing "Good and Bad Government." But the Sienese school reached a crisis during the 15th century: Sassetta (fl. 1423–50), who tried to fuse Sienese abstractionism with Florentine naturalism; Domenico di Bartolo (1400–49); Vecchietta (1412–80); and Matteo di Giovanni (1435–95), in whom Florentine influence is felt still more decisively. However, at the end of the 15th century the elegant, spiritualized, traditional style enjoyed a final revival in the work of Neroccio de' Landi (1447–1500). The last major Sienese painter is the mannerist Beccafumi (1485–1551), whose ambiguous space, morbid *sfumato,* and capricious subject matter could not be further from the once great Sienese tradition. Since the 16th century, except for Francesco Vanni and the Caravaggiesque Rutilio Manetti in the 17th century, Siena has produced no painters who could be considered great.

Bibliography: E. CARLI, *Sculttura lignea Senese* (Florence 1951). G. H. and E. R. CRICHTON, *Nicola Pisano and the Revival of Sculpture in Italy* (New York 1938). G. H. EDGELL, *A History of Sienese Painting* (New York 1932). M. MEISS, *Painting in Florence and Siena after the Black Death* (Princeton, N.J. 1951). W. HEYWOOD and L. OLCOTT, *Guide to Siena: History and Art* (2d ed. Siena 1924). J. POPE-HENNESSY, *Introduction to Italian Sculpture,* 3 v. (London 1955–62); *Sienese Quattrocento Painting* (New York 1947). A. VENTURI, *Storia dell'arte italiana,* 11 v. in 25 (Milan 1901–40). C. H. WEIGELT, *Sienese Painting of the Trecento* (New York 1930).

[I. GALANTIC]

SIERRA LEONE, THE CATHOLIC CHURCH IN

The Republic of Sierra Leone is a tropical, largely agricultural country on the west coast of Africa, bordered on the southeast by LIBERIA, on the south and west by the North Atlantic Ocean, and on the north and northeast by the Republic of GUINEA. Hot and humid through most of the year, the region is characterized by coastal swamps rising to wooded hills, thence to a plateau region and mountains in the far east. Natural resources include diamonds, titanium, bauxite, iron ore, gold and chromite. Agricultural production, which is threatened annually by dusty harmattan winds blowing westward from the encroaching Sahara, include rice, coffee, cocoa, palm, peanuts, livestock and fish.

A British colony from 1808 and protectorate from 1896, Sierra Leone became an independent and sovereign

Capital: Freetown.
Size: 27,925 sq. miles.
Population: 5,232,625 in 2000.
Languages: English, Mende (south), Temne (North), Krio (lingua franca).
Religions: 156,980 Catholics (3%), 2,354,680 Muslims (45%), 366,285 Protestants (7%), 2,354,680 follow indigenous beliefs.
Archdioceses: Freetown and Bo, with suffragans Kenema and Makeni (created 1961).

member of the British Commonwealth of Nations in 1961. A settled government became established by 1970, although as a result of the famine, ethnic tensions and government corruption that characterized the 1980s, a military coup under General Valentine Strasser gained power in April of 1992. After working to end corruption and reform the region's economy, the government removed the ban on political parties in 1995. The first democratic elections were held in 1996 and a civilian president elected. The region's mineral wealth—particularly its diamond mines—prompted a decade of civil war in an effort to unseat the government by the Revolutionary United Front. In addition to the negative impact on the economy as a result of the forced closure of mines, thousands were killed and another 2,000,000 made refugees by 2000 as a result of the continued violence. A peace agreement signed in 1999 and the deployment of U.N. peacekeeping forces in the region boded well for a return to peace.

History. After the Portuguese exploration of the region's coast *c.*1462, there followed many attempts at evangelization among the Temne and other tribes that left little permanent trace. The depredations of pirates and a flourishing slave trade kept mission efforts at bay through the 16th and 17th centuries. In 1858 the vicariate apostolic of Sierra Leone was detached from the vicariate of the Two Guineas and confided to the Society of the AFRICAN MISSIONS, whose founder MARION-BRÉSILLAC came to start the mission, but soon died of yellow fever, along with his four companions. The HOLY GHOST FATHERS then assumed charge, and sent two missionaries in 1864. The St. Joseph Sisters of Cluny arrived soon after. The mission made modest but steady progress, but did not gain converts in the same manner as British Protestants, who had established a haven for destitute British slaves along the Sierra Leone coast in 1787 and continued to work to abolish slavery as well as to evangelize. After 1815, as British colonization of the area increased, British warships sent ashore at Freetown all slaves captured on foreign ships.

By the mid-20th century the Catholic mission gave much attention to education, which was supported by the British government. The hierarchy was created in 1964, at which time there were no native priests. The diocese of Makeni was entrusted to the Xaverians of Parma.

By 2000 there were 37 parishes tended by 52 diocesan and 70 religious priests. Other religious included approximately 40 brothers and 60 sisters, who ran the country's 386 primary and 48 secondary Catholic schools. Although freedom of religion was guaranteed under the constitution promulgated on Oct. 1, 1991, that changed during a short-lived military coup took control of the government in 1998 and Catholic missionaries became the target of kidnappers and other violence. In January of 1999, five months before a peace agreement was reached between the government and rebel leaders, Freetown Archbishop Joseph Ganda was taken in a rebel raid, although he managed to escape shortly thereafter. Church leaders remained active in efforts to free hostages and orchestrate a lasting peace in the region, and joined Caritas International in that organization's efforts to return the 330,000 refugees who fled the country to their homes. Three thousand rebels turned over their weapons to the government in June of 2001, signaling the potential for a lasting peace in Sierra Leone. Diplomatic relations with the Holy See were established in 1996.

Bibliography: K. S. LATOURETTE, *A History of the Expansion of Christianity,* 7 v. (New York 1937–45) v.3. *Bilan du Monde* 2:790–792. *Annuario Pontificio* has information on all diocese. For additional bibliog. *see* AFRICA.

[J. BOUCHAUD/EDS.]

SIFFRIN, PETER

Liturgist; b. Bildstock (Saar), Germany, Oct. 1, 1886; d. Trier, June 6, 1963. He studied the humanities at Prüm, and philosophy and theology at the seminary of Trier. He was ordained Aug. 1, 1912, and was named curate at Kyllburg. In 1913 he joined the Benedictine monastery of St. Joseph, Gerleve (Westfalen); he moved to Dormition Abbey, Jerusalem, in 1928; and he lived at St. Matthias Abbey, Trier, until 1941 when it was suppressed by the Nazis. In 1949 he went to Rome and was subsequently appointed a consultor of the Congregation of Rites and for Vatican Council II; at the same time he taught liturgy and served as a member of the Liturgical Institute at St. Anselmo, Rome, and as an extraordinary member of the Abt-Herwegen Institute for liturgical and monastic research at the Abbey of Maria Laach, Germany. He was awarded an honorary doctorate in theology by the theological faculty of Trier in 1960. He created a complete alphabetical index of the *initia* of the Latin prayers of medieval liturgical books, especially the Sacramentaries. He collaborated with K. MOHLBERG in editing the Leonine and Gelasian Sacramentaries, the *Missale Francorum, Missale Gallicanum Vetus,* and the *Missale Gothicum.* Very useful are his concordances to these Sacramentaries and his word index to the Leonianum. He wrote numerous articles on liturgical subjects in *Ephemerides Liturgicae, Jahrbuch für Liturgiewissenschaft, Enciclopedia Cattolica,* and the second edition of the *Lexikon für Theologie und Kirche.*

Bibliography: L. EIZENHÖFER, *Ephemerides liturgicae* 78 (1964) 63–65.

[L. EIZENHÖFER]

SIGEBERT OF AUSTRASIA, ST.

Merovingian king, b. 631; d. Feb. 1, 656. The son of Dagobert I, Sigebert became king when he was three years old. Precise sources for his reign are lacking. It was marked by a war against Duke Radulphus, to whom Dagobert had entrusted the defense of Thuringia and who had revolted. Sigebert was defeated and barely escaped massacre. He was baptized by St. AMANDUS and in general showed deference toward the Church, but he resisted the bishops when he felt his royal prerogatives were at stake. He showed particular favor to the two abbeys of St. Remaclus, STAVELOT and MALMEDY. He was buried at Saint-Martin-devant-Metz, a monastery whose benefactor he had been. In 1552–53, his relics were transferred to Nancy; he became patron of the city. His *vita* was written by SIGEBERT OF GEMBLOUX. He is invoked for protection against inclement weather.

Feast: Feb. 1.

Bibliography: Sources. *Acta Sanctorum* (Paris 1863–) Feb. 1:231–242. ''Historia Francorum,'' *Monumenta Germaniae Historica: Scriptores rerum Merovingicarum* (Berlin 1826–) 2:215–328. ''Chronica Fredegarii,'' *Monumenta Germaniae Historica: Scriptores rerum Merovingicarum* (Berlin 1826–) 2:1–193. Literature. E. LAVISSE, ed. *Histoire de France,* 9 v. (Paris 1900–11) 2.1:163–165. U. CHEVALIER, *Répertoire des sources historiques du moyen-âge. Biobibliographie,* 2 v. (2d ed. Paris 1905–07) 2:4241. B. KRUSCH, ''Der Staatsstreich des fränkischen Hausmeiers Grimoald I,'' *Historische Aufsätze Karl Zeumer zum sechzigsten Geburtstag als Festgabe* (Weimar 1910) 411–428. *Cambridge Medieval History,* 8 v. (London-New York 1911–36) v.2. ABBÉ GUISE, *Saint Sigisbert* (Paris 1920). A. BUTLER, *The Lives of the Saints,* rev. ed. H. THURSTON and D. ATTWATER, 4 v. (New York 1956) 1:229.

[É. BROUETTE]

SIGEBERT OF GEMBLOUX

Teacher, hagiographer, historian; b. *c.* 1030; d. Gembloux, Oct. 5, 1112. He entered the Benedictine monas-

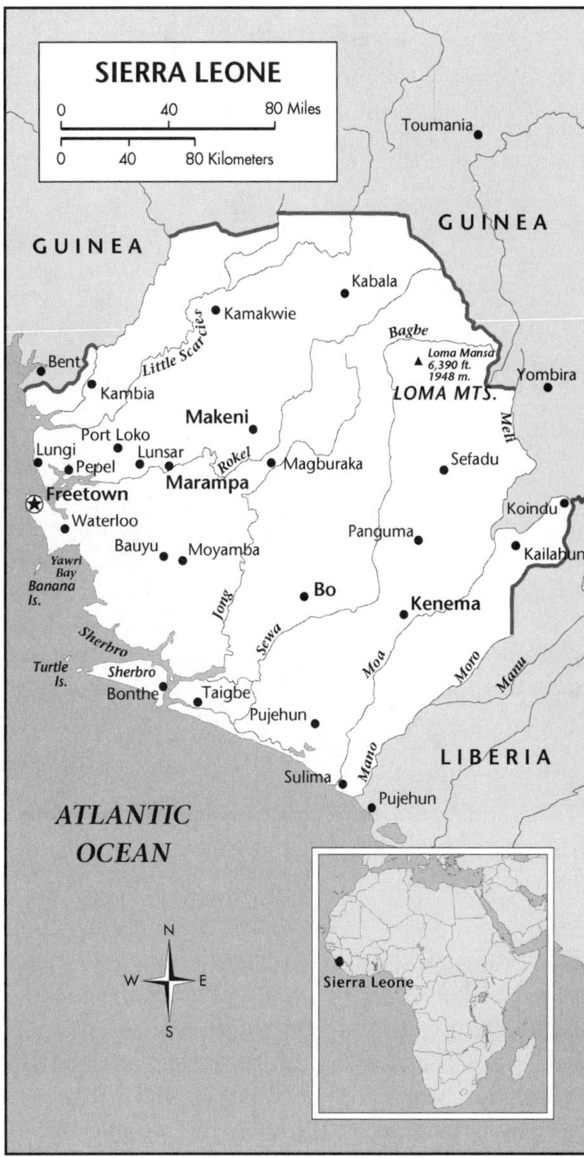

tery of GEMBLOUX as a child and was trained by Abbot Olbert (d. 1048), who conducted a good school and systematically built up an excellent library. At the request of Folcwin, Abbot of St. Vincent's, Sigebert went to Metz, where he was schoolmaster for 20 years and where his long literary career began with composing the *Lives* of the saints of Metz, of the *Passion* of St. Lucia, and the *Sermon* on her translation. Late in 1070 Sigebert returned home. He then began a series of hagiographical and historical works for his own monastery, Gembloux, and his diocese, Liège. The lengthy *Passion of the Theban Martyr Legion,* in hexameters, shows not only his vast acquaintance with classical and Christian literature but also some genuine poetic expression. Sigebert's *Life* of Wicbert, founder of Gembloux, and the lives of other local notables are found in the *Gesta* of the Abbots of Gem-

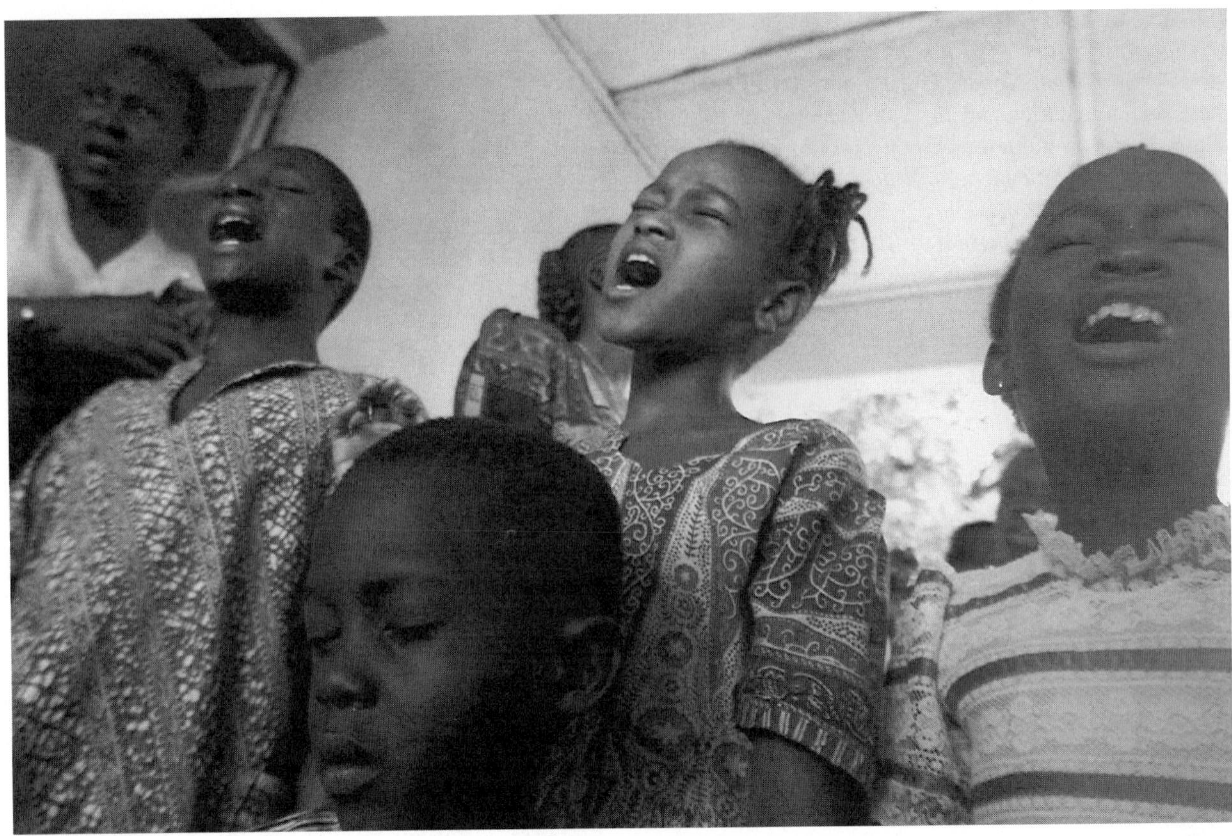

Children practice prayer songs before a live performance at Flaming Bible Children's Church, Freetown, Sierra Leone. (AP/Wide World Photos)

bloux. Although Sigebert wrote only three tracts (*Monumenta Germanica Libelli di Lite* 2:436–464) during the 30 years the INVESTITURE STRUGGLE was at its height, his position is made clear through his extant letter of 1075 in which he charges Pope GREGORY VII with the ills produced by his innovations. Further, Sigebert's letter directed against Pope PASCHAL II (1103) upholds the clergy of Liège and supports royal and imperial investiture against usurping popes. It was in his last decade that he produced two major works to crown his scholarly career. The *Chronica* (*Monumenta Germanica Scriptores* 6:300–374) attempted to establish a correct chronology of historical events from 381 to 1111 (but failed), while the *De viris illustribus* sought to provide a compendium of all important ecclesiastical writers as had the similar works of St. JEROME and GENNADIUS. Sigebert's *De viris illustribus* is one of the most important works of its kind in the Middle Ages and ranks with the *summae* of ABELARD and GRATIAN.

Bibliography: *Patrologia Latina* 160:57–834, works. *Geschichte der lateinischen Literatur des Mittelalters* 3:332–350. É. DE MOREAU, *Histoire de l'Église en Belgique* (2d ed. Brussels 1945) 2:95–99, 156–158, 277–281. *Deutschlands Geschichtsquellen im Mittelalter* 1.4:727–737. A. BOUTEMY, *Deutches Archiv für Erforschung des Mittelalters* 10 (1953) 534–535. J. LECLERCQ, *Lexikon für Theologie und Kirche* [2] 9:746.

[S. WILLIAMS]

SIGER OF BRABANT

Aristotelian and Averroist philosopher; b. Duchy of Brabant, *c.* 1240; d. Orvieto, between 1281 and 1284. He was a secular cleric and canon of St. Paul in Liège.

Life. After studying the liberal arts in Paris, Siger became master of arts and taught philosophy at the university. In 1266 he was cited by the papal legate, Simon of Brion, as the leader of a rebellious faction in the arts faculty. At about the same time he became the leader of a group of professors, among whom were BOETHIUS OF SWEDEN (Dacia) and Bernier of Nivelles, who taught an ARISTOTELIANISM influenced by Averroës and on some points contrary to the Christian faith. In 1270 the bishop of Paris, Étienne TEMPIER, condemned some of their teachings. Despite the official action against his doctrines, Siger's influence at the university grew. In 1271 he was again involved in a dispute in the faculty of arts, this time over the election of the rector of the university. On Nov. 23, 1276, Simon du Val, the inquisitor of France, summoned Siger of Brabant, Bernier of Nivelles, and Goswin of La Chapelle to appear before him to answer the charge of heresy. On March 7, 1277, the bishop of Paris condemned 219 propositions, among which are the heterodox teachings of Siger's Latin Averroism. Siger fled to the papal curia at Orvieto, where he died, stabbed by a demented secretary.

Siger was a philosopher of importance in the thirteenth century. He was called Siger the Great (*Magnus*), and Dante placed him among the wise men in paradise, with St. Thomas Aquinas speaking his eulogy. According to A. NIFO, writing about 1500, Siger was the founder of the Averroist school of philosophy.

Teaching. Like Averroës, Siger separated philosophy from religion. While accepting the truth of the Catholic faith, he insisted on the right of the philosopher to follow human reason to its inevitable conclusions, even though, in his view, it sometimes contradicts revelation. For example, he taught the eternity of the world as a necessary conclusion of philosophy, though it is contrary to faith. He did not acknowledge a double truth, one for philosophy and another for religion; however probable or even necessary he thought philosophical conclusions contrary to faith may be, he never called them true. The aim of the philosopher, he said, is not so much to discover the truth but what the great philosophers of the past, and especially Aristotle, thought (*De anima intell.* 7, ed. P. Mandonnet 2:164). St. Thomas opposed this conception of philosophy: ''It is not the aim of philosophy,'' he wrote, ''to know what men have thought but what the truth of things is'' (*In 1 cael.* 22.8).

Siger's doctrine of being or reality is that of Aristotle as interpreted by Averroës. Opposing St. Thomas, Siger denied a composition of essence and existence in creatures. Existence, he said, is of the essence of creatures; for example, it is essential for man to exist. All species are eternal and necessary; individuals in the species are alone contingent. Siger granted a distinction between the terms ''thing'' (*res*) and ''being'' (*ens*), but in his view they signify the same reality in different ways. When one says that something is a being or exists, he means that it enjoys actuality; when he calls it a reality, he means that it possesses being in a stable manner.

Siger's notion of man and the human soul is also derived from Averroës's interpretation of Aristotle. According to Siger, each man is a substance composed of matter and a form, or soul, endowed with vegetative and sense powers. The intellect is an eternal, spiritual substance, separate from matter, and possessed in common by the human race. It is composed of two parts, the agent and possible intellects. This intellect may be said to belong to each man because it operates in him and uses his sense powers. The will, a faculty of the separate intellect, is passive and determined by motives presented to it by the intellect. The intellect is immortal, but individual souls of men are not. There are moral sanctions in the present life but not in a future one; good deeds are their own reward; evil ones bear their own punishment.

In a lost work, *De intellectu,* Siger later held that God is the agent intellect. The human intellective soul is composed of the possible intellect, which is one for all men, and the human cogitative power. Because of this union, the intellect is multiplied and diversified, and it can be said to be the substantial form of man, giving him his specific rational being. In another lost treatise, *De felicitate,* Siger, following Averroës, held that man's supreme happiness in this life consists in the possible intellect's knowledge of the essence of the agent intellect, or God.

Works. Commentaries on Aristotle: *Quaestiones in physicam, in metaphysicam, in tertium de anima; Compendium de generatione et corruptione.* Questions on Aristotle's *Libri naturales* and *Politics* are lost. A collection of seven other commentaries on Aristotle in maunuscript Munich 9559 is of disputed authenticity. Independent treatises are as follows: *Quaestiones logicales; Quaestio utrum haec sit vera: homo est animal, nullo homine existente; Impossibilia; Sophisma ''Omnis homo de necessitate est animal''; Quaestio de necessitate et contingentia causarum; Quaestiones naturales; Quaestio de aeternitate mundi; Tractatus de anima intellectiva; Quaestiones morales.* Lost treatises are as follows: *De intellectu; De motore primo; Liber de felicitate.*

See Also: AVERROISM, LATIN; DOUBLE TRUTH, THEORY OF.

Bibliography: Editions. P. F. MANDONNET, *Siger de Brabant et l'averroïsme latin au XIII*[e] *siècle,* 2 v. (2d ed. Les Philosophes belges 6–7; Louvain 1908–11). F. VAN STEENBERGHEN, *Siger de Brabant d'après sea oeuvres inédites,* 2 v. (*ibid.* 12–13; Louvain 1931–42). *De aeternitate mundi,* ed. W. J. DWYER (Louvain 1937). *Questions sur la métaphysique,* ed. A. GRAIFF (Louvain 1948). Literature. F. VAN STEENBERGHEN, ''Nouvelles recherches sur Siger de Brabant et son école,'' *Revue philosophique de Louvain* 54 (1956): 130–147. A. MAIER, ''Nouvelles questions de Siger de Brabant sur la Physique d'Aristote,'' *ibid.* 44 (1946): 497–513. A. ZIMMERMANN, *Die Quaestionen des Siger von Brabant zur Physik des Aristoteles* (Doctoral diss. U. of Cologne 1956). J. J. DUIN, *La Doctrine de la Providence dans les écrits de Siger de Brabant* (Louvain 1954). G. DA PALMA, *La dottrina sull'unità dell'intelletto in Sigieri di Brabante* (Padua 1955). B. NARDI, *Sigeri di Brabante nel pensiero del Rinascimento italiano* (Rome 1945). A. MAURER, *Medieval Philosophy* (New York 1962). É. H. GILSON, *History of Christian Philosophy in the Middle Ages* (New York 1955). F. C. COPLESTON, *History of Philosophy,* v. 2. *Medieval Philosophy, Augustine to Scotus* (Westminster, Md. 1950). L. HÖDL, *Lexikon für Theologie und Kirche,* 10 v. (Freiburg 1957–65) 9:746–747.

[A. MAURER]

SIGFRID, ST.

Missionary bishop in Sweden and Norway; fl. first half of the 11th century. The near-contemporary chronicler Adam of Bremen reported that Sigfrid came to the North from England. Later legends and chronicles embellished this fact by adding that he baptized King Olaf (Skötkonung) and that he was the first bishop of Växjö (southern Sweden), where he had labored with his three nephews (Ss.) Unaman, Sunaman, and Vinaman, who were killed by the pagan population and whose heads he carries in icons. Two Offices for his feast have survived: one is partly prose and partly rhythmical, the other is more properly a *historia rhythmica;* three sequences were also composed in his honor. His feast, observed throughout Sweden, is also celebrated in other Scandinavian countries, especially in Roskilde, Denmark, and in lands to which the Bridgettines had spread. In art, Sigfrid is depicted in bishop's attire, usually carrying the three heads of his martyred nephews.

Feast: February 15.

Bibliography: T. SCHMID, *Den helige Sigfrid* (Lund 1931); "Till Sigfrids officiets utveckling," *Nordisk tidskrift för Bok- och Bibliotheksväsen* 20 (1933) 34– ; "Trois légendes de Saint Sigfrid," B. DE GAIFFIER, *Analecta Bollandiana* 60 (1942) 82–90. *Scriptores rerum Suecicarum Medii Aevi,* 3 v. in 6 (Uppsala 1818–76) v.2.1. *Analecta hymnica* (Leipzig 1886–1922) v.25, 42. M. RYDBECK, *Den helige Sigfrid* (Lund 1957). A. ÖNNERFORS, *Die Hauptfassungen des Sigfridoffiziums* (Lund 1968). J. GALLÉN, *Lexikon für Theologie und Kirche*, ed. J. HOFER and K. RAHNER, 10 v. (2d, new ed. Freiburg 1957–65) 9: 742.

[T. SCHMID]

SIGILLOGRAPHY

The study of SEALS, sigillography or sphragistic(s) was originally a branch of DIPLOMATICS, with which it still shares much of its subject matter, though the sigillographer's approach is primarily technical and archaeological.

Sealing, as a means of authenticating written matter, has been practiced from remotest antiquity: in western Europe it enjoyed its greatest vogue between the 12th and the 15th century, when the principals in most transactions could not (or at least did not) validate their acts by signature. During this period seal owners were to be found at every level of society, and the great had needs and functions for which one seal might be insufficient.

The matrix by means of which the seal impression was made was most commonly metal: latten, a brasslike alloy, was normal, with precious metals used by the rich and lead by the poor. Jet, engraved gems (often survivals from classical antiquity specially mounted in metal), ivory, bone, and even wood were also used. The device and its circumambient legend were incised in reverse on the matrix, the back of which (on a single-sided seal) was shaped to form a handle, with or without a ring. The matrices of a double-sided seal were flat slabs, sometimes hinged but oftener having projecting pierced lugs through which pins were passed vertically to secure correct register.

In the papal Curia (imitated in this respect by some other Mediterranean chanceries) the impression took the form of a bulla, a ball of lead squeezed flat between two matrices. So-called bulls of gold and silver, used for documents of exceptional ceremoniousness, are seldom or never true seals; when they are not casts, they consist of thin leaves of metal stamped in shallow relief and soldered together. But the overwhelming majority of surviving medieval seal-impressions are in a material normally composed of roughly two parts of beeswax to one of resin. Chalk or ashes might be added to this mixture to harden it and to combat warmth later. Apart from white, which occurs before 1100, red and green were the earliest and the commonest variations on the natural color of this compound; but black, brown, and (rarely) blue are also found. Impressions in natural wax were sometimes coated with a dark varnish. Colors were occasionally combined in a single seal, as when the impression is borne on a layer of wax set in a "saucer" of wax of another color. There may be significance in the color used; for example, in both England and France royal grants in perpetuity were sealed in green.

The commonest shapes for medieval seals are the circle and the oval, the latter frequently pointed at top and bottom and especially affected by ladies and ecclesiastics, who were conventionally portrayed on their seals in a standing position. Other shapes are rare: even the "Gothic shield," which lent itself to the much-favored armorial device, is seldom found.

Within any one country the great seal (or seal of majesty) of the sovereign tends to be at any given time preeminent in size and to grow progressively larger, reaching a diameter of about 4 ½ inches in France at the end of the 15th century; the seals of subjects were ordinarily much smaller. Privy or "secret" seals were smaller still; they were used either to warrant the employment of the owner's great seal or to make a counter-impression in the back of a single-faced great seal and thus identify the seal owner personally with his act.

The devices on medieval seals are so diverse that the most thorough classification leaves a large category of "arbitrary" or "miscellaneous" charges outside the more readily defined types, such as the enthroned monarch, the patron saint, the mounted knight, the standing figure, the coat of arms, or the stylized castle. But all alike provide a rich source for the study of medieval art in general.

Legends, usually in Latin but occasionally in the vernacular, run clockwise around the circumference from a point right of top center. They generally proclaim the ownership and nature of the seal in formal language, but allusive, punning, and pious mottoes may also be found. The lettering develops from crude Roman capitals to ''Lombardic'' in the late 12th century and from Lombardic to ''black letter'' about 200 years later.

Wax seals might be applied directly to the surface of the document, which was often prepared by incisions or other means of fully engaging wax and parchment. Applied seals of the 15th century are frequently covered by a layer of paper interposed between matrix and wax at the moment of sealing. Bullae and double-sided wax seals were necessarily pendent. They hung either on a tongue, provided by almost severing the bottom margin of the document, or on tags, strings, or laces passed through slits or holes in the margin. The papal bulla was borne on hempen strings on letters of justice and by silk on letters of grace. Pendent wax seals are sometimes protected by woven bags or small boxes of wood or metal known as skippets.

Bibliography: H. JENKINSON, *Guide to Seals in the Public Record Office* (London 1954). J. H. ROMAN, *Manuel de sigillographie française* (Paris 1912). H. BRESSLAU, *Handbuch der Urkundenlehre für Deutschland und Italien,* ed. H. W. KLEWITZ, 2 v. (2d ed. Leipzig 1912–31) v. 2. A. DE BOÜARD, *Manuel de diplomatique française et pontificale* (Paris 1929) 333–351, an admirably clear and concise summary. M. TOURNEUR-NICODÈME, *Bibliographie générale de la sigillographie* (Besançon 1933), for sigillographic works pub. in Europe, particularly strong on the copious French literature. Y. METMAN, in *L'Histoire et ses méthodes,* ed. C. SAMARAN (Paris 1961) 393–446.

[L. C. HECTOR]

SIGISMUND, ST.

King of Burgundy (France), reputed martyr; d. *ca.* 524. The son of King Gundebald of Burgundy, an Arian, Sigismund was converted *ca.* 499 to the orthodox faith by Bp. AVITUS OF VIENNE, even though he persisted for some time longer in his old ways of life. He succeeded to the Burgundian throne in 516. In remorse for having ordered his own son strangled to death in a fit of anger (522), Sigismund became the effective founder of the monastery of SAINT-MAURICE in the present-day Valais canton of Switzerland. He sent for monks from LÉRINS, Gigny, Ile-Barbe, and SAINT-CLAUDE, endowed the community liberally, and initiated there the *laus perennis,* i.e., the continuous chanting of the Divine Office. About 523 Sigismund was defeated at the Battle of Agaune by the three kings of France, all sons of CLOVIS, who were intent on gaining the Kingdom of Burgundy and on revenging their maternal grandfather, King Chilperic, who had been put to death by Sigismund's father. Sigismund escaped to the vicinity of Saint-Maurice, where he became a hermit, but he was soon captured by King Clodomir and, despite AVITUS's remonstrances, was drowned in a well. Tradition ascribes miracles to Sigismund; his cult spread in southern France and among the West Franks. His body was taken to Saint-Maurice; in 676 his skull was taken to St. Sigismund's in Alsace (today in Matzenheim). Since 1354 part of his relics have been preserved in the cathedral at Prague, while others were taken to the Diocese of Freising in Germany and to the cathedral in Płock, Poland.

Feast: May 1.

Bibliography: *Monumenta Germaniae Historica: Scriptores rerum Merovingicarum* (Berlin 1826–) 2:333–340; 7.2:775–776. C. J. VON HEFELE, *Histoire des conciles d'après les documents originaux,* tr. and continued by H. LECLERQ, 10 v. in 19 (Paris 1907–38) 2.2:1017–22, 1031–42. A. BUTLER, *The Lives of the Saints,* rev. ed. H. THURSTON and D. ATTWATER, 4 v. (New York 1956) 2:209–210. R. FOLZ, ''Zur Frage der heiligen Könige: Heiligkeit und Nachleven in der Geschichte des burgundischen Königtums,'' *Deutsches Archiv für Erforschung des Mittelaltars* 14 (Cologne-Graz 1958) 317–344. J. M. THEURILLAT, *L'Abbaye de St-Maurice d'Agaune, des origines à la réforme canoniale,* 515–830 (Sion Switz, 1954); *Lexikon für Theologie und Kirche,* ed. J. HOFER and K. RAHNER (Freiburg 1957–65); suppl., *Das Zweite Vatikanishe Konsil: Dokumente und Kommentare,* ed. H. S. BRECHTER et al. (1966) 9:748–749.

[B. B. SZCZESNIAK]

SIGISMUND, HOLY ROMAN EMPEROR

King of Hungary, 1387; King of the Romans, 1410; King of Bohemia, 1419; Holy Roman Emperor, May 31, 1433; b. Nuremberg, Germany, Feb. 12, 1368; d. Znojmo, Czechoslovakia, Dec. 9, 1437. The son of Emperor Charles IV and Elizabeth, daughter of Boguslav, Duke of Polish Pomerania, Sigismund was educated chiefly at the Hungarian Court. In 1385 he married Maria, daughter of King Louis the Great of Poland-Hungary and heir to Hungary; he had been rejected by Hedwig, the young Queen of Poland. In 1378 he had succeeded his father to the Mark of Brandenburg; on March 31, 1387, he was crowned King of Hungary. He also claimed the Mark of Moravia, which was under the rule of Duke Jobst, his cousin. His Hungarian reign was marked by domestic wars and failures in foreign policy (e.g., his defeat by the

Turks at Nicopolis in 1396). Because of his involvement in the political skirmishing of German and other European princes for the Roman imperial crown, Sigismund lost any real influence in Hungary after 1396; but upon the forced resignation of Emperor WENCESLAUS IV, his stepbrother, he became vicar of the Holy Roman Empire in 1400. However, Rupert III, elector palatine of the Rhine, received the German crown despite Sigismund. These defeats precipitated new domestic wars with his Hungarian magnates, who ''deposed'' and actually imprisoned him for a short time in 1401. These skirmishes were followed by wars with Venice and with King Ladislaus of Naples, who sold the Dalmatian cities claimed by Hungary to the Republic of Venice. In 1401 Sigismund imprisoned Wenceslaus, who was still King of Bohemia, but was able to rule there in his stead for only 19 months before Wenceslaus escaped and returned. In 1410, after the death of Emperor Rupert, Sigismund was finally elected German king, that is, king of the Romans. Coronation was impeded by the wars among factions of German princes; but finally, on Nov. 8, 1414, he was crowned king at Aachen.

In his new role Sigismund attempted to achieve the unity of the Empire and the Church. To end the disorder of the Church occasioned by the WESTERN SCHISM and particularly by the election of antipope John XXIII at the Council of PISA, he pressured the convocation of the Council at CONSTANCE (1414–18). Later, with Pope MARTIN V, he convoked the Council at BASEL (1431). As imperial protector of the Church, Sigismund exercised a dominant influence in the councils; with his support, the contesting popes at Constance resigned, and reunion under Martin V was achieved. Sigismund was popularly held responsible for the Council's condemnation of John HUS, Bohemian religious reformer and agitator, to the stake.

In 1419 Sigismund became king of Bohemia also, but the actual ruler was the widow of Wenceslaus, Queen Sophie.

The HUSSITE wars in Bohemia (*c.* 1420–36) and the second victory of the OTTOMAN TURKS, who were invading Hungary's Danubian province (1426–27), considerably augmented Sigismund's difficulties in uniting all German princes under his rule. To strengthen his camp of princely supporters, Sigismund made Frederick I, a Hohenzollern, the burgrave of Nuremberg, margrave of Brandenburg, and an elector of the Empire (1415); but in 1424 Frederick joined the opposition. With this Sigismund lost any real authority over the German princes; however, he was able to retain control of the Italian domains. On Nov. 25, 1431, he was crowned king of the Lombards at Milan; on May 31, 1433, Pope Eugene IV crowned him Holy Roman Emperor. Finally, the estates of Bohemia formally recognized him as their king.

When Sigismund died (he was buried at Oradea, Rumania), he had not achieved the basic goal of his life, the unification of Christendom under his authority to fight the Turks, who constituted the gravest danger to the existence of the Byzantine Empire and Western Christendom. Upon his death, the house of Luxembourg became extinct; his only daughter, Elizabeth, from his second wife, Barbara of Cile, married the Hapsburg Duke Albert V of Austria, the future German King Albert II, Sigismund's successor.

Bibliography: J. VON ASCHBACH. *Geschichte Kaiser Sigmunds,* 4 v. (Hamburg 1838–45). W. BERGER, *Johannes Hus und König Sigmund* (Augsburg 1871). E. WINDECKE, *Denkwürdigkeiten zur Geschichte des Zeitalters Kaiser Sigmunds,* ed. W. ALTMANN (Berlin 1893). A. MAIN, *The Emperor Sigismund* (London 1903). M. SPINKA, *John Hus and the Czech Reform* (Chicago 1941). L. R. LOOMIS, tr., *The Council of Constance,* ed. J. H. MUNDY and K. M. WOODY (New York 1961). A. POSCH, *Lexikon für Theologie und Kirche*, ed. J. HOFER and K. RAHNER, 10 v. (2d, new ed. Freiburg 1957–65) 9:749–750.

[B. B. SZCZESNIAK]

SIGN

A sign is anything that represents to a knowing power something other than itself. For example, the color white, which is not itself joy, is a sign of joy in the Latin rite. A sign, then, is always distinguished from the thing signified; it is not a matter of the volitional or emotional orders, but of the cognitive. Nevertheless, the knowing power need not be the INTELLECT; the sign is a reality of the brute-animal world as well as of the human.

Types of Sign. There are six traditional types of sign: natural or artificial, instrumental or formal, imaging or nonimaging. A natural sign receives its significative force from nature itself, as smoke is a sign of fire. An artificial or arbitrary sign, on the other hand, receives its significative force from those using the sign, as a white color signifies joy for some people. When an artificial sign is imposed by tradition, it is sometimes called a customary sign; otherwise, it is a conventional sign. An instrumental sign is one that must be known apart from and before the thing signified. Thus one must first learn of the connection between smoke and fire, between white and joy, before smoke and white can become signs. When a sign is known together with the thing signified, on the other hand, it is a formal sign. An example is a bird's danger cry, which conveys its meaning at once, even though it may never have been heard before. An instrumental sign requires previous education and experience; a formal sign is grasped intuitively. An imaging sign is one that pictures the thing signified, as in picture writing; a nonimaging sign is one that does not picture the thing signified, as in writing employing an alphabet.

Uses of Sign. The sign plays a role in philosophy and theology, as well as in formal disciplines. In philosophy, realists consider the CONCEPT or IDEA as the natural and formal sign of extramental reality, and the TERM or WORD as the artificial and instrumental sign of the concept. For this reason the universal term is called *universale in significando,* i.e., the universal as it is a sign (*see* UNIVERSALS). In theology, sign is indispensable for discussing the SACRAMENTS and the LITURGY, although for the latter SYMBOL is frequently used as synonymous with sign. Modern mathematicians and logicians restrict their use of symbol to artificial, nonimaging signs, usually written, such as ''*p*,'' or ''*q*,'' (*see* LOGIC, SYMBOLIC). In linguistic analysis, discussions of meaning are basically discussions of signs and what they signify (*see* SEMANTICS; SEMIOTICS).

[E. BONDI]

SIGNS OF THE TIMES

The Biblical expression ''signs of the times'' has been used with a general meaning of significant events and trends in many languages for centuries. It was given a specific theological meaning at Vatican II in the Pastoral Constitution on the Church in Today's World: *Gaudium et spes* (art. 4). There it refers to those events in history characteristic of an epoch, which, if properly read, can reveal the presence or the absence of God.

History of the Term at the Council. ''Signs of the times'' was first used in a theological context by Pope John XXIII in the Bull *Humanae salutis* (Dec. 25, 1961), in which he convened the Vatican Council, to meet in the next year. After dismissing those who see only darkness burdening the face of the earth, the Pope stated:

> We renew our confidence in our Savior who has not left the world he redeemed. Instead we make our own the recommendation that one should know how to distinguish the signs of the times (Mt 16:4) and we seem to see now in the midst of so much darkness a few indications that argue well for the fate of the Church and humanity (sec. 3).

While the Council was in session, Pope John published the encyclical letter *Pacem in terris* (April 13, 1963) in which the term ''Signs of the Times'' was used three times, not however in the text of the letter, but as the sub-titles to three distinct sections (par. 29, 126, 142). Under this heading the pope noted three events in particular as being significant for the knowledge of God and religion: the progressive development of the working classes, the growing role of women in public life, and the gradual disappearance of colonialism.

A year later, Pope Paul VI used the term in *Ecclesiam suam* (Aug. 6, 1964), where he spoke of the ''signs of the times'' as part of a dialogue between the Church and the world.

From the time of *Pacem in terris* the term ''signs of the times'' was used in successive drafts of sections of the pastoral constitution. ''Signs of the Times'' was the name given to a subcommission preparing the Introductory Statement of the Constitution.

Origin and Meaning. The origin of the term''signs of the times'' is the Gospel (Mt. 16.1.3):

> The Pharisees and the Sadducees came along; and as a test asked Jesus to show them some sign in the sky. He gave them this reply: 'In the evening you say ''Red sky at night, the day will be bright'' but in the morning, ''Sky red and gloomy, the day will be stormy.'' If you know how to interpret the look of the sky can you not read the signs of the times (semeia tou kairon)? An eager faithless age is eager for a sign but no sign will be given it except that of Jonah.' With that he left them (NAB).

In this context, the ''signs of the times'' are the person and activity of Jesus which signify that these days are decisive for repentance and judgment. They are clear indications of the coming of the Kingdom, signs which should be able to be read by all. In a more general context, the ''signs of the times'' could be said of events which, by qualities within the events themselves, manifest the presence and activity of God and call the Church to faith and deeper understanding.

The Biblical context is both christological and eschatological. World Council of Churches observers and some fathers of the Council objected to the use of the term for contemporary events. For this reason, the subcommission removed the term from the text submitted to the third and fourth sessions of the Council. It was inserted in the final text without, however, its Biblical citation; the term was to be understood only in the sense in which Popes John and Paul had used it.

Understood sociologically the ''signs of the times'' are those events in human history which, by their widespread or frequent appearance, or by some dramatic quality so characterize an era that in them the needs, achievements, and aspirations of men and women present themselves. Reflected in the light of the Gospel, they are signs of the divine saving will in history. From these ''signs of the times'' the Church is able to understand its teaching better, to express it more clearly and fully, and to adapt its pastoral action.

The most telling weakness in any theory of interpreting events as signs of God's presence is its optimism: it fails to take into account the ambiguity which baffles any interpretation of human history. Pastor Lukas Vischer, a World Council of Churches observer at Vatican II, wrote the subcommission:

. . . to recognize the signs of the times one ought to distinguish the voice of God from any other voice no matter how persuasive it might be. Furthermore, the world is ambiguous and evil is mixed up with the good . . . evil is powerful in this moment of history; and when we compare it to the proclamation of the Reign of Christ it has an extraordinary power

The Council suggested no criteria for this prophetic task except study, discussion, prayer, and the assistance of the Holy Spirit in the Church (art. 44). Nor was this ever assumed to be easy.

Motivated by this faith it labors to decipher authentic signs of God's presence and purpose in the happenings, needs, and desires in which this people has a part along with other men of our age. . . . The Council wishes to assert in the light (of faith) those values which are most highly praised today and to relate them to their divine source. For insofar as they stem from endowments conferred by God on man, these values are exceedingly good. Yet they are often wrenched from their rightful function by the taint in man's heart and we stand in need of purification (art. II).

In the years that have followed the Council the phrase ''signs of the times'' has been applied frequently to descriptions of contemporary events which have an impact on the life of faith or on the Church. Papal letters and statements of the Synod of Bishops offer an analysis of contemporary events in the manner of *Gaudium et spes* as a preface or introduction, especially if the document deals with questions of social doctrine. However the term ''signs of the times'' is rarely used of this description. Almost nothing has been written about ''signs of the times'' as a font of revelation or a source of theology since the studies published in 1967–69 immediately after the Council, by the theologians who played a role in the preparation of the Pastoral Constitution when the concept was new and exciting.

Bibliography: C. MOELLER, ''History of the Constitution'' and ''Preface and Introductory Statement,'' *Commentary on Documents of Vatican II*, v. 5, *Pastoral Constitution on the Church in the Modern World* (New York 1969) 1–114. M.-D. CHENU, ''Les Signes des Temps,'' 87 *Nouvelle Revue Theologique*, 29–39.

[M. HEATH]

SIKHISM

An indigenous Indian religion, found predominantly in the Punjāb region of India; founded by Gurū Nānak (1469–1538), a Hindu raised under Muslim rule and influence, who combined Hindu and Islamic beliefs to achieve religious and social harmony. According to his doctrine, there is but one True God (Ik Onkar), a transcendent and almighty Creator. Everything on earth is determined by the will of God (hukam). God can be approached from the interior of one's heart, without the need for elaborate rituals and ceremonies. Sikhism emerged as a distinct religion because of Gurū Nānak's personal rejection of pilgrimages, his stress on living the good life on earth, and his appointment of a successor as the master (*guru*) for his disciples (*sikhs*).

Of the succeeding gurus, Angad (1539–52) developed the Gurmukhi script in which to record Nānak's life and doctrine; Amar Dās (1552–74) fixed Sikh funeral and marriage rites, forbade intoxicants and cruel Hindu customs, and established 22 centers of worship and missionary activity; Rām Dā (1574–81) built the most famous Sikh shrine, the Amritsār; and Arjun (1581–1606) compiled the *Ādi Granth* (First Book), the canon of hymns and sayings of Gurū Nānak and his successors, to be revered by the Sikhs. Gobind Singh (1675–1708), the 10th and last guru, completed the transformation of the Sikhs into a militant community to defend against Muslim incursions. In 1699, he established the Khālsa, the sworn brotherhood of fighting Sikhs, with its initiation, distinctive marks, and sanctions. Having lost his sons in war, he provided for the succession to the guruship by prescribing obeisance and offering to the *Granth Sāhib* (Sacred Book; an enlargement of the *Ādi Granth* with his own writings), as ''the visible guru'' and by exalting the Khālsa as the embodiment of the guru.

A long period of internal strife ended under Ranjīt Singh (1780–1839), who founded the Sikh kingdom in the Punjāb. At his death, however, the Sikhs rapidly declined in power and deviated from the teachings of the gurus by tolerating widow burning (*satī*), cow veneration, and caste division among Sikhs. In 1848 they fell under British rule. Later, when Christian and Hindu missionaries became active, the Singh Sabhā society was formed to foster education and teach the *Granth Sāhib,* missionaries were appointed, and the Khālsa Tract Society was organized to distribute religious literature.

Bibliography: G. SINGH, *The Religion of the Sikhs* (New York 1971). W. O. COLE, *Sikhism and Its Indian Context, 1469–1708: The Attitude of Guru Nanak and Early Sikhism to Indian Religious Beliefs and Practices* (London 1984). W. H. MCLEOD, *The Sikhs: History, Religion, and Society* (New York 1989). M. MACAULIFFE and K. SINGH, *The Sikhs: Their Religion, Gurus, Sacred Writings, and Authors* (Oxford 1989). G. R. THURSBY, *The Sikhs* (Leiden-New York 1992). W. COLE and P.S. SINGH, *Sikhism and Christianity: A Comparative Study* (New York 1993). K. SINGH, *A History of the Sikhs* (Oxford 1999). J. P. SINGH UBEROI, *Religion, Civil Society and the State: A Study of Sikhism* (New York 1996). W. H. MCLEOD, *Sikhs and Sikhism* (New York 1999). W. H. MCLEOD, *Exploring Sikhism: Aspects of Sikh Identity, Culture and Thought* (Oxford 2000). G. S. MANN, *The Making of Sikh Scripture* (Oxford/New York 2001). C.

Gilded Plaque at the Golden Temple. A scene of Gurū Nānak accompanied by Mardana, Amritsar, India. (©Michael Freeman/ CORBIS)

SHACKLE, G. SINGH and A.-P. SINGH MANDAIR, *Sikh Religion, Culture and Ethnicity* (Richmond, Surrey, England 2001).

[A. S. ROSSO/EDS.]

SILAS (SILVANUS)

Important figure in the apostolic Church and frequent companion of St. Paul. The two names, Silas (used throughout Acts) and Silvanus (found in the Epistles: 2 Cor 1.19; 1 Thes 1.1; 2 Thes 1.1; 1 Pt 5.12), assuredly belonged to the same man. Either he had two names, as Paul (who is also called Saul), or Silas is a Greek form of the Latin Silvanus.

Silas enjoyed Roman citizenship (Acts 16.37). He is first mentioned as one of the ''leading men'' of the Church at Jerusalem (15.22). After the Council of Jerusalem he was selected, together with Judas Barsabbas, as the bearer of the decree of the Council to Antioch (15.27). At Antioch they encouraged the Christians in their faith and exercised the office of ''prophets'' (15.32). Silas remained there, while Judas returned to Jerusalem (15.34–35). Some time later, Silas was chosen to accompany Paul on his second missionary journey, after the disagreement between Paul and Barnabas over John Mark (15.40). At Philippi, because they exorcised a girl possessed by a divining spirit, Paul and Silas were treated badly by the citizens and beaten with rods. They were imprisoned, but a midnight earthquake opened the doors of the jail. Instead of escaping, they calmed the jailer and converted his whole family. When the magistrates of the city wanted to release them secretly, Paul and Silas demanded redress for the unjust treatment accorded them even though they were Roman citizens (16.19–40). They went on to preach the gospel in Thessalonica, but soon the jealousy of the Jews forced them to go on to Beroea (Acts 17.4, 10). Silas stayed there with Timothy while

Paul went on to Athens (17.14). Later they joined Paul in Corinth and were with him when he wrote the two letters to the Thessalonians (1 Thes 1.1; 2 Thes 1.1). There is no record of Silas's further activity with Paul. He must have joined St. Peter at some later time, however, for he served as St. Peter's secretary or even as coauthor of 1 Peter (1 Pt 5.12).

Legend says Silas was the first bishop of Corinth and died in Macedonia.

Feast: July 13.

Bibliography: A. STEGMANN, *Silvanus als Missionar und "Hagiograph"* (Rottenburg 1917). L. RADERMACHER, "Der erste Petrusbrief und Silvanus," *Zeitschrift für die neutestamentliche Wissenschaft und die Kunde der ärlteren Kirche* 25 (1926) 287–299.

[S. MUSHOLT]

SILOAM INSCRIPTION

A six-line Hebrew inscription accidentally discovered in 1880 in the rock wall of the lower entrance to the tunnel of King Hezechiah that connects the Virgin's Pool ('Ain Sitti Maryām), outside Jerusalem, with the pool of Siloam (Birket Siloam; Siloe: Jn 9.7), inside Jerusalem. The inscription had been chiseled out of the rock about 19 feet from the Siloam end. Above it the rock was dressed for a considerable space as though it had been prepared for more text. In 1890 the inscribed rock was hewn out to be brought to the museum, but it broke into six or seven pieces; the restored inscription is in the Museum of the Ancient Orient in Istanbul.

The text describes an incident in the boring through of the tunnel: the crews of miners that started from opposite ends successfully effected a junction that permitted the flow of water from the spring to the pool. The several lacunae in the text and an obscure *hapax legomenon* preclude a full understanding of the contents, but the following version does not differ in substance from others that have been proposed (brackets indicate words missing from the text; parentheticals are explanatory):

> [When] it (the tunnel) was being bored through, this was the manner in which it was bored through. While . . . the pick-axe, each man toward his fellow, and while there were still three cubits to bore through, [there was heard] the voice of a man calling to his fellow, for there was a fissure(?) in the rock on the right [and on the left]. And when it was bored through, the quarrymen struck toward each other, pick-axe against pick-axe, and the water flowed from the spring toward she reservoir for 1,200 cubits. And the height of the rock above the heads of the quarrymen was 100 cubits.

Among scholars there is agreement that the tunnel was the work of King Hezechiah (*c.* 715–686 B.C.), who, according to 2 Chr 32.2–4, as a precaution against a possible siege, brought water from the only natural spring near Jerusalem by a channel through the rock to a secure place within the city. In 2 Kgs 20.20 it is stated that he "made a pool and a conduit and brought water into the city" (*see* Sir 48.17). Hence, both the aqueduct and the inscription must date *c.* 700 B.C. The orthography points to the same conclusion. The forms of the letters are more cursive than those of the MESHA INSCRIPTION (*c.* 840 B.C.), and some of the letters are palpably different. Final vowels are represented by consonants, but internal long vowels are not written fully unless they come from diphthongs, e.g., *'wd,* from *'aud.* Written in good Hebrew prose, the inscription reads like a passage of the Old Testament.

Bibliography: D. DIRINGER, *Le inscrizioni antico-ebraiche palestinesi* (Florence 1934) 95–102, with extensive bibliog. up to 1932. W. F. ALBRIGHT, tr., J. B. PRITCHARD, *Ancient Near Eastern Texts Relating to the Old Testament* (Princeton 1955) 321. H. DONNER and W. RÖLLIG, *Kanaanäische und aramäische Inschriften,* v.2 (Wiesbaden 1964) 186.

[M. J. DAHOOD]

SILOS, ABBEY OF

Santo Domingo de Silos, Spanish Benedictine monastery in southern Burgos founded by Fernán González on July 3, 954. It was almost deserted and in ruins in 1041, when Ferdinand I sent DOMINIC OF SILOS to restore it. Dominic made arrangements for the material needs, built the church, began the cloister, enriched the library, and instituted a scriptorium that produced such codexes as the MS of the *Etymologies* of ISIDORE OF SEVILLE, now in the Paris Bibliothèque Nationale, and the wonderfully illuminated MS of the Commentary on the Apocalypse of BEATUS OF LIÉBANA, now in the British Museum. Dominic was buried in the cloister at the time of his death (Dec. 20, 1073). The translation of his relics to the church in 1076 by King, prelates, and people was equivalent to canonization. The name of the monastery was then changed from San Sebastián to Santo Domingo, and the tomb became the most important pilgrimage center in Castile.

As a result, the monastery prospered. A splendid transept was added to the church *c.* 1100, the cloister was expanded, and throughout the 12th century the library was increased. From Silos came Grimaldus, who wrote an account of Dominic's life and miracles *c.* 1088, and the historian in León who wrote the chronicle known as *Silense.* Donations from princes and the faithful brought

Silos dozens of churches, towns, and priories—such as San Frutos in Segovia. In 1118 Pope Gelasius II made Silos immediately subject to the Holy See. When Paschasius was abbot (1170–84), St. DOMINIC (GUZMÁN), who was named for the founder of Silos and educated in the monastery, was born nearby. Rodrigo Iñiguez Guzmán, Silos's most illustrious abbot of the 13th century (1242–76), came from the same family. In this period Gonzalo de Berceo wrote a life of St. Dominic of Silos in Castilian verse, and Pero Marín composed an enchanting account of the saint's miracles. A visitation ordered by Benedict XII (1338) showed that Silos had 30 monks and a revenue of 39,000 maravedis. Several nearby hermits, the sick in the hospital of San Lázaro, eight lay brothers, 60 servants, and two women in seclusion (or confinement) depended on the abbey, which in the years just previously had suffered great losses. There was a material and spiritual decline until Silos joined the Congregation of Valladolid in 1512. Thereafter it prospered in all aspects for 300 years. During the Napoleonic Wars, Dominic Moreno, later bishop of Cadiz, saved Silos from ruin, but it could not survive the suppression of religious orders in 1833. Its rich collection of medieval MSS was scattered, mostly to London and Paris, but the buildings were preserved, thanks to French monks who began a restoration under Abbot Guépin in 1880.

Silos in 1964 was a flourishing abbey of the Congregation of SOLESMES with some 20 old MSS in its archives, several excellent gold treasures (such as the chalice St. Dominic had made), and the Romanesque altar front of wrought copper. One wing of the old transept remains with its excellent original art. The rest, however, was ruined in the 18th century when the monks raised over it a baroque church after the plans of Ventura Rodriguez. Fortunately the Romanesque cloister, one of the most beautiful in the world, is intact with its two stories, 74 capitals, and eight corner reliefs that offer, in some of the most striking sculpture of the Middle Ages, a complete survey of Romanesque art in the late 11th and early 12th century. The upper cloister and the reliefs of the Annunciation and the tree of Jesse date from the early 12th century. The realistic ceiling decoration of the lower cloister, with its assorted paintings by a mudéjar of few scruples, is from the late 14th century.

Bibliography: *Enciclopedia universal ilustrada Europeo-Americana* (Barcelona 1908–30) 54:377–393. M. FÉROTIN, *Histoire de l'abbaye de Silos* (Paris 1897); ed., *Recueil des chartes de l'abbaye de Silos* (Paris 1897). L. DELISLE, "Les Manuscrits de Silos dans la Bibliothèque Nationale de Paris," *Mélanges de paléographie et de bibliographie* (Paris 1880) 53–116. E. M. THOMPSON, ed., *Catalogue of Additions to the Manuscripts in the British Museum in the Years 1876–1881* (London 1882). W. M. WHITEHILL and J. PÉREZ DE URBEL, "Los manuscritos del real monasterio de S. Domingo de Silos," *Bolotín de la Real Academia de la Historia* 95 (1929) 521–601. E. ROULIN, *L'Ancien trésor de l'Abbaye de Silos* (Paris 1901); "Les Claustres de l'Abbaye de Silos," *Revue de l'art chrétien* 59 (1909); 60 (1910). A. M. HUNTINGTON, ed., *Initials and Miniatures of the IXth, Xth, and XIth Centuries From the Mozarabic Manuscripts of Santo Domingo de Silos in the British Museum* (New York 1904). R. DE PINEDO, *Ensayo sobre el Simbolismo Religioso en las construcciones ecclesiásticas de la Edad Media* (Burgos 1924). J. PÉREZ DE URBEL, *El Claustro de Silos* (Burgos 1930); *Historia del condado de Castilla,* 3 v. (Madrid 1945). H. LECLERCQ, *Dictionnaire d'archéologie chrétienne et de liturgie*, ed., F. CABROL, H. LECLERCQ and H. I. MARROU (Paris 1907–53) 15.1:1452–54. L. H. COTTINEAU, *Répertoire topobibliographique des abbayes et prieurés* (Mâcon 1935–39) 2: 3036–37.

[J. PÉREZ DE URBEL]

SILVA, ATENÓGENES

Mexican archbishop and preacher; b. Guadalajara, Aug. 26, 1848; d. there, Feb. 26, 1911. He was the son of a Portuguese father, Joaquín Silva, and a Mexican mother, Ignacia Alvarez Tostado. Silva was ordained in 1871, received the doctorate in theology in 1878, then served for several years as professor and vice rector of the seminary. In 1880 he was sent to the parish of Zapotlán el Grande and in 1884, was named theologian of the cathedral of Guadalajara. He was made bishop of Colima in 1892, and in 1900, archbishop of Michoacán. This important diocese was made famous in its early days by the saintly sociologist Vasco de QUIROGA, whose name and works are still revered by the people and admired by scholars four centuries later. Silva was outstanding for his apostolic zeal, keen understanding, wide knowledge, generous and charitable spirit, and unusual talent for oratory. A notable sermon that he preached before a select audience in the Church of La Profesa in Mexico City, on the third centenary of St. Philip Neri in 1895, earned him an appointment to the Mexican Academy of the Language. He was made an Arcadian of Rome with the name Egeneo Senopeo. He promoted and took part in the Plenary Council for Latin America (Rome 1899). There, in the church of San Nicolás in Carcere before all the council fathers, he delivered a sermon on the Virgin of Guadalupe, the papacy, and the Mexican nation. Silva was devoted to the miracle of Tepeyac, and on another solemn occasion in 1904, in the Basilica of Guadalupe, he preached on the influence of the Virgin of Guadalupe on Mexican civilization. The same year, in commemoration of the 50th anniversary of the proclamation of the Immaculate Conception, Archbishop Silva organized a great religious celebration and announced a literary contest. The prize went to a Catholic layman, Francisco ELGUERO, for his important work *La Inmaculada: Disertación histórico-filosófica*, (Mexico 1995). The archbishop was instrumental in having the Holy See elevate to the rank of collegiate church the secular sanctuary of Pátzcuaro, where a statue of Our Lady of Good Health had been venerated since the time of Vasco de Quiroga. The solemn dedication was celebrated in 1908. The royal family of Spain sent gifts to mark the occasion, and Alfonso XIII awarded the Grand Cross of Isabella the Catholic to Archbishop Silva. Many sermons, letters and other writings of the archbishop are found in separate pamphlets. A collection of his works appeared as *Obras literarias, pastorales y oratorias* (Guadalajara 1898). It contains two academic addresses, three funeral eulogies, ten sermons, eight pastoral letters and edicts, five allocutions, and six circular letters. Nothing seems to have been published later except for a few pastoral letters that are not readily available.

See Also: GUADALUPE, OUR LADY OF.

Bibliography: E. VALVERDE TÉLLEZ, *Bio-bibliografía eclesiástica mexicana, 1821–1943,* 3 v. (Mexico City 1949).

[A. JUNCO]

SILVEIRA, GONÇALO DA, VEN.

Jesuit missionary of the Far East and Africa; b. Almeirim, Portugal, between 1521 and 1524; martyred, Africa, March 11, 1561. His parents were Luis da Silveira, first Count of Sortelha, and Beatrice Coutinho, daughter of Fernando Coutinho, Marshal of the Kingdom of Portugal. On June 9, 1543, Gonçalo entered the Society of Jesus at the University of Coimbra. He brilliantly completed the course of studies. In 1556 (St.) Ignatius of Loyola confirmed his appointment as provincial of the Jesuits in India. Silveira managed the Jesuit mission in the Far East until Antonio de Quadros relieved him in 1559. Shortly afterward he departed for Africa, where he founded a mission among the Monomotapa on a tributary of the Zambesi River. He converted their chief and many tribesmen, but Arabs from Mozambique convinced the chief that he should be killed. On March 11, 1561, he was strangled. No one came to take his place, and his work among the Monomotapa died with him.

Bibliography: H. CHADWICK, *Life of Ven. Gonçalo da Silveira* (New York 1911). F. RODRIGUES, *História da Companhia de Jesus na Assistência de Portugal* (Porto, Port. 1931–). B. LEITE, *D. Gonçalo da Silveira* (Lisbon 1946). L. KOCH, *Jesuiten-Lexikon: Die Gesellschaft Jesu einst und jetzt,* (Paderborn 1934) 1645–46. C. SOMMEVOGEL et al., *Bibliothèque de la Compagnie de Jésus,* 11 vol. (Brussels-Paris 1890–1932) 7:1731–33.

[G. R. AVELLAR]

SILVERIO OF ST. TERESA

Writer, general of the Discalced Carmelites; b. Julian Fernández Gómez, Escóbados de Arriba, Burgos, Spain, March 8, 1878; d. Mazatlán, Mexico, March 10, 1954. He was the first of 13 children, eight of whom entered the Discalced Carmelite Order. After finishing his philosophical studies in the diocesan seminary of Burgos, he was professed in the Discalced Carmelites in Larrea (July 5, 1896) and was later ordained in Burgos (July 27, 1902). He became editor of the review *El Monte Carmelo*, and was appointed general historian of the Discalced Carmelites in 1912.

This work was interrupted by the preparation of his critical editions of the works of St. Teresa (1915–25) and St. John of the Cross (1927–30). Father Silverio then dedicated himself to his *Historia del Carmen Descalzo en Espãna, Portugal y America*. His strenuous literary labors did not free him from the burden of administrative office. At various times he was prior, provincial of Burgos, general definitor, vicar-general, and finally (1947–54), general of the Discalced Carmelites. During his generalate he sought to improve studies in the order, built the new International College in Rome, and visited almost all the provinces of the order. While visiting Mazatlán, Mexico, he died; his remains were transferred to the International College (1955).

The complete list of his writings, which Father Simeon de la Sgda. Familia compiled in *Zelo Zelatus Sum* (Rome 1952, 65–152), numbers 565 titles. His literary work centered on three major enterprises: *Biblioteca Mistica Carmelitana* (20 v.); *Historia del Carmen Descalzo* (15 v.); *La Carmelita Perfecta* (3 v.). He gathered a large number of documents related to the history of the Discalced Carmelites. These are preserved in Burgos under the title *Archivo Silveriano*.

Bibliography: VALENTIN DE LA CRUZ, *Fr. Silverio de Sta. Teresa: Su vida, su obra y su gobierno* (Burgos 1962). N. J. OTILIO, ''Bodas de oro de la profesión religiosa de N. M. R. P. Silverio de Sta. Teresa, Vicario General,'' *El Monte Carmelo* 50 (1946) 408–412.

[O. RODRIGUEZ]

SILVERIUS, POPE, ST.

Pontificate: June 8, 536 to 537, d. Palmaria, probably Dec. 2, 537. When Rome learned of the death of Pope AGAPETUS I, King Theodatus imposed the son of Pope Hormisdas, the subdeacon Silverius, on the Roman clergy as a means of thwarting Byzantine intrigue by means of a pro-Gothic pope. The clergy who opposed him acquiesced reluctantly with the king's decision. The council for which Pope Agapetus had called before his death was duly held in Constantinople under the presidency of Patriarch Mennas and with the pope's suite in attendance. ANTHIMUS was condemned, as were the Monophysites SE-

VERUS OF ANTIOCH and Peter of Apamea. The disappointment of the Empress THEODORA (1), who saw her desire for a restoration of the Monophysites undone, apparently led her to bargain with the Roman deacon Vigilius, papal apocrisiary in Constantinople since 533, for the election of a pope who would depose Mennas and restore Anthimus. It is not known what kind of agreement was reached, but some plan seems to have been agreed upon between the two, for Vigilius was ambitious. Theodora at first tried to win over Pope Silverius; but when he refused to restore Anthimus, she sent Vigilius to Italy with orders for the general BELISARIUS to find an excuse for deposing the pope and installing Vigilius in his stead. Vigilius arrived in Rome shortly after Belisarius entered the city; but soon Belisarius found himself besieged in turn by the Ostrogothic King Vitiges, who invested Rome for a whole year, cutting off the aqueducts and doing considerable damage to the catacombs and cemeterial basilicas outside the walls.

Belisarius was at first reluctant to carry out the orders of the empress, for he had been kindly received by Silverius, who had convinced the civic authorities to admit the Byzantine army into Rome to avoid blood shed. But the general's wife, Antonina, a confidante of Theodora, saw to it that the imperial will prevailed. Letters were forged to implicate Silverius in an attempt to deliver the city to the Goths, and the unfortunate pope was summoned to appear before Belisarius in the latter's palace on the Pincian Hill.

What appears to be an authentic version of the facts states that, accompanied only by the deacon Vigilius, Silverius penetrated to an inner chamber, where he found Antonina reclining on a couch with Belisarius at her feet. She upbraided him for attempting to betray them to the Goths; and while she was speaking, a subdeacon ripped off the pope's pallium and took him into another room, where his clothes were removed and replaced by a monk's garb. It was then announced that the pope had been deposed and a new election would be necessary (March 537). Vigilius's complicity in this affair cannot be excused. Silverius was secretly taken out of the city and banished to Patara, in Lycia. Evidently the emperor, Justinian I, was not accurately informed by his wife about what had taken place. When he found out from the bishop of Patara, he ordered the pope returned to Rome and tried. If he had been guilty of writing the traitorous letters, he was to be free to live as a bishop in exile in any city of the empire; but if the letters were forgeries, he was to be restored to his see.

Silverius was accordingly brought back to Italy; but when he arrived at Rome, Vigilius, now pope, had him dispatched to the island of Palmaria (Ponza), in the Tyrrhenian Sea. His resignation was extorted on Nov. 11, 537; and he died shortly thereafter, probably of starvation. The Byzantine historian Procopius reports that Antonina was also involved in this plot, reasoning that Silverius's death on the island would obviate any embarrassing trial. There is no trace of any veneration being paid to him in Rome before the fourteenth century. He is first listed among the saints in the eleventh century. His remains, apparently, were never removed from the island of Palmaria.

Feast: June 20.

Bibliography: *Patrologia Latina*, ed. J. P. MIGNE (Paris 1878–90) 66:85–88, spurious letters. L. DUCHESNE, *Liber pontificalis* (Paris 1886–92) 1:290–295; 3:91–92. E. CASPAR, *Geschichte de Papsttums von den Anfängen bis zur Höhe der Weltherrschaft* (Tübingen 1930–33) 2:229–233, 769. H. LECLERCQ, *Dictionnaire d'archéologie chrétienne et de liturgie* (Paris 1907–53) 13.1:1218–20. G. SCHWAIGER, *Lexikon für Theologie und Kirche*, ed. J. HOFER and K. RAHNER (Freiburg 1957–65) 9:757. R. U. MONTINI, *Le tombe dei papi* (Rome 1957). H. JEDIN, *History of the Church* (New York 1980) 2:452. J. N. D. KELLY, *Oxford Dictionary of Popes* (New York 1986) 59–60. J. RICHARDS, *Popes and Papacy the Early Middle Ages* (London 1979) 128–133. W. KOHL, *Biographisch-Bibliographisches Kirchenlexikon* 10 (Herzburg 1995).

[J. CHAPIN]

SILVESTER GUZZOLINI, ST.

Abbot, founder of the Sylvestrine Benedictines; b. Osimo, Italy, 1177; d. Montefano, Nov. 26, 1267. Silvester, born of the noble Guzzolini (or Gossolini) family, studied law at Bologna and Padua and then was ordained. In 1227 he renounced his benefice and became a hermit. Many disciples joined him, and in 1231 he built a monastery at Montefano, near Fabriano, Italy, founding the so-called Blue or Sylvestrine BENEDICTINES, who were approved by Innocent IV in 1247. At the death of the founder when be was about 80 years old, the new congregation had at least 11 monasteries. Later there were as many as 56 in Italy, Portugal, and Brazil. The Sylvestrine Congregation still exists in Italy (152 monks) and in Ceylon (43 monks), where they have charge of the missionary Diocese of Kandy (Ann Pont 1963). Silvester was canonized by Clement VIII in 1598.

Feast: Nov. 26.

Bibliography: His life, written between 1275 and 1280 by his successor Abbot ANDREW DE GIACOMO, was printed 1772 in Jesi, Italy, in *Vita di S. Silvestro Abate* by C. S. FRANCESCHINI. A. M. ZIMMERMANN, *Kalendarium Benedictinum: Die Heiligen und Seligen des Benediktinerorderns und seiner Zweige*, 4 v. (Metten 1933–38) 3:358–360. A. M. CANCELLIERI, *S. S. Abate . . .* (Matelica, Italy 1942). A. BUTLER, *The Lives of the Saints*, rev. ed. H. THURSTON and D. ATTWATER, 4v. (New York 1956) 4:422–423.

[M. A. HABIG]

SILVESTRELLI, BERNARD MARIA OF JESUS, BL.

Baptized Cesare, Passionist priest; b. Nov. 7, 1831, Rome, Italy; d. there Dec. 9, 1911, in Morricone Monastery.

Cesare was born into Roman nobility, the third of the seven children of Gian Tommasso and Teresa Silvestrelli. Cesare attended Jesuit schools, including the Collegio Romano. Although he entered the Passionist novitiate on Monte Argentaro (1854), he was forced to leave because of ill health. He continued his studies and was ordained a secular priest (1855). Four months later he asked and was given permission to re-enter the Passionists at Morrovalle, where he was given the name Bernard Maria of Jesus (Apr. 28, 1857) and studied with St. Gabriel Possenti.

Following the completion of his studies, Father Bernard Maria served the Passionists in various capacities: novice master (1865–69) and rector of the new Scala Santa (''Holy Stairs'') monastery next to the Lateran (1869–75); provincial consultator (1875–76); and vice-provincial (1876–78). Silvestrelli was elected and re-elected superior general (1878–84, 1884–89, 1893–99, 1899–1905, 1905–07) and instituted a number of reforms within the order.

To maintain the order's ideals, he published the *vitae* of the companions of St. Paul of the Cross. Additionally, he established preparatory schools to form future candidates for the novitiate. As superior general, he expanded the congregation into Spain, Mexico, and Latin America, established a novitiate in Bulgaria, and founded the international house of studies at Saints John and Paul in Rome. Silvestrelli visited all the Passionist provinces, including those in northern Europe, Spain, and, in 1896, the United States to better understand the difficulties pursuant to Passionist life in these localities. He was a man known for his prudence, gentleness, and charity.

Pope John Paul II beatified Silvestrelli on Oct. 16, 1988.

Feast: December 9 (Passionists).

Bibliography: F. GIORGINI, *Bernardo Maria Silvestrelli Passionista* (Rome 1988); English tr. P. ROGERS (Rome 1990). F. G. ZICCHETTI, *Padre Bernardo M. Silvestrelli Passionista* (Recanati 1988).

[K. I. RABENSTEIN]

SIMEON BARSABAE, ST.

Martyr, bishop of Seleucia-Ctesiphon, Mesopotamia; d. Karkha de Ledan, Mesopotamia, April 17, 344. *Bar sabb'ē* signifies the son of a dyer, but Simeon is first mentioned in the acts of a synod under Dadischo in 424 as an opponent of Papa bar 'Aggai, Bishop of Seleucia. Although elected to succeed the deposed Aggai, be took office only upon the latter's death. He is possibly the object of the denunciation in St. APHRAATES' demonstration (14.8.9.25). As bishop Simeon faced internal difficulties and the persecution of Sapor II, who suspected him of Byzantine leanings on religious grounds, imprisoned him under penalty of paying ransom, and eventually put him to death together with two priests, Abdhaikla and Hanania; the eunuch, Gushtahazad; Simeon's sister, Tarbo; and the chief of the royal artisans, Puseik; who formed the first group of Persian martyrs under the Sassanid dynasty. The *passio* supplying the details of his death seems authentic in both the simplicity of its narration and the absence of miraculous happenings. The date of his death, between 341 and 344, is disputed, and SYNAXARY of CONSTANTINOPLE varies between April 14 and 17 for his feast.

Feast: April 14.

Bibliography: J. P. KIRSCH, *Lexikon für Theologie und Kirche*, ed. M. BUCHBERGER, 10 v. (Freiburg 1930–38) 9:574. MARUTA, *Acta sanctorum martyrum orientalium,* ed. S. E. ASSEMANI, 2 v. (Rome 1748) 1:10–36. P. BEDJAN, ed., *Acta martyrum et sanctorum,* 7 v. (Paris 1890–97) 2:123–130. M. KMOSKO, tr. and ed., *Martyrium Beati Simeonis Bar Sabba'e* (*Patrologia syriaca*, ed. R. GRAFFIN et al., 3 v. [Paris 1894–1926] 2; 1907) 715–960. J. LABOURT, *Le Christianisme dans l'empire Perse* (Paris 1904). P. PEETERS, ''La Date du martyre de S. Syméon,'' B. DE GAIFFIER, *Analecta Bollandiana* (Brussels 1882–) 56 (1938) 118–143.

[A. PENNA]

SIMEON OF DURHAM

English chronicler; d. *c.* 1130–38. He entered the Benedictine monastery at JARROW probably soon after 1071. When Jarrow was transferred to Durham (1083), Simeon made his profession there, in 1085 or 1086. He eventually became precentor. According to the monastery's obituary, Simeon died on October 14, between 1130 and 1138. Between 1104 and 1108 Simeon compiled the *Historia Ecclesiae Dunelmensis.* This work traces the history of the See of DURHAM from its beginnings to 1096, when Abbot William of St. Cerilef died. It depends on BEDE's *Ecclesiastical History of the English People* and *Life of St. Cuthbert.* Simeon's history of England, *Historia Anglorum et Dacorum,* is divided into three sections. The first covers the period from 732 to 957, and is based primarily on the *Annales Alfredi* of ASSER; it contains valuable information on the north country. The second section extends to 1119, and utilizes the *Chronicon* of FLORENCE OF WORCESTER. The third section (covering 1119–29) is an original work on contemporary history. Some minor works and letters are now lost. All his works have been edited by Thomas Arnold; his historical writings have been translated into English by Joseph Stevenson.

Bibliography: *Symeonis Monachi opera omnia,* ed. T. ARNOLD, 2 v. (*Rerum Brittanicarum medii aevi scriptores*; 1882–85). J. STEVENSON, "S. of D.," *The Church Historians of England,* v.3.2 (1855). C. GROSS, *The Sources and Literature of English History* (2d ed. London 1915). C. L. KINGSFORD, *The Dictionary of National Biography from the Earliest Times to 1900,* 63 v. (London 1885–1900) 18:254–255. F. L. CROSS, *The Oxford Dictionary of the Christian Church* (London 1957) 1256. P. H. BLAIR, "Some Observations on the *Historia* . . . ," *Celt and Saxon: Studies in Early British Border,* ed. K. H. JACKSON et al. (Cambridge, Eng. 1963) 63–118.

[M. A. MULHOLLAND]

SIMEON OF POLIRONE, ST.

Hermit, later a Benedictine; d. Polirone, near Mantua, Italy, July 26, 1016. According to a legendary vita, published soon after his death, Simeon was originally from Armenia (hence he is sometimes called Simeon the Armenian). Abandoning his wife and family, he became a Basilian monk and hermit. He undertook many arduous pilgrimages throughout Palestine, France, and Spain, and came to Rome (*c.* 983), where he was charged with being a heretic. By order of Benedict VII he was examined and found to be orthodox. He was renowned for his piety and heroic charity, and for numerous miracles performed during life and after death. His cult was approved by Benedict VIII (1024) and Leo IX (1049). In 1913 his relics were solemnly exposed.

Feast: July 26.

Bibliography: P. JAFFÉ, *Regesta pontificum romanorum ab condita ecclesia ad annum post Christum natum 1198,* ed. S. LÖWENFELD et al., 2 v. (2d ed. Leipzig 1881–88; repr. Graz 1956) 1:4055, 4310, 4729. *Acta Sanctorum* July 6:319–337. G. D. GORDINI, *Lexikon für Theologie und Kirche*, ed. J. HOFER and K. RAHNER, 10 v. (2d, new ed. Freiburg 1957–65); suppl., *Das Zweite Vatikanische Konzil: Dokumente und Kommentare*, ed. H. S. BRECHTER et al., pt. 1 (1966) 9:762. A. BUTLER, *The Lives of the Saints*, rev. ed. H. THURSTON and D. ATTWATER, 4v. (New York 1956) 3:190. A. M. ZIMMERMANN, *Kalendarium Benedictinum: Die Heiligen und Seligen des Benediktinerorderns und seiner Zwiege,* 4. (Metten 1933–38) 2:500–501.

[F. D. LAZENBY]

SIMEON OF SYRACUSE, ST.

Byzantine monk, recluse at Trier, Germany; b. Syracuse, Sicily, *ca.* 970; d. Trier, June 1, 1035. At the age of seven he moved to Constantinople, where his father, a Greek, held a military position. After considerable success in studies, he journeyed to Jerusalem and at Bethlehem was ordained deacon. He then entered the monastery of Mt. Sinai. In 1027 his abbot sent him to collect alms promised by Duke Richard of Normandy. Near Alexandria he was almost killed by pirates, but he escaped to Antioch, where he was well received by the patriarch. There he met Richard, Abbot of VERDUN-SUR-MEUSE, on his way to the Holy Land. On Richard's return, Simeon traveled with him to Rome and then arrived in Verdun about the end of October 1027. After visiting the Duke of Normandy, he went to Trier with Eberwin, abbot of Saint-Martin in Trier, whom he had also met in Antioch. In 1028 he accompanied Abp. Poppo of Trier to the Holy Land. On their return, *ca.* 1030, Simeon established himself as a hermit in a tower near the Porta Nigra in Trier. There he died, and according to letters of Pope Benedict IX to Abp. Poppo, he seems to have been canonized about Christmas of that same year. His life, written by Abbot Eberwin, is noted for its authenticity, and is a valuable historical source for precrusade pilgrim routes (*see* ITINERARIA).

Feast: June 1.

Bibliography: *Acta Sanctorum* June 1:85–104. P. THOMSEN, "Der heilige Symeon von Trier," *Zeitschrift des deutschen Palästinavereins* 62 (1939) 144–161. H. DAUPHIN, *Le Bienheureux Richard: Abbé de Saint-Vanne de Verdun* (Louvain 1946). M. COENS, "Un Document inédit sur le culte de S. Syméon moine d'Orient et reclus à Trèves," B. DE GAIFFIER, *Analecta Bollandiana* 68 (1950) 181–196.

[G. T. DENNIS]

SIMILARITY

Similarity or likeness (Gr. ὁμοίωσις Lat. *similitudo*) denotes some agreement between two or more things, something short of absolute identity, a partial sameness, as in "not exactly the same but similar." Thus similarity indicates some shared unity of entities somewhat the same, and similitude means any relative sameness. This article sketches, in successive paragraphs, various uses of the notion in epistemology, metaphysics, patristic theology, and Thomistic theology.

In KNOWLEDGE, the distinction of the knower and the known is more evident than their relative sameness. Yet a similitude of the thing somehow present to the knower re-presents the thing, and the comparison of the knower's possession and the thing's offering furnishes the known identity called TRUTH. SCIENCE itself is based on the causality of this likeness as provided by objects and present in subjects, and thus explains how man knows something to be so, and also why it is so—such explanation also accounting for his CERTITUDE. (*See* EPISTEMOLOGY.)

In distinguishing the properties of the basic CATEGORIES OF BEING (*Cat.* 11a 15–19), ARISTOTLE shows likeness to be the first feature of QUALITY. With further precision, in the *Metaphysics* (1018a 15–19; 1021a 10–14; 1054b 51055a 2) he coordinates ''the similar'' with the basic traits of all ''being,'' ''one,'' and ''same,'' and thus discloses various degrees of UNITY. ''One'' applied to such variations of being as substance, quantity, and quality renders the basic notions of ''same,'' ''equal,'' and ''similar,'' respectively. But since ''same'' extends beyond things substantially one (or numerically the same: as Plato and ''the author of the *Timaeus*''), a further distinction may be made between things specifically the same (Plato and Socrates), those generically the same (Plato and his dog), and finally, those analogically the same (Plato and Pluto)—with greatest identity in the first and the least in the last. Thus, a second view of ''similar,'' under the title of sameness, escapes the limits of the accidental unity of quality to apply to three degrees of relative sameness that depart from the absolute, or numerically self-same. So Aristotle provides two usages: the univocal, based on quality, and the analogical, based on any formal qualification. The latter furnishes the basic intentional unities: SPECIES naming similitude in nature or form (disregarding the numerical diversity of individuals); GENUS denoting a more remote similitude (by prescinding from specific differences); and the analogical unity of those not so obviously alike intrinsically, but manifesting similitude in acting alike or affording a basis for being understood similarly (*see* ANALOGY).

The Greek Fathers seem to have read with Philo's eyes the creation account of man as made ''to the image and likeness'' of God (Gn 1.26–27; Septuagint εἰκωνόμοίωσις). IRENAEUS took image for nature, and likeness for grace; ORIGEN, with most Platonists, gave image a dynamic character terminating in assimilation to God by likening, thus contrasting image and likeness as beginning and end of human life. This likening by resemblance assumes in St. CLEMENT OF ALEXANDRIA the function of grace in Irenaeus, supplying the supernatural perfection lacking to nature. GREGORY OF NYSSA sees here two aspects of the same reality: εἰκόν naming the static terms of beginning and end; ὁμοίσωις giving the dynamic advance from the one to the other, the progressive retrieving of the divine image once had, but lost by sin.

St. THOMAS AQUINAS finds image (*Summa theologiae* 1a, 35) the proper title for the Son; he sees man created to image the Trinity just by being human, in knowing and loving (1a, 93) and fulfilling (1a2ae, prol.) his destiny by assimilation (i.e., with increasing likeness to God) through a life of virtue, aided by the exemplarity of Christ (3a, prol.). The various facets of likeness are brilliantly displayed in the view of beings unequally sharing in the absolute perfection of existence (1a, 4), inherently seeking greater realization of that perfection (1a, 5–6), and tending toward reunion with their principle (1a, 42–46) by imitating their cause (1a, 50.1; 103.4; 1a2ae, 109.6; etc.), with similitude as the cause of love (1a2ae, 27.3) and all delight (32.7). The patterns of similitude measured between model and copy are disclosed in the tracts on ideas (1a, 15) and exemplarity (1a, 44.3); the dynamism of assimilation is seen in *C. gent.* 3.19–21.

See Also: EXEMPLARISM; IMAGE OF GOD; JESUS CHRIST, ARTICLES ON; RELATION.

Bibliography: V. MIANO, *Enciclopedia filosofica* (Venice-Rome 1957) 4:784–786. P. T. CAMELOT, ''La Théologie de l'image de Dieu,'' *Revue des sciences philosophiques et théologiques* 40 (1956) 443–471. C. FABRO, *Participation et causalité selon S. Thomas d'Aquin* (Louvain 1961).

[B. M. MATTINGLY]

SIMON, APOSTLE, ST.

One of the TWELVE chosen by Jesus. In the lists of the 12 APOSTLES, Simon (Σίμων, a genuine Greek name, but used by the Jews as a Hellenized form of the Hebrew name *šim'ōn,* Simeon) is named in the 11th place in Mt 10.4 and Mk 3.18, in the 10th place in Lk 6.15 and Acts 1.13. In the first two Gospels he is called ''the Cananean'' (ὁ Καναναῖος), in Luke and Acts, ''the zealot'' (ὁ ζηλωτής). These titles were apparently added for the purpose of distinguishing him from the chief Apostle Simon Peter. The word ζηλωτής is the Greek translation of the Aramaic word *qan'ānai,* which is merely transliterated in Mt 10.4; Mk 3.18 as ὁ Καναναῖος, both words meaning zealot. Some MSS in Mt 10.4 and Mk 3.18 have incorrectly ὁ Κανανίτης, which has been understood as meaning the man from Cana (so, e.g., by St. Jerome, *Patrologia Latina* 23:763; 26: 63), and therefore Simon was identified by some of the Church Fathers with the unnamed bridegroom of Jn 2.9. In any case, neither Καναναῖος nor Κανανίτης has anything to do with the word Canaanite. It is not certain why Simon was given this epithet; it was probably either because he had belonged to the Jewish party of the ZEALOTS before he became an Apostle, or because of his zeal for the Mosaic Law (cf. the use of the term in Acts 22.3; Gal 1.14).

Very little is known about this Apostle. Many would identify him with Simon the brother of Jesus (Mt 13.55; Mk 6.3), but this identification does not seem likely. The latter is the same as Simon son of Clopas who succeeded

James, ''the brother of the Lord,'' as bishop of Jerusalem (A.D. 62) and was crucified under Trajan *c.* A.D. 107; see Hegesippus as quoted by Eusebius (*Historia Ecclesiastica* 3:11; 32.1–2). According to later legends, particularly in the apocryphal *Acts of Simon and Jude,* Simon the Apostle preached in various parts of the Near East and was martyred by being sawed in two (a motif borrowed from the apocryphal Martyrdom of Isaiah). In iconography he is usually represented with a saw, the supposed instrument of his martyrdom, though sometimes with a book, probably in reference to his zeal for the law. In legend and in iconography he is generally associated with St. JUDE THADDEUS.

Feast: Oct. 28 (Western Church); May 10 (Eastern Church).

Bibliography: J. BLINZLER, ''Simon Zelotes,'' *Lexikon für Theologie und Kirche*, ed. J. HOFER and K. RAHNER (Freiburg 1957–65) 9:772–773; ''Simon, Bruder Jesu,'' *ibid.* 9:765; ''Simon der Apostel, Simon der Herrenbruder, und Bischof Symeon von Jerusalem,'' *Passauer Studien: Festschrift für Bischof Dr. Simon Konrad Landersdorfer, OSB* (Passau 1953) 25–55.

[J. A. LEFRANÇOIS]

''The Apostle Simon,'' painting by Nicolaus Alexander Mair von Landshut, 1496. (©Alexander Burkatowski/CORBIS)

SIMON, RICHARD

Often referred to as the ''father of Biblical criticism''; b. Dieppe, May 13, 1638; d. there, April 11, 1712. Simon, of a middle-class working family, completed the course of studies at the *collège* of Dieppe with distinction, lived some time in Paris, and then, in 1662, entered the Congregation of the Oratory. He became regent of philosophy at the *collège* of Juilly, was ordained on Sept. 20, 1670, and then took up residence at the Oratory in Paris on the Rue Saint-Honoré. After a period in which he applied himself to the study of the Eastern Churches and Judaism, he published his *Histoire critique du Vieux Testament* (Paris 1678). This work provoked the opposition of J. B. BOSSUET and of many other theologians, both Catholic and Protestant, and led to his expulsion from the Oratory. In retirement, first at Bolleville (in the Diocese of Rouen), he published several works under pseudonyms: *Histoire de l'origine et des progrès des revenus ecclésiastiques* (Frankfort 1684), *Histoire critique du texte du N.T.* (Rotterdam 1689), *Histoire critique des versions du N.T.* (Rotterdam 1690), *Histoire critique des principaux commentateurs du N.T.* (Rotterdam 1693), *Le N.T. de N.S.J.-C. traduit sur l'ancienne édition latine, avec des remarques littérales et critiques* (Trévoux 1702), and others.

Exceptionally learned in a number of fields (Biblical criticism, Eastern languages and literature, history of ecclesiastical institutions), Simon was clearly gifted with rare genius for critical study. Working independently of B. Spinoza and animated by a quite different spirit, he alone of the Christians of his time discovered and attempted to resolve the problem of the composition of the Pentateuch. In spite of his deep and genuine attachment to the Catholic faith, many regarded his views with suspicion. He had no disciples, and his work had no influence on the history of exegesis.

Bibliography: A. BERNUS, ''Richard Simon'' in *Essai de bibliographie oratorienne,* ed. A. INGOLD (Paris 1880–82). J. STEINMANN, *Richard Simon et les origines de l'exégèse biblique* (Bruges 1960).

[P. AUVRAY]

SIMON, YVES RENÉ MARIE

Catholic philosopher; b. Cherbourg, France, March 14, 1903; d. South Bend, Ind., May 11, 1961. Yves, the son of Auguste Simon and Berthe Porquet la Ferronnière, received his secondary education at Cherbourg. After one year at the Lycée Louis-le-Grand, he continued at the University of Paris and at the Catholic Institute of Paris to receive his doctoral degree. Among his distinguished professors were Abbé Lallement and Jacques Maritain.

Although a man of enormous erudition, it is safe to say that the works of St. Thomas Aquinas and of P. J. Proudhon (1809–65) exerted a profound influence on Simon. In 1930 he married Paule Dromard, who was studying Thomism at Paris. His concern with the growth of the intellect in the service of moral life are evident in *Philosophy of Democratic Government* (Chicago 1951) and *A General Theory of Authority* (Notre Dame 1962), both of which may be regarded as classics in political philosophy. In purely speculative philosophy his greatest work is *Introduction à l'ontologie du connaître* (Paris 1934). After eight years at the University of Lille, he went to the U.S. to serve as professor of philosophy at the University of Notre Dame and at the University of Chicago. Most of his students would agree with Simon's widow: "A non-specialized philosopher by principle, he, nevertheless, made his mark principally in metaphysics, logic, and political philosophy" [*The New Scholasticism* 37 (1963) 501]. Her comment is in an article, "The Papers of Yves R. Simon," that analyzes Simon's philosophical inquiries and proposes the posthumous publication of several major works in varying stages of readiness when death overtook him.

Bibliography: M. HOEHN, ed., *Catholic Authors* (Newark 1948). Data on Simon's manuscripts are available at the Maritain Center, University of Notre Dame, Ind.

[G. J. MCMORROW]

SIMON BALLACHI, BL.

Dominican; b. *c.* 1258; d. *c.* 1329. He entered the Dominican house at Rimini as a lay brother at the age of 27. Biographers in the 17th century identified him as the son of Count Rodulfus de Ballochi of S. Archangelo, a town near Rimini, but no local document or historian of the period confirms this information. Simon, employed principally in the monastery garden, also taught catechism to the young children. He lived a life of great humility and disciplined his body with corporal penances for the conversion of sinners. As a result of his penances, he became blind at 59. He lived thus with such courage and cheerfulness for 12 years that from the day of his death he was regarded as a saint. His body was buried in the Dominican church of St. Cataldus at Rimini. After several translations, Simon's relics were finally interred in the church of S. Archangelo on July 3, 1817. PIUS VII in 1820 confirmed his cult for the Diocese of Rimini and for the Dominican Order.

Feast: Nov. 3.

Bibliography: *Summarium probationum ad cultus confirmationem obtinendam* (Rome 1820). *Acta Sanctorum* Nov. 2.1:209–212. J. L. BAUDOT and L. CHAUSSIN, *Vies des saints et des bienheureux selon l'ordre du calendrier avec l'historique des fêtes,* ed. by the Benedictines of Paris, 12 v. (Paris 1935–56) 11:101. A. BUTLER, *The Lives of the Saints*, rev. ed. H. THURSTON and D. ATTWATER (New York, 1956) 4:254–255. G. LÖHR, *Lexikon für Theologie und Kirche*, ed. J. HOFER and K. RAHNER, 10 v. (2d, new ed. Freiburg 1957–65) 9:574.

[M. G. MCNEIL]

SIMON DE GHENT

English medieval scholar and bishop; b. London; d. London, April 2, 1315. He was born of Flemish merchant stock. The first record of Simon is from 1268 when Abp. WALTER GIFFARD of Canterbury admitted him to the rectory of Wilford (Nottinghamshire) to help defray his educational expenses, presumably at Oxford. From 1284 to 1297 he was archdeacon of Oxford. He incepted at Oxford as doctor of theology probably *c.* 1290–91 and was regent master there when elected chancellor of the university (1291–93).

He was consecrated bishop of SALISBURY in 1297 and devoted himself with indefatigable zeal to the spiritual and temporal administration and reform of his diocese. His itineraries alone fill almost 20 pages (xxvii-xlvi) of the introduction to his *Registrum.* He called a synod to reform his cathedral statutes; its work covered the whole field of cathedral legislation and is still recognized (*V. C. H. Wiltshire* 3:172–173). He made provision for the housing and teaching of the choristers. He established a guildhall for the city of Salisbury (as bishop he held the lordship of the city) and licensed its fortification by ditch and walls. He dealt vigorously with the many abuses that were rampant within the diocese, e.g., unrepaired and unconsecrated churches, absenteeism, pluralism, etc. Outside his diocese, he was frequently called upon to act as arbitrator. He took the side of the barons in their war against King EDWARD II and proclaimed the "Ordinances" in St. Paul's churchyard in 1311. In the last years of his life, his health failed rapidly and his activities were much reduced.

Of his scholastic work, little has survived beyond a few notes in the Assisi MS; a sermon preached when he was chancellor, Ash Wednesday, Feb. 11, 1293 (ed. F. Pelster, *Oxford Theology . . . ,* 205–215); a short *Meditatio de statu praelati;* and his Latin translation of the *ANCRENE RIWLE* (ed. F. M. Powicke). His reputation for sanctity is evidenced by pilgrimages to his tomb (in Salisbury cathedral).

Bibliography: *Registrum Simonis de Gandavo,* ed. C. T. FLOWER and M. C. B. DAWES, 2 v. (Canterbury and York Society 40–41; 1934) v.1, introd. *The Victoria History of the County of Wiltshire,* ed. R. B. PUGH and E. CRITTALL (London 1953) v.3. *A Bio-*

graphical Register of the University of Oxford to A.D. 1500 2:759–760.

[T. C. CROWLEY]

SIMON DE LONGPRÉ, MARIE CATHERINE OF ST. AUGUSTINE, BL.

Baptized Catherine, virgin of the Hospitallers of Mercy of St. Augustine; b. May 13, 1632, Saint-Sauveur le Vicomte, France; d. May 8, 1668, Québec, Canada. Catherine's vocation was awakened by her grandparents, who lovingly tended the sick and poor in their own home. She joined a new order of Augustinian hospitaller sisters and received the habit, Oct. 24, 1646, the same day her biological sister pronounced her vows. Marie Catherine made her own vows on May 4, 1648. The two sisters were among the first to respond to the call for women religious to minister in New France (now Canada). Marie Catherine set sail the day before her sixteenth birthday. Despite the hardships of colonial life, the young sister remained cheerful as she cooked for and tended the sick, sharing with them her medical knowledge and spiritual wisdom. Before her death at 36, she was novice mistress for her community (1665–68). Pope John Paul II beatified Sister Marie Catherine on Apr. 23, 1989.

Feast: May 8 (Canada).

Bibliography: G. BOUCHER, *Dieu et Satan dans la vie de Catherine de Saint-Augustin, 1632-1668* (Tournai 1979). A. MERLAUD, *L'épopée fantastique d'une jeune Normande: Catherine de Longpré* (Paris 1981).

[K. I. RABENSTEIN]

SIMON FIDATI OF CASCIA, BL.

Augustinian friar, preacher, and spiritual author; b. Cascia, Umbria, 1295; d. Florence, Feb. 2, 1348; buried in Cascia. Simon first studied natural philosophy in Cascia. As a result of a conversion experience that probably was occasioned by the Franciscan spiritualist Angelo Clareno, Simon turned to theology and joined the Augustinians. Until Clareno died in 1337, he remained Simon's spiritual advisor. Simon was an active and successful preacher, traveling between Florence and Rome, helping the persecuted Clareno maintain contact with his spiritual followers by transmitting messages between them. On Sept. 6, 1338, he moved to Rome, and from that time until almost the end of his life he worked on a commentary on the Gospels under the title *De gestis domini salvatoris*. His version of the life of Christ contain treatises on John the Baptist, Mary, the sermons and miracles of Jesus, the testament of love, and the suffering and resurrection of Jesus, as well as commentaries on Christian justice and rule. This work was circulated widely outside of Italy and exercised a continuing influence on the spirituality of the late middle ages.

In his writings, Simon urged his readers to a life modeled on Christ (*cristiformitas*). His interpretation of the Scriptures had a devotional, rather than a academic, goal. Simon strongly emphasized Jesus Christ, faith, grace, and Holy Scripture as the norms of theology. He also rejected mixing quotes from Scripture with philosophical propositions. Simon influenced Martin Luther's *Aristoteleskritik*, and probably Luther's general theological approach, although the latter has not been proved.

Feast: Feb. 16.

Bibliography: W. ECKERMANN, ed., *De gestis domini salvatoris: Erstveroffentlichnung durch Johannes con Salerno Nach dem Tode Simons (kritische Edition)* (Wurzburg and Rome 1998). N. MATTIOLI, *Epistolarium: Briefsammlung in lateinischer und italienischer Sprache* (Rome 1898) 259–519. Literature. W. ECKERMANN, ''Simon Fidati con Cascia, Europaische Theologie im lateinischen Mittelater,'' *Augustiniana* 47 (1997) 339–356. G. CASCIANO, *Beato Simone Fidati* (Tern 1993). W. ECKERMANN and F.-B. STAMMKOTTER, ''Die Rezeption des S. Fidati con Cascia,'' *Analecta Augustiniana* 55 (1992) 221–246.

[W. ECKERMANN]

SIMON HINTON

English Dominican theologian. He received a bachelor's degree at Oxford by 1239, the doctorate in theology *c.* 1248, and until 1250 or 1254 acted as master at the Oxford Dominican priory, probably succeeding RICHARD FISHACRE. He served as provincial of the English Dominicans (1254–61), but was removed from office by the general chapter for failure to comply with regulations of the order. The issue involved a refusal to accept foreign students at the studium of the order at Oxford. When sent to lecture at the Dominican school at Cologne, he was permitted to return to England within a year. A theologian of the Augustinian school, Hinton was not an outstanding thinker. His works, however, are useful in shedding light on instructional methods at mid-13th-century Oxford. His writings include scriptural treatises, theological works, and a manual for study. Besides several *Quaestiones disputatae,* he has left scriptural commentaries and glosses, and postils on the Minor Prophets. The *Summa ad instructionem iuniorum* was a manual of practical theology and enjoyed wide usage from the 13th to the 15th century.

Bibliography: A. DONDAINE, ''La Somme de Simon de Hinton,'' *Recherches de théologie ancienne et médiévale* 9 (1937)

5–22, 205–218. B. SMALLEY, ''The *Quaestiones* of Simon of Hinton,'' *Studies in Medieval History Presented to Frederich Maurice Powicke,* ed. R. W. HUNT et al. (Oxford 1948) 209–222. A. WALZ, ''The *Exceptiones* from the *Summa* of Simon of H.,'' *Angelicum* 13 (1936) 283–368. A. B. EMDEN, *A Biographical Register of the University of Oxford to A.D. 1500* (Oxford 1892–1921) 2:937.

[J. F. HINNEBUSCH]

SIMON ISLIP

Archbishop of Canterbury; b. probably at the village of Islip, near Oxford, England; d. Mayfield, Sussex, April 26, 1366. He prepared himself in both canon and civil law at Oxford and entered into a career as a lawyer in the ecclesiastical courts. He served the court of the bishop of Lincoln and later the Court of ARCHES, whose principal officer he became in 1344. He held canonries in Lincoln, Lichfield, and London cathedrals as well as other benefices. When both JOHN DE OFFORD and THOMAS BRADWARDINE were successively struck down in the plague of 1349 shortly after their appointments to the See of Canterbury, Islip was provided at the King's request; his consecration took place on Dec. 20, 1349. He took action to remedy the dislocations caused by the plague epidemics and earned the unpopularity of the secular clergy by keeping their salaries at the preplague level. In 1361 Islip founded Canterbury Hall at Oxford to be supervised by the monks of Christ Church, Canterbury. Its charter of 1363 provided for a warden and 11 fellows, both secular and regular (including four monks of Christ Church). In 1365 Islip's statutes altered the college's nature and made it a secular college, and Master John WYCLIF became its new warden. Moreover, Islip settled by amicable agreement the long-standing controversy between Canterbury and York over the latter archbishop's carrying his cross in the southern province. Authorship of the *Speculum regis Edwardi* was at one time attributed to Islip but is now more properly attributed to Abp. SIMON MEPHAM. Two years before his consecration Islip was in the King's service as keeper of his privy seal and, as archbishop, he was used on several diplomatic missions by Edward III. His body was buried before the rood in Canterbury cathedral not far front the body of his nephew, Abp. William Whittlesey.

Bibliography: W. F. HOOK, *Lives of the Archbishops of Canterbury,* 12 v. (London 1860–84). J. TAIT, ''On the Date and Authorship of the *Speculum Regis Edwardi,*'' *English Historical Review* 16 (1901) 110–115. T. F. TOUT, *The Dictionary of National Biography from the Earliest Times to 1900,* (London 1885–1900) 10:511–514. J. R. L HIGHFIELD, ''The English Hierarchy in the Reign of Edward III,'' *Transactions of the Royal Historical Society,* 5th ser., 6 (1956) 115–138. *A Biographical Register of the University of Oxford to A.D. 1500* (Oxford 1957–59) 2:1006–08. M. MCKISACK, *The 14th Century, 1307–1399* (Oxford 1959).

[F. D. LOGAN]

SIMON LANGHAM

Archbishop of Canterbury; b. probably Langham, Rutlandshire, England; d. Avignon, July 22, 1376. By 1339–40 he was a monk of Westminster Abbey, and from 1346 to 1348 he studied at Oxford. He was elected prior and then abbot of Westminster in the spring of 1349, the year of the Black Death. His economic skill was quickly shown by his reorganization of the abbey's finances, which was so successful that he was able to rebuild the cloisters. In 1360 Edward III appointed him treasurer of England. Elected bishop of ELY in 1361 he refused to change to London, to which he was also elected in the same year. Soon he was appointed chancellor of England (1363), an office he resigned in 1366 on his election to Canterbury, but not before he had begun the custom whereby the chancellor's speech at the opening of Parliament is delivered in English. As primate of England, Langham introduced legislation against pluralism, though ironically he was to become an extreme exponent of it. He removed WYCLIF from the headship of Canterbury Hall, Oxford. Since Langham had offended the king by accepting the title of cardinal priest in 1368 without the king's permission, he resigned his archbishopric and became a leading diplomat of the AVIGNON PAPACY. He was rewarded with many preferments in England and the title of cardinal bishop of Palestrina (1373). By the time of his death he had accumulated books, plate, and ornament calculated as equivalent to $840,000 in 1955 currency (Knowles). He left everything to Westminster Abbey, hence his title as the second founder of the abbey and his remarkable tomb designed by Henry Yevele.

Bibliography: A. B. EMDEN, *A Biographical Register of the University of Oxford to A.D. 1500* 2:1095–97. J. A. ROBINSON, ''S. L., Abbot of Westminster,'' *Church Quarterly Review* 66 (1908) 339–366. D. KNOWLES, *The Religious Orders in England* 2:54–56. C. L. KINGSFORD, *The Dictionary of National Biography from the Earliest Times to 1900* 11:540–541. M. MCKISACK, *The Fourteenth Century, 1307–1399* (Oxford 1959).

[D. NICHOLL]

SIMON MAGUS

A magician of Samaria converted to Christianity by PHILIP THE DEACON (Acts 8.9–24). The title Magus, given him in tradition, is from the Greek μάγος (a loanword from Persian) meaning an astrologer, diviner, sorcerer. While μάγος is not found in the account in Acts, Luke writes that Simon was ''practising magic'' (μαγεύων) and that many were ''bewitched'' by his ''sorceries'' (μαγείαις). *See* MAGIC.

The conversion of Samaria was a significant development in the early Church. It marked an important step in the fulfillment of the Lord's promise, "You will be witnesses for me in Jerusalem and in all Judea and Samaria and even to the very ends of the earth" (Acts 1.8). After the death of Stephen, which marked the beginning of a period of persecution for the Church, Philip preached the gospel to the SAMARITANS with extraordinary success. This was impressive in view of the fact that the people of Samaria were much given over to sorcery under the leadership of a certain Simon, who had previously astounded everyone by his magical powers. Luke tells us that "Simon also himself believed, and after his baptism attached himself to Philip; and at the sight of the signs and exceedingly great miracles being wrought, he was amazed" (Acts 8.13).

When the Apostles in Jerusalem heard of Philip's success in preaching to the Samaritans, who were not regarded as belonging to the Jewish community, they sent Peter and John to them. On their arrival, "they laid hands on them, and they [the converts] received the Holy Spirit" (v. 17). When Simon saw that the Apostles had this special power, he offered Peter and John money so that they would give it to him also; they refused and judged him worthy of God's wrath (v. 20). Simon thereupon repented and asked their prayers that God might not punish him. The story of Simon's attempt to buy spiritual power has produced the word SIMONY, traffic in sacred things.

From the NT we know nothing more of Simon Magus. Justin Martyr (2d Christian century) goes beyond the story in Acts, stating that Simon claimed to be a god and attracted many disciples in a false sect that endured until Justin's time (*1 Apol.* 26). After Justin, later writers, especially Irenaeus (*Adversus Haereses* 1.23), describe him as the founder of the Simonians, a gnostic sect, and as the archetype of heretics. Some even portray him as the Antichrist. Several legends are told of him in apocryphal literature, e.g., of his dispute with Peter and Paul before Nero, in which Simon, to prove his divinity, tries to fly to heaven but falls to his death (Pseudo–Marcellus).

Bibliography: É. AMANN, *Dictionnaire de la Bible,* suppl. ed. L. PIROT et. al. 1:499–500. G. KLEIN, *Die Religion in Geschichte und Gegenwart*[3] 6:38–39.

[J.A.GRASSI]

SIMON MEPHAM

Archbishop of Canterbury; b. Mepham, Kent, England; d. Mayfield, Sussex, Oct. 12,1333. He studied at Oxford, acquiring his M.A. by 1295 and becoming a doctor of theology by 1315. Consecrated archbishop of Canterbury in June 1328, he held provincial councils at St. Paul's, London, January-February 1329 (where he proclaimed the Feast of the IMMACULATE CONCEPTION); at Winchester March 11, 1330, and at Mayfield, Sussex, July 27, 1332. In 1329 he refused to install Annibale da Ceccano, Archbishop of Naples, as rector of Maidstone, was subsequently cited to the Curia, and was suspended by Pope JOHN XXII. A visitation of his own diocese in 1329 led to a conflict with the Abbey of SAINT AUGUSTINE, Canterbury. The nuncio adjudicated the case in favor of the abbey after Mepham refused to comply with the citation of the nuncio. As a result, Mepham was suspended from office in 1330 and excommunicated. Politically, Mepham had been one of the key figures in 1328–29 when King Edward III attempted to assert his independence at the court still dominated by Mortimer. His own appointment as archbishop, engineered by Henry, Earl of Lancaster, had been directed against Bp. Henry Burghersh of Lincoln, who was Mortimer's choice. Mepham was instrumental in bringing about Lancaster's submission to the young King's grace at Bedford, in January 1329. Mepham died excommunicate, but his body received absolution Oct. 26, 1333, and was buried in Canterbury cathedral, in St. Peter's chapel in the south ambulatory of the choir.

Bibliography: J. TAIT, "On the Date and Authorship of the *Speculum Regis Edwardi,*" *English Historical Review* 16 (1901) 110–115, work of Mepham? T. F. TOUT, *The Dictionary of National Biography from the Earliest Times to 1900,* 63 v. (London 1885–1900) 13:260–263; *Chapters in the Administrative History of Mediaeval England,* 6 v. (New York 1920–33). A. B. EMDEN, *A Biographical Register of the Scholars of the University of Oxford to A.D. 1500,* 3 v. (Oxford 1957–59) 2:1261.

[V. MUDROCH]

SIMON OF AULNE, BL.

Cistercian lay brother; b. *c.* 1145; d. Aulne (Belgium), Dec. 6, 1229. Although he was related to the counts of Geldern, Simon joined the abbey of AULNE-SUR-SAMBRE as a simple lay brother and was believed to possess the extraordinary gifts of discernment of spirits and prophecy. According to tradition, he was consulted by INNOCENT III. Simon was buried at Aulne and his relics soon became objects of veneration, although he has never been canonized.

Feast: Feb. 24.

Bibliography: S. LENSSEN, *Hagiologium cisterciense,* 2 v. (Tilburg 1948–49; suppl. 1951) 1:297–299.

[L. J. LEKAI]

SIMON OF BISIGNANO

Canonist; b. early 12th century, Bisignano in Calabria; date and place of death unknown. He was a student at Bologna, quite possibly of Gratian, and *magister* there. In addition to numerous *glossae* on the *Decretum* of GRATIAN he left a *Summa* covering all parts of that work except the *De poenitentia*. It belongs to the late 1170s (possibly 1177–1179). It is a work of great originality and the product of a competent and mature canonist. Simon is responsible for introducing an extensive use of the newer papal legislation since the time of Gratian. On more than 175 occasions he cites excerpts from the decretals of which more than 60 are of Alexander III. Simon seems to have regarded the *Decretum* of Gratian as the ancient law that could be and must be brought up-to-date by present and future legislators. Abrogations, derogations, modifications to the law of the past are to be expected. In this he was followed by SICARDUS OF CREMONA, the *Summa Lipsiensis*, HUGUCCIO, and all later canonists. It is interesting also to note that by more than 50 references to the *Decretum* of BURCHARD OF WORMS he testifies to the continuing use of that work and also indicates the view that Gratian did not contain all the ancient law. Though he made use of the teaching of earlier DECRETISTS he rarely refers to them by name. The *Summa* exercised considerable influence upon the development of the canonical method and has survived in at least eight manuscripts. An edition is being prepared.

Bibliography: S. KUTTNER, *Repertorium der Kanonistik* 148–149. J. F. V. SCHULTE, *Die Geschichte der Quellen und der Literatur des kanonischen Rechts* 1:140–142. J. JUNCKER, "Die Summa des Simon von Bisignano und seine Glossen," *Zeitschrift der Savigny-Stiftung für Rechtsgeschichte, Germanistische Abteilung* 15 (1926) 326–500. T. P. MCLAUGHLIN, "The Extravagantes in the Summa of Simon of Bisignano," *Mediaeval Studies* 20 (1958) 167–176. W. HOLTZMANN, "Zu den Dekretalen bei Simon von Bisignano," *Traditio* 18 (1962) 450–459.

[T. P. MCLAUGHLIN]

SIMON OF CRAMAUD

Cardinal; b. Diocese of Limoges, France, *c.* 1360; d. Dec. 14, 1422. He first studied law at Orléans and was licensed there; later he received a doctorate of jurisprudence from Paris and became a noted canonist and influential orator. He greatly admired the University of Paris and championed its cause in connection with the WESTERN SCHISM. He served as chancellor for the Duke of Berry for ten years. His was a brilliant career: on May 30, 1382, he was named bishop of Agen; in 1383, bishop of Béziers; in 1385, bishop of Poitiers, and finally on May 27, 1390, archbishop of Sens. On March 17, 1391, he was raised to the rank of titular patriarch of Alexandria and was made administrator of Avignon by Pope CLEMENT VII, whom he served during the Western Schism. In 1409 he was made archbishop of Reims and was elected president of the Council of PISA, where he proclaimed that both BENEDICT XIII and GREGORY XII should be deposed and championed the election of ALEXANDER V. In a council at Rome convoked in 1413 by John XXIII, he was named a cardinal. There he assisted in condemning the writings of J. HUS and J. WYCLIF. He was a forerunner of Gallicanism in that he staunchly supported temporal authority, At the Council of CONSTANCE he showed himself violently opposed to the Hussites. After MARTIN V was elected pope in 1417, Simon lost his influence in Church affairs, and for the rest of his life was the administrator of the diocese of Poitiers. His tomb was found in the cathedral of Poitiers in 1859.

Bibliography: K. A. FINK, *Lexikon für Theologie und Kirche*, ed. J. HOFER and K. RAHNER, 10 v. (2d, new ed. Freiburg 1957–65) 9:765–766. L. SALEMBIER, *Dictionnaire de théologie catholique*, ed. A. VACANT, 15 v. (Paris 1903–50; Tables générales 1951–) 3.2:2022–26. C. J. VON HEFELE, *Histoire des conciles d'après les documents originaux,* tr. and continued by H. LECLERCQ, 10 v. in 19 (Paris 1907–38) 6.2:1193–95; 1210–26.

[F. D. LAZENBY]

SIMON OF SAINT-QUENTIN

French Dominican missionary, fl. mid-13th century, author of *Fratris Simonis historia,* an account of a journey to Tatary. He is known only through VINCENT OF BEAUVAIS. Simon's *Historia* is lost but its substance has been preserved in the *Speculum historiale* of Vincent (29.69–89, 95; 30.26, 32–50; 31.2) who supplements Simon's information with extracts drawn from the work of the Franciscan, JOHN DA PIAN DEL CARPINE. After the Council of LYONS (1245), Innocent IV sent six missionaries into Tatary: two Franciscans, Carpine and Benedict the Pole; and four Dominicans: the Lombard ASCELLINO, the Poles Alexander and Alberic, and the Frenchman Simon, almost certainly a native of Saint-Quentin. The Franciscans traveled by way of Bohemia, Poland, and Russia, while the Dominicans took the Acre, Armenia, Georgia, and Persia route. When the Dominicans arrived at the court of the prince of the Tatars, Bajothny (Bacin, Bochin, or Batu Khan), they would not offer presents and thus earned bitter reproaches. They also refused to accord him divine honors and would have been massacred, had not one of the prince's six wives interceded for them. Simon's account gives the letter of Bajothny to the pope and dwells on the sufferings and bad treatment the Dominicans had to endure, but it is vague in its description of the country and its inhabitants. This mission to Tatary lasted from 1245 to July 1248 or 1249 and the friars are believed to have spent two years and six weeks in the country.

Bibliography: J. QUÉTIF and J. ÉCHARD, *Scriptores ordinis praedicatorum* (New York 1959) 1.1:122. J. A. FABRICIUS, *Biblio-*

theca latina mediae et infimae actatis, 6 v. in 3 (Florence 1858–59) 3:586. M. DAUNOU, *Histoire littéraire de la France* 18 (1835) 400–402. B. ALTANER, *Die Dominikanermissionen des 13. Jh.* (Habelschwerdt 1924). *Bibliotheca missionum* (Freiburg 1918–) 4:9–10.

[J. DAOUST]

SIMON OF SUDBURY

Archbishop of Canterbury, chancellor of England; b. Sudbury, Suffolk; d. London, July 14, 1381. Simon studied in Paris where he graduated as doctor of laws. Having been appointed chaplain to Pope Innocent VI, he proved his skill as a diplomat when sent as nuncio to EDWARD III in 1356. As a reward for this and similar services, he was made bishop of London in 1361 by papal PROVISION. For the next 20 years he took a leading part in English politics, siding with John of Gaunt, Duke of Lancaster, and incurring the accusation of being too lenient toward Gaunt's protégé, John WYCLIF. In 1375 Sudbury was transferred by papal bull to Canterbury. As archbishop he crowned Richard II (1377); as chancellor (1380–81) he helped shape royal policy, yet he was overshadowed constantly by the energetic William COURTENAY, his successor as bishop of London. It was Courtenay who forced him to examine Wyclif at Lambeth Palace in 1378. When the peasants revolted in 1381, Sudbury was a target of their hatred. They released their priest, John BALL, from the archbishop's prison at Maidstone, then seized the archbishop in the Tower of London and executed him. Before dying Sudbury granted absolution to the headsman.

Bibliography: W. HUNT, *The Dictionary of National Biography from the Earliest Times to 1900,* 63 v. (London 1885–1900) 19:146–149. A. B. EMDEN, *A Biographical Register of the Scholars of the University of Oxford to A.D. 1500,* 3 v. (Oxford 1957–59) 3:2218. W. L. WARREN, "Reappraisal of S.S.," *Journal of Ecclesiastical History* 10 (1959) 139–152.

[D. NICHOLL]

SIMON OF TOURNAI

Theologian; b. Tournai *c.* 1130; d. *c.* 1201. If he was the reporter of the second half of Odo of Soissons' (Ourscamp's) *Quaestiones*, as seems likely from the language and technique, he was doubtless the master of Odo's school and his successor in the chair of theology from 1165. Before that he taught the arts for ten years. He used Aristotle's *Physics, Metaphysics*, and *De anima*, newly translated from the Arabic, and admired Abelard and Gilbert de la Porrée. He excelled in dialectics and in clarifying and classifying concepts. Accusations of blasphemy, heresy, and incontinence, made some years after his death, have been discredited. The chronology and relationship of his works with those of other Porretani, especially Alain of Lille and Raoul Ardent, and with Peter of Poitiers are not yet established. His following works have been printed: *Disputationes, Expositio super Simbolum,* a sermon on the antiphon *O Sapientia* (by J. Warichez, Louvain 1932); *Expositio Symboli S. Athanasii* [in *Bibliotheca Casinensis. Florilegium,* 4 (Montecassino 1880) 322–346]; and the Trinitarian portion of his *Institutiones in sacra pagina* [M. Schmaus, *Recherches de théologie ancienne et médiévale,* 4 (1932) 59–72, 187–198, 294–307]. The sacramental portion of the latter was copied from Ps.-Hugh, *Speculum ecclesiae* (*Patrologia latina* 177:335–380), and the *Summa decretorum* of Rufinus.

Bibliography: D. VAN DEN EYNDE, "Deux sources de la Somme théologique de Simon de Tournai," *Antonianum* 24 (1949) 19–42. P. GLORIEUX, *Dictionnaire de théologie catholique* 14.2:2124–30. A. M. LANDGRAF, *Einführung in die Geschichte der theologischen Literatur der Frühscholastik* (Regensburg 1948); revised as *Introducción a la historia de la literatura teológica de la escolástica incipiente* (Barcelona 1956). J. N. GARVIN, "Peter of Poitiers and Simon of Tournai on the Trinity," *Recherches de théologie ancienne et médiévale* 16 (1949) 314–316. P. S. MOORE et al., eds., *Sententiae Petri Pictaviensis,* 2 v. (Notre Dame, Ind. 1943–50) v.2. M. CAPPUYNS, *Revue d'histoire ecclésiastique* 49 (1954) 564–565.

[J. N. GARVIN]

SIMON (SIMEON) OF TRENT

Alleged boy martyr; d. Trent, Italy, March 23, 1475. Son of a tawer, he was found murdered near his home at the age of 20 or 30 months, allegedly by Jews during the celebration of the Pasch on Maundy Thursday. Upon discovery of the body, a trial was instigated; the proceedings, assembled by Bp. John Hinderbach and approved by Pope Sixtus IV on June 20, 1478, who suspended Simon's cult, are not considered reliable inasmuch as torture was employed to exact testimony. Numerous miracles were attributed to the boy (curing of the dumb, the blind, and the paralyzed, and restoration to life of the dead), which led to the Pope Sixtus V's authorization for the continuation of his cultus (1588). He was probably considered a saint, and his feast day was celebrated annually at his tomb in the church of St. Peter at Trent, until the cult was forbidden by order of Abp. A. M. Gottardi of Trent (Oct. 28, 1965) and his name removed from the Roman Martyrology. This is the unique example of ritual child murder recognized in the Martyrology; it was first listed as a commemoration in a missal in 1487 and picked up in a martyrology dated 1584. The incident still awaits critical historical investigation.

See Also: MEDIEVAL BOY MARTYRS.

Bibliography: J. M. TIBERINUS, *Die Geschicht vnd Legend von dem seyligen Kind vnd Marterer genannt Symon, von den Juden zu Trientt gemarteret vnd getöttet* (Augsburg after April 4, 1475) U. PUSCULUS, *Brixieñ duo libri Symonidos* (Augsburg 1511). B. BEN A. ANAU, *Sefer Masa ge hizayon* (s.l. 1965). L. DONATI, *L'inizio della stampa a Trento ed il beato Simone* (Trent 1968). E. S. TESSADRI, *L'arpa di David: storia di Simone e del processo di Trento contro gli ebrei accusati di omicidio rituale* (Milan 1974). A. ESPOSITO and D. QUAGLIONI, *Processi contro gli ebrei di Trento (1475–1478)* (Padua 1990). R. P. HSIA, *Trent 1475: Stories of Ritual Murder Trial* (New Haven 1992). W. TREUE, *Der Trienter Judenprozess: Voraussetzungen, Abläufe, Auswirkungen* (Hannover 1996). *Acta Sanctorum* March 3:493–500. *Bibliotheca hagiographica latina antiquae et mediae aetatis,* 2 v. (Brussels 1898–1901; suppl. 1911) 2:7762–72. A. BUTLER, *The Lives of the Saints,* ed. H. THURSTON and D. ATTWATER, 4 v. (New York 1956) 1:671–672. *Analecta Bollandiana* 23 (1904) 122–124. I. ROGGER, *Lexikon für Theologie und Kirche,* ed. J. HOFER and K. RAHNER, 10 v. (2d, new ed. Freiburg 1957–65) 9:772.

[F. D. LAZENBY]

SIMON STOCK, ST.

General of the Carmelite Order; b. England; d. Bordeaux, France, May 16, 1265. The only contemporary evidence seems to be a notice in *Vitae fratrum (ca.* 1260) of Gerard of Frachet; "Simon, the prior of this Order, a religious and veracious man"; it seems to indicate also that he was in the Holy Land (1237). Two 14th-century necrologies attest to his English origin, his generalate, his death, and his reputation for sanctity. In the earliest redaction of the Catalogues of Saints of the Carmelites about the same time, he is called Simon of Gascony; his generalate is not mentioned, but the reference is undoubtedly to Simon Stock. The earliest (ca. 1400) list of Carmelite generals by John Grossi, places his generalate from 1200 to 1250, but Grossi's chronology has no historical basis. The commonly accepted report that Simon was elected general at the chapter of Aylesford in 1247 (or 1245) cannot be maintained, because in 1249 a certain Geoffrey was general; consequently the change of the Carmelite rule from eremitical to mendicant in 1247 was not the work of Simon. He was perhaps elected at the chapter of the order in London in 1254. The year of his death as 1265 is first recorded at the end of the 15th century but is corroborated by the foundation of the convent of Bordeaux shortly before and by the election of his successor in 1266. In iconography and from the *Catalogues of Saints,* Simon is chiefly known for his famed scapular vision. While he was praying to Our Lady for privileges for his order, she appeared to him, holding the Carmelite SCAPULAR in her hand and saying: "This is your privilege: whoever dies in it, will be saved." The obvious sense is that whoever lives and dies as a Carmelite, will not be lost. This account helped spread the devotion of the scapular among the faithful, especially from the 16th century onward. The so-called documents of Swanyngton concerning this vision are a 17th-century fabrication. Other particulars of Simon's life, such as his living in a hollow tree, his joining the Carmelite Order in England, and performing various miracles, can be discarded as 15th-century legends. During the Middle Ages his feast was celebrated in several Carmelite convents; the whole order accepted it only in 1564, when the feast was approved by the Vatican. He has not been officially canonized; however, his relics are venerated in the cathedral of Bordeaux and in the Carmelite monastery of Aylesford, England.

Feast: May 16.

Bibliography: *Acta Sanctorum* May 3:650–651. B. M. XIBERTA Y ROQUETA, *De visione Sancti Simonis Stock* (Rome 1950).

[A. STARING]

SIMONETTA

A noble family, originally from Calabria, that played a prominent part in Milanese and papal affairs during the 15th and 16th centuries.

Francesco, humanist and statesman; b. Caccuri, Catanzaro, Italy, 1410; d. Milan, Aug. 30, 1480. He served on the Royal Council of Naples before entering the service of the Sforzas. During the regency of Bona of Savoy, widow of Galeazzo Maria, Duke of Milan, and the minority years of Gian Galeazzo Sforza, Francesco served as minister of state (1476–79). The accession of Ludovico il Moro, which brought about a new regime, led to Francesco's capture and decapitation.

Giovanni, brother of Francesco, historian and statesman; b. Caccuri, Catanzaro, Italy, *c.* 1415; d. Rome, 1491. He entered the service of Francesco Sforza, first as his secretary (1444) and later as chancellor of Milan (1453). He wrote a Latin account of Milanese history from 1421 to 1466, which paid tribute to Francesco and which was entitled *Commentarii rerum gestarum Francisci Sfortiae . . . .* It is generally considered an excellent example of Italian humanistic history. With the accession of Ludovico il Moro (1479), Giovanni was forced to flee into exile, where he died.

Bonifacio, nephew of Francesco and Giovanni, abbot of San Stefano in Corno; b. unknown; d. San Stefano, 1492. He is remembered chiefly for his works on the early Christian persecutions, *Christianae persecutiones* (Milan 1496).

Giacomo, son of Giovanni, cardinal; b. Milan 1475; d. Rome, Nov. 1, 1539. A lawyer in the Roman Consistory, he served as an auditor of the Rota during the Fifth Lateran Council (1512–17). Appointed bishop of Pesaro in 1529 by Clement VII, he was raised to the cardinalate by Paul III (1535). He also administered, at different times, the Dioceses of Perugia, Lodi, and Nepi. He was sent as legate *a latere,* with Cardinals Lorenzo Campeggio and Girolamo Aleandro, to a council, summoned at Vicenza, that was eventually prorogued (1538).

Ludovico, nephew of Giacomo, cardinal; b. Milan, 1500; d. Rome, April 30, 1568. His uncle Giacomo renounced the See of Pesaro in Ludovico's favor in 1537. He was referee of the papal segnatura (1540), and was present at the Council of Trent (1546–47). He was appointed bursar of the Vatican in 1560. A year later he was named cardinal and papal legate to Trent by Pius IV. At Trent he frequently led the opposition to the theological proposals of Cardinal Girolamo Seripando, president of the Council.

Bibliography: H. JEDIN, *History of the Council of Trent,* tr. E. GRAF, v.1–2 (St. Louis 1957–60); *Geschichte des Konzils von Trient,* 2 v. (Freiburg 1949–57; v.1 2d ed. 1951). H. JEDIN, *Lexikon für Theologie und Kirche,* ed. M. BUCHBERGER, 10 v. (Freiburg 1930–38) 9:580–581; *Papal Legate at the Council of Trent: Cardinal Seripando,* tr. F. C. ECKHOFF (St. Louis 1947).

[P. S. MCGARRY]

SIMONY

The term simony is derived from Simon Magus, who tried to buy the gift of the Holy Spirit from the Apostles (Acts 8.18–24).

Theology. Modern authors usually adopt the definition of THOMAS AQUINAS: ''A deliberate design of selling or buying something spiritual or annexed to the spiritual'' (*Summa Theologiae* 2a2ae, 100 ad 1). This definition covers simony of divine law but not of ecclesiastical law (1917 *Codex iuris canonici* c. 727). We are concerned here with the former, which constitutes a real SACRILEGE. The gravity of the offense lies in equating spiritual with temporal goods. Also, insofar as an element of belief is involved, those who commit simony become suspect of heresy.

To commit the *sin* of simony, the intention alone suffices. However, for the *delict* of simony (a crime subject to ecclesiastical penalties) there must be some external agreement with one or more persons (1917 *Codex iuris canonici* cc. 2195, 2218, 2228), although this may be tacit or implied. The temporal price can be other than money. The traditional definition originated with GREGORY I (cf. *Corpus iuris canonici* c.1 q.1 c. 114): *munus a manu,* i.e., a monetary gift or one that is calculable in monetary

Sixteenth-century wooden statue of St. Simon Stock receiving scapular from Virgin Mary, holding Infant Jesus.

terms; *munus a lingua,* i.e., praise, promises, recommendations; *munus ab obsequio,* i.e., the rendering of undue services. ''Spiritual'' refers to those things that exist for the good of the soul, such as grace, the Sacraments, prayer, sacramentals, indulgences, ecclesiastical authority and jurisdiction. ''Annexed'' objects are such things as church benefices, sacred vessels, relics, and the right of patronage. To sell these things is simony of divine law. Slightness of matter is not admitted—except in simony of ecclesiastical law; thus the sin is mortal in every instance.

There are numerous practices that are not simoniacal (Iorio, 37–39). Thus it is lawful and proper for a priest to receive a stipend or offering on the occasion of performing his sacred duties, e.g., Mass offerings, marriage and burial fees, and he may demand such where permitted (Lk 10.7; 1 Cor 9.13). Blessed objects, such as rosaries, chalices, and crucifixes, may be sold provided the price is not increased on that account. Nor is it simony to give someone a gift to persuade him to accept some spiritual advantage. However, scandal should be avoided.

History. In the first three centuries simony was uncommon. But after the Edict of Milan (313), when the Church began to accumulate wealth and power, positions were eagerly sought. Despite attempts at suppressing this abuse, it continued throughout the Middle Ages. The worst period was from the 9th to the 11th century when simony pervaded the monasteries, the lower clergy, the episcopacy, and even the papacy. Thus GREGORY VI (1045–46) was accused of simony and NICHOLAS II's famous decree on papal election (1059) was directed at simony principally. In the later Middle Ages the abuse, especially the traffic in indulgences and relics, was attacked by WYCLIF and other reformers. Lay princes as well as churchmen were responsible for these practices.

Simony did not go unchallenged. Countermeasures consisted of theological tracts and conciliar, papal, and synodal legislation, much of which passed into the canonical collections. An important canon was CHALCEDON (451), cap. 2, which ordered bishops who ordained for money to be deposed (Jedin, *Conc. Oec. Dec.* 63; *Corpus iuris canonici* C.1 q. 1 c.8). Papal letters, especially of LEO I (P. Jaffé, *Regesta pontificum romanorum ab condita ecclesia ad annum post Christum hatum 1198,* ed. F. Kaltenbrunner 410, 544), INNOCENT I (the famous *Ventum est, ibid.* 303), and Gregory I (*ibid.*, ed. P. Ewald, 1743, 1744, 1747, 1859), imposed deposition and excommunication, but with little success.

The commonest form of simony was the buying and selling of Holy Orders. From Gregory I onward this was referred to as the heresy of simony (*simoni aca haeresis*) but simony was not held to be a HERESY *simpliciter*, certainly not in the 11th century when the phrase was most used. Yet this discussion raised the question of whether simoniacal orders and sacraments were valid. Some modern authorities have argued that the doctrine was defective from the 10th to the 12th century. The opinion of the author is that simoniacal orders were regarded as valid but illicit. Some of the GREGORIAN reformers may have followed the extreme views of HUMBERT OF SILVA CANDIDA, but not the majority. The orthodox view was expressed by PETER DAMIAN and generally adopted (*see* REORDINATION).

Although the theological and canonical treatment of simony (the Paris school) continued on sound lines down to Aquinas, we should note that the Bolognese school taught differently about simoniacal ordinations, that is, debating whether they were valid or not. The disputes were generally settled by the 13th century.

Elimination of the abuse, however, was not so successful. Injunctions and prohibitions continued. Thus in 1464 PAUL II in his bull *Cum detestabile* decreed excommunication *latae sententiae* against those guilty of simony in granting benefices, together with their mediators. Yet simony remained a major abuse down to and after the Council of TRENT. However, the council legislated against the worst of the simoniacal transactions that had been common (cf. Session 21, *De Reform.* can. 1, 9; Session 24, *De Reform.* can. 14, 18). This together with the renewal of the inner life and the increasing separation of Church and State made possible the eventual elimination of all simony.

Bibliography: N. A. WEBER, *A History of Simony in the Christian Church* (Baltimore 1909). R. A. RYDER, *Simony* (Washington 1931). H. NOLDIN and A. SCHMITT, *Summa theologiae moralis,* v. 2 *De Praeceptis* (28th ed. Heidelberg 1944–). J. LECLERCQ, "Simoniaca Heresis," *Studi Gregoriani* 1 (1947) 523–530. D. M. ROSATI, *La teologia sacramentaria nella lotta contro la simonia e l'investitura laica del secolo XI* (Tolentino 1951). T. A. IORIO, *Theologia moralis* (5th ed. Naples 1960–) v.2. H. G. KRAUSE, "Das Papstwahldekret von 1059 und seine Rolle im Investiturstreit," *Studi Gregoriani* 7 (1960). J. GILCHRIST, "*Simoniaca Haeresis* and the Problem of Orders from Leo IX to Gratian," *Proceedings of the Second International Conference of Medieval Canon Law Held at Boston, August 1963* (Vatican City 1964).

[J. GILCHRIST]

SIMOR, JÁNOS

Cardinal, primate of Hungary; b. Székesfehérvár (Stuhlweissenburg), Hungary, Aug. 23, 1813; d. Esztergom (Gran), Jan. 23, 1891. Son of a wealthy family, he was ordained (1836), taught theology (1839–50) in Budapest, Vienna, and Esztergom, and became court chaplain (1850) and counselor for Hungarian affairs in the ministry of public worship and education in Vienna (1851). He became bishop of Györ (March 19, 1857), archbishop of Esztergom and prince-primate of Hungary (Feb. 22, 1867), and cardinal (Dec. 22, 1873). He was outstanding for his pastoral, organizational, and building activities and still more for his work to restore his diocese and clergy to closer union with the pope and the Roman Curia after JOSEPHINISM had alienated so many. Also, as leader of the Hungarian ecclesiastical autonomy movement, he sought to free the Church in Hungary from traditionally strong royal influence, which after 1868 was exercised mainly by liberal ministers. At VATICAN COUNCIL I he opposed as inopportune the definition of papal infallibility, but later supported and publicized the conciliar decrees in his diocese and throughout Hungary, and contravened attempts to submit them to the royal *placet.*

Bibliography: J. KÖHALMI-KLIMSTEIN, *Johann Simor* (Bratislava 1886). C. BUTLER, *The Vatican Council,* 2 v. (New York 1930). C. GREINZ, *Lexikon für Theologie und Kirche,* ed. M. BUCHBERGER, 10 v. (Freiburg 1930–38) 9:583–584. T. VON BOGYAY,

Lexikon für Theologie und Kirche, ed. J. HOFER and K. RAHNER, 10 v. (2d, new ed. Freiburg 1957–65) 9:776.

[F. MAASS]

SIMPLICITY, VIRTUE OF

In ordinary speech the word "simplicity" sometimes designates an undesirable characteristic, namely, an incapacity for dealing with ideas or situations of any complexity, an inadequacy that stems from either a defect of intelligence or a want of native shrewdness. In reference to the spiritual life, however, simplicity has two uses, in both of which it signifies commendable qualities. One of these is necessary to the virtuous man, and the other is of counsel. As a necessary quality, it is a disposition firmly opposed to deceit, double-dealing, hypocrisy, dissimulation, and duplicity of every kind. Jesus noted this trait in Nathaniel (Jn 1.47; for other scriptural references, *see* Jb 1.1; Prv 2.21–22). As a counsel of perfection, simplicity signifies the indivision of heart and the singleness of purpose of those who are free from voluntary imperfection and who seek God with great purity of INTENTION. By those who lack this quality, God is not loved perfectly, *ex toto corde;* the eye of the soul is not full of light (Mt 6.22); and intentions that are less worthy, even if they are not strictly opposed to the love of God, clutter the heart.

[P. K. MEAGHER]

SIMPLICITY OF GOD

The divine attribute that excludes from God's being all composition, whether physical, metaphysical, accidental, or merely logical. The Catholic Church, whose tradition finds expression in the Scriptures, in the witness of the Fathers, in the liturgy, and in the exercise of her teaching prerogative, has ever maintained that the being of God is, in the deepest sense of the term, simple. This article explains the Church's teaching in two stages: the first is devoted to establishing the fact of God's simplicity, the second to exploring theologically its significant meaning. Procedure on this latter point relies largely upon philosophical considerations (appropriated in a ministerial function by theology) and involves determining the nature of simplicity, then arguing that God is intrinsically simple, and finally establishing the consequential truth that God cannot enter into the composition with the world.

Fact of Simplicity. Yahweh's revelation of Himself to the Israelites as "Who Is" focuses upon His oneness and His "otherness." The latter attribute is presented largely in terms of God's holiness (*agios*), which renders Him inaccessible and separate from the world. In this it is strongly suggested that God is spirit and is incorporeal, though such concepts are not sufficiently clear to include explicitly the concept of simplicity. Indeed, the Old Testament abounds with corporeal metaphors employed for the most part to establish beyond doubt the concrete actuality of God. On the other hand, God's command to Moses prohibiting graven images of Himself (Ex 20.4) can readily be seen as expressive of His immateriality. The New Testament expressly speaks of God as a "spirit" (Jn 4.24; 2 Cor 3.17), who "has not flesh and bone" (Lk 24.39) and is thus "invisible" (Jn 5.38; 6.46). He is not located and worship of Him does not depend upon place (Jn 4.20–24). Further, He is His own truth and life (Jn 14.6) by way of a real identity and does not merely possess these.

If the concept of simplicity is not explicitly stated, the Fathers of the Church remedy this. Origen speaks of God's "perfect simplicity," which "excludes all addition and all intrinsic diversity" (*Periarch.* 1.1.6); Athanasius calls it "absolute simplicity which excludes every quality and every kind of composition properly so called" (*Epist. ad Afros episcopos* 8, *Patrologia Graeca,* ed. J. P. Migne, 26:1043); Gregory of Nyssa sees the divine nature as so one and simple in itself that man cannot conceive of it (*Contra Eunom.* 12.2, *Patrologia Graeca* 45:1069, 1077, 1104). Much of the concern of the Fathers is directed to showing how neither the Incarnation of the Word nor the real distinction of the divine Persons is in any wise injurious to God's simplicity.

The liturgy for the Mass of Trinity Sunday refers to the Trinity as "a simple Unity." In due time, the teaching authority of the Church gave express formulation to this attribute of God, especially in the Councils of Toledo (H. Denzinger, *Enchiridion symbolorum,* ed. A. Schönmetzer, 566), Rheims (*Enchiridion symbolorum* 745), Lateran IV (*Enchiridion symbolorum* 800), and Vatican I—the last council condemning, in particular, various forms of pantheism as implying composition between God and the world (*Enchiridion symbolorum* 3001, 3023–24).

Notion of Simplicity. Everything confronting man in experience admits of composition of some kind; thus one's procedure in arriving at the notion of simplicity is necessarily negatory. The concept itself signifies a negation of composition: a simple thing is something that lacks parts or really distinct elements. Simplicity likewise implies indivisibility, since only composites admit of division.

There is truth to the observation that in the created order the complex is more perfect than the simple, as man is more perfect than a stone. This, however, is a simplicity of imperfection or of lack of being. The simplicity of God is rather a simplicity of perfection; it consists in being all perfections, not distinctly, but by way of real identity.

Arguments for God's Simplicity. The demonstration of God's simplicity is effected by the successive elimination of all forms of compositions: first, real composition, either substantial (physical or metaphysical) or accidental; and second, rational or logical composition.

Physical Simplicity. The most obvious composition is that proper to bodies and radicated in matter as necessarily subject to EXTENSION. Three characteristics are verifiable of all corporeal substance: mobility, quantitative divisibility, and (in terms of mere corporeity as such) inanimation. For, (1) no body as such can be the cause of its own motion, since what is only capable of motion must receive its motion extrinsically; (2) every body as extended must admit of the possibility of division; and (3) mere corporeity cannot be explanatory of life, else every body would necessarily be animate.

Each of these characteristics of body is, however, incompatible with the authentic concept of God—as unmoved mover, as totally actual, as pure perfection. God is not receptive of motion, not passive to division, not lifeless but living. These nominal definitions of God are not presupposed, moreover, but are arrived at by a true deductive process originating with external phenomena. They are conclusions to the classical ''five ways'' whereby Saint Thomas establishes God's existence (*see* GOD, PROOFS FOR THE EXISTENCE OF). The human intellect then is logically constrained to deny body of God, to conceive Him as transcending the structure necessary to the very notion of body. The metaphors of Sacred Scripture must therefore be understood as metaphors, and not as implying that God is truly possessed of a body.

The foregoing argument does not merely remove from God material composition of parts in space; it implicitly precludes any notion of God as a form-matter composite (*see* MATTER AND FORM). For a material element in God would still imply POTENCY; it would merely participate in the perfection of the form, and God would not be a pure agent cause, since matter is operative only in virtue of its form.

Metaphysical Simplicity. The denial of matter in God leads readily to the removal of another form of composition—that between nature, or essence, and individual. God *is* His own nature by a real identity and cannot be thought of as a subject who *has* a common nature in which others may possibly share in individually distinct ways. Any nature involved in matter (as man's) is thereby necessarily subject to individuating determinations so that the individual is something over and above, and thus distinct from, the nature it shares in common with many (*see* INDIVIDUATION). The immateriality of God means that His essence is individuated of itself, and not in virtue of a composition with really distinct singularizing elements. God does not possess His Godhead (as a man does his humanity), He *is* that Godhead.

Profounder still is the identification in God of essence and existence (*see* ESSENCE AND EXISTENCE). God's ''being-ness'' is not to be thought of as the emergence, or ''standing out'' (*ex-sistentia*) of a prior essence. This would necessarily contract His being to that of the finite order and make it univocal with creaturely existence. There is always and necessarily a real distinction between the ESSENCE (that which is) and the EXISTENCE (the act of existing) of a creature; indeed in this does its very creatureliness consist. But such a distinction itself implies that the existence in question is a caused one, that it is an ultimate perfecting of the nature to which it accrues, and that the nature realizes its own being by way of a PARTICIPATION in pure, unreceived Being. But nothing in God is caused—indeed there are no causes prior to Himself; His totalness of being is such that it admits of no further perfecting; and as absolutely first Being He cannot participate any being prior to Himself. God is thus the very act of being itself in its absolute purity. This is His very essence; His name is ''He Who Is.''

Accidental Composition. Catholic faith ascribes to God perfections without number—intelligence, will, power, justice, mercy, operation, the whole array of divine attributes. Their inclusion in Him is real and authentic. Yet these perfections are not to be conceived as really distinct qualities that are accidentally added to the divine being, enriching God, as it were, from without. Every finite essence is receptive not only of the substantial perfection of existence but also of multiple accidental qualifications that enjoy existence in the essence as its various modifications. Yet these accidents are necessarily posterior (in nature, if not in time) to the essence they modify and are caused either by an extrinsic agent or by the intrinsic principles of the essence whence they emanate, the latter in the case of properties. To have such accidental modifications is in direct opposition to God's primacy of being and to His being the uncaused cause of all.

A more ultimate reason for this impossibility lies in the recognition of God as pure subsistent Being. [*See* ASEITY (ASEITAS); SUBSISTENCE.] Speaking precisely, no essence as such admits of additions to itself; the very supposition of such intrinsic addition would mean the destruction of the essence in question and the origin of a new essence. To add a unit to the number five is to eliminate the number five and substitute a new mathematical essence, that of the number six. Accidents, then, do not reside in, and belong to, the essence; they are modifications of the individuals who possess the essence. Baldness happens not to humanity but to certain individual males. But God is not a subject *having* his nature and thus capable of receiving further accidental qualifications. Rather He is His intelligence, His will, His mercy, etc. Accidental composition is as repugnant to Him as substantial composition.

It follows from this that God cannot bear in Himself any real RELATION to the world, for a real relation is an accidental being. He is not a being among beings, subject to the inevitable and limiting complexus of interrelationships and dependencies. This is not to deny that God is really Creator, Provider, etc., but only to deny that such real causality implies any real intrinsic accidental mutation of the divine transcendence.

Logical Composition. So total is the divine simplicity that the human mind cannot (without falsifying its object) impose upon that simplicity a composition entirely of its own making. And any placing of God in logical categories proper to rational thought amounts to just such a composing. As long as there is some foundation in God Himself for so doing, the mind can and indeed must employ distinctions not really found in God. To compose generic and specific elements, however, in fashioning the very concept of God has no such justification. For one thing, a GENUS must be prior to what it contains, but God's primacy of being (not so much a primacy in time as in excellence) means that nothing can be prior to Him, either really or in meaning. Also if God were to be considered as in a genus, this would have to be that of "being." But, as Aristotle observes, being cannot be a genus since the difference of a genus must lie outside it and outside being there is only nothingness. Even more cogent, perhaps, is the necessity of distinguishing the QUIDDITY from the existence of whatever is contained within a genus—a distinction nowise allowable in God. Each SPECIES has the same generic quiddity as every other species of the same genus, but obviously must have its own distinct act of being. This is only to say that logical composition is dependent upon prior metaphysical composition. The impossibilities here cannot be avoided by saying that God belongs to a genus reductively—i.e., not as contained therein but as an external principle thereof—for in such a case the principle cannot extend beyond the genus it principles, and God is much more than any category of being that might be excogitated.

Since definitions are arrived at by establishing the generic elements and then discerning the specific difference, it follows that there can be no proper DEFINITION of God. This, in its turn, accounts for the impossibility of an a priori demonstration of God's existence.

Extrinsic Simplicity. It is further impossible for God to enter into composition with other things. He cannot be in any fashion the formal principle of the world; even less plausibly can He be its material principle. The decisive reason for this is that a cause cannot be confused with its effect. Could God truly be composed with the world either He would become His own effect or the world would become its own cause—all of which is a denial of the notion of God as first cause. It must be noted well that this is no denial of the possibility of union between God and creature. The INCARNATION is precisely a union with a created humanity, indeed a substantial union. Accidental unions are numberless and varied, occasioned by every exercise of divine causality and creaturely mutation. Union is a relation to God as a totally extrinsic agent or term. Composition, by contrast, renders God an intrinsic part of something —potency or act, matter or form, substance or accident. God is present to and in the universe, but He is nowise a part of it.

The transcendental theism of Christianity, then, is at a far remove from PANTHEISM of whatever kind—either that which sees God becoming the world, as does Eastern religion, especially HINDUISM, and classical pantheism extending from PARMENIDES and HERACLITUS down to B. SPINOZA, or that which sees the world becoming God, as does the materialistic pantheism of E. Haeckel or the idealistic pantheism of G. W. F. HEGEL (see the condemnations of Vatican Council I, H. Denzinger *Enchiridion symbolorum*, ed. A. Schönmetzer, 3023–25). Equally inimical to Catholic faith is the more prevalent PANENTHEISM of such moderns as C. S. PEIRCE, A. N. WHITEHEAD, W. JAMES, M. Buber, A. Schweitzer, and P. Weiss, which represents God as including the world in His own actuality (see C. Hartshorne and W. L. Reese, *Philosophers Speak of God,* Chicago 1953).

Ultimately, the Christian position rests upon a concept of God as the PURE ACT of being, transcending His creation.

See Also: GOD, ARTICLES ON

Bibliography: THOMAS AQUINAS, *Summa theologiae* 1a, 3, Eng. ed. v.2, *Existence and Nature of God,* ed. and tr. T. MCDERMOTT (New York 1964); *C. gent.* 1.17–27, tr. A. C. PEGIS, *On the Truth of the Catholic Faith,* book 1 (New York 1955). R. GARRIGOU-LAGRANGE, *God: His Existence and His Nature,* tr. B. ROSE, 2 v. (St. Louis 1934–36) v.2. E. MANGENOT et al., *Dictionnaire de théologie catholique*, ed. A. VACANT et al., 15 v. (Paris 1903–50) 4:948–1300. K. JÜSSEN, *Lexikon für Theologie und Kirche*, ed. J. HOFER and K. RAHNER, 10 v. (2d, new ed. Freiburg 1957–65) 3:745–46.

[W. J. HILL]

SIMPLICIUS, POPE, ST.

Pontificate: March 3, 468 to March 10, 483. "Born at Tivoli, his father Castinus" (*Liber pontificalis*), Simplicius seems to have been chiefly a spectator of events, in contrast to his immediate predecessors. During his tenure, the last shadowy emperor of the West was relegated to a comfortable villa at Naples and the imperial insignia sent to Constantinople by Odoacer, who assumed the title of king of Italy, under the vague suzerainty of the Eastern emperor (476). A series of barbarian kingdoms, all Arian, had established themselves on the ruins of the Western Empire. The Church's relations with the new rulers were generally good; only in Spain and Africa was there real persecution.

The unsuccessful attempt by Acacius, patriarch of Constantinople, to win the pope's approval for canon 28 of Chalcedon colored Acacius's later attitude toward the Roman Church. In spite of the imperial government, the Monophysites succeeded, for a time, in gaining control of the important Sees of Alexandria, Jerusalem, and Antioch. Under the usurper Basiliscus (475–476), who needed their support, they were openly favored. The encyclical issued by Basiliscus, in an attempt to reconcile the orthodox and the Monophysites, condemned Chalcedon and Leo's Tome. Acacius, afraid of the usurper and angered by the pope's attitude toward canon 29, failed to keep him informed about events. Simplicius wrote to both Basiliscus and Acacius expressing concern about the restoration to Alexandria of the Monophysite Patriarch TIMOTHY AELURUS, but to no avail.

The return to power of the Emperor ZENO seemed to assure the triumph of Chalcedonian orthodoxy. Although the pope obtained an imperial decree banishing Timothy, who died before it arrived in Alexandria (477), he could not obtain the support of either Zeno or Acacius for the removal of Timothy's successor, the Monophysite Peter Mongus. The Monophysite Peter the Fuller was also obliged to leave Antioch, but only for a time.

Both the emperor and patriarch were intent on pursuing a policy of religious conciliation. The skillfully drawn up HENOTICON, prepared by Acacius with the help of Peter Mongus and issued as an imperial edict in 482, was superficially orthodox, but it failed to cover the main point at issue: it was silent on Chalcedon and Leo's Tome. Peter Mongus was recognized as the lawful patriarch of Alexandria following the death of the orthodox Timothy Salophaciolus (February 482). Acacius left the pope in ignorance of the latest developments, in spite of repeated appeals for information from Rome. Simplicius died, after a long illness, before any action could be taken about the Henoticon.

The policy of delegating papal authority was extended to Spain, when Bishop Zeno of Seville was appointed papal vicar for that country and charged with seeing that the decrees of the Apostolic See were observed there. Under Simplicius occurred the first instances of adapting public buildings in Rome for use as churches. A hall on the Esquiline, erected by the consul Junius Bassus, was dedicated to St. Andrew (S. Andrea in Catabarbara). The most important foundation of the reign was the construction on the Coelian hill of the architecturally interesting round church of S. Stefano in Rotondo, formerly thought to have been an earlier building transformed into a church. Recent examination and restoration have shown that it was erected in one building about this time. In addition, a small basilica was erected to St. Bibiana in the gardens of Gallienus (S. Bibiana).

The *Liber pontificalis* records that Simplicius designated priests from certain of the Roman titular churches to assist with the services at the greater basilicas of St. Peter, St. Paul, and St. Lawrence on a weekly rotation basis. The system was later extended to the basilica of St. Mary Major, while the Lateran Basilica was served by the suburbicarian bishops. Simplicius was the first pope to be portrayed with a square nimbus, indicating that he was still living at the time (in a mosaic in the apse of S. Bibiana, no longer extant). He was buried in the portico of St. Peter's. The 9th-century Martyrology of Ado was the first to commemorate him (the date of his death is wrongly given in the Roman Martyrology as March 2, following the *Liber pontificalis*).

Feast: March 10.

Bibliography: *Clavis Patrum latinorum*, ed. E. DEKKERS (Streenbrugge 1961) 1664, and *Patrologiae cursus completus, series latina*, suppl., ed. A. HAMMAN (Paris 1957—) 3:443–444, editions. *Patrologia Latina*, ed. J. P. MIGNE (Paris 1878–90) 58:35–62. A. THIEL, ed., *Epistolae romanorum pontificum* (Braunsberg 1868—) 1:175–2:14. *Liber pontificalis*, ed. L. DUCHESNE (Paris 1886–92) 1:249–251; 3:86–87. E. CASPAR, *Geschichte de Papsttums von den Anfängen bis zur Höhe der Weltherrschaft* (Tübingen 1930–33) 2:14–25, 746. H. LECLERCQ, *Dictionnaire d'archéologie chrétienne et de liturgie* (Paris 1907–53) 13.1: 1210–11. É. AMANN, *Dictionnaire de théologie catholique*, ed. A. VACANT et al. (Paris 1903–50) 14.2:2161–64. O. BERTOLINI, *Roma di fronte a Bisanzio e ai Longobardi* (Bologna 1941) 19–30. T. G. JALLAND, *The Church and the Papacy* (Society for Promoting Christian Knowledge, 1944) 314–317. E. SCHWARTZ, *Publizistische Sammlungen zum Acacianischen Schisma* [Abhandlungen der Akademie (Gesellschaft, to 1940) der Wissenschaft NS 10; 1934]. R. U. MONTINI, *Le Tombe dei papi* (Rome 1957) 104. W. ULLMANN, *The Growth of Papal Government in the Middle Ages* (New York 1962). G. B. LADNER, *Die Papstbildnisse* (Vatican City 1941–) 1:60–61. R. VIELLIARD, *Recherches sur les origines de la Rome chrétienne* (Rome 1959) 89–91. M. REDIES, "Die Usurpation des Badiliskos (475–476) im Kontext der aufstiegenden monophysitischen Kirche," *Antiquité Tardive. Revue Internationale d'Histoire et Archéologie (IVe-VIIIe siècle)* 5 (Paris 1997) 211–221. J. RIST, *Biographisch-*

Bibliographisches Kirchenlexikon 10 (Herzberg 1995). G. SCHWAIGER, *Lexikon des Mittelalters* (Munich-Zurich 1994–1995).

[J. CHAPIN]

SIMPSON, RICHARD, BL.

Priest, martyr; *alias* Highgate; b. *c.* 1553 at Well, Ripon, Yorkshire, England; hanged, drawn, and quartered July 24, 1588 at Derby. After a short time as a Protestant minister, his journey to the Catholic Church caused him to be imprisoned. Released (or exiled) he began his studies for the priesthood at Douai in 1577, where he was ordained a priest. Thereafter Simpson was sent to England. He labored in the mission field for almost ten years prior to his arrest and banishment. He returned furtively, but was caught passing from Lancashire to Derbyshire. He was reprieved at the Lenten assizes of 1588 and almost conformed. His fellow inmates, Nicholas GARLICK and Robert LUDLAM, comforted and encouraged him to hold fast to the faith. He repented of his inconstancy and was condemned for high treason because he was an unlawful priest. All three were beatified by Pope John Paul II on Nov. 22, 1987 with George Haydock and Companions.

Feast of the English Martyrs: May 4 (England).

See Also: ENGLAND, SCOTLAND, AND WALES, MARTYRS OF.

Bibliography: R. CHALLONER, *Memoirs of Missionary Priests,* ed. J. H. POLLEN (rev. ed. London 1924). J. H. POLLEN, *Acts of English Martyrs* (London 1891).

[K. I. RABENSTEIN]

SIMULATION

Simulation is a special form of untruthfulness. It is an acted lie; for while the lie, properly speaking, is untruthfulness in speech, simulation is untruthfulness in deed.

Simulation is sinful, having the same kind and degree of malice as a lie; i.e., in itself it is venially sinful, but according to circumstances (e.g., when it causes another person grave injury) it can be mortal. However, its sinfulness is not quite so obvious as that of the lie. Words have definite meanings; and so if certain words are used that are contrary in meaning to what one has in mind, it is evident that a lie is being told. But actions are not so definitely significative. Except for a few conventional gestures, actions have no set meaning. Here it is the intention that counts. A woman may dye her hair, not wishing to deceive anyone or to appear what she is not, but simply to beautify herself, which, within certain limits, she has every right to do. Another may do exactly the same thing, but with the definite intention to deceive, e.g., to be taken for another woman. Here the intention vitiates the act, and the result is a sin of simulation.

Simulation can manifest itself in a variety of ways and spring from a multiplicity of motives. A man by affectations in demeanor or speech or dress may pretend to a culture or knowledge or wisdom that is not his own. Another may simulate a professional competence, as in the case of the quack or even of the legitimate doctor who poses as a specialist in areas of medicine other than his own. Another may simulate spiritual gifts and virtues, as does the fortune-teller, the clairvoyant, or the hypocrite. Still another may protest a love and respect for one whom in reality he despises. All of this may be from motives of monetary gain, reputation, power, or simply from uncontrolled feelings of inferiority. Ignorant of his own worth and potential, a man puts on a mask that he might appear in the power and worth of another.

It may seem that there are cases in which simulation is legitimate and even virtuous. For instance, one who is sick may act as though he were quite well so as not to cause inconvenience to others; or he may affect ignorance when he feels that a display of knowledge might embarrass another. These are cases not of simulation but of dissimulation. There is no real pretense here springing from a desire to deceive, but simply silence in order to keep one's secret. In ordinary circumstances one need not speak all one knows, and has no obligation to declare to others the state of his body or soul. By the same token one has a right to dissemble, i.e., to act in such a way as to ward off the curiosity of others. However, if being sick, one should simulate health in order to get a job in which health is required, or if one should pretend ignorance to avoid an obligation, which otherwise would be legitimately imposed upon him, then he would be committing the sin of simulation. For he would not simply be forestalling the curiosity of others, but actually and positively deceiving them.

Bibliography: J. A. MCHUGH and C. J. CALLAN, *Moral Theology,* rev. E. P. FARRELL, 2 v. (New York 1958) 2:2403–04.

[S. F. PARMISANO]

SIN (IN THE BIBLE)

The concept of sin, which underwent a gradual change toward increasing clarity and refinement, can be understood in the meanings of the term in the books of the Bible. Sin will be treated as it is described in the Old Testament, and in various sections of the New Testament.

"Temptation of Adam and Eve," painting c. 1550 by Titian. (©Francis G. Mayer/CORBIS)

Sin in the Old Testament

Sin in the Old Testament is portrayed rather graphically and concretely without recourse to theological speculation. It will be treated under four headings, its nature, causes, effects, and in its later development in Judaism.

Nature of Sin in the Old Testament. The words used for sin have generally to do with human relations. The most commonly used root is *ḥaṭṭā'*, meaning to miss the mark (morally, to be deceived, fall short of the goal). In sin the goal is a person, and hence it is a failing toward someone, a violation of the bond uniting persons to one another. Sin is therefore a personal failing as regards God, a failing of Him, a falling short of the mark God sets for us. The less frequent but more theological word *peša'* indicates defiance toward God. It denotes a transgression, the violation of the rights of others, setting the rebellious sinner against God as it sets people one against another. It is a word reserved for Israel's sin.

Ancient Dynamistic Notion. Once Israel came to know God, sin was taken as a personal offense, rebellion or revolt against the covenant God. Yet before Israel became the people of God, it shared the attitude of its neighbors toward God and sin, regarding sin as a violation of the domain of the numinous, and it took a long time before this dynamistic concept of sin died out or was reinterpreted. This taboo-consciousness is patently present in older sections of the Old Testament. For instance, when "Oza put forth his hand to the ark of God, and took hold of it because the oxen kicked and made it lean aside . . . and he [God] struck him for his rashness. And he died there before the ark of God" (2 Sm 6.6–7). Thus, even though sin was considered a violation of the will of God, contact with God or what belonged to Him (holy things) was dangerous, and the notion of sin was still considered a material violation, something outside oneself, not spiritualized. The prohibition of blood meat, the distinction between clean and unclean animals, the rules for ritual purification probably stem from dynamistic backgrounds. Following upon these are the notions of immediate retribution (mentioned above), of collective guilt (Nm 16.32), of guilt for involuntary transgressions of ritual (Lv 4.3), and the notion of *ḥērem*—claimed exclusively for YAHWEH (Joshua 6.17–18). Yet as the Israelite's understanding of God grew, so did his awareness of sin as first of all "against God" [Ps 50(51).6].

Sin as a Personal Offense against God. The word offense itself is rare in the Old Testament as well as in the New Testament. When it is found, however, as in the book of Job, the notion of God's transcendence is more than safeguarded: "If you sin, what injury do you do to God? Even if your offenses are many, how do you hurt him?" (Job 35.5–6). By sin man may despise or contemn the precepts of God and in a sense God Himself. It follows that the sinner acts against God but cannot do anything to God. St. Thomas wisely comments that the sinner acts against God insofar as he contemns His commandments and injures himself or another who is under God's protection.

Alongside the notion of offense against God can be considered that of saddening God within the wider context of SALVATION HISTORY (HEILSGESCHICHTE). The background for this seems to be the above mentioned primitive notion of sin whereby something is actually taken away from the divinity by a sinful act, whatever it be. Vestiges of this can be found in 1 Samuel 5.7–9; 6.19–20; 24.7, 11, 13; 2 Samuel 1.14–16. The authentic notion of sin as an offense against God, however, cannot be drawn from these taboo-breaking narratives.

The personal character of sin as an offense against God is brought out by the sacred writer in his account of David's sin (2 Sm 11–12) and in the Judaic tradition regarding Psalm 50(51). David shows himself ungrateful to God, despising His word, even despising God Himself (2 Sm 12.7, 9–10). David finally acknowledges: "I have sinned against the Lord" (12.13). The King thought that it was only against a man, and one who was not even an

Israelite, and consequently it was not a grave sin; he did not realize that God identifies His cause with every man, in this case, that of Uria.

But despite his confession, David's punishment follows according to the *lex talionis* (12.14); i.e., the child is to die (*see* RETRIBUTION). Thus sin reaches God insofar as it hurts man, whom God loves.

In God's design it was left to the prophets to inculcate the proper sense of sin, not as a simple violation of a taboo or external transgression, but rather as a personal offense against God: ". . . it is your sins that make him hide his face so that he will not hear you" (Is 59.2). They made the people of God aware of the personal relationship between God and them. Within the pattern of the COVENANT, Israel became more aware of the refusal involved in sin, its hardness of heart (Is 46.12; Ez 2.4), its ingratitude: "An ox knows its owner, and an ass, its master's manger; but Israel does not know, my people has not understood" (Is 1.3).

By breaking the covenant, Israel offended against God personally, for the prophets often expressed the covenant relationship as that of a marriage between God and His people. In graphic terms the prophet Hosea's marriage to a harlot wife represented the relation of God to Israel: just as a man is offended by his wife's infideli ties, so Yahweh is offended by the infidelities of Israel, who was betrothed to Him. Israel's infidelity takes the form of idolatry and oppression of the poor. Hosea (ch. 11) expresses God's love and its frustration in a most tender manner: "When Israel was a child I loved him, out of Egypt I called my son. The more I called them, the farther they went from me, sacrificing to the Baals and burning incense . . . yet, though I stooped to feed my child, they did not know that I was their healer" [Hos 11.1–2, 4; cf. Is 5; Jer 2.2; 3.1–5, 20; Is 50.1; 54.6; Ps 44(45); Ez 16].

Notion of Sin in Primeval History. The first chapters of Genesis emphasize the spiritual degeneration of man as a result of the sin of Adam. Man was made in God's image; he lived in communion with Him. Adam's sin was essentially one of disobedience or breaking the covenant law, consciously and deliberately opposing the will of God; it was an external act of rebellion proceeding from within according to the suggestion of the serpent: ". . . you will be like God, knowing good and evil" (Gn 3.5). Doubting His infinite generosity, man defied God in striving for something above himself and thus perverted the notions of man, a creature, and of God who lacks nothing and can only give. When he lost access to the tree of life as well as his Father-son relationship, death followed as a result.

Man's sinfulness increased according to the following chapters of Genesis. His insubordinate pride set man against man, splitting the family and leading to fratricide (Gn 4.3–8), to mass murder and brutality (Gn 4.23–24). The evil was conceived as growing unbearable to God and reaching its climax in the wickedness that brought about the deluge (Gn 6.5–7). After the flood story the sacred editors used the TOWER OF BABEL episode to express man's continued pride and its consequent disunity (Gn 11.1–9). Thus did primeval history present the universality of sin (*see* PRIMEVAL AGE IN THE BIBLE). Sin and unhappiness go together. The first sin separated man from God, aroused shame, drew punishment, multiplied pain and suffering.

Sin as a Revolt against God. Adam's act makes it clear that sin is a revolt (*peša'*). This term provides the theological depth of the Biblical notion of sin. It is a revolt against God and His covenant. It is not a mere mistake or failure since it involves willful disobedience. The verb and noun forms are also used to express rebellions against nations or transgressions against men (1 Kgs 12.19; Am 1.3). The word takes on the idea of trampling on the rights of another, going beyond the limits set for one.

Although missing in Genesis, this word appears in Exodus to denote a new quality of sin in God's people. It is a revolt, a direct attack on God, who by His covenant makes Israel His special possession, His people. The word is later reserved for Israel's sin, especially in the Prophets; e.g., "Woe to them, they have strayed from me! Ruin to them, they have sinned against me!" (Hos 7.13; cf. 8.1–2); "Your first father sinned; your spokesman rebelled against me . . ." (Is 43.27; cf. Mi 1.5; Jer 2.8; Ez 2.3; etc.). Although *peša'* does not occur as frequently as other terms, e.g., *ḥaṭṭā',* it is the strongest word for sin and its meaning is adopted by the New Testament.

The depth of revolt is magnified by the notion of Israel as the spouse and Yahweh, the faithful husband: ". . . she played the harlot. And I thought, after she has done all this she will return home. But she did not return. . ." (Jer 3.6–7); "Return, rebel Israel, says the Lord, I will not remain angry with you. . ." (Jer 3.12). Thus it was the deepest meaning of the covenant that the prophets developed as opposed to sin. The covenant morality was the mind and heart responding to the will and the law of Yahweh. Eventually, with a new mind and heart the true Israelite would be able to live according to God's word, to return to God with a covenant loyalty prompted by God's covenant love and fidelity.

Causes of Sin. The Old Testament generally accuses man as the cause of sin, but other factors outside him also are indicated.

Origin of Sin within Man. The Old Testament as a whole presents evil as beginning in man himself. The OT authors did not speculate but rather traced the source of sin existentially in human life. Sin came from the corrupt heart of man: ". . . this people draws near with words only and honors me with their lips alone, though their hearts are far from me. . ." (Is 29.13). From man's evil heart came all sin: "When the Lord saw . . . that man's every thought and all the inclination of his heart were only evil,. . ." (Gn 6.5). Only when God gave man a new heart would he be able to live by His statutes and carefully observe His decrees (Ex 36.26–27). For the Israelites, it was the heart, the seat of the understanding and will, that had rebelled against God. They said: ". . . we will follow our own devices; each one of us will behave according to the stubbornness of his evil heart!" (Jer 18.12).

Outside Influence. Gn (ch. 3) clearly states that sin came upon earth at the instigation of a superhuman power. The serpent was no mere animal; it was the incarnation of a fundamental element of disorder, the source of revolt and insubordinate pride. He enticed Eve to judge that God's command was not absolute, and thereby caused her to doubt God's word and to suspect that the command was not for man's good but for God's jealously guarded excellence [Gn 3.5; *see* SERPENT (AS SYMBOL)].

In 1 Chronicles 21.1 Satan moved David to sin: "And Satan rose up against Israel and moved David to number Israel" (but cf. 2 Sm 24.1). He also tried to make Job blaspheme God (Job 2.5–8). The Satanic origin of sin is mentioned in the Old Testament, however rarely. The latest Old Testament book, obviously commenting on Genesis 3, states it clearly: "But by the envy of the devil, death entered the world . . ." (Wis 2.24).

Possible Allusions to Concupiscence. Although there is no mention in the Old Testament of a state of personal sin having been inherited from Adam, the inclination to sin is evident: "Indeed in guilt was I born, and in sin my mother conceived me" [Ps 50(51).7]. Concupiscence or tendency to evil comes with the uncleanness of birth. It is ascribed to the children of Adam and Eve. Its result is murder, attempted deception of God, revenge, polygamy, revolt, and complete apostasy from God.

A noticeable change appears in man immediately following his sin before any explicit punishment; though man and woman were naked before the sin, they felt no shame; but after the sin they were ashamed. Previously man had conversed familiarly with God; now he fled from Him (Gn 2.25 and 3.7–8).

Analysis of Sin. Beyond the account of Genesis 3, the Old Testament does not analyze sin psychologically. As mentioned above, the Old Testament writers approach sin concretely as it appeared in human life. Yet, the Old Testament certainly provides distinction between sins. Besides sins of thought, word, and deed there are sins of omission and commission, e.g., Heli's sin by not correcting his sons (1 Sm 3.13). More important, however, is the distinction between serious sins, e.g., sins committed "with an uplifted hand," i.e., defiantly (Nm 15.30), and slight sins; between crimes and hidden sins, i.e., those done with full deliberation in open revolt against God and those incurred by human weakness and inadvertence. Some of the more serious sins were: IDOLATRY (Ex 22.19), MAGIC (Ex 22.17), DIVINATION (Lv 19.26; etc.), and BLASPHEMY (Lv 24.11–16). Some sins punishable by death were: murder (Ex 21.12–14), striking or cursing parents (21.15, 17), kidnapping (Ex 21.16), ADULTERY, INCEST, homosexuality, and bestiality (Lv 20.10–16). Other sins, serious though not punishable by death, were: stealing (Ex 21.37–22.3), slandering one's wife (Dt 22.13–19), seducing a virgin (Ex 22.15–16), etc. Sins of youth were considered lesser sins because of inexperience [Job 13.26; Ps 24(25).7].

Effects of Sin. Sin left its mark on the sinner, on nature itself, and on all men universally.

Guilt. As a result of revolt against God, a sense of guilt arose. The Old Testament generally did not distinguish between sin and resultant guilt. The most frequent term for expressing guilt was *'āwōn* denoting all the disorder, deviation, and falseness that sin involves. Its most common note is the burden whose weight bears down on the sinner. Another word *'āšām* (to be guilty) could also mean guilt offering. In Leviticus and Numbers it refers to becoming guilty as a result of cultic transgressions and reflects the dynamistic background of sin. In some places the root conveys the notion of moral guilt (Prv 30.10; Gn 26.10; Jer 2.3; 51.5; etc.).

Evil Effect on Creation. Creation manifests God's power and wisdom (Is 40.12; Job 28.23–27; 38–39); His majesty shines through His creation [Ps 8; 18 (19).1–7; 103(104)]. Yet after Adam's sin the ground was corrupted because of man:

> Cursed be the ground because of you; in toil shall you eat of it all the days of your life; Thorns and thistles shall it bring forth to you, and you shall eat the plants of the field. In the sweat of your brow you shall eat bread, till you return to the ground, Since out of it you were taken; for dust you are and unto dust you shall return (Gn 3.17–19).

What was intended for man's good and happiness now became his chastisement. Calamities involving creation itself followed man's sin: the Deluge, the plagues of Egypt, and the curses on unfaithful Israel (Dt

28.15–46). In the end nature would undergo total transformation and renewal (Is 11.6–9; 65.17–25; 66.22).

Universality of Sin. The Hebrew tradition was firm: all men were considered sinners. Although just and wicked men were always distinguished, the universality of sin was the cause of the Flood (Gn 6.5–8), and man's heart was inclined to evil from his youth (Gn 8.21). The prophets considered the nation as a whole sinful, evil, laden with wickedness (Is 1.4; Ez 2.5; Mi 7.2; Jer 5.1). The psalmists and sages proclaimed this universality: "All alike have gone astray; they have become perverse; there is no one who does good, not even one" [Ps13(14).3]; ". . . yet there is no man on earth so just as to do good and never sin" (Ecc 7.20). The wisdom writers especially emphasized the universality of sin. The antithesis of the just and the wicked occurred frequently in their works (Prv 11.21; 21.29; etc.). Job, although his innocence was necessary to establish the author's point, realized that he could not be sure of his sinlessness (Job 9.21). In fact, the whole of the Old Testament is a massive denunciation of sin as an offense against God.

In Judaism. In JUDAISM the Law was especially important in determining the notion of sin. Every transgression of the Law was a sin, a rebellion against God's will. There was some effort, however, to maintain the Old Testament distinction of sinning defiantly and sinning through ignorance. Since the 6th century B.C., because of Jeremiah and Ezekiel, the tendency was to put the burden of guilt on the individual as well as on the community. Generally Judaism considered sin as universal and coextensive with mankind having had its origin in the sin of Adam and Eve. Sin was a controlling power over the world. By observing the Law man could overcome the inclination to sin. Following upon sin was punishment including sickness, death, and eternal damnation. Repentance and return to God, however, was always possible because of God's mercy.

Sin in the New Testament

The most prominent word for sin in the New Testament is ἁμαρτία, which renders *ḥaṭṭā'* in the Septuagint, indicating deviation from the good. In the classical authors it indicated "missing of a target." It could refer to wrong done to man, but above all it expressed sin against God. 'Αμαρτία itself referred to a single act, a characteristic of human nature, or a personal power. In the Synoptics and Acts this word is almost always used as the object of forgiveness, more often in the plural. John and Paul employed the plural especially in formulas referring to remission of sins and to Christ's death for sins. The singular often indicates the sinful state of the world (John) or the power of sin (Paul).

A related term is ἀνομία, meaning lawlessness, iniquity, or a lawless deed. The term usually indicates a state of hostility toward God and His salvific revelation, and reveals the depth of sin. In this sense the one who sins rejects his Christian vocation and communion with God and submits to the devil's domination.

In the Synoptics. Every vestige of the taboo notion of sin has vanished together with the legalistic and impersonal notion (Mk 7.1–23; cf. Mt 15.1–20).

In Matthew 7.23, 13.41, and 24.12 the word ἀνομία (iniquity) is used in an eschatological context: "Depart from me, you workers of iniquity!" Christ refers to the Pharisees as full of iniquity (Mt 23.28). Sin is usually, however, presented in the context of forgiveness. In the parable of the prodigal son (Lk 15.11–32) the sin consisted in the son's leaving his father to enjoy a life of debauchery. The offense was a desertion of the father along with a squandering of the father's wealth in loose living. In forgiving, the father showed mostly his joy at his son's return and never even mentioned the injuries he suffered. The son recognized his sin as an offense against heaven and his father whereby he destroyed his own sonship. The miserable servitude he suffered was the natural consequence of his sin. His father recognized that by his return the son has passed from death to life. Sin then was slavery and death as well as an offense against God.

Christ's life and mission destroyed Satan's reign of slavery and death and replaced it with freedom and life in the Father's house. Following His victory over the devil in the desert, Jesus drove out devils from the possessed, cured ills caused by unclean spirits, and restored the health of a paralytic to prove He had the power to forgive sins (Mt 9.2–8). Sin then was considered as the source of all these ills of mankind.

In the Pauline Epistles. Paul usually referred to sin as something internal and stable in man. Except in certain formulas, ἁμαρτία does not usually signify an act of sin, but almost a personal force in man that acts through his body. It entered into the world with Adam's sin and exercised its deadly work by means of the Law. Thus in Paul sin is similar to what iniquity means in 1 John 3.4. Paul also used iniquity in the Johannine sense in the phrase, "the mystery of iniquity" (2 Thes 2.7). Sin then was not just an act of disobedience to God's will and law; it was open revolt against Him, the result of which was a state that was inimical to God and would lead to death. For the act of sin, other terms were generally used, literally signifying transgression or overstepping.

In Romans (ch. 5) Paul showed that sin permeates the whole human race through death, but its power is not equal to Christ's grace and justice: "For if by reason of the one man's offense death reigned through the one man, much more will they who receive the abundance of the grace and of the gift of justice reign in life through the one Jesus Christ. . .'' (5.17). By being baptized into Christ's death and Resurrection man is freed from sin and begins to live by Christ's life. ''For we were buried with him by means of Baptism into death, in order that, just as Christ has risen from the dead through the glory of the Father, so we also may walk in newness of life'' (6.4). Thus through Baptism the Christian is conformed to Christ so that after Baptism the ''old man'' and the ''body of sin'' cease to be the instruments of sin. Now the Christian has a new ''mode of being,'' a new ''mode of acting.'' He is no longer in the service of sin; the Holy Spirit is present in him. The new man is inspired, motivated by the Spirit to fight against the flesh; he passes from the carnal state to a spiritual state. The opposition between the flesh and spirit indicates the nature of sin, for sinful flesh is thus described as God's enemy while the spirit is God's gift. Sin, then, is a personal force by which man is opposed to God, and sinful deeds are its works.

These principles concerning the nature of sin are concretized in Romans 1.18–3.20, 23, where Paul speaks of the sin of all mankind, Jew and Gentile alike. The Gentile refuses to acknowledge God as the author of all good. Hence he no longer cares to depend on God, the invisible source of all visible things; he turns away from Him, excites His wrath, and is delivered by Him to all kinds of sinful passions. And the Jew is no better; although he knows God and His Law, he does not honor Him by keeping it. In fact, because of the Law, he becomes more conscious of sin and guilt, and should be more conscious of his need for justification, whereas he is not. Paul sums up his doctrine on the role of sin in the mystery of salvation in Romans 3.22–23: ''For there is no distinction [between Jew and Greek], as all have sinned and have need of the glory of God'' (cf. Rom 7.7–25). Even sin plays its role in God's plan: it makes man cry out in his misery, ''Who will deliver me from the body of this death?'' (Rom 7.24).

In Johannine Writings. Although the Synoptics generally speak of sin in the plural, John speaks of it more often in the singular (13 times; three times in the plural). John's notion of sin is that of a separation from God ending in hatred of God and servitude to the devil.

By way of opposition, the nature of sin is seen in the Lord's way of destroying it. Christ takes away the sin of the world (Jn 1.29; 1 Jn 3.4–10) by cleansing with the Holy Spirit (Jn 1.33), by a rebirth from on high, from the Spirit (Jn 3.3–8; 1.12–13), by giving His disciples the freedom of the Son (Jn 8.31–36), by giving them His peace through His return to the Father by way of the Cross (Jn 14.27–31). Christ can take away sin because He is the light of the world (Jn 8.12; 12.35–36); in contrast, sinners and sin belong to the realm of darkness (Jn 3.19–21; 9.3–5). According to 1 John sinners are the devil's children (3.8, 10; cf. Jn 8.38–47). Christ has come: ''that he might destroy the works of the devil'' (1 Jn 3.8). The Christian, born of God, does not commit sin because God's seed, Christ, abides in him. The sinner is the devil's son, the devil's slave, a murderer as he was from the beginning, he who ''has not stood in the truth because there is no truth in him.'' When he tells a lie he speaks from his very nature, for he is a liar and the father of lies (Jn 8.44). Jesus, in contrast, is the truth (8.45; 14.6; 1.14, 17–18) and the life (14.6; 3.14–16, 36; 5.21, 24–29; 6.48–60; 11.25). He opposes the devil who brings sin and death (8.21–21; 44) and casts him out by His own death (12.31–33).

Sin is also hatred: ''For everyone who does evil hates the light, and does not come to the light, that his deeds may not be exposed'' (Jn 3.20). This hatred leads the Jews to hate Christ and to have Him killed. Consequently, ''now they have no excuse for their sin. He who hates me hates my Father also'' (Jn 15.22–23). Thus they do the work of their father, the devil (Jn 8.41).

By counteracting sin, hatred, and the devil, Jesus gives the supreme revelation of the New Testament: that God is love (1 Jn 4.8). Jesus' one command to His disciples, then, is to love one another as He has loved them (Jn 13.34–35; 15.12–17). Whoever hates his brother is still in darkness; he is a murderer and a liar (1 Jn 2.11; 3.15; 4.20).

John presents the Passion as instigated by the devil (Jn 13.2, 27; 14.30); but Christ overcomes the devil and sin: ''Now is the judgment of the world; now will the prince of the world be cast out'' (12.31; cf. 16.7–11; 14.30–31). Revelation puts it this way: ''And that great dragon was cast down, the ancient serpent, he who is called the devil and Satan, who leads astray the whole world. . .'' (12.9). Thus Jesus in the very act of laying down His life for His sheep cries out: ''It is consummated!'' (Jn 19.30; 10.17–18). His peace has come to the world through the Holy Spirit and the power to forgive sins for all who believe (20.20–23, 29–31).

Characteristics of Sin in the New Testament. The New Testament writers generally understand sin as a concrete reality. Christ mingles with its perpetrators like a physician among the sick (Mk 2.15–17; Lk 7.34). For Jesus those who commit sin are the lost whom He seeks to find and save (Lk 19.9–10; 15.1–10); they are the dead to whom He offers life and merriment (Lk 15.22–24, 31–32). Sin is a canker of the heart and from the corrupt heart come all sorts of evil deeds: ''For from within, out of the heart of men, come evil thoughts, adulteries, immorality, murders, thefts, covetousness, wickedness, deceit. . . . All these evil things come from within and defile a man'' (Mk 7.21–23). The new law goes more deeply into man to root out the hidden causes of sin (Mt 5.21–48). The greatest sin is to reject the Spirit, to refuse the light (Mt 12.31–32; Jn 9.39–41). Sin, then, is a real disease that demands a radical cure and a complete change in one's way of thinking (μετάνοια, change of mind, REPENTANCE, Mk 1.15).

For Paul sin is so real that it acts as a force conditioning the world. This idea stems from Paul's profound experience described in Romans 7.13–25. There he saw that sin's only cure was the ''grace of God through Jesus Christ our Lord.'' Paul personifies the notion of sin and portrays its tyranny over mankind, as that of a master over his slave with death as the sinner's wages. Only Christ can destroy the effect of sin, a sting that brings death (1 Cor 15.55–57). In Baptism the Christian dies with Christ to sin and rises with Him to life (Rom 4.25); he becomes a new being (Rom 6.4), a new creation: ''If then any man is in Christ, he is a new creature: the former things have passed away; behold, they are made new!'' (2 Cor 5.17). He is no longer in the flesh but in the Spirit (Rom 7.5; 8.9). The mystery of divine wisdom is that God made the sinless Christ to be ''sin'' so that man might become God's justice (2 Cor 5.21).

Besides tracing all sin back to Adam, the New Testament considered SATAN a source of sin. He tempted Christ Himself (Mt 4.3–11); he tempts Christians: ''Be sober, be watchful! For your adversary the devil, as a roaring lion, goes about seeking someone to devour'' (1 Pt 5.8; cf. Eph 6.12; Jn 13.2; Acts 5.3).

The immediate cause of sin, however, is man himself: ''All these evil things come from within, and defile a man'' (Mk 7.23). St. Paul speaks of an inner tendency to evil expressed by the term ''flesh.'' The flesh sets man against what good reason or the Law prescribes. It leads man to evil and to death: ''For the inclination of the flesh is death, but the inclination of the spirit, life and peace'' (Rom 8.6; cf. 6.19; 13.14; Gal 5.16–17, 24). Paul speaks of sinful flesh (Rom 8.3) and the body of sin (Rom 6.6); ''I am carnal, sold into the power of sin'' (Rom 7.14). Hence man is in sin's power as long as he has not received Christ's Spirit. All men are subject to the ''power of sin'' because of Adam's sin (Rom 5.19).

The flesh, then, is the internal factor for sin, while the Law is an external factor making man aware of his sinfulness. The Law cooperated with the flesh to bring man to sin consciously. Even though the Law expressed God's will, it was incapable in itself to effect salvation. When sinful flesh clashes with the Law that prohibits sin, sin abounds the more (Rom 5.20). Yet in the plan of God the Law, by its increasing of transgressions, serves His purpose; His justice and glory is proclaimed by His Son's sacrifice and all human self-glorification is destroyed: ''By sending his Son in the likeness of sinful flesh as a sin-offering, he has condemned sin in the flesh in order that the requirements of the Law might be fulfilled in us, who walk not according to the flesh but according to the spirit'' (Rom 8.4).

Sin, then, is the normal human situation: ''If we say that we have no sin, we deceive ourselves, and the truth is not in us'' (1 Jn 1.8). But John also says: ''Whoever is born of God does not commit sin, because his [God's] seed abides in him and he cannot sin, because he is born of God'' (1 Jn 3.9). The Christian therefore cannot remain in the state of sin and continue to be God's son. His divine sonship is directly opposed to the state of lawlessness. It follows that while man is still in the world, still in the body, he must war against sin. Likeness to Christ and spiritualization come by justification, but the battle is not over; one must still put to death one's sinful inclinations (Col 3.1–5). Only in the heavenly Jerusalem will the threat of sin be no more (Rv 21.27; 22.14–15). Hence the Sacrament of Penance, having the permanent power of Christ's Blood and infinite mercy, is given for the remission of sins: ''Receive the Holy Spirit; whose sins you shall forgive, they are forgiven them; and whose sins you shall retain, they are retained'' (Jn 20.23). The need for a continual source of forgiveness is indicated in Luke's version of the Lord's prayer: ''Forgive us our sins, for we also forgive everyone who is indebted to us'' (Lk 11.4). The Christian, once he shares in Christ's victory over sin, must still work out his salvation ''with fear and trembling'' and manifest God's works in him by will and performance (Phil 2.12–13).

With the coming of Jesus, God made His ultimate intervention in salvation history, and the salvation brought by Him was from sin: ''. . . and thou shalt call his name Jesus, for he shall save his people from their sins'' (Mt 1.21); ''And thou, child, shall be called the prophet of the Most High, for thou shalt go before the face of the Lord to prepare his ways, to give his people knowledge of salvation through forgiveness of their sins . . .'' (Lk 1.76–77); ''Behold, the Lamb of God, who takes away the sin of the world!'' (Jn 1.29). Since there is no sin in Him, He is its conqueror (1 Jn 3.5). Jesus overcame the world and the devil (Jn 12.31; 16.33). His birth, life, death and Resurrection were for this purpose: the conquering of sin and the giving of life: ''I came that they may have life, and have it more abundantly'' (Jn 10.10).

Although He did not make sweeping statements concerning the universality of sin, Christ considered all men sinful. He saw sin in the hearts of the strict observers of the Law and denounced them (Mt 12.34–35; 16.4; 23.33). Even His disciples were included in this perverse generation (Lk 9.41). Christ Himself showed His solidarity with man's sinfulness in accepting baptism and the cross although He was sinless (Mt 3.13–15; 2 Cor 5.21; Rom 8.3; Gal 3.13; Heb 4.15; 7.26–27; 1 Pt 1.19; 2.21–25; 1 Jn 3.5; Is 53.6–8).

Following the pattern of the Wisdom literature, Paul clearly portrays the universality of sin: "For we have argued that Jews and Greeks are all under sin. . ." (Rom 3.9; cf. 6.16–23; Tm 3.3). Hence all men are sinners and in need of Christ's redemption.

According to John, Christ came to take away the sin of the world (Jn 1.29). That all are subject to sin is implied in the use of the singular, "sin" of the world. "If we say that we have no sin, we deceive ourselves, and the truth is not in us," but man's universal problem has a solution, for "If we acknowledge our sins, he is faithful and just to forgive us our sins and to cleanse us from all iniquity" (1 Jn 1.8–9).

See Also: GUILT (IN THE BIBLE); ORIGINAL SIN

Bibliography: *Encyclopedic Dictionary of the Bible*, tr. and adap. by L. HARTMAN (New York 1963), from A. VAN DEN BORN, *Bijbels Woordenboek* 2218–32. S. J. DE VRIES, G. A. BUTTRICK ed., *The Interpreters' Dictionary of the Bible*, 4 v. (Nashville 1962) 4:361–76. J. HASTINGS and J. A. SELBIA, eds., *Dictionary of the Bible*, rev. in 1 v. ed. F. C. GRANT and H. H. ROWLEY (New York 1963) 916–22. G. KITTEL, ed., *Bible Key Words* (New York 1951). P. RIGA, *Sin and Penance* (Milwaukee 1962). X. LÉON-DUFOUR, ed., *Vocabulaire de theologie biblique* (Paris 1962) 774–87. P. DELHAYE et al., *Theologie du péché* (Tournai 1960). S. LYONNET, *De notione peccati,* v.1 of *De peccato et redemptione* (Rome 1957–). J. GUILLET, *Themes of the Bible,* tr. A. J. LAMOTHE (Notre Dame, Indiana 1960). J. GIBLET, *The God of Israel: The God of the Christians,* tr. K. SULLIVAN (New York 1961) 149–63. H. RONDET, *The Theology of Sin,* tr. R. W. HUGHES (Notre Dame, Indiana 1960). C. R. SMITH, *The Bible Doctrine of Sin and the Ways of God with Sinners* (London 1953). L. MORALDI, *Espiazione sacrificale e riti espiatori . . .* (*Analecta biblica* 5; Rome 1956).

[J. LACHOWSKI]

SIN (PHENOMENOLOGY OF)

Sin is a notion that indicates most emphatically disruption of what is religiously sanctioned or required. Although as a rule the disruption takes place through man, sin always indicates the result of a power of evil that exceeds man's capabilities or it indicates that power itself; hence, special care is needed to avoid or to free from sin (*see* PURIFICATION; EXPIATION). Sin implies more or less strongly an ethical notion. Everywhere words for sin occur that denote moral transgressions, and the ethical nature of sin depends on the religious tradition of a community. At the same time, notions of sin imply impurity or religious defilement; "sinful" and "impure" are synonymous concepts in all civilizations with a cultic tradition. The contents of the notions for sin depend on their opposites—purity, justice, wholeness, sanctity, the sacred. Because of their peculiarly religious character and function within a religious setting, notions of sin are, as a rule, more comprehensive than an exclusively ethical notion of "bad" or "unacceptable," or any other specialized concept. This is particularly clear in most primitive religions where the same words can be rendered by "to heal" (a wound) or "to liberate" (from a magic spell), and the evil that makes purification imperative relates to what for us would be distinct realms—the physical, moral, spiritual.

The polarity between sin and its opposite is related to the inner ambivalence of the sacred itself. Greek ἅγιος, meaning consecrated, pure, or holy, occurs also in the opposite sense of dangerously desecrated, impure, damned. Latin *sacer* shows a comparable ambivalence. Different, but not unrelated, the polarity of impurity (sinfulness) and purity functions in the Brahmanic ritual; special ceremonies dissolve the sins of the sacrificer, thus preparing him for the sacred rite. Yet similarly, a ceremony takes place at the end for his return to ordinary life, as if it were an equally necessary desanctification.

Origin of Awareness of Sin. Generally held views on concepts of sin in the history of religions have been unduly affected by evolutionistic presuppositions. First, the assumption was too often made that personal awareness of right and wrong and a corresponding consciousness of guilt were late phenomena in the history of man. Secondly, until very recently, little or no sense of sinfulness was ascribed to primitive religions, other than for specific moral transgressions. Both views have proved to be erroneous. The former has been refuted in recent ethnology (especially by Jensen). Many hunter cultures naturally honor the successful hunter; yet the act of killing the game is regarded as a sin which requires special purification. The latter view has been opposed by a more careful study of myths; paradise and fall myths are widespread among the primitives and indicate a consciousness not only of individual wrongdoings, but more generally an awareness of man's *sinful state.*

Forms and Aspects of Sin. The various concepts and forms of sin in various philological contexts, and on different cultural levels, cannot be distinguished as stages in a historical process. However, we may discern aspects that are of greater clarity in some settings than in others.

Moral Sins. These are fundamental to the religions of most primitive societies because of the idea of physical results. Thus barren women may confess their moral infidelities in order to stop their barrenness, which is attributed to their transgressions. The typically Greek concept of sin, ὕβρις, known particularly as "pride" (or rather "wanton overestimation of oneself" or "disproportionate good fortune") is used also (in Homer and even later, e.g., in Theognis) in reference to moral offenses. Religions that have developed elaborate cults and theological acumen never abandon the religious notion of moral sins. In the Egyptian *Book of the Dead* (ch. 125) a long list of sins is mentioned, which the (deceased) king declares that he has not committed. Manichaeism also produced lists of sins; they occur in confessional forms used in the liturgy. Here and elsewhere, however, moral and doctrinal transgressions are mentioned side by side.

The Breaking of a Taboo. This is regarded as particularly sinful. The sense of this type of guilt is by no means limited to primitive cultures, in which, for instance, a man is not allowed to speak to his mother-in-law. Modern Western man considers some offenses, such as grave-robbing, particularly heinous, although the moral reason why they would be worse than many other offenses is obscure. The reason for such sense of guilt at the breaking of a taboo is to be sought in a commonly held profound reverence (as expressed by German, *Ehrfurcht*).

Mythical and Cultic Aspects. Almost all religious traditions recall in some sense a state of perfection at the beginning of creation; creation myths are often interwoven with paradise myths. Hence the cultic forms in which sins or man's sinful state play a role are connected with cosmogony. A sinful deed—or the breaking of a taboo—is to be understood as the forgetting of the divine, mythical process, which is the model for rightful human activity. Often the sinner is required to perform an expiatory sacrifice, which is modeled on the primordial sacrifice—in that divine mythical process—in order to bring to mind precisely that which was forgotten (Jensen). Likewise, the mythical origin of evil may be related to man's sin or sinfulness. Egypt portrayed the prototype of evil in the harm done by Seth to Osiris in mythical time. This evil (*dw-t*) is more than individual transgression, but the same word occurs also in that sense. In Egypt and many other places the ultimate measure of sin or evil is associated with the powers of chaos that are overcome by the creator; this victory is preserved in the justice of the king. For that reason breaking the king's law is a religious and cultic offense. A close connection of religious and moral sin is particularly striking in the cults of the mystery religions (*see* MYSTERY RELIGIONS, GRECO-ORIENTAL).

Speculative and Theological Reflections. In religious systems with great emphasis on individual efforts to attain sacred liberating knowledge, sin is regarded principally as obstructing impurity [*see* ASCETICISM; GNOSTICISM] or demerit (*see* BUDDHISM; JAINISM; HINDUISM). In classical Indian YOGA the aspirant must master first of all five "restraints" *yamas* (not to kill, not to lie, not to steal, sexual abstinence, not to be avaricious). In all ascetic and gnostic life certain "sins" must be conquered, even if they are such as are tolerated in common life. In all ascetic and gnostic systems, a strong awareness exists of an evil greater than any individual transgression. A precosmic fall is an object of theological reflection both in Gnosticism and in MANICHAEISM. The Indian religions emphasize impurity and its results as a generally human conditioning (*see* INDIAN PHILOSOPHY). In *Bhakti* and other forms of devotional religion in which God's grace is supreme, man's relation to God is sometimes longed for or exulted in to such an extent as to make the sinful and imperfect state seem of no significance by contrast.

See Also: SIN (IN THE BIBLE); SIN (THEOLOGY OF).

Bibliography: H. FRANKFORT, *Ancient Egyptian Religion* (New York 1948). H. ABRAHAMSSON, *The Origin of Death: Studies in African Mythology* (Uppsala 1951). M. ELIADE, "Nostalgia for Paradise in Primitive Traditions," in his *Myths, Dreams, and Mysteries,* tr. P. MAIRET (New York 1960); *Yoga: Immortality and Freedom,* tr. W. R. TRASK (New York 1958). A. E. JENSEN, *Myth and Cult among Primitive Peoples,* tr. M. T. CHOLDIN and W. WEISSLEDER (Chicago 1963); "Über den sittlichen Gehalt der primitiven Religionen," *Paideuma* 3 (1949) 241–256. H. JONAS, *The Gnostic Religion* (2d ed. rev. Boston 1963). R. CAILLOIS, *L'Homme et le Sacré* (2d ed. Paris 1953). O. F. BOLLNOW, *Die Ehrfurcht* (Frankfurt a.M. 1958). G. MENSCHING, *Die Idee der Sünde, ihre Entwicklung in den Hochreligionen des Orients und Okzidents* (Leipzig 1931). H. BAUMANN, *Schöpfung und Urzeit des Menschen im Mythus der afrikanischen Völker* (Berlin 1936). L. J. CAZEMIER, "Het begrip zonde in de Pyramideteksten," in G.v.d. Leeuw Festschrift *Pro Regno Pro Sanctuario* (Nijkerk 1950) 101–113. É. DES PLACES, "Péché. dans la Grèce Antique," *Dictionnaire de la Bible,* suppl. ed. L. PIROT, et al. 7 (Paris 1962) 471–480. H. B. ALEXANDER et al., J. HASTINGS, ed., *Encyclopedia of Religion & Ethics,* 13 v. (Edinburgh 1908–27) 11:528–570, old, but still useful.

[K. W. BOLLE]

SIN (THEOLOGY OF)

Sin is an evil human act. But an act is evil, bad, or wanting in the goodness or perfection it should have, because it is out of conformity with its proper norm, or standard. With regard to the human act, the norm, or standard, from a philosophical point of view, is man's rational nature; and from the theological point of view, God's nature and the eternal law. This article, being concerned with the theology of sin, considers sin mainly as an offense against God, and can therefore take as its starting point St. Augustine's classical definition of it as a word, deed, or desire in opposition to the eternal law of God (*C. Faust.* 22.27).

''Sloth,'' in kitchen, mid-19th-Century drawing by Louis Boilly. (©Historical Picture Archive/CORBIS)

This definition applies primarily and univocally to personal, mortal sins, a mortal sin being a fully deliberate act involving a sinner's choice of some created good as a final end in preference to the Supreme Good, with a consequent loss of sanctifying grace if, prior to the sinful act, the sinner possessed that grace. In other uses the term is analogical, and as such is applied to: (1) venial sin, in which the idea is not fully realized, either because the act is imperfectly deliberate or because the matter with which it is concerned involves no disruption of man's orientation toward his final end and is therefore compatible with sanctifying grace; (2) original sin, which is not an act, but an inherited defect of sanctifying grace and is antecedent to and independent of personal voluntary action; (3) habitual sin, which is not an act, but a state in which the sinner is without grace because of his personal sin; and (4) concupiscence, which is not an act, but a tendency or imbalance in the psychological integrity of the human composite, and which is not, in the words of the Council of Trent, ''sin in the true and proper sense, but [is called sin] only because it is from sin and inclines to sin'' (H. Denzinger, *Enchiridion symbolorum*, ed. A. Schönmetzer, 1515).

Material and Formal Sin. There are two ways of looking at an action that is in disaccord with God's law. It can be considered objectively and in its kind or subjectively, as it is in the consciousness of the individual who performs it. From the objective point of view, the act of feeding poison to another is out of accord with the eternal law, but a person doing so could be innocent of subjective fault if he is inculpably ignorant of the fact that the food he offers is poisoned and hence is unaware of the true nature and consequences of his act. The performance of an objectively evil act is called by theologians a material sin; when all the conditions necessary to subjective imputability are present, the act is said to be a formal sin. The determination of the objective sinfulness of an action is made on the basis of divine revelation as interpreted by the magisterium of the Church and also on the basis of the rational analysis of the nature of the act. This is properly a theological or a philosophical question. The determination of subjective responsibility is more immediately a psychological question. Contemporary interest, with its existential orientation, tends to center more on the latter question than on the former, and an anti-intellectualism that fails to distinguish between the two problems leads to moral relativism and situational ethics. It also brings confusion to any discussion of the role of conscience in moral activity. Although all are acutely conscious of the problem of the erroneous conscience and the obligation (not the right) to follow its dictates, the contemporary existentialist tends to be blind to the prior obligation to form an upright conscience, the only kind, according to reason and revelation, that confers the right to follow its dictates.

Sin as an Act. Sin is to be distinguished not only from the morally good act and habit to which it is opposed, but also from the morally bad habit, or VICE, which is not uncommonly its habitual source. Properly speaking, vices are not sins, but habits, whereas a sin is a voluntary act and does not necessarily demand a vicious habit any more than a good moral act demands a virtue for its source. Otherwise the vicious man could never perform a good act, nor could the virtuous man ever sin, an error condemned by the Council of Trent (*Enchiridion symbolorum* 1540). Moreover, a sin is a HUMAN ACT, and precisely as such requires the exercise of both intellect and will. When this is lacking, a man's act is amoral and cannot be described as human, or virtuous, or vicious, or sinful. Basically, therefore, sin is a deliberate and voluntary act. Even in the so-called sin of omission, the omission to be sinful must be traceable to a positive act of will, the object of which is either not-to-act or to do something incompatible with the omitted obligation. And in either case there is an act marked by a want of conformity with the law of God.

Reference to God. The elaboration, therefore, of the theological notion of sin must begin not with the sinner, but with God. Pius XII decried as one of the errors of modern times the misrepresentation of ''the whole nature of original sin, and indeed of sin in general, considered as an offense against God . . .'' (*Enchiridion symbolorum* 3891). Since the theologian is concerned with creatures only inasmuch as God is their principle and goal, human activity becomes theologically significant in accordance with its orientation to God. Man is made to pursue his happiness, and ultimately this can be achieved only in the attainment of the Supreme Good, which is God. His human activity must be directed to this goal, and even such part of it as has other more immediate and proximate objectives must be ultimately subordinated to the ultimate, supreme goal, which is desirable above all things and answers objectively to the full amplitude of human desire.

But man's end in reaching toward happiness and God's purpose in creating man are really identical. For God, who is perfect, complete, self-contained in Himself, was not urged or drawn to the creation of man by the hope of acquiring new perfection for Himself, for there is nothing good or desirable that was not already contained in His own infinite goodness. It was not, then, for the sake of increasing but of diffusing His goodness that He created. On His part, the object of creation could be nothing but the giving of Himself, the communicating of His goodness. The gain had necessarily to be on the part of the creature. In the ultimate communication of a participation in His own happiness, the extrinsic glory of God that is said to be the purpose of creation is realized. [*See* GLORY OF GOD (END OF CREATION).] It follows that man, by nature a rational being and a free agent with the power of selective activity, must deliberately and consciously direct himself to the attainment of God, or to the glory of God, as his ultimate end. Deliberately to choose some other goal than God as an ultimate is to take something from God that is due Him, to twist the whole order of creation, and to usurp God's place by substituting a human will and a human order for the divine. In this way every sinner imitates in his own fashion the sin of Lucifer.

A further precision, providing a more profound insight into the nature of mortal sin, is possible to theologians who take, as most Catholic theologians have taken, the intellectualist position of St. Thomas Aquinas with respect to divine law. This, however, is beyond the grasp of those such as Calvin and voluntarists generally, who in their concern to preserve the transcendent and even autocratic supremacy of God, have held that the ultimate norm of what is right and wrong is simply the good pleasure of God. The eternal law, as seen from the intellectualist position, is not arbitrary or whimsical, nor can it be divorced from the nature of things. The eternal law is reducible ultimately not to the divine will but to the divine intellect. It is the plan and pattern of created nature as God's intellect sees this in His vision of Himself. Consequently, the sinner who deviates from the eternal law does violence to his individual nature and to the created order of things of which he is a part. For the voluntarist, the eternal law is a barricade or a leash confining the liberty of individual men who are constrained through fear to observe it. It is much easier from the intellectualist position to love God's law because the intellectualist sees in it a sorely needed gift that God in His mercy has dispensed to men. It is easier to see sin not only as a violation of God's law, but as an act of self-mutilation and self-destruction. Man reaches his perfection and fulfillment in an orderly way by taking his place within God's plan of love, which is manifest to him by the natural and the positive divine law. The voluntary act by which he withdraws from God's plan and substitutes one of his own is sinful because it is the rejection in fact and in deed of God's love. Thus the proportionate remedy for sin, whether it be described as repentance, reconciliation, remission, or justification, is the appreciative love of God, the act of perfect love, which also effects the restoration of the sinner to his proper place in creation, or to the state of grace.

It is possible to express the malice involved in mortal sin in various ways: it breaks the ties of love binding man to God and is the rejection of the divine goodness; as an aversion from God and a conversion to some created good in His place, it is a kind of idolatry; it involves contempt of God and of His precepts; it is an injustice to Him in denying Him His rights; it breaks the new covenant of mercy and love made by God through Jesus Christ (cf. Hebrews 10.28–29); it is an act of base ingratitude to God, who has been so good and generous to man.

The Question of the Philosophical Sin. The distinction between sin as an offense against God and sin as a violation of nature makes it possible for one to ask whether a sinner can be guilty of sin in the theological sense of the term if in sinning he is conscious only that his act is out of harmony with his rational nature. Such a person, according to an opinion advanced by François Musnier in 1686, would be guilty only of a philosophical sin, but not of an offense against God. This opinion was proscribed by Alexander VIII in 1690 as scandalous, temerarious, offensive to pious ears, and erroneous (*Enchiridion symbolorum* 2291). All theologians are agreed that, objectively speaking, all sin is sin in the theological sense. Whether this is also true of all sin, considered from the point of view of subjective responsibility, has been disputed by some authors. In the opinion of most theologians, who see the authority of God as the proximate basis of moral obligation, every sin, even when considered subjectively, must be a sin in the theological sense because in their opinion no true moral obligation can exist for one who does not know himself to be bound to the observance of moral law by the authority of God. Thus, if one can suppose that a man is invincibly ignorant of God's existence, he would not, in this view, be capable of moral action in the proper sense of the word, and however advanced he might be in years, he would be morally in the condition of a child who has not yet reached the age of reason. This was, for example, the opinion of L. Billot, who was willing to admit that there are many of adult age in that situation [*De Deo uno* (Rome 1931) 50]. However, the recognition of the authority of a divine lawmaker who is offended by sin need not be clear and explicit. It seems to be implicit in all true moral judgment.

Constitutive Elements. In every sin it is possible to distinguish two elements, one positive and the other negative, or, more exactly, privative. The positive element consists in the sinner's conversion to some created good, ''good,'' that is, in the sense that it so attracts him that he prefers the satisfaction to be found in it to the divine good. Converting thus to a created good, the sinner by the same act turns away from God and is deprived of his orientation to God along with sanctifying grace and its attendant gifts. This ''aversion'' from God constitutes the privative element in sin. Which of the two elements is more formal in sin has been debated by theologians, the Thomists generally making the ''conversion'' the constitutive element and the Scotists holding that the privation is more formal. However, the more common Thomist opinion does not deny that the privative element belongs essentially to the sinful act, which would not indeed be a sinful conversion to a created good if it did not entail aversion from God and the privations associated with such aversion.

The distinction of these two elements helps to clarify the psychology of the sinful act, which would be difficult to explain if sin were simply the choice of evil and nothing else. Moreover, it provides an answer to the protest of the sinner who declares that he did not think about offending God when he gave himself up to his sinful deed. But he did seek an illicit good, one to which a privation is inseparably attached, and in doing this he indirectly intended the privation.

Distinction of Sins. The practice of sacramental confession, as required by Canon Law (1917 *Codex Iuris Canonicis* c.901) and the Council of Trent (*Enchiridion symbolorum* 1679–81), requires the confession of all mortal sins committed after Baptism according to their kind and number. This practice makes the specific and numerical discrimination of sins a matter of practical importance to the Catholic theologian. The species of a sin is the kind, or class, into which sin falls, whereas the numerical distinction of sins is simply the number of distinct occurrences. Theologians distinguish two kinds of species: the moral and the theological. Moral species depends on the specific type of malice manifest in a sin and distinguishing it from other kinds of sin, as for example, theft is distinguished from blasphemy. The difference of theological species is based on the gravity of sins. There is one essential difference between sins in this respect, and thus there are two theological species, namely, mortal and venial.

The essentially distinguishing factor in the determination of the moral species for those who hold that the formal constitutive of sin is not the privative element but the positive conversion of the sinner to something illicit, is the object considered in the moral order, that is from a moral point of view. This includes not merely what is done (the *finis operis*), but also the sinner's purpose in doing it (the *finis operantis*), as well as the CIRCUMSTANCES that give a new kind of moral quality to what is done. That is not to say, however, that the motive or the circumstances change the moral character of what is done; blasphemy is blasphemy, and murder is murder, whatever be the motive. But the motive (or *finis operantis*) is itself an object of the will, and circumstances can so modify an object that it acquires a new kind of morality in addition to that which it has of itself. An act that is single in its physical entity can be multiple from a moral point of view. Thus the theft of a sacred object is at once an act of theft and an act of sacrilege. A lie told for the purpose of seduction is an offense against both veracity and chastity. For those who see the essence of sin to consist more formally in a privation, other norms had to be found to differentiate one sin from another. Some have based the distinction on opposition to different virtues, others on the difference of the laws or precepts violated.

The numerical distinction of sins, though relatively simple in principle, is sometimes complicated in the application of the principle, especially with regard to internal sins of thought and desire. The basic principle is that there are as many sins as there are morally distinct acts of the will.

Connection of Sins. Vices and a fortiori sinful acts are not interconnected in the same way as are the virtues. The acquired moral virtues, in their perfect state, are all connected in prudence, and the infused virtues are connected in charity, so that the possession of any one perfect virtue guarantees the possession of the others as well. Such is not the case where sins are concerned. Virtue tends to unify and focus all activity upon moral goodness; vice and sin, on the contrary, scatter and dissipate man's moral act. The morally good act is in conformity with the moral law. The possibility of variety in nonconformity or difformity is endless.

Some sins are opposed to others by a relationship of contrariety, for example, prodigality and miserliness, and one therefore is exclusive of the other. Moreover, the intention of the sinner is not directly to depart from the rule of reason or the law of God, but to realize something that he sees as good to himself. Sins would be interconnected if their objects were connected, but manifestly they are not.

Nevertheless, it must be admitted that there is some connection between sins. In some cases, what are virtually different sins are joined in the same act, as an offense against justice and one against chastity in the sin of adultery. Sometimes one sin can dispose a man to the commission of another of a different kind, as when drunkenness leads to quarreling. Some sins are the effects of other sins, as when pride begets envy, and in this way all the capital SINS have a numerous progeny. Again, by grievous sin the infused virtue of prudence is lost and acquired prudence is weakened, and because of this one becomes less capable of virtuous action and less able to stand firmly and constantly against the temptation to other sin. Furthermore, one who cuts himself off from the love of God and has overcome the fear of being separated from Him is deprived of a most effective motive against any sin, and may the more readily fall victim to temptation. Still one sin cannot be said to contain all others except in the sense that it disposes more or less remotely to their commission (St. Thomas Aquinas, *Summa theologiae* 1a2ae, 73.1).

Comparative Gravity of Sins. Not all sins are equal in their gravity. This is the teaching of the Scriptures (Jn 19.11; Ez 16.44–58; Jer 7.26; Lam 4.6) and of all Catholic theologians. Although sin consists in a privation, it is not a pure or total privation, but one that admits of more or less. The gravity of sin is measured objectively and specifically by the extent of the disorder and aversion caused by the sinful object and its consequences, and subjectively by the intensity of the will's act and the dispositions of the sinner.

First and foremost, the gravity of sin is measured against a scale of values in which God is highest; the substantial good of man, intermediate; and external goods, lowest. These values are secured and protected by the virtues, the comparative excellence of which is judged by reference to the same scale. It is possible and convenient, therefore, to measure the gravity of a sin by considering the comparative excellence of the virtue to which it is opposed and the manner of its opposition (e.g., by excess or by defect). Generally speaking, spiritual sins are more serious than carnal sins because the element of aversion from God is more pronounced in them and because they involve more directly the good of the soul, which is greater than the good of the body, and because, being less influenced by passion, they are less excusable. Whatever weakens the judgment of reason or lessens a sinner's liberty of action diminishes the gravity of a sin because it makes the act less voluntary.

Harmful consequences, to the extent that they are forseen, also aggravate the gravity of a sin; and the dignity, character and reputation of the person sinning, as well as the person sinned against, may have a bearing on the seriousness of a sin. For example, other things being equal, venial sins, when indeliberate, are less serious in a person of greater, as compared with a person of lesser, virtue, because they have a greater element of the involuntary in them. Deliberate sins, however, are worse in a person of greater virtue, partly because they are less excusable, since virtue should make resistance to sin easier, and partly because there is more ingratitude to God and scandal to neighbor in them. The sin of defamation, on the other hand, committed by one known to be a liar, does less harm than it would if it were committed by a person with a reputation for veracity.

Subject of Sin. Under this heading theologians discuss the faculty or power to which sin is attributed as to a source or principle. It is, of course, the person who sins, not the part, or member, or faculty of the human composite. Nevertheless, an act proceeds from a person through the operation of some power or faculty; and inquiring into the subject of sin, theologians seek to identify the powers in which the sinful act can originate. Sin is found primarily in the will, which is the principle of all human action; when it is attributed to other powers, it is only as they are subject to voluntary control and yet retain in themselves a capacity for disordered activity. Sin is not attributed to the external members of the body that move in complete subjection to the will, for they are simply the instruments through which the commands of the will are put into effect. Besides the will itself, the sense appetite and reason qualify as subjects of sin inasmuch as in their activity they are subject to disorder that could and should be controlled. [*See* EMOTION (MORAL ASPECT); THOUGHTS, MORALITY OF.]

Internal Causes of Sin. Sin can be considered in two ways: materially, in its physical entity, or formally, in its defectiveness, its disorder, its disaccord with moral law. Sin viewed in its physical being must have a direct efficient cause, but the identification of the cause of what is formally evil in it is more difficult. Since the disorder of sin is not mere negation, but a privation of something that should be present, it requires a cause. Because evil as evil is not per se appetible, the activity of its cause will not be directed immediately to the evil, the disorder, of the sin, but rather to some positive goal that entails the privation and disorder. As a human act, sin must proceed from the will as from a cause. The will, ''lacking the direction of the rule of reason and of the divine law, and intent upon some mutable good, causes the act of sin directly and the inordinateness indirectly and without intending it. The lack of order in the act results from the lack of direction in the will'' (Aquinas, *Summa theologiae* 1a2ae, 75.1). This defect in the direction of the will can be caused by the defect in the will itself that is called malice, or by a defect of knowledge in the intellect called ignorance, or by a defect in the sense appetite called weakness.

Psychologically, choice by the will follows a judgment of reason on the goodness of the proposed object. This judgment may be vitiated by ignorance either of general principles or of the right application of principles. Very often, however, it is not in its speculative but its practical role that the mind fails. The judgment that precedes sin is a practical judgment, and it is influenced by factors operative here and now, existential in the truest sense of the word. Whatever colors the practical judgment influences the will and is in that sense a cause of sin. In particular, the emotional state of a man at any particular moment unconsciously and even consciously affects his estimate of the value of a proposed action. An angry or terrified man does not think and act like a tranquil one. He judges a thing according to the advantages it appears to offer him here and now, and this judgment so occupies his mind that he is distracted from the use of his moral knowledge.

Sins arising from neither passion nor ignorance are traceable to the malice of a will prepared deliberately to choose the disorder and spiritual loss involved in sin rather than forego some temporal satisfaction. Malice makes a sin graver, because it is a disposition of the will itself and is a more enduring source of disorder than passion.

External Causes. Factors external to the sinner himself may also contribute to his sin. In their consideration of the mystery of iniquity, theologians have given much attention to the question of God's causality with respect to the sinful act of the creature. God, the Supreme Good, wills indirectly physical evil incidental to the total perfection of creation and the penal evil that is incidental to the fulfillment of divine justice, because these evils are not directly opposed to His honor and glory; but He cannot will the moral evil of sin in any way, because it is contradictory to His love. Just as He cannot make anything hating it, neither can He make anything to hate Him. All things come from Him, and are made to return to Him, not to move away from Him. Yet men do sin, and they could not do this without God's help. Theologians distinguish between the physical entity of a sin, which comes from God as does the whole of created being and all its modes; and what is human in the sin, which is from God and from the free will; and what is defective, which is not from God in any way but from the defect of the creature. A radical defectibility is inevitable in the creature precisely because it is not an absolute. But God could preserve the creature from all sin. He has not willed to do this, but this fact cannot be understood to make Him the cause of what is formal in sin, because He does not owe such preservation to the creature. Moreover, the privation that is formal in sin requires for its explanation not an efficient but a deficient cause; in a sense it is something not caused rather than something caused. But God, as First Cause, lacks nothing. From no point of view can He be conceived as the cause—efficient, exemplary, or final—of the sinful disorder of the act of the will. (For the treatment of this problem in its proper context, *see* EVIL.)

The devil cannot be considered the cause of sin in the sense that he directly moves man's will to sin. At most he is able to tempt men to sin by operating upon their internal senses, causing them to think of sinful things and to focus their attention on the desirability of illicit pleasures. Not all temptation need be explained in terms of diabolical activity, however; the world and the flesh can account for most of the temptations that men experience. In a general sense, nevertheless, because the devil was instrumental in causing original sin, which has left men prone to evil, he can be considered an indirect and partial cause of all sin.

Man can be the cause of sin in another by inducing him to sin by means of persuasion, suggestion, command, example, etc. (*see* SCANDAL), or by cooperating in his sin (*see* SIN, COOPERATION IN; for the causal influence of certain kinds of sin upon other sins, *see* DEADLY SINS).

Effects of Sin. The act of sin produces certain psychological, spiritual, and even physical effects, which, although foreseen, are not intended by the sinner. Theologians speak of the loss of both natural and supernatural good.

Man's essential natural good, his existence, the integrity and essential capacity of his natural powers, is not lost in consequence of either original or personal sin. But the human good that consists in an inclination to virtue, a natural characteristic of a rational being, is lessened, but not completely destroyed, by sin. Some diminution of this good is a result in man of original sin. This wound in nature is not healed in man's present state by sanctifying grace. Personal sin aggravates and deepens this wound, making further sin easier to commit and virtue more difficult to practice.

The principal effect of sin, however, is the loss of supernatural good and the incurrance of guilt. Mortal sin deprives the soul of sanctifying grace; and with the deprivation of grace, its attendant supernatural gifts, capacities, and privileges are lost. It is because of this that mortal sin is referred to as the ''death'' of the soul, which, in effect, ceases to have being on the supernatural level. GUILT is the state or condition of being at fault (*reatus culpae*) and so deprived of supernatural life, the absence of the splendor of which is a stain (*macula peccati*) on the soul, and also the state or condition of being liable to the penalty due in punishment for the fault (*reatus poenae*).

Venial Sin. The words ''mortal'' and ''venial'' in connection with sin are not found in the Scriptures, but the distinction between the two types of sin is clearly affirmed. There are sins that exclude from the kingdom (Eph 5.5; Gal 5.19–21) and sins that do not exclude from it (Jas 3.2; 1 Jn 1.8; Eccl 7.21). In the 4th century Jovinian claimed that all sins were equal and therefore deserving of the same punishment. St. Augustine took a strong stand against this doctrine [see J. Mausbach, *Die Ethik des hl. Augustinus* (Freiburg 1909)]. Wyclif, and after him Martin Luther, Calvin, and others among the Reformers, rejected the distinction so far at least as it supposed a difference in the sin rather than the sinner. Pius V in 1567 condemned a proposition of Baius repudiating the distinction (*Enchiridion symbolorum* 1920). The Council of Trent spoke of mortal sin, which the just man can avoid, and venial sin, which he cannot avoid without special grace (*Enchiridion symbolorum* 1573); of mortal sin that must be confessed in the Sacrament of Penance and venial sin that need not be confessed (*Enchiridion symbolorum* 1707); of mortal sin by which one falls from justice and venial sin by which the sinner does not cease to be just (*Enchiridion symbolorum* 1537).

According to St. Thomas Aquinas, the difference between mortal and venial sin follows upon the diversity of the disorders that constitute the essence of the sin. There are two kinds of such disorder, one that destroys the very principle of order and one that leaves the principle but introduces inordinateness among things consequent to it. The principle of the entire moral order is the last end. Hence when a soul is so disordered that it turns away from its last end, which is God, to whom it has been united by charity, there is mortal sin; and when there is disorder in the soul without its turning away from God, there is venial sin. St. Thomas likened the aversion from God in mortal sin to death, in which the principle of life is lost, and the disorder of venial sin to sickness, which is a reparable condition because the principle of life remains (*Summa theologiae* 1a2ae, 72.5).

From this it is evident that the term sin is not applied univocally to mortal and venial sin as to two species contained under a common genus. The disorder involved in venial sin is different, and so also the offense to God, and it makes a man liable to quite a different penalty.

St. Thomas thought that venial sin was not so much against the law of God (*contra legem*) as outside the law (*praeter legem*) (*Summa theologiae* 1a2ae, 88.1 ad 1). St. Thomas wanted, as did other outstanding theologians of his time, to include under the heading of sin as defined by St. Augustine only those acts in which the idea of sin was fully realized. The restrictive interpretation of these theologians was due to the severity of the early scholastics who thought that any voluntary and deliberate transgression of the divine will was worthy of eternal punishment. The later scholastics sought to get around the rigor of this doctrine by finding formulas that made venial sin seem something less than an outright violation of the divine law. Thus Scotus, for example, is alleged by some, although this is disputed by others, to have taught that venial sin is a violation of a counsel rather than a precept. St. Bonaventure and St. Albert the Great used the same formula as St. Thomas and declared that venial sin is not *contra* but *praeter legem.* However, they did not mean this in the sense that it was opposed to no law, but that it was not opposed to the law of charity that obliges one to love God above all things and to seek Him alone as a final end. A venial sin does not make it impossible for one to be intent upon God as an ultimate end. It disorders a man, not with respect to his end, but with respect to the means employed in the pursuit of his end. But if the law of God is understood in its full amplitude as it regards not only end but means, venial sin cannot be said to be only *praeter legem.*

Venial sin differs from mortal sin in the punishment due to it: it merits a temporal rather than an eternal penalty. It may be declared in confession, but need not be, for it can be expiated by many other remedies (*Enchiridion symbolorum* 1680). Venial sins dispose a man to mortal sin because, by inordinate preoccupation with means, he can become so attached to them that they begin to assume a major importance in his life, or because, being undisciplined in little things, he can grow bolder and become less ready to subject himself to God's law in graver matters (Aquinas, *Summa theologiae* 1a2ae, 88.3). Nevertheless, venial sin does not directly cause a diminution of charity or of sanctifying grace (*op. cit.* 2a2ae, 24.10).

Bibliography: THOMAS AQUINAS, *Summa theologiae* 1a2ae, 71–89; *De ver.* 15, 25, 28; *De malo* 2–5, 7–8. Commentaries on Thomas Aquinas, especially C. R. BILLUART, *Summa Sancti Thomae,* 10 v. (new ed. Paris 1874–86). Manuals of moral theology, especially B. H. MERKELBACH, *Summa theologiae moralis* (8th ed. Paris 1949) v.1. Various dissertations on special points. B. A.

BROWN, *Numerical Distinction of Sins in Franciscan Schools* (Washington 1948). E. F. DURKIN, *The Theological Distinction of Sins in the Writings of St. Augustine* (Mundelein, Illinois 1952). J. R. MALONEY, *The Formal Constituent of a Sin of Commission* (Somerset, Ohio 1947), bibliography. E. MOORE, *Los principios constitutivos de la materia leve* (Granada 1956). P. V. O'BRIEN, *Emotions and Morals* (New York 1950). V. RIMSELIS, *Natura et peccatum* (Rome 1952). W. E. ORCHARD, *Modern Theories of Sin* (London 1909). J. G. MCKENZIE, *Guilt: Its Meaning and Significance* (London 1962). Special treatises. P. LUMBRERAS, *De vitiis et peccatis* (Rome 1935). E. J. MAHONEY, *Sin and Repentance* (New York 1928), reprinted in the *Teaching of the Catholic Church,* ed. G. D. SMITH, 2 v. (New York 1948) 2:919–54. M. ORAISON et al., *Sin,* tr. B. MURCHLAND and R. MEYERPETER (New York 1962). J. REGNIER, *What is Sin?,* tr. U. MORRISSY (Westminster, Maryland 1961). H. RONDET, *The Theology of Sin,* tr. R. W. HUGHES (Notre Dame, Ind. 1960). P. PALAZZINI, *Sin: Its Reality and Nature,* tr. B. DEVLIN (Chicago 1964), 2 more v. by various authors proposed. For a survey, see P. SIMON, *La Littérature du péché et de la grâce . . . depuis 1880* (Paris 1957). T. DEMAN, *Dictionnaire de théologie catholique,* ed. A. VACANT et al., 15 v. (Paris 1903–50) 12.1:140–275. For additional bibliography, see F. ROBERTI et al., *Dictionary of Moral Theology,* ed. P. PALAZZINI et al., tr. H. J. YANNONE et al. From 2d. Italian edition (Westminster, Maryland 1962) 1313–52.

[I. MCGUINESS]

SIN, COOPERATION IN

Cooperation is an action or operation carried out jointly with another or others. Cooperation in sin consists in being a cause with another of a sinful action. A cooperator in sin gives aid to the sinful action of another. Cooperation in sin is not the same thing as giving scandal, for scandal does not give aid to the sinful action of another but rather merely influences his will, moving him to will something sinful (*see* SCANDAL). A scandalized person makes up his mind to sin only after scandal has been given; cooperation is given to one who has already decided to commit sin.

Cooperation in sin, then, is the action of aiding another in carrying out his sinful purpose. It presupposes the other's evil will and helps him to put it into execution. When the cooperation is in the sinful act itself of another, it is immediate cooperation. If the cooperation merely provides aid through other acts or objects not so immediately connected with the sin of another, the cooperation is said to be mediate. Mediate cooperation can be either proximate or remote. It is proximate when the action or aid given to the sinful action of another is intimately connected with that action, as is the help given by an anesthetist to a doctor performing a sinful operation. When the action is not so closely connected with the sin committed, it is remote cooperation. Thus, for example, the cooperation of a nurse who prepares the instruments to be used in the surgery is remote.

Moral theologians consider it important to distinguish also between formal and material cooperation. Cooperation is formal when the cooperator shares in some way in the intention and purpose of the sinner whom he assists. He can do this either by wanting the evil act performed and doing something to help bring it about or by making an unambiguous contribution to the performance of the act, that is, by contributing help that of its nature has no other purpose than to make the sin possible or to facilitate its commission, for example, to fetch and set up a ladder when a burglar asks this help in order to gain entrance to a house. In this case the cooperator cannot reasonably disavow a part in the intention of the thief.

Cooperation is material when it avoids participation in the evil intention of the sinner. The material cooperator does not want the sinful action to take place, and there is an ambiguity about what he actually does. His assistance may in fact contribute to the sin, but it is not of its nature or in the circumstances exclusively ordained to the commission of the sin. To sell a bottle of whiskey may contribute to the drunkenness of the one who buys it; but whiskey has other than sinful uses, and the shopkeeper does not necessarily enter into the intentions of his customers who want to intoxicate themselves.

Formal cooperation in the sin of another is always sinful because it involves, virtually at least, a sharing in a sinful purpose. Material cooperation, on the other hand, is considered permissible under certain conditions, namely, that the action of the material cooperator is not evil in itself, that his intention is good, and that he has a proportionately grave reason for doing something that may contribute in some way to the sin of another. The rendering of any aid whatever to the commission of sin is a thing to be avoided; but if the aforesaid conditions are verified, the principle of DOUBLE EFFECT is applicable, and an action can be performed even though it is foreseen that an evil effect may ensue. If it were obligatory to avoid material cooperation in such circumstances, it would be because of the duty in charity to prevent another's wrongdoing; but one is not bound to this at the cost of serious inconvenience to himself.

In estimating the proportionate gravity of the reason for cooperating materially in the sin of another, the immediacy or mediacy, the proximateness or remoteness, of the influence of the cooperation upon the sin should be taken into consideration, as well as the necessity of the cooperation to the commission of the sin. Obviously it requires a less grave reason to justify the doing of something that only mediately and remotely lends aid in the commission of sin than something that is proximately and immediately involved in the sinful act. Similarly, a form of cooperation readily available from other sources would be easier to justify than cooperation that no other could supply.

Although it is possible to justify material cooperation in sin in some circumstances, it is not always clear in concrete cases that the conditions necessary for licit cooperation are verified. The goodness of a particular action may be open to doubt, and the sufficiency of the reason that calls for cooperation may be questionable. Moreover, it sometimes requires wisdom and prudence to determine how closely the cooperation touches the sinful action, how necessary the cooperation is to the commission of the sin. Because personal interest may intervene to distort an individual's judgment upon such a matter, it is generally advisable for one who finds himself perplexed with a problem regarding cooperation to seek the advice of a prudent counselor, e.g., his confessor.

Bibliography: THOMAS AQUINAS, *Summa Theologiae* 2a2ae, 78.4. ALPHONSUS LIGUORI, *Theologia moralis,* ed. L. GAUDÉ, 4 v. (new ed. Rome 1905–12) 2.59–80. D. M. PRÜMMER, *Manuale theologiae moralis,* ed. E. M. MÜNCH, 3 v. (Freiburg-Barcelona 1955). N. NOLDIN, *Summa theologiae moralis* (Innsbruck 1961–62) 2:116–129. H. DAVIS, *Moral and Pastoral Theology* (New York 1958) 1:341–352. E. DUBLANCHY, *Dictionnaire de théologie catholique,* ed. A. VACANT, 15 v. (Paris 1903–50; Tables générales 1951–) 3.2:1762–70.

[F. E. KLUEG]

SIN, OCCASIONS OF

An occasion of sin is circumstance of person, place, or thing, extrinsic to the potential sinner involved, that draws him to sin and gives him an opportunity of committing it. Inclinations toward sin found within a man, such as bad habits and passions, because they are intrinsic to himself, are thus not what a moral theologian would call occasions of sin. Nor is an occasion to be confused with a danger of sin. A danger of sinning is more general and includes various internal dispositions, such as temptations, natural weakness, and the like, that can exist independently of any ''occasion'' as the term is here understood.

An occasion of sin is said to be remote or proximate, according to the degree of influence it exercises on the person whose sin it may occasion. If the attraction it exerts is not strong, or there is only a relatively small probability of its leading to sin, the occasion is remote; if the attraction is powerful, or the probability of sin is serious, the occasion is proximate. Remote occasions abound in the lives of most people, and there is no obligation to try to avoid them. An occasion of sin can be proximate for everyone and in that case is called an absolute proximate occasion. Other occasions are proximate only for certain individuals because of their weaknesses and particular dispositions, and these are said to be relative.

The relative frequency of lapses in the exposure to a certain occasion that requires its classification as proximate is a matter of dispute among theologians. Some are of the opinion that one must fall more frequently than not in a particular type of occasion before it becomes proximate. Others hold that fewer lapses would suffice to make the occasion proximate, agreeing with St. Alphonsus that if an individual sins four out of ten times in a given situation, that situation should be considered a proximate occasion of sin for him. All agree, however, that it is imprudent for a person to place himself in an occasion in which he frequently sins.

A proximate occasion of sin may be freely and voluntarily entered upon, or it may be necessary in the sense that it cannot be avoided, or at least cannot be avoided without serious difficulty. Thus, if they are occasions of sin, reading certain books, frequenting particular places, associating with particular people would, generally speaking, be considered voluntary occasions. Military service, living at home or in prison, on the other hand, may be necessary or unavoidable occasions.

Everyone is under a grave obligation to avoid proximate occasions of grave sin as far as that is possible. To remain without sufficient reason in a proximate occasion of serious sin implies a willingness to commit that sin. As long as a person freely remains in, or will not undertake to avoid such an occasion, he is not properly disposed for absolution, for he lacks the firm PURPOSE of amendment essential to CONTRITION. Just as it is evil to expose oneself needlessly to the risk of grave injury or physical death, so is it seriously sinful to expose oneself needlessly to spiritual death through mortal sin.

As to necessary or unavoidable occasions, it should be noted that the necessity that characterizes them is not a necessity of sinning but a necessity of remaining in the physical situation that has been or could be a proximate occasion of sin. When a person is confronted with such a necessity, he should take steps to reduce the probability of sin by arming himself against the dangers inherent in the situation. This course can so alter the occasion that it ceases to be proximate and becomes remote. Spiritual means of effecting this change include a frequent reception of the Sacraments of Penance and the Eucharist, prayer, mortification, and reflection that tends to activate one's love of God and to increase one's awareness of the evil of sin and of its consequences. In addition to these spiritual countermeasures, ingenuity can often discover physical means of one kind or another, depending on the nature of the occasion, to make the danger of sin more remote.

Bibliography: E. THAMIRY, *Dictionnaire de théologie catholique,* ed. A. VACANT, 15 v. (Paris 1903–50; Tables générales 1951–) 11.1:905–915. B. MERKELBACH, *Questiones de variis poenitentium categoriis* (Liège 1928). M. FÁBREGAS, "De obligatione vitandi probabile periculum peccandi," *Periodica de re morali canonica liturgica* 30 (1941) 20–45. J. C. FORD and G. A. KELLY, *Contemporary Moral Theology,* v. 1 (Westminster, MD 1958) 141–173.

[F. E. KLUEG]

SIN AGAINST THE HOLY SPIRIT

Unlike all other sins and blasphemies (Mk 3.28), the "blasphemy against the Holy Spirit" that is mentioned in Mt 12.31–32; and Lk 12.10 is characterized by Jesus as unforgivable (Mk 3.29). According to Mark's explanation (Mk 3.30), certain scribes committed this sin by attributing the works that Jesus had done by the Holy Spirit's power to an unclean spirit. The same saying is found in Lk 12.10b among a group of disconnected sayings, addressed, however, not to the scribes, but to the disciples (Lk 12.1). Matthew, in a context similar to Mark's (cf. Mt 12.24), has two versions in tandem; cf. Mt 12.31 with Mk 3.28–29 and Mt 12.32 with Lk 12.10.

The Fathers of the Church and later the theologians were concerned to identify this blasphemy or sin, to apply the concept to sins analogous to it, and to account for the unforgivableness of these sins. St. Augustine, who found great difficulty in the scriptural passages referring to this sin (see *Sermo 2 de verbis Domini,* 5), understood the irremissibility to be absolute. Now the only sin to which absolute irremissibility can be attributed is final impenitence; even God cannot forgive an unrepented sin, and this Augustine understood to be the sin against the Holy Spirit. Subsequent theologians followed him in this to the extent that they generally admitted that final impenitence is a sin against the Holy Spirit, although they usually added others to the category. This view, however, need not be understood in contradiction to a more literal interpretation of the specific malicious act that Jesus called blasphemy against the Holy Spirit, i.e., the insult to the Holy Spirit committed by those who attributed His works to an unclean spirit. St. Augustine was more concerned with explaining why the sin was unforgivable, and the reason for this was that the Pharisees would have no change of heart, but would obdurately continue in their sin until death. However, the final impenitence of one dying with other kinds of sin unrepented would also be a sin against the Holy Spirit in the sense that it would frustrate the remission of sins, a work appropriated to the Holy Spirit.

Later theologians extended the concept of this sin by including under the heading certain sins that are unforgivable only in the sense that they put an obstacle in the way of forgiveness, but they do not make its attainment impossible because the obstacle is not such that it cannot be overcome by the grace of God. The obstacle arises from one of two sources.

(1) Some sins are committed with no extenuating circumstances to call for or to make appropriate a remission of the penalty. They leave the sinner, so to speak, with no grounds for appeal to the divine clemency. Three inner sources or causes of sin were recognized by the medieval scholastic theologians: ignorance; passion or weakness; and deliberate malice (*certa malitia*). Sins caused by human weakness or frailty, and those caused by ignorance have a certain element of excusability lacking to the sin that comes of pure malice. Sins of weakness, because weakness is opposed to power, were said to be against the Father, to whom power was appropriated; sins of ignorance were against the Son, to whom, as the Word of God, wisdom and knowledge were appropriated; and sins of malice were against the Holy Spirit, to whom goodness was appropriated. Thus sins *ex certa malitia* came in medieval theology to be associated or even identified with the sin against the Holy Spirit, but they were thought to be unforgivable only in the sense that no extenuating circumstance appealed to the divine mercy for forgiveness; but this by no means made it impossible for the divine mercy to move the sinner gratuitously to repentance and so to pardon.

(2) Other sins were accounted unpardonable (in a limited sense) because, of their nature, they choked off or put a stop to efforts on the part of the sinner that might bring him to repentance and forgiveness, or cut him off from access to God. Thus, just as an illness would be fatal if it impeded one from taking the measures necessary to stay alive, so presumption and despair, or the deliberate rejection of divine truth, or the repudiation of the workings of grace, can be considered irremediable in the sense that they close the way to God through whom forgiveness could be had. Such a sin is "against the Holy Spirit" because it opposes the working of the Spirit.

Thus in medieval theology the sin against the Holy Spirit came to be considered as a genus containing, in the listing of Peter Lombard, six species. These are: despair, presumption, impenitence or a firm determination not to repent, obstinacy, resisting divine truth known to be such, and envy of another's spiritual welfare.

Bibliography: THOMAS AQUINAS, *Summa Theologiae* 2a2ae, 14.3; *In 2 sent.* 43.1.2. T. DEMAN, *Dictionnaire de théologie catholique,* ed. A. VACANT, 15 v. (Paris 1903–50; Tables générales 1951–) 12.1:199. G. MANISE, F. ROBERTI et al., *Dictionary of Moral Theology,* ed. P. PALAZZINI et al., tr. H. J. YANNONE et al., from 2d Ital. Ed. (Westminster, MD 1962) 1138.

[P. K. MEAGHER/C. BERNAS]

SIN OFFERING (IN THE BIBLE)

A form of expiatory sacrifice prescribed by the Pentateuchal PRIESTLY WRITERS of the Old Testament (Heb. *ḥaṭṭā't*). The date of its origin is not known with certainty, but Ezekiel mentions it as a familiar practice (Ez 40.39; 42.13), a fact that disproves a postexilic origin. Its purpose was to make expiation [*see* EXPIATION (IN THE BIBLE)] for material, not formal, sin [*see* SIN (IN THE BIBLE)], i.e., infractions against God's commandments or against the laws of ritual purity (*see* PURE AND IMPURE). For a sin committed with a ''high hand'' (defiantly) there could be no atonement by a sin offering. The distinction between a sin offering and a guilt offering (Heb. *'āšām*) was not always clear (cf. Lv 5.17–19 with Nm 15.22–29), and at times the expiatory rite was called indifferently either a sin offering or a guilt offering (e.g., Lv 14.10–20; Nm 6.9–12).

Chapters 4 and 5 of Leviticus enumerate the different victims to be offered by various classes of the people. A priest and the whole community must offer a bull (Lv 4.3, 14); a ruler, a male goat (4.23); the ordinary citizen, a female goat (4.28); the poor, two turtledoves or two pigeons (5.7); and the destitute, a very small amount of flour (5.11). No one was exempt from offering at least some small sacrifice in expiation for his sin.

The place for expiatory sacrifice was the forecourt of the TENT OF MEETING on the north side of the altar. The slaughtering was performed by the offerer (an indication of the primitiveness of the practice), except for national offerings (2 Chr 29.24). The offerer's action of placing his hands on the head of the victim was not intended (contrary to an opinion that has now been almost universally abandoned) to signify the transfer of the sin to the victim, for this would only have made the victim impure and, therefore, unsuitable for sacrifice. The action signified rather that the offerer initiated the sacrificial rite and thus confessed his guilt and sorrow. The manipulation of the sacrificial blood (*see* BLOOD, RELIGIOUS SIGNIFICANCE OF) formed the most important part of the sin offering, since Yahweh Himself had designated it as a proper means for cleansing the person, place, or thing made unclean even by inadvertent sin, thus for reestablishing communion with the holy God (Lv 17.11). On the Day of ATONEMENT (Yom Kippur) the Holy of Holies was entered and the sacrificial blood of the national sin offering was sprinkled on the ark of the covenant, where Yahweh was invisibly enthroned, in order to have it come as close to Him as possible in its cleansing power.

In the New Testament Christ is identified as the ultimate sin offering in Rom 8.1–4; 2 Cor 5.20–21, and especially throughout the Epistle to the Hebrews (*see* Heb 10.1–18).

See Also: SACRIFICE, III (IN ISRAEL); SACRIFICE, IV (IN CHRISTIAN THEOLOGY).

Bibliography: R. DE VAUX, *Ancient Israel, Its Life and Institutions,* tr. J. MCHUGH (New York 1961) 418–421. *Encyclopedic Dictionary of the Bible,* translated and adapted by L. HARTMAN (New York, 1963) 2239–41. L. MORALDI, *Espiazione sacrificale e riti espiatori. . .(Analecta Biblica* 5; Rome 1956) 133–157.

[R. J. KUJAWA]

SINAI, MOUNT

The mountain of revelation, called Mt. HOREB in the Deuteronomic source, where Moses received the revelation of the Law and the people of Israel entered into solemn covenant with Yahweh. It is traditionally located at the southern end of the Sinai Peninsula.

The origin and meaning of the name Sinai (Heb. *sînai*) is uncertain. Some scholars connect it with the Hebrew word *s^eneh,* which is translated as bush in the account of the vision that Moses had of the bush that was aflame but not consumed by the fire (Ex 3.1–4). Actually, in this passage the place of the vision is not called Sinai, but ''Horeb, the mountain of God.'' Other suggestions are that the name Sinai is connected with that of the Babylonian moon-god Sin or that it is related to the Desert of Sin to the northeast. Not only the mountain but the surrounding desert is called Sinai in the Old Testament. The name is now used also for the peninsula or triangle of desert land that lies between the south of Palestine, the Suez arm of the Red Sea, and the Gulf of Aqaba. This peninsula, an area of about 10,000 square miles, was the scene of most of the 40-year wandering of the Israelites after the Exodus from Egypt. At its southern point is a group of dominating peaks, the highest of which are Jebel Serbāl (6,759 feet), Jebel Katerîn (8,652 feet), Jebel Mûsā (7,497 feet). The Egyptians considered these mountains sacred from antiquity.

Although most scholars agree that the traditional identification of Mt. Sinai with Jebel Mûsā (Mountain of Moses), attested as early as *c.* A.D. 400 by the pilgrim Silvia, is correct, the location has been doubted by some. Because of Moses' dealings with the Madianites and because of the volcanic activity of the mountain El Bedr in Madianite territory to the east of the Gulf of Aqaba, J. Garstang identified Sinai with this mountain. J. Wellhausen, relying on his interpretation of Dt 33.2, ''The Lord came from Sinai and dawned from Seir upon us,'' as well as for other reasons drawn from literary criticism, put the place of the revelation of the Law at Cades, and not at Sinai. Some, therefore, have identified Mt. Sinai with Jebel Helal, a hill to the west of Cades. Most scholars, however, agree on regarding Rās es-Ṣafṣafeh (6,937

Moses receiving the Ten Commandments. (Archive Photos)

ft), one of the twin peaks of Jebel Mûsā, as the mountain of the Ten Commandments. Rās es-Ṣafṣafeh accords well with the data found in Exodus. The mile-and-a-half plain at the foot of the mountain would have been ideal for the year's encampment that the Israelites, with their herds and flocks, made at Sinai.

In the 6th century, the Byzantine Emperor Justinian the Great had the Monastery of St. Catherine built on the shady northern slope of Jebel Mûsā, the traditional site of the burning bush. This monastery, with its ancient manuscripts and priceless works of art, still remains as a relic of an age long passed. Because of the monastery's isolation, its icons escaped the iconoclastic ravages of the 8th century. Its collection of manuscripts, more than 3,000 of them, are written in Greek, Arabic, Syriac, Georgian, Slavonic, and other languages. The renowned Bible manuscript, Codex Sinaiticus, dating from the 4th century, was found there by C. Tischendorf in 1844.

Bibliography: G. E. WRIGHT, *The Interpreter's Dictionary of the Bible* (Nashville 1962) 4:376–378. *Encyclopedic Dictionary of the Bible,* translated and adapted by L. HARTMAN (New York, 1963) 2232–33. M. J. LAGRANGE, ''Le Sinaï biblique,'' *Revue Biblique* 8 (1899) 369–392. F. M. ABEL, *Géographie de la Palestine,* 2 v. (Paris 1933–38)1:391–396. D. BALY, *The Geography of the Bible* (New York 1957) 5–6. E. G. KRAELING, *Rand McNally Bible Atlas* (2d ed. New York 1962) 107–113. M. DU BUIT, *Géographie de la Terre Sainte* (Paris 1958) 111–115. G. H. FORSYTH, ''Island of Faith in the Sinai Wilderness,'' *National Geographic Magazine* 125 (1964) 82–106.

[C. MCGOUGH]

SINGAPORE, THE CATHOLIC CHURCH IN

Singapore is an island republic in Southeast Asia located at the tip of the Malay peninsula. The capital, Singapore City, is a major commercial center and one of the world's busiest ports. Written accounts of ancient Singapore are sketchy. It is featured in Javanese chronicles as an uninhabited island called Temasek. Its Sanskrit name, Singapura (''Lion City'') had come into common use by the end of the fourteenth century. Sir Stamford Raffles gained possession of the island for the British in 1819 to secure its merchant fleet and forestall further advance of the Dutch in the area. The British developed the uninhabited island into a major entrepot harbor and military base. During the Second World War it was occupied by the Japanese; but in 1946, after the war, it became a British crown colony. In 1959 it became a self-governing state. In 1963 Singapore joined the Federation of Malaysia, but withdrew in 1965, becoming an independent republic within the British Commonwealth.

The history of the Catholic Church in Singapore began with British colonization in 1819. In 1821 a missionary in transit found some 12 Catholics, and in 1829 there were about 200. By the time the first bishop established a residence there in 1838 there were about 500. Portuguese missionaries arrived in Singapore in 1825, and a few years later the Paris Foreign Mission Society (MEP) sent missionaries who established places of worship and educational centers. One of them, Jean-Marie Beurel (1813–72), became known as the founder of Catholic Singapore. He built the Cathedral of the Good Shepherd, a school for boys staffed by the Brothers of the Christian Schools, and one for girls run by the Sisters of the Infant Jesus. From the beginning the Catholics came under two jurisdictions: Catholics of the Portuguese mission were under the *Padroado* archbishop of Macau, and those of the French mission under the the Vicar Apostolic of Ava and Pegu (Burma). In 1888, Singapore became part of the re-established Diocese of Melaka, with the exception of the existing *Padroado* mission in Singapore, which remained under the archbishop of Macau. In 1972 Pope Paul VI made Singapore a separate archdiocese under the direct jurisdiction of the Holy See. In 1977, the Bishop of Macau agreed to relinquish his authority over the *Padroado* mission in Singapore to the archbishop of Singapore, a decision which the Holy See ratified in 1981. Singapore belongs to the Catholic Bishops' Conference of Malaysia-Singapore-Brunei, itself a part of the Federation of Asian Bishops' Conferences. Religious congregations with the archdiocese support many schools, a hospital and a hospice, several nursing homes and a children's home. In 1989, at the direction of the Vatican, the St. Francis Xavier Major Seminary for the training of local clergy was officially opened. Pope John Paul II visited Singapore on Nov. 20, 1986. A multiracial crowd of 63,000 attended the Mass he celebrated in the National Stadium.

Capital: Singapore.
Size: 225 sq. miles.
Population: 4.3 million. About three-fourths of the population are ethnic Chinese, followed by Malays, Indians, Eurasians and others.
Languages: Chinese (official), Malay (official and national), Tamil (official), English (official).
Religions: More than half of the population observe a mix of Buddhism, Taoism and Confucian ancestor worship. Almost one-fifth of the population are Muslims, predominantly of the Sunni School. Hinduism and Sikhism are practiced mainly by the small ethnic Indian community. Christians constitute a small but significant minority, counting about one-tenth of the population as adherents. Almost 90% of the Christians are ethnic Chinese. Protestants outnumber Catholics by two-to-one.
Archdiocese: Singapore.

Bibliography: CATHOLIC BISHOPS' CONFERENCE OF MALAYSIA-SINGAPORE-BRUNEI, Official Catholic Church Directory (published annually).

[J. FERNANDEZ/EDS.]

SINGIDUNUM, MARTYRS OF

SS. Hermylus and Stratonicus are connected with the ancient city of Singidunum near Belgrade and were martyred during the persecution of Licinius (308–323). The *passio* narrating their ordeal is untrustworthy except as a source for their names and as witness to their early cult. Two further martyrs, Montanus and Maxima, are associated with Singidunum, but they were decapitated in SIRMIUM. A church in Constantinople was erected in honor of St. Stratonicus. Among the Greeks, Hermylus and Stratonicus are commemorated on January 13; but the Martyrology of St. Jerome mentions St. Hermylus on August 2.

Bibliography: *Analecta Bollandiana* 31 (1912) 254–257. H. DELEHAYE, *Les Origines du culte des martyrs* (2d ed. Brussels 1933).

[A. PENNA]

SINNER, HABITUAL

One who has a habit of committing a specific sin and, by repeated lapses, has developed a strong inclination to it. The presence of a habit is indicated by frequent and regular moral failures of the same kind. It is impossible, however, to classify a person as a habitual sinner simply on the basis of the number of lapses, because circumstances make each individual case different. Moralists agree that as a general rule sins committed once a week are to be considered habitual, except where grosser sins

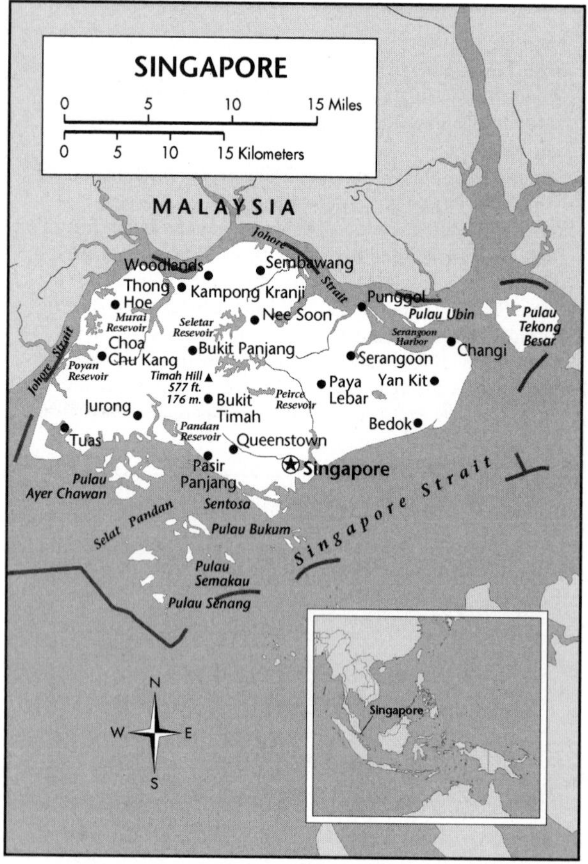

are concerned, in which case a sin committed as often as once a month might be considered habitual. A habit of sinning can be contracted more easily in some matters than in others; for example, where gluttony, lust, blasphemy, or cursing are concerned, notable pleasures or strong emotions may be involved that cause the habit to be formed more quickly and to resist more stubbornly the breaking of it.

The effect of habit upon the morality of the vicious act that comes of it may be either to mitigate or to aggravate its malice. As a consequence of the force of passion that often plays a part in habitual sin, the sinner's freedom and responsibility is often diminished, and so also the malice of what he does. When the sinful habitual disposition, voluntarily acquired, is voluntarily retained, even the impetus of passion does not lessen the malice of the act, for this is itself voluntary, and as such indicates a will bent with greater determination upon evil. In this sense St. Thomas Aquinas could say that whoever sins out of habit sins *ex certa malitia* (*Summa theologiae* 1a2ae, 78.2).

Since habit is something learned, i.e., acquired by learning, it can be unlearned. That is to say, it can be reduced or even eliminated by learning. Since a sinful habit is a cause of sin, a penitent has an obligation to rid himself of the habit, or at least to have the sincere intention of doing so. This intention should include the purpose of taking whatever steps are necessary to overcome the inclination to sin that he has acquired. Hence, the habitual sinner may be absolved if he shows signs that he is truly contrite and has a firm purpose of amendment. Repeated lapses after repentance are not a certain indication that these necessary conditions were lacking. Just as a sinner's repudiation of his sin is possible, so also is his later repudiation of a repentance that was sincere at the time it was made. Moreover, when a sinful habit has been sincerely repudiated by the will, the disposition to repeat the sinful act that may remain after repentance is involuntary, and as such is no longer a vice, or a sinful habit, in the full sense of the term. If the penitent through weakness falls back into his sin, the existence of the involuntary disposition is a mitigating circumstance unless he also falls back into a voluntary acquiescence in his inclination to sin.

In dealing with a habitual sinner, and in distinguishing him from a recidivist, a confessor will look especially for a willingness on the part of the penitent to use the means by which the habit can be broken.

Bibliography: H. DAVIS, *Moral and Pastoral Theology,* rev. and enl. ed. by L. W. GEDDES (New York 1958) 3:286–288, D. M. PRÜMMER, *Manuale theologiae moralis*, ed. E. M. MÜNCH, 3 v. (Freiburg-Barcelona 1955) 1:62. N. HALLIGAN, *The Administration of the Sacraments* (New York 1963) 260–261. T. ORTOLAN, *Dictionnaire de théologie catholique*, ed. A. VACANT et al., (Paris 1903—50) 6:2.2016–19; 2019–26.

[F. E. KLUEG]

SINNICH, JOHN

Jansenist theologian at Louvain; b. Cork, 1603; d. Louvain, May 8, 1666. He matriculated at Louvain in 1624, received his master's degree on Oct. 2, 1625, and his doctorate in theology on Sept. 27, 1639, at the time of the printing in Louvain of Jansenius's *Augustinus.* Sinnich collaborated in this publication, providing the table of contents, and indices for the three volumes. He was a Jansenist from the inception of the movement, and profited by this fact. In 1641 he became president of the College of the Holy Spirit; and was made a member of the faculty of theology in 1642. In 1643 he became semestral rector of the university, and was several times dean of the faculty of theology. His Augustinian convictions strengthened his stubborn defense of Jansenius. To this end he spent three years in Rome (1643–45). He also took part in the Jansenist controversy through pamphlets, often published anonymously. His best-known work is

St. Andrews Cathedral, Singapore. (©Robert Holmes/CORBIS)

the *Sanctorum Patrum Trias* (series 1; 1648). In *Goliathismus profligatus* (Louvain 1657), he became an apologist against Protestantism. His *Saulus Exrex* (2 v. Louvain 1666–67) is a sort of manual for Catholic princes. In volume one, he inserted a long diatribe against laxism. His name occurs several times in the *Index librorum prohibitorum.*

Bibliography: F. DEININGER, *Johannes Sinnich: Der Kampf der Löwener Universität gegen den Laxismus* (Düsseldorf 1928). H. WILLEMS, ''Les Publications du Père Lucien Ceyssens concernant le jansénisme,'' *Augustiniana* 13 (1963) 55–56. J. CARREYRE, *Dictionnaire de théologie catholique,* ed. A. VACANT, 15 v. (Paris 1903–50; Tables générales 1951–) 14.2:2165–66.

[L. CEYSSENS]

SINZIG, PEDRO

Editor in Brazil; b. Linz, Germany, Jan. 29, 1876; d. Düsseldorf, Sept. 12, 1952. Having completed his studies in the humanities, he went to Brazil in 1893, was ordained (1898), and as a member of the Franciscan province of the Immaculate Conception began an intense apostolate throughout Brazil. Sinzig was a pioneer in all Catholic cultural activities in his adopted land. He founded or edited 12 periodicals, including *A Resposta, A Tela, Vozes, Beija Flor,* and *A União* (with Felício dos Santos). Another journal, *Múica Sacra* (1941), which he founded and edited, was one of his contributions to music; others were his *Dicionário Musical* (1947), *Sei Compor* (1946), and *O Organista.* He also organized and taught influential summer courses in the Pro-Arte Brasil. Sinzig's novels, among them *Não desanimar* (1912) and *Pela Mão de uma Menina* (1913), are noteworthy, as are such critical studies as *Caricatura na Imprensa Brasileira* (1911), *Em Plena Guerra* (1912), and *Através dos Romances* (1928). In 60 years of intense apostolic activity, this authentic Christian humanist made unique contributions to the religious and cultural life of Brazil.

Bibliography: P. SINZIG, *Reminiscências d'um Frade* (Petrópolis 1911). L. L. BEUTENMUELLER, Frei Pedro Sinzig, O.F.M. (Petrópolis 1955). R. KOEPE, ''Em memória de Frei Sinzig, O.F.M.,'' *Música Sacra* 13 (1953) 2–4. F. M. KOHNEN, ''Frei Sinzig Pedro Sinzig, O.F.M., o pionerio,'' *Vozes de Petrópolis* 11 (1953) 1–18.

[A. STULZER]

SIOUX CITY, DIOCESE OF

The diocese of Sioux City (*Sioupolitana*), Iowa, was established Jan. 15, 1902. A suffragan of the Metropolitan See of Dubuque, it embraces the 24 northwest counties of Iowa, an area of 14,518 square miles.

History. Catholics first settled in the area around the middle of the nineteenth century. The first Catholic service was celebrated in November of 1850 by a Jesuit missionary, Father Christian Hoecken. Dubuque's first bishop, Mathias Loras, assigned the first resident pastor to northwest Iowa in 1857 at Corpus Christi Parish of Fort Dodge. From 1850 to 1920, as the agricultural frontier moved across the Midwest, Northwest Iowa received many thousands of European immigrants. The earliest were Irish, and about 75 Irish-born priests served during the era. The numbers of Irish were rivaled only by the Germans, and several towns contained both English-speaking and Germanic parishes. Other nationalities of Catholic immigrants, several of which formed ethnic parishes, were French, Bohemian, Polish, Italian, Syrian, Lithuanian, Croatian, and Luxembourger. After the 1980s, the diocesan Catholic population became more diverse, with the immigration of significant numbers of Vietnamese, Laotian, Cambodian, and Hispanic immigrants.

Bishops. The first bishop of the Diocese of Sioux City, Philip Joseph Garrigan (1840–1919), an Irish immigrant, had served as the first vice-rector of The CATHOLIC UNIVERSITY OF AMERICA, Washington, D.C., before being named as the first Bishop of Sioux City, May 25, 1902. The newly established diocese had a Catholic population of about 50,000 served by 116 parishes (84 with resident priests). During his administration, the number of schools doubled, and three of every four children were enrolled in Catholic schools.

Irish-born Bishop Edmond Heelan (1868–1948) spent nearly his entire priestly life in Sioux City. He was appointed auxiliary to Bishop Garrigan in 1918 and succeeded to the See on March 8, 1920, after Garrigan's death. Bishop Heelan witnessed the slowing of the flow of immigrants and the hardships brought by world and national events in the wake of World War I, but carried on the expansion of parishes, missions, and schools begun by Garrigan. He also helped establish Briar Cliff College in Sioux City in 1929.

Joseph Maximillian Mueller (1894–1981), a native of St. Louis, was named coadjutor in 1947 and became the Ordinary of the diocese on Sept. 20, 1948. Bishop Mueller was widely recognized for the bold and highly successful consolidation of high schools, and a tremendous building campaign of parish plants. He also founded the diocesan newspaper, *The Globe*.

Frank Greteman (1907–1987) was consecrated as auxiliary bishop of Sioux City on May 26, 1965, at the Cathedral of the Epiphany in Sioux City, and became the Ordinary in 1970. Born in Willey, Iowa, he was the first priest native to northwest Iowa to become a bishop and the first Iowa priest to serve his home diocese as bishop. Bishop Greteman completed the consolidation of the diocesan high schools and carried out re-organization of the diocesan elementary schools.

The Episcopal ordination of Bishop Lawrence Soens (born 1926), a native of the Diocese of Davenport, took place on Aug. 17, 1983, at the Cathedral of the Epiphany. He established and expanded many religious programs in the diocese. Upon Soens' retirement, Bishop Daniel DiNardo (born 1949), a native of the Diocese of Pittsburgh, was ordained for the diocese on Oct. 7, 1997, and became the sixth Ordinary in 1998.

[R. RODER]

SIOUX FALLS, DIOCESE OF

The diocese of Sioux Falls (*Siouxormensis*) comprises about 35,000 square miles lying east of the Missouri River in the state of SOUTH DAKOTA. It is a suffragan of the metropolitan See of ST. PAUL-MINNEAPOLIS. In the 1880s, the Benedictine missionary bishop, Martin Marty, OSB, who had served as vicar apostolic of Dakota Territory since 1879, left Yankton for Sioux Falls, choosing the latter as his See because he rightly assumed that it would become and remain the state's largest city. The diocese was erected in 1889 when the Territory was divided into and admitted to the Union as North and South Dakota. Ill health prompted Marty's transfer to the bishopric of St. Cloud just over a year before his death in 1896 at the age of 62. He had burned out as a circuit rider throughout the Territory's vast expanse (77,000 square miles) where he traveled constantly by horseback and wagon in all kinds of inclement weather to visit the far-flung Indian reservations, and the 150 towns and villages where his parishioners needed his attention.

Marty was succeeded in Sioux Falls by Thomas O'Gorman, who died in 1921. Bernard J. Mahoney then served the diocese until his death in 1939 when William

O. Brady succeeded him. Brady became Archbishop of St. Paul in 1956, dying in 1961 in Rome while preparing for Vatican Council II as one of the papal consultors. Lambert Hoch served as bishop from 1956 until his retirement in 1978 when he was succeeded by Paul Dudley. His successor, Robert J. Carlson was consecrated in 1994.

The diocese has 144 priests, and 35 permanent deacons serving 151 parishes and nine Catholic hospitals. A record 33 men are studying in out-of- state seminaries. There are two Catholic colleges, Mount Marty, in Yankton, sponsored by the Benedictine Sisters who opened the school in 1936, made it co-ed in 1969 and now boasts over 1,000 students on three campuses and in classes at Yankton's Federal Prison Camp. The Presentation Sisters first opened a junior college in Mitchell in 1922, transferring it to Aberdeen in 1951 where it became a four-year college. Courses are also offered in a branch school on a reservation.

Several motherhouses of women and one of men are located in the diocese. The Benedictines in the Yankton monastery (150 nuns) were a Swiss group who had settled first in Maryville, Missouri. They had responded to Marty's call to assist him in the Native American ministry in what became North and South Dakota. Their novitiate was moved from Zell to Yankton where it opened in 1887. Later Bishop O'Gorman asked them relocate in Vermillion so that the first Catholic hospital, Benedictine-sponsored, could be opened in their Yankton monastery. Eventually the nuns returned in 1908 to their permanent residence on Mount Marty—continuing to staff Sacred Heart Hospital and dozens of parish schools, their own high school and later also a college. In 1961 a daughter-house (Mother of God Monastery) was opened in Pierre, which later transferred to Watertown.

The Presentation Sisters originated in Ireland. They came to the Territory originally in 1880, later transferred to Fargo, North Dakota. Some Sisters returned when, in 1882, Bishop Marty and a pastor, Father Robert Haire, requested their assistance in Aberdeen. They opened a school there and later a hospital when, continuing the health care they had begun when an epidemic prompted them to minister to the sick brought to their convent. They also staffed a nursing school there, admitting the first men to enroll in 1942 during World War II. A four-year School of Nursing is now a department in their college.

Franciscan Sisters from North Dakota opened a convent at Gettysburg in 1970. They later transferred to Mitchell. The community of Oblates of the Blessed Sacrament, a branch of Mother Katharine Drexel's Pennsylvania congregation, was established in 1935 by the Benedictine missionary, Father Sylvester Eisenman, who arranged the admission of seven young Native American women to be admitted as postulants to the new religious community at Marty Mission near Wagner. It was 1949 before it was formally established as a religious congregation. The Oblates also serve the Native American population in Rapid City where home visits to those in need constitute their ministry. Other schools for Native American children are located in Chamberlain—under the supervision of the Sacred Heart Fathers from Hales Corners, Wis., and Stephan, formerly staffed by the Benedictine nuns and monks. The Benedictine nuns of Yankton and the Presentation Sisters of Aberdeen have recently united in co-sponsoring the major Catholic hospitals and care centers in the diocese, institutions which they had established and formerly community-sponsored. They operate under the umbrella of the Avera Health organization. Contemplative nuns are at Alexandria—a recent foundation.

In the mid-19th century, the Benedictine monks of St. Meinrad, Ind., built a monastery near Marvin, to enable them to be closer to the reservations and facilitate their ministry to the Native Americans. Before the close of the 20th century, however, the Sioux Falls diocese assumed the obligation of filling the vacancies left by the monks who are no longer in that apostolate. Jesuits still minister at the Rapid City Diocesan reservations traditionally filled by them when Marty, the first bishop, could no longer recruit Benedictine monks from the abbeys in Indiana and Missouri.

Although the numbers are relatively small, the areas huge, the Catholics of the diocese, overwhelmingly of German, Irish, Czech, or Polish ancestry, are committed to furthering Catholic education for their children, health care for those in need, social services of all kinds, and reconciliation with the fast-growing Native American population.

Bibliography: R. KAROLEVETZ, *With Faith, Hope and Tenacity* (Sioux Falls 1989); *Bishop Martin Marty: Black Robe Lean Chief* (Yankton 1980). A. KESSLER, "First Catholic Bishop of Dakota," in *South Dakota Leaders,* H. HOOVER et al., eds. (Vermillion 1989); "Mount Marty College," in *From Idea to Institution,* eds. H. HOOVER et al. (Vermillion 1989); *Benedictine Men and Women of Courage* (Yankton 1996); "Valiant Women," with S. PETERSON in *South Dakota Leaders,* H. HOOVER et al. eds. C. DURATSCHEK, *Beginnings of Catholicism in South Dakota* (Washington, D.C. 1943); *Crusading along Sioux Trails* (St. Meinrad, Ind. 1947); *Under the Shadow of His Wings* (Yankton 1971); *Builders of God's Kingdom* (1985).

[A. KESSLER]

SIRACH, BOOK OF

The name of one of the Wisdom books of the OT in many Bibles. The book is now generally called WISDOM OF BEN SIRA.

[A. A. DI LELLA]

SIRICIUS, POPE, ST.

Pontificate: Dec. 15 or 22 or 29, 384 to Nov. 26, 399. Siricius, a Roman by birth, was ordained a lector, then deacon by Pope LIBERIUS. On the death of Damasus (December 11, 384) he was elected pope despite the candidacy of Ursinus, who during the election of Damasus 18 years earlier, had incited bloody strife, and that of (St.) JEROME, who had enjoyed the favor of Damasus and seemed to cherish the hope of being raised to the Roman See (*Epist.* 45.3).

Letters. The papacy of Siricius is not well documented, nor does it appear to have been particularly distinguished. In 390 the Pope consecrated the newly reconstructed basilica of St. Paul on the Ostian Way, and several of his letters contain ''the first papal decrees'' that are listed as pontifical documents in canonical collections. On February 10, 385, Siricius wrote to Himerius of Tarragona, who had referred several points of discipline to Damasus (*Epist.* 1; P. Jaffé *Regesta pontificum romanorum ab condita ecclesia ad annum post Christum natum 1198,* 255). On January 6, 386, he wrote to the bishops of Africa on the decisions of a council that had met in Rome ''above the relics of St. Peter.'' This is the first known ''council of the Vatican'' (*Epist.* 5; P. Jaffé 258). In 386 he wrote to Anysius of Thessalonica on the subject of episcopal ordination in Illyricum (*Epist.* 4; P. Jaffé 259). About 390, in an address to ''the orthodox in the provinces,'' apparently the Italian bishops, he points out certain abuses that had been creeping into the rite of ordination (*Epist.* 6; P. Jaffé 263). In 390 (St.) Ambrose replied (*Epist.* 42) to a circular, addressed to the Church of Milan, that forwarded the decision of a Roman council condemning Jovinian and the others who denied the perpetual virginity of Mary (*Epist.* 7; P. Jaffé 260). Letter 9 in this collection, dealing with the case of Bonosus, belongs to Ambrose, and Letter 10, *ad Gallos,* was written by Damasus.

These letters are of importance in the history of ecclesiastical discipline. They settle pastoral problems, stating, for example, that heretics, both Arians and Novatians, are not to be rebaptized, but should be reconciled by the laying on of hands (*Epist.* 1.1.2). Except in cases of necessity or for infants, Baptism is to be bestowed at Easter or Pentecost, not on Christmas (*Epist.* 1.2.3). Episcopal consecration may not be bestowed by a single bishop; there must be several consecrators (*Epist.* 5.2.1). A bishop should not ordain a cleric of another church, nor accept one deposed by another church (*Epist.* 5.2.6, 7). Very precise regulations concern the age of those being ordained (*Epist.* 1.8) and, especially, the continence of clergymen: priests and deacons are bound ''by the everlasting law of continence'' (*Epist.* 1.6, 7–7.8, 9); severe punishments are set for the guilty, as also for monks and nuns who fall into incontinence. Clerics should not live with women except in circumstances mentioned by the Council of Nicaea (*Epist.* 1.10). Other regulations concern the discipline of Penance, which remained harsh (*Epist.* 1.4, 12). A baptized man who embraced the ''*cingulum militiae saecularis*'' (civil office as well as more explicit military service) could not be admitted to the clerical state (*Epist.* 5.2.3).

Papal Authority. More important than their content is the testimony of these decrees regarding the growing authority of the Apostolic See, particularly in the West. Siricius is the first pope to claim that the Apostle Peter spoke through him: ''We bear within us the burdens of all who are weighed down, but it is rather the Blessed Apostle Peter who bears these burdens in us, since, as we trust, he protects us in all the matters of *his* administration and guides us as his heirs'' (*Epist.* 1.1). References to the double foundation of Rome (Peter and Paul) fade away as only the Petrine foundation is seen to be important. The bishops should address the Roman Church as head of their body (*Epist.* 1.15.20). The pope replies to their queries: *rescripsimus* (a technical term of the imperial chancellory) with complete authority; i.e., we command, we decree (*jubemus, decernimus*). His decisions are the *Statuta Sedis Apostolicae* and have the same authority as those of the revered councils (*Epist.* 1.15.20); bishops who do not obey them separate themselves from the solidity of the apostolic rock, on which Christ built the universal Church (*Epist.*1.2.3).

This authority was imposed at first upon the bishops of rural Italy over whom Siricius had immediate supervision: no episcopal election could be accomplished ''without the knowledge of the Apostolic See'' (*Epist.* 5.2.1). Beyond that area, Siricius forwarded the decisions of the Roman council to the Church of Milan and addressed the bishops of Gaul, Spain, and Africa with full authority, but the Gauls had reservation and the Africans typically accepted only what they agreed with. He intervened likewise in the problems over PRISCILLIANISM and sided with the bishops who had refused communion with Ithacus and Idacius after they had persuaded the usurper Maximus that it was legitimate to put Priscillian to death (P. Jaffé 262; Mansi 3:1005). He made Anysius of Thessalonica his vicar in Illyricum to protect the province from the influence of Constantinople. No episcopal ordination could take place there without the consent of Anysius (*Epist.* 4). At the request of Ambrose (*Epist.* 56.7) Siricius attempted to solve the schism of Antioch but failed.

Siricius was a strong personality but not a thinker. He distrusted the new breed of ascetic intellectuals. He acquiesced in the expulsion of Jerome from the city of Rome, and he distanced himself from Paulinus of Nola. His approach to theological questions was to cite Roman tradition and authority. Yet this firmness often placed him in good stead. Siricius played an important part in the promotion of the authority of the Apostolic See. He was buried in the basilica of St. Silvester in the cemetery of Priscilla, where pilgrims were still venerating his tomb in the seventh century (*Martyrologium Romanum* 547).

Feast: November 26.

Bibliography: SIRICIUS, *Patrologia Latina,* ed. J. P. MIGNE (Paris 1878–90) 13:1131–1202. É. AMANN, *Dictionnaire de théologie catholique,* ed. A. VACANT et al., 15 v. (Paris 1903–50; Tables générales 1951–) 14.2:2171–74. P. JAFFÉ *Regesta pontificum romanorum ab condita ecclesia ad annum post Christum natum 1198,* ed. S. LÖWENFELD et al., 2 v. (2d ed. Leipzig 1881–88, repr. Graz 1956) 1:40–42. A. DIBERARDINO, *Patrology* (Westminster, Md. 1986) 4:580–581. E. FERGUSON, ed., *Encyclopedia of Early Christianity* (New York 1997) 2:1064. H. JEDIN, *History of the Church* (New York 1980) 2:254–256. J. N. D. KELLY, *Oxford Dictionary of Popes* (New York 1986) 35–36. C. PIETRI, *Roma Christiana* (Rome 1976) 468–474, 888–909. J. CURRAN, ''Jerome and the Sham Christians of Rome,'' *The Journal of Ecclesiastical History* 48: 213–29. R. GIULIANI, ''Un'interessante novità epigrafica della catacomba della ex vigna Chiaraviglio sulla via Appia Antica. Ancora sull'attività dei presbiteri Proclino e Urso a S. Sebastiano,'' in *'Domum Tuam Dilexi'. Miscellanea in onore di Aldo Nestori* (Vatican City 1998) 375–97. P. LAURENCE, ''Rome et Jérôme: des amours contrariées,'' *Revue Bénédictine* 107: 227–49.

[P. T. CAMELOT]

SIRLETO, GUGLIELMO

Cardinal, Tridentine scholar, Vatican librarian; b. Guardavalle, Calabria, Italy, 1514; d. Rome, Oct. 7, 1585. After studying at Naples, where he became proficient in Greek, he continued his researches at the Vatican Library. Here he made the acquaintance of Cardinal Marcello Cervino (later Pope MARCELLUS II), presiding official at the intial phases of the Council of Trent. While remaining at Rome, Sirleto prepared extensive memoranda on many of the important questions discussed at the council. He similarly collaborated with the other cardinal legates, particularly Cardinal Girolamo Seripando, at the later phases of the council. As head of the Vatican Library, he catalogued all its Greek manuscripts. In 1565 he was made a cardinal; in 1566, bishop of San Marco, Calabria; and in 1568, bishop of his native diocese of

Guglielmo Cardinal Sirleto.

Squillace. However, even after his episcopal consecration he almost always resided in Rome. Here he was the central figure in editing the publications decreed by the council: the revised Missal and Breviary, the Roman Catechism, the *Corpus Iuris Canonici,* and the official texts of the Latin Vulgate and the Greek Septuagint.

Bibliography: H. HURTER, *Nomenclator literarius theologiae catholicae,* 5 v. in 6 (3d ed. Innsbruck 1903–1913); v.1 (4th ed. 1926) 3:258–261. J. MERCIER, *Dictionnaire de théologie catholique,* ed. A. VACANT, 15 v. (Paris 1903–50; Tables générales 1951–) 14.2:2174–75. W. KOCH, *Lexikon für Theologie und Kirche,* ed. M. BUCHBERGER, 10 v. (Freiburg 1930–38)[1] 9:596–597. G. TACCONE GALLUCCI, *Monografia del cardinale Sirleto nel secolo 16* (Rome 1909). S. MERKLE, ''Kardinal Sirleto,'' *Beiträge zur Geschichte des christlichen Altertums und der byzantinischen Literatur: Festgabe, Albert Erhard* (Bonn 1922).

[L. F. HARTMAN]

SIRMIUM

Ancient city of Pannonia on the River Sava, the site of modern Hovatzka Mitrovitza in Bosnia. The city was conquered by the Romans under Caecina Severus in the 1st century A.D. and became the capital of Pannonia II under Diocletian. Its early Christian colony included the FOUR CROWNED MARTYRS, Pollius the lector, and

Irenaeus of Sirmium (d. 309). In the 4th century it served as the metropolitan see for western Illyricum. In the Arian quarrel its bishop, Photinus (d. 343), made himself the champion of the radical Arianism of Eunomius of Cyzicus (Anomoeanism): ''The Word is dissimilar to the Father.'' This doctrine was condemned, along with Photinus, at Antioch (344), Milan (345), and Sirmium (348, 351); the last-named synod deposed Photinus. His successor, Germinius, held a synod (summer of 357) and with Valens of Mursa and Ursacius of Singidunum adopted the ''Second Formula of Sirmium,'' which held that the Son was inferior and subordinated to the Father, that the Holy Spirit existed through the Son, a statement that Hosius of Córdoba signed, and that became for a time the official doctrine of Imperial orthodoxy. It was condemned by the Emperor Gratian (378), by Pope DAMASUS I (375), and by the Synod of Aquileia (381).

Destroyed by the Avars (582), the city was rebuilt around the Oriental monastery of St. Demetrius and was called Dmitrovica, while Sirmium (Croatian Sriem) became the name of the region between the Sava and the Danube Rivers. Pope ADRIAN II in 869 attempted to form an archdiocese of Sirmium with jurisdiction over the central Danubian area, but political intrigue frustrated the project. In 1229 GREGORY XI made it a diocese, with the former Benedictine monastery at Bonostar as its seat. It was troubled with heretical movements from the so-called Bosnian heresy of the PATARINES to Calvinism, and counted many apostates to Islam.

Bibliography: W. KOCH, *Lexikon für Theologie und Kirche,* ed. M. BUCHBERGER, 10 v. (Freiburg 1930–38) 9:597–598. D. FARLATI, *Illyricum sacrum,* 8 v., v. 5–8 ed. G. COLETI (Venice 1751–1819) 7:449–571. J. ZEILLER, *Les Origines chrétiennes dans les provinces danubiennes* (Paris 1918).

[P. JOANNOU]

SIRMOND, JACQUES

Jesuit historian and patristic scholar; b. Riom, Auvergne, France, Oct. 12, 1559; d. Paris, Oct. 7, 1651. He studied at the Jesuit college of Billom, and became a Jesuit (1576) and a priest. From 1581 to 1590 he taught literature at Pont-à-Mousson and Paris (where SS. Francis of Sales and Peter Fourier were his students), and from 1590 to 1608 he was secretary to the Jesuit general C. Acquaviva in Rome, also aiding Cardina Baronius in his historical works. In 1608 he returned to Paris and in 1617 became rector of the college of Clermont there. From 1637 to 1643 he was confessor to Louis XIII. As one of the most learned men in France in his day, he edited the texts of many early authors, especially those pertaining to the history of France, such as texts of Geoffrey of Vendome, Flodoard of Reims, Sidonius Apollinaris, Paschasius Radbertus, Avitus of Vienne, Hincmar of Reims, and Theodulf of Orleans; the lives of Leo IX and Charles of Flanders; the capitularies of Charles the Bald, and the *Concilia antiqua Galliae.* His editions of works of Eusebius of Caesarea, Theodoret of Cyr, and FULGENTIUS OF RUSPE are noteworthy. He also discovered and edited the ecclesiastical constitutions of the Theodosian Code. Many of his texts were later adopted for the collections of LABBE, MANSI, and MIGNE. Sirmond's distinction between Dionysius the Areopagite and PSEUDO-DIONYSIUS was an important correction of traditional opinion. He wrote or published other works of interest in the history of dogma and theology, e.g., on predestination, public penance, and the Sacraments of Confirmation and the Eucharist.

Bibliography: *Opera,* ed. J. DE LA BAUME, 5 v. (Paris 1696, Venice 1728), including a biography. C. SOMMERVOGEL, *Bibliotèque de la Compagnie de Jésus,* 11 v. (Brussels-Paris 1890–1932) 7:1237–61,11:1910–11. P. GALTIER, *Dictionnaire de théologie catholique,* ed. A. VACANT, 15 v. (Paris 1903–50; Tables générales 1951–) 14.2:2186–93.

[F. X. MURPHY]

SISINNIUS, POPE

Pontifcate: Jan. 15 to Feb. 4, 708; b. Syria, date unknown; d. Rome. His exact birthplace is unknown, but the *Liber pontificalis* states that he was a native of Syria, the ''son of John.'' There is no information on his education. He seems to have been a man of both practical ability and noble generosity. In January 708 Sisinnius was elected successor to JOHN VII by the clergy and nobility of Rome, as was the custom. His pontificate of 20 days was complicated by the exactions of the Byzantine exarch at Ravenna, the encroachment of the LOMBARDS, and the menace of the Moslem advance from the south. As pope, his first act was to order the reinforcement of the walls of Rome. He held one ordination and consecrated a bishop for Corsica. He was buried in St. Peter's.

Bibliography: L. JAFFÉ, *Regesta pontificum romanorum ab condita ecclesia ad annum post Christum natum 1198,* ed. P. EWALD 1:247. *Liber pontificalis,* ed. L. DUCHESNE, (Paris, 1958) 1:388. H. K. MANN, *The Lives of the Popes in the Early Midlle Ages from 590 to 1304* (London 1930–32) 1.2:124–126. E. CASPAR, *Geschichte de Papsttums von den Anfängen bis zur Höhe der Weltherrschaft* (Tübingen 1930–33) 2:620. G. H. BAUDRY, *Catholicisme hier aujourd'hui demain,* 14 (Paris 1994). J. N. D. KELLY, *Oxford Dictionary of Popes* (New York 1986) 85–86.

[M. A. MULHOLLAND]

SISINNIUS I, PATRIARCH OF CONSTANTINOPLE

Episcopacy: 426 to 427, saint; d. Constantinople, Dec. 24, 427. Sisinnius, a priest working in the suburb of Elaia in Constantinople, was selected patriarch on Feb. 26, 426 by popular acclamation. The people recognized his piety and love for the poor, and preferred him to the clergy's candidates, Proclus, secretary of the deceased Patriarch Atticus, and Philip, presbyter of Side, who later criticized Sisinnius in his *Christian History*. In a synod held soon after his consecration, Sisinnius condemned the lax discipline with which the Messalians were treated by Beronicianus of Perga. He also vindicated the reputation of Proclus by selecting him as bishop of Cyzicus, but the people of Cyzicus claimed the right to elect their own bishop and chose Dalmatius instead. Upon Sisinnius' sudden death, at a time when the Church was divided over the nature of Christ, the bishops, clergy and monks could not decide on a successor. The decision was left to the Emperor Theodosius II, who selected the Antiochian priest Nestorius. Pope Celestine I praised Sisinnius' simple faith and orthodoxy.

Feast: Oct. 11.

Bibliography: *Acta Sanctorum Sedis* 627–629. SOCRATES SCHOLASTICUS, *Historia ecclesiastica* (Patrologia Graeca 67) 7:26–28; tr. A. C. ZENOS (A Select Library of the Nicene and Post-Nicene Fathers 2.2; 1890) 1–178. MARCELLINUS COMES, *The Chronicle of Marcellinus,* tr. B. CROKE (Sydney 1995) 14, 77. THEODORE LECTOR, *Theodore Anagnostes, Kirchengeschichte,* ed. G.C. HANSEN (Berlin 1971) 324–326. THEOPHANES, *The Chronicle of Theophanes Confessor,* tr. C. MANGO and R. SCOTT (Oxford 1997) 136–137. L. DINDORF, ed., *Zonaras* (Leipzig 1868–75), 13.22. G. BARDY, *Histoire de l'église depuis les origines jusqu'à nos jours,* ed. A. FLICHE and V. MARTIN (Paris 1935) 4:161–162. G. DAGRON, *Naissance d'une capitale, Constantinople et ses institutions de 370 à 451,* (Paris 1974) 470, 492. A. DI BERARDINO, ed. *Encyclopedia of the Early Church,* tr. A. WALFORD (Cambridge 1992).

[F. NICKS/A. PENNA]

SISINNIUS II, PATRIARCH OF CONSTANTINOPLE

Reigned 996 to 998; d. Constantinople, Aug. 24, 998. Distinguished for his medical knowledge and his eloquence, Sisinnius succeeded the Patriarch Nicholas II after a four-year interval. He was responsible for at least three synodal decisions on marriage, one of which extended the impediment of affinity to the fifth grade, while the second and third dealt with impediments and second marriages. Some doubt exists regarding the authenticity of the latter two. He opposed the abuse called the *Charisticariate,* whereby monasteries were deeded to lay people or to other monasteries, which practice was originally intended as a means of preserving their financial stability. He wrote a treatise on the apparition of St. Michael the Archangel (*Acta apparitionis in Chonis*) and a panegyric in honor of the martyr SS. Kerykos (Cyriacus) and Julitta, as well as a controversial *Tome on Marriage* (Feb. 21, 997). His part in renewing difficulties between Rome and Constantinople by the republication of an anti-Latin encyclical of PHOTIUS is disputed.

Bibliography: H. G. BECK, *Kirche und theologische Literatur im byzantinischen Reich* (Munich 1959) 88–89, 136, 554. V. GRUMEL, ed., *Les Regestes des actes du Patriarcat de Constantinople,* v.2 (Constantinople 1936) 231–239; "L'Encyclique de Photius . . . et Sisinnius II . . . ," *Échos d'Orient* 34 (1935) 129–138. V. LAURENT, "Réponses canonique inédites," *ibid.* 33 (1934) 302–305; "Charisticariat et commende à Byzance," *Revue des études byzantines* 12 (1954) 100–113. E. HERMAN, *Dictionnaire de droit canonique,* ed. R. NAZ, 7 v. (Paris 1935–65) 3:611–617.

[A. PENNA]

SISTER FORMATION MOVEMENT

An international movement, founded to promote the spiritual, intellectual, social and professional development of women religious by providing a program of advanced education for them comparable to, though of shorter duration than, the formation given to candidates for the priesthood.

Early Formation of Apostolic Women Religious. Prior to Vatican Council II, the advanced education of women religious committed to Catholic education and/or health care was highly restricted by the Church authorities and was dependent primarily upon the limited resources of the individual religious congregations. The founding of The Catholic Sisters' College at The Catholic University in 1911 (discontinued in 1950) provided one of the earliest opportunities for major superiors to obtain advanced education for their members within a Catholic environment. Catholic universities at this time were almost exclusively male oriented—administration, faculty, staff and student body. Most of them offered a few classes for women, both religious and lay, in the late afternoon or evening and during the summer.

After state and regional certification requirements in 1918 gave impetus to what was already a deeply felt need, some major superiors were able, with the special permission of their bishops, to send their sisters to secular universities to obtain certification and/or advanced degrees. For the next two decades, the higher education of women religious in both secular and Catholic colleges experienced slow if steady growth.

The publication in 1941 of *The Education of Sisters,* the doctoral thesis of Sister Bertrande Meyers, DC, drew attention to the effects on women religious of what had become large-scale attendance at Catholic and secular colleges and universities. The book revealed widespread dissatisfaction of major superiors with the education of their sisters, which was still obtained for the most part by attending late afternoon, Saturday and summer classes while working full time in schools or hospitals, and with the marked dichotomy between the sisters' spiritual and intellectual maturation. Meyers proposed a plan for integrating the four facets of a sister's formation— the spiritual, intellectual, social and professional— through the founding of colleges specifically designed for the needs of sisters.

National Catholic Education Association. At the National Catholic Education Association (NCEA) convention in 1949, a symposium entitled ''The Education of Sister Lucy'' included a paper by Sister Madeleva Wolff, CSC, entitled ''The Education of Young Religious Teacher'' that decried the piecemeal education of sisters. This event marked an early national, public acknowledgement of a growing concern among many members of apostolic congregations.

In December 1950, the Holy See called an international congress of men and women religious to discuss mutual concerns, among them the programs of education for sisters. The following year Pius XII in his Discourse to the Teaching Sisters stated:

> Many of your schools are being described and praised to us as being very good. But not all. It is our fervent wish that all endeavor to become excellent. This presupposes that your teaching Sisters are masters of the subjects they expound. See to it, therefore, that they are well trained and their education corresponds in quality and academic degrees to that demanded by the State.

At the NCEA convention of 1952, Sister Mary Emil Penet, IHM, led a panel that addressed Pius XII's concern for better Catholic schools and better-trained teachers. The first Congress of Major Superiors, held at Notre Dame University in South Bend, Indiana, the following summer focused on ways of accomplishing this ideal.

The following year, SFC was officially launched as a committee within the College and University Department of NCEA. After holding more than 250 regional meetings, the leaders of the movment developed a plan for establishing postnovitiate houses of study to be known as ''juniorates.'' These programs would comprise three years of formative study intended to ensure the development of a well-integrated, mature, holy and effective religious, prepared for active ministry.

Sister Formation Conference. By 1957, the organization of the Sister Formation Conference was completed with a national chairman, vice-chairman, executive secretary, and a national leadership group of sisters and a consultative committee of priests. They now operated under the aegis of the Conference of Major Superiors of Women Religious (CMSW), and in 1964 they achieved the status of a separate committee within the CMSW. At this time their staff status within NCEA was terminated.

In addition to sponsoring in-service workshops for teachers and administrators, the Sister Formation Conference published a quarterly bulletin. The *Sister Formation Bulletin* (1955–1972) under the leadership of Sister Rita Mary BRADLEY, SFCC, exerted a formidable influence upon the lives of most American women religious in the second half of the twentieth century.

In addition to providing for the education of American women religious, SFC made an outstanding contribution to the universal church by arranging for qualified sisters from Africa, India and South America to be accepted into juniorates and Catholic women's colleges throughout the United States.

In 1971, SFC became a separate national conference independent of LCWR (formerly CMSW). The leadership of the SFC adopted a new set of bylaws by means of which they hoped to widen the sphere of their influence. SFC now admitted as members both men and women, individuals and groups, non-canonical communities and secular institutes from within and outside the United States. Five years later, in 1976, the conference changed the name of the organization to the Religious Formation Conference to reflect the new makeup of its membership.

The RFC retained its commitment to initial formation while expanding efforts to include ongoing formation and continuing education. One outgrowth of their dedication to religious life has been their effort to foster and nourish a vital community life in which new members may find daily support and encouragement.

Bibliography: Proceedings of the Sister Formation Regional Conferences. *The Mind of the Church in the Formation of Sisters* (New York 1956); *Spiritual and Intellectual Elements in the Formation of Sisters* (New York 1958); *Planning for the Formation of Sisters* (New York. 1958); *The Juniorate in Sister Formation* (New York 1960). B. MEYERS, DC, *Sisters for the 21st Century* (New York 1965). A. WALTERS, CSJ, ''Religious Life: Yesterday and Tomorrow,'' *New Catholic World* (March/April 1972) 74–75; H. M. MALONEY, SC, ''Formation: Where Has It Been?'' *Sister Formation Bulletin*, 18(4) (summer 1972) 5. Papers of SFC/RFC are held in Marquette University Archives, as are the personal papers of pioneers Sister R. Bradley, SFCC (1917–2000) and Sister A. Walters, CSJ (1910–1978).

[M. R. MADDEN]

SISTERS, FAITHFUL COMPANIONS OF JESUS

(FCJ, Official Catholic Directory #4048); a congregation with papal approbation, founded in Amiens, France, in 1820 by Marie Madeleine Victoire de Bonnault d'Houet, née De Bengy. Following the death of her husband in 1805, Madame d'Houet devoted herself to raising her son and contemplated founding a religious community for the education of children. With the help of three companions, her plan began to materialize in 1820. By the time of her death in 1858, 20 houses had been established, and her community gradually spread to England, Switzerland, Italy, Scotland, Ireland, and Belgium. At the end of the 19th century the sisters had extended their work to North America and Australia. From Canada, where the sisters were working in the native missions of the Northwest, they came to the U.S. in 1896 and established themselves in Fitchburg, MA. Two more foundations were later made in Rhode Island. The generalate is in Broadstairs, Kent, England. The U.S. provincialate is in Portsmouth, RI.

[Z. O'CONNELL/EDS.]

SISTERS ADORERS OF THE PRECIOUS BLOOD

(APB, Official Catholic Directory #0110); a cloistered, contemplative community with papal approbation, founded in Canada in 1861 for the twofold purpose of adoration of the Precious Blood and the salvation of souls. The foundress, Catherine Aurélie Caouette, and three companions began the congregation at St. Hyacinthe, Quebec Province, with the approval of Bp. Joseph LaRocque (1860–65) and under the direction of Msgr. J. S. Raymond. Mother Catherine Aurelia of the Precious Blood, as she was known in religious life, died July 6, 1905. The constitutions of the community were approved by Leo XIII in 1896, after several foundations had been made in Canada and one in the United States, in Brooklyn, NY (1890).

The sisters pray the Liturgy of the Hours in common, and participate in prayers for reparation of the world and special hours of adoration before the Blessed Sacrament. The sisters also engage in making altar breads, vestments, and altar linens and in doing art work.

At the beginning of the 21st century, there were nineteen monasteries of the Precious Blood: six autonomous houses belonging to the American Federation; four houses belonging to the French Generalate of Canada, seven belonging to the English Generalate of Canada, and two independent monasteries in Japan.

Bibliography: *The Life of Mother Catherine Aurelia of the Precious Blood* (St. Louis 1929).

[M. M. RYAN/EDS.]

SISTERS FOR CHRISTIAN COMMUNITY

Founded, 1970 in response to Vatican II and to the desire of a number of committed women for a flexible lifestyle to facilitate ministry. The Sisters For Christian Community (SFCC) is an international community with a committed membership in all continents of the world. The sisters seek to be present wherever there is a need for Christian love and community witness. The community reflects the journey of women called to be co-foundresses, co-equals, and co-responsible for all aspects of this form of religious life, which is non-canonical and ecumenical, with a self-supporting membership.

The vision of the community was formulated by Lillanna Kopp, Ph.D, then Sister Audrey Kopp, a sociologist and member of the Sisters of the Holy Names (SNJM), who had been teaching at Maryhurst College and who was very active in the renewal of religious communities of women during the 1960s. Her vision was of a new form of religious life that would embody the values and principles of the Second Vatican Council. She was urged by several bishops who were involved in the renewal of religious communities to carry out this vision. A number of women religious, leaders in their congregations, encouraged her to be the catalyst in forming the community and, with Lillanna, became the founding group of the Sisters for Christian Community.

The mission and goals of the Sisters for Christian Community are clearly stated in the SFCC *Profile.* The apostolic goal of SFCC is to promote and witness Christian community; and, the sisters strive through all means available to forward the realization of Christ's prayer, ". . . that all may be ONE . . . ." that they may be Community. To achieve this goal, they seek to bring together into a community Christ-committed women who give witness to collegial community with the mission of building the body of Christ through helping to build dynamic Christian community wherever they live their calling. Each sister determines her own ministry on the basis of her personal call within the community, her training and interests, and the movement of the Spirit.

The vows of poverty, chastity, and obedience (expressed in terms of serving and sharing; celibate love; and listening to the guidance of the Spirit) are lived in accord with the special ministry of the sister. The sisters are found in nearly every professional field in faith-based ministries; in public, private, and corporate organizations; in university, diocesan, and parish settings; in such works areas as education, social work, and health; with the homeless, the elderly, the poor, and the sick. All are concerned with issues of social justice and the bonding of women.

The organizational structure of the community is simple. The sisters live alone or with others. Community transcends distance. It is experienced through personal contacts, local, regional, and international gatherings, and newsletters. Community decisions are made collegially, through a process of consensus. Mutual support and accountability are most tangibly experienced at the regional and local levels.

Since its inception in 1970, SFCC has been a community in process, refining its international communications network under the inspiration of the Holy Spirit. By the end of the 20th century, membership exceeded 470 and had expanded into 19 regions, each with a regional communications coordinator who is selected through a process of discernment whereby the sisters call forth a member to assume the service role. SFCC numbers over 470 members and the sisters are currently exploring new forms of membership at the Annual International Assemblies.

[M. V. JOSEPH]

SISTERS OF CHARITY, FEDERATION OF

A number of Roman Catholic Institutes of Consecrated Life and Societies of Apostolic Life are inspired by the charisms of St. VINCENT DE PAUL (1581–1660), St. LOUISE DE MARILLAC (1591–1660) and, in the United States, St. Elizabeth Ann Bayley SETON (1774–1821). In 1965 several took the first steps in forming the predecessor to the Sisters of Charity Federation, a voluntary association of sisterhoods that share the common Vincentian heritage of the Common Rules of the Daughters of Charity (Paris, 1672). The founding communities trace their roots to the Sisters of Charity of Saint Joseph's founded by Mother Seton near Emmitsburg, Maryland. This article describes the origin of the Vincentian Tradition in France, its adaptation by Mother Seton in United States and the communities she inspired, the development and structures of the federation, and finally brief descriptions of each of the member congregations.

French origin of the Vincentian tradition. In his *Conferences to the Daughters of Charity,* St. Vincent explained on Sept. 29, 1655, that he and Saint Louise cofounded the *Confraternity of the Charity of the Servants of the Sick Poor of the Parishes* (whose members the people of Paris called *Daughters of Charity*) ''to honor the great charity of Our Lord Jesus Christ'' through service to persons who were sick and poor [Joseph Leonard, ed., trans., *Conferences of Vincent de Paul to the Daughters of Charity,* 4 v. (Westminster, Md. 1939) 3:98]. The Company of the Daughters of Charity, founded on Nov. 29, 1633, developed from the parish-based Confraternities of Charity and became the first successful institute of non-cloistered religious women to serve in the active apostolate in France. As such, the *Common Rules of the Daughters of Charity* became a prototype. The rule developed by Louise de Marillac and Vincent de Paul was first explained to the sisters on July 31, 1634, and refined over time on the basis of the lived experience of the sisters who sought to live a lifestyle for mission characterized by humility, simplicity, and charity. According to Saint Louise, ''If humility, simplicity, and charity which gives support are well-established among you, your little Company will be composed of as many saints as there are persons in it'' [Louise Sullivan, trans., *Louise de Marillac Spiritual Writings* (New York 1991) 532].

Saint Vincent invited the sisters to sign the *Act of Establishment of the Company* on Aug. 8, 1655. His immediate successor as superior general, Very Reverend René Alméras, CM, (1613–1672; superior general 1661–1672), reorganized the original text of 43 articles that constituted the primitive rule. Alméras arranged them into chapters, with the assistance of Sister Mathurine Guérin (1631–1704) and included some unpublished oral traditions. This edition, in effect for the Daughters of Charity from 1672 until after Vatican II, reflects the thinking and collaboration of both Saint Louise and Saint Vincent.

In imitation of Saint Vincent's first Daughters of Charity, many congregations throughout the world carry the title ''Sisters of Charity'' and seek to live in their time the Vincentian mission having what Vincent de Paul described on Aug. 24, 1659, ''for cloister the streets of the city, for enclosure obedience, going only to the homes of the sick and to places necessary for their service'' (Leonard 4:264). The mission of the Company of Charity required a structure and lifestyle that circumvented the 17th-century requirement of enclosure for religious women. Louise explained in a letter to the Abbé de Vaux on June 29, 1649 that she and Vincent established the Daughters of Charity as ''just a secular family'' (Sullivan 293), ''for whoever says *religious* says *cloistered,* and Daughters of Charity should go everywhere,'' as Saint Vincent explained to the Company of Charity on June 29, 1649 (Leonard 4:261).

The Daughters of Charity confirmed their commitment to mission through annual, private vows of poverty, chastity, obedience, and service of poor persons. The cloister would have prevented the sisters from doing their mission, which, according to Saint Vincent's explanation on May 30, 1659, called them to a *state of charity* through ministry among the sick poor, rather than a state of perfection through perpetual, public vows. The Daughters of Charity of Saint Vincent de Paul first received (1646) ecclesiastical approval by the archbishop of Paris, but that approbation, together with the royal letters patent, were inexplicably lost. Louise de Marillac wished to preserve the integrity of the Vincentian charism and to protect the Company of the Daughters of Charity from ecclesiastical interference. At her insistence, the substitute document was revised to place the Daughters of Charity under the perpetual direction of Saint Vincent and his successors as superior general of the Congregation of the Mission. Cardinal de Retz, archbishop of Paris, gave his approval on Jan. 18, 1655. The statutes of the company were confirmed in the name of Pope Clement IX by his legate, Cardinal Louis de Bourbon, duke de Vendôme, on July 8, 1668.

American origin of the Setonian tradition. Reverend Louis William Dubourg, SS (1766–1833), had desired to expand educational programs for girls in Baltimore since 1797. He met Elizabeth Bayley Seton about 1806 in New York and invited her to that city, where she served for one year as school mistress. She established (1808) a small boarding school for girls beside the Sulpician institution Saint Mary's College & Seminary on Paca Street. This plan enjoyed the enthusiastic support of John Carroll (1735–1815), first bishop of the United States and first archbishop of Baltimore (1789–1815). Carroll's primary concern was to provide educational opportunities for lay leaders and to develop native clergy for the Catholic Church in America.

The Sulpician priests of Baltimore offered to assist Elizabeth in formulating plans that would be beneficial to the welfare of her children. They expected women to join Elizabeth in forming a sisterhood modeled on the French Daughters of Charity under their direction. Elizabeth entrusted such a project to Divine Providence. In a letter dated Feb. 20, 1809 to Rose Stubbs of New York, Elizabeth explained that she would be forming apostolic women who ''choose to lead a Religious life devoted to the education of poor children in the Catholic faith . . . [with] the prospect of receiving many [spiritual] daughters.'' Describing her vision of mission to Julia Sitgreaves Scott of Philadelphia in a letter dated March 23, 1809, Elizabeth exclaimed enthusiastically about ''the joy'' of her ''soul at the prospect of being able to assist the Poor, visit the sick, comfort the sorrowful, clothe little innocents, and teach them to love God!'' Two days later on March 25, Elizabeth pronounced vows of chastity and obedience to Bishop Carroll for one year in the lower chapel at Saint Mary's, after which the archbishop bestowed the title ''Mother'' on her.

The Sulpicians actively recruited the first candidates who joined the germinal community named at Baltimore between December 1808 and June 1809. Among them were the Misses Cecilia O'Conway (1788–1865), Anna Maria Murphy-Burke (*c.* 1787–1812), and Mary Ann Butler (1784–1821) all of Philadelphia; Susan Clossey (1785–1823) of New York; and Catherine (Kitty) Mullen (1783–1814), and Mrs. Rosetta (Rose) Landry White (1784–1841), a widow, of Baltimore. Elizabeth's youngest sisters-in-law arrived from New York and accompanied her to Emmitsburg in June of 1808. Cecilia Seton (1791–1810) was already a convert, and by September that year Harriet Seton (1787–1809) was also received into the Catholic Church.

Samuel Sutherland Cooper (1769–1843), a wealthy convert and seminarian at Saint Mary's Seminary, Baltimore, wished to address the needs of poor persons. Cooper donated $6,961 to purchase 269 acres of land from Robert Fleming for Mother Seton and her new community. Cooper designated the property, near Emmitsburg in Frederick County, Maryland, for education, care of the elderly, and employment training. Initially Elizabeth considered naming the community the Sisters of Saint Joseph but in recognition of the Vincentian tradition, she expanded its title to be the Sisters of Charity of Saint Joseph's.

The Sisters of Charity of Saint Joseph's. The community of the Sisters of Charity of Saint Joseph's was founded July 31, 1809, at the Stone House in Saint Joseph's Valley near Emmitsburg, Maryland, and from there launched their apostolate of education and charity, trusting all to Divine Providence. *The Provisional Regulations for Saint Joseph's Sisters* (1809) was the primitive governing documents of the new community. In mid-February of 1810 the sisters moved into the newly constructed Saint Joseph's House (the White House). There 86 candidates joined the new sisterhood during Elizabeth's lifetime. The women were courageous in their mission despite the ravages of illness and premature death, which first claimed her sisters-in-law, Harriet and Cecilia Seton, then her oldest and youngest daughters, Anna Maria (1795–1812) and Rebecca (1802–1816). Elizabeth also buried 18 young Sisters of Charity during the 12 years she lived in Saint Joseph's Valley.

Under the guidance of Archbishop Carroll and the Sulpicians, Mother Seton and the early members of the Sisters of Charity of Saint Joseph's shaped the first native sisterhood in the United States, creating a truly American community. Despite their humble beginning, the American Sisters of Charity launched multi-faceted ministries and became trailblazers in many fields, especially in education. They established the first free Catholic school for girls staffed by sisters in the United States (Emmitsburg, 1810). As the prototype of the Catholic school, Saint Joseph's Academy and Day School laid the foundation for a national network of quality Catholic education through the parochial school system, which developed later in the century. After Mother Seton's death, the Sisters of Charity of Saint Joseph's also began the first Catholic hospital in the United States (St. Louis, Mo. 1828).

The second Sulpician superior of the Sisters of Charity of Saint Joseph's, Reverend John Baptiste David, SS (1761–1841), commissioned (1810) Benedict Joseph Flaget, SS, (1763-1851), bishop-elect of Bardstown, Kentucky, to obtain French Daughters of Charity during his trip to Paris. David's goal was for the French sisters to establish themselves at Emmitsburg and train the American women in the Vincentian way of life, incorporating them as members of the Company of the Daughters of Charity of Saint Vincent de Paul. Mother Seton expressed her grave concerns about the implications of David's plans in a letter dated May 13, 1811, to Archbishop Carroll. ''What authority would the [French] Mother they bring have over our Sisters (while I am present) but the very rule she is to give them? — and how could it be known that they would consent to the different modifications of their rule which are indispensable if adopted by us . . . How can they allow me the uncontrolled privileges of a Mother to my five darlings? — or how can I in conscience or in accordance with your paternal heart give up so sacred a right.''

Mother Seton and Dubois modified the original French rule to address the urgent needs of the Church in early nineteenth-century America. Their rule was based on a manuscript copy of the Alméras edition of the *Common Rules of the Daughters of Charity* (Paris, 1672), which Flaget had brought when he returned to America. John Carroll approved *The Regulations for the Society of the Sisters of Charity of America* (Emmitsburg, 1812).

The Sisters of Charity responded to the urgent need for female education in America and initially made it their primary ministry. The American rule is the root foundational document of the majority of the congregational members of the Sisters of Charity Federation. Article Four of *The Constitutions of the Sisters of Charity in the United States of America* (1812) specified membership criteria and outlined stipulations regarding parental obligations of widows with minor children. In the same letter to Carroll, Mother Seton expressed her sentiments about the exemption granted her as a mother with five dependent children, then ranging from 10 to 16 years old. ''The constitutions proposed have been discussed by our Rev. Director [Dubois] and I find he makes some observations on my Situation relative to them but surely an Individual is not to be considered where a public good is in question— and you know I would gladly make every sacrifice you think consistent with my first and inseparable obligations as a Mother.''

Eighteen Sisters of Charity pronounced private, annual vows for the first time on July 19, 1813. They committed themselves to ''Poverty, Chastity, and Obedience to God and our Reverend Superior General until the 25th of March next'' and engagement in ''the corporal and spiritual service of the poor sick . . . [and] the instruction of those committed to our charge.'' The vow day was the feast of the Annunciation each year.

Mother Seton seemed pleased to give progress reports to Antonio Filicchi on the missionary efforts of the Sisters of Charity in Philadelphia and New York and at Mount Saint Mary's College and Seminary near Emmitsburg. In October of 1814 she first sent Sister Rose White, accompanied by Sister Susan Clossey and Sister Theresa Conroy (1780–1823), on mission to Philadelphia to manage Saint Joseph's Asylum, the first Catholic orphanage in the United States. The next August, Sister Bridget Farrell (1765–1847), Sister Ann Gruber (1779?–1840), and a novice, Sister Anastasia Nabbs (1788–1823), began supervision of the infirmary and domestic services at Mount Saint Mary's near Emmitsburg. In August of 1817, Sister Rose White, Sister Cecilia O'Conway, and Sister Felicitas Brady (1784–1883) launched the New York Catholic Benevolent Society, which became the New York City Orphan Asylum (later Saint Patrick's Orphan Asylum).

Reverend Simon Bruté, SS (1779–1839, later first bishop of Vincennes, Indiana, 1834–1839) first came to Mount Saint Mary's (1811). He became chaplain to the Sisters of Charity and spiritual director for Mother Seton. Bruté guided the inculturation of the Vincentian charism among the Sisters of Charity, advising Mother Seton to read and translate the lives of Vincent de Paul and Louise de Marillac and their spiritual writings. Elected the first Mother of the new community, Elizabeth Bayley Seton remained in office until her death on Jan. 4, 1821.

Change. By 1830 the sisters had begun the care of young male orphans on an emergency basis. As a result of recurring problems, however, the council at Emmitsburg made several unsuccessful attempts to limit the age and length of time boys would be in care, but they finally concluded (1845) that the sisters would no longer have boys in their institutions. This decision paved the way for conflict between Louis-Regis Deluol, Sulpician superior general of the Sisters of Charity of Saint Joseph's, and John Hughes (1797–1864), archbishop of New York. The result was the withdrawal of 30 Sisters from Emmitsburg to establish an independent congregation of diocesan right, the Sisters of Charity of Saint Vincent de Paul of New York.

Regis Deluol, fearing that the New York separation could set a precedent for other bishops, continued his pursuit of a union between the French Daughters of Charity and the Sisters of Charity of Saint Joseph's. These efforts were also precipitated by directives (1829 and 1845) from Sulpician major superiors in Paris that the Sulpicians in America divest themselves of any ministry not directly connected with their mission of formation and education of candidates for the priesthood. After meeting with Reverend Mariano Maller, CM (1817–1892), visitor of the Vincentian province of the United States (1846–1850), Deluol wrote in his diary on April 26, 1849 that a decision had been made to unite the Emmitsburg community with the Daughters of Charity in France in order to obtain the assistance of the Congregation of the Mission "Vincentian priests" for the Community.

In her formal request to Father Etienne, CM, on June 19, 1849, Mother Etienne Hall stated that the pending union was "the wish of the kind and venerable Superior [Deluol] who for so many years has labored at the welfare of our Community, and he it is who at this present time continues to make all the efforts in his power to bring about the union so important and so necessary for us." The earliest reference to the union with France occurs in *The First Council Book,* after arrangements had already been finalized: "On this day [March 25, 1850] the renewal of the Vows has taken place . . . The Sisters have used the same Formula which is used yearly by the Daughters of Charity throughout the world . . . have . . . consummated the Union with the Daughters of Charity of Saint Vincent de Paul" (§324). Almost 100 years later the Daughters of Charity of the United States convened the first meeting of the Conference of Mother Seton's Daughters, which later became the Sisters of Charity Federation in the Vincentian and Setonian Tradition.

Development of federation. The apostolic delegate to the United States, Amleto Giovanni Cardinal Cicognani (1883–1973), recommended that the spiritual daughters of Elizabeth Bayley Seton collaborate to further the cause for canonization of this convert, who was a wife, mother, widow, sole parent, foundress, and spiritual leader. Despite growing pains the Sisters of Charity continued to develop and blossom into independent new congregations in North America: New York (1846), Cincinnati (1852), Halifax (1856), Convent Station (1859), and Greensburg (1870). The conflict-ridden circumstances surrounding the initial separations from Emmitsburg were a source of pain for all involved, especially after French émigré priests belonging to the Society of Saint Sulpice (Sulpicians) of Baltimore arranged for the Sisters of Charity of Saint Joseph's to join (1850) the Company of the Daughters of Charity of Saint Vincent de Paul (DC) of Paris, France.

In a spirit of reconciliation, Sister Isabel Toohey, DC (1893–1979), provincial of the Eastern Province of the Daughters of Charity in the United States, visited the major superiors of the congregations that developed historically from the 1809 Emmitsburg foundation. Sister Isabel asked pardon of them for any role the Sisters of Charity of Saint Joseph's and the Daughters of Charity at Emmitsburg may have had in contributing to strained relations among the spiritual daughters of Elizabeth Bayley Seton over the years. She invited them to meet and discuss collaborative strategies for the Seton cause for canonization.

Historical Perspective. The historic first meeting of the Conference of Mother Seton's Daughters, held at Emmitsburg, Maryland, from Oct. 28 to 29, 1947, proposed: "to strengthen the bond of union among the member congregations and to work together in advancing the cause of Mother Elizabeth Ann Seton." John Michael McNamara (1878–1960), auxiliary bishop of Baltimore (1928–1948) and Washington, D.C. (1948–1960), served as moderator and invited attendees to work together "through a unity of charity in the spirit of Christ." A zealous supporter of the Seton cause, McNamara presided during future sessions as long as his health permitted.

Beginning with the third meeting of the conference, when possible, the vice-postulators for the cause, who were Vincentian priests (Congregation of the Mission), also participated in the meetings: Reverend Salvator M. Burgio, CM (vice-postulator, 1939–1959); Reverend John P. McGowan, CM (vice-postulator, 1959–1968); and Reverend Sylvester A. Taggart, CM (vice-postulator, 1968–1975). The vice-postulators, appointed by the postulator general of the Congregation of the Mission and the Daughters of Charity, updated members about reported miracles and issues regarding the Seton cause.

Purpose. The Conference of Mother Seton's Daughters functioned (1947–1965) with minimal organizational structure until it became the Federation of the Daughters of Blessed (later Saint) Elizabeth Ann Seton (1965). This change responded to the directive of Vatican II (*Perfectae Caritatis,* §22) that congregations possessing the same general spirit and origin should form a federation for mutual support and development. Members shortened the name of the organization to The Elizabeth Seton Federation (1990), which remained its legal title when incorporated in the state of New York (1995). They adopted the following purposes and a new name, the Sisters of

Charity Federation in the Vincentian and Setonian Tradition (1996):

> To support the commitment of its members to the mission of Charity expressed through the diversity of their specific congregational charisms.
> To foster ongoing study and reflection on the Tradition of Charity.
> To facilitate collaboration in projects related to ministry and other areas of common concern.
> To foster ongoing study and reflection on the charism and Tradition of Charity in its seventeenth-century origin and in its flowering in many congregations founded in North America.

Until 1975 the federation focused almost exclusively on promoting the Cause of Elizabeth Bayley Seton for sainthood. Many of these projects were publicized by the Mother Seton Guild, an organ of the Postulation, which helped to spread devotion to Elizabeth Bayley Seton and raise funds to advance the cause.

Cause. The Seton cause was introduced in Rome in 1940. Blessed John XXIII declared Mother Seton venerable on Dec. 18, 1959, and also presided at her beatification on March 17, 1963. Pope Paul VI canonized her as Saint Elizabeth Ann Seton on Sept. 14 during the Holy Year of 1975 and the International Year of the Woman. The Holy See accepted three miracles through her intercession: the cures of Sister Gertrude Korzendorfer, DC (1872–1942), of Saint Louis, of cancer; a young child, Ann Theresa O'Neill (b. 1948), of Baltimore, from acute lymphatic leukemia; and Carl Kalin (1902–1976), of New York, from a rare form of encephalitis. Exhumed prior to the beatification, the remains of Saint Elizabeth Ann Seton repose in the Basilica of the National Shrine of Saint Elizabeth Ann Seton, in Emmitsburg, Maryland.

Pope Paul VI announced Elizabeth Seton's canonization on Dec. 12, 1974. At that time, Sister Hildegarde Marie Mahoney, SC, major superior of the Sisters of Charity of Saint Elizabeth (1971–1979) and chair of the Federation of Blessed Elizabeth Ann Seton, remarked that "Elizabeth Seton now belongs to all people. Her life speaks to all those who seek sincerely to follow God's Will—in whatever faith; to all who have known human love of husband, wife, family and friends—and the inevitable suffering that is part of that love." Sister Katherine O'Toole, SC (1935–1990), then superior general of the Sisters of Charity of Halifax (1972–1980), reflected on Elizabeth's final admonition to her sisters, "Be children of the Church," with the comment: "When there are so many questions and such confusion . . . the words are a timely reminder of the solidarity that is needed among all of us . . . religious, priests and lay people . . . who are involved in the ongoing process of redemption."

In planning for the event, federation members, keenly conscious of the needs of the starving people of the world, desired that the canonization festivities be marked by simplicity. Among the gifts the federation presented to Pope Paul VI on this occasion was a contribution of $200,000 to a World Hunger Fund, drawn on the Bank of New York with which Elizabeth's husband William Magee Seton (1768–1803) and his father William Seton (1746–1798) had been associated, and a calligraphy manuscript of Saint John's Gospel. Sister Hildegarde Marie had the honor of being a lector at the liturgy of canonization, the first woman to ever read at a papal Eucharistic celebration. Lectors representing the various stages of the life of Elizabeth Bayley Seton read the general intercessions. International media covered the event and U.S. President Gerald R. Ford, in accordance with Senate Joint Resolution 125, designated Sunday, Sept. 14, 1975, as National Saint Elizabeth Seton Day, and he called for such memorials and other observances as are appropriate to the occasion. She was the first person born in the United States to be canonized a saint.

Federation focus. After their successful collaboration on the cause for canonization, the federation focused on joint projects related to charism, formation, and mission. Member congregations explored the triadic base of renewal recommended by Vatican II—the Gospel, the signs of the times, and the original spirit of the founders—and came to a new awareness of and appreciation for their shared heritage and stewardship responsibility for the Vincentian and Setonian charism expressed through the Tradition of Charity (Cf., *Perfectae Caritatis,* §1–2).

Charism. Members focused on the Seton legacy of education as a springboard for exploring collaborative possibilities through annual conferences of Setonian colleges (1967). The federation also used special anniversaries to promote Seton celebrations in conjunction with the bicentennial year of the birth of Elizabeth Ann Seton (1974), and the bicentennial of the United States (1976).

Among its earliest intercongregational projects were a newsletter, observances of the feast of Blessed Elizabeth Ann Seton, special gatherings at professional meetings, and the publication of reports related to social justice advocacy and local ministries among persons oppressed by poverty. Members assisted the Mother Seton Guild with public relations and promotion of the Seton cause (1969) and served as docents at the Seton Shrine in Emmitsburg. Members also launched drives to seek approval for a Seton stamp from the Citizens Stamp Advisory Committee of the United States Postal Service (1977). Representatives gathered informally as Charity Connections to share reflections and to write occasional essays on the charism, later published (1988) in booklet format, *Living the Charity Charism.*

The federation has also undertaken some major publication projects. Sister Hildegarde Marie Mahoney, SC (New Jersey), was commissioned in 1991 to prepare a manuscript on the history of the Federation, but failing eyesight necessitated her withdrawal from the project. Sister Geraldine Anthony, SC (Halifax), completed *A Vision of Service* (1997), which was published during the fiftieth anniversary of the federation.

In order to make the writings of Saint Elizabeth Ann Seton more available, the federation appointed (1996) Sister Regina Bechtle, SC (New York), and Sister Judith Metz, SC (Cincinnati), as co-editors for the publication of the corpus of the Seton papers found in numerous archives in the United States and Canada. Ellin M. Kelly, Ph.D., transcribed these documents and served as the manuscript editor along with federation representatives who comprised an advisory committee for the three-volume work, *Collected Writings/Elizabeth Bayley Seton* (Hyde Park, N.Y. 2000).

Federation members desired to forge links with other groups in the Vincentian Family and appointed (1969) Sister Mathilde Comstock, DC, (1901–1997) and later (1984) Sister Rosemary Fleming, SC (Greensburg), as the official representatives of the group to serve on the national board of the Ladies of Charity of the United States. The Ladies of Charity, begun in Paris (1634), developed from the first foundation by Vincent de Paul at Châtillon-les-Dombes, France (1617). Louise de Marillac was actively involved with the Ladies of Charity from which the Daughters of Charity developed. Over time an awareness of the extended Vincentian Family evolved along with the federation's desire to strengthen intercongregational networking and collaboration. Sister Theresa Capria, SC (New York), represented the federation at the 1998 General Assembly of the Congregation of the Mission in Rome.

Formation. The mistresses of initial formation were the first group invited to convene through the federation (1966). This led to the ongoing discussion about formation practices and sponsorship of formation programs (1985), *The Roots Program* (1986), *Roots on-the-Road* (1987), *Roots Revisited,* and a final vow retreat (1989). Later the Sisters of Charity of New York and the Sisters of Charity of Saint Elizabeth established a joint novitiate (1990), which became (1992) a collaborative novitiate with the additional involvement of the Sisters of Charity of Seton Hill, the New York and Boston Provinces of the Sisters of Charity of Halifax, and later other federation members. An annual gathering of formators evolved (1989) into the Company of Charity Formation Personnel (CCFP), which affiliated (1992) with the federation as a formal subgroup.

During the annual meetings of the federation, members considered strategies to make their shared charism more effective in the modern world, especially in the areas of social justice, spirituality, and renewal programs (1974). One result was the initiation (1988) of *Charity: A Shared Vision,* an ongoing formation program. A later outcome was the first of several scholarly symposia to explore the historical and theological relevance of *The Seton Legacy* (1992). The Vincentian Studies Institute collaborated with the federation and published the proceedings of the symposia and annotated listings, by repository, of the writings of Elizabeth Bayley Seton in *The Vincentian Heritage.*

Mission. Federation members committed themselves to seeking effective strategies for human development, to promoting investment in minority enterprises, and to making corporate responses to social justice issues as early as 1973. Subsequently, members sought ways to study unmet human needs and resources (1979) with the goal of coordinating and networking among already existing ministries which respond to neighbors in need (1987). In order to be more effective advocates on peace and justice issues, the Federation gained recognition as a Non-Governmental Organization (NGO) at the United Nations in 1997. Sister Maria Elena Dio, SC (Halifax), was the first representative of the Federation to the Department of Public Information at the United Nations.

Organizational structure. The canonization in 1975 marked the achievement of the federation's founding purpose. After again revising the statutes and bylaws (1976), the federation adopted a new purpose: "to bring together in love and friendship the various congregations that are inspired by the charism of their common foundress, Saint Elizabeth Ann Seton; and thus be enabled to discover more fully the life and mission of a Sister of Charity today."

The bylaws were amended (1982) to allow for two categories of membership: full membership for those with common origin in the Emmitsburg foundation and associate membership for those that derive their spirit and inspiration from Saint Elizabeth Ann Seton. These were later modified (1985, 1988) to allow equality of status among members and to admit congregations within the Tradition of Charity that do not have a direct connection to Elizabeth Seton.

The federation continued updating and refining its structure and restated (1991) its purpose as follows: To bring together "in love and friendship"congregations that trace their roots to Emmitsburg; have a Seton connection and share her spirit; or share the spirit of Vincent de Paul and Louise de Marillac through adaptation of the *Common Rules of the Daughters of Charity.* The American Sisters of Charity inculturated the Vincentian charism in North America by modifying the seventeenth-century French rule of Louise and Vincent to suit the needs of the nineteenth-century Church in the United States. The Setonian tradition developed from the Vincentian tradition.

In 1996 the Sisters of Charity Federation in the Vincentian and Setonian tradition adopted a new name and clarified that congregations must meet one of two key criteria for membership: trace their characteristic spirit and charism to the Tradition of Charity of Vincent de Paul, Louise de Marillac, and Elizabeth Ann Seton; and trace the influence of the Vincentian Rule (*Common Rules of the Daughters of Charity*) in their documents and in their lifestyle.

The Sisters of Charity of the Immaculate Conception (1979) and Les Religieuses de Nôtre Dame du Sacré-Coeur (1986), both of Canada, were the first additional communities to seek admission as associate members. In 1988 the associate status was deleted in favor of full membership and the following congregations were admitted: Vincentian Sisters of Charity of Pittsburgh (1989); Vincentian Sisters of Charity of Bedford (1990); Sisters of Charity of Nazareth (1991); Sisters of Charity of Our Lady of Mercy of Charleston (1994); and Sisters of Charity of Leavenworth (1995).

Membership. *Daughters of Charity of Saint Vincent de Paul (DC) of the United States* (Official Catholic Directory #60) was founded in 1633 in Paris by Vincent de Paul and Louise de Marillac as a lay confraternity to serve Jesus Christ in persons who are poor and marginalized. Today in the United States this society of apostolic life traces its roots to the 1809 foundation by Elizabeth Bayley Seton under the direction of the French Sulpicians of Baltimore. After receiving orders for the Sulpicians to return to their principal work of conducting seminaries, Deluol accelerated strategies to unite the Sisters of Charity of Saint Joseph's with the Company of the Daughters of Charity of Saint Vincent de Paul of Paris, France. The Sisters of Charity of Saint Vincent de Paul of New York (1846) and the Sisters of Charity of Cincinnati (1852) developed directly from the Emmitsburg foundation. The Daughters of Charity of the United States was one of six congregations that were founded (1947) by the Sisters of Charity Federation in the Vincentian and Setonian tradition.

Sisters of Charity (SC) of New York. It (Official Catholic Directory #0650) originated in the 1809 foundation by Elizabeth Bayley Seton and began (1817) in New York City as a mission from Emmitsburg to educate and care for children and perform other works of charity. It became autonomous (1846) under the sponsorship of Bishop John Hughes of New York (1797–1864) with Mother Elizabeth Boyle (1788–1861) as the first superior (1846–1849). She had been formed by Mother Seton in the Emmitsburg community and in a letter dated Oct. 25, 1820, Mother Seton referred to Elizabeth Boyle as ''dearest old partner of my cares and bearer of my burdens.'' This congregation is rooted in the *Regulations for the Society of the Sisters of Charity of America,* which it modified to allow for the care of male orphans. This congregation later assisted in establishing the Sisters of Charity of Saint Vincent de Paul of Halifax, the Sisters of Charity of Saint Elizabeth, and the Sisters of Charity of the Immaculate Conception. This institute of diocesan right was a founding member of the Sisters of Charity Federation.

Sisters of Charity (SC) of Cincinnati. It (Official Catholic Directory #0440) originated in the 1809 foundation by Elizabeth Bayley Seton and began (1829) in Cincinnati, Ohio, as a mission from Emmitsburg. It became an independent institute (1852) under Archbishop John Baptist Purcell (1800–1883). Mother Margaret Cecilia Farrell George (1787–1868) was the first superior (1853–1859). She had also been a prominent member of the Emmitsburg community. Mother Seton wrote her a prophetic letter dated May 28, 1819, in which she told Margaret George: ''You have so much to do for our Lord.'' The Cincinnati community retained the *Regulations for the Society of the Sisters of Charity of America* but added the care of male orphans. This congregation assisted with the establishment of the Sisters of Charity of Saint Elizabeth and the Sisters of Charity of Seton Hill. It became a pontifical institute (1927) and was a founding member of the Sisters of Charity Federation.

Sisters of Charity (SC) of Saint Vincent de Paul. It (Official Catholic Directory #0640) was founded in 1856 in Halifax, Nova Scotia, Canada, by William Walsh, bishop of Halifax (1844–1858), with the assistance of the Sisters of Charity of New York, who had established (1849) a mission in Halifax and supplied the first sisters and officers for the new institute. Mother Basilia McCann (1811–1870), who had formerly belonged to the Emmitsburg community (1830–1847), was the first superior (1849–1855; 1855–1858). Their rule, derived from the *Regulations for the Society of the Sisters of Charity of America* and based on that of the New York institute, was modified for Canada. This congregation became a pontifical institute (1913) and was a founding member of the Sisters of Charity Federation.

Sisters of Charity (SC) of Saint Elizabeth. It (Official Catholic Directory #0590) was founded in 1859 in Newark, New Jersey, by James Roosevelt Bayley (1814–1877), bishop of Newark and a half-nephew of

Elizabeth Bayley Seton. Sister Margaret George, who had lived with Mother Seton, directed the formation of the first novices, who were trained in Ohio by the Sisters of Charity of Cincinnati. The Sisters of Charity of Saint Vincent de Paul of New York sent Sister Mary Xavier Mehegan (1825–1915, superior 1859–1915) and Sister Mary Catherine Nevin (d. 1903, mother assistant 1859–1903) to organize the new institute in New Jersey. They both later opted to join the Sisters of Charity of Saint Elizabeth when it became autonomous (1859). The institute is rooted in the *Regulations for the Society of the Sisters of Charity of America.* This congregation was a founding member of the Sisters of Charity Federation and later became a pontifical institute (1957).

Sisters of Charity (SC) of Seton Hill. At the request of Bishop Michael Domenec, CM (1816–1878), bishop of Pittsburgh, the Sisters of Charity of Seton Hill (Official Catholic Directory #0570) was officially established (1870) as a separate congregation for the Pittsburgh diocese. Mother Regina Mattingly (1826–1883) of the Sisters of Charity of Cincinnati installed Mother Aloysia Lowe (1836–1889, superior 1870–1889). The first novices were trained by the Sisters of Charity of Cincinnati. Originally the Sisters of Charity of Cincinnati had anticipated that their sisters who were sent to Altoona would eventually return to Ohio; gradually, most of them were recalled. In 1888, however, upon the advice of Bishop Richard Phelan (1828–1904) of Pittsburgh, Mother Aloysia and Sister Ann Regina petitioned the superiors of the Cincinnati motherhouse for permission to remain permanently with the new foundation. The permission was granted. This congregation is rooted in the rule from Cincinnati derived from the *Regulations for the Society of the Sisters of Charity of America.* It was a founding member of the Sisters of Charity Federation and later became a pontifical institute (1957).

Sisters of Charity of the Immaculate Conception (SCIC). It (Canadian Religious Conference 119) was founded in 1854 in Saint John, New Brunswick, Canada, by Honoria Conway (Sister Mary Vincent, 1815–1892) to care for children left orphaned after a cholera epidemic. The foundress, a novice with the Sisters of Charity of Saint Vincent de Paul of New York, volunteered to go to Saint John at the urgent request of Bishop Thomas Connolly, OFM (1815–1876). Sister Ermelinda Routanne (1822–1894), who previously had belonged to the Sisters of Charity of Saint Joseph's at Emmitsburg (1842–1848?), became a founding member of this congregation (1854) and was known as Mother Mary Frances (second superioress, 1862–1865). This congregation is rooted in the *Regulations for the Society of the Sisters of Charity of America.* This congregation became a pontifical institute (1908) and joined the Sisters of Charity Federation in 1979.

Les Religieuses de Nôtre Dame du Sacré-Coeur (NDSC). It (Canadian Religious Conference 177) was established in 1871 as a mission at Bouctouche in New Brunswick, Canada, of the Sisters of Charity of the Immaculate Conception to minister to French-speaking Acadians in order to help them preserve language, culture, and faith. Encouraged by Bishop Edward Alfred LeBlanc (1870–1935), Suzanne Cyr (Soeur Marie Anne, 1850–1941), an Acadian, and 52 other Sisters of Charity of the Immaculate Conception formed (1924) an independent congregation. This congregation is rooted in the *Regulations for the Society of the Sisters of Charity of America* and was founded as a pontifical institute. It joined the Sisters of Charity Federation in 1986.

Sisters of Charity of Nazareth (SCN). It (Official Catholic Directory #0500) was established 1812 in Nazareth, Kentucky, by Reverend John Baptist David, SS (second bishop of Bardstown, Kentucky, 1832–1833), and cofounder Mother Catherine Spalding (1793–1858, superior 1813–1819; 1824–1831; 1838–1844; 1850–1856) to minister to Catholic families on the frontier. Simon Bruté, SS, made a handwritten copy of the *Regulations for the Society of the Sisters of Charity of America* for the Nazareth community. Six sisters withdrew (1851) to establish a new congregation, the Sisters of Charity of Nashville, Tennessee, which later became the Sisters of Charity of Leavenworth, Kansas. This congregation became a pontifical institute (1911) and joined the Sisters of Charity Federation in 1991.

Sisters of Charity of Our Lady of Mercy (OLM). It (Official Catholic Directory #0510) was established in 1829 at Charleston, South Carolina, by Bishop John England (1786–1842) to teach young girls, instruct African-American slaves, and care for the sick and infirm. Bishop England obtained the *Regulations for the Society of the Sisters of Charity of America.* His successor Bishop Ignatius Reynolds (1798–1855), who had served previously as chaplain and second superior of the Sisters of Charity of Nazareth (1833–1835), modified the rule according to England's recommendations. This institute of diocesan right joined the Sisters of Charity Federation in 1994.

Sisters of Charity of Leavenworth (SCL). It (Official Catholic Directory #0480) developed from a mission of the Sisters of Charity of Nazareth at Nashville, Tennessee, under Bishop Pius Miles, OP (1791–1860), and initially became the Sisters of Charity of Nashville (1851). After a misunderstanding, the sisters left Nashville and went to Leavenworth at the invitation of Bishop John Baptist Miège, SJ (1815–1884), vicar apostolic of Indian Territory, Kansas, and continued to follow the same constitution under the title of the Sisters of Charity of Leavenworth (1858). Mother Xavier Ross (1813–1895), formerly of the Sisters of Charity of Nazareth, was the first superior (1858–1862; 1865–1877) of the Leavenworth community. The institute received the *Regulations for the Society of the Sisters of Charity of America* through Bishop John Baptist Purcell of Cincinnati. This congregation became a pontifical institute (1915) and joined the Sisters of Charity Federation in 1995.

Vincentian Sisters of Charity (VSC) of Pittsburgh. It (Official Catholic Directory #4160) was established 1902 in Braddock, Pennsylvania, as a foundation from the Sisters of Charity of Saint Vincent de Paul of Satu-Mare, Romania, by Mother Emerentiana Handlovits (1869–1935, superior 1902–1935) to serve immigrant peoples from Eastern (now Central) Europe. Voted (1938) to become independent from the parent congregation in Romania and received pontifical status (1951). Traces its roots through the Sisters of Charity of Satu-Mare (1842), Vienna (1843), Zams (1823), and ultimately Strasbourg (1734). John Francis Regis Canevin (1852–1927), bishop of Pittsburgh, renamed this institute, giving it the current title since the Sisters of Charity of Seton Hill were already in the same diocese. This congregation joined the Sisters of Charity Federation in 1989.

Vincentian Sisters of Charity (VSC) of Bedford. It (Official Catholic Directory #4170) was established in 1928 in Bedford, Ohio, by Joseph Schrembs, (1866–1945), bishop of Cleveland, to minister to Slovakian immigrants in that diocese with the intention of starting a new province from the foundation at Pittsburgh. Sister Mary John Berchmans Fialko (1898–1959) was the first superior (1933–1959). This congregation became autonomous (1939) from Pittsburgh as an institute of diocesan right and joined the Sisters of Charity Federation in 1990.

Conclusion. The Federation honors the particular history of each member congregation and their common charism rooted in the founding spirit of Louise de Marillac and Vincent de Paul who instructed the early servants of the poor on Nov. 24, 1658: ''How consoled you will be at the hour of death for having consumed our life for the same purpose as Jesus did! It was for charity, for God, for the poor'' [Marie Poole, ed., trans. et al., *Vincent de Paul Correspondence, Conferences, and Documents,* v. 1–8 (New York 1983–2000) 7:397]. In instructions and meditations, Elizabeth Seton reminded her companions of the significance of their name, Sisters of Charity, exhorting them to be faith-filled women of mission. ''No personal inconvenience should prevent Sisters of Charity [from] doing what duty and charity require'' (Council, Aug. 20, 1814). The members of the federation provide mutual support to one another in living their mission of charity in the modern world through their shared legacy of the Vincentian and Setonian tradition.

Bibliography: Excerpts from Elizabeth Bayley Seton Papers and community documents are due to the courtesy of Archives Saint Joseph's Provincial House, Daughters of Charity of Saint Vincent de Paul (Emmitsburg, Maryland) and the Archives of the Archdiocese of Baltimore, Maryland. G. ANTHONY, *A Vision of Service* (New York 1997). R. BECHTLE and J. METZ, eds., *Collected Writings/Elizabeth Bayley Seton* v. 1 (Hyde Park, N.Y. 2000); v. 2–3 (forthcoming). P. COSTE, *Vincent de Paul Life and Works* (New York 1987). JOSEPH DIRVIN, *Louise de Marillac* (New York 1970). A. DODIN, *Vincent de Paul and Charity* (New York 1992). T. O. HANLEY, ed., *The John Carroll Papers,* 3 v. (Notre Dame, Ind. 1976). R. P. MALONEY, *The Way of Vincent de Paul* (New York 1992). J. LEONARD, ed., trans., *Conferences of Vincent de Paul to the Daughters of Charity,* 4 v. (Westminster, Md. 1939). A. M. MELVILLE, *Elizabeth Bayley Seton, 1774–1821* (New York 1951). B. A. MCNEIL, *The Vincentian Family Tree: A Genealogical Study of Institutes of Consecrated Life, Societies of Apostolic Life, Lay Associations, and Non-Catholic Religious Institutes* (Chicago, Ill. 1996). M. POOLE, ed., trans. et al., *Vincent de Paul: Correspondence, Conferences, and Documents,* v. 1–8 (New York 1983–1999); v. 9–14 (forthcoming). L. SULLIVAN, trans., *Louise de Marillac Spiritual Writings* (New York 1991).

[B. A. MCNEIL]

SISTERS OF CHRISTIAN DOCTRINE, MARTYRS OF, BB.

Angeles Lloret Martí and companions; religious of the Institute of Sisters of Christian Doctrine; d. Paterna, Valencia, Spain, September to November 1936; beatified Oct. 1, 1995, by Pope John Paul II.

The third decade of the twentieth century in Spain was characterized by a social and political turmoil and antagonism toward the Catholic Church. The Sisters of the Institute of Christian Doctrine, founded by Mother Micaela Grau in 1880, devoted themselves to teaching catechism even in the midst of the difficult political climate. Dedicated to evangelization, the sisters followed the poor Christ by living in poverty and working arduously to alleviate the anguish of the poor.

While some of the sisters had been able to take refuge with their relatives, others who had no families, the elderly sisters, and their caretakers remained in the Mother House. The sisters who remained kept correspondence with the dispersed sisters during years 1931 to 1936, which intensified in the latter months. These letters witness that they were conscious of the events happening and the imminent danger.

On July 19, 1936, they were forced to abandon the Mother House in Valencia. They remained a community led by Mother Angeles de San José and supported one another. Mother Amparo Rosat and Sister María del Calvario were executed on Sept. 26, 1936, having been incarcerated at Carlet. During the month preceding their death, the sisters continued to trust in God and do works of charity, even knitting jerseys for their captors. On Nov. 20, 1936, a bus came to collect the sisters, ultimately taking them to their death. They are:

Angeles (Francisca D. H. Lloret Martí), superior general; b. Villajoyosa, Alicante, Jan. 16, 1875.

María del Safragio (Antonia María del Sufragio Orts Baldó); b. Altea, Alicante, Feb. 9, 1888; vicar general and novice mistress.

María de Montserrat (María Dolores Llimona Planas), b. Molins de Rey, Barcelona, Nov. 2, 1860; superior general from 1892 to 1931; advisor general in 1936.

María Teresa de San José (Ascensión Duart y Roig); b. Benifayó, Valencia, May 20, 1876; novice mistress and local superior of the Generalate when the revolution broke out.

Isabel (Isabel Ferrer Sabriá); b. Vilanova y la Geltrú, Barcelona, Nov. 15, 1852. Inspired by the ideals of the foundress Mother Micaela, she collaborated in the foundation of the Institute.

Amparo (Teresa Rosat Balasch); b. Mislata, Valencia, Oct. 15, 1873. Superior of the Colegio de Carlet, Valencia; martyred with María del Calvario on September 26, in the station at Llosa de Ranes, Valencia.

María de la Asunción (Josefa Mangoché Homs); b. Ulldecona, Tarragona, July 12, 1859.

María Concepción (Emilia Martí Lacal); b. Carlet, Valencia, Nov. 9, 1861.

María Gracia (Paula de San Antonio); b. Valencia, June 1, 1869.

Corazón de Jesús (María Purificación Gómez Vives); b. Valencia, Feb. 6, 1881.

María del Socorro (Teresa Jiménez Baldoví); b. San Martín de Provençal, Barcelona, March 13, 1885.

María Dolores (Gertrudis Suris Brusola); b. Barcelona, Jan. 17, 1899.

Ignacia del Santísimo Sacramento (Josefa Pascual Pallardó); b. Valencia, 1862.

María del Calvario (Josefa Romero Clariana); b. Carlet, Valencia, April 11, 1871.

María del Rosario (Catalina Calpe Ibáñez); b. Sueca, Valencia, Nov. 25, 1855.

María de la Paz (María Isabel López García); b. Turía, Valencia, Aug. 12, 1885.

Marcela de Santo Tomás (Aurea Navarro); b. Provincia de Albacete; a novice.

Feast: November 20.

Bibliography: V. CÁRCEL ORTÍ, *Martires españoles del siglo XX* (Madrid 1995). J. PÉREZ DE URBEL, *Catholic Martyrs of the Spanish Civil War*, tr. M. F. INGRAMS (Kansas City, Missouri 1993). *L'Osservatore Romano*, Oct. 29, 1995.

[A. ROS]

SISTERS OF DIVINE PROVIDENCE

(CDP, Official Catholic Directory #0990); founded in 1851 by Bishop Wilhelm Emmanuel von KETTELER of Mainz, Germany. Amelia Fanny de la Roche, one of the original group of five members, became the first superior of the community, which adopted the title of Sisters of Divine Providence. In 1873, during the KULTURKAMPF, the German government prohibited their teaching in government schools and forbade the acceptance of new members. Three years later six sisters made the first United States settlement in Pittsburgh, Pennsylvania. The congregation's rules and regulations, drawn up by Ketteler and modeled on those of St. Vincent de Paul, were later revised and received papal approbation in 1935. The members bind themselves by the three vows of religion and exercise their apostolate primarily through educational and nursing activities.

At the beginning of the 21st century, there were three provinces in the United States: St. Peter's (established 1876) with headquarters at Allison Park, Pennsylvania; St. Louis (established 1930), at Hazelwood, Missouri; and Our Lady of Divine Providence (established 1957), at Kingston, Massachusetts. The generalate of the congregation is in Rome, Italy.

[M. A. WINSCHEL/EDS.]

SISTERS OF DIVINE PROVIDENCE OF KENTUCKY

(CDP, Official Catholic Directory #1000); established in 1889 at Newport, KY, by members of the Congregation of the Sisters of Divine Providence, founded in Lorraine, France, in 1762, by John Martin MOYË, parish priest of the Diocese of Metz. Moyë desired ''to form Sisters who would go alone into the hamlets and isolated country places, there to teach school and catechism to neglected children.'' His plan became effective Jan. 14, 1762, when Marguerite Lecomte opened the first school in Vigy, near Metz. When the French Revolution disrupted the schools, Moyë and a group of about 30 sisters under Sister Rose Methains, Superior General of the congregation, became exiles in Trier, Germany. After the Revolution the sisters returned to France and opened a novitiate in Insming (1803), Hommarting (1812), and St. Jean de Bassel (1827), the present motherhouse general of the Sisters of Divine Providence of Metz. Despite disturbed political conditions, the congregation grew steadily and in 1888, Rev. Mother Anna Houlne, Superior General (1885–1903), became interested in extending the congregation's work to the U.S. With the approval of Bp. Camillus Paul Maes of Covington, KY, the first house of the congregation in the new world was established at Mt. St. Martin Convent, Newport, KY. Subsequently, an academy and a novitiate were opened there. Under the constitutions, definitively approved by the Holy See in 1943, teaching and nursing are the principal works of the congregation.

Since 1919, St. Anne Convent, Melbourne, KY, has served as provincial house and novitiate. In the U.S., the sisters are engaged in the fields of academic education, catechetics, homes for working women, retreat centers, parish ministry, pastoral ministry, healthcare and social services.

Bibliography: Archives, Sisters of Divine Providence of Kentucky, St. Anne Convent, Melbourne, Kentucky. R. PLUS, *Shepherd of Untended Sheep,* tr. J. ALOYSIUS and M. GENEROSA (Westminster, MD 1950).

[M. S. BRAUCH/EDS.]

SISTERS OF DIVINE PROVIDENCE OF TEXAS

(CDP, Official Catholic Directory #1010); a congregation of pontifical rite engaged in teaching, nursing, and social service work in the southwest United States and Mexico. It is a branch of the institute founded (1762) by John Martin Moyë in Lorraine, France, for the education of poor children, particularly in country places.

In 1866, in answer to Bishop Claude Dubuis's appeal, two Sisters of Divine Providence of the Congregation of St. Jean-de-Bassel, Lorraine, arrived in Texas to staff a parochial school in Austin, erected to comply with the decrees of the Second Plenary Council of Baltimore. A provincial motherhouse of the American group was established at Castroville (about 20 miles west of San Antonio) and received both natives and European vocations until 1886, when it became an independent diocesan congregation. In 1898 the motherhouse was transferred to San Antonio. The sisters also engaged in work among the African-Americans in Louisiana (1887); the Native Americans in Oklahoma (1902); and the Spanish-speaking population of the Southwest, whose need for organized catechetical instruction resulted in the founding of the Missionary Catechists of Divine Providence (MCDP). This branch of the congregation received papal approval in 1946. The congregation has been pontifical since 1907.

Bibliography: M. G. CALLAHAN, *The History of the Sisters of Divine Providence, San Antonio, Texas* (Milwaukee 1955); *The Life of Blessed John Martin Moyë* (Milwaukee 1964).

[M. G. CALLAHAN/EDS.]

SISTERS OF MERCY

The title *Sisters of Mercy* (RSM) pertains to a number of religious congregations of women which were founded by and embrace the charism of Catherine McAuley (1778 to 1941) and whose constitutions can be traced to the original (1841) Sisters of Mercy *Rule and Constitutions.* With one exception, the Diocesan Sisters of Mercy of Portland, Mercy congregations are of pontifical jurisdiction. Characteristic of the Sisters of Mercy is their fourth vow of service to the poor, sick and ignorant. The three principal groupings of Sisters of Mercy in the United States are:

> Sisters of Mercy of the Americas (Official Catholic Directory #2575); Religious Sisters of Mercy of Alma, Michigan (Official Catholic Directory #2519); Diocesan Sisters of Mercy of Portland, Maine (Official Catholic Directory #2655).

Historical Foundations

The Institute of Our Lady of Mercy was established in Dublin, Ireland, on Dec. 12, 1831, by Catherine Elizabeth MCAULEY; in the 20th century her followers formed the largest English-speaking group of religious women in the world, embracing various unions and independent congregations of Sisters of Mercy.

Institute of the Sisters of Mercy (RSM). As early as 1822 Catherine McAuley had worked out a successful system of distributing food and clothing to the needy, of instructing and training poor girls, and of performing other works of mercy. In 1824, on a site in south Dublin, she planned a center for her charitable endeavors, which, designated by Archbishop Daniel Murray as the House of Mercy, opened on Sept. 24, 1827, the feast of Our Lady of Mercy. Although its personnel consisted mainly of women of means who felt an attraction to the religious life, Miss McAuley herself had no desire to be a religious. She did, however, place her estate in a trust, with the proviso that the Baggot Street property should be under the control and management of the archbishop of Dublin.

St. Mary's Boarding School, Sacred Heart Mission, Macon, Illinois.

Moreover, for the sake of economy and uniformity, she sanctioned the adoption of a uniform dress and the observance of a horarium modeled on that of religious communities. Some of the clergy and laity of Dublin opposed this charitable organization as unorthodox and regarded it as an unfriendly rival of the Irish Sisters of Charity, an institute founded by Mary AIKENHEAD. As prejudice and opposition to her House of Mercy mounted, Miss McAuley expressed her willingness to turn the institution over to the Sisters of Charity. In an effort to resolve the situation, Archbishop Murray insisted that she either embrace the religious life or determine to continue the work along secular lines.

Despite her personal antipathy to the idea of starting a religious congregation, Miss McAuley finally selected the Presentation Convent at George's Hill, Dublin, as the place where she and two companions would receive their canonical training in preparation for the founding of a new institute. Her choice was influenced by the fact that Nano NAGLE, foundress of the Presentation sisters, had held ideals similar to her own with regard to work among the sick poor. After 15 months of preparation, during which the future foundress of the Institute of Our Lady of Mercy was subjected to many trials, the first three Sisters of Mercy pronounced the simple vows of poverty, chastity, and obedience on Dec. 12, 1831. Returning to the House of Mercy, Mother Catherine McAuley, Sister Elizabeth Harley, and Sister Anne Doyle were welcomed by the seven women who had continued the work of serving the poor in their absence and who in turn were eager to receive the religious training that would qualify them to become Sisters of Mercy.

Rules and Constitutions. In drawing up the rules and constitutions for the institute, the foundress used the rule of the Presentation sisters, which was based on that of St. Augustine as adapted by St. Thomas of Villanova. She composed two original chapters that dealt with the visitation of the sick and the care of distressed women. Since the Presentation sisters' rule adhered to the monastic form, it was necessary to make some modifications with regard to enclosure. Gregory XVI approved the institute on March 24, 1835; he gave final confirmation to its rule in June 1841.

Growth. Mother McAuley personally directed the establishment of 12 convents in Ireland and two in England, where uniformity of observance was practiced. After her death on Nov. 11, 1841, however, each house became independent. The first overseas foundation was

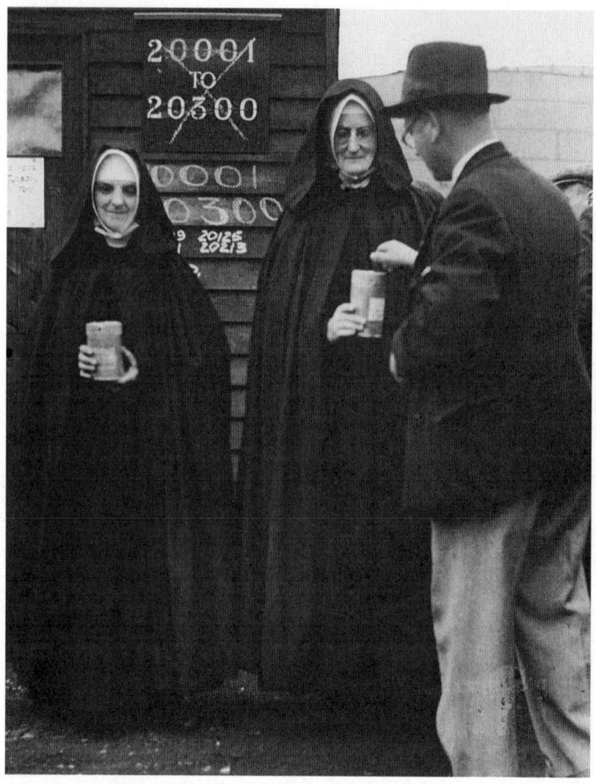

Sisters of Mercy collecting money, 1941. (©Hulton-Deutsch Collection/CORBIS)

made from the Convent of Mercy, Dublin, in 1842, when Sister Frances Creedon, a native of Newfoundland, and two other sisters left Ireland to begin work in Newfoundland under Bishop Michael Fleming. The following year Mother M. Francis Xavier WARDE and six companions from Carlow made the first foundation in the United States at Pittsburgh, Pennsylvania. Within the next 15 years other foundations were made at New York (1846) from the parent house, Dublin; Little Rock, Arkansas (1851), from Naas; and San Francisco, California (1854), and Cincinnati, Ohio (1858), from Kinsale. These, together with the foundation at Middletown, Connecticut, made from Ennis in 1872, were the centers of subsequent American growth.

In 1846 Mother Ursula Frayne (who had been one of the three to undertake the Newfoundland mission) arrived at Perth in western Australia with six sisters from Baggot Street to make a foundation in that newly developing country. Sisters of Mercy also reached New South Wales in the 1850s; they made foundations from Westport, Charleville, Ennis, Rochford Bridge, and Callan in Ireland, and also from Liverpool, England. From Perth a group was sent to Victoria in 1857, and three years later a group from Baggot Street under Mother Xavier Maguire sailed for Geelong. When additional sisters were needed in Victoria, the houses of Swinford, Carlow, and Carrick-on-Shannon, Ireland, responded generously. After Queensland became a separate colony from New South Wales (1859), its capital Brisbane received a contingent of Baggot Street sisters under the able leadership of Mother Vincent Whitty. Others went from Athy, and London supplied many more. South Australia and Tasmania also benefited by foundations in their emerging urban centers. The bishops in the areas to which the sisters went, most of whom were Irish-born, were convinced that the growth of the Church was dependent on the education of youth.

The first foundation in Scotland was made in 1849 from Limerick under Mother Elizabeth Moore, but its growth was less rapid and extensive than elsewhere. In 1850 Mother Cecelia Maher and four sisters from Carlow made the first of several foundations at Auckland, New Zealand. In 1856 Mother Evangelist Fitzpatrick and eight sisters from Dublin went to Buenos Aires, Argentina, where they worked until they were expelled in 1880, only to be recalled a decade later. A foundation made at Barbados, British West Indies, by sisters from Middlesex, England, was relinquished in 1894 to the Ursulines, when the Sisters of Mercy went to Charlestown, Demarara, British Guiana. In 1883 Belize, British Honduras, welcomed its first Sisters of Mercy from the United States, when Mother Teresa Austin Carroll and five companions from New Orleans, Louisiana (founded in 1869 from St. Louis, Missouri, which had been established from New York in 1856), went to assist the Jesuit missionaries. Sisters from Bermondsey, England, opened a mission at Jamaica, British West Indies, in 1890; and in 1897 a group from Strabane, Ireland, went to Mafeking, South Africa.

The Sisters of Mercy from Pittsburgh took up missionary activities in San Juan, Puerto Rico, in 1941. In 1946 sisters from Belmont, North Carolina, inaugurated a successful apostolate on Guam, where native sisters soon extended the works of the institute. First among Mother McAuley's daughters on the continent of Asia were the sisters from Merion, Pennsylvania, who established Mater Misericordiae Hospital at Jamshedpur, India. Sisters from St. Maries-of-the-Isle, Cork, Ireland, and from Buffalo, New York, engaged in missionary endeavors in the Philippine Islands. In 1959 the province of Providence, Rhode Island, sent sisters to La Ceiba, Honduras, and a year later missionary activity, sponsored by the province of Chicago, Illinois, was initiated in Sicuani, in the Peruvian Andes.

Apostolate. Throughout the history of the institute, the Sisters of Mercy have undertaken a variety of works to extend the interests of the Church. The outbreak of Asiatic cholera in Ireland in 1832, and again in the 1850s in Ireland, England, and the United States, provided many opportunities for the sisters to relieve the afflicted. During the Crimean War (1854 to 1855), sisters from England and Ireland served in British military hospitals at Scutari and Koulali in Turkey and at Balaclava in Russian terrain, caring for sick and wounded soldiers. Sisters from communities in New York; Chicago, Illinois; Baltimore, Maryland; Cincinnati, Ohio; Little Rock, Arkansas; Pittsburgh, Pennsylvania; and Vicksburg, Mississippi, ministered to both Union and Confederate soldiers during the American Civil War (1861 to 1865). Many victims of the Chicago fire of 1871 were aided by the Sisters of Mercy, whose hospital became a house of refuge. During the Boer War (1899 to 1902), sisters at Mafeking, who diverted their efforts from education to hospital care, ministered to Boer and Briton alike.

The Sisters of Mercy bind themselves to observe the three simple vows of religion and the requirements of their constitutions. The characteristic works of the institute include the education of the young, the visitation of the sick in homes, the care of the sick in hospitals, the care of girls and of women, of the aged, and of orphans. The spirit of the institute is mercy, theologically defined as love in the face of misery; it permits such an extension of the works of mercy as human needs may necessitate. The importance of a collective approach through service was emphasized by Mother McAuley, who stressed also the careful observance of the constitutions so that her followers, nourished through the liturgy and private prayer, would express their love for Christ in His Mystical Body through service to everyone.

Sisters of Mercy of the Union in the United States. During the period of rapid growth and development, the institute was characterized by close adherence to its rule and spirit among the many scattered communities. Until the promulgation of the 1917 Code of Canon Law, legislation promulgated by the then Congregation of Religious, particularly with regard to the training of postulants and novices, was not always followed; pioneer life frequently led to irregularities. In 1902 and 1905 attempts were made to urge the Sisters of Mercy in the United States to consider the adoption of general government as a means of more effective fulfillment of their religious purpose. In 1907 the Sisters of Mercy in Victoria and Tasmania amalgamated; they received approval of their revised constitutions in 1918. A similar revision, submitted by the sisters in the Dioceses of San Francisco, Monterey-Fresno, and Los Angeles, California, and of Tucson, Arizona, received approval in 1922. In 1929, under the guidance of Archbishop Pietro Fumasoni-Biondi, then Apostolic Delegate, 39 of the 60 independent motherhouses in the United States amalgamated to form the Institute of the Religious Sisters of Mercy of the Union in the United States of America, with Mother Carmelita Hartman as first mother general. The number of provinces grew from the original six to more than three times that number in the ensuing decades. In 1931 the generalate was located at Bethesda, Maryland (near Washington, D.C.). Revised constitutions were approved by Pius XI in 1931 and confirmed by Pius XII in 1940.

By the mid-1960s, more than 7,000 Sisters of Mercy belonged to the Union and there was almost an equal number attached to 17 independent motherhouses, each enjoying papal approbation. In the same period, the total world membership of the Sisters of Mercy was more than 27,000, including approximately 5,000 in Ireland, 4,000 in Australia, 2,500 in Great Britain, and 1,000 in New Zealand.

Developments since Vatican II

Since the Second Vatican Council, the Mercy Sisters, both in the United States and worldwide, have expanded the range of their ministries, most still connecting with both the spiritual and corporal works of mercy. The Sisters both promote systemic social change and respond in more immediate ways to current needs by establishing and/or staffing emergency housing shelters, food banks, soup kitchens, and centers for housing assistance, as well as developing ministries focused on persons with AIDS, chemically dependent persons, those in prison, and immigrants for whom English is a second language. The Sisters of Mercy of the Americas sponsor ministries such as the McAuley Institute, an organization that provides technical assistance, advocacy, and funding for groups nationwide working to provide low-income housing. In 1971, the Sisters of Mercy established Mercy Action, Inc., as a funding resource corporation. Its purpose is to empower people in ministry with the poor to carry on the works of mercy that improve the quality of life, effect positive changes in attitudes, and change structures that perpetuate inhuman and unjust conditions.

Many of the congregations have members ministering in developing nations: the Irish, in several African and South American nations; North Americans, in the Caribbean, Central, and South America, and the Pacific; Australians and New Zealanders, in the Pacific and Southeast Asia. Catherine McAuley's preferential concern for women continues to motivate the Sisters of Mercy as they strive to promote the dignity of women and their full participation in both Church and society.

Amalgamation and Consolidation. Although the Mercy congregation was founded as a pontifical institute, because of the social and ecclesial considerations of the times Catherine McAuley established new foundations as autonomous houses with direct ties to local diocesan bishops. This practice prevailed throughout the remainder of the nineteenth century wherever the sisters went. During the early twentieth century, because of the perceived need for a stronger organization, more uniform discipline, regularized novitiates, and a higher quality leadership, Church authorities and many congregational superiors encouraged unification on diocesan and eventually national scales.

As noted above, the most comprehensive union prior to the Second Vatican Council occurred with the 1929 formation of the Religious Sisters of Mercy of the Union of the United States of America. It involved some 42 autonomous congregations, over two-thirds of the number of Mercy congregations then in existence in the United States.

The Second Vatican Council's decree on the renewal of religious life, *Perfectae caritatis*, exhorted religious institutes to rediscover the spirit of their founders; it further directed congregations belonging to the same family to form federations and possibly unions. This decree, together with the growing realization that the Mercy Sisters' trend toward autonomy in its foundations was not tied inseparably to Catherine McAuley's original inspiration but rather was the method that suited well the time of expansion, sparked worldwide movements toward restructuring.

Initially, in North America this renewed sense of commonality resulted in the 1965 establishment of the Federation of the Sisters of Mercy of the Americas, replacing the less inclusive and less structured Mother McAuley Conference formed some ten years earlier. The Federation strengthened bonds between the autonomous congregations of the United States and Canada and the Sisters of Mercy of the Union. The 1967 establishment of the non-governmental Conference of the Sisters of Mercy of Australia encompassed sisters in two other groupings: the Australian Union (formed 1953) and the Australian federation (formed 1957). In 1968, the establishment of the Federation of the Sisters of Mercy of New Zealand encompassed that nation's four existing congregations: Auckland, Wellington, Christchurch and Dunedin. Renamed as the Federation of the Sisters of Mercy of Aotearoa New Zealand, these Sisters of Mercy serve in Aotearoa-New Zealand, Western Samoa, Fiji, Tonga, Vietnam, South Africa, Chile, Jamaica and Australia.

Comprehensive Restructuring Efforts. The experience of various national groupings of Sisters of Mercy during the late 1960s and 1970s and the rapidly changing demographics compelled leadership to initiate movement toward more comprehensive restructuring.

Great Britain. In 1976, a new religious Institute was formed, the Union of the Sisters of Mercy of Great Britain, comprised of the Birmingham Amalgamation (formed 1932) and the Westminster Amalgamation (formed 1922) and governed by a General Superior and Council. In addition to serving in England, Scotland and Wales, Union Sisters of Mercy served in Peru.

In 1983, the Institute of the Sisters of Mercy, with houses in England, Peru and Kenya came into existence with a governance structure comprised of a Superior General and a Council with four provinces. In 1996, the governance structure was altered with the provinces being dissolved and an Institute Leader and Leadership Team designated to govern the entire Institute. Over the years a non-governmental Federation type structure has also been attempted. The first Federation formed in 1969 yielded to a second formed in 1988 that presently is comprised of approximately 16 percent of the Mercy Sisters in Great Britain.

Australia. Between 1975 and 1980, the Conference of the Sisters of Mercy of Australia conducted extensive consultations with membership concerning the formation of a governmental structure to unite the Australian Union of the Sisters of Our Lady of Mercy (formed 1953) and the Australian Federation of the Religious Sisters of Mercy (formed 1957). On Dec. 15, 1981, with the convening of its inaugural chapter, the Institute of the Sisters of Mercy of Australia came into existence. This new entity, with each of the 17 congregations remaining autonomous, and with foundations in Papua New Guinea and Pakistan had membership extending to sisters in the Australian Aboriginal settlement on the edge of the Great Sandy Desert, Thailand, Cambodia, Hong Kong, Ethiopia, and the Philippines.

The Australian governance structure includes several central but no centralizing bodies, i.e., the National Chapter, the National Executive Council (a national president and council) and the National Plenary Council (the general superiors of the member congregations and the National Executive Council).

The Americas. In 1981, as the Australians were inaugurating their new institute, the Federation of the Sisters of Mercy of the Americas began to consider the topic of restructuring. Initial conversation included all autonomous member congregations, the Sisters of Mercy of the Union, and the Canadian-based Sisters of Mercy of Newfoundland, whose joint members served in North America, the Caribbean, Central America, South America, Guam, and the Philippines.

Between 1981 and 1985, the Federation's consultation with the membership and the Roman Curia's Congregation for Religious produced a governance structure that served as the basis for a decision-making process used by the Federation's United States congregations; because of geographic, cultural, and other concerns, the Newfoundland congregation decided to discontinue participation in the restructuring project.

On July 20, 1991, the Institute of the Sisters of Mercy of the Americas came into existence with the convening of the First Institute Chapter. The founding members of this Mercy institute included the 16 former autonomous congregations and the former Sisters of Mercy of the Union with its nine provinces. The Institute's governance structure includes the Institute Chapter, the Institute President and Council, and the Institute Leadership Council comprised of the Institute President and Council and 25 regional presidents.

Not included in this 1991 foundation were 12 Sisters of Mercy of Portland, who refused membership in the new institute and became the Diocesan Sisters of Mercy of Portland, and about 40 Mercy sisters, who comprised the Religious Sisters of Mercy of Alma, Michigan, a congregation that was formed after ten sisters terminated membership in the Sisters of Mercy of the Union in 1973.

The Republic of Ireland and Northern Ireland. In 1985, the national Assembly of the Sisters of Mercy in Ireland (the general superiors and elected delegates from each congregation) formed an association, ''Mercy Ireland,'' which was commissioned to explore the feasibility of the 26 Irish congregations becoming a single institute with canonical status. Between 1985 and 1990, Mercy Ireland consulted with membership to determine the type of governance structure desired. Overwhelmingly, the sisters opted to form a single institute as their United States counterparts had done. On July 14, 1994, with the convening of the first congregational chapter, the Congregation of the Sisters of Mercy of Ireland came into existence. The 26 former autonomous Irish congregations and one autonomous congregation centered in Johannesburg, South Africa, formed this single institute. The Sisters of Mercy of Ireland consists of four Irish provinces, a South African province and a United States province. Kenya is a vice-province; Canada, Nigeria, Peru and Zambia are regions; while Brazil, Dundee (S.A.), Peru and Rwanda and Zambia are mission areas. The 1994 governance structure included a Congregational chapter, a Congregational Leader and Team, and a Plenary Conference consisting of the provincial leaders and the Congregational Leader and Team.

Establishment of Non-Juridical Structures. In addition to the official governmental structures, the Sisters of Mercy have also supported less formalized structures to enhance the effectiveness of their mission of mercy and justice. In so doing, links were made over both congregational and national boundaries. For instance, in 1979, the United States-based Sisters of Mercy of the Union founded the Latin American Caribbean Conference (LACC) to enable its sisters serving in that geographic region to network among themselves. At the first meeting, the sisters voted to open LACC up to all Mercy Sisters in ministry in that part of the world regardless of countries/congregations of origin. LACC includes sisters serving in the Caribbean (the Bahamas, Belize, Guyana, Haiti, Jamaica), Central America (Guatemala, Honduras, Panama), and South America (Argentina, Brazil, Chile, Peru).

Likewise, in 1989, the Institute of the Sisters of Mercy of Australia and the Federation of the Sisters of Mercy of New Zealand formed Mercy Pacific as a means to network the sisters working in Tonga, Samoa, Fiji, Papua New Guinea, New Zealand, and Australia. Similar structures—usually ministry-related—have been formed to provide networking opportunities for the sisters and their partners in ministry. Justice networks, e.g., the Mercy Justice Network of the Sisters of Mercy of the Americas, the Australian Mercy Aboriginal Justice Network, and Mercy Refugee Service, provide mechanisms for the Sisters of Mercy to address social ills.

Mercy International Association. A unifying force for all Sisters of Mercy is the Mercy International Association (MIA) which is a group comprised of the leader of each of the Mercy Congregations, Institutes, or Federations worldwide. The purposes of MIA are to increase our awareness and experience of our interdependence and to foster unity of heart and mind among Sisters of Mercy; to facilitate collaboration for the sake of ministry and justice and to encourage and nurture the Mercy charism within the various cultures of the world. MIA sponsors two ongoing activities—Mercy Global Concern which is the Mercy presence at the U.N. and Mercy International Justice Network which is a network of sisters around the world working on justice issues.

Associate Members. Since the 1980s, most Mercy congregations have embraced some form of associate lay involvement through which non-vowed women and men share formally the mission of the Sisters of Mercy. In the United States alone, approximately 1,247 women and men are associate members of the Sisters of Mercy.

Founder Honored. On April 9, 1990, the Congregation for the Causes of Saints declared Catherine Elizabeth McAuley as venerable, the first step in the effort to advance her cause for canonization. In July 1994, the House of Mercy in Dublin, opened by Catherine McAuley on Sept. 24, 1827, was rededicated as the Mercy International Centre. This newly renovated facility is sponsored by Sisters of Mercy worldwide.

Conclusion. During the nineteenth and twentieth centuries, the Sisters of Mercy were instrumental in the shaping the systems of education, health care, and social services in various countries. In the United States today, strengthened by formation of health care systems and greater appreciation of the role of the laity in their institutions, the Sisters of Mercy are one of the nation's leading health care providers. In addition to hospitals and other healthcare facilities, they sponsor colleges and high schools, elementary schools and other centers of learning and childcare.

Bibliography: H. AMOS and H. BURNS, "Restructuring the Sisters of Mercy," *Human Development* 12 (1991) 16–20. M. B. BAUMAN, *A Way of Mercy: Catherine McAuley's Contribution to Nursing* (New York 1958). A. BOLSTER, *Catherine McAuley: Venerable for Mercy* (Dublin 1990). E. A. BOLSTER, *The Sisters of Mercy in the Crimean War* (Cork 1964). M. C. BOURKE, *A Woman Sings of Mercy* (Sidney 1987). B. BRENNAN, *"It Commenced with Two": The Story of Mary Ann Doyle* (Ireland 2001). R. B. SAVAGE, *Catherine McAuley: The First Sister of Mercy* (Dublin 1949). A. CARROLL, *Leaves from the Annals of the Sisters of Mercy*, 4 v. (New York 1895). C. DARCY, *The Institute of the Sisters of Mercy of the Americas: The Canonical Development of the Proposed Governance Model* (Lanham, Maryland 1993). M. B. DEGNAN, *Mercy Unto Thousands: Life of Mother Mary Catherine McAuley* (Westminster, Maryland 1957). H. DELANEY, *The Evolution of the Governance Structures of the Sisters of Mercy in Australia, 1946–1990* (Ottawa 1991). K. HEALY, *Frances Warde: American Founder of the Sisters of Mercy* (New York 1973). E. HERRON, *The Sisters of Mercy in the United States, 1843–1928* (New York 1929). M. HOGAN, *Pathways of Mercy in Newfoundland, 1842–1984* (St. John's 1986). M. J. GATELY, *The Sisters of Mercy: Historical Sketches, 1831–1931* (New York 1931). H. MULDREY, *Abounding in Mercy. Mother Austin Carroll* (New Orleans 1988). M. I. NEUMANN, *The Letters of Catherine McAuley, 1827–1941* (Baltimore 1969). J. REGAN and J. KEISS, *Tender Courage* (Chicago 1988). SISTERS OF MERCY, *Trees of Mercy: Sisters of Mercy of Great Britian from 1839* (Wickford, Essex 1993). M. SULLIVAN, *Catherine McAuley and the Tradition of Mercy* (Dublin and Notre Dame, Indiana 1995). M. SULLIVAN, "Catherine McAuley's Theological and Literary Debt to Alfonso Rodriguez: The 'Spirit of the Institute' Parallels," *Recusant History* 20 (1990) 81–105. M. SULLIVAN, *The Friendship of Florence Nightingale and Mary Clare Moore* (Philadelphia 1999). I. SUMNER, *Angels of Mercy: An Eyewitness Account of the Civil War and Yellow Fever*, ed. M.P. Oakes (Baltimore 1998). R. WERNTZ, *Our Beloved Union. A History of the Sisters of Mercy of the Union* (Westminster, Maryland 1989).

[M. MC A. GILLGANNON/C. C. DARCY]

SISTERS OF PROVIDENCE

(SP, Official Catholic Directory #3340); a diocesan congregation whose motherhouse is in Holyoke, Massachusetts (Diocese of Springfield). This religious community stems from a congregation founded in 1861 in Kingston, Ontario, Canada (SP, Official Catholic Directory #3350), a community that was, in turn, a branch of the Sisters of Charity of Providence of Montreal (founded in 1843). A group of four sisters from Kingston came to St. Jerome's parish in Holyoke on Nov. 7, 1873, invited by the pastor, Patrick J. Harkins. In 1874 they established the first Catholic hospital in western Massachusetts. One year later another group of six sisters arrived to teach in St. Jerome's parish school for boys. In August 1892 the community in Holyoke separated itself from the Kingston foundation and became a diocesan institute as a result of the negotiations carried out by the first bishop of Springfield, Patrick T. O'Reilly (1870–92). Their religious life was based on the rule that St. VINCENT DE PAUL wrote for the Daughters of Charity. The congregation is engaged in the ministries of healthcare, geriatrics, catechetics, pastoral ministries and social outreach.

[M. L. DONOVAN]

SISTERS OF PROVIDENCE OF ST. MARY-OF-THE-WOODS

The Sisters of Providence of Saint Mary-in-the-Woods (SP; Official Catholic Directory #3360) came to the United States in 1840 from Ruillé-sur-Loir, France at the request of Simon Bruté, the first bishop of the Diocese of Vincennes, Indiana. They were asked to establish a novitiate for the formation of new members and open an academy for young women.

The French community of the Sisters of Providence of Ruillé had been founded in 1806 by Jacques-François Dujarié, in response to the dire needs of the people of the countryside as a result of the French Revolution and its aftermath. By the 1830s the little community was flourishing and generously responded to the needs of the American frontier. After a long and arduous journey, Mother Theodore GUÉRIN and her five companions arrived in the midst of the Indiana forest on Oct. 22, 1840.

Four prospective candidates awaited them in the farmhouse, home to the Thralls' family. This frame building, which they would purchase from the Thralls family within the next month, was to serve for 13 years as the first Providence convent. In November 1840, Bishop Celestine de la Hailandière formally opened the novitiate with the reception of three of the original American postulants. In July 1841, St. Mary's Female Institute admitted its first students in the fine brick academy that Hailandère had built.

In the beginning, the community operated under the French Rule of 1835. Modifications to the original rule were made in 1843 and again in 1863. Finally in 1894 Leo XIII gav definitive approval to the Constitutions and established the American congregation as a papal institute.

After the death of Mother Theodore in May 1856, the Congregation continued to grow. Because education was the crying need of the frontier, the sisters were unable to pursue their traditional commitment to healthcare. At the time of the Civil War, however, some sisters were temporarily withdrawn from the schools to assist in the military hospitals in Indianapolis and Vincennes. For a brief time, they administered the St. John's Home for Invalids in Indianapolis, a facility founded to care for wonded veterans.

At the beginning of the 20th century, the increased influx of immigrants drawn to the large industrial cities of the Midwest reemphasized the need for parochial schools. The Congregation expanded to Michigan, Chicago, and beyond. In November 1920, six Sisters of Providence, under the leadership of Sr. Marie Gratia Luking, opened the first American missionary school for girls on mainland China. In 1929, Sr. Marie Gratia founded an auxiliary congregation of young Chinese women, the Providence Catechist Society. For the next 30 years, the Providence Catechist Sisters remained under the guidance of the Sisters of Providence, but in 1962 they achieved canonical status as an autonomous congregation.

In the United States the Sisters of Providence continued to grow, staffing elementary and secondary schools in New Hampshire, Maryland, Massachusetts, North Carolina, Indiana, Illinois, Oklahoma, Texas, California, and Washington, D.C. They also maintained St. Mary-of-the-Woods College and Immaculata Junior College in Washington, D.C., as well as Providence College of Liberal Arts and Sciences in Taiwan. Of these institutions of higher learning, only St. Mary-of-the-Woods continues in existence in the 21st century.

At the beginning of the third Christian millennium, the Sisters of Providence are engaged in various ministries throughout the U. S. and Taiwan, serving as educators, pastoral associates, healthcare givers, hospital chaplains, and home visitors to the aged and infirm. On Oct. 25, 1998, Pope John Paul II beatified Mother Theodore Guerin.

Bibliography: M. B. BROWN, *The History of the Sisters of Providence of Saint Mary of the Woods, Vol. 1 1806–1856* (New York 1949). E. LOGAN, *The History of the Sisters of Providence of Saint Mary of the Woods, Vol II 1856–1890* (Saint Mary-of-the-Woods, Indiana 1978). M. R. MADDEN, *The Path Marked Out: history of the Sisters of Providence of Saint Mary-of-the-Woods, Vol. III 1890–1926* (Saint Mary-of-the-Woods, Indiana 1991). A. C. WOLF, *Against all Odds: Sisters of Providence Mission to the Chinese, 1920–1990* (Saint Mary-of-the-Woods, Indiana 1990).

[M. R. MADDEN]

Mother Theodore Guérin.

SISTERS OF THE ADORATION OF THE BLESSED SACRAMENT

The Congregation of the Sisters of the Adoration of the Blessed Sacrament (SABS), a congregation of religious women within the SYRO-MALABAR CHURCH, was founded at Champakulam in 1908 by Bishop Thomas Kurialacherry, with the assistance of its first member Mother Mary Chantal. After the death of Bishop Kurialacherry in 1925, Father J. Kandathiparampil directed the Congregation. In 1930 the Congregation was introduced in the Archdiocese of Ernakulam. Independent diocesan communities of the Congregation which were established in the various Syro-Malabar dioceses were united under a Superior General in 1963. The Congregation was raised to the pontifical status by Pope Paul VI in 1968.

Prime importance is given to the Eucharistic apostolate. Each day every SABS spends one hour of eucharistic adoration before the Blessed Sacrament. The whole Congregation is taken as a single unit to have a chain adoration both day and night throughout the year. Besides the Eucharistic apostolate, SABS extends their services in the fields of education, care of the sick, pastoral ministry and other social welfare activities when and where need arises. The Sisters wear a white habit, white coif, black veil, and a medal of the Blessed Sacrament.

By the end of 2000, the Congregation had grown to over 4000 members including a few from outside Kerala, distributed in seven provinces, six vice-provinces and two regions.

Bibliography: *The Silver Jubilee of the Sisters of Adoration and the Inaguration of Perpetual Adoration, Mannanam,* 1936. SR. METILDA SABS, *Oru Kudumbathinte Kadha,* ''The Story of a Family'' in Malayalam (Aluva 1991). *SABS Constitution* (Aluva, 1991). *Indian Christian Directory,* (Kottayam 2000), 1288.

[A.M. MUNDADAN]

SISTERS OF THE MOST HOLY SACRAMENT

(MHS, Official Catholic Directory #2940), a congregation with papal approbation (1935), whose motherhouse is in Lafayette, LA. This community, which follows the Rule of St. Augustine, stems from the Sisters of Perpetual Adoration of the Most Holy Sacrament, founded in 1851 by Aloysius Faller, parish priest of Bellemagny in Alsace, France. In 1872, at the request of Abp. Napoleon J. Perche of New Orleans, LA (1870–83), four sisters came to the U.S. Two years later they began their work for the education of children in New Orleans.

Until 1892 Bellemagny remained the motherhouse of the entire community. In that year the U.S. houses organized themselves into a distinct congregation, with its own motherhouse in New Orleans. As the work of education grew more arduous, the practice of perpetual adoration was discontinued, but daily exposition of the Blessed Sacrament was maintained in the motherhouse. The sisters, thereafter, adopted the name of Sisters of the Most Holy Sacrament. In 1924, at the request of Bp. Jules B. Jeanmard of Lafayette (1918–56), the motherhouse and novitiate were transferred to Lafayette. The sisters are engaged in the field of education, catechetics, pastoral care and homes for the aged.

[M. E. MARTIN]

SISTINE CHAPEL

The most famous chapel in the papal palace. It was built for Pope SIXTUS IV for papal functions and serves as palatine and court chapel. (*See* VATICAN; VATICAN CITY.) The design by the architect Giovannino de'Dolci is a rectangular brick structure with travertine corners and window projections. It has six arched windows on each of the two main walls and a barrel-vaulted ceiling, and contains a simple interior space which is divided into choir and nave by a screen. On the right side is the *cantoria* for the Sistine Choir.

On Oct. 27, 1481, after the completion of construction, a contract for its decoration was drawn between the Pope's architect, Giovannino de'Dolci, and the painters Rosselli, Botticelli, Ghirlandaio, and PERUGINO. Other painters—Signorelli, Bartolomeo della Gatta, Pintoricchio, and Fra Diamante—assisted in the project. The vaulted ceiling was painted to simulate a blue heaven studded with gold stars. Between the windows at the top of the walls were placed portraits of popes, standing in shell niches. Below these, as the main feature of the decoration, was painted a series of scenes from the life of Moses and of Christ complementing each other on the left and right walls, respectively, as one faces the altar. An ''Assumption of the Virgin'' originally painted on the altar wall above two of the scenes was later removed, together with the two scenes, to make room for MICHELANGELO'S *Last Judgment.* These wall decorations were dedicated on the feast day of the Assumption, 1483.

In 1508 Pope JULIUS II finally persuaded Michelangelo to undertake the redecoration of the vaulted ceiling. This monumental project was completed in 1513. In this gigantic enterprise Michelangelo attempted to blend the Christian doctrine of the fall of man and his need for salvation with Neoplatonic ideas current in Renaissance Italy, ideas that are present also in Michelangelo's own sonnets. The Christian doctrine of the hopelessness of man when left to himself is illustrated in nine scenes running down the center of the ceiling, beginning with the creation and ending with the drunkenness of Noah. In the temptation episode man chooses to disobey the command of God. In the Noah scene he cannot even control his personal behavior.

God's intervention to save man is then illustrated in scenes at the four corners of the ceiling vault, depicting episodes from the Old Testament in which the Hebrews were delivered from disaster. The theme is then carried on by the huge figures of the Prophets and their classical counterparts, the sibyls, enthroned along the lower edge of the vault. The Prophets and the Cumean sibyl had announced the coming of a deliverer. Christ Himself does not appear in the ceiling decoration. However, in the lunettes along the top of the walls are groups of figures presumably representing His ancestors. The scenes from the life of Christ along the right wall, already mentioned, then take their place in the entire scheme that is concluded by Michelangelo's huge Last Judgment on the end-wall, painted many years later in 1548. The Neoplatonic element injected into the decoration of the ceiling is present in the restless, ideal, nude figures of youths seated on the pedestal projections of the illusionistic architectural framework for the scenes along the center of the ceiling. Renaissance Neoplatonism saw in the beauty of the human form a reflection of God's beauty from which the

"The Creation," 1508-12 by Michelangelo.

forms emanated. Their restlessness suggests their unhappiness in the human shell and their desire to be reabsorbed into God, the source from which they issued.

Bibliography: E. STEINMANN, *Die Sixtinische Kapelle,* 2 v. (Munich 1901–05). C. DE TOLNAY, *Michelangelo,* v. 2, 5 (Princeton 1960). E. T. DEWALD, *Italian Painting 1200–1600* (New York 1961) 325–331, 378–394.

[E. T. DEWALD]

SISTINE CHAPEL, RESTORATION OF

On Dec. 11, 1999, Pope JOHN PAUL II presided at a prayer service to mark the completion of the restoration of the SISTINE CHAPEL. The fifteenth-century chapel takes its name from Pope SIXTUS IV (1471–1484) who commissioned it and engaged notable Italian artists of the day to decorate it: Rosselli, Botticelli, Ghirlandaio, and Perugino. Early in the sixteenth century, Pope JULIUS II persuaded MICHELANGELO to redo the vaulted ceiling, a project that was finished in 1513. Over the centuries, the elements, dust, and candle-smoke dimmed the colors of the frescoes and caused them to deteriorate.

An ambitious restoration program, begun in 1964, went through several phases during the pontificates of Paul VI, John Paul I, and John Paul II, including the cleaning and repair of the fifteenth-century frescoes, which depicted scenes from the lives of Moses and Christ, the roof and battlements, and the frescoes on the entrance wall that continued the fifteenth-century cycle. In 1980 the project turned to the portraits of the popes and of Michelangelo's frescoes, successively the lunettes, the ceiling frescoes, and the *Last Judgment.* The final phase of the work, completed in 1999, repaired the cycle of murals by artists of the Florentine and Umbrian schools.

Means and Method of Restoration. The climax of the work was reached in April of 1994 with the ceremoni-

Fresco by Botticelli in the Sistine Chapel, in foreground, the "Purification of the Leper," center background, façade of the Hospital of the Holy Ghost founded by Sixtus IV; upper background, three scenes from the "Temptation of Christ."

al unveiling of the *Last Judgment.* Pope John Paul II celebrated a Mass in the chapel in honor of the event (April 8, 1994), using the opportunity to highlight the theology enshrined in Michelangelo's frescoes.

The decision to clean Michelangelo's paintings was made after examination of the lunette of Eleazar and Nathan detected tiny cracks in the color fabric of the whole ceiling. They were caused by the shrinking of the covering of glue that pulled away the layers of originally luminous color. Previous restorers had used the glue to revive the frescoes darkened by dust and soot. After research, experiment, and a trial cleaning in June of 1980 on the figure of Eleazar, the frescoed surfaces of the ceiling in the Sistine were cleaned by a method using the solvent known as AB57, applied briefly and removed with a sponge soaked in distilled water. The few parts retouched by Michelangelo *a secco* (after the plaster had set, thus sensitive to water) were cleaned last with specific organic water solvents fixed with a solution of Paraloid B72. Watercolor was used for some modest pictorial restorations. Because Michelangelo had used the delicate lapis lazuli in coloring and a more *a secco* technique for the *Last Judgment,* it called for different cleaning methods, including washings with distilled water and treatments with a solution of water and ammonium carbonate. All the stages of the work were scrupulously filmed. The chapel was kept open for the public to see the progress of the enterprise since the scaffolding covered the ceiling frescoes only partially at any one time.

The program of cleaning rid the frescoes in the Sistine Chapel of the polluting conditions chiefly responsible for their deterioration. To counter continuing pollution, however, experts decided to eschew the use of resinous or other protective substances on the frescoes, to install a conditioning system with a monitored annual cycle for air filtration, and to lay dust-retaining carpeting on the stairs leading to the Chapel from the Vatican Museums.

Michelangelo's Genius Rediscovered. During the cleaning, a photogrammetic survey of the ceiling and the *Last Judgment* revealed fresh details about their state of preservation and shed new light on Michelangelo's technical procedures and virtuosity. About 6,000 specialists and scholars from the fields of art and culture examined the outcome of the restoration carefully. Many of them approved of the astonishing results, but some art historians reacted with strong criticism.

The cleaning of the frescoes in the Sistine, originally both chapel and fortress, revealed long-lost or unobserved details of Michelangelo's work. The architectural design of the ceiling, which ingeniously divided one dramatic scene from another, became powerfully evident. Because the myriad of figures from the family scenes in the lunettes to the protesting saints in the *Last Judgment* was more clearly delineated, the emotions of tenderness, fear, and fury registered in their gestures and expressions became more apparent. The meticulous painting of the ceiling histories from the first scene of the Creation to the Drunkenness of Noah was found to contrast sharply with the rapid execution of the lunettes, some of which had been left almost as studies. This discovery led scholars to deduce that for the lunettes, Michelangelo did not use cartoons and did the painting without using his assistants. Michelangelo's skilled use of traditional Tuscan *buon fresco* for the vault and the lunettes also became manifest. This demanding technique requires the painting of complete details of entire sections of the work onto fresh plaster. Art scholars could detect his sudden decisions to make changes in his figures by noting where he removed the frescoed plaster and applied a new layer on which to paint. The restored clarity of the *Last Judgment* revealed the strength and audacity of Michelangelo's brushstrokes, the mastery of his composition, the intellectual and pictorial brilliance of his balancing of mass and space, and the detailed expression of his mischievous or macabre humor.

The restoration and cleaning of the Sistine Chapel opened the way for many years of further study and appreciation. Worldwide attention focused on the need to reassess Michelangelo's place in the development of Renaissance painting and of his aims and achievements as a colorist and draftsman. He was perceived as well situated in the lineage of Tuscan painting, beginning in the studio of Ghirlandaio in Florence and influencing such younger Florentine painters as Rosso and Pontormo. Michelangelo used colors on the ceiling of the Sistine Chapel to model his figures. His varied shades created immense light and startling shimmering effects: gleaming white, flesh tints, yellows, and greens. His use of abrupt juxtapositions of violets, greens, and yellows in the lunettes produced wonderful impressions of light and shade. After veils of grime were removed from the *Last Judgment,* the colors appeared incandescent, with the figures rising and falling in a space of blue so luminous that the wall on which they were painted seemed to have dissolved.

The ''rediscovery'' of Michelangelo as a painter vastly different from the somber artist previously perceived was accompanied by scholarly reappraisals of other aspects of his life, his complex personality, and his always surprising art: spiritually resonant poetry, original architecture, and expressive sculpture in stone.

Bibliography: Detailed bibliographies on the cleaning of the Sistine Chapel have been published in the *Monumenti, Musei e Gallerie Pontificie* series. Other recent publications on Michelangelo and/or the cleaning of the Sistine Chapel include: G. COLALUCCI, ''Brevi considerazioni sulla tecnica pittorica e la problematica di restauro degli affreschi michelangioeschi della volta Sistina'' in *Problemi del restauro in Italia,* ed., CAMPANOTTO (Udine 1988); ''The Frescoes of Michelangelo on the Vault of the Sistine Chapel. Original Technique and Conservation,'' in *The Conservation of Wall Paintings,* Proceedings of a Symposium organised by the Courtauld Institute of Art and the Getty Conservation Institute (London, July 13–16, 1987), ed. S. CATHER (Singapore 1991). DE MAIO, *Michelangelo e la Controriforma* (Roma-Bari 1981). M. HALL, *Michelangelo—The Sistine Ceiling Restored* (New York 1993). F. HARTT, G. COLALUCCI, F. MANCINELLI, (and D. SCHLESAK in the German edition), *La Cappella Sistina,* 3 v.: v. 1, *La preistoria della Bibbia*; v. 2, *Gli antenati di Cristo*; v. 3, *La storia della Creazione* (Milan 1989–90; Paris, 1989–90; Luzern 1989–91; Anversa 1990–91; Tokyo 1990–91; New York 1991; Warsaw 1991). R. HATFIELD, *Trust in God: The Sources of Michelangelo's Frescoes on the Sistine Ceiling* (Florence 1991). F. MANCINELLI, ''La pulitura degli affreschi di Michelangelo nella Cappella Sistina,'' in *Il problema della Cappella Sistina,* ed. ISTITUTO SUPERIORE DI ARTE SACRA (Rome 1987). J. D. OREMLAND, *Michelangelo's Sistine Ceiling: A Study of Creativity* (Madison, Conn. 1989); *The Sistine Chapel: Michelangelo Rediscovered,* Eng. ed. (Great Britain 1986). ''All Salvation History Leads to Christ,'' *L'Osservatore Romano,* English edition (December 15, 1999).

[G. A. BULL]

SITUATION (SITUS)

A situation is one of the ten Aristotelian CATEGORIES OF BEING (Gr. κεῖσθαι, Lat. *situs*) describing how a body is disposed or situated. It designates the arrangement of

''Pope St. Marcellus I,'' fresco by Ghirlandaio, Sistine Chapel. (Alinari–Art Reference/Art Resource, NY.)

parts of a body in place, and is a further determination of the category location. The latter is commensurate with place, part to part, but does not specify the arrangement of parts. The separate category of situation is therefore postulated specifically to account for this arrangement.

See Also: LOCATION (UBI); PLACE.

[P. R. DURBIN]

SIVA

One of the names under which the Supreme Being is worshipped in Hinduism. Together with Brahma and Vishnu he forms the *trimūrti,* the triple form of the deity, conceived as the Creator, Preserver, and Destroyer of the world. Siva is a complex figure and his cult has a long history. Originally a non-Aryan fertility god, he was later identified with the Vedic god Rudra, the god of storm and thunder who is also the ''lord of cattle'' (*paśupati*). An early seal from Mohenjo Daro showing a yogi sitting cross-legged in meditation surrounded by animals is believed to be the earliest representation of Siva. Besides being the god of fertility, whose symbol is the linga, Siva is also the great ascetic who holds the world in being by his power of austerity. He is conceived as the reconciler

"Consegna Delle Chiavi (The Consigning of the Keys)," fresco by Perugino and Luca da Signorelli, early Renaissance, masterpiece restoration project in the Sistine Chapel. (AP/Wide World)

of opposites. He is the Destroyer of the world, who haunts the cremation grounds and wears a necklace of skulls, but he is also the divine physician who recreates the world at the end of time. He is absolutely inactive as the pure source of Being, but he also sustains the world as *natarāja* in the cosmic dance. Furthermore he is both male and female, and is sometimes represented as half man and half woman. Yet this strange ambivalent deity has come to be regarded as the Supreme Being, the Father and Creator of the world; as a personal god who is immanent in all things, dwelling in the heart of man and assisting him by his grace.

[B. GRIFFITHS]

SIXTUS I, POPE, ST.

Pontificate: 117 or 119 to 126 or 128. Sixtus (Xystus) was the sixth successor to Peter (*see* CLEMENT I). The Liberian catalogue dates his reign 117 to 126. Virtually all lists and Eusebius (*Histoire ecclesiastique* 4.4, 5; 5.6, 24) indicate a ten-year episcopate. The *Liber pontificalis* says that he was a Roman, son of a certain Pastor but the name Xystus is Greek. It also attributes to him a garbled disciplinary decree that is intelligible only in early sixth-century terms, a decree that sacred vessels should not be touched except by the ministering clergy, and a decree that the people should chant the Sanctus with the priest. He probably was not a martyr. His reputed burial near the body of Peter in the Vatican has not been substantiated by modern excavations.

Feast: April 6.

Bibliography: *Liber pontificalis*, ed. L. DUCHESNE (Paris 1886–92) 1:ccviii, 54–57, 128. É. AMANN, *Dictionnaire de théologie catholique*, ed. A. VACANT et al., (Paris 1903–50) 14.2:193–94. J. N. D. KELLY, *Oxford Dictionary of Popes* (New York 1986) 9. E. FERGUSON, *Encyclopedia of Early Christianity* (New York 1997) 2:1065. E. KETTENHOFFEN, *Biographisch–Bibliographisches Kirshcenlexikon*, 10 (Herzburg 1995).

[E. G. WELTIN]

SIXTUS II, POPE, ST.

Pontificate: Aug. 30, 257 to Aug. 6, 258; martyr. Sixtus succeeded Stephen I during the first phase of the Vale-

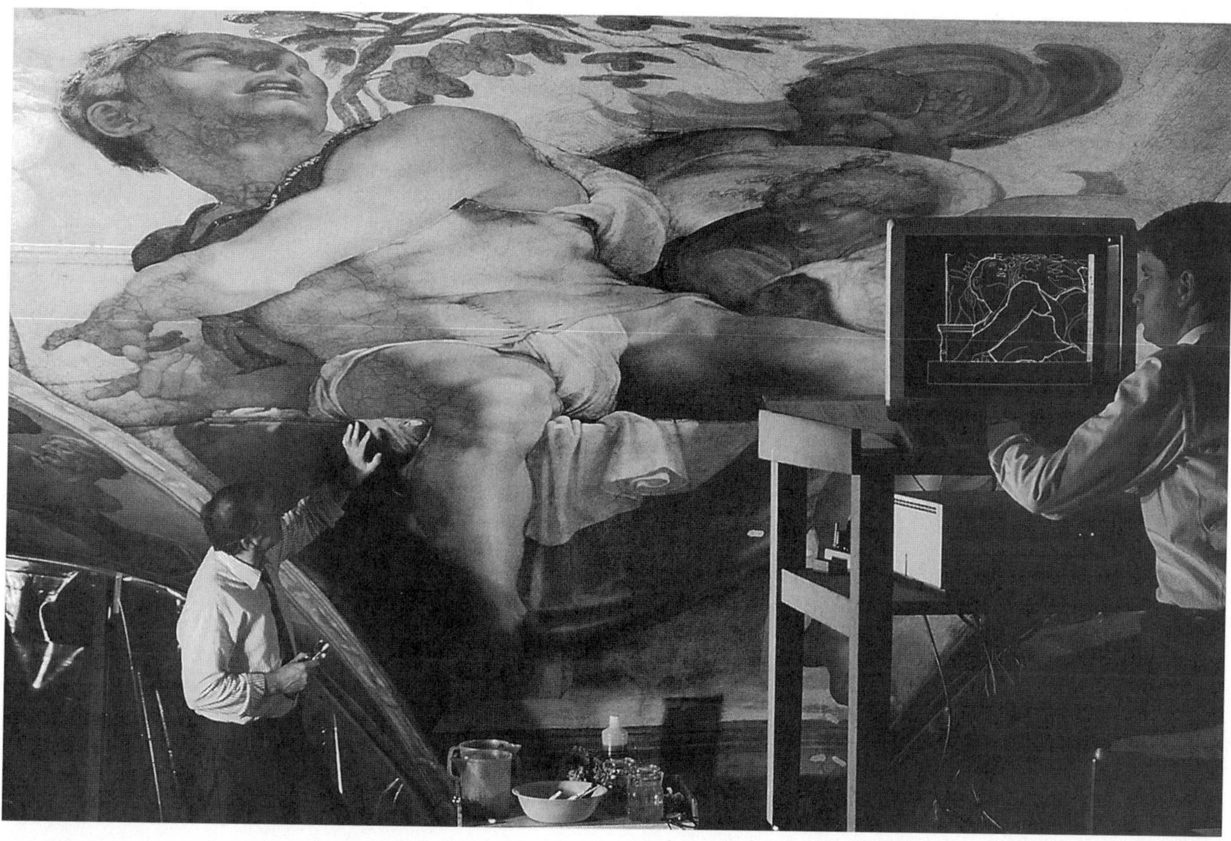

Conservators using computer technology in the restoration of Michelangelo's frescoes in the Sistine Chapel, 1989. (©Vittoriano Rastelli/CORBIS)

rian persecution (257). While Sixtus was conducting services in the cemetery of Praetextatus, Roman troops came to arrest him. Realizing that if he tried to escape, there would be a general massacre as the troops came after him, this true pastor identified himself to the troops. He and four deacons, Januarius, Vincent, Magnus, and Stephen, were seized and beheaded; two other deacons, Felicissimus and Agapetus, were also probably martyred the same day, and St. Lawrence four days later. Sixtus was buried in the cemetery of Callistus, and 100 years later Pope DAMASUS (366–384) composed his epitaph from which Prudentius erroneously concluded that Sixtus had been crucified.

During his reign Sixtus dealt with the controversy over the validity of baptism by heretics. He supported the view of his predecessor that baptism by heretics was valid, but apparently influenced by Dionysius of Alexandria, he adopted a tolerant policy toward the divergent rebaptism policies of the Eastern Churches. He also sent envoys to Cyprian of Carthage, Stephen I's adversary in this problem. The claim that Sixtus wrote the treatise *Ad Novatianum* cannot be established. He is thought by some to have been the composer or at least the editor of the Pythagorean Sentences of SEXTUS translated by RUFINUS OF AQUILEIA, but this attribution is doubtful. Sixtus is commemorated in the Canon of the Mass.

Feast: Aug. 6.

Bibliography: EUSEBIUS, *Ecclesiastical History.* 7.5, 9, 27. É. AMANN, *Dictionnaire de théologie catholique*, ed. A. VACANT et al., (Paris 1903—50) 14.2:2194–96, E. KOTTING, *Lexikon für Theologie und Kirche*, ed. J. HOFER and K. RAHNER (Freiberg 1957–65) 9:809. E. FERGUSON, ed., *Encyclopedia of Early Christianity* (New York 1997) 2.1065. J. N. D. KELLY *Oxford Dictionary of Popes* (New York 1986) 21–22. F. SCORZA BRACELLONA, *Lexikon des Mittelalters,* 7 (München-Zürich 1994–1995).

[E. G. WELTIN]

SIXTUS III, POPE, ST.

Pontificate: July 31, 432 to Aug. 19, 440. This pope was a Roman, the son of Xystus, and a priest at the time of his election. He was well known to (St.) AUGUSTINE and seems to have sympathized with PELAGIUS until the issuance of the *Tractoria* of Pope ZOSIMUS. Sixtus then abandoned Pelagius and was reminded of the limits of prudence and charity by Augustine.

"St. Lawrence Receiving the Treasures of the Church from Pope Sixtus II," detail of fresco cycle "The Lives of Saints Stephen and Lawrence" by Fra Angelico in the Chapel of Pope Nicholas V, Vatican Palace, Rome. (Alinari–Art Reference/Art Resource, NY)

Sixtus encouraged the negotiations, following the Council of EPHESUS (431), between CYRIL OF ALEXANDRIA and JOHN OF ANTIOCH, who finally reached agreement regarding the two natures in Christ; the pope wrote to congratulate them (433). During his pontificate, friendly relations between Rome, Constantinople, and Alexandria had all but liquidated the Nestorian problem, until PROCLUS succeeded Maximian as bishop of Constantinople and attempted to impose the decisions of a Constantinopolitan council on the bishops of Illyricum. Sixtus wrote to Bp. Anastasius of Thessalonica confirming his office as papal vicar and warning the Illyrian bishops against the jurisdictional encroachments of Proclus. At the same time, he requested Proclus not to tolerate appeals to Constantinople from the Illyrian bishops. On the other hand, when Iddua, the bishop of Smyrna, appealed to Rome against a sentence rendered by Proclus as metropolitan of Asia Minor, the pope refused to interfere, thus indicating his determination to uphold the system of vicariates. The matter remained a thorny one in Roman-Constantinopolitan relations.

Probably relying on the memory of old sympathies, the exiled Pelagian, JULIAN OF ECLANUM, attempted to persuade Sixtus to allow him to return to his see in Italy (439), but the pope was warned against such a gesture by the deacon (later pope) Leo.

The name of Sixtus III is linked with several of Rome's outstanding churches and monuments, and modern scholars speak of a Sixtine Renaissance. He rebuilt the Lateran BAPTISTERY, giving it the form that it has retained ever since: the inscription on the marble beams around the font extols grace and the theology of baptism to mark the Church's triumph over the heresy of Pelagius. His most important undertaking was a complete reconstruction of the Liberian Basilica of Saint Mary Major on the Esquiline Hill and its dedication to the Virgin Mary (the first, and for many years the only, church to be so dedicated in Rome). Its majestic mosaics commemorated the triumph of the Church over the heresy of Nestorius.

A second basilica was joined to the Constantinian church of St. Lawrence Outside the Walls. The Roman Emperor VALENTINIAN III was persuaded to contribute costly silver and gold ornaments to the basilicas of St. Peter, St. Paul, and the Lateran to replace what had been carried off by the Visigoths.

The first monastery in Rome was established at St. Sebastian's to ensure the daily recitation of the Divine Office, and in the papal crypt at St. Callistus the pope erected an important inscription or plaque on which were listed the names of the bishops and martyrs buried there. Sixtus himself was buried in St. Lawrence, although the exact location of his tomb is unknown. Ado of Sens was the first to include him in his ninth-century version of the Roman MARTYROLOGY under the date of March 28.

Feast: March 28.

Bibliography: *Patrologia Latina,* ed. J. P. MIGNE (Paris 1878–90) 50:581–618. *Patrologiae cursus completus, series latina*; suppl., ed. A. HAMMAN (Paris 1957—) 3:21–22, for eds. of letters. *Liber pontificalis,* ed. L. DUCHESNE (Paris 1886–92) 1:232–237; 3:85. H. LECLERCQ, *Dictionnaire d'archéologie chrétienne et de liturgie* (Paris 1907–53) 13.1:1204–10. É AMANN, *Dictionnaire de théologie catholique,* ed. A. VACANT et al. (Paris 1903–50) 14.2:2196–99. G. FERRARI, *Early Roman Monasteries* (Rome 1957) 162. R. U. MONTINI, *Le tombe dei Papi* (Rome 1957) 100. R. KRAUTHEIMER, "The Architecture of Sixtus III," *Essays in Honor of Erwin Panofsky,* ed. M. MEISS, 2 v. (New York 1961). A. DIBERARDINO, *Patrology* (Westminister, Md. 1986) 4:589. E. FERGUSON, ed., *Encyclopedia of Early Christianity* (New York 1997) 2:1065. H. JEDIN, *History of the Church* (New York 1980) 2:263–264. R. KRAUTHEIMER, *Rome: Profile of a City* (Princeton 1980) 33–58. J. N. D. KELLY, *Oxford Dictionary of Popes* (New York 1986) 42–43. C. PIETRI, *Rome Christiana* (Rome 1976) 955–966, 1139–1147. R. DELBRUECK, "Notes on the Wooden Doors of Santa Sabina," *Studies in Early Christianity* 18 (New York & London 1993) 13–21. M. V. MARINI CLARELLI, "La Controversia nestoriana e i mosaici dell'arco trionfale di S. Maria Maggiore," in *Bisanzio e l'Occidente. Arte, Archeologia, Storia, Studi in onore di Fernanda de'Maffei* (Rome 1996) 323–42.

[J. CHAPIN]

SIXTUS IV, POPE

Pontificate: Aug. 9, 1471, to Aug. 12, 1484; b. Francesco DELLA ROVERE, in Celle near Savona, Italy, July 21, 1414; d. Rome. Belonging to an impoverished Ligurian family, he was educated by the Franciscans, and joined the Conventual FRANCISCANS. He taught at several Italian universities, acquiring a wide reputation through his works on theology and philosophy and through his excellence as a preacher. In 1464 he became minister-general of his order; three years later he was made cardinal. After a short conclave he was elected pope to succeed PAUL II. The reign of Sixtus IV opened one of the saddest periods in papal history. During that era the concern of the popes with family affairs and political ambitions far overshadowed their interest in their duties as spiritual leaders of the Church. In fact, the contributions to the life of the Church made by Sixtus IV were few. He celebrated a HOLY YEAR in 1475, which drew numerous pilgrims to Rome, and he greatly increased the privileges of the Conventual Franciscans. He shared his order's devotion to the Blessed Virgin and supported the teaching of her Immaculate Conception. Although he tried to summon a crusade against the Turks, other European states failed to support him, and with Venetian and Hungarian aid he succeeded only in recapturing the Italian town of Otranto from the OTTOMAN TURKS. The chief interest of Sixtus remained the aggrandizement of his family. His numerous relatives were given benefices in profusion as well as high church offices. Two nephews, Giuliano Della Rovere (later Pope JULIUS II) and Pietro Riario, were made cardinals. Another nephew, Girolamo RIARIO, planned to carve a principality for himself out of Italy and involved the Pope in almost continuous disputes and wars with the other Italian states. The most infamous affair into which he drew Sixtus was the PAZZI conspiracy of 1478 against Lorenzo and Giuliano de' MEDICI. As a result of the pope's nepotism and political activity, finances fell into increasing disorder. Despite his efforts to create new sources of revenue, such as the doubling of venal curial offices, Sixtus left a large deficit to his successor. In 1482 Abp. Andrea ZAMOMETIČ attempted unsuccessfully to convoke at Basel a council before which the pope would have to justify himself.

As ruler of Rome and as patron of humanists and artists, Sixtus must be judged more favorably. He began the rebuilding of Rome on a large scale, having streets opened, widened, and paved. He erected the churches of S. Maria della Pace and S. Maria del Popolo, and, above all, the SISTINE CHAPEL, decorated by the outstanding artists of the time, including Botticelli and PERUGINO. He drew to Rome Pinturicchio, Ghirlandaio, and many other painters and sculptors. The rearranged and enlarged VATICAN LIBRARY was opened to scholars during his reign. The tomb of Sixtus, done by Pollaiuolo and situated in the grottoes of SAINT PETER's Basilica in Rome, is one of the finest monuments of Italian Renaissance art. The theological works of Sixtus include *De sanguine Christi, De potentia Dei*, and *De futuris contingentibus* (Rome 1470–72).

Bibliography: L. PASTOR, *The History of the Popes from the Close of the Middle Ages* (London-St. Louis 1938–61) v.4. A. TEETAERT, *Dictionnaire de théologie catholique,* ed. A. VACANT et al. (Paris 1903–50)14.2:2199–2217. A. MATANIĆ, "Xystus Pp. IV scripsitne librum *De conceptione beate virginis Marie?*" *Antonianum* 29 (1954) 573–578. F. X. SEPPELT, *Geschichte der Päpste von den Anfängen bis zur Mitte des 20. Jh.* (Munich 1954–59) v.4. G. SCHWAIGER, *Lexikon für Theologie und Kirche*, ed. J. HOFER and K. RAHNER (Freiburg 1957–65) 9:810–811. L. EGMONT, *Sixtus IV and Men of Letters* (Rome 1978). L. PUSCI, "Profilo di Francesco Della Rovere, poi Sixto IV," *Storia e cultura al Santo*, ed. A. POPPI (Vincenza 1976) 279–88.

[E. G. GLEASON]

SIXTUS V, POPE

Pontificate: April 24, 1585, to August 27, 1590; b. Felice Peretti at Grottammare, near Montalto, in the March of Ancona, December 13, 1520 (or in 1521 according to some). His father was a field laborer. His uncle Salvatore, a Franciscan Conventual, took him under protection and sent him to school in Montalto. Felice entered the Franciscans at the age of 12. Between 1540 and 1546 he continued his studies in Fermo, Ferrara, Bologna, Rimini, and Siena, being ordained in Siena in 1547. In 1548 he received the doctorate in theology from the University of Fermo and began teaching in the Order's convent school in Siena (1549). His reputation as a preacher attracted the notice of Cardinal Carpi, the protector of the Franciscans, who brought him to Rome in 1552. There his Lenten sermons recommended him to Julius III. Interest in Church reform led to his becoming acquainted with Cardinal Giampietro Caraffa (later Paul IV) and Cardinal Michele Ghislieri (later Pius V). Some of the sermons he gave at Perugia were printed. In 1557 Paul IV made him inquisitor in Venice. He was unpopular there and, after the death of Paul IV, withdrew to Montalto. Pius IV, however, reappointed him as inquisitor in Venice in 1560. Because of his sternness, the Republic soon officially requested that he be recalled. He was also named as theologian for the Reform Commission. Soon he was chosen as procurator-general of the Franciscans, while at the same time he served on a commission preparing a new edition of Gratian's *Decretum.* In 1565 he went to Spain with Cardinal Ugo Buoncampagni (later Gregory XIII) to review the proceedings against Bartolomé de CARRANZA, Archbishop of Toledo, on charges of heresy. He and Buoncampagni did not get on well together. The

Spanish mission was interrupted by Pius IV's death; the resulting conclave chose Cardinal Ghislieri, who took the name of Pius V. Peretti was soon made vicar-general of the Franciscans and in 1566 bishop of Sant'Agata dei Goti, at which time he began to use Montalto as a surname. Thus when Pius V made him cardinal in 1570, he was known as Cardinal Montalto. In 1571 he was transferred from the Diocese of Sant'Agata to that of Fermo. When Gregory XIII became Pope, Montalto fell into disfavor, and he withdrew to the villa he was building on the slopes of the Esquiline. Gregory XIII suspended the pension granted him by Pius V, but the loss was repaired by the Grand Duke of Tuscany. In retirement Montalto prepared an edition of the works of St. Ambrose, but unfortunately this work had many scholarly flaws. On the death of Gregory XIII in April 1585, the Sacred College was divided by rival factions under Cardinals Alessandro de' Medici and Alessandro Farnese, as well as by the conflicting interests of Spain and France. Montalto emerged as the man whom all, however they might differ, might join in supporting. His election on April 24 was unanimous. The new Pope took the name of Sixtus V, in memory of the preceding Fransciscan Pope, Sixtus IV.

Papal Reforms. Devoted to church reform and centralization, he moved quickly to impose stern discipline upon the clergy of the churches and colleges of Rome. This accomplished by his vigorous action, he undertook to tighten up clerical discipline throughout the world. The decree of the Council of Trent against simony and plurality of benefices was strictly applied. A bull of December 20, 1585, reestablished for all bishops the visit "ad limina Apostolorum," requiring further that they make detailed reports concerning their dioceses. Residence of bishops and pastors was enforced. In the bull of December 3, 1586, he set a limit of 70 members on the College of Cardinals and promulgated regulations for the cardinals, some of which still apply. In January 1588 he established 15 congregations of cardinals to carry out the administration of the Church and of the Papal States. It was feared that nepotism might again become offensive when he made his grandnephew a cardinal at the age of 14, but neither this nephew nor other relatives influenced Sixtus in his official policies or decisions.

Among the religious orders he favored the Franciscans, not only in the appointments he made among them, but by honoring them through the canonization of Diego of Alcalá and the proclamation of St. Bonaventure as a Doctor of the Church. Before his death he was thinking of requiring the Jesuits to change their name and of having a commission review the Jesuit constitution. In the dispute between the Jesuits and Dominicans over grace, he imposed mutual silence. He gave strong support to the missions, being especially aware of the conversions being made in China and Japan because an embassy from Japan was in Rome at the time of his election. He was attentive to the Dominican and Franciscan missions in South America and in the Philippines. Sixtus created additional tribunals of the Inquisition and brought more offenses within its jurisdiction. A new Index of Prohibited Books, whose preparation he had ordered, was not printed before his death. The edition of the Vulgate that he sponsored was faulty and was subsequently withdrawn. Sixtus reestablished the feast of the Presentation of the Blessed Virgin Mary.

Administration of the Papal States. Sixtus succeeded brilliantly in eradicating the banditry that had grown prevalent in the Papal States under Gregory XIII, by recourse to repressive measures. An unflinching harshness, shown by the exposure of bandit's heads on the Sant'Angelo Bridge, caused some to censure him, but in general he was praised for ridding Rome of a scourge that involved even great families. Although the coffers of the treasury were empty when his reign began, through economies, new taxes, sale of offices, and the floating of new loans (*Monti vacabili* and *Monti non vacabili*), he created a reserve of more than five million crowns. He carefully administered the provisioning of Rome, promoted the silk and wool industries, encouraged agriculture, began the draining of the Pontine marshes, and constructed new aqueducts (including the rebuilding of that of Alexander Severus, which was then called Acqua Felice).

Monumental construction in Rome included the Lateran Palace, enlargement of the Quirinal, completion of the dome of St. Peter's, building of that section of the Vatican in which the popes reside, a new building for the Vatican Library, and placing four great obelisks, including one in St. Peter's Square. Sixtus was very generous to the University of Rome.

International Diplomacy. His greatest problem in foreign policy concerned France. Sixtus wanted to halt the spread of Protestantism, but he also wanted to uphold the political balance so that Spain would not dominate all Europe. If the civil and religious struggle in France should end with Huguenot control, it could mean the end of Catholicism throughout a great part of Europe. But if the Huguenots were subdued by the power of Spain, it could mean the end of the Church's political independence. So Sixtus tried to reconcile all French Catholics to Henry III. However, the King vacillated and gave way to his personal distrust of the Guises. Moreover, the Catholic League under the Guises became affiliated with PHILIP II, King of Spain. When the Duke of Guise and his brother the cardinal were murdered by Henry III's order, Sixtus issued a stern *monitorium* and excommunication against the King. Yet he did not sanction revolt of the League's members against their legitimate King. When Henry III was assassinated, Sixtus allied with Philip II against the Huguenot Henry of Navarre (later King HENRY IV). The Pope knew that one thing could still achieve his original aims, namely, the conversion of Henry of Navarre. This, however, did not occur until 1593, nearly three years after Sixtus's death. In regard to England, Sixtus was solicitous for MARY STUART, Queen of Scots, but there is no proof that he was involved even indirectly in the Babington plot. After Mary's execution in 1587, Sixtus aided Spain in building the ARMADA. Upon the destruction of that fleet, however, the Pope abandoned further actions against England. He longed to crusade against the Turks, conjecturing that such a crusade could take the form of an assault on Algiers, action in the Mediterranean by a great alliance that would include Venice or, possibly, even action based on Poland in the East. None of these projects was ever launched. Sixtus favored Maximilian of Hapsburg in his attempt to achieve the Polish crown after the death of King Stephen BÁTHORY (1586). Maximilian's failure was partially compensated by the conversion to Catholicism of the Margrave of Baden.

Vigorous, eloquent, and stern, Sixtus had devoted himself unsparingly to the defense and advancement of the Church, including the promotion of missionary work in Latin America and Asia. This primary concern underlay his wide and intricate diplomacy. As an administrator he was talented, exacting, energetic, able in finance, resolute in enforcing public order, and munificent in his patronage of art and learning. A year after his death (1591), his remains were placed in the Sistine Chapel he had constructed in Santa Maria Maggiore.

Bibliography: U. BALZANI, *Sisto Quinto* (Geneva 1913); "Rome under Sixtus V," *Cambridge Modern History* (London-New York 1902–12) 3:422–455. J. A. VON HÜBNER, *Sixte V é d'après des correspondances diplomatiques inédites*, 3 v. (Paris 1870), Eng. *The Life and Times of Sixtus the Fifth . . .*, tr. H. E. H. JERNINGHAM, 2 v. (London 1872). J. A. ORBAAN, *Sixtine Rome* (London 1910). L. PASTOR, *The History of the Popes from the Close of the Middle Ages* (London-St. Louis 1938–61) v.21, 22. L. PASTOR, *Sisto V: il creatore della nuova Roma* (Rome 1922). L. M. PERSONNÉ, *Sisto V: Il genio della potenza* (Florence 1935). A. TEETAERT, *Dictionnaire de théologie catholique*, ed. A. VACANT et al., 15 v. (Paris 1903–50; Tables générales 1951–) 14.2:2217–38. G. SCHWAIGER, *Lexikon für Theologie und Kirche*, ed. J. HOFER and K. RAHNER, 10 v. (2d, new ed. Freiburg 1957–65) 9:811–812, S. BORSI, *Roma di Sisto* (Rome 1996). I. DE FEO, *Sisto V* (Milan 1987). G. PORISCIANI, *Sisto V e la sua Montalto* (Padua 1986) F. SARAZANI, *Roma di Sisto V* (Rome 1979). M. L. MADONNA, *Roma di Sisto* (Rome 1983).

[D. R. CAMPBELL]

SIXTUS OF SIENA

Biblical scholar; b. Siena, 1520; d. Genoa, 1569. Converted from Judaism in his youth, he first became a Franciscan, but later, when convicted of heresy and condemned to death, he was spared through the intercession of Michael Ghislieri, OP (later Pius V), who persuaded him to recant and become a Dominican (1551). In 1559 he was appointed censor of Hebrew books by Pius V, and in this office he was able to save many valuable works from destruction. In 1566 he published at Venice his celebrated *Bibliotheca Sacra,* containing eight "books" in two volumes: (1) division and authority of Scripture, (2) alphabetic and historical indexes, (3) interpretation of the inspired books, (4) alphabetic list of Catholic interpreters, (5) hermeneutics [also published separately as *De arte interpretandi sacra volumina* (Cologne 1577)], (6) and (7) exegetical interpretations, and (8) apologia. Some later editions arrange the eight books in a different order. Since it was based on scientific principles, this work is considered to be the first of the modern Biblical introductions. In it were used for the first time the terms protocanonical and deuterocanonical that later became standard for distinguishing respectively the OT books that are regarded as canonical by Jews and Protestants as well as by Catholics and those that are so regarded only by Catholics.

Bibliography: J. QUÉTIF and J. ÉCHARD, *Scriptores Ordinis Praedicatorum,* 5 v. (Paris 1719–23); continued by R. COULON (Paris 1909–); repr. 2 v. in 4 (New York 1959) 2.1:206–208. *Dictionnaire de la Bible,* ed. F. VIGOUROUX, 5 v. (Paris 1895–1912) 5.2:1799–1800.

[A. SMITH]

SKARGA, PIOTR

Eminent Polish preacher, theologian, and apologist; b. Grójec, Mazovia, 1536; d. Cracow, Sept. 27, 1612. He attended the parish school at Grójec, went on to the University of Cracow (B.A. 1554), was ordained at Lvov (1564), and entered the Jesuit novitiate. He studied theology in Rome (1564–71) and was appointed professor at Pułtusk College (1571). He abandoned his teaching career for preaching and missionary activities (he converted the Radziwill princes and their Lithuanian subjects) and founded or enlarged Jesuit colleges in Ryga, Dorpat, Połock, Nieśwież, and Lublin. He was first rector of the Academy (university) of Vilna (1579–84).

To uphold Catholicism and to convert Protestants and schismatics, Skarga wrote many treatises, usually in Polish, such as *Pro Ssma. Eucharistia* (1576; Eng. tr. Milwaukee 1939) and *O Jednosci Kościoła Bożego*

(1577, On the Unity of the Church of God). The Union of Brest (1596), which united the schismatic Ruthenians with Rome, was widely attributed to the influence of Skarga's apologetic treatises.

Zywoty Swietych (1579, Lives of the Saints) has been most widely read by Poles through the centuries. Rather than simply translate, Skarga artistically transformed Lippomano's hagiographic work by adapting it to the Polish mentality, adding original commentaries, and including new biographies. Outstanding for philosophic depth and finesse of style is *Kazania na Niedziele i Swięta* (1595, Sermons for Sundays and Holidays). Skarga published his powerful *Kazania o Siedmiu Sakramentach* (1600, Sermons on the Seven Sacraments), together with *Kazania Przygodne* (Sermons on Various Occasions) and his prophetic *Kazania Sejmowe* (Sermons Preached to the Diet). The last work, a national examination of conscience, greatly influenced Polish literary and patriotic thought, particularly in the 19th century.

Skarga's profound eloquence combined with piety and humility to win him the name of the Polish Bossuet. He founded many charitable societies in major Polish cities: *Bractwo Miłosierdzi* (the Brotherhood of Charity), *Bractwo Betanii Sw. Łazarza* (the Brotherhood of St. Lazarus of Bethany) to care for the sick, *Skrzynka Sw. Mikołaja* (St. Nicholas' Chest) to shield young girls, and especially the *Bank Pobożny* to protect the poor from usurers. He spent the last 24 years of his life as King Zygmunt III's preacher, using his prestige and power solely for the good of his Church and his country, to which he had given a salutary program for reform.

Bibliography: P. SKARGA, *Pisma wszystkie*, 5 v. (Warsaw 1923–30); *Les Sermons politiques . . .*, tr. A. BERGA (Paris 1916). S. WINDAKIEWICZ, *P. Skarga* (Cracow 1925). A. BERGA, *Un Prédicateur . . . Pierre Skarga . . .* (Paris 1916). G. M. GODDEN, *P. Skarga, Priest and Patriot* (London 1947).

[T. F. DOMARADZKI]

SKEHAN, PATRICK W.

Old Testament and Semitics scholar; b. New York, N.Y., Sept. 30, 1909; d. Wash., D.C., Sept. 9, 1980. Patrick William Skehan received his B.A. from Fordham University (1929), studied theology at St. Joseph's Seminary, Yonkers, N.Y., and was ordained a priest Sept. 23, 1933. He studied Scripture and Semitic Languages at The Catholic University of America, Wash., D.C., where he obtained an S.T.D. in the Old Testament (1938). He taught in the Department of Semitic Languages at CUA from 1938 until his retirement in August 1980, often serving as departmental chairman. On several occasions he served as visiting lecturer/professor to the Oriental Seminary of The Johns Hopkins University, and was annual professor at the American School of Oriental Research, Jerusalem (1954–55), serving as director there from 1955 to 1956. Skehan was Catholic Biblical Association Visiting Professor to the Pontifical Biblical Institute, Rome, 1969–70, where he was named consulter to the Pontifical Biblical Commission (1965–71).

Msgr. Skehan is perhaps best known for his work on the DEAD SEA SCROLLS, some of which he edited for publication, and the New American Bible translation. His contribution to the latter is inestimable, for he meticulously edited all parts of the Old Testament, as well as translating extensive sections himself. Skehan was a charter member of the Catholic Biblical Association, its president from 1946 to 1947, and treasurer from 1977 until his death. He was several times associate editor of the *Catholic Biblical Quarterly*, associate editor of *Old Testament Abstracts*, and editor of the association's monograph series (1973–75). A retiring man, he was revered by his colleagues for his scholarly care and integrity, and by his students for the generous and unassuming care he lavished on them.

Bibliography: A. A. DI LELLA, "Patrick William Skehan: A Tribute," *The Catholic Bibical Quarterly* 42 (1980) 435–437. Bibliography of Skehan's publications up to 1971: P. W. SKEHAN, *Studies in Israelite Poetry and Wisdom*; *The Catholic Bibical Quarterly MS* 1 (Wash., D.C. 1971) 254–260. Bibliography of Skehan's publications from 1971 until his death: *The Catholic Bibical Quarterly* 43 (1981) 96–98.

[J. JENSEN]

SKEPTICISM

The term skepticism (Gr. σχέπτομαι, to examine) designates a variety of approaches to philosophical problems. According to popular usage, a skeptic is a person who, as a general rule, or in a particular instance, hesitates or refuses to accept the truth of propositions. Skepticism may be a mere psychological attitude, or a deliberate doctrine; it may be systematic or unsystematic, partial or total. Philosophical skepticism usually implies more than mere caution or a readiness to examine problems; otherwise most philosophies would have to be termed skeptical, since they involve methodical reflection on man, knowledge, and being. Rather it has come to be indissolubly associated with DOUBT, i.e., an inability to form one's judgment; thus doubt is the skeptic's characteristic reaction in the face of theoretical problems.

While a number of names in the history of philosophy have been identified with skepticism, historians generally fail to acknowledge the extent of their influence on the development of philosophical thought. For this reason, the present treatment first sketches the historical development of skepticism, and then gives a systematic analysis of its basic concepts and presuppositions.

Historical Development of Skepticism

The history of skepticism fits naturally into three main divisions, corresponding to those used to describe the evolution of philosophy itself. Its foundations were laid by the Greeks; it was revived, largely under fideist influences, in the medieval and Renaissance periods; and it emerged as a philosophical system, although with many variations, during the early development of modern philosophy.

Greek Skeptics. Ancient skepticism was fostered by two schools, one Pyrrhonian and the other Academic. It traces its origins, with some justification, to the difficulties, controversies, hesitations, and perplexities of pre-Socratic philosophers. The most immediately palpable influence is that, of DEMOCRITUS of Abdera, who taught that the world is made up of atoms and the void, and that qualitative diversity is a mere illusion of the senses. Truth, in such an atomistic materialism, can be gauged only by the intellect or mind, in conformity with the old Parmenidean opposition between sensation and intelligence. Through Metrodoros of Chios and Anaxarchos, a direct descendence is traceable from this doctrine to Pyrrho of Elis, the founder of Greek skepticism.

Pyrrhonians. Pyrrho is generally believed to have lived between 365 and 275 B.C. Influenced by the imperturbability and indifference of the Indian Magi or gymnosophists, he came to regard peace of mind as an end to be achieved through steadfast opposition to all dogmatic assertions. Since Pyrrho left no written works, his thought has been transmitted by the writings of his disciple, Timon of Phlius (*c.* 320–230). It seems quite evident, from the fragments of Timon, that the basic elements of skepticism were already present, at least in primitive form, in the teachings of Pyrrho. (*See* PYRRHONISM.)

Later skeptics developed and systematized Pyrrhonian philosophy. Unfortunately, we know practically nothing about their lives. Some ancient authors say that the succession lapsed after Timon, to be taken up again later by Ptolemy of Cyrene. Others (see Diogenes Laertius, 9:115–16) establish an unbroken line of succession from Timon to Saturninus, the successor of Sextus Empiricus. Two authors, besides Sextus Empiricus, are singled out for their work in elaborating and systematizing the tropes (Gr. τρόποι), or ways of achieving suspension of judgment: Aenesidemus (sometime between 80 B.C. and A.D. 130) compiled the ten trope setting forth the relativity and the unreliability of sense cognition; Agrippa (no date known) worked out the five logical tropes challenging the validity of all argumentation.

Academicians. The Pyrrhonians, however, were not alone in their skeptical claims. Arcesillaus of Pitane (*c.* 315–241), the successor of Crates and founder of the Middle Academy, developed the elements of doubt inherent in Platonic thought (*see* PLATONISM). He is even credited by some authors, such as J. Burnet, with having been the first to formulate the skeptical τρόποι. Despite complete suspension of judgment in theoretical matters, Arcesilaus met the need for taking a stand in practical matters by defining a criterion of reasonableness (Gr. εὔλογον), founded on the convergence of representations with respect to a given judgment.

The Middle and New Academies, stemming as they did from the great Platonic tradition, did not join forces with Pyrrhonians whose theoretical views were practically identical with their own. The later Pyrrhonians suspected the Academicians of insincerity and of harboring an esoteric dogmatism; Academic skepticism was represented as being little more than a test of one's worthiness to be initiated in the hidden dogmas of the Academy.

In any case, it seems that the continuity of the Pyrrhonian school was interrupted, or at least that its influence was sporadic, during the period when academic skepticism developed. But it is more than probable that latter-day Pyrrhonism, which developed largely in connection with medical practice, owed much of its subtle dialectic and its boundless arsenal of skeptical tropes to the work of its Academic forebears.

Carneades of Cyrene (*c.* 219–129) defined a new criterion of persuasiveness or verisimilitude (Gr. πιθανόν) based on a single representation. The suspension of judgment, or ἐποχή, tended to be less pronounced as the Academy progressed. Eusebius quotes Numénius as saying that Arcesilaus was a Pyrrhonian in everything save in name (*Praep. Ev.* 14.6, *Patrologia Graeca*, ed. J. P. Migne, 21:1202). In Carneades's teaching there seems to have been an ambiguity that one of his disciples, Clitomachos, resolved in the sense of a complete ἐποχή; another, Metrodoros, interpreted Carneades as opening the way for the possibility of speculative judgment. In the end Academic skepticism practically disappeared in Greece, but according to Cicero, it continued to flourish in Rome.

Medieval and Renaissance Skeptics. Medieval mystics, as a rule, tended to disparage the capabilities of unaided reason. In the later Middle Ages, doubt was thus thrown on the validity of rational proofs of God's existence and similar matters.

Ockhamists. JOHN OF MIRECOURT, for example, judged propositions such as God's existence and the causal dependence of creatures to be incapable of demonstrative proof. His philosophy amounts to a form of probabilism [F. C. Copleston, *History of Philosophy*; v.3, Ockham to Suárez (1953) 3:129–34]. NICHOLAS OF AUTRECOURT, another Ockhamist, denied the possibility of inferring the existence of one thing from that of another, or the cogency of holding that accidents inhere in substances. He even invoked the well-known skeptical argument of the ''future adversary'' (viz, some future thinker may be able to refute what one now considers to be irrefutable) to urge caution regarding his own probable theories.

Renaissance Origins. A number of factors contributed to the rise of skepticism in the RENAISSANCE, among which one might mention the Reformation, with its challenge to the traditional criteria of religious and philosophical truth; the revival of interest in ancient literature, particularly in Cicero; the rediscovery and translation of the works of Sextus Empiricus; and the invention of printing, which diffused such works as the Pyrrhonian corpus of Sextus, the *Lives* of Diogenes Laertius, and Cicero's *Academica.*

Pyrrhonian and Academic doubt gained numerous followers in the period that stretches from the beginning of the 14th century to the advent of modern philosophy, though few proponents of skepticism fully adopted the radical principles of their ancient models. Systematic doubt became an effective way of expressing one's sense of personal freedom and worth, as well as a general feeling of contempt for the philosophical dogmatism of the Middle Ages.

NICHOLAS OF CUSA (1401–64) was an anti-Aristotelian whose work on ''learned ignorance'' (*De docta ignorantia*) presented wisdom as consisting in a recognition of one's own ignorance. Desiderius ERASMUS (1467–1536) in his *De libero arbitrio* expounds a form of fideistic skepticism (of which the Renaissance offers countless varieties) as a ''basis for remaining within the Catholic Church'' (Popkin, 5). His *In Praise of Folly* emphasizes the contradictions and excesses of scholastic systems. The Italian philosopher P. POMPONAZZI (1462–1525), though quoting Aristotle and St. Thomas Aquinas throughout his *Tractatus de immortalitate animae* and making constant use of scholastic terminology, refuses to admit that the immortality of the soul can be proved (ch. 15). Pomponazzi's approach amounts to a sort of philosophical probabilism in which Christian revelation exercises a normative role.

Cornelius Agrippa of Nettesheim (1486–1534), a German alchemist and philosopher who is said to have influenced the French humanist Montaigne, wrote a work *De incertitudine et vanitate omnium scientiarum* in which he asserted that nothing is more pernicious to human salvation than the arts and sciences (1726 ed., 7). Agrippa's skepticism, like that of most Renaissance skeptics, was fideistic in orientation. He likens knowledge to the serpent of the Garden of Eden. Revelation offers the sole means of overcoming the handicap arising from original sin.

Both Cardinal Sadoleto and Guy de Bruès wrote books intended to refute the arguments of the skeptics, but in such an indecisive manner as to reinforce the claims of skepticism.

Later Thinkers. Michel Eyquem de MONTAIGNE (1533–92) expressed a variety of philosophical attitudes in the *Essais* that give a running account of the evolution of his thought from 1572 to his death. Fideistic skepticism certainly marked an important phase of his development. Systematic doubt pervaded much of the intellectual life of the times, and Montaigne obviously made use of skeptical arguments to discredit immoderate dogmatic claims in all areas of knowledge (See Essais, Bk. 2, ch. 12). Pierre CHARRON (1541–1603), a disciple of Montaigne, advocated in his work *De la sagesse* a ''universal and total freedom of mind, as regards judgment and will'' (1606 ed., Bk. 2, ch. 2). He advised suspension of judgment in all matters save ''divine truths revealed by eternal wisdom'' and the actions of practical life (*ibid.*, 292). However, the general tenor of his assertions, e.g., on God and moral virtues, seems to contrast with his skeptical principles. Skepticism was considered by many apologists such as St. FRANCIS DE SALES (1567–1622) and J. P. Camus (1582–1653), Bishop of Belley, to be a potent weapon in the fight for Catholic orthodoxy, however strange this may appear to present-day Catholics.

Francisco SANCHES (1550–1623), a Portuguese (or Spanish) philosopher and physician, published in 1581 his *Tractatus de multum nobili et prima universali scientia quod nihil scitur.* All of his writings end with the question *Quid?*—to underline the fact that when all is said the basic question still remains unanswered. ''The more I think, the more I doubt,'' Sanches wrote. ''What can I say,'' he asked, ''that is not open to suspicion? For to me, all human affairs are suspect, even the very things I write at this moment'' [*Quod nihil scitur*, ed. J. de Carvalho; *Opera philosophica* (Coimbra 1955) 8]. God alone knows all. Hence faith and the holy Scriptures must be set apart from the things to be doubted (*ibid.*, 49), and so Sanches falls into the fideistic pattern of Renaissance skepticism.

Modern Philosophy. As philosophy moved into the modern era, the influence of ancient skepticism seemed to increase rather than diminish. Blaise Pascal's skeptical cry *''Le Pyrrhonisme est le vrai,''* with its fideistic orientation, does not seem particularly original in itself, nor does René Descartes's arsenal of skeptical arguments in the *Discours de la méthode* and the *Méditations sur la philosophie première.* Viewed in the context of Renaissance skepticism, Descartes's initial doubt comes into focus not as a set of personal problems, but as the expression of stock arguments that had been bandied about by countless philosophers for the previous 200 years at least, and that were still popular with his contemporaries.

Revival of Sextus Empiricus. Pierre GASSENDI (1592–1655), though not a full-fledged skeptic, was impressed with the works of Sextus Empiricus. Bayle's *Dictionnaire* (see below) refers to a summary of Sextus Empiricus in Gassendi's *De fine logicae* that greatly influenced contemporary thought (*Dict.*, 2306). The last chapter of the second book of Gassendi's *Exerci tationes paradoxicae adversus Aristoteleos* (Amsterdam 1649) is entitled: *Quod nulla sit scientia et maxime Aristotelea.* F. de la Mothe le Vayer (1588–1672) and S. J. Sorbière (1615–70), a disciple of Gassendi's, carried on the skeptical tradition well into the Cartesian period. In his *Opuscule ou Petit Traité sceptique,* published in Paris in 1646, towards the end of Descartes's career, the former extols the Pyrrhonian ἐποχή as the only reasonable attitude (*Opuscule,* 170). He believes that skepticism, of which he considers Sextus to have been the prime exponent [cf. *Cincq Dialogues* (Mons 1671) 1], is in full accord with the condemnations of worldly wisdom by St. Paul and Isaiah (Opuscule, 197–98) and therefore harmonizes best with Christian revelation (*ibid.,* 200–01).

In the modern period, skepticism has often assumed the role of an indispensable prolegomenon to critical philosophical speculation, or has served to clear the way for reliance on the new methods of science. No doubt the thorough going skeptics of antiquity would have frowned on such fideistic or positivistic orientations.

Huet and Bayle. Pierre Daniel HUET (1630–1721), a French bishop who severely criticized Descartes's philosophy, wrote a work on the weakness of the human mind (*Traité philosophique de la faiblesse de l'esprit humain,* Amsterdam 1723). In it he expresses admiration for Pyrrhonism [ed. of London (1741) 125–31], which lays bare the imperfections of human knowledge (*ibid.,* 20–21) and forces men to acknowledge the role of faith as an aid to the ''faltering understanding.''

Pierre BAYLE (1647–1706), author of the famous *Dictionnaire historique et critique,* was a fervent reader of Montaigne's *Essais.* On the subject of Pyrrhonism, he assures his readers that most physicists of his day are convinced of the incomprehensibility of nature, and thus agree with Pyrrhonism and the Academy (2d ed., 2306). Like Pascal and Saint-Cyran, he sees skepticism as a chastening experience by which men are led to the Christian faith (2d ed., 2308).

Others. David Hume's critique of substance and causality leads to a phenomenalistic philosophy that owes much to reflection on the methods of the physical sciences. Immanuel Kant's *Critique of Pure Reason* presupposes Hume's attack on traditional concepts, and pronounces the NOUMENA or natures of things to be unknowable. Critical philosophy appears as the crowning achievement of the mind, presupposing an earlier skeptical phase. Further inquiries would reveal skeptical components or prerequisites in other modern and contemporary philosophical systems, such as LOGICAL POSITIVISM, and Herbert Spencer's or Francis Herbert Bradley's peculiar brands of AGNOSTICISM.

Nature Of Skepticism

Sextus, whom most authors acknowledge to have been the major exponent of Pyrrhonism, defines skepticism as a mental attitude or a capacity (Gr. δύναμις) to recognize the opposition of appearances and judgments, thence to suspend judgment, and finally to achieve the mental tranquillity that dogmatists vainly seek to attain by rash assertions (*Pyrrh. Hyp.*, 1.6). The word δύναμις in the Greek text is meant to indicate that skepticism of the Pyrrhonian variety refuses to be considered as a speculative system or as a philosophy. Renaissance and modern skeptics (e.g., Montaigne, Sanches, Pascal, and Hume) tend to differ from their ancient counterparts in that suspension of judgment becomes for them a steppingstone to something else. This certainly accounts for the greater earnestness of modern skeptics. They do not seek suspension of judgment merely for the sake of tranquillity, but to make the mind receptive to revelation, to science, or to some great philosophical intuition.

Basic Concepts. A careful reading of Sextus reveals three main components of the skeptic attitude: equipollence, suspension of judgment, and tranquillity. The first means the equality of arguments on both sides of any question. It presupposes contrariety in man's perception of reality, and controversy in the accounts given of the same things by different people. The second, suspension of judgment, results from equipollence and controversy. It involves negative attitudes to definition (Gr. ἀοριστία), external expression (Gr. ἀφασία), and inclination (Gr. ἀρρεψία). The third component of the skeptic attitude or method is tranquillity (Gr. ἀταραξία). The resolve to suspend judgment removes the mental anguish or uneasiness attendant on a dogmatist search for truth. Applied to the passions, tranquillity becomes apathy or metriopathy, or again, indifference—the external expression of Pyrrhonian quietude.

Sextus tries to avoid the contradictions of ἀφασία or ἐποχή by stating that his propositions are not meant to be dogmatic assertions or judgments, but mere expressions of what appears to him. He is no more attached to them than to their opposites. The very phrase ''no more this than that'' (οὐδέν μᾶλλον) cancels itself out, along with everything else (*Pyrrh. Hyp.* 1.7, 18, 19).

Tropes are systematic means of ensuring suspension of judgment. Sextus lays great store by the ten tropes of Aenesidemus, directed mainly against sensation, which he develops at great length (*ibid.,* 1.14). The reliability of sense impressions is questioned because of (1) differences in animals, which make for differences in the impressions they receive from the same objects; (2) differences in men; (3) differences in the senses of an individual man; (4) differences in the circumstances or states of a man; (5) the different positions and places occupied by a person; (6) diverse relationships and mixtures in which an object is implicated when it impinges on a sense; (7) diverse conditions or underlying structures of the object; (8) the general relativity of all things, which precludes statements as to their natures; (9) differences in one's perception of an event as a result of its frequent or rare occurrence; and (10) in ethical matters, differences of laws, habits, and customs.

Agrippa's five dialectical tropes present a sequence of logical traps designed to thwart any attempt at valid reasoning (*Pyrrh. Hyp.* 1.15). The first trope sets forth the fact of controversy, which prevents the mind from giving assent to anything. If one tries to prove the truth of an opinion, he must prove the premise of his proof and so on ad infinitum (2d trope). He may wish to avoid infinite regress in any one of three ways, immediate experience, hypothesis or postulate, and circular reasoning, but these are blocked off by the remaining three tropes. Immediate experience is relative to the subject and does not make known the being of the object. There is no justification for assuming a given hypothesis rather than its opposite. And finally proving the same by the same amounts to no proof at all. Diogenes's account follows the same order. Sextus presents two further tropes on the impossibility of apprehending an object (*ibid.*, 1.16) and eight other modes against causal explanation (*ibid.*, 1.17).

Evaluation. It is impossible to evaluate generally all authors who manifest some affinity or admiration for the skeptical attitude. Hence the judgment here bears primarily on the form of skepticism commonly regarded as the most radical, the most influential, and the most highly developed, i.e., that expounded by Sextus Empiricus.

Careful scrutiny of the works of Sextus reveals two distinct phases, or aspects, in the total attitude. The first stems directly from the difficulties experienced in man's knowledge of reality and the endless controversies among proponents of various explanations. It involves uneasiness and frustration of the mind in its search for truth. Doubt and suspension of judgment flow from an incapacity to unravel the difficulties of being and cognition. Pascal or Hume probably never got much beyond this stage. However the Pyrrhonians, confronted as they were with the stupendous dogmatic constructions of the Epicureans and Stoics, came to look upon their ἐποχή as something to be nurtured and valued, particularly as compared to the rash opinions of other thinkers.

Unwittingly, a second phase or aspect then took form. Principles such as that of equipollence reflect a crystallization of doubt. Suspension of judgment becomes a systematic reaction to all opinions, thus stifling the search for truth, Ἐποχή, which ordinarily gives no cause for rejoicing, produces peace of mind.

The elements of both phases combine to constitute the final attitude. The skeptic sees himself as still searching for truth, but the systematization of doubt in the many tropes, the willingness to reject arguments on the a priori ground that some future thinker may be able to prove them invalid, reveal basic contradictions in his radical skepticism. Many texts express an uneasy awareness of these incompatible elements. The numerous attempts to correct the apparent dogmatism of language, the use of analogies such as that of the ladder (which is toppled after an ascent), of the fire (which consumes itself), of the cathartic (which eliminates itself along with body wastes), these and many others represent efforts to reconcile the inner contradictions of radical skepticism.

The problems of practical living represent the major stumbling block of skepticism. The mind may refuse assent in speculative matters, but the requirements of everyday life are incompatible with a universal ἐποχή or with the sophistic tendencies inherent in equipollence.

However, historians owe a debt of gratitude to skeptics for the wealth of materials relating to ancient thought they preserve in their writings. Again, their relentless attacks on DOGMATISM impresses upon the nonskeptic the limitations of human knowledge, the importance of moderation in judgment, and the necessity of a rigorous method in the search for truth.

See Also: CERTITUDE; EPISTEMOLOGY; KNOWLEDGE; KNOWLEDGE, THEORIES OF; TRUTH.

Bibliography: SEXTUS EMPIRICUS, *Opera,* ed. H. MUTSCHMANN and J. MAU, 3 v. (Leipzig 1958); tr. R. G. BURY, 3 v. (*Loeb Classical Library* 1933–36). DIOGENES LAERTIUS, *Lives of Eminent Philosophers,* tr. R. D. HICKS, 2 v. (*Loeb Classical Library* 184, 185; rev. ed. 1942) bk. 9. CICERO, *De natura deorum; Academica,* tr. H. RACKHAM (*Loeb Classical Library* 268; 1956). R. H. POPKIN, *The History of Scepticism from Erasmus to Descartes* (Assen 1960). E. R. BEVAN, *Stoics and Sceptics* (Oxford 1913). A. GOEDECKEMEYER, *Die Geschichte des griechischen Skeptizismus* (Leipzig 1905). V. C.

L. BROCHARD, *Les Sceptiques grecs* (2d ed. Paris 1923). F. C. COPLESTON, *History of Philosophy* (Westminster, Md. 1946–); v.3, Descartes to Leibniz (1958).

[V. CAUCHY]

SKILLIN, EDWARD SIMEON

Editor and publisher; b. New York City, Jan. 23, 1904; d. Montclair, New Jersey, Aug. 14, 2000. Skillin attended school in Glen Ridge, New Jersey, and at Phillips Academy in Andover, Massachusetts. He graduated Phi Beta Kappa from Williams College in 1925. In 1933 he completed an M.A. in political science at Columbia University, where he studied under Cornelius Clifford, a noted lecturer in theology who ''opened before me the wealth and depth of the [Catholic] tradition, and the full meaning of the Mass.'' Clifford encouraged Skillin to acquaint himself with Portsmouth Priory, the Benedictine foundation in Rhode Island, and eventually Skillin became a lifelong Benedictine Oblate. In 1945, Skillin married Jane Anne Edwards; they had five children and seven grandchildren.

Years at *Commonweal.* In 1933, Skillin joined the *Commonweal,* an independent Catholic journal of opinion founded in 1924 by Michael Williams. He spent his professional career over 60 years with the review.

Under the tutelage of managing editor George N. SHUSTER, Skillin learned the rudiments of professional journalism. Shuster left the magazine in 1937 because of his disagreement with Williams's support of Franco during the Spanish Civil War. In 1938, Skillin and fellow junior editor Philip Burnham purchased *Commonweal* for $9,000. They paid off the magazine's creditors and reversed its editorial support for Franco, becoming one of the few Catholic journals in the United States to espouse a neutral position. Under Skillin's long editorship, *Commonweal* placed greater emphasis on social justice and the social implications of the Christian message. In this regard, Skillin credited Virgil Michel, OSB, the founder of the liturgical movement in America, with stressing the connection between the liturgy and social action, and the French philosopher Jacques Maritain. In 1967, he resigned the post ''in favor of the stimulating views of the younger editors'' and to devote himself entirely to the duties of publisher.

Skillin wrote more than 3,000 articles, editorials, and book reviews for *Commonweal,* on topics ranging from worker cooperatives to racism, disarmament, food policy, ecumenism, human rights, liturgical reform, foreign affairs, and economic justice. Under his leadership, the magazine became deeply involved in such controversies as the Senator Joseph McCarthy affair, opposition to the Vietnam War, the debate over the papal encyclical *Humanae vitae* and theological dissent in the Church, and the abortion and euthanasia issues. Skillin remained principal owner of the magazine until 1984 when he donated his stock to the newly formed, nonprofit Commonweal Foundation.

Skillin was known for his kindliness and spiritual tranquillity, his physical resiliency and intellectual acumen even at an advanced age, his financial stewardship that kept the precarious *Commonweal* afloat, his solicitude for the less fortunate, and his dedication to justice and the common good.

Bibliography: R. VAN ALLEN, *The* Commonweal *and American Catholicism* (Philadelphia 1974); *Being Catholic:* Commonweal *from the Seventies to the Nineties* (Chicago 1993).

[P. JORDAN]

SKY AND SKY GODS

In all ages and in all religions the sky was regarded as a symbol and manifestation of the divine (cf. the distinction between sky and heaven). Knowledge of the mythology, *Weltanschauung,* social order, and environment is of fundamental importance for understanding the function of heaven and the gods of heaven. Three types of function are distinguished, which often overlap.

Heaven is conceived as the symbol and name of the Supreme Being. This is the case among the Chinese (*Tien*), Mongols (''by the power of the eternal Heaven,'' ''Heaven has commanded me''), the Sumerians (An), and especially, among the inhabitants of the Afro-Asiatic steppes and the herding peoples. The Indo-European languages employ the terms *Devah, Dyaus, Die, Tivar, Zeus, Deus, Diespiter,* and *Jupiter* to designate the creator and lord of all things. Side by side with the active worship of the Supreme God of Heaven there is a tendency to make him a *Deus otiosus* (as in Africa) and to concentrate on the active worship of other religious phenomena that seem to be closer and to play a more central role in daily life.

Heaven is viewed as the realm (often arranged in tiers) or dwelling place of the Supreme Being and of other supraterrestrial powers or of the dead. Heaven is the place of sacred action. Its gradation and the composition of its inhabitants are often based on the syncretistic merging of the individual gods of conquered or foreign peoples: in Egypt, *Hathor, Maut, Nut, Neith,* and *Isis;* among the Aztecs, *Tezcatlipoca, Tlaloc, Quetzalcoatl, Huitzilopochtli.* Among the Pygmies, their god *Epilipili* lives in the sky because men were unworthy of him. The Iro-

Sculpture of a 17th-century Sun God. (©Macduff Everton/CORBIS)

quois relate that the daughter of their Celestial Chief fell through a hole in the sky to the earth and became the mother of their culture-heroes. The shamans visit the celestial realms.

Heaven is thought of also as a cosmic world-principle. The union of heaven (mostly masculine) and earth (always feminine) determines, for example, the Taoistic world order (*Ying-Yang*). In Polynesia, through this union (*Rangi-Pépé*) the world is born. Both are fertility principles (as is clear from the rock pictures of the Yoruba in West Africa). The visible heaven is a representative of the divine. Accordingly, the natural phenomena connected with it are frequently the symbols or hypostases of divinity. Among the Haida Indians, the term Sins means heaven, air, storm, and weather. The identification of heaven with rain (*Jupiter pluvius*) or with thunder (among the Semang on the Malacca peninsula, the combination *Ta Ped'n-Karei*) is very commonly made.

The assumption that the Supreme Being is the personification of the material heaven or sky (the view of R. Pettazzoni) runs counter to the scientific evaluation of the evidence. The phenomena mentioned above are best explained by supposing the presence of an original idea, founded in the nature of man, but variously modified and hypostatized in individual cases.

Bibliography: J. HAEKEL, *Lexikon für Theologie und Kirche,* ed. J. HOFER and K. RAHNER, 10 v. (2d, new ed. Freiburg 1957–65) 5:352–354. S. MORENZ, *Die Religion in Geschichte und Gegenwart,* 7 v. (3d ed. Tübingen 1957–65) 3:328–331. M. ELIADE, *Patterns in Comparative Religion,* tr. R. SHEED (New York 1958) 38–123, an excellent treatment with copious bibliog. G. FOUCART, J. HASTINGS, ed., *Encyclopedia of Religion & Ethics,* 13 v. (Edinburgh 1908–27)11:580–585. R. PETTAZZONI, *The All-Knowing God* (New York 1956). F. HEILER, *Die Religionen der Menschheit* (Stuttgart 1959).

[W. DURPÉ]

SLAVERY, I (IN THE BIBLE)

Although slavery existed in Israel on only a small scale, it was an integral part of the ancient Semitic culture; basically, it was an economic institution that remained unchanged in a stable economy.

Enslavement. In Israel the following were reduced to slavery: captives taken in raids (Am 1.6, 9), insolvent debtors (Am 2.6; 2 Kgs 4.1; Neh 5.5, 8), convicted thieves unable to make retribution (Ex 22.2), young girls sold by their fathers into conditional slavery (Ex 21.7-11), and non-Israelite prisoners taken in war (2 Chr 28.8-15). The captives taken in war might become Temple slaves, domestic slaves, or state slaves. It was customary to dedicate some of the captives to Temple service (Nm 31.25–47; Jos 9.21–27); some became slaves in private households; others were made to work as slaves on state projects. The insolvent debtors mentioned above were sold into slavery to satisfy their creditors. To avoid the danger of wholesale population drift of small-scale farmers into slavery as a result of insolvency, the Law limited such slavery to a maximum of six years (Ex 21.2; Dt 15.12); at the end of this service, they were to be provided with the means necessary for returning to normal life (Dt 15.13–18). A Hebrew who had sold himself into slavery to escape poverty was to serve till the JUBILEE YEAR. If his master was a foreigner, he could either purchase his freedom or ask to be redeemed by one of his relatives any time before the Jubilee Year (Lv 25.47–55). Yet this humanitarian legislation of 7th-year release and jubilee-year liberty remained largely theoretical, as is seen in the unfulfilled pledge given the Hebrew slaves at the time of the Babylonian siege (Jer 34.8-22; see Mendelsohn, 86–87).

Legislation. Legally, the slave was property, without name or genealogy, a commodity to be sold, bought, or inherited. However, OT legislation, especially the Deuteronomic code, mindful of Israel's slavery in Egypt (Dt 5.15; 15.15; 24.18) and increasingly considerate of the individual, aimed at keeping the number of Hebrew slaves to a minimum and mitigating the severities in their life. A man who was married when he became a slave could take his wife back with him at the end of his service, but if he was single at the beginning of his service and was given a wife by his master, the wife and any children born of the couple belonged to the master (Ex 21.3-4). A significant difference between Hebrew and foreign slaves was that the latter could be held in servitude permanently and handed on with other family property (Lv 25.44–46). Religious privileges were accorded also to slaves; Hebrew and non-Hebrew slaves were to be circumcised (Gn 17.12) and enjoy the Sabbath rest (Ex 20.11; 23.12; Dt 5.14). A woman captured in war and taken as a wife, if later divorced, could neither be sold nor again reduced to slavery; her husband had to allow her to go free (Dt 21.10-14). The death penalty was prescribed for a man who deceitfully sold a fellow Israelite into slavery (Dt 24.7). The OT codes limit their legislation to domestic slaves; no prescriptions are given for the state or Temple slaves mentioned in nonlegal texts.

Role in OT Economy. Slavery, as such, was not a prominent feature of the Israelite economy. The agricultural projects were too small to lend themselves to the exploitation of slave labor; the hired laborer did this work more economically. There were no private industrial projects of great scope in Israel, nor was there a continued international commerce. Yet the nation had its building programs and, for a time, a metal industry. Israel's most outstanding use of state slaves was in the copper smeltery and foundry built by King Solomon at Asiongaber [see N. Glueck, *Bulletin of the American Schools of Oriental Research* 79 (1940) 2–18]. Some slaves were attached to the Temple throughout Israel's history (Jos 9.23, 27; Ezr 8.20). But the majority of Israel's slaves were found in private homes performing domestic chores.

Place in New Testament Ethics. The attitude of the NT toward the institution of slavery was primarily religious, not social. Christ and His Apostles did not give new legislation to oppose the system of existing slavery, but preached principles that would logically lead to its abolition. If all are children of the same Father, no essential distinction can remain between slave and free man (1 Cor 12.13; Gal 3.28; Col 3.11).

The Apostles did not intend an immediate change in social institutions; theirs was a religious message with the primary intention of making their converts obedient to God's revelation in Christ (Eph 6.5–9; Col 3.22–4.1; 1 Pt 2.18). Paul does not command Philemon to free his slave, although he implicitly recommends this in reminding him that Onesimus is his brother in Christ and is to be treated as such (Phlm 15–16). Moreover, he exhorts the slaves of the Corinth Church not to be impatient with their station, but to accept it, recognizing that they have a higher life in Christ (1 Cor 7.21–24). Nevertheless, in the NT the foundations were laid for a slow but effective social revolution that eventually caused the abolition of slavery in Christian countries.

Bibliography: I. MENDELSOHN, *The Interpreters Dictionary of the Bible,* ed. G. A. BUTTRICK et al. (New York 1951–57) 4:383–391; *Slavery in the Ancient Near East* (New York 1949). R. SALOMON, *L'Esclavage en droit comparé juif et romain* (Paris 1931). M. ROBERTI, *La lettera di S. Paulo a Filemone e la condizione giuridica dello schiavo fuggitivo* (Milan 1933). P. HEINISCH, ''Das Sklavenrecht in Israel und im alten Orient,'' *Studia catholica* 11 (1934–35) 201–218. R. DEVAUX, *Ancient Israel, Its Life and Institutions,* tr. J. MCHUGH (New York 1961) 80–90.

[H. C. FRANCO]

SLAVERY, II (AND THE CHURCH)

Slavery is here understood to signify a social and economic institution in which one human being is the legal property of another, or, as the condition of such a human being who is thus become a *res non persona,* a human chattel without rights or privileges.

For the understanding of the Church's attitude to slavery and for balanced judgment on the morality of slavery, two things must be kept in mind: the Church's attitude toward social questions in general, and the fact that slavery has existed under different forms.

The Church was born into a world in which slavery was universally accepted as a social and economic institution pertaining to the very structure of society, just as today the system of remunerated employment is taken for granted. As in modern society no one would be likely to contemplate seriously the abolition of the existing system, so neither did it occur to Christians of the early Church to advocate the abolition of slavery. The Church did, however, from the beginning, urgently insist on the mutual rights and duties existing between masters and slaves, just as in our times she emphasizes the mutual rights and duties of employers and employees. God became man and founded His Church, not in order to usher in a new social, economic, or political order, but rather to change the hearts of men according to the prophecy of Ezekiel: ''I will give them a new heart and put a new spirit within them; I will remove the stony heart from their bodies, and replace it with a natural heart, so that they will live according to my statutes, and observe and carry out my ordinances'' (Ez 11.19–20). The Church took men and society as she found them and did her utmost to transform them. Thus St. Paul wrote to the Galatians: ''For all you who have been baptized into Christ, have put on Christ. There is neither Jew nor Greek; there is neither slave nor free-man; there is neither male nor female. For you are all one in Christ Jesus'' (Gal 3.2728; see also 1 Cor 12.13; Eph 5.9; Col 3.22–24; 1 Pt 2.28). An instructive concrete case of Paul's conception of things, and of the Church's constant attitude ever since toward the master-slave relationship, and later to the employer-employee relationship, is afforded by Paul's one-page letter to Philemon.

Different Forms. The term ''slavery'' did not always have the odious connotation that it has today. The history of slavery shows that two quite distinct forms of it have existed side by side, depending for their distinction less upon juridical institution than upon the virtue of the owners. In the form known as symbiotic slavery, master and slave worked together for their mutual good as human beings. In this form there was, on the part of the slave, fidelity, devotedness, and willing service, all in keeping with true human dignity; and, on the part of the master, kindness, respect, and even true charity, while between master and slave there often existed real friendship. The slave was part of the household and was treated as such from the moment he came into the service of his master until he died. The second historical form of slavery has been called parasitic, and in this form the master or owner exploited the labor of the slave for his own private advantage and pleasure. In this form there was inhumanity, brutality, and vice in both masters and slaves. Slavery in this form was obviously diametrically opposed to the spirit of Christianity and, as such, was always condemned by the Christian Church.

The first form of slavery the Church never opposed directly, but sought rather to transform it from within. The idea of one human being belonging to another as a piece of property was always repugnant to the Christian concept of human dignity. By changing the minds of men, masters and slaves, and legislators, the Church contributed efficaciously, although indirectly, to the total disappearance of slavery in the strict sense in all Christian lands before the 13th century.

It can be said that some men are naturally disposed, not indeed to be slaves, that is, to be the property or chattels of other men, but to serve, that is, to work under direction for their own good and for the common good of all. Moreover, in the Christian view of things, work and service are noble activities fully in keeping with true human and Christian dignity. Christ Himself came on earth to do the will of His Father (Jn 4.34; 6.8; Heb10.7, 9) and to be obedient unto the death of the cross (Phil 2.8) out of love for His Eternal Father and out of love for mankind (see St. Thomas, *Summa Theologiae* 3a, 46.2). St. Thomas maintained that a life of free service in this sense would have been part of human life in the state of original justice before the fall (ST 1a, 96.3); but in no wise would a life of penal servitude (*ibid.,* ad 1 and art. 4), which was regarded by him and by many of the Fathers of the Church as a consequence of sin (see St. Augustine, Civ. 19.15). St. Augustine makes the same point with regard to work: from being a glad and even effortless sharing in God's creative activity, it becomes as a result of sin a painful toil and labor (*Gen. ad litt.* 8.8). St. Thomas's teaching that between master and slave strict justice could not exist (see ST 2a2ae, 57.4, and passim) has been frequently grossly misinterpreted through being understood out of its true historical and doctrinal context. Historically, slavery in the strict sense no longer existed in Christian lands in the time of St. Thomas. Doctrinally, St. Thomas was trying to explain that the virtue governing the master-servant relationship is not mere justice but something greater, for the simple reason that between master and servant there are mutual rights and duties that last as long as the relationship remains. By insisting precisely on these mutual rights and obligations, the Church was instrumental in bringing about the abolition of slavery in the strict sense, transforming it gradually into a state of noble service on the part of the inferior and of conscientious care on the part of the superior or master. She insisted over and over again on the inalienable right of man to freedom, to guide his own life, to marry, to enter religion, and to take Orders. She insisted that servants should be given free time to attend to their own lives and families, and forbade, for instance, at the Council of Auxerre in 578 all unnecessary work on Sundays (c.16, J. D. Mansi, *Sacrorum Conciliorum nova et amplissima collectio* 9.913). On the other hand, she condemned most severely those who, under one pretext or another, incited the servants to revolt against their masters (see c.3 of the Council of Gangres in the middle of the 4th century, Mansi 2.1102). Instances of such legislation could be given without number.

The Slave Trade. The great geographical discoveries by Spain and Portugal in the 15th and 16th centuries brought in their train the recrudescence of slavery so that the problem of the morality of slavery and enslavement again became acute. After a brief period of hesitation and uncertainty, caused by inaccurate information on conditions in Africa and the two Americas, and by a desire to avoid greater evils, the Church unreservedly condemned colonial slavery, and every type of slave trade, as inhuman and immoral. The slave trade as such was not something new. It had been practiced long before Christian times and the Church, from the beginning, regarded it as immoral. Numerous documents attest to the fact. The following are easily accessible. In 873, John VIII wrote to the rulers of Sardinia exhorting them and ordering them to restore freedom to slaves bought from the Greeks (H. Denzinger, *Enchiridion symbolorum* 668). In 1537, Paul III excommunicated those who enslaved the Native Americans and confiscated their property (Denzinger 1495). In 1838, Gregory XVI condemned all forms of colonial slavery and the slave trade, calling it *inhumanum illud commercium* (Denzinger 2745-46). In a letter to the bishops of Brazil (May 5, 1888), Leo XIII recalled the Church's unceasing efforts in the course of centuries to get rid of colonial slavery and the slave trade and expressed his satisfaction that Brazil had at last abolished it (Acta Leonis XIII, 8, 169–192). From the 15th century Catholic missionaries, theologians, and statesmen never ceased to strive for the abolition of ignominious traffic in human beings. During the French Revolution, at the instigation of a Catholic priest, the Abbé H. Grégoire, the National Assembly in 1794 decreed the abolition of slavery and the slave trade in all French colonies. In1890, Cardinal LAVIGERIE founded the antislave league of France for combatting of slavery and the slave trade on an international basis. In a radio message to the workers of Spain, March 11, 1951, Pius XII stated succinctly the Church's constant attitude to slavery in all its forms. ''The Church,'' he said, ''never preached social revolution, but everywhere and at all times, from the letter of Paul to Philemon up to the great social teachings of the popes in the 19th and 20th centuries, she did her utmost to see that consideration was taken more of man himself than of economic and technical advantages so that all men might have the possibility of living a life worthy of a Christian and of a human being'' (*Acta Apostolicae Sedis* 1951, 214). Today the Church still spares no effort to save men from the crypto-slavery of the modern industrial world.

See Also: LAS CASAS, BARTOLOMÉ DE.

Bibliography: H. A. WALLON, *Histoire de l'esclavage dans l'antiquité,* 3 v. (2d ed. Paris 1879). J. HÖFFNER, *Christentum und Menschenwürde* (Trier 1947). M. LENGELLÉ, *L'Esclavage* (Paris 1955). A. KATZ, *Christentum und Sklaverei* (Vienna 1926). L. HANKE, *The Spanish Struggle for Justice in the Conquest of America* (Philadelphia 1949); *Aristotle and the American Indians* (London 1959).

[C. WILLIAMS]

SLAVERY, III (HISTORY OF)

Although slavery was found among all peoples of antiquity, an account of its development until its abolition in the most advanced countries during the 19th century can be limited to the Christian Era, beginning, that is, when Rome ruled the entire Mediterranean world.

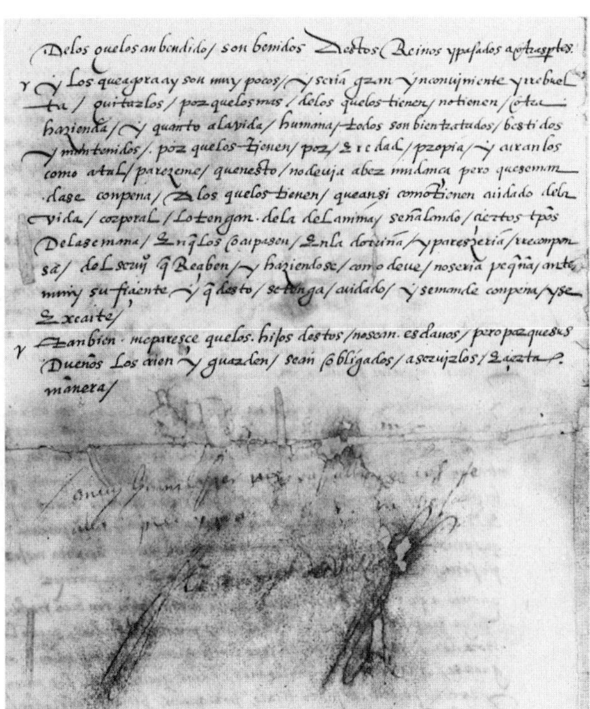

Letter to King Charles V of Spain, 1542, from Hernando Cortez in which Cortez advises putting natives of the colonies under the protection of the Crown to prevent their enslavement.

Slavery in the Roman Empire. The legal status of the slave improved measurably toward the end of the Roman Republic and especially under the ROMAN EMPIRE. The powers of masters were reduced by law. It was forbidden to deliver a slave to wild beasts without a formal judicial sentence, and any master who mistreated a slave was obliged to sell him. An ailing or aged slave who was abandoned by his master was freed *ipso facto.* By degrees, the magistrate replaced the master as judge in slave proceedings. The idea of the slave as a person, still vague, gradually became more precise. These innovations reflected the theories of STOICISM that had begun to exert an influence in the first century before the Christian Era. In the early Empire, SENECA maintained that slavery was merely corporal and that the spirit remained *sui juris.* Ideas such as these soon infiltrated the works of jurists, as can be seen in the well-known text of Florentinus: ''Slavery is a creation of the *ius gentium,* by which a man is subjected, contrary to nature, to ownership on the part of another'' (*Corpus iuris civilis, Digesta* 1.5.4). The entire law of servitude was considered to be a matter of the *ius gentium.* Tryphoninus declared: ''Liberty is contained in the natural law; domination was introduced by the *ius gentium*'' (*ibid.* 12.6.64). Ulpian added, in a passage frequently quoted in medieval acts of manumission: ''Manumissions are also comprised in the *ius gentium* . . . seeing that by natural law all were born free, and manu-

Under the Roman Yoke: The Iberians driven under the yoke and sold as slaves by the Romans. Engraving from a painting by R. Cogghe. (©CORBIS)

Abraham Lincoln (left, center) at first reading of the Emancipation Proclamation.

mission was not known because slavery itself was unknown; but when slavery came in through the *ius gentium,* there followed the relief given by manumission'' (*ibid.* 1.1.4). Another passage from Ulpian shows the position on slavery that classical roman law attained: ''According to the civil law, slaves have no rights; it is not the same according to natural law, for according to natural law all men are equal'' (*ibid.* 50.17.32). Although the Stoics helped to humanize legislation concerning slavery, they never dreamed of furthering the abolition of the institution. Their philosophy aimed to humanize relations among men without altering the traditional order.

Early Christian Views. The early Church entertained ideas about slavery somewhat similar to those of the Stoics. For St. Paul as for Seneca, slavery was merely external. It did not exist in the moral and spiritual domain. Although the Apostle excluded slave merchants from the numbers of the just (1 Tm 1.10), he nonetheless regarded slavery as a legitimate institution: ''Let every man remain in the calling in which he was called. Wast thou a slave when called? Let it not trouble thee.'' (1 Cor 7.20–21). Furthermore he advised slaves to serve their masters ''with fear and trembling'' (Eph 6.5). His well-known letter to Philemon, to whom he returned a fugitive slave in whose regard he recommended indulgence, illustrates clearly the attitude of the early Church. [*See* SLAVERY (IN THE BIBLE); SLAVERY (AND THE CHURCH).]

AMBROSIASTER, commenting on the Epistle to the Colossians (4.1), made a very lucid presentation of patristic teaching. Masters, he wrote, had duties toward their slaves. God had created only free men, but because of worldly wickedness it was possible that men born free might be reduced to slavery as a consequence of war (a situation considered as commonplace). Slavery as the result of war could not exist in the eyes of God; sin alone could be the source of this social evil. Among the Fathers of the East, St. GREGORY OF NYSSA opposed the legitimacy of slavery in his homily on Ecclesiastes, but the theory of slavery as a consequence of sin perdured. The Western Fathers went further, and St. AUGUSTINE looked upon slavery as an expression of the divine order: ''It is clear, then, that sin is the primary cause of servitude in the sense of a social status in which one man is compelled to be subjected to another man. Nor does this befall a man, save by the decree of God, who is never unjust and who knows how to impose appropriate punishments on different sinners'' (*Civ.* 19.15). If doctrinally the Church seemed uninterested in changing social conditions, in practice she was inclined to favor freeing the slaves. From this point of view, one of the most efficacious instruments was the *manumissio in ecclesia,* legally approved in 321 under Constantine; it was, however, a charitable work devoid of any obligatory power. About 358 the Council of GANGRA anathematized anyone who, under the pretext of religion, taught slaves to resist their masters, to flee their service, or not to obey willingly and with all deference.

There was a recrudescence of slavery in the third, fourth, and fifth centuries, accompanying the decline of the *pax romana* and the renewed wars against the barbarians. SALVIAN, for example, noted (*De gubernatione Dei* 4.14) that bands of slaves supervised by *actores* and *silentiarii* continued to exist. Under the influence of the colonate the condition of some slaves was ameliorated, but slavery in its full rigor was in evidence everywhere while the German states were being built on the ruins of the Roman Empire. In these states, as in the Empire, enslavement had its source in war, even in war between Christians. The slave trade was equally important. The *Vita* of St. ELIGIUS, Bishop of Noyon in the seventh century, makes it clear that ships bearing more than 100 slaves were not unusual at this time.

Slavery in Medieval Europe. Every European country accepted slavery for a more or less extended period during the Middle Ages. Even in countries in which social development was most rapid, slavery did not disappear before the tenth century. There was general progress, however, toward what is called, for want of a better or more generally accepted term, servitude or semifreedom. (*See* FEUDALISM.) The semifree could no longer be sold at the block. Servitude developed both in countries in which slavery lasted until the end of the Middle Ages or well beyond, i.e., the Mediterranean countries, and in others. The transition from slavery to servitude was first accomplished in Western Continental countries, but slavery continued alongside servitude in the maritime regions where Christian peoples were in contact with heterodox populations, as well as in central and eastern Europe, where the Slavs, still pagan, were often reduced to servitude. Even in Great Britain, prisoners taken during the wars among the Anglo-Saxons, Welsh, Irish, and Scots were for a long time reduced to slavery. As late as 1102 a council held in London saw fit to decree: ''Let no one hereafter presume to engage in that nefarious trade in which hitherto in England men were usually sold like brute animals.'' In reality slavery had by this time become rare in Britain and was found only in a very small segment of British society in frontier territories. When political unity was accomplished, slavery disappeared just as it had in other western European nations that had been inhabited by several different peoples but governed by a central authority.

Evolution of the Term in the Middle Ages. The Latin word *sclavus*—common source of the words slave, *esclave* (Fr.), *esclavo* (Sp.), *escravo* (Port.), *schiavo* (It.), and *Sklave* (Ger.)—was not yet in use during the early medieval period when slavery was common throughout Europe. Medieval slavery was then the heir of the ancient institution, the continuity of which was still in question. The slave was still the *servus,* the *mancipium,* as in Rome. It was not until slaves began to be recruited from entirely new sources that new terms appeared to describe those who were not free. Among these terms *sclavus,* derived from the ethnic name of the Slavic peoples, was widely accepted. In its Latin form it first appeared in Germany in the tenth century. At the same time a similar Arabic form, *siklābi* (pl. *sakāliba*), was in use in Muslim Spain. This was because an important trade route brought to the Spain of the Caliphs of CÓRDOBA, and from there to the rest of the Muslim world, large numbers of Slavs who were captured or bought on the eastern frontiers of Germany and transported across western Europe. The trade ceased in the 11th century, and the semantic evolution of *sclavus* and *siklābi* was arrested, in the sense of interest here, in the countries where these terms had first appeared. *Sclavus* disappeared altogether and *siklābi* came to be restricted to the nonfree eunuch.

In the 13th century, however, *sclavus,* meaning slave, reappeared in Italy, whence it spread over Europe. At this time the Italians were in effect at the beginning of a new trade route that served especially the Mediterranean world. Enslaved Slavs from southeastern Europe and the shores of the Black Sea began to be imported into Italy. The Slavs once again became the object of a very active trade, with the result that their name was soon used to describe all the nonfree. From Italy, Slavic slavery spread through the south of France into eastern Spain, where the Catalan *sclau* came into general use in the 14th century. On the other hand, there were never any enslaved Slavs in the Castilian political complex or in Portugal, since these countries participated very little in Mediterranean economic life. As a result the term *slave* appeared there only much later.

Origins of the African Slave Trade. Enslavement following a war against unbelievers was very common on the Iberian Peninsula as long as the Christian kingdoms were at war with Muslim nations. In central Spain the struggle lasted until the conquest of Granada in 1492, the year America was discovered. Even later, however, Muslims captured at sea were regularly sent to slave markets in Spain, as on their side the Muslims took Spanish and other Christian captives to North Africa. Also, until the middle of the 13th century, prisoners taken in frontier raids between Christian Portugal and her Muslim neighbors were enslaved. However, when the Portuguese reconquest became an accomplished fact and no independent Moors remained in the country, slaves could be obtained only outside the boundaries of the kingdom.

During the 14th and 15th centuries, when a number of African islands were discovered, the search for slaves was immediately renewed. Portuguese and Castilians sought the Guanches, a Canary Island people now extinct; but they bought still more slaves who were natives of the interior of the African continent. For a long time these black slaves were brought across the Muslim territory of Africa into southern Europe. During the 14th century a special caravan route was opened from the Sudan across the Sahara as far as the peninsula of Barca in Cyrenaica. The Portuguese, just as they later established a direct maritime line for the spice trade in the time of Vasco da Gama, now established an African slave route under Henry the Navigator, eliminating the need for intermediaries along the caravan routes or in the North African ports. The Portuguese themselves loaded the slaves at their ports of call in Senegal or Guinea. After the death of Henry the Navigator, Diogo Cão reached the Congo, where, as in Angola, increasing numbers of slaves were procured and sent, first to Europe, and then to America when the sugar plantations began to grow in importance. Beginning in the 15th century, the Portuguese government granted *asientos,* or permits, for the slave trade. The slave trade continued for four centuries in spite of its condemnation by the papacy, beginning with Pius II, on Oct. 7, 1462.

The trade along the African coast at the end of the Middle Ages underwent a transition to colonial slavery in America. Since the American aborigines who had been reduced to slavery at the beginning of Spanish colonization in the West Indies died out very quickly, they were replaced by Africans imported according to the rules established by the permits of the Middle Ages. The change from medieval slavery in the Mediterranean and in western Europe to colonial slavery in America was hardly noticed; it was a matter of simple continuity.

Slavery in Spanish America. In America the problem of the enslavement of the native inhabitants arose almost immediately. In Spanish America, as in Spain during the last centuries of the reconquest, native slavery quickly became a phenomenon characteristic of the frontier, that is, of any region adjacent to a still unsubdued indigenous population. At the same time, as in Spain itself, slaves originally taken on the frontier were imported into the interior of the imperial territory. This did not particularly surprise the subdued native peoples, since the tribal societies of America, like others, knew slavery as a consequence of war. Nevertheless, as the unsubdued areas gradually disappeared and the bulk of the native population was integrated into the Spanish empire, enslavement of the native peoples following frontier wars diminished and finally disappeared altogether. In one instance, in southern Chile, however, the Spanish Crown acted contrary to its general policy of suppressing the practice of subjection of the natives. The frontier war against the indomitable Araucanians continued to the end of the 17th century, and yielding to the plea of the local colonists, the Crown permitted the enslavement of prisoners. In general, however, the Spanish government envisaged colonial peace as its goal. Just as it saw no place within its realm for internecine war, it saw at the same time no advantage in slavery; and through the efforts of the Dominican friar Bartolome de LAS CASAS and the theologians F. de VITORIA and F. SUÁREZ, it had been brought at an early date to recognize in its slave law the inherent dignity of the slave as a person. This is not to say that it did not continue to treat the indigenous population very badly, but at the time the European peasant class did not always fare better.

There were similar conditions of servitude or its derivatives on both sides of the Atlantic. These conditions in America and especially in Spanish America, affecting practically the entire native population, differed from those prevailing in Europe in that the racial differences between the colonist or proprietary landowner and the Indian who tilled the soil were associated with the perpetuation of colonial customs that kept the semifree natives in a condition of hardship long outmoded in all, or most, of Europe.

Slavery and Colonization. Contrary to what is generally believed, no colonial society has been able to subsist while reducing into slavery the indigenous population, that is, the one inhabiting the colony. In the final analysis slavery and colonization proved to be in contradiction, at least with respect to the aborigines of colonized countries. Unfortunately, however, colonization did not exclude the enslavement of the nonindigenous, that is, of imported slaves; and it was thus that black slavery was introduced into the economy of colonial America.

In Africa, Europeans did not really penetrate inland between the 15th and the 19th centuries. They set up agencies along the coast where whites or blacks themselves lived by trading with inland peoples. This situation persisted throughout the *ancien régime* as well as during a great part of the 19th century, when colonial slavery flourished in America. During this time there was little thought of questioning the legitimacy of reducing Africans to slavery. Except with respect to black slavery in America, serious discussion of abolishing the slave trade began only after the colonial powers occupied the African interior. Then relations in Africa between colonizers and colonized became what they had long since been in America: the enslavement of the native African population became incompatible with the desire to establish and develop colonies. Great abolitionists such as William Wilberforce had not yet put an end to black slavery, but their efforts aided the cause. The necessity of establishing colonial peace in Africa in order to permit its exploitation made possible the triumph of their ideas. In the 19th century the black continent opened its inland wealth to the appetites of colonial powers, which then had to abolish the African slave trade (in which the Muslims had also engaged) to be in a position to exploit Africa.

Economic Effects of Abolition. The emancipation of slaves was proclaimed in the U.S. on Jan. 1, 1863, during the Civil War; but it was not until 1871 that the Spanish Cortes decided to prohibit slavery, after 1880, in what remained of the Spanish empire. It is true that Spain had forbidden the slave trade in 1820, whereas Portugal had not decided to do so until 1836, even after Brazil, its former colony, had set an example in 1831. The last Brazilian emperor, Peter II, decreed in 1871 the law of ''free birth'' that assured freedom at birth for all children of slaves, and in 1888 he proclaimed full emancipation, a move that cost him his throne.

In the West Indies, where at the very beginning of the 19th century HAITI had forged in blood the political freedom of a nation of emancipated slaves, the progressive suppression of slavery created numerous difficulties for which remedy was sought by the importation of nonindigenous people, mostly from Asia. Legally these were not slaves, although their economic condition was hardly better. There were even attempts to return to the importation of Africans called ''free workers'' whose misery was such that they were easily recognized as new victims of the slave trade. The apparent similarity, recognized by international opinion, was sufficient reason to end the forced migration. It had lasted long enough, however, to substitute for slavery on the plantations a multiracial labor force with living standards that were extremely low. More and more, emancipated Africans were subordinated, just as the Native Americans were, in those zones of the Americas where the plantation economy was maintained or developed by diversification of crops. Sugar, in effect, was no longer king; the elevation of European living standards resulting from industrialization created markets for new agricultural produce of the plantation regime. At the same time, this produce was no longer an American monopoly, since plantation farming had spread to other tropical and subtropical regions both in Asia and in Africa. Thenceforth, the plantation worker, regardless of the color of his skin, was to belong first to the agricultural proletariat, then to the industrial, as production was intensified by technological development. The amelioration of living conditions became dependent on technical advances, the progress of which led to the lessening of physical hardship and at length to an increase in wages.

Historic Roots of Slavery. It is generally believed that colonial slavery, and especially plantation slavery, was a product of the modern period found particularly in America. This is not the fact. Colonial slavery—distinguished by the use of nonfree manual labor of distant origin, with physical and religious characteristics different from the colonizers—existed in the eastern Mediterranean long before a plantation regime was developed in colonial America. Slaves had worked on the sugar plantations of Cyprus and in the alum mines of Phocaea on the Anatolian coast, as they did later on the sugar plantations of Brazil and the West Indies and the tobacco plantations of Virginia. In the East these slaves were not always black, but either Slavs or Muslims; in Virginia, white indentured servants worked side by side with black slaves.

Moreover, it is important to note that slavery antedated the coming of Europeans in all countries occupied during the period of colonial expansion. This was true in America, Africa, and Asia. Slavery as an institution was not introduced by Europeans, although the number of slaves increased in a frightening manner after their arrival. In the slaves' native lands population decreased as a result of the raids made by slave hunters, many of whom were themselves natives. The wholesale transportation of slaves could be effected only to those countries that were sufficiently far away to remove the possibility of escape and return of the slave to his native land. During the period in which colonial slavery underwent its greatest development, that is, from the 16th to the 19th century, these countries could be reached only by sea. Therefore, nations in a position to dominate or monopolize maritime transportation, especially intercontinental transportation, retained a monopoly of the slave trade. These were the same nations that established colonial empires across the ocean, which they succeeded in doing for the very reason that enabled them to carry on their trade on a large scale—they had achieved technical superiority in the area of maritime transportation.

In ancient times, whenever an ethnic group or nation achieved a superiority that gave it ascendancy over other ethnic groups or nations with sufficiently different physical or religious traits, the slave trade flourished. This was especially true if its victims were on a lower rung of general technical development, without arms or other means of defense sufficiently effective to afford them permanent protection. Thus Arab navigation dominated the Indian Ocean before the arrival of Vaseo da Gama and the Portuguese. Long before the arrival of Europeans, the Swahili principalities on the eastern coast of Africa organized forays into the interior and filled the Arab ships with heavy cargoes of black slaves who were sent to various parts of the Muslim world. On the other hand; the Islamic conquests spread with surprising rapidity into the Sudan and Guinea after the end of the 11th century. In less than 50 years, Islam took over all western Africa, from which black captives were sent to Muslim Spain. The Africans were thus reduced to slavery in the Islamic world before the arrival of Europeans, although this in no way alters the fact that African slavery was most highly developed when the Portuguese, Spanish, and later the Dutch and English, with occasional localized French competition, achieved the dominion of the seas. Not surprisingly, since Islamic law always recognized slavery, as long as European colonization did not penetrate into the interior of eastern or central Africa, the Arab trade in Africans continued to be very active. It was not until the colonial powers gained ascendancy in these regions in the last quarter of the 19th century, that this trade, too, died out.

Bibliography: W. L. WESTERMANN, *The Slave Systems of Greek and Roman Antiquity* (Philadelphia 1955). E. MEYER, *Die Sklaverei im Altertum* (Dresden 1898). W. W. BUCKLAND, *The Roman Law of Slavery: The Condition of the Slave in Private Law from Augustus to Justinian* (Cambridge, Eng. 1908). M. ROBERTI, *La lettera di S. Paulo a Filemone e la condizione guiridica dello schiavo fuggitivo* (Milan 1933). C. VERLINDEN, *L'Esclavage dans l' Europe médiévale,* v. 1 *Péninsule Iberique, France* (Bruges 1955); ''L'Origine de sclavus—esclave,'' *Archivum latinitatis medii aevi* 17 (1943) 97–128; ''Pax Hispanics en la America colonial,'' *Historia* no. 12 (Buenos Aires 1958) 5–17; ''Esclavage médiéval en Europe et esclavage colonial en Amérique,'' *Sorbonne, Cahiers de l'Institut des Hautes Études de l'Amerique latine* 6 (1963) 29–45.

[C. VERLINDEN]

SLAVIC RELIGION

Slavic paganism was animistic, worshiping all the essential elements of Slavic life. Since the daily life of the Slavs revolved around the house, yard, and stables and their agricultural, hunting, and fishing pursuits, their religious concepts developed against the background of the home life, fields, rivers, lakes, and forests among which they lived. Various spirits dwelt in all these places and the goodwill of those spirits had to be propitiated. Sacrifices were offered to them as well as to the spirits of ancestors.

The pagan Slavs believed in future life, a fact emphasized by the great attention paid to funeral rites and their great complexity: the immolation of wives, slaves, and animals that were supposed to accompany the souls of the dead into the future life, the funeral banquet called *tryzna,* the offering of food deposited at the graves, and the belief in the close association of the ancestral spirits with the everyday life of their living descendants. This belief explains also the great role of ancestral spirits in Slavic folklore and popular tradition, and it survives into modern times.

The early method of disposing of corpses was cremation, which was replaced by inhumation toward the end of the pagan period under the influence of Christianity. In the grave were placed ornaments, arms, tools, and other objects of daily life. Like so many other primitive peoples, the Slavs often killed old people unable to work and unwanted children. In some more remote and backward areas, this practice survived until the 14th century. Another common practice was the *postrigi,* or *postrizini,* a ritual performed on male children when they reached the age of seven. It consisted of a solemn cutting of hair of the child and symbolized the transfer from the authority of the mother to that of the father.

Over and above the household spirits, there was a group of supreme deities headed by Perun, the god of storm, thunder, and lightning. Procopius (6th century) and Helmold (11th century) both emphasize this supreme role of Perun in the Slavic pantheon. There were other great deities. Svarog was the god of the sun, fire, and light. The fire as such was considered to be a Svarozic, son of Svarog. The name of Svarog shows a close affinity to the Indo-European root *svar,* meaning heat, brilliance. The Eastern Slavs worshiped the sun also under the name of Dazbog, meaning ''the giver.'' Volos, or Veles, was the god of cattle and possibly of agriculture in general. Stribog (the god of wind), Khors, and Mokos (a female deity personifying mother earth) were worshiped particularly by the Eastern Slavs, but their attributes are less clear. All of them show a close affinity to similar deities of the Iranian and Vedic pantheons.

There was usually no definite priestly caste, and worship was offered usually by the village or family elders. There is very little indication of temples or great centers of worship except among the Slavic tribes on the Baltic (Arcona, Radgost), where there was also a priestly caste, and among the Russians.

Bibliography: N. REITER, ''Mythologie der alten Slaven.'' in *Wörterbuch der Mythologie,* ed. H. W. HAUSSIG (Stuttgart 1961–) Abt.1.2.1, fasc.6, 163–208. J. VENDRYÈS, E. TONNELAT, and B. O. UNBEGAUN, *Les Religions des Celtes, des Germains, et des anciens Slaves* (''Mana'' Series 2.3; Paris 1948) 387–445.

[O. P. SHERBOWITZ-WETZOR]

SLAVOPHILISM

The romantic ultranationalistic ideology of a group of 19th-century Russian right-wing reformers who fervently predicted a brilliant future for Russia. They held forth in the endless debates inevitably occasioned by Russia's victory over Napoleon I in 1812. For them that future depended upon the restoration of Russia's legitimate past. They scorned St. Petersburg, Russia's ''German'' capital and the memory of the man who built it, Emperor PETER I. The Slavophiles, as they came to be known, were the philosophers of nationality (*narodnost'*). For them nationalism was something more than a Russian subject's manifestation of patriotic loyalty to St. Petersburg's laws, policies of the moment, and international commitment to the concert of Europe. To the Czar's alarm Slavophilism logically developed into a cultural and political pan-Slavism with dangerous messianic visions of Great Russia. The Slavophiles were interested primarily in the Slavonic race and also in the land and the faith of the Russian people (*narod*). Russian nationality was the object of Slavophile veneration. It was to them a grass roots ''folkishness,'' a complexus of a God-bearing apolitical people's traditions and preoccupations: the commune (*mir*), religion and worship, the things of the soul (*dusha*) in general. Slavophiles opposed serfdom because formerly Russians were freemen. The definitive stand of the Slavophiles against their ideological enemies, the Westernizers, was crystallized in the summer of 1836 when the brilliant P. Y. Chaadaev's *First Philosophical Letter* appeared in Nadezhdin's *Teleskop.* The visiting Marquis Astolphe de Custine later published scathing observations in *La Russie en 1839.* Emperor NICHOLAS I promptly declared Chaadaev officially insane, and the Slavophiles rushed to defend Russia, whose past, present, and future had been so grossly slandered by both son and outlander. Because they championed the wrong Russia, so to speak, Slavophiles were often jailed by Nicholas I. Ironically, they were frequently in material agreement with their professed enemies, the Westernizers, as Herzen and Bakunin were to note.

Conservative Slavophiles were deeply religious and supported the Orthodox Church; religion was the basis of their bias. They made their own the phrase perhaps first used by a journalistic supporter, S. P. Shevyrëv: ''the rotting West'' (*gniloĭ zapad*). For men such as their talented leaders, A. S. Khomyakov and K. S. Aksakov, the West was deteriorating because of the false principles on which Europe's culture rested, the eclecticism and individuality of its thinkers, and the worldly political concerns of its philosophers and citizens. I. V. Kireevskiĭ and others drew up long lists of contrasts between East and West, always to the disadvantage of the latter. Slavophile theological thought was hostile to both Catholicism and Protestantism. Supported by M. P. Pogodin and F. I. Tyutchev, the Slavophiles Y. Samarin, I. S. Aksakov, and their followers all logically demanded that Russia halt the process of her contamination by the West, and quarantine herself spiritually and politically in the splendid Muscovite isolation of Holy Russia of a bygone age.

Bibliography: N. L. BRODSKIĬ, *Rannie slavyanofily* (Moscow 1910). F. FADNER, *Seventy Years of Pan-Slavism in Russia* (Washington 1962). N. V. RIASANOVSKY, *Russia and the West in the Teaching of the Slavophiles* (Cambridge, MA 1952).

[F. L. FADNER]

SLAVORUM APOSTOLI

Pope JOHN PAUL II's fourth encyclical letter, ''The Apostles of the Slavs,'' issued June 2, 1985, commemorating the eleventh centenary of the evangelizing work of Sts. Cyril and Methodius. In the Introduction, Pope John Paul recalls and expands on his apostolic letter *Egregiae virtutis* (1980), in which he named the brother-saints as co-patrons of Europe along with St. Benedict, as well as letters of his predecessors. In a personal note, John Paul acknowledges that he felt ''a particular obligation'' to pay tribute to Cyril and Methodius, being ''the first Pope called to the See of Peter from Poland, and thus from the midst of the Slav nations'' (3).

The encyclical looks back at the apostolic lives and work of evangelization of Cyril and Methodius. Part 2 presents a biographical sketch of the two saints. Part 3 recalls their evangelizing activity. Part 4 emphasizes their vision of the Church as one, holy, and universal. Part 5 proposes that their catechetical and pastoral method remains ''instructive for the Church today.'' Part 6 cites their work as a model of inculturation—''the incarnation of the Gospel in native culture and also the introduction of these cultures into the life of the Church'' (21). Part 7 explains the significance of the Christian millennium to the common culture of the Slavic world. Cyril and Methodius ''made a decisive contribution to the building of Europe not only in Christian religious communion but also to its civil and cultural union'' (n. 27).

Woven throughout the encyclical are reflections on the method the brothers used in evangelizing Europe and the contributions they made to Slavic culture. The words of Christ, ''Preach the Gospel to the whole creation'' (Mk 16:15) inspired their missionary work, and they tried to adopt the customs and language of the people to whom they were preaching. Among their principal contributions were the composition of a new alphabet and their translation of the sacred literature into the Old Slavonic language. Their profound work in orthodox doctrine and their zeal gained a great deal of admiration from Roman pontiffs, patriarchs of Constantinople, and Byzantine emperors. Because of their ability to stay in touch with both the patriarch of Constantinople and the Roman See, Cyril and Methodius bridged the Eastern and Western traditions which come together in the one, universal Church.

Despite misunderstandings—the price they had to pay for their work—Cyril and Methodius served as instruments of unity in places where there was not unity between individual communities. Their approach was based on the reality that every individual and all cultures and nations have their place in God's mysterious plan of salvation.

In the conclusion of the encyclical Pope John Paul states that Cyril and Methodius by their words and life, sustained by the charism of the Holy Spirit, gave an example of a fruitful vocation not only for past time, but also for the centuries that are to come.

Bibliography: For the text of *Slavorum apostoli,* see: *Acta Apostolicae Sedis* 77 (1985): 779–813 (Latin); *Origins* 15, no. 8 (18 July 1985): 113–25; *The Pope Speaks* 30 (1985): 252–75 (English).

[D. CLOONEY]

Saint Cyril of Belozersk, Apostle to the Slav, tempura on gesso over wood panel, early 16th century. (©The State Russian Museum/CORBIS)

SLIPYJ, JOSYF

Cardinal, archbishop, leader of Ukranian Catholics; b. Zazdrist in the Ukraine, Feb. 17, 1892; d. Rome, Sept. 7, 1984. Josyf Kobernyckyj-Dyckowskyj Slipyj (also spelled Slipyi) was born in the Western Ukraine (Galicia) when it was still a part of the Austro-Hungarian Empire. He received his theological education and seminary training in Lvov (Lviv, Lemberg), Innsbruck and Rome. Ordained a priest in 1917, in 1922 he was appointed to the faculty of the Major Seminary in Lvov (now part of Poland), and became president of the newly founded Theological Academy. He started a respected theological quarterly *Bohoslovia* that he later (1963) revived in Rome, after a long lapse, as a yearly publication.

In 1939 Slipyj was made coadjutor to Metropolitan Szeptyckyj of Lvov, whom he succeeded as head of the Uniate Ukrainian Church in 1944. The difficulties he had with the Nazi occupation during the first few months of his tenure were nothing in comparison to what he suffered at the hands of the Bolsheviks who took over the next year (1945), annexing the Western Ukraine to the Soviet Union. Arrested and condemned for unspecific crimes, Slipyj spent 18 years in prison, labor camps and exile in Siberia (1945–63). His church was officially annihilated through forced union with the Russian Orthodox Church (Synod of Lvov 1946).

Slipyj was allowed to leave the Soviet Union in 1963 as a result of initiatives that had been set in motion by Pope John XXIII. He spent the rest of his life in Rome as a witness to the vitality of the Church in the Ukraine, notwithstanding the long years of repression. He spoke of a ''church in the catacombs'' in terms which, to some, sounded exaggerated, but later were found to be quite accurate.

Role in the West. Pope Paul VI gave Slipyj the title *Major Archbishop* of the Ukrainian Church, with right and privileges similar to those of a patriarch. The title, newly created by Vatican II, was the source of misunderstanding and much friction between the Holy See and Ukrainians in the West. Many thought that *patriarch* was the more rightful title for the head of the large and long-suffering Ukrainian Church. The appointment of Slipyj as a cardinal in 1965 did not satisfy pressure groups within the Ukrainian community, and at times Slipyj himself seemed to speak and act as an opponent of the Vatican's *Ost Politik.* Although his actions and movements were restricted, Slipyj visited most Ukrainian communities in Europe and America, and held two Synods of Ukrainian bishops in Rome (1971, 1980). He was also outspoken on behalf of his persecuted people. Some of his strong statements caused an exchange of letters between Patriarch Pimen of Moscow and Pope John Paul II (1980–81).

Josyf Archbishop Slipyj, Ukrainian Primate, conducting the Divine Liturgy at the Cathedral of the Holy Name, Bombay, India, 1964. (AP/Wide World Photos)

The cultural activity of the Ukrainian cardinal was also remarkable. He played a principal part in the establishment of the faculty of St. Clement of Rome, a Ukrainian Catholic University (1963), and the construction of St. Sophia, the Ukrainian Catholic Cathedral (1969), modeled in part on that of Kiev. Both are located in the Eternal City. He wrote highly speculative treatises on the doctrine of the Holy Trinity, and he appeared as quite an expert on problems of Unionism, Ukrainian church history and liturgy. Shortly before his death at the age of 92, a new edition of his *Omnia Opera* appeared.

Bibliography: J. SLIPYJ, *Omnia Opera Card, Josephi (Slipyj Kobernyckyj-Dyckovskyj) Archiepiscopi Majoris*, 13 v. (Rome 1968–83) [Volume 14, with contributions by a number of authors, was added after his death (Rome 1984)]. M. MARUSYN, *Mitropolit Josif Slipyj* [in Ukrainian] (Rome-Brussels 1972); *Cristiani d'Ucraina. Un popolo dilaniato ma non domato* (Rome 1983). G. CHOMA, ''La vita e le opere del Cardinale Slipyj,'' *Euntes Docete* 38 (1985) 217–236. G. CAPRILE, ''Il Card: Josif Slipyj Pastore e Studioso,'' *La Civilta Cattolica* (1985) 400–404. J. PELIKAN, *Confessor between East and West: A Portrait of Ukrainian Cardinal Josyf Slipyj* (Grand Rapids, MI 1990).

[G. ELDAROV]

SLOMŠEK, ANTON MARTIN, BL.

Slovenian archbishop, educator, writer, poet; b. Nov. 26, 1800, Slom, Ponikva, Lower Styria, Slovenia; d. Sept. 24, 1862, Maribor, Slovenia.

Born into a prosperous peasant family, he received his secondary education in Celje (Zilli in Old Austria, now Slovenia), Ljubljana, and Senj. Slomšek finished his theological studies in the Carinthian capital of Klagenfurt and was ordained (1824). He ministered in two Slovene parishes in Styria and was appointed (1829) spiritual director at the theological seminary in Klagenfurt, where he also taught the Slovene language.

In 1846, he became archbishop of the Lavant Valley (Carinthia), but in 1859 was transferred to Maribor (or Marburg, as the Austrian Germans called it) in the Slovene part of Styria. Slomšek was devoted to raising the cultural and moral level of the Slovene population. Schools were in a precarious state because of the Austrian suppression of the national language and the introduction of foreign teachers. Slovenian literature was forbidden out of fear of Panslavism. Following the adoption of the Constitution of 1848, granting national rights, he helped to found many schools, in which he also taught. His most important work, however, was the founding (1851–52) of the St. Hermagoras Society (*Druzba svetega Mohorja*), whose aim was to distribute inexpensive and good books among the people.

Working as a Christian moralist and educational author, he published in 1834 *Keršansko devištvo* (*Christian Charity*). In the same lucid Slovene prose (the best of the period) was the educational narrative *Blaže in Nežica v nedeljski šoli* (1842, *Little Blase and Agnes in the Sunday School*), as well as essays and other books on a great variety of subjects. In 1846, he began the educational weekly *Drobtinice* (*Crumbs*), designed to serve village priests and teachers. In 1849, his collection of sermons, *Apostolska Hrana* (*Apostolic Food*), appeared. Slomšek was also, although less prominently, a poet. As a young priest of 26 he translated Schiller's *Das Lied von der Glocke*, and in 1833 was responsible for a collection of Slovene folk songs sung in Carinthia and Styria. His own poems are didactic, serene, and close to the style and rhythm of folk song. Although Slomšek was a zealous nationalist, his humility, childlike simplicity, and kindness won the admiration of foreigners.

Pope John Paul II beatified Slomšek on Sept. 19, 1999, at Maribor, Slovenia. The pope praised Slomšek, the first Slovenian to be beatified, for his work of evangelization and his ecumenical efforts.

Feast: Sept. 24.

Bibliography: A. SLOMŠEK, *Zbrani spisi*, 5 v. (Celje 1876–90), collected works; *Izbrani spisi za mladino* (Celje 1924), selected works for youth. J. AMBROZIC, *Pastorale familiare di Mons. Anton Martin Slomsek* (Rome 1981). V. HABJAN, *Anton Martin Slomsek* (Ljubljana 1992). F. HRASTELJ, *Otrok luci: zgodovinska povest o Antonu Martinu Slomsku* (Ljubljana 1999). S. JANEZIC, *Slomsek in nas cas* (Maribor 1992). I. JERIC, *Moji spomini* (Murska Sobota 2000). M. KLUN, *Fürstbischof Anton Martin Slomsek in Kärnten* (Klagenfurt 1969). F. KOSAR, *Anton M. Slomšek, Fürstbischof von Lavant* (Marburg 1863). F. KOVACIC, *Sluzabnik bozji A. M. Slomšek*, 2 v. (Celje 1934–35). D. MEDVED, *Knezoškof Lavantinski A. M. Slomšek* (Cakovec 1900). J. POGACNIK, *Kulturni pomen Slomskovega dela* (Maribor 1991). B. ZAVRNIK, *Anton Martin Slomsek* (Ljubljani 1990).

[J. LAVRIN/K. I. RABENSTEIN]

SLOVAKIA, THE CATHOLIC CHURCH IN

Capital: Bratislava.
Size: 18,928 sq. miles.
Population: 5,407,956 in 2000.
Languages: Slovak (official), Hungarian.
Religions: 3,244,774 Roman Catholics (60%), 216,318 Greek Orthodox (4%), 432,765 Protestants (8%), 965,199 other (18%), 548,900 without religious affiliation.
Archdioceses: Bratislava-Trnava, with suffragans Nitra and Banská Bystrica; Košice, with suffragans Spiš and Rožňava. The episcopal see of the Byzantine-rite Greek Catholic Church is in Prešov, with an apostolic exarchate in Košice.

Part of the former Czechoslovakia, the Slovak Republic is located in eastern Europe. Bound on the northwest by the Czech Republic with which it was formerly united, Slovakia is bound on the northeast by Poland, on the east by Ukraine, on the southeast by Hungary, and on the west by Austria. Featuring a mountainous landscape dominated by the Carpathians to the south, Slovakia is heavily forested, with some steppe regions in the lowlands to the southeast. Natural resources include coal, timber, and small quantities of iron, copper and manganese ore. The transition from a planned economy under communism to a modern economy was a difficult one due to international debt, unemployment and inflation. Over half of Slovakia's exports of machinery, fuels and other manufactured goods are shipped within the European Union, which it hoped to join after achieving economic stability.

Together with the historic lands of the Czechs in Bohemia and Moravia, with Silesia, and with Carpathian Ruthenia, Slovakia was part of the Austro-Hungarian Empire since medieval times. Czechs and Slovaks shared ethnic roots and spoke languages very closely allied to one another. Because of the frequent cultural exchanges they had shared for centuries, they united politically in 1918 to form their own independent state, the Republic of Czechoslovakia. When the Communists seized power in 1948, the region was termed a People's Republic, and in 1960 it became the Czechoslovak Socialist Republic. After the region achieved independence in 1989, Slovakia agitated for independence from her neighbor to the north; the Czech Republic was founded in January of 1993, leaving Slovakia an independent nation as well.

Within Slovakia there are two relatively independent organizational structures of the Catholic Church with different liturgical and juridical traditions: the Roman Catholic Church and the Byzantine (Greek) Catholic Church. Under communism, Byzantine-rite Catholics were absorbed into the Czechoslovak Orthodox Church, but by the 1970s the Byzantine Church had resumed functioning in Slovakia. The Eastern and Roman Churches fully respect each other and work together; bishops from all seven Slovak dioceses form the Bishops' Conference of Slovakia, the office of which is in Bratislava.

Christianity in Slovakia to 1918

Slovakia was subject to the archbishop of SALZBURG until 829, and then to Passau. After the destruction of the Empire of Great Moravia (907), Slovakia was incorporated into Hungary, where it remained until 1918.

Medieval Period. Slovakia was gradually exposed to Germanic, Celtic and Roman peoples, and missionaries entered the area in the 8th century. Within the fortified towns that grew up in the region, Slavonic culture and liturgy were gradually replaced by Latin culture and liturgy, although in the more remote valleys of eastern Slovakia the Byzantine-Slavonic rite continued to be observed. The immigration of Valachians (Rumanians) and Ruthenians, belonging to the same rite, increased the number of its adherents in the following centuries. For the most part these two groups were assimilated by the Slovaks, but a small Ruthenian (now Ukrainian) national group retained its separate identity well into the 20th century.

In 880 the Diocese of Nitra was built; it would continue to be active save for the century between the Hungarian invasion and its restoration (1024) by the sainted King STEPHEN I, who had established a Latin hierarchy in his realm by this time. In addition to Nitra, Slovakia included the See of Eger (founded *c.* 1009) and the Archdiocese of Esztergom (*c.* 1000, now located in Hungary). This ecclesiastical organization lasted for several centuries. Important contributions to Slovakia's civilization were made by the BENEDICTINES, whose monasteries included ZOBOR (founded *c.* 1000), Sv. Beňadik (1075) and Opátska (1143); as well as by the CISTERCIANS, who founded the monasteries of Lipovník (1141) and Štiavník

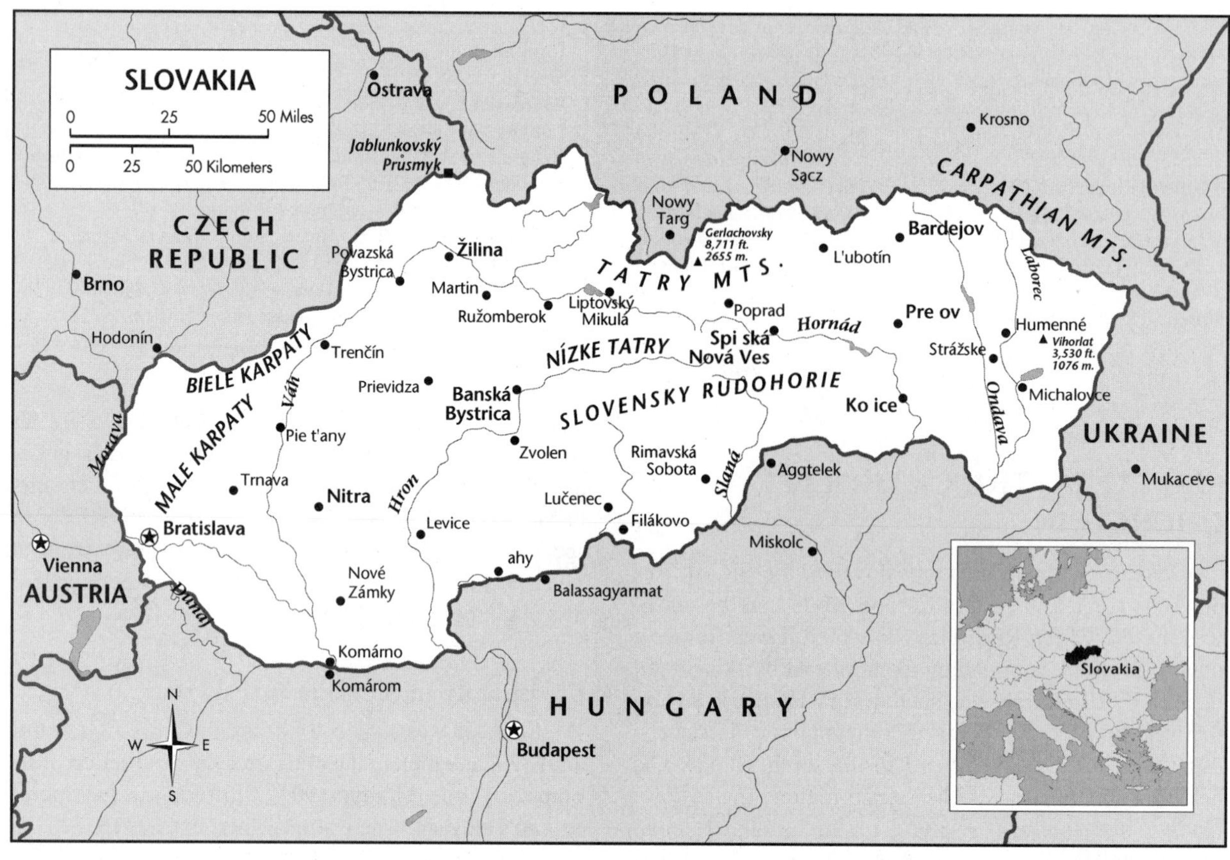

(1223); and by the PREMONSTRATENSIANS, whose houses included Bzovík (1130) and JASOV (1220).

In 1241 Tartars from Russia moved southwest into Slovakia, invading and devastating the country (*see* MONGOLS). To expedite reconstruction, King Bela IV encouraged colonists from Germany by granting these immigrants a number of privileges. The Germans founded several cities and promoted trade and commerce, but they lived and worked in close association with one another, thus preserving their own national enclaves through many generations. In 1930 Slovakia's German population numbered 147,500, but after 1945 almost all of them were forced to leave.

Reformation and Catholic Restoration. In the 16th century the Germans were the first in Slovakia to embrace Protestantism. The new doctrine also spread rapidly among the nobility, who then imposed it upon their feudal subjects. Because ecclesiastical discipline was decadent and ecclesiastical organization inadequate, Protestant doctrine was widely accepted by the clergy as well. After the Turks conquered the primatial See of Esztergom in 1543, the archbishop and the metropolitan chapter relocated in Trnava, where they remained for the next three centuries. It was at Trnava that Archbishop Miklós Olahus (OLÁH, 1553–68) began the work of Catholic restoration by convoking provincial synods and by introducing the Jesuits to Trnava in 1561. After his successor's death, however, the see remained vacant for 34 years. By 1600 almost all of Slovakia was, to all appearances, Protestant. Cardinal Peter PÁZMÁNY (1616–37) took as his charge the restoration of Catholicism in Slovakia. In addition to winning many nobles back to the faith, Pázmány founded the University in Trnava (1635) and entrusted it to the Jesuits.

The work of Catholic restoration proved extremely difficult, in part because Slovakia was a battleground throughout the 17th century. Turks occupied the southern section until the Christian victory at Vienna (1683). In other sections the Catholic armies of the Hapsburgs fought the Protestant troops of the princes of Transylvania. But by the 18th century the political situation had become more peaceful, and when Emperor Joseph II decreed the act of tolerance in 1781, the religious situation was stabilized. Since that time, Protestants—predominately Lutherans, but also some Calvinists—formed only a small percent of the population. The Union of Užhorod, which was tentatively settled in 1646, was concluded by the mid-18th century and helped strengthen the Church by obtaining the accession of the Orthodox members of the Byzantine rite. To improve the ecclesias-

Bratislava Castle and city of Bratislava, Slovakia. (©Adam Woolfitt/CORBIS)

tical structure, the Dioceses of Banská Bystrica, Rožnava and Spiš were erected in 1776, the Diocese of Košice in 1804, and the Byzantine-rite Diocese of Prešov in 1818.

National Awakening. For many years Slovakia had existed as a province of the Austro-Hungarian empire. However, as a result of philosophical changes brought on by the European Enlightenment and the rise of the Napoleonic vision, the beginnings of a national consciousness arose *c.* 1800. This striving for a national identity received the support of many Slovak priests, notably linguist Anthony Bernolák (1762–1813), poet John Hollý (1785–1849) and Bishop Stephan Moyses (1797–1869). Some Lutheran clergymen and laymen of both confessions were also prominent. In 1870 Andrew Radlinský founded the Society of St. Adalbert (Spolok Sv. Vojtecha) to spread popular Slovak Catholic literature.

To destroy the first glimmerings of a Slovak national consciousness, the Hungarian government began a program involving political and ethnic persecution in 1867. This harassment, along with social and economic unrest, caused hundreds of thousands of Slovaks to immigrate, principally to North America. So large was the movement that the percentage of emigrants in relation to total population was higher in Slovakia than anywhere else in Europe except in Ireland and Norway. In order to turn the Slovaks into Hungarian Magyars, the government ordered that all secondary schools use the Hungarian language by 1875, and by 1907 all primary school teachers in Slovakia were required to present their lessons in Hungarian as well. These laws had the effect of preventing the development of a Slovak intellectual class, as few could read the works of native writers. By 1900 the majority of Slovak intellectuals could be found only among Catholic priests and, to a lesser extent, Lutheran ministers. The most outstanding among these priests was Monsignor Andrew Hlinka (1864–1938), who founded the Slovak Catholic People's Party in 1905. For this activity

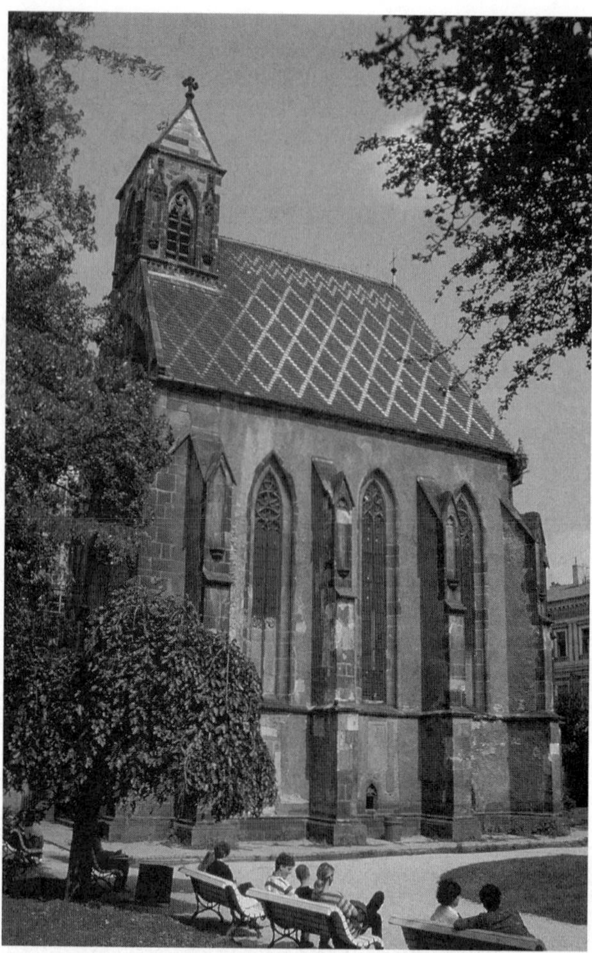

St. Michael's Church, Košice, Slovakia. (©Carmen Redondo/ CORBIS)

Hlinka spent several years in prison, where he translated the Bible into Slovak. By the time Slovakia was separated from the collapsed Austro-Hungarian Empire in 1918, the denationalization process was almost complete.

Upheaval Follows World War I. In 1919 Slovakia joined with the Czech region to the north and formed the republic of Czechoslovakia. During the critical years following World War I, all incumbent Slovak bishops were forced to give up their sees, except Augustine Fischer-Colbrie (d. 1922) of Košice, who retained his diocese despite his German extraction. The first three Slovak bishops were consecrated in Nitra on Feb. 13, 1921. Fortunately, unlike the situation in other parts of the former Austro-Hungarian Empire, anticlerical intellectual circles were uncommon, and the clergy retained its influence over the people. The Slovak Catholic People's party became the largest political party due to its platform of Slovak autonomy and preservation of the Slovak religious heritage. It continued to gain support, despite the anti-Catholic spirit of the central government.

The papal document *Ad ecclesiastici regiminis* issued on Sept. 2, 1937 adjusted the southern boundaries of Slovakia but did not make a final settlement concerning the Apostolic Administration of Trnava, which had been created in May of 1922 from those parishes formerly belonging to the Hungarian Archdiocese of Esztergom but situated in Slovakia. The *modus vivendi* provided that Slovak dioceses should be united in one ecclesiastical province and that a second metropolitan see should be erected for Byzantine-rite Catholics in eastern Czechoslovakia. However, a new political upheaval in Europe would prevent such plans from being carried out.

The expansion of Germany's National Socialist agenda during the late 1930s directly affected Czechoslovakia due to both its proximity and cultural ties to Germany. Under the terms of the Munich Pact signed between the Czechoslovakian government and Germany in the fall of 1938 Slovakia lost its southern districts to Hungary and the former Soviet Union. Changed to a federated state of the Third Reich on Oct. 6, 1938, the republic of Czechoslovakia was forcibly dissolved six months later, and Slovakia was proclaimed an independent republic on March 14, 1939.

Slovakia's altered southern and eastern boundaries disturbed the ecclesiastical organization once more, because Hungary now encompassed the Dioceses of Košice and Rožnava, while Užhorod, residence of the Byzantine rite bishop of Mukačevo and the Latin apostolic administrator for the parishes of Satu-Mare, was part of the former Soviet Union. Parishes of the three Latin-rite dioceses remaining in Slovakia were now placed under an apostolic administrator stationed in Prešov. The Byzantine rite parishes that had belonged to the Diocese of Mukačevo were now administered by the Byzantine rite bishop of Prešov. Political power was exercised mostly by the Slovak Catholic People's party headed by Monsignor Jozef Tiso (1887–1947), who was prime minister and president of the Nazi-collaborationist state from 1939–45. Tiso's administration was disturbed by Nazi interference, both with regards to the Jewish question and in other matters. After fleeing the country in 1945, he was captured by the Allies in Germany and delivered to the Communist-controlled Czechoslovak government, which condemned him to death and executed him in Bratislava on April 18, 1947. After his death, the Slovak people continued to hold Tiso in high esteem, and as late as 1999 the city of Zilina was condemned by Catholic, Jewish and Lutheran leaders for its desire to publicly commemorate Tiso with a plaque.

Church under Communism. In 1948 a communist government under Klement Gottwald took power in the reunited Czechoslovakia. During the four decades of authoritarian rule that followed, the Church suffered great persecution. Repressive government policies gave rise to a vigorous underground Church served by bishops and priests who were ordained clandestinely. One of them, Ján Chryzostom Korec, a Jesuit, had been secretly ordained a bishop in 1951 at the age of 27. He served the underground church until 1960, when upon discovery he was sentenced to a 12-year prison term. Released in 1968 during a brief respite from oppression known as the "Prague Spring," Korec worked in Bratislava as a laborer while founding a new clandestine ministry. In 1976, in an effort to placate the anticlericism of Czechoslovakian president Husák, a Vatican envoy ordered Korec to cease his underground activities and stop ordaining priests, but there was no letup in government repression. Other clandestine bishops continued to ordain priests, many of whom were married men because their wedded state would make them beyond suspicion of government agents. Nikolaus Krett ordained several women during this period.

The underground Church was made even more necessary after 14 June 1950, when all diocesan seminaries in Czechoslovakia were closed by the government. In their stead the government opened one seminary for the Czech lands, located in Prague, and another in Bratislava for Slovakia. Both of these state-controlled institutions were termed theological faculties, and their students were in constant suspicion of teachers who promoted a communist-controlled curriculum. During the Communist regime, Rome was allowed to appoint only three "compromise-minded" bishops to Vatican II, which met for the first of four sessions in 1962.

Despite the efforts of the government to exacerbate tensions between the two groups, Czechs and Slovaks united in efforts to frustrate Communist repression of political and religious liberties. Resistance to the Communist regime stiffened in the wake of the police assault on peaceful Catholic demonstrators on March 25, 1988. Known as "the Good Friday of Bratislava," the Husák regime viciously attacked the thousands of Slovaks who had come to pray and in Hviezdoslavovo Square. The incident prompted international protests and solidified the will of the people to resist. In November of 1989, during a period dubbed the "Velvet Revolution," many Slovaks joined in the creation of Verejnost Proti Násiliu ("Public against Violence"), an umbrella organization linking parts of the resistance community. On Oct. 22, 1991, the bishops of the Czech Slovak Federal Republic gathered in St. Vitus Cathedral in Prague for a Mass celebrating the 13th anniversary of the installation of Pope John Paul II. Archbishop Miloslav Vlk of Prague greeted an assembly that included many revolutionary leaders as well as the principal celebrant, underground bishop Korec, now Archbishop of Bratislava and newly created cardinal. By the end of 1991 Husák had lost power and communist rule in Czechoslovakia had come to an end.

Although Czechs and Slovaks had united in their opposition to the Communist regime, the elections of 1992 foreshadowed the changes that would take place in the region. While a new government was established under Czech leader Václav Havel and separate legislative councils were established for both the Czechs and the Slovaks, Slovakia reasserted its independence on Jan. 1, 1993. The Church would develop a good relationship with the new Slovak government, and in June of 1995 Pope John Paul II visited the country. Two years later, Slovak President Michal Kovac made his third visit to the Holy See in four years.

Liberated Church Enters 21st Century. After the division of the two countries, the Church in Slovakia maintained open contacts with the Church in the Czech Republic. According to their statutes and encouraged by the Holy See, the episcopal conferences in both countries met annually in plenary session to discuss common problems and keep each other abreast of developments in their respective lands. One problem common to both countries was how to deal with the bishops and priests—particularly those who were married—who had been ordained in the underground church during the communist era. Fortunately, the Byzantine-rite Church had a tradition of accepting married clergy; coming forward in response to a call from the Pope in 1997, many priests who had been ordained clandestinely were re-ordained by the Greek Catholic bishop in eastern Slovakia and permitted to minister to congregations in both the Latin and Greek rites. The ordination of women remained invalid.

The regeneration of the Church in Slovakia began in 1989, when the Church was finally able to implement the liturgical reforms of the Second Vatican Council. During the 1990s, this regeneration became full-blown: religious communities opened schools, publishing companies reopened, Christian associations once again operated in the open, and the religious once again set themselves to the task of evangelization. Chaplains were once again able to resume their ministry in Slovakia's army, prisons and hospitals. As bishop of Nitra, Cardinal Korec estimated that he opened over 70 new churches and ordained 100 priests in the decade following Slovak independence. In 1996 bishops began a program to reacquaint adult Catholics with the catechism as a way to combat the dearth of religious participation that had occurred under communism. In addition, many Church buildings confiscated by the communist government earlier in the century were returned to the Church, while new seminaries and theological faculties, such as a private Catholic university established in Ruzomberok in 2000, sprang up to replace those institutions that had been destroyed. Unfortunately, many buildings were returned in poor condition and parishes and religious houses often found themselves without sufficient funds for repairs. While the return of Church property remained an issue into 2000—in part because of Slovakia's current economic downturn—a resolution was anticipated that would allow the Church to be made "whole."

By 2000 there were 1,440 parishes ministered to by 1,750 secular and 503 religious priests. In addition, 202 brothers and 3,101 sisters worked within their communities as teachers, caregivers and in other areas of social outreach. Among the most pressing social ills that Catholic leadership hoped to address were the evangelization of youth, the welfare of the Catholic family, stopping the outbreaks of racial violence focused against the region's Roma minority and combating the spiritual inertia of an increasingly secularized and materialistic society. In November of 2000 the Holy See signed a "fundamental accord" with the Slovak government that would, in the words of Pope John Paul II, "safeguard the cultural patrimony" of the country's Catholics. Although some commentators saw the accord as providing preferential treatment of Catholic interests within Slovakia, bishops answered such complaints by noting that the agreement will in fact help all churches within the country.

Because of its long history in Slovakia, the Roman Catholic Church proved invaluable in helping not only Catholics but all Slovaks to recapture the cultural traditions their nation adopted from the West. The presence of the Byzantine Catholic Church, with its spirituality and liturgy, also reminded Slovaks of their centuries-old connection with the East. The continued unity of the two Slovak Catholic Churches, despite the religious and cultural differences that exist, illustrated the potential for unity within a secularized and diversified post-communist culture. As John Paul II commented of the importance of the Slovak Church in eastern Europe, it continued to serve as an example to all Catholics of how to "breathe by both lungs."

See Also: CZECH REPUBLIC, THE CATHOLIC CHURCH IN.

Bibliography: F. DVORNIK, *The Slavs, Their Early History and Civilization* (Boston 1956); *The Slavs in European History and Civilization* (New Brunswick, NJ 1962). R. ŘÍČAN, *Das Reich Gottes in den böhmischen Länderň* (Stuttgart 1957). E. VARSIK, *Husiti a reformaceja na Slovensku do Zilinské dohody* (Bratislava 1932). G. L. ODDO, *Slovakia and Its People* (New York 1960). P. YURCHAK, *The Slovaks* (Whiting, IN 1946). J. M. KIRSCHBAUM, *Slovakia: Nation at the Crossroads of Central Europe*(New York 1960). J. KVACALA, *Dejiny reformácie na Slovensku,* 1517–1711 (Lipt 1935). J. ŠPIRKO, *Cirkevné dejiny: Sosobitným zretal'om na vývin cirkevných dejín Slovenska* (Turč 1943). *Slovenska republika,* ed. M. ŠPRINGC, (Scranton, PA 1949) A. MIKUŠ, *Slovakia: A Political History 1918–1950* (Milwaukee 1963). T. J. ZÚBEK, *The Church of Silence in Slovakia* (Whiting, IN 1956) M. LACKO, "The Forced Liquidation of the Union of Uzahorod," *Slovak Studies,* 1 (Rome 1961) 145–185. J. BROUN, *Conscience and Captivity: Religion in Eastern Europe* (Washington DC 1988). R. ROBERSON, *The Eastern Christian Churches: A Brief Survey* (3d ed.; Rome 1990). G. WEIGEL, *The Final Revolution. The Resistance Church and the Collapse of Communism* (New York 1992).

[M. LACKO/M. FIALA/EDS.]

SLOVENIA, THE CATHOLIC CHURCH IN

Part of the former Yugoslavia, the southeastern European Republic of Slovenia is bordered on the north by Austria, on the northeast by Hungary, on the east and south by Croatia, and on the west by Italy. It is landlocked except for a short strip of coastline in the southwest that provided access to the Gulf of Venice; among the rivers crossing Slovenia is the Sava, running from the Julian Alps to the north southwest to Croatia. Within its wooded alpine regions and fertile valleys, Slovenia enjoys a mild climate that becomes Mediterranean along the coast. Natural resources include lignite coal, lead, zinc, mercury, uranium and silver; its primary exports are manufactured goods and machinery and transportation equipment. Agricultural products include sugar beets, potatoes and cereals.

Except for an initial period under Slovene rulers, historical and political circumstances caused Slovenes in almost all the eastern section of Austria to fall under German domination from the beginning of Austro-Hungarian overlordship (907–955) through the time of the Napoleonic Illyrian Republic (1809–13). Slovenia was incorporated into the duchy of Carantania by Frankish Emperor Otto I in 952; later rulers split the duchy into Carinthia, Carniola and Styria. In 1278 Slovenia fell to the Austrian Habsburgs, who controlled it until 1918, when Slovenia joined the Serbs and Croats in forming what would become Yugoslavia in 1928. Political independence was reestablished in 1991.

The Early Church. A Slavic people, the Slovenes entered the region from the east during the fifth and sixth centuries and settled in the Julian Alps, in the ancient Roman provinces of Pannonia and Noricum. The Franks overran the region in the late eighth century and along with them came Christianity, via both the Patriarchate of AQUILEIA and the See of Salzburg (the Drava River would divide these ecclesiastical jurisdictions until the 1700s). In response to the request of Chotimir (753–769), the Slovenes' second Christian prince, for a bishop to evangelize his people, St. Virgilius of Salzburg sent Chorbishop Modestus, who resided near what is now Klagenfurt, in the Austrian province of Carinthia, near the church of Sancta Maria from 760 to 763. The Prince's residence was in the same neighborhood, at Karnburg.

Under Charlemagne (742–814), German nobles began ensuring that the Slovenes and German missionaries baptized them in the Latin rite. During the ninth century CYRIL and Methodius worked among the Pannonian Slavs at the request of Prince Kocel, who intended to withdraw his lands from German influence by joining them to the Slav archdiocese of St. Methodius (created in 869) and by introducing the Slavonic liturgy. However, Koce's efforts resulted in a Slavic renaissance that was short-lived, as the Latin-rite continued to predominate.

The See of Ljubljana, created in 1461, became the first diocese in Slovenian territory. In 1788 the diocese of Lavant was expanded to include Slovenian territory, and was transferred to the city of Maribor in 1857. The Archdiocese of Gorizia (Gorica in Slovene) was erected in 1751; that see is now in Italy.

When the Ottoman Turks plundered the region during the 16th and 17th centuries, many Slovenes were forced to abandoned their homes and band together, often in churches around which they had raised bulwarks for protection. The Turkish conquest of the Balkans hurt the Slovenian economy, with the result that German nobles' demands for feudal obligations incited numerous peasant revolts from 1470 to the late 16th century.

From Reformation to Enlightenment. While encouraging the spread of Protestantism within the region, the most significant impact of the Reformation was in sparking Slovenia's cultural awakening. In Tübingen, Germany, Protestant writer Primož Trubar published the first Slovenian-language catechism and abecedarium in 1550; these would be followed six years later by a translation of the New Testament, as well as by 20 other books in both Latin and Cyrillic scripts. While Ljubljana had a printing press by 1575, the authorities closed it when Jurij Dalmatin tried to publish a Slovenian translation of the Bible. Dalmatin moved to Germany, and published his Bible in 1584, complete with a glossary enabling Croats to read it.

Promotion of the Slovenian language was important to both Catholics and Protestants, the former as a means of retaining Sloveninan cultural autonomy in a Protestantized society, and the latter as a way to break the hold of centuries-old power bases. Many German nobles living in the Slovenian provinces of Carinthia, Carniola and Styria supported the reformation solely as a means of

Capital: Ljubljana.
Size: 7,897 sq. miles.
Population: 1,927,593 in 2000.
Languages: Slovenian; Serbo-Croatian is also spoken.
Religions: 1,388,590 Roman Catholics (71%), 28,910 Sunni Muslims (1.5%), 48,189 Serbian Orthodox (2.5%), 18,567 Protestants (1%), 443,337 practice other faiths or are without religious affiliation.
Archdiocese: Ljubljana, with suffragans Koper and Maribor.

breaking the hold of the Catholic Church and gaining political autonomy. However, the Catholic Counter-reformation eventually gained influence and by 1628 the Austrian emperor was giving Slovenian Protestants the choice between Catholicism and exile. Slovenian-language elementary schools were dismantled in cities and gradually died out in rural areas. Jesuit counter reformers burned Slovenian Protestant literature and took other measures that, while stalling the spread of Slovenian nationalism, failed to stifle it completely. Meanwhile, Capuchin friar Janez Svetokriški published volumes of Slovenian sermons, and other Religious followed suit, determined to defend the Slovenian language against a Germanicization of the litergy that reflected an increasingly liberalized post-reformation culture. In 1769 Augustinian monk Marko Pohlin would publish a Slovene grammar that would further revive the language.

During the 17th and 18th centuries, Slovenia developed a strong economy and living conditions improved due to increased trade within Europe, although the power of the Church slowly eroded as Austrian emperors used their authority to take possession of monastic lands. By the beginning of the 19th century, Slovenia possessed a generation steeped in the views of the Enlightenment and an intellectual class trained in Catholic schools and writing in Slovenian about the ideal Slovenian culture. In 1809, following victories in Austria, Napoleon Bonaparte incorporated the three Slovenian provinces as part of the Slavic Illyrian Provinces, its capital at Ljubljana. Promoting the ancient state of Illyria as a unifying force among Slovenes, Croats and Serbs planted the first seeds of a possible Slavic unification. The French, issuing proclamations in Slovenian as well as in German and French, instituted reforms that included new roads, the establishment of Slovenian-language schools and the appointment of Slovenes to government positions.

While Austria rescinded these French reforms after regaining power in Slovenia in 1813, intellectuals continued to debate the ramifications of Slovenian nationalism. To counter this line of thought, philologist and pioneer linguist Jernej Kopitar created a Slovenian literary language through which he hoped to strengthen support for

the status quo: the Austrian-Habsburg monarchy and the Catholic Church. Despite a 1848 revolution ending serfdom, the nationalist momentum gained little headway, and the Church used its renewed control of the region's schools to promote the Serbian language within a Catholic context. Their efforts ended in 1866, after control over non-religious elementary and secondary education reverted to the state. From 1879 to 1893 the Austrian government allowed Slovenian to be used in schools and in some local governments. Slovenes controlled the local assembly of Carniola after 1883, and Ljubljana had a Slovenian mayor after 1888.

To promote Catholic culture among the populace, the Society of St. Hermagoras was founded in the 19th century in Celovec; its headquarters were moved to Celje in 1918. Battling a growing liberal nationalist ideology, the Church attempted to return education, the media and many social structures to a Catholic base, and restore Slovenia's Catholic culture. However, events early in the next century would undermine their efforts.

The Rise of Yugoslavia. In October of 1908 Austria annexed the southern Slav provinces of Bosnia and Herzegovina, a move many Slovenians viewed as a step toward formation of a South Slav union. Ten years later, at the close of World War I, Slovenia joined the Kingdom of Serbs, Croats and Slovenes, renamed the Kingdom of Yugoslavia in 1929. The region's wealthy Catholics aided fellow Catholics harmed during the war in Serbia and Macedonia by sending priests and financial and humanitarian aid. By the early 1920s Slovenian society was so homogenous that an estimated 96 percent declared themselves Catholic; among the most popular periodicals of the era was the Catholic monthly *Mladika* (1924–32), edited by Father Franc Saleški Finzgar, which was published in Slovenian.

Within the Kingdom of Yugoslavia, Slovenia soon realized that the Serbian majority dominated, despite policy opposition from Croats, Macedonians and other minorities. Although the Yugoslav constitution guaranteed freedom and equality to all faiths, the government favored the Orthodox Serbian Church, prompting many to join that faith and resulting in a decline in the Roman Catholic population in southern Yugoslavia. In 1922 Slovenia supported the Yugoslav government's negotiations with the Holy See intended to create corresponding diocesan and state borders and establish the Roman-Slavonic liturgy in all regions where so desired. While an agreement was reached in 1935, the Parliament bent to the will of the Orthodox Church and refused ratification.

During World War II Slovenia was occupied by German forces north of the Sava River and by Italian forces south of it. In 1946 it joined the socialist Federal People's Republic of Yugoslavia, proclaimed in 1945 by Communist leader Josip Broz Tito. Although the republic's Nov. 30, 1946 constitution guaranteed religious liberty, the new Yugoslavian government demonstrated its opposition to religion by open persecution. Ljubljana Bishop Gregorij Rožman, forced to flee in May of 1945, was marked as a fascist and traitor to his people. Almost all Catholic schools, as well as other church properties, were nationalized or destroyed; religious instruction was prohibited in public schools; the Catholic media was curtailed; and faith-based associations were suppressed.

An ideological disagreement between Yugoslavia and the former Soviet Union in 1948 prompted government officials to establish a policy of toleration with regard to religious groups. After 1956 they permitted the Holy See to appoint new bishops, suspended charges against the clergy, allowed some religious periodicals to resume publication and permitted some minor seminaries to reopen. In 1961 Ljubljana became an archdiocese without suffragans. In 1962 all bishops received permission to attend Vatican Council II. These conditions strengthened religious life in some measure; they by no means destroyed it. On June 25, 1966 the government signed a protocol with the Vatican that improved Church-state relations still further, and diplomatic relations were restored between Yugoslavia and Rome on Aug. 14, 1970.

The Slovenian region that returned to the newly socialist Yugoslavia in 1945 had been enlarged by the annexation of Slovenian portions of the Istrian peninsula under the care of the Italian-based Archdiocese of Gorizia and Diocese of Trieste. Because Italian Church leaders were not permitted in Yugoslavia, the Holy See first appointed two apostolic administrators; in 1964 Rome reduced this administration to one bishop.

The Modern Era. By the mid-20th century Slovenia was the most economically viable and politically stable republic in Yugoslavia. When a new 1974 constitution outlined federal budgeting procedures forcing Slovenia to support Yugoslavia's underdeveloped republics, the region grew increasingly critical of the amount of Serbian influence in government. Slovenia also condemned Serbian oppression of ethnic Albanians in Kosovo and the Serbian majority's push for one man-one vote elections. By 1989 several noncommunist political groups had developed in Slovenia, multiple-candidate elections were held, and open discussion of all issues was encouraged. On Sept. 27, 1989, the Slovenian parliament voted itself the right to secede from Yugoslavia. Shortly thereafter, the Slovenian League of Communists renamed itself the Party of Democratic Renewal. In 1990 it became the first Yugoslav republic to hold multiparty elections, and it declared itself independent of Yugoslavia on June 25, 1991, under a six-party coalition led by newly elected reformist president Milan Kucan. Although scattered fighting followed, Yugoslavian president Slobodan Milošević agreed to follow the ruling of the European Community and withdrew his forces.

While Slovenian independence was welcomed by the Church, a rift soon developed between the liberal government that came to power after Kucan and Church leaders over the reintroduction of religious education as part of public school curriculum, the return of confiscated Church properties and the role of the Church in Slovenian society. Under liberal Prime Minister Janez Drnovsek, state restitution for confiscated Church property quickly came to a standstill, and by 1999 only a third of all property issues had been resolved. The election of conservative president Andrej Bajuk in 2000 was viewed as encouraging by the Church. Other issues remained between conservative Catholics and the liberal minority, one of which involves the treatment of affluent Catholics alleged to be Nazi sympathizers, who were either killed or evicted from Slovenia, their property confiscated by the state, between 1946 and 1948.

Under the new constitution of Dec. 23, 1991, the government recognized freedom of religion, allowing for a regeneration of the Church. By 2001 Slovenia had over 800 parishes, tended by 835 secular and 300 religious priests. In addition, 810 sisters and 45 brothers tended to Church-run education and other community and health-based needs. During a visit from Pope John Paul II in May of 1996, the pontiff celebrated Mass in Ljubljana, and expressed joy at ''being in independent Slovenia at the dawn of the new age of its history.''

Bibliography: *Monumenta spectantia historiam Slavorum meridionalium* (Zagreb 1868—), 46 v. to 1951. M. SPINKA, *A History of Christianity in the Balkans* (Chicago, IL 1933). R. RISTELHUEBER, *Histoire des peoples balkaniques* (Paris 1950). P. D. OSTROVÍC, *The Truth about Yugoslavia* (New York 1952). W. MARKERT, *Jugoslawien* (Cologne 1954). F. DVORNIK, *The Slavs: Their Early History and Civilization* (Boston 1956); *The Slavs in European History and Civilization* (New Brunswick, NJ 1962). K. S. LATOURETTE, *Christianity in a Revolutionary Age: A History of Christianity in the Nineteenth and Twentieth Centuries,* 5 v. (New York 1958–62) v.1, 2, 4. F. MACLEAN, *The Heretic: The Life and Times of Josip Broz-Tito* (New York 1957). M. KOS, *Zgodovina Slovencv* (Ljubljana 1955). A. L. KUHAR, *The Conversion of the Slovenes* (New York 1959). S. P. RAMET, *Nihil Obstat: Religion, Politics, and Social Change in East-Central Europe and Russia* (Durham, NC 1998). J. MATL, *Lexikon für Theologie und Kirche*[2], eds., J. HOFER and K. RAHNER, 10 v. (Freiburg 1957–65) 5:1191–94. B. SPULER and H. KOCH, *Die Religion in Geschichte und Gegenwart* [3], 7 v. (3d ed. Tübingen 1957–65) 3:1054–60. *Bilan du Monde,* 2:914–928. *Annuario Pontificio* has annual data on all dioceses.

[P. SHELTON]

SMALDONE, FILIPPO MARIANO, BL.

Priest and cofounder of the Congregation of the Salesian Sisters of the Sacred Hearts (*Congregazione delle Suore Salesiane dei Sacri Cuori*); b. Naples, Sicily, Italy, July 27, 1848; d. Lecce, Apulia, Italy, June 4, 1923. The eldest of the seven children of Antonio Smaldone and Maria Concetta de Luca, Filippo had decided by age 12 to become a priest, despite the persecution the Church was experiencing. He entered the minor seminary in Rossano Calabria (1862). His specific apostolate was determined while he was still a student following a encounter with the mother of a deaf child in Saint Catherine's Church in Naples. From that time he evangelized and taught the deaf.

Overcoming some difficulties that required his transfer to the archdiocese of Naples, Smaldone was ordained in 1871. While ministering to plague victims, Smaldone contracted the disease, but was miraculously healed through the intercession of Our Lady of Pompeii. Frustrated by his inability to help the deaf sufficiently, Smaldone considered undertaking a foreign mission; however, his spiritual director convinced him to recommit himself to his apostolate in Naples. On March 25, 1885, Smaldone cofounded an institute in Lecce with Father Lorenzo Apicelia and some specially trained Grey Sisters, who became Salesian Sisters of the Sacred Heart dedicated to the education of the deaf. Other institutes followed for the deaf in Bari (1897) and throughout Italy, as well as centers for the blind, abandoned, and orphaned.

Smaldone's love for the Blessed Sacrament was demonstrated by his founding the Eucharistic League of Priest Adorers and Women Adorers. In addition to his charitable activities and spiritual direction of many priests, seminarians, and religious communities, Smaldone served as superior for the Congregation of the Missionaries of Saint Francis de Sales and canon of the Lecce cathedral.

He died at age 75 of cardiac complications from diabetes, and was declared venerable July 11, 1995. Pope John Paul II beatified Smaldone on Aug 16, 1996.

Feast: June 4.

Bibliography: *Acta Apostolicae Sedis* (1996): 551–53. *L'Osservatore Romano,* no. 20 (1996): 1; 21 (1996): 4–5. *L'Osservatore Romano,* English edition, no. 29 (1995): 5.

[K. I. RABENSTEIN]

SMARAGDUS OF SAINT-MIHIEL

Benedictine abbot of that monastery, where he died after 825. He was probably of Irish origin. While teaching Latin grammar at the abbey of Castellion, he compiled his commentary on the manual of DONATUS, the *Liber in partibus Donati,* a work that had considerable influence. After becoming abbot, he moved from Castellion to the monastery of SAINT-MIHIEL, which he established near the Meuse. With abbatial solicitude he exhorted his monks to the practice of virtue in the *Diadema monachorum* (after 805) drawn largely from patristic writings. In preparation for the Council of AACHEN of 809, Smaragdus wrote a justification from Scripture of the Frankish position in the FILIOQUE controversy. Among other duties he performed at the council, he formulated its conclusions in a letter from CHARLEMAGNE to Pope LEO III. As a member of the three-man delegation sent to Rome to have the Pope impose Frankish custom on the Church, he reported the proceedings of the fruitless interview with the Pope. To Emperor LOUIS the Pious he addressed the *Via regia,* a work on the spiritual formation of a prince, with particular emphasis on the virtues of piety and justice. Monastic reform was the concern of his *Expositio in regulam s Benedicti,*. written after the Council of Aachen of 817. A simple commentary on the rule, it presents an accurate picture of monastic life in the time of Louis the Pious and of the influence exerted by the reform of BENEDICT OF ANIANE. His last work, the *Collectiones in epistolas et evangelia* or *Liber comitis,* is a series of patristic texts to serve as a commentary on the Epistles and Gospels of Sundays and feasts of the year and some other Masses. His acknowledgments reveal the broad expanse of his erudition and reading and his knowledge of patristic authors.

Bibliography: *Patrologia Latina* 102:1–970. *Monumenta Germania Poetae* 1:605–619; 2:918–924. M. L. W. LAISTNER in *Speculum* 3 (1928) 392–397. J. SCHARF, "Studien zu S. und Jonas," DeutschArch 17 (1961) 333–384. D. MISONNE, *Lexikon für Theologie und Kirche* [2] 9:836–837.

[J. M. O'DONNELL]

SMART, RODERICK NINIAN

Philosopher, historian of Comparative Religion; b. Cambridge, England, May 6, 1927; d. Lancaster, England, Jan. 29, 2001.

Ninian Smart was born to an academic family. His father, William M. Smart was an astronomer, his mother was poet Isabel Carswell, and his elder brothers were J. C. Smart (Philosophy) and Alastair Smart (Art History). In 1954 he married Libushka Baruffaldi, with whom he had four children.

Scottish Epicopalian, Smart studied at Glasgow Academy. While serving in World War II as a Captain in the Royal Army Intelligence Corps (1945–48), he studied Cantonense and was introduced to Thervadan Buddhism in Sri Lanka. After the war he studied at Queen's College, Oxford (Classics and Philosophy, 1948–54), then lectured in Philosophy at University College of Wales, Aberystwyth (1952–55), Yale (including studies of Pali and Sanskrit, 1955–56), and also at King's College, London (1956–61). He served as H. G. Wood Professor of Theology at Birmingham University (1961–67), founding Professor of Religious Studies, University of Lancaster (1967–82), and Professor of Religious Studies, University of California, Santa Barbara (1976–1998).

Professor Emeritus at the Universities of Lancaster (1989) and California (1998), his academic career included honorary professorships and degrees, numerous visiting professorships and lectures across the globe (including the Gifford Lectures), executive positions with various academic societies, consulting work (including editor of *The Long Search Series*), and appointments as director of Schools Council Project on Secondary and Primary Religious Education (1969–1979), centered at the University of Lancaster, and vice- chancellor of that institution (1969–72).

A pioneer in the comparative study of religion, Smart was a prolific writer and lecturer. His early work focused on issues in the philosophy of religion, including substantial comparative explorations of Indian philosophy. This included a linguistic analysis of religious doctrines and concepts that distinguishes between patterns of religious discourse and practice according to particular experiential types: the numinous, the mystical, and the incarnational. This ''logical strand'' model of religion draws on examples from Hinduism, Buddhism, and Christianity to illustrate how religious propositions and practices are contextualized in terms of these particular doctrinal systems.

He later went on to frame cross-cultural expositions of these and other religions in terms of various dynamic and interacting ''dimensions'' that are distinguished under the general categories of belief and practical manifestation. The former division of this dimensional model of religion includes: the doctrinal and philosophical; the mythic and narrative; and the ethical or legal. The latter involves: the ritual or practical; the experiential or emotional; the social, institutional or organizational; and the material or artistic.

Smart also extended his studies of religion to include ''worldview analysis,'' arguing that secular ideological orientations (such as Marxism, scientific humanism, nationalism, and democratic liberalism) significantly resemble religious traditions in the way in which they are empowered through their own ritual, symbol, and myth. He advocated an ''interactive pluralism'' committed to tolerance and openness in inter-religious and even inter-ideological dialogue and comparative study, with the goal of enhancing and refining one's own worldview through the phenomenological study of others. In regard to methodology, he stressed an attitude of ''informed empathy'' and advocated a ''polymethodic'' approach to the study of religion. Smart argued that the scientific study of religion ought to include the various academic disciplines, and refrain from imposing values and beliefs on the subject in question.

He also distinguished the scientific study of religion from various religious theologies. While theological approaches espouse and defend truth claims of religious faith, religious studies, Smart observed, maintains a neutrality on these questions. Nevertheless, the two disciplines are often mutually engaged: theology is a major subject of religious studies and religious studies provides much helpful material for theologians. Indeed, Smart himself co-authored a substantial ecumenical work of systematic theology, one that explores essential elements of Christian faith in light of contemporary developments in religious studies.

Ninian Smart was a highly influential figure in the philosophy of comparative religion and in the method and theory of religion. He played a key role in the worldwide development of religious education and the discipline of religious studies. He founded the first religious studies department in the United Kingdom and was a major force in the international expansion of the discipline. But he is best known for his survey texts on the world's religions and secular ideologies. These, as well as his other books, demonstrate Smart's vast breadth of cultural and historical knowledge, his sharp eye for comparative detail and significance, and his keen philosophical insight into religious traditions and other worldviews.

Bibliography: Books by Ninian Smart: *Reasons and Faiths* (London 1958); *A Dialogue of Religions* (London 1960), reprinted as *World Religions: A Dialogue* (Harmondsworth 1966); *Historical Selections in the Philosophy of Religions* (London 1962); *Philosophers and Religious Truth* (London 1964); *Doctrine and Argument in Indian Philosophy* (London 1964); *The Teacher and Christian Belief* (London 1966); *Secular Education and the Logic of Religion* (London 1968); *The Yogi and the Devotee* (London 1968); *The Religious Experience of Mankind* (New York 1969, new edition 1984), new edition published as *The Religious Experience* (New York 1991); *The Philosophy of Religion* (New York 1970, new edition 1979); *The Concept of Worship* (London 1972); *The Science of Religion and the Sociology of Knowledge* (Princeton 1973); *The Phenomenon of Religion* (London 1973); *Mao* (London 1974); *Background to the Long Search* (London 1977), published also as *The Long Search* (Boston 1978); *The Phenomenon of Christianity* (London 1979), published also as *In Search of Christianity* (New

York 1979); *Beyond Ideology* (London 1981); *Worldviews, Cross-cultural Exploration of Human Beliefs* (New York 1983); *Prophet of a New Hindu Age* (London 1985); *Concept and Empathy*, ed., D. WIEBE (New York, 1986); *Religion and the Western Mind* (London 1987); *The World's Religions* (Englewood Cliffs 1989); *Christian Systematic Theology in a World Context* (London, 1991); *Buddhism and Christianity* (Honolulu 1993); *Religions of Asia* and *Religions of the West* (Englewood Cliffs 1993); *Dimensions of the Sacred* (Berkeley 1996); *Reflections in the Mirror of Religion*, ed., J. P. BURRIS (New York 1997); *World Philosophies* (New York 1999). For a chronological listing of Smart's publications and professional activities, as well as a detailed biographical sketch to 1993, see: the Appendix and P. MAGEE, "Roderick Ninian Smart—A Biographical Sketch," eds., P. MASEFIELD & D. WIEBE, *Aspects of Religion: Essays in Honour of Ninian Smart* (New York 1994).

[M. STOEBER]

SMEDT, CHARLES DE

Belgian Bollandist; b. Gand, April 6, 1831; d. Brussels, March 4, 1911. Educated at Louvain, De Smedt entered the Society of Jesus in 1851 and taught at Namur and in the scholasticate at Tronchienne (1857). Upon joining the church history faculty at Louvain in 1864, he quickly recognized the need for purging Catholic historical writing of its use of doubtful sources and of an exaggerated reliance on the supernatural element in human affairs. Sent to Paris in 1869 as an editor of the *Études religieuses,* he published a series of articles on the principles of historical criticism, later edited as a book, *Principes de la critique historique* (Paris 1883). He served as a fellow of the society of Bollandists from 1870 and was made a member in 1876 on the death of V. de Buck. Two series of lectures delivered at Louvain were published as *Introductio ad historiam ecclesiasticam critice tractandam and Dissertationes selectae in primam aetatem historiae ecclesiasticae.* The latter work outlined a reordination of the *Acta Sanctorum,* giving greater importance to primary sources by publishing the original documents. As head of the society of Bollandists (1882–1911) he inaugurated the periodical *Analecta Bollandiana* as an instrument for the publication of hagiographical documents and critical apparatus. He likewise reorganized the use of subsidiary historical disciplines including the employment of inventories, almanacs, catalogues, and bibliographies. He discovered an unknown manuscript of the *Gesta episcoporum cameracensium* (1092–1138) and published an outstanding ascetical treatise, *Notre vie surnaturelle* (2 v. 3d ed. Brussels 1920). His reorganization of the work of the Bollandists slowed down the publication of the *Acta Sanctorum* but immeasurably added to their value. De Smedt became a correspondent of the Académie des Inscriptions (1894) and a member of the Académie Royale de Belgique (1900).

Bibliography: H. LECLERCQ, *Dictionnaire d'archéologie chrétienne et de liturgie* 15.1:1516–18. *Le R. P. Charles de Smedt, Analecta Bollandiana* 30 (1911) I-X. H. DELEHAYE, *L'Oeuvre des Bollandistes à travers trois siècles 1615–1915*, (2d ed. Brussels 1959), with bibliog. 166–189; Eng. (Princeton 1922). R. AIGRAIN, *L'Hagiographie* (Paris 1953) 346–350. A. CAUCHIE, *Revue d'histoire ecclésiastique* 12 (1911) 347–358. M. COENS, *Lexikon für Theologie und Kirche* [2] 9:837.

[J. BEAUDRY]

SMET, EUGÉNIE DE, BL.

Foundress of the HELPERS OF THE HOLY SOULS; b. Lille, France, March 25, 1825; d. Paris, Feb. 7, 1871. Eugénie was the daughter of Henri and Pauline (Taverne de Mont-d'Hiver) de Smet, a family of the landed gentry. She was educated at the convent of the Sacred Heart in Lille, and then she devoted some years to charitable works. After seeking the counsel of the Curé d'Ars (St. Jean VIANNEY), she resolved her doubts concerning her religious vocation and decided to establish a congregation of religious women dedicated to charitable endeavors and to assistance of the souls in purgatory by prayers, sufferings, and labors. She arrived in Paris on Jan. 19, 1856, and with the aid of Hippolyte Basiau, SJ, founded her community, with a rule modeled on that of the JESUITS. In religion Smet was known as Marie de la Providence. She shared fully the squalor of the poor among whom the young community worked. She was assisted and encouraged by Pierre OLIVAINT, SJ. Smet was beatified on May 26, 1957.

Feast: Feb. 7.

Bibliography: M. RENÉ-BAZIN, *She Who Lived Her Name, Mary of Providence* (Westminster, MD 1948). M. C. BUEHRLE, *I Am on Fire: Blessed Mary of Providence* (Milwaukee 1963). J. L. BAUDOT and L. CHAUSSIN, *Vies des saints et des bienheureux selon l'ordre du calendrier avec l'historique des fêtes,* ed. by the Benedictines of Paris, 12 v. (Paris 1935–56); v. 13, suppl. and table générale (1959) 13:176–182.

[M. C. BUEHRLE]

SMETANA, BEDŘICH

Romanticist composer considered the founder of modern Czech music; b. Litoměřice, Bohemia, March 2, 1824; d. Prague, May 12, 1884. Although he wrote little church music, he was a figure of spiritual as well as historic importance in the development of romanticism and Czech nationalism. While studying at the Praemonstratensian Gymnasium at Plezeň he revealed exceptional pianistic gifts, and thereafter was active as virtuoso and chamber player. He became a friend of Robert and Clara

Schumann and a disciple of LISZT, and participated enthusiastically in romanticist and liberal movements. After five years in Göteborg, Sweden, he returned to Prague in 1861 to lead the National Theater orchestra and establish a conservatory. Bearing with nobility both personal affliction (total deafness from 1874; later, mental illness) and public calumniation, he emerged a national artist-hero. Best known for his comic opera *The Bartered Bride,* the cycle of six symphonic poems *My Fatherland,* and the string quartet *From My Life,* he composed also eight other operas, additional chamber and symphonic works, and a quantity of vocal, choral, and piano music, while active as conductor, critic, and educator. Devotion to family and fatherland and a joyous optimism animated his life and art alike.

Bibliography: V. HELPERT, *Die schöpferische Entwicklung Friedrich Smetanas,* Ger. tr. (from Czech) B. LIEHM (Leipzig 1956). E. RYCHNOVSKY, *Smetana* (Berlin 1924). Z. NEJEDLÝ, *Frederick Smetana,* 4 v. (Prague 1924–33); abr. Eng. tr. 1 v. (London 1924). R. NEWMARCH, *The Music of Czechoslovakia* (London 1942). R. NEWMARCH and G. ČERNUŠAK, *Grove's Dictionary of Music and Musicians*, ed. E. BLOM 9 v. (5th ed. London 1954) 7:843–849. P. ANDRASCHKE, ''Über die Gestaltung von Smetanas *Vyšehrad,*'' *International Journal of Musicology* 1 (1992) 127–37. T. BARFOOT, ''*Dalibor*'' in *International Dictionary of Opera* 2 vols., ed. C. S. LARUE (Detroit 1993). J. CLAPHAM, *The New Grove Dictionary of Music and Musicians* ed. S. SADIE (New York 1980). C. HEADINGTON, ''*The Bartered Bride*'' in *International Dictionary of Opera,* ed. C. S. LARUE (Detroit 1993). R. PECMAN, ''Smetanovská Miscellanea,'' *Sborník Prací Filosofické Fakulty Brnenské University* 4 (1969) 130. M. STROEHER, ''Bedrich Smetana's *Dalibor:* A Study in Czech Cultural Nationalism,'' *The Opera Journal* 24/2 (1991) 3–23.

[F. J. BURKLEY]

Bedřich Smetana.

SMITH, ADAM

Scottish economist and moral philosopher; b. Kirkcaldy, Scotland, June 5, 1723; d. Edinburgh, Scotland, July 7, 1790. Having been educated at Glasgow and Oxford, he became professor of moral philosophy at the University of Glasgow in 1752 and seven years later published his first book, *A Theory of the Moral Sentiments.* That book, at first widely read and admired, soon fell almost into oblivion; thus, unfortunately, the psychological and ethical insights expressed in it have rarely been taken into account, as they should be, in interpreting Smith's theory of economics and his advice about economic policy, as presented in his great work on the wealth of nations. Before writing the latter, he traveled on the Continent from 1764 to 1766, and while in France met some of the Physiocrats, whose important contributions to economics partially anticipated his own; but his indebtedness to them was limited. After returning in 1766 to the University of Glasgow, he labored there for ten years more and brought out, in 1776, his masterwork, *An Inquiry into the Nature and Causes of the Wealth of Nations.* In 1778 he was appointed commissioner of customs for Scotland. Little more of note happened in the remaining 12 years of his life. His *Essays on Philosophical Subjects,* written relatively early in his life (before 1752), were found among his papers and published posthumously in 1795.

Smith's place in the age-long history of the development of political economy must be estimated as very high, although not as high as was widely supposed in the early nineteenth century. He was by no means the founder of that science, the beginnings of which go back at least to Aristotle, and to which numerous scholastic and other writers in the medieval and early-modern centuries made important contributions. Smith was one among many great economists in his own century. Yet he stands above the others not as being more original, or brilliant, or penetrating, or invariably correct in his observations and reasonings, but by virtue of the nearly all-comprehensive breadth of his outlook and knowledge, and the surpassingly realistic, well-balanced, and moral wisdom of his treatment of the vast subject of his famous *Inquiry.* This work in its way sums up the main fruits of most previous research and thinking in its field, and con-

Adam Smith, an engraving. (©Bettmann/CORBIS)

tains the germs of many, if not most, of the advances that have since been achieved.

The generally prevailing impression, however, of the supposed central thesis of the *Wealth of Nations* has always been somewhat incorrect. This is so in part because there has been general neglect of the relevant psychological and ethical views expressed in Smith's earlier work on the moral sentiments, and in part because, as ''capitalism'' and attacks upon it, and diverse political ideologies, went on developing throughout the nineteenth century, it became the fashion to attribute to Smith the original sponsorship of the crude, dogmatic, unqualified, and biased laissez-faire gospel of later generations of conservative businessmen. The economic liberalism—in his phrase, ''system of natural liberty'' for all individuals—that Smith really sponsored had behind it both his ethical and humane concern for equal rights and opportunities for all men, and his economic analysis of the requirements of an optimal growth of their common wealth and welfare. In his early treatise, he argued that citizens of a free society could be led by their human-natural, humane, reciprocal ''sympathies'' and sensitivities to each others' moral judgments to develop a moral consensus and (to implement that) a just legal order, impartially defining the just rights and freedoms of all severally, and allowing none to infringe the rights of others. In his subsequent economic treatise, presupposing the existence (in a good approximation) of such a moral climate and legal order, he went on to argue that, *within it,* a generally competitive economic system could function in such a way that all in maximizing their private gains would also be maximizing their contributions to the aggregate wealth of the nation and the world. The wisdom of that outlook can be questioned, but its true meaning, grounds, and implications as elaborated in Smith's own writings need and deserve careful study and just appraisal undistorted by confusions of it with propaganda. Nor is his program for creating a harmony of individual (suitably modified) self-interests and the common welfare the whole or main substance of his economics. His immortal *Inquiry* in its time was, and even today remains, an inexhaustible mine of wisdom about the processes and conditions of on-going growth of aggregate and per capita wealth or economic welfare in and throughout all nations.

Bibliography: O. H. TAYLOR, *Economics and Liberalism* (Cambridge, Mass. 1955); *A History of Economic Thought* (New York 1960). R. B. HALDANE, *Life of Adam Smith* (London 1887). G. R. MORROW, *The Ethical and Economic Theories of Adam Smith* (New York 1923). J. RAE, *Life of Adam Smith* (New York 1895). F. A. NEFF, *Adam Smith and His Master Work* (Wichita, Ks. 1940).

[O. H. TAYLOR]

SMITH, HENRY IGNATIUS

Orator and educator; b. Newark, NJ, Aug. 25, 1886; d. Washington, DC, March 8, 1957. He was the oldest of the eight children of Michael and Loretta (Gaskins) Smith, four of whom became Dominican priests. After study in New Jersey and Ohio, he entered The Catholic University of America, Washington, DC, where he was ordained June 27, 1910, and received his Ph.D. in 1915. After teaching philosophy and sociology from 1913 to 1916 in the Dominican House of Studies, Washington, DC, he was appointed national director of the Holy Name Society and of the Third Order of St. Dominic. He served also as editor of the *Holy Name Review* and the *Torch,* which he founded in 1916, and as prior and rector of St. Catherine of Siena Church in New York, NY. In 1920 he returned to Catholic University as an instructor in philosophy, acting also as prior (1922–28) of the Dominican House of Studies. He was promoted to associate professor in 1926 and professor in 1947, and appointed to succeed Msgr. Edward A. Pace as dean of the School of Philosophy in 1936. Smith developed the School of Philosophy and made it a chief center of Thomism in the U.S. He was also responsible for the establishment of the Preachers' Institute. Renowned for his abilities as a speaker, he preached countless sermons, conducted many retreats and missions, and gave numerous talks to lay organizations. His training and interests were not those of the specialized scholar, but in addition to his doctoral dissertation, *The Classification of Desires in St. Thomas Aquinas and in Modern Sociology* (1915), he produced a number of articles and pamphlets on religious and philosophical subjects. They include ''Aquinas and Some American Freedoms,'' ''St. Thomas Aquinas and Human Social Life,'' ''The Militant Christian Virtues,'' ''Justice,'' ''Education for Patriotism,'' ''Benedict XV and the Historical Basis for Thomistic Study,'' and ''The Place of Authority in St. Thomas.'' For the old *Catholic Encyclopedia* he wrote the article, ''Dominican Rite,'' and seven biographical articles. Upon his retirement on Aug. 31, 1956, he was awarded the papal medal *Pro Ecclesia et Pontifice* and named to the newly established position of dean for religious communities. A bronze bust, presented by friends to the University on his retirement, stands in McMahon Hall.

Bibliography: J. K. RYAN, ed., *Philosophical Studies in Honor of the Very Reverend Ignatius Smith, O.P.* (Westminster, MD 1952). Archives, The Catholic University of America.

[J. K. RYAN]

Henry Ignatius Smith.

SMITH, JAMES

Journalist; b. Skolland, Shetland, July 11, 1790; d. Oakley, Fife, Jan. 5, 1866. He was brought up a Presbyterian and trained as a solicitor before the Supreme Courts in Edinburgh. He was converted to Catholicism and, in the public controversy over the Catholic Emancipation Bill of 1829, lectured and wrote in support of Catholic claims. He married Catherine Mackenzie (1812), a cousin of Bp. Alexander MacDonell of Kingston, Ontario; and his own son, William, became archbishop of St. Andrews and Edinburgh (1885). In 1831, some of Smith's controversial lectures, *Dialogues on the Catholic and Protestant Rules of Faith,* were published and, in 1832, he founded and edited the first Catholic Scottish monthly; the *Edinburgh Catholic Magazine.* It appeared from April 1832 to November 1833, then fell silent until February 1837. In April 1838, ''Edinburgh'' was dropped from the title, and it continued as the *Catholic Magazine* until December 1842.

One of the reasons for the journal's eventual failure (and a typical source of weakness in Scottish periodical literature) was that the editor migrated to London. There he continued his journalistic activities, editing two successive issues of the *Dublin Review* (1837, 1838), and launching the *Catholic Directory* on the lines of John MACPHERSON's directory in Scotland. Smith's publication superseded the old *Laity's Directory* and still continues as the national Catholic directory for England and Wales. Smith continued a prominent role in religious controversy and Catholic public life, acting for a time as secretary to the Catholic Institute of Great Britain. Toward the end of his life he returned to his native land.

[D. MCROBERTS]

SMITH, JOHN TALBOT

Author; b. Saratoga, N.Y., Sept. 22, 1855; d. Dobbs Ferry, N.Y., Sept. 24, 1923. He was the son of American-born parents, Bernard, a railroad worker, and Brigid (O'Donnell) Smith. After early education at the Christian Brothers' school, Albany, N.Y., he entered St. Michael's College and Seminary, Toronto, Canada, where he was ordained in 1881 for the Diocese of Ogdensburg, N.Y. After serving the diocese as curate in Watertown and pastor at Rouses Point, he was released by his bishop in 1889 and went to New York City, where he devoted himself mainly to literary work for nearly 20 years. During most of that period he was chaplain to the Christian Brothers at De La Salle Academy, and from 1901 to 1904 to the Sisters of Mercy at St. Catherine's Convent. His first publication was a novel, ''A Woman of Culture,'' that ran serially in the *Catholic World*, as did some of his later writing. He was the author of a number of novels, some on the juvenile level; a biography of Brother Azarias, FSC (1897); some short stories; and a *History of the Diocese of Ogdensburg* (1885). He edited (1889–92) the *Catholic Review*, a weekly paper, and contributed, sometimes anonymously, to various other papers. His *History of the Catholic Church in New York* (1906), written for the centenary of the archdiocese, remains the only book on the subject. In *Our Seminaries* (1896), reprinted as *The Training of a Priest* (1908), his scathing criticism of the entire system of clerical training in America caused lasting resentment, partly because so much of what he said was true. He was a founder and president (1905–09) of the Catholic Summer School of America, and he established the first Catholic camp for boys as an adjunct to it. He founded also the Catholic Writers Guild and the Catholic Actors Guild. An excellent lecturer and preacher, he was in demand for special occasions. In September 1908, he was appointed pastor of Sacred Heart parish, Dobbs Ferry, N.Y. Before his death there, he destroyed all his personal papers.

Bibliography: *Catholic World* 64 (Dec. 1896) 419–420. T. MCMILLAN, *ibid.* 118 (Nov. 1923) 218–220.

[F. D. COHALAN]

SMITH, JOSEPH

Founder and first president of the Mormon Church; b. Sharon, Vt., Dec. 23, 1805; d. Carthage, Ill., June 27, 1844. His parents, Joseph and Lucy (Mack) Smith, were poor and migrated to upstate New York about 1816. Joseph claimed visions from 1820 on and in 1830 published *The Book of Mormon* as a divinely rediscovered scripture linking pre-Columbian civilizations with the ancient Hebrews. On April 6, 1830, he founded the Church of Jesus Christ of LATTERDAY SAINTS (Mormons) at Fayette, N.Y. He started Mormon communities in Kirtland, Ohio; Independence and Far West, Mo.; and Nauvoo, Ill. His movement evoked considerable opposition. The Kirtland effort ended in financial disaster, and the Saints were driven from Missouri by mob action. In Illinois, Joseph and his brother Hyrum were murdered in the Carthage jail by a mob that included uniformed militia. Heroism in death made Smith a martyr as well as a prophet to his followers. The revelations he claimed, *The Book of Mormon, A Book of Commandments* (1833), *Doctrine and Covenants* (1835), and *Pearl of Great Price* (1842) are, together with the Bible, accepted as scripture by the Mormon Church.

Bibliography: F. M. BRODIE, *No Man Knows My History* (New York 1945). W. A. LINN, *The Story of the Mormons* (New York 1902). T. F. O'DEA, *The Mormons* (Chicago 1957).

[T. F. O'DEA]

SMITH, RICHARD

Distinguished theologian of the English Reformation period; b. Worcestershire, 1500; d. Douai, July 9, 1563. Smith was elected probationer fellow of Merton College, Oxford, in 1527. In 1535 he was appointed the first Regius professor of divinity at Oxford when the chair was founded by Henry VIII. He held many ecclesiastical preferments under Henry VIII. Under Edward VI he at first adopted an equivocal attitude toward the Reformation and for a time succeeded in retaining office, but he was eventually deprived and fled abroad. Under Mary he was restored to his former position and actively supported Mary's persecution of the Protestants, bearing witness personally against Thomas CRANMER and taking part in the public disputes with Nicholas RIDLEY and Hugh Latimer. On the accession of Elizabeth I in 1558 he again lost his position and was placed under arrest, but he succeeded in escaping to the Continent. Philip II of Spain appointed him dean of St. Peter's at Douai in the Spanish Netherlands, and when the University of Douai was founded in 1562 Smith became the first chancellor and a few months later, professor of theology. He was a prolific writer and published a number of theological treatises, mostly in Latin.

Bibliography: T. COOPER, *The Dictionary of National Biography from the Earliest Times to 1900,* 63 v. (London 1885–1900) 18:509–510. H. TOOTELL, *Dodd's Church History of England,* ed. M. A. TIERNEY, 5 v. (London 1839–43).

[A. F. ALLISON]

SMITH, RICHARD

Bishop of Chalcedon, second vicar apostolic of England; b. Hanworth, Lincolnshire, 1569; d. Paris, France, March 18, 1655. Smith, of non-Catholic parents, went to Oxford but left without taking a degree, probably on becoming a Catholic. In 1586 he went to the English college, Rome, to train for the priesthood, and he was ordained there in 1592. For several years he taught philosophy at the English colleges at Valladolid and Seville. He took his doctorate in theology at the University of Valladolid. From 1603 to 1609 he was on the English mission in Sussex. In 1609 he made a journey to Rome to try to obtain certain concessions from the Pope for the English secular clergy. After this he settled in Paris, where he helped to found Arras College, a small establishment of controversial writers drawn from the English clergy. In 1611 he entered the household of Richelieu, whom he instructed in theological controversy. After the death of William BISHOP in 1624, Urban VIII appointed him bishop for England with the title of bishop of Chalcedon. Like his predecessor, Smith claimed the full rights and privileges of an ordinary. In so doing, he came into conflict with the Jesuits and Benedictines on the mission and alienated a considerable portion of the laity. Though Rome decreed in 1627 that he was not ordinary, the conflicts continued until he withdrew to France in 1631, resigning his position. Rome accepted the resignation and though Smith afterward wished to withdraw it, refused to allow him to return to England. He lived thenceforward under Richelieu's patronage until the latter's death in 1642, when he retired to the convent of the English Augustinian Canonesses at Paris. Rome did not appoint a successor till 1685.

Bibliography: H. TOOTELL, *Dodd's Church History of England,* ed. M. A. TIERNEY, 5 v. (London 1839–43). P. HUGHES, *Rome and the Counter-Reformation in England* (London 1942). T. A. HUGHES, *The History of the Society of Jesus in North America* 3 v. in 4 (New York 1907–17). *A Literary and Biographical History or Bibliographical Dictionary of the English Catholics from 1534 to the Present Time* 5:5:11–514. J. G. ALGER, *The Dictionary of National Biography from the Earliest Times to 1900,* 18:510–511. A. F. ALLISON and D. M. ROGERS, *A Catalogue of Catholic Books in English . . . 1558–1640,* 2 v. (London 1956). A. F. ALLISON, ''John Gerard and the Gunpowder Plot,'' *Recusant History* 5.2 (1959–60); ''Richard Smith, Richelieu and the French Marriage,'' *ibid.* 7.4 (1963–64).

[A. F. ALLISON]

Joseph Smith.

SMITH, WILFRID CANTWELL

Historian and comparativist of religion, minister; b. July 21, 1916, Toronto, Ontario, Canada; d. Feb. 7, 2000, Toronto. The younger of two sons of Sarah Cory Cantwell and Victor Arnold Smith, as a youth Smith attended Upper Canada College of Toronto and spent extended periods in France, Spain, and Egypt. He obtained an Honours B.A. in Oriental Languages at University College, University of Toronto (1939), and subsequently studied Christian theology and Arabic and Islamic history at Cambridge, England (1938–40). Following missionary work in India, both as a teacher of Islamic and Indian history and as a minister of the United Church of North India (1940–46), Smith went on to obtain a Ph.D. in Oriental languages at Princeton University (1948), and was appointed W. M. Birks Professor of Comparative Religion at McGill University (1949). In Montreal he established and directed the McGill Institute of Islamic Studies (1951–1964) before moving to Harvard University as the director of the Center for the Study of World Religions (1964–73). He later founded the Department of Comparative Religion at Dalhousie University in Halifax (1973–78), returned briefly to Harvard University (1978–84), and then settled in Toronto as professor emeritus at Trinity College, Toronto School of Theology, University of Toronto (1985–2000). Throughout his academic career he held executive positions with various professional associations. His books have been translated into more than ten languages.

Trained as a specialist in Islamic studies, Smith broadened his areas of historical expertise to include other major religious traditions, and explored issues in the comparative study and method and theory of religion. In his early research in Islam and in his seminal work, *The Meaning and End of Religion: A New Approach to the Religious Traditions of Mankind* (1962), Smith began to develop a personalist, comparativist approach to the study of religion. Over his prolific career, his carefully researched analyses focused on the major themes of faith, belief, history, religion, transcendence, cumulative traditions, world theology, and religious pluralism.

In his exploration of the dynamics of faith, Smith responds critically to trends in the philosophical theology of his time. These tended to concentrate in the analysis of faith on the propositional truth claims of creedal belief that are given in narrowly systematized and institutionalized contexts. Supported by his detailed historical research into various religious traditions, Smith argues that faith is essentially an intimate relationship of love and commitment to God that profoundly influences a person's way of being and acting in the world. Questions concerning religious truth are only answered in reference to a particular orientation of faith. Faith is a personal experience of individuals that expresses the dynamics of the human encounter with ultimate Reality, in the unfolding of religious meaning and personal transcendence.

The historically developed expressions of this common and primary feature of religious life are the many different religious traditions of the world. Smith observes that religion, understood as a unified and fixed institutional system of beliefs and practices, is a recently developed intellectual abstraction that does not correspond to a concrete reality and tends to adversely depersonalize the subject of study. He deconstructs the idea in light of his analysis of faith and speaks rather of specific, diverse, and dynamic cumulative traditions. These various religious traditions, which Smith shows to be historical, interconnected, interdependent, and continuously constructed, provide the multifarious data for the scholar of religion. But for Smith it is faith that provides the common thread in the development of a world theology of different religious traditions.

Smith's comparative methodology hopes to transcend parochial and absolutist attitudes of earlier interreligious relations by stressing personal engagement in interfaith dialogue. He insists in his ''religious pluralism'' that in the global and corporately communal context of modern life means that comparativists must be unassumingly self–conscious and cognizant both of the historical construction of religious traditions and their interconnected nature. In a world theology, religious traditions must be studied on their own terms and from a perspective that recognizes the universally salvific power of God or the Ultimate and the mutual intelligibility of diverse religious views and practices.

Smith's work has drawn much attention and many responses from diverse circles in religious studies and theology, which speak to the originality and substance of his contributions. Regarded as ''the 'father' of the *pluralist model* in Anglo-American theology'' (Grüschloß, 359), he has significantly influenced contemporary understandings of certain key concepts and categories in religious studies and theology. Moreover, he has helped in the process of bridging the methods of religious studies and theology, and has stimulated and influenced the direction of comparative religion and interfaith dialogue into the 21st century.

Bibliography: W. C. SMITH, *Modern Islam in India: A Social Analysis* (Lahore 1943); *Islam in Modern History* (Princeton 1957); *The Meaning and End of Religion: A New Approach to the Religious Traditions of Mankind* (New York 1962); *The Faith of Other Men* (Toronto 1962), revised and republished as *Patterns of Faith around the World* (Oxford 1998); *Modernisation of a Traditional Society* (Bombay 1965); *Questions of Religious Truth* (New York 1967); *Religious Diversity: Essays by Wilfred Cantwell Smith,* ed. W. G. OXTOBY (New York 1976); *Belief and History* (Charlottesville 1977), republished as *Believing—An Historical Perspective* (Oxford 1998); *Faith and Belief* (Princeton 1979), republished as *Faith and Belief: The Difference between Them* (Oxford 1998); *On Understanding Islam: Selected Studies* (The Hague 1981); *Towards a World Theology: Faith and the Comparative History of Religion* (Philadelphia 1981); *What is Scripture?—A Comparative Approach* (London 1993); *Modern Culture from a Comparative Perspective,* ed. J. W. BURBIDGE (Albany, N.Y. 1997). R. T. MCCUTCHEON, ''Wilfred Cantwell Smith: A Chronological Biography,'' ed. M. DESPLAND and G. VALLÉE, *Religion in History: The Word, the Idea, the Reality* (Waterloo, Ontario 1992). A. GRÜNSCHLOß, *Religionswissenschaft als Welt-Theologie: Wilfred Cantwell Smiths interreligiöse Hermeneutik* (Gottingen 1994). *Method & Theory in the Study of Religion* 4 (1992) 1–105.

[M. STOEBER]

SMITH, WILLIAM ROBERTSON

Protestant exegete, Semitic philologist, student of comparative religion; b. Keig, Aberdeenshire, Scotland, Nov. 8, 1846; d. March 31, 1894, Cambridge, England. After receiving his elementary education at home, he studied at Aberdeen University and at Free Church College, Edinburgh; he concluded his formal studies in Germany at Bonn and Göttingen. In 1870 he was appointed professor of Old Testament exegesis and Oriental languages at the Free Church college in Aberdeen. In 1875 he was made a member of the revision committee that produced the Revised Version of the Bible published in 1885. His articles on ''angels'' and ''Bible'' in the ninth edition of the *Encyclopaedia Britannica* (1875) were regarded with suspicion and disliked by authorities in his church. A prolonged public trial by the Free Church Presbytery of Aberdeen for alleged heresies gained him great popularity; but although acquitted, he was removed from his position. His lectures were published as *The Old Testament in the Jewish Church* (1881) and *The Prophets of Israel* (1882). As editor-in-chief of the *Encyclopaedia Britannica* from 1881 to 1888 he was commissioned to complete the ninth edition; to this edition he contributed many articles on Biblical topics. Appointed professor of Arabic at Cambridge University (1883), he fostered the study of comparative religions with his *Kinship and Marriage in Early Arabia* (1885), and he popularized the notion of sacrifice as communion with God in his *Religion of the Semites* (1889).

Bibliography: *The Dictionary of National Biography from the Earliest Times to 1900,* 63 v. (London 1885–1900) 18:568–570. W. NEIL, ''The Critical and Theological Use of the Bible 1700–1950,'' *The Cambridge History of the Bible,* ed. S. L. GREENSLADE (Cambridge, Eng. 1963) 287–288. J. S. BLACK and G. W. CHRYSTAL, *The Life of William Robertson Smith* (London 1912).

T. K. CHEYNE, *Founders of Old Testament Criticism* (New York 1893) 212–225.

[R. L. ZELL]

SMOTRYTS'KYĬ, MELETIĬ

Author and noted advocate of Church union; b. Smotryc, Ukraine, *c.* 1578; d. Dermansky Monastery, Volhynia, Ukraine, 1633. He was educated at the Orthodox Academy in Ostrog and at the Jesuit college in Vilna. In the ecclesiastical conflicts provoked by the Union of BREST he was in the beginning an Orthodox partisan and wrote several polemical tracts, the best known of which is *Threnody* (Vilna 1610), in which he laments the state of the Ukrainian Orthodox Church after mass conversion to Catholicism. His grammar of Church Slavonic (1619) was important for Slavic philology. He was consecrated Orthodox bishop of Polotsk, and in 1623 was a representative in the Polish parliament during discussions for the reconciliation of the churches. He took refuge among the Cossacks when persecuted by Polish authorities. After a stay in Constantinople he returned to the Ukraine and, when his efforts for compromise and reconciliation of the churches failed, he joined the Eastern Catholics in 1627. In 1628 at the Orthodox Council in Kiev he was denounced and forced to leave.

Bibliography: D. DOROSHENKO, *History of the Ukraine,* tr. H. CHIKALENKO-KELLER, ed. G. W. SIMPSON (Edmonton, Can.1939). M. HRUSHEVSKY, *A History of Ukraine,* ed. O. J. FREDERIKSEN (New Haven 1941). J. MIRTSCHUK, *Lexikon für Theologie und Kirche*, ed. M. BUCHBERGER, 10 v. (Freiburg 1930–38) 9:640.

[G. J. PRPIC]

SMUGGLING

The clandestine importation or exportation of goods in violation of the civil law. Those who engage in it do so for the purpose of evading the payment of duty or customs charges, or of circumventing absolute prohibitions on the export or import of certain commodities. That smuggling is widespread cannot be doubted, although the secrecy with which the smuggler operates makes it impossible to obtain accurate statistics.

There is no difficulty for the moralist in the case of those products that are legally forbidden as harmful or dangerous, e.g., narcotics. Smuggling such goods is clearly sinful since the legal prohibition is, in most cases at any rate, declarative of natural law. But with regard to secret importation or exportation of goods to avoid the payment of taxes, moralists are not agreed. Some insist that all civil laws impose a true obligation in conscience (provided they are just laws), at least by reason of legal justice, or, as some would say, SOCIAL JUSTICE. This opinion was at one time the general teaching of moralists, before the development of the theory of purely penal law and is still defended by many authorities. Others hold that many civil laws are purely penal—that is, they oblige in conscience only to the payment of the penalty if one is caught, and not to obedience to the law itself. All advocates of this opinion number indirect taxes, of which customs charges are a prime example, among those laws that are purely penal. These authors hold that smuggling itself does not involve moral fault. Apart from scandal, bribery, or some other immoral circumstances, one who evades the payment of these charges by smuggling is not guilty of sin. This more lenient opinion is probable enough to be used in practice.

Whatever their teaching on smuggling in general, however, moralists are agreed that one who engages in smuggling as a profession cannot be excused from moral fault. Great harm is done to civil society and to the common good by an attitude of habitual disregard for the law. Moreover, a professional smuggler places himself in danger of bringing harm upon himself and his dependents. And finally, professional smugglers are ordinarily so disposed that they are prepared to defend themselves, even by use of violence, against legitimate guardians of the law.

Nor is there any disagreement among moralists in stating that those who make use of BRIBERY or fraud to evade customs taxes are guilty of sin against legal and also commutative justice.

Bibliography: R. BROUILLARD, *Catholicisme* 3:146–148. M. T. CROWE, *The Moral Obligation of Paying Just Taxes* (Catholic University of America Studies in Sacred Theology 84; Washington 1944). J. MCCARTHY, *Problems in Theology,* 2 v. (Westminster, MD 1956–60) v. 2 *The Commandments,* 308–311, 324–329, 400–403.

[J. P. BROWNE]

SMYTH (SMITH), JOHN

Reputed founder of the English General Baptists and known as the Se-Baptist, because he baptized, or, as he said, ''churched'' himself; b. *c.* 1554; d. 1612. He was educated at Christ's College, Cambridge, and ordained in the Church of England. Preaching strict observance of the Jewish Sabbath, he set up in Gainsborough, 1606, a separate congregation, and later left for Amsterdam, where in 1608 he solemnly baptized himself and 40 others. An able but discourteous disputant, quick to change his opinions, he soon declared this to have been an error and was excommunicated by the majority of his followers. With the rest (30 or 40) he applied to join the Mennonites but was refused. He resorted to services in the Great Cakehouse, Amsterdam, until he died of consumption in 1612; then a group of his associates returned to London to establish the first Baptist Church in England. The popular notion that he is the father of the English Baptists rests on such early writings as *The Differences of the Churches of Separation* (1608).

Bibliography: *Works,* ed. W. T. WHITLEY, 2 v. (Cambridge, Eng. 1915). A. C. UNDERWOOD, *A History of the English Baptists* (London 1947). T. COOPER, *The Dictionary of National Biography from the Earliest Times to 1900,* 63 vol. (London 1885–1900) 18:476–478. W. T. WHITLEY, *A History of British Baptists* (2d ed. London 1932).

[G. ALBION]

SNOW, PETER, BL.

Priest, martyr; b. at Ripon, Yorkshire, England; hanged, drawn, and quartered June 15, 1598 at York. He entered the seminary at Rheims in 1589 and was ordained at Soissons, France, 1591. After working in Yorkshire for about seven years, he was arrested about May 1, 1598, while traveling to York with Bl. Ralph GRIMSTON. Snow was condemned and executed for his priesthood. He was beatified by Pope John Paul II on Nov. 22, 1987 with George Haydock and companions.

Feast of the English Martyrs: May 4 (England).

See Also: ENGLAND, SCOTLAND, AND WALES, MARTYRS OF.

Bibliography: R. CHALLONER, *Memoirs of Missionary Priests,* ed. J. H. POLLEN (rev. ed. London 1924). J. H. POLLEN, *Acts of English Martyrs* (London 1891).

[K. I. RABENSTEIN]

SOBORNOST

Derived from the Russian *sobiratj,* meaning ''to gather'' or ''a state of being united.'' It is identified with Alexy Khomyakov's concept of the church as a theandric organism of love, effecting its unity as a free association of all peoples in Christ, patterned on the communal unity of the first Christians (Acts 2.42), and corresponding to the Greek term κοινωνία. Between what it considers a kind of mechanical unity based upon exterior authority—this it attributes to the Roman Catholic Church—and the individualistic excess of liberty—this it attributes to Protestantism—the Orthodox Church considers that it realizes a synthesis of such opposites in its characteristic of a free communion of all in charity. Its catholicity, termed *sobornaja,* equivalent to the Greek καθολικη, is interior; it diverges from the concept of external authority as vested in the person of the pope, whose prerogatives of primacy and infallibility are, according to the Orthodox, immanent to the church as a whole. The covenant principle of sobornost goes beyond the usual idea of conciliarity by seeing the government and sovereign magisterium of the church as residing in the college of bishops, equal in dignity and rights, who only when assembled in a universal synod legislate on matters of faith or regulate affairs of ecclesiastical government affecting the universal church. While C. Lialine associated this idea only with ''dialectical solidarity'' in the Oecumene, G. Dejaifve considered the concept of sobornost to be more than mere feeling and fellowship; he claimed that when rightly understood it is compatible with the hierarchical principle, even with that of a supreme papal authority.

Bibliography: G. DEJAIFVE, ''Sobornost ou Papauté? La Notion de l'église dans l'orthodoxie contemporaine,'' *Nouvelle revue théologique* 74, 355–371; Eng. version, '''Sobornost' or Papacy?'' *The Eastern Churches Quarterly,* 10 (1953–54) 28–38, 75–85, 111–124, 168–176. G. FLOROVSKY, ''Sobornost in the Church of God,'' *An Anglo-Russian Symposium* (London 1934) 53–74. S. BOLSHAKOFF, ''Patristic Foundations of Khomyakov's Theology,'' *The Eastern Churches Quarterly* 10 (1953–54) 233–237. C. LIALINE, ''Nouvelles précisions sur le Conseil Oecuménique des Églises,'' *Irénikon* 24 (1951) 37–54. N. ZERNOV, *Three Russian Prophets: Khomyakov, Dostoievsky and Soloviev* (New York 1944). N. ZABOLOTSKY, ''Esprit communautaire et conciliarité (sobornost'),'' in *Procès-verbaux du Deuxième Congrès de théologie orthodoxe à Athènes* (Athens 1978) 129–140. M. G. RITCHEY, ''Khomiakov and his theory of Sobornost,'' *Diakonia* 17 (1982) 53–62. A. UGOLNIK, ''An Orthodox hermeneutic in the West,'' *Saint Vladimir's Theological Quarterly* 27 (1983) 93–118. C. D. H. DOHERTY, *Sobornost: Eastern Unity of Mind and Heart for Western Man, rev. ed.* (Combermere, Ont. 1992).

[L. NEMEC/EDS.]

SOBREVIELA, MANUEL

Missionary, explorer, author, and the mapper of the Amazon Basin; b. Epila, Aragon, Spain, date unknown; d. San Francisco de Lima, 1803. He arrived in Peru in 1785 and for eight years was an active and prudent superior at the Colegio de Propaganda Fide of Ocopa, building up its library with several thousand volumes. With the help of excellent collaborators, he concentrated his work on the missions in the Peruvian Amazon up to the Chanchamayo and Pachitea Rivers, achieving his greatest success in the Apurimac, Huallaga, and Ucayali River regions. He founded and organized towns, built roads, and established schools, granges, and shops, thus promoting the river and land trade between civilized regions and the jungle missions. All this formed a base for more solid and lasting evangelical work. With the same purpose in mind, Sobreviela published numerous reports and accounts of the earlier and contemporary Franciscan work in the Peruvian jungle with descriptions of territories, rivers, tribes, and land and river passages, together with a minute analysis of the causes for the flourishing or decay of the missionary centers in which more than 50 missionaries had already perished at the hands of the natives. As an assiduous correspondent of the *Mercurio peruano* of Lima, he published in that periodical the synthesis of these studies, some of them translated later into English and French. The most valuable of his various maps, *Plan del curso de los ríos Huallaga y Ucayali y de la Pampa del Sacramento* (*Mercurio peruano,* 1791) has had repeated editions, with successive improvements made by Ocopa missionaries and various scientists.

Bibliography: M. DE MENDIBURU, *Diccionario históricobiográfico del Peru,* 11 v. (Lima 1931–34) 10:224–228. B. IZAGUIRRE ISPIZUA, *Historia de las misiones franciscanas . . . ,* 14 v. (Lima 1922–29).

[O. SAIZ]

SOBRIETY

Sobriety is a term that may be used in a broad sense to signify moderation of any kind, but in its strict sense indicates the virtue, a species of temperance, whose function is to moderate and control the sense appetite with respect to alcoholic drink or other intoxicating substances. The older theologians were familiar with no intoxicants except fermented drink, and sobriety for them was simply temperance as applied to the desire and use of such drink. It was distinguished from abstinence, which was temperance in the use of food and nonintoxicating drink. A virtue in addition to abstinence was considered necessary where intoxicants were concerned, because the desire for them constituted a distinct form of appetition, difficult yet important to keep under reasonable control. Today, however, when a great variety of substances are used to produce a condition morally indistinguishable from alcoholic intoxication, the scope of the virtue of sobriety must be broadened to include moderation in the use of intoxicants in every form.

The use of intoxicants is not per se or essentially evil (see 1 Tm 5.23; Sir 31.27). But if, as the son of Sirach states, wine was created to promote joy of heart, good cheer, and merriment, it has in fact proved the ruin of many, and its abuse is certainly sinful.

As in the case with other moral virtues, sobriety consists in a mean between excess and defect. The defect of sobriety is drunkenness; the vice by way of excess has been given no special name, but it consists in an unreasonable unwillingness to use intoxicants even when health requires them. Total abstainers are not guilty of a culpable excess of sobriety unless their abstention is unworthily motivated. For those prone to alcoholic addiction, the reasonable mean is total abstention. In contemporary life, when powerful intoxicants, especially distilled spirits, are in common use, and when social customs lead many into excess, total abstinence, under ordinary circumstances, is a commendable, though not an obligatory, measure to safeguard the observance of temperance. Moreover, the mean of the infused virtue of sobriety is measured by higher considerations than those that determine what is reasonable from the point of view of the natural, acquired virtue. The sacrifice of otherwise legitimate satisfactions for a supernatural motive can be praiseworthy and meritorious, as is evident in the case of virginity or celibacy undertaken for the sake of virtue, or in the case of fasting.

See Also: TEMPERANCE, VIRTUE OF; TEMPERANCE MOVEMENTS.

Bibliography: THOMAS AQUINAS, *Summa theologiae,* 2a2ae, 149.

[P. K. MEAGHER]

SOCIAL CONTRACT

Social contract is a concept used variously to explain, on consensual grounds, the origin, limits, conditions, and purposes of political AUTHORITY and obligation. The contract is usually deduced from some conception of NATURAL LAW, which serves as the basic reason and ultimate sanction for the agreement, although it has also been put forth on utilitarian grounds to explain political authority in purely conventional terms.

History. The Greek SOPHISTS and the philosophy of EPICUREANISM equated nature with self-interest, denied any intrinsic moral virtues, and explained the STATE as formed by men to obtain security on the basis of a tacit agreement neither to inflict nor to suffer harm. Against this, CICERO and the Roman lawyers argued that JUSTICE is an intrinsic good, that political authority arises from the collective power of the people, and that it is always subject to natural law.

Medieval Theories. In medieval Europe the contractual basis of political obligation was implied in FEUDALISM and in the patristic principle that law and government, to be legitimate, must always subserve justice. In the 11th century MANEGOLD OF LAUTENBACH preached that a people establishes a ruler that he may govern justly; if he violates the agreement, they are absolved from obedience. St. THOMAS AQUINAS distinguished (1) the *principium,* or substance, of authority, which is divinely ordained; (2) the *modus* or form of government, which is determined by the corporate people; and (3) the *exercitium* of authority, which must accord with natural law and which is conferred, and can be revoked if misused, by the people. Unlike the Sophists and Epicureans, Aquinas, though regarding the specific form as a matter of free choice, saw government as a dictate of natural law. In the 15th-century conciliar dispute, NICHOLAS OF CUSA wrote that "if by nature men are equally strong and equally free, the ruler having equal natural power could be set up only by the choice and consent of the others, just as law also is set up by consent" (*De Concordantia Catholica* 2.14).

Calvinist Theories. During the Protestant REFORMATION the idea of contract took systematic form and became a theory of action for beleaguered minority confessions. Depending on their situations, Calvinists and Catholics resorted to it as a weapon against the theory of the DIVINE RIGHT OF KINGS and as a principle of legitimacy (the Calvinists giving it a strong theological basis). The Huguenot treatise *Vindiciae Contra Tyrannos* (1581) answered the question of what obedience was due from a Christian to a prince commanding action contrary to divine law by arguing for the existence of a twofold contract—one between God and the people binding the people to obey God's will and one between the prince and the people binding the people to obey the prince as long as he obeys God's law. If the prince acts in violation of the second contract, resistance is obligatory, but it is exclusively an aristocratic function. English Puritan theory of the 16th century was connected, in good part, with the federal COVENANT THEOLOGY and in the 17th century was carried in this form to New England, where it served as the basis of the various compacts establishing new communities.

Counter Reformation Theories. On the Catholic side, the work of the Jesuits Robert BELLARMINE, Francisco SUÁREZ, and Juan de MARIANA was most prominent. In extending the arguments of Aquinas, Suárez maintained that the state is a purely natural phenomenon originating in a voluntary union of heads of families by which each assumes the obligation to subserve the common good. The state depends on God's ordination only insofar as does all of creation. Political power derives from the community; when it is used to contravene the common good or any other injunction of natural law, it may be resisted. Coupled with the indirect theory of papal power to intervene in temporal affairs, the formulation of Suárez (and of Bellarmine) tended to exalt the divine right of the pope and to set the state apart from theology by explaining it in naturalistic terms. More radical, although not novel, was Mariana's deduction that private citizens have the right to kill usurpers of temporal power.

Hobbes. In the 17th century the idea of contract was joined to an individualistic theory of autonomous natural law (*see* NATURAL LAW IN POLITICAL THOUGHT). Thomas HOBBES, in his *Leviathan,* hypothesized a state of nature wherein men are radically egotistic, perpetually seeking power, and subject to no law, divine or natural. This leads to a *bellum omnium contra omnes* in which life is "solitary, poor, nasty, brutish and short." Impelled by the desire of self-preservation to seek security and order, men contract with each other to set up a common sovereign to whom they relinquish all their rights. Thus by artifice is set up that "mortal god," the state, which exists not as in the classical tradition as a dictate of nature to help men become good, but as a convention to ensure existence. The desire to be is the fundamental natural right; natural law and the social contract are deductions therefrom that are merely definitive of the conditions of ordered existence. The only real limitation on the sovereign—be he one, few, or many—is the amount of power he can effectively command at any moment. Hobbes's notion of obligation is rooted in interest. Law is the command of the sovereign and is limited only insofar as one is not obliged to obey an order violative of the basic right of self-preservation.

Locke. John LOCKE, in his second *Treatise of Civil Government,* propounded a contractual theory that proceeded from assumptions similar to Hobbes's but within the framework of transcendent natural law. Locke's state of nature is a condition in which men are free and equal and subject to natural law, the terms of which each judges and enforces. Because of the lack of a common impartial judge and executive, uncertainties and inconveniences arise that can issue in a state of war. To remedy this, men contract to form civil society to protect their property in their lives, liberty, and estates. Government is then set up on a fiduciary basis to protect property; when it acts to the contrary as manifested in a concerted pattern of abuses and usurpations, the people, with the majority as the motive force, may resist. Locke's philosophy underlies the American Declaration of Independence and constitutions of government; it differs from Hobbes's thought in holding that natural rights can never be surrendered to the state but serve as limitations on political authority. Whereas Hobbes's contract theory issued in ABSOLUTISM, Locke's issued in constitutionalism.

Hume, Rousseau, and Kant. In the 18th century David HUME attacked the theory that political obligation may be binding only if it is accepted voluntarily, arguing that the obligation to civil obedience cannot be derived from the obligation to keep an agreement but that both are binding because without them an ordered society cannot be attained and that allegiance develops on habitual grounds, reinforced by education. After Hume the idea of contract lost ground in England; it retained vigor in America until attacked in the 19th century by men such as John C. Calhoun. On the Continent Jean Jacques ROUSSEAU postulated the social contract as a means whereby men retain their original freedom while creating morality by establishing as sovereign the general will of the community. Each surrenders himself entirely to the community with all his rights and property and by giving himself to the whole surrenders to no one. Thus civil society is constituted by the agreement between men to subserve the general will, which leaves each as free as before because he subscribes only to his transformed or ideal will. Because Rousseau recognized no fixed ends in man's nature, the general will is purely formal; its only limitation lies in the requirement of its generality. Accepting Rousseau's premises, Immanuel KANT viewed the social contract in a metaphysical sense as an instrument relating men to each other so that the freedom of each is compatible with the freedom of all. In this view the social contract is a social imperative prescribing the conditions of free social life rather than a call to action. In the 19th century the idea of contract lost attractiveness because of the growth of historical studies and idealist and evolutionist philosophies.

Critique. The idea of a social contract contains two elements, the *pactum unionis,* which forms the body politic, and the *pactum subjectionis,* which organizes political authority in a constitution and government. Catholic thought in the Middle Ages and Calvinist thought emphasized the latter; Hobbes, Locke, Rousseau, and the rationalists emphasized the former; and Catholic scholastic thought, in developed form (Bellarmine, Suárez), does not separate the two but regards the will to common life in political society as realized in a concrete constitutional order. Hobbes, Locke, and Rousseau deny any teleological necessity for the origin of the state in man's nature, seeing authority as rising solely from the wills of the contracting individuals. Catholic thought presupposes families as the basic social units and regards the state as a moral necessity whose concrete realization and organization is the product of man's will. The contract does not create political authority but designates how and by whom it shall be exercised. The state is seen as part of the objective moral order, with human intelligence and will having a role in its construction. It follows that obligation to obedience is not, as with Hobbes, Locke, and Rousseau, rooted in the contractual promise or in individual interest, but in the objective natural law, which indicates the moral necessity of authority. That history shows that many states were established by force and exist by sheer power and that specific conscious acts of consent by all within a community rarely, if ever, occur, does not vitiate the contract theory as a normative explanation of the origin and continued existence of the state. Modern constitutionalism based on the dignity of man recognizes this fact in the emphasis it places on the consensual factor as a legitimating and operational principle.

Bibliography: O. F. VON GIERKE, *Natural Law and the Theory of Society, 1500–1800,* tr. E. BARKER (Boston 1957); *Political Theories of the Middle Ages,* tr. and introd. F. W. MAITLAND (Boston 1958). E. BARKER, ed., *Social Contract: Essays by Locke, Hume, and Rousseau* (New York 1948). J. N. FIGGIS, *Studies of Political Thought from Gerson to Grotius* (Cambridge, Eng. 1960). G. SABINE, *A History of Political Theory* (New York 1961). T. HOBBES, *Leviathan,* ed. and introd. M. OAKESHOTT (Oxford 1957). S. J. BRUTUS, *A Defense of Liberty against Tyrants,* ed. and introd. H. J. LASKI (London 1924). H. A. ROMMEN, *The State in Catholic Thought* (St. Louis 1945). L. STRAUSS, *Natural Right and History* (Chicago 1953). J. F. FENTON, *The Theory of the Social Compact and Its Influence upon the American Revolution* (New York 1891). D. HUME, *Theory of Politics,* ed. F. WATKINS (New York 1951).

[A. J. BEITZINGER]

SOCIAL GOSPEL

The movement in American Protestantism, beginning in the 1870s, that endeavored to answer the challenges presented by the abuses of industrialism. It was also a corrective to the theological individualism and economic conservativism of the churches of that epoch, and an assertion that from the teachings of Jesus Christ the institutions of a just social order can be deduced. Although its theological premises were different, the moral idealism of the social gospel movement and its goals paralleled those of Christian socialism in England, and the efforts of Continental Catholicism that culminated in Leo XIII's encyclical *RERUM NOVARUM* of May 1, 1891. The social sympathies of UNITARIANS and the utopian perfectionism of TRANSCENDENTALISM earlier in the 19th century undoubtedly contributed to the emergence of the social gospel, as did the momentum of the antislavery crusade. These humanitarian protests came at a time when labor leaders, socialists, and reformers were attacking Christianity as a class religion concerned primarily with protecting property and ignoring widespread human misery. Moreover, science was eroding the beliefs of theological fundamentalism, and the recognition was growing that the shocking disparities of wealth were not to be cured by appeals to middle-class piety. A new interpretation of the Christian message was probably inevitable, one addressing itself to the changed world and its problems of the sweatshop, the slum, the company town, and unemployment.

A social order reflecting the fatherhood of God and the brotherhood of man was the essential demand of the social gospel. The ideas of Horace BUSHNELL directly influenced Washington Gladden, who, along with W. D. P.

Bliss, gave a new orientation to American Protestantism at the end of the century. Their voices were subsequently joined by those of George D. Herron, Walter RAUSCHENBUSCH, and Shailer MATHEWS. In a movement climaxed in December 1908, the overwhelming majority of churches of the evangelical tradition formed the NATIONAL (originally called Federal) COUNCIL OF CHURCHES OF CHRIST IN THE U.S.A. to secure, as the preamble to its Constitution declared, ''a larger combined influence for the Churches of Christ in all matters affecting the moral and social condition of the people, so as to promote the application of the law of Christ in every relation of human life.''

The reforms advocated by the exponents of the social gospel were gradual ones. Their goals, partly because of the moral energy they released, have been incorporated into national legislation. Their overly simple belief in the essential goodness of man and in his responsiveness to moral suasion, along with their lack of realism as to the magnitude and complexity of the problems they optimistically analyzed and prematurely ''solved,'' ultimately weakened confidence in the social gospel. Its energies were dissipated in efforts to impose national prohibition. Attacks on its theological adequacy by the disciples of Karl Barth, and on its political naïveté by Reinhold Niebuhr, further weakened the movement. But its activist emphasis and its concern for justice among men left a characteristic stamp on American Protestantism.

Bibliography: R. H. GABRIEL, *The Course of American Democratic Thought* (2d ed. New York 1956). F. E. JOHNSON, *The Social Gospel Re-examined* (New York 1940). J. A. HUTCHISON, *We Are Not Divided* (New York 1941). C. H. HOPKINS, *The Rise of the Social Gospel in American Protestantism, 1865–1915* (New Haven 1940). A. S. NASH, *Protestant Thought in the Twentieth Century: Whence and Whither?* (New York 1951). W. A. VISSER 'T HOOFT, *The Background of the Social Gospel in America* (New York 1929).

[E. DUFF]

SOCIAL JUSTICE

The VIRTUE that ordains all human acts toward the common good. It is a special virtue, specified and distinguished from other virtues, but like charity it is also a general virtue because ordered to it under a certain aspect are all acts of other virtues and not only acts of JUSTICE in the particular sense of the term. It is appropriate to outline the historical development of this expression and to define its meaning.

Origins of the Term. The term social justice has been employed in ecclesiastical teaching only recently. St. Thomas Aquinas referred to the same reality as general, or legal, justice. Referring to general justice he wrote: ''Now it is evident that all who are included in a community, stand in relation to that community as parts to a whole; while a part, as such, belongs to a whole, so that whatever is the good of a part can be directed to the good of the whole. It follows therefore that the good of any virtue, whether such virtue direct man in relation to himself, or in relation to certain other individual persons, is referable to the common good, to which justice directs: so that all acts of virtue can pertain to justice, insofar as it directs men to the common good. It is in this sense that justice is called a general virtue.'' Then, using the term legal justice, St. Thomas adds, ''Since it belongs to the law to direct to the common good, as stated above, it follows that the justice which is in this way styled general, is called *legal justice,* because thereby man is in harmony with the law which directs the acts of all the virtues to the common good'' (*Summa theologiae* 2a2ae, 58.5).

The expression social justice was introduced into the vocabulary of Catholic writers by Luigi TAPARELLI D'AZEGLIO, SJ [*Saggio teoretico di diritto naturale* (2v. Palermo 1840) no. 353]. Others who used the term, often imprecisely, were Édouard de Léhen, SJ [*Institutes du droit naturel privé et public et du droit des gens* (Paris 1866) 535], and later the French Catholic social thinkers C. H. R. LA TOUR DU PIN and Albert de Mun. Some people distrusted the expression and suspected those who used it of inclinations toward statism and equalitarian socialism. Undoubtedly La Tour du Pin invited such criticism by appearing to confuse social justice with distributive justice or with the obligations imposed by the state as legislator. In Germany, the Jesuits of *Stimmen aus Maria Laach,* particularly Viktor CATHREIN, sought at first to restore use of the term legal justice. However, in spite of the efforts of Heinrich Pesch to avoid the restriction of legal justice to the distributive justice exercised by the state, contemporary writers were too inclined toward this confusion to allow acceptance of the Thomistic term.

In the end the term social justice imposed itself. The new expression was found in the writings of René du Bouays de la Bégassière, SJ (*c.* 1895), of Charles Antoine, SJ [*Cours d'économie sociale* (2d ed. Paris 1899)], and of A. Pottier [*De jure et justitia* (Liège 1900)]. At the Semaines sociales de France, A. G. SERTILLANGES, OP, spoke of ''general justice or social justice destined to safeguard the common good'' [Proceedings 8 (1911) 98]. In Germany as early as 1905, in a development seemingly inspired by Antoine, Pesch used the term *soziale Gerechtigkeit.* The idea spread little by little but without gaining full acceptance. Arthur VERMEERSCH, SJ, who had referred to ''legal or social justice'' at least as early as 1921, was still uncertain about the term on the eve of the encyclical *QUADRAGESIMO ANNO.* He wrote at the time that ''social justice is an imprecise expression that designates an end rather than a virtue, an end in which different virtues meet'' [*Il XL anniversario della enciclica Rerum Novarum* (Milan 1931) 556]. But was this not exactly the general justice of St. Thomas?

Use in Early-Twentieth-Century Papal Teaching. Pius XI definitively incorporated the term social justice into the teaching of the Church, giving it, it seems, exactly the same meaning as general and legal justice. The latter expressions may have been abandoned because they were poorly understood, especially legal justice, which was too easily confused with the rule of the positive legislator. Some years before Pius X had extolled St. Gregory the Great as the ''public champion of social justice'' because he had resisted the unjust pretensions of the Byzantine emperors [*Jucunda sane, Acta Sanctae Sedis* 36 (1904) 515]. Pius XI gave the term a more technical meaning as early as 1923, recalling that St. Thomas had formulated with exactitude ''the principles of legal or social justice'' [*Studiorum Ducem, Acta Apostolicae Sedis* 15 (1923) 322]. The expression soon appeared in the writings of Cardinal Pietro Gasparri, papal Secretary of State, who in a letter to Eugène Duthoit on the occasion of the Semaine sociale of 1928 termed social justice ''this virtue which orders toward the common good the external acts of all the others'' [Proceedings 20 (1928) 11].

In *Quadragesimo anno* Pius XI employed the term eight times. In discussing the just distribution of goods, he identified social justice with respect for the ''good of the whole community'' [*Acta Apostolicae Sedis* 23 (1931) 196, 197]. He mentioned it again in insisting on the urgency of reforms to ensure wage levels adequate for family needs and so regulated as to maximize opportunities for employment (*ibid.* 200, 202). The Pope condemned as a violation of ''right order'' capital's use of labor ''without any regard to the human dignity of the workers, the social character of economic life, social justice and the common good'' (*ibid.* 210). On this principle also, institutions for social assistance are required by social justice. In general, an enduring economic order must be subject to the norm of social justice. Free competition ''cannot be an adequate controlling principle in economic affairs''; there must be recourse to nobler principles of ''social justice and social charity'' (*ibid.* 206). The Pope adds that ''the public institutions of the nations should be such as to make all human society conform to the requirements of the common good, that is, the norm of social justice'' (*ibid.* 212). Social reform must proceed ''according to the mind of the Church on a firm basis of social justice and social charity'' (*ibid.* 218).

The encyclical *DIVINI REDEMPTORIS* (1937) contains the most explicit definition of social justice: ''It is of the very essence of social justice to demand from each individual all that is necessary for the common good. But just as in the living organism it is impossible to provide for the good of the whole unless each single part and each individual member is given what it needs for the exercise of its proper functions, so it is impossible to care for the social organism and the good of society as a unit unless each single part and each individual member . . . is supplied with all that is necessary for the exercise of his social functions'' [*Acta Apostolicae Sedis* 29 (1937) 92].

Even after *Quadragesimo anno,* some still questioned the appropriateness of the term social justice. J. Tonneau, OP, suggested that it was a vague expression taken from the language of the people and regretted ''that the qualified representatives of moral theology, who should have a truly scientific care to use only a well-developed terminology, were not able to provide the magisterium with a body of technical formulas, if not more expressive, at least more logically articulated'' [*Bulletin thomiste,* 4 (1934–36) 498]. In Tonneau's view, there had been a confusion of the obligations of general justice and of distributive justice; his interpretation was undoubtedly related to his own inclination to consider as simple distributive justice that which belongs at the same time to general justice or (according to the new term) to social justice. Pius XII did not use social justice very frequently; but when he did, he used the term in the sense of ordination to the common good.

Underlying Problem. Under the influence of individualist and liberal philosophies, many 19th- and early 20th-century Catholics restricted their view of justice to commutative justice between individuals. This species of justice is concerned with the equivalence of reciprocal payments beyond which nothing can be strictly owed and beyond which there is room only for charity (understood in the narrow sense that has brought it into disrepute). As a result, the Church sought to reaffirm its traditional doctrine that there can be no justice in the full meaning of the word without an ordination of parts to the whole, of individuals and all their acts to the common good. Assuredly, the common good is not unrelated to particular goods. It is the ''community of the good'' that enables each member of the community to participate in ''all possible good.'' This end cannot be attained without the mediation of a ''good of the community''—a common good in the usual meaning of the term—that is imposed on individuals and binds them to various duties in view of the common participation of all in the greatest possible good. Social justice is the virtue that subjects men to the ''good of the community'' in view of the ''community of the good'' [Gaston Fessard, *Autorité et bien commun* (Paris 1944) 55].

Social justice is achieved by the acts of all other virtues, especially, however, by the acts of ''particular'' justice, either commutative in the relation of person to person or, distributive in the distribution of the common good among diverse individuals. This distribution is accomplished by reference to the common good, for each man participates in the good of the community; to consider distributive justice in isolation would be to deprive it of its ultimate norm. To reduce social justice to distributive justice, on the other hand, would risk giving distributive justice an arbitrary or simply equalitarian character. Both commutative justice and distributive justice are related to social justice as to their ultimate norm.

Recent Developments. In the era after Vatican II, common understandings of the meaning of social justice have evolved considerably. The term has come to be something of a rallying cry for a variety of efforts to improve society and enhance the equitable treatment of all people, especially the poorest. The increase in prominence of this term may be attributed in part to several pivotal church documents and to the courageous leadership of recent popes. The tone for the developments of recent decades was set by the strong words of the Vatican II document *Gaudium et spes* (Pastoral Constitution on the Church in the Modern World) which elucidated a communal vision that embraces all of humankind and noted ''the pressing need to reform economic and social structures'' (par. 86) so that all people benefit from prosperity. The social encyclicals of Pope Paul VI, particularly *Populorum progressio* (1967), spoke prophetically about the necessity of assisting the needy, not merely as a desirable act of voluntary charity but as an absolute demand of justice. Social justice is appropriately applied not only within given societies, but on the global level, where rich countries experience an obligation to aid the development of their poorer neighbors. The 1971 Synod of Bishops reaffirmed both the seriousness and international dimension of the obligations of social justice with its document *Justice in the World.*

Pope John Paul II has also spoken forcefully about social justice, particularly in his social encyclicals *Sollicitudo rei socialis* (1987) and *Centesimus annus* (1991). He has particularly emphasized the fact of global economic interdependence which underlines the importance of the virtue of solidarity which motivates acts of social justice. Like several of his predecessors, John Paul II seeks to inform Catholics about the requirements of social justice in light of the ''signs of the times'' (such as the fall of Communism and the phenomenon of globalization) and to respond to new realities in ways consistent with the Gospel. Bishops' conferences in many parts of the world have interpreted the universal call for social justice for their own national contexts. The bishops of the United States addressed numerous concerns about social justice in the American context in the 1986 Pastoral Letter *Economic Justice for All.*

Finally, recent Catholic reflections on social justice have benefitted from the influence of several important movements, both intellectual and popular in nature. Liberation theology has added many rich themes to contemporary religious discourse on proper social order. Its call to enact a ''preferential option for the poor'' has inspired not only constructive scholarship on social obligations to those in need but also concrete praxis aimed at the advancement of social justice. Other contributors include academics who engage in political theology, those who take part in intentional alternative communities such as the Catholic Worker and labor activists who seek greater equity in work arrangements and remuneration. Catholicism, with its distinctive vision of the communal nature of human life, will surely continue to play a pivotal role in inspiring and enacting social justice.

See Also: SOCIETY; STATE, THE

Bibliography: J. Y. CALVEZ and J. PERRIN, *The Church and Social Justice: The Social Teachings of the Popes from Leo XIII to Pius XII, 1878–1958,* tr. J. R. KIRWAN (Chicago 1961) 133–61. P. VALLIN, ''Aux origines de l'expression justice sociale,'' *Chronique Social de France* 68 (1960) 379–92. W. FERREE, *Introduction to Social Justice* (New York 1948), pamphlet. J. MADIRAN, *De la justice sociale* (Paris 1961).

[J. Y. CALVEZ/T. MASSARO]

SOCIAL SERVICE, SISTERS OF

(SSS), a congregation of women religious founded in 1923 in Budapest, Hungary, for social service work. In 1926 the first American foundation (the Sisters of Social Service of Los Angeles, Official Catholic Directory #4080) was made in Los Angeles, CA; it became a motherhouse for U.S. and Canadian foundations in 1956. Another branch of this congregation was established as a diocesan congregation with its motherhouse in Buffalo, NY (Official Catholic Directory #4090). Its special objective is to engage in social and pastoral activities at parish and diocesan levels. The sisters are engaged in education and literacy programs, catechetics, retreats, counseling, spiritual direction, camps for children and youth, ministries to the elderly, immigrants and ethnic minorities, legal services and social outreach programs for the poor, as well as justice and peace work.

[J. M. RENFRO/EDS.]

SOCIAL SIN

The concept of social sin is derived from the biblical account of Israel's struggle to remain faithful to the terms of the ancient covenant. Torah committed Israel to a life of society free of the inequality and exploitation that characterized its own existence in the Egyptian land of bondage. Whenever Israel tolerated the oppression of the poor, of orphans, widows and immigrants, the prophets accused the people of collective infidelity to God. To know God was to do justice (Amos, Jeremiah, Isaiah). Jesus himself included in his mission the release of captives and the liberation of the oppressed (Lk 4.18–19).

De-privatization. The concept of social sin has come to the fore in post–Vatican II Catholic theology, especially political theology and LIBERATION THEOLOGY, and has assumed a prominent place in the Church's social teaching. One of the principal tasks of political theology, according to J.-B. Metz, is the ''de-privatization'' of the Christian message, i.e., the overcoming of the inherited individualistic interpretation of sin, conversion, and new life, and the retrieval of the original social dimension of the Good News. Sin has both a personal and a social dimension; and the two are interrelated. One of the tasks of Latin American liberation theology is the analysis of the structures of marginalization that inflict misery and hopelessness on the people of that continent. In *A Theology of Liberation*, G. Gutierrez argues that institutionalized injustice reveals the collective dimension of human sin.

Since post–Vatican II Catholic social teaching based itself, not on the inherited natural law theory, but on biblical revelation and, guided by its light, on human reason, the ecclesiastical documents began to use theological terms to designate the violations of justice. Institutions that violate justice are called sinful.

Influenced by the perspective of the Medellin Conclusions (Latin American Bishops Conference 1968), the statement ''Justitia en mundo'' published by the 1971 Synod of Bishops, spoke of ''recognizing sin in its individual and social manifestation'' (n. 51) and acknowledged that the dynamism of the gospel ''frees men from personal sin and from its consequences in social life'' (n. 5). The statement recognized ''the network of domination, oppression and abuses'' (n. 3) that was being built around the world and that stifled freedom and kept the greater part of humanity excluded from power and resources.

Institutional Injustice. The Church itself is not altogether free of social sin. The same statement demanded that the Catholic Church critically evaluate its own self-organization (nn. 40–48).

> Within the Church rights must be preserved . . . (n. 41). We also urge that women should have their own share of responsibility and participation in community life . . . of the Church (n. 42). The Church recognizes everyone's right to suitable freedom of expression and thought. This includes the right of everyone to be heard in a spirit of dialogue which preserves a legitimate diversity within the Church (n. 44).

Social sin refers to institutionalized injustices. At Medellin the bishops spoke of situations that were so massively unjust that they had to be called ''institutionalized violence.'' The Canadian bishops, following John Paul II, spoke of the plague of unemployment as a ''moral evil'' and as ''symptomatic of a basic moral disorder'' (*Ethical Reflections on the Economic Crisis,* n. 3; cf. *Redemptor hominis*, n. 52). In their pastoral, ''Economic Justice for All'' (1986), the North American bishops defined injustice as the structured exclusion of people from political, economic, and cultural participation in society (n. 77). Since these patterns of exclusion are created by free human beings, ''they can be called forms of social sin'' (n. 77).

The notion of social sin has not yet been fully explored theologically. Since the term ''sin'' usually refers to a personal option, how can one speak of sinful institutions or sinful structures? Replying to this question, the Vatican Instruction on Christian Freedom and Liberation (1986) recognized that sin in the primary sense refers to voluntary acts, but because unjust structures are created by sinful humans, it is possible to speak of ''sinful structures'' and ''social sin'' in a derived and secondary sense (n. 75).

Source and Consequence. How do structures become sinful? The ecclesiastical documents offer several suggestions. First, and most obviously, structures may be sinful because they have been created by sinful men to institutionalize exploitation and discrimination. More often, however, institutions are created to serve a good purpose. How, then, do they become sinful? In *Redemptor hominis* (n. 15), John Paul II introduced dialectical thinking into Catholic theological reflection. He argued that what humans produce with the best of intentions often turns against them in the long run. Instruments and institutions created to serve human purposes may actually come to control their masters and exercise dehumanizing influence. It follows from this that it always remains necessary to test structures to see if they still serve their purpose or if they have come to damage human life. If the latter is true, personal sin enters the situation only when those in charge refuse to be critical and rebuild the inherited structures. ''Acquiescence with sinful structures or failure to correct them when it is possible to do so is a sinful dereliction of Christian duty'' (*Economic Justice for All,* n. 77).

This dialectic reveals how even holy institutions, such as the Church, created in accordance with the demands of justice and love, can become tainted by social sin. Administrative structures set up to serve the life of the community may, after a period of time, actually become obstacles to the Spirit-guided unfolding of this life. The sin is then not in the founders of these structures but in those who refuse to recognize the present damage and resist efforts to reconstruct them.

Personal sins, then, generate social sin. Conversely, social sin multiplies personal sins. Marginalization creates conditions that foster resentment and despair in the victims and thus easily provoke irrational responses. More than that, since institutionalized injustice affects *all* members of society, it creates conditions that facilitate personal sin on all levels. Social sin distorts people's perception of reality; it makes them see the structures of marginalization as natural and necessary; it falsifies their moral conscience. That is why the Medellin Conclusions (*Justice* nn. 17, 20, 23) included ''conscientization'' in the Church's pastoral mission, i.e., the raising of people's consciousness in regard to the historical obstacles that prevent them from assuming responsibility for their lives. Social sin, often hidden by the dominant culture, must be made visible.

Bibliography: G. BAUM, *Religion and Alienation* (New York 1975). D. DORR, *Option for the Poor* (Maryknoll, NY 1983) J.-B. METZ, *Theology of the World* (New York 1973). P. KERANS, *Sinful Social Structures* (New York 1974).

[G. BAUM]

SOCIAL THOUGHT, CATHOLIC

Social thought is an inclusive term that refers to any expression of ideas concerning the conduct of relations among men, particularly ideas concerning the comprehensive system of relations that is SOCIETY. According to this usage, Catholic social thought includes not only the official teaching of the Church affecting the organization of society but all social ideas that can be attributed to Catholic inspiration, whether these ideas are taught formally or only exemplified in the social institutions and popular traditions of a given period of history. The introduction to this article defines the more restricted official concern of the Church with the morality of social life. The historical sketches in the succeeding parts outline the development preceding the systematic formulation of Catholic social teaching that began with Leo XIII (*see* SOCIAL THOUGHT, PAPAL). Thus the Bible itself is seen to be rich in social concepts and social implications, although obviously the sacred writers were not professedly concerned with social theory. The Fathers of the Church and the medieval theologians addressed themselves formally to numerous social questions (e.g., the social nature of man, forms of government, the morality of interest), but they did not recognize a distinctive corpus of social doctrine as such. Concern with the theory of society is a development of the modern period and particularly of the 19th century, when Catholic moralists and others and ultimately the magisterium of the Church had to take account of divergent social philosophies and ideologies and of the fundamental changes in social life that were initiated by industrial capitalism. Meanwhile, social philosophy and social science and their specialized branches had become the explicit concern of scholars. These disciplines have become increasingly important in their own right and as means for the understanding of complex situations that must be evaluated by the teaching Church.

1. Introduction

The basic assumption of the Church's teaching on social questions is that man is a social being (*see* MAN, 3). By nature he is dependent on others at every stage of life, for existence and for the fulfillment of spiritual, intellectual, emotional, physical, and social needs. Peace and order in human society require the conformity of individual members to certain expectations in their interaction with each other, individually and collectively. Conformity to role expectations in family life, education, economic behavior, participation in the political community, and all daily interaction is universally deemed essential for the common good. The ultimate concern of the Church is the salvation of men's souls, for which both guiding principles and specific means must be provided. Since salvation is won or lost during life on earth and since it depends not only on internal dispositions but also on conformity with a code of conduct prescribed for human interaction, the Church is of necessity concerned with social morality. What is morally right and what is morally wrong in social institutions and human behavior patterns? What are men's basic moral rights and responsibilities toward each other as individuals and in groups? What are the mutual rights and responsibilities of social groups such as families and political or economic communities? The body of principles applicable to these and similar questions that has been developed through the centuries is known as Catholic social teaching. It is logically necessary to inquire why the Church is concerned with social morality, what the sources are from which teaching on social questions is derived, how the doctrine is developed, and why it differs from other codes of social morality that may be current from time to time.

Authority of the Church. The bases of the Church's concern were clearly stated by Pius XI in a well-known paragraph of *QUADRAGESIMO ANNO:*

> That principle which Leo XIII so clearly established must be laid down at the outset here, name-

> ly, that there resides in Us the right and duty to pronounce with supreme authority upon social and economic matters. Certainly the Church was not given the commission to guide men to an only fleeting and perishable happiness but to that which is eternal. Indeed "the Church holds that it is unlawful for her to mix without cause in these temporal concerns;" however she can in no wise renounce the duty God entrusted to her to interpose her authority, not of course in matters of technique for which she is neither suitably equipped nor endowed by office, but in all things that are connected with the moral law. For as to these, the deposit of truth that God committed to Us and the grave duty of disseminating and interpreting the whole moral law, and of urging it in season and out of season, bring under and subject to Our supreme jurisdiction not only social order but economic activities themselves [*Acta Apostolicae Sedis* 23 (Rome 1931) 190].

Although there are some who consider morality to be completely divorced from religion, it is nevertheless true that in the traditional Catholic view the Church is the only authoritative custodian and interpreter of the moral code in all its aspects, social morality included.

Sources of Catholic Teaching. The Church's teaching on social questions is derived from the same sources as on all matters of faith and morals. These sources are usually classified as mediate, or remote, and immediate, or proximate.

Natural Law. One mediate source is the NATURAL LAW comprising all moral principles that can be known through reason. A considerable proportion of the Church's teaching on social questions is based essentially on natural law principles, e.g., teaching on such important issues as the right of the worker to a living wage for himself and his family, the right to organize labor unions and political parties, the responsibilities of qualified citizens to vote, and the like. A remarkable development of these principles began with the pontificate of Leo XIII (1878–1903). Revolutionary changes in the way men earn their living and support their families and in the manner in which they wish to be governed, as well as human problems arising out of rapid scientific and technological developments, call for continuing reexamination by the teaching Church of the application of the natural law to the new situations and human problems. The natural law does not change, but its principles are developed through specification and application to new human problems as they arise. The Church claims the exclusive right to determine such specifications and applications, usually through the pronouncements of the popes and the general councils of Church Fathers.

Revelation. A second mediate source of Catholic social teaching is revelation. As understood by Catholics this includes both the Sacred Scriptures and tradition (*see* REVELATION, THEOLOGY OF). Many important moral principles are derived directly from the revealed word of God. The demands of charity, particularly as they apply to man's attitudes toward and interaction with his fellowmen serve as a prime illustration. The Church insists that true peace and order in society cannot be achieved until the ideals regarding love of neighbor that were preached by Christ are realized. Other social principles implicit in the natural law regarding justice in all its forms, e.g., the right to ownership and the durability of marriage, are strongly supported by the revealed word of God. Even the Church's teaching on interracial relations is based in large measure on Sacred Scripture.

Magisterium. The immediate source of Catholic social teaching is the magisterium of the Church, or the Church as the divinely authorized teacher in the realm of faith and morals. Here it is necessary to distinguish between the ordinary and extraordinary teaching power of the Church. Since the latter usually involves solemn and inspired declarations by the sovereign pontiffs or by a general council of the Church acting in union with the pope, relatively few Catholic social principles are placed in this category. Certainly some of the Church's social teaching, e.g., on man's ultimate goal and the measures to achieve it and on the nature of marriage as a Sacrament, has been solemnly defined by the Church and has the standing of doctrine that must be accepted as a matter of faith. But most of the recent development in Catholic social teaching, including the principles and directives on social questions that have emanated principally from the Holy See since the time of Leo XIII, cannot be taken as infallible but rather as an expression of the ordinary magisterium of the Church. Pronouncements in this category are not infallible in the sense that they must be believed, in the theological meaning of the term.

It is common opinion among theologians, however, that ordinary teaching of the magisterium must be accepted, even internally, and obeyed. The assumption is that although the Holy See or a general council does not usually make infallible pronouncements on questions that involve what are in essence specific applications of the natural law, the role of the teaching Church as the authoritative custodian and interpreter of the whole moral code, nevertheless, requires that directives and prescriptions on social questions must be accepted and obeyed by all Catholics. There is some disagreement as to the specific virtue involved here, but most authorities seem to agree that OBEDIENCE, at the very least, is certainly involved.

Distinctiveness of Catholic Social Teaching. Why and how does Catholic social teaching differ from other codes of social morality? This is a complex question that cannot be resolved satisfactorily here. The Church's position on most social questions is identical with, or at least approximates, that of all denominations in the Judeo-Christian tradition. It differs most in its fundamental premise that the natural moral law is one, universal, invariable, and immutable and that the Catholic Church is its official custodian and interpreter. The Church cannot agree with the proposition that social morality, in any objective sense, is ultimately dictated by the mores of particular societies or that social morality is determined by men rather than ultimately by the Creator. Because of this position, the Church's teaching on such issues as divorce with the right to remarry and artificial birth control may differ markedly from that of other religious groups in the Judeo-Christian tradition. Needless to say, its teaching on social questions differs to a considerable degree from that of religions that are not in this tradition.

Bibliography: J. MESSNER, *Social Ethics*, tr. J. J. DOHERTY (St. Louis 1964). E. WELTY, *A Handbook of Christian Social Ethics*, tr. G. KIRSTEIN, rev. J. FITZSIMONS (New York 1960—).

[T. J. HARTE]

2. In the Bible

The concept of the people of God is basic in biblical thought. In the Old Testament (OT) justice is the social principle that gives solidarity to this people; in the New Testament (NT) justice is transcended by love. This article treats the application of these principles to the family, the economy, labor, slavery, and loans.

The People of God. In all creation, man is the only being created in the image of God and therefore free—free in all things, even to rebel against his Creator. A group of men chosen by God form Israel, a people consecrated to God, bound to Him by a COVENANT, established as a juridical person for a universal mission, the spread of monotheism. As children of a single God, all men are brothers, equals, to be loved, as they await the Messiah to unite them more closely. When Israel turns this divine privilege into opposition, to other nations, the prophets remind it of its solidarity with them, joining, at the center of life in common, love with the worship of God and love with the service of men. Yahweh is not pleased with fasting and sacrifice unless accompanied by works of mercy toward brethren in need.

The Law of Moses implies the duties of ''releasing those bound unjustly, untying the thongs of the yoke, setting free the oppressed, . . . sharing bread with the hungry, sheltering the oppressed and homeless, clothing the naked'' (Is 58.5–7); for ''to do what is right and just is more acceptable to the Lord than sacrifice'' (Prv 21.3). The king also is bound to such justice, and therefore he must be ''a kinsman, not a foreigner . . . . He may not have a great number of wives, . . . nor may he accumulate a vast amount of silver and gold;'' every day he must read and meditate on the Law, that he may learn to keep all its commandments, ''lest he become estranged from his countrymen through pride'' (Dt 17.15–20).

When this communion among the Israelites is in danger of being broken by grievous inequalities, the conscience of the people reacts against it, especially through the prophets, so that the rich are identified with the wicked, the poor with the pious, and the obligations of the Decalogue are again called to mind: to worship God, to honor parents, not to kill, not to commit adultery, not to steal, not to lie, not to covet another's possessions. Such solidarity is expressed at times, in ''the assembly of the people of God'' (Jgs 20.2), by the sharing of the income with those in need. This is the symbolic meaning of the precept that the first fruits and tithes are to be eaten in a sacred meal, ''in Yahweh's presence,'' together with the poor and the strangers, the widows and the orphans (Dt 14.29; 16.11, 14; 24.19–21; 26.12–13; etc.); hence also, the importance of almsgiving.

In the NT the new people of God, now baptized and no longer circumcised, and therefore freed from limitations of race and territory, keep the character of ''the assembly of God'' (ἡ ἐκκλησία τοῦ θεοῦ: Acts 20.28; 1 Cor 1.2; 10.32; 11.16; etc.), with the priestly mission of ''a chosen race, . . . a holy nation'' (1 Pt 2.9), for the purpose of mankind's unification—''that all may be one'' (Jn 17.21).

In the OT the authority that rules the state and the various communities comes from God and obeys His law. This law commands the rulers not to be proud, not to make selfish misuse of power, not to be influenced by bribery, not to overburden the subjects, and to give justice to the innocent. In other pre-Christian regimes politics includes religion; in Israel religion includes politics. Therefore, a sacral character is impressed on government. (*See* THEOCRACY).

Jesus recognizes a lay element in government: ''Give to Caesar what belongs to Caesar, and to God what belongs to God'' (Mk 12.17 and parallels). Between the two He makes a distinction, but not a separation; both come forth from God. If political authority orders actions contrary to the law of God, God, rather than man, is to be obeyed (Acts 5.29). The opposition can reach the point of active persecution and the dualism of the Apocalypse: the City of the Lamb (Jerusalem, the Church) as opposed to the City of the Beast (Rome, the Empire). But this does not lead to any overthrow. The Christian religion may be worn away by the spirit, but not by externals, not by any hostile structures.

The Social Principle. The centripetal social principle of the OT is justice, as contained in the Law, the synthesis of divine and human rights. (*See* JUSTICE OF GOD; JUSTICE OF MEN.) The Law also commands love. Yet actually, the sense of solidarity is limited to fellow members of religion and race, even though the prophets often urge a going beyond these narrow limits.

In the NT love plays the predominant role; it becomes the new commandment that overthrows all 613 prescriptions of the OT. In this sense Jesus does not abolish the law; he completes it: "It was said to those of old: 'Thou shalt love thy neighbor and shalt hate thy enemy' [cf. Lv 19.18; Nm 35.19–20]. But I say to you: Love your enemies, do good to those who hate you" (Mt 5.43–44). Love is life—the life of God who is love; hatred is the spirit of Satan, murder. Love unifies: "In one Spirit we were all baptized into one body, whether Jews or Gentiles, whether slaves or free" (1 Cor 12.13). Christ insists, above all, on unity, through which there is born a spiritual living together in which distinction of race, class, or sex is no longer valid, with a resulting social economy in which, all being "of one heart and one soul," there is a sharing of material goods, so that no one is in want (Acts 4.32, 34). Love is God's justice that surpasses man's justice, as illustrated in the parable of Lazarus and the rich man, the parable of the laborers in the vineyard, the episode of the woman taken in adultery, etc. Human justice gives to each one his due; love gives of oneself, one's very life. [*See* LOVE (IN THE BIBLE).]

The main source of profit in Israel is agriculture, not war. God loves peace. Among the Israelites, soldiers are allowed to return home for work and for feastdays and even because of fear; their military law is shot through with humaneness. When the army goes on a campaign, before a city is besieged it is offered terms of peace. The Bible champions peace without end, which will be realized by the Messiah, "the prince of peace," "with right and justice" (Is 7.14; 9.5–6), when "they shall beat their swords into ploughshares, and their spears into pruning hooks; one nation shall not raise the sword against another, nor shall they train for war any longer" (Mi 4.3). [*See* WAR (IN THE BIBLE).]

The NT opens with the announcement of peace to men of good will, it puts forgiveness in place of quarrels, it urges the overcoming of evil with good, it ranks peacemaking as one of the beatitudes, and it warns that "all those who take the sword will perish by the sword" (Mt 26.52).

The Family. The Bible has important teachings on the family, which is the nucleus of society. For the preservation of family life, adultery and other sexual sins are condemned. [*See* ADULTERY (IN THE BIBLE); SEX (IN THE BIBLE).] Contrary to the Code of Hammurabi, Israelite Law protects the personality and rights of children: "Fathers shall not be put to death for their children, nor children for their fathers; only for his own sin shall a man be put to death" (Dt 24.16). The sacrifice of the firstborn, a common practice of the neighboring peoples, is condemned. Children are to receive a strict education. WOMAN is of the same nature as man: "God created man in his image, . . . male and female he created them" (Gn 1.27). Yet in several respects Israelite society is androcratic. A husband may divorce his wife, but a wife may not divorce her husband. Adultery consists only in sexual intercourse between a married woman and a man other than her husband, not in illicit relations of a married man with a woman other than his wife. A woman is juridically subject to her father or husband or nearest male relative; she cannot hold property in her own name, unless there is no male heir [*See* INHERITANCE (IN THE BIBLE).] Limited polygamy is permitted in the patriarchal period; later custom is opposed to it. King Solomon is censured for taking many wives, although primarily because they were pagans who led him to offer pagan sacrifices. The wisdom literature frequently sings the praises of the virtuous wife and condemns the adulterous woman (Prv 11.16; 12.4; 19.14; 22.14; 30.20; 31.10–31; Eccl 7.26–28; Sir 7.19; 25.12–25; 26.1–4, 6–18; 42.9–14; etc.)

In the NT the Blessed Virgin Mary carries out with dignity a unique task: it falls to her, a young woman, to proclaim in her MAGNIFICAT the Christian revolution—the putting down of the mighty and the exalting of the lowly, the scattering of the proud, the filling of the hungry with good things and the sending away of the rich empty—the realization of the OT messianic ideals.

Jesus treats all women, even the much-married Samaritan woman, with deference. He condemns divorce and adultery equally of the husband and the wife. He declares the marriage bond sacred: "What God has joined together let no man put asunder" (Mk 10.9). In the NT marriage is an indissoluble union between one man and one woman, similar to the mystical union between Christ and His Church and therefore called "a great mystery" (Eph 5.29–32). This similarity is also the reason why the husband should love his wife, and the wife should be subject to her husband (Eph 5.22–28). Second marriages are regarded with disfavor, and celibacy is praised. [*See* MATRIMONY.]

Widows, Orphans, and Strangers. The most unfortunate persons in the ancient world were widows and orphans, who were economically helpless without the aid of a male head of the family. But the God of Israel "executes justice for the orphan and the widow, and befriends the alien, feeding and clothing him" (Dt 10.18). Like the

OT, the NT also inculcates charity to those unfortunate creatures: ''Religion pure and undefiled before God the Father is this: to give aid to orphans and widows in their tribulation, and to keep oneself unspotted from this world'' (Jas 1.27). [*See* WIDOW (IN THE BIBLE).] Charity must be shown also to the resident alien (Heb. *gēr*), who, without landed property, would find it hard to earn a livelihood: ''When an alien resides with you in your land, do not molest him. You shall treat the alien who resides with you no differently than the natives born among you; have the same love for him as for yourself; for you too were once aliens in the land of Egypt'' (Lv 19.33–34). The NT abolishes the religious distinction based on race or nationality: ''You know it is not permissible for a Jew to associate with a foreigner or to visit him; but God has shown me that I should not call any man common or unclean'' (words of Peter regarding his visit to the Gentile Cornelius in Acts 10.28).

Wealth. All wealth comes from the divine Creator and is to be used according to His will, that is, for the benefit of all men. In keeping with the OT ideal, there would be no poverty: ''There should be no one of you in need'' (Dt 15.4). Should an Israelite be in need, his fellow Israelites were commanded to help him, at least by giving him an interest-free loan of ''enough to meet his need'' (Dt 15.7). A sharing of the goods given by the heavenly Father is demanded by the sense of solidarity among His children on earth. Realistically aware that there will always be some poor people (Mt 26.11), the Law ordains: ''The needy will never be lacking in your land; that is why I command you to open your hand to your poor and needy kinsman in your country'' (Dt 15.11). Avarice is condemned. Ownership, particularly of farm land, is relative, provisional; it is more an occupancy than a possessing. Yahweh says to Israel: ''The land is mine, and you are but aliens who have become my tenants'' (Lv 25.23). If landed property is sold, it must be restored to the original owner in the JUBILEE YEAR (Lv 25.13–17). The purpose of this law is to prevent the accumulation of vast estates in the hands of a few people (Is 5.8) and to permit the economic recovery of impoverished families.

''Woe to you rich!'' (Lk 6.24); for ''it is easier for a camel to pass through the eye of a needle than a rich man to enter the kingdom of heaven'' (Mt 19.24). These are the words of Jesus, who calls the poor blessed (Lk 6.20), the poor in spirit (Mt 5.3), whose hearts are detached from the MAMMON of iniquity (Mt 6.24; Lk 16.9, 11, 13), ''for a man's life does not consist in the abundance of his possessions'' (Lk 12.13). Jesus wishes the goods of this world to circulate for the benefit of all. Without material poverty there is no spiritual perfection: ''If thou wilt be perfect, go, sell what thou hast and give to the poor, and thou will have treasure in heaven'' (Mt 19.21). He who has more than enough should give to him who is in need, ''that there should be equality'' (2 Cor 8.13–14).

The Christian social order is born from a union of faith and good works, founded on the principle of the Incarnation of the God-Man, Jesus Christ. The LORD'S PRAYER associates our Father in heaven with our bread on earth (Mt 6.9–11). The Church, following the example of Jesus, is concerned with the corporal and temporal as well as the spiritual and eternal. The importance of material food is shown in the institution of the first seven DEACONS, who serve at table before they preach the Gospel (Acts 6.1–7).

Labor. God has prescribed work for man, to subdue the earth and to have dominion over the animals (Gn 1.28). Labor, which is natural for man, has become burdensome for him as a punishment for sin (Gn 3.17–19). Since work is the God-ordained means of man's subsistence, man has both the duty and the right to work. If a man works for another, he has a right to a just wage: ''The laborer deserves his wages'' (Lk 10.17; 1 Tm 5.18). The prophets inveigh against ''those who defraud the hired man of his wages'' (Mal 3.5; Jer 22.13; Lv 19.13; Jas 5.4). Of all work, farming is the best: ''Hate not laborious tasks, nor farming, which was ordained by the Most High'' (Sir 7.15). The wisdom literature has many warnings against sloth (Prv 6.6–11; 13.4; 19.15; 20.4; Eccl 10.18; Sir 22.1–2). Labor, however, is mitigated by the SABBATH rest, which, with its freedom from work every seven days, refreshes both the body and the soul of man. The blessings of the Sabbath are to be shared in by the slaves, the strangers, and even the domestic animals.

The NT presents its greatest figures as laborers—Joseph, Jesus, and the Apostles. St. Paul reechoes the OT refrain against laziness: ''If any man will not work, neither let him eat'' (2 Thes 3.10). ''He who was wont to steal, let him steal no longer; but rather let him labor, working with his hands at what is good, that he may have something to share with him who suffers need'' (Eph 4.28).

Slavery. The ancient Israelites used slave labor, as did the rest of the ancient world; but their slaves were mostly foreigners who had been captured in war or foreigners bought from other lands (Lv 25.44–46). Sirach takes a realistic view of the hardship of a slave's life: ''Food, correction, and work for a slave. Make a slave work, and he will look for his rest; let his hands be idle, and he will seek to be free. Force him to work that he be not idle, for idleness is an apt teacher of mischief. Put him to work, for that is what befits him; if he becomes unruly, load him with chains. But never lord it over any human being, and do nothing unjust'' (Sir 33.27–30). The humane attitude of Israel toward slaves is seen in the fact that asylum was given to fugitive slaves: ''You shall not hand over to his master a slave that has taken refuge with you. Let him live with you wherever he chooses, in any one of your communities that pleases him. Do not molest him'' (Dt 23.16–17).

Slavery of an Israelite to a fellow Israelite was limited by the Law, which considered this an abuse: ''If your kinsman, a Hebrew man or woman, sells himself to you, he is to serve you for six years, but in the seventh year you shall dismiss him from your service, a free man. When you do so, you shall send him away empty-handed'' (Dt 15.12–13). Only if a Hebrew slave freely requests to remain a slave may his master keep him indefinitely (Dt 15.16–18). If an Israelite is forced by poverty to sell himself into slavery to a foreigner, his fellow countrymen are urged to redeem him (Lv 25.47–55).

In the NT also the institution of slavery is taken for granted. But the teachings of the NT contain the seed that ultimately grew into the abolition of slavery in Christendom. Paul sends back Onesimus, a fugitive slave, to his Christian master; but he urges the latter to receive him back, not as a slave, but as a ''brother'' in Christ (Phlm). In the urgency of the forthcoming return of Christ, it matters little if one is a freeman or a slave (1 Cor 7.17–21). Among those who have been baptized into Christ ''there is neither slave nor freeman'' (Gal 3.28; Col 3.11), for a baptized slave is ''a freeman of the Lord,'' and a baptized freeman is ''a slave of Christ'' (1 Cor 7.22). On the relationship among Christians between a slave and his master, see Eph 6.5–9 and Col 3.22–4.1. [*See* SLAVERY (IN THE BIBLE).]

Loans. Among the ancient Israelites, as among all other peoples, loans were taken for granted. It was mostly poor farmers, impoverished after a bad season, who were forced to take out loans. If they could not repay the debt, they had to sell themselves as slaves to the creditors. The Mosaic Law had various provisions for alleviating this unfortunate situation. A Hebrew slave could regain his freedom after six years of service (Dt 15.12); every Sabbath year all loans were cancelled (Dt 15.1–2). Although interest could be demanded on a loan to a foreigner, no interest could be asked on a loan to a fellow Israelite (Dt 23.20–21), since an Israelite would ordinarily not take out a loan unless forced by necessity. The taking of a pledge for a debt was limited: a mantle thus taken had to be returned before sunset, since it was used also as a blanket (Dt 24.12); a hand mill could not be thus taken at all, since it was needed for daily bread (Dt 24.6). [*See* PLEDGE (IN THE BIBLE).]

In the NT, which is not concerned with commercial loans, the giving of a loan to one in need is regarded as an act of charity: ''Do good and lend, not hoping for any return, and your reward shall be great, and you shall be children of the Most High, for he is kind toward the ungrateful and evil'' (Lk 6.35).

Jesus Christ and the Apostles sum up the social thought of the messianic expectations in their teaching, which they first practice themselves, of love for all without distinction, of justice and peace, and of economic solidarity on the basis of communion that meets every need of body and soul. They affirm the dignity of the human person, whether master or slave, rich or poor, man or woman. They condemn the deprivation of freedom and the exploitation of human beings. They make the prime function of authority the service of mankind, and they put all things and all men in dependence on God. Social relationships are simplified by equating man with Christ, as quaintly stated in one of the *Logia Jesu:* ''See your brother, see the Lord.''

Bibliography: R. H. KENNETT, *Ancient Hebrew Social Life as Indicated in Law, Narrative and Metaphor* (London 1933). J. W. GASPAR, *Social Ideas in the Wisdom Literature of the Old Testament* (Washington 1947). R. G. NORTH, *Sociology of the Biblical Jubilee* (Rome 1954), bibliog. ix–xlvi. I. GIORDANI, *Il messaggio sociale del cristianesimo* (Rome 1963).

[I. GIORDANI]

3. Patristic and Medieval

Christian thinkers of the patristic and medieval periods developed no comprehensive and autonomous systems of social thought, but they did produce an extensive and often perceptive social commentary. Their thought, in the main, proceeded along two lines: (1) the examination of social institutions in the light of the Christian comprehension of the nature of man and his destiny; (2) the examination of social practices in the light of Christian ethical standards.

The Patristic Age (*c.* 200–600). In background and education, the FATHERS OF THE CHURCH were closely associated with the aristocracy of ancient society, the curial or senatorial class of substantial landowners. Steeped in the same literature, even educated in the same schools as their pagan counterparts, the Fathers accepted without question established social institutions. They further believed that the promise of Christianity was in personal reform, not social reform, and this reinforced the conservative bent of their thought. But the Fathers still faced the problem of reconciling the authority of the state, the existence of private property, and resultant social inequality with the fundamental Christian assumption that all men are equally the children of God and heirs of His kingdom.

Authority of the State. ARISTOTLE had maintained that man was by nature a political animal, and this naturalistic interpretation of the STATE was repeated by LACTANTIUS (*Divinarum Institutionum Libri VII* 6.8, following Cicero; 6.10) and even by St. AUGUSTINE (*De civitate Dei* 19.12; *Bon. coniug.* 1). But the more favored patristic opinion—from the Epicureans, repeated by Lactantius, AMBROSE, Augustine, GREGORY I (the Great), and ISIDORE OF SEVILLE among others—was that the state was not natural. It was rather the product of a SOCIAL CONTRACT or convention among men for the repression of evil. The state became necessary when men, through ORIGINAL SIN, lost their pristine innocence and became prone to evil; it was itself an evil, but a necessary one. St. Paul, however, had laid the basis for a more positive interpretation of authority (Rom 13.1–7). The king was the minister of God appointed as a correction for sin, a *remedium peccati*. In the 4th century, EUSEBIUS OF CAESAREA, in his *Panegyric on Constantine*, declared that the emperor was not alone God's steward but His earthly counterpart, providentially appointed to the sacred functions of ruling His people, protecting His Church, and promoting the salvation of souls. This exalted interpretation paralleled Hellenistic ideas on the sacred character of kingship and struck deep roots in the Eastern Empire, where it served as one of the foundations of Byzantine CAESAROPAPISM.

The most original and influential patristic interpretation of authority was undoubtedly Augustine's profound exploration of the societal implications of the Christian dogma of GRACE. Augustine maintained that grace not only sanctified the individual but introduced him into a new spiritual fellowship, the City of God. With his acute sense of psychology, Augustine discerned the basis of all societies in a union or harmony of wills (*De civitate Dei* 19.24). The City of God was composed of those who, through grace, loved God more than themselves. Its counterpart was the Earthly City, made up of those who loved themselves more than God.

Augustine's political dualism dominated all subsequent discussion of authority during the Middle Ages. His own attitude toward secular power was, however, ambivalent. The coercive authority of the state resulted from evil, but in the *City of God* Augustine urged the good Christian to be subordinated to it, even to pray for its welfare, in order to make use of its peace. On the other hand, in his tracts against the Donatists, Augustine maintained that the state should help the Church in the repression of heresy and therefore be subservient to its interests. This ambiguity meant that Augustinian principles could be used to support quite different attitudes toward authority during the Middle Ages.

Property. In regard to private PROPERTY, the common opinion of the Fathers, expressed by Ambrose (*De off.* 1.28; *De Nabuthae* 1, 2; *Exp. ev. sec. Luc.* 7.124), Lactantius (*Divinarum Institutionum Libri VII* 5.5, 5.6), and Augustine (*In evang. Ioh.* 6.25) was that this too, like the state, was not natural to men but resulted from sin. The Fathers were, however, in no sense communists, nor did they consider a community of possessions a practical arrangement for fallen men. Lactantius (*Divinarum Institutionum Libri VII* 3.21), Ambrose (*Epist.* 63, 92), Augustine (*C. acad.* 20.2), and HILARY OF POITIERS (*Com. in ev. Matt.* 19.9) all expressly recognized the right of private ownership. The Fathers, however, constantly warned of the dangers of avarice and taught that the rich had a positive duty to relieve through alms the sufferings of the poor. [*See* ALMS AND ALMSGIVING (IN THE CHURCH).]

Slavery. Concerning slavery, Augustine expressed the characteristic patristic opinion when he declared (*De civitate Dei* 19.15) that, although it was contrary to nature, it was a punishment for sin that had to be accepted accordingly. [*See* SLAVERY (AND THE CHURCH).]

Commerce. Concerning commercial activities, the Fathers expressed fear at the temptations to avarice and deceit associated with them and forbade clerics to participate in them, but they never denied to merchants the possibility of salvation. Breaking with the tradition of Roman law that permitted USURY, or profit on a loan, Fathers such as Augustine, Ambrose, JEROME and LEO I (THE GREAT) condemned it as contrary to biblical commands. In more general terms, Ambrose (*De off.* 3.6, 3.9) argued that no commercial profit could be made at public injury. But the Fathers on the whole paid slight attention to commercial transactions, and their statements did not go much beyond large and often vague exhortations to justice.

Significance of Patristic Social Thought. The historical importance of patristic social thought is difficult to evaluate. Interested in personal reform rather than social reform, the Fathers promoted such social virtues as frugality, diligence, self-restraint, self-discipline, and fairness. Undoubtedly too, in praising manumission as a virtuous act, in proclaiming the human dignity of slaves and the social dignity of the labor they performed, the Fathers facilitated the transition to the peasant economy of the Middle Ages, based, in a way the ancient economy had never been, upon willing labor. The Fathers confirmed the solidarity of the family; the position of woman in later epochs—a subordinate but honorable one—owed much to their influence. Intellectually, they transmitted to the Middle Ages many of the seminal social ideas of pagan antiquity. But they contributed almost nothing to the methods of social analysis, since their thought was confined to speculation concerning the religious purposes of social institutions and they had no interest in empirical approaches. They did, however, advance the proposition that a society's institutions ought to be considered and judged not by the interests of an aristocracy but by the JUSTICE imparted to all its members. This has remained a lasting ideal within the tradition of Christian and Western social thought.

The Middle Ages (*c.* 600–1500). Appreciation of the social thought of the MIDDLE AGES has often been obstructed by persistent misconceptions concerning it. One such misconception is that medieval social thought was monolithic and unchanging, devoted to the defense of a land-based and rigidly stratified feudal society dominated and regulated in all particulars by an omniscient Church. Another is that medieval thinkers were unalterably opposed to a free economy, to economic individualism, and to the commercial, capitalistic activities associated with it.

The truth is more complex. Medieval social thought changed greatly, as medieval society and the position of the scholar within it themselves changed. Up to the 11th century, the medieval economy remained overwhelmingly agrarian (*see* FEUDALISM), and intellectual activity was carried on largely within the disciplined and ascetic milieu of the monasteries. The few writers who commented upon social institutions— JONAS OF ORLÉANS, SMARAGDUS OF SAINT-MIHIEL, Sedulius Scotus, and HINCMAR OF REIMS among the more important—did little more than repeat patristic commonplaces.

From the 11th century, however, the equilibrium of the medieval economy and society was shaken by many forces: population growth, geographic and commercial expansion, the rise of towns and the extension of capitalistic techniques, the growth of effective administrative institutions in both church and state. These dynamic conditions confronted medieval thinkers with social and political problems that the Fathers had scarcely anticipated. The thinkers themselves changed. Supported by the new universities, aided by a new familiarity with ancient philosophy and law, they became full-time, professional scholars, constituting a true intelligentsia, confident in and committed to systematic rational analysis.

Church and State. These thinkers greatly developed the social ideas of the Fathers. The INVESTITURE STRUGGLE in the late 11th century and subsequent conflicts between church and empire inspired an abundant polemical literature and energetic efforts to analyze the nature of power (*see* CHURCH AND STATE). The imperial supporters explored at length the patristic idea that the emperor was directly God's minister; and the papalists, including GREGORY VII himself, responded that the state was the result of sin and should be subject to higher spiritual authority. The hierocratic theme later achieved its most forceful expression in the works of the papal publicists GILES OF ROME (d. 1316) and AUGUSTINE (TRIUMPHUS) OF ANCONA (d. 1328). They claimed for the pope a plenitude of power; all authority and even all property upon earth belonged to him. Their systems exemplified admirable philosophical and juridical reasoning, paradoxically advanced at a time when the reality of papal power was already declining. Paradoxically too, in their analysis of absolute power, they rank among the apostles of the modern idea of monistic and unlimited SOVEREIGNTY, although the secular state, not the papacy, was to benefit from it.

Theory of the State. Besides enlarging upon patristic ideas, medieval social thought also changed in its fundamental assumptions and even in its methods. In his *Policraticus* (finished in 1159), JOHN OF SALISBURY mentioned the spiritual purposes of society but concentrated his attention upon how the political community was actually constituted and how its parts were interdependent. He likened the body politic to the body physical, and advised princes and statesmen how to assure its proper coordination. John thus revealed a new social consciousness and even preached a new social responsibility, manifest particularly in his famous proposition that the good citizen had the right, even the duty, to assassinate a tyrant.

To this growing interest in the natural foundations and structure of the state, the *Politics* of Aristotle, available in western Europe by the 2d decade of the 13th century, made two fundamental contributions: (1) it presented for the first time to medieval thinkers a mature and intellectually compelling naturalistic theory of the state; (2) it introduced a strong element of empiricism into medieval social thought. Aristotelian naturalism directly challenged the Augustinian assumptions of earlier social theory. What, if anything, did a state established by nature owe to the Church, which existed through grace? This problem occupied the greatest scholastic thinkers of the 13th century, St. ALBERT THE GREAT and St. THOMAS AQUINAS. St. Thomas conceded that the state was natural and autonomous, but held that its sovereignty was limited by NATURAL LAW and, in religious matters, by ecclesiastical authority. Thomistic political and social thought, which must be reconstructed from numerous scattered passages, is perhaps too intricate and in points even obscure. But Thomas's full acceptance of the autonomy and dignity of the natural order has remained a premise of modern Catholic social thought, and Thomas himself serves as a model of openness to new ideas, of moderation, balance, and prudential wisdom.

The opponents of papal theocracy also made use of Aristotelian principles. Prominent among them were JOHN

(QUIDORT) OF PARIS, who in 1302 wrote the *Treatise on Royal and Papal Power*, and the more radical WILLIAM OF OCKHAM and MARSILIUS OF PADUA. The latter's *Defensor Pacis* (1324) ranks as one of the most original of medieval political tracts. Marsilius was less interested in the purpose of power than in its origin and nature. He maintained that it derived from the people, and his theory is the most rigorous expression of medieval populism. The authority of the people, or of their ''greater and healthier part,'' was limited neither by natural law, which the people themselves created, nor by ecclesiastical authority, to which Marsilius denied any substance. Marsilius, along with his great opponents, the papal hierocrats, was a pioneer of modern conceptions of sovereignty as monistic, absolute, and unlimited.

Property. In regard to property and economic matters, medieval social thought both developed patristic ideas and struck out in entirely new directions. The patristic notion of a state of communism before the Fall figured in many heretical and social-revolutionary movements in the later Middle Ages [CATHARI, APOSTOLICI, Beghards (*see* BEGUINES AND BEGHARDS), and many others]; these groups demanded a return to the communistic regimen God had originally intended for men. But the true originality of medieval social thought was its adoption of Aristotelian naturalism and empiricism.

St. Thomas, for example, accepted the patristic notion that private property was the result of original sin (*Summa theologiae* 1a2ae, 98.1 ad 3). But he sought also to show its practical necessity in the functioning economy: it assured peace, maintained order, provided incentive, and guaranteed proper care of belongings (*Summa theologiae* 2a2ae, 66.2). Property had to be administered, however, not for the owner's benefit but for the good of society. The owner was similarly obligated to CHARITY, but the chief virtue to be cultivated by him was LIBERALITY. Liberality meant not so much generosity as the willingness freely and appropriately to use property in the primary interest of the common welfare.

Economic Justice. Toward commercial activities, St. Thomas still betrayed a traditional suspicion, as he discerned therein ''something base'' (*Summa theologiae* 2a2ae, 77.4). But under the influence of Aristotelian naturalism and empiricism and confronting a rapidly developing and ever more complicated economy, St. Thomas and later scholastics—DUNS SCOTUS, NICHOLAS ORESME, St. BERNARDINE OF SIENA, St. ANTONINUS OF FLORENCE—undertook an ever more penetrating economic and social analysis. They sought principally to accomplish two things: (1) to find a basis in natural law for such traditional ethical teachings as the usury prohibition or the requirement of justice in pricing; (2) to define what was ethical and not ethical within the multifarious and highly complex operations of the marketplace.

The scholastics were thus drawn to examining such basic economic concepts as the nature of money and value, and the factors that determine price. Nicholas Oresme, for example, in attempting to show the injustice of monetary debasements, wrote between 1350 and 1360 the tract *De moneta*, which anticipated many of the ideas of the 16th-century economist Jean Bodin. Scholastic thought was also less rigid and more favorable to a free economy than is frequently asserted. The common scholastic opinion was, for example, that the just price was under normal conditions the free-market price; while maintaining the usury prohibition, the scholastics did not obstruct the development of alternate ways of channeling credit: through partnerships and companies, annuities, and bills of exchange. Scholastic thought through the later Middle Ages and into the early 17th century reveals an ever stronger empirical emphasis in its analysis and an ever more sympathetic comprehension of the activities of the marketplace.

Significance of Medieval Social Thought. The historical importance of medieval social thought is again difficult to define. Medieval thinkers wanted to establish justice in social affairs, but the extent to which they were successful is beyond assessment. On a more practical level, their early suspicions of commercial activities probably worked to channel effort and investment into agriculture rather than trade; but given the predominantly agricultural character of the early medieval economy, it would be hard to call this result unfortunate. And it would also be hard to say that the usury prohibition for long delayed the development of a capitalistic economy, so varied were the ways of circumventing it. Scholastic thought did have a clear impact on medieval economic institutions, and it strongly influenced banking practices and the economic policies of cities and states. The time has long since passed when the scholastics could be dismissed as unimportant in the history of European social thought. Scholastic social analysis forms an initial and integral chapter within the larger effort of Western man to understand, and hopefully to improve, his society and its institutions.

Bibliography: G. LE BRAS, ''Conceptions of Economy and Society,'' *Cambridge Economic History of Europe*, v.3 (Cambridge, Eng. 1963) 554–575. I. GIORDANI, *The Social Message of the Early Church Fathers* (Paterson, NJ 1944). I. SEIPEL, *Die wirtschaftsethischen Lehren der Kirchenväter* (Vienna 1907). P. H. FURFEY, *A History of Social Thought* (New York 1942). R. W. and A. J. CARLYLE, *A History of Mediaeval Political Theory in the West*, 6 v. (New York 1950). G. DE LAGARDE, *La Naissance de l'esprit laïque au déclin du moyen âge*, 5 v. (Louvain 1956–63). J. A. SCHUMPETER, *History of Economic Analysis*, ed. E. B. SCHUMPETER

(New York 1954). J. W. BALDWIN, *The Medieval Theories of the Just Price* (Philadelphia 1959). R. DE ROOVER, ''The Concept of the Just Price: A Theory of Economic Policy,'' *Journal of Economic History* 18 (1958) 418–438. J. T. NOONAN, *The Scholastic Analysis of Usury* (Cambridge, MA 1957). E. TROELTSCH, *The Social Teaching of the Christian Churches*, tr. O. WYON, 2 v. (New York 1931). B. JARRETT, *Social Theories of the Middle Ages, 1200–1500* (Westminster, MD 1942). G. A. O'BRIEN, *An Essay on Mediaeval Economic Teaching* (New York 1920).

[D. J. HERLIHY]

4. Modern

Social movements, in the sense of practical programs for political and economic reform in the interest of the general welfare, are relatively modern phenomena. They were particularly characteristic of the 19th century and arose out of a heightened consciousness of the importance of society in the lives of individual men. This social consciousness was derived from the revolutions wrought by DEMOCRACY, nationalism, and industrialism. The democratic revolution, set in motion in the U.S. and France, replaced the older aristocratic political structures with a new one centered on the masses. In Germany the nationalist revolution, which came into being by way of opposition to Napoleonic dominance, influenced economics, law, and philosophy as well as politics. The industrial revolution, originating in England, substituted a system of production based on factories for the previous simple, cottage-housed, rural industry. Each of these revolutions contributed in its own way to a keener awareness of social reality and social problems. This was particularly true of the industrial revolution. Factories themselves became miniature societies; industrial cities were new and larger social groupings; and at national and international levels social interdependence was fostered by developments in banking, finance, transportation and general communications of the industrial era.

The Challenge of Freedom. Despite their different origins, immediate interests, and emphases, these revolutionary changes developed from a common philosophy. It was summed up in the one word liberty—liberty through political representation, national independence, and economic initiative. In the domain of politics the way was prepared by the writings of the 18th-century ENCYCLOPEDISTS and the *philosophes*, for whom individual FREEDOM was the highest human value. In the sphere of nationalism the new spirit made the 19th century an era of turmoil and rebellion. But LIBERALISM in the form of economic INDIVIDUALISM was most significant, to the extent that the basic economic outlook of the 19th century was termed *laissez-faire*. The glorification of freedom in every realm led to many and grave abuses, particularly in economic matters. In this field the doctrine of freedom, often expressed by the phrase ''every man for himself,'' allowed the strong to oppress the weak. In the absence of trade unions, then regarded as threatening individual freedom, capitalist manufacturers imposed miserably low wage rates on employees. In like manner, with the state standing by and refraining from interference, exceptionally bad working and living conditions became the order of the day. In short, what began to be called the proletariat, that is, the propertyless, wage-earning class, was reduced to a state little better than slavery. Paradoxically, the 19th century, despite its insistence upon liberty for all men and all nations, produced at first a new bondage for the working man.

Catholic Traditionalism. One of the most striking things about this development is that the Christian churches, at least officially, made virtually no attempt to stem the evil effects of early industrialism. As far as Protestantism was concerned, the opposite was the case. Those countries in which industrial capitalism made its first headway were precisely the Protestant countries and regions of Europe. So much so that Max WEBER, R. H. Tawney, and others have advanced the thesis that the Protestant ethic, particularly in its Calvinist form, was an important impetus to the growth of industrial capitalism. Although it is true that an earlier form of commercial capitalism had developed in the 14th and 15th centuries, insofar as it was related to religion it was a reflection of Europe's waning faith and indifference to the Church's condemnation of usury; it was not something that received support from official Catholic teaching. The case of industrial capitalism vis-à-vis Puritan Protestantism was quite different; for material success was linked with the possession of virtue and the promise of salvation, and vice with general fecklessness and moral evil. Many Christian statesmen and economists felt that it would be flaunting Providence to attempt to change the situation in the name of social reform.

For decades the Catholic Church also remained inactive, with near-disastrous consequences. In retrospect, it seems clear that the Church should have developed a body of social thought and a program of social reform much earlier than it did. There were extenuating factors that explain, although they do not justify, this failure. In particular, the European Church was intensely preoccupied with the problems raised by the democratic revolution. Indeed, her fear of its consequences as manifested in the ATHEISM and RATIONALISM of the FRENCH REVOLUTION, the seizure of Church lands, and the imposition of the CIVIL CONSTITUTION OF THE CLERGY became almost a Catholic obsession. Although alleviated for a time by the Napoleonic Concordat, the reaction was prolonged by Napoleon's annexation of the States of the Church, concern for which later occupied the attention of the papacy during the period of the Italian RISORGIMENTO. The intensity of the reaction was manifest in the Church's rejection of Félicité Robert de LAMMENAIS (1782–1854) and the Liberal Catholics, whose interests, though predominantly political, included some attention to social reform. In England, the leading industrial country, where the evils of liberal capitalism were most in evidence, the Church was especially weak. In 1800 there were only about 60,000 Catholics in the country. By 1850 the number had risen to about a million, but both the leaders of the Church and the faithful were without much social or political influence. Moreover, both in England and on the Continent, there was a Catholic traditionalist conservatism that resisted awareness of the need for radical social reform. An aspect of this attitude was displayed by CHATEAUBRIAND, who extolled the glories of a past age in his *Genius of Christianity* when he should have been leading Catholics to face contemporary problems.

Growth of Secularism. The outcome was a lamentable division of European men into two blocks of opinion, two closed and mutually exclusive compartments, the Christian and the secular. Of course the growth of SECULARISM is not to be attributed entirely to the failure of organized religion to come to grips with the social injustice of the period. The apathy of the churches was indeed an important contributing factor, but the rise of atheism and disbelief was influenced directly by other factors, such as the rationalism and freethinking of the *Aufklarung* (Enlightenment). The social situation was nevertheless a cause, and an important one. This being the case, it is not at all surprising that the first formal movements for social reform came from secular sources and, as a result, had an irreligious and even antireligious character. Their object—to achieve the equality that was intended to go hand in hand with liberty—was conceived in a variety of ways by diverse thinkers; but it is generally covered by the term socialism, one wing of which was moderate and democratic in its aims, whereas the other, communism, was very extreme.

Rise of Catholic Social Movements. Modern Catholic social thought in general began in a series of unrelated and sporadic efforts rather than as the official program of a full-fledged movement. In France it had its beginnings in opposition to the Young Socialists after the abortive revolution of 1830. Its chief representatives were Frédéric OZANAM (1813–53), who launched a successful organization for the relief of the poor, the Society of ST. VINCENT DE PAUL; LACORDAIRE (1802–61), who preached in Notre Dame against the worst evils of capitalism; and MONTALEMBERT (1810–70), who, as member of the Chamber of Deputies, was responsible for the first French factory legislation. Together with the Workers' Circles and study circles promoted by Albert de Mun and LA TOUR DU PIN, these initiatives represented the only French Catholic social thought and activity until the last decade of the century.

In Germany similar figures appeared in opposition to the Communists after the revolution of 1848. These were Adolf KOLPING (1813–64), the journeyman worker become priest, who established a string of hostels for immigrant peasant workers in the new industrial cities; Emmanuel von KETTELER (1811–77), civil servant and bishop of Mainz, who preached sermons and wrote treatises condemning *laissez-faire;* and Ludwig WINDTHORST (1812–91), who, like Montalembert in France, was a member of the Reichstag and sponsored the first German factory acts.

Two defects in these developments are immediately apparent. For one thing, they originated defensively, in opposition, that is, to socialism of one kind or another. Certainly they were founded in a consciousness of the need for justice, but this consciousness was not experienced with the intensity needed for action until the socialist movement had begun to draw thousands of workmen away from the faith. Second, they sought amelioration rather than thoroughgoing reform. In general, the existence of the captialist system with all its shortcomings was accepted and ways and means were sought to bandage the afflicted, when what was needed was a sort of preventive social medicine.

These proponents of a committed social Catholicism, however, laid the bases of the now widespread and successful Catholic social movements. They were at least a generation behind the early socialists, such as the Comte de SAINT-SIMON, Robert Owen, and Charles Fourier. Moreover, socialism was first to organize at the international level—the Socialist International was founded in 1864—whereas the Catholic social movement first became international in scope in 1885. In that year Cardinal Gaspard MERMILLOD (1824–92) founded the Fribourg Union to provide a link between the independent efforts in different countries and the development of a common body of Catholic social thought. This was progressively hammered out at meetings of the Fribourg Union and through the force of concrete example in the practical attitudes of men such as Cardinals Henry MANNING (1808–92) and James GIBBONS (1834–1921). The revival of Thomistic philosophy about 1880 led to a systematic effort in social philosophy, particularly on the part of German Jesuits such as Viktor CATHREIN (1845–1931) and Heinrich Pesch (1854–1926), whose theories of SOCIETY and the STATE were based upon applications of natural law in economic and political thought.

These developments were given status and authority in 1891 by the encyclical *RERUM NOVARUM* of Leo XIII, reinforced in later decades by *Quadragesimo anno* (1931) and the social encyclicals of Popes John XXIII, Paul VI, and John Paul II. Here, the most recent popes develop carefully nuanced positions on the themes of property and wages, trade unionism and industrial relations, the role of the state in socioeconomic affairs, international economic development, and new challenges to the advancement of the common good in society. The papal social encyclicals constitute a tradition of reflection that at once builds upon the biblical, philosophical, and theological traditions treated above and exhibits an openness to new ideas (such as the imperative to end colonialism), trends of thought (such as personalism), and empirical data (such as the end of communism and the Cold War). In so doing, these documents take up the challenge offered by the Second Vatican Council ever to take seriously ''the duty of scrutinizing the signs of the times and of interpreting them in the light of the gospel'' (*Gaudium et spes*, 4).

Contemporary Catholic social thought is not restricted, of course, to papal teachings and magisterial documents emanating from national episcopal conferences and regional or occasional synods of bishops. Besides these magisterial social teachings there is also a less well-defined but vitally influential body of unofficial Catholic social thought. Some of this ethical guidance is associated with the literature and social involvements of lay movements, from the predominantly European Catholic Action (encouraged especially during the pontificate of Pius XI) to the Catholic Worker Movement (active mainly in North America since the 1930s) to the base Christian communities (primarily a Latin American phenomenon) associated with liberation theology. These and many other popular movements serve as indispensable contributions to Catholic social thought, for they help form the laity and assist in organizing social action on behalf of justice in an increasingly complex and interdependent world.

Bibliography: J. NEWMAN, *The Christian in Society* (Baltimore 1962). D. A. O'CONNOR, *Catholic Social Doctrine* (Westminster, MD 1956). H. SOMERVILLE, *Studies in the Catholic Social Movement* (London 1933).

[J. NEWMAN/T. MASSARO]

SOCIAL THOUGHT, PAPAL

The social teaching of the Church as promulgated by the popes. This article indicates the historical background of the remarkable development of this teaching that began in the 19th century and outlines the basic concepts involved.

1. History

Direct papal involvement in the systematic, positive development of Catholic teaching on social questions is a relatively recent phenomenon, beginning with the pontificate of LEO XIII (1878–1903). It is clear, nevertheless, that the papacy has always had, at least since the patristic period, an important role in the evolution of doctrinal and disciplinary positions bearing in some degree, directly or indirectly, on society and its problems. One example can be found in its well-known role in the INVESTITURE STRUGGLE and in the determining of the relations of CHURCH and State in general. Similarly, although the concern of the early popes with marriage and the family was essentially doctrinal and disciplinary, their decisions had important social ramifications. As early as the 5th century INNOCENT I and LEO I issued decisions on divorce and remarriage that had far-reaching effects. Beginning in the 8th century, the papacy was increasingly involved in untangling the confusion surrounding cousin marriages, both for consanguineal and affinal relationships. It is difficult to determine the papacy's exact role in the elimination of SLAVERY in the Roman Empire, in the development of Christian principles pertaining to the morality of WAR, or in the resolution of problems related to charging interest for financial loans—USURY. Yet in these and other matters, to the extent that papal approval was given to the acts of official Church councils, both general and local, it can be concluded that the popes had a significant role in the development of Christian social thought, at least in a broad sense. [*See* SOCIAL THOUGHT, CATHOLIC.]

Papal Conservatism in the 19th Century. The 19th century was a period of radical political, economic, and social change. After the FRENCH REVOLUTION the Church was confronted with new or changing structures. It faced many problems involving its own status in relation to the new secular governments and, as an aftermath of the industrial revolution, new social and economic problems with complex moral implications. Most serious of all was the fact that the spirit initiating the momentous social upheavals was that of RATIONALISM (and later, LIBERALISM). The tenets of these new philosophies were often diametrically opposed to traditional Catholic teaching. Throughout the first three-quarters of the century, however, there were many eminent Catholics, both clerical and lay—among them J. B. H. LACORDAIRE, C. F. R. de MONTALEMBERT, and Frédéric OZANAM in France; Bp. Emmanuel von KETTELER in Germany; Cardinal Henry Edward MANNING in England; and Cardinal Gaspard MERMILLOD in Switzerland—who clearly recognized that the new trends were irreversible and that the Church would have to go beyond its traditional teaching and even in some measure reverse its historic position vis-à-vis other social institutions.

The reactions of the popes to the changes of this period were in general negative. They fought to stem the tide and to restore the old order. Their attitude was most clearly reflected in GREGORY XVI's *Mirari vos* (1832), which condemned the teachings of H. F. R. de LAMMENAIS and the *L'Avenir* group in France, and in the *QUANTA CURA* (1864) and accompanying SYLLABUS OF ERRORS of PIUS IX (1846–78). The latter condemned many propositions of rationalists that had social implications, among them those pertaining to religious freedom and separation of Church and State. The papacy, shorn of its temporal power and in apparently bitter opposition to almost everything equated with enlightened progress, suffered a diminution of prestige. Indeed the prestige of the Church was at a low ebb at the time of the papal election of 1878.

Role of Leo XIII. Leo XIII made it apparent in his first encyclical, *Inscrutabili* (1878), that although he had no intention of compromising basic philosophical or theological principles to placate progressives, neither would he admit that the Church was an outdated institution in the modern world. On the contrary, he asserted that the Church favored true progress in all areas, as it had in the past, and that, far from impeding it, the Church would promote and support social progress in all possible ways. This became a recurrent theme in his great encyclicals and in those of his successors. They emphasized the need of society for the moral leadership of the Church, just as the Church in turn was seen to be dependent upon other social structures and institutions in every age.

It was not until ten years after his election to the papacy that Leo XIII issued his first fully developed pronouncement on one of the most controversial issues of the day, the nature of human liberty. His *LIBERTAS* (1888) must be considered as one of the most basic social documents of the Holy See in modern times inasmuch as it laid down the fundamental principles for papal teaching regarding marriage and the family, the nature of the state and of relations between Church and State, the rights and duties of management and labor, the right of the Church to freedom in the fulfillment of its mission, and the right of peoples to be free to determine the form of government exercising rule over them. Leo wrote in effect that, far from being opposed to human liberty in all areas, the Church supported the ideal of freedom while opposing license as a perversion of freedom.

Papal Teaching on Marriage and the Family. In some areas there have been only slight changes or developments in papal social thought. Thus, Catholic teaching has always held the family to be the basic unit of society and all modern popes have been solicitous in defense of the marriage bond and the rights of parents in the education of children. PIUS XI, in *CASTI CONNUBII* (1930), included a discussion of the problem of birth control, a subject not even mentioned in Leo XIII's *ARCANUM* (1880). Continuing attention to this problem and to the morality of rhythm (periodic abstinence) can be found in the discourses of PIUS XII. Pius XII also opened new vistas in addresses on the role of women in modern society [*see* WOMEN AND PAPAL TEACHING]. Paul VI's *Humanae vitae* (1968) not only reaffirms the Church's prohibition of artificial birth control but also treats many aspects of family life, such as the value of spousal fidelity. John Paul II's *Familiaris consortio* (1981) and *Letter to Families* (1994) advanced Catholic reflection on the relationship between the genders and underlined the importance of family life by frequently referring to the family as "domestic church."

Defense of Human Dignity. Only shortly before the appearance of *Libertas* Leo XIII's encyclical *In plurimis* (1888) had reiterated the position of the Church on the morality of slavery as it developed after the latter part of the 15th century. One of the more useful features of the encyclical was its treatment of the historical application of the Church's official teaching on the capture of African slaves, the slave trade, and the enslavement of natives in the New World. Leo pointed with obvious pride to the denunciations of these practices by PIUS II (1458–64), LEO X (1513–21), PAUL III (1534–49), URBAN VIII (1623–44), BENEDICT XIV (1740–58), and PIUS VII (1800–23). Leo's immediate successor, St. PIUS X (1903–14), found it necessary to address himself to the same problem in his *Lacrimabile statu* (1912).

On the broader problem of racism, the teachings of Leo XIII, Pius XI, Pius XII, and JOHN XXIII have been most explicit. In 1938 the famous condemnation by the Congregation of Seminaries and Universities of eight racist propositions, all referring to the teachings of National Socialism, summarized the official Roman attitude toward this heresy. Many of the major pronouncements of Pius XII, his *SUMMI PONTIFICATUS* (1939), for example, and John XXIII's *MATER ET MAGISTRA* (1961) and *PACEM IN TERRIS* (1963) also developed the Church's position on racism in the course of their consistent emphasis on world unity. In *Populorum progressio* (1967), Paul VI also denounced any structures, whether economic, political or social in nature, that divide the human race by race or class and thereby diminish the recognition and dignity that should be accorded to all. John Paul II has consistently used the term *solidarity* as a summary of the ethical principles and moral virtues that enhance the achievement of equal dignity for all humans. In *Sollicitudo rei socialis* (1987), John Paul II denounces "the various forms of exploitation and of economic, social, political and even religious oppression of the individual and his or her rights, discrimination of every type, especially the exceptionally odious form based on differences of race'' (no. 15).

Freedom of Religion. Some modifications and clarifications of Leo's ideas on liberty appeared in the pronouncements of later popes. One of the most important was in the area of FREEDOM OF RELIGION. Leo XIII took the position that governments could tolerate evil, false religions, for example, in the interests of the common good. Pius XII, in his *Ci riesce* (1953), held the coexistence of a plurality of religions on an equal basis to be not a matter solely of permissiveness but, where conditions required, a moral imperative. John XXIII in *Pacem in terris* (1963) removed this question from the realm of mere ''tolerance'' when he insisted on the right of every human being ''to honor God according to the dictates of an upright conscience, and therefore the right to worship God privately and publicly'' (14). After the Second Vatican Council's *Dignitatis humanae* (Declaration on Religious Freedom) definitively expressed the church's support of civil freedom in religious matters, subsequent popes have spoken eloquently of their unwavering support for the principles of religious freedom and respect for individual conscience in every social context.

Democratic Government. There has been in fact a marked progression in papal teaching on the nature and function of the STATE, particularly with regard to the acceptance of democratic forms of government. In his *IMMORTALE DEI* (1885) and in *Libertas* Leo XIII readily admitted DEMOCRACY among the many forms of government acceptable to Catholic teaching. Pius XII in his Christmas message *Benignitas et humanitas* (1944) remarked that people at the time were convinced that only democracy could provide protection against dictatorship and secure world peace. He proceeded to discuss the rights and responsibilities of free citizens, rulers and subjects, under a democratic regime. John XXIII strongly implied in *Pacem in terris* that democratic political organization should be the ultimate goal even for emerging nations. The Second Vatican Council's *Gaudium et spes* (no. 31) all but endorsed democracy when it affirmed, ''Praise is due to those national procedures which allow the largest possible number of citizens to participate in public affairs with genuine freedom.'' Subsequently, Popes Paul VI and John Paul II have viewed democracy in a positive light, although have stopped short of providing an uncritical endorsement of all features of modern democratic societies. For example, in nos. 46–49 of his 1991 encyclical *Centesimus annus*, John Paul II intersperses his appreciation of democratic principles (''The church values the democratic system . . .'') with reminders of potential shortcomings of democratic societies (as when he calls upon citizens of democracies to ''overcome today's widespread individualistic mentality'').

Approach to the Social Question. Leo XIII pioneered in his *RERUM NOVARUM* (1891) by laying down a set of broad principles pertaining to the rights and obligations of workers, employers, and the state, in the kind of wage economy that had emerged in Europe and America after the industrial revolution. These principles, based essentially on NATURAL LAW, ran counter to the prevailing principles of economic and political liberalism. Stressing the dignity of the worker as a human being, Leo developed the rights flowing from this fact: the worker's right not to be treated as a mere commodity in the productive process; the right of the state to intervene in private industry when necessary to protect the worker against exploitation and to ensure his or her rights to self-development; the right of the worker to a just wage because individual labor is both personal and necessary in a wage economy; the right of workers to organize for group protection; and the right and necessity of private ownership for all.

Pius XI's *QUADRAGESIMO ANNO* (1931) took its place with *Rerum novarum* as one of the great papal social documents. It developed further the principles of Leo XIII, especially through its emphasis on the concept of the common good of society and on the responsibility of the state to promote the temporal well-being of every segment of society. The principle of intervention by public authority is balanced by another principle, that of SUBSIDIARITY. Pius XI also introduced two new concepts, those of SOCIAL JUSTICE and social charity, the implementation of which he considered essential to the reconstruction of society. He emphasized, as had Leo XIII, the substitution of the principle of cooperation for that of conflict in the relationship between management and labor. To this end he proposed the establishment of a form of industry council plan calling for the reorganization of all industries and professions along vertical rather than horizontal class lines. He also suggested as feasible the introduction of some form of partnership contract whereby workers might share in ownership or management and also in profits. Finally, he emphasized the role of the LAITY as indispensable for the restoration of social order. His successors have placed ever-increasing emphasis on the importance of the lay apostolate.

The concept of private PROPERTY received further clarification in *La solennità* (1941), a radio message of Pius XII. One of the most basic of human rights is that of every human being to access to whatever material goods he needs for his full development as a human being. This individual right cannot be suppressed, even by other clear and undisputed property rights. The ultimate justification of the institution of private property is to protect and promote this individual right, and it is a weighty duty of public authority to protect and implement the right.

John XXIII's contributions on economic questions were numerous and varied, not the least being his excellent historical summary and interpretation of preceding papal teaching in the first part of *Mater et Magistra.* He made particular contributions in two areas, namely, in his insistence that the farmer and the farm worker should share in the material and social rewards of progressively industrialized societies and in his demand that all classes in developing areas—workers, especially—should be given assistance and opportunity to share in the benefits of the more highly developed nations in accordance with the demands of the principle of subsidiarity. Pope Paul VI and John Paul II have extended their predecessors' concerns about social order by repeating calls for the equitable sharing of the world's material resources. Paul VI affirmed that the new global nature of human interdependence calls for a recognition of new social duties, such as his hope, expressed in his 1967 encyclical *Populorum progressio* (no. 49) ''that the superfluous wealth of rich countries should be placed at the service of poor nations.'' John Paul II also frequently notes the increase in global economic interdependence, a fact of modern life which makes all the more relevant his 1987 reminder that ''private property, in fact, is under a social mortgage, which means that it has an intrinsically social function'' (*Sollicitudo rei socialis*, no. 42).

Popes and International Order. On the subject of war, Benedict XV bemoaned the horrors of World War I, particularly in his *Ad Beatissimi* (1914), as did his successor, Pius XI, in his *Ubi arcano Dei* (1922). Pius XII, who was very much involved in the problems of World War II, stated in 1939 that ''nothing is lost by peace. Everything may be lost by war'' (*Un'ora grave*). Again in *Benignitas et humanitas* he called on peoples everywhere to make war on war. John XXIII in *Pacem in terris* summed up his discussion of the need for worldwide disarmament by declaring that ''it is hardly possible to imagine that in the atomic era war could be used as an instrument of justice'' (127).

In *Ubi arcano Dei,* Pius XI touched on the broader question of the international community more or less in passing when he pointed to excessive nationalism, which overlooks the fact that all peoples are members of the universal human family, as a major cause of world unrest. His successor, Pius XII, was very much concerned with this problem from his first encyclical, *Summi Pontificatus,* in which he considered the denial of the unity and solidarity of the human race as one of the major heresies of modern times. He returned repeatedly to this subject, stressing first of all that there is a natural international community that embraces all peoples, and secondly that there is a very real need for a juridically established international organization as a *sine qua non* of peace in the modern world (see especially, *Benignitas et humanitas* and *Ci riesce*). The name of John XXIII will be forever identified with the quest for international unity and world peace. It was he who first saw clearly that world unity is unattainable unless there is, if not total religious unity, at least greater tolerance among religious groups of all kinds (*Pacem in terris*). To this end he convened Vatican Council II, to which he invited as observers representatives of all major Christian denominations. His successors picked up John's mantle as defenders of peace. Both Paul VI and John Paul II acted frequently and heroically to bring together warring parties, to defuse global conflicts and to use their good offices for the peaceful arbitration of differences. Both issued encyclicals that treated not only the proximate causes of armed conflict, but also more remote causes, such as economic underdevelopment (see Paul's *Populorum progressio*, nos. 76–7 and John Paul's *Centesimus annus*, no. 52, both of which note that ''another name for peace is development''). In numerous statements released during the Persian Gulf War of 1990–91 and the several Balkan conflicts of the 1990s, John Paul II subjected to rigorous moral scrutiny the repeated appeals to the just war theory on the part of armed parties. The effect of John Paul's rejection of any facile appeal to the principles of just war was an authentic development of doctrine which renewed the early church's overwhelming presumption against the use of force and challenged modern nations to reconsider whether their option for war was genuinely a last resort motivated by the highest principles, as opposed to opportunistic ventures in national aggrandizement.

Bibliography: M. C. CARLEN, *A Guide to the Encyclicals of the Roman Pontiffs from Leo XIII to the Present Day* (New York 1939); *Dictionary of Papal Pronouncements: Leo XIII to Pius XII, 1878–1957* (New York 1958). T. J. HARTE, *Papal Social Principles: A Guide and Digest* (Milwaukee 1956). L. STURZO, *Church and State,* tr. B. B. CARTER (New York 1939).

[T. J. HARTE/T. MASSARO]

2. Basic Concepts

The magisterium of the Church has not defined its social teaching in systematic form, once and for all. Instead, especially under Leo XIII and his successors, it has gradually enucleated this teaching from its sources in revelation and tradition, elucidating it in relation to new situations and almost always in the solution of problems emerging from social evolution. On this account, real difficulties can arise in attempts to determine which elements of the teaching are essential and which are only relative to the historical situations in which they are formulated. One possible solution is that of holding as essential only those elements that are frequently repeated and reaffirmed in varying historical situations, but an absolute value cannot be attributed to this criterion. It is more to the point to note that there has always been in the magisterium of the Church a consciousness of the need to distinguish clearly, especially in the social field, between the specific and direct object of its teachings and the motives by which it justifies these teachings. It is, for example, an essential element in the social teaching of the Church that private ownership of goods, productive goods included, is a natural right; but the motives that are cited by the pontiffs to justify the natural character of this right are not always the same—they have different values and some are mere expressions of opinion. (*See* ENCYCLICAL; SOCIAL THOUGHT, CATHOLIC, 1.)

It is evident that, in its general scope, the social teaching of the magisterium comprises both metaphysical and moral elements, that is, elements that explain what social reality is and elements that indicate how men ought to live in SOCIETY. When referring precisely to the social *DOCTRINE* of the Church and its specific content, scholars are not in unanimous agreement, although the opinion that the specific content of this doctrine is metaphysical in nature continues to gain support. In this view, the problems of doctrinal concern are such as the following. What is social reality? What are the elements that form it and the subjects that work in it? What are the fundamental principles on which it is built and that regulate the relationships of which it is composed?

It is true that the magisterium of the Church alternates metaphysical and moral teachings in one and the same document; in fact, frequently the former are developed in the latter. This characteristic approach is explained by the very mission of the Church, which is to guide men and women to the attainment of their last end, an end reached outside time, if during the earthly phase of his or her existence a person has acted justly. Since there is an intrinsic connection between being and acting, once the nature of social reality is defined, it is logical that the magisterium of the Church should deduce from it the norms according to which people, especially the faithful, are obliged to act and that it should encourage the observance of these norms.

In outlining the basic concepts of the social doctrine of the Church presented by modern popes from Leo XIII to Paul VI, this article follows, although not rigidly, the opinion of those who hold that the specific content of the Church's social doctrine is metaphysical.

Dignity of Man. A human being, in all the relationships of society, in all institutions and in all environments, can never be considered as a chattel or a mere instrument; he must instead always be considered and treated as a person [*see* PERSON (IN PHILOSOPHY)]. In discussing economic relationships, Leo XIII declared in the encyclical *RERUM NOVARUM:* ''Workers are not to be treated as slaves; justice demands that the dignity of human personality be respected in them, ennobled as it has been through what we call the Christian character. . . . It is shameful and inhuman to use men as things for gain and to put no more value on them than what they are worth in muscle and energy'' [*Acta Sanctae Sedis* 23 (1890–91) 649]. Leo's successors have repeated this principle and applied it to all sectors of society. The individual, proclaimed Pius XII in his Christmas message of 1944, ''so far from being the object and, as it were, a merely passive element in the social order, is in fact, and must be and continue to be, its subject, its foundation and its end'' [*Benignitas et humanitas, Acta Apostolicae Sedis* 37 (1945) 12]. John XXIII confirmed the same concept in *PACEM IN TERRIS*:

> Any human society, if it is to be well-ordered and productive, must lay down as a foundation this principle: that every human being is a person; his nature is endowed with intelligence and free will. By virtue of this, he has rights and duties of his own, flowing directly and simultaneously from his very nature, which are therefore universal, inviolable and inalienable.
>
> If we look upon the dignity of the human person in the light of divinely revealed truth, we cannot help but esteem it far more highly; for men are redeemed by the blood of Jesus Christ, they are by grace the children and friends of God and heirs of eternal glory. [*Acta Apostolicae Sedis* 55 (1963) 259.]

Nobility of Work as Expression of Personality. The work of human beings can never be placed on the same level as the forces of nature and therefore can never be assigned a monetary value as can merchandise. It is a free and conscious human activity, an expression of the personality of the worker. Therefore, it is always noble, even when expressed in modest forms and in economic activity. In the words of Leo XIII, ''If we hearken to natural reason and to Christian philosophy, gainful occupations are not a mark of shame to man, but rather of respect, as they provide him with an honorable means of supporting life'' (*op. cit.*).

Certainly work is a human activity, carried out according to the laws of the immediate and specific ends that it is meant to attain. If one wishes to produce economic wealth, one must know and respect the laws that govern economic activities and one must also know and respect the laws that govern the specific activity in which one intends to engage. It is true that economic laws are always the same, but each of the innumerable activities of the economic world has also laws of its own; e.g., the laws that one must respect in building houses are different from those that apply to making clothes or preparing food. But any work, whatever the nature of its specific and immediate end, is also and always an expression of the personality of the worker. In his activities he must obey the laws governing his work, but he is also obliged to obey the moral law, which is founded on God and leads to God. Pius XI developed this thought in *QUADRAGESIMO ANNO*:

> Even though economics and moral science employs each its own principles in its own sphere, it is, nevertheless, an error to say that the economic and moral orders are so distinct from and alien to each other that the former depends in no way on the latter. Certainly the laws of economics, as they are termed, being based on the very nature of material things and on the capacities of the human body and mind, determine the limits of what productive human effort cannot, and of what it can attain in the economic field and by what means. Yet it is reason itself that clearly shows, on the basis of the individual and social nature of things and of men, the purpose which God ordained for all economic life.
>
> But it is only the moral law which, just as it commands us to seek our supreme and last end in the whole scheme of our activity, so likewise commands us to seek directly in each kind of activity those purposes which we know that nature, or rather God the Author of nature, established for that kind of action, and in orderly relationship to subordinate such immediate purposes to our supreme and last end. If we faithfully observe this law, then it will follow that the particular purposes, both individual and social, that are sought in the economic field will fall in their proper place in the universal order of purposes, and we, in ascending through them, as it were by steps, shall attain the final end of all things, that is God, to Himself and to us, the supreme and inexhaustible Good. [*Acta Apostolicae Sedis* 23 (1931) 190–191.]

What is stated in this passage with respect to economic science and the moral law can be affirmed for all human activity. When there is a question of human activity in the field of art, it is carried out according to the laws of art but also governed by the moral law. The same can be said of human activity in the fields of law, politics, culture, health, or any other field.

Multiplicity of Values in Work. A multiplicity of values is implicit in every form of work. First of all there is the value of the objects sought. An economic work tends to realize an economic value, an artistic work an artistic value, a political work a political value, a scientific work a scientific value, and so on; considering work in relation to its objects the possible values to be realized are limitless. But work is carried out in harmony with the moral law, which is the law governing the worker. Since it is or should be the fulfillment of duty, work possesses a moral value.

Further, the moral law has its foundation in the relationship that exists between man and God and imposes obligations upon man in this most profound of all relationships. Therefore, work is the recognition and respect of the order established by God, an act of homage to Him, a contribution toward the fulfillment of His providential plan in history. Through work a religious value can be realized. This is worth so much more when men, united to Christ as branches to the vine (Jn 15.5), live their work as a continuation of the work of Christ Himself. As Pius XII reminded a group of Italian civil servants, ''Work done with God and for God is human work transformed into the Divine. It is prayer'' [*Abbiamo avuto recentemente, L'Osservatore Romano* 161 (May 19–20, 1952) 1]. Or, more amply,

> Labor is a service of God, a gift of God, the vigor and fullness of human life, the gauge of eternal rest. Lift up your heads, and hold them up, workers. Look at the Son of God, Who, with His eternal Father, created and ordered the universe; becoming man like us, sin alone excepted, and having grown in age, He enters the great community of workers; in His work of salvation He labors, wearing out his earthly life.
>
> It is He, the Redeemer of the world, Who by His grace, which runs through our being and our activity, elevates and ennobles every honest work, be it high or low, great or little, pleasant or tiresome, material or intellectual, giving it a meritorious and supernatural value in the sight of God, and thus gathering every form of multifarious human activity into one constant act of glorifying His Father Who is in heaven. [*Ancora una quinta volta, Acta Apostolicae Sedis* 36 (1944) 16]

Every human being in each instant of his work life is confronted with two alternatives that can be formulated in the question of whether personality should be sacrificed to work or be enriched by work. Many theories have been elaborated that accept the first alternative. Man's being is identified with his work, bounded as it is by time and space. Many forces in modern civilization, which is characterized by the prevalence of scientific and technical elements, impel men toward such an identification. On the other hand, the magisterium of the Church speaks with clarity and insistence for the second alternative. Man's work is only a moment of his existence, it is carried out for the efficacious attainment of the immediate ends that correspond to his specific nature, but at the same time it can assure his perfection and lead him to the attainment of his celestial and eternal destiny [John XXIII, *Mater et Magistra, Acta Apostolicae Sedis* 53 (1961) 460–463].

Just Remuneration of Work. Work is an obligation, not only because the members of the human race can perfect themselves through their work, but also because it enables them to enjoy a decent standard of living, meet their family responsibilities, and fulfill their social obligations. But if work is an obligation, it is also a right, because every duty imposed by one's conscience and by God presupposes a corresponding right in human society (*Pacem in terris, loc. cit.* 264). There is, therefore, an objective and intrinsic relationship between work and the means of livelihood, that is to say, the moral law assigns a specific end to work that cannot be arbitrarily misunderstood or violated; it is that of being the natural source from which a man draws his livelihood.

It follows that the remuneration of work cannot be left to the changing laws of the market, nor can wages be fixed by an arbitrary decision of those occupying high places in the economic order or by those invested with civil authority. Wages must be determined according to criteria of justice. This is a doctrinal line constantly affirmed and progressively clarified by the teachings of the Church. Leo XIII affirmed that justice demands that the remuneration of work must be sufficient to enable the worker to live with dignity:

> Let it be granted then that worker and employer may enter freely into agreements and, in particular, concerning the amount of the wage; yet there is always underlying such agreements an element of natural justice, and one greater and more ancient then the free consent of contracting parties, namely, that the wage shall not be less than enough to support a worker who is thrifty and upright. If, compelled by necessity or moved by fear of a worse evil, a worker accepts a harder condition, which although against his will he must accept because the employer or contractor imposes it, he certainly submits to force, against which justice cries out in protest. [*Op. cit.* 662]

Pius XI taught that in determining wages it is necessary to consider, as a criterion of justice, what is sufficient for the support of the worker and his or her family, the conditions of any particular business, and the exigencies of the common good (*op. cit.* 200–202). Pius XII reiterated frequently the same directives, while John XXIII in *Mater et Magistra* included also the personal contribution of the worker to production and the exigencies of the universal common good, that is, the common good of the entire human family.

This doctrine concerning the remuneration of work finds confirmation in the actual development of the economy. A better way of life for the working classes has accompanied the progressive growth of production. The modern economy, founded on science and technical knowledge and characterized by the assembly line, tends naturally to produce goods and services in increasing quantities; that is, it gives rise to mass production. Mass production demands mass consumption, without which the whole system is disrupted, and collapse and disintegration follow. Mountains of unsold goods would destroy their producers. In turn, therefore, mass consumption depends on the purchasing power of the working classes that alone can consume the vast amount of commodities produced. The three elements mass production, mass consumption, and mass purchasing power are interdependent.

Economic development, therefore, demands social progress, and social progress promotes economic development. When the modern economy is studied objectively, the demands of justice are seen to be suggested and obtained by the inherent logic of its interior growth, rather than by any imposition from without. On this point, history has refuted the Marxist thesis of the progressively increasing distress of the working classes.

The immanent tendency of economic development, however, understood in terms of experience since the early 19th century, is realized only after a long period of fluctuation and periodic crises that have immediate and acutely negative effects on the social classes that are economically weak. In order to limit these fluctuations and their repercussions, the more politically mature communities with market economies have made more and more effort to regulate management-labor relations, above all in the medium and larger businesses, through collective bargaining and the introduction of social insurance and social security systems. After World War II, these states developed economic and social policies expressed in many forms of intervention but directed toward the same fundamental objective of insuring comparable development in the social and the economic order. This implies that the division of wealth with respect to the remuneration of labor should be carried out according to the criteria of justice mentioned above.

John Paul II and Human Labor. The most extensive papal statement on work to date is John Paul II's 1981 encyclical *Laborem exercens*. In marking the 90th anniversary of the first modern social encyclical *Rerum novarum*, John Paul offers a detailed treatise which addresses not only the conditions under which human labor proceeds, but also the overarching issue of the meaning of human work, in its subjective as well as objective dimensions.

John Paul repeats many of the concerns voiced by his predecessors: that just wages prevail, that laborers' rights to collective bargaining be respected, that workers in all sectors (agricultural as well as industrial and service workers) face favorable working conditions, and that public authorities fight the scourge of unemployment. New concerns are added to previous lists, such as the impact of work on family life in general and women in particular (no. 19), provision for the physically and mentally disabled to work according to their capacity (no. 22), and an insistence that legislators in all nations respect the rights of those who emigrate in search of work (no. 23). John Paul introduces (in nos. 16–17) a novel term, the ''indirect employer,'' to express the new awareness of the complex interdependence of our new economic system, where many systemic factors influence the terms of employment and turn the seemingly private contract between workers and management into truly public matters which impact all members of society and reflect a wide range of social conditions. In this new environment, regional and national economic planning is not only a viable option, but truly a necessity to protect the rights of workers. Although it should not lead to excessive centralization, a carefully planned labor policy may prevent unemployment and poverty and promote the security of all families.

The most original aspect of *Laborem exercens* lies in the way it evokes the themes of personalism to portray the subjective dimensions of labor as supremely important, indeed as ''the essential key to the whole social question'' (no. 3). In order to prevent the alienation of workers from their work and to advance the achievement of social justice, we must insure against impersonal centralization ''which makes the worker feel that he is just a cog in a huge machine moved from above, that he is for more reasons than one a mere production instrument rather than a true subject of work with initiative of his own'' (no. 15). The right ordering of labor arrangements will recognize the priority of labor over capital and place people above the production process, so that an ethic of ''being'' over ''having'' may prevail in society. Work holds the promise to be far more than just a source of income to support the worker and his or her family; work at its best is an expression of the worker's personality, the performance of a service to others and the locus of one's contribution to the good of society.

The encyclical concludes with a section entitled ''Elements for a Spirituality of Work'' that seeks to link the foregoing philosophical considerations to the life of the church and its tradition. Rich connections are drawn to scriptural materials to portray Christ as the ''man of work'' who preached a ''gospel of work'' (no. 26) to encourage all humankind to become co-creators with God, participants in God's plan for the universe (no. 27). In subsequent encyclicals, John Paul II continues to emphasize the relation of work to human dignity, underlining his observation in *Laborem exercens* that ''in the first place work is for man, and not man for work'' (no. 6).

Private Property. Private ownership, even of productive goods, is a natural right, a right that belongs to man by virtue of his dignity as a person and not because of any concession by public authority. This right is man's because he is spiritual, intelligent, and free and responsible for his own livelihood and destiny; each man is responsible for the support and government of the family he decides to form and bound to contribute personally to the common good.

This doctrinal position has been constantly reaffirmed by the magisterium of the Church. Leo XIII stated, ''To own goods privately . . . is a right natural to man, and to exercise this right, especially in life in society, is not only lawful, but clearly necessary'' (*op. cit.* 651). Adverting to unjust claims of both capital and labor with respect to the distribution of goods and income, Pius XI reaffirmed ''that the division of goods which results from private ownership was established by nature itself in order that created things may serve the needs of humankind in fixed and stable order'' (*op. cit.* 196). Pius XII noted that ''the right of the individual and of the family to the private ownership of property is a direct consequence of their human personality, a right due to their dignity as persons, a right to which social obligations are attached but which is not only a social function'' [*Mit Freuden kommen Acta Apostolicae Sedis* 44 (1952) 792]. And John XXIII reiterated in *Mater et Magistra* that ''the right of private property, including that pertaining to goods devoted to enterprises, is permanently valid. Indeed, it is rooted in the very nature of things, whereby we learn that individual men are prior to civil society, and hence, that civil society is to be directed toward man as its end'' (*loc. cit.* 427).

Individual Functions. The motives that the magisterium of the Church usually cites to justify the natural character of the right of private ownership of goods, productive goods included, apply to individuals, to the family, and to society. From the point of view of the individual, the right of private ownership is based on the fact that the individual is prior to society. This priority is derived from the individual's existence, his work, and the hierarchical relationship between his final end and the end of society. Private ownership of property is a necessity of the spiritual nature of man ''under the eternal law, and under the power of God most wisely ruling all things'' (Leo XIII, *op. cit.* 643). The same right finds its principal source and constant support in the fruitfulness of labor; it is also a stimulus to the exercise of responsibility in all fields of society, and it is a defense and guarantee of the fundamental expression of human liberty. In *Mater et Magistra* John XXIII observed that "experience and history testify that where political regimes do not allow to private individuals the possession also of productive goods, the exercise of human liberty is violated or completely destroyed in matters of primary importance. Thus it becomes clear that in the right of property, the exercise of liberty finds both a safeguard and a stimulus" (*loc. cit.* 427).

Familial Functions. In the familial order, private ownership is considered an element of stability, serenity, and efficiency in the pursuit of the ends proper to the family unit. Possessing a patrimony, even a modest one, the individual can face with fewer preoccupations the responsibility inherent in the creation of a new family; disastrous and painful separations of husband and wife, parents and children are less frequent; children are better nourished, better educated, and more fittingly prepared to face life. The argument is found in *Rerum novarum* that the "right of ownership . . . bestowed on individual persons by nature, must be assigned to man in his capacity as head of a family. Nay, rather, this right is all the stronger, since the human person in family life embraces much more" (*loc. cit.* 645–646.) Pius XII, in a happy expression, called private ownership the "vital space" of the family: "If today the concept and the creation of vital spaces is at the center of social and political aims, should not one, before all else, think of the vital space of the family and free it of the fetters of conditions which do not permit even to formulate the idea of a homestead of one's own?" (*La solennita, Acta Apostolicae Sedis* 33 (1941) 224).

Societal Functions. In the society in general, the social function of private ownership has a double aspect, constitutive and operative. The first follows from the fact that the resources of nature and the economic world are preordained by Providence to provide for the dignified support of the human family. However, this end can be reached only if there is a lasting and fruitful order in social relationships, an order that includes as one element the institution of private ownership of goods, productive goods included. This is recalled in *Quadragesimo anno* as the traditional teaching on the twofold aspect of ownership: "Nature, rather the Creator Himself, has given man the right of private ownership, not only that individuals may be able to provide for themselves and their families but also that the goods which the Creator destined for the entire family of mankind may through this institution truly serve this purpose. All this can be achieved in no wise except through the maintenance of a certain and definite order" (*loc cit.* 191–192; see also St. Thomas Aquinas, *Summa theologiae* 2a2ae, 66.2 ad 7).

The second aspect flows necessarily from the first. It is found in the truth that while one pursues his own interests in the exercise of this right he contributes also to the common good; the goods he owns can also be used for the needy and for the accomplishment of noble works without compromising the owner's way of life and his economic and social position (*Mater et Magistra, loc. cit.* 430–431). In consideration of the relationship between private ownership and concrete possibilities for the integral development of human beings; between private ownership and stability, serenity, and family preferences; between property and an orderly and fruitful progress in society; the magisterium of the Church constantly engages in various efforts to ensure the proper division of goods. As John XXIII maintained, "It is not enough, then, to assert that man has from nature the right of privately possessing goods as his own, including those of productive character, unless at the same time, a continuing effort is made to spread the use of this right through all ranks of the citizenry" (*ibid.* 428).

Not only individuals and their respective families but other organized groups, intermediate associations, and public agencies, whether administrative or political, can also lawfully own private property, even productive property; and they can be owners insofar as it is necessary for the effective attainment of their specific goals and the common good. *Mater et Magistra,* in a passage noting that the doctrine of private property obviously "does not preclude ownership of goods pertaining to production of wealth by states and public agencies" (*ibid.* 429), cites *Quadragesimo anno* to the effect that this is true especially "if these carry with them power too great to be left in private hands, without injury to the community at large" (*loc. cit.* 214).

Without ever disputing the validity of the basic principle of private property, recent popes have insisted upon the advisability in certain circumstances of exceptions to a regime of what is sometimes termed "possessive individualism." The right to private ownership of property is not an absolute and unconditional right that may disregard the urgent needs of others and numerous concerns for the common good. The popes of the late 20th century staked out several carefully nuanced positions regarding the competing values of the common good and the legitimate private ownership of productive and personal property. In nos. 51–67 of *Mater et Magistra*, Pope John XXIII noted how improvements in technology, transportation and communication were creating a more interdependent world. He referred to these trends as "the multiplication of social relationships," a circumlocution which has since been generally referred to as the phenomenon of ''socialization.'' Because we are increasingly interdependent in our economic and social lives, the intervention of public authorities is more often necessary in order to coordinate social relations. From time to time, it becomes necessary to restrict the free exercise of property rights, such as when a government invokes the principle of eminent domain to secure land for road construction or expansion of public utilities such as energy production or distribution. At other times, vital industries that impact the welfare of all people (such as oil, electricity, and communications) are subject to regulation or even nationalization in order to provide for the common good. John XXIII and subsequent popes understand these departures from a regime of private property not as excuses for crass collectivization, but as the employment of prudent measures to insure accountability to universal well-being.

Pope Paul VI addressed a more dire instance of the need for societal restriction of property rights. During his pontificate, several nations in Latin America witnessed heated disputes over the issue of land reform. Desperately poor and landless workers were demanding the expropriation of large estates (*latifundia*), many of which not only contained disproportionate shares of the most fertile land, but often lay fallow while nearby *campesinos* faced starvation. In his 1967 encyclical *Populorum progressio*, Paul VI first notes the principle that ''private property does not constitute for anyone an absolute and unconditional right'' (no. 23) and then proceeds to apply this timeless church teaching to his contemporary situation: ''If certain landed estates impede the general prosperity because they are extensive, unused or poorly used, or because they bring hardship to peoples or are detrimental to the interests of the country, the common good sometimes demands their expropriation'' (no. 24). This teaching neither refutes the principle that private holdings are legitimate nor justifies a totalitarian state, but it does update the church's understanding of the role and functions of public authorities in securing the common good. Paul VI thus reiterated the church's recognition of the social nature and purpose of property, an aspect of Catholic social philosophy since many of the figures of the patristic era emphasized the universal destination of all material goods. John Paul II contributed a new way to express this insight when he used the phrase ''social mortgage'' in no. 42 of his 1987 encyclical *Sollicitudo rei socialis*: ''The good of this earth are equally meant for all. The right to private property is valid and necessary, but it does not nullify the value of this principle. Private property, in fact, is under a social mortgage.''

Authority Essential to Moral Order. Human society is consistent with the dignity of human beings when the moral law is recognized, respected, and lived, that is, when the rights of the individual are recognized, obligations are fulfilled and, in countless forms of collaboration with others, each man acts on his own responsibility. Under such conditions, a society is based on truth, realized in justice, vivified and integrated by love, and accomplished in liberty (*Pacem in terris, loc. cit.* 265–266). It is indispensable that there be in this society an authority and a power to command according to right reason (*ibid.* 269). This authority is invested in the civil powers according to the needs of the historical situation. The right to command is required by the moral law to ensure the observance of that law in a sufficient degree so that social living can be human, dignified, and fruitful. As stated by Pius XII, ''the absolute order itself of beings and purposes, which shows that man is an independent person, namely the subject of inviolable duties and rights, who is the source and end of his own social life, comprises the state also as a necessary society endowed with authority, without which it could neither exist nor live'' (*Benignitas, loc. cit.* 15). The right to command is required by the moral law, and it follows that those who hold authority may not exercise it in violation of the moral law; should they attempt to do so, their decrees would carry no obligation and if their orders were intrinsically immoral there would be an obligation to resist rather than to obey. (*See* AUTHORITY, CIVIL.)

God the Foundation of the Moral Law. The moral law is a universal law, immutable and absolute; it can therefore find its basic goal and its final explanation only in the relationship between man and God—the true God, transcendent and personal, existing Truth, highest Good, supreme Justice. For this reason human authority can and must be held as a participation of the divine authority. Pius XII continues: ''And since that absolute order, in the light of right reason, and in particular of the Christian faith, cannot have any other origin than in a personal God, our Creator, it follows that . . . the dignity of political authority is the dignity deriving from its sharing in the authority of God'' (*ibid.*).

The derivation of human authority from God through the moral law, while it explains the power of the authority to oblige man in conscience, constitutes also a safeguard for the dignity of his person. In fact, obedience to public authority is not obedience to men but an act of homage to God, the provident Creator, who has decreed that men's dealings with one another should be regulated by an order that He Himself established. Obeying God, man does not debase himself but rather is ennobled, for to serve God is to rule (*Pacem in terris, loc. cit.* 271).

Common Good. The common good of the political community is not identical to the sum of the individual goods of its respective citizens (*Summa theologiae* 2a2ae, 58.7). It is characterized by its specific content, which, however, cannot be conceived in its essential aspects and still less determined in its historical elements unless man as a person is considered in relation to the totality of his material needs and spiritual necessities. The common good ''embraces the sum total of those conditions of social living whereby men are enabled more fully and more readily to achieve their own perfection'' (*Mater et Magistra, loc. cit.*417).

Individuals as well as intermediate groups and social enterprises are obliged to contribute to the interests of the common good, and they do contribute when they pursue their own special interests in true harmony and without damage to the common good. However, the public authority is especially obliged to guarantee the common good; in fact, the realization of the common good is the reason for the existence of this authority, and the goal toward which it must work. In modern times the public authority pursues its proper end above all when it acknowledges, respects, coordinates, and effectively and harmoniously defends the rights of the individual and when it promotes these rights contributing positively to create an atmosphere where each one may more easily carry out his duties (*Pacem in terris, loc. cit.* 273–274).

During recent decades the pontiffs have been identifying a new doctrinal principle regarding the attainment of the common good. They have begun to affirm more clearly the existence of an intrinsic relationship between the historical content of the common good, on one hand, and the juridical structure and operation of the public authority, on the other. Since authority is required to effect the common good, the moral law demands that this authority should be efficient for the attainment of this goal. In this matter Pius XII observed that according to reason political communities must be built democratically: ''If then, we consider the extent and nature of the sacrifices demanded of all the citizens, especially in our day when the activity of the state is so vast and decisive, the democratic form of government appears to many as a postulate of nature imposed by reason itself'' (*Benignitas, op. cit.* 13). John XXIII, in his turn, stressed the fact that the juridical political organization of the human community, founded in a convenient division of powers corresponding to the three principal functions of the public authority, ''affords protection to the citizens both in the enjoyment of rights and in the fulfillment of duties'' (*Pacem in terris, loc. cit.* 277). As for that which concerns the universal common good, he declared that it presents problems so vast, complex, and urgent that they can be solved only by a public authority capable of operating efficiently on a world basis. From this he concluded that the moral order itself ''demands that such a form of public authority be established'' (*ibid.* 293). Both Paul VI and John Paul II continued this pattern of reflection regarding the legitimate role of government as the privileged agent of the common good, treating a range of new economic and cultural conditions which threaten to abridge the full attainment of the common good and calling upon public authorities, in cooperation with the institutions of civil society, to address these concerns and injustices.

Intermediate Associations. Human society is, by its nature, pluralistic. In the natural order there are three centers possessing universal and inviolable rights: individuals, the family, and the political community. The Church, not founded by men but established by God through Jesus Christ, is also a center of universal and inviolable rights, but as a supernatural society, founded for a supernatural end that must be reached by supernatural means. In addition, according to a doctrinal line consistently advanced by the magisterium of the Church, social life cannot develop in an orderly and fruitful manner if between individuals and their respective families, on the one hand, and the political community, on the other, there is not found a scale of organized groups or intermediate associations. The number of these groups or associations will be in proportion to the needs of a community. Whether in the economic, professional, recreational, hygienic, political, cultural, religious or other fields, they find their source in the natural law, which impels individuals and their respective families to associate themselves in order to attain ends that they could not otherwise attain. On the other hand, in relation to these ends, the action of public authority is not indispensable or even advantageous; on the contrary, its action for such ends would only be burdensome and therefore unproductive. Consequently, the autonomy of intermediate associations, which corresponds to the true ends for which they were organized, must be recognized. This implies that in the field of their specific activity they move by their own initiative and responsibility and employ suitable methods to render their actions effective. (*See* ASSOCIATION.)

Solidarity and Collaboration. Every human being is a person and therefore by nature social. This is proved by the fact that human beings live normal lives when they mutually assist each other; it is also true that each one succeeds in perfecting himself when with the same activity he contributes to the perfection of others. It follows that force cannot be accepted as the supreme criterion in the government of human relations, as in the liberal doctrine of free competition, the Marxist doctrine of class warfare, or the doctrine of group pressure or economic or political superiority. Social relations must be governed instead according to the principles of solidarity and mutual collaboration in truth, justice, love and freedom. Pius XI wrote:

> Just as the unity of human society cannot be founded on an opposition of classes, so also the right ordering of economic life cannot be left to a free competition of forces. . . . But free competition, while justified and certainly useful provided it is kept within certain limits, clearly cannot direct economic life—a truth which the outcome of the application in practice of the tenets of this evil individualistic spirit has more than sufficiently demonstrated. Therefore, it is most necessary that economic life be again subjected to and governed by a true and effective directing principle. This function is one that the economic dictatorship which has recently displaced free competition can still less perform, since it is a headstrong power and a violent energy that, to benefit people, needs to be strongly curbed and wisely ruled. But it cannot curb and rule itself. Loftier and nobler principles—social justice and social charity—must, therefore, be sought whereby this dictatorship may be governed firmly and fully. [*Op. cit.* 206]

What Pius XI indicated as the criterion according to which human relationships in the economic order should be governed, John XXIII reaffirmed in application to all the relationships of human society, whatever their content, extent, or nature: ''The society of men must not only be organized but must also provide them with abundant resources. This certainly requires that they recognize and fulfill their mutual rights and duties; it also requires that they collaborate together in the many enterprises that modern civilization either allows or encourages or demands'' (*Pacem in terris, loc. cit.* 265).

Principle of Subsidiarity. Individuals, families, intermediate groups, and public authority are the units present and working in society. The problem arises: what is the principle or the criterion used to decide the sphere of action proper to each group? The magisterium of the Church usually calls this the principle of SUBSIDIARITY, according to which intermediate associations and public authority do not claim to do those things that individuals and families are able to accomplish unaided and public authority does not claim to do those things that intermediate associations can and in fact do accomplish.

This principle was first proposed in explicit form by Pius XI in *Quadragesimo anno,* as a principle according to which the spheres of action of individuals, organized groups or intermediate associations, and public authority in the socioeconomic field, should be decided (*loc. cit.* 203). While John XXIII in *Mater et Magistra* affirmed its validity in the same field, in the encyclical *Pacem in terris* he maintained that this principle must be considered valid even in delineating the spheres of action proper to the political authority of the individual political communities and those of the political authority of the world community:

> Just as within each political community the relations between individuals, families, intermediate associations and public authority are governed by the principle of subsidiarity, so, too, the relations between the public authority of each political community and the public authority of the world community must be regulated by the same principle. This means that the public authority of the world community must tackle and solve problems of an economic, social, political or cultural character which are posed by the universal common good. For because of the vastness, complexity, and urgency of those problems, the public authority of the individual states are not in a position to tackle them with any hope of a positive solution. [*Loc. cit.* 294]

The principle of subsidiarity is proposed as a principle of action or as a criterion for the effective resolution of concrete problems; it is rooted in the nature of the relations between human beings and the society of which they are members. Human beings create or maintain a society not for the purpose of being absorbed by it, but in order to reach goals that otherwise they would not be able to reach, goals that they foster and pursue as means of affirming their own personality. This is what Pius XI held in the first formulation of the principle: ''For every social activity ought of its own very nature to furnish help to the members of the body social, and never destroy and absorb them'' (*op. cit.* 203). The same idea is advanced by John XXIII in *Pacem in terris* in applying the principle to the relations between individual political communities and the world community: ''The public authority of the world community is not intended to limit the sphere of action of the public authority of the individual political community, much less to take its place. On the contrary, its purpose is to create, on a world basis, an environment in which the public authorities of each political community, its citizens and intermediate associations, can carry out their tasks, fulfill their duties and exercise their rights with greater security'' (*loc. cit.* 294–295). Pope John Paul II, particularly in the 1991 encyclical *Centesimus annus*, has called attention to the prudent limits to centralized activities of the state, which should act in such a way as to empower private, local and voluntary associations, never to impinge on their legitimate operations or threaten their rightful autonomy and initiative (see nos. 39–51).

Unity, Growth, and Purpose of Papal Social Teaching. Like any tradition, modern papal social teaching has grown and developed over time in ways that could not have been predicted at the time of its origin. Succeeding popes have responded to new political and economic conditions and new social and cultural challenges. Although some might prefer to emphasize either the elements of change or those of continuity, an honest observer of papal social encyclicals over the past century detects both elements at work. It would be as false to claim that each pope is idiosyncratic in his social concerns as it would be to claim that a stable complex of ideas passed unchanged from papal mind to papal mind over the decades. Rather, it is perhaps best to interpret this tradition as a response to the call all Christians receive, in the words of the Second Vatican Council, to take seriously "the duty of scrutinizing the signs of the times and of interpreting them in the light of the gospel" (*Gaudium et spes*, 4).

The distinctive aspect of papal social thought is that it is promulgated as an authentic teaching of the Catholic Church. These reflections on the ethical meaning and implications of human life in society are proposed as genuine sources of moral guidance for all members of the church. Because they draw from deep sources of the Christian tradition such as scripture and Doctors of the Church, papal social encyclicals enjoy the presumption of authentic truth that adheres to similar magisterial statements. Yet because they so often deal with changing temporal phenomena, in those instances where prudential judgments are offered on political and economic realities, there is room for disagreement even on the part of faithful Catholics of good will. To accord to papal social teaching a different type or level of authority than any given statement on "the social question" intends would be to misconstrue its nature as some sort of blueprint for society, to be followed slavishly and without appropriate adaptation in every corner of the world.

In his 1971 apostolic letter *Octogesima adveniens*, Pope Paul VI offers these suggestions for the local application of papal social teachings: "In the face of such widely varying situations it is difficult for us to utter a unified message and to put forward a solution which has universal validity. Such is not our ambition, nor is it our mission. It is up to the Christian communities to analyze with objectivity the situation which is proper to their own country, to shed on it the light of the Gospel's unalterable words and to draw principles of reflection, norms of judgment and directives for action from the social teachings of the Church" (no. 4). Similarly, Pope John Paul II in no. 41 of his 1987 social encyclical *Sollicitudo rei socialis* explained how the notion of the "hierarchy of truths" applies to papal social teaching. He begins by insisting that "the church does not have technical solutions to offer" regarding complex economic problems; its expertise is of the moral variety. The aspiration of popes when they address complex social issues is to see that "the church fulfills her mission to evangelize" by "proclaiming the truth about Christ, about herself and about man, applying this truth to a concrete situation." In taking seriously the messages of papal social teaching, faithful Catholics (and indeed all people of good will) answer their call and fulfill their moral duty to discern the meaning of social justice and to act to advance the common good in our complex contemporary world.

Bibliography: J. N. MOODY and J. G. LAWLER, eds., *The Challenge of Mater et Magistra* (New York 1963). J. Y. CALVEZ and J. PERRIN, *Église et societé économique,* 2 v. (Paris 1959–63), v.1 *The Church and Social Justice . . . Leo XIII to Pius XII,* tr. J. R. KIRWAN (Chicago 1961). J. F. CRONIN, *Social Principles and Economic Life* (Milwaukee 1959). L. J. DE MESQUITA, *As enciclicas socials de Joao XXIII* (Rio de Janeiro 1963). E. M. GUERRY, *The Social Doctrine of the Catholic Church,* tr. M. HEDERMAN (New York 1961). T. J. HARTE, *Papal Social Principles: A Guide and Digest* (Milwaukee 1956). Instituto social Leon XIII, ed., *Commentarios a la "Mater et Magistra"* (Madrid 1962); *Commentarios a la "Pacem in terris"* (Madrid 1963). R. KOTHEN, *L'Enseignement social de l'Église* (Louvain 1949). D. A. O'CONNOR, *Catholic Social Doctrine* (Westminster, Md. 1956). P. PAVAN, *L'ordine sociale* (Turin 1963); *Dalla Rerum novarum alla Mater et Magistra* (Rome 1963). J. VILLAIN, *L'Enseignement social de l'Église,* 3 v. (Paris 1953–54). C. VAN GESTEL, *La Doctrine social de l'Église* (Paris 1952). E. WELTY, *A Handbook of Christian Social Ethics,* tr. G. KIRSTEIN, rev. J. FITZSIMONS (New York 1960–). P. BIGO, *La Doctrine sociale de l'Église* (Paris 1965).

[P. PAVAN/T. MASSARO]

SOCIALIZATION, RELIGIOUS

Religious socialization may be broadly described as a process that encompasses the varying dynamics of religious group membership and the patterns of commitment which such membership can engender (Roberts 1984:133–148). It is a process potentially life-long in scope, and until quite recently it was a process thought virtually inevitable in churches and traditional religious groups, as the latter could assume both ongoing commitments in an unchanged society and the gradual incorporation of individuals into the religious group, whether from birth onward (as was the case of Roman Catholics and many mainline Protestants) or from the point of a conversion experience with its strong emotional power (the case of many sects and evangelical traditions). However, as churches and other social groups have been touched by increased levels of social and institutional change (Roof and McKinney 1987), and as CULTS and newer religious groups have become prominent in American society (Chalfont, Beckley and Palmer 1987:191–220), commitment patterns have become tenuous, and religious socialization has become a subject of specific and—on the part of churches—self-conscious concern (see the discussions by Westerhoff 1974; Groome 1980; Marthaler 1980; Phillibert and O'Connor 1982; Princeton Research Center 1986).

A concern with religious socialization has also been evident in the literature of social science. Since the mid-

1970s, social scientists (e.g., McGuire 1981; Roberts 1984; Chalfont, Beckley and Palmer 1987) have refocused the theoretical grounding of religious socialization and directed research efforts to the study of conversion as the illustrative case of this theoretical regrounding. This essay addresses religious socialization from within the context of these concerns. It begins with a discussion of the "problems" of religious socialization; it then identifies key efforts on the part of researchers who have attempted to resolve these problems; and finally, it closes with an overview of selected issues which are implied by, but yet underdeveloped within, the current religious socialization literature.

"Problems" of religious socialization. In the literature of social science, there are at least two problems that have beset the study of religious socialization during the period since the mid and late 1960s. The first problem is what one might term the "absence of boundary questions," or the absence of those questions which set limits on the object of one's study. They include the following: First, what is religious socialization? And second, what is it not? Is it a study of the effects of a process? Or is it the study of the process itself?

These questions are, at first glance, apparently obvious, but as one reviews the early literature on religious socialization, one finds that the latter is a general topic about which much is said, but about which little is actually made clear. Merton Strommen's (1971) extended anthology, *Research on Religious Development,* illustrates this point. It has 22 literature review entries grouped under the general headings of "religion and research," "personal and religious factors in religious development," "religion, personality and psychological health," "dimensions of religious development," etc., that survey the effects of several presumed "agents" of religious socialization (whether church-based or secular) in their efforts to communicate and/or transmit aspects of religion to individuals who constitute the captive audience for these attempts. There are, however, almost no entries (save that by Greeley and Gockley) that address the religious socialization process per se, or any that attempt to explain how individuals and agents together enter into and engage in the process of people "becoming religious." Rather, one finds the assumed postulates of this process and discussions about its varying and far-reaching correlates and effects (see Fairchild and Elkind).

This point is important, for in such an approach one makes two methodological mistakes. First, one equates a study of the process with a study of (presumably) its effects. Second, one lets stand what Long and Hadden (1983:2) describe as the "core theorem of socialization," namely, the "equation of socialization with internalization."

Unless these errors are clearly identified, they generate a tautological framework for both the conceptualization and analysis of the religious socialization process. Further, they can preclude a clear distinction between the study of religious socialization and the study of religiosity, or the various ways in which individuals express their involvement and attachment to religious phenomena, e.g., the knowledge of specific religious teachings, the types and levels of participation individuals may have in religious organizations, their adherence to faith tenets, etc. (See Chalfont, Beckley and Palmer 1987:58–76 for an overview of recent research literature).

The first problem of religious socialization, therefore, is to establish clear boundaries concerning the object of one's study, for without such boundaries, both the process and its effects become confused, and "theory" follows the circular logic of tautology. A second problem is the tendency of researchers to conceptualize by means of analogy, or to adopt selected general assumptions about socialization and then transfer them uncritically to the sphere of religion. This problem is related to the first, for it too identifies socialization with internalization. However, this second problem differs in that it roots the equation in assumptions that stem from functionalist (and/or social system) theory. Put differently, this second problem focuses socialization in terms of its integrating function for social systems, and as assumptions about socialization are applied to the sphere of religion, the internalization equation and its tautological outcomes are again affirmed.

By way of illustration, in the general socialization literature it is typically assumed that socialization entails the internalization of what is external to subjective consciousness (Berger and Luckmann 1966:129–163), since socialization is a life-long process "by which individuals acquire the attitudes and behaviors which are appropriate for [membership] in [their] society" (Taylor, et al. 1987:66; Clausen 1968:5–9). Further, it is assumed that this process is best studied through discipline-specific analyses (i.e., anthropological, sociological and psychological studies), since the phenomena to be internalized include cultural norms and symbols, institutionally based social roles, and those factors that shape the development of individual personality structures (Clausen 1968:18–72).

However, as DiRenzo (1977) points out, neither discipline-specific perspectives nor standard functional assumptions are helpful for understanding the actualities of socialization. Virtually all of the social sciences equate socialization with internalization, and functional approaches do no more than characterize its systemic effect, i.e., system integration. More pointedly, functional perspectives do not define socialization, or rather, when they do, they do so in terms of internalization. Thus, whether the categories of discussion are ''socialization'' per se (the sociological term of reference) or ''culturation'' and ''enculturation'' (the anthropological terms of reference), or lastly ''personality development'' and/or ''maturation'' (the psychological terms of reference), they are all terms that assume the transferral of externalities into human consciousness, or the equation of socialization with internalization. Thus, as this mechanism of system integration is detailed, it is done via the assumption ''of a relatively simple material object [internalization] with varied formal objects [discipline specific terms of reference]'' (DiRenzo 1977:265).

DiRenzo dubs this strategy a ''simplistic labeling of [one's] appropriate disciplinary heritage'' (1977:264) and identifies it as the ''crux'' of many conceptual issues attached to contemporary socialization theory. Alternatively, the functional/discipline-specific approach is an orientation that clouds the understanding of religious socialization, as again, the socialization-internalization equation is affirmed, and a tautological framework generated.

One additional assumption from the general literature also bears mention. This assumption is the distinction between primary and secondary socialization or the idea that socialization occurs in two stages: primary socialization, which begins at birth and continues through early childhood, and secondary socialization, which is ''role specific'' and picks up at the close of primary socialization and continues throughout life (Berger and Luckmann 1966:163–173)

While this assumption is valid insofar as socialization does occur throughout the life cycle (Brim 1966; Dion 1985), it is not particularly helpful, at least as it presently stands, for it implies that secondary socialization is either only role-specific learning, or that learning is borne only of primary socialization experiences. In short, this two-stage approach lends itself to a deterministic or ''oversocialized'' (Wrong 1961) approach to human, social learning. Further, it is contradicted by the research literature on ''adult socialization'' and the findings of symbolic interactionists (Stryker and Statham 1985), which suggest that every experience is a socialization experience and that new learning, or learning unrelated to primary socialization, can and apparently does take place (Stryker and Statham 1985).

The second problem of religious socialization, therefore, is the tendency to theorize by analogy or the tendency to adopt general assumptions about socialization as if they could apply (without qualification) to the sphere of religion. Its main defect is its enhancement of the socialization-internalization equation and the tautological framework that this equation engenders. This problem, in conjunction with religious socialization's lack of clear boundaries, leads inevitably to the following questions: What actually is entailed in the study of religious socialization, and how might the latter be studied?

The answers are obvious. The study of religious socialization entails the study of a process (rather than the presumption of its outcomes), and the study of this process through categories that permit a descriptive account of how individuals enter into and engage in the process of becoming religious. Further, if this is the task that constitutes the study of religious socialization, then research efforts need to be directed to a context that permits the fulfillment of these criteria.

The study of religious conversion affords the occasion to meet these criteria, and its articulation through the framework of symbolic interactionism meets to the request of describing the process of religious socialization apart from its religion specific ''contents'' or outcomes, i.e., expressions of religiosity. In sociological terms this is the study of religious affiliation and disaffiliation or the study of the dynamics encompassed in religious group membership and the patterns of commitment that they can engender.

Conversion and religious socialization. In the study of religious socialization, it is helpful to begin with a discussion of two seemingly disparate topics: cult recruitment and symbolic interaction theory. The literature on cult recruitment stems largely from research by John Lofland (1977) who, with Rodney Stark and others (Lofland and Stark 1977; Lofland and Skonovd 1981), has presented a seven-step description of ''conversion,'' or recruitment to cult membership. The model is premised upon the conditions of both psychological ''tension'' and ''religious seekership'' (i.e., an inclination to solve such problems from a religious rather than non-religious perspective), and while its particulars need not be spelled out here (see Roberts 1984:148–156), two emphases within it merit mention. First, in spite of the tension-based predisposition that characterizes it, the model indicates clearly that recruitment to new religious groups is based on extensive cult member and potential new member interaction and the gradual movement of an individual from diffuse to close-knit (new) group associations. Second, the model indicates that such movement involves a general movement away from competing groups and toward the new group as a primary reference group or context for identity.

These emphases are important, for although the Lofland model has been criticized in terms of its initial stages and the assumption of a tension-based experience that generates the process (Snow and Phillips 1980; cf. Roberts 1984:153–156), it has occasioned a re-thinking of the classical imagery attached to religious conversion. Several sources are important in this vein. First is the Hoge and Roozen (1979:48–49) discussion of ''factors affecting church commitment,'' which highlights the difficulty of testing deprivation-based theories in general and conversion deprivation-based theories in particular.

Second, as Snow and Machalek (1984) point out, the methodological difficulties in conversion research are only one aspect of the problem. Of equal importance is the conceptualization of conversion. It has been described generally within the literature, as either ''radical personal change . . . the core of all conceptions of conversion, whether theological or social scientific'' or a ''change in one's universe of discourse.'' The latter is the framework that informs Snow and Machalek's own research (1983), and for them, it suggests something that ''concerns not only a change in values, beliefs, and identities, but more fundamentally and significantly . . . the displacement of one universe of discourse by another or the ascendance of a formerly peripheral universe of discourse to the status of a primary authority'' (Snow and Machalek 1984:170–171).

Third is James Richardson's (1985) survey of recent conversion research literature, which he characterizes as caught in the midst of a paradigm conflict. Although his own research on conversion is extensive (Richardson 1978; 1980; 1985), it is his 1985 discussion that proves to be most compelling. It attempts to dispel the so-called passive qualities view assumed in religious conversion, so that a more activist and interactive approach to both conversion and the activity of potential converts may be developed.

Richardson begins his discussion with a summary of the major characteristics that attach to the ''old paradigm'' for conversion research, i.e., the experience of Paul on the road to Damascus. These characteristics are generally well known. First, the experience of conversion is typically assumed to be sudden, dramatic, and emotional, and often, irrational in quality. Second, it is an event that is perceived as external to the recipient. Third, it is both individualized and psychologized in that it is an event thought to change one's life completely. Fourth, this change is (in Richardson's words) ''static'' and ''deterministic,'' as the event involves a total break with one's past—or more particularly, the negation of one's old self into a new self. Fifth, because this event was (and is) perceived from within the context of the one true church (i.e., Christianity), it is an event that is a ''once-in-a-lifetime experience'', or an experience never to be repeated and, of ever-greater significance, never needing to be repeated. Finally, because Paul's experience entailed an apparent change in his own belief structure, conversion was defined in cognitive terms such that ''behaviors follow beliefs'' and not beliefs behaviors.

It is against this type of thinking that Richardson marshals his argument for the adoption of a more activist and interactive perception of conversion, since, on the one hand, the interactive model presented initially by Lofland has had significant and expanding confirmation without reference to a tension and/or problem-solving basis (cf. literature cited by Richardson: Pilarzyk 1969; Gerlach and Hine 1979; Bromley and Shupe 1979) and, on the other hand, theoretical frameworks such as that of symbolic interaction and humanistic sociology (e.g., the sociology of knowledge) suggest an alternative context for interpreting conversion.

In particular, Richardson draws attention to the concept of alternation, as developed by Berger and Luckmann (1966) and Travisano (1970). Alternation implies a less definitive and externally directed change of identity and a more initiative and interactive role of converts with potentially new reference groups. This view is based upon Meadian social psychology (Blumer 1969; Hewitt 1983), and especially Mead's notion of role-taking and self-other interaction as the bases of identity development.

According to Mead, individuals develop through interaction with others and in the light of mutually constructed symbols or—to borrow from Berger and Luckmann (1966:34–46)—mutually agreed upon significations of human behavior. These significations are both behavioral and linguistic, and according to Mead, they are the media through which interaction takes place. Further, they are the bases of his concept of role taking, for as both gestures and linguistic significations merge, identifiable role structures become obvious, and individuals can opt to ''take on the role'' of others or engage in imaginative imitation of these persons. Children engaged in ''let's pretend'' play are Mead's illustration of this point, for as children imagine themselves as others, whether doctor, ''mommy'' or ''daddy,'' they not only see these others as distinct from themselves, but they also anticipate the behavior of these others and enact it. Thus as children play, they takes on the roles of others and to a greater or lesser extent, appropriate them for their own purposes.

Participation in structured games is a second illustration that Mead uses to unfold his notion of role taking, for in contrast to play (or imitative behavior), games come replete with rules, differentially structured roles, and more often than not, competition. Thus, as the child enters into a game, she or he must anticipate not only multiple role relations, but also their sequenced and potentially patterned relationships. To make the point concretely, Mead cites team play in baseball: it is interactive, it involves the capacity to "take on the role" of many others simultaneously, and it is a game that must be played in terms of rules, or behavioral norms that transcend the identities of individual players.

Mead's concept of role taking is important, for while it acknowledges the eventual possibility of routinized or automatic role enactment, it nonetheless recognizes that role learning is a dynamic and interactionally based negotiation, or a phenomenon that involves common participation by all engaged parties. His notion of the self as a social process involving both an "I" and a "Me" further expands this point.

As already indicated, the self develops through interaction with others through the process of role taking. However, this self is not an undifferentiated stream of consciousness. Rather it is a process of engagement with others, wherein the individual is self-reflective, or able to distinguish present consciousness from past experience. Put differently, as the process called "self" develops, it does so as an "I" (the active and responsive dimension of self) in dialogue with several "Me's" (past experience or the many composites of previous "I's" together with society's responses to them). Put in yet another way, the self is an ongoing process that interprets both others and the responses of others to itself. It is a process that organizes these responses internally and then knows them as recognizable realities, that is, as "Me's".

It is precisely these Meadian emphases on role taking and the social basis of identity that undergird Richardson's discussion of conversion. Richardson (1985:171) notes that a symbolic interactionist perspective permits the depiction of conversion as a series of alternations within and among religious groups, or as a career-like phenomenon involving the serial and periodic construction of one's religious-social self. More graphically, the symbolic interaction framework permits the depiction of conversion as a "conversion career" (Richardson 1980; 1984), or a series of identity adaptations grounded in the "I-Me" dialectic of role-taking vis-à-vis "old and new" religious groups. Thus for Richardson, symbolic interactionism permits a better image of conversion because it suggests that conversion involves alternation rather than the once in a life-time event of the Pauline paradigm; and it permits a more accurate description of conversion because it illumines the interaction of individuals with identity defining roles and significations in a manner that exhibits the partial control that potential converts appear to have (and retain) over their old and new religious identities. Thus it challenges the external assumptions of the traditional paradigm, with its character of sudden dramatic event, of individualized and "deterministic" qualities, and of distinctive cognitive bias. These emphases are all implicit in the symbolic interaction framework that underlies the literature cited by Richardson, and hence his advocacy of the activist rather than passive paradigm for conversion research.

Wider implications. There are three sets of wider implications that follow from this understanding of religious socialization as a process that involves the dynamics of religious group membership and the patterns of commitment that such membership can engender: those concerning the "activist" paradigm itself; those concerning important differences between cults and mainline churches; and finally, those concerning the sociology of religious commitment, about which the literature is relatively silent.

First, as regards the development of an activist or interactive paradigm for the study of conversion (and by extension religious socialization), Richardson is correct in noting that conversion research is presently in a state of paradigm conflict because active and passive images are both supported in varying degrees by past and present literature (see Rambo 1982 which contains a detailed conversion bibliography through 1981). However, the weight of the evidence seems to be in favor of Richardson's activist paradigm. The Lofland research points to this as does the work of Snow and Machalek, who suggest that conversion studies should focus on the analysis of "rhetorical indicators" such as "biographic reconstruction, adoption of a master attribution scheme, suspension of analogical reasoning and the embracement of the convert role" (Snow and Machalek 1984:173ff.). Further, as Chalfont, Beckley and Palmer (1987:44) indicate, the current cult recruitment/conversion literature (including Richardson's own) seems to suggest that conversion (however it is imaged) is but one *type* of religious socialization. In their judgment, religious socialization may involve not only "conversion," but "a series of affiliations and disaffiliations," or "alternations" in Richardson's terms. Indeed, Chalfont, Beckly and Palmer take Richardson's position as a given. This is important, for it underscores the potentially life-long and variegated character of religious socialization.

If such alternations are endemic to the life-long course of religious socialization, then it would appear that the study of religious socialization should be undertaken concomitantly with the study of religious and social change, since the unidirectional assumptions of traditional (and often tautological) frameworks have less bearing than one might imagine. If religious socialization is based instead on interactive and processually based interpretive processes, then dynamic rather than static conceptual frameworks need specification, and research needs to be directed to the interplay between organizational, confessional, and locally based reference groups, or what sociologically are church politics, historically normative frameworks (including "dogmas" and worship), and ethnic or otherwise configured parish and/or congregational memberships.

Second, although cults and churches differ significantly, e.g., the former generally access individuals who are older and frequently in marginal contexts, whereas churches frequently begin socialization in early childhood and within established class contexts, they are, nonetheless, both groups that seek to engage persons in interpretive interaction vis-à-vis their respective spheres. Thus, whether one is speaking about evangelization (a mainline analog to cult recruitment) or recruitment by membership birth, one is still addressing religious socialization vis-à-vis the "institutional," "meaning," and "reference group" factors (Roberts 1984:325–372) that typify church based socialization efforts and/or contexts, or the interplay of both religious and social demographics that underlie the significations attached to these spheres.

It is this latter emphasis that is underdeveloped within the literature, but the seeds of its future development are present within the notion of the activist paradigm, for change and the presence of overlapping social worlds are inherent to the paradigm. In particular, in a mobile, information based and pluralistic society, it is necessary to consider the social and demographic bases of mainline churches and denominations, and by way of specifics, their overlap with traditional and modified family and educational structures, such ascribed characteristics as age, race, and gender, achieved characteristics such as occupational and political networks (with their associated ethics and worldviews), and a host of personal psychological variables, including perceived values of success, failure, self-image, power, responsibilities to others and the like. In short, it is necessary to consider the full range of those social-organizational variables that undergird the mainline churches and their structures, for it is these latter variables that provide the warp and woof of activist and interactive spheres.

This last consideration brings us to the subject of commitment, the third of the wider implications for religious socialization, but one largely unaddressed by the cult recruitment/conversion literature, save the assumption that commitment entails conformity to group norms or acquiescence to the eventuality of routinized role behavior and their associated cognitive enclaves (Berger 1967).

In the general literature on religious socialization, the subject of commitment has largely been underdeveloped, save for isolated studies that address commitment in particular institutional frameworks, such as religiously affiliated schools (Greeley and Rossi 1966; Greeley and Gockel 1971) or institutions involving socialization to religious professions (Schoenherr and Greeley 1974; Potvin 1976). One explanation for this is that as Kanter (1968; 1972) has noted, commitment is multidimensional. That is to say, it involves (at least) three different dimensions, i.e., "instrumental" (or organizational) commitment, "affective" commitment (or commitment to group members), and "moral" commitment (ideational or ideological commitment). Extended theoretical work is needed, however, if the study of commitment is be advanced, for although Kanter's work details these three types of commitment and the mechanisms that seem to facilitate them, it is based on the study of utopian (or closed) communities and not denominational or open, voluntary associations. Rather, for an understanding of commitment in these spheres, attention must be directed (again) to the situationally specific bases of religion (viz., the variables of social organization) and their interplay with local church reference groups, large-scale church bureaucratic structures, and denominationally specific theological emphases (i.e., confessional ideations).

Finally, if the study of commitment is to be undertaken independently (but not completely apart from) the study of religiosity, it will be necessary to connect the activist paradigm to the concerns of socialization within non-religious spheres, since the carrying over of religious values—and particularly service to those in need—into spheres not formally defined as religious is still the goal of churches and traditional religious associations.

Bibliography: P. BERGER, *The Sacred Canopy* (New York 1967). P. BERGER and T. LUCKMANN, *The Social Construction of Reality* (New York 1966). H. BLUMER, *Symbolic Interaction: Perspective and Method* (New Jersey 1969). O. BRIM and S. WHEELER *Socialization After Childhood: Two Essays* (New York 1966). D. BROMLEY and A. SHUPE, JR., "Just a Few Years in a Lifetime: A Role Theory Approach to Participation in a Religious Movement," L. KRISBERG, ed. *Research in Social Movements: Conflict and Change* (Conn. 1979) 159–186. H. P. CHALFONT, et al., *Religion in Contemporary Society* (California 1987). J. CLAUSEN, ed. *Socialization and Society* (New York 1968). K. DION, "Socialization in Adulthood," v. 2 *The Handbook of Social Psychology*, G. LINDZEY and E. ARONSON, eds. (New York 1985) 123–148. G. DIRENZO, "Socialization, Personality and Social Systems," *Annual Review of Sociology* 3 (1977) 261–295. J. DITTES, "Beyond William James," C. GLOCK and P. HAMMOND, eds. *Beyond the Classics* (New York 1978) 291–354. A. GREELEY and G. GOCKEL, "The Religious Effects of Parochial Education," *Research on Religious Development*, M. STROMMEN ed. (New York 1971) 265–301. A. GREELEY and P. ROSSI, *The Education of Catholic Americans* (Chicago 1961). T. H. GROOME, *Christian Religious Education* (New York 1980). D. R. HOGE and D. ROOZEN, eds. *Understanding Church Growth and Decline* (New York 1979). J. HEWITT, *Self and Society: A Symbolic Interactionist Social Psychology* (3d ed. Boston 1983). R. M. KAN-

TER, ''Commitment and Social Organization: A Study of Commitment Mechanisms in Utopian Communities,'' *American Sociological Review* 33 (1968) 499–517; *Commitment and Community* (Cambridge, Mass. 1972). J. LOFLAND, *Doomsday Cult* (enlarged edition New York 1977). J. LOFLAND and NORMAN SKONOVD, ''Conversion Motifs,'' JScStRel 20 (1981) 373–385. J. LOFLAND and R. STARK, ''Becoming a World-saver: A Theory of Conversion to a Deviant Perspective,'' *American Sociological Review* 30 (1965) 863–874. T. LONG and J. HADDEN, ''Religious Conversion and the Concept of Socialization: Integrating the Brainwashing and Drift Models,'' JScStRel 22 (1983) 1–14. B. L. MARTHALER, ''Handing on the Symbols of Faith,'' *Chicago Studies* 19 (1980) 21–33. M. MCGUIRE, *Religion: The Social Context.* (Belmont, Calif. 1981). P. PHILLIBERT and J. P. O'CONNOR, eds., ''Adolescent Religious Socialization: A Study of Goal Priorities According to Parents and Religious Educators,'' RevRelRes 23 (1982) 225–316. T. PILARZYK, ''Conversion and Alternation Processes in Youth Culture,'' *Pacific Sociological Review* 21 (1978) 379–406. R. POTVIN, ''Role Uncertainty and Commitment Among Seminary Faculty,'' *Sociological Analysis* 37 (1976) 45–52. Princeton Research Center, *Faith Development and Your Ministry* (Princeton 1986). D. RAFKY, ''Phenomenology and Socialization: Some Comments on the Assumptions Underlying Socialization Theory,'' *Recent Sociology No. 5: Childhood and Socialization*, H. P. DREITZEL, ed. (New York 1973) 44–64. L. RAMBO., ''Current Research on Religious Conversion,'' *Religious Studies Review* 8 (1982) 147–159. K. A. ROBERTS, *Religion in Sociological Perspective* (Illinois 1984). W. C. ROOF, ''Traditional Religion in Contemporary Society: A Theory of Local-Cosmopolitan Plausibility,'' *American Sociological Review* 41 (1976) 195–208. W. C. ROOF and W. MCKINNEY, *American Mainline Religion: Its Changing Shape and Future* (New Brunswick 1987). J. T. RICHARDSON, *Conversion Careers* (Beverly Hills 1978); ''Conversion Careers,'' *Society* 17 (1984) 47–50; ''Studies of Conversion: Secularization or Reenchantment?'' *The Sacred in Secular Age*, P. HAMMOND, ed. (Berkeley 1984) 104–121; ''The Active and Passive Convert: Paradigm Conflict in Conversion/Recruitment Research,'' *Journal for the Scientific Study of Religion* 24 (1985) 163–179. R. A. SCHOENHERR and A. GREELEY, ''Role Commitment Processes and the American Catholic Priesthood,'' *American Sociological Review* 39 (1974) 407–426. D. A. SNOW and C. PHILLIPS, ''The Lofland-Stark Conversion Model: A Critical Assessment,'' *Social Problems* (1980) 430–447. D. SNOW and R. MACHALEK, ''The Convert as a Social Type,'' *Sociological Theory*, R. COLLINS, ed. (California 1983) 259–289; ''The Sociology of Conversion,'' *Annual Review of Sociology* 10 (1984) 167–190. S. STRYKER and A. STATHAM, ''Symbolic Interaction and Role Theory,'' v. 1 *The Handbook of Social Psychology*, G. LINDZEY and E. ARONSON, eds. (3d ed. New York 1985) 311–378. M. C. TAYLOR, et al., *Introduction to Sociology* (New York 1987). J. H. WESTERHOFF, *Will Our Children Have Faith?* (New York 1976). J. H. WESTERHOFF and G. N. KENNEDY, *Generation to Generation* (Philadelphia 1974). D. WRONG, ''The Oversocialized Conception of Man in Modern Sociology,'' *American Sociological Review* 26 (1961) 183–193.

[M.-P. WALSH]

SOCIETAS LITURGICA

Societas Liturgica came into existence by the initiative of Wiebe Vos, a pastor of the Netherlands Reformed Church. In 1962 he had founded *Studia liturgica*, ''an international ecumenical quarterly for liturgical research and renewal.'' In 1965 he convened a conference of 25 liturgists from Europe and North America at the Protestant community of Grandchamp, in Neuchâtel, Switzerland. With J. J. von Allmen in the chair, the conference discussed Christian initiation and resolved to found a Societas Liturgica, ''an association for the promotion of ecumenical dialogue on worship, based on solid research, with the perspective of renewal and unity.'' As an ecumenical society, membership is open to all Christians who are engaged in teaching and doing research in liturgical and related studies, as well as those who make significant contributions to the liturgical life of their churches.

The foundation meeting of Societas Liturgica took place at Driebergen, Holland, from the 26th to the 29th of June, 1967. That meeting studied Vatican II's Constitution on the Liturgy and recent work on worship by the World Council of Churches' Faith and Order. Thereafter the Societas has held congresses at two-yearly intervals. The papers delivered at these congresses have been published in English in its journal *Studia Liturgica.*

Bibliography: E.S. BROWN, ''New Faces on the Scene: Societas Liturgica,'' *Christian Century* 84 (Aug. 23, 1967) 1080–1082. D.S. HENDERSON, ''First International Conference of Societas Liturgica,'' *Studia Liturgica* 6:4 (1969) 189–190. W.L. MCCLELLAND, ''Societas liturgica: from Grandchamp to Montserrat, 1965–1973,'' *Studia Liturgica* 10:3–4 (1974) 77–87. T. BERGER, ''The International Congresses of Societas Liturgica: A Bibliographical Survey,'' *Studia Liturgica* 19 (1989) 111–114. G. LAPOINTE, ''The Societas Liturgica: Towards International Ecumenical Research in Liturgy,'' *Ecumenism* 122 (1996) 28. B. BÜRKI, ''Societas Liturgica: Tracing Its Journey So Far,'' *Studia Liturgica* 27 (1997) 129–151.

[G. WAINWRIGHT]

SOCIETY

A union of individuals, particularly of human beings, among whom a specific type of order or organization exists, although not all are agreed on its formal constitutive. This article first analyzes the nature of society from the viewpoint of Catholic social philosophy and then outlines theories of society that are proposed in the science of sociology.

Philosophical Analysis

Society may be defined as the permanent union of men who are united by modes of behavior that are demanded by some common end, value, or interest. Analyzed semantically, the term denotes a union of one kind or another. Its notion differs from that of community in that community is a form of society in which men are more intimately bound by specific ends and natural forces. Society itself is not possible, however, unless based upon some common moral and legal understanding with social laws and controls to sustain it; hence some characteristics of the community are found also in society.

Nature. Guided by experience, and thus by the findings of the social sciences, the social philosopher regards it as empirically established that man can attain the full development of his nature only in association with others. Human nature therefore constitutes the ontological ground for society; it manifests this through its biological, psychological, and teleological tendencies. Biologically, man's nature is ordered to marriage and the family. Psychologically, the impulse to be a member of a social group and to be appreciated as such is characteristically human. Teleologically, man seeks both happiness and conformity with the NATURAL LAW; both of these, in turn, urge him to establish an order of social life guaranteeing freedom and common utility as conditions for the achievement of a fully human existence. In consequence, viewed ontologically, human nature needs social supplementation for its integration; again, since different potentialities are found in individual humans, human nature is capable of bringing about such supplementation. Hence man is by nature a social animal (ζῷον πολιτικόν for ARISTOTLE; *ens sociale* for St. THOMAS AQUINAS).

Since this is the design of the Creator, it is in human nature itself that one can recognize the will of the Creator with regard to the fundamental ordering of society. The fact that one can philosophically ascertain the will of the Creator in ''the nature of things'' needs emphasizing in contemporary Catholic social philosophy; while until recently there was a lack of contact with the empirical social sciences, there is currently a precipitous tendency to theologize concerning Christian social theory. It must be emphasized, too, that Catholic social doctrine does not depend simply upon ethical postulates; rather, its ethical principles are ontologically grounded in the natural law.

Unity of Society. Because MAN is a composite of body and soul, and hence a PERSON who is responsible for his own conduct, the society he forms is, unlike other unities, unified by an intrinsic principle, the self-binding will of its members. In this specific sense, society is a unity resulting from an actualized moral order (*unitas ordinis*). Nevertheless, society rests also on an extrinsic formative principle that adds to the note of order one of organization. The reason for this is not only that the self-binding will of its members is to some extent defective, but also that the concrete demands of society's intrinsic end are not fully recognizable by all of its members, and, furthermore, that the lasting realization of the social end from one generation to another can be secured only by organizational means, such as legal and administrative institutions.

Function of Society. The function of society is to actualize its inherent end, the common good, viz, the conditions that make a fully human existence possible for all of its members. Because the individual depends on others to bring about the end of society (principle of solidarity), the individual good is part of the common good.

Only when the common good has been established as an ontological criterion can the true functions of society be ascertained. For this reason, in line with the thought of St. Thomas Aquinas, the present exposition of society focuses on the idea of ends (*ordo finium*) rather than on the idea of value found in modern social theory. When the idea of ends implicit in human nature is given equal prominence with that of value, three problems that beset the philosophical and ethical theory of value become more amenable to solution. First, the connection of value with objective being becomes more readily apparent, for in modern theory the recognition of value is made a matter of feeling or of mere a priori insight. Second, the obligatory character of moral values in the personal and social sphere can be shown more easily; this follows from their being related to inherent tendencies in human nature (*inclinationes naturales,* in *Summa theologiae* 1a2ae, 94.2), whose intrinsic ends indicate the will of the Creator. Third, in this way the standards for defining the order of values and the scale of values in the life of both the individual and the community can be established. Apart from these considerations, moreover, an ontologically founded teleological order makes it apparent that man, as a member of the community, has to achieve ends or realize values on his own responsibility (principle of SUBSIDIARITY) as far as this is possible.

Instead of ends and values, one may speak of interests (e.g., general or public interests, group interests, individual interests); even in this terminology, however, the ontological idea of ends is indispensable for an objective evaluation of subjective claims based on interests.

Reality of Society. The common good is a reality over and above the good that individuals can achieve separately; consequently, in realizing the common good, society emerges as a reality of a special kind. Predicamentally this reality cannot be defined simply in terms of the disjunction between SUBSTANCE and ACCIDENT (*see* CATEGORIES OF BEING). Society is not a substance, but neither is it a mere ontological accident. The interpretation of the good of the individual as part of the common good of society, which had far-reaching implications for Aquinas, has been concretized by those social scientists who give equal importance to nurture and nature in forming the fully human existence of the individual as a person. They see in nurture the culture or the civilization of the society by which the individual's psychic, mental, moral, and religious predispositions are largely formed. In view of their analysis, the category of RELATION is not sufficient to describe the being of society, for it would suggest that society is a structure consisting in relations between fully developed persons, whereas man reaches the fullness of his human existence only through social interaction. This is especially true during adolescence, but it is true too in later life; as Aquinas also taught, only the completely matured person is morally permitted to leave society and to live in solitude. Society's ontological nature is also obscured when it is reduced to an ''I-Thou'' relationship or to a ''we'' relationship or to a ''dialogue'' form of human existence, even though such attempts contain elements of truth and may serve to illustrate man's social nature and responsibility. In Aquinas's thought, the relation *ad alium singulariter* is given due consideration, but emphasis is laid on the relation *ad alium in communi,* i.e., on the community as such (*Summa theologiae* 2a2ae, 58.5). Other attempts are deficient in accounting for the supra-individual reality of society as this is actualized in the process of realizing the common good. It is, however, equally certain that the existence of society does depend upon the existence of man who ontologically is a substance. As a person he is also a supersocial being with supersocial ends; it is here that his rights to freedom, which are not to be violated by society, are grounded.

Structure. Since the ends to be realized through social cooperation are many, society necessarily has a pluralistic structure. This pluralism is of two kinds. The first is derived directly from the social nature of man in which are rooted not only such vital structures as the family and the state, but also the territorial as well as the vocational community and the ethnic-cultural group. Because they are based directly upon human nature as such, they are found everywhere in mankind and its history in one form or another. The second kind of social pluralism is based indirectly on human nature, namely, on common purposes open to man's free CHOICE. This kind of pluralism intensifies in proportion to the growth of population and to the development of civilization. It results from the articulation and particularization of both material and mental ends and values, whose pursuit results in an increasing variety of associations and in a growing measure of socialization, i.e., closer interdependence among men. The pluralism existing in the modern democratic society derives its peculiar character from its causes; these lie in the mechanism of decision-making in the parliamentary process and in the striving for influence on government and parliament by pressure groups.

From what has been said about the structure of society, a further important characteristic emerges, namely, that it is always historically patterned. Only the fundamentals of social order are implicit in human nature; more cannot be found in such nature even for the family community, still less for larger elements of society and for the state. In their concrete aspects, the forms of society change as human nature changes, which, though invariable in its essence, is otherwise mutable (*Summa theologiae* 2a2ae, 57.2 ad 1).

Social Process. It follows from the fact that common ends are constitutive of society that a power of direction must be vested in some AUTHORITY. To the extent that social ends are ontologically implicit in human nature, authority is itself ontologically grounded; otherwise, it is established by the agreement of wills of those who freely unite themselves for the pursuit of a common goal. Authority is necessary not only because the realization of common ends by a self-determining group requires coordination, but also because a governing power must determine concrete objectives pertaining to the common good as well as methods to attain them. The mode of exercising authority and the extent of its competence depend very largely on the form of society in which it operates. It is practically confined to a rule of custom in the case of the homogeneous ethnic community living as a national minority, whereas it is comprehensive in the case of a heterogeneous society such as a large territorial state, for this must rely to a great extent on organizational means.

Capacity for Action. Only the person is capable of having responsibility and of acting accordingly. Society as a whole is responsible for actualizing its own ends, and it carries out this responsibility through various organs (e.g., states conclude treaties and trade unions make contracts). Society, therefore, is a person; but because its bond of unity consists in a common responsibility, it is called a moral person, to distinguish it from the physical person of individual man. It is also called a juridical person because it possesses natural rights by reason of its responsibilities and is capable of legally relevant action. In consequence, society is a person not merely in a metaphorical sense but by strict ANALOGY.

In a similar manner, society may be called an organism; in fact, one is accustomed to speak of the body politic, its members, and its organs. The organic theory of society lays stress on a community of responsibility to attain common intrinsic ends, whereas the mechanistic theory sees society either as a harmony of self-balancing interests (individualism) or as a unity to be organized for extrinsic ends by a ruling group (collectivism). Aquinas refers to the Church as a person (*Summa theologiae* 2a2ae, 83.16 ad 3) and a body (*ibid.* 3a, 8.4).

Types. A major consideration of social philosophers is the relation between a society and its members; these latter may be individuals or they may be smaller societies. Hence, the first classification is that of the all-embracing society, such as the STATE or the organized society of nations. Particular societies are referred to as intermediate structures because they serve as social units between the individual and the all-embracing society through their particular ends, responsibilities, and rights. Another division is that into necessary communities, relatively necessary communities, and free associations. Necessary communities, examples of which are the family and the state, are indispensable to human existence and are based directly on human nature; they also impose indisputable moral obligations. Relatively necessary societies also are based directly on human nature, but they are structures with limited functions, such as ethnic groups. Free associations (e.g. the literary club and the stock company) are based on human nature only indirectly; they have their origin in the free choice of their members and are limited to serving man in various spheres of culture.

All of the foregoing social units belong to the natural sphere, as distinct from the supernatural. The Church, by reason of its divine mandate for salvation and its life of grace, forms the MYSTICAL BODY OF CHRIST, a supernatural society. A society that affords all the requisites for the full development of human nature is called a perfect society: examples are the state in the natural order and the Church in the supernatural order. Imperfect societies are the smaller societies; these are capable of performing their functions only as members of a perfect society. The free society, in which the state fully recognizes human rights, particularly that of free public opinion, is to be differentiated from the totalitarian society, in which the government assumes unlimited dominance over the individual. The free society is an open society to the extent that it allows COMMUNICATION with individuals and associations outside its domain in an unhampered way. A closed society excludes such communication. In a different sense, one speaks of a closed society when a traditional social morality (H. Bergson) or *Ethosform* (M. Scheler) prevails to unite its members in an intimate spiritual bond. Finally, the juridical society may be differentiated from the amicable society. The first rests upon legal provisions (e.g. a municipality or a business corporation), whereas the second rests upon a good-will agreement on the part of the members (e.g. a sports club or charitable organization).

Narrower Sense. Society is sometimes used in a narrower sense to designate relative autonomies as compared to the more absolute autonomy of the state. The distinction is of crucial importance for social philosophy and social ethics. In the narrower sense, society is composed of individuals and smaller social units with their own particular ends and responsibilities; the state, on the other hand, has an all-embracing end and effects the basic ordering of social functions in the over-all society. This is the common understanding in English social theory, in contrast to Hegel's theory in which society is absorbed by the state (cf. E. Barker, *Political Thought in England 1848–1914* [Oxford 1942] 66).

F. Tönnies (1855–1936) uses the word ''society'' in a still narrower sense as designating only associations based on free choice and generally with material purposes, to distinguish these from the community as a biological-spiritual unit, especially the family, the ethnic group, and the nationality. As an example of the first, he would cite the modern market society that is formed by commercial exchange in balancing supply and demand. Influenced by Tönnies as well as by Marx, not a few regard the state itself as a purely functional social entity. There is an element of truth in Tönnies's distinction, easily recognized in present pluralistic democracies. Yet in light of the principles of social philosophy pointed out above, the state is much more than an arbitrary structure; it is grounded in the social nature of man and can subsist as a political society only if it is rooted in consent with respect to common values. This has been the thought of political theorists from Cicero, Augustine, Aquinas, and Edmund BURKE down to the rise of individualism. One who sets society altogether apart from community, as does Tönnies, overlooks the fact that society in any form must rest on a sharing of values, particularly those values that man finds revealed in his nature as morally binding for life in society.

Other philosophical theories. In the latter part of the Middle Ages, NOMINALISM set the stage for the undermining of the ontological and metaphysical concept of society. It held that only individual things are real, hence also only individual human beings; for the nominalist, therefore, society could exist only in mind as an idea, not as a reality. The so-called fictive theory of society is believed to be traceable to Pope INNOCENT IV, who, referring to social grouping, used the expression *fingatur una persona;* what he meant by this, however, was only that society is a *res incorporalis,* for he was concerned with establishing the difference between a juridical and a physical person.

Under the influence of nominalism, the doctrine developed that society depends exclusively on the will of the people, giving rise to the theory of the SOCIAL CONTRACT. According to T. HOBBES (*De Cive,* 1642; *Leviathan,* 1651), the natural state of man is a struggle of each individual against the other. Fear and self-preservation lead to the social contract, by which men establish an order that guarantees a limited amount of freedom for all. J. J. ROUSSEAU (*Contrat social,* 1762), advocated the opposite theory, namely, that man in his natural state lived in freedom and equality, both of which were destroyed by the introduction of property, to be followed by strife and war. Order was established by means of the social contract, and thus by the will of the people, with the result that each man obeys himself, having cooperated in establishing law and authority.

According to G. W. F. HEGEL (*Grundlinien der Philosophie des Rechts,* 1821), society is ''the realization of the substantial will'' expressing ''the objective spirit,'' the moral consciousness made effective in group life; participating in this spirit, individual man attains fully human existence, but this is only an ''accidental'' being. In K. MARX's theory of dialectical materialism (*Zur Kritik der politischen Ökonomie,* 1859), society is patterned on the ''mode of production of material life''; hence every advanced precommunist society must be a class society, if only because of the ''social power'' inherent in the private ownership of production.

In spite of manifest discrepancies, some element of truth is to be found in all these theories. They are not so much concerned with society, however, as they are with the justification of the state and its authority; yet all of them presuppose that association is necessary for man and even essential to his nature. This is the basic problem in social philosophy; it still calls for analysis and explanation. Moreover, since these theories take as their starting point an inadequate notion of the person, they reach false conclusions, such as those on which individualism and collectivism are based, and continue to have detrimental consequences in the development of modern society. The element of truth to be found in the social contract theory is that society and its order rest upon the individuals' responsibility to comply with the demands of human nature and thus upon a union of wills (or upon what Aquinas, following Cicero and Augustine, calls a *iuris consensus, Summa theologiae* 1a2ae, 105.2). The basic mistake of any social contract theory is the notion of absolute sovereignty, which Hobbes situated in monarchy and Rousseau in the people. Hegel was right in emphasizing that society requires a spiritual basis of unity and that only by participating in it can man achieve a fully human existence; this is akin to the scholastic doctrine that the individual good is but a part of the common good. However, Hegel left too little room for the individual, particularly when the supersocial and superpolitical ends of the human person are to be considered. For Marx, social (and consequently the individual) human consciousness are formed wholly by the material world with its technical and economic means of production; moreover, he too finds no room for the individual's own being and responsibility as a person, having disavowed the ''dualism of spirit and matter.'' On the other hand, there is an element of truth in his theory of society, particularly in its emphasis on political economy as the most important socially uniting bond; the latter's relative importance as an integrating factor was acknowledged by Aquinas as well.

Bibliography: J. MESSNER, *Social Ethics: Natural Law in the Modern World,* tr. J. J. DOHERTY (new ed. St. Louis 1965). E. WELTY, *Man in Society,* v. 1 of *A Handbook of Christian Social Ethics,* ed. J. FITZSIMONS, tr. G. KIRSTEIN (New York 1960–), bibliog. B. A. PAPARELLA, *Sociality and Sociability: A Philosophy of Sociability according to St. Thomas Aquinas* (Washington, D.C. 1955). J. MARITAIN, *The Person and the Common Good,* tr. J. J. FITZGERALD (New York 1947); *Moral Philosophy: An Historical and Critical Survey of the Great Systems* (New York 1964). J. F. CRONIN, *Catholic Social Principles* (Milwaukee, Wis. 1950). M. J. WILLIAMS, *Catholic Social Thought* (New York 1950). A. F. UTZ, *Die Prinzipien der Gesellschaftslehre,* v. 1 of *Sozialethik* (Heidelberg 1958—), international bibliog. G. GUNDLACH et al., *Staatslexikon* 3:817–823, 842–847.

[J. MESSNER]

Sociological Theories

The effects of nominalistic and individualistic theories of society upon social institutions were already evident when the modern science of sociology was first proposed and named by Auguste COMTE (1798–1857). His work and that of other early sociologists was in part a reaction against the dissolution of traditional groupings in the course of the FRENCH REVOLUTION. There remained, so it seemed, no intermediary groups between the individual and the STATE, and this condition heightened the importance of a distinction between society and the state that had not been made explicit up to that time. Sociology was conceived as a means for the discovery of laws of societal structure and change through the application of which a new social solidarity could be attained. Since ontological and metaphysical concepts of society had been abandoned, the search for such laws could be undertaken only with the method of ''positive science.'' As the field developed, the original POSITIVISM became the object of a critique from within as well as from without, but the inductive study of society remained the distinctive task of sociology. Thus, although sociologists are aware that assumptions about the nature and reality of society affect the models, methods, and techniques that they employ, these assumptions are not their primary concern. Their attention is given to the observable fact of society.

Definition. The sociologist begins with the observation that individuals interact with reference to pluralities or collectivities of various types. Among these are some that are broadly inclusive and are called societies (assuming that they can be distinguished empirically from other types). Some definitions identify a society in this macroscopic sense as a plurality possessing a common CULTURE, while others refer to a common territory or a common government. In general, these definitions are deficient because they do not distinguish sufficiently between society, culture complex, community, and nation. Marion J. Levy has attempted a conceptually precise and empirically relevant definition of society as ''a system of action in operation that (1) involves a plurality of interacting individuals of a given species (or group of species) whose actions are primarily oriented to the system concerned and who are recruited at least in part by the sexual reproduction of members of the plurality involved, (2) is at least in theory self-sufficient for the actions of this plurality, and (3) is capable of existing longer than the life-span of an individual of the type (or types) involved'' (*Structure of Society* [Princeton, N.J. 1952] 113). In a human society, the ''given species'' is *Homo sapiens* and the system itself consists in the patterned, organized regularities observable in the interaction of men who are primarily oriented to the system and influenced by it.

In theory, animals may form societies according to this definition, but this does not imply that the anthill or elephant herd is of the same type or order as human society. Human interaction is empirically distinct. It involves symbols and meanings that have both subjective and cultural dimensions. It produces a specifically different kind of plurality with its own internal problems of order and its own dynamism of development (deriving ultimately from human rationality and freedom).

A society is not simply the sum of discrete interactions. Rather, its members or parts are organized in such a way that an emergent whole is maintained and develops, remains static, or disintegrates. ''American society,'' for example, has meaning with reference to its past development, its present state, and its prospects for the future. Although the whole is the product of interaction, it is nonetheless a system of patterned relationships and institutions that influence behavior, even so-called unstructured or deviant behavior.

The members of a society vary as to the extent and the exclusiveness to which their actions are oriented to this system. Citizenship, which constitutes membership in the state, is not the basic criterion for membership in a society. A member is one whose actions are oriented more toward the major institutions of one society, especially the institutions that define its goals, than toward those of another. Most often contemporary societies and nation-states are coextensive, but they need not be.

The restriction that a society's members must be recruited at least in part through sexual reproduction excludes such pluralities as the ASSOCIATION or collectivities that are prisons and religious communities. It implies further that a society must be composed of members of both sexes and must provide institutional regulation of sexual relations.

The norm of self-sufficiency requires that a society be capable of supplying ''from within'' all the adaptive and integrative institutions needed for its existence and operation. This excludes such partial systems as the family or the church that need the help of other institutions if they are to function. (The Catholic Church is a perfect society in the theological and canonical, not the sociological, meaning of the word.) Self-sufficiency in this context does not imply that a society must not import goods or services, but only that it must have the necessary structures to obtain what it needs.

Moreover, a society must be capable of existing beyond the life-span of its individual members. In effect this means that some provision has to be made for the effective socialization of the young. The society must possess the structural facilities—through its families, religious institutions, social classes, schools, etc.—to transmit the beliefs, values, and norms required for the survival of its institutions.

Theories and models. Although sociologists have relatively little difficulty in isolating a society from other types of social pluralities, they have not reached consensus on the analysis of its structure and functions. Is society simply a more complex organization of microsystems such as interactional encounters? Or is it a macrosystem in its own right with emergent structures and processes unique to its own level? If society is a whole made up of parts, how are these parts put together and how do they work? Is this whole an on-going process, a BECOMING, or a BEING? In attempting to answer these questions, sociologists have proposed various models or general images, often developed through analogy, about the kinds of units, the patterns of their relations, and the type of whole that is society. The literature is replete with models inspired by physics, biology, psychology, and even mathematics. Thus there are atomistic, organic, evolutionary, conflict, equilibrium, and statistical models. The extent to which any one of these models exhausts the sociological reality of society is still debatable since each seems to present some aspect of that reality. A completely adequate model that is more than an eclectic juxtaposition is still to be developed.

Comte. In some ways Comte prefigured most of the currently available approaches to the study of society. Although he never defined the term, he equated it with the whole of the human species. He considered the species to be one organism to be studied in itself, since a whole is better known than its parts. In practice, he tempered this extreme macroorientation by stressing the reciprocal influence between individuals, families, and pluralities of lesser scope than total humanity. He insisted that the family is the basic unit of society and gives birth to feelings of solidarity among men but that in turn ''wise men,'' men with ideas, are needed to unite families together into tribes and nations. Although he postulated a basic antagonism between forces of innovation and conservatism, he viewed society as an order based on a universal consensus, the foundation of unity as well as of the division of labor. In another perspective, however, that which he called social dynamics, he referred to society as primarily a process of growth from a militaristic through a legalistic to an industrial stage of organization. Unfortunately, Comte never integrated his static and his evolutionary models, nor did he fully incorporate the functions of ideas and of conflict into his organic model. Each of his approaches seems to have had a ''life of its own'' prefiguring one of the competing theories to follow, just as his concern with these several approaches prefigured the more eclectic or synthesizing theories of contemporary sociologists.

Spencer. Perhaps Herbert SPENCER (1820–1903) was the most extreme among the early sociologists in his use of the organic-evolutionary model. He defined society as a superorganism progressing inevitably from homogeneity to heterogeneity, and he conceived it as an entity formed of permanently arranged units analogous to the arrangement of the parts of a biological organism having its own sustaining, distributive, and regulating organs or institutions. As a society grows its units become more differentiated. The result is an increase of structure as well as of mass. The process is similar to the growth of an organism even though the basic parts of society (individuals) are discrete and do not form a concrete whole. Spencer's macromodel assumes, in spite of some denial on his part, that societal laws are merely special cases of biological laws.

Durkheim. Such extreme forms of bio-organicism have long since disappeared from sociology, but more moderate models have persisted, to a great extent because of the influence of Émile DURKHEIM (1855–1917). While he retained Spencer's macrosociological approach, he stripped it of all biologism. In his theory the social fact of solidarity is the essential characteristic of society, but solidarity is conceived as an emergent reality arising from the association of individuals and not reducible to the mere sum of their actions. Society has a consciousness (*conscience collective*) that creates a system of values and norms binding upon the individual. The resultant solidarity has in one sense a life of its own; it progresses from a mechanical to an organic form as the collective consciousness becomes less imperative and the division of labor increases because of rising population density and effective communication. But even in a society characterized by organic solidarity, individual actions are only incidents within the large-scale social process in which society exists.

Tönnies. This undiluted macroorientation seems to postulate a substantial reality for society, a position that Ferdinand Tönnies (1855–1936) found unacceptable. Although conceiving society as a type of collective person, he defined it as a product of single persons, the will of one affecting another and vice-versa, with a collective will developing from this interaction. His theory suggests the possibility of microanalysis within a macrosociological framework. In fact, his societal types, *Gemeinschaft* and *Gesellschaft,* are explained in terms of human willing. The first is a union of persons relating to each other through a natural, unconditional volition, such as the love of a mother for her child, while the second is a plurality of individuals interacting as a consequence of ''rational will,'' a sort of calculating volition whereby appropriate means are chosen for specific ends. In general, Tönnies saw society as changing from a *Gemeinschaft* to a *Gesellschaft* much in the same way that Durkheim saw mechanical solidarity being replaced by organic solidarity.

Simmel. Georg Simmel (1858–1918) retained the microanalytical approach but rejected the organic overtones. He defined society as a function and a process manifest in the relationships and interactions of men. He was not a reductionist, however, at least in the strict meaning of the term, since in his system individual interaction, while remaining discrete, is synthesized into the unity of society as each element (the content) is related to the others through forms (in the Kantian sense). Simmel posited the existence of society in the consciousness of its members, but the individual is not the group and therefore must become ''generalized'' by a postulated call or vocation. This helps to explain why quantitative growth can lead to qualitative changes in society, but Simmel did not discuss the process, perhaps because of his failure to attack the problem of macroanalysis.

Marx. Most of these theorists, in spite of their different views, were preoccupied mainly with the problem of unity or order. Karl Marx (1818–83) preferred a conflict-evolutionary model in his analysis of society. He defined it as a dialectical process of warring classes wherein economic factors determine the structure and development. The nature of this determinism has been the subject of much controversy, even among so-called orthodox interpreters, but the notion of conflict remains central to Marxian thought. Each stage of society is held to contain within itself the seeds of its own destruction and to prepare the next state until the final end of evolution, a classless order, is attained. Others before Marx noted the fact of conflict, but Marx postulated that the process itself and its resolution are the very core of society.

Sumner. This notion of conflict was taken up by William Graham Sumner (1840–1910) but recast in the framework of social Darwinism and Spencerian organicism. Sumner maintained that the basic law of society is the law of evolution that receives its impetus from the struggles for existence. Society is basically a system of forces arising primarily from the pressure of population and economic growth and generating through trial and error specific folkways (or ways of doing things). In his early thought Sumner believed that these customs could be modified by man to a very limited extent only, but later he seemed to allow man a larger role in the structuring of society.

Small. Sumner's idea was further developed by Albion W. Small (1854–1926), who defined societal conflict in terms of man's interests and society as the product of individual efforts to fulfill interests, resulting in a continuous process of conflict constantly resolving itself into cooperation. Like the organic model before it, the conflict model of society was slowly transformed into a more psychological conception, but one in which both conflict and order assumed prominence.

Ward. It was Lester F. Ward (1841–1913) who projected man into the evolutionary process. He conceived of society in terms of a psychological-evolutionary model. Attributing spontaneous evolution (genesis) to blind forces, he believed the process was bifurcated with the appearance of mind. Thus he defined ''social forces'' as psychic forces or feelings and assigned a crucial role to man's purposive actions (telesis). Recognizing that social forces could give rise to conflict, he held them to be checked by ''synergy,'' the basic principle behind evolution, and molded into structures and society. In this way, Ward retained the notion of conflict but subordinated it to equilibrium.

Trend Toward Psychological Models. With the decline of the evolutionary school, the psychological model became more microoriented. In the thought of Gabriel Tarde (1843–1904) the fundamental elements of society are belief and desire and the basic processes are imitation or repetition, opposition, and adaptation. For him society could not be studied as such. Gustave Le Bon (1841–1931) accepted this proposition but attempted to reconcile it with Durkheim's stress on the collectivity, an effort at integration that influenced the work of James Baldwin (1861–1934) and George Mead (1863–1931) and found its sociological expression in the theories of Charles Horton Cooley (1864–1929) and William I. Thomas (1863–1947).

Cooley defined both society and individual as ''simply collective and distributive aspects of the same thing'' (*Human Nature and the Social Order* [New York 1902] 2). The basic social fact, he maintained, resides in the imagination each person has of the other. He conceded, however, that social reality is not simply the product of agreement between individuals but the result of organization. Unfortunately, he never explained what he meant by organization. While sharing Cooley's basic orientation, Thomas was somewhat more specific. He postulated attitudes and values as the elements of society, but among the latter he included social norms that coalesce into institutions and social organization. This marked the beginning of a return to macroanalysis by theorists using psychological models.

Weber. This trend is pronounced in Max WEBER (1864–1920). Even though he believed the individual and his actions to be the basic units of study, he carried forward his analysis to all levels of social life. While Cooley reduced society to a socio-psychic complex, Weber postulated a continuum of social categories ranging from the individual actor to society. He saw the social relationship in which actors take account of and are oriented to each other as capable of patterning in different ways and of forming different pluralities, including society. His concern, however, focused on the subjective meaning of action; it is ''meaning'' that becomes patterned and expected in certain situations, so that in spite of the macrosociological scope of his historical studies, Weber remained strongly nominalistic and conceived of society mainly as a category of human interaction. This did not preclude his analyzing the evolution of social structures as the result of tension between the principles of traditionalism, rationality, and charisma, or his seeing a general trend of increasing rationality in the development of societies.

Pareto. With the renewed concern for macroanalysis it was inevitable that the organic model should return to favor. In a sense the equilibrium paradigm of Vilfredo Pareto (1848–1923) represented an attempt to incorporate elements of most previous approaches without reducing society to any one type of phenomenon. Pareto's notion of equilibrium was taken from physics and mechanics but he rejected the outright physicalism of a Henry Carey (1793–1879), who saw man as a molecule of society and society as a variation of the law of molecular gravitation. In spite of his terminology Pareto was more a moderate organicist than a mechanist. He conceived of society as a system whose form and state of equilibrium are determined by the elements acting upon it, which elements in turn are influenced by society. This type of system analysis implies both micro- and macrosociological orientations. Reciprocal causality is operative.

If some change is introduced and affects the form of society, a reaction occurs tending to restore the form to its original state. Pareto, however, does not rule out all change of the system since the "sentiment" of resistance (an innate human tendency manifested in interests, knowledge, "residues," and "derivations") may not be operating for some reason. In fact, since there are two principal types of elites in a society, a governing and nongoverning elite, they can and do succeed each other and thus give birth to conservative and progressive phases. Thus Pareto's theory incorporates an element of change, but change of society is explained in terms of change within society.

Variant Tendencies. In effect Pareto achieved a partial synthesis of previous models. Although most contemporary sociologists follow his lead, a few remain committed to the early models. Leopold von Wiese (b. 1876), for example, is basically microoriented. For him all plurality patterns, including societies, are nothing more and nothing less than neuropsychic patterns. Georges Gurvitch (b. 1894), on the other hand, insists that societies cannot be adequately analyzed unless the collective mind that operates through individual minds is recognized as the immediate social reality. George Lundberg (b. 1895) reduces society to physical phenomena, a field of force wherein individuals are attracted or repulsed as particles of an atom. George Vold (b. 1896) sees it as a congeries of conflicting groups and V. Gordon Childe (b. 1892) continues the tradition of the biological-evolutionary school wherein Darwin's theory of variation is transferred from organic to social evolution. But, for the most part, today's theorists have developed more complicated models of society.

Contemporary attempts at integration. The insights of Durkheim, Weber, and Pareto have been combined by the "social action–functionalist school." The basic unit of society is taken to be meaningful social action, i.e., an action that has meaning for the actor because it takes into account the behavior of others. Florian Znaniecki (1882–1958) termed this concern the "humanistic coefficient of cultural data," while Robert MacIver (b. 1882) drew attention to the "dynamic assessment" of the situation made by the actor. Both of these men defined society as an emergent reality and recognized that in some way the "whole" has causal priority over the part. Znaniecki subsumed the concept of social action under the concept of system and prepared the way for the study of a society as an inclusive "system of systems." MacIver proposed different levels of causal analysis and stressed the need to study the "teleological aspects of social phenomena." For him, while social facts are products of individual meanings, they may be distributive phenomena (activities of a like nature), collective phenomena (conjoint actions), or conjunctural phenomena (unpurposed results of activities by interdependent groups or individuals). Society includes all of these phenomena. Thus are joined in one model the micro- and macrosociological, the psychological and the organic approaches. MacIver added an evolutionary dimension. Society, while constituted by meaningful acts, is forever unfolding, and this process manifests itself in greater division of labor and increasing differentiation of associations and institutions.

Sorokin. In a sense Pitirim Sorokin (b. 1889) belongs to this school, although he denies any association with functionalism. His analysis is in terms of an idealistic organic model, but again, meaningful interaction is at the basis of society. Such interaction can be understood, however, only in terms of the total sociocultural system in which all the parts are mutually interdependent, some of which must be "logico-meaningfully" integrated. Sorokin denies neither the existence of unintegrated or neutral and contradictory or antagonistic elements nor the existence of congeries or elements related to the system only in terms of mechanical adjacency, but he does insist that every society is characterized by a central theme that is either sensate (equating truth with sense knowledge), ideational (equating truth with faith), or idealistic (equating truth with reason). In every society these central themes are forever changing. While MacIver sees a trend toward structural differentiation, Sorokin concludes to cycles of sensate, ideational, and idealistic themes.

Merton and Homans. The implications of Znaniecki's model have been developed by Robert Merton (b. 1910) and George Homans (b. 1910). Merton, influenced by Radcliffe-Brown and Malinowski, defines functions as the consequences of any act, aim, or purpose within an organic-type system, including society. These may serve to maintain or to disrupt the system, and society thus becomes not only an integrated whole, but a net balance of integration and deviance that in turn affects the individuals composing it. Homans, on the other hand, isolates the structural components that contribute to the whole: activities, interactions, sentiments, and norms, some of which are oriented to solving problems arising from the environment, others of which are oriented to the internal problem of integration and differentiation. Society therefore is composed of an external system and an internal system, which interact with each other and set the stage for its survival or collapse.

Parsons. Perhaps the most comprehensive model of society in contemporary sociology is that of Talcott Parsons (b. 1902). He postulates a homology of small and large systems, a continuity between two-person interaction and society. His model is based upon (1) a voluntaristic conception of social action with psychological overtones, (2) the physicalist notion of action space and the law of inertia, (3) the mechanistic idea of equilibrium, and (4) the organismic postulate of functional requisites. Therefore the model combines micro- and macroanalysis.

Parsons defines society as a system of interaction, and the relations between actors (status-role reciprocities) compose its structure. In a sense the system is superior to its units and ''calls'' for structural contributions for its functioning. A society must meet all the essential functional requisites for survival through its own resources and must not be a differentiated subsystem of a larger plurality or, more precisely, collectivity. In other words, it must be a relatively self-sufficient system and possess a common culture to coordinate differentiated units that in the long run depend on human individuals as actors. In effect, this means that a society must have the needed institutions to meet the requirements of goal attainment, adaptation to the environment, pattern maintenance (socialization and tension management), and integration.

While society as defined by Parsons cannot be equated with nation, the boundaries of a society tend to coincide with the territory under control of the highest-order political organization. This holds true in spite of increasing structural differentiation, the specialization of function and separation of the kinship system, the economy, religion, the legal system, and the polity because, in effect, any institution whose orientation is primarily cultural rather than societal lacks the legitimate authority to prescribe values and enforce norms for the society. Nonetheless, in Parsons' model each institution contributes to the maintenance of society and is involved in a process of exchange by which equilibrium is maintained. These intermeshing processes deal with decisions about the disposition and allocation of resources that, from the point of view of the system, are consumed, and with media of control that, like power, circulate from one unit to another. In effect, Parsons sees the dynamics of society mainly as the processing of information.

But this equilibrium-maintaining process does not imply a static structure. Society is a cybernetic system of control over behavior, and structural change is inevitable in the equilibrating process because roles are continuously being played by new actors and strains are inevitable in the exchange between societal units. Control can resolve these problems up to a point; but when a cumulative process begins, change in the normative structure results and its general direction is toward functional differentiation and increasing complexity of the system.

Evaluation. Contemporary theorists seem agreed that Parsons' model of society helps to resolve many of the differences between the so-called individualistic and collectivistic points of view, but that the two have not been fully integrated. Significant objections have been based upon the model's failure to explain adequately the basic fact of conflict and its contribution to the ''state of the system.'' Another objection is that the evolutionary nature of society is not really explained. Some sociologists, such as Lewis Coser and Ralph Dahrendorf, maintain that society is not in the harmonious balance implied by an equilibrium model. In their view, dissension arising from competition rather than consensus is a basic condition of society and a dialectical model of some sort is needed. Wilbert Moore insists that the notion of equilibrium either forecloses discussion of change or predicts change in one direction only, the restoration of society to a steady state. He suggests the use of a tension-management model, but one that makes no presumption that tensions or strains are in fact ''managed.'' Moore would make both order and change problematical and normal.

Pierre van den Berghe, while recognizing that societies show a tendency toward equilibrium and solidarity, argues that they generate the opposites as well and require other mechanisms of integration than consensus. Moreover, he agrees that the equilibrium model does not account for endogenous change through conflict and contradiction. He suggests that there is need for a dialectical model (one that does not reduce social reality to polarized opposites), but he also recognizes that social dialectics alone cannot account for change through differentiation and adaptation nor account for consensus. He therefore proposes a functional-dialectical model wherein both conflict and consensus are basic.

Such a model has not been developed but may be promising. The juxtaposition of the two approaches is not as arbitrary as it might seem. In a sense, interdependence contains its own dialectic and dialectical conflict and is based on some assumption of equilibrium. The model of structural-functional analysis postulates that society is a system composed of interrelated parts but, whether institutions or actors, the parts are to some extent relatively autonomous. These parts may adjust or react so that equilibrium and interdependence cannot be equated. Adjustment itself occurs within a tension system wherein autonomy and control interact dialectically (in the broad sense of the word) so that consensus or stability cannot be a permanent or total state of the system. And reaction occurs within a system of interdependence in which equilibrium forces are operative so that society cannot be adequately defined in terms of simple conflict or change. As a system of relatively autonomous but organized elements, society is empirically a whole whose equilibrium implies a tension system and whose dialectics imply an evolving synthesis. As such, strain and deviancy are as much its components as harmony and conformity, and change as much its feature as stability.

Such a model, which might be called an evolving dialectical-equilibrium model, would seem to reunite the major insights of past theorists and resolve many of the contemporary objections to the structural-functional analysis of society. It would incorporate into one synthesis actor-interaction as well as holistic processes, conflict and consensus, stability and change as *facts* of society. Whether such a model is adopted sooner or later, the contemporary trend seems to point in such a direction.

Bibliography: H. E. BARNES and H. BECKER, *Social Thought from Lore to Science,* 2 v. (2d ed. Washington, D.C. 1952). L. A. COSER, *The Functions of Social Conflict* (Glencoe, Ill. 1956). S. N. EISENSTADT, ''Social Change, Differentiation and Evolution,'' *American Sociological Review* 29 (1964) 375–386. A. INKELES, *What Is Sociology?* (Englewood Cliffs, N.J. 1964). M. J. LEVY, *The Structure of Society* (Princeton, N.J. 1952). W. E. MOORE, *Social Change* (Englewood Cliffs, N.J. 1963). T. PARSONS et al., eds., *Theories of Society,* 2 v. (New York 1961). P. A. SOROKIN, *Contemporary Sociological Theories* (New York 1928). H. R. WAGNER, ''Displacement of Scope: A Problem of the Relationship between Small-Scale and Large-Scale Sociological Theories,'' *American Journal of Sociology* 69 (1964) 571–584. P. L. VAN DEN BERGHE, ''Dialectic and Functionalism,'' *Americn Sociological Review* 28 (1963) 695–705. D. MARTINDALE, *The Nature and Types of Sociological Theory* (Boston, Mass. 1965).

[R. H. POTVIN]

SOCIETY (CHURCH AS)

The term society has been in use to designate the Church throughout the history of Western Christian thought. However, it is only within the last two centuries that the term, with its corresponding systematic conceptualization, has found widespread favor and use in ecclesiology.

Patristic Era. Among the Fathers, St. Augustine often applied the term society to the Church. The term in St. Augustine, corresponding to his whole philosophical and religious spirit, has a strong emphasis on the interiority of the intrapersonal society involved, on the community of life being actually what it seems to be, and not merely fair seeming. The basic reason for this emphasis is his conviction that the Holy Spirit, who is ''the society of the Father and of the Son'' within the Trinity, is also the ground of the Church as a society:

> . . . the society of the unity of the Church of God, outside of which there is no forgiveness of sins, is, as it were, the proper work of the Holy Spirit (the Father and the Son, to be sure, working together with Him), because the Holy Spirit Himself is in a certain sense the society of the Father and of the Son (*Serm.* 71.20.33; *Patrologia Latina* 38:463).

''The society by which we are made the one Body of God's only Son, is the Spirit's role'' (*ibid.* 17.28; *Patrologia Latina* 38:461). ''. . . no one can achieve eternal life and salvation apart from the society of Christ, which is realized in Him and with Him, when we are bathed in His Sacraments and incorporated into His members'' (*Pecc. merit.* 3.11.19; *Corpus scriptorum ecclesiasticorum latinorum,* 60:145). Augustine asks, ''How should the city of God . . . originate, develop, and attain its destiny, if the life of the saints were not a social life?'' (*Civ.* 19.5; *Corpus Christianorum. Series latina* 48:669.) Even ''the peace of the heavenly city,'' which is the glorious Church of heaven, is called ''the perfectly ordered and harmonious society of those who find their joy in God and in one another in God'' (*ibid.* 19.13; *Corpus Christianorum. Series latina* 48:679). Augustine's generic understanding of what a society is can be gathered from a phrase of the *City of God:* ''. . . an assemblage of reasonable beings joined in society by their harmonious sharing in the object of their love'' (*ibid.* 19.24; *Corpus Christianorum. Series latina* 48:695).

Medieval and Later Scholasticism. Notwithstanding Augustine's patronage, the term society was slow to become one of the abstract collective names commonly used to designate the Church. Rather these were in large measure derived from the name *ecclesia,* which the Fathers and the scholastics explained etymologically as God's ''convocation'' of His people, with the ''congregation'' of the faithful resulting from God's calling (see St. Isidore of Seville, *De eccles. off.* 1.1.2; *Patrologia Latina* 83:739–740).

The following are examples of the continuing, though relatively minor, use of the term society. St. Thomas Aquinas, who uses the term rather infrequently, says that the grace of the Eucharist is ''the Mystical Body of Christ, which is the society of the saints'' (*Summa theologiae,* 3a, 80.4), thus intimately linking the society or communion of the saints with the Eucharistic Communion. In an Augustinian phrase St. Thomas calls the heavenly Church ''the well ordered society of those who enjoy the vision of God'' (*C. gent.* 4.50); it is St. Thomas's view that citizenship in the city of God ''will not be annulled in the future world but perfected'' (*In 3 sent.* 33.1.4). For a similar use of the term society with respect to the heavenly Church, (see *Summa theologiae,* 1a2ae, 4.8; *De carit.* 2; *De vit. spir.* 2; *In 1 Cor.* 10. *lect.* 5; *In 3 sent.* 19.5.1). In St. Thomas the concept society emphasizes the community of life, the interdependence (the *ordo ad invicem*) of those who share in the same common good (here the *ordo ad Deum*).

Among the controversialists St. Robert Bellarmine uses the term society only rarely (see *De eccl. mil.* 5, 12). It is interesting to note that Bellarmine employs the concept society as an argument for the VISIBILITY OF THE CHURCH. "The Church is a society, not of angels or of souls, but of men" (*De eccl. mil.* 12). Hence, as a society made up of men, it must be structured visibly, with visible criteria for membership, so that its members can know who their fellows are.

Modern Era. The importance that the term and concept society have in the ecclesiology of the last two centuries can be judged by examining their use in Church documents and also in the unofficial, though historically important, two schemata on the Church prepared for Vatican I.

Pius IX's *Syllabus errorum* (Dec. 8, 1864) stresses that the Church is "a true and perfect society, wholly free" (H. Denzinger, *Enchiridion symbolorum,* 2919). Since the *Syllabus* was to set the guidelines for the theological commission in working up the preliminary drafts for Vatican I (see J. D. Mansi, *Sacrorum Conciliorum nova et amplissima collectio,* 49:621), the theme of the Church as "a true and perfect society, wholly free," not unexpectedly had a prominent place in the first schema on the Church, and also, in a lesser degree, in the second schema.

The first schema (*ibid.* 51:539–553) uses the term and concept society as its main theme. The Church is portrayed as "the society of salvation" (ch. 8), "the society of life" (ch. 9), the unique repository of Christ's light and grace, wholly competent within its own resources to achieve its mission, and totally independent of any tutelage of the state. Hence it is "a true and perfect society" (ch. 3). Although a visible human society, it belongs to an order wholly transcending the purely natural level, because the indwelling Holy Spirit is the ground of its unity and life. As a society it is a sign to the nations, discernible from other religious groupings that challenge its unique mission. It is a society that requires a harmonious coexistence with the state.

The anti-Protestant orientation of this development is clear. Over against the traditional Protestant theme of the invisible, or hidden, church, the schema teaches that the Christian religion is not un-churched, but divinely incorporated in a true society, which is not optional but the one peremptory means of SALVATION for all men. In the face of a more recent development in Protestant ecclesiology, dating from the 18th century, in which many Protestant theologians and jurists, often under the spirit of the Enlightenment, and using categories taken from the philosophy of society, presented the empiric national church as a man-made institution and conceded the state a hegemony over this church, the schema reacts with like categories, drawn from the philosophy of society, proposing, however, entirely opposite doctrines on the nature of the Church as a society.

The second revised schema (*ibid.* 53:308–317) was drawn up by Joseph Kleutgen, SJ, to meet the criticisms that the Fathers had made of the first schema. Responsive to their wishes, Kleutgen greatly curtailed in frequency and emphasis the use of the term society. However, despite this deemphasis, "it has been judged wholly advantageous," Kleutgen wrote in his covering report on the revised schema, "to state in the constitution in so many words that the Church is a true and perfect society" (*ibid.* 53:318). Moreover, "it is not alien to the Church's language to call the Church a society," for St. Augustine himself "often" (*ibid.*) used the term of the Church.

Leo XIII, who was present at Vatican I, made repeated use of the theme society in several encyclicals dealing with the Church, both in itself and in its relation to the city of man. See, e.g., *SATIS COGNITUM*, June 29, 1896 [*Acta Sanctae Sedis,* 28 (1895–96) 724–725; see H. DENZINGER, *Enchiridion symbolorum* 31 1959]. It is to be noted that the pope strongly emphasized the supernatural life of the Church as a society, and grounded its social life primarily in the "life of Jesus Christ [which] . . . nurtures and sustains each member, keeps them joined together and directed to the same end, amid all the variety of action of the single members" [*Sapientiae christianae,* Jan. 10, 1890; *Acta Sanctae Sedis,* 22 (1889–90) 392].

The social theme is worked through the whole of Pius XII's encyclical *MYSTICI CORPORIS* (June 29, 1943). Phrases such as "social body," "social members," "social activity," and "society" occur with notable frequency. The following points of the encyclical deserve mention:

1. All social members of the Body "ought to serve in common Christ and His saving work" (i.e., the application of Christ's merits to men through the Church), "all 'who are saved and who save from One and through One'" (par. 57). In other words, the whole Church, acting jointly, is *mater ecclesia* (12, 43, 86).

2. In this work "the divine Savior with His social Body constitutes only one mystical person . . . the whole Christ" (67, cf. 78).

3. This common work and service is due primarily to an inward principle, "the divine Spirit who . . . fills and unites the whole Church" (60, cf. 68–69).

4. There is no radical dissociation, or even any uneasy precarious alliance, between a "society nurtured and formed by love," and a "juridic society"; on the contrary these two aspects "mutually complement and perfect each other" (63).

For the Church as a society of worship, see Pius XII, *MEDIATOR DEI* [Nov. 20, 1947, *Acta Apostolicae Sedis,* 39 (1947) 538; *Enchiridion symbolorum,* 3841].

Conclusion. Vatican II's *Lumen Gentium* expressed an ecumenical position that emphasized simultaneously the visible and invisible dimensions of the Church: "the society equipped with hierarchical structures and the mystical body of Christ, the visible society and the spiritual community, the earthly church and the church endowed with heavenly riches, are not to be thought of as two realities. On the contrary, they form one complex reality comprising a human and a divine element" (8). The tendency to highlight one of these dimensions over the other underlies much contemporary ecclesiological debate. On the one hand lies the danger of reducing the Church to a merely psychological or sociological reality by underemphasizing its mystical and transcendent dimensions. On the other hand lies the danger of ignoring the historical and social dimensions of the Church in favor of a mystified or overly idealized view.

The Church considered as a society is like other societies in that it has certain structures and laws; unlike most other societies, however, its essential structures are believed to be of divine origin. Although the Church is to be distinguished from the kingdom of God in its fullness, *Lumen Gentium* says that "the church . . . is, on earth, the seed and the beginning of that kingdom" (5). *Gaudium et Spes* describes the role of the Church in the world, "to be a leaven, and, as it were, the soul of human society in its renewal by Christ and its transformation into the family of God" (40).

See Also: MYSTICAL BODY OF CHRIST; SOUL OF THE CHURCH; CHURCH, ARTICLES ON.

Bibliography: N. MONZEL, *Struktursoziologie und Kirchenbegriff* (Bonn 1939). T. GEPPERT, *Teleologie der menschlichen Gemeinschaft* (Münster 1955). A. RADEMACHER, *Die Kirche als Gemeinschaft und Gesellschaft* (Augsburg 1931). Y. CONGAR, "Peut-on définir l'Église?" *Sainte Église* (Paris 1963) 21–44. U. VALESKE, "Die Kirche als Gemeinschaft und als Gesellschaft," *Votum Ecclesiae* (Munich 1962) 115–127. D. M. DOYLE, "Henri de Lubac and the Roots of Communion Ecclesiology," *Theological Studies* 60:209–227. J. A. KOMONCHAK, "Ecclesiology and Social Theory: A Methodological Essay," *The Thomist* 45:262–283.

[F. X. LAWLOR/D. M. DOYLE]

SOCIETY (THEOLOGY OF)

In the Constitution on the Church in the Modern World Vatican Council II outlined some general principles for a theology of society. They concerned the social nature of man, the interrelationship between individual and community and between the primacy of the person and a notion of the common good as "the sum total of social conditions which allow people, either as groups or as individuals, to reach their fulfilment more fully and more easily" (*Gaudium et spes* 25–26).

Resources: The Social Sciences. For these very general observations to become the subject of a systematic reflection on society, theologians must make use of the resources and conclusions of the social sciences. They will, first of all, have to take account of the almost bewildering variety which empirical research has discovered in social relationships and orders both across generations and across cultures. Secondly, they will have to reflect on what might be called "the dialectic of social existence," by which the very societies which men have produced themselves become the producers of men.

The latter interest will first see societies as human products, produced and constituted by shared meanings and values. Social relationships and orders are the effects of exercises of human intelligence and freedom, and not the inevitable products of a preconscious "human nature" nor of a cosmic or merely "natural" order.

Such social orders have their own "objectivity." They confront the individual born or reared within them with a massive inertial force. The "real world" into which he is introduced is the world as it has been shaped and interpreted by earlier generations and his own possibilities for self-realization are limited by the resources of his society and its communities. It is their language through which the world is mediated to him and which moulds and orients his own consciousness. It is their taken-for-granted stock of knowledge which constitutes the largest part of what he comes to "know." It is in terms of their roles and institutions and in pursuit of the values they honor that he learns to orient his freedom. In all these ways, the individual is a social product; the self is socially mediated.

Society: Theological Object. So understood, the social order itself becomes an object of theological investigation and evaluation. The society, policy, economy are not premoral givens within which individuals privately live, and the Christian message does not concern only their privatized lives. The social order is another of the ambiguous works of man, and its moulding and orienting influence on those born and reared within it is no less ambiguous. The Gospel does not address individuals in the abstract, but only the persons who exist, all of whom are social products. Thus, for example, contemporary theologians speak of "sinful social structures" or of "social sin" to describe the larger context of evil to which the Gospel must be addressed, and seek to explain how the "reign of sin" shows itself there as well as in the minds and hearts of individuals.

Such reflections lead easily enough into a POLITICAL THEOLOGY. This is not simply a ''theology of politics,'' but an attempt to rethink the Christian message in terms of the fundamental and even constitutive role which societies play in the development of individuals. The search for meaning and value, which defines man, is seen to be a ''political'' enterprise, first in the sense that this search, like every other human endeavor, is inescapably marked by the social conditions under which it is undertaken, and, secondly, in the sense that the discovery of the revealed meanings and values of the Gospel has immediate political and social implications.

A critical theology of society, then, must (1) start from the social matrix of individual existence; (2) critically explore the relationship between that essential freedom which the Church has always defended as ''free will'' and its effective realization in concrete individuals; (3) interpret the meaning of the Gospel and the role of the Church in the light of the social dialectic; (4) elaborate effective hermeneutical principles by which the Gospel may be made to evaluate social orders; and (5) learn how to collaborate with the social sciences in bringing the Gospel's redemptive truth and power to bear upon concrete social orders and situations.

Bibliography: P. BERGER and T. LUCKMANN. *The Social Construction of Reality* (New York 1980). J. GREMILLION, *The Gospel of Peace and Justice: Catholic Social Teaching since Pope John* (Maryknoll, NY 1976). G. GUTIERREZ, *A Theology of Liberation: History, Politics and Salvation,* tr. C. INDA and J. EAGLESON (Maryknoll, NY 1973). B. LONERGAN, *Method in Theology* (New York 1972). J. B. METZ, tr., W. GLEN-DOEPEL, *A Theology of the World* (New York 1969).

[J. A. KOMONCHAK]

SOCIETY FOR PROMOTING CHRISTIAN KNOWLEDGE (SPCK)

The oldest Anglican mission society, SPCK was founded in 1698 by Rev. Thomas Bray and four lay supporters, ''to promote and encourage the erection of charity schools in all parts of England and Wales; to dispense, both at home and abroad, Bibles and tracts of religion; and in general to advance the honour of God and the good of mankind, by promoting Christian knowledge both at home and in the other parts of the world by the best methods that should offer.'' An appeal from Maryland for help in the colony's ecclesiastical organization made Henry Compton, Bishop of London, choose Bray as his commissary. Bray sought missionaries to join him and worked out a scheme for free libraries in Maryland. The support he received made him try out the library scheme in England with success. This and other educational and literary projects led to the foundation of the SPCK. After long legal delays, Bray set sail for Maryland, arriving in March 1700. Though well received, he returned almost immediately, convinced he could serve the Maryland church better from England. Finding that the SPCK had developed rapidly, Bray founded the SOCIETY FOR THE PROPAGATION OF THE GOSPEL (1701) for the foreign missions. This and the National Society for the Education of the Poor in the Principles of the Established Church (1811) have since shared the work of the SPCK, but the latter has set up Church of England schools and teachers' training colleges both at home and abroad. The SPCK is best known now for its publications on theological and other subjects. It holds the distinction of being the third oldest publishing house in England, after Oxford and Cambridge.

Bibliography: W. O. B. ALLEN and E. MACCLURE, *Two Hundred Years: The History of the Society for Promoting Christian Knowledge, 1698–1898* (London 1898). W. K. L. CLARKE, *A Short History of S. P. C. K.* (London 1919). M. CLEMENT, *The S.P.C.K. and Wales, 1699–1740* (London 1954). W.A. BULTMANN and P.W. BULTMANN, ''The Roots of Anglican Humanitarianism : A Study of the Membership of the SPCK and the SPG, 1699–1720,'' *Historical Magazine of the Protestant Episcopal Church* 33 (Mar 1964) 3–48. M.A.C. WARREN, ''The Missionary Expansion of Ecclesia Anglicana,'' in *New Testament Christianity for Africa and the World* (London 1974) 124–140. C. ROSE, ''The Origins and Ideals of the SPCK 1699–1716,'' in *The Church of England c. 1689–c. 1833* (Cambridge 1993) 172–190. P.J. POSAN, ''The Society for Promoting Christian Knowledge: Past, Present, and Future,'' *American Theological Library Association: Summary of Proceedings* 52 (1998) 247–254.

[G. ALBION/EDS.]

SOCIETY FOR THE PROPAGATION OF THE GOSPEL

More commonly known as the SPG. This society (full title, Society for the Propagation of the Gospel in Foreign Parts) was founded under royal English charter in June 1701 as the official overseas missionary body of the Church of England. Its leading promoter was Rev. Thomas Bray (1656–1730), also one of the founders of the SOCIETY FOR PROMOTING CHRISTIAN KNOWLEDGE (SPCK), who had been Ecclesiastical Commissary for Maryland in 1699–1700. The impulse for the SPG's organization came from a belated but nonetheless fervent Anglican recognition of the need to carry the Christian Gospel beyond England. In this sense it was a part of the great worldwide Christian revolution, which eventuated in the emergence of Christianity as a genuine universal faith during the following 200 years. According to the terms of its charter the SPG was incorporated for the purposes of (1) ''providing a maintenance for an orthodox

Clergy in the plantations, colonies, and factories of Great Britain beyond the seas, for the instruction of the King's loving subjects in the Christian religion''; (2) ''making such other provisions as may be necessary for the propagation of the Gospel in those parts;'' and (3) ''receiving, managing, and disposing of the charity of His Majesty's subjects for those purposes.'' During most of the 18th century the Society's activities were confined to the British colonies of North America where it was active not only among European colonists but undertook the conversion of Black slaves and Native Americans. Prevented by the terms of its charter from continuing in the United States after the American Revolution, the SPG shifted its activity, first, to Canada and, after 1823, to non-Christian regions of Asia and Africa. On the whole, the SPG tended to develop the community type of mission and usually carried on its activities under the direct superintendence of the diocesan bishop in the mission field. Its close identification with Anglo-Catholicism during much of its history and the founding by the Anglican evangelicals of the Church Missionary Society in 1799 somewhat limited the Society's activities. Nevertheless, during the course of the 19th century it spread extensively into South Africa (1821), Bengal and South India (1823), Borneo (1848), Pacific Islands (1862), North China (1863), Japan (1873), Korea (1899), Manchuria (1892), and Siam (1903). Its greatest mission successes were won in India where it still has great influence. The 20th century has witnessed some diminution of the Society's activities as the former holdings of the British Empire have contracted. Even so, it continues to play an active and effective role as a mission agency in the British Commonwealth.

Bibliography: H. P. THOMPSON, *Into All Lands* (London 1951). C. F. PASCOE, *Two Hundred Years of the S.P.G., 1701–1900* (London 1901). R. P. S. WADDY, ''250 Years of *Patrologia Graeca*,'' *International Review of Mission* 40 (1951) 331–336. B. C. ROBERTS, ''SPG: How It Works,'' *Church Quarterly Review* 157 (1956) 136–143. W. A. BULTMANN and P. W. BULTMANN, ''The Roots of Anglican Humanitarianism: A Study of the Membership of the SPCK and the SPG, 1699-1720,'' *Historical Magazine of the Protestant Episcopal Church* 33 (Mar 1964) 3–48. G. J. GOODWIN, ''Christianity, Civilization and the Savage: The Anglican Mission to the American Indian,'' *Historical Magazine of the Protestant Episcopal Church* 42 (June 1973) 93–110. M. A. C. WARREN, ''The Missionary Expansion of Ecclesia Anglicana,'' in *New Testament Christianity for Africa and the World* (London 1974) 124–140. B. HOUGH, ''Archives of the Society for the Propagation of the Gospel,'' *Historical Magazine of the Protestant Episcopal Church* 46 (1977) 309-322. R. H. S. BOYD, ''The *Patrologia Graeca* in Ahmedabad: 1830–1851,'' *Indian Church History Review* 12 (June 1978) 54–66. A. K. DAVIDSON, ''Colonial Christianity: The Contribution of the Society for the Propagation of the Gospel to the Anglican Church in New Zealand 1840–1880,'' *Journal of Religious History* 16 (Dec. 1990) 173–184.

[S. BURRELL/EDS.]

SOCIETY OF CATHOLIC COLLEGE TEACHERS OF SACRED DOCTRINE

Founded in 1953 as a national association of Catholic university and college professors of theology whose main objective is the improvement of the teaching of sacred science as a liberal (that is, nonprofessional) study above the secondary or high school level. In 1967, the society adopted a new name, the COLLEGE THEOLOGY SOCIETY. This entry describes the history of the society from 1953–1967.

After much criticism in private circles, university workshops, and journals of the impoverished quality of religion courses then offered on Catholic campuses, this society began in 1953 as a constructive effort to remedy the situation. After preliminary meetings of small groups of teachers in Washington and Philadelphia, representatives of 47 eastern colleges meeting at Fordham University, New York City, Feb. 24, 1954, agreed on a provisional constitution.

The title chosen for the group (generally abbreviated to Sacred Doctrine Society) is self-explanatory. The word *doctrine* was chosen as being general enough to refer both to theology and the content of religion courses. At that time, a controversy was raging among college educators, dividing them into those who favored the academic learning of theology and those inclined to stress the pedagogical aspect of communicating religious truth. The Society was committed to be an open forum, uncommitted to either side of the controversy.

The ultimate purpose of the Society, according to its original constitution, was the assurance of a high academic level for its special discipline and assistance to professors for imparting solid and effective instruction in sacred science. This original intention was further explicated in more proximate aims that included: (1) the formulation of the proper and immediate aim and content of sacred doctrine curricula for Catholic colleges within the context of the total aim of Christian higher education; (2) the investigation of the suitability of sacred doctrine as a principle of interdisciplinary integration; (3) assistance in the development of programs genuinely intellectual in content and method, yet designed to take into account actual student needs and capacities; (4) discussion and evaluation of methods of teaching; (5) the encouragement of teacher preparation both in the graduate schools and in in-service training; (6) the providing of opportunity for meeting with experts in the various areas of the science; (7) serving as a forum for the communicating of pedagogical experience and information.

The accomplishment of these aims was attempted through a variety of means. For example, the quarterly newsletter, *Sacred Doctrine Notes* (originally called *Magister*), offered both member and nonmember subscribers news, discussion, book reviews, and bibliographies. The *Proceedings* of the annual national conventions proved to be a valuable source for expert theological articles.

While the membership was largely from the U.S., Canada had a substantial membership and even non-English-speaking countries had representatives. Membership was restricted to priests, religious, and Catholic laity who were qualified by training or teaching experience for the instruction of college students in theology. Although the society attempted to encourage attempts to better high school religion courses, its focus was consistently that of education leading to college degrees.

The national conventions, held Easter Monday and Tuesday, showed the development of the society, the status of theology in the college and of theology itself. The first convention (1955) was devoted to a study of proposed curricular plans, and used a society survey of curricula in use. A year later, the concern was with the finality of theology and the student; another year, the relation of theology to other disciplines. From 1958 to 1960 the topics became more technical, with increasing emphasis on scriptural study. The years following until the 10th anniversary presented special area studies in ecumenism, liturgy, and spiritual theology. Finally, in 1964, the convention, after visiting major American cities, returned to Washington for a realistic appraisal of present status and future needs. The society demonstrated its advancing maturity by its ability to formulate more specific resolutions on teacher preparation, on the equality of status for religious and secular subjects, on minimum time requirements, on implementation of Vatican Council II's decrees on renewal of church and theology.

For developments from 1967, see: COLLEGE THEOLOGY SOCIETY.

[U. VOLL/EDS.]

SOCINIANISM

An antitrinitarian movement on the margins of Protestantism. Three phases of thought are distinguished: (1) that of two members of a Sienese family of juris-consults, Laelius and Faustus Socinus (Sozzini); (2) that of the Socinianized Minor (Reformed) Church of Poland from 1579 to 1605; and (3) evangelical rationalism, especially after the suppression of the Minor Church in Poland in 1658.

Socinianism originated in Italy as an amalgam of Valdesian Erasmianism, Florentine Platonism, Paduan Aristotelianism, and Protestant Biblicism. In Poland it was augmented and altered by specifically Calvinist and Anabaptist ingredients. Diffused in Germany, Holland, and Great Britain, it showed affinities with 17th-century philosophy. In all three phases Socinianism was characterized by a rationalistic scriptural literalism (with a predilection for the New Testament) and by an acceptance of Jesus as the definitive revelation of God (*interpres divinae voluntatis*), but solely as a man, born of the Virgin, resurrected from the dead, in confirmation of his exemplary obedience, and deputed to rule as King, Priest, and Prophet over the world and the church. Socinianism espoused toleration for all. Mutually disciplined members looked forward, after the death of the soul with the body (mortalist heresy), to the final resurrection of the soul of the righteous only and of their investment with spiritual bodies to enjoy the immortality that was the reward of all who had persevered in observing all of Jesus' commandments ''through the power of the Spirit.''

Laelius and Faustus Socinus. Laelius Socinus, born in Siena in 1525, was a student and seeker, who established close contacts with P. Melanchthon, J. Calvin, and H. Bullinger, and also with the Rhaetian radical Camillo Renato. Suspected of heresy by Bullinger, Laelius was obliged to prepare an (ambiguous) Confession of Faith, one of the few extant documents from his hand. At death in 1562 in Zurich he left his library and papers to his nephew Faustus.

Faustus Socinus, born in Siena in 1539, became a student of logic and law, and a member of the local academy and of the court in Florence; he first clearly manifested his rejection of Catholicism in a letter of 1563, arguing against the unconditional IMMORTALITY of the soul. A major work followed on hermeneutics, *De auctoritate sacrae scripturae* (1570). His treatise on Christology and soteriology, *De Jesu Christo servatore* (1578), clarified his view that the ascended Christ, though not divine *by nature,* was divine *by office* and might therefore be properly addressed in prayer. At this time a faction under Franz DÁVID in the Unitarian Reformed Church in Transylvania had moved to the more extreme position of disallowing such prayer. The more moderate faction under Giorgio BLANDRATA invited Socinius to their side. On his journey thither he was persuaded to make Poland his permanent home.

The Socinianized Minor Church (1579–1658). In this second phase of development, the theology of Faustus was fused with that of the antecedent antitrinitarian and partly anabaptist Minor (Reformed) Church. Raków, the communitarian settlement and spiritual center northeast of Cracow, developed a *gymnasium bonarum artium* at one time attracting 1,000 students, and a publishing house turning out tracts and books in a score of languages. Faustus defended the Minor Church on the issues of war and political authority, although he declined on principle to become a communicant member because he refused to submit to the practice of believers' baptism (anabaptism) by immersion. Socinus was nevertheless co-commissioned to revise the *Catechesis* (1574) of Raków, published in Polish as the *Racovian Catechism* in 1605, a year after Socinus's death in Lucławice (German and Latin editions, 1609). Among the faculty of the academy and the pastorate of the synod that met annually in Raków the most prominent were Faustus's own grandson, Andreas Wiszowaty (d. 1678), Stanislas LUBIENIECKI, who wrote *Historia Reformationis Polonicae,* and converts from German Protestantism such as Christoph Ostorodt (d. 1611) and Johann Crell (d. 1631). The academy and press at Raków were suppressed in 1638; and in 1658 the Warsaw Sejm threatened Socinians with death if they would not become Catholic within three years.

Evangelical Rationalism. Socinians were established in the Netherlands and Germany well before the extinction of the Minor Church in Poland. Ernst Soner (d. 1612) made the University of Altdorf a center of diffusion. At Amsterdam the basic works of the movement were printed in 1688, as the *Bibliotheca Fratrum Polonorum* in eight volumes. Christoph Sand (d. 1680) compiled the *Bibliotheca Antitrinitariorum.* In England Socinian rationality, LATITUDINARIANISM, and mortalism variously appealed to Arminian prelates, to Oxford rationalists, to Cambridge Platonists, to scientist-theologians (such as Isaac Newton), and to the first *avowed* native Socinians: John BIDDLE ("the father of English Unitarianism") and Stephen Nye, whose *History of Unitarianism* commonly called *Socinianism* set off the Trinitarian Controversy in the Established Church of England in 1687.

Bibliography: L. CRISTIANI, *Dictionnaire de théologie catholique,* ed. A. VACANT, 15 v. (Paris 1903–50; Tables générales 1951–) 14.2:2326–34. B. STASIEWSKI, *Lexikon für Theologie und Kirche,* ed. J. HOFER and K. RAHNER, 10 v. (2d, new ed. Freiburg 1957–65) 9:928–931. E. M. WILBUR, *A History of Unitarianism* 2 v. (Cambridge, MA 1945–52). D. CANTIMORI, *Eretici Italiani del '500* (Florence 1939), German *Italienische Haeretiker der Spätrenaissance* (Basel 1948). L. CHMAJ, *Faust Socyn* (Warsaw 1963). S. KOT, *Socinianism in Poland,* tr. E. M. WILBUR (Boston 1957). W. J. KÜHLER, *Socinianisme in Nederland* (Leiden 1912). H. J. MCLACHLAN, *Socinianism in 17th Century England* (New York 1951). J. TEDESCHI, ed., *Italian Reformation Studies* (Florence 1965), esp. for genealogy of Sozzini family.

[G. H. WILLIAMS]

Faustus Socinus.

SOCRATES

Greek philosopher, teacher of PLATO; b. the son of a stonemason and a midwife, Athens, *c.* 469 B.C.; d. Athens, 399 B.C.

Life. Socrates's life spanned the great outburst of Athenian activity and culture triggered by the Greek victory over Persia (480–479) and ending in the long war of attrition with Sparta that brought Athens to ruin. He married, perhaps twice and rather late in life, leaving young sons when he died at the hands of the restored democracy, which found in him a scapegoat for Athenian failings during the recent war.

In early life he showed interest in the physical speculations of his time and is said to have associated with Archelaus, who was a close follower of ANAXAGORAS. Aristophanes's *Clouds* (423 B.C.) links him, in comic fashion, with the SOPHISTS and speculators on cosmology. In the *Phaedo* (97C), Plato represents him as pleased with the view of Anaxagoras that Mind arranges and is the cause of all things, but as disappointed with Anaxagoras's subsequent explanation of the universe through physical causes. Certainly at some time during his life, possibly around the outbreak of the Peloponnesian War, Socrates turned his attention almost exclusively to questions of human conduct and virtue. It was a change con-

Socrates, drinking hemlock.

sonant with the increased importance and responsibility of the individual under the new Athenian democracy and paralleled by the search for a systematic higher education that gave the Sophists their opportunity to practice as itinerant teachers. Socrates's ascetic habits, extreme self-control, and refusal to take fees, together with his great courage and striking appearance, gave personal weight to his emphasis on care of the soul and his quest for moral definition. He served with bravery at Potidaea (432), Delium (424), and Amphipolis (422); as one of the Council of Presidents he refused to sanction simultaneous trial of eight generals after Arginusae (406); and he disobeyed an order of the Thirty that would have involved him as an accomplice to murder (403).

Teaching. Sources for the teaching of Socrates are various. He wrote nothing himself, reckoning dialogue as far superior to the written word, but in Plato's *Apology* and in the early ''Socratic'' dialogues perhaps the historical Socrates is fairly substantially represented, although Plato allows himself considerable liberty in dramatic setting, casting, and literary embellishment. Another contemporary source is Xenophon, who gives a more matter-of-fact account of Socrates in his *Memorabilia, Apology,* and *Symposium.* Aristotle gives some assessments in the *Metaphysics* and *Nicomachean Ethics* that are confirmed in the *Magna Moralia,* and there is a life of Socrates in Diogenes Laertius.

Chaerephon, a lifelong friend of Socrates, is said to have asked the oracle of Apollo at Delphi whether anyone was wiser than Socrates and to have received a negative reply. To test the truth of the oracle, Socrates is represented (*Apol.* 21C–22E; Diog. Laert. 2.5.37) as constantly searching for persons of wisdom, but as disappointed in his quest, and hence concluding that he must be wiser than others because he knew himself to be ignorant, whereas they thought themselves wise and were not. Socrates is portrayed as a frequent visitor to the market place, where he was ready to converse with all comers in an attempt to turn their attention from externals to themselves and to the virtues of the soul. The typical procedure (e.g., *Charmides, Euthyphro, Meno, Mem.* 4.2.8–39) was for Socrates to lead on his acquaintance to make some assertion concerning a particular virtue or virtue in general, and then to question the accuracy of his observations. After several attempts at definition, the dialogue usually ends in indecision, but much has been accomplished. The person engaged in conversation has recognized his own lack of precision and mere assumption of knowledge where true knowledge was none. He leaves convicted of ignorance and perhaps stimulated to search further for a satisfactory answer. All the while, Socrates, with gentle irony, protests his own ignorance and his desire to learn from his interlocutor.

ARISTOTLE is insistent that Socrates considered virtue to be knowledge. In a sense, knowledge is the only good, ignorance the sole evil. There is no such thing as the problem of incontinence—i.e., knowing what is good, but failing to do it because of the lure of pleasure (*Eth. Nic.* 1145b 21–1146b 5). Socrates analyzes this so-called problem and pronounces it to be a failure in the correct estimate of the relative balance of pleasure and pain or of good and evil (*Prot.* 353–7). Aristotle summarizes the achievement of Socrates by ascribing to him inductive reasoning and the quest for universal definitions in matters of human conduct (*Meta.* 987b 1–4). Perhaps the wisdom of Socrates was truly a ''human'' wisdom (*Apol.* 20D).

Aristotle remarks that Socrates did not separate his universal definitions from particular things (*Meta.* 1078b 30, 1086b 3–5), and it is clear from the *Meno* (80D–81E) that Plato first puts forward the theory of preexistence and recollection in order to justify Socrates's confidence in inquiry and to save him from the horns of Meno's dilemma. The theory of Ideas is a development of Socrates's thought that must be ascribed to Plato.

Appreciation. Socrates was a religious man, who saw clearly the limits of human reason and the need to consult the gods in matters beyond the grasp of men (*Mem.* 1.1.4–9). He was accused of ''introducing strange deities'' only because of his constant reference to a spiritual warning that always stopped him from a proposed course of action but never positively encouraged him to act. It is clear that this was, in his view, something distinct from the mere voice of conscience, and Socrates was too rational a man to be given to hallucinations. Of personal immortality he was unsure. Death was either a dreamless sleep or a migration of the soul to another place where it would be immortal and happier than here (*Apol.* 40D–41C).

The CYNICS are connected with Socrates via Antisthenes, an admirer of his poverty and frugality (*Symp.* 4.34–44); the CYRENAICS through Aristippus, whom Xenophon portrays in discussion with Socrates on the question of pleasure (*Mem.* 2.1); and the Megarian school of eristic disputation through Euclides. But none of these minor schools can strictly be called Socratic in tradition.

See Also: GREEK PHILOSOPHY.

Bibliography: A. E. TAYLOR, *Varia Socratica* (Oxford 1911); *Socrates* (New York 1933). E. DUPRÉEL, *La Légende socratique et les sources de Platon* (Brussels 1922). A. K. ROGERS, *The Socratic Problem* (New Haven 1933). R. HACKFORTH, *The Composition of Plato's Apology* (Cambridge, Eng. 1933). A. D. WINSPEAR and T. SILVERBERG, *Who Was Socrates?* (New York 1939). V. DE MAGALHÃES-VILHENA, *Le Problème de Socrate* (Paris 1952). A. H. CHROUST, *Socrates, Man and Myth* (London 1957). G. FAGGIN, *Enciclopedia filosofica* 4:742–749. F. UEBERWEG, *Grundriss der Geschichte der Philosophie*, ed. K. PRAECHTER et al. 1:129–158. *Paulys Realenzyklopädie der klassischen Altertumswissenschaft*, ed. G. WISSOWA et al. 3A.1 (1927) 804–893. F. C. COPLESTON, *History of Philosophy* (Westminster, Md.) 1:96–115.

[W. H. O'NEILL]

SOCRATES, BYZANTINE HISTORIAN

Byzantine Church historian; b. Constantinople, *c.* 380; d. *c.* 450. Socrates, known also as Socrates Scholasticus, was educated by the pagan grammarians Helladius and Ammonius; he became a lawyer in Constantinople and is the first known layman in the field of ecclesiastical historiography. At the request of Theodore, identified only as ''a sacred man of God,'' he continued Eusebius's *Historia ecclesiastica* in seven books beginning with the year 305 and ending with 439. Each book covers the reign of an emperor and takes into account secular history and events in Constantinople, as well as matters of purely ecclesiastical interest.

Socrates's *Historia ecclesiastica* has been preserved in a second edition. It uses as its sources EUSEBIUS OF CAESAREA; the treatises and letters of St. ATHANASIUS, GREGORY OF NAZIANZUS, RUFINUS OF AQUILEIA; conciliar acts collected by the Macedonian Sabinus of Heraclea; lists of bishops; and letters of prelates and emperors. The first edition of the first two books (only fragments in an Armenian translation survive) was drastically revised when the inaccuracies of Rufinus were detected.

Socrates's work is particularly valuable because of verbatim quotation of sources. His *Historia ecclesiastica,* completely extant, is an objective account, uninvolved in theological controversy, nonpartisan and fair in its treatment of heresies (especially the Novatianists, *see* NOVATIAN AND NOVATIANISM), yet in full accord with orthodox teaching. The work of Socrates was the chief source for his younger contemporary SOZOMEN, for THEODORE LECTOR of the early 6th century, and for the Epiphanius-Cassiodorus *Historia tripartita* of the later 6th century.

Bibliography: J. QUASTEN, *Patrology* 3:532–534. R. HANSLIK, *Die Religion in Geschichte und Gegenwart*[3] 6:127–128. L. SZYMANSKI, *The Translation Procedure of Epiphanius-Cassiodorus in the ''Historia Tripartita''* (Washington 1963). *Handbuch der Kirchengeschichte* 1:22. *The Armenian Adaptation of the Ecclesiastical History of Socrates Scholasticus*, tr. R. W. THOMSON (Sterling, VA 2001).

[H. DRESSLER]

SODALITIES OF OUR LADY, NATIONAL FEDERATION OF

The National Federation of Sodalities of Our Lady in the U.S. was erected by the bishops of the U.S. at the annual meeting of the National Catholic Welfare Conference (NCWC), November 1956, in response to the expressed wish of Pius XII. At the time thousands of sodalities in the U.S., canonically erected and affiliated with the Prima Primaria Sodality in Rome, were serving the Church under their local ordinaries. In approving the national federation, the American hierarchy wished to provide a structure that would unify these singular and individual sodalities, represent them on national and international levels, and enable them to cooperate in approved work of other organizations.

First Sodality. The first Sodality of Our Lady was established in Rome in 1563 by Father John Leunis, SJ, for students attending the Roman College. In its initial years, this organization for men developed and practiced the distinctive marks of sodality life that have been perpetuated through the centuries. Thereafter, for 400 years, the sodality, proposing a Christian way of life through a well-defined program of spiritual formation, tried to implement and unify the sacramental nature of the Christian at prayer and the Christian in action. Its characteristic mark has been service of the Church under the patronage of Our Lady and the direction of the hierarchy.

After the erection of the first sodality, similar groups were formed in other Jesuit institutions in Europe. In 1584 Gregory XIII canonically erected the Annunciation Sodality at the Roman College as the Prima Primaria Sodality and empowered it to affiliate other sodalities willing to adhere to the rules approved by the Holy See. Women were admitted as sodalists in 1751.

The Sodality in the Americas. The first sodality in the New World was founded in 1574 at the Colegio Maximo in Mexico City. In March 1739, Clement XII issued a papal bull approving the sodality founded in 1730 at the Ursuline school in New Orleans, Louisiana. The first sodality within the geographical area of the U.S. after its emergence as a new nation, was at Georgetown University in Washington, D.C. This sodality was affiliated with the Prima Primaria in 1833, but had been established and functioning since shortly after the founding of the college in 1789.

During the latter part of the 19th century and the first few decades of the 20th century, the Sodality of Our Lady was widely used in the U.S. by pastors as a basic parish organization for women and young girls. These sodalities developed during the era when the Church was stressing monthly corporate Mass and Communion for the laity. Although a monthly meeting provided for some spiritual and apostolic development of the members, many of the groups lost sight of the nature and purpose of sodalities as defined in the common rules.

In 1910, when the common rules of sodalities were revised, there was need to promulgate them. In 1913, the general of the Society of Jesus asked Jesuits in various countries to begin publication of sodality magazines for their nations. In the U.S. the task was committed to the Missouri province. Under the guidance of Rev. Edward F. Garesché, SJ, the *Queen's Work* was launched to encourage directors and sodalists to honor the Queen of Sodalities through fidelity to the common rules of the sodality.

Aware of the need to meet sodalists personally, Garesché held meetings and conventions across the country. In many localities he was successful in organizing diocesan unions of sodalities, and he appealed to the bishops to appoint diocesan sodality directors.

In 1925 Daniel A. Lord, SJ, who as a Jesuit scholastic had worked with Garesché, was assigned to succeed him as editor of the sodality periodicals. For more than a quarter of a century, Father Lord exercised an important influence on the development and promotion of sodalities. In 1929 he organized the National Parish Sodality Advisory Board, composed of lay sodalists from many dioceses. While this board served in an advisory capacity, it was a formative step toward national sodality unity, and its effectiveness led to the establishment of a national advisory board for high school sodalists. In 1931, in response to the official call to Catholic Action issued by Pius XI, Lord instituted the Summer Schools of Catholic Action (SSCA). These were originally designed for leaders of sodalities so they could assume their rightful responsibility in the apostolic programs of their bishops.

From 1913 to 1963 the Jesuits and laity of the *Queen's Work*, St. Louis, Missouri, promoted sodalities through publications and in national and local training sessions. Gradually, more bishops gave approval for the establishment of diocesan federations of sodalities and appointed diocesan sodality directors. In 1939 the diocesan directors, with the help of the sodality promoters at the *Queen's Work*, began to meet annually. These informal meetings resulted in the formation in 1956 of the National Diocesan Sodality Directors Conference. Rev. Erwin A. Juraschek of San Antonio, Texas, was elected the first president.

U.S. Federation. On July 2, 1953, Pius XII juridically established the World Federation of Sodalities whose general aim was to assure union of sodalities everywhere and more effective cooperation in the lay apostolate throughout the world. One of the approved means for doing this was the establishment of national federations of sodalities. Under the World Federation of Sodalities, the first World Sodality Congress was held in Rome in 1954. In November 1956, the American bishops in their annual meeting approved the National Federation of Sodalities and named Cardinal Joseph Ritter (then Archbishop) of St. Louis as episcopal moderator and Bp. Leo. C. Byrne of St. Paul, Minn. as executive episcopal moderator.

The first convention of the U.S. federation was held in St. Louis in January 1957, with 17 diocesan federations or unions present. Robert Graffy, a Cleveland, Ohio, businessman was elected president, and seven lay sodalists formed the executive council, with Juraschek as national director. In 1959, the National Federation of Sodalities (NFS) was host to the second World Sodality Congress in Newark, New Jersey. An American sodalist from New York, Mary I. DiFonzo, was elected secretary of the World Federation. The need for stronger unity in the national federation demanded that it embrace sodalities of all kinds and classes, as well as all directors and all movements.

This next organizational step was undertaken by a committee of lay sodalists and directors under the leadership of Bishop Byrne. A new constitution was adopted at the fourth biennial convention held in Cleveland, October 1963, which transformed the NFS into an organism representative of all parts of the sodality movement. Three councils within the framework of the NFS include one representative of all sodalities, whether or not these are organized into diocesan federations; another for the bishops' representatives and diocesan directors; and a third representative of all directors and moderators of sodalities, whether they be clergy, religious, or lay.

In the organizational structure of the NFS the president of the council of lay sodalists was, ex officio, the president of the federation. Major responsibility was placed in the hands of the laity who constitute a majority of the executive council. The council of lay sodalists, within the NFS, reflected the results of the apostolic constitutio *Bis saeculari,* issued by Pius XII in 1948. The challenge of the social apostolate emphasized in *Bis saeculari* brought new depth and vitality to existing adult sodalities, and influenced the establishment of many sodalities for professional adults, such as teachers, lawyers, doctors, and business people. Through the apostolic spirituality of the common rules and the *Bis saeculari* of Pius XII, the NFS also guided the laity to the mature Christian thought and action enjoined on them by Vatican Council II.

In 1971 Pope Paul VI promulgated revised norms for the organization and changed the name for sodalities of Our Lady to Christian Life Communities.

Bibliography: Archives, National Sodality Service Center, St. Louis, Mo. E. VILLARET, *Abridged History of the Sodality of Our Lady,* tr. W. J. YOUNG (St. Louis 1957). B. WOLFF, *The Sodality Movement in the United States, 1926–36* (St. Louis 1939) W. B. FAHERTY, "A Half-Century with the *Queen's Work,*" *Woodstock Letters* 92:2 (April 1963) 99–114.

[A. J. CONLEY/EDS.]

SODALITIUM PIANUM

Sodalitium pianum, or the Sodality of St. Pius V, known also as *Sapinière,* was a more or less secret Catholic society or federation of secret societies founded by Umberto BENIGNI in 1909, to implement the condemnations of PIUS X against Modernism. It turned out to be a chief instrument of INTEGRALISM, one of whose leaders was Benigni. On three occasions (July 5, 1911, July 8, 1912, and July 6, 1914) Pius X (1903–14) endorsed *Sapinière's* generic aims, but the pope never gave a formal, definitive approval. The Sodalitium's activities were supposedly known to higher ecclesiastical authorities; but the clandestine nature of this work has left the movement's history very imperfectly known, even to the present. In its anti-Modernistic zeal the Sodalitium raised suspicions concerning the orthodoxy of several reputable Catholic scriptural scholars, theologians, philosophers, and ecclesiastical historians. These condemnatory judgments were published in *La Correspondenza* and *Agence internationale de Rome,* newsletters founded by Benigni in 1909 and 1912 and copied by European Catholic newspapers. Opponents of Catholic Liberalism and Christian Democracy also used *Sapinière* as a rallying point.

After Pius X's death, the organization disbanded for a year, and then revived despite the warning of BENEDICT XV (1914–22) against restricting free discussion within the Church (Nov. 1, 1914). During World War I the German occupation troops in Ghent, Belgium, seized documents revelatory of *Sapinière's* work. These were transmitted to the Holy See (1921) and were largely instrumental in the suppression of the *Sodalitium* (November 1921) by the cardinal prefect of the Congregation of the Council, who acted seemingly at the Pope's urging. The sole public explanation was that the organization had served its purpose and was no longer needed. Some French leaders of the Sodalitium were believed to have joined ACTION FRANÇAISE.

The investigation by the Congregation of Rites preceding Pius X's beatification delved into the Sodalitium's activities. The results were published in the historical

Disquisitio which supplies a fairly detailed history of the Sodalitium.

Bibliography: F. ANTONELLI and G. LÖW, *Disquisitio circa quasdam objectiones modum agendi servi Dei Pii X respicientes in modernismi debellatione cum summario additionali ex officio compilato* (Vatican City 1950). O. WEISS, *Modernismus und Antimodernismus im Dominikanerorden: zugleich ein Beitrag zum "Sodalitium pianum"* (Regensburg, Germany 1998).

[G. J. O'BRIEN/EDS.]

SODEPAX

SODEPAX is the acronym for *Société, Développement, Paix*. SODEPAX was established as the Committee on Society, Development and Peace of the Programme Unit *Justice and Service* of the World Council of Churches (WCC) and the Pontifical Commission *Justice and Peace* of the Holy See, its official parent bodies. SODEPAX was a liaison body whose task was to promote development, justice, and peace by means of study and reflection programs. Based on the social thinking and teachings of the WCC, these programs were for ecumenical use in the Churches and were developed in close conjunction with the WCC and the Catholic Church. In this way, SODEPAX was intended to be a significant ecumenical instrument of the WCC's and the Catholic Church's common witness to Christian concern for development, justice, and peace in the world.

SODEPAX was established on an experimental basis in 1968, in the spirit of Vatican Council II and the WCC's Geneva Conference on Church and Society (1966). Its offices were located in the Ecumenical Centre in Geneva. By agreement, the General Secretary was a Catholic, the Associate General Secretary a Protestant. In its first phase, 1968–71, SODEPAX organized a number of large international conferences on development and peace, in addition to sponsoring many regional meetings and organizing national chapters in several countries. Its second mandate, 1972–75, was notable for activity in the Far East on development and an important conference which brought together Protestant and Catholic representatives from Northern Ireland to discuss avenues to peace. The third mandate of SODEPAX, 1976–78, saw the launching of an ecumenical program entitled *In Search of a New Society: Christian Participation in the Building of New Relations among Peoples*. From 1973 onward, SODEPAX published a journal of documentation, news and articles, in French and English, called *Church Alert*.

In addition to its program function of reaching out to the Churches and the world, SODEPAX carried on a continuous liaison function between its parent bodies, seeking to draw them closer together in both reflection and action. It kept in close touch with the Secretariat for the Promotion of Christian Unity and the JOINT WORKING GROUP of the World Council of Churches and the Roman Catholic Church, while acting as a kind of ecumenical and social conscience for the Churches, and especially its parent bodies. Perhaps most important of all, it attempted, despite its slim resources, to be the effective symbol of the Churches' commitment to unity and to the Christian service of humanity.

In the late 1970s, SODEPAX was caught in the dilemma of being regarded as a "third entity" that overshadowed its sponsoring institutions, the WCC and the Vatican. Under considerable pressure, it reduced its operations, and in 1980 its experimental mandate was terminated.

Bibliography: H. A. JACK, "SODEPAX Program: Guidelines for Peace and Christian Action," *Christian Century,* 87 (1970) 675–677. H. A. JACK, "SODEPAX as a Thriving Union," *Christian Century,* 87 (1970) 709–710. G. H. DUNNE, "Principes et activités de Sodepax," in *Oecumenisme en mission,* eds. J. KEMPENEERS, J. MASSON, and G. H. DUNNE (Paris 1970) 23–39. J. J. SPAE, "SODEPAX: An Ecumenical and Experimental Approach to World Needs," *Ecumenical Review,* 26 (1974) 88–99. L. J. NIILUS, "Efforts for Human Rights of the World Council of Churches and of SODEPAX," *The Church and the Rights of Man* (*Concilium 124*) (New York 1979) 86–91. "Some Lessons from the Ending of SODEPAX," *African Ecclesiastical Review,* 23 (1981) 258–259. P. LAND, "SODEPAX: An Ecumenical Dialogue," *Ecumenical Review,* 37 (1985) 40–46.

[J. LUCAL/EDS.]

SÖDERBLOM, NATHAN

Lutheran archbishop, historian of religion, theologian, leader in the ECUMENICAL MOVEMENT, principal promoter of the LIFE AND WORK movement; b. Trönö, Sweden, Jan. 1, 1866; d. Uppsala, July 12, 1931. Son of a Pietist pastor, he was ordained a Lutheran minister (1893), and served as pastor of the Swedish congregation in Paris from 1894 until he received his doctorate from the Sorbonne (1901), where he specialized in the study of comparative religion, especially Persian religion. From 1901 to 1914 he was professor of the history of religions at the University of Uppsala and also at Leipzig University (1912–14). From 1914 to 1931 he was archbishop of Uppsala and primate of the Church of Sweden. His engaging personality won him a very wide circle of international friendships, also among Catholics, whose liturgy and piety appealed to him, although he was sharply critical of the "Roman system." As a theologian he was much influenced by Louis SABATIER, RITSCHL, and other Liberal Protestants and to some extent by proponents of Modernism, such as LOISY, TYRRELL, and Von HÜGEL. His ability, industry, and outstanding oratorical qualities made him the leading force in the Swedish Church and in European Protestantism, despite conservative opposition. His intervention in behalf of war prisoners and displaced persons during World War I and his advocacy of peace won him the Nobel peace prize (1930).

Söderblom's interest in Christian reunion began during his student years and increased during a visit to the U.S. (1890) and journeys elsewhere. He sought the cooperation of all Christian denominations in solving social problems and in serving society without consideration of doctrinal differences. Largely because of him the Universal Christian Council on Life and Work came into being. This movement formed one of the two main streams that in 1948 merged in the WORLD COUNCIL OF CHURCHES.

Söderblom's numerous writings, few of which have been translated into English, include *La Vie future d'après Mazdéisme* (1901), *Humor och Melankoli* (a study of Luther, 1919), and *Einigung der Christenheit* (1938). His translated books include *The Nature of Revelation* (1933), *Christian Fellowship* (1923), and *The Living God* (1933).

Bibliography: N. KARLSTRÖM, ed., *N. Söderblom in memoriam* (Stockholm 1931), with bibliog. P. KATZ, *Nathan Söderblom: Ein Führer zur kirchlichen Einheit* (Halle 1925). T. ANDRAE, *Nathan Söderblom* (Berlin 1938), originally pub. in Swed. R. ROUSE and S. C. NEILL, eds., *A History of the Ecumenical Movement, 1517–1948* (London 1954).

[S. J. MILLER]

Nathan Söderblom (r).

SODOR AND MAN, ANCIENT SEE OF

The Ancient See of Sodor and Man is a bishopric formed by the union of the two old Celtic dioceses of the Isles, or Sudreys (Latin, *Sodor;* Norse, *Suðreyjar,* the Southern Isles, as distinct from the northern isles of Orkney, Shetland, and the Faroes), and Man, both of which had been disorganized by the Scandinavian invasions of the 8th and 9th centuries. Its foundation date is uncertain, but it occurred after the conquest of both the Isles and Man by Magnus III of Norway about 1098, and before Eugene III placed it under the jurisdiction of the Archdiocese of Trondheim (Norway) in 1152. Its seat was established at Peel on the Isle of Man, St. German's cathedral being built on the site of an earlier church associated with St. German, the disciple of St. Patrick, who is said to have first brought Christianity to Man. The political hegemony that the early Manx kings exerted over this whole archipelago of islands lying between northeast Ireland, southwest Scotland and northwest England, however, led them and their Norwegian overlords into conflict with the kings of England and Scotland, and on July 2, 1266, Magnus IV of Norway was forced to cede Man (but not the Southern Isles) to Alexander III of Scotland. Later (1334) Man passed into English hands. These changes in political loyalties are reflected not only in the number of Norwegian, Scottish, and English bishops appointed to the see, but also in the fact that, when under Scottish control, it reverted to its old title of "The Isles," and its bishops rejected the metropolitan claims of YORK upon them. The matter was settled on July 11, 1458, when Callistus III transferred the see from the jurisdiction of Trondheim to that of York, a decision that was confirmed later by Henry VIII in 1542. The CISTERCIANS had an abbey at Rushen (colonized from Furness), Cistercian nuns lived at Douglas, and Franciscan friars were at Becmachen. These houses were dissolved at the time of the Reformation, when St. German's cathedral was abandoned to ruin. The Church of England, however, retained the bishopric with its title of Sodor and Man, although today it includes only the Isle of Man.

Bibliography: *Chronica regum Manniae et insularum. The Chronicle of Man and the Sudreys,* ed. P. A. MUNCH and A. GOSS,

2 v. (Douglas, Isle of Man 1874). W. HARRISON, *An Account of the Diocese of Sodor and Man. . .* (Douglas 1879). W. CUBBON, *A Bibliographical Account of Works Relating to the Isle of Man,* 2 v. (London 1933–39); *Island Heritage* (Manchester 1952). R. H. KINVIG, *A History of the Isle of Man* (2d ed. Liverpool 1950). D. KNOWLES and R. N. HADCOCK, *Medieval Religious Houses: England and Wales* (New York 1953), map appendices. F. M. POWICKE and E. B. FRYDE, eds., *Handbook of British Chronology* (2d ed. London 1961) 254–256. A.W. MOORE, *Sodor and Man* (London 1893). A. ASHLEY, *The Church in the Isle of Man* (London 1958).

[L. MACFARLANE/EDS.]

SOGLIA CERONI, GIOVANNI

Cardinal, secretary of state; b. Casola Valsenio near Imola (Bologna), Italy, Oct. 11, 1779; d. Osimo (Ancona), Aug. 12, 1856. He became secretary of the Congregation of Studies early, and as a member of the papal household of PIUS VII was imprisoned at Fenestrelle when that pontiff was dispossessed by Napoleon. He also followed Pius VII to Savona. Leo XII made him titular archbishop of Ephesus and privy almoner. Gregory XVI made him Latin patriarch of Constantinople, secretary of the Congregation of Bishops and Regulars, and cardinal (1839). Meanwhile he governed the See of Osimo and Cingoli very capably. Pius IX appointed him secretary of state (June 4, 1848) and president of the Council of Ministers. The latter post normally had merely nominal authority, but Soglia, following the pope's wishes, often acted independently of the lay ministers and came into conflict with them. After Pius IX's flight to Gaeta (Nov. 24, 1848), Soglia resigned as secretary of state (November 29) and spent the remainder of his life directing the Diocese of Osimo.

Bibliography: W. SANDFUCHS, *Die Aussenminister der Päpste* (Münich 1962).

[A. RANDALL]

SOKA GAKKAI

A modern lay Buddhist movement, Soka Gakkai means ''value-creating society.'' It arose and has its principal strength in Japan, but has followers in the U.S. and other countries as well. Originally associated with Nichiren Shoshu, one of several groups based on the reinterpretation of Buddhism by the Japanese teacher Nichiren Daishonin (1222–82). Soka Gakkai's origins go back to 1930, when its founder, Tsunesaburo Makiguchi (1871–1944), published the first of four volumes of his *Value-Creating Pedagogical System.* It was formally organized in 1937 in Tokyo and by 1941 had some 3,000 members. Refusal to support Shintoism during World War II brought virtual destruction of the movement, however, and Makiguchi died in prison.

In 1946 the movement was revived by his chief disciple, Josei Toda (1900–58). In the wake of national defeat, Soka Gakkai appealed to many Japanese as a new religious force, but one that, unlike Christianity, was deeply rooted in Japanese history. A stress on health and prosperity gave mass appeal, and members were offered a wide array of cultural activities. Counting membership in households, and never subtracting those who may have drifted away, Soka Gakkai reported growth from 3,000 families in 1951 to 750,000 in 1957, to more than 6 million by the end of the 20th century. Meanwhile it had become involved in politics, electing its first representatives to the Diet in 1956 and organizing its political arm, Komeito (Clean Government Party), in 1964.

Its organizational discipline led some outsiders to fear it was reviving the spirit of militarism. And it disturbed many Japanese by its outspoken intolerance of other religions and its aggressive *shakubuku* (break and subdue) methods of winning converts. Talk of converting all Japan and building a national temple disturbed those who considered the idea of a state religion detrimental. But these particular goals were deemphasized under Daisaku Ikeda, Soka Gakkai leader after Toda, and some of the militancy subsided.

Since the seventies the Komeito was Japan's third largest party. It stresses nationalism, world peace, and opposition to corruption. It calls for a somewhat vaguely defined Buddhist democracy, rejecting both liberal and Marxist democracy. Soka Gakkai spiritual life centers on chanting Nichiren's phrase *Nam-myoho Renge-kyo* (devotion to the wonderful lotus sutra), and each household is given a replica of the Dai-gohonzon, the sacred tablet on which Nichiren is said to have written the phrase. The original is in the chief Nichiren Shoshu temple at Taisekiji, at the foot of Mt. Fuji.

In the U.S. Soka Gakkai's initial adherents were primarily Japanese immigrants, including a number who had married U.S. servicemen. In some cases the American spouses became members, and Soka Gakkai subsequently won considerable numbers of other American converts. Since 1964 Soka Gakkai in the U.S. has gone under the name Nichiren Shoshu.

Bibliography: T. KUBO, *The Development of Japanese Lay Buddhism* (Tokyo 1986). D. A. METRAUX, *The History and Theology of Soka Gakkai: A Japanese New Religion* (Lewiston, NY 1988). J. D. HURST, *Nichiren Shoshu Buddhism and the Soka Gakkai in America: The Ethos of a New Religious Movement* (New York 1992). D. A. METRAUX, *The Soka Gakkai Revolution* (Lanham, Md. 1994). P. E. HAMMOND and D. W. MACHACEK, *Soka Gakkai in America: Accommodation and Conversion* (Oxford/New York 1999). D. W. MACHACEK and B. R. WILSON, *Global Citizens: The Soka Gakkai Buddhist Movement in the World* (Oxford/New York 2000).

[T. EARLY/EDS.]

SOLANO, FRANCIS, ST.

Franciscan missionary; b. Montilla, Spain, March 1549; d. Lima, Peru, July 14, 1610. Solano was born of a moderately wealthy family in Andalusia. His secondary studies were made in the local Jesuit college. As a youth, he must have met frequently with Garcilaso Inca, the Peruvian writer, who went to Montilla to live in 1561. Solano entered the Franciscan Order in the local friary and was professed in 1570. He worked 20 years in Spain and 20 years in the Americas. In Spain, he was novice master, teacher, and superior. He was also a preacher with a boundless compassion for the ailing in society, as evidenced by his labors among the plague-stricken in Montoro. In 1589 his superiors sent him to America with a band of missionaries intended for Tucumán in Argentina. After landing in Lima, he journeyed overland to Santiago del Estero on foot, arriving in 1590. He had hardly passed a year among the natives of Socotonio and La Magdalena, when he was appointed custos of Tucumán and Paraguay. Upon the completion of the term, he was recalled to Peru (1598), where he spent the remaining years of his life as superior in Lima and Trujillo.

His biographers often picture him as a hermit of the desert rather than as a Franciscan from Andalusia, whose primary aim was to model his life after St. Francis of Assisi. Those who knew him best called him *Franciscus redivivus.* A gifted man with a fine voice and training on the Spanish violin, he was fond of composing songs and dances in honor of the Christ Child and the Blessed Mother. On occasion, he would snap his fingers to imitate the castanets of his native province. Knowledgeable in medical lore, he insisted on isolation of the victims of the plague and on burning the garments worn by those who had recovered. His passion was to make Christ known and loved by all men, and to this end he never spared himself. When his novices asked how they could become saints, he told them by accepting the disappointments of everyday life, especially those that came from their friends. He was a man of prayer and a lifelong student, especially of the writings of St. Bonaventure, a select library of whose works he always carried with him. Unfortunately, his writings, carols, and songs were all sent to Rome for the process of his beatification and then lost. Clement X beatified him in 1675 and Benedict XIII canonized him in 1726. His body rests in the Franciscan church in Lima, but his portable altar is in Buenos Aires; his ritual, in Córdoba; his miraculous spring, in Salta; his chasuble, in Tucumán; one cell, in la Rioja, and another, together with his garments, in Santiago del Estero, thus justifying in a way his title as apostle of South America.

Bibliography: J. G. ORO, *San Francisco Solano: Un hombre para las Americas* (Madrid 1988). M. F. WINDEATT, *Saint Francis Solano: Wonder Worker of the New World and Apostle of Argentina and Peru* (Rockford 1994).

[A. CAGGIANO]

SOLER, MARIANO

Catholic polemicist and intellectual; b. San Carlos, Maldonado, Uruguay, March 25, 1846; d. at sea, Sept. 26, 1908. He studied in Santa Fé, Argentina, and at the South American College in Rome, where he received the degrees of doctor of theology and canon law. He was ordained Dec. 20, 1872. In Uruguay he was appointed ecclesiastical attorney. In 1875 he founded and directed the Liceo Universitario. He combated the very active liberal campaign of the Ateneo and the Sociedad Universitaria. In 1879 he entered the House of Representatives. Combative and well versed in sacred and profane learning, Soler directed the campaign against the irreligious attacks of the government of Gen. Máximo Santos. This campaign found expression in the daily *El Bien Público,* edited by the poet Juan Zorrilla de San Martín, and through the Catholic Club, dominated by the powerful eloquence of Francisco Bauzá. The pulpit of the church of El Cordón, of which Soler was pastor, was a focal point of resistance that elicited governmental objections since Church and State were united. In 1886 Soler went to Europe; he visited also the Orient and several Latin American republics. When Bp. Inocencio María Yéregui died in 1890, Soler acted as apostolic administrator of the diocese, and on Feb. 8, 1891, he was consecrated the third bishop of Montevideo. When Montevideo was raised to an archbishopric on April 19, 1897, Soler was appointed the first metropolitan archbishop. To his apostolic ministry and a militant defense of Catholic doctrine, Mariano Soler brought the gifts of a facile writer, skillful in answering his opponents. He was a powerful dialectician who treated a wide variety of subjects, many of which were forced on him by circumstances and had to be developed without the time for careful study. His writings were numerous, and his intellectual reputation is still in the forefront of Catholicism in Uruguay.

[A. D. GONZÁLEZ]

SOLESMES, ABBEY OF

The Abbey of Solesmes, or Abbaye Saint–Pierre, in the village of Solesmes (Sarthe), France, was founded *c.* 1000 by Geoffroy de Sablé as a priory of the Benedictines dependent on the abbey of La Couture. In the 12th century it was given a relic of the CROWN OF THORNS, which is still an object of great veneration. The priory was de-

Interior of Abbey of Solesmes. (©John Heseltine/CORBIS)

stroyed during the Hundred Years' War by the English (1425) but was soon reconstructed. During the Renaissance the 11th–century church was rebuilt and adorned with magnificent statues, called ''the saints of Solesmes.'' The monastery was placed in COMMENDATION (1556–1773), and aggregated to the Benedictine Congregation of St. Maurus, or MAURISTS (1664). During the French Revolution it was suppressed and put up for sale, and the monks dispersed (1791). Prosper GUÉRANGER, then a curate in Sablé, purchased the property (1833) and reestablished Benedictine life. Pope Gregory XVI raised it to the status of an abbey (1837), named Dom Guéranger as first abbot (1837–75), and made it head of the new Benedictine Congregation of France, known also as the Congregation of Saint–Pierre de Solesmes. Under Guéranger Solesmes became a famed center of religious renewal. The French government expelled the monks in 1880 and again from 1882 to 1896. Dom Paul Delatte, abbot (1890–1920) succeeding Dom Charles Couturier, regained possession of the abbey and began large scale construction until the laws against religious (1901) sent the monks into exile to QUARR ABBEY on the Isle of Wight. Dom Germain Cozien, fourth abbot (1920–59) led the community back to Solesmes (1922). The monastery has gained world renown for its role in the liturgical movement and the restoration of Gregorian chant. In addition to Guéranger it has produced such well–known scholars as Cabrol, FEROTIN, LECLERCQ, MOCQUEREAU, PITRA, Pothier, and QUENTIN. Among the most notable publications of the monks have been editions of the writings of St. Gertrude, St. Mechtild, William of Saint–Thierry, St. John of the Cross, John of St. Thomas, Bérulle, and the English mystics. Current projects include the publication of the works of Pseudo–Dionysius the Areopagite, and papal documents (*Collection Les Enseignements Pontificaux*), and a series of phonographic records of Gregorian chants.

Bibliography: L. H. COTTINEAU, *Réertoire topobibliographique des abbayes et prieurés,* 2 v. (Mâcon 1935–39) 2:3055–57. O. L. KAPSNER, *A Benedictine Bibliography: An Author–Subject Union List,* 2 v. (2d ed. Collegeville, Minn. 1962): v. 1, author part; v. 2, subject part. 2:5253–99. P. GUÉRANGER, *Essai historique sur l'Abbaye de Solesmes* (Le Mans 1846). H. QUENTIN, *Notice historique sur l'Abbaye de Solesmes* (Tours 1924). Benedictines of Solesmes, *Le Monastère Saint–Pierre de Solesmes* (Solesmes 1955); *Les Saints de Solesmes* (Paris 1951). A. SAVATON, *Dom Paul Delatte, Abbé de Solesmes* (Paris 1954). J. HOURLIER, *Les Églises de Solesmes* (Paris 1951). P. SCHMITZ, *Lexikon für Theologie und Kirche,* ed. J. HOFER and K. RAHNER, 10 v. (2d, new ed. Freiburg 1957–65) 9:864.

[L. ROBERT]

SOLIDARISM

A social philosophy based on Catholic philosophic principles whose leading proponent was Heinrich Pesch, SJ, the famous German economist. Rejecting both socialism and individualism, solidarism finds in the nature of society and man a principle of order for the economy as a whole. Society is a moral organism presenting not the unity of oneness but the union of the many. The economy is an organic-moral unity of many autonomous economic units bound together by the goal and the authority of society. It is a community of free citizens striving for the common welfare of all. The variety, freedom, particular aims, autonomy, and self-responsibility of the individuals and private enterprise are to be encouraged and furthered and also are to be subordinated to the fulfillment of the common task. The state is not a necessary evil, but a necessary good. Its function is to direct, supervise, stimulate, and restrain the activities of the economic units to the extent that the common welfare requires it.

In solidarism the individual is not a mere member of the whole or a mere means by which a state-designated goal is achieved, but he is a person for whom all the activities of all the members of society and of the state are directed. The profit motive is not rejected but merely restrained so that it aids rather than hinders the attainment of the goal of the economy. More generically, self-interest is recognized as a legitimate, natural instinct, a force for good, which must, however, be ordered so that both the individual and community are satisfied.

Solidarism recognizes the importance of freedom in the economic sphere. While it rejects a compulsory planned economy, it also disavows absolute freedom. It fears that unlimited, unbridled freedom will hinder the achieving of the goal of the economy unless it is subject to the demands of justice. Only the acceptance of authority develops and guarantees that degree of justice required by freedom. Solidarism's freedom is the freedom of order.

Both the individualistic, irresponsible, absolute concept of private property and the socialistic concept of state ownership are rejected. Solidarism justifies private ownership and limits it by invoking the principle that ''the goods of the earth should serve all mankind.'' In the last resort the state has the duty and the right to see that this is achieved.

Just as solidarism is a middle way between socialism and individualism, it stresses the establishment in society of groups that will take their place between the individuals and the state. These are organizations embracing all who are engaged in a particular profession or performing a particular service for the nation. All performing the same function in society, though divided by different personal interests, belong to the same group. These functional groups are organs of society that operate as the representatives of the group and as self-governing authorities for the particular profession of industry in keeping with the principle of SUBSIDIARITY. While not essential to the political society, in the sense that society could not exist without them, they are necessary for its perfection. The particular form that these functional groups may adopt will vary according to the economic, social, and political conditions of the nation.

Bibliography: R.C. MULCAHY, *The Economics of Heinrich Pesch* (New York 1952). F. H. MUELLER, *Heinrich Pesch and His Theory of Solidarism* (St. Paul 1941).

[R. E. MULCAHY]

SOLIDARITY

Solidarity, as defined by Pope JOHN PAUL II, represents ''a firm and persevering determination to commit oneself to the common good; that is to say for the good of all and of each individual, because we are all really responsible for all'' (*Sollicitudo rei socialis,* no. 38). Solidarity is a recurring theme in the writings of John Paul II. In the encyclical *CENTESIMUS ANNUS* he says that the term describes ''one of the fundamental principles of the Christian view of social and political organization,'' and notes that previous popes have identified the same principle under the name ''friendship'' (Leo XIII), ''social charity'' (Pius XI), and ''the civilization of love'' (Paul VI) (no. 3). John Paul II's repeated appeal to this principle in a variety of contexts makes it clear that solidarity is neither a vague feeling of compassion or commiseration, nor the union of one group in society over against another. Though the pope uses the word to describe the union of workers against the degradation of their work (*Laborem exercens,* no. 8), he insists that solidarity ''aims at the good of social justice,'' and is not undertaken ''for the sake of 'struggle' or in order to eliminate the opponent'' (ibid., no. 20). It is a human and Christian virtue, describing the commitment to the common good. It has three principal manifestations, according to whether the common good is taken to refer to goods, activities, or the communion of persons. This same division is found in the treatment of solidarity in the Catechism of the Catholic Church, nos. 1940–1942.

According to John Paul II, the common good can consist of goods, realized in individuals, that share a common species. Because of our common humanity we can say that we share a common status, in the sense that no person is more or less human than another; that there are perfections common to us all, such as health, knowledge, and religious devotion; and that there are things whose use is inherently common, such as money, food, and technology. Each of these can be the ground of moral and legal rights, and thus can express a reason for solidarity. In *SOLLICITUDO REI SOCIALIS* the ''virtue'' of solidarity is described initially as the willingness to make a moral response to common goods described in this way (no. 38). Likewise the Catechism says, ''Solidarity is manifested in the first place by the distribution of goods and remuneration for work'' (no. 1940). Solidarity thus described recognizes and is committed to the virtue of distributive justice, not only on the part of the state, but also on the part of other social groups: families, unions, business enterprises.

The common good can also be realized in the common activity of individuals. John Paul applies this idea to the domestic political order, international relations, the initiatives of intermediate societies, and economic life (cf. CCC 1941). In *Centesimus annus* he writes:

> By means of his work a person commits himself, not only for his own sake but also for others and with others. Each person collaborates in the work of others and for their good. One works in order to provide for the needs of one's family, one's community, one's nation, and ultimately all humanity. Moreover, a person collaborates in the work of his fellow employees, as well as in the

> work of suppliers and in the customers' use of goods, in a progressively expanding chain of solidarity. (No. 43; cf. *Laborem exercens,* no. 8)

Insofar as the common good is constituted by common activity, having its own inherent perfection and value, the supplanting of that activity through the intervention of ''higher'' powers results in the loss of the good itself. The good is not simply the external result (e.g., the just distribution of goods), but the collaborative activity whereby the external result is produced. Pope John Paul speaks also, in the same vein, of the ''subjectivity'' of society, constituted by ''structures of participation and shared responsibility'' (*Centesimus annus,* no. 46); totalitarian societies invariably bring about ''the destruction of the true subjectivity of society and of the individual citizens''—not because the State does a poor job of distributing common goods equitably, but because in such a society the individual and the people as a whole are reduced to objects.

The principal meaning of ''common good'' is found in the theological concept of communion: the greatest common good is the communion of persons. Papal and conciliar documents speak of ''communion'' typically in reference to those means by which the individual becomes part of, or grows in, the body of Christ (e.g., marriage, Eucharistic fellowship, baptism). It is this understanding of ''common'' that governs the others. In *Sollicitudo rei socialis* John Paul says:

> Beyond human and natural bonds, already so close and strong, there is discerned in the light of faith a new model of the unity of the human race, which must ultimately inspire our solidarity. This supreme model of unity, which is a reflection of the intimate life of God, one God in three Persons, is what we Christians mean by the word ''communion.'' (No. 40)
>
> The Catechism (no. 1942) likewise speaks of solidarity involving the communication of spiritual goods. This communion has often, throughout Christian history, been the inspiration for the fostering of solidarity in temporal goods, impelling souls then and now to the heroic charity of monastic farmers, liberators of slaves, healers of the sick, and messengers of faith, civilization, and science to all generations and all peoples for the sake of creating the social conditions capable of offering to everyone possible a life worthy of man and of a Christian (Ibid., quoting a discourse of Pius XII).

Solidarity therefore involves charity as well as justice: communion in common goods and activities finds a root in the common nature of man, but it is ultimately secured by the recognition that every person is called to share in the communal life of the Trinity.

With this notion of solidarity, John Paul II has marked out the basis for an understanding of social and political life that challenges the distinctively modern notion of the political good. The revolutions of the nineteenth century produced an aggressively secularist and monistic notion of solidarity achieved by, or exemplified in, the state; in certain species of liberalism, on the other hand, a mechanistic notion of the market is given primacy. In *Centesimus annus* John Paul II criticizes any system that would ''suffocate'' the human person ''between two poles represented by the State and the marketplace'' (no. 49); in *Evangelium vitae* he warns that authentic solidarity is not compatible with the way the democracies understand themselves today. Contrary to their own constitutions, some human lives are deemed unworthy of protection. The ''civilization of love'' bases the social good on solidarity: the authentic interdependence of persons, leading to communion.

Bibliography: R. HITTINGER, ''Making Sense of the Civilization of Love,'' *In The Legacy of Pope John Paul II: His Contribution to Catholic Thought* (New York 1999).

[R. HITTINGER]

SOLIGNAC, ABBEY OF

Former BENEDICTINE monastery of St. Peter and St. Paul, on the Briance River, in the Diocese and *arrondissement* of Limoges, Haute-Vienne, France. Solignac (Lat. *Solemniacum*) was founded in 631 at the request of St. ELIGIUS OF NOYON (d. 659), a minister of King Dagobert. The first monks came from LUXEUIL; St. Remaclus, who later became bishop-abbot of STAVELOT- MALMÉDY, was Solignac's first abbot (632–642). The abbey soon grew to 150 monks. In 675 it founded Brageac in the Diocese of Clermont-Ferrand. Solignac was plundered several times and had to be restored in 840 and 1100. Its dependent priories included Arton (Haute-Vienne) and Agumont (Corrèze). In 1571 it was ravaged by the Calvinists. Though incorporated into the Congregation of Saint-Maur in 1619 (*see* MAURISTS), the abbey had only nine monks in 1768. It was suppressed during the French Revolution, but the buildings were preserved, and sheltered in succession a boarding school, a porcelain factory, and finally a major seminary of the OBLATES OF MARY IMMACULATE. The abbey church, a masterpiece of romanesque art, has been made a national historical monument.

Bibliography: *Gallia Christiana,* v.1–13 (Paris 1715–85), v.14–16 (Paris 1856–65) 2:566–575. BEAUNIER, *Abbayes et prieurés de l'ancienne France,* ed. J. M. L. BESSE, 12 V. (Paris 1905-41) v.5. L. H. COTTINEAU, *Répertoire topobibliographique des abbayes et prieurés,* 2 v. (Mâcon 1935–39) 2:3058-59. ''Solignac,'' *Bulletin de la société archéologique et historique du Limousin* 77

(1937) 155–179. P. MOREL, ''Les Archives de S.,'' *ibid.* 84 (1953) 169–180. F. BAIX, ''L'Hagiographie à Stavelot-Malmédy,'' *Revue Bénédictine* 60 (1950) 120–162.

[J. DE LA C. BOUTON]

SOLIPSISM

Solipsism is a term that seems to have been first used by G. W. LEIBNIZ; derived from the Latin *solus* (alone) and *ipse* (self), it designates the philosophical teaching that a person can know only himself and that there are no grounds for acknowledging the existence of anything apart from SELF. The general theory of knowledge that overemphasizes the subject of knowledge while depreciating its OBJECT is IDEALISM; most types of idealism also imply subjectivism, either total or partial. Solipsism is the ultimate reach of total subjectivism, for it shuts man up within himself and equates his personal experience with the totality of existence.

The idealistic thesis that knowing is an immanent action within man and therefore that man cannot transcend his own mind has dominated modern philosophy. It has led many to the conclusion, unwarranted though it may be, that man cannot know things in themselves. The logical conclusion of such thinking is solipsism, however much its proponents deny this. It is not in any sense a new insight into the problem of knowledge, but simply an old mistake revived. Implicit in the view of the early Greek SOPHISTS, it is later found in the SKEPTICISM of the Platonic academies. ARISTOTLE was aware of it and deals with it in his *Metaphysics,* where he complains that men who think this way reduce themselves to the level of plants (1006a 15). In modern thought, the faulty definition of the idea by J. LOCKE reintroduced it; G. BERKELEY applied it to man's knowledge of matter; and D. HUME applied it finally to all things, turning it into a corrosive skepticism that seemed insane even to its author. Hume can hardly be called a conscious solipsist, but he would have become one had he carried his thought to its logical outcome.

The obvious difficulties of such an extreme position preclude any general support on the part of philosophers, even among idealists; and the term solipsism, rarely if ever self-applied or willingly acknowledged, is usually pejorative. Solipsism, moreover, being hardly defensible in itself, is attributed to the extreme varieties of subjective idealism less as a primary position than as an inevitable consequence of these doctrines if pursued to their logical conclusion. It is thus held up as the absurd situation to which subjective idealism must be driven by its own principles: the ultimate *reductio ad absurdum* of extreme idealism.

See Also: KNOWLEDGE; KNOWLEDGE, THEORIES OF; EPISTEMOLOGY.

Bibliography: P. COFFEY, *Epistemology,* 2 v. (New York 1917; repr. Gloucester, Mass. 1958). L. M. RÉGIS, *Epistemology,* tr. I. C. BYRNE (New York 1959). J. MARITAIN, *Distinguish to Unite, or the Degrees of Knowledge,* tr. G. B. PHELAN (New York 1959). R. HOUDE and J. P. MULLALY, eds., *Philosophy of Knowledge* (Philadelphia 1960).

[G. C. REILLY]

SOLITUDE

Solitude, in Christian usage, a condition, or state, of deliberate separation from others in order to devote oneself, without the distractions of company, to prayer. Following the example of Christ, who often went alone to pray, Christians desirous of being close to God have, from earliest times, sought solitude as a condition for continued prayer. In mid-3d century, the first monks found solitude in the desert. In the 4th century, hermitages were scattered through the Christian world (*see* MONASTICISM, 1). Hermits' cells grouped around a common place of worship developed into monasteries, in which solitude of soul was achieved by silence.

Authors of religious rules have considered solitude necessary for RECOLLECTION and aimed at it by the practice of silence. In modern times the CARTHUSIANS and CAMALDOLESE achieve relative solitude in their monasteries; the Discalced CARMELITES are permitted occasional periods of complete solitude; all religious communities insist on some solitude, through retreats and times of silence each day.

Bibliography: H. HEMMER, *Dictionnaire de théologie catholique,* ed. A. VACANT et al., 15 v. (Paris 1903–50; Tables générales 1951) 1.1:1134-42. H. J. WADDELL, tr., *The Desert Fathers* (New York 1936). M. WOLTER, *The Principles of Monasticism,* tr. B. A. SAUSE (St. Louis 1962).

[P. MULHERN]

SOLLICITUDO REI SOCIALIS

Pope JOHN PAUL II's seventh encyclical letter, issued Dec. 30, 1987, marking the twentieth anniversary of *POPULORUM PROGRESSIO,* Pope Paul VI's encyclical on the development of peoples. John Paul II presents a series of reflections on the requirements of authentic human development, the international duty of solidarity, and the social responsibility of the church. In considering the relevance of the earlier document's themes for the present era, the pope aims both to pay homage to his predecessor and to set forth the tradition of Catholic social teaching (nos. 1–4).

The pope begins by characterizing *Populorum progressio* as an application of the teachings of the Second Vatican Council, and in particular the social tenets of the Pastoral Constitution GAUDIUM ET SPES, to the problem of the development of peoples (nos. 5–7). The encyclical, he states, is original in three respects: its bringing to bear of an authoritative ethical perspective on a problem often viewed as social and economic, its transferral of the "social question" to a global context, and its exposition of the proposition that "Development is the new name for peace" (nos. 8–10).

The next section surveys conditions in the contemporary world and comments on their implications for a renewal of the teachings of *Populorum progressio.* After discussing such indicators as world poverty; the divisions between East and West, North and South, and the First, Second, Third, and Fourth Worlds; and cultural ills such as illiteracy, social and religious oppression, and the suppression of economic initiative, the pope concludes that Paul VI's hopes for development have remained unmet and that, indeed, the situation has worsened (nos. 11–16). Because global interdependence determines that the levels of development of all nations are intertwined, even developed countries have come to manifest signs of underdevelopment, in the form of a housing crisis and burgeoning under- or unemployment. Moreover, loans to developing nations, originally intended to contribute to their development, have instead aggravated underdevelopment by producing a system of international debt (nos. 17–19). In analyzing the causes of these failures, the pope focuses on political factors, criticizing the ideological conflict between East and West and its impact, via the mechanisms of neo-colonialism, on the developing world; the "disorders" of arms production and the arms trade; and population control policies rooted in an "erroneous and perverse" concept of human development (nos. 20–25). This largely negative balance, he adds, should not overshadow hopeful signs such as increasing respect for human rights, a growing sense of international solidarity, and the spread of "ecological concern" (no. 26).

The "true nature of the development of peoples" forms the subject of the subsequent section. This concept is distinguished from both a naive, Enlightenment belief in progress and a purely economic conception of development leading, in practice, not only to underdevelopment but to a nexus of consumerism, materialism, and anomie the pope terms "superdevelopment." Authentic human development, by contrast, retains an economic component, but subordinates the "having" of goods to the "being" of the person (nos. 27–28). Its essence, meanwhile, is moral and theological: as the pope shows in a reflection on the creation accounts in Genesis, "full" development is rooted in the human participation in the image of God and the vocation to obey the divine law, to work, and to serve others that flows from it (nos. 29–30). Christian faith, with its vision of the Kingdom, at once found a new assurance regarding the attainability of development and mandates that the church has an obligation to work toward it; this obligation, indeed, is shared by all individuals as well as the various communities including religious ones in which they find themselves, and it is mirrored in the right of all peoples or nations to full development (nos. 31–32). The moral character of authentic development is exhibited in its intrinsic commitment to the spectrum of human rights, including social, economic, political, personal, and collective rights; to the values of solidarity, freedom, and love of God and neighbor; and to respect for nature (nos. 33–34).

The pope next brings this account of development to bear on a "theological reading of modern problems." In keeping with development's primarily moral character, he asserts, the chief obstacles to development are also of a moral nature, and consist in such failings as an "all-consuming desire for profit," a widespread "thirst for power," and, building on such attitudes, "structures of sin" (nos. 35–37). In order to overcome these evils, a profound change in spiritual attitudes for Christians, a conversion is necessary, leading to the embrace of the virtue of solidarity: "a firm and persevering determination to commit oneself to the common good." The pope's exposition of the functions of solidarity both within and among societies demonstrates it to be a core value of Catholic social teaching, intimately bound up with such notions as peace, justice, the common good, the option for the poor, and the universal destination of the goods of creation. Solidarity is, he further notes, a Christian virtue, closely related to charity and, in its commitment to human unity, modeled on and symbolic of the Trinity and Christian communion (nos. 38–40).

A penultimate section presents particular guidelines for addressing the problem of development. Since the church does not profess to offer a "third way" between liberal capitalism and Marxist collectivism, these guidelines are not technical but moral and theological in character. Drawing on Catholic social teaching regarding the primacy of the poor, the universal destination of goods, and the "social mortgage" on private property, the pope calls for reforms involving the international trade and monetary systems, international organizations, and technology exchanges. Invoking the Catholic social doctrine of participation, he further counsels developing nations to promote the literacy, self-sufficiency, and political involvement of their citizens and to cooperate with one another in regional associations (nos. 41–45).

In his conclusion, the pope, making reference to Latin American liberation theology, identifies a strong link between authentic development and ''true'' liberation. Both values are manifested in the exercise of solidarity, a virtue the pope exhorts all religious people to exhibit. The letter closes with a reflection on the sacrament of the Eucharist and an appeal for the intercession of Mary (nos. 46–49).

Bibliography: For the text of *Sollicitudo rei socialis,* see: *Acta Apostolicae Sedis* 80 (1988) 513–86 (Latin); *Origins* 17, no. 38 (Mar. 3, 1988): 642–60 (English); *The Pope Speaks* 33 (1988): 122–55 (English). For commentaries and summaries on *Sollicitudo rei socialis,* see: J.-Y. CALVEZ,''Sollicitudo rei socialis,'' in J. A. DWYER, ed. *The New Dictionary of Catholic Social Thought* (Collegeville, MN 1994) 912–917. P. HENRIOT, E. P. DEBERRI, and M. J. SCHULTHEIS, *Catholic Social Teaching: Our Best Kept Secret* (Maryknoll, NY 1988) 74–82.

[W. BARBIERI]

SOLMINIHAC, ALAIN DE, BL.

Reforming bishop of Cahors, France, canon regular of St. Augustine (OSA); b. Nov. 25, 1593, Belet (near Périgueux) France; d. Dec. 31, 1659, Mercuès (near Cahors), Quercy, France. Named abbot of Chancelade (a foundation of CANONS REGULAR OF ST. AUGUSTINE near Périgueux) in 1614, Alain gradually corrected the physical and spiritual deterioration of his monastery. He was consecrated bishop of Cahors on Sept. 27, 1637, and worked vigorously and successfully for the reform of this huge but spiritually impoverished diocese. He was strongly pro-papal in the Gallican conflicts and actively anti-Jansenist. He was regarded as a saint by VINCENT DE PAUL and others. The cause of his beatification was introduced in 1783. Pope John Paul II, during the beatification ceremony (Oct. 4, 1981), praised Solminihac for his ''courage to evangelize the modern world fearlessly.''

Feast: Jan. 3.

Bibliography: *Acta Apostolicae Sedis* 74 (1982): 261–63. *L'Osservatore Romano,* English edition, no. 41 (1981): 1, 12. L. CHASTENET, *La Vie de Monseigneur Alain de Solminihac Eveque Baron, et Comte de Caors, et Abbé régulier de Chancellade* (Cahors 1663). C. DUMOULIN, *Au service de Dieu et de sa gloire* (Paris 1981). E. SOL, *Un prélat ultramontain du XVIIe siècle, Alain de Solminihac et le Saint–Siège* (Aurillac, France 1927); *Alain de Solminihac . . . : Lettres et documents* (Cahors 1928); *L'Église de Cahors à l'époque moderne* (Paris 1947).

[M. A. ROCHE]

SOLOMON

Son and successor of DAVID as king (*c.* 961-922 B.C.) of all Israel. According to 2 Sm 12.25, his name seems originally to have been Jedidia (Heb. *y^e^dîdyâ,* beloved of Yahweh), and the name Solomon (Heb. *š^e^lōmōh,* often associated with *šālôm,* peace, but probably an abbreviation of a longer name meaning something like ''may Yahweh guard his welfare'') was probably adopted on his accession to the throne.

Solomon's mother was Bathsheba, David's partner in adultery (2 Sm 11.2-5), but the precise details of his birth and early life are not clear, because of the complex nature of the Biblical record. For instance, it is usually assumed that he was the second son of David and Bethsabee, the first having died as punishment for the sin of adultery (2 Sm 12.13–25); but elsewhere (1 Chr 3.5; 14.4; 2 Sm 5.14) he is listed as their fourth son. In David's time there was no strict rule of primogeniture determining royal succession. Accordingly, David did no one any injury in selecting Solomon as his heir. That he did so is certain, but the details are confused. Solomon, having obtained the crown through the intercession of his mother and of the Prophet NATHAN, consolidated his position by the ruthless removal of those who stood in his way.

More space in the Bible (1 Kgs 1.1–11.43; 2 Chr 1.1–9.31) is devoted directly to Solomon than to any other king except David, but curiously he does not emerge as a clearly delineated person. Most of the material deals with the Temple of Jerusalem [*see* TEMPLES (IN THE BIBLE)] and his building operations; and the rest, partly owing to the complex nature of the literary form, tells relatively little about the man himself. Even his celebrated wisdom, the tradition of which provides the basis for the later ascription to him of most of the SAPIENTIAL BOOKS of the Bible (Proverbs, Ecclesiastes, Song of Songs, Wisdom, and certain Psalms), is dealt with mostly in general terms. The single specific illustration, the story of the two mothers (1 Kgs 3.16–28), is a familiar theme in Oriental folklore. It is unlikely, however, that his reputation as the wise king is entirely without foundation.

Solomon's fabled magnificence, alluded to by Jesus (Mt 6.29), is probably exaggerated; in any case, it was purchased at too high a price in excessive taxation, forced labor, and the destruction of tribal loyalties—all of which helped pave the way for the division of the kingdom immediately after his death.

All in all, however, Solomon was an outstanding king. Taking advantage of the momentary weakness of Egypt and Assyria, he consolidated his already strong position and even extended his sphere of influence by skillful diplomacy rather than war. It is especially as a peaceful king that Christian tradition sees in him a type of Christ. Despite his very real shortcomings he seems to have been sincerely devoted to the service of God; yet he apparently did not grasp the full implications of uncompromising monotheism.

King Solomon's Temple, drawing by John W. Kelchner, 1913.

Many events of Solomon's life as described in the Bible have provided themes for Christian art. These include the encounter between Solomon and Bethsabee (1 Kgs 2.19–24), Solomon's dream (3.4–15), the judgment for the two mothers (3.16–28), and the meeting with the Queen of Sheba (10.1–13), as well as the Temple and its furnishings. Sometimes the motif is given a typological interpretation, as when Solomon's invitation to Bethsabee to share his throne is understood to foreshadow Mary's crowning at the hand of Christ or when his judgment is set in relation to the Last Judgment. The earliest example of Solomon in Christian art is the bas-relief of Solomon's judgment on the silver reliquary of the cathedral of Milan (end of the 4th century).

Bibliography: *Encyclopedic Dictionary of the Bible,* translated and adapted by L. HARTMAN (New York, 1963) 2260–63. M. REHM and A. LEGNER, *Lexikon für Theologie und Kirche,* ed. J. HOFER and K. RAHNER, 10 v. (2d, new ed. Freiburg 1957–65) 9:272–275. J. BRIGHT, *A History of Israel* (Philadelphia 1959) 190–208. L. RÉAU, *Iconographie de l'art chrétien,* 6 v. (Paris 1955–59) 2.1:286–299.

[B. MCGRATH]

SOLOV'EV, VLADIMIR SERGEEVICH

Russian mystic, theologian, philosopher, poet, journalist, ecumenist (also known as Solovyiev, Solovyev, Solowjew); b. Moscow, Jan. 16 (28), 1853; d. Uzkoe, near Moscow, July 31 (Aug. 13), 1900. Although reared in a devout Russian Orthodox home, Solov'ev became an atheist while in secondary school after reading the lives of Christ written by David STRAUSS and RENAN. He also became devoted to the MATERIALISM of Ludwig Büchner (1824–99) and the NIHILISM of Pisarev. During his university years in Moscow (1869–74), he experienced another religious crisis. From SPINOZA he gained a living sense of God's reality and a clear experience of the total spiritual unity of the world. Other influences on the development of his religious thought were SCHOPENHAUER, Eduard von HARTMANN, SCHELLING, and HEGEL. He attended the Theological Faculty of Moscow (1873–74) and published his widely acclaimed dissertation against COMTE and POSITIVISM, *Crisis of Western Philosophy* (1874). After lecturing at the university, Solov'ev studied mysticism and THEOSOPHY in London (1875). He then went to Egypt, where he claimed to have had a vision of Sophia, or Wisdom. In 1876 he resumed teaching but soon left Moscow University because of a dispute concerning SLAVOPHILISM. In St. Petersburg he served on the Scholarly Committee of the Educational Ministry and delivered 12 lectures on Godmanhood (1877). He thought the essence of Christianity consisted of the union of God and man in the Incarnate Word, but that Eastern Orthodoxy neglected man, while Western Christianity tended to forget God. These lectures attracted much attention. The audience included DOSTOYEVSKY and TOLSTOI. The former had been a friend of the lecturer since 1873 and seemingly fashioned the character Alyosha in *Brothers Karamazov* after Solov'ev. Tolstoi's denial of Christ's resurrection caused Solov'ev to be wary of him. *A Critique of Abstract Principles* (1880), Solov'ev's doctoral dissertation, met wide acclaim, but its author was compelled to retire from teaching in 1881 because he had publicly sought clemency for Alexander II's assassins.

This proved to be a turning point in Solov'ev's life. Thereafter he devoted himself entirely to writing and the ECUMENICAL MOVEMENT. He described himself as an eternally wandering, homeless pilgrim seeking the heavenly Jerusalem. Friends were never lacking, however, to provide him with hospitality. Some of his writings at this time concerned contemporary problems, but his most significant works had to be published abroad because of his growing sympathy with the Roman Church. These tendencies occasioned a break with his slavophile friends, especially KHOMIÂKOV and Kireyevsky. In his *Great Dispute and Christian Policy* (1883) he defended the papal primacy. His *History and Future of Theocracy* (1884) indicated that he had been little influenced by Chaadayev's slavophile views about the kingdom of God. During Solov'ev's travels in Croatia (1886–88), his association with Bishop STROSSMAYER strengthened his desire for reunion with Rome. In 1887 he lectured in Paris on the Russian Church, and in 1889 he published *La Russie et l'église universelle,* which met a very hostile reception in Russia. The HOLY SYNOD forbade him to write further on religious topics.

In 1896 he made a profession of faith, confessed to a Catholic priest, and received Holy Communion. He hoped to see all men united religiously in Christianity (which would be in practice a theocracy under the pope) and politically, under the czar. His thought became more eschatological in *Three Conversations* (1889–90), as he became increasingly pessimistic and concerned with the problem of evil and of the ANTICHRIST. On his deathbed Solov'ev received the Last Rites from a Russian Orthodox priest. Since he believed that Roman Catholicism and the ORTHODOX churches remained mystically united despite their outward separation, he apparently considered intercommunion justifiable. His action, therefore, was apparently not based on disregard for canon law. So broad was his erudition that Solov'ev has been called the Russian Newman. Several of his works have been translated into English.

Bibliography: Collected works in Russian, 9 v. (St. Petersburg 1901–07; 2d. ed., 10 v. 1911–14); Collected letters in Russian, 4 v. (St. Petersburg 1908–23); *A Solovyof Anthology,* ed. S. L. FRANK, tr. N. DUDDINGTON (London 1950). M. D'HERBIGNY, *Vladimir Soloviev, A Russian Newman,* tr. A. M. BUCHANAN (London 1918). D. STREMOUKOV, *Vladimer Soloviev et son oeuvre messianique* (Paris 1935). K. PFLEGER, *Wrestlers with Christ,* tr. E. I. WATKIN (London 1936). N. ZERNOV, *Three Russian Prophets: Khomyakov, Dostoievsky and Soloviev* (New York 1944). V. V. ZEN'KOVSKIĬ, *History of Russian Philosophy,* tr. G. L. KLINE, 2 v. (New York 1953). E. MUNZER, *Solovyev, Prophet of Russian-Western Unity* (London 1956). L. MÜLLER, *Lexikon für Theologie und Kirche,* 10 v. (Freiburg 1957–65) 9:869–870.

[J. PAPIN]

SOMALIA, THE CATHOLIC CHURCH IN

Somalia is located on the horn of the east coast of Africa, and is bordered on the north by Djibouti and the Gulf of Aden, on the east by the Indian Ocean, on the southwest by Kenya and on the west by Ethiopia. Largely semi-desert, with the exception of irrigated areas along the two rivers, Juba and Shabele, in the south, the region is plateau, rising to hills in the north. Natural resources, which are under-exploited, include uranium, iron ore, tin, gypsum, copper, bauxite and salt. Most of the population are nomadic farmers who raise livestock; other agricultural products include bananas, sorghum, corn, sugarcane, sesame seeds and mangoes.

In 1960 Somalia became an independent republic formed by the union of the British Somaliland Protectorate to the north and the Italian trusteeship territory of Somalia to the south. Subsequent border disputes with Kenya and Ethiopia were eventually resolved, and in 1969 the region became a Marxist dictatorship under General Muhammad Siyad Barrah (1911–95) as the Somali Democratic Republic. By 1988 the economy was in tatters due to drought and civil wars, resulting in a humanitarian disaster as thousands died due to famine and disease. In 1991 a rebel Muslim faction took control of the former British protectorate, but fighting continued in the south, despite U.N. efforts at a ceasefire. In 1995 General Muhammad Aidid declared himself president. Aidid was killed in 1996 and the presidency claimed by his son, Hussein Aidid, although with no end to the violence. The inhabitants are mostly Somalis, a Hamitic people, who are almost all Sunni Muslims. There are also Arab and Egyptian minorities, as well as small Indian, Pakistani, Italian and British populations. Most of the population is pastoral nomads. The country was again visited by

Capital: Mogadishu.
Size: 258,000 sq. miles.
Population: 7,253,137 in 1975; large nomadic populations, famine, and ethnic warfare precluded 2000 estimates.
Languages: Somali, Arabic, Italian, English.
Religions: (Estimated) 200 Catholics, 100 Protestants; almost all others are Sunni Muslim.
Diocese: Mogadishu, immediately subject to the Holy See.

drought in 2000, increasing the humanitarian tragedy in this region. At the start of the 21st century there was no functioning government in Somalia.

History. The region was crossed by Muslim and Arab trading routes from the 7th century, and by the 10th century Somali nomads inhabited the interior regions. The British entered the region after occupying Yemen, and the region was divided into British and Italian spheres of influence. Successive civil administrations restricted Catholic missionary activity to the spiritual care of immigrants. Capuchin missionaries labored in the northern part from 1891 until 1910 when the British expelled them. From 1904 TRINITARIANS and then CONSOLATA MISSIONARY FATHERS were entrusted with the southern, Italian-occupied section until 1930 when the Franciscans took charge. In 1904 the Prefecture Apostolic of Benadir was created in southern Somalia, while Northern Somalia became part of the Vicariate of Arabia under the Capuchins. In 1927 southern Somalia was constituted the Vicariate of Mogadishu.

The ''Somali Socialistic Revolution'' brought Mohamed Siyad Barre to power on Oct. 21, 1969. For the first three years of this government the Catholic Church continued its social activities, mainly in the fields of education and health, as well as its pastoral commitments. In December of 1971 northern Somalia was separated from the vicariate of Arabia and became part of the vicariate of Mogadishu; on Nov. 20, 1975, the vicariate became the diocese of Mogadishu.

In 1972 the Marxist government nationalized all 15 of the country's Catholic schools, and other properties were confiscated. Under threats of violence from Islamic extremists many Christians of all denominations left the country. Franciscans were reduced from 30 to 10, and the Consolata sisters from 95 to 35, and there was also a reduction in the number of lay missionaries. Religious sisters continued to work after this time in government hospitals. The general situation of Somalia continued to worsen as a consequence of the Ogaden war (1977–78), which was lost by Somalia. In response to the requests of the government, Mogadishu Bishop Colombo was able to bring in more sisters—the St. Joseph of Tarbes sisters and the Mother of Carmel sisters—from India to work as nurses in Mogadishu hospitals.

The influx of hundreds of thousands of refugees from the Ogaden war saw the Church in the frontline of service. Bishop Colombo founded Caritas Somalia in 1980 as the instrument of the Catholic community in helping refugees, providing hundreds of wells for drinking water, constructing a hospital in Qorioley and contributing to agricultural and forestation projects. During the 1980s an interreligious library was opened at the Mogadishu Cathedral. The liturgy was translated into Somali, and catechetical books in Somali were also produced. There was also collaboration with Protestants, who used to conduct religious services in the two Catholic churches of Mogadishu.

On July 9, 1989, Bishop Colombo was murdered, and replaced by apostolic administrator G. Bertin. The rebellion against the regime of Siyad Barre reached Mogadishu in late December of 1990, and the cathedral was ransacked and destroyed by fire within weeks. The civil war that followed destroyed all the properties of the Church in the country and obliged all the missionaries and most Christians to leave Somalia. Only a few dozen Somali Christians remained underground, due to the strong threat of Muslim fundamentalists. One of the last missionaries to remain, Father Turati, was murdered in February of 1991. Apostolic administrator Bertin, with the last four Consolata sisters, took refuge in Nairobi, Kenya, from where he attempted to minister to the few remaining Catholics in Somalia and guide the work of Caritas Somalia. The sisters eventually returned to Mogadishu.

The 1990s saw the destruction of the Somali state, the secession of the northern regions as the Republic of Somaliland, anarchy, famine, and banditry. For humanitarian reasons the international community intervened with ''Operation Restore Hope,'' followed by UNOSOM 2, a United Nations operation, which remained in the region from 1995 until violence forced them to leave two years later. The Church, along with other nongovernmental organizations, remained active in Somalia, attempting through the Caritas network to alleviate the terrible consequences of the region's human disaster.

By 1998 a priest and the four Consolata sisters were all that remained in the country. The sisters operated a hospital in Mogadishu where they provided maternity care and treated 500 children per week. After one sister was kidnapped on Sept. 10, 1998, the sisters—the last Catholic missionaries in Somalia— were forced to leave the country. Islam was considered the state religion, despite the absence of an organized government. Shari'a (Islamic Law) was increasingly implemented in civil

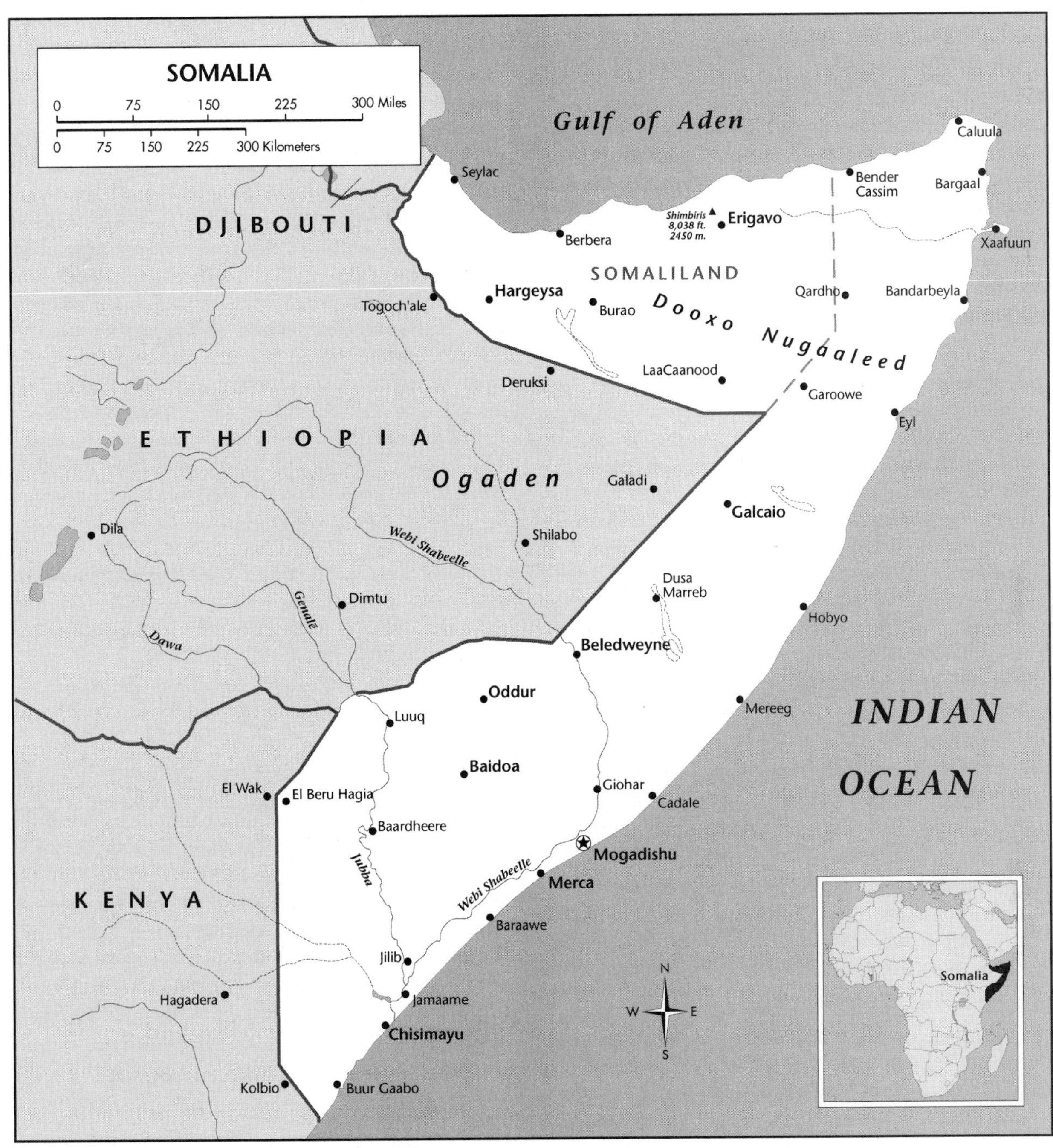

governments throughout the region, particularly in the radicalized north, and proselytization was considered a criminal offense.

Bibliography: *The Catholic Directory of East and West Africa 1961* (Nairobi 1961). *Le missioni cattoliche: Storia, geographia, statistica* (Rome 1950) 208, 92–93. *Bilan du Monde* 2:793–795. *Annuario Pontificio* has information on all diocese.

[T. A. WHITE/G. BERTIN/EDS.]

SOMASCAN FATHERS

(Clericorum Regularium Somaschensium, CRS, Official Catholic Directory #1250); also known as Order of St. Jerome Aemilian. The Order of Clerics Regular of Somascha, a religious community of men was begun at Venice, Italy, in 1528 by St. Jerome EMILIANI to care for orphan children and to teach Christian doctrine. The founder, who remained a layman, died in Somasca (from which the order took its name), a town near Bergamo, Italy, on Feb. 8, 1537. In the beginning the order was called the Society of Servants for the Poor, and its membership included both clerics and laymen. On June 6, 1540, the society was approved by Paul III. In 1547 Paul IV, the former Gian Pietro Caraffa, who had been the confessor of Emiliani, united the society with the THEATINES. This union lasted only until 1555, because of differences in ideals between the two groups. An attempt was made also for union with the Jesuits, but without success. On Dec. 6, 1568, Pius V promoted the society to a religious order, gave it its present title, and extended its activities to work in seminaries, colleges, academies, and parishes.

During the 17th century the order experienced growth and progress. Some of its distinguished institutions at that time were: the seminary in Venice; the Cardinal Gallio College in Como, Italy; and the Clementine College in Rome, where Prospero Lambertini (later Benedict XIV) was a student. In 1616 Paul V united the Congregation of Christian Doctrine of France, at the request of its members, to the Somaschi Fathers—a union that lasted until 1647. Urban VIII in 1626 approved definitively the constitutions of the order. Among the notable members of the community were: Angiolmarco Gambarana (1498–1573), outstanding for his sanctity; Giacomo Stellini (1699–1770), philosopher; and Francesco Soave (1743–1806), a teacher who had among his students the famous Alessandro Manzoni. During the 19th century the Somaschi Fathers, like all other religious, suffered greatly from suppression and confiscation in Europe. In the early 20th century, it recovered and established houses in Switzerland, Spain, El Salvador, Guatemala, Honduras, Mexico, Brazil, and the U.S.

The Somascan Fathers established their first foundation in Manchester, NH, with a program aimed at the needs of youth. The U.S. headquarters is in Suncook, NH; the generalate is in Rome.

Bibliography: P. BIANCHINI, *Origine e sviluppo della Compagnia dei Servi dei Poveri* (Milan 1941). S. RAVIOLO, *Lineamenti di storia dei CC. RR. Somaschi* (Rome 1957).

[P. BIANCHINI/EDS.]

SON OF DAVID

A messianic title describing Jesus Christ as man, a SAVIOR of His people who would bring Israel the full enjoyment of God's promises. It is based on God's assurance to DAVID (2 Sm 7.13–29) that his kingship would last forever. Time proved that these words could not be understood literally, but Jewish hope transcended time and gave the promise an eschatological dimension. Men believed that a king would inaugurate this blessed era in this world. '''I have made a covenant with my chosen one, I have sworn to David my servant: Forever will I confirm your posterity and establish your throne for all generations''' [Ps 88(89).45].

The exile of Israel strengthened this interpretation. Jeremiah wrote: ''On that day, says the Lord of hosts . . . they shall serve the Lord, their God, and David, their king, whom I will raise up for them'' (30.8–9). According to Ezekiel, all Israelites will be united forever in one kingdom under David (Ez 37.24–26). Psalm 2 describes the submission of all nations to the king appointed by the Lord. Some expected a civil ruler, a prince of peace (Zec 9.9–10); others believed that he would be a warrior who would rule with ''a rod of iron,'' as in the Psalms of Solomon (17.26). This latter work (17, 18) suggests that Son of David was a messianic title favored by the Pharisees, who taught that he would expel pagans from Jerusalem, purify the city, and restore the Davidic kingdom. A popular opinion about the return of David's Son prevailed in Palestine at the time of Christ (Mt 12.23; Jn 7.41–42). The synoptists used this title in the cure of the blind Bartimaeus (Mt 20.30–31; Mk 10.47–48; Lk 18.38–39). Matthew introduced it in the genealogy (1.1), cure of two blind men (9.27), crowd (12.23), Syro-Phoenician woman (15.22), Palm Sunday (21.9), Temple (21.15). Jesus did not welcome the title and tried to open men's minds to another concept of the Messiah. Paul used the phrase ''born of the seed of David'' and linked it with the statement that Jesus is the SON OF GOD (Rom 1.3–5). This relationship was recognized in the primitive Church (Lk 1.26–38; Acts 13.16–41; Ignatius *Ad Eph.* 20.2; *Ad Smyrn.* 1.1). In the *Epistle to Barnabas* (12.10–11) ''Son of David'' is rejected as heretical and Jesus is called instead the Son of God. This is in harmony with Jesus' own teaching. Just as He invited men to look beyond the restoration of the earthly kingdom long associated with David, so the primitive Church was not content with ''Son of David'' but preferred to use ''Son of God.''

See Also: JESUS CHRIST, III, 7; MESSIANISM.

Bibliography: B. VAN IERSEL, ''Fits de David et Fils de Dieu,'' *La Venue du Messie* (Recherches Bibliques 6; Louvain 1962). V. TAYLOR, *The Names of Jesus* (New York 1953). O. CULLMANN, *The Christology of the New Testament,* tr. S. GUTHRIE and C. HALL (Philadelphia 1959). E. LOHMEYER, *Gottesknecht und Davidsohn* (Göttingen 1953).

[K. SULLIVAN]

SON OF GOD

The concept is first considered according to its Biblical employment (with attention given here to the relevance of other Near Eastern usage); it is then treated for its significance in subsequent theology.

IN THE BIBLE

The term son of God was used (1) in the ancient Near East to express a variety of relationships of man or the world to God or the gods; (2) in the Old Testament for the people or the king as chosen and called to special intimacy with God; (3) in later Judaism for the pious or just; (4) in the New Testament of Jesus as the chosen, the Messiah, and Son of God in a new sense illumined by His teaching and especially by His Resurrection, and given theological precision by the Epistles of Paul and the Fourth Gospel.

In the Ancient Near East. Here theophoric names expressive of a man's relation of sonship to a particular god were widespread: e.g., Ben-Hadad, meaning son of (the god) Hadad; Bar-Rekub, son of (the god) Rekub; Abiel (1 Sm 9.1), meaning (the god) El is my father; Abiah, Yahweh is my father (1 Sm 8.2; 2 Chr 13.20); Abibaal, Baal is my father. These names were meant to express confident trust in the god's fatherly protection, the sonship being conceived, at most, as adoptive.

When appropriated by kings, the term son of God was frequently understood to express a really divine character in its bearer. This was particularly true of the kings of Egypt, who called themselves the sons of Ra; the Ptolemies took the title θεὸς ἐκ θεῶν (god of the gods). By New Testament times the Roman emperors had taken over the Near Eastern practice. Inscriptions from Pergamum, Magnesia, and Tarsus give Augustus and his successors the title son of god, θεοῦ υἱός (*divi filius*).

''Madonna and Child,'' painting by Sandro Botticelli. (©Francis G. Mayer/CORBIS)

There was a growing tendency to attribute divine qualities to exceptional men. A prophet or a wonder-worker of the Hellenistic world was called a divine man or son of god. In this way in the HERMETIC LITERATURE, a man who undergoes a rebirth may become ''a god, a child of god.'' Counter to this seeming devaluation of the transcendence of the god, certain philosophical circles spoke of the created cosmos, or of its archetype, or of the LOGOS, as the only true son of god—using the title in a clearly metaphorical sense for the mediating or emanating essences through which the supreme god creates the world, through which he may also be known. Nevertheless, the distinction between the divine and the human spheres eventually wore thin [''Man on earth is a mortal god; god in heaven is an immortal man''; *Corpus Hermeticum* 10(key).25].

In the Old Testament. The king was understood in the Old Testament to stand in a special relation of sonship to God, and although the title son of God is never given to the king explicitly, Yahweh is frequently depicted as calling him ''my son'' (2 Sm 7.14; 1 Chr 22.10; Ps 2.7), ''my firstborn'' [Ps 88(89).28]. This unique relationship was rooted in Yahweh's choice (1 Chr 28.6) and was acknowledged at the king's enthronement: ''You are my son; this day I have begotten you'' (Ps 2.7). The king was thus understood to sit on Yahweh's throne (1 Chr 29.23), to be His representative and the witness of God's love and care for His people (2 Chr 9.8). Although divine wisdom is sometimes attributed to the king (2 Sm 14.20; 1 Kgs 3.12, 28), and a court poet goes so far as to call him *'ĕlōhîm,* ''god'' [in the same sense that the judges are so called in Ps 57(58).2; 81(82).1, 6], the king was never given divine worship in Israel, and the Prophets felt free to criticize the ruler as one who was himself subject to God's judgment (2 Sm 12.5–12). Hence, the tendency to exalt the king as God's son was tempered by that other more ancient tradition according to which the people of Israel itself is God's son in virtue of Yahweh's choice, deliverance, and covenant (Ex 4.22; Jer 31.9; Hos 11.1; Wis 18.13; *See* SONS OF GOD).

In Later Judaism. The Israelite in later Judaism who practiced the virtues, especially generosity to the poor, was ''like a son to the Most High'' (Sir 4.10); but

"Resurrection of Christ," ca. 1503, High Renaissance style painting by Raphael. (©Francis G. Mayer/CORBIS)

notably the title described the just man who excited the envy and malice of the wicked and was subjected by them to revilement and torture to try his patience (Wis 2.15–18); or the just whom God's fatherly providence chastised for their own good (Psalms of Solomon 13.8; 17.30; 18.4). At this period the royal Psalms [Ps 2; 44(45); 71(72); 109(110)] were interpreted as referring to the MESSIAH, and although the earlier idea of the king as son of God could be implicitly transferred, nowhere is the Messiah directly called the son of God. (In 4 Ezra 7.28, "my Son, the Messiah," is probably not original; and at any rate 4 Ezra is not pre-Christian.) There is hesitation (evident in the Aramaic translations of the Old Testament) in using this title even for the king or for the people for fear of its polytheistic connotations. Consequently, at the time of Jesus, Son of God was not a common title for the Messiah, although it is used at times in the New Testament in this sense (Mk 12.35–37; 14.61; Lk 4.41). Judaism never attributed a divine nature to the Messiah; the SON OF MAN (Dn 7.13–14) was interpreted in Enoch (ch. 46, 48, 52) as the Messiah, but was given preexisting, heavenly traits, quite out of keeping with the traditional earthly character and origin of the Davidic Messiah. When the rabbis said that the Messiah existed eternally with God, they meant merely that God knew from all eternity who the Messiah would be.

In the New Testament. In contrast to the Old Testament usage, the title Son of God in the New Testament differs both in frequency and in content. For the purposes of the present discussion, it is not possible to leave aside such other usages as "the Son," "His Son," "a Son," "My Son," "My beloved Son," and "the [His] only-begotten Son." Treatment will be made here of the New Testament depiction of Jesus' consciousness of His divine sonship, the conception of the primitive Christian community of His sonship, the theological clarifications of St. Paul, and the Johannine development.

Jesus' Consciousness of Divine Sonship. In the Synoptic Gospels Jesus, who frequently calls Himself Son of Man, never applies to Himself the title Son of God. Others, however, use it frequently of Him (nine times in Matthew; five times in Mark; six times in Luke). From this it does not follow that the conception of Jesus' divine sonship derived uniquely from the faith of the Christian community. The Synoptics attest that the primitive Christian faith in the divinity of Jesus was rooted, not merely in the fact of the Resurrection, but also in the illumination this brought concerning Jesus' own statements and deeds during His public ministry, which His Disciples at first did not adequately understand. That Jesus conceived of Himself and presented Himself as the Son of God in a unique and preeminent sense appears repeatedly in the Synoptic tradition. An allusion appears in the Parable of the Vinedressers, in which a qualitative difference is stressed between the servants and the son, the heir (Mk 12.1–12 and parallels). If this is discounted as merely stressing the preeminence of the Messiah over His forerunners, the same cannot be said of the question concerning the origin of the Messiah: if David calls his son Lord, how can He be merely his son? (Mk 12.37). Jesus' deliberate usage of "your Father" when speaking of His Disciples' relation to God, as contrasted with "my Father" when speaking of His own (Mt 7.21; 10.32–33; 11.27; 12.50; Lk 2.49; 10.22), and the conspicuous absence of the term "our Father" applying to both together evidence a clear distinction between the two. The passage of Mt 11.27 (parallel to Lk 10.22) is important in this context: "All things have been delivered to me by my Father; and no one knows the Son except the Father; nor does anyone know the Father except the Son, and him to whom the Son chooses to reveal him." The statement portrays a claim to a knowledge by Jesus of God in His personal relationship, a knowledge that the Son alone possesses and that corresponds to the Father's personal knowledge of the Son, a knowledge that the Son alone can communicate. Particularly interesting is the logion of Mk 13.32 concerning the Last Day: "But of that day or hour no one knows, neither the angels in heaven, nor the Son, but the Father only." The authenticity of this passage can hardly be questioned, for a community bent on exalting its Lord would scarcely have constructed a saying in which He confesses ignorance. In this text Jesus uses ''Son'' of Himself, not as men or angels are sons, but as He alone stands as Son in His distinctive relationship with God.

Primitive Christian Concept of Jesus' Divine Sonship. Although Jesus was conscious of His divine sonship, this divine sonship in the strict sense was not so clear from the beginning to His contemporaries or His Disciples; hence the importance of distinguishing the meaning of the term Son of God when used in the original life situation of Jesus and the enriched meaning perceived by the Evangelist, in the redaction of the account. At the more primitive stages of the New Testament tradition, the title Son of God frequently is used or is shown to be understood in less profound senses. (1) It is not always clear what the term means when spoken by the demons; it may mean only man of God (Mt 8.29 and parallels; Lk 8.28; Mk 3.11; Mk 1.25 and parallels: the Holy One of God), but in Lk 4.41 it clearly means the Messiah. (2) Used by the centurion at the Crucifixion, it seems to have meant only a just man (cf. Mt 27.54 and Mk 15.39 with Lk 23.47). (3) In the INFANCY NARRATIVES the child to be born shall be called the ''Son of the Most High'' [Ps 81(82).6] because the ''Lord God will give him the throne of David, his father'' (Lk 1.32), i.e., He will be the Davidic Messiah; and He will be called the Son of God because He is conceived by the Holy Spirit and the power of the Most High (Lk 1.35). The ''Son of the living God'' in Peter's Matthaean confession (Mt 16.16) seems to modify Mk 8.29, in which Peter confesses Jesus' messiahship. (4) In the accounts of the baptism and the Transfiguration of Jesus, the voice from heaven declaring Jesus to be God's only-begotten Son reveals the highest point of intimacy with the Father. The two events are connected certainly with Jesus' messianic mission (see also Mt 3.17 and parallels; 17.5 and parallels). (5) In Mark's account of the trial of Jesus, the high priest asks ''Art thou the Christ, the Son of the Blessed One?'' (Mk 14.61). Is the second title an appositive of the first, or does it mean the divine sonship in a higher sense? Matthew's version of the question has ''Christ, the Son of God'' (Mt 26.63). Luke's version makes two separate interrogations: ''If thou art the Christ, tell us'' (Lk 22.66), and after Jesus' prophecy concerning the Son of Man, ''Art thou, then, the Son of God?'' (22.67). Luke seems clearly to distinguish the two titles. The evidence that Son of God was not a current title for the Messiah, that the claim to mere messiahship could hardly have been a pretext for the accusation of blasphemy, and that the teaching of Jesus (which John assures his readers was a major object of the trial: Jn 18.19) had laid much more stress on the religious nature of His mission than on His earthly sonship of David—all this points to the fact that Son of God, particularly as qualified by the Son of Man statement in the context, was understood by the Sanhedrin to be something quite beyond messiahship, namely, Jesus' claim to an intimacy with God given to no other mortal.

It was in the Resurrection that the Disciples recognized Jesus as ''the Son of God in power'' (Rom 1.4), and thereafter the title is charged with a new significance. In their report of the earthly life of Jesus, which Mark entitles ''the good news about Jesus Christ, the Son of God'' (Mk 1.1), the Synoptic Evangelists portray His divine power more by what Jesus did than by what He said. That the demons are subject to Him (Mt 8.28–34 and parallels) is proof that God's royal power is manifest in Him (Mt 12.28). He assumes the divine prerogative of forgiving sinners on His own authority (Mk 2.5, 7). He is not bound to the limits of Scripture and tradition in His teaching, as are the Scribes and Pharisees, but teaches with full authority (Mk 1.22; Mt 7.28–29), not hesitating to improve on the divine law (Mk 10.1–12; Mt 5.21–48). His word abides forever (Mk 13.31), a claim which the Old Testament had reserved for the word of God (Is 40.8).

The Resurrection of Jesus and the descent of the Holy Spirit strengthened the originally weak faith of the Disciples (Mk 8.17–21; 6.51–52; Mt 14.33) and clarified what had originally been a stumbling block for them (Mk 8.32), namely, that it was indeed the divine plan for Jesus to enter His glory by way of suffering and death (Lk 23.26, 46; 1 Pt 1.11), that in order to fulfill the prophecies concerning the Messiah and the conception of the glorious Son of Man, He would first fulfill those that told of the Suffering Servant of Yahweh (Acts 4.27, 30; Mk 9.12; 10.45; Mt 17.12; *see* SUFFERING SERVANT, SONGS OF). The Resurrection thus appeared as the reversal of the judgment of the Sanhedrin and as the instatement of Jesus in the fullness of His glory as Lord and Messiah (Acts 2.36; 5.31). As this glory is something strictly divine, the term Son of God now connotes the enthronement in a royal dignity that is also divine. To Christ are now applied statements reserved to Yahweh in the Old Testament: salvation through invoking the name of Jesus (Acts 4.10, 12); coming at the end of time to judge the living and the dead (Acts 10.42;17.30). The consciousness that such a dignity belonged to Christ by right and by preexistence becomes clearer, but it is St. Paul who gives the theological precision.

St. Paul's Theological Clarifications. In the Pauline Epistles, Lord is the preferred title for expressing the divine glory of the risen Christ. Paul does not hesitate to transfer to the Person of Christ this title reserved to Yahweh in the Old Testament: ''God has exalted him and bestowed on him the name which is above every name [in the Old Testament this could only be Yahweh], that at the name of Jesus every knee should bend, in heaven and on earth and under the earth, and every tongue confess, to the glory of God the Father, that Jesus Christ is Lord'' (Phil 2.9–11). It is in the same vein that in Rom 1.4 Paul states that God's Son was ''constituted Son of God by an act of power in keeping with the holiness of his spirit, by resurrection from the dead.'' From Paul's doctrine elsewhere, it can be seen that this text does not imply that Jesus became Son of God at the Resurrection, but that the Resurrection manifested His divine sonship and instated Him in its fullness. (1) Christ's lordship, like Yahweh's in the Old Testament (Is 40.22–26; 45.18–24), is associated with creative power (1 Cor 8.16; Col 1.13–17). He was ''begotten before every creature'' (Col 1.15). (2) The ''sending'' of the Son implies His preexistence (esp. Gal 4.4; cf. Rom 8.3). (3) Christ ''was in the form of God from the start'' (Phil 2.6). The noun μορφή and the participle ὑπάρχων make it clear that Christ possessed the divine character essentially before His entry into time. (4) The Trinitarian texts (e.g., Eph 4.4–6; 1 Cor 12.4–6; 2 Cor 13.13) put the Son on the same level as the Father. In the prayer of 2 Thes 2.16–17, the Lord Jesus Christ is addressed before the Father, and the plural subject is preceded by a singular intensive pronoun (''himself'') and followed by singular verbs (see also 1 Thes 3.11). The Resurrection is the full expression of Christ's divine sonship, while at the same time it gives Him the power of becoming the principle of resurrection to His members, who are adopted sons of God (Rom 8.11). Hence, Paul gives precision to the Synoptic theology, but he takes for granted that he is not introducing anything novel into the Christian tradition (1 Cor 15.11; Rom 1.1–4). It is even probable that the passage of Phil 2.6–11 is a primitive hymn of a Palestinian Christian community incorporated by St. Paul in this letter. Nevertheless, in Paul the divinity of Christ is always considered in relation to the Father, who remains the first principle (1 Cor 3.22–23; 11.3; 15.24–27).

Johannine Development. In the Gospel of St. John, twice the title Son of God means nothing more than Messiah. Thus Nathanael's confession of faith, ''Rabbi, thou art the Son of God, thou art King of Israel!'' (Jn 1.49) regards the two as equivalent (see also 11.27). Or again ''the Son'' may be related to the concept of Son of Man and His mission (3.14–17). However, in ch. 5, the strife with the Jews begins over Jesus' curing on the Sabbath and ''calling God his own Father, making himself equal to God'' (5.18). The climax of the accusation comes in 19.7: ''We have a Law, and according to the Law he must die, because he has made himself the Son of God.'' The title here goes beyond messiahship and affirms the uniqueness of relationship between Son and Father that the entire Gospel of John describes. With the Synoptics, John portrays Jesus distinguishing ''my father'' and ''your father,'' adding ''my God'' and ''your God'' (20.17). But in John alone in the New Testament is the term only-begotten (Son) used of Jesus (1.14, 18; 3.16, 18). ''The Father is in me and I in the Father'' (10.38); seeing Jesus is seeing the Father (14.9), and Father and Son are embraced in one act of faith (12.44), because ''I and the Father are one'' (10.30). The Jews interpret this as blasphemy, ''You, being a man, make yourself God'' (10.33).

On the preexistence of the Son of God, John is clearer than any other New Testament author. If some of the statements (8.56; 12.41; 17.5, 24) can be interpreted as describing merely the glory that was foreseen by Abraham or Isaiah or that was predestined by the Father from all eternity, the same cannot be said of statements such as 6.63: ''What then if you should see the Son of Man ascending to where he was before?'' and 8.58: ''Before Abraham came to be, I am.'' The intentional contrast here between an existence that had a beginning and one that transcends time and history, coupled with the use of the divine name revealed to Moses, witnesses to a claim to full divinity, and the Jews are shown to understand the claim by their attempt to stone Him (8.59). Similarly, in the words of the Baptist, ''After me there comes one who has been set above me, because before me he was'' (1.30), the stress is on the verb relegated to the end of the clause, which predicates a transcendent existence to Christ. The progression of faith in the Disciples is climaxed in Thomas's post-Resurrection confession: ''My Lord and my God!'' (20.28).

The prologue is a synthesis of Johannine theology of the Son of God. Calling the preexisting Son the WORD, the text in swift strokes attributes to Him eternal preexistence (''In the beginning was the Word''), personal distinction from the Father (''and the Word was with God''), and divine nature (''and the Word was God'' —1.1). Then it evokes His role in the creation of absolutely everything (1.2). He is the principle of all being, the source of all life, and the light that enlightens every man (1.4–9). Then, touching on the shadow of rejection by His own, which will lengthen as the Gospel unfolds, John goes on to portray the gift of ''becoming sons of God'' given to those who received the Word when He came (1.11–12). The Word was made flesh, and in His human nature ''we saw his glory—glory as of the only-begotten of the Father'' (1.14). Glory in John expresses the manifestation of the divine nature of the only-begotten Son of God, which takes place already during His earthly life (2.11). It is the mission of the only-begotten to reveal the Father (1.18), and this expression of the Father to men partially explains John's choice of

Word as Jesus' title in the prologue. But the term Logos is more than functional. "His work is to reveal God to men, but this is itself founded upon the very nature of Christ; before all revelation He was already in a certain sense the Word of God (just as the sapiential books say of Wisdom that she was Wisdom in God even before the work of creation), He was in a certain sense the expression of the thought of God" (M. É. Boismard, 94). The prologue thus prepares and introduces the theme of the whole Gospel, namely, that the entire earthly career of Jesus is a projection on the plane of time of the eternal relationship between the Son and the Father.

The history of the term Son of God illustrates the attempt of the early Church to articulate a new experience for which it continually found the Old Testament and Hellenistic vocabulary and thought patterns inadequate. But other tools it did not have. It would be naïve to expect a Nicaean definition of those who first sought to translate into human words their experience of incarnate divinity. "Divinity is felt before it is named, and when it is named, the words are inadequate" (V. Taylor).

Bibliography: A. GELIN et al., *Son and Saviour,* tr. A. WHEATON (2d ed. Baltimore 1960). J. DE FRAINE, *Encyclopedic Dictionary of the Bible,* tr. and adap. by L. HARTMAN (New York 1963), from A. VAN DEN BORN, *Bijbels Woordenboek* 2264–70. V. TAYLOR, *The Names of Jesus* (New York 1953) 52–71. J. LEBRETON, *Dictionnaire de la Bible,* supplmental ed. by L. PIROT, et al. (Paris 1928–) 4:1025–34. E. HUNTRESS, "*Son of God* in Jewish Writings Prior to the Christian Era," *Journal of Biblical Literature* 54 (1935) 117–123. M. J. LAGRANGE, "Les Origines du dogme paulinien de la divinité du Christ," *Revue biblique* 45 (1936) 5–33. C. P. CEROKE, "The Divinity of Christ in the Gospels," *The Catholic Biblical Quarterly* 24 (1962) 125–139. B. M. F. VAN IERSEL, *"Der Sohn" in den synoptischen Jesusworten: Christusbezeichnung der Gemeinde oder Selbstbezeichnung Jesu?* (*Novum Testamentum* Supplement 3; 1961), with extensive bibliography. M. J. LAGRANGE, *Évangile selon saint Jean* (8th ed. Paris 1948) cxliv–clx. M. É. BOISMARD, *St. John's Prologue,* tr. CARISBROOKE DOMINICANS (Westminster, Maryland 1957). C. H. DODD, *The Interpretation of the Fourth Gospel* (Cambridge, England 1960) 250–262.

[G. T. MONTAGUE]

IN THEOLOGY

The place of Son of God in CHRISTOLOGY is the subject that will now be considered.

Christology. Concerned with the theological analysis and synthesis of the Church's faith in Jesus Christ, Christology is controlled by the dogmatic definition of the Council of CHALCEDON, 451: ". . .one and the same Christ, Son, Lord, only-begotten, proclaimed in two natures, without confusion, without change, without division, without separation. . ." (H. Denzinger, *Enchiridion symbolorum*, ed. A. Schönmetzer 302). In the classical theology of the West this statement of the Church's doctrine about Jesus Christ is developed by using the categories of formal ontology; the concepts of Person and nature are used, according to the analogy of proportionality, to interpret the formula of Chalcedon. Son of God within this setting is seen as the subject possessing, though in different manners, the divine nature and the human nature. From this position are drawn the soteriological consequences of the satisfactory and meritorious value of Jesus Christ's earthly actions, especially of His voluntary death; it also follows that Jesus Christ is the object of the supreme form of worship, adoration. The static character of the categories employed by classical Christology make for intellectual clarity in the theological statement of Son of God, and in this way the problems raised by Son of God can be appreciated. But these categories do not easily lend themselves to the interpretation of the significance of Son of God, which is the point of interest today (Leeming, 696).

Investigation into the origins of prescientific Christology, especially into the Christology of the New Testament writings, reveals an essentially dynamic approach to the understanding of the Person of Jesus Christ. The conclusion reached by C. H. Dodd (123) is that even in its developments New Testament Christology goes back to a primitive body of testimonies from the Old Testament, seen as declaring "the determinate counsel of God," now fulfilled in the events that constituted the life of Jesus Christ. J. Jeremias (30) takes this same dynamic approach to the understanding of the Person of Jesus Christ beyond the apostolic KERYGMA about Christ to the historical Jesus. In the very way in which Jesus speaks of God as ABBA, Father, this author (27) sees Jesus bearing witness to Himself as Son of God precisely because of the unique way in which He knows God: God has revealed Himself to Him as only a father can reveal himself to his son. Modern theologians, using existential categories (here given the precise meaning of the categories thrown up by the philosophic analysis of spiritual, personal being), are working to interpret the Christological formula of Chalcedon in such a way that Son of God is seen in a dynamic way. The purpose of this endeavour is not to replace classical Christology but to carry it through to another dimension.

Bibliography: A. MICHEL, *Dictionnaire de théologie catholique: Tables générales* (Paris 1951–) 2548–2655. R. SCHNACKENBURG and R. LACHENSCHMID, *Lexikon für Theologie und Kirche,* ed. J. HOFER and K. RAHNER, 10 v. (2d, new ed. Freiburg 1957–65) 9:851–857. O. CULLMANN, *The Christology of the New Testament,* tr. S. C. GUTHRIE and C. A. M. HALL (rev. ed. Philadelphia 1963). C. H. DODD, *According to the Scriptures* (New York 1953). J. JEREMIAS, *"Abba": The Central Message of the New Testament* (London 1965). K. RAHNER, "Current Problems in Christology," *Theological Investigations,* tr. C. ERNST (Baltimore 1961–) 1:149–200. B. LEEMING, "Reflections on English Christology" in A. GRILLMEIER and H. BACHT, *Das Konzil von Chalkedon: Geschichte und Gegenwart,* 3 v. (Würzburg 1951–54) 3:695–718. R. SCH-

NACKENBURG, ''Der Abstand der christologischen Aussagen des N.T. vom chalkedonischen Bekenntnis nach der Deutung Rudolf Bultmanns,'' *ibid.* 675–693.

[E. G. HARDWICK]

SON OF MAN

This title is of special interest because it was the one more particularly employed in the New Testament to designate Jesus and His mission. The import it had in His teaching is to be determined by the associations it already had in His day and the new content with which He endowed it. Accordingly, this article will investigate the Old Testament background of the term, its use in Jewish apocryphal writings, and its use in the New Testament.

Old Testament Background. The phrase ''son of man'' is a literal rendering of the Hebrew *ben 'ādām* (Aramaic, *bar 'ĕnāš;* Greek, υἱὸς ἀνθρώπου), an expression that more exactly means ''a man,'' or ''a human individual'' (see ADAM). It is not the common expression for man, but is used especially in poetic parallelism with more usual words for ''man'' (e.g., Nm 23.19; Is 51.12; 56.2; Ps 8.5). The prophet Ezekiel is addressed frequently (more than 90 times) by this title by God, a usage intended to accentuate his human state before the majesty of God.

The most important Old Testament occurrence of this expression is found in Dn 7.13. The interpretation of the apocalyptic vision of Daniel ch. 7 as it now stands is fairly clear (*see* DANIEL, BOOK OF). The four beasts who come up from the sea (7.1–7) represent the succession of world empires. While the judgment passed upon them represents the negative element of God's saving intervention, the positive element is seen in the establishment of God's rule, the messianic kingdom (*see* MESSIANISM), represented by the investiture of ''one like a son of man'' with dominion, glory, and kingship. The human figure represents a collectivity, ''the holy ones of the Most High'' (7.18, 27); just as the beasts were apt for symbolizing the pagan empires, so a human figure was apt for symbolizing God's kingdom. However, just as in this vision the four beasts can be understood, almost indifferently, to represent kings (7.17) or kingdoms (7.23), so also the human figure could symbolize the individual who rules and represents the kingdom of God. The figure in this vision is hardly to be identified with the Davidic Messiah, for he is a celestial being rather than a mortal; the clouds of heaven ''on'' or ''with'' (Aramaic *'im*) which he comes are commonly the vehicle of Yahweh and an element of divine theophanies. A. Feuillet, J. Coppens, and others have emphasized the fact the apocalyptic expectation looked for a kingdom established from above rather than a resurgence of the Davidic line.

There are some who think that the Son of Man did not appear for the first time in Dn 7.13, but was well-known in earlier, non-Israelite speculation; the human figure in this vision, according to these authors, would not need to be interpreted strictly within the framework of this chapter. Those who suggest such a prehistory (e.g., E. Sjöberg, S. Mowinckel) think especially of Iranian, Chaldean, and Gnostic myths of a primordial man (Anthropos, Gayomart), a cosmological and eschatological figure, the archetype of all men, who will come as a redeemer of men on the last day. Some non-Israelite prehistory of the Son of Man cannot be ruled out, but neither has it been proved. Most scholars hold that the structure of Daniel ch. 7 and standard Biblical imagery explain the appearance of the human figure, which, it is to be noted, is referred to in a rather indeterminate way: ''one like a son of man.'' Even if a new creation motif may be seen here (the raging sea, animals placed under dominion of a human figure with divine characteristics—cf. Gn 1.2, 26–28), the imagery and thought is still that drawn from the Bible.

Apocryphal Works. The Book of Enoch also, in the section called Parables or Similitudes (ch. 37–71), speaks of a celestial man who is closely connected with the establishment of God's kingdom. There are, however, difficult problems of original language, time of composition, and textual transmission of this book [*see* CANON, BIBLICAL].

In the Parables of Enoch (possibly 1st century B.C.) the Son of Man clearly emerges as an individual rather than as a symbol for a collectivity, as the Danielic figure was, although intimately united to the elect community. He is preexistent (48.2–3), will appear at the end of the world (62.4–5) to sit upon the throne of God (51.3) and exercise judgment (62.1). He is identified with the Messiah (48.10; 52.2) and in many passages is referred to as ''the Elect One.''

The question arises as to whether the Son of Man of Enoch can be explained simply as an evolution from the figure in Daniel, or whether non-Biblical ideas have entered in. Again there is a division of opinion. Mowinckel believes that the Son of Man in Enoch, where he is clearly an individual, goes back directly to the Anthropos myth, while Daniel's figure, a symbol for a collectivity, is a reinterpretation of the same myth. Thus the Enoch figure would not depend on that of Daniel, but both would depend on earlier tradition. Against this is the fact that the figure in Enoch does not have the nature of an archetype at all; while he is clearly an eschatological figure, there is nothing to connect him with the beginning except his preexistence. P. Grelot and others, therefore, accept Daniel ch. 7 as the point of departure for Enoch's Son of Man, while conceding that there has been a great deal of advance. The Parables of Enoch demonstrate very clearly that there existed in some circles of Judaism, probably before the time of Jesus, belief in a transcendent Messiah who could be referred to by the title Son of Man.

The same concept appears in 4 Ezra, in which "as it were the form of a man" rises from the sea and travels with the clouds of heaven (13.3), destroys the wicked with his breath (13.10–11, 27), and gathers together the lost ten tribes (13.12–13, 39–42). Like the Son of Man in Enoch, he has been kept by God for many ages to deliver creation (13.26) and is identified with the Messiah (cf. 13.32, 37, 52 with 7.28), who is referred to as God's Son. This apocalypse, probably composed near the end of the 1st Christian century, neither influenced the composition of the Gospels nor was influenced by them. Yet it does bear further witness to speculation concerning the Son of Man in Jewish circles near the time of Christ.

In the New Testament. It is most likely that the Christian community did not invent the title Son of Man and apply it to Jesus, but that He applied it to Himself, a title He preferred above all others and used almost exclusively. The title is found, for all practical purposes, in the mouth of Jesus alone. The rare exceptions are hardly true exceptions: in Jn 12.34 the crowd is quoting Him, and in Acts 7.56 Stephen sees the words of Christ in Mk 14.62 fulfilled; see also Rv 1.13 and 14.14. The usage is found in all strata of the Gospel tradition: Mark, the common source of Matthew and Luke, the materials proper to Matthew and Luke, respectively, and John (*see* SYNOPTIC GOSPELS).

It is clear from the discussion above that Son of Man was considered a messianic title in at least some circles. (For Jewish interpretation of the Danielic figure in a messianic sense during the rabbinic period, see texts given in Strack-Billerbeck on Mt 8.20.) Yet there are many who doubt that this usage was widely spread; no example of it has been found at Qumran, for instance. It is also true that while Jesus avoided the title Messiah (*see* MARK, GOSPEL ACCORDING TO), He freely used Son of Man. Part of the explanation probably lies in the nationalistic overtones the title Messiah had acquired in popular expectations and in political overtones that would have been a threat to His mission.

Jesus never mechanically adopted earlier traditions, but always transformed them to conform to His own original conception of His mission. Thus it is necessary to seek the meaning the term Son of Man took on in the light of His teaching and ministry. Scholars often distinguish various classes of Son of Man sayings: those in which the title refers to the glory and power of Jesus, hidden during His earthly ministry, but to be revealed at His Parousia (e.g., Mk 2.10; 8.38; 13.26–27; 14.62; Mt 10.23; 16.27; 19.28; 25.31); those in which the title recalls the humble circumstances of His ministry (e.g., Mt 8.20; 11.19); and those which refer to suffering and death (e.g., Mk 8:31; 9:31; 10:33). The first series builds in part upon the figure of Dn 7.13 (glory, power, clouds of heaven), but also goes beyond it (the Son of Man sits upon the throne of glory and judges), perhaps building upon the usage the Son of Man in Enoch. The second series of texts finds no parallels in earlier literature mentioning the Son of Man; however, the basic expression was apt for expressing the condition of human weakness (cf. its use in Ezekiel) in which the Savior had come, as well as the suffering He would endure in the absolute obedience by which He redeemed mankind. In the third series, Jesus brought a whole new content to the term Son of Man by applying to Himself under this rubric what had been said of the Servant of the Lord (*see* SUFFERING SERVANT, SONGS OF). At the Last Supper He said, "The Son of Man indeed goes his way, as it is written of him" (Mk 14.21, and see 9.11); the Scripture referred to is almost certainly Is 53.1–12 (cf. also 1 Cor 15.1–3; see Mk 10.45). The sayings that combine predictions of the Passion [*see* PASSION OF CHRIST, I (IN THE BIBLE)] and the Resurrection likewise find their natural source in the Servant of the Lord oracles. In thus combining two currents of thought under one title, the New Testament immeasurably enriched both: the Servant of the Lord, who by His obedient suffering and death would redeem Israel and all the world, was also the Son of Man who would one day be revealed in glory as God's Son and judge of all men. Both Old Testament figures find their fullest and most natural explanation as corporate personalities and so illustrate well the relationship of the faithful to Jesus: by incorporation into Christ the believer shares in that absolute obedience to the will of God which destroys sin and enables him to share in the glory of the second coming.

In the fourth Gospel also, Passion and glorification are both referred to in Son of Man passages, but here the tendency is to unite the two concepts more strictly, even to the extent of seeing the Passion already the beginning of Christ's glorification. This is done especially by the play on words in which "to be lifted up" (Jn 3.14; 8.28; 12.23, 34) signifies both His being raised up in crucifixion and His exaltation in one and the same act (*see* JOHN, GOSPEL ACCORDING TO ST.). St. John also puts a certain emphasis on Our Lord's preexistence in heaven (3.13; 6.63; 17.5; cf. 1.1–2); while this is a necessary corollary of faith in His divinity, it is possible that the formulation owes something to the teaching of Enoch. [*See* JESUS CHRIST (IN THE BIBLE).]

While the evangelists place all these "Son of Man" sayings in the mouth of Jesus, there is little doubt that the faith of the early Church developed the nucleus of sayings attributed to Jesus and enriched them with new insights from Christian faith. The degree to which this has been done is impossible to determine.

St. Paul does not use the term Son of Man, but he does speak of Jesus as "the Man" (the actual meaning of the longer phrase) in Rom 5.12–21, and as the "last Adam" in 1 Cor 15.45–49, in such a way as to link up with the Jewish speculation on Adam that was closely akin to and possibly dependent on myths concerning primordial man. Paul, however, clearly distinguishes and separates the figures (the first earthly, the second heavenly) that non-Christian thought had tended to identify. See further, O. Cullmann in bibliography.

Bibliography: *Encyclopedic Dictionary of the Bible,* translated and adapted by L. HARTMAN (New York, 1963) 2270–79. S. E. JOHNSON, G. A. BUTTRICK, ed., *The Interpreters' Dictionary of the Bible,* 4 v. (Nashville 1962) 4:413–420. E. SJÖBERG, *Der Menschensohn im äthiopischen Henochbuch* (Lund 1946). J. COPPENS and L. DEQUEKER, *Le Fils de l'homme et les Saints du Très-Haut en Daniel VII, dans les Apocryphes et dans le Nouveau Testament* (2d ed. Paris 1961), with ample bibliog. O. CULLMANN, *The Christology of the New Testament*, tr. S. C. GUTHRIE and C. A. M. HALL (Philadelphia 1959) 137–192. S. O. MOWINCKEL, *He That Cometh*, tr. G. W. ANDERSON (Nashville 1956) 346–450. C. H. DODD, *The Interpretation of the Fourth Gospel* (Cambridge, England 1953) 241–249. P. GRELOT, "Le Messie dans les Apocryphes de l'Ancien Testament," *La Venue du Messie*, ed., E. MASSAUX et al. (Bruges 1962) 19–50. A. J. B. HIGGINS, "Son of Man-Forschung since The Teaching of Jesus," *New Testament Essays; Studies in Memory of T. W. Manson, 1893–1958*, ed. A. J. B. HIGGINS (Manchester 1959) 119–135. A. FEUILLET, "Le Fils de l'homme de Daniel et la tradition biblique," *Revue Biblique* 60 (Paris 1892–) 170–202, 321–346. T. W. MANSON, "The Son of Man in Daniel, Enoch, and the Gospels," *The Bulletin of the John Rylands Library* 32 (Manchester 1949–50) 171–193. V. TAYLOR, "The Son of Man Sayings Relating to the Parousia," *Expository Times* 58 (Edinburgh 1946–47) 12–15. D. R. BURKETT, *The Son of Man Debate: A History and Evaluation* 107 (Cambridge and New York 1999). G. W. E. NICKELSBURG, "Son of Man," *Anchor Bible Dictionary* 6:137–150. J. A. FITZMYER, "Some Implications of the New Henoch Literature from Qumran," *Theological Studies* 38 (1977) 221–45.

[J. JENSEN]

SONG OF SONGS

The Song of Songs, or Canticle of Canticles, is a canonical book of the OT. The title means "the greatest song," and the book is the first of the *m^egillôt* or "scrolls" used in the liturgy of the Synagogue. This article treats of its author, date, and canonicity; its literary structure; its content; and its interpretation.

Authorship. The authorship is unknown; the mention of Solomon in 3.7; 8.11 probably is a reason why this postexilic work was ascribed to him. Although some of the songs are doubtless pre-exilic (as suggested by the reference to Thersa, the early capital of the Northern Kingdom, in 6.4), the form of the language, as a whole, suggests a late date. Early Jewish tradition indicates that there was some opposition before the first Christian century to its inclusion in the canon [see W. Rudolph, *Zeitschrift für die alttestamentliche Wissenschaft* 18 (1942–43) 189–199]. Among Christians, Theodore of Mopsuestia is alleged to have opposed the work; but the condemnation of Theodore at Chalcedon V in 553 is aimed at his views concerning the inspired character of the book, not at the so-called naturalistic interpretation attributed to him [see R. E. Murphy, *The Catholic Biblical Quarterly* 15 (1953) 502–503; A. Brunet, *Études et Recherches* 9 (Ottawa 1955) 155–170]

Literary Structure. Although there are refrains in the work (2.7; 3.5; 8.4; etc.), there has been no general agreement on the division into poetic units. A. Bea finds seven; the CCD has 24 subheadings. As the book now stands, several songs have been combined into a loose unity. Some scholars (e.g., F. Delitzsch) have interpreted it as a drama, with two leading characters, Solomon and the Sulamite girl (cf. Ct. 7.1). Others (e.g, H. Ewald; W. Pouget-J. Guitton) have recognized three characters: the girl, her rustic lover, and Solomon, whose blandishments the girl resists. But the dramatic interpretation has not been able to overcome its own subjective and arbitrary explanations. There is no example of any drama in all of ancient Semitic literature, and in this book any conflict between the alleged suitors necessary for true drama seems to be absent. The truth in this view is that the Song is in a certain sense dramatic, since it is a dialogue, as the ancients recognized and as the Hebrew text itself makes clear; hence, modern translations (e.g., CCD) supply marginal rubrics to indicate the speakers.

Contents. As a collection of love lyrics, this book is not easy to summarize. The poems follow no logical sequence; rather, they express the various moods of love: the joy of union, the pain of separation. There are protestations of love and fidelity, reminiscences of courtship, descriptions of each other's beauty. The mood of mutual love is sustained throughout, but a high-point is reached in 8.6–7, "Set me as a seal on your heart. . . ." The imagery is spontaneous and varied: gazelles and hinds, pomegranates and mandrakes, myrrh and spices, vineyards and wine. The rich use of geographical references suggests the disparate origins of the lyrics: Cedar, Engaddi, Lebanon, etc.

Interpretation. If identifying the literary structure is difficult, the interpretation of the meaning is more so. Both Christian and Jewish interpretations have agreed on a religious meaning: this book describes the love of Yahweh and Israel (or Christ and the Church) in terms of human marriage, thus continuing the theme inaugurated by Hosea (ch. 1–3) and echoed in many later prophets (Is 1.21–22; 62.5; Jer 3.1–10; Ez ch. 16, 23).

As Parable or Allegory. In detail, this interpretation is worked out as a parable, or as an allegory. The parabolic view is presented by D. Buzy, who claims that the work as a whole deals with the covenant relationship under the guise of human marriage. One should not press the details here; they serve to create the marriage atmosphere and to carry on the theme. Others argue that the Song is an allegory; the details have each a transferred meaning, referring to various aspects of Yahweh's dealings with Israel. This approach was first given a strong philological and exegetical basis by P. Joüon, and it has been supported by the method of *style anthologique,* applied by A. Robert. The ''anthological style'' refers to the Biblical practice (e.g., in Prv ch. 1–9, Sir, Wis) of composing a work in phrases and diction borrowed from earlier Biblical works; presumably the allusions to the previous books betray the intention of the writer of this book.

As Cultic Songs. Another interpretation, by such scholars as T. Meek, M. Haller, H. Ringgren, H. Schmökel, finds in this book cultic songs of the pagan myth of Tammuz and Ishtar. Presumably these could have been sung in the temple (e.g., during the reign of Manasseh) and might later have entered the Passover liturgy. But the contacts that are pointed out between the Song and the myth are not sufficient to establish this interpretation. Nor can one easily imagine that Israel would have glossed over such origins in eventually accepting the poems into the canon. Any similarity is more easily explained by the influence that popular beliefs might have had on the love poetry and the wedding imagery of the Israelites themselves.

As Extolling Human Love. In recent times several Catholic scholars have criticized both the allegorical and parabolic approach. The principal reason for this criticism is that the obvious meaning of the Song is human love. When human love is used in the prophetical writing as referring to Yahweh and Israel, the explanation of the symbolism is always given. Hence we may not presume that the intent of this book goes beyond the obvious and direct meaning. The use made by the prophets is usually in terms of Israel as the adulterous spouse (Hos 2.18–22; Is 62.5; etc. are clear exceptions), but the Song presents a picture of idyllic love. The elaborate use of anthological style by A. Robert and A. Feuillet has not convinced many, especially for the reason that there is no indication in the Song of alleged mercy toward an unfaithful spouse.

There is a strong trend among recent Catholic scholars to agree with many of their Protestant colleagues (H. H. Rowley, W. Rudolph, etc.) that the literal sense of this book is the extolling of love and fidelity between man and woman; so say J. P. Audet, A. Dubarle (at the Louvain *journées bibliques* of 1963), M. van den Oudenrijn, and others. Comparison of this book with the love poems of the ancient Near East, especially Egypt, shows a common atmosphere and similarity of theme. The Song would be the ''voice of the bridegroom'' and the ''voice of the bride'' mentioned in Jer 7.34 (Audet). Such praise of love is entirely consonant with inspiration, since God himself is the author of that love (Gn 1.27).

In line with this deeper understanding of love, these scholars also allow that a higher sense, fuller or typical, can be found here. Human love is a participation in divine love, to which it is oriented; the family reflects the people of God. Here exegesis would join the age-old interpretation that sees in the Song the description of the love between God and his People. Christian tradition has developed this theme, already found in the NT (Eph 5.23–25, marriage compared to the relationship between Christ and his Church). The famous medieval writers, such as St. Bernard, and the mystical writers, such as St. John of the Cross, have exploited the richness of this interpretation.

Bibliography: For surveys, see R. E. MURPHY, ''Recent Literature on the Canticle,'' *The Catholic Biblica Quarterly* 16 (1954) 1–11. H. H. ROWLEY, *The Servant of the Lord and Other Essays on the Old Testament* (London 1952). A complete and up-to-date bibliography is to be found in the two recent commentaries: A. ROBERT et al., eds. and trs., *Le Cantique des cantiques* (Études bibliques; Paris 1963) 29–39 and G. GERLEMAN, *Ruth, Das Hohelied* (Biblischer Kommentar: Altes Testament 18.2; Neukirchen 1963) 85–92. D. BUZY, ed. and tr., *Le Cantique des Cantiques* (Paris 1950). T. MEEK, *The Song of Songs, The Interpreters' Bible*, ed. G. A. BUTTRICK et al. (New York 1951–57) 5:91–148. W. RUDOLPH, *Das Buch Ruth, Das Hohe Lied, Die Klagelieder* (Kommentar zum Alten Testament 17:1–3; Gütersloh 1962). For comparisons with ancient Near Eastern literatures, cf. the excursus in the volume by Robert, et al. 339–421. A history of interpretation is to be found in F. OHLY, *Hohelied-Studien* (Wiesbaden 1958). Two important articles are: A. M. DUBARLE, ''L'Amour humain dans le Cantique des cantiques,'' *Revue biblique* 61 (1954) 67–86. J. P. AUDET, ''Le Sens du Cantique des cantiques,'' *Revue biblique* 62 (1955) 197–221.

[R. E. MURPHY]

SONNET, RELIGIOUS USE OF

After some centuries of existence as a light love lyric, the sonnet began to find profound religious use in late 16th-century England. After *Tottel's Miscellany* introduced, in 1557, the sonnets of Thomas Wyatt (1503–42) and the Earl of Surrey (1517?–46?), the Petrarchan tradition of languishing lovers complaining of cruel mistresses in 14 lines of closely rhymed iambic pentameter verses flourished, and collections of sonnet sequences flooded the literary market. But a number of writers began to experiment with the form as an expression of religious thought and feeling. In the last decade of the century, the Protestant Barnabe Barnes (1570?–1609) and the Catholic Henry Constable (1562–1613) turned out undistinguished collections of *Spirituall Sonnettes.* A far better poet, Sidney, in his ''Leave me, O love which reachest but to dust,'' used the sonnet to celebrate the progress from mortal love to ''Eternall Love.'' Shakespeare, in sonnets such as his 116, 129, and 146, echoed the religious insights of St. Paul. In Sonnet 116 (''Let me not to the marriage of true minds / Admit impediments''), for example, Shakespeare embodied much of ch. 13 of 1 Corinthians, and followed Paul's thought so far as to state that if there were no love (in the full Pauline sense of the unselfish willing of the good of another), both literature and life would be meaningless: ''If this be error and upon me proved, Solidus never writ, nor no man ever loved.''

The first complete flowering of the religious use of the sonnet came with DONNE'S *Holy Sonnets,* written in the early years of the 17th century. Here for the first time a great poet demanded that sonnets set forth carefully articulated Christian dogma, sometimes with enormous power (''Batter my heart, three-personed God'') and sometimes with profound tenderness (''Immensitie cloysterd in thy deare wombe'').

In two famous sonnets, Milton's ''soul-animating strains'' expressed religious conviction: ''On his blindness,'' which accepts God's providence in spite of appearances, and ''Thy martyred saints,'' which foretells the triumph of God's justice.

Wordsworth's Treatment. For the next century and a half, interest in the sonnet waned, and not until Wordsworth joined in the attempts to revive the Petrarchan tradition did the religious use of the sonnet by a great poet appear once again. The results here were largely unfortunate. In some of his good sonnets, such as ''The World is too much with us,'' Wordsworth expressed his conviction that a response to natural beauty will evoke also a religious response—though to him this may mean no more than bringing oneself to an experience of one's own spirituality. But Wordsworth called upon the sonnet to express dogmatic facts in historical sequence in his long *Ecclesiastical Sonnets,* a history of the Anglican Church.

These poor, warped poems fail to express any profound grasp of Christian dogma, to say nothing of the bathetic things they do with history. They clumsily and grotesquely attack the Catholic Church at times, as in the section (xix–xvii) depicting the dissolution of the monasteries and shrines during Henry VIII's reign. Here monks and nuns sit on either side of a huge hearth quaffing beer and roaring, ''Our kingdom's here.'' The dismissal of the saints and of idolatry, after being noted and approved, is sentimentally mourned. The sonnet often included in Catholic anthologies, ''The Virgin'' (xxv), with its much-quoted line, ''Our tainted nature's solitary boast,'' appears at this point. Its statement, ''Thy image falls to earth,'' often glossed as a Protestant poet's tribute to Mary's influence, in context means merely, ''Your statue, your graven image, forbidden by God, fails to the ground.'' But, the poem goes on to say, the idolatry of Catholics might merit forgiveness because of the beauty of the Ideal Woman—scarcely a Catholic or an Anglican attitude. A careful reading of the poem will disclose that Wordsworth is really writing about a goddess whose beauty he admires, not about the Mother of God.

Hopkins's Achievements. The highest point for the religious use of the sonnet comes between 1875 and 1889, the productive years of one of England's great religious poets, Gerard Manley HOPKINS. Like Wordsworth, Hopkins set forth, as in ''God's Grandeur,'' a response to natural beauty, but in and beyond nature he responded also to God, the dynamic Creator and Sustainer of nature. Hopkins, too, drew upon Christian dogma for the elements of his sonnets; and in ''The Windhover: To Christ our Lord'' and ''As Kingfishers Catch Fire,'' he echoed St. Paul far more pointedly and profoundly than did Shakespeare, expressing the Catholic insight of the identity of Christ and Christian in the Mystical Body— ''I live now, not I, but Christ lives in me.''

The success of Donne and Hopkins (and Wordsworth's failure) in using the sonnet for religious ends may indeed, as Louis Martz suggests in his study of the poetry of meditation, owe something to the activity of Ignatian meditation influencing the artistic vision and techniques of those artists (or failing to do so, as in Wordsworth's case). More likely, however, is the supposition that the power of Catholic tradition added to the vigor and depth of Catholic belief (qualified but not destroyed in Donne's vision) provided the added element rare in our literature to account for the bias and the success of these poets in their religious sonnets.

Bibliography: L. L. MARTZ, *The Poetry of Meditation* (New Haven 1954; repr. pa. 1962).

[R. BOYLE]

SONS OF DIVINE PROVIDENCE

Filii Divinae Providentiae (FDP; Official Catholic Directory #0410), a congregation of priests with papal approbation (1944 and 1954), founded by Don Luigi Orione in 1903. It is one of five communities that comprise Orione's Little Work of Divine Providence; there are communities of priests, brothers, hermits, and two of sisters (the LITTLE MISSIONARY SISTERS OF CHARITY, and the Perpetual Adorers of the Blessed Sacrament; the members of the latter group are blind persons). Orione began his apostolate as a seminarian at Tortona, Italy, in 1892, and after ordination he established a series of oratories for the care and education of neglected boys. The bishop of Tortona gave initial approval to Orione and his companions on March 21, 1903, under the name Sons of Divine Providence. The first foundation in the United States was established at Boston, Massachusetts, in 1949. The generalate is in Rome.

Bibliography: D. SPARPAGLIONE, *Vita di Don Orione* (Venice 1942). D. HYDE, *God's Bandit* (Westminster, Maryland 1957).

[J. COSS/EDS.]

SONS OF GOD

The title sons of God was used outside Israel for beings that belonged to the divine sphere or for men who worshiped a given deity, and in Israel, for beings, heavenly or earthly, who were in some way associated with divine functions; for the members of Israel as objects of the divine election, and for the pious. In the New Testament it is used for those who do God's will and imitate His love for all men, and for those chosen and adopted by God who accept through faith the Redemption by Christ.

Outside Israel. The term sons of God was a common term in the mythologies of the ancient Near East for the divine offspring of a certain god or goddess. Thus, in the Ugaritic texts, EL and his consort Asherah are clearly designated as the parents of the gods who are collectively designated as the ''seventy children of Asherah'' (II *Anchor Bible* VI 46), ''the generation [circle, family] of El,'' (III K III 17–19), or the ''circle of the sons of El,'' (2:17, 34; 107:2). Similarly, in Babylonia, Apsu and Tiamat are the begetters of the gods, Anu is Anshar's firstborn, etc. (see J. B. Pritchard, *Ancient Near Eastern Texts Relating to the Old Testament*, 61).

The term is likewise used of demigods, whether these are represented as the offspring of god and man (Gilgamesh being depicted as two-thirds god and one-third man), or as a kind of god incarnate, as were the kings of Egypt, or the Phoenician Keret, a mortal hero or king who addresses El as his Father (I K 41, 59, 76, 169) and is called ''the son of El'' and ''the offspring of the Beneficent and Holy One'' (II K I–II 10–11, 20, 21).

The worshipers of a national god are called the sons of this god, who was considered to be the head of the tribe, family, or house (whence the term ''the lord of the house'' among the Aramaeans of the 9th and 8th centuries B.C.). Early in the 1st millennium the Aramaeans named their children ''Son of (the god) Hadad,'' a custom that later became very popular among the pagans of Syria and Mesopotamia in the early Christian age. An echo of this widespread practice is found in Nm 21.29, where the worshipers of Chamos, god of the Moabites, are called his sons and daughters (see also Jer 2.27).

Finally, in keeping with the Semitic usage of the word son in the sense of one belonging to a class or group, the title sons of God may stand for the whole assembly of divine beings, for those who belong to the sphere of the divine.

In Israel. In adapting the title sons of God to its monotheistic faith, the Old Testament used it with various meanings.

Applied to the Angels. The title most frequently refers to those heavenly beings who form the court of God, who serve Him, act as His messengers and at times do battle for Him, who were later given the technical title angels [Jb 1.5; 2.1; 38.7; Ps 28(29).1; 88(89).7; Dn 3.24; see also 1 Kgs 22.19; Gn 35.7]. This general usage invites taking sons of God in the controverted passage Gn 6.1–4 in the same sense, particularly in virtue of the contrast there between sons of God and daughters of men. The Septuagint (LXX), later Judaism (esp. the book of Enoch 5.1–10.17), and nearly all the Fathers of the first three centuries concur in this interpretation. The other interpretation that sees in these sons of God the Sethites and in the daughters of men the Cainites dates from the 4th century and is influenced by theological concern for maintaining the spirituality of the angels (H. DENZINGER, *Enchiridion symbolorum,* 428). For the same reason and also because they find it difficult to admit that the sacred author could have made use of material from a pagan myth, many modern Catholic scholars hold to the latter interpretation. Yet it is generally admitted today that the principle of Biblical inspiration does not exclude the possibility that the sacred author picked up and reworked a preexisting popular tale about a race of giants before the flood. Babylonian and Greek mythologies speak of the gods having intercourse with mortal women; the monotheistic author who used the expression sons of God and the Israelite who heard this section recited would certainly have understood the term in a way compatible with Israelite monotheism, and hence as meaning the angels rather than gods. Far from approving the practice, the sacred author rather uses the tale to climax his illustration of the progression of wickedness upon the earth, which prepares the flood. Moreover, by upsetting the natural order in what is left of the tale (vv. 1, 2, 4, 3), the author reveals his intention to deny these illicit relationships any proper causality in the phenomenon of giants. Thus the author may be said to have used the materials of a myth to reverse the myth's original proposition: a claim to immortality by the physical, procreative transmission of the divine spirit of the gods. Such a claim is impious, for man's spirit is from Yahweh (v. 4), who may withdraw it or limit it at will. (*See* ANGELS, 1.)

A similar problem is raised by Dt 32.8–9: ''When the Most High assigned the nations their heritage, when he parceled out the descendants of Adam, He set up the boundaries of the peoples after the number of the sons of God; while the Lord's own portion was Jacob, His hereditary share was Israel.'' The Masoretic Text has ''sons of Israel,'' but the LXX reading, ''sons of God,'' has been confirmed by the Hebrew manuscript of Deuteronomy found in Cave 4 at Qumran. Here again the imagery is borrowed from the ancient conception of the pantheon dominated by the ''Most High'' God, who apportions to each of the members of the divine court the territories of the different peoples who will be their wards. But that this is a mere poetic device with no intention to admit polytheism is seen from the poem itself, which conceives Yahweh Himself as the Most High and master of human destiny and reduces the gods to ''no-gods'' (v. 21). Here again, Israel's tradition would have understood sons of God as the angels (Jb 1.6), the members of the heavenly court (as in Dt 32.43), the guardian angels of the nations (Dn 10.13).

Applied to the Judges. The title is applied to men; and, in particular, to the judges, who in God's name render a judgment to those who present their cases ''to God'' [Ex 18.15–19; 22.8–9; Ps 57 (58).2; 81(82).1]; even though they bear the titles *'ĕlōhîm* (gods) and *b^enê 'elyôn* (sons of the Most High), they too will be judged [Ps 81 (82). 6–8].

Applied to Israel and Its King. In Ex 4.22 Yahweh says, ''Israel is my son, my first-born.'' Thus the people of God stand in a relation of sonship to Yahweh [Dt 14.1; 32.5; Jer 31.9; Ps 72(73).15]. The Prophets recall this adoption (Hos 11.1; Jer 31.20) to justify the divine complaint that the sons Yahweh has reared have disowned Him (Is 1.2) and have become lying and rebellious sons (Is 30.1, 9; Jer 3.14, 19). After the captivity God will bring back His sons from distant lands (Is 43.6), and they shall then be called ''sons of the living God'' (Hos 2.1); for the corollary on God's fatherhood (see Is 63.16; 64.8).

The king also is addressed by Yahweh, ''You are my son'' (Ps 2.7). Yet never does the Bible use the term ''Son(s) of Yahweh.'' In the creation account of Genesis, man in virtue of his creation is ''in the image, after the likeness of *'elōhîm*'' (Gn 1.27), but he is notably not given the title son of God. Any polytheistic idea of a direct or equal sharing in the divine nature is thus avoided. Creation is not procreation. Men are not sons of God in virtue of their creation; in the case of Israel and its king, the instatement to sonship supposes a special divine election.

A similar thought underlies the application of the title in later Judaism to individual Israelites who lived virtuous lives in accordance with God's will (Sir 4.10; Wis 2.16–20; 5.5; Job 1.23–25; Enoch 62.11; Psalms of Solomon 13.9; 17.27).

In the New Testament. The Synoptic tradition gives the title sons of God to the peacemakers (Mt 5.9), to those who return good for evil (Mt 5.45; Lk 6.35), and to the just in their risen state (Lk 20.36).

St. Paul, using the legal figure of adoption, identifies the Christian community as the New Israel, object of God's gratuitous election (Gal 4.5, where the obviously intentional use of the article before the abstract υἱοθεσία not only recalls a well-known truth, but also most probably connects Christian sonship with that of Israel as type and antitype; see also Rom 9.4). It is specifically faith that has made Christians the sons of God (Gal 3.26), and this new title brings with it God's interior gift of the Spirit by which we cry with God's own son, ''ABBA, Father'' (Gal 4.4–6; Rom 8.15). That the title is no longer purely juridical appears in its close relationship with the efficacious Spirit and in the obviously intentional switch from υἱός (son, as one with recognized status and legal privileges) to τέκνον (son or child, as one who has origin or descent or personal relation) in Rom 8.12–18. In Rom 8.23, if the traditional reading ''the adoption of sons'' is correct, it expresses the final consummation looked forward to, but the apparent absence of υἱοθεσία from the recently published P46 (3rd century) in support of the later D and G manuscripts, makes it highly questionable that Paul used the term in the future sense.

The Johannine literature likewise attributes Christian sonship to a power from God by which those who receive Christ, that is, believe in Him, are made sons of God (Jn 1.14). The idea of God's free election is likewise present (''born of the will of God''), but it is also stressed that ''children of God'' is not just a title but a reality (1 Jn 3.1–2).

See Also: SON OF GOD.

Bibliography: P. VAN IMSCHOOT, *Encyclopedic Dictionary of the Bible,* tr. and adap. by L. HARTMAN (New York 1963), from A. VAN DEN BORN, *Bijbels Woordenboek,* 2281–83. J. L. MCKENZIE, *Divine Sonship in the Old Testament* (Weston, Mass. 1946); ''Divine Sonship of Man in the O.T.,'' *The Catholic Bible Quarterly,* 7:326–339; ''Divine Sonship and Individual Religion,'' *ibid.* 32–47; ''The Divine Sonship of the Angels,'' *ibid.* 5:293–300. B.

S. CHILDS, *Myth and Reality in the O.T.* (Naperville, Ill. 1960) 49–57. M. H. POPE, *El in the Ugaritic Texts* in *Vetus Testamentum* (Suppl. 2; 1955), 47–49. J. B. BAUER, ''Videntes filii Dei filias hominum,'' *Verbum Domini,* 31:95–100. J. E. COLERAN, ''The Sons of God in Gn 6.2,'' *Theological Studies,* 2:488–509. E. G. KRAELING, ''The Significance and Origin of Gn 6.1–4,'' *Journal of Near Eastern Studies,* 6:193–208. P. JOÜON, ''Les Unions entre les *Fils de Dieu* et les *Filles des hommes* (Gn 6.1–4),'' *Recherches de sciences religieuses* 29:108–112. H. JUNKER, ''Zur Erklärung von Gn 6.1–4,'' *Biblica* 16:205–212. C. ROBERT, ''Les Fils de Dieu et les filles de l'homme,'' *Revue Biblique,* 4:340–373, 525–552. M. W. SCHOENBERG, ''Huiothesia: The Adoptive Sonship of the Israelites,'' *American Ecclesiastical Review,* 143:261–273; ''St. Paul's Notion on the Adoptive Sonship of Christians,'' *Thomist* 28:51–75.

[G. T. MONTAGUE]

SONS OF MARY HEALTH OF THE SICK

(Filii Mariae Salutis Infirmorum, FMSI, Official Catholic Directory #1270); a diocesan congregation founded in 1952 in the Archdiocese of Boston by Edward F. GARESCHÉ, with the approval of Archbishop (later Cardinal) Richard J. Cushing, for medical, catechetical, and social work in home and foreign missions. Besides the sanctification and mission work of its own members, the society has as its special purpose the training of qualified lay people for catechetical and medical work in order to reach large numbers of persons in need of religious instruction and medical attention. On March 26, 1955, a decree from Rome recognized the diocesan status of the congregation. Its first priest was ordained Jan. 29, 1956. The generalate is in Framingham, Masschusetts.

[J. COSS/EDS.]

SOPHISTS

The term sophist (Gr. σοφιστής), meaning an expert either in practical or theoretical matters, was initially equivalent to σοφός (wise man). In the fifth and fourth centuries B.C. it designated one who possessed wisdom and virtue and for a livelihood made a profession of teaching these to others (Plato, *Prot.* 348E; Xenophon, *Memorab.* 1.2). The name gradually assumed a derogatory meaning, largely through the Platonic and Aristotelian writings in which the Sophists are portrayed as professors of apparent, not true, wisdom (*Prot.* 312C–313C; *Soph. elen.* 165a 19–24). Thus in time it came to signify a quibbler or one who employs specious arguments (sophisms), the sense it still has in nontechnical usage (*see* FALLACY).

Characterization. The Sophists first appeared in Greece in the fifth century B.C. as traveling teachers of political virtue to the sons of wealthy families, for which they received substantial fees. With them a new kind of *paideia* was introduced into Greece, dictated by the exigencies of the social order. The Sophists imparted the prized arts of eloquence and persuasion, and the more eminent among them also instructed their charges in arithmetic, geometry, music and astronomy. Thus they contributed to the development of disciplines later to be known as the trivium and quadrivium. In extensive travels throughout Greece they served the cause of Panhellenism well; they also emphasized the conventional character of the social and political institutions of the individual Greek city-states.

Of the writings of the Sophists only a few fragments remain, more rhetorical than philosophical in content. The Sophists wrote chiefly for their contemporaries, and later Greeks did not preserve their works as productions of permanent value. Historians of philosophy depend greatly on Plato's dialogues, especially the *Protagoras, Gorgias* and *Theaetetus,* for knowledge of their doctrines. Aristotle also supplies important information about them. Both are reliable sources, though somewhat prejudiced. The Sophists were individualists, but they did have a common Eleatic, Heraclitean and Democritean background. Avoiding the cosmological speculation of the pre-Socratics, they concentrated on problems of man, his knowledge and society.

Sopristic philosophy was a radical phenomenalistic RELATIVISM that denied a knowledge of things in terms of being (ἐπιστήμη) and satisfied itself with mere opinion (δόξα) as sufficient for practical human needs. Although philosophy inherited little from the Sophists, without their challenge Socrates, Plato and Aristotle would not have achieved their masterly solutions to the problems of knowledge.

Protagoras. Protagoras of Abdera (*c.* 590–420 B.C.) was the first Sophist. Very little is known of him except that he visited Athens on several occasions. Some ancient writers testify that he was an associate of DEMOCRITUS, though this is questionable. According to Diogenes Laertius (9.55), Protagoras wrote several treatises, of which only a few scattered fragments remain. As a teacher of political virtue he trained his charges in the art of making the weaker cause appear the stronger (Aristotle, *Rhet.* 1402a 23–24). He held the opinion that two contradictory accounts can be given about everything (Diogenes 9.51). How he developed this point is not known. Earlier ZENO OF ELEA employed the same technique in his arguments against motion and plurality. Protagoras is most famous for his statement that ''man is the measure of all things, of existing things that they exist and of non-existing things that they do not exist'' (Sextus Empiricus, Against the Logicians 1.60). Philosophers have variously interpreted this as meaning either the individual or collective man. Plato (*Theaet.* 152A–154B) takes it to mean individual man; Aristotle (*Meta.* 1062b 12–15) and Diogenes Laertius agree. For Plato it meant that things are as the individual knower perceives them to be, and he relates it to the universal flux of HERACLITUS. Aristotle reduces it to a denial of the principle of CONTRADICTION. The statement most probably refers to the second part of ''The Way of Seeming'' of PARMENIDES. In another statement attributed to him, Protagoras seems to profess complete agnosticism: ''About the gods, I have no way of knowing whether they exist or do not exist, nor of what form they are; for there are many things which hinder knowledge, the obscurity and the shortness of man's life'' (*Die Fragmente der Vorsokratiker: Griechisch und Deutsch,* 80B, 4).

Gorgias. Gorgias of Leontini (*c.* 480–380 B.C.), an eminent Sicilian, had been a pupil of EMPEDOCLES and was himself the master of Isocrates. Most of Gorgias's writings were rhetorical in nature, but his chief work, ''On Not-Being or On Nature'' (περὶ τοῦ μὴ ὄντος ἤ περὶ φύσεως), was philosophical. It contains three nihilistic statements, together with a proof of each: (1) nothing is; (2) even if anything is, it is unknowable to man; and (3) even if anything is knowable, it is incommunicable to others (Sextus Empiricus, *ibid.* 1.65–87). Various interpretations have been given, namely, that they are facetious statements, that Gorgias was merely displaying his rhetorical skill, that they represented an anti-Eleatic polemic, that they were intended to abolish the copula ''is,'' or finally that they expressed the tragedy of human reason. Since the ancients understood them in a serious way, they can hardly be facetious. They are the logical result of Eleatic dialectic pushed to its limit, expressing a radical intellectual pessimism.

Hippias of Elis. Plato is the chief source of information about this rhetorician in the *Protagoras* and *Hippiss Maior* (probably authentic). A younger contemporary of Protagoras, Hippias was a prodigious polymath with a most versatile mind, but boastful and vain. Very little is known of his philosophical doctrines, for all his writings have disappeared. According to Plato he set up a radical opposition between nature and law (*Prot.* 337D). This was a view common to the Sophists.

See Also: GREEK PHILOSOPHY.

Bibliography: F. C. COPLESTON, *History of Philosophy* (Westminster, Md 1946–) v.1. J. OWENS, *A History of Ancient Western Philosophy* (New York 1959). K. FREEMAN, *The Pre-Socratic Philosophers* (2d ed. Cambridge, Mass. 1959); tr., *Ancilla to the Pre-Socratic Philosophers* (Cambridge, Mass. 1957). W. W. JAEGER, *Paideia: The Ideals of Greek Culture,* tr. G. HIGHET (2d ed. New York 1945–) v.1. M. UNTERSTEINER, *The Sophists,* tr. K. FREEMAN (Oxford 1954). H. DIELS, *Die Fragmente der Vorsokratiker: Griechisch und Deutsch,* ed. W. KRANZ, 3 v. (8th ed. Berlin 1956); v.1 (10th ed. Berlin 1960–61).

[L. A. BARTH]

SOPHRONIUS, ST.

Patriarch of Jerusalem, b. Damascus, Syria, ca. 560; d. Jerusalem, March 11, 638. Most probably to be identified with Sophronius Sophistes (''the Sophist''), he was a monk in Egypt (ca. 580), then in the Jordan area, and from 619 at the Theodosius Monastery at Jerusalem. He accompanied John MOSCHUS on his journey to Rome, and Moschus dedicated his Λειμών (*Pratum spirituale*) to him. In 633 Sophronius went to Alexandria to combat, but without success, the Monothelite doctrine of Cyrus of Phasis, Patriarch of that city. In the same year he traveled to Constantinople in order to persuade the patriarch SERGIUS I, the leading figure among the Monothelites, to accept the Orthodox position, but this mission likewise ended in failure. Shortly after his own election to the Patriarchate of Jerusalem (634–638), he addressed his famous *Synodical Letter* to the other patriarchs, explaining his own teaching on the two natures in Christ. His death was undoubtedly hastened by the tragic event of the preceding year, the surrender of Jerusalem to the Saracen conqueror the Caliph Omar. In addition to his *Synodical Letter,* he composed a *Florilegium* (not extant) in two books in which he cited some 600 passages from earlier ecclesiastical writers in support of Dyothelitism. Earlier in his career, he wrote an *Encomium* on the Alexandrian martyrs, Cyrus and John, a *Vita* (not extant) of the Alexandrian patriarch, Joannes Eleemon (d. 619), and 23 Anacreontic Odes in Classical meter on the Christian feasts. Of his 11 extant sermons, in part in Latin translation, that delivered on Christmas 634 has special historical interest, as it indicates that the Saracens were already in possession of Bethlehem.

Feast: March 11.

Bibliography: F. L. CROSS, *The Oxford Dictionary of the Christian Church* (London 1957) 1272. B. ALTANER, *Patrology,* tr. H. GRAEF from 5th German ed. (New York 1960) 628–629. H. G. BECK, *Lexikon für Theologie und Kirche,* ed. J. HOFER and K. RAHNER (Freiburg 1957–65); suppl., *Das Zweite Vatikanishe Konsil: Dokumente und Kommentare,* ed. H. S. BRECHTER et al. (1966) 9:888–889. H. G. BECK, *Kirche und theologische Literatur im byzantinischen Reich* (Munich 1959) 434–436, critical study, with bibliog. G. BARDY, *Dictionnaire de théologie catholique,* ed. A. VACANT et al., (Paris 1903–50; Tables générales 1951–) 14.2:2378–83. O. BARDENHEWER, *Geschichte der altkirchlichen Literatur* 5. (Freiburg 1913–32) 36–41. C. VON SCHÖNBORN, *Sophrone de Jérusalem* (Paris 1972). H. DONNER, *Die anakreontischen Gedichte Nr. 19 und Nr. 20 des Patriarchen Sophronius von Jerusalem* (Heidelberg 1981).

[M. R. P. MCGUIRE]

SORA (SOR), ABBEY OF

Benedictine foundation near the city of Sora, southeast of Rome, at the junction of the Liri and Fibreno Rivers, in the Diocese of Aquino, Pontecorvo, and Sora. The abbey was built on the traditional site of a Ciceronian villa by St. DOMINIC OF SORA, a native of Foligno and a monk of MONTE CASSINO, at the request of the Lombard duke, Pietro di Rainerio, probably about 1011. Dominic became abbot and it was there that he died in 1031. The monastery failed to develop economically or spiritually, and in view of its rapid decline by 1222 Pope HONORIUS III placed it under the nearby Cistercian establishment of Casamari. The CISTERCIANS installed their own prior, and the ancient abbey was reduced to a simple dependency and followed the fate of its motherhouse. In the 19th century Ferdinand II of Bourbon, King of Naples, granted the revenues of the monastery to the Chapter of St. Peter's in the Vatican. Little remains of the original church consecrated by PASCHAL II in 1104; it was restored frequently, the last time in the 18th century. The body of its holy founder is still preserved in this church.

Bibliography: L. H. COTTINEAU, *Répertoire topobibliographique des abbayes et prieurés,* 2 v. (Mâcon 1935–39) 2:3062. A. LAURI, *Il mio paese natio* (Sora 1905).

[I. DE PICCOLI]

"God sending the Word and Holy Spirit to the soul," by Ángeles Sorazu.

SORAZU, ÁNGELES

Franciscan conceptionist nun, mystic, and mystical writer; b. Zumaya, Guipúzcoa, Spain, Feb. 22, 1873; d. Valladolid, Aug. 28, 1921. Florencia, as she was christened, grew up in an atmosphere of Christian virtue, but she had much poverty and other misfortune to endure in her childhood, and her education was limited. At the age of 15, when she was in Tolosa working in a hat factory, she went through a brief period of worldly attachment and minor dissipation. Converted from this, she consecrated herself totally to God. At 18 she was received into the Franciscan monastery of the Purisima Concepción. She took the name María de los Ángeles, though she was commonly known simply as Sister—or later, Mother—Ángeles. She was elected abbess of her monastery in 1904, and remained in that office until her death. She is chiefly remembered for her interior life, of which she left an account in works written in obedience to her directors and published after her death. The more important of these were: *La vida espiritual coronada por la triple manifestación de Jesucristo* (Valladolid 1924); *Autobiografia* (Valladolid 1929); *Exposición de varios pasajes de la Sagrada Escritura* (Salamanca 1926). Three volumes of letters she wrote to her principal director, Mariano de Vega, OFMCap, were published in Madrid (1942, 1952, 1958). Her spirituality was influenced by her devotion to the mysteries of Christ, to Our Lady, and by her interest in the Gospels and the catechism. Her descriptions of transforming union, of the soul's participation in the divine attributes, and of contemplation are, according to the judgment of some, not unworthy of comparison with the writings of St. TERESA OF AVILA and of St. JOHN OF THE CROSS.

Bibliography: L. VILLASANTE CORTABITARTE, *La sierva de Dios, M. Ángeles Sorazu: Concepcionista franciscana, 1873–1921,* 2 v. (Bilboa 1950) v.1 *Estudio místico de su vida.* "El caso de la Madre Sorazu," *Verdad y Vida* 14 (1956) 105–114. M. LÉDRUS, "Le Cas de la Mère Sorazu," *Gregorianum* 35 (1954) 656–659. J. M. DE BUCK, *Révérende Mère Angelés Sorazu, conceptioniste* (Paris 1937), translation and adaptation of the *Autobiografia.*

[L. VILLASANTE]

SORBON, ROBERT DE

Theologian and founder of the Sorbonne, first endowed college of the University of Paris; b. Sorbon, near Rethel, Champagne, France, Oct. 9, 1201; d. Paris, Aug. 15, 1274. He became a master theologian *c.* 1236, and as a master regent taught at the University of Paris from 1254 to 1274. His teaching career covered the period in which secular and religious teachers engaged in fiery discussions concerning religious perfection (WILLIAM OF SAINT-AMOUR and GERARD OF ABBEVILLE, 1254–56), the great school strike, and Latin AVERROISM (SIGER DE BRABANT). Robert was a contemporary and colleague of THOMAS AQUINAS, BONAVENTURE, ALBERT THE GREAT, and GILES OF ROME. Named chaplain of Cambrai (*c.* 1250) and in 1258 at Notre Dame de Paris, he belonged to the circle of friends of Louis IX, who regarded him as a man of great wisdom and chose him as his confessor. J. de Joinville has preserved his memory in a series of vignettes that give evidence of his simplicity and kindliness.

Among his works are a number of frequently revised treatises that deal with moral and spiritual matters rather than with learned speculation: *De conscientia, De tribus dietis, De matrimonio, De confessione,* and *De saporibus* (unpublished). He also left about 85 remarkably simple but concrete sermons delivered between 1260 and 1265. Robert de Sorbon's renown, however, does not stem from his works. Having himself experienced the difficulties of poor students in the pursuit of theological studies, he undertook the foundation of a college for ''poor lay theology students'' that was not to be a mere student hostel but a true house of studies such as those provided by the Dominicans and Franciscans. His project won the interest of the king, the bishops, and even the pope, and he opened the college in October 1257. After a well–organized search for suitable property, he bought almost all the houses (62 at the time of his death) in the neighborhood of Rue Coupe Gueule, a site still occupied by the Sorbonne. He gave the institution carefully planned statutes that provided for the recruitment, common life, and studies of the students who were to live *collegialiter, socialiter, moraliter, scholariter,* and to participate in the various duties and responsibilities of the house under the direction of the headmaster. Master Robert's college, which usually numbered about 30 theology students, soon became the center of attraction at the Faculty of Theology. The large classrooms conducive to the meetings and scholarly discussions characteristic of the Sorbonne, and the library open to outsiders, contributed to its growth and soon made its name synonymous with the Faculty of Theology and its professors, the arbitrators of orthodoxy.

Bibliography: P. GLORIEUX, *Dictionnaire de théologie catholique,* ed. A. VACANT et. al. 14.2:2883–85. P. GLORIEUX, *Répertoire des maîtres en théologie de Paris au XIIIe siècle* 1:340–342. A. L. GABRIEL, ''Robert de Sorbonne,'' *Revue de l'Université d'Ottawa* 23 (1953) 473–514.

[P. GLORIEUX]

SORETH, JOHN, BL.

Carmelite reformer; b. Caen, *c.* 1395; d. Angers, July 25, 1471. He studied at Paris, where he received his doctorate in theology in 1438. Superior of the province of Francia (1440–51), he was elected prior general of the order in 1451 and remained in that office until his death. As general he worked for reform, and was particularly successful in the Low Countries, the Rhineland, and northern France. He sought to improve religious life in general within his order, especially by establishing stricter observance on a voluntary basis. At the Brussels chapter of 1462, he promulgated new constitutions for his order that were approved by the Orléans chapter in 1469. He was the founder of the second order of cloistered Carmelite nuns, and received from Nicholas V the bull *Cum nulla* giving canonical status to various women's groups affiliated with the order (Oct. 9, 1452). He personally established some convents, among them the foundations at Liège (1457), Dinant (1455), Haarlem (1466), and Vilvoorde (1469). With the collaboration of Bl. FRANCES D'AMBOISE he introduced Carmelite nuns into France, establishing a house at Vannes in 1464. Bl. Soreth drew up the constitutions for the nuns. Similar foundations were established in Italy during Soreth's generalate. He visitated extensively as prior general, insisting everywhere upon the renewal of the liturgy. He was noted for his love of the Blessed Sacrament, and is pictured in art with a pyx in his hand, recalling his defense of the Eucharist from profanation when Charles the Bold attacked Liège. He was beatified by Pius IX in 1866.

Bibliography: M. REUVER, ''Prima biographia B. Joannis Soreth e codice Viennensi *Novale Sanctorum* (12709) transcripta,'' [by Joannes Taye, a contemporary] *Carmelus* 5 (1958) 73–99. G. MEESTERS, ''Carmelite Spirituality according to Blessed John Soreth,'' *The Sword* 16 (1953) 323–335. M. ARTS, ''The Work of John Soreth,'' *ibid.* 15 (1952) 457–466. P. M. DE LA CROIX, ''Une Précieuse découverte: Les Constitutions des Carmélites de Vannes (Nazareth),'' *Carmel* 44 (1961) 61–70. G. MEESTERS, ''Johannes Soreth und sein Werk,'' in *Karmel: Gesetz und Geheimnis,* ed. A. DECKERT and O. MERL (Cologne 1959) 55–68. *Carmelus* 10 (1963), special number on *Las monjas Carmelitas hasta Santa Teresa de Jesús,* has much on Soreth and the nuns, e.g., A. STARING, ''The Carmelite Sisters in the Netherlands,'' 56–92, V. WILDERINK, ''Les Premiers monastères de Carmélites en France,'' 93–148.

[E. R. CAROLL]

SORIN, EDWARD FREDERICK

Founder of the University of Notre Dame, South Bend, Ind.; b. Ahuillé, France, Feb. 6, 1814; d. Notre Dame, Oct. 31, 1893. He entered the diocesan seminary at Le Mans, France and was ordained May 27, 1838. He later joined the Congregation of the HOLY CROSS, founded by Basil Anthony MOREAU, a professor at the Le Mans seminary, and was professed Aug. 15, 1840. When Bp. Célestine de la Hailandière of Vincennes, Ind., on a visit to France in 1839, asked Moreau for missionaries for his diocese, Sorin and six brothers volunteered. Reaching Vincennes in October 1841, they settled first at St. Peter's, in Daviess County. The following year Hailandière offered Sorin a plot of land near South Bend on condition that he start a college within two years. The land's original owner, the missionary Stephen T. BADIN, called the site Ste. Marie des Lacs. Sorin accepted the condition, appealed to France for more men, and began to build. On Jan. 15, 1844, the General Assembly of Indiana granted him a charter for the University of NOTRE DAME DU LAC, and the first building was completed in time for commencement that June. Sorin was president until 1865; he also served as provincial superior, and took care of the missions in northern Indiana and southern Michigan.

In 1843 he received a group of Sisters of Holy Cross from Le Mans, and established them the following year at Bertrand, Mich. The site of the present motherhouse was secured in 1854 for the sisters' convent and academy. He brought to the community Eliza Maria GILLESPIE, who, as Mother Angela, guided and inspired the sisters after their separation into a distinct community. At his direction, priests and sisters cared for the soldiers during the Civil War. In 1865 he began publication of the magazine *Ave Maria.* He was elected superior general of the Congregation of the Holy Cross in 1868, and thus supervised the community's educational and missionary activities in France, Canada, and Bengal, as well as in the U.S. In 1883 he suggested the establishment of the Laetare Medal award. Sorin retained the presidency of the trustees of Notre Dame until his death.

Bibliography: E. F. SORIN, *Journal* and ''Missions Attended from Notre Dame,'' Notre Dame Provincial Archives. T. E. HOWARD, *History of Saint Joseph County, Indiana,* 2 v. (Chicago 1907). Notre Dame University, *Brief History of the University of Notre Dame du Lac, Indiana from 1842 to 1892* (Chicago 1895). E. and T. CATTA, *Basil Anthony Moreau,* tr. E. L. HESTON, 2 v. (Milwaukee 1955). A. J. HOPE, *Notre Dame: One Hundred Years* (Notre Dame 1943). W. MCNAMARA, *Dictionary of American Biography,* ed. A. JOHNSON and D. MALONE, 20 v. (New York 1928–36; index 1937; 1st suppl. 1944; 2d suppl. 1958) 17: 399–400.

[T. T. MCAVOY]

SORROWS OF MARY

The spiritual martyrdom of Mary, Blessed Virgin, and her compassion with the sufferings of her divine Son are referred to as her sorrows (or dolors). Underlying all consideration of the sorrows of Mary by Christians is the fact of her presence ''by the cross of Jesus'' (Jn 19.25). St. Luke, who recorded Simeon's prophecy concerning the sword that would pierce her soul (Lk 2.35), does not mention Mary's presence on Calvary. The preceding verse, however, shows that the sword refers to Mary's sorrow at the contradictions her Son would meet. At least implicitly, then, it refers to her sorrow when these came to climax in His redemptive Passion and death.

Fathers. Except for St. Ambrose, who portrayed Mary standing with courage beneath the cross, conscious of the Redemption of mankind and of the Resurrection to follow (*De inst. virg.* 7; *Patrologia Latina,* ed. J.P. Migne, 16:318), the Latin Fathers who considered these New Testament texts explained them in terms of Mary's sorrow without much elaboration. It was not properly until the 11th and 12th centuries that the theme of Mary's compassion was fully developed in the West.

Following Origen (*Hom. in Luc.* 17), during three centuries the Eastern Fathers quite universally held the sword of Lk 2.35 to indicate Mary's supposed doubt or infidelity during the Passion. St. Romanus Melodus (d. 556) in a liturgical poem in the form of a dialogue between the suffering Christ and Mary seems the first in the East to show her keeping faith during her sorrow [ed. Pitra, *Anal. sacra* 1 (Paris 1876) 101–07]. From the 6th to the 10th century, and thus before the West, the East considerably developed the theme of Mary's sorrow.

Devotion to the Seven Sorrows. Traceable to the early 14th century, devotion to the seven sorrows even in the 15th century varied in the specific sorrows and was paralleled by devotion to 5, 15, etc. Devotion to a fixed number of sorrows followed and was modeled on devotion to a fixed number of Mary's joys. The unvaried sorrows of today (Simeon, Egypt, loss in the Temple, carrying of the cross, Crucifixion, taking down from the cross, burial) are the result of the spread of confraternities of the seven sorrows in the Low Countries toward the end of the 15th century by a priest, John of Coudenberg. Latin distichs on these seven sorrows were part of the devotions of this confraternity [*Analecta Bollandiana* 12 (1893) 339–46]. In 1607 Paul V granted the SERVITES, apostles of this devotion, exclusive power to erect these confraternities everywhere.

Liturgical Feasts. Until 1960 two feasts of the Seven Sorrows of Mary existed. The feast until then celebrated on the Friday after Palm Sunday found early precedent in a Mass decreed by a Synod of Cologne in 1423. Sixtus IV composed the liturgical Mass in 1482 and had it inserted in the Roman Missal. First conceded to individual religious orders and countries, the feast was extended to the whole Latin Church by Benedict XIII in 1727. The sequence *STABAT MATER* was added at this time. The rubrics of 1960 reduced the feast to a commemoration. The second feast originated in 16th-century devotions led by the Servites. About 1600, a Mass and procession on the third Sunday of September became popular, and in 1668 Innocent XI granted the feast to the Servites. In 1672 the Servite Prosper Bernardi composed the Mass and Office. After partial concessions, in 1814 Pius VII extended the feast to the Latin Church, to be celebrated on the third Sunday of September. In 1908 St. Pius X raised the feast to the second class, and in 1913 fixed the feast on September 15, except for the Servites, who retain the Sunday. The 1969 reforms of the liturgical calendar designate a single Feast of Our Lady of Sorrows, to be celebrated as an obligatory memorial on September 15.

Bibliography: A. M. LÉPICIER, *Mater Dolorosa: Notes d'histoire, de liturgie et d'iconographie . . .* (Spa 1948).

[J. C. GORMAN/EDS.]

SORTES HOMERICAE, VERGILIANAE, BIBLICAE

Divination by the use of tablets containing letters of the alphabet, which were drawn at random from a receptacle, and usually by a child, was practiced at ancient Praeneste in Italy and elsewhere. The tablets with individual letters were replaced subsequently by others containing phrases selected from books inspired by the Muses, especially books of Homer, Hesiod, and Vergil, or from collections of divinely inspired oracles. This form of divination was called rhapsodomancy. Finally, in place of such extracts, it became customary to open a copy of Homer or Vergil at random and to regard the first words to catch the eye as giving an answer to the problem of the consultant. In the *Historia Augusta* (*Vita Hadr.* 2.8) it is recorded that Hadrian, in consulting Vergil in this manner, hit upon *Aeneid* 6.808–812 and felt these lines indicated that he enjoyed the favor of Trajan and was to be his successor. In the same work (*Vita Sev. Alex.* 14) it appears that Alexander Severus also consulted Vergil and chanced upon *Aeneid* 6.848–854; he interpreted the passage to mean that he was to become emperor. The Vergilian *sortes* have had a long history. R. Ganszyniec found 169 examples of their use in the 16th century. Charles I (1625–49) of England was persuaded to consult them at Oxford and chanced upon *Aeneid* 4.615–621, the curse of Dido. D. A. Slater has shown that they are still being consulted in the present century.

The term *Sortes Biblicae* is employed to designate a similar Christian practice, noted from the early 4th century. The most famous ancient example is that described by Augustine in his *Confessions.* When he opened a codex of the New Testament at random, the first passage to meet his eye—and one most appropriate under the circumstances—was Rom 14.1 (*Conf.* 8.12.29). However, he realized the dangers of such consultations and warned against them in *Letter* 55.37.

The term biblical *sortes* is used rather loosely to include the similar employment also of liturgical texts and lives of the saints. P. Courcelle has listed a number of examples (see bibliography) and he has indicated the role played by children, and particularly by young lectors, either official or chosen for the occasion. In late antiquity and into the Carolingian age, widespread use of the biblical *sortes* in various matters of importance included that of the election of bishops and other ecclesiastical officials. Naturally, such a procedure led to abuses, and the use of the *sortes,* especially of the collection known as the *Sortes Sanctorum,* which should not be confused with the biblical *sortes* proper, was repeatedly condemned by medieval councils.

The use of the biblical *sortes* declined from the beginning of the Carolingian age, but persisted sporadically; it occurs as an individual aberration in the spiritual realm even in recent times.

See Also: DIVINATION.

Bibliography: A. BOUCHÉ-LECLERCQ, "Divination," C. DAREMBERG and E. SAGLIO, *Dictionnaire des antiquités grecques et romaines d'après les monuments* (Graz 1962–63) 2.1:292–319, esp. 302. D. A. SLATER, *"Sortes Vergilianae" or Vergil Today* (Oxford 1922). H. A. LOANE, "The *Sortes Vergilianae,*" *Classical Weekly* 21 (1927–28) 185–189. R. GANSZYNIEC, "Vergiliana: De sortibus Vergilianis," *Eos* (1930–31) 194, 201, 597, 650. H. LECLERCQ and H. I. MARROU, *Dictionnaire d'archéologie chrétienne et de liturgie,* ed. F. CABROL, H. LECLERCQ and H. I. MARROU, 15 v. (Paris 1907–53) 15.2: 1590–92. P. COURCELLE, "L'Enfant et les 'sorts bibliques'," *Vigiliae Christianae* 7 (Amsterdam 1953) 194–220, with copious examples and bibliog. C. DU CANGE, *Glossarium ad scriptores mediae et infimae latinitatis* (Niort 1883–88) 7:532–534.

[M. R. P. MCGUIRE]

SOTER, POPE ST.

Pontificate 162 or 168 to 170 or 177. Eusebius may have been mistaken when he placed Soter's accession in the eighth year of Marcus Aurelius, 168 (*Chron.; Hist. Eccl.* 4.21–23, 30; 5.1, 6, 24), and his dates are not certain. The *Liber pontificalis* states that Soter was a Campanian from Fondi (although he had a Greek name) and that he ordered non-ordained monks not to touch altar cloths or offer incense in church. It gives two accounts of his burial: one in the Vatican, which modern excavations have not borne out; and in the cemetery of Calixtus, which, at least in name, did not exist in Soter's time. Eusebius preserved a letter from DIONYSIUS OF CORINTH to Soter stating that an earlier epistle of Soter's, which was read in the Church of Corinth for its wholesome consolation and advice, commended Rome for its charity to the needy everywhere and its solicitude for those laboring in the mines. This letter identifies Clement I as the author of the Roman letter to the Corinthian community, written some 75 years earlier. The fifth-century report (*Praedestinatus* 1.26) is not credible where it reports that Soter wrote against the heretic Montanus, who was then active in Asia Minor.

Feast: April 22.

Bibliography: *Liber pontificalis*, ed. L. DUCHESNE (Paris 1886–92, 1958) 1:58–59. É. AMANN, *Dictionnaire de théologie catholique*, ed. A. VACANT et al., (Paris 1903–50) 14.2:2422–23. W. C. VAN UNNIK, *Die Religion in Geschichte und Gegenwart* (Tübingen 1957–65) 6:148–149. E. FERGUSON, *Encyclopedia of Early Christianity* (New York 1997), 2:1079. J. N. D. KELLY, *Oxford Dictionary of Popes* (New York 1986).

[E. G. WELTIN]

SOTERIOLOGY

The term soteriology is derived from the Greek words σωτηρία (deliverance, salvation) and λόγος (word, thought). It designates in a general sense the study of salvation.

The Christian faith proclaims the fact of man's SALVATION, which is accomplished by the merciful act of God's love in Christ, who, by means of His life, death, and Resurrection, delivers man from the evil of sin and reunites man in grace with God. The term salvation names the mystery. The term soteriology names the effort of Christian theologians to investigate the mystery for some understanding of the data of revelation and to shape these understandings into a coherent, organic system. Soteriology is both a special field of sacred doctrine and a special focus of theological research.

The Christian faith in its totality is the salvific event, the saving encounter of God with sinful men. From this point of view the study of any subject of revelation could be called soteriology. The field of soteriology would be as wide as revelation itself. But in accepted theological usage, the term refers most properly to the study of God's saving action as performed in and through the work of the Incarnate Word. Soteriology considers the work of Jesus Christ in its finality of delivering mankind from sin and restoring man to divine grace. Soteriology conceives the Incarnate Word in His redemptive role; it is the dynamic and practical aspect of CHRISTOLOGY.

To the redemptive work of Christ, soteriology addresses questions to understand in what salvation consists, in what manner the life, death, and Resurrection of the Redeemer accomplish salvation, how man's salvation is achieved by God's activity and man's response. Soteriology is also the effort to adduce those theological principles both of exposition and of proof that will attempt a systematization of the many subjects, the divergent issues, and the multirelated facts that are included in and related to the mystery of salvation as achieved by the work of Christ.

See Also: REDEMPTION.

Bibliography: K. RAHNER, *Lexikon für Theologie und Kirche,* ed. J. HOFER and K. RAHNER, 10 v. (2d, new ed. Freiburg 1957–65) 9:894–897. J. GNILKA and W. DETTLOFF, H. FRIES, ed., *Handbuch theologischer Grundbegriffe,* 2 v. (Munich 1962–63) 1:303–319. E. MASURE, ''Le Rédempteur,'' *Le Christ,* ed. G. BARDY and A. TRICOT (Paris 1946) 518–551. J. RIVIÈRE, *Dictionnaire de théologie catholique,* ed. A. VACANT, 15 v. (Paris 1903–50; Tables générales 1951–) 13.2:1912–2004. F. BAMMEL et al., *Die Religion in Geschichte und Gegenwart,* 7 v. (3d ed. Tübingen 1957–65) 2:584–599.

[E. L. PETERMAN]

SOTO, DOMINGO DE

Theologian; b. Segovia, 1494; d. Salamanca, Nov. 15, 1560. He received his early education in Segovia. Poverty forced him to seek employment as a sacristan in the church of a neighboring village, Ocando, where he began to develop a true spirit of piety and a love of study. At the University of Alcalá he studied logic and philosophy under THOMAS OF VILLANOVA and became a close friend of Pedro Fernandez de Saavedra, who later became a missionary to America. After his studies at Alcalá, De Soto attended the University of Paris, received his baccalaureate, and immediately began his theological studies; but a longing for Spain cut short his stay in Paris and he returned to Alcalá. The chair of philosophy was vacant and De Soto won an appointment to it in 1520. He established himself as a brilliant scholar, pitting Aristotelian thought against the nominalism of his day.

Quite suddenly he resigned his post and made a retreat at the Benedictine Abbey of Montserrat. His original intention was to become a Benedictine but the retreat master directed him to the Dominicans. He made his profession in the Dominican priory of Burgos on July 23,

1525. Domingo de Soto was immediately assigned to the house of studies in Segovia as a professor of dialectics. He taught there for seven years and during that time compiled a manual of logic, *Summulae F. Dñci Soto Segobiensis, Ord. Praed. Magistri* (Burgos 1529). This treatise was renowned for its simplicity, precision, and clarity. In 1532 his superiors sent him to Salamanca to occupy one of the order's chairs at the University in that city.

The Emperor Charles V selected him to be his imperial theologian at the Council of Trent. De Soto's work at the Council was varied. He won recognition as a man of sterling character, true piety, and deep learning. He labored diligently in the task of formulating *schemata* and solving difficult questions. He defended the doctrines of original sin, predestination, justification, merit, and others against the attacks of the Protestant theologians. He also wrote the treatise *De Natura et Gratia* (Venice 1547) and dedicated it to the conciliar fathers. In the meantime, he acted in another capacity. When the Dominican master general Albertus Casuas died before the opening of the Council, De Soto was appointed to serve as the order's representative during the first four sessions. Although a new general was elected in 1546, De Soto continued to serve as the Dominican representative during the fifth and sixth sessions.

When in 1547 the Council was interrupted, Charles requested that De Soto be appointed his confessor and spiritual advisor. He also sought to nominate De Soto for the vacant See of Segovia, but De Soto refused the honor and returned to Salamanca in 1550. Here he was elected prior of the ancient Dominican priory founded in the time of St. Dominic. In 1552, when Melchior CANO resigned from the first chair of theology at the University of Salamanca in order to accept a bishopric, De Soto was chosen to succeed him, a choice approved by the university and student body. This was his crowning glory, and he taught with success the doctrines of St. Thomas Aquinas and St. Augustine. He retired from his professorship in 1556.

His principal works are: *In dialecticam Aristotelis commentarii* (Salamanca 1544), *Commentarii in libros Physicorum* (*ibid.* 1545), *In tres libri De anima* (unedited), *Quaestiones in libros Physicorum* (*ibid.* 1545), *Deliberatio in causa pauperum* (Venice 1547), *In Epistolam divi Pauli ad Romanos commentarii* (Antwerp 1550), *In quartam sententiarum commentarii* (Salamanca 1557), and *De institia et iure* (*ibid.* 1556).

Bibliography: J. QUÉTIF and J. ÉCHARD, *Scriptores Ordinis Praedicatorum*, 5 v. (Paris 1719–23) 2.1:171–174. A. M. VIEL, "Dominique Soto 1494–1560: Étude historico-doctrinale," *Revue thomiste* (Paris 1893–) 12 (1904) 151–166; 13 (1905) 174–193. A. TOURON, *Histoire des hommes Illustres de l'ordre de St. Dominique*, 6 v. (Paris 1743–49) 4:205–216. V. BELTRÁN DE HEREDIA, *Dictionnaire de théologie catholique*, ed. A. VACANT et al., 15 v. (Paris 1903–50; Tables Générales 1951–) 14.2:2423–31.

[F. D. NEALY]

SOTO, PEDRO DE

Theologian; b. Córdoba, Spain, 1500; d. Trent, Italy, April 22, 1563. He was born of noble parents, and as a youth displayed superior intelligence and a remarkable memory. He entered the Order of Friars Preachers and made his profession in 1519 at St. Stephen's Priory, Salamanca, Spain. During his student days he made an assiduous study of sacred doctrine, showing a special interest in patrology and in a study of the councils of the Church.

In 1542 Charles V of Spain selected him for his adviser and confessor. This association was severed six years later because of a disagreement on the INTERIMS, the three provisional arrangements for the adjustment of religious differences between the Catholics and Protestants of Germany. During his service to the emperor, De Soto and another Dominican, Gabriel de Guzmans, were credited by Paul III as being highly successful in arranging a peace between Charles V and Francis I of France.

The association with the emperor also introduced De Soto to the reality of Lutheranism, and he became enthusiastic over the project of preaching in the areas greatly influenced by Lutheranism. With the help of his friend Cardinal Otto Truchses of Augsburg, he succeeded in restoring the chair of theology at the University of Dillingen. De Soto himself occupied the chair (1549–53). During his tenure as professor of theology he stressed the teachings of St. AUGUSTINE and St. THOMAS AQUINAS.

In 1554 De Soto and a fellow Dominican, Juan de Villagracia, were sent to England at the request of Philip II in the hope that they would be instrumental in effecting the return of the faith to the universities of Oxford and Cambridge. Far from meeting with success, they were forced to flee England upon the death of Queen Mary in 1558.

The Dominicans also made use of De Soto's talents. He was appointed the superior of the German province of the order, acting as commissar of the master general, Franciscus Romeus (1546–52), who tried to restore a real vitality to the province.

De Soto's last assignment was his appointment as Pius IV's theologian at the Council of Trent. He died while attending the council.

His major works include *Institutiones Christianae* (Augusta 1548), *Defensio catholicae confessionis et scholiorum circa confessionem ducis Wirtenbergensis nomine editam adversus prolegomena Joannis Brentii* (Antwerp 1557), *Manuale Clericorum* (Dillingen 1558), *Methodus confessionis* (Antwerp 1553), *Doctrinae christianae compendium in ultimum plebis recte instituendae* (Ingolstadt 1549), and *Assertio catholicae fidei* (Cologne 1555).

Bibliography: J. QUÉTIF and J. ÉCHARD, *Scriptores ordinis praedicatorum* (New York 1959) 2.1:183–184. D. A. MORTIER, *Histoire des maîtres généraux de l'ordre des Frères Prêcheurs,* 8 v. (Paris 1903–20) 5:463–469, 504–505, 525–529. A. TOURON, *Histoire des hommes illustres de l'ordre de Saint Dominique,* 6 v. (Paris 1743–49) 4:216–230. V. D. CARRO, *Dictionnaire de théologie catholique,* ed. A. VACANT et al. (Paris 1903–50) 14.2:2431–43.

[F. D. NEALY]

SOUBIRAN, MARIE THÉRÈSE DE, BL.

Foundress of the Society of Mary Auxiliatrix; b. Castelnaudary, near Carcassonne, France, May 16, 1834; d. Paris, June 7, 1889. Sophie Thérèse Augustine Marie, as she was named, came of a family that traced its ancestry, directly or collaterally, to St. LOUIS IX, St. ELZÉAR OF SABRAN, St. ELIZABETH OF HUNGARY, and Pope Bl. URBAN V. Her parents, Joseph and Noémi (de Gélis) de Soubiran la Louvière, afforded a pious but stern family atmosphere; and her uncle, canon Louis de Soubiran, took firm control of her spiritual direction. At the age of 14, she made a private vow of chastity and aspired to join the Carmelites, but in 1854 her uncle convinced her to join the BEGUINES at Ghent, Belgium. In 1855 she established a *béguinage* at Castelnaudary. This community was bound to common life, ran an orphanage, and was devoted to nocturnal adoration.

In September 1864, with the assistance of a Jesuit, Paul Ginhac, Mère Thérèse instituted a new religious congregation, the Society of Mary Auxiliatrix, at Toulouse; it received diocesan approval (1867) and the approval of the Holy See (1868). The constitutions were patterned on those of the JESUITS. The sisters were to engage in works of charity and to practice perpetual adoration of the Blessed Sacrament. The institute soon expanded to Amiens and Lyons, but during the Franco-Prussian War (1870), the sisters fled to London. After their return to Bourges (1871), Mére Marie Françoise de Borgia (1830–1921) became very influential in the congregation. As assistant superior general, she convinced Mère Thérèse, the superior general, to embark on a disastrous expansion of houses. By 1874 the congregation was in difficulty and Mère Françoise discredited. Domineering, unstable, and ambitious, she reacted by blaming Mère Thérèse and even succeeded in turning Father Ginhac, the archbishop of Toulouse, and the sisters against her. On Sept. 20, 1874, the foundress was expelled from the society.

She sought vainly to join the Visitation Nuns and the Carmelites. Eventually accepted by the Sisters of Our Lady of Charity of the GOOD SHEPHERD at Paris, she made her profession in this congregation (1877). Mère Françoise's autocratic rule even forced the expulsion of Mère Thérèse's sister, Marie Xavier (January 1881). Within a year of Mère Thérèse's death, however, her persecutor was deposed and expelled from the congregation. The new superior general, Mère Élisabeth de Luppé, exonerated the foundress, and recalled Mère Xavier. Mère Thérèse was beatified on Oct. 20, 1946. Her remains rest in the motherhouse in Paris.

Feast: Oct. 20.

Bibliography: *Bl. Marie-Thérèse de Soubiran: A Study in Failure,* ed. H. MONIER-VINARD, tr. T. BAILY (London 1944). W. LAWSON, *A Life of Blessed Marie Thérèse de Soubiran* (London 1952). J. L. BAUDOT and L. CHAUSSIN, *Vies des saints et des bienheureux selon l'ordre du calendrier avec l'historique des fêtes*, ed. by the Benedictines of Paris (Paris 1935–56) 6:140–143. A. BUTLER, *The Lives of the Saints,* rev. ed. H. THURSTON and D. ATTWATER (New York 1956) 4:157–161.

[T. JOYCE]

SOUBIROUS, BERNADETTE, ST.

B. Lourdes, southwestern France, Jan. 7, 1844; d. Nevers, France, April 16, 1879. Bernadette was the eldest of nine children of the miller Françoise and Louise (Castérot) Soubirous. Because of her family's poverty and her own poor health, she was not sent to school. Delay in her instruction meant that she was unable to receive her First Communion until June 3, 1858. Bernadette is reputed to have had 18 visions of the Blessed Virgin Mary between Feb. 11 and July 16, 1858. While collecting firewood close to a grotto called Massabielle, by the River Gave near LOURDES, she saw a young girl dressed in white and holding a rosary. Her account of her vision met with disbelief from her pastor, M. Peyramale. She also suffered much misunderstanding from her family and the townsfolk. In subsequent apparitions she first called the young girl "the lady," but during the 16th apparition, on the feast of the Annunciation, the visitor identified herself in the dialect of Lourdes as the IMMACULATE CONCEPTION. The doctrine of Mary's conception without the stain of original sin had been formally defined by Pius IX shortly before this (Dec. 8, 1854). On the feast of Our Lady of Mt. Carmel (July 16), the final apparition occurred.

After the apparitions Bernadette was educated as a day and boarding student with the Sisters of Charity and Christian Instruction of Nevers at Lourdes (*see* CHARITY, SISTERS OF). In 1866 she joined the congregation at the

St. Bernadette Soubirous.

motherhouse in Nevers. In religion she kept her baptismal name, Marie Bernarde. Even after the bishop of Tarbes rendered a favorable judgment on the authenticity of the apparitions, Bernadette continued to experience much misunderstanding. Tuberculosis of the bone kept her always in weak health in the convent, where she performed the duties of assistant in the sacristy and infirmary. Bernadette was beatified on June 14, 1925, and canonized on Dec. 8, 1933. The immense popularity of Lourdes as a pilgrimage center has helped make her one of the most popular of modern saints (*see* VISIONS).

Feast: Feb. 18.

Bibliography: H. PETITOT, *The True Story of Saint Bernadette,* tr. a Benedictine of Stanbrook Abbey (Westminster, Md. 1950). R. CRANSTON, *The Miracle of Lourdes* (New York 1955), popular. L. VON MATT and F. TROCHU, *St. Bernadette: A Pictorial Biography,* tr. H. REES (Chicago 1957).

[T. F. CASEY]

SOUILLAC, ABBEY OF

Former Benedictine monastery of St. Mary, Souillac, canton and *arrondissement* of Gourdon (Lot), France, Diocese of Cahors, on the Borrèze River (Latin, *Solliacum, Sordillacum, Sublacum*). According to tradition, the abbey was founded by ELIGIUS OF NOYON in 655. In 806 it needed restoration by Louis I, the Pious. After the NORMAN invasions, it was reendowed in 927 by Frotard, Viscount of Cahors; in 960 it was restored by Gerald of Saint-Céré, Abbot of AURILLAC. In 1660 Souillac was united to the Congregation of Saint-Maur (*see* MAURISTS). At one time it had over 80 priories and parishes dependent on it. The 12th-century Romanesque abbey church, which is now a national historical monument, is perfectly preserved and recalls Saint-Front of Perigueux in size and Byzantine style. A former portal of the church, now inside, is one of the most interesting pieces of southern French romanesque sculpture.

Bibliography: *Gallia Christiana,* v.1–13 (Paris 1715–85), v.14–16 (Paris 1856–65) 1:179–182. L. H. COTTINEAU, *Répertoire topobibliographique des abbayes et prieurés,* 2 v. (Mâcon 1935–39) 2:3069. M. AUBERT, ''Souillac,'' *Congrès archéologique de France* 90 (1927) 261–270. G. CANY, ''Les Chapiteaux historiés du choeur de Souillac, Lot,'' *Annales du Midi* 62 (1950) 209–214. G. CANY and M. LABROUSSE, ''L'Église abbatiale de . . . Souillac . . . ,'' *Bulletin monumental* 109 (1951) 389–404.

[J. DE LA C. BOUTON]

SOUL

In its most ordinary present-day usage, the term ''soul'' (Gr. ψυχή; Lat. *anima*), when used alone, refers to the human soul; to say soul is to mean human soul. If one intends to speak about other sorts of soul, he uses expressed qualifiers; e.g., he says plant soul, or animal soul. There is nonetheless a use of the term ''soul'' that means simply a principle of life, or a source of life activities, at least that of nourishing. According to this usage, soul designates the mark of a living thing, or what separates the living from the nonliving; soul in this sense is the concern of this article.

Early Greek Views. The Greek predecessors of Aristotle fastened on two characteristic marks that distinguish what has soul in it from what has not: (1) movement, and (2) sensation or knowledge; each of these is traceable to their views on the first principles of things (see Aristotle, *Anim.* 403b 25–28). Those who paid special attention to movement thought that soul ought to be identified with the first principle, which is most capable of originating movement. DEMOCRITUS, e.g., held that soul is composed of spherical atoms, which because they are spherical are most suited for motion, and hence are most in a state of motion. Diogenes's argument was in form identical with that of Democritus; but for Diogenes, air was the element most capable of originating movement, because it is the finest in grain. Anaxagoras's view, though obscure in many respects, seems to have been that soul is the source of movement, without itself being in

Abbey Church of Souillac, France. (Marburg Art-Reference, Art Resource, NY)

motion; seemingly, therefore, it is a first principle in some respects unlike what is material or a body.

Those who expressed a view on soul from the viewpoint of sensation or knowledge had, as a basic conviction, that like is known only by like. Thus, if one analyzes what soul knows, one can say what soul is. According to EMPEDOCLES, the soul knows all natural things, and natural things can be analyzed into four intrinsic constituents, namely, fire, air, water, and earth, and two extrinsic principles, namely, Love and Strife. Soul, therefore, is a combination of the six. Otherwise, it would be difficult to see how soul can know these things. According to PLATO, soul knows not only natural and changing things, but also changeless things—the Numbers, the Forms or Ideas, and the Geometricals. Since all things have whatever reality they possess because of a participation in the Numbers, and since soul knows all things, soul must be a number. Another way of showing that the soul is a number (or a combination of numbers) is to consider the fact that soul knows in different ways: (1) by intuition (hence the number one is of the nature of the soul, since intuition grasps in a single flash); (2) by science (hence the number two, since in science the soul moves from one thing to a second, i.e., from premises to a conclusion); (3) by opinion (hence the number three, since soul here moves from premises to a conclusion but with the fear that some third thing, rather than the conclusion, may be true); and (4) by sense (hence the number four, because it takes four points to determine a body, and the soul knows bodies by sense).

A brief reflection on the views just recorded reveals a third characteristic mark of soul, namely, incorporeity. But two senses of incorporeity can be discerned: (1) a strict sense, as in the case of Plato's Numbers, which are neither material nor bodies; this is perhaps also implied in Anaxagoras's view of soul as the origin of motion, itself not in motion, hence possibly itself not a body; and (2) a looser sense, as in the case of Democritus's spherical atoms and Diogenes's air—in the sense of something subtle or rarefied, but nonetheless a body or material.

Preliminaries to a Definition. Of the many criticisms ARISTOTLE makes of his predecessors' views on the soul (*Anim.* 403b 20–411b 31), two are quite basic: (1) If one is to have a complete account of soul from the viewpoint of MOTION, one ought to investigate all that is implied in motion. If there is motion, then there is both a mover and a moved; in the mover there must be the ability to move, i.e., to originate motion; in the moved, the ability to be moved. The mover in this case is said to be the soul; the moved, the body. Thus, one ought not simply to put his finger on the source of soul's ability to move the body, e.g., Democritus's spherical atoms or Diogenes's air; one should also try to put his finger on the source of the body's ability to be moved by the soul. One should perhaps ask such questions as: What are the structural specifications of a body moved by soul? None of the views of Aristotle's predecessors looks to the condition of the body qua moved by the soul; all of them look only to the condition of the soul qua mover of the body. (2) Aristotle observes that all the views on soul proposed by his predecessors fail to take into account all types of soul. To say something about soul from the viewpoint of local movement, or of sensation or knowledge, or of respiration, is not to talk about all kinds of soul, for it is obvious that not all living things move about locally, nor do all of them sense, nor do all of them breathe. A complete account of soul ought to consider all types of soul. And this is why Aristotle begins his own account of soul by proposing a common definition of soul, i.e., one applicable to all its types without specifying what is distinctive of any given type; and why he carefully specifies the sort of body that is the appropriate subject having a soul (see *Anim.* 412a 2–414a 28).

The question, What is it?, which is fundamental for philosophers and which asks for a DEFINITION, is not properly asked about a thing until one knows that there is such a thing. But to ask: Is there such a thing as soul? presupposes having assigned a meaning to soul. Now, if soul is taken to mean the source or principle of life activities, namely, whatever there is in all things we call living that distinguishes them from those we call nonliving, then it is clear that the question: Is there such a thing as soul? is answered by answering the question: Are there living things? It is clear therefore that there is such a thing as soul, because it is clear that there are living things.

What follows is a brief presentation of Aristotle's two common definitions of soul, as commented on by St. THOMAS AQUINAS, and as clarified with examples from modern science, wherever they are of service. Aristotle's method is that of division. He begins by laying out two sets of distinctions. The first set:

1. What exists, i.e., BEING, is either a SUBSTANCE, i.e., an independently existing subject, like Jack; or an ACCIDENT, i.e., something that exists in an independently existing subject as some sort of modification of it, like Jack's height.
2. Substance, according to its meanings or senses, is either MATTER, which is POTENCY and as such does not exist; or FORM, which is ACT, and as such does not exist, but which accounts for the existence of matter and of the composite (such a form is said to be a substantial form—*see* MATTER AND FORM); and the composite (i.e., what is composed of matter and form), which is the actually existing thing, such as Jack.
3. Actuality or ENTELECHY is either like knowledge possessed (this is first actuality) or like considering knowledge possessed (this is second actuality).

The second set:

1. Substance, according to its types, is either a body (i.e., a corporeal substance) or a SPIRIT (things such as an angel or God). (*See* ANGELS, 2.)
2. A body is either natural, which is such that both its matter and its form are substantial; or artificial, which is such that only its matter is substantial, its form being accidental. The form of an artificial body is man-given. A natural body is more perfectly a substance than an artificial body, since both its matter and its form are substantial.
3. A natural body is either nonliving, such as a stone, or living, such as Jack. Anything that at least vegetates, i.e., keeps itself in existence by absorbing nourishment from its environment, is said to be a living body.

First Definition. From the second set of distinctions, it is easy to see that a living body is a natural body and a substance. Since a living body is an actually existing thing, such as Jack, a living body is a substance in the sense of a composite (see substance in the first set). Therefore, a living body has a natural and substantial matter and a natural and substantial form; a form that accounts for its being alive, and a matter that is its potentiality for being alive. Thus, soul is the form or actuality of a natural body with a potentiality for being alive. Indeed, soul is the first actuality of such a body. Soul is actuality in the sense in which knowledge possessed is actuality; for soul is presupposed to life activities. Life activities are actualities in the sense in which actually considering what one knows is actuality; actually considering what one knows presupposes what one knows. To say that soul is the first actuality of such a body is to say that soul is such a body's substantial form.

But life activities presuppose not only soul. They presuppose also a certain sort of natural body, a body having life potentially in it. Such a body is composed of certain sorts of natural elements and compounds, and is productive of certain others whose natural activities contribute to life activities. For example, digestion is performed through the natural activities of HCl, among others. Such a body is also an organized body. Witness those things, i.e., plants, in which are found what men take to be the minimum manifestations of life. The plant has diverse bodily parts ordered to diverse functions. Functionally ordered parts are organs; and a body with such parts is said to be an organized body or organism.

In light of this analysis, it can be said that natural organized body stands in the same relationship to soul as potency does to actuality. But this proportion must be properly understood. There are two senses of the potency-actuality relationship: (1) the sense in which marble, for example, before the change in which it becomes a statue, is in potency to the shape; it is as something perfect*ible* in relation to the perfection (the shape) it is about to acquire; (2) the sense in which the marble, after the change has been completed, is in potency to the shape it has acquired; it is as something perfect*ed* in relation to the perfection it possesses, the perfection being no part of the marble as such. Natural organized body, as it appears in the definition of soul, is in potency to soul in the second sense just distinguished.

Second Definition. Aristotle's second common definition of soul, namely, the *primary* principle whereby we live, sense, move, and understand, is formulated in order to be used as a middle term for arriving at the first common definition by the method of DEMONSTRATION.

Types of Soul. There are three types of soul, distinguished in terms of the extent to which activities commonly attributed to living things transcend the activities of matter in its nonliving states; or, in another way of putting it, in terms of the extent to which these activities transcend anything that is found in the makeup of the natural organized body of a living thing (see St. Thomas, ST 1a, 78.1). There is an activity of soul that so transcends anything in the makeup of a natural organized body, that it is not even performed by any bodily organ; this is the activity of the *intellectual* soul (*see* SOUL, HUMAN). Below this, there is an activity of soul performed by a bodily organ, but not through the natural activities of the elements and compounds that constitute the organ; this is the activity of the *sensitive* soul. Of course, such elements and compounds and their activities are required for this activity of soul, not in such a way that it takes place by the power of these elements, but only for keeping the organ properly disposed. Lastly, there is an activity of soul that is performed by a bodily organ and by the activities of certain natural elements and compounds; this is the activity of the *vegetative* soul. The transcendence of this activity is seen clearly in nourishment; it is seen even more clearly in the process of reproduction.

Parts of Soul. Since soul performs diverse sorts of activity, it is often said that soul has diverse parts, a part for each sort of activity. Since soul is not a body, but the first entelechy of a body, these parts of soul cannot be quantitative parts; hence soul is not quantitatively divisible into them. These parts are nothing other than the potencies or powers the soul has for performing diverse sorts of life activity; thus, if one says that soul is divisible into these parts, the meaning is simply that these parts are distinguishable from each other by definition; each is defined in terms of its object (*see* FACULTIES OF THE SOUL). These parts are often called power parts, to distinguish them from quantitative parts; and the soul, a power whole. The following will make clear the difference between power parts and quantitative parts: (1) quantitative parts are ''spread-out'' parts, whereas power parts are not; (2) quantitative parts are homogeneous, whereas power parts are heterogeneous—there being as many different sorts of parts as there are different activities; and (3) quantitative parts are intrinsic constituents of the whole, whereas power parts are not, since the soul is something substantial and the powers of the soul are merely accidents.

Modern Thought. In modern thought, say from the time of R. DESCARTES to the present, man's concern with the problem of soul has been: (1) a concern with the human soul, largely with the problem of the relation between man's body and soul (*see* SOUL-BODY RELATIONSHIP); and (2) a concern with the problem of LIFE, turning mainly about the issue of mechanism versus vitalism (*see* MECHANISM, BIOLOGICAL; VITALISM).

See Also: SOUL, HUMAN; IMMORTALITY; SOUL, HUMAN, ORIGIN OF.

Bibliography: J. E. ROYCE, *Man and His Nature* (New York 1961). A. M. HOFFSTETTER, ''Viruses: Are They Alive?'' *New Scholasticism* 31 (1957) 297–316. R. TAYLOR, *Metaphysics* (Englewood Cliffs, N.J. 1963). M. J. ADLER, ed., *The Great Ideas: A Syntopicon of Great Books of the Western World,* 2 v. (Chicago 1952); v. 2, 3 of *Great Books of the Western World* 2:791–810. C. MAZZANTINI, *Enciclopedia filosofica,* 4 v. (Venice-Rome 1957) 1:222–239. R. EISLER, *Wörterbuch der philosophischen Begriffe,* 3 v. (4th ed. Berlin 1927–30) 3:1–22.

[J. BOBIK]

SOUL (IN THE BIBLE)

Soul in the OT is *nepeš,* in the NT, ψυχή. The definitions and the use of these terms will be treated in this article.

Old Testament. *Nepeš* comes from an original root probably meaning to breathe. Thus the noun form means neck or throat opened for breathing, thence, breath of life. Since breath distinguishes the living from the dead, *nepeš* came to mean life or self or simply individual life. *Nepeš* is used in regard to both animals and humans. If life is human, *nepeš* is equivalent to the person, the ''I.'' After death, the *nepeš* goes to SHEOL.

The above summary indicates that there is no dichotomy of body and soul in the OT. The Israelite saw things concretely, in their totality, and thus he considered men as persons and not as composites. The term *nepeš,* though translated by our word ''soul,'' never means soul as distinct from the body or the individual person. Other words in the OT such as SPIRIT, FLESH, and HEART also signify the human person and differ only as various aspects of the same being.

In Ps 68(69).2, the phrase, ''the waters threaten my life,'' is literally ''waters come up to *nepeš*'' (cf. Jn 2.6; Is 5.14; Prv 23.2). The sense of throat for *nepeš* is apparent in these places. The word *nepeš* means breath in Jb 41.13: ''His breath [*nepeš*] sets coals afire; a flame pours from his mouth.'' In 2 Kgs 17.22, it means breath of life, ''And the soul [*nepeš*] of the child returned into him and he revived'' (cf. 2 Kgs 17.21; 2 Sm 1.9; Jer 38.16).

In Gn 9.4, ''But flesh with its life [*nepeš*]—that is, its blood—you shall not eat,'' the comparison shows more of an abstract meaning for *nepeš* as life in general without signifying breath or breathing (cf. Lv 17.11; Dt 12.23). Finally, *nepeš* means the individual being itself whether of animals or men. In Gn 2.7, ''Then the Lord God . . . breathed into his nostrils the breath of life, and man became a living being,'' the Hebrew word for being is *nepeš*. Of animals, Prv 12.10 says, ''The just man takes care of his beast,'' literally, ''the *nepeš* in his beast.''

As a human life, *nepeš* can be identical with the personal pronoun or the reflexive pronoun (Gn 27.4, 25; Lam 3.24, where ''says my soul'' could be just as correctly translated ''say I,'' etc.). As the ''I,'' the *nepeš* performs all the sensations of an individual. The *nepeš* hungers, thirsts, hopes, longs, loves, and hates.

At death, the *nepeš* goes to Sheol, a place of an insensitive, shadowy existence. Many psalms pray for the rescue of one's *nepeš* from death, where the rescue means to be saved from dying, not to be raised from the dead. Happiness after death is known only in late OT revelation.

New Testament. The term ψυχή is the NT word corresponding with *nepeš*. It can mean the principle of life, life itself, or the living being. Through Hellenistic influence, unlike *nepeš,* it was opposed to body and considered immortal.

The psyche in Mt 10.28, ''And do not be afraid of those who kill the body but cannot kill the soul [psyche]; but rather be afraid of him who is able to destroy both soul and body in hell,'' means a life that exists separately from the body. The meaning of psyche in our Lord's statement, ''[T]he Son of Man has not come to be served but to serve, and to give his life [psyche] as a ransom for many,'' is obviously His mortal existence (Mt 20.28; Jn 10.11). As a living being, subject to various experiences, it can refer to animals, ''And every live thing [psyche] in the sea died'' (Rv 16.3), or to humans, ''Fear came upon every soul [psyche]'' (Acts 2.43; Rom 2.9; 13.1). Thus the psyche feels, loves, and desires. In this connection it can be used to mean the personal or reflexive pronoun, as in Jn 10.24, ''How long dost thou keep us [our psyches] in suspense?''

Thus far, ψυχή is quite similar to the Hebrew *nepeš,* except for Mt 10.28. Under the Greek influence, however, it was gradually opposed to body and was used for the immortal principle in man (Rv 6.9; 20.4).

In summary, the Hebrew *nepeš* generally is connected with the concrete sign of life in the individual, the ''I'' that feels, wills, pants for, etc. Its end is Sheol. The Greek counterpart, ψυχή, includes many of the meanings of *nepeš;* but it has added to the concept ''I,'' the immortality of later philosophy and revelation.

See Also: MAN, 1; LIFE, CONCEPT OF (IN THE BIBLE).

Bibliography: *Encyclopedic Dictionary of the Bible* (New York 1963) 2286–90. J. P. E. PEDERSEN, *Israel: Its Life and Culture,* 4 v. in 2 (New York 1926–40; reprint 1959) 1:99–181. R. BULTMANN, *Theology of the New Testament,* tr. K. GROBEL (New York 1951) 1:190–259. C. TRESMONTANT, *A Study of Hebrew Thought,* tr. M. F. GIBSON (New York 1960) 83–124.

[W. E. LYNCH]

SOUL, HUMAN

Intuitively and almost universally man acknowledges an essential difference between living and nonliving things. The intrinsic force, or principle of movement, by which certain things are living is commonly called the soul (see Aristotle, *Anim.* 413a 20–21). The human soul, essentially different from other souls, is that internal principle by which man lives, perceives, and thinks (*Anim.* 414a 12–13). All cultures and civilizations have been convinced that man is not a purely material being; rather, they recognize that man possesses within himself some element that is relatively independent of the body, giving life and power to the body. The nature of this principle was not always clearly understood. Often it was compared or identified with air, wind, breath, or spirit. Some

Soul parts with dead body, illustration by William Blake. (©Historical Picture Archive/CORBIS)

considered the soul to be a single simple principle; others distinguished between the soul, the principle of bodily life, and the intellectual powers by which man thinks (*see* FACULTIES OF THE SOUL). The origin of the human soul has often been explained by myths, by superstitious belief, by natural causes, or by religion. Consideration of its survival and ultimate destiny have given rise to many beliefs.

The human soul is considered here under five titles: (1) Oriental and Greek conceptions; (2) patristic and medieval writers; (3) modern and contemporary thought; (4) philosophical analysis; and (5) theology.

1. Oriental and Greek Conceptions

Long before the earliest philosophers discussed the human soul in philosophical language, ancient peoples of the East spoke of the soul in the language of myth and primitive religion. While philosophical analysis was the greatest contribution of the Greeks, the non-philosophical and mythical approach of ancient religions cannot be neglected.

Nonphilosophical thought. In Chinese tradition a distinction is made between the lower, sensitive soul that disappears at death and the *hun,* or rational principle, that survives the grave and is the object of ancestor worship. The ancient Egyptians spoke of at least two souls: the *ka,* or breath, the ''double'' of man, born with him but surviving death and remaining close to the tomb, and the *ba,* or spiritual part, which alone proceeded to the region of the dead to be judged by Osiris. The Greek epics of Homer represented the soul as the breath of life, something airy, or ethereal, so that when Achilles saw the spirit of Patroclos, he was able to recognize him but unable to embrace him (*Iliad* 23:99–104).

In India the religious philosophical treatises of Brahmanism, the *Upanishads* (*c.* 650–500 B.C.), present the first extensive account of the origin, nature, and destiny of the human soul. According to this account, which is essentially monistic, BRAHMAN, the original source, generated the world and individual souls that enter bodies and are caught up in the world of *maya,* i.e., illusion and suffering. Birth is considered a misfortune, since the body is the prison of the soul. Salvation requires withdrawal from the body, even in this life, through knowledge of the All, the Absolute, in everything, and through an asceticism that strips off individuality and particular existence. If one has achieved this salvation, death brings extinction to him as an individual and a return to the Absolute; for one not purified by knowledge and asceticism, death brings a transmigration to another body and further suffering. In Brahmanism, the soul not only existed before the body, but it is somehow an emanation from Brahman, individualized and implanted in the world of phenomena. When purged and purified, the soul loses its individuality and merges once more with the Absolute. In a more pessimistic vein, BUDDHISM denied even substantiality to the individual soul, reducing it to a mere chain of sensations.

What was implied in Brahmanism became explicit in the cosmogony of ORPHISM among the Greeks. As a religious reform movement, about which authorities are not agreed, Orphism seems to have adapted older legends to account for the origin of man. According to one account, the evil Titans, sons of Earth, who had been gods before Zeus, killed and devoured the infant Dionysos; in punishment Zeus hurled a thunderbolt upon them to burn them up. From their ashes came forth the human race, in whom the divine, good element derived from Dionysos is mingled with the earthy, evil element derived from the Titans. The soul of man was thus considered a remnant of a god, but his body was a child of earth. Nevertheless the human soul, which apparently was considered to be an individual, could not return to the divine realm until it had sloughed off, in a series of transmigrations, all taint of what Plato later called ''the old Titanic nature'' (*Laws* 3:701C). Orphism, Pythagoreanism, the κάθαρμοι, or purifications of EMPEDOCLES, the catharsis of Plato—all sought to provide a means of deliverance from the ''wheel of births.'' (*See* PYTHAGORAS AND PYTHAGOREANS; MYSTERY RELIGIONS, GRECO-ORIENTAL.)

Greek philosophers. Not without reason has it been said that Orphism introduced into Greek philosophical thought the notion of soul as something divine, a quasi-incorporeal, immortal substance that existed before the body and sojourns a while on earth in the prison of the body. Not all Greek philosophers, however, were impressed by this mystery religion, and not all were inclined to accept its teachings on the soul. Instead, many philosophers tried to study human nature in terms of natural causes and events.

Early philosophers. The pre-Socratic philosophers generally considered man within the larger framework of φύσις, the basic principle, or source, of all growth and movement. As a result, they tended to define the soul as something that causes movement and to identify it with whatever element they considered primarily responsible for movement in the universe: fire, water, air, or ether. Since no one suggested that it was made out of earth (Aristotle, *Anim.* 405b 8–10), pre-Socratic philosophers, it would seem, attributed a tenuous, non-bodily character to the soul. This does not imply that any of the pre-Socratics attained to a concept of the spirituality of the soul. In all their descriptions, they spoke of the soul as something material. Anaximenes (fl. 542B.C.) described the soul as having an air-like nature that guides and controls the living being. ANAXAGORAS did not escape an implicit MATERIALISM, even though he introduced the notion of mind both for the universe and for man. Materialism is more evident in HERACLITUS, for whom the soul was fire, and in DEMOCRITUS, who considered it to be made of the finest atoms.

Plato. It was not until SOCRATES and PLATO that Greek thought rose to the notion of immateriality. Even when Plato employed mythology to describe creation, he considered the human soul an incorporeal substance, made from the same elements as the WORLD SOUL, akin to the gods and yet part of the world of change and becoming (*Tim.* 41). Being composed, the soul has within itself the roots of conflict—implied in the myth of the charioteer and the two winged horses (*Phaedrus* 246A–248D). If the earthy part of the soul triumphs over the divine, the soul falls from happiness to union with the body, which is its prison rather than its natural abode. Since the body is composed of ''the turbulent and opposing mob of elements,'' man is the seat of constant inner conflict, from which he must be delivered by the catharsis of philosophy. To explain the sources of this inner conflict Plato suggested that man has three souls or one soul having three parts: rational, irascible, and appetitive (*Tim.* 69D–72B; *Phaedo* 80B; *Rep.* 4.444B). Harmony is attained only when the rational part, the ''man within man,'' is able to attain mastery over the lower forces. The dependence of Plato's doctrine on Orphism is a matter of conjecture, although there is a striking resemblance between the two.

Aristotle. In his early writings ARISTOTLE accepted the myth of the soul as a divine sojourner on earth; the lost *Eudemus* apparently dwelt at length on this theme. But as Aristotle grew to intellectual maturity he abandoned this outright dualism of body and soul. At first he adopted a theory of close collaboration between the two without considering them elements of one unique reality. Finally in the *De anima,* he described the soul as an entelechy, or form, ''inseparable from its body, or at any rate, certain parts of it are'' (*Anim.* 413a 4–5). But even when Aristotle proposed his doctrine of the substantial unity of body and soul, he wondered whether mind (νοῦς), the power of thinking, may not be ''a widely different kind of soul, differing as what is eternal from what is perishable'' (413b 25–26). He stated that ''it alone is capable of existence separated from all other powers'' (413b 26–27). However, in later chapters he suggested a distinction between νοῦς that is the power of becoming all things through knowledge and νοῦς that is active, ''separable, impassible, unmixed'' (430a 14–19). Aristotle's obscure explanation of the precise relation between the active and passive intellects occasioned many divergent and contradictory explanations of his doctrines [see W. D. Ross, *Aristotle* (New York 1959) 128–151].

Later Philosophers. Aristotle's doctrine in the *De anima* seems to have been unknown to the Epicureans and Stoics, both of whom, despite vast differences, had a materialistic concept of the soul. For EPICURUS, the soul is composed of Democritus's atoms that disperse after death. The Stoics considered it a particle of the divine fire, or Logos, without deciding whether it survives this life or not (*see* STOICISM). Platonic dualism of soul and body was revived in the 1st century B.C. by the Stoic Poseidonius of Apameia (d. *c.* 51B.C.) and by the Platonist Antiochus of Ascalon (d. *c.* 68B.C.). Both considered the soul to be preexistent and immortal, and Poseidonius regarded it as distinct from the corporeal spirit that confers sentient and appetitive life. In the early Christian era, Middle Platonism helped to shape the Christian concept of a spiritual soul. PLOTINUS and NEOPLATONISM, representing the last philosophical movement among the Greeks, saw the soul not as entelechy (*Enneads* 4:7:8, against Aristotle's doctrine), but as an emanation from Soul, ψυχή, the third divine hypostasis. Though it was forced to descend to the body by way of punishment, or, as other passages suggest, came voluntarily to put order and beauty into matter, the human soul is never quite separated from Soul or wholly immersed in matter (*Enn.* 4:3:12–13). Its union with the body is natural and necessary, although it does not form with the body a new reality (*Enn.* 4:3:19). Plotinus went so far as to say that man is the soul; everything else is merely accidental (*Enn.* 4:7:1; 4:4:18).

Arabian falasifa. Significant developments in Aristotelianism took place among the Muslim philosophers, the *falasifa,* when they tried to solve the ancient problem of the two intellects. From Alexander of Aphrodisias (fl. A.D. 198–211) they borrowed an interpretation that identified the active intellect with God, who accordingly caused the material, or possible, intellect of man to pass from potentiality to the actuality of knowledge possessed. Since Arabian philosophers professed a Neoplatonic kind of Aristotelianism, they were inclined to identify the agent intellect with the last of the intelligences, or intellectual emanations from the One. From this tenth intelligence, according to AVICENNA, emanates the human soul, which is essentially intelligent, immaterial, indestructible, and immortal. Although the soul came into existence with the body, it has a life and operation of its own so that union with the body is not of the essence of the soul but rather a temporary situation. Avicenna explained knowledge as the infusion of intelligible forms by the separated agent intellect. Sense knowledge, for him, merely disposes the human intellect to receive such forms.

The problem implicit in Avicenna became acute when AVERROËS undertook to comment on the *De anima* of Aristotle. The human soul, according to Averroës, is a substance brought into being by human generation, and it perishes at death. Man possesses by nature only a material, passive, intellect, sometimes called *vis aestimativa,* or particular reason. For Averroës, the spiritual faculty of knowing and the agent intellect are both separated from individual men and are common to all men (*see* INTELLECT, UNITY OF). Since knowledge is achieved only by a kind of union, continuation, or conjunction of the individual with the separated intellects, the human soul is not essentially an intellectual one (*anima intellectiva*), but only a corruptible actuality of matter. This doctrine of Averroës, a matter of great concern in scholasticism after 1260, was one of the principal tenets of Latin AVERROISM.

See Also: GREEK PHILOSOPHY; ARABIAN PHILOSOPHY.

Bibliography: I. C. BRADY, *A History of Ancient Philosophy* (Milwaukee 1959). J. OWENS, *A History of Ancient Western Philosophy* (New York 1959). C. TRESMONTANT, *La Métaphysique du christianisme et la naissance de la philosophie chrétienne* (Paris 1961). L. PETIT, *Dictionnaire de théologie catholique* 1.1:1006–16 (Paris 1950). C. MAZZANTINI, *Enciclopedia filosofica* 1:222–226.

[I. C. BRADY]

2. Patristic and Medieval Writers

The Christian concept of a spiritual soul created by God and infused into the body at conception to make man a living whole is the fruit of a long development in Christian philosophy. Only with Origen in the East and St. Augustine in the West was the soul established as a spiritual substance and a philosophical concept formed of its nature. Even then, no adequate theory of the relationship between soul and body was achieved before the development of scholasticism.

Greek Fathers. The early Fathers were not directly concerned with the nature of the human soul, although they could not avoid treating this question at least implicitly when discussing the soul's immortality (*see* IMMORTALITY, 1. HISTORY OF PROBLEM).

Athenagoras. The apologist Athenagoras (*c.* 177), who called himself ''a Christian philosopher of Athens,'' perhaps attained more clarity than others in his ''On the Resurrection of the Dead.'' There he taught that God made man both to reveal His own goodness and wisdom and for man's sake. Since such reasons are permanent, there is no reason for man's total annihilation. Yet since man's nature is composed of an immortal soul and a body, neither of which is intended by God to exist apart, these elements will be reunited at the resurrection (ch. 12–15). Here one finds a clear emphasis on the Christian view of man as a unit, a living whole, even if the immortal soul is the more important element.

Irenaeus. In somewhat the same spirit St. IRENAEUS attacked the notion of preexistence and transmigration, arguing that God confers on each individual body its proper soul, to which it will be rejoined in the resurrection. In this, Irenaeus was an early witness to the Christian dislike for the Platonic notion of immortality, which implied that the soul was in some sense divine. The parable of Dives and Lazarus (Lk 16:19–31) induced Irenaeus to conclude that the departed soul preserves the same form or character as the body to which it was united and retains the figure of the man so that it is recognizable, as Dives recognized Lazarus (*Adversus haereses* 2:34). That this implied, for him, a certain materiality in the soul is confirmed by his earlier remark that souls are adapted to bodies and so possess the form of the body (*ibid.* 2:19). Such materiality, however, is not necessarily corporeality, since Irenaeus sharply distinguishes between body and soul; souls are immortal and incorporeal in comparison to bodies, which are subject to death (*ibid.* 5:7). If at times Irenaeus seems to distinguish in man body, soul, and spirit, this should not be understood as implying a real difference between the psyche and nous, soul and intellect, for these are identical in being (2:29). Rather it refers to the union of soul and Spirit that produces the perfect man, the spiritual man made to the likeness of God (5:6; cf. J. Quasten, *Patrology* 1:308–310).

Clement. The first of the Fathers explicitly to borrow from the Greek tradition on the soul was CLEMENT OF ALEXANDRIA. For him, philosophy can be judiciously used by the Christian as an aid to wisdom and the defense of the faith; whatever any school rightly teaches can be used by the Christian gnostic (*Strom.* 1:7, 1:13; *Patrologia Latina* 8:732D, 756B). What little Clement had to say on the nature of the soul, usually within the framework of Genesis, ch. 1 and 2, betrays such eclecticism. At times he was inclined to adopt the Platonic teaching of the tripartite soul, or posit a composition in man of body, soul, and spirit (*Paedag.* 3:1, *Patrologia Graeca* 8:556A; *Strom.* 3:9, *Patrologia Graeca* 8:1166C). Yet he seems to have preferred a Stoic analysis whereby the soul is said to have ten parts: the five senses, the power of speech, the generative faculty, a corporeal spirit, another spirit that is the ruling power (*hegemonikon*) of the soul, and lastly the Holy Spirit, who comes to those who have the faith (*Strom.* 6:16, *Patrologia Graeca* 9:360A). By ''corporeal spirit'' Clement evidently meant the vegetative-sentient soul (*ibid.* and 7:12, 509A). The ruling power, identified as the mind (nous), is not generated but introduced from without by God (6:16; 5:14). The lower elements are subordinate to such ''ruling power,'' through which man is said to be alive (6:16), which bestows on him his true dignity, and in which is found the image of God (6:16; 6:9). Do these two spirits form one soul? Clement did not say. On the one hand, he considered man as made up simply of body and soul (*ibid.* 4:26, *Patrologia Graeca* 8:1373A, C). Yet, since the ''corporeal spirit'' can rebel with the flesh against the soul (Gal 5:17), it is hardly identical with the latter, which is ''subtle and simple, and can even be called incorporeal'' (*Strom.* 6:6, *Patrologia Graeca* 9:273C). In such a doctrine Clement mingled elements from both Scripture and Greek thought, but he did not succeed in obtaining a clear concept of soul as one spiritual substance possessed of many powers. Instead, he seemed to favor a kind of trichotomy in man of body, soul (as principle of sentient life), and spirit or mind.

Origen. Only with ORIGEN, Clement's most famous pupil, did the soul emerge as a spiritual rational substance identified with spirit or mind. Since it was within the same context of ''flesh rebelling against the spirit'' (Gal 5:17) that Origen considered the question of two souls or soul and spirit in man, he likely had Clement's doctrine before him (*De principiis* 3:4, *Patrologia Graeca* 11:319–325). Is there, he asked (323C), another soul in man, an *anima carnis,* besides the heavenly and rational soul? Advancing arguments for both sides, he modestly let the reader decide (325C). Yet he himself evidently thought there was but one soul, a conclusion bolstered by his earlier interpretation of soul and spirit (2:10:7, 239). The latter is either the Holy Spirit or the ''better part of the soul,'' that made to the image and likeness of God but not separate from the substance of the soul, or even the spirit or angel assigned to man as guardian. The ''Discussion with Heraclides,'' discovered only in 1941, corroborates the identity of soul and spirit, since Origen here proposes that ''spirit'' is really a part of man (J. Quasten, *Patrology,* 2:62–64). This one soul in man is a rational substance (*De prin.* 2:6:3–5, *Patrologia Graeca* 11:211D, 213C), a simple intellectual nature that ''needs no bodily place or physical magnitude, color, or aught else that is proper to body or matter,'' and grows only in ''intelligible magnitude'' as it increases in knowledge (1:1:6, 125A–126C). ''Let those who think the mind and soul is a body tell me, if this were so, how it could receive and understand reasonings which are often difficult and subtle, and contemplate and know things invisible and incorporeal'' (1:1:7, 126C). Such intellectual knowledge, in marked contrast to sense knowledge (127B), forces one to conclude that mind or soul is superior to all corporeal nature. Lastly, to claim that mind is corporeal is to offer insult to God, since the mind is the intellectual image of God and has thereby a certain affinity to Him who is wholly spiritual and intellectual in nature (128A) and is the source of every intellectual being (125A; cf. *Exhortatio ad martyrum* 47, *Patrologia Graeca* 11:629B).

Such a position, established by arguments valid in their own right, marked a decided advance that was maintained by Origen's successors. Unfortunately, in his own thought it was intimately bound up with a theory on the origin of the soul that exceeded the limits of orthodoxy. For Origen, all rational creatures were created at once, in the beginning, pure, equal, and alike; since they were without body or matter, and invisible and intelligible by nature, they could rightly be called intelligences. But because they were creatures, they were mutable and equally capable of good and evil; and when God put them to the test, all fell in some degree, except the soul of Christ. The result was the diversity and hierarchy of rational creatures: angels, souls, and demons. The human soul was thus originally a nous, a purely spiritual being, which became a soul (psyche) "because it waxed cold [*psychesthai*] from the fervor of just things" (*De prin.* 2:8:3, *Patrologia Graeca* 11:223B). The proximate cause of such diversity was to be found in the type of body each nous received as chastisement and remedy for the fall [*ibid.* 2:9, *Patrologia Graeca* 11:225–233; for details, see J. Daniélou, *Origen* (New York 1955) 209–219, and C. Tresmontant, 395–518].

Gregory of Nyssa. This theory did not go unchallenged by such anti-Origenists as Peter of Alexandria and Methodius of Olympus. Yet the orthodox elements of Origen's thought lived on in the two Christian psychologists of the 4th century: St. GREGORY OF NYSSA and Nemesius of Emesa. Both made considerable use of Greek psychological writings, though always with the critical eye of a Christian. Gregory was much more the theologian, while Nemesius was primarily the philosopher in his approach. In the first complete definition of soul to be found, it would seem, in a Christian writer, Gregory saw soul not only as the life-giving principle but also as identical with mind: "Soul is a produced, living, rational substance, which imparts of itself to an organic body capable of sensation the power of life and sensation, as long as the nature capable of such things exists" (*Macrinia,* or *De anima et resurrectione, Patrologia Graeca* 46:29B). The Pauline distinction of body, soul, and spirit is primarily a moral one (*De hominis opificio* 8, *Patrologia Graeca* 44:145), and there is no question in man of two or three souls welded together: "the true and perfect soul is one in nature, intellectual and immaterial, and endowed with powers it imparts to the material body" (*ibid.* 14, 176B). Such is the remarkable union of this spirit with matter that all the lower powers serve the higher (8–10), from which they receive life; while the intellect itself is dependent on the senses for communication with the outer world (10, 14). The question of the origin of the soul was much discussed, Gregory said, in the churches of his day (*ibid.* 28, 229B), an echo of the Origenist controversies. That soul was created before the body he labeled fantastic and absurd, a fable borrowed from Greek philosophy. That soul is made after the body he held as contrary to manifest experience. Therefore both come into existence together, though Gregory was at a loss to explain how. He was content to believe that somehow the power of God intervenes to change the sperm into a most wondrous living thing (*Catechesis* 33, *Patrologia Graeca* 45:84D; cf. 11, 44A and *Macrinia, Patrologia Graeca* 46:120CD, 121A, 125A).

Nemesius. The first Christian to write a full summa on the nature of man (which scholastics knew under the name of Gregory), NEMESIUS OF EMESA began by examining the all-important question: what do we mean by soul? Is it identical with mind, or does mind come to soul? (*De natura hominis* 1, *Patrologia Graeca* 40:504A). The answers of Plotinus, Aristotle, and Plato he rejected as insufficient. Plotinus would make mind and soul two distinct entities; Aristotle posits a double nous, one coming from without; while Plato identifies nous and man, defining the latter as "a soul using a body." What Nemesius considered the soul to be is evident only indirectly, through his long survey and criticism (2, 556–589) of ancient opinions, including a devastating attack on Aristotle (560–569). He concluded that the soul is an incorporeal substance, subsistent in itself, not dependent on something else for its being, yet intended for union with the body (589AB, 592A). Bolder than his predecessors, Nemesius undertook to answer "the difficult question" how soul and body are joined (3, 592–608). Of all solutions offered, that of Ammonius Saccas (593B), as expressed by Porphyry, seemed to him best: "It cannot be denied [quoting Porphyry] that some substance can be assumed as complement to another substance and so become part of a being that, while remaining in its own nature, it both completes the other substance and becomes one with it and yet keeps its own identity. Moreover, without suffering any change itself, it may by its presence transform those things in which it is into means of its own activity" (604A). To illustrate such a union Nemesius found an apt analogy in the union of the Word of God and man in the Incarnation (601A). Much of what he said in succeeding chapters on the body, the outer and inner senses, the lower powers of the soul, and the passions, is an agglomerate from many sources: Aristotle, the Stoics, Galen, etc. This, with the lengthy analysis of the will, dependent in part on Aristotle's *Ethics,* is a new and important contribution to the Christian philosophy of man.

Other Influences. Since Maximus Confessor and St. John Damascene did little more than summarize earlier writers, Nemesius marked the climax of Greek patristic thought on the soul. The resulting doctrine of the soul as a substance made for union with the body, yet subsistent in itself, rational, incorporeal, simple, and immortal, was far different from the teaching of the early Greek philosophers. Plato and Aristotle seem to have had little direct influence in the formation of such a concept; when their doctrine was adduced, it was usually subject to criticism. Neoplatonism received less attention than one might expect. It is more probable that Middle Platonism, which flourished in the first Christian centuries, furnished Clement, Origen, and later writers with key ideas. At the same time, the Fathers were concerned with establishing a concept in accord with the Christian doctrine of immortality as well as of the Incarnation. Frequently, it seems they read Scripture with Greek minds, interpreting certain Semitic expressions in terms of their own backgrounds.

Latin Fathers. Africa, not Rome, provided the first Latin writers in the Church. Of those who wrote on the soul, the most important include Tertullian, Arnobius, Lactantius, Augustine, and a few later thinkers.

Tertullian. A lawyer and apologist, not too apt a philosopher, TERTULLIAN undertook in his *De anima* to summon up every human opinion on the soul [ch. 58; ed. J. H. Waszink (Amsterdam 1947) 80], using ''God's letters'' to test its worth (ch. 2). His documentation is poor, since much of his information is derived from Soranus the Stoic (ch. 6). Stoicism led him into one famous error, that the soul though a spirit is at the same time a body (ch. 5); this, he thought, was the only explanation of Dives and Lazarus (ch. 7). From it proceeds his TRADUCIANISM: that Adam's soul alone was created by God, while all other souls come into being by the act of generation (ch. 23–27, 36). Despite such errors, Tertullian's position was often solidly Christian, e.g., his approach to the body and its functions (*De resurrectione carnis* 4–6), the close union of body and soul (*ibid.* 7–10, 15–16), and the identification of soul and mind (*De anima* 12–13). He was the first Latin to see the powers not as parts of the soul but as *vires et efficaciae,* evidently a translation of the Greek *energiae* (*ibid.* 14). The influence of his *De anima* was extremely slight, perhaps because it was too polemical.

Arnobius. Of less importance was ARNOBIUS, whose ''Case against the Pagans'' (*Adversus nationes*) is of interest only for its attack on the immortality of the soul, a doctrine that turned the soul into a god (2:14–15). In his view, men are merely animate beings not greatly different from beasts, and for the most part do not act according to reason (16–17); this fickleness would show that the soul is not made by God (36, 45).

Lactantius. In contrast, LACTANTIUS dwelt on the real differences between man and beast as revealing God's special providence (*Div. institut.* 7:4; *De opificio Dei* 2–4). He rejected Tertullian's traducianism, since spirit cannot beget spirit (*De opif.* 17–19); for him, souls are produced by God at the time of conception.

Augustine. St. AUGUSTINE is the first of the Latin Fathers to have a clear concept of soul as a spiritual substance intimately united to the body. His doctrine, which became standard in the West until the late 12th century, owed much (including some shortcomings) to Neoplatonism, yet was much more strikingly Christian in approach and content. His thought begins with man created by God as a whole, a rational substance composed of body and soul (*Trin.* 15:7:11; *Serm.* 150:4). How these are united is beyond the comprehension of man (*Civ.* 21:10), but the union is natural and not penal (*ibid.* 13:16; *Epist.* 164:7), substantial and not accidental (*Civ.* 13.24). The soul is the active principle, the body the passive, in the living whole that is man (*ibid.* 22, 24), since the body subsists through the soul and receives form and life from it (*ibid.* 13.2; *Immort. anim.* 15–16), while soul is so merged with body that it does not lose its identity (*Epist.* 166:2). All this is possible only because the soul is a completely immaterial substance, *res spiritualis, res incorporea,* and close to the substance of God (*In psalm.* 145:4). The incorporeality of the soul, Augustine wrote to St. Jerome (*Epist.* 166:2), is something difficult to prove to those who are slow of wit—as is evident from his controversies over the question—but it is something of which he was wholly convinced. In proof he offered especially man's intellectual knowledge of the immaterial (*Quant. anim.* 13–14, 27–28), as well as self-consciousness (*Gen. ad litt.* 7:19–21). Later, between 467 and 472, his position was defended and reinforced by Claudianus Mamertus (*De statu animae*) against Faustus, Bishop of Riez, who ascribed a corporeal nature to both souls and angels [on this problem, see P. Glorieux, *Autour de la spiritualité des anges* (Tournai 1959)].

While Augustine was sure of the incorporeality of the soul, he was unable to reach a definitive position on its origin. Adam's soul was created directly by God (*Gen. ad litt.* 7:28); but as to the origin of all others, he confessed his inability to choose between opposing opinions (*Retract.* 1:1:3; *C. Iulian. op. imperf.* 2:178). Traducianism he regarded as a perverse theory that destroys the spiritual character of the soul (*Epist.* 190:4); creation of individual souls at conception seemed preferable, yet it hardly explained the transmission of original sin (*Epist.* 166:8). Could all souls have been created at once and then either be sent by God in due time to be united to bodies or come of their own accord? This is possible, yet it does not provide a solid reason for union with the body (*Epist.* 166:3). At most, Augustine was sure that God is the creator and maker of every soul, and that the soul is not an emanation from the divine substance but a creature made to God's image.

Later Thinkers. Augustine was not alone in such difficulties. St. GREGORY THE GREAT considered the question of the origin of soul difficult and beyond human comprehension (*Epist.* 52, *Patrologia Latina* 77:990A). St. ANSELM OF CANTERBURY regretted on his deathbed (1109) that he had not been able to elucidate the question (*Patrologia Latina* 158: 115B). On the other hand, St. Leo the Great (447), reproving the ''fable'' of preexistence, stated plainly that the Catholic faith constantly and truly teaches that the souls of men do not exist before they are breathed into their bodies, being placed there by God alone, who is the creator of souls and bodies (*Epist.* 15.10, *Patrologia Latina* 54:685A). Among the scholastics, following Peter Lombard (*Sent.* 2:18:7), St. Jerome was considered the patristic authority for creationism, since he said that God daily fashions souls and does not cease to be the creator (*Patrologia Latina* 23:372; on this problem, see Tresmontant, *La Métaphysique du christianisme et la naissance de la philosophie chrétienne,* 577–612).

Scholastics. Very little originality was shown in all the treatises on the soul that fill the early Middle Ages. Cassiodorus, Licinianus, Alcuin, Rabanus Maurus, Hincmar of Reims, and Ratramnus of Corbie were content to repeat Augustine and sometimes one another, even when they engaged in fresh controversies on soul and body. An exception was John Scotus Erigena, who translated Gregory of Nyssa's *De hominis opificio* and introduced certain of its themes into his *De divisione naturae.*

Twelfth-century Mystics. The renaissance of the 12th century saw a whole new approach to the soul from the viewpoint of MYSTICISM. Psychology became a prelude to the ascent to God. Such an approach had been that of St. Augustine, who in his search for God had proceeded from the external world to the inner world of the soul, and ascended through it to God (*Conf.* 7:17; 10:6–8). His dialectic became the inspiration for HUGH OF SAINT-VICTOR: ''To mount upward to God is to enter into oneself; and not merely so to enter but in an ineffable way to transcend self within'' (*De vanitate mundi* 2, *Patrologia Latina* 176:715B). The Cistercian school, after St. Bernard, was a more striking example of this trend. Almost every one of its writers composed a treatise in some form or other ''On the Soul'' as the key to, and formulation of, his mysticism [see J. M. Déchanet, *Guillaume de Saint-Thierry, Oeuvres choisies* (Paris 1944) 51]. What sets many of these treatises apart from previous works was the fusion of the Latin tradition of Augustine with the theology of the Greek Fathers, especially Gregory of Nyssa and Pseudo-Dionysius, as well as the incorporation after 1140 of medical and psychological material from newly translated Greek and Arabic sources. William of Saint-Thierry is an example of the former, since his treatise *De natura corporis et animae* (*Patrologia Latina* 180:695–726) is largely and literally Gregory's work supplemented by Cassiodorus, Claudianus Mamertus, and a few pieces of Augustine (see Déchanet, 71–). Later writers of the school, St. Aelred of Rievaulx, Isaac of Stella, Alcher of Clairvaux (the supposed author of *De spiritu et anima*), and William of Conches, who was not a Cistercian, were much preoccupied with classifying the powers of the soul and discussing the organs of the body and the ventricles of the brain. Their work, especially Isaac's *Epistola de anima* and the anonymous *De spiritu et anima* (which incorporates much of the former) influenced some scholastics of the 13th century. The question of the identity of soul and powers, for example, stems from their writings (cf. Lottin, 1:483–502). Again, Isaac's theory that the union of soul and body is effected through the medium of the imagination was accepted by some and rejected by others, including St. Augustine [see *Epist., Patrologia Latina* 194:1881D; *De spiritu et anima* 14, *Patrologia Latina* 40:790; and P. Michaud-Quantin, ''La classification des puissances de l'âme au XIIe siècle,'' *Revue du moyen âge latin* 5 (1949) 15–34].

Greek and Arabian Influence. The foregoing writers belong to what is sometimes called pre-scholasticism, the period uninfluenced by the new philosophical literature, Greek and Arabian, that began to appear in the West after 1150 (see Van Steenberghen). The advent of ARISTOTLE, AVICENNA, and later AVERROËS, and the appearance of the *De anima* of DOMINIC GUNDISALVI, or perhaps more likely of Ibn David, produced a whole new approach to psychological problems. Faced for the first time with a purely philosophical definition of the soul free from ethical or mystical aspects, and a metaphysical and not merely psychological theory of the relation of soul and body, the schoolmen were forced to reexamine their Christian traditions and decide whether or not they would and could accept the hylomorphism of Aristotle.

Those who came to grips with the problem early in the 13th century (e.g., JOHN BLUND, PHILIP THE CHANCELLOR, and JOHN OF LA ROCHELLE) usually took Avicenna as their guide in interpreting Aristotle's definition, since with Roger Bacon they considered him ''the principal imitator of Aristotle and next to him the leader and prince of philosophy.'' For Avicenna, the soul is both a spiritual substance and the perfection of the body. But, in an all-important distinction, he differentiated between the essence of the soul and its role in the body: ''The term 'soul' is not given this spiritual being because of its substance but by reason of its relation to the body, just as in defining a workman we must include his trade, but we do not do so in defining 'man''' [*Anim.* 1:1 (Venice 1508) fol. 1c]. On this basis some scholastics, St. Albert the Great among them, claimed that the spiritual soul could be considered the perfection of the body without being a form in the strict sense, since a form is always immersed in matter and has no existence of its own. Out of this viewpoint grew the theory, in Odo Rigaldus and St. Bonaventure and his school, of the *colligantia naturalis,* the natural bond, between body and soul. Soul is united as ''perfection'' to the body as ''that which is perfectible''; but both are considered complete substances existing and acting independently of each other. To explain how the soul is capable of subsisting in itself, the school adopted the theory of a composition of spiritual matter and form proposed by AVICEBRON. The body, on the other hand, is constituted as body by some form or forms that precede the union with the soul and perdure in that union. Notwithstanding their individual substantiality, soul and body are made for mutual union. There is a natural bond between them from which there results a natural union, but not that proposed by Aristotle. At most, Aristotelian HYLOMORPHISM was a help in understanding that union; the doctrine itself was rejected because it seemed to contradict the Christian teaching of the soul as a spiritual substance.

Thomas Aquinas. All such theories St. THOMAS AQUINAS rejected as useless obstructions to the true approach to the problem. For him, to speak of spiritual matter was to contravene the obvious and established meaning of matter. To posit a plurality of forms in the human body or in any body was to weaken, if not destroy, the metaphysics of actuality and potentiality, of matter and form, and to abandon the principles of true philosophy. To distinguish with Avicenna between soul as spirit and soul as form or perfection was to reduce its union with the body to one of ''contact of power'' and to make man ''a being by accident'' (*C. gent.* 2.57). Instead, St. Thomas undertook to show that Aristotle's doctrine on soul as form and its hylomorphic union with the body was the only adequate interpretation fitting the facts of experience: ''If anyone does not wish to say that the intellectual soul is the form of the body, let him find a theory whereby the act of understanding is the action of this man, for everyone knows by experience that *he* understands'' (*Summa theologiae* 1a, 76:1).

Yet, to establish this, Thomas had to meet a more formidable adversary than the semi-Aristotelian scholastics; he had to oppose and refute Averroës, the Commentator of Aristotle, and the group in the Paris faculty of arts who chose to follow the mighty Muslim. For Averroës every form is completely immersed in matter and is thus purely and simply material. From this it follows that no immaterial intellectual substance can be the form of a body. While man possesses a soul that is a material perishable form, the intellect is not part of that soul but is somehow a separate unique substance. The burden lay on St. Thomas to prove against such a position (advanced in the name of Aristotle) that the soul and intellect are one, that this intellectual soul can be and is the form of the body and yet transcends the body in its intellectual power, and that this is the only true interpretation one can give to Aristotle's doctrine (see Pegis, ''St. Thomas and the Unity of Man,'' 153–173).

In answering both extremes St. Thomas refused to see the problem as psychological or spiritual, as perhaps other scholastics were inclined to do, but regarded it, with Averroës, as primarily and fundamentally metaphysical. The solution, whether of the question of spiritual matter and form, of the plurality of forms, or of the union of soul and body, was so intrinsically bound up with his metaphysical doctrine that it provoked opposition on this ground in many quarters. In the last quarter of the 13th century the scholastic world was full of controversies that arose out of refusal to accept Aquinas's position. Among the theologians of Paris there was open and outspoken criticism of his teaching on the unicity of form in man. Among the 219 propositions condemned at Paris in 1277 some touched it indirectly, while among the 30 proscribed shortly after at Oxford it was mentioned very specifically. The controversy continued into the 14th century, as is evident in Duns Scotus's doctrine of the form of corporeity. Yet throughout, Aristotle's definition was accepted; the differences arose over particular metaphysical interpretations.

Peter John Olivi. Connected with this is the peculiar theory of PETER JOHN OLIVI on the constitution of the soul itself. In the human body, he held, there are other forms (e.g., vegetative and sensitive) besides the soul; yet with the latter such forms make up but one complete form [*Quaest. in 2 sent.* 50 (Quaracchi 1924) 35]. From this he concluded that the intellective part of the soul is not as such the form of the body, since otherwise it could not be intellectual, free, immortal, and separable (*ibid.* 51, 111); yet at the same time it is the form through the sensitive part (59, 539). In the Council of Vienne (1311) many of Olivi's positions were attacked; yet the decree *Fidei Catholicae fundamentum,* defining that the intellective or rational soul *per se et essentialiter* is the form of the body

(Denz 900), apparently did not concern his doctrine, though William of Alnwick seems to have interpreted it to be so [Greg 30 (1949) 268; cf. C. Partee, ''Peter John Olivi,'' *Franc Studies* 20 (1960) 241–253].

Finally, the discussion over the relation of the soul to its powers, which had its rise in the mid-13th century, gathered momentum after the time of St. Thomas and HENRY OF GHENT, especially among the disciples of Duns Scotus (see Piana). Interest in the 14th century, however, shifted from the soul itself to questions of man's knowledge of it and of knowledge in general.

See Also: AUGUSTINIANISM; FORMS, UNICITY AND PLURALITY OF; SCOTISM; THOMISM.

Bibliography: C. MAZZANTINI, *Enciclopedia filosofica* 1:222–239. J. BAINVEL, *Dictionnaire de théologie catholique,* 1.1:977–1006 (Paris 1950). É. H. GILSON, *History of Christian Philosophy in the Middle Ages,* (New York 1955). F. C. COPLESTON, *History of Philosophy* v.1–2 (Westminster, Md. 1950). A. C. PEGIS, ''St. Thomas and the Unity of Man,'' *Progress in Philosophy,* ed. J. A. MCWILLIAMS (Milwaukee 1955) 153–173; *St. Thomas and the Problem of the Soul in the Thirteenth Century* (Toronto 1934). O. LOTTIN, *Psychologie et morale aux XII*[e] *et XIII*[e] *siècles,* 6 v. in 8 (Louvain 1942–60). THOMAS AQUINAS, ''Commentary,'' Aristotle, *De anima, in the Version of William of Moerbeke,* tr. K. FOSTER and S. HUMPHRIES (New Haven 1951). A. FREMANTLE, ed., *A Treasury of Early Christianity* (New York 1953). F. VAN STEENBERGHEN, *Aristotle in the West,* tr. L. JOHNSTON (Louvain 1955). C. TRESMONTANT, *La Métaphysique du christianisme et la naissance de la philosophie chrétienne* (Paris 1961). C. PIANA, ''La controversia della distinzione fra anima e potenze ai primordi della scuola scotista,'' *Miscellanea del Centro di Studi Medievali* (Milan 1956) 65–168.

[I. C. BRADY]

3. Modern and Contemporary Thought

Although the word soul continued to be widely used until the 19th century, the scholastic view of it as the principle of existence, of life, and of all levels of activity, as that which constitutes the individual man as one corporeal human existent, had already been lost before the origin of modern philosophy with Descartes. This part of the article therefore begins with doctrines concerning the soul that are typical of the Renaissance, continues with notions that were prevalent in the modern period, and concludes with a survey of the status of the concept of soul in contemporary philosophy.

Renaissance thought. Because of their nearness to the Averroist struggle over the unity of the intellect, Renaissance philosophers were concerned more with personal immortality and free will than with the substantiality of the soul. Thus M. FICINO, a Platonist, defended personal immortality. In his five degrees of being, related successively as cause and effect, the soul is the third or middle essence and the ''fountain of motion.'' The higher soul comprises the power of contemplation (mind), shared with God and the angels, and reason, unique to man. The soul, with two tendencies, one toward the body and related to sense, the other toward God and associated with the rational soul, is free to oppose or be misled by the senses. Because of reason, man is unable to attain final perfection on earth. That the general ontological principle (no natural desire can be in vain) be not contradicted, the human soul must know and enjoy God in afterlife. The natural inclination of the body also will be satisfied when the soul possesses its own body made everlasting, a natural condition in which the soul finds eternal rest.

P. Pomponazzi, heir to Averroist and Italian ARISTOTELIANISM, tried to make the soul a material inhabitant of an orderly universe. To be consistent with revelation, which states that the soul is immortal, the intellective soul must be entirely separate; if it is, it cannot be a FORM or else the union is of two independent elements. If the soul is the form of the body, it gives the body being as well as operation and is an immersed form. The human soul is thus essentially mortal and relatively immortal. The Aristotelian form or soul is here viewed univocally, not analogically. The act of existence of the soul is different from that of man the composite. The soul is a bodily function generated by the parents, not by special creation, and is incapable of operating or existing without the body. Later Pomponazzi declared that, philosophically speaking, the soul is mortal, and, lacking simplicity and spirituality, is exactly like any material form; only by faith can it be seen as immortal.

B. Telesio, while recognizing in the bodies of men and animals a SPIRIT or pneuma—an emanation of the warm element passed through the body by the nerves—felt that man could not be totally analyzed in biological terms. In his view, there must be present in man a *forma superaddita,* an immortal soul that informs body and spirit and is capable of union with God. This divine soul understands, but only those things the natural spirit presents to it.

G. Bruno, lacking a concept of ANALOGY, was unable to distinguish between SUBSISTENCE and ASEITY (*aseitas*). Particular finite substances are only modes of the unique divine substance. Every existent is animated by the WORLD SOUL, an infinite continuum in one sense, and yet, in another sense, discontinuous and infinitely divisible. The human soul is an individual soaring to the utmost spiritual development congruent with its own nature, imbued with the divine spirit, whereby the whole infinity of discrete and independent souls is fused into a unity transcending their discrete separateness. While immortality of a kind is thus guaranteed for the intellectual principle in man, man's individuality is lost, since union through love is comparable to the identification of a substance with its attributes.

Modern period. With the growth of the scientific attitude and the sterility of scholastic philosophy in the 17th century, scholastic terms were no longer used with their medieval connotations. This prepared for a variety of explanations consonant with rationalist, empiricist, and idealist philosophical positions.

Cartesianism. The *Cogito* of R. DESCARTES split man into two separate substances: one a thinking substance, the other, the body, an extended substance that is mechanical in nature and operation and thus like the rest of the material world. J. KEPLER and G. GALILEI had banished animation from inorganic nature, but the Cartesians went one step further and conceived the entire organic realm as subject to mechanical laws. Those who supported animism did so to support religious dogmas, particularly belief in an afterlife. The soul was regarded as a thinking substance, but the vitalizing, vegetative, and sensory functions implicit in the Thomistic concept were denied to it. Vitalism proposed a life principle in no way linked to the thinking, willing soul, the ground of all individual consciousness as described by Descartes. The soul, to him, located in the pineal gland, is an immaterial unextended being interacting with the body through the medium of the brain and nervous system only. The separation of the conceptions of vitalizing principle and thinking principle thus became complete.

Descartes's bold assertion that animal and bodily behavior are mechanical hastened the view of man's behavior as a mechanical response to stimuli and laid the grounds for the theoretical justification of conditioning therapies. The two aspects of the soul—that of thinker (*res cogitans*) and of thought (*res cogitata*) further complicated the mind-body problem. A. GEULINCX and N. MALEBRANCHE attempted a solution with their doctrine of OCCASIONALISM, which held that a change in either soul or body was the occasion for God to bring about a corresponding change in the other.

Leibniz and Spinoza. G. W. LEIBNIZ refused to admit intercausal relation. Man is composed of a superior monad (the soul) and an aggregate of inferior monads (the body). Both are so constructed that they register alike in their experiences but independently of each other, much as two clocks run together in preestablished harmony. The term soul applies to those created monads whose perception is more distinct than that of simple substances. Rational soul or mind, which distinguishes man from mere animals, gives reason and raises man to a knowledge of himself and of God. For Leibniz, thinking is the proper activity of the human soul. Ultimately, thinking becomes its *only* activity—with no causal relation to the body. While souls act according to final causes (thus implying the presence of a DYNAMISM in the soul), bodies act according to the laws of efficient causality. The two realms of causality are in harmony, not in contact, with each other.

For B. SPINOZA, mind and body are but two reflections of one clock seen at different angles. Thought, soul, or mind, and extension are but two of many attributes of one Real Substance, God. The soul is one with the cosmos; the mind, an activity of the Divine Mind.

Empiricism. J. LOCKE, too, rejected the soul as a substantial form. The conception of an immaterial soul, for him, involved no more obscurity than that of material substance. Soul is as unknown as is substance, but the notion of ''spiritual substance'' seemed to him more reasonable, probable, and in harmony with religious belief.

The ambiguous connotations of the soul as both subject of thinking and object of thought persisted for a century. G. BERKELEY was convinced of the reality of the spirit, mind, or soul as a perceiving active being—not one's ideas, but something distinct from ideas in which ideas exist or whereby they are perceived. Spirit is that which thinks, wills, and perceives. The soul always thinks. Such an active uncompounded substance cannot be dissolved by natural forces; therefore, Berkeley concluded, the soul of man is naturally immortal.

D. HUME denied the substantiality of spirit. In place of the word soul he used the term self, that to which impressions and ideas are supposed to have a reference. Through habit man merely ascribes constancy and identity to a bundle of perceptions (called self) in much the same way as he ascribes a causal relationship to a mere sequence of events. If substance is defined as something that may exist in itself; and, if man has no idea of substance, only of perceptions; and if perceptions do not appear to need support, then the question as to whether perceptions inhere in a material or spiritual substance is meaningless. So, too, is the question of the relation of the soul to the body.

J. O. de La Mettrie brought to its ultimate conclusion this examination of the metaphysical concept of soul and the effort to verify it empirically by calling soul ''an empty symbol of which one has no conception and which a sound mind would use only to indicate that which thinks in man.''

Kantianism. I. KANT faced the ambiguity implicit in the connotation of soul as both thought and thinker. He claimed that reason *regulates* ideas, validly, but that reason may *constitute* ideas, invalidly. The ultimate synthetic principles of reason are soul, world, and God. Attempts to prove the soul's immateriality, spirituality, immortality, personality, and its animation of a body amount to paralogisms or formal errors in reasoning. "*I* as thinking am an object of the internal sense, called a soul." That which is object of the external senses is called body. In pure reason, one confuses the logical subject with the real substrate when trying to prove the substantiality of the soul. The soul as an unconditioned real unity of all phenomena of the inner sense can neither be proved nor refuted, but it can be a valuable heuristic principle for investigating the interconnections of the psychical life. The object of psychology is the determinable self or thought; of philosophy, the determining self or thinker. Only for practical or moral purposes are the freedom and immortality of man to be believed. They can never be known. Man can believe that the soul is immortal because ethical consciousness demands the highest GOOD that is beyond the order of nature. Philosophically, it is not clear how Kant's noumenal ego or self is related to the scholastic term soul.

The role of reason as regulator of phenomenal experiences changed imperceptibly, however, into the view that the mind constitutes knowledge. The Kantian school continued to propagate in crude form the doctrine that neither the object in itself nor the subject in itself is knowable but only the world of CONSCIOUSNESS. The object gives the manifold of the material; the subject imposes the synthetic unity of the form. Soul, like all forms, is a logical construct imposed by the subject on a series of phenomena to preserve the unity of man. That the intrinsic unity of man may be due to the soul as a formal metaphysical principle is simply not present in Kantian thought.

Reactions to Idealism. In reaction to post-Kantian IDEALISM, J. F. Herbart developed the theory of the "reals" (*Realen*) that reciprocally disturb each other in order to be preserved. These self-preservations are the means by which the unknown "real" of the human soul maintains itself against disturbance by other "reals." As a simple substance, the soul is naturally unknowable; psychology, as a science, studies only its self-preservations, for these constitute the soul. The soul merely furnishes the indifferent stage for the coexistence of the ideas. The psychical life or life of the soul is one of reciprocal tension of ideas.

A. SCHOPENHAUER, still keeping Kant's doctrine of the noumenal and the phenomenal, held that the thing-in-itself is the WILL. In men and animals, the will appears as motivation determined through ideas; in instinctive and vegetative life, it appears as susceptibility to stimulation, and in the rest of the nonconscious world, as mechanical processes. For Schopenhauer, the ABSOLUTE is world-will.

The result of this line of thought was that human soul was no longer considered as it is in itself but rather as it can be investigated in its activities. MAINE DE BIRAN, J. G. FICHTE, and Schopenhauer located the essential nature of man in the will—although they did not explicitly identify soul with will itself.

Hegelianism. The dialectical method of Fichte and G. W. F. HEGEL challenged the immortality of the soul. In their systems of perpetual becoming and of passing from one form to another, the finite personality could scarcely be a substance in itself, and thus the strongest argument for immortality was undermined.

Hegel presented his philosophy of spirit in three parts, the first two dealing with finite spirit or soul and the last with Absolute Spirit. In anthropology, the soul is merely a sensing and feeling spirit, enjoying self-feeling but not reflective self-consciousness. It is embodied; the body is merely the external aspect of the soul. After this study of an undifferentiated subjective spirit, Hegel investigated the phenomenology of consciousness wherein the subjective spirit is confronted first by the other, external to it, and then by itself in reflective self-consciousness. Ultimately it rises to universal self-consciousness wherein other selves are recognized as both one with itself and yet distinct.

Contemporary philosophy. Granted the difficulty of drawing a dividing line between modern and contemporary thought regarding the soul, the principal movements within contemporary philosophy may be discussed under the headings of phenomenology, Marxism, neopositivism, American philosophy, and existentialism.

Phenomenology. M. SCHELER opposed Kant's ideas on the noumenal ego and maintained that the ego is merely another object of knowledge. E. HUSSERL, on the other hand, extended Descartes's doubt to the absolute certainty of mind as thinking substance. By transcendental reflection, he bracketed the existence of the world and his thoughts and thus reached the transcendental ego, the source from which all objective phenomena derive their meaning. In Husserl's transcendental reflection, man looks at himself as the thought. Man is thus still split into the psycho-physical "I," the "I" of lived immanent events, and the transcendental ego. The sharp distinction between mind and soul persists in Husserl's thought; the principle that gives rise to man's rational and volitional life is still considered as quite apart from psychical effects.

M. MERLEAU-PONTY viewed man as the unfolding of the body-subject. The relation between the body and the soul, for him, is one in which the first constituted layer of meaning, the body, serves as the starting point for the higher "given" of meaning, the soul. The body is below the conscious subject. It is another subject, preconscious and impersonal, and does not derive its subjective character from a principle other than itself. It is a self-transcending movement. The natural "I" understands the world before and better than the conscious "I." The "I-body" is neither pure matter, pure spirit, nor a merger of the two. The concepts soul and body are relative. Fixed existence and human self-movement are two aspects of the soul reality, the body-subject.

Marxism. K. MARX described a profound self-alienation in the socioeconomic sphere, for he regarded man only as matter. To N. LENIN, mind or consciousness was an epiphenomenon. In the Marxist-Leninist view, consciousness is a product of the brain and the soul as a spiritual substance is not even considered. (*See* MATERIALISM, DIALECTICAL AND HISTORICAL.)

Neopositivism. Neopositivists and logical positivists continue the emphasis on verifiability raised by the empiricists. B. RUSSELL claims that mental events are more real to him than matter, which is not immediately given but must be established by deduction and construction. At the same time he denies the existence of a substantial soul because, as he maintains, mental phenomena are totally dependent on physiological phenomena. Neopositivists, in general, hold that intersubjective VERIFICATION is possible only of empirical experience, only of the body and its movements. The concept of soul, not open to intersubjective verification, is meaningless. Statements in classical philosophy, such as, "The soul is immortal, free, and a substance," express feelings but assert nothing.

American Philosophy. For W. JAMES, the soul or pure ego and the will are outside the realm of empirical psychology. They can neither be affirmed nor denied by psychology, although the notions of soul and will may help in systematizing philosophical thought. J. Dewey, influenced by the theory of evolution, regarded the mind merely as an adaptive function of the body. While A. N. WHITEHEAD affirmed the existence of spirit, he could regard it as substance no more than he could regard the body as substance. Both are events. Consciousness is a function, the bipolar event seen from within. The immortality of the soul can be maintained only on the evidence of something like religious experience.

Existentialism. In reaction to SCIENTISM, to extreme DUALISM, and to idealism, H. BERGSON, the existentialists, and the personalists sought to restore either the spiritual aspect of man, or his unity, or his presence in the world, or all three. They, too, avoided the word soul and substituted for it such terms as besouled body, body-subject, incarnated consciousness, and person. Discussion here is limited to the forms of EXISTENTIALISM proposed by Jaspers, Marcel, Sartre, and Heidegger.

Karl JASPERS holds that there are four spheres of reality in the world: matter, life, the soul as inner experience, and spirit, the rational soul of traditional philosophy. None can be subsumed under a single unifying principle. Mythical language calls it the soul, whereas philosophical terminology calls it "existence," a being that stands out against the totality of the world's being.

Gabriel MARCEL starts with man's presence in the world. To be a man is not only to "have" a body but to "be" a bodily incarnate being. In fact, men's souls are made or unmade by the quality of response to being and bodily trials.

J. P. SARTRE denies that man has a nature or fixed essence. He is a useless passion for whom there is no potentiality. The questions of God and the soul are problems for metaphysics since one questions about the soul only in relation to particular things. If the study of apparential presence in consciousness is identified with ontology, the principle of causality is excluded from both the real and the intentional order. This ontology is not required to infer an immaterial principle of life or soul. Sartre's denial of essences is ambiguous, however, for it is not clear whether he refers to the metaphysical or to moral aspects of man when he states that man's free choices constitute his essence.

Martin HEIDEGGER possibly substitutes the notion of spirit for that of soul. He deplores the reinterpretation of spirit as intelligence or mere cleverness. The spirit, to him, is the sustaining, dominating principle in which all true power and beauty of the body, all courage, authenticity, and creativity are grounded. Upon the power or impotence of the spirit depends the rise and fall of these qualities and activities of man. "Spirit is a fundamental knowing resolve toward the essence of being." Where spirit prevails, this being becomes ever more so, for the spirit is the mobilization of the powers of being. Spirit, moreover, is not world reason.

Summary. NOMINALISM and the rise of empirical and mathematical science gradually emptied the concept of soul of its original meaning as substantial form of living beings. With the confusion of the metaphysical and empirical levels of knowledge and the transfer of the scientific criteria of validation to metaphysics, the concept of soul as substance, knowable by man, was challenged by Locke and Hume and ultimately by Kant. The subject-object split in man's knowledge, begun by Descartes and accentuated by Kant, led to idealism and MATERIALISM.

In reaction, philosophers became less concerned with probing the nature of man's unity of body and spirit (i.e., the essence of man). Rather they sought a view of man as incarnated consciousness, besouled body, and body-subject whose existence is quite different from the being of all other reality, since only man can stand out (*ex-sistere*) against the world by acts of responsible decision. The consequent disuse of the term soul is not so much a rejection of the concept of a dynamic organizing principle of unity in man as it is a rejection of a concept of man as split in two—a view that is apt to occur when man is described as a union of body and soul. The shift in attention is thus from the essence of man to his existing—his mode of being in the world. That man is spiritual may be implied by many of the existentialists when they attribute to man a form of existence different from other existents. Related notions, such as FREEDOM and spirituality (but not immortality), seem to be implicit in the thinking of Marcel, E. Mounier, Heidegger, Jaspers, M. Buber, perhaps even of Merleau-Ponty. Yet the term soul itself seems to be ignored by contemporary philosophers and to be used primarily in theological and moral circles.

See Also: PERSONALISM; SELF, THE; SPIRIT; SPIRITUALISM; SUBJECTIVITY.

Bibliography: F. C. COPLESTON, *History of Philosophy,* (Westminster, Md. 1963). R. EISLER, *Wörterbuch der phiosophischen Begriffe,* 3 v. (4th ed. Berlin 1927–30) 3:1–22. J. D. COLLINS, *A History of Modern European Philosophy* (Milwaukee 1954). S. STRASSER, *The Soul in Metaphysical and Empirical Psychology* (Pittsburgh 1957). W. ELLIS, *The Idea of the Soul in Western Philosophy and Science* (New York 1940). E. CASSIRER, *The Individual and the Cosmos in Renaissance Philosophy,* tr. M. DOMANDI (New York 1964). E. CASSIRER et el., eds., *The Renaissance Philosophy of Man* (Chicago 1948). P. O. KRISTELLER, *Renaissance Thought* (New York 1961). B. SNELL, *The Discovery of the Mind: The Greek Origins of European Thought,* tr. T. G. ROSENMEYER (Cambridge, Mass. 1953). H. SPIEGELBERG, *The Phenomenological Movement,* 2 v. (The Hague 1960). R. C. KWANT, *The Phenomenological Philosophy of Merleau-Ponty* (Pittsburgh 1963). W. A. M. LUIJPEN, *Existential Phenomenology* (Pittsburgh 1960).

[M. GORMAN]

4. Philosophical Analysis

One cannot ask about the nature of the human soul without having first asked and answered the question about its existence. Moreover, the question about its existence cannot be meaningfully pursued unless one has first assigned a meaning to ''human soul.'' This is simply an application of the Aristotelian-Thomist doctrine that the question *quid est* (which asks for a DEFINITION, i.e., a statement of a thing's nature) is not properly asked unless one has answered the question *an est* (which asks whether there is such a thing); and that the question *an est* cannot be pursued unless one has answered the question *quid est quod dicitur* (which asks for a meaning for the word or expression used to designate the thing to be investigated, i.e., a *quid nominis*).

Existence. If one agrees that ''human soul'' will be taken to mean ''source of thought activity,'' and gives a careful account of the meaning of ''thought activity,'' he is in a position to ask: Are there human souls? It is then easy to see that the question: Are there human souls? is answered by answering the question: Are there things that think? Of the two direct methods available for answering the latter question—that of sense observation and that of INTROSPECTION—introspection can serve here as the primary, though not exclusive, method. One confronts a thinking being in the awareness of his own thought activity; that is, introspection makes man aware of his own existence as a thinking being. Further, by noticing that language is used to communicate thoughts, man comes to recognize that thinking beings other than himself exist. Sense observation plays a primary role in this recognition. (Direct method is used here by way of opposition to indirect method; in the latter—in addition to sense observation or introspection—there is also a reasoning process, as, e.g., in proofs for God's existence. In the direct method, one has an immediate cognitive contact, either in sense observation or in introspection, with the thing in question, so that reasoning is not required as a mediating activity; all one needs is a *quid nominis.*)

Nature. Apropos of the nature of the human soul, it is important to consider the following points: (1) the human soul is man's substantial form; nonetheless (2) it is to some extent completely immaterial, i.e., it is a subsistent form, or a spirit; but (3) it is not complete as to species; (4) though it is essentially and quantitatively simple, it is dynamically composed; (5) some of its powers require habits for their perfection; and (6) even though it is to some extent completely immaterial, it is even to that extent, though from a different viewpoint, dependent on the human body. These points are considered in order.

Substantial Form. The human soul, like any sort of soul, is the first actuality of a natural organized body, and as first actuality it is a substantial form (*see* SOUL; ENTELECHY). It is thus not a substance, but only part of a substance.

Immaterial. To say that the human soul is completely immaterial is to say both that matter is not a part of what it is and that it is independent of matter for its existence. This becomes clear when one considers that a thing can be said to be immaterial if it is such that matter is not a part of what it is, even though such a thing may be dependent on matter for its existence; e.g., substantial forms, or the accidental form of QUANTITY. A thing is completely material only if it depends on matter for its existence and has matter as part of what it is—a definition that is verified of composed substance. Substantial forms, therefore, can be said to be material, since they depend on matter for existence, and immaterial as well, since matter is not a part of what they are. But the completely immaterial neither has matter as part of what it is nor depends on matter for its existence.

The claim that the human soul is completely immaterial can be established as follows. In the realm of physical changes, both substantial and accidental, the forms received are individual forms, because what receives them is individual matter. An individual form is a form that is one, countably one, among several of a type. A type, considered as such, e.g., manness, is neither one (countably one) nor more than one. Man can be one or many only if found in something divisible in such a way that its actually being divided yields a countable or numerical plurality; in the physical universe this is clearly three-dimensional extendedness. It is because the matter of the physical universe is three-dimensionally extended that it can be divided into diverse parts, each of which can be counted as one (this is what is meant by ''individual matter''), and into each of which, subjected to an appropriate natural process, a form of some type can be introduced.

It is to be noticed that wherever matter is found, it is found as three-dimensionally quantified; moreover, it is circumscribed to being just so much (i.e., actually divided into diverse parts) as is found in what one calls an individual thing. If matter were not quantified and actually divided into diverse parts, the forms of things in the physical universe could not be numerically multiplied (*see* INDIVIDUATION).

Thus, in the realm of physical changes, whether substantial or accidental, the forms received are individual forms, because the recipient is individual matter. The same thing is to be noticed in the realm of sensitive activity. The sensible form received into the sense is received into a bodily organ, such as the eye, an organ that is three-dimensionally quantified and circumscribed to being just so much; this is why the form received is an individual form. Thus, one can see that, universally speaking, if the recipient of a form is individual matter, the form received is an individual form. So that, if man can discover in an examination of the contents of his knowing experiences a form that is not an individual form, it will follow that there is in him a power that is not the power of some bodily organ.

It is not difficult to discover such a form, for the human soul performs the activity of UNDERSTANDING. To understand is to receive the forms (essences) of things absolutely, i.e., as separated from, as abstracted from, individuality. For example, to understand ''man'' is to have grasped this: something composed of flesh and bones and soul—understood absolutely or with no qualifications. Existing men are individual men; each man is something composed of this flesh and these bones and this soul. It is the presence in the existing individual of quantified matter circumscribed to being just so much that accounts for its being an individual. But one's understanding, i.e., his intellectual knowledge, of that to which he attaches the word ''man'' is simply this: something composed of flesh and bones and soul; and the qualifiers ''this'' and ''these'' are not included.

Even though each human soul is an individual soul, it cannot have matter as part of what it is. For it is clear that whatever is received into something must be received according to the mode (capacity) of the recipient. Since the human soul, in knowing what things are, receives the forms (essences) of things absolutely, i.e., since its mode of reception in intellectual knowledge is absolute, the human soul likewise must be an absolute form.

If the human soul were composed of matter and form, it would follow that the forms of things received in knowledge would be received into it as individuals, as is the case in sensation and in physical change generally. The same thing would follow if the intellectual soul were held to operate through some bodily organ, e.g., the brain, in the way in which the power of sight operates through the bodily organ that is the eye. The bodily matter of the organ would individualize the form received. Thus, the human soul is totally free of matter; not only does it not have matter as part of what it is, but it neither exists nor operates with a dependence on matter (St. Thomas Aquinas, *Summa theologiae* 1a, 75.5).

The complete IMMATERIALITY of the human soul must be properly understood. It is a complete immateriality that is at the same time partial. The human soul is the form (substantial form) of the human body; and as the form of a living body, it is the source of vegetative and sensitive activities, which take place with a dependence on the matter of the human body. Thus, the human soul has activities, hence powers or parts, that are material, in the sense of dependent on matter. In some of its powers or parts, therefore, the human soul is dependent on the body. In its intellectual part, it is independent of the body. This is what is meant by describing the complete immateriality of the human soul as a partial one.

The above has shown that the human soul is a subsistent form or a spirit, i.e., that it operates and exists independently of matter as of a subject. Now, matter is the proper subject for substantial form; there is no subject but matter in which such a form can exist (*see* MATTER AND FORM). Thus, if the existence of the human soul is independent of matter as of a subject, it exists in the way proper to a SUBSTANCE; it is subsistent. But it is subsistent only partially, i.e., to the extent that it has an intellectual power or part.

Incomplete in Species. Though the human soul is a subsistent form, it is a subsistent form that is also a substantial form. From this it is clear that the human soul, though complete as an existent, is nonetheless not complete as to SPECIES. Only the composite of human body and human soul, the man, is complete as to species.

Essentially Simple, but Dynamically Composed. Although the human soul is essentially simple (i.e., not composed of matter and form), and hence quantitatively simple (i.e., not composed of quantitative parts), it is nonetheless said to be dynamically composed. That is, it has a multiplicity of parts or powers, ordered to a multiplicity of life activities; it has as many powers as it has diverse sorts of activity. These are often called power parts or dynamic parts; and thus the soul is sometimes said to be dynamically composed, i.e., to have dynamic parts (*see* FACULTIES OF THE SOUL).

Although the soul is dynamically composed, there is but one soul in each one man, which is clear from the fact that soul is a substantial form. If a living thing had a plurality of souls, each taken as the source of a diverse sort of activity—e.g., if man had a vegetative soul as source of nourishing, growing, and reproducing, and also a sensitive soul as source of seeing, hearing, etc., and lastly an intellectual soul as source of thought activity—it would follow that a man would be simultaneously more than one thing. For a substantial form is what constitutes a thing a being.

Powers and Habits. Some of the powers of the human soul can be made to operate more easily, more perfectly, and more efficiently by means of habits. Habits are acquired qualities (as opposed to powers, which are innate) that dispose these powers to easier and more efficient operation (*see* HABIT). Knowledge is such a quality of the intellect; virtue, of the will and of the sense appetites—e.g., temperance is a virtue of the concupiscible APPETITE. Not all powers can be perfected by habits, nor are all of them in need of such perfecting, e.g., the powers of nourishing and growing. Nonetheless, some aspects of these powers are so perfectible, e.g., one can acquire the habit of proper and deep breathing. Generally speaking, man's rational powers, and any of man's lower powers, to the extent that they come under the domination of the rational powers, are so perfectible.

Dependent on Body. It is important to understand that, although the human soul is completely immaterial in its intellectual part, it is nonetheless, and qua intellectual, dependent on the body, in particular on the brain and on the organs of the external senses. This dependence is twofold: originative and concomitant.

Man is born with an INTELLECT that is as a blank tablet; it is a power or capacity to know, but it possesses no knowledge. Man's first intellectual knowledge is about things in the sense-perceivable world. His intellect forms its ideas about things in the real world with a dependence on his senses. Man's intellectual knowledge thus originates in his sense experience of the real world; nevertheless the intellect itself, by its own power and not by that of any sense, produces its ideas; for an idea is an absolute form. This is what is meant by the originative dependence of the intellect on the bodily organs of sensation.

But even after the intellect is in possession of some knowledge, it remains dependent on a bodily organ, viz, the brain; for the brain is the bodily organ of the IMAGINATION, which produces and stores the sensible forms of things originally perceived by the external senses. These stored forms are called images or phantasms. Like the sensible species that are individualized by the bodily matter of the organs of the external senses, the phantasm is individualized by the bodily matter of the brain. By means of phantasms man is in cognitive contact with things not here and now being perceived by external sense. Thus, by means of phantasms, the intellect is provided an object to think about. The intellect carries on its thought activities, therefore, with a dependence on accompanying or concomitant brain-produced phantasms. To be sure, the intellect thinks by its own power, for to think is to entertain an absolute form; but the phantasm provides the object about which it thinks. Ordinarily the concomitant phantasm is visual, or auditory, or olfactory, etc., i.e., a reproduction of the external sensation(s) from which the idea was originally abstracted. For example, a visual phantasm of the body of a man ordinarily accompanies one's thinking about what a man is. Often, however, especially in highly abstract thinking, the concomitant phantasm is a phantasm, usually visual or auditory, of the word, expression, or symbol attached to the concept. For example, a visual or auditory phantasm of the word ''essence'' often accompanies one's thinking about what it is to be an essence; or, visual phantasms of the symbols for ''is equal to'' (=), ''is greater than'' (>), ''is less than'' (<), etc., often accompany one's mathematical thinking. This is what is meant by the concomitant dependence of the intellect on the body.

Other views. Although materialistic views of the nature of man—views denying the existence of the human soul—have the obvious advantage of simplicity and of not having to consider the problem of the soul-body relationship, they nonetheless do not take into account, among other things, the fact that knowledge of absolute forms is an indisputable element of man's knowing experience. The very formulation of such a denial is itself an instance of knowledge of absolute forms.

Platonic views of man's nature—views that identify man with his soul and claim that soul's relationship to body is accidental and simply that of a tenant to his room or that of a prisoner to his cell—also have the advantage of simplicity. However, they have no adequate way of accounting for things such as: (1) the effects that conditions or states of the body have on the soul's thinking and willing, e.g., the effects of brain damage in impairing thought activity or causing its total cessation, or the role of bodily conditions and states in the phenomena of split personality, hysteria, and amnesia; (2) the introspectively experienced unity of a man as the single source of the activities attributed to his body as well as of those attributed to his soul. Idealistic views of man's nature—views that deny the existence of matter and maintain that all bodies exist only as thoughts in some mind—are subject to the same inadequacies.

Other views of man's nature, such as interactionism, epiphenomenalism, the dual-aspect theory, parallelism, occasionalism, and preestablished harmony, are attempts to come to grips, but without success, with the great problems emerging from treating the human body and the human soul as two different things (*see* SOUL-BODY RELATIONSHIP). In the Aristotelian-Thomist account, the soul is not one thing and the body another. Neither is a thing at all. The man is the thing, the one thing, with a soul related to the body as the body's first actuality.

See Also: FORM; MAN, 2; SPIRIT.

Bibliography: C. MAZZANTINI, *Enciclopedia filosofica* 1:222–239. R. EISLER, *Wörterbuch der philosophischen Begriffe* 3:1–30 (4th ed. Berlin 1927–30). F. HARTMANN, *Die Religion in Geschichte und Gegenwart* 4:287–291 (3rd ed. Tübingen 1957–63). J. E. ROYCE, *Man and His Nature* (New York 1961). R. J. CONNELE, ''The 'Intus Apparens' and the Immateriality of the Intellect,'' *The New Scholasticism* 32 (1958) 151–186.

[J. BOBIK]

5. Theology

There is no unanimous Christian teaching on every point concerning the human soul. We seem to live in an era in a very long evolution of the anthropological dogma, i.e., of the believing understanding of the mystery of man in his body and soul. As a result of controversy and the development of Biblical anthropology, there is a growing tendency to consider man in his unity and personality and to interpret him from the historico-salvational and Christological point of view (Christ the ideal of man; see H. Denzinger, *Enchiridion symbolorum,* ed. A. Schönmetzer 301, 554, 900, etc.). This is being done in a manner as free as possible of any preconceived philosophical mentality (e.g., Orphic or Platonic understanding of the human soul), the projection of which upon the revealed data could oversimplify, impair, or destroy rather than save and elucidate to the faithful the mystery of man in the totality of his being. Besides, today in theology the accent lies correctly on the eternal life of the whole man after resurrection in Christ, rather than on the salvation of the immortal soul, because it is the whole man in his totality who is saved by the merciful God [note the definition of the Assumption of Mary ''to the glory of heaven both in body and soul'' (*ibid.* 3903)]. As a result, the distinction between the superior and inferior, more and less noble, or precious, part, in man (*ibid.* 815) is vanishing, because theologians realize that man is an IMAGE, partner, child, mystery, etc. of God in the totality of his being rather than in his soul only.

Soul and Body. This article considers the soul first according to the teaching of the solemn magisterium and then according to that of the ordinary magisterium.

Solemn Magisterium. Interpreting officially the witness of the Scriptures and tradition concerning the human soul, the teaching authority of the Church solemnly affirms that the Triune God is the creator of the human creature ''constituted, as it were, alike of the spirit and the body'' (Lateran Council IV in 1215: *ibid.* 800; cf. Vatican Council I: *ibid.* 3002); ''that man has one rational and intellectual soul'' (Council of Constantinople IV in 870: *ibid.* 657; there the doctrine of the two souls in man was condemned as heretical); ''that the rational or intellective soul is the form of the human body in itself and essentially'' (Council of Vienne in 1312 against Peter John Olivi: *ibid.* 902, cf. 900, 1440); and that the human soul is ''immortal and multiple according to the multitude of bodies into which it is infused, multiplied, and to be multiplied . . .'' (Lateran Council V in 1513 against some humanistic Aristotelians who renewed the Averroistic monopsychism: *ibid.* 1440). These decisions of the ecumenical councils tried to save the true unity of man and simultaneously to point out his metaphysical constitution and not the historico-salvational, biological, or (experimental) psychological dimensions in which man must be considered primarily as a psychosomatic whole. Besides, the councils did not recognize officially the Thomistic doctrine of the unicity of the substantial form or Aristotelian HYLOMORPHISM, but, in the language most convenient at that time, only tried to defend the mystery of man in the plurality of his dimensions and the unity of his being. The definition of the soul's personal immortality (*ibid.* 1440) leaves open the question whether it is naturally immortal because of its spiritual quality, or supernaturally because of a special gift of God (however it is stated that Christ makes men participators in His immortality: ibid. 413).

Ordinary Magisterium. Man is so substantially one, according to the ordinary teaching authority of the Church, that his unity (which is not accidental) has ontological priority before the real and irreducible plurality of his being. He is one in origin (*see* CREATIONISM; TRADUCIANISM), being, and final destiny (*Enchiridion symbolorum* 502, 2828, 3005, 3221–22, 3224). Therefore each consideration of a part or one aspect of man implies repercussions concerning all parts and aspects. Any division of man is always inadequate, because as a microcosm (*ibid.* 3771) he must be considered as a whole. However, since there is an essential difference between matter and SPIRIT (*ibid.* 3891; cf. 3022–24), there is a real plurality of realities in man which are irreducible to each other. Thus the spiritual soul is not an emanation or a part of man's matter or body (*ibid.* 3022, 3220–21, 3896), and it is equally true that the matter cannot be deduced from or reduced to the finite human spiritual soul. Both need a special creative act of God in order to exist, because they are ontologically different (*ibid.* 360, 3896). Thus man possesses the vital (*ibid.* 2833) and constitutive principle of his being, i.e., one spiritual, simple, and substantial soul (*ibid.* 791, 801, 900, 1440), which despite the substantial unity of being in man, is in its being and meaning essentially different and independent of matter (*ibid.* 1007, 3002, 3022, 3220–24, 3896), and immortal (*ibid.* 1440). Since the soul is spiritual in itself, man is not composed of three different realities, i.e., body, soul, and spirit, but is a substantial unity in body and spiritual soul only (as opposed to all sorts of trichotomy: *ibid.* 301, 502, 657, 900, 902, 1440–41, 2828). The approval by the ordinary magisterium of the Thomistic theses concerning the human soul (*ibid.* 3613–22) must be understood as a favorable reception of them as one of the best illustrations of the mystery of man.

See Also: MAN, ARTICLES ON; RESURRECTION OF THE DEAD, 2; SOUL, HUMAN; IMMORTALITY; SOUL, HUMAN, ORIGIN OF; SOUL-BODY RELATIONSHIP.

Bibliography: J. BAINVEL et al., *Dictionnaire de théologie catholique,* ed. A. VACANT, 15 v. (Paris 1903–50; Tables générales 1951–) 1.1:968–1041. J. HAEKEL, et al., *Lexikon für Theologie und Kirche,* ed. J. HOFER and K. RAHNER, 10 v. (2d, new ed. Freiburg 1957–65) 9:566–574. A. HALDER, *ibid.* 4:611–614. A. HALDER, et al., *ibid.* 1:604–627; 7:278–294. "Tod," *ibid.* v.10. "Leib," "Seele," "Tod," K. RAHNER and H. VORGRIMLER, *Kleines theologsches Wörterbuch* (Freiburg 1961). J. B. METZ, H. FRIES, ed., *Handbuch theologischer Grundbegriffe,* 2 v. (Munich 1962–63) 2:30–37, bibliog. J. BRINKTRINE, *Die Lehre von der Schöpfung* (Paderborn 1956) 220–256. W. B. MONAHAN, *The Psychology of St. Thomas Aquinas and Divine Revelation* (Worcester 1938). D. R. G. OWEN, *Body and Soul* (Philadelphia 1956). K. RAHNER, *On the Theology of Death,* tr. C. H. HENKEY (Quaestiones disputatae 2; New York 1961). P. OVERHAGE and K. RAHNER, *Das Problem der Hominisation* (Quaestiones disputatae 12–13; Freiburg 1961). K. RAHNER, *Schriften zur Theologie* (Einsiedeln 1954–) 2:211–225; 4:428–437. H. W. ROBINSON, *The Christian Doctrine of Man* (Edinburgh 1911). J. A. T. ROBINSON, *The Body: A Study in Pauline Theology* (Chicago 1952). F. RÜSCHE, *Das Seelenpneuma* (Paderborn 1933). M. J. SCHEEBEN, *Handbuch der katholischen Dogmatik* (v.3–4; 3d ed. Freiburg 1961) 3 § 146–157. M. SCHMAUS, *Katholische Dogmatik,* 5 v. in 8 (5th ed. Munich 1953–59) 2.1 § 128–130; J. SCHMID, "Der Begriff der Seele im NT," *Einsicht und Glaube,* ed. J. RATZINGER and H. FRIES (Freiburg 1962). A. SERTILLANGES, *Les Grandes thèses de la philosophie thomiste* (Paris 1928). S. STRASSER, *Le Problème de l'âme* (Paris 1953). THOMAS AQUINAS, *Summa Theologiae* 1a, 75–90; *De anim.* J. TYCIAK, *Zwischen Morgenland und Abendland* (Düsseldorf 1949). T. WARE, *The Orthodox Church* (pa. Baltimore 1963), R. C. ZAEHNER, *Matter and Spirit: Their Convergence in Eastern Religions, Marx, and Teilhard de Chardin* (New York 1963). A. AHLBRECHT, *Tod und Unsterblichkeit in der evangelischen Theologie der Gegenwart* (Paderborn 1964). R. HEINZMANN, *Die Unsterblichkeit der Seele und die Auferstehung des Leibes* (Münster 1965).

[P. B. T. BILANIUK]

SOUL, HUMAN, ORIGIN OF

Christians are in fairly general agreement that each human soul begins to exist by a direct creative act of God at the moment of its union with matter to form the new human being, with no previous existence. Various other theories have been held, however, and Catholic scholars are still divided as to whether the soul originates at the moment of conception or later during gestation. This article discusses the problem involved and the diversity of solutions offered concerning both the manner of the soul's origin and the time at which this occurs.

Manner of Soul's Origin

Historically, emanationism and traducianism are the two major theories opposing orthodox teaching concerning the origin of the human soul. Recent Catholic discussion, while presupposing the doctrine of CREATIONISM, has centered about the degree of immediacy of God's action in the creative process.

History. EMANATIONISM was held by pantheists, Pythagoreans, Stoics, and early heretics such as the Gnostics, Manichees, and Priscillianists. They believed that the human soul emanates or flows from the divine substance as a particle or offshoot of God. This theory has been rejected as contrary both to the nature of God and to the nature of the soul. If God is a perfectly simple spiritual substance, He cannot be divided or have parts; conversely, the soul lacks many of the characteristics proper to divine substance, such as eternal self-subsistence and total lack of change. Moreover, this position militates against the individuality of the human soul.

TRADUCIANISM holds that the human soul is produced by the generative act of the human parents. This explanation supposes a seed or sprout, which may be either material or spiritual. Totally materialistic theories of evolution and other denials of the spirituality of the soul naturally imply that all of man originates through organic generation. A spiritual soul cannot come wholly from material germ cells. TERTULLIAN seems to have held such a theory. More palpable is the spiritual traducianism of the Apollinarists, which postulates the origin of the human soul from the souls of the parents.

In Oriental Christianity the orthodox tradition has consistently taught creation of the human soul. The Western tradition was similar, except for Tertullian, up until the Pelagian heresy. The motivation for some to hold spiritual traducianism at that time was an attempt to explain the transmission of original sin in the human race. St. AUGUSTINE seems to have remained doubtful on the point, along with Fulgentius, ISIDORE OF SEVILLE, and others. Martin LUTHER and a scattering of both Catholic and Protestant theologians over the past four centuries have favored spiritual traducianism.

Catholic Teaching. Contemporary Catholics appeal both to philosophical reasoning and to the pronouncements of the Church (H. Denzinger, *Enchiridion symbolorum*, ed. A. Schönmetzer [Freiburg 1963] 190, 360, 455–456, 685, 1007, 1440, 3024, 3896) to support the doctrine that the soul is created immediately by God. Scriptural proofs are difficult and only suasive, because of contextual problems. The Biblical words for soul usually mean total person. [*See* SOUL (IN THE BIBLE).] Scriptural texts favor placing more stress on the flesh-spirit composite, both in activity and origin, than appears in many post-Cartesian formulations.

The substantial forms (or "souls") of other animals below man, having no existence apart from that of the composite, have no cause other than the causes of the animal itself; but the human soul cannot arise wholly by generation, since it is spiritual and not within the potentialities of matter. The Apollinarists argued that there is no need to postulate the origin of the human spiritual soul by a material process, as the parents' souls could act as a spiritual cause producing a spiritual effect. However, serious difficulties arise in the attempt to explain precisely how this would happen. The soul is simple and could not be compounded from something received from each parent. There is no evidence that it arises simply from one parent, to say nothing of the problems arising if one attempted to designate which one. The parent's soul is simple and spiritual; so there is no possibility of dividing off a piece of it for the child's soul. The new soul could not be educed from the potency of spiritual substance, for spirit does not contain a principle of SUBSTANTIAL change analogous to primary matter in material being. The parents' souls would have nothing to work on, nothing out of which to make the soul.

One might consider whether it is necessary to talk of the parents' souls making the new soul "out of" any preexisting subject, i.e., whether they could simply produce it by their sheer reproductive activity. Aside from the fact that the parental reproductive activity is entirely biological, this solution is rejected because no created cause makes something simply to be rather than not be. Since only the First Cause has being of Itself and hence dominion over existence, only God can give being absolutely, rather than cause what already exists to be in another way. The human soul can originate only through creation by God (St. Thomas Aquinas, *Summa theologiae* 1a, 90.2–3; *C. gent.* 2.87). The human soul is intrinsically independent of matter in its becoming; i.e., the generative act of the parents is only the extrinsic cause setting the time and place for the origin of the soul. Since an efficient cause is always distinct from its effect, the soul cannot be God, or a part of God. Creation is the antithesis of PANTHEISM.

One might object that the body is in potency to the soul, and therefore the soul must be educed from the potency of matter. This does not follow, for to be in potency to a form is not necessarily to have that form in potency. Matter is in potency to any form that can actuate it, and the human soul does this. But only material forms can be educed from the potency of matter. (*See* MATTER AND FORM.)

God's Activity. This doctrine of creation might seem to detract from the fullness of parenthood, since the parents do not generate the soul, but their offspring are truly theirs nonetheless, for it is not necessary that one produce all the component parts in order to be the true cause of a thing. Relations such as father and son are said of the PERSON, not of the part.

However, the precise nature of the cooperation between God and the human parents is more complex and intimate than suggested by the older formula "God creates the soul, the parents make the body." Man is one being, not two. Both God and parents contribute to this unique act of existence. Moreover, acceptance of evolution among theologians has turned attention to the notion that all creatural causality is an instrument of God (St. Thomas, *De pot.* 3.7), a doctrine neglected in the centuries of vigorous opposition to OCCASIONALISM. TEILHARD DE CHARDIN and Karl RAHNER applied this thinking to the origin of the first man. The same reasoning can be used regarding the origin of all other human souls; but in both cases it seems more logical to posit union with the human zygote at the moment of conception, rather than holding mediate animation or that the first man was originally subhuman.

The degree of immediacy of God's action in creating the human soul, whether the first or subsequent ones, is hence controversial. One can detract neither from the unique role of God nor from the vital, if secondary and instrumental, role of the parents. God's causality is not one link in a long chain of causality, but basic to, and cooperating with, all others. Similarly, one can avoid neither the unique nature of the human soul as the terminus of the divine action nor the existential unity of man as a composite produced by the complex cooperation of many causes.

Time of Soul's Origin

ORIGEN, PRISCILLIAN, and other Neoplatonists taught that human souls existed separately before being united with matter. This opinion is considered heretical (*Enchiridion symbolorum,* 403, 456).

Arguments Against Preexistence. Unlike an angel whose nature it is to exist by itself as a complete substance, the human soul has as its proper role union with matter to form this man and no other. Hence any existence previous to the man is contrary to the very meaning of soul as substantial form (*Summa theologiae* 1a, 90.4). The separate existence of the soul after death does not contradict this, since the soul retains previously acquired knowledge, a transcendental relation to matter, and even a certain exigency to be united with matter; but before actual union with matter to form a body it has no such relation. The notion that God has a supply of souls that are not anybody's in particular until He infuses them into human embryos is entirely unwarranted by any evidence. Such souls would have no individuality, no personal human identity, and would be in an unnatural state because of their inability to acquire any knowledge in the way proper to man. The theory that man is born with ideas carried over from a previous life has little to support it, and much evidence against it (*see* METEMPSYCHOSIS). The soul is created by God at the time it is infused into matter, i.e., when it is substantially united with an embryo appropriately disposed to receive it and form a man.

Time of Infusion. Exactly when this happens is more controversial, and still an open question with scholastic philosophers of high standing on both sides. All agree that since the soul is the principle of vital operations, the human soul is present when there is specifically human operation. Because there is evidence of specifically human operations from the first moment of conception, a majority assert that the human soul is present then.

Aristotle thought that he was unjustified in asserting true human life in the male before the embryo was 40 days old and in the female, before 80 to 90 days. St. Thomas followed him in teaching a succession of forms, the embryo having first a vegetative soul and later a sensitive one, before the human soul finally arrives. Modern studies in embryology reveal that at the moment sperm and ovum unite and the two pronuclei fuse, an orderly process of development begins with a definiteness governed by the pattern of the DNA molecule. The new individual is characterized by the resulting unique constellation of genes and chromosomes before the zygote divides for the first time. This organization is not only intricate and vital; it is specifically human. The chromosomes contain determiners for specifically human eyes and ears, not just animal eyes and ears in general. The offspring of all vertebrates may go through the same stages of embryological development, and in similar ways, but each goes through those stages in ways that are characteristic and peculiar to its own species. Embryology considers the living body from the one-cell stage onward to be a human individual, not some general plant or animal that will become human in 40 or 80 days.

If one were to wait for clear evidence of *rational* activity before concluding belief in the existence of a human soul, it would not be a matter of days, but of years. As long as the embryo is clearly the product of human generation, it has a human nature even if severe organic defect prevents it from ever exercising any rational activities, as in the case of some developmentally disabled individuals. Examination of the fetus through its early stages gives no clue as to when one can draw the line. The available evidence seems to force one back to the very moment of conception.

A minority view points to the problems of fragmentary life, transplants, divisibility of lower animals such as worms, and human identical twins as arguments in favor of the mediate animation held by St. Thomas Aquinas, which seems to handle these difficulties more neatly.

The problem of when the human soul is created received renewed attention in the latter half of the twentieth century with the rise of modern reproductive technologies and the growing possibility that human embryos might be made the object of scientific experimentation. In vitro fertility laboratories, in an effort to increase the efficiency of their procedures, began producing many more human embryos than they actually needed for implantation, leading to the frozen storage of tens of thousands of human embryos in laboratories throughout the developed world. The emergence of this problem convinced the Vatican that new statements of concern over this practice were necessary and these included renewed calls for the world community to respect the dignity of the human being from the moment of conception.

The debate over whether the soul is immediately infused or arrives at some later point in embryological development was not the most pressing moral problem faced by the Church during the rise of legalized abortion. Nonetheless, the much referenced footnote 19 of the *Declaration on Procured Abortion* (1974) took note of the debate between proponents of immediate and delayed hominization and stated that:

> It is not within the competence of science to decide between these two views, because the existence of an immortal soul is not a question in its field. It is a philosophical problem from which our moral affirmation remains independent . . . supposing a later animation, there is still nothing less than a *human* life, preparing for and calling for a soul in which the nature received from parents is completed.

One finds here two important points: the question of when the soul is infused is not one that can be decided by any empirical means, and even if the soul were to be infused at some later point in embryological development, the zygote that is present at fertilization is surely a human life. As such it deserves the same respect as is due to any other human being.

With the discovery of human genome, and the recognition that it contains the entire code for the epigenetic unfolding of the human being, there was a growing conviction among many Catholic theologians that personhood must begin at conception. Others, in spite of this new evidence, insisted that the lack of individuality in the early embryo, which is capable of twinning in its earliest stages, or the supposed absence of a proper material foundation to support the human soul, such as the ''primitive streak'' (primitive spinal cord and brain), which appears at approximately 14 days, left the question at best undecided or perhaps even settled in favor of delayed hominization on scientific grounds.

In 1987 the Congregation for the Doctrine of the Faith entered this debate with *Donum vitae: Instruction on Respect for Human Life in its Origin and on the Dignity of Procreation.* The document addressed a panoply of moral issues related to modern reproductive technologies, but it took special note of the question of the origin of the human soul. The Congregation stated that it was ''aware of the current debates concerning the beginning of human life, concerning the individuality of the human being and concerning the identity of the human person'' and then, calling attention to recent findings of science that indicated that a ''new human individual'' is constituted at the moment of conception, remarked:

> Certainly no experimental datum can be in itself sufficient to bring us to the recognition of a spiritual soul; nevertheless, the conclusions of science regarding the human embryo provide a valuable indication for discerning by the use of reason a personal presence from this first appearance of a human life: how could a living human creature not be a human person? The Magisterium has not expressly committed its authority to an affirmation of a philosophical nature, but it constantly reaffirms the moral condemnation of any kind of procured abortion. [I.1]

Thus, while leaving the door open for the possibility of later animation, *Donum vitae* placed the weight of the Vatican on the side of those who view a personal presence in the human zygote; however, because this document did not make its judgment definitive, the debate on this important topic continues. What is clear beyond any doubt is that, in the view of the Church, ''the fruit of human generation, from the first moment of its existence, that is to say from the moment the zygote is constituted, demands the unconditional respect that is morally due to the human being in his bodily and spiritual totality.''

The prospect of so-called therapeutic human cloning, in which human clones are made and destroyed for research purposes, and the desire among certain members within the scientific community to exploit the unfortunate plight of frozen human embryos, has greatly heightened the stakes in this debate and promises to keep the question at the forefront of philosophical and theological discussion well into the twenty-first century.

See Also: SOUL, HUMAN; IMMORTALITY.

Bibliography: P. OVERHAGE and K. RAHNER, *Das Problem der Hominisation* (Freiburg 1961). R. LACROIX, *L'Origine de l'âme humaine* (Quebec 1945). R. NORTH, ''Teilhard and the Problem of Creation,'' *Theological Studies* 24 (1963) 577–601. M. FLICK, ''Problemi teologici sull' 'ominazione','' *Gregorianum,* 44 (1963) 62–70. M. HUDECZEK, ''De tempore animationis foetus humani secundum embryologiam hodiernam,'' *Angelicum* 29 (1952) 162–181. A. MICHEL, *Dictionnaire de théologie catholique*, ed. A. VACANT et al., (Paris 1903–50) 15.1:1350–65.

[J. E. ROYCE/E. J. FURTON]

SOUL-BODY RELATIONSHIP

In the context of scholastic teaching that man is composed of body and soul, the question arises how the relationship between these two elements is to be conceived. (Although modern nonscholastic authors rarely use the term soul, they do speak of the mind-body problem, and in so doing ask essentially the same question in a less philosophical way.) The answer can be investigated generally, as applied to all species of living organisms, or it can be investigated only in relation to humanity, where it raises particularly difficult problems. Man's soul being spiritual in nature, how can such a spiritual principle be related to the matter of the human body? The disproportion between matter and spirit seems so great that it is difficult to conceive how both can be joined in man to form an essential unity.

Greek Thought. As long as GREEK PHILOSOPHY considered only the material cause, as Aristotle noted, no major difficulty of this type arose. With the discovery of a spiritual dimension to reality, as in Plato's world of ideas, however, the problem immediately came into focus: how can something spiritual, characterized as it is by its independence from matter, be essentially bound to something material? Such a union seems contrary to the very nature of spirit. Influenced by this line of thought, PLATO considered the union to be a punishment for some sin committed by the soul in a former life. The relation of the soul to the body, in his view, was that of a prisoner to his prison (*Phaedrus* 250; *Phaedo* 80–83). In other texts, Plato compared the relation to that between a ship and the pilot, insofar as the soul moves and directs the body as a pilot does a ship—a relationship that remained somewhat extrinsic and accidental.

ARISTOTLE criticized this teaching of his master as inconsistent with the facts. Man is one substantial reality, not an accidental union of two different substances. Yet how can he be one substance, if two such different elements as a material body and a spiritual soul are found in him? Aristotle saw the solution in his doctrine of HYLOMORPHISM. He defined the soul as the first act of a physical organic body (*Anim.* 412a 20–28). Unfortunately, this cryptic definition seemed to imply a contradiction, because a physical organic body, as something determined, was already conceived as in act, and thus it was hard to see how the soul could be its "first" act. The difficulty, it turns out, is largely terminological; an adequate explanation of the Aristotelian formula can be given, although it is not easy to comprehend (*see* SOUL; ENTELECHY). Possibly because of its concise and somewhat elliptic formulation, it has been regarded by many as not giving a satisfactory and adequate solution to the problem.

Thomistic Explanation. St. THOMAS AQUINAS, and most scholastic philosophers, took over the Aristotelian formula and used it to derive a more accurate conception. (1) The basic reality to account for, as Aquinas saw it, is the essential unity of man. This unity is clearly demonstrated by the fact that the same concrete man who is given to one's phenomenological experience in his bodily presence is also a person who thinks. The spiritual activity of thinking and the material givenness of the body are both manifestations of one and the same human reality. (2) Again, the transcendence of the spirit over material reality is manifested by the immateriality of thinking; this means that the soul, having an activity that is intrinsically independent of material conditions, cannot have a mode of being inferior to its mode of acting. In other words, it must be essentially independent of matter. (3) On the other hand, man is really material, and this not only accidentally: the body belongs essentially to his nature. How can one reconcile all three seemingly contradictory, but equally certain, data?

Soul-Body Union. Taking into account all three aspects, St. Thomas proposed a precise and ingenious solution. He refused to admit a contradiction between the spirituality of the soul and its union with a material body. This union, he argued, need not be understood as implying an essential dependence on matter. The soul, as spiritual, really exists on its own account and in its own right. In other words, it is not dependent on matter in the very fact of existing. This, in turn, does not entail that the body belongs to man only accidentally. The body is a real and essential part of man's nature, but not in such a way that the soul is essentially subjected to it or ontologically dependent upon it. On the contrary, the body is dependent upon the soul and exists in virtue of the soul's existence. As Thomas puts it: "Human existence pertains to corporeal matter as receptive and as subjected to something above it; it pertains to intellectual substance as to a principle, and according to the demands of its proper nature" (*C. gent.* 2.68). This describes an intimate, ontological relationship between body and soul, destroying neither man's substantial unity, nor the spiritual character of his soul, nor the body as an essential part of his nature.

Solution of Difficulties. Is this, however, only a clever theoretical construction, or is it an interpretation of man that conforms to genuine human experiences? Does the human soul really enjoy the type of superiority over the body that this ontological interpretation implies? Does experience not show, on the contrary, that man's spiritual soul is dependent upon his body in many ways? Man comes into being through biological conception and birth; the very existence of his soul seems thus to be conditioned by his body. And what about fatigue, illness, and death? In all these cases is not the soul subject to the law of the body? How can one bring such arguments in harmony with the Thomistic conception of a soul that exists in its own right, in ontological independence of the body?

It may be noted that, apart from these instances of negative interplay between body and soul, innumerable instances of a positive relation between the two are equally evident in authentic human experience. The body appears as an instrument of the soul, for example, in acquiring knowledge or in executing decisions of the will; or it simply appears as an expression of the soul, e.g., in language, in gestures, in a smile or in a tear. The main thing to be noted about these experiences, however, whether they be positive or negative, is that the Thomistic explanation does not conceive these as an interplay between two realities, but rather a mutual conditioning of two constitutive principles in one reality. Thus the soul is conditioned by the body, just as the body is conditioned by the soul. Yet the fact that the body is dependent upon the soul need not entail that the soul is also dependent upon the body. If the soul really assumes the body into its own existence, as Thomists maintain, the body cannot be considered as alien to the soul. It is the soul's body, and nothing else. The whole bodily condition, with all its implications, positive and negative, is assumed by the soul as its own. The soul cannot be said to depend upon the body, but it can be said to have assumed as its own a bodily condition. The soul does not participate in the existence of the body, but the body is assumed in the existence of the soul. Thus, although body and soul really coincide in man's substantial unity, and in a total mutual conditioning, there is a one-way dependence in the strict sense of the word, namely, that of the body upon the soul.

This delicate, subtle, and finely balanced conception of the soul-body structure gives due account of the concrete human situation, which, however materially conditioned, is marked by the absolute primacy of the spirit and of spiritual values. It is also in accord with the image of man that is presented in divine revelation.

Other Explanations. The value of this particular interpretation of the soul-body relationship may be confirmed by a brief comparison with alternative solutions.

Extreme monistic solutions, such as those reducing man to mere spirit or not taking the reality of the body seriously (e.g., PLATONISM), or those reducing man to matter alone, considering the soul to be a manifestation of matter (e.g., MATERIALISM), do not explain the real man as given in experience. Nor does an exaggerated DUALISM, such as that of DESCARTES, account for the subtle complexity and unity of man as manifested in personal and intersubjective experiences.

Again, man cut as it were in two parts—the phenomenal and the noumenal, as KANT presents him—does not furnish an adequate explanation. Similarly, the positivist approach to the question reduces the delicate and complex ontological problem to a psychophysical parallelism in which the spiritual dimension of man disappears, to be replaced by a superfluous and meaningless epiphenomenon of physiological processes.

A newer and sounder conception of man's duality has been proposed in PHENOMENOLOGY, particularly by M. MERLEAU-PONTY and by Gabriel Marcel (*see* EXISTENTIALISM, 4). Though thinking in very different categories, confining themselves more to phenomenological description than to ontological analysis, these thinkers have rediscovered the intimate, indissoluble union of body and mind in their conception of man as *esprit incarné.* Marcel concentrates on the question, "Am I body or do I have a body?" and, distinguishing between the *corps objet* and the *corps sujet,* affords new evidence for a conception of man akin to that of traditional scholasticism. Though the deeper ontological view is lacking in such phenomenological approaches, they represent a great progress over positivist conceptions and can lead to a fuller understanding of man in terms of the soul-body relationship.

See Also: SOUL, HUMAN; IMMORTALITY; MAN, 3, 4.

Bibliography: N. A. LUYTEN, "The Significance of the Body in a Thomistic Anthropology," *Philosophy Today* 7 (1963) 175–193; "Das Leib-Seele Problem in philosophischer Sicht," *Geist und Leib in der menschlichen Existenz* (Naturwissenschaft und Theologie 4; Munich 1961) 150–214. G. SIEWERTH, *Der Mensch und sein Leib* (Einsiedeln 1953).

[N. A. LUYTEN]

SOUL OF THE CHURCH

The early Christian creeds point to a faith in the life-giving Spirit (H. Denzinger, *Enchiridion symbolorum,* ed. A. Schönmetzer 42, 150) present in the Church and in the saints, quickening and sanctifying them (*ibid.* 44, 46, 48, 60, 62, 63). The historical reasons why the Church was originally inserted among the items appended to the third member of the Trinitarian-structured creeds have not been clarified. However, the logic of Christian life soon associated the mention of the Church with the mission of the Spirit, precisely because the Church was paramount among "the realities that could be, and were, regarded as the fruits of the Spirit in action" [J. N. D. Kelly, *Early Christian Creeds* (2d ed. London 1960) 155]. The Fathers, with a copious range of imagery, present the Spirit as the prime inward principle of all life and unity in Christ's Body, the Church [see S. Tromp's florilegia: *De Spiritu Sancto anima: I. Testimonia e PP. graecis* (2d ed. Rome 1948); *II. Testimonia e PP. latinis* (Rome 1932)]. St. Augustine, in particular, compared the Spirit's role in the Church with that of the soul in the human body, thus striking off a fresh analogy destined to influence the whole Western Church; see especially two sermons on the mystery of Pentecost (267.4, *Patrologia Latina,* ed. J. P. Migne 38:1231; 268.2, *ibid.* 1232). As for the Eastern Church, *see Chrysostom*'s commentary on Eph 4.3 (*Hom.* 9.3; *Patrologia Graeca* 62:72).

The Augustinian theme became a commonplace of medieval and later Western theology. However, speculation concerning the headship of Christ interested scholastic theologians much more than the question of the Spirit's role as the soul of the Body.

In recent times this traditional analogy of metaphor has been taken into the Church's documents. [*See* Leo XIII's DIVINUM ILLUD MUNUS (May 9, 1897: *Enchiridion symbolorum* 3328).] Pius XII (MYSTICI CORPORIS, June 29, 1943: *ibid.* 3807–08) presents Christ's Spirit as the prime inward principle, one and indivisible, of all SUPERNATURAL life and growth, energies and powers, of Christ's Body (Pius XII *Mystici Corporis,* pars. 54, 68); a transcendent principle, "infinite and uncreated" (60), which, without prejudice to its transcendence, is an immanent principle, abidingly present and active in the whole Body (55, 60), thus forming the one, holy and living Body of Christ (55). Christ the Head, by communicating His Spirit to the Body, joins and assimilates the Body to Himself (51, 54, 78) with an immediacy of union that establishes His Body, analogically, in a theandric order. Christ is in His members, and they in Him, through His Spirit (77), with a measure of unity such that He is become the bearer, the "sustainer" (52) of His Body; and thus "the whole Christ" (78), Head and Body together, comes into being to serve Christ's work in the world of men.

Bellarmine, although continuing the traditional doctrine, inaugurated another way of employing the body-soul metaphor that found widespread favor in apologetic writing. He compared the soul of the Church to "the interior gifts of the Holy Spirit," while the body became "the exterior profession of faith and the sharing in the Sacraments" (*De ecclesia militante* ch. 2). However, any maladroit use of this theological construct creates the impression that there is a dissociation between body and soul in the Church. The lasting dissatisfaction with this usage, especially since *Mystici corporis,* has ensured its obsolescence.

As for its basis in Scripture, it may be said that the metaphor of the Spirit as soul is not biblical, the nearest approach being Eph 4.4 and 1 Cor 12.13. St. Paul used the "Body" theme in a Semitic sense, with Body signifying the whole concrete Person. Hence, only after the Fathers had taken over the Greek dualism of body and soul did it become feasible to elaborate a body-soul development in ecclesiology.

See Also: MYSTICAL BODY OF CHRIST; HOLY SPIRIT; CHURCH, ARTICLES ON.

Bibliography: P. DE LETTER, "The Soul of the Mystical Body," *Sciences Ecclésiastiques* 14 (1962) 213–234. C. LIALINE, "The Holy Spirit and the Mystical Body of Christ," *The Eastern Churches Quarterly* 7 (1947–48) 69–94. F. MALMBERG, *Ein Leib-ein Geist* (Freiburg 1960). S. TROMP, *De Spiritu Christi anima* (1960), v. 3 of *Corpus Christi quod est ecclesia,* 3 v. (Rome 1937–60).

[F. X. LAWLOR]

SOULERIN, JEAN MATHIEU

Founder of the University of St. Michael's College, Toronto, Canada; b. Ailhon, Ardèche, France, June 6, 1807; d. Annonay, Ardèche, Oct. 17, 1879. Educated at the Basilian College in Annonay, he joined the Congregation of Priests of St. Basil in the first decade of its history and was ordained Dec. 20, 1834. While serving as director of the College at Annonay, he was chosen in 1852 to head a mission band of five sent to Canada to found a school at Toronto that has since grown into the University of St. Michael's College. He also established St. Basil's parish and a novitiate in Toronto. Elected superior general of the Basilian Fathers in 1865, he returned to France and in 1878 published the French text of the constitutions of his congregation. During his years as superior general the Congregation of St. Basil reached its peak in France, and developed rapidly in America.

Bibliography: L. K. SHOOK, "St. Michael's College: The Formative Years, 1850–1853," *Canadian Catholic Historical Association, Report 1950* (Ottawa 1950) 37–52.

[R. J. SCOLLARD]

SOUTH AFRICA, THE CHURCH IN

The Republic of South Africa, located at the southern tip of Africa, is bordered on the north by Botswana and Zimbabwe, on the northeast by Namibia, on the east by Mozambique and Swaziland, on the southeast and south by the Indian Ocean and on the southwest by the South Atlantic Ocean. The region also includes the Prince Edward Islands, located southwest of the mainland in the Atlantic. The region is semiarid except for a subtropical region along the eastern coast. A narrow plain along the southern coast rises to a large plateau region, rising to hills to the north. The wealth of South Africa is in its natural resources, which include diamonds, gold, platinum, chromium, coal, iron ore, manganese, nickel, uranium and copper. Despite the long periods of drought experienced in much of the country, agricultural products include corn, sugar cane, wheat, fruits and vegetables and wool.

From 1910 until 1961 the region was a self-governing colony of the United Kingdom, formed by uniting the Cape, Natal, Free State and Transvaal provinces. Most Europeans are Afrikaners, descendants from Dutch, Huguenot and German settlers who arrived during

Capital: Pretoria (administrative), Bloemfontein (judicial), Cape Town (legislative).
Size: 472,494 sq. miles.
Population: 43,421,010 in 2000.
Languages: Afrikaans, English; native languages are spoken in various regions.
Religions: 3,830,150 Catholics (8.8%), 5,000,000 Dutch Reformed (11.5%), 868,420 Muslims (2%), 654,980 Hindus (1.5%), 8,439,200 Protestants (20%), 24,628,260 followed indigenous or Zionist faiths or were without religious affiliation.

the early 18th century. The discovery of diamonds and gold between 1867 and 1886 resulted in the subjugation of the native population by a white minority elite which maintained its social and economic dominance by the rigid policy of racial segregation called apartheid. Due to increasing international condemnation of South Africa's racist policies and the work of nationalists, black rule returned to South Africa in the 1990s.

Catholic Origins and Development. The Catholic Church first came to South Africa when Portuguese explorers arrived late in the 15th century seeking a shorter route to the Orient. In 1488 Bartholemew Dias rounded the Cape of Good Hope. The Portuguese planted stone crosses (*padroes*) in several locations along the coast. Cape Cross, St. Blaise Bay, Conception Bay, St. Lucia Bay, Port Natal and other places still bear Catholic names bestowed on them by the Portuguese. Joan de Nova built a small hermitage near St. Blaise Bay in 1501, and in 1635 a Catholic church was built at the mouth of the Umzimkulu River on the Natal coast. However, the Catholic presence in the region ended by the mid-17th century, after Jan van Riebeeck founded Cape Town in 1652. Dutch Calvinists (called Boers) immigrating to the region were bitterly intolerant of Catholicism and expelled all priests and missionaries, causing the disappearance of Catholic life until the 19th century.

England occupied the Cape in 1795, receiving permanent possession by the Treaty of Paris in 1814. Evicted from the region, Boers traveled north in what became known as the Great Trek, founding the republic of Transvaal and Orange Free State. In 1804 three Dutch priests arrived, and one of them, Joannes Lansink, was appointed prefect apostolic. However, the British expelled all three priests in 1805. British tolerance of the Church increased in the next decade, and in 1818 Edward Bede Slater, OSB, of Ampleforth, England, was named vicar apostolic for the Cape of Good Hope, Madagascar and neighboring islands (including Australia and New Zealand). Unable to reside at Cape colony, he was appointed the first vicar apostolic of MAURITIUS in 1819. Slater visited the Cape in 1820, and left Father Scully, an Irishman, who built the first church in 1822, in charge of the mission. In 1837 the Vicariate of the Cape of Good Hope was separated from Mauritius, and Patrick GRIFFITH, OP, became the first resident bishop.

With the bishopric established, evangelization of the native South African population began. As the congregations grew, the vicariate of the Cape was separated into eastern and western sections in 1847, and the vicariate of Natal was created in 1850 and entrusted to the OBLATES OF MARY IMMACULATE (OMI). Bishop Marie Jean Allard, OMI, Vicar Apostolic of Natal (1850–73), inaugurated missionary efforts among the Zulu and Basuto tribes. In 1879 the Jesuits assumed charge of the Zambezi mission north of the Limpopo River. With the discovery of diamond mines and gold fields, immigrants from many countries arrived in South Africa after 1867, and in 1886 the Vicariate Apostolic of the Orange Free State and the Prefecture Apostolic of Transvaal were created. In 1910, following the Boer Wars, all colonies in the region were united under British rule, and 12 years later Pius XI established an apostolic delegation for South Africa, headquartered in Pretoria. The present hierarchy was established in 1951. In 1991 a group called Afrikaans Apostolate completed a 29-year undertaking by publishing the first Afrikaans Sacramentary and Lectionary.

Church Confronts Apartheid. In the 1947 elections, a right-wing party took power in South Africa. The policy of apartheid (officially known as "plural democracies") was introduced in 1952 by Prime Minister D. F. Malan, and touted as a means of preserving the cultural identity of each of the many "nations" that constituted the region by keeping the races separate. The brutal shooting of blacks during the Sharpesville Massacre, which occurred in 1960, concurrently with South Africa's struggle for independence, served as a symbol to the world of the severe repression under this system. In 1977 the government proposed a plan whereby the black majority was to be distributed among nine "homelands" which the government claimed would become independent nations. This scheme failed to receive international recognition, being regarded as unjust, a denial of human rights, and a ruse to perpetuate white domination in South Africa. Apartheid was confronted by such moderate groups as the Christian Institute and Black Consciousness, as well as the African National Congress (ANC), which began campaigns of civil disobedience that would extend for over four decades as it gained in power.

In September of 1977 Black Consciousness leader Stephen Biko died of wounds received while in police custody. The government moved to suppress the rioting and criticism of Biko's death by jailing almost all black leaders except those appointed by the government itself, and by banning several influential white critics. (Banning orders forbade, among other activities, speaking in public or writing for publication.) Among the imprisoned black leaders was Father Smangaliso Mkhatshwa, acting secretary-general of the South African Catholic Bishops' Conference (SACBC). After four months of imprisonment, Mkhatshwa and several others were released, but severe restrictions were placed regarding his movements and activities. In February of 1977 the SACBC called for drastic changes in the organization of South African society, as well as advocating reforms within the Church itself. On racism they declared that "the only solution . . . consists in conceding full citizen and human rights to all persons in the Republic, not by choice on the false grounds of color, but on the grounds of the common humanity of all men, taught by our Lord Jesus Christ."

The announced policy of Church leaders was contrary to government policy and even illegal in several significant ways. In addition, conflict existed within the Church itself between adherents of the Black Consciousness Movement (including many black priests) and white Church authorities that centered around questions of the extent to which the Church should take a political stance against the government. The South African Catholic Defense League presented an organized objection to the Church's position in support of school integration. Meanwhile, other religious communities also struggled with such conflicts. In April of 1978, the Dutch Reformed Church of South Africa cut its ties with its "Mother Church," the Dutch Reformed Church of the Netherlands, which had been critical of South Africa's racial policies despite its South African congregations's support of the government. Because of these conflicts, during the 1970s and 1980s Church leaders were expelled from the country, sometimes even arrested and tortured for their views.

International public opinion combined with a more moderate white government succeeded in bringing an end to apartheid before the end of the century. In the early 1990s came the work of dismantling the apartheid apparatus, and in April of 1994 the White congress voted itself into history. A new constitution went into effect and on May 10, ANC leader Nelson Mandela was sworn in as the first black president of South Africa at the head of a coalition government. In 1996 the country produced a new constitution, which, like the one it replaced, guaranteed religious freedom. In 1997 the Church admitted that, although not active in supporting apartheid policies, it could have done more to prevent them.

Into the 21st Century. By 2000 there were 746 parishes in South Africa tended by 398 diocesan and 749 religious priests. Other religious included 215 brothers and approximately 2,940 sisters, each of whom served the region's growing Catholic population and some of whom ran the Church's 249 primary and 115 secondary schools throughout the country. Despite the end of apartheid, Church leaders now found themselves forced to publicly confront racism against South Africa's growing Muslim population, which had become the focus of scattered violence by 2000. The midlands area also continued to be visited by violence as Zulu extremists rebelled against the current political system. Ironically, the Church also began to break with the new mixed race government. The government's liberal views involved legalizing abortion in 1996 and the Church responded with a "right to live" campaign. However, despite such conflicts, relations between Church and state remained amicable. During a 1998 meeting between President Mandela and Pope John Paul II, Mandela commented that "No one among us can forget what the Church has done in teaching and health care for our children, when no one else was doing the same thing."

Archdioceses	**Suffragans**
Bloemfontein	Bethlehem, Keimoes-Upington, Kimberley, Kroonstad
Cape Town	Aliwal, De Aar, Oudtshoorn, Port Elizabeth, Queenstown
Durban	Dundee, Eshowe, Kokstad, Mariannhill, Umtata, Umzimkulu
Pretoria	Johannesburg, Klerksdorp, Lydenburg, Pietersburg, Rustenburg, Tzaneen, Witbank

There is an apostolic vicariate at Ingwavuma and a military ordinariate in South Africa.

Bibliography: J. E. BRADY, *Trekking for Souls* (Cedara, Natal 1952). W. E. BROWN, *The Catholic Church in South Africa from Its Origins to the Present Day* (New York 1960). K. S. LATOURETTE, *A History of the Expansion of Christianity,* 7 v. (New York 1937–45) v.5. K. S. LATOURETTE, *Christianity in a Revolutionary Age: A History of Christianity in the Nineteenth and Twentieth Centuries,* 5 v. (New York 1958–62) v.3, 5. *Bilan du Monde* 2:25–36. *The Catholic Directory of South Africa* (Capetown 1917–). *Annuario Pontificio* has annual data on all dioceses.

[J. E. BRADY/EDS.]

SOUTH CAROLINA, CATHOLIC CHURCH IN

The Diocese of Charleston began the 21st century under the leadership of Robert J. Baker, who was appointed as the 12th bishop of the diocese on July 13, 1999 by Pope John Paul II. Baker was consecrated in Charleston on September 29, 1999 and installed in the Cathedral of Saint John the Baptist. The diocese, established by Pope Pius VII on July 11, 1820, comprises the land area of the entire state, and with Richmond, Virginia, was the first diocese created in the South.

At the beginning of the new millennium the diocese included about 122,000 Catholics, representing 3.25 percent of the state's population. The diocese is served by 94 active priests (of whom 34 are members of religious orders), 69 permanent deacons, and 184 religious brothers and sisters serving in 85 parishes, 30 missions, and 10 pastoral centers. The diocese sponsors two hospitals, seven social service centers, a retirement center, 25 parochial schools, and two high schools.

The first act of Christian worship in what is now South Carolina was probably a Mass celebrated by Catholic priests accompanying the explorations of Lucas de Ayllon and Hernando de Soto through the area in the first half of the 16th century; but it was not until more than 250 years later that the Church began to develop in the region. The English Crown gave eight lords proprietors

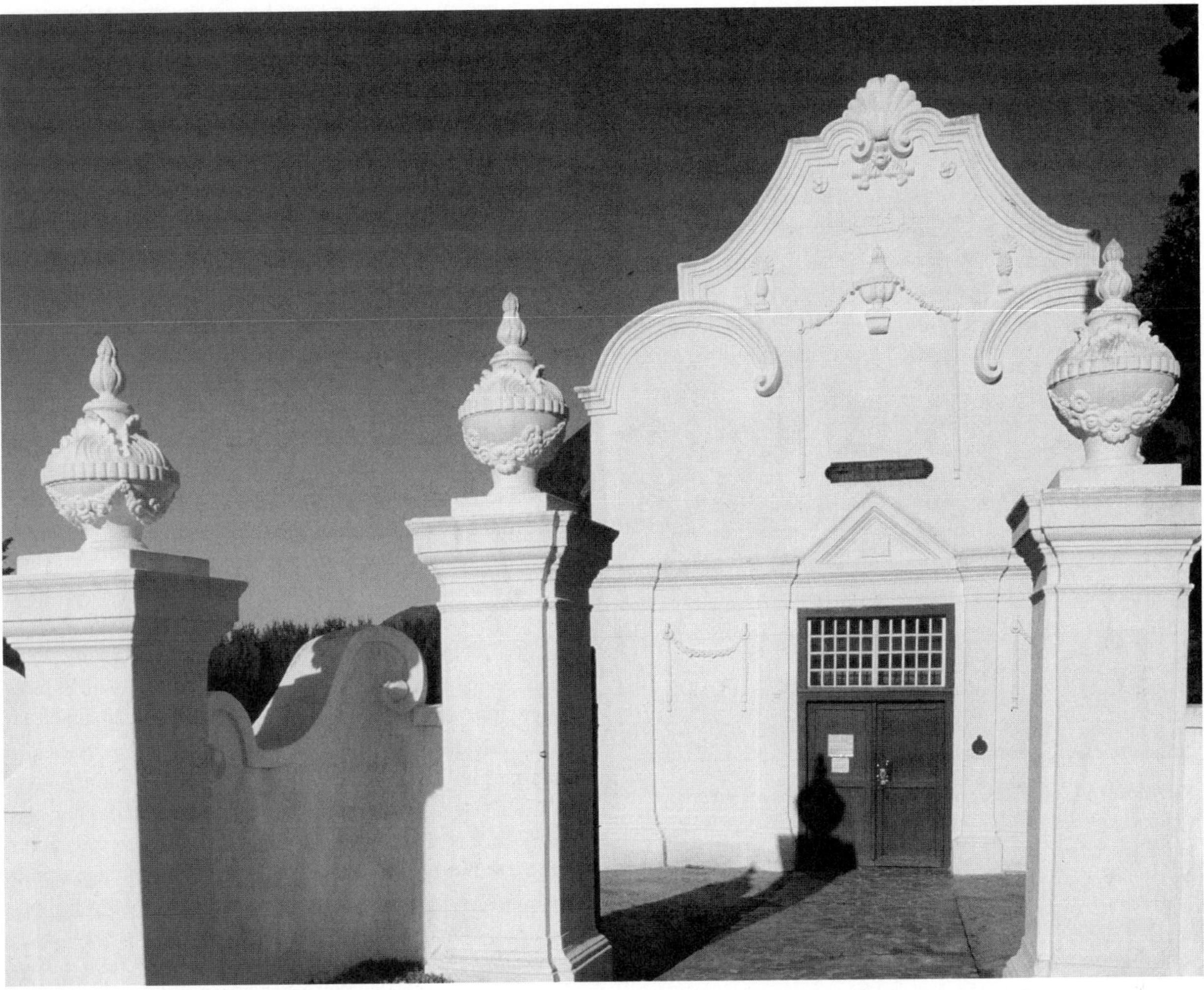

Decorative mouldings embellish the facade of a South African church. (©Hans Georg Roth/CORBIS)

a charter in the 17th century to develop the colony of Carolina. Charleston, the see city of the diocese, was settled in 1670 when the first English colonists arrived with their slaves from Barbados. The English, reflecting European political divisions, adopted a policy prohibiting the immigration of Catholics and all manifestations of their religion. Carolina's royal governor observed in 1770 that there was religious freedom for everyone in the colony ''except Papists.'' The Church took root in the state only after the success of the American Revolution during which the Church of England was disestablished. An Italian priest celebrated the first Mass in Charleston in 1788 as he was passing through the city on a ship bound for South America.

Matthew Ryan was the first priest assigned to minister to the small Catholic population in Charleston. Father John Carroll of Baltimore, the first ecclesiastical superior in the emerging nation, sent the Irish priest to Charleston in 1788. The fledgling congregation acquired a building on Hasell Street in 1789 and established Saint Mary's Church. Charleston was an important seaport on the southern Atlantic coast, and the number of Catholics increased as the city grew with immigration from Ireland and other European nations.

French Catholics arrived in Charleston from the Caribbean after a slave revolution in Haiti led to the flight of many residents from Haiti and Santo Domingo. Among them were two daughters of Admiral le comte de Grasse, a French naval hero of the American Revolution. Both girls died in Charleston in 1799 and their bodies were laid to rest in Saint Mary's churchyard.

Simon Felix Gallagher, an Irish priest with a degree from the University of Paris, came to Saint Mary's in 1793. Gallagher was an important figure in the Charleston community as well as at Saint Mary's during the 30 years he lived in the city. He was a member of the faculty of the College of Charleston, and served as its president

Exterior of Llandaff Oratory, the world's smallest Catholic Church, Van Reenen, Transvaal, South Africa. (©Nik Wheeler/ CORBIS)

on two occasions. He founded a school called the Athenian Academy, and was a founder of an association of Irishmen called the Hibernian Society that is still in existence.

Both Gallagher and the congregation at Saint Mary's were often embroiled in conflicts with the ecclesiastical authority. The congregational disputes reflected the republican disposition of the young nation and a desire for independence from outside control from afar. The bishop received frequent complaints from Charleston Catholics about Gallagher's personal behavior. Carroll warned Gallagher on more than one occasion about using inappropriate language during services, and for celebrating Mass in an inebriated condition.

The congregation at Saint Mary's decided that it wished to have a voice in the selection of bishops chosen to serve in Charleston as well as elsewhere in America. When its proposals to have a veto power over the selection of bishops were thwarted, the congregation made attempts to recruit a bishop of its own liking from among Old Catholic separatists or from one of the Eastern Orthodox Churches in an effort to establish an ''Independent Catholick Church'' in America. The mission was unsuccessful, but problems continued until closer ecclesiastical supervision could be established.

Many priests came to America from France to escape the dangerous effects of the French Revolution. Their immigration resulted in a disproportionately large number of French clergy in the American church. Disputes arose within the Church as many Catholics of Irish origin thought that too many French clerics were appointed to positions of authority. The tension was heightened in South Carolina where the Church was predominately Irish from the earliest days, but where there was also a significant French Catholic population.

Carroll, now Archbishop of Baltimore, sent a French priest to Charleston in about 1810 to assist Gallagher. Joseph Picot Limoelan de la Clorivière had been a royalist officer at the beginning of the French Revolution and was forced to leave France. When he returned to France after the Revolution, Clorivière was implicated in a plot to assassinate Napoleon Bonaparte. He escaped execution for his involvement in the affair only because his uncle, the head of the Society of Jesus in France, was able to arrange his secret emigration to America. Clorivière arrived in Baltimore, attended Saint Mary's Seminary, was ordained to the priesthood, and assigned to Saint Mary's in Charleston. He was not acceptable to Gallagher or to many in the congregation, which led to further fragmentation of the parish, and Saint Mary's was placed under an interdict by Carroll's successor, Archbishop Leonard Neale of Baltimore, in 1817.

The Diocese of Charleston was created on June 20, 1820, and John England, a native of Cork, Ireland, was nominated its first bishop. England was consecrated in Ireland on September 1, and arrived in Charleston on December 30 with his sister, Joanna Monica England, and a priest, Denis Corkery. The first Mass celebrated by a bishop of Charleston occurred at Saint Mary's Church on Dec. 31, 1820.

The newly erected Diocese of Charleston comprised three states, North Carolina, South Carolina, and Georgia, and covered 142,000 square miles which contained no more than five churches and less than 400 Catholics. Bishop England wasted no time establishing a coherent diocesan organization. He established the Cathedral of Saint Finbar on Broad Street in Charleston, giving it the same name as that of his home parish in Cork. The bishop opened a seminary, Saint John the Baptist, adjacent to the cathedral, and its first student was Andrew Byrne who later became the first bishop of Little Rock, Arkansas. England established the *United States Catholic Miscellany*, the first Catholic publication of general circulation in the nation. He wrote a constitution for the diocese that enabled lay people to participate in the affairs of church governance through state and diocesan conventions of elected representatives. The bishop and his sister, Joanna, were instrumental in founding a religious order for women known as the Sisters of Charity of Our Lady of Mercy, and he invited a community of Ursuline nuns to Charleston where they founded a non-sectarian school that was perhaps the first such school in the state. England founded schools in Charleston for slaves, free blacks, and mulattos to promote education among the African American population. Saint Peter's Church, established in Columbia, the state's capital city, was one of the first parishes in the midlands of the state. It was dedicated by England on Dec. 12, 1830. Churches were established wherever there were Catholics to support them as the population moved farther into other parts of the state. The Church was firmly established in South Carolina by the time Bishop England's ministry ended with his death at age 56 in 1842. From his first days in America, he preached a message of tolerance among all people, and worked to make Catholicism acceptable in the emerging nation. He appreciated American democracy and endeavored to present it as compatible with the Catholic faith. The essentially Irish character of the Church that emerged in the diocese continued until well into the 20th century.

Ignatius A. Reynolds became the second bishop of the diocese. A native of Bardstown, Kentucky, Reynolds was consecrated in Cincinnati and arrived in Charleston on April 3, 1844. Under Reynolds's leadership the diocese continued to expand beyond the city of Charleston as more Catholics settled in the region. He raised funds to pay debts incurred by Bishop England, and organized plans to build a new cathedral, which was consecrated in 1854. The Sisters of Charity of Our Lady of Mercy prospered and opened a hospital in Charleston in 1852. Schools were opened in Columbia where Saint Joseph's Church was established in 1854. The diocese was reduced in territorial size when the Diocese of Savannah, including the entire state of GEORGIA, was erected in 1850. Reynolds served until his death on March 6, 1855.

A local priest, Patrick Neison LYNCH, became the diocesan administrator upon the death of Reynolds, and was soon appointed the third bishop of the diocese. Born in Ireland, Lynch became the first bishop consecrated in the diocese. Bishop Lynch's episcopate was engulfed by the disruption and turmoil of the Civil War that began when South Carolina seceded from the Union on December 20, 1860.

A devastating fire struck the city of Charleston on December 11, 1861, that added to the wartime destruction. The Charleston fire destroyed the cathedral, the bishop's residence, the Catholic Institute Hall, the seminary library, and an orphanage near the cathedral. The state's separation from the Union brought about the change of the name of the *U.S. Catholic Miscellany* to the *Charleston Catholic Miscellany*, and its last edition was published on December 14, 1861, three days after the fire. The population of the city was endangered and church property damaged by hostile shelling during a siege by northern forces from 1863 to 1865. The Ursuline convent in Columbia was severely damaged by a fire in 1865. Several Sisters of Our Lady of Mercy joined the war effort as nurses supporting the Confederate Army. During the war, the westward expansion of the diocese continued as more Catholics settled the Carolina backcountry.

The ruins of a Catholic cathedral damaged during the Civil War in Charleston, South Carolina, 1865. (©CORBIS)

Lynch became an advocate for the Confederate cause and, like some of the other southern bishops, was a slave owner. He defended the institution of SLAVERY and justified its existence on moral grounds, and felt that the proper treatment and education of slaves by the Catholic Church was necessary to sustain it. Jefferson Davis, the president of the Confederacy, asked Lynch to represent the rebellious southern government on a diplomatic mission to the Holy See. The bishop agreed to undertake the assignment and arrived in Rome in June 1864 as a "Special Commissioner of the Confederate States of America to the States of the Church," for the purpose of seeking the diplomatic recognition of the Confederate government by Pope Pius IX. He had an audience with the Pope and presented his credentials as "Minister of the Confederate States," but his petition evidently did not proceed beyond that point. He was unable to return to the diocese because he was declared *persona non grata* by the United States government. Lynch was pardoned by President Andrew Johnson after taking an oath of allegiance to the United States before the ambassador in Paris on Oct. 14, 1865, thus enabling him to return to South Carolina. The bishop returned to the diocese to find much destruction and the need for substantial funds for rebuilding the fabric of the Church and the community.

A vicariate apostolic was established for North Carolina in 1868, separating it from the Diocese of Charleston and relieving Bishop Lynch of further responsibilities there. Lynch spent much of his time during Reconstruction away from the diocese raising funds in the North for rebuilding. He also developed ideas and plans for the assimilation of former slaves into the Church and society. Economic stability was not achieved in the South until many years after the Civil War, and there was much to be done to restore the spirit of the people and church property when Lynch's episcopate ended upon his death on Feb. 26, 1882.

The period between the Lynch's death and World War I was one of steady growth and progress in the diocese. Henry P. Northrop, the only native of the city of Charleston to be named bishop of the diocese, became the fourth bishop on March 11, 1883. He had been serving in North Carolina as the vicar apostolic. A time of religious and minority intolerance followed the Civil War. The Reconstruction era brought with it the establishment of such organizations as the KU KLUX KLAN and the enactment of Jim Crow laws throughout the region. The Catholic Church unfortunately became the target of more than its share of vitriolic language and behavior by many whites.

Another natural disaster visited the coastal area of the diocese when a severe earthquake hit Charleston in 1886. It caused damage to church property in the city and surrounding area requiring renewed fund-raising efforts to repair the damage.

A synod of the diocese, the first since the time of Bishop England, was called in 1887 and attended by 16 priests. A new wave of immigrants from predominantly Catholic European countries and from Lebanon led to a sharp increase in the number of communicants in the diocese around the turn of the 20th century. The Lebanese brought the Maronite Rite with them, but they were soon largely assimilated into the Latin Rite Catholic population. The demography of the diocese began to shift with the new immigration from one of traditional Irish dominance to one with broader cultural diversity. There were about 9,000 Catholics in South Carolina at the turn of the century, and many improvements were made in the fabric of the diocese as the economic hardships of the Reconstruction era began to subside. A cathedral school was opened in 1887, and new churches were established across the diocese to accommodate the increasing numbers of Catholics.

Northrop's episcopate, the longest in the history of the diocese, was marked by steady progress in the development of diocesan institutions. Saint Angela's Academy opened in Aiken in 1900, a branch of the Knights of Columbus was organized in Charleston in 1902, the Holy Name Society was established, and Bishop England High School was founded in 1915. James Cardinal Gibbons, the archbishop of Baltimore, celebrated a Mass of dedication on April 14, 1907, for the reconstructed cathedral on the 25th anniversary of Bishop Northrop's consecration. And in about 1910, a new motherhouse for the Sisters of Charity of Our Lady of Mercy began operation at Queen and Legare Streets in Charleston.

Northrop's death came on June 17, 1916. He was succeeded by William T. Russell of Washington, D.C. Installed on March 22, 1917, Russell continued the development of mission work throughout the diocese and blessed many new parishes. Saint Francis Xavier Hospital was organized in Charleston where the bishop died in 1927.

Russell's successor was Emmet Michael Walsh, a much beloved native son of the diocese who came from Atlanta and was installed as the sixth bishop of Charleston on Sept. 22, 1927. Walsh served in Charleston until his appointment as coadjutor bishop of the Diocese of Youngstown, Ohio, in 1949. Catholic hospitals were established in Charleston, Greenville, Rock Hill, York, Columbia, and Dillon. Bishop Walsh founded a Council of Catholic Women, a Council of Catholic Men, and a Catholic Youth Council. Camps for children were organized, and a parish for African Americans was begun in Columbia.

Bishop Walsh developed an innovative program for the development of new church buildings. A standard church building design was developed with the help of a priest at Belmont Abbey in North Carolina to provide the diocese with simple, dignified church buildings of wooden frames on brick pillars with cedar shingles on the outside walls. These simple buildings were designed to include all the necessary furnishings and fixtures down to the curtains for the confessionals. The standard design made it possible to construct identical buildings any place in the diocese where a church was needed at low cost in a minimal time. At least 12 of these structures were put into service, including church buildings at Myrtle Beach, Union, Dillon, Bennettsville, Bishopville, and Saint Patrick's in Columbia.

Mepkin Abbey was established in the diocese in 1949 by the Order of Cistercians of the Strict Observance (Trappist). Clare Booth Luce and her husband, Henry Luce, whose bodies lie at rest on the Abbey grounds, gave the order 3,000 acres of land for the abbey in Berkeley County, just north of Charleston. The first monks arrived at Mepkin in the fall of 1949 under the leadership of Dom Anthony Chassagne. The leadership of Abbot Francis Kline (1990–) continued the tradition of making the abbey and its monastic community an important part of the life of the local diocese.

From the departure of Bishop Walsh in 1949 to 1963 three bishops were appointed to the see of Charleston, and all were transferred elsewhere. John J. Russell was installed in 1950 and appointed bishop of Richmond, Virginia, in 1958; Paul J. Hallinan was installed in 1958 and became archbishop of the new Province of Atlanta in 1962; Francis F. Reh was installed in 1962 and became rector of the North American College in Rome in 1963.

Joseph L. Bernardin, a native of Columbia, was ordained in the Charleston cathedral in 1953 and became Bishop Russell's secretary. He served as a priest in the diocese for 14 years after his ordination until his appointment as auxiliary bishop of Atlanta. A distinguished son of the diocese, Bernardin later served as general secretary to the National Conference of Catholic Bishops and cardinal archbishop of Chicago.

A new publication, the *Catholic Banner*, was inaugurated in 1951 to provide a newspaper for the diocese for the first time in many years. In 1959, the motherhouse of the Sisters of Charity of Our Lady of Mercy moved to a new site on James Island, overlooking Charleston Harbor, and Cardinal Newman High School was dedicated in Columbia in 1961. Upon the departure of Bishop Reh in 1963, Joseph L. Bernardin became the diocesan administrator until the installation of Ernest L. Unterkoefler as the 10th bishop of the diocese on February 22, 1964.

The episcopate of Unterkoefler was marked by a strong voice from the Church on matters of racial justice and social concerns. Unterkoefler courageously led public civil rights marches in the diocese in the 1960s in order to demonstrate the commitment of the Church to the achievement of social justice for everyone in America. He also strongly supported ecumenical activities with other Christian bodies.

David B. Thompson became the 11th bishop of the diocese in 1990 and promptly set about the task of improving the Catholic school system, and took steps to insure a racial balance in all the educational institutions of the diocese. The name of the diocesan newspaper was changed to the *New Catholic Miscellany* to honor Bishop England's founding of the first general publication for Catholics in the nation.

The church in South Carolina was racially segregated until the mid-1960s. There were several parishes in the diocese, Saint Patrick's in Charleston, Saint Martin de Porres in Columbia, Saint James at Ritter, and others that specifically served the African-American Catholic population. Immaculate Conception in Charleston was a high school for African-American students. Under the leadership of Unterkoefler the parishes, schools, and other diocesan institutions were successfully desegregated.

Bishop Thompson convened a synod in 1995, called the Synod of Charleston, to plan and empower the participation of lay people in the work of the Church. The Synod, involving lay people and clergy, led to the renewal of participation by lay people in the parishes of the diocese as lectors, cantors, eucharistic ministers, and pastoral associates. It also encouraged the development of new religious education and peace and justice programs.

The cultural diversity of the Church in South Carolina continued to broaden as the American population became more mobile in the 20th century. By the end of the millennium the Irish dominance of the Church in earlier times had given way to a Catholic population reflecting the attributes of the rich cultural heritage of America. These changes along with the reforms of the Second Vatican Council have placed the Diocese of Charleston in the mainstream of American Catholicism.

Bibliography: G. ACCAME, producer, "Fire Tried Gold" (film) (Kensington, Md. 2000). THE REV. S. J.-A. BUCHANAN, "Catholicism in the Carolinas and Georgia: 1670–1820," *Dissertatio ad Licentiam in Facultate Historiae Ecclesiasticae* (Rome 1998). P. GUILDAY, *The Life and Times of John England, First Bishop of Charleston (1786–1842)*, 2 v. (New York 1927). R. C. MADDEN, *Catholics in South Carolina* (Lanham, N.Y. 1985). J. J. O'CONNELL, *Catholicity in the Carolinas and Georgia* (New York 1879). T. TISDALE, *A Lady of the High Hills: Natalie Delage Sumter* (Columbia, S.C. 2001). Also see the web site of the Diocese of Charleston, www.catholic-doc.org.

[T. TISDALE]

SOUTH DAKOTA, CATHOLIC CHURCH IN

Bordered by North Dakota, Minnesota, Iowa, Montana, Wyoming, and Nebraska, South Dakota comprises over 77,047 square miles with two dioceses, that of Sioux Falls east of the Missouri River and Rapid City which includes the Black Hills and the area west of the river. Major cities are Sioux Falls, Rapid City, and Aberdeen. Pierre is the capital. Agriculture and tourism contribute most to the economy although more industrial and service enterprises are locating in the state. The poorest areas are on the reservations although the upsurge in gambling casinos on most of them has provided funds for more educational and social services. The population of this state (which derives its name from the Dakota Sioux) is over 725,000, of whom about 125,000 of these are Catholic. The two Catholic dioceses in South Dakota, RAPID CITY and SIOUX FALLS, are suffragan sees of the Archdiocese of ST. PAUL–MINNEAPOLIS.

Catholicism arrived with French-Canadian fur traders in the 18th century, but it was not until the Belgian Jesuit missionary, Pierre Jean De Smet journeyed through the area in the mid-19th century that a baptism was recorded. Although the missionary catechized and was beloved by the Native Americans who, at that time, still populated almost half of the state's area, it was not until the arrival of Martin Marty, a Swiss Benedictine abbot who came to Dakota Territory from Indiana in 1876 to minister to the Native Americans that the church was organized on and off the reservations. Small rural and town parishes had been under the jurisdiction of the bishop of Omaha, Neb. which also governed the parishes just across the Missouri from Yankton.

Within two years of his arrival, Marty was appointed Vicar Apostolic to the area which then included what is now North and South Dakota and small sections of the present Montana and Wyoming borders. Marty came to Yankton and the Standing Rock Reservation shortly after Custer's defeat by the Sioux at Little Big Horn on the Wyoming-Territory border. Prominent in that battle were two Native American leaders from the Dakota Territory: Crazy Horse and Sitting Bull. Marty eventually journeyed to Canada to encourage the refugees, Sitting Bull, a Hunkpapa Teton Sioux, and his followers, to return to the territory's reservations in order to avoid starvation. Although they refused at the time, the crops were still good and buffalo and deer plentiful, ultimately drought, depletion of the wildlife, and famine as well as Canadian policy that they be self-sufficient, forced them to return. Sitting Bull was later accidentally killed by Native American police commissioned by reservation agents to transfer him from one reservation to another.

The Dakota Vicariate had been assigned to the Benedictine missionary in 1879 making him Dakota Territory's first bishop. After division into North and South Dakota and admission to the Union in 1889, Bishop Marty decided that Sioux Falls, the fastest growing town, should be the new diocesan See. He left his Yankton residence (which still stands) where he had based his ministry. Yankton had formerly served as the territorial capital when he had arrived to minister to the Native Americans.

It was Marty who, as a circuit rider, on horseback or wagon, in inclement weather of all kinds, had had churches built on most of the reservations, regularly visited the small rural parishes, and established dozens of new ones. He baptized numerous children and adults, opened parish schools and mission schools for the Native American children who spoke Dakota, Lakota or Nakota. However, government policy mandated English only be used by the Sioux and their teachers in the reservation schools. To date about 50% of the more than 25,000 Native Americans on eight reservations are Catholic. One of them, Marty Mission near Wagner, founded after his death, is named for the first bishop. It also supports a school for Native American children, funded originally by Mother (now St.) Katharine Drexel, who responded to Bishop Marty's pleas for financial assistance and sisters to staff the school.

It was this first bishop who brought the Benedictine Sisters to Yankton and Sturgis (now at Rapid City) primarily to educate Native American children, as well as the Presentation Sisters to Aberdeen where they operated a parish school and, when an epidemic prompted them to care for the sick, a hospital which has become one of the largest in the state. Transferred to St. Cloud, Minn., because of declining health, Marty died in 1896 at age 62 shortly after attending the South Dakota Indian Congress which he had organized years earlier. (A later Tekakwitha Conference has somewhat replaced that although gatherings of Native Americans in the Dakotas are still frequent). In 1891, he had agonized over the infamous Massacre of Wounded Knee on the Pine Ridge Reservation. That reservation, Rosebud, Crow Creek, Lower Brule and the southern area of Standing Rock all later became part of the new diocese of Lead, founded in 1902, (which transferred to Rapid City in 1930). State-wide and diocesan apologies and reconciliation efforts concerning the Native Americans have served to heighten an awareness among the Catholics of the need for justice and more spiritual as well as material assistance for native tribespeople.

Catholic Institutions. South Dakota has five motherhouses of religious nuns and sisters. Benedictines are in Yankton and Rapid City; Presentations in Aberdeen;

Oblates of the Blessed Sacrament in Marty; Franciscans in Mitchell, formerly Gettysburg; and contemplative Carmelites in Alexandria. The only Benedictine abbey near Marvin, S.D., was founded in the 1950s by monks from ST. MEINRAD ARCHABBEY in Indiana, to enable them, working as missionaries to the Native Americans, to have a motherhouse nearer their ministries. The Sioux Falls diocese has assumed the obligation of serving the parishes formerly filled by the monks whose paucity of numbers has obliged them to withdraw from Native American ministry except at the abbey itself, and in a nearby parish. Another fast growing minority, the Hispanics, are also being served with the opening of Our Lady of Guadalupe parish in Sioux Falls. It is staffed by a recently ordained native Spanish-speaking priest from South America. South Dakota, although not populous, has a vibrant Catholic presence that is apparent wherever one travels across the state.

The state has two Catholic colleges, Mount Marty in Yankton and Presentation in Aberdeen; nine Catholic hospitals; four diocesan and parish high schools and 23 Catholic elementary schools. Schools primarily for the Native American population are on the reservations, at Marty Mission, and Chamberlain.

Bibliography: R. KAROLEVETZ, *With Faith, Hope and Tenacity* (Sioux Falls, 1989); *Bishop Martin Marty: Black Robe Lean Chief* (Yankton, 1980). A. KESSLER, ''First Catholic Bishop of Dakota'' in *South Dakota Leaders,* eds H. HOOVER et al. (Vermillion 1989); ''Mount Marty College,'' in *From Idea to Institution,* eds. H. HOOVER et al. (Vermillion 1989); C. DURATSCHEK, *Beginnings of Catholicism in South Dakota,* (Washington, D.C. 1943); *Crusading along Sioux Trails* (St. Meinrad, Ind. 1947).

[C. DURATSCHEK/A. KESSLER]

SOUTHERNE, WILLIAM, BL.

Priest, martyr; b. *c.* 1579 at Ketton, Co. Durham; d. April 30, 1618 at Newcastle-under-Lyme under James I. Following his studies at Douai and Valladolid, he was ordained and returned to England. There he worked for 14 years, primarily among the poor of Staffordshire, particularly at Baswich, which then belonged to a branch of the Fowler family. He was arrested while saying Mass and sentenced in his vestments for being a priest and refusing the Oath of Supremacy. He remained in Stafford prison for six days after his condemnation because no one was willing to hang him. Finally he was strangled, then drawn and quartered. His head was stuck on one of the gates of Stafford. He was beatified by Pope John Paul II on Nov. 22, 1987 with George Haydock and companions.

Feast of the English Martyrs: May 4 (England).

See Also: ENGLAND, SCOTLAND, AND WALES, MARTYRS OF.

Bibliography: R. CHALLONER, *Memoirs of Missionary Priests,* ed. J. H. POLLEN (rev. ed. London 1924). J. H. POLLEN, *Acts of English Martyrs* (London 1891).

[K. I. RABENSTEIN]

SOUTHWELL, NATHANAEL (BACON)

Jesuit bibliographer; b. Sculthorp, near Walsingham, Norfolk, England, 1598; d. at the Gesù, Rome, Dec. 2, 1676. He studied the humanities at the College of English Jesuits, Saint–Omer, and entered the English College at Rome, October 1617, under the assumed name Southwell. He was ordained Dec. 21, 1622, and sent to England. Later he was recalled to Rome as minister and procurator of the college there. In 1637 he was appointed spiritual father and confessor of the college. Then he went to the Gesù where for more than 20 years he was secretary to five generals of his order: V. Caraffa (1646–49), F. Piccolomini (1649–51), A. Gottifredi (1652), G. Nickel (1652–64), and J. P. Oliva (1664–81). Even after his retirement in 1668 he remained admonitor to Oliva. He revised and continued the great work of Pedro de RIBADENEYRA, *Bibliotheca Scriptorum Societatis Jesu* (1676). He also compiled *A Journal of Meditations for Every Day of the Year. Gathered out of Divers Authors,* first published 1669, with a second edition, 1674, and a third edition, 1687. The work was translated from the original Latin by Edward Harvey, alias Mico, SJ, who died in prison in 1678.

Bibliography: T. COOPER, *The Dictionary of National Biography from the Earliest Times to 1900,* 63 vol. (London 1885–1900) 18:700. J. GILLOW, *A Literary and Biographical History or Bibliographical Dictionary of the English Catholics from 1534 to the Present Time,* 5 vol. (London-New York 1885–1902) 1:95–96.

[H. S. REINMUTH, JR.]

SOUTHWELL, ROBERT, ST.

English poet and martyr; b. Horsham St. Faith, near Norwich, toward end of 1561; d. Tyburn, London, Feb. 21, 1595. His father, Sir Robert Southwell, was a Catholic, but later conformed to the new religion; his mother's family (Copley) remained staunchly Catholic, as did his relatives, the Shelleys, Gages, and Cottons. When sent abroad for his education, he lived first among the English Catholic exiles at DOUAI, attending classes at the Jesuit college there. Later he went to Paris, where he came under the influence of the Jesuit Thomas Darbyshire, who had been an eminent divine under Queen Mary. Southwell, scarcely 17, sought admission into the Society of Jesus at Paris, but was refused because of his youth. He went on foot to Rome, and was there admitted in the autumn of 1578. Before and after ordination in 1584, he lived at the newly founded English College in Rome, where he acted as tutor and spiritual instructor to the students.

In 1586 Southwell left Rome for England with Henry GARNET; they landed near Folkestone on July 7. In London, which Southwell reached a few days later, he narrowly escaped capture: it was the time of the Babington Plot (*see* MARY STUART, QUEEN OF SCOTS), which Southwell later exposed in his *An Humble Supplication to Her Majestie* (1595). He worked mostly in London, living first at Arundel House in the Strand, the home of the countess, whose husband (St.) Philip HOWARD was a prisoner in the Tower. To Howard, Southwell addressed the spiritual letters that he later expanded into *An Epistle of Comfort,* which is one of the finest prose works of the late Elizabethan Age. Among his other writings, most of them printed at a secret press that he and Garnet directed, were *Mary Magdalen's Funerall Teares* (1594) and *A Short Rule of Good Life* (1598). The best known of his poems are *The Burning Babe* and *St. Peter's Complaint* (1595), in which he made experiments in verse that were followed or developed by others, including Shakespeare. He has been compared with Philip Sidney in his style and conceits.

In June 1592 Southwell was captured by an agent of the crown, Richard Topcliffe, at Uxenden, Harrow, the home of the Bellamy family, and was tortured in his captor's lodgings adjoining the Gatehouse prison in London. Later he was transferred to the Tower and finally to Newgate. In all he was tortured ten times. He was condemned for his priesthood, hanged, drawn, and quartered; his execution shocked the court and the whole country. He was beatified by Pius XI on Dec. 15, 1929 and canonized in 1970 as one of the Forty Martyrs of England and Wales.

Feast: Oct. 25 (Feast of the 40 Martyrs); Dec. 1 (Jesuits); May 4 (Feast of the English Martyrs in England).

See Also: ENGLAND, SCOTLAND, AND WALES, MARTYRS OF; OATHS, ENGLISH POST-REFORMATION; RECUSANT LITERATURE.

Bibliography: C. DEVLIN, *The Life of Robert Southwell: Poet and Martyr* (New York 1956). P. JANELLE, *Robert Southwell, the Writer* (New York 1935). H. FOLEY, *Records of the English Province of the Society of Jesus,* 7 v. (London 1877–82) *passim.* M. FITZ HERBERT, *An Epistle of Comfort* (London 1965).

[P. CARAMAN]

SOUTHWORTH, JOHN, ST.

Priest, martyr; b. Lancashire, 1592; d. Tyburn June 28, 1654. He belonged to the family of Southworths of Sameesbury near Preston. He entered the English College, Douai, on July 4, 1613; was ordained in 1618; and left for the English mission on December 13 the following year. He returned to Douai in March 1624, but in July 1625 left again for England, where he worked for five years in his native Lancashire. In 1627, he was arrested and was imprisoned in Lancaster Castle at the same time as Edmund ARROWSMITH, whom he absolved on his way to execution on Aug. 28, 1628. He was condemned for his priesthood but reprieved, and was next heard of in the Clink prison, Southwark, in March 1630. His name was included in an order for the banishment of priest prisoners, but it is uncertain whether he left the country. Henceforth his apostolate lay in London, where he showed heroic courage during the plague of 1636 to1637. With Henry MORSE he organized the relief for the Catholic poor, who by their religious profession were excluded from the assistance given by the parishes. He worked mostly in the Westminster district, where his activity aroused the jealousy of the curate of St. Margaret's, who in October 1636 secured his arrest and imprisonment in the Gatehouse. There he continued his work for the plague-stricken. He was released in June 1637 but recommitted the following November. His name occurs again among the prisoners in the Clink in June 1640. His movements are obscure between his last release in July that year and 1654, when he was seized in bed, condemned to death, and executed at Tyburn on June 28. The Spanish ambassador conveyed his quartered body to Douai, where it remained in the chapel of the English College until the confiscation of the seminary by the French revolutionary forces. It was then secretly removed, reburied elsewhere in the building, and in 1927 discovered by workmen excavating on the site. After identification it was transferred first to St. Edmund's College, Ware, and after Southworth's beatification on Dec. 15, 1929, to Westminster Cathedral, where it is now exposed for veneration. He was canonized by Paul VI on Oct. 25, 1970 as one of the Forty Martyrs of England and Wales.

Feast: Oct. 25 (Feast of the 40 Martyrs of England and Wales); May 4 (Feast of the English Martyrs in England).

Bibliography: A. B. PURDIE, *The Life of Blessed John Southworth . . .* (London 1930). E. E. REYNOLDS, *John Southworth . . .* (London 1962). R. CHALLONER, *Memoirs of Missionary Priests,* ed. J. H. POLLEN (rev. ed. London 1924). A. BUTLER, *The Lives of the Saints* 2:662–664.

[G. FITZHERBERT]

SOUVIGNY, ABBEY OF

Former Cluniac priory, burial place of the dukes of Bourbon, located at Souvigny. Founded in the tenth century by the then obscure feudal lord of the Bourbonnais, the monastery became a center of pilgrimage after the burial there of two famous abbots of Cluny, St. MAJOLUS (d. 994) and St. ODILO (d. 1049). The dukes of Bourbon alternately protected and attacked Souvigny. In the 13th century Robert, the youngest son of LOUIS IX, married the heiress of Bourbon; from this marriage HENRY IV derived his claim to the French throne in 1589. From the time of Duke Louis II (d. 1410) the family was buried there. In the 15th century the prior, Dom Chollet, restored the church by constructing a beautiful flamboyant Gothic nave on the sturdy Romanesque basilica. The tombs of Duke Charles and Duchess Agnes, sculptured by Jacques Morel (d. 1459?), are found in the new chapel. In the 16th century commendatory abbots collected the revenues but made no contribution to the development of Souvigny, which suffered also from internal decay. In the 17th century, however, the prior Nicolas des Mesgrigny renewed the spirit of the monastery and contributed to its history by collecting documents which form the *Thesaurus silviniacensis,* an incomplete but precious *corpus* for the history of the monastery. Souvigny was suppressed in 1791; two years later the Terror destroyed the house and the artistic accumulation of nine centuries.

Bibliography: S. MARCAILLE, *Antiquitez du prioré (sic) de Souvigny* (Moulins 1610). *Thesaurus silviniacensis,* ed. N. DE MESGRIGNY (1652). *Gallia Christiana,* v.1–13 (Paris 1715–85), v.14–16 (Paris 1856–65) 2:377–380. A. ALLIER, *L'Ancien Bourbonnais,* 2 v. (Moulins 1833–38); ed. M. FAZY in 4 v. (1934–38). A. BRUEL, ed., *Recueil des chartes de l'abbaye de Cluny,* 6 v. (Paris 1876–1903). N. DE NICOLAY, *Générale description du Bourbonnais,* ed. A. VAYSSIÈRE, 2 V. (Moulins 1889). G. DE VALOUS, *Le Temporel et la situation financière des établissements de l'ordre de Cluny du XIIe au XIVe siècle* (Paris 1935). L. CÔTE, *Contributions à l'histoire du prieuré clunisien de Souvigny* (Moulins 1942); *Moines, sires, et ducs* (1965).

[L. CÔTE]

SOVEREIGNTY

Sovereignty is a species of AUTHORITY, namely, political authority, the moral right of ultimate decision within a legitimately constituted STATE. Whether this supreme societal power is vested in the one, the few, or the many, it includes the right to direct by laws and other institutions and instrumentalities of GOVERNMENT, not excluding that of physical coercion, the activities of persons, families, and other subordinate societies toward the attainment of the common good. It embraces legislative, executive, and judicial power, the right of life and death, of war and peace. On the international level it demands the juridical independence of the state and its acceptance as an equal in the community of nations. Ideas such as these embraced by the term are as old as the state itself,

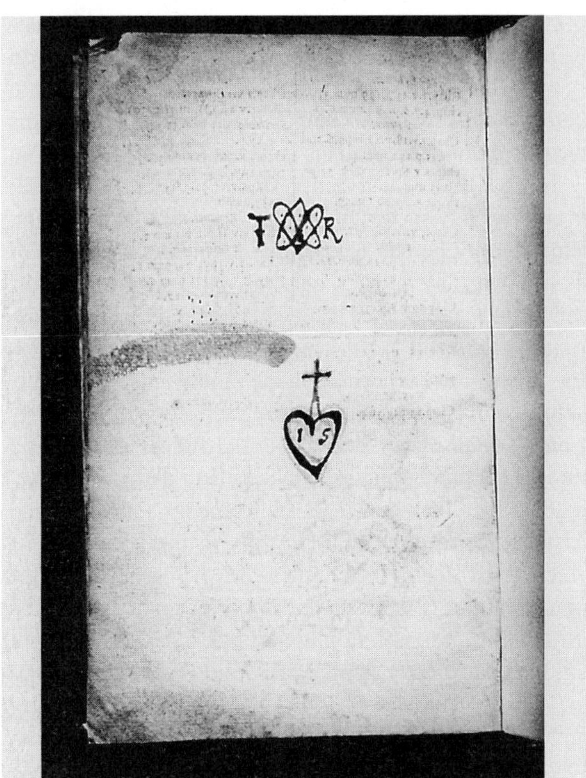

Book inscription, heart with initials J.S., reportedly a gift from John Southworth to his servant John Lillie.

and they were known to the Greek political philosophers and the Roman jurists, for example. However, sovereignty as a philosophical term came into use during postmedieval political developments, notably in the works of Jean Bodin (1530–96), alleged father of the term, Thomas HOBBES (1588–1679), and Jean Jacques ROUSSEAU (1712–78).

Origin. Sacred Scripture, papal teaching, and Catholic philosophy declare that sovereignty ultimately derives its origin from God. St. Paul, instructing the faithful on human dignity and the duty to obey civil authority, wrote, ''Let everyone be subject to the higher authorities, for there exists no authority except from God'' (Rom 3.1–7;1 Pt 2.13–17 and Jn 19.9–11). The *Syllabus* of Pius IX and the encyclicals of Leo XIII, Pius XI, Pius XII, and John XXIII present the Church's doctrine in regard to the origin, function, and limitations of sovereignty. In these documents sovereignty is ascribed to God, the author of man's nature. ''Every civilized community,'' Leo XIII said, ''must have a ruling authority and this authority, no less than society itself, has its source in nature and consequently has God for its author. It follows, then, that all power must proceed from God'' [*Immortale Dei, Acta Sanctae Sedis,* (Rome 1865–1908) ed. 18 (1885) 162].

The philosophical arguments of Catholic philosophers lead to the same conclusion. In them, MAN has been viewed consistently as a social and political being not merely by his own free choice but by the exigency of his intrinsic human nature. This is to say that man is obliged by the NATURAL LAW to accept or create right social order or civil society in which he may achieve the perfection demanded by human nature, that is, the development of his physical, intellectual, cultural, and moral potentials. This natural goal can be achieved only in and through association with his fellow men. Consequently, membership in SOCIETY, especially in the family and the state, is natural to man. It is an expression of his dynamic nature. It answers an essential demand and fulfills an intrinsic need of his human nature. Since human nature demands the existence of the state, it simultaneously requires the existence of all elements essential to the state, one of which is sovereignty. God, therefore, being the author of human nature, is likewise the author of the state and the origin of sovereignty. Edmund BURKE (1729–97) put the argument succinctly in his *Reflections on the Revolution in France:* "He who gave our nature to be perfected by our virtue willed also the necessary means of its perfection: He willed, therefore, the state" [*Works* (Boston 1881) 3.361].

Limitations. In accordance with this philosophical theory, in exercising sovereignty the state performs a twofold service function. First, it directs its activities toward the realization of the common good, while at the same time safeguarding the inviolable rights of the human person. Secondly, it maintains a stable order of peace and prosperity in and through which man, in the enjoyment of his God-given rights, may pursue within the confines of the common good his happiness and perfection. Sovereign power, therefore, although supreme and final in the direction of society toward the common good, is not absolute and unlimited. It is limited by its purpose, the common good, by the inviolable rights of the human person, and by the dictates of the natural law and the divine law. Any law or activity of the sovereign power that would deprive a person of his natural rights to ownership of property, to marry, or to worship God, for example, would be contrary to the will of God and the inviolable rights of the person and therefore *ultra rites,* not only immoral but also illegal. Political philosophers who deny that man is social and political by nature and those who advance positivistic theories of sovereignty are forced to posit the free will of man as the sole source of political society and sovereignty. Consequently, they are unable to establish a sound, objective justification either for man's obedience to or for any theoretical limitations on sovereignty. If the supreme authority of the state, sovereignty, is derived solely from the free will of man, there is no objective order of rights or any higher law to which both man and the state are subject. Nor is there any valid protection against the abitrary use of sovereignty and the creation of the absolute state. To say that God is the author of sovereignty is not to deny men the right in the actual formation or change of government to choose the form of government under which they wish to live and to locate sovereignty.

Bibliography: H. A. ROMMEN, *The State in Catholic Thought* (St. Louis 1945). L. STURZO, *Church and State,* tr. B. B. CARTER (New York 1939). J. MARITAIN, *Man and the State* (Chicago 1951). G. BOWE, *The Origin of Political Authority* (Dublin 1955). J. LECLERQ, *The Two Sovereignties* (New York 1952). THOMAS AQUINAS, *On Kingship, to the King of Cyprus,* tr. G. B. PHELAN, ed., I. T. ESCHMANN (Toronto 1949). F. SUÁREZ, *Selections from Three Works,* tr. G. L. WILLIAMS, 2 v. (Oxford 1944), contains *De Legibus, Defensio fidei,* and *De triplici virtute theologica.* R. BELLARMINE, *De laicis, or The Treatise on Civil Government,* tr. K. E. MURPHY (New York 1928).

[A. A. NORTH]

SOZOMEN

Greek Church historian; b. Bethelia near Gaza, Palestine, *c.* 400; d. Constantinople, *c.* 450. He was born of a Christian family converted by St. Hilarion. Salaminius Hermias Sozomen received his primary religious education in a monastery, studied law at Beirut, and practiced law in Constantinople under Theodosius II. He speaks of a historical epitome covering the history of the Church from the birth of Christ to the defeat of Licinius (323), but this work is lost. His Ecclesiastical History, written between 439 and 450 and dedicated to THEODOSIUS II, covers the period from 324 to 439 in nine books; however, the years 425 to 439 are missing. Sozomen frequently follows his contemporary SOCRATES, Historian, almost verbatim, but interpolates archival and Syriac material unknown to Socrates, for example, the persecution of the Christians in Persia under Sapor II, evidently based on the Acts of the Persian Martyrs. Stylistically, his work is superior to that of Socrates, but it is less critical and occasionally incorporates legendary material. A possible explanation for his less-critical sense arises from his desire to present monasticism as a guideline for his history of the Church.

Bibliography: *Patrologia Graeca,* ed. J. P. MIGNE (Paris 1857–66) 67:844–1630. R. HUSSEY, ed., *Ecclesiastica historia,* 3 v. (Oxford 1960). J. QUASTEN, *Patrology,* 3 v. (Westminster, Md. 1950–) 3:534–536. B. ALTANER, *Patrology,* tr. H. GRAEF from the 5th German ed. (New York 1960) 274. G. BARDY, *Dictionnaire de théologie catholique,* ed. A. VACANT, 15 v. (Paris 1903–50; Tables générales 1951–) 14.2:2469–71. N. H. BAYNES, *Journal of Theological Studies* 49 (1948) 165–168. W. TELFER, *ibid.* 50 (1949) 187–191. P. BATIFFOL, "Sozomène et Sabinos," *Byzantinische Zeitschrift* 7 (1898) 265–284. G. SCHOO, *Die Quellen des Kirchen-*

historikers Sozomenos (Berlin 1911). J. BIDEZ, *La Tradition manuscrite de Sozomène et la Tripartite de Théodore le Lecteur (Texte und Untersuchungen zur Geschichte der altchristlichen Literatur* 32.2b; 1908). W. ELTESTER, *Paulys Realenzyklopädie der klassischen Altertumswissenschaft,* ed. G. WISSOWA, et al. (Stuttgart 1893–) 3A.1 (1927) 1240–48.

[F. CHIOVARO]

SPACE

The term space, derived from the Latin *spatium.* has a variety of meanings both in ordinary language and in philosophical and scientific usage. While corresponding etymologically to the Greek στάδιον, it has a much wider meaning than the latter; thus it can signify distance or length, place, temporal duration or interval, or other types of dimensionality. In the Greek language there is no term corresponding to this broad signification of the Latin and modern term. It is difficult, then, to speak about the historical development of the concept of space. Rather one must speak about various concepts and problems that are more or less connected with the meanings attributed to the word in modern usage. This article proposes to do so by a philosophical analysis of the concept.

Philosophical Analysis. A philosophical analysis of the concept of space distinguishes a threefold aspect or usage of the concept, viz, the psychological, the mathematical, and the physical.

Psychological Aspect. According to the investigations of contemporary psychology, the representation of space is gradually formed in the consciousness of the child through a complex experience that begins from the very early months of his life. The senses principally involved in this experience present a whole field wherein single objects are perceptible; this forms, as it were, a unitary and permanent picture wherein individual objects appear and disappear. The unitary and permanent picture gradually becomes distinct and separate from the individual objects and, notably in the imagination, is established as something independent and existing in itself. Thus, by successive integrations, there is formed visual, tactile, imaginary, etc., space.

By reason of its very origin, the space pertinent to perception and imagination has an essential unity, an absolute center of reference, and privileged directions of up and down, length, width, and depth. With the extension of infantile experience, the space relevant to perception, initially limited to present perception, is progressively broadened and identified first with the space of familiar surroundings, places of travel and play, and the region about the horizon of one's own experience. Finally, by way of information gleaned from stories and schooling, it is identified with terrestrial space, wherein the earth, with its complex of mutually similar objects, constitutes the privileged and absolute platform on which bodies exist and physical phenomena develop and about which the celestial sphere moves with the stars.

This geocentric representation, which has formed the space of humanity for thousands of years, has the same characteristics of absoluteness and independence of individual bodies, together with unity, center, and privileged directions, as the primitive representation in the child. When the Copernican revolution substituted the heliocentric system for the geocentric, it did not make essential modifications in the representation of space. A more decisive and revolutionary step was taken shortly afterward: this resulted from the recognition of the sun's equality with other stars, the recognition of equivalence in inertial systems, and the definitive renunciation of privileged centers and direction—all associated with the beginnings of modern mechanics, especially the work of Galileo GALILEI. Did these developments imply a renunciation of all systems of extrinsic reference for the position and movement of bodies or of all stable platforms for the description of physical phenomena? In the 17th century an affirmative answer would have demanded an audacity of which a genial poet might possibly have been capable, but not a methodical and reflective scientist such as Isaac Newton. A man of his times, Newton restricted himself to the path that seemed safer and less risky for him. For the egocentric, geocentric, and heliocentric platform, he substituted the notion of absolute space, existing by itself, always conformed to itself, and immobile, infinite, and eternal, without being dependent upon particular terrestrial and heavenly bodies.

From the psychological point of view, Newton's absolute space constitutes the projection of imaginary space into the world of physical reality, while maintaining the same characteristics of unity, absoluteness, and necessity. In fact, although the fantasy can imagine that it is suppressing all existing bodies, it cannot suppress imaginary space. This is a matter however, of psychological necessity deriving from the fact that the imagination is an organic faculty and, therefore essentially spatial. However, as a spiritual faculty, the intellect—which has being as such as its object—can discern (that is, judge, and not merely imagine) that the world and space itself would not exist if matter were totally annihilated. The intellect, then, can recognize that imaginary space is fictitious entity lacking reality in itself, independent of material bodies. This realization opens the door to a more rational consideration of space through the sciences of mathematics and physics.

Mathematical Aspect. Mathemathical space, which is the proper object of classical geometry and its more recent generalizations, can be defined as pure EXTENSION. Absolutely considered in its essence, abstracting from all the concrete conditions of its realization, as well as from every relation, either of dependence or of content, to real bodies. As such, it is absolutely possible extension.

Mathematical space received a systematic treatment, admirable for its logical rigor and completeness, in the *Elements* of Euclid about the year 300 B.C. Transmitted through Arabian culture to medieval Europe, this treatise still constitutes the nucleus of geometric knowledge for the person of ordinary culture. At the basis of this teaching there is a natural, uncritical, and directly realistic conception taking fundamental notions (point, line, surface, etc.) from spontaneous intuition. It proceeds from principles held as evident and necessary truths, and it claims that all its propositions contain absolute truth. Euclidean space is three-dimensional, homogeneous, and isotropic, as well as infinite, or rather, indefinite. In it, parallel straight lines are equi-distant; there is the possibility of similar figures, and the form of geometric things is independent of their position and extension. In short, Euclidean space is straight, having no curvature.

All the properties of Euclidean space can be deduced by introducing a postulate, namely, Euclid's fifth postulate, which states in substance that through a point external to a straight line one and only line can be drawn parallel to that line. The evidence and necessity of this postulate, and equivalent statements that have been substituted for it, have been disputed since the time of Euclid's first commentators. In fact, it constitutes an extrapolation from immediate intuition, lacking logical justification. The critique of Euclidean geometry, through the work of many mathematicians, such as K. F. Gauss, J. Bolyai (1802–60), N. I. Lobachevskiĭ, and G. F. B. Riemann, has led to the conclusion that Euclid's postulate does not have an intrinsic and exclusive logical necessity, since it is possible to substitute opposite postulates for it. These lead to concepts of curved, hyperbolic, or elliptical spaces having properties different from those of Euclidean space, yet logically coherent and free from internal contradictions. This development has led to a generalization of the concept of mathematical space, further elaborated by the consideration of nonisotropic and differential spaces, of hyperspaces having more than three dimensions, and of functional spaces having infinite dimensions, etc.

The evolution of geometry, then, has shown the need for distinguishing the question of absolutely possible mathematical spaces from that of a really existing physical space. Rene DESCARTES and classical physicists deemed these questions to be identical.

Physical Aspect. By physical space is meant the first, fundamental, dimensional quantity that, along with time, enables one to describe the emotion of bodies, define velocity as the derivative of space with respect to time, and, consequently, determine the position of the body at the term of its motion. Two questions are posited in reference to physical space: (1) Does physical space haven an existence distinct from the bodies that fill it (or can there be space without matter)? And (2) What are the properties of physical space?

As regards the first question, the Greek atomists, in opposition to PARMENIDES, claimed that the void exists together with the plenum and that this is necessary for the multiplicity and motion of atoms. This teaching was restored by Pierre GASSENDI during the 17th century, in opposition to Descartes; the latter, identifying the essence of bodies with their extension, denied all possibility of empty space. Aristotle, and scholastic philosophers generally, deny the possibility of an absolute void; as a mere nonentity, this cannot exist in itself. Aristotelians explain the multiplicity and movement of bodies in terms of real divisibility of matter, itself made intelligible by the concept of potency. There would seem to be no validity Isaac Newton's arguments in favor of an absolute space independent of sensible bodies or fixed stars, since the position and movement of bodies can be explained in reference to the complex of sensible bodies or fixed stars, without recourse to a system of uncontrollable and purely imaginary reference. Physical space, then, is identical with the complex of extended bodies constituting the universe—not only directly sensible bodies, that is, solids, liquids, and gases, but also ether and the fields of modern physics.

As regards properties, man has always asked whether physical space is finite or infinite. According to the Ptolemaic conception, it was easy to deem physical space to be finite and limited by the outermost celestial sphere; according to the Copernican conception, however, one was led to think of space as open and infinite. More recently, equilibrium considerations in celestial mechanics and deductions from the theory of general relativity lead scientists to conceive of physical space as finite. In recent times a question has also arisen as to whether physical space is Euclidean or non-Euclidean. There is no absolute answer to this question, since all physical measurements for ascertaining the geometry of space are approximate and imprecise; one can speak only of a greater or lesser approximation to a geometric space. Within the limits of attainable measures and terrestrial experiments, physical space constitutes a good approximation to Euclidean space. Where astronomical distances are involved, however, it is more exact to say (in keeping with the theory of general relativity) that physical space is what Riemann has described it to be—elliptical, curved in its totality, and enclosed within itself, as a spherical hypersurface.

Finally, as regards the relations between space and time, the theory of special relativity rejects the absolute separation of these categories and claims the existence of a sole spatial-temporal physical reality, the space-time continuum, wherein spatial and temporal relations among various bodies and events depend upon the state of reciprocal movement.

See Also: CONTINUUM; PLACE; TIME; MOTION

Bibliography: M. J. ADLER, ed., *The Great Ideas: A Syntopicon of Great Books of the Western World,* 2 v. (Chicago 1952) 2:811–25. C. B. GARNETT, *The Kantian Philosophy of Space* (New York 1939). M. JAMMER, *Concepts of Space* (Cambridge, Mass. 1954). G. BACHELARD, *L'Experience de l'espace dans la physique contemporaine* (Paris 1937). L. P. EISENHART, *Reimannian Geometry* (Princeton 1949). F. GONSETH, *La Geometrie et le probleme de l'espace,* 6 v. (Neuchatel 1945–55). F. SOCCORSI, *Quaestiones scientificae cum philosophia coniunctae: De geometriis et spatiis non euclideis* (Rome 1960). A. EINSTEIN, *Relativity,* tr. B. W. LAWSON (15th ed. London 1953). A. S. EDDINGTON, *Space, Time and Gravitation* (Cambridge, Eng. 1920). H. MARGENAU, *The Nature of Physical Reality* (New York 1950). D. NYS, *La Notion de'espace* (Brussels 1922). F. SELVAGGI, *Cosmologia* (Rome 1962); *Scienza e metodologia* (Rome 1962).

[F. SELVAGGI]

SPADAFORA, DOMINIC, BL.

Dominican preacher; b. Randazzo, near Mt. Etna in Sicily, 1450; d. Monte Cerignone in Urbino, Dec. 21, 1521. He entered the Order of Preachers at St. Zita's Priory in Palermo. After ordination, he went to Padua, where he taught for several years. He then returned to Palermo, as the center of missionary work among the people of Sicily, for eight years. In 1487 he obtained the degree of master in theology and was called to Rome as assistant to Master General Joachim Torriani. Together they worked on the reform of the order until 1491, when Spadafora was commissioned to found a monastery of strict observance at Monte Cerignone near the shrine of Our Lady of Grace, and thus he was spared involvement in SAVONAROLA's tragic course toward execution for sedition and heresy. For 30 years he served as prior at the monastery and as missionary preacher to the people of central Italy. He was memorable for his wisdom, his ascetic spirit, and the constancy of his zeal for souls. Benedict XV beatified him Jan. 12, 1921.

Feast: Oct. 12, formerly Oct. 3.

Bibliography: A. BUTLER, *The Lives of the Saints,* rev. ed. H. THURSTON and D. ATTWATER (New York, 1956) 4:21–22. J. QUÉTIF and J. ÉCHARD, *Sciptores Ordinis Praeddicatorum,* 5 v. (Paris 1719–23); repr. 2 v. in 4 (New York 1959) 2.1:333. G. GIERATHS, *Lexikon für Theologie und Kirche,* ed. J. HOFER and K. RAHNER, 10 v. (2d, new ed. Freiburg 1957–65) 3:483. *Acta Apostolicae Sedis* 13 (1921) 104–108. R. DIACCINI, *Vita del B. Domenico Spadafora* (Foligno 1921).

[G. M. GRAY]

SPAIN, THE CATHOLIC CHURCH IN

Located on the Iberian peninsula in Europe, Spain (Estado Español) is bordered on the north by the Bay of Biscay and the French Pyrenees, on the east by the Mediterranean Sea, on the south by Morocco and the Strait of Gibraltar, and on the west by Portugal and the North Atlantic Ocean. Spain also includes the Balearic Islands in the Mediterranean and the Canary Islands in the Atlantic Ocean off the coast of Africa. With most of its land comprised of a flat plateau region, Spain has a strong agricultural base, producing grains, olives, grapes, and other crops, as well as beef, poultry, and pork. Predominately an industrial and service industry economy, Spain was plagued by higher-than-acceptable unemployment rate through much of the late 20th century. Governed as a socialist dictatorship following World War I, Spain reverted back to a monarchy in 1975.

Two-thirds of Spain's population live in the coastal regions. Although there are noticeable regional and linguistic diversities, the Spanish people are basically homogeneous in race and culture. The only true racial minority in Spain are the Gypsies whose number is estimated at several hundred thousand. Barcelona, Valencia, Seville, and Madrid are among the major cities.

The Spanish mainland has 15 geographic and historic regions that generally correspond to what were once Christian and Moorish kingdoms. The predominant religion in Spain is Roman Catholicism. Most non-Catholic Christians are Protestant, and among the newer sects the Jehovah Witnesses, by aggressive proselytizing, are most conspicuous. Among non-Christians, the Jewish community is prominent.

The four-part essay that follows deals with (1) the early history of Spain until A.D. 711, under Roman and Visigothic rule; (2) the medieval kingdoms, 711 to 1474; (3) the rise of modern Spain from 1474 to 1939; and (4) the close of the Spanish Civil War to 2000.

[EDS.]

Early History. Although first colonized by Phonecian and Greek peoples, Spain was christianized following its inclusion in the Roman Empire, *c.* 201 B.C., and its episcopacy organized along Roman lines. The conquering Germanic Visigoths, who ruled the region during the 4th century, supported Arianism until they were converted to Catholicism in 587. Visigoth rule was marked

Capital: Madrid.
Size: 194,419 sq. miles.
Population: 39,320,000 in 2000.
Languages: Castilian Spanish; regional dialects include Catalan, Galician, and Basque.
Religions: 33,028,800 Catholics (84%), 450,000 Muslims (1%), 786,400 Protestant and other denominations (2%), 5,054,800 without religious affiliation (13%).

by an important amalgam of Roman and Gothic law and by one of the most flourishing cultural periods of Spanish history, during which the episcopacy took an active part in the political affairs of the country.

Roman Rule. While no positive proof remains, it is believed that St. Paul planned to take the gospel to Spain, which had been incorporated into the Roman Empire by the time of Emperor Augustus. Both St. Irenaeus and Tertullian testified that there were Christians in Spain before A.D. 200. In 254 St. CYPRIAN OF CARTHAGE mentioned the bishops of Leén-Astorga, Mérida, and Saragossa and alluded to other unnamed sees. His letter revealed the close relationship that existed between Christians in Spain and in North Africa. In 259 St. FRUCTUOSUS and two of his deacons were martyred at Tarragona. At the Council of ELVIRA (*c.* 304), 43 bishops and priests represented 37 communities, all but five in south Spain. The great persecution begun by DIOCLETIAN (303–304) apparently claimed Christian martyrs in all five provinces of Spain: Galicia, Tarraconensis, Baetica, Carthagena, and Lusitania.

After establishing peace under Emperor Constantine, the Church increased in numbers despite being infiltrated with pagan influences. Spain produced several remarkable bishops and theologians in the 4th century, among them Hosius of Córdoba, Potamius of Lisbon, GREGORY OF ELVIRA, and PACIAN OF BARCELONA. This period also saw the rise of the Emperor THEODOSIUS I, the poets Juvencus and PRUDENTIUS, and probably the Virgin Aetheria, whose account of her travels to the East is of great interest.

A late 4th-century controversy caused by PRISCILLIAN reflected the difficulties encountered throughout western Europe by the monastic movement, although in this instance the struggle was exacerbated by the doctrinal insecurity betrayed by insistence on apocryphal writings. Priscillian's execution in 385 only encouraged the growth of PRISCILLIANISM, which survived in Galicia as a powerful movement until the late 6th century. Councils to combat Priscillianism were convoked at Saragossa (380) and at Toledo (400).

Visigothic Rule. The 5th century, with its wars and invasions, remains obscure. In 409 Spain was invaded by the barbarian ALANS, VANDALS, and Suevi. Vandals and Alans who survived the subsequent attack of the Germanic Visigoths in 418 moved to North Africa, while the Suevi withdrew to Galicia and part of modern Portugal. The main Visigothic movement into Spain took place in 496 and again after their loss of most of south Gaul to the Franks in 507. In 554 the Visigoths established their capital in Toledo. Baetica, which had resisted conquest by the barbarians, welcomed the Byzantines (552), who were expelled finally from south Spain only in 629. There is little evidence of religious persecution of the Church by the Arian Suevi or Visigoths. In the 6th century a number of councils were held, mostly in east Spain: Tarragona (516), Gerona (517), Toledo (527), Barcelona (540), Lérida (546), and Valencia (549). These councils, which reformed abuses, mark a revival of religious life, which was evident also in Christian literature. The Arian Suevi were converted to Catholicism by St. MARTIN OF BRAGA, who inspired two Councils of Braga (561, 572). The conversion of the Visigoths to Catholicism followed a civil war between King Leovigild and his Catholic son, St. HERMENEGILD, in Seville (580–584). After Leovigild's victory he conquered the Suevi, incorporating their kingdom into the Visigothic. After the murder of Hermenegild in 585 and the death of Leovigild a year later, Hermenegild's younger brother, King Recared, became a Catholic and in 589 officially brought the Visigoths into the Church.

The 7th century was the great age of Catholic Spain under the Visigoths. It saw an apparent Romanization of the Visigoths and a renaissance of Latin literature in cathedral and monastic schools, which produced such luminaries as St. ISIDORE OF SEVILLE (d. 636), St. BRAULIO OF SARAGOSSA (d. 651), St. EUGENE II (III; d. 657), St. ILDEFONSUS (d. 667), and St. JULIAN OF TOLEDO (d. 690). National and provincial councils were regularly held at Toledo from 589 to 702. The acts of provincial councils at Narbonne (589), Seville (590, 619), Huesca (598), Barcelona (599), Egara (614), Mérida (666), Braga (675), and Saragossa (691) also are preserved. The kings and some of the nobility attended the national councils, whose legislation was in large part intended to invest royal authority with moral force. The initiative lay with the kings, as with the emperors in Byzantium.

The Spanish Visigothic Church comprised 77 bishoprics in six provinces, under the archbishops of Toledo, Tarragona, Seville, Braga, Mérida, and Narbonne. Narbonne included several sees in Septimania; part of south Gaul was still subject to the Visigoths. The Church in Spain became increasingly nationalistic, more closely identified with the monarchy, suspicious of papal intervention (though recognizing papal primacy in theory), and more amenable to the persecution of the Jews, who were required to choose between baptism and slavery (694). By 681 the head of the Church was the archbishop of Toledo, who participated in all episcopal nominations as deputy of the king. The Church was governed by the *HISPANA COLLECTIO*, a collection of Canon Law drawn up by ISIDORE OF SEVILLE and revised by Julian of Toledo. This collection influenced Carolingian legislation, and Isidore's many writings were continually quarried and copied by later generations, beginning with the Irish in the 7th century. There was a strong monastic movement in Spain, both in the cities and in the countryside. In Galicia it was influenced by Irish asceticism and dominated by such figures as St. FRUCTUOSUS OF BRAGA (d. 667) and the hermit St. VALERIO OF BIERZO (d. *c.* 690). The Mozarabic liturgy, drawn up in the 6th and 7th centuries, was revised by Julian. The creeds of the Councils of Toledo signaled a step forward in the development of doctrine. Church architecture displayed interesting Byzantine influences.

The Visigothic kingdom, elective from 636 and weakened by incessant civil wars betwen factions of nobles, eventually succumbed to the Arab invasion from North Africa (711–714). The Church had tried to stabilize and support a strong monarchy; but in the last decades, it, too, became weak. Only in north Spain did Christian elements hold out. Elsewhere, the Church lived according to its tradition, dealing as best it could with Islam and heterodox Christian movements.

Bibliography: *Patrologia Latina*, ed. J. P. MIGNE (Paris 1878–90) 84. *Concilios visigóticos e hispano-romanos,* ed. J. VIVES et al., v.1 of España Cristiana (Barcelona 1963). J. VIVES, in *Miscellanea L. Ferotín* (Madrid 1965), Varones Apostólicos; *Inscripciones cristianas de la España romana y visigoda* (Barcelona 1942). K. ZEUMER, ed., *Leges visigothorum* (*Monumenta Germaniae Historica: Leges* (Berlin 1826–) 1.1; 1902). M. C. DÍAZ Y DÍAZ, *Index scriptorum latinorum medii aevi hispanorum,* 2 v. (Salamanca 1958–59). A. FÁBREGA GRAU, *Pasionario hispánico,* 2 v. (Madrid 1953–55), acts of martyrs. R. MENÉNDEZ PIDAL, ed., *Historia de España* (Madrid 1935–), v.2, *España romana* (1935), and v.3, *España visigoda* (Madrid 1940). P. B. GAMS, *Die Kirchengeschichte yon Spanien,* 3 v. in 5 (Regensburg 1862–79). Z. GARCÍA VILLADA, *Historia eclesiástica de España,* 3 v. in 5 (Madrid 1929–36). J. FERNÁNDEZ ALONSO, *La cura pastoral en la España romanovisigoda* (Rome 1955). J. N. HILLGARTH, "Coins and Chronicles: Official Propaganda in Sixth-Century Spain," *Historia* 14 (1965); "Visigothic Spain and Early Christian Ireland," *Royal Irish Academy: Proceedings* 62.C (1962) 167–194. R. AIGRAIN, A. FLICHE and V. MARTIN, eds., *Histoire de l'église depuis les origines jusqu'à nos jours* (Paris 1935–) 5:231–267. A. K. ZIEGLER, *Church and State in Visigothic Spain* (Washington 1930). J. M. LACARRA, in *Settimane di studio* v.7.1 (Spoleto 1960) 353–384. A. MUNDÒ, "Il monachesimo nella penisola iberica fino al sec. VII," *ibid.* v.4 (Spoleto 1957) 73–108. J. PÉREZ DE URBEL, *Los monjes españoles en la edad media,* 2 v. (Madrid 1933–34). A. ECHÁNOVE, "Precisiones acerca de la legislación conciliar toledana sobre los judíos," *Hispania sacra* 14 (1961) 259–279, Jews. P. B. HUGUET and H. SCHLUNK, *Ars Hispaniae* v.2 (Madrid 1947).

Metropolitan Sees	**Suffragans**
Burgos	Bilbao, Osma-Soria, Palencia, Vitoria
Granada	Almería, Cartagena, Guadix, Jaén, and Málaga
Madrid	Alcalá des Henares, Getafe
Mérida-Badajoz	Coria-Cáceres, Plasencia
Oviedo	Astorga, León, Santander
Pamplona y Tudela	Calahorra y La Calzada-Logroño, Jaca, San Sebastián
Santiago de Compostela	Lugo, Mondoñedo-Ferrol, Orense, and Tui-Vigo
Seville	Cádiz y Ceuta, Córdoba, Huelva, Canary Islands, Jerez de la Frontera, San Cristóbal de la Laguna, or Tenerife
Tarragona	Girona, Lleida, Solsona, Tortosa, Urgell, Vic
Toledo	Albacete, Ciudad Real, Cuenca, Siguenza-Guadalajara
Valencia	Iviza, Majorca, Minorca, Orihuela-Alicante, Segorbe-Castellón de la Plana
Valladolid	Ávila, Ciudad Rodrigo, Salamanca, Segovia, Zamora
Zaragoza	Teruel y Albarracín, Barbastro-Monzón, Huesca, Tarazona

[J. N. HILLGARTH]

MEDIEVAL SPAIN

The Visigothic kings, unable to command the loyalty of their subjects even with the occasional support of Spanish bishops, fell quickly before the sudden invasion of Arabs and Moors from North Africa in 711. One by one, lords and cities fell to the conquerors, except for groups in the northern mountains, one of which, in the Asturias, would eventually lay claim to the Visigothic inheritance. The region's new Arab governors—most of whom were subject to the emir of al-Qayrawān, who in turn depended on the caliph in Damascus—governed amid civil war from the strategic location of Córdoba in

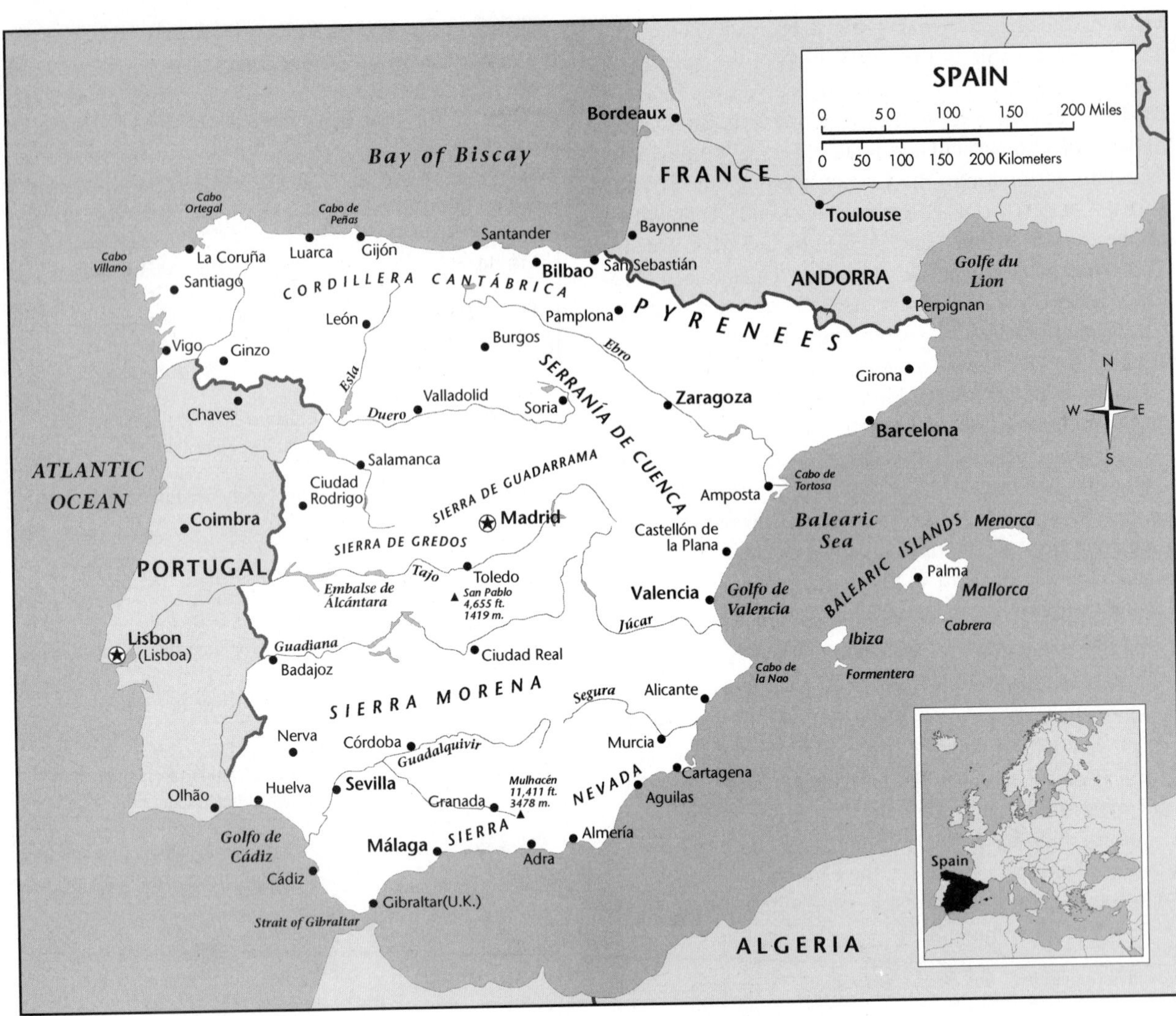

upper Andalusia. Their rule continued until 755 when Abd ar-Rahman I, refugee scion of the fallen UMAYYADS of Damascus, established a dynasty in Córdoba that lasted as an independent power in the Muslim world to 1031. The conquered land alloted to Arab tribes in 745 extended from Algarye to Murcia, and the levy of troops under Emir Mohammed I (852–886) came from an even smaller area; Córdoba itself was excluded from the allotment and the levy. Córdoba's control of the Meseta and the Mediterranean and Atlantic coasts was never strong or direct.

Christians under Muslim Rule. The Christian church, having deeper and stronger roots in the peninsula than the Visigoths, survived under the Muslims, the bishops retaining much of the administrative authority they acquired during the Roman Empire. At least 29 bishoprics survived under the Muslims, and seven ''national'' councils in Toledo (792), Seville (782, 823), and Córdoba (839, 852, 860, 862) dealt freely with matters of common interest in the absence of bishops from the Christian north.

Possibly because of efforts to accommodate the two religions and perhaps as a result of the influence of Christians of Syria, the Church in Spain suffered throughout Muslim rule from errors in discipline and doctrine, for the most part christological. Pope ADRIAN I (772–795), now allied with the new Frankish power which had been victorious at Tours (732) and elsewhere, felt enough concern to send letters and the missionary Egila to the Spanish bishops. But the bishops acquitted themselves before the Pope, while Egila fell victim to the heterodox teachings of the Spaniard Migetius, who was condemned by a council in Seville in 782 presided over by Abp. ELIPANDUS OF TOLEDO. In his attempt to maintain the primacy of Toledo (the last-known effort before its reconquest in 1085) and in his obstinate defense of ADOPTIONISM and of the traditional Spanish liturgy (*see* MOZARABIC RITE), Elipandus may have weakened the authority of Toledo and caused a division in the Spanish episcopate. He faced opposition from BEATUS OF LIÉBANA and Bp. Eterius of Osma, the authors of a lengthy treatise more important for the view it offers of Christian life and thought in the Asturias than for its refutation of Elipandus. Beatus compiled a commentary on REVELATION, the MSS of which offer an important link between early Christian and medieval art. ANTICHRIST figured prominently in the writings of Beatus and in a later work by Albar of Córdoba. In 851 EULOGIUS OF CÓRDOBA praised Bp. Wistremirus of Toledo, "the lamp of all Spain," for sanctity and learning. The bishops of Córdoba, despite their residence in the Muslim capital, do not seem to have exercised jurisdiction over the traditional metropolitans of Toledo, Seville, and Mérida.

The great achievement of Visigothic rule, the *Liber iudicum,* an amalgam of Roman and Visgothic law, continued, alongside the edicts of the emirs and decrees of church councils, to be the law of the Christians in Muslim areas. Some Christians apostatized from their Latin Christian heritage to accept Arabic culture and Islam, which enjoyed official precedence. Many Christians, however, were bilingual and knowledgeable in Islam as well as in their own religion, and into the mid-9th century a sufficiently large number of Muslims and apostate Christians identified themselves as Christians as to alarm the Muslims of Córdoba. Contemporary with the CAROLINGIAN RENAISSANCE, which attracted a number of Spaniards (THEODULF OF ORLÉANS, CLAUDIUS OF TURIN, AGOBARD OF LYONS, PRUDENTIUS OF TROYES), a renaissance of Latin learning in Córdoba began with Abbot Esperaindeo and flowered in his pupils Eulogius and Albar, whose works constitute the most important historical sources of early Muslim Spain. The strong cultural and religious competition that developed in Córdoba erupted in the martyrdom, in part voluntary, of some 50 Christians between 850 and 859. The martyrdoms disturbed Umayyad rule in Andalusia and coincided with a disruption of communications between Córdoba and Muslim Saragossa during this period, leaving the land between prey to brigands. The Abbot Samson's lengthy theological *Apologeticus* (864), dealing with cosmology, ANTHROPOMORPHISM, and PANTHEISM, prefigures the later philosophical literature of the Latin West that would also wrestle with Arabic ideas. Christian Córdoba collected texts, especially a corpus dealing with the prophet MUHAMMAD and Islam. Whether the renaissance there was without issue depends on what influence it had on later Mozarabic scriptoria and on later Arabic letters in Córdoba.

As a rule, the rebellions against Córdoba were based on issues of municipal independence, as had been the case under the Visigoths, rather than on religious or cultural differences. But Omar ibn Hafsun (d. 917), who returned to Christianity from a renegade family, in 879 stirred up a rebellion, motivated in part by religion, that his sons continued to 932.

The holy image of Montserrat, "Black Virgin."

Although Arabic letters flourished in Córdoba in the 9th century, extant Arabic works from Spain date from the late 10th century, when the glory of the caliphate, established in 929, was a thing of the past. Recemundus, a learned bilingual Christian, chancellor-ambassador of Abd ar-Rahman III (912–961), bishop of Granada, and author of an Arabic Christian liturgical calendar dedicated to the Caliph al-Hakam II (961–976), appeared at the court of Emperor OTTO I, where he struck up a friendship with LIUTPRAND OF CREMONA. Mozarabic scriptoria flourished at this time, and Córdoba was a center visited by Christian pilgrims. Christians fared well enough under Muslim rule until the reconquest of Toledo in 1085. The 25 or more petty municipal kingdoms (*taifas*), which had succeeded the caliphate in 1031, were overwhelmed by the Muslim Almoravid religious zealots from southern Senegal. These invaded Spain in 1086 and recaptured the

Interior view of Mudejar ceiling detail, geometric interlace pattern with the lion of Castile in center, built by Isabella and Ferdinand, 1510, San Juan de los Reyes Monastery, Toledo, Spain. (©CORBIS)

strategic port of Valencia from the Cid of Castile in 1102, while European crusaders were taking Jerusalem. Almoravid invasions (1146–1212) harmed Spain's Mozarab communities under the influence of the Church to the north and influenced by the GREGORIAN REFORM. Some Mozarabs immigrated to the north while others were deported to North Africa, much of their distinctive and traditional culture thus stamped out. In 1212 a united crusade of Spanish, French, and military orders broke Almohad power at Las Navas de Tolosa. Córdoba (1236) and Seville (1248) were reconquered, and only the kingdom of Granada, a link with North Africa, remained until 1492.

The Reconquest. The Reconquest (*Reconquista*) of Muslim Spain by the Christian kings of northern Spain characterizes most of medieval Spanish history. Although efforts to restore peninsular unity in the Visigothic tradition and assert the supremacy of Christianity figure prominently in the Reconquest, self-interest better explains many actions. Agricultural and commercial development, the growth of towns, the corporate enterprise of religious and military orders, centralized monarchies, and the universal papacy were among the goals of those who supported dispossessing the Moors to the south. Aragon wished to control the Mediterranean, from which she sought to exclude Castile. Castile hoped to control the major part of the peninsula and thus make others depend on her; her ambitions to expand in North Africa were restrained by Aragon, Portugal, and France. For many Spanish, however, reconquest would be achieved by the conversion of the Moors to Christianity.

In the north Christians reorganized the conquered peninsula into the kingdoms of Portugal, Castile, and Aragon. In 1139 Portugal became a separate kingdom independent of Castile. In 1037 Castile absorbed the kingdom of León and in 1479 united with Aragon under Ferdinand and Isabella. In 1162 Aragon joined with Catalonia (Barcelona) and became a maritime power with extensive Mediterranean interests. Navarre survived as a more or less independent state until it was absorbed by Aragon and France in 1512.

After Emperor Nicephoras II Phocas added Antioch to the Byzantine Empire in 969, the Fatimid caliphs of Tunisia moved to Cairo and the Umayyad caliphs of Córdoba extended their authority in the Moghreb. Diplomatic efforts by Córdoban kings were followed by sudden attacks against the Muslim frontier in northern Spain,

Segovia Cathedral visible through trees at left, designed by Juan Gil de Hontanon and Rodrigo Gil de Hontanon, built c. 1525–1590, and 1678, Segovia, Spain. (©Macduff Everton/CORBIS)

which were answered, especially after the death of Caliph al-Hakam II (976), by al-Manzor using auxiliary troops from North Africa. The Reconquest then moved down from the Pyrenees and, with French help, had by 1085 taken Toledo, thereafter the capital of the Reconquest. After the conquests of the Balearic Islands (1229), Valencia (1238), Córdoba (1236), and Seville (1248), the Reconquest was complete except for the Moorish principality of Granada.

While some lands reconquered from the Muslims suffered little, others had to be resettled and defended. Initially repopulation was overseen by bishoprics and monasteries; later settlement was effected by the efforts of Cluniacs, Cistercians, and the Cistercian-affiliated military orders. Grants of *fueros* (privileges, franchises, and immunities), beginning in the 11th century, attracted settlers and provided law and government for areas far from royal control. The *fueros*, which reached a peak in the 12th and 13th centuries and declined *c.* 1300, modified the Visigothic *Fuero juzgo,* which Alfonso II (793–842) had restored as the basic law of the Reconquest. Under the influence of revived Roman law, efforts were made at legislative unity from the time of Ferdinand III (1217–52). The maze of charters and liberties accumulated in the peninsula over several centuries would be among the problems faced by Ferdinand and Isabella.

Papal Relations. In 918 Pope JOHN X sent a legate to Santiago to inspect the ancient Spanish (Mozarabic) rite. While the rite was approved in a Roman synod of 924 and at the Council of Mantua in 1067, Rome wanted it replaced by the Latin. The decree of the cardinal legate Richard and Alfonso VI (1078) was officially confirmed by the Council of Burgos (1080), and the Mozarabic rite survived only in chapels in Toledo and Salamanca. The popes also intervened in Spain because of civil wars and royal marriages within the forbidden degrees of kinship. Alfonso Enriquez of Portugal and Peter II of Aragon made themselves vassals of the Holy See and established special ties with Rome. Henry II of Castile and Peter IV of Aragon were neutral in the WESTERN SCHISM, which began in 1378, but collected papal revenues in Spain until the congresses of Alcalá and Barcelona chose to support the Avignon popes. Spain supported the Spanish-born Benedict XIII until 1416 (after his death in 1423 his relics were reported to work miracles.) The election of bishops, as a rule the privilege of cathedral chapters, by the 14th century came to be reserved to the popes with the kings having the right of presentation. Popes gave generously

Loyalist firing squad takes aim at statue of Jesus Christ surmounting cluster of religious figures, 1936, Cerro de Los Angeles, Spain. (AP/Wide World Photos)

from the Church's wealth, derived from voluntary contribution and tithes, to assist the kings in their wars against the Moors. The royal third (two-ninths of the tithes) given to Alfonso X by Gregory X was made a perpetual gift by Alexander VI. More than 130 church councils were held in Spain between 711 and 1474.

Culture and Literature during the Medieval Period. During the early years of the Reconquest, Church cultural activity was at first generally restricted to copying MSS in monastic scriptoria, especially in Bobadilla, Cardeña, Silos, Berlangas, Cuxa, Gerona, and Vich. The Visigothic script was used until suppressed by the Council of León in 1091, although Caroline minuscule appeared in Catalonia in the 9th century. As the frontier moved south and as relations with the rest of Europe increased, in part because of the pilgrimage route to Santiago de Compostela, cultural activity expanded and increased from the 11th century. Noteworthy Romanesque monasteries and churches were built in Ripoll, San Juan de las Abadesas, Lérida, Tarragona, Leyre, Jaca, Loarre, León, Palencia, and Santiago. In the 13th century Gothic cathedrals of note appeared in Burgos, Toledo, León, Barcelona, Palma de Majorca, and Gerona. Bishops sought to raise the level of their clergy through cathedral schools. Under Abp. Raymond of Toledo (1126–52) a school of translators transmitted Arabic learning into Latin. Under royal patronage universities were founded, replacing the cathedral schools: Palencia (1212), Salamanca (1220), Seville (1254), Valladolid (1260–64), Alcalá de Henares (1293), Lérida (1300), Huesca (1354), Perpignan (1354), Gerona (1446), and Saragossa (1474).

While the 13th century saw the founding of universities, mendicant orders fostered zeal, and RAYMOND OF PEÑAFORT opened a *studium arabicum* in Tunis (1250). Missionary activity was promoted not only for Moors and Jews in the peninsula but also for carrying the Gospel to

Unfinished interior of Gaudi's Sagrada familia, Barcelona, Spain. (©Macduff Everton/CORBIS)

foreign lands. Spanish missionary activity in Morocco was almost continuous from at least the 13th century. Mysticism and asceticism informed much of the spiritual life. Heretical and heterodox movements also appeared. Lucas of Tuý (d. 1249), a chronicler in León, wrote a treatise against the ALBIGENSES, who made some headway in Aragon and Catalonia. BEGUINES, FRATICELLI, and divers POVERTY MOVEMENTS appeared in Narbonne, Gerona, Barcelona, Tarragona, Valencia, Majorca, and elsewhere: disciples of PETER JOHN OLIVI, JOACHIM OF FIORE, Arnold of Villanova (d. 1311), and Philip of Majorca (d. *c.*1340). In response, Pope Gregory IX would begin the INQUISITION by asking Abp. Espárrago de Barca of Tarragona (d. 1233) to act against the heretics. The Inquisitor General Nicholas Eymerich (d. 1399) compiled a famous *Directorium inquisitorum.* The vernacular came to be a frequent vehicle for writings.

Although much of the literature translated from Arabic was philosophical and philosophy and theology were of great importance in the universities, no outstanding Spanish theologians emerged during the early Middle Ages; Spanish literature for the most part consisted of historical chronicles and practical religious writings, apologetical or polemical treatises against Judaism and Islam, the vitae and miracles of saints, and sermons or treatises promoting a more perfect Christian life. Works of the 8th and 9th century may be regarded as Mozarabic, but thereafter Christian writings seem to come almost entirely from Christian Spain. Until the Reconquest was completed near the 13th century, Christian works, somewhat sparse, consisted mainly of HAGIOGRAPHY.

Judaism contributed substantially to Spanish letters, inasmuch as it occasioned many apologetical and polemical works and several converted Jews were prominent authors in the late Middle Ages. The *Introduction to the Duties of Hearts* by 11th-century Jew Bahya ibn Paqûda, of Córdoba or Seville, is a spiritual work of great value. Salvus (d. 972), abbot of ALBELDA, composed a rule for nuns and several liturgical writings. Oliva (d. 1046), abbot of Ripoll, founder of MONTSERRAT, and bishop of Vich, was a literary figure. Peter Alfonsi (1062–1140), a converted Jew of Huesca, composed a *Disciplina clericalis* in the form of a fabliau as well as a Latin dialogue against Judaism. Peter of Compostela imitated Augustine, Boethius, and Isidore of Seville in his *De consolatione rationis* (1140–50). The translator DOMINIC GUNDISALVI showed the influence of Arab philosophy in his *De anima* and *De processione mundi.* MARTIN OF LEÓN (d. 1203) left a large corpus of sermons.

FRANCISCANS and DOMINICANS were prominent in Spain in the later Middle Ages. In the former group, Raymond LULL (1232–1315) dominated the period, writing prolifically on a variety of subjects. John Gil of Zamora (*c.* 1300) composed a number of works in Latin and Castilian on the Blessed Virgin and saints. ALVARO PELAYO (1275–1349) wrote exhaustively in the interest of general Church reform. Francis Eximenis (1340–1409) composed mystical works in Catalan and Latin. The reformer Lope de Salinas (d. 1463) wrote spiritual guidance in Castilian. Among the Dominicans, founder St. DOMINIC GUZMAN (d. 1221) was himself a Spaniard. The famous Orientalist RAYMOND MARTINI (d. 1286), a converted Jew, composed among other works a treatise against Moors and Jews. Rodrigo el Cerratense (d. 1290) compiled a collection of vitae of Spanish saints that influenced later periods. The *Vergel de consolación del alma o Viridario* of James of Benavento (d. 1350), a study of sin and virtue, was influential in the development of Spanish literature. John of Monzon (d. 1412) and Sancho Porta (d. 1429) left works on the Blessed Virgin. Miracle worker St. VINCENT FERRER (1346–1419) composed a number of sermons and treatises. Cardinal Juan de TORQUEMADA (d. 1468) wrote a series of spiritual and theological works, while Antonio de Canals (d. 1418), Alfonso de San Cristobal (d. 1440), and Juan López (d. 1490) wrote on penitence and the spiritual life.

The Carthusian Boniface Ferrer (d. 1417), brother of St. Vincent, translated the Bible into Valencian for the first time, but as it lacked critical notes the edition was burned in 1478. Carmelites Guido Terrena (d. 1342), Francis Bacó (d. 1372), Juan Ballester (d. 1374), Francis Marti (d. 1390), and Philip Ribot (d. 1391) wrote sermons and works on the spiritual life, the Blessed Virgin, and on heretics and infidels. The Augustinian Bernard Oliver (d. 1348) composed an *Excitatorium mentis ad Deum* and a *Tractatus de inquisitione Antichristi;* and Lope Fernández de Minaya (d. after 1475) wrote on penitence and the spiritual life. The Mercedarian PETER PASCUAL (d. 1300), defender of the Immaculate Conception, left extensive apologetical writings in the vernacular; Antonio Tajal (d. 1417) composed a *Rosa ad auroram* on the Immaculate Conception. Lope de Olmedo (d. 1433) and Alfonso of Oropesa (d. 1478) wrote sermons and works of importance for Hieronymites.

Diego Garcia (1140–1218), chancellor of Castile, composed a *Planeta* in seven books in which, while discussing Christ the King, the Blessed Virgin, St. Michael, and peace in the Church, he criticized the morals of his time. The spiritual poetry of Gonzalo de Berceo (d. after 1246) is the earliest poetry in Castilian. The works of Alfonso de Valladolid (d. 1346), the first converted Jew to use the vernacular to defend his new faith, gave new impetus to preaching in Burgos. Pedro de Luna, Antipope BENEDICT XIII (d. 1423), left a *Vitae humanae adversus omnes casus consolationes,* a *Liber de consolatione theologiae,* and a *Tractatus de horis dicendis per clericos.* Pablo de Santa Maria (d. 1435), a converted rabbi and bishop of Cartagena and Burgos, turned to Holy Scripture to defend the Eucharist and the Blessed Virgin. His son, Alfonso of Cartagena (1384–1456), who succeeded him as bishop of Burgos, dealt with historical and religious matters in his works. The learned Alonso TOSTADO DE MADRIGAL (d. 1455), bishop of Ávila, was a prolific author of commentaries on Holy Scripture and treatises on the Mass. Alfonso Martínez of Toledo (d. 1470), archpriest of Talavera, is known chiefly for his satire on women, *El Corbacho.* Rodrigo Sánchez de ARÉVALO (d. 1470) composed the first history of Spain arranged according to papal reigns. The *De confessione* of Peter of Osma (d. 1480) was condemned by Sixtus IV for doctrinal errors. Pedro López de Ayala (1332–1407), chancellor of Castile whose contemporary chronicle deals with social institutions, was also a translator of works of Pope St. Gregory I, St. Isidore, and Boethius. The lay poet Juan de Mena of Córdoba (d. 1456) composed pieces on Virtues and Vices, on the Seven Deadly Sins, and a *Laberinto* in imitation of Dante. The works of Fernand Pérez de Guzmán (d. 1460), humanist, moralist, and poet, are also of religious interest.

Kingdom of Navarre. The people of the western Pyrenees, led by the kings of Pamplona, had retained their independence of Romans, Visigoths, Franks, and Moors; their land was both a buffer state and a bone of contention between Asturias-León-Castile and Aragon. Charlemagne razed Pamplona in 778 as he returned to the Saxon wars from his bootless expedition to Saragossa, but his rear guard was decimated by Basques in the pass of Roncevalles. Iñigo Arista in the early 9th century began a Christian dynasty that came to prominence with Sancho I Garcés (905–925). With Ordoño II of León in 917 Sancho defeated the emir of Córdoba and in 918 raided the upper Ebro valley. In 920 the emir defeated the two kings in the battle of Valdejunquera, sacked Pamplona, and replaced the Banu Kasi dynasty of Saragossa with the

Tuchibis. In 924 Sancho founded the monastery of Albelda, which soon became the cultural center of the Rioja; his son and daughter married into the dynasties of Aragon and Castile.

Beginning with Queen Tota's regency of her son Garcia I Sánchez (925–970), Navarre intervened in the affairs of Castile and became allied with Muslim and Christian alike in an effort to obtain hegemony among the northern Christian kingdoms, siding with León and Castile in the victory over Córdoba at Simancas in 939. Sancho II Garcés (970–995), who enjoyed peace with Córdoba, endowed the monasteries of San Pedro de Siresa (971), San Andres de Cirueña (972), and San Juan de la Peña (983, 987), meanwhile extending Navarre's influence east to Ribagorza. The mother of Caliph Hisham II of Córdoba (976–1013) came from Navarre; and al-Manzor, actual ruler of Córdoba (981–1002), married princesses from León and Navarre. Almost all northern Spain was ruled by Sancho III Garcés the Great (1000–35), who introduced the CLUNIAC REFORM to San Juan de la Peña in 1020, restored the monastery of San Victorian and the bishoprics of Roda and Pamplona, and granted fueros to cities. He divided his realm among four sons: Ferdinand I in Castile, Ramiro I in Aragon, Garcia III in Navarre, and Gonzalo in Sobrarbe and Ribagorza. Garcia III Sánchez (1035–54), who made a pilgrimage to Rome, was slain by his brother Ferdinand in the battle of Atapuerca; and Sancho IV Garcés (1054–76), who allied with Aragon against Castile, was assassinated. The Navarrese then elected as king Sancho Ramírez (1076–94) to put an end to the invasion of their land by Alfonso VI of Castile. In 1060 the Council of Jaca was presided over by (St.) Austinde (1042–68), Archbishop of Auch. Auch was a metropolitan see having jurisdiction over Navarre and Aragon until the restoration of the See of Tarragona in 1118.

Sancho Ramírez, Peter I (1094–1104), and Alfonso I (1104–34) ruled Aragon and Navarre. García Ramírez (1134–50) and Sancho VI (1150–94) kept Navarre independent of Aragon and Castile. Sancho VII (1196–1234) traveled to Morocco in 1198 and 1199 to ally with the sultan against a Castile-Aragon alliance, and in 1202 he made an alliance with King John of England; but he sided with Castile in the victory over the Moors at Las Navas de Tolosa in 1212. On his death the Navarrese repudiated his agreement that Navarre should pass to James I of Aragon and elected as king his nephew, Thibault I of Champagne (1234–53), who favored the CISTERCIANS and made Pamplona a center of troubadors. Thibault II (1253–70) married Isabelle, the daughter of LOUIS IX OF FRANCE, and followed the French king on his crusades. From the marriage of Joan I (1274–1305), Thibault's niece, to PHILIP IV OF FRANCE in 1284 Navarre was ruled by the kings of France through French governors. The Évreux dynasty began with Philip III (1329–43), whose wife Joan waived her claims to the French throne. During the Hundred Years' War Charles II the Bad (1349–87) centralized the administration of Navarre and took an active part in events in France and Spain. In 1377 the Navarrese company under Louis of Évreux conquered Albania and then took over the conquests of the Catalan company in Greece, but its power declined by 1402. Under Charles III the Noble (1387–1425) Navarre enjoyed peace and justice. Charles's daughter Blanche (1425–42) was succeeded by her husband, John I (1442–79), the son of Ferdinand I of Aragon and a member of the Castilian house of Trastamara, and their son Charles of Viana (1442–61).

Amid civil war in Navarre John I succeeded in disinheriting Charles, who fled to Naples in 1455 but was unable to obtain help from Alfonso V, who died in 1458 leaving Aragon to John. Charles then tried to marry Isabella, sister of Henry IV of Castile, but was imprisoned by John; he was released after a general protest, but died suddenly. His sister and heir, Blanche, imprisoned by John, died in 1464. John was succeeded in Aragon by his son Ferdinand II, who had married Isabella of Castile in 1469, and in Navarre by his daughter Leonore (1479), married to the Count of Foix. Leonore was succeeded by her grandson Francis I (1479–83) and granddaughter Catherine (1483–1515), both minors under the regency of their mother Madeleine, sister of Louis XI of France. Catherine's marriage to Jean d'Albret in 1486 led to the occupation of Navarre by Ferdinand of Aragon and the loss of its independence (1512–15). The part of Navarre north of the Pyrenees went to France.

Asturias and León. The history of the Asturian kings is seated on a rivalry between Galicia and the Asturias and between the Church and the Crown. Alfonso I (739–757) reconquered lands stretching from Galicia to Castile, restoring episcopal sees and devastating areas he could not hold to leave a no-man's-land between Christians and Muslims that lasted through most of the Reconquest. Under Aurelius (768–774) there was an uprising of slaves against their masters, and Silo (774–783) had peace with the Moors "because of his mother." Alfonso II (793–842), friend of Charlemagne, resumed the war against the Muslims. He founded the See and cathedral of Oviedo, where he built churches and palaces in an attempt to make it the successor of Visigothic Toledo. During his time the tomb of St. JAMES (SON OF ZEBEDEE) was discovered in Santiago. Christian arms had great success under Alfonso III (866–909); during his reign Oviedo became a metropolitan see (874) and the basilica of Compostela was built (899). He abdicated and left his realm, comprising Galicia, León, and the Asturias, to his three sons. In 924 the three kingdoms were reunited under León.

Ramiro II of León (931–951), who built the monastery of San Salvador in León, defeated the new caliphate of Córdoba at Simancas (939) and at Talavera (950) but could not control the counts of Castile. The first *cortes*—a gathering of nobles and clergy—were held in León in 934 and 937. Sancho I the Fat (956–966) was cured of obesity in Córdoba (959) and obtained for León the relics of the martyr St. Pelagius of Córdoba (d. 925). Under Alfonso V (999–1028), who resumed the Reconquest after the death of al-Manzor, the politicoreligious Council of León (1020) granted the famous fuero of León. The royal dynasty became extinct at the death of Bermudo II (1028–37), and León went to Ferdinand I of Castile.

The counts of Castile, known from 824, had become independent of León as Fernán González (923–970) was closing his career. Sancho Garcés (995–1017), who made an entry into Córdoba in 1009 at the end of the caliphate, granted many fueros to towns. At the death of García Sanchez (1017–28) Castile reverted to Sancho III of Navarre (1028–35) and his wife. Their son Ferdinand I (1037–65), confirmed the fueros of Castile at the reform Council of Coyanza (1050). The Muslim rulers of Badajoz, Saragossa, Toledo, and Seville did homage to him. In 1062 Ferdinand obtained from Seville for his capital León the relics of St. ISIDORE, the father of Spanish learning. Ferdinand died besieging Valencia.

When Sancho II of Castile was treacherously killed at Zamora, Alfonso VI (1065–1109) returned from his refuge in Muslim Toledo. In 1085 he took Toledo, giving Valencia as a fief to its dispossessed ruler, receiving homage from a number of Muslim rulers, and calling himself "Emperor of the Two Religions." The Almoravid Muslim zealots, called in from North Africa to stop the rout of Islam, devoted themselves to reorganizing a Muslim monarchy in the south and left Alfonso, who failed to take Saragossa in 1086, free in his own lands. There Alfonso supported the official change from the Visigothic or Mozarabic rite to the Roman. Valencia, taken in 1094 by Alfonso's estranged vassal, El Cid, was yielded to the Almoravids in 1102 by El Cid's widow. Alfonso died at the age of 79, the year after his only son was slain in the battle of Uclés (1108). The prowess of the half-legendary Cid (b. Burgos, *c.* 1040; d. Valencia, 1099), known through the *Cantar* or *Poema de mio Cid* and through later chronicles, was compared in an epitaph by Alfonso X with that of imperial Rome, King Arthur, and Charlemagne.

The heiress of Alfonso VI, Urraca (1109–26), daughter of Alfonso's second wife, Constance of Burgundy, and widow of the count of Galicia, Raymond of Burgundy (d. 1107), had one of the most complicated reigns in Spanish history. She had to deal with the threat of Aragon in the person of her spouse, Alfonso I, until the annulment of their marriage in 1114; with revolt in Galicia, centering around the powerful archbishop of Santiago, Diego Gelmírez; and with the claims of Portugal, a county founded after the Almoravid victory at Lisbon in 1094 as a vassal of Galicia. Alfonso VII (1126–57), called *Imperator* of all Spain at the cortes of León in 1135, moved the frontier south to the Guadiana River. In 1142 at the peace of Zamora he recognized the independence of Portugal. He took Córdoba (1146) and, with help from Pisa, Genoa, and Montpellier, also Almeria (1157), but he lost them to the fierce and destructive Almohads from North Africa who entered Spain to halt once again the march of Christian arms. Alfonso left his realm to two sons, Sancho II of Castile (1157–58) and Ferdinand II of León (1157–88).

Alfonso VIII of Castile (1158–1214), founder of the University of Palencia (1212), withstood a confederation of Navarre, Aragon, and León in 1191 and led Christians to a lasting victory over the Almohads at Las Navas de Tolosa in 1212. Neither León nor Portugal sent troops for the famous battle; and many French, Germans, and Italians left the widely proclaimed crusade in Spain that had won the support of INNOCENT III. When Alfonso died, the hegemony of Castile in Spain was clear. After 14-year-old Henry I (1214–17) was killed at play, his sister Berenguela abdicated in favor of her son by Alfonso IX of León, Ferdinand III (1217–30). Alfonso IX (1188–1230), founder of the University of Salamanca, had serious conflicts with the papacy over his marriages with Bl. THERESIA of Portugal and Berenguela of Castile.

The late Middle Ages in Castile were introduced by the triumphal reign of (St.) FERDINAND III, who, after its capture in 1248, made Seville his residence. Having defeated the Moorish fleet, he prepared to invade Morocco but was prevented by death. His last years were contemporary with the Crusade to Palestine and Egypt (1248–54) of Louis IX of France, son of Blanche of Castile (d. 1252). While an uprising of Andalusian Moors prevented ALFONSO X (1252–84) from invading Morocco, he also worked vainly to obtain the HOLY ROMAN EMPIRE (1256–75). When Alfonso's support of the succession of his grandson Ferdinand de la Cerda over his second son Sancho caused him to be deposed in 1282, he allied with Morocco and France against Sancho, who found a ready ally in Aragon. Alfonso died in Seville. Sancho IV (1284–95) repelled an invasion from Morocco as Philip III of France, with papal blessing, led his ill-fated invasion of Aragon in retaliation for Aragon's seizure of Sicily after the Sicilian Vespers (1282). Ferdinand

IV (1295–1312), king at the age of nine, was succeeded by Alfonso XI (1312–50), who became king at one year of age. A Moroccan invasion of Spain was defeated on land and sea by Alfonso with help from Aragon and Portugal in 1340. With Abp. Gil ALBORNOZ of Toledo he reorganized Castile (1344–50), especially in the *Ordenamiento* of Alcalá (1348). In 1348 the Black Death took a heavy toll in Spain. On Alfonso's death at the siege of Gibraltar his policies were reversed under Peter I (1350–69), king at the age of 15.

Peter warred without success from 1356 against Aragon, France, Bertrand du Guesclin's free companies, and his rival Henry, eldest illegitimate son of Alfonso XI, of the house of Trastamara, which was to succeed also to the crown of Aragon in 1412. After slaying Peter and gaining the throne of Castile, Henry II Trastamara (1369–79) then had to fight against several Spanish cities—Portugal, Granada, Navarre, Aragon, and John of Gaunt (Duke of Lancaster)—all of which took advantage of the irregularity of his succession. He sent the Castilian fleet to aid France against England in the Hundred Years' War and was planning to complete the Reconquest when he was murdered. John I (1379–90), who became king at 21, continued naval aid to France and recognized the Avignon pope in the Western Schism. In 1383 he replaced the Spanish Era with the normal Christian chronology (A.D.), and in 1385 lost a chance to unite Spain and Portugal in the brutal battle of Aljubarrota. John died after falling from his horse. The accession of Henry III (1390–1406), who came to the throne at 11, was marked by massacres of Jews by the people of Seville, Córdoba, Toledo, and elsewhere (1391). Henry cleared the straits of Gibraltar of pirates (1400); sent embassies to the Ottoman Bajacet I and Tamerlane (1403); and added to the crown (1402–05) the Canary Islands, discovered in 1341. John II (1406–54), who became king at age two, continued the war against Granada. Ferdinand, his uncle and regent, became Ferdinand I of Aragon (1412–16); in 1418 John married Ferdinand's daughter Maria. Henry IV the Impotent (1454–74), king at 30, kept a large army but did little fighting against the Moors. With a claim to the throne of Navarre through his first wife Blanche, he offered his sister Isabella in marriage to Charles of Viana. The marriage of Isabella to Ferdinand of Aragon in 1469 augured that Castile's future lay with Aragon and its Mediterranean interests rather than with Portugal and its Atlantic and African discoveries. In 1470 Henry, who had repudiated Joan (*la Beltraneja*), born to his second wife Joan of Portugal, declared her legitimate and heir to Castile; but later he was reconciled with his sister Isabella.

Monarchical authority grew strong under Ferdinand III, who made Castilian the official language, published the *Fuero juzgo* in Castilian, and began work on a general legal code. Alfonso X and Alfonso XI continued this tradition; but the power of the nobles increased during the frequent regencies because of illegitimate royal offspring and royal protection of the families of concubines and favorites. The cortes, representing the main cities, the nobility, and the clergy, reached a peak under John I but declined under Henry IV; those of Castile and León continued to meet separately until 1301. Towns of democratic origins and seeking freedom from nobles and bishops reached a peak in the 13th and 14th centuries but declined in the 15th under the influence of Roman law. *Hermandades* or leagues of towns, originating in the fuero of Salamanca (*c.* 1200) and its association of 13 towns, were prohibited by the cortes of 1252; but in 1282 a hermandad of prelates and nobles was thriving. Hermandades of laborers, of public peace, and of ports on the Bay of Biscay also existed. The cortes of Guadalajara (1390) created a standing army. The regent Ferdinand used gunpowder and many machines of war at Zahara in 1408. From the time of Alfonso X, Castile, whose navy was stronger than that of the English, kept two fleets, one in the Bay of Biscay and one in the south.

The Crown of Aragon. The 9th-century county of Aragon, which derived its name from the Arrago River, became independent of Navarre in 1035, and had Saragossa as its capital after 1118. In 1137 it was united with Catalonia (Barcelona), whose counts had absorbed the Spanish March of the Carolingians. Aragon's basic interests were peninsular, Catalonia's Mediterranean. With the inclusion of Majorca (1229), Valencia (1238), Sicily (1282), Sardinia (1324), Athens (1311), and Naples (1442) Aragonese history became that of several kingdoms known as the Crown of Aragon.

Catalonia. Augustus had ruled the Roman Empire temporarily from Tarragona, capital of Tarraconensis; while Barcelona, Arian under the Visigoths, had close ties with Vandal North Africa. After Clovis broke Visigothic power in Gaul (507), the Ostrogoths of Italy intervened to divide France's Mediterranean coast between themselves and the Visigoths. Visigothic Septimania (Narbonne) and Tarraconensis were not successfully ruled from Toledo; the Arabs took Saragossa *c.* 713 and moved quickly down the Ebro to the sea. Count Fortunius of Tarragona became a Muslim and founded the Banu Kasi dynasty of Saragossa (replaced by the Tuchibi in 924), which became, in fact, an independent kingdom nominally dependent on Moorish Córdoba. Both Banu Kasi and Tuchibi married Christians and allied with Christians. After Charlemagne organized the kingdom of Aquitaine for Louis the Pious, the Franks began to attack Catalonia. Whole districts of refugee Visigoths migrated and settled Septimania by *aprisiones,* the occupation of land abandoned for 30 years, living under the Visigothic *Forum iudicum.* The Franks took Gerona in 785 and Barcelona in 801, building a road and establishing counties as they advanced.

Although Christian rule in Catalonia was interrupted only for about 80 years, extant hagiographical and liturgical traditions derive from sources mostly later than the 9th century. The civil and ecclesiastical reorganization was the work of Christians of the north under the Frankish king and the metropolitan of Narbonne; the Visigothic Church was not restored. Apparently, only Urgel's episcopal succession continued uninterrupted; bishops of Saragossa under Muslim rule appeared intermittently. Monastic foundations date from the 9th century, and a new church architecture, with Frankish influence, appeared. Dating according to the regnal years of French kings lasted until 1180. To offset Frankish influence Catalonia maintained ties with Córdoba, whose gold coinage was used in Barcelona.

As Carolingian power declined, the counts became hereditary and assumed sovereign prerogatives. Wifred, the first count of Barcelona free of the Franks, united the counties of Barcelona, Urgel (873), Gerona (894), and Cerdagne (895); took Montserrat from the Moors; gave charters to towns; founded the monastery of San Juan de las Abadesas (875); and revived that of Ripoll. The dynasty he founded lasted until 1410. Meanwhile, Visigoths and Mozarabs in Catalonia were seeking independence of the metropolitan of Narbonne. Count Borrell II (966–993), Gerbert of Aurillac, and Bp. Ato of Vich went to Rome in 970 and obtained metropolitan status and the pallium for Vich, Tarragona being still under the Moors; but the metropolitan dignity was not retained. Catalan relations with Capetian France (987), north Italy, and the papacy increased in the late 10th century. Under Ramón Berenguer I (1035–76) Barcelona's rule, through marriages, extended from the Ebro to the Rhone. In 1064 he supported the peace and the truce of God in a promulgation to an assembly of bishops, clergy, and laity. The *Usatges,* the customary law of Catalonia, were promulgated before 1068 and compiled after 1076 by a judge of his court.

The incongruous joint reign of Ramón Berenguer II, ally of Muslim Seville against Muslim Murcia in 1076, and Berenguer Ramón II, ally of Muslim Lérida against Muslim Saragossa in 1078, each to rule for six months of the year, ended with the former's assassination in 1082. Berenguer Ramón allied with Saragossa against El Cid's Valencia in 1089 and put himself in the service of Alfonso VI of Castile in 1092; in 1096, accused of his brother's murder by Ramón Berenguer III and defeated in trial by battle at Alfonso's court, Berenguer was deposed and joined the First Crusade to Palestine. Ramón Berenguer III (1096–1131), Count of Provence by marriage in 1112 and ally of Genoa, Pisa, and his mother's Norman Sicily, in 1118 restored the metropolitan See of Tarragona, to which the Norman Robert de Aquilo brought colonists and was made prince. In 1130 Abp. Olegarius brought the TEMPLARS to Catalonia. Ramón Berenguer IV married Petronilla of Aragon in 1137, and their son Alfonso II of Aragon began his rule in 1162.

Aragon. The county of Aragon, known from the 9th century, became a kingdom by the last testament of Sancho III of Navarre in 1035. The bishops of Aragon and Navarre, suffragan to Auch, called themselves bishops of Aragon until the reconquest of Huesca (1096), even though Jaca became a see in 1063. They were itinerant and followed the royal court in the Reconquest. Sancho I (1063–94), who succeeded Ramiro I (1035–63) and divided Navarre with Alfonso VI of Castile, granted many fueros to Christians who repopulated towns under him. Opposite Huesca, Sancho built (1086–89) the fortress monastery of Monte Aragon, subsequently one of the most important in Aragon. In 1071 he introduced the Roman liturgy in San Juan de la Peña and in 1073 his brother-in-law in Champagne, Ebles of Roucy, organized an impressive crusade against the Moors of Spain; the land he hoped to reconquer was to become a fief of the Holy See. Aragon became a papal fief in 1089, and documents thereafter were dated according to the regnal years of the popes, the feudal lords. With papal approval, Sancho distributed churches and monasteries in areas reconquered from the Moors favoring CLUNY; his authority was the basis for the kings of Aragon and Spain to claim tithes. Sancho died while besieging Huesca. Peter I (1094–1104) took Huesca (1096) and Barbastro (1101), occupied by the bishop of Roda with the authority of the old See of Lérida. In 1095 Urban II gave Peter and his successors exemption from episcopal authority for chapels and monasteries on which the king's warriors depended for their support. During Peter's reign the papacy intervened in a dispute between the canons of Saint-Sernin in Toulouse and monks of San Juan de la Peña over a church in Pamplona.

Alfonso I (1104–34), husband of Urraca of Castile, attacked the bishops of Burgos, León, Palencia, and Toledo and replaced the abbot of Sahagún with his brother Ramiro (1112). When he confiscated Church treasure, the people turned against him. He took Saragossa in 1118 with the aid of Frankish troops. On an appeal from the Christians of Andalusia *c.* 1125 he penetrated as far as Murcia and returned with 10,000 "Mozarabs" whom he resettled with fueros. Without heirs and on bad terms with Cluny and the monasteries of Castile and Aragon, Alfonso left Aragon to the Templars, KNIGHTS OF

MALTA, and KNIGHTS OF THE HOLY SEPULCHER, who were defending the frontier. Indignant nobles and clergy brought his brother Ramiro II (1134–37) out of the cloister, where he may have received major orders, and elected him king at the cortes of Monzon. Without papal dispensation Ramiro married the daughter of the Duke of Aquitaine, and their daughter Petronilla in 1137 was given in marriage to Ramón Berenguer IV (1131–62) of Barcelona. In 1156 Ramón recognized his vassalage to the Holy See.

Aragon and Catalonia. In 1156 Ramón Berenguer fixed the south border of Murcia as the limit of Aragon's Reconquest. He died en route to the court of Emperor FREDERICK I in Turin to acknowledge Provence as a fief of the Empire. Alfonso II (1162–96) ended Aragon's vassalage to Castile by helping Castile conquer Cuenca and moved the royal pantheon from Ripoll to the Cistercian abbey of Poblet (founded 1150). Peter II (1196–1213), whose sister Constance, widow of the King of Hungary, married Emperor FREDERICK II, recognized Aragon as a fief of the Holy See when he was crowned by Innocent III in Rome (1204). After taking part in the victory of Las Navas de Tolosa (1212), he died at Muret defending the count of Albigensian Toulouse and several of his vassals against French crusaders, and Aragon's influence in southern France came to an end. James I (1213–76), who became king at six, was married to the daughter of the King of Hungary; he maintained commercial relations with Morocco and Tunis and restricted Genoese shipping in 1227 by forbidding Catalan cargos to travel on foreign ships for Ceuta, Syria, or Alexandria. He replaced Latin with Catalan as the official language. In 1229, despite Aragonese reluctance, he conquered Majorca, as RAYMOND OF TOULOUSE surrendered to the French regent Blanche of Castile in the treaty of Paris, and as Pope Gregory IX began a crusade against Frederick II. Valencia was reconquered (1232–38) and in 1244 a new treaty fixed the Castile-Aragon border for the Reconquest. After the marriage (1262) of James's heir, Peter, to Constance, daughter of Manfred of Sicily, over the objections of the Pope, of Louis IX, and of Alfonso X of Castile, an uprising of Moors took place in Andalusia and in Murcia (1263) that James and Alfonso put down by 1266. Peter III (1276–85), whose daughter married Denis of Portugal, held gages of peace with both Castile and France by his custody of the widow (Blanche of France) and the heirs of Ferdinand de la Cerda (d. 1277), claimant to the throne of Castile. In 1280 he set up a quasi protectorate over Tunis and in 1282 occupied Sicily after the Sicilian Vespers overthrew Charles of Anjou. In 1285 Philip III invaded Aragon with an army of 240,000 men, including 6,000 papal mercenaries, and took Gerona; but Aragon's victory over the French fleet, disease, and guerrilla warfare brought the expedition to ruin. Charles of Anjou, Philip III, Peter III, and Pope Martin IV all died in 1285.

Alfonso III (1285–91) was succeeded by his brother JAMES II OF ARAGON (1291–1327), who left his brother Frederick in Sicily to war against the house of Anjou. Thanks to Boniface VIII, James made a treaty with the Angevins in 1295 and in 1297 gained Corsica and Sardinia as well as the titles Admiral and Captain General of the Church. The end of the fighting in Sicily (1302) left Aragonese forces free to go to the East and begin the Catalan Company, which established the Duchy of Athens under the King of Sicily (1311–88). In 1312 the Templars were suppressed, their goods going to the Hospitallers; and in 1317 the KNIGHTS OF MONTESA were founded in Valencia with the goods of both Templars and Hospitallers. Alfonso IV (1327–36) had to deal with a Genoese attack on Sardinia, which Aragon never held with success. Peter IV (1336–87) annexed the Balearics in 1344 and defeated a union of Aragonese nobles backed by Valencia in 1348. He reorganized the court of Aragon and sought to introduce Alfonso X's *Siete Partidas* into Aragon, but met strong feudal opposition. His Catalan translation of the *Partidas,* however, weakened the feudal position. John I (1387–95) fostered French art and vogues in his court. His brother Martin I (1395–1410) died without heirs, his son having died (1409) of poison in the war against Genoa in Sardinia. Delegates from Catalonia, Aragon, and Valencia in the Compromise of Caspe then chose as king Ferdinand of Antequera (1412–16), Regent of Castile, at a moment when the monarchy had become dominant in Aragon. Alfonso V (1416–58) used Aragon as a source of revenue for his wars in south Italy. The son of John II (1458–79), Ferdinand, married Isabella of Castile.

Majorca. The kingdom of Majorca (1276–1344), comprising the Balearics and the mainland counties of Roussillon, Cerdagne, and Montpellier, was the vassal of Aragon until annexed by Peter IV. It depended on Catalonia for its cortes and its coin, but the royal court in Perpignan was dominated by French influence. Majorca, where Raymond Lull founded a school of Oriental languages for missionaries, was an important cartographical center, participating in the Atlantic discoveries. A highly prized atlas of 1375, probably by the Majorcan Jew Abraham Cresques, described coasts in detail but gave little information on hinterlands. Jafuda Cresques, converted to Christianity in 1391, directed Prince Henry the Navigator's school at Sagres (Portugal). When Aragon lost Mediterranean naval supremacy to Italian cities and to the Turks, Majorca's prosperity declined.

The Crown of Aragon differed from Castile in that the monarchy was oligarchic rather than democratic. Its smaller but better-organized nobility never attempted to change the hereditary succession, but fought only to obtain more liberties for themselves. The important institution of the *Justicia* of Aragon, arbitrator between the king and his subjects, declined in time and became nominal. The question of Aragon's vassalage to the Holy See disturbed Church affairs in Aragon but did not affect orthodoxy. After introducing the Roman rite and the Gregorian reform, papal legates to Spain generally turned to keeping peace and organizing the ecclesiastical hierarchy under the feuding metropolitanates of Toledo, Tarragona, Braga, and Santiago. They later devoted themselves to the restoration of sees and to the organization of the war against the Moors. After 1100, relations increased between Rome and Spanish bishops, who grew stronger at the expense of Cluny and the Benedictines. The Cistercians, closely affiliated with Rome, arrived in Spain *c.* 1150 from Morimond and Clairvaux (later from Cîteaux), going first to the west of the peninsula and later to the east. The military orders, at their peak *c.* 1300, were associated with the Cistercians. Cathedral chapters in Aragon elected bishops until *c.* 1250, when episcopal appointments came into the hands of the popes and the kings. With the crown of Sicily, Aragon obtained the *patronato* of churches in the Holy Land. In 1318 Saragossa became a metropolitan see separate from Tarragona.

Bibliography: R. BEER, *Handschriftenschätze Spaniens* (Vienna 1894). *España sagrada* (Madrid 1747–). J. L. VILLANUEVA, *Viage literario á las iglesias de España,* 22 v. (Madrid 1803–52). E. R. ST.-HILAIRE, *Histoire d'Espagne depuis les premiers temps historiques jusqu'à la morte de Ferdinand VII,* 14 v. (rev. ed. Paris 1844–79). Consejo Superior de Investigationes Científicas, *Estudios de Edad Media de la Corona de Aragón* (Saragossa 1945–). H. FINKE, ed., *Acta aragonensia,* 3 v. (Berlin 1908–22). P. F. KEHR, ed., *Papsturkunden in Spanien,* 4 v. (Berlin 1926–28). D. MANSILLA, ed., *La documentación pontificia hasta Inocencio III, 965–1216* (*Monumenta Hispaniae Vaticana* 1; Rome 1955). J. M. CASTROVIEJO BLANCO CICERÓN, *Galicia: Guía espiritual de unatierra* (Madrid 1960). F. VALLS-TABERNER and F. SOLDEVILA, *Historia de Cataluña,* 2 v. (Barcelona 1955–57). H. J. CHAYTOR, *A History of Aragon and Catalonia* (London 1933). J. PLA, *Cataluña* (Barcelona 1961). F. SOLDEVILA, *Història de Catalunya,* 3 v. (Barcelona 1962–). A. Lambert, *Dictionnaire d'histoire et de géographie ecclésiastiques,* ed., A. BAUDRILLART et al. (Paris 1912–) 3:1378–86; 6:734–747. *Encyclopedia of Islam,* ed., M. T. HOUTSMA et al., 4 v. (Leiden 1913–38) F. J. SIMONET, *Historia de los mozárabes de España* (Madrid 1897–1903). M. GÓMEZ-MORENO, *Iglesias mozárabes: Arte español de los siglos IX a XI,* 2 v. (Madrid 1919). F. R. FRANKE, "Die freiwilligen Märtyrer von Cordova und das Verhältnis der Mozaraber zum Islam . . . ," *Gesammelte Aufsätze zur Kulturgeschichte Spaniens* 13 (Span. Forschungen der Görresgesellschaft; 1958) 1–170. I. DE LAS CAGIGAS, *Minorías étnico-religiosas en la Edad Media española,* I. *Los mozárabes,* II. *Los mudéjares,* 4 v. (Madrid 1947–49). E. P. COLBERT, *The Martyrs of Córdoba, 850–859: A Study of the Sources* (Washington 1962). R. M. PIDAL, *La España del Cid,* 2 v. (4th ed. Madrid 1947). L. VÁZQUEZ DE PARGA et al., *Las peregrinaciones a Santiago de Compostela,* 3 v. (Madrid 1948–49). M. DEFOURNEAUX, *Les Français en Espagne aux XIe et XIIe siècles* (Paris 1949). *La reconquista española y la repoblación del país* (Saragossa 1951). J. G. GAZTAMBIDE, *Historia de la bula de la cruzada en España* (Vitoria 1958). *Acts of the Asturian Kings,* ed. L. BARRAU-DIHIGO, in *Revue hispanique* 46 (1919) 1–191; 52 (1921) 1–360. A. C. FLORIANO CUMBREÑO, *Estudios de historia de Asturias: El territorio y la monarquía en la alta edad media asturiana* (Oviedo 1962). J. V. SUBIRATS, *Alfons "el Cast": El primer comte-rei* (Barcelona 1962). J. GONZÁLEZ, *Alfonso IX,* 2 v. (Madrid 1944); *Elreino de Castilla en la época de Alfonso VIII,* 3 v. (Madrid 1960). F. PIÉTRI, *Pierre le Cruel* (Paris 1961). L. S. FERNÁNDEZ, *Castilla, el cisma y la crisis conciliar, 1378–1440* (Madrid 1960). J. M. LACARRA, *Orígenes del condado de Aragón* (Saragossa 1945). A. D. GUDIOL, *La Iglesia de Aragón durante los reinados de Sancho Ramírez y Pedro I, c.1062–1104* (Rome 1962). C. M. LÓPEZ, *Leyre: Historia, arqueologiá, legenda* (Pamplona 1962). H. C. LEA, *A History of the Inquisition of Spain,* 4 v. (New York 1906–07). J. B. VINCKE, *Zur Vorgeschichte der spanischen Inquisition: Die Inquisition in Aragon, Katalonien, Mallorca, und Valencia während des 13. und 14. Jahrhunderts* (Bonn 1941). B. LLORCA, *La inquisición en españa* (3d ed. Barcelona 1954). J. VANCE, *The Background of Hispanic-American Law: Legal Sources and Juridical Literature of Spain* (Washington 1937). R. B. DONOVAN, *The Liturgical Drama in Mediaeval Spain* (Toronto 1958).

[E. P. COLBERT]

SPAIN IN THE MODERN ERA

Ferdinand and Isabella unified the entire Iberian peninsula except for Portugal, which came under Spanish rule later (1580–1640). They organized political, religious, and cultural life more extensively than they had ever been; and Spain and Portugal built colonial empires that remained important in world history until the 19th century. After the Catholic sovereigns, Charles V combined Spain's military might and the wealth of the New World with Hapsburg power in central Europe to establish hegemony in Europe. Philip II elected to pursue this same goal from Spain, meanwhile developing the overseas possessions without serious threat from other powers. After Philip's death in 1598, however, Spain's empire in Europe declined, while England, France, and the Netherlands began to build colonial empires to compete with the Spanish-Portuguese monopoly. In the mid-17th century, France crushed Spain as a power in Europe, reducing Spain's role to that of a guerrilla force and an ally of occasional critical importance to the major powers.

The Bourbon accession to the throne of Spain in 1700 extended Castilian administration to all Spain and introduced an era of economic reform, especially under the enlightened despot Charles III. French military occupation of the peninsula and Napoleon's disrespect for the Spanish monarchy provoked the War of Independence (1808–14), which sapped France's effort to establish an empire in Europe. As a result of these years of war, Spain's overseas possessions became independent, except Cuba, Puerto Rico, and the Philippines, which were lost in the war of 1898. The Bourbon dynasty, interrupted between the constitutionally restive reign of Isabella II

(1833–68) and that of Alfonso XII (1875–85), came to an end with the exile of Alfonso XIII (1886–1931). The political, social, and economic troubles of the 20th century gave rise to the dictatorship of Primo de Rivera (1923–30), the Republic (1931–36), the Civil War (1936–39), and the government of Francisco Franco. For much of the period after 1600 Spain's history is mainly that of a traditionalist nation dealing with liberal forces that had well-springs outside the peninsula.

Reform of Ferdinand and Isabella: 1474–1517. The Catholic sovereigns Ferdinand and Isabella made Spain the prototype of the modern state and instituted a profound religious and ecclesiastical reform that served as a solid basis for the reform of the Church sought by all Christendom since the 14th century. Their focus on a close union of politics and religion illustrates the determining influence that the religious ideal of the Reconquest, terminated in 1492 with the conquest of Granada, played in the formation of Spain. Their esteem for the medieval religious ideal of unity was the historical justification for the decree of 1492 which expelled from Spain all 165,000 Jews who would not become Catholics, as well as for the policy whereby they obtained the mass conversion of the Moriscos in 1502 (*see* MARRANOS). (Despite this forced conversion, the religious, social, and political problem presented by the Moriscos would not be solved until the reigns of Philip II [1556–98] and Philip III [1598–1621].) The desire for unity was the basis for the sovereigns' decision to extend to all of Spain the tribunal of the Inquisition, conceded by Sixtus IV in 1478.

In their intrusion in ecclesiastical affairs Ferdinand and Isabella were supported by royal rights whose juridical bases, attested since the *Siete Partidas* of Alfonso X (1252–84, were recognized by the popes. Believing in the supreme power of the popes, they made it a point always to obtain not only papal agreement but papal support in bulls and briefs for everything they thought had to be done in the religious sphere. They regarded the people's private rights as an obligation of service, to foster and defend the purity of the Church. They submitted requests to the pope, albeit with the understanding that they had a right to what they requested. What conflicts they had with the Holy See did not violate this doctrinal basis, making their religious policy substantially different from that which had been pursued in the Crown of Aragon by Ferdinand's father, John II, and that eventually sought by 18th-century Regalists.

Thanks to this spirit and to the great churchmen who worked with the sovereigns—Hernando de Talavera, Diego de Deza, Cardinal MENDOZA, and especially Cardinal XIMÉNEZ DE CISNEROS—Spain achieved a profound ecclesiastical reform, as well as a real and productive approach to the new spirit of the Renaissance and humanism that was in perfect accord with the spirit of Christianity. The laicization of culture characteristic of the Italian and European Renaissance hardly showed itself in Spain. Such a basis made Spain the solid bastion of the COUNTER REFORMATION and the model state for the defense of Catholicism in Europe during the political-religious crisis of the 16th and 17th centuries, until the Peace of Westphalia in 1648.

Clerical Reform. The religious reform that began with the secular clergy was fostered and directed personally by the sovereigns. First, the feudal episcopacy was reformed. The bishops, some of whose lives were completely secular, had participated in the anarchy of the last previous reigns, intervening at times decisively in civil conflicts and court intrigues (e.g., Abp. Alfonso Carrillo of Toledo). These bishops, along with other nobles, were put down skillfully and forcefully. But the reform of the sovereigns, especially of Isabella, was more pastoral than political. From the beginning of her reign (Jan. 15, 1475) she outlined a plan of "appeal" to the pope in the matter of filling bishoprics and benefices "as seems best for the service of God and the good of the churches, and for the souls of all and the honor of the realm, and those appointed will be educated persons." Moreover, those chosen were almost without exception native Spaniards who resided in the country and devoted themselves to their pastoral duties. Many of the candidates, who had to be reputable persons, came from the middle class. In the defense of their "right" of presentation, the sovereigns came at times into quite violent conflict with popes: with Sixtus IV over the choice of his nephew Girolamo RIARIO for the See of Cuenca in 1482 and with Innocent VIII over Rodrigo BORGIA for that of Seville in 1484. In 1482 they came to a partial agreement with the papal legate Dominic Centurione without obtaining the right of *PATRONATO*, which was granted in 1483 by Innocent VIII for Granada, confirmed in 1493 by Alexander VI, and extended in 1523 by Adrian VI to CHARLES V for all Spain.

The result of this policy, at a time when little could be expected from the popes in the way of reform, was the high moral and cultural level of Spanish bishops, who in turn reformed the lower clergy after a plan outlined by the national assembly of the clergy convoked by the sovereigns in Seville in 1478 and by the cortes of Toledo in 1480. Many reformers were zealous, and a multitude of synods were held. The provincial synod of Aranda called in 1473 by Alfonso Carrillo, the synods of Toledo convoked in Alcalá and Talavera in 1497 and 1498 by Cisneros, and the synod of Palencia in 1500 summoned by Deza were especially noteworthy. The majority of bishops shared the positive ideals of clerical reform, fostering spiritual and cultural life and the reorganization of pastoral care. To carry out the reform, many colleges for the training of priests were founded: Sigüenza in 1476, Toledo in 1485, Granada in 1493, Seville in 1506, Alcalá in 1513, Salamanca in 1510 and 1517, and many more in the 16th century.

The reform of the religious, after an initial move inspired by Talavera (1475–92), began on a grand scale after 1495 under Cisneros with many bulls and briefs from Alexander VI. Directed primarily to Franciscans, it extended also to Cistercians, Benedictines, Dominicans, Augustinians, and, to a lesser degree, to Premonstratensians, canons regular, and others.

Cultural Advance. Cultural life too received a vigorous stimulus that lasted into later reigns, giving Spain a hegemony in theology and the humanities to accompany its political eminence. The central figure again was Cisneros, who in 1508 founded the University of Alcalá, the most important center of Spanish humanism, where the Church had access to the achievements of the Renaissance in literature, philology, and humanism and where free criticism and a wide representation (chairs of NOMINALISM and SCOTISM as well as THOMISM) were introduced into the teaching of philosophy and theology. The ideas of ERASMUS, whom Cisneros invited in vain to teach at Alcalá, had free scope. The Complutense POLYGLOT BIBLE (1502–14) was a typical example of this spirit.

All these elements brought about the introduction, on the spiritual plane, of the DEVOTIO MODERNA and the Erasmian "philosophy of Christ" that so influenced later Spanish spirituality. The ideas were widely diffused even outside universities thanks to the new invention of printing, and people came into direct contact with Holy Scripture, the Fathers, and the best ascetic-mystic authors.

Isabella died in 1504, Ferdinand in 1516, and Cisneros in 1517. In less than 50 years (1474–1517) there had occurred in the ecclesiastical sphere a gigantic achievement that in retrospect appears to be the germ from which grew the Church of Spain (and Spain itself), especially in the 16th and 17th centuries.

Reform and Counter Reform: 1517–1700. The theological and spiritual renovation begun at Alcalá spread year by year. One of its merits was that it occasioned the reform of method and the institution of a theological dialogue in the University of Salamanca through the work primarily of Francisco de VITORIA (1480–1546) after 1526. This method was characterized by a criterion independent of and above the various schools, by the use of St. Thomas' *Summa* as a text, by recourse to sources (Holy Scripture, acts of councils, Church teaching, etc.) and all the aids employed by the Renaissance and humanism, by simplicity of exposition, and by concern for problems of the time (the conquest of America, just war, etc.). Melchior CANO, OP (1509–60), systematized this method, and Domingo de SOTO, OP (1494–1560), composed the first great moral treatise. From this center in Salamanca went forth the great theological reform that produced figures such as Domingo BAÑEZ, OP (1528–1604), Diego LAÍNEZ, SJ (1512–65), Alfonso SALMERÓN, SJ (1515–85), Francisco SUÁREZ, SJ (1548–1617), and Alfonso de Castro, OFM (1495–1558), who systematized penal law. The profundity of Spanish theology was confirmed at the Council of Trent and is suggested by the number of Spaniards teaching in the Universities of Paris, Coimbra, Louvain, Rome, Ingolstadt, Prague, and others. This was one of Spain's most important contributions to the reform of the universal Church.

The spiritual movement of Cisneros came to flower in the ascetic-mystic splendor of such figures as the Franciscans BERNARDINO OF LAREDO (d. 1565), Alfonso of Madrid (d. 1545), and FRANCIS OF OSUNA (d. 1540); the Dominican LOUIS OF GRANADA (d. 1568); the Carmelites St. TERESA (d. 1582) and St. JOHN OF THE CROSS (d. 1591); the Jesuits St. IGNATIUS (d.1556), Alfonso RODRÍGUEZ (d. 1616), Luis de la Palma (d. 1616), ALVAREZ DE PAZ (d. 1620), and Luis de la Puente (d. 1624); the Benedictine abbot of Montserrat, García de CISNEROS (d. 1510); the Augustinians St. THOMAS OF VILLANUEVA (d. 1555) and Luis de LEÓN (d. 1591); and the secular priest Bl. JOHN OF ÁVILA (d. 1569), confessor of saints. The reform of religious orders continued, Franciscans by St. PETER OF ALCÁNTARA (d. 1562) and Carmelites by St. Teresa and St. John. New orders were founded, the Jesuits by St. Ignatius and the clerics of Pious Schools by St. JOSEPH CALASANCTIUS (d. 1648).

A byproduct of the mysticism fostered by Cisneros was the heterodox Illuminist Movement of the *ALUMBRADOS* among the masses and converted Jews and Moors, especially in New Castile, suppressed by the Inquisition from 1524. The Erasmian spirit of reform dominant in the *bourgeoisie* and intellectual circles determined the religious policy of Charles V (1516–56) in the Empire, through the influence of Erasmus himself and the Spanish Erasmists Juan Luis Vives, Alfonso and Juan de VALDÉS, and Vice Chancellor Miguel May, educated in Barcelona.

Charles V. Charles's plan of empire did not entail a universal empire or monarchy, but rather the hegemony of an emperor who maintains peace among Christians to be able to war against infidels, an ideal shaped by Ferdinand and Isabella in their testaments and proposed to Charles in 1516 by First Secretary of State Pedro de Quintana. In 1520 Charles declared Spain to be "the fortress, defense, wall, refuge, and final security'' of his other realms and lands; and all the spiritual and material resources of Spain, including gold from America, did service for the religious policy of the emperor. This policy, based on the ideals of Erasmus, sought a reconciliation among Christian princes and between Catholics and Protestants, while promoting an ecclesiastical reform to restore religious unity. But Spanish and imperial policy failed in both respects. France, German princes, and even the popes opposed the political aims of the emperor, who was only partly successful against them in wars in France, Germany, and Italy. In the religious sphere the Protestant position became radical in Calvinism, supported by German princes and the French king, who saw in Protestant particularism the basis for the struggle of autonomous states against Charles's pet idea of empire. Important but relative triumphs were the convocation of the Council of Trent by Paul III, the first two stages of which (1545–49, 1551–52) constituted the last attempt at religious conciliation; and the uncertain but generally positive course of the war against the Turks. The treaty of Passau (1552) and the religious peace of Augsburg (1555) made the religious division of Europe definite, and thus ruined the imperial policy of Charles V. With this bitter medicine, in 1556 he abdicated from the Empire and left Spain and its dominions to his son Philip II.

Philip II. The failure of the conciliatory policy resulted in loss of status for Erasmists in Spain. They gained a political victory in Valladolid in 1527, but opposition to them increased until, in 1530, the Inquisition began to investigate charges of illuminism and Lutheranism against large numbers of Erasmists. A fear of Protestant infiltration developed, reaching its height under Philip II, whose religious policy was modeled completely on the Counter Reformation, the product of the third stage of Trent (1562–63) and the inevitable consequence of the collapse of the ideals of empire. Spain, cooperating closely with Archduke Ferdinand I, who succeeded to the Empire, became a kind of fortress and paladin state in the fight against Protestantism and the infidel Turks. The Inquisition, spurred on and supervised by the king, suppressed the only Protestant centers of any importance, Valladolid and Seville, in 1559–60 and, with a zeal explained only by the great fear, prosecuted anything that indicated connivance with the ideas of Luther and Erasmus: such as Holy Scripture in the vernacular, commentaries on Scripture for the laity, ascetic and mystical writings tainted with illuminism.

Along with persons and movements undoubtedly of Protestant origin or heterodox tendency (the *alumbrados* of Llerena, 1574–78), persons undeniably orthodox (Bl. John of Ávila, St. Teresa, St. John of the Cross, Luis de León) were subjected to the scrutiny of the Inquisition. A typical example of the fear and the impassioned religious fervor then prevalent in Spain appears in the dramatic trial of Abp. Bartolomé de CARRANZA of Toledo (d. 1576), which offered an outlet for the personal enmity of the Inquisitor Fernando de Valdés, Melchior Cano, and others, while providing Philip II with the opportunity to defend the Spanish Inquisition with regard to the papal tribunal. Philip's prohibition against Spaniards studying in universities abroad in 1559 (renewed in 1568) may have kept heresy out, but it also isolated Spain from the current of European thought until the 18th century. The Wars of Religion fought all over Europe were a gigantic effort and had some spectacular victories, but they had no chance of bringing about the triumph of the Christian policy of Philip ''the Prudent.'' The only substantial victory, the naval defeat of the infidel Turks at Lepanto (Oct. 7, 1571), was not lasting. The Moriscos, constantly conspiring with the Turks against the security of the Spanish state, were more a political than a religious problem. Philip II's attempt to handle them by mass conversion not only failed but worked against him. Philip III's expulsion of about 300,000 of them between 1609 and 1614 was also more for political than for religious reasons.

Philip's concern for domestic church matters appears in his negotiations with the Holy See to obtain new dioceses: Orihuela (1564), Barbastro and Jaca (1571), Teruel (1577), Solsona (1593), Valladolid (1595), and the division of Albarracín and Segorbe (1577). The decrees of the Council of Trent, officially received on July 12, 1564, were applied through provincial councils: Tarragona in 1564; Toledo, Valencia, Salamanca, Granada, and Saragossa in 1565; and Toledo in 1581–82. Spain's great reform bishops at Trent were Martín López de Ayala, Bernardo de Sandoval y Rojas, Pedro Guerrero, and Bernal Díaz de Luco. Among others deeply moved by spiritual and pastoral zeal for reform who were not at Trent should be noted Abp. Juan de Ribera of Valencia (d. 1611).

The Council of Trent was accepted ''saving the rights of king and country'': meaning except rights linked to the *patronato real* over dioceses and certain benefices; the royal exequatur and placet introduced by Charles V in 1523, 1528, and 1543; *recursos de fuerza,* or appeal from ecclesiastical to civil tribunals; and other items. All this constituted the basis of the Regalism thought out and scientifically systematized by Diego Covarrubias (d. 1577) and later canonists, which, sponsored by the state, gave rise to serious conflicts with the Holy See in the 17th century, especially under Philip III (1598–1621) and Philip IV (1621–65). The most serious crisis, that caused by the defense of the Spanish crown in Rome by Bp. Domingo Pimentel of Córdoba and Juan Chumacero y Carrillo in 1633, led to the breaking of relations and the closing of the papal nunciature in 1639. The Facchinetti concordat ended the crisis with a concession by the Holy See with regard to the privileges of its nunciature. Civil courts were showing themselves more and more opposed to ecclesiastical immunities.

Decline. Meanwhile Spain's economic and political fall was in course: the defeat at Rocroy in 1643, the Peace of the Pyrenees in 1659, the Portuguese independence of 1640 finally recognized in 1668. Spain's European religious policy came to ruin with the treaties of Westphalia in 1648. The theological idealism represented in Spain's combined defense of Catholicism and of the supremacy of the state was cause enough for her general collapse. Still, Spain's religious spirit lasted well into the 17th century and inspired another golden century of the arts, expressed in the transcendent painting of El Greco (d. 1614), the polychrome sculptures of Gregorio Fernández (d.1636), Martínez Montañés (d. 1649), and their disciples, and the writings of priests Lope de Vega (d. 1635), Tirso de Molina (d. 1648), and Calderón de la Barca (d. 1681). There also unfortunately existed an inordinate concern among bishops for precedence and prestige, an excessive number of clerics, inadequately trained and lacking apostolic zeal, and an abundance of superstition among an inadequately instructed laity. To offset this laxity, prelates such as Ven. Juan de PALAFOX Y MENDOZA (d. 1659) worked zealously to evangelize their dioceses, fostering FORTY HOURS DEVOTION to the Eucharist, sponsoring groups such as the School of Christ to encourage piety and prayer, and making special use of religious orders for missions and teaching (St. VINCENT DE PAUL's Congregation of the Mission, St. Philip NERI's Oratory). Popular missions were preached by Jesuits Baltasar Gracián (d. 1658), Jerónimo López (d. 1658), and Tirso GONZÁLEZ (d. 1705), the last a Jesuit general known for his opposition to probabilism in moral theology. The widely known mystic teachings of Ven. Mary of ÁGREDA (d. 1665) inspired the painting of J. Ribera (d. 1659), F. Zurbarán (d. 1662), and B. Murillo (d. 1682).

Regalism and Enlightenment: 1700–1808. The heightened Bourbon Regalism, given perfect expression by Melchor de Macanaz, produced a deep split in the Spanish episcopacy that would last until the late 19th century. When Philip V (1700–46) broke relations with the Holy See in 1709, the split became open. Opposed to the king were the primate, Cardinal Portocarrero of Toledo; the archbishops of Seville, Granada, and Santiago; and in particular Bp. (future cardinal) Luis Belluga of Cartagena (d. 1743). In conflict with these ultramontanes were bishops who championed the most blatant regalism, actively represented by Francisco de Solís (d. 1716), Bishop of Lérida and later of Córdoba. A middle group, called Jansenists later in the century, while Regalist and influenced by the Enlightenment, maintained a true Christian spirit and a deep devotion to the Church. This spiritual synthesis differentiated the Spanish from the general European Enlightenment. The crisis of 1709 embittered the movement against clerical privilege and ecclesiastical immunity. After the sterile concordats of 1717 and 1737, that of 1753 recognized the *patronato real* in its fullest extension in return for insignificant concessions by the Spanish government.

This Christian Enlightenment was guided by Benijo Feijoo (d. 1764), who spearheaded the enormous historicoecclesiastical work of a generation of scholars. The belief in the right of the state to many of its claims against ecclesiastical immunity and in the ideals of progress and patronage of culture under an enlightened despot—the best example of which was Charles III (1759–78)—were shared by many Christians. They were also shared by some members of the clergy and bishops, such as those who in 1765 endorsed the *Tratado de la regalía de amortización* by statesman and economist Pedro Rodríguez de Campomanes (1723–1803) and those who approved the expulsion of the Jesuits in 1767. Perhaps the best representative of this group was Bp. Philip Bertrán of Salamanca (d. 1783), who was supported by many close associates, such as Bp. José Climent of Barcelona (d. 1782) and Abp. Francisco Armañá of Tarragona (d. 1803). Marked by great pastoral zeal, they were concerned with the education of the clergy, preaching, and the catechetical instruction of the faithful. Seminaries thrived, especially after the expulsion of the Jesuits, many of whose houses were converted to seminaries. Preaching became simpler and more practical, prompted by the keen criticism of José Francisco de Isla, SJ (d. 1781). Models of the new style were the Jesuit Pedro of Calatayud (d. 1773) and the Capuchin Bl. DIEGO OF CÁDIZ (d. 1801). The clergy were numerous (172,231 according to a census of 1797), but only about 20,000 devoted themselves to pastoral care; the faithful held the rural pastor in very high esteem. Several religious orders did service in education and social work, areas to which the state still paid little heed.

Moderates lost ground with the outbreak of the French Revolution in 1789. In the last years of Charles IV (1788–1808) religious policy was determined by extremist Regalist ministers, supported by Félix Amat (d. 1824), titular Archbishop of Palmyra, the priests Joaquin Lorenzo Villanueva and J. A. LLORENTE, and others. Such clergy, espousing Regalist and episcopalist (even heterodox) views, almost provoked a national schism in 1799.

Years of Violence: 1808–1936. Spaniards continued to be both good Christians and attached to the traditional ways and institutions of the Church, as they showed in the War of Independence against Napoleon (1808–13), when they defended their religious ideas as well as their country. But in the constitution of the *cortes* of Cádiz in 1812 the extremist ideas of the French Revolution triumphed over those of enlightened despotism. More than half the 2,128 monasteries were suppressed, freedom of the press was declared, and the Inquisition was abolished. While Ferdinand VII (1813–33), on his return in 1814, abrogated these measures and installed unrestrained absolutism, six years later revolutionists forced the reimplementation of the constitution of Cádiz with all its consequences: the Jesuits were again expelled, many bishops were exiled, and relations with the Holy See were broken. In 1823 absolutism was restored with French intervention (the 100,000 sons of St. LOUIS IX). Things were made worse by the dynastic war between Carlists and liberals, who in 1835 renewed the measures against monasteries, further restricted ecclesiastical liberties, and issued laws of amortization, confiscating much church property; it was the final act of a campaign by the state that had gone on for centuries and had been especially hard in the 1700s. Convents were burned, religious were murdered in Madrid (1834), Saragossa, Murcia, Barcelona, and elsewhere (1835), and several bishops were exiled in the bloody persecution of the Church.

The Concordat of 1851 made Catholicism the only recognized religion in Spain and revised the map of Spanish dioceses; the Church renounced the amortized property, and the state agreed to subsidize cult and clergy; the king retained his right of *patronato* unrestricted. In the Liberal period 1854 to 1856 persecution was renewed, and the revolts of 1868 and the fanatic character of the first Republic (1873–74) made the concordat practically useless. The situation of the Church became more difficult with the political-religious split of Catholics and clergy into traditionalists (liberal conservatives or liberal Catholics) and integrists. Neither the advice of great thinkers such as Jaime BALMES (d. 1848) and J. F. DONOSO CORTÉS (d. 1853), nor the good intentions of certain governors, nor the warnings of Pius IX and Leo XIII could mend the split. The most important cultural and political figures of the late 19th and early 20th century were shaped in the Free Institute of Education, founded by Francisco Giner de los Ríos, which introduced new pedagogical methods into Spain and provoked a real cultural renaissance. Unfortunately, it was basically laicist and antireligious. Apologetics and polemics dominated the Catholic field, the greatest positive contribution being by M. Menéndez y Pelayo (d. 1912).

A spiritual and cultural renaissance of the Church marked the end of the 19th century, thanks especially to religious orders: the Augustinian university in the ESCORIAL (1893), the Jesuit Faculties of law and letters in Deusto (1886), the pontifical university of Comillas (1890), and the pontifical Spanish college in Rome (1892). St. Anthony M. CLARET (d. 1880) and P. Tarín, SJ (d. 1910), were apostles of the people. Catholic socialism had a forerunner in Anthony Vincent, SJ (d. 1912), but neither he nor his followers could form a unified organization or infuse the Christian spirit into worker movements, which since 1843 had drifted away from the Church. The only organized general movement, albeit composed of minorities, was that conceived by Angel Ayala, SJ, and put into practice by Angel Herrera, Bishop of Malaga after 1947, who founded the national Catholic Action of Propagandists (1909) and organized Catholic Action (1924)—both events of prime importance in the religious life of 20th-century Spain.

In the first decades of the 20th century, popular manifestations of Catholicism alternated with persecution by anticlerical governments. After the dictatorship of Primo de Rivera (1923–30) brought years of religious peace, the Republic was installed in 1931. Its fanatic character quickly appeared in the burning of convents in Madrid, Málaga, and elsewhere (May 1931). A discriminatory constitution was voted into law, the Jesuits were dissolved, the cardinal primate of Toledo was expelled, and the state confiscated all church goods. A Catholic reaction in 1933 under José María Gil Robles was annulled in February 1936 by revolutionary forces who began a regime of anarchy and terror.

National Movement: 1936–39. The National Movement begun on July 18, 1936, under General Francisco Franco was designed to remedy the political and social situation created by the Republic. Begun as a military insurrection to restore legality and order, it evolved into the Spanish Civil War (1936–39). For many it also became a religious war in defense of Catholicism and the Church, as the episcopate solemnly declared in a common letter in 1937. In response, violent religious persecutions were systematically carried out. Under José Giral (July 20–Oct. 4, 1936) 2,600 secular priests (12 bishops), 1,200 religious, and 100 nuns were murdered. Under Largo Caballero, the ''Spanish Lenin'' (Oct. 4, 1936–May 18, 1937), 1,400 priests, 1,130 religious, and 150 nuns were murdered. Countless laymen died simply because they were Catholics; to carry a religious object (crucifix, medal, rosary) was reason enough to be killed. By the end of the war 6,832 clerics (4,184 secular, 2,365 religious, and 283 nuns) were dead, called genuine martyrs by Pius XI. Meanwhile a clandestine ecclesiastical and religious life was organized; Mass was celebrated, the Sacraments administered, and mutual aid provided, in areas such as the Dioceses of Madrid and Barcelona, with an extraordinary precision in organization.

The common letter of the episcopate noted, in 1937: "The Church, although peaceful of nature and neither desiring nor participating in the war, could not be indifferent in the struggle. . . One side seeks to suppress God, whose work the Church is to do in this world, and works great harm to the Church in persons, things, and rights, such as probably no institution in history has suffered. The other side, despite human deficiencies, is the force seeking to preserve the old life, Spanish and Christian." Accordingly, Catholic forces joined Franco's National Movement, excepting only separatist Basque Catholics seeking autonomy. Pius XI (Sept. 14, 1936) blessed "those with the difficult and dangerous task of defending and restoring the rights and honor of God and religion, that is to say, the rights and dignity of men's consciences." In the months following, pastoral letters on the spiritual value of the Movement multiplied: "The Two Cities" by Bp. Play Deniel of Salamanca (Sept. 30, 1936); the many documents of Cardinal Isidro Gomá. of Toledo, among them "The Case of Spain" (Oct. 23, 1936), "Spain's Lent" (Jan. 30, 1937), and "Lessons of War and Obligations of Peace" (Aug. 8, 1939). But the Church did not intend to"guarantee the conduct, aims, or intentions that in the present or future might disfigure the noble visage of the National Movement in its origin, its course, and its ends."

Bibliography: L. G. DE VALDEAVELLANO, *Historia de España* (Madrid 1947–1952). R. B. MERRIMAN, *The Rise of the Spanish Empire in the Old World and the New,* 4 v. (New York 1918–34). E. A. PEERS, *Spain: The Church and the Orders* (London 1945); *The Mystics of Spain* (London 1951); ed., *Spain: A Companion to Spanish Studies* (4th ed. London 1948). J. H. ELLIOTT, *Imperial Spain, 1469–1716* (Toronto 1963). R. T. DAVIES, *The Golden Century of Spain, 1501–1621* (London 1937). J. RUBIÓ et al., *Fernando el católico y la cultura de su tiempo* (Saragossa 1961). R. GARCÍA Y GARCÍA DE CASTRO, *Virtudes de la Reina Católica* (Madrid 1961). T. DE AZCONA, *Isabel la Católica* (Madrid 1964). M. BATAILLON, *Erasmo y España,* tr. A. ALATORRE, 2 v. (Mexico City 1950). J. E. LONGHURST, *Erasmus and the Spanish Inquisition* (Albuquerque 1950). A. S. TURBERVILLE, *The Spanish Inquisition* (London 1932). M. BOYD, *Cardinal Quiroga, Inquisitor General of Spain* (Dubuque 1954). J. LYNCH, *Spain under the Habsburgs,* v.1. *Empire and Absolutism, 1516–1598* (New York 1964). R. ALTAMIRA Y CREVEA, *Ensayo sobre Felipe II. hombre de estado* (Madrid 1959). J. H. ELLIOTT, *The Revolt of the Catalans: A Study in the Decline of Spain, 1598–1640* (Cambridge, Eng. 1963). I. MARTIN, *Figura y pensamiento del cardenal Belluga a trayes de su memorial antirregalista a Felipe V* (Madrid 1960). R. HERR, *The Eighteenth-Century Revolution in Spain* (Princeton 1958). V. RODRÍGUEZ CASADO, *La política y los políticos en el reinado de Carlos III* (Madrid 1962). E. DE TAPIS OZCARIZ, *Carlos III y su época: Biografía del siglo XVIII* (Madrid 1962). J. BECKER, *Relaciones diplomáticas entre España y la Santa Sede durante el siglo XIX* (Madrid 1908). P. DE POLNAY, *A Queen of Spain: Isabella II* (London 1962). C. A.M. HENNESSY, *The Federal Republic in Spain: Pi y Margall and the Federal Republican Movement, 1868–1874* (New York 1962). C. M. RAMA, *La crisis española del siglo XX* (2d ed. Mexico City 1962). G. BRENAN, *The Spanish Labyrinth: An Account of the Social and Political Background of the Spanish Civil War* (New York 1943). A. M. MORENO, *Historia de la persecución religiosa en España, 1936–39* (Madrid 1961). P. BROUÉ and E. TÉMIME, *La Revolution et la guerre d'Espagne* (Paris 1961). *La Guerra de liberación nacional* (Saragossa 1961). H. THOMAS, *The Spanish Civil War* (New York 1961). D. T. CATTELL, *Communism and the Spanish Civil War* (Berkeley 1955); *Soviet Diplomacy and the Spanish Civil War* (Berkeley 1957). J. M. SANCHEZ, *Reform and Reaction: The Politico-Religious Background of the Spanish Civil War* (Chapel Hill, NC 1964). D. A. PUZZO, *Spain and the Great Powers, 1936–1941* (New York 1962). Instituto de Estudios Politicos, *El nuevo estado español: Veinticinco años de movimiento nacional, 1936–1961* (Madrid 1961). J. DELPECH, *Oppression of Protestants in Spain,* tr. T. and D. JOHNSON (Boston 1955). *Bilan du Monde* 2:318–333. *Guía de la Iglesia en España* (Madrid 1954–). *Annuario Pontifico* (Rome 1912–) has annual data on all dioceses. Archivo de la Corona de Aragón (Barcelona). Archivo histórico nacional (Madrid). Archivo general de Simancas (Valladolid). Archivo general de Indias (Seville). B. SANCHEZ ALONSO, *Fuentes de la historia española e hispanoamericana,* 3 v. (3d ed. Madrid 1952); *Historia de la historiografía española,* 3 v. (Madrid 1941–50). *Al-Andalus* (Madrid 1933–). *Anuario de historia del derecho español* (Madrid 1924–). *Boletín de la Real Academia de la Historia* (Madrid 1877–). *Bulletin hispanique* (Bordeaux 1899–). *Hispania sacra* (Madrid 1948–). *La Ciudad de dios* (Valladolid 1881—). *Revista de Archivos, Bibliotecas y Museos* (Madrid 1871). B. LLORCA et al., *Historia de la Iglesia Católica,* 4 v. (*Biblioteca de autores christiano* (Madrid 1945–) 1955), v.1, A. BALLESTEROS BERETTA, *Historia de España y su influencia en la historia universal,* 12 v. (2d ed. Barcelona 1943–). R. M. PIDAL, ed., *Historia de España* (Madrid 1935–). L. P. GARCIA and C. S. SERRANO, *Historia de España,* 6 v. (Barcelona 1958–62). F. SOLDEVILA, *Historia de España,* 8 v. (Barcelona 1952–59). R. FOULCHÉ-DELBOSC, *Manuel de l'hispanisant,* 2 v. (New York 1920–25). J. VIVES, "Bibliografía hispanica de ciencias históricoecclesiásticas" in *Analeta Sacra Tarracon Ensia* (Barcelona 1925–) v.9–27 (1928–54). *Indice histórico español* (Barcelona 1953–). M. MENÉNDEZ V PELAYO, *Historia de los heterodoxos españoles,* 8 v. (new ed. Madrid 1946–48). C. M. AJO and G. Y SÁINZ DE ZÚÑIGA, *Historia de las universidades hispánicas* (Madrid 1957–). C. R. POST, *A History of Spanish Painting,* 12 v. (Cambridge, MA 1930–58). E. LAMBERT, *L'Art en Espagne et en Portugal* (Paris 1945).

[J. FERNÁNDEZ-ALONSO]

THE CHURCH SINCE 1939

When the Spanish Civil War ended on April 1, 1939 and the authoritarian regime of Franco began, the Church faced the difficult task of material and spiritual reconstruction. New government legislation promoted the restoration of Christian life and the repeal of the antireligious laws of the Republic on civil marriage, secularization of cemeteries, "religious denominations and congregations," divorce, and the budget for cult and clergy; special laws were issued for the reconstruction and restoration of churches. While a new concordat was being prepared to replace the abrogated concordat of 1851, special arrangements were made with the Holy See regarding presentation for the election of bishops, provision for benefices not consistorial, state subsidies for seminaries and church universities, restoration of the Rota tribunal of the nunciature in Madrid, and military jurisdiction and religious service for the armed forces. Politically, Spain navigated the tumultuous 1940s by retaining non-belligerent status during World War II, and distancing herself from communist leaders.

The Concordat of 1952. According to the nation's new concordat, signed Aug. 27, 1953, Catholicism"continue[d] to be the only religion of the Spanish nation" and would enjoy official protection; no one would be molested because of his beliefs, but the public cult of other religious denominations would not be allowed (art. 6 of the Charter of Spaniards, incorporated as appendix 7 to the concordat); the principles regulating relations between Church and State according to the code of Canon Law were also recognized. A reconfiguration of the Spanish ecclesiastical map was done in 1956 as a consequence of the signing of the Concordat of 1952. The criterion used was to adapt the ecclesiastical boundaries as closely as possible with the civil ones.

By 1953 Franco had insured stability and taken steps to improve the Spanish economy. The improved situation was signaled by the signing of a new concordat between Spain and the Holy See in 1953 and an agreement with the United States that established four U.S. military bases in Spain in exchange for financial assistance and trade concessions. The economic nationalism favored by the right-wing, fascist *Falange* movement was gradually replaced by a capitalist system administered by technocrats, many of whom were members of Opus Dei.

A Peaceful Political Transition. The final decade and half of Franco's rule played out against the background of Vatican II and Franco's own efforts to prepare the country for a peaceful transfer of power. In 1969 he designated Prince Juan Carlos, grandson of Alfonso XIII, as his successor. Upon Franco's death in 1975 Juan Carlos became chief of state. Working closely with the premier, Adolfo Suárez González, King Juan Carlos steered the country toward parliamentary democracy. In the election that followed Suárez's Democratic Center received a plurality, but the party was swept out of office in 1982 with the stunning victory of the Socialist Party.

Vatican II and Its Implementation. The critical and creative drive of the world Church during the years 1965–75 contrasted with the stasis characteristic of the Spanish Church during Franco's dictatorship, and the country's religious foundations were eventually brought into question. The convocation of the Second Vatican Council by John XXIII in 1962 took the Church in Spain by surprise. Under Franco Spain had been politically and religiously isolated, and the council's decrees initially produced disorientation and inconvenience. During the conciliar sessions, the contribution of the Spanish episcopate (80 bishops whose median age was 65) was lackluster compared with the participation of bishops from other countries. Yet when the council ended, the Church in Spain took charge of conciliar implementation with enthusiasm and resolution, launching very significant applications in civil life, such as the legal modification of religious freedom in line with Vatican II, which challenged assumptions of Franco's regime.

Efforts to implement the conciliar decrees in Spain proved difficult. Tension resulted from the self-critical and renewal-oriented spirit as exemplified in the Joint Assembly of Bishops and Priests, held in September 1971. Although endorsed and presided over by the hierarchy and ratified by Rome as a "positive and dynamic event for the Church," the assembly was strongly contested by the more conservative sectors who relied on support from Franco. The controversy drastically reduced its pastoral impact. The dynamism of change that culminated in the joint assembly gave way to a long series conflicts between 1965 and the early 1970s. The struggle on the part of the Church to become more independent of the Franco government was described by some as disengagement and faulted by others as opportunistic. In reality, it was a consequence of the global application of conciliar dynamism, which in Spain acquired special contours before Franco's ideology became obsolete. The distancing of the Church from the government inevitably degenerated into religious-political conflict. There were fines for homilies, suspension of ecclesial assemblies by civil authority, and the creation of a jail for clergy in Zamora. Church-state relations approached the point of open rupture in 1974 with the Añoveros case. Monsignor Antonio Añoveros, bishop of Bilbao, approved a homily to be read in the churches of his diocese that drew attention to the rights of the Basques. The government placed the bishop under house arrest, demanding that he be transferred to another diocese and that in the future bishops should submit an advance text of any sermon touching on "temporal" issues. Both the Vatican and the Spanish hierarchy rejected the government's demands.

Internal ecclesial conflicts also abounded during the latter part of Franco's reign. The ministerial tradition of Christianity was questioned, and a crisis resulted from the drop in the number of priests due to laicization and the simultaneous decline in the number of vocations. Apostolic movements experienced trouble, in particular Acción Católica, many of whose leaders resigned. Each one of its agencies relied either on the political support Franco's government or on the left and its corresponding organizations. Tension between adherents of traditional devotional practices and more modern practices sowed seeds of polarization among the faithful. In spite of the many conflicts that dominated the period, however, ecclesial renewal presented a positive image in Spanish civil society. The Church demonstrated a critical capacity for modernization and an historical sensibility that was lacking in the political regime.

From Dictatorship to Democracy. Following the death of Generalissimo Franco in November 1975, the ''Spanish Miracle''—the peaceful end of 40 years of dictatorship—paved the way to democratic institutions, pluralism in political parties, and the consolidation of a State of Law. Consistent with positions it had taken during the final decade of Franco's regime, the Church aided in transition efforts and made a positive contribution to the new state of affairs, despite its loss of status as the established religion.

In a homily delivered on Nov. 27, 1975 at the ceremony inaugurating the reign of Juan Carlos I, Cardinal Tarancón (d. Nov. 28, 1994), president of the episcopal conference and archbishop of Madrid, proposed peace and reconciliation to Spanish society as a way to transcend its splintered, post-civil war conscience. Tarancón called for the acceptance of pluralism, democracy, and the endorsement of the State of Law and offered the Church's collaboration with the government, beginning with a principal of mutual independence. The new situation allowed for a strengthening of the leadership of the Spanish Church. In the years that followed, Church leadership was characterized by Cardinal Tarancón himself. His style, popularly known as taranconismo, was inspired by Vatican II in its independence, moderation, and tolerance both in church-state relationships and with regard to social issues. Both Cardinal Tarancón and the episcopal conference depended on the backing of Pope Paul VI and Monsignor Luigi Dadaglio, the long-time apostolic nuncio to Spain (1967–80). They had already found substantial support in previous years with regard to the implementation of Vatican II and the conflicts that arose with Franco's government. By renouncing political privilege, the Church sought to achieve greater moral and religious credibility.

A New Constitution. Two events of major importance for the Church in Spain during the transition period were the approval of a new constitution (Nov. 27, 1978) and new church-state agreements. The constitution established a parliamentary monarchy, guaranteed human and civil rights, and affirmed the nondenominational stance of the state. Article 16.3 included a specific reference to the Catholic Church: ''No denomination will have a state character. Public authorities will take into account the religious beliefs of Spanish society and will maintain the resulting cooperative relations with the Catholic Church and the other denominations.''

The organization of Spanish territory into seventeen autonomous communities after the Constitution of 1978 introduced new variations and produced a greater disparity between civil and ecclesiastical demarcations. Thus, there arose anomalous situations that produced frequent confrontations and protests, such as the various *arciprestazgos* of Aragon in the diocese of Barbastro that actually belonged to the Catalunian diocese of Lérida. Other readjustments of territorial boundaries sought were autonomous ecclesiastical provinces for the Basque dioceses and the various islands of the Balearic and Canary archipelagos.

Despite reservations on the part of some bishops and groups of Catholics, the Church officially accepted the new constitutional plan. In January 1979, the Catholic hierarchy and the Spanish state signed four agreements replacing the 1953 concordat that had caused difficulty for both sides, especially after Vatican II. With the new agreements, the Crown relinquished the privilege of appointing bishops it had enjoyed from time immemorial. The practice had become a stumbling block and the root of most of the tensions between the Holy See and Franco's regime. The new constitution and the church-state agreements defined the Church's public presence in Spanish society more in line with the vision of Vatican II. The Church accepted the fact that modern society is shaped by ideals of democratic liberty and political pluralism and secular, consumer, and permissive features beyond its control.

The Spanish Church deliberately renounced its claim to denominational hegemony and its privileged ties to the state in order to emphasize its identity as a community of believers. Taking its cue from Vatican II the Spanish Church decided not to rely on any specific political party, not even those of Christian orientation, in the ensuing elections. The decision of the bishops to keep the Church at the margin of political contention was inspired not only by conciliar doctrine, but also by the arduous and hostile experience of the civil war in which the religious question became a factor of social opposition.

Socialist Change. In the general parliamentary elections of October 1982, the Partido Socialista Obrero Español (PSOE) garnered ten million votes. The 1982 victory was followed, with a gradual decline in the percentage of votes, by electoral victories over the next decade. The triumphant election of 1982, besides being fully democratic, was historic because it brought a left-of-center government to power in Spain for the first time since before the civil war of 1936–39. The socialists launched a program of radical change with regard to politics, ethics, and culture.

The Church, for its part, accepted the socialist victory with grace and did not resist its political agenda. Many Catholic voters supported the socialist platform that offered an attractive promise of much desired change. While the PSOE did not resurrect the anticlerical streak characteristic of past Spanish socialism, it did devalue the Christian tradition and religion in general. In its effort to reduce religion to the purely private sphere of the conscience, the government showed itself insensitive to maintaining harmonious relations with the Church, with Christian traditions, and the religious feelings of the vast majority of the people. In this sense, the POSE went beyond the nondenominationalism of the 1978 constitution of 1978 to a kind of ''anti-denominationalism.''

Church-State Tensions. Despite grudging collaboration with the Church and formally appropriate but clearly unproductive relations with the Catholic hierarchy, the policies of the socialist government were a cause of friction. Conflict occurred most noticeably in the areas of education; financial support of the Church; the media and mass communications; in policies related to the family, marriage, and youth; and in general questions of ethics and morality. According to the agreements of January 1979 the government budgeted an annual subsidy to support the Church and its various ministries. The socialist government changed the policy of budget endowment to a tax allowance, more in accord with a pluralist, democratic society. On one side, the Church did not garner a sufficient revenue with the new arrangements; and on the other, the socialist government displayed insensibility to the claims of the Church, freezing year after year the percentage of its taxes that contributors had freely decided to assign to the Catholic Church.

The media and mass communications controlled by the state were equally a frequent source of tension and resistance during the socialist term of office. In the case of television, it had the character of a monopoly until late in the socialist period. The Church regularly objected to the media's aggression toward Catholic religious sentiment, whose respect had been guaranteed in the Agreement of 1977. The Church protested programming that frequently promoted ethical standards and behaviors contrary not only to Christian morality, but also to the moral tradition of Spain.

The most significant points of contention between the Catholic Church and Spain's socialist government involved family life, education, and sexual mores. A particularly bitter conflict arose when the government introduced legislation permitting the legalization of abortion in face of the Church's traditional teaching condemning abortion as a crime against life. The Church also opposed legal initiatives on sex education and the use of drugs. While the Church was free to express its teaching, the socialist government hardly listened to it, governing and legislating in accord more with trends detected in polls than with principles.

Following the passage of the laws of education reform, Ley Orgánica del Derecho a la Educación (LODE) in 1985 and Ley Orgánica de Ordenación General del Sistema Educativo (LOGSE) in 1990, engaged in a tenacious struggle with the Church. The Church denounced what it saw as the systematic marginalization of religious education and the socialist tendency toward state control over education that favored public schools over private schools, thus creating a disequilibrium that violated the constitutional rights of parents and students regarding freedom of education and religion. The long and bitter battle portended the gradual strangulation of religious schools and the slow death of religion in public schools.

In the years after Vatican II, Catholic education changed and the influence of the Church in the field of education declined. Among the causes were the Constitution of 1978 which broke the Church's prior monopoly and promoted the general secularization of society. The two legislative pillars of the socialist government, LODE and LOGSE, furthered the trend toward lay teaching and state-controlled education. Government policy imposed serious and increasing difficulties for both private education and for its Catholic orientation. Although enrollments trended downward trend, by the mid-1990s there were 6,215 Catholic education centers in Spain, the majority run by religious, with enrollments in the millions. Four Catholic universities—in Salamanca, Comillas, Deusto, and Navarra—provided advanced studies in theology, philosophy, and other disciplines, while private Catholic universities also were established. The majority of public school students continued to exercise their choice for Catholic instruction guaranteed by the Constitution.

Continuing the Influence of the Church. Following a trend worldwide, the Catholic Church in Spain saw its leadership in various social arenas through the 20th century. However, both the clergy and the pope continued to provide guidance to the faithful in an increasingly secular society. Responding to the continued unrest caused by Basque demands for political autonomy, Bp. José Maria Setien Alberro volunteered to mediate the longstanding dispute, although his offer was declined by the government in 1998. Bombing incidents and other violence relating to Basque demands was condemned by Pope John Paul II as ''an abomination,'' and on Jan. 13, 2001 he appealed directly to Basque terrorists to stop the violence that ended the lives of 23 Spaniards in 2000.

In the modern history of the Church of Spain, the Spanish Episcopal Conference (CEE) held a place of distinction. From 1921 to 1965 the Spanish metropolitan archbishops met regularly in conference, but the CEE itself grew out of Vatican II. Its first statutes were passed in March 1966 by the plenary assembly of the episcopacy and ratified by Pope Paul VI. The CEE possessed both an ecclesiastical, juridical structure and a civil one by virtue of the agreement between the Spanish state and the Holy See. Membership included bishops and their auxiliaries, the military ordinary, and retired bishops, the last who could attend meetings but could not vote. The CEE was composed of three governing bodies: the executive committee, the permanent commission, and the plenary assembly, which held annual meetings in the spring and autumn. The publication of doctrinal and pastoral texts and documents was integral to the CEE's mission to govern and guide the Spanish Catholic community.

Papal Visits. The visits of Pope John Paul II to Spain continued to be significant to the Church. The first took place in October 1982, shortly after the socialists gained control of the government. The pope travelled widely through the regions of Spain, his messages bolstering a revitalization of faith among Spaniards, the stimulus to the recovery of its spiritual fecundity, and a clear incitement to be actively present in the new society of socialist change that had just begun.Visits in 1989 to Santiago de Compostella to take part in the WORLD YOUTH DAY, and again in June 1993 to Sevilla and Heulva to solemnize the fifth centenary of the discovery and evangelization of America, allowed the pope to propound his vision of a new evangelization. The pope's call for a Churchwide "examination of conscience" as the world approached the Jubilee Year 2000 sparked a reconsideration of the Spanish Inquisition and prompted some to ask for God's pardon. Revisionist historians, reviewing that period in preparation for a Vatican conference on the Inquisition, posited that anti-Catholic propaganda during the Reformation exaggerated the violent effects of the movement, which had as its ultimate goal the prevention of civil war.

Lay Movements and Global Outreach. The Church hierarchy traditionally coordinated apostolic movements, associations of the faithful, and Third Orders through the Comisión Episcopal de Apostolado Social (CEAS). Another group focusing on lay activities, Acción Católica underwent a crisis of purpose in 1967, after which it was unable to recover its past ecclesiastical importance. In the postconciliar period, new associations more in harmony with the times took hold among the laity. Communion and Liberation and the Focolare movement were part of international movements; other lay groups have included OPUS DEI, education movements, devotional groups, service and charitable societies, and associations oriented according to life experience: business leaders, teachers, youth, missions, journalists, senior citizens. By 2000 approximately four million Catholics were involved in a Church-related lay association.

The Church of Spain always zealously promoted social welfare and ministered to those in need. While by the 1990s other organizations within Spain began to become more involved in social work, the social ministry of the Church also increased in intensity and scope. In 2000 religious orders ran some 3,000 hospitals, dispensaries, old age homes, and other centers, administering to the needs of over 2,000,000 people. AIDS, old age, substance abuse, and special education were among the most pressing social concerns moving into the third millennium. On a worldwide level, the ecclesial agency CARITAS functions and develops programs both in Spain and wherever an emergency situation calls for its aid. Other institutions channel humanitarian aid to Third World countries, among them Manos Unidas.

Catholics in a Media Age. The area wherein Church influence declined most drastically following Vatican II was social communications. The loss of influence over the daily press, periodicals, and newer media such as television, contributed, in the opinion of many, to declining traditional values and the eclipse of Catholic culture in the late 20th century. The Church's influence was eventually limited to its radio station COPE—remembered as one of the most stable and influential stations on the national scene during the Franco years—which broadcasted throughout much of Spain and had a direct relationship to the conference of bishops. An effort to suspend one of COPE's regional broadcast licenses was shot down by the courts in 1989. In addition to some direct media access, and a proliferation of Catholic-focused web sites on the Internet, the Church's message continued to be conveyed through numerous Catholic publications distributed locally by dioceses and religious congregations. Despite its frustrations at influencing contemporary society via media channels, the Spanish Church continued to play a crucial role in conserving and promoting the historical and artistic legacy of Spain. The Church held about 80 percent of the national patrimony in buildings for worship, museums, archives, and libraries available for study and appreciation of both experts and the general public.

Although no longer the official state church, Catholicism continued to be the religion of the majority of Spaniards in 2000. Claiming as followers 84 percent of the country's population, the Church oversaw a total of 22,102 parishes served by 18,976 secular and over 9,000 religious priests. Despite the government's move to become a secular state in 1975, the Church retained several privileges that by the millennium had sparked protest among Spain's minority religions. In addition to denying Spain's various Protestant and other sects with tax-exempt status, a chance to receive a small percentage of monies owed the government via the country's annual income tax return, and other benefits, the government began a policy of investigating what it termed ''destructive sects'' in 1989, in at least one instance identifying the Salvation Army among such allegedly destructive religious groups.

Bibliography: AA.VV., ''Cincuenta años: Historia y balance de la Iglesia en España (1941–1991),'' *Ecclesia* 2509 (1991); *Iglesia y Sociedad en España 1939–1975* (Madrid 1977); *Diez años en la vida de los españoles* (Madrid 1986). BIBLIOTECA DE AUTORES CRISTIANOS, *La hora de Dios: Visita pastoral de Juan Pablo II a España* (Madrid 1993). F. BLAZQUEZ, *La tradición de los clérigos en la España de Franco* (Madrid 1991). M. L. BREY, *Coversaciones con el cardenal Tarancón* (Madrid 1994). CONFERENCIA EPISCOPAL ESPANOLA, *Juan Pablo II en España* (Madrid 1983). C. CORRAL and L. DE ECHVERRIA *Los Acuerdos entre la Iglesia y España* (Madrid 1980). C. CORRAL and J. LIST, *Constitución y Acuerdos Iglesia-Estado* (Madrid 1988). J. L. M. DESCALZO, *Tarancón, el cardenal del cambio* (Madrid 1977). M. J. FRANCES, *España 2000 ¿cristiana?* (Madrid 1990). A. HERNANDEZ, *Crónica de la cruz y de la rosa. Los socialistas y la Iglesia hoy* (Barcelona 1984). INSTITUTO PAOLO VI, *Pablo VI y España* (Brescia 1995). J. IRIBARREN, *Documentos Colectivos del episcopado español 1870–1974* (Madrid 1974); *Documentos de la Conferencia Episcopal española 1965–1983* (Madrid 1984). J. M. LABOA, *El Posconcilio en España* (Madrid 1988). V. MANUEL ARBELOA, *Aquella España católica* (Salamanca 1975). OFICINA DE ESTADISTICA Y SOCIOLOGIA DE LA IGLESIA, *Estadísticas de la Iglesia Católica 1992* (Madrid 1992); *Guía de la Iglesia Católica en España* (Madrid 1993). J. L. ORTEGA, ''La Iglesia española des de 1939 hasta 1976,'' in *Historia de la Iglesia en España,* v. 5 (Madrid 1979); ''La España del Posconcilio,'' in *Vida Nueva* 1000 (1975); ''Iglesia, Estado, Sociedad en el decenio socialista,'' in *El Decenio Gonzalez* (Madrid 1992). V. PEREZ DIAZ, *La primicía de la sociedad civil. El proceso de formacíon de la España democrática* (Madrid 1993). J. RUIZ GIMENEZ, *Iglesia, Estado y Sociedad en España 1930–1982* (Madrid 1984). J. J. RUIZ RICO, *El papel político de la Iglesia Católica en la España de Franco* (Madrid 1977). SECRETARIO NACIONAL DEL CLERO, *Asamblea Conjunta Osbispos Sacerdotes* (Madrid 1971). J. J. TOHARIA, *Cambios recientes en la sociedad española* (Madrid 1989). J. TUSELL and G. GARCIA QUIPO DE LLANO, *El catolicismo mundial y la guerra civil española* (Madrid 1993). F. YSART, *Quien hizo el cambio* (Barcelona 1984).

[J. L. ORTEGA/EDS.]

SPALATIN, GEORG

Humanist, reformer, and partisan of Martin LUTHER; b. G. Burckhardt in Spalt, Bavaria, Jan. 17, 1484; d. Altenburg, Jan. 26, 1545. In 1499 he was graduated at Erfurt, where he possibly met Martin Luther for the first time. As a member of the humanist circle he associated with Heinrich Urbanus and Crotus Rubianus. He taught at the monastery of Georgenthal in 1508 and was ordained. In 1509 he became tutor, librarian, and historian for the elector of Saxony, Frederick III. In the chancery after 1516 he was occupied with the affairs of the church and the university, which, with Luther and Melanchthon, he sought to reform. As private secretary, spiritual adviser, and court preacher, he could influence the elector to protect Luther. He translated the Latin writings of Luther, ERASMUS, and MELANCHTHON for Frederick. The elector died in 1525, and Spalatin became pastor in Altenburg, and married Katharina Steubel. He continued as religious adviser for the electors Johann and Johann Frederick and he was zealous in the visiting of churches and schools throughout Electoral and Albertine Saxony. Of importance is his *Annales reformationis* (ed. E. S. Cyprian, Leipzig 1718). Although many of his letters appear in *Georg Spalatins historischer Nachlass und Briefe* (ed. C. G. Neudecker and L. L. Preller, Jena 1851), those written to Luther have never been found.

Bibliography: E. ENGELHARDT, *Georg Spalatins Leben* (Leben Der Altväter der lutherischen Kirche 3; Leipzig 1863). I. HÖSS, *Georg Spalatin* (Weimar 1956); *Die Religion in Geschichte und Gegenwart,* 7 v. (3rd ed. Tübingen 1957–65) 6:221.

[P. L. HUGHES]

SPALDING, CATHERINE, MOTHER

The cofounder of the SISTERS OF CHARITY of Nazareth; b. Charles County, Md., Dec. 23, 1793; d. Nazareth, Ky., March 20, 1858. She migrated to Kentucky in 1799 with the Thomas Elder family, her mother, and her sister Ann. When Bp. Benedict J. Flaget of Bardstown and his future coadjutor John Baptist David announced their plans for a religious community to instruct frontier youth, Catherine, Teresa Carrico, and Elizabeth Wells responded to the call in December 1812. In March 1813 Catherine was elected first superior of this third congregation for religious women founded in the U.S. Their first convent was a log cabin on St. Thomas Seminary farm about five miles southeast of Bardstown. Their early years were marked by poverty and hard work, but by 1829 they had obtained a charter of incorporation from the Commonwealth of Kentucky and the congregation had begun to expand. At the time of Mother Catherine's death, the original membership had grown to 145, and there were 16 convents located in Kentucky and Tennessee.

Bibliography: A. B. MCGILL, *The Sisters of Charity of Nazareth, Kentucky* (New York 1917). C. FOX, *The Life of the Right Reverend John Baptist Mary David, (1761–1841)* (U.S. Catholic Historical Society 9, New York 1925).

[A. G. MCGANN]

SPALDING, JOHN LANCASTER

First bishop of Peoria, Ill., educator; b. Lebanon, Ky., June 2, 1840; d. Peoria, Aug. 25, 1916. He was the first of nine children born to Richard Martin and Mary Jane (Lancaster) Spalding. The Spaldings had emigrated from Lincolnshire, England, to St. Mary's County, Maryland, in the 17th century; the Lancasters lived in Maryland during the colonial period and began to migrate to Kentucky in 1788.

Early Career. After obtaining his early education (1852–57) at St. Mary's College near Lebanon, Spalding was sent (1857) to Mt. St. Mary's College, Emmitsburg, Maryland. Influenced by his uncle, Bp. Martin John SPALDING of Louisville, Kentucky, he decided to study for the priesthood. In 1858 he enrolled at Mt. Saint Mary's of the West, Cincinnati, Ohio, a college and seminary that had recently (1856) been founded by Abp. John B. Purcell, a graduate of Mt. St. Mary's and an associate of Bishop Spalding. After graduating as valedictorian of his class (B.A. 1859), Spalding was sent to the newly opened American College at the Catholic University of Louvain, Belgium, where he received his S.T.B. degree (1862) and his S.T.L. (1864). He was ordained by Cardinal Englebert Sterckx, Archbishop of Malines, Belgium, on Dec. 19, 1863. Following a brief visit to Freiburg, Germany, he journeyed to Rome for further studies in Canon Law, returning to the U.S. in 1865.

Although his uncle, who had become archbishop of Baltimore, Maryland, tried to obtain his services, Spalding remained attached to the diocese of Louisville. After a brief period as assistant at the Cathedral of the Assumption, Louisville, he acted as secretary to Bps. Peter J. Lavialle and William G. McCloskey, while performing numerous other duties as diocesan chancellor (1871), editor of the diocesan newspaper, pastor of the African American parish of St. Augustine, and head of the cathedral school. In 1866 he attended the Second Plenary Council of Baltimore as theologian to Abp. Francis N. Blanchet of Oregon City, Oregon. There he worked on behalf of the establishment of a Catholic university in the U.S., an idea first suggested by his uncle who presided over the council as apostolic delegate. The council failed to act on this project, but Spalding continued to write on its behalf for the next two decades.

Bishop. In 1872, following the death of his uncle, Spalding went to New York City to work on *The Life of the Most Rev. M. J. Spalding,* published in 1873. He found time, too, to serve as director of schools for St. Michael's parish and to bring out a book of *Essays and Reviews* (1876) based on his articles, sermons, and lectures. By 1877 he had acquired sufficient reputation to be appointed first bishop of Peoria. Consecrated on May 1 by Cardinal John McCloskey of New York, he presided over a diocese that embraced 18,000 square miles in north central Illinois and a Catholic population of 45,000. As bishop he placed much emphasis on the development of parochial schools, which increased during his administration (1877–1908) from 12 to 70 in number and from 2,010 to 11,360 in enrollment. He also supported academies for girls and founded a boys' high school, Spalding Institute, in 1899.

National Leader. Much of Spalding's time was devoted to national causes. Along with Bp. John IRELAND of St. Paul, Minnesota, he was an ardent sponsor of the IRISH CATHOLIC COLONIZATION ASSOCIATION, of which he became president (1879). He furthered its effort to encourage settlement of Irish immigrants on Western farmlands, as an alternative to their concentration in Eastern cities and as an impetus to the spread of American Catholicism, by making extensive lecture tours in the East and by publishing his well received *Religious Mission of the Irish People and Catholic Colonization* (1880).

In Education. He was a strong advocate among the hierarchy for a Catholic institution of higher learning. When financial difficulties led to the temporary closing of Mt. St. Mary's Seminary of the West (1878), he suggested that the bishops assume control of the seminary and establish there a national center of theological study. Cardinal McCloskey rejected this proposal, but Spalding continued to preach on the subject, to promote its discussion in Catholic newspapers and magazines, and to enlist the support of Abp. (later Cardinal) James GIBBONS of Baltimore. During his *ad limina* visit to Rome in 1882, he worked to secure papal approval for a university or, failing this, for another plenary council. Leo XIII ordered preparations for such a council the following year and Spalding obtained from Mary Gwendoline CALDWELL a grant of $300,000 to finance a prospective university.

At the opening of the council in Baltimore on Nov. 16, 1884, Spalding delivered a noted sermon on "The Higher Education of the Priesthood" setting forth his case for a Catholic university. While he praised the professional training available at Catholic seminaries, he regarded them as intellectually sterile and inadequate in training Catholic spokesmen capable of influencing contemporary controversies. A school of intellectual culture, offering courses in philosophy and theology as the nucleus of a complete university program and flourishing in the atmosphere of American freedom, was necessary for the effective defense of the faith and reform of American life. Pressing his arguments during the council, he secured the approval of the hierarchy and the appointment of a committee to handle the details. Spalding was an active member of the committee during its five years of planning and fund-raising and delivered the address at the laying of the cornerstone of the CATHOLIC UNIVERSITY OF AMERICA, Washington, D.C., on May 24, 1888. His speech, delivered before President Grover Cleveland and about 30 bishops, was full of praise for the American political system and for its separation of Church and State. The message was not without its critics among both the members of the Congregation of the Propaganda in Rome and the conservative-minded members of the American hierarchy, who regarded it as too liberal. Spalding himself refused a proferred appointment as rector, but he gave the university consistent attention and supported the appointment as rector of Bp. John J. KEANE, whose ''liberalism'' caused his dismissal in 1896.

The creation of a Catholic university was only one facet of Spalding's interest in education. He produced a number of books on the subject, including *Education and the Higher Life* (1890), *Things of the Mind* (1894), *Means and Ends of Education* (1895), *Thoughts and Theories of Life and Education* (1897), and *Religion, Agnosticism, and Education* (1902). In all his works he opposed state interference in education and urged Catholics to support a parochial school system without seeking state financial aid. Spalding was intimately concerned with the school controversy of the 1890s, involving the relations of public and private school systems. Although he counseled moderation in the quarrel, he joined the other Illinois bishops in condemning the Edwards Law, which placed certain restrictions on attendance and teaching in parochial schools. Regarding the law as an unconstitutional assault upon freedom of worship, he joined in the pastoral letter on education issued by the bishops of the Province of Chicago, Illinois, and defended its views in the press. The election of 1892 resulted in victory for the Democrats and Gov. John P. Altgeld, and in quick repeal of the Edwards Law. Spalding also participated in the controversy over Archbishop Ireland's FARIBAULT PLAN to integrate parochial schools into the public school system. Despite a decision by a papal commission to tolerate the plan, Spalding was fundamentally opposed to it and remained critical of the exclusion of religion in the public schools. He insisted upon further development of the independent Catholic school system enjoined by the Third Plenary Council of Baltimore, which had required the establishment of parochial schools in every parish where that was possible.

Among persistent themes in Spalding's educational writings were encouragement of research in an atmosphere of freedom, improved education of the clergy, and education for women. He gave his support to Trinity College for women in Washington, D.C., opened in 1900, and to Rev. Thomas E. Shields's plan for the Sisters College of the Catholic University of America, opened in 1911. Spalding's status as an educator was recognized by the American archbishops who placed him in charge of the Catholic educational exhibit at the World's Columbian Exposition of 1893 in Chicago. He also served (1884–1907) on the board of trustees of the Catholic University, and he was awarded honorary degrees by Western Reserve University, Cleveland, Ohio, and Columbia University, New York City. His work earned the praise of professional educators, who credit him with broadening the outlook of Catholic education, which had been confined by nationalistic and linguistic interests; with cultivating the intellectual virtues; and with changing its focus from the past to the present.

Other Issues. Americanism was a frequent theme in Spalding's speeches, notably his sermon in the Church of the Gésu, Rome, on March 21, 1900. His criticism of European culture and glorification of American institutions were purely patriotic; they were in no way infected with the doctrinal errors known as AMERICANISM condemned by Leo XIII's *Testem benevolentiae* (1899). The practical Americanism of Spalding was illustrated in 1902, when President Theodore Roosevelt appointed him to the arbitration commission in the coal strike. The miners, many of whom were Catholic, suggested the appointment, and Spalding was instrumental in arranging a satisfactory settlement of the dispute. He enjoyed a reputation as a critic of business abuses and a friend of labor until he suffered a paralytic stroke in 1905. Three years later he resigned as bishop of Peoria, but remained in that city as titular archbishop of Scitopolis until his death in 1916.

Publications. As perhaps the premier American Catholic essayist of his day, Spalding was the author of numerous books, among which were *Opportunity and Other Essays* (1898–1900), *Aphorisms and Reflections* (1901), *Socialism and Labor and Other Arguments* (1902, 1905), *Glimpses of Truth* (1903), and *Religion, Art, and Other Essays* (1905). He also published several volumes of poetry, among which were *America and Other Poems* (1885); *The Poet's Praise* (1887); *Songs Chiefly from the German,* written in 1896 under the pseudonym of Henry Hamilton; and *God and the Soul* (1901). *A Kentucky Pioneer,* his major narrative poem, was not published until 1932.

Bibliography: J. T. ELLIS, *John Lancaster Spalding* (Milwaukee 1962). M. E. HENTHORNE, *The Irish Catholic Colonization Association of the United States* (Champaign, Ill. 1932). J. J. COSGROVE, *Most Reverend John Lancaster Spalding, First Bishop of Peoria* (Mendota, Ill. 1960).

[J. L. MORRISON]

SPALDING, MARTIN JOHN

Archbishop, church historian, and apologist; b. Rolling Fork, Ky., May 23, 1810; d. Baltimore, Md., Feb. 7, 1872. He was the third son of the thrice-married Richard and his first wife, Henrietta (Hamilton) Spalding, and was the most outstanding of his father's 21 children. The

Spalding family had arrived in Maryland in 1657 and had migrated with other Catholic families to Kentucky in 1790.

Early Career. Spalding's early education (1821–26) was under Rev. William Byrne at his pretentiously named St. Mary's College, Lebanon, Kentucky; he achieved frontier fame for his mathematical proficiency, serving as a student instructor under the Lancastrian system used by Byrne. At St. Thomas Seminary, Bardstown, Kentucky (1826), Spalding came under the influence of Bps. B. J. FLAGET and J. B. DAVID and the Roman-trained F. P. KENRICK, later archbishop. In 1830 Flaget, seeking to develop a ''Little Propaganda of the West,'' sent Spalding and a classmate to the Urban College, Rome, where the rector and vice rector (later cardinals), Karl von REISACH and Paul CULLEN, broadened the outlook of the raw frontier youths. In spite of serious illness involving the loss of a major portion of a school year, Spalding was the first American to win his doctorate in theology (1834); he was ordained (Aug. 13, 1834) and appointed (1835) pastor of St. Joseph's Cathedral, Bardstown.

To his pastoral duties and philosophy classes at St. Joseph's College, Bardstown, Spalding added literary efforts, first with the short-lived *St. Joseph's College Minerva* and more lastingly as an editor of the *Catholic Advocate,* first issued Feb. 13, 1836. Frontier pastoral experience, dissatisfaction with oral controversies, and a bent for historico-apologetic study inclined Spalding to use lectures and articles in newspapers and journals to inform the well-disposed rather than to challenge the anti-Catholic extremist of the day. These attitudes set the pattern of his future writings. He served as president of St. Joseph's College from 1838 to 1840, when he was appointed administrator of St. Peter's in Lexington, Kentucky, with a wide circuit of 11 mission stations and with many lecture opportunities. When the see was transferred to Louisville (1841), he was recalled to Bardstown, serving four mission stations there.

Spalding gained national prominence by writing *D'Aubigné's ''History of the Great Reformation in Germany and Switzerland,'' Reviewed* (1844), later expanded into *The History of the Protestant Reformation* (1860). In October 1844, after publishing his *Sketches of the Early Catholic Missions of Kentucky* (1844), he became vicar-general of Louisville, where, as a result of Flaget's age and Chabrat's increasing blindness, Spalding had to exercise unobtrusively the major administrative functions of the diocese. His lectures in the cathedral formed his next book, *General Evidences of Catholicity* (1847). At the Sixth Provincial Council of Baltimore (1846) he was unsuccessful in his endeavor to have a national tract society established. On Sept. 10, 1848, despite initial opposition from Flaget because of poor health, too close attachment to his many relatives, and the need for an outsider to lead the diocese (later archdiocese) of LOUISVILLE, Spalding was finally consecrated coadjutor; he succeeded to the see Feb. 11, 1850. His *Sketches of the Life . . . of . . . Flaget* was published in 1852.

Bishop of Louisville. As the tide of Irish and German immigration filled up the former missionary territory, the diocese urgently needed a more efficient administrative organization on all levels, as well as more priests, brothers, and sisters to staff parishes, schools, orphanages, and hospitals. The new bishop continued work on the cathedral begun by Chabrat (1849), consecrating it Oct. 3, 1852, and he entrusted the financial affairs of the diocese to his brother Rev. B. J. Spalding (1812–68), who handled them ably until his death. He settled the dispute over the jurisdiction of the Covington area by having it erected into a new see (1853). Spalding was close to Archbishop Kenrick at the First Plenary Council of Baltimore (1852), where he preached the memorial sermon for the deceased bishops, and he became familiar with the intricacies of gaining approval for national legislation for the Church. This, joined to practical knowledge from his frequent diocesan synods and extensive participation in the first three Provincial Councils of Cincinnati, Ohio, became a valuable preparation of his own conciliar activities. His visit to Europe from November of 1852 to April of 1853 helped to solve other diocesan problems; he recruited ten clerics, made provisions for the XAVERIAN BROTHERS to come to Louisville (1854), secured financial aid from the Lyons Society for the Propagation of the Faith, and laid the groundwork for the American College at Louvain, Belgium, which, with Bp. Peter P. LEFEVERE of Detroit, Michigan, he founded in 1857. After his return he established a chancery office in Louisville and developed an efficiently functioning diocese.

The spread of the Church and the increase of foreign-born in Kentucky sparked anti-Catholic demonstrations during the visit of Abp. G. BEDINI to Louisville (1853), presaging the outbreaks of violence culminating in the ''Bloody Monday'' riots of Aug. 5, 1855. Although more than 20 people were killed on this day, the toll in lives and property would have been much higher had it not been for the calm leadership of Spalding, who put the burden of control on the mayor. By dispassionate reasoning in *An Address to the Impartial Public on the Intolerant Spirit of the Times* (1854) and lectures correcting the calumnies of S. F. B. Morse and of G. D. Prentice of the *Louisville Journal,* later published with other articles in *Miscellanea* (1858), Spalding was able to restore some harmony among the groups. He gained grudging respect from his opponents, established an atmosphere that recalled the Irish and Germans to Louisville, and even secured a token indemnity bill from the Know Nothing-dominated legislature (*see* KNOW-NOTHINGISM). Spalding continued to establish churches, schools, and orphanages, and introduced into his diocese a house for Magdalens, and a conference of the St. Vincent de Paul Society (1854), as well as the Franciscan Fathers, the Brothers of Christian Instruction, the Ursulines, and the Sisters of Notre Dame. He was also energetic in supporting the NORTH AMERICAN COLLEGE in Rome at its foundation (1855–59) and especially in securing its endowment in 1869.

In the Civil War period Spalding reflected the attitude of his area, favoring first the neutrality policy of Kentucky and preferring the Church in general to follow an impartial course of action while performing works of charity for both sides. He opposed the Kentucky test-oath bill, which was vetoed by Gov. B. Magoffin; when it became law, Spalding took it under protest of unconstitutionality. He supplied chaplains and nursing sisters for North and South and endeavored to maintain strict impartiality himself in his spoken and written words. He was understanding of, but opposed to, the extreme position of some bishops, protesting to Rome in 1863 when he felt they were putting the Church in a bad light by their partisanship. A coolness developed between himself and Abp. J. B. PURCELL over the attitude of the *Catholic Telegraph* of Cincinnati, but never an open break. Spalding himself suspended the *Louisville Guardian* during the war. The apparent delay between the death of Kenrick (July 8, 1863) and Spalding's installation as archbishop of Baltimore (July 31, 1864) was caused reputedly by Secretary of State William Seward's alleged protest to Rome over sending one of doubtful loyalty to the powder-keg city of Baltimore.

Archbishop of Baltimore. In Baltimore Spalding scrupulously maintained his neutrality, supplying chaplains both for Federally occupied territory and for Confederate prisoners. He decreed public mourning after the assassination of President Abraham Lincoln, but would not directly intercede in behalf of assassin Mrs. Mary SURRATT, although he did petition the government to allow the return of Bp. Patrick Lynch to Charleston, South Carolina. When peace came, he sought to heal the scars of war as quickly as possible, appealing for and administering financial help to the people of the South. Within one year in his archdiocese he began 20 new churches. He completed the cathedral, organized conferences of the St. Vincent de Paul Society, began St. Mary's Industrial School as a protectory under the Xaverian Brothers, established homes for the Sisters of the Good Shepherd and the Little Sisters of the Poor, and welcomed the Passionist Fathers to the archdiocese. His major effort was as apostolic delegate for the Second Plenary Council of Baltimore of 1866 (*see* BALTIMORE, COUNCILS OF). After months of preparation with his theologian advisers, he presented a unified and cohesive outline, updating previous legislation and adapting it to current circumstances, yet leaving it broad enough for individual bishops to apply it as needed in their own jurisdictions. Unusual agreement was reached in all areas except that concerning Spalding's project of entrusting the mission work among the African Americans to special prefects apostolic. In this he was strongly opposed by Abp. P. R. KENRICK of St. Louis, Missouri, who feared a divided authority, and Kenrick's views prevailed. With few modifications, the 534 decrees were approved by the Congregation of Propaganda on Jan. 24, 1868. The decrees, with some changes at the Third Plenary Council of Baltimore (1884), formed the basis of American ecclesiastical law and set the pattern of administrative development of the Church in the U.S. The manner of preparation and discussion became a model for later Church councils.

In 1867 Spalding was in Rome at the centenary of SS. Peter and Paul when Pius IX convoked Vatican Council I (1869–70). On Aug. 16, 1868, he consecrated as vicar apostolic of North Carolina James Gibbons, his protégé and secretary since 1865. The sudden death (Aug. 6, 1868) by fire of his brother Benedict and the difficulty in settling his affairs led to strained relations with the bishop of Louisville, William MCCLOSKEY; it also caused problems later for his nephew John Lancaster SPALDING. At Vatican Council I Spalding was elected to the Commission on the Faith, having previously been appointed to the Commission on Postulata, which examined all matters proposed for deliberation before they were presented to the Council. Although Spalding at first desired the doctrine of papal INFALLIBILITY to remain implicitly defined, he later came out strongly in favor of explicit definition. In Rome he wrote his pastoral *On Papal Infallibility* (1870), clearing up some of the confusion that had attended the American position. After his return, using Michael O'Connor, SJ, as his agent, Spalding secured the first priests of St. Joseph's Society, formed in England by Rev. (later Cardinal) Herbert Vaughan, for the work of the conversion of the African Americans (*see* JOSEPHITES). Shortly after welcoming them to Baltimore on Dec. 5, 1871, he went into his final illness.

Bibliography: J. L. SPALDING, *The Life of the Most Reverend M. J. Spalding* (New York 1873). B. J. WEBB, *The Centenary of Catholicity in Kentucky* (Louisville 1884). A. G. MCGANN, *Nativism in Kentucky to 1860* (Washington 1944). R. F. TRISCO, *The Holy See and the Nascent Church in the Middle Western United States, 1826–1850* (*Analecta Gregoriana* 125; 1962). A. A. MICEK, *The Apologetics of Martin John Spalding* (Washington 1951).

[P. E. HOGAN]

SPANGENBERG, AUGUSTUS GOTTLIEB

Bishop and chief organizer of Moravian missionary activities in America; b. Klellenberg-Hohenstein, Germany, July 15, 1704; d. Berthelsdorf, Germany, Sept. 18, 1792. He was the son of a Lutheran pastor, and he studied at the University of Jena, where he received his M.A. in 1726. In his student days he was deeply influenced by PIETISM and in 1730 visited Herrnhut, the estate of Count Nikolaus Ludwig von ZINZENDORF, Moravian leader. Coming increasingly under Moravian influence, Spangenberg was dismissed from his professorship of religious education at Halle and joined the Herrnhut community. He went to Georgia (1733), but moved to Philadelphia, Pa. (1736), with a view to making it a center for Moravian missions. He returned to Germany (1739), where he developed missionary organization. Chosen bishop in 1744, he went to Bethlehem, Pa., where he organized the Pilgrim (missionary) and Home Congregations (*see* MORAVIAN CHURCH). In 1752 he settled in North Carolina and petitioned for legislation to protect Indian rights. Five years later he reorganized the missions and from 1759 to 1762 disbanded the communal economy at Bethlehem. He returned to Herrnhut in 1762, but continued to supervise foreign missions. He wrote *A Concise Historical Account of the Unitas Fratrum* (London 1775) and a life of Count Zinzendorf (Barby 1775), as well as *Idea fidei Fratrum* (Leipzig 1789).

Bibliography: G. NEISSER, *A History of the Beginnings of Moravian Work in America,* tr. W. N. SCHWARZE and S. H. GAPP (Bethlehem 1955). E. E. GRAY, *Wilderness Christians: The Moravian Mission to the Delaware Indians* (Ithaca 1956). E. LANGTON, *History of the Moravian Church* (London 1956).

[R. K. MACMASTER]

SPANHEIM, EZECHIEL AND FRIEDRICH

Ezechiel, Calvinist savant and diplomat; b. Geneva, Dec. 7, 1629; d. London, Nov. 7, 1710. During his theological studies at Leiden, where his father had been invited as a professor in 1642, Spanheim developed a scholarly interest in antiquities. He became a professor of eloquence at Geneva (1651), but resigned his academic post to be a tutor at the ducal court at Heidelberg (1656–61). His study *Discours sur les affaires d'Allemagne et sur le vicariat le l'Empire* involved him in the controversy over the vicariate of Palatinate-Bavaria, and he was sent to Rome to represent the Palatinate (1661–65). His close affiliation with the scholarly society sponsored by Queen Christina of Sweden was a decisive factor in his scientific development. While at Rome he published his eminent work on numismatics, *Dissertationes de praesentia et usu numismatum antiquorum* (1664). This was followed by a long period of diplomatic service: between 1665 and 1680 he was the Palatinate ambassador in Paris, Cologne, and London; he served the Brandenburg court at Paris (1680–90 and 1697–1702) and at London (1702–10). Spanheim as a politician was without distinction. Though he performed his office with integrity, he lacked the ambition of a statesman (Löwe). At the outbreak of the Franco-Palatine war, he was recalled to Berlin (1690–97), where he worked for refugee Huguenots, founding a society, named after him, that became the precursor of the Berlin Academy of Sciences. During these years he corresponded with G. W. Leibniz on the subject of union between Lutherans and Calvinists and wrote *Juliani imperatoris opera quae supersunt omnia* (1696), *Ezechielis Spanheim in Callimachi hymnos observationes* (1697), *Orbis romanus seu ad constitutionem Antonii imperatoris. . . exercitationes duae* (1697).

Friedrich, Calvinist theologian and historian; b. Geneva, May 1, 1632; d. Leiden, May 18, 1701. As did his brother Ezechiel, Friedrich, too, studied theology in Leiden, where he received an M.A. degree on Oct.17, 1548. He taught theology at the University of Heidelberg from 1655 until 1670, when he was invited to succeed Johannes Cocceius (1603–69) in the chair of theology at Leiden. In his strong defense of Calvinist orthodoxy against ARMINIANISM, he wrote *Dissertatio theologica de quinquarticulanis controversiis pridem in Belgio agitatis,* defending the decisions of the Synod of Dort (1618–19). (*See* CONFESSIONS OF FAITH, PROTESTANT.) The polemical disputes with Thomas Hobbes, Lord Herbert of Cherbury, and Baruch Spinoza produced his *De novissimis circa res sacras in Belgio dissidiis epistola ad amicum responsoria* (1677), where his theological position shows the effects of the conciliatory Academy of Saumur. He affirms the differentiation between fundamental and nonfundamental creed formulas and displays a relaxation in his earlier rigid orthodoxy. In 1671 Spanheim was appointed to the professorship of ecclesiastical history and composed historical works, of which three are of special merit: *Summa historiae ecclesiasticae* (1689), *Geographia sacra et ecclesiastica* (1698), and *Brevis introductio ad historiam sacram utriusque testamenti ac praecipue christianam.*

Bibliography: Ezechiel. V. LÖWE, *Ein Diplomat und Gelehrter, Ezechiel Spanheim* (Historische Studien 160; Berlin 1924). E. MURET, *Geschichte der französischen Kolonie in Brandenburg-Preussen* (Berlin 1885). A. VON HARNACK, *Geschichte der königlich-preussischen Akademie der Wissenschaften* (Berlin 1900). H. V. PETERSDORFF, *Allgemeine deutsche Biographie* 35:50–59. A. M. KOENIGER, *Lexikon für Theologie und Kirche,* ed. M. BUCHBERGER,

10 v. (Freiburg 1930–38) 9:702–703. W. DELIUS, *Die Religion in Geschichte und Gegenwart,* 7 v. (3d ed. Tübingen 1957–65) 6:223–224. Friedrich. *Opera,* 3 v. (Lyons 1701–03). O. RITSCHL, *Dogmengeschichte des Protestantismus,* 4 v. (Göttingen 1908–27) v.4. P. TSCHACKERT, *Allgemeine deutsche Biographie* 35: 60–61. L. ZSCHARNACK and O. WEBER, *Die Religion in Geschichte und Gegenwart,* 7 v. (3d ed. Tübingen 1957–65) 6:224.

[J. KRASENBRINK]

SPANN, OTHMAR

Austrian social philosopher; b. Altmannsdorf, near Vienna, Oct. 1, 1878; d. Neustift, Burgenland, July 8, 1950. After study at the universities of Vienna, Zurich, Bern, and Tübingen, Spann received his doctorate from the last in 1903. Employment in a center for private social work at Frankfurt am Main led to statistical, economic, and sociological publications. He was admitted to teach at the technical institute at Brünn (Moravia) in 1907 and was promoted to ordinary professor in 1911. In 1919 he was called to Vienna as professor of economics and sociology. The Nazi regime deprived him of his title in March 1938, and he was imprisoned on political grounds; he was not permitted to return to his position at the end of World War II.

Spann's theories were in sharp contrast to dominant scientific tendencies. Appealing to Plato and Aristotle, Meister Eckhart and St. Thomas Aquinas, and to German idealism and romanticism, he opposed empiricism, positivism, and materialism in philosophy, and atomism, individualism, and collectivism in social science. His system of ''universalism'' lent itself to use by proponents of social reconstruction and—partly misunderstood—became the object of political controversy. Spann himself had no political ambitions.

The problem Spann set for himself was to confront contemporary empiricism on its own ground with a new, nonempirical method. Moreover, he sought to establish the applicability of this method to broader scientific fields and to philosophy itself. He began with a concept of society as ''spiritual and acting totality,'' affirming that no member of society can be isolated from other members, but that he can develop only in spiritual community with others. Spann proposed as fundamental concepts: (1) the existence of partial wholes or subtotalities in all spheres of finite being, (2) a mutuality between parts that links them with the whole and, in the realm of the infinite, with the highest totality, (3) reorganization of the ever-changing subtotalities in time, and (4) the ordering of totalities according to content, degree, and precedence as discerned in reality. To Spann this concept of order was not based upon value judgments but upon analysis; he thought that, far from precluding empirical research, it elucidated and illuminated its results. Further, since the actual could always be compared to the norm—the systematically perfect totality—the method could lead to knowledge of the degree of perfection attained in concrete reality. Given the variety of his sources and the difficulty of their identification, it is not surprising that the adherents of his universalism are to be found more outside than within the realm of the social sciences.

Bibliography: *Gesamtausgabe der Werke von Othmar Spann,* ed. W. HEINRICH et al. (22 v. in preparation). B. LANDHEER, ''The Universalistic Theory of Society of Othmar Spann and His School,'' *An Introduction to the History of Sociology,* ed. H. E. BARNES (Chicago 1948) 385–399. D. VIKOR, *Economic Romanticism in the Twentieth Century: Spann's Attempt to Revolutionize Economic Theory* (New Delhi 1964).

[W. HEINRICH]

SPECIES

From the Greek εἶδος, having several meanings: (1) a logical relation of universality, the second of the PREDICABLES enumerated by Porphyry in his *Isagoge;* (2) a unit of taxonomy in biological classification; (3) the natural species as the QUIDDITY of sensible things and the proper object of the human mind; (4) the intentional species, a likeness or representation of the object in which the thing is made present to the knowing power; and (5) one of several names for Plato's unchanging, eternal Ideas. This article considers only the first three meanings; for the others, *see* SPECIES, INTENTIONAL; IDEA.

Logic. Species meant first the shape or visible FORM, and since anything was best recognized by its visible form, the same term was extended to designate its common intelligible character. In logic it meant the universal said in answer to ''What is it?'' of many that differ in number (''man,'' of Plato and Socrates). The species whose immediate inferiors are individuals is species only and is called the *infima species* (Gr. εἶδος εἰδικώτατον). The species is also related to the GENUS, which can be said of it as a direct quidditative predicate. Species in each category that fall between the supreme genus and the lowest species are, from alternate points of view, either species or genera; they are called subaltern species.

More recent logic speaks of classes rather than species. In mathematics especially they are called sets. Thus, a class is a group of individuals each having certain properties in virtue of which they are said to be its members. The attributes constitute the intention of the class; the members determine the extension. Classes of individuals are called classes of the first order, and these are grouped in classes of the second order, etc.

The question remains whether such classes are real entities independent of the human mind, or only common names, or concepts in the mind. A. N. WHITEHEAD and B. RUSSELL describe them as ''merely symbolic or linguistic conveniences, not genuine objects as their members are if they are individuals'' [*Principia Mathematica* (3 v. Cambridge, Eng. 1910–13) 1:75]. The problem dates from the classic questioning in Plato's *Parmenides* on how the universal idea that is one can be in its many instances. (*See* UNIVERSALS.)

Classification and Natural Species. In the natural sciences, species are units of classification between the genus and the subspecies. ARISTOTLE used this term in natural history. A common criterion for determining a natural class is descent from a common stock and indefinite fertility among the members. Problems in this area are those of the fixity and the evolution of species. (*See* EVOLUTION)

Distinct from the logical ordering of the relations of species and genera is the question of the objective fundament of these species. If there is a diversity of species in the corporeal world, manifested by the activity of bodies, to what extent can these be known? Does man have quidditative knowledge, real definitions of the species of any natural substance? Of man only? Of a relatively small number? Of very many? At what point in classification do the differences become merely accidental ones? These questions are commonly debated among scholastics and Thomists, with little consensus on the answers given.

See Also: INTENTIONALITY; DEFINITION; QUIDDITY.

Bibliography: G. DALLA NORA, *Enciclopedia filosofica* (Venice-Rome 1957) 4:846–852. M. J. ADLER, *Problems for Thomists* (New York 1940). A. C. COTTER, *Natural Species* (Weston, Mass. 1947). I. M. BOCHEŃSKI, *A History of Formal Logic,* ed. and tr. I. THOMAS (Notre Dame, Ind. 1961).

[W. BAUMGAERTNER]

SPECIES, INTENTIONAL

A term that designates the immaterial mode of existence an OBJECT acquires when it is united to the INTELLECT in the act of UNDERSTANDING. It is also used to designate the mode of existence of an object in the external and internal SENSES. While practically all modern Thomists refer to intentional species and to impressed or expressed intelligible species, St. THOMAS AQUINAS did not use these expressions. He frequently used intention and SPECIES (and also FORM) interchangeably; and while he used intention as synonymous with concept, he distinguished intention from intelligible species. In view of such a diversity in usage, this article first explains the notion of intentionality in the teaching of St. Thomas and then treats of the later scholastic development of intentional species, the importance of intentional species in scholastic philosophy, and the rejection of the notion in modern philosophy.

Thomistic Notion. St. Thomas's theory of knowledge rests on a principle accepted by all scholastics, namely, that the intellect is a faculty of an immaterial and subsistent soul (*see* FACULTIES OF THE SOUL). In light of this principle, the CONCEPT, or intention, whereby the intellect understands a thing must have the same mode of existence as the intellect itself; namely, it must have an immaterial existence. Furthermore, because the intellect is immaterial, the ESSENCE of a material object as understood is identically the same essence for every individual object that possesses the same specific nature. For instance, the concept man is used to designate a particular individual and every human person. Thus the concept is said to be universal (*see* UNIVERSALS). As opposed to this, the intentional species in the external senses and IMAGINATION, while immaterial to a certain degree, are not universal; they are merely individual intentions because the faculties involved are bodily faculties.

Intelligible Species. Thus, one must understand the analogous manner in which St. Thomas refers to a spiritual transmutation of a sensory organ, as when the eye is affected by something visible ''when it receives the intention of color'' (*Summa theologiae* 1a2ae, 22.2 ad 3). When the eye beholds gold, the gold is not in the eye, although its intention is. Thus the union of gold and the eye cannot possibly be conceived as a material union. Similarly, the imagination forms an intention of gold that enables the knower to image the gold in its absence. And just as the intention of gold must exist in the imagination in a manner different from that in which it exists in the external sense, so the intention of gold must exist in the intellect in a manner appropriate to the intellect. Therefore, the intellect must immaterialize, as it were, the sensible species found in the imagination. From the image in the imagination, the intellect must abstract an intelligible species. And it is by means of the intelligible species that the intellect forms a universal intention.

It should be noted that the concept has a nobler existence in the intellect than the image has in the imagination. Hence, the imagination can in no way be considered the efficient cause of a concept, since no agent can produce an effect nobler than itself. Reflections such as these on the causality involved in the formation of a concept led Aristotle to develop a theory of ABSTRACTION that has become traditional among scholastics. The efficient cause that alone is capable of producing the concept as its proper effect is the intellect itself; the image in the imagination is only a material cause, while the intelligible species is an instrumental cause.

Intentions. Contrary to the teaching of many scholastic textbooks, St. Thomas makes a distinction between the intelligible species and the intention, as mentioned above. For Aquinas, the intelligible species is the means whereby the intellect understands the intention, which is the terminus or term of the abstractive process: "Now since this intention as understood is the terminus of the intellectual operation, it is distinct from the intelligible species . . . which should be considered as the principle of the intellectual operation" (*C. gent.* 1.53). The intelligible species is a PRINCIPLE not as an efficient cause but as the first act of the intellect in the order of understanding.

Furthermore, St. Thomas divides concepts into first intentions and second intentions (*In 1 sent.* 23.1.3, 26.1.1 ad 3). The first intention is a concept that has an immediate foundation in reality, as the concept of man, tree, dog, etc.; whereas the second intention has only an indirect foundation in reality, such as the concept of universal, species, etc. (*see* LOGIC). Thus St. Thomas's understanding of intention in the intellectual order remains distinct from that of the intelligible species. Only during the later scholastic development of his doctrine did the intelligible species come to be identified with the intentional species.

On the other hand, St. Thomas frequently uses the terms "species," "form," and "intention" to signify the same thing. This is particularly evident when he treats of the manner in which the object is represented by the various internal senses, i.e., the imagination, memory, CENTRAL SENSE, and the COGITATIVE, or estimative, power. For instance, in arguing for a distinction between each of these powers, he states that "the power that receives the species of sensible things must be distinct from the power that preserves them" (*Summa theologiae* 1a, 78.4). Then, in the same context, he uses the terms "form" and "intention": "The phantasy or imagination is ordered to the retention and preservation of these forms . . . and the ESTIMATIVE POWER is ordered to apprehending intentions that are not received through the senses" (*ibid.*).

Scholastic Development. The later scholastic philosophers simplified the manner of specifying the way in which the object is received and represented by various powers, or faculties, by adding the qualifying terms "impressed" and "expressed" to their designations of sensible species and the intelligible species. Since the external senses are passive with respect to their objects—for the change a sense undergoes is in the order of an impression only—they held that there is only an impressed sensible species in the external senses. In the internal senses, on the other hand, since the object is both received and understood, there must be both an impressed sensible species and an expressed sensible species. Likewise, in the intellect there must be an impressed intelligible species and an expressed intelligible species, the latter corresponding to the intention or concept of St. Thomas.

These usages had been fairly well established before the time of JOHN OF ST. THOMAS, who used them in his interpretation of St. Thomas's theory of abstraction. Contemporary Thomists follow John of St. Thomas in this respect, standardizing scholastic terminology along the lines just indicated. In a still later development, the intention itself was designated as the intentional species. The expression intentional species came to be current among scholastic philosophers when it became necessary to defend the entitative character of intentions in the intellect against thinkers who reduced all knowledge to a sensory level (see M. Maher, *Psychology: Empirical and Rational* [New York 1930] 52).

Importance. In Thomistic EPISTEMOLOGY it is of utmost importance to emphasize that the intentional species, or concept, as a formal SIGN of something in reality, does not have any signification other than the thing itself. Thus it cannot be viewed as a mere instrumental sign, having a signification of its own apart from what it represents in reality. When something is said to have an intentional mode of existence, this manner of speaking signifies that the object in reality is understood by the intellect. In this way it is maintained that the intellect does not understand the concept as such, but that the intellect understands the object in reality through an intentional being such as a concept. To maintain that the intellect understands the concept as such would be to profess, at least implicitly, CONCEPTUALISM or IDEALISM, positions that St. Thomas took pains to avoid in elucidating his theory of knowledge. A correct interpretation of the intentional species, on the other hand, enables the REALISM of Thomistic philosophy to be preserved.

Modern Philosophy. The intentional species is rejected by those modern philosophers who make no distinction between mind and matter, namely, proponents of MATERIALISM, SENSISM, naturalism, etc. It is rejected also by existential phenomenologists who adopt a purely empirical approach to reality. It is rejected too by American pragmatists, such as W. JAMES and J. Dewey, whose theories of knowledge are confined to sensory experience. It is further rejected by those who disavow the so-called faculty theory of knowledge, as does A. N. WHITEHEAD.

Whenever intentional species are rejected, the only alternative is a nominalistic interpretation of concepts in their relation to objects: terms as arbitrary symbols derive a meaning only when they are applied to individual objects. For scholastics, the opposite is true: terms derive their meaning from objects. In symbolic logic, the term ''intention'' refers to the meaning that arbitrary signs acquire when viewed in relation to each other; the relation of such signs to reality is regarded as more descriptive than existential (*see* LOGIC, SYMBOLIC). As a further difference from usage within the scholastic tradition, the term is spelled differently, as ''intension.''

See Also: INTENTIONALITY; KNOWLEDGE, PROCESS OF; KNOWLEDGE, THEORIES OF; NOMINALISM.

Bibliography: J. E. ROYCE, *Man and His Nature* (New York 1961). R. E. BRENNAN, *Thomistic Psychology* (New York 1956). J. MARITAIN, *Distinguish to Unite, or The Degrees of Knowledge,* tr. G. B. PHELAN (New York 1959); *Bergsonian Philosophy and Thomism,* tr. M. L. and J. G. ANDISON (New York 1955). JOHN OF ST. THOMAS, *Cursus philosophicus thomisticus,* ed. B. REISER, 3 v. (new ed. Turin 1930–37).

[R. J. MASIELLO]

SPEDALIERI, NICOLA

Apologist; b. Bronte (Cantania), Dec. 5, 1740; d. Rome, Nov. 26, 1795. He studied at the seminary in Monreale, Sicily, where he took his doctorate in theology. He was ordained in 1764 and was admitted to the Arcadia under the name of Melanzio Alcioneo. He cultivated also poetry, music, and paintings.

His published works are *Analisi dell'esame critico del Sig. Nicola Ferret sulle prove del Christianesimo* (Rome 1778), a defense of the authenticity and veracity of the New Testament, and *Confutazione dell'esame critico del Christianesimo fatto dal Sig. Edoardo Gibbons* (Rome 1784), a treatise against the rationalist theories of Gibbons. The principal work, however, is still *Dei diritti dell'uomo,* in which he shows the Christian religion to be the most secure guardian of the rights of man (Rome 1791). In it he combatted deism, atheism, the so-called natural religion proclaimed by the French Revolution, Jansenism, and Freemasonry; he also developed the thesis that sovereignty resides in the people, who in order to avoid confusion and tyranny, entrust it to the governing body as depository. The work was proscribed by all the courts. The libertine philosophers did not like it because it reconciled the rights of man with the Gospel. The liberals were against it because it held that only religious ideas were capable of procuring the people's well-being. Some Catholic theologians were opposed to it because it admitted the licitness of regicide, even if only in extreme cases.

Bibliography: H. HURTER, *Nomenclator literarius theologiae catholicae,* 5 v. in 6 (3d ed. Innsbruck 1903–13) 5.1:323–324.

[C. TESTORE]

SPEE, FRIEDRICH VON

German poet, moral theologian, and pioneer opponent of trials for witchcraft; b. Kaiserswerth, near Düsseldorf, Feb. 25, 1591; d. Trier, Aug. 7, 1635. He entered the Society of Jesus at Trier in 1610 and after completing his studies at Fulda and Würzburg was ordained in 1622. After he served as a professor of philosophy at Paderborn (1623–26), he spent the next two years in teaching and missionary work, especially at Cologne and Wesel. While preaching near Peine, he was attacked and severely wounded by a fanatical opponent of Catholicism. He returned to Paderborn and was appointed professor of moral theology there in 1630, but found time to engage in pastoral work, which included giving spiritual help and comfort to those condemned and executed on the charge of witchcraft. From 1631 to 1633 he was professor of moral theology at Cologne, and from 1633 to 1635, at Trier. In the storming of that city by the imperial forces, he ministered zealously to the sick and wounded of both sides. He died of the plague, contracted in this charitable activity.

Among his works, three merit special mention. His *Trutznachtigal,* a collection of religious lyrics, composed in 1629, but first published in full in 1649, and his *Guldines Tugendbuch,* a poetic treatment of the theological virtues, composed in 1631, but again not published until 1649, give him a high place in German religious poetry. The second work was praised in the highest terms by Leibniz, and both have been repeatedly printed. He deserves to be remembered above all, however, for his *Cautio criminalis,* in which, with a psychological insight far in advance of his times, he attacked courageously and eloquently the terrible abuses of the witch trials and witch hysteria and advocated a whole series of reforms. This work, published in 1631, anonymously and apparently without the author's permission, involved him in temporary difficulties with his superiors and raised a storm of criticism against him. However, the *Cautio,* from the first, exercised a powerful influence against the evils it described, and was repeatedly published in new editions and in translation.

Bibliography: R. NEWALD, *Lexikon für Theologie und Kirche* [1] 9:713–714. R. BROUILLARD, *Dictionnaire de théologie catholique* 14.2:2474–77. *Bibliothèque de la Compagnie de Jésus* 7:1424–31. B. DUHR, *Geschichte der Jesuiten in den Ländern deutscher Zunge,* 4 v. in 5 (Freiburg 1907–28) 2.2:745–766. E. ROSENFELD, *Friedrich Spee von Langenfeld* (Berlin 1958). H. WOLTER, *Lexikon für Theologie und Kirche* [2] 9:956.

[M. R. P. MCGUIRE]

SPEECH, INDECENT AND VULGAR

St. James states that "if anyone does not offend in word, he is a perfect man" (Jas 3.2). There are many ways in which one may offend by speech. BLASPHEMY is a direct insult of God; cursing, in the strict sense, CALUMNY, DETRACTION, the uncharitable slur, and the like are sins against the neighbor (and hence, against God). Of inherently lesser evil is the type of speech called indecent or vulgar, and of these two, the kind called vulgar is generally less morally reproachable than indecent speech.

Vulgar speech, of its nature, is not more than a flouting of social custom. Words once in current usage, even in good society, have come (by a shift in custom, a perhaps heightened refinement in social intercourse) to be unacceptable as a means of expression in normally polite society. Such, for example, are the so-called four-letter words. Many of them can be found, used quite naturally and not for any shock value, in the works of Chaucer and Shakespeare. They generally cannot be so used in our age without almost certainly causing raised eyebrows or the unhealthy snigger. But the words themselves, taken as vocables, are not necessarily sinful. Circumstances may make them sinful: if they are used in a deliberate effort to shock or disedify; if their use scandalizes; if their use leads the young and impressionable to consider that this is the way they should talk.

The word "decent," derives from the Latin *decere,* which means in its adjectival form (*decens*) "becoming, proper, fitting." Even if one were to think that off-color jokes, "dirty" stories, habitual vulgar language are not in themselves sinful, their use would still be unbecoming for all who believe in human dignity, and above all for all who profess to follow Christ, from whose mouth there never issued an unbecoming word.

Bibliography: H. C. GARDINER, *Norms for the Novel* (rev. ed. Garden City, N.Y. 1960).

[H. C. GARDINER]

SPEED, JOHN, BL.

Lay martyr; *alias* Spence; b. Durham, England; d. hanged there Feb. 4, 1594. John Speed diligently escorted St. John BOSTE from house to house as he ministered to his scattered flock. He was arrested in the Brancepeth (Durham) home of William and Grace Claxton with them and Boste. All were condemned, but Mrs. Claxton was reprieved because she was pregnant. John Speed died with constancy for aiding an illegal priest. He was beatified by Pius XI on Dec. 15, 1929 as one of the Martyrs of Durham.

Feast of the English Martyrs: May 4 (England).

See Also: ENGLAND, SCOTLAND, AND WALES, MARTYRS OF.

Bibliography: R. CHALLONER, *Memoirs of Missionary Priests,* ed. J. H. POLLEN (rev. ed. London 1924; repr. Farnborough 1969), I, 100ff. J. H. POLLEN, *Acts of English Martyrs* (London 1891); *English Martyrs* 1584–1683 (London 1908), 239.

[K. I. RABENSTEIN]

SPEER, ROBERT ELLIOTT

Presbyterian lay mission leader; b. Huntingdon, Pennsylvania, Sept. 10, 1897; d. Philadelphia, Pennsylvania, Nov. 23, 1947. He was of Scotch-Irish background. Speer graduated from Princeton University, New Jersey, in 1889 and spent his entire career in the Presbyterian Board of Foreign Missions (1891–1937). He was an accomplished administrator and scholar, whose efforts more than doubled the scale of Presbyterian mission work. He withstood the conservative attacks of J. G. Machen on Presbyterian missions and, from the opposite side, the critique of William E. Hocking and associates in *Rethinking Missions* (1933). With John R. MOTT, leader of the STUDENT VOLUNTEER MOVEMENT, and in cooperation with the Young Men's Christian Association, Speer led his own denomination and Protestant mission work as a whole into the age of world mission, inspired by the slogan, "The Evangelization of the World in This Generation." In 1927, as moderator of the General Assembly of the Presbyterian Church in the U.S.A., he played a reconciling role at the height of the Fundamentalist-Modernist dispute. He published a total of 66 books, as well as numerous articles.

Bibliography: W. R. WHEELER, *A Man Sent from God . . . Robert E. Speer* (New York 1956), complete list of writings, 312. J. A. MACKAY "Robert Elliott Speer: A Man of Yesterday Today." *Princeton Seminary Bulletin* 60 (1967) 11–21. The Library of Princeton Theological Seminary contains a substantial collection of materials concerning Speer and his career.

[E. A. SMITH]

SPELLMAN, FRANCIS

Cardinal; b. Whitman, Massachusetts, May 4, 1889; d. New York, Dec. 2, 1967. He was the son of William and Ellen Conway Spellman. After attending public elementary and secondary schools in Whitman, Spellman entered Fordham College, where he received a bachelor of arts degree in 1911. With the approval of Archbishop William O'Connell of Boston, he entered the North American College in Rome. In 1916 he received a doctorate in theology, and on May 14 of the same year he was ordained a priest in the Church of St. Apollinaris in Rome. He returned to Boston and was assigned as an assistant pastor at All Saints Church in Roxbury, Massachusetts. He was appointed assistant chancellor of the archdiocese in 1922 and became archivist a year later.

Spellman accompanied a Holy Year diocesan pilgrimage to Rome in 1925 and remained there to direct playgrounds presented to the Holy See by the Knights of Columbus. The same year Pope Pius XI appointed him to the Vatican Secretariat of State. It was there that he became friendly with Cardinal Eugenio Pacelli, the future secretary of state and later Pope Pius XII. Pope Pius XI named him auxiliary bishop of Boston, and he was consecrated in St. Peter's Basilica by Pacelli on Sept. 8, 1932. Spellman returned to Boston where he became pastor of Sacred Heart parish in Newton Center. When Pacelli visited the United States as papal secretary of state in 1936, Spellman accompanied him on his visits throughout the country.

On April 15, 1939, the recently elected Pope Pius XII appointed Spellman as archbishop of New York, and on Feb. 18, 1946 named him cardinal. Under Spellman the Archdiocese of New York underwent years of extraordinary expansion and development. During his first year in New York, he refinanced a $28 million debt incurred by the diocese and the parishes during the Depression. Also in 1939 he established the Building Commission to supervise and advise on building projects throughout the archdiocese. The Institutional Commodity Services was established in 1941 as a central purchasing agency for the churches and institutions of the archdiocese, thereby saving them more than $1.5 million a year in purchases.

Under Spellman the Catholic Charities of the archdiocese underwent enormous expansion. Spellman constructed or renovated more than 370 elementary and secondary schools at a cost of $500 million, earning for him the title, ''cardinal of education.'' Recognizing the value of television in education, he purchased the RCA color broadcast equipment at the New York World's Fair and established the Instructional Television Center in 1966. He sponsored the publication of the *Catholic Encyclopedia for School and Home* (1965), and the *New Catholic Encyclopedia* (1967). Under his direction St. Joseph's Seminary was completely renovated.

Spellman was also military vicar of the Armed Forces, consisting of more than two million servicemen and their families and 2,700 chaplains. From 1942 until 1966 he journeyed throughout the world visiting military installations, and was preparing his 17th annual Christmas pastoral visit when he died. As a national figure, the cardinal was outspoken in support of racial justice and equality and of the rights and interests of Catholic students at every level. His statements on communism, immorality, and education received international attention.

In 1960 Pope John XXIII appointed him to the Central Preparatory Commission for the Second Vatican Council. He was also appointed by Pope Paul VI to the Central Post-Conciliar Commission to implement and interpret the decrees of the council. He spoke frequently during the four sessions of the council and was especially influential in the formulation of the Declaration on Religious Freedom during the third and fourth sessions. He was among the first American bishops of the country to implement the decrees of the council concerning reforms in the liturgy, the establishment of episcopal vicars in areas of the archdiocese, and the formation of a senate of priests to assist the archbishop.

Bibliography: J. COONEY, *The American Pope: The Life and Times of Francis Cardinal Spellman* (New York 1984).

[G. E. TIFFANY]

SPENCER, HERBERT

English social philosopher and pioneer sociologist; b. Derby, April 27, 1820; d. Brighton, Dec. 8, 1903. His father was William George Spencer, a Quaker schoolmaster; his mother, Harriet Holmes, was of Huguenot and Hussite ancestry. After a sketchy private education, Spencer taught for a year at the age of 16, worked as a railroad engineer from 1837 to 1848, except for a period in journalism between 1841 and 1844, then became subeditor of the *Economist* from 1848 to 1853 before resigning to do freelance writing. He remained unmarried.

Works. As early as 1843, Spencer published a pamphlet of essays entitled *The Proper Sphere of Government.* His first book, *Social Statics* (1851), attracted considerable attention. Thereafter, despite dyspepsia, neurasthenia, and insomnia in later life, he published a wide variety of books and essays. His second book, *Principles of Psychology* (1855), was later incorporated in his ambitious ten-volume *Synthetic Philosophy,* first publicized in 1860. This included *First Principles* (1862), *The Principles of Biology* (2 v. 1864–67), *The Principles of Psychology* (rev. 2 v. 1870–72), *The Principles of Sociology* (3 v. 1876–82), and *The Principles of Ethics* (2 v. 1879–93). Besides writing, revising, and enlarging several editions of each of these large works, Spencer published collections of essays in 1858, 1863, and 1874, as well as several other books. After *Education* (1861) and *The Study of Sociology* (1873), there appeared *Descriptive Sociology* (8 v. 1873–81), in which Spencer classified and arranged data compiled by others on various historical and primitive peoples; additional volumes were compiled after his death with money he left for that purpose. His last works were *The Man versus the State* (1884), *Facts and Comments* (1902), and *An Autobiography* (2 v. 1904), published posthumously.

Religious and Ethical Views. Spencer called himself an agnostic, considering God unknowable. In *Principles of Sociology* he propounded his well-known theory of the ''ghost origin'' of religion (manism), holding that early man feared the spirits of nature, practiced nature worship, and then adopted successively ancestor worship, polytheism, and eventually monotheism. He maintained that fear of the dead is the root of religious control, and fear of the living, the root of political control.

Spencer adopted the ethics of UTILITARIANISM. In additon, he was passionately in favor of individual liberty and went to great lengths to develop and defend a doctrine of laissez faire. In politics he espoused ''radical'' reformist ideas. In his view man was solitary by nature and compelled only by population growth to live in organized social life. Not only did he reduce the function of the State to minimal protective duties, but he denied the State's right to provide for education and welfare, looking forward to the time when human progress would make the State superfluous.

Herbert Spencer.

Social Evolutionism. Spencer's extreme individualism was associated with both evolutionary and organic views of SOCIETY. He accepted Lamarck's belief in the inheritance of acquired characteristics, and in *Social Statics,* nine years before Darwin's *Origin of Species,* he proposed human perfection as the outcome of a long process of adaptation to the environment by means of natural selection. In psychology he tried to combine the EMPIRICISM of LOCKE, maintaining that the mind derives all knowledge from experience through the senses, and the RATIONALISM of DESCARTES, who considered ideas to be innate. In Spencer's view, ideas transcend the experience of the individual, being transmitted by inheritance from the experience of the race.

The guiding principle of Spencer's philosophy was evolutionism. Later he invented the term, often associated with Darwin, of the ''survival of the fittest.'' According to his view of the evolutionary adaptive process, the organic nature of society made cooperation inevitable and necessary for progress, as no part of society can develop faster than another. He opposed state welfare programs not only in the name of individual liberty but because he believed that they impeded the operation of the law of natural selection and because they necessitated taxation, thus depriving individuals of the means to take part in productive enterprise. His economic individualism did not always make him callous, however, for he extolled sympathy and in developing his argument held that government aid to the poor would usurp the role of natural sympathy and private charity.

Influence. Spencer popularized individualism and laissez-faire economics in England and the United States. He inspired many sociologists to adopt an organismic conception of society, promoted the idea of unilinear evolution, and contributed to the development of what is known as social Darwinism. He called attention to problems of methodology involved in the inductive study of society. His analysis of institutions and especially ceremonies proved to be very fruitful in sociology. Indeed, he influenced a number of sociologists, including L. T. Hobhouse in England, Emile Durkheim in France, Franz Müller-Lyer in Germany, and W. G. Sumner in the United States, to use anthropological and other cultural data and to adopt the comparative method of studying society. Some value may still be derived by examining Spencer's work, now chiefly of historical interest.

Bibliography: E. BARKER, *Political Thought in England from Herbert Spencer to the Present Day* (New York 1915). D. DUNCAN, *The Life and Letters of Herbert Spencer,* 2 v. (New York 1908). H. S. R. ELLIOT, *Herbert Spencer* (London 1917). F. J. C. HEARNSHAW, ed., *The Social and Political Ideas of Some Representative Thinkers of the Victorian Age* (London 1933). J. RUMNEY, *Herbert*

Spencer's Sociology (London 1934). A. W. TILLETT, *Spencer's Synthetic Philosophy* (London 1914); *Herbert Spencer Betrayed* (London 1939).

[E. J. ROSS]

SPENER, PHILIPP JAKOB

Founder of PIETISM; b. Rappoltsweiler, Upper Alsace, Jan. 23, 1635; d. Berlin, Feb. 5, 1705. He studied at Strasbourg and became pastor of the Lutheran church at Frankfort on the Main. Here Spener began to gather a group of his parishioners about him on Sundays for further prayer, pious songs, spiritual reading, and discussion. The term Pietist finds its root in these *Collegia pietatis* or Guilds of Piety as the meetings came to be called. In 1675, Spener published his *Pia desideria* or *Heartfelt Desires for a God-pleasing Reform of the True Evangelical Churches.* Herein he proposed his program for Christian reform: private gatherings, like the Guilds of Piety, should be formed to improve the believer's understanding of the teachings of Scripture. He emphasized universal priesthood, the necessity of virtuous living, and the perfect union of Christians in prayer, good example, and calm discussion. He also advocated the reform of seminary training to provide greater emphasis on spiritual reading and scriptural study. The *Pia desideria* was greeted by some with enthusiasm; others feared its deemphasis of dogma.

In 1686, Spener became preacher to the court at Dresden. At the same time a short-lived seminary on the Spener plan was established at Leipzig. Trouble at Dresden led him to welcome the pastorate of St. Nicholas in Berlin in 1691. His writings indicate that he was not at peace there either. However, he was able to organize the faculty of theology at Halle, from whence the gospel of Pietism was to spread throughout Europe.

Bibliography: L. CRISTIANI, *Dictionnaire de théologie catholique*, ed. A. VACANT et al., 15 v. (Paris 1903–50; Tables Générales 1951–) 12.2:2084–89. P. GRÜNBERG, *Philipp Jacob Spener,* 3 v. (Göttingen 1893–1906).

[H. J. MULLER]

SPENGLER, OSWALD

German philosopher of history; b. Blankenburg (Harz), May 29, 1880; d. Munich, May 8, 1936. Spengler studied mathematics and philosophy at Halle, Munich, and Berlin. His main work, *Der Untergang des Abendlandes* (2 v. Munich 1918–22; tr. C. F. Atkinson, New York 1926–28), is an all–inclusive, cyclical philosophy of history that is presented also as *the* authentic philosophy of the West. In Spengler's view, the prime forms of history are the great cultures, each lasting 1,000 years. Cultures are organisms that have their childhood, youth, manhood, and old age. The destiny idea governs every phase of a culture with absolute necessity; there is no freedom but the ''freedom'' to affirm the inevitable. Cultural phenomena, including philosophy and religion, are relative expressions of the basic idea, or soul, of a culture. There are no eternal truths. A comparative morphology of great cultures lays bare the primitive culture form that underlies them all.

Spengler writes with prophetic power, reminiscent of F. W. NIETZSCHE. Brilliant insights occur amid dubious generalizations. His cyclical theory is naturalistic, relativistic, and fatalistic; but it compels reflection on the inadequacies of rationalistic or positivistic views of history.

Bibliography: A. HILCKMAN, *Enciclopedia filosofica* 4:865–867. H. S. HUGHES, *Oswald Spengler: A Critical Estimate* (rev. ed. New York 1962). R. T. FLEWELLING, *The Survival of Western Culture* (New York 1943). G. MÜLLER, ''Oswald Spenglers Bedeutung für die Geschichtswissenschaft,'' *Saeculum* 13 (1962) 380–393.

[P. L. HUG]

SPENSER, WILLIAM, BL.

Priest, martyr; b. *c.* 1555 at Gisburn, Yorkshire, England; hanged, drawn, and quartered on Sept. 24, 1589 at York. His maternal uncle, Bl. William Horne, sent him (1573) to Trinity College, Oxford, where he earned his master's degree in 1580. He used his position as a fellow at Oxford to influence his pupils regarding the truth of Catholicism, but he delayed his formal reconciliation with the Church until 1582 when he was received into communion at Rheims. He then began his seminary studies. After presbyteral ordination (1583), on Aug. 29, 1584, he was sent to England, where he worked in Yorkshire. One of his greatest accomplishments was the reconciliation of his parents and uncle, who later became a priest. Spenser voluntarily gave himself up to authorities at York Castle in order to assist those imprisoned there. He was condemned for his priesthood and was executed with Bl. Robert HARDESTY. He was beatified by Pope John Paul II on Nov. 22, 1987 with George Haydock and companions.

Feast of the English Martyrs: May 4 (England).

See Also: ENGLAND, SCOTLAND, AND WALES, MARTYRS OF.

Bibliography: R. CHALLONER, *Memoirs of Missionary Priests,* ed. J. H. POLLEN (rev. ed. London 1924). J. H. POLLEN, *Acts* *of English Martyrs* (London 1891), 273–78; *English Martyrs 1584–1603* (London 1908), 34, 35.

[K. I. RABENSTEIN]

SPERANDEA, ST.

Benedictine nun; b. Gubbio, Umbria, central Italy, *c.* 1216; d. Cingoli in the Marches, Sept. 11, 1276. She has no connection with either the Abbot St. Sperandeus (also a native of Gubbio) or the Congregation of St. Santuccia. For 10 years she wandered through central Italy preaching penance. She was especially renowned for her charity, piety, rigorous mortifications, and strict observance of the ascetic life. She restored the Benedictine convent of St. Michael (later St. Sperandia) at Cingoli in 1265 and served as abbess. Very shortly after her death, she became patron saint of Cingoli. Her body, buried there, long remained incorrupt; her cult was approved by JOHN XXII in 1325.

Feast: Sept. 11.

Bibliography: *Acta Sanctorum* (Paris 1863–) Sept. 3:890–913. A. MERCATI and A. PELZER, *Dizionario ecclesiastico,* 3 v. (Turin 1954–58) 3:939. A. M. ZIMMERMANN, *Kalendarium Benedictinum: Die Heiligen und Seligen des Benediktinerorderns und seiner Zwiege,* 4. (Metten 1933–38) 3:42–45. G. MALAZAMPA, *Vita di s. Sperandea, vergine, protettrice di Cingoli* (Cingoli 1901). *Bibliotheca hagiographica latina antiquae et mediae aetatis,* 2 v. (Brussels 1898–1901; suppl. 1911) 2:1133. A. POTTHAST, *Bibliotheca historica medii aevi* (2d ed. 1896; repr. Graz 1954) 2:1581. U. CHEVALIER, *Répertoire des sources historiques du moyen-âge. Bio-bibliographie,* 2 v. (2d ed. Paris 1905–07) 2:4312. L. H. COTTINEAU, *Répertoire topobibliographique des abbayes et prieurés,* 2 v. (Mâcon 1935–39) 1:784. G. SPAHR, *Lexikon für Theologie und Kirche,* ed. J. HOFER and K. RAHNER (Freiburg 1957–65) 9:960.

[F. D. LAZENBY]

SPEYR, ADRIENNE VON

Medical doctor, mystical writer, stygmatic; b. La Chaux-de-Fonds, Switzerland, Sept. 10, 1902; d. Basel, Switzerland, Sept. 17, 1967. She was born into one of Basel's oldest families and schooled in the Protestant tradition. A three-year bout with tuberculosis preceded her study of medicine. She worked her way through medical school to become a doctor in 1928. In 1927 she married Emil Dürr, a widower with two small sons, and a professor at the University of Basel. His death in 1934 drove her to the brink of suicide. In 1936 she married Werner Kägi also a professor of history. She maintained a busy practice, seeing up to 80 patients a day, until failing health compelled her to restrict, and eventually give up, her practice in the mid-1950s.

Interior Life. This active exterior was accompanied by an intense interior life. She records that as a child and adolescent she was aware of the presence of angels, had encounters with IGNATIUS OF LOYOLA, and a vision of the Virgin Mary. In spite of these extraordinary occurrences she suffered distress from the pain of her unfulfilled religious search. Her meeting in the autumn of 1940 with Hans Urs von BALTHASAR, then chaplain at the University of Basil, and her subsequent conversion to Catholicism ended the quest which had thus far characterized her inner life. Von Balthasar, who became her confessor, writes of a ''veritable cataract of mystical graces'' which ''poured over Adrienne in a seemingly chaotic storm'' (Balthasar, p. 33) immediately after her conversion. Experiences of a mystical nature intensified. In 1941 during Holy Week she began experiencing the interior sufferings of Jesus. Von Balthasar attests to exterior stigmatization occurring in 1942. Her self-forgetting availability for the Word of God seemed to enable her to ''travel''—to be transported in prayer to various parts of the world where she comforted the physically tortured and the spiritually suffering (von Balthasar, pp. 39, 40).

Oswald Spengler. (©Bettmann/CORBIS)

Mystical Writings. Von Speyr's meeting with von Balthasar marked the beginning of a lifelong friendship of mutual respect and cooperation which had significant impact on the life of each. Citing her extensively in some of his major works, von Balthasar repeatedly speaks of her influence on his theology: ''Today, after her death, her work appears far more important to me than mine, and the publication of her still unpublished writings takes precedence over all personal work of my own'' (Balthasar, p. 13). Von Speyr's understanding of her mission to establish a secular institute with von Balthasar was the occasion that caused him to leave the Jesuit Order. If she was an inspiration for him, she needed him as a catalyst in the moment of her conversion, and as a co-founder of the secular institute, but most importantly she needed him as a confessor who over a period of 27 years listened to her insights, wrote them down, and was instrumental in the publication of what to date includes some 63 volumes.

Meditative commentaries on the Bible make up a major portion of von Speyr's work, reflecting her conviction that Christian mysticism necessarily proceeds from Holy Scripture. Each word must be considered as containing the infinity of the divine Word, the entire Christ, the trinitarian source.

Experience, rather than scholarship in the conventional sense, is the basis of her writings which she composed in a state of mystical intensity, never remembering what she had already dictated. Thus it is not surprising that mysticism and the visionary have a predominant place in her work. In her commentary on the Apocalypse and in her two-volume work on objective and subjective mysticism (which von Balthasar has termed ''experiential dogmatics'') we find a systematization of her thought. In contrast to the Gospels in which ''the truth of God assumed the form of a human being'' (*Apokalypse*, p. 16), the vision takes place in a realm in which time is suspended, neither in heaven or on earth, but in an indeterminate third place. It reveals an absolute, not a ''relative'', ''incarnational'' truth, such as we find in the Gospels. As such it can only be revealed to a human being in a state of ecstasy in which the mystic ''becomes a pure instrument of registering'' (*Apokalypse*, p. 17). The defenseless availability of the mystic makes possible a perfect obedience to God and to her confessor, God's representative for the individual. Von Balthasar tells how von Speyr was granted the gift of testing the authenticity of mystics such as Theresa of Avila, John of the Cross, Ignatius of Loyola, and many others by ''reliving them'' when ''under obedience'' to him as her confessor.

Bibliography: A. VON SPEYR, *Apokalypse* (Einsiedeln 1950); *Das Wort und die Mystik* (Einsiedeln 1970); *Confession*, tr. D. W. STOTT (San Francisco 1985); *The Gates of Eternal Life*, tr. C. SHARP (San Francisco 1983). H. U. VON BALTHASAR, *A First Glance at Adrienne von Speyr*, tr. A. LAWRY and S. ENGLUND (San Francisco 1981).

[P. KIRK]

SPIEGEL, FERDINAND AUGUST

Archbishop of Cologne; b. Canstein, in Westphalia, Dec. 25, 1764; d. Cologne, Aug. 2, 1835. He was ordained and made dean of the cathedral in Münster (1799), became count of Desenberg (1816) and archbishop of COLOGNE (1824) after Pius VII refused to confirm his nomination to the See of Münster (1813). Spiegel was the last German bishop molded by the Catholic ENLIGHTENMENT and was an intimate friend of WESSENBERG for a time. Despite this and despite his rearing in the tenets of FEBRONIANISM and his lifelong adherence to moderate episcopalism, he conformed to the ecclesiastical restoration after the Napoleonic period. Spiegel circumspectly reorganized his archdiocese, severely damaged by the secularizations of 1803, and fostered clerical education, religious instruction of the faithful, and timely reforms. He had also a share in the reconstruction of other dioceses. Charges that he was oversubservient to Prussia have been exaggerated. In his dealings with this government his tenacity won many of the church's claims, and his tact avoided conflicts. Only late in life did he go to excess in placating the Protestant state when he made a secret arrangement, with the consent of his suffragans, dispensing with the requirement that Catholic parties in mixed marriages receive a guarantee that all their children would be educated as Catholics, as demanded by Pius VIII (1830). Thereby, he set the stage for the celebrated dispute under his successor, DROSTE ZU VISCHERING (*see* COLOGNE, MIXED MARRIAGE DISPUTE IN). The archbishop's favoring of the teachings of HERMES, condemned by Rome in 1835 soon after Spiegel's death, permitted these errors to become deeply rooted in Cologne.

Bibliography: H. BASTGEN, ''Erzbischof Graf Spiegel von Köln und der Heilige Stuhl,'' *Römische Quartalschrift für christliche Altertumskunde und für Kirchengeschichte* 39 (1931) 507–605, separately pub. (Freiburg 1932). W. LIPGENS, *Lexikon für Theologie und Kirche* 2 9:965–966.

[R. LILL]

SPINA, GUISEPPE

Cardinal, diplomat; b. Sarzana (La Spezia), Italy, March 12, 1756; d. Rome, Nov. 12, 1838. After studying law at Bologna and Rome and serving as referendary of the papal *segnatura,* he was ordained (1796) and consecrated titular archbishop of Corinth (September 1798). He accompanied Pius VI into exile and administered to him on his deathbed at Valence (1799). Charged with negotiating a concordat with France, he arrived in Paris (Nov. 15, 1800) and with BERNIER sought to establish the basis of an agreement. Although Cardinal CONSALVI, who was called in to prevent a rupture in the proceedings, had the honor of concluding the CONCORDAT OF 1801, Spina's prudence and skill deserve no less credit for preparing the way. After being created cardinal and archbishop of Genoa (1802), he was conciliatory to such an extent that he joined the "red" cardinals who attended the second marriage of NAPOLEON I with Marie Louise (1810) and the French national council (1811). After the restoration of the STATES OF THE CHURCH, Spina resigned his archbishopric (1819). He was papal legate to Forli (1816) and then to Bologna (1818–24). As plenipotentiary of the Holy See at the Congresses of Laibach (1821) and Verona (1822) he refused to lend Metternich military help from the Holy See in return for quelling the revolution in Naples and renounced a projected central police commission and postal union for Italy, which favored Austrian hegemony.

Bibliography: J. H. BRADY, *Rome and the Neapolitan Revolution of 1820–21* (New York 1937). *Spiegel und das Verhältnis von Kirche und Staat* (Münster 1964). H. SCHRÖRS, *Die Kölner Wirren* (Bonn 1927).

[J. LEFLON]

SPINELLI, FRANCESCO, BL.

Priest, founder of the Sisters of Perpetual Adoration of the Blessed Sacrament; b. Apr. 14, 1853, Milan, Italy; d. Feb. 6, 1913, Rivolta d'Adda (near Cremona), Italy. While he was still very young, Francesco moved with his family from Milan, where he was baptized (Apr. 15, 1853), to Cremona. The family spent summers at Vergo (near Bergamo), where Francesco was cured of a severe spinal problem in 1871. His priestly vocation was fostered by the charity and devotion of his mother, his uncle, Peter Cagliaroli, and a friend, Luigi Palazzolo. Soon after his ordination (Aug. 14, 1875) at Bergamo, Spinelli made a pilgrimage to Rome, where he was inspired to create an order of nuns dedicated to prayer before the Blessed Sacrament for atonement and reconciliation. Upon returning to Bergamo, he met Gertrude Caterina COMENSOLI, who was pursuing the same calling. With Comensoli he founded the Sacramentine Sisters (1882). When the new congregation met with financial difficulties, the bishop of Bergamo severed Spinelli's connection with the sisters in the diocese. Spinelli was welcomed by Bishop Geremia Bonomelli of Cremona. At Rivolta d'Adda Spinelli founded (1889) the Sisters of Perpetual Adoration of the Blessed Sacrament, which is independent of the Sacramentine Sisters but uses the same Rule. Personally Spinelli was compelled by his love of the Eucharist to meet the needs of the suffering and marginalized, even while he himself was sick or troubled. Spinelli's process for beatification, opened Jan. 25, 1952, concluded with his beatification at Caravaggio, Italy, by John Paul II, June 21, 1992.

Bibliography: P. G. BORGONOVO, *Il prête Francisco Spinelli*, (Milan 1939). E. LINGIARDI, "A quarant'anni dalla santa morte. Il venerabile. Francesco Spinelli verso la gloria degli altari," *La vita cattolica* (Cremona, 5 February 1955): 4. *Acta Apostolicae Sedis* (1952): 638–40; (1992): 764.

[K. I. RABENSTEIN]

SPÍNOLA, CRISTÓBAL ROJAS DE

Bishop of Wiener-Neustadt, noted for his attempts to unite Catholics and Protestants; b. Gheldern, Flanders, 1626; d. Wiener-Neustadt (Austria), March 12, 1695. After receiving his training as a Franciscan, he entered the service of Emperor Leopold I. At the Viennese court his chief work was dedicated to the restoration of Church unity. He made many visits throughout the princely courts of Germany, acted as an imperial agent in Spain, and made three trips to Rome. As a reward for his services he was made bishop of Knin (Yugoslavia) and subsequently (1685) bishop of Wiener-Neustadt. His fame lies in his irenic negotiations with Molanus, Lutheran Abbot of Loccum, and with the philosopher Leibniz. Spínola proposed (1) an ecumenical council preceded by a series of colloquia between Catholic and Protestant theologians that were to settle major dogmatic differences; (2) recognition of the ministry of Protestant clergy who would accept papal authority; and (3) granting the chalice to the laity and the right of clerical marriage to those who requested it. His Church union plans were not successful because of the rigid confessionalism of the 17th century and because of the hostility of French foreign policy.

Bibliography: S. J. T. MILLER and J. P. SPIELMAN, *Crístobal Rojas y Spínola* (Philadelphia 1962). P. HILTEBRANDT, *Die Kirchlichen Reunionsverhandlungen* (Rome 1922). I. BOG, in *Jahrbuch für fränkische Landesforschung* 14 (1954). G. HASELBECK, "Der Ireniker Padre C. de Rojas y S.," *Der Katholik,* 4th ser. 12 (1913) 15–37, 385–405.

[S. J. T. MILLER]

SPÍNOLA Y MAESTRE, MARCELO, BL.

Also known as Marcello of Seville, cardinal archbishop, founder of the Conceptionist Handmaids of the Divine Heart; b. Jan. 14, 1835, Isla de Spinola, San Fernando (near Cádiz), Spain; d. Jan. 19, 1906, Seville. Marcelo, the son of the Marquis Juan de Spinola and his wife Antonia Maestre, was a lawyer prior to his ordination as a diocesan priest (Mar. 21, 1864). On Mar. 21, 1871, he was appointed parish priest of San Lorenzo in Seville, where he engaged in pastoral work and instituted pro-

Baruch Spinoza.

grams for the sick and abandoned until Cardinal Archbishop de la Lastra y Cuesta named him cathedral canon (1879). Upon his consecration as auxiliary bishop of Seville (1881), he adopted the motto: ''Either sanctity or death.'' Three years later (1884) he was named bishop of Caria in Cáceres, then transferred to the see of Málaga (1886) until his appointment as archbishop of Seville (1896). As archbishop, Spínola concerned himself especially with educational reforms. To further this goal, he founded the Handmaids of the Divine Heart for the education of girls, an order that combines the active and contemplative life. This bishop, known for his devotion to duty, defense of the interests of the Church, and his concern for the poor, was named cardinal in 1905, but died before receiving the red hat. He was beatified by John Paul II, March 29, 1987.

Bibliography: J. M. JAVIERRE, *El arzobispo mendigo: biografía de Marcelo Spínola* (Madrid 1974); *Don Marcelo de Sevilla* (Barcelona 1963). *Acta Apostolicae Sedis* (1987): 598. *L'Osservatore Romano,* English ed. 14 (1987): 1–2.

[K. I. RABENSTEIN]

SPINOZA, BARUCH (BENEDICT)

Jewish philosopher and foremost exponent of RATIONALISM; b. Amsterdam, Nov. 24, 1632; d. The Hague, Feb. 21, 1677. It may have been fear of the Inquisition that caused his grandfather, Abraham, to leave Vidigueira, Portugal, and settle in Holland. The Union of Utrecht had granted the greatest religious freedom to all sects, and Abraham was there able to profess openly the religion of his ancestors. Soon he had acquired the esteem of his coreligionists and a large fortune. His son Michael, the father of Baruch, was principal of the Jewish community school in Amsterdam.

Life and Studies. Details of Baruch's childhood are almost entirely unknown. He lost his mother at the age of six, and in school he showed a lively and open mind. Since his teachers, devoted to the Talmud, could not give satisfactory answers to his religious difficulties, he attempted to probe alone the problem of his eternal destiny. Yet until his father's death (1654), he practiced Judaism faithfully. Then he no longer observed the rituals and began to criticize the various dogmas more and more openly. After vain attempts to bring him back to orthodoxy, religious authorities excommunicated him on July 27, 1656.

Influence of Jewish Philosophy. The notoriety of the excommunication brought Spinoza many admirers and disciples. Under pressure from the synagogue at Ouwerkerk he was banished from the capital but returned some months later to study the great Jewish philosophers. Moses MAIMONIDES, who showed him how religion can be formed by reason, made the deepest impression; in fact, Spinoza transcribed long passages of Maimonides's *Guide for the Perplexed* and presented them as his own. Another philosopher, LEVI BEN GERSON, encouraged him to break completely with the tradition of his ancestors—to deny the creation of the world and to explain miracles by the forces of nature. Certain passages of Levi's works may be found almost exactly in Spinoza's *Tractatus theologicus-politicus* (ch. 2). Hasdai CRESCAS taught Spinoza to conceive of space as an attribute of God and free will as mere immunity from constraint. Leo Ebreo (1463-?), in his doctrine on intellectual love, gave an affective complement to Spinoza's philosophy. Finally Abraham ben Esra (1092–1167) showed him how God may be conceived both as a unity and as a totality in the pantheistic sense.

Other Intellectual Influences. In order to study other philosophers, Spinoza learned Latin under the guidance of Francis van den Enden, who taught him the elements of scholastic philosophy, which he himself had learned in his 14 years as a Jesuit. (Van den Enden was expelled from the Society before ordination because of his errors against the faith; he led an incredibly adventurous life that ended on the gallows in France, under charge of being a political conspirator, in 1674.) Instead of reading the more respected scholastics, however, Spinoza contented himself with manuals by obscure compilators, such as Heerbord and Kekermann. He must have known little of the works of St. THOMAS AQUINAS, for he imputes to Thomas ideas he never had. Still less did he know PLATO and ARISTOTLE; for his knowledge of Greek was inadequate, as he himself confessed (*Tract. theol.-pol.* ch. 10), and the Latin translations available were incomplete and imperfect. Of all the systems of classical antiquity, he was most familiar with STOICISM, which he could study in CICERO and SENECA. No doubt the philosopher he knew best was R. DESCARTES, to whom he owed his theory of knowledge, his geometrical method, and his physics.

In an effort to find the meaning of his destiny, Spinoza studied Christianity also. Of its representatives in Holland, he preferred the Mennonites and the Collegiants, who were strongly influenced by rationalism and naturalism. His most intimate friends, most faithful disciples, and best collaborators were of this religious persuasion.

Work and Character. Since he had no source of income, Spinoza began to polish optical glass, a work in which he achieved rare skill. He also painted, but as an amateur. In 1660 he settled in Rijnsburg, but three years later moved to Voorburg, then in 1670 to The Hague, where he remained. These three places became successively the centers of numerous visits paid him by illustrious scholars such as C. Huygens and G. W. LEIBNIZ. He led a sober, peaceful, and hardworking life and stoically accepted his suffering from tuberculosis. His virtue, however, did not merit the title of saint that some lavished on him, nor did his vices suggest a comparison with the devil. According to S. von Dunin-Borkowski, Spinoza ''had no idea of self-criticism, and so considered himself an infallible oracle; self-sufficiency often made him partial and impolite, and sometimes arrogant and autocratic'' [*Stimmen aus Maria Laach* (1902) 28]. He died in the presence of a doctor who was an intimate friend. The theory of suicide has never been completely proved, although it remains plausible.

Teaching on Truth and Method. The end of philosophy, says Spinoza, is to teach one to form true ideas and to distinguish these infallibly from false or doubtful ideas. But in what does the truth consist? It does not consist in the ''correspondence of resemblance'' between the idea and its object, since, for example, the idea of a mechanic who has conceived a machine to build is said to be true although the machine does not, and may never, exist. So also the ideas that the mathematician develops are truly independent of all reference to the objective order. Truth is something intrinsic to the idea. In order to grasp truth, man needs a method that does not stop at the periphery of things but penetrates to the interior of the idea and assists at its birth. Such a method is a priori and deductive. Experience as such reaches ideas only through the modifications produced by the exterior object on the senses; thus it gives a mediate, indirect, and relative knowledge. Experience registers facts, describes them, classifies them, and that is all; in sum, it is only a ''story.'' As much can be said of the knowledge given by hearsay or faith.

The philosopher, therefore, should follow the geometric method. To begin with, let him take some self-evident ideas or axioms. Applying these to definitions that he has chosen well and determined well, he then deduces *more geometrico* propositions whose truth need no longer be questioned. The train of ideas implied in this deduction has nothing to do with the psychological or the physiological trains that are at the basis of the association of ideas by the imagination and the memory. In fact, the knowledge that such association gives is always imperfect and inadequate. It is knowledge of the first degree. General ideas also belong to this degree, including TRANSCENDENTALS (e.g., being and thing) or UNIVERSALS (e.g., man and horse). Such ideas are only confused agglomerations of sense impressions.

Concept of Being, Substance, and God. To avoid all danger of error, Spinoza built his system starting with the idea of BEING as the clearest and the simplest available. Such an idea, for him, does not lend itself to approximation or to ANALOGY. It excludes all multiplicity and is unique. As such it does not comply with the traditional division of being into created and uncreated. Considered as the ultimate ground of intelligibility, i.e., as ''that whose concept does not require, for its formation, any other concept'' (*Eth.* 1, def. 3), this unique being is at the same time SUBSTANCE.

In virtue of its uniqueness, substance is also infinite since nothing exists to limit it. Infinite as it is in all lines of being, however, substance is known only under two attributes: thought and space.

The relation between substance and God is easily explained by Spinoza. In his view, everyone conceives God as the absolutely infinite being, the substance with infinite attributes (*ibid.* def. 6). And substance is by its essence unique. Thus God is identical with substance. The universe is God's infinite mode, and the particular things that make up the universe are His finite modes. But although He is extended, God is nonetheless indivisible and simple, because all division produces multiplicity. And the infinite is essentially unique. It cannot degrade itself in a collection of other finite beings. In this way also it is incorporeal, for a body is nothing other than a finite area. The same reasoning shows that God is not a spirit.

He is simply thought, whose finite modes are particular human spirits.

As God is infinite in all lines of being, He is also infinite in action. But the effect of this activity remains necessarily within Him, since He exists alone. Thus God is always an immanent, and never a transitive, cause. As a cause He is supremely free; for, existing by Himself, He can suffer no constraint from outside. Just as mathematical properties flow from a triangle in an infallible, eternal way that does not alter its essence, so also an infinitely long and rich train of modes (creatures) proceeds necessarily from God. Thus creation is at the same time free and necessary. The modes of God (e.g., man) cannot be free, since they are determined to be and to act through God-substance.

Notions of Morality and Religion. Philosophers traditionally regard morality as based on two postulates as its *sine qua non* condition, viz, FREE WILL and the existence of moral GOOD. But Spinoza completely rejected free will and considered the notions of good and evil as mere fictions of the imagination. He conceived these only in relation to the end, which for him is only the last term of the activity that is developed independently of man's free will. In Spinoza's view, the moral problem lies in the area of the metaphysics of being. It is transposed into ontological terms: man acts morally well if his action is developed according to the second or third degree of knowledge. Thus also does man deliver himself from the yoke of passions, his dutiful companions at the first degree.

What is commonly called natural law is, for Spinoza, only the manner of being of the individual; it merges with his nature. It extends as far as does his physical power. In the state of nature everything is permitted. However, since men could not live long in anarchy, they had to come to an agreement, to renounce the violence of their individual appetites, and to conform themselves to the will of their chief (*Eth.* 4.37). All must execute every one of the chief's commands, even the most absurd (*Tract. theol.-pol.* ch. 16), and he himself is limited by no law. He can command whatever he wills—and in every matter, especially in religious affairs. The whole community belongs to him, as does all that it possesses: land, houses, etc. This explains why Communists feel justified in considering Spinoza as "the father of Bolshevism" (A. Deborin).

In Spinoza's system there is no room for a positive religion, especially not for Christianity. In his view, one could never deduce the truths it teaches mathematically, as from necessary principles. Such truths imply the idea of grace, which, in its turn, is inextricably associated with a supremely free choice. This perhaps explains why historic Christianity seemed to Spinoza a superstition unworthy of discussion.

Critique. A refutation of Spinoza and his philosophy is not difficult. It suffices to examine closely the notions that Spinoza candidly accepted as "clear and distinct" and on which he based his entire metaphysics, viz, truth, methodology, being, and substance. The arguments of centuries weigh heavily against his simplistic solution.

See Also: CARTESIANISM; PANTHEISM; RATIONALISM.

Bibliography: Works. *Opera,* ed. C. GEBHARDT, 4 v. (Heidelberg 1924); *The Chief Works of Benedict de Spinoza,* tr. R. H. M. ELWES, 2 v. (London 1883–84; repr. in 1 v. New York 1951); *Spinoza Selections,* ed. J. WILD (New York 1930); *The Principles of Descartes' Philosophy,* tr. H. H. BRITAIN (Chicago 1905). Studies. F. C. COPLESTON, *History of Philosophy* (Westminster, MD 1946–) 4:205–263. A. GUZZO and V. MATHIEU, *Enciclopedia filosofica* (Venice-Rome 1957) 4:873–888. J. D. COLLINS, *A History of Modern European Philosophy* (Milwaukee 1954) 199–251. P. SIWEK, *Spinoza et le panthéisme religieux* (rev. ed. Paris 1950); *Au Coeur du spinozisme* (Paris 1952); *L'Âme et le corps d'après Spinoza* (Paris 1930). S. VON DUNIN-BORKOWSKI, *Der junge De Spinoza* (Münster 1910); *Spinoza,* 2 v. (Münster 1933–36); *Spinoza nach dreihundert Jahren* (Berlin 1932). H. A. WOLFSON, *The Philosophy of Spinoza,* 2 v. (Cambridge, Mass. 1934; repr. in 1 v. 1948). E. L. SCHAUB, *Spinoza: The Man and His Thought* (Chicago 1933).

[P. SIWEK]

SPIRATION

A theological term derived from the concept of Spirit as used in Jn 3.8. The term is applied to the second procession in the Holy TRINITY, the procession of the Holy Spirit from the Father and the Son—or through the Son, according to the Greek Fathers (H. Denzinger, *Enchiridion symbolorum* [Freiburg 1963] 1301). Spiration is taken actively as the act of love and passively as the love proceeding, or the Holy Spirit.

The Old Testament mentions the Spirit of Yahweh, the Spirit of God, and the Holy Spirit, but never in a personal sense. In the New Testament the Holy Spirit is presented as a Person, equal to the Father and the Son (Mt 28.19). The Holy Spirit is called the Spirit of the Father (Mt 10.20) and the Spirit of the Son (Gal 4.6). These and many passages referring to the divine MISSIONS of the Son and the Holy Spirit are the basis for the doctrine of spiration.

The Trinitarian doctrine of the early Christian centuries emphasized the essential unity and the absolute equality of the three Divine Persons. The pseudo-Athanasian creed (*Enchiridion symbolorum* 75) excludes the concepts of generation and FILIATION from the second procession. Thus, there is an absolute and essential difference between the two processions.

St. Augustine discerned that the second procession in the Trinity is one of mutual love of the Father and the Son (*Enchiridion patristicum,* ed. M. J. Rouët de Journel [Freiburg im Breisgau 1960] 1665). Thus, to love, or the act of love of the Father and of the Son, is active spiration, and the Love proceeding from the Father and the Son is the Holy Spirit, or passive spiration (St. Thomas Aquinas, *Summa theologiae* 1a, 36–38).

The Holy Spirit proceeds from the Father and the Son as from one principle and as by one spiration (*Enchiridion symbolorum* 850). This procession is from the Persons of the Father and the Son (*Enchiridion symbolorum* 804–806), as the divine nature (remote principle) and the divine will (proximate principle) are formally in the Father and formally in the Son. As the Father is the Father only in relation to the Son (*Enchiridion symbolorum* 528), the paternal spiration is the voluntary diffusion of His goodness to the Son, or paternal love; and, as the Son is the Son only in relation to the Father, the filial spiration is His voluntary conformity to the Father or filial love (whence the conformity of Christ: Jn 5.30; 6.38; 14.31). Hence, the Holy Spirit ''is known as the love or the sanctity of both'' the Father and the Son (*Enchiridion symbolorum* 527). This love of the Father and the Son is a mutual, complementary love, spirating the Holy Spirit, who as a distinct Person proceeds eternally from the Father and the Son in the immanent life of the Trinity.

See Also: HOLY SPIRIT; PROCESSIONS, TRINITARIAN; ACTS, NOTIONAL; TRINITY, HOLY, ARTICLES ON.

Bibliography: LEO XIII, ''Divinum illud munus'' (encyclical, May 9, 1897) *Acta Apostolicae Sedis* (Rome 1909–) 29 (1896–97) 644–658, Eng. *Catholic Mind* 36 (May 8, 1938) 161–181. A. PALMIERI, *Dictionnaire de théologie catholique*, ed. A. VACANT et al., (Paris 1903—50) 5.1:676–829; Tables générales 1:1254–63.

[G. M. GREENEWALD]

SPIRIT

Primitive terms used to designate spiritual reality, such as the Sanskrit *atman,* the Hebrew *rûaḥ,* the Greek πνεῦμα, and the Latin *spiritus,* originally referred to air as breathed from the lungs; the soul left the body at death almost as air escaped from the mouth. This primary meaning is retained in the expression πνεῦμα ψυχικόν (animal spirit) found in Greek medical treatises such as those of Galen, and used in medicine and philosophy to signify a fluid and vaporous material element dispersed from the heart or brain throughout the body, and accounting for vital interactions. This use was made common by Renaissance philosophers such as G. Cardano (*De subtilitate* 14.585), B. TELESIO (*De rerum natura* 5.13, 17), F. BACON (*De digitate* 4.3; *Historia vitae et mortis,* Intentions, 1), and R. DESCARTES (*Les Passions de l'âme* 1.10, ed. Adams and Tannery 11:334–335); it remained in common use until the 18th century.

As employed in philosophy, spirit means any reality that in its nature, existence, and activity is intrinsically independent of matter, is not subject to determinations of time and space, is not composed of parts spatially distinct from one another, and is, or is related to, an original source of such activities as are centered on being under the universal aspects of truth, goodness, and beauty. Such a notion is analogical, capable of being verified in different beings in different ways and to different degrees. These differences may bear on the mode of subsistence (complete or incomplete), on the degree of independence from matter (perfect or imperfect), or on the manner of exercise of the activities characteristic of spirit.

For some thinkers, spirit is primarily identified either with reality as a whole in its inner nature (spiritualistic monism), with an objective order of transcendent realities (Platonism), or with impersonal and collective realms of being (values, group-spirits).

Christian Concept. For those of the Christian tradition, spirit is always personal and subjective, and all other manifestations of spirit can be reduced to their source in the person. Within this tradition, the radical and essential manifestation of spirit has been variously singled out as: creative activity, self-consciousness, interiority or subjectivity, intelligence, reason, knowledge of universals, love, freedom, and communication (dialogue). These are activities by which the presence of spirit may be known, and they furnish a clue to the nature of spirit in itself as a form of subsistent being.

Christian thought also recognizes three main kinds of spirit: (1) the human soul, incomplete in its mode of subsisting and extrinsically dependent on the body; (2) pure finite spirit, i.e., the angel, perfectly subsisting and independent of matter; and (3) Absolute Spirit, or God, infinite, utterly pure, and fully actual being (subsistent existence) without any limitation. Man's primary apprehension of these forms of spirit is gained through self-knowledge. The spiritual being most proportionate to his way of knowing is his own soul, manifesting its nature through activities that are immediately present to his consciousness. His knowledge of other spiritual realities is in turn based on such knowledge (cf. St. Thomas Aquinas, *C. gent.* 3.46).

Human Spirit. The spirituality of the human soul can be discerned from its characteristic intellectual activities of understanding and judgment, from its voluntary activity, and according to some, from its objectivating of such activities in permanent external forms.

Regarding intellectual activities as such, it should be noted that all KNOWLEDGE implies a degree of IMMATERIALITY, of superiority over every merely material manner of receiving forms. Yet the transsubjectivity of knowledge, by which the knower is identified psychically with the known precisely as it is other than the knower, is found also in SENSE KNOWLEDGE and is not of itself evidence of spirituality. Sense knowledge is characterized by reference to time and space and to the external appearances of things and, of itself, is entirely directed to action; it has a primarily biological function, since it attains its objects precisely as they act on the animal. Thought, on the contrary, transcends such limitations, for it is not centered on self or on objects seen merely as useful or harmful to the knower. It implies a power of being present to other beings in a purely objective way and is open to all possible modes of being. It attains things not simply in their biological reference to the knower but as in themselves, in their interiority and intimacy.

Understanding. Evidence of such superiority to sense knowledge is found in UNDERSTANDING, the manner of knowing that is proper to the INTELLECT. Here the CONCEPT is obtained by ABSTRACTION, without the aspects of "this, here, now," and refers to the QUIDDITY of things, so that the meaning of the word and something of the nature of the things known are grasped. Understanding is free from the relativity of sense; it has an absolute character, and it alone can make sense knowledge objective. It can know what perception is, distinguishing it from other activities as well as from its object.

Objects known as to their essential nature, and as freed from the particularity of their concrete manner of existing in the world, are attained as UNIVERSALS—called such because what is represented in the concept is predicable of many things that, though differing individually, are of the same nature. The concept exhibits a specific kind of being, an ESSENCE, and may be predicated of each and all the members of a class by identity, whereas no individual may be predicated of another. Moreover, thought can know what is meant by abstract and universal.

Not only the manner of knowing, but also the kind of objects known by thought, shows the superiority of intellect to sense. Man can know relations precisely as they are relations (or kinds of order), objects that cannot exist in reality (logical intentions, such as GENUS), and even negations (NONBEING) or privations (EVIL and blindness). He forms concepts of thought, substance, and cause that say nothing of the outward or spatiotemporal appearances of things. He can think about such immaterial realities as truth, goodness, and virtue. Above all, he can know things as real, as having determinate natures, as sharing the fundamental characteristic of BEING, the primary aspect under which everything is known by mind. Man is unique in this relation to other things, to the world as a whole, which phenomenologists describe as his universal horizon.

Judgment. Understanding leads to the more perfect act of the intellect, JUDGMENT, by which the knower returns to the object known in its concrete and existential reality. One can distinguish here (1) intentional judgment, bearing on an object distinct from the knower and his act of knowing, and (2) reflexive judgment, bearing on either the act itself or on the knower.

As the primary object of understanding is being as essence, the primary object of judgment is being as existent, since existence, as actualizing actuality, is adequately attained by the mind only in the act of judging. It is this prerogative of the intellect, its power to grasp existent being as such, that is its essential activity and the principal and sufficient evidence of its spirituality. The explication of such knowledge is carried out (with constant recourse to experience) through the use of FIRST PRINCIPLES, formulated in dependence on the primordial grasp of being. The interpretation of experience by means of such principles gives rise to the sciences, in which a further mental activity is employed, that of REASONING. All these activities are proper to man and point to his spirituality. Among the sciences, METAPHYSICS stands out as supremely witnessing to the spirituality of man; it is no accident that philosophers who see no essential difference between the souls of men and of animals inevitably deny the validity, or the meaningfulness, of metaphysics as the scientific knowledge of being as such. It is metaphysics alone that can justify man's knowledge of the existence of God. The fact and the object of such knowledge clearly show its spirituality.

The intellect, centered on being as such, can know its own act (which is a being) and thus arrive at some knowledge of its own nature as well as of its own existence and of that of the ego (*see* REFLECTION). It can know the relation of its act to its object, its power to attain that object as it is in itself, and thus know TRUTH and ERROR. Man can know himself as a subject, as a subsistent source of spiritual acts that attain being as such. He is, as M. Heidegger insists, that being in which being becomes conscious of itself and whose inner nature is to be an affirmation of being (*Sein und Zeit* [Halle 1927] 12–15).

Voluntary Activity. The WILL reveals the same openness to being in all its universality that one finds in the intellect. Man can love all that shares in, or is thought to share in, the goodness that is consequent upon being as such. It can tend to others as others with that pure and disinterested activity proper to human love, as best appears in the power to treat another human being as another, in his own intimacy and interiority, that is, as a person, and to love God in and for Himself.

Man as intelligent and loving is a PERSON; the interpersonal relationships of COMMUNICATION, dialogue, and encounter (''I-Thou''), through which he lives as a person, show his distinctive spiritual nature. Because he can love goodness in all its fullness, he is free with regard to all that is only to a limited extent good and he has access to the world of values. As intelligent and free he can direct his actions to ends that are preconceived and deliberately chosen; his activity is marked by rational finality.

The actualization of value is possible to man because he is free; it is incumbent upon him because, being free, he is responsible for his actions. The free and responsible guidance of his life in accordance with values consciously known and accepted raises his activity to the domain of MORALITY, where man is the subject of rights and duties and is ruled by law. As a person he can enter social groupings on various levels. The distinctive character of his spiritual activity shows itself in what one may call its perfectional trend, since in contrast with his biological life fixed within definite limits, no limits can be set to his spiritual perfection in knowledge, art, morality, and love. This is true above all in regard to moral perfection, by which man's spiritual nature is at once most evidently signified and most completely attained, especially when his existence is ennobled by RELIGION through adoration of God.

Objective Spirit. It is doubtful that distinct evidence of spirit can be found in what M. SCHELER and N. HARTMANN call objective spirit, namely, the world of opinions, outlooks, and attitudes shared by many persons in common, in matters of religion, law, politics, morals, taste, and art; an impersonal spirit, in the sense in which one here understands spirit, is a contradiction.

What W. DILTHEY calls objective spirit is better named objectivated spirit by Hartmann. It signifies things (e.g., sounds, books, stones, and canvases) on which spirit has engraved its signature, as in language, literature, plastic and musical works of art, monuments, tools, arms, utensils, myths, philosophical systems, and codes of law. These are the external depositaries of the spiritual activities referred to above and imply reference to spirit both as to their origin and as to that for which alone they have meaning. CULTURE and civilization betray the presence of the spiritual element in man's being; they are the voice of spirit recorded in history, a voice that can be heard only by spirit. One may also appeal to history itself as showing signs of providential guidance (St. AUGUSTINE and J. B. BOSSUET) or also of rational pattern (G. VICO, J. G. von HERDER, and G. W. F. HEGEL) pointing to human or to divine activity.

Angels. The conviction, expressed in many religions, of the existence of spiritual beings that mediate between God and man, finds support in the teaching of many philosophers. Of the ancients it will suffice to quote Aristotle, who posits beings separate from all matter, not subject to alteration, enjoying an excellent and eternal life, as movers of the heavenly bodies (*Meta.* 1073a 13–1074b 14; *Cael.* 279a 19–23). St. THOMAS AQUINAS argues that the perfection of the universe, in order to manifest more completely the ways in which the Creator may be imaged, demands the existence of pure spirits (ST 1a, 50.1, 3). Among contemporary writers one may refer to Eugenio D'Ors (1882–1954) in Spain, who held that the world of angels is the most authentic one created and that man tends to the state of angels as to perfection (*Introduccion a la vida angélica,* Madrid 1941; *El secreto de la filosofia,* Barcelona 1947). (*See* ANGELS)

Absolute Spirit. The supreme objective evidence for the existence of spirit is that which moves the mind to conclude to the existence of GOD, who alone can ultimately explain the origin of finite forms of spirit.

Of the characteristics of the universe that have been regarded by philosophers as pointing to the existence of spirit, characteristics that find their full explanation only in reference to a Creator, the one that has been stressed is the order of the universe—the rational design apparent in the harmonious interrelation and interaction of the bodies that compose one system, and of their movements (*see* UNIVERSE, ORDER OF). Closely connected with this order is the finality, internal and external, apparent in living beings. Philosophers such as F. W. J. von SCHELLING found evidence of spirituality in such natural phenomena as polarity (recalling the subject-object opposition of consciousness), artistry (natural objects as embodying ideals), and evolution toward higher forms. Others, such as I. Kant, marveled at the adaptation of the world of nature to the exercise of moral activity.

The rationality of the universe is most stressed by the idealists. What is most acceptable in their theories is that they point to the undeniable fact of a deep affinity between mind and the whole material universe. Since that universe is actually knowable, it must be somehow proportioned to mind; and this can ultimately be explained only by postulating that both mind and matter have a common source in the intellectual activity of the Creator. The recognition of this fact, however obscure, lies at the root of the well-nigh universal fact of religious worship among men, a fact that bears eloquent witness to the existence of spirit in man and in his creative source.

See Also: GOD, PROOFS FOR THE EXISTENCE OF; SOUL, HUMAN; IMMORTALITY; SPIRIT (IN THE BIBLE); SPIRIT, MODERN PHILOSOPHIES OF; SPIRITISM; SPIRITUALISM.

Bibliography: S. STRASSER, *The Soul in Metaphysical and Empirical Psychology* (Pittsburgh 1957). W. A. M. LUIJPEN, *Existential Phenomenology* (Pittsburgh 1960). B. MILLER, *The Range of Intellect* (London 1961). M. F. SCHELER, *Man's Place in Nature,* tr. H. MEYERHOF (Boston 1961); *On the Eternal in Man,* tr. B. NOBLE (New York 1960). J. DE VRIES, *La Pensée et l'être,* tr. C. DE MEESTER DE RAVENSTEIN (Louvain 1962). A. MARC, *L'Etre et l'esprit* (Paris 1958). K. RAHNER, *Geist im Welt,* ed. J. B. METZ (2d ed. Munich 1957). H. CONRAD, *Die Geistseele des Menschen* (Munich 1960). M. F. SCIACCA, ed., *L'Anima* (Brescia 1954).

[A. J. MCNICHOLL]

SPIRIT (IN THE BIBLE)

The word spirit is the usual translation of the Hebrew word *rûaḥ* and of the Greek word πνεῦμα. This article treats of the various meanings and uses of these terms in their original context under three main headings, in the Old Testament, in late Judaism, and in the New Testament.

In the Old Testament. Under the first heading, *rûaḥ* will be considered as life breath, as the seat of human experience, in its opposition to flesh and the Greek concept of spirit, and in its nature.

Rûaḥ as Life Breath. The basic meaning of *rûaḥ* in the Old Testament is breath or wind and by extension it came to mean the breath as signifying life and thence spirit, mind, and life principle. In creatures with lungs, breathing is a natural sign of life, and in many languages the term connoting physical breath takes on the meaning of what it signifies, life. So in Hebrew, *rûaḥ* came to mean breath as significative of life in men (Gn 6.17; Ez 37.10) and in animals [Gn 7.22; Ps 103 (104).29]. It was often used in synonymous parallelism with *n*^{e}*šāmā* (breath of life, Gn 2.7) and *nepeš* (throat opened to breathe, thence, life, seat of emotions, self or person; cf. Judges 15.19, *rûaḥ,* with Lam 1.11, 16, *nepeš*). The absence of *rûaḥ* connotes the lack of vital force (Jer 10.14; 51.17). Since God is the life-giver, life breath comes from Him and man lives as long as God's breath remains in him (Jb 27.3; Is 42.5; Zec 12.1). When God withdraws His breath, man and all flesh return to the ground [Ps 145 (146).4; Jb 34.14; Eccl 12.7]. During man's existence life breath may wax or wane (Gn 45.27; Jgs 15.19).

Rûaḥ as the Seat of Human Experience. This use is frequent. Hebrew awareness of the concrete observed that strong feelings affected respiration. Thus, dejection, sadness, astonishment, anger, patience, pride are all expressed by corresponding changes in a man's breathing (Jos 2.11; 1 Kgs 10.5; 1 Sm 1.15; Gn 26.34; Mi 2.7; Prv 16.18; Eccl 7.8; etc.). *Rûaḥ* is then the subject of human emotions, and good and evil habits (Ex 35.21; Is 19.3a; Jer 51.11; etc.). The modern, Western concept of spirit fits these situations but only in a very extended acceptance of the word.

Rûaḥ in Opposition to Flesh. In Is 31.3, man is contrasted to God as flesh is to spirit. Man then is flesh, weak and perishable, while spirit is divine, strong, and enduring. In this opposition can be seen the concrete Hebrew grasp of the numinous, mysterious power that man shares, participates in, while he lives, but does not control. It belongs to the divinity who gives of it to man, but who can and does take it away. This contrast is obviously not that of the material and immaterial, the body and spirit, as found in Greek categories, for it is God's *rûaḥ* that gives whatever degree of permanency man's flesh (*bāśār*) enjoys (Gn 6.3). God controls man's destiny and life by the power of His spirit (Jb 10.12; Is 42.5).

Rûaḥ as Opposed to Immaterial Spirits. Until late Judaism and New Testament times, *rûaḥ* is never used of an immaterial spirit, whether demon, angel, or ghost. In 1 Kings 22.21, the Prophet Micaiah describes the spirit commissioned by Yahweh to deceive Ahab. Here there is a personification of the prophetic spirit that God changes into a lying spirit to achieve His punishment of Ahab through his own sycophantic seers. In other cases the original meaning of breath persists. In Judges 9.23, the evil spirit that God puts between Abimelech and the Sichemites is correctly translated by the CCD translation as "God put bad feelings . . . ." The evil spirit from the Lord that troubled Saul in 1 Samuel 16.14 is a mysterious, abnormal feeling—an attempt to describe the source of his psychopathic melancholy. Other frequent uses of spirit modified by substantives such as knowledge, fear, and fornication, express either special powers from God or subjective attitudes, evil, good, or indifferent, of an individual (Is 11.2; Hos 4.12; etc.).

The Nature of the Old Testament Spirit. To arrive at a common notion of *rûaḥ* from its concrete, particularized use is a very difficult task. One may, however, conclude to at least this common theological notion that transcends its merely physical usage—that it comes from God as a creative, life-giving, superhumanizing force (Gn 1.2; 2.7; 41.38; Ex 31.3; 1 Sm 16.13; Jgs 3.10; Nm 24.2; Is 42.1; 59.21). Its extraordinary effusion will characterize the Messianic age and will make men share in special charismatic gifts (Zec 4.6; 6.8; Nm 11.29; Jl 3.1–2; Acts 2.16–21). Most of all, it will create a New Alliance and become an interior source of justice and peace in man's heart through the ministry of the Messiah who will transmit it to His faithful (Ez 36.26–27; 37.14; Is 32.15–19; 44.3; Zec 12.10; Is 11.1–3; 42.1; 61.1). This notion of spirit as a participation in God's power is still real and concrete and is never taken as an empty, unreal abstraction (*see* SPIRIT OF GOD).

Spirit in Late Judaism. In the two centuries preceding the Christian Era and in subsequent Jewish tradition, due to Persian and Greek influence, there is a noticeable development of thought concerning spirit and spirits. The Biblical indications of this development are found in the important Book of Wisdom, 2 Mc, and the Greek version of Nm 16.22. In Wisdom 7.22–23, wisdom's spirit is described as the source of many qualities in ''all spirits, though they be intelligent, pure and very subtle.'' The Book of 2 Maccabees and the Greek version of Numbers speak of the divinity as the ''Lord of spirits'' (2 Mc 3.24; Nm 16.22). The same development is evident in extra-Biblical Jewish literature, especially in the Book of Henoch 22.3–13, where the deceased are described as ''the spirits of the dead.'' Good and evil spirits, spirits of fornication, uncleanness, and error, are also mentioned in this apocryphal literature. All these spirits are taken as persons and not merely as subjective attitudes in man. Nevertheless, this evolution did not lead to a philosophical analysis of spirit or spirits in Judaism. The particularized concept of spirit remained dominant and, as will be seen, appears again in the New Testament.

In the New Testament. The basic meaning of spirit as breath or wind is found in the New Testament, but its derived meanings are, of course, more common and important (2 Thes 2.8; Jn 3.8).

Man's Spirit. As the principle of life (Mt 27.50) it exists after death (Lk 8.55) and goes to the underworld (1 Pt 3.19) or to the heavenly Jerusalem (Heb 12.23). It is the seat of man's feelings (Mk 2.8; 2 Cor 2.13) and mental attitudes, in contrast to the flesh (Mt 26.41) or the body (1 Cor 5.3; 2 Cor 7.1). Sometimes it has merely a pronominal use (Gal 6.18). Spirit (πνεῦμα) and SOUL (ψυχή) are often used interchangeably, although the tripartite division of man in 1 Thessalonians 5.23 may indicate that the spirit is of a higher order than the soul and more amenable to God's influence, whereas soul would pertain more to man's rational nature. However, this division is unique in Paul and the New Testament and is certainly not evidence of an elaborated psychology.

When spirit is governed by a modifier, it expresses a disposition or mental state rather than life principle (Gal 6.1; 1 Pt 3.4), although in Paul it is difficult to determine whether he uses spirit as man's natural faculties or as a special disposition that can easily receive the Holy Spirit's influence (1 Cor 2.4–16, *passim;* 2 Cor 4.13).

Spirit, Flesh, and the Law's Letter. Paul often contrasts spirit with flesh (Gal 3.3–6; Rom 8.4–13). Spirit is the vital, justifying principle while flesh is weak and corruptive. The spiritual man is opposed to the carnal (1 Cor 3.1) and the merely human or psychic man (1 Cor 2.14). So also, the spiritual body and not the psychic will inherit incorruptibility (1 Cor 15.35–58). These contrasts are also evident in Jude 19; James 3.15, and especially in John (4.23–24; 3.10–12, 27–36; 7.37–39).

The Pauline opposition between spirit and the Law (Rom 2.29; 2 Cor 3.4–18) is not that between a shallow and a deeper appreciation of God's Law. In Paul's conception the Law is external to man, a letter and not an interior vital force like the spirit. The Law makes one aware of what should be done but, in contrast to the spirit, does not give the ability to do what is right, and therefore serves only to make one more aware of guilt and its consequence, death. Thus, the Law kills man by making him conscious of sin, whereas the spirit sets him free (Rom 7.5–12).

The spirit then is the source of a new creation (Gal 15.16–26; Rom 8.1–4) and the fulfillment of the Old Testament promise (Jer 31.31–34; Ez 36.36–39) of a new covenant written in man's heart. It is a life-giving reality as its source is the ''life-giving spirit'' (1 Cor 15.45; cf. Jn 3.5; 6.63–64).

Good and Evil Spirits. The use of the word spirit to refer to superhuman beings or good spirits, i.e., angels, is not common in the New Testament (Acts 23.8–9; Heb 1.14; Rv 4.5). The Synoptic Gospels and Acts; however, frequently speak of evil or unclean spirits (Mt 12.43; Acts 5.16; etc.). These DEMONS or DEVILS as Luke and Matthew often call them (Lk 4.33; 8.27; Mt 9.33–34; etc.) know something of the mystery of Jesus, but when they are cast out by Him, they are not allowed to reveal to others that He is the Messiah (Mk 1.23–28).

Spirit as Characteristic of God. In John 4.23–24, God is called spirit not simply because He is immaterial and not bound by place, but because He is the source of a new life and worship that is totally different from the previous dispensation. The worship He desires, therefore, is in spirit and in truth, i.e., the worship of men who are born from on high, of the water that is the Spirit (Jn 3.3–13), of those who by receiving and believing in His unique Son become His own sons, sharing in the gratuitous covenant love and truth of Jesus Christ (1.13–18). Thus the living waters that Christ offers the Samaritan woman and all who come to Him and believe is the participation in the Divinity, in His Spirit, by which, henceforth, man can offer the only true worship to God (4.10–14; 7.37–39). This promise is fulfilled when Jesus breathes forth His spirit from the cross and on His Disciples after the Resurrection (19.30; 20.19–23).

Bibliography: *Encyclopedic Dictionary of the Bible*, tr. and adap. by L. HARTMAN (New York 1963), from A. VAN DEN BORN, *Bijbels Woordenboek* 2294–99. E. KÄSEMANN, *Die Religion in Geschichte und Gegenwart*, 7 v. (3d ed. Tübingen 1957–65) 2:1268–79. W. EICHRODT, *Theology of the Old Testament*, tr. J. A.

BAKER (London 1961–) v.1. P. VAN IMSCHOOT, *Théologie de l'Ancien Testament,* 2 v. (Tournai 1954–56). E. SCHWEIZER et al., ''Spirit of God,'' tr. A. E. HARVEY, *Bible Key Words,* ed. G. KITTEL (New York 1961) v.3.2.

[L. A. BUSHINSKI]

SPIRIT OF GOD

The expressions ''the spirit of Yahweh'' (*rûaḥ Yhwh*) and ''the spirit of God'' (*rûaḥ 'Ĕlōhîm*) are common in the Old Testament. ''His holy spirit'' and ''Your holy spirit'' (in reference to God) are also found. The absolute use, ''the spirit'' or ''spirit,'' seldom occurs. In late Judaism it was a practice to avoid use of the divine name by means of circumlocutions. Thus in the Greek versions of the Old Testament there are found such expressions as ''divine spirit,'' ''the holy spirit,'' or simply, ''holy spirit.'' The most common expression in the New Testament is ''the Holy Spirit'' (τὸ πνεῦμα τὸ ἅγιον). ''Holy Spirit'' (πνεῦμα ἅγιον) and simply ''the Spirit'' (τὸ πνεῦμα) or ''Spirit'' (πνεῦμα) are also found. God's spirit was originally called ''holy'' in the same way as His word [Jer 23.9; Ps 104(105).42], His arm [Is 52.10; Ps 97(98).1], and His name (Am 2.7; Ez 36.20) were called holy, because God is by nature holy. ''Holy spirit,'' therefore, means ''divine spirit.''

This article treats the spirit of God as it is presented in the Old Testament and Judaism, and in the New Testament. Consideration is given in each of these sections to the spirit of God as a power and as a Person.

Spirit of God in the Old Testament

The specific implications of the phrase ''Spirit of God'' must be deduced from the operations ascribed to it in the Old Testament.

God's Spirit as a Power. ''Spirit of God'' is used in the Old Testament to signify ''God's breath'' (Jb 33.4). Just as the ancient Israelites spoke anthropomorphically of God's arm, hand, and face, so they also spoke of His breath, i.e., His vital power or spirit, which was as active and as efficacious as God Himself. This use has its foundation in the original meaning of the word *rûaḥ*—''breath'' or ''wind.'' The breath, which was regarded by the ancients as the vital force in man and animals, and the wind, which in Palestine can blow with sudden violence, were looked upon as mysterious, powerful, and terrifying forces. Consequently, it is not surprising that they attributed to the breath or spirit of God the manifestations of extraordinary mysterious powers in man or in nature.

A Power Affecting Man's Soul or Mind. Certain individuals manifested occasional extraordinary power (e.g., Jgs 14.6, 19), heroic courage (e.g., Jgs 3.10), or the gift of prophecy (e.g., 1 Sm 10.6–13). These transitory phenomena were regarded by the Israelites as manifestations of God's spirit. In other cases God's spirit appeared as a permanent force bestowed on individuals because of their office. This was true of the great founders of the nation: Moses (Nm 11.17, 25), Joshua (Dt 34.9), David (1 Sm 16.13; 2 Sm 23.2). It was particularly the messianic king upon whom the spirit would rest (Is 11.2; 42.1). Finally, the spirit of God was the organ that, through the Prophets as intermediaries, constantly delivered Yahweh's orders to His people (Zec 7.12; Neh 9.30), and for the same purpose it was also imparted to the sages (Wis 7.7). It is noteworthy that the psychic rather than the moral activity of God's spirit was emphasized. However, there are moral overtones, for by these transitory or permanent gifts God made fit His chosen instruments to establish and preserve His covenant. There is a similar substratum in Acts ch. 1–2.

A Life-giving and Creative Power. The concept that the breath of life comes from God is very old (Gn 2.7; 6.3). However, it is only in relatively late texts that one finds God's spirit as the cause of man's normal life and activity (Ez 37.1–14; Jb 27.3; 33.4; 35.14–15). God's spirit as a creative force is more commonly found in poetic passages where it is synonymous with ''wind'' (Ex 15.8, 10; Jdt 16.17).

A Morally Effective Force. According to the Old Testament, the chief characteristic of the future new covenant would be a religious and moral transformation of all mankind. So the Prophets, particularly Isaiah (61.1–4; 32.15–20), frequently spoke of God's spirit accomplishing this work in the coming new age. Not only the community, but every individual would be morally re-created by the spirit of God (Is 59.21; Ez 36.25–27). The Psalmist [Ps 50(51).12] prayed that this inner re-creation should be accomplished in his own time; however, as in Wis 1.4–5, this renewal was asked for only the just man. In Ezechiel and in the New Testament a change from a sinner to a just man was envisaged. In other Old Testament passages, God's spirit is conceived more as a teacher or guide—the source of all intellectual and spiritual gifts—than as an efficacious force [Ps 142(143).10; Neh 9.20; Dn 5.15].

God's Spirit Not Presented as a Person. The Old Testament clearly does not envisage God's spirit as a person, neither in the strictly philosophical sense, nor in the Semitic sense. God's spirit is simply God's power. If it is sometimes represented as being distinct from God, it is because the breath of Yahweh acts exteriorly (Is 48.16; 63.11; 32.15). Very rarely do the Old Testament writers attribute to God's spirit emotions or intellectual activity

(Is 63.10; Wis 1.3–7). When such expressions are used, they are mere figures of speech that are explained by the fact that the *rûaḥ* was regarded also as the seat of intellectual acts and feelings (Gn 41.8). Neither is there found in the Old Testament or in rabbinical literature the notion that God's spirit is an intermediary being between God and the world. This activity is proper to the angels, although to them is ascribed some of the activity that elsewhere is ascribed to the spirit of God.

Spirit of God in Judaism. In Judaism God's spirit was generally called ''the holy spirit'' (without capital letters because no personification is indicated). It was regarded primarily as the divine power that gave the Prophets insight into the future and knowledge of hidden things (Sir 48.24–25) and inspired the writers of sacred books (4 Esdras 14.22–48). To it also were ascribed extraordinary psychic phenomena, such as ecstasy and prophetic vision (Enoch 71.11; 4 Esdras 5.22). God's spirit was frequently the divine power that was granted to the pious Patriarchs to strengthen them in the exercise of virtue (Testament of Simeon 4.4); it will be poured out on all Israelites at the messianic renewal (Testament of Juda 24.2; Testament of Levi 18.11). It was generally thought that the holy spirit belonged to the past, having been withdrawn from Israel at the close of the ministry of Haggai, Zechariah, and Malachi (1 Mc 9.27). The sins of Israel were assigned as the cause of this disappearance of the spirit. It was hoped that the messianic age would bring with it prophecy and the renewal of heart.

Spirit of God in the New Testament

As in the Old Testament, so also in the New Testament, the spirit of God comes down from on high (Mk 1.10). He ''falls'' or is ''poured out'' upon those who believe in Christ (Acts 10.44–45; 11.15), for He is ''sent'' or ''given'' by the Father (1 Jn 3.24; Gal 4.6). He ''fills'' a man (Lk 1.15) and He ''dwells'' in him (Rom 8.9).

God's Spirit as a Power. As a result of the teaching of Christ, the definite personality of the Third Person of the Trinity is clear. However, in most cases, the phrase ''spirit of God'' reflects the Old Testament notion of ''the power of God.''

God's Spirit Acting on Man's Soul. In the New Testament, the holy spirit effects such wonders as the expulsion of devils (Mt 12.28) and a miraculous pregnancy (Mt 1.18,20; Lk 1.35). He also effects such supernatural phenomena as the CHARISMS, and the miracle of Pentecost (1 Cor 12.4–11; Acts 2.4; 19.6; Lk 1.67). Such manifestations of the spirit, however, are usually transitory. The holy spirit is especially instrumental in the right exercise of certain offices, and in these cases the recipients are permanently endowed with the divine spirit. This is especially true in the case of the Apostles in fulfillment of the promise of Christ (Jn 14.16–17, 26; (*see also* Acts 1.8; 6.5–11; 1 Cor 12.28). Indeed, by the Apostles, the Holy Spirit governs the Church (Acts 1.8; 13.2; 15.28; 1 Tm 4.14; 2 Tm 1.6).

A focal point in Biblical history, given prominence in the summaries of Jesus' work (e.g., Acts 10.36–41), was His baptism. It was then that He was solemnly installed in His office as the ''anointed'' and ''chosen'' by the descent of the Holy Spirit (Mt 3.16; Mk 1.10; Lk 3.22; Acts 10.38). (At Christ's baptism, the Holy Spirit was symbolized by a dove.) His work began and remained under the influence of the Holy Spirit (Jn 1.33; Mt 4.1; Mk 1.12; Lk 4.1, 18). All this was in fulfillment of the words of the Prophets and the expectations of His contemporaries (Is 11.2; 42.1; 61.1).

God's Spirit as a Sanctifying Power. John the Baptist is presented in the New Testament as the link between the Old and New Testaments. He prepared a faithful remnant of Israel for the messianic baptism (Mt 3.11)—a baptism by the Holy Spirit and fire (baptism by fire meaning a great messianic purification). The messianic baptism brought about the moral and religious re-creation of the people of the new covenant that was promised by the Prophets (Ez 36.35-27; Jer 31.31–34). The actual outpouring of this Holy Spirit at the first Christian Pentecost was a sign for the Apostles that the final days had come (Jl 2.28; Is 44.3; Acts 2.17) and that Jesus, who had bestowed on them power from heaven, was revealing His royal power at the right hand of the Father (Acts 1.8; 2.33). It is especially in the theology of St. Paul and St. John that the possession of the spirit is a sign that the old relationship to God had been abolished and that an entirely new world had been born. The Holy Spirit had not been given previous to Pentecost, for Jesus was not yet glorified (Jn 7.39); but, from the day of Pentecost onward, the Spirit has been active (1 Cor 2.12–16), primarily as the one who brings eternal life (1 Cor 6.11; Jn 3.5–8). The Spirit is said to be the ἀρραβών, the ''pledge,'' that guarantees our full inheritance, eternal glory (Eph 1.13; 2 Cor 1.21–22). The new covenant is characterized by this Spirit, not by the letter of the law (2 Cor 3.6). A Christian has the Spirit of Christ (Rom 8.9) and the love of God that is poured forth in his heart by the Holy Spirit (Rom 5.5); God dwells in him (Rom 8.9, 11), and he is led by the Spirit (Rom 8.14). There is such an intimate connection between Christ and the Holy Spirit in the act of sanctification that they can be spoken of interchangeably (cf. 1 Cor 1.2 and Rom 15.16).

There is conferred on man a new life by Baptism (Rom 6.3–11). Man, however, who is flesh and blood, cannot be elevated to this life, unless he is born again from on high of a divine principle, namely, the Spirit (Jn 3.3, 5; Ti 3.5). The Holy Spirit also comes upon the baptized by the laying on of hands (Acts 8.17; 19.6) in order to confer special charismatic gifts (cf. 1 Tm 4.14).

The Spirit of God as a Person. Although the New Testament concepts of the spirit of God are largely a continuation of those of the Old Testament, in the New Testament there is a gradual revelation that the Spirit of God is a Person.

In the Synoptic Gospels. The majority of New Testament texts reveal God's spirit as something, not someone; this is especially seen in the parallelism between the spirit and the power of God. When a quasi-personal activity is ascribed to God's spirit, e.g., speaking, hindering, desiring, dwelling (Acts 8.29; 16.7; Rom 8.9), one is not justified in concluding immediately that in these passages God's spirit is regarded as a Person; the same expressions are also used in regard to rhetorically personified things or abstract ideas (see Rom 8.6; 7.17). Thus, the context of the phrase ''blasphemy against the spirit'' (Mt 12.31; cf. Mt 12.28; Lk 11.20), shows that reference is being made to the power of God. The only passage in the Synoptic Gospels that clearly speaks of the person of the Holy Spirit is the Trinitarian formula in Mt 28.19.

In the Acts of the Apostles. In Acts, the use of the words ''Holy Spirit,'' with or without an article, is rich and abundant. However, again, it is difficult to demonstrate a personality from the texts. The Spirit continues the work of Jesus and is the link between the earthly and heavenly Jesus. The same Spirit that descended upon Jesus at His baptism is given to the Apostles ''in parted tongues as of fire'' (Acts 2.1–4) and is transmitted beyond these original witnesses to all members of the Church by means of chosen leaders such as Paul, Barnabas, Stephen, and Philip. Reception of this power by the faithful is the principal testimony to the truth of the apostolic preaching. The Spirit is manifested by ''tongues,'' prophecy, and other unusual phenomena. Emphasis is placed on the role of the Spirit in the spread of the Church (Acts 1.8). The statement in Acts 15.28, ''the Holy Spirit and we have decided,'' alone seems to imply full personality.

In the Pauline Epistles. St. Paul uses the word πνεῦμα 146 times. Sometimes it means man's natural spirit, but more often it signifies the divine sanctifying power (2 Cor 3.17–18; Gal 4.6; Phil 1.19). However, the Trinitarian formulas employed by St. Paul (e.g., 2 Cor 13.13), indicate a real personality.

In the Theology of St. John. St. John's theology of the Holy Spirit is very rich in meaning. The Holy Spirit is the Spirit of truth (Jn 14.17; 15.26; 16.13; cf. 1 Jn 4.6; 5.6), and ''another helper,'' the ''Paraclete'' (Jn 14.16). The Spirit is ''another'' helper because, after Christ's Ascension, He takes Christ's place in assisting the disciples, in teaching them all that Jesus Himself had not yet told them, in revealing the future to them, in recalling to their minds that which Jesus had taught them, in giving testimony concerning Jesus, and in glorifying Him (14.26; 16.12–16; 15.26; 1 Jn 2.27; 5.6). So clearly does St. John see in the Spirit a person who takes Christ's place in the Church, that he uses a masculine pronoun (ἐκεῖνος) in reference to the Spirit even though πνεῦμα is neuter in gender (16.8, 13–16). Consequently, it is evident that St. John thought of the Holy Spirit as a Person, who is distinct from the Father and the Son, and who, with the glorified Son and the Father, is present and active in the faithful (14.16; 15.26; 16.7).

See Also: TRINITY, HOLY (IN THE BIBLE).

Bibliography: G. KITTEL, *Theologisches Wörterbuch zum Neuen Testament* (Stuttgart 1935–) 1:104–107. W. EICHRODT, *Theology of the Old Testament,* tr., J. A. BAKER (Philadelphia 1961–) 1:210–220. E. JACOB, *Theology of the Old Testament,* tr. A. W. HEATHCOTE and P. J. ALLCOCK (New York 1958) 121–127. P. VAN IMSCHOOT, *Théologie de l'Ancien Testament,* 2 v. (Tournai 1954–56) 1:183–194. J. GUILLET, *Themes of the Bible,* tr., A. J. LA MOTHE (Notre Dame, Ind. 1960) 225–272. M. BURROWS, *Outline of Biblical Theology* (Philadelphia 1946). L. JOHNSTON, ''The Spirit of God,'' *Scripture* 8 (1956) 65–74. N. H. SNAITH, ''The Spirit of God in Hebrew Thought,'' *The Doctrine of the Holy Spirit* (London 1937). F. J. CRUMP, *Pneuma in the Gospels* (Washington 1954). A. BENSON, *The Spirit of God in the Didactic Books of the Old Testament* (Washington 1949). W. L. MCCELLAN, ''The Meaning of Ruah 'Elokim in Genesis 1, 2,'' *Biblica* 15 (1934) 517–527. J. GUILLET, ''La Révélation progressive du Saint-Esprit dans l'Écriture,'' *Lumen Vitae* (French ed.) 8 (1953) 18–32. J. DE BAIOCCHI, ''Comment reconnaître la personnalité du Saint-Esprit?'' *Nouvelle revue théologique* 77 (1955) 1025–49. L. J. LUTKEMEYER, ''The Role of the Paraclete (Jn. 16:7–15),'' *The Catholic Biblical Quarterly* 8 (1946) 220–229. W. F. ARNDT and F. GINGRICH, *A Greek-English Lexicon of the New Testament and Other Early Literature,* tr. and adapt. of W. BAUER'S *Geriechische-Deutsches Wörterbuch* (Chicago 1957) 680–685.

[L. A. BUSHINSKI]

SPIRITISM

Belief in the possibility of communication with the spirits of the departed, and the practice of attempting such communication, usually with the help of some person (a medium) regarded as gifted to act as an intermediary with the spirit world. In popular speech the word ''spiritualism'' is more commonly employed to express this meaning, but its use is here avoided to prevent confusion with SPIRITUALISM in its philosophical sense.

Moral Evaluation. Catholic theologians reject the idea that disincarnate spirits can be evoked at will, but they do not, in general, favor any particular interpretation of the phenomena that spiritists claim have occurred. Catholic moralists are agreed that to participate in spiritistic activities is gravely illicit for the following reasons. (1) Spiritistic organizations often constitute a heretical sect that professes doctrines entirely opposed to divine revelation. Frequently spiritists incline to pantheism or some form of theosophy; they generally admit the permanent existence of human personality after death, but they teach a form of metempsychosis for all and deny an eternity of punishment. They consider Christ and the Prophets as only ''mediators'' of a natural religion. Needless to say, they are opposed to other organized religions, considering them to have only an indifferent value. (2) Sacred Scripture expressly forbids the practice of trying to summon up the souls of the deceased (See Dt 18.10–12; Lv 19.31; Lv 20.6, 27). (3) Catholic moralists point to the possibility that many of the things reported in spiritistic séances could be due to diabolical influence, so that to engage in spiritistic practice could, in effect, amount to a kind of trafficking with evil spirits. (4) Spiritistic activity not infrequently causes damage to the health of body and mind.

It is not lawful to have recourse to spiritism as a means of therapy even if a physician thinks that it can produce possible beneficial effects on the psychoneurotic patient. Psychiatry today possesses other shock therapeutic methods that are effective, lawful, and advisable. It is also held to be gravely sinful to act as a medium or to consult one with the intention of finding out something that is not known. It is basically a form of divination, and as such, is contrary to the law of God.

Decrees of the Church. A decree issued by the Congregation of the Inquisition on July 30, 1856, mentioned ''evocation of departed spirits and other superstitious practices of spiritism,'' and exhorted the bishops to employ every effort to suppress these abuses. The reason it called for strenuous and swift action on the part of the bishops was stated: ''that the flock of the Lord may be protected against the enemy, the deposit of faith safeguarded, and the faithful preserved from moral corruption.'' When asked ''whether it is allowed either through a so-called medium or without one, and with or without hypnotism, to assist at any spiritualistic communications or manifestations, even such as appear to be blameless or pious, either asking questions of the souls or spirits, or listening to their answers, or merely looking on, even with a tacit or express protestation that one does not want to have anything to do with evil spirits?'' the Holy Office replied in the negative to all points in the inquiry on April 26, 1917 (*Acta Apostolicae Sedis* 9–269; T. L. Bouscaren and J. I. O'Connor, *Canon Law Digest* 1.155).

It is understood, however, that what is condemned is superstitious abuse and that there was no intention to preclude legitimate scientific study, provided there is no recourse to means that are essentially immoral or specifically forbidden.

Bibliography: A. WIESINGER, *Occult Phenomena* (Westminster, MD 1957). R. OMEZ, *Psychical Phenomena,* tr. R. HAYNES (New York 1958). A. FLEW, *A New Approach to Psychical Research* (London 1953). C. M. DE HEREDIA, *Spiritism and Common Sense* (New York 1922). H. THURSTON, *The Church and Spiritualism* (Milwaukee 1933). A. H. M. LÉPICIER, *The Unseen World* (new ed. enl., London 1929). J. LILJENCRANTS, *Spiritism and Religion* (New York 1918).

[M. D. GRIFFIN]

SPIRITUAL COMBAT

A treatise on the spiritual life, especially in its ascetical aspects. *Spiritual Combat* first appeared anonymously in Venice in 1589. In Genoa, in 1610, it was first published under the name of Lorenzo SCUPOLI, a Theatine, who died that year. Shortly thereafter many editions appeared in the various European languages and in Latin. It is a book on spiritual strategy presenting a simple and practical method for bringing souls to perfection, principally by interior mortification.

The central section, the core of the work, gives the book its name and constitutes a valuable contribution to spiritual literature. Here the author considered the nature and the use of the faculties of the soul, and principally of the will, in achieving union with God (ch. 10–26). There are Ignatian traces, but the ascetical note is much more marked and detailed than in the *Exercises.*

The book has been ascribed to different authors, especially to a Spanish Benedictine, John of Castagniza, and to an Italian Jesuit, Achille GAGLIARDI. As it stands today, the work contains traces of Spanish asceticism and also of Ignatian and Franciscan spirituality. The first editions contained only 24 chapters; later versions had 33, 37, 47, and 66 chapters. As the editions grew in size, the work lost its earlier simple grace and unction. Today historians generally agree that the basic chapters were written by Scupoli and were added to later (not to their benefit) by writers of widely varying schools.

The popularity of the book was due in large part to the recommendation given it by St. Francis de Sales. He is said to have received a copy of the first edition from Scupoli. At any rate, it was his self-confessed favorite, and he read from it every day for 18 years (see Camus, 37). Its teaching on the place of the will in self-denial was of capital importance in the development of Salesian spirituality (see Bremond, 53).

Bibliography: J. MERCIER, *Dictionnaire de théologie catholique,* ed. A. VACANT, 15 v. (Paris 1903–50; Tables générales 1951–) 14:1745–46; H. BREMOND, *Histoire littéraire du sentiment réligieux en France depuis la fin des guerres de religion jusqu'à nos jours,* 12 v. (Paris 1911–36) 7:52–57. J. P. CAMUS, *The Spirit of St. Francis de Sales,* tr. C. F. KELLEY (New York 1953) 37. P. POURRAT, *Christian Spirituality,* tr. W. H. MITCHELL et al., 4 v. (Westminster, MD 1953–55) v.3.

[P. MULHERN]

SPIRITUAL EXERCISES

A systematic series of meditations composed by St. IGNATIUS OF LOYOLA, and one of the great classics of Christian spirituality. St. Ignatius was the originator neither of the spiritual retreat nor of methodical prayer—in which fields he was the heir of an already existing tradition—but he did nevertheless make a significant contribution in both respects through the *Spiritual Exercises.*

History. The *Exercises* was not written at a single time. It was composed between 1521 and 1548. Ignatius began with a notebook of quotations put together during his spiritually decisive convalescence at Loyola after the battle of Pamplona. Shortly afterward, in Manresa in 1522, he roughed out his work, and completed it in Paris in 1534. This edition he revised slightly in 1548. The Spanish original of the *Exercises* has been lost. There is one copy called ''autograph'' because Ignatius himself made corrections in it, and three Latin translations: the *versio prima,* done, it would seem, by Ignatius himself at Paris in 1528; the *vulgata* of André des Freux, printed in 1548; and the *versio litteralis* of Jean Roothaan, done during the first part of the 19th century. The *vulgata* is considered the official text, although the autograph has gained general favor, especially with modern translators. The paragraph numbering used by all recent editors was introduced by A. Codina in the handbook edition published at Turin in 1928.

Three major influences contributed to the *Exercises:* Ignatius' reading of the *Vita Christi* of Ludolph of Saxony, the *Flos Sanctorum* of James of Voragine, and the *Ejercitatorio* of García de Cisneros; his spiritual experiences during his conversion; and the mystical graces received at Manresa and noted in his autobiography (nn. 28–30). Ignatius' later studies, especially at Paris, and his knowledge of budding Protestantism provided a significant complement to these earlier influences.

Contents. The book contains instructions, admonitions, warnings, meditations, examinations of conscience, and other practices, together with the method of arranging the different exercises for their fruitful use by the exercitant. The work was not composed with any thought to elegance of style or easy readability. Indeed, it was not intended for light reading, and was not written so much for the exercitant as for the retreat master. It was conceived as a kind of vade mecum to aid the latter in directing persons making the exercises. The various exercises can be used more or less completely according to the spiritual needs of the exercitant and the time he can devote to solitude and prayer. By its more or less integral use the *Exercises* provides a basis for what amounts, in effect, to different kinds of retreats. It can be used over a period of months by those who have only a short time each day to give to its program, but for those who are able to withdraw from other activities and give themselves entirely to the making of the exercises, they are designed to take about 30 days. Apparently Ignatius himself did not foresee the short retreat that condensed the whole of the exercises. This practice was begun by St. Peter CANISIUS in 1588 and became quite popular. Similarly Ignatius did not think of giving the exercises in their entirety to assembled groups. His retreat was intended for individuals, not for groups, and it was the function of the retreat master or director to adapt the various exercises to the needs of the exercitant and to the action of the Lord in him. The Ignatian exercises were, in fact, intended to be a personal enterprise of the exercitant, and the director was expected neither to preach nor to suggest decisions to him; he was merely to provide the retreatant with ''points'' on subjects of meditation, and to help him, through the DISCERNMENT of spirits, to understand what was taking place in his soul during the course of the retreat.

When the exercises are used in their complete form, the first week is given to the systematic consideration of sin and its consequences, the second to the kingdom of Christ, the third to the Passion, and the fourth to the risen and glorified Christ. The meditations appeal to the retreatant's sense impressions, imagination, and understanding in a way calculated to move his will toward decision in the pursuit of perfection.

Development. The *Exercises* is a delicate instrument, difficult to handle with unfailing fidelity to its original intent. Soon after the death of Ignatius deviant tendencies began to appear among Jesuits. A need for establishing authoritative norms was felt, and a directory was drawn up, which was published in 1599 by C. Aquaviva, General of the Society. This document was more practical than theological in character, and while it made possible a return to the Ignatian method, it did not contribute much to a profound understanding of the *Exercises,* or to a uniform application of its principles.

The work of retreats grew. At the end of the 16th century the colleges of the Society reserved accommodations for the making of the exercises, and soon houses were built for this ministry exclusively. Individual retreats, however, especially those lasting a month, tended to disappear. In the 17th and especially in the 18th centuries there were mass retreats and popular missions, which no doubt accomplished a great good, but in many cases strayed from the Ignatian concept. At the end of the following century, the exercises were often reduced to a short span of three days.

While J. Roothaan was general of the Society, at the beginning of the 19th century, a renewal began, the effects of which are still being felt. An effort was made to discover the full meaning of the *Exercises* by studying the text itself and by reference to other works of St. Ignatius that had long remained unknown. Studies appeared, such as those of P. I. Casanovas and those of the *Collection de la Bibliothèque des Exercices* published by H. Watrigant; critical studies also have appeared, such as that of A. Codina in the *Monumenta Historica Societatis Jesu* and that of P. J. Calveras in manual form; reviews dedicated to Ignatian spirituality have been founded (e.g., *Manresa, Christus*); congresses have been held in various countries. There has been a serious effort to discern the theology latent in the text of the Exercises and to give to the exercises their full spiritual efficacy.

Constitutive Elements of the Ignatian Exercises. The *Exercises* is not a product of the work of the mind; it is rather the fruit of an experience through which St. Ignatius lived during the year of his spiritual conversion. In the words of G. da Camara, a confidant of Ignatius, at the end of the *Autobiography* (n.99), ''Certain things which he observed in his soul and which he found useful, seemed to him to have a possible value to others, and thus he wrote them down.'' Ignatius saw that his experience had an objective value and could be communicated in its essentials to other human beings. This prompted him to write the *Exercises.* Thus it is important, in understanding it, to bring out the elements of this experience that the exercitant in turn undergoes. Ignatius read the lives of Christ and the saints and then fell into a prolonged meditation, in which he experienced a struggle between good and evil for his soul. He was under interior pressure to give himself generously to God, then came mystical graces through which he received illumination of mind with regard to the Trinity, Creation, the Eucharist, the humanity of Christ and the Blessed Virgin Mary. Finally, a transforming illumination seems to have revealed to him, in synthesis, the design of God for the world. From these experiences, all intimately linked, the essential traits of the *Exercises* are derived.

Prayer. In the Ignatian retreat, prayer in various forms plays a major role. The exercises are really something to be done or performed. The exercitant is called upon to devote himself to interior activity, under divine action, to enter into the supernatural world, to experience what it means to be a Christian. Every day he must make either four, or more often five exercises, each lasting a whole hour, from the brief indications given by the director. In the evening he should recall, as he is retiring, the subject on which he will meditate after his sleep, and on rising he gives all his attention to this subject. At the beginning of each exercise he puts himself in the presence of God, to whom he makes an act of reverence. In his mind's eye he pictures the subject on which he will meditate; he leaves himself open to the message it bears, he asks for the grace that awaits him and that he desires with his whole being. During the prayer, in which intelligence, will, the heart are engaged, and docility is an operative force, he pauses at particular points where he finds what he was seeking; he ''tastes things interiorly,'' to fill himself with them (n.2). After completing the exercise he reviews it in order to observe what took place in his soul. First place is given to the interiorization of the subjects that have been meditated upon. For each day there are only one or two subjects for the five exercises, the fourth and fifth being a ''repetition,'' and the last an ''application of the senses,'' a very intimate contact with the contemplated mystery. The Ignatian retreat is a time of profound prayer, of generous receptivity. Thus St. Ignatius asks the exercitant to bring his particular examination of conscience to bear on his faithfulness in assuring the success of his prayer in whatever way this depends upon himself.

Interior Struggle. A successful prayer is one in which interior motion has taken place, whether it be in the form of what Ignatius calls ''consolations'' or ''desolations.'' Faced with supernatural mystery, the exercitant feels either peace or trouble, light or dark, attraction or repulsion, for God and Satan are at work in a soul that has placed itself completely in the hands of the Creator. If the exercitant is not thus moved during the exercises, St. Ignatius felt there is cause for concern and asks the director or retreat master to examine the case more carefully. Indeed this is the function of the Ignatian director. To give the exercises requires above all the discernment of spirits in order to bring the exercitant to understand and distinguish the activity of God and of Satan in his own soul. To enable the director to do this, St. Ignatius provided two series of rules for the discernment of spirits.

Discovery of God's Will. The Spirit of the Lord manifests His designs for the exercitant and the course He wishes him to pursue. St. Ignatius thought of God as active in the world, as having a design for each individual soul, as personally calling the soul to His service. The exercitant makes the exercises expressly to discover the design God has for him, to seek and find the divine will in the disposition of his life (n.1). So also Christ voices a call, reveals His holy will to the soul contemplating His mysteries, and the love that moves and causes one to choose descends from above, that is, from the love of God (n. 184). This choice is concerned with a state of life or with the amendment of a state already chosen. Ignatius designed his exercises particularly for those who must reach a decision with regard to their state of life, but they are also profitable to one who is at a turning point of his spiritual life. What matters is that the exercitant should offer to his Creator and Lord all his will and liberty, that His Divine Majesty dispose of him and all he possesses, according to His most holy will (n.5).

The meditation in which the choice one is called to make becomes evident, centers upon the history of salvation revealed in the Bible. Of the four weeks into which the exercises are divided, only the first is concerned with the sinful condition of man, and the three others are taken up with the consideration of the life of Christ: His hidden life and public life, His Passion, Resurrection, and Ascension. The Trinity is clearly invoked in the meditation on the Incarnation and is prominent in the triple colloquy that St. Ignatius introduces at crucial moments in the exercises: one prays to Our Lady, then through her to the Son, and through the Son to the Father, always in the "Spirit who directs and governs us." At the center of the exercises one finds Jesus Christ, "Eternal Lord of all things" who guides souls "to the glory of His Father" (nn.98, 95), in His Eucharistic mystery that is shared during the days of the exercises, in the give and take of love (n.234). He is present throughout. In the first exercise, where the theme is sin, He appears in the colloquy as Creator made man to die for man's sins (n.53); during the second, third, and fourth weeks, the mysteries are entered into in order to follow Him into the way of Incarnation-Death-Resurrection. He is the Kyrios of St. Paul, the Lord lifted up from earth, whom St. John reveals. The four weeks of exercises unfold the complete mystery of the Kingdom, which is at the root of the exercises (nn.91–98).

To make the exercises is thus to contemplate the mystery of salvation and to discover therein the divine will for oneself. The Ignatian exercitant ponders in prayer the great facts of divine revelation; he perceives in it the design of God for man; he seeks in the debate that the Spirit and Satan awake in his nature, the particular way in which he is to participate in the plan of God, his way as God sees it, of taking part in the work of Christ here on earth. The exercises introduce the retreatant into a total spiritual experience: he lives the revelation realized in Christ, an interior dialogue with God, a sovereign act of liberty that engages his person and his destiny. During his 30 days of retreat, he personally submits himself to the initiative of the Lord.

Objections to the Ignatian Exercises. The exercises have been charged with not respecting the liberty of the exercitant, of being an instrument of pressure on the part of the director, of autosuggestion on the part of the one who makes them, a powerful psychological machine. Certainly a retreat, especially in the form of the Ignatian exercises, which require solitude and silence, tends to be a precise framework, and some of its provisions with respect to behavior can lead to abuse under a willful and dominating director, or in the case of a retreatant with strong emotions. But this danger is not inherent in the exercises. St. Ignatius wished the retreat master to be retiring and "permit the Creator to deal directly with His creature" (n.15), to adapt the exercises to the condition of him who is to engage in them (nn.18–20), to apply only the directions and regulations that will be helpful (nn.130–229). On the other hand, though St. Ignatius demanded much generosity and effort on the part of the exercitant, he clearly gave priority to grace, to the work of the Holy Spirit, to an attitude of spiritual receptivity.

Another complaint, related to the foregoing, is that the exercitant is expected to be sanctified in a month through the exercises, as though they had an automatic efficacy and amounted to a kind of spiritual magic. The fact is that although St. Ignatius justifiably expected that a serious retreatant would receive light and inspiration from God, he did not suppose for a moment that the exercitant would be confirmed in sanctity at the conclusion of the exercises. Like other retreats, the exercises reorient the soul, without, however, bringing it immediately to the perfection of Christian life. St. Ignatius desired that after the exercises one should assiduously practice the examination of conscience and try steadfastly to live in union with the Lord.

Finally, the exercises have been accused of fostering individualism. No doubt the Ignatian retreat, as it is understood by an individual, will always be conceived as addressed to his particular self; it is a matter of converting the retreatant himself. But he is nevertheless led to see himself in his relation to all of creation and to the Church. He is invited to consider all things on the face of the earth (see n.23, *First Principle and Foundation*). In the first week, he integrates himself to the whole story of sin in creation; hell reminds him that all human beings are judged with reference to the central event in the history of humanity, which is the coming of Jesus Christ (n.71); the *Kingdom of Christ* presents the "whole world" to him, which he helps the Lord to conquer (n.93). The second week in the contemplation of the Incarnation he sees the Three Divine Persons looking down upon the whole of the earth, and decreeing that in the fullness of time the Word would become man to save the human race (n.102). The *Two Standards* depict to him Christ and Satan addressing themselves ''to all the world'' and to every person (nn.141, 145); *Contemplation to Attain the Love of God* invites him to serve the Lord in all things, the Lord who lives in all, works in all, showers them with his goods (n.235–237); at the end of the text, the rules show him that he must think with a ''militant Church'' (n.352), which is the ''Spouse of Christ our Lord'' and ''our holy Mother Church who is ruled and governed'' by the Spirit (n.365). Individualism is a strange charge to level against a spirituality so charged with apostolic spirit.

Commendation. If some few critics have spoken unfavorably of the *Exercises,* many others—theologians, masters of the spiritual life, saints—have taken a different view, and with this substantial majority the authority of the Church has always sided. Even during the lifetime of Ignatius, Paul III, in his brief *Pastoralis Officii* of July 31, 1548, approved and praised the *Exercises.* Other popes have done the same: Clement VIII, Gregory XIII, Alexander VII, Innocent XI, Benedict XIV, Pius IX, Leo XIII, Plus X, and Benedict XV. In his apostolic constitution *Summorum pontificum* of July 25, 1922, Pius XI proclaimed St. Ignatius celestial patron of spiritual exercises, and in 1929, in the encyclical, *Mens nostra* he recommended to all the practice of the Ignatian exercises. Pius XII confirmed the praise of his predecessors in the encyclical *Mediator Dei* of Nov. 20, 1947.

Bibliography: Texts. *Exercitia Spiritualia Sancti Ignatii de Loyola,* ed. A. CODINA (*Monumenta historica Societatis Jesu*; 1919); *Ejercicios espirituales, Directorio y Documentos,* ed. P. J. CALVERAS (Barcelona 1944). Various English translations, especially by L. J. PUHL (Westminster, Maryland 1951) and T. CORBISHLEY (New York 1963). History. A. BROU, *Les Exercices spirituels de saint Ignace de Loyola* (Paris 1922). I. IPARRAGUIRRE, *Historia de los ejercicios de San Ignacio,* 2 v. (Rome 1946–55). H. PINARD DE LA BOULLAYE, *Les Étapes de rédaction des Exercices de S. Ignace* (Paris 1945). C. D. PLATER, *Retreats for the People* (St. Louis 1912). Commentary. J. RICKABY, *The Spiritual Exercises: Spanish and English, with a Continuous Commentary* (2d ed. New York 1923). H. D. EGAN, *The Spiritual Exercises and the Ignatian Mystical Horizon.* (St. Louis, 1976). D. L. FLEMMING, *The Spiritual Exercises of Saint Ignatius: A Litera Translation and a Contemporary Reading* (St. Louis, 1978). Studies. G. FESSARD, *La Dialectique des Exercices spirituels de saint Ignace de Loyola* (Paris 1956). A. GOODIER, *The Life That Is Light,* 3 v. (London 1935); *St. Ignatius Loyola and Prayer* (London 1940). P. LETURIA, *Estudios Ignacianos,* 2 v. (Rome 1957). H. RAHNER, *The Spirituality of St. Ignatius Loyola,* tr. F. J. SMITH (Westminster, Maryland 1953). *Spirituality of St. Ignatius Loyola: An Account of its Historical Development* (1968). *Directoria Exercitiorum Spiritualium,* ed. I. IPARRAGUIRRE (*Monumenta historica Societatis Jesu*; 1955). Papal documents. C. H. MARÍN, *Spiritualia Exercitia secundum Romanorum Pontificum Documenta* (Barcelona 1941). Other editions and literature, J. JUAMBELZ, *Bibliografía sobre la vida, obras, y escritos de San Ignacio de Loyola 1900–1950* (Madrid 1956) 1–100, 832–2397.

[J. LEWIS]

SPIRITUAL THEOLOGY

It has become common to use the term ''spiritual theology'' to indicate the portion of theology that in older terminology was called ascetical and mystical. It is called ''spiritual'' in order to emphasize forcefully that it has to do with the application of Christ's redemptive work to the individual soul and with the manner by which each soul receives and cooperates with it. It embraces the part of sacred doctrine that treats of the ''spiritual life,'' i.e., the life according to the spirit understood in the sense of the New Testament, especially of St. Paul, in opposition to a life according to the ''flesh.'' Joseph de GUIBERT defined spiritual theology as ''the science which deduces from revealed principles *what* constitutes the perfection of the spiritual life and *how* man can advance towards and obtain it.'' It is thus the task of spiritual theology to establish the true nature of Christian perfection and to determine the means, both in general and in particular, that are to be used in the soul's advance on the way of perfection.

The Spiritual Life. The growth and development of the spiritual life has been divided into three ways, or stages. This does not mean that there are three parallel or divergent ways, but rather that there are three stages, or degrees, of the spiritual life that souls must traverse on the way to perfection. This division into the purgative, illuminative, and unitive ways is a traditional one, and comes from pre-Christian sources through Pseudo-Dionysius. Another, mentioned by Origen and used by St. Thomas Aquinas (*Summa theologiae* 2a2ae, 24.9; 183.4) divides the spiritual life into the states of the beginner, the proficient, and the perfect. St. Augustine provided a division based on love. Since perfection consists in love, he noted three degrees in the practice of this virtue: incipient, growing, and full-grown or perfect. St. Bernard considered three degrees in the love of God: the first is the love man has for God because of His gifts; then he begins to love God for His own sake; and finally, his love for God is altogether disinterested.

The work of the purgative way is to purify a man from his faults and to strengthen him against committing them in the future. Only the pure in heart will see God, perfectly in heaven, imperfectly and through faith here on earth. Prayer, meditation, mortification, and the practice of the virtues are required to obtain this purity and to strengthen the soul in virtue.

After the work of purification, the soul must ''put on Christ.'' It must strive to make its own the mind and the heart of Christ by a more generous and constant practice of the moral and theological virtues. The great desire of the soul then is to become more and more like Christ in thought, word, and action. Prayer now becomes more affective. The soul is now in the illuminative way.

As the soul progresses, a time comes when under the action of the Holy Spirit, working through His gifts, the desire for a more intimate union with God will become more intense. Seeking Him everywhere and at all times, the soul clings to Him and finds its greatest happiness in His presence. The gifts of the Holy Spirit are now more manifest, and prayer is much more simple, consisting in a loving thought of God and of things of God. This is the unitive way.

Ascetical and Mystical Elements. The development of the life of grace in man has two elements, one ascetical and the other mystical. Both are essential to every form and degree of the spiritual life. The ascetical element (from the Greek verb ἀσκεῖν, which signifies personal effort, physical and mental training) includes everything that man does, with the help of ordinary grace, toward his spiritual perfection. It is concerned especially with the uprooting of vices or defects and the practice of the virtues. It might be called the active element of the spiritual life. The first Christians who devoted themselves to the practice of mortification and the exercises of piety and who observed perfect continence or virginity were called ascetics. Ascetical theology is the part of sacred science that treats the nature of Christian perfection and the different means to be used to acquire it. It is a practical science, having for its end to guide and direct the soul in its striving for holiness.

The mystical element consists in a deepening of the spiritual life under a more pronounced action of the Holy Spirit through His gifts, thus elevating the soul to a more intimate, hidden knowledge of God, resulting from a more intimate union with Him. The action of the Holy Spirit is especially manifest in the passive purifications of the soul and in the interior illuminations that it receives. For the old authors mystical theology was a knowledge of God and of divine things acquired by the soul in the highest form of contemplation. St. Thomas considered it to be a most perfect and exalted contemplation of God and a "fruitive" and very savory love of Him possessed in the depths of the soul. It is a practical or quasi-experimental knowledge of God acquired in contemplation. J. GERSON said that "mystical theology has for its object the experimental knowledge of the things of God produced by the intimate union of love." Mystical theology today is defined as the part of sacred science that treats the more hidden and mysterious things of God, such as the intimate union between the soul and God; the transitory phenomena, such as ecstasy, that sometimes accompany certain degrees of union; and extraordinary graces, such as visions and private revelations.

The sources of both mystical and ascetical theology are Sacred Scripture, tradition, the teachings and definitions of the Church, and the common teaching of the Fathers and the theologians of the Church. The ascetical and mystical writings of the saints and the Doctors of the Church such as SS. Augustine, Bernard, John of the Cross, and Teresa of Avila offer excellent material for practical and descriptive mysticism.

Ascetical and mystical theology is the practical application of theology in the direction of souls to a more intimate union with God. There is an interplay of the ascetical and the mystical life, and it is difficult to determine precisely where the one stops and the other begins.

Distinction Between Ascetical and Mystical. Until the 17th century spiritual theology was considered as a unit, a whole. It was not divided into ascetical and mystical, nor was it considered to be a science distinct from the rest of theology. The spiritual life was considered as received at Baptism with sanctifying grace, and it was to grow and develop by the exercise of the supernatural organism, i.e., the infused virtues, both theological and moral, and the gifts of the Holy Spirit, by the practice of prayer and mortification and by the reception of the Sacraments, until it reached the end to which it was directed, namely, intimate union with God. There is a unity in this conception of the spiritual life, and it sees the mystical life as the normal development of the ascetical. There is no separation or division of the two, but rather an ordering of the one to the other. They are not two distinct divisions of theology, but two aspects of spiritual theology that show the spiritual life in its beginnings, its progression, and in such perfection as it can have upon earth. This was the traditional teaching.

Another school of thought arose in the 17th and 18th centuries. Some theologians of this period thought it necessary to divide spiritual theology into ascetical and mystical. G. B. SCARAMELLI (1687–1752) was one of the first to make this division, and he was followed by many authors of that time. Thus appeared the *Mystical Directory* and *Ascetical Directory.* Ascetical theology according to the teaching of these authors should treat the "ordinary" Christian life, whereas mystical theology should consider only extraordinary graces, such as visions and revelations, as well as infused contemplation, the passive purifications, and the mystical union. Although there continue to be authors who hold this division, the general tendency is to return to the traditional teaching expressed by the use of the term spiritual theology in place of the terms ascetical and mystical.

Since the matter treated in spiritual theology is the same as that treated separately under the headings of ascetical and mystical theology, the sources are the same as those given above: the Old and New Testaments and tradition as it is expressed in the writings of the Fathers and the theologians. The autobiographies and lives of the saints provide excellent material for this subject.

The conclusions of experimental and religious psychology also can be used by spiritual theology. Spiritual theology has for its end to teach souls how to acquire perfection. It is a practical science. It employs a combination of the doctrinal, or deductive, and the experimental, or inductive, methods. To use either the doctrinal or the experimental method exclusively would be to run the risk of error. The doctrinal method must be employed because it is only from revelation that the existence, nature, and causes of the perfection at which it aims can be certainly known. From the revealed truths that are its principles and from the infallible teaching of the Church in explanation of these truths, spiritual theology makes deductions concerning its own object, i.e., spiritual perfection.

The deductive method alone does not suffice. Spiritual theology must know how to apply the general theological deductions to individual cases, taking account of all particular circumstances. The experience of the saints and of other fervent souls concerning the means they used to attain perfection, as well as the trials and sufferings that God asked of them will enable one to form a judgment with regard to efficacy of a certain means of sanctification, both its advantages and its dangers.

Spiritual as Related to Other Parts of Theology. St. Thomas and the other theologians of the Middle Ages treated theology as a whole. It was only in the 17th century that theology began to be divided into different parts for the purpose of facilitating its study. The subject matter of dogmatic theology is also treated by spiritual theology: the revealed mysteries of the Blessed Trinity, the Incarnation, the Redemption, the Sacraments, and the Last Things. It is not only to know and contemplate these mysteries that spiritual theology considers them, but above all to make known how man can participate in them, share in them, and thus be united to God.

Moral theology as it was understood by the early theologians and as it is found in the *Summa theologiae* of St. Thomas Aquinas contains the principles necessary for leading souls to the highest sanctity. However, all authors do not agree concerning the relationship between spiritual and moral theology. For some, moral theology considers the commandments and virtues as they are of obligation and precept, whereas spiritual theology considers the same subject—human acts, virtues, and counsels—as means for acquiring perfection. The difference, however, depends less on a divergence of opinion regarding the nature of spiritual theology than it does on the discrepant views that may be taken of MORAL THEOLOGY. If moral theology is understood to be concerned exclusively with the differentiation of what is sinful from what is not, then spiritual theology must necessarily be regarded as a distinct science. If, on the other hand, moral theology is understood, as it was by older theologians and still is by many among modern theologians, as the science of the attainment of God, then it must include spiritual theology within its scope, and it differs from spiritual theology only as a whole differs from its part. Even those who take this latter view, however, generally admit that pedagogical reasons make it desirable to teach and study the two disciplines separately.

The Liturgy. There is a very intimate connection between spiritual theology and the liturgy. It is the liturgy that makes present the mysteries of the life of Christ. It does so in order that men may participate in them in a real way and thus become more fully assimilated to Christ. ''In the liturgy the sanctification of man is signified by signs perceptible to the senses, and is effected in a way which corresponds with each of these signs; in the liturgy the whole public worship is performed by the mystical body of Jesus Christ, that is by the Head and His members. . . . Recalling thus the mysteries of redemption, the Church opens to the faithful the riches of her Lord's powers and merits, so that these are in some way made present for all time, and the faithful are enabled to lay hold upon them and become filled with saving grace'' (Vatican Council II, *Constitution on the Sacred Liturgy*). The same constitution makes it clear that the spiritual life is not limited solely to participation in the liturgy. Private, secret prayer, unceasing prayer by which one bears in his body the dying of Jesus so that His life may be made manifest in him, is of great profit to one's spiritual life. The study of sacred liturgy is to be a major course in seminaries and religious houses of studies, and it is to be taught under its spiritual aspect. The professors of such subjects as dogmatic and spiritual theology will show connections between their own subjects and the liturgy. Clerics are to be given a liturgical formation in their spiritual life.

Historical Development. As in the case of theology in general, spiritual theology developed slowly in regard to its subject matter, to the determining of its proper object, and to its method. Sacred Scripture, in both the Old and the New Testaments, is the primary and the most exalted source of the teaching concerning the spiritual life. It is from this source that the Fathers drew the matter for their sermons and writings. In the letters of such men as Jerome and Augustine, and in the Rules of Pachomius, Basil, Benedict, and Augustine, the spiritual life was given much attention. Clement of Alexandria (150–217) and his famous pupil, Origen (1852–55), did much to systematize the study of the spiritual life and to provide it with a philosophical foundation and orientation. The teaching of Origen was characterized by his love of

Scripture and its spiritual meaning. His mysticism was founded on the gifts of the Holy Spirit, and he surpasses all his precursors by the extensive use he makes of the gifts in explaining the perfect Christian life. The *Theologia mystica* of Pseudo-Dionysius has held first place in the field of spiritual theology for nearly 1,000 years. The Middle Ages made immense contributions to the history of spiritual theology by the writings of the foremost members of the Benedictine, Cistercian, Carthusian, Franciscan, and Dominican orders, as well as of the Canons Regular. After the Reformation, St. Ignatius expressed his teachings on the spiritual life in his *Spiritual Exercises.*

The great mystics SS. John of the Cross and Teresa of Avila have enriched the study of spiritual theology by their works, which have become classics in this field. In modern times men such as A. Poulain, SJ; J. G. Arintero, OP; R. Garrigou-Lagrange, OP; A. Gemelli, OFM; and A. Stolz, OSB, have contributed in no small way to make known the ineffable riches of the spiritual life.

See Also: SPIRITUALITY, CHRISTIAN; SPIRITUALITY (HISTORY OF).

Bibliography: J. G. ARINTERO, *The Mystical Evolution in the Development and Vitality of the Church,* tr. J. AUMANN, 2 v. (St. Louis 1949–51). J. BONSIRVEN, *The Theology of the New Testament,* tr. S. F. L. TYE (Westminster, Md. 1963). E. C. BUTLER, *Western Mysticism* (2d ed. London 1927). J. DE GUIBERT, *The Theology of the Spiritual Life,* tr. P. BARRETT (New York 1953). R. GARRIGOU-LAGRANGE, *Christian Perfection and Contemplation,* tr. M. T. DOYLE (St. Louis 1937); *The Three Ages of the Interior Life,* tr. M. T. DOYLE, 2 v. (St. Louis 1947–48). W. K. GROSSOUW, *Spirituality of New Testament,* tr. M. W. SCHOENBERG (St. Louis 1961). C. JOURNET, *The Dark Knowledge of God,* tr. J. F. ANDERSON (London 1948). J. LEBRETON, *The Spiritual Teaching of the New Testament,* tr. J. E. WHALEN (Westminster, Md. 1960). A. MAGER, *Mystik als Lehre und Leben* (Innsbruck 1934). A. MEYNARD, *Traité de la vie interieure . . . ascetique et mystique* (Clermont-Ferrand 1885). P. P. PARENTE, *The Ascetical Life* (rev. ed. St. Louis 1955); *The Mystical Life* (St. Louis 1956). A. POULAIN, *The Graces of Interior Prayer,* tr. L. L. YORKE SMITH, ed. J. V. BAINVEL (St. Louis 1950). A. ROYO, *The Theology of Christian Perfection,* ed. and tr. J. AUMANN (Dubuque 1962). A. STOLZ, *The Doctrine of Spiritual Perfection,* tr. A. WILLIAMS (St. Louis 1938). A. TANQUEREY, *The Spiritual Life,* tr. H. BRANDERIS (2d ed. Tournai 1930; repr. Westminster, Md. 1945).

[T. A. PORTER]

SPIRITUALISM

The term ''spiritualism'' seems to have been coined by 17th-century theologians to signify erroneous forms of mysticism, but was taken over by V. COUSIN to denote his own eclectic philosophy. Its use in philosophy became common in the 19th century, both in the wider sense of systems opposed to materialism, as with T. S. Jouffroy (1796–1842) and MAINE DE BIRAN, and in more restricted contexts, as referring for instance to trends of thought originating with St. Augustine. In general usage, thinkers are termed spiritualist if they maintain the existence and primacy of a reality that is distinct from, and not derived from, matter, that of itself is not subject to the determinations of time and space, and that, in its existence, is independent of a bodily frame. Such reality may be conceived as an impersonal, universal cosmic force, or as personal, either in a supreme being or in finite beings; it may be regarded as the only reality, implying the negation of matter; or it may be affirmed as coexistent with matter and associated principally with certain aspects or regions of reality, such as essences or values, or the order and structure of the universe. Under the heading of spiritualism one may therefore include such diverse systems as pantheism, deism, theism, idealism, immaterialism, personalism, and many forms of realism.

Idealism provides the spiritualist philosopher with many valid arguments in favor of the reality and superiority of spirit, without implying that all forms of being are fundamentally spiritual in the sense of being limited manifestations of one primal spirit, or that they are inconceivable except as objects essentially related to, if not immanent in, the act of thought. Catholic philosophy sees such implications as exaggerations of the truths that all finite being proceeds from the creative knowledge of God and that the formal element in all creatures may be seen as the external realization of a divine idea as its prototype. Material beings may, moreover, be seen as relative to mind since they are formally true only for mind and are endowed with higher perfection in the mind when they are known. The affinity of being with thought does not imply that being is essentially either spiritual or immaterial, but that both created thought and created being have their source in the creative knowledge of God.

Forms of realism that teach the evolution of spirit from matter deny in practice the principle of CAUSALITY. They also imply the denial of the validity of KNOWLEDGE. But such a denial is itself knowledge, and therefore, if it does not contradict itself, it at least deprives itself of any right to be heeded. The denial of the spirituality of man is itself an act of the mind of man and implies the very spirituality that is denied. If it be granted that thought is not spiritual and is nothing more than the result of the play of material forces, there can no longer be any question of truth for man, in which case the initial supposition cannot be regarded as true. The denial of spirituality thus involves a latent contradiction.

See Also: SPIRIT; SPIRITISM; PANPSYCHISM; IDEALISM.

Bibliography: J. MACQUARRIE, *Twentieth-Century Religious Thought* (New York 1963). A. DONDEYNE, *Contemporary Europe-*

an Thought and Christian Faith, tr. E. MCMULLIN and J. BURNHEIM (Pittsburgh 1958.). J. D. COLLINS, *God in Modern Philosophy* (Chicago 1959). É. H. GILSON, *Being and Some Philosophers* (2d ed. Toronto 1952); *The Unity of Philosophical Experience* (New York 1937). A. G. SERTILLANGES, *Le Christianisme et les philosophies,* 2 v. (Paris 1939–41). M. F. SCIACCA, *Il problema di Dio e della religione nella filosofia attuale* (3d ed. Brescia 1953). L. BRUNSCHVICG, *Les Âges de l'intelligence* (3d ed. Paris 1947). R. VANCOURT, *Pensée moderne et philosophie chrétienne* (Paris 1957). N. A. BERDÎAEV, *Esprit et réalité* (Paris 1943). F. TULOUP, *L'Âme et sa survivance, depuis la préhistoire jusqu'à nos jours* (Paris 1947).

[A. J. MCNICHOLL]

SPIRITUALISTS

Those who believe that the dead can make contact with the living through the person of a medium (*see* SPIRITUALISM; SPIRITISM). The Spiritualist movement in America originated (1848) in Hydesville, later Rochester, New York. Margaret and Kate Fox heard strange knockings and began to interpret them as sounds coming from spirits of the other world. Earlier, Andrew Jackson Davis had published a book, *Nature's Divine Revelations* (1847), from which the basic principles of Spiritualism are taken. Within a few years after the Fox sisters went on tour, giving demonstrations of their extraordinary abilities, there were thousands of mediums holding séances throughout the country.

Spiritualists took some time to become firmly established as a sect. In general they consider themselves to be Christian, with churches, ministers, and a basic doctrine. Christ, though not considered to be God, is the great medium, while the Annunciation is looked upon as a communication with the spirit world, and the Resurrection as a proof of the existence of the continued life of the spirit beyond the grave. The doctrinal position for most Spiritualists is set forth as follows:

> We believe in Infinite Intelligence; and that the phenomena of nature, both physical and spiritual, are the expression of Infinite Intelligence.
>
> We affirm that a correct understanding of such expressions and living in accordance with them constitute the true religion; that the existence and personal identity of the individual continue after the change called death; that the communication with the so-called dead is a fact scientifically proved by the phenomena of Spiritualism.
>
> We believe that the highest morality is contained in the Golden Rule: "Whatsoever ye would that others do unto you, do ye also unto them."
>
> We affirm the moral responsibility of the individual, and that he makes his own happiness or unhappiness as he obeys or disobeys Nature's physical and spiritual laws.
>
> We affirm that the doorway to reformation is never closed against any human soul, here or hereafter.

Spiritualists hold worship services patterned generally on the Protestant worship service, with the addition of messages from the spirits of the departed. Members are encouraged to make private, even daily, contact with the spirit world. For this a medium, not necessarily a minister, is employed. The medium is usually a highly psychic person, usually a female, though there are some male mediums. Contact is made at a séance, or group meeting, in which the medium goes into a trancelike state to communicate with the spirits. Responses are had through knocks, voices, or the emission of a vaporous substance, called ectoplasm.

The main Spiritualists organizations in the United States include the International General Assembly of Spiritualists (1936), with headquarters in Norfolk, Virginia, a federation to charter local groups throughout the world; the National Spiritualist Association (1893), at Chicago, Illinois, the largest of the Spiritualist denominations in the United States, with more than 8,000 members adhering to the doctrinal and religious practices cited above; the National Spiritual Alliance (1913), at Lake Pleasant, Massachusetts, "emphasizes subnormal and impersonal spirit manifestations"; and the Progressive Spiritual Church founded (1907) in Chicago by the Reverend G. Cordingly, which holds essentially to the doctrinal position stated above, with the addition that the Sacred Scriptures are recognized as the necessary guide for spirit communication. The major stronghold for the movement has been Latin America, especially Brazil, where a large segment of the population practices Spiritualism in some way.

Bibliography: J. A. HARDON, *The Protestant Churches of America* (rev. ed. Westminster, Maryland 1962). NATIONAL SPIRITUALIST ASSOCIATION, *Spiritualist Lyceum Manual,* comp. V. K. KUHLIG (Washington 1944). G. WEIGEL, *Churches in North America* (Baltimore 1961). W. J. WHALEN, *Faiths for the Few* (Milwaukee 1963).

[J. TARAN/EDS.]

SPIRITUALITY, CHRISTIAN

The spiritual life is the Christian life lived with some intensity. It is the serious response of man to the revelation of God's love in Christ and consists in loving knowledge and service of God and one's fellow men in the Mystical Body of Christ. Christian spirituality begins when God's word is accepted in faith. It manifests itself in the expression and the development of the love of God in prayer and action. It is the subjective assimilation and living in charity of the objective, theological realities of revelation.

Since its object, origin and goal is God in His personal life, Christian spirituality is interpersonal; it is the life of man with God. Men are given this new relationship with the Trinity gratuitously, and they express it in acts that are at once human and transcendent. The open, free, and in some sense unlimited human spirit can express itself only in dependence on the material, the finite and particular, hence little by little and in time. This particularized condition of existence is reinforced in Christianity by the fact that grace is union with a historical person, Christ (Acts 2.38), and a participation in the sacred events called mysteries in His life. At the same time the new life in Christ is transhistorical and supernatural (Gal 2.20); it is nothing less than the life of the Holy Spirit, the Spirit of the Son, in man (Rom 8.14–16).

This brief identification of Christian spirituality has three distinguishing features that will be examined separately. They are the interpersonal, the historical, and the transcendent aspects of Christian spirituality.

Interpersonal Life

The meaning of interpersonal life can best be examined by considering the encounter with which it begins and the community or fellowship of life that follows.

Encounter. Men as children of Adam are born estranged from God. Christian spirituality begins for them with their encounter with God who comes to them in Christ. This encounter is not a mere psychological construction, like an imagined visit with an absent person. The encounter is primarily ontological, founded on the real, objective, superconscious union with God in grace (Gal 3.2–5). But encounter in the spiritual life is more than ontological union. It is the intellectual and affective realization of the I-thou relationship of grace as well, the conscious experience of God who calls in love and is answered in faith. This experience or consciousness is not necessarily immediate and direct, like the feeling of God's presence in the classical mystical experience of God. It takes many forms, but basically it is an awareness and conviction that God is a person, that He is real and His love is real, and that this love freely accepted makes man a friend of God sharing God's own life.

Christian spirituality is neither abstract knowledge nor mere moralism (1 Cor 13.1–3). It is not a human system of self-perfection, even in the moral or religious order, nor a program of psychological conditioning to induce certain "states of soul." Christian spiritual life involves knowledge, moral effort, and spiritual exercises, but essentially it is a person-to-person contact between God who speaks to man in His Word and man who responds in the Word in loving faith (1 Thes 2.13). It is a dialogue with God in love—life with the Father, in the Son, through the Holy Spirit. The spiritual life is eternal life and consists in knowledge and love of the Father and the Son (Jn 17.3) and in living as sons in the Son in fraternal love (1 Jn 4.7–8; Jn 15.4–10).

The personal response to God in faith and love is the "theologal" life, the concrete expression of the theological virtues. The theologal life can be compared to the moral or ascetical life as later and earlier stages of spiritual growth, corresponding to the ancient distinction between contemplative and active life. Such stages describe states of soul in which either the theological or the moral elements are more obvious, but both elements are part of every degree of spirituality. Otherwise there would be the error of psychologism or moralism, both of which are counterfeit spirituality. The first consists in a superficial consciousness of God independently of the orientation of faith, hope, and charity, which may or may not be present. This is more akin to aesthetic feeling than to true religion. Moralism is moral effort without relation to God. In authentic Christian spirituality, the theological virtues unite the soul with God, while moral virtues dispose for this union by removing obstacles and by executing the commands of love. Moral virtues purify spiritual vision by allowing the light of faith to enlighten and manifest the Mystery of Christ (Eph 4.17–24); at the same time they strengthen the capacity for personal commitment and love by removing voluntary self-centered attachments that close the soul to God.

For the Christian there is no value in pure asceticism, unrelated to friendship with God, or in a self-redemptive, external observance of the law. The law in fact is a shackle if it is performed for its own sake (Rom 7.13–23). Christian law supplies guidelines only and exists because of the imperfect spiritualization of the faithful. The local dynamism of the Christian life is found not in particular forms or laws, but in charity and the Holy Spirit, who leads the sons of God in perfect freedom (Rom 8.14–16). But virtuous works are the good fruit produced by the Holy Spirit and a witness to His presence (Gal 5.22–26). The Church today wisely interprets heroic VIRTUE to be proved by the constant and faithful fulfillment of duty. It reasons that given the weakness and instability of fallen man, only the gifts of the Holy Spirit are a sufficient explanation of perfect perseverance in good works [Gabriel of St. Mary Magdalen, "Present Norms of Holiness," in *Conflict and Light* (New York 1952) 154–169].

Community. Man encounters God in the Word of God (1 Thes 2.13). The Word is not only the saving actions of God, apostolic preaching, or the inspired accounts in Sacred Scripture; it is especially and above all Christ Himself, the Substantial Word of the Father (Jn 1.14; 6.35, 54). He is the living Word that vivifies and brings to fulfillment the words and acts of the past and in Whom in the economy of his redemption man makes his personal response to God's love. Concretely the Word comes to us through the Church; the Church is the fundamental sacrament revealing and communicating the Word to men.

The consequences of this truth in the spiritual life are manifold, as will be seen in the next section. Here one central implication is singled out, the fact that encounter with God occurs in community, in the fellowship of Christ's Body, the Church.

The Christ in whom men meet the Father is not the Christ of memory alone, but one who lives on mystically and sacramentally in His followers (Acts 9.5; 1 Cor 8.11–13). The Church is Christ acting now, sanctifying men and offering men access to the Father (Eph 2.18). The Church is constantly reliving the life of Christ, especially the paschal mystery of ''passing over'' to the Father (cf. Jn 13.1; 1 Cor 5.7). Liturgically it makes present this passage, and historically its members recapitulate in their own lives the journey from sin to grace.

Life with the Father is life in the Son; life in the Son is a communal existence with other sons in the Son, hence with one's brothers. An individualistic God-and-I relationship is foreign to an informed Christian consciousness. Liturgical life, the source and summit of Christian life, is communal by nature, since the liturgy is the Mystical Body, Head and members together, worshiping the Father and sanctifying men. Private prayer likewise demands fraternal unity (Mt 5.23–24). Charity itself is necessarily social, since the same one virtue is exercised toward God and toward one's fellowmen (Mt 25.35–40). The Christian cannot afford to seek the transcendent God in contemplation and avoid Him in those who share His life. God dwells among men (Jn 1.14) as well as in inaccessible light (1 Tm 6.16), and neither presence can be neglected without compromising Christian life. This does not automatically spell out the forms the engagement to one's fellowmen will take. The call may be to silence and solitude in canonical contemplative life, which according to Pope Pius XII is ''intrinsically apostolic'' [*Acta Apostolicae Sedis* 43 (Rome 1951) 32]. Or it may be a vocation to social action in the world. Whatever the vocation there is no sanctification independently of the visible community and no love of God without a genuine, personal love of neighbor, for ''if anyone says he loves God and hates his brother, he is a liar'' (1 Jn 4.20).

Historical Nature

Christianity is a historical religion; it is a Person (Christ) and His saving deeds (Acts 10.37–42), especially His death and Resurrection, the paschal mystery, before it is a philosophy or a theology. Only by union with that Person through faith and Sacrament, only by reliving and assimilating the sacred events of His life, does the Christian make contact with God, undergo the transforming influence of grace, and achieve perfect friendship with God. From this point of view Christian spirituality is the living of the mystery of Christ.

The Mystery of Christ. St. Paul calls the full divine plan revealed in the New Testament the mystery of Christ (Col 1.25–27; Eph 1.8–10; Rom 16.25–27). This mystery is Christ in His personal identity and in saving acts, especially the paschal mystery of His death and Resurrection. Salvation history culminates in the paschal mystery. Its final act will be the Parousia, the unveiling of the mystery. In the present time, between the Ascension and the Second Coming, the mystery of Christ consists in the subjective application of Christ's work to men. The mystery now is the Risen Christ, who having been lifted up on the cross draws all men and all creation to Himself (Jn 12.32). It is ''Christ in you, your hope of glory'' (Col 1.27).

In a certain transhistorical sense Christians are already redeemed (Rom 8.24–25; 31–39). The baptized have gone down into the tomb with Christ and died to sin; they have risen with Christ to newness of life (Rom 6.2–11). Union with Christ glorified is so vivid in Paul's mind that he sees his fellow Christians already enjoying their risen status and seated at the right hand of God (Eph 2.5–6). This has been called the constitutive aspect of redemption in Christ. It is salvation in mystery, in signs that witness though they do not fully reveal the reality; it is mystical identification with Christ. (See Albert Plé, *Mystery and Mysticism* (London 1956) 1–17, and other essays in this volume.)

But in point of historical fact there is also a progressive assimilation of the paschal mystery. Mystical identity must be translated into moral action. 'Therefore,'' says Paul, ''if you have risen with Christ, seek the things that are above'' (Col 3.1). Liturgical reliving of the death and Resurrection must be complemented by the actual crucifixion of one's sins and vices (Gal 5.24) and the effort to follow the lead of the Holy Spirit. Because it is the Cross, the process involves suffering; because it is the Resurrection, there is joy. The sacrifice of self expressed symbolically in the Mass of the liturgy becomes the self-surrender to God's will in the free choices of daily life; the Mass and life together achieve the sanctification of the Christian and the worship of God.

In liturgical celebration and daily life Christians make their passage from flesh to spirit, from separation from the Father to communion with Him. This progressive transformation, which is the Christian's pasch or passage to the Father (Jn 14.4), takes place in company with Christ and the people of God. The Christian goes out of this world to the Father not in the sense that he leaves this world materially (Jn 15.18–19), but insofar as he rejects the isolated, independent world at enmity with God and embraces the redeemed world that takes its meaning from the Spirit. In other words the pasch is not a movement away from people or terrestrial realities to abstraction and immateriality, but a commitment to God's people and the abandonment only of selfishness and egoism. This process is the work of the Spirit; the Christian cooperates by discerning, approving, and implementing the movements of grace. In this way the whole Body of Christ is brought "to perfect manhood, to the mature measure of the fullness of Christ" (Eph 4.13) and the kingdom of Christ is established in the cosmos (Eph 1.10).

Application of the Mystery. The mystery of Christ is mediated to men through the visible structures of Christian life, all of which are found in the Church. The Church is the Bride of Christ and in this capacity it sees Mary as its perfect archetype and mother of all who answer the call of the Bridegroom. The Church looks to Mary as model because of her "fiat," which was a total surrender to God's will, and it goes to her as the Mother of grace who forms men in the image of the Son (Jn 19.25–27). In its ministry of word and Sacrament the Church presents the Word to men and conveys the response of her children back to the Father (Eph 5.25–27). Christian spirituality is stamped by all these characteristics. Christocentric through and through, it is ecclesial, Marian, Biblical, and liturgical. Each note is necessary, though the forms and their coordination in a given synthesis of Christian life will vary. Different spiritualities are possible in the Church, precisely because there are different ways of applying and interrelating the dogmas of the faith.

The living of these dogmas is not achieved completely and perfectly in the first act of acceptance. Modern authors (e.g., P. Fransen, M. Flick, Z. Alszeghy, and K. Truhlar) present a dynamic picture of man's personal growth in grace by appealing to the two kinds of will acts suggested by S. Kierkegaard. The fundamental option is made in favor of God revealed in Christ by faith and Baptism, but it is deepened by the daily choices of Christian life. Free choices are ineluctable for man, and every choice strengthens or weakens his ultimate orientation toward God or self, toward freedom or servitude. The "person" emerges from his experience; he is the product of the infinite ways he has chosen to direct his energies and consent to or dissent from grace. In this way the Christian gradually "puts on Christ" (Rom 13.14), builds himself as the temple of the Holy Spirit (1 Cor 6.20), and grows in the likeness of Christ (2 Cor 3.18). The most important element is the constant in the process, the fundamental option; the Bible calls it the heart of man (Rom 5.5; 6.17; 8.27); it is the person who is evolving. Yet the particular choices are likewise important since they are building up or tearing down this basic option and no choice goes uncounted. The present choice builds on past ones and prepares for future ones. Only the last choice of man's life, the final option, which takes place in the moment of death, is believed to express fully the heart of man because it sums up and recapitulates his whole life.

The contrary of the love of God is selfishness, which is voluntary opposition to the movements of grace. This willful selfishness diminishes with growth in grace, because the love of God brings the virtues in its train. The virtues bring reason and order into the faculties of the soul, at once humanizing and spiritualizing the psychophysical structure. They place the whole man at the service of charity. The sign of perfect transformation is perfect conformity of will with God, even to the point where the first movements of the soul are directed toward God (St. John of the Cross, *Spiritual Canticle* B, 28.5). Such persons are completely possessed by the Holy Spirit.

Does the presence of contrary movements in the psyche of man even though they are nonvoluntary argue to less than complete spiritualization and perfection? This question, one aspect of the relationship between the psychic and the spiritual, is not adequately answered as yet. Nonvoluntary movements as such are not opposed to virtue, since VIRTUE is a voluntary condition, a "habitus." But how is one to gauge the voluntary and nonvoluntary in these psychic factors? Moreover they at least occasion disordered choices by drawing the will after them. In the practical order psychic weaknesses can make striving after perfection very difficult; extreme instability or imbalance may even make sanctity impossible not because of an intrinsic but only an extrinsic connection. Psychic health, on the other hand, while negative in sanctifying power, places fewer obstacles in the way and supplies a good natural base for the reception of grace. Emotional maturity easily becomes natural virtue, and natural virtues, such as authenticity, honesty, courage, and community spirit, clear the underbrush for the freer growth of grace. But one must proceed cautiously in theorizing about these areas. Above all, the psychic (or the "natural" generally) must not be confused with the spiritual. But the two areas touch at many points. The relationships between the soul and the psyche, between maturity and sanctity, between neurosis and sin, are at present subject to different opinions among the experts and need further research and reflection.

The regime of the spirit extends into all the areas of human life. Growth does not automatically mean a reduction of human commitments or withdrawal from human engagements. The spiritual man enters within himself in the sense that he possesses himself at the core of his being and can dispose of himself in greater liberty toward God and men and the cosmos. The journey within is the journey into reality.

The interior life, meaning the life of prayer, is not the whole spiritual life. For contemplatives it is the principal part of their vocation and it is an element in every Christian life. But the spiritual life is service as well as knowledge and love of God. It is human life metamorphized, the body-soul composite animated by the Holy Spirit; the spiritual life is not the natural life of the immaterial soul. Spiritual has this meaning in Sacred Scripture (e.g., 1 Cor 2.13–14) and it is contrasted to carnal, which describes fallen man who lacks grace, the unregenerated man considered on any level of his life, whether of instinct, emotion, intellect, or will. Pride of intellect is carnal, whereas Christian marriage is spiritual. The temporal order, social action, the apostolate in all its forms are part of Christian spirituality. The whole of life ideally comes to be looked at as a function of charity and each act a response of the new creature to the Word of God.

Supernatural Quality

Everything human is to be renewed and integrated into the new creation by the power of the Holy Spirit (2 Cor 5.17; Gal 6.15), yet no created form, effect, or manifestation exhausts or confines or even adequately expresses the life of the Spirit. God acts in and affects the particular and the finite: this is the ongoing, incarnational aspect of salvation history. The apostle John alludes to this aspect when he writes: ''Behold what manner of love the Father has bestowed upon us, that we should be called children of God; and such we are'' (1 Jn 3.1). But just as God is beyond any of His acts or effects in history, so the life of grace is a supernatural relationship that places it beyond any of its particular expressions. This is its transcendent ''eschatological'' aspect that will be fully revealed in the Parousia: ''Beloved, now we are the children of God, and it has not appeared what we shall be. We know that, when he appears, we shall be like to him, for we shall see him just as he is'' (1 Jn 3.2).

The spiritual life is Trinitarian life, essentially supernatural, hence beyond any creature's abilities or demands. It is a spiritual life of knowledge and love that belongs to God's own level of existence. Because it is God's life, its every expression in man—the moral act, the religious experience, the apostolic service—falls short of the divine reality, even though these individual acts are the workings of the Spirit. God is greater than any finite knowledge of Him, more lovable than any created love can envisage. There is no perfect correlation, therefore, between grace and human behavior or grace and any human experience. A Christian's knowledge, love, and service of God are incarnations of the Trinitarian life he shares; but God is greater than the incarnations, and union with Him is what is sought. A description of this supernatural quality and an indication of its implications in the matter of prayer and self-denial in Christian spirituality now follows.

Life of Grace. Scripture uses many analogies to convey the meaning of this mystery. The life of grace is a participation in divine life (2 Pt 1.4; Gal 2.20), sonship (Rom 8.14–16.23), friendship (Jn 15.14–15), and possession by the Spirit (Rom 8.9; Eph 1.13) or by the indwelling God (Jn 14.23; 1 Jn 4.12–13; 1 Cor 3.16). The Scriptural as well as the patristic perspective centers on Uncreated Grace, an approach that serves to bring out the transcendent quality of Christian spirituality. So the spiritual life is the Spirit received, and sanctifying grace, the effect of this Presence, a ''being possessed'' (Latin ''habitus'') by God, who first possesses the soul. Possession by God is the same as the divine INDWELLING, according to the Scriptures (cf. 1 Kgs 8.27–30; 9.3). When God fully possesses the person, the spiritual activity is closest to God's own. He is attained in ever purer faith and love with the accompanying, proportionate affective detachment and poverty of spirit. To move toward God is to move out of a world measured by the created and finite and into God's world where He Himself is the measure (1 Cor 3.22).

Just as the transcendent God was ''truly in Christ, reconciling the world to himself'' (2 Cor 5.19), so He is in the world of men in the continued mediations of Christ's presence. Men will find Him in proportion as they are transformed in God by grace, i.e., in proportion as they rise above themselves. Thus the spiritual life is fully achieved when the Christian attains God, while remaining himself with his own knowledge and love, his own intimacy and conscious friendship with God; this occurs when he is lost, transformed, and identified with God, without losing his own identity.

A profound exposition of this is to be found in the transforming union of St. John of the Cross (e.g., *The Ascent of Mount Carmel* 2.5), which we follow here, in the conviction that this is the universal goal of Christian life. St. John attributes the transformation to love. Perfect love produces perfect likeness, indeed it produces identification in the intentional order. Thus perfect love makes one know and love not only like the Beloved but as one with Him. When a man is no longer a prisoner in the closed universe of the merely human, and his life is open and transparent to the influence of God, God can communicate Himself to him like the sun that pours through a clear windowpane, and he can truly live by God's own light. God is the sun and man the windowpane. The cleaner the glass, the more illumination it receives; if it is perfectly clear, it seems dissolved in the light. In a similar way the purified and illuminated soul is transformed in God. "All the things of God and the soul are one in participant transformation; and the soul seems to be God rather than a soul, and is indeed God by participation; although it is true that its natural being, though thus transformed, is as distinct from the Being of God as it was before" (*op. cit.* 2.5, 7).

This transformation is not an abandonment of one's creature status or use of the world, but a rising above the limitations of the created. It is divinization by grace and implies the removal of all selfishness, that is, any inordinate activity or attachment to what is less than God. Affective detachment is required here, since the deified man in no way rejects or neglects the finite and particular forms that are part of his vocation. Creatures as such are no obstacle to divine union; only those human activities that are opposed to the work of the Holy Spirit—the "carnal" activities mentioned by St. Paul (Gal 5.16–26)—are incompatible. With growth in sanctity there is a deepening, an interiorization in one's human activity. This is a shift in awareness and concern from exterior aspects to the interior, from the moral to the theological, from the letter to the spirit. The first term is not canceled in favor of the second; rather there is a penetration of the finite to the divine meaning, a communion with God and His world together (1 Cor 10.31).

Prayer and Self-denial. Transformation is the goal toward which all spiritual activity tends and the root from which such activity flows. This contemplative union with God is the soul of all Christian life. It corresponds to the Christian's "heart," the fundamental orientation discussed above.

The concrete expressions are multiple and varied. There are prayer and action, penance and apostolate, internal and external acts, liturgical and nonliturgical functions. This activity is arranged and structured into the various "mysticisms" of Christian life, each of which emphasizes a particular incarnation of the transcendent goal and lays down appropriate means to attain that goal. So there is a mysticism of prayer, of action, of suffering. There are schools of spirituality that systematize a particular synthesis. But even within the schools there will be the splendor of variety, because ultimately spirituality is a personalized and particularized relationship. This very variety is a sign that grace is only partially incarnated in given acts of men, not only because it is man's fundamental option, but also and especially because it is supernatural. Each Christian is a witness to his all-holy Master, but no witness, not even all the witnesses together, can fully express Him.

Two forms deserve special stress as implementations of the supernatural union of grace. These are PRAYER and SELF-DENIAL. Both are immediate applications of the contemplative union of knowledge and love. Prayer expresses that knowledge and love by conversation; self-denial is a rejection of a selfish preference in favor of God's will.

Manuals of piety in the past tended to reduce the spiritual life to these two operations. This was in line with the eschatological rather than incarnational emphasis that characterized spiritual writing till recent years. The liturgy and the apostolate, especially action in the temporal order, which Pius XII called the "consecration of the world," were not sufficiently integrated into this picture. The transcendent emphasis presented the world only as a hazard and not as already partially redeemed and on its way to fuller redemption (Rom 8.18–22); the apostolate was a distracting duty, in a sense a necessary evil, in which "one left God for God."

Today the apostolate is not conceived as leaving God at all. There is, instead, a growing literature on the spirituality of action, of involvement in the world of responsibility for the tasks of men. This modern stress, which is inspired by the realism of the Incarnation and expressed in response to the appeals of the popes and the needs of the times, takes as its point of departure the community rather than the individual, the liturgy rather than private prayer, holiness "in" as well as "not of" this world. These are valid additions that do not deny the necessity of prayer and self-denial.

Both the incarnational and the eschatological elements of Catholic dogma must be translated into action and a balance struck between the antinomies of withdrawal and engagement, renouncement and use. The incarnational emphasis promotes action, the eschatological favors CONTEMPLATION. But both action and contemplation are necessary according to one's vocation; in the saint they interpenetrate. But for the journey to the goal different articulations and coordinations of the two activities are possible. Traditionally, contemplation comes first and leads to action and to the apostolate. But there seems to be no good reason why the process could not be inverted, as some modern writers suggest. In such a case, engagement in the world of men would be the first act, in which and through which one would contact God in contemplation. Action and contemplation would thus have a different place and role in the Christian's life.

In a similar way self-denial is as necessary as the cross, the negative term of the paschal mystery. Both the transcendent nature of Christian life and the fallen condition of man demand this effort if man is to avoid the hazards and rise above the limitations of a closed universe. But whether the purification is sought by material renouncement and withdrawal to the desert or by the self-forgetfulness demanded in the spending of oneself and being spent for others (2 Cor 12.15) is a secondary question.

Conclusion. Christian spirituality is complex, because it is both human and supernatural. It is the highest activity of man, the life of his spirit, but it is rooted in his historical existence. While the life is his own vital activity, it is above and beyond him, because it is supernatural. This second factor, more than the body-soul dimensions of human existence, is the reason for the antinomies, the paradoxes, and the dialectical nature of Christian life. Christian spirituality cannot be reduced to one simple category, both because it is life and especially because it is the life of God lived by men in the Body of Christ.

Bibliography: H. U. VON BALTHASAR in *Geist und Leben* 31 (1958) 340–352, summarized in *Theology Digest* 10 (1962) 189–195. L. BOUYER, *Introduction to Spirituality,* tr. M. P. RYAN (New York 1961). P. FRANSEN, *Divine Grace and Man,* tr. G. DUPONT (rev. ed. New York 1965); ''Toward a Psychology of Divine Grace,'' *Cross Currents* 8 (1958) 211–232. F. ROUSTANG, *Une Initiation à la vie spirituelle* (Paris 1963). G. THILS, *Christian Holiness,* tr. J. L. FARRAND (Tielt, Belgium 1961).

[E. E. LARKIN]

SPIRITUALITY, CHRISTIAN (HISTORY OF)

A history of spirituality is a history of the problem, always newly posed in a dynamic and changing civilization, of how the soul may live as integrally as possible the life of Jesus Christ. This article presents a general survey of ancient sources and early forms of spirituality and of the evolution and formation of multiple currents in the schools of spirituality from early ages to the present.

Scriptural origins. The Jewish religion was above all the religion of the covenant. This covenant was the source of unshakable trust in God's divine power and of the nearness of God, who condescended to make Himself the companion of His people. The prayers of the Jewish religion were permeated with the sense of God's nearness and at the same time of His elevation.

Jesus' first preaching was the good news of the Reign of God. This reign was revealed as the re-creating intervention of God, offering to every man the grace of being made a child of God. In Jesus the divine perfection, the perfection of the love that gives itself totally, was put within man's reach. He expressed this total self-giving by taking on Himself the weight of the sins of men and redeeming them from those sins through His death on the cross. The poverty involved in total self-giving, which is the *AGAPE* of the Gospel, makes one blessed. Blessedness was to be the result of carrying the Messiah's cross, His easy yoke and light burden.

In the preaching of the primitive Church, the Resurrection was seen as the fruit of the cross and the principle or source of the effusion of the Spirit into men's souls. St. Paul taught that by Baptism man is made one with Christ in assimilation to His death, in view of His Resurrection. St. John, on the other hand, frequently used the images of life and light. He taught that the Word is the life proper to God, the life which God communicated by creating through the Word, the life which He came to restore and which is also the light.

Patristic period. The principal consideration of Christian spirituality in the beginning was the problem of eschatology, the expectation of Christians of Christ's second coming. By the end of the 2d century, it was realized more clearly than before that the Christian life is situated in a paradoxical intermediate state. In the risen Christ, the Church has already gained everything that it is to possess after the last times.

Martyrdom. Martyrdom was for the first Christian generations the ideal instance of union with Christ in trial, leading to perfect union with Him in the life of charity. The importance of martyrdom arose from the fact that it offered a possibility, by assimilation to Christ dead and risen again, of attaining and, in a certain sense, of anticipating the eschatological event. It was Jesus whom the martyr sought (*see* MARTYRDOM, THEOLOGY OF).

After the persecutions, the question arose whether there was not some substitute for martyrdom as a way of being united to Christ, and Origen maintained that a fervent preparation for death, being a life of self-sacrifice, could be a true though unbloody martyrdom. And Clement of Alexandria pointed out that anyone could make his death a martyrdom if he prepared for it with the fitting dispositions.

Gnosis. In the meeting with Hellenism, Christianity had to cope with the dualistic and intellectualistic views on which Hellenic spirituality was based. By its intellectualism GNOSTICISM thought to find salvation simply in the recognition of a radical opposition between the world of spirit, fundamentally good, and the world of matter, essentially imperfect. St. Irenaeus (d. 120) became the great spokesman of the Church's rejection of this heretical pseudo-gnosis. According to gnosis in its orthodox form, everything, matter as well as spirit, is to be saved. Orthodox gnosis is intimate knowledge of and participation in the love that is communicated by God to men through Christ; and it surpasses all natural knowledge to lose itself in the fullness of God.

The Alexandrian School. The Christian school of Alexandria, particularly as represented by Clement and Origen, had great importance in the field of spirituality. For CLEMENT OF ALEXANDRIA (150?–215?), the supreme state is that in which one knows the God of love by loving as He loves. The attainment of the summit of the gnostic life, i.e., assimilation to God, was made possible by *apatheia,* a term he introduced into Christian language. By this term, he meant a domination, acquired through grace, over everything that is opposed to charity. The resulting stable condition is, as it were, a foretaste of eternity.

ORIGEN (185?–254?) taught that the soul must struggle to uproot itself from the world in which it is buried by its egoistic desires. This struggle is carried out by an imitation of and participation in the life of Christ. Like Clement, Origen wrote about vocal prayer, saying that as it is interiorized, it goes beyond itself into the prayer of silence, which characterizes the state of union with God and liberation from the body.

Formerly, persecutions caused faithful Christians to retire to the desert and there freely lead a life of the most precarious kind. As the State made its peace with the Church, a world that without changing its ways had become friendly to Christianity led many Christians to return to the desert to find once more the detachment, austerity, and fervor they had known but could no longer know in a life suddenly become too easy.

The retreat of early Christians to the deserts of Egypt did not express just a simple desire for tranquillity, leisure, or extended contemplation in the sense the term had in Greek philosophy. The monk went to the desert to fight against the devil. Solitude allowed him to discover and face all the obscure forces he bore within himself. These religious men knew that one must suffer to be a monk, but they did not hesitate to condemn rigorous austerities whenever, instead of freeing the spirit, they weighed it down. The asceticism particularly of Egyptian monasticism was an exercise of liberation, of disengagement from the bonds of the flesh and of the world.

But in Syria austerities took forms unknown in Egypt. Stylites lived on columns; hermits used iron chains to inflict punishment on themselves, or had themselves buried alive. Solitaries exposed themselves to the elements. Yet, rather than suffering, it was indifference to everything unessential that was sought.

Monasticism. Gradually hermits were joined by others to whom they communicated what they had received. Around the idea of the abbot, or spiritual father, the transition was made from pure anchoritism, with its complete solitude, to mitigated anchoritism, in which solitaries were grouped about a spiritual father, and finally to cenobitism (*see* MONASTICISM). In the beginning the abbot had no official function. He was simply the perfected spiritual man.

It became a theme, traditional until the end of the Middle Ages, that the monastic was the continuation of the apostolic life. And the apostolic life was understood by all antiquity as primarily a life in which Christians persevere together in prayer, in community of goods, and in the breaking of bread. In the period when monasticism in general came to be organized, the practice of consecrating one's virginity to Christ was solemnized by profession and public consecration before the Church. By VIRGINITY the Christian sought to achieve the reality of which marriage offers an image: the union of Christ and the Church.

Two or three generations had gone by before monasticism provided itself with a theological teaching. This teaching came through the Cappadocians. They rectified and broadened the thought of Origen and furnished monasticism with a well-wrought theory. The influence of the Cappadocians, and particularly of St. GREGORY OF NYSSA (330?–395?), on monasticism has not always been as clear as now. Gregory of Nyssa's thought was transmitted in two different ways: one was more learned, and the other was more popular and practical. In Syria what was most personal in this thought came to be the seed of a new development: the Areopagitical writings.

According to PSEUDO-DIONYSIUS (4th or 5th century), the soul finds God by going beyond itself, by rejecting all particular knowledge and by being united to Him, who is transcendent, in the luminous darkness where He awaits it. Spiritual writers were very numerous in the East during the 5th and 6th centuries, and certain of them were masters whose influence was considerable throughout the later history of spirituality. But only with St. MAXIMUS (580?–662) was a new departure sketched out: that of Byzantine spirituality.

St. Augustine. Meanwhile, St. AUGUSTINE (354–430) had been dependent on the whole spiritual heritage of the Christian East. But his manner of rethinking and synthesizing was often so personal and creative that his work became the starting point of a renewed tradition. Moreover, the works of Augustine had a preface, so to speak, in the works of SS. AMBROSE and JEROME. Augustinian wisdom is something other than the gnosis of the Greek Fathers, in spite of certain affinities. It is distinguished particularly by its psychological, reflexive orientation. It does not deal directly with the mystery of God in Christ, but with the mystery of men's selves that Christ helps them to discern. The sense of the meditation on Scripture was changed in his spirituality. An element of anthropocentrism was introduced.

Augustine's work included significant endeavors regarding monastic life. When he had become bishop, he organized the whole life of the clergy around him in a quasi-monastic fashion. This example of Augustine was fruitful in propagating a new type of monasticism. Side by side with this new monasticism in the West, however, the older type also spread. There were monasteries of laymen, strangers both to the concern for intellectual culture that had always been Augustine's and to the pastoral care that would be added later on.

Cassian. It was John CASSIAN (360?–435?) who transmitted to the West the monastic practices and types of organization first developed in the East, as well as the best distillation of its teaching. Throughout the whole work of asceticism, the monk is not to seek anything but the kingdom of God. He will attain this kingdom by purity of heart, which is the condition and counterpart of the full development of charity. The summits of Cassian's mysticism are described by him as a constant prayer, a prayer of fire wholly inspired by the Gospel.

St. Gregory. From the time of the invasions in the 6th century, a new world began in the West. The life and action of St. GREGORY THE GREAT (540–604) pertain to the patristic period, but the doctrine he elaborated in contact with this tradition became the principal source from which the Middle Ages drew its spiritual program. By its simplicity, its lack of speculation, Gregory's doctrine was suited to the needs of the new people of the barbaric world after the invasions.

Middle Ages. The spirituality of the early Middle Ages was necessarily that of the cloisters, for it had developed in the dark ages, when conditions were such that civilized life hardly existed elsewhere. During the period from the pontificate of St. Gregory to the middle of the 8th century, monks maintained a high ascetical ideal and gave an example of prayer profitable to the laity, clerics, and bishops. These centuries in which the new Christian peoples arose out of barbarism manifested an intense need for exterior penance. Devotions at this time were directed to the cross, the relics and tombs of the saints, and the Mother of God.

Carolingian Period. In the Carolingian epoch the influence of the Benedictine Rule became almost exclusive. Among the laity, groups of penitents, oblates, and fervent Christians were organized; they became especially numerous around the monasteries. The two traits that marked Carolingian piety were interest in the Bible and love of the liturgy.

The 10th and 11th Centuries. In the 10th and 11th centuries, to prevent abuse and obtain the spiritual freedom necessary to carry on the tasks of the Church, the abbeys began to join in groups, but they were bound by very loose juridical bonds. These federations were made around key monasteries and gave rise to congregations of monasteries and to the first religious order, the Order of Cluny. The life of the medieval monk consisted in keeping present before the world the value of Pentecost: the holiness of God communicated to men. All his asceticism and the entire system of observances that constrained him had as their goal his liberation.

In Italy, attempts were made to organize a quasi-eremitical form of life. SS. ROMUALD at Camaldoli and elsewhere, JOHN GUALBERT at Vallambrosa, and PETER DAMIAN established groups of followers who led lives of austerity, perpetual silence, and strict enclosure, without manual labor.

At this time, too, men filled with violent passions turned more spontaneously toward extreme forms of penance. Long, tiring pilgrimages and self-flagellation were ways of showing one's love, generosity, and desire for martyrdom.

Meanwhile, John of Fécamp (d. 1079) was one of the most widely read spiritual writers up to the end of the Middle Ages. In his system, quiet meditative reading occupies the mind with thoughts about God; the thoughts give rise to acts, to affective prayer, and this in turn becomes simplified until it merges into a contemplative prayer.

The Cluniac movement in the course of time made many additions to the original Benedictine Office, and as a result manual labor practically ceased (*see* CLUNIAC REFORM). The Cistercian Order founded by St. ROBERT OF MOLESME in 1098 removed most of these additions and returned to the primitive manual labor of the fields.

Although Cistercian spirituality was fundamentally the same as that of the black monks, the early Cistercian writers, such as St. BERNARD and WILLIAM OF SAINT-THIERRY, cultivated a theology of the mystical life. St. Bernard (1091–1153) considered the soul as the image of God because of its gift of free will; but when it is in sin this likeness is obscured. The soul can turn again to the Word to be reformed in itself and conformed to Him. This conformity weds the soul to the Word. Already like Him by nature, it shows its likeness to Him through its will, loving even as it is loved. In his sermons to his monks, Bernard was intensely concerned with Christ in

His infancy and in His Passion; this gave him the reputation of having introduced devotion to the humanity of Christ into the spiritual life.

The institution of the Carthusian Order by St. Bruno in 1098 established on a wider basis the quasi-eremitical life begun earlier in Italy. Instances of extraordinary phenomena are to be found in the German nuns SS. HILDEGARDE and ELIZABETH OF SCHÖNAU in the 12th century, and SS. GERTRUDE and MECHTILD in the 13th century.

The 12th Century. In the 12th century, Saint-Victor, outside Paris, became a well-known theological and spiritual center and also the birthplace of a congregation of canons regular. The intellectual movement of scholasticism had some impact on the writers of this school, who are known as the Victorines (*see* VICTORINE SPIRITUALITY); nevertheless, they remained within the monastic tradition. Their symbolist view of the universe, taken from St. Augustine, led to an intuitive rather than a dialectical method of approaching God and naturally to greater emphasis on contemplation. The principal writers of this school were HUGH OF SAINT-VICTOR, RICHARD OF SAINT-VICTOR, and THOMAS GALLUS.

There also appeared in the 12th century a kind of exasperated reaching toward the pure ideal of the Gospel. Social, political, and religious leaders were pushing to extremes the demands of radical poverty and an opposition to all formalism and legalism. By the 13th century, sections of the laity were criticizing the existing social conditions and the lives of the clergy, and they were fostering a neo-Manichean movement represented first by the Waldenses and then by the Albigenses.

The 13th Century. SS. FRANCIS (1181?–1226) and DOMINIC (1170–1221) remedied these spiritual ills through their ideal of the practice of poverty and the active service of the Church. Dominic provided his Preachers with a background of traditional cloister life that was to serve as a safeguard and a source of strength. Accordingly, St. THOMAS AQUINAS (1224–1274) taught that the highest life was that which combined contemplation with preaching: *contemplata aliis tradere.*

St. Francis' original idea had been the imitation of the life of Christ in all its simplicity and poverty. As the number of the Franciscan friars increased, organization became necessary. St. BONAVENTURE (1221–1274) established the balance. There were to be three elements in the Franciscan way of life: following Christ through the evangelical counsels, especially poverty; laboring for the salvation of souls by preaching and hearing confessions; and contemplation. Likewise, in the footsteps of Bernard and Francis, a movement of Christocentric and affective piety stirred Europe in the 12th and 13th centuries.

The 14th Century. About the beginning of the 14th century, a new current in spirituality began in the Rhineland, the Low Countries, and England, involving a new attitude toward contemplation and an attempt to analyze it. The greatest influence on the new school was that of Pseudo-Dionysius. Because of his identification with the Areopagite mentioned in the Acts of the Apostles (17.34), his works had a quasi-apostolic authority throughout the Middle Ages, but it was only after Thomas Gallus had translated and commented on these works in the 13th century that they began to exercise a strong influence in the West. Those mainly influenced were three German Dominicans (Meister ECKHART, TAULER, and HENRY SUSO) and the Flemish RUYSBROECK, a canon regular of St. Augustine. The chief concern of these men was the soul's union with God, which was at its fullest in contemplation. Thus they made a highly intellectual analysis of contemplation based on theological principles. They demanded as necessary preparation for this union the abandonment of all thought of creatures.

The unknown English author of *The CLOUD OF UNKNOWING* gave perhaps the clearest practical exposition of this. A group of other English spiritual writers during this century, such as Richard ROLLE and Walter HILTON, belonged essentially to this same school. A little later, the northern school found its most coherent theorist and efficient propagandist in the Franciscan HENRY OF HERP, better known as Harphius.

Spiritual writers up to the 14th century were interested more in the conditions of contemplation than in its redemptive effects. St. CATHERINE OF SIENA (1347–80), however, was more obsessed by the needs of the Church. Yet she was always aware that her prayer and penance did more for the Church than her public acts.

The need for widespread reform in the Church by the end of the 14th century began to be met in the Low Countries with the formation of the BRETHREN OF THE COMMON LIFE by Gerard GROOTE. The spirituality of this movement was known as the DEVOTIO MODERNA. Instead of speculative analyses of contemplation, affective and empirical spirituality engaged its interests. The one great work the movement produced was *The IMITATION OF CHRIST* by THOMAS À KEMPIS.

Renaissance. The years that witnessed the upheavals of the humanist Renaissance and the Protestant Reformation were fertile in spirituality, but medieval tendencies actually continued for a long time, and new ideas were grafted into them without violence. Attempts to organize private prayer began to be faced and achieved a decided advance at the beginning of the 16th century with García de CISNEROS, the Benedictine reformer. St. IGNATIUS OF LOYOLA (1491–1556) brought a technique to its full perfection of form in his *SPIRITUAL EXERCISES*. The fundamental elements of this systematized prayer were a methodic use of the imaginative powers, deliberate incitement of the affections, and ascetic and moral application.

Many of the Christian humanists were sympathetic toward mysticism; and, faithful to its heritage of the Middle Ages, mysticism persisted throughout the century. Christian humanists were also working in their own fashion toward a restoration of the Christian life. Love for classical antiquity and an optimistic view of human nature characterize what has been called devout humanism. The spiritual works of ERASMUS (1467–1536) provide an example.

The ideas of Erasmus found firm support in Spain and began to join with the vigorous mystical tendencies of the ALUMBRADOS. After 1525, in Spain, the antimystical reaction took the form of suspicion. The Index of Valdes (1559) proscribed all the Rheno-Flemish mystics and also the majority of vernacular books on spirituality. In the first decades of the century, the writings of FRANCIS OF OSUNA and BERNADINO OF LAREDO gave free expression to mysticism, but later the writings of LOUIS OF GRANADA, Bl. JOHN OF AVILA, and Luis de LEÓN, etc., were more restrained in regard to mysticism. In 1583 Cardinal Quiroga published an Index that was more liberal; this made possible the appearance of works left unpublished by SS. Teresa and John of the Cross.

St. TERESA (1515–1582), a mystical writer of the first rank, has left a fine analysis of the stages of prayer, which has had an exceptional influence upon subsequent theologians. However, since for Teresa prayer consists essentially in an exchange of love with God, she insisted upon the concrete proof of this love, upon the soul's effort to practice the virtues, leaving to God the communication of His extraordinary graces, when and how He wishes.

St. JOHN OF THE CROSS (1542–1591), a companion of Teresa in her work of reform within the Carmelite Order, is held by many to be the greatest of the mystical writers. The importance of his contribution lies in his analyses of the soul's active and passive purifications, and his explanations of the life of union with God.

Spanish spirituality became theoretical and scientific with and after John of the Cross, but Italian spirituality was more practical. There were fervent groups in Italy desirous to reform the Church, revive interior life, and inspire the clergy with a sense of their duties. Models of this type of spirituality were SS. Philip NERI and Charles BORROMEO. CATHERINE OF GENOA (1447–1510) had a marked influence throughout two centuries. The substance of her writings seems to have come from notes taken by another during her ecstasies. She compared the state of the souls in purgatory to the trials of the mystical life. Some other Italian writers of this period were SS. Mary Magdalen dei PAZZI, CATHERINE OF RICCI, and Robert BELLARMINE. There is noticeable in many of the Italian writers a tendency to aspire to God through the contemplation of creation and its wonders, and also a kindly feeling for human nature.

Post-Reformation. Spirituality in France, because of the troubles that so long divided it, remained more or less underground. The saintly Mme. Acarie (1566–1618) became a center of devout circles in Paris. The extraordinary phenomena of her life, together with the influence of her holiness, helped to gather around her a group of spiritual persons, including such figures as Benet of Canfield, Dom Beaucousin, and Cardinal de BÉRULLE (1575–1629), who became the origins of the religious spring that revived French Catholicism in the early years of the 17th century.

The task of bringing the piety of the cloister into the world fell to St. FRANCIS DE SALES (1567–1622), a representative of the Counter Reformation who frequented the entourage of Mme. Acarie. He sought to show Christians that, whatever their place in society, their lives must be imbued with the religion they profess.

Devotion to the Word Incarnate and a special regard for the virtue of religion are traits of Bérulle's teaching. His most famous disciples were Charles de CONDREN, St. VINCENT DE PAUL, Jean Jacques OLIER, St. John EUDES, and St. GRIGNION DE MONTFORT. These representatives of the French school were fiery opponents of Jansenism. Jansenism was a reaction away from the spirituality of St. Francis de Sales toward rigorism, exaggerating the austerity and the more threatening aspects of Christianity.

The prayer of simplicity was practiced almost everywhere in France about 1670. Among its most famous advocates was a Carmelite lay brother, LAWRENCE OF THE RESURRECTION. Many spiritual authors, however, regarded this prayer as mystical and recommended it to all indiscriminately, thus unwisely impelling them to passive prayer.

FÉNELON's teachings on pure love and the absolute sacrifice of salvation were condemned by the Holy See in 1699, but his errors were not as gross as those of the Spanish quietist, Miguel de MOLINOS, or of Mme. GUYON. Molinos taught that nonresistance to temptation is allowable to contemplatives and he also contrived a general system based on the total inertia of the soul that has attained the ''interior way.'' In opposition to the quietists, BOSSUET (1627–1704) taught that, rightly understood, abandonment makes the soul apply itself energetically to its religious exercises and other duties.

After the condemnation of Fénelon, many thought the best thing to do was not to talk about mysticism at all. Since the censuring of the quietists was considered a personal victory for the Jansenists, Jansenistic spirituality spread its influence widely. At the very time when quietism was corrupting the traditional idea of Christian piety and Jansenism was making fear the only motive for moral activity, Our Lord revealed the treasure of love in His heart to St. Margaret Mary at Paray-le-Monial, and asked that religious veneration be made publicly to His divine Heart.

St. ALPHONSUS LIGUORI (1696–1787) has been called an Italian Francis de Sales. His spiritual writings, which restored the true idea of piety that Jansenist pessimism had deformed, are mainly affective and give much attention to divine love.

Modern period. After David Augustine BAKER (1575–1641) revived mystical traditions in England, there were few English spiritual writers until the 19th century. One of the causes of the Oxford Movement was the longing for closer contact with God. Devotion to the Holy Spirit was characteristic of the Oxford converts, who felt the hidden action of the Spirit guiding them toward truth. The inspiration for the writings of Frederick William FABER (1814–1863) was drawn from the Italian and French schools. Cardinal Newman (1801–1890), however, preferred English habits of devotion and belief. Though spirituality was not a special concern of his intellectual activity, Newman touched upon it in his sermons and writings.

During the 19th century, mysticism and holiness inspired a prodigious apostolic activity of re-Christianization. There existed on all sides an extraordinary effervescence of religious and spiritual works: instruction in schools, care for the sick, catechizing, foreign mission work, and care of the poor. Through these works, souls expressed their love of Christ and reached union with God. Many congregations of sisters devoted to education were founded, and the work of education attracted many generous souls. A French saint active in the Christian revival at this time was Jean VIANNEY, curé of Ars (1786–1859), to whose confessional came hundreds of thousands. His spiritual life was characterized by a deep hatred of sin and an acute, intense sadness, like that Our Lord knew during His agony.

At the end of the 19th century, the errors of Americanism were pointed out by Leo XIII, and a little later impassioned disputes over the boundaries of mysticism and asceticism began after Augustin POULAIN, SJ, published his *Graces of Interior Prayer.*

The spiritual biography that surpassed all others in popularity was that of St. THÉRÈSE OF LISIEUX (1873–97). Her ''little way of spiritual childhood'' has won many followers and has become the source of deep theological studies.

Under the influence of modern individualism, the worship of the Church had been increasingly relegated to the background. Spiritual life had assumed a largely subjective and private character. Thus there arose the effort to regain what had been set aside; this became known as the liturgical movement and spread throughout the world.

The findings of modern psychology also brought new insights to the field of spirituality through deep analyses of human behavior and understanding of the values of interpersonal relationships. Finally, scientific and technological advances made man master of the universe in ways that were not previously imagined. No longer were many areas of existence regarded as outside man's personal responsibility. There developed in consequence what might be called the spirituality of involvement. The Christian came more to regard his professional life, his work in organization, commerce, production, and science, if done according to God's will, as a true contribution to the building up of the city of men. It became clear that when Christians love one another and bear together the burden of building the community, God reveals Himself to them as Lord, Redeemer, and Father.

Late twentieth century. The most striking and perhaps also the most significant effect of the renewal inaugurated by Vatican Council II has been an intensified interest and desire to share in the spiritual life. The average practicing Catholic has been most affected by the reform of the liturgy. The Mass was always fairly central in Catholic spiritual practice, but its pervasive influence in the lives of the faithful has been greatly enhanced with the general introduction of the vernacular and other reform measures. Previous to Vatican II, a relatively small number were directly nourished by the liturgical texts and action. When the priest came down from the high altar to a small table facing the people and invited them to sing popular hymns, do the readings, lead the congregation, bring the gifts, generally plan the liturgy, and sometimes even have the liturgy in their own living rooms, more and more of the faithful began effectively to hear the Word of God proclaimed and to interiorize the sentiments of the liturgical action. One result has been a renewed study and use of the Scriptures in the private devotional lives of Catholics. Concomitantly with the renewal of the Mass form came a more independent attitude on the part of the lay Catholic in moral judgment, leading to an increased freedom in receiving the Eucharist. The emphasis on this as a shared meal rather than an awesome communion with the Transcendent has also greatly affected the role the Eucharist plays in Catholic spirituality today, reducing those practices which largely emphasized adoration: exposition, benediction, processions. In great measure what elements remained in the Western liturgy of mystery and awe before the Almighty have been eliminated and spirituality has been centered more on an incarnate God within community. The renewal of the Sacraments with their emphasis on communal participation and celebration has fostered the same attitude. The transformation of Extreme Unction into the Sacrament of the Sick has even brought the lonely act of dying more into the supportive presence of the Christian community and opened the way to communal healing services (*see* HEALING, CHRISTIAN). The most recent reform, the new rites of Penance, which has become the Sacrament of Reconciliation, has not yet had impact, but may, especially in its communal celebration, help the Catholic community to refind ways of expressing conversion and self-denial that have generally been lost with the end of most of the common obligations of fast and abstinence. More important perhaps is the opportunity this renewed rite offers to refind the value of the personal guidance and care of a spiritual father, the need for which many Christians have been discovering in the charismatic community with its emphasis on ''headship,'' in Eastern religious traditions, or just in a sincere quest for a deeper prayer life. The American Jesuits especially have been trying to respond to the need through the establishment of several programs for the formation of competent spiritual guides.

The Charismatic Movement. Undoubtedly the liveliest spiritual movement in the American Catholic Church since Vatican II has been the charismatic movement. The ecumenical impetus that opened the Catholic community to a wide use of Protestant hymns in the renewed liturgy and a greater emphasis on scriptural reading, study and prayer, also opened a certain segment of people to a particular form of evangelical enthusiasm that broke in on American Protestantism early in the 20th century—the willingness to receive and use certain of the gifts of the Spirit commonly seen among the faithful since the first days of the Church, praying and singing in tongues, prophecy, and healing. The renewal for the most part has for Catholics blended well with the renewal of liturgical piety. The communal element has been greatly emphasized, the place of Scripture in spiritual formation and prayer is almost exaggerated, and Mass and the Sacraments are celebrated with an unparalleled fullness (*see* CHARISMATIC RENEWAL, CATHOLIC).

The Meditation Movement. Only a segment of the Catholic community has been attracted to the lively, extraverted form of piety that has characterized the charismatic movement in the Church. Unfortunately little was being offered to those who were attracted to a more quiet, interior experience of the Transcendent. Catholic retreat centers had suffered a period of decline and are only now beginning to experience new vitality as centers of prayer. Contemplative monasteries have been attracting large numbers, but their teaching programs are virtually nonexistent. The result has been that large numbers of young Christians, and those not so young, have turned to Eastern religions and traditions to satisfy their desires in this direction. The movement is having one notable semantic effect. For the Catholic ''meditation'' has usually signified a discursive process of reflecting on a truth to evoke affective and volitional response, while ''contemplation'' meant a quiet, loving ''presence to.'' In the Eastern traditions the words are used in the opposite sense, contemplation being a discursive process and meditation involving the silent presence, though not usually including love because of the absence of interpersonal relationship. So pervasive has been the influence of the Eastern meditation movements in the West that now even among Christians, the term ''meditation'' is coming to be the prevalent name used for inner prayer and presence and the term ''contemplation'' is falling somewhat by the wayside.

Only gradually is the Christian community beginning to recover its contemplative dimension, which was largely lost in the 16th century, and respond to this spiritual attraction. The Cistercians as the strongest contemplative group in the Church have been taking a lead. To foster the return to Christian sources, they began publishing the great 12th-century spiritual and mystical texts that stand at the head of their tradition (*The Cistercian Fathers Series*) and the classic texts of monastic spirituality through the centuries (from EVAGRIUS PONTICUS and Dorotheos of Gaza to Jules Monchanin—*The Cistercian Studies Series*) to complement the *Fathers of the Church* series (The Catholic University of America) and the *Ancient Christian Writers* series (Newman-Paulist). The way had thus been prepared for the very significant series inaugurated by the Paulist Press in January of 1978: *The Classics of Western Spirituality.* In 1973 in collaboration with Western Michigan University, the Cistercians established the Institute for Cistercian Studies and three years later the Center for Contemplative Studies. In the following year the Paulists, joining hands with the Jesuits, opened in Boston the Isaac Hecker Institute of Applied Spirituality to come to grips with the notion and reality of a distinctive American spirituality and also to further the integration of the values and methods of Eastern traditions that have come to be very present in America.

The Cistercians, especially those of Saint Joseph's Abbey, Spencer, Massachusetts, had been pioneering in this area of integration of spiritualities, bringing to America the fruits of the study and experience of Jean-Marie Déchanet, OSB, (*Christian Yoga*), Francis Ancharya, Dom Bede GRIFFITHS, OSB, Abhisktananda (Father Henri Le Saux), William Johnston, SJ (Christian Zen) and E. Lassalle, and working in collaboration with Swami Satchidananda (Integral Yoga Institute), Joshua Sasaki Roshi (Mount Baldy Zen Center), and the TRANSCENDENTAL MEDITATION movement of the Maharishi Mehesh Yogi. In June of 1977 at the request of the Secretariat for Non-Christian Religions, the Spencer monks organized the Petersham Meeting, which led to the establishment of the North American Board for East-West Dialog. A symposium of spiritual masters West and East was held in June of 1978, and an international seminar on the use of Eastern methods in Christian prayer was scheduled for August of 1979. The aim of all these activities was not only to foster the evolution of a global spiritual culture to give a base to worldwide political, economic, and ethical accord, but to help the large number of Christians who have found values in Eastern spirituality to integrate these in a renewal of their Christian faith.

Perhaps the most significant contribution of the Spencer monks to the recent evolution of Catholic spirituality in America has been the promotion in collaboration with the Conference of Major Superiors of Men USA and other similar Catholic organizations of a Christian meditation movement. A simple method for entering into nonconceptual prayer that belongs to Western Christian tradition is now being taught in centers across the country. This particular method arises from Saint John Cassian, finds its most popular expression in *The Cloud of Unknowing,* and is commonly called Centering Prayer, a name drawn from the writings of Thomas MERTON—undoubtedly the most popular and influential Catholic spiritual writer in English of the age. The English Benedictines have taken up this method and are teaching it in centers in England and Canada. It is gradually moving into other language areas within the Church and other similar methods are being developed (*see* PRAYER, CENTERING).

Balancing Factors. Within the Christian meditation movement much of the emphasis in the quest for spiritual perfection has centered on the search for experience of the Transcendent, with the conviction that such experience will humble, enlighten, and lead to the growth of all the virtues. But side by side with this popular current there remains a faithful and strong advocacy of the ways of the Carmelite Doctors of the 16th century, of Saint Ignatius Loyola—whose more contemplative methods are being rediscovered and whose 30-day program is quite popular, especially among religious—and some of the other particular schools of spirituality. Centers of Jesuit, Carmelite, and Franciscan studies have been established and programs for publishing the classics of these traditions and studies on them are actively being carried out.

George Maloney, SJ, of the John XXIII Center, Fordham University, has been a leader in promoting a balanced and fruitful use of Eastern Christian prayer within the American Catholic community. The Jesus Prayer especially has become popular through the publication of *The Way of the Pilgrim.* Very valuable insights from the behavioral sciences, especially from the field of psychology, have been effectively applied to the spiritual life in a popular way by such writers as John Powell, SJ, Henri Nouwen, and Morton Kelsey. At the same time, there are those who look upon this emphasis on prayer and spiritual development as excessive and insist on the Christian way of fraternal love and service as having, if not the primacy, at least a predominant role in the quest for spiritual perfection. This is found especially among the active religious of the United States and has led recently to a fraternal warning from their brother and sister religious of Canada who have affirmed that ''Religious life has a future among us if it is *the experience of God shining forth in all we do* . . .'' (Third Interamerican Conference of Religious, Montreal, November 1977).

In theory, there is no controversy as to what spiritual perfection ultimately means for the Christian, but there is relatively little theorizing today. The way to attaining it is centered in practice and experience. The social and political emphasis of the 1960s expressed itself in an emphasis on finding God in creation, in one's brethren who are to be loved and served. With the waning of the hopes of the 1960s, there has been a turning to seeking the transcendent, immediate experience of God in himself. Meditation, prayer, is seen as the surer and more practical way to right action, universal brotherhood, peace on earth—whatever perfection man can hope to attain. As usual the large institutions—the hierarchy, the clerical ministry, the religious orders—are slow in moving with these popular shifts. In this they help the Christian community to preserve a more balanced outlook, so that the pendulum does not swing to extremes and a truer picture of what integral Christian holiness is remains to guide the faithful and have its overflowing effect on all persons of good will.

Bibliography: P. POURRAT, *Christian Spirituality,* tr. W. H. MITCHELL et al., 4 v. (Westminster, Md. 1953–55). L. BOUYER et al., *A History of Christian Spirituality* (New York 1963—), tr. F. CAYRÉ, *Spiritual Writers of the Early Church,* tr. W. W. WILSON (New York 1959). G. SITWELL, *Spiritual Writers of the Middle Ages* (New York 1961). L. COGNET, *Post-Reformation Spirituality,* tr. P. H. SCOTT (New York 1959). E. O'BRIEN, *Varieties of Mystic Experience* (New York 1964). J. WALSH, *Spirituality through the Centuries* (New York 1964). H. BRÉMOND, *Literary History of Religious Thought in France,* tr. K. L. MONTGOMERY, 3 v. (New York

1928–37). H. C. GRAEF, *The Light and the Rainbow* (Westminster, Md. 1959). F. VERNET, *Dictionnaire de spiritualité ascétique et mystique* (Paris 1932—) 1:625–659. C. BARAUT et al., *ibid.* 4:1089–1192. J. DE GUIBERT et al., *ibid.* 1:936–990. J. FONTAINE et al., *ibid.* 5:785–997. J. LEBRETON et al., *ibid.* 2:1643–2193. F. CAYRÉ, *Patrologie et histoire de théologie,* v.3 (2d ed. Paris 1950). J. M. DÉCHANET, *Christian Yoga,* tr. R. HINDMARSH (London 1960). D. GOLEMAN, *The Varieties of the Meditative Experience* (New York 1977). B. GRIFFITHS, *Vedanta and Christian Faith* (Lower Lake, Cal. 1973); *Return to the Center* (Springfield, Ill. 1977). G. A. MALONEY, *The Breath of the Mystic* (Denville, N.J. 1974); *Inward Stillness* (Denville, N.J. 1976). H NOUWEN, *Reaching Out* (New York 1975); *The Spirituality of Compassion* (New Haven, Conn. 1977). M. B PENNINGTON, ''Looking East-Seeing West,'' *America* 134 (1976) 180–182; ''Spirituality for a World Culture,'' *ibid.* 137 (1977) 100–103; *Daily We Touch Him* (New York 1977); ed., *Prayer and Liberation* (Canfield, Ohio 1977). L. J. SUENENS, *A New Pentecost?* (New York 1974).

[K. KAVANAUGH/M. B. PENNINGTON]

SPIRITUALITY, FRENCH SCHOOL OF

''French School'' is a popular term applied to a doctrine of spirituality that developed in France during the 17th century. Cardinal de BÉRULLE and Charles de CONDREN of the French Oratory, along with Jean Jacques OLIER, founder of the Sulpicians, were the masters of the school. In addition to these three leaders, two other men developed specific aspects of French School theology into Catholic devotional life: St. John EUDES, the devotion to the Sacred Heart; St. Louis Marie Grignion de Montfort, true devotion to the Blessed Virgin.

General Characteristics. The founders of the French School shared an extraordinary love of the priesthood, and were entirely dedicated to the work of priestly sanctification. To accomplish their high purpose, these men were inspired to explore deeply and profoundly St. Paul's doctrine of the MYSTICAL BODY. Their teaching constitutes a considerable development of this doctrine. They were able to synthesize CHRISTOLOGY and SPIRITUALITY by proposing man's incorporation into Christ as a code of perfection, and in this were innovators in a postscholastic, post-Reformation Latin Church. Both in spirit and in expression the French School writers were closer to patristic times, to St. Augustine and the Greek Fathers, than to theologians and writers of their own time.

Even the slightest sketch of the spiritual doctrine of the French School must include the following points: Christianity is a mystery; the events of Christ's life are mysteries; the heart of each mystery is that inner state or disposition of Christ in the mystery; of these various states the most fundamental of all is Christ's state of ''infinite servitude'' to God in the HYPOSTATIC UNION.

From these premises the masters of the French School drew the most characteristic principles and practices of their spiritual teaching: their markedly Christocentric and theocentric concept of religion; their special insight into the doctrine of the Mystical Body in terms of Christ's ''heavenly sacrifice,'' His priestly and victim life in heaven and in the Church; and finally, their Christian way of life and prayer as an actual sharing in the mysteries of Christ.

The Christian Mysteries. Christianity is before all else a mystery in St. Paul's sense of the term. As mystery, Christianity is a divine action. This divine action is essentially the Incarnation, life, death, and Resurrection of Jesus Christ, as realized in the person of Christ and in His Mystical Body, the Church.

Each event in the life of Christ, e.g., His death and Resurrection, is also a mystery insofar as it is a sign containing and communicating an inner reality and a principle of grace for men.

In every mystery or event of Christ's life there is an exterior aspect, the sign, and an interior aspect, the reality that is signified and communicated. There is the historical fact, the event, that took place in time and under definite circumstances; Christ was born, He lived in Nazareth, He taught, He suffered, He died, He rose from the dead. This exterior aspect of the mystery was passing and transitory; it took place and now it is over. The inner aspect of the mystery is the state or disposition that Christ had in His soul when He lived the mystery.

These inner states or dispositions of Jesus are simply what He is in the Incarnation and what He has as an immediate consequence of what He is. Jesus is first of all Son of God. Always in the bosom of the Father, He is Son. In His Incarnation He is Son by the communication of His person to a human nature. This is His condition and state in the very depth of His being.

By the same communication of the Word to His human nature Jesus is constituted, at one and the same time, perfect worshiper of his Father, priest and victim of His sacrifice, prophet and king. These are the states of Jesus in the most typically Berullian sense.

The State of Servitude. The French School writers singled out as central and fundamental to all Christ's states His state of servitude. In the complete possession of Christ's humanity by the divinity wherein the humanity of Christ lacks its own subsistence, its own personality, they saw the absolute condition of self-renouncement and clinging to God. From this state of ''infinite servitude'' they drew the most fundamental characteristic of their spirituality—the deep, total renunciation of self that is at the same time total adherence to Christ and being possessed by Him.

Jesus is subsisting religion; simply by being what He is He establishes the creatural position of man before God, which is adoration. Adoration, then, in the Berullian sense, is a persisting state of renunciation, of self-surrender, a constitution of the creature in the most elemental condition of its being. This state exists independently of any thought or act, and by the very value it has as being, gives worship to God.

In its development of the concept of the state of adoration, the French School penetrated more deeply into the central mystery of divine grace in the soul. By the simple fact that he is in the state of grace, a Christian is already in a state of adoration; he is already in some way ''consumed in God.'' Habitual grace in him is a created copy of the state of servitude of Christ in the hypostatic union.

Through its concept of the state of servitude, the French School probed more deeply into the relationship of Christ to His Mystical Body. As head of His body, Christ is the spiritual ''subsistence'' of all its members; He is a ''divine capacity for souls.'' In the supernatural order and in a mystic way, the members of Christ's body bear to Him the same relationship that a perfect human nature bears to its own proper subsistence. The members of the Church need Christ and require Christ as an individual nature needs and requires its own act of subsistence, its own personality. In the Mystical Body the relationship of the members to the head is a created copy of the relationship of Christ's own humanity to the Person of the Word in the hypostatic union. They depend on Him, and are perfected by Him as His own humanity depends upon and is perfected by the Person of the Word.

Christ's Priestly and Victim State. The writers of the French School celebrated Christ as head of His Mystical Body most of all in terms of His priestly and victim state in heaven, in terms of the ''heavenly sacrifice'' of Jesus. They cherished the heavenly life of Jesus as that phase of His life most complete and effective for God, for Himself, and for man. In His risen life Jesus returns to His Father as priest and victim, bearing in all its fullness the accomplishment of perfect religion, to give to God for all eternity the glory and worship that accrues from His life and His sacrifice. In His risen life Jesus returns to His Father as victim and conqueror, to have declared for His humanity all the glory that was His and was always due Him as Son of the Father. In His risen life Jesus, priest and victim, becomes the source of all life and grace He has merited on earth for men.

Participation in the Mysteries. In the most complete sense of the word, then, the French School conceived the way of Christian perfection to be the actual living of the life of Christ, by participation in the mysteries of His life. Christ and His members form one single living victim offered to the glory and the praise of God. Jesus, the head, traveling the course rigorously marked out by religion and sacrifice, became the victim of God. In His death He was immolated and returned to His Father to be made forever gloriously a priest and victim in heaven. It is His desire, and the inexorable pattern of religion and sacrifice, that His members go with Him through the same course. There is no other way. For this He sends His Spirit to consecrate them in Baptism as members of His body and to reproduce in them a most intimate sharing in all of His mysteries.

In virtue of this union of members with head in the Mystical Body, the sacred humanity of Christ is the efficient cause of grace in men. Christ in His humanity, made available to men in the Church especially through the sacramental signs, is not only a moral cause of their sanctification. The humanity of Christ working through His mysteries operates in men as an efficient, instrumental cause, actually producing grace. Living in communion with Christ, adhering to the states of the Incarnation, of itself actually causes grace in men. In addition, each mystery is also an exemplary cause of grace; each mystery contains and confers its own special grace, especially at the time of the celebration of that mystery.

Man cooperates with the Spirit of Jesus, producing in himself the states of Jesus by using his faculties of mind, heart, and will to yield himself to the Spirit of Jesus, to abandon himself to Him, to appropriate the states of Jesus, and to express them in daily living. In this union the person desires to make Christ's life flourish in him at the expense of his own. This is the work of prayer and the practice of virtue.

The form of prayer of the French School is admirably adapted for participating in the mysteries of Christ. It consists simply in ''having our Savior before the eyes, in the heart, and in the hands.'' As Olier says (''Introduction,'' 4.62): ''Christianity consists in these three points; . . . to look upon Jesus, to unite oneself to Jesus, and to act in Jesus. The first leads us to respect and to religion; the second to union and to identification with Him; the third, to an activity no longer solitary, but joined to the virtue of Jesus Christ, which we have drawn upon ourselves by prayer. The first is called adoration; the second, communion; the third, cooperation.''

Olier easily summarized the spiritual vision of the French School in an ''elevation'' characteristic of the style of the school. The entire design of Christ, our head, is ''to make of the whole world but one Church, to make of all men but one adorer, to make of all their voices but one voice of praise, and to make of all their hearts but one victim in himself, who is the universal and unique adorer of God, his Father'' (J. J. Olier, *Grand' Messe,* 8.3.433).

Bibliography: Sources. P. DE BÉRULLE, *Oeuvres complètes,* ed. J. P. MIGNE (Paris 1856). C. DE CONDREN, *Oeuvres complètes,* ed. L. M. PIN, 2 v. (Paris 1857–58), v.1 *Lettres.* J. J. OLIER, *Oeuvres complètes,* ed. J. P. MIGNE (Paris 1856). General Studies. P. BROUTIN, *La Réforme pastorale en France aux XVIIIe siècle,* 2 v. (Paris 1956), esp. 2:413–429. H. BRÉMOND, *Literary History of Religious Thought in France from the Wars of Religion down to Our Own Times,* tr. K. L. MONTGOMERY, 3 v. (New York 1928–37), v.3 *The Triumph of Mysticism.* L. COGNET, *Les Origines de la spiritualité française au XVIIe siècle* (Paris 1949). J. DAGENS, *Bérulle et les origines de la restauration catholique* (Bruges 1952), excellent bibliog. J. G. GAUTIER, ed., *Some Schools of Catholic Spirituality,* tr. K. SULLIVAN (New York 1959). H. C. JUDGE, ''Congregation of the Oratory in France in the Late 17th Century,'' *The Journal of Ecclesiastical History,* 12:46–55. P. POURRAT, *Christian Spirituality,* tr. W. H. MITCHELL et al., 4 v. (Westminster, Md. 1953–55) 3:332–401. A. SQUIRE, ''The Human Condition: A Study of Some 17th Century French Writers,'' *Life of the Spirit,* 16 (Nov. 1961) 166–182. Special Studies. L. COGNET, *Post-Reformation Spirituality,* tr. P. H. SCOTT (New York 1959). A. LAPLANTE, *Le Vertu de religion selon M. Olier* (Montreal 1953). J. E. MENARD, *Les Dons du Saint-Esprit chez M. Olier* (Montreal 1951). P. MICHALON, *La Communion aux mystères de Jésus-Christ selon Jean Jacques Olier* (Lyons 1942). E. A. WALSH, *The Priesthood in the Writings of the French School: Bérulle, de Condren, Olier* (Washington 1949). J. SAWARD, '''The Earthly Home of the Eternal Father': The Holy Family in the Spirituality of the French School,'' *The Holy Family in Art and Devotion,* ed. J. F. CHORPENNING (Philadelphia 1998), 54–66. R. DEVILLE, *The French School of Spirituality: An Introduction and Reader* (Pittsburgh 1994). *Bérulle and the French School: Selected Writings,* ed. W. M. THOMPSON, trans. L. M. GLENDON (Mahwah, N.J. 1989).

[E. A. WALSH]

SPIRITUALITY, RHENISH

Though there were other German mystics, such as HILDEGARDE (d. 1179), this term is applied to the school inaugurated by Meister ECKHART and represented by him, Johannes TAULER, HENRY SUSO, and their disciples, mostly Dominicans but also other religious, secular priests, and laymen. In addition to relying on the thought of St. Thomas, the masters of this school were strongly influenced by Neoplatonic ideas. Their mysticism, preoccupied with supernatural contemplation, has been called speculative, or mysticism of the essence, since, through speculation on man's experience of God and his union with Him, it sought to express in rational terms spiritual truths that transcend reason, namely, what God is, what His life consists of, what His relations to the world and the soul are, what the soul is and how it is united to God. These mystics speculated in view of practice; union with God was attained by the double way of theoretical abstraction and practical self-abnegation.

The doctrine of the school is trinitarian, based on the idea of God's transcendence. The absolute and infinite being of God, being in its purity and plenitude, lies at the heart and source of being in all other things, particularly the human soul. United in its profoundest depths to God; the soul can never be entirely outside Him; yet it may choose to concentrate on itself and withdraw from God, or it can renounce itself and turn totally toward Him. To achieve union with God, it must seek Him beyond creatures and itself. In renouncing self and clinging to God, the soul finds itself and true liberty and reaches its own purest essence. This is achieved in the ''spark'' or ''ground'' of the soul, its highest or innermost part, the point of intimate contact with God. Total stripping of self, abandonment of one's will, and perfect submission to God dispose the soul for union. Nudity of intelligence, i.e., complete turning away from all sensible and intellectual images, is the condition of union, which is reached when the soul returns to God, the One.

Exponents. In each of the masters of the school, these ideas had a distinctive coloring. Eckhart was the most speculative; Tauler, the most practical. Even while acknowledging the passive elements of mystical life, Tauler inculcated a laborious, prayerful, and charitable life. Suso was both speculative and practical, but above all affective. His *Little Book of Truth,* an introduction to speculative mysticism, is the only *ex professo* treatise of the school's spirituality. In Suso tender devotion to Christ expressed in the language of human love (a characteristic almost absent from the works of Eckhart and Tauler) finds its poet.

The teaching of Eckhart, Tauler, and Suso influenced the nuns of the Dominican monasteries of the Rhineland, Switzerland, and Upper Germany. Under the direction of such masters, the spiritual life of these monasteries came to maturity in the early 14th century. The intensity and character of the mysticism of the nuns was expressed in a series of works and chronicles. From the monastery of Maria-Mödingen in Bavaria came the *Revelations* of Margaret Ebner (d. 1351); from Engeltal in Swabia, those of Adelaide Langmann (d. 1375) and the *Visions and Revelations* of Christine Ebner (d. 1356), who probably also wrote the *Little Book of Grace,* recording the biographies of the nuns. Similar ''Lives'' under slightly varying titles were written at Adelhausen by Anna of Munzingen (1318), at Unterlinden by Catherine of Guebwiller (d. 1330), and at Katharinental in Diessenhoven, Ottenbach near Zurich, Kirchberg near Sulz, Weiler near Esslingen, and Töss in Switzerland. The latter ''Lives'' were written by Elizabeth Stagel (d. 1360), the spiritual daughter and biographer of Suso. Many of the nuns experienced visions, ecstasies, and private revelations, but unlike that of the friars their mysticism was affective rather than speculative.

Friends of God. Closely allied to the school were the FRIENDS OF GOD, pious folk of all ranks of society:

laymen, diocesan priests, monks, friars, and nuns. Held together in loose association by their spiritual interests and by their distress at the political and social evils of the day, they sought to live lives of intense union with God. Through Suso and Tauler, their two most prominent leaders, the Friends of God also came indirectly under the influence of Eckhart's spirituality. Notable among them were the two Ebners and their spiritual director Henry of Nördlingen, the friend of Suso and Tauler. His exchange of letters with Margaret Ebner is the oldest collection of letters in the German language and a monument of Rhenish spirituality. Also prominent among the Friends of God was Rulman Merswin (d. 1382), a rich merchant of Strassburg and one of Tauler's penitents. He composed pious romances and a partial autobiography, which was his only original work. His language and imagery owed much to Eckhart and Tauler, but his manner of borrowing discolored much of their teaching. The enigmatic Friend of God of the Oberland, who figures in documents and was the reputed author of spiritual treatises, was a fictitious character created probably by Merswin to symbolize God's voice.

The anonymous *Book of Spiritual Poverty,* long attributed to Tauler, developed the Rhenish themes of spiritual detachment as a way to true liberty, imitation of Christ, and union with God. The *THEOLOGIA GERMANICA* written toward the end of the century, though sometimes suspected of pantheism and quietism, actually presented the classical themes of the school without much originality but with more insistence on Christ's mysteries. Jan van RUYSBROECK (d. 1381) was much influenced by Eckhart. Though he has usually been catalogued under the Rhenish school, there are solid reasons also for labeling him the founder of the SPIRITUALITY OF THE LOW COUNTRIES.

Orthodoxy. With the papal condemnation in 1329 of propositions drawn from Eckhart's writings, the suspicion of pantheism and quietism fell over the Rhenish school. These doubts have been persistent and have involved not only Eckhart but also Suso and Tauler, who defended and handed on the master's basic doctrines, though purged of his exaggerated formulas. The reputation of the school suffered again when Luther unjustifiably appealed to the *Theologia Germanica* and Tauler in support of his attack on good works. Apart from certain passages in Merswin, the *Book of Spiritual Poverty,* and *Theologia Germanica,* and obscure, exaggerated, or ill-sounding expressions in Eckhart, who was certainly orthodox in intention, the Rhenish school was orthodox. Eckhart's works can be safely read when accompanied by adequate explanations. The doctrine of Suso, Tauler, and the Dominican nuns is above challenge.

The doctrines of the school exercised a wide influence. NICHOLAS OF CUSA was much attracted to the thought of Eckhart. Through Tauler and Suso, Eckhart's ideas reached the Dominicans VENTURINO OF BERGAMO and Louis CHARDON, the Carmelites JOHN OF SAINT-SAMSON and JOHN OF THE CROSS, the Jesuit Peter CANISIUS, and the Capuchin Benet of Canfield, the Benedictines John of Castel and BLOSIUS, the Carthusians Denis of Rijckel (*see* DENIS THE CARTHUSIAN), LUDOLPH OF SAXONY, and Lawrence SURIUS, the Spanish Franciscan JUAN DE LOS ANGELOS, and PAUL OF THE CROSS, founder of the Passionists.

Bibliography: J. M. CLARK, *The Great German Mystics* (Oxford 1949). J. ANCELET-HUSTACHE, *Master Eckhart and the Rhineland Mystics,* tr. H. GRAEF (pa. New York 1958). P. POURRAT, *Christian Spirituality,* tr. W. H. MITCHELL et al., 4 v. (Westminster, MD 1953–55) 2:213–251. J. LECLERCQ et al., *La Spiritualité du moyen âge* (Histoire de la spiritualité chrétienne 2; Paris 1961) 448–486. É. H. GILSON, *History of Christian Philosophy in the Middle Ages* (New York 1955) 438–446. A. WEEKS, *German Mysticism from Hildegard of Bingen to Ludwig Wittgenstein: A Literary and Intellectual History* (Albany 1993). H. GRUNDMANN, *Religious Movements in the Middle Ages: The Historical Links between Heresy, the Mendicant Orders, and the Women's Religious Movement in the Twelfth and Thirteenth Century, with the Historical Foundations of German Mysticism,* trans. S. ROWAN (Notre Dame, IN 1995). A. DE LIBERA, *Introduction à la mystique rhénane: D'Albert le Grand à maître Eckhart* (Paris 1984).

[W. A. HINNEBUSCH]

SPIRITUALITY OF THE LOW COUNTRIES

Whether there is spirituality peculiar to the Low Countries is disputed. Some regard Devotio Moderna as the sole distinctive spirituality of the Low Countries. They assign Bl. Jan van RUYSBROECK to the Rhenish school and limit his influence in the Netherlands to the introduction of Flemish as a medium of mystical expression (e.g., J. Huijbens). Writers after Ruysbroeck represent an affective, ascetic, moralizing, even anti-speculative doctrine scarcely influenced by him. When he is claimed for Low Countries spirituality, two divergent trends are found, his speculative system and the ascetico-practical teaching of the DEVOTIO MODERNA. A third opinion considers Ruysbroeck a central figure who, inheriting spiritual elements from Flemish predecessors, developed an ordered spirituality that served as a cohesive principle uniting writers of the region, despite differences of sensibility and emphasis in their teaching, into a distinct school for centuries thereafter. Even writers of the Devotio Moderna owed much to his mysticism. Ruysbroeck's essential ideas—a trinitarian-inspired exemplarism, introversion, and the life of union—keep reappearing subsequently in the works even of writers such as Gerlac Peters, manifesting strong ascetical tendencies (S. Axters).

Origins. Low Countries spirituality, which gave the Church the feasts of the Trinity and Corpus Christi and the final forms of the ROSARY and the Way of the Cross, originated in the hagiographical literature of the Merovingian age. The Carolingian period produced a spiritual literature of striking liturgical inspiration and developed the literary genre of ''spiritual elevations'' (St. Anscar, d. 965, and Rather of Verona, a monk of Lobbens, d. 974). The 11th- and 12th-century Benedictines, e.g., Lawrence of Liège, Rudolph of St. Trond, and especially RUPERT OF DEUTZ, whose spirituality centered on Christ triumphant, taught a hieratic spirituality redolent of the spirit of the Fathers. From the late 12th into the 13th century, under Cistercian influence, the spirituality of the Low Countries became intimate and warmhearted, concerned with the problem of divine love. It manifested itself in Ida of Nivelle's (d. 1231) devotion to the Trinity, in LUTGARDIS of Tongres's (d. 1246) devotion to the Sacred Heart and, with BEATRICE OF NAZARETH (d. 1268), to Our Lady, and in the devotion of Juliana of Cornilion (d. 1258) and Ida of Louvain (d. 1300) to the Eucharist. Elias of Coxide (d. 1203) found in Christ Crucified all his logic, all his physics, and all his ethics. The *Quinque incitamenta* of Gerard of Liège (*c.* 1250) is, from a psychological point of view, an extremely penetrating treatise on the love of God.

With Beatrice of Nazareth's autobiography (which is entire in the Latin version of William of Affighem and which comprises one chapter in the vernacular *Seven Ways or Degrees of Love*), a trend toward introversion and speculative mysticism entered the spirituality of the Low Countries; yet her teaching preserved a nuptial emphasis. The mid-13th century Hadewijch, whose letters, poems, and accounts of her visions are still stamped with Beatrice's idea of love and an authentic Christocentrism, developed a metaphysical exemplarist spirituality of the soul's return to God, a progress motivated by the search of the soul for the divine Threefold. Gerard Applemans' commentary on the ''Our Father'' carried Hadewijch's introversion and exemplarism forward: all creation returns to God; the Father begets the Word in the depths of the soul, which grasps His message only when it listens spiritually. Ruysbroeck, taking the metaphysical intuitions of Hadewijch and Applemans, built a trinitarian exemplarism by which the soul attains consciousness through introversion and flowers in a union with the Triune God that he called the ''common life.''

Currents. Just before Ruysbroeck's death, the spirituality of the Low Countries divided into two streams, one marked by speculative interest in mysticism, the other by concern with the ascetical life. The latter blossomed in Devotio Moderna, a spirituality that influenced most contemporary and subsequent schools. The Dominican Dirk van Delf (d. after 1404) went his own way. His *Table of Christian Faith,* one of the first vernacular summas, scarcely bothered with speculative themes and was content to describe the mystical state on the basis of experience.

The representatives of the mystical current were effected by the ideas of Ruysbroeck, especially his disciple John of Leeuwen (d. 1374), who produced a score of tracts that clarified his master's doctrine. John of Schoonhoven (d. 1432), after an initial interest in speculative mysticism, turned toward asceticism, perhaps under the influence of Windesheim. The Carthusian Gerard of Hérinnes (or of Sainctes), in a prologue to a collection of five of Ruysbroeck's works, expounded some of his most difficult pages. DENIS THE CARTHUSIAN (van Rijkel or van Leeuwen, d. 1471, the most scholastic of the Flemish mystics, gave special place in his *De fonte lucis* to the doctrines of Ruysbroeck. The Franciscan HENRY OF HERP, (d. 1477) in his *Mystica theologia* and *Mirror of Perfection,* handed on in an affective manner the speculative ideas of Ruysbroeck, especially his exemplarism, introversion, and Trinitarian orientation. His personal contribution was a theory of the efficacy of repeated aspirations of faith and love, and the development of the doctrine of mortification and renunciation. Herp exercised an influence well into the 17th century, especially on his fellow Franciscan Francis Vervoort (d. 1555), who mourned over the suffering Christ, as did the earlier unknown author of *Indica mihi* and John Brugman, OFM (d. 1473), in his meditations on the life of Christ. The Capuchins John Evangelist (d. 1635) and Luke of Malines (d. 1652), whose works are marked by strong introversion, also were influenced by Herp.

The writings of the 16th-century beguines, notably *The Gospel Pearl,* written before 1540, bear a strong Christiform stamp. Christ is born mystically in the soul, which lives His various states and conditions in faith and love. Claesinne of Nieuwlant (d. 1611) spoke of self-emptying and a corresponding unreserved union with Christ. Her director, Peregrine Pullen (d. 1608), wrote of identification with Christ, of contemplation achieved in Him, of seeing God in and through Him.

Francis Louis Blosius (de Blois; d. 1566), on a basis of introversion, developed a simple, warm, Christocentric spirituality that stressed the Eucharist as the indispensable food for the journey toward the Trinity. The Carmelite mystics, Mary of St. Teresa (d. 1677) and Michael of St. Augustine (d. 1684), taught a Mariform doctrine that contemplated Mary's life and virtues and brought the soul through her to union with Christ and God.

Bibliography: S. AXTERS, *The Spirituality of the Old Low Countries,* tr. D. ATTWATER (London 1954). J. HUIJBEN, ''Y a-t-il une spiritualité flamande?'' *La Vie spirituelle* 50 (Paris 1937) 129–147. J. LECLERCQ et al., *La Spiritualité du moyen-âge* (Histoire de la spiritualité chrétienne 2; Paris 1961) 430–438, 478–481. S. MURK-JANSEN, *Brides in the Desert: The Spirituality of the Beguines* (Maryknoll, NY 1998). P. VERDEYEN, *Ruusbroec and His Mysticism*, trans. A. LEFEVERE (Collegeville, MN 1994). L. DUPRÉ, *The Common Life: The Origins of Trinitarian Mysticism and its Development by Jan Ruusbroec* (New York 1984).

[W. A. HINNEBUSCH]

SPIRITUALS

Religious folk songs that originated among evangelical Protestant groups on the American frontier (from Kentucky westward) and spread to the rural South during the revivalist or second GREAT AWAKENING period (early 19th century).

White Spirituals. Although black spirituals are better known, the so-called white spirituals comprise the older repertory. Calvinist teaching permitted the singing of only the 150 Psalms of David and of such scriptural canticles as the *Benedictus* and *Magnificat* in public worship. Early in the 18th century, however, congregations in both England and New England began singing ''hymns and spiritual songs'' as well as the time-honored metrical psalms. (*See* PSALTERS, METRICAL.) Isaac Watts's *Hymns and Spiritual Songs* (1707) started a trend that in America took added impetus from the ''spiritual songs'' published by Samuel Hall (Newport, Rhode Island 1766), John Peak (Windsor, Vermont 1793), and Joshua Smith (Norwich, Connecticut 1794). In the early 1800s folkish melodies to which ''spiritual'' words had been adjusted pervaded the camp meetings of Methodists and Baptists in frontier America. If not traceable folk songs from the British Isles, the melodies in such typical collections as Jesse Mercer's *The Cluster of Spiritual Songs* (1823), James P. Carrell's *The Virginia Harmony* (1831), William Walker's *Southern Harmony* (four editions 1835–54), and B. F. King's *The Sacred Harp* (1844) almost always had a folkish ring.

The millennial excitement of the 1840s fanned the production of numerous song books containing ''revival'' spirituals that appealed especially to the blacks, who were often invited to participate in camp meetings. The *Evangelist,* a New York weekly, published an article in October 1856 (later reprinted in *Dwight's Journal of Music*) recording the presence of hundreds of whites and blacks together ''at a camp meeting in the woods.'' According to the writer, upon joining in the chorus of such a hymn as Watts's ''When I Can Read My Title Clear, To Mansions in the Sky,'' the hearer was raised ''from his feet by the volume and majesty of the sound.''

Black Spirituals. As early as 1755 to 1758 Watts's ''hymns and spiritual songs'' were the singing staple of slave congregations being formed in Virginia by the pioneer Presbyterian missionary Samuel Davies. It was not, however, the sober psalm tunes current in the 18th century that caught the blacks, but the exciting verse-refrain (leader-group) tunes spread abroad in frontier America by early 19th-century revivalists. The earliest published collections—*Slave Songs of the United States* (1867), *Jubilee Songs* (1872), *Cabin and Plantation Songs* (1874)—contained numerous tunes for which cognates can be found in white-spiritual song collections of a generation earlier. The overwhelming success of the touring Fisk University and Hampton Institute singers sent North and to England and Europe on money-raising tours reflected the pleasure with which white listeners in the 1870s received back their discarded folk repertory, now dramatized with a stronger rhythmic pulse, occasional syncopations, exaggeration of the primitive shout that city congregations had grown too polite to utter, more exciting pitch discrepancies, and other dialectical idosyncrasies of African provenante. Many black spirituals, however, have no counterpart in the revivalist repertory but represent rather a synthesis of African chant forms, calypso (West Indian) motifs, plantation melos, and the Christian themes they had absorbed.

Since the form of Christianity to which most blacks were initiated was biblically oriented, their spirituals are predominantly biblical in text. Particularly before Emancipation blacks identified spontaneously with the captive Hebrews. ''Let My People Go'' typifies this stress on freedom from oppression. The theme of glory also was suited to the needs of a suffering people, and the Book of Revelation, as well as Old Testament apocalyptic passages (e.g., Elijah), provided sources of imagery. This empathy toward scriptural narratives has been noted by the Biblical scholar A. Gelin, who suggests that a play such as *Green Pastures,* in the style of spirituals, can help clarify Old Testament literary genres. Other spirituals are directly hortatory (e.g., against the evil of drink) or sociocritical (against the evil of slavery or discrimination).

In recent years ethnomusicologists have made extensive use of electronic equipment to record spirituals in their natural habitat—usually rural church settings—and to produce analytical studies of their findings. Long before that, however, Thomas Wentworth Higginson had collected texts of 35 black spirituals while commanding a regiment of black soldiers during the Civil War. For ''Hail Mary,'' which contained the lines ''O hail Mary, hail [*three times*] To Help me bear the cross,'' Higginson postulated a Catholic origin: ''. . . as I had several men from Saint Augustine who held . . . to that faith.'' He noted also that ''We'll Soon Be Free'' and similar spirituals were given a nonspiritual meaning, and conversely, that any newly made-up profane one might be called a "speritual"; that blacks with their histrionic flair turned every scriptural incident into a bold drama (e.g., "Wrestling Jacob"); that they changed texts they did not understand ("gird on the armor" became "guide on the army").

They make the "minor-keyed pathos" of their spirituals a passport to the "sublime scenery of the Apocalypse," Higginson observed. The 19th-century black spirituals best known today, however, are major-keyed, pentatonic melodies such as "Nobody Knows the Trouble," "Swing Low, Sweet Chariot," and "Were You There." The fate that T. P. Fenner prophesied for them in 1874 has become reality: black congregations have stopped using them, along with other reminders of a slave past. The more recent "composed" spirituals, such as "Russia, Leave That Moon Alone," and the anonymous civil-rights anthem, "We Shall Overcome" (with a melody akin to the Sicilian fisherman's hymn *O Sanctissima*), leave the plaintive past and strike a vigorous and warlike note.

Since Vatican Council II black spirituals have inspired composed Masses by the black Catholic priest Clarence Rivers and others. Earlier, Daniel Gregory Mason, of the distinguished family of American musicians, composed a string quartet on black spiritual themes. And DVOŘÁK, during his stay in the United States, steeped himself in Black melodies (his student H. T. Burleigh, composer and transcriber usually identified with the poignant "Were You There," was frequently called upon to sing old plantation songs for him) and embodied their spirit and occasionally even their tunes in his "American" compositions, notably the symphony "From the New World."

Bibliography: G. P. JACKSON, *White Spirituals in the Southern Uplands* (Chapel Hill 1933); *White and Negro Spirituals: Their Life Span and Kinship* (New York 1944). D. YODER, *Pennsylvania Spirituals* (Lancaster, Pa. 1961). A. M. BUCHANAN, ed., *Folk Hymns of America* (New York 1938). S. E. ASBURY and H. E. MEYER, "Old-Time White Camp-Meeting Spirituals," *Texas Folklore Society Publications* 10 (1932) 169–85. D. LARSON, "'When We All Get To Heaven': The Ecumenical Influence of the American Gospel Song," *Restoration Quarterly* 36:3 (1994) 154–72. P. K. MAULTSBY, "The Use and Performance of Hymnody, Spirituals, and Gospels in the Black Church," *The Hymnology Annual* (Berrien Springs, Michigan 1992) 11–26. C. M. HAWN, "A Survey of Trends in Recent Protestant Hymnals: African-American Spirituals, Hymns, and Gospel Songs," *Hymn* 43 (January 1992) 21–28. M. BURNIM, "The Performance of Black Gospel Music as Transformation," in *Music and the Experience of God* (Edinburgh 1989) 52–61. C. DIXON, *Negro Spirituals: From Bible to Folk Song* (Philadelphia 1976). K. WATKINS, "A Few Kind Words for Fanny Crosby," *Worship* 51 (May 1977) 248–59. P. K. MAULTSBY, *Afro-American Religious Music: A Study in Musical Diversity* (Springfield, Ohio 1981). J. R. HILLSMAN, *The Progress of Gospel Music: From Spirituals to Contemporary Gospel* (New York 1983). J. LOVELL, *Black Song: The Forge and the Flame: The Story of how the Afro-American Spiritual Was Hammered Out* (New York 1986). M. P. BANGERT, "Black Gospel and Spirituals: A Primer," *Currents in Theology and Mission* 16 (1989) 173–79. J. H. CONE, *The Spirituals and the Blues: An Interpretation* (Maryknoll, New York 1991). A. C. JONES, *Wade in the Water: The Wisdom of the Spirituals* (Maryknoll, New York 1993).

[R. M. STEVENSON/C. J. MCNASPY/EDS.]

SPIRITUS PARACLITUS

Encyclical letter of Pope BENEDICT XV concerning Biblical study, in commemoration of the 15th centenary of St. Jerome's death, published Sept. 15, 1920. Its background, contents, and results are treated here.

At the turn of the 20th century a lively discussion was in progress among Catholic Biblical scholars. The progressive school of thought, aware of the necessity of reassessing some commonly accepted notions regarding the historicity of the Bible, proposed various theories. One theory, for which the support of St. Jerome and Leo XIII's *PROVIDENTISSIMUS DEUS* was claimed, was that of historical appearances: the sacred writers wrote history as found in the popular traditions of their contemporaries. Another was the theory of tacit quotations: the sacred writer quotes without acknowledgment and without assuming responsibility for the content of the quotation. The third was the method of literary forms. By means of these theories the progressive school hoped to discover what the Biblical authors really teach, and thereby to know what is really inerrant. The weakness in these theories consisted in their tendency to determine *a priori* what is taught and what is not taught.

The conservative wing persisted in treating the Bible as a series of propositions: asserted or not, every statement must be accepted. They refused to grant that the Bible may have error, i.e., mistaken notions of the sacred authors that are not taught by them. In 1905 and 1909 the PONTIFICAL BIBLICAL COMMISSION carefully circumscribed the employment of the methods of "tacit quotations" and "historical appearances" (*Enchiridion biblicum* 160, 161, 336–343; H. Denzinger, *Enchiridion symbolorum* 3372–73, 3512–19).

The purpose of the encyclical is to promote study and reading of the Bible in the light of St. Jerome's teaching and example. After a brief biography of the Saint, the encyclical summarizes his doctrine on the inspiration and inerrancy of the Bible, and contrasts it with some modern views. According to the Great Doctor, the Bible is inspired whole and entire and, as such, is inerrant. Some recent opinions, however, falsely claiming to stem from St. Jerome, tend to admit error in the Bible. The encyclical repudiates the theory that asserts *a priori* that only the religious element is taught and that, consequently, this element alone is inerrant. It likewise rejects the application of the principles outlined in *Providentissimus Deus* for the solution of difficulties in the field of natural sciences to problems created by historical research. It cautions, further, against the abuse of sound methods of exegesis, such as that of literary forms, tacit quotations, and pseudohistorical narratives.

St. Jerome's example is held up for our imitation. Great love for the Bible impelled him to study it constantly and deeply. According to the encyclical we must follow him in his humble docility to his predecessors and his obedience to the Church. Turning to the present, the encyclical praises the work of the Society of St. Jerome for its encouragement of daily reading of the New Testament. It exhorts priests to study the Bible, and bishops and religious superiors to send men to study at the Biblical Institute in Rome.

The next section deals with practical benefits deriving from greater knowledge of the Scriptures: spiritual life will be deepened, and the defense of faith made more secure; preaching, which should be simple and primarily concerned with the literal sense, becomes more effective.

The encyclical finally enumerates some of the effects of Biblical study: one experiences internal joy and consolation, one's love for the Church and apostolic zeal increase, and union with Christ grows in intensity. The Holy Father concludes by expressing the hope that greater knowledge and love of Jesus Christ found in the pages of the Bible will stem the waves of godlessness and bring peace among men.

While not condemning the method of literary forms and not affirming the inerrancy of every sentence in the Bible that is in the indicative mood, *Spiritus Paraclitus* did not open the door to a freer Biblical research among Catholics. The fear of modernism was as yet too strong.

Bibliography: BENEDICT XV, ''Spiritus Paraclitus,'' *Acta Apostolicae Sedis* 12 (1920) 385–422; tr. *Rome and the Study of Scripture* (5th ed. St. Meinrad, Ind. 1953). *Enchiridion biblicum* (Rome 1956) 444–495. J. LINDER, ''Die absolute Wahrheit der hl. Schrift nach der Lehre der Enzyklika Papst Benedikts XV 'Spiritus Paraclitus,''' *Zeigeist für katholische Theologie* 46 (1922) 254–277. J. M. VOSTÉ, *De Scripturarum veritate iuxta recentiora Ecclesiae documenta* (Rome 1924). W. DRUM, ''The Encyclical of Pope Benedict XV on the Fifteenth Centenary of St. Jerome,'' *Homiletic and Pastoral Review* 21 (1920) 278–291.

[A. M. AMBROZIC]

SPOHR, LOUIS (LUDWIG)

Romanticist violinist and composer; b. Brunswick, Germany, April 5, 1784; d. Kassel, Oct. 22, 1859. Born into a musical atmosphere, he became a leading violin virtuoso who was no less gifted as conductor and composer. Although chiefly remembered for his violin and clarinet concertos, he was active in opera, oratorio, art song, and symphony and wrote much interesting chamber music. His expression was conservative in many respects; yet his harmonic audacities anticipated those of LISZT and WAGNER. Despite his hostility to Catholicism (see the diatribes against Gregorian chant and the Church in his autobiography), he composed a *Mass for Ten Voices, Op. 54 (1820),* after his examination of Thibaut's collection of Renaissance sacred music. In the Mass, which was not intended for liturgical performance, he attempted to combine the techniques of Renaissance polyphony with the harmonic style of MOZART's later works. His oratorios *The Last Judgment* (1826) and *Calvary* (1835) were extremely popular; and their chromatic harmonies, often excessively sentimental, had a strong influence on the sacred works of MENDELSSOHN and the Victorian composers.

Bibliography: L. SPOHR, *Selbstbiographie,* 2 v. (Kassel 1860–61); *Musical Journeys,* tr. and ed. H. PLEASANTS, (Norman, Okla. 1961). P. H. LÁNG, *Music in Western Civilization* (New York 1941). *Baker's Biographical Dictionary of Musicians*, ed. N. SLONIMSKY (5th, rev. ed. New York 1958) 1548–49. J. BERRETT, in *International Dictionary of Opera,* ed. C. S. LARUE (Detroit 1993). C. BROWN, *Louis Spohr: A Critical Biography* (Cambridge 1984). D. M. RANDEL, ed., *The Harvard Biographical Dictionary of Music* (Cambridge 1996). M. WEYER in *The New Grove Dictionary of Music and Musicians* ed. S. SADIE (New York 1980). M. WULFHORST, *Louis Spohr's Early Chamber Music (1796–1812), A Contribution to the History of Nineteenth-Century Genres* (Ph.D. diss. City University of New York, 1995); ''Louis Spohr and the Modern Concept of Performance,'' *Journal of the Conductors' Guild* 18 (1997) 66–75.

[R. M. LONGYEAR]

SPONDANUS, HENRI (DE SPONDE)

Ecclesiastical author, reforming bishop; b. Mauléon (Basses-Pyrénées), Jan. 6, 1568; d. Toulouse, May 18, 1643. A Calvinist, Spondanus, after an excellent education in humanities and law, became *maître des requêtes* of Henry, King of Navarre. In 1595, led by his brother Jean's conversion, Robert BELLARMINE's writings, and Jacques-Davy du Perron's influence, he became a Catholic. After moving to Rome in 1600, he made learned friends, and was ordained in 1606. He was assigned duties at the Roman Curia and made rector of Saint-Louis des Français; he was esteemed for his knowledge, virtue, and aid to diplomats. Made bishop of Pamiers (Ariège) in 1626, he labored diligently for peace, pastoral reform, and conversion of Protestants. In 1637, ill and weary, he retired to Paris, where he continued his writings. These include apologetics, history, biography, and pastoral works. The most noteworthy are *Les Cimetières sacrés* (1597; fuller Latin ed., 1638), *Epitome* of Caesar Baronius' *Annales* (1613), *Annales sacri . . .* (1637), and *Annalium . . . Baronii continuatio . . .* (1641).

Bibliography: J. CONTRASTY, *Cinq visites ''ad limina'' aux XVIe-XVIIe siècles* (Paris 1913). J. M. VIDAL, *Henri de Sponde, recteur de Saint-Louis des Français, évêque de Pamiers 1568–1643* (Paris 1929). P. BROUTIN, *La Réforme pastorale en France au XVIIe siècle,* 2 v. (Tournai 1956) 1:141–153. J. MERCIER, *Dictionnaire de théologie catholique,* ed. A. VACANT, 15 v. (Paris 1903–50; Tables générales 1951–) 14.2:2550–51.

[W. H. PRINCIPE]

SPONSORS

A sponsor is one who binds himself to answer for another. According to Canon Law, sponsors are required at BAPTISM and CONFIRMATION.

Baptism. In accordance with ancient custom a sponsor is to be employed in Baptism whenever possible (CIC c. 872; CCEO c. 684). The Latin code states that there should be but one sponsor of either sex; at the most two sponsors, one male and one female, are employed (c. 873).

For sponsorship: (1) The sponsor must be so designated and have the intention of fulfilling this function. (2) The sponsor generally should have completed the sixteenth year. (3) The sponsor must be a fully initiated Catholic who leads a life of faith. (4) The sponsor may not be bound by any canonical penalty legitimately imposed or declared. (5) Finally, the sponsor may not be the father or mother of the one to be baptized. A non-Catholic Eastern Christian may be admitted to the role of sponsor in a Catholic baptism, but always in addition to a Catholic sponsor (CCEO c. 685 §3). A baptized Christian belonging to a non-Catholic ecclesial community (e.g., Lutheran, Methodist, Presbyterian communions) may not function as a sponsor, but may be admitted as a witness to the baptism if a Catholic sponsor is also had (CIC c. 874 §2).

Spiritual relationship is a bond arising between certain persons from the Sacraments of Baptism and Confirmation. In the Eastern Catholic Churches, the spiritual relationship resulting from Baptism constitutes a diriment impediment to marriage (CCEO c. 811).

Sponsors assist in preparation for Baptism, testify to the faith of an adult candidate or profess the Church's faith with the parents of a child to be baptized, and help the new Christian persevere in faith after Baptism (ChrInitGenIntrod 8–9).

Louis Spohr. (©Bettmann/CORBIS)

Confirmation. A sponsor should be present at Confirmation insofar as possible (CIC c. 892). There should be only one sponsor for each person confirmed.

The qualifications required of a confirmation sponsor are the same as those required for a baptismal sponsor (CIC c. 893 §1). It is desirable that a person's baptismal sponsor also serve as the sponsor for confirmation (CIC c. 893 §2). This stresses the unity of the two Sacraments. It is also possible to choose a sponsor other than one's baptismal sponsor.

Bibliography: J. C. BENNINGTON, *The Recipient of Confirmation* (Washington 1952). T. L. BOUSCARON and A. C. ELLIS, *Canon Law* (3d rev. ed. Milwaukee 1957). H. DAVIS, *Moral and Pastoral Theology,* 4 v. (rev. ed. New York 1958) v.3. R. J. KEARNEY, *Sponsors at Baptism* (Washington 1925). J. F. WALDRON, *The Minister of Baptism* (Washington 1942). S. WOYWOD, *A Practical Commentary on the Code of Canon Law* (New York 1963).

[E. H. SULLIVAN/L. MICK]

SPONTANEOUS GENERATION

Also referred to as abiogenesis, the theory that living things arise *de novo* without living parents from lifeless matter, held almost universally until mid-17th century. After careful observation of the habits of animals and the life cycles of plants, ARISTOTLE concluded that some insects arise from putrefying earth or vegetable matter, oysters from slimy mud, lice from the flesh of animals, and so on. I. Newton, W. Harvey, and R. DESCARTES were among the eminent scientists who accepted the theory without question.

The attempt of the ancients and medievals to explain the origin of lower forms of life from natural causes, rather than attributing it directly to a supramundane or divine power, was scientifically respectable. Without microscopes, these men could see neither the minute eggs of many of the invertebrates nor the spores of plants or other reproductive structures of lower animals and plants. Their scientific frame of mind demanded that they account for the change from the inanimate to the animate by proximate or proper causes; the only alternative to this, in their way of thinking, was belief in a special creation for each organism. The medievals preferred spontaneous generation for much the same reasons that 20th-century scientists seek to explain the origin of life from concatenations of molecules in the oceans of the primitive earth.

St. THOMAS AQUINAS accepted the spontaneous generation of living things from decaying matter. He also accepted the ancients' postulate that the active principle for such a power resides in some way in a celestial body. Since the sun's heat has a beneficial effect on the growth and development of living things, he thought that such heat could communicate the power of life to the slime of the earth. Not regarding the heavenly bodies as animated, however, he held that they could produce living things only in virtue of some higher power (*De pot.* 6.6 ad 10).

In Aquinas's terminology, the sun, not being determined to produce any one kind of animal or plant, is referred to as a universal cause (*Summa theologiae* 1a, 115.3 ad 3). The species of animals produced by such a cause are determined by the proportionate composition of elements in the decaying organic matter (*ibid.* 1a2ae, 60.1).

The forms of such organisms are not in the sun, any more than the forms of new animals or plants are in the gametes that give rise to them (*ibid.* 1a, 118.1 ad 4). Rather they are educed from the potency of matter, just as the form of water can be said to be educed from the potentiality of hydrogen and oxygen (*see* MATTER AND FORM).

To avoid a disproportion between cause and effect, St. Thomas argued that just as a living canine parent must empower the seed or gamete to produce another dog, so some living being must empower a celestial body to bring forth life. In his analysis, angels could fulfill this function, since they have more knowledge of, and greater power over, celestial and terrestrial operations than man (*De pot.* 3.11 ad 13; 6.3). In light of man's rapidly increasing control over matter and energy, it would be in accord with such an analysis to hold that man might be able to dispose matter in such a way as to educe from it a living form. The living thing produced would then be the result of NATURE as well as of man's art (cf *Summa theologiae*. 3a, 75.6 ad 1).

See Also: LIFE.

Bibliography: R. F. NIGRELLI, ed., ''Modern Ideas on Spontaneous Generation,'' *Annals of the New York Academy of Sciences* 69 (1957) 257–376. J. B. CONANT et al., eds., *Harvard Case Histories in Experimental Science,* 2 v. (Cambridge, MA 1957) v. 2.

[A. M. HOFSTETTER]

SPONTINI, GASPARE

Romanticist conductor and composer; b. Majolati (Ancona), Italy, Nov. 14, 1774; d. Majolati, Jan. 24, 1851. Although destined for the priesthood, the boy studied instead at the Turchini conservatory in Naples, in which city his first opera was produced in 1796. He was active successively in Rome, Palermo (as maestro to the Naples court in exile), Venice, and Paris, where he became *compositeur particulier* to Empress Josephine (1804). In Paris he produced his best opera, *La Vestale* (1807), and introduced MOZART's *Requiem, Don Giovanni* (original version), and other compositions. In 1819 he became court composer to Friedrich Wilhelm III and music director in Berlin. The *première* of Carl M. von WEBER's *Der Freischütz* in 1821 threatened the reign of Italian opera, and Spontini's highhanded and dilatory ways were unpopular, but the King remained loyal until his death in 1840. His successor, Friedrich Wilhelm IV, proving less sympathetic, Spontini returned to Paris in 1841, and in 1850 retired to his birthplace. Spontini was an ambitious man whose career was a series of feuds, rivalries, and litigations; yet he was capable of great generosity. After Weber's death he conducted *Der Freischütz* as a benefit for the composer's widow and children, and he gave his retirement years and all his possessions to the needy. His operas and church works (mostly very early) were mounted in the grand ''revolutionary style'' of the time of Napoleon, with rich orchestration and majestic choruses.

Bibliography: C. BOUVET, *Spontini* (Paris 1930). A. GHISLANZONI, *G. Spontini* (Rome 1951). G. ABRAHAM, ''The Best of Spontini,'' *Music and Letters 23* (1942) 163–171. R. EITNER, *Quellen-Lexikon der Musiker und Musikgelehrten,* 10 v. [Leipzig 1900–04; New York n.d. (1947)] 9:230–233. T. BARFOOT, ''*La Vestale*'' in *International Dictionary of Opera,* ed. C. S. LARUE (Detroit 1993); ''Gaspare (Luigi Pacifico) Spontini,'' *ibid.* K. H. COCHRAN, *The Genesis of Gaspare Spontini's ''Agnes von Hohenstaufen'': A*

Chapter in the History of German Opera (Ph.D. diss. University of North Carolina at Chapel Hill, 1995). P. FRAGAPANE, *Spontini* (Florence 1983). D. LIBBY in *The New Grove Dictionary of Music and Musicians,* ed. S. SADIE (New York 1980). N. SLONIMSKY, ed., *Baker's Biographical Dictionary of Musicians* (New York 1992).

[W. C. HOLMES]

SPORER, PATRITIUS

Franciscan moral theologian; b. Passau, *c.* 1620; d. Passau, May 29, 1683. Sporer entered the Strasbourg province of the Strict Observance in 1637 and after his ordination in 1644 immediately became teacher of philosophy and later of theology. He was also preacher and penitentiary of the cathedrals of Augsburg and Passau. He is remembered chiefly for his textbooks of moral theology, which were in use inside and outside of the order for more than 100 years. His more important works are *Tyrocinium theologiae moralis conscientiam, actum humanum et peccatum in genere moraliter explicans et applicans* (Würzburg 1660–61), *Seraphim moralis: Amor Dei super omnia theologico-practice explicatus* (*ibid.* 1662), and *Tyrocinium sacramentale practicum ad instructionem ordinandorum et curandorum* (Salzburg 1681–82). After Sporer's death these works were revised and, partly with the aid of his manuscripts, completed and repeatedly edited under the new title *Theologia moralis super decalogum et sacramenta.* In 1724 Kilian Katzenberger added two *Supplementa.* The last revised edition is the work of Irenaeus Bierbaum (Paderborn 1901–05). Sporer admitted that he had learned more by practice than by formal schooling; and his writings are practical rather than theoretical. He was a probabilist and lenient in his judgments. St. Alphonsus of Liguori considered him an authority.

Bibliography: H. HURTER, *Nomenclator literarius theologiae catholicae* (Innsbruck 1926) 4:944. A. GOETZELMANN, ''Das Studium marianum theologicum im Franziskanerkloster zu Dettelbach,'' *Franzisfanische Studien* 6 (1919) 345–365. J. H. SBARALEA, *Supplementum et castigatio ad scriptores trium ordinum S. Francisci a Waddingo* (Rome 1906–36) 4:284. *Syllabus Scriptorum Provinciae Argentinae,* ed. B. LINS (Analecta Franciscana 8; 1946) 563–565. A. TEETAERT, *Dictionnaire de théologie catholique*, ed. A. VACANT et al., (Paris 1903–50) 14.2:2551–53.

[G. GÁL]

SPORTELLI, CAESAR, VEN.

Redemptorist preacher of missions, companion and counselor of St. Alphonsus LIGUORI; b. Mola di Bari, Italy, June 19, 1701; d. Pagani, April 19, 1750. As the son of distinguished parents, he studied law and practiced with success in Naples. Deeply religious, he sought spiritual direction from Thomas Falcoja, who later became bishop of Castellamare di Stabia. Through Falcoja, Sportelli came to know (St.) Alphonsus, whom he joined in April 1733. Because of difficulties concerning a title for ordination, he was not a priest until May 5, 1737. Meanwhile he taught in the schools of the Redemptorist foundations at Scala and Villa Liberi. As a missionary his fame was widespread. Besides natural eloquence, he possessed a frankness, optimism, discretion, and piety that touched the most hardened sinner. The Redemptorist houses at Pagani and Caposele were stabilized during his regime as superior. Stricken with apoplexy, he increased his renown for sanctity by his resignation to a long illness. Alphonsus wished to see the process of Sportelli's beatification begun during his own lifetime, but the cause was not introduced until 1899.

Gaspare Spontini, 19th-century painting by Nicoli Luigi. (©Archivo Iconografico, S.A./CORBIS)

Bibliography: C. SPORTELLI, *Epistolae Ven. Servi Dei Caesaris Sportelli,* ed. C. HENZE (Isola del Liri, Italy 1935). G. LANDI, *The Life of. . . C. Sportelli* (The Saints and Servants of God; London 1849).

[M. J. CURLEY]

SPRINGFIELD IN MASSACHUSETTS, DIOCESE OF

The Diocese of Springfield in Massachusetts (*Campifontis*) is a suffragan of the metropolitan See of BOSTON, established June 14, 1870, from the five central and western counties of Massachusetts; in 1950 when the Diocese of WORCESTER was erected, Springfield was reduced to four counties, an area of 2,822 square miles.

The area lacked a church and a resident priest until 1836, when Rev. James FITTON built Christ Church in Worcester. The pioneer Catholics were Irish immigrants working on canals and railroads; Worcester, where Fitton resided from 1836 to 1843, was the first Catholic center. The next church in Cabotville, now Chicopee, was built in 1843 by John D. Brady, the first resident priest in western Massachusetts. By 1870, when the diocese was erected, there were nearly 100,000 Catholics, 38 parishes, and 43 diocesan priests, as well as the Sisters of Mercy in Worcester and the Notre Dame Sisters in Chicopee and Holyoke. Holy Cross in Worcester, founded in 1843 as the first Catholic college in New England, has been closely associated with the growth of the diocese.

Patrick Thomas O'Reilly, a native of Ireland, was consecrated the first bishop of Springfield, Sept. 25, 1870. He had been ordained for the Boston diocese Aug. 15, 1857, and was, when appointed bishop, 37 years old and gifted with an imposing presence and an uncommon measure of tact and capacity for work. He was succeeded by Thomas Daniel Beaven (1892–1920), a native of Springfield, and Thomas Mary O'Leary (1921–49), a native of Dover, N.H. The Catholic population had more than doubled by 1900, and it nearly doubled again during the next five decades. The fourth bishop, Christopher Joseph Weldon, was appointed Jan. 28, 1950; the diocese then had a population of 285,000, which was 46 percent of the total population of the four counties that remained after Worcester was detached. These Catholics, mainly descendants of diverse immigrant stock of the 19th century, included Irish, French-Canadians, Poles, Lithuanians, Italians, Slovaks, and Syrians. National parishes were founded to serve them. Although national parishes were needed, they were conducive to disunity. (*see* POLISH NATIONAL CATHOLIC CHURCH).

Educational institutions included Assumption College (1904), since 1950 in the Worcester diocese; Our Lady of the Elms, Chicopee, a college for women (1928); Cranwell Preparatory, Lenox, a private school operated by the Jesuits (1939); Ursuline Academy for girls, Springfield (1955); and Cathedral High School. The diocese's charitable institutions included a home for children, West Springfield (1954), and the new Providence Hospital in Holyoke (1958), both under the Sisters of Providence, active in the area since 1873. The *Catholic Mirror,* a monthly that began in 1920, was replaced in 1954 by the weekly *Catholic Observer.* In 1977, when Bishop Weldon resigned after more than a quarter century of devoted service, the diocese of Springfield had grown in population but continued to retain the same number of parishes and priests. Under his successors, Bishop Joseph E. Maguire (1977–91) and Bishop John A. Marshall (1991–94) the diocese has seen a decline in the number of priests as well as in the overall Catholic population. In 1995, Thomas Dupre was named to succeed Bishop Marshall.

Bibliography: J. J. MCCOY, *History of the Catholic Church in the Diocese of Springfield* (Boston 1900). K. F. MULLANEY, *Catholic Pittsfield and Berkshire,* 2 v. (Pittsfield, Mass. 1897–1924).

[W. L. LUCEY/EDS.]

SPROTT, THOMAS, BL.

Priest, martyr; *alias* Parker; b. *c.* 1571 at Skelsmergh (near Kendal), Westmoreland, England; hanged, drawn, and quartered on July 11, 1600 at Lincoln, England. After studying at Douai, he was ordained in 1596 and sent on the English Mission that same year. During a search for robbers in a Lincoln inn, authorities found holy oils and breviaries among the possessions of Sprott and his companion Bl. Thomas HUNT. They were arrested. During the trial Judge John Glanville directed the jury to find them guilty, though they neither confessed nor were proven to be priests. He was beatified by Pope John Paul II on Nov. 22, 1987 with George Haydock and companions.

Feast of the English Martyrs: May 4 (England).

See Also: ENGLAND, SCOTLAND, AND WALES, MARTYRS OF.

Bibliography: R. CHALLONER, *Memoirs of Missionary Priests,* ed. J. H. POLLEN (rev. ed. London 1924), nos. 118, 119. J. H. POLLEN, *Acts of English Martyrs* (London 1891).

[K. I. RABENSTEIN]

SPURGEON, CHARLES HADDON

English Baptist minister and preacher; b. Kelvedon, Essex, June 19, 1834; d. Mentone, Jan. 31, 1892. Of Dutch ancestry, Spurgeon was reared in the Independent (Congregationalist) tradition, but became a Baptist in 1850. Although he had little formal education, Spurgeon early displayed extraordinary preaching ability and became pastor of Waterbeach, Cambridge (1852). In 1854 he was called to a run-down London parish at New Park

Street, Southwark, where he quickly drew such enormous crowds that the Metropolitan Tabernacle, Newington, London, accommodating 6,000, was built in 1861 for him. There he preached to crowded congregations until his death. Many charitable institutions grew up around the Tabernacle, including an orphanage, a pastors' training college, and organizations for the distribution of religious tracts. At 22 he was the most popular preacher in England. His success was due partly to his youth, but also to his spontaneous humor, intense earnestness, and direct appeal to the individual conscience. His rigid Calvinism led him into many controversies with evangelical Anglicans and with fellow Baptists. The growing indifference to Orthodoxy and the rationalistic tendencies in liberal Biblical criticism disturbed him. Some 2,500 of his sermons have been published in 50 volumes in *The Tabernacle Pulpit* collection. Many have been translated into other languages. Among his better-known publications are *The Saint and the Saviour* (1857) and *Commenting and Commentaries* (1876). His four-volume autobiography (1897–1900) was compiled by his wife and Rev. W. J. Harrald, his private secretary, from his diary, letters, and records. A condensed version, edited by D. O. Fuller, appeared in 1946.

Bibliography: G. H. PIKE, *The Life and Work of C. H. Spurgeon,* 3 v. (London 1892–93). J. C. CARLILE, *C. H. Spurgeon: An Interpretative Biography* (London 1933). W. Y. FULLERTON, *C. H. Spurgeon* (London 1920). A. R. BUCKLAND, *The Dictionary of National Biography from the Earliest Times to 1900,* 63 v. (London 1885–1900) 18:841–843.

[W. HANNAH]

SRI LANKA, THE CATHOLIC CHURCH IN

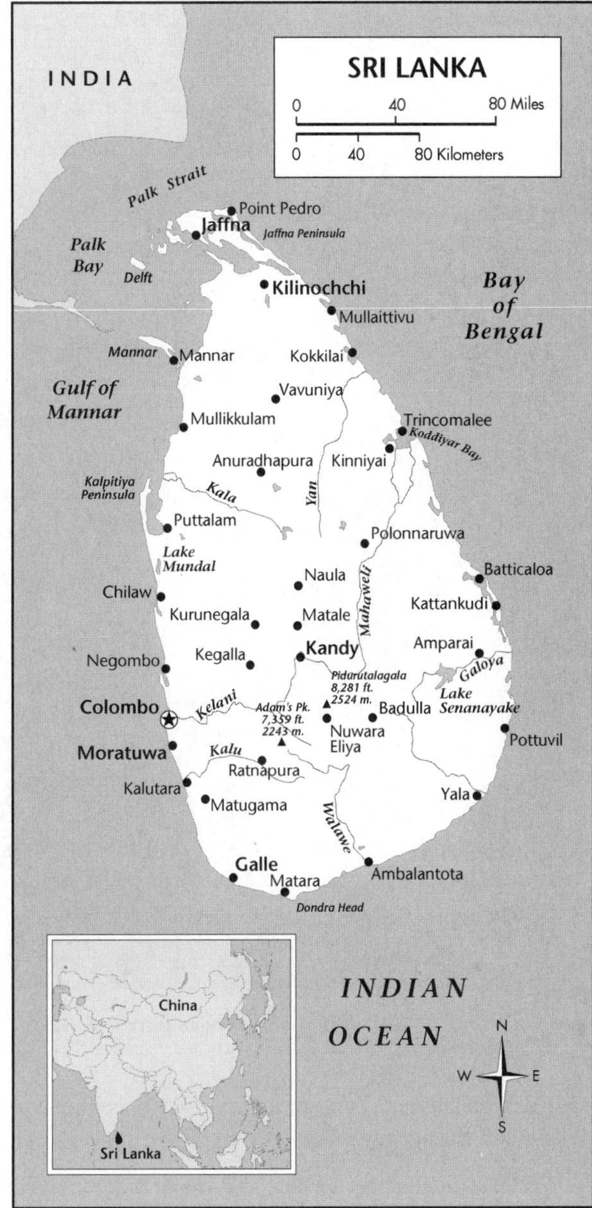

The Democratic Socialist Republic of Sri Lanka is an island country of the Indian Ocean, located southeast of the tip of the Indian subcontinent. Connected to the Indian mainland through a narrow, intermittent causeway, the island consists of low rolling plains rising to mountains in the interior. Visited by monsoons in winter and summer, the climate is tropical; agricultural crops include rice, sugarcane, grains, spices and tea, although agriculture is slowly being replaced by textile and garment manufacture as the region's main export. Natural resources include limestone, graphite, gems and phosphates; Sri Lanka is also located near the major Indian Ocean shipping lanes, which has fueled the government's recent efforts to boost trade.

Once known as Ceylon, the region was inhabited mainly by Sinhalese and Tamils who migrated from India. The island was discovered by the Portuguese in 1505, and captured by the Dutch in the 17th century. In 1796 it was occupied by Great Britain and was made a Crown colony in 1802. The region was granted independence as a member state of the British Commonwealth in 1948. Ethnic violence broke out in the early 1980s, and continued unabated into 2000. From 1985 to the end of the 20th century 50,000 Sri Lankans lost their lives in the fighting. The population in 1960 showed the Buddhist Sinhalese population at 69 percent and the Hindu Tamil population at 23 percent Tamil; by 2000 the exodus of hundreds of thousands of Tamils had shifted those percentages to 75 and 15 percent respectively. Other ethnic groups include Ceylon and Indian Moors, Burghers (Eur-

Catholic Church in Galle, Sri Lanka. (©Arvind Garg/CORBIS)

asian descendants of Portuguese and Dutch colonists), Malays and Europeans.

Ecclesiastically, Sri Lanka has its Archdiocese in Colombo, with suffragans at the ancient city of Anuradhapura, as well as at Badulla, Chilaw, Galle, Jaffna, Kandy, Kurunegala, Mannar, Ratnapura and Trincomalee-Batticaloa. The island's minority Roman Catholic population is concentrated in the west coast of the island, with pockets in the central highlands, around east coast ports, and in the northern peninsula.

The following essay is divided into two parts. Part One covers the history of the Church in Sri Lanka from its beginnings through Vatican II. Part Two completes that history through 2000.

The Early Church

A center of Buddhist civilization from the 3rd century B.C., Sri Lanka was first evangelized by Portuguese Franciscans, but the mission was not systematically organized before 1543. Although most attention was given to the west coast across from India, a mission was established in the north at Mannar, although the King of Jaffna presumably massacred the 600 Christians there in 1544. St. Francis XAVIER sent a missionary to the island in 1544, but never visited there himself. The Franciscans had exclusive charge of Sri Lankan missions until the arrival of the Jesuits in 1602, and of the Dominicans and Augustinians soon after. By the middle of the 17th century there were 170 churches and 120 missionaries on the island.

Reformation, then Freedom. The arrival of the Dutch in 1658 led to serious difficulties for the Sri Lankan Church. Priests were immediately expelled, and the Dutch Reformed Church became the only recognized form of Christianity. No priest worked on the island until Joseph VAZ, a member of the Oratory of Goa, arrived secretly in 1687 to begin reorganizing the Church. Of those

ORATORIANS who followed him, the most outstanding was J. Gonçalvez (d .1742), who was a pioneer in the development of Christian literature in Singhalese and Tamil. By the end of the Dutch period (1796), Catholicism, though still officially prohibited, was tolerated in practice, and Catholics outnumbered Protestants on the island.

With the advent of British rule in 1802, anti-Catholic laws were abolished (1806), and Governor Thomas Maitland officially proclaimed freedom of conscience and worship. In 1809 there were 83,595 Catholics in the island, which the British named Ceylon. The Church continued to grow and in 1836 the Vicariate of Ceylon, with headquarters at Colombo, was separated from the Diocese of Cochin, on the Indian coast. The Oratorians, unable to supply priests for the growing mission, were obliged to ask for European missionaries. In 1848 the vicariate was divided, and the Silvestrine Benedictines were entrusted with the Vicariate of Jaffna. The Benedictines confined their activity to the Vicariate of Kandy after 1857, while the Oblates of Mary Immaculate assumed responsibility for Jaffna (1857) and Colombo (1883). The hierarchy was established in 1886 with COLOMBO as the metropolitan see and Jaffna and Kandy as suffragan sees. Dioceses were erected at Galle and Trincomalee (1893) and entrusted to the Jesuits, who at the same time founded a pontifical seminary at Kandy to serve both India and Sri Lanka. In 1939 the Diocese of Chilaw was erected and entrusted to secular clergy under the first Sri Lankan bishop. The great organizer of the Sri Lankan Church in the 19th century was C. E. Bonjean, the Oblate bishop of Colombo (1883–92), who established a network of parochial missions and Catholic schools, encouraged native vocations and recognized the value of a Catholic press. His aim was more a revival of faith among Catholics than an attempt at mass conversions.

The island achieved independence from Great Britain on Feb. 4, 1948, after suffering heavy bombing by the Japanese during World War II. At independence, despite racial tensions that had been growing in the region since the 1930s, president, Don Denanayeke established a balanced government. Over the next three decades, however, the Church's position became increasingly threatened by nationalism, a Buddhist revival and a series of leftist governments. In 1956 the Nationalist Freedom Party swept the elections, and Sinhalese was made the official language of government.

In the face of rising Sinhalese nationalism, attempts to appease the Tamil minority were met with communal rioting and the assassination of Prime Minister Bandaranaike in 1959. In 1961 Catholic primary schools were nationalized, and funding was withdrawn from all Church-run schools. Sisters were required to leave the hospitals in 1963. Foreign missionaries were prevented from entering the country, and those already in Sri Lanka were required to pay large fees to apply annually for residency status. Fortunately, the Church possessed a high percentage of native clergy; the Archbishop of Colombo, Cardinal Thomas Cooray, was Sri Lankan, as were his auxiliary and the bishops of Chilaw, Jaffna and Kandy. English-speaking Christians lost their jobs in the civil service and in the armed forces after an attempted coup in 1962 by military officers, among whom Catholics figured prominently.

Bibliography: F. DE QUEYROZ, *The Temporal and Spiritual Conquest of Ceylon,* tr. S. G. PERERA, 3 v. (Colombo 1930). S. G. PERERA, *The Jesuits in Ceylon in the XVI and XVII Centuries* (Madura, Ind. 1941). R. BOUDENS, *The Catholic Church in Ceylon under Dutch Rule* (Rome 1957). J. ROMMERSKIRCHEN, *Die Oblatenmissionen auf der Insel Ceylon* (Hünfeld, Ger. 1931). W. L. A. PETER, *Studies in Ceylon Church History* (Colombo 1963). H. HAAS, "Zur gegenwärtigen Lage der katholischen Kirche auf Ceylon," *Neue Zeitschrift für Missionswissenschaft,* 19.4 (1963) 300–311. *Bilan du Monde,* 2:210–215.

[R. BOUDENS]

Vatican II and Beyond

Sri Lanka's nationalist ruling party equated their victory in the parliamentary general election of 1960 with the supremacy of both the Sinhalese race and the Buddhist religion. This quickly translated into laws that favored the rural Sinhalese majority over the colonially favored Tamils and the minority English-speaking Christians. By the end of the 1960s the Church saw the erosion of its privileged colonial position and separate eurocentric religio-cultural identity, which it had protected and reproduced mainly through its educational institutions.

Influence of Vatican II. The teachings of Vatican II on INCULTURATION and the use of the vernacular, the role of the laity, interreligious dialogue and the social mission of the Church were received in Sri Lanka against a troubled ethnic and socio-economic background. With regard to clergy and religious, most sisters, priests and bishops were indigenous Sri Lankans, a result of the immigration restrictions in place on the island. After Vatican II new dioceses were erected in Anuradhapura, Mannar, Kurunegala and Badulla. Parish councils and various forums of clergy and laity at the diocesan level organized local church affairs. The first national diocesan synod was held in 1968.

In the spirit of Vatican II the Church attempted to Asianize itself and find a common identity with the rest of the nation. Despite efforts at inculturation and use of the Sinhal and Tamil vernaculars, the pervasive nationalism promoted by the ruling Sinhala nationalists caused the Church, composed mainly of Sinhalese and Tamils, to ultimately split along divisive communal lines.

The 1968 Pastoral Convention commissioned a report on the nation's deteriorating social and economic situation and suggested ways the Church could progress its spiritual and social mission. Many ideas, however, were slow to be implemented. The role and impact of the laity in Sri Lanka, first enhanced by the schools crisis, eventually found expression in the increased lay involvement in catechetical work, social projects and organized critical debate on the Church's organization, teachings and role in society. Dialogues with other Christian groups as well as with the island's non-Christian faiths, such as Buddhism, were stepped up.

In 1971 a failed insurrection led by a group of educated, unemployed and mainly rural Sinhalese youth in the south known as the Peoples Liberation Front (JVP), brought the social mission of the Church into sharp focus. While the majority of bishops called the youthful leaders of the JVP "misguided," some in the clergy and laity, supported by then bishop of Kandy, Leo Nanayakkara, saw the rebellion as a sign that the hierarchy was failing to respond to the needs of the times. A variety of social justice and dialogue groups were organized, among them the Center for Society and Religion, Satyodaya, Tulana Research Centre and the Janavabhodhi Kendraya. Bishop Nanayakkara also attempted to create new forms of pastoral life and priestly formation in the "experimental" new diocese at Badulla.

In the 1970s Catholic and other Christian groups formed throughout the mainly Hindi Tamil north to address the minority question. Social justice and dialogue groups in the predominantly Sinhalese south also addressed the question of rights for the Tamils.

Political Shift under New Constitution. A republican constitution was introduced in 1972, renaming the country and cutting all remaining ties with the British crown. A new government elected in 1977 set the country on a development policy driven by free market economics, and on Aug. 16, 1978 the constitution was altered to provide for an all-powerful executive presidency. Relations between the Sinhalese and the Tamil communities quickly deteriorated, resulting in a series of pogroms that reached an irreversible climax in 1983 when the violence, fanned by a group of Sinhala racists, became particularly intense. A longstanding, hitherto minority claim for a separate Tamil homeland in the north and east of the island found wide Tamil support, as both sides chose the military option. In the midst of the war between Tamil separatists—called the Liberation Tigers of Tamil Eelam (LTTE)—and the Sri Lankan government, the Church found itself divided on the race issue and the bishops' conference was unable to produce a unified response. A second JVP uprising (1989–91) in the south saw atrocities and human rights violations committed by both the state and the JVP. The Church was paralyzed with silence as the violence escalated, leaving it to the members of radical Christian and interreligious groups to raise protests, demand justice and openly criticize both sides, often at risk to their own lives.

Other groups, formed within the Catholic, Anglican and Methodist churches in the mid-1970s, called for radical social, political and spiritual solutions to the country's serious ethnic and socio-economic problems. They argued that the social teachings of Vatican II were not taken far enough in Sri Lanka. In calling for theological renewal, they explored interreligious relations and dialogue with other ideologies. Creative new contextual theologies and liturgical practices emerged from this radical fringe of the Church based mainly around an Asian perspective on the theology of liberation and dialogue with Buddhism and Hinduism.

Into the 21st Century. A change of government occurred in 1994 when, after 17 years of rule by the United National Party, the coalition People's Alliance, led by the Freedom Party, was elected into office. While the new government promised a negotiated settlement of the Tamil issue and curtailment of the excesses of the free market, it was unable to end racial violence, and by 1995 the violence had escalated. A state of emergency was declared in Sri Lanka in 1996, and the violence caused many Tamil to flee to surrounding areas.

A minority faith within a predominately Buddhist nation, the majority of Sri Lankan Catholics remained faithful to the teachings of the Church with regard to doctrine, liturgy, church organization and the living of a Catholic life in a secular or non-Christian culture, although by the late 1990s they were forced to confront the possibility of legalized abortion due to pending government legislation. In the wider society, fringe groups, though small in number, were influential, some pushing for a return to the devotion and ritual of a pre-Vatican II Catholicism. The charismatic Pubuduwa movement, founded in 1973, retained a large lay following from all sectors of the Church. Initially a purely spiritual movement with no interest in politics, it became active in human rights and economic issues after 1982, was critical of clericalism, showed itself to be significantly different from other interdenominational lay groups like the Christian Workers Fellowship (CWF), a worker-led, church-related ecumenical movement founded in 1958 with a strong interreligious and socialist flavor.

In 2000 there were 384 active parishes in Sri Lanka, with 568 diocesan and 308 religious priests. In addition,

246 brothers and 2,237 sisters worked in various capacities. Religious active on the island included the indigenous Rosarians, founded by P. T. Thomas, OMI, in 1928, and the Rosarian nuns, founded in 1950. The Young Christian Workers and the LEGION OF MARY were also active in the towns. A Catholic weekly, *The Ceylon Catholic Messenger,* published in Sinhalese and Tamil as well as in English, represented mainstream church views. A Catholic college, the Catholic University College, was located in Colombo. Catholic schools continued to provide an alternative to the religious education mandatory in state-run public schools, where the parent's choice of faith was presented in an academic, rather than spiritual manner.

The Catholic Bishops' Conference took a vocal role in denouncing the racial war in their country, issuing numerous statements in response to the continued bombings, massacres and other acts of terrorism, including a 1999 attack by the LTTE of a church in Madhu that resulted in nearly 100 casualties. The Holy See supported the bishops' efforts to stop the violence in Sri Lanka. In August of 1996, one year after his visit to Sri Lanka to beatify the Indian-born priest Joseph Vaz, "Apostle of Ceylon," Pope John Paul II noted: "Only dialogue can safeguard inviolable human rights, including the legitimate rights of minorities." Hope for a peaceful resolution grew stronger in May of 2001 when the government announced an agreement reached with LTTE leaders that would establish peace talks, although a cease-fire was not implemented.

Bibliography: U. DORNBERG, *Searching through the Crisis* (Colombo 1992). K. MALALGODA, *Buddhism in Sinhalese Society* (Berkeley 1976). F. HOUTART, *Summary of the Survey of the Catholic Church in Ceylon* (Colombo 1971); *Attitudes toward Development among Catholics in Sri Lanka* (Colombo 1980). E. HARRIS, *Crisis, Competition, and Conversion: The British Encounter with Buddhism in 19th-Century Sri Lanka* (Colombo 1993). CENTRE FOR SOCIETY AND RELIGION, *Statements of the Catholic Church in Sri Lanka 1988* (Colombo 1989).

[R. CRUSZ/EDS.]

STABAT MATER

A hymn that was traditionally sung during Lent. It was also prescribed as a SEQUENCE for the Feast of Our Lady of Sorrows. It was suppressed at the Council of Trent, but was restored to the Mass in 1727. This venerable poem is probably of 13th-century origin, but its authorship is attributed variously to St. BONAVENTURE, JACOPONE DA TODI, and even to Pope INNOCENT II, who lived a century earlier. A notable number of scholars point to Da Todi as author, since two 14th-century codices and the 1495 edition (Brescia) of the sequence attribute it to him. While it cannot be denied that the composition's general tone and sentimentality parallel that of Da Todi's poems, strictly stylistic comparisons yield uncertain and even disputable results. Recent scholars, such as M. Casella and L. Russo, are not impressed by the arguments in favor of Jacopone's authorship.

The chant setting uses the simplest of melodic lines, applied in strophic fashion with the same tune for each single versicle. Although early sequences, devised as they were to conform to the Jubilus of a preexistent alleluia, were unrhymed and of irregular meter, the *Stabat Mater,* as a late sequence, evidences the regular meter (most often trochaic) and more intricate rhyme scheme that most scholars date from the 12th century. Again, like all true sequences, the poem is cast in double versicles, or couplets. The rhyme scheme of the first couplet, AAB-CCB, is duplicated in each of the nine subsequent couplets:

> Stabat Mater dolorosa/ Juxta crucem
> lacrimosa/ Dum pendebat Filius.
> Cuius animam gementem/ Contristatam et
> dolentem/ Pertransivit gladius.

The end rhyme of the versicles is supplemented by additional rhymes between the first two segments of each versicle.

Bibliography: F. J. E. RABY, *A History of Christian-Latin Poetry from the Beginnings to the Close of the Middle Ages* (Oxford 1953) 436–442. G. REESE, *Music in the Middle Ages* (New York 1940). G. REESE, *Music in the Renaissance* (New York 1959).

[L. E. CUYLER]

STAFFORD, JOHN

Archbishop of Canterbury, chancellor of England; d. Maidstone, Kent, England, May 25, 1452. He was the natural son of Sir Humphrey Stafford of Southwick Court, Wiltshire. A doctor of Canon Law and a protégé of Abp. Henry CHICHELE, he was advocate in the court of ARCHES (1414) and auditor of causes (1419). Like Chichele, he became chancellor of Salisbury (1420) after being archdeacon. He was made dean of Wells (1423), then bishop of BATH AND WELLS (1424). He was keeper of the privy seal (1421–22), treasurer (December 1422 to 1426), and chancellor of England during the most difficult period of the Lancastrian regime (1432–50). A number of diplomatic commissions fell to him: to France (1419), Brittany (1420), and Scotland (for the release of James I in 1423). He accompanied King Henry VI to France in 1430 and attended him at his coronation in Paris (1436). He supported Henry BEAUFORT and later the unpopular William de la Pole, Earl of Suffolk. Still, Stafford's care and moderation as chancellor and the high opinion formed of him as a judge were sufficient to outweigh all criticism when he was appointed (Aug. 1, 1450) a member of the commission of *oyer* and *terminer* after Cade's rebellion. Tito Livio of Forli extolled Stafford's beneficence and sympathy in a poem; on the other hand, Stafford was detested by Thomas Gascoigne, who charged him with having illegitimate offspring by a nun. The best testimonial to Stafford was in the two letters written by Chichele to Henry VI and to Pope EUGENE IV in 1442, recommending him for the archbishopric of Canterbury, *ut patrem maxime meritum*, on grounds that in administering justice to Henry's subjects, he "had emerged greatly loved of all" *(plurimum dilectus evaserit)*. The pope assented (1443), but in 1445–46 the new archbishop had the task of defending the country from the attempt of the pope to enforce a crusading tenth against the Turks and of making it clear that the termination of the French War had—for the English Council—priority over the defense of Constantinople and the security of the Mediterranean. He was successful in this, his tact avoiding strictures from Rome such as had fallen upon his master, Chichele.

Bibliography: Stafford's Canterbury Register is in the Lambeth Palace Library. *The Register of John Stafford, Bishop of Bath and Wells*, 1425–1443, ed. T. S. HOLMES, 2 v. (Somerset Record Soc. 31–32; 1915–16). *The Register of Nicholas Bubwith, Bishop of Bath and Wells*, 1407–1424, ed. T. S. HOLMES, 2 v. (*ibid.* 29–30; 1914). J. H. RAMSAY, *Lancaster and York*, 2 v. (Oxford 1892). E. F. JACOB, "Archbishop J. Stafford," *Transcripts of the Royal Historical Society ser.* 5, v.12 (1962) 1–23. A. B. EMDEN, *A Biographical Register of the University of Oxford to A.D. 1500*, 1750–52.

[E. F. JACOB]

STAGEL, ELSBETH (ELBETHE)

Dominican nun, chronicler, and spiritual daughter of Bl. Henry Suso; b. *c.* 1300; d. Töss, Switzerland, 1360. She entered the Dominican monastery of Töss at an early age and became its first chronicler. Using data gathered from the archives and from older sisters, she wrote the biographies of about 40 sisters who had lived in the convent from its founding in 1233 until 1340. Elbethe ardently sought perfection and sought help in the works of mystical writers. Finding the works of John Tauler too difficult for a beginner, she wrote to Suso for direction. To console her in an illness he revealed his own mystical experiences, which, without his knowing it, she wrote down from memory. These memoirs and their correspondence form the bulk of Suso's *Life* and *Book of Letters.* Their relationship is explained in the prologue and in Part II of the *Life.* She is remembered not only for her saintly life but especially for the influence she exerted on Suso, and for giving to the world the experiences of that renowned German mystic.

Bibliography: J. ANCELET-HUSTACHE, *La Vie mystique d'un monastère de Dominicaines au moyen âge* (Paris 1928). H. SUSO, *The Exemplar,* tr. A. EDWARD, 2 v. (Dubuque 1962).

[C. HAHN]

STAINED GLASS

To understand the nature of this art one needs to consider the material components of the stained-glass window and the various ways in which these are assembled; the architectural factors that govern the luminosity of stained glass and the resources of the medium for exploiting different degrees of luminosity; and the reasons for the singularly entrancing effect of 12th- and 13th-century stained glass. From the time of its origin to the present day the art of stained glass has undergone an interesting evolution.

Fabric of the Stained-glass Window. The art of making stained glass is not now and probably never was—for the designer, painter, or fabricator of stained-glass windows—essentially an art of coloring or literally staining glass. The technique of making colored glass is one thing, and the art of designing and making stained-glass windows out of such glass is quite another. The two skills stand in exactly the same relation as do the manufacture of oil paints and the art of easel painting.

Like nearly all other kinds of glass, stained glass is colored by the addition of various metal oxides to its basic ingredients while the glass is in a molten state. The glass is then made into sheets approximately 20 by 30 inches in size by an ancient technique that gives it very much the appearance of medieval glass. Hence its common trade name "antique" glass. The glassblower gathers an amount of molten glass on the end of a blowpipe and blows a bubble, which he manipulates into the shape of a bottle. He next cuts the end off the bottle, slits the remaining cylinder down one side, and then places the glass into an annealing oven, where it is gently flattened into a sheet. All glass made in this way is transparent and colored throughout with one basic color. Because it varies slightly in thickness, however, its color will often vary in depth, adding greatly to the beauty of the glass.

The basic steps in the making of a typical 13th-century stained-glass panel, "The Prophet Ezekiel," are as follows: From the design, or cartoon, a pattern is made, showing the exact shapes and sizes of the pieces of glass to be cut, and indicating the color for each piece, namely, *R* for ruby, *W* for white, and so on. A piece of glass of the proper color is selected for each area and cut to shape with a small interval of space between it and all adjacent pieces to allow for the leading. The details of the design—features, drapery, or whatever—are then ''traced,'' often literally, onto the various pieces of glass with a dense, colorless enamel consisting of oxides and ground glass and mixed with a purely temporary aqueous glue binder, such as gum arabic. This paint can be applied either opaquely or in thin films so as to overlay the basic color of the glass with a purely tonal shading. While much of the shading has disappeared from the earliest windows or merged with the patina on the glass, it can be clearly seen in the very early and unusually well-preserved ''Head of Christ'' from Wissembourg. After the pieces are painted they are placed in a kiln and fired at a temperature that is not high enough to melt the glass but high enough to cause the glass paint to vitrify and fuse to its surface. When all the glass has been selected, cut, painted where necessary, and fired, it is assembled with flexible preformed strips of lead. These have an ''H'' cross section with grooves on either side to take the glass. They are fitted around all the pieces, and the joints are soldered, first on one side of the panel, then on the other. The panel is then waterproofed by scrubbing or pressing a putty compound under the leads. It is then completed and ready for installation in a window.

All but the very smallest stained-glass windows must, for purely structural reasons, be made in several sections and installed in some kind of frame or armature from which they will derive sufficient rigidity to withstand the pressures of wind and their own cumulative weight from top to bottom. This frame, far from being a mere structural necessity, has always been exploited by the most competent designers as a transitional link between the purely internal, pictorial, or ornamental composition of the window itself and the larger rhythms of its architectural setting. As will be seen below, the evolution of the stained-glass armature is one of the basic distinguishing characteristics of the art from century to century.

In the 13th century it was true without exception that each piece of glass consisted of but one basic color, so that each change of color in the image could be effected only by the introduction of another piece of glass of the second color and a line of lead between it and the first color. The skill with which the artisans of the period incorporated this leading into their designs is apparent when one compares almost any medieval window with a typical panel of the 16th century, e.g., the ''Triumph of David,'' from the Abbey of Marienwald; but since this is essentially a problem of style, it is taken up in a later section of the article.

Two ways of modifying the color of a single piece of glass were discovered in the later Middle Ages. First,

Stained glass windows depicting life of Thomas Becket, including scenes with King Henry II, North Aisle, Trinity Chapel, Canterbury Cathedral, Canterbury, England. (©Angelo Hornak/CORBIS)

in the 14th century it was discovered that glass could in fact be stained one color, yellow, with silver salts applied and fired like the vitreous glass paint already in use. Then in the 15th century two processes, flashing and abrasion, were combined to create another technique. Flashed glass is glass consisting of a basic color, usually somewhat light, upon which a thin film of a stronger color has been superimposed during the process of its manufacture. The glassblower creates it dipping his first bubble of glass into a second color before blowing the bottle from which the sheet of glass is made. From earliest times ruby glass had to be made in this manner because of the density of its coloring agent—hence the famous ''streaky'' rubies of the 12th- and 13th-century windows, which actually consist of several alternate layers of ruby and white. By grinding away parts of the flashed surface color it is possible to create patterns of the two colors, the flash and the base color, on a single piece of glass, which, moreover, can also be stained yellow and painted with tones and lines of the glass paint already described. In the 19th century the laborious technique of removing flashed colors by abrasion gave way to the much superior technique of etching them away with hydrofluoric acid. Except for this late refinement all of the practicable techniques of color

A craftsman makes the cartoons or original designs for stained glass windows to be placed in a Catholic church. (©Hulton Getty/ Liaison Agency)

manipulation now known were perfected in the Middle Ages. The most significant 20th-century contribution to the craft was the development of two new materials that make possible the assembly of stained-glass panels without leads: slab glass and epoxy resin.

If instead of being blown into sheets of antique glass in the traditional manner (sheets that usually vary in thickness from one-eighth to three-sixteenths of an inch), glass is cast in slabs more nearly a full inch in thickness, it becomes almost another material—a rocklike, jewellike substance that can be chipped and faceted and cast into panels with cement. Since a panel made in this way is actually a piece of masonry itself, it readily takes its place in the masonry wall as a very congenial and substantial part of it.

While epoxy resin is sometimes used as a binder in slab glass and concrete windows in lieu of lime, still another, more radical, use is made of the glue. Pieces of antique glass are cut, painted, and fired exactly as if they were to be leaded; but instead of being joined by leads, the pieces are glued to a sheet of plate glass with a clear variety of the resin. This provides them with a completely invisible support. Not only is the need for an opaque structural lead or concrete element within the stained-glass panel eliminated, but it is possible also to make the individual sections of an epoxy window several times as large as those of the leaded or slab glass window. The significance of this technique is still more of a promise than an actuality; but there is every indication that, just as slab glass has extended the range of the medium in the direction of massiveness, this technique will be used to create far lighter and more evanescent windows than have ever been technically possible heretofore. The architectural significance of these new techniques will become apparent in the next section.

Chartres Cathedral, rosette and stained glass window. (Corbis)

Luminosity. Light is a uniquely pervasive and dynamic force in man's life. Since time immemorial the polarity of light and darkness has been almost universally felt and consciously accepted as a reflection of life versus death, awareness versus ignorance—as a natural counterpart of good versus evil, however these were culturally defined. Delight, dread; enlightenment, superstition; clarity, obscurity; brilliance, dullness—the complexities of man's attraction to light are so mingled that the expression of them cannot be affected by a truism. Nevertheless even the truism enables one to understand why stained glass, properly designed to exploit light in its particular architectural setting, can be so powerful an art form.

The normal range of light values within a stained-glass window is between 10 and 15 times as great as the range possible in the most vigorous opaque painting; in absolute brightness the white or clear glass in a stained-glass window is not uncommonly as much as 125 times as bright as even a white wall adjacent to it.

The apparent brightness of a stained-glass window is governed not by its absolute brightness, however, but by the difference between the amount of light that comes through it from the outside and the amount of light, natural or artificial, that strikes its inner surfaces. When indoors, one's eyes are adjusted not to the full intensity of daylight but to the general level of illumination indoors. In a typical 12th-century church, where the window openings are generally quite small and widely spaced, the basic interior light level, even with clear or unglazed windows, is quite low. The pupils of one's eyes must dilate considerably for him to see anything at all. The daylight that comes through its windows therefore appears brighter to the eye than it ever does out of doors or in a lighter interior. The apparent brightness of any window opening varies inversely with the light level inside it; and this light level is determined by the design of the space itself, by the relative amount of its wall surface opened up in order to admit light. It is the architect, therefore, more than the artist, who actually determines how luminous a stained-glass window can be. The darker the space he creates, the more brilliant a light source he creates for stained glass; the lighter the space, the more muted the light source will be.

Neither of these situations is inherently better than the other; but the failure to grasp the necessary relation between dark interiors and colors dense enough to avoid harsh, overbrilliant effects on the one hand, and light interiors and colors light enough not to become dull and murky on the other, might almost be called the lost art of stained glass. Contrary to popular belief, there is no color in medieval glass that glassmakers have not been able to match very closely for at least 100 years. As long ago as 1868 Viollet-le-Duc, restoring the French cathedrals, could claim that his workmen had "completed ancient windows with such a perfection of imitation that one cannot distinguish the restorations from the old parts." There is no question that the artists and architects of the Middle Ages understood this basic relation of dark-to-dark and light–to-light, for it is only where one finds a later window inserted into an earlier space, for example in the 15th-century Vendome Chapel in the 13th-century nave of Chartres, that one finds a medieval window out of key with its setting.

Given the brilliant, even harsh light created by the dark interiors of the 12th and 13th centuries, the glassmen of the time very logically worked with a schema of deep, saturated colors or, where only white glass could be afforded, painted the glass with a fine overall pattern of "grisaille" that breaks up and subdues the light. Later, as the walls of the high and late Gothic churches were opened up to admit more and more light, the point was soon reached where the difference between the outside and inside light levels was no longer great enough to illuminate fully the ruby-and-blue windows of the earlier churches. The artists of the 14th and 15th centuries were therefore obliged to work out a viable palette of lighter colors, colors that needed less light to bring them to life; it was the English who, utilizing yellow stain and white glass to maximum advantage, evolved in the 15th century the gold-and-silver windows, which are the final and logical major development in medieval stained glass.

It is obvious from the foregoing that what the newly developed techniques of slab glass and transparent epoxy have done is to extend the range of light controls within the medium, at the disposal of the artist, in both directions. Stained glass is thus technically a far more versatile art now than it ever was in the past.

Stained Glass of the 12th and 13th Centuries. To grasp what an overwhelming effect the stained glass of the 12th and 13th centuries must have had in its day, one has to visualize it in the context of a largely agrarian world dominated not by the paints, inks and dyes, electric lights, and neon signs of urban industrialized civilization, but rather by homespun and weathered wood, the greens and browns of the countryside. It was a world that had, in the words of Aldous Huxley, "a passionate thirst for bright, pure colors," and these the stained-glass windows in the early churches provided in an altogether unprecedented richness and abundance. It is evident also that for men such as Abbot Suger of Saint-Denis the splendor of stained glass must have had a significance over and above that of its particular subject matter. In his writings there are passages such as the following: "When—out of my delight in the beauty of the house of God—the loveliness of the many-colored stones has called me away from external cares, and worthy meditation has induced me to reflect, transferring that which is material to that which is immaterial, on the diversity of the sacred virtues: then it seems to me that I see myself dwelling, as it were, in some strange region of the universe which neither exists entirely in the slime of the earth nor entirely in the purity of Heaven; and that, by the grace of God, I can be transported from this inferior to that higher world in an anagogical manner.''

To account for the continuing hold of these magnificent works on even the most casual visitor to the great cathedrals requires some analysis of their form as well as of their color and their luminosity. The predominant colors in them, ruby and blue, are deployed in a distinctive and powerfully affective way that can be almost transporting in itself: each of the principal colors keeps shifting its status in the composition of the windows from figure to ground or ground to figure in relation to the other. Scenes with blue backgrounds, for example, alternate with border areas in which figurative blue ornamental motifs are set off against a ruby background; and the artist has contrived to place bits of figurative blue or ruby adjacent to background blue or ruby. The result is an interlaced pattern of colors that one is forced to keep interpreting and reinterpreting from point to point and that never resolves into any one fixed and final form.

This is but one of the seemingly endless devices that the artisans of the time hit upon to imbue each part of their work with the quality of its opposite, and it was the indispensable formal device for linking their stained-glass windows with the larger architectural settings in which they were placed. Not only are the narrative medallions in 13th-century windows deployed ornamentally in the windows, but the armatures that support the glass reflect the adjacent structural order of the wall; also, the lyricism of the windows is echoed in the detailing of the stonework that frames them. To continue the sequence, the sculpture of the portals, though endlessly subtle in detail, is grouped architecturally, whereas the towers of the cathedrals are treated sculpturally; the manifold variety of silhouettes of the cathedral is resolved in its overall monumentality; and it stands, for all its complexity, as a landmark on the horizon.

Evolution of Stained Glass. The art of stained glass as it is now known begins with the five ''Prophet'' windows in the clerestory of Augsburg cathedral, thought to be the work of the monks of Tegernsee in the year 1065. Rigidly frontal, these windows seem to derive not only from the Italo-Byzantine mosaics of Rome, Venice, and Ravenna, but in drawing and to some extent color, from the Celtic manuscripts of St. GALL in Switzerland. They are predominantly ruby, green, yellow, and wine-colored, with only a relatively small amount of pale blue in them, and are the only existing windows that predate the ruby-and-blue color scheme that was practically universal during the 12th and 13th centuries.

The most complete ensemble of 12th-century windows extant are those in the west façade of the cathedral of Chartres, dating from midcentury. Like the famous ''La Belle Verriere'' in the south aisle of the cathedral and the surviving glass of this period in Bourges and elsewhere, these windows are dominated by an incredibly luminous blue, against which are played ruby and a deep rose color and secondary accents of white, green, yellow, and a ruddy flesh tint. The windows were painted in the vigorous calligraphic manner of the Wissembourg ''Head of Christ.'' The iron armatures had not yet become an actively ornamental device but were simply employed to divide the windows into panel-sized squares or rectangles. Within these squares, however, the individual episodes in a narrative window are usually framed by exuberantly ornamented borders in which the figure-ground status of the major colors is manipulated in the manner already described.

The 13th century saw the ruby and blue windows brought to their ultimate refinement. The wrought-iron armatures of the windows became an actively ornamental device in their own right, dividing the windows first into simple circular medallions, as in the very early example from Canterbury, and later into very handsome patterns of alternating or interlaced circles, lozenges, and quatrefoils. The 13th-century blue is generally a deeper, graver blue than that of the 12th century, although it is still a very saturated color; and the development of distinctive secondary color schemes within the basic ruby and blue is present. Thus, for example, in the nave of Chartres one window is largely green, white, and wine-colored in its secondary colors, whereas the next one emphasizes a smoky yellow and white, and so on.

After the heroic scale and rigorous order of the 12th and 13th centuries came the langorous windows of the 14th century. The window openings were subdivided into lancets and tracery of stone rather than ornamental ironwork, and the international ruby and blue color scheme gave way to a range of alternate schemes that took on increasingly regional characteristics as the century progressed, particularly after the hiatus caused by the Black Death (1350). Nearly everywhere there is more use of white, partially in order to let more light into the churches; partly to take advantage of the newly discovered technique of yellow staining; perhaps also because of a shortage of ruby and blue glass; and probably in simple reaction to a mood and style that had dominated the art for at least five or six generations. The figures and figure compositions became generally much larger and less complex than in the earlier medallion windows, and they were framed in canopies, which sometimes, as in Gloucester, became as elaborate as the figures themselves. The touchstone of 14th-century stained glass is the ''Gothic sway'' in the stance of its figures and in the simple flow of their garb, as in the detail from a choir window, Koenigsfelden.

By the end of the 14th century the die was cast. French stained glass, which had dominated the field for more than two centuries, began to slip into a hard, joyless competence from which it did not recover. German, Austrian, and Swiss stained glass was both retrospective, in its retention of the medallion composition and diapered backgrounds of the 13th century, and at the same time advanced, in adopting certain perspective devices from the proto-Renaissance art of Italy. For the 15th century, therefore, it is to England that one turns in order to follow the most purely medieval, and most genuinely creative, evolution of the art for another 100 years.

If the stained glass of the 13th century may be called a cathedral art because of its jewel-like richness and overall formality, that of the 15th century seems to be essentially an art of chapels and of parish churches, less architectonic, more intimate, and more concerned with the expression of human feeling. In the words of Émile Mâle, ''the high Middle Ages rarely chose to depict any but the triumphant Christ; the thirteenth century found in the teaching Christ the subject for its greatest works; the fifteenth century saw in God the Man of Sorrows. The Passion had always been at the center of the Christian faith, but formerly the death of Christ had been a dogma that addressed itself to the intellect. Now it was a moving image that spoke to the heart.'' There was a return in the windows of Norfolk and York to the depiction of such elaborate group subjects as the ''Last Supper'' and the ''Entry into Jerusalem,'' and an increasing interest in the depiction of individual rather than generalized types; the ruddy flesh tint of earlier periods was abandoned in favor of a pure white, which gives the otherwise intimate figures a curious spectral quality. In the south of England the treatment of the figure remained somewhat more hieratic, as in the ''Virgin and Child'' in the east window of Merton College Chapel, Oxford, and the portraits of Edward IV and his consort in Canterbury; the essentially linear style had already partially given way to an extremely sensitive tonal modeling. But beyond such works as these neither the medieval conception of man nor the art of stained glass could be extended.

The conquest of naturalism, the development of easel painting to the level of a fine art, and the subjugation of all other media except sculpture to the role of minor arts were the proud, and at the same time tragic, achievements of the next two centuries. There was in 16th-century stained glass at its best a kind of robust athleticism; at its worst, an indifferent aping of Raphael and Michelangelo. The leading was no longer treated as an integral part of the design but was regarded as nothing but a structurally necessary evil. The more purely pictorial the design became, the more alien and obtrusive the leading became, overemphasizing in haphazard fashion certain contours of the subject matter and altogether abandoning others, as can be seen in the ''Triumph of David.'' The smoothly rendered modeling of the effects of light and shade gave the glass a dull parchment-like appearance; and the ability to make larger and flatter, more evenly colored, and less textured pieces of glass than in the Middle Ages was also exploited to the detriment of the art. This, along with the introduction of translucent colored enamels, finally reduced the art to such travesties as Sir Joshua Reynolds's ''Virtues'' in the New College Chapel, Oxford. In these windows Reynolds got rid of the leads completely, only to have his armatures become ''prison bars,'' which, when they deign to bend with a knee or elbow, seem positively fatuous.

From the mid-16th century until the mid-19th century there was scarcely a thing in stained glass that was not slavishly derived from easel painting or the graphic arts, little that had not been far more easily and excellently achieved in these other media. The revival of the art that has since taken place may be divided into four distinct though overlapping phases.

First, there was the rediscovery, analysis, and restoration of the ancient windows, which may be placed roughly in the three decades from 1840 to 1870. In England Charles Winston, a lawyer by profession, became enamored with medieval stained glass and proceeded during the 1840s and 1850s to make a most thorough study of the succeeding styles, painting techniques, and types of glass used in English windows. From this labor of love came two still valuable books, his *Hints on Glass Painting,* which he published anonymously in 1847, and his *Memoirs,* which were published posthumously in 1865 (see bibliog.). Winston was among the first to recognize how inadequate the glass of the early 19th century was for stained-glass windows, and it was largely through his efforts in England that the manufacture of antique glass was revived. In France, Eugène Viollet-le-Duc supervised the restoration of several of France's greatest medieval structures, including Notre Dame in Paris, and published in 1868, in the ninth volume of his monumental *Dictionnaire raisonné de l'architecture française,* an article on stained glass that emphatically demonstrates the ''logic'' of medieval stained glass. Even though the theories in ''Vitrail'' have since come under criticism (see bibliog.), there is no question about the validity and timeliness of Viollet-le-Duc's essential point: ''Different processes, different conditions, different branches of art. . . . In an opaque painting the radiation of the colors is absolutely under the control of the painter, who . . . can diminish or augment it at will. The radiation of transparent colors in glass cannot be thus modified by the artist whose whole talent consists in profiting by it to work out a harmonic scheme on a single plane, like a rug.''

Second, there was an increasing effort on the part of the makers of stained-glass windows to recapture some of the qualities of medieval stained glass, which began at about the same time and resulted, by the 1870s and 1880s, in the ability of the better studios to turn out technically competent but almost universally lifeless and sentimental neo-13th-, 15th-, and even 16th-century windows. This movement flourished with the great wave of architectural revivals that began in the Victorian period and was finally broken only by the Great Depression of the 1930s. The names of this movement are less the names of individual designers than of the studios that were founded or enlarged to meet the great demand for such stained glass—firms more or less competent in their ability to imitate the windows of earlier periods, more or less motivated by purely commercial interests.

Third, there was the periodic effort on the part of artists not initially trained as stained-glass designers to free the art from its bondage to historical styles and ineffectual variations on historical styles. This effort began very largely with two men, William Morris and Sir Edward Burne-Jones, who met as undergraduates at Oxford in 1853 and formed a lasting alliance based upon a common philosophy of art. Within the aesthetic limits of the pre-Raphaelite movement, Morris, with Burne-Jones as his chief designer, largely succeeded during the 1870s and 1880s in realizing his objectives. In the judgment of Sir Herbert Read, ''his selection of colours is admirable, and he was not afraid of using colours to achieve effects unknown to previous ages. In the use of leads to emphasize design he is masterly, and we must again go back to the 13th century for an adequate comparison.''

In America the artists John LaFarge and Louis Comfort Tiffany were leaders a generation later in the development of a distinctively American style, using an iridescent, milky, ''opalescent'' glass—a style that, especially in the case of Tiffany, was *art nouveau* in character and was employed not only in church windows but in secular settings of every conceivable kind. Tiffany was that rare combination, the consummate craftsman and the born entrepreneur, and he was among the comparatively few American artists of his time to achieve international recognition.

In Germany in the 1920s Jan Thorn-Prikker, Karl Schmidt-Rottluff, and Josef Albers (later moved to the U.S.); in Holland Joep Nicolas; and in Ireland Erie Hone began to create work of integrity; but the generally conservative architecture of that decade, followed by the worldwide Depression of the 1930s and then by World War II, all conspired to postpone the further development of stained glass for another 25 years.

The postwar period provided the indispensable conditions for the fourth and final phase in the revival of stained glass as a living art form: an experimental architecture capable of producing two such completely opposite yet equally masterful and original settings for stained glass as Dominikus Böhm's Church of Maria Königin in Cologne and Le Corbusier's Notre Dame du Haut in Ronchamp; the need to build buildings of every kind on an unprecedented scale; the willingness and ability of outstanding painters such as Fernand Léger, Henri Matisse, and Alfred Manessier to create stained-glass windows conceived purely in terms of the medium; and finally, talented younger men turning to stained glass as their principal medium of expression.

To achieve ''a design of imaginative worth free from the cramping influence (and the mere imaginative insufficiency) of the craftsman, and a technical execution of this design free from the craft amateurishness of the imaginative artist'' (Sir Herbert Read) was the goal that William Morris set for himself in mid-19th century; this goal has never been more achievable than in the mid-20th century.

Bibliography: THEOPHILUS, called also RUGERUS, *On Divers Arts: The Treatise of Theophilus,* ed. and tr. J. G. HAWTHORNE and C. S. SMITH (Chicago 1963), thought to have been written between 1110 and 1140, contains the most complete medieval description of stained-glass techniques. C. WINSTON, *An Inquiry into the Difference of Style Observable in Ancient Glass Paintings, Especially in England: With Hints on Glass Painting* (Oxford, Eng. 1847); *Memoirs Illustrative of the Art of Glass-Painting* (London 1865). E. VIOLLET-LE-DUC, ''Vitrail,'' *Dictionnaire raisonné de l'architecture française du XIe au XVIe siècle,* 10 v. (Paris 1854–68) 9:373–462, pub. serially in Eng. in *Stained Glass* 26–28 (1931–32). C. W. WHALL, *Stained Glass Work* (London 1931), still the most complete craft manual in Eng. C. J. CONNICK, *Adventures in Light and Color* (New York 1937), lavish but dated elaboration on the theories of Viollet-Le-Duc, with some excellent color and light studies of medieval windows. J. R. JOHNSON, *The Radiance of Chartres* (New York 1965). R. SOWERS, *Stained Glass: An Architectural Art* (New York 1965), more detailed exposition of material contained in first three sections of this article, illustrates approximately 50 French, German, and American windows created since 1955. M. AUBERT et al., *Le Vitrail françis* (Paris 1958). J. BAKER and A. LAMMER, *English Stained Glass* (New York 1960). G. MARCHINI, *Italian Stained Glass Windows* (New York 1956). H. WENTZEL, *Meisterwerke der Glasmalerei* (Berlin 1954).

[R. SOWERS]

STANBROOK ABBEY

Called also Our Lady of Consolation, of Benedictine nuns; in Worcester, England. In 1625 in Cambrai, Flanders, nine English ladies, who included three descendants of St. Thomas MORE and kinswomen of other English martyrs, founded the abbey, which has remained under the jurisdiction of the English Black Monks. The teachings of D. A. BAKER, for nine years spiritual director of the community, were preserved thanks to the nuns' copyist work. Dispossessed by the French Revolution in 1793, the community spent 18 months in prison in Compiègne, where four of them died. The others were released in April 1795. They returned to England penniless and clad in the secular attire of their fellow prisoners, the Carmelite martyrs of COMPIÈGNE. After various wanderings they settled in 1838 in Stanbrook, where by 1880 they had built a monastery and restored full monastic observance with papal enclosure. In 1911 three Brazilians trained and professed at Stanbrook, established the Benedictine Santa Maria in São Paulo, from which several daughterhouses have been founded in South America.

Bibliography: *In a Great Tradition: Tribute to Dame Laurentia McLachlan by the Benedictines of Stanbrook* (New York 1956). T. B. SNOW, comp., *Obit Book of the English Benedictines from 1600 to 1912,* ed. H. N. BIRT (Edinburgh 1913). C. HEYWOOD, ''Records of the Abbey of Our Lady of Consolation at Cambrai, 1620–1793,'' ed. J. GILLOW, *Publications of the Catholic Record Society* 13 (Miscellanea 8; 1913) 1–85. *Stanbrook Abbey: A Sketch of Its History 1625–1925,* by a nun of the same abbey. (London 1925).

[F. CORRIGAN]

STANGASSINGER, KASPAR, BL.

Also called Gaspar or Caspar; Redemptorist priest and teacher; b. Unterkälberstein (near Berchtesgaden), Bavaria, Germany, Jan. 12, 1871; d. Gars am Inn, Upper Bavaria, Sept. 26, 1899. Stangassinger was the second of 16 children of a farmer who owned a stone quarry and participated in local politics. At school in Freising he encountered difficulties in his studies, but his vocation to the priesthood remained strong. During summer vacations he organized friends for group religious activities: Mass, pilgrimages, and common prayer. He began his theological studies in the diocesan seminary at Freising, but he transferred to the Redemptorist seminary at Gars because of his desire to become a missionary. He was ordained in Regensburg (Germany) on June 16, 1895. Although he preferred missionary work, out of obedience he dedicated himself wholeheartedly to his assignment as vice-director of the minor seminary of Dürrnburg (near Hallein) where he taught and provided spiritual direction to his students. On weekends, he served nearby parishes, preparing his homilies in front of the Blessed Sacrament and often preaching on the consolation available in the Eucharist. In 1899 (age 28), he was appointed director of the order's new seminary in Gars. Shortly after the opening of the school year, he died of peritonitis.

When his cause for canonization was opened in 1935, his body was translated to the side chapel of the church of Gars. During the beatification Mass on April 24, 1988, Pope John Paul II noted that Stangassinger ''did not seek the extraordinary, but wanted 'to do what the day demanded.'''

Feast: Sept. 26 (Redemptorists).

Bibliography: *Der selige Kaspar Stanggassinger (1871–1899) in Selbstzeugnissen und im Urteil seiner Zeitgenossen,* ed. O. WEISS (Rome 1995). *L'Osservatore Romano,* English edition, no. 16 (1988): 12. *Positio super causae introductione* (Rome 1959). *Positio super virtutibus* (Rome 1978). A. CUMMINGS, *A Shining Light. The Story of Fr. Kaspar Stanggassinger* (Dublin 1963). O. GAMBI, *Vida do Padre Gaspar Stanggassinger* (Aparecida 1991). J. HEINZMANN, *Suchen was droben ist* (Freiburg, Switzerland 1988). H. PFEILSTETTER, *Pater Kaspar Stanggassinger. Annäherungen* (Gars 1988). M. STÖBENER, *Du forderst mich heraus. Eine briefliche Begegnung mit Kaspar Stanggassinger* (Munich 1988). F. TATARELLI, *Un canto sulle Alpi: vita del servo di Dio P. Gaspare Stanggassinger, Redentorista* (Rome 1963). F. WETTER, *Leben und Wirken eines Seligen. Hirtenbrief zur Fastenzeit 1988* (Munich 1988).

[K. I. RABENSTEIN]

STĂNILOAE, DUMITRU

Romanian Orthodox priest, theologian, spiritual father, professor; b. Vlădeni, Transylvania, Nov. 15, 1903; d. Bucharest, Romania, Oct. 5, 1993. Stăniloae, who single–handedly transformed Romanian Orthodox theological thinking in the post–war period, is widely recognized as one of the most important ORTHODOX theologians of the twentieth century. His work is characterized by a return to the patristic sources, a close relationship between theology and spirituality, and an effort to help his church adjust to conditions imposed by the communist government that ruled Romania from 1947 to 1989.

Stăniloae began studies in the faculty of theology at the University of Cernăuţi, Bukovina, in 1922 and received his doctorate in 1928. He was ordained a priest in 1932 while serving on the faculty of the Sibiu Theological Academy (1929–1947). He published a study of the life and teachings of Gregory Palamas in 1938 that is credited with heralding the modern revival in palamite studies, and in 1943 he finished a seminal work in Christology.

In 1947 he moved to Bucharest, where he served as a member of the faculty of the Bucharest Theological Institute until his retirement in 1973. Although a married priest with two children, Stăniloae was the prime instigator of the hesychastic renewal of monastic life in Romania in the mid–1950s. He published a series of Romanian translations of the *Philokalia,* which by the time of his death had reached twelve volumes. In 1958, as part of a crackdown on the monastic renewal, he was imprisoned by the communist authorities.

After his release from prison in 1964, Stăniloae rejoined the faculty of the Bucharest Theological Institute and focused his energies in three main areas. First, he set out to develop a contemporary Orthodox theology that takes ecumenical concerns into account. This included a re–articulation of patristic doctrines in language accessible to the laity, as well as the development of the notion of ''open sobornicity,'' an understanding of the catholicity of the Church open to the insights of other Christian confessions. Secondly, he elaborated an Orthodox theology of the transfiguration of creation and the consequent need for the Church to be open to the world. Thirdly, he attempted to draw out the cultural and social implications of Christian faith by showing the link between faith and love and by proposing the Trinity as the supreme model for human relations.

Stăniloae's most important work was his three–volume *Orthodox Dogmatic Theology,* published in 1978. Translations of sections of it have since appeared in several languages. Here he provides a majestic synthesis of all the main themes in Christian theology and their relationship to one another. Other major works include *Orthodox Spirituality* (1981), *Spirituality and Communion* (1986), and a new Christological opus, *The Immortal Image of God* (1987).

After the fall of the Ceauşescu regime in December 1989, Stăniloae joined the ''Reflection Group for the Renewal of the Church,'' which sought to facilitate the Romanian Orthodox Church's transition to a post–communist society. Under the new conditions Stăniloae's achievement could be officially recognized: he was named a member of the prestigious Romanian Academy in 1990.

See Also: ROMANIA, THE CATHOLIC CHURCH IN.

Bibliography: *Persoană şl comuniune: Prinos de cinstire Părintelui Professor Academician Dumitru Stăniloae la împlinirea vârstei de 90 de ani* (Sibiu 1993). M.–A. COSTA DE BEAUREGARD, *Dumitru Staniloae: Ose comprendre que je t'aime* (Paris 1983). D. STĂNILOAE, *Theology and the Church,* trans. R. BARRINGER (Crestwood, NY 1980). The first part of Stăniloae's *Orthodox Dogmatic Theology* has appeared in English as *The Experience of God* (Brookline, MA 1994). D. CIOBOTEA, ''Une dogmatique pour l'homme d'aujourd'hui,'' *Irénikon* 54 (1981) 472–484.

[R.G. ROBERSON]

Miracle performed by St. Stanislaus of Cracow, fresco by an artist of the School of Giotto, in lower church of the basilica of St. Francis of Assisi, Italy

STANISLAUS OF CRACOW, ST.

Patron of Poland; b. Szczepanów, Poland, *c.* 1030; d. Cracow, April 11, 1079. He was educated at the cathedral schools of Gniezno, then capital of Poland, and at Paris, later becoming canon and preacher at Cracow. Pope Alexander II nominated him successor to Bishop Lambert in the Diocese of Cracow in 1072. As a result of the prolonged expedition of King Boleslaus (Bolesław) II the Daring against the Grand Duchy of Kiev in 1069, the political situation in Poland was antagonistic to the king. Consequently, Bishop Stanislaus (Słanistaw) joined the magnates of the opposition, led by the king's brother Ladislaus (Wladysław); the king accused him of being a traitor, and condemned him to death by dismemberment. Stanislaus was actually slain subsequently by Boleslaus himself in St. Michael church, Cracow; the exact motivation of the king's action is still disputed. With this ''martyrdom'' of the bishop, Boleslaus lost all chances of defeating his opposition in Poland and escaped to his royal relatives in Hungary. There he spent his life as a penitent in the Benedictine abbey at Osiak, and the 11th-century martyrology of the Polish Benedictines refers to the king as *Beatus Boleslaus rex penitens.*

In the meantime reputed miracles and legends spread the cult of the martyred bishop to Lithuania, Byelorussia, and the Ukraine. Stanislaus became patron of the commonwealth of Poland. The most popular legend asserted that Stanislaus had brought Knight Peter back from the grave to witness Stanislaus' innocence to the king. In 1088 Stanislaus' body was transferred by his successor, Bishop Lambert III, to the cathedral church in Cracow, which was renamed for him; his body still rests in the main altar. Pope Innocent IV canonized him in Assisi in 1253. The earliest preserved biographies are the *Vita minor, c.* 1230, and the *Vita major, c.* 1260 [*Bibliotheca hagiographica latina antiquae et mediae aetatis*, 2 v. (Brussels 1898–1901; suppl. 1911) 7832–35] by Dominicans of Cracow priory.

Feast: April 11 (formerly May 7).

Bibliography: *Monumenta Poloniae historica,* 6 v. (LVOV and Cracow 1864–93) 4:238–438. *Acta Sanctorum* May 2:196–277. D. B. NUNIS, ed., *Saint Stanislaw, Bishop of Kraków* (Santa Barbara, Calif. 1979). T. GRUDZINSKI, *Boleslaus the Bold, Called Also the Bountiful, and Bishop Stanislaus*, tr. L. PETROWICZ (Warsaw 1985). M. W. LODÝNSKI, *Uzaleznienie Polski od papiestwa a kanonizacjasw Stanislawa* (Krakow 1995). J. KUREK, *Eucharystia, biskup i król* (Wroclaw 1998). *Grand Universal Encyclopedia* (in Polish) (Warsaw 1902) 31:477–478. G. KORBUT, *Polish Literature* (in Polish), 4 v. (Warsaw 1929–31) 1:3–4. A. BUTLER, *The Lives of the Saints*, rev. ed. H. THURSTON and D. ATTWATER, 4v. (New York 1956) 2:244–246. G. SPAHR, *Lexikon für Theologie und Kirche*, ed. J. HOFER and K. RAHNER, 10 v. (2d, new ed. Freiburg 1957–65) 9:1018.

[B. B. SZCZESNIAK]

STANYHURST, RICHARD

Irish historian, polemicist, devotional writer, priest; b. Dublin, 1547; d. Brussels, Belgium, 1618. Richard, son of James Stanyhurst, a zealous Irish Protestant, was educated at University College, Oxford (B.A. 1568) and studied law at Lincoln's Inn. By temperament and training a classicist, he abandoned law for historical and literary study. With (St.) Edmund CAMPION, an Oxford acquaintance, as his tutor, Richard returned to Ireland, where they collaborated on a history of Ireland that was published as part of Raphael Holinshed's *Chronicles* (1577). This work and Stanyhurst's *Description of Ireland* were accused of having a pro-English bias. After the death (1579) of his young wife, Janet Barnewall, Stanyhurst went to the Netherlands, where he embraced Catholicism (1581?), and never returned to the British Isles again. In the Netherlands, he devoted himself to translating Vergil's *Aeneid* (Leyden 1582). His translation met with such a storm of criticism that from that time on, he confined himself to Latin prose. His historical works *De rebus in Hibernia gestis* (Antwerp 1584) and *De vita S. Patricii Hyberniae Apostoli* (Antwerp 1587) mix history, legend, and theology indiscriminately. Politics and medicine were other Stanyhurst occupations which he practiced both in the Netherlands and in Spain, visited in 1590. The death of his second wife freed him to seek ordination (1602). Stanyhurst, a pensioner of Spain, was appointed chaplain to the rulers of the Netherlands, Archduke Albert and Archduchess Isabella. He devoted his remaining years to the writing of history, verse, devotional treatises, and polemical tracts including a refutation of the work of his own nephew, James USSHER, later Protestant archbishop of Armagh.

Bibliography: K. F. H. BERNIGAU, *Orthographie und Aussprache in Richard Stanyhursts englischer Übersetzung der Äeneide (1582)* (Marburg 1904). C. LENNON, *Richard Stanihurst the Dubliner* (Blackrock, Ireland 1981). A. J. LOOMIE, *The Spanish Elizabethans . . .* (New York 1963). E. WAUGH, *Edmund Campion* (New York 1935).

[P. S. MCGARRY]

STAPHYLUS, FRIEDRICH

German theologian; b. Osnabruck, Aug. 27, 1512; d. Ingolstadt, March 5, 1564. After receiving his M.A. at Wittenberg, he was encouraged by Melanchthon to translate the works of Diodorus of Sicily. As a theologian at Königsberg in 1546, he disputed with W. Gnaphaeus and A. OSIANDER, and published a work in 1553 in which he insisted upon agreement with the tradition of the Church and maintained that the Church alone could give authentic interpretation to Holy Scripture. He was converted to Catholicism during an illness in Breslau in 1552 and later opposed Melanchthon at Worms and attacked Protestant disunity in his *Theologiae M. Lutheri trimembris epitome* (1558). At the request of Peter CANISIUS, and by papal dispensation, since he was a married man, Staphylus became a professor of theology and Canon Law in 1559. He reformed the university and took part in the Catholic Restoration in Bavaria and Austria. He held that reunion would come about if both sides would recognize one Biblical text, so he urged the printing of the Greek text of the Vaticanus. His last work, *On the Great Apostasy* (*Lutheranism*) *before the Coming of Antichrist,* stresses the need for a living magisterium in the Church. His works were edited by his son (Ingolstadt 1613).

Bibliography: P. TSCHACKERT, *Allgemeine deutsche Biographie* 35:457–461; J. J. HERZOG and A. HAUCK, eds., *Realencyklopädie für protestantische Theologie,* 24 v. (3d ed. Leipzig 1896–1913) 18:771–776. É. AMANN, *Dictionnaire de théologie catholique,* ed. A. VACANT, 15 v. (Paris 1903–50; Tables générales 1951–) 14.2:2563–66.

[G. J. DONNELLY]

STAPLETON, THOMAS

Theologian and controversialist; b. Henfield, Sussex, England, July 1535; d. Louvain, Belgium, Oct. 1598. Stapleton was a son of William Stapleton, steward to the Bishop of Chichester and a member of the Carlton family of Stapletons. His early studies were at Canterbury and Winchester. Elected a fellow at New College, Oxford, he received a B.A. degree in 1556. Near the close of Mary's reign, he was appointed prebendary of Woodhorne in Chichester Cathedral.

His staunch Catholicism forced him into exile in the Low Countries early in the reign of Elizabeth. At LOUVAIN he studied theology; later, at Paris, he pursued ancient languages. He returned to England in 1563, but because of his refusal to deny papal authority he suffered in his ecclesiastical status and lost the prebend at Chichester. Returning to Louvain, Stapleton worked with William Allen in the establishment of the English College at DOUAI. In 1571 he received the doctor of divinity degree, and was rector of the University of Douai 1574–75. In 1584 he entered the Society of Jesus, but ill health forced him to leave within a short time. In 1590 he was appointed to the royal chair of theology at Louvain and became rector of the University in 1595. In recognition of his ability, Clement VIII twice offered him positions in Rome, which Stapleton refused, but in 1597 he was made protonotary apostolic.

Stapleton's reputation spread throughout Europe and he became deeply engaged in polemic contests. Among his theological works are the *Principiorum fidei doctrinalium demonstratio* (1578) and the *Auctoritas ecclesiasticae defensio* (1592), directed against William Whitaker of St. John's College. These and other writings on controversial subjects were of vast influence, for Stapleton was one of the most learned Catholics of his time.

He also translated Bede's *Ecclesiastical History of the English People,* the first English translation since that of Alfred the Great. His apologetic purpose was evidenced in the words of his dedication to Queen Elizabeth: "In this history it shall appear in what faith your noble realm was christened."

One of his last writings was a biography of Thomas More, compiled from authentic and unpublished sources, and from his own recollections of his early years when he was associated with friends of More. He willed his literary productions, including valuable manuscripts, to the English College at Douai.

Bibliography: H. HOLLAND, *Vita Thomae Stapletoni,* in v.1 of *T. Stapletoni. . . . opera. . . omnia,* 4 v. (Paris 1620). BEDE, *Ecclesiastical History* 2 v., tr. J. E. KING based on the version of T. STAPLETON (Loeb Classical Library; New York 1930). T. COOPER, *The Dictionary of National Biography from the Earliest Times to 1900* (London 1885–1900) 18:988–991. Other information may be found in *The First and Second Diaries of the English College, Douay* (London 1878). G. THILS, *Les Notes de l'église dans l'apologétique catholique depuis la réforme* (Gembloux 1937). W. ALLEN, *Letters and Memorials . . .* (London 1882). *Correspondance d'Ottavio Mirto Frangipani, Premier Nonce de Flandre, 1596–1606,* v.1 ed. L. VAN DER ESSEN (Rome 1924), v.2–3 ed. A. LOUANT (Rome 1932, 1942). A. C. SOUTHERN, *English Recusant Prose, 1559–1582* (London 1950). G. ALBION, "An English Professor at Louvain: T. S. (1535–1598)," *Miscellanea Historica Alberti de Meyer* (Louvain 1946) 895–913. M. R. O'CONNELL, *Thomas Stapleton and the Counter Reformation* (New Haven 1964).

[A. M. SAWKINS]

STATE, THE

The independent (and sovereign) political community. The term is derived from the Roman-law concept of *status rei Romanae,* i.e., the public law of the Roman Republic. Beginning in the 15th century (e.g., Stato di Firenze), it replaced the original terms, the Greek *polis* and the Latin *res publica, civitas,* and *regnum corpus politicum* (*mysticum*). The state has elements of both community and ASSOCIATION, in the sense of the distinction made by the sociologist Ferdinand Tönnies. As a political community it is included in the most comprehensive and highest SOCIETY, mankind, which has its proper common good, its specific "international" law, and its historically variable forms of organization. As a body politic the state has its own supreme internal order of POSITIVE LAW, ordered to a distinct common good that is the ultimate AUTHORITY within its order, binding a people who inhabit a defined territory. Although each state claims SOVEREIGNTY and independence from other societies of the same order, states are interdependent and bound to recognize the community of nations (mankind) and its public international law, and of course the NATURAL LAW, which is ultimately the foundation of the state and the critical norm for all manmade positive law. States (including VATICAN City, or the APOSTOLIC SEE) are thus primary subjects of public international law, regardless of their internal constitutions, whether unitary or federal, republican or monarchic, national or multinational (*see* GOVERNMENT).

Concept

Three basic elements of the state are commonly distinguished: (1) a distinct territory with more or less strictly determined boundaries; (2) a multitude of people already individualized by language, tribal customs, religion, or other cultural forms of living together; and (3) a positive constitutional and legal order that determines, legitimizes, and limits the one political authority and the basic relations between ruler and ruled—in public law—

and between the citizens—in private (civil) law—that together form the "bond of law" (*vinculum juris*). Some scholars add as a qualification of the first element the wealth of the nation, i.e., its raw materials, soil fertility, climate, and all economically relevant abilities and skills of the inhabitants. The state is distinguished from the Church by a distinction of ends and means, since, in scholastic language, each is a "perfect" society possessing and controlling all the means necessary for the realization of its specific end. In relation to the many other societies creatively produced by man in the course of his intellectual, moral, socioeconomic, and cultural growth and differentiation, the state is the ordering and unifying authority, the *unitas ordinis* of the common good in which all individual persons and their many free associations participate and through which they enjoy legal security and self-fulfillment in the stability and tranquility, i.e., the PEACE, of the public order.

More than any other temporal community, the state, as the name implies, tends toward perpetuity and survival into an indefinite future. A people conscious of itself and its historical individuality often longs for political existence. As individual persons and families follow each other in an unceasing sequence, they appear to be the ever-changing matter of an enduring form. This has led more than a few thinkers to hypostatize the state, to ascribe to it not merely legal personality but physical personality and substance, as did G. W. F. HEGEL, R. Kjellen, A. Schäffle, and J. J. von Uexcüll, for example. But in its mode of BEING the state is accidental, not substantial; it does not exist independent of, outside, or above the persons who are organized within it, but wholly in them. It cannot act except through the persons who have competence, whose acts are imputed to the state; thus, although a collective criminal guilt is impossible, there may very well be a collective liability of the whole for the unjust acts of its agents. Nor is the end of the state so much its own and so independent of the ends of the persons forming it that their lives, rights, and fortunes can be unlimitedly sacrificed for its end or good. Instead, the rights of individual persons are themselves essential parts of the end of the state, which, like all societies, must ultimately serve the ends of its individual members.

State and Society. Although the formal distinction between state and society is of relatively recent date, as a practical distinction it is actually very old, since it is implicit in the traditional distinctions between public law and private or civil law, and between commutative JUSTICE, specifying relations between persons and groups of persons, and legal and distributive justice, specifying duties of citizens to political authority and duties of the authority to citizens. In all states, regardless of the form of government, the political authority monopolizes the power to enforce laws in order to establish justice, protect personal and civil rights, ensure domestic tranquility, and provide for external defense. No individual or group can take the law into its own hands. The security of the public order, the protection of rights (except in immediate self-defense), and the enforcement of the legal order, especially the administration of criminal justice, are prerogatives of civil authority.

Since he who has power is always tempted to abuse it, this monopolized power must be limited, that is, subjected to strict procedural forms, or channeled, as it were, by a higher law. In other words, it must be exercised within constitutional limitations. Important among these are the limitations placed upon the state as the administrator of criminal justice by bills of rights and by legal principles that provide for trial by a jury of one's peers or that prohibit ex post facto legislation; arrest for crime or imposition of punishment without previous law; arrest without a warrant; or deprivation of life, liberty, or property without due process of law. Principles such as these have been included since the early Middle Ages in the many charters of rights of which the MAGNA CARTA is the prototype. These charters often guaranteed also the rights of association, of free movement, of taxation only by consent of the estates, etc. Other limitations on the state were found in the participation of the people in legislative bodies, in the widespread self-government of towns and of guilds of artisans and merchants, and in the liberties and privileges of the universities. Thus, under the protection of the public order in the West, there developed over many centuries a rich life of many groups and associations free from the arbitrary intervention of political power. After the downfall of ABSOLUTISM with its petty bureaucracy and economics of mercantilism, the third estates insisted on a sphere of free economic, cultural, and academic activities of citizens that was circumscribed and protected by the formal bills of rights found in modern constitutionalism. Within this sphere citizens form by free initiative economic, social, cultural, educational, religious, or other associations characteristic of the free and pluralistic society of modern times. Their proper role is distinguished from that of the state by the principle of SUBSIDIARITY. During bellicose occupation or complete subjugation of a belligerent nation (*debellatio*), society continues to exist under the protection of international law while the state is inoperative and even destroyed. For war is directed against the state and its armed forces, not against society and its institutions, the peaceful life of its families and the private life of its private persons, and their properties and rights under civil law. The real distinction between state and society, and between public and civil law, is essential for the free state as well as for the free society. Although the line of separation between the two is not rigid and defined once for all, but fluid, shifting the line radically in favor of society results in anarchy, and shifting it radically in favor of the state results in totalitarianism.

State and Nation. State and NATION are not necessarily coterminous. During the 19th century the principle of national self-determination established by the FRENCH REVOLUTION became a kind of ideal of European public law. It was a consequence of the democratic movement that developed in contrast to the historic multinational state of monarchic legitimacy. The new principle led to the unification of Germany and Italy and, after 1918, to the reestablishment of the Polish state and the dissolution of the multinational Austro-Hungarian Empire. Actually, the new states in central Europe were not themselves nation-states, but contained within their borders ''national'' minorities that the minority treaties of 1919 (avoiding the term ''national'') were intended to protect. Similarly, few of the new states that have arisen as a result of the abolition of colonialism in Africa and Asia are true nation-states; because the former colonial borders were not established with respect to the older tribal territories, in most of the new states nations are still to be formed.

Historically, it is significant that the first nation-states—France, England, and Spain (even in the case of the *reconquista*)—resulted from the struggle against the universalism of Christendom, of the *sacrum imperium* and the Church universal. Kings claiming to be emperors in their territories were assisted against emperor and pope by the growing national consciousness of the ruling groups, namely, the aristocracy, clergy, universities, and jurists. The Protestant REFORMATION strengthened this consciousness. But modern secularized nationalism is the product of the French Revolution and the democratic sovereignty of the nation.

The nation as a product of historical forces is a stable community of persons and families who have developed a common CULTURE—a common language, literature, customs, and often a common religion—as well as a distinct feeling of belonging together and of being different from neighboring communities, a common awareness of a historical destiny, and a consensus of accepted value preferences often but not necessarily based on ethnobiological factors. All these factors need not be present together to produce the ''daily plebiscite'' that makes a nation. Mexico and Argentina speak the same language but are different nations. Poland and Ireland lived for generations without statehood, yet continued to exist as nations, thanks mainly to the bond of religion. The nation-state is not the only legitimate political form of an independent state. Indeed, Ignaz SEIPEL regarded it as an inferior form because of its tendency to promote doctrinaire, quasi-religious nationalism. The best way for neighboring nations to find a home in one state without succumbing to this tendency is federation, toward which the old nations of Europe now tend; their example might well be salutary for newer nations. In the contemporary world the narrowly conceived unitary sovereign nation-state is more and more anachronistic.

The State in Catholic Thought. The state as exemplified in the Greek *polis* or the Roman, Egyptian, Persian, or Chinese empires is older than Christianity. When what Tacitus contemptuously called the *Secta Christianorum* spread from its birthplace in the Roman-occupied religio-political community of the Jews into the Helleno-Roman Empire, which was then seeking to save itself by an ideological assertion of the divinity of the emperor, the Christians were neither socially nor politically revolutionary. They accepted the empire; they prayed for the powers above them; they paid their taxes; they served in the legions. They were accused of ''atheism,'' however, because they refused to acknowledge the national gods and the worship of the emperor, and thus they were persecuted. Already in the writings of the Church Fathers and especially in those of the apologetes, Christians began to make the political community the subject of their thinking, critically studying Greek and Stoic political philosophers and accepting what did not contradict the Gospels, the faith, and the experience of the new Ecclesia. Slowly, there developed in Christian intellectual circles a political philosophy that was to be systematically elaborated through the great scholarly effort of SCHOLASTICISM in the high Middle Ages. It remains a philosophy of man that is valid for all men and not only for believers.

According to Catholic tradition, the state belongs to human culture and to the secular order. Its root is in the social nature of man. Its end is temporal felicity (HAPPINESS). Therefore it is taught by all that the essential mutual rights and duties of citizens and of political authority are independent of the state of GRACE. Baptism does not change these rights and duties, although it exalts them into the realm of grace by means of supernatural motives. Certainly the state cannot be a virtually omnipotent pedagogue, the only master of moral life; the contention that the state is such a master leads necessarily to a Hegelian divinization of the state and to the servitude of the Church, if not to the Church's destruction in the totalitarian state. Once this is said, however, it is to be remarked that this traditional political philosophy does not use theological method; its principles are based not on theology but on natural reason and on the great tradition of natural law. Viktor CATHREIN has rightly called it a natural-law political philosophy. The term ''Catholic political philosophy'' means only that this political philosophy, as part of the *philosophia perennis,* has always had a home and a refuge in the Church's intellectual institutions and in the utterances of her magisterium.

Origin

The philosophical problem of the origin of the state must be distinguished sharply from inquiries into the factual historical beginnings of individual states or from ideal constructions of how these beginnings ought to have occurred. It refers rather to the essential properties of man's nature that make life in a political community—be it ultimately even that of a world state—a necessity in the sense of Aristotle's dictum that the stateless man is either a demigod or a beast. True, history proves empirically that man has always lived in "states" and that all attempts to live in anarchy, i.e., without law and authority and motivated exclusively by mutual love, have failed. What Aristotle meant was that man is by his very nature not only a social but also a political being. Only by establishing a stable and enduring order of peaceful and protected personal life and social cooperation can he fully realize all his potentialities. He is an "incarnate person" in a "world" that he himself helps to form and shape into an ever more favorable and less unfriendly environment through the social process of progressive civilization, developing culture and technical control of the powers of "nature." Christianity did not change the fundamental requirements of this process, although it gave it a new dignity and made it the object of new motives as the field in which man *in statu viatoris,* participating in the "visible" sacramental order of grace, works in the world for the salvation of his immortal soul.

Family as the Basic Unit. Political theory recognized at its beginning two natural societies, the family and the state. The family is based on the bisexual nature of man as a rational being. Each individual is born into a family, needing education, protection, and bodily care; growing, maturing, founding a family, and caring and working for those who are nearest and dearest. The "natural" authority in the family from the great patriarchal forms to the modern is the *parentes* or one of them, truly *auctores* with their natural rights and duties. In the first stages of social evolution families increased to tribal multitudes that settled in particular territories. Agriculture developed as the first form of the rational, technical use of nature. The first stable and immovable homes were built, and a new form of human living together became necessary. This form was a superfamilial, sociojuridical order supplying a stable authority to judge in conflicts, to protect against breaches of the peace and violence to members or their property, and to protect against dangers from foreigners while extending hospitality to guests. In this perspective, experience itself proved the family insufficient for the full realization of man's social nature; it was in this respect *imperfecta.* A "more perfect union," a *societas perfecta,* was demanded, a social organization that in a continuous process of perfection would be able to care for and to improve the superfamilial multitude by its own means.

The Primitive State. This organization exists in the inchoate state of primitive societies. It is a necessity of human nature, but it is established through the free will of rational beings. The state is not the result of a blind biological urge, as is an animal herd. However necessary it is from the point of view of man's nature, ultimately it cannot be formed without free human acts. Aristotle found this development of the human social process only in the *polis,* the city-state, so that he termed "barbarians" those who were not members. Contrariwise, the theologians of the age of discovery, at least the majority, regarded the "newly discovered Indians" as states despite the primitive condition of some of them. These theologians (e.g., F. de VITORIA, F. SUÁREZ) protested when a Sepúlveda used the Aristotelian theory of the barbarian as the natural slave of the citizen to justify enslavement of the native peoples and confiscation of their lands. As a matter of fact, primitive civilizations (considered both as early and as simple) were and are organizations of citizens. They form civil societies intellectually and morally, and with their customary law and their religious beliefs are by no means "animal-like" (*see* LAW, PRIMITIVE). Fritz Kern shows that they practically "lived natural law" (*Beginn der Weltegeschichte* [1953]). Their religious beliefs are often monotheistic; their social life often confirms Kropotkin's thesis that mutual help and aid are anterior and superior to a ruthless "struggle for existence." Anthropologists of the 19th century, viewing them, were too much under the influence of Hegel and Charles DARWIN.

Concept of the State of Nature. Nor can a primitive organization be equated with the celebrated *status naturalis* from which it was once thought that solitary primitive man entered into the *status civilis,* as in the theories of Thomas HOBBES, John LOCKE, or Jean Jacques ROUSSEAU or in those of some of the Greek sophists. Actually, neither Aristotle nor any of the scholastics (except Juan de MARIANA) indulged in the description of a *status naturalis* of the individual man. They did distinguish—as do their successors—the *status familialis* with its specific authority from the *status civilis* with its different specific authority. For them the social process that produced the state was based on the rational dynamic activity of man and on his creative ability to meet new situations and to understand the necessities demanded by his nature, more than on irrational biological urges. The state was thus seen neither as merely the result of an arbitrary free contract nor as an ethically indifferent invention of the strong seeking to transform might into right and conformity into the duty of free obedience.

Theory of the Social Contract. Hobbes, Locke, and Rousseau, for the purposes of their characteristic political theories, postulated a SOCIAL CONTRACT. For Hobbes all rights except that of self-preservation were transferred by the contract to the sovereign. Locke held that inalienable rights were retained but that their protection was guaranteed by the state. In Rousseau's theory the natural rights were transferred to the sovereign people and granted back as civil rights. The main aim of these contract theorists—even of Hobbes—was the protection of the very individualistically conceived natural rights that to them was the *raison d'être* of the state. Yet even they thought of this social contract not as a solemn formal agreement but as a postulate of reason accounting for the transition from the *status naturalis* to the *status civilis.*

That the rights and duties of the first natural society, the family, differ from those of the *status civilis* was and is the *opinio communis.* How the *status civilis* came to have moral and juridical validity therefore requires explanation. Was this an unconscious growth, or must it be assumed that the change from one form of social life into a qualitatively different one could not have occurred without the mediation of human reason directing the wills of the heads of families? If the latter, then a moral-legal form providing this mediation must be identified. Ancient writers proposed as the mediating agency the idea of a *pactum,* a consensual agreement or meeting of minds, enabling the realization of the higher form of social life, a good life demanded by natural human initiative and therefore by the natural law. This theory was accepted by some of the Church Fathers and by medieval thinkers and was developed especially by the great writers of the 16th to 18th centuries, as Peter Tischleder has shown. Later it was abandoned by many to avoid confusion with the theories of Hobbes and Rousseau, but it has again gained many adherents.

Unlike Rousseau, for example, scholastic theory defined the pact in terms of *status.* The new rights and duties of the *status civilis* were seen as demanded objectively by natural law. Man was not considered able arbitrarily to enter into or to avoid the pact once it was demanded by social conditions, or able to determine arbitrarily or to change the basic rights and duties imposed by the *status civilis.* As St. Robert BELLARMINE explained, the political order of legal justice, with its mutual rights and duties of governor and governed, is in its *existence* dependent on the free acts of consent of those uniting in the body politic; in its *essence,* however, that is, in its foundation and final cause and in the rights and duties that it imposes by virtue of the natural law, it is independent of human will. What obliges and empowers is not the juridical fact of consent but the natural law, which is perpetual and immutable (*De Laicis* ch. 2). Thus persons born after the formation of the pact also are bound by the essence and final cause of the natural law.

Theories of the Reformers. Neither *quoad essentiam* nor *quoad existentiam* is the state a consequence of sin, original or personal. Some schoolmen asked whether in the state of pure or integral nature (before the fall of man) the political community would have been necessary. They affirmed that although the coercive power of authority would not have been necessary, the directive authority to establish order would have been necessary. For the Reformers—Martin LUTHER, John CALVIN, Huldrych ZWINGLI—and for spiritualist groups such as the ANABAPTISTS, the state was a result of ORIGINAL SIN. Their view of the latter exaggerated its destructive influence on the intellect and will of man and, in consequence, exaggerated man's necessary sinfulness (*simul justus et peccator*).

Luther. If men were truly Christian and redeemed, Luther said, there would be no need for the state; but since their nature is evil, since they cannot recognize a natural law, the state is necessary as ''God's stickmaster and hangman.'' In this view, the state and its authority and power are only instrumental causes through which God Himself maintains peace and law; they are not secondary efficient causes with their own initiative, responsibility, and relative autonomy, as in scholastic theory. The foundation and the justification of the state and its authority are found neither in God-given human nature, to be realized ever more fully through the state, nor in natural law under the aspect of the order of creation, but only in God's revealed word in the sinful world. The state is thus singly and wholly the instrument of the hidden and incomprehensible will of God in its infinity and absolute omnipotence. The state and its authority in their ever-changing forms are, from man's point of view, accidental, but are nevertheless divine instruments to which is owed humble obedience. All powers are in their mere factuality God's instruments, so that this factuality itself clearly demands submission; a right to active resistance against political authority is a moot question. The one tormenting question for Luther was how man, always and from the beginning a sinner, might find the merciful God. This is not to say that Luther did not acknowledge and now and then use natural-law doctrine, but for him it had in no way the importance it still had in the political thought of WILLIAM OF OCKHAM, for example.

Calvin. Calvin held a similar, theologically founded doctrine. For him the state and its authority were based on the positive will of God revealed in the Bible. His legalistic approach to the Old Testament and his predilection for the THEOCRACY of the Book of Judges show that he regarded the Scriptures as a collection of permanently binding laws expressing the only valid absolute will of the one Sovereign, God. He could not accept human nature, including rational insight into the natural law, as *in se* a valid and sufficient moral basis for the state and its authority. The latter appeared rather, in whatever forms they were found to exist, as instruments of God's sovereign will. In this concept, too, the state is God's rod, and self-negation and penitence are the proper attitudes of Christians. Calvin's doctrine of the right of resistance of the ''inferior magistrates'' was not the medieval theory of the *valentior pars* of the people justifying eventual active resistance against tyrannical authority. Like Luther, Calvin made furious attacks against the Anabaptists with their spiritual individualism and anarchical millenarianism.

Post-Reformation Developments. Because the Reformers left no systematic political theory, their followers were more or less free to develop eclectic doctrines and even to radicalize the original Anabaptist tendencies. The theory of the DIVINE RIGHT OF KINGS, concerned principally with the origin of political authority, was definitely a ''protestant'' doctrine based on biblical grounds. It was too unhistorical to be acceptable to Catholic thought. The arguments for the theory, not unknown during the early medieval dispute between the emperor and the pope of the one Christendom, would have subordinated the Church universal to kings as heads of Erastian state churches. Although a similar defense of the principle of monarchy was attempted later by Joseph de MAISTRE and Louis de BONALD, its argument was much more historical and was based upon the constitution of the papal Church rather than upon the Bible.

During the ENLIGHTENMENT, references to the natural law in the thought of Philipp MELANCHTHON were revived by Samuel von Pufendorf and John Wise, among others. Later, inspired by German idealism, Karl Holl (1866–1926) promoted an idealistic interpretation of Protestant political theory. Others incorporated idealism into this theory through a Christian interpretation of Hegel's philosophy. Subsequently, after a period of ''secularization'' that produced liberal Protestantism, the dialectical theology of Karl BARTH returned to the original inspirations of Luther and Calvin. But BARTHIANISM revived also the ambiguity of their theology of creation (*Schöpfungsordnungen*) and of their rejection of natural law in favor of exclusively biblical argumentation.

Marxism. Marxist theory traces the origin of the state to the class struggle caused by the development of private PROPERTY. This view is so in contradiction with traditional doctrine and the faith that even the few Christian writers who have accepted Karl Marx's critique of capitalism (e.g., Wilhelm Hohoff) have never accepted the typical Marxist theory of the state as a mere superstructure or the chiliastic hopes of the withering away of the state and the rise of the classless society. Although historically the state as an institution may sometimes be the prize in violent group conflicts and there may be a certain degree of class struggle, especially in laissez-faire capitalism, the Marxist view is so barren of ethical considerations as to be unacceptable on either philosophical or theological grounds.

Legal Positivism. Legal positivism, as part of a general positivist philosophy and a special scientific method, either excludes all ethical problems of the state and its authority as irrelevant for the jurist or disqualifies them as ''unscientific.'' The state, its origin, and its authority are merely facts for the positivist. Only positive law and imperative commands issuing from the legislator, whatever his constitutional form, and enforced by the organs of the state, its police, and administrative bureaucracy are ''laws.'' Natural law and divinely revealed biblical law are thus not ''laws.'' They may be subjectively valid moral or religious norms, and they may be motives for the individual's external conformity to the law as the will of the sovereign. But because they imply value judgments, they are regarded as irrelevant for ''science.'' What matters is not the ethically relevant content of the positive law but merely the form, namely, that it issue in a constitutionally correct form from the sovereign, or supreme authority, that does not recognize any superior and receives ''habitual obedience'' from the greatest number of citizens (*obedientia facit imperantem*). Law is not reason, nor is it legitimized by its ordination to the common good; nor is obedience a virtue of free men who can render only ''reasonable'' obedience.

In the face of tyranny positivism is helpless with its slogan that law is law, for the tyrant ''legalizes'' his regime. The judge has no other criterion than this legality; he cannot find, for instance, that the law is arbitrary or commands acts that are evidently against humanity and the basic values that transcend positive law, e.g., justice. The argument that law is law actually means that might is right. But might decrees only a ''must,'' not an ''ought''; it cannot be the basis of a valid obligation. The positivist concept of law, although neat and easily identified, neglects the whole ambiance of the law, the intimate relation between the legal and the moral order, the hunger and thirst for justice in and from the law, the ethical consensus of the consciences of the citizens and its vital influence on the values to be realized by positive law. A satiated peaceful or apathetic society can afford positivism, but in times of crisis ethical values and the natural law demand recognition. Positivism, furthermore, is intimately related to the closed sovereign nation-state, in which the power element, i.e., the ability to enforce external conformity by whatever means, is superior. Thus it is basically unable to recognize international law and canon law as genuine law. (*See* POSITIVISM IN JURISPRUDENCE.)

Form of Unity

A fundamental concept of MAN that affects understanding of the specific form of unity of the state is implied in the thesis that man is a sociopolitical being and that in the social process of the realization of this nature he produces an increasingly complex, gradated order of social forms for the attainment of his truly human goals. These extend to the political community and ultimately to the community of nations, or mankind, in the temporal order, with which the Church universal is coordinated. Man is an incarnate person, a master of his own acts, with an inborn initiative deriving from his intellect and will; and he is thus free and responsible to God, his Maker, and to his fellowmen. His sociality reaches into his inner life, into the center of his person, despite the ''ultimate solitude'' there that is open only to the Creator. A person is the highest form of being; it is as a person that man is created in the image of God. The intentional character of the acts of a person demands fulfillment by a ''Thou'' and an original dialogue and awareness of ''we.'' Man is a speaking being; he has something to communicate from his more or less rich inner subjective world. Love in its various forms—from love of neighbor, friendship and comradeship, conjugal love, civic friendship, and patriotism to the highest form of selfless love (*agape*)—is manifested by intentional personal acts that distinguish the person from all animals. ''Man has intellect and hands''; man is *homo faber.* Through various forms of cooperation he transforms the ''natural'' world, as its master and owner, into an ever more favorable material, moral, spiritual, and cultural ''hominized'' world.

Basic Principles. It follows as a first principle of social philosophy, coordinate with that of the sociopolitical nature of man, that all social forms exist to serve persons. They fulfill their meaning and their ends only insofar as they are means to the fuller development of persons in the production and perfection of what more pious, less materialistic eras called *humanitas* and *humaniora* and of what, in view of Christ's mission, ought to be called *humanitas Christiana.* There is a corresponding theological principle that supernatural grace presupposes human nature and perfects it (*see* GRACE AND NATURE). Thus a table of objective values follows, descending from the highest values—the glory of the personal triune God and the salvation of the soul; the freedom of the person and of conscience—which are the foundation of intellectual, moral, and cultural values, down to biological, economic, and comfort values produced by common social efforts and thus by specific ''functional'' groups within the peace and security of the public order, the state.

Subsidiarity. A third basic principle is that of subsidiarity. According to it, the state as the public authority should leave to the individual person what the person through initiative and competence can regularly and reasonably do and perform in the private sector. Similarly, it should leave to the family and then to the many associations that persons and families produce for their improvement the functions that they can adequately serve. The state should afford to these groups legal status in private and social law, and it should protect their ''self-government'' and provide rules to resolve conflicts of competencies and interests. This principle is directed against collectivism as well as against totalitarianism, each with its depersonalization and *Vermassung.*

Solidarity. A fourth principle, solidarity, follows from the sociality that has been described and affirms a fundamental mutual relationship between individual persons and the community. The first are ordered to the latter, and the latter exists only in and for the persons in mutual solidaristic obligations. The common good of a community, e.g., of the state, embraces the rights of the citizens to the extent that the wanton arbitrary deprivation of the rights of a member of a racial or religious group is a mutilation of the common good itself.

Social Justice. SOCIAL JUSTICE as a fifth principle augments the three classical forms of justice, legal, distributive, and commutative. It is the dynamic element that demands a continuous effort to adapt the positive sociolegal order to ever-changing conditions of life and to the more clearly conceived ideals of justice as they grow in the community. Each age has its ''social questions'' through which men become aware that de facto the static positive order has become unjust, inasmuch as whole groups within the community have become its victims while others have gained unjustifiable advantages exclusively from it. In such an eventuality social justice demands that objectively unjust but legally correct rules should be changed and that a more just positive order should be established. Thus, social legislation has been employed to correct the injustice of the predominance of property rights over the personal rights of the unprotected worker selling his labor as a ''commodity.'' All these principles are principles of the order of being and therefore ethical-legal principles governing man's social activity.

The State as a Unity of Order. Although the state may be called a *communitas communitatum,* its unity is not that of a biological organism or of a racially defined substantial being as in the Nazi formula of *Volk-Blut-Rasse,* according to which the *Volk* was all and the individual nothing and the so-called pure Aryan race had the right to exterminate mongrel races. Nor is the state merely the positive legal order as in the ''pure'' theory of law of Hans Kelsen. For the state lives in the ethical order as well as in the legal; it is a sociological form that exists in the informal consensus and in the spirit of civil friendship of the citizens as well as in positive law. The state is a unity of order, and the common good is the good and end of this order.

Catholic thinkers also, under the influence of the Pauline *Corpus Christi mysticum,* have often used the term ''corporate,'' or ''organic,'' in defining the state. Suárez, following some late medieval writers, among them Baldus de Ubaldis, Lucas de Penna, and Jean GERSON, called the state a *corpus politicum mysticum.* The term can best be translated as moral organism, indicating that the character of the bond as well as the end of the *corpus* is not physical but moral. That is, it includes ethical virtues such as civic friendship, obedience, and mutual help in numerous freely formed associations and legal virtues such as the spirit of solidarity, mutual responsibility, and duty, or obligation. All these underlying virtues support the ''visible'' legal order, which is directed to the good common life, to the concrete realization of the common good in which all participate, and which guarantees that the persons united in it are able to reach the natural felicity that ''opens'' upon their supernatural end, known by God's revelation. There are thus two *ordines,* two mystical bodies, two supreme authorities, independent of each other yet destined to serve the same persons as citizens of the state and as members of the Church universal.

The ''organic view'' sees the state as a whole as a functional structure of many associations serving the varied human goals that develop with the progress of civilization, of the *civitas humana.* All these functional associations are protected in their initiative and self-government within the legal order; they fulfill their own particular common goods and yet in so doing serve in their diversity the common good of all as a whole. The term ''organism'' denotes a *universitas* having a *telos* and end in itself and being able to fulfill this *telos* by its own organization. It is this character that makes the state (like the Church) a perfect society.

This view is opposed to the so-called individualist-mechanist view, which holds that the state integrates exclusively the ''interests'' of individuals who out of regard for their interests are forced either by the sovereign (Hobbes) or by the mechanism of the competitive economic market (Adam Smith's ''invisible hand'') to bring into being the optimal organization of the state-society. Or the state becomes a kind of umpire of the struggle for survival charged with keeping a minimum of public peace (Herbert Spencer) or the instrument of the exploiting class in the historical process of the class struggle (Marx).

Finally, in the organic view the active element that obtains the cooperation of the members and directs it is not an external principle, e.g., the ruler. If this were the case, the *forma rei publicae* would be constituted by political authority alone, commanding from above, as it were, to organize the whole. The *forma,* the *causa formalis* that is at the same time the *causa finalis* of the state, is the political common good. Its realization is the result both of the acts of the authority and of the members' acts of assent and of faithful fulfillment of their various functions in many associations. Thus it is the *common good* and its realization *hic et nunc* that is the norm of *legitimacy* for the laws of the ruler as well as for the due obedience of the free citizens. It is one of the (few) principal rules of natural law that the realization of the (political) common good is to be assisted and not obstructed. This rule binds all, ruler and ruled alike. It allows no divine right of kings or transhistorical monarchical legitimacy.

The Common Good as the End of the State

If man is ontologically a social and political being, his natural potentialities, inclinations, and longings for the full realization of his God-given nature as a rational, free, self-determining, and thus responsible person can be realized only through a series of increasingly varied social forms. This culminates (in the natural order) in the state and in mankind, the highest community. The ''goods,'' or values, to be realized by this functionally differentiated structure of social life constitute national cultures and ultimately human culture. It follows that the political community as, in a sense, the *communitas communitatum* must have a distinctive communal end, the common good. This is a good in which all participate, at least in principle. It is not merely the sum of the individual goods and interests of the persons that form the community. Furthermore, between the original natural societies, the family and the state and, beyond, the community of states, numerous forms of social life are products of man's unrelenting active drive toward happiness, toward a more perfect life in the *civilitas humana.* This is a drive for the creation, protection, and development of spiritual, moral, cultural, artistic, and material values that the bodybound spiritual being needs and desires.

The Realization of Justice and Public Peace. The life of the free, value-producing, and value-preserving persons and their many corresponding societies or groups presupposes an order of public peace and security. This is an order of positive law that rests upon the moral order of justice and is secured by the constituted organs of the political community. It guarantees and protects not only the persons but also all the free and autonomous groups within it. Thus the common good is a *bonum ordinis,* an order of positive law, security, protection, peace, and mutual help that approximates justice. The legal order organizes and limits public power; protects rights; enforces internal peace as constitutional law; grants persons the legal forms of private, or civil, law essential for the development of socioeconomic and cultural life; and secures and protects the network of legal relations through civil and criminal courts. Since the order of law must be protected against a foreign invader or aggressor, a common defense of the order of peace is implied. By natural reason and by the Scriptures, the *jus vitae ac necis* and the *jus pacis et belli* are given political authority in defense of the common good. It is easy to see that the preambles of constitutions provide in fact good definitions of the political common good, as does the preamble to the Constitution of the United States, setting forth as the purposes of the document, ''to form a more perfect Union, establish Justice, insure domestic Tranquillity, provide for the common defence, promote the general Welfare and secure the Blessings of Liberty.'' It is just, following Aristotle and Thomas Aquinas, to say that the common good is the realization of justice and public peace in and by the positive legal order in its entirety.

The Common Good and the Person. Since the natural rights of persons and of groups of persons organized as corporate bodies are integral parts of the order of law, there is no irreconcilable conflict between the good of the person and the common good. As Suárez wrote, *bonum commune consurgit ex bonis singulorum.* The common good may demand the risk of life in its defense, not only out of *pietas* but in justice. The duty of justice is perfectly fulfilled in the supreme sacrifice. The relations between the political authority and those who owe obedience to it, including the duties of the authority to its subjects, are ruled by distributive and legal justice; and the exchange of goods and services between private persons is ruled by commutative justice. All are embraced in the justice demanded by the common good. In contradistinction to the principle of equality between persons and between goods and services exchanged, this justice takes account of standing in relative importance and closeness to the realization of the common good; thus it requires, for example, a more intense loyalty from a civil servant or a judge than from a private citizen. In the same way, a higher salary for a judge than for a janitor is justified because the profession of the judge, and consequently his or her loyalty, is nearer to and more important for the common good. This is so even in the most egalitarian society. Conversely, an income tax with a reasonable (i.e., neither confiscatory nor economically unsound) progression is justified because the security of the legal order is proportionally more important to the owners of large fortunes than to propertyless workers.

The Common Good and Free Associations. The common good and its specific form of justice, in its positive realization in history, is correlative with the structure of society. If society becomes more complex, if the differentiation of vocations and professions in economic life requires a high degree of integration because of increasing interdependence, an increase in social legislation and administrative law is demanded. This may be necessary in particular if social and economic institutions prevent the participation of a whole group or class in the fruits of the common good. Social security is a general human quest. If the social structure prevents its attainment by the working class, social legislation must guarantee it to this class in principle, because without it the active participation of persons in the cultural and public life of society would be hindered. The realization of the common good of the state thus presupposes the realization of the individual common goods of many free associations that owe their existence to the free, creative initiative of persons for whom to be active means *to be,* to create what is called significantly civilization, culture. These groups and corporate bodies have rights to autonomy and to self-government and development within the order of law according to the principle of subsidiarity. A free state favors them, helps them by improving the order of law, by tax exemption, etc.; for although the state is not primarily the creator of values and culture, it must further the works of persons in their free associations because they make possible and perfect the common good. In this much, the common good is inseparable from public welfare in the literal sense. All states are welfare states, but none should become an all-providing state, a state that by its administrative agencies assumes all the freely created social and cultural functions. The administered person is unfree, and the administered culture becomes sterile.

The Common Good as the First Principle of the State. The common good and its optimal realization *hic et nunc* is the principle that determines the legitimacy of forms of government, laws and decrees, even war. The tyrant, the illegitimate ruler, is he who injures gravely the common good, the first and foremost right of the people. Some modern philosophers identify the state itself with the positive legal order, forgetting that the state lives and acts in the more comprehensive orders of international law and natural law, and forgetting also that the state lives essentially by the sociopolitical virtues, such as patriotism, civil friendship, mutual aid, respect and love of neighbor, and willingness to subordinate private interests to the common good, since the optimal concrete realization of the common good of a state is the *conditio sine qua non* of the freedom, rights, and private interests of the citizens. The positive legal order can operate efficiently and with approximate justice only if these ethical virtues constantly support it. The common good is the end of these virtues, and the positive legal order lives by them. Traditionally, the end of the state, the common good, has been held to embrace justice, social welfare, and culture. This is still a good description, but one that must be enlarged and refined with changes in the political order both inside and among states.

Political Authority

Primitive peoples usually ascribe political authority to their deities just as they attribute their laws to these deities. This interpretation of authority and law recedes with the "awakening" of critical reason, which must then explain satisfactorily the problem of political authority. This is the *majestas tremenda* of rulers and judges in any state regardless of its form or the historical phase of development of the people whose political life form the state is. In harsh reality, the state is the armed police, the military barracks, the criminal court, or the hangman; and in all ages there have been pleas that men should live together without coercive rule, without *arche,* that is to say, anarchically. Humanitarian or religiously inspired love, an imputed fundamental urge toward mutual help (Kropotkin), or human altruism have been proposed as foundations for new communal movements. Yet all such experiments have failed after a period of initial enthusiasm. Certainly love is a great inspiration, but man must live—and love—in the security of legal order. This security implies that all participants in the order may rely upon it without risk and that all will conform to the order, if need be as subjects of coercive power and public punishment.

Necessity of Authority. No human community can have enduring life without law: *ubi societas ibi jus,* but also *ubi jus ibi auctoritas.* Communities less inclusive than the state must be able to rely on the possibility of an appeal to the final authority, the common legal order with ultimate power of decision. Political authority has a monopoly of coercive power, enforcing legislative enactments as a coercive executive and administrator of criminal justice and as a judicial body. It protects the mutual rights and duties of all, their lives, liberties, and properties, including the rights and duties created by free contracts, etc. The imposition of obligations and the binding of consciences has always been and is still a foremost ethical and political problem, because it is in the hands of fallible men, subject to the highest of all temptations, that of power. Those in authority and in power have the right to demand obedience, the free assent of free men; but if authority is gravely abused by the tyrant, by arbitrary and unjust laws, there is presented the severe problem not only of passive but of active resistance. Such an authority and power over equal, rational free persons (wholly different from the *patria potestas*) must ultimately come from Him who is the Creator and Author of all men and Who is all-wise, all-just, and omnipotent. This has been recognized in all civilizations not expressly atheistic. Parenthetically, it explains why divine-right theories could be accepted by reasonable men.

Origin of Authority. Christian tradition has always taught that political power comes from God. He who gave man his nature and gave him reason and free will to shape his own forms of living together is the origin of political authority as He is the origin of the state. But just as the state came into existence only through the reason and will of those who first formed it and continues in existence by a daily plebiscite and indisputable moral necessity, so political authority was not given by God immediately in a concrete legitimate form. Because anarchy is an impossibility, even in the *status naturae integrae,* political authority was born in the same moment that the state was born. It is mediately from God; immediately its form, its constitution, is determined by men who as free persons may never owe "blind" obedience to any human authority. In constituting political authority, men must order its competencies, form, etc., to the common good, which is the only source of the legitimacy of political authority and of all its acts.

What eventually came to be called the constituent power rested originally with the people who constituted themselves as the state. No individual could by any particular gift of character or wisdom have a "natural" inborn right to political authority; the only means by which this authority might be conferred was a pact, a consensus of fellowmen. Naturally, once an individual or a "collegium" of elders, a "senate," was established to rule, all owed obedience to laws and commands, so long as these served the common good, the realization of which is the categorical duty of rulers and ruled alike. In the writings of the Church Fathers, the schoolmen, and theologians before the French Revolution two pacts were distinguished: the pact of union, by which the state came into existence as a direct democracy, and the pact of subjection, by which a particular form of government (regime) was established by the original holder of political authority, the people themselves. In consequence, all rulers distinct from the whole people hold their authority by positive law. There is neither a divine right of monarchy nor a natural right of democracy. Forms of government are historical forms, to be judged according to the service they render for the realization of the common good of a people in a given stage of development.

All forms of government are limited thus by natural law (and divine law) and by the natural rights of persons that are indelibly part of the essential content of the common good. Furthermore, the constituent power is returned to the people in a justifiable revolution or in the event of collapse of the public order. An illegitimate ruler is legitimized, not by prescription, but by the consensus of the people who sanction his regime because and insofar as he actually serves the common good. Thus it is evident that the concrete actual realization of the common good is the objective principle of legitimacy, not only tradition or majority opinion, which is all too often manufactured.

''Indifference'' of the Church to Forms of Government

The ''partner'' of the Church universal is historically and in principle not so much the abstract state as the pluralism of concrete states, each having its historical form, development, and constitutional law. To speak of eras of absolute monarchies or of aristocratic feudalism, for example, is to refer to historical tendencies, to Weberian ''ideal-types,'' rather than to concrete forms that were everywhere identical. Although the democratic principle of legitimacy has become dominant (see the *Universal Declaration of Human Rights*, art. 18–21), so that even totalitarian states must formally proclaim it, the concrete forms of government not only vary but vary considerably. The Church universal, called to teach and baptize all nations through the history of civilization, is only by historical accident, not by nature, Occidental. The Church can and must accommodate its religious activity as *mater et magistra* to various cultures, civilizations, and political forms. In all these the Church must claim its liberty (*Ut* [*ecclesia*] *tibi serviat secure libertate*). Political forms that leave to the Church universal this field of secured liberty are indifferent to the Church. The field is greater in a ''neutral'' democracy than in an antireligious ''laicist'' democracy or in an absolutist (e.g., Gallican) regime. Totalitarian states guarantee no such field constitutionally, and in them the Church becomes the suffering underground Church of Silence.

Supernatural Vocation of the Church. The Church always opposes a fanatic devaluation of the world as essentially sinful, as the realm of the Prince of Darkness. It opposes as well its own definite identification with historically specific forms of political life, born out of the freedom of man to organize his political and social life in independence. Admittedly, on certain occasions such an identification has been avoided only at the last moment. Ruling classes have often tried to identify their transitory interests with the Church in order to gain perpetuity for themselves, and churchmen have often been deceived or have succumbed to temptations of power. But a full identification has always been avoided, else the Church would have disappeared with past forms. Her indifference to legitimate political forms has its ultimate reason in her supernatural vocation.

This indifference of the Church universal to forms of government, as long as and insofar as they respect the *libertas ecclesiae* that permits the Church to fulfill her supernatural end through the millennia and within the various civilizations and cultures, does not absolve the Christian theorist from studying the profound and universal trends found in these civilizations. The present era is witness to the slow and difficult growth of a world civilization toward political forms that are called democratic. These embody the demands for the self-determination of mature nations that need neither temporal nor ecclesiastical guardians. Even the ''new'' nations demand effective bills of rights, representation based on universal suffrage, equality before the law, and democratic legitimacy (consent of the ruled). The latter demand is generally accepted in theory even by totalitarian regimes, and the others have been enunciated in the Universal Declaration of Human Rights and acknowledged in the 1944 Christmas message of Pius XII and in an encyclical of John XXIII, PACEM IN TERRIS.

The Church and Democracy. The ''new'' democratic trends at least imply a new relationship between state and Church as compared with older forms of union with all their dangers of GALLICANISM and jurisdictionalism in relation to the freedom of the Church. The modern trend has been toward the free Church in the free state, toward FREEDOM OF RELIGION in constitutional law, and toward a friendly form of ''separation'' in societies that have become or are becoming religiously and culturally pluralistic. Throughout the 19th century the basic issue was subordinated to others that were less important, e.g., the challenge to the temporal power of the papacy, once a protection of the *libertas ecclesiae,* as a result of the demand for Italian national union on a semidemocratic basis. During the great controversy over the reform of laissez-faire capitalism and the demands of workers for equal rights as citizens, workers apostatized in great numbers wherever the older ''union of throne and altar'' still existed or was held as the ideal. Catholic social movements could not help but become ''liberal'' and ''democratic'' as they freed themselves from the tutelage of paternalistic employers, princes, and parish priests. Until the dispute over integralism, priests continued to hold to the fiction of a Christian, i.e., Catholic society, although the ''real'' society as distinguished from the ''legal'' was threatened by the progressive mass apostasy of intellectuals and workers. Also, post-Reformation ecclesiology had stressed the institutional and juridical aspect of the monarchical papal Church so that ''democratic'' thinkers were suspect as antiecclesiastical. This occurred despite the fact that state and Church do not and cannot have univocally the same constitutional principles and despite what Joseph de Maistre and other conservative thinkers sought to prove.

The 19th century was thus an era of fictional identifications, at least in Europe. In the name of liberty, doctrinaire liberal democrats repudiated the Church and the faith; and in the name of faith and the union of throne and altar, Catholic Christians repudiated liberal democratic demands for social justice and political reform. The Body of Christ was torn apart; on the ''left'' was His justice, on the ''right'' was His truth. But truth without justice too easily becomes tyranny; and justice without truth, anarchy. Since 1914 these false identifications have more and more disappeared. The once-repudiated demands of Liberal Catholics and of the ''democratic'' Catholic social movements have become the program of Christian democracy, with the consent of the overwhelming majority, even of conservatives, and with the approval of the popes of the 20th century (except, perhaps, St. Pius X).

Bibliography: THOMAS AQUINAS, *Selected Political Writings,* ed. A. P. D'ENTRÈVES, tr. J. G. DAWSON (Oxford 1948). J. F. CRONIN, *Catholic Social Principles* (Milwaukee 1950). J. EPPSTEIN, *The Catholic Tradition of the Law of Nations* (London 1935). J. MARITAIN, *Man and the State* (Chicago 1951). J. MESSNER, *Social Ethics: Natural Law in the Modern World,* tr. J. J. DOHERTY (new ed. St. Louis 1964). A. J. OSGNIACH, *The Christian State* (Milwaukee 1943). *Philosophy of the State* (*American Catholic Philosophical Association. Proceedings of the Annual Meeting* 15; 1939). *Philosophy and Order* (*ibid.* 17; 1941). F. J. POWERS, comp. and ed., *Papal Pronouncements on the Political Order* (Westminster, Md. 1952). H. A. ROMMEN, *The Natural Law,* tr. T. P. HANLEY (St. Louis 1948); *The State in Catholic Thought* (St. Louis 1945). Y. SIMON, *Philosophy of Democratic Government* (Chicago 1951).

[H. A. ROMMEN]

STATES OF THE CHURCH

When the concept of papal temporal rule came into existence in the 8th century, it was a mixed one, in which elements of papal patrimonial rights, of former imperial jurisdiction, and of the traditional supremacy of the Roman bishops existed side by side. To the high Middle Ages the question whether the popes ought to be rulers of a given territory in central Italy did not really present itself. For the first time in the early 14th century Pierre Dubois posed the problem in these terms. The Middle Ages knew the papal territory as *terrae seu patrimonium ecclesiae.* The imperial donors spoke of papal lands as being *in iure principatu et ditione ecclesiae Romanae;* OTTO I swore to defend the *terra sancti Petri.*

It is impossible to treat the Papal State on a purely regional and territorial basis. On the one hand its history is inseparable from that of the papal theocracy and the papal Curia; on the other, one cannot make a clear distinction between Papal State policy, and papal temporal policy elsewhere in Italy or indeed in Europe. It is also hard to draw a line between developments of the papal bureaucracy that affected the Papal State and those that did not. From the early 14th century the Apostolic Camera was both the financial and juridical bureau for the Papal State and that for the Roman Church in general. Financial and Papal State policy were always closely related.

Origins of the Papal State. From the time of the Peace of the Church the Roman see possessed great landed wealth, both in Italy and elsewhere as far afield as Asia Minor. The use of this wealth was primarily to maintain the Roman churches and shrines and to support the social welfare of the Roman people. For the latter purpose the PAPACY from the late 6th century assumed many responsibilities formerly met by the imperial government. An elaborate organization existed to run the papal estates, and the ''rectors'' and ''defenders'' influenced later administrative developments.

The Papal State emerged out of the quarrel between the Holy See and the imperial government at the time of the controversy over ICONOCLASM. In 725–726 GREGORY II put himself at the head of regional Italian resistance to the taxation of the emperor LEO III. Some scholars have suggested that his actions and those of later 8th-century popes were part of a long meditated plan prepared by the papal bureaucracy; others have suggested that the military pressure of the LOMBARDS and Byzantine impotence to resist it were the decisive factors. In 739 GREGORY III sent an embassy to CHARLES MARTEL, the Frankish mayor of the palace, referring to him as *PATRICIUS ROMANORUM* and asking for help. In 749 the approval given by Pope ZACHARY to PEPIN's usurpation of the Frankish crown was the turning point. When STEPHEN II faced a Lombard threat from King Aistulf in 752 he wrote to Pepin for aid. In 753 he traveled to Francia and met Pepin at Ponthion in Champagne. The Frankish king swore to restore the Exarchate of RAVENNA and the rights and territories of the *res publica* (*see* DONATION OF CONSTANTINE). There were then two Frankish campaigns against Aistulf, who in 756 was made to swear to return to the Romans the Exarchate of Ravenna, most of Pentapolis, and towns in Emilia and Umbria. A papal territory may be said to have existed from this point.

Some scholars emphasize the care that the 8th-century popes took, in spite of the iconoclast controversy, not to derogate explicitly from Byzantine sovereignty.

The territorial interests and ambitions of the Roman nobility, who were strongly represented in the Roman clergy, also probably played a part. The juridical position of the new state was for long unclear, complicated by these factors and others, such as the confusion between papal patrimonies or landed estates in the strict sense and other lands occupied by "Romans."

Development and Early Constitution. The first period of the history of the Papal State probably ended with the tragic death of JOHN VIII (882). The state entered into treatylike relations with the Carolingians that left it as an autonomous region under Frankish protection. Political turbulence in Rome, sometimes abetted by the popes, led Louis the Pious to direct his son Lothair in 824 to issue the *Constitutio Romana* which imposed a stricter regime of protection on Rome and its surrounding territories. The *Constitutio* called for papal and Frankish *missi* to sit together in Rome and to hear appeals against officers of the papal administration. The Romans, moreover, but not the popes, had to swear allegiance to the Frankish emperor. Within a generation, however, the political dissolution of the Carolingian empire, factional squabbling in Rome, and Muslim attacks combined to leave Carolingian protection a dead letter and papal territorial authority severely curtailed. A second period ran from the early 10th century to the era of the Gregorian reforms. This period was marked by a continuous but weak German presence in Rome and by the frequent subjection of the Papal State to factions among the Roman nobility—notably the CRESCENTII and TUSCULANI. But it was significant also by the emergence of a more truly autonomous Papal State, no longer impeded by Carolingian officials, and showing some consciousness of its powers in its appointments of rectors, and in the legal formulas used by papal officials in the exercise of their jurisdiction. Although under the dynasty of MAROZIA and the rule of Alberic of Spoleto, *princeps et senator* (932–954), the Papal State was subject to an aristocratic clique, its administrative foundations were being laid. The restoration of Ottonian power in Italy after 962, however, placed important checks on the Papal State. While OTTO III recognized that the popes exercised *potestas legalis* in their dominions, he claimed for himself the *jus publicum et legitima potestas.*

One must distinguish between the areas over which the popes had treaty rights and those that they effectively governed. There is no reliable text of any treaty made between the popes and the Frankish government prior to that of 817, but it is probable that from the promises made by Pepin from 754 onward, the Franks tended to guarantee Roman rule over areas wider than Roman power was able to administer. It may be that the early papal-Frankish treaties were based on the frontiers between the Byzantine Empire and the Lombards, at periods in the 7th or early 8th century when Byzantine power was relatively strong. This would explain the papal claim, mentioned in the *LIBER PONTIFICALIS*, to the area south of a line from Luni in Liguria to Monfelice on the Adriatic.

The core of the Papal State was the former Byzantine duchy of Rome. The Franks imposed a compromise territorial settlement on the papacy. To the north of Rome, the popes asked for Venetia and Istria, Ravenna and the Pentapolis, and all of Lombard Tuscany. Charlemagne declined to hand over Venice and Istria, permitted shared rule in Ravenna among the popes, the patriarch of Ravenna, and himself, and added a slice of southern Tuscany to the duchy of Rome while retaining the rest of Tuscany as part of the Lombard kingdom. In central Italy, Charlemagne extended papal rule into the Sabina, added some lands around Perugia to effect communications between Rome and the northeast, and advanced papal territory to the south into the Liri valley. He did not assign the duchy of Benevento to the papacy. Effective papal power in Emilia and in the Exarchate of Ravenna dwindled almost to nothing in the late 9th century; and there was a similar decline of power in Pentapolis, as is made clear in the donation of eight counties there by Otto III to SYLVESTER II.

Growth of the Papal State. The policies of LEO IX and his successors in the GREGORIAN REFORM were vital to the temporal power, particularly in their results for southern Italy. The papal court was beginning to be acutely affected by feudal law. The reform policy of active intervention on the southern borders of the Papal State and of establishing feudal sovereignty over the new Norman principalities strengthened papal authority in the Papal State proper, as did also the reform emphasis on the patrimonial and financial rights of the Holy See. Benevento became a papal enclave (1050).

In the 12th century the Papal State was still essentially the area "from Acquapendente to Ceprano." In this zone the rights of the Church were interpreted in an increasingly feudal sense, while the Holy See showed itself willing to acquiesce to some extent in the setting up of communes. The most important exponents of the "feudal" policy were Adrian IV and his chamberlain, Cardinal BOSO. Although 12th-century popes had not abandoned their claims to the eastern lands (particularly Ferrara) and had added to them the claim to the allodial lands of MATILDA OF TUSCANY, effective papal rule was nevertheless sometimes reduced to Rome. And in Rome and the district, the new commune that had come into existence in 1143 made the task of the popes more difficult.

The foundations of the later Papal State were laid by Innocent III. To the existing area of effective rule he added the duchy of Spoleto (in its late imperial sense) and the march of Ancona. To administer the state he set up rectorates in these areas and in the other provinces of Campagna-Marittima, Sabina, and the Patrimony of St. Peter in Tuscany. Building on this basis, subsequent 13th-century popes set up a machine of provincial taxation and justice. By mid century parliaments existed in most provinces for conciliar, financial, and legislative purposes. Particularly after the acquisition of Romagna in 1278, the new state possessed a modest but appreciable military and financial power.

By 1300 most of the essential governmental organs of the later Papal States were in existence. In spite of the severe strain placed on the state by the absence of the popes during the AVIGNON PAPACY, and by their long and costly struggles with the Ghibelline tyrants of north Italy (*see* GUELFS AND GHIBELLINES), the administrative machine held its ground and developed. By mid-14th century most of the communes were too weak to oppose the formidable attempt to centralize and rationalize the institutions of the state effected by the Spanish Cardinal Gil ALBORNOZ. Many minor tyrannies, however, remained to be a source of disorder until the 16th century.

The work of Albornoz was advanced by later Avignon popes (notably GREGORY XI), only to be all but undone by the effects of the WESTERN SCHISM. Fifteenth-century popes (notably MARTIN V and NICHOLAS V) had to rebuild the Papal State with financial and political resources far inferior to those of the Avignon popes. Under SIXTUS IV and especially under ALEXANDER VI, an exaggerated nepotism became the aim rather than the instrument of papal policy.

The declining international position of the papacy was offset in the Papal State by increasingly centralized administration and by the inability of all but the largest units, whether feudal lordships, communes, or tyrannies, to resist central pressure. Tyrants such as the MALATESTA of Rimini succumbed largely from economic debility. Finally, under the new strains placed on them by the wars of France and Spain in Italy, most of the remaining semi-autonomous communes or seigniories were reduced to obedience. Bologna and Perugia, the ESTE of Ferrara, and the Montefeltro of Urbino all lost their old positions in the first half of the 16th century. The action of PIUS IV against the CARAFA and the COLONNA marked the end of the old style of baronial nepotism. His attempt at a root and branch reform of the Papal State was abortive; but reorganization of the various provincial legations and of central justice and finance nevertheless took place in the course of the century.

Economic and Demographic Factors. The economic power of the early Papal State was closely related to the patrimonial wealth of the Roman see and the application of that wealth on behalf of the Roman people through the agency of the Roman deaconties and *xenodochia.* In the period from Zacharias to Leo III the papal patrimonies were partly reorganized into larger units (*domuscultae*). This reorganization was much resented by the Roman nobles, who wished to be granted Church property at nominal rents.

The influence of the nobles prevailed after the death of John VIII; in the late 9th and early 10th centuries most of the huge papal estates were feudalized and fell into the hands of the great Roman families. At the same time, the value of many of the great estates experienced a decline, because of Arab raids, political disorders, and the effects of these on the productivity of the soil. It is, however, disputed whether the decline in agricultural production was as great as was once thought. The turnover to grazing in many parts of south Italy probably preceded this period. Many papal and Roman estates, however, were lost, e.g., those in the Neapolitan *campagna* and probably most of those that were in the area around Ravenna.

In spite of the reorganization of the finances of the Roman see during the reform period, demesne and Papal State revenues were slow in expanding, and the great alienated estates were never recovered. The *LIBER CENSUUM,* compiled at the end of the 12th century, shows a wide variety of patrimonial and feudal dues, but mostly of a residual nature and amounting in all to only a modest revenue. Only after the great expansion of the Papal State in the 13th century, particularly with the absorption of such rich areas as the march of Ancona, with its port of Ancona, did the state acquire a respectable revenue. It is true that military expenditure often exceeded income, but the same was true of many European states.

Although after depression, plague, and war in the 14th century the population and wealth of the Papal State decreased, the government became stronger, which suggests that revenues were on the whole larger. In 15th century the Papal State revenues began to form an even larger proportion of total papal revenue, and this tendency was accentuated in the 16th century by more centralized government and by the increased prosperity of Rome, which rose from 30,000 to 100,000 inhabitants in that century.

Bibliography: W. ULLMANN, *The Growth of Papal Government in the Middle Ages* (2d ed. New York 1962). O. BERTOLINI, "Il problema delle origini del potere temporale dei papi," *Miscellanea Pio Paschini,* 2 v. (Rome 1948–49) 1:103–171. K. JORDAN, "das Eindringen des Lehnswesen in das Rechtsleben der römischen Kurie," *Archiv für Urkundenforschung* 12 (1931) 13–110. L. M. HARTMANN, "Grundherrschaft und Bureaukratie im Kirchenstaate vom 8. bis zum 10. Jahrhundert," *Vierteljahrschrift für Sozial- und Wirtschaftsgeschichte* 7 (1909) 142–158. D. P. WALEY, *The Papal*

State in the Thirteenth Century (New York 1961). J. GUIRAUD, *L'État pontifical après le grand schisme* (Paris 1895). P. PARTNER, *The Lands of St. Peter* (Berkeley and Los Angeles 1972). P. TOUBERT, *Les structures du Latium médiévale,* 2 v. (Rome 1973). M. CARAVALE, *Lo Stato pontificio da Martino V a Pio IX* (Turin 1978). M. LAUFS, *Politik und Recht bei Innocenz III* (Cologne 1980). T. F. X. NOBLE, *The Republic of St. Peter: The Birth of the Papal State, 680–825* (Philadelphia 1984). F. MARAZZI, *I 'Patrimonia Sanctae Romanae' nel Lazio (secoli IV–X): Struttura amministrativa e prassi gestionali* (Rome 1998).

[P. PARTNER/T. F. X. NOBLE]

1600 to 1796. Following years of consolidation and centralization, the two centuries prior to the French invasion of 1796 witnessed a progressive decline in the Papal State, culminating in its temporary disappearance in 1798. The change from the previous period was notable.

Sixteenth-century popes had succeeded in transforming their authority over their realms into a system of absolute monarchy. They regained the large, quasi-independent fiefs and neutralized or abolished the political and judicial power of the feudal families. Through the instrumentality of the papal secretary of state and the Cardinal Camerlengo, charged with administering the temporal domain, the popes made their authority effective in the provinces, or legations, where they named the resident functionaries. They created specialized central administrative organisms, which functioned suitably. The college of cardinals was fragmented into specialized congregations and lost its collegial power, which had once rivaled papal authority. Brigandage declined with the decline of the feudatories, who used to profit well by protecting brigands. Giovanni Botero wrote in 1595: ''The ecclesiastical state is more peaceful today than formerly, and the authority of the ruler greater than ever.'' The danger was that this machine, well designed for a state expanding economically and socially, would become outmoded; this happened in the ensuing period when internal and international factors conspired to jeopardize its future.

Internally, the Roman aristocracy and families owing their wealth and honors to nepotism, such as the Pamphili, Rospigliosi, Chigi, Ottoboni, and Pignatelli, amassed great political influence and economic power, to the detriment of the central authority. Innocent XI (1676–89) attempted to remedy these evils by eliminating the post of cardinal legate, by combating small-scale nepotism, and by introducing rigid economies to ward off bankruptcy. His successors tried to unify the provinces administratively. In this work Cardinal Giulio ALBERONI distinguished himself by his energy when, as legate to Ravenna under Clement XII (1730–40), he sought to eliminate the existing autonomies of medieval origin and annexed the ancient republic of SAN MARINO to the States of the Church, at least temporarily. Bologna completely lost its ancient municipal autonomy in 1788.

Political Decline. These attempts at internal renovation failed to stem the state's growing political weakness. Internationally the balance of power preserved an equilibrium of sorts among the states of the peninsula, but left all of Italy vulnerable to outside pressure from the national monarchies. These powers took advantage of this situation by impertinently, even brutally, seeking to extort from the papal government renunciations of some of its rights and prerogatives, to force it to support their selfish political interests, and to introduce changes conformed to their own juridical and anticurial views. LOUIS XIV, king of France (1638–1715), used strong pressure, and at times violence, to humiliate this state and its rulers. Thus when the duke of Créqui, the French ambassador, unjustifiably insisted on extending the diplomatic ''right of quarters'' beyond his dwelling in Rome to embrace an area ''as far as his eye could behold,'' an incident occurred between his entourage and the Corsican guards, which the French government used to impose its will on Alexander VII (1662). Innocent XI (1676–89), however, refused to bow to a repetition of these pretensions; and Alexander VIII in 1691 caused Louis XIV to renounce these claims, tolerated in no other capital. More extreme were the pressures applied to Clement XIII (1758–69) and Clement XIV (1769–74) by the Bourbon courts to break down papal resistance to the suppression of the JESUITS. Besides severing diplomatic relations, France occupied Avignon and Venaissin; and Naples seized Benevento and Pontecorvo.

Economic Decline. Agriculture, industry, and trade remained static or deteriorated. The same was true of social conditions. Decline was especially marked in Latium, a region almost denuded of population, where the rule was large-scale ownership, concentrated almost entirely in the hands of the Roman aristocracy, whose income derived largely from rents paid by shepherds for pasturage. The plain neighboring on Rome, the *agro romano,* occupied 485 square miles, but its ownership was limited in 1789 to a mere 113 families. The Borghese family alone possessed 55,000 acres; the Sforza, 27,000. Instead of improving conditions and exploiting these holdings efficiently, the wealthy proprietors were content to see their lands leased, subleased, and then subsubleased to wretched *contadini* weakened by disease contracted from the undrained, malaria-breeding Pontine marshes. Their primitive methods eked the barest subsistence from their tiny parcels. The wheat crop barely sufficed for local consumption; its export was forbidden.

The only industries of any size were the alum mines at Tolfa and the foundries at Canino, Bracciano, and

Conca employing about 300 to smelt the iron ore mixed on the island of Elba. Outside of these the shops were small, family-run affairs. The Marches were relatively prosperous, especially Ancona, which became a free port in 1732, and Senigallia, which attracted merchants from Italy and abroad to its famous fair. Foreign trade was, however, minimal in quantity. Despite the number of small towns no real middle class developed.

Rome always remained an important commercial center because of the constant flow of ecclesiastics, pilgrims, and tourists. A cultural capital, it was a magnet for artists in search of inspiration, scholars in search of the past, and collectors in quest of purchases. In 1768 Rome had some 159,000 inhabitants; the entire state about 2 million.

Papal Attitudes. No help could come from the sovereign or the state. The popes, who supported a court, a diplomatic corps, festivals, building construction, and maintenance, had to bear all the expenses of a great power with the revenues of a poor one. Rome itself absorbed the meager income. At the death of Clement XIV (1774), who was a good administrator, the public debt totaled 74 million scudi, although the annual revenue was only 2.5 million. When financial distress became more acute, sumptuary expenses were trimmed, but profitable, long-term investments were impossible. There was no policy for inaugurating great public works. The draining of the Pontine marshes scarcely passed the planning stage. Economic development was a very minor preoccupation of the popes, who did not wish to overload their subjects with taxes, and remedied misery by increasing alms when they could.

The governmental and administrative system finally became dilapidated. Papal departments were encumbered with inactive employees, said to number 30,000 by 1800. The clientele of cardinals and the great families could not be allowed to starve. Papal officialdom, like Roman beggary, was an institutionalized form of parasitism. The most enlightened and energetic reformer would have wasted his efforts, because the basic difficulty was economic and social sluggishness.

Peace was preserved in the States of the Church during these two centuries, but it was often accompanied by humiliation and internal disorder. It was disturbed mainly by the endemic brigandage. Public order was not seriously ruffled, save for occasional quarrels concerning diplomatic precedence or squabbles between the Romans and the dependents of foreign ambassadors. The outbreak of the French Revolution quickly altered this situation. During the 19th century disturbances and movements originating outside this state caused ever-increasing public disorders and dissatisfaction within it.

French Intervention, 1796 to 1815. Neither the economic recession of the 17th century, the economic stagnation of the 18th, the critique of the Enlightenment, nor the slow deterioration of governmental and administrative organisms had sufficed to disturb seriously the States of the Church. A tremor of adequate magnitude came from abroad, started by the FRENCH REVOLUTION in 1789. It was so powerful that this state, even were it better equipped, would not have remained shockproof, any more than other European states. French revolutionists soon occupied the papal territories of AVIGNON and Venaissin lying within French borders; and the Constituent Assembly decreed their annexation to France (Sept. 14, 1791). Rome became the refuge of numerous *émigrés* following the condemnation of the Civil Constitution of the Clergy by the papal bull *Charitas.* Their tragic tales filled the Roman Curia and, still more, the populace with terror and detestation of the Revolution. At the same time many republican agents arrived in Rome to propagate revolutionary ideas and found admirers in educated circles influenced by the doctrines of the ENLIGHTENMENT and sympathetic toward Freemasonry. The first revolutionary associations arose as well as popular antirevolutionary outbursts. One of these resulted in the assassination of the French diplomat Nicolas de Bassville (1793); and another in the murder of General Mathieu Duphot (1797).

Active French intervention began with the descent into Italy of an army under General Napoleon Bonaparte in 1796 (*see* NAPOLEON I). He proposed to the Directory that he lay hands on Loreto, containing "the immense treasures that superstition has amassed during 15 centuries. They are valued at one million pounds sterling." In May 1796 Bonaparte received orders to occupy Rome; but he took only the legations (Bologna, Ferrara, Ravenna) in June. Bonaparte proved a prudent governor, because he foresaw his later need for papal cooperation to regulate the affairs of the Church in France. "The influence of Rome is incalculable," he declared; "I ambition more the title of savior than that of destroyer of the Holy See." Once more the Papal State became involved in the general history of the Church. Bonaparte evacuated Ravenna, Faenza, and Ancona (June 23) after 33 million francs were paid to the Directory. Despite the size of this ransom, Rome expressed relief.

After the Austrians were badly defeated in 1797, PIUS VI, who had manifested hostility toward France, had to sign the Treaty of Tolentino (Feb. 19, 1797), ceding Avignon, Bologna, and Ferrara to France, and Romagna to the Cisalpine Republic, an emanation of French power. After Duphot's murder General Berthier seized Rome under orders from the Directory (February 1798). Five days later a group of "patriots" took advantage of the presence of French arms and proclaimed the birth of the Roman Republic and the demise of papal temporal power. Pius VI was carried off a prisoner to Tuscany, then to Valence in southern France, where he died (Aug. 29, 1799). Defeats in the War of the Second Coalition forced the French to evacuate Rome (Sept. 30, 1799), ended the Roman Republic, and led to the restoration of the States of the Church, minus the legations, according to the Treaty of Lunéville (Feb. 9, 1801). The Neapolitan government, whose army had delivered Rome, continued acting as sovereign there; but in 1800 it turned over the city to the newly elected Pius VII (1800–23). The French victory at Marengo (June 14, 1800) would have threatened this fragile restoration of papal authority, had not Napoleon been eager to restore religious peace to France and to arrange the CONCORDAT OF 1801. It was he who obliged the Austrians to abandon their claims to the legations, and the king of Naples to evacuate the States of the Church, including Benevento and Pontecorvo. The Cisalpine Republic, however, was restored and soon was called the kingdom of Italy (Jan. 26, 1802). This placed the northern boundary of the States of the Church along the line established by the Treaty of Tolentino.

First Restoration. Pius VII was now sovereign of a territory reduced in size and economically less viable than before. He sought first a reorganization of the whole government and administration and designated four commissions to elaborate a plan. The papal bull *Post diuturnas* (Oct. 10, 1800), which promulgated the reforms, reflected two diverse currents of opinion evident in these commissions. The traditionalists regarded all the recent French innovations as diabolical and wanted only a return to the old state of affairs. The second group considered the former organization outmoded and a fresh start essential. The papal decision favored the conservatives, with few exceptions. Such improvements as were introduced were rendered inoperative by the passive resistance of the prelates assigned to the new posts. The statute did, however, envision the confiding of some positions to laymen, i.e., to representatives of the nobility. All that remained of this first restoration was the noble guard.

Another measure, which might have produced good results, was the freeing of commerce, up to then practically a state monopoly. But lack of ports or industry left the States of the Church unable to develop commerce in the near future. A timid agrarian reform was inaugurated, which aimed to divide the latifundia and make it possible for cultivators to purchase the land. But these poor persons lacked the capital to buy. Structural reforms hesitantly outlined, devoid of means or will to put them into effect, represented the extent of the restoration in 1800. The States of the Church continued to vegetate during their remaining decades of life.

Relations with Napoleon I. When Bonaparte became Emperor Napoleon I (1804), he allowed Pius VII to consecrate him but did not intend to leave to the pope the least liberty of political option as a temporal sovereign, even that of declaring his neutrality in European conflicts. Napoleon sought to impose the Continental System upon the Papal State. Pius VII thought otherwise and refused to put the boycott into effect in his territory. This led to a crisis that began with the French occupation of Ancona (1805), continued with the seizure of Civitavecchia (1806), the Marches (1807), and Rome itself (1808). Pius VII was placed under arrest (June 5, 1809) and kept in captivity at Savona and Fontainebleau until 1814. An imperial decree annexed the States of the Church to the French Empire and announced the formation of a commission (*Consulta*) charged with administering the former papal realm (1810). The region was then divided into the two departments of Tiber and Trasiméne. Rome was proclaimed second city of the empire after Paris; and Napoleon's son became king of Rome, a post once held by his father. Though a prisoner, the pope still urged passive resistance. The reactions of the Romans varied. Most ecclesiastics observed the papal instructions; most of the nobles collaborated with the French in the hope of saving their wealth and position. The mass of the populace maintained a stubborn, malevolent opposition because of affection for the pope, the influence of the religious, and discontent with increased taxes and the suppression of charitable institutions, which used to distribute the indispensable alms. Young men fled military conscription and formed wandering bands, always ready to take to highway robbery.

French laws of the Civil Code were applied in the region. De Tournon, a capable administrator, was named prefect of Rome and undertook considerable public works, such as the restoration of ancient monuments, urban planning, the laying out of the Pincio as a public park, clearing the Tiber's channel, highway improvements, and draining marshes. Napoleon was eager to revive the old Rome and build a new one and to improve economic conditions, but he lacked time and was too much preoccupied with his perennial wars. From 1814 the French Empire was in its death throes.

Pius VII was liberated and reentered Rome (May 24, 1814), where he was hailed with enthusiasm. A second restoration was about to begin but immediately faced imposing obstacles. Murat, king of Naples, coveted the States of the Church but lost his claim and his throne when he allied with Napoleon who returned from Elba. Then the Congress of Vienna, which aimed to give a territorial status to Europe after Napoleon's downfall, refused for a while to recognize the papal temporal sovereignty. Austria wanted to annex part of Italy and install in power princes devoted to her. Due in good part to the diplomatic skill of Cardinal E. CONSALVI, papal secretary of state, the Congress permitted the pope to regain his former states, save for some alterations of borders and the permanent loss of Avignon and Venaissin (June 1815).

1815 to 1870. This final period presents two aspects. One concerns domestic events in the papal realm; the other deals with developments outside this region. In a sense the *RISORGIMENTO,* the movement for Italian unification, combined the two and was largely responsible for the disappearance of the papal temporal power.

Second Restoration. Upon returning from his long imprisonment Pius VII confronted the problem of administrative realignment, since the French occupation, for all its unpopularity, had roused middle-class aspirations for a more modern regime. Consalvi favored these demands within limits and was largely responsible for the promulgation of a constitutional charter in 1816, which marked some progress, although it still bore close resemblance to the privileges accorded by enlightened despots in mid-18th century. Opposition to these modest innovations in curial and aristocratic circles was strong enough to impede the effecting of substantial reforms. This, coupled with the worsening economic situation in 1816 and the impact of the *Risorgimento,* led to the formation of numerous secret societies such as the CARBONARI, especially in Romagna. These found a strong following among the lesser nobility and bourgeoisie eager for opportunities to hold public office and participate in the government. Soon after this restoration started, sectarian influences caused incidents in the legations and Marches.

Gregory XVI. Counterrevolutionary forces regained full strength under Leo XII (1823–29), Pius VIII (1829–30), and GREGORY XVI (1831–46). Following the July Revolution in Paris (1830), the Carbonari joined forces with the liberals against the papal temporal power, in the hope that France would impose on the HOLY ALLIANCE respect for the principle of nonintervention. Insurrection broke out in Bologna (Feb. 4, 1831) and spread rapidly to Umbria, Romagna, and the Marches. It gave rise to several provisional governments, which were unified under Terenzio Mamiani. The revolt failed only because of Austrian and French armed intervention, which quickly restored the papal authority. The great powers (France, Great Britain, Austria, Russia, and Prussia) met in conference and in a memorandum cataloged the reforms required in the Papal States to avert further revolutionary outbursts.

Gregory XVI refused to accept most of its proposals such as the admission of the laity to positions of authority, enforcement of the 1816 constitution, organization of consultative representative assemblies on the municipal and provincial levels, and creation of an auditor's office. Minor changes were introduced in 1832, notably the establishment of a corps of Swiss soldiers, but the memorandum was essentially shelved in the Vatican archives. Since papal authority was based on divine right, criticisms were regarded as disrespect toward God Himself, and revolutionary attempts as sacrilegious. The papacy found it difficult, if not impossible, to introduce the requested political and administrative reforms in its state. This was reinforced by the fact that the papacy considered its temporal and spiritual power inextricably intertwined and therefore feared that limitations on the former would inevitably impinge on the latter.

Final Quarter Century. PIUS IX (1846–78) appeared to Italian patriots for a short time to herald a new era. He had earlier outlined a reformist program for the temporal power in his "Thoughts on the Public Administration of the Papal States" (1845). Once pope, he granted a generous amnesty to political offenders, organized a lay council (Consulta di Stato) and a civil guard, permitted limited press freedom, and protested against Austrian occupation of Ferrara. All this gave further impetus to the movement for Italian unification and to constitutional tendencies. By the Fundamental Statute (March 14, 1848), the pope provided his subjects with a constitution. He also allowed the papal banner to be adorned with the tricolor cockade and sent troops to guard the Po River during the hostilities between Piedmont and Austria.

As spiritual head of all Catholics, however, the pope could not make war on Austria; and this impossibility was reaffirmed in the papal allocation of April 29, 1848. This alienated both liberals and patriots and made difficult his relations with the legislature, which opened on June 5, and with the constitutional ministry presided over by Mamiani. Pellegrino ROSSI, who succeeded Mamiani early in September, was not acceptable to conservatives because of his constitutional convictions or to liberals because of his opposition to involving the Papal States in warlike enterprises. Rossi's opposition to the Piedmontese requests for a military league against Austria increased the hatred of the radicals, by whose hands he was assassinated (Nov. 15, 1848).

The ensuing popular tumults forced Pius IX to flee Rome (Nov. 24, 1848) and take refuge at Gaeta in the kingdom of Naples. Revolutionaries proclaimed the Roman Republic (Feb. 9, 1849), soon placed under the control of a triumvirate composed of Mazzini, Saffi, and Armellini, who determined to resist the imminent invasion by Catholic France, Austria, Spain, and Naples, which accepted the petition of Cardinal G. ANTONELLI for aid. With Austrian troops pressing from the north and

French forces besieging Rome, the republic collapsed. Pius IX reentered his capital (April 1850), but French soldiers remained in the city and Austrian ones in the legations. It was now clear that papal temporal power could continue only with foreign military aid. The events of 1848–49 deeply troubled the pope, who believed that his good will had been unworthily abused. Henceforth he was hostile to all liberal programs.

The final years of the States of the Church formed an episode in the unification of the Italian peninsula. Because of this movement the papal territory lost the legations (1860). After the papal volunteer army of ZOUAVES met defeat at Castelfidardo (Sept. 18, 1860), Italy annexed the Marches (with 133,000 votes favoring it in a plebiscite and 1,200 opposed) and Umbria (with 97,000 votes favoring it and 380 opposed). Rome was proclaimed capital of the new kingdom of Italy (1861) by Cavour. Napoleon's troops protected the remaining papal territory, but the French emperor sought to evacuate them as soom as possible. By the September Convention of 1864, concluded between the Paris government and the Italian kingdom without papal consultation, the French forces were to be withdrawn within the course of the next two years. This prompted Pius IX to issue the encyclical *Quandra cura,* deploring contemporary developments, to which was attached the Syllabus of Errors. French troops returned to stop Garibaldi's intrusion into the Papal States in 1867, remaining there until 1870. Once the Franco-Prussian War demanded the withdrawal of the French garrison, the Italians invaded the state and took Rome after some hours of bombardment, breaching the Porta Pia (Sept. 20, 1870). A plebiscite in the small area in papal hands recorded 133,681 votes in favor of annexation to Italy, 1,507 opposed. VICTOR EMMANUEL II in October proclaimed the annexation of Rome and the surrounding area. Thus ended the States of the Church. In the opinion of some the impending demise of the temporal power played a part in the bolstering of the spiritual power, and the proclamation of papal infallibility in July 1870, during the Vatican Council.

The principal states continued to recognize the personal sovereignty of the pope, admitting among other things his active and passive right to diplomatic representation. When the Law of GUARANTEES proved unacceptable to Pius IX and his successors, the Roman Question continued to be a major problem for Italy until its definitive settlement in the LATERAN PACTS (1929). The State of VATICAN CITY, which then originated, is not, however, a resurrection of the former States of the Church.

Bibliography: M. CARAVALE and A. CARACIOLO, *Lo stato pontifico da Martino V a Pio IX* (Turin 1978). P. PRODI, *The Papal Prince: The Papal Monarchy in Early Modern Europe,* tr. S. HASKINS (Cambridge 1987); *Lo sviluppo dell'assolutismo nello Stato pontificio* (Bologna 1968). M. BROSCH, *Geschichte Kirchenstaats* (Gotha 1882). A. D. WRIGHT, *The Early Modern Papacy: From the Council of Trent to the French Revolution, 1564–1789* (London 2000). S. ANSELMI, ed., *Economia e società: le Marche tra XV e XX secolo* (Bologna 1978). J. DELUMEAU, *Vie économique et sociale à Rome dans la seconde moitié du XVI*e *siècle,* 2 v. (Paris 1957–59); "Le Progrès de la centralization dans *l'État pontifical au XVI* e *siècle,*" *Revue historique* 226 (1961) 399–410; *L'Alun de Rome, XV* e*–XIX*e *siècle* (Paris 1963). G. CAROCCI, *Lo Stato della Chiesa nelle seconda meta del secolo XVI* (Milan 1961). L. DAL PANE, *Lo Stato pontificio e il movimento riformatore del Settecento* (Milan 1959). F. VENTURA, "Elementi e tentativivi di riforma nello Stato pontificio del Settecento," *Rivista Storica Italiana,* 75 (1963) 778–817; *Settecebti rifornatore,* v. 1–3 (Turin 1972–79). H. GROSS, *Rome in the Age of the Enlightenment* (Cambridge 1990). M. ANDRIEUX, *La Vie quotidienne dans la Rome pontificàle au XVIII*e *siècle* (Paris 1962). G. MOLLAT, *La Question romaine de Pie VI à Pie IX* (2d ed. Paris 1932), copious bibliog. J. LEFLON, *La Crise révolutionnaire 1789–1846* (A. FLICHE and V. MARTIN, eds., *Histoire de l'église depuis les origines jusqu'à nos jours* [Paris 1935–] 20; 1949). R. AUBERT, *Il Pontificato di Pio IX* (Turin 1969). A. DUFOURCQ, *Le Régime jacobin en Italie (1798–1799)* (Paris 1900). L. MADELIN, *La Rome de Napoléon* (Paris 1932). F. HAYWARD, *Le Dernière siècle de Rome pontificale, 1769–1870,* 2 v. (Paris 1927–28). M. PETROCCHI, *La restaurazione: Il cardinale Consalvi e la riforma del 1816* (Florence 1941); *La restaurazione romana, 1815–1823* (Florence 1943). A. VENTRONE, *L'amministrazione dello Stato Pontificio dal 1814 al 1870* (Rome 1942). M. M. O'DWYER, *The Papacy in the Age of Napoleon and the Restoration, Pius VII, 1800–1823* (New York 1985). A. ROVERI, *La Santa Sede tra rivoluzione francese e restaurazione* (Florence 1974). M. FANTI, "Bologna nell'eta moderna," *Storia di Bologna* (Bologna 1978). F. J. COPPA, *The Modern Papacy since 1789* (London 1998); *Cardinal Giacomo Antonelli and Papal Politics in European Affairs* (Albany, N.Y. 1990). A. J. REINERMAN, *Austria and the Papacy in the Age of Metternich and Revolution, 1830–1838* (Washington, D.C. 1989). M. LUPI, *Il clero a Perugia durante l'episcopato di Guiacchini Pecci (1846–78): Tra Stato Pontficio e Stato Unitario* (Rome 1998). G. MARTINA, *Pio IX (1846–50)* (Rome 1974); *Pio IX (1851–66)* (Rome 1986); *Pio IX (1867–78)* (Rome 1990); "La fine del potere temporale nella coscienza religiosa e nella cultura dell'epoca in Italia," *Archivum Historiae Pontificiae IX* (1971) 309–376. O. CHADWICK, *A History of the Popes, 1830–1914* (Oxford 1998). C. T. MCINTIRE, *England against the Papacy, 1858–61: Tories, Liberals and the Overthrow of the Papal Temporal Power during the Italian Risorgimento* (New York 1983). M. TEDESCHI, *Francia e Ingilterra di fronte alla questione romana, 1859–1860* (Milan 1978). P. DALLA TORRE, *L'opera riformatrice ed amministrativa di Pio IX dal 1850 al 1870* (Rome 1945). D. DEMARCO, *Una rivoluzione sociale: La Repubblica Romana del 1849* (Naples 1944). A. M. GHISALBERTI, *Roma da Mazzini a Pio IX* (Milan 1958). S. JACINI, *Il tramonto del potere temporale nelle relazioni degli ambasciatori austraici a Roma (1860–1870)* (Bari 1931). A. QUACQUARELLI, *La ricostituzione dello Stato Pontificio* (Bari 1945). N. MIKO, *Das Ende des Kirchenstaates* (Vienna 1961–).

[E. JARRY/R. MOR/F. J. COPPA]

STATIONAL CHURCH

Those churches, particularly in Rome, that have been designated for the celebration on set days of the "liturgical station,'' that is, the pontifical service of the local bishop. This article treats etymology, ancient stational churches outside Rome, Roman stational origins, Roman stational churches, earlier Roman stational rites, and liturgical stations since the fourteenth century.

Etymology. The term *station* (Gr. στατίων; Lat. *statio*) was used by the early Christians in two senses, both of obscure origin. Fundamentally the Latin *statio* derives from *stare* (to stand, halt, take up a position), and it came to mean a gathering at a fixed place for any fixed purpose. *Statio* was certainly used to describe a strictly liturgical assemblage in the Luciferian *Libellus precum* of 384 (*Patrologia Latina* 13:83). Whether the convocations of clergy and laity called *stationes* by Cyprian and Cornelius were liturgical gatherings is not so clear [Cyprian, *Epist.* 44.2; 49.3 (*Corpus scriptorum ecclesiasticorum latinorum* 3.2:598, 612)].

Statio in the secondary sense meant a partial fast or day of partial fast, as distinguished from a day of full fast (*jejunium*). The *statio* normally ceased at the ninth hour, while the *jejunium* was prolonged to vespertide. Wednesdays and Fridays were days of customary if not obligatory Christian fast by the beginning of the second century (Didache 8). Fifty years later the expressions ''to maintain a station'' and ''to maintain a fast'' were interchangeable (Pastor Hermae, *Similitudo* 5.1.2). And by the beginning of the third century *statio* was the accepted synonym for a day of partial fast (Tertullian, *De oratione* 19; *Patrologia Latina* 1:1181–83). Several theories have been advanced to explain how *statio* acquired this penitential connotation. Most plausible, perhaps, is the conjecture that since the days of semifast were also in many places days of liturgical observance, the term *station* came to be popularly applied to the day's fast as well as the day's rite.

Statio also had the meaning, in military language, of an outpost and the sentinels assigned to it. Ambrose, in the fourth century, seemed quite sure that the Church had deliberately applied the military term to liturgical assemblies because Christians were the ''militia of Christ'' who gathered for prayerful vigil (*Sermo* 21 *de sancta Quadragesima* 5; *Patrologia Latina* 17:644). But Tertullian, writing about the year 200, accepted this derivation with less conviction (*De oratione* 19; *Patrologia Latina* 1:1181–83).

Ancient Stational Churches outside Rome. As residential bishops witnessed the increase in the number of church buildings under their jurisdiction, they naturally found reasons for celebrating the solemn liturgy now at one, now at another of these churches. The Spanish nun Egeria, who made a pilgrimage to the Holy Land around 386, has left an account of the current stational practice there, although she does not use the word *statio*. A similar procedure was followed in Antioch, in Oxyrhynchus, Egypt, and doubtless in other dioceses of the Near East and Egypt. Many of the larger Christian dioceses in the West had stational liturgies: for example, Carthage, Milan, Vercelli, Ravenna, Lìege, Paris, Tours, Cologne, Mainz, Metz, and Strasbourg. Tours had its stational rites by 460 (Gregory of Tours, *Historia Francorum* 10; *Patrologia Latina* 71:566–567). The stational cycle observed in Metz by 766 was patterned on that of Rome (Chrodegang, *Regula canonicorum* 33; *Patrologia Latina* 89: 1117).

Roman Stational Origins. In addition to suburban cemeterial basilicas, Rome had an early multiplicity of city churches. The primitive *domus Dei*—churches in private homes—became, after the persecutions had ended, the *tituli,* or parish churches, which numbered 25 by the fifth century. To these were added, under the Christian emperors, the major basilicas and a number of lesser church edifices. In establishing a cycle of stational visits, the bishops of Rome, like other bishops who followed this policy, saw in it an apt symbol of the unity of the shepherd with his flock. For although the whole diocesan community could not attend the stational Mass, this Mass would still be the official diocesan liturgy, and delegations would be on hand to represent the various city districts, with their own clergy to minister to them. If the priest in charge of a *titulus* was absent, the celebrant would send to him, as a sign of Eucharistic union, the FERMENTUM, a portion of his own consecrated Host.

It is not known which were the original Roman stational churches, but the popes may have started the practice as early as the third century. Gregory the Great reorganized the existing schedule at the beginning of the seventh century (Joannes Diaconus, *Vita* 2.18.19; *Patrologia Latina* 75:94). The oldest known lectionary, the ninth-century Würzburg *Comes,* gives the stational calendar as it stood in Gregory's time. During the reign of Gregory II (d. 731) other churches were added to fill out the cycle of Lenten stations. The Tridentine Missal (1570) retained this eighth-century schedule substantially unchanged, indicating the station at the head of each stational Mass.

Lent and Easter Week had the most complete series of station days. Less complete series were assigned to Advent and Christmastide, and to the Ascension and Whitsuntide. Ember and Rogation Days also had stational services. The eventual total was 89 stational services on 87 stational days, at 42 station churches.

Roman Stational Churches. The traditional Roman stational churches (those italicized are the ancient Roman *tituli*) were *S. Anastasia,* S. Apollinaris, SS. Apostoli, *S.*

Balbina, S. Caecilia, S. Cyriacus (now replaced by S. Maria in Via Lata), *S. Clemens,* SS. Cosmas et Damianus, *S. Chrysogonus,* S. Crux in Jerusalem, *S. Eusebius,* S. Georgius in Velabro, S. Joannes in Laterano, *SS. Joannes et Paulus,* S. Joannes ante Portam Latinam, *S. Laurentius in Damaso,* S. Laurentius extra Muros, *S. Laurentius in Lucina,* S. Laurentius in Paneperna, *SS. Marcellinus et Petrus, S. Marcellus, S. Marcus,* S. Maria in Domnica, S. Maria Maggiore, S. Maria ad Martyres, *S. Maria trans Tiberim,* S. Nicolaus in Carcere, S. Paulus extra Muros, S. Petrus in Vaticano, *S. Petrus ad Vincula, S. Praxedes* (transferred in the Middle Ages to *Nereus et Achilleus*), *S. Prisca, S. Pudentiana, SS. Quattuor Coronati, S. Sabina, SS. Silvester et Martinus* (church now called S. Martino ai Monti), *S. Xystus,* S. Stephanus in Caelio monte, *S. Susanna,* S. Trypho (now replaced by S. Agostino), and *S. Vitalis.* Certain other Roman churches have been designated as station churches by apostolic privilege, apparently to facilitate the gaining of the stational indulgences by providing alternate places for the required visit.

Early Roman Stational Rites. The stational rite proper was a pontifical Mass. In order that this Mass might be celebrated at all the stations with equal splendor, Pope Hilary (d. 468) provided a special set of chalices and other utensils that were carried out to each day's station (*Liber pontificalis* 1:244–247). For the ordinary stational Mass, the pope and his train went in state to the appointed church where the clergy and faithful from all the *tituli* awaited him. On penitential days when there was to be a *letania* or procession, the pope went first to another church that had been designated as the rendezvous for the formation of the procession and was therefore called the *collecta,* for example, S. Georgius in Velabro, collecta for *S. Caecilia,* S. Hadrianus (in the Forum Romanum), *collecta* for S. Maria Major. Here he initiated the day's rite with special prayers, concluding with the *oratio ad collectam* (prayer for the assembly). Then the procession, led by one bearing the wooden stational cross, set out for the station. Following the cross bearer were the clergy and faithful from the seven ecclesiastical districts of Rome, and the pope and his clergy in black vestments (*Ordo Romanus* 21; M. Andrieu, *Les 'Ordines Romani' du haut moyen-âge* 3:247–249).

Since the Litany of the Saints chanted by the procession concluded with a triple Kyrie, the Mass at the station had no Kyrie of its own. The stational rite itself was the ceremonious papal liturgy prescribed by the Roman Ordinals of the seventh to eleventh centuries (*Ordines* 1, 4, 5, 6 in Andrieu's series). The clergy of the *tituli* originally concelebrated with the pope and administered Communion to their own parishioners in attendance. At Communion time the archdeacon announced the station church for the next station day, and the *collecta* if there was to be a procession. The announcement was greeted by a *Deo gratias.* Since the rite at the *collecta* usually began about 3 P.M., the day's penitential fast ended with the conclusion of the stational Mass.

The beautiful Masses composed for the stational liturgy were frequently written with the station church in mind. Thus SS. Cosmas and Damian are mentioned in Collect of the Mass celebrated in their church, and the lesson read in the stational Mass of S. Susanna is the story of Susanna and the elders, from the Book of Daniel.

After the popes took up residence in France in 1305, the stational program fell into disuse, and upon their return to Rome in 1378 it was resumed only on a much diminished scale. Sixtus V, in the constitution *Egregia* of Feb. 13, 1586, attempted to renew the custom more fully, but his efforts met with slight success. After the fall of Rome in 1870, the popes, as voluntary prisoners of the Vatican, could not have revived the papal stational visits even if they had desired to do so. Pius XI, freed from this "captivity" by the Lateran Pacts of 1929, did not personally undertake the stational visits; but he did encourage the revival of the general stational practice and granted indulgences to those who participated (April 12, 1932: *Raccolta* 780). Credit for its revival is due to Carlo Respighi (d. 1947), prefect of the apostolic ceremonies and *Magister* of the *Collegium Cultorum Martyrum,* a Roman archeological and devotional society. Successive popes from Pope John XXIII have participated in stational visits.

Bibliography: I. P. KIRSCH, "L'Origine des Stations liturgiques du Missel Romain," *Ephemerides liturgicae* 41 (1927) 137–150. J. A. JUNGMANN, *The Mass of the Roman Rite,* tr. F. A. BRUNNER, 2 v. (New York 1951–55). D. G. MORIN, "Le Plus ancien *Comes* ou lectionnaire de l'église Romaine," *Revue Bénédictine* 27 (1910) 41–74. J. A. GURRIERI, "The Stational Liturgies of the Paschal Season," in *The Cathedral: A Reader,* ed. R. E. RAMBUSCH (Washington, D.C. 1979). J. F. BALDOVIN, *The Urban Character of Christian Worship: The Origins, Development, and Meaning of Stational Liturgy* (Rome 1987).

[R. F. MCNAMARA/EDS.]

STATIONS OF THE CROSS

Also known as the Way of the Cross. As practiced today, the devotion centers on 14 chosen representations of the sufferings of Christ on his way to Calvary. The devotion originated as a pious imitation of the pilgrims who traveled to the Holy Land to visit the places hallowed by Christ's sufferings.

Origins and Early History. Pilgrimages to the holy places began in the early centuries of Christianity. St. Jerome and other early Christian writers attested to this fact. The custom may have grown from the tradition that the Blessed Virgin visited these places after Christ's Ascension and related this to St. Brigid in a vision [Adrichomius, *Theatrum Terrae Sanctae et biblicarum historiarum cum tabulis geographicis* (Cologne 1590)].

Devotion to the Passion of Christ, which became widespread in the 12th and 13th centuries, was promoted by many veterans of the Crusades who erected tableaux at home representing various places they had visited in the Holy Land. This devotion became known as the Little Jerusalem (Kneller, 56).

The first coherently related stations built outside Palestine were erected at the church of San Stefano in Bologna in the 5th century. The idea of a series of shrines commemorating places and events in the Passion became fairly general in the 15th century. Bl. Alvarez of Cordova, OP, erected such a series at his monastery near Cordova. The Augustinians, Peter and John da Fabriano, did the same, and stations were installed in the cemetery of the Franciscan friary at Antwerp at about the same time, or perhaps even earlier in the century. At Antwerp the stations represented the Seven Sorrows of Our Lady.

When the Franciscans took over custody of the holy places in 1342 they saw it as part of their mission to promote devotion to these places and to the Passion of Christ, and this, as the practice became more common, found expression in devotion to the Stations of the Cross. It became general in the monasteries, friary chapels, and churches the Franciscans served throughout the world, and from these places it spread to parish churches. In the 18th century St. LEONARD OF PORT MAURICE promoted the devotion so enthusiastically and successfully that he became known as the "preacher of the Way of the Cross." He is said to have erected more than 572 stations between 1731 and 1751. The number of stations in each series, the place and circumstances of their erection, and the mode of practicing the devotion became stabilized by the monita issued under the authority of Clement XII in 1731.

Number and Titles of Stations. There was originally a considerable variety with regard to the number and titles of the stations. William Wey, an English pilgrim to the Holy Land in 1458 and 1462, testified that the number varied in many places. Wey was the first to use the designation "station" (stop, standing, halt) in connection with the devotion. In 5th-century Bologna there were five "stops"; in Antwerp there were seven. Sometimes there were as many as 20, 30, or even more. Adrichomius set the number at 12, and these 12 correspond to the first 12 of the 14 in use when the form of the devotion eventually became settled. The number 14 first appeared in manuals of devotion published during the 16th century in the Low Countries. The determination of this number seems due to the choice of devotional writers rather than to the actual practice of pilgrims in Jerusalem, for during the 16th century the Turkish authorities permitted no halting or external acts of veneration at any of the holy places. The act of the Holy See settling the number at 14 appears to have been simply an approval of popular custom; and for some time, at least, it seems not to have been regarded as mandatory, since in 1799 a special set of 11 stations was ordered for use in the Diocese of Vienne.

The subjects represented by the stations show a similar variation. In earlier series having more numerous stops, events and places were commemorated that were only distantly connected with the Via Dolorosa, if at all: for example, the house of Dives, the probatic pool, the houses of Herod and Simon the Pharisee. The number of falls has varied from one to seven. Some of the incidents common on earlier lists, e.g., the Ecce Homo scene on the balcony, have been dropped, but the meeting with Veronica, on the other hand, is a later inclusion.

The accepted 14 stations today are: (1) Christ is condemned to death by Pilate; (2) Jesus is made to carry the cross; (3) Jesus falls the first time; (4) Jesus meets His blessed Mother; (5) the cross is laid on Simon of Cyrene; (6) Veronica wipes the face of Jesus; (7) Jesus falls the second time; (8) Jesus speaks to the women of Jerusalem; (9) Jesus falls the third time; (10) Jesus is stripped of His garments and receives gall to drink: (11) Jesus is nailed to the cross; (12) Jesus dies on the cross; (13) Jesus is taken down from the cross; (14) Jesus is laid in the sepulcher. In some places, a 15th station has been added for meditation upon the Resurrection, a practice that has yet to find universal acceptance.

Pictures and Images. From the earliest times there have been artistic representations of the scenes and events recalled at the different stations. Artists have vied in creating appropriate tableaux. These are helpful in assisting the faithful to center their thoughts upon the incident to be recalled, and so are commonly found in churches and oratories where the stations have been erected, but they are not essential to the devotion itself. Strictly speaking, the wooden crosses themselves hung in the nave of the church constitute the stations, not the artistic representations.

Erection of the Stations. According to the first concessions granted by the Holy See, the stations could be erected only in churches subject to the Friars Minor Observants. In fact, in the earliest concessions it was stated that only those who had some connection with the order, e.g. tertiaries, could gain the indulgences. Later, Benedict XIII extended all the indulgences "to any one of the faithful . . . in no manner subject to the Minister General . . . who makes the pious exercise of the stations privately . . .'' (*Inter plurima,* 1726). Clement XII in a brief issued in 1731 extended the privilege to other churches, oratories, and hospices ''not subject to the Order.'' In the monita issued the same year under authority of the same pontiff it was declared that stations could be erected in the open (*subdio*), provided they originated or ended at a church. Today, stations can be erected in churches, oratories, chapels, cemeteries and religious places of pilgrimage. For many centuries they were set up in a manner the reverse of that customary now. Instead of following Christ from the praetorium or Pilate's palace, the people would begin at Calvary and trace their steps back to the palace or Gethsemane. In all probability the present custom goes back to St. Leonard of Port Maurice.

Bibliography: M. SLEUTJES, *Instructio de stationibus S. Viae Crucis,* ed. B. KURTSCHEID (5th ed. Quaracchi-Florence 1927). G. GOLUBOVICH, *Bibliotheca bio-bibliografica della Terra Santac . . .*, 5 v. (Quaracchi-Florence 1906–27) 4:7–8. H. THURSTON, *The Stations of the Cross* (New York 1906). K. A. KNELLER, *Geschichte der Kreuzwegandacht* (Freiburg 1908). M. J. MATHIS and N. W. MEYER, eds., *The Pastoral Companion* (12th ed. Chicago 1961).

[B. BROWN/EDS.]

STATUTA ECCLESIAE ANTIQUA

A canonical compilation from southern Gaul, made between 442 and 506, by a priest with reforming tendencies who enjoyed the privileges of his order. Hence this is not an African collection (4th Pseudo-Council of Carthage in which the *Statuta* are mentioned in the canonical collections), nor is it a Spanish collection, a work of Caesarius of Arles, nor even a strictly Arlesian work. The compiler, if not the author, was probably Gennadius of Marseilles. The most probable date is 476 to 485, the last years of Euric's reign.

The *Statuta* is known to us in a threefold tradition: Gallic, Italian, and Spanish (with interpolations). The tripartite ordering and the succession of the primitive canons has been preserved and indicates that it followed the *HISPANA COLLECTIO.* It includes: (1) prologue (examination of the candidate elected to the episcopacy and *professio fidei* that distinguishes the *De ecclesiasticis dogmatibus* of Gennadius of Marseilles); (2) disciplinary canons (cc. 1–89) following the plan of the APOSTOLIC CONSTITUTIONS; (3) succinct but very precise ritual of ordinations and of benedictions of persons (cc.90–102), following the Western non-Roman and so-called Gallican style—bishop, priest, deacon, subdeacon, acolyte, exorcist, lector, porter, psalmist, virgins, widows, spouses. The *Statuta* constitute a major document for Canon Law and the liturgy of the 5th century in the Gallo-Roman Church. It is a work of reform, whose orientation is ascetical, presbyteral, and antidiaconal, addressed to the episcopate and clergy of Provence. Its presence in the canonical collections assured its wide dissemination.

Bibliography: C. F. ARNOLD, *Caesarius von Arelate und die gallische Kirche seiner Zeit* (Leipzig 1894). B. BOTTE, ''Le Rituel d'ordination dans les Statuta ecclesiae antiqua,'' *Recherches de théologie ancienne et médiévale* 11 (1939) 223–241. F. X. VON FUNK, ''Analekten,'' *Theologische Quartalschrift* 693–696. A. MALNORY, ''La Collection canonique des Statuta ecclesiae antiqua rapportée à son véritable auteur, Saint Césaire, évêque d'Arles,'' in *Congrès scientifique international des catholiques tenu à Paris du 8 au 13 avril 1888,* 2 v. (Paris 1889) 2:428–439; *Saint Césaire, évêque d'Arles* (Paris 1894). G. MORIN, ''Hierarchie et liturgie dans l'Église gallicane au Ve siècle,'' *Revue Bénédictine* 8 (1891) 97–104. F. PETERS, ''Les Prétendus 104 canons du concile de Carthage de l'an 398,'' in *Compte rendu du troisième Congrès scientifique international des Catholiques tenu à Bruxelles du 3 au 8 Septembre 1894,* 9 v. in 3 (Brussels 1895) 1:220–231. J. B. THIBAUT, *L'Ancienne liturgie gallicane, son origine, et sa formation en Provence aux Ve et VIe siècles* (Paris 1929). C. MUNIER, *Les Statuta ecclesiae antiqua* (Paris 1960), critical ed. of text and studies; repr. in *Corpus Christianorum* 148A (Turnhout, Belgium 1963) 162–188.

[C. VOGEL]

STAUPITZ, JOHANN VON

Vicar-general of the German Augustinians at the time of Martin LUTHER's revolt and personal counselor of Luther; b. probably at Motterwitz, near Leisnig, 1468–69; d. Salzburg, Austria, Dec. 28, 1524. There is little certain knowledge about his early years. He studied at Cologne and Leipzig from 1483 to 1489 and entered the AUGUSTINIAN order perhaps at Munich. Made doctor of theology in 1500 he took a leading role in founding the University of Wittenberg, where in 1502 he was named professor and first dean of the theological faculty. Staupitz was elected vicar-general of the order in 1503. From 1508, he was on close personal terms with Luther at Wittenberg. He acted as Luther's spiritual director, recommended Biblical study and later ceded to him his own chair of theology. Staupitz taught him, Luther said, to regard the love of God and of his justice as the starting point and not the goal of all true penance and therefore to understand true penance as above all a change of heart. Hence his crusade against the contemporary preaching of indulgences that Luther thought overemphasized satisfaction, ''the vilest part of penance.'' Staupitz at first supported Luther in the ensuing controversy, but he gradually withdrew from the ranks of his partisans. Resigning as vicar-general in 1520, Staupitz signed a statement of his submission to the Pope and moved to Salzburg, where in 1522 he entered the Benedictine

Order. Eventually he was elected abbot of St. Peter's Abbey. Luther was much affected by the desertion of Staupitz, but in his last letter to Staupitz, Sept. 17, 1523, disavowed any hard feelings against the man who, he said, had led him to the light of the gospel.

Staupitz did not share Luther's heterodox views, and he even called for their condemnation as heresy. A Thomist and a mystic, he was a prominent director of souls, a noteworthy preacher, and a pious, kindhearted man. He was of a gentle and compromising nature, however, and this explains the ambiguous and uncertain role he played during the critical years of Luther's break with the Church.

Bibliography: A. JEREMIAS, ed., *Johann von Staupitz, Luthers Vater und Schüler* (Berlin 1926). H. WRIEDT, *Gnade und Erwählung: Eine Untersuchung zu Johann von Staupitz und Martin Luther* (Mainz 1991).

[T. S. BOKENKOTTER]

STAVE CHURCHES

Dating mostly from the 12th and 13th centuries, stave churches are a unique Norwegian contribution to medieval architecture. They are constructed in the country's traditional building material, wood, and incorporate structural principles that antedate the coming of Christianity to Norway. In plan they owe much to the Romanesque basilicas of western Europe, being divided into nave, choir, and apse; the manner in which the main roof is raised above the aisles and the handling of the inner columns, with carved capitals and round arches in between, are additional evidence for this view. There is, however, nothing comparable to their complicated wooden framing system in the contemporary architecture of western Europe; it is this system, together with the exceedingly rich decoration, that gives stave churches their distinctive character and historical importance. The heavy wooden posts (or staves) are fitted together within a vertical and horizontal framework. The horizontal foundation beam, resting on a stone sill, supports the vertical corner posts, which are fastened together by, and bear the weight of, an upper crossbeam. The walls consist of thick planks, the ends of which are sunk in the lower and upper crossbeams and are fitted together by a tongue-and-groove method. This scheme is repeated upward in diminishing scale so that the church has a pronounced verticality within its generally pyramidal shape. A great deal of cross bracing of various types also is employed. While on the interior, space soars upward through the different levels, the exterior is covered with shell-shaped wooden shingles. These, combined with the numerous dragons' heads, give the whole structure a fantastic appearance.

The essential elements are the four great corner posts, or staves. These were traditionally made from a special type of pine tree having much red marrow and little sap, with the convenient virtue of rarely splitting or cracking. The inner columns also were called staves, but these might be of a different type of wood. The entire system is in a certain sense analogous to Gothic architecture in that it utilized a static skeleton that could undertake the dual task of framing the walls and supporting the roof. The sources, however, are to be sought not in the sophisticated masonry techniques of the continent but in the native building traditions of Norway. These were developed by the Vikings in the early Middle Ages, and can be seen well in such relics as the Oseberg and Gokstad ships. Many analogies can be drawn between stave churches and Viking sea vessels. Strzygowski is the chief exponent of this connection; he went so far as to call these buildings "mast churches." Recent scholarship, while accepting his general contention, has not been quite so insistent on a maritime derivation of the structure. Nonetheless, it is true that the central space of the stave church was usually called "skipet" or ship. Furthermore, the structure, like the boats that sailed to North America, was designed to withstand the fierce storms that are a feature of the Norwegian climate.

While the stave churches are generally alike in their basic structural scheme, they vary widely in plan, form, and decoration. Urnes on the Sognefjord is the oldest; parts of it may date from about 1030, shortly after the introduction of Christianity. This church is notable also for the fine carvings around the north portal. The theme of these carvings clearly owes much to Viking precedent; it closely resembles that of the Oseberg ship. The portal decorations show the strange animals of Norse myth and fable, interlocked in bold coils and carved in high relief. The carvings exhibit a blend of elegant rhythm and powerful movement characteristic of the best Norwegian art in every period. Similar work, though not of the same quality, is found in other stave churches.

The most elaborate series of paintings is probably to be found in the Torpo stave church dating mostly from the mid-13th century. Here the choir vault is covered by an elaborate painting with a fairly conventional iconographic scheme: Christ in majesty surrounded by symbols of the four evangelists and the twelve apostles. Below is depicted the martyrdom of Saint Margaret of Antioch. In technique and subject matter the work is much closer to the art of western Europe than are the Urnes carvings. Painted altar frontals may be found at Heddal in East Norway and at Ulvik.

The golden age of the stave church occurred in the 12th century when the sons of King Magnus ruled in Norway. At this time a sound economic background had been laid by the introduction of tithes under King Sigurd Jorsalafar, and the church grew to a real power in the land with the institution of a native Norwegian archbishopric. This happy interlude of stable government was broken by the arrival of the priest Sverre, who split the country into warring factions. Heathen times were still so close that the oldest members of the community could describe them to their sons and grandsons. Much of the pagan spirit still survived, and the building of stave churches up and down the land may therefore be viewed as one aspect of a crusade. They were intended to provide a home for the new Christian faith from seacoast towns to remote interior valleys. Like the early Christian basilicas of ancient Rome, they were often built on sites consecrated to pagan worship. A few even incorporate parts of older structures. Apparently between 500 and 600 churches were built, of which about 25 remain. These are an eloquent testimonial of the building art in medieval Norway.

Bibliography: J. STRZYGOWSKI, *Early Church Art in Northern Europe* (New York 1929). *Norwegian Architecture throughout the Ages,* ed. E. ALNAES et al. (Oslo 1950), chiefly illustrative with a historic survey by G. ELIASSEN. A. R. BUGGE, *Norwegian Stave Churches,* tr. R. CHRISTOPHERSEN (Oslo 1953). *Norway: Paintings from the Stave Churches* (UNESCO; New York 1955), pref. R. HAUGLID, introd. L. GRODECKI. G. KAVLI, *Norwegian Architecture, Past and Present* (London 1958).

[L. K. EATON]

Stave Church, 1150 A.D., Borgund, Norway. (©Elio Ciol/ CORBIS)

STAVELOT, ABBEY OF

Benedictine monastery in Belgium, Diocese of Liège [Latin, *Stabela(c)us*]. Founded *c.* 650 in the forest of the Ardennes, it was endowed with a large domain by the Merovingian King Sigebert III. Its first abbot, St. Remaclus, a monastic bishop, was likewise the abbot of the sister abbey, MALMÉDY. Both abbeys were abolished during the French Revolution, and Stavelot's last abbot—the 69th successor of Remaclus—His Highness Dom Célestin Thys, was exiled to Germany, where he died in 1796. In 870 this royal abbey, which had been under the protection of Louis the German, became part of the Holy Roman Empire. As an imperial abbey it remained free and exempt, its abbot, who was elected by the chapter and confirmed by the pope and the emperor, being a prince of the Empire. Stavelot was reformed by Abbots Odilo (d. 954), POPPO (d. 1048), the builder of the large abbey church that was destroyed in 1801, WIBALD (d. 1158), a humanist and promoter of Mosan art, and William of Manderscheid (d. 1546). The abbey's schools and scriptorium were important during the Middle Ages. The extensive monastic buildings, all built during the 18th century, were secularized and exist today. In 1950 the Benedictine priory of Saint-Remacle was founded at Wavreumont-Stavelot.

Bibliography: Sources. Archives de l'État, Liège. Bibliothèque royale, Brussels. Literature. U. BERLIÈRE, *Monasticon belge,* v.2 (Gembloux 1928). W. LEGRAND, ''L'Église abbatiale de Stavelot,'' *Bulletin de la société d'art et d'histoire du diocèse de Liège* 43 (1963) 183–226.

[W. LEGRAND]

STEBBINS, H. LYMAN

Lay activist, Knight of St. Gregory, first president of Catholics United for the Faith; b. New York, Sept. 1911; d. New Rochelle, N.Y., Feb. 19, 1989. Stebbins' great grandfather, Henry George Stebbins, was president of the New York Stock Exchange and one of the founders of the Metropolitan Museum of Art. His father, Rowland Stebbins, left Wall Street in 1929 to become a producer on Broadway. Lyman Stebbins was educated at St. Bernard's in New York City, St. Paul's in Concord, and Yale University, class of 1933. The Yale years were lived without any particular religious commitment, the nominal Episcopalianism of his childhood having given way to a moral and spiritual vacuity. Upon graduation from Yale, he ratified family expectations and entered the brokerage house of DeCoppet and Doremus.

Stebbins' conversion to Roman Catholicism followed a literary turn. C. S. LEWIS' works moved him to Anglo-Catholicism, while Jacques MARITAIN's *The Things That Are Not Caesar's* provided a cogent explanation of papal prerogatives and the nature of the teaching office of the Roman pontiff. After taking instruction from Fr. Vincent Holden, CSP, he was received into the Catholic Church in London in 1945.

During the 1950s and 1960s, Stebbins led a life of quasi-retirement and solitude, becoming a Benedictine oblate. He was attracted by the contemplative life, and, in particular, the singing of Gregorian chant with the religious and with his brother and sister oblates at Mount Savior Monastery in Elmira, N.Y., and the convent Regina Laudis in Bethlehem, Conn. His meditative disposition was given a philosophical and theological focus through contacts with Catholic scholars, such as Baldwin Schwarz and Dietrich von Hildebrand. Stebbins served as friend and editor to both of these men, helping to make their works known to a wider public.

Catholics United for the Faith. In September of 1968, Stebbins was invited by the advisory board of the newly created group Catholics United for the Faith to serve as its president. The immediate crisis precipitating the formation of CUF was the dissenting posture adopted by American theologians and the other signatories of a document that challenged Pope Paul VI's restatement in *HUMANAE VITAE* of the Church's ban on contraception. ''Unstinting loyalty shown to the Holy Father had been a hallmark of American Catholicism,'' Stebbins argued, yet this loyalty was now threatened by the ''widespread spectacle of dissent.'' Drawing upon his ''novitiate'' of reading and praying practiced in the years after his conversion, Stebbins saw his summons to be the formation of a group apostolate of the laity that would rally to the side of the pope while also being formed according to the mind of the Church in the spirit of the Second Vatican Council. The council's *Decree on the Apostolate of the Laity (Apostolicam actuositatem)* had left a deep impression upon him.

The organizational structure of CUF developed to include an international headquarters in New Rochelle, N.Y., with a network of 110 chapters in the United States, Canada, Australia, New Zealand, Ghana, and Myanmar, comprising a membership of 16,000. In July of 1994, the international office was relocated to Steubenville, Ohio. Each chapter was urged to follow a tripartite scheme of prayer, study of the faith, and action. Stebbins worked earnestly to convince members affiliated with CUF that any ''action'' undertaken for the good of the Church would need to be preceded by prayer and study of the faith. Cardinal Newman became a central influence in the development of the CUF spirit, especially with reference to his enjoinder that ''the laity know just where they stand,'' and that ''they know their faith.'' Stebbins's stress on piety and the call to holiness caused some Catholics of a more truculent spirit to fall away from the association, while his resolute support of Paul VI and the pontiff's reform of the sacred liturgy led to the eventual termination of chapters in Georgia and North Carolina that had declared support for Archbishop Marcel Lefebvre.

Throughout the 1970s and mid-1980s, Stebbins faced the delicate issue of the relationship of individual lay members of CUF and their bishops. Writing in CUF's monthly publication *Lay Witness,* Stebbins recalled the immense dignity of the episcopal office, yet he did not shy away from stressing ''the obligations which bishops owed to the faithful.'' If, however, after respectful implorations from the laity, the bishop still seemed obdurate, ''then the matter should be peacefully and confidently left in the hands of Christ.''

While many Catholics were looking to CUF as a principal vehicle to reform the Church in America, Stebbins was reminding everyone that true renewal had to start at home. Speaking to the National Sacred Heart Congress in Hazelton, Pa., in 1978, he underscored the fact that the priesthood of the faithful was to be exercised in a special way by the laity in the home, the domestic church. Such a role remained quite distinct from the ministerial priesthood, yet was indispensable. Pope John Paul II conferred on Stebbins the Knighthood of the Order of St. Gregory on Jan. 10, 1989.

Bibliography: P. ALLITT, *Catholic Intellectuals and Conservative Politics in America, 1950–85* (Cornell 1993). H. L. STEBBINS, *The Priesthood of the Laity in the Domestic Church* (New Rochelle 1978); ''The Responsibility of the Laity to the Bishops and Vice Versa,'' *Lay Witness* (March 1985). J. A. SULLIVAN, ''H. Lyman Stebbins: The Planting of a Seed,'' *Catholic Free Press*, March 17, 1989; ''Catholics United for the Faith: Dissent and the Laity,'' in *Being Right: Conservative American Catholics,* ed. M. J. WEAVER and R. S. APPLEBY (Bloomington, Ind. 1995).

[J. SULLIVAN]

STECK, FRANCIS BORGIA

Historian; b. St. Louis, Mo., July 11, 1884; d. Quincy, Ill., July 5, 1962. He was the son of Bernard and Mary

(Schwietering) Steck and was baptized Henry. After early education in the parochial schools of St. Louis and five years at St. Joseph Seminary, Teutopolis, Ill., he entered the Franciscan Order in 1904, receiving the name Francis Borgia, and was ordained in 1911. During the six years (1913–19) he taught at St. Joseph Seminary in Teutopolis, he wrote *The Franciscans and the Protestant Revolution in England* (1920) and *Glories of the Franciscan Order* (1920). From 1924 to 1927 he pursued doctoral studies in history at The Catholic University of America, Washington, D.C., and wrote *The Jolliet–Marquette Expedition, 1673* (1928, published originally as a doctoral dissertation 1927). In 1933 he joined the faculty of Catholic University and for the next 14 years taught courses in Spanish American History. Failing health caused his retirement in 1947 to Quincy College, where he continued his scholarly pursuits. He translated from the Spanish *Motolinia's History of the Indians in New Spain* (1951) and wrote *Essays Relating to the Jolliet-Marquette Expedition*, 1673 (1953) and *Marquette Legends* (1960) (*See* MARQUETTE, JACQUES).

In *Marquette Legends* Steck, contrary to the commonly held tradition, maintained that Marquette was not the leader of the Jolliet expedition down the Mississippi River in 1673; the *Narrative* of this expedition was not written by Marquette, but by Claude Dablon, SJ, in 1678 (three years after Marquette's death); the *Journal of the Second Voyage* (to the Illinois country in 1674–75) was not written by Marquette and was not known to exist before 1844; the *Narrative* of the 1673 expedition and the *Journal of the Second Voyage* to the Illinois country were not among the manuscripts preserved at the Hotel-Dieu in Quebec and returned to the Jesuits at Montreal in 1844; the Kaskaskia Mission was not founded by Marquette in 1675, but by Claude Allouez, SJ, in 1673; and finally that the priesthood of Marquette must be considered doubtful.

[A. REYLING]

STEFAN (SEMEN ÎAVORSKIĬ)

Russian theologian; b. Javor, near Lvov, Russia, 1658; d. Moscow, June 12, 1722. He was born of Ukranian parents; he studied at Kiev, Lvov, and in the Jesuit schools in Poland at Lublin, Vilna, and Posen. In 1684 he entered the Roman Catholic Church, but in 1687 returned to Orthodoxy. On becoming a monk, he changed his name to Stefan. He became from 1689 successively professor, prefect, and rector of the Academy of Kiev. In 1700 he was named bishop of Ryazan; and in 1701, exarch or representative of the Moscow patriarch. When PETER I (the Great) suppressed the patriarchate (1721), Stefan was appointed the first president of the newly established HOLY SYNOD. Stefan's principal book, *Petra fidei* (Keystone of Faith), appeared originally in Latin (1728) and was directed against the Protestant tendencies introduced into Russia, especially by Feofan PROKOPOVICH. Stefan accepted the Czar's political reforms, but vigorously opposed his Protestant leanings and his church policies, which intruded the state into the realm of Orthodox teachings and discipline.

Bibliography: M. JUGIE, *Theologia dogmatica christianorum orientalium ab ecclesia catholica dissidentium,* 5 v. (Paris 1926–35) 1:583–584. J. LEDIT, *Dictionnaire de théologie catholique,* ed. A. VACANT, 15 v. (Paris 1903–50; Tables générales 1951–) 14.1:326–329; Tables générales 2421–22. B. STASIEWSKI, *Lexikon für Theologie und Kirche,* ed. J. HOFER and K. RAHNER, 10 v. (2d, new ed. Freiburg 1957–65) 5:885.

[J. PAPIN]

STEIN, EDITH (TERESA BENEDICTA OF THE CROSS), ST.

Martyr; Carmelite nun; philosopher and pedagogue; b. Wrocław (Breslau in Prussian Silesia), Poland, Oct. 12, 1891; d. Birkenau section of Auschwitz concentration camp, Aug. 9, 1942. Born of devout Jewish parents, Edith gave up her faith as a teenager and became interested in philosophy after dissatisfaction with her studies in psychology. She read the important philosophical treatise *Logical Investigations of Edmund Husserl,* the founder of PHENOMENOLOGY, and went to Göttingen University to study with him. Her acquaintance with Catholicism began there with the Munich phenomenologist Max SCHELER. After several years of searching, and after reading the autobiography of St. Teresa of Avila, she asked to enter the church and was baptized on Jan. 1, 1922. She accepted a teaching post at a girls' school run by Dominican teaching sisters in the cathedral city of Speyer. Along with her teaching duties, she acquainted herself with Catholic philosophy and translated the treatise *On Truth* by St. Thomas Aquinas.

Stein traveled to several German–speaking countries to address Catholic audiences, especially on women's and educational topics. Her growing reputation led her to leave the school at Speyer to teach at a more specialized institution of higher learning. In 1932 she became a lecturer at the German Institute for Scientific Pedagogy in Münster, but in the next calendar year she had to leave this post because of anti–Semitic legislation introduced by the Nazi Party. Convincing her spiritual director the time had come, she now acted on a long–cherished wish and entered the Carmel of Cologne, taking the name of Sister Teresa Benedicta of the Cross. After her initial training at Cologne her monastic superiors invited her to

St. Edith Stein. (©Bettmann/CORBIS)

resume writing. She transformed an earlier philosophical essay, developed in an unsuccessful effort to obtain a university position a few years previously, into her major opus *Finite and Eternal Being,* in which she attempted to synthesize the philosophy of St. Thomas with modern thought, especially with phenomenology. From her monastery she remained a faithful correspondent with former colleagues, among them the Polish phenomenologist Roman Ingarden.

Soon after the Nazi persecution of the Jews turned violent in the nationwide Kristallnacht pogrom of November 9–10, 1938, she left Germany for exile in the Dutch Carmel of Echt on the last day of the year. Here she wrote another important work, *The Science of the Cross,* a presentation of the life and teaching of St. John of the Cross. This contains several passages that incorporate the phenomenological method. Nazi Germany invaded the Netherlands in 1940 and both Sr. Teresa Benedicta and her sister Rosa Stein, now living at the Echt Carmel as a lay assistant, had to comply with anti–Semitic regulations. SS agents arrested them both on a day she was putting the finishing touches on her *John of the Cross* manuscript (which was published posthumously). That round–up on Sunday, Aug. 2, 1942, led to deportation of several hundred priests and religious and Catholic laity of Jewish origin as a reprisal for an outspoken pastoral letter written by Dutch bishops condemning the anti–Semitic measures of the German occupation forces. One week later they arrived at the Auschwitz concentration camp, where she and her sister died in the gas chamber.

Official introduction of her cause for canonization took place in 1962, leading to her beatification at Cologne by Pope John Paul II on May 1, 1987. He canonized her at St. Peter's Basilica in the Vatican on Oct. 11, 1998. In the same week he recommended reading her works in his encyclical *Fides et Ratio.* The following year the pope declared her copatron of Europe, the only 20th–century saint to be so honored.

Bibliography: Works by Edith Stein: *Life in a Jewish Family* (Washington 1986); *Essays on Woman,* rev. ed. (Washington 1997); *On the Problem of Empathy,* 3d ed. (Washington 1989); *The Hidden Life* (Washington 1992); *Self–Portrait in Letters, 1916–1942* (Washington 1993); *Knowledge and Faith* (Washington 2000); *Philosophy of Psychology and the Humanities* (Washington 2000); *Edith Stein: Selected Writings,* tr. S. BATZDORFF (Springfield, Ill. 1990); *Edith Stein: Day Book,* tr. S. BATZDORFF (Springfield, Ill. 1994); *The Science of the Cross,* tr. H. GRAEF (Chicago 1960). Works about Edith Stein: S. BATZDORFF, *Aunt Edith: The Jewish Heritage of a Catholic Saint* (Springfield, Ill. 1998). *Never Forget: Christian and Jewish Perspectives on Edith Stein,* tr. S. BATZDORFF (Washington 1998). C. BASEHEART, *Person in the World: Introduction to the Philosophy of Edith Stein* (Dordrecht 1997). *Holiness Befits Your House,* ed. J. SULLIVAN (Washington 2000).

[J. SULLIVAN]

STEIN AM RHEIN, ABBEY OF

Former Benedictine abbey in the canton of Schaffhausen, Switzerland. Its patron was St. George. It was founded in the latter half of the 10th century on the Hohentwiel by Duke Burkhard II of Swabia and his consort Hadwig and was moved to Stein *c.* 1020 by the Emperor HENRY II, Hadwig's nephew. Relics of SS. George and Cyril were brought there. In 1007 the monastery was given to the Diocese of Bamberg. Bishop OTTO OF BAMBERG (d. 1139) favored the introduction of statutes of HIRSAU. In 1223 Pope HONORIUS III confirmed all the rights of monastery. The advocates of the monastery were the Zähringer (14th-century Dukes of Austria, then Dukes of Klingenberg), and after 1478, the city of Zurich. Stein was suppressed in 1525 during the Reformation but had two further abbots. Zurich impounded the holdings in Switzerland, and the abbey's German possessions were taken over in 1698 by the abbey of PETERSHAUSEN. The monastery, a fine Gothic structure of the 15th and 16th centuries, has been used as a museum since 1927.

Bibliography: L. H. COTTINEAU, *Répertoire topobibliographique des abbayes et prieurés,* 2 v. (Mâcon 1935–39) 2:3087–88. R. HENGGELER, *Professbücher der Benediktinerabteien . . . St. Georg zu Stein am Rhein* (*Monasticon-Benedictinum Helvetiae* 4; August 1957) 387–409, with bibliog. U. ENGELMANN, *Lexikon für Theologie und Kirche,* ed. J. HOFER and K. RAHNER, 10 v. (2d, new ed. Freiburg 1957–65) 9:1029.

[P. VOLK]

STEINER, RUDOLF

Founder of ANTHROPOSOPHY; b. Kraljević, Austria, Feb. 27, 1861; d. Dornach, near Basel, Switzerland, March 30, 1925. His formal schooling in natural science at the University of Vienna was supplemented by extensive reading, notably in GOETHE, whose complete works he edited (1889–96). For a time he was coeditor of *Magazin für Literatur.* His bent for occultism led him from Catholicism into THEOSOPHY. In 1902 he became head of a German section of the Theosophical Society, although he reacted against its dominantly Oriental associations. In 1912 he organized the Anthroposophical Society as an autonomous branch of theosophy and built the Goetheanum as international headquarters at Dornach, where the center of the Anthroposophical Society remains. Steiner's extensive lectures were later published in book form. *Die Philosophie der Freiheit* (1894; Eng. tr. 1916) was his most important book. His other best-known works were *Das Christenthum als mystische Tatsache* (1902), *Die Geheimwissenschaft* (1910), *Vom Meschenrätsel* (1916), and *Von Seelenrätseln* (1917). His autobiography, *Story of My Life* (1925; Eng. tr. 1928), gives the clearest insight into his complex character. Steiner claimed to have discovered the secret of man's search for the divine by his theory of spirit cognition, innate in everyone. According to him, most people are blinded by attention to material phenomena and are liberated from this materialism through contact with the reality of a spiritual world. His system differs from the more familiar Eastern philosophies in that he admits the existence of things less than spirit. He further postulates that not only the whole cosmos but all history and culture verify the same levels of existence that the human spirit can penetrate through its native intuition without books, teachers, or other external aids. Steiner inspired numerous activities and movements, such as the Waldorf school program, homes and schools for impaired children, the biodynamic method of farming, centers for science research, and academies for the fine arts. Most of these projects have no direct connection with anthroposophy. The Anthroposophical Society has published several of Steiner's books in English translation.

Bibliography: A. P. SHEPHERD, *A Scientist of the Invisible* (London 1954). G. WACHSMUTH, *The Life and Work of Rudolf Steiner,* tr. O. D. WANNAMAKER and R. E. RAAB (2d ed. New York 1955).

[J. A. HARDON]

STELE

An upright block of stone with or without an inscription, erected to commemorate an important person or event or to function as a sacred object. As a commemorative gravestone or sacred object, the more precise terms "pillar" and the Hebrew *maṣṣēbâ* (plural *maṣṣēbôt*) are apt to be used by the archeologist, with the word "stele" reserved for the stone slab, essentially secular in character, that is inscribed with records of victories, alliances, treaties, laws, or decrees. However, the Greek word στήλη, from which the English word is derived, was used for all these meanings.

All ancient peoples of the Near East erected steles. They are found from Mesopotamia to Egypt. One of the best-known steles is the one that is inscribed with the code of laws of HAMMURABI (Hammurapi), in the Louvre Museum, Paris. The Egyptians were particularly fond of steles and at times went to great lengths to produce them, as is evidenced in the famous Egyptian obelisks, which are essentially steles or more technically *maṣṣēbôt.*

The Israelites erected memorial gravestones (Gn 35.20; 2 Sm 18.18), and frequent mention was made of sacred *maṣṣēbôt* that caused no end of concern for the religion of Yahweh. As yet, however, no commemorative stele, strictly so-called, of Israelite origin has been unearthed. Nevertheless, several steles have been found that have had profound effect on the understanding of the general background of the biblical period and in some cases of the biblical text itself. The importance of steles is easily appreciated because of the contribution the inscriptions have made to the fields of history, linguistics, and religion.

Important steles that have had a direct bearing on the understanding of the Bible are the following: of Egyptian origin—the stele of Mer-ne-Ptah, four royal stelae from the Egyptian garrison town of Beth-San, the stele of SESAC I found at MAGEDDO, and a stele of Thutmose III or Amenhotep found at Chenereth in Galilee; of Canaanite origin—the MESHA INSCRIPTION, known also as the Moabite stone, and the stele of Balu'ah; of Mesopotamian origin—the stele of Hammurabi and the Black Obelisk of Salmanasar III.

Bibliography: *Encyclopedic Dictionary of the Bible,* translated and adapted by L. HARTMAN (New York, 1963) 2322–24, with bibliog. on the individual historical steles. J. SCHARBERT, *Lexikon für Theologie und Kirche,* ed. J. HOFER and K. RAHNER, 10 v. (2d, new ed. Freiburg 1957–65); suppl., *Das ZweiteVatikanische Konzil: Dokumente und kommentare,* ed. H. S. BRECHTER et al., pt. 1 (1966) 9:1035. K. GALLING, *Die Religion in Geschichte und Gegenwart,* 7 v. (3d ed. Tübingen 1957–65) 6:352–353. K. GALLING, *Biblisches Reallexicon* (Tübingen) 500–503.

[T. H. WEBER]

STENSEN, NIELS, BL.

Also known as Nikolaus or Nils Steensen, Steno, Stens, or Stenonis; pioneer in the field of anatomy, founder of scientific paleontology, geology, and crystallography, bishop; b. January 11, 1638, Copenhagen, Denmark; d. December 5, 1686, Schwerin, Germany.

His parents were Lutheran; his father, a goldsmith, was the descendent of a long line of Lutheran pastors in Scania. At an early age Niels showed a strong interest in mathematics and science, and he began to study medicine in 1656 at the University of Copenhagen. His first discovery (1660) in Amsterdam was the excretory duct of the parotid gland (Steno's duct); it was followed by many more discoveries after he moved to Leiden (July 27, 1660). These are described in the *Observationes anatomicae* (Leiden 1662) and *Observationum anatomicarum specimen* (Copenhagen 1664).

After the University of Copenhagen passed him over, the University in Leyden granted him the degree of doctor of medicine *in absentia* in 1664. In Paris (1665), in the house of M. Thévenot, he delivered his *Discours sur l'anatomie du cerveau* (Paris 1669) to the forerunners of the Académie des Sciences. There he gained a reputation as an embryologist and brain anatomist. The following year he was well received at the court of the Medici, and among the members of the Accademia del Cimento, which had been founded in the spirit of Galileo; he resumed anatomical research at the Ospidale de S. Maria Nuova in Florence. By sectioning the head of a large shark and by stating the organic origin of the *glossopetrae* (fossilized shark teeth) he was led to basic discoveries in the fields of paleontology and geology. These discoveries he published succinctly and hurriedly in the *Elementorum myologiae specimen seu musculi descriptio geometrica* (Florence 1667) and *Prodromus de solido intra solidum naturaliter contento* (Florence 1669).

While residing in the Netherlands he had begun to question Lutheran doctrines. A Corpus Christi procession in Livorno, Italy deeply impressed him and he decided to become a Catholic; and on November 7, 1667 he entered the Church. Shortly after, he received a letter from the crown of Denmark calling him home and offering him a high annual salary. But it was too late; he did not feel that he could return to Denmark as a Catholic.

After a journey covering half of Europe in 1669 and 1670, he returned to Italy for a time, then served as royal anatomist in Copenhagen from 1672 to 1674. Discerning a call to the priesthood, he went back to Italy and was ordained in Florence before Easter 1675. He was appointed tutor of the crown prince of Florence, but upon request of Duke Johann Friedrich of Hanover, Innocent XI made him vicar apostolic for the Nordic Missions on August 21, 1677, and he was consecrated bishop of Titiopolis on September 19. His territory extended to the north of Norway, but it contained very few Catholics. In his dealings with Protestants in Hanover he showed both determination and mildness (e.g., his discussions with G. W. Leibniz).

After Johann Friedrich's death, Prince-Bishop Ferdinand von Fürstenberg of Paderborn requested Stensen as auxiliary bishop of Münster (appointed October 7, 1680). With great zeal he continued the work of reform begun by C. B. von Galen. His vibrant preaching led many back to Catholicism. In his *Parochorum hoc age* (Florence 1684) he exhorted both clergy and laity to follow the example of the early Church. In 1683 he left Münster in protest against a simoniacal election. After two years of strenuous activity in Hamburg, he spent the last year of his life as a missionary in Schwerin.

Stensen ranks with the most eminent scientists. Among other things, he discovered many glands and glandular ducts in the eye, mouth, nose, skin, chest, and the mucous canal system of fish. He described the structure in general and in particular muscles such as those of the tongue and esophagus. He pioneered in declaring the heart to be a muscle and in stating the function of the uterus and ovaries, and in new methods of research on the brain. His chief contributions were his scientific explanations of fossils, geological stratification, the development of mountains, the difference between organic and inorganic growth, and the law of the constancy of crystalline angles.

Stensen became a model for all times through his desire for certitude, combining, happily, the most exacting inductive method with ingenious deductive conclusions. Though enthusiastic about mechanical and mathematical methods, he contradicted Descartes from the biological point of view, and referred Spinoza, the friend of his youth, to the *philosophia perennis* in his *Epistola ad novae philosophiae reformatorem de vera philosophia.* His coat of arms reflect his ideals (a heart crowned with a cross), and his most quoted saying is: ''Pulchra quae videntur, pulchriora quae sciuntur, longe pulcherrima quae ignorantur'' (''Beautiful are the things that are seen; more beautiful are the things that are known; and most beautiful of all are the things that are not known'').

As priest and bishop, Stensen was a reformer. He became most influential through his own personal striving for sanctification in poverty, strict asceticism, and a deep union with God. Of his 16 theological works the more interesting are his *Epistola de propria conversione* (Florence 1677) and *Defensio et plenior elucidatio epistolae de propria conversione* (Hanover 1680).

His nine years of difficult labor in northern Germany eroded his health. When he died at age 48, he was venerated as a saint in the diocese of Hildesheim. After his death, Cosimo III had his remains transferred to the crypt of St. Lorenzo in Florence, from where they were solemnly removed to a chapel in the transept of this basilica in 1953. His canonization process was begun in Osnabrück in 1938. Pope John Paul II beatified him October 23, 1988.

Feast: December 5.

Bibliography: Works. *Opera philosophica,* ed. V. MAAR, 2 v. (Copenhagen 1910); *Opera theologica,* ed. K. LARSEN and G. SCHERZ, 2v. 2d ed. (Copenhagen 1944–47); *Epistolae,* ed. G. SCHERZ, 2 v. (Copenhagen 1952); *The Prodromus,* tr. and ed. J. W. WINTER (New York 1916); *The Earliest Geological Treatise,* tr. C. CARCHARIAE, ed. A. GARBOE (New York 1958); *Chaos-manuscript, Copenhagen, 1659,* ed. A. ZIGGELAAR (Copenhagen 1997). Studies about Stensen: R. ANGELI, *Niels Stensen anatomico, fondatore della geologia, servo di Dio* (Florence 1968). M. BIERBAUM, *Niels Stensen: Anatom, Geologe u. Bischof,* 2d ed. (Münster 1979). R. CIONI, *Niels Stensen: Scientist-Bishop,* tr. G. M. CAMERA (New York 1962). A. GARBOE, *Nicolaus Steno and Erasmus Bartholinus* (Copenhagen 1954). U. HEIDA, *Niels Stensen und seine Fachkollegenin* (Berlin 1986). A. D. JÖRGENSEN, *Niels Stensen,* ed. G. SCHERZ, 2d ed. (Copenhagen 1958). T. KARDEL, *Steno: Life, Science, Philosophy* (Copenhagen 1994); tr., *Steno on Muscles* (Philadelphia 1994). V. MAAR, *To uudgivne Arbejder af Nicolaus Steno fra Biblioteca Laurentiana* (Copenhagen 1910). J. METZLER, *Die Apostolischen Vikariate des Nordens* (Paderborn 1919). H. MOE, *Nicolaus Steno: An Illustrated Biography,* tr. D. STONER (Copenhagen 1994). E. K. PÅLSSON, *Niels Stensen, Scientist and Saint,* tr. M. N. L. COUVE DE MURVILLE (Dublin 1988). W. PLENKERS, *Der Däne Niels Stensen* (Freiburg 1884). K. J. PLOVGAARD, *Niels Stensen: Anatom, Geologog Biskop* (Copenhagen 1953). N. QUATTRIN, *Nicola Stenone scienziato e santo (1638–1686)* (Vicenza 1987). S. DE ROSA, *Niccolò Stenone a Volterra, 1668,* tr. G. LAZZERI (Florence 1996). G. SCHERZ, *Dansk biografisk leksikon,* ed. C. F. BRICKA et al., v.22 (Copenhagen 1942); *Vom Wege Niels Stensens* (Copenhagen 1956); *N. Steno and His Indice* (Copenhagen 1958), with biography and essays on his scientific work; *Niels Stensen* (Würzburg 1962); *Pionier der Wissenschaft* (Copenhagen 1963), list of sources; *Niels Stensen: Forscher und Denker im Barock* (Stuttgart 1964); *Niels Stensen: The Goldsmith's Son from Copenhagen . . . ,* tr. R. SPINK (Copenhagen 1988).

[G. SCHERZ]

STEPHEN (PROTOMARTYR), ST.

First deacon and apologist for the Christian faith. After considering the Biblical data, found in Acts 6.1–8.2, this article treats of the cult and iconography of the saint.

Biblical Data. Stephen (Στέφανος, crown) was a HELLENIST, one of the Greek-speaking Jews of the DIASPORA, many of whom came to visit or dwell in Palestine. More liberal in their education and views concerning the Jewish faith, they had their own SYNAGOGUES in Jerusalem (Acts 6.9). A great number of them became Christians (6.1). The most distinguished of the Hellenist converts was Stephen, ''full of faith and the Holy Spirit'' (6.5).

Leader of Hellenist Christians. The complaint of the Hellenist widows against Hebrew Christians that they did not receive daily food and alms led the Apostles to ordain DEACONS, a new order of ministry, conferred through the imposition of hands and prayer of the Apostles. By this means Stephen, first of the seven chosen by the assembly, received power and grace (Acts 6.6, 8). Stephen did not limit his service to works of charity; he preached the faith with zeal and ''worked great wonders and signs among the people'' (6.7).

In the Hellenist synagogues of Jerusalem, Christian and non-Christian Jews prayed and worshiped together. Christian Jews, with Stephen as their leader and apologist, were eager to preach Christ. Their opponents, desirous of being considered equal to the native Hebrews in zeal for the Law and the traditions, resented the teaching of salvation through faith in Jesus. They ''disputed with Stephen, but were not able to withstand the wisdom and the Spirit who spoke'' (6.10). In content, his arguments were without doubt similar to those contained in his discourse before the Sanhedrin.

Nature and Purpose of Stephen's Final Sermon. Stephen's discourse is a sublime apology for the Christian faith. It recalls the principal phases of Israel's history and interprets them in the light of the present. It is a theology of Israel's history in which the continuity of divine revelation, begun with Abraham, is shown to be fulfilled in Christ. At the same time it exposes Israel's progressive opposition to God's word through failure to obey it. The principal arguments are these: (1) God is not limited to one person (Moses) for His covenant (Acts 7.2–17) or to one place (the Temple in Jerusalem) for worship (7.44–50). The Law and the Temple made with hands are to pass away and to be replaced and spiritualized in Christ (cf. Jn 4.21–24; Acts 17.24–28; Rom 12.1–3; 1 Pt 2.5). (2) Ingratitude, failure to understand (7.25), disobedience even to Moses (7.39), idolatry (7.40–43), persecution of

"St. Stephen Distributing Alms" 15th-century fresco by Fra Angelico in the chapel of Nicholas V, Vatican Palace, Rome.

the Prophets, betrayal and murder of the Just One, failure to keep the Law (7.52–53)—these showed the accusers of Stephen, rather than himself, to be guilty of blasphemy and crime against the Law and the Temple.

Stephen's judgment of history is prophetic; that of his opponents is legalistic. Stephen's fidelity to revelation makes him "full of grace and power"; the infidelity of his opponents makes them "stiff necked and uncircumcised in heart and ear, always opposing the Holy Spirit" (7.51). The purpose of the discourse is to show, as Christ did (Mt 5.17), that the new religion is the divinely ordered fulfillment of the old, and that the history of the Jews condemns them and their forefathers for disobedience to divine revelation and for persecution of the Prophets and of the Just One (cf. Mt 23.31–39). Stephen's discourse affirms and defends the universality of salvation through faith in Jesus Christ.

Martyrdom. The arrest of Stephen, the incitement of the crowds against him, his arraignment before the Sanhedrin, the bribed witnesses, and the false charges of speaking against the Holy Place and the Law (Acts 6.12–14) were now climaxed by the onrush of the tumultuous crowd who "cast him out of the city and stoned him" (7.58), while he prayed like his Master, "Lord, do not lay this sin against them" (v. 60). Significant is the mention of the youth, Saul of Tarsus, whose approval of Stephen's death (Acts 22.20) and consequent hatred and persecution of Christians were changed, through the blood of the martyr, into zeal and love for Christ and for the Church of Paul the Apostle (Acts ch. 9). As St. Augustine cryptically expressed it: "If Stephen had not prayed, the Church would not have Paul."

Stephen's life and death were a true witness to Christ, in whom he believed, whom he loved, and whose teaching he proclaimed by word and example. This Saint's teaching marked the beginning of the great first–century controversy between Judaism and Christianity that resulted in the victory of the Council of JERU-

SALEM, just as his martyrdom introduced the era of persecution that won so many saints for the Church.

Cult. ''Devout men took care of Stephen's burial and made great lamentation over him'' (Acts 8.2). No indication of the place of burial is given. The cult of Stephen is evidenced by the power and influence of his example on the army of martyrs who followed him. Eusebius (*Ecclesiastical History* 2.28; 5.2; *De Martyribus Palest.* 3) shows the frequency with which Stephen's prayer for his persecutors was imitated. Veneration of Stephen continued beyond the era of persecution. It increased with the widespread cult of martyrs in the fourth century and became universal after the priest Lucian discovered, at Kefr Gamla in 415, Stephen's remains along with those of Gamaliel, Nicodemus, and Abibas (*Epist. Luciani ad omnem Ecclesiam de revelatione corporis Stephani martyris primi et aliorum; Patrologia Latina*, ed. J. P. Migne [Paris 1878–90] 41:807–18).

Relics and Churches. Most of the remains of St. Stephen were brought to the Church of Sion in Jerusalem and were thence transferred to the Church of the Stoning of Stephen north of Jerusalem. This church was replaced by the basilica that the Empress Eudoxia built in 460. It was later destroyed. After its ruins were rediscovered in 1882, the present Basilica of St. Stephen of the ÉCOLE BIBLIQUE was erected on the ancient foundations. (A later tradition located the site of Stephen's martyrdom in the Kidron Valley to the east of Jerusalem, so that the eastern gate of the Old City is now commonly called St. Stephen's Gate.) Some relics of St. Stephen were taken to Constantinople (560), some to Rome (San Lorenzo in Campo Verano), and some to other churches, that later became popular sanctuaries of the saint.

Such a shrine was in Hippo, where St. Augustine wonderfully propagated devotion to St. Stephen and required that public testimony be given to the miracles wrought. Similar miraculous shrines in Africa existed at Calama and at Uzali, a colony near Utica [*De Civitate Dei* 22.8, in *Basic Writings of St. Augustine,* v.2 (New York 1948) 625–628]. A similar shrine existed on the Isle of Minorca (see letter 5 of Bishop Severus, *Patrologia Latina* 41: 821–832). In Italy a shrine of St. Stephen at Ancona claimed to have a rock used in the stoning of Stephen even before the priest Lucian discovered the saint's body. There were numerous other churches, such as those in Rome (the Basilica on the Via Latina; the Church of SS. Rotundo on the Celian Hill), Ravenna, and Naples. From the close of the fourth century and until the middle of the fifth, three churches were erected in Constantinople. Thereafter churches in honor of St. Stephen began to multiply everywhere.

Feasts. The date of death of St. Stephen is unknown. Among the list of Biblical saints in the early Church, Stephen is closely related to Christ because he was the first to give witness to Him through his blood. Accordingly, the feast of Stephen became associated with the birth of Christ and was observed on December 26, the day after Christmas, according to numerous testimonies, such as that of Gregory of Nyssa in the late fourth century (*In laudema fratris Basilii; Patrologia Graeca*, ed J. P. Migne [Paris 1857–66] 46:789), and the Sacramentaries, Calendars, and Martyrologies of the West. In the Eastern Church the veneration of the parents of Jesus on December 26 caused the feast of St. Stephen, from the early seventh century, to be observed on the following day (Sophronius or Jerusalem, *Oratio* 8 *in SS Apost. Petrum et Paulum; Patrologia Graeca* 87:3361).

The feast of the finding of the body of St. Stephen by the priest Lucian is celebrated on August 3 in the Latin Church, though it was not in the Missal prior to the nineth and tenth century. The reason for the feast seems to have been the dedication of a church in the Saint's honor. Since 1955 this is no longer a feast for the universal Church of the Roman rite. The Greek Church celebrates on August 2 the transfer of the relics of St. Stephen to Constantinople (*Bibl. hagiogr. Lat.* 7857–58; *Bibl. hagiogr. Graeca,* 1649–51). In the list of the Apostles and martyrs mentioned after the Consecration of the Mass, Stephen appears in both the Roman and the Ambrosian Mass.

Legends. An apocryphal account of Stephen's martyrdom (*Discourse of Gregory, Priest of Antioch*) in a Greek text, now lost, exists through a tenth–century Georgian translation from Athos (*Patrol. orient.* 19: 689–699) and a 17th–century Slavonic version in two forms [J. Franko, ed., *Monum. linguae necnon litter. ukrano-russic,* v.3 (1902) 28–33, 256–258]. The Georgian and second Slavonic text omit the final trial of Stephen and the conversion of Pilate and his family; the first Slavonic form includes both. The Georgian MSS does not mention the death of Gamaliel and companions.

The account is as follows: controversies in Jerusalem over the birth, death, and Resurrection of Jesus have attracted teachers from distant parts. Stephen's discourse in defense of these mysteries and of the signs of Christ's Second Coming brings mistreatment from attendants, but sympathy and defense from Pilate, the Roman Procurator, who is baptized with his wife and children. In a three-day controversy Stephen confounds his opponents with his wisdom. Priests dispatch Saul of Tarsus among Caesarean Christians with a search warrant. Saul has his cousin Stephen appear before him and violently upbraids him. Stephen replies, foretelling Saul's conversion and in turn is struck with a stick by Saul. Rabbi Gamaliel defends Stephen with such Christian sentiments that the ancients are provoked to demand Stephen's death. Aided by an angel, Stephen is victorious in his sufferings—a miracle, which occasions many conversions. He meets Christ at the Mount of Olives, recalling the agony in Gethsemane. Stephen's discourse occasions his arrest and a hearing before Alexander the Scribe. A voice from heaven and a brilliant light reassure Stephen on the eve of his condemnation by the Sanhedrin. Many, including Abibas, Gamaliel, and Nicodemus, besides Pilate and his family, are faithful to him. Fearing the increase of Christians, Saul demands Stephen's death; he is infuriated at the executioners' hesitation, removes the garments of the servants, and orders the stoning. Stephen exclaims: "Saul, Saul, what you are doing to me today you will suffer tomorrow from the same Jews, and you will think of me." When Saul gives the signal for the execution, Gamaliel and companions try to protect Stephen with their bodies, but are killed with Stephen by a dense volley of stones that even obscure the sunlight.

This apocryphon originated outside of Palestine, most probably after the above mentioned universally received testimony of Lucian the priest (415) concerning the finding of the body of Stephen, and those of Gamaliel, Abibas, and Nicodemus. If the Slavonic version mentions the martyrdom of Gamaliel and companions with Stephen, the Georgian MSS does not. The former obviously invented it to explain the discovery of their bodies with that of Stephen the protomartyr.

Iconography. Among the early and varied representations of St. Stephen are those that depict him robed as a deacon. Stones at his head or shoulder or in the air recall the manner of his martyrdom. An example is the central portion of P. F. Bissoli's triptych (16th century) in the Brera Gallery, Milan. The painting of St. Stephen in Rome's Borgese Gallery shows him kneeling with his head bleeding as he prays during his martyrdom. Representation with the deacon and martyr St. Lawrence is evidently intended to express their association as patrons of deacons and the common cult surrounding the twin tombs guarding their relics in the Roman Basilica of San Lorenzo.

Of special interest are the cycle representations of the life of St. Stephen: one by Bl. Angelico (15th century) in the Cappella Nicolina, Vatican, including six scenes (Stephen is ordained, distributes alms, preaches, is condemned, led out to martyrdom, and stoned); and another of four scenes by V. Carpaccio (16th century), among them the Disputa now in Milan's Brera Gallery. There is also Raphael Sanzio's Disputa of the Blessed Sacrament representing Stephen among companion saints in the court of heaven. The 18th–century dual series of frescoes of SS. Stephen and Lawrence in the San Lorenzo Basilica is the work of C. Fracassini and others. It was destroyed in the bombardment of Rome (1943), but has since been reproduced.

Feast: Dec. 26.

Bibliography: E. MUSSNER, and K. BEITL, *Lexikon für Theologie und Kirche*, ed. J. HOFER and K. RAHNER (Freiberg 1957–65) 9:1050–52. F. M. ABEL, *Dictionnaire de la Bible,* suppl. ed. L. PIROT et al. (Paris 1928–) 2:1132–46. *Encyclopedic Dictionary of the Bible*, tr. and adap. by L. HARTMAN (New York 1963) 2324–25. M. SIMON, *St. Stephen and the Hellenists in the Primitive Church* (New York 1958). C. MENCHINI, *Il discorso di S. Stefano protomartire nella letteratura e predicazione cristiana primitiva* (Rome 1951). H. LECLERCQ, *Dictionnaire d'archéologie chrétienne et de liturgie*. ed. F. CABROL, H. LECLERCQ and H. I. MARROU (Paris 1907–53) 5.1:624–671. M. J. LAGRANCE, *St. Étienne et son sanctuaire à Jérusalem* (Paris 1894). V. L. KENNEDY, *The Saints of the Canon of the Mass* (Vatican City 1938) 145–148. K. KÜNSTLE, *Ikonographie der christlichen Kunst* (Freiburg 1926–28) 2:544–547. L. RÉAU, *Iconographie de l'art chrétien* (Paris 1955–59) 3.1:444–456.

[S. J. HARTDEGEN]

STEPHEN, KING OF ENGLAND

Stephen, king of England (1135–1154, born before 1101). Stephen was the third son of Count Stephen of Blois and his wife, Adela, a daughter of William the Conqueror. By 1113, Stephen had joined the court of his uncle, King Henry I of England. He and his brother, Count Theobald of Blois, became the king's most trusted allies in Henry's struggle to hold Normandy against the machinations of his nephew, William Clito, and King Louis VI of France. Stephen was rewarded for his loyalty with the honors of Eye and Lancaster, the county of Mortain, and a splendid marriage to Matilda, the daughter and heiress of Count Eustace III of Boulogne.

Since Henry I's son, William, had perished in the wreck of the White Ship in 1120, the king named his daughter, the widowed Empress Matilda, as his heir and forced the barons to swear an oath to support her claim. Stephen gave his word at that time, even indulging in a friendly quarrel with the king's illegitimate son, Robert of Gloucester, for the honor of being the first to swear.

However, when Henry died unexpectedly in 1135, Stephen rushed to England, where he had himself crowned king on December 22. One of Stephen's first acts as king was to grant an unprecedented charter of liberties to the English Church, guaranteeing ecclesiastical rights and property and promising to curb the abuses of royal officials.

But while Stephen was establishing himself in England, his cousin, Matilda, and her husband, Count Geoffrey of Anjou, invaded Normandy to secure Matilda's inheritance. In addition, Stephen immediately faced rebellions in the West Country and in Wales, and invasions by King David I of Scotland. While Stephen concentrated on the siege of Exeter, he dispatched lieutenants to deal with the situation in Wales. This decision proved to be a costly mistake, for their failure to accomplish anything alienated the Marcher lords, including Earl Robert of Gloucester.

Stephen made another crucial mistake in 1139, when he arrested bishops Roger of Salisbury, Alexander of Lincoln and Nigel of Ely on charges of treason, alienating the English episcopacy, including his own brother, Bishop Henry of Winchester. In the same year, the empress invaded England. For two years the parties skirmished unsuccessfully, but in February 1141 the empress defeated the royal army at Lincoln and captured Stephen himself. While the king languished in prison, the Empress Matilda enjoyed a triumphal entry into Winchester, escorted by the bishop of Winchester. She then traveled to London for her coronation, but the Londoners, remembering their long and mutually beneficial relationship with Stephen as count of Boulogne, and spurred on by the pleas of Stephen's wife, Matilda, rose in rebellion and drove the empress from their city. This event caused Henry of Winchester to rejoin the royal party. The angry empress besieged the bishop in his castle at Winchester, but the royal army, commanded by Queen Matilda and the Flemish mercenary, William of Ypres, routed her supporters and captured Robert of Gloucester. Faced with this fatal loss, the empress agreed to an exchange of prisoners, so King Stephen regained his freedom in November 1141, and the political situation returned to what it had been before the battle of Lincoln.

Although Geoffrey of Anjou succeeded in conquering Normandy in 1148, the stalemate in England continued, with sporadic fighting, until Geoffrey and Matilda's son, Henry Plantagenet, invaded in 1153. King Stephen, grieving for the sudden death of his son, Eustace, and pressured by his barons to make peace, readily agreed to the Treaty of Winchester. The agreement allowed him to retain the crown during his lifetime, but stipulated that upon his death, Henry of Normandy was to become king. When Stephen died in 1154, the terms of the treaty were honored, and Duke Henry succeeded to the English throne as HENRY II.

Bibliography: D. CROUCH, *The Reign of King Stephen, 1135–1154* (Harlow, England 2000). E. KING, *The Anarchy of Stephen's Reign* (Oxford 1994). K. J. STRINGER, *The Reign of Stephen: Kingship, Warfare and Government in Twelfth Century England* (London 1993). R. H. C. DAVIS, *King Stephen, 1135–1154* (London 1990). K. R. POTTER, *Gesta Stephani* (Oxford 1976). M. CHIBNALL, *The Ecclesiastical History of Orderic Vitalis,* v. 6 (Oxford 1978). E. KING and K. R. POTTER, *William of Malmesbury: The Historia Novella* (Oxford 1998).

[J. TRUAX]

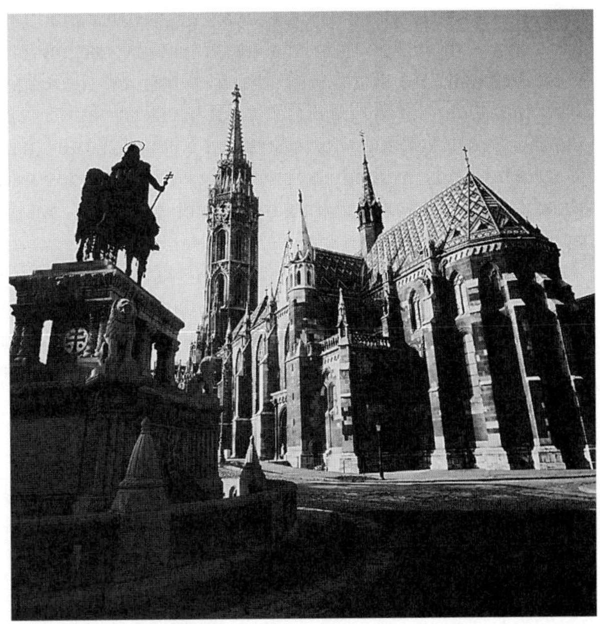

Statue of King Stephen I, sculpture by Frigyes Schulek Alajos Strobl, outside of Matthias Church, Budapest, Hungary. (©Paul Almasy/CORBIS)

STEPHEN I, KING OF HUNGARY, ST.

Reigned 997 to Aug. 15, 1038; b. Esztergom, between 970 and 975; (translation of relics to Buda celebrated in Hungary, August 20). Stephen is generally considered the real founder of the state of HUNGARY. A descendant of Árpád, conqueror of the country, Stephen was the son of Géza, ruler (*dux*) of Hungary. Born a pagan and called Vajk, he was baptized in his early youth and received the name Stephen (in Hungarian, *István*). He married Gisela, sister of the future Emperor HENRY II. In 997 Stephen succeeded his father, and on Christmas day 1000, he had himself crowned king with a crown sent, at his request, by Pope SYLVESTER II. By conviction as well as from political considerations, Stephen was a fervent Christian and a staunch supporter of the Church. BENEDICTINES were entrusted with the task of converting the Hungarians and with the organization of the Hungarian Church. By the time of Stephen's death two archbishoprics, Esztergom (Gran) and Kalocsa; eight bishoprics [Csanád, Eger, Bihar (Nagyvárad), Pécs, Györ, Fehérvár (Alba Julia), Veszprém, and Vac]; and numerous monasteries bore witness to their activity. Stephen was aware that his seminomadic people could survive only if they embraced Christianity. He eliminated all the pagan representatives of the old order with grim determination and quite ruthless methods to achieve this integration into the Christian commonwealth; he transformed the tribal state into a ''modern'' feudal state of Western pattern (*see* FEUDALISM). Nothing shows Stephen's genius better than that, while relying heavily on foreign missionaries and knights, he could assert Hungary's independence from its neighbors. Stephen was canonized in 1083. The *Legenda maior* (late 11th century), the *Legenda minor* (early 12th century), and the legend written by a Bishop Hartvik deal with his life. Stephen is conventionally credited with the authorship of a moralizing *Mirror of Princes,* written for the use of his son.

Feast: Sept. 2.

Bibliography: A. F. GOMBOS, *Catalogus fontium historiae Hungaricae,* 3 v. (Budapest 1937–38). G. BÓNIS, *István király* (Budapest 1956), best monograph but it neglects the religious aspects. B. HÓMAN, *Szent István* (Budapest 1938). *Archivum Europae centro-orientalis* 4 (1938), contains relevant articles in Eng., Fr., Ger., Ital. and Lat. J. L. BAUDOT and L. CHAUSSIN, *Vies des saints et des bienheureux selon l'ordre du calendrier avec l'historique des fêtes,* ed. by the Benedictines of Paris, 12 v. (Paris 1935–56); v. 13, suppl. and table générale (1959) 9:48–52. D. SINOR, *History of Hungary* (New York 1959). J. BAK, *Lexikon für Theologie und Kirche,* ed. J. HOFER and K. RAHNER (Freiburg 1957–65) 9:1048.

[D. SINOR]

STEPHEN I, POPE, ST.

Pontificate: March 12, 254 to Aug. 2, 257. A Roman by birth, Stephen is commemorated in the *Depositio episcoporum* as buried in the cemetery of Callistus, but the early Roman liturgy does not record his cult as a martyr. This claim was first made in a sixth-century *passio* that confused the notice of the end of the reign of SIXTUS II with that of Stephen. His short pontificate was disturbed by problems of government and doctrine, information for which is preserved mainly in the letters of St. CYPRIAN (*Epistles* 67–75; *Corpus scriptorum ecclesiasticorum* 3.2.738–827).

At the close of the Decian persecution, two Spanish bishops, Martial of Mérida and Basilides of León Astorga, were accused of accepting certificates indicating that they had sacrificed (*LIBELLATICI*) and deposed from their sees. Basilides personally appealed to Pope Stephen and obtained rehabilitation for himself and Martial. Upon being apprised of this papal action, Cyprian and the African bishops in council advised the Spanish churches not to reinstate the two bishops. When later, in two letters to Cyprian, Bp. Faustinus of Lyons denounced Marcian of Arles as a schismatic in communion with NOVATIAN, Cyprian wrote to Stephen, who had shown reluctance to intrude, asking him to depose Marcian.

The conflict between Cyprian and Stephen over the validity of baptism administered by heretics was more serious. In North Africa, Antioch, and Asia Minor, the baptism performed by heretics was generally regarded as invalid. In Rome, Alexandria, and Palestine, however, such baptisms were held to be valid, and heretics were reconciled with the Church through absolution given by the imposition of hands. At the request of the layman Magnus (*c.* 255), Cyprian wrote a treatise to prove his contention that as heretics were outside the Church, they could not forgive sins, and the Council of CARTHAGE in 255 supported him. Some African bishops, however, objected, defending the Roman position. After another council of 71 bishops in 256, Cyprian sent the synodal decree to Rome. His envoys were treated as heretics, and a split between Rome and Carthage threatened. Cyprian wrote to Stephen asserting that every bishop was master in his own see. Stephen's reply was an order to obey: ''If anyone comes to us from any heresy at all, let nothing new be done (*innovetur*), but abide by tradition and let there be an imposition of hands for penance; for the heretics themselves do not baptize those who come to them, but grant them communion.'' On Sept. 1, 256, eighty-seven African bishops in council again supported Cyprian and wrote to Bp. FIRMILIAN OF CAESAREA in Cappadocia. Cyprian's letter to Firmilian is not extant, but Firmilian's reply is a violent attack on the pope and the Roman teaching on baptism by heretics. Whether Stephen went through with his threatened excommunication is not known. St. DIONYSIUS OF ALEXANDRIA wrote to Stephen calling for moderation; and VALERIAN began a persecution of the Christians. Stephen died, probably not, as the *Liber pontificalis* reports, a martyr. His successor, Sixtus II, restored peaceful relations with Carthage and Cappadocia, and by the beginning of the fourth century North Africa had adopted the Roman usage.

Stephen is the first bishop of Rome after VICTOR I (*c.* 190) known to have tried to exercise supervision over the whole Church and the first, with the possible exception of CALLISTUS I, to refer explicitly to Matthew 16.18 (Thou art Peter...) to justify the pope's authority to impose Roman traditions on other sees. This text would dominate later exercises of papal authority, but unfortunately scholars know little about the Roman understanding of this text before Stephen's use of it in this controversy.

Feast: Aug. 2.

Bibliography: EUSEBIUS, *Histoire Ecclesiastique* 7.2, 3, 5. DUCHESNE, *Liber pontificalis*, 1:XCVI–XCVIII, CCXLVII, 68–69, 154. J. QUASTEN, *Patrology* (Westminster, Md. 1950—) 2:237–239. A. CLARVAL, *Dictionnaire de théologie catholique*, ed. A. VACANT et al., (Paris 1903–50) 5.1:970–973. J. P. BURNS, ''On Rebaptism: Social Organization in the Third Century Church,'' *Journal of*

Early Christian Studies 1 (1992) 367–403. E. FERGUSON, ed., *Encyclopedia of Early Christianity* (New York 1997) 2.1089. S. G. HALL, "Stephen of Rome and One Baptism," *Studia Patristica* 17.2 (1982) 796–798. J. N. D. KELLY, *Oxford Dictionary of Popes* (New York 1986) 20–21. M. BÉVENOT, "'Primatus Petro datur': St. Cyprian on the Papacy," *Studies in Early Christainity* 13 (1993) 341–57. H. KIRCHNER, "Der Ketzertaufstreit zwischen Karthago und Rom und seine Konsequenzen für die Frage nach den Grenzen der Kirche," *Studies in Early Christianity* 11 (1993) 414–31. J. ŚRUTWA, "Ewangelia św. Mateusza (16, 16–19) jako argument papieża Stefana I na rzecz prymatu papieskiego," *Analecta Cracoviensia* (1995) 323–28.

[E. G. WELTIN/J. F. KELLY]

STEPHEN II, POPE

Pontificate: March 752, reigned for four days. Stephen, a Roman priest elected to succeed Pope ZACHARY, who died as the Lombard peril neared its crisis in Italy, was installed at the Lateran but died before his episcopal consecration. Since, in the 8th century, consecration was thought to mark the official beginning of a pope's reign, Stephen is not listed among the popes by his contemporaries or by most medieval and modern historians. However, since modern Canon Law holds that a pope's pontificate begins with his election, the *Annuario pontificio* from 1961 on, took cognizance of Stephen II and renumbered all subsequent popes of this name with alternate numbers, e.g., Stephen's successor is referred to as Stephen II (III). Recent works tend to accept the validity of Stephen's extremely short pontificate but refuse to accept the renumbering of his successors. Despite the adjustments involved in a double set of numbers for popes of this name, there is no doubt that this man who exercised the pontifical power for even so short a time should be recognized by historians as Pope Stephen II (*see* POPES, LIST OF).

Bibliography: *Liber pontificalis*, ed. L. DUCHESNE (Paris 1886–92) 1:440. *Annales Nazariani, Monumenta Germaniae Historica: Scriptores* (Berlin 1826)1:23–31, 40–44. A. FLICHE and V. MARTIN, eds., *Histoire de l'église depuis les origines jusqu'à nos jours* (Paris 1935) 5:423. H. K. MANN, *The Lives of the Popes in the Early Middle Ages from 590 to 1304* (London 1902–32) 1.2:290–291. R. L. POOLE, "The Names and Numbers of Medieval Popes," *English Historical Review* 32 (1917) 465–478. R. THIBAUT, "Noms et chiffres pontificaux," *Nouvelle revue théologique* 72 (1950) 834–838.

[P. J. MULLINS]

STEPHEN II (III), POPE

Pontificate, March 26, 752 to April 26, 757. Stephen II was a descendant of Roman nobility who prior to his election to the papacy entered the clerical ranks and served in the papal administration. His social status and his service in papal governance marked the convergence of the interests in controlling the papal office held by two groups which had grown increasingly powerful in Rome during the century prior to 752: the landed aristocracy which dominated the military establishment and the civil administration of the duchy of Rome and the clerical officials directing the papal administration. As a consequence of the resourcefulness of Stephen's immediate predecessors in both religious and secular affairs and of the increasing inability of the imperial government in Constantinople to exercise effective political authority in Italy and to enforce its policy of iconoclasm, the papacy had by mid-eighth century established *de facto* control over Rome and its environs and was able to assert considerable influence in central and southern Italy beyond Rome. However, as imperial power in Italy deteriorated, the aggressiveness of the Lombards increased, reaching a climax just before Stephen was elected when King Aistulf (749–756), driven by an ambition to unite Italy under LOMBARD rule, seized Ravenna and other key imperial cities and threatened to establish his authority over Rome itself.

Immediately after his election Stephen persuaded Aistulf to agree to a 40-year truce, but the Lombard king soon resumed his aggression. Stephen continued his diplomatic efforts to restrain Aistulf and sought aid from Emperor CONSTANTINE V. When those measures proved fruitless, he took a fateful step: he initiated measures intended to persuade PEPIN III, king of the Franks, to come to the aid of St. Peter and his people. Earlier, Pope GREGORY III (731–741) had unsuccessfully appealed to the Franks, but now things had changed. Not only had papal influences in Francia expanded, chiefly through papal support of BONIFACE in his missionary and reforming activities, but also Pepin was indebted to the papacy because of Pope ZACHARIAS's approval in 751 for Pepin to deprive the MEROVINGIAN dynasty of the Frankish throne and to bestow the crown on his own family, the CAROLINGIANS. As a consequence of the king's favorable response to the Pope's appeal, Stephen, accompanied by a Frankish escort, was able to depart Rome in October 753 for a trip to the Frankish kingdom. The party stopped briefly in Pavia for one more fruitless effort to make peace with Aistulf.

In January 754 Stephen met Pepin at Ponthion and began a series of negotiations extending over several months. The exact details of these proceedings have been subject to considerable disagreement. At Ponthion Pepin promised under oath to accede to Stephen's request for protection and to restore territories that rightly belonged to St. Peter. That promise was part of an alliance of friendship, peace, and love entered into by pope and king, creating bonds deeply rooted in religious convictions. After their initial meeting Stephen went to the abbey of ST. DENIS to spend the winter. Pepin tried unsuccessfully through a series of diplomatic exchanges to persuade Aistulf to concede territories claimed by the pope, making it increasingly obvious that a military campaign would be necessary. Before undertaking such a campaign Pepin had to win the support of significant numbers of Frankish magnates who were reluctant to abandon the long-standing friendship between the Lombards and the Franks and uneasy about any move that would enhance the power of their new king and his family. But Pepin won the day, perhaps helped by the presence of the pope to remind the nobles of the plight of St. Peter. At a general assembly held at Quierzy in April 754 the Frankish magnates approved the Italian campaign. On that occasion Pepin also spelled out in detail the territories claimed by the pope. That list, involving most of central and southern Italy and embracing both Lombard and imperial territory, must surely have been compiled with the advice of Stephen. Perhaps Stephen's thinking about what belonged to the papacy was influenced by a famous forgery, the Donation of Constantine, which came into existence in Rome about this time. In July 754 the final actions in shaping the Frankish-papal alliance unfolded at the abbey of St. Denis. Stephen solidified Pepin's claim to the Frankish throne by anointing him, his queen, and his sons and by forbidding anyone except a member of Carolingian family from ever wearing the Frankish crown. He also bestowed on Pepin and his sons an enigmatic title, *patricius Romanorum,* apparently intended to provide the legal basis for Pepin's protectorate over St. Peter and his people.

In 755 Pepin led his army into Italy and easily defeated Aistulf. A peace treaty involving the papacy, the Franks, and the Lombards was arranged requiring Aistulf to surrender to the pope territories he had recently seized. Hardly had Pepin departed Italy when Aistulf resumed his attacks on territories claimed by the Pope and threatening Rome itself. Stephen wrote letters to Pepin and to the Frankish clergy, magnates, and army, pleading with them to fulfill their promise to protect the papacy; one of these letters purported to have been written by St. Peter himself. The result was a second Frankish campaign in 756 in which Aistulf was again defeated. During the course of that campaign Pepin was approached by a legate of the emperor in Constantinople demanding the return to their rightful owner of the territories which Aistulf had seized from the empire, a plea that the king rebuffed on the grounds that he could not alienate what belonged to the church of St. Peter, out of love for whom he was acting. Instead, as part of treaty ending the campaign, Pepin commissioned a Frankish agent to oversee the surrender of numerous cities and territories in the Exarchate of Ravenna, the Pentapolis, and Emilia. These territories were then granted in perpetuity to St. Peter in a document that came to be called the Donation of Pepin. Although not embracing all that Pepin had promised at Quierzy in 754, the new acquistions, when added to the Duchy of Rome, constituted the core of an entity often referred to as the "Republic of the Romans" belonging to St. Peter and directed by his vicar, the pope. An independent Papal State destined to endure until the nineteenth century had come into existence.

Stephen had still one more opportunity to strengthen the papal position against the Lombards. When Aistulf died in December 756, a dispute arose over succession to the Lombard throne. Stephen played a decisive role in settling the succession in favor of DESIDERIUS, who in return promised to restore still more territory to the Republic of St. Peter. The pope's death in April 757 marked the end of remarkable pontificate. By his skillful diplomacy Stephen II forged an alliance with the ascending Carolingian dynasty willing to act as protector of the Republic of St. Peter and to support its acquisition of territorial possessions sufficient to allow its survival as an independent state. In the immediate setting that success saved the papacy and Rome from absorption into the Lombard kingdom. In a larger sense that alliance in effect severed the bonds that had long linked the papacy to the eastern Roman Empire and cast its lot with the western European Christian community in the process of formation.

See Also: DONATION OF CONSTANTINE.

Bibliography: Sources. *Le Liber Pontificalis,* ed. L. DUCHESNE, 3 v., 2d ed. (Paris 1955–1957) 1:440–462 [Eng. tr. in *The Lives of the Eighth-Century Popes (Liber Pontificalis). The Ancient Biographies of Nine Popes from A.D. 715 to A.D. 817,* tr. with intro. by R. DAVIS, (Liverpool 1992) 51–76]. *Regesta Pontificum Romanorum ab condita ecclesia ad annum post Christum MCXCVIII,* ed. P. JAFFÉ, 2 v., 2d ed. (Leipzig 1885–1888) 1:271–277. *Codex Carolinus,* Epp. 4–11, ed. W. GUNDLACH, *Monumenta Germaniae Historica: Epistolae Merowingici et Karolini aevi,* v. 1 (Berlin 1892) 487–507. *Clausula de unctione Pippini regis,* ed. W. ARNDT, *Monumenta Germaniae Historica: Scriptores rerum Merovingicarum* 1 (Hannover 1884) 465–466. *The Fourth Book of the Chronicle of Fredegar, with its Continuations,* Continuationes, chs. 36–38, ed. tr. with intro. J. M. WALLACE-HADRILL (London) 104–108. *Annales regni Francorum,* a. 753–756, ed. F. KURZE, *Monumenta Germaniae Historica, Scriptores rerum Germanicarum in usum scholarum* (Hannover 1885) 10–14 (Eng. tr. in *Carolingian Chronicles. Royal Frankish Annals and Nithard's Histories,* tr. by B. W. SCHOLZ [Ann Arbor, Mich. 1970] 39–42). *Annales Mettenses priores,* a. 753–756, ed. B. SIMSON, *Monumenta Germaniae Historica, Scriptores rerum Germanicarum in usum scholarum* (Hannover and Leipzig 1905) 44–49. **Literature.** L. DUCHESNE, *The Beginnings of the Temporal Sovereignty of the Popes, A.D. 754–1073,* tr. A. H. MATTHEW (London 1908) 13–48. E. CASPAR, *Pippin und die römische Kirche: kritische Untersuchungen zum fräish–päpstlichen Bunde im VIII. Jahrhundert* (Darmstadt 1914; reprinted, 1973). L. LEVILLAIN, "L'avénement de la dynastie carolingienne et les origines de l'État pontifical (749–757),'' *Biliothèque de l'École des chartes* 94:225–293. F. X. SEPPELT, *Geschichte des Papsttums. Eine Geschichte der Päpste von den Anfängen bis zum Tod Pius X.*, v. 2 (Leipzig 1934) 115–136. O. BERTOLINI, *Roma di fronte a Bisanzio e ai Langobardi, Storia di Roma 9* (Bologna 1941) 515–582. L. BRÉHIER and R. AIGRAIN, *Grégoire le Grand, les États barbares et la conquête arabe (590–757),* Histoire de l'Église depuis les origines jusqu'a nos jours, ed. A. FLICHE and V. MARTIN (Paris 1947) 412–430. J. HALLER, *Das Papsttum: Idee und Wirklichkeit,* v. 1 (Basel 1951) 412–441. W. ULLMANN, *The Growth of Papal Government in the Middle Ages. A Study in the Ideological Relation of Clerical to Lay Power* (London 1955) 44–86. O. BERTONLINI, ''Le origini del potere temporale e del domino temporale dei papi,'' in *I Problemi dell'occidente nel secolo VIII,* Settimane di studio del Centro italiano di studi sull'alto medioevo 20 (Spoleto 1973) 1:231–255, 319–325. W. H. FRITZE, *Papst und Frankenkönig. Studien zu den päpstlich–fränkischen Rechtsbeziehungen von 754 bis 824,* Vorträge und Forschungen, Sonderband 10 (Sigmaringen 1973). D. H. MILLER, ''The Motivation of Pepin's Italian Policy, 754–768,'' *Studies in Medieval Culture,* 4: 44–54. D. H. MILLER, ''The Roman Revolution in the Eighth Century: A Study of the Ideological Background of the Papal Separation from Byzantium and Alliance with the Franks,'' *Medieval Studies* 36:79–133. J. JARNUT, ''Quierzy und Rom. Bemerkungen zu den *Promissiones Donationis* Pippins und Karls,'' *Historische Zeitscrift* 220:265–297. A. DRABEK, *Die Verträge der fränkischen und deutschen Herrscher mit dem Papsttum von 754 bis 1020,* Veröffentlichungen des Instituts für österreichische Geschichtsforschung 22 (Vienna, Cologne, Graz, 1978) 13–29. A. ANGENENDT, ''Der geistliche Bündnis der Päpste mit dem Karolingern (754–796),'' *Historisches Jahrbuch,* 100 (1980) 1–94. M. KERNER, ''Die frühen Karolinger und das Papsttum,'' *Zeitschrift des Aachener Geschichtsvereins* 88/89:5–41. J. T. HALLENBECK, *Pavia and Rome: The Lombard Monarchy and the Papacy in the Eighth Century,* Transactions of the American Philosophical Society 72/4 (Philadelphia 1982) 39–90. T. F. X. NOBLE, *The Republic of St. Peter. The Birth of the Papal State, 680–825* (Philadelphia 1989) 71–103, 256–276. O. ENGELS, ''Zum päpstlich-fränkischen Bündnis im VIII. Jahrhundert,'' in *Ecclesia et Regnum. Beiträge zur Geschichte von Kirche, Recht und Staat im Mittelalter. Festschrift für Franz-Josef Schmale zum seinem 65. Geburtstag,* ed. D. BERG and H.-W. GOETZ (Bochum 1989) 21–38. P. LLEWLLYN, *Rome in the Dark Ages* (London 1993) 199–228, especially 207–217 P. ENGELBERT, ''Papstreisen ins Frankenreich,'' *Römische Quartalschrift für christliche Altertumskunde und Kirchengeschichte* 88:77–113.

[R. E. SULLIVAN]

STEPHEN III (IV), POPE

Pontificate, Aug. 7, 768 to Jan. 24, 772. A Sicilian by birth, Stephen came to Rome at an early age and became a priest serving in the papal bureaucracy under Popes STEPHEN II (752–757) and PAUL I (757–767). During their pontificates the clerical element governed the Papal State with a strong hand and played a key role in establishing a peace in Italy that met the interests of the papacy, the LOMBARDS, and the FRANKS. With the death of Pope Paul I, a crisis developed within the Papal State that placed its very existence in jeopardy.

The crisis began with a disputed election to replace Paul I. Dissatisfied with clerical domination and anxious to have a larger voice in selecting the official who now controlled the Papal State, a faction representing the military aristocracy, led by Duke Toto of Nepi, used force to elevate to the papal office a laymen, Constantine, Toto's brother, who was hastily ordained as deacon to qualify him for the papal office. In the face of what they considered an illegitimate election, the leaders of the clerical party, the *primicerius* of notaries Christopher and his son Sergius, fled Rome and sought support from the Lombard king, Desiderius. Anxious to gain influence in Rome by controlling the papal office, Desiderius provided troops which allowed Christopher and Sergius to recapture Rome and depose Pope CONSTANTINE (II) after a pontificate lasting a year. Thereupon, the priest Waldipert, an agent of Desiderius who accompanied the Lombard forces that ousted Constantine, arranged for the election of a certain Philip to the papal office. Christopher soon rallied sufficient support to depose Philip and arrange for the election of Stephen, a representative of the clerical party in Rome.

Stephen III's election was followed by violent measures taken against the faction who had elected Constantine as pope. Among the victims were Constantine himself, who was blinded, and Waldipert, the agent of Desiderius, whose murder made the Lombard king a bitter enemy of Christopher and his party. Stephen remained passive in the face of these atrocities, suggesting that he was under the influence of Christopher and Sergius. One of the new Pope's first acts was to send a letter to PEPIN III, king of the Franks, asking him to confirm the Frankish-papal alliance and to send bishops to Rome to participate in a synod that would deal with Constantine. Pepin was dead when the papal message reached Francia, but his successors, CARLOMAN and CHARLEMAGNE, agreed to Stephen's requests. With thirteen Frankish bishops participating the Lateran synod of 769 condemned the election of Constantine and nullified all his acts. Measures were adopted to limit eligibility for the papal office to a restricted number of clerics and to allow only the clergy to participate in papal elections; members of the laity were assigned only a ceremonial role in the election process. Although these provisions marked an immediate victory for the clerical bureaucracy, they failed to take into account the social and political realities in the Papal State and thus deepened the tensions between the clerical bureaucracy and the military aristocracy. The synod also condemned the acts of the council of Hiereia (754), which had reaffirmed the policy of iconoclasm pursued by the imperial government in Constantinople.

Other problems emerged to threaten the security of the Papal State. Papal authority in Ravenna was challenged by a newly elected archbishop anxious to assert his autonomy and extend his control over the territory surrounding Ravenna. He won the support of DESIDERIUS, who became increasingly hostile toward Rome after his rebuff when Stephen was elected. More ominous were developments in the Frankish kingdom which put in doubt the Frankish protectorate over the Papal State and Frankish aid in gaining possession of territories which the papacy claimed were owed to St. Peter. Before his death in 768 Pepin III created a kingdom for each of his sons, Carloman and Charlemagne. The new kings soon became rivals. One of the results of that rivalry was a move, perhaps initiated by Desiderius, to form an alliance between the Franks and the Lombards to be sealed by a marriage arrangement that would link the two royal families, a prospect that Desiderius certainly welcomed as a way of undermining the Frankish-papal alliance. When Stephen heard of this possibility, he wrote to Carloman and Charlemagne, bitterly denouncing the Lombards as loathsome, diabolical barbarians unworthy of association with the Franks and reminding the kings that they already had wives who could not be set aside according to canon law. His effort came to naught; in 770 Bertrada, the mother of the Frankish kings, made a journey to Pavia and Rome during which she arranged such an alliance to be sealed by the marriage of Charlemagne to the daughter of Desiderius. Bertrada was able to convince Stephen III that the alliance offered advantages to the Pope, including Desiderius' willingness to restore lands to the Papal State and Charlemagne's support for papal rights in Ravenna. In fact, these conditions were met in early 771, assuring the papacy of continued Frankish protection of the Papal State from the Lombards.

In Rome the formation of the Frankish-Lombard alliance was opposed by Christopher and Sergius, who now sought the support of Carloman as way of sustaining the Frankish presence in Rome. Some evidence suggests that Stephen accepted the Frankish-Lombard alliance because it offered an opportunity to escape domination by Christopher and Sergius. Perhaps as a result of the efforts of the papal chamberlain, Paul Afiarta, an agent of Desiderius, Stephen became convinced that Christopher, Sergius, and Carloman's agent in Rome were conspiring to murder him. As a result the pope met Desiderius in person to initiate actions that resulted in the deposition of their common enemies, Christopher and Sergius. Their fall opened the way for the ascendancy of Paul Afiarta, who aspired to assume the papal office and who seemed to dominate Stephen during the last months of his pontificate. During those same months the scene changed elsewhere. Desiderius, described by the pope only shortly before as ''his most excellent son,'' refused to make any restitutions to the Papal State. His cause suffered a setback when Charlemagne repudiated his Lombard wife, thus breaking the Frankish alliance with the Lombards. When Carloman died in December 771, Charlemagne assumed his kingdom, disregarding the claims of Carloman's sons who, with their mother, sought refuge at the Lombard court. When Stephen III died in January 772, the future of the Republic of St. Peter was far less certain than it had been when he was consecrated pope.

See Also: ICONOCLASM

Bibliography: Sources: *Le Liber Pontificalis,* ed. L. DUCHESNE, 3 v., 2nd ed. (Paris 1955–1957), 1:468–485 (Eng. tr. in *The Lives of the Eighth-Century Popes (Liber Pontificalis). The Ancient Biographies of Nine Popes from A.D. 715 to A.D. 817,* tr. with intro. R. DAVIS [Liverpool, 1992] 85–106). *Regesta Pontificum Romanorum ab condita ecclesia ad annum post Christum MCXCVIII,* ed. P. JAFFÉ, 2 v., 2nd ed. (Leipzig 1885–1888) 1:285–288. *Codex Carolinus,* Epp. 44–48, ed. W. GUNDLACH, *Monumenta Germaniae Historica: Epistolae Merowingici et Karolini, v. 1* (Berlin 1892) 558–567. *Epistolae Langobardorum collectae,* ed. W. GUNDLACH, *Monumenta Germaniae Historica: Epistolae Karolini Aevi,* v. 1 (Berlin 1892) 711–715. *Concilia,* v. 2: *Concilia aevi karolini,* v. 1, part 1, ed. A. WERMINGHOFF, *Monumenta Germanicae Historica: Leges,* Sectio III (Hannover and Leipzig, 1906) 74–92. **Literature:** L. DUCHESNE, *The Beginnings of the Temporal Sovereignty of the Popes, A.D. 754–1073,* tr. A. H. MATTHEW, (London 1908) 70–86. C. J. HEFELE, *Histoire des conciles d'après les documents originaux,* tr. H. LECLERCQ, v. 3, part 1 (Paris 1905) 730–740. F. X. SEPPELT, *Geschichte des Papsttums. Eine Geschichte der Päpste von den Anfängen bis zum Tod Pius X,* v. 2 (Leipzig 1934) 149–157. O. BERTONLINI, *Roma di fronte a Bisanzio e ai Langobardi, Storia di Roma 9: 614–653.* ÉMILE AMANN, *L' Époque carolingienne, Histoire de l' Église depuis les origines jusqu'a nos jours,* ed. A. FLICHE and V. MARTIN 6 (Paris 1947) 32–49. O. BERTONLINI, ''La caduta del primicerio Cristoforo (771) nelle versioni dei contemporanei e le correnti antilongobarde e filolongobarde in Roma alla fine del pontificato de Stefano III (771–772),'' *Rivista di storia della chiesa in Italia* 1: 227–262, 340–378. J. HALLER, *Das Papsttums: Idee und Wirklichkeit,* vol. 1 (Basel 1951) 441–448. D. H. MILLER, ''The Motivation of Pepin's Italian Policy, 754–768,'' *Studies in Medieval Culture* 4: 44–54. J. T. HALLENBECK, ''Pope Stephen III: Why Was He Elected?'' *Archivum Historiae Pontificiae* 12: 287–297. J. T. HALLENBECK, *Pavia and Rome: The Lombard Monarchy and the Papacy in the Eighth Century,* Transactions of the American Philosophical Society 72/4:90–140. T. F. X. NOBLE, *The Republic of St. Peter. The Birth of the Papal State, 680–825* (Philadelphia 1989) 112–127. P. LEWELLYN, *Rome in the Dark Ages* (London 1993) 194–228. J. JARNUT ''Ein Bruderkampf und seine Folgen: Die Krise der Frankenreichen (768–771),'' in *Herrschaft, Kirche, Kultur: Beiträge sur Geschichte des Mittelalters: Festscrift für Friedrich Prinz zu seinem 65. Geburtstag,* Monographien zur Geschichte des Mittelalters 37 (Stuttgart, 1993) 165–176.

[R. E. SULLIVAN]

STEPHEN IV (V), POPE

Pontificate: June 22, 816 to Jan. 24, 817. A member of a noble Roman family, Stephen IV served from his youth in the papal administration and was ordained deacon by his predecessor, Pope LEO III (795–816). Not only because of the tumult marking the last days of Leo III's pontificate but also because Stephen was the first pope elected since the renewal of the Roman Empire in the West, the beginning of Stephen's pontificate was marked by uncertainty. Of crucial importance in clarifying the situation were the intentions of Emperor Louis the Pious, who had succeeded to Charlemagne only two years earlier and whose first measures as emperor left doubts about his willingness to follow his father's policy toward the papacy. One of Stephen's first acts was to exact an oath of obedience to the emperor from the Roman people. Then Stephen sent legates to Louis informing him of his election and announcing that he was coming to Francia, in the words of the papal biographer, ''to reaffirm peace and the unity of the holy church of God.''

Stephen and Louis met at Reims in October 816. Their negotiations led to highly important consequences. In a carefully staged public ceremony Stephen consecrated and anointed Louis, placing on his head a crown that the pope had brought from Rome and that allegedly once belonged to the Emperor Constantine the Great. By this act Stephen added a religious dimension to the title and the office that Louis had originally received from his father without the involvement of an ecclesiastical official. The religious sanction involved in the papal coronation and anointment was particularly important to Louis and his chief advisers, who were in the process of exalting the imperial office with its connotation of unity as the focal point of Louis's regime. This occasion also served as a precedent for future papal participation in legitimizing succession to the imperial office. No less important, Stephen and Louis worked out the details that led to a renewal of the friendship alliance between papacy and the Frankish ruling house, which dated back to 754. Their agreement, known as the *Pactum Ludovicianum,* marked an important step in clarifying the place of the Papal State in the Carolingian Empire. The territorial claims of the papacy as set forth in previous donations by Frankish rulers dating back to the agreement between Pope Stephen II and King PEPIN III in 754 were restated in detail. Papal sovereignty in administrative and judicial functions in that territory was reaffirmed, except for the emperor's right to hear appeals in carefully defined cases. The emperor's pledged to protect the Papal State and to allow complete freedom of papal elections. In effect, the *Pactum Ludovicianum* drew the Papal State into the structure of the Carolingian Empire but gave to it and its ruler, the pope, a privileged place in the Empire.

Stephen died soon after returning to Rome from his meeting with Louis. The official ratification of the *Pactum Ludovicianum* was left to his successor, Pope PASCAL I. For his part in negotiating that agreement Stephen deserves credit for an important contribution to a clearer definition of the relationship of the Papal State and the papacy to the secular state and its ruler.

Bibliography: *Liber Pontificalis,* ed. L. DUCHESNE, 3 v., 2nd ed. (Paris 1955–1957), 2: 49–51 (Eng. tr. in *The Lives of the Eighth-Century Popes). The Ancient Biographies of Nine Popes from AD 715 to AD 817,* tr. R. DAVIS, *Translated Texts for Historians* 13 (Liverpool 1992) 231–236. *Regesta Pontificum Romanorum ab condita ecclesia ad annum post Christum MCXCVIII,* ed. P. JAFFÉ, 2 v., 2nd ed. (Leipzig 1885–1888) 1:316–318. *Annales regni Francorum,* a. 816, ed. F. KURZE, *Monumenta Germaniae Historica, Scriptores rerum Germanicarum in usum scholarum* (Hannover 1989), (Eng. tr. in *Carolingian Chronicles: Royal Frankish Annals and Nithard's Histories,* trans. B. W. SCHOLZ; Ann Arbor, MI 1970). *Theganus, Gesta Hludowici Imperatoris,* chs. 16–17, and *Astronomus, Vita Hludowici Imperatoris,* chs. 26–27, both in *Thegan, Die Taten Kaiser Ludwigs; Astronomus, Das Leben Kaiser Ludwigs,* ed. and tr. E. TREMP, *Monumenta Germaniae Historica, Scriptroes rerum Germanicarum in usum scholarum* 64 (Hannover 1995) 196–198, 364–372 (an Eng. tr. of the passage from the Astronomer in *Son of Charlemagne. A Contemporary Life of Louis the Pious,,* tr. A. CABANISS [Syracuse, NY 1964] 59–62). ''Ermold le Noir, Poème sur Louis le Pieux et épitre au roi Pépin,'' Bk. II, lines 846–1137, ed. and tr. E. FARAL, *Les classiques de l'histoire de France au Moyen Age* 14 (Paris 1932) 67–89. Literature. F. X. SEPPELT, *Geschichte des Papsttums. Eine Geschichte der Päpste von den Anfängen bis zum Tod Pius X,* v. 2: *Das Papsttums im Frühmittelalter. Geschichte des Päpste von Regierungsantritt Gregors des Grossen bis zum Mitte des ll. Jh.* (Leipzig 1934) 200–204. É. AMANN, ''L'Époque carolingienne,'' *Histoire de l'Église depuis les origines jusqu'a nos jours,* ed. A. FLICHE and V. MARTIN 6 (Paris, 1947) 204–206. W. ULLMANN, *The Growth of Papal Government in the Middle Ages. A Study in the Ideological Relation of Clerical to Lay Power* (London 1955) 119–166. W. H. FRITZE, ''Papst und Frankenkönig. Studien zu den päpstlich-fränkischen Rechtsbeziehungen von 754 bis 824,'' *Vorträge und Forschungen, Sonderband* 10 (Sigmaringen 1973) *passim,*, especially 15–45. A. HAHN, ''Der Hludowicianum. Die Urkunde Ludwigs des Frommen für des römischen Kirche von 817,'' *Archiv für Diplomatik* 21 (1975) 15–135. A. DRABEK, ''Die Verträge der fränkischen und deutschen Herrscher mit dem Papsttum von 754 bis 1020,'' *Veröffentlichungen des Instituts für österreichische Geschichtsforschung* 22 (Viena, Cologne, Graz, 1978) 33–43. T. F. X. NOBLE, *The Republic of St. Peter. The Birth of the Papal State, 680–825* (Philadelphia 1984) 299–308. J. FRIED, ''Ludwig der Fromme, das Papsttum und die fränkischen Kirche,'' in *Charlemagne's Heir. New Perspectives on the Reign of Louis the Pious (814–840),* ed. P. GODMAN and R. COLLINS (Oxford 1990) 31–273. P. DEPREUX, ''Empereur, empereur associe et pape au temps de Louis le Pieux,'' *Revue belge de philologie et d'histoire* 70 (1992) 893–906.

[R. E. SULLIVAN]

STEPHEN V (VI), POPE

Pontificate: Sept. 885 to Sept. 14, 891; Roman priest elected by the people, but rejected by Emperor Charles the Fat, who sent his legate Liutward to depose him. Stephen proved the validity of his election, and no action was taken. In November 887, Charles was deposed by his subjects and the Carolingian empire disintegrated. In

Italy the power was claimed by Berengar I of Friuli, great–grandson of Charlemagne, but Guido III of Spoleto, the actual ruler of the major part of the peninsula, was crowned emperor by Stephen in 891. In the course of the preceding year the pope had summoned Arnulf, later crowned emperor, who held power in the greater part of the Frankish empire, to rescue Italy from the devastations of ''pagans and evil Christians.'' Arnulf did not come to Italy until after Stephen's death; meanwhile Guido's son Lambert (*see* LAMBERT OF SPOLETO) had been crowned by Stephen's successor, FORMOSUS, who reaped the tragic fruits of this disastrous expediency. The vacillating character of Stephen was again tested in the matter of the Slavonic liturgy introduced among the Moravians by SS. CYRIL AND METHODIUS. Methodius had been twice summoned to Rome, where he had received from ADRIAN II and JOHN VIII approval of his missionary work and liturgical practice. Wiching, the suffragan of Methodius, received from Stephen sanction for the organization of the Moravian Church according to the wishes of the German hierarchy. The Slavonic liturgy was forbidden, and the disciples of Methodius fled to Bulgaria, where their rite continued to be celebrated. There is no evidence that Stephen failed to recognize the second patriarchate of PHOTIUS.

Bibliography: P. JAFFÉ, *Regesta pontificum romanorum ab condita ecclesia ad annum post Christum natum 1198*, ed. S. LÖWENFELD (repr. Graz 1956) 1:427–435. *Liber pontificalis*, ed. L. DUCHESNE (Paris 1886–92) 2:191–198. LIUTPRAND, *Antapodosis, Monumenta Germaniae Historica: Scriptores rerum Germanicarum* (Berlin 1826) 38:1–158. A. FLICHE and V. MARTIN, eds., *Histoire de l'église depuis les origines jusqu'à nos jours* (Paris 1935) 7:15–19. A. FLICHE, *L'Europe occidentale de 888 à 1125* (Paris 1930). F. DVORNIK, *The Photian Schism* (Cambridge, England 1948). P. VIARD, *Catholicisme. Hier, aujourd'hui et demain* (Paris 1947–) 4:588–589. D. JASPER, ''Die Roller der Querimonia Egilmari und der Responsio Stephani V (JL 3464) im Osnabrüker Zehnstreit unter Heinrich IV,'' *Zeitschrift für Kirchengeschichte* (Stuttgart 1976) 202–220. G. SCHWAIGER, *Lexikon des Mittelalters* 8 (Munich-Zurich 1996). A. SPICKER-WENDT, *Die Quaerimonia Egilmari episcopi und die Responsio Stephani papae. Studien zu den Osnabrücker Quellen der Karolingerzeit* (Cologne 1980). F. STAAB, ''Die Wurzel des zisterziensischen Zehntprivilegs. Zugleich: Zur Echtheitsfrage der 'Querimonia Egilmari episcopi' und der 'Responsio Stephani V papae''' *Deutsches Archiv für Erforschung der Mittelalters* (1984) 21–54. J. N. D. KELLY, *Oxford Dictionary of Popes* (New York 1986) 113–114.

[P. J. MULLINS]

STEPHEN VI (VII), POPE

Pontificate: May or June, 896 to July or August 897; b. Rome. Although already bishop of Anagni, Stephen was elected pope, contrary to the current law, which forbade the transfer of a bishop from one see to another. Victim of the political factions of his day, Stephen cooperated with LAMBERT OF SPOLETO in the posthumous trial of his predecessor, Pope FORMOSUS, who, after crowning Lambert as Emperor in 892, had subsequently bestowed the same honor upon the Frankish ruler, Arnulf of Carinthia. Nine months after his death, Formosus' body was disinterred from the papal crypt and arraigned for trial before a ''cadaveric'' council, at which Stephen presided. The deceased pope was accused of inordinate ambition for the papal office and all his acts were declared invalid because he had been excommunicated under JOHN VIII and had previously held the episcopal See of Porto. The corpse was stripped of pontifical robes; the fingers of the right hand were amputated, and the mutilated body was eventually cast into the Tiber. The Holy Orders conferred by Formosus were pronounced void; by this declaration Stephen's prior appointment as bishop of Anagni was invalidated and he was thus freed from the irregularity of transferring from one see to another. Within a few months a violent reaction ended the pontificate of Pope Stephen; he was deprived of the pontifical insignia, imprisoned, and strangled. He was succeeded by ROMANUS, then THEODORE II (897) and JOHN IX (898).

Bibliography: Sources. LIUTPRAND, *Antapodosis, Monumenta Germaniae Historica: Scriptores rerum Germanicarum* (Berlin 1826) 41:1–158. AUXILIUS OF NAPLES, *In defensionem sacrae ordinationis papae Formosi* in E. DÜMMLER, ed. *Auxilius und Vulgarius* (Leipzig 1866) 59–95. C. J. VON HEFELE, *Histoire des conciles d'après les documents originaux*, tr. H. LECLERCQ (Paris 1907–38) v. 4. L. DUCHESNE, *The Beginnings of the Temporal Sovereignty of the Popes,* A.D. *754–1073,* tr. A. H. MATHEW (London 1908). H. K. MANN, *The Lives of the Popes in the Early Middle Ages from 590 to 1304* (London 1902–32) 4:76–85. A. FLICHE, *L'Europe occidentale de 888 à 1125* (Paris 1930). A. FLICHE and V. MARTIN, eds., *Histoire de 'église depuis les origines jusqu'à nos jours* (Paris 1935) 7:25–26. A. DUMAS, *Dictionnaire d'histoire et de géographie ecclésiastiques,* ed. A. BAUDRILLART et al. (Paris) 15: 1196–97. R. BENERICETTI, *La cronologia dei Papi dei secoli IX–XI secondo le carte di Ravenna* (1999) 29–30. G. SCHWAIGER, *Lexikon des Mittelalters* 8 (Munich-Zurich 1996). J.N.D. KELLY, *Oxford Dictionary of Popes* (New York 1986) 115–116.

[P. J. MULLINS]

STEPHEN VII (VIII), POPE

Pontificate: January 929 to February 931; b. Rome. In the last years of his pontificate, Pope JOHN X (904–928) had incurred the wrath of MAROZIA, the *Donna Senatrix* of Rome, and had been imprisoned and assassinated. Marozia then conferred the papacy on Pope LEO VI, who died after six and a half months in office. Stephen VII succeeded him, probably through the influence of Marozia. As cardinal priest at St. Anastasia in Rome, he had been faithful to his duty and kind to the poor. During his two years as pope, he was powerless under the domination of Marozia. He extended privileges to monasteries in Italy and France; ODO, Abbot of Cluny, was promoting the CLUNIAC REFORM throughout Europe. Stephen was buried in St. Peter's Basilica.

Bibliography: P. JAFFÉ, *Regesta pontificum romanorum ab condita ecclesia ad annum post Christian natum 1198,* ed. S. LÖWENFELD 1:453–454. *Liber pontificalis,* ed. L. DUCHESNE, v. 1-2 (Paris 1886–92), v. 3 (Paris 1958) 2:242. *Patrolgia Latina,* ed. J. P. MIGNE, 217 v., indexes 4 v. (Paris 1878–90) 132:1049–56. A. CLERVAL, *Dictionnaire de théologie catholique,* ed. A. VACANT et al., 15 v. (Paris 1903–50; Tables générales 1951–) 5.1:980. H. K. MANN, *The Lives of the Popes in the Early Middle Ages from 590 to 1304,* 18 v. (London 1902–32) 4:189–190. R. BENERICETTI, *La cronologia dei Papi dei secoli IX–XI secondo le carte di Ravenna,* (1999) 38. M. HEIM, *Lexikon des Mittelalters,* 8 (Munich-Zurich 1996). J. N. D. KELLY, *Oxford Dictionary of Popes* (New York 1986) 122–123.

[M. A. MULHOLLAND]

STEPHEN VIII (IX), POPE

Pontificate: July 14, 939 to Oct. 942; b. Rome. Like his predecessors JOHN XI and LEO VII and his successors MARINUS II and AGAPETUS II, Stephen was a protégé of MAROZIA's son Alberic (II) of Spoleto, dictator of Rome. He was educated in Germany. After his return to Rome, he was cardinal priest of the church of SS. Silvester and Martin until his election to the papacy. Stephen offered no opposition to Alberic's control of the STATES OF THE CHURCH. His private life was blameless; his public life, devoted to peace. In 942 Stephen sent a Bishop Damasus as his legate to France with letters recognizing Louis IV d'Outremer, son of Charles the Simple, as the Frankish king. Louis, who had been crowned in 936 by the archbishop of Reims, was facing a formidable rebellion of powerful French and Burgundian nobles; however, under Stephen's threat of excommunication, it collapsed. In Rome the peace between Hugh of Provence, King of Italy, and Alberic II was broken once again in 942. Stephen requested ODO OF CLUNY to negotiate yet another peace. The CLUNIAC REFORM continued throughout Stephen's pontificate. He was buried at the Vatican.

Bibliography: P. JAFFÉ, *Regesta pontificum romanorum ab condita ecclesia ad annum post Christum natum 1198,* ed. S. LÖWENFELD (repr. Graz 1956) 1:457–458. *Liber pontificalis,* ed. L. DUCHESNE (Paris 1886–92) 2:244. H. K. MANN, *The Lives of the Popes in the Early Middle Ages from 590 to 1304* (London 1902–32) 4:212–217. F. X. SEPPELT, *Geschichte der Päpste von den Anfängen bis zur Mitte des 20. Jh.* (Munich 1954–59) 2:357. R. AUBERT, *Dictionnaire d'histoire et de géographie ecclésiastiques,* ed. A. BAUDRILLART et al. (Paris 1912) 15:1198. R. BENERICETTI, *La cronologia dei Papi dei secoli IX–XI secondo le carte di Ravenna,* 40. M. HEIM, *Lexikon des Mittelalters,* 8 (Munich-Zurich 1996). J. N. D. KELLY, *Oxford Dictionary of Popes* (New York 1986) 124.

[M. A. MULHOLLAND]

STEPHEN IX (X), POPE

Pontificate: Aug. 3, 1057 (consecration, Rome) to March 29, 1058 (Florence); b. Frederick of Lorraine (father Duke Gozelo), he came to Rome in 1050 after the election of Pope Leo IX whose aims of church reform he supported. His brother, Godfrey III the Bearded, was Duke of Lorraine and, by marriage to Beatrice of Canossa, Duke of Tuscany. Frederick's noble birth and kinship with Leo IX marked him for high office. He studied at Liège, where he became a canon, then archdeacon of the chapter of the cathedral of Saint-Lambert. Leo nominated him chancellor and librarian of the Roman Church (before March 12, 1051), thus making him one of the leading papal advisers. Together with Cardinal-Bishop Humbert of Silva Candida and Archbishop Peter of Amalfi he was a member of the ill-fated legation to Constantinople in 1054 when the schism between the Latin and Greek Church became evident, but it is not known how much or even whether he contributed to the anti-Greek polemics current at that time. On account of the conflict between his brother Godfrey and Emperor Henry III he entered the abbey of MONTECASSINO upon his return where he was elected abbot (May 23, 1057) at the urging of HUMBERT OF SILVA CANDIDA and Hildebrand (later GREGORY VII). On June 14, Victor II made him cardinal-priest of St. Chrysogonus. Within two months Victor was dead and Frederick elected in his place. Prior approval of the Empire was not sought possibly because of the presence of Stephen's brother Godfrey and the minority of Emperor Henry IV, whose mother Agnes served as Empress-Regent. Although most historians have interpreted this event as a first step toward freeing the papacy of imperial control, it has been overemphasized, and it is safer to assume that the intention was primarily to avoid any interference by the Roman nobility and to secure the protection of Duke Godfrey and his troops for the papacy. Empress Agnes subsequently gave her approval to the election. As pope, Stephen continued the reform and centralization of the Church. He promoted Peter Damian and Humbert of Silva Candida to positions of authority and used Hildebrand on missions. Like Leo IX he tried to fight against Norman inroads in southern Italy and once again sought to settle the Eastern schism in 1058.

He died in Florence was buried in the Church of S. Reparata. Despite his brief pontificate he may be accounted with Leo IX and Nicholas II as one of the decisive personalities in the early stages of the GREGORIAN REFORM.

Bibliography: G. DESPY, ''La Carrière lotharingienne du pape Etienne IX,'' *Revue belge de philologie et d'histoire* 31 (1953) 955–972. E. GOEZ, *Beatrix von Canossa und Tuszien (Vorträge und Forschungen Sonderband 41)* (Sigmaringen 1995). J. LAUDAGE, ''Stephan IX,'' *Lexikon der Päpste und des Papsttums* (Freiburg-Basel-Vienna 2001) 375. W. PETERS, ''Papst Stephan und die Lütticher Kirche,'' in *Papstgeschichte und Landesgeschichte* (Festschrift H. Jakobs, Cologne 1995) 157–176. R. SCHIEFFER, ''Stephan IX,'' *Lexikon des Mittelalters* 8 (Munich-Zuirch 1996) 118. G. TELLENBACH, *The Church in Western Europe from the Tenth to the Early Twelfth Century*, translated by T. REUTER (Cambridge, England 1993).

[J. GILCHRIST/U.–R. BLUMENTHAL]

STEPHEN BAR-SŪDHAILĒ

Syrian mystic and heretical theologian; b. Edessa, Syria, *c.* 500; d. *c.* 550. Stephen became a monk in Edessa and migrated to the desert of Egypt, where he composed books that betray the influence of the Origenist EVAGRIUS PONTICUS, prompting the Monophysite Jacob of Serugh (d. 521) to warn him not to believe with Evagrius that the punishments of the damned have an end. PHILOXENUS OF MABBUGH states that Stephen had to flee Edessa *c.* 512 to 515 and, finding no support in Philoxenus, had gone to the deserts of Jerusalem. By 541 to 543 he had returned to Edessa and oblivion.

Stephen's only extant work, *Liber de occultis mysteriis domus Dei* (*The Book of Hierotheus*), written in Syriac, survived because it was later attributed to the Hierotheus whom PSEUDO-DIONYSIUS the areopagite had earlier claimed as his master. Its doctrine, however, is a radically pantheistic development of the thought of Evagrius Ponticus: a world created after the Fall and the reascent of the soul toward (in Stephen) virtual unity with God. Philoxenus says Stephen wrote on the wall of his cell: ''Every nature is consubstantial with the divine essence.'' Stephen's work had little influence on later times.

Bibliography: *Works,* ed. and tr. F. S. MARSH (London 1927). H. ERHARTER, *Lexikon für Theologie und Kirche,* ed. J. HOFER and K. RAHNER, 10 v. (2d, new ed. Freiburg 1957–65) 9:1042. H. G. BECK, *Kirche und theologische Literatur im byzantinischen Reich* (Munich 1959) 351, 395. A. GUILLAUMONT, *Dictionnaire de spiritualité ascétique et mystique. Doctrine et histoire,* ed. M. VILLER, et al. (Paris 1932–) 4:1481–88; *Les ''Kephalaia gnostica'' d'Evagre le Pontique* (Paris 1963). I. HAUSHERR, *Orientalia Christiana* 30 (1933) 176–211.

[D. B. EVANS]

STEPHEN HARDING, ST.

Third abbot of CÎTEAUX; b. near Porlock, England; d. March 28, 1134. Like other Anglo-Saxon monks after the Norman Conquest, Stephen, a member of SHERBORNE ABBEY, Dorset, fled to Scotland and thence to Paris where he continued his studies. On his return from a pilgrimage to Rome, during which he came in contact with the monastic tradition of CAMALDOLI and VALLOMBROSA, Stephen joined the abbey of ROBERT OF MOLESME in the Diocese of Langres. The desire for a more austere life and a more literal interpretation of the BENEDICTINE RULE, encouraged by Hugh, archbishop of Lyons, led to his secession with 20 other monks to Cîteaux, Diocese of Chalon-sur-Saône, where a new monastery was founded, March 21, 1098. Here he acted as prior until the death of Alberic (1109), when he was elected abbot. In the early days the community suffered many privations, and it was on the point of extinction when St. BERNARD with 30 companions joined the abbey and ensured its future success. New foundations followed quickly: LA FERTÉ (1113), PONTIGNY (1114), CLAIRVAUX and MORIMOND (1115), and Preuilly (1118). To keep these abbeys united and to preserve the early spirit and discipline, strong organization was needed, and this Stephen provided.

Until recent years he was thought to have written the *Charta caritatis,* the *Exordium parvum,* and the *Instituta capituli generalis,* but manuscript research has shown that these documents, in their present form, belong to a later date, and are the product of a gradual evolution in Cistercian legislation. At the foundation of Pontigny, Harding laid down three points: Cîteaux was to exercise spiritual jurisdiction over its filiations, but to leave them financially independent; the Benedictine Rule was to be observed exactly as at Cîteaux; liturgical books, customs, and chant were to be uniform in all abbeys. A little later the abbots were commanded to attend an annual chapter at Cîteaux where breaches of discipline could be dealt with, the abbot of Cîteaux having power to depose unworthy superiors of his filiations. Before 1119 the relationship between mother- and daughter-houses was fixed, and the system of visitation, general CHAPTERS, and elections was perfected. These, and later elaborations, were done in consultation with the evergrowing number of abbots. The *Exordium Cistercii* (1118–19), composed for presentation to Pope Callistus II, is probably the work of Stephen, but the *Instituta* may be the fruit of collaboration. Hence, though Stephen had a controlling hand in this legislation, he can no longer be considered as having issued a complete and final code defining the constitution of the CISTERCIAN ORDER. In fixing a uniform text for liturgical hymns and the Bible he played a paramount part; his Bible, corrected by recourse to Jewish scholars and completed at Cîteaux in 1112, is preserved at Dijon. Three of his letters are extant, two concerning ecclesiastical affairs in France, a third written to the abbot of Sherborne shortly before his death. He was canonized in 1623.

Feast: April 17; July 16 (Cistercians).

Bibliography: *Acta Apostolicae Sedis* April (Rome 1909–) 2:496–501. WILLIAM OF MALMESBURY, *Gesta regum Anglorum,* ed. W. STUBBS, 2 v. (*Rerum Britannicarum medil aevi scriptores,* 244

v. (London 1858–96; repr. New York 1964–) 90; 1887–89) 2:380–385. BERNARD OF CLAIRVAUX, *Epistolae, Patrologia Latina,* ed. J. P. MIGNE (Paris 1878–90) 182:149–152, 157–158. C. H. TALBOT, ''An Unpublished Letter of Stephen Harding,'' *Collectanea ordinis Cisteriensium Reformatorum* 3 (Rome 1937). J. B. DALGAIRNS, *Life of St. Stephen Harding,* ed. J. H. NEWMAN (new ed. London 1898). L. J. LEKAI, *The White Monks: A History of the Cistercian Order* (Okauchee, Wis. 1953). D. KNOWLES, *Great Historical Enterprises* (New York 1963) 198–222, with a bibliog. of the numerous articles by J. A. LEFÈVRE. M. B. D'ARNEVILLE, *Saint Étienne* (Tours 1964). J. B. VAN DAMME, *Les trois fondateurs de Cîteaux* (Roybon, IsSre 1966). M. RAYMOND, *Three Religious Rebels: The Forefathers of the Trappists* (Boston, MA 1991, c1986).

[C. H. TALBOT]

Saint Stephen Harding, reliquary bust. (©Francis G. Mayer/ CORBIS)

STEPHEN LANGTON

English theologian, archbishop of Canterbury; b. Langton-by-Wragby, Lincolnshire, *c.* 1155; d. Slindon, Sussex, July 9, 1228. As a young man he went to Paris to study arts and theology, attending the lectures of John Beleth (fl. 1165) and PETER COMESTOR. Becoming a master in theology around 1180, he taught for more than 20 years at the University of Paris. Among his disciples were Guérin of Corbeil, Richard Poore (d. 1237 as bishop of Durham), Thomas Marlborough (d. 1236 as abbot of Evesham), and most probably Godfrey of Poitiers, whose *Summa,* written between 1213 and 1215, shows heavy dependence on Stephen. During his teaching years, Stephen was canon of York and of Notre Dame and became a close friend of Lothar of Segni, later Pope INNOCENT III. Called to Rome, he was made cardinal by Innocent on June 22, 1206. On the death of HUBERT WALTER, the monks of Canterbury elected rival candidates for the position of archbishop. Innocent, displeased with both King John's candidate, JOHN DE GREY, and the younger monks' candidate, REGINALD OF CANTERBURY, declared the election void and ordered a new election in Rome. At the pope's suggestion, the delegation of Canterbury monks elected Stephen Langton in December 1206. On June 17, 1207, Innocent consecrated Stephen at Viterbo and conferred the pallium. The King's displeasure kept him in exile at the Cistercian abbey of Pontigny, France, for the next seven years. When King John surrendered his kingdom to Innocent, becoming his vassal on May 15, 1213, Stephen returned to England to absolve the King from excommunication on July 20. On August 25, according to Roger of Wendover, he preached an important sermon to the clergy and barons at St. Paul's, London, and afterward engaged the barons in a conversation concerning the possibility of regaining their lost liberties from the King. This culminated in the signing of the MAGNA CARTA at Runnymede, June 15, 1215. Pope Innocent III, misunderstanding this settlement between the king and barons, suspended Langton for more than two years, during which time he lived in Rome. The suspension was eventually revoked, on condition that he would not return to his see. After the death of Innocent and John, HONORIUS III permitted Langton to return to Canterbury in the spring of 1218. During the next ten years he became an increasingly dynamic and powerful ruler of the Church in England. He enforced the decrees of the Fourth Lateran Council and convoked a provincial council at Oxford in April 1222 that heralded a new era in the history of Church law in England (J. D. Mansi, *Sacrorum Conciliorum nova et amplissima collectio,* 31 v. (Florence-Venice 1757–98); reprinted and continued by L. Petit and J. B. Martin 53 v. in 60 (Paris 1889–1927; repr. Graz 1960–) 22:1147–68). Stephen died in his manor at Slindon, and was buried in his cathedral church at Canterbury.

As a teacher and writer, Langton was not only prolific, but popular and influential. His most permanent contribution was the division of the Bible into chapters, which, although not the first or only division, is the one followed today. His stature as a schoolman has led some historians to rank him as the greatest teacher between PETER LOMBARD and ALEXANDER OF HALES, a period of nearly a century.

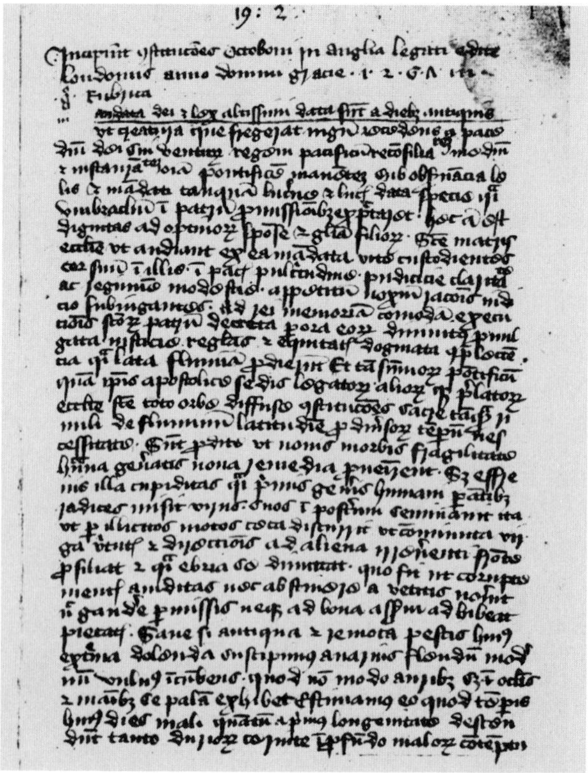

Manuscript folio from 15th-century manuscript of "Constitutiones" of various archbishops of Canterbury from 1120–1343, including those of Stephen Langton.

By far the greatest and most important part of his writings is his commentaries on the whole of the Bible, which, for the most part, have not yet been published [see P. Glorieux, *Répertoire des maîtres en théologie de Paris au XIIIe siècle (Paris 1933–34)]; v.17–18 of Bibliothèque Thomiste 1:238–260).* Besides commenting directly on the Bible, he wrote at least two commentaries on the *Historia scholastica* (one before 1187, the other in 1193) and a gloss on the Magna glossatura of the *Pauline Epistles* by Peter Lombard (between 1200 and 1203). He wrote also a substantial *Summa theologiae* (c. 1180–85) and published his *Quaestiones disputatae,* held in the schools (c. 1203–06). The importance of these questions is evident from their influence on Langton's successors in the schools, notably ALEXANDER NECKHAM, Godfrey of Poitiers, ROBERT OF COURÇON, WILLIAM OF AUXERRE, HUGH OF SAINT-CHER, and ROLAND OF CREMONA. Known to his contemporaries and successors as Doctor nominatissimus, Stephen was one of the most widely quoted masters of his day. More than 500 sermons are extant in numerous MSS, besides his series on the *Ave maris stella.* He wrote also the hymn *Veni Sancte Spiritus* for the Mass of Pentecost and a *Psalterium Mariae* in 150 strophes [*Psalteria Rythmica,* ed. G. M. Dreves (Leipzig 1900) 35:153–171].

Bibliography: F. M. POWICKE, *Stephen Langton* (Oxford 1928). G. LACOMBE et al., "Studies on the Commentaries of Cardinal Stephen Langton," *Archives d'histoire doctrinale et littéraire du moyen-âge* 5 (1930) 52–66. P. GLORIEUX, *Dictionnaire de théologie catholique*, ed. A. VACANT et al., 15 v. (Paris 1903–50; Tables Générales 1951–), Tables générales 1299. K. NORGATE, *The Dictionary of National Biography from the Earliest Times to 1900*, 63 v. (London 1885–1900; repr. with corrections, 21 v., 1908–09, 1921–22, 1938; suppl. 1901–) 11 563–569.

[L. ANTL]

STEPHEN OF DIE, ST.

Also known as Stephen of Châtillon, Carthusian bishop; b. Châtillon-lez-Dombes, France, Diocese of Lyons, *c.* 1150; d. Sept. 7, 1208. Born of a famous family of Châtillon, Stephen very early in life gave signs of his religious vocation by his fasting and penances. When he was 26 he became a CARTHUSIAN at Portes. After 25 years as an exemplary monk he was elected prior of his charter-house. In 1207 when the See of Die became vacant, the people and canons acclaimed Stephen their new bishop, but he refused to accept until enjoined to do so by Pope Innocent III and the general of the Carthusians. He devoted his short episcopate to a reform of the diocese. He was credited with several miracles during his lifetime and with so many more after his death that in 1231 Pope Gregory IX was asked to proclaim him blessed. His beatification in the 13th century remains doubtful, but in 1852 Pius IX authorized his cult in the diocese of Die and in 1857 extended it to the Carthusians.

Feast: Sept. 7.

Bibliography: V. LECLERC, *Histoire littéraire de la France* (Paris): v. 1–12, ed. Maurists (1733–68); v. 13–38, ed. Académie des Inscriptions et Belles-Lettres (1814–1941); v.1–29 (repr. 1865–) 21:575. *Acta Sanctorum* (Antwerp 1643–) Sept. 3:175–201. J. L. BAUDOT and L. CHAUSSIN, *Vies des saints et des bienheureux selon l'ordre du calendrier avec l'historique des fêtes,* ed. by the Benedictines of Paris, 12 v. (Paris 1935–56); v. 13, suppl. and table générale (1959) 9:156. A. M. SOCHAY, *Dictionnaire d'histoire et de géographie ecclésiastiques,* ed. A. BAUDRILLART et al. (Paris 1912–) 15: 1220–22.

[J. A. CORBETT]

STEPHEN OF GRAVESEND

Bishop of London; d. Bishop Stortford, Hertfordshire, England, April 8, 1338. A native of Kent, he was probably a nephew of RICHARD OF GRAVESEND, Bishop of London, and grand-nephew of RICHARD OF GRAVESEND, Bishop of Lincoln. Having studied probably at Oxford and Paris, he became bishop of London in January 1319. At first he took the barons' side against King Edward II, but later tried to mediate between he and Queen Isabella. The rebel Londoners who murdered WALTER DE STAPELDON, Bishop of Exeter (1326), plotted against Gravesend, but he escaped and denounced them publicly. He protested in Parliament against Edward's deposition (1327), and supported efforts to free King Edward III from Roger Mortimer's influence. Although imprisoned in connection with the conspiracy of Edmund, Earl of Kent (1330), he was released. His episcopate was marked by controversies with Abp. WALTER REYNOLDS and with the CANTERBURY monks. Disputatious and sometimes misguided, Gravesend nevertheless exemplified honesty and courage at a time when many English bishops were self-seeking or easily intimidated.

Bibliography: London, Canterbury and York Society, *Registrum Radulphi Baldock. . . et Stephani Gravesend, episcoporum Londoniensium. . .*, ed. R. C. FOWLER (London 1911). C. L. KINGSFORD, *The Dictionary of National Biography from the Earliest Times to 1900,* 63 v. (London 1885–1900) 8:443–444. K. EDWARDS, ''The Political Importance of the English Bishops during the Reign of Edward II,'' *English Historical Review* 59 (1944) 311–347. A. B. EMDEN, *A Biographical Register of the Scholars of the University of Oxford to A.D. 1500,* 3 v. (Oxford 1957–59) 2:805–806.

[R. W. HAYS]

STEPHEN OF MURET, ST.

Founder of the Order of GRANDMONT; b. Thiers, Auvergne, France, *ca.* 1045; d. Muret, the Limousin, France, Feb. 8, 1124. The son of the viscount of Thiers, a nobleman of the Auvergne, Stephen went on pilgrimage to southern Italy when he was a young man, perhaps to the shrine of Monte Gargano. In the course of his travels he acquired the friendship of a partisan of the GREGORIAN REFORM, Abp. Milo of Benevento, and made the acquaintance of some of the eremitical communities that were flourishing in the region of Calabria at that time. Impressed by their way of life, he decided to introduce it into his native country, where it was then little known. About 1080 he settled in a secluded forest at Muret, in the mountains north of Limoges. His sanctity quickly gained him a considerable reputation; some people came to him for spiritual advice, others, seeking to follow the life he led. The latter he welded together in a communal life that developed into the Order of Grandmont, which for some time spread rapidly, especially in western France. Stephen's way of life was austere, involving a concept of poverty that anticipated that of the MENDICANT ORDERS. His teaching, recorded in the *Liber sententiarum* (*Patrologia Latina*, ed. J. P. Migne, 217 v., indexes 4 v. [Paris 1878–90] 204:1085–1136), reflects the influence of the Gospels and the works of Gregory I the Great. His relics were translated from Muret to the new motherhouse of the order at Grandmont on June 25 in or about 1166. He was canonized in 1189, at the insistence of King Henry II of England.

Feast: Feb. 8.

Bibliography: *Vita, Patrologia Latina*, ed. J. P. MIGNE, 217 v., indexes 4 v. (Paris 1878–90) 204:1005–46. J. BECQUET, *Dictionnaire de spiritualité ascétique et mystique. Doctrine et histoire*, ed. M. VILLER et al. (Paris 1932–) 4.2:1504–14.

[J. C. DICKINSON]

STEPHEN OF NARBONNE, ST.

Inquisitor (known also as Stephen of Saint-Thibery); d. Avignonet, France, May 29, 1242. Stephen, a Franciscan, had been appointed an inquisitor by Gregory IX in 1237 (*see* INQUISITION). In May 1242 he was sent to Avignonet with the vigorous Dominican inquisitor, WILLIAM ARNAUD, apparently to moderate Arnaud's decisions. The village of Avignonet, located in the lands of Count Raymond VII of Toulouse, was a center of the CATHARI. While there, the inquisitors stayed at the house of Count Raymond, whose agent, Raymond of Alfar, rounded up local accomplices and massacred the whole inquisitorial court during the night of May 28, 1242. Stephen's remains were buried in the Franciscan church at Toulouse. His cult was confirmed by Pius IX in 1866.

Feast: May 29.

Bibliography: *Acta Sanctorum* May 7:177–179. J. GUIRAUD, *Dictionnaire d'histoire et de géographie ecclésiastiques*, ed. A. BAUDRILLART et al. (Paris 1912–) 5:1154–62.

[J. A. CORBETT]

STEPHEN OF OBAZINE, BL.

Founder and first abbot of OBAZINE (Corrèze, France); b. Vierjo near Limoges, *c.* 1085; d. Bonaigue, March 8, 1159. A secular priest of humble origin, Stephen became a hermit under the influence of a disciple of Robert of Arbrissel. In the forest of Obazine, he founded a community that in 1142, after having adopted the Rule of St. Benedict, became Obazine Abbey. Under Stephen's direction, this prosperous abbey founded several daughter abbeys and a convent for nuns; in 1147, the whole group joined the Cistercian Order. Stephen died in Bonaigue, one of his later foundations, but was buried in an ornate sarcophagus at Obazine where his body remains intact. He was never officially canonized, but his immemorial cult was approved by Clement XI in 1701.

Feast: March 11.

Bibliography: *Acta Sanctorum* March 1:799–808. G. MÜLLER, ''Der Gründer der Abtei Obazine,'' *Cistercienser–Chronik* 40

(1928). S. LENSSEN, *Hagiologium cisterciense,* 2 vol. (Tilburg 1948–49) 1:92–96.

[L. J. LEKAI]

STEPHEN OF SALAGNAC

Dominican historian; b. Grand-Bourg de Salagnac, near Perigueux, France, *c.* 1210; d. Limoges, Jan. 8, 1291. Stephen entered the Dominican Order at Limoges in 1230 and was prior there from 1249 to 1259, then prior at Toulouse from 1259 to 1261. He was made visitor to the Scottish province of the order (1261–65), then prior again at Limoges from 1265 to 1271. Subsequently he became prior at Annecy and LePuy before returning to Limoges where he died. During his years as prior, and on his numerous trips as visitor or as representative of his house at the Dominican chapters, Stephen was close to the events of the order. He wrote the *De quatuor in quibus Deus predicatorum ordinem insignivit* and the *De tribus gradibus prelatorum.* Both are of great value because of the documents that they reproduce. The first, which Stephen completed in 1278, was reworked and completed by BERNARD GUI. The second has not been published.

Bibliography: STEPHEN OF SALAGNAC and BERNARD GUI, *De quatuor in quibus Deus praedicatorum ordinem insignivit,* ed. T. KAEPPELI (*Monumenta Ordinis Fratrum Praedicatorum historica,* 22, 1949). J. QUÉTIF and J. ÉCHARD, *Scriptores Ordinis Praedicatorum* (New York 1959) 1.1:415–417. R. AUBERT, *Dictionnaire d'histoire et de géographie ecclésiastique,* ed. A. BAUDRILLART et al. (Paris 1912–) 15:1261. A. AUER, *Ein neuaufgefundener Katalog der Dominikaner-Schriftsteller* (Paris 1933).

[J. A. CORBETT]

STEPHENS, THOMAS

Jesuit missionary and poet in Marathi-Konkani; b. Clyffe Pipard (Wiltshire), England, 1549; d. Goa, Portuguese India, 1619. Stephens was the son of Thomas Stephens (Stevens) of Bushton, a merchant; he was elected scholar of Winchester in 1564 and probably attended New College, Oxford. After conversion to the Catholic faith, he proceeded to Rome and was admitted to the Society of Jesus on Oct. 20, 1575.

The Portuguese had settled (1510) in Goa, and the conversion of Hindus followed the arrival of Francis XAVIER as papal nuncio in 1542. But the converts often remained devoted to their old religious literature and traditional ritualistic practices, a situation that caused the institution of the INQUISITION in 1560.

Stephens sailed from Lisbon on April 4, 1579, and arrived at Goa by way of the Cape of Good Hope on October 24, being, perhaps, the first Englishman thus to reach India. An account sent to his father in England of his voyage and of Portuguese commercial ventures in the East acquired wide currency; it was included or referred to in the travel books of Hakluyt, Purchas, and John Hamilton Moore, and may have occasioned the incorporation (1599) of the East India Company.

Stephens spent approximately 40 years in Goa, where he was widely known as Padre Estevao, and served for a time as rector of Salsette College. He quickly learned Konkani, the spoken dialect of the region, and composed a grammar (*Arte de Lingua Canarin,* 1640) and a manual of Christian doctrine (*Doutrina Christã em lingua Bramana-Canarin,* 1622) for the benefit of his Konkani flock. He also mastered both Sanskrit and literary Marathi, the language of the medieval Maharashtra saints, Jnānēshwar and Nāmadēv.

Stephens thought that a new native Christian literature in literary Marathi, seasoned with living Konkani speech, could wean converts from the old pagan literature. As a beginning, he composed a voluminous work, *Discorso sobre a Vinda de Jesus Christo,* a *Krista* [Christian]-*Purana* narrating in epic detail the coming of Jesus Christ the Savior into the world. Based on the Old and New Testaments, this treatise, in two parts of 36 and 59 cantos, totals more than 11,000 strophes in the *ovi* meter. Stephens was clearly acquainted with the work of Jnānēshwar and of his own contemporary, Ēkanāth (1548–99), whose major works also were in the *ovi* meter. *Krista-Purana,* first published in the Roman script in 1616, was well received, and two more editions appeared in 1649 and 1654.

Like Costanzo BESCHI's *Tēmbāvani* in Tamil, *Krista-Purana* is more than a tour de force; it is a high poetic achievement that opens new vistas on the landscape of the spirit and demonstrates the singular flexibility of the modern evolved Indian languages to meet the impact of new themes and inspirations. Encouraged by the success of *Krista-Purana,* other Puranas appeared—one on St. Peter, by Étienne de la Croix, and one on St. Anthony, by Antonio Saldanha. With a growing native Christian literature to sustain them, converts less frequently provoked the rigors of the Inquisition by indulging in reading that was frowned upon. *Krista-Purana* thus appeared at a crucial time and made history in more than one sense.

Bibliography: T. STEPHENS, *The Christian Purana,* ed. J. L. SALDANHA (Mangalore 1907). M. K. NADKARNI, *A Short History of Marathi Literature* (Baroda 1921). C. SOMMERVOGEL et al., *Bibliothèque de la Compagnie de Jésus* (Brussels-Paris 1890–1932) 2:468–469; 12:281–282. G. SCHURHAMMER, "Thomas Stephens, 1549–1619," *Month* NS 13 (1955) 197–210.

[K. R. SRINIVASA IYENGAR]

STEPINAC, ALOJZIJE VIKTOR, BL.

In English: Louis or Aloysius Victor, cardinal, archbishop of Zagreb, martyr; b. May 8, 1898, at Brezaric (near Krašić), Croatia; d. Feb. 10, 1960, in Kraší.

Stepinac was the eighth of twelve children of wealthy farmers, Barbara Penic and Josip Stepinac. Upon graduation from the Gymnasium in Zagreb (1916), he was drafted into the Austrian army. As second lieutenant he fought on the Italian front (1917–18). Taken prisoner by the Italians (September 1918), he joined the South Slav volunteers to fight against the Hapsburg rulers. Returning to CROATIA (1919), by then a part of Yugoslavia, he studied agriculture in Zagreb. In 1924 he enrolled in the German College, Rome, and attended classes at the Gregorian University. In 1930, he obtained doctorates in philosophy and theology and was ordained a priest in Rome (October 26).

After returning to Zagreb in 1931 he was assigned to the chancery office, from which he administered several parishes and initiated the establishment of Caritas in the archdiocese. He became coadjutor of Zagreb in 1934 (the youngest bishop in the world at the time), and archbishop in 1937.

As archbishop he promoted Catholic charities and Catholic Action, defended the Church's rights, and denounced Communism and National Socialism. On Dec. 31, 1938, he founded the Relief Action for Refugee Jews under his protection. In April 1941 he welcomed the Croatian State, but continuously opposed the regime of Ante Pavelić, especially for its forced conversions and racial persecution. Thousands of persecuted Jews, Slovenes, and Serbs received his help.

After the government was taken over by the Communist party in 1945, Stepinac and his fellow bishops refused to accede to the new regime's desire for a ''national Catholic Church,'' independent of Rome, and spoke out against the persecution of the Church by the communists. He was arrested for denouncing the execution of priests by militant communists and later released.

Josip Tito's government arrested him again in 1946 and tried him on trumped-up charges of collaborating with the Germans, Italians, and the fascist Ustasha regime. He was sentenced to 16 years' imprisonment. For five years he was kept in Lepoglava prison; in 1951 Tito released him on house arrest in Krašić because of his health.

Systematically harassed and urged by Tito to leave the country, Stepinac remained with his flock. When he was made cardinal by Pope Pius XII in 1953, he declined to go to Rome to receive the cardinal's hat, fearing that he would not be allowed back into Yugoslavia. He did not attend the conclave after Pius XII's death, for the same reason. During these years of internment and isolation he continued his practice of exercising his ministry in part through extensive letter-writing (more than 5,000 letters in all).

Alojzije Cardinal Stepinac (left) under guard. (Catholic News Service)

Stepinac's faith was nurtured by daily meditation on the whole rosary and Holy Scripture—practices he recommended to the faithful. His spirituality is marked by gratitude for God's gifts, a desire to compensate for the sins of blasphemy and abortion, zeal for the Eucharist, and filial devotion to the Blessed Mother. He predicted that ''Russia will be converted, and the statue of the Mother of God will be put in the Kremlin.''

He died in 1960 of a rare blood disease (*polycythemia rubra vera*) from which he suffered acutely since 1953. He was buried behind the main altar in the cathedral in Zagreb. Stepinac was beatified by John Paul II when the pope visited the Marian shrine of Marija Bistrica, near Zagreb, Oct. 3, 1998.

Bibliography: *Alojzije Kardinal Stepinac, Nadbiskup Zagrebacki*, documentation for canonization (Zagreb 1996). S. ALEXANDER, *The Triple Myth* (New York 1987). D. BATON, *Mladi Stepinac. Pisma zarucnici* (Rome 1975). E. BAUER, *Aloisius Kardinal Stepinac* (Recklinghausen 1979). T. DRAGOUN, *Le Dossier du Cardinal Stepinac* (Paris 1958). F. ETEROVIC, *Aloysius Cardinal Stepinac: A Spiritual Leader* (Chicago 1970). N. ISTRANIN, *Stepinac-un innocenta condemnatio* (Vicenza 1982). A. H. O'BRIEN, *Archbishop Stepinac: The Man and His Case* (Westminster, Md. 1947). R. PATTEE, *The Case of Cardinal Aloysius Stepinac* (Milwaukee 1953). E. PEZET, *Stepinac-Tito* (Paris 1959). M. PIOVANELLI, *Un vincitore all'Est* (Milan 1962). I. PRCALA and S. SKRTIC, *The Man of God and His People* (Cleveland 1961). M. RAYMOND, *The Man for this Moment: The Life and Death of Aloysius Cardinal Stepinac* (New York 1971). M. A. RIVELLI, *L'arcivescovo del genocidio* (Milan 1999).

[G. J. PRPIC/K. I. RABENSTEIN]

STERCKX, ENGELBERT

Archbishop of Mechelen; b. Ophem (Brabant), Nov. 2, 1792; d. Mechelen, Dec. 4, 1867. He came of peasant stock. After ordination (Jan. 18, 1815) he taught logic and ethics at the major seminary in Mechelen (1815–21) and was also attached, from 1813, to the archbishop's secretariate. He became pastor at Bouchout in the Province of Antwerp (1821) and vicar-forane of Antwerp (1824). In the Archdiocese of Mechelen (Malines) he was named vicar-general (1827); vicar-capitular (Jan. 15, 1831); archbishop (Feb. 24, 1832); and cardinal (1838). Before becoming archbishop he was noted for his diligence, pastoral zeal, and skill at conciliation. He had acted as mediator in the lengthy conferences (1825–30) between the Belgian episcopate and the Dutch government to assure liberty for Catholic worship and education.

When BELGIUM became independent (1830), he immediately accepted, despite some opposition from Rome, the liberal institutions imposed on the country by the constitution. He discovered in them the means of favoring the Catholic faith. Some based their opposition to modern liberties on the encyclical *Mirari vos* of GREGORY XVI, and on Pius IX's *QUANTA CURA* and SYLLABUS OF ERRORS. Sterckx, however, remained loyal to the constitution despite the proponents of ultramontanism and some governmental secularizing intrigues. It was in these circumstances that he published his *Lettres sur la Constitution* (1864), which led the Holy See to accommodate itself to modern liberties. His moderation and competence won from the Belgian public authorities acceptance of a practice favorable to the Catholic religion, yet on the fringe of separation between church and state.

Once the politico-religious tasks were accomplished, Sterckx reorganized his diocese, multiplying parishes, Catholic schools, and good works. He summoned congresses at Mechelen in 1863, 1864, and 1867, which systematized the lay apostolate. Agreements with the state to assure the teaching of religion in public schools in the primary (1842) and secondary (1854) grades met his approval. He played an important role in the reopening of the University of LOUVAIN and in its reorganization (1834).

Conscious of his authority, he centralized all priestly activity in his diocese, although sometimes without taking into account the canonical rights of religious. He succeeded in unifying all the apostolic efforts of the Belgian hierarchy, proving by his prestige and diplomacy that he was truly primate of Belgium.

Bibliography: A. SIMON, *Le Cardinal Sterckx et son temps,* 2 v. (Wetteren 1950).

[A. SIMON]

STERZINGER, FERDINAND

German Church historian; b. Lichtwehr in the Tyrol, May 24, 1721; d. Munich, March 18, 1786. He entered the Theatines in 1740 and taught moral theology, canon law, and church history in various houses of that order. In 1759 Sterzinger went to Munich to teach and remained there until his death. In 1776 he produced his continuation of the work of Christian Pfeffel, the *Chronologische Einleitung in die Kirchengeschichte*, which he nevertheless opposed in 1780 in his *Nothwendige Beiträge zur chronologischen Einleitung* (*Necessary Contribution to the Chronological Introduction*). He is noteworthy for his opposition to the witchcraft trials so numerous in his time in southern Germany. He wrote the academic discourse *Von dem gemeinen Vorurtheile der thätigen und wirkenden Hexerei* (*On Common Prejudice Concerning the Effectiveness of Witchcraft*; Munich 1766) against them. His book met with much opposition, even from his own colleagues, e.g., Agnellus März, OSB. Sterzinger defended his discourse in 1767 and wrote other works on the subject. The majority of his writings lie unedited in the State Library at Munich.

Bibliography: H. HURTER, *Nomenclator literarius theologiae catholicae,* 5 v. (3rd ed. Innsbruck 1903–13) 5.1:397–400. E. FREYS, *Lexikon für Theologie und Kirche,* ed. J. HOFER and K. RAHNER, 10 v. (2d new ed. Freiburg 1957–65) 9:816–817. É. AMANN, *Dictionnaire de théologie catholique,* ed. A. VACANT et al., 15 v. (Paris 1903–50) 14:2612. REUSCH, *Allgemeine deutsche Biographie,* (Leipzig 1875–1910) 36: 124–125.

[G. J. DONNELLY]

STEUART, ROBERT HENRY

Jesuit spiritual writer; b. Reigate, Surrey, April 13, 1874; d. London, July 9, 1948. Father Steuart, a Scot, claimed descent from Robert Bruce, who defeated the English at Bannockburn in 1314. He was educated with the Benedictines, and was destined for the Navy, but was failed for a trivial physical cause. This was a bitter disappointment; but he eventually found his vocation as a Jesuit. He served as chaplain to the forces in World War I, and wrote a moving account of life in the trenches called *March, Kind Comrade.* He was superior at Farm Street, London (1926–35). As a retreat master Steuart clothed the Ignatian Exercises with his own very original thought and expression, and inspired many to move forward on the path to perfection. His teaching was Christocentric, his favorite theme ''I live; now not I, but Christ liveth in me.'' He had dry humor, clear vision, and a keen insight into souls. He was a pioneer in encouraging the formation of modern secular institutes, and anticipated the Church's return to constant invocation of the Holy Spirit. Above all, he is remembered as a master of the life of prayer.

Bibliography: R. H. J. STEUART, *The Inward Vision* (New York 1929); *Temples of Eternity* (New York 1931); *Diversity in Holiness* (New York 1937); *The Two Voices,* ed. C. C. MARTINDALE (Westminster, Md. 1952); *Spiritual Teaching,* ed. K. KENDALL (Westminster, Md. 1952). K. KENDALL, *Father Steuart: A Study of His Life and Teaching* (London 1950).

[K. KENDALL]

STEUERNAGEL, CARL

Protestant Old Testament scholar and Hebrew grammarian who contributed to the development of Pentateuchal criticism in the early years of the 20th century; b. Hardegsen, near Göttingen, Germany, February 17, 1869; d. Greifswald, Germany, March 4, 1958. Following upon the work of J. Wellhausen, Steuernagel's general introduction to the Bible and series of monographs arrested the attention of scholars for more than a decade [see *Theologische Rundschau* 1–11 (1897 or 1898–1908)]. He published his critical commentary on Deuteronomy in 1898, a work he revised in 1923. In 1903 Steuernagel published the first edition of his Hebrew grammar; that the work subsequently passed through many editions, including posthumous publication, attested to its popularity. In 1912 he published his voluminous and detailed *Lehrbuch der Einleitung in das Alte Testament.* He edited surveys of Hauran and the northern Transjordan by G. Schumacher, as well as the account of the same scholar's work at Tell el-Mutesellim, the site of ancient MEGIDDO. For a quarter of a century he edited the *Zeitschrift des Deutschen Palästina-Vereins,* a learned review of contemporary research in Palestine. Professor Steuernagel was attached to the Evangelical theological faculties of the Universities of Halle, Breslau, and, finally, Greifswald.

Bibliography: M. NOTH, *Zeitschrift des deutschen Palästinavereins* 74 (1958) 1–3. W. SCHMAUCH, *Theologische Literaturzeitung* 83 (1958) 547–550.

[T. W. BUCKLEY]

STEVENSON, JOSEPH

Scottish Jesuit priest and historian; b. Berwick-on-Tweed, Nov. 27, 1806; d. London, Feb. 8, 1895. He was educated at Durham and Glasgow University but renounced his intention of becoming a minister of the Church of Scotland. From 1831 he was employed on historical manuscripts at the British Museum and the Record Office. He married Mary Ann Craig of Glasgow in 1831, and on becoming librarian of Durham Cathedral in 1842 took Anglican orders. From 1849 to 1862 he was vicar of Leighton Buzzard, Bedfordshire, during which period he continued to publish numerous editions and translations of medieval literary and historical texts. He took a leading part in the inception of the Rolls Series, to which he contributed four volumes. His studies led him to enter the Catholic Church in 1863. Although compelled to resign from the Record Office, he continued to work for the Historical Manuscripts Commission in Birmingham, where, after the death of his wife, he was ordained priest in 1872. Work for the British government in the VATICAN LIBRARY was followed by his entry into the English Province of the Society of Jesus in 1877. He resumed his historical work in London, and published altogether more than 50 volumes besides numerous articles, reports, and miscellaneous papers.

Bibliography: E. F. SUTCLIFFE, comp., *Bibliography of the English Province of the Society of Jesus, 1773–1953* (London 1957). J. H. POLLEN, *In Memoriam. Father Joseph Stevenson, S.J. A Biographical Sketch, with a List of His Published Works* (London; reprinted from *Month,* March-April 1895). D. KNOWLES, *Great Historical Enterprises* (Edinburgh 1963).

[F. COURTNEY]

STIGMATINE FATHERS

(CSS, Official Catholic Directory #1280); the Congregation of the Sacred Stigmata was founded by (Ven.) Gaspare Bertoni (1777–1853), a priest of the Diocese of Verona in northern Italy. His early years in the priesthood were divided between teaching in the seminary and working as a parish priest. Aware of the need to salvage youth from the moral breakdown of society, he began to devote his energies to education. Gradually other priests joined him, and on Nov. 4, 1816, the group adopted a rule of life under the leadership of Bertoni. This was the foundation of the Stigmatine Congregation, which took its name from their residence, *Le Stimate,* formerly owned by a pious confraternity but given to Bertoni for his work. Because of the name, it is sometimes assumed that the Stigmatines were connected with St. Francis or the Franciscans, but in fact the early rule was based on that of the Jesuits. Having been modified through the years, the rule no longer prescribes as lengthy a scholastic discipline as the Jesuits have. On Sept. 15, 1890, the congregation was approved by Leo XIII, and on Nov. 16, 1916, the rule and constitutions received approval from Benedict XV.

In Italy, the Stigmatines are known mainly as educators—staffing seminaries, schools, and boarding colleges—but they are engaged also in other forms of priestly work. On Jan. 5, 1910, the first group of Stigmatine missionaries to South America arrived in Brazil, and in 1925 the Stigmatines answered the call for missionaries to China, where they labored until the expulsion of all missionaries from that land.

During the first 15 or 20 years after their arrival in the U.S. (1905), a few Stigmatine priests were scattered from Massachusetts to the Midwest, rarely seeing one another and suffering loss of identification from lack of community life. In the early 1920s they decided to concentrate their forces and to labor in the more restricted area of Massachusetts and New York, and to establish a minor seminary for American candidates. This was inaugurated in 1924, in Waltham, MA, in the Archdiocese of Boston. Ten years later the first U.S. Stigmatine was ordained in Rome, Italy; all were ordained there before the outbreak of World War II. In September of 1940, a major house of studies was opened in Wellesley, MA, and the following year the community in the U.S. was established as a separate province by Pius XII.

The initial work in the U.S. was the care of Italian parishes, but it is no longer exclusively parochial activity nor is it restricted to Italians. The Stigmatines now educate youth in summer camps and engage in preaching and retreat work. The U.S. provincialate is in Waltham, MA; the generalate is in Rome.

[J. E. MULLEIN/EDS.]

STIGMATIZATION

Term derived from the Greek root stigma, meaning mark and, in particular, a brand impressed by iron. It was used in antiquity to refer to marks branded on cattle, on all slaves in the Orient, and on fugitive slaves in Greece and Rome. Soldiers also, of some Eastern countries, wore stigmata. In modern times, the term was introduced into medical science to signify characteristic symptoms of mere illnesses, e.g., hysteria and syphilis.

A religious significance was first attached to the term when Herodotus used it to signify the tattooing practiced in certain ancient religions (2.13). The word appears in only one passage of Scripture, where St. Paul writes, "I bear the marks of the Lord Jesus in my body" (Gal 6.17). By this he designated the marks, on his body, of what he suffered for Christ. In medieval times, the meaning of the stigmata was restricted to wounds some people bore on hands, feet, and sometimes the side, shoulder, or back. They were considered a visible sign of participation in Christ's Passion. This conception of the stigmata is easily understood in the light of the times. The devotion to Christ crucified, which in the first centuries of Christianity had emphasized Christ's triumph over the kingdom of evil, took on in medieval times a character of compassion with His sufferings. Medieval preachers and ascetical writers, particularly St. Bernard of Clairvaux (1091–1153), spread this devotion with zeal and success. For some of them, the devotion was the way par excellence of reaching mystical contemplation (see St. Bonaventure, *Itinerarium mentis ad Deum,* prol.). Some people, such as Bl. Mary d'Oignies (d. 1213) and Robert de Monferrant (d. 1234) went so far in the practice of compassion and resemblance with Christ that they themselves deliberately reproduced on their own bodies the marks of Christ's Passion. They did this either in or out of a state of ecstasy.

Occurrences in Christian History. When St. FRANCIS OF ASSISI died (1226), his friends and followers could see the stigmata on his hands, feet, and side. He had received them in an ecstatic vision two years before, as St. Bonaventure testified in his *Legenda S. Francisci* (13.5, 8). From that time, the number of persons with the stigmata increased considerably. A catalogue of them, containing 321 names, was compiled by A. Imbert-Goubeyre, M.D. in *La Stigmatisation* (2 v. Clermont-Ferrand 1894–95; 2 ed. 1908).

However, no reliable list of stigmatized persons exists. The catalogue just mentioned has serious defects. J. Lhermitte contemptuously calls it a Gilded Legend (*Legende Dorée*). H. Thurston, SJ, considers it "irritating both from its entire lack of historical criticism and from its pretension to constitute a complete record" (223). Moreover, it includes doubtful cases of stigmatization. Many mentioned in it had only what are now commonly called invisible stigmata, that is, intense pains localized in those places of their bodies in which, in other stigmatics, wounds were visible. This is the kind of stigmatization that St. CATHERINE OF SIENA and St. TERESA OF AVILA had. St. FRANCIS DE SALES explains them as a strong emotion of compassionate love, which an ecstatic person experiences when contemplating the Passion of Christ (*Treatise on the Love of God,* 6.15).

Imbert-Goubeyre's list of stigmatics gives no satisfactory account of the circumstances in which stigmata first appeared, or of the details of the lives of the stigmatics, and in particular of their health before and after they became marked, or of their attitude with regard to the stigmata, and so on. All these particulars are important in an attempt to explain the stigmata. For purposes of scientific or theological study, only those cases should be considered that are accessible to direct observation or are founded on really irrefutable testimony.

In this kind of study one enjoys full liberty. There is no a priori decision of the Church on the matter, and as to the liturgical commemorations of the stigmata of certain canonized saints, this ''does not commit us,'' says C. C. Martindale, SJ, ''to belief in them any more than we are committed to all that is said in the second nocturn, to the origin of successive translations of the Holy House of Loreto, or the carrying of St. Catherine of Alexandria's body by angels to Mount Sinai'' (660). For Pius XI, the stigmata of St. Francis of Assisi were a historical fact, proved by irrefutable testimonies, but not an article of faith. [See *Acta Apostolicae Sedis* 26 (1924) 362–365]. Still more instructive is the official document of the Church regarding St. Gemma Galgani. The Church refused to pass judgment on her stigmata, as well as on other marvelous phenomena that abounded in her life [*ibid.* (1932) 57].

Theories. Some think that stigmatization is attributable to a particular action of God, if the stigmatic person is distinguished for his piety; otherwise it must be regarded as caused by the intervention of the devil. This solution supposes as evident that stigmatization always surpasses the powers of nature. Such a position is untenable. Moreover, according to Catholic doctrine, there exists no intrinsic connection between sanctity and stigmatization. God can grant charisms, such as stigmata, to any person, even one in the state of mortal sin or one outside the Church (Benedict XIV).

Another theory, which is now held by many theologians and Catholic scholars, is that stigmatization is attributable to purely natural causes, so long as the contrary has not been proved. Such an attitude seems to correspond best with the reluctance of the Church to settle this problem. Outstanding theologians caution us not to be hasty in attributing stigmatization to a miracle; for psychophysiological sciences may in the future show such attribution to be untenable. It seems that St. Francis de Sales had already accepted this cautious attitude in respect to stigmatization, for in the final draft of the *Treatise on the Love of God,* he omitted the word miracle, to which he had attributed the stigmata of St. Francis of Assisi in the MSS of the first edition. A. Gemelli, OFM, believed that St. Francis of Assisi's stigmatization was unique (*caso unico*), being a fleshy, nail-like neoformation. Other cases of exterior stigmatization must have been conscious or unconscious artifacts.

''St. Francis Receiving the Stigmata,'' painting by Jan van Eyck. (©Francis G. Meyer/CORBIS)

All scholars agree that stigmata are connected with ecstasy that, considered psychologically, is an emotional state. If it is really God who miraculously produces the stigmata, why would He have imposed ecstasy as an indispensable condition? Ecstasy in itself does not possess any supernatural character. It is a kind of weakness, an imperfection of human nature, incapable of supporting the strong movements of soul caused by love, contemplation, vision, etc. Why should God never grant the stigmata to persons who contemplate the Passion of Christ with all the intensity of mystical life but without ecstasy? Why did He not grant such a favor to SS. Francis Xavier, Vincent de Paul, and others, especially since many of inferior piety and morality have possessed the stigmata? Again, why should God never grant the stigmata at the very moment the ecstasy begins, but only after a notable lapse of time? Moreover, why should He not produce them at once, in their perfection, rather than by degrees? Several weeks before Theresa NEUMANN's stigmata appeared, the doctor discovered a pronounced sensibility in the places where the wounds later developed. The wound on the back of her right hand developed only eight days after the stigmata on the back of her left hand and on the palms of her hands the following year. This occurrence has been observed in many other stigmatics.

It is notable also that as a rule the exterior stigmatization is preceded by the "invisible stigmata," as in the case of PADRE PIO. All these facts are understandable in our hypothesis that the wounds are traceable to organic functions and that all natural processes must operate for some time to produce an overt symptom such as a wound. Sometimes they result in incomplete stigmata (in Mary B. Schumann, Pirona Hergods, Mary Agnes Steiner, etc.). Again, if stigmata are the effect of a miracle, why is it that a nervous weakness or even hysteria is a necessary condition for their appearance? All stigmatized persons whose lives we know in some detail gave evidence of this illness.

Among the stigmatics, some (SS. Catherine of Ricci, Joanna of Jesus and Mary, Veronica Juliana, Louise Lateau, Theresa Neumann, etc.) had the body wound on the left side, whereas many others had it on the right side. Yet Christ had the wound on one side, not on two. This inconsistency can be explained. When a person in a cataleptic state (induced, e.g., by hypnosis) is asked to repeat the movements executed before him, he will repeat them mirrorwise; that is, if the left arm is extended, he will invariably extend his right arm. In the same way, an ecstatic person reproduces Christ's wounds seeing Christ before him. Furthermore, in modern times, under the influence of the devotion to the Sacred Heart, the trend has been in favor of the left side, the side of the heart. The stigmatic who shares this view will instinctively reproduce the wound on the left. Again, in some stigmatics, the wounds correspond exactly to those depicted on the image of the Crucified before which they are accustomed to pray. This is asserted by the biographers of Catherine Emmerich (Schomeger) and St. Gemma Galgani (Father Germanus). Moreover, the shape of the stigmata varies: sometimes they are square, sometimes round. They may disappear for varying periods of time.

Dr. von Arnhard speaks of the frequent stigmata observed among Muslim ascetics who immerse themselves in contemplation of the life of Muḥammad. These stigmata correspond to the wounds received by the prophet during his battles for the spread of the faith [A. Abadir, *Sur quelques stigmatisés . . .* (Paris 1932)]. The occurrence of stigmatization among the Jansenists has been reported also.

Natural or Supernatural? There are no convincing reasons for holding that stigmatization, considered in itself, necessarily surpasses all the powers of nature or that it is strictly miraculous. The stigmata seem to be rather the effect of ecstasy. Ecstasy as such is not a supernatural event. But if, in a determined case, it is produced by a supernatural contemplation or vision, ecstasy can be called supernatural in cause (*supernaturalis quoad causam*). The stigmata then, which are a connatural effect of ecstasy, can also be called "supernatural in cause."

Consideration must be given to the objection that stigmatization cannot be healed by any remedy. It is questionable, however, whether a suitable remedy has really been used. In the case of Theresa Neumann a number of authors affirm that it was. Nevertheless, on only two occasions did Dr. Seidl apply salve to Theresa's stigmata, and on each occasion the application was removed a few hours later.

Bibliography: R. BIOT, *L'Enigme des Stimatises* (Paris 1955). M. FREZE, *They Bore the Wounds of Christ: The Mystery of the Sacred Stigmata* (Huntington, Ind. 1989). T. HARRISON, *Stigmata: A Medieval Mystery in a Modern Age* (New York 1994). H. OHLY, "Stigmatisierung: Wunder oder Betrug," *Jensiets der Erkenntnis* (Frankfurt 1977) 66–83. B. RUFFIN, *Padre Pio, the True Story*, (Huntington, Ind. 1991). I. WILSON, *Stigmata: An Investigation into the Mysterious Appearance of Christ's Wounds in Hundreds of People from Medieval Italy to Modern America* (San Francisco 1989).

[P. SIWEK]

STILLA, BL.

Twelfth-century German ascetic, virgin. She was somehow related to the counts of Abenberg, but the only other substantiated fact of her life is her construction of a small church dedicated to St. Peter at Abenberg, near Nuremberg, Germany. She hoped eventually to establish beside it a monaster for nuns that she intended to enter, but she died before accomplishing her plan. Her brothers, monks in the Cistercian abbey of HEILSBRONN, which they had founded (1132), were eager—according to the 16th-century legend—to bring her body to their abbey for burial; but the horses refused (a commonplace in medieval hagiography), turning instead to her own church of St. Peter, where she was buried in a grave marked by a 12th-century tombstone with her effigy. MARIENBERG ABBEY was later built on the spot (*c.* 1495) for AUGUSTINIAN NUNS. Her cult, first attested in 1480, was approved by the bishop of Eichstätt in 1897 on the grounds that it antedated 1534, and later (1927) it received papal approval. Stilla's many favors (the BOLLANDISTS list 55 miracles) have been acknowledged, especially by wax votive images.

Feast: July 19.

Bibliography: *Acta Sanctorum* July 4:656–663. A. BUTLER, *The Lives of the Saints,* rev. ed. H. THURSTON and D. ATTWATER, 4 vol. (New York 1956) 3:149–150. A. BAUCH, *Lexikon für Theologie und Kirche,* ed. J. HOFER and K. RAHNER, 10 v. (2nd new ed. Freiburg 1957–65) 9:1082–83.

[C. M. AHERNE]

STILLINGTON, ROBERT

Chancellor of England, bishop of Bath and Wells; d. between April 8 and May 15, 1491. The son of John Stillington of Nether Acaster, near York, England, he was educated at Oxford, where he became a doctor of civil law by 1443. Before 1448 he entered the royal service and held office as keeper of the privy seal (July 1460–June 1467) and as chancellor of England (June 1467–June 1473, except during King Henry VI's restoration). He was rewarded with valuable ecclesiastical preferments, including the London deanery of St. Martin-le-Grand, which he retained after his provision in October 1465, to the See of BATH and Wells, a diocese he visited only twice in 25 years. A timeserver in politics, he supported King Richard III by drawing up the bill declaring Edward IV's issue illegitimate. Although pardoned by King Henry VII in 1485, he was imprisoned in 1488–89 for suspected complicity in rebellion. "Ce mauvais évesque," as Comines called him, had a discreditable political record and seems to have been wholly indifferent to his diocesan responsibilities.

Bibliography: R. STILLINGTON, *Registers,* ed. H. C. MAXWELL-LYTE (Somerset Record Society 52; Somerset 1937). C. L. SCOFIELD, *The Life and Reign of Edward the Fourth,* 2 v. (New York 1923). A. B. EMDEN, *A Biographical Register of the Scholars of the University of Oxford to A.D. 1500,* 3 v. (Oxford 1957–59) 3:1777–79.

[C. D. ROSS]

STÖCKLEIN, JOSEPH

Jesuit mission historian; b. Öttingen, Bavaria, July 30, 1676; d. Graz, Austria, Dec. 28, 1733. He entered the Society of Jesus Oct. 9, 1700, and received his theological training and was ordained in Vienna. As a priest he was chief field chaplain (1714–18) with Prince Eugene in Serbia. In this capacity he saw action in 11 field battles. Later he was rector at the College of Vienna-Neustadt (1720–23) and preacher at the court. He is best known for his writings, especially for his *Der Neue-Weltbott* (1728–61), a compilation of reports from Jesuit missionaries in the East Indies, the New World, and other overseas lands, forwarded to Europe from 1642 to 1726. The collection is one of the most important sources for the history of the Catholic missions of the 18th century. The first volume, comprising the first eight parts, was published by Stöcklein in Augsburg in 1726. This collection, greatly indebted to the *Lettres Edifiantes* of Charles Gobien, SJ, was extended later to include 38 parts. Stöcklein collected the first three volumes (24 parts), which were published in 1736. After Stöcklein's death, other Jesuits carried on the work. Thus, Peter Probst brought out parts 25 to 28 in 1748; Francis Keller issued parts 29 to 36 in 1758; and Francis Xavier Socher completed the work by 1761. Keller (1700–62) wrote a letter on the life and death of Joseph Stöcklein that appears at the end of part 29 (n. 572). R. STREIT gives a complete listing of the letters and descriptions contained in *Der Neue-Weltbott.*

Bibliography: C. SOMMERVOGEL et al., *Bibliothèque de la Compagnie de Jésus,* 11 v. (Brussels-Paris 1890–1932; v.12, suppl. 1960) 7:1585–86; 12:821. R. STREIT and J. DINDINGER, *Bibliotheca missionum* (Freiburg 1916–) 1:838, 942, 976, 994. M. A. BLANKENBURG, "German Missionary Writers in Paraguay," *Mid-America* 29 (1947) 45–61.

[J. J. HOLLOHAN]

STOHR, ALBERT

Bishop and liturgical leader; b. Friedberg (Oberhessen), Germany, Nov. 13, 1890; d. Seligenstadt, June 4, 1961. He studied theology at Mainz and was ordained there in 1913. From 1914 to 1920 he served as a curate and taught religion. He then pursued higher studies in several German universities and in Rome. He taught Church history (1924) and dogma (1926) at the major seminary of Mainz. In 1935 he was appointed bishop of Mainz, and he became one of the most important German bishops of the war and postwar eras. The German bishops made their youngest member head of the youth apostolate in 1937, and in 1941 (together with Bishop Landersdorfer of Passau) of the liturgical commission. In both capacities Stohr's dynamic, pastoral personality achieved excellence; with a sure hand, he helped to lead the German Catholic youth and the liturgical movement through the crises of the 1940s. He fought vigorously for the maintenance of the privilege of the so-called German high Mass, but he did not live to see it extended by Vatican Council II to the whole world. A third area of his endeavor was the ecumenical dialogue to which he devoted much of his energy and love. He was the first bishop to request and obtain permission to ordain married converts from the Protestant ministry.

Bibliography: J. WAGNER, *Litugisches Jahrbuch* 11 (1961) 193–202. L. LENHART, *Lexikon für Theologie und Kirche,* ed. J. HOFER and K. RAHNER, 10 v. (2d, new ed. Freiburg 1957–65) 9:1086–87.

[B. FISCHER]

Zeno of Citium.

STOICISM

A philosophical school named after the stoa (στόα), i.e., the porch, or painted colonnade where Zeno of Citium (*c.* 366– *c.* 264 B.C.), its first exponent, used to teach in Athens. Stoicism stresses the seriousness of life. It emphasizes the individual and the concrete in opposition to Platonic ideas or Aristotelian universals. Among its characteristics, some of which it shares with other contemporary schools, are the primacy of the practical, the ideal of ataraxy or mental tranquillity, a pervading MATERIALISM, and, generally, a marked affinity for Oriental values and attitudes. This article treats of Stoicism in two parts, the first dealing with its philosophical teachings, the second with the influence of these on Christian thought.

Stoic Philosophy

Although Stoicism took many forms during its long existence, its principal thinkers are usually classified as belonging to one of three groups, viz, the Ancient Stoa, the Middle Stoa, and the Later Stoa.

Proponents and Their Works. Among the Ancient Stoa are enumerated three outstanding philosophers, Zeno of Citium, Cleanthes of Assos, and Chrysippus of Soloi. Zeno founded the school after studying under the Cynic Crates, the Megarians Stilpo and Diodorus, and the Platonist Xenocrates. His pupil Cleanthes (*c.* 331–232) became head of the school at Zeno's death. Chrysippus (*c.* 282–206) was referred to as the second founder of Stoicism. The Middle Stoa are represented by two main figures, Panaetius of Rhodes and Poseidonius of Apamea. Panaetius (*c.* 185–109) was influenced by the philosophy of Plato, whom he considered to be the wisest and holiest of men, the Homer of philosophers (Cicero, *Tusc. disp.* 1; see Van Straaten, 83). Poseidonius (*c.* 135-50) appears, on some points at least, to have been more strongly swayed by PLATONISM than even his master Panaetius. The Later Stoa developed largely in Rome. Its chief representatives were L. Annaeus SENECA (A.D. 4–65), Nero's preceptor; EPICTETUS of Hierapolis (*c.* 50–138), a liberated slave, whose *Discourses* and *Enchiridion* (published by his disciple Arrianus) are classics of moral philosophy; and the Roman emperor MARCUS AURELIUS (121–180).

The works of the ancient and middle Stoics exist only in fragmentary form. Hans Von Arnim collected these fragments in a monumental work that is the chief instrument for the study of Stoic philosophy. The works of the later Stoics, being mainly concerned with ethics, are of little help in determining the nature of Stoic physics and logic as expounded in the numerous writings of the school (Chrysippus alone is known to have written more than 700 works). Cicero's philosophical treatises have preserved a large number of fragments, while Plutarch (in his disputations against the Stoics), Galen, Sextus Empiricus, and Diogenes Laertius have transmitted countless other texts. Unfortunately for positive understanding, the doctrines of the Stoics are known largely through the polemical works of their adversaries. (*See* SKEPTICISM.)

Doctrines. The Stoics, with some minor exceptions, divide philosophy into logic, physics, and ethics (Diogenes Laertius, 7.39) and conceive these as closely interrelated. One Stoic analogy compares philosophy to an animal, logic constituting the bones and nerves; ethics, the flesh; and physics, the soul. Zeno and Chrysippus taught logic before physics and physics before ethics. Others preferred to teach the three parts at the same time (Diogenes, 7.40) or followed different orders.

Logic. Logic examines the elements of discourse or reasoning with their properties and relationships. Of presentations (φαντασίαι), some derive from sensations, others only appear to come from the senses, still others take their origin in reason, such as the incorporeals (τὰ ἀσώματα) and other products of the mind (Diogenes, 7.51). The criterion of truth is the comprehensive presentation (φαντασία καταληπτική), which involves the firm conviction that it could not be so perceived by the mind if the reality were not such as it is represented to be. This criterion bore the brunt of countless attacks on the part of Pyrrhonians and Academics (*see* PYRRHONISM). The comprehensive presentation makes the difference between ignorance and science, because through it men communicate with nature; in the words of Cicero *natura quasi normam scientiae et principium sui dedisset* (Von Arnim, 1:66). The implications of the empirical presentations are developed by means of a logic of propositions that differs from the Aristotelian logic of terms (Diogenes, 7.69–83). *See* LOGIC, HISTORY OF.

Physics. Stoic physics deals with the cosmos, its principles and elements, space and the void, the gods, and their existence and their nature. Since everything natural, whether active or passive, is thought to be material, Stoic materialism has been aptly though paradoxically described as a ''spiritualistic materialism.'' The activities and properties of matter are given enough range to allow for distinctions and operations that other philosophies place in the immaterial order. However, even the Stoic concept of the incorporeal does not involve a distinct spiritual domain. The incorporeal is divided into four categories: expressibles or λεκτά (such as mental terms or propositions), void, place, and time (Sextus Empiricus, *Adv. math.* 10.218). It can neither act nor be acted upon and always originates in the body; e.g., the λεκτὸν stating that something is burning depends on the physical fact of burning. In any case, the incorporeals depend on the body and are inseparable from it.

The world is one and is made up of four elements: fire, air, water, and earth. God, who seems to be more or less identified with primal fire, creates the elements out of himself through processes reminiscent of the pre-Socratic cosmogonies. Some parts (those partaking more fully of the primal element) are active (τὸ ποιοῦν) and divine, whereas the rest of matter is passive (τὸ πάσχον). According to most Stoics, the entire cosmos moves in a fore ordained manner, throughout time, from states of fuller material differentiation to reabsorption into primal fire (ἐκπύρωσις).

Fire is like a seed or germ having in itself the reasons of all things (σπερματικοὶ λόγοι) and the causes of what was, is, and shall be (*see* SEMINAL REASONS). It is the vital principle from which all plants and animals spring. At any stage of natural development god remains as a living force, molding and dominating passive matter in view of further progress (Diogenes, 7.136, 148). Thus the entire world is animate, rational, and divine (*see* WORLD SOUL). The first men were generated by the sun's fire (Von Arnim, 1:124) and made up of the four elements. The Stoics reasoned that the soul was corporeal, being that inner material breath (πνεῦμα) whose departure causes the body to be dead (*ibid.* 137). The human soul is but a fragment of the soul that animates the totality of matter (Diogenes, 7.142–143); its separate existence is annihilated in the process of ἐκπύρωσις. Most Stoics divide the soul into eight parts: the hegemonikon or ruling part, the five senses, the faculty of speech, and the generative faculty.

God is fire and logos diffused throughout the cosmos. The law of nature is his material presence in the universe. As cosmic reason he is *ipso facto* PROVIDENCE (πρόνοια), ordaining all things, and FATE (εἱμαρμένη), imposing upon man a physical determinism that allows for freedom merely as man's inner acceptance of cosmic necessity.

Ethics. The Stoic conception of nature and of man's place in it necessarily leads to a science of human behavior. Self-preservation is an animal's first impulse (ὁρμή); it can be realized only by living in conformity with nature (Diogenes, 7.87). Similarly, the end of man coincides with the virtuous or rational life. Pleasure is not valued for its own sake but merely follows upon the attainment of the GOOD. Most Stoics restrict the good to virtue and to what partakes of virtues (Diogenes, 7.94), defining virtue as the quality of a spirit in perfect harmony with itself (Von Arnim, 3:197–200). The virtues are so connected that to possess one is to possess all.

Things that are neither good nor evil, i.e., neither virtuous nor vicious, are termed indifferent (ἀδιάφορα). Some of the latter can be used to good advantage (e.g., wealth, fame, and health) and are said to be ''preferred'' (προηγμένα). Others (e.g., poverty, disease, and weakness), without being evil in themselves, are classified as not-preferred (ἀποπροηγμένα). A third category of ''indifferent things'' is purely neutral (e.g., the number of hairs on one's head) and gives rise neither to preference nor to rejection.

Corresponding to the division of things into good, bad, and indifferent, and of the latter into preferred, not-preferred, and neutral, one finds in the subjective order a distinction between virtue, vice, and the sense of suitability (καθῆκον). The last enables one to discriminate between the indifferent things and to behave in a fitting manner with respect to them. The Stoics generally consider the passions to be irrational and unnatural movements of the soul or, again, excessive impulses (Diogenes, 7.110). The wise man is free from all passions, but the Stoic is quick to point out that the apathy of the wise is not to be confused with that of the callous or evil man. The Stoic wise man is happy, free, godlike, never errs and—unlike his Epicurean counterpart—does not spurn political action.

Stoicism helped to establish cosmopolitan attitudes in ancient society through a conception of the individual's moral value that ignored national or class distinctions. Perhaps the best illustration of this lies in the fact that the former slave Epictetus and the Roman emperor Marcus Aurelius were equally honored as great exponents of the doctrines of the Later Stoa.

Appreciation. Though Stoicism as established by Zeno continued to exist as a major school of thought for about 800 years, it underwent many changes and adaptations. The most important of these, perhaps, was the shift from an explicit formulation of logic in the Ancient Stoa to what appears to have been an exclusive preoccupation with ethics in the Later Stoa. Despite a basic agreement on the nature of the cosmos and the requirements of human behavior, Stoics appear to have disagreed among themselves on a number of matters, such as the nature of logic, the divisions of philosophy, the relative immortality of human souls, or the possibility of dividing the category of preferred things.

Stoicism expounded a new outlook on personal dignity and on the nature of law, together with a new conception of the state as reflecting world order and as leading men of all origins and classes to personal fulfillment. It may be said that this philosophy not only presented a moral alternative to Christianity, but also that it helped develop a climate in which Christian teaching could take hold more firmly. Many of its doctrines were transposed into Christian thought by the Fathers of the Church (see below) and have become important aspects of modern civilization and thought.

See Also: GREEK PHILOSOPHY.

Bibliography: Sources. H. F. VON ARNIM, *Stoicorum veterum fragmenta,* 4 v. (Leipzig 1903–24), v.1 *Zeno et Zenonis discipuli,* v. 2–3 *Chrysippi fragmenti,* v.4 Index. M. VAN STRAATEN, *Panaetii Rhodii Fragmenta* (Leiden 1952). DIOGENES LAERTIUS, *Lives of Eminent Philosophers,* tr. R. D. HICKS, 2 v. (Loeb Classical Library London-New York-Cambridge, MA 184, 185; rev. ed. 1942) v.2, bk.7. Literature. F. C. COPLESTON, *History of Philosophy* (Westminster, MD 1946–) v.1. B. MATES, *Stoic Logic* (Berkeley 1953). É. BRÉHIER, *Chrysippe et l'ancien stoïcisme* (rev. ed. Paris 1951). E. R. BEVAN, *Stoics and Sceptics* (Oxford 1913; repr. New York 1959).

[V. CAUCHY]

Influence on Christian Thought

Despite its wide diffusion around the 1st century, Stoicism left little mark on Sacred Scripture. The Book of Wisdom, wrought in the cosmopolitan milieu of Egypt, sometimes borrowed its terminology when speaking of the pneuma (7.22–24; 8.1). St. Paul used some terms, the images of city, construction, and body, and the processes of the Cynic-Stoic diatribe. He developed some related theses—equality of all men by the pneuma, absolute freedom of man, and natural knowledge of God—but in such a way that the independence and Christian authenticity of his message were not put into question. Conversely, one may presume that Seneca and Epictetus were influenced by the new religion; certainly the Christianity of the Middle Ages laid claim to them.

However, a deep incompatibility existed between Christianity and Stoicism in its religious form. The Stoic ascetic effort resulted in an autarchic fulfillment of the personality. This was only temporary, however, since man's terminus was, after all, a return to primitive elements, while the Christian opened himself to the infinite and sought an eschatological conclusion. On the other hand, the God of the Portico was always the soul of the world, and the relationship of men to God was physical. This excluded true divine transcendency, the supernatural, and redemptive Incarnation.

Early Patristic Thought. In the patristic era the influence of this philosophy was pronounced until about 230 and became sporadic thereafter. In bk. 2 of his *Paidagogos,* CLEMENT OF ALEXANDRIA made at least 15 textual borrowings from Musonius; in the same work he sometimes used the text of Epictetus. Seneca provided a few lines for St. CYPRIAN and MINUCIUS FELIX, but the effect of Stoicism is clearly noticeable in the theses they elaborated.

Man. The anthropology of all the Fathers had Stoic elements, although none omitted the presence of a supernatural reality in man. Almost all divided the human composite into body and soul in Stoic fashion, and TERTULLIAN saw in it a ''mixture'' of two elements. The soul itself was considered corporeal by IRENAEUS and Tertullian, the latter supporting his position with the Stoic principle: ''nihil si non corpus.'' The psychology of Clement of Alexandria had a materialistic bent, especially that in the *Excerpta ex Theodoto.* Finally, TATIAN and Irenaeus noted in the soul an element shared with universal life and thus reattached man to the cosmos. Tertullian and Clement of Alexandria presented many other Stoic ideas in treating medical questions, developments relating to generation and heredity, and particularly theories of knowledge with their emphasis on the senses and ''common notions.'' Finally ethics was frequently related to Stoicism in its terminology and in certain of its themes: indifference (JUSTIN MARTYR, ATHENAGORAS, Tatian, Minucius Felix, Tertullian, and, with some variations, Clement of Alexandria), apathy and intellectualism (Justin, Athenagoras, Irenaeus, and especially Clement of Alexandria), conformity to the logos and to nature (Clement of Alexandria), NATURAL LAW (Justin, the Apostolic Constitutions, Clement of Alexandria, and particularly

Tertullian), equality of man and cosmopolitanism (particularly Tertullian, Cyprian, and Minucius Felix), the model of the wise man (Tatian and Clement of Alexandria, for whom the wise man became the gnostic), and all of the themes of the diatribe.

God. There was less Stoic influence on matters relating to God. Some Fathers emphasized God's rational nature (Athenagoras, Minucius Felix, and Tertullian), others His material nature (Tertullian). Almost all, and especially Clement of Alexandria, noted His impassibility. All proved His existence rationally, usually taking the order of the universe as their point of departure. Their theories of the *logos-pneuma* also exhibited a Stoic aspect, and this apart from the terminology used: e.g., God's corporeal nature (Tertullian and the *Excerpta ex Theodoto*) and His cyclic unfolding in the Incarnation (the paschal homily attributed to Hippolytus). One may even detect an animistic concept of the world in Tatian and THEOPHILUS OF ANTIOCH, and secondarily in Tertullian, Irenaeus, Hippolytus, Novatian, and Clement of Alexandria, but for all these thinkers the pneuma of the world, instead of being God, became some ill-defined intermediate. Finally, Minucius Felix and Clement of Alexandria made the logos the law and order of the world. In all this God was viewed more as present in the universe than as functioning in His redemptive work.

The World. Despite their theses about the initial creation, the Fathers sometimes saw the world as undergoing a cyclic evolution. They unanimously praised its beauty, order, and harmony, from Pope St. CLEMENT I OF ROME all the way to Clement of Alexandria, who was filled with wonder at the cosmos. The imperfection of detail in the universe contributes to the perfection of the All (Tertullian and Clement of Alexandria), which perfection results from the complementarity of opposites (Irenaeus, Tertullian, NOVATIAN, and Clement of Alexandria). For these writers, as for the Stoics, the world was at the disposal of man and was explained in anthropomorphic terms with a disconcerting optimism. Finally, the universe itself constituted a great All (Irenaeus, Tertullian, and Novatian), one "vast body" (Tatian and Tertullian); Tertullian's universal materialism unhesitatingly encompassed angels, the soul, and God. Many Fathers had materialistic leanings on the question of angels (Tatian, Minucius Felix, and Clement of Alexandria), and the meeting of body and spirit (in anthropology, the Incarnation, grace, and the matter of the Sacraments) presented no difficulty for any of them. Finally, everything was conceived in a spatiotemporal framework, even man, who was seen as subject to a uniform law of the cosmos. This law was seen variously as a "sympathy" among all spirits (Athenagoras and Clement of Alexandria), an essential connection (Tertullian and particularly Minucius Felix), and a "combined effort uniting all in harmony" (Novatian). Everything was historically linked, physically (Athenagoras and Clement of Alexandria) or rationally (Tertullian), with a determinism that extended to astral fatalism (*Excerpta ex Theodoto* and especially BARDESANES).

A brief account does not permit the necessary references or useful precisions, but the fact is that a Stoic current ran through Christian thought before 250. In this the Fathers were influenced by the surrounding climate of opinion, adjusting themselves to the ideas of their pagan auditors and refuting the generally Platonic tendencies of the heretics, especially the Gnostics. But their philosophy was in the service of a Christian theology that was rarely betrayed.

Later Patristic Thought. A second era in patristic thought extends from about 230 to the beginning of the Middle Ages; its thought may be explained in terms of the principal theses and their application.

Theses. In this second period, which was dominated by Platonism, Stoic ethics remained influential. It left countless definitions in the works of ORIGEN and St. BASIL, intelligently adapted by St. AMBROSE (whose *De officiis* is clearly Stoical) and by St. AUGUSTINE. The bipartite division of the moral universe into "what is within man's power and what is not," with the supremacy of "free choice" (προαίρεσις) over the "indifferents," passed from Origen and Basil to JOHN CHRYSOSTOM, who composed a discourse entitled "Who does not injure himself cannot be injured by anyone" (*Patrologia Graeca,* ed. J. P. Migne 52: 459–480) and incessantly repeated these ideas; from him the division passed on to monasticism. Stoicism transmitted its positions on virtue: autarchy (LACTANTIUS and Ambrose), the necessary connection of the virtues (Origen, Ambrose, GREGORY OF NYSSA, John CASSIAN, EVAGRIUS PONTICUS, and Pope St. GREGORY I), and the grouping of the four cardinal virtues, following Athenagoras and Clement of Alexandria (Basil, Ambrose, JEROME, Augustine, Cassian, Gregory, and ISIDORE OF SEVILLE). The notion of apathy, applied to God, to Christ, and especially to the Christian, received special emphasis; baptized from the time of Origen, it was used by all writers, particularly in treatises on anger, and became the ideal of the monk, the basis of his contemplation. The theme of the wise man was taken up especially by Lactantius, Ambrose, and BOETHIUS who, with GREGORY OF NAZIANZUS, also used the classical themes relating to consolation.

Stoicism also provided elements on the physical and metaphysical plane. Analyzed in Stoic terms by NEMESIUS OF EMESA, man was the center of the universe for Ambrose, who attributed his anthropocentrism to the Stoics. Man's fate was sometimes linked to the evolution of the

All (the *De Incarnatione* attributed to ATHANASIUS; Basil and Gregory of Nyssa). The materialistic pneumatology was repeated by Lactantius and MACARIUS the Egyptian and left its traces in Augustine, who made frequent use of seminal reasons and never completely rejected the concept of world soul. NATURE (''common notions,'' natural knowledge, and natural law) occupied a prominent place. Central to most thought was the All, wherein the detail evident in the universe found its meaning and evil its place in the harmony of opposites (Origen and Augustine). Many other Stoic elements were intermingled in Christian thought, although Stoicism never appeared as the dominant philosophy except for Lactantius.

Adaptations. Christians often simply adopted the ethical works of the Stoics. MARTIN OF BRAGA borrowed freely from Seneca. A treatise close to Epictetus, Christianized on the surface, figures at the head of the *Philocalia,* entitled ''Exhortation of Our Holy Father Anthony the Great'' (Athens 1893, 1:2–16). The *Enchiridion* itself, with minor modifications, has been attributed to NILUS OF ANCYRA (*Patrologia Graeca,* ed. J. P. Migne 79:1285–1312). Another adaptation of the *Enchiridion,* improperly called ''Christian Paraphrase'' (ed. J. Schweighäuser, *Epictetae Philosophiae Monumenta* 5:10–94) also reproduces the text of Epictetus, Christianized and with a few touches relating to monastic life. Finally this last text has been the object of a Christian commentary, still unedited, that appears in 15 manuscripts but is not complete in any of them. These undertakings between the 5th and 10th centuries testify to the success some Stoics had with the monks.

Medieval Thought. The Middle Ages that Christianized Epictetus and Seneca took little from the Stoic system of thought. Stoic writers were represented by manuscripts of their entire works, FLORILEGIA, and various scholia. Byzantine thought was little influenced by Stoicism (ARETHAS OF CAESAREA and Kekaumenos), and the Latins were only a bit more sensitive to it. The *Moralium dogma philosophorum,* very likely the work of WILLIAM OF CONCHES, is a florilegium of Cicero, Seneca, Sallust, and some Fathers. JOHN OF SALISBURY was sympathetic to Stoicism in all his works, while John of Damback wrote a *Consolatio theologiae* that was greatly imbued with this philosophy and Barlaam of Seminara wrote an *Ethica secundum Stoicos.* Many moralists, moreover, mentioned Seneca by name.

Modern Thought. From the rediscovery of Stoicism with the first translators of Epictetus, N. Perotti in 1453 and A. Poliziano in 1497, Christian thinkers made use of Stoic doctrines, particularly against EPICUREANISM. Among these may be mentioned Petrus Crinitus (P. Ricci), *De honesta disciplina* (1508); G. Budé, *De contemptu rerum fortuitarum* (1520); J. Clichtove, *De doctrina moriendi opusculum* (1538); A. Steucho, *De perenni philosophia* (1540), who even made use of the metaphysics; and T. Kirchmaier, called Naogeorgius, who wrote a translation and commentary of Epictetus with the meaningful title, *Moralis philosophiae medulla* (1554). Spiritual writers, both Protestant and Catholic, did not escape its influence. Trace are noted in the *Spiritual Exercises* of St. IGNATIUS LOYOLA (the ἀδιάφορα and the notion of conformity with God), while the biographers of SS. Charles BORROMEO, ALOYSIUS GONZAGA, and John BERCHMANS mention their interest in this philosophy. LOUIS OF GRANADA made frequent use of it in all his works, including his sermons. While denouncing its polytheism, apathy, and pride, FRANCIS DE SALES made much of the Portico and showed great sympathy for the ''poor soul, Epictetus,'' whose spirit of poverty he particularly admired. Among the Reformers, H. ZWINGLI, A. de Rivaudeau, P. DUPLESSIS-MORNAY, and S. Goulard, illogically enough, were inspired by the Stoics. As early as 1532, J. CALVIN wrote a quite eulogistic commentary on the *De clementia* of Seneca.

At the juncture of the 16th and 17th centuries, Stoicism assumed a dominant place with J. LIPSIUS, K. SCIOPPIUS, Guillaume du Vair, P. CHARRON, and F. de Quevedo y Villegas. Many religious writers took great advantage of its teachings. According to J. E. d'Angers, who has devoted some 20 articles to them, some are Christian humanists who use Stoic texts but refute the errors of the system, whereas others are Christian Stoics who, at the price of misinterpretation and scorn, put the pagan masters at the service of Christianity without reservation, even in defining sovereign good, wisdom, and virtue. The famous Bishop of Belley, J. P. Camus, illustrated this twofold attitude in the evolution of his *Diversités* (1609–18), which were published in the order of their composition. Among the Christian humanists are numerous Capuchins (Jacques d'Autun, Zacharie de Lisieux, Léandre de Dijon, Georges d'Amiens, and Yves de Paris); Jesuits (R. Ceriziers, J. Hayneuve, and F. Garasse); the Franciscan J. du Bosc; the Oratorian J. F. Senault; and the Carmelite LEO OF ST. JOHN. The Christian Stoics include the Jesuits B. Castori, N. Caussin, É. BINET, P. Lescalopier, and M. Mourges; the Cistercian John of St. Francis; the Franciscan tertiary Jean Marie de Bordeaux; the Capuchin Sebastian de Senlis; and the Recollect Pascal Rapine de Sainte Marie, who even discovered in the Stoics the notions of purgatory, penance, and the resurrection of the dead.

A naturalist and rationalistic, indeed a Semi-Pelagian, tendency lay hidden behind this literature of confidence in man; on this account, it was denounced by the Jansenists, including B. PASCAL. The latter, in fighting its "presumption," exposed the philosophy of Epictetus with great admiration, exclaiming: "I dare say that he would be worthy of adoration had he known his powerlessness" (*Entretien avec M. de Saci sur Epictète et Montaigne*). Stoicism waned before the end of the century. In the course of Christian thought it knew two great periods: the first 2 centuries, in which it seems to have set the tone; and the 16th and 17th centuries, when it again found favor despite strong opposition, particularly from JANSENISM, which negated its basic theses.

Bibliography: R. STOB, "Stoicism and Christianity," *Classical Journal* 30 (1934–35) 217–224. M. POHLENZ, "Paulus und die Stoa," *Zeitschrift für die neutestamentliche Wissenschft und die Kunde der älteren Kirche* 42 (1949) 69–104. A. JAGU, "Saint Paul et le Stoïcisme," *Revue des sciences religieuses* 32 (Strasbourg 1958) 225–250. M. SPANNEUT, *Le Stoïcisme des Pères de l'Église de Clément de Rome à Clément d'Alexandrie* (Paris 1957); *Reallexikon für Antike und Christentum,* ed. T. KLAUSER [Stuttgart 1941 (1950)–] 5:599–681. J. STELZENBERGER, *Die Beziehungen der frühchristlichen Sittenlehre zur Ethik der Stoa* (Munich 1933). G. VERBEKE, *L'Évolution de la doctrine du pneuma du Stoïcisme à s. Augustin: Étude philosophique* (Louvain 1945). J. E. D'ANGERS, "Étude sur les citations de Sénèque et d'Épictète dans *L'Institutione civile christiana* de B. Castori, S.J., 1622," *Mélanges de science religieuse* 17 (Lille 1960) 81–130. J. N. SEVENSTER, *Paul and Seneca* (Leiden 1961).

[M. SPANNEUT]

STOLE

A band of material worn by bishops, priests, and deacons for all liturgical services; bishops and priests wear it about the neck and with the ends loose or crossed over the breasts; deacons, across the breast from left shoulder to right waist. The origin of the stole is obscure. It was already in use in the East in the 4th century as an insignia for the lower clergy, and was adapted apparently from Imperial civil services. In the West it had made its appearance in Spain by the 7th century; thence its use spread throughout the Carolingian realm, until by the 12th century it was accepted at Rome. Theories supporting the derivation of the stole from a towel for serving at table or a neck-cloth for warmth can no longer be held. From the first record of its use the stole is always mentioned in conciliar and synodal decrees as a distinctive mark for deacons, later for priests and bishops. The name was given to it in Gaul and is derived from the Greek designating a white robe of distinction. Furthermore it was originally worn over the other vestments.

The stole was always white until the 16th century when it became customary to match its color to that of the chasuble or dalmatic and embroider a cross on it. It must be worn by the clergy when they administer any sacrament or exercise their order during any liturgical function. The custom of having deacons wear the stole from the left shoulder to the right waist originated in the 12th century. Though the practice of crossing the stole over his breast is attested already in the 7th century, it did not become universal until the promulgation of the *Missale Romanum* by Pius V in 1570. In the wake of the Second Vatican Council, and the frequency of concelebration, the ancient practice of clergy wearing stole freely over the alb was revived.

Bibliography: H. NORRIS, *Church Vestments* (London 1948). E.A. ROULIN, *Vestments and Vesture*, tr. J. MCCANN (Westminster, MD 1950). J. BRAUN, *Die liturgische Gewandung im Occident und Orient* (Freiburg 1907). J. MAYO, *A History of Ecclesiastical Dress* (London 1984). D. HINES, *Dressing for Worship: A Fresh Look at What Christians Wear in Church* (Cambridge 1996). D. PHILIPPART, ed., *Clothed in Glory: Vesting the Church* (Chicago 1997).

[M. MCCANCE]

STOLLENWERK, HELENA, BL.

In religion, Maria, and later as Adoration Sr. Maria Virgo, co-foundress of the Congregation of Missionary Sisters, Servants of the Holy Spirit (SSpS); b. Nov. 28, 1852, in Rollesbroich (northern Eifel Region), Germany; d. Feb. 3, 1900, at Steyl, the Netherlands.

Raised in a religious farm family headed by Johann Peter Stollenwerk and his third wife, Anna Maria Bongard, Helena had early aspirations to evangelization. In the autumn of 1881, she wrote to Bl. Arnold JANSSEN, founder of the Divine Word Missionaries, to help her realize her own dream of taking the Good News to China. He promised her nothing but accepted her as a kitchen maid in the Divine Word Seminary he had founded at Steyl. From 1882–89, she served in the kitchen with three other women who shared her missionary vocation.

With Helena Stollenwerk and Hendrina Stenmanns, Janssen founded the Congregation of Missionary Sisters, Servants of the Holy Spirit on Dec. 8, 1889, in response to a call from Argentina for sisters. Stollenwerk became its first superior general when she received the religious habit and the name Sr. Maria in 1892. She professed her vows on Mar. 12, 1894. As superior she remained in Steyl while the first sisters went to Argentina in 1895.

In 1896, Janssen founded the cloistered Holy Spirit Adoration Sisters with a small group of Missionary Sisters. Stollenwerk expressed a desire to join the new branch immediately, but it was not until two years later he asked her to make the transfer and begin a second novitiate with the name Sr. Maria Virgo. Although she had hesitated between her missionary vision and a desire for a more contemplative life, her humility and obedience are demonstrated by her uncomplainingly relinquishing of her position as superior and her desire to become a missionary.

Her motto indicates the depth of her spirituality: ''To God the honor, to my neighbor the benefit, and to myself the burden.'' At the time of her transfer to the Adoration Sisters she encouraged the sisters in Argentina: ''If you find things difficult at any time in the future, be comforted by the thought that, like Moses in the Old Testament, there is a Sister before the tabernacle raising her heart and hands to Heaven for you.''

Stollenwerk professed as a Holy Spirit Adoration Sister three days before she died. She was beatified by John Paul II, May 7, 1995.

Bibliography: *Acta Apostolicae Sedis* (1995): 564. *L'Osservatore Romano,* Engish edition, no. 19 (1995): 2, 4. A. GRÜN, *Treue auf dem Weg. Der Weg der Helena Stollenwerk* (Münsterschwarzach 1995); *Faithful to the Spirit,* Eng. tr. P. G. LAFORGE (Techny, IL 1997). F. C. REHBEIN, *Helena Stollenwerk, A Charism Nurtured: Mission and Surrender* (Rome 1995). O. STEGMAIER, *M. Maria Stollenwerk: Aufzeichnungen* (Rome 1987); *M. Maria Stollenwerk: Berufsgeschichte* (Rome 1987), Eng. tr. *Mother Maria's Vocation* (Rome 1990); *M. Helena Stollenwerk Reifung und Sendung der Mitgründerin der Steyler Missionsschwestern im Licht ihres Christusbildes* (Augsburg 1994); *Brought Forth into Freedom,* Eng. tr. L. J. MULBERGE (Rome 1995).

[K. I. RABENSTEIN]

STOLZ, ANSELM

Theologian; b. Erkrath, near Düsseldorf, Jan. 28, 1900; d. Rome, Oct. 19, 1942. In 1918 he became a Benedictine at Gerleve, Germany. He studied theology at St. Anselm's in Rome, where from 1928 he was professor of dogma. A charismatic teacher, Stolz attracted many pupils. His theology is the expression of old monastic spirituality in its extraordinary union of asceticism, liturgy, mysticism, teaching, and speculation. Stolz stands at the beginning of the new theology with its accent on the anthropological value of revelation, yet he does not neglect speculative theology. Stolz' particular strength lies in the organic, historico-dogmatic inclusion of patristics in a theology stamped with clear, methodological principles. His early death prevented him from satisfying the extensive requests for a Biblically oriented theology. His chief works were: *Glaubensgnade und Glaubenslicht nach dem hl. Thomas* (Rome 1933), *The Doctrine of Spiritual Perfection* (St. Louis 1938), *Anselm von Canterbury* (Munich 1937), the incomplete *Manuale theologiae dogmaticae* (Freiburg 1939–41), and ''Theologia kerygmatica,'' *Angelicum* 17 (1940) 337–351.

[A. ROTH]

STONE, JAMES KENT

Theologian, Passionist missionary; b. Boston, Mass., Nov. 10, 1840; d. San Mateo, Calif., Oct. 4, 1921. His father, Dr. John Seely Stone, was a prominent churchman and dean of the Episcopal Theological School, Cambridge, Mass.; his mother, Mary Kent, was the daughter of jurist James Kent, chancellor of New York and author of the standard *Commentaries on American Law.* James interrupted his undergraduate studies at Harvard University to spend a year at Göttingen University, Germany. After graduating from Harvard in 1861, he served as a lieutenant in the Union Army and saw action in the Battle of Antietam. He was appointed in 1863 as an instructor in Latin at Kenyon College, Gambier, Ohio. He also pursued studies in theology, and in June 1866 was ordained an Episcopalian minister. The following year he was made president of the college. Having become involved in a controversy between ''high-church'' and ''low-church'' theologians over the dogma of the Incarnation, he resigned from Kenyon and accepted the presidency of Hobart College, Geneva, N.Y., in 1868.

The sudden death of his young wife, Cornelia Fay, whom he had married in 1863, and his long study of Catholic teachings disposed Stone for conversion. He entered the Church Dec. 8, 1869, joined the Paulists, and was ordained on Dec. 21, 1872. He was, however, attracted to a more austere monastic life and transferred to the Congregation of the Passion, taking his vows Aug. 11, 1878, and receiving the name Fidelis of the Cross. For the next 44 years he held office as professor, superior, master of novices, provincial, and consultor. Much of his life after 1881 was given to the South American apostolate, erecting Passionist houses and preaching missions in Chile, Argentina, and Brazil. He returned to the U.S. in 1889 to speak at the opening of the Catholic University of America, Washington, D.C., and again from 1894 to 1897, for a preaching tour. He was stationed in the U.S. from 1899 to 1908, when he was named provincial for South America. After he was barred from Mexico by the Carranza regime in 1914, he labored in Cuba and Texas before his retirement in 1917. Despite his reputation as a theologian and preacher, Stone's only publications were an apologia, *The Invitation Heeded* (1870), which had 17 editions, and its autobiographical sequel, *An Awakening and What Followed* (1920), written at the end of his life.

Bibliography: W. G. and H. G. SMITH, *Fidelis of the Cross (James Kent Stone)* (New York 1926). K. BURTON, *No Shadow of Turning* (New York 1944). R. J. PURCELL, *Dictionary of American Biography,* ed. A. JOHNSON and D. MALONE (New York 1928–36) 18:76–77.

[C. J. YUHAUS]

STONE, JOHN, ST.

English Augustinian friar, martyr; b. date, place unknown; hanged, drawn, and quartered at Canterbury, probably Dec. 27, 1539. Nothing is known of Stone's early life. In the absence of evidence to the contrary it may be assumed that he became an Augustinian friar at the house of the order founded in 1318 at Canterbury, where it is not unlikely that he was born; two namesakes of his were monks of Christ Church in the same city. In April 1534 Henry VIII, as a step preparatory to the suppression of the friaries, appointed Thomas Cromwell's friend, George Browne, prior provincial of the Augustinians, with a commission to visit all houses of the order and obtain the individual acknowledgment of every inmate to the validity of Henry's marriage to Anne Boleyn and to his headship over the Church in England. The following November the Act of Supremacy made it treason to deny this. Shortly afterward the Treason Act extended the penalty to all who might ''maliciously'' desire to deprive the king of his title of supremacy. Somehow Stone avoided taking the oath, but when in December 1538 Richard Ingworth, suffragan bishop of Dover and agent of Cromwell, took possession of the Augustinian friary at Canterbury in the name of the king, he forced the community to sign a deed of surrender that contained an explicit acknowledgment of the king's supremacy. Stone refused to sign. On December 15 Ingworth, in a letter to Cromwell, wrote of Stone that ''he still held and still wills to die for it that the king may not be head of the Church of England, but it must be a spiritual father appointed by God.'' Stone stood alone among the Augustinians in his resistance; the same day he was taken to London, where in the Tower he was interviewed by Cromwell, who, perhaps hoping that Stone would die in prison, did not hasten to bring him to trial but waited until the following December, when Stone was returned to Canterbury and there sentenced to be hanged, drawn, and quartered. The historian Nicholas Harpsfield wrote that ''before [his execution] having poured forth prayers in prison to God and fasted continuously for three days, he heard a voice, though he saw no one, which addressed him by name and bade him be of good heart and not to hesitate to suffer death with constancy for the belief which he professed.'' The delay in his execution was due to the preparations at Canterbury for the arrival of Anne of Cleves, Henry VIII's fourth bride. Stone was executed either shortly before or on the day of Anne's arrival at Canterbury (Dec. 29, 1539). He was beatified by Leo XIII on Dec. 9, 1886, and canonized by Paul VI on Oct. 25, 1970 as one of the Forty Martyrs of England and Wales.

Feast: May 12; October 25 (Feast of the 40 Martyrs of England and Wales); May 4 (Feast of the English Martyrs in England).

A woman bends over a sacred stone at the entrance to Hazrati Shah-i-Zinda (Shrine of the Living King), Samarkand, Uzbekistan. (©Francesco Venturi/CORBIS)

See Also: ENGLAND, SCOTLAND, AND WALES, MARTYRS OF.

Bibliography: B. HACKETT, *Blessed John Stone* (Postulation Pamphlet; London 1961). A. BUTLER, *The Lives of the Saints,* rev. ed. H. THURSTON and D. ATTWATER, 4 v. (New York 1956) 2:292. R. CHALLONER, *Memoirs of Missionary Priests,* ed. J. H. POLLEN (rev. ed. London 1924; repr. Farnborough 1969).

[G. FITZHERBERT]

STONES, SACRED

From prehistoric times stones have played an important role, and on a worldwide basis, in religion and magic. Stones symbolize power and duration, and have served many purposes as instruments. However, they were usually venerated as symbols of, or as dwelling places of, divinity rather than as objects of worship in themselves. Stones were set up as funeral monuments to give peace and protection to the soul or spirit of the dead. In the case of violent death, the monument was often erected on the spot where the victim was killed. This monument, the dwelling place of the dead, could either help the living or prevent the spirit of the dead from harming him.

In many cultures, certain stones, according to their form, were venerated as symbols of the male generative power and of female fecundity. Meteorites, as "stones fallen from heaven," were especially important in this respect, as manifestations of divinity, bringers of rain, and efficacious sources of fertility for the women who touched them.

Naturally stones were most appropriate for altars, and either as altars or as sacred objects were usually associated with sacred trees and springs in holy places. The notion that a certain stone deserved special veneration as the *omphalos,* or navel of the universe, is common not only among the early Greeks but among other peoples as well.

Bibliography: J. GOETZ, *Religionswissenschaftlichens Wörterbuch,* ed. F. KÖNIG (Freiburg 1956) 835–836. K. GALLING, *Die Religion in Geschichte und Gegenwart,* 7 v. (3d ed. Tübingen 1957–65) 6:348–350. E. S. HARTLAND et al., J. HASTINGS, ed., *Encyclopedia of Religion & Ethics,* 13 v. (Edinburgh 1908–27) 11:864–877. M. ELIADE, *Patterns in Comparative Religion,* tr. R. SHEED (New York 1958) 216–238, an excellent treatment with copious bibliog.

[M. R. P. MCGUIRE]

STONES, SACRED (IN THE BIBLE)

As among many other ancient peoples, so among the Israelites, too, sacred stones played an important cultic role. The Old Testament uses the term *maṣṣēbâ* (literally, an erected thing) to designate such a sacred stone, usually in the form of an uninscribed stele. Sacred stones were regarded approvingly in early Old Testament texts; later they were forbidden because of their association with idolatrous Canaanite rites.

Sacred stones were used during the ceremonies of covenant ratification at Sinai (Ex 24.4). Moses erected 12 *maṣṣebôt* as a sign of the acceptance of Yahweh's covenant by the 12 Israelite tribes. A stone became sacred also by reason of its association with a theophany. After his vision at Bethel, Jacob took the stone on which he had slept, anointed it with oil, and set it up to commemorate his vision (Gn 28.18). When Bethel later became a popular sanctuary, anointing the stone became part of the rites celebrated there (Gn 35.14).

The *maṣṣebôt,* however, were not always directly related to divinity. Sometimes they were used as funeral monuments (Gn 35.20) or as steles commemorating an agreement, like that of Jacob and Laban (Gn 31.44–54). The erection of stones was a natural method of delimiting the sacred territory around a sanctuary; eventually the stones themselves came to be regarded as sacred. For example, after crossing the Jordan into Palestine, Joshua ordered the erection of 12 stones from the Jordan as a memorial (Jos 4.19). These stones may have been used to enclose the area around the Galgal (Gilgal) sanctuary, for in Hebrew, *gilgal* means circle of stones.

In monarchic Israel the *maṣṣebôt* took on evil connotations because of their relation to Canaanite fertility cults at the high places. The characteristic appurtenances of these sites were the sacred stone pillar (*maṣṣēbâ*) and the sacred wooden pole (*'ašērâ*). Sacred pillars have been found in Palestinian archeological sites, such as Mageddo, Beth-San, and Sichem. The pillar, sometimes in phallic form, was linked to the pagan male deity; the pole, with the female. Such associations made the use of the *maṣṣebôt* repugnant to orthodox Yahwism. Numerous texts forbade the erection of *maṣṣebôt* (e.g., Lv 26.1; Dt 16.22) and ordered their destruction (Ez 23.24; 34.13; Dt 7.5; 12.3). The diatribes of the Prophets against idolatrous worship also implied the condemnation of *maṣṣebôt— see* Mi 5.10–13; Hos 4.13; 10.1–2; Jer 2.20.

On the Ka'bah, the sacred stone of the Muslims, *see* MECCA; ḤAJJ; ISLAM.

Bibliography: R. DE VAUX, *Ancient Israel, Its Life and Institutions,* tr. J. MCHUGH (New York 1961) 285–287, 290, 303, 314, 414.

[A. SUELZER]

STORER, FRANZ

Missionary; b. Jan. 17, 1617, Konstantz, Germany; d. after 1658. He entered the Jesuits in 1635 and was professor of mathematics and Hebrew at Ingolstadt. Storer traveled with Father Henry Roth through Asia Minor and Persia to Goa, and served as missionary in India. In 1656 he traveled from Mokka (the Red Sea) to Gondar, the capital of Abyssinia. Anti-Catholic persecution handicapped his ministry, but he did serve as physician at the imperial court. His last letter known to be extant is of 1658; after this date there is no more trace of him. The letters were published by C. Beccari, *Rerum aethiopicarum scriptores* (v. 13 Rome 1913).

Bibliography: R. STREIT and J. DINDINGER, *Biblioteca missionum* (Freiburg 1916–) 16:458–459, 893, 940.

[J. WICKI]

STORY, JOHN, BL.

Lay martyr; b. Salisbury, England, 1504; d. hanged, drawn, and quartered at Tyburn (London), June 1, 1571. Story earned his doctorate in law from Oxford and became known as "the most noted civilian and canonist of his time." The year he married, he also became president of Broadgates Hall (now Pembroke College), Oxford (1537–39). He practiced as a barrister, then became a member of Parliament (1547–49) for Hindon, Wiltshire.

On Jan. 24, 1548, he was imprisoned for opposing the Bill of Uniformity. Upon his release (March 2, 1549), he fled England with his family to Louvain. Upon the accession of the Catholic Queen Mary, he returned to England (August 1553), and became chancellor to Bishop Bonner. He again sat in Parliament for Wiltshire (1553–60) until he was imprisoned at the Fleet (May 20, 1560) for incurring the displeasure of Queen ELIZABETH I for his outspoken opposition to the Bill of Supremacy. He escaped, but was caught and committed to the Marshalsea (1563).

Once again he escaped and managed to reach Antwerp, where he renounced his English citizenship in favor of Spain and took a customs position in Flanders under the duke of Alva. In August 1570, he was kidnapped at Bergen-op-Zoon, taken to London, and imprisoned in the Tower. There he courageously endured torture. He was indicted at Westminster, May 26, 1571, for conspiring to assassinate the queen and aiding the Northern rebels while at Antwerp. He declared his innocence and that, as a Spanish subject, the court had no jurisdiction over him. Undaunted by that fact, his judges condemned Story on May 27.

He was beatified by Pope Leo XIII on Dec. 9, 1886.

Feast of the English Martyrs: May 4 (England).

See Also: ENGLAND, SCOTLAND, AND WALES, MARTYRS OF.

Bibliography: B. CAMM, ed., *Lives of the English Martyrs,* (New York 1905), II, 14. R. CHALLONER, *Memoirs of Missionary Priests,* ed. J. H. POLLEN (rev. ed. London 1924; repr. Farnborough 1969). J. H. POLLEN, *Acts of English Martyrs* (London 1891).

[K. I. RABENSTEIN]

STOWE MISSAL

Manuscript; Dublin, Royal Irish Academy D.II.3. This manuscript is dated the end of the 8th century. The Missal is important because of the pre-Gregorian material it contains. It is Roman in style and content but has affinities with the Mozarabic rite. It has preserved a diaconal litany that was said after the sermon, before the Offertory, and some notable early readings in the Canon of the Mass. The Stowe Missal is by no means the oldest extant manuscript of the British Isles. That honor belongs to the so-called Irish palimpsest Sacramentary that dates probably from 640–685. The most interesting aspect of the Irish palimpsest Sacramentary is the primitive non-Roman institution narrative that forms a part of the Mass of Christmas.

See Also: CELTIC RITE.

Bibliography: Critical Editions: *The Stowe Missal,* 2 v., ed. G. F. WARNER (London: 1906, 1915). *Das Irische Palimpsestsakramentar im CLM 14429 der Staatsbibliotek München,* eds. A. DOLD and L. EIZENHÖFER (Beuron 1964). **Studies:** B. MACCARTHY, "On the Stowe Missal," *Royal Irish Academy Transactions* 27 (1886) 135–268. T. F. O'RAHILLY, "The History of the Stowe Missal," *Eriu* 10 (1926) 95–109. For overview and further bibliographies, see: C. VOGEL, *Medieval Liturgy: An Introduction to Sources* (Washington, D.C. 1986); and E. PALAZZO, *A History of Liturgical Books: From the Beginning to the Thirteenth Century* (Collegeville, Minn. 1998).

[H. ASHWORTH/EDS.]

STRACHAN, JOHN

First Anglican bishop of Toronto, Canada; b. Aberdeen, Scotland, April 12, 1788; d. Toronto, Nov. 6, 1867. He attended the University of St. Andrews and received his M.A. from the University of Aberdeen (1796). After immigrating to Canada in 1799, he studied theology privately and was ordained in 1803. He served first as rector at Cornwall (1803), then successively as rector (1812), archdeacon (1825), and first bishop of the newly created Diocese of Toronto (1839). As an advocate of Protestant church unity, Strachan envisioned a united Canadian church in communion with the See of Canterbury; he consistently proposed an ecclesiastical establishment in Canada similar to England's. He also fought for church control of all education and resigned in protest as first president of King's College (later University of Toronto) when the state reorganized it. He then founded the University of Trinity College, Toronto. Among his better known writings is his *Journal of Visitation,* a detailed account of his pastoral travels, valuable for its descriptions of Canadian frontier life.

Bibliography: A. N. BETHUNE, *Memoir of the Rt. Rev. John Strachan* (Toronto 1870). T. B. ROBERTON, *The Fighting Bishop* (Ottawa 1926).

[T. HORGAN]

STRADELLA, ALESSANDRO

Baroque composer of opera and sacred music; b. Montefestino, Italy, 1642; d. Genoa, Feb. 25?, 1682.

Much obscurity and legend surround the events of his life. He seems to have studied at Modena and at various times to have been active in Rome, Venice, Turin, and Genoa; but he did not hold a continuous position in any one place. An amorous liaison in Venice resulted (1677) in his being wounded by order of the woman's family. He later was assassinated in Genoa; the causes of his murder are uncertain. As a musician he was industrious and serious, and may rightly be considered the most progressive dramatic composer of the mid-17th century, the link between the Venetian school of CAVALLI and the Neapolitan school of A. SCARLATTI. Among his compositions are operas and oratorios, numerous chamber and church sonatas, serenatas, and instrumental sonatas that resemble the early concerto in form and style. His oratorio *La Forza dell'amor paterno* (Genoa 1678; new ed. 1931) is considered his masterpiece by A. Gentili, who discovered the score in Turin in 1927.

Bibliography: O. H. JANDER, *A Catalogue of the Manuscripts of Compositions by Alessandro Stradella Found in European and American Libraries* (Wellesley, Mass. 1960). A. GENTILI, *Alessandro Stradella* (Turin 1936). R. GIAZOTTO, *Vita di A. Stradella,* 2 v. (Milan 1962). G. RONCAGLIA, *Le composizioni strumentali di A. Stradella* (Milan 1942), repr. from *Estratto dalla Rivista musicale italiana* 46.1 (1942) 57–88. S. GODDARD *Grove's Dictionary of Music and Musicians*, ed. E. BLOM 9 v. (5th ed. London 1954) 8:106–107. M. F. BUKOFZER, *Music in the Baroque Era* (New York 1947). A. J. B. HUTCHINGS, *The Baroque Concerto* (New York 1961). O. H. JANDER, *Die Musik in Geschichte und Gegenwart*, ed. F. BLUME (Kassel-Basel 1949–) 12: 1418–22. K. A. CHAIKIN, ''The Solo Cantatas of Alessandro Stradella (1644–1682)'' (Ph.D. diss. Stanford University, 1975). H. DIETZ, ''Musikalische Struktur und Architektur im Werke Alessandro Stradellas,'' *Analecta Musicologica* 9 (1970), 78–93. C. GIANTURCO, ''Alessandro Stradella'' in *The New Grove Dictionary of Music and Musicians*, vol. 18, ed. S. SADIE (New York 1980) 188–193; *Alessandro Stradella (1639–1682), His Life and Music* (Oxford 1994). O. HUGHES JANDER, ''The Minor Dramatic Works of Alessandro Stradella'' (Ph.D. diss. Harvard University, 1963). D. M. RANDEL, ed., *The Harvard Biographical Dictionary of Music* (Cambridge 1996) 874. N. SLONIMSKY, ed., *Baker's Biographical Dictionary of Musicians*, Eighth Edition (New York 1992) 1798.

[F. J. GUENTNER]

STRADIVARI, ANTONIO

Foremost among violin makers; b. Cremona?, Italy, 1644?; d. Cremona, Dec. 18, 1737. A violin dated 1666 contains his name and states that he was a student of Nicola Amati. Later he inscribed his age on the violin labels, and from this the year 1644 is generally accepted as the date of his birth. He went through several more or less well-defined phases in the construction of his violins: 1666 to 1684, years when the Amati influence was predominant; 1684 to 1700, years of progress toward perfection through experiments in form, length, and balance. In 1690 there first appeared the ''Long Strad,'' which was capable of producing more forceful tones. The finest instruments date from 1700; the average length of the instruments of this period was 14 inches, as opposed to the 14 3/16 inches of the ''Long Strad.'' He made also guitars, lutes, viols, and mandolins. With the collaboration of two of his 11 children, Francesco and Omobono, he is estimated to have produced 1,116 instruments, of which 540 authentic violins, 50 violoncellos, and 12 violas are extant. Five of the finest were given to the Library of Congress by the Gertrude Clarke Whittall Foundation and are used by the resident chamber players during their weekly public concerts.

Bibliography: W. H. HILL et al., *Antonio Stradivari* (London 1902; repr. New York 1963). E. N. DORING, *How Many Strads?* (Chicago 1945). C. BEARE, ''Antonio Stradivari'' in *The New Grove Dictionary of Music and Musicians,* ed. S. SADIE (New York 1980). G. GIANPAOLO, *La chitarra Giustiniani Antonio Stradivari (1681)*(Cremona 1998). S. POLLENS, *The Violin Forms of Antonio Stradivari* (London 1992). D. M. RANDEL, ed., *The Harvard Biographical Dictionary of Music* (Cambridge 1996). N. SLONIMSKY, ed., *Baker's Biographical Dictionary of Musicians* (New York 1992).

[F. J. GUENTNER]

STRAHOV, MONASTERY OF

PREMONSTRATENSIAN abbey in the city of Prague known as the Czech Mt. Sion. It was founded possibly before 1140 by Bp. Henry Zdík of Olomouc with canons perhaps from the Holy Land, and was confirmed in 1140 by Ladislaus II. Strahov was settled in 1143 by Abbot Gezo (1143–60) with monks from Steinfeld, near Cologne, and in turn founded Litomysl (1145), Hebdow (1149), Louka (1190), TEPL (1193) and Zabrdovice (1200) and directed the convent of Doksany (founded 1143). In 1294 Strahov founded four houses in Hungary. Its school was known for learning by 1150. In 1341 Abbot Peter II Vojslai received the *pontificalia.* The monastery was burned in 1258 and destroyed by HUSSITES in 1420, and languished until Abbot Johann LOHELIUS (1586–1612) from Tepl revived it. Strahov in turn revived several other abbeys: Nova Říše in 1596; Allerheiligen in 1601; Zeliv and Milevsko in 1622; Geras in 1627; Jerichow in 1628; and Gottesgnaden, Ilfeld, and Magdeburg in 1629. In 1627 the reformer Abbot Caspar of Questenberg translated the relics of St. NORBERT from Magdeburg to Strahov. In 1691 Abbot Vitus II Seipel reintroduced the order into Hungary. Strahov had many famous members in the 17th and 18th centuries. Emperor JOSEPH II reduced the abbey to a parish church. After the suppression of PRÉMONTRÉ in 1789, Austrian and Czech abbeys formed a circary under Strahov in 1859. The

Czech character of the abbey assured it of favor under the Czechoslovak Republic after 1918, but the Communists suppressed it in 1950. The last abbot, Bohulaus II Jarolímek (1942–58) died in prison. The excellent library of 110,000 volumes, 2,000 MSS, and 1,200 incunabula and the art gallery of 1,100 paintings became part of the state museum.

Bibliography: N. BACKMUND, *Monasticon Praemonstratense,* 3 v. (Straubing 1949–56). L. NEMEC, *Church and State in Czechoslovakia* (New York 1955). A. HUBER, *Lexikon für Theologie und Kirche,* ed. J. HOFER and K. RAHNER, 10 v. (2d, new ed. Freiburg 1957–65) 9:1102–03.

[L. NEMEC]

STRAMBI, VINCENZO MARIA, ST.

Bishop, preacher; b. Civitavecchia, Italy, Jan. 1, 1745; d. Rome, Jan. 1, 1824. At the seminary in Bagnoregio, he became rector while still a deacon, and was ordained in 1767. He entered the PASSIONISTS (1768), and became one of Italy's leading pulpit orators, renowned as a preacher of missions, and also a professor of sacred eloquence. Named bishop of Macerata and Tolentino (1801), he retained unaltered his life of prayer, poverty, and penance. He devoted himself particularly to the sick, aged, and orphaned, and promoted the spiritual rejuvenation of his diocese by capable administration, good example, and concern for the progress of his clergy in learning and sanctity. He personally supervised his seminary, screened candidates, conducted examinations, and gave retreats. His organization of clergy and laity to act as instructors made him a precursor of the modern catechetical movement. Rather than take the oath of fealty demanded by NAPOLEON I but disapproved by PIUS VII, he suffered exile and imprisonment in Novara and Milan (1808–14). In 1823 LEO XII allowed him to resign his see, but brought him to Rome as his adviser. During a critical illness of the pope, Strambi offered to God his own life in exchange for the pontiff's return to health. Leo XII recovered, but Strambi died shortly after. He was beatified April 26, 1925, and canonized June 11, 1950.

Feast: Sept. 25.

Bibliography: S. DELL'ADDOLORATA, *S. Vincenzo Maria Strambi* (Rome 1949). A. BUTLER, *The Lives of the Saints*, rev. ed. H. THURSTON and D. ATTWATER, 4v. (New York 1956) 3:644–645.

[C. J. YUHAUS]

STRANSHAM, EDWARD, BL.

Priest martyr; sometimes given as Transham; *alias* Barber; b. *c.* 1554, Oxford, England; hanged, drawn, and

Antonio Stradivari. (Archive Photos)

quartered at Tyburn (London), Jan. 21, 1586. After receiving his B.A. from St. John's College, Oxford, Edward studied for the priesthood at Douai (1577) and Rheims (1578–80) with a brief interruption due to illness. Six months after his ordination in Soissons, France (December 1580), he was sent to the English mission with Bl. Nicholas WOODFEN. Two years later he returned to Rheims accompanied by 12 converts from Oxford. There his tuberculosis worsened. He spent about 18 months recuperating in Paris before returning to London, where he was arrested in Bishopgate Street Without while saying Mass (July 17, 1585). He was tried and condemned for being an illegal priest. He was beatified by Pius XI on Dec. 15, 1929.

Feast of the English Martyrs: May 4 (England).

See Also: ENGLAND, SCOTLAND, AND WALES, MARTYRS OF.

Bibliography: R. CHALLONER, *Memoirs of Missionary Priests,* ed. J. H. POLLEN (rev. ed. London 1924; repr. Farnborough 1969). J. H. POLLEN, *Acts of English Martyrs* (London 1891).

[K. I. RABENSTEIN]

Strahov Monastery library, Prague.

STRAUSS, DAVID FRIEDRICH

Protestant theologian of the Tübingen school, the principal representative of the mythological interpretation of the Gospels through the application of the dialectic of G. W. F. HEGEL; b. Ludwigsburg, Germany, Jan. 29, 1808; d. there, Feb. 8, 1874. During his early years, Strauss embraced Hegelianism and made it the basis of all his subsequent speculative thought. His monumental two-volume work *Das Leben Jesu kritisch bearbeitet* (Tübingen 1835–36) profoundly affected Gospel scholarship of the following century. Beginning with Hegel's rationalistic a priori philosophic tenets and prejudices against the supernatural, Strauss extended the mythological theory of W. de Wette to the Gospels by asking whether it is possible to accept their testimony as historical. Strauss answered in the negative. The Christ of faith exists as the product of a credulous myth–creating community. The Evangelical myth falls into two types: (1) pure myth arising from the messianic portrait of the OT and from the application of this portrait to Jesus; (2) historical myth consisting of highly mythologized stories embodying the popular aspirations of the community. Christianity is not destroyed in its internal essence, according to Strauss, by the Evangelical myth since all religion is based on ideas, not facts. These extreme views provoked a reaction that produced the liberal school (e.g., J. E. RENAN, A. von HARNACK) that vainly attempted to recover the historical Jesus and ended in finding only an ideal, dynamic personality. In turn, there arose the eschatological school (still under the influence of *Leben Jesu*) that forever lost hope of recovering the historical Jesus (e.g., A. Schweitzer). Other important works of Strauss were: *Der alte und neue Glaube* (Leipzig 1872) and *Der Christus des glaubens und der Jesus der Geschichte* (Berlin 1865) mit *Nachwort* (1873).

Bibliography: F. MUSSNER, *Lexikon für Theologie und Kirche* 2 9:1108–09. E. SCHOTT, *Die Religion in Geschichte und Gegenwart* 3 6:416–417.

[J. E. LAZUR]

STRAVINSKY, IGOR FEODOROVICH

Russian composer; b. Oranienbaum, near St. Petersburg, Russia, June 17, 1882; d. New York, April 6, 1971. Although Igor's father, Feodor Stravinsky, was a bass in the St. Petersburg Imperial Opera, Igor was permitted to devote himself to music only after four desultory years as a law student. He worked under the tutelage of Nicolai Rimsky Korsakov from 1903 until the latter's death in 1908. Stravinsky's friendship and collaboration with the choreographer Sergei Diaghilev led to the three ballets that established the composer's reputation: *The Firebird* (1910), *Petrushka* (1911), and *The Rite of Spring* (1913).

He left Russia for good in 1914, and spent the period between the world wars in Switzerland and then France, a time corresponding to Stravinsky's so-called ''neoclassical'' period, during which he generally employed smaller performing forces (although this was in part due to economic necessity, especially during the World War I years) and compositional techniques that seemed conservative compared to the revolutionary *Rite of Spring.* He subsequently settled in Hollywood and became a U.S. citizen. With an output in excess of 100 works, he dominated the world of music for more than half a century. His own musical language never ceased to grow and develop; all centuries provided him with musical and literary source matter, which he assimilated into his own technique. His adoption of serialism in the 1950s was no conversion to doctrinaire academic avant-gardism, but the absorbtion of the technique within his own musical language.

Stravinsky wrote a number of sacred compositions, or pieces on religious subjects, several of which rank among his major works. His earliest sacred piece, the *Pater Noster* (1926) for unaccompanied chorus, is a simple setting in the style of Russian liturgical chant. It has been published with both the Latin and Old Slavonic texts. With it belong his *Credo* (1932) and *Ave Maria* (1934). Among his most popular works is the *Symphony of Psalms* (1930), a three-movement setting of Latin Psalm texts for chorus and orchestra. In addition, he wrote *Mass* (1948), *Canticum Sacrum* (1956), *Threni* (1958), *A Sermon, A Narrative, and A Prayer* (1962), *Noah and the Flood* (1962), *Abraham and Isaac* (1964), and *Requiem Canticles* (1966). Stravinsky, a lifelong Russian Orthodox, insisted that a composer of sacred music must himself be a believer. He had a special regard for the great composers of sacred music, from the Renaissance masters to Bach. Of his own works, only the *Mass* was written with the possibility of liturgical use in mind, but all are profound and significant contributions to the sacred repertory. Latin intrigued him; in addition to the sacred works, he used a Latin libretto in *Oedipus Rex* (1927), a translation by Jean Daniélou fron Jean Cocteau's original. He was decorated by Pope Paul VI in 1965.

In 1947 Stravinsky took on as his musical assistant the young American conductor Robert Craft. Craft also became his mentor's amanuensis; six volumes of dialogues between the two appeared, the major source for Stravinsky's thoughts and presumably in the composer's own words. The accuracy of some of these dialogues, especially the later ones, has occasionally been questioned, and Lillian Libman, Stravinsky's concert manager, has published an account of the composer's last years that differs on some points with Craft, while shedding some light on the latter's personality. Future research may clarify these matters, especially when Stravinsky's papers become available to scholars.

Bibliography: I. STRAVINSKY, *Stravinsky: An Autobiography* (New York 1936); *The Poetics of Music* (Cambridge, Mass. 1948). I. STRAVINSKY and R. CRAFT, *Conversations with Igor Stravinsky* (Garden City, N.Y. 1959); *Memories and Commentaries* (Garden City, N.Y. 1960); *Expositions and Developments* (Garden City, N.Y. 1962); *Dialogues and a Diary* (Garden City, N.Y. 1963); *Themes and Episodes* (New York 1966); *Retrospectives and Conclusions* (New York 1969). R. CRAFT, *Stravinsky: Chronicle of a Friendship* (New York 1972). L. LIBMAN, *And Music at the Close: Stravinsky's Last Years* (New York 1972). E. W. WHITE, *Stravinsky: The Composer and His Works* (Berkely, Calif. 1966). R. VLAD, *Stravinsky* (2d ed. New York 1967). B. BORETZ and E. T. CONE, *Perspectives on Stravinsky* (New York 1972). E. H. BUXBAUM, "Stravinsky, Tempo, and *Le Sacre,*" *Journal of the Conductors' Guild* 13 (1992) 32–39. J. KNJAZEVA, "Jacques Samuel Handschin – Igor Stravinskij: Eine noch unbekannte Seite des Dialogs," *Die Musikforschung* 52 (1999) 207–211. A. SOPART, "Der Einfluss des russischen Theaters um 1910 auf die dramaturgische Technik von Stravinskijs *Renard,*" *Die Musikforschung* 53 (2000) 60–68. P. TRUMAN, "An Aspect of Stravinsky's Russianism: Ritual," *Revue Belge de Musicologie* 46 (1992) 225–246.

Vincenzo Maria Strambi.

[A. DOHERTY]

STREIT, KARL

Founder of ecclesiastical cartography; b. Dittersbäckel, Aug. 5, 1874; d. Maria Enzersdorf, Austria, May 31, 1935. He was associated with William Schmidt, SVD, in producing and promoting the magazine *Anthropos.* In 1930 he founded the Cartographical Institute to study geographical and statistical aspects of the Catholic Church. For a great portion of his active life he lived at Steyl, Holland. He published his *Katholische Missionsatlas* in 1906. This is a mission atlas, with a statistical supplement. It gives detailed statistics of every mission area and mission-sending society, population, baptized Catholics, priests, brothers, sisters, catechists, schools, etc. His second well-known work was *Atlas Hierarchicus* (1913, 2nd ed. 1929). This is a survey of all the Catholic dioceses of the world with their divisions, indexing 20,000 cities and mission stations. It has 36 large-scale maps. This monumental work has been translated into five languages. It is a most complete collection of statistics concerning the Catholic Church, with historical and

Igor Feodorovich Stravinsky. (Archive Photos)

ethnological notices. He also wrote: *Sprachfamilien und Sprachenkreise der Erde* (1926). Streit was a member of the Society of the Divine Word.

Bibliography: J. DINDINGER, *Lexikon für Theologie und Kirche,* ed. J. HOFER and K. RAHNER, 10 v. (2nd ed. Freiburg 1957–65) 9:862–863.

[J. A. MCCOY]

STREIT, ROBERT

Pioneer in Catholic mission science; b. Fraustadt (Posen), Germany, Oct. 27, 1875; d. Frankfurt am Main, July 31, 1930. In 1895 he entered the Oblates of Mary Immaculate. After ordination he became editor of the mission periodical of the Oblates. In this position he conceived the idea of starting a movement for the scientific investigation of the missionary apostolate. His first important treatises on missiology were *Die Theologisch-wissenschaftliche Missionskunde* (1909) and *Die Missions in Exegese und Patrologie* (1910). At the German Catholic Congress held at Breslau in 1909, there was established a missionary commission of which he was a member. When this commission met in Berlin in 1910, the idea for a scientific missionary periodical was raised. Through Streit's influence, Joseph SCHMIDLIN founded the first scientific mission journal in German.

Streit's principal work was the *Bibliotheca Missionum,* a bibliography of all literature concerning the missions. Documents, letters, pamphlets, and the like are described in detail with scholarly references and editorial comment. One volume appeared each year. Seven had appeared before Streit's death in 1930. After his death, J. Dindinger, who had collaborated with him and who succeeded him as prefect of the Pontifical Library of Missions, continued the work. There were more than 20 volumes in the series by 1964.

At the request of Pope Pius XI, Streit produced *Die Weltmission der Katholischen Kirche, Zahlen und Zeichen* (1927), a study of the Vatican Mission Exposition of 1925. This amazing array of facts about every mission area in the world was published in five languages. The English version, *Catholic Missions in Figures and Symbols,* was published in 1927. Streit's other important works are *Opfer der Hottentotten* (1907); *Katholische deutsche missionsliteratur* (1925), a history of German Catholic mission literature from 1800 to 1925, with a bibliography; and *Missionspredigten* (3 v. 1914–1918).

Bibliography: R. STREIT and J. DINDINGER, *Bibliotheca missionum* (Freiburg 1916–) 6:IX–XIII. J. PIETSCH, *P. Robert Streit, Pionier der Missionswissenschaft* (Beckenried 1952).

[J. A. MCCOY]

STREPA, JAMES, BL.

Franciscan missionary and archbishop; b. Poland, *c.* 1350; d. *c.* 1409–11. The facts of Strepa's early life, other than his noble Polish parentage, are uncertain. As a Franciscan he preached to the pagan Lithuanians, Walachians, and dissident Russians, was guardian of the friary in Lvóv, and was vicar of the Societas pro Christo Peregrinantium, a band of itinerant Dominicans and Franciscans founded to make contact with the Orthodox Russians. When appointed to the see of Halicz (1391) in Galicia, he built churches in remote areas and secured pastors from Poland; set up religious houses, schools, and hospitals; and governed his large and difficult diocese with prudence and zeal. PIUS VI confirmed his cult in 1791; in 1795 his remains were transferred from Halicz to the cathedral of Lvóv, which had become (1414) the metropolitan see.

Feast: Oct. 21 (formerly June 1).

Bibliography: O. HALECKI, *Collectanea Theologica* 8 (1937) 477–532. LÉON DE CLARY, *Lives of the Saints and Blessed of the Three Orders of St. Francis,* 4 v. (Taunton, Eng. 1885–87). A. BUTLER, *The Lives of the Saints*, rev. ed. H. THURSTON and D. ATTWATER (New York 1956) 4:172. G. FUSSENEGGER, *Lexikon für Theologie und Kirche*, ed. J. HOFER and K. RAHNER (Freiberg 1957–65) 5:847–848.

[M. F. LAUGHLIN]

STRITCH, SAMUEL ALPHONSUS

Cardinal archbishop of Chicago; b. Nashville, Tenn., Aug. 17, 1887; d. Rome, May 27, 1958. He was the seventh of eight children of Garrett Stritch, a native of Ireland, and of Katherine (Malley) Stritch, born in America of Irish parents. After graduating at 14 from high school, he attended St. Gregory's Minor Seminary in Cincinnati for two years, the American College in Rome for six, and the Urban College of Propaganda, where he received the doctorate in philosophy (1906) and theology (1910). He was ordained, under canonical age, at St. John Lateran, Rome, by Cardinal Pietro Respighi on May 21, 1910. On returning to the U.S., he was assistant pastor first of Assumption Church in Nashville, then of St. Patrick's in Memphis. He was appointed secretary to Bp. Thomas S. Byrne in 1916 and chancellor of the diocese two years later; he was also superintendent of schools and rector of the Nashville cathedral.

On Aug. 10, 1921, he was named bishop of Toledo, succeeding Joseph Schrembs, first bishop of the 11-year-old see, and was consecrated on November 30 by Abp. Henry Moeller of Cincinnati. The youngest member of the American episcopate, he proved to be a capable administrator and educator. In 1924 he opened the first diocesan teachers' college in the country and in 1928, Central High School, which he staffed by bringing together members of several religious orders, a novel idea at that time. In 1926 he initiated construction of Holy Rosary Cathedral; 24 other churches were built in Toledo during his tenure. After the death of Milwaukee's fourth archbishop, Sebastian MESSMER, Stritch was promoted to that metropolitan see on Aug. 26, 1930. Faced with problems arising from the Great Depression, he acted energetically to expand Catholic charitable undertakings. He also inaugurated a comprehensive program of activities for young people of the archdiocese and introduced the Catholic Youth Organization. To strengthen the Catholic press, he negotiated a merger of the old diocesan weekly with a privately owned newspaper to form the *Catholic Herald Citizen* (*see* MILWAUKEE, ARCHDIOCESE OF).

Ordinary of Chicago. On Dec. 27, 1939, Stritch was transferred to the metropolitan see of Chicago, the most populous diocese in the U.S., as successor to Cardinal George MUNDELEIN. He was installed the following March 7 by Apostolic Delegate Abp. A. G. Cicognani. One of his first actions was to reorganize the archdiocesan weekly, the *New World,* and to increase its circulation. He instituted the Confraternity of Christian Doctrine and directed the program of religious guidance known as the Parish High School of Religion. He promoted the postwar surge of diocesan construction and supported the Back-of-the-Yards Council and the Cardinal's Conservation Committee, both designed to improve urban living conditions. Within the framework of Catholic charities he introduced specialized services for the deaf and blind, a guidance center for children, and the Peter Maurin house for alcoholics. In 1951 he realized an ambition he had cherished for 30 years when he opened Cardinal Stritch Retreat House for diocesan priests on St. Mary of the Lake Seminary grounds. He appointed an archdiocesan commission on sacred music in 1953 and four years later set up an archdiocesan office for radio and television. From his youth he was a friend to minority groups; he founded a unit of the Catholic Interracial Council and fostered integration. To help solve problems posed by the influx of Mexicans and Puerto Ricans, he established the Cardinal's Committee for the Spanish-Speaking in Chicago. In 1950 he received the Leo XIII Award of the Shell School of Social Studies for "outstanding devotion to the cause of Christian social education," and six years later an award "for bettering race relations and the cause of brotherhood" from the George Washington Carver Memorial Institute (*see* CHICAGO, ARCHDIOCESE OF).

National Leadership. In 1935 Stritch was elected to the administrative board of the National Catholic Welfare Conference and was chairman of its Department of Catholic Action Study until 1939 when he was elected chairman of the board. After five successive terms on the board, he was ineligible in 1940, but was reelected the following year and was vice chairman and treasurer for four years, and chairman again in 1945. While archbishop of Milwaukee he had become vice chancellor of the Catholic Church Extension Society, and as archbishop of Chicago he was chancellor. In 1941 he was elected chairman of the American Board of Catholic Missions. He was also on the board of trustees of the Catholic University of America and of the North American College in Rome. He collaborated with Abp. John T. MCNICHOLAS of Cincinnati to organize the Catholic Commission on Intellectual and Cultural Affairs to foster emphasis on the liberal disciplines in Catholic scholarship. He was president of the board of the National Catholic Community Service (a United Service Organization agency) during World War II and visited USO clubs in many cities. After helping to create War Relief Services in 1943, he was chairman of its governing committee for a year following the war.

As chairman of the American Bishops' Special Committee on the Pope's Peace Plan, he strove to enforce Pius XII's principles, advocating justice and charity toward defeated nations. He placed great hope in the United Nations Organization, favored the Marshall Plan and other forms of foreign aid, and urged the American people to accept their responsibilities in international affairs. He supported the Catholic League for Religious Assistance to Poland and in 1948 received an award from the Friends of American Relief for Poland. He shared in founding the American Commission on Italian Migration and in 1957 was presented with Italy's highest decoration, the Grand Cross of Merit, for his efforts. In 1955 he recommended a more liberal U.S. policy in the Refugee Relief Program and relaxation of immigration restrictions, while using the facilities of his see for resettlement of displaced persons. He was awarded the Pro-Hungaria Medal of the Knights of Malta for his work with Hungarian refugees in Chicago after the 1956 revolt. He censured anti-Semitism and decried persecution of the Jews. Non-Catholics held him in esteem, and in 1958 he was awarded the Unitas Medal of St. Procopius Abbey, Lisle, Illinois, in recognition of his efforts "for the extension and preservation of Catholic unity." Shortly before the 1954 Evanston assembly of the World Council of Churches, he issued a pastoral letter (June 29, 1954) in which he forbade the clergy and laity to participate in such conferences. Alert to the dangers of Marxism and of the welfare state, he warned against extreme encroachments of government in social assistance and was opposed to the substitution of entirely public agencies for partly private charities. He considered secularism the gravest threat to the nation and frequently inveighed against a materialistic concept of life. At the same time he was zealous for social justice; he was known as a friend of organized labor and was called by labor leader George Meany "a champion of the working man."

Cardinal. In the first secret consistory held after World War II, Pius XII named him a cardinal priest along with three other U.S. archbishops and bestowed the red hat on him on Feb. 18, 1946. At his request St. Agnes Outside the Walls was designated his titular church. In 1958 he was asked by Pius XII to accept the office of pro-prefect of the Congregation for the Propagation of the Faith, replacing the aged and nearly blind Cardinal Pietro Fumasoni-Biondi. He was the first U.S. citizen to be called to head a congregation of the Roman Curia, and the third non-Italian named to the Propaganda since its founding in 1622. Despite his consuming solicitude for home and foreign missions, it was admittedly "with a heavy heart" that he left Chicago. While en route to Rome, occlusion of the major artery of his right arm necessitated amputation upon his arrival. During recovery from surgery, he suffered a stroke that brought death within a week. After obsequies in Rome his body was flown back to Chicago and interred on June 3d in Mount Carmel Cemetery, Hillside, Illinois.

Short of stature, portly, and always slightly Southern in manner, Stritch impressed all who knew him with his kindliness, piety, and intelligence. He was an eloquent orator who could extemporize by drawing on the large store of knowledge that he kept replenished by constant reading and discussion. Although a gifted administrator, he disliked being confined to a desk and accepted numerous invitations to public functions. While he had a penetrating mind that quickly grasped all aspects of a problem, he was often slow to arrive at a decision. His fatherly, gracious concern for each individual won him the loyalty of his priests and people.

Bibliography: M. C. BUEHRLE, *The Cardinal Stritch Story* (Milwaukee 1959).

[R. F. TRISCO]

STROBL, ANDREAS

Missionary; b. Schwandorf (Bavaria), Jan. 23, 1703; d. Agra, March 3, 1758. He entered the Society of Jesus in 1721. At the invitation of the Sovereign of Jaipur, Jai Singh II, he traveled with Father Anthony Gabelsberger to India in 1736. He worked in 1737 at Goa and in 1740 at Jaipur, where he learned the Persian language while serving as the sovereign's teacher. After the death of the prince in 1743 he took up missionary work at Agra, moved in 1745 to Delhi, and in 1749 founded the mission of Narwar (Gwalior). In 1753 he was appointed visitor of the missions in the Mogul Empire, where he remained until his death.

Bibliography: A. STROBL, Letters in *Der neue Welt-Bott,* ed. J. STÖCKLEIN and F. KELLER, 5 v. (Augsburg-Graz-Vienna 1726–61) 5, nos. 641–650, 806–807. E. D. MACLAGAN, *The Jesuits and the Great Mogul* (London 1932). R. STREIT and J. DINDINGER, *Biblioteca missionum,* (Freiburg 1916–) 6:95, 564.

[J. WICKI]

STROSSMAYER, JOSIP JURAJ

Bishop and promoter of the union of Churches; b. Osijek, Croatia, Feb. 4, 1815; d. Djakovo, April 8, 1905. After completing his secondary education at the Gymnasium in Osijek, Strossmayer attended seminaries in Djakovo and Budapest, obtained his Ph.D. (1834), and was ordained (1838). After receiving a doctorate in theology at the Augustineum, Vienna, he taught at Djakovo seminary, then became chaplain at the imperial court in Vienna (1847–49), and bishop of Djakovo (November 1849). As an ardent patriot, he strove for a federation of the Hapsburg empire and resisted the absolutist policies of Vienna and Budapest. He was a member of the Croatian Diet (1860–73). Constantly he worked for the autonomy and unification of all Croatian lands. As a leading promoter of religion and culture, he spent vast sums building the beautiful cathedral of Djakovo, and erecting seminaries, convents, secondary schools, and libraries. He was instrumental in establishing a new university, the South Slav Academy, and a national gallery of art in Zagreb. At VATICAN COUNCIL I he was a leading opponent of a definition of papal infallibility, but later accepted the conciliar decision. His views stemmed partly from a desire to gain the conversion of Russia, toward which he worked with the Russian philosopher Vladimir SOLOV'EV. His friendship with the Russians won a rebuke from Emperor Francis Joseph (1888), but the pope upheld him. Hoping for a reunion of the Orthodox and Catholics, he contacted Serbs, Montenegrins, and Bulgarians. The Croatians still honor him as a great religious and national leader whose motto was ''All for the Faith and Fatherland!''

Bibliography: A. KADIĆ ''Vladimir Sloviev and Bishop Strossmayer,'' *The American Slavic and East European Review* 20 (1961) 163–188. R. SCHUTZ, *Dictionnaire de théologie catholique,* ed. A. VACANT, 15 v. (Paris 1903–50; Tables générales 1951–) 14.2:2630–35. B. HURST, ''The Founder of Modern Croatia,'' *Catholic World* 81 (1905) 773–789.

[G. J. PRPIC]

STRUCTURALISM

Structuralism refers to a movement that became fashionable in French intellectual circles and with the French public in the mid-1960s. Structuralism, or structural analysis, is above all a method applicable to a wide range of disciplines (but it should not be confused with E. B. Titchener's structuralist psychology). Although not its founder, the anthropologist Claude Lévi-Strauss is generally considered the most notable exponent of the movement.

Structuralism and the Notion of Structure. Structuralism, as the term indicates, has to do with structures, but the word structure was used long before anybody dreamed of calling himself a structuralist.

Originally ''structure,'' a derivative of the Latin *struere,* to build, designated the manner or act of building, constructing, or organizing; something built or constructed such as a building or dam; the interrelationship of parts in an organized whole. The building metaphor was extended to include the structure of rocks, plants and animals, chemical structures, the structure of a sentence or of society, and even the way in which the elements of consciousness were organized.

Hence, structure means what an internal analysis of a given whole reveals, viz, elements, relationships among elements, and the arrangement or system of these relations. Structures thus defined are observable empirical entities, and structure, organization, arrangement, and ordering are all synonymous. In this sense nearly everything possesses a structure, and we do not need structuralism to tell us so.

Traditional notions of structure involve eliminating differences and emphasizing similarities. Structuralism proper begins when we admit that differing wholes can be brought together not despite but by virtue of the differences we then seek to order.

Structuralism involves a plurality of organized wholes, but this does not indicate a structure proper to each whole, nor an ideal structure of a plurality of wholes. The structure is essentially the syntax of transformations that enables us to pass from one variant to another.

The contemporary structuralist sees structure as the means of making different wholes appear as variants of one another. In each organized and systematized whole there exists a more restricted configuration that defines the whole both in its singularity and its comparability, since it is the variability of this configuration that situates it among other wholes defined according to the same procedure [*Pouillon, Les Temps Modernes* (Nov. 1966) *passim*]. This configuration is not a privileged part of the organization, nor its skeleton, as would be implied in the traditional definition of structure. The structure is both a reality (this configuration discovered by analysis) and an intellectual tool (the law of its variability). This duality is expressed by the French adjectives *structurel* and *structural.* A relation is *structurel* when considered in its determining role at the heart of a given organization; *structural* when considered susceptible of being realized in several different and equally determining ways in several organizations. *Structurel* refers to structure as reality; *structural* refers to structure as syntax.

Piaget summarizes the progress of this study of structures in mathematics, logic, physics, biology, psychology, linguistics, the social sciences, and philosophy in a single unifying definition of structure as ''a self-regulating system of transformations'' (p. 36).

Origins and Development. Thus defined, the first-known structure to be studied was the 19th-century mathematical discovery of ''group.'' But most structuralists recognize Ferdinand de Saussure as the founding father of the method. If so, structuralism can be dated from 1916 when Saussure's students published their lecture notes under the title of *Cours de linguistique générale.*

Saussure makes a number of important distinctions. First of all, a particular language (*langue*) should not be confused with human speech in general (*langage*). ''Language . . . is a self-contained whole and a principle of classification'' (p. 9). Language should be considered as a system of functions on one level (*langue*) as opposed to the shifting actualizations of speech on another (*parole,* utterance). A linguistic sign is the whole resulting from the association of the signifier (*significant,* the sound image) and the signified (*signifié,* the concept or meaning). Linguistics must study these arbitrary signs not in a historical or comparative way (diachronically) but in a single language at a single moment in time (synchronically). Finally, a linguistic system (Saussure did not use the word ''structure'') ''is fundamentally one of contrasts, distinctions and ultimately oppositions, since the elements of language never exist in isolation but always in relation to one another'' (Lane, p. 28).

Roman Jakobson later improved Saussure's linguistic model and influenced Lévi-Strauss's application of it to ethnological data. In 1945 their fruitful collaboration led to Lévi-Strauss's article on structural analysis in linguistics and anthropology (*Word* 1.2, ch. 2 of *Structural Anthropology*). Through an analysis of phenomena such as kinship (*Elementary Structures of Kinship*) and ritual and myth (*Totemism, The Raw and the Cooked, Ashes and Honey, Table Manners*), Lévi-Strauss discerned a certain number of recurring types of mental operations, a structure or hidden order of human behavior. Social organization and myth were studied as languages having syntactical and grammatical characteristics; they were also thought to result from a limited number of inherent categories according to Lévi-Strauss.

Such conclusions regarding human nature coupled with Sartre's attack in the *Critique de la raison dialectique* and Lévi-Strauss's counterattack in *The Savage Mind* sparked popular interest in structuralism. Thus the 1960s witnessed a flurry of publications by or about structuralists in France. *Esprit* devoted its May 1963 issue to a treatment of *La pensée sauvage* and a roundtable discussion involving Lévi-Strauss, Paul Ricoeur, Mikel Dufrenne, Jean Cuisenier, and others. The Nov. 1966 issue of *Les Temps Modernes* (a review under Sartre's direction) dealt with the problems of structuralism in mathematics, history, Marx, and literary criticism as well as an attempt at definition. The May 1967 issue of *Esprit* (p. 771) declared structuralism officially ''à la mode'' and named its ''four'' musketeers: Lévi-Strauss, Jacques Lacan (whose psychoanalytical *Ecrits* show the unconscious to be structured like a language), Louis Althusser (whose *Lire le Capital* and *Pour Marx* translate Marx into structuralist terms), and Michel Foucault (whose *Les Mots et Les Choses* credits structuralism not only with the death of the human sciences but also with the death of man). Equally notable were the publication of *Yale French Studies* 36–37 (*see* Ehrmann) and the proceedings (*see* Macksey) of an international symposium held in Baltimore in Oct. 1966 where structuralist participants included the literary critic Roland Barthes, the philosopher Jacques Derrida, the genetic structuralist Lucien Goldmann, and Jacques Lacan. The decade also saw the extension of structural analysis to art, cinema, the James Bond novels, Corneille's ''Cinna,'' Racine, and Genesis.

But the popularity of the movement has not prevented a growing controversy centered on Lévi-Strauss and also involving the very definition of structuralism. Edmund Leach, a British anthropologist and one-time disciple of Lévi-Strauss, has criticized him for insufficient field experience and an overreliance on Jakobson's linguistic model, largely outdated by Chomsky's work. On the other hand, it would seem that Lévi-Strauss's generative and transformational rules for myth analysis parallel Chomsky's generative and transformational grammars. Jean Paul Sartre and Henri Lefevre, among others, have criticized the philosophical and ideological implications of Lévi-Strauss's work. Consequently, most discussions of structuralism define it under the double heading of ''method and theory'' or the triple classification of method, philosophical transposition, and ideological use.

Structuralism as Method. Although the structuralist methodology varies somewhat in its application to different disciplines, there are certain features common to all structuralists. They include the attempt to reduce a multiplicity of expressions to one language or the view that all human social phenomena can be treated as languages; the emphasis on wholes or totalities and the logical priority of the whole over its parts; the search for structures below or behind empirical data; a belief in the innate structuring capacity of man which limits the possible number of available structures; the concern with synchronic structures whose relations reduce to binary oppositions; and the rejection of causal laws for laws of transformation.

Philosophical and Religious Implications. When the structuralist methodology is transposed into philosophy, we are confronted with a world view and an interpretation of human nature that competes not only with existentialism but also with Marxism and Christianity. The scientific hypotheses of man's innate structuring capacity and the limited number of mental categories echoes Kant and implies the primacy of essence (a single human nature) over existence (freedom). Sartre sees the structuralist emphasis on synchrony as ''bourgeoisie's last stand against Marxism, an attempt to set up a closed inert system where order is privileged at the expense of change'' [*New York Times Magazine* (Jan. 28, 1968) 40]. Some misinterpret structures to be Platonic ideas. Others charge structuralism with atomism, formulaism, positivism, scientism, static relativism, and antihumanism—charges vigorously refuted for the most part.

Günther Schiwy views the movement as both useful and challenging to the contemporary Christian. The *structurel-structural* distinction might remind the believer to avoid the temptation of identifying his world view or ''model'' with reality itself (pp. 23–24). Roland Barthes' description of literary criticism as metalanguage can also apply to religious discourse (p. 72) and dogmatic formulations (p. 81). Finally, ''the structuralistic thesis that the individual is embedded in a certain system of relationships and must be understood in terms of this system is a challenge to Christianity to reflect anew on its own original catholicity'' (p. 47).

Bibliography: R. BARTHES, *Elements of Semiology* (London 1964). J. A. BOON, *From Symbolism to Structuralism: Lévi-Strauss in a Literary Tradition* (New York 1972). R. T. and F. M. DEGEORGE, eds., *The Structuralists: From Marx to Lévi-Strauss* (New York 1972). J. EHRMANN, ed., *Structuralism* (New York 1970). M. FOUCAULT, *The Order of Things: An Archeology of the Human Sciences* (New York 1971). H. GARDNER, *The Quest For Mind: Piaget, Lévi-Strauss, and the Structuralist Movement* (New York 1973). M. LANE, ed., *Introduction to Structuralism: A Reader* (New York 1970). E. R. LEACH, *Genesis as Myth and Other Essays* (New York 1969). C. LÉVI-STRAUSS, *The Savage Mind* (Chicago 1966); *Structural Anthropology* (New York 1963). R. MACKSEY and E. DONATO, eds., *The Languages of Criticism and the Sciences of Man: The Structuralist Controversy* (Baltimore 1970). J. PIAGET, *Structuralism* (New York 1970). F. DE SAUSSURE, *Course in General Linguistics* (New York 1959). G. SCHIWY, *Structuralism and Christianity* (Pittsburgh 1971). F. WAHL, ed., *Qu'est-ce que le structuralisme?* (Paris 1968).

[J. M. MILLER]

STRUMI, ABBEY OF

Former Vallombrosan monastery in the Casentino district, two miles from Poppi, Italy, in the province and Diocese of Arezzo. It was founded at Strumi in the 10th century by Count Teugrimo of the Guidi family and was dedicated to San Fedele. About the end of the 11th century the original BENEDICTINES were replaced by VALLOMBROSANS, whose first abbot was Andrew of Strumi, and the eighth, John of Strumi, who was made antipope under the name Callistus III by Emperor FREDERICK BARBAROSSA. The old abbey was abandoned by the monks towards the end of the 12th century as struggles between GUELFS AND GHIBELLINES rendered its position hazardous; a new one was erected at Poppi, and likewise dedicated to San Fedele. Monastic life flourished there until the 15th century when the abbey was granted in COMMENDATION to the bishop of Florence. It was restored to Vallombrosan control in 1510; it was suppressed in 1809. The church of San Fedele still exists at Poppi; its valuable paintings include one on wood that is a Madonna of the 13th-century Tuscan school. Of the original abbey at Strumi there remain only a few traces of the foundations and the choir of the church, now used as a farmhouse.

Bibliography: *Chartularium abbatiae Strumensis* (Poppi, Biblioteca comunale, cod. 36, 13th cent. MS). *Chartularium Puppiense* (Florence Archivio di Stato, conventi soppressi, v.227, 18th cent. MS). P. F. KEHR, *Regesta Pontificum Romanorum. Italia Pontifia,* 8 v. (Berlin 1906–35) 3:169–170. G. DOMENICI, ''La badia di S. Fedele di Strumi presso Poppi,'' *Rivista storica benedettina* 10 (1915) 72–92. L. H. COTTINEAU, *Répertoire topobibliographique des abbayes et prieurés,* 2 v. (Mâcon 1935–39) 2:2337–38, 3097.

[S. OLIVIERI]

STUART, HENRY BENEDICT MARIA CLEMENT

Cardinal, Jacobite Duke of York, last legitimate heir of the royal house of Stuart; b. Rome, March 6, 1725; d. Frascati, Italy, July 13, 1807. He was the second son of James Stuart (the Old Pretender) and grandson of JAMES II OF ENGLAND [*See* JACOBITES (ENGLISH)]. When his elder brother Charles (the Young Pretender) invaded Scotland (1745), Henry was placed in command of an army at Dunkirk that never left French soil. He returned to Rome (1746), was created cardinal by Benedict XIV (1747), and was ordained a priest (1748). His ecclesiastical vocation was genuine, but it caused a rift with his brother and displeased Stuart sympathizers in England. It enabled him to maintain his family's cause at the Vatican. At his father's death he tried to have Clement XIII recognize his brother Charles as king of Great Britain. When Charles died (1788), Henry had medals struck with Latin inscriptions: ''Henry IX, King of Great Britain; not by the will of men but by the grace of God.'' In the Roman Curia he held important posts, including that of archpriest of St. Peter's (1751), vice-chancellor of the Roman Church (1763), and dean of the College of Cardinals (1803). He was also titular archbishop of Corinth (1758) and bishop of Frascati (1761). When the army of the French Revolution reached Rome, it sacked his palace. The cardinal lost his fortune and was forced to flee to Naples and then to Venice (1800). King George III was advised of the cardinal's plight and offered him a pension. In gratitude the cardinal of York, as he was called, willed the crown jewels of James II to the Prince of Wales (George IV). He was known as a constant patron of the arts and benefactor of the poor.

Bibliography: B. FOTHERGILL, *The Cardinal King* (London 1958). *The Dictionary of National Biography from the Earliest Times to 1900,* 63 v. (London 1885–1900) 9:561–562.

[B. FOTHERGILL]

STUART, JANET ERSKINE

Educator and spiritual writer, superior general of the Society of the Sacred Heart; b. Cottesmore, Rutland, England, Nov. 11, 1857; d. Roehampton, Oct. 21, 1914. Janet's father, Andrew Stuart, was the Anglican rector in Cottesmore. At the age of 21 she sought instruction in the Catholic faith from Peter Gallwey, SJ, and was received into the Church March 6, 1879. Three years later she entered the Society of the Sacred Heart, Roehampton, London. From early in her noviceship and for a period of nearly three decades, she served first as secretary to, and then as associate of, the mother superior, Mabel Digby. Immediately after her profession, Feb. 12, 1889, Mother Stuart assumed the duties of submistress of novices, and in 1892 became novice mistress, a post she held at intervals throughout the next 19 years. She rose to the position of superior of the community in Roehampton in 1894, and then to superior vicar of England, and on Aug. 27, 1911, she was made superior general of the society. She directed the society's administration from the motherhouse, which was at Ixelles, Brussels, until 1914. During her tenure of office she traveled extensively, visiting convents of her spiritual daughters around the world from Europe to Egypt, Australia, Japan, Canada, and the U.S. The German occupation of Brussels in August 1914 caused her to leave Ixelles for Roehampton. Her published works include: *The Society of the Sacred Heart* (1915); *Highways and By-Ways in the Spiritual Life* (1923); *Poems* (1924); *Prayer in Faith* (1936); and *The Education of Catholic Girls* (first published in 1912 and reprinted in 1964). She is best known to the public, however, through M. Monahan's *Life and Letters of Janet Erskine Stuart* (London 1946), the definitive biography in which her common sense and deep spiritual insight are revealed.

Bibliography: *Tablet* 124 (Oct. 31, 1914) 594–595. *America* 97 (April 20, 1957) 71–72.

[M. FITZGIBBON]

STUDENT VOLUNTEER MOVEMENT

A foreign mission organization that originated at a conference held July 1886 at Mt. Hermon, MA. The conference, called by the Young Men's Christian Association, with the Protestant evangelist Dwight Lyman MOODY as leader, was attended by 251 men from 89 colleges and universities in the United States and Canada. When the conference closed, 100 of the group, led by Robert P. Wilder, of Princeton University, N.J., had decided to become foreign missionaries. In the ensuing year Wilder and a companion toured colleges, universities, and theological seminaries, seeking to enlist others. An organization was formed, with John Raleigh MOTT, who had been at Mt. Hermon, as chairman of the executive committee. For 33 years Mott directed the movement. Students became members of the movement by signing the declaration: "it is my purpose, if God permits, to become a foreign missionary." Their watch-word, "the evangelization of the world in this generation," expressed their belief that all Christians had the duty of making the Gospel known to their contemporaries throughout the world. Student Volunteer "bands" were organized at many colleges, universities, and theological seminaries throughout the United States Wilder carried the message also to the British Isles and the Continent of Europe, and similar movements arose in several countries. Beginning in 1891, quadrennial conventions, as they were called, were held to present foreign mission work to successive generations of students. In 1959 the Student Volunteer Movement became the Commission on World Mission of the National Student Christian Federation, a division of the NATIONAL COUNCIL OF THE CHURCHES OF CHRIST in the U.S.A.

[K. S. LATOURETTE]

STUDION (STUDIU)

Studion (Studiu) was the most important monastery of Byzantine Constantinople. It was situated in the western part of the city not far from the Golden Gates. The Roman consul, Studios, after whom it was named, founded it in 463 and dedicated its church to St. John the Baptist. In 798 the monks from the newly founded (781) monastery of Saccoudion, called *Acoemetae* (sleepless), being devoted to perpetual prayer, took refuge from the Saracens in Studion and, under the leadership of the Abbot Plato and his nephew St. THEODORE THE STUDITE, quickly raised its membership to 700.

Theodore blended the basic cenobitic rule of St. BASIL with Palestinian spirituality and liturgical practice to produce a model of cenobitic monastic rule that found its way to MOUNT ATHOS; from there into Russia through ALEXIUS THE STUDITE (1025–43); and thence into the whole of Slav monasticism. A fragment of this *typikon,* or rule, has been preserved [*Patrologia Graeca,* ed. J. P. MIGNE, 161 v. (Paris 1857–66) 99:1703–20]. Theodore also established schools of manuscript copyists famous for their calligraphy. From the 8th to the 11th centuries the monks of Studion produced a wealth of liturgical hymns that are still used throughout the BYZANTINE LITURGY. Studion during the rule of the Iconoclast (*see* ICONOCLASM) emperors stood as the unflinching protector of icon veneration. Many of the monks laid down their lives for this. NICETAS STETHATOS, a famous Studite monk of the 11th century, became known for his polemical and theological writings against the Latins.

In 1204 the monastery was destroyed by the Crusaders but was rebuilt in 1290, only to be destroyed again during the sack of the city by the Turks in 1453. Today the only parts of the monastery still standing are remnants of the Church of St. John the Baptist, which form part of a Turkish mosque.

Bibliography: E. MARIN, *De Studio coenobio* (Paris 1897). E. SPULER, *Die Religion in Geschichte und Gegenwart*³ 7 v. (Tübingen 1957–65) 6:430. H. G. BECK, *Kirche und theologische Literatur im byzantinischen Reich* (Munich 1959) 127, 209, 491–496.

[G. A. MALONEY]

STUDIOUSNESS, VIRTUE OF

The virtue of studiousness is a disposition to diligence in the pursuit of knowledge. The attainment of knowledge is indispensable to the human good. Therefore its pursuit can be a matter of moral obligation. It is primarily from this point of view that studiousness is considered a virtue. Its function is to regulate the desire for knowledge, so that this is neither inadequate to enable one to meet the requirements of duty or of moral fitness, nor so exaggerated as to exceed the bounds of reason.

An individual has an obligation to acquire the knowledge necessary for leading a good moral life, for eternal salvation, and for the performance of the duties of his state. In the concrete the obligations of individuals vary considerably in accordance with their differences of intellectual ability, opportunity for learning, and other circumstances. There is a large area of knowledge that for most people could be considered optional. There is no particular obligation to know, yet the knowledge may be useful or reasonably desired for any number of reasons. In this matter it is fitting that one should follow his tastes and inclinations, provided this involves no neglect of duty nor unseemly waste of energy on the trivial at the expense of what has greater human value.

Like other moral virtues that consist in moderation, studiousness has to deal with conflicting tendencies on the part of the student. The commonest tendency that needs moderation is an inclination against study because of the tediousness and the difficulty involved. To yield to this inclination in a situation in which there is an obligation to learn involves a certain amount of sinful negligence.

Normally, the spirit of inquiry is laudable in life. However, there are circumstances in which its indulgence would be unreasonable. For example, it would be imprudent to pursue unnecessary knowledge to the neglect of duty, or to study with a vehemence that constituted a notable hazard to health. Moralists usually classify immoderation by way of excess in this matter under the heading of CURIOSITY, the commonest instances being the unjust invasion of the privacy of others, or the illegitimate investigation of secrets.

Because studiousness consists in the moderation of an impulse, St. Thomas considers it to be a potential part of the virtue of temperance (*Summa theologiae,* 2a2ae, 166.2).

Bibliography: THOMAS AQUINAS, *Summa theologiae,* 2a2ae, 166. F. L. B. CUNNINGHAM, ed., *The Christian Life* (Dubuque 1959) 737–739.

[T. C. KANE]

STUHLMUELLER, CARROLL

Biblical scholar, author, editor; b. Hamilton, OH, April 2, 1923; d. Chicago, IL, Feb. 21, 1994. The son of William and Alma (Huesing) Stuhlmueller, Carroll Stuhlmueller was baptized William Ignatius, taking the name Carroll when he entered the novitiate of the Congregation of the Passion in 1942. After his ordination to the priesthood in 1950, he began graduate studies first at the Catholic University of America in Washington, D.C., and later at the Pontifical Biblical Institute in Rome. He completed work for a doctorate in sacred scripture (S.S.D.) in 1968, publishing his dissertation under the title *Creative Redemption in Deutero-Isaiah* (1969). He held faculty positions at the Passionist seminary in Louisville, Kentucky, (1954–65); St. Meinrad Seminary (1965–66); and the Catholic Theological Union at Chicago from 1968 until his death. Stuhlmueller was in great demand as a lecturer, retreat-master, and teacher. In addition to summer courses at several Catholic colleges and universities in the United States, he lectured in South Africa, the Philippines, Latin America, South Korea, and Japan and was visiting professor at the *École Biblique* in Jerusalem during the winter and spring of 1973. He served as president of the Catholic Biblical Association (1978–79) and was a member of the Faith and Order Commission (1970–73) and of the Roman Catholic/ Southern Baptist dialogue. Stuhlmueller was the only male on the steering committee for the first Women's Ordination Conference, at which he spoke.

Acclaimed as a writer and editor, Stuhlmueller was the author of 23 books and scores of articles published in both professional and popular journals. He contributed entries to the *New Catholic Encyclopedia*, the *Jerome Biblical Commentary*, and numerous other reference works. He was a member of the editorial board of the *Catholic Biblical Quarterly* (1970–73) and *Journal of Biblical Literature* (1987–92). A lifelong member of the editorial board of *The Bible Today*, he served as an associate editor, general editor (1981–85), and to the time of his death as Old Testament book review editor. Stuhlmueller, a first-class scholar, had the enviable knack of popularizing the best in biblical research for the general public and inspiring in his students a lasting appreciation of the sacred text.

Bibliography: D. SENIOR, "Carroll Stuhlmueller, C.P. (1923–1994)," *The Bible Today* 32 (1994) 197–206.

[B. L. MARTHALER]

STURMI, ST.

Benedictine, founder and first abbot of FULDA; d. Fulda, Dec. 17, 779. Sturmi, of Bavarian extraction, joined (St.) BONIFACE and became his favorite disciple. Having made his novitiate at Fritzlar *ca.* 735, he was ordained *ca.* 740 and devoted himself to missionary work among the Hessians. Commissioned by Boniface, he founded the monastery of Fulda (March 12, 744) and visited the great Italian Benedictine abbeys of SUBIACO, MONTE CASSINO, and St. Andrew (747–748) to learn their organization and way of life. During his tenure of office Fulda flourished economically and as an intellectual and cultural center. A dispute with Abp. LULL OF MAINZ over Fulda's EXEMPTION was followed by Sturmi's banishment by King Pepin to the Abbey of JUMIÉGES (763), but he was permitted to return and resume work at Fulda (766). Charlemagne granted Sturmi a part of the newly won Saxon lands as missionary territory. While accompanying Charlemagne's Saxon campaign (779), he fell ill. He returned to Fulda, died, and was buried there. He was canonized (1139) at the Second Lateran Council.

Feast: Dec. 17.

Bibliography: *Vita s. Sturmi,* ed. G. H. PERTZ, *Monumenta Germaniae Historica* (Berlin 1826–), Scriptores 2:365–377. *Patrologia Latina*, ed. J. P. MIGNE, 217 v., indexes 4 v. (Paris 1878–90) 89:1257–64. F. FLASKAMP, *Westfälische Lebensbilder* 2 (1931) 1–14; *Die Religion in Geschichte und Gegenwart*, 7 v. (3d ed. Tübingen 1957–65) 6:444. W. HESSLER, "Zur Abfassungszeit von Eigils Vita Sturmi," *Hessisches Jahrbuch für Landesgeschichte* 9 (1959) 1–17.

[D. ANDREINI]

STURZO, LUIGI

Social theorist, historian, and political leader; b. Caltagirone, Sicily, Nov. 26, 1871; d. Rome, Aug. 8, 1959. After his ordination in 1894, Sturzo decided on an academic career and proceeded to Rome for advanced study. It soon became clear to him, however, that his real interest lay in the world of hard political and social facts. Fortunately, his love of learning and his passion for ideas stayed with him, increasing rather than diminishing in strength as he became more and more immersed in practical affairs. In later years he praised Giambattista VICO for divining "the intimate relationship between doing and knowing." This dedication to a life of action on the part of one given to reflection and contemplation was extraordinary, considering that Sturzo was also artistically inclined, showing exceptional talent in poetry and a marked inclination toward music.

During his years of reorientation, Leo XIII's *RERUM NOVARUM* served him as a practical handbook for social action. The teachings of the economist Giuseppe TONIOLO also proved invaluable in helping him to formulate his own ideas. From 1905 to 1920 Sturzo served as deputy mayor of Caltagirone. By 1919 he was in the national limelight as the moving spirit behind the Partito Popolare, forerunner of the Christian Democratic party. This was his master stroke in politics, for it gave Italy a democratic mass party of Catholic orientation. Moreover, by refusing to make religion a divisive factor in politics, the Popular Party paved the way for a normal development of political life between the extremes of clericalism and anticlericalism. Unfortunately, fascism proved too strong for it, for reasons which Sturzo treats in *Italy and Fascism* (New York 1927). Historians, awaiting archival evidence, attribute Sturzo's resignation from party leadership in 1923 to pressure from the Vatican. By 1926, when the party was dissolved by royal decree, Sturzo had been living in exile for two years. His prodigious effort to liberate democratic forces among the Catholics of Italy seemed to have come to nought, but he had laid the groundwork for the eventual triumph of Christian Democracy. It was the Christian Democratic party founded by Sturzo's former lieutenants that formed a democratic government after the defeat of fascism in World War II. In addition, his party served as an inspiration and model for other Christian Democratic parties in Europe and Latin America.

In 1946, after more than 20 years in England and the U.S., Sturzo returned in triumph to Italy and settled in Rome. In 1952 the President of the Republic of Italy named him a senator for life. His years of exile had proved beneficial in one way at least, for they had given him the leisure to gather in the fruits of a rich and many-sided experience and to formulate his ideas and theories on society and history.

The general orientation of Sturzo's thought can be found in *Inner Laws of Society* (New York 1944), first published in French, under the title *Essai de sociologie* (Paris 1935). This work deals with society, not as an abstraction, but as a concrete reality evolving in time. Thrown into sharp relief is the view that there can be no true doctrine of man that ignores the historico-sociological dimension, since human personality itself is in continuous evolution within a developing society. *The*

International Community and the Right of War (New York 1930) throws light not only on the historical evolution of the international community, but also on the historico-sociological roots of war. *Church and State* (New York 1939) reveals the new polarization of forces introduced into Western life and culture through the appearance of a sociological novelty: an autonomous Church. This polarization is seen to explain the dynamism of Western culture and the immense liberation of energies resulting from the confrontation of the religious and the secular, mysticism and philosophy, faith and science, contemplation and action, love and logic, experience and intellectuality. In the *True Life* (Washington, D.C. and Paterson, N.J. 1943), Sturzo shows how the universal process becomes meaningful when seen in its polarization to divinity. In such a universe the Incarnation takes on its fullest cosmic and historical significance. A new perspective on religious life is opened by showing that it is not outside but well within the cosmic and historical process. The intimate connection between love of God and creative activity is revealed.

Bibliography: *Opera omni* (Bologna 1954–). A. R. CAPONIGRI, ''Don Luigi Sturzo,'' *Review of Politics* 14 (1952) 147–165. N. S. TIMASHEFF, *The Sociology of Luigi Sturzo* (Baltimore 1962).

[R. C. POLLOCK]

STYLIANOS OF NEOCAESAREA

Ninth-century Byzantine archbishop. One of the most bitter opponents of the Patriarch PHOTIUS, Stylianos, also known as Mapas, refused to recognize Photius as legitimate patriarch even after the latter's reconciliation with Rome in the Union Council (879–880). He denied the validity of ordinations made by Photius and tried to justify his intransigent position in two letters addressed to Pope STEPHEN V that are preserved, in a biased form, in the anti-Photianist collection. After the abdication of Photius (886), Stylianos refused to accept the new patriarch Stephen, brother of the Emperor LEO VI, because he had been ordained a deacon by Photius. He abandoned the obstinately schismatic ''Little Church'' probably in 899, as is learned from a letter addressed to him by Pope JOHN IX. The compiler of the anti-Photianist collection who preserved this correspondence and interpreted it in his own way, reproached Stylianos for ''straying from the path of truth.'' Stylianos is the author of a short treatise on the Holy Trinity.

Bibliography: B. DE MONTFAUCON, *Bibliotheca Coisliniana* (Paris 1715) 88–90, Holy Trinity. J. D. MANSI, *Sacrorum Conciliorum nova et amplissima collectio* (Graz 1960–) 16:425–442, correspondence with Rome. F. DVORNIK, *The Photian Schism* (Cambridge, Eng. 1948); *The Patriarch Photius in the Light of Recent Research* (Munich 1958).

[F. DVORNIK]

STYLITES

Stylites were ANCHORITES who lived on top of pillars, hence, ''pillar saints''; a phenomenon of 5th–century penitential custom. Stylitism began in Syria and spread to Mesopotamia, Egypt, Palestine, and Greece. In the 2nd century A.D., Lucian (*De Syria Dea,* 28–29) testified to the existence at Hieropolis of a pagan ascetic who mounted a column twice a year to spend two weeks in contemplation. But the beginnings of the Christian stylite tradition can be seen in the shepherd–monks, such as James and Abraham of Cyr, who imposed upon themselves the sentence of standing in the open all their lives (Theodoret, *Hist. Relig.* 17–21). Palladius records that a Palestinian hermit inhabited a cave on the top of a mountain and never turned his face to the west for 25 years (*Hist. Laus.* 48); and one hermit is known to have spent ten years in a tub hanging in mid–air from poles (Theodoret, *Philotheus* 28).

St. Simeon Stylites the Elder took up residence atop a column in 423 to escape the crowds that followed him (*Phil.* 1464). St. Nilus, a contemporary of Simeon, was the author of two letters to another stylite, Nicandrus [*Patrologia Graeca,* ed. J. P. Migne, 161 v. (Paris 1857–66) 79; 250]. Simeon's disciple, St. Daniel Stylites, took up residence on a column near Constantinople *c.* 495, where Emperors LEO I and ZENO visited him; and St. Simeon the Younger (d. 596) lived near Antioch. A contemporary of St. Simeon the Younger, St. Alipius, having lost the use of his feet after 53 years of standing on his pillar near Adrianopolis, spent his final 14 years on the pillar lying on his side.

St. Luke the Younger (*c.* 946) lived as a hermit on Mt. Joannitsa near Corinth. Many stylites mitigated the austere practices of Simeon and Alipius by building a small hut on top of a pillar, or, as in the case of some Monophysites, by living inside a hollow column (*see* MONOPHYSITISM).

The custom of stylitism never took root in the West but lasted throughout the East into the 12th century; as late as the 19th century in Russia stylitism was practiced by Seraphim de Sarov (d. 1833) who lived three years (1,000 nights) on a rock exposed to the elements.

Bibliography: H. DELEHAYE, *Les Saints Stylites* (Paris 1962). A. J. FESTUGIÈRE, ed., *Les Moines d'Orient* (Paris 1961) v. 2. P. VAN DEN VEN, ed., *La Vie ancienne de S. Syméon le Jeune* (Brussels 1962–). T. ŠPIDLÍK, *Dictionnaire d'historie et de géographie ecclésiastiques,* ed. A. BAUDRILLART et al. (Paris 1912–) 15:766–771.

[T. ŠPIDLÍK]

SUÁREZ, FRANCISCO

Philosopher and theologian; b. Granada, Spain, Jan. 5, 1548; d. Lisbon, Portugal, Sept. 25, 1617. At the age of 14, he was sent to Salamanca to study Canon Law; there he joined the Society of Jesus in 1564. He continued his philosophical and theological studies until 1571 and was ordained in 1572. From 1571 to 1574 he taught philosophy at Ávila and Segovia; and from 1574 to 1580, theology at Ávila, Segovia, and Valladolid. He then taught for five years in the Roman College. After returning to Spain because of bad health, he continued teaching at Alcalá (1585–93) and Salamanca (1593–97). In 1597, he received the doctorate at Evora and, at the invitation of Philip II, accepted the chair of theology at the University of Coimbra, where he remained until 1615, adding to his teaching career the activities of a writer and consultant, especially in moral and canonical matters. At the request of Paul V, he wrote a tract, *De defensione fidei* (1613), against James I of England, and *De immunitate ecclesiastica contra Venetos* (1615). His piety, which was intense yet tranquil, is manifest in his writings. St. John Eudes called him a very pious theologian. On his deathbed he exclaimed, "I would never have thought it was so sweet to die."

Works. Suárez was the most prolific of modern theologians. The Venetian edition (1747) of his works filled 23 volumes, while the Parisian edition (1856) numbered 28. From the beginning the publication of his treatises (continued after his death by Balthasar Alvarez) was recognized to be an important event. There were also editions printed in Lyons, Mainz, Cologne, and Geneva. In less than a century, 18 editions of his *Disputationes metaphysicae* appeared.

Suárez's works, while they were the fruit of his teaching, were not simply his university classroom lectures in Coimbra. He undertook ample commentaries on the *Summa* of St. Thomas (1590–95, 1602–03). Later he wrote other treatises, more ample and not limited to mere commentary: *Varia opuscula theologica* (1599), *De religione* (v.1, 2 in 1608; v.3 in 1624; v.4 in 1625), *De legibus* (1612), *De gratia* (v.1, 3 in 1619; v.2 in 1651), and *De angelis* (1620). Realizing that he could not explain all theology in the same extensive manner, he began to prepare the rest in more succinct form: *De Deo uno et trino* (1606), *De fide, spe et caritate* (1621), and *De ultimo fine* (1628).

In 1859 Malou published six of his theological opuscula, and in 1948 the University of Coimbra published a two-volume work, *Conselhos y pareceres.* A few other unedited works have not been published, but considerable work was done in the 1950s and 1960s toward publication of his letters. His commentaries on Aristotle have never been found.

Doctrine. Suárez was the principal exponent of the doctrinal thought of the Jesuits, and was called Doctor Eximius by Paul V, Alexander VII, and Benedict XIV, and Pius XII. He followed the methodical tradition begun by Francisco de Vitoria in Salamanca. His knowledge of the Fathers was thorough; no contemporary writer had so firm a control of former philosophical and theological thought. Suárez's work was distinguished by the range of the subject matter, its scientific depth, and the clarity of exposition. His procedure was analytic, but it is not lacking in synthetic comprehension. He was an effectual organizer of tracts, such as those on Mariology, grace, religion, law, and metaphysics. The internal unity of his theology and philosophy resulted in an impression of novelty in his day, but a good part of Suárez's contribution has since become part of the common fund of theology. Although he deviated in no small degree from the current of Thomistic thought, the fact that he was fundamentally Thomistic was recognized by Cardinal Z. González and M. Grabmann.

The doctrines characteristic of Suárez are not only those of his own originating, but also that he accepted in substance from earlier scholastic tradition and enriched with his own insights. His essential originality appears in his method. Somewhat unreasonably, it has been branded as eclecticism because he did not adhere unconditionally to any of the existing systems. Instead, he examined them critically before proposing his own.

Theology. Suárez's doctrine on the Trinity is based on ANALOGY, the application of human concepts to the study of the divinity with the help of a nonreciprocal virtual distinction between the absolute and relative. For this reason he does not admit the universal validity (embracing all being) of the principle of triple identity (viz., *A* is *B; B* is *C;* therefore *A* is *C*) in the sense of real identity. He thus resolves (though in a negative way) the fundamental difficulty in the mystery of the Trinity.

Analogy helps him to penetrate the notions of procession, relation, and person, which are the principles of distinction in the Godhead. Notice should be taken of his elaboration on the question of the formal principle (*principium quo*) of the processions, God's knowledge and will; and of his insights regarding the intellectual generation of the Word. With regard to the procession of the Holy Spirit he does not admit that active spiration forms part of the unique spirating principle (*principium quod*). Divine relation as subsistent, and, as such, constitutive of the Divine Persons, denotes infinite perfection—not absolute, but relative (because the relation is *esse ad*), not *simpliciter simplex* but *simplex non simpliciter.* With this Suárez distinguishes in the Trinity relative perfections, existences, and subsistences formally distinct from the absolute existence and subsistence that belong to the divinity as such. He presents the Holy Spirit's indwelling as demanded by the friendship implied by sanctifying grace.

In the celebrated discussion concerning the motive of the Incarnation, the involved position of Suárez, thanks to the distinction between the order of intention and the order of execution, maintains everything positive in the opposing Thomistic and Scotist tendencies. He explains the HYPOSTATIC UNION by the lack in the humanity of Christ of the mode of SUBSISTENCE constitutive of the created person, which is replaced by the substantial union with the divine Word.

The teaching on the supernatural order and grace is, without doubt, the most fully elaborated part of Suárez's speculative theology. He vigorously defended the absolute transcendence of the order of grace as supernatural and brought greater precision to the question. To explain the existence of the supernatural, he admitted an obediential potency that is not only passive but active. For him original justice is essentially constituted by sanctifying grace, which forms the radical basis for the preternatural gifts; in his last explanation of these gifts, however, he postulates a special providence. Suárez greatly limited the effects of original sin in the transcendent order without admitting that the *peccatum naturae* in no way affected human nature considered in its essential constituents and in the providence that connaturally corresponds to it. The true nature and extent of fallen man's weakness in observing the moral law received a treatment at Suárez's hands that is yet to be surpassed; in general he initiated an increased appreciation of the moral cause.

Suárez used the criterion of pre-Tridentine theologians for establishing the entitative supernatural quality of all salutary acts, and also affirmed the supernaturalness of the formal object of every act in this order. Contrition, as the immediate disposition for justification, is produced, according to Suárez, not by the same sanctifying grace, but by a previous actual grace. The opposition between sanctifying grace and sin is one of contrariety, not contradiction, and although the expulsion of sin is demanded by grace as a secondary formal effect, their coexistence is not absolutely repugnant. Suárez defended the increase of supernatural virtues by reason of any act however remiss, as in general he accentuated the difference between supernatural and natural habits.

Suárez also developed the theology of merit. In particular, he insisted on positing commutative justice in God, analogous, of course, to the same virtue in man and based on a free divine institution. Merit for good acts essentially requires no other orientation to man's last end or other imperative of charity than that which the supernatural work brings with it.

The supernaturalness of the intuitive vision of God was expressly underscored by Suárez; he denied it to be connatural in any created nature. His thought on this vision was conditioned by his philosophical doctrine about knowledge in general. As a vital act of the creature, this vision is a formal assimilation of the divine essence, intentional but real, the terminus of an action shared by the created intellect and by God present in Himself with the light of glory as His instrument.

Although Suárez did not personally intervene in the public disputations *de Auxiliis,* throughout the controversy he was the adviser of the Jesuit theologians (*See* CONGREGATIO DE AUXILIIS). His writings are the choicest pieces of the dossier composed for the Jesuit side. The best and most definitive foundation for the basic principles of MOLINISM is due to him: liberty as active indifference, simultaneous concurrence and knowledge of future conditionals (*scientia media*), and the accentuation of the voluntary element in the grace efficacious for the predefinition of a salutary act. It has been recently made clear that Suárez did not at first accept *scientia media* nor efficacious grace explained in this manner; later he became its most ardent defender and systematized Molina's ideas in the formula *gratia congrua,* which in a general sense is the common opinion of Molinist theologians. With Robert Bellarmine he taught formal predefinition in the strictest sense together with its corollary, formal predestination to glory *ante praevisa merita,* a position that is usually called CONGRUISM.

Suárez's influence in moral theology has been considerable; Alphonsus Liguori cites him as one of his principal authors. Suárez was one of the theologians who developed the probabilist system begun by Medina. For Suárez, mortal sin consisted essentially in man's loving a creature virtually more than God. Venial sin, on the other hand, is a sort of delay on the road to our ultimate end; thus does he interpret St. Thomas's *praeter legem.* Suárez's thick volumes on the virtue of religion presented a novelty in scholastic theology, for they embraced questions pertaining to the spiritual life in all its manifestations, both interior and exterior; the religious life and states of perfection; the Society of Jesus and the Exercises of St. Ignatius. In these volumes one should note his profound analysis of contemplation and sinless moral imperfection.

Philosophy. His *Disputationes metaphysicae,* used in Protestant universities of the 17th century and recently the object of renewed interest, was the first systematic treatment of this science not based exclusively on the texts of Aristotle. This and the *De anima* are his main philosophical treatises, although other works, such as *De angelis,* contain material of interest to philosophers.

Suárez's philosophy was a personal interpretation of perennial philosophy; he drew on the common heritage of epistemological, cosmological, anthropological, and metaphysical doctrines, and at the same time developed a new concept of being as the object of metaphysics. Negatively, his system may be characterized by his rejection of the realist application of the teaching on potency and act to being, of Scotist formalism, and of nominalist conceptualism. Positively, it is based on an idea of being that sees it as having a confused unity and as enjoying nonmutual distinction from its different manifestations; it is transcendent and implied in all instances of determinate being. His teaching is based also on the analogy of intrinsic attribution, an analogy founded on the necessity of being's plenitude in Being *per essentiam,* and its derivation to all other beings by casual participation, with full dependence on Being itself. Thus the first division of being is that of Being by essence and being by total participation; from these notions are deduced their differentiating properties. Other conclusions also follow; e.g., existence is identified with essence as the latter's actuality or realization; individuation and multiplication of an essence are effected by its limitation, making recourse to matter for this individuation unnecessary. As a result, Suárez attributes proper existence to primary matter and to accidents.

Suárez's theory of physical mode is characteristic of his metaphysics; it is a purely modal entity, a simple, ultimate, and formal determination of a subjective indifference. This provides his philosophical explanation of subsistence, of union, of action as identified with passion, and of ubication. Efficient causality also holds a special place in his metaphysics; its actuation is extrinsic to the agent and as such is that of active potency, not passive. This permits him to say that liberty is the active indifference of the will without the need of determination by the practical judgment or of physical premotion.

Suárez devoted special attention to the category of relation. Real relation denotes a reality—not only in the sense of *esse in* but also in the sense of *esse ad.* It is not truly distinct from its foundation. Suárez holds the so-called transcendental relation to be a true real relation, and characterizes as relations *secundum dici* those predicates that are absolute in themselves but that cannot be expressed by man except as relations.

According to Suárez, knowledge is based on immediate intellectual apprehension of the material singular. The impressed species (not a formal, but a virtual image of the object) is not required for the knowledge of universals, but rather for the spirituality and perfect immanence of knowledge. Intellectual knowledge is a reproduction or formal likeness of the object, and knowing is itself a vital assimilation of the object. Thus the mental word is not really distinct from the act of knowing; nor is it the *medium in quo,* but rather the *medium quo.* Nevertheless, Suárez introduces a modal distinction between the producing of the word and the word itself, on the basis that every action is so distinct from its term. Universal concepts have objective reality by reason of their foundation, but their universal form consists alone in precisive and abstract knowledge.

Disputations 29 and 30 of Suárez's metaphysics, together with the tracts *de Auxiliis,* form his natural theology. God's existence is effectively proved by contingency and the principle of causality, the argument from physical motion being rejected. The divine attributes are proved by means of the notion of necessary being or of being by essence. Among the attributes one should note that divine ubiquity results from God's immensity, and is therefore not formally an action, though this is presupposed as its foundation. Suárez's attempt to reconcile God's freedom with His simplicity and immutability is interesting. Divine freedom does not imply a distinct intrinsic determination or contingency in the entity of an infinite being, but only in its termination in this or that object. Immediate divine concurrence in every creatural act is not previous to, but simultaneous with, the act itself; this is necessitated by the contingency of created being and its full and immediate domination by the first cause. The concurrence with the free action of the creature is indifferent *in actu primo,* but is identified with the action of the creature *in actu secundo.*

Law. Suárez's influence in the field of law, in general, and in international law, in particular, has recently been evaluated by the studies of J. Brown Scott, H. Rommen, and C. Barcia Trelles, and is now generally recognized. He was esteemed as a canonist, and even today, despite the changes in ecclesiastical legislation, is still consulted by canonists.

In his systematic exposition of juridical doctrine, especially the concept of law and its consequences, Suárez stresses the voluntary element, without disassociating it from the intellectual. This voluntarism has nothing to do with the irrational arbitrariness in legal matters that sometimes goes by the same name. Although he was not the originator of the theory of penal law, he explained it as imposing a true obligation according to the rational will of the legislator. He also made a profound study of the juridical value of custom.

His political theory is without doubt the most personal part of his juridical doctrine, judging from the depth with which he explained and enlarged the Christian principles concerning civil society. The end of civil society, required by its very nature, is the common good in some way disassociated from the good of the individual. The virtue proper to civil authority is general or legal justice. Tyranny is unjust because it is contrary to the common good. A perfect civil society admits connaturally lesser corporations for particular ends and must grant them those prerogatives required for their proper function. When the state intervenes it must keep in mind the principle of subsidiarity. With Robert Bellarmine, Suárez has been regarded as the representative of the traditional doctrine on the immediate origin of civil society and its authority (essentially different from the family society with its dominative authority) in the free consent of the families or members of society. This presupposes its natural necessity and its ultimate foundation in God. Civil society as a perfect society is supreme in its own order, but by reason of the supernatural end of the Church civil society is subordinate to her through her so-called indirect power, which Suárez elaborated in his polemic against James I of England.

Finally, international law claims Suárez as its founder along with De Vitoria. This is based on Suárez's doctrine on the law of peoples and his grandiose idea of the natural community of nations. The human race, though naturally divided into different nations or states, maintains a certain quasi-political and moral unity; the signs of this are the precept of love for all and the mutual needs of all the classes. Therefore, though perfectly independent, they do not cease being members of a certain community of nations. The mutual relations of these nations are governed by the *ius gentium* or law of peoples, developed by Suárez, as a law between natural law properly so-called and fully positive law. The law of peoples, intimately based on nature, is constituted by an aggregate of practices established more by tradition and custom than by exact treaties. Today it is called international law.

Bibliography: See the bibliographical indices published in 1948, the 4th centenary of Suárez birth, in the special volumes of *Razón y Fe, Estudios eclesiásticos,* and *Pensamiento. Miscelánea Comillas* 9 (1948). R. DE SCORRAILLE, *François Suárez de la Compagnie de Jésus,* 2 v. (Paris 1912–13). P. MONNOT et al., *Dictionnaire de théologie catholique*, ed. A. VACANT et al., 15 v. (Paris 1903–50; Tables Générales 1951–) 14.2:2638–2728. K. WERNER, *Franz Suárez und die Scholastik der letzten Jahrhunderte,* 2 v. (Regensburg 1889). K. SIX et al., *P. Franz Suárez: Gedankenblätter zu seinem 300 jährigen Todestag* (Innsbruck 1917). M. GRABMANN, *Mittelalterliches Geistesleben* (Munich 1926). P. DESCOQS, ''Qués-tions de métaphysique: Le Suarézisme,'' *Archives de philosophie* 2 (1924) 187–218; ''Thomisme et Suarézisme,'' *ibid.* 4 (1926) 434–544. H. ROMMEN, *Die Staatslehre des Franz Suárez* (München-Gladbach 1927). K. ESCHWEILER, ''Die Philosophie der spanischen Spätscholastik auf den deutschen Universitäten des XVIII. Jahrhunderts,'' *Gesammelte Aufsätze zur Kulturgeschichte Spaniens* 1 (1928) 251–325. J. B. SCOTT, ''Suárez and the International Community,'' *Francisco Suárez: Addresses in Commemoration of His Contribution to International Law and Politics,* ed. H. WRIGHT (Washington 1933). F. STEGMÜLLER, *Zur Gnadenlehre des jungen Suárez* (Freiburg 1933). C. BARCIA TRELLES, *Internacionalistas españoles del siglo XVI: Francisco Suárez (1546–1617)* (Valladolid 1934). C. C. RIEDL, ''Suárez and the Organization of Learning,'' *Jesuit Thinkers of the Renaissance,* ed. G. SMITH (Milwaukee 1939). H. GUTHRIE, ''The Metaphysics of Francis Suárez,'' *Thought* 16 (1941) 297–311. J. HELLIN, *La analogía del ser y el conocimiento de Dios en Suárez* (Madrid 1947). J. M. ALEJANDRO, *La gnoseología del Doctor Eximio (Suárez) y la acusación nominalista* (Comillas 1948).

[J. DALMAU]

SUAREZIANISM

A doctrine within SCHOLASTICISM inspired by the *Metaphysical Disputations* of F. SUÁREZ. Existing within the broad area of THOMISM, it has special features resulting from the personal way in which Suárez rethought earlier problems and their historical solutions. This article sketches the origins of the system, details its characteristic teachings, and concludes with a brief summary of its influence and a critique.

Historical Origins. Suarezianism originated in Spain in the time of the late humanistic and Renaissance culture of early baroque and the Counter Reformation. It presents a wealth of detail respecting the historical sources of Catholic philosophy and theology, and a positive and critical analysis of previous thinkers, from Aristotle and his commentators through the Fathers of the Church, the scholastics of the golden age, the nominalists of the 14th and 15th centuries, and the Spanish revivers of scholasticism in the 16th century. [*See* R. De Scorraille, *François Suarez* (Paris 1912); J. Iturrioz, *Estudios sobre la Metafísica de Francisco Suárez* (Madrid 1949)].

Characteristic Teaching. The main points of Suarezian doctrine may best be summarized under headings that present its teaching on analogy, essence and existence, matter and form, modes, quantity, ubication, predicamental relations, and obediential active potency.

Analogy. That beings are extremely numerous and diverse is explicable by the analogous nature of being. The primary case of being is that which exists by right of its very nature; this being is God. God is essentially existent (*ens per essentiam*), while His imitability by secondary and dependent beings (*entia per participationem*) is the explanation of the possibility of creatures, and His omnipotent free choice explains their actuality.

Formal similarity in a common note possessed, essential diversity in the manner in which the note is possessed, and the relationship of priority and dependence (*per prius—per posterius*) in the possession of the note by the diverse subjects constitute the analogousness of the notes common to God and creature and of being with respect to substance and accident. Suárez (*Disp. meta.* 2; 28) calls this the analogy of intrinsic attribution. (*See* J. Hellín, *La Analogía del Ser y el Conocimiento de Dios en Suárez,* Madrid 1947). *See* ANALOGY.

Essence and Existence. Nothing can be real by something really distinct from itself; and whatever is real is, as such, existent. The contingency of an actual creature gives man the foundation for conceiving a distinction between its essence and its existence, but the actual essence of a creature is not really distinct from the existence. To account for a creature's limited perfection, it suffices that the creature's existence be caused by God. As to the intrinsic principle of this limitation, Suárez says (*Disp. meta.* 31.13.18): ''Just as actual essence is formally limited by itself or by its own intrinsic principles, so also created existence is limited by the essence, not that the essence is a potency into which existence is received, but because existence is really nothing else but the actual essence itself.'' [*See* J. Hellín, ''Sobre el ser esencial y existencial en el ser creado,'' *Actas* of the *Congreso Internacional de Filosofía* (Barcelona 1948) 2. 519–561; ''Sobre la raíz de la limitación del ser según el P. Suárez,'' *XIII Congresso Luso-Espanhol para o Progresso das Ciências* (Lisbon 1950) 7.69–110]. *See* ESSENCE AND EXISTENCE.

Matter and Form. Corporeal substances are composed of really distinct potency and act: primary matter and substantial form. Primary matter is pure potency in the order of form, but it is not altogether pure potency in the order of being since, as real, it has its own act of existence. Absolutely speaking, God could miraculously preserve matter in existence without any form. Still, matter and form are transcendentally related to each other and have an actual exigency for each other. The actual communication of form to matter is accounted for by a substantial union, a modal being, distinct from the two components.

Suárez holds the unicity of substantial form in any given being (*Disp. meta.* 15.10); but a leading Suarezian, L. Fütscher, points out [*Akt und Potenz* (Innsbruck, 1933) 283–284] that the pluralism of substantial forms, at least as a possibility, cannot be ruled out by Suarezian principles. Suárez also denies (*Disp. meta.* 5.6.17) that primary matter is the principle of INDIVIDUATION. [*See* J. Hellín, ''Nociones de la potencia y del acto, y sus mutuas relaciones, según Suárez,'' *Las Ciencias* 17 (1952) 91–118; ''Naturaleza de la Materia Prima en Suárez,'' *La Materia: Tercera Reunián de Aproximación Filosófico-Científica* (Saragossa 1961) 2.154–182]. *See* MATTER AND FORM.

Modes. The fact that a being exists does not, of itself, account for the fact that it is something subsistent, or an accident, or an actual component of some composite being. The final determination in these respects is contributed by the mode of SUBSISTENCE, of inhesion and, in the case of components, of union. A physical MODE is really distinct with a real, minor distinction, from its subject. It is utterly inseparable from its subject, but the subject is not inseparable from it.

A supposit is a whole, made up of the mode of subsistence united to a complete nature. The nature is conceived after the manner of a form received in the supposit and inadequately distinct from it as a form is from a whole. For Suárez this inadequate distinction is real, since subsistence is really distinct from the complete nature. For some Suarezians (e.g., J. B. FRANZELIN) the distinction is only conceptual, since for them subsistence and nature are only conceptually distinct. [*See* J. Alcorta, *La Teoría de los Modos en Suárez* (Madrid 1949); Iturrioz, *op. cit.* ch. 5].

Quantity. According to Suarezians (appealing to *Disp. meta.* 40.3–4, and to *De Euch.* 48.1.20–21) the primary formal effect of QUANTITY does not give a substance actual EXTENSION, whether this is considered as actually occupying place or not; rather, it gives a material substance ''aptitudinal extension,'' or the exigency for having parts outside of parts. This aptitudinal extension has integrating parts that are actually gathered in a point of space, but have a proximate exigency for being outside one another. Christ is present in the Eucharist with actual quantity, but not with actual extension. [*See* J. Hellín, *Cosmologia, Philosophiae Scholasticae Summa* (Madrid 1955) 2.58–69]. That this view is that of Suárez himself is challenged by P. Hoenen [*Cosmologia* (4th ed. Rome 1949) 48–50].

Ubication. For Suárez, everything whatsoever has an absolute ubication, or absolute presence. In creatures this is an intrinsic modal entity existing prior to and furnishing the foundation for relative presence to or distance from another being. In God ubication, or absolute presence, is the divine immensity and is not a modal accident, but a substantial perfection, viz, the exigency of God's substance for being present, by omnipresence or relative presence, to all nondivine realities if and when such realities exist, even in the absurd hypothesis that these exist without God's creating them or operating on them. [See J. Hellín, ''Sobre la inmensidad de Dios en Suárez,'' *Estudios Eclesiásticos,* 22 (1948) 227–263.]

Predicamental Relations. Suarezians hold that predicamental relations are not really distinct from their foundation. Some of them say that this foundation is exclusively in the subject and that the term of the relation is required, not as a constituent of the relation, but as something extrinsically connoted. Other Suarezians claim that the relation is identical with the foundation adequately taken and that this is both in the subject (aptitudinally related) and in the term (whose presence actuates the aptitudinal relation of the subject). [*See* J. Iturrioz, *Metaphysica Generalis, Philosophiae Scholasticae Summa,* (Madrid 1953) 1.797–807; J. Hellín, ''Essencia de la relación predicamental según Suárez,'' *Las Ciencias,* 23 (1958) 648–696]. *See* RELATION.

Obediential Active Potency. Suárez holds that any creature can, by reason of an obediential active potency, be instrumentally elevated by God to exercise any efficient causality on another creature. There seems to be no reason why a creature cannot contribute to the production of something supernatural, e.g., grace or supernatural acts of the virtues. The Sacraments thus do not cause a mere disposition for grace but the grace itself. [*See* F. Basabe, ''Exposición Suareciana de la causa instrumental,'' *Pensamiento* 16 (1960) 189–223]. *See* INSTRUMENTAL CAUSALITY; POTENCY.

Historical Influence. Suarezianism spread very rapidly during the 17th century and became the accepted teaching of many Catholic and Protestant universities. It was studied a little by R. DESCARTES and a great deal by G. W. LEIBNIZ. B. SPINOZA, C. Wolff, G. BERKELEY and A. SCHOPENHAUER read Suárez. Giambattista VICO steeped himself in the *Disputations* to get a sense of the history of metaphysical thought.

Suarezianism is not, and never has been, the official doctrine of the Jesuits, but its influence has naturally been prominent in Jesuit philosophers and theologians, particularly among the Spanish (*see* De Scorraille, *op. cit.*). Among the more prominent Suarezians one can list, for Italy: Domenico PALMIERI, Salvatore TONGIORGI, Camillo MAZZELLA, Santo Schiffini, Nicola Monaco; for France: Théodore de Regnon, Charles Delmas, Gabriel Picard, Pedro Descoqs, and Paul Dumont; for Germany and Austria: J. B. Franzelin, Josef Müller, Christian and Tilmann PESCH, Josef Donat, and Lorenz Fütscher; for Spain and Latin America: Luis de Lossada, J. J. URRÁBURU, Jesús Iturrioz, José Alejandro, Eleuterio Elorduy, José Hellín, and Ismael Quiles.

The 1948 celebration of the quadricentennial of Suárez's birth witnessed to the interest in and lasting value of Suarezianism. (See the publications officially sponsored that year by the Spanish government; also the proceedings of the International Philosophical Congress at Barcelona, and the great number of important studies written, especially in Spain, for the leading philosophical and ecclesiastical periodicals of that year.)

Critique. For the first time and on a large scale, Suárez presented metaphysics as an organic and systematic whole and not mainly as a commentary and digression on Aristotle. He did not, however, write for beginning students of philosophy, but for theologians who needed to refresh their memories with a synthetic exposition of philosophical presuppositions. He did not mean his manner of presentation to be the pedagogical norm for the teaching of philosophy. The popularity of his work, however, quickly led others to go beyond his own intentions. They stressed a deductive and synthetic approach to all philosophy at the very outset of a pupil's philosophical education and consequently underestimated the importance of Aristotle's *Physics* as propaedeutic to metaphysics [*See* P. Descoqs, *Institutiones Metaphysicae Generalis* (Paris 1925) 1.34–35].

The stricter Thomists think that most of Suárez's original contributions and interpretations are erroneous, both as doctrines and as interpretations of St. Thomas Aquinas [*See* N. Del Prado, *De Veritate Fundamentali Philosophiae Christianae* (Fribourg 1911) 165–209; R. Garrigou-Lagrange, *Reality, a Synthesis of Thomistic Thought,* tr. P. Cummins (St. Louis 1950) 37–57]. Seeking for the underlying causes of what they consider defective in Suarezianism, certain critics focus upon the influence they believe NOMINALISM exerted upon Suárez (*See* L. Mahieu, *François Suarez, sa philosophie et les rapports qu'elle a avec sa théologie* (Paris 1921); C. Giacon, *Guglielmo di Occam* (Milan 1941) 2.679–689]. For reflections upon this criticism, *See* P. Descoqs, in *Archives de Philosophie,* 2.2:123–154, and 4.4:82–192; J. Iturrioz, *Estudios,* 199–277; and J. Alejandro, *La Gnoseología del Doctor Eximio y la Acusación Nominalista* (Comillas 1948).

It is sometimes claimed that Suárez's greatest and most lasting value lies in the realm of his political and legal philosophy.

See Also: NEOSCHOLASTICISM AND NEOTHOMISM; SCHOLASTICISM, 2.

Bibliography: R. F. HARVANEK, ''Suarezianism,'' Catholic University of America, Workshop on Teaching Thomism Today, *Teaching Thomism Today,* ed. G. F. MCLEAN (Washington 1964) 81–96. P. DUMONT, *Dictionnaire de théologie catholique*, ed. A. VACANT et al., (Paris 1903–50) 14.2:2649–91. F. C. COPLESTON, *History of Philosophy* (Westminster, Md. 1946–) 3:353–379. M. COLPO, *Enciclopedia filosofica* (Venice-Rome 1957) 2:686–691. C. C. RIEDL, ''A Suarez Bibliography,'' *Jesuit Thinkers of the Renaissance,* ed. G. SMITH (Milwaukee 1939) 227–238. P. MÚGICA, *Bibliografía suareciana* (Granada 1948). ''Bibliografía suareziana (desde 1917 a 1947),'' *Estudios Eclesiásticos* 22 (1948) 603–671. J. ITURRIOZ, ''Bibliografía suareciana,'' *Pensamiento* 4 (1948) 603–638, special issue.

[A. J. BENEDETTO]

SUBDEACON

In the Western Church, the lowest of the two major orders that led to the priesthood. The origin of the subdiaconate has been the subject of much historical and theological speculation. The earliest mention of subdeacons, as distinguished from deacons, is found about the middle of the third century. Originally, the rite of subdiaconate resembled that of the order of acolyte, the highest of the four minor orders. As the functions of the subdeacon became more important, and the obligations of perpetual chastity and the recitation of the Divine Office became attached to his state, the rite for this order gradually assumed its present form. No one was permitted to receive the subdiaconate unless he had already received the tonsure and the four minor orders. However, the words of admonition addressed to the candidates at the beginning of the ceremony suggest that at one time laymen may have been admitted immediately to the subdiaconate.

The rite of subdiaconate comprised two parts: (1) the giving of the empty chalice and paten, and (2) the giving of the book of Epistles. In receiving the subdiaconate, the cleric was clothed for the first time in vestments characteristic of his office, from the amice to the tunic, with an appropriate formula for each vestment. Of these vestments, the one that is strictly proper to the subdiaconate was the maniple. The functions of the subdeacon were performed principally in the Eucharist, during which he chanted the Epistle and assisted at the Offertory.

In the motu prioprio, *Ministeria quaedam* dated Sept. 14, 1972 (effective Jan. 1, 1973), Pope Paul VI abolished the orders of Porter, Exorcist and Subdeacon.

Bibliography: A. MICHEL, *Dictionnaire de théologie catholique* 14.2:2459–66. P. DE PUNIET, *The Roman Pontifical: A History and Commentary*, tr. M. V. HARCOURT (New York 1932) 141–169. J. H. MILLER, *Fundamentals of the Liturgy* 483–485. A. BAUMEISTER, *Lexikon für Theologie und Kirche* [1] 9:874–875.

[T. J. RILEY/EDS.]

SUBIACO, MONASTERIES OF

Subiaco is a commune 50 miles east of Rome, whose name derives from NERO's villa *Sublaqueum* (beneath the lake). Of 14 Benedictine monasteries in the neighborhood, 12 were built by St. BENEDICT. Two of these, St. Scholastica and Sacro Speco, still flourish. The probable names of the other monasteries of St. Benedict are: S. Angelo, S. Maria di Morrabotte (S. Lorenzo), S. Girolamo, S. Giovanni Battista, S. Clemente, S. Biagio (S. Romano), S. Michele Archangelo, S. Vittorino, S. Andrea or S. Donato, Vita Eterna, and S. Salvatore di Communacqua. In 529 St. Benedict left Subiaco for MONTE CASSINO.

Sacro Speco, the cave where Benedict dwelt alone for three years, has since been venerated as a sanctuary, although he did not build there. Cenobitical life began there under Abbot Romanus (1192–1216), and the extant buildings date from the 13th and 14th centuries. The priory was dependent on St. Scholastica, with whose fate it was linked.

The abbey of St. Scholastica, a national monument since 1873, was not the first monastery of Benedict, who for his earliest disciples used a building of Nero's villa (S. Clemente, destroyed by an earthquake in the 13th century). But since the 8th century it has been regarded as the most important Subiaco monastery. The oratory of St. Sylvester, the original patron, may be the small church recently discovered beneath the floor of the present church. In the 7th and 8th centuries the names of SS. Benedict and Scholastica were added to the title of St. Sylvester, which soon disappeared. It has been called St. Scholastica since 1400. The first centuries of its history are obscure. During the pontificate of Gregory IV (827–844) and probably in 876–877, it was destroyed by Saracens; but the monastic tradition was not interrupted. The feudal period began under Abbot Leo III (923–961), who was especially favored by Popes John X, Leo VII, John XII, and by the Prince of the Romans, Alberic II. Within 80 years the monastery increased its property sixfold. It flourished especially from 1050 to 1150 under Abbots Humbert (1050–69), who built the Romanesque belltower, and John V (1069–1121), *Gloriosissimus abbas,* a learned administrator known for moral and spiritual qualities, who led the monastery to the peak of its glory. Abbot Lando (1219–43) built the artistic Cosmatan cloister. Innocent III (1198–1216), who visited Subiaco (1202), enriched Sacro Speco and left a bull of reform. Gregory IX (1227–41) rented the castle of Jenne, which belonged to the abbey, and visited Subiaco several times, certainly in 1232. Alexander IV (1254–61), born at Jenne, inherited from his father the title ''lord'' held by his ancestors and so, as cardinal and pope, was the feudatory of the monastery. In 1260 he was at Subiaco and Jenne for two months, and left the monks an important apostolic constitution containing instructions on the religious life. The 14th century was a period of disorder and decline with only a short respite of peace and prosperity. Abbot Bartholomew of Siena (1363–69) reformed the abbey with many German monks and compiled the *Consuetudines Sublacenses.*

After ''manual-curial'' abbots, appointed by the popes, the Holy See in 1456 placed the abbey in COMMENDATION. The first commendatory abbot, Juan de TORQUEMADA, governed well and took in two German printers, Konrad SWEYNHEYM and Arnold Pannartz, who set up the first printing house in Italy in the abbey. Other

Rooftops of Abbey of St. Scholastica, Subiaco, Italy.

commendatory abbots were Popes Alexander VI (1492–1503), Pius VI (1775–99), Pius IX (1846–78), and Pius X (1903–14), the last such abbot.

In 1915 Benedict XV in the apostolic constitution *Coenobium Sublacense* restored to the abbey the privileges of an abbey *nullius* (Sublacensis), and made the abbot an ordinary with quasi-episcopal jurisdiction, stipulating that the abbey church with its regular chapter should have the title, privileges, and honor of a cathedral.

Bibliography: L. ALLODI and G. LEVI, eds., *Regesto Sublacense del secolo XI* (Rome 1885). C. MIRZIO, *Cronaca Sublacense,* ed. P. CROSTAROSA and L. ALLODI (Rome 1885). R. MORGHEN, ed., *Chronicon Sublacense* (593–1369) (Bologna 1927). P. EGIDI et al., *I monasteri di Subiaco,* 2 v. (Rome 1904). G. DRINKWATER, *History of the Monastery of Subiaco in the Middle Ages* (Chicago 1932). B. CIGNITTI and L. CARONTI, *L'abbazia nullius Sublacense: Le origini, la commenda* (Rome 1956). P. CAROSI, *Il primo monastero benedettino* (*Studia anselmiana* 39; 1956). S. ANDREOTTA, *La famiglia di Alessandro IV e l'abbazia di Subiaco* (Rome 1963). L. H. COTTINEAU, *Répertoire topobibliographique des abbayes et prieurés,* 2 v. (Mâcon 1935–39) 2:3099–3100. O. L. KAPSNER, *A Benedictine Bibliography: An Author-Subject Union List,* 2 v. (2d ed. Collegeville, MN 1962): v.1 author part; v.2, subject part 2:5310–31. *Annuario Pontificio* (Rome 1964) 732.

[S. ANDREOTTA]

SUBJECT

Subject is a term derived from the Latin *subiectum,* meaning what is thrown under or underlies and signifying a substrate or foundation that is determined or specified by something else, whether the determiner be a predicate, an attribute or property, an accident, or an object. It has various meanings in different disciplines. In logic the subject is that to which some predicate is attributed or of which some PROPERTY is scientifically demonstrated. *See* PREDICATION; SCIENCE (SCIENTIA). In the philosophy of nature the subject may be either the substratum that underlies accidental CHANGE, viz, substance or secondary matter, or that which underlies SUBSTANTIAL CHANGE, viz, primary matter (*see* MATTER AND FORM). In psychology the subject is the individual who experiences a psychological state (the SELF) or who is the object of clinical or experimental study; the term may also refer to a POTENCY or to the soul or one of its FACULTIES as the proper locus of a particular ACT or HABIT. In metaphysics the subject is something that subsists in itself and does not depend upon another as the material cause of its existence; this is SUBSTANCE as distinguished from ACCIDENT (*see* SUBSISTENCE). In epistemology the subject is the knower, distinguished precisely as such from the thing known, or OBJECT (*see* KNOWLEDGE). In social and political philosophy the subject is either the individual PERSON who comes under the AUTHORITY of another or the physical or moral person bound by a particular LAW.

Subjective is a derivative of subject and is also used in many senses. It may refer to the personal, as opposed to the impersonal, and accent the feelings, tastes, and desires that affect a particular action or judgment. It may signify what occurs in the human mind or in a knowing subject as opposed to what exists objectively and independently of the knowing process, particularly when emphasizing the apparent, the unreal, and the illusory. It may refer to the content of CONSCIOUSNESS, stressing the latter's interiority as opposed to its exteriority. It may indicate, finally, something characteristic of the PHENOMENA, the data of sense experience, as opposed to the reality of the thing-in-itself.

See Also: RELATIVISM; IDEALISM.

Bibliography: P. FOULQUIÉ and R. SAINT-JEAN, *Dictionnaire de la langue philosophique* (Paris 1962) 697–699. A. LALANDE, *Vocabulaire technique et critique de la philosophie* (8th ed. Paris 1960) 1036–41, 1066–69. R. EISLER, *Wörterbuch der philosophischen Begriffe,* 3 v. (4th ed. Berlin 1927–30) 2:165–172. A. GUZZO and V. MATHIEU, *Enciclopedia filosofica,* 4 v. (Venice–Rome 1957) 4:759–764. W. B. SELBIE, J. HASTINGS, ed., *Encyclopedia of Religion and Ethics,* 13 v. (Edinburgh 1908–27) 11:908–909. J. M. BALDWIN, ed., *Dictionary of Philosophy and Psychology,* v. 2 (New York 1928) 607–610.

[B. A. GENDREAU]

SUBORDINATIONISM

The generic term for a heresy that taught that the Son and Holy Spirit are inferior to the Father. This heresy found support in certain passages of scripture wherein Christ indicated his inferiority to the Father (Jn 14.28; Mk 10.18, 13.32, etc.), as well as from middle Platonism which viewed the logos as an intermediary between the transcendent divinity and the world. Subordinationist tendencies can be found in Hermas, Justin Martyr, Irenaeus, Tertullian, Clement of Alexandria and Origen. The classic forms of subordinationism are the following:

Arianism. Arius (d. 336), a priest of Alexandria, denied that the Son was either coeternal or coequal with the Father. He taught that the Son (Logos, Word) is not of the same nature as the Father; he is not begotten of the substance of the Father but made freely by the Father out of nothing. The Son, he said, did not exist from eternity: ''there was a time when he was not.'' He is a mere creature (ποίημα) of the Father, created before all other creatures and exalted above them, an instrument used by the Father for creation. The Son is not God, but can be called God in an improper sense; God not by nature but by grace, because He was adopted by God as Son. Arianism was condemned at the Council of NICAEA I (325), which defined Jesus Christ as ''the Son of God, begotten of the Father . . . God from God . . . begotten not made . . . consubstantial (homoousios) with the Father.''

Semi-Arianism. The Nicene definition was opposed not only by the strict Arians but by Semi-Arians and others, who refused to subscribe to the HOMOOUSIOS (of the same substance) because it seemed to them Sabellian. They maintained that the Son was not homoousios with the Father but only homoiousios or like the Father in substance (Acacius of Caesarea, Aetius). A bitter struggle followed Nicaea in the years leading to the Council of CONSTANTINOPLE (381), and Arian and Semi-Arian emperors brought such pressure to bear on bishops that Jerome could write of the Council of Ariminum (359): ''the whole world groaned and marvelled to find itself Arian.'' The open persecution of the Catholics by the Emperor Valens had the good result of making clear the real issues and putting an end to confusion about terminology. When Valens was succeeded by a Catholic, THEODOSIUS I, the way was open for an unambiguous acceptance of what had been defined at Nicaea.

A council was held in 381 in Constantinople, which repeated homoousios, named and condemned different forms of Arianism, and affirmed that there is one divine substance in three Persons in God, and that the Second Person became man. By this formula, which was a triumph for the great Cappadocian bishops, Basil, Gregory of Nazianzus, and Gregory of Nyssa, the Council condemned not only Arianism, but also the heresy known as Macedonianism.

Macedonianism. Arius had treated explicitly only of the Son, but his teaching was extended to the Holy Ghost by, it is said, Macedonius, Semi-Arian bishop of Constantinople (deposed 360). The Holy Ghost was declared not to proceed from the Father, but to be a creature made by the Son, by whom ''all things were made'' (Jn 1.3; 15.26). Against the Macedonians (Pneumatomachi, enemies of the Spirit, as Athanasius called them) Athanasius, Didymus the Blind, and the Cappadocian Fathers upheld orthodox doctrine. The General Council of Constantinople I (381), defined (indirectly) the divinity of the Holy Ghost and his consubstantiality with the Father and Son by calling him ''Lord'' and ascribing certain divine attributes to him: the giving of life, adoration and glory such as are due to Father and Son, and illumination of the Prophets.

Bibliography: G. BARDY, *Dictionnaire de théologie catholique,* ed. A. VACANT, 15 v. (Paris 1903–50; Tables générales 1951–) 15.2:1625–29. J. LEBRETON, A. FLICHE and V. MARTIN, eds.,

Histoire de l'église depuis les origines jusqu'à nos jours (Paris 1935–) 2:88–91, 319–324, 337–344; *Revue d'histoire ecclésiastique* 19 (Louvain 1923) 481–506; 20 (1924) 4–37. J. TIXERONT, *History of Dogmas,* tr. H. L. BRIANCEAU, 3 v. (St. Louis 1910–16) v. 1. J. N. ROWE, *Origen's Doctrine of Subordination: A Study in Origen's Christology* (Berne and New York 1987). R. P. C. HANSON, *The Search for the Christian Doctrine of God* (Edinburgh 1988).

[P. J. HAMELL/EDS.]

SUBSIDIARITY

The principle of subsidiarity is broadly concerned with the limits of the right and duty of the public authority to intervene in social and economic affairs. The term was first used and explicitly defined by PIUS XI in his encyclical *Quadragesimo anno:* ''It is a fundamental principle of social philosophy, fixed and unchangeable, that one should not withdraw from individuals and commit to the community what they can accomplish by their own enterprise and industry. So, too, it is an injustice and at the same time a grave evil and a disturbance of right order, to transfer to the larger and higher collectivity functions which can be performed and provided for by lesser and subordinate bodies. Inasmuch as every social activity should, by its very nature, prove a help to members of the body social, it should never destroy or absorb them'' (79). This doctrine, though not by name, was taught in the earlier encyclicals of LEO XIII, *Immortale Dei* and *Rerum novarum,* and is contained in the writings of Thomas Aquinas about the nature of law and the state. Subsequently, PIUS XII and JOHN XXIII quoted with strong approval PIUS XI's enunciation of the principle.

Right to Intervene. That the principle of subsidiarity contains a positive statement of the right and duty of the public authorities to intervene was recognized by John XXIII in *Mater et Magistra:* ''This intervention of public authorities that encourages, stimulates, regulates, supplements, and complements, is based on the *principle* of subsidiarity as set forth by Pius XI in his encyclical *Quadragesimo anno*'' (53). John XXIII then continued to quote the passage from the encyclical given above. There can be no doubt, however, that he had in mind also the paragraph that immediately follows in *Quadragesimo anno* for the idea and the wording are almost identical: ''The state should leave to these smaller groups the settlement of business of minor importance. It will thus carry out with greater freedom, power, and success the tasks belonging to it, because it alone can effectively accomplish these, directing, watching, stimulating and restraining, as circumstances suggest or necessity demands. Let those in power, therefore, be convinced that the more faithfully this principle be followed, and a graded hierarchical order exist between the various subsidiary organizations, the more excellent will be both the authority and the efficiency of the social organization as a whole and the happier and more prosperous the condition of the state'' (80).

However, because the emphasis in the original formulation of the principle of subsidiarity is negative, some wish to interpret it in the spirit of 19th-century liberalism. According to this view, the state is an evil, though perhaps a necessary evil, and its intervention in social and economic affairs must be limited to cases where subordinate bodies are unable or unwilling to perform their own proper function. Thus, a role proper to the state alone is not recognized and its activity theoretically could be reduced to nothing.

Nature of State and Society. To arrive at a proper understanding of the principle of subsidiarity, one must look to the nature of the state and society. Man is a social person, who achieves his perfection only in society. The state exists to help the persons who live within the society. This is the meaning of the Latin word, *subsidium,* aid, help. Normally, this aid is indirect by the care of the complex of conditions that enable the subordinate societies and the individuals to care for their own needs. This complex of conditions is what has been traditionally called the ''common good.''

In the words of *Mater et Magistra,* the common good ''embraces the sum total of those conditions of social living whereby men are enabled more fully and more readily, to achieve their own perfection'' (65). *Pacem in terris* explains more explicitly and concretely what is involved in the total of these conditions: ''It is agreed that in our time the common good is chiefly guaranteed when personal rights and duties are maintained. The chief concern of civil authorities must therefore be to insure that these rights are acknowledged, respected, co-ordinated with other rights, defended and promoted, so that in this way each one may more easily carry out his duties'' (60).

While accepting the duty of the state to intervene to further, protect, and promote personal rights some have such a narrow concept of what these personal rights include that they ascribe a very limited role to the state. How widespread in reality is the proper role of the state is made clear in *Pacem in terris:* ''It is therefore necessary that the administration give wholehearted and careful attention to the social as well as to the economic progress of citizens, and to the development, in keeping with the development of the productive system, of such essential services as the building of roads, transportation, communications, water supply, housing, public health, education, facilitation of the practice of religion, and recreational facilities. It is necessary also that governments make efforts to see that insurance systems are made available to the citizens, so that, in case of misfortune or increased family responsibilities, no person will be without the necessary means to maintain a decent standard of living. The government should make similarly effective efforts to see that those who are able to work can find employment in keeping with their aptitudes, and that each worker receives a wage in keeping with the laws of justice and equity. It should be equally the concern of civil authorities to insure that workers be allowed their proper responsibility in the work undertaken in industrial organization, and to facilitate the establishment of intermediate groups which will make social life richer and more effective. Finally, it should be possible for all the citizens to share as far as they are able in their country's cultural advantages'' (64).

All these tasks are included in the complex of conditions necessary to enable the individual to achieve his own social and economic welfare. These then would be the primary and direct concern of the public authority in helping the individual members of society to attain their full development. Moreover, there can be circumstances when lower social bodies may be deficient or even nonexistent, so that the state must be directly concerned with the welfare of the individual. Here, according to *Quadragesimo anno,* the public authorities must remember they are to aid the lesser society or the individual, but not to destroy them by permanently taking over their function.

Related Questions. The principle of subsidiarity also has applicability to various related questions of social philosophy. For example, a planned economy determining prices, wages, production and investment quotas, and the like, violates the principle of subsidiarity, for the public authority would thus be making decisions that should be the concern of individuals or private enterprise. On the other hand, economic planning, determining monetary and fiscal policy, antitrust regulations, and the like, which affect the general economic environment, is consistent with subsidiarity.

Nationalization, as a principle, violates the principle of subsidiarity, because it claims for the state the right to manage economic enterprises and denies this right to individuals. However, applied *ad hoc* to special circumstances in which a particular private enterprise is detrimental to the common good nationalization can be in keeping with the subsidiarity principle.

In the context of American government, the principle of subsidiarity is often recognized as being effected through the historically developed system of federalism, that is, the sharing of responsibilities on the federal, state, and local levels of counties and municipalities. Not to be neglected is the working of civil society, that ensemble of numerous private and voluntary associations, as the locus of the achievement of the majority of social functions, from economic production and distribution to the cultural and religious life of a people. To recognize the ordinary functioning of civil society as the ''center of gravity'' of social relations is implicitly to acknowledge the natural right of free association and the wisdom of broad institutional pluralism. It is only when social tasks (such as the protection of rights and care for the common good) are not adequately fulfilled on the local and voluntary levels that resort to government intervention is rightly made. The U.S. Bishops' 1986 pastoral letter, *Economic Justice for All*, calls all Americans to respect the principle of subsidiarity in assigning social and economic tasks to various appropriate levels and bodies within our society (see esp. nos. 99–101, 124, 303–311, 323–325). JOHN PAUL II reiterated the importance of this guiding norm in his 1991 encyclical *Centesimus annus*, particularly in treating the scope and reach of centralized state bureaucracy (nos. 44-48). The *Catechism of the Catholic Church* (no. 1885) also notes that ''the principle of subsidiarity is opposed to all forms of collectivism. It sets limits for state intervention. It aims at harmonizing the relationship between individuals and societies. It tends toward the establishment of true international order.''

This latter observation indicates a trend in more recent Catholic social teaching whereby the principle of subsidiarity has increasingly been applied not only to the various levels of national politics, but now also to the relationship between individual nation-states and global authorities. Various references to subsidiarity (both implicit and at times explicitly using the term) in the social teaching documents of Popes PAUL VI and John Paul II emphasize the interplay of the rightful autonomy of states and the simultaneous limits to that autonomy in the interest of correcting global imbalances and resolving conflicts. Building upon John XXIII's observation that ''nations are reciprocally subjects of rights and duties'' in the worldwide community (*Pacem in terris*, no. 80), recent popes have urged the development of an appropriate sharing of global authority through international agencies and bodies (such as the United Nations, the International Court of Justice and various organizations that treat economic, social and environmental concerns) oriented to advancing the global common good. When Paul VI in 1967 observed that ''the social question has now become worldwide'' (*Populorum progressio*, no. 3), he ushered in a renewed papal perspective on a broader interpretation of subsidiarity. John Paul II's frequent treatment of the theme of global solidarity implies the need for global institutions to regulate social relationships that now cross national borders, and this increasingly globalized order calls for a renewed application of the principle of subsidiarity. Catholic reflection on the new division of labor in addressing worldwide problems relates particularly to the task of economic development, as John Paul II notes in his 1987 encyclical *Sollicitudo rei socialis* (see nos. 21 and 26) when he calls upon international institutions to foster authentic development in those countries requiring assistance in the task of effecting economic progress.

Bibliography: J. Y. CALVEZ and J. PERRIN, *The Church and Social Justice,* tr. J. R. KIRWAN (Chicago 1961). O. VON NELLBREUNING, *Reorganization of Social Economy,* tr. B. W. DEMPSEY (Milwaukee 1936) ch. 9–10. J. MESSNER, ''Freedom as a Principle of Social Order,'' *The Modern Schoolman* 28 (St. Louis 1951) 97–110.

[R. E. MULCAHY/T. MASSARO]

SUBSIDIARITY IN THE CHURCH

In the encyclical *Quadragesimo anno* (1931), Pius XI taught that the principle of subsidiarity, which had become a staple teaching among Catholic thinkers, was applicable to society at large on the basis of the natural law. The formulation of the principle was urgent at the time, given the emergence of various European totalitarian states. In 1946, Pius XII informed the College of Cardinals that the principle of subsidiarity was applicable not only to society at large but to the Church as well. Pius XII reiterated his teaching in 1957. At Second Vatican Council, the ecclesiological principle of subsidiarity seemed more assumed than expressly enunciated. The only explicit references were to the principle as one of Catholic social theory (*Gravissimum educationis* 3 and 6 and *Gaudium et spes* 86). Nonetheless, the Synod of Bishops in 1967 and 1969 called for the implementation of the principle in a proposed new edition of the Code of Canon Law and in understanding and implementing episcopal collegiality. But when the new Code appeared in 1983, the principle was never cited or invoked. This neglect of what many considered a secure teaching of the Church led to a further challenge of the principle at the extraordinary assembly of the Synod of Bishops in 1985. There, further clarification was called for regarding the meaning and applicability of subsidiarity in the Church. In response, the last 15 years have resulted in many helpful studies of the principle.

Meaning of the Principle of Subsidiarity. Three aspects of the meaning and limits of subsidiarity emerge in *Quadragesimo anno* (aa. 79–80). First, Pius XI insists on the primacy of the individual person. Second, he emphasizes the priority of small groups vis-à-vis larger, more complex, state-sponsored agencies. Finally, he points to the necessity of assistance on the part of the state when either an individual or smaller social units cannot achieve their purposes. Taken together, these general ideas constitute ''the principle of subsidiarity.'' Although Pius XII invoked the principle in respect to the Church, he never addressed the question of how these three aspects interact and modify one another.

W. Bertrams and F. Klüber highlighted how the principle of subsidiarity is bound up with an entire anthropology, whether philosophical (Klüber) or theological (Bertrams). Klüber also stressed the mutual coordination of three fundamental principles: the principle of the person (radical dignity and hence primacy of the person), the principle of social solidarity (radical openness of the person to others), and the principle of subsidiarity, which mediates between the first two principles and truly effects them. Two distinct functions of the principle emerge clearly. On the one hand, when an individual can achieve a goal necessary for his full development, the individual, in freely assumed and more or less spontaneous relationships, retains the right to self-determination of the goal and the means to achieve it. On the other hand, in those instances where mutual social activity is rendered difficult or impossible, the next higher group of individuals or agents must assume this responsibility. Higher or more complex agencies assume functions that can no longer be met adequately by individuals or small groups of individuals.

Postsynodal Clarifications. In light of the call of the Synod of Bishops for clarification regarding the applicability of the principle of subsidiarity to the Church, a number of important ideas have surfaced. Some theologians have claimed that Vatican II's enunciation of an ecclesiology of communion have rendered the teaching of subsidiarity in the Church redundant. By insisting on the Church as the People of God, the council abandoned the older theology of the Church as a *societas inaequalium*, i.e., a society based on the distinction between the ''hierarchy'' (higher) and the ''faithful'' (lower) founded in the will of Christ. Another group of scholars, however, pointed to Vatican II's continued teaching on the Church as *societas*. Though the Church is a *mysterium*, the category of *societas* emphasizes its genuine historicity and social location or concreteness. These authors argued that ecclesial *communio* runs the risk of becoming an ineffectual panacea when it is not anchored in juridically established institutions or laws. *Communio* itself needs to be specified, since the council used it in two distinct though related senses: *communio* of the People of God and hierarchical *communio*. In ecclesiology, both the christological and the pneumatological dimensions of the Church demand expression as they mutually effect the Church as *mysterium*. The Church is always both universal sacrament of salvation (in Christ) and communion in grace, or the mystery of divine self-communication (in the Spirit). In a word, the modern traditional teaching of the Church as *societas* has not been abandoned but reordered, with the result that the role of subsidiarity in the Church continues to occupy an important place. Finally, several writers have pointed to the analogical character of the role of subsidiarity in the Church when compared with secular society. Like other societies, the Church is structured, but this structure must be such as to enable the Church to accomplish its distinctive mission. The principle of analogy suggests that the place of subsidiarity in the Church is ''never less'' than that which it holds in the Church's social theory for society in general. Yet ecclesial subsidiarity is unique by reason of the specific mission of the Church, and so is not simply interchangeable with the social determinations of any given society but is free to rethink them in the light of the gospel.

Bibliography: W. BERTRAMS, ''Das Subsidiaritätsprinzip in der Kirche,'' *Stimmen der Zeit* 160 (1957) 252–67. J. BEYER, ''Principe de subsidiarité ou 'juste autonomie' dans l'Église?,'' *Nouvelle revue théologique* 108 (1986) 801–22. J. J. BURKHARD, ''The Interpretation and Application of Subsidiarity in Ecclesiology: An Overview of the Theological and Canonical Literature,'' *Jurist* 58 (1998) 279–342. P. DU FAY DE CHOISINET, ''La subsidiarité, un principe juridique contesté?,'' *Praxis Juridique et Religion* 7 (1990) 55–66. J. L. GUTIÉRREZ, ''El principio de subsidiariedad y la igualidad radical de los fieles,'' *Ius Canonicum* 11 (1971) 413–43. W. KASPER, ''Der Geheimnischarakter hebt den Sozialcharakter nicht auf. Zur Geltung des Subsidiaritätsprinzips in der Kirche,'' *Herder-Korrespondenz* 41 (1987) 232–36; ''Zum Subsidiaritätsprinzip in der Kirche,'' *Internationale katholische Zeitschrift Communio* 18 (1989) 155–62. F. KLÜBER, *Lexikon für Theologie und Kirche*, 2d ed., s.v. ''Soziallehre.'' M. KREBS, *Subsidiarität und kirchliches Leben. Das Subsidiaritätsprinzip in Anwendng auf die Kirche nach Pius XII*, S.T.D. dissertation (Rome 1991). A. LEYS, *Ecclesiological Impacts of the Principle of Subsidiarity*, tr. A. VAN SANTVOORD (Kampen 1995). O. VON NELL-BREUNING, ''Subsidiarität in der Kirche,'' *Stimmen der Zeit* 111 (1986) 147–57. J. N. SCHASCHING, ''Das Subsidiaritätsprinzip in der Soziallehre der Kirche: Reflexionen zu einer Anfrage,'' *Gregorianum* 69 (1988) 413–33.

[J. BURKHARD]

SUBSISTENCE

From the Latin *subsistere,* meaning to stand under, or to stand still, subsistence is ''that mode of existence which is self-contained and independent of any subject, and also a being that exists in this manner, synonym of *hypostasis, res subsistens, persona,* i.e., both that which exists for itself and not in another and also the manner of existence . . .'' [L. Deferrari, M. I. Barry, and J. McGuiness, *A Lexicon of St. Thomas Aquinas,* (Washington, 1948) 1063]. Used as an abstract noun, subsistence denotes an order to per se existence that is proper to substances, as distinct from accidents, which depend upon a sustaining subject in order to exist (*see* SUBSTANCE; ACCIDENT). Used as a concrete noun, subsistence denotes a substantial essence in its relationship to proportionate existence.

Related Terminology. Supposit is another term for subsistence concretely understood. Derived from the Latin *supponere,* meaning to put or to place under, it signifies that which underlies and supports accidental being, namely, substance with its own order to self-contained being independent of any subject. Supposit and subsistence concretely considered differ only etymologically.

HYPOSTASIS similarly designates the same reality as supposit and subsistence used as a concrete noun. It differs from supposit only in its derivation from Greek (ὑπόστασις) instead of from Latin.

PERSON, from the Greek πρόσωπον, meaning face, is reserved for a supposit having an intelligent nature, whether divine, angelic, or human; thus no infra-intelligent supposit is a person. Person and supposit are related as the less inclusive (person—an intelligent supposit) to the more inclusive (supposit—very subsistent reality).

NATURE is closely connected with the notions of subsistence, supposit, etc., but is really different from them. The term nature designates a thing's specific identity, its essence. Nature answers the question What is this? and indicates the essential, dynamic constitution of a thing. Yet nature as such has no per se or immediate reference to the existential order and is defined independently of existence. But reference to the existential order enters decisively into the notion of subsistence, which cannot be defined save in terms of a certain manner of existential actuality.

Historical Development. Only in the context of early doctrinal discussions of the Incarnation did the term subsistence acquire the technical meaning, equivalent to hypostasis, that it has long enjoyed in theology and philosophy. The earliest formulations of Christian faith were all expressed in the Greek language, where, necessarily, person and hypostasis were used to express the union between Christ's divine and human natures. The union is personal, hypostatic, because in Him there is but one hypostasis subsisting in both natures.

Meeting the Western need to express Christian faith in Latin terms, ecclesiastical writers first tended to translate hypostasis as *substantia,* substance. BOETHIUS actually defines person or hypostasis in terms of individual substance (*De duabus naturis* 3, *Patrologia Latina*, ed. J. P. Migne, 64:1343). Even the great Augustine uses *substantia* as synonomous with person (*Trin.* 7.47–7.5.10,

Patrologia Latina 42:941–943). Later, the Lateran Council of 649 under Pope Martin I followed this usage, calling the hypostatic union a ''substantial union of natures'' (*naturarum substantialem unionem,* H. Denzinger, *Enchiridion symbolorum,* ed. A. Schönmetzer, 508).

But substance is, in this context, ambiguous, a potential source of confusion; for it can signify both nature and suppposit. It can be said that in Christ there are two substances (natures) and one substance (person, supposit). The same Council that describes Christ's ''substantial [personal] union of natures'' asserts of Him ''a substantial difference of natures'' (*Enchiridion symbolorum* 507), a juxtaposition that nicely suggests the ambiguity implicit in this use of substance.

A less equivocal usage did not gain ground until about the beginning of the 5th century. RUFINUS OF AQUILEIA seems to have been the first ecclesiastical writer to translate hypostasis as *subsistentia* and to distinguish clearly between subsistence taken in the concrete and substance (*Ecclesiastical History* 1.29, *Patrologia Latina* 21:499–500), thereby removing the terminological difficulty at its root. Half a century earlier, MARIUS VICTORINUS had used the term subsistence, but not as a precise Latin equivalent of hypostasis or person (*Adv. Arium* 1.30, *Patrologia Latina* 8:1062–63). FAUSTUS OF RIEZ, like Rufinus, very precisely distinguished between *substantia* and *subsistentia,* using only the latter as an accurate translation of hypostasis (*Epist.* 7, PL 58:858). The same is true of Paschasius the Deacon (*De Spiritu Sancto,* 1.4, *Patrologia Latina* 62:13) and of Rusticus, who explicitly identified *persona* and *subsistentia* in their distinction from *natura* (*C. Acepholos disp.; Patrologia Latina* 67:1192–99, 1238, etc.).

As subsistence came to be commonly used to express the union of the Incarnation, it appeared also in documents of the magisterium. The first of such documents is the dogmatic letter of Pope John I explicitly equating *subsistentia* with person or hypostasis in Christ (*Enchiridion symbolorum* 401). The Council of Rome (680) teaches that ''. . . Jesus Christ . . . subsists in two substances . . . meeting in one person and one subsistence'' (*Enchiridion symbolorum* 548), so restricting the term substance to nature. The same Council speaks of ''the subsistential union'' (*subsistentialem adunationem*) in Christ (*ibid.*). In his preface to the translation of the acts of the seventh General Council, Anastasius the Librarian (d. 879) points out that he translates hypostasis as *subsistentia* and contrasts his usage with that of authors who had employed *substantia* to designate person or hypostasis (*Interp. synodi* 7 *gen., praef.; Patrologia Latina* 129:197). Eventually the conviction became universal among Latin ecclesiastical writers that whereas substance, as equivalent to hypostasis, could lead to misunderstanding, subsistence involved no such danger but carried the precise meaning of the Greek term, a conviction embraced by Pope Eugene IV and the Council of Florence (*Enchiridion symbolorum* 1339–46).

The supplanting of ''substantial'' by ''subsistential'' in describing the union of natures in Christ had both theological and philosophical advantages. Theologically the unambiguous *subsistentia* removed the danger of a monophysitic interpretation conceivably lurking in the formula: ''In Christ is a substantial union of natures.'' Philosophically the new terminology pointed to the need for investigating the relationship between substance, understood as nature, and subsistence or supposit, and existence. These investigations have not by any means resulted in agreement among philosophers about these relationships, and over the centuries many opinions have developed. Here only three more widely accepted opinions are considered, viz, the Thomistic explanation and the explanations of Scotus and Suárez.

Thomistic Explanation. Nowhere does St. THOMAS AQUINAS treat subsistence systematically or completely. His opinion must be pieced together from passages in his various works, but the following points explicitly taught by him are basic in the Thomistic account of subsistence. (1) ''In things composed of matter and form . . . nature or essence and supposit differ''; the difference is real because the supposit adds extraneous elements to the nature or definition, notably individual matter (*Summa theologiae* 1a, 3.3). (2) In created immaterial substances (e.g., angels), there is some real distinction between the nature and the supposit because the supposit somehow includes existence and other predicable accidents. ''In an angel they [nature and supposit] are not the same because the angel has accidents over and above what pertains to its species; the very existence of the angel is other than its essence or nature; and it has other accidents that certainly pertain to the supposit but not to the nature'' (*Quodl.* 2.2.2). In general, therefore, ''in creatures the essence is really distinct from the supposit'' (*In 1 sent.* 5.1.1). (3) Only in God are supposit and nature really identical. ''In God alone there is no accident outside His essence, because His existence is His essence . . .; therefore in God supposit and nature are the same'' (*Quodl.* 2.2.2), although they are ''rationally distinct'' (*Summa theologiae* 3a, 2.2). St. Thomas's general norm is clear; namely, supposit is really distinct from nature when the nature is not its own existence, but is identical with nature in God, because God's nature is His existence. (4) Nevertheless the supposit is not to be confused with existence. ''Existence is not included in the notion of supposit,'' although ''existence pertains to the supposit'' in a way in which it does not pertain to nature (*Quodl.* 2.2.2 ad 2).

(5) As between supposit and existence, the latter is posterior in the order of nature. ''Existence follows the person or supposit'' (*Summa theologiae* 3a. 17.2 ad 1). Hence, the order of nature is first individual nature, then subsistence, and finally existence.

From these insights Thomistic commentators, e.g., John Capreolus and Tommaso de Vio CAJETAN, constructed a theory of subsistence favored by Thomists generally. Subsistence is described as really distinct from essence, or nature, in the sense that to nature it adds a real MODE, namely, a transcendental order or relationship to existence. Abstractly considered, subsistence is this order to existential actuality; concretely considered, it is the essence so ordered. The notion of nature-ordered-to-existence has analogous unity as applied to divine, angelic, human, and infrahuman natures, so that while the relationship itself may be different in each case, the common notion is proportionately verified in all substantial natures.

Cajetan expressly teaches that in created, material natures supposit really differs from nature because, for one thing, supposit includes something real, but extrinsic to itself, which the nature does not include, namely existence, for existence is the act of the supposit. Similarly as to created, immaterial substances, ''because in them . . . existence really differs from nature, which [existence] is primarily the act of the supposit, it follows that in them supposit differs from nature'' (*De ente et essentia,* 5.9). Supposit includes esse per se ''as its proper act through which it would have to be defined, but the nature . . . does not'' (*Comm. in Summa theologiae* 1a, 3.3). Reference to existential actuality is (and defines) the supposit; the formality of nature abstracts from all such reference. Even in divinity the Persons, or supposits, are constituted by distinct relationships of origin, i.e., of actual being, within the one divine nature. The divine nature as ordered to being begotten is the Son; the same nature as ordered to begetting is the Father; and the identical divinity as ordered to being breathed forth in love is the Holy Spirit. In the entire reach of subsistence from the most material reality to the all-spiritual God, subsistence names natures as ordered to actual being.

Yet the relationship is different as the hierarchy of beings differ. Because in God the existence to which His nature is ordered in distinct ways is really identical with His nature, each Person is really identical with the divine essence. Among angels, the supposit really differs from the nature precisely because the existence to which it orders nature is really distinct therefrom. As potency is really distinct from, but related to, act, so is the supposit vis-à-vis existence. Among material substances, subsistence is even more complex. Even prior to ordering nature to existence, it brings to nature a termination making it apt for existential ordination. So the material supposit includes as intrinsic to itself the principles that individualize the nature, real modifications of the material substance, yet distinct from its essence. Hence material subsistence has the twofold function of terminating nature and of ordering it to existence (see Cajetan, *loc. cit., Comm. in Summa theologiae* 3a, 4.2; Capreolus, *In 1 sent.* 4.2.1, *In 3 sent.* 5.3.3).

Scotus and Suárez. In the view of DUNS SCOTUS, subsistence, or personality, is nothing positive but a simple negation of dependence in being, such dependence as characterizes accidental realities. ''Human nature is not completely personated (*personata*) by anything positive. . . . For personality is required ultimate aloneness (*solitudo*), or the negation of actual and aptitudinal dependence on a person of another nature'' (*In 3 sent.* 1.1.17; cf. *Quodl.* 19.3). In this view, whatever is so independent in its actual being as to be incommunicable to another is a supposit; subsistence is the lack of dependence called incommunicability. This independence Scotus conceived as ''not . . . anything positive'' but a simple ''negation of dependence.'' Because Christ's humanity was and is communicated to, and dependent upon, the being of the Son of God, that humanity has no human subsistence, or personality. Other humans are human persons because *de facto* their human nature is not communicated, or communicable to another.

With this opinion F. SUÁREZ disagrees. For him subsistence is not a mere negation ''but comes formally from some positive *ratio* which . . . is added to the nature as a nature actually existing.'' With Thomists, Suárez agrees that subsistence is a positive perfection; contrary to them he holds that it is posterior to existence (*De Incarn.* 11.3), even though existence means ''to have entity in physical reality and outside the causes [of the existent]'' (*Disp. meta.* 34). To a substance as actually existing, subsistence can be added because existence itself is quasi-potential. It can be either independent of any sustaining subject—the mode of existence found in substances and called subsistence—or an existence that is dependent upon a sustaining subject, verified of accident and called *inesse* or inherence (*ibid.*). Therefore subsistence is incommunicability ''that excludes only communication to another, as to the ultimate term of existence, which term in created things is conceived as necessary to the complement of existence'' (*De Incarn.* 11.3) in the sense already indicated, viz, that existence is determinable to either an independent or dependent mode. Subsistence, for Suárez, is the final term or complement not of a substantial essence but of existence itself (*est ultimum complementum in ratione existendi*). Whether subsistence be considered existence plus the mode of incommunicability, or merely the mode itself, is a mere ''disagreement about words'' (*Disp. meta.* 34).

Philosophical Relevance. Scholastic discussions about subsistence, the person, and the supposit can seem to moderns so abstract, metaphysical, and obscure as to have nothing in common with present philosophical moods and interests. These latter emphasize the existential, the contingent, the empirical; and no one has ever experienced a mode or empirically encountered ''the order of nature to existence.''

Yet the centuries-old discussions concerning subsistence have value for modern philosophical thinking. In the first place, scholastic theories about subsistence are honest human efforts to account for an aspect of reality. The experienced world is an intriguing combination of the necessary and the contingent, the constant and the variable, the empirically encountered and the purely intelligible. For natures are universal; yet every encountered nature is both singular and contingent. Essences are constant and immutable, yet all experienced reality is variable. In science and philosophy men look for meaning, intelligibility, and truth; yet what they seek lies beyond the ambit of empirical methodology. Subsistence is, for the scholastics, the real bridge between the world of immutable, intelligible, universal essences and the world empirically encountered, the world of contingency, of flux, and of the singular. Admitting the respective validity of each order—the essentialist and the existentialist—the scholastic finds in subsistence a highly intelligible and reasonable reconciliation of the two facets of reality, the order of the one to the other.

Second, much modern philosophizing is homocentric, preoccupied especially with the limitations and urgent problems of the human condition. The doctrine of subsistence implies that every person, every supposit is actually, formally constituted by confrontation with existential, transsubjective reality. The person, the ''I,'' is dynamic relationship to existential actuality, to the world of anguished limitations. Since, according to scholastic accounts of subsistence, this is the metaphysical constitutive of the person and the supposit, it follows that in the operational order the person, as such, is more or less perfected according to his more or less total and realistic acceptance of, and adjustment to, the real situation in which subsistence places him. This outlook gives a reasonable, metaphysical basis to the modern philosophical yearning for perfection achieved through commitment to the existential condition.

Most significant is the scholastic doctrine of person as verified of the Persons of the divine Trinity. Supposit, or subsistence, in general means the relevance or order of nature to existence; proportionately, divine supposits, or Persons, are constituted by divine relationships of origin, that is, by the divine nature's having really, mutually distinct relationships to divine being. In effect, each divine Person is constituted by a relationship to the other Person or Persons; without this note of relationship to another, divine Persons, or supposits, are inconceivable. And the distinct relationships are rooted in God's understanding and love. If to this one adds the revealed truth that created persons are to the image of divine Persons, he gains the insight that every created person can achieve his own fulfillment and perfection only in relation to other persons, specifically the relations of understanding and of love. This is at once ancient Christian truth and the most modern doctrine, rendered divinely meaningful and intelligible.

See Also: SUBSISTENCE IN CHRISTOLOGY.

Bibliography: G. ROVES and A. GAZZANA, *Enciclopedia filosofica*, 4 v. (Venice-Rome 1957) 4:1053–55. A. MICHEL, *Dictionnaire de théologie catholique*, ed. A. VACANT et al., 15 v. (Paris 1903–50) 7:369–437. R. P. PHILLIPS, *Modern Thomistic Philosophy,* 2 v. (Westminster, Md. 1934; repr. 1945). J. GREDT, *Elementa philosophiae Aristotelico-Thomisticae,* ed. E. ZENZEN, 2 v. (13th ed. Freiburg 1961). F. P. MUÑIZ, *El constitutivo formal de la persona creada en la tradición tomista* (Salamanca 1947). U. DEGL' INNOCENTI, ''Il Capreolo e la questione sulla personalità,'' *Divus Thomas* 17 (1940) 27–40. M. DUQUESNE, ''Personne et existence,'' *Revue des sciences philosophiques et théologiques* 36 (1952) 418–35, 626–55.

[T. U. MULLANEY]

SUBSISTENCE (IN CHRISTOLOGY)

The use of the term ''subsistence'' in Christology is highly dependent upon philosophy, especially the developments of medieval scholasticism (see previous article).

Subsistence Christology is the name given to the second of the three main trends PETER LOMBARD identified in theological attempts to explain the INCARNATION. This line of thought sought to protect the unity of person in Christ and in doing so found its firm anchor in the tradition in the dogmatic statement of the Council of Chalcedon. Gilbert of Porrée was its strong advocate in the 12th century. He distinguished between the *id quod* and the *id quo* of any being. The *id quod* refers to the existent being: the subsistent, existing reality. The *id quo* refers to the qualities that enable a subsistent being to be that particular being. In the incarnate Christ there is one *id quod*, the person of the Word of God. After the incarnation the Word existed through two *id quo*, two modes of being, the divine nature and the human nature. Critics of this position questioned whether Christ was truly human if he were not a particular subsistent reality as a human being. However, if in his humanity Christ is a subsistent human being, then there are two beings in Christ, a position in which the echoes of Nestorianism were heard.

Thomas Aquinas refined this position in the 13th century and eventually claimed that it was the only orthodox position of the three Peter Lombard outlined. Aquinas reworked the position by further refining Boethius's definition of a person as an individual substance of a rational nature. He recognized that in most beings there is only one nature which subsists in that particular being as its essence. However, in some beings there also exist things beyond the essence, either accidents or individuating matter. Thus a person can include things beyond its essential nature. In becoming human, the Word did not become a second being, a second subsistence. He remained the subsistent reality of the Word of God but took on the mode of being which is appropriate to human nature. This human mode of being subsists in the one being of the eternal Word of God.

The shift away from scholastic categories in the 20th century has resulted in this theory falling out of use. Those who seek to reinterpret and explain the Chalcedonic formula struggle with a major shift in terminology which would force further developments in any modern version of the subsistence theory. The term "person" has undergone great modification because of the development of such themes as self-consciousness, personal freedom, the psychological self, and the temporal nature of the human. To the modern mind human nature implies personhood. To affirm that the humanity of Christ possesses no created subsistence or personality appears to many to rob it of any genuine participation in the life of man.

St. Thomas's solution parallels that found in the Greek tradition, especially in the thought of Leontius of Byzantium. The humanity of Christ is not *hypostasis*, nor is it *anhypostatos*; it is *enhypostatos*. Similarly one may say: the humanity of Christ is not desubsistentialized by the hypostatic union but subsistentialized-in-the-Word. Far from representing privation, this subsistence-in-the-Word brings consummate fulfillment (cf. *Summa theologiae* 3a, 4.2 ad 2). The ultimate reason why this is possible is the transcendent perfection of God, the fullness of creative being. "God is not opposed to anything; therefore, in taking over all that is in human nature, He does not exclude or impair anything" (Mersch, 220; cf. St. Augustine, *Fid. et Symb.* 7; *Patrologia Latina* 40:185). It is the prerogative of the divine creativity to be able to constitute the creature in an autonomy that is in direct, not inverse, proportion to its total dependence on God (cf. Rahner, 162). In Jesus the human person comes to its fulfillment through its union with the divine. The point is of the highest relevance for Christian life as well as for Christian thought, for it assures the Christian that the Incarnational economy, far from withdrawing a human individual from human existence, invites a person to exercise it more fully.

Bibliography: E. MERSCH, *The Theology of the Mystical Body*, tr. C. VOLLERT (St. Louis 1951) 202–216. F. MALMBERG, *Uber den Gottmenschen* (Quaestiones disputatae 9; Basel 1960) 44–61. K. RAHNER, "Current Problems in Christology," *Theological Investigations*, v. 1, 149–200. K. RAHNER, "On the Theology of the Incarnation," *Theological Investigations*, v. 4, 105–120. W. KASPER, *Jesus the Christ*, 238–252. W. PANNENBERG, *Jesus—God and Man*, 295–296. D. LANE, *The Reality of Jesus*, 109–129.

[T. E. CLARKE/M. B. RASCHKO]

SUBSTANCE

No common statement on the nature of substance is acceptable to all philosophers, the more famous of whom range from a full treatment of its nature to an outright rejection of its existence. From the variety of their views, however, a descriptive statement of the meaning of substance can be pieced together: it is something basic and independent in existence, standing under other realities, and a source of activity. To explain and develop a fuller definition, this article presents the early history of the term substance, a detailed analysis of its nature according to St. Thomas Aquinas, a survey of the views of modern philosophers, and a summary critique and evaluation.

EARLY HISTORY OF THE TERM

The word "substance" is a transliteration of the Latin *substantia,* the components of which give the root meaning of standing under. In popular usage, substance is often interchanged with ESSENCE since both terms have the same general connotation. This popular usage of the term witnesses to a constant factor in the historical development of the philosophical notion.

Greeks. Early GREEK PHILOSOPHY was a search for something basic or fundamental in the cosmos, something that would explain stability within the context of change. The primary formulation of the term to express this reality was the work of PARMENIDES, who denied change and affirmed the real as unchanging. To express this unchanging reality Parmenides used various forms of the verb "to be," εἶναι.

Pre-Socratic philosophers, while accepting change as real, continued to refer to a stable reality in some derivative form of εἶναι. Decisive formulation in the tradition of εἶναι was given by PLATO in his attempt to solve the problem of stability versus change. Confining the stable and unchanging to his world of Ideas, Plato named such things οὐσία, from the feminine participle of εἶναι.

The Platonic term οὐσία with its connotation of perfect stability was, however, inapplicable to various entities that, although substances, are subject to substantial change. To allow for the dynamic character of substance, Aristotle therefore expanded the meaning of οὐσία and applied it to things in the sensible, changing world. He applied οὐσία in a fourfold way: to the essence, τὸ τί ἦν εἶναι; to the universal, τὸ καθόλον; to the genus, τὸ γένος; and to the subject, τὸ ὑποκείμενον (*Meta.* 1028b 33–35). This last term is translated into Latin as *subjectum.* Concerning it, Aristotle says, ''. . . for that which underlies a thing primarily is thought to be in the truest sense its οὐσία'' (Meta. 1029a 3).

Latins. The term οὐσία, especially with the Aristotelian connotation of underlying or basic, is the word the Latins rendered philosophically as *substantia* (Seneca, *Epist.* 58). St. Augustine writes that ''essence [οὐσία] usually means nothing else than substance in our language'' (*Trin.* 7.4.7).

St. Augustine emphasized not only the sustaining role of substance, but also its mutability. Because he regarded mutability as proper to substance, he considered it an abuse to call God a substance. Properly God is called an essence (*Trin.* 7.5.10), ''to whom existence itself, whence is derived the term essence, most especially and most truly belongs'' (*Trin.* 5.2.3).

SUBSTANCE ACCORDING TO ST. THOMAS AQUINAS

In treating of substance, St. THOMAS AQUINAS provides for both the mutable and the immutable, the composite and the simple. While he appears merely to repeat Aristotle in many of his divisions of substance, and especially in the division of being into substance and accident, Thomas introduces a distinctive difference. The perfection of being for Thomas is EXISTENCE (*esse*), and in all finite beings existence is other than essence. St. Thomas contributed to the clarification of the notion of substance by a synthesis of this special insight with the various insights of Plato, Aristotle, and Augustine. For him, the reality in any thing that is substance must be primary and fundamental and thus the basic and independent source of its subsequent and dependent characteristics and properties. St. Thomas does not demonstrate that nature exists, since this is manifest to the senses (*In 2 phys.* 1.8). But he does demonstrate that in any thing there must be something basic, primary, and independent to account for the unity of that thing. The alternative is a meaningless regression to infinity. That which is the basic and independent source of a thing's unity and the ultimate subject of all predication is substance (*Summa Theologiae* 1a, 11.1 ad 1; *In 4 meta.* 7.630).

Definition. St. Thomas thus acknowledges the supporting or underlying role that substance plays in reference to accidents, but he does not identify this as primal. ''There are two things proper to substance as a subject. The first is that it does not need an extrinsic foundation in which it is sustained, but is sustained in itself; and thus it is said to subsist, as existing per se and not in another. The second is that it is itself a foundation sustaining accidents; and as such it is said to stand under (*substare*)'' (*De pot.* 9.1). The primary characteristic is embodied in his definition: ''Substance is essence to which per se existence is proper'' (*Summa Theologiae* 1a, 3.5 ad 1). The definition emphasizes the absolute and independent character of substance. It also gives the reason for substance's capacity for supporting accidents, whereas the etymology of the term emphasizes only its function of support.

In the definition both essence and existence appear. Hence the definition must be judged in the context of St. Thomas's position on being. For him, in all things other than God existence is other than essence (*Summa Theologiae* 1a, 44.1; *Quodl.* 3.8.20); thus, in all substances other than God, the substance is other than its existence (*De subs. sep.* 8). He states, ''To exist per se is not the definition of substance; because by this we do not manifest its quiddity, but its existence; and in a creature its quiddity is not its existence'' (*In 4 sent.* 12.1.1.1 ad 2).

The proper formality in a finite substance is therefore identified as the essence in its capacity for per se, or independent, existence. By so identifying the formality of substance in the creature, St. Thomas provides the basis for distinguishing finite substance from God as substance and for distinguishing substance from essence, nature, and accident (*Summa Theologiae* 3a, 77.1 ad 2).

Distinctions. The creature substance is distinguished from God as substance in that every finite substance has its existence as ACT in relation to which substance is POTENCY, whereas ''only in God is His substance the same as His existence'' (*Summa Theologiae* 1a, 54.1; *C. gent.* 2.53).

Substance is distinguished from essence in that substance signifies the basic principle in a thing in its reference to a per se mode of existence, whereas essence signifies reference to existence without specifying independent or dependent mode. Hence essence, as such, is applicable both to substance and to accident, though primarily to substance (*De ente* 2).

Substance is distinguished from NATURE in that nature signifies the substance as a principle of activity. Hence, in one and the same thing substance, essence, and nature can express the same reality but differ in connotation by a virtual distinction (*see* DISTINCTION, KINDS OF).

Substance is, however, really distinct from ACCIDENT, which it underlies and sustains, and by which substance is enabled to operate and manifest itself in a variety of ways. The precise difference between the two is that substance is of such perfection that it can exist per se, whereas accident is so imperfect a principle that it has need to exist in another (*In 4 sent.* 12.1.1.3 ad 2).

But if substance is other than accident and finite substance is other than its existence, this does not mean that existence is an accident. "The substantial existence of a thing is not an accident, but the actuality of an existing form, either without matter or with matter" (*Quodl.* 12.5.1). The existence is contingent but not an accident.

Characteristics. Strength and durability are often considered as characteristic of substance, but this judgment, if unqualified, is false. A soap bubble is as truly substance as is a steel bar. And a subatomic particle with its minimal duration does not cease to qualify as a substance, whereas the intellect with its immortal duration is still a power of the soul, and hence an accident. Substance should therefore be considered in its proper formality, which permits a variety of substances with proportionate properties and characteristics. The fact that substance, essence, and nature express the same reality in a thing provides a basis for understanding substance as dynamic and varied.

The basic reality that is the essence or substance is not constituted by some element called substance plus some other element whereby this element is made specific. "For when we say that some substance is corporeal or spiritual, we do not compare spirituality or corporeity to substance as forms to matter, or accidents to a subject; but as differences to a genus. Thus it is that a spiritual substance is not spiritual through something added to its substance, but is such through its own substance. In the same way, corporeal substance is not corporeal through something added to substance, but according to its own substance" (*De subs. sep.* 8).

Substance and Accident. A substance is always a specific substance in existing reality. Furthermore, every finite existing substance has need of further perfections that are called accidents. But finite substance and accident must be considered in correlation. Accident, in St. Thomas's teaching, is neither a perfect being nor an individually existing being, but a principle that complements substance and together with it, through their existence, constitutes the individually existing thing. An accident is a being of a being.

The substances of human experience are existing things with varieties of accidental perfections. As is detailed below, the errors about substance in modern philosophy stem in part from a singular failure to treat of substance and accident in this mutual relation. To treat of substance either exclusively in terms of its basic perfection of subsisting or exclusively in terms of its etymological signification of standing under is thus to distort the finite reality that is the existing substance. The finite substance does not simply subsist; it needs proper and common accidents. But it must not be considered merely as a support for PHENOMENA. It is much more than a foundation for a kind of superstructure of accidents. Substance as cause of accidents gives them entitative support; the existence (*esse*) of accidents is existence in (*inesse*). In finite, natural conditions, accidents are never present without their substance. And even in cases of supernatural intervention and support of accidents, as in the Holy Eucharist, accidents do not cease to have an aptitude for inherence in a subject. They never cease to be accidents (*Summa Theologiae* 3a, 77.1 ad 2).

Presence in Things. It is the nature of substance to be in every part of a thing as whole and entire. As foundational for a thing's independent existence, substance is present wherever the thing is in independent existence, which is total. Even in the phenomenal or accidental phases of its being, the thing in its substantial existence sustains the accidental existence (*C. gent.* 4.14). Substance, therefore, should be understood as neither exclusively interior nor exclusively exterior, but everywhere present to the thing. To speak of stripping off accidents from the substance is without meaning (Descartes, *Réponses aux quatrièmes objections*) for that could happen only if there could be an existence in self simultaneously and essentially committed to existence in other. Even in divine intervention these two opposites are not united.

First and Second Substance. The proper focus for understanding both finite substance and accident is to consider them as correlated, as mutually involved. This is how they exist in reality. St. Thomas stresses this by teaching that all idea of substance is taken from substance of actual existence, which he calls first substance. First substance is the individually existing substance with all its attributes and accidental modifications. When precision is made from individual existence and substance is taken in the abstract as a class or category, as universal, it is called second substance.

Complete and Incomplete Substance. A complete substance is one that can exist per se. This terminology can be misleading because substance is said to be essence in its capacity for independent existence, and this would seem to apply to any substance. However, there are composite substances, as evidenced by SUBSTANTIAL CHANGE, and as a consequence there must be substantial components. Further, the reconciliation of a plurality of substantial components with a unity of substantial nature requires that there be only two components, one of which is potential, the other actual. The one is primary matter, the other substantial form (*see* MATTER AND FORM). Each requires the other for actual existence. Each by itself is incapable of actual existence. Each is thus called an incomplete substance because by itself it cannot exist per se. The composite substance is a complete substance.

There is another type of complete substance—a simple substance or one that lacks composition in its essence or nature. Such a substance is spiritual, and its nature is perfect enough to exist per se. In this class are angels and also the human soul. The latter, however, constitutes a special case. The human soul is complete as substance since it can exist per se when separated from matter, but it is incomplete as to species since only with matter does it constitute a complete human nature (*see* SOUL, HUMAN, 4).

Person and Subsistence. PERSON is intimately related to substance—a relation that has special interest because of the doctrine of the INCARNATION. The theology of the Incarnation teaches that there is a complete human nature in Christ in hypostatic union with the Second Person of the Blessed Trinity. There is no human person in Christ. As already noted, any specific substance is the same reality as the essence, or nature, of the thing. Moreover, St. Thomas accepts the definition of person by Boethius: ''An individual substance of a rational nature'' (*Summa Theologiae* 1a, 29.1). The question centers therefore on the precise formality of person and its real distinction from substance.

Despite the variety of answers proposed by scholastic theologians and philosophers, there is general agreement that what is called supposit at the infrahuman level is called person in the human species. A supposit is an individually existing substance. When a particular substance is a human nature the supposit is a person.

SUBSISTENCE is generally accepted by theologians and philosophers as that which together with substance constitutes the supposit. At the human level, subsistence and substance constitute the person. St. Thomas, Duns Scotus, and F. Suárez differ as to the precise meaning of subsistence. Among the followers of St. Thomas, different developments of his teaching are made by CAJETAN, L. BILLOT and J. MARITAIN.

SUBSTANCE IN MODERN PHILOSOPHY

Much of contemporary philosophy tends to dismiss substance as irrelevant. This dismissal is the culmination of a variety of teachings in modern philosophy wherein the notion of substance was either distorted, its nature considered unknowable, or its existence denied. Common to this variety of rejections of substance is a constant failure to treat of substance in its mutual relation with accident, while yet preserving the proper distinction between the two. This fault is actually an inheritance from late scholasticism out of which modern philosophy developed. Suárez, for example, taught an exaggerated view of the individuality and absolute character of accident. ''Being (*ens*) can be predicated absolutely and without qualification of the accident'' (*Disp. meta.* 32.2.18). The scholastic philosophy known to modern philosophers from the 16th to the 18th centuries was principally the philosophy of Suárez. Descartes and Leibniz both read him, and Kant knew his teaching through the *Ontologia* of C. WOLFF. Wolff unfortunately presented the teaching of Suárez as though it were the same as that of St. Thomas.

Descartes. Substance is a key notion in the philosophy of R. DESCARTES. Inspired by the clarity and certainty of mathematics, Descartes searched for a new philosophy whose criterion of truth would be the clarity and distinctness of ideas. He defined substance as ''a thing which so exists that it needs no other thing for existence'' (*Principles of Philosophy* 1.51). His criterion was applied to kinds of substance, and he concluded that there are ''two ultimate classes of real things—the one is intellectual things, . . . the other is material things'' (*ibid.* 1.48). For ''there is always one principal property of substance which constitutes its nature and essence, and on which all the others depend. . . . Thought constitutes the nature of thinking substance. . . . Extension in length, breadth and depth, constitutes the nature of corporeal substance. . . . For all else that may be attributed to body presupposes extension, and is but a mode of this extended thing'' (*ibid.* 1.53).

Descartes made two errors whose influence has been decisive in modern philosophy. First, he equated substance and its property, allowing only a logical distinction between them (*ibid.* 1.60–62). Second, he applied his notion of substance to man's nature and concluded that man is constituted of two substances, soul and body, which are so distinct that man has no direct access to knowledge of the corporeal world (*Meditations* 3, 5, 6). Much of modern philosophy is an attempt to solve the problem of knowledge thus posed by Descartes. The reality and notion of substance have suffered distortion in the process.

Spinoza and Leibniz. B. SPINOZA corrected the notion of a soul too distinct from body by making the Cartesian thought and extension two modes of one infinite substance. For him, multiplicity and finiteness are mere modifications of the two attributes of the one substance that is divine. Thus there is only one substance, which he defined as ''that which is in itself and is conceived through itself, that is, the concept of which does not need the concept of another thing by which it ought to be formed'' (*Ethics* 1, def. 3).

For G. W. LEIBNIZ, substance is a ''being capable of action'' (*Principles of Nature and Grace* 1 [ed. Wiener, 522]). He called the substance a MONAD to emphasize its unity. He proposed an elaborate system, a calculus of reality, in which each monad is self-contained with its particular function, without direct causal interaction among monads and without direct perception of the rest of the universe. Sensation is only the occasion for the intellect's development of innate truths whose whole cause is in the understanding. As Descartes justified man's intellectual knowledge of corporeal reality by an appeal to the divine veracity, and Spinoza by a type of PANTHEISM, so Leibniz guaranteed the truth by a divinely preestablished harmony with God as ''a perfect Geometer'' (*On a General Principle,* ed. Wiener, 66; *New System of Nature and of the Communication of Substances,* ed. Wiener, 114–15).

Locke and Berkeley. British empirical philosophy reacted to the RATIONALISM of the Cartesian philosophy. John LOCKE rejected Descartes's innate ideas and sought his answers to reality in terms of the senses and a mind that are acted upon by sensible objects. In treating of substance and accidents, Locke sought to avoid the Cartesian identification of substance with its property while accepting Descartes's criterion of clear and distinct ideas. When he applied this criterion to quality as distinct from substance, Locke concluded that quality could be considered absolutely by itself and that consequently substance was unknowable in itself. Since ''qualities cannot be the real essence of . . . a substance, man does not know what substance is in itself.'' Substance is an unknown ''standing under or upholding'' of qualities (*Essay Concerning Human Understanding* 2.31; 2.2).

George BERKELEY probed Locke's thought on quality. Since Locke explained primary qualities, such as color and sound, as the product of man's sensations and rejected any role for quality in providing for the knowability of substance, Berkeley went a step further and denied the need for any material substance. ''From what has been said it is evident there is not any other Substance than Spirit, or that which perceives'' (*Treatise Concerning Principles of Human Knowedge* 1.7).

Hume. David HUME took the question still further by challenging the need of any substance to account for the qualities. Like Descartes, Locke, and Berkeley, Hume taught that the immediate object of knowledge is one's perceptions or ideas (*A Treatise of Human Nature,* 1.2.6). Hume then contrasted the perception or impression with what is called substance and concluded that substance is unknowable. He reasoned: ''For how can an impression represent a substance, otherwise than by resembling it? And how can an impression resemble a substance since, according to this philosophy, it is not a substance, and has none of the peculiar qualities or characteristics of substance? . . . We have no perfect idea of any thing but a perception. A substance is entirely different from a perception. We have, therefore, no idea of substance'' (*ibid.* 1.4.5). By concentrating his analysis on perceptions as the only objects of knowledge, Hume rejected the ''opinion of the double existence of perceptions and objects. . . . For as to the notion of external existence, when taken for something specifically different from our perceptions, we have already shown its absurdity'' (*ibid.* 1.4.2).

Finally, Hume turned the definition of substance back upon its proponents. He declared that the same definition could apply to both substance and accident and that since ''every perception may exist separately, and have no need of anything else to support their existence, they are therefore substances, as far as this definition explains a substance'' (*ibid.* 1.1.5).

Kant. Hume carried empiricist philosophy to the dead end of SKEPTICISM with his doubt of the existence of an objective world beyond the knower. Rationalism in the person of Descartes and Leibniz confidently affirmed the existence of such an objective world. But both the empiricists and the rationalists were in agreement that man had no immediate intellectual access to the object outside the knower. Immanuel KANT tried to find a middle path between EMPIRICISM and rationalism by his critique of the grounds of knowledge. Yet his final conclusion had this in common with the extremes he sought to mediate: man has no immediate intellectual access to the thing in itself. Modern philosophy thus found common ground in making the perception or the idea the object of knowledge. Kant wrote: ''Now since without sensibility we cannot have any intuition, understanding cannot be a faculty of intuition. But besides intuition there is no other mode of knowledge except by means of concepts. . . . Since no representation, save when it is an intuition, is in immediate relation to an object, no concept is ever related to an object immediately . . .'' (*Critique of Pure Reason* A 68, B 92–93). By restricting man's immediate knowledge to the realm of sensibility, and this sensibility to the phenomena or appearances only, Kant rejected human knowledge of the thing in itself, the noumenon or substance (*see* NOUMENA). ''How things may be in themselves, apart from the representations through which they affect us, is entirely outside our sphere of knowledge'' (*ibid.* A 190, B 235).

CRITIQUE AND EVALUATION

The problem of substance in modern philosophy is basically the problem of an adequate theory of knowledge. Empiricism, rationalism, and Kant's critical philosophy all fail to evaluate the data of both sense and understanding in terms of the evident unity of man as knower. St. Thomas, using Aristotle's insight of man as a substantial composite, could deal realistically with the problems that are raised by sense knowledge but that remain unanswerable at the sense level. Man is not hopelessly divided into two realms of sensibility and understanding. The solution to the apparent division and opposition is found in the unifying function of the soul as form of the body, with the human intellect serving as a power of the soul (*Summa Theologiae* 1a, 85.1).

False Conceptions. A corollary of modern philosophy's inability to know the thing in itself was its repeated characterization of substance as an unknown, inert, and permanent underlying ground of phenomena, appearances, or qualities. This false description of substance has contributed in large measure to its rejection by recent philosophy (see *The Problem of Substance,* University of California Publications in Philosophy, v. 9, 1937). As Henri BERGSON noted, the rejection turns against the false stereotype. ''I reject an ego-thing, that is, an immobile ego, and in a general way a substance which would be an inert and undefinable support. But to define substance and the ego by their very mobility, this is not to deny them.''

St. Thomas's definition and analysis of the meaning of substance provides sufficiently both for the mobility that Bergson stressed and the permanent subject within the manifold of alterations called for by Kant (*Critique of Pure Reason* A 182, B 225). Unlike both Bergson and Kant, Aquinas provides for an intellectual knowledge of specific substance by ABSTRACTION. There is a hierarchy of substances, some of which are simple, some composite. The composite, whether of short or long duration, are mobile. Yet they serve as a subject of manifold developments. Moreover, substance as a real principle within the concrete reality of the finite individual nature is always to be treated in relation to its various accidents. Far from being static or abstract, the actual substance is dynamic and concrete. St. Thomas repeatedly warns that it is a falsification to identify the mode of existence of a thing in nature with the mode of existence it has within the mind in abstraction.

However, a false conception of substance continues to be dominant in contemporary philosophy. As a result, substance is not so much denied as ignored. Substance for linguistic analysis is a ''factually meaningless verbalism.'' Science and naturalism in philosophy speak more of system than of substance. But within their systems there are entities, particles, which continue to be designated by the descriptive terms once used to describe substances. The philosophical problem of science is how to reconcile the unity of a nature with the plurality of particles (*see* ATOMISM). As St. Thomas stressed, only substance can so guarantee unity as to prevent a meaningless regression to infinity.

Role in Theology. In theology, substance is important not only for the doctrine of the Incarnation, as noted above, but it is also central to an intelligible expression of the mystery of the Holy Eucharist. The Council of Trent, treating of the EUCHARIST, teaches the ''change of the whole substance of the bread into the Body and of the whole substance of the wine into the Blood . . . (of Our Lord Jesus Christ) which change the Catholic Church most suitably calls transubstantiation'' (H. Denzinger, *Enchiridion symbolorum* 1652). Pope Pius XII, in *HUMANI GENERIS*, took occasion to remind Catholic teachers of the validity of the notion of substance as used in the doctrine of TRANSUBSTANTIATION and warned against rejecting substance as though it were ''an antiquated philosophic notion.''

See Also: BEING; CATEGORIES OF BEING; KNOWLEDGE, THEORIES OF; REALISM.

Bibliography: C. ARPE, ''Substantia,'' *Philologus* 94 (1940) 65–78. G. CAPONE BRAGA, *Enciclopedia filosofica,* (Venice-Rome 1957) 4:804–815. H. BLUMENBERG, *Die Religion in Geschichte und Gegenwart* (Tübingen 1957–65) 6:456–458. R. E. MCCALL, *The Reality of Substance* (Washington, D.C. 1956). C. A. HART, *Thomistic Metaphysics: An Inquiry into the Act of Existing* (Englewood Cliffs, N.J. 1959). L. DE RAEYMAEKER, *The Philosophy of Being,* tr. E. H. ZIEGELMEYER (St. Louis, Mo. 1954). M. M. SCHEU, *The Categories of Being in Aristotle and St. Thomas* (Washington, D.C. 1944). A. J. OSGNIACH, *The Analysis of Objects* (New York 1938). J. OWENS, *The Doctrine of Being in the Aristotelian Metaphysics* (Toronto, Ont. 1951). T. J. RAGUSA, *The Substance Theory of Mind and Contemporary Functionalism* (Washington, D.C. 1937). A. J. RECK, ''Substance, Language and Symbolic Logic,'' *The Modern Schoolman* 35 (March 1958) 155–171. L. RUMBLE, ''Science, Substance and Sacrament,'' *Homiletic and Pastoral Review* 59 (1959) 638–648.

[R. E. MCCALL]

SUBSTANTIAL CHANGE

Substantial change (Lat. *generatio simpliciter*) or absolute BECOMING (Lat. *fieri absolute, fieri simpliciter*) is the passage in a subject from absolute nonbeing to being that is SUBSTANCE. This passage is necessarily produced in the indivisible instant in which a substance both comes to be and exists in itself. For example, when Socrates becomes man, in contrast to his becoming pale or suntanned, there is no time or instant in which Socrates himself begins to exist and yet does not already exist. As a substance, he does not admit of being more or less. He can, however, be more or less pale or suntanned, and become so through a becoming that, unlike substantial change, is MOTION in the strict sense, successive and measured by time. Because substantial change is a change between contradictories (being and nonbeing), wherein there is no intermediary, it is not simply a change according to place, or according to quality, or according to quantity, or merely some combination of these. Such changes affect an already existing substance only in some respect and not absolutely. There is always, however, a motion in the strict sense that precedes the instantaneous generation of a substance and terminates at the moment of generation. And in every substantial change there is involved not only the absolute generation of a substance that did not exist before, but also the absolute corruption of a substance that did exist before. The change of quality of this preceding composite of subject and substantial form, called alteration, terminates (1) at an ultimate qualitative disposition incompatible with the preceding substance, (2) at the corruption of this substance, and (3) at the production of the substance that now comes to be absolutely—and terminates at all three in the same instant.

Terminological Distinctions. The following distinctions of meaning in the use of the expression ''absolute becoming'' are indispensable for understanding substantial change, for sometimes the word ''absolute'' refers to the becoming itself, sometimes to the term of the becoming, and sometimes to both.

''Absolute becoming'' can mean: (1) becoming in the strict sense, which is a motion, measured by time, such as ''being in the process of whitening''; (2) becoming, again in the strict sense, but attributed to a substance, such as Socrates, as to its term but before this term is attained; (3) becoming that is according to contradictories and therefore instantaneous, whether in the order of ACCIDENT or that of substance; (4) the becoming of a substance, such as Socrates, where the term signifies both the alteration that precedes Socrates and his instantaneous becoming; or (5) the instantaneous becoming of an absolute being, which is called ''becoming'' with respect to the preceding movement of alteration, and ''absolute'' by reason of that which comes to be, namely a being absolutely or a substance.

The permanent subject required for becoming as such—something that the earliest philosophers acknowledged—is called MATTER, by analogy with that ''from which'' and ''out of which'' artificial objects are made, as a table is made out of wood, and is regarded as a potency in relation to the act or form acquired in becoming. This subject, common to both terms of the becoming and permanent throughout it, must be part of the substance generated, and must have been part of the substance now corrupted. This is necessary if the substance now generated, say Socrates, is truly to have come to be according to what he is absolutely, and is not merely to have become pale or suntanned, either of which requires that he himself already have come to be and, now existing, can become this or that.

Greek Problematic. The difficulty of accounting for the difference between substantial change and accidental change, and of accounting for the sensibly evident multiplicity and variety of things in the world and the unity and unchangeableness that things have in the mind, finds its first expression in ancient Greece. The pre-Socratic philosophers puzzled over the problem of the one and the many, seeking to account for changes in a way that yet allowed for unchanging knowledge. Driven to extreme positions in their quest for a truth that proved unexpectedly difficult, some, like PARMENIDES of Elea (515–440 B.C.), argued that true knowledge and science must be possible, that only being that is one is real, but that change is an illusion. Others, like Cratylus of Ephesus (5th century B.C.), a disciple of HERACLITUS the Obscure (530–470 B.C.), argued that being was the illusion, change the only reality, and hence true knowledge and science were impossible. Further attempts to reconcile these extreme views proved unsatisfactory. The skepticism of the SOPHISTS finally provoked a sincere new effort to resolve the dilemma and preserve the truths already attained.

Socrates's arguments with the Sophists and Plato's further development of theory and reflective thinking prepared the way for a flowering of logic in the thought of Aristotle. Aristotle's solution was that there is a permanent subject of the forms that succeed each other in change, and that this subject is a potency that lacks at first the form of the composite produced at the end of the change. In substantial change, the subject must be a pure potency in itself lacking any form, but able to be the subject of any form it lacks. A substance, then, does not come to be from sheer nothing, but from being in potency (not being in act). It thus becomes possible to have true knowledge and science even of changeable things by knowing their necessary principles, causes, and elements; material individuals themselves, however, are known in sensation and remain perishable in time.

Although Aristotle's solution to the problem of being and becoming is conclusive, it is by no means a conclusion of man's perennial pursuit of wisdom to satisfy his wonder. Nor do later philosophers always accept it as the foundation of further research and explanation.

Medieval and Modern Thought. In the Middle Ages, Aristotle's most famous commentator, St. THOMAS AQUINAS, imparted a new momentum to the reintroduction of Aristotle's teachings into the stream of Western thought. He affirmed again the dependence of knowledge in the order of learning on experience of the sensible world, reiterated the principles enunciated by Aristotle, and elaborated upon them in arguing against the Platonist view of reality that placed the primary emphasis on a priori forms of human thought. The ancient dilemma of being and becoming, of the noetic problem of the one and the many, found further controversial expression in the rationalistic thought of DESCARTES and his followers in the rise of British EMPIRICISM. Kant's critical idealism sought anew to resolve the same basic problem by distinguishing between things in themselves and their ''appearances in sensuous representation'' or a priori intellectual formation. The Platonist view persevered, only to be countered by continued insistence from empiricists upon the reality of changing phenomena to the exclusion of intellectual certainty.

The German idealist philosopher, HEGEL, meditating on the paradox of instantaneous becoming and substantial change, denied that it was a paradox, and affirmed the identity of being or substance in thought with its contradictory opposite, nonbeing or nothing. He regarded the very antithesis of reason as the only reasonable principle to hold; contradiction itself was the source of all being and becoming.

Problems from Modern Science. The rapid development of natural science and experimental method, of modern physics and atomic theory, presented new difficulties. Real substantial differences and substantial changes in the world first seemed to give way to differences merely in atomic or nuclear structure of basically unchanging but rearrangeable fundamental particles. But these protons, electrons, neutrons, and other newly discovered or manufactured particles themselves soon exhibited the capacity to be transformed.

Nuclear isomerism, which refers to atomic nuclei with the same mass and charge but with different nuclear properties such as observably different half-lives, pointed to differences between isomers of the same element that might qualify as ''accidental'' in terms of Aristotelian principles. The destruction of chemical bonds between molecular atoms due to isomeric transitions characterized by energy emission, or to other radioactive transformations, pointed to changes that might be ''substantial'' or ''accidental.'' But to think of such changes as occurring on the microscopic level of the atomic and subatomic worlds, where unimaginable waves and particles dissolve one into the other, leads to the use of ambiguous and misleading language. Ordinary terminology becomes equivocal when thus transferred to the context of modern physics and chemistry.

In their employment of measurement to get at the quantitative aspects of things, and in their mathematical formulation of results, the concrete branches of modern science necessarily abstract from the basic problem and its solution. However important are the problems the experimental sciences attempt to resolve, the philosophical problem of substantial change lies outside the scope of their direct concern. And whether physical substances are made of protons and electrons or of the elements of the ancients, perennial philosophy still regards substances as capable of coming to be from being in potency, and not from being in act, and as existing in themselves and not in something else. It holds, moreover, that some certain knowledge of their nature and properties can be had in terms of their necessary principles, causes, and elements.

See Also: ATOMISM; HYLOMORPHISM; HYLOSYSTEMISM; MATTER AND FORM.

Bibliography: V. E. SMITH, *General Science of Nature* (Milwaukee 1958). P. H. J. HOENEN, *The Philosophy of Inorganic Compounds,* tr. P. COHEN (West Baden Springs, Ind. 1960). C. DE KONINCK, ''UB Paradoxe du devenir par contradiction,'' *Laval Théologique et Philosophique,* 12 (1956) 9–51. A. MANSION, *Introduction à la physique aristotélicienne* (Louvain 1946). A. D. SERTILLANGES, *La Philosophie de St. Thomas d'Aquin,* 2 v. (new ed. rev. and enl. Paris 1940). H. VEATCH, ''Aristotelianism,'' *A History of Philosophical Systems,* ed. V. T. A. FERM (Patterson 1961) 106–117. F. C. COPLESTON, *History of Philosophy* (Westminster, Md. 1946–) v. 1, Greece and Rome (1946; 2d ed. 1950).

[A. ROBINSON]

SUDAN, THE CATHOLIC CHURCH IN

The Republic of the Sudan is located in east Africa. Straddling the Nile River, it is bound on the north by Egypt, on the east by the Red Sea, Eritrea and Ethiopia, on the south by Kenya, Uganda and the Democratic Republic of the Congo, on the west by Chad and the Central African Republic, and on the northwest by Libya. Cotton, Sudan's main economic resource, is cultivated by means of massive irrigation projects near the Nile. Apart from the Nile banks, northern Sudan is an arid plateau or desert. The south is fertile with abundant rainfall, but economically unexploited. Livestock production has been increasing. Mineral resources, which are poor, include petroleum, as well as small quantities of iron ore, copper, chromium, zinc, mica, silver and gold.

An independent republic since 1956, the Sudan (literally ''country of the blacks'') has alternated between periods of colonization from Egypt and periods of independence. In 1898, Lord Kitchner, a Britisher, crushed a massive revolt against Egyptian rule, and the Anglo-Egyptian condominium was established that would rule for over half a century. Ethnically the populace represents the results of centuries of invasion and migration. In the north live Arabs or ''arabized'' Hamites and Nubians, while to the south the inhabitants come from 56 major tribal groups, the most important of which are the Azande

Capital: Khartoum.
Size: 967,500 sq. miles.
Population: 35,079,815 in 2000.
Languages: Arabic, Nubian, Ta Bedawie, English; Nilotic, Nilo-Hamitic dialects and Sudanic languages are spoken in various regions.
Religions: 1,052,380 Catholics (6%), 26,309,000 Sunni and other Muslims (75%), 1,049,880 Protestants (3%), 800,000 Orthodox (2%), 5,868,555 follow indigenous beliefs.
Archdioceses: Khartoum (created 1974), with suffragans El Obeid (1974); Juba (1974), with suffragans Malakal (1974), Rumbek (1974), Tombura-Yambio (1974), Torit (1983), Wau (1974), and Yei (1986).

and the Fung. One-third of the population concentrates in one-tenth of the land area along the Nile. Since 1993 civil war between the Arab Muslim north and the Black Christian south has resulted in a massive loss of life, a floundering economy and harsh criticism from international humanitarian organizations.

Early History. Egypt began its colonizing to the south in 2700 B.C. Roman influence brought Christianity to Dongola and Khartoum in the 4th century and created Christian islands that survived successive invasions by Muslim bedouins from Arabia, who entered by way of Egypt beginning in the 7th century. The Abbasids, the Fung Empire and other Muslim states ruled the area in succession, with the result that Christianity had disappeared completely by 1600. The northern Sudan came to embrace Islam, but ANIMISM retained its hold on the south, even after the chiefs introduced ISLAM. Egyptian Pasha Mehemet Ali conquered the Sudan in 1820–22. A few Jesuits and Austrian diocesan missionaries vainly tried to begin evangelization in 1846; Franciscan efforts in 1861 fared no better.

The newly founded Verona Fathers succeeded in establishing a mission in 1872, but the regime of Mahdi Muhammad Ahmed (1881–98) ruined their work. In 1881 a massive revolt erupted under Ahmed's government that was successfully put down by Lord Kitchener in 1898. The Verona Fathers immediately renewed their work in the Sudan with 250 Catholics. By 1931 the Catholic population had increased to 39,416. In 1933 the MILL HILL MISSIONARIES joined the Verona Fathers in the south, where the Church worked among the native tribes.

A year after Kitchner's military intercession, the Egyptian and British governments signed the Anglo-Egyptian Condominium Agreement, under which they jointly governed the Sudan. Northern and southern Sudan were isolated from one another thus creating dramatic cultural differences. British influence lasted until 1950, amid a growing nationalist movement by the region's Egyptian population to the north. A three-year transitional period led to Sudanese independence in 1956 under a preliminary Sudanese government elected in 1953.

An Independent Sudan. As was typical of many newly created African nations, factional conflicts began almost immediately; in Sudan's case between the north and the south. Civil warfare between the northern and southern Sudanese led the British government to close the 161 mission schools in the south temporarily in 1955. The new Sudanese Republic allowed them to reopen in 1956, but expelled several missionaries on charges of complicity in the southern revolt. In 1957 all schools were nationalized as part of a national unification policy that aimed at the progressive Islamicization of the south. A military coup led by General Ibrahim Abboud took control of the government in 1958, continuing the policy of Islamicization and imposed martial law. In 1962 the Missionary Societies Act (MSA) severely restricted religious freedom, its main target the Christian churches of the south. The building of churches was forbidden, and freedom of opinion and expression was curtailed. The law, rigidly enforced only in the south, resulted in the expulsion of foreign missionaries. By the end of 1964 when more than 200 Comboni priests and sisters were indiscriminately deported, all Christian missionaries, save for a few Sudanese, had been driven from the south, and all mission schools were closed. In the north, where Christian proselytizing was not attempted, missionaries continued to engage in educational work and to minister to small expatriate communities. 1965 saw the establishment of the Sudan Council of Churches, an organization that would be involved in major relief and reconstruction work in the south during the decades to come.

In 1969 Prime Minister Abboud was deposed by Colonel Jafaar Muhammad al-Nimeiry, who governed under a revolutionary council and became Sudan's first elected president via elections held three years later. In 1974 the hierarchy was established, and a Sudan Episcopal Conference (SCBC) was formed. When Archbishop Baroni of Khartoum retired in 1981, the SCBC became the first national episcopal conference in modern church history to be made up entirely of African-born bishops.

While President Nimeiry's Addis Ababa agreement created a fragile peace between north and south that lasted from 1972 to 1983, his economic policies failed, resulting in growing unrest. In 1983 civil war broke out anew under the leadership of the Marxist Sudan People's Liberation Army (SPLA), a non-Muslim group based in the south. Missionaries who had returned after the Addis Ababa accord now came under the attack of both the SPLA and the government. Missions were sacked and priests and sisters held hostages for months by the SPLA.

Later, pressured by a new international political climate, the SPLA abandoned its ideology and allowed church personnel to work in the areas under its control.

The growing climate of violence and political unrest culminated in a bloodless military coup in April of 1985. Following a brief reign by Sadiq al-Mahdi, Lieutenant General Omar Hassan Ahmed al-Bashir became prime minister, and political parties were banned. Islam became the state religion in the north, while penal codes for the entire country were Islamicized as early as 1984. The devastating conflict in Southern Sudan continues to be fueled by cultural differences, ethnic fragmentation and economic underdevelopment. The war situation and the continuous relocation of the displaced people deeply marked the life of the Christian communities and caused the failure of many pastoral initiatives.

In a letter to the new government in 1986, Sudanese bishops repeatedly asked that the MSA be repealed, noting that ''Christian Sudanese will never enjoy freedom of religious profession and practice, neither public nor privately, as long as the 1962 MSA exists.'' The government did not respond. On the occasion of the visit of Pope John Paul II to Khartoum in February of 1993 Sudan

Catholic Church, Wau, Sudan. (©Paul Almasy/CORBIS)

President Bashir, in a spirit of goodwill, promised to repeal the MSA, but this did not occur.

Focuses on Humanitarian Efforts. It was estimated that between 1983 and 1994, at least a million and a half southern Sudanese died, and four and a half million more became refugees or displaced, living outside their traditional homelands and in nearby Zaire, Uganda and Kenya due to the combined actions of the civil war and the recurrent droughts. Throughout the 1990s, conditions continued to deteriorate, as the SPLM waged war on the Muslim government. In 1990 missionaries were expelled from South Kordofan, and in 1992 from Juba. In the north, missionaries who were mainly engaged in educational work and in ministry to communities of foreigners were allowed to stay.

Beginning in 1989 the presence of the Church in the areas held by the rebels grew perceptibly, and the work of evangelization, rehabilitation and humanitarian assistance was carried out under the leadership of two bishops and an apostolic administrator. Their activity included advocacy at all levels (other episcopal conferences and international political organizations). They were assisted in this by People for Peace in Africa, a pacifist ecumenical organization based in Nairobi that began in response to the Sudan problem. In February of 1990 Catholics joined Sudan's other Christian churches in forming the New Sudan Council of Churches (NSCC) to unify ongoing humanitarian efforts to assist war victims.

In addition to aiding residents in militarized areas, the Church dedicated itself to working among the refugees and displaced, making Catholic missions a lifeline for many thousands who would otherwise live on leaves and grass in the famine-stricken region. Around the outskirts of Khartoum, where about a million and a half displaced southern Sudanese lived, SUDANAID was active. The Church established Multipurpose Centers (MPC) in rented houses or constructed them in squatter's camps with mud and straw. Run by catechists or lay-leaders aided by a committee, the MPC's offered educational and religious programs: kindergarten for children, women's education, reading programs, an organized catechumenate and prayer meetings on Sundays. By 2000 these camps were being dismantled by the government, the one on the outskirts of Khartoum razed and its residents forced into the desert. The Church was also present in the refugee camps of Zaire, Uganda and Kenya with missionary personnel and the NSCC. Pope John Paul II's short visit to Khartoum on Feb. 10, 1993 was a historic event in support of the Church's efforts. In his sermon the pope spoke of the long suffering of the people of Sudan and of the experience of the South as ''a living Calvary.''

Into the 21st Century. The special status given to Islam under Bashir's government fostered discriminatory practices against Christianity and other non-Islamic religions in the country. The right to practice a Christian faith continued to be constrained into the 1990s, and a new constitution promulgated in 1999 did little to promote religious tolerance, proclaiming Shari'a and Islamic custom to be the source of all legislation. Catholic leaders responded with an attitude of openness and expressed a desire for dialogue as a means of promoting peace efforts, human dignity and mutual respect, but rejected the imposition of an Islamic state. Because Christianity had become a symbol of resistance to the imposition of this state, Catholic priests continued to be the focus of harassment by police, and were sometimes subject to false arrest. In 1998 two priests were charged with a bombing attempt in Khartoum but were later released. In 2000 an armed police squad entered the priests's residence of Comboni College secondary school to ostensibly search for illegal immigrants. Other areas of concern were the taking of slaves—usually Christians or practitioners of indigenous faiths—in the southern war zone and their transport to northern Sudan. By 1998 it was reported that the Church was buying back orphaned children away from their captors.

By 2000 the Catholic community continued to reside in southern Sudan, and consisted of four rites: Armenian, Chaldean, Maronite and Roman. There were a total of 104 parishes, tended by 188 diocesan and 123 religious priests. Other religious, who aided in humanitarian efforts and operated the country's 206 primary and 22 secondary Catholic schools. The three primary Orthodox

Churches in the region were the Coptic, the Ethiopian Orthodox Church and the Armenian Orthodox Church, all of which had adherents living near Khartoum. Housing the government, Khartoum became a focus of anti-Christian action, razing Christian churches, schools and other structures, confiscating Church property, and refusing permits for new construction. A peace agreement reached in 1997 negotiated a southern self-determination referendum by 2001, although the terms of the agreement were later disputed.

Bibliography: J. DEMPSEY, *Mission on the Nile* (New York 1956). *Le missioni cattoliche: Storia, geographia, statistica* (Rome 1950) 93–96. *Annuario Pontificio* has data on all diocese.

[J. A. BELL/R. K. SESANA/EDS.]

SUENENS, LEON-JOSEPH

Ecumenist and cardinal archbishop of Mechelen-Brussels, Belgium; b. Brussels, July 16, 1904; d. Brussels, May 6, 1996; studied at the Gregorian University in Rome (1921–1929) and was ordained a priest for the Mechelen (Malines) archdiocese in 1927.

In 1930 Suenens was appointed professor of philosophy at the seminary of Mechelen and then vice-rector of the Catholic University of Louvain in 1940, and in 1945 he became auxiliary bishop to Cardinal Van Roey, whom he succeeded as archbishop of Mechelen and primate of Belgium (1961). Suenens was responsible for the division that resulted in the creation of the new diocese of Antwerp. Pope John XXIII named him a cardinal in 1962, and soon after a member of the Central Commission for Vatican II. Suenens then presented the pope an outline of the themes he felt had to be dealt with at the council. This outline was endorsed by Pope John and warmly supported by a number of influential cardinals, including G. B. Montini, the future Pope Paul VI. There is no doubt that it decisively influenced the further proceedings of Vatican II.

Vatican II. Pope Paul VI appointed Suenens as one of the four moderators who guided the proceedings of the Council. His three main interventions promoted the ideas of a permanent diaconate, proposed an age limit of 75 for bishops, and stressed the value of charisms conferred upon the laity. Friendly contacts with non-Catholic observers at the council resulted in Suenens' deep and personal involvement in ecumenical relationships. Year after year he was invited to the U.S. and to Britain by a wide diversity of ecclesiastical organizations as a leading figure of the post-conciliar Church. Meanwhile he pursued his efforts to defend the legacy of Vatican II, ''keeping guard at the doors opened by the Council'' (Methodist Bishop Corson). At the first Synod of Bishops (1967) Suenens recommended the creation of an International Theological Commission, which was established soon thereafter. This same concern prompted him to publish his book *Co-Responsibility in the Church* (1968), which made a considerable impact. He later raised the same issue in two interviews which appeared in the French press. There ensued a heated controversy, in which Suenens had to vindicate his loyalty to the Holy See in the face of public criticism from high-ranking prelates. His ideas on collegiality received, however, a wide support in the Second Synod of Bishops.

No less controversial was his proposal in the Third Synod (1971) that the ordination of married men be considered in regions where celibate priests were lacking. Throughout his episcopacy, Suenens had been acutely aware of contemporary social trends and seeds of spiritual renewal for the Church. Hence interest in and support of the LEGION OF MARY, MARRIAGE ENCOUNTER, and from the early 1970s, the CHARISMATIC RENEWAL. At the request of Pope Paul VI, he became the unofficial but very efficient shepherd of Catholic charismatic groups and communities throughout the world, a role that contributed in a decisive way both to their acceptance by the hierarchy and to the preservation of their Catholic identity. He also stressed the value of a spiritual renewal for ecumenical rapprochement. Suenens' wide range of interests and untiring pastoral zeal is best evidenced in the impressive series of books he authored: *Theology of the Legion of Mary* (1954); *The Right View of Moral Rearmament* (1954); *The Gospel to Every Creature* (1957); *Mary, the Mother of God* (1959); *The Nun in the World* (1962); *Love and Self-Control* (1962); *Christian Life Day by Day* (1964); *Co-Responsibility in the Church* (1968); (with Archbishop M. Ramsey) *The Future of the Christian Church* (1970); *A New Pentecost?* (1975); *Ecumenism and Charismatic Renewal* (1978; with D. H. Camara); *Charismatic Renewal and Social Action* (1979); and *Renewal and the Powers of Darkness* (1982).

When Cardinal Suenens reached the age of retirement in 1979, he resigned his see, but continued to promote charismatic renewal, always faithful to the motto on his coat of arms: *In Spiritu Sancto.* When he died at the age of 91, Pope John Paul II recalled the important role Suenens played at the Second Vatican Council.

Bibliography: L.-J. SUENENS, ''Aux origines du Concile Vatican II,'' *Nouvelle revue thé'ologique* 107 (1985): 3–21, with first-publication of original documents. E. HAMILTON, *Cardinal Suenens: A Portrait* (London 1975). P. WEBER, ''Le Cardinal Suenens,'' *La foi et le temps* 16 (1985–6): 400–422.

[P. LEBEAU]

SUETONIUS

Roman biographer, b. Rome? *c.* A.D. 69 of an equestrian military family; d. *c.* 140. Gaius Tranquillus Suetonius was dismissed as a private secretary under Hadrian *c.* 121 for reasons unknown. A reference in the letters of his friend PLINY THE YOUNGER and an article in Suidas are the main sources for his life. He wrote much in Latin and Greek, but only the *Lives of the Twelve Caesars* and fragments of *De viris illustribus* (*Famous Men*) survive. From the latter work (*c.* 106–113) the lives of Terence, Horace, Lucan, and Pliny are substantially preserved. The *Lives* of the Caesars from Julius to Domitian is a garrulous, uncritical work but fills a void in knowledge of the early Empire; Suetonius's racy style makes his characters come alive. His motive in writing would seem to have been to show the frailty of the Julio-Claudian line. An interesting but garbled reference puts Christ at the time of Claudius (*Claud.* 25.4). Suetonius exercised an influence on JEROME's *Lives* and, centuries later, on EINHARD's *Life of Charlemagne.*

Bibliography: G. FUNAIOLI, *Paulys Realenzyklopädie der klassischen Altertumswissenschaft,* ed. G. WISSOWA, et al. (Stuttgart 1893–) 4A.1:593–641. J. ROLFE, *The Oxford Classical Dictionary,* ed. M. CARY et al. (Oxford 1949) 865–866. M. SCHANZ, C. HOSIUS and G. KRÜGER, *Geschichte der römischen Literatur,* 4 v. in 5 (Munich 1914–35) 3:48–67. J. W. and A. M. DUFF, *A Literary History of Rome in the Silver Age . . .* (2d ed. London 1960), bibliography.

[H. MUSURILLO]

SUFFERING

Connected with the problem of THEODICY, or why the just God allows evil in the world, is the problem of suffering, or why the good God permits man to have physical, mental, and spiritual afflictions. This article first treats the ideas of the Sacred Scriptures and then those of post-Biblical Christian thought on the problem of human suffering.

In the Bible

The sacred writers, focusing their attention on the various aspects of suffering, look on it as an evil whose origins are to be traced to sin, especially the sin of Adam; also, as God's RETRIBUTION for national or personal sin; and most significantly, beginning with Second Isaia, as vicarious expiation effectual by reason of human solidarity [*see* EXPIATION (IN THE BIBLE)].

In the Old Testament. The most significant attitude toward suffering in the Old Testament was that it was God's punishment for sin; in postexilic Judaism this position was challenged and modified by new revelation.

Suffering as Punishment for Sin. Although everything, good and evil, comes from God (Am 3.6; Is 45.7; Jb 2.10), the ultimate cause of suffering is to be related somehow to ORIGINAL SIN [*see* SIN (IN THE BIBLE)]. According to Genesis ch. 2 and 3, man's first parents were created in the state of innocence and happiness, but by the sin of disobedience they brought on themselves suffering and death. The effort of providing their daily bread and the pain of childbearing are singled out as outstanding features of the suffering that resulted from their fallen condition (Gn 3.16–19). Because of the solidarity of the human race, subsequent suffering in the world is essentially related to this first sin. The Mosaic Law, presupposing strict retribution as God's way of dealing with sin, sanctioned the punitive aspect of suffering and applied it to individuals as well as to the entire nation (Lv 26; Dt 27–28). Hence, individual crimes were punished by law (Ex 21.12, 17–25); suffering was considered just retribution for sin (Nm 12.1–15; 2 Chr 26.16–21); and an apostate nation would be punished with extreme sufferings (Dt 8.28; 28.15–68). The Prophets in particular attributed Israel's calamities to her unfaithfulness to Yahweh (Is 3.16–26; 22.1–14; Jer 2.19; 4.18). Because of Israel's corporate solidarity, the whole family or even the whole nation would suffer for the sin of one of its members (Jos 7.10–15; 2 Sm 24.10–17; 1 Kgs 17.1; 2 Kgs 21.10–15). But suffering also had a medicinal purpose, for God did not want to destroy but to convert His people (Lv 26.40–45; Dt 4.30–31). Thus, their sufferings became the birth pangs of a new era of restoration (Is 25.8; 35.4–10; Jer 31.15–20, 31–34).

Postexilic Crisis about Suffering. Ezekiel was the first who explicitly applied the doctrine of retribution to the individual (31.29–30): the individual during his lifetime was to be rewarded or punished for his own behavior, not for that of his parents or nation. This doctrine was consistently repeated in Proverbs, some of the Psalms, and later in Sirach. But such teaching, rigidly applied, contradicted everyday experience, which showed that the wicked often prospered and the just often suffered. And so the just, almost scandalized by the apparent injustice, cried to God [Ps 6.4; 34(35).17; 87(88).15; 88(89).47], vehemently expressed sorrow (Jer 20.14–18; Jb 3.3–12), and protested the prosperity of sinners (Jer 12.1–4). The books of Job and Ecclesiastes and some of the Psalms [Ps 36(37); 48(49); 72(73)] attempted to reconcile the suffering of the just with God's providence and wisdom; yet the final solution could come only with the revelation of eternal reward and punishment in the life hereafter (Wis 1–5; Dn 12.1–3; 2 Mc 7.9, 11, 14, 23). In searching for this final solution, the Jews also recognized that suffering tested man's virtue and his fidelity to God (Sir 2.4; Wis 3.5) and enabled him to atone for others. The idea of vicarious suffering was fully developed by Isaiah in his Songs of SUFFERING SERVANT (Is 42.1–4; 49.1–7; 50.4–11; 52.13–53.12).

In the New Testament. The suffering of Christ is presented in the New Testament as a wholly vicarious suffering, necessary for effecting man's Redemption; the Christian, in turn, as a redeemed member of Christ's Mystical Body, must share in his Lord's suffering if he wishes to participate in His glory.

Suffering of Christ. In the life of Jesus suffering found its full meaning. Christ did not suffer for suffering's own sake. Indeed, he was distressed at the thought of it (Jn 12.27), prayed that it might pass away (Lk 22.42), and felt it acutely on the cross (Mt 27.46). Yet He accepted it voluntarily out of love for His Father and friends (Jn 14.31; 15.13; Gal 2.20). Hinting at it (Jn 3.14; 12.32) and openly predicting it (Mk 8.31–33; 10.33–34), He taught clearly that His suffering the ordeal of death was absolutely necessary for man's Redemption and His own glorification (Mk 8.31–33; Lk 24.25–26). The early KERYGMA went on to attest that by His suffering Christ merited man's Redemption and fulfilled the Isaian prophecies of the Suffering Servant of the Lord (Acts 2.23–24; 3.13–14; 4.10–12; 1 Jn 2.2; 4.10). In the words of St. Paul, Christ's death expiated man's sins (Rom 5.9; 1 Cor 15.3; 2 Cor 5.21; etc.), reconciled man to God (Rom 5.9; 2 Cor 5.19; 1 Tm 2.5–6), and merited His own glorification (Eph 1.20–23). The author of Hebrews represents the suffering Christ as the High Priest who sacrificed Himself for man ''once for all'' (Heb 2.9; 7.27; 9.26–28), learned obedience by His suffering (Heb 5.8), and became compassionate with man (Heb 2.17–18). According to St. Peter, Christ, by His vicarious suffering, not only effected man's salvation but also left an example (1 Pt 2.21–25; cf. Is 52.13–53.12).

Suffering of the Christian. Suffering pertains to the essence of the Christian life (Mt 5.10–12). Like Christ, the disciple will be persecuted (Mt 10.24; Jn 15.19–21). Following Christ, he must deny himself (Mt 16.24; Mk 8.34–35; Lk 9.23), must learn to suffer unjustly (1 Pt 4.15–19), with joy (Jas 1.2; 1 Pt 4.13), for Christ's sake (2 Cor 4.9–11; Phil 1.29). So the Apostles rejoiced that they were found worthy to suffer for the name of Christ (Acts 5.41; 2 Tm 1.8, 12; 2.9, 12). Yet man's present suffering cannot be compared to his future glory (Rom 8.18). St. Paul adds another reason: the suffering of the Christian benefits not only himself but the whole MYSTICAL BODY. Paul rejoiced in his suffering, for it gave consolation to others (2 Cor 1.4–7) and effected their salvation (2 Tm 2.10). In Baptism he died to sin (Rom 6.1–11), carried the marks of Christ's suffering in his own body (Gal 6.17), and longed for the fellowship of the suffering of Christ (Phil 3.8–10) in order to fill up what was wanting in the suffering of Christ for the Church (Col 1.24).

Bibliography: *Encyclopedic Dictionary of the Bible*, tr. and adap. by L. HARTMAN (New York 1963), from A. VAN DEN BORN, *Bijbels Woordenboek* 2340–45. O. A. PIPER, G. A. BUTTRICK ed., *The Interpreters' Dictionary of the Bible*, 4 v. (Nashville 1962) 4:450–53. E. F. SUTCLIFFE, *Providence and Suffering in the Old and New Testaments* (London 1955). J. A. SANDERS, *Suffering as Divine Discipline in the Old Testament and Post-Biblical Judaism* (Rochester, New York 1955). J. SCHARBERT, *Der Schmerz im Alten Testament* (Bonn 1955). C. R. NORTH, *The Suffering Servant in Deutero-Isaiah* (2d ed. London 1956). J. J. STAMM, *Das Leiden des Unschuldigen in Babylon und Israel* (*Abhandlungen zur Theologie des Alten und Neuen Testaments* 10; 1946). H. H. ROWLEY, *Submission in Suffering and Other Essays on Eastern Thought* (Cardiff 1951). J. KREMER, *Was an den Leiden Christi noch mangelt* (Bonn 1956).

[J. BUKOVSKY]

Christian Attitude

Traditional Christian ascetical theory and practice have been shaped by the scriptural teaching set forth above; and a distinctively Christian attitude toward the suffering, adversity, and death that are inseparable from the human lot, as well as toward voluntary SELF-DENIAL and works of mortification, developed and has been maintained in spite of wide differences in the particular manifestations in which it has found expression.

Baptism. The Christian has been baptized into Christ, into His death and Resurrection, symbolically but really, through the Sacrament of Baptism (Rom 6.3–5). Just as a man who is submerged into the water dies of drowning, but when he is pulled up, he is saved from death, so does Baptism work spiritually in the soul of the Christian. Baptism gives the Christian life in Christ, but it does not liberate him from an internal state of struggle. There is another tendency in him that drives him away from the love of God and neighbor, that inclines him to listen to temptation. The period until the coming of Christ at the end of time is one of struggle (Rom 7.21–25) and calls for self-denial and control (1 Cor 9.27; Eph 4.22). Thus is the Christian faced with a paradox: although as one who has accepted and believed in Christ he already has a share in Christ's life even here on earth and in that sense is ''saved,'' he must nevertheless mortify his bodily members (Col 3.5). Like St. Paul, he sees the need of ''chastising his body and bringing it into subjection'' (1 Cor 9.27). He is one of those to whom Christ referred when He said: ''After the bridegroom has been taken away, the disciples will fast'' (Mt 9.15).

The paradox is resolved by the fact that Christian fasts and self-denial take on an eschatological meaning. Those who believe in Christ are saved, but they have not yet reached their final goal. They still move through a valley of tears and are beset with danger. But above all, Christians endure suffering and even undertake voluntary austerities ''because the bridegroom has been taken away.'' They long for the day when they will ''see Him as He is''; the messianic banquet—Christ—is not theirs yet, and they must wait in patience and love, but prudent as serpents against the enemy, the devil, who ''goes about seeking whom he may devour'' (1 Pt 5.8). The Christian's patient endurance of tribulation and the fasting and other mortifications he undertakes become, then, an appeal to the invisible Spouse to speed the day of His coming. By their endurance and by their mortification, by their prayers and sacrifices, by mysteriously ''filling up those things which are lacking in the passion of Christ,'' Christians help bring closer the second glorious coming of Christ.

Voluntary Suffering. Christian tradition has seen the aspect of the voluntary submission of affliction and works of self-denial also as a way of imitating Christ's own love. The Christian is in a sense the prolongation of the presence of Christ in space and time, and as such he must continue Christ's actions in his own life (see Vatican II, *Constitution on the Sacred Liturgy,* ch. 1–5). Christ died for all men because He loves all men; Christians must continue this loving suffering and mortification for those who are, either potentially or in fact, their brothers in Christ. In his apostolic letter *Salvifici doloris* (1984), John Paul II said that Christ's passion ''raised human suffering to the level of redemption'' (19): Christ has become a ''sharer in all human suffering'' and each person who suffers discovers ''new content and new meaning'' in his suffering, through faith (20).

Bibliography: *Christian Asceticism and Modern Man,* tr. W. MITCHELL et al. (New York 1955). P. R. RÉGAMEY, *The Cross and the Christian,* tr. A. BOUCHARD (St. Louis 1954). G. BOYD, *God at War: The Bible and Spiritual Conflict* (Downers Grove 1997). D. A. CARSON, *Divine Sovereignty and Human Responsibility* (Atlanta 1981). E. GERSTENBERGER and W. SCHRAGE, *Suffering* (Nashville 1977). J. HICK, *Evil and the God of Love* (rev. ed.; New York 1978). B. L. WHITNEY, *Theodicy: An Annotated Bibliography on the Problem of Evil, 1960–1991* (Bowling Green, Ohio 1998). JOHN PAUL II, *Salvifici doloris* (Vatican City 1984).

[P. RIGA/EDS.]

SUFFERING SERVANT, SONGS OF THE

Title generally applied to certain prophecies in Deutero-Isaiah, that is, the second part of the Book of ISAIAH (ch. 40–55). Each of these oracular poems concerns a mysterious figure called the Lord's ''servant.'' The NT finds these songs fulfilled in Jesus Christ, the Servant of the Lord par excellence.

Old Testament Concept

Very different interpretations of the mysterious figure of the Servant have been put forward; before discussing these, however, it is necessary to investigate the title itself and the extent and content of the songs of Deutero-Isaiah that are the subject of the present article.

Servant of the Lord as a Title. The expression Servant of Yahweh (Heb. *'ebed yhwh*) or Servant of the Lord is not peculiar to these Isaiahan songs; it is frequently found elsewhere in the OT as a title of honor given to those whom God has chosen to be His assistants in carrying out His plan for the chosen people and for mankind. The expression is applied to Abraham (Gn 26.24), to Isaac (Gn 24.14), to Jacob (Ez 37.25), to all three Patriarchs together (Ex 32.13; Dt 9.27), to Moses (Ex 14.31; Nm 12.7), to Joshua (Jos 24.29), to David (2 Sm 7.8; 1 Kgs 8.24–25), to the Prophets (1 Kgs 18.36; Am 3.7; Jer 7.25), to the future shepherd-king of the line of David who shall rule when the Lord makes a new covenant with His people (Ez 34.23–24; 37.24–25), to Zerubbabel (Hg 2.23; Zec 3.8), to Israel as a nation [Ps 104(105).6; Jer 30.10; 46.27; Ez 28.25], and even to NEBUCHADNEZZAR, KING OF BABYLON (Jer 27.6; 43.10). In Deutero-Isaiah (ch. 40–55), apart from the Songs of the Suffering Servant, the title is frequently applied to Israel as a whole (Is 41.8–9; 42.19; 43.10; 44.1–2; 45.4; 48.20; 49.3) and occasionally to faithful Israelites (54.17). Deutero-Isaiah does not explicitly use the term for CYRUS, King of Persia, liberator of the exiled Jews, though similar titles are given to him (44.28: ''my shepherd''; 45.1: ''his anointed'').

Extent of the Songs. The difficulties connected with determining the extent of the Songs of the Suffering Servant arise from the nature of the composition of Isaiah ch. 40–55 in which they are found. Though the separate songs are discernible, there are problems in determining their exact extent.

Exegetes agree on distinguishing four Servant songs. There is no serious problem as to the beginning of these poems, but the exact ending of the first three is disputed. The first song certainly includes 42.1–4; many commentators extend it to include v. 5–7. The extent of the first song, then, is at least 42.1–4, at most 42.1–7. The second song certainly includes 49.1–6; v. 7 with its new introduction, ''Thus says the Lord,'' probably does not belong to the original song. The third song poses less difficulty. It includes 50.4–9. The two following verses (v. 10–11) are probably an addition, a reflection on the preceding verses. The fourth song can easily be discerned, though it is related to its immediate context; it extends from 52.13 to 53.12.

Content of the Songs. Before endeavoring to interpret the Songs of the Suffering Servant and to evaluate their significance, an analysis of their content follows.

First Song. In the first song (42.1–7) the Lord presents His Servant as "my chosen one with whom I am well pleased." The Lord has put His spirit upon him, as he gave His spirit to Moses (Nm 11.17–25), Joshua (Nm 27.18), and David (1 Sm 16.13), and especially as He gave it to Prophets who proclaimed His word (Zec 7.12; Neh 9.30; see Is 48.16). Endowed with the charism of God's spirit, the Servant teaches "justice" (religious principles, God's will and order) to the nations (Gentiles). He does so with gentleness, in contrast to the vehemence usually found in protesting Orientals, until justice is established throughout the world. In the following verses (5–7) Yahweh, as creator and ruler of all, who gives and sustains life, speaks to His Servant. This introduction prepares the reader for the greatness of the creative work that Yahweh will perform through His Servant. The Servant is told (v. 6) that through him the Lord intends to bring about justice and right order in the world. God has formed him and set him "as a covenant of the people." The "people" are either Israel alone or all mankind, including Israel. The meaning of setting the Servant "as a covenant" is uncertain; perhaps the notion that the Servant will unite God and man in the permanent relationship of covenant is implied. The Servant is to be a "light for the nations"; he will enlighten the blind (see 42.16, 18) and will liberate prisoners. Some maintain that v. 6–7 refer to Cyrus, the Persian king who freed the exiled Jews, since the preceding chapter (41) concerns him.

Second Song. In the second song (49.1–6) it is the Servant who speaks. He addresses all nations, telling them that he was claimed by the Lord from his mother's womb (cf. Jer 1.5). The Lord protected him and prepared him to be an effective weapon for the manifestation of His glory (v. 1–3). The Servant's mission has not yet been successful (v. 4). His task is now extended, beyond that of restoring Israel, to include being a light to the nations and a bearer of the Lord's salvation to the ends of the earth (v. 5–6). Verse 7 speaks of the restoration and exaltation of humiliated Israel, apparently distinct from the Servant.

Third Oracle. In the third song (50.4–9) the Servant speaks of the help he has received from the Lord; he has received a well-trained tongue to rouse the weary and is given inspiration day by day. He has not refused to cooperate with Yahweh in spite of the abuses he must endure (v. 4–6). The Servant goes on to state his assurance of divine assistance and his conviction that God will justify him in the face of his enemies (v. 7–9). An addition (v. 10–11) warns the people that, if they do not walk in the light that comes through the Servant, they will perish in the fire of their own light.

Fourth Oracle. This song (52.13–53.12), the most important of the Songs of the Suffering Servant, is unique in many ways: its vocabulary has a large number of words that are unusual in Deutero-Isaiah; the form of the song is difficult to determine, being neither clearly that of a thanksgiving hymn, nor a funeral song, nor a liturgical poem, though it has traces of all three. All this serves to make its extraordinary theme—the vicarious suffering of the Servant of the Lord—more striking. In the first lines (52.13–15) Yahweh speaks of the exaltation that follows the great humiliation of His Servant. The nations (including Israel, it seems) are startled at the wonder that has been worked through the Servant. In 53.1–10 this wonder is described by the "many nations" themselves: God made the Servant unattractive to men and afflicted him in such a way that men avoided him as they do a leper (v. 1–3). The poem goes on to speak of the suffering that the Servant endured "for many" ("for us," "for his people"). Without offering resistance, he was led like a lamb to the slaughter and "cut off from the land of the living" (v. 7–8), expressions that, to most Catholic exegetes, indicate the death of the Servant (cf. Jer 11.19). If these terms are taken literally, they do mean death; but they can also be taken metaphorically, as are similar expressions often used in the Psalms of supplication (*see* PSALMS, BOOK OF), to indicate the nearness of death. Whether the passage is taken literally or metaphorically, the Servant's willingness to die for others is clear. The Servant is innocent, he does not die for his own sins; it is for the guilt of others that he accepts his affliction (v. 9–10). Yahweh will reward him for his deed—He will give him life again, happiness, offspring, honor, and prosperity (v. 10–12).

Interpretation of the Songs. There is hardly another point of OT exegesis more difficult to solve than the interpretation of these songs and the identity of the Servant. A clear and definitive answer to all the problems posed by the songs is not possible; what follows is a summary of the more significant views taken by scholars.

A preliminary question should be answered: do all four songs refer to one and the same Servant of the Lord? Not all exegetes agree. E. Kissane, for example, holds that the figure of the first two songs is Israel; in the third, the Prophet-author himself; and in the fourth, the Messiah. The majority of commentators, however, maintain that one and the same figure is the subject of all four songs. That is the position adopted here. In what follows only those verses that are certainly part of the songs are taken into consideration.

Significance of the Servant. The Servant announces Yahweh's justice (religious principles, will, law) that the world awaits; gently, without violence, he must work until his mission is accomplished (42.1–4) in Israel and the whole world. In fulfilling his mission of bringing the

Lord's salvation to the world he meets with opposition (49.1–6). This opposition turns into abuse, yet the Servant does not despair or cease his work; he trusts in the Lord's assistance (50.4–9). Salvation comes to the world through the suffering and death that the Servant undergoes for the sins of others. His willing sacrifice atones for the offenses of many; in reward, Yahweh greatly exalts him and gives him life. The vicarious suffering of the Servant, so vividly brought out in the fourth song, is a completely new concept at this point in the history of the Bible; new also in these four songs is the Servant's mission to the nations.

Interpretations. Three general categories of interpretation can be outlined, designated as collective, individual, and corporate personality.

The collective interpretation considers the Servant to be either historical Israel or ideal Israel. In Deutero-Isaiah, Israel is repeatedly designated as the Lord's servant. It would be faulty exegesis to rule out that identification in the four Songs of the Suffering Servant. Moreover, the Servant bears undeniable resemblances to Israel as a whole: he is despised, rejected, and humiliated as Israel was by its enemies; he is later exalted and given the respect of the nations, as Israel was to be raised up and honored by them; the mission of the Servant is to announce God's rule to the world, a mission similar to that of Sion (Is 2.2–4). This interpretation, however, does not give enough importance to the distinction that the author makes between the Servant and Israel as a whole. The Servant is docile, guiltless, humble, and a light to the nations; he atones for the sins of others. But Israel is described in Deutero-Isaiah, even in these four songs, as stubborn, sinful, haughty, and blind, and it is punished for its own offenses. Moreover, the Servant performs his great deed for Israel as well as for the nations (see 49.6; 53.8). Though it cannot be denied that the role and experience of the Servant is similar to and related to Israel's, they are nevertheless distinct. Some scholars maintain that the Servant should not be understood in terms of historical Israel, but in terms of faithful Israel, the ideal Israel. This position is supported especially by the identification of Israel and the Servant in 49.3 (a reading that cannot be rejected on the grounds that it is omitted in one Hebrew MS). In Is 54.17 the faithful Israelites of the restoration are called the "servants [plural] of the Lord." This qualitative Israel, however, is more ideal than real; it existed more in theory than in fact. It cannot be denied that both these collective interpretations have a basis in the songs, but they do not seem to consider all the data.

The individual interpretation finds its support in that the Servant, throughout the four songs, is presented in terms that suggest an individual person rather than a group. The arguments of the so-called collective interpretation, as presented above, show the weakness of this position; yet it cannot be denied some validity.

The collective interpretation is held by exegetes who recognize the so-called collective or corporate character of the Servant as well as his individuality. These commentators (especially H. W. Robinson) base their thesis on the Biblical notion, which they refer to as corporate personality, according to which a given individual can stand for a group (e.g., a father for his family and descendants, a king for his people), and the group is in some way identified with the individual. These exegetes claim that the individual-vs.-collectivity debate over the Servant is resolved if the Servant is seen as an individual who sums up Israel (the collectivity) in himself. Israel manifests itself in the mission and person of the Servant, and the Servant always remains the representative of Israel. Although some critics feel that this view is too sophisticated to be attributed to Israelite authors, it continues to be popular. In spite of its complexities, the corporate-personality theory has thrown a good deal of light on some of the problems in other parts of the Bible, e.g., the fluctuating singulars and plurals in the Psalms.

Identification of the Servant. Attempts to identify the Servant of the Lord with an individual abound. He is related to persons of the past, present, or future. Various individuals of the past are suggested: Moses, the giver of the Law and intercessor for his people (or a future "second Moses" whose mission is extended to the whole world); a Prophet, such as Jeremiah with whom the Servant has much in common (cf. his call, mission to the nations, suffering: Jer 1.4–5; 11.19; 18. 19–20; his intercession: 7.16; 11.14; 14.11; 15.1, 11). However, the work of Jeremiah could never be equated (even in poetry) with that of the Servant. Jeremiah's mission ended in failure; his preaching was never actually to the nations; the popularity of the Prophet's message among the Jews after his death can hardly be called a great exaltation by the Lord. Some consider the Servant to be the Prophet himself who uttered these songs (e.g., S. Mowinckel and S. Smith). Others, mainly Scandinavian scholars, hold that the Servant is presented as a king. This position is rejected by most scholars, even though the Servant of the first song could be construed as a royal figure. Still others identify the Servant with Cyrus. Cyrus, however, hardly fits the dimensions of the Servant, especially in the fourth song. Catholic exegetes, for the most part, see the Servant of the Lord as God's instrument in establishing His justice and His rule (kingdom) in the world, much as the MESSIAH is sometimes given this role as God's viceroy on earth. The Servant, however, does not clearly show forth the kingship that is usually associated with the Messiah in earlier texts. Understood in a messianic sense, the Servant is seen by Christians as foreshadowing Jesus Christ.

In all this there is an element of mystery, a quality of the Songs of the Suffering Servant that the author may well have intended. There is at least some truth in all the positions taken about the Servant; yet no one of them taken in isolation seems completely satisfactory. If the author saw the Servant as Israel's Messiah, he was giving to the Messiah a dimension hitherto unknown in the Bible. As Servant, the Messiah becomes an unattractive victim for the sins of the world before he is exalted or obtains a distinction that could be called kingly. The Messiah-King is freed of all nationalistic and mundane traits; his work becomes universal and spiritual—preaching justice and suffering for the sins of the world. There is some evidence, even in pre-Christian times, of an old Jewish interpretation of the Servant that saw in him something of both Israel and the Messiah.

To many Christians of all ages the solution to the problem of identifying the Servant has been clear: He foreshadows Jesus of Nazareth, who is at once the Messiah, a Prophet greater than all other prophets, the new Israel, the Lamb who died for the sins of man, and whom God raised up and made exalted, Lord and King.

New Testament Application

The NT sees in the mystery of the life, death, and Resurrection of Jesus the fulfillment of the Songs of the Suffering Servant.

In the Early Kerygma. Among the earliest texts of the NT are found several references to Jesus Christ as the Servant of the Lord. In Acts 3.12–18 Peter speaks to the Jews of God's ''servant'' (τὸν παῖδα αὐτοῦ) Jesus, the ''Just One'' (cf. Hebrew text of Is 53.11), whom they ''delivered up'' (cf. Greek text of Is 53.6, 12). Peter presents the work of Jesus as the accomplishment of what the Prophets had foretold about the sufferings that the Christ should endure. The prayer of the community after the release of Peter and John from their arrest by the Sanhedrin gives Jesus the title of God's ''holy servant'' (Acts 4.27). The most explicit application of the fourth Servant song to Jesus is found in the explanation that the Deacon Philip gives to the Ethiopian who asks concerning Is 53.7–8: ''I pray thee, of whom is the prophet saying this? Of himself or of someone else?'' (Acts 8.34). Philip ''beginning from this scripture'' preached Jesus to him.

In the Gospels. The Evangelists refer to the Servant songs at the most important points in the life of Jesus. At the BAPTISM OF THE LORD in the Synoptics (Mk 1.9–11; Mt 3.13–17; Lk 3.21–22), the voice from heaven, ''Thou art my beloved Son, in thee I am well pleased,'' echoes Ps 2.7 and the first Servant Song (Is 42.1). The variations in the words from heaven as they are found in Matthew only serve to make the reference to Is 42.1 clearer. The Fourth Gospel reports the Baptism indirectly; yet the words of the Baptist allude to the fourth song: ''Behold the Lamb of God, who takes away the sin of the world'' (Jn 1.29, 36, compared with Is 53.7, ''like a lamb led to the slaughter'' and Is 53.12, ''he shall take away the sins of many''). Though this allusion is not accepted by all scholars, it finds added strength in a possible Aramaic form behind the Greek ''Lamb of God'': the Aramaic expression *ṭalyā' dē'lāhā'* could be translated ''Servant of God'' as well as ''Lamb of God.'' In all four Gospels the descent of the Spirit upon Jesus at the Baptism recalls Is 42.1. The same text is alluded to in the account of the TRANSFIGURATION of Jesus in Mt 17.5. The three predictions of the Passion (Mk 8.31–33; 9.29–31; 10.32–34, and parallels) describe the coming suffering of Jesus in terms that reflect Is 53.1–9. The words of Jesus at the Last Supper, ''This is my blood of the new covenant, which is being shed for many,'' are given with variants (Mk 14.22–25, and parallels; 1 Cor 11.23–27); but present in each account are influences from the fourth song: the notion of vicarious suffering (''for many,'' ''for you,'' ''for many unto the forgiveness of sins''), and possibly (as O. Cullmann suggests) the idea of reestablishing the covenant with God, implied in the Servant's role as reconciliator (Is 49.5), mentioned explicitly in Is 42.6 and possibly referred to in Is 49.8. In Luke, Jesus ends His words after the Last Supper with an explicit quotation from Is 53.12: ''And he was reckoned among the wicked.'' The Gospel according to St. John sees the fulfillment of the Servant of the Lord prophecies in the life, death, and Resurrection of Jesus. These three form a mysterious unity in which John sees the glorification of Jesus accomplished. In a passage that links the life and ministry of Jesus with His death and Resurrection (Jn 12.37–41), John refers to Is 53.1 and states that Isaiah had seen the glory of Jesus (i.e., the suffering and exaltation of Jesus as the Servant of the fourth song).

In the Epistles. Several passages that reflect understanding of the mystery of Jesus in the light of the Servant of the Lord are found in the NT Epistles. Though Paul's Christology does not center on the Servant theme, and though he has given this theme a new use (see Stanley), he clearly knows and hands on the primitive Servant theology (1 Cor 15.1–3; Rom 4.25). Writing to the Philippians (Phil 2.5–11), he describes the Incarnation as a ''taking the nature of a slave [servant].'' In 1 Pt 2.18–25, the author admonishes servants to be subject even to severe masters and gives them the example of Christ who suffered for them unjustly. In his admonition he quotes from Is 53.9 and alludes to Is 53.4–4. The Epistle to the Hebrews (Heb 9.28) explains that Christ offered Himself ''to take away the sins of many.''

Place of Servant Theology in Teaching of Jesus. The theology based on the Servant theme is certainly one of the oldest Christologies of the NT. Its presence in the NT cannot be adequately explained unless one realizes that it was first applied by Jesus to Himself and taught by Him to His disciples: ''Whoever wishes to be first among you shall be the slave of all; for the Son of Man also has not come to be served but to serve, and to give his life as a ransom for many'' (Mk 10.44–45). From the earliest to some of the latest texts in the NT, Jesus is understood in terms of the Servant of the Lord. The most obvious application is that of the fourth song to His death and Resurrection, since it perfectly foreshadowed the vicarious suffering and exaltation of the Lord Jesus. But even the cures and good works of Jesus in His public life are seen in the light of the songs; cf. Mt 8.16–17 with Is 53.4, and Mt 12.15–21 with Is 42.1–4. The consistency with which the NT understands Jesus as the fulfillment of the Servant-of-the-Lord prophecies is difficult to explain unless it is admitted that Jesus Himself understood His mission as that of the Servant of the Lord.

Bibliography: W. ZIMMERLI and J. JEREMIAS, *Theologisches Wörterbuch zum Neuen Testament* by G. KITTEL (Stuttgart 1935) 5.653–713; *The Servant of God,* tr. H. KNIGHT et al. (Studies in Biblical Theology 20; Naperville, Ill. 1957). O. CULLMANN, *The Christology of the New Testament,* tr. S. GUTHRIE and C. HALL (Philadelphia 1959) 51–82. J. DE FRAINE, *Adam et son lignage* (Bruges 1959) 158–171. C. R. NORTH, *The Suffering Servant in Deutero-Isaiah* (2nd ed. London 1956). J. LINDBLOM, *The Servant Songs in Deutero-Isaiah* (Lund 1951). C. LINDHAGEN, *The Servant Motif in the O.T.: A Preliminary Study to the 'Ebed-Yahweh Problem' in Deutero-Isaiah* (Uppsala 1950). E. J. KISSANE, *The Book of Isaiah* (Dublin 1941). J. VAN DER PLOEG, *Les Chants du serviteur de Jahvé dans la seconde partie du livre d'Isaïe* (Paris 1936). H. GUNKEL, *Ein Vorläufer Jesu* (Bern 1921). S. MOWINCKEL, *Der Knecht Jahwäs* (Giessen 1921). A. FEUILLET, *Dictionnaire de la Bible,* suppl. ed. L. PIROT, et al. (Paris 1928) 4:690–714. J. E. MÉNARD, ''*Pais Theou* as Messianic Title in the Book of Acts,'' *The Catholic Biblical Quarterly* 19 (1957) 83–92. D. M. STANLEY, ''The Theme of the Servant of Yahweh in Primitive Christian Soteriology and Its Transposition by St. Paul,'' *ibid.* 16 (1954) 385–425. R. T. A. MURPHY, ''Second-Isaias: The Servant of the Lord,'' *ibid.* 9 (1947) 262–274. H. CAZELLES, ''Les Poèmes du Serviteur,'' *Recherches de sciences religieuse* 43 (1955) 5–55. R. J. TOURNAY, ''Les Chants du Serviteur dans la seconde partie d'Isaïe,'' *Revue biblique* 59 (1952) 355–384, 481–512. J. JEREMIAS, ''Zum Problem der Deutung von Jes. 53 im palästinischen Spätjudentum,'' *Aux Sources de la tradition chrétienne* (Paris 1950). H. H. ROWLEY, ''The Suffering Servant and the Davidic Messiah,'' *Oudtestamentische Studiën* 8 (1950) 100–136. I. ENGNELL, ''The 'Ebed Yahweh Songs and the Suffering Messiah in 'Deutero-Isaiah',''*The Bulletin of the John Rylands Library* 31 (1948) 54–93. H. W. ROBINSON, ''The Hebrew Conception of Corporate Personality,'' *Werden und Wesen des A.T.,* ed. J. HEMPEL, *Zeitschrift für die alttestamentliche Wissenschaft* Beiheft 66 (1936) 49–62. W. H. BELLINGER and W. R. FARMER, eds., *Jesus and the Suffering Servant: Isaiah 53 and Christian Origins* (Harrisburg, Penn. 1998). J. ALOBAIDI, *The Messiah in Isaiah 53: The Commentaries of Saadia Gaon, Salmon ben Yeruham and Yefet ben Eli on Is 52:13 53:12* (Bern 1998).

[M. A. GERVAIS/EDS.]

SUFFICIENT REASON, PRINCIPLE OF

The principle of sufficient reason states that everything that exists has a sufficient reason for its existence. Originally proposed by G. W. LEIBNIZ, it has been incorporated into neoscholastic thought and is commonly listed among the FIRST PRINCIPLES. Opinion is divided as to its proper formulation and ultimate validity.

Leibniz's Formulation. In his systematization of philosophy Leibniz sought a principle that would govern the world of existence or of actual fact just as the principle of CONTRADICTION governs the realm of the possible. Such would be a principle ''of sufficient reason, in virtue of which we hold that no fact can be genuine or existent and no proposition true unless there is a sufficient reason why it should be so and not otherwise, although for the most part these reasons cannot be known by us'' (*Monadology* 31–32; confer, *Principles of Nature and Grace,* 7; *Theodicy,* 1.44).

Thus stated, the principle of sufficient reason has two aspects. As applied to things, it means that everything existent either exists of its nature or has been brought into being by something else that is the reason of its existence. As applied to statements, it means that every true proposition is either a necessary proposition or follows from other true propositions that give the reason of its truth. It is probable that Leibniz regarded all apparently contingent facts and truths as derivatively necessary, for he held that the objects of creation were determined by their belonging to the best possible world, which God was of His nature necessitated to create. If so, the principle of sufficient reason was for Leibniz a principle of universal necessity; he might not have said this explicitly so as not to come into conflict with Christian orthodoxy.

Other Interpretations. Thus understood, Leibniz's principle represents the point of view of systems seeing all reality and history as the unrolling of an intelligible NECESSITY, for example, STOICISM, some forms of NEOPLATONISM and the philosophy of SPINOZA. Equally it looks forward, for example, to Hegelianism. But the principle has also a weaker, but more acceptable meaning in which ''sufficient'' is distinguished from ''determining.'' In this sense it is compatible with the occurrence of free CHOICE in creatures and with God's FREEDOM to create.

Taken in this way, it is, in its application to contingent things, equivalent to the principle of CAUSALITY. In its universality it says in effect that everything that exists is either caused or is such as to need no cause. As applied to statements it is equivalent to the principle of INTELLIGIBILITY. It means that all true statements could ideally commend themselves to the mind by being seen either as necessarily true or as having adequate grounds for being true. This is approximately what scholastics meant by saying that all reality possesses ontological TRUTH (*omne ens est verum*). Understood in this way, the principle becomes an acceptable reformulation of something that had always been held in scholastic metaphysics.

Kant and the Principle. C. WOLFF and A. G. Baumgarten (1714–62) attempted a proof of Leibniz's principle of sufficient reason. In his early *Principiorum primorum cognitionis metaphysicae nova dilucidatio* (Königsberg 1755), I. KANT, while rejecting their proof, tried to offer another. In his critical writings Kant regarded the principle of sufficient reason as the fundamental synthetic a priori proposition, paralleling the principle of contradiction as the fundamental analytic proposition. He states that "the principle of sufficient reason is the basis of possible experience, that is, of the objective knowledge of phenomena, in respect of their relationship in the time-series" (*Critique of Pure Reason,* A200-1; B246).

In this view, the principle of sufficient reason is valid only within the realm of PHENOMENA as an indispensable means of making them intelligible, and has, in relation to phenomena, a character similar to that attributed to it by Leibniz in relation to real being. As a principle of intelligibility, it means for Leibniz that things are in themselves intelligible and for Kant that we cannot think of things without imposing an intelligible order upon them, which is precisely the general contrast between these two thinkers.

Scholastic Views. Scholastic philosophers usually accept the principle of sufficient reason in the weaker sense described above. They differ, however, about whether its evidence is primary or can in some way be derived from a prior principle and, more generally, about its relationship to other principles.

Some, like R. GARRIGOU-LAGRANGE, hold that the principle of sufficient reason is reducible to the principle of contradiction or the principle of IDENTITY. Such authors usually reject the Kantian distinction between analytic and synthetic a priori propositions as misleading, and if willing to use the term analytic at all, describe all self-evident propositions as analytic. They mean in this case that it is impossible in the concrete to contemplate the notion of being adequately without perceiving its radical intelligibility. Being would not be being unless it had all that was needed in order to be, that is, unless it had a sufficient reason for its being. Hence the principle of identity and the principle of sufficient reason are inseparable; the latter is merely an unfolding of what is involved in the former.

Others, like J. Laminne and P. Descoqs, are willing to accept the Kantian distinction of analysis and synthesis, although they regard true synthetic a priori judgments as valid for reality and not only for phenomena in the Kantian sense. On this basis they point out that the notion of reason is not contained in the notion of being and cannot be derived from it. Hence, while the principles of identity and contradiction are analytic, the principle of sufficient reason, introducing in the predicate the notion of reason that is not contained in the subject, is synthetic. It is a self-evident and necessary truth, but its evidence is its own, and it cannot be reduced to any other principle.

These two schools of thought nevertheless have in common that they attribute fundamental importance to the principle of sufficient reason and regard the principle of causality as an application of it to contingent or temporal being. Yet other neoscholastics, like J. Geyser, are less interested in Leibniz's principle and find a primary and independent evidence in the principle of causality.

Critical Evaluation. If the principle of sufficient reason is interpreted as a principle of universal necessity, it is evidently unacceptable in any philosophy that upholds FREE WILL in creatures and God's free choice in creation. But, in the wider and looser sense in which it is generally held, its precise logical status is still in need of discussion.

What does one mean when he speaks of the sufficient reason of a thing's existence? There can be no doubt that he usually means its causes. Yet one speaks of God as being the sufficient reason of His own existence. Here it can mean only that His existence, so to say, makes sense without reference to anything other than God. But this is merely to say that God needs no cause; He exists necessarily. What foundation, then, has the distinction between God as the sufficient reason for His own existence and God as existing? In the ontological order, the two are absolutely identical. Hence, when one says that everything that exists has a sufficient reason for its existence, he seems to say that everything that exists is either caused or needs no cause. But this is an empty formal dichotomy. One can, therefore, sympathize with those authors who devote their chief attention to causality, and seek to arrive at principles that offer a criterion of the sort of being that needs to be caused, that is, the contingent, the temporal and the finite.

There is more to be said for Leibniz's formula if it is understood as stating that everything that exists is intelligible. Here one asserts an actual or potential relationship to thought that is applicable even in the case of God. He is saying that, if he understands anything and insofar as he understands anything, he understands how it is that it is so, either because he sees that it is necessarily so or because he finds what has made it so. In principle, however great may be man's ignorance in particular cases, reality responds to the demands of thought. There is harmony between thinking and being. Even so one may judge that this was sufficiently expressed in the older assertion of the ontological truth of things and need not be surprised that the principle of sufficient reason was not formally enunciated by ARISTOTLE or St. THOMAS AQUINAS, but was left for Leibniz to formulate.

What modern scholastics have taken the principle of sufficient reason to mean is no doubt true. The question is simply whether its explicit statement adds much or little to what had been stated in other ways before. If an unfavorable view has been suggested here, it must be remembered that other writers have thought otherwise. Difference of opinion is likely to continue.

See Also: FIRST PRINCIPLES; TRUTH; CERTITUDE.

Bibliography: J. E. GURR, *The Principle of Sufficient Reason in Some Scholastic Systems: 1750–1900* (Milwaukee 1959). D. J. B. HAWKINS, *Being and Becoming* (New York 1954). R. GARRIGOU-LAGRANGE, *God, His Existence and His Nature,* tr. B. ROSE, 2 v. (5th ed. St. Louis 1934–36) 1:181–191. P. DESCOQS, *Institutiones metaphysicae generalis* (Paris 1925). A. SCHOPENHAUER, *On the Fourfold Root of the Principle of Sufficient Reason, and on the Will in Nature,* tr. K. HILLEBRAND (rev. ed. London 1907). W. M. URBAN, *History of the Principle of Sufficient Reason: Its Metaphysical and Logical Foundations* (Princeton Contributions to Philosophy 1; Princeton 1900) 1–87.

[D. J. B. HAWKINS]

ṢŪFĪSM

This term is the Europeanized form of the Arabic *taṣawwuf.* According to Muslim authors, several etymologies are possible: *ṣafā'* (purity), *ṣuffa* (the "bench" of Medina, where the "Companions of Muḥammad" sat). But it seems simpler and more accurate to translate *taṣawwuf* by: leading the life of the *ṣūfī,* of the man clothed in wool (*ṣūf*).

Taṣawwuf or Ṣūfīsm is a Muslim mysticism, i.e., the rules of life and the doctrines of the Muslims "athirst for God," straining in pursuit of union with God. It appears as a complexus of schools and tendencies, sometimes accepted but more often condemned by the official teachings of ISLAM. However, it did have at several stages a profound influence on Muslim life and piety, and it sometimes found written expression in literary masterpieces of the highest importance. Its poems and treatises were written primarily in Arabic, often in Persian, and to a lesser degree in Turkish, Urdū, and other languages.

Origins and Early Forms. The influences that helped shape Ṣūfīsm have been studied many times by Orientalists, whose various theses are in conflict. Miguel Asín Palacios insists that there were Christian influences, and explains the very origins of Ṣūfīsm in terms of these. (Conversely, he affirms that later Ṣūfīsm in turn influenced subsequent Christian mysticism, especially that of St. John of the Cross.) Iranian sources and themes (myths of ancient Iran) were given greater stress by E. Blochet, and in more recent time by H. Corbin. Indian influences are emphasized by I. Goldziher, R. A. Nicholson, and others. Without denying these various contributions, we should stress that Ṣūfīsm is first of all a Muslim phenomenon, and a debt of gratitude is owed to L. Massignon for having clearly pointed this out (see bibliography).

Indeed, even in the early days of Islam, there were believers who could not be satisfied merely with the testimony of faith in the One God, the Creator and Master of Judgment. However, the QUR'ĀN teaches that God, through His Prophets, has communicated His Word to men, that He is "very close to man whom He created," that He knows "what his soul suggests to him," and is "closer to him than his jugular vein" (Qur'ān, 34.50; 50.16). How could sincere hearts not be eager to live this Word in the depths of their being, and hence go forward to meet the Speaker? Very early, two Qur'ānic texts (3.31; 5.54) that suggest mutual love between God and man served as the basis for Ṣūfī meditations. It can be said that Ṣūfīsm was one of the virtualities that presented itself from the earliest centuries to Muslim souls. The opposition it encountered among jurists and doctors and the condemnations it received must not make us forget this fact.

Muslim mysticism has a long history. During the 1st century of the Muslim era (from A.D. 622) it became rooted in the ascetical tendencies of certain "Companions of the Prophet," such as Abūl-Dardā' and especially Abū Dharr al-Ghifarī. Meanwhile the preaching of various ascetics, sermonizers, and "weepers" incited the people to repentance and piety. But the first ascetics, clothed either in patched tunics or wool robes, quickly organized themselves into small group of disciples united around the "master," the *shaykh.* The outstanding names of the first two Muslim centuries are Ḥasan al-Baṣrī, the poet of the "desire for God" (*'ishq*), and Rābi'a, the converted woman flute-player, who celebrated divine love (*ḥubb*). In the 3d Muslim century, special mention must be made of an isolated figure, Abū Yazīd al-Bisṭāmī, who, through a radical intellectual self- stripping, set up the pure "I"—the pure act of being "without attribute or form"—face to face with the inaccessible divine Essence. Whereas Ḥasan al-Baṣrī and Rābi'a announced a mysticism of union through love, Bisṭāmī's way has been compared to certain negative dialectics of Indian yoga.

Official Opposition. During the first two Muslim centuries, the Ṣūfīs were not opposed by the doctors of the Law, and some of them even sprang from the most traditional circles. Even Bisṭāmī, in his mountains of Tabaristān (Persia), was not called upon to answer for his doctrine before constituted authority. But the 3d century H. (of the Hijra: from about A.D. 820) saw the decisive rupture between *taṣawwuf* and official Islam. Dhū 'l-Miṣrī was persecuted in Egypt; Muḥāsibī, the master of the "examination of conscience," was sent into quasi-banishment in Kūfā; Ibn Karrām, the philosopher, was imprisoned; Sahl Tustarī, the apostle of continual attrition, died in exile at Baṣra; and finally Nūrī was brought before the tribunals with several of his disciples for having taught divine love (not without a certain self-affliction), and was released only because of his firm attitude.

In the face of so many arrests and persecutions, Junayd sought refuge in a prudent solution of esotericism, and Shiblī withdrew into calculated eccentricity. But the second half of the 3d century H. was dominated by the great figure of Ḥallāj, whom Massignon has thoroughly studied. Al-Ḥusayn Ibn Manṣūr al-Ḥallāj was born in Fars (Persia) *c.* 244 H. (A.D. 858). He was a disciple of Junayd (who was to repudiate him), a pilgrim and hermit at Mecca, a traveler on the distant routes of Sind, and a fiery preacher in the *sūq* (marketplace) of Baghdad. The "carder of consciences," which is what his name Ḥallāj signified, was denounced to the public authorities. After a long trial, he was condemned to death under false political pretexts, and executed in 309 H. (A.D. 922). On his gibbet, scourged and mutilated, Ḥallāj bore witness to the God who is Love, and to the possibility of a union of love between God and His human creature, though they are as far removed from each other as "the Eternal and the perishable contingent" can be. The mere mention of Ḥallāj remains, in the bosom of Islam, as it were, an unceasingly repeated question.

Literary Expression. However, the position of Ṣūfīsm in relation to official Islam was to change during subsequent centuries. An indication of this is seen in the growing success of a didactic teaching provided by the manuals. Suffice it to mention the *Luma'* of Sarrāj, the *Kitāb al-ta'arruf* of Kalābādhī (written about 50 years after the execution of Ḥallāj), Qushayrī's *Risāla,* Abā Tālib al-Makkī's *Qūt al-qulūb,* Anṣārī's *Manāzil al-sā'irīn;* many others might be cited. In the end it was ALGAZEL (Abū Ḥāmid al- Ghazzālī) who had the distinction of making the notion of love of God (*maḥabba*) acceptable in the religious climate of Islam. His conversion to Ṣūfīsm is famous; he expatiated on it in his autobiography, and the last part of his great work *Iḥyā' 'ulūm al-dīn* (Revivification of the Sciences of Religion) bears witness to it. Thanks to Ghazzālī, *taṣawwuf* became a "religious science," no doubt very controversial and reserved to the few, but taught nonetheless as an optional subject in certain great mosques.

The efforts of the authors of manuals proved only partially successful in assuring to Ṣūfīsm the stamp of orthodoxy. In the 6th century H. (12th century A.D.), the secular arm once again exercised bloody coercion against 'Ayn al-Quḍāt al-Hamadhānī, who was executed in 525 (1131); and against Suhrawardī, "master of the doctrine of illumination," which is still professed in Iran. The latter was condemned to death by SALADIN (Ṣalāḥ al-Dīn), but it is certainly true that political questions were also involved in this condemnation. While Suhrawardī probably was, as Massignon says, "the last of the nonmonistic Ṣūfīs," his disciples crossed the threshold into monism.

Powerful Neoplatonic influences had made themselves felt, especially through AVICENNA; and they were accompanied or followed by Indian influences, whether direct or brought in by the MONGOLS. Beginning with about the 7th century H., Ṣūfīsm tended to express itself under cover of a sapiential gnosis, which was the basis of several great literary works. Certainly the traditions of the first centuries were not forgotten. They appeared dominant here or there, but more often remained submerged by the search for an interior experience conceived as a realization of substantial identity.

From the 7th to the 9th centuries H. (13th to 15th centuries A.D.), Islamic literature produced a constellation of great mystical poets and writers. Suffice it to mention 'Umar Ibn al-Fāriḍ, "prince of Lovers," who was born and died in Cairo, and whose beautiful poetic work has been studied by Msgr. di Matteo, R. A. Nicholson, and C. A. Nallino; and the Andalusian Muḥyī al-Dīn IBN 'ARABĪ, who left more than 200 works, especially the *Futūḥāt al-makkiyya* and *Fuṣūṣ al-ḥikam,* and whose theories of the logos and of the "Perfect Man" strongly influenced all subsequent gnoses. (He has been studied by Asin Palacios and Nicholson, among others.) Also to be mentioned are the masters of the Maghribi school of the Shādhilīs, namely, Ibn 'Ata' Allāh of Alexandria, and Sha'rānī. Ibn 'Abbād of Ronda belongs to the Shādhilī school. He has remained famous for his "letters of spiritual direction," a collection of which has recently been edited by Father Paul Nwyia. There was also Jalāl al-Din al-Rūmī, the founder of the "whirling dervishes," who wrote in Persian and was the author of *Mathnāvī,* one of the greatest literary glories of Iran; also 'Abd al-Karīm Jīlī, for whom the myth of the "Perfect Man," on which he wrote a long poem, transcends its own dimensions and encompasses those of the cosmos (also studied by Nicholson). At least 100 other names could be cited here.

Thus, the Ṣūfīs of this era left us works of literary merit, of which Arabo- or Irano-Muslim humanism is rightly proud. However, the increasing dominance—except among certain Shādilīs—of the monist thesis of the "Unicity of Being" should be noted. The creature is viewed as a necessary emanation of the Creator, and willed by Him; the world is God "expressed," and the spiritual creature, whether man or angel, belongs by nature to the "divine." When Hallāj speaks of "identification" (*ittiḥād*), this must be understood, not as substantial, but as intentional identification, through a union of love. Beginning with Ibn 'Arabī, mystical union becomes, or tends to become, an "identification" in which the empirical personality of the Ṣūfī is, as it were, volatilized to the advantage of a divine "I"; this is in a sense an echo of the "Thou, thou art That" of Indian mysticism.

Formalism and Decline. Concurrently with the great literary works, Ṣūfīsm found expression in the everyday life of the ISLAMIC CONFRATERNITIES (*ṭarīqa*, pl. *ṭariqāt*). One of the most famous founders was the Ḥanbalite doctor 'Abd al-Qādir al- Jīlānī (6th/11th century). We have mentioned Jalāl al-Dīn al-Rūmī and his "DERVISHES"; this movement was to grow in intensity beginning with the 15th or 16th centuries A.D., from the Maghrib to India and southeast Asia; it became diversified in a great number of confraternities and profoundly influenced popular piety. Yet the absence of any doctrinal criteria left the door open more than once to excesses and deviations. The exaggerations of the Oriental dervishes or "fakirs," and of Maghribi "Maraboutism" are well known. Too often the confraternities in their decadent form became the only image of Ṣūfīsm in modern times. In fact, condemnation of the confraternities, to the mind of many Muslim critics, has become tantamount to impugning Ṣūfīsm itself.

Beginning in the 16th century, Ṣūfīsm underwent a progressive decline. With few exceptions, the period of great writings was at an end. Meanwhile the position of Ṣūfīsm remained ambiguous, or at least marginal, in Islam. A twofold temptation constantly threatened it. First, an intellectual preoccupation with the allurement of gnostic themes such as "Muḥammadan light" or the "Perfect Man" tended to reinforce and amplify the doctrine of "monism of Being." Secondly, a quasi exclusive use of the *dhikr* became widespread, i.e., the tireless and rhythmic repetition of a divine Name or an ejaculatory prayer. Whether or not the *dhikr* was accompanied by certain physical postures and respiratory exercises, it was transformed from a method into a technique, an efficacious technique that guaranteed the attainment of certain spiritual "states" (*aḥwāl*).

Basic Tendencies. To sum up, the history of Ṣūfīsm has shown two great trends. The first prevailed during the 2d and 3d centuries of the Hijra, and then declined without completely disappearing. Ḥallāj was its typical exemplar. It corresponded to what was called "the Unicity of Testimony" (waḥdat al- shuhūd). In other words, it is God who validly bears witness to Himself in the heart of the faithful. The union extolled was a union of the will through love, and—for Ḥallāj among others—the way to it was suffering, accepted and loved. Therefore union was accomplished by a divine presence, which, if it was authentic, had to be a supernatural presence of grace, as understood within the frame of reference of Christian theology. This is not to imply that Christian mysticism and Muslim mysticism must always be juxtaposed. One should beware of equivalences in literary images or procedures; and this is especially true with regard to the works of later Ṣūfīsm. For example: the similarity which Asín Palacios stresses between Ibn 'Abbād and St. John of the Cross in the night-day metaphor, and which he interprets as at least an indirect influence of the Andalusian Ṣūfī upon the Christian saint, is not very convincing. It would seem valid on the phenomenological level, but does not penetrate to the actual structure of their experience.

The second tendency gained strength only in the 7th century H., although preliminary signs of it can be discerned during the first few centuries. These were the Neoplatonic and Oriental influences that provided its mode of expression. It is clearly prefigured in Ibn 'Arabi. It is the tendency characterized as the "Unicity of Being" (*waḥdat al-wujūd*), in which created being annihilates itself and is transmuted into the divine, and in which the world is God manifested and set forth. Here the spiritual technique of the *dhikr* tends to become, more than once, a sort of substitute for the gift of God. Looking at it within the frame of reference of Christian theology, it would perhaps be fitting to speak of a natural experience directed toward a natural term, toward the grasping of the substantial actuality of the soul—a created absolute that the Ṣūfī, within the monotheistic climate of Islamic opinion, continued to call God. The vocabulary of both tendencies was often identical, but here and there it referred to very diverse experiences. Hence, it is necessary to study each case individually and to situate each ease within the total context.

An understanding of Ṣūfīsm and of its history demands the knowledge and careful historical study of its relations through the centuries with the offficial teaching of Islam. For the Muslim, God reveals His word in the Qur'ān, but does not reveal Himself; and the doctors long taught that the human will can and must love the law, the gifts, the commandment of God, but not God Himself. The mystics who strove to go to God through love thus advanced in a certain respect beyond the explicit data of their faith. And since God never refuses grace to humble and sincere souls, the Ṣūfī who authentically penetrated to the depths of the divine Life under the impulsion of grace was justified—granted the religious climate in which he lived—in making his own personal experience his criterion of religious rectitude. But what happens when this criterion is measured by experiences less pure? The mistrust of many jurists representative of the established Community can readily be understood.

One can understand also the strength of the temptation toward ''monism of Being.'' But in the measure that Muslim mysticism tended toward the God who is love and to a personal union with Him through love, the crux was that, in the Ṣūfī's heart, this could not be subject to an exterior criterion of faith. It is to be hoped that its most beautiful canticles and its noblest exemplars may be, as it were, testimony to the mysterious ways of divine grace.

Bibliography: A. J. ARBERRY, *Sufism: An Account of the Mystics of Islam* (New York 1951); *An Introduction to the History of Sufism* (New York 1943). M. SMITH, *The Ṣufī Path of Love: An Anthology of Ṣufīsm* (London 1954); *Rābi'a the Mystic and Her Fellow-Saints in Islam* (New York 1929); *Studies in Early Mysticism in the Near and Middle East* (New York 1931). R. A. NICHOLSON, *The Mystics of Islam* (London 1914); *Studies in Islamic Mysticism* (Cambridge, Eng. 1921). L. MASSIGNON, *La Passion d'al-Ḥosayn-ibn-Mansour al-Ḥallāj: Martyr mystique de l'Islam,* 2 v. (Paris 1922); *Akhbar al Ḥallāj* (Études musulmanes 4; 3d ed. Paris 1957). L. GARDET and M. M. ANAWATI, *Introduction à la théologie musulmane* (Paris 1948). T. J. E. ANDRAE, *Islamische Mystiker* (Stuttgart 1960). O. BIEHN, *Lexikon für Theologie und Kirche* 9, ed. J. HOFER and K. RAHNER, 1149–50. B. SPULER, *Die Religion in Geschichte und Gegenwart* 6 (3d ed. Tübingen 1957–65) 517–518.

[L. GARDET]

SUGAR, JOHN, BL.

Priest, martyr; *alias* Cox; b. *c.* 1558 at Wombourne, Staffordshire, England; hanged, drawn, and quartered July 16, 1604 at Warwick under James I. Sugar, described as *clerici filius* (son of a clergyman), studied at Merton College, Oxford; however, he did not receive his degree because he objected to swearing the Oath of Supremacy. Nevertheless, he became a Protestant minister at Cannock (Cank), Staffordshire. After converting to Catholicism, he studied at Douai, was ordained there in 1601, and immediately returned to England. He worked in Warwickshire, Staffordshire, and Worcestershire. On July 8, 1603, he was arrested with Bl. Robert GRISSOLD at Rowington, Warwickshire. After a year's imprisonment at Warwick, Sugar was condemned on July 14 for his priesthood. He was beatified by Pope John Paul II on Nov. 22, 1987 with George Haydock and companions.

Feast of the English Martyrs: May 4 (England).

See Also: ENGLAND, SCOTLAND, AND WALES, MARTYRS OF.

Bibliography: R. CHALLONER, *Memoirs of Missionary Priests,* ed. J. H. POLLEN (rev. ed. London 1924), 2, nos. 135, 136. J. FOSTER, *Alumni Oxonienses* (Oxford 1892). J. H. POLLEN, *Acts of English Martyrs* (London 1891), 321.

[K. I. RABENSTEIN]

SUGER OF SAINT-DENIS

Abbot of the royal Abbey of SAINT-DENIS; b. Saint-Denis or Argenteuil, *c.* 1081; d. Saint-Denis, Jan. 13, 1151. He was the friend and adviser of LOUIS VI and LOUIS VII, and the regent of France during the Second Crusade. In the rebuilding of his abbey church, he introduced Gothic art and architecture to western Europe. The name of his father, Helinandus, is all that is known of his background, presumably a very humble one, since he was given as an *oblatus* to Saint-Denis at the age of ten. At the abbey school he became a close friend of Prince Louis, later Louis VI, and remained an intimate of the royal family for the rest of his life. At 26 he represented the abbey's interests before Pope PASCHAL II and began his administrative career as prior of Berneval in Normandy. In 1122 he was elected abbot of Saint-Denis; he instituted a reform in 1127 and began the rebuilding of the church *c.* 1135. The western entrance with royal portals was dedicated June 9, 1140, and the choir, illuminated by stained-glass windows, June 11, 1144. The slender supports, the ribbed vaults, the open space that unites the choir, and the colored light reflected from glittering altar decorations proclaimed a new style, which spread rapidly through the royal domain and ultimately throughout the Western world, as *opus modernum,* or *opus francigenum,* to be dubbed Gothic in the 17th century. He was a patron of the arts rather than an artist, a statesman and an able administrator; his writings are those of a historian—he recorded the life of King Louis VI, the consecration of his church, and details of his own administration. Inspired by the Neoplatonic *Celestial Hierarchy* of PSEUDO-DIONYSIUS the Areopagite, whom he identified as his patron saint, he also sought to reconcile the earthly claims of church and state. His epitaph says of him: ''Small of body and family, constrained by a twofold smallness,/ He refused, in his smallness, to be a small man.''

Bibliography: *Oeuvres complètes de Suger*, ed. A. LECOY DE LA MARCHE (Paris 1867), Latin texts of all writings, letters, related documents; *Vie de Louis VI le Gros*, ed. and tr. (into Fr.) H. WAQUET (Paris 1929); *Abbot Suger: On the Abbey Church of St. Denis and its Art Treasures*, ed. and tr. E. PANOFSKY (Princeton 1946), Eng. tr. of selected portions of the *De administratione*, the *De consecratione*, and the *Ordinatio; Suger: Comment fut construit Saint-Denis*, Fr. tr. of *De consecratione* by J. LECLERCQ (Paris 1945). O. CARTELLIERI, *Abt Suger von Saint-Denis, 1081–1151* (Berlin 1898). M. AUBERT, *Suger* (Paris 1950). S. M. CROSBY, *L'Abbaye royale de Saint-Denis: Cent Trente photos de Pierre Devinoy* (Paris 1953). O. VON SIMSON, *The Gothic Cathedral* (2d ed. New York 1962).

[S. MCK. CROSBY]

SUHARD, EMMANUEL CÉLESTIN

Cardinal, archbishop of Paris; b. Brains-sur-les-Marches (Mayenne), France, April 5, 1874; d. Paris, May 30,1949. He studied theology at Laval and Rome, gained a doctorate in theology, and was ordained (Dec. 18, 1898). For the next 30 years he was a professor in the major seminary in Laval. He was chosen bishop of Bayeux and Lisieux (July 6, 1928) and promoted to the archiepiscopal See of Reims (Dec. 23, 1930), where he vigorously promoted seminaries, religious communities, Catholic Action, and charitable works. Two years after becoming cardinal (Dec. 16, 1935) he saw the complete restoration of his cathedral, severely damaged during World War I, consecrated the edifice (Oct. 18, 1937), and presided as papal legate at the official inauguration (July 8–10, 1938). He succeeded Cardinal Verdier in the See of Paris (May 1940). During the enemy occupation in World War II, Suhard did his utmost to alleviate the people's sufferings and to avert the dangers menacing them. Unjust vexations did not cease with liberation. The cardinal drew attention to them in a series of widely heralded pastoral letters, some of which were published and some translated into English and other languages. In his zeal to evangelize the de-Christianized segments of the populace, Suhard advocated new apostolic methods and created the Mission de France, whose seminary was placed in his former Diocese of Lisieux near the shrine of St. Thérèse of the Child Jesus. He set up the Mission de Paris, a prelude to the WORKER PRIESTS. He also recommended community life for the clergy, constructed new churches, developed Catholic Action, and promoted devotion to the Blessed Sacrament.

Bibliography: Works. *The Church Today: The Collected Writings of E. C. Suhard* (Chicago 1953); *Growth or Decline? The Church Today,* tr. J. A. CORBETT (South Bend, Ind. 1948), tr. of *Essor ou déclin de l'Église* (Paris 1947); *Priests among Men,* tr. L. BÉGIN et al. (New York 1949), tr. of *Le Prêtre dans la cité* (Paris 1949); *The Meaning of God* (pa. Notre Dame, Ind. 1963), tr. of *Le Sens de Dieu* (Paris 1948). Literature. J. RUPP, *Histoire de l'Église de Paris* (Paris 1948).

[R. LIMOUZIN-LAMOTHE]

SUICIDE

A term derived from the Latin *suicidium,* meaning the taking of one's own life. In the broadest sense it is applied to any voluntary act by which one causes his own death. In the strictest moral sense it means an unlawful moral act, positive or negative, by which one directly causes his own death.

One can cause his own death voluntarily either by a positive act of self-destruction or by refusing or neglecting to do something known to be necessary for the preservation of one's life. The difference between a positive act and an omission is notable from a physical point of view, but it is of little moral consequence. To fail to do something physically and morally necessary to the preservation of life is the moral equivalent of a positive act of self-destruction. A man who bleeds to death because he will not close an open artery is no less a suicide than one who opens an artery with the intent of taking his own life.

Morality. Catholic moralists are generally agreed that direct suicide is intrinsically evil, and they hold therefore that no circumstances can ever justify it. Examples of suicide in cases in which its malice is less apparent have been the subject of much discussion. Samson's deed as recorded in Jgs 16.29–30 and that of Eleazar as recorded in 1 Mc 6.46 would seem to be examples of indirect rather than direct suicide, although the distinction between the two was not clearly drawn by older authors who found difficulty in explaining the incidents. The deaths of Saul and Ahithophel (1 Sm 31.2–6 and 2 Sm 17.23) are recorded in the Scriptures without comment, and there is no need to justify them. The same is true of the suicide of Razis (2 Mc 14.41–46); although the incident is narrated sympathetically, it is possible to regard suicide as an objectively wicked thing, but committed in inculpable ignorance of its malice.

If suicide is intrinsically evil, God could not command it, and it is not true, as some have alleged, that direct suicide is permissible if it is committed in response to a special inspiration of God, the Lord of life and of death. This is a solution proposed by some to explain the suicides of certain holy virgins, venerated as saints and martyrs, who killed themselves in defense of their virtue. However, virtue can be adequately defended by other means than suicide, and a person who is forcibly violated does not, on that account, lose her or his virtue.

Surrendering One's Life. It is important to distinguish between the willing surrender of one's life and the deliberate taking of it. It has been common for some writers to refer to the former as *indirect suicide* and to apply the principle of double effect to justify it as in cases when a person knowingly gives up his life in the pursuit of some good end or to prevent some grave wrong. Examples are the soldier who throws himself on a hand grenade to protect those around him, the truck driver who chooses to steer his vehicle over a precipice to avoid a collision with a school bus, the action of St. Maximillian KOLBE who volunteered to take the place of a fellow prisoner who was sentenced to be executed, or an individual who dies on a hunger strike as part of a non-violent response to social injustice. More and more, writers avoid speaking of indirect suicide because such actions reflect neither the true nature of suicide as a choice to end one's life, nor an appropriate application of the principle of double effect. Rather, these examples embody the supreme charity of willingly sacrificing one's life for others in imitation of him who taught that there is no greater love than to lay down one's life for one's friends (Jn 15, 13).

Pastoral Considerations. Although the 1917 Code of Canon Law denied ecclesiastic burial to individuals who committed suicide (*c.* 1240), the Church's pastoral attitude grew more lenient over time. While recognizing suicide is objectively (''materially'') sinful, the culpability of the act depends on the state of mind of the individual. Illness or depression, for example, may diminish the person's freedom in acting. Great discretion is allowed the pastor in determining culpability, and in allowing the full rites of Christian burial.

Another question, both practical and urgent, that is difficult to resolve apart from knowing the particular requires concerns individuals engaged in guerilla activities, espionage, or other operations employed in modern warfare. If captured by the enemy, they may face the probability or even the certainty of interrogation under torture so artfully contrived that no one could be reasonably expected to endure it without breaking. People likely to be put in such a situation are not uncommonly given a capsule of poison to be used in case of capture. Can it be argued that a person, when captured under such circumstances, is on the point of becoming, in a material sense at least, an unjust aggressor against those whose secrets he possesses, and as such, may he be slain if there is no other way to control his aggression? Again, if an individual sees himself faced with the immediate prospect of becoming an aggressor in this way, can he legitimately take his own life? These and related questions require deep reflection and great sensitivity on the part of pastoral ministers.

See Also: EUTHANASIA; HEALTH, CARE OF.

Bibliography: THOMAS AQUINAS, *Summa Theologiae* 2a2ae, 64.5. M. P. BATTIN, *Ethical Issues in Suicide* (Englewood Cliffs, N.J. 1982). A. SALVATORE, ''Professional Ethics and Suicide: Toward an Ethical Typology,'' *Ethics, Law, and Aging Review* 6 (2000): 257- 69.

[T. C. KANE/J. F. TUOHEY]

SULPICIANS

The Society of the Priests of St. Sulpice was founded at Paris in 1642 by Father Jean Jacques OLIER, in response to the seminary legislation of the Council of TRENT. It is an association of diocesan priests, released by their bishops to the society primarily to ''devote themselves to the discernment of vocations [and] to the initial and ongoing formation of priests.'' Although the basic principles governing the society were formulated by Olier, it was his successor, Alexandre Ragois de Bretonvilliers, who drafted the original constitutions that received ecclesiastical approval on Aug. 3, 1664. With later additions and revisions, the constitutions were approved temporarily by the Holy See in 1921; Pius XI approved them definitively on July 8, 1931. The Second Vatican Council occasioned another major reexamination of the Sulpician charism and approach to priestly formation in the light of the council documents and contemporary needs. This found expression in a major revision of the Sulpician Constitutions, published in 1982.

Early Growth. Determined to establish a seminary according to the mind of Trent, Olier and two (later three) companion priests took possession of a small house in the village of Vaugirard, a suburb of Paris, on Dec. 29, 1641. Within months the experiment had attracted favorable attention and by March 1642 seminarians were in residence; priests and students shared a common schedule of work, study, and prayer. Circumstances soon dictated the removal of the Vaugirard community to Paris. On Aug. 11, 1642, Olier became pastor of the parish of St. Sulpice in Faubourg St. Germain; four days later the entire community, 12 seminarians and 4 priests, joined him there (hence the name Priests of St. Sulpice). The seminarians, besides their normal duties, participated in all the activities of the parish; the more advanced students followed the theological courses at the Sorbonne.

As the number of students increased, two new buildings were added to the rectory, which had served as the original seminary. Olier gave special attention to candidates who expressed a desire to remain with him in seminary work. They made up the inner core of the seminary and were the nucleus of the Society of St. Sulpice. By a decree in November 1645, the society was granted official state recognition and accorded all the privileges en-

Exterior addition of Theological College of the Sulpician, 1963, by Johnson & Boutin, architects, Washington, D.C. (The Catholic University of America)

joyed by other religious societies within the realm. In 1652 Olier relinquished his pastoral office to devote the remainder of his life to the seminary. During these years he assigned priests of his community to four other seminaries: Nantes (1649), Viviers (1650), Le Puy (1652), and Clermont (1653). Olier died on April 2, 1657, at Issy, outside Paris, where later the Paris seminary was transferred, and where candidates for the society spent a year of novitiate before their formal acceptance into the society.

After Olier's death, both GALLICANISM and JANSENISM disturbed seminary life, but the record of the society was remarkably preserved from blemish through the history of these troubled issues. The French Revolution broke over the society with the same destructive force it exerted on other religious societies. During this critical period the society was governed by Father Jacques André ÉMERY, perhaps the greatest of Olier's successors, and the "restorer of the Society of St. Sulpice." Seminaries were closed; members of the society were scattered; and persecution was visited on those who remained. Not one of them took the oath to the Civil Constitution of the Clergy, and 18 members died for the faith.

19th and 20th Centuries. During the 19th century, the society recovered from the reverses suffered during the Revolution, and continued to grow in both membership and number of seminaries, which totaled 26 in 1900. The 20th century began with the most insidious assault yet launched against the freedom of the Church in France. For the society, this came to a climax in 1904 with a circular written by the anticlerical minister J. L. Combes, declaring that Sulpicians were unfit to teach in seminaries. Despite oppression, the society continued its work quietly, and sometimes secretly, wherever possible. In the revival of religion following World War I, the society regained all that had been lost. By 1963 there were 330 Sulpician priests and 36 houses of clerical training in France. In addition, the French Sulpicians maintained a seminary in Hue, Vietnam, and two seminaries in Africa, one in Koumi, Upper Volta, and the other in Ouida, Dahomey.

Canadian Foundations. Olier had had a vital interest in the missionary efforts of the Church and had sent four of his disciples to Montreal in 1647. Somewhat later the Sulpicians undertook the administration of schools and seminaries, including the College de Montreal (1767), the Grand Seminaire de Montreal (1840), and the House of Philosophy in Montreal (1894). From the beginning, the work of the Canadian Sulpicians was characterized by diversity; it expanded to include parochial work, college teaching, and the administration of seminaries. In 1963 the Canadian province included more than 163 Sulpician priests and was responsible for three seminaries outside Canada: one in Fukuoka, Japan (1933), one in Manizales, Colombia (1950) and one in Bogota, Colombia (1961). In 1990 the Canadian province assumed responsibility for St. Joseph Seminary in Edmonton,

Alberta, in collaboration with Newman Theological College.

U.S. Foundations. In 1790 Bishop John Carroll of Baltimore, Maryland, while in England for his consecration, negotiated with Father Émery for the opening of a seminary in his see city. Four Sulpicians led by Francis Charles NAGOT arrived in Baltimore on July 10, 1791. A house was purchased on what became 600 North Paca Street, classes were begun in October with students who had accompanied the priests from France. It was the beginning of St. Mary's Seminary, which despite early difficulties due to the scarcity of seminarians, saw 30 of its graduates ordained priests by Bishop Carroll by 1815. Because of the small number of students in the early years, many of the Sulpicians at that time were diverted from seminary work to parochial and missionary ministry in the United States. Gradually, however, the seminary prospered. In 1822 the Holy See empowered St. Mary's to grant pontifical degrees. The theology division was relocated to Roland Park in Baltimore in 1929.

In 1799, when the future of the original seminary looked dim, a college also called St. Mary's was built alongside the seminary to accept secular students. This was discontinued in 1852. Another college, Mount St. Mary's, was established in Emmitsburg, MARYLAND, in 1808 by a Sulpician, John Dubois, in hope of supplying candidates for the theological school in Baltimore. In 1826 the Sulpicians withdrew from the institution, which has continued as Mount St. Mary's College and Seminary. In 1831, on ground donated by Charles Carroll of Carrollton, who witnessed the laying of the cornerstone, St. Charles College, a preparatory seminary, was built at Ellicott City, Maryland. Consumed by fire in 1911, the institution was rebuilt in Catonsville, Maryland. In 1884 St. John's Seminary, in Brighton, Massachusetts, was entrusted to the Sulpicians, and in 1896 they assumed charge of St. Joseph's Seminary, in Dunwoodie, New York. The society later disengaged itself from both seminaries, St. Joseph's in 1906, and St. John's in 1911.

New foundations continued to mark the society's history in the United States. In 1889 the Sulpicians were entrusted with Divinity College attached to the CATHOLIC UNIVERSITY OF AMERICA, and in 1919 they built the Sulpician Seminary of Washington, D.C., adjacent to the campus of Catholic University. This seminary was incorporated as the Theological College of the University in 1940 when the university assumed responsibility for all theology courses as well as for the Basselin Foundation, a philosophy program for seminarians on full scholarship. The society had moved to the Far West in 1898 in response to the invitation from the archbishop of San Francisco to take direction of St. Patrick's Seminary in Menlo Park, California. The latter served as both a preparatory and major seminary until 1924 when St. Patrick's became the major seminary only, and the society accepted responsibility for the newly built preparatory seminary, St. Joseph's in Mountain View, California.

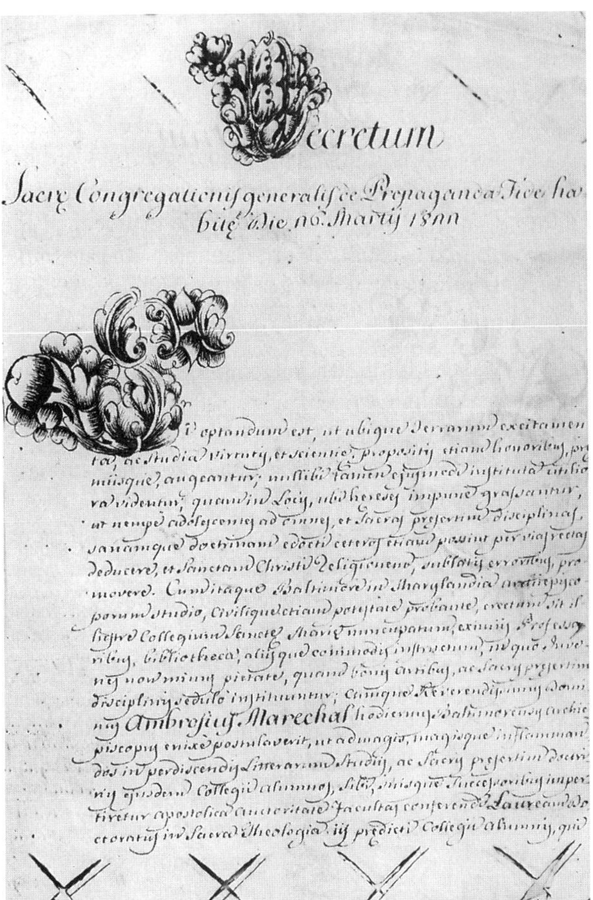

Decretum

Sacræ Congregationis generalis de Propaganda Fide habitæ die 16. Martii 1822

Original decree constituting St. Mary's Seminary a Pontifical Seminary, May 1, 1822.

In Seattle, Washington, St. Edward's Seminary, built to serve as the seminary of the archdiocese, began as a preparatory seminary but eventually included the major seminary program as well, both under the direction of the society. In 1958 a new major seminary was erected on the same grounds as the St. Thomas Seminary of Seattle, while St. Edward's continued as the preparatory seminary. In 1946 the society accepted responsibility for conducting St. Stephen's Preparatory Seminary in Honolulu. Three years later, it agreed to direct, as well, the provincial theological seminary in Plymouth, Michigan, St. John's Provincial Seminary, serving the dioceses of the province of Detroit. In Kentucky the archbishop of Louisville entrusted its own St. Thomas Preparatory Seminary to the society in 1952.

Post-Vatican II Developments. The decades following the close of the Second Vatican Council witnessed very positive developments in the society as well as some decidedly less positive. In the spirit of the council's ecumenical initiative, and encouraged by Cardinal Sheehan of Baltimore and the Right Reverend Harry Lee Doll, Episcopal bishop of Maryland, the Ecumenical Institute was founded at St. Mary's Seminary, Roland Park. It offered evening theology classes for Catholics, Protestants, and Jews, clergy and lay people.

As the need for greater ongoing formation of priests became increasingly evident, in 1971 the Vatican II Institute for Priests was founded under the sponsorship of the bishops of Region XII and was located on the seminary campus in Menlo Park, California. It provides a three-month sabbatical program for diocesan and religious priests from the United States and other countries as well. In 1976 Sulpicians in cooperation with the Jesuit School of Theology at Berkeley began a doctor of ministry program, which was then part of the Jesuit School of Theology in Berkeley, and later moved to St. Mary's Seminary in Baltimore. The degree program eventually gave way to a variety of programs allowing priests a choice of different designs and duration, and in 1996 St. Mary's completed a large continuing education center on its grounds not only for priests, but also lay men and women.

Another important development after the council was the commitment of the U.S. province, following the example of the French and Canadian provinces, to aid sister churches in mission areas by supplying trained formators for initial and ongoing formation of priests. Beginning in 1965, Sulpicians were sent to Argentina, Guatemala, Panama, and Samoa. In 1989, two Sulpicians were sent to the national seminary in Zambia in Central Africa, with a longer commitment in mind. Three years later more Sulpicians were sent forth, allowing a Sulpician presence in the Emmaus Spiritual Center, St. Augustine's Philosophy Seminary and St. Dominic's Theologate. Sulpicians also participated in leading seminars for rectors and spiritual directors, sponsored by the Congregation for Evangelization of Peoples in both West and East Africa. In 1995 the bishops of Zambia entrusted Emmaus Spirituality Center to the society, and since that time they have released several Zambian priests to join the society. Finally, while not specifically a mission operation, with the growth of the number of Hispanic Catholics in the United States and the consequent need for multicultural priestly formation, the society was happy to accept the invitation to send Sulpicians to join the faculty of Assumption Seminary in San Antonio, Texas, in 1994. Currently there are three Sulpicians there, including one as rector.

Since 1971 the society has accepted responsibility for three parishes with a priestly formation dimension: the first was established in the archdiocese of Seattle with the chapel of St. Thomas Seminary serving both as chapel for the seminarians and as parish church for the rapidly growing neighborhood. The second is St. John the Evangelist parish in San Francisco, California, a working-class parish with many immigrants, which serves also as a center for prospective seminarians who are discerning a possible priestly vocation. The third is Our Lady of the Angels at the Charlestown Retirement Community in Catonsville, Maryland, with over 2,000 people, where seminarians work in a pastoral placement under the direction of the Sulpician pastor.

The decline in the number of seminarians throughout the United States in the early 1970s resulted in the closing of many seminaries, and the return of many Sulpicians to their home dioceses. In 1969 the high school division of St. Charles College was closed, and the philosophy program at St. Mary's Seminary on Paca Street was merged with the first two college years at St. Charles College on the latter's campus, but under the name of St. Mary's College. The following year St. Thomas Preparatory Seminary in Louisville, Kentucky, closed. In 1971 the Sulpicians withdrew from St. John's Provincial Seminary in Plymouth, Michigan. This period was painfully symbolized in 1975 by the demolishing of the historic buildings of the nation's first seminary on Paca Street, leaving the chapel, St. Elizabeth Seton's house, and the convent now operating as a spirituality center. That same year the society withdrew from the high school division of St. Joseph's College in Mountain View, California. St. Edward's Seminary in Seattle closed in 1976 sending the college students to the neighboring theologate building of St. Thomas Seminary, which itself closed in 1977. That same year St. Mary's Seminary College closed after eight years on the Catonsville, Maryland, campus. The earthquake in California in 1989 damaged the structures of St. Joseph's College in Mountain View beyond repair, eventually causing the bishop to close the seminary.

In 2000 there were three major seminaries under the Sulpician direction: St. Mary's in Baltimore; St. Patrick's in Menlo Park, California; and the Theological College of the Catholic University of America, all of which have their own pre-theology programs, in addition to Theological College's Basselin philosophy program. Furthermore, the society is making a significant contribution of formators in the major seminaries of San Antonio, Texas, and Zambia, Central Africa. The province also has responsibility for two parishes, one in Baltimore, and the other in San Francisco.

[C. J. NOONAN/E. J. FRAZER]

SULPICIUA OF BOURGES, SS.

Two early medieval bishops of Bourges.

Sulpicius I ''Severus,'' d. 591, was bishop of Bourges from 584 to 591. GREGORY OF TOURS, recalling his noble origin, praised his rhetorical and poetic skill and recorded his appointment to the See of Bourges and his convocation of a provincial synod at Clermont. Sulpicius also was present at the synod of Mâcon (585).

Feast: Jan. 29.

Sulpicius II, the Pious, d. *c.* 647, was bishop of Bourges from 624 to *c.* 647. He attended the synod of Clichy in 627 and in 630 consecrated DESIDERIUS OF CAHORS, whose correspondence contains several letters that passed between the two. He is best known as the titular saint of the church of Saint-Sulpice in Paris and as the patron of the SULPICIANS.

Feast: Jan. 17.

Bibliography: GREGORY OF TOURS, *Historia Francorum* 6:38–39, 10:26, Eng. tr. O. M. DALTON, 2 v. (Oxford 1927). *Monumenta Germaniae Historica* (Berlin 1826–), Concilia 1:164, 200, 203. *Monumenta Germaniae Historica* (Berlin 1826–), Scriptores rerum Merovingicarum 4:364–380. *Patrologia Latina*, ed. J. P. MIGNE, 217 v., indexes 4 v. (Paris 1878–90) 80:591–594; 87: 254–255, 260. *Bibliotheca hagiographica latina antiquae et mediae aetatis*, 2 v. (Brussels 1898–1901; suppl. 1911) 2:7927–34. J. L. BAUDOT and L. CHAUSSIN, *Vies des saints et des bienheureux selon l'ordre du calendrier avec l'historique des fêtes*, ed. by the Benedictines of Paris, 12 v. (Paris 1935–56); v. 13, suppl. and table générale (1959) 1:581–582, 354–355. É. BROUETTE, *Lexikon für Theologie und Kirche*, ed. J. HOFER and K. RAHNER, 10 v. (2d, new ed. Freiburg 1957–65) 9:1160–61. A. BUTLER, *The Lives of the Saints*, rev. ed. H. THURSTON and D. ATTWATER, 4v. (New York 1956) 1:202–203, 111–112.

[G. M. COOK]

SULPICIUS SEVERUS

Church historian and hagiographer; b. *c.* 363; d. *c.* 420. Sulpicius, son of a distinguished Aquitanian family, made the most of the fine schooling then available in Gaul. He studied presumably in Bordeaux and met his lifelong friend PAULINUS OF NOLA, along with whom he was baptized (*c.* 390). Promptly successful in the law, Sulpicius then married into a well-to-do family. The early death of his wife and the promptings of Paulinus and of Martin, already for two decades bishop of Tours, directed him to a life of ascetic retirement, which he led first at Eluso, near Toulouse, and then at a place called by Paulinus Primuliacum and not satisfactorily located. Sulpicius remained in close association with MARTIN OF TOURS until the latter's death and later with several of the saint's disciples. A dozen letters to Sulpicius found in the correspondence of Paulinus witness the busy exchange between the two friends, but no letter from Sulpicius to Paulinus survives. In Gennadius's brief biography (*De vir. ill.* 19) Sulpicius is called a presbyter, a statement otherwise unsupported but not to be rejected. Through confusion with another Sulpicius (Severus), 6th-century bishop of Bourges, Sulpicius of Primuliacum stood for a time in the Roman Martyrology (Jan. 29).

About half of Sulpicius's preserved writing is devoted to an enthusiastic and artistic rehearsal of the life of Martin of Tours. Three different literary forms are employed. The *Life* proper, written substantially before Martin died, is a narrative with dedication and preamble. As supplements there are, first, three *Letters.* Of these the second and third were occasioned by the saint's death, which is movingly narrated in the third. Latest of the three in date is the first letter, which, like many another passage in the *Martiniana,* is a defense of the bishop against detractors. The final supplements are the two *Dialogues* (more commonly divided as three), which present a two-day reunion at Primuliacum; the talk is mainly of miracles, many just reported from the East, with new ones of Martin's to match them.

Recent studies reveal Sulpicius's literary aims in these hagiographical compositions that in part may be said to stand close to the historical novel; they betray a Sulpicius who is to be distinguished from the critical author of the *Chronica.* Whatever their motivation, the *Martiniana* enjoyed an early and lasting popularity and had a substantial influence on later hagiography.

Little-known in the Middle Ages and preserved to modern times in a single manuscript are the two books of the *Chronica,* an abridgment of sacred history from creation to the author's own time. In *Chronica* 1 and 2.1–26 Sulpicius presents OT history; *Chronica* 2.27 to the end gives the postapostolic history of the Church to the first consulship of Stilicho (A.D. 400). Certain parts of these concluding chapters have primary historical value, especially those dealing with the case of PRISCILLIAN and the courageous part taken in it by St. Martin. In the *Chronica* Sulpicius makes fullest use of classical models and achieves his most polished style.

Bibliography: Editions. K. HALM, ed., *Corpus scriptorum ecclesiasticorum latinorum* 1 (Vienna 1866). B. M. PEEBLES, ed. and tr., *The Fathers of the Church: A New Translation* 7 (1949) 77–254, *Martiniana. Clavis Patrum latinorum*, ed. E. DEKKERS (2d ed. Streenbrugge 1961) 474–477. *Series latina* (Turnhout, Belg. 1953–). Literature and commentary. P. HYLTÉN, *Traditio* 19 (1963) 447–460; *Studien zu Sulpicius Severus* (Lund 1940), on style and text. N. K. CHADWICK, *Poetry and Letters in Early Christian Gaul* (London 1955). J. FONTAINE, in *S. Martin et son temps* (*Studia anselmiana* 46; 1961), 189–236, *Martiniana.* É. GRIFFE, *Bulletin de littérature ecclésiastique* 62 (1961) 114–118; in *Mélanges offerts à Mademoiselle Christine Mohrmann* (Utrecht 1963) 84–95; *Ana-*

Bl. Nunzio Sulprizio.

lecta Bollandiana 81 (1963) 31–58. G. LAMPL, in *Jahresbericht des Kollegium Petrinum* (Linz 1951–58). M. J. MCGANN, *Archivum latinitatis medii aevi* 32 (1962) 91–94. G. RESTA, ed., *Vita S. Martini di Anonimo* (Padua 1964), medieval Latin verse rendering of some of the *Martinana.* S. PRETE, *I Chronica di Sulpicio Severo* (Rome 1955). H. MONTEFIORE, *Historia* 11 (1962) 156–170. M. L. W. LAISTNER, *Classical Philology* 35 (1940) 241–258. P. FABRE, *Essai sur la chronologie de l'oeuvre de saint Paulin de Nole* (Paris 1948). *Clavis Patrum latinorum*, ed. E. DEKKERS (2d ed. Streenbrugge 1961) 746, 741, 479, 758, for seven (eight) spurious letters. A. KAPPELMACHER, *Paulys Realenzyklopädie der klassischen Altertumswissenschaft*, ed. G. WISSOWA et al. 4A.1 (1931) 863–871. H. LECLERCQ, *Dictionnaire d'archéologie chrétienne et de liturgie*, ed. F. CABROL, H. LECLERCQ, and H. I. MARROU, 15 v. (Paris 1907–53) 14.2:1781–98, on Primuliacum. G. BARDY, *Dictionnaire de théologie catholique*, ed. A. VACANT et al., 15 v. (Paris 1903–50; Tables Générales 1951–) 14.2:2760–62. J. A. FISCHER, *Lexikon für Theologie und Kirche*, ed. J. HOFER and K. RAHNER, 10 v. (2d, new ed. Freiburg 1957–65) 9:1161–62. J. FONTAINE, *Dictionnaire de spiritualité ascétique et mystique. Doctrine et histoire*, ed. M. VILLER et al. (Paris 1932–) 5:789–797.

[B. M. PEEBLES]

SULPRIZIO, NUNZIO, BL.

Youth, b. Pesco Sansonesco near Sulmona in central Italy, April 13, 1817; d. Naples, May 5, 1836. Nunzio was the son of a poor cobbler; Domenico, and Domenica Rosa (Luciani) Sulprizio. Orphaned at the age of nine, he was first cared for by a grandmother, and later went to live with an uncle, a blacksmith. For six years Nunzio suffered patiently and meekly the harsh treatment and abuse of his coarse and brutal guardian. Worked beyond the strength of his weak constitution and often deprived of food, he was reduced to a pitiful condition and suffered particularly from a painful sore on his foot. In 1832 another uncle brought Nunzio to Naples and, through the kindness of Col. Felix Wochinger of the Royal Guard, had him placed in the hospital of St. Maria del Popolo for incurables. He never recovered fully, and at the age of 19 died at the home of Col. Wochinger where he had been taken. He was beatified on Dec. 1, 1963 by Pope Paul VI.

Feast: May 5.

Bibliography: V. SARDI, *Storia della vita del Ven. Nunzio Sulprizio* (Rome 1892). A. MARENA, *Dall'incudine all'Altare* (Rome 1963).

[F. G. SOTTOCORNOLA]

SUMMA PARISIENSIS

An early anonymous *Summa* on the Decretum of GRATIAN. It constitutes an important link in the development of the science of Canon Law. A modern edition of the only known manuscript (Bamberg) has been published. The Parisian origin of the work, knowledge of which is based upon a close examination of its contents, has never been questioned. The author's references to northern Italy, to the laws of the Lombards, and especially to the *magistri Boloniensis* suggest that he was a student in that area, probably at Bologna. His references to France in general, to the French language and usages, to the general region of Paris—Sens, Saint-Denis, etc. and his adherence to the teaching of the "Paris School," as well as his knowledge of the Parisian teachers of the time, are clues that he was writing at Paris.

The work can be dated about 1160. The style, the method of referring to the *Decretum,* the *paleae,* the absence of any mention of the legislation of Alexander III, the authorities quoted, and other internal evidence point to an early date in the decretist writings. The work contains no commentary on the *De consecratione* or on *Causae* 27–29. The remarks on the *De poenitentia* are limited to eight lines. The author had firsthand knowledge of older collections such as the FALSE DECRETALS and those of IVO OF CHARTRES. He did not cite BURCHARD OF WORMS. He used the *Summa Rolandi* and had the *Summa* of PAUCAPALEA always at hand. He did not use the *Summa* of RUFINUS. Among the 12th-century writers whom he quoted are Gerlandus, PETER LOMBARD, Magister P. or Pe. (PETER OF POITIERS?), Gilbert of Poitiers, Gerard Pucelle, Magister G. (Gandulphus?) and Magister C. The author had considerable knowledge of the Roman law of Theodosius and Justinian and cited commentators on the latter—Placentinus, Martinus, Roger, and especially Bulgarus. The work was used by the Pseudo-Rufinus, by the *Summa* ''Antiquitate et tempore,'' the ''Distinctiones Monacenses,'' and perhaps by Stephen of Tournai.

Bibliography: *The Summa Parisiensis on the Decretum Gratiani,* ed. T. P. MCLAUGHLIN (Toronto 1952), with references to earlier studies of Maasen, Schulte, Gillmann, etc. T. P. MCLAUGHLIN, ''The Formation of the Marriage Bond according to the Summa Parisiensis,'' *Mediaeval Studies* 15 (1953) 208–212. S. KUTTNER, *Repertorium der Kanonistik* (Rome 1937) 177–178. C. LEFEBVRE, *Dictionnaire de droit canonique,* ed. R. NAZ, 7 v. (Paris 1935–64) 6:1230–31.

[T. P. MCLAUGHLIN]

SUMMI PONTIFICATUS

The first encyclical letter of PIUS XII, on the function of the state in the modern world, issued Oct. 20, 1939, to members of the Catholic hierarchy throughout the world. Pius XII had been elected pope on March 2, 1939, only a few months before the outbreak of World War II. His preoccupation with the world crisis is apparent throughout this important encyclical. Its four principal parts include an introduction in which Pius rededicates his pontificate to the Sacred Heart, thus emulating the action taken by LEO XIII 40 years earlier in his *Annum Sacrum* (1899); a second section outlining the causes of the existing disastrous conditions; a third part treating the errors resulting from the prevailing new morality; and finally a presentation of basic principles for the establishment of a new order after the restoration of peace.

The pope singled out as a fundamental cause of all the grave social problems of the time a widespread denial of a universal norm of morality. According to the encyclical, two major errors have resulted from the abandonment of an objective moral law. The first is a denial of the unity and solidarity of the human race. On this point the encyclical provides a concise but complete philosophical and theological justification for the ''oneness'' of mankind, despite racial and ethnic diversity. The second error condemned is the secularization of the modern state, manifest in the separation of civil authority from any connection with divinity. From this results the omnipotent, absolute, autonomous state that considers itself the final end of all things.

Pius declared it imperative that the postwar social order should be founded on principles of natural law and divine revelation, that such evils as economic instability and the unequal distribution of wealth should be corrected, and that mankind should be reeducated in religious and moral values. He appealed for freedom of action for the Church so that it could make its contributions to social unity and lasting peace. In concluding, he reviewed the efforts of the Holy See to prevent the war and begged for charity toward the victims of war.

Sculpture of Pharoah Akhenaton, with his wife Nefertiti, making offerings to the sun god, Aton. (©Sandro Vannini/CORBIS)

Bibliography: *Acta Apostolicae Sedis* 31 (1939) 413–453, 538–564, gives Lat. text and Eng. tr. For other Eng. tr., see *Catholic Mind* 37 (1939), 889–918, and pamphlet eds. pub. by the National Catholic Welfare Conference and America Press. M. C. CARLEN, *Guide to the Documents of Pius XII* (Westminster, Md. 1951), comment.

[T. J. HARTE]

SUN WORSHIP

Since the sun is present in some way in most myths, worship of the sun or elements of sun worship are found in almost all religions. God-Sun worship or Sun-God worship—a clear distinction is not always possible—seems to be a common feature in the early stages of the higher cultures. This is probably to be explained by the fact that the sun as a concrete phenomenon fits in so well with institutional preoccupations, especially with the establishment of divine kingship as a unifying and sacredly founded central authority. Among the planting or food-gathering peoples, sun worship is mostly on the fringes of mythology and cult, or it is one element within a basically broader and more comprehensive system of worship. Thus, to promote fertility, sun wheels are placed in fields, fire wheels are rolled over declivities, and solstices and eclipses of the sun are marked with religious rites in order to renew the powers of the sun. On the other hand, men try through their worship to protect themselves from the sun. In any case, the sun is not the supreme being, nor does the sun exercise the latter's functions.

Many examples may be cited to illustrate the point that the sun is often not the only or even the main object of worship. In China, offerings were made to the sun along with those made to the eight gods. In the Temple of Heaven (Tian Tang) at Beijing, there was an altar to the sun. The worship of the sun by Indo-European peoples is well attested, e.g., by the sun chariot of Trundholm, and by Stonehenge. Thus, the sun in the form of a wheel was carried about on a wagon drawn by war horses, and mimetic sun dances (a form of sympathetic magic), morning greetings of the sun, ball games, wheel games, and offerings to the sun on sun feast days, etc., were common. In India the temple at Konarak in Orissa (built in the 10th century A.D.) was the center of a comprehensive sun cult. In the *Gāyatrī* rite, every Hindu began his day with a prayer and a hymn of praise to the sun (*Sūrya*), the giver (feminine) of light, heat, and fruitfulness. The sun worship of the non-Aryans, with sun ritual and accompanying sacred meal and sacrifice, may have been even more fervent.

The religions of the Babylonians and Assyrians, the cult of Mithras (the cult of the *sol invictus*), and Zoroastrianism, were all sun-centered forms of worship. The Babylonian sun god, Shamash (in Sumerian, Utu or Babbar, the Shining One) was worshipped at Larsa, and the cult was promoted later at Sippar by Hammurabi. Shamash was the god of justice, a hero and conqueror of death, who was praised in hymns (cf. the stories of Gilgamesh and Marduk).

Highly developed sun cults were characteristic of Mexico and Egypt. The Aztecs worshipped Tonatiuh, and the other gods who assumed his traits, with the heart's blood (as a nourishment for the sun) of the noblest human victims. The ball game called *Ollama* was dedicated to him. The Incas made heart-offerings (mostly animal hearts) to their sun god Inti. At the great sun feasts held at the solstices, they offered burnt sacrifices, and they enkindled the sacred fire. The sun was regarded as the ancestor of the Inca rulers, who were therefore declared sacred. Since the conquered peoples were frequently familiar with solar divinities, these rulers enjoyed a religious sanction. This phenomenon is found repeatedly elsewhere. In Japan, the emperor was worshipped as the descendant of the sun-goddess Amaterasu. The Thracians worshipped a sun king, from whom they believed they had descended. The Natchez Indians called their chief, "Great Sun," "Brother of the Sun." The mummies of dead Inca rulers were placed on seats in the sun temple of Cuzco, and thus continued to hold court as formerly in life.

In Egypt the cult of the sun god, Ra, of Heliopolis was made an official religion from the Fourth Dynasty, and the Pharaoh was worshipped as the son of Ra. With the ascendancy of Thebes under the Twelfth Dynasty, the cult of Ra was combined with that of Amon of Thebes into the cult of Amon-Ra. The sun worship in Egypt reached its highest point under Amenhotep IV (Akhnaton), one of the last kings of the Eighteenth Dynasty. The sun god was represented as a solar disk with many rays, each ending with beneficent or gift-giving hands, and he was invoked in hymns that were often very beautiful.

See Also: AZTEC RELIGION; INCA RELIGION; EGYPT, ANCIENT, 1.

Bibliography: F. VON OEFELE et al., J. HASTINGS, ed., *Encyclopedia of Religion & Ethics,* 13 v. (Edinburgh 1908–27) 12:48–103. M. ELIADE, *Patterns of Comparative Religion,* tr. R. SHEED (New York 1958) 124–153 with good bibliog. J. G. FRAZER, *The Worship of Nature* (London 1926). G. LANCZKOWSKI, *Die Religion in Geschichte und Gegenwart,* 7 v. (3d ed. Tübingen 1957–65) 6:137–139, with good bibliog.

[W. DUPRÉ]

SUNDAY

Christians have from the earliest times come together on Sunday to anticipate the second coming of the Lord, to encounter the risen Christ in the Eucharist, and to gratefully recall to mind the death and Resurrection of Jesus. One reads in Acts: "On the first day of the week, when we had met for the breaking of bread. . ." (20.7). St. Paul speaks of collections of money to be made on the first day of the week (1 Cor 16.2), and in Rv 1.10 mention is made of the Lord's day.

Theme. The Christian Sunday is essentially a weekly festival of the Resurrection of Christ. Probably the weekly Easter of Sunday came into general observance some time before there were annual Holy Week and Easter festivities. Sunday did not arise out of the Jewish Sabbath. In fact, the first Christians kept both Sabbath and Sunday. Rather, Sunday is a creation of Christian inspiration and is filled with uniquely Christan meaning.

First Day. Whereas the last day of the week was sacred to the Jews as the day on which creation was completed, the first day is sacred to the Christians as the day of the new creation begun in the Resurrection of the Lord. As Eusebius of Alexandria says, ''It was on this day that the Lord began the first-fruits of the creation of the world, and on the same day He gave to the world the first-fruits of the Resurrection'' (*Sermo* 16; *Patrologia Graeca.* ed. J. P. Migne [Paris 1857–66] 86:416). Sunday is not only a day of rest, it is also a day for celebrating Baptism and the Eucharist. Although Sunday is not a Christian Sabbath, nonetheless Sunday brings together and transcends the two great themes of the Jewish Sabbath—memorial of creation (Ex 20.8–11) and memorial and sign of the Old Testament covenant (Ex 31.13). For the Sunday assembly and Eucharist of the Church are a celebration of a renewed humanity in the New Adam and of the New Testament covenant made in the blood of Jesus.

Day of the Sun. The Fathers of the Church also exploited the symbolism based on the Greco-Roman (originally Egyptian) name for this day, namely, *dies solis* (day of the sun), from which the Anglo-Saxon name Sunday is derived. Justin Martyr constructs a parallel between the name and what God did on that day: ''We come together on the day of the *sun* on which God, changing *darkness* and matter created the world, and on which Jesus Christ our Savior arose from the dead'' (1 *Apol.* 67.7; J. Quasten, *Monumenta eucharista et liturgica vetusissima* [Bonn 1935–37] 20). In the same vein Eusebius of Caesarea remarks: ''It was on this day that at the time of creation when God said, 'Let there be light,' there was light; and on this day also the Sun of Justice arose on our souls'' (*Comm. in psalmos* 91; *Patrologia Graeca* 23:1172). St. Jerome acquiesced in this coincidence between revelation and pagan terminology: ''If it is called the day of the sun by the pagans, we willingly accept this name, for on this day arose the Light of the world; on this day shone forth the Sun of Justice in whose rays is health'' [*In die dominica paschae;* G. Morin, *Anecdota Maredsolana* (Maredsous 1897) 3.2:418].

Eighth Day. As early as the first half of the second century Christian writers began calling Sunday the ''eighth day.'' Pseudo-Barnabas uses the expression to indicate the substitution of the New Testament for the Old. He portrays God as resting on the Jewish Sabbath from His work of creation, and then accomplishing the New Creation, the Church, on the eighth day: ''The present Sabbaths are not acceptable to me, only the Sabbath which I have made, in which, after giving rest to all things, I will make the beginning of the eighth day, that is, the beginning of another world.'' Therefore, says Pseudo-Barnabas, ''we . . . celebrate . . . the eighth day on which Jesus arose from the dead, was made manifest, and ascended into heaven'' [*Letter of Barnabas* 15.8–9; *The Fathers of the Church* (New York 1947) 1:216].

The eschatological symbolism implicit in Pseudo-Barnabas is brought out by Origen: ''The number eight, which contains the virtue of the Resurrection, is the figure of the future world'' (*Selecta in psalmos* 118.164; *Patrologia Graeca* 12:1624). In like manner Ambrose gives the number eight the meaning of redemption: ''The number eight is the fulfillment of our hope'' (*Expos. in evang. sec. Lucam* 5.49; *Patrologia Latina*, ed. J. P. Migne [Paris 1878–90] 15:1735). ''According to the Mosaic law a male child had to be circumcised on the eighth day after his birth, while in the New Testament Christ arose from the dead on the eighth day'' (*De Abraham* 2.11; *Patrologia Latina* 14:494).

Hence by this term patristic writers teach that Sunday represents the definitive stage of creation, which began with the Resurrection. It is a day taken out of time to emphasize the fact that the events of the Redemption have already initiated for Christians the timeless life of heaven.

Lord's Day. The name *dies dominica,* appearing for the first time in Rv 1.10, was quickly taken up by Christians, and in time replaced *dies solis* as the legal name for the day. It is preserved to our own day in the romance languages as *domenica, domingo,* and *dimanche.*

The reason for the success of this term is that it aptly summarizes the Christian theology of Sunday. ''The Lord's Day'' refers to Christ the Lord (Kyrios), the Conqueror and Master. He became Lord and Master effectively through His Resurrection, which occurred on Sunday. ''The Lord's Day,'' then, represents for Christians the marvelous intervention of God whereby He redeemed them in Christ, initiated His kingdom with them as Christ's Body, and prepared them for ultimate glory in heaven. Hence, it is the memorial of the Resurrection, the day for assembling the members of Christ's Body and making His redeeming presence actual, and the anticipation of the Parousia.

Celebration. Given the unique place of Sunday in the Christian dispensation, it bore from the very beginning a joyous character. All signs of penance and sorrow, such as kneeling and fasting (Tertullian, *De corona militis* 3; *Patrologia Latina* 2:79), were set aside. In fact, doing penance on Sunday was considered sinful (*Didascalia Apostolorum* 5.20.11; F. X. Funk, ed., *Didascalia et constitutiones apostolorum* [Paderborn 1905] 1:298).

Mass. The Eucharistic celebration is without doubt the chief characteristic of a Christian's observance of Sunday. No hard-and-fast rule existed in the early Church; attendance at Sunday Mass was simply taken for granted [Acts 20.7; Didache 14.1 (J. Quasten, *Monumenta eucharista et liturgica vetusissima* [Bonn 1935–37] 12); Justin, 1 *Apol.* 67.3 (*ibid.* 19)]. Only in the sixth century was there formulated an explicit law regarding the obligation to assist at Mass on Sunday; it came from the Council of Agde in 506 (Guiniven 23).

The Church is the assembly of the people of God. At Sunday Mass the Church becomes visible in her members gathered about the Lord's table to celebrate the Eucharist. This meal creates the Church as the Mystical Body of Christ as her members make present the Lord's redemptive action. Such an assembly gives the individual the sense of belonging to a family whose Father is God, whose elder brother is Christ, and whose joy is to live for each other. To absent oneself from the Sunday gathering without reason is to run the risk of weakening the tie with the body of Christians and of depriving oneself of the necessary spiritual nourishment.

Sunday Rest. The Sunday rest has an uneven history. Before the fourth-century decrees of legal toleration and later establishment of Christianity, Sunday was a workday; Christians worshiped in the night and early morning hours. The Church long maintained a healthy fear of idleness; the cessation of work on Sunday was introduced less to allow for rest than to clear the way for intense spiritual activity. This was clearly Origen's point of emphasis: ''On Sunday none of the actions of the world should be done. If, then, you abstain from all the works of this world and keep yourself free for spiritual things, go to church, listen to the readings and divine homilies, meditate on heavenly things'' (*Homil. 23 in Numeros* 4; *Patrologia Graeca* 12:749). Sunday rest from the labor that characterizes the other days of the week is a sign of freedom and redemption of a soul destined for God. Contemporary Catholic practice allows the use of Sunday for reasonable recreation, repose, charitable activity, and work that is truly necessary; primary emphasis, however, should be put on the worship of God.

Baptism. Traditionally, this Sacrament is a Sunday event. This practice is highly appropriate, since from very early times the custom of the Church was to baptize at Easter, and, even now, the baptismal water is blessed during the Easter Vigil. As we have seen, Sunday prolongs Easter through the year and is the weekly celebration of the Resurrection. Sunday is the proper day for administering this Sacrament, for the human race is buried to sin with Christ and rises with Him to newness of life in Baptism. The custom of the celebrant passing among the people before the principal Sunday Mass to sprinkle them with blessed water also provides a remembrance of Baptism and an echo of the Easter Vigil (see: ASPERGES).

Vatican II. Vatican Council II's Constitution on the Sacred Liturgy contains an expanded description of the significance of Sunday in the life of the faithful. The description focuses on the day itself and the action of the Church community. ''By an apostolic tradition which took its origin from the very day of Christ's resurrection, the Church celebrates the paschal mystery every eighth day'' (*Sacrosanctum Concilium* 106). Thus the Council Fathers articulated the memorial nature of the Sunday observance. The description continues: ''For on this day Christ's faithful should come together into one place so that, by hearing the word of God and taking part in the Eucharist, they may call to mind the passion, the resurrection, and the glorification of the Lord Jesus'' (ibid.). The document further notes that: ''[the faithful] may thank God who 'has begotten us again, through the resurrection of Jesus Christ from the dead, unto a living hope''' (ibid.). The consequence of such a memorial day with its community action makes the Lord's day the original feast day. The Council urges that this observance should be part of the piety of the faithful in order that Sunday would become in fact a day of joy and freedom from work. Drawing these thoughts into a specific norm, the document continues: ''Other celebrations, unless they be of overriding importance, must not have precedence over this day, which is the foundation and nucleus of the whole liturgical year'' (ibid.).

The revised Roman Calendar (1969) translated these guiding thoughts of the Constitution on the Sacred Liturgy into practical norms. The calendar's table of liturgical days according to their order of precedence ranks the Sundays of the year sixth (CalendRom 4). The following specific norms are presented.

(1) ''Because of its special importance, the celebration of Sunday is replaced only by solemnities or feasts of the Lord. The Sundays of Advent, Lent and the Easter season, however, take precedence over all solemnities and feasts of the Lord'' (ibid. 5).

(2) ''By its nature, Sunday excludes the permanent assignment of another celebration'' (ibid. 6). Nevertheless, the document continues to note two categories of exceptions.

''Nevertheless (a) Sunday within the octave of Christmas is the feast of the Holy Family; (b) Sunday following January 6 is the feast of the Baptism of the Lord;

(c) Sunday after Pentecost is the solemnity of the Holy Trinity; (d) the last Sunday of the liturgical year is the solemnity of Christ the King (ibid. 6). In those areas where the solemnities of Epiphany, Ascension, and Corpus Christi are not observed as holydays of obligation, they are assigned to a Sunday'' (ibid. 7).

(3) Sundays of the year do yield their place to feasts of the Lord which are found in the general calendar, proper solemnities, solemnities of the Lord, the Blessed Virgin Mary and saints listed in the general calendar (ibid. 59).

(4) ''For the pastoral advantage of the people, it is permissible to observe on the Sundays of the year those celebrations which occur during the week and which are popular with the faithful, provided they take precedence over these Sundays in the table of liturgical days'' (ibid 58).

The revised calendar contains three directives for the development of particular (local) calendars. Among these there is an insistence that ''the temporal cycle . . . in which the mystery of the redemption is unfolded during the liturgical year must be preserved intact and maintain proper preeminence over particular celebrations'' (ibid. 50). The framers of the revised general calendar indicate strongly that the particular calendars are not to be enlarged disproportionally. Hence saints are to have only one feast in the liturgical calendar.

The expanded description of Sunday found in the Constitution on the Sacred Liturgy and the practical norms of the revised calendar move in the direction of recognizing Sunday as ''the original feast day'' (ibid. 4; *Sacrosanctum Concilium* 106). This is very consistent with current liturgical spirituality which is centered on the person of Jesus in his passion, resurrection, and glorification, i.e. on the paschal mystery.

Bibliography: J. A. JUNGMANN, *The Meaning of Sunday* (Notre Dame, Ind. 1961). N. M. DENISBOULET, *The Christian Calendar,* tr. P. HEPBURNE-SCOTT (New York 1960). A. G. MARTIMORT, *L'Église en prière* (Tournai 1961) 673–685.T.J. TALLEY, *The Origins of the Liturgical Year* (Collegeville, 1991); A.J. MARTIMORT, ed. *The Church at Prayer IV: The Liturgy and Time* (Collegeville 1986); A. ADAM, *The Liturgical Year: Its History and Its Meaning After the Reform of the Liturgy* (New York 1981).

[W. J. SHERZER/P. R. COONEY/EDS.]

SUNDAY, WILLIAM (BILLY) ASHLEY

Evangelist; b. Ames, Iowa, Nov. 19, 1863; d. Winona Lake, Ind., Nov. 6, 1935. During a successful eight-year baseball career (1883–91) that included a record number of stolen bases, Sunday displayed little religious interest until 1887 when, after hearing a street preacher, he decided to commit himself totally to God. Encouraged by his wife Helen, Sunday left baseball in 1891 and took a position with the Chicago Young Men's Christian Association. Subsequently he was ordained a Presbyterian minister. His evangelistic career, begun in Garner, Iowa (1895), at the invitation of some associates, was characterized by his unusual acrobatic antics. Sunday was a popular evangelist for about 15 years and reached his peak during the pre-Prohibition era. He has been called the greatest single influence in arousing sentiment in behalf of the prohibition by law of the manufacture, transportation, and sale of alcoholic beverages.

Bibliography: F. G. BEARDSLEY, *Heralds of Salvation* (New York 1939). W. T. ELLIS, *''Billy'' Sunday: The Man and His Message* (Philadelphia 1936), authorized ed.

[T. HORGAN]

SUNDAY AND HOLYDAY OBSERVANCE

According to the present discipline of the Church the faithful are obliged on Sundays and other holydays of obligation to participate at Mass, ''to abstain from those works and affairs which hinder the worship to be rendered to God, the joy proper to the Lord's day, or the suitable relaxation of mind and body'' (*Codex iuris canonicis* c.1247). The Second Vatican Council emphasized the importance of Sunday observance, and its preeminent position in the Church's liturgical year:

> The Lord's Day is the first holy day of all and should be proposed to the devotion of the faithful and taught to them in such a way that it may become in fact a day of joy and of freedom from work. Other celebrations, unless they be truly of greatest importance, shall not have precedence over the Sunday, the foundation and core of the whole liturgical year (*Sacrosanctum concilium,* 106).

History of the Observance

The obvious analogy between the Jewish SABBATH and Christian Sunday and the influence of the former on the latter make it necessary to say something about the historical connection between the two.

Sabbath and Sunday. The Sabbath, or 7th day of the week, was observed among the Jews as a day sacred to Yahweh. As the law was enunciated in Ex 20.8, it was positive in form—''Remember to keep holy the Sabbath day''—but the manner in which this was to be done was described negatively in the context. It was to be sanctified by abstinence from work because God had rested on the 7th day after having carried out all the work for the creation of the world, and God had blessed and sanctified that day. Nevertheless, there were positive aspects to the observance. The Sabbath was a joyful feast day and one on which the Jews visited sanctuaries (Is 1.13; Hos 2.13) or went to consult a prophet of God (2 Kgs 4.23). It was a day of special sacrifice (R. de Vaux, *Ancient Israel, Its Life and Institutions*, tr. J. McHugh, 469), and in postexilic times it was celebrated by attending instruction and prayer gatherings in the synagogues.

It was made clear to the early Christians that they were not bound by Jewish practices as such (Acts 15.28–29). Among the observances regarded as abrogated under this rubric was the keeping of the Sabbath. Possibly, as is believed by some on the basis of Mt 24.20, the early Christian community at Jerusalem, and perhaps early generations of Judeo-Christians elsewhere, continued to observe the Sabbath, but St. Paul did not impose the obligation on the communities he established outside Palestine (Col 2.16; Gal 4.10; Rom 14.5).

Worship. There is evidence that even during the time of the Apostles Sunday enjoyed a preeminence among the days of the week because of its association with the Lord's Resurrection; and already, at the time the Book of the Revelation was written, it was known as the Lord's day (Rv. 1.10). The emphasis put by the four evangelists on the fact that the Resurrection took place on the first day of the week suggests that even when the Gospels were being written, Sunday was regarded as sacred to Christ. While the celebration of the Eucharist was not limited to Sunday, there are indications in the NT significantly coupling its celebration with the first day of the week. The contribution that St. Paul exhorted the Corinthians to make each first day of the week for the poor in Jerusalem was probably associated with a weekly assembly for divine worship on that day. In Acts 20.7 it is said: "And on the first day of the week, when we had met for the breaking of the bread, Paul addressed them . . . ." These passages do not prove that the faithful of the Pauline churches met every Sunday for the celebration of the Eucharist, but they indicate the probability of such a practice. This is confirmed by an ordinance contained in the Didache—"On the Lord's day come together and break bread and give thanks (offer the Eucharist), after confessing your sins that your sacrifice may be pure" (14.1)—which shows that the practice of sanctifying the Lord's day by the celebration of the Eucharistic meal was firmly established in postapostolic times. St. Ignatius of Antioch some time in the first years of the 2d century wrote: "Christians no longer observe the Sabbath but live in the observance of the Lord's day on which our life rose again" (*Ep. Ad Magnes.* 9). Other important evidence is to be found in St. Justin's description of the worship of Christians on the day of the Lord (*Apol.* 1.67).

There is nothing to indicate that the practice of coming together on Sundays for the Eucharistic celebration was regarded as obligatory under pain of sin during the first three centuries of the Christian era. Only gradually did the idea of obligation emerge. The Council of ELVIRA in the first years of the 4th century declared that anyone who neglected to come to Church for three Sundays was, for his correction, to be excommunicated for a short time. This penalty seems too severe to have been imposed for anything not regarded as a serious transgression of the law. The APOSTOLIC CONSTITUTIONS, dating from the latter part of the same century, attributed the precept to the Apostles and suggested therefore that it was seriously binding. The ordinance regarding attendance at Mass in Codex Iuris Canonicis c.1247 goes back to the Decretal of Gratian (*c.* 1150).

Rest. The observance of Sunday as a day of rest was a later development, possibly because in the more primitive Church many of the faithful were of low station in life, or even slaves, and hence were not in a position to take a holiday when they wished. But as the faithful grew in numbers, the situation changed, and there were more who could find leisure at set times. As greater insistence began to be laid upon attendance at worship as a duty, and as services grew longer, the desirability became apparent of securing leisure for worship by the general observance of Sunday as a day of rest. Moreover, familiarity with the stress laid by the OT upon the Sabbath rest, which some held to have been transferred to Sunday under the New Law, and the example of pagan festivals that were celebrated as holidays turned popular thought in the direction of a Sunday holiday. There was also a general dissatisfaction with the provision for rest and recreation that prevailed in the Roman empire at that time. There was no lack of holiday festivals, but the intervals between them were irregular, and they did not provide the periodically recurrent interruptions of work necessary to meet human needs for rest and leisure. There was little resistance even from pagan sources, therefore, when Constantine in 321 decreed a weekly holiday on the "venerable day of the Sun."

The Sabbatarian idea, expressly repudiated by St. Jerome and condemned by the Council of Orléans in 538 as Jewish and non-Christian, was clearly stated in Charlemagne's decree of 789, which forbade all labor on Sunday as a violation of the Third Commandment. From that time onward the identification of the Sabbath and the Sunday rest was more or less taken for granted, and there was a tendency to draw conclusions of increasing severity from it, all based on the fundamental assumption that the Sunday rest was an institution of divine positive law.

The first written ecclesiastical law on the subject of Sunday rest appears to have been that of the Synod of Laodicea toward the end of the 4th century. The synod was content to prescribe that on the Lord's day the faithful were to abstain from work as far as possible. From the 8th century onward the law was formulated by local councils more or less as it is today. As a general law of the Church it goes back to the Decretals of Gregory IX (1234).

The Fathers from Irenaeus to Augustine used the term ''servile'' in an allegorical sense to signify sin and used ''rest'' to signify freedom from sin. The Sunday rest was therefore, before all else, a cessation from sinful activities. This explains why, as the Sabbatarian movement gathered strength, attention was given to abstinence not only from work but also from various forms of recreation and amusement. Before the 15th century, however, there were few restrictions placed on the amusements in which the people indulged on Sundays. Sinful abuses of leisure and increasing Sabbatarian sentiment gave rise to strong puritan reaction in Protestant countries (*see* SABBATARIANISM), and local councils in the Counter Reformation era also protested vehemently and attempted restrictive legislation. In the common law of the Church, however, no general regulation of Sunday recreation has ever been formulated.

Other Feasts. In the 4th century, feasts on days other than Sunday began to be celebrated in the Church. Over the course of the centuries the list of such feasts became quite lengthy. From the 13th to the 17th centuries there were dioceses in which the Sundays and other feasts on which the faithful were expected to attend Mass and abstain from work amounted to more than 100 days in the course of a year. Urban VIII in 1642 greatly reduced the number, leaving 36 feasts of obligation exclusive of Sundays, and limited the right of bishops to introduce new feast days. Later there were further reductions made for particular countries, followed by general reductions applicable to the whole Latin Church.

According to the present discipline of the Church there are ten feasts or holydays of obligation exclusive of Sundays. These are Christmas, the Epiphany, the Ascension, the Body and Blood of Christ, Mary, Mother of God, her Immaculate Conception and her Assumption, St. Joseph, SS. Peter and Paul, and All Saints (*Codex iuris canonicis* c.1246 §1). However, with the permission from the Holy See, ''the conference of bishops can suppress some of the holy days of obligation or transfer them to a Sunday'' (*Codex iuris canonicis* c.1246 §2). In the U.S., the solemnities of the Epiphany and the Body and Blood of Christ are transferred to Sundays, while the feasts of St. Joseph, and SS. Peter and Paul are not observed as holydays of obligation. Whenever January 1 (Mary, Mother of God), August 15 (the Assumption) or November 1 (All Saints) fall on a Saturday or a Monday, the obligation to attend Mass is suppressed. In the U.S., the decision whether to transfer Ascension to the Seventh Sunday of Easter is left to each ecclesiastical province.

Moral Obligation

Observance of Sundays and holy days of obligation requires two different things of the faithful, namely, participation in the Mass and rest from unnecessary work. These duties should be considered separately.

Participation in the Mass. The faithful are bound by Codex Iuris Canonicis c.1247 to be present at Mass on all Sundays and holy days of obligation. At minimum, participation entails physical presence and consciousness. While the precept to participate in the Mass may be fulfilled on the evening before the Sunday or holyday of obligation, the precept of rest from unnecessary work has to be observed on the day itself. The common teaching of canonists and moral theologians is that the obligation is a grave one, and the deliberate missing of Mass without excuse is considered a grave transgression of ecclesiastical law. The precept is fulfilled by attendance at Mass celebrated in any Catholic rite (see *Codex iuris canonicis* c.1248 §1). The obligation may be satisfied at any time during the 24 hours of the Sunday or holy day of obligation, or on the preceding evening. Here, ''evening'' is understood as anytime from 4:00 p.m. onwards (see Pius XII, *Christus Dominus* VI, Jan. 6, 1953, in AAS 45 (1953) 14–24).

Abstinence from Work. The obligation regarding the work that must be omitted is more difficult to define and to apply. The traditional prohibition against ''servile,'' labor on Sunday is traceable in this connection to St. Jerome's faulty translation of the Hebrew *m^{e}leket 'aboda* used in a number of OT passages regarding the cessation of work on holydays as *opus servile.* The servile work of the Vulgate was interpreted by some of the Fathers as sin, but between the 6th and 12th centuries local councils, popular preachers, religious chapters, devotional treatises gradually but firmly established a more literal interpretation. Some theologians from the 13th to the 16th century thought that the purpose for which a work is performed, i.e., whether or not it is done for earthly gain, ought to be considered in the determination of its servility. From the latter part of the 16th century, however, the influence of Cajetan and Suárez, and later of Alphonsus Liguori and Busenbaum, prevailed, and theologians came commonly to distinguish servile from nonservile work simply on the basis of the nature of the work alone. A work was to be classified as servile simply because it was a mechanical, arduous, physical sort of work, a sort of work that would be left to slaves or servants if that were possible. Examples of servile work would be sowing, plowing, cutting wood, making clothes. Servile work was understood in distinction to liberal work, or work that employs the mental powers chiefly, and to ''mixed'' or common work that requires both physical and mental effort but with the mental predominating. Servile work, so understood, was regarded as forbidden on Sundays and holydays, while liberal and common work was not. Over time, a long and increasing list of exceptions was admitted by most authorities under the title of custom, necessity, public utility, charity, piety, emergency, or even the obligation of avoiding idleness likely to prove a proximate occasion of sin.

In the 20th century considerable dissatisfaction was expressed, not with the law itself, but with the outmoded concept of servility enshrined in it, a concept elaborated for a social and religious milieu so different from that which prevails in the modern world. The prohibition of servile as opposed to liberal work was well enough suited to the social conditions of earlier times. It effectively outlawed Sunday and holy day work on the great landed estates and so accomplished something of religious and social value. But the interpretation has become increasingly difficult to apply to contemporary conditions and situations. The difference between what is servile and what is liberal has lost much of its relevance, and the stress upon hard physical toil appears less important in a world in which workers are generally in less need of rest from hard physical labor than relief from the monotony, cares, and frustrations involved in the liberal or common types of work by which they earn their living.

Canonists argued that the rest required by Sunday and holyday observance can best be secured by interpreting it with less attention to the historical question of what kind of work was once done by slaves and serfs, and what kind by free citizens and with more attention to the ever actual purpose of the law, which is to give to all, time to worship God, to hear the word of God, to regain spiritual and physical strength, and to enjoy family life. The preoccupation with work precludes one from all of the foregoing, whatever that may be and regardless of whether it is liberal, mixed, or servile.

All these factors led to a rewording of the 1983 Code of Canon Law. Whereas c. 1248 of the 1917 Code obliged the faithful on Sundays and other holy days to attend Mass and to abstain from servile work, from judicial proceedings, and unless legitimate customs or special indults make exceptions, from public markets, fairs, and other public buying and selling, the 1983 Code avoids the use of the phrase ''servile work.'' Canon 1247 states the obligation as follows:

> On Sundays and other holy days of obligation, the faithful are obliged to participate in the Mass. Moreover, they are to abstain from those works and affairs which hinder the worship to be rendered to God, the joy proper to the Lord's day, or the suitable relaxation of mind and body.

Those who are employed in jobs that require them to work on Sundays and/or holy days are excused from the observance of rest, but not necessarily from the obligation to participate in the Mass. In individual instances when one finds it impossible, or impossible without extreme inconvenience to attend Mass, one is morally excused from the obligation without the need for a dispensation. Where there is a ''just cause'' for the inability to participate in the Mass on Sundays and holy days, those who are affected may seek a dispensation or commutation under *Codex iuris canonicis* c.1245, which provides that: ''Without prejudice to the right of diocesan bishops mentioned in can. 87, for a just cause and according to the prescripts of the diocesan bishop, a pastor can grant in individual cases a dispensation from the obligation of observing a feast day or a day of penance or can grant a commutation of the obligation into other pious works.'' Here, ''individual cases'' include both a one-off case, as well as an ongoing situation. In the latter case, the preference is for commutation rather than outright dispensation.

Bibliography: J. M. NIELEN, *Das Zeichen des Herrn: Sabbat und Sonntag in biblischer und urchristlicher Bezeugung* (Freiburg 1940). M. ZALBA, ''De conceptu operis servilis,'' *Periodica de re morali canonica liturgica* 52 (1963) 133–63, 261–319. V. J. KELLY, *Forbidden Sunday and Feast Day Occupations* (Washington 1943). J. T. SULLIVAN, *The Sunday Rest* (Rome 1952). B. HÄRING, *The Law of Christ,* tr. E. G. KAISER, v.2 (Westminster, Md. 1963) 296–338. J. A. QUIGLEY, ''Changing Concept of Servile Work,'' *Catholic Theological Society of America. Proceedings* 12 (1957) 145–55. L. L. MCREAVY, ''Servile Work: The Evolution of the Present Sunday Law,'' *Clergy Review* 9 (1935) 269–84; ''Servile Work: Criticism and Suggestions,'' *ibid.* 453–66; ''Sabbatarianism and the Decalogue,'' *ibid.* 20 (1941) 498–508. E. J. MAHONEY, ''Bondsman or Free,'' *ibid.* 1 (1931) 333–45. P. O'NEILL, ''The Meaning of Servile Work,'' *The Irish Ecclesiastical Record* 52 (1938) 646–47. J. BEAL et al, *New Commentary on the Code of Canon Law* (New York-Mahwah, N.J. 2000).

[M. HERRON/EDS.]

SUNNITES

The vast majority of the Muslims professing belief in the unicity of God and the apostleship of MUḤAMMAD. They derive their title from the Arabic word *sunna,* meaning custom, use, or statute. In the development of ISLAM the term took on the meaning of the standard practice derived from Muḥammad and the early Muslim community; as such it was opposed to innovation (*bid'a*). In the various crises that arose and split the Muslim community, the majority steered a middle course between extremes and labeled themselves the ''people of the Sunna and the community.''

Basic Principles. The peculiar constitution of the Muslim community, which developed without any clear distinction either between politics and religion or between morality and law, precludes any facile comparison with Christianity. The roots of Muslim faith are found in the QUR'ĀN, the Sunna of the Prophet, and the consensus of the community. The institution of consensus, in a society without central religious control or a priesthood, allowed for the incorporation of the historical process of development and customary uses that had no roots in the Qur'ān or the Sunna. At the same time, it set the limits of orthodoxy by rejecting developments that jarred the sensibility of the tradition-centered community. As a result, it is difficult to define clearly the dogmas of the orthodox community or to record any universally valid creed. There are creeds in abundance, but they are the product of individual reflection or group beliefs.

Like all Muslims, the Sunnites accept the ''Five Pillars'' of Islam: witness to one God and His apostle Muḥammad, prayer, alms, the fast of RAMAḌĀN, and the *ḤAJJ*, or *pilgrimage*, to MECCA. But in the elaboration of these basic beliefs and practices distinctions arise.

Perhaps the clearest distinction setting off the Sunnites from the other major sects is found in the constitutional theory of the caliphate (*see* CALIPH). The Khawarij (Seceders) at one extreme maintained the elective principle, leaving the community free to set up or depose whomsoever they wished. The SHĪ'ITES, at the other extreme, claimed that divine right limited succession to the offspring of 'ALĪ and Fatima, Muḥammad's daughter. The Sunnites, avoiding the anarchy of Kharajism and the exclusiveness of Shī'ism, held that the caliph must be of Muḥammad's tribe of the Quraysh and incorporated a theory of election that was flexible enough to accept historical facts and was symbolized in the oath of allegiance that the community offered to the *de facto* caliph. Although the caliphate, for all practical purposes, disappeared in 1258, the community division it occasioned remained firm. Earlier and later crises left their stamp on orthodoxy, but divisions were smoothed over by deeper loyalties.

Different Schools of Thought. Within the community thus defined, law and religious practice carry more significance than dogma and belief. The Sunnites accept as orthodox the four schools of law: Ḥanafite, Mālikite, Shāfi'ite and Ḥanbalite (*see* ISLAMIC LAW). But in the matter of belief, divisions are less clear. Two main tendencies remain constant: the stubborn traditionalist position of Ḥanbalite theology, which allows little room for reason, and the moderate theologizing position of the Ash'arite school, which uses reason and its categories to safeguard revelation. A third, rationalistic tendency, defeated by orthodoxy in the Middle Ages, is evident again today in the attempts to restate Islam in modern terms. However, political, social, and economic problems tend to obscure theology; accordingly, it would be temerarious to define Sunnite orthodoxy in other than historical terms.

Early contact with Christianity, Hellenism, and Iranian religious thought gave rise to theological questions often complicated by political overtones. Faith, sin, and free will became the focus of early discussions. Based on the Qur'ān and early tradition, the orthodox maintained that faith (*imān*) is distinct from membership in the community (*islām*). The latter comprises outward adherence, while the former comprises, in addition, submission of heart and good works. Though dispute continued on whether faith admitted of degrees, the consensus held that faith was not lost by grave sin, and that a sinner who believed in God's unicity would be rescued from hell by Muḥammad's intercession.

Triumph of Traditionalism. The main theological dispute, which ranged over three centuries, pitted the traditionalist theologians against the MU'TAZILITES, who had adopted Greek categories and logic in the defense of Islam. The general dispute was between a literal acceptance of the Qur'ān and tradition, and a rational theology seeking to safeguard the unity and justice of God. The specific questions debated were God's attributes, the Qur'ān, free will, and the vision of God. In the 9th century the Mu'tazilite doctrine of a created Qur'ān was forcibly imposed by the Caliph Ma'mūn, but he and his immediate successors succeeded only in hardening the opposition that centered around Aḥmad ibn Ḥanbal, the eponym of the fourth school of law and the advocate of an uncompromising traditionalist theology. Again in the 10th century, under the Shī'ite dynasties in Iraq, Mu'tazilism had a free rein. The Ḥanafite law school tended to identify itself with a Mu'tazilite theology, and the Shāfi'ite school with a moderate position using the theology (*KALĀM*) of the Mu'tazilites, while defending the attributes of God, the uncreatedness of the Qur'ān, and the absolute power of God over good and evil. This latter, the Ash'arite school, derived its name from Abū al-Ḥasan 'Alī al- ASH'ARĪ (d. 935). He personally appears to have renounced Mu'tazilism for anbalism, but his followers developed a *via media.* It is usually claimed that Ash'arism, under the Sunnite revival of the SELJUK Turks in the 11th century, became the orthodox theology, but more recent studies make clear the persistance of Ḥanbalite traditionalism content to describe God as He describes Himself in the uncreated Qur'ān, without asking how or why. Reason as advocated by the Mu'tazilites was driven from orthodoxy and found its home with the Shī'ites.

Later, philosophy suffered the same defeat, but the resulting emphasis on the transcendence of God cleared the way for the spread of an ascetical mysticism emphasizing God's immanence. ALGAZEL (al-Ghazzālī; d. 1111), philosopher, theologian, and mystic, symbolizes the fusion that took place. He found philosophy sterile and theology useful only for defense. True knowledge came through mystic experience. ṢŪFĪSM did develop anomistic and monistic branches, but there remained a legitimate mysticism that flowered into brotherhoods spread across the face of Islam to serve a social as well as a religious function (*see* DERVISHES).

Shift in Authority. While Islam has undergone continuous development throughout its 14-century history, making any model of a ''golden age'' followed by a ''decline'' and then a ''revival'' untenable, movements within Islam in the modern era of the 19th and especially the 20th centuries have taken unprecedented directions. Though such movements had previously arisen out of the dynamic of Muslim religious renewal, a decisive new factor that molded movements after 1800 was the progressive integration of the Muslims into the modern world. With the European colonial intrusion, the Muslims' situation was transformed for the first time from that of an independent universe into that of a minority in a non-Muslim world. The continuing political dominance of the European powers, coupled with widespread technological, educational, and other structural changes set in motion by the European colonial endeavor, led to a profound transformation of the discourses of Islam and their meanings.

The most salient development in Islam, which has become especially acute in the 20th century, is the unprecedented weakening of traditional religious leadership and the resulting plurality of sources of authority. The classical *'ulamā'* held a near monopoly not only on religious authority but also over education, writing, intellectual activity, and popular approval. The rulers were weak and unable to mobilize the people to build institutions of the modern state. With the arrival of European colonization, this situation changed. Rulers like Muḥammad 'Alī in Egypt (ruled 1805–48), supported by European advisers, were able to seize the sources of income of the *'ulamā'* from charitable foundations to send students to Europe to study European knowledge, which was more advanced in the scientific field, and generally to strengthen the state by establishing official institutions. This compromised the monopoly of the *'ulamā'* on education in the first degree.

At the same time, science and modernism also directly influenced the thinking of the *'ulamā'*. In Egypt, for example, Rifā 'ah al-Tahtāwī (1801–73) represented the beginning of a development culminating in Muḥammad 'Abduh (1849–1905), who emphasized the texts of the Qur'ān and prophetic traditions (*ḥadīth*) at the expense of jurisprudence, insisted on the right of the scholar to interpret texts (ijtihād) independently, deemphasized Ṣūfīfism, and accepted materialist explanations of the Qur'ān that reduced the supernatural element. Soon such ''reformist'' trends were bring promoted throughout the Muslim world, from Indonesia to Morocco, often with the usually intended effect of reducing the authority of the more traditional *'ulamā'*. In India, a similar trend can be seen in the teachings of Sayyid Amad Khān (1817–1898).

Conservative *'ulamā'* responded to the modernist challenge by repudiating modernism, as at the ancient mosque of al-Azhar in Egypt (founded 974) or the modern academy at Deoband in India (founded 1867), but their own arguments were subtly altered by the new situation. Thus, the Deobandis, although adhering to the Ḥanafi school of jurisprudence, continued the revival of the *ḥadīth* begun by Shāh Walī al-Dihlāwī (1703–62), thereby contributing to the spread of textualism that has characterized much of Islam in the 20th century. Although they also maintained Ṣūfīfism, it received less attention than before. Most portentously, the Deobandis enthusiastically established religious discourse in the vernacular Urdu, changing the unique status of Arabic as the sole medium of religion. The unprecedented use of the vernacular languages for religious purposes, including Friday sermons, has continued to grow down to the present.

Impact of Secular Education. No other single factor had such an impact in undermining the authority of the *'ulamā'* as the spread of secular education. By 1900, secular-educated Muslims and their governments desired to set up schools in the European model in their homelands as soon as possible. Thus, Cairo University was founded in 1908. Generally, Muslim graduates of European-style schools were strongly under the influence of prevailing patterns of European thought. While these were a threat to the *'ulamā'* in the sense that they tended to treat the received tradition of Islam with disdain and to promote modern thinking, they did not significantly challenge the *'ulamā'* on the latter's own ground of religion. Indeed, such graduates of modern institutions often did not give much heed to religion, viewing it as their European contemporaries did—a problem to be contained—in order to establish the supremacy of the state for their nationalist state-building projects. The *'ulamā'* did battle with the modernists, but the elite nature of the latter and their alienation from the culture of the Muslim world in the first half of the 20th century did not seriously threaten the status of the '*ulamā*' with the people as the sole legitimate interpreters of the faith.

This began to change, however, once the shock of the first encounter with the West had begun to wear off. For their part, many of the '*ulamā*' who had adopted modernist positions began to return to a more conservative construction of Islam, such as 'Abduh's famous pupil, Muḥammad Rashīd Riḍa (1865–1935). Once the exact nature of the West's technical superiority and political hegemony had been clearly understood through a careful study of the West itself, and the technical gap began to be narrowed, it could be seen that it was not necessary to make as many concessions as had been thought at first. Thus, Riḍa retreated from some materialist interpretations of scripture and also reaffirmed the role of Islam in government.

But while such development was happening with some of the '*ulamā*', many of the modern-educated Muslims also began to have doubts about the West and modernism. Some of them ardently returned to Islam, where they were welcomed as allies by the traditional '*ulamā*', except when they attacked the '*ulamā*' head-on with charges of backwardness or obsequiousness to the government. But such exchanges were the exception rather than the rule, and relations of the conservative modern-educated with the conservative '*ulamā*' were on the whole cordial.

Nevertheless, the rise of a class of modern-educated intellectuals ardently committed to Islam constituted a far more serious challenge to the ' *ulamā*' than that of the secular intellectuals and led to a serious decline in the authority of the '*ulamā*'. The intellectuals, trained in modern knowledge, could see the flaws in the information of the '*ulamā*' about the world, and this perception would spread as modern education was gradually extended to the masses everywhere. Thus, although no one questioned their knowledge of classical religious texts, the '*ulamā*' were no longer the scholars and intellectuals in other fields as they had been in premodern times.

A Rereading of Islam. On the other hand, the committed intellectuals could and did study the source books of the religion, unconsciously bringing the critical attitude fostered by their modern education with them. This enabled them to engage in a massive rereading of Islam based on the Qur'ān, usually without much emphasis on the *ḥadīth*, which was very large, diffuse, and difficult to access. Thus, *ḥadīth* remained largely the preserve of the '*ulamā*'. Because the intellectuals spoke and wrote in the language of the people, their works were widely read. Though they often did not claim the title of *tafsīr* (exegesis) for their efforts, their works tended to replace the scholarship of the traditional '*ulamā*' at the popular level. Such works include the commentaries of Sayyid Quṭb of Egypt (1906–66), Sa'īd awwa of Syria (1935–89), Abū al-A'ā al-Mawdūdī of India and Pakistan (1903–79), and Hamka of Indonesia (1908–82), the latter two in vernacular languages. Thus, the previous longstanding monopoly of the '*ulamā*' on scriptural interpretation was decisively breached. No less important, the appeal to the modern mind and the political and social activism that characterized the new works clearly departed far from the methods and content of the traditional interpretations.

Indeed, all of the above mentioned commentators were involved in Muslim mass political movements in their respective countries and spent time in prison, where Sayyid Quṭb was executed. Their ideas even attracted many of the traditional '*ulamā*', such as Muḥammad al-Ghazālī (b. 1917) and Yūsuf al-Qardāwī (b. 1926) in Egypt, where the Muslim Brotherhood became a major political force from the 1940s through the 1960s before it was suppressed by the government. Meanwhile, the intellectuals themselves tended to become more conservative the more they studied the received heritage of Islam. Many were described as *salafī*, meaning that they abandoned the traditional schools of law for a more *ḥadīth*-based approach. They were also highly critical of Ṣūfīfism. This fitted well with the doctrine backed by the Saudi Arabian religious establishment, which tried to influence the new movements to remain non-revolutionary, with mixed success.

Bibliography: H. A. R. GIBB, *Modern Trends in Islam* (Chicago 1947). H. LAMMENS, *Islām: Beliefs and Institutions,* tr. E. D. ROSS (London 1929). A. J. WENSINCK, *The Muslim Creed* (New York 1932). R. J. MCCARTHY, *The Theology of al-Ash'ari* (Beirut 1953). H. LAOUST, *La Profession de foi d'Ibn Baṭ ṭa* (Damascus 1958). G. MAKDISI, *Ibn'Aqīl et la réurgence de l'Islam traditionaliste* (Damascus 1963). L. GARDET, *Le Cité musulmane: Vie sociale et politique* (2d ed. Paris 1961). W. C. SMITH, *Islam in Modern History* (Princeton 1957). A. AL-AHSAN, *Ummah or Nation? Identity Crisis in Contemporary Muslim Society* (Leicester 1992). J. L. ESPOSITO, *The Islamic Threat: Myth or Reality?* (New York 1992); J. L. ESPOSITO, ed., *Voices of Resurgent Islam* (New York 1983). F. RAHMAN, *Islam and Modernity: Transformation of an Intellectual Tradition* (Chicago 1984).

[J. J. DONOHUE/K. Y. BLANKINSHIP]

SUÑOL, GREGORIO MARÍA

Apostle of Gregorian chant; b. Barcelona, Sept. 7, 1879 (baptized Ramón); d. Rome, Oct. 26, 1946. A Benedictine of MONTSERRAT, the artistically gifted monk studied there and at SOLESMES under MOCQUEREAU, equipping himself to promote his abbey's work of restoration of the Gregorian liturgy. He was choir director from 1907 to 1928 and prior from 1915 to 1931, when he was asked by Cardinal SCHUSTER to administer the Scuola Superiore di Musica Sacra in Milan. In 1938 he succeeded FERRETTI as president of the Pontificio Istituto di Musica Sacra in Rome, where he introduced important scientific criteria during his eight-year leadership. Among his scholarly works are *Método completo de Canto gregoriano* (ten editions in Spanish; also in French, German, Italian, English, and Braille); *Introducción a la paleografía gregoriana* (1925; augmented in French, 1935); and *Antiphonale missarum juxta ritum sanctae ecclesiae mediolanensis* (1935), an edited transcription of the liturgical books of AMBROSIAN CHANT. He also transcribed 14th-century folk music and composed a number of popular songs and melodies adapted from ancient codices. An untiring propagator, he was the soul of the national congresses on sacred music held at Seville (1908) and Barcelona (1912); he also lectured at many conferences and *cursillos* and on radio, and was a permanent collaborator on *Revista Montserratina, Vida Cristiana,* and several other periodicals.

Bibliography: G. M. SUÑOL, *Text Book of Gregorian Chant according to the Solesmes Method,* tr. from 6th Fr. ed. by G. M. DURNFORD (Tournai 1930). H. ANGLÈS, ''Le Chant grégorien et l'oeuvre de Dom Suñol,'' *Revue Grégorienne* (1948) 161–173. E. CATTANEO, ''L'abate Gregorio Maria Suñol,'' *Ambrosius* 22 (1946) 121–130. M. QUEROL, *Die Musik in Geschichte und Gegenwart* v.13. *Enciclopedia de la Religión Católica* 6:1552–54. O. CUNILL, ''Un apóstol del gregorianismo: Dom Gregorio Suñol,'' *Musica sacra españolo* (Montserrat 1947).

[B. MORAGAS]

SUPEREROGATION, WORKS OF

Virtuous acts surpassing what is required by duty or obligation. They are compared to other works not as good to evil, but as better works to good works. The term—based on the Latin term *erogare,* to pay out or to expend—is found in the Vulgate version of the Bible. In the parable, the Good Samaritan tells the innkeeper, ''Whatever thou dost spend besides . . . ,'' *quodcumque supererogaveris* (Lk 10.35). The generosity of Zacchaeus in giving half his possessions to the poor and in quadrupling whatever he owed in restitution (Lk 19.8, 9) and the work of St. Paul in supporting himself as a tentmaker (Acts 20.34; 1 Thes 3.8, 9) are seen as examples of supererogation (cf. St. Thomas Aquinas, *Summa Theologiae* 1a2ae, 108.2 ad 3; 2a2ae, 62.3 ad 2).

The counsels of Christian perfection, especially the evangelical COUNSELS of POVERTY, CHASTITY, and OBEDIENCE, have been commonly considered in Catholic theology as supererogatory works. The traditional basis for these counsels and their distinction from precepts or commands is seen in such scriptural passages as St. Paul's recommendation of virginity (1 Cor 7.7) and Christ's invitation to the rich young man to renounce his possessions (Mt 19.16–22). Christian perfection, however, does not consist in these counsels, but in charity (*see* PERFECTION, SPIRITUAL). Neither are they the chief means to attain it; but the counsels are concerned with things good in themselves—and therefore not opposed to charity or perfection—that may provide obstacles to a greater development of charity (cf. St. Thomas, *Summa Theologiae* 1a2ae, 108.4; 2a2ae, 184.3).

Among medieval theologians, such as Alexander of Hales and St. Thomas Aquinas, the term ''supererogatory'' works had a precise, almost technical, meaning. Aquinas contrasted them with works of necessity (*C. impug.* 4 ad 5), or those that pertain to salvation (2a2ae, 88.2), and describes them as acts to which all are not held (2a2ae, 85.4). In fact, he notes that some may not have the necessary dispositions to follow the evangelical counsels (1a2ae, 108.4 ad 1). These counsels may be made a matter of obligation through vow (2a2ae, 185.6). In one place, St. Thomas distinguished two types of supererogatory works. One kind is simply such, and he listed the Pauline exhortation to virginity as an example. Other works, such as fasting, are not the matter of precept as such, but may be made so by competent ecclesiastical authority (*In 4 Sent.* 15.3.1.4 ad 2).

Many of the reformers rejected this doctrine. Thus article XIV of the Anglican Thirty-Nine Articles states that ''the works of supererogation cannot be taught without arrogancy and impiety.'' Calvin rejected the distinction between counsel and precept and insisted that anything commended by Christ is commanded by Him.

Some Catholic theologians, especially those with a personalist or existential outlook, have called for a reexamination of the question. They stress the individuality of God's gifts of grace and the universal application of the law of love.

Bibliography: ANTONINUS OF FLORENCE, *Summa Theologica* (Venice 1480), pt. 3, title 16, ch. 1. FRANCIS DE SALES, *Treatise on the Love of God,* tr. V. KERNS (Westminster, MD 1963), bk. 8, ch. 6, J. SCHWANE, *De operibus supererogatoriis et consiliis evangelicis in genere* (Münster 1868). E. DUBLANCHY, *Dictionnaire de théologie catholique,* ed. A. VACANT, 15 v. (Paris 1903–50; Tables générales 1951–) 3.1:1175–82. R. SCHNACKENBURG and B. HÄRING, *Lexikon für Theologie und Kirche,* ed. J. HOFER and K. RAHNER, 10 v. (2d, new ed. Freiburg 1957–65) 3:1245–50.

[J. HENNESSEY]

SUPERNATURAL

Supernatural realities figure on every page of the New Testament, as also ubiquitously in tradition. They appear under such key words and phrases as Redemption, salvation kingdom of God, everlasting life, Christ and life in Christ, holiness, faith, rebirth, adoptive sonship, indwelling Spirit, grace, charity, and mystery.

Besides, the supernatural becomes historically tangible and visible in Christianity, which surpasses (just as it is diametrically opposed to) all natural religions, because of its origin, its sublimity of means, and its orientation: they are man-made, man's groping toward the Infinite; it is God-given, the descent of the Father through Christ and the Church to deify man in view of the BEATIFIC VISION. In the concrete, the supernatural designates Christianity itself and its treasures of SALVATION.

Consequently, the concept of the supernatural is on a footing of equal importance with the concepts Incarnation, Sacrament, and revelation—with which last it is closely connected. For the supernatural can be known only through revelation received in FAITH.

Like *Incarnation, Sacrament,* and *revelation* the word supernatural is, of course, current in modern theology, where, especially in the last three centuries, it has become a shorthand term of capital importance. It has acquired many nuances of meaning, as may be seen by consulting theological manuals, in which one will find numerous qualifying words and phrases such as *simpliciter, absolute, quoad substantiam, ontologice, entitative, secundum quid, relative, quoad modum.* There is a certain fluidity in their usage.

Our aim is quite simple: to throw into prominence what may be considered (not all will agree) the supernatural in its strictest sense. Taken thus, it may be provisionally described as embracing all redemptive gifts positively conducive to the winning of the beatific vision and given through Christ Jesus and the Church.

HISTORY OF THE WORD AND ITS MEANING

As background to the understanding of the strictly supernatural we offer a few notes on the history of the word and its meaning.

Word. Neither the adjective *supernaturale* nor the adverb *supernaturaliter* was used by the classical writers of ancient Rome. However, Cicero, Tacitus, and Seneca did have equivalent expressions to describe extraordinary effects: *divinitus, supra naturam excedens.*

The corresponding Greek adjective ὑπερφυής was used by classical authors for overgrown, enormous, monstrous, extraordinary, marvelous. Likewise the adverb ὑπερφυῶς was common enough for wonderfully, exceedingly.

In the New Testament, in the patristic writings of the first centuries, in the ancient texts of the liturgy, one searches for the word in vain.

With the Greek Neoplatonists the stable meaning of *superior substance* begins to emerge. St. Proclus of Constantinople (d. 446) and, more important, Pseudo-Dionysius (*c.* 500) head a long tradition of labeling all spiritual beings—especially God but also angels and even human souls—with the Greek equivalents of *supernatural.*

In a famous text, St. Cyril of Alexandria (d. 444), breaking up the Greek adjective into its components of noun and preposition, gets very close to the modern notion of the strictly supernatural—a fact that is not surprising when one recalls the exceptional richness of Cyril's theology of grace. Treating of our adoptive sonship, he presents it as our elevation through Christ to a dignity surpassing not only human nature but Nature *tout court:* εἰς τὸ ὑπὲρ φύσιν ἀξίωμα διὰ Χριστόν. The summons to the supernatural is: πρὸς τὸ ὑπὲρ φύσιν (*In Joan. evang.* 1.12, *Patrologia Graeca*, ed. J. P. Migne, 73:153; cf. *Dial. 4 de Trin., Patrologia Graeca* 75:882; St. Maximus, *O, LXV ad Thal., Patrologia Graeca* 90:769).

In the 9th century, through translations of the works of Pseudo-Dionysius made principally by John Scotus Erigena (*c.* 850), *supernaturalis* makes its debut in the theology of the West. It has the sense of superior being.

More than anyone else St. Thomas Aquinas deserves the credit of launching the word into theological circulation. Thus in a single article (*De ver.* 12.7) one can count upward of 20 usages. Sometimes St. Thomas employs the word in its Greek acceptation. Thus he presents the beatific vision as a contemplation of *supernatural* Truth where modern theology would prefer *subsistent* Truth—". . . contemplatio patriae, qua supernaturalis veritas per essentiam videtur" (*Summa theologiae* 2a2ae, 5.1 ad 1)—and God as the supernatural principle of our faith (*ibid.,* 6.1). Far more commonly (a complete tally would hardly be feasible) St. Thomas applies *supernatural* not to superior substances but to surpassing effects.

However, only in the last three centuries did the word reach the first flight of importance as a technical term. Evidence for this assertion can be found by glancing through the indexes of the famous editions of the Fathers or of the medieval theologians: the word scarcely appears. Not till Pius V's condemnation of the 21st and 23d proposition of Baius in 1567 (H. Denzinger, *Enchiridion symbolorum*, ed. A. Schönmetzer, 1921, 1923) did the magisterium officially adopt it. Its apotheosis came in 1870 when Vatican I embodied it for the first time in a conciliar decree (*Enchiridion symbolorum* 3008).

Meaning. Outside modern technical theology, in popular speech and literature, supernatural is a word of wide application. Its chief content seems to be whatever is beyond the ken of the senses or unaccountable for in the categories of experiential observation and the physical sciences. All that is metaphysical or simply inexplicable to the rationalist, or transcendent, or outside the routine workings of cause and effect, is commonly dubbed supernatural. It is a label put indiscriminately on ghosts and spirits good or bad, on God, on miracles and prodigies, on the unnatural and the violent.

If one scans this list more closely, one will remark that supernatural phenomena divide into two classes: (1) that of superior *substances;* (2) that of surpassing *effects.*

The first class bears witness to the persistence in popular circles of the Greek tradition, which was also the prevalent theological usage up to the 13th century. As we saw, it crops up in St. Thomas, although it is especially the weight of his authority that swings the scales in favor of the second class. Henceforward this latter predominates in theological literature. From it develops the strictest technical sense. However, even after St. Thomas the first class keeps on rallying support. It recurs frequently among the mystics of the 14th century. In the 17th century it flares up in a sort of sickly brilliance with J. M. de Ripalda's theory of a supernatural substance. Most theologians showed good sense in rebutting Ripalda (1594–1648), whom H. de Lubac censured in withering terms [*Surnaturel* (Paris 1946) 294, 299].

As we understand it, the strictest acceptation of supernatural does not exactly square with either of the two classes above. It borrows from each, perhaps, but is a concept far richer in meaning than either.

In the strictest, technical sense, then, supernatural does not mean (1) superior substances such as angels or God taken in their lofty isolation, invisibility, and absoluteness; nor does it mean (2) merely wonderful, surpassing effects such as miracles and prodigies. Rather it is reserved to signify a new relationship of God to man, a fresh contact between Infinite and finite, a real descent of God to a personal creature.

In order to penetrate more deeply the meaning of this notion, we must pause over the correlatives of the supernatural, to wit, NATURE and natural.

CORRELATIVES: NATURE, NATURAL

The theology of the supernatural was bound to remain stunted until a satisfactory philosophy of nature had been evolved. This was achieved thanks to Saints Albert the Great and Thomas, under the aegis of Aristotle. Pre-Thomistic writers such as Anselm, Bernard, and Peter Lombard fight shy of the word supernatural, largely because of the inadequacies of their philosophy of nature.

History. Nature, before being established by the scholastic theologians as antithesis to supernatural, had gone through three main stages of historical growth. They may be rapidly and roundly sketched in as follows.

Greek Philosophy. With Greek thinkers, especially Aristotle, Nature and the universal laws springing from the inflexible essences of things were conceived as the sole and peremptory norm for every happening in the world. God was regarded either as wholly aloof from the world or as producing it according to inexorable necessity. Contemplating the beauty of Nature and its unswerving regularity, God might display a certain Olympian complacency; but never might He show toward individual men the slightest trace of selective, personal love. Such a philosophy, precluding in principle the very possibility of the supernatural, was radically pagan and anti-Christian.

St. Augustine. Realizing the need to remedy this deep defect, St. Augustine went to the opposite extreme. He refused to define natures by reference to the necessary laws of essences. Instead, he reduced natures to what God wanted things to be, to the mere objects of God's good pleasure. Thus, giving everything to God, Augustine easily accounted for miracles and for God's personal intervention in the world. But his philosophy labors under serious drawbacks: if created natures are not stable principles of action possessed of intrinsic necessity, we are living in the dreamworld of the nominalist philosophers (*see* NOMINALISM); natural science and secondary causality vanish; and one cannot draw the essential line of demarcation between ordinary and extraordinary (supernatural) events.

Saints Albert and Thomas. The *via media* between the rigid, self-enclosed naturalism of the Greeks and the VOLUNTARISM of Augustine was laid down by St. Albert the Great and, above all, St. Thomas. On the one hand they admitted that natures are abiding principles of activity endowed with internal necessity; on the other they denied that nature contained all the clues to the understanding of the whole of reality. The personal God, in the initiative of sheer love, could always enter onto the stage of history, transcending the demands of nature and outstripping its forces. Thus was shaped a philosophy of nature in harmony with Christian revelation. A landmark had been reached. The theology of the supernatural was now able to advance.

Senses. *Supernatural* evokes *natural,* which in its turn evokes *nature.* We need to note a quartet of senses for *nature-natural,* because they all bear, though unequally, on *supernatural.*

Genetic Sense. This is what is given with nature from the start, or belongs to one from one's birth; the endowments of one's origin, even though some of these may in fact be transcendent. In this sense, common in early Church documents, man is considered not philosophically but historically, i.e., according to the condition of his actual creation. Thus Adam's ORIGINAL JUSTICE was natural (*Enchiridion symbolorum* 239, 389, 396; Augustine, *Spir. et litt.* 27.47; Leo, *Serm.* 12.1) and ORIGINAL SIN was a wound inflicted in human nature (*Enchiridion symbolorum* 371, 400).

Specific, Abstract Sense. The ontological type communicable to many, the sheaf of essential attributes leaving out of account their realization in individuals, is the specific, abstract sense of nature. The value of this abstract concept calls for comment owing to recent controversies centering on the supernatural. In order to demonstrate the gratuity of the supernatural, a common procedure was to appeal to the hypothetical state of PURE NATURE, in which man would exist fully equipped with all natural resources and end, but shorn of any supernatural influence whatsoever. Certain modern thinkers [H. de Lubac, ''Le Mystère du surnaturel,'' *Recherches de science religieuse* 36 (1949) 80–121] challenged such a procedure as futile: proving the gratuity of the supernatural in a state of pure nature does not prove its gratuitousness in the present order, where man, intrinsically affected by the supernatural, is necessarily totally other than he would be in any such phantom state. This attitude, while showing an excellent appreciation of the deep, inward resonance in man evoked by his call to the beatific vision, does not do equal justice to the abstractive power of the intellect with its ability to shape a single concept valid for human nature wheresoever found or howsoever postulated. For the supernatural, no matter how inwardly and deeply it influences and transforms human nature, cannot change it substantially but only accidentally. The example of sex is instructive: its influence is far-reaching and intrinsic; the differences between men and women are not only anatomical and physiological but also emotional and psychological. Yet the differences of sex are accidental, not substantial; and the abstract concept of human nature fits both men and women perfectly. Similarly, whether man is assigned a natural commensurate goal or a supernatural and surpassing one, the abstract concept of human nature is left unaffected.

Individual Sense. If there is little difficulty in forming an abstract concept of human nature, it is another matter when one tries to fashion a satisfactory concept of human nature in the individual, e.g., the human nature of Christ. The shadow of the supernatural lies across this path. The concept of concrete human nature must be built up from various sources: sensation, intelligence, self-consciousness, and history (this illustrates the forces and resiliency of a concretely existing nature). The fact that the last page of human history has yet to be written suggests a certain incompleteness—which may not be serious. However, what is more troubling is the fact that the lives of all men have been led in a supernatural order; this has wrapped man around like the air he breathes and has affected him within and without. Hence when one studies existing human nature, one studies it as somehow supernaturalized. But to know the supernatural as such and delineate it against the natural is beyond unaided reason. Revelation is needed [J. P. Kenny, ''Human Nature under the Influence of the Supernatural,'' *Australasian Catholic Record* 33 (1956) 11–21].

Cosmic Sense. This is the universe and everything in it—Nature with a capital *N:* φύσις or τὰ φυσικά in Greek, *rerum natura* in Latin. However, different senses are attached to Nature according as one is a physicist or metaphysician. The former limits Nature to the sense-perceptible; the latter extends it to embrace the whole gamut of creation, the spiritual as well as the sensory. When the theologian speaks of the supernatural as transcending the demands of Nature he means Nature in the metaphysical sense.

STRICTEST TECHNICAL SENSE

As a proximate preparation for our definition, we must weigh the force of three assertions about the supernatural in the strictest technical sense: (1) It surpasses all the demands and forces of nature; (2) it involves something infinitely more precious than miracles or preternatural gifts; and (3) it connotes with metaphysical necessity a created gift.

First Assertion. To say that the supernatural surpasses all the demands and forces of nature is to make a complex statement.

Unowed to Human Nature. It means, first, that the supernatural is unowed or gratuitous to the particular nature of man. A grasp of what is unowed to man's nature is best gained by considering what is owed. Human nature needs: body and soul—these are structurally owed (*constitutive debita*); spiritual and sensory faculties of action—these are consequently owed (*consecutive debita*), for without them man's nature would be nonsensically crippled; outside aids such as providence, concursus, proportioned goal, appropriate sanctions and rewards for right behavior (*exigitive debita*). In none of these senses is the supernatural owed to nature. Casting this in parallel phraseology we say that the supernatural surpasses all nature's demands and forces.

Unowed to All Created Nature. Second, not only is the supernatural unowed to the particular nature of man, exceeding all his exigencies, it is likewise unowed to the whole of created Nature, exceeding all its exigencies. The carving of a ''Moses'' is beyond the capacities of the block out of which it is hewn. Nevertheless it is not supernatural. It is well within the scope of Michelangelo's genius. The supernatural surpasses not only the capacities of every individual creature, even of an archangel; it further surpasses the powers of the aggregate of all created natures and of the cosmos itself. Indeed it exceeds not only all actual creatures and creation but also all conceivably possible creatures and creations. Nothing created or creatable can be thought of that the supernatural does not outstrip.

Priority of Creation. It has been pointed out, third, that the supernatural implies a new relationship, a fresh contact between God and man or angel, a divine descent and union with a creature. Therefore, in the very concept of the supernatural in this strictest technical sense is implied the preexistence of its term and of the universe. Man cannot be elevated to the supernatural unless he exists. This does not necessarily mean that a time interval must separate man's creation from his elevation. Both may take place simultaneously. But creation enjoys a priority of order; unless one respects this, one makes man's elevation unintelligible. This priority is picturesquely and felicitously hinted at in Genesis, ch. 2, where Yahweh is presented as first creating man in a desert and then establishing him in Eden (symbol of a privileged condition). Both the patristic and the Thomistic traditions maintain that Adam received original justice at the very moment of creation.

Just as man's particular creation logically precedes his supernatural elevation, so *a fortiori* the general creation of the universe anticipates everything supernatural. Of course, without the preexistence of the world, man himself cannot be imagined: he is essentially an inhabitant requiring a habitat. But seeing that the creation of the world itself is presupposed to the supernatural, its creation cannot properly be described as supernatural—and this despite the fact that its creation manifestly exceeds its own demands and forces. If then earlier writers, such as St. Bonaventure, describe creation as *supernaturalis mutatio* (*In 2 sent.* 1.1.1.2 concl. ad 1), they are employing the term in a broader sense where any effect whose unique cause is God can be so styled. The supernatural, being a relative notion, has to take for granted the existence of men, angels, and the cosmos—as much as it has to presuppose the existence of God Himself.

Exigencies and Forces. Fourth, the supernatural surpasses both exigencies and forces taken together. Exigencies: the creation of a human soul is beyond the reach of creatures; nevertheless it is natural, because it is necessarily joined with the procreation of a human body; nature demands the soul's creation and infusion. Forces: a particular personal choice is outside natural exigencies; yet it is natural, because it is the upshot of the normal resources of a being endowed with free will.

Second Assertion. The supernatural in the strictest sense is something higher than miracles or preternatural gifts. A miracle (called by some authors *supernaturale quoad modum*), e.g., the sudden mending of a shattered bone, restores a perfectly natural gift of health; the wonder of it lies sheerly in the instantaneousness of the recovery—explainable only by an almighty efficient Cause.

A preternatural gift (sometimes listed as *supernaturale relativum*) is one that, though unowed and therefore gratuitous, nevertheless perfects a nature within the range of the nature's own perfectibility. Adam's immunity from concupiscence and his bodily immortality are cited as examples. Bodily immortality means prolongation of a quite natural life; however, it comes gratuitously to a being naturally liable to decay. Preternatural gifts, according to Thomistic doctrine, spring from GRACE, which is strictly supernatural. Consequently the grace-endowed man has some ultimate summons both to integrity and immortality of the flesh. A preternatural gift, while it is bound up with the supernatural, is nevertheless far below it in excellence.

Third Assertion. As the supernatural spells a new descent of God to a creature, bringing about a new relationship and contact, it clearly gives birth to a new union. Now the very reality of this union exacts, with metaphysical necessity, some real change somewhere. Such change is unthinkable in God (Jas 1.17). Therefore it must be in the creature (*C. gent.* 3.51). But what is received in the creature must itself be created. Hence unless we are prepared to admit some created gift lodged in the creature, we jeopardize the very reality of the supernatural. Of course, we also sadly underestimate it if we leave out of account the Uncreated Gift involved. So sublime is the supernatural that nothing created suffices to explain it; one must postulate the Uncreated. The supernatural is a descent of God, a new contact with God, a new union between God and the creature. Justice must be done to both gifts: created and Uncreated. The former serves this vital function of being at once the disposition for, upshot to, and guarantee of the latter.

The created gift is the foundation of a new relationship between God and His spiritual creature. In one sense it may be described as absolute, for it is a quality inhering in the creature. In another sense, however, it is relative—in so far as it is the foundation of a real relation (*relatio realis*) of the creature to God. The relation of God to the creature is, on the contrary, only one of reason (*relatio rationis*); the immutability of God forces us to adopt this position. The inequality of these relations (real from the creature's side toward God, logical only from God's side toward the creature) makes no special difficulty for the supernatural, for it is often paralleled elsewhere, e.g., in the relationship existing between Creator and creature, the Word and His human nature, Mary and Christ: on her side the mother-Son reference is real; on His (according to SS. Thomas, Bonaventure, and a host of others) it is logical only.

DEFINITION—REALIZATION

We have come, finally, to the definition itself of supernatural. After enunciating it, and explaining its elements, we shall go on to indicate those realities in which it is verified.

Supernatural Defined. In the strictest technical sense, the supernatural (1) connotes (2) the Self-gift (3) of the Three-Personed God, Father, Son, and Holy Ghost, (4) to a personal being (5) out of love and friendship. Each member of this definition calls for comment.

Connotes. We do not say *is* because we do not simply identify the supernatural with God's loving self-communication. Sometimes the two may be identical; at other times the supernatural is rather an exigency for, and positively conducive to, God's self-communication without precisely being identical with it. So a Catholic once in the state of grace but now in mortal sin has driven the Triune God from his soul; nevertheless he is still possessed of strictly supernatural gifts: faith, hope, and actual membership in the MYSTICAL BODY OF CHRIST.

Self-gift. The supernatural implies God giving God to a creature. The initiative is sheerly divine. The supernatural is primarily some*body* (God) and only see ondarily some*thing* (created gift). The created coefficient is wholly subordinated to the advent of the Uncreated. Those two elements mutually imply one another. Their interconnection, especially in the field of grace and glory, has been brilliantly set forth by M. de la Taille and K. Rahner.

Three-Personed God. The supernatural is not simply an episode of creation-history, or precisely an aspect of God's ubiquity, or an impersonal juxtaposition of Creator with creature. Rather, directly or indirectly, it pivots around a loving, personal union between Father, Son, and Holy Ghost on the one hand, and, on the other, a personal creature. It is wholly ordered to the cultivation by the creature of a trio of special relations, an I-Thou dialogue with each member of the Blessed Trinity.

Personal Being. God cannot thus give Himself to stock or stone, to tree or horse, but only to a personal being, e.g., angel or man. The infrapersonal world is not open toward, lacks OBEDIENTIAL POTENCY for, the supernatural. A fetus or a baby, though as yet incapable of making up its own mind, is nevertheless a person and, therefore, open to the supernatural. The choice of *personal being* rather than *person* in the definition is dictated by the HYPOSTATIC UNION, which, of course, is preeminently supernatural. In this union the Second Divine Person assumes a human, i.e., a personal or intellectual, nature.

Love and Friendship. This phrase underscores the salient difference marking off God's presence in the supernatural from His OMNIPRESENCE in the natural order. By very title of Creator, God is everywhere, in the inorganic as well as in the organic worlds, in the sinner as well as in the saint, in hell as well as in heaven, in the damned as well as in the elect. By contrast, the supernatural belongs to another sphere and climate: that of CHARITY and FRIENDSHIP. And because the Friend and Lover in question is almighty, the new union and friendship that He establishes between Himself and the creature can never be pegged down to the affective, intentional order alone. It is also real, physical, ontological—and the proof of this lies, as we have noted, in the created endowment always given as an integral part of the supernatural (*see* FRIENDSHIP WITH GOD).

Realization. The supernatural in the strictest technical sense—where is it realized—De Lubac answers: it is above all the vision of God (243). A. Tanquerey speaks for many theologians when he contends that there are only three examples of it: Hypostatic Union, grace, and glory. Our own longer list is as follows.

1. Incontestably the Hypostatic Union is not only supernatural but also the prime analogate of the supernatural.
2. Beatific vision—its right to a place on the list is beyond discussion.
3. Deification here on earth, for this is the ontological prerequisite for glory.
4. But if the two radical gifts (created and uncreated) of deification, forming reborn man's new quasi-nature, are supernatural, the same must be asserted about the other gifts that are structurally related to deification and serve as man's new quasi-faculties: the theological and infused moral virtues, the seven gifts of the Holy Ghost.
5. Internal actual graces of illumination to the mind or inspiration to the will are clearly supernatural when given to one who is already an adoptive son of the heavenly Father. But they are also supernatural when, leading to conversion, they are given to an unbeliever or one in the state of mortal sin. They are then best conceived as a fleeting visitation of God to the soul, motivated by the desire for intimate friendship. This, indeed, is adumbrated in Rv 3.20. The imagery of the meal shared in by friends is a classical Scriptural illustration of heaven.
6. Plainly one must list as strictly supernatural the

visible Church, Christ continued down the avenues of history, His Mystical Body whose soul is the Holy Ghost (*see* SOUL OF THE CHURCH), treasurehouse of all redemptive grace, one ark of salvation.

7. Likewise the Mass and the Sacraments, in which Christ is today operative and which bring grace and the Holy Ghost into souls.

8. The sacramental characters are supernatural, because they link us with Christ the High Priest, give basic membership or higher status in the Church, and are the point of contact between the Holy Ghost as soul of the Mystical Body and each individual cell of that Body.

9. Perhaps other elements of the Christian economy merit the title of strictly supernatural. Assuredly this is so of revelation, whose correlative is faith in man (*see* REVELATION, THEOLOGY OF). Here once again there is a wedding of Uncreated (the authoritative utterance of Subsistent Truth) with created (act or virtue of faith in man), of *testimonium externum* with *testimonium internum.* One recalls that for St. Thomas faith is *inchoatio visionis* (cf *De ver.* 14.2; H. Denzinger, *Enchiridion symbolorum,* ed. A. Schönmetzer, 1532).

See Also: ANIMA NATURALITER CHRISTIANA; DESIRE TO SEE GOD, NATURAL; ELEVATION OF MAN; GRACE, ARTICLES ON; GRACE AND NATURE; JUSTICE OF MEN; MAN 3; NATURAL ORDER; PRETERNATURAL; SUPERNATURAL EXISTENTIAL; SUPERNATURAL ORDER.

Bibliography: A. MICHEL, *Dictionnaire de théologie catholique,* ed. A. VACANT et al., 15 v. (Paris 1903–50) 14.2:2849–59. ''Übernatürlich,'' *Lexikon für Theologie und Kirche,* ed. J. HOFER and K. RAHNER (2d, new ed. Freiburg 1957–65) v.10. F. DANDER, F. KÖNIG ed., *Religionswissenschaftliches Wörterbuch* (Freiburg 1956) 892–96. H. KUHN, S. OTTO, and H. FRIES ed., *Handbuch theologischer Grundbegriffe* (Munich 1962–63) 2:211–21. C. E. BOYER, *Tractatus de Deo creante et elevante* (5th ed. Rome 1957). V. DE BROGLIE, *De fine ultimo humanae vitae* (Paris 1948) 126–62, 245–64. H. KÜNG, *Rechtfertigung: Die Lehre Karl Barths und eine katholische Besinnung* (Einsiedeln 1957). H. DE LUBAC, ''Remarques sur l'histoire du mot *surnaturel,*'' *Nouvelle revue théolgique* 61 (1934) 225–49, 350–70. H. RONDET, *Gratia Christi* (Paris 1948). M. DE LA TAILLE, ''Actuation créé par acte incréé,'' *Recherches de science religieuse* 18 (1928) 253–68; Eng. *The Hypostatic Union and Created Actuation by Uncreated Act,* tr. C. VOLLERT (West Baden, Indiana 1952). G. COLOMBO, ''Il problema del soprannaturale negli ultimi cinquant'anni,'' *Problemi e orientamenti di teologia dommatica,* 2 v. (Milan 1957) 2:545–608. P. DE LETTER, ''The Theology of God's Self-Gift,'' *Theological Studies* 24 (1963) 402–22. K. RAHNER, *Schriften zur Theologie* (Einsiedeln 1954–) 1:347–75; Eng. *Theological Investigations,* tr. C. ERNST (Baltimore 1961–) 1:319–46. *Australasian Catholic Record* 31 (1954) 106–18, 212–22. *Clergy Monthly* 27 (1963) 54–60. *American Ecclesiastical Review* 98 (1938) 401–13; 146 (1962) 47–56. *Heythrop Journal* 2 (1961) 318–32. J. P. KENNY, *The Supernatural: Medieval Theological Concepts to Modern* (New York 1972). J. BORELLA, *The Sense of the Supernatural,* tr. G. J. CHAMPOUX (Edinburgh 2000).

[J. P. KENNY]

SUPERNATURAL EXISTENTIAL

According to some theologians, something SUPERNATURAL lodged in man anticipating the subjective Redemption of GRACE. In this concrete, SUPERNATURAL ORDER, even prior to his first grace, man is different from a sinner in a state of PURE NATURE. Before Baptism or the free self-surrender to Christ of faith, man is driven by a positive, unconditional, internal, sheerly gratuitous and strictly supernatural orientation to the BEATIFIC VISION. Supernatural existential may be commended as a postulate that enables one to avoid nominalism while doing justice to such converging considerations as the following:

1. God has summoned man to vision as to his sole and obligatory last end. This divine call runs the risk of being an empty fiction unless it affects man through and through, awakening some real response within him even before his first gift of grace. At God's command something springs into being: ''For he spoke, and it was made'' [Ps 32 (33) 9].

2. Man enters this world having ORIGINAL SIN *within* him [''omnibus inest unicuique proprium'' (H. Denzinger, *Enchiridion symbolorum,* ed. A. Schönmetzer, 1513)]. This inwardness of sin seems to imply the thwarting of some intrinsic orientation to vision.

3. The punishment of loss, the capital catastrophe of hell, is best interpreted as a disjointedness within the damned springing from the deathless, supernatural dynamism planted in his soul and driving him toward a vision of God that forever eludes his grasp.

4. Although the individual cannot be saved except through a personal appropriation of Christ's grace either within or without the Sacrament, it is nevertheless true that all men are redeemed by the death of Christ. The reality of this objective Redemption seems to demand something supernatural in man anticipating the subjective redemption of grace.

5. Hence the efficacy of God's universal salvific will means more than a salvific intention locked away in God's bosom, more than the fact that every man will eventually get a chance of salvation. Even before grace comes, each man is conditioned by God's salvific will.

6. Man, even when stripped of grace, shows signs of some real and absolute orientation toward vision. To construe this as a natural exigency is forbidden by the doctrine of the gratuity of the supernatural—which is wholly safeguarded if the orientation is itself supernatural.

7. Had God not been born as man, man would have had a different self-experience, even inwardly (K. Rahner).

See Also: ANIMA NATURALITER CHRISTIANA; DESIRE TO SEE GOD, NATURAL; DESTINY, SUPERNATURAL; ELEVATION OF MAN; FAITH, BEGINNING OF; MAN, 3; NATURAL ORDER; OBEDIENTIAL POTENCY.

Bibliography: K. RAHNER, *Lexikon für Theologie und Kirche*, ed. J. HOFER and K. RAHNER (Freiberg 1957–65) 3:1301; *Schriften zur Theologie* (Einsiedeln 1954–) 1:323–345; 3:35–46; v.1 tr. C. ERNST, *Theological Investigations* (Baltimore 1961) 297–317. H. KÜNG, *Rechtfertigung: Die Lehre Karl Barths und eine katholische Besinnung* (Einsiedeln 1957). J. P. KENNY, ''Reflections on Human Nature and the Supernatural,'' *Theological Studies* 14 (1953) 280–287.

[J. P. KENNY]

SUPERNATURAL ORDER

That suitable arrangement by God of proportionate means in view of man's attainment of his supernatural DESTINY. Its author and architect is the Father who, through Christ in the Holy Ghost, makes men His adoptive sons (Gal 4.4–8; Eph 1.3–14) and joint heirs with Christ (Rom 8.17) to the patrimony of the BEATIFIC VISION. Its beneficiary is man. All the public and visible means for reaching the goal are held by the Church, membership in which is the authentic way of being in Christ and of enjoying also the private and hidden means of SALVATION: GRACE, infused VIRTUES, and the seven gifts (*see* HOLY SPIRIT, GIFTS OF). Because the Word took flesh, all reality has an Incarnational structure, and the Church is the continuation of Christ in history.

The magisterium frequently alludes to some distinction between natural and supernatural orders (H. Denzinger, *Enchiridion symbolorum*, ed. A. Schönmetzer 1934, 1936, 1938, 2439, 2441, 2623, 3236, 3238, 3891); indeed its denial would jeopardize the very concept of the SUPERNATURAL. To acknowledge a distinction, however, is not to affirm a real separation. In fact, never has man existed in a purely NATURAL ORDER; never has his end been other than supernatural, to gain which he has had at hand sufficient means (1 Tm 2.3–7; Jn 1.9). The supernatural is embedded in the natural: grace needs the soul to lodge in; FAITH, the mind; CHARITY, the will. Between natural and supernatural, while there is ceaseless traffic, there is no pantheistic fusion (*Enchiridion symbolorum*, 3814): deified man is still man, not God. If his will maliciously forfeits charity, he tends toward his natural level. Faith and hope may maintain man in the supernatural order, in which, besides, he is anchored by his summons to the beatific vision and any sacramental character he may possess. The supernatural order so trenches on the natural as to (1) supplant man's connatural end; (2) to affect even the infrapersonal world, which, existing for man's sake, is mysteriously caught up into the travail of human history (Rom 8.19–25) and restored to equilibrium under Christ [ἀνακεφαλαιώσασθαι τά πάντα ἐν τῷ χριστῷ (Eph 1.10)]; and to (3) make it precarious for reason unenlightened by revelation to ascertain what is purely natural in the concrete.

See Also: DESIRE TO SEE GOD, NATURAL; ELEVATION OF MAN; GRACE AND NATURE; MAN, 3; OBEDIENTIAL POTENCY; PURE NATURE, STATE OF; SUPERNATURAL EXISTENTIAL; TEMPORAL VALUES, THEOLOGY OF.

Bibliography: A. MICHEL, *Dictionnaire de théologie catholique*, ed. A. VACANT et al., (Paris 1903—50) 14:2849–59. K. RAHNER, *Schriften zur Theologie* (Einsiedeln 1954–) 1:323–345; 3:35–60; v.1 tr. C. ERNST, *Theological Investigations* (Baltimore 1961) 297–317. J. P. KENNY, *Australasian Catholic Record* 33 (1956) 11–22.

[J. P. KENNY]

SUPERSTITION

An irrational or abject attitude of mind toward the supernatural, nature, or God, proceeding from ignorance, unreasoning fear of the unknown or the mysterious, or from morbid scrupulosity; a belief in magic or chance; or any misdirected or misinformed attitude toward nature that would be subversive of true or pure religion.

Scope. The moralist confines the concept of superstition to the vice that is contrary to religion and considers contempt for the things associated with the worship of God as the vice of irreligion. Aquinas thought that since religion is a moral virtue especially concerned with common or public worship, its contrary would involve any falsehood either on the part of the worshipper or in the manner in which worship is offered (*Summa theologiae* 2a2ae, 92.1). He further subdivided the species of superstition into those involving an undue mode in the act of worship and those involving an undue object such as idolatry, divination by spirits, or religious observances contrary to the precepts of God regarding the object of worship (*Summa theologiae* 2a2ae, 92.2).

Practical moralists further confine their interest in superstition to sins of commission rather than omission since the latter are nothing but the neglect of a given religious duty. Among sins of superstition are classed actions that involve either undue cult of the true God or some superfluity in the matter of cult. False cult includes such things as liturgical ceremonies of the Old Testament, which pointed to a Messiah to come and hence would now be meaningless from the viewpoint of time signified; the proposal of false miracles or spurious revelations offered to confirm the faith; and the offering of false relics for veneration.

Morality. Generally speaking, all such acts of false cult would be seriously sinful, for they attempt a grave injustice to God, falsify the honor due to Him, or have a deleterious effect on the true religion. For the most part, vain or superfluous acts that are superstitious per se would be only slightly sinful for the simple reason that no grave irreverence to God or the Church is intended. Superfluity would include such things as the veneration of images that are not approved by the Church, the addition by the priest of private prayers and rubrics in the celebration of Mass, the odd predilection of some of the faithful for Masses celebrated by a particular priest, or some singularity about just what candles are to be lighted. To this list of oddities one might add eccentricities of a more common but less serious nature, such as incongruous devotions that do not have the approval of the Church, or the unwarranted conviction that unusual stances during prayer or particular numerical sequences or accumulations of devotions are especially effective with the divinity.

It is conceivable that the ordinary faithful would be unaware of the odious tinge the Church attaches to such superfluities and would thus be exempt from moral fault of any kind. As a matter of fact, such superstitions can be practiced on a national scale. However, when the clergy are superstitious there is a possibility that their superfluities, especially private rubrics and prayers during the Canon of the Mass, can be seriously scandalous and looked upon with grave displeasure by the Church.

Apparently human nature has a fundamental need for the tangible things of sense in relating to God and things divine. This is one of the traditional explanations for Christ's provision of the sacramental system. Through the years the Church also has appreciated this basic human need and the possibility that it will sometimes seek expression in unreasonable practices. Some of the more usual symptoms of typical superstition are fascination for the primitive, illogical reasoning, a false conception of the powers of nature, a blind obsession with the sinister powers of fate, a fear of ungodly forces that threaten one's life, and an antisocial and egotistical attitude that leads one to view commonly accepted practices of religion as inadequate.

See Also: MAGIC; IDOLATRY; DIVINATION; SPIRITISM.

Bibliography: THOMAS AQUINAS, *Summa theologiae* 2a2ae, 92–96. L. G. FANFANI, *Manuale theoretico-practicum theologiae moralis ad mentem S. Thomae*, 3 v. (Rome 1950–51) 3:142–155. D. M. PRÜMMER, *Manuale theologiae moralis,* ed. E. M. MÜNCH (Freiburg-Barcelona 1955) 500–525.

[J. D. FEARON]

SUPPOSITION (LOGIC)

The word supposition (Lat. *suppositio*) originally meant substitution, and commonly indicates an assumption, HYPOTHESIS, or THEORY. In logic, the notion of substitution is retained in the first meaning of supposition, which is the same as that of signification, that is, ''the name stands for the thing—*nomen supponit pro re*.'' As Aristotle observes, ''it is impossible in a discussion to bring in the actual things discussed; we use their names as signs instead of them'' (Soph. elen. 165a 5). St. Thomas Aquinas points out that what the name stands for is called the substance of the name, namely, that which underlies the name (*In 3 sent. 6.1.3*).

Supposition and the Proposition. Thus initially understood, supposition takes on a further meaning when one considers the name as part of a proposition. Although the name is made to stand for what is named, whether within or apart from a proposition, yet when it is a part of a proposition and the proposition is to be true, the substance of the name will not be indifferent to the time expressed by the verb. For example, to say that ''Caesar is'' in the sense of ''exists'' would be false, since Caesar no longer exists. In other words, there is a discrepancy between the substance of the name ''Caesar,'' which no longer exists but in memory, and the tense of the verb ''to be,'' which here stands as both copula and predicate. On the other hand, to say that ''Caesar is praiseworthy'' is true, for what is predicated here is not ''existence'' but ''praiseworthy.'' We thus arrive at the second logical meaning of supposition: the verification of a name in a proposition in accordance with the requirements of the verb copula.

The verb as mere copula must signify with present time. For example, ''Caesar was,'' logically analyzed, implies that it is true (at the present time) that he was. In other words, if a proposition was true in the past (there was a time when it was true to say: ''Caesar is''), but now no longer is true, it must nonetheless now be true that it was true. All propositions, whether about the present, the past, or the future, are formed in the present.

The logic of supposition stretches back to ancient Greece. Thus as Aristotle points out, ''Homer is something, say, a poet. Is it therefore true to say also that Homer is, or not? The 'is' here is predicated accidentally of Homer, for the 'is' is predicated of him with regard to the fact that he is a poet, not in itself.'' (*Interp.* 21a 25–28.) In the Middle Ages, the doctrine of supposition was developed extensively. At first, it was discussed in terms of a parallel with grammatical structure (namely, imposition), for example by ABELARD and JOHN OF SALISBURY. Later it was treated more formally as a distinctive logical doctrine, in extensive detail, by such medieval authors as Peter of Spain (Pope JOHN XXI), WILLIAM OF OCKHAM and JOHN BURIDAN; still later by St. VINCENT FERRER and JOHN OF ST. THOMAS.

Kinds of Supposition. Only some principal kinds of supposition are here mentioned, considering first supposition in a proposition as determined by the way in which the predicate is attributed, and then supposition on the part of the predicate itself.

Material Supposition. This is the use of a word to stand for itself with respect to its oral or written aspect; thus, ''Man is a name''; ''Man is of one syllable.''

Personal Supposition. This is the normal use of names as they stand for subjects of propositions. Thus in the proposition ''Man is an animal,'' ''man'' is used so as to stand both for what can be said of any individual of the nature signified by the word, and for this nature taken universally. The designation ''personal'' derives from the more known instance of a name's standing for individual persons as well as for the nature; this meaning is extended to the individuals of any nature and not just to individual human beings, who are persons. Personal supposition is further divided into universal (*Every man* is wise), particular (*Some man* is wise), indefinite (*Man* is wise) and singular (*Peter* is wise).

Simple Supposition. This is the use of a name to stand for what it immediately signifies, the nature as known, without including the individuals of that nature. Thus in ''Man is a species'' (whether a natural or predicable species), ''man'' stands for the nature as known by the mind, excluding the individuals of that nature, for no individual man is a species.

The Predicate. Supposition on the part of the predicate is taken either *universally* (distributed) or *particularly* (undistributed), the latter in the sense of ''some.'' Every *negative* proposition has the predicate standing universally, for in a negation the predicate is always denied universally of the subject. Every *affirmative* proposition, on the contrary, always has a predicate standing particularly. Thus, in the proposition ''Every man is an animal,'' the predicate cannot be taken universally, otherwise one would assert that every man is every animal and that each man is every animal.

Other divisions of supposition, as well as the relation of supposition to ampliation, restriction, alienation, diminution and appellation, are discussed in logic textbooks (for example, see bibliography).

Relevance of Supposition. The logical doctrine of supposition is as significant now as it has been in the past. To ignore it leads to weird logical paradoxes. The role of supposition calls attention to the fact that words, being restricted to the limitations of a material medium, cannot adequately or fully convey the expression of thought. Indispensable though sense signs and symbols are to man's thinking and the expression of it, nevertheless his thought cannot be identified with a linguistic system. Supposition manifests the suppleness of the human intellect in dealing with words. It brings out the manner in which the mind, while attending to the meaning a word has, can still *use* the word to stand for various things in a variety of ways (*see* SEMANTICS).

Moreover, sound reasoning depends upon the correct supposition of terms. A valid SYLLOGISM, for example, must retain the same supposition of terms throughout; a shift in supposition renders an argument fallacious. The supposition of terms is particularly relevant for the relations between propositions as expressed in the square of OPPOSITION. Attempts to invalidate the rules of truth and falsity for contrariety, subcontrariety and subalternation fail to take into account that the supposition of names in propositions must be applied consistently, particularly with respect to the kind of existence signified. Neglect of supposition in logic invites inconsistency in thinking and an oversimplification of the function of language as expressing thought.

It may also be noted that the logic of supposition is particularly crucial in understanding the theology of the Trinity.

See Also: LOGIC; LOGIC, HISTORY OF; TERM (LOGIC); PROPOSITION.

Bibliography: J. A. OESTERLE, *Logic: The Art of Defining and Reasoning* (2d ed. Englewood Cliffs, N.J. 1963). G. GIANNINI, *Enciclopedia filosofica,* 4 v. (Venice-Rome 1957) 4:1050–51.

[J. A. OESTERLE]

SUPRALAPSARIANS

From Latin supra, above, and *lapsus*, fall, 16th- and early 17th-century Calvinistic adherents of a view of predestination in which God, for His glory, elected some men to salvation and condemned others to damnation before the Fall of Adam. An opposing view of the time was held by the INFRALAPSARIANS who declared that the divine decree of predestination came after the Fall. John CALVIN, out of whose doctrine of predestination Supralapsarianism developed, was neither a Supralapsarian nor an Infralapsarian. He was concerned to establish that the division of men into believers (who would be saved) and unbelievers (who would be condemned) depended upon the absolute decree of God. Since Calvin's view was sufficiently indefinite, both parties claimed him as favoring their view. In further support, the Supralapsarians pointed to the *Consensus Genevensis* (1551–52), written by Calvin to combat Jerome Bolsec (d. 1584) as Supralapsarian, while the Infralapsarians claimed the Gallican Confession (1559), whose first draft was the work of Calvin, as favoring their view. Theodore BEZA, the successor of Calvin, was a strong Supralapsarian, and the Synod of Dort (1618–19) in the Dutch Reformed Church upheld Supralapsarianism vigorously, but the doctrine was never popular, and it was soon eclipsed by the more moderate view.

See Also: CALVINISM; CONFESSIONS OF FAITH, PROTESTANT; PREDESTINATION (IN NON-CATHOLIC THEOLOGY).

[R. MATZERATH]

SUPREME BEING, CULT OF THE

A religious belief established during the FRENCH REVOLUTION by a decree of the National Convention (May 7, 1794). The feast of the Supreme Being was celebrated on June 8, 1794, to replace Pentecost Sunday. Maximilien ROBESPIERRE and his supporters, particularly Georges Couthon, who claimed that atheism was aristocratic and belief in a Supreme Being was republican, inaugurated the new cult with an elaborate ceremony in the Tuileries Gardens. Jacques David, the official painter of the Revolution, and Gardel, ballet master at the opera, designed the pageant, which the National Convention and a large concourse of Parisians attended. Robespierre presided as pontiff, although some of his colleagues referred to him as dictator or tyrant. This function marked the apex of Robespierre's domination; even during the ceremony murmurs assailed him. The cult was based on the ideas of ROUSSEAU and had two tenets: the existence of a Supreme Being and the immortality of the soul. The temple of this Being was the universe; nature was His priest. The only worship to be rendered to this Supreme Being was the practice of ''the duties of man''; chief among these were detestation of tyranny and defense of the oppressed. The cult was philosophically and theologically weak, and it depended on rhetoric to gain adherents.

Extreme radicals considered the cult reactionary, since it burned atheism in effigy and replaced it by a fireproof symbol of wisdom. Some naïve Catholics concluded that the cult marked the end of the Revolution's period of dechristianization. The city proletariat was not convinced by this spiritualist propaganda. Even the Parisians who participated in the cult's inauguration considered it part of the religion of patriotism. They had grown accustomed to references to the Supreme Being in official statements since 1789. The official cult was short-lived; when Robespierre fell (July 28, 1794), it quickly disappeared. A similar cult, THEOPHILANTHROPY, replaced it. Both used Volney's *Catéchisme du citoyen* as their handbook.

Bibliography: F. AULARD, *Le Culte de la raison et de l'être suprême (1793–94)* (Paris 1892). A. SICARD, *À la recherche d'une religion civile* (Paris 1895). A. MATHIEZ, *Contributions à l'histoire religieuse de la révolution française* (Paris 1907). R. R. PALMER, *Twelve Who Ruled* (Princeton 1941). A. LATREILLE, *L'Église catholique et la Révolution française,* 2 v. (Paris 1946–50). G. LEFEBVRE, *The French Revolution*, tr. E. M. EVANSON et al., 2 v. (New York 1961–64).

[M. LAWLOR]

SURIN, JEAN JOSEPH

Jesuit spiritual writer; b. Bordeaux, France, Feb. 9, 1600; d. Bordeaux, April 22, 1665.

Surin was the son of a *conseiller* to the Parlement of Bordeaux and studied at the Jesuit college of that city. At 16 he entered the novitiate of the Society of Jesus, then was sent for his theological studies to the college of Clermont in Paris. His formation culminated in the year of tertianship (1629–30) he made under the direction of Louis LALLEMANT, who was an opponent of Jansenism.

In 1634 Surin was sent, at the request of Cardinal Richelieu, to Loudun, a small city in the Province of Poitou. For two years strange phenomena had been taking place in a community of Ursuline nuns, the victims, apparently, of diabolical possession. Surin was named exorcist and was given special charge of the prioress, Jeanne des Anges. His mental equilibrium did not withstand this ordeal, which lasted three years. From 1635 to about 1656 he was subject to abnormal phenomena and believed himself possessed by the devil; at the same time he was favored with signal graces. It is impossible to distinguish clearly the supernatural graces from the pathological elements. He seems to have had a true manic-depressive type of breakdown, which was for him, however, the occasion of genuine spiritual progress. Despite his sickness or mental fatigue, Surin wrote numerous works. One finds in them the influence of St. Ignatius Loyola and Lallemant, as well as quotations from numerous other Jesuit spiritual writers. Surin has been criticized for placing too much importance on the extraordinary sensible manifestations of the mystical life. He has also been accused of quietism. An Italian edition of his *Catéchisme spirituel* was even placed on the Index in 1695. Bossuet, however, energetically approved and defended the orthodoxy of Surin. Fénelon also had much esteem for him.

He insisted on the interior and free character of the spiritual life. That life ought not be subject to exterior constraints or to selfish motives, but solely to what he called, using an expression borrowed from St. Ignatius, ''the interior law of charity and love.'' Surin emphasized the role of the inspiration of the Holy Spirit in the spiritual life. He distinguished the ''common gifts'' of grace from the ''interior and mystic way,'' known only by the ''disciples of the Holy Spirit.''

One of the best methods of prayer, he thought, is that which he called ''ordinary contemplation,'' a ''simple repose of the soul'' that tastes spiritual realities interiorly and holds itself without effort in the presence of God. But Surin did not neglect the use of other methods in prayer. He recommended the prayer of St. Ignatius as the way toward spiritual liberty and mystical contemplation, which is according to him perfectly compatible with the apostolic ministry.

Absolute detachment and the perfect acquiescing in the will of God held an important place in his spiritual doctrine and in the exercise of his spiritual direction. He insisted on the disinterestedness of our love for God, but distinguished his teaching from that of Fénelon on ''pure love'' by showing that one must also practice the virtues of hope, fear of God, and apostolic zeal.

Surin had a great influence on such Jesuit spiritual writers of the 18th century as J. P. de CAUSSADE, J. N. GROU, and P. de CLORIVIÈRE.

Bibliography: H. M. BOUDON, *L'Homme de Dieu* (Chartres 1683). This, the only complete life of Surin, is very unsatisfactory. It was republished by M. Bouix under the title *Vie du Père Jean-Joseph Surin* (Paris 1876). H. BRÉMOND, *Histoire littéraire du sentiment réligieux en France depuis la fin des guerres de religion jusqu'à nos jours* (Paris 1911–36) 5:148–310. J. DE GUIBERT, *La Spiritualit de la Compagnie de Jésus*, ed. E. LAMALLE (Rome 1953). E. DE GREEF, ''Succédanés et Concomitances psychopathologiques de la 'Nuit obscure' (Le cas du Père Surin),'' *Études Carmélitaines* 23.2 (1938) 152–176. M. OLPHE-GALLIARD, ''Le Père Surin et les Jésuites de son temps,'' *ibid.* 177–182. J. DE GUIBERT, ''Le Cas du Père Surin: Questions théologiques,'' *ibid.* 183–189. F. ACHILLE-DELMAS, ''À propos du Pére Surin et de M.-Th. Noblet,'' *ibid.*, 235–239. M. DE CERTEAU, ''Jean-Joseph Surin,'' *Month* NS 24 (1960) 340–353. M. OLPHEGALLIARD, *Dictionnaire de théologie catholique*, ed. A. VACANT et al., 15 v. (Paris 1903–50; Tables Générales 1951–) 14.2:2834–42.

[F. COUREL]

Capital: Paramaribo.
Size: 63,251 sq. miles.
Population: 431,303 in 2000.
Languages: Dutch, Suriname.
Religions: 94,895 Catholics (22%), 84,110 Muslims (19.5%), 110,645 Hindu (27%), 107,794 Protestants (25%), 33,859 practice indigenous faiths.
Diocese: Paramaribo (created 1958), suffragan to Port of Spain, Trinidad and Tobago; Paramaribo shares its metropolitan with dioceses in Barbados, Guyana, and Aruba. Together with the diocese of Cayenne, French Guiana, Paramaribo was formerly subject to the Holy See through the apostolic nuncio of Venezuela

SURINAME, THE CATHOLIC CHURCH IN

Formerly known as Dutch Guiana, the Republic of Suriname is located in northern South America, and is bordered on the north by the Atlantic Ocean, on the east by French Guiana, on the south by Brazil and on the west by Guyana. Part of the region between the mouth of the Amazon and that of the Orinoco River that was once known as Guiana, Suriname is characterized by northern mountains falling to a forested plateau and savannah through which cross many rivers. Rice, citrus, bananas and sugarcane grown near the coast account for much of the region's agriculture, while natural resources include bauxite, gold, iron ore and aluminum. The southernmost portions of the country, consisting of a nature reserve in the Amazon basis, have yet to be fully explored.

Formerly a part of the Netherlands realm of South America, Suriname gained independence in 1975. The region's mixed population includes blacks descended from 17th- and 18th-century slaves and East Indians descended from 19th-century immigrants. The Christian Churches include Roman Catholic, Moravian, Dutch Reformed, Lutheran and Episcopalian. There are also Muslims and Hindus represented in the area.

History. The region is named for the Surinen, its original inhabitants, although they had abandoned the region by the 16th century. In 1593 Spanish explorers entered the region, followed by Dutch settlers in 1602. Although a British settlement was well established in the area after 1651, the Treaty of Breda granted Suriname to the Dutch in 1667 (the British received the region that would later be called New York in exchange). Catholicism was introduced along the coast in 1683, but the strong post-reformation Dutch influence as well as the presence of slavery proved discouraging to missionary activity. Although Great Britain intermittently wrested control of the region away from the Netherlands, a series

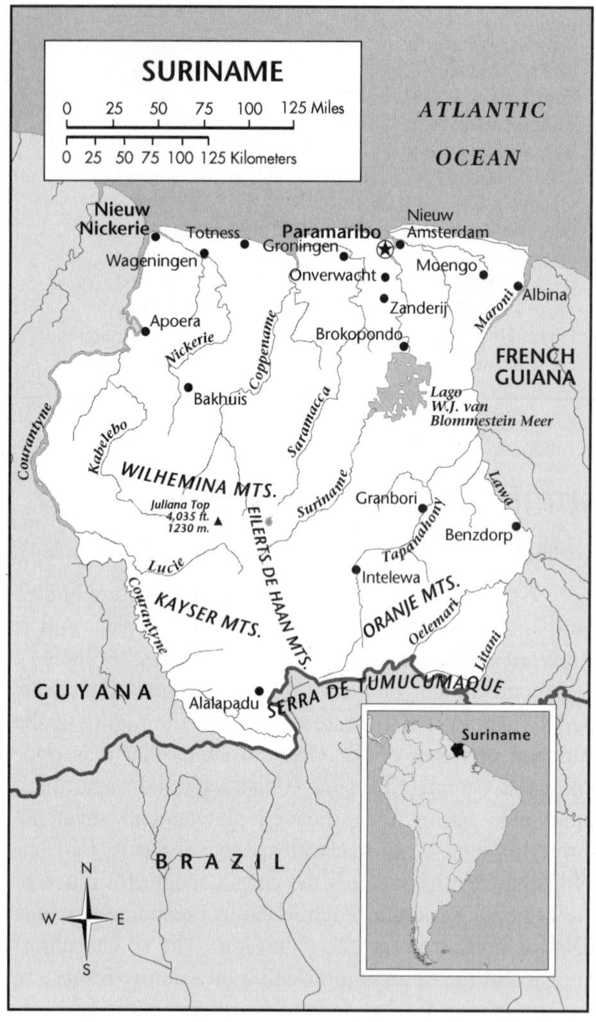

of new treaties ultimately returned the region to the Dutch in 1816. During the 19th century a large majority of Suriname's African workers were converted to the Moravian Church, which by 2000 counted among its adherents 16 percent of the population (*see* DONDERS, PETER). Catholic evangelization also began in earnest *c.* 1817.

As Dutch Guinea, the region became part of the Netherlands in 1948, and two years later was granted limited home rule. In 1954 Suriname became an autonomous territory of the Netherlands, and as the result of ethnic violence and economic problems it was granted full independence on Nov. 25, 1975. Within five years the civilian government was toppled by a military regime let by Col. Dési Bouterse, who ruled until 1990. Ethnic violence by various guerilla groups continued to flare during the 1980s, and a subsequent coup during 1990 resulted in free elections the following year; a formal peace treaty was signed with the region's assorted guerilla groups in 1992. The new civilian government's attempts to tackle Suriname's economic woes were ineffective, and by 1997 the inflation rate stood at a staggering 70 percent. In 2000 a new coalition government was elected in hopes that it would improve the economy, which then boasted a 20 percent unemployment rate.

Acknowledging the region's tradition of religious diversity, the Surinamese government allowed for freedom of worship, and religious groups were not required to register with the state. By 2000 there were 27 parishes tended by six secular and 15 religious priests. Nine brothers and 23 sisters, who aided in the operation of the 58 primary schools and 11 secondary schools run by the Church, administered to the humanitarian needs of the region. While the Church continued its evangelical efforts, U.S.-sponsored Baptist missionaries were increasingly active in the region. Tragically, in August of 1996 a fire of suspicious origin destroyed the archives of the Catholic diocese, although its main target was believed to be the country's House of Parliament, situated nearby. Drug and gun trafficking, as well as money laundering, continued to be among the problems addressed by the Church as it sought ways to stabilize Surinamese society after decades of political unrest.

Bibliography: E. M. DEW, *The Difficult Flowering of Suriname: Ethnicity and Politics in a Pluralistic Society* (Netherlands 1991). *Annuario Pontificio* has data on all dioceses.

[J. HERRICK/EDS.]

SURIUS, LAWRENCE

Carthusian spiritual writer; b. Lübeck, 1522; d. Cologne, May 23, 1578. Surius took the degree of master of arts at Cologne in 1539 and became a Carthusian the following year. At the time of the Reformation the Carthusians were doing little original work, but, especially at Cologne, they were active in translating, editing, and printing the works of the great ascetical and mystical authors of the Rheno-Flemish School and of the *Devotio Moderna.* Surius compiled from available sources a voluminous hagiographical work, *De probatis Sanctorum historiis* (Cologne 1570–75). Remarkably critical for its time, this work was useful to the Bollandists, especially after George Garnefelt, also of the Cologne charterhouse, published a revised edition of it that carefully indicated the sources Surius had used (Cologne 1617–18). Revised, enlarged, abridged, and translated into various languages, the editions of the *Lives of the Saints* are countless. The last Latin edition, in 13 volumes, was published at Turin (1875–80). Surius also translated and edited the *Meditations on the Life of Christ,* and *Pearl of the Gospel,* and the works of Henry SUSO, Johannes TAULER, and Jan van RUYSBROECK. These translations of the Rhenish and Flemish mystics are valuable because they reflect the interpretation of these authors current at the time of the Reformation. Historically, they were important also for their contribution to the revival of interest in the spiritual life in the Counter Reformation period. Surius's total literary production amounted to 36 volumes.

Bibliography: S. AUTORE, *Dictionnaire de théologie catholique,* ed. A. VACANT, 15 v. (Paris 1903–50; Tables générales 1951–) 14.2:2842–49.

[B. DU MOUSTIER]

SURPLICE

A form of the alb but unlike it, having large sleeves and worn loose at the waist as choir dress. The use of the surplice originated in the 11th century in England or France, where it was worn over a tunic or cassock lined with furs for warmth in churches unheated in winter. Like the alb, the early surplices were made of linen and were full length, but by the end of the 18th century this garment had lost its nobility. Lace had been substituted for linen, and the length had been so reduced that it barely covered the hips. The rochet is similar to the surplice in appearance but is distinguished from it by the shape of its sleeves, which are always tight-fitting. The surplice is less frequently worn today, giving way to the alb, which requires no cassock as an undergarment.

Bibliography: H. NORRIS, *Church Vestments* (London 1948). E.A. ROULIN, *Vestments and Vesture*, tr. J. MCCANN (Westminster, MD 1950). J. BRAUN, *Die liturgische Gewandung im Occident und Orient* (Freiburg 1907). J. MAYO, *A History of Ecclesiastical Dress* (London 1984). D. HINES, *Dressing for Worship: A Fresh Look at What Christians Wear in Church* (Cambridge 1996). D. PHILIPPART, ed., *Clothed in Glory: Vesting the Church* (Chicago 1997)

[M. MCCANCE]

SUSANNA

Heroine of the story in Daniel ch. 13. Susanna (Heb. *šôšannâ,* lily) was the beautiful and God-fearing wife of the wealthy Joakim of the Jewish Diaspora in Babylonia. When two elders and judges of the Jewish community tried to seduce her and she resisted their efforts, they accused her before the community of having been caught in the act of adultery with a young man. The elders' words were received without question, and Susanna was condemned to death. As she was being led out to execution, God raised up a young boy named Daniel who protested against the unjust sentence that had been passed without prior examination of the evidence. The case was reopened, and the witnesses were questioned by Daniel, who showed they were lying. Susanna was acquitted, and the elders were made to undergo the death sentence that had been passed on Susanna.

St. John Vianney wearing a dark cassock and white surplice.

The oldest extant text of the story is in Greek in two somewhat variant forms, one of the Septuagint (LXX) and one of the so-called Theodotion recension. For differences between these forms, refer to *Dictionary of the Bible* (1963) 4:631. Puns on certain Greek words in v. 54–55 and 58–59 have led some scholars, since the time of Julius Africanus (*c.* A.D. 200), to believe that the story was composed in Greek. Most scholars, however, now favor a Semitic (Hebrew or Aramaic) original. The puns in the Greek text may be imitations of puns in the original, or they may be due to a free-handed Greek translator.

The story of Susanna should be classed as pious HAGGADAH, a Jewish literary genre whose purpose was edification or moral instruction. It first circulated independently of the Book of DANIEL and only later was attached to it. Since it is not in the Hebrew Bible, it is reckoned as one of the apocrypha by non-Catholics, but it is held as inspired and canonical (deuterocanonical) by Catholics.

Certain folkloristic elements, two in particular, have been identified in the narrative. These are the theme of

Susanna and the Elders, portrayed as a lamb between two wolves, fresco in the Cemetery of Pretestato, Rome, c. A.D. *350.*

the faithful wife who is calumniated and later vindicated (cf. the Genoveva tale) and that of the unjust sentence righted by the ''wise child.'' These motifs are present in Oriental literature, e.g., the ''Thousand and One Nights,'' [W. Baumgartner, *Archiv für Religionswissenschaft* 27 (1929) 187–188; G. Huet, *Revue de l'histoire des religions* 65 (1912) 277–284]. The Susanna story seems to have used the same motifs. Nevertheless, it is also permeated with biblical language and doctrine.

It is not certain what purpose the author of the story had in mind. He may have intended merely to edify or teach a moral. He may also have been addressing himself to some contemporary abuse within the Jewish community. Under Simeon ben Shetah (*c.* 100–67 B.C.), the PHARISEES were advocating the introduction of a more just judicial procedure than that of their enemies, the SADDUCEES, which consisted in examination of the witnesses and the infliction of the death penalty for perjury in capital cases, even if the accused escaped execution. Both these points are made in the story, and since N. Brüll's *Jahrbuch für jüdische Geschichte und Literatur* 3 (1877) 1–69; some scholars believe that the story was composed to show the desirability of Simeon ben Shetaḥ's proposed reforms. This view, while possible, has not won general assent.

Despite the Babylonian locale, the narrative was probably composed in Palestine. Unless it was written at the time of Simeon ben Shetaḥ, no more precise date than 2d or 1st century B.C. can be assigned to it.

Scenes from the story of Susanna are depicted in catacomb frescoes from the 2d to the 4th centuries. In the cemetery of Pretestato (mid-4th century) Susanna is portrayed as a sheep between two wolves. The narrative is dramatized on certain Roman and Gallic sarcophagi and on the glass disc of Lothair II (A.D. 860). The frescoes of Baldassare Croce (early 17th century) in the Church of St. Susanna, Rome, cover the entire account; other painters of the period restrict themselves to the attempted seduction scene.

Bibliography: *Encyclopedic Dictionary of the Bible*, tr. and adap. by L. HARTMAN (New York 1963) 2368. F. DINGERMANN and H. SCHLOSSER, *Lexikon für Theologie und Kirche*, ed. J. HOFER and K. RAHNER (Freiburg 1957–65) 9:1194–96. M. WEISE, *Die Religion in Geschichte und Gegenwart* (Tübingen 1957–65) 6:532. R. H. PFEIFFER, *History of N.T. Times* (New York 1949) 448–454, with bibliog. O. EISSFELDT, *Einleitung in das A. T.* (Tübingen 1964) 797–800, with latest bibliog. W. BAUMGARTNER, ''Susanna: Die Geschichte einer Legende,'' *Archiv für Religionswissenschaft* 24 (1927) 259–280. R. A. F. MACKENZIE, ''The Meaning of the Susanna Story,'' *The Canadian Journal of Theology* 3 (1957) 211–218. H.

LECLERCQ, *Dictionnaire d'archéologie chrétienne et de liturgie* (Paris 1907–53) 15.2:1742–52.

[M. MCNAMARA]

SUSANNA, ST.

Roman martyr, first mentioned by the pagan poet Claudius Claudianus in 401 (*Monumenta Germaniae Historica* [Berlin 1826–], Auctores antiquissimi 10.340), if the reference is authentic, which can be doubted. In the MARTYROLOGY OF ST. JEROME she is recorded on August 11 ''ad duas domos,'' beside the Diocletian Baths, where the Church of St. Susanna still stands. A ''Titulus of Gaius'' is mentioned in the Roman Synod of 499; and in that of 595 it is recorded as that of Susanna. In the sixth century the name of Susanna appears in a legendary *passio,* according to which Susanna was the daughter of the priest Gabinius, brother of Bishop Gaius, and cousin of the Emperor Diocletian. When asked in marriage by the emperor's son, she refused and was beheaded.

This does not determine the identity of Susanna venerated in the Titulus. L. Duchesne proposed the Susanna of Daniel 13, and denies the historical existence of the martyr Susanna. No itinerary or other document except the *passio* speaks of her tomb. Lanzoni and H. Delehaye suggested the Susanna mentioned in Luke 8.3; while Franchi de'Cavalieri maintained that she was confused with a nonmartyr, daughter of the priest Gabinius and buried in the same titulus; the invasion of the Goths destroyed the tomb and the cult (537). This hypothesis has been rejected by A. Amore. The evidence thus far adduced indicates that at the titulus ''ad duas domos'' there was a tomb of a Susanna, the daughter of the priest Gabinius, and it was believed that she was a martyr. The modern church, a 17th-century partial reconstruction by Cardinal Carlo Moderno, is conducted by the Paulist Fathers as the Church for American Catholics in Rome.

Feast: Aug. 11.

Bibliography: *Bibliotheca hagiographica latina antiquae et mediae aetatis*, 2 v. (Brussels 1898–1901; suppl. 1911) 2:7937. *Acta Sanctorum* Aug. 2:624–632. L. DUCHESNE, *Mélanges d'archéologie et d'histoire* 36 (1916–17) 27–42. L. RÉAU, *Iconographie de l'art chrétien*, 6 v. (Paris 1955–59) 3.3:1240–41. F. LANZONI, *Revista di archeologia cristiana* 2 (Rome 1925) 228–234. H. DELEHAYE, *Les Origines du culte des martyrs* (2d ed. Brussels 1933) 435. P. FRANCHI DE'CAVALIERI, ''S. Susanna el il Titulus Gai,'' *Note agiografiche* 7 (Studi e Testi 49; Rome 1928) 185–202. A. AMORE, *Lexikon für Theologie und Kirche*, ed. J. HOFER and K. RAHNER, 10 v. (2d, new ed. Freiburg 1957–65); suppl., *Das Zweite Vatikanische Konzil: Dokumente und Kommentare*, ed. H. S. BRECHTER et al., pt. 1 (1966) 9:1196; *Antonianum* 39 (1964) 37–42;.

[E. HOADE]

Saint Susanna, sculpture by Jean de Chartres, c. 1500. (©Archivo Iconografico, S.A./CORBIS)

SUTRAS

A Sanskrit term used to designate in Hinduism, Jainism, and Mahāyāna Buddhism a vast class of texts of a didactic, mnemotechnic character. The word *sūtra,* originally meaning ''thread,'' is found in the UPANISHADS in the sense of ''a short treatise, to be learned by heart.'' A first group of *sūtras,* called as a whole ''Supplement to the Vedas,'' is devoted respectively to phonetics, ritual, grammar, etymology, metrics, and astronomy, all disciplines that are necessary for reciting the sacred hymns correctly. In addition, and less dependent on the hymns, there are the great *sūtras* on ritual: (1) *Shrauta-sūtras,* dealing with the great sacrifice, in which three fires or more are necessary; (2) *Shulva-sūtras,* which give the rules of measuring the place of sacrifice, of building the altar, etc.; (3) *Grhya-sūtras,* dealing with the daily duties of man and personal rites from conception to death and burial; (4) *Dharmasūtras,* expounding the priestly and secular law.

The last group of Hindu *sūtras* has a philosophical character. Each of the four systems of Hindu philosophy in its classical age has its own *sūtras:* (1) The *Vaisheshika-sūtras* aim at liberating man by revealing to him the principle of his self. (2) The *Nyāya-sūtras,* although concerned with logic, also aim at liberating man by fighting error. (3) The *sūtras* called *Samkhyakarika* deal with physics. (4) The *Yoga-sūtras* are concerned with mental concentration.

See Also: HINDUISM; JAINISM; BUDDHISM; INDIAN PHILOSOPHY; and the bibliographies at the end of these articles.

[J. DUCHESNE-GUILLEMIN]

SUTRI, COUNCILS OF

Two early councils of the GREGORIAN REFORM era, held at Sutri, a diocesan seat north of Rome. (1) When Emperor HENRY III went to Italy in 1046, he was met at Piacenza by GREGORY VI, who had become pope by bribing BENEDICT IX to resign. At Henry's instance, Gregory convoked a council at Sutri (December 20), to which he explained that he had purchased the office in order to reform it. Nonetheless the bishops in council declared that such action constituted SIMONY, and Gregory accordingly was deposed, with their approval. At the same time, Gregory's rival, the antipope Sylvester III, was deposed also, lest he still have some claims on the papal office. Finally, the unworthy Benedict IX himself was deposed at Rome on December 23–24, and CLEMENT II was made pope. (2) Pope NICHOLAS II, after election in Siena, opened his pontificate by attempting to expel his rival, the antipope BENEDICT X, from Rome. He held a council at Sutri (January 1059), attended by his lay protectors and the bishops of Lombardy and Tuscany. They discussed the antipope, but no decisions are recorded; having thus assembled forces, however, their army advanced on Rome, and Benedict fled.

Bibliography: C. J. VON HEFELE, *Histoire des conciles d'après les documents originaux,* tr. and continued by H. LECLERCQ, 10 v. in 19 (Paris 1907–38) 4.2:986–991 (year 1046),1133–38 (year 1059). A. FLICHE, *La Réforme grégorienne,* 3 v. (Louvain 1924–37) 1:107–110. G. B. BORINO, ''L'elezione e la deposizione di Gregorio VI,'' *Archivio della Società Romana di Storia Patria* 39 (1916) 142–252, 295–410; ''Invitus ultra montes cum domno Papa Gregorio abii,'' *Studi Gregoriani,* ed. G. B. BORINO 1 (1947) 3–46.

[R. KAY]

SUTTON, ROBERT, BL.

Priest, martyr; b. *c.* 1545 at Burton-on-Trent, Staffordshire, England; hanged, drawn, and quartered July 27, 1588 at Stafford. He received his master's degree from Christ Church, Oxford (1567). In 1571, he was the Anglican rector of Lutterworth, Leicestershire, but was converted to Catholicism by his younger brother William, who later became a Jesuit. The 30-year-old Robert and his 25-year-old brother Abraham arrived together at the English College of Douai on Mar. 23, 1575. They were ordained priests at Douai and left for England on Mar. 19, 1578. Robert labored in Staffordshire until his arrest and banishment in 1585. Upon his return, he was apprehended, tried, and condemned for high treason because he was a seminary priest. Catholics were able to secure part of his remains as relics. His thumb is now at Stonyhurst College. This *beatus* is the second English martyr of this name; the other, the companion of Bl. William HARTLEY. This Robert Sutton was beatified by Pope John Paul II on Nov. 22, 1987 with George Haydock and Companions.

Feast: July 27; May 4 (Feast of the English Martyrs in England).

See Also: ENGLAND, SCOTLAND, AND WALES, MARTYRS OF.

Bibliography: R. CHALLONER, *Memoirs of Missionary Priests,* ed. J. H. POLLEN (rev. ed. London 1924), I, no. 44. J. FOSTER, *Alumni Oxonienses* (Oxford 1892). J. H. POLLEN, *Acts of English Martyrs* (London 1891), 323–26.

[K. I. RABENSTEIN]

SVETLOV, PAVEL IAKOVLEVICH

Modern Russian theologian; b. 1861; d. Kiev, 1942. Svetlov studied at the Ecclesiastical Academy of Moscow and received the title of archpriest in 1890 when he was named professor of theology at the Institute of History and Theology of Nezhin and at the University of S. Vladimir in Kiev. In his early studies, he concentrated on Christology and wrote a valuable dissertation on *The Meaning of the Cross in the Work of Christ* (Kiev 1893; 2d ed. augmented, 1907). He produced a great number of articles for journals on dogmatic and moral theology, on apologetics and exegesis. In conjunction with the theologians V. V. Bolotov and A. A. Kireev, he furthered the efforts begun at Bonn in 1874 for a union between Catholics, Anglicans and Orthodox. He adopted a conciliatory position on controversial points between East and West, such as the procession of the Holy Spirit and the Immaculate Conception. He said explicitly that he did not see a substantial difference between the Oriental expression *Spiritus a Patre per Filium* and the Occidental *A Patre Filioque procedit*; and he believed that the addition of the FILIOQUE to the Creed was not the cause of the schism but its pretext. In general, however, his theological thinking was influenced by A. S. Khomiakov. His principal works are: *Christian Doctrine Presented in Apologetical Form* (2 v., 2d ed. Kiev. 1912); *The Idea of the Reign of God in Its Significance for a Christian Concept of the World* (Serghiev Possad 1905); *The Origin of the Current Opinion Concerning the Opposition between Faith and Reason* (St. Petersburg 1896); *The Eastern Orthodox Church and the Old-Catholic Church* [in French: *Revue internationale de théologie* 29 (1899) 27]; and *On the Reform of Religious Teaching in Russia* (St. Petersburg 1906). Besides reforms in the ORTHODOX Church he promoted religious liberty for Catholics and Protestants in Russia.

Bibliography: N. LADOMERSKY, *Dernières déviations sotériologiques dans la théologie russe* (Rome 1945). M. JUGIE, *Theologia dogmatica christianorum orientalium ab ecclesia catholica dissidentium* v.1–4.

[P. MAILLEUX]

SWASTIKA

The Sanskrit name (*svastika*) for the gamma-cross, a figure consisting of four capital gammas, joined at right angles. One of the most common of ancient symbols, it is found in almost universal use in the cultures or civilizations of Eurasia, and it may have had an independent origin in Africa and the Americas. The Sanskrit term means well-being (from *su,* well, and *asti,* is). The swastika, accordingly, was a symbol of good omen, a bringer of luck, prosperity, fertility, protection, and long life. It was employed also as a symbol of fire, lightning, and of the heavenly bodies and their motions. It has a prominent place in the various forms of Buddhism, and in Hinduism and Jainism. Christianity took it over as a form of cross and used it in a Christian signification. However, it has never been a favored Christian symbol. Its employment among the ancient pagan Germanic peoples—although not original with them—led the founders of German National Socialism (1933–45) to make it their militant party emblem.

See Also: CROSS.

Bibliography: J. HASENFUSS, *Lexikon für Theologie und Kirche,* ed. J. HOFER and K. RAHNER, 10 v. (2d, new ed. Freiburg 1957–65); suppl., *Das Zweite Vatikanische Konzil: Dokumente und kommentare,* ed. H. S. BRECHTER et al., pt. 1 (1966) 4:1327–28. J. DE VRIES, *Die Religion in Geschichte und Gegenwart,* 7 v. (3d ed. Tübingen 1957–65) 3:31–32. G. D'ALVIELLA, "Cross 3," J. HASTINGS, ed., *Encyclopedia of Religion & Ethics,* 13 v. (Edinburgh 1908–27) 4:327–328. P. THOMSEN, *Reallexikon der Vorgeschichte,* ed. M. EBERT, 15 v. (Berlin 1924–32) 5:20–21.

[P. SCHMIDT]

SWAZILAND, THE CATHOLIC CHURCH IN

A former British territory located in Africa, the Kingdom of Swaziland is bound on the northeast by Mozambique and on all other sides by the Republic of South Africa. A hilly region, Swaziland's terrain rises to mountains in the east and falls to sloping plains, leaving little land available for large-scale farming. Natural resources include asbestos, coal, clay and timber; once-rich iron ore deposits were depleted by 1980. Unlike similarly situated Lesotho, Swaziland exports little of its labor to South Africa but supplies a great deal of sugar, wood pulp and fruit to the surrounding region.

Guaranteed political autonomy by the British in the late 19th century, Swaziland was part of the British High Commission territory from 1906 to 1968, when it achieved independence. Due to the toll of AIDS as well as continued drought in the region, the average life expectancy for a Swazi was 40.4 years in 2000.

History. Inhabited by the Swazi tribes since the 16th century, the region received its first Catholic missionaries in the mid-19th century, when the OBLATES OF MARY IMMACULATE were sent from the Vicariate Apostolic of Natal. A shortage of missionaries retarded development in the region, and after the British took control following the second Boer War, the SERVITES (OSM) were entrusted with the area in 1913. The Prefecture Apostolic of Swaziland, erected in 1923, became a vicariate in 1939 and a diocese in 1951, whose name was changed from Bremersdorp to Manzini in 1961. Bishop Attilius Barneschi, OSM, who worked within the country from 1939 until 1965, built a cathedral at Manzini and established a seminary and a novitiate for African sisters.

On Sept. 6, 1968, the country gained its independence, and its first king, Sobhuza II. While the original constitution was suspended within a few years with the intention of revising it, no revision had been put in effect by 2000, although the Swazi government respected freedom of religion. While the fact that the country was almost totally inhabited by one ethnic group, the Swazi, allowed Swaziland to maintain civil peace in contrast to many of its African neighbors, political unrest developed. The lack of political parties prompted student activists, with support from Church leaders, to agitate for reforms that would create a government more responsive to the people. In 1992 the Holy See established relations with the country's King Mswati III; the following year the country held quasi-parliamentary elections, although the results were considered by many to be suspect.

Into the 21st Century. By 2000 Swaziland had 15 parishes tended by eight diocesan and 30 religious

Capital: Mbabane.
Size: 6,704 sq. miles.
Population: 1,083,290 in 2000.
Languages: English, siSwati.
Religions: 216,650 Catholics (20%), 108,320 Muslims (10%), 259,990 Protestants (24%), 433,320 (40%) Zionist (indigenous belief), 65,010 follow other faiths.
Diocese: Swaziland is a single diocese whose African bishop lives in Manzini. Manzini is suffragan to the archdiocese of Pretoria, South Africa.

priests. Other religious included nine brothers and approximately 60 sisters. In addition to 45 primary and 12 secondary schools, the Church also operated several hospitals, dispensaries, orphanages and hostels in the country. The bishop, a member of the South African Bishops' Conference, joined in that organization's efforts to bring about racial peace and justice in the whole of southern Africa. The spread of HIV/AIDS also presented the Church with a pressing challenge; in 2000 over one fourth of all adults were HIV-positive. In 2000, to help stop the spread of this disease, the government passed a law banning girls ten years and older from wearing miniskirts in schools.

Bibliography: J. E. BRADY, *Trekking for Souls* (Cedara, Natal 1952). W. E. BROWN, *The Catholic Church in South Africa from Its Origins to the Present Day* (New York 1960). *The Catholic Directory of South Africa* (Capetown 1917–). *Annuario Pontificio* (1964) 262.

[J. E. BRADY/EDS.]

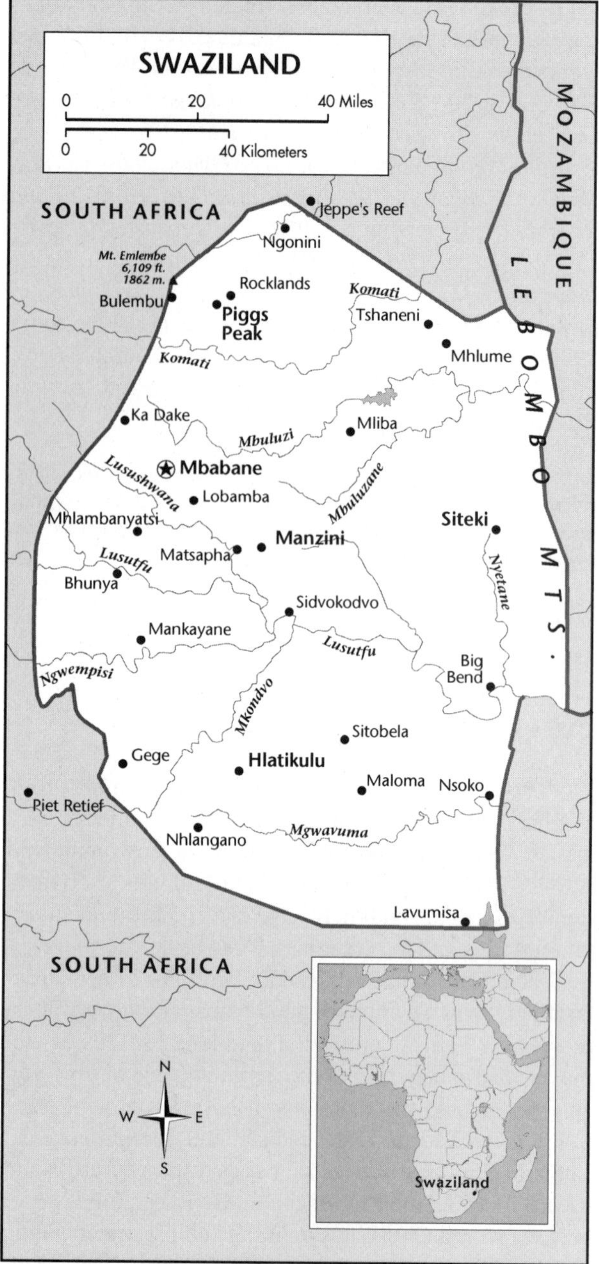

SWEDEN, THE CATHOLIC CHURCH IN

A kingdom in northern Europe, Sweden encompasses the larger section of the Scandinavian Peninsula. It is bordered on the north by Norway, on the east by Finland and the Gulf of Bothnia, on the southeast and south by the Baltic Sea, and on the southwest by the Kattegat, which separates it from Denmark. A land of many lakes and rivers, Sweden's lowlands are mostly forested, with timber joining hydropower and mining as its export base. The country's skilled labor force allowed Sweden to compete in high-tech industries, and its literacy rate was among the highest in Europe in 2000.

Sweden is a parliamentary democracy with a hereditary king. Until the 17th century the three southernmost provinces of Skåne, Blekinge and Halland belonged to Denmark; Bohuslän and Jämtland in the west were held by NORWAY. Noted for its neutral stance in both world wars of the 20th century, Sweden became a member of the European Union in 1995.

Christianity to 1500. Scandinavia was settled before 5000 B.C. as the glacial ice receded. There is evidence that during the Bronze Age (1500–500 B.C.) sun worship was practiced. From *c.* 500 the chief gods were Oden, Thor and Frey; sacrifices consisted of horses, but at times human sacrifice was practiced; the most important temple was at Uppsala. The first recorded Christian mission, to Birka near Stockholm in 830, was that of the Frankish monk ANSGAR, who was later archbishop of Bremen-Hamburg. This see subsequently claimed ecclesiastical jurisdiction over the country (directly or via Lund). Other missionaries came from England. St. SIG-

FRID baptized King OLAF I *c.* 1000. Christian influence possibly also entered Sweden from Russia, which was colonized partly by Swedes in the 9th century. The discovery of rural stone churches dating from *c.* 1100 provide evidence of a stabilized Christian mission; the majority of Sweden's parish churches dated from Catholic times even in 2000.

Early episcopal sees were established at Sigtuna (eventually moved to Uppsala) and Skara. Later sees included those of Linköping, Strängnäs, Västerås and Växiö. In 1164 Uppsala became an independent province. Important papal legations, under Nicholas Breakspear (1152) and William of Sabina (1248), introduced clerical CELIBACY.

Monastic life came to Sweden through the efforts of the CISTERCIANS. ALVASTRA and Nydala were founded in 1143, soon to be followed by three other monasteries and six convents. Later the KNIGHTS OF MALTA, the CARMELITES, the CARTHUSIANS and the Hospitallers of St. Anthony entered the country.

The clergy was educated either at cathedral schools or abroad. Uppsala, Linköping and Skara maintained houses at the University of PARIS during the 14th century, but later the University of Prague and the German universities were favored. The cathedral school at Uppsala was successively enlarged until it was raised to the status of University of Uppsala in 1477.

Considerable Christian influence was exerted in Sweden's growing civilization, including that of the codification of its own laws, but the system of Roman law was never accepted, nor did Roman law enter Sweden through the medium of Canon Law. Church-State relations were on the whole harmonious. With few exceptions no serious attempts at undue influence arose from either direction. Recruitment of the higher clergy was not restricted exclusively to the nobility, as was common elsewhere. Schools, hospitals, old age homes, hostels and the support of the poor were practically all maintained by the Church, whose endowments were not excessive in relation to the work that needed to be done.

Among the earliest works of Swedish literature is the 13th-century biography of the German mystic CHRISTINA OF STOMMELN, written by the Swedish Dominican Peter of Dacia (d. 1288). The best-known literary figure, whose influence was widely felt, was St. BRIDGET OF SWEDEN (1303–73). Her *Revelations* were widely read, and she gained fame for her attempts at influencing the popes to abandon Avignon and return to Rome (*see* AVIGNON PAPACY). The BRIGITTINE SISTERS, which she founded, spread to many countries and had their motherhouse at Vadstena; their first abbess was CATHERINE OF SWEDEN, the daughter of Bridget.

Capital: Stockholm.
Size: 173,394 sq. miles.
Population: 8,873,052 in 2000.
Languages: Swedish; Lapp and Finnish are spoken in small immigrant populations.
Religions: 159,714 Catholics (1.8%), 7,719,555 Lutherans (87%), 488,020 other (5.5%), 505,763 without religious affiliation.
Archdiocese: Stockholm.

While several Swedish clerics gained positions of importance in the academic world abroad, none were of lasting renown save the brothers Johannes and Olaus MAGNUS, Catholic archbishops of Uppsala in exile, who were famous for their history and geography of Scandinavia published in 1554–55.

Protestant Reformation. At the end of the Middle Ages Sweden was one of the most Catholic countries in Europe. The educational standard of the clergy was high; by 1480 more than 300 clerics had received academic training. Priories and monasteries continued to be founded, including houses of Carmelites and Carthusians, while churches were enlarged and decorated with frescoes. Though no overt signs of religious decline existed, there was political unrest, which contributed to the easy acceptance of Protestantism. The union of the Scandinavian countries (1389–1520) begun under Margaret, Queen of DENMARK (1375), and Norway (1387) was never firm in Sweden. It grew increasingly unpopular after the Union of Kalmar (1397) because of control by Denmark (which was often under German princes), combined with the influence of the Hanseatic League.

The continuous struggle to break loose finally succeeded in 1521 when Gustavus (Eriksson) Vasa led the peasants of Dalecarlia to victory over Christian II of Denmark and was elected king by the Diet of Strängnäs; he ruled until 1560. During his reign Lutheranism evolved as the favored faith. Most of the sees were vacated, and Archbishop Gustav Trolle of Uppsala, who had upheld Christian II, was exiled. Gustavus influenced the nomination of bishops and other clergy, especially as Rome showed little interest. At the Diet of Västerås (1527) King Gustavus Vasa obtained complete economic power over the Church and thereby gained great influence over its internal policy. The subservience of the nobility was obtained by returning to them estates that had been bequeathed to the Church by their relatives.

Although the diet did not favor Protestant reformers, it prepared the way for later development in that direction. Until 1539 no one was persecuted for reasons of faith, but major changes in ecclesiastical personnel, were

effected by the king for political reasons. The rupture with Rome widened after attempts were made to introduce the Germanesque, state-dominated Lutheran Church (1539–50). Education of the Catholic clergy became virtually impossible after Gustavus began supplying schools with Protestant-trained teachers. By 1536 practically all monasteries had been suppressed. Catholics reacted strongly, but their strength dissipated after a series of local rebellions were suppressed, their leaders killed, exiled or made submissive by clever grants of clemency.

While the reformation made inroads into Sweden, it was not until 1593 that the AUGSBURG CONFESSION (1530) was officially accepted at the Assembly of Uppsala. This delay was due partly to the temporary reconciliation of King John III (1560–93) with Rome, brought about in 1578 by Laurentius NIELSEN and Antonio POSSEVINO. John's Catholic son, Sigismund III, King of Poland, succeeded to the Swedish throne in 1593, but hopes for a Catholic restoration were destroyed six years later when he was defeated at Stångebro by his uncle, Charles, Duke of Södermanland (crowned Charles IX, 1604; *see* REFORMATION, PROTESTANT).

The slow and unsystematic development of Protestantism in Sweden accounts for the retention of such Catholic elements as vestments and the episcopacy in the Swedish Lutheran Church. Both the Wittenberg-trained Laurentius Petri, Archbishop of Uppsala (1531–73), who drew up a church ordinance that was accepted in 1572, and his elder brother Olaus PETRI, by his doctrinal tracts and disputes, were major figures in the formation of the Swedish Church. Codification of Church-State relations occurred in 1686, but no act of supremacy was ever passed. The Church's legal position remained unclear even into the 20th century, and this ambiguity continued to be one source of difficulty in its relation with the civil power.

During the 17th century strict Lutheran orthodoxy became the religion of the land. After King Gustavus II Adolphus entered the THIRTY YEARS' WAR as the protector of the interests of the Danish King, Christian IV, Sweden symbolized Lutheran resistance to the oppression of the Catholic Emperor. Gustavus's daughter, Queen Christina, was converted to Catholicism after her abdication (1654), but this act had no religious significance within Sweden.

Lutheranism since 1700. The influences of the 18th-century ENLIGHTENMENT and 19th-century philosophical and theological LIBERALISM served to weaken the established Swedish Church and caused, by way of reaction, an upsurge of PIETISM and EVANGELICALISM. When these two movements met strong clerical opposition and restrictive legislation, some groups seceded from the State Church and formed a number of sects. One result was agitation for religious freedom, which proved beneficial to Catholics. The sects and nonconformist groups, notably the PENTECOSTAL CHURCHES, remained a significant influence in Swedish life, despite declining memberships after World War I.

Until Jan. 1, 2000 persons born in Sweden were automatically considered members of the State-supported

St. Birgitta's Church, Vadstena, Sweden. (©Macduff Everton/CORBIS)

Lutheran Church, unless official notification to the contrary was given. Such notification involved a procedure that did little to deter Catholics and other minority faiths. During the 20th century considerable tensions developed both within the Lutheran Church itself and between the Church and the State. Conservatives and liberals battled over a politically motivated decision in 1957 to permit the ordination of women. By 1995 the Swedish Parliament voted to end its affiliation with the Lutheran Church, once again leaving the appointment of bishops to Church leaders and ending all financial subsidies. Despite this break with the government, in 2000 almost 90 percent of all Swedes remained affiliated with the Lutheran faith. New Testament scholarship at the University of Uppsala continued to merit international renown into the 21st century, supplying a counterbalance to theological liberalism within Protestant sects. The University's work was inspired in the mid-1900s by a High Church movement and a regeneration of Lutheran orthodoxy. Among modern Lutheran churchmen of international renown have been Archbishop Nathan SÖDERBLOM, the exegete Bishop Anders Nygren, and ecclesiastical historian Archbishop Yngve Brilioth.

Catholic Church since the Reformation. The Swedish Church suffered by being cut off from the rest of the Catholic world after the Reformation, one of the effects of which was a cultural decline in Sweden. Although the JESUITS established colleges along the southern shores of the Baltic that were attended for a time by upper-class Swedish youths, the government strongly discouraged this practice. Legislation became increasingly restrictive until the presence of Catholicism was completely forbidden (1617). Two Catholics were executed for their faith in 1624. Chaplains at foreign embassies were the only priests to be found from 1617 until 1781, when King Gustavus III issued a decree of tolerance for foreign Catholics after a visit with Pope Pius VI. In 1783 the Vicariate Apostolic of Sweden (which included Norway until 1868) was constructed; it became the Diocese of Stockholm in 1953.

Of primary importance for Catholic revival were the marriage in 1823 between Oscar I (King 1844–59) and the Catholic Josephine Beauharnais, and the work of her chaplain, Jacob Studach, Vicar Apostolic (1833–73). St. Eugenia's church in Stockholm, built in 1837, was the first modern church allowed to be constructed on the Scandinavian Peninsula. In 1873 Swedes gained the legal right to leave the Lutheran Church and join another Christian community by a decree of tolerance enacted principally under nonconformist pressure. Indicative of the slow progress of Catholicism despite such freedom was the fact that in 1923 Sweden had only 11 priests and five parishes. After World War II traditional prejudices against the Church began decreasing, and the number of converts rose to about 100 a year. An influx of refugees and foreign workers during the 1970s and 1980s also augmented Catholic ranks, necessitating the establishment of new parishes in the provinces. The Church worked to reach Sweden's widespread population through both radio and television programming and printed publications, including the diocesan biweekly *Katolsk Kyrkotidning*, the bi-monthly *Credo*, and several publications for children. Major Catholic associations included Academicum Catholicum (affiliated with Pax Romana) and the youth-group Sveriges Unga Katolikers.

Looking to the Future. After 1952 the country enjoyed almost complete religious freedom despite the existence of a state-sanctioned faith; this too would end in 2000. In 1953 the Church hierarchy was restored, its one diocese reestablished in Stockholm. Despite a continuing interest in Catholicism among Swedes, progress in conversions was impeded by limited resources, lack of native clergy—Swedish seminarians continued to study abroad, as Scandinavia lacked a regional seminary—and the sheer size of the country. As occurred elsewhere in Europe during the late 20th century, an increasingly widespread lack of interest in religion also worked to erode the work of the Church ministry. Nonetheless, the country's Catholic population continued to grow. While statistics from 1964 reported 21 parishes and 45 religious and 20 secular priests in Sweden, by 2000 those same figures had increased to 38 parishes and 131 total priests.

In November of 1998 Pope John Paul II named Anders Arborelius as the first Swedish-born bishop since the Reformation to the position of the leader of the country's church. Although born in Switzerland, Bishop Arborelius was of Swedish parentage and was raised in the Swedish city of Lund. The pope's action reflected an increasing stability in the Swedish Church, a stability that would be increased during the early 21st century as the liberal Swedish government passed reform legislation intended to restore basic rights such as land ownership and legal protections to all the nation's churches.

Bibliography: H. HOLMQUIST, *Handbok i Svensk kyrkohistoria,* 3 v. (Stockholm 1948–52). B. GUSTAFSSON, *Svensk kyrkohistoria* (2d ed. Stockholm 1963). *Die Kirche in Schweden,* ed. F. SIEGMUND-SCHULTZE, (*Ekklesia* 2.5; Gotha 1935). I. ANDERSSON, *A History of Sweden,* tr. C. HANNAY (New York 1956). C. J. A. OPPERMANN, *The English Missionaries in Sweden and Finland* (*Society for Promoting Christian Knowledge,* 1937). G. SCHWAIGER, *Die Reformation in den nordischen Ländern* (Munich 1962). J. MARTIN, *Gustave Vasa et la Réforme en Suède* (Paris 1906). H. BIAUDET, *Le Saint-Siège et la Suède durant la seconde moitie du XVIe siècle,* 1570–76 (Paris 1907). O. GARSTEIN, *Rome and the Counter-Reformation in Scandinavia,* v.1, 1539–83 (New York 1964). J. METZLER, *Die Apostolischen Vikariate des Nordens* (Paderborn 1919). A. V. PALMQVIST, *Die römisch-katholische Kirche in Schweden nach 1781,* 2 v. (Uppsala 1954–58). H. M. WADDAMS, *The Swedish Church* (London 1946). J. WORDSWORTH, *The National Church of Sweden* (Milwaukee 1911). J. TESCHITEL, "Schweden in der Gesellschaft Jesu, 1580–1773," *Archivum historicum Societatis Jesu,* 21 (1952) 329–343. K. S. LATOURETTE, *Christianity in a Revolutionary Age: A History of Christianity in the Nineteenth and Twentieth Centuries,* 5 v. (New York 1958–62) v.2, 4. J. GALLÉN, *Lexikon für Theologie und Kirche*[2], eds., J. HOFER and K. RAHNER, 10 v. (2d, new ed. Freiburg 1957–65) 9:537–539. S. GÖRANSSON et al., *Die Religion in Geschichte und Gegenwart*[3], 7 v. (3d ed. Tübingen 1957–65) 5:1592–1605. *Bilan du Monde* 2:804–809. *Annuario Pontificio* (1964) 428.

[L. ROOTH/EDS.]

SWEDENBORG, EMANUEL

Swedish philosopher and scientist; b. Stockholm, Jan. 29, 1688; d. London, Mar. 29, 1772. His parents were Jesper Swedberg, a Lutheran court chaplain and later professor of theology at Uppsala University and bishop of Skara, and his first wife Sara (née Behm).

Early Years. As a boy Emanuel distinguished himself by his intelligence and quick apprehension, and as early as 1699 he entered the University of Uppsala, where he studied most of the subjects offered (though not, apparently, theology and law). After his dissertation in 1709, he went abroad to study languages and mechanical crafts in London, Oxford, Amsterdam, and Paris (1710–14), and for some years he lived as an amateur inventor and natural scientist. In 1716 King Charles XII appointed him extraordinary assessor of the Royal Board of Mines, and from 1724 to 1747 he worked as an ordinary assessor of that institution. In 1719 he was ennobled by Queen Ulrika Eleanora, and he assumed the name of Swedenborg.

His mining and engineering experiences he described in a huge work *Opera philosophica et mineralia* (3 v. Leipzig 1733), the first volume of which, the *Prin-*

cipia rerum naturalium, contained a mathematical, mechanical explanation of the universe and its origin. For unknown reasons, Swedenborg, while seeing the book through the publication process, seems to have abandoned the materialistic philosophy expressed in it, and the next year he published *Prodromus philosophiae ratiocinantis de infinito et causa finali creationis,* developing a neoplatonic philosophy, which was similar to and by no means independent of that proclaimed by sixteenth- and seventeenth-century Protestant mystics. In order to demonstrate its truth, Swedenborg then devoted himself to the task of proving the existence of the soul ''by experience, geometry and reason,'' that is, by finding the laws governing the soul's interaction with the body. For this purpose he went abroad to study anatomy and embryology in Paris, Venice, and Rome (1736–39), and he finally published his results in the *Oeconomia regni animalis* (two parts, Amsterdam 1739), still a principal work in the history of anatomy. At the same time it is a systematical representation of his philosophy, though not yet applied to the Christian religion. Here his doctrine of series and degrees is developed: the soul, which is the particle of life from the infinite and the formative force causing the body, must descend into matter by four degrees, into four different ''auras'': (1) the material for the organism of the soul, (2) the intellectual mind, (3) the animus (the seat of sensuous desires and imagination), (4) the external sense and motor organs. An ethical theory was included in the work: man, according to Swedenborg, in his rational mind has the ability to choose between good (philanthropic) and evil (selfish) deeds, and has a free will.

Conversion and Doctrine. When Swedenborg wrote the *Oeconomia,* he had for several years been suffering from strange dreams and visions, especially visions of light—a psychological peculiarity, inherited from his father. After 1739 the frequency of his dreams and visions increased, and at the same time he was gradually attracted by the Christian religion. From 1743 to 1745, he went through a mental crisis, and having had a vision of Jesus Christ (1744), he felt confirmed in his conversion and spent the rest of his life expounding the doctrines of ''the true Christian religion,'' which should perhaps rather be called a Neoplatonic philosophy admitting the historical figure of Jesus Christ. The theological characteristic of orthodox Swedenborgianism, exhibited in a series of commentaries to the Bible (e.g., *Arcana celestia* 8 v. 1749–56) and doctrinal works, such as the *Vera Christiana religio* (1771), is the denial of the doctrines of the Holy Trinity and of the vicarious atonement: God, the invisible, spaceless and timeless, is one; in Jesus Christ God manifested Himself in time, thus causing a kind of trinity composed of the soul (from the eternal Father), the body (as the son of Mary), and the Holy Spirit (as the action caused by the union of both). Man's spirit is eternal, and after the death of the body it lives according to its earthly justification; spirits of philanthropic, God-loving men gather in heavens, and spirits of the selfish seek the company of their equals in hells.

Emanuel Swedenborg.

After his conversion, Swedenborg believed himself to be in constant communication with spirits who dictated the revelations of the next world to him. Unbiased scholars (Lamm, Benz, Lindroth) tend to believe that Swedenborg's visions were manifestations of a mental disease (paranoia), subconsciously developed to confirm the theories that he had already worked out. In this light, Swedenborg's not too original philosophical and religious theories stand out as typical and pleasant representatives of eighteenth-century mercantilistic and philanthropic ideals. His influence, however, has been considerable, affecting particularly the philosophy and literature of the Romanticists, and the development of the psychical sciences. Although Swedenborg did not found a church, his religious followers organized themselves in 1787 into a body known as the New Church or NEW JERUSALEM CHURCH, based upon his writings.

Bibliography: *Autographa . . . ,* ed. R. L. TAFEL, 10 v. (Stockholm 1869–70) and 18 v. (*ibid.* 190–16). J. J. G. HYDE, *A Bibliography of the Works of Emanuel Swedenborg, Original and*

Jan Pieters Sweelinck.

Translated (London 1906). M. LAMM, *Swedenborg* (Stockholm 1915). G. TROBRIDGE, *Swedenborg: Life and Teaching* (4th ed. New York 1955). H. DE GEYMULLER, *Swedenborg et les phénomènes psychiques* (Paris 1934). C. S. L. O. SIGSTEDT, *The Swedenborg Epic* (New York 1953). E. BENZ, *Emanuel Swedenborg: Naturforscher und Seher* (Munich 1948). S. LINDROTH, *Ny illustrerad svensk litteraturhistoria,* ed. E. N. TIGERSTEDT, 5 v. (Stockholm 1955–58) 2:177–199; bibliog. 600–602. S. TOKSVIG, *Emanuel Swedenborg: Scientist and Mystic* (New Haven 1948). G. GOLLWITZER, *Die Religion in Geschichte und Gegenwart,* 7 v. (3d ed. Tübingen 1957–65) 6:535–556.

[T. D. OLSEN]

SWEELINCK, JAN PIETERS

Renaissance organist and church composer (called also Jan Pieterszoon); b. Deventer, Holland, May 1562; d. Amsterdam, Oct. 16, 1621. His father, Pieter, was organist at the Oude Kerk (Catholic) in Amsterdam, and Jan succeeded to the post about 1577 and retained it until his death. He was an organist and teacher of uncommon brilliance, and vestiges of his style may be traced through many pupils into many countries. His vocal music, though eclipsed by his great contribution to the development of a new instrumental style, reflects the finest of late Renaissance style and texture, especially in the four books of Psalms, and in the transitional protobaroque Latin motets comprising the *Cantiones sacrae* of 1619. His harpsichord music won its way into such anthologies as the Fitzwilliam Virginal Book. His organ music shows him at the height of his powers as an innovator in such forms as the toccata and the chorale variation, the latter serving to carry the earlier *cantus firmus* techniques into the mainstream of baroque music.

Bibliography: *Complete Works,* ed. M. SIEFFERT, 10 v. (Amsterdam 1894–1901). B. VAN DEN SIGTENHORST MEYER, *Jan P. Sweelinck en zijn instrumentale muziek* (The Hague 1934; repr. 1946); *De vocale muziek van Jan P. Sweelinck* (The Hague 1948). P. H. LÁNG, *Music in Western Civilization* (New York 1941). G. REESE, *Music in the Renaissance* (rev. ed. New York 1959). A. ANNEGARN, *Die Musik in Geschichte und Gegenwart,* ed. F. BLUME (Kassel-Basel 1949). T. A. ANDERSON, *The Metrical Psalmody of Jan Pieterzoon Sweelinck, with a Practical Performing Edition of the Livre Quatrième et Conclusional des Pseaumes de David (1621)* (Ph.D. diss. University of Iowa, 1968). P. DIRKSEN, *The Keyboard Music of Jan Pieterszoon Sweelinck: Its Style, Significance, and Influence* (Utrecht 1997). F. NOSKE, *Sweelinck* (Oxford 1988). D. M. RANDEL, ed., *The Harvard Biographical Dictionary of Music* (Cambridge 1996). N. SLONIMSKY, ed., *Baker's Biographical Dictionary of Musicians* (New York 1992). R. H. TOLLEFSEN in *The New Grove Dictionary of Music and Musicians,* ed. S. SADIE (New York 1980).

[D. STEVENS]

SWEYNHEYN, KONRAD

Originally of Mainz, protoprinter in Italy, who established a press at the Benedictine Abbey of St. Scholastica, SUBIACO, apparently upon invitation of Cardinal Juan de TORQUEMADA; fl. 1465 to 1477. His first work, a Latin grammar of Donatus, has not survived. The first dated book was LACTANTIUS's *De divinis institutionibus* (1465). After completing Augustine's *De civitate Dei* (1467), he moved to Rome where he produced 28 classic and religious works by 1472, notably (1471–72) a five–volume Italian commentary on the Bible by Nicolaus de Lyra and an edition of St. Jerome's letters (1476). His printings averaged 275 copies. Another printer, Arnold Pannartz (*c.* 1465–76), was associated with Sweynheym in these undertakings.

Bibliography: E. VON RATH, "Spread of Printing in the 15th Century," *A History of the Printed Book,* ed. L. C. WROTH (New York 1938). W. D. ORCUTT, *The Book in Italy during the Fifteenth and Sixteenth Centuries Shown in Facsimile Reproduction* (New York 1928).

[E. P. WILLGING]

SWIFT, JONATHAN

Anglo-Irish satirist, poet, patriot; b. Dublin, Nov. 30, 1667; d. there, Oct. 19, 1745.

He was born of English parents; his early education at Kilkenny Grammar School included a rigorous Anglican training, as did his undergraduate years at Trinity College, Dublin. There he did well in literature but badly in the barren, abstract philosophy of the period (with its heavy emphasis on logic) and in formal rhetoric, though his writing was to be shaped by his ironic use of these disciplines. His formation continued in the household of Sir William Temple at Moor Park, Surrey (1689–94, 1696–99). While acting as secretary to Temple, he attended Oxford, earning a Master of Arts degree in 1692. Poems of this period reveal the characteristics of his later work—deliberate avoidance of the ''poetic''; moral IDEALISM; opposition to dissent, deism, and the naturalism of contemporary science; and scorn for the aridities of formal logic. He was ordained in 1695 and held the prebend of Kilroot, Ireland. But parishes in physical ruin and a primarily Presbyterian flock were intolerable to the ambitious and Anglican Swift. He returned to Surrey (1696), edited Temple's correspondence, and worked on his own first major efforts, *A Tale of a Tub* and *The Battle of the Books* (1704).

After Temple's death, Swift held several unimportant benefices in Ireland. He received the degree of D.D. from Dublin University in 1701, the year in which Esther Johnson (''Stella''), with whom he had formed a tutor-student attachment at Moor Park, came to Ireland. Whether he married her or not, their attachment was close, but no evidence exists that they were ever alone together. She died in 1728.

This period (1701–14) was interrupted by trips to England, some on church business, some occasioned by Swift's growing involvement in English politics. He was active in Whig circles until 1710, but such works as *Sentiments of a Church of England Man* (1708) and the ironic *Abolishing of Christianity* (1708, published in 1711) reflect his belief that Whig attempts to repeal the Test Act sacrificed the Establishment to dissenters and deists. In disgust, he joined the Tories. Meanwhile, he engaged in a humorous campaign against the astrological quack John Partridge with the ''Bickerstaff'' letters (1708–09).

Though he expected a bishopric, his reward from the Tories was the deanery of St. Patrick's, Dublin (1713). With Queen Anne's death and the collapse of the Tories (1714), he settled unhappily in Dublin, revisiting England occasionally to renew friendships and oversee the publication of *Gulliver's Travels* (1726). His championing of the Irish against English repressions culminated in the *Drapier Letters* (1724–25) and the bitterly ironic *Modest Proposal* (1729). Ménière's disease, not insanity, began to afflict him about 1736. He was declared legally insane in 1742.

The highly colored picture of the scabrous, mad misanthrope, faithless priest, and heartless lover has given way to a more balanced view. Recent critics, alert to Swift's method of speaking behind the ''mask'' of an arrantly mistaken contemporary, see Swift's satires as essentially exposures. *The Battle of the Books* exposes ''modern'' man's arrogant assumption of superiority over the ancients. The *Tale of a Tub* explores the Reformation and its aftermath through the eyes of a modern hack, enemy of humanistic values, friend of scientific naturalism, and admirer of intellectual and spiritual decay. The result is the exposure of a Catholic Church intellectually and morally sick (as an Anglican, Swift also ''exposes'' the Church's dogmatic and disciplinary claims), the anarchic anti-intellectualism of dissent, the mechanization of Anglicanism itself, and the naturalism—scientific and humanistic—of the age. *The Abolishing of Christianity* exposes the friendly ''defender'' of an Anglicanism sapped of its religious content and reduced to mere structure. *The Modest Proposal,* written by an ''economist,'' exposes the mindless amorality of a science that solves the problem of Ireland's poverty by eating its children.

Jonathan Swift.

Gulliver's Travels, his best-known work, exposes Gulliver, blind to his own venality, yet increasingly repelled by the world's malice, the frivolity of its intellectual concerns, and the ugliness of man's departures from the norms of his rational nature. In reaction, Gulliver yearns for the ''angelistic,'' stoic calm of the Houyhnhnms—a solution that Swift, the Christian, despised. Swift's poetry has alienated readers because of its coarseness, but it has the same force and energy that characterize his prose and is based on much the same assumptions.

Bibliography: *Prose Works,* ed. H. DAVIS, 15 v. (London 1939–); *Correspondence of Jonathan Swift,* ed. H. WILLIAMS, 3 v. (New York 1964); *Journal to Stella,* ed. H. WILLIAMS, 2 v. (New York 1948); *Poems,* ed. H. WILLIAMS, 3 v. (2d ed. New York 1958). H. CRAIK, *The Life of Jonathan Swift, Dean of St. Patrick's Dublin,* 2 v. (2d ed. London 1894). K. WILLIAMS, *Jonathan Swift and the Age of Compromise* (Lawrence, Kan. 1958). P. HARTH, *Swift and Anglican Rationalism* (Chicago 1961). M. PRICE, *Swift's Rhetorical Art* (New Haven 1953).

[E. J. CHIASSON]

SWINT, JOHN JOSEPH

Fourth bishop of Wheeling, W.Va.; b. Florence, near Pickens, W.Va., Dec. 15, 1879; d. Wheeling, Nov. 23, 1962. He was the son of Peter, an emigrant from Luxembourg, and Bavarian-born Caroline (Winkler) Swint. Religion was a dominant influence in the Swint home, which in lieu of a church, was the center of Catholicity in the Pickens area. Three of Swint's sisters entered religious life. After early education in nearby one-room schools, he entered (1893) St. Charles College, Ellicott City, Md. He graduated in 1899 and began his studies for the priesthood that same year at St. Mary's Seminary, Baltimore, Md. He was ordained June 23, 1904, in St. Joseph's Cathedral, Wheeling, by Bp. Patrick J. Donahue and appointed to assist at the Wellsburg, W.Va., parish for the summer months. In September 1904 he was sent to the Apostolic Mission House, Washington, D.C., to prepare himself for missionary work in the Diocese of Wheeling. Recalled in April 1905, he was appointed pastor of Hinton, where he remained for three years. In 1908 he established the Diocesan Mission Bank, with offices at DeSales Heights Academy, Parkersburg. For the next 14 years he gave missions throughout the diocese, sometimes alone, sometimes with the assistance of other priests, notably James M. Gillis, CSP, and Joseph H. Steinbrunner, of Cincinnati, Ohio. In 1914 Swint's mission work was curtailed, but not ended, when he was made pastor of St. Patrick's parish, Weston. On Feb. 22, 1922, he was named auxiliary bishop of Wheeling, to assist the ailing Bishop Donahue. He was consecrated on May 11, 1922, as titular bishop of Sura, by Abp. Michael J. Curley of Baltimore and succeeded to the See of Wheeling, Dec. 11, 1922, following the death of Donahue. Swint was honored by being made an assistant at the pontifical throne (June 14, 1929), and he received the personal title of archbishop from Pius XII (March 12, 1954).

During Swint's 40-year episcopate, an unusual material development accompanied the spiritual growth of the diocese. In addition to the cathedral, 101 churches were built, as well as 35 elementary schools, eight high schools, one college, three new hospitals (not including two that were purchased and four that were substantially enlarged), five schools of nursing, two homes for the aged, and numerous convents, rectories, and other smaller structures. Outstanding as a preacher, he published upon request several volumes of his sermons, among which are *Forgotten Truths* (1941), *Back to Christ* (1941), and *The Sweetest Story Ever Told* (1947). For his religious, civic, educational, and humanitarian leadership, he was awarded honorary degrees by Duquesne University, Pittsburgh, Pa.; Georgetown University, Washington, D.C.; Wheeling College; and the University of West Virginia, Morgantown.

[D. KIRWIN]

SWISS GUARDS

During the Middle Ages, it became the practice for Swiss soldiers to hire themselves as mercenaries to fight wars in other countries. From the 15th century until the 19th, such mercenary activity came to be regulated by treaties between the Swiss cantons or districts and various foreign states. These treaties, called capitulations, involved payment for the employment of such military forces. It is said that Francis I of France employed up to 150,000 Swiss mercenaries in his military campaigns against Emperor Charles V. At the Battle of Pavia (1525), the personal guard of Francis I, called the Hundred Swiss, died in a futile effort to protect the French king from being captured by the Spanish. On Aug. 10, 1792, 500 members of the Swiss Guard of King Louis XVI died in their effort to protect the Tuileries palace from the invading mob aroused by the French Revolution. The *Lion of Lucerne,* an impressive monument by Bertel Thorvaldsen commemorates the Swiss soldiers who gave their lives on that day. Beginning in 1803, Napoleon I made use of several regiments of Swiss mercenaries, although many died in his ill-fated Russian campaign of 1812. Swiss regiments continued to be used by the French during the Bourbon restoration, but after the July Revolution of 1830, such forces ceased to be employed. The Swiss constitution of 1874 prohibited all military capitulations and the recruitment of Swiss forces by foreign powers with one exception: the Swiss Guard of the papacy.

While Swiss soldiers had been used by the popes since the late 14th century, it was not until the pontificate of JULIUS II (1503–13) that the Papal Swiss Guard was officially formed. Through Cardinal Matthäus SCHINER, Julius II negotiated a treaty with the cantons of Zurich and Lucenne, and on June 21, 1505, he requested that 200 soldiers be sent to Rome with Peter von Hertenstein as *condottiere* [captain] and Caspar von Silenen as commander. On Jan. 21, 1506, they arrived in Rome and were received by Julius II who extended a solemn blessing upon them in the Piazza S. Pietro. This was the beginning of the Pontifical Swiss Guard (*Schweizergarde, Guardia Svizzera*), a stable and disciplined corps of Swiss soldiers, entrusted with the protection of the Roman Pontiff and the Apostolic Palaces.

Over the centuries, the Pontifical Swiss Guard has shared in the vicissitudes of the papacy itself, and there have been times of suspension and decline, especially during periods when the popes have suffered exile and captivity. During the tragic sack of Rome, on May 6, 1527, 147 members of the Swiss Guard died while the other 42 were successful in saving Pope Clement VII who made his way along a secret corridor to Castel Sant'Angelo. In commemoration of this historic sacrifice, on May 6 of each year, there is a solemn ceremony which includes the swearing in of the new members of the Swiss Guard. In an oath taken in one of four different Swiss languages—German, French, Italian and Ladino—the soldiers raise three fingers of their right hand in honor of the Trinity and place their left hand on the flag of the Swiss Guard Corps. This flag is made up of a large white Swiss cross and three shields representing the coat of arms of the present pope, Pope Julius II, the founder of the Guard, and the current commander. Traditionally, the commander of the Guard has been a member of the Swiss nobility, but in recent years this tradition has not been followed. The oath taken on May 6 pledges fidelity to the pope, his successors and to the College of Cardinals when the See of Peter is vacant. The members of the Guard likewise pledge to dedicate themselves to the service and defense of the popes even, if necessary, by the sacrifice of their lives.

Following the trials of the papacy under the French Revolution and Napoleon I, the Pontifical Swiss Guard became more stable during the 19th and 20th centuries. Contracts were established between the Holy See and the canton of Lucerne by Leo XII in 1825, and by Pius IX in 1850. A reorganization of the corps was effected by Pius X on March 13, 1914, and again by John XXIII on Aug. 6, 1959. On Sept. 15, 1970, Pope Paul VI decreed that the Swiss Guard would become the only pontifical military corps, and it would fall directly under the Holy Father's supervision. Thus, he abolished all other Vatican military units, including the Noble Guard and the Palatine Guard. By this decision, the protection of the Apostolic Palace was confided exclusively to the Swiss Guard, but Vatican City State would also have its own police force.

Swiss Guard stands on duty at Vatican City, Rome. (©Kelly-Mooney Photography/CORBIS)

The Swiss Guard is presently composed of 110 men. There is one commander, one chaplain, three officers, 25 lesser officers (*Unteroffizieren*) and 80 guards or halbardiers. For acceptance into the Guard, the men must be unmarried, between 19 and 30 years of age and at least 5 feet, 8 inches tall (174 cm). They must be Swiss citizens, Catholic, possessed of a good reputation and have graduated from either an apprenticeship or secondary school to the second degree. In addition, they must have completed their military training in a ''recruitment school'' (*Rekrutenschule*) and show signs of the physical and psychological requisites of the military profession. There is a minimum commitment of two years of service, and during these initial years, the guards must remain celibate. Those who commit themselves for extended service can marry, but since all the guards reside within the Vatican, permission is contingent on whether there are enough apartments for the married available. During their first years of service, the guards study Italian, receive training in firearms and self-defense and familiarize themselves with the organizational structure and residents of the Vatican. They also participate in sports on the athletic fields of the various foreign seminaries outside the Vatican. The Swiss Guard is under the patronage of Saints Nicholas of Flüe, Martin and Sebastian. They have their own chapel of Saints Martin and Sebastian within the Vatican, which was remodeled and dedicated by Cardinal Angelo Sodano, the Secretary of State, on Nov. 11, 1999.

The principal function of the Swiss Guard is the protection of the person of the Holy Father. Hence, they are given the title, *Cohors pedestris Helvetiorum a sacra custodia Pontificis* [Infantry guard of the Swiss for the sacred protection of the Pontiff]. The members of the Guard are responsible for the custody of the entrances of the apostolic palaces, the papal apartments and the pope's summer residence of Castelgandolfo when he resides there. They protect the pope during solemn pontifical ceremonies, during which they also guard the chapels. In years past, six members of the Guard would flank the Pope as he was carried on the *sedia gestatoria*. Today, when the Roman pontiff travels abroad, several plain-clothed members of the Swiss Guard accompany him, along with members of the Vatican police. The ceremonial weapon of the Guardsmen is the seven-foot-long medieval boarding pike or halberd. However, when they are with the pope during his foreign visits, they often carry a personal revolver.

The Renaissance uniform of the Swiss Guard consists of dark blue, red and yellow colors with a white collar. Traditionally, Michelangelo is credited with the design, but some dispute this claim. Tourists frequently wish to have their photographs taken with members of the Guard. However, Guardsmen are instructed to allow this only when security risks are minimal.

One of the most recent tragic events of the Swiss Guard's history occurred on the evening of May 4, 1998. Colonel Alois Estermann and his wife, Gladys Meza Romero, were killed by Cedric Tournay, a vice-corporal of the Guard, who then committed suicide. The murders and suicide took place within the Vatican apartment of the couple.

Efforts to restore morale and confidence in the Swiss Guard following the murder-suicide of 1998 include the establishment in 1999 of ''The Foundation for the Pontifical Swiss Guard at the Vatican.'' This Foundation seeks to provide material and social assistance to the Guard by help in recruitment, public relations and efforts towards the improvement of the infrastructure of the Guard itself. The Foundation's council is made up of numerous Swiss personalities from the Church, the military, higher education and public life. On May 5, 1999, Pope John Paul II spoke to members of the Swiss Guard, including the new members who would be sworn in the next day. He reminded them of the importance of their spiritual life and of their commitment ''to a very honorable and responsible task in the very heart of the universal Church.''

Bibliography: E. HAMPOOLE, ''The Papal Swiss Guards,'' *American Catholic Quarterly Review* 37 (1912) 286–309, 369–387. L. VON MATT, *Die päpstliche Schweizergarde,* text, P. KRIEG (Zurich 1948). J. REPOND, *Le Costume de la Garde Suisse Pontificale et la Renaissance italienne* (Rome 1917). ''Murder and Suicide, and. . . ,'' *The Catholic World Report* (June 1998) 6–7. D. WILEY, ''The Pope's Private Army,'' *The Tablet* (June 20, 1998) 809–810. *The Columbia Encyclopedia* (6th ed. New York 2001). JOHN PAUL II, ''Use Time in Rome for Christian Growth,'' *L'Osservatore Romano,* Eng. ed. (May 19, 1999):7,. ''The Drama and Drudgery of a Swiss Guard's Life,'' *L'Osservatore Romano* (April 30, 1990) 6–7.

[R. FASTIGGI/E. D. MCSHANE]

SWITHBERT (SUIDBERT, SUITBERT), ST.

Anglo-Saxon bishop and missionary in the Netherlands; d. Kaiserswerth, Germany, *ca.* 713. A Northumbrian by birth, he became a monk and went to Rathmelsigi in Ireland to be under the tutelage of EGBERT OF IONA. He was one of the band who accompanied WILLIBRORD to Frisia in 690 to evangelize the pagans. He labored in the southern part of the present-day Netherlands. In 693 he went back to England to receive consecration as bishop from WILFRED OF YORK. Upon his return he seems to have devoted himself to the conversion of the peoples northeast of the Rhine. Pepin of Heristal gave him an island in the Rhine (modern Kaiserswerth) as a monastic base. During the pagan counterattack on the Rhineland missions, Swithbert retired to his monastery and died there, to be succeeded by (St.) WILLAIK. Evidence of his scholarship exists in a manuscript of Livy now in Vienna, which probably was in his possession and in which he is described as bishop of Duurstede. In ecclesiastical art he is represented as a bishop holding an eight-rayed star between his hands.

Feast: March 1.

Bibliography: BEDE, *Ecclesiastical History* 5.9–11. M. BATESON, *The Dictionary of National Biography from the Earliest Times to 1900*, 63 v. (London 1885–1900; repr. with corrections, 21 v., 1908–09, 1921–22, 1938; suppl. 1901–) 19: 155. F. FLASKAMP, *Suidbercht* (Duderstadt 1930). W. LEVISON, *England and the Continent in the Eighth Century* (Oxford 1946) 57–62. T. SCHIEFFER, *Lexikon für Theologie und Kirche*, ed. J. HOFER and K. RAHNER, 10 v. (2d, new ed. Freiburg 1957–65); suppl., *Das Zweite Vatikanische Konzil: Dokumente und Kommentare*, ed. H. S. BRECHTER et al., pt. 1 (1966) 9:1159.

[J. L. DRUSE]

SWITHIN OF WINCHESTER, ST.

Anglo-Saxon bishop; b. after 802; d. July 2, 862. Educated at Winchester and ordained a priest, he was chosen by King Egbert of Wessex as tutor for his son Ethelwulf. Upon the latter's accession (839) Swithin (Swithun) served as chief spiritual advisor. When Bishop Helmstan died, Swithin was consecrated, with royal approval, for the See of Winchester by Archbishop Ceolnoth of Canterbury on Oct. 30, 852. An energetic and virtuous bishop during very disturbed times, he is remembered especially for a remarkable humility. His cult arose a century after his death in the age of monastic revival. In 971, as the result of a vision, his remains were translated on July 15, 1093, from a neglected grave in the churchyard to the newly restored cathedral, thereafter called St. Swithin's. WILLIAM OF MALMESBURY recounts the bishop's request to be buried ''where the footsteps of passerby and dripping rains from the eaves above would make the spot unpleasant.'' This statement may indicate that St. Swithin's legend already existed in the 12th century: that the weather will continue fair or foul as it is on St. Swithin's day for the next 40 days. His shrine, demolished at the Reformation, was restored in 1962.

Feast: July 2; July 15 (translation); Oct. 29 (ordination, Winchester).

Bibliography: *Acta Sanctorum* July 1:321–37. WILLIAM OF MALMESBURY, *Gesta pontificum Anglorum,* ed. N. E. S. A. HAMILTON *Rerum Britannicarum medii aevi scriptores*, 244 v. (London 1858–96; repr. New York 1964–), ordinarily called Rolls Series (52:1870) 2.75. FLORENCE OF WORCESTER, *Chronicott ex chronicis,* ed. B. THORPE, 2 v. (London 1848–49) 1:68–69, 79, 141. J. EARLE, *Gloucester Fragments,* 2 v. (London 1861) v.1, fac. of some leaves on St. Swithin pub. with elucidations and an essay. AELFRIC, Abbot of Eynsham, *Lives of Three English Saints*, ed. G. I. NEEDHAM (rev. ed. Exeter 1976). J. EARLE, *Gloucester Fragments* (Folcroft, Pa. 1974)

[R. D. WARE]

SWITZERLAND, THE CATHOLIC CHURCH IN

The Swiss Confederation (Helvetica) is a republican federation composed of 22 states or cantons. Located in the central European Alps, Switzerland borders Germany on the north, Austria and Liechtenstein on the east, Italy on the south and France on the west. A landlocked, mountainous region possessing many rivers and lakes, Switzerland encompasses the Jura Mountains in the west and the Swiss Alps in the south and east; the highest point in Switzerland is at 15,217 ft. A central plateau region is characterized by rolling hills leveling to plains. The climate is temperate, with humid summers. Agricultural products include wheat, rye, sugar beets, tobacco and wine. Natural resources consist of timber and salt. International banking and tourism account for much of Switzerland's gross domestic product.

Switzerland under Roman Rule. The territory of modern Switzerland has no recorded history prior to the Roman conquest. The first identifiable inhabitants, the Gallic Helvetians, were defeated by Julius Caesar near present-day Autun in 58 B.C. and thereby incorporated into the Roman Empire. The mountain tribes in the east were not conquered until the time of Augustus (15 B.C.), after which Latin language and civilization spread rapidly, especially in the west. Roman occupation lasted for 500 years, with government seated at Aventicum (Avenches). The more important centers were the colony of Augusta Raurica, near present-day Basel, and the military camp of Vindonissa (now Windisch). Well-built roads that stretched throughout the country were strategically important for the Romans, especially in a border and buffer province against the Germanic tribes.

Beginnings of Christianity. The first Christian missions to Switzerland occurred under Roman rule, the first witness to the gospel coming most likely from zealous Christians who reached Helvetia as merchants, artisans or even slaves. While Christianity had already gained a foothold in some places as early as the 3d century, the first documented traces of the Christian faith date from the 4th century, when the Roman Empire in the West was becoming progressively Christianized. Several 20th-century archeological discoveries point to a gradual penetration of the country by Christianity. The earliest Christian monuments that can be dated are two monograms of Christ, the first on a fibula found in 1958 in a tomb in Basel, the second on the inscription of Pontius Asclepiodotus, dating from A.D. 377, now in the town hall in Sion. The oldest Christian church known to exist in Switzerland was a chapel built by Bishop Theodore of Octodurus, between 386 and 392, over the tomb of the THEBAN martyrs in Agaunum (*see* SAINT-MAURICE, ABBEY OF). The fragmentary remains of the oldest altar on Swiss territory were discovered in the late Roman church of St. Germanus in Geneva and dated from about A.D. 400.

The 346 decrees of an anti-Arian synod of Colonia Agrippina (Cologne) were signed by Justinianus, Bishop of the Rauraci. Geneva, as capital of an administrative district (*Civitas Genavensium*), also had its bishop, the first-known being Isaac, *c.* A.D. 400. Chur likely had a bishop as early as the 4th century, since it was the seat of government for the Province of Rhaetia I from 310. However, the first mention of a bishop in Chur, Asinio by name, dates from A.D. 451. No names of early bishops were recorded for Aventicum, capital of the *Civitas*

Capital: Bern.
Size: 15,944 sq. miles.
Population: 7,262,372 in 2000.
Languages: German; French, Italian, Romansh are spoken in various regions.
Religions: 3,195,572 Catholics (44%), 2,905,048 Protestants (40%), other 1,161,752 (15%), 508,365 without religious affiliation.
Dioceses: Basel, Chur, Lausanne-Geneva-Fribourg, Lugano, Sankt Gallen, and Sion, all of which are immediately subject to the Holy See. In addition, there are two exempt abbeys: Saint-Maurice and Maria Einsiedeln. The Diocese of Chur, which formerly included Liechtenstein Catholics in its domain, was redistricted by the Vatican in 1997.

Helvetiorum, because Aventicum was sacked by the Alamanni in 265 and 350 and the whole region was devastated from the 5th century. During the 5th and 6th centuries Helvetian bishops resided in the stronghold of Vindonissa.

Traces of Christianity are more numerous from the 5th century onward, and have been discovered in excavated strongholds and *castra* built by the Romans from the 4th century as defenses against the advancing Germanic tribes and containing small Christian churches. In all probability there were small late Roman churches also within the fortification walls of other strongholds, such as Oberwinterthur, Irgenhausen, Solothurn and Yverdon.

Christianity during the Barbarian Invasions. Located at the heart of Europe, Switzerland was affected by the invasions of the Barbarian nations, which inspired its linguistic and cultural character. Helvetica was settled gradually by two radically divergent and mutually hostile peoples: from the north the pagan Alamanni advanced to take possession of the central portion; from the west the Burgundians penetrated into Switzerland. But the advance of these two peoples developed in quite different fashion. In the west, Roman General Aetius settled the Burgundians (after A.D. 400) as military colonists in Sapaudia to protect the Empire against new thrusts by the Germanic tribes, and these Burgundians rapidly adopted the Latin language and civilization. They were Arians (*see* ARIANISM) who identified more with the older Catholic Gallo-Roman population than with the pagan Alamanni. Burgundian King SIGISMUND (d. 524) converted to Catholicism and restored the monastery of Saint-Maurice at Agaune in 515, thus helping Christianity gain a firm foothold in the west through monastic foundations. Sigismund's convocation of a Burgundian imperial council at Epao in 517 was further evidence that Christianity persisted without a break in that part of Switzerland settled by the Burgundians.

Central Switzerland as far as the Alps, and in some places even beyond, was occupied by the Alamanni in a much less peaceful fashion. The Alamanni advanced into the region only after being defeated by the FRANKS under CLOVIS in A.D. 496–497. Through a slow infiltration of clans and individual families, they occupied the area to the Reuss, and later to the Saane, making that river the dividing line between German and French speech. Because the Alamanni at first avoided the walled Roman towns, Christianity continued to survive more or less precariously along with Roman institutions in such late Roman strongholds as Arbon, Eschenz, Pfyn, Oberwinterthur, Pfäffikon, Zurich, Vindonissa (an episcopal see), Zurzach, Augst, Basel, Olten, Solothurn and Aventicum. During this period Grammatius signed decrees of the two synods of Orléans (541 and 549) as bishop of the *civitas* and church of Vindonissa. The episcopal See of Vindonissa was later transferred to Aventicum and thence to Lausanne. Meanwhile, the Alamanni extended their military expeditions into northern Vaud. The monastery of Romainmôtier and the church erected in 587 in Payerne were destroyed *c.* 600 as a result of Alamanni attacks.

The valleys of Churrhaetia withstood the advancing Alamanni, thus maintaining their Romance dialects, Romansh and Ladin, and Christianity persisted without a break. From the 6th to the 8th century the office of governor and that of bishop were in the hands of the powerful family of the Victoridae.

The occupation of Switzerland by Germanic tribes split the region into three political units—Burgundy, Alamannia and Churrhaetia—which continued to exist after the Franks added Switzerland to their growing Empire, subjugated the Alamanni (496), then the Burgundians (534) and finally Churrhaetia (536). The three areas enjoyed a certain independence under the MEROVINGIANS (481–752) and, to some extent, even under the CAROLINGIAN DYNASTY.

Conversion of Alamannic Switzerland. While the Alamanni repressed Christianity in the areas they had occupied, they did not annihilate it. Nevertheless, the Alamannic portion of Switzerland had to be Christianized a second time, in contrast with Burgundy and Churrhaetia. This conversion, undertaken by Irish and Frankish monks, progressed very slowly between the 6th and 9th centuries, the achievement of St. GALL and the Irish FRIDOLIN being most notable However, the gradual conversion of the Alamanni was due less to the effort of individual missionaries than to the permeation of the country by Christian settlers from the Frankish kingdom and the activity of the monasteries. As early as the 7th century, the monasteries of Moutier, Grandval, Saint Ursanne, and Vermes had been established in the Swiss Jura

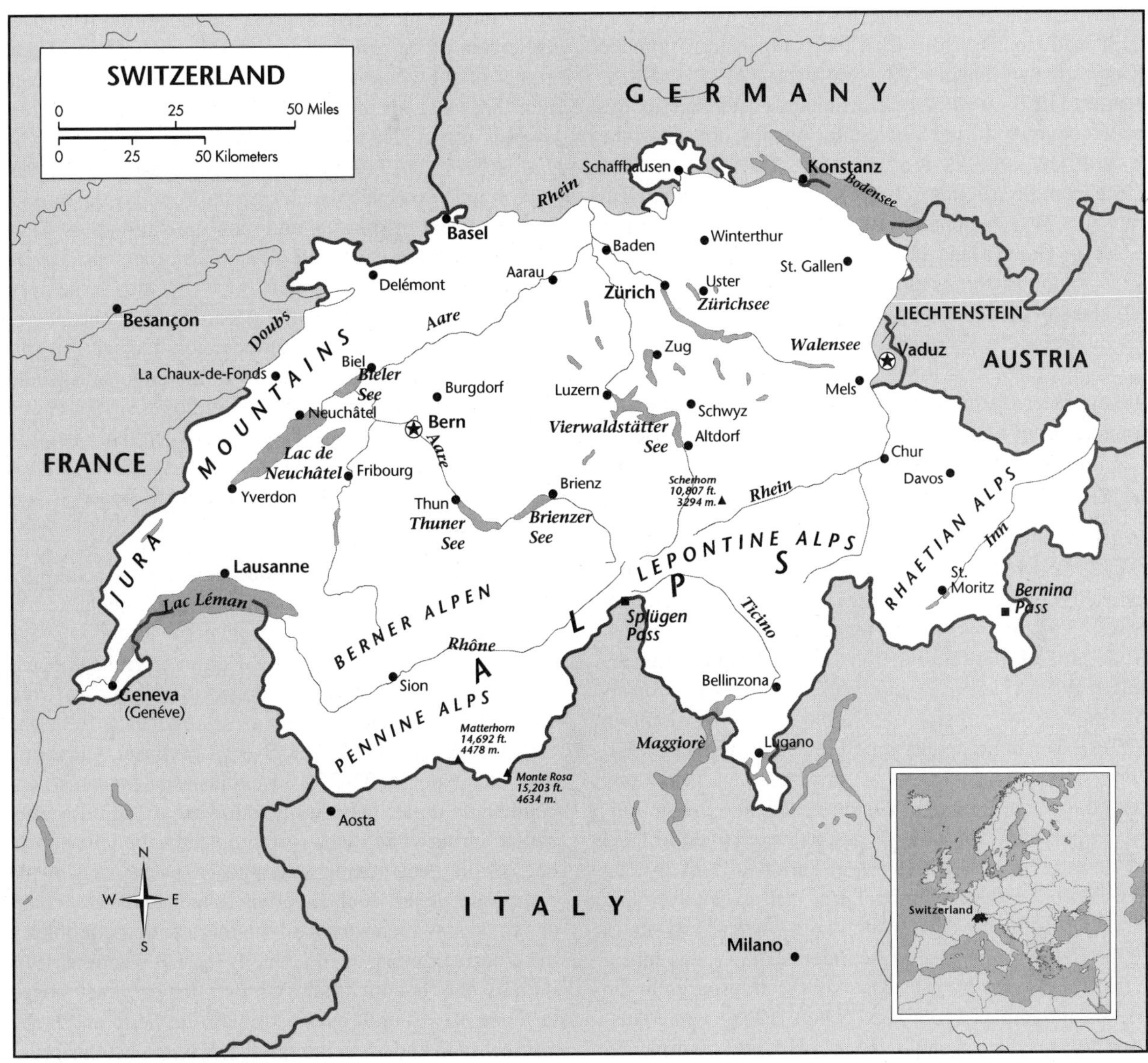

area from LUXEUIL, Columban's chief foundation. SANKT GALLEN was the most important monastery in the eastern region, while the abbey founded about 724 on the Island of REICHENAU by St. Pirmin was also influential. The Monastery of DISENTIS was founded in the 8th century via the Lukmanier, a Benedictine monastery was founded in Lucerne about the middle of the 8th century, and the Abbey of EINSIEDELN was founded in 934. The Diocese of Constance, founded in the early 7th century, became the bastion of Christianity among the Alamanni.

Switzerland in the Middle Ages. Initially Switzerland was a part of the Carolingian Empire. With the collapse of the Carolingians, Burgundy became independent in 888. Alamannia claimed independence in 917 as the Duchy of Swabia, but as early as 919 was incorporated into the new German Empire, along with Burgundy in 1033. Thenceforth the entire territory of present-day Switzerland was a part of the German Empire (*see* HOLY ROMAN EMPIRE). The six ancient dioceses of Basel, Lausanne, Geneva, Sion, Chur and Constance, which had been founded by the early 7th century, remained essentially intact throughout the Middle Ages, the only changes being in diocesan boundaries and assignment of metropolitan sees. The CLUNIAC REFORM penetrated into Switzerland as early as the 10th century. Romainmôtier joined the monastic federation and experienced a new upsurge. The Burgundian Queen Bertha founded Payerne as a Cluniac monastery (962). The Monastery of All Saints in Schaffhausen received the Customs of Cluny in 1079 from the south German reform Monastery of HIRSAU. MURI was founded in 1027 and Engelberg in 1120.

The CISTERCIANS also made foundations in Switzerland. In 1123 BERNARD OF CLAIRVAUX sent 12 monks to

Bonmont near Nyon, while HAUTERIVE was settled in 1138 with monks from Cherlieu, who in turn founded Kappel on the Elbe in 1183. Saint Urban (1190) and WETTINGEN (1227) were the most famous Cistercian abbeys of the country. In the 13th century, many houses of the MENDICANT ORDERS were founded. The FRANCISCANS came from Strasbourg to Basel in 1231; they were in Zurich in 1240, in Schaffhausen before 1253, in Bern in 1255, in Geneva and Fribourg in 1256, in Lausanne in 1256, and in Lucerne before 1269. POOR CLARES were established in Paradies, above Schaffhausen in 1235 and in Kleinbasel at St. Klara in 1275. The double MONASTERY of Königsfelden was founded in 1310 by the consort and the daughter of the murdered Emperor Albert. The Dominicans made foundations in Zurich in 1229, Basel in 1233, Lausanne in 1234, Geneva in 1262, Bern in 1269, Chur in 1277 and Zofingen in 1286 (*see* DOMINICANS).

Origin of the Swiss League. The Swiss League, or *Eidgenossenschaft,* was founded during a time of upheaval following the overthrow of the Hohenstaufen Emperors. The cantons on the Vierwaldstättersee recognized Rudolph I of Hapsburg as ruler of the Empire after the Interregnum (1250–73), but refused to become subjects of a HAPSBURG principality. On the death of Rudolph in 1291, a pact in perpetuity renewed between Schwyz, Uri and Nidwalden to throw off the Austrian hegemony served as the founding document of the Swiss *Eidgenossenschaft.* These three cantons were joined in 1332 by Lucerne, in 1351 by the city of Zurich, in 1352 by Zug and Glarus, and in 1353 by Bern, then a rapidly rising city, to become the eight cantons and cities or city-states of the Eidgenossenschaft. Federation territory was subsequently extended by victories over the Hapsburgs in the battles of Sempach (1386) and Näfels (1388), while Austrian Aargau was conquered in 1415 and Thurgau in 1460. To these initial ''Common Domains,'' others were later added, reaching into southern Switzerland (Ticino), as well as the abbey and city of Sankt Gallen (Saint Gallen), the Toggenburg and the cities of Solothurn, Fribourg and Biel, which formed the so-called ''associates'' (*Zugewandten*). During the Burgundian Wars (1474–77) the confederates eliminated Burgundy as a major power. Solothurn and Fribourg joined the confederacy in 1481, and in the Swabian War (1499), the confederates made themselves *de facto* free of the German Empire. In the north, Basel and Schaffhausen joined the confederacy in 1501, and Appenzell joined in 1513. Thus the confederacy of 13 members took definite form. In 1536 Bern conquered the Vaud from Savoy, expanding the Eidgenossenschaft into the form it would maintain until the French Revolution of 1798.

The Church in the Old Confederation. After the rise of the Eidgenossenschaft, ecclesiastical relations altered only to the extent that the confederation took over the rights of the Austrian archdukes; the privileges and rights of the churches and monasteries were respected and there was no illegal seizure of Church property. Of special importance to the position of the Church was the *Pfaffenbrief* of 1370, an accord that forbade any appeal to foreign, especially ecclesiastical, courts via foreign clerics except in spiritual and matrimonial matters. During the WESTERN SCHISM (1378–1418), the confederates initially adhered to the Roman pope and later to the pope of the Pisan obedience, while Austria was on the side of the Avignon popes. The confederates managed in this way to secure new privileges from the pope, and would later be particularly successful under Popes SIXTUS IV and JULIUS II, who were dependent on Swiss military help. In 1506 the 100-member SWISS GUARD was formed by Pope Julius II as the personal bodyguard of the pope.

The Reformation in Switzerland. In Switzerland, as in neighboring Germany, conditions for a schism were present in the 16th century. Continuing efforts at reform begun in the late 15th century had come to nothing. The efforts of Bishop of Constance, Hugo von Hohenlandenberg (1496–1532) at reform during the Synod of Constance in 1497 encountered great resistance from the clergy of Switzerland. The Bishop of Basel, Christoph von Utenheim (1502–27), an enthusiastic humanist, encountered similar opposition following a 1503 diocesan synod during which were promulgated excellent reform decrees: implementation was opposed, particularly by the cathedral chapter. Such experiences incited the city councils to occupy themselves all the more with the problems of reform, although such councils did not desire, at least initially, any break with the Church. Instead, they hoped to renew the Church by prescribing the Scripture as the norm of faith and of divine service. It is against this background that the Reformation in Switzerland must be understood.

Martin Luther was in the foreground of the Reformation, and it was only later that Huldrych ZWINGLI, the real reformer of German Switzerland, took Luther's place. Zwingli began by criticizing liturgical customs and practices not founded on Scripture and by attacking genuine abuses. He hoped to advance his cause in Zurich by means of two religious debates in 1523. The new doctrine was then introduced in Zurich the following year, after wholesale and ruthless destruction of images. The monasteries were dissolved, and in 1525 celebration of the Mass was forbidden. From Zurich the new doctrine spread especially in east Switzerland; the original cantons of Lucerne, Zug and Fribourg, however, rejected it decisively. At their instigation, the diet announced a religious debate whereby the Catholic localities hoped, with the help of the state, to preserve religious unity against

Zwingli by theological argument. The religious debate took place in mid-1526, in Baden and ended with the triumph of the Catholics.

Zwingli won his greatest triumph when Bern, the largest member of the Eidgenossenschaft, introduced the Reformation in 1528. Bern's example set the style for Basel which went over to the new doctrine in 1529; Schaffhausen embraced the new faith in the same year as Basel. However, Zwingli's attempt to advance the Reformation by force in central Switzerland was repulsed in the second battle near Kappel (1531), where he was killed. The defeat of the Reformers at Zwingli's death put an end to the spread of the Reformation in German Switzerland and ensured the continued existence of the Catholic faith in dependent areas as well.

In west Switzerland the Reformation was closely connected with the struggle of the city of Geneva to free itself from the Dukes of Savoy, who had filled the episcopal See of Geneva with princes of their house since the 15th century. To obtain freedom from Savoy, Geneva attached itself to Bern, under which protection the new faith was proclaimed first in Neuenburg (1530) and then in Geneva, which openly adopted it in 1535. After Savoy tried to subdue the city by force of arms, Bern rushed to Geneva's aid, conquered Vaud in 1536 and introduced the new doctrine there as well. Reformer John CALVIN would later make Geneva the center of international Protestantism.

Counter Reformation and the Last Wars of Religion. Before the Council of TRENT, reform in Catholic regions was in the hands of the secular governments where it did not make the progress it should have made. Then, in 1570 the Archbishop of Milan, Charles BORROMEO, as "Protector of Catholic Switzerland," visited the interior of Switzerland, and turning the tide for Catholic reform. Borromeo sent JESUITS into Switzerland to found colleges in Lucerne (1574), Fribourg (1582, by St. Peter CANISIUS), Pruntrut (1591), Pollegio (1622), Sion (1625), Bellinzona (1646), Brig (1662) and Solothurn (1668). The Archbishop did not rest until the Catholic regions had been given a papal nuncio of their own. Giovanni Francesco Bonhomini worked in Switzerland from 1579–81 as first nuncio; he tried to implement the Tridentine reform and also promoted the entry of the Capuchin FRANCISCANS into the region. Capuchin monasteries were founded in Altdorf (1581), Stans (1582), Lucerne (1583), Schwyz (1585), Solothurn and Appenzell (1588), Baden (1593), Frauenfeld and Zug (1595) and elsewhere. The most outstanding reform bishops were Christopher BLARER of Wartensee in Basel (1575–1608) and St. FRANCIS DE SALES in Geneva (1602–22).

This period saw alliances form between the Catholic cantons and Savoy (1577) and with Bishop Blarer of Basel (1579). Especially important was the mutual defensive pact of the seven Catholic cantons, the Golden League (1586), and the alliance with Spain's King Philip II (1587).

The reformed cantons developed still closer ties with the Alsatian cities of Mühlhausen and Strasbourg, prompting a deep-seated opposition that led finally to the two Wars of Religion of Villmergen (1656–1712). By the terms of the peace that marked their conclusion the five Catholic cantons lost administrative control of important subject territories. The division of Switzerland into two confessional camps extended into the 18th century; it was only under the influence of the ENLIGHTENMENT, which came to Switzerland from France, that "enlightened" Catholics began to collaborate with "enlightened" Protestants in matters of Swiss culture and politics. ABSOLUTISM, JOSEPHINISM, and the ideal of a state-controlled church also were imitated in Switzerland. The Lucerne statesman J. A. F. Balthasar (d. 1810) composed the treatise *De Helvetiorum iuribus circa sacra,* in which he attempted to formulate a code of Church-State law for the country. The disastrous effects of this treatise would be revealed only too clearly in the ecclesiastico-political strife of the 19th century.

Fall of the Old Confederation. The old order in Switzerland collapsed in 1798 under the influence of the revolutionary upheavals in neighboring France. France invaded Switzerland, imposed a new constitution, and proclaimed the Helvetian Republic, consisting of 19 cantons enjoying equal rights. The Helvetic constitution (1798–1802), distinguished by its anti-ecclesiastical and antireligious spirit, caused all monasteries to be dissolved and their holdings to be declared national property. As a result, more than 130 monasteries were nearly forced out of existence. In 1803 a new constitution, the Act of Mediation imposed by Napoleon I, restored the old confederation of states and added six new cantons to the earlier 13: Saint Gallen, Graubünden, Aargau, Thurgau, Vaud and Ticino. Most of the monasteries were restored; only the Abbey of Sankt Gallen remained suppressed. Unfortunately, the Church's situation was less favorable than it had been before the revolution, as Napoleon reintroduced State control of the Church.

The 19th Century and the Kulturkampf. After the political upheavals of the 18th century, diocesan boundaries were redrawn with the aim of separating various nationalities and native bishops were placed in charge. In 1815, to checkmate the influence of the Vicar-General of Constance, Ignaz von WESSENBERG, Pius VII detached the Swiss part of the Diocese of Constance and placed it under an administrator. The Diocese of Basel was erected in 1828; its seven cantons included parts of the Swiss section formerly belonging to Constance and the remains of the prince bishopric of Basel. Urschweiz was provisionally placed under the administration of the bishop of Chur in 1819. Saint Gallen and Chur united in 1823 to form a double diocese, but this union was dissolved in 1836, when Saint Gallen became a separate bishopric. In western Switzerland the canton of Geneva was placed under the bishop of Lausanne (1819), but the episcopal residence remained at Fribourg, whose collegiate church of St. Nicholas became the cathedral in 1924. The canton of Ticino belonged to the Dioceses of Como and Milan until 1884; four years later it became an administration apostolic, with its own bishop.

During the Kulturkampf (1870–86), Church activities were severely restricted by the liberalism and radicalism dominant in many cantons, and Catholics polarized into ultramontanes and Catholic liberals. The Baden Articles (1834) were a concerted effort to subordinate the Church to the State, and although condemned by Pope Gregory XVI attempts by some cantons to implement them let to further conflicts. Monasteries were dissolved in the canton of Aargau in 1841, whereas Lucerne called in the Jesuits in 1844 to take over the theological college. In 1845 the Catholic cantons concluded an alliance (*Sonderbund*) to defend religious liberty, and their refusal to dissolve this alliance led to a civil war in which they were defeated (1847). As a result, more monasteries were dissolved, and the Jesuits were banned from Switzerland. The federal constitution, adopted in 1874 during the Kulturkampf, contained special decrees regulating the Catholic Church. Dioceses could be erected only with the federal government's approval. New monasteries could not be created, nor could dissolved monasteries be restored. Liberals and radicals so harassed the Catholic minority that for a long time the Church was forced into a purely defensive position.

In defense of the Church and its interests, Catholics founded a great variety of associations and organizations. Most important were the Pius Verein (1857) and the Society for Home Missions (1863), the latter which devoted itself mainly to Catholics in the diaspora. Despite their losses, Catholics developed new enterprises. The outstanding social apostle Theodosius FLORENTINI founded the Teaching Sisters of the Holy Cross in 1844 and the Sisters of Mercy of the Holy Cross in 1856, which grew to be the largest congregations of women in the country. Over 1,000 new churches were built in the diaspora regions. A Christian worker movement developed, and the Union of Fribourg, founded under the leadership of the future Cardinal MERMILLOD, did preliminary work toward resolving the worker question. To replace the suppressed Jesuit colleges, new schools were started by Benedictines, Capuchins, Augustinian Canons and secular priests. The most important educational accomplishment was the foundation of the Catholic University of Fribourg by Georges Python in 1889.

The Modern Church. Despite the suppressions of the 19th century, many religious houses remained in operation by 1900. The BETHLEHEM FATHERS engaged in foreign mission work, while Switzerland's brothers and sisters conducted numerous Catholic schools on the primary and secondary levels. During the 20th century, aided by Switzerland's position of neutrality during both world wars, the missions gained in strength, and by 2000 there were 300 brothers and 7,000 sisters tending to humanitarian needs in orphanages, hospitals and other outreach centers. In 1920 a papal nuncio was established in Bern. Three Catholic colleges educated Catholic teachers. The University of Fribourg maintained a Faculty of Catholic Theology, Lucerne. Catholic seminaries existed in Chur, Fribourg, Lugano, Lucerne, Sion, Solothurn and Sankt. The bishops' conference met twice annually.

The Industrialization of the late 19th century caused large population movements, one result of which was a notable intermingling of religious groups in the cantons. In most, the Catholic Church was among the officially recognized regional Churches (*Landeskirchen*) and enjoyed the right to a church levy in those cantons that imposed it. (Ironically, during the 1990s church membership declined as some Swiss renounced membership in their church as a means of avoiding payment of this tax.) Despite the exclusion article in the federal constitution of May 29, 1874, the Church was free to develop associations, the two largest being the Swiss Catholic Volksverein and the Swiss Catholic Women's League, both supporters of Catholic Action. The faith predominate in the canton was taught in public schools, although students would be exempted at the request of their parent.

By 2000 there were 1,691 parishes in Switzerland, with 1,950 secular and 1,392 religious priests working among them. In the late 1990s both the Church and the Swiss government addressed the issues surrounding the Holocaust era, as accusations surfaced regarding anti-Semitism, the redistribution of Jewish-held property during World War II and the closing of Swiss borders to Jewish refugees in 1942. In 1997 the Swiss bishops admitted that the Church was once hostile to Jews, but noted that ''we admit the guilt that occurred then and ask the heirs of those affected for forgiveness, as Pope John Paul II has done in light of [Jubilee 2000].'' The government continued to support freedom of religion, although by the late 1990s the activities of Scientologists and the appearance of more than 400 denominations in the region prompted requests for the regulation of sects.

Bibliography: H. BARTH, *Bibliographie der Schweizer Geschichte . . . bis Ende 1912,* 3 v. (Basel 1914–15); *Bibliographie der*

Schweizergeschichte, 1913–1919, as suppl. to *Anzeiger für schweizerische Geschichte;* 1920– as suppl. to *Zeitschrift für schweizerische Geschichte.* H. AMMANN and K. SCHIB, *Historischer Atlas der Schweiz* (2d ed. Aarau 1958). H. NABHOLZ et al., *Geschichte der Schweiz,* 2 v. (Zurich 1932–38). T. SCHWEGLER, *Geschichte der katholischen Kirche in der Schweiz* (2d ed. Stans 1943). F. STAEHELIN, *Die Schweiz in römischer Zeit* (3d ed. Basel 1948); *Die Schweiz im Frühmittelalter* (*Repertorium der Ur- und Frühgeschichte der Schweiz,* 5; Basel 1959). R. PFISTER, *Kirchengeschichte der Schweiz,* v.1 *Von den Anfängen bis zum Ausgang des Mittelalters* (Zurich 1964). O. VASELLA, *Reform und Reformation in der Schweiz* (Münster 1958). J. G. MAYER, *Das Konzil von Trient und die Gegenreformation in der Schweiz,* 2 v. (Stans 1901–03). F. STEFFENS and H. REINHARDT, *Die Nuntiatur des G. F. Bonhomini, 1579–1581,* 4 v. (Solothurn 1906–29). A. CHÈVRE, *Jacques-Christoph Blarer de Wartensee* (Bibliothèque Jurassienne 5; Delémont 1963). U. LAMPERT, *Kirche und Staat in der Schweiz,* 3 v. (Basel 1929–39), F. STROBEL, *Die Jesuiten und die Schweiz im 19. Jahrhundert* (Freiburg 1954). K. S. LATOURETTE, *Christianity in a Revolutionary Age: A History of Christianity in the Nineteenth and Twentieth Centuries,* 5 v. (New York 1958–62) v.1, 2, 4. B. MEYER and R. PFISTER, *Die Religion in Geschichte und Gegenwart*[3], 7 v. (3d ed. Tübingen 1957–65) 5:1608–18. F. EHRLER *Lexikon für Theologie und Kirche*[2], eds., J. HOFER and K. RAHNER, 10 v. (2d, new ed. Freiburg 1957–65) 9:541–545. *Bilan du Monde,* 2:809–817. *Annuario Pontificio* has annual data on all dioceses.

[J. B. VILLIGER/EDS.]

SWORD OF THE SPIRIT

A movement founded in October 1940, by Cardinal Arthur HINSLEY, Archbishop of Westminster; its objectives were to uphold the British cause in World War II, to combat the evils of totalitarianism, and to unite all men of good will to secure a Christian peace. Through lectures and discussion groups, it caught the imagination and gained the support of many non-Catholics as well as Catholics. Groups were formed among the Allies and eventually there were French, Belgian, Polish, and Czech sections. Unfortunately, the Catholic body in England was not prepared for the movement, and Cardinal Hinsley, having launched it without prior consultation with other members of the hierarchy, found their support lacking in enthusiasm. The original inspiration came from Christopher Dawson, and the movement rallied the best of the Catholic laity in Britain.

The climax of this effort in Christian cooperation was reached in 1942 in the form of a joint pledge by the Church of England, the Church of Scotland, the Free Churches, and the Sword of the Spirit, to work ''through parallel action in the religious field, and joint action in the sphere of social and international ethics.'' After the war the movement's influence declined (as did cooperation), but it was revived in 1950 when Cardinal Bernard GRIFFIN, Hinsley's successor, gave it a new mandate: to educate Catholics in international affairs. Since then it has concentrated on spreading information—through public meetings, publication of literature, and organization of high school groups—concerning European unity, aid to developing countries, and the United Nations.

[J. E. FITZSIMONS]

SYKES, EDMUND, BL.

Priest, martyr; b. at Leeds, Yorkshire, England; hanged, drawn, and quartered March 23, 1587 at Tyburn in York. He completed his seminary studies at Rheims, where he was ordained in 1581. He labored in his native Yorkshire until 1585 when he was betrayed by an apostate, Arthur Webster. He was captured and imprisoned for about six months in the York Kidcot. Weakened by an illness, he consented to attend a Protestant service, but he refused to do so a second time. Banished to the Continent, he made his way to Rome. He made his way back to England in June of 1586 and six months later, he was betrayed by his brother in whose home he was apprehended. He was held as prisoner at York Castle until arraignment at the Lenten assizes, when he was condemned for his priesthood. He was beatified by Pope John Paul II on Nov. 22, 1987 with George HAYDOCK and companions.

Feast of the English Martyrs: May 4 (England).

See Also: ENGLAND, SCOTLAND, AND WALES, MARTYRS OF.

Bibliography: R. CHALLONER, *Memoirs of Missionary Priests,* ed. J. H. POLLEN (rev. ed. London 1924). J. MORRIS, ed., *The Troubles of Our Catholic Forefathers Related by Themselves,* 3 v. (London 1872–77), v. 3. J. H. POLLEN, *Acts of English Martyrs* (London 1891).

[K. I. RABENSTEIN]

SYLLABUS OF ERRORS

''Syllabus of Errors'' is the shortened version of the title of a document issued together with the encyclical *QUANTA CURA* on Dec. 8, 1864, containing errors condemned by Pius IX. The full title is: ''A syllabus containing the most important errors of our time which have been condemned by our Holy Father Pius IX in allocutions, at consistories, in encyclicals and other apostolic letters.''

History. Pope Pius IX was petitioned by the Provincial Council of Spoleto in 1849 to draw up a constitution that would list the principal prevailing errors and condemn them. In 1852 he commissioned Cardinal Fornari to formulate the list; the cardinal enumerated 28 errors, but two years later the project was transferred to the commission that had drawn up the bull defining the Immaculate Conception. This work was abruptly ended when in 1860 P. Gerbet, Bishop of Perpignan, published in his diocese a ''pastoral instruction on various errors of the present''; this document with its 85 theses so satisfied the Pope that he organized a new commission under the leadership of Cardinal Caterini to formulate a syllabus with this instruction as its framework. This new commission drew up a list of 61 errors with their theological qualifications. It was presented for approbation to an assembly of 300 bishops gathered in Rome for the canonization of the Japanese Martyrs in 1862. The anticlerical Turin newspaper *Il Mediatore* disclosed the errors and their theological notes and caused a storm of hostility against the Church; thus Pius IX refrained from promulgating this list. A new commission was appointed and compiled the final syllabus of 80 theses (H. Denzinger, *Enchiridion symbolorum,* 2901–2980); the wording of the errors was drawn from the allocutions, encyclicals, and apostolic letters of Pius IX. When the syllabus was sent to the bishops of the world, it was accompanied by an official communication from the secretary of state, Cardinal Antonelli; it was not signed by Pius IX.

The publication raised a furor that had been long expected. The Italian and French governments allowed the press to publish and comment upon it, but denied the ecclesiastical authorities equal freedom in explaining the propositions; and so misconceptions about the condemned errors became widespread, especially since many of the errors had specific reference to the Italian situation. For example, condemned proposition 80 reads: ''The Roman pontiff can and should reconcile and harmonize himself with progress, with liberalism, and with recent civilization.'' This condemnation was drawn from the allocution *Jamdudum cernimus* (March 18, 1861), which had reference to the Piedmontese government's idea of progress and civilization, i.e., closing of religious houses, enforcement of secular education, secularism, and anticlericalism. Other nations had different views on progress, liberalism, and civilization, and misinterpreted the meaning of the pope; Catholics became confused about some of these condemnations, although many were very clear, e.g., those with reference to the denial of Christ's divinity and to atheism.

Contents. The syllabus is composed of ten sections under which the 80 theses are arranged: (1) pantheism, naturalism, and absolute rationalism (theses 1–7); (2) moderate rationalism (8–14); (3) indifferentism and religious latitudinarianism (15–18); (4) a paragraph condemning socialism, communism, secret societies, Bible societies, and clerical-liberal societies; (5) errors about the Church and its rights (19–38); (6) errors on the State and its relation to the Church (39–55); (7) errors on natural and Christian ethics (56–64); (8) errors on Christian matrimony (65–74); (9) errors on the temporal power of the pope (75–76); and (10) errors of modern liberalism (77–80).

The condemned propositions under the first heading either identify God with the universe or totally exclude God from it (No. 2) and exalt human reason in a way that does away with revelation; e.g., ''All the truths of religion derive from the natural force of human reason; hence reason is the principal norm by which man can and must attain knowledge of all truths of any kind whatever'' (No. 4). The condemned propositions of the second title, however, exaggerate the possibilities and independence of philosophy to such an extent that they would admit of no judge of philosophy, whether it be the Church or supernatural revelation. The Church is accused of preventing the advance of science, holding onto archaic methods and principles of theology that do not meet the needs of the times. The indifferentism condemned in section 3 places all religions on a par with one another as means of salvation. The condemned propositions of section 5 deny the freedom of the Church and its nature as a true and perfect society, subjecting it rather to the laws and authority of the State. The Church's power solemnly to define its unicity is denied (No. 21). Temporal power, direct or indirect, is refused the Church (No. 24) as well as any native right to acquire and possess any material goods (No. 26). Bishops have no right to promulgate apostolic letters without permission of the government (No. 28), the ecclesiastical and clerical immunities are said to originate from civil law alone (No. 30), and clerical exemption from military service can be abrogated if civil progress so requires (No. 32). The inherent right of the Church alone to direct the teaching of sacred doctrine is denied (No. 33), and it is asserted that national Churches, freed of the authority of the Roman pontiff, can be established (No. 37). This section of the syllabus is the longest because of the contemporary widespread attack on these rights of the Church.

The errors enumerated in section 6 about civil society are numerous for the same reason. The State is granted limitless power in them because it is the origin and font of all rights (No. 39), and among them is at least an indirect negative power in matters of religion (Nos. 41, 44). Civil law must always prevail in conflicts of the power of Church and State (No. 42). The State has the right to rescind concordats concerning ecclesiastical immunities without seeking the consent of the Holy See (No. 43). The State has the exclusive right to decide all questions in schools in which Christian youth are educated (No. 45), and even the method of studies used in seminaries is subject to civil authority (No. 46). The right of civil authority to prevent bishops and the faithful from communicating with the pope is asserted (No. 49). Lay authority per se has the right to present bishops, install them, and depose them (Nos. 50, 51) and is not obliged to obey the laws of the Church as regards the constitution of bishops. The government is able in its own right to change the laws of the Church concerning ages for religious profession and to demand that its permission be sought before anyone be admitted to solemn vows (No. 52). Kings and princes are exempted from the jurisdiction of the Church (No. 54), and there must be separation of Church and State (No. 55).

Among the errors on ethics, it is stated that human laws do not need to conform to the law of nature or to receive divine sanction (No. 56); only those powers rooted in matter are to be acknowledged (No. 58), and authority is nothing other than numbers and the sum of material powers (No. 60). It is licit to rebel and withdraw obedience from legitimate princes (No. 63). The errors in section 8 about Christian matrimony would deny the sacramental character of matrimony, asserting that the sacramental aspect consists in a blessing only (No. 66). The matrimonial bond is said to be dissoluble of its very nature, and the State can allow divorce in the strict sense (No. 67). Only civil authority has the right to state diriment matrimonial impediments; those that the Church determined were done so not by the authority of the Church, but by the power received from the State (Nos. 68, 69). The canons of the Council of Trent censuring those who deny the Church the right to declare diriment impediments either are not dogmatic or must be understood in the sense of the Church's power coming from the State (No. 70). The form of marriage determined by Trent does not oblige, under pain of invalidity, if the State has decided upon another form (No. 71). Matrimonial cases by nature are to be adjudicated in civil courts (No. 74).

The two errors in section 9 say that the compatibility of the temporal with the spiritual power of the pope is disputed among Catholics (No. 75) and that the abrogation of the civil power that the Holy See has acquired would be most conducive to the liberty and well-being of the Church (No. 76). In the final part against liberalism, error 77 reads that it is no longer expedient that the Catholic religion be the only religion of the State, and proposition 78 commends the fact that in some regions Catholic in name, laws provide that immigrants may publicly exercise any cult they choose.

Interpretation. The interpretation of these theses requires examination of the writings of Pope Pius IX from which they were compiled and of the condemned books in which they were originally found; otherwise grave misinterpretations will result. For example, the clerical-liberal societies condemned in thesis 18 refer to those government-supported groups of the Piedmontese clergy opposed to the papal attitude against the closure of monasteries, etc.; by ignoring the context of this thesis some have thought it was directed against Montalembert and his followers in France. Condemned proposition 15 reads: ''Everyone is free to adopt and profess that religion which he, guided by the light of reason, holds to be true.'' The meaning of this proposition, contained in the apostolic letter *Multiplices inter* of June 10, 1851, is that given by Vigil, a Peruvian priest, in his *Defensa.* Vigil asserted that man was to rely on his own powers of reason and not on the authority of God in the acceptance of religious truths, and it is in this sense alone that thesis 15 must be understood; for when the words are considered by themselves apart from the context, they contain a truth.

Theologians dispute the authority of the condemnations in the syllabus itself, although there is unanimity that the errors are condemned if not in the syllabus, at least in the papal documents from which they were taken. Some theologians attribute infallible teaching authority to the syllabus itself, while others deny this. Nevertheless, the syllabus must be accepted by all Catholics, since it comes from the pope as universal teacher and judge, according to the official communication from Cardinal Antonelli accompanying it. Its contents cannot be challenged by Catholics, and they are to give assent to it, holding the opposite of the condemned propositions. To find out the general position held by the Church in the matters repudiated by the syllabus, one need simply preface the errors by ''It is not true that . . . .'' Care must be used, however, not to draw false conclusions about the Church's positions; e.g., in denying that the State has the absolutely exclusive right to control schools one must not conclude that their control is not at all within the power of the State. Attention must always be paid to the exact wording to ascertain the precise sense of the condemnation.

Importance. The syllabus enjoys an important role in the history of the Church because of its attack on the rationalistic currents of the 19th century that sought to undermine religion, the Church, and the true nature of civil society. While defending the basic rights and privileges of the Church, the syllabus sought to prevent the havoc being caused by the confusion of freedom with license and of progress with error, and by the excessive claims being made for the power of reason. In the name of freedom the liberals were casting aside everything that had any connotation of restraint, oblivious to the fact that freedom does not allow man to act against his nature and supernature, and that freedom and law are not mutually opposed but complementary. By repudiating these errors that eradicate the influence of the Church from the life of the individual, family, and nation, the Syllabus of Errors called to the attention of mankind the nature and mission of the Church in this world. By pointing out the errors into which mankind was falling through the use of reason alone, the syllabus has served to recall to man a proper appreciation of the role of human reason when used in harmony with faith and to prepare the way for the decrees of Vatican Council I.

Bibliography: R. AUBERT, *Le Pontificat de Pie IX* (Paris 1952). G. F. H. and J. BERKELEY, *Italy in the Making,* 3 v. (Cambridge, Eng. 1932–40). L. BRIGUÉ, *Dictionnaire de théologie catholique,* ed. A. VACANT et al., 15 v. (Paris 1903–50; Tables générales 1951–) 14.2:2877–2923. R. CORRIGAN, *The Church and the Nineteenth Century* (Milwaukee 1938). E. E. Y. HALES, *Pio Nono* (New York 1954). S. W. HALPERIN, *Italy and the Vatican at War* (Chicago 1939). G. MOLLAT, *La Question romaine de Pie VI à Pie IX* (Paris 1932). T. F. WOODLOCK, ''‘Liberalism’ and the Church,'' *Month* 167:493–503; ''Liberals and the Syllabus,'' *Catholic Mind* 42:12–20.

[W. F. HOGAN]

SYLLOGISM

A syllogism is an artificial, logical arrangement of a natural deductive process known as argumentation. It was invented and perfected by ARISTOTLE, although other Greek thinkers, particularly Theophrastus, the Stoics and the Megarians, made substantial additions. In the Middle Ages the syllogism became identified with SCHOLASTIC method, and it was much ridiculed by the founders of modern science in the 17th century. Recent studies, however, including those in symbolic LOGIC, have vindicated the concern of ancient and medieval thinkers for this instrument of human thought. In its apodictic form, or DEMONSTRATION, the syllogism is man's most powerful device for the attainment of TRUTH and CERTITUDE (*see* LOGIC, HISTORY OF).

Nature and Kinds of Syllogism. The argumentation expressed by a syllogism involves three elements: the antecedent, or truth already known; the conclusion or new truth; and the inference of the mind connecting these two. In the syllogism, the antecedent is made up of propositions called premises, usually two in number. The conclusion is also a proposition, preceded by a ''therefore'' to signify the act of inference. While inference itself is not artificial, since it is a natural act of the mind (called REASONING), the forced disposition of the antecedent and conclusion according to logical laws *is* artificial, that is, it is imposed on the mind by mind itself in order to attain truth more easily and with less error. Thus syllogism is a logical tool that makes the natural deductive process more accurate, much as learning to eat correctly is an artificial imposition that assists the natural process of nutrition.

The two principal types of syllogism are the categorical and the hypothetical. The difference lies in the formal structure and the type of inference, as is explained below.

Categorical Syllogism. The categorical syllogism is defined as an argumentation in which two terms are compared with a third term in the antecedent, and the conclusion states that the two terms agree or do not agree with each other. An example is the following:

> All things composed of matter are corruptible.
> But all men are things composed of matter.
> Therefore all men are corruptible.

In this example, the first two propositions constitute the antecedent; the proposition ''Therefore all men are corruptible'' is the conclusion. The subject term of the conclusion, ''men,'' is the minor term and the premise that contains this term is called the minor premise. The predicate term, ''corruptible,'' is the major term and the premise that contains it is called the major premise. The term repeated in both premises but not found in the conclusion, that is, ''things composed of matter,'' is known as the middle term.

The categorical syllogism is validated by two basic principles of logic, the so-called *dictum de omni* and *dictum de nullo.* The first states that whatever is distributively and universally predicated of some subject must be affirmed of all included under that subject; the second states that whatever is universally and distributively denied of a subject must be denied of all included under that subject (*see* PREDICATION). These principles are similar to the mathematical propositions: two things equal to a third are equal to each other, and two things not equal to a third are not equal to each other.

Rules for the Syllogism. From the nature of the categorical syllogism certain laws follow that govern its use. These may be summarized as follows: (1) There can be only three terms in such a syllogism, one of which (the middle term) cannot appear in the conclusion. From this law, logicians deduce that only four ''figures'' of the categorical syllogism are possible. The following shows the four figures of the categorical syllogism and the possible arrangements of the subject term (S), the predicate term (P) and the middle term (M):

First Figure
M is P
S is M
———
S is P

Second Figure
P is M
S is M
———
S is P

Third Figure
M is P
M is S
S is P

Fourth Figure
P is M
M is S
S is P

(2) A TERM in the conclusion cannot have a wider extension than in the premises, for the effect cannot be greater than the cause. (3) The middle term must be used universally at least once, otherwise one cannot be certain that this subject term is included under this predicate term. (4) If one premise is negative or particular, the conclusion must be negative or particular. (5) When both premises are negative or particular, no conclusion is possible.

Mnemonics and the Laws. When these rules are applied to the various figures of the categorical syllogism, only a limited number of forms, or moods, are found to be valid within each figure. These valid moods can be recognized with the aid of the following mnemonics or memory aids, devised by logicians for this purpose:

First Figure: *Barbara, Celarent, Darii, Ferio.*
Second Figure: *Cesare, Camestres, Festino, Baroco.*
Third Figure: *Darapti, Felapton, Disamis, Datisi, Bocardo, Ferison.*
Fourth Figure: *Bamalip, Calemes, Dimatis, Fesapo, Fresison.*

The first three vowels in these mnemonics indicate whether the major premise, the minor premise, and conclusion, in order, are *A, E, I,* or *O* (*see* PROPOSITION). Some of the consonants, similarly, indicate how various moods can be reduced to the four basic moods of the first figure. The first figure is considered the most perfect, because it best illustrates the principles on which the categorical syllogism is based, while the mood *Barbara,* being composed of three universal affirmative propositions, is regarded as the most perfect form of the first figure.

Related Forms. The polysyllogism is a series of categorical syllogisms so arranged that the conclusion of the previous syllogism becomes a premise of the next. The enthymeme is a categorical syllogism with one premise merely implied; it is employed with great effect in RHETORIC. The singular syllogism, called an expository syllogism if the singular term is the middle term, is a post-Aristotelian development; its validity as a form of categorical syllogism is controverted. The sorites is a categorical syllogism resulting from a concatenation of middle terms. The modal syllogism is made up of propositions that have a modality apart from being true or false, such as, necessary, possible, or problematical; while not much discussed in traditional logic, it is undergoing extensive development in symbolic logic (*see* LOGIC, SYMBOLIC; MODE).

Hypothetical Syllogism. The hypothetical syllogism is defined as an argumentation that has a hypothetical proposition as a major premise. Hence the basic forms of this syllogism derive from the forms of the hypothetical proposition, namely, conditional, disjunctive and alternative. The conditional syllogism, most important among the hypotheticals, has two valid figures: one posits the condition in the minor premise, and then posits the conditioned in the conclusion; the other denies the conditioned in the minor premise, and denies the condition in the conclusion. The frequent use of the other possibilities constitutes the FALLACY of consequence.

See Also: DEDUCTION; FIRST PRINCIPLES; PROOF;

Bibliography: I. M. BOCHENSKI, *A History of Formal Logic,* tr. I. THOMAS (Notre Dame, Ind. 1961). S. CARAMELLA, *Enciclopedia filosofica,* 4 v. (Venice-Rome 1957) 4:615–620. R. EISLER, *Wörterbuch der philosophischen Begriffe,* 3 v. (4th ed. Berlin 1927–30) 2:757–771. J. A. OESTERLE, *Logic: the Art of Defining and Reasoning* (2d ed. Englewood Cliffs, N.J. 1963). V. E. SMITH, *The Elements of Logic* (Milwaukee 1957). E. D. SIMMONS, *The Scientific Art of Logic* (Milwaukee 1961).

[E. BONDI]

SYLVESTER I, POPE, ST.

Pontificate: Jan. 31, 314 to Dec. 31, 335. After an interval of 21 days, Sylvester, the presbyter of the *titulus Equitii* on the Esquiline, succeeded Pope MILTIADES. According to the *LIBER PONTIFICALIS,* Sylvester was ''Roman by birth, his father was Rufinus.'' He was consecrated, according to the Liberian catalogue, on Jan. 31, 314.

The Church and the Roman State. Sylvester's pontificate corresponds roughly to the reign of the Emperor CONSTANTINE I, who exercised a dominant role in the ecclesiastical as well as the political affairs of the Roman Empire. The Emperor heard the complaints of bishops, summoned councils, participated in dogmatic discussions, and treated the bishops as brothers, occasionally assuming the title ''bishop of external affairs'' (*episkopos ton ektos*), according to Eusebius. Under Constantine, the Christian Church was not merely tolerated, but in keeping with the tradition of the Roman state, religion was used as an instrument of state policy. The Christian clergy were exempted from public services (*munera civilia*), as were the pagan priesthoods (313); the churches were authorized to accept legacies (321); and the deci-

"Pope Sylvester I Carried in the Sedia Gestatoria, with His Retinue," chalk drawing by Raphael. Isabella Stewart Gardner Museum, Boston. (©Burstein Collection/CORBIS)

sions of episcopal courts were given binding force equal to the civil courts in certain areas (333). Sunday was declared an official holiday (321). The policy of close union with the Church forged by Constantine, later called CAESARO-PAPISM, was intensified after his defeat of Licinius at Adrianople and accession as sole ruler (324). He transferred the seat of power to CONSTANTINOPLE (330), and there came under the influence of Eastern churchmen, such as the Arian-sympathizer EUSEBIUS OF NICOMEDIA, who replaced the Western orthodox Hosius of Córdoba, a close confidant of Constantine's early years.

The bishop of Rome seems to have had little value in Constantine's eyes. When the African Donatists refused to abide by the decision of the Roman synod (313) and appealed to the Emperor, Constantine summoned 130 bishops to ARLES to a council that was attended by two priests and two deacons as representatives of the Bishop of Rome (August 314); again the decision went against the Donatists. Another fruitless appeal was heard in person by Constantine at Milan (316). The letter in which the bishops at Arles communicated their decisions to Pope Sylvester, while full of deference for his person and veneration for his see, seems to betray a sense of embarrassment about the anomalous position into which they had been forced by the strong will of the Emperor. The text is partly corrupt. It is not clear whether the words "you who hold the greater dioceses" (*qui maiores dioeceses tenes*), in the passage requesting the Pope's cooperation, refer to his metropolitan position in Italy, his patriarchal authority over the West (Pierre BATIFFOL, Erich Caspar based on canon 6 of Nicaea I), or possibly the authority of Constantine (C. TURNER).

Constantine and the Pope. Some 250 bishops were summoned to Nicaea by the Emperor for the first ecumenical council (May 325); they accepted the HOMOOUSIOS approved by Rome, condemned ARIUS, and agreed upon the date of Easter according to Roman and Alexandrian usage. Hosius guided the discussions, but the Emperor himself presided over impressive opening and closing ceremonies and was in effect the president of the assembly. The acts were signed by the Roman priests Vito and Vincentius, after Hosius, and before the other bishops.

Ten years later this triumph of Roman and Alexandrian orthodoxy seemed to have been all but erased. At councils in Tyre and JERUSALEM (354) summoned by Constantine, (St.) ATHANASIUS was deposed from the Alexandrian see by Arian-sympathizers, and banished to TRIER; and the rehabilitation of Arius himself seemed imminent. At Ancyra two years later the Emperor was baptized on his deathbed by Eusebius of Nicomedia; he was laid to rest as an "Equal of the Apostles" (*Isapostolos*) in a mausoleum he had constructed next to the church of the Apostles in Constantinople.

Sylvester was dead by then and had been buried, according to the *Depositio Episcoporum,* on Dec. 31, 335, in the Cemetery of Priscilla on the Via Salaria. A basilica built either by himself or one of his successors stood there. The ruins were excavated and partially restored in 1907. His remains (or possibly only his head) appear to have been moved by Pope PAUL I (762) to the church of S. Silvestro in Capite within the city walls. His sarcophagus, or what was regarded as such, stood within the medieval basilica of St. Peter's, but all traces of it were subsequently lost.

The life of Pope Sylvester in the *Liber pontificalis* gives a catalogue of Constantine's magnificent foundations in Rome and its vicinity, including the cemeterial basilicas of Old St. Peter's on the Via Ostiensis, S. Lorenzo fuori le Mura and S. Agnese, and one that has disappeared, that of SS. Peter and Marcellinus on the Via Labicana. Within the city the LATERAN basilica with its BAPTISTERY was built close to the palace of the Laterani, which had been recently sequestered as imperial property, and was then given to the bishop of Rome as an official residence, later known as the *Patriarchium.*

Later generations found it difficult to believe that under Constantine the bishop of Rome had played an insignificant role in these happenings; and they surrounded his memory with legends. The earliest was the "Acts of

Blessed Sylvester,'' purportedly a work of EUSEBIUS OF CAESAREA, but actually a Roman compilation of about 460 (Caspar). Written in a popular style, it is a romantic account of Sylvester's life, which starts with his youth when he looked after the pilgrims who came to Rome. It continues with his ordination by Pope Miltiades, the persecution of the Church by Constantine (*sic*), Sylvester's withdrawal to Mt. Soracte (*Syraptim*), a vision of the Apostles Peter and Paul, the Emperor's Baptism in the baptistery of the Lateran Palace (not yet built), and Constantine's cure from leprosy. It also contains St. HELENA's regrets that her son had been converted to Christianity and not to Judaism, a debate between Sylvester and a rabbi, and Helena's finding of the holy CROSS in Jerusalem. A pseudo-Constantinian decree that ''all bishops of the whole world shall be subject to the pope as the magistrates are to the emperor'' clearly reflects a date later than the 4th century. Two other forgeries, the ''Constitution of Sylvester'' and the ''Council of 275 bishops,'' a collection of 20 decrees allegedly promulgated by the Pope in a council at Rome in 326 that confirmed the Council of NICAEA I, form part of the Symmachan Forgeries, compiled *c.* 500 during the Laurentian schism. The most famous of these documents, the DONATION OF CONSTANTINE, was not compiled until the eighth century. Once regarded as authentic, these legends had an enormous influence on medieval thought.

Feast: December 31.

Bibliography: *Liber pontificalis,* ed. L. DUCHESNE, 1 (Paris 1886–92):cix–cxx, clii–cliv, 170–201; 3 (Paris 1938):76–81. H. LECLERCQ, *Dictionnaire d'éologie chrétienne et de liturgie,* ed. F. CHABROL, H. LECLERCQ, and H. I. MARROU, 15 v. (Paris 1907–53) 13.1:1197–98, 15.1:1455–57. É. AMANN, *Dictionnaire de théologie catholique,* ed. A. VACANT et al., 15 v. (Paris 1903–50; Tables générales 1951–) 14.2:2068–75. *Clavis Patrum latinorum,* ed. E. DEKKERS (2d. ed. Streenbrugge 1961) 2235, for eds. Of *Actus Silvestri papae.* G. WOLF, ''Gloriosissimus papa,'' *Zeitschrift der Savigny-Stiftung für Rechtsgeschichte, Kanonistische Abteilung,* 44: 350–352. R. U. MONTINI, *Le Tombe dei papi* (Rome 1957), 89–91. R. VIELLIARD, *Recherches sur les origines de la Rome chrétienne* (Mâcon 1941; repr. Rome 1959) 57. L. D. DAVIS, S.J., *First Seven Ecumenical Councils* (Collegeville, Minn. 1990) 33–80. E. FERGUSON, ed., *Encyclopedia of Early Christianity* (New York 1997) 1:1097. J. N. D. KELLY, *Oxford Dictionary of Popes* (New York 1986) 27–28. C. PIETRI, *Rome Christiana* (Rome 1976) 68–186. M. R. BARNES, ''One Nature, One Power; Consensus Doctrine in Pro-Nicene Polemic,'' *Studia Patristica* 29: 205–223. M. J. EDWARDS, ''The Arian Heresy and the 'Oration of the Saints'rdquo; *Vigiliae Christianae* 49: 379–87.

[J. CHAPIN]

SYLVESTER II, POPE

Pontificate: April 4, 999 to May 12, 1003. Thanks in no small part to his surviving correspondence from both before and after he assumed the pontificate, Sylvester II represents one of the most accessible and interesting figures of the tenth century.

Gerbert was born in the early 940s near Aurillac (southern France) and probably entered the monastery of Saint-Gerard as a child. As a young man he must have demonstrated a particular intelligence and ability, for in the late 960s he was brought to Catalonia by Count Borrell of Urguel to study under the guidance of Bishop Hatto of Vich. In Catalonia, at the library of Santa Maria de Ripoll, he would have had access to a great collection of classical Latin works and perhaps even some translations of Arabic works in astronomy, geometry, and arithmetic. Three years later, in 970, he accompanied Borrell and Hatto to Rome where he impressed first the pope and then Emperor OTTO I with his knowledge of the quadrivium. When Borrell and Hatto returned home, they left Gerbert behind as the teacher of Otto's son, the future Emperor OTTO II.

In the early 970s, at the invitation of Archbishop Adalbero of Reims, Gerbert moved north to study dialectic with Gerannus, archdeacon of the cathedral and master of its school. Over the next decade students flocked to study with Gerbert and Gerannus, and Reims flourished as one of the leading intellectual centers in Europe. Gerbert's innovative teaching of the liberal arts and exchanges with other thinkers distinguish him as perhaps the foremost intellectual of his day. As such, in 981 while accompanying Adalbero on a trip in Italy, he met Otric, master of the school of Magdeburg, in Ravenna where the two engaged in a great philosophical debate over the division of knowledge. Gerbert's former pupil, Otto II, had arranged this debate and, after Gerbert's impressive showing, retained him in his service. In 982, Otto made him abbot of Bobbio (northern Italy), but Gerbert quickly found himself in conflict with local nobles and, in June of 983, left the monastery for the imperial court in Pavia. Otto II died shortly thereafter. The widowed empress struggled to ensure the succession of her young son (Otto III) against the boy's kinsman (Henry the Quarrelsome) who sought the throne for himself. Gerbert worked to secure support for the young king from important churchmen east of the Rhine before he left for Reims to resume his teaching.

Back in Reims, early in 984, Gerbert returned to his students and his books—he was an avid collector—but as Adalbero's secretary, he would continue to be intimately involved in secular politics. Like Gerbert, Adalbero supported the Ottonians in their time of dynastic crisis, but his political imperatives and family's interests in Lotharingia brought him (and thus Gerbert) into conflict with the west Frankish king Lothar. After the death

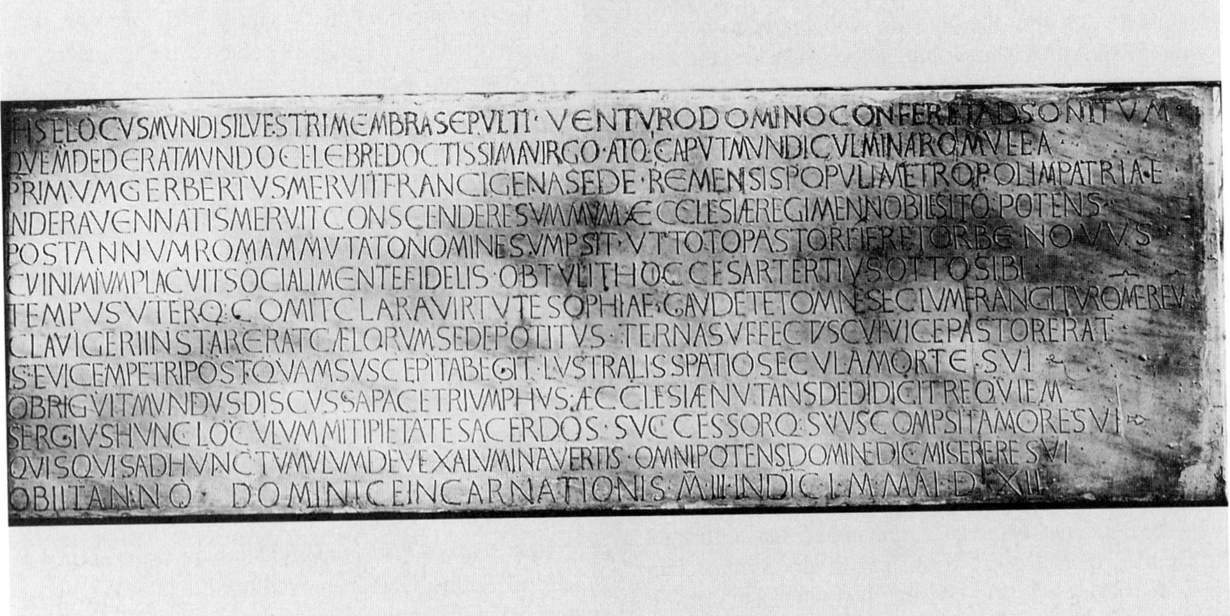

Epitaph of Pope Sylvester II, in the basilica of St. John Lateran, Rome.

of the king in 986 and, in the following year, of his son, they supported the election of Hugh Capet as king. Hugh's accession would come to mark the end of Carolingian rule in west Francia, but his election was challenged by Lothar's brother Charles, duke of Lotharingia, who claimed the throne for himself and, with growing support, was threatening to take Reims when Adalbero died in 989. Gerbert expected to succeed Adalbero—he claims to have been assured that he would—and was disappointed when Hugh made Charles' nephew Arnulf archbishop. Arnulf betrayed Hugh and joined his uncle's rebellion, but the conflict ended with the capture of the rebels two years later. When Arnulf was deposed at a synod held at Saint-Basle in 991, Hugh made Gerbert archbishop of Reims. During his episcopacy (991–998), Gerbert was forced to defend (against papal challenges) the legitimacy of Arnulf's deposition at the synod and thus his own appointment. Ultimately he failed to do so and left Reims, as he had Bobbio, for the Ottonian court where he devoted himself principally to his studies. And in the spring of 998, at OTTO III'S behest, Pope Gregory V made Gerbert archbishop of Ravenna. But before Gerbert had much of a chance to settle into this important office, Gregory died and, in early April 999, Otto had his former secretary made pope.

Gerbert took the name Sylvester II. He established the first archiepiscopal see in Poland in 999; for Hungary, when he anointed King Stephen in 1001, he established two archbishoprics and eight episcopal sees; and he seems to have been in communication with recently baptized leaders of more still distant peoples (Prince Vladimir of Kiev and King Olaf Trygvvesön of Norway). During his brief tenure as pope, Sylvester held several synods and also issued a number of privileges and decrees. Perhaps his most famous edict came in January 1001 when he renounced the so-called DONATION OF CONSTANTINE, an eighth-century forgery in which Constantine was supposed to have left to Sylvester I (and thus the papacy) dominion over all lands of Italy and the west. While he would not support that fiction, he did administer papal lands in Italy for the four years of his papacy, which drew to a close with his death on the 12th day of May 1003.

Bibliography: Gerbert's letters have been edited on several occasions, most recently (together with a French translation) by P. RICHÉ and J. P. CALLU as Gerbert d'Aurillac, *Correspondance*, 2 v. (Paris 1993); they have also been translated into English by H. P. LATTIN as *The Letters of Gerbert with His Papal Privileges as Sylvester II* (New York 1961). For his mathematical works, see Gerbert, *Opera Mathematica*, ed. by N. BUBNOV (Berlin 1899). And for his accounts of the synods held concerning the deposition of Arnulf of Reims, see *Monumenta Germaniae Historica,* 3: 655–693. Most of our information about Gerbert's teaching comes from the work of RICHER OF REIMS, *Histoire de France,* ed. and French tr. by R. LATOUCHE, 2 v. (Paris 1930, 1937), newly edited by H. HOFFMANN as Richer von Saint-Remi, *Historiae* (Hannover 2000). And for a selection of relevant documents and scholarly commentary on them, *see* O. GUYOT JEANNIN and E. POULLE, eds., *Autour de Gerbert d'Aurillac: le pape de l'an mil* (Paris 1996). For more detailed studies and bibliographic orientation, see also P. RICHÉ, *Gerbert d'Aurillac, le pape de l'an mil* (Paris 1987); ''Gerberto scienza, storia e mito. Atti del *Gerberti Symposium* (Bobbio 25–27 iuglio 1983)'' (Bobbio 1985); and U. LINGREDEN, *Gerbert von Aurillac und das Quadrivium* (Weisbaden 1976).

[J. GLENN]

SYLVESTER III, POPE

Pontificate: Jan. 10 to March 1045; b. John of Sabina, birthdate unknown; d. before 1063. In September 1044, an opposition party drove the last Tusculan pope, BENEDICT IX, from Rome. With Benedict gone and after what appears to have been some bitter infighting, the Stephanian branch of the Crescentian family managed to have their local bishop, John of Sabina, elected pope. John took the title of Sylvester III, but his reign was short lived. After a little more than one month had elapsed, Benedict returned to Rome and reclaimed his throne. Never having been deposed officially, Benedict worked quickly to undermine Sylvester's authority and was able to excommunicate him. Yet Benedict himself did not remain pope for long. Perhaps realizing that his own position was untenable, Benedict IX sold the papal office by May 1045 for an inordinate sum of money to John Gratian, who assumed the title Pope Gregory VI. His action may not have constituted simony in the strict sense. He may have been trying to induce Benedict's abdication rather than buying the office outright. But whatever the truth may be, John was permitted to assume the name Gregory VI only after Benedict received a pension.

Sylvester III did not bother to challenge the validity of the new pope. Rather, he appears to have recognized Gregory's legitimacy and returned to his bishopric in Sabina, where his Crescentian ties enabled him to carry out his episcopal duties. Emperor Henry III, however, was not convinced of Gregory's right to the papacy, and in 1046 he ordered Benedict, Sylvester, and Gregory to appear before a synod that was held at Sutri, where all three were deposed. Sylvester himself was condemned as an invader of the Holy See and was sentenced to confinement in a monastery. But since records indicate that he continued to serve as the Bishop of Sabina until at least 1062, the sentence against him was probably never enforced. Most likely Sylvester III died sometime before 1063, and his right to be recognized as a pope is questionable, although he is listed as one in the *Annuario Pontificio 2001.*

Bibliography: G. BARRACLOUGH, *The Medieval Papacy* (New York 1968) 71. J. N. D. KELLY, *Oxford Dictionary of Popes* (Oxford 1986) 144; F.X.SEPPELT, *Geschichte der Päpste*, 2 (Munich 1955) 414–417.

[J. A. SHEPPARD]

SYLVESTER IV, ANTIPOPE

Pontificate: Nov. 18, 1105 to April 12 or 13, 1111. Little is known of Maginulf, archpriest of St. Angelo, until he emerges in 1105 as the favored candidate for antipope among opponents of Pope Paschal II (1099–1118). This group may not have been purely old partisans of antipope Clement III (1080–1100)—like those who had elected Theodoric (1100) and Albert (1102)—because they appear to have had imperial support through Count Werner, who administered the royal holdings in Ancona and Spoleto. They met in Santa Maria Rotunda (the Pantheon), and elected Maginulf pope after accusing Paschal of simony and heresy. Count Werner brought troops to Rome while Paschal was outside the city, and Maginulf was consecrated Sylvester IV in the Lateran. Fighting broke out upon Paschal's return. For a time Paschal could only occupy an island in the Tiber that was owned by the Pierlioni family, but he soon forced Sylvester to flee the city, first for Tivoli and then for Osimo (in Ancona).

Nothing substantive is known of Sylvester until 1111, when Henry V (1106–25) occupied Rome with an imperial army. In an effort to pressure Paschal to end the INVESTITURE Controversy, Henry brought Pachal to his camp and threatened to replace him with Sylvester if pope and emperor could not come to an agreement. After Paschal's arrangement with the emperor was rejected by his own cardinals, Henry took him away from Rome and soon secured from Paschal the right to invest his bishops with ring and staff (the so-called Privilege of Ponte Mammolo). As a result, on April 12 or 13, 1111 Henry ordered Sylvester to renounce his claim to the papacy and do homage to Paschal. Sylvester complied and lived the rest of his life at Ancona under the protection of Count Werner.

Bibliography: L. DUCHESNE, ed. *Liber Pontificalis* (Paris 1886–92; repr. 1955–57) 2.298, 345–48. P. JAFFÉ, *Regesta pontificum Romanorum* (Leipzig 1885–88; repr. Graz 1956) 1.773–74. *Forma abrenuntiationis Silvestri IV Antipapae*, in *Monumenta Germaniae historica, Constitutiones* 1.146–47. *Annales ceccanenses*, in *Monumenta Germaniae historica, Scriptores* 19.281–82. C. SERVATIUS, *Paschalis II* (Stuttgart 1979) 43, 71–74, 220, 232, 245, 251. J. N. D. KELLY, *The Oxford Dictionary of Popes* (New York 1986) 162–63. G. TELLENBACH, *The Church in Western Europe* *from the Tenth to the Early Twelfth Century* (Cambridge 1993) 253–64.

[P. M. SAVAGE]

SYLVIUS, FRANCIS (DU BOIS)

Theologian; b. province of Hainault, Belgium, 1581; d. Douai, France, Feb. 27, 1649. He studied the humanities at Mons and later took up philosophy at Louvain. He then moved to the University of Douai, which had been founded in 1559 by Philip II. After teaching there for a time, he received the doctorate in theology in 1610. Sylvius succeeded William Estius in the chair of theology at the university in 1613. In 1618 he became canon, and in 1622, dean of the collegiate church of Saint-Amé. This latter office brought with it the rank of vice chancellor of the university.

Sylvius's writings show him to have been a thorough and penetrating disciple of St. Thomas Aquinas. His most important work was his commentary on the *Summa theologiae* of Aquinas, which was first published at Douai during the years 1620 to 1635. This four-volume commentary required a second edition almost immediately (1622–48). Jean Paquot probably exaggerates when he says Sylvius's commentary on the *Summa* is superior to any other, but it does, nonetheless, have distinctive merit. Sylvius produced several other works defending and explaining Thomistic doctrines, e.g., *Explicatio doctrinae S. Thomae et confirmatio thesium ex eodem de motione primi motoris* (Douai 1609); *Liber sententiarum . . . de statu hominis post peccatum* (Douai 1614).

In addition to his speculative work, he retained a lively interest in the practical application of theological ideas. To this end he translated the Rule of St. Benedict into French, prepared new editions of the pastoral instructions of St. Charles Borromeo (1616; 1624), and of the practical manual *Petri Binsfeldii enchiridium theologiae pastoralis locupletatum* (1622).

In the work entitled *Resolutiones variae* (1640; 1644) Sylvius practices the art of casuistry, i.e., the application of general principles in moral theology to hypothetical concrete cases. His treatment of these questions is often excessively complex, and in this he reflects the spirit of his day. Generally speaking, he favors the system described as ''moderate probabilism'' as a practical norm in moral judgments.

From his earliest days as a theologian, Sylvius stood firmly against the opinions put forward by Jansenius [see, e.g., *Litterae eximiorum DD. G. Colvenerii, F. Sylvii et V. Rendour . . . quibus testantur se Jansenii doctrinam semper proscriptam voluisse* (1648)]. His later works show that he became much concerned with the dangers inherent in the thought of Jansenius. Not long before his death, he sent an urgent letter to the Holy See, warning of the Jansenist peril confronting the Church.

Sylvius, along with his predecessor in the chair of theology, Estius, brought much honor to the newly established University of Douai. In the midst of bitter theological controversy he maintained a delicate balance in attitude as well as doctrine. Sylvius must be described as one of the better Thomists of the early 17th century. (*See* THOMISM.)

Bibliography: É. AMANN, in *Dictionnaire de théologie catholique,* ed. A. VACANT et al., 15 v. (Paris 1903–50; Tables générales 1951–) 14:2923–25.

[M. KELLEY]

SYMBOL

Etymologically, the word ''symbol'' can be traced to the Greek, συμβάλλειν, which means to throw together or simply to place together, as when two things are juxtaposed for the purpose of comparing them. In one of its noun forms, the comparing or setting together refers to the custom of tallying or dovetailing the two halves of a broken coin, called ''symbols,'' in order to establish the identity of one or both of the persons possessing the matching halves. The abstract and more general use of the term still retains this notion of one thing (usually material and visible) calling forth its complement or better half (usually something that is immaterial and unseen). Thus, HUGH OF SAINT-VICTOR describes the symbolic process as ''a comparison of the visible forms for the showing forth of the invisible'' (*In hierarch. coel.* 2.1.941; *The New Schaff-Herzog Encyclopedia of Religious Knowledge,* 11:204a). Throughout the medieval period symbolism plays an important role not only in architecture, heraldry and art but also in military and mercantile enterprises. The fundamental conception always includes a movement from the material symbol to something in a spiritual or suprasensible order.

In the patristic era the liturgical creeds pronounced by candidates at the time of Baptism were called symbols, probably because they were collections of dogmatic statements ''brought together'' as succinct expressions of basic Christian truths (*see* CREED). More recently, the study of the various beliefs and doctrinal tenets of the different Christian denominations has given rise, among Protestants, to a branch of theology known as comparative symbolics.

Symbol as Representative Form. While most of the contemporary uses of the word reflect the original idea of a comparison or juxtaposition of two things, the variety of symbols is so great that it is almost impossible to provide a definition that will satisfy every instance. Perhaps the best way to define the symbol is to contrast it with other representative forms that, like the symbol, stand for or point to something beyond themselves:

Images (pictures, statues, photos, etc.) imitate what they represent, whereas symbols need not resemble what they symbolize. It is sufficient if the symbol suggests or is associated with its meaning.

Signs (dinner bell, traffic light, smoke) announce some fact or give notification. Their role is practical and instrumental (*see* SIGN). Save for mathematical symbols, which some authors call signs, the typical symbol provides inspiration rather than notification. It functions as a rallying point for meaning, representing what is complex in a simple way. This is especially true of emblems, flags, or conventionalized drawings.

Gestures (shrugging the shoulders, bowing the head) express or embody their meaning as spontaneous, visible extensions of inner attitudes. While many gestures are symbolic, not all symbols are gestures or actions.

Analogues involve some perfection common to several beings of different orders, with the shared perfection being found either formally or causally in each but with references to one (*see* ANALOGY). With symbols, however, the perfections to which they refer need not be present in the symbol either formally or causally. A flag neither causes nor contains the ''spirit'' of a nation. By association and convention, this colored bit of cloth comes to represent that spirit, but of itself the cloth neither participates in nor causes the quality it stands for. On the other hand, some symbols involve a tacit analogy, as when ritual ablutions are understood to bring about spiritual purification on the analogy of the cleansing properties of ordinary water. It should be apparent that symbols based on an underlying analogy that is ontologically rooted in the nature of things are bound to be richer and more fertile than those resulting from convention or casual association. If Sacraments, like Baptism and the Eucharist, make use of water or bread, it is because these elements are natural symbols for spiritual cleansing and nourishment, and the implied analogy is clear.

Kinds of Symbol. Of the endless variety of symbols, three categories may be singled out for special attention.

Arbitrary Symbols. These symbols are not found in nature but are established by decree, for example, the plus sign in mathematics or the notation used in music. They are sometimes called stenographic or code symbols.

Associative Symbols. Here the symbol and its meaning are joined in virtue of an implicit middle term with which they are connected either naturally or because of some historical event. Thus, a key is a natural and almost inevitable symbol for authority because of its association with ownership or stewardship. The dove and the olive branch stand for peace, no doubt because of the story of Noah.

Evocative Symbols. These symbols suggest their meaning by engendering certain attitudes and feelings rather than by direct statement. Symbolists, both in art and literature, seek to communicate an impression in a nonconceptual way by the use of color or word combinations, as when a lurid green is employed to suggest envy.

There are also instances in which symbols symbolize still other symbols, as when the printed word symbolizes the spoken word, while the spoken word symbolizes thought that, once again, represents something beyond itself. One might even say that all finite beings symbolize and point to something beyond themselves, and that God alone is a nonsymbolic Being. It should be noted, however, that symbolism alone does not provide a conclusive argument for the existence of God. Symbolism can be effective only when the symbol and its meaning are known or at least vaguely suspected; otherwise the symbol is incapable of eliciting an affective response. If we know that God exists, ritual gestures and symbolic rites can deepen our understanding of divine things. But an atheist cannot appreciate the significance of most religious actions since he is not convinced that they refer to anything real.

The Religious Symbol. Since symbols need not imitate what they represent, and since they usually refer to something that is in a different and higher category, they are ideally suited for expressing not only abstract notions and mental operations but also spiritual and religious truths—none of which can be pictured in any literal way. While some symbols are so conventionalized and instrumental that they are totally unlike what is symbolized, the majority of symbols do bear some natural relationship to their meaning. Moreover, they usually have an emotive quality whereby they evoke in the knower not simply an intellectual assent but a nonneutral or affective response. Now it is precisely in the area of these ''charged'' symbols that we find forms that have the greatest elevating thrust or power of self-transcendence. Here must be situated the various kinds of liturgical and sacramental symbols that are so indispensable in communicating a sense of the sacred. Gestures (lifting the arms in prayer, prostration, the ritual kiss), as well as various material elements (water, fire, oil, incense, breath), all lend themselves spontaneously to the process of religious intention.

If the most pregnant religious symbols stand somewhere between the extremes of iconic (pictorial) and stenographic (code) representation, the reason should be evident. Pictorial symbols are too literal; they leave little to the imagination. Therefore, they do not elicit the kind of inner activity that projects the subject beyond what is immediately seen or heard. On the other hand, while code symbols are active creations of the human mind and while they do prescribe difficult mental operations, they are affectively neutral and lacking in depth. Useful in solving technical problems because of their univocity and invariability, they do not plunge the spectator into the mystery of being.

But primordial elements like water and fire are suggestive of cosmic forces. It is not this particular water or this particular fire that cleanses or purges. It is the very essence of water or fire as an expression of God's creative power that is invoked. A symbol, or a symbolic gesture like prostration, immediately and directly portrays man's essential and existential relationship to the Creator and it is a relation of total dependence and subordination. Nothing equals the spontaneous power of the appropriate symbol to project the mind towards the ABSOLUTE, and not only the mind but the heart as well; for religious symbols are nonneutral, that is, they are charged with affectivity and intelligibility. For this reason any spirituality that tries to eliminate symbolism in its cult tends to diminish man himself, since it is an attempt to reduce the human spirit to a naked intelligence. The Incarnation of the Son of God and the dispensation of the Sacraments as visible signs of invisible grace are but two of the many divine accommodations to the needs of man in his spatiotemporal condition.

Since symbolism avoids the complexities of formal analogy and since it provokes an immediate ascent or movement of transcendence in the beholder, it offers one of the simplest and most powerful vehicles for expressing man's spontaneous attitudes and affections in his secular as well as in his religious life.

See Also: LOGIC, SYMBOLIC.

Bibliography: P. FOULQUIÉ and R. SAINT-JEAN, *Dictionnaire de la langue philosophique* (Paris 1962) 703–704. G. FAGGIN and A. COLOMBO, *Enciclopedia filosofica,* 4 v. (Venice-Rome 1957) 4:622–627. A. MICHEL, *Dictionnaire de théologie catholique,* ed. A. VACANT et al., 15 v. (Paris 1903–50) 14.2:2925–39. R. EISLER, *Wörterbuch der philosophischen Begriffe,* 3 v. (4th ed. Berlin 1927–30) 3:194–196. J. M. SOMERVILLE, "Language as Symbolic Function," *American Catholic Philosophical Association. Proceedings of the Annual Meeting,* 34 (1960) 139–151. H. MUSURILLO, "History and Symbol: A Study of Form in Early Christian Literature," *Theological Studies,* 18 (1957) 357–386. G. VANN, *The Paradise Tree: On Living the Symbols of the Church* (New York 1959).

[J. M. SOMERVILLE]

SYMBOL IN REVELATION

In the restricted meaning here in question, SYMBOL is a particular type of SIGN: a sensible reality (word, gesture, artifact, etc.) that betokens that which cannot be directly perceived, properly described, or adequately defined by abstract CONCEPTS. The symbol, by its suggestive capacity, thus discloses something that man could not otherwise know, at least with the same richness and power.

Symbol in General. The meaning of symbol is grasped not by discursive reasoning but by a kind of synthetic insight. Frequently symbols do not have any one determinate meaning, but evoke a whole gamut of related significances. The cross, for example, is symbolic of a crisis to be faced, a burden to be carried, adversity, suffering, death; for the Christian, it implies patience, trust in Providence, sacrifice, reconciliation, and Redemption. Because of its capacity to unify such diverse elements, symbolism has an integrating function: it binds up the shattered, alienated existence of individuals and societies.

Symbolism derives its power from the fact that it speaks not only to the reflective intelligence but to the entire human psyche. It arouses deep emotional experience, releases hidden energies in the soul, gives strength and stability to the personality, establishes strong loyalties, and disposes a man for consistent and committed action. By reason of these properties, symbols are of great importance in art and literature (image, metaphor, etc.), in psychotherapy (e.g., dream analysis), in the cementing of human societies (e.g., the flag), and in religious worship (the icon, ritual, etc.).

As mediations of the divine, symbols have a certain foundation in the ANALOGY of being, which implies that material realities are partial expressions and reflections of the attributes of God. The common experience of the human race gives further specification to realities such as fire, water, sun, air, bread, wine, enriching their symbolic capacity. According to Carl Jung and his disciples, the pervasive symbolism of the great religions rests also upon the archetypes of the collective unconscious, but psychologists of other schools deny the need of such an appeal to racial memory.

Because they communicate levels of meaning and reality that are not accessible through immediate experience or conceptual thought, symbols as such are in some sense revelatory. They would therefore seem to have special aptitude to serve as vehicles of SUPERNATURAL revelation, should God be pleased to disclose Himself personally to man. The Judeo-Christian religions are based on the conviction that He has done so.

Theology of Symbol. The revelatory role of symbol has been variously appraised by Christian theologians over the centuries. Under the influence of Biblical and Platonic thought, the early Greek Fathers, especially the Alexandrian school (Clement, Origen, etc.), took a highly symbolic view of the Scriptures and of the universe as a whole (*see* ALEXANDRIA, SCHOOL OF). In this they were followed in the West by Ambrose, Augustine, and Gregory the Great, whose symbolic cast of thought is manifest in their allegorical exegesis. In the Middle Ages symbolism in religious art and literature became progressively more exuberant. Certain theological schools, notably the Victorines (*see* VICTORINE SPIRITUALITY) and the Franciscan mystics (*see* FRANCISCAN SPIRITUALITY), developed what M. D. Chenu, OP, has aptly called a ''symbolic theology.'' In the late Middle Ages and in modern times, symbolism has retained its dominant position in mystical theology (*see* SPIRITUAL THEOLOGY).

In the post-Reformation period, a decidedly Aristotelian brand of THOMISM established itself in the schools, and revelation was regarded primarily as a communication of doctrine. Some Catholic theologians, as well as ''orthodox'' Protestants, came close to the view of B. Spinoza and G. W. F. Hegel that imagery was at best a pragmatic expedient to impress on untutored minds truths that a cultivated intelligence could translate into clear and distinct ideas. Reacting against this theological rationalism, which tended to suppress all mystery, the romantics of the 19th century, followed by the Catholic Modernists and the Protestant Symbolo-Fideists of the early 20th century, espoused the view that revelation consists in symbols alone. Symbols, moreover, were for them thoroughly subjective and emotional modes of expression, devoid of truth value. The 20th century gave renewed attention to symbol, considered as yielding a special but authentic type of religious knowledge. This revival of symbolic theology has been assisted by recent work in the fields of depth psychology, comparative religion, and literary criticism. A number of recent Catholic and Anglican theologians, without minimizing the doctrinal component in revelation, insist on the indispensability of symbol. Symbolism, they maintain, is uniquely suited to convey revelation, i.e., to express in a vivid and concrete way what God may wish to manifest of Himself to a creature such as man.

Symbolic Realities in the Bible. The SALVATION HISTORY that forms the principal theme of both Testaments consists of the great symbolic deeds by which God manifests His power and mercy. These deeds may be called God's gestures in history. Miracle, according to the Biblical conception, is a particularly striking deed of God. (*See* MIRACLES (IN THE BIBLE).) Events such as the crossing of the Red Sea, the manna in the desert, the entry into the Promised Land, and the dedication of the Temple, viewed in the perspectives of salvation history, are charged with symbolic overtones that give them undying significance.

In the NT the Incarnate WORD is the absolute, unsurpassable earthly embodiment of God, and hence the supreme religious symbol. But for Him to be effectively a symbol for man, He must be manifested as such. Christ's miraculous deeds, His ritual actions (e.g., the Last Supper), His sacrifice on Calvary, and God's acceptance of that sacrifice in the Resurrection and Ascension, symbolically disclose His mission and Person. In Christ and the Church all the symbolism of the OT is recapitulated and fulfilled.

Symbolic Language in the Bible. The Prophets and other Biblical writers describe divine things in highly figurative speech. Some of the images are taken from cosmic realities—fire, water, rock, etc. Others are borrowed from the social life of Israel—e.g., God as father, king, judge, shepherd, vinedresser, and spouse. Under the impact of salvation history, the images themselves took on a history. Through calamities such as the collapse of the Davidic monarchy, the destruction of the Temple, and the Babylonian Exile, the images were purified, detached from their terrestrial moorings, universalized, and thus made available to carry a higher spiritual meaning. Providential transformations of this sort made it possible to forge the pregnant images found in the later books of the OT, such as the New Covenant, the ''circumcision of the heart,'' the Suffering Servant, and the heavenly Son of Man.

Images such as these were taken up with added power in the NT. Christ Himself described His status in terms of the OT figures and preached to the people in the form of parables. The Johannine Gospel, the most symbolic of the four, is built around dominant images such as the good shepherd, the true vine, the manna, the living water, and the light of the world. Such symbols, as C. H. Dodd remarks, ''retire behind the realities for which they stand, and derive their significance from a background of thought in which they had already served as symbols for religious conceptions'' [*The Interpretation of the Fourth Gospel* (Cambridge, Eng. 1953) 137]. The same is true in varying degrees of other NT writings.

Revelatory Value of Symbols. The importance of symbol in revelation follows from the fact that revelation is historical and interpersonal. It does not simply put us in touch with God in an abstract way, as He might be known in philosophy. General statements in cold abstract language would be powerless to effect personal encounter. But God reveals Himself concretely, incarnating His very self in historical gestures and realities and in the tenor of the speech that He inspires. The Church, assisted by the Holy Spirit, achieves a mysterious contact with the God of faith through the veils of these symbolic manifestations. Making full use of the flexibility and inexhaustible fecundity of the Biblical symbols, the Church continually brings forth from her treasure "things new and old" (cf. Mt 13.52).

See Also: MIRACLES (THEOLOGY OF); PROPHECY (IN THE BIBLE); PROPHECY (THEOLOGY OF); REVELATION, CONCEPT OF (IN THE BIBLE); REVELATION, THEOLOGY OF.

Bibliography: I. G. BARBOUR, *Myths, Models, and Paradigms* (New York 1974). C. A. BERNARD, *Theologie symbolique* (Paris 1978). L. M. CHAUVET, *Symbol and Sacrament* (Collegeville, Minn. 1995). F. W. DILLISTONE, *The Power of Symbols in Religion and Culture* (New York 1986). A. DULLES, *Models of Revelation*, 2d ed. (Maryknoll, N.Y. 1992). M. ELIADE, *Images and Symbols*, tr. P. MAIRET (New York 1961). T. FAWCETT, *The Symbolic Language of Religion* (Minneapolis 1971). K. RAHNER, "Theology of the Symbol," *Theological Investigations 4* (Baltimore 1966), 221–52. W. M. URBAN, *Language and Reality* (London 1939).

[A. DULLES]

SYMBOLISM, EARLY CHRISTIAN

The use of signs, both literary and material, to represent spiritual reality. It is now generally recognized that, similar to the development of the primitive Christian theology, of which it was an essential part, the symbolism of the early Christian Church was a continuation of Judaic practice, both in the literary sphere and in the sphere of plastic representation.

Judeo-Christian Symbolism

The New Testament is replete with symbols that express the reality of the mystery of God's presence in the world and in the Church. In preaching the Gospel, Christ frequently used symbolic words and actions to point a lesson or exhibit His divine power. He made mud of spittle to cure the man born blind (Jn 9.6); in healing the deaf mute He put his fingers into the man's ears, and spitting, He touched the mute's tongue (Mk 7.33); and He referred to the fountain of living water to describe eternal life for the Samaritan woman (Jn 4.13–15). In the Gospels, likewise, He used a series of symbols to describe the reality of the Church: the planted field, and the seed that becomes a tree; the vine and its branches; yeast for leaven, and a kingdom. St. Paul in his Epistles spoke of the Church as the body of Christ, and described its members as the hands, feet, and eyes, with Christ as the head (1 Cor 12.12–27; Col 1.18).

Theological Substratum. Besides these realistic symbols, however, the Epistle to the Hebrews and Revelation in particular abound in symbolic representations, both prophetic and explanatory, that have their roots almost solely in the Old Testament. The theological continuity between the two Testaments was thus exemplified in a striking fashion; its actuality is further expressed in the early liturgy, and supported by archeological evidence.

The principal feasts of the Jewish religion were centered in the Passover, the Feast of Tabernacles, or Sukkoth, Rosh Hashana, and Yom Kippur; they are ceremonial manifestations of a symbolism that points to eschatological fulfillment that, in later Judaism, expressed itself in a rising hope in Messianic deliverance and immortality. Likewise, the Old Testament funerary monuments and ossuaries, as well as the synagogues, were decorated with significant symbols whose history and meaning, though still not fully understood, depict a deep theological substratum and development in late Hebraic thought.

Liturgy and Archeology. The Judaic themes of deliverance and eschatological fulfillment are reflected in the primitive Judeo-Christian theology and appear early on Christian monuments with, for example, the palm leaf, the anchor, and the cross, accompanied by brief inscriptions or legends. In the catacombs as well as in the earliest ecclesial assembly rooms (*see* DURA-EUROPOS), representations characteristic of the synagogue are rare; but the ORANS and the GOOD SHEPHERD were used as indicative of Christian piety, and of hope in God and in a Savior interested in mankind. It is not certain whether both the Orans and the Good Shepherd were adopted immediately from Jewish use, for both symbols were widely employed in the Greco-Roman milieu.

Eschatological Hope. It is in the liturgy that the true connection between the Old and New Testament symbolism is found; and this connection is reflected in the 3rd and 4th century plastic arts on monuments and in church decoration. In his Commentary on Zechariah, Jerome is a witness to this development (*Comm. in Zach.* 3) even though he considered the Jewish interpretation of the Feast of Tabernacles as a false pre-figuration of an earthly millennium. The prophet had spoken of "Yahweh standing on the Mount of Olives"; he described "living waters that shall go out from Jerusalem" and predicted that "the remnant of the nations will return yearly to keep the Feast of Tabernacles" (Zec 14.4–16). The earlier Jews celebrated the feast during eight days, living in huts or arbors surrounded by rustic greenery that symbolized the Garden of Eden. To this earthly paradise the people hoped to return in the restored Jerusalem. The living waters were the river of Paradise flowing in four directions; and the *ethrog,* or citron, and the *lulab,* or nosegay of myrtle, palm, and willow, carried in their hands, represented the fruit of the tree of life. The early Christians were familiar with these eschatological symbols and used them freely. This is clearly exemplified in the *Shepherd of* HERMAS, which in the early Church was considered as possibly a canonical book similar to Revelation.

Modern investigation indicates that there is a connection between the details of the Transfiguration and the description of the Feast of Tabernacles in Zechariah. The appearance of Christ and the three disciples on a mountain suggests the Prophet's reference to Yahweh's manifestation of His glory on the Mount of Olives; and Peter's reaction, "It is good for us to be here" (Lk 9.33), and his proposal to build three huts or arbors seem directly connected with the hope nurtured by the symbols of an eschatological state of enjoyment and life in the new paradise.

METHODIUS OF OLYMPUS reflects this attitude when he speaks of "celebrating a feast to God, adorning my bodily tabernacle with good deeds" (*Convivium* 9.17); and EPHREM says that he saw the "tents of the righteous" in paradise; the greater a "man's struggle to be virtuous, the more beautiful will be his tabernacle" (*Hymn Parad.* 5.6). The Second Epistle to the Corinthians (2 Cor 5.1, 4) and 2 Peter (1.13) had spoken of the body as a tabernacle, whereas IRENAEUS OF LYONS referred to the resurrection of the body when he described the "raising of the tabernacle of David" (*Demonstration* 38; 62).

Palestinian Ossuaries. Archeological evidence on Jewish and Paleo-Christian ossuaries in Palestine, as collected by E. Goodenough and more recently by E. Testa and B. Bagati and commented on by J. Daniélou, confirms the use of these symbols on Judaic funerary monuments in the Greco-Roman period, and particularly the use of the symbols of the *lulab* and *ethrog,* the *menorah* or seven-branched candlestick, and the *shophar* or ram's horn used as a trumpet. In the synagogue at Dura-Europos there is reason to believe that the frescoes have a direct relation to the Feast of Tabernacles and the dedication of the Temple. A fresco surrounding the niche of the Torah depicts the seven-branched candlestick, the *lulab* and *ethrog,* and the sacrifice of Isaac, overshadowed by the tree of life, a table, and throne, all of which have been interpreted by R. Wischnitzer as a reference to the eschatological temple of Zechariah (14.16).

Specific Symbols

The theological relationship between the two Testaments is illustrated by a series of specific symbols whose description here may serve as an introduction to the development of Christian thought in the early Church, indicating in a summary fashion its complexity and

Grave marker, good shepherd, gold glass, 4th century, Cemetery of Pamphilia, Rome.

profundity. These examples do not exhaust the rich storehouse of ideas contained in the archeological evidence and patristic literature.

The Palm and the Crown. TACITUS described the Jewish priests wearing crowns of ivy during the Feast of Tabernacles (*Hist.* 5.5), thus confirming the Book of Jubilees (16.30), which prescribed that during the feast, "Israel should celebrate by living in arbors, with wreaths on their heads, and carrying leafy boughs and branches of willow." There is an obvious connection between these customs and Christ's triumphal entrance into Jerusalem, as well as the mocking ceremony in which He was crowned with a wreath of thorn branches.

The *Shepherd of Hermas* described a vision of the Judgment in which the angel of the Lord adorned the men with crowns "seemingly of palm leaves, after they had surrendered their branches bearing buds and fruit" (*Sim.* 8.2.1). The *Odes of Solomon*, describing apparently the rite of Baptism, refers to the crowning of the neophyte with a garland (*Ode* 20.7–8), and this custom was preserved in the Syro-Christian rite. Both the Testament of Levi (8.4–9) and the Gnostic Book of *Jeû* (47) refer to an olive branch and a crown of garlands in relation to the baptismal ceremony.

Tomb inscription, Greek "Fish of the Living," anchor, two fish, detail, Licinia, ca. 200.

The crown of life is a symbol of immortality on the late Jewish funerary monuments according to Goodenough; in the Epistle of James (1.12), 1 Peter (5.4), the Revelation (2.10), and the apocryphal Ascension of Isaiah (7.22; 8.26) and Testament of Levi (4.1) there is direct reference to the "crown of life" and the "crown of glory." This symbolism seems to be inspired by a Jewish ideology independent of St. Paul's reference to the crown given to the victor (1 Cor 9.25), which reflects Hellenistic practice. TERTULLIAN repudiated the use of crowns for Christians, but his objection was based on the connection with the worship of the emperor as a god, exemplified in the triumphs celebrated by the military (*De corona mil.*). Later Christian writers frequently employed the crown to symbolize the rewards of eternal life.

The Vine, the Tree, and the Cross. In describing the Church, Christ used a series of symbols that have their root in the Old Testament, and that are reflected all through patristic exegesis. Isaiah had spoken of the Israelites as the vine of Yahweh (5.1–7); Christ spoke of his Church as a plantation or vineyard (Mt 21.33–41). This symbolism appears in the *Shepherd of Hermas* (5.5, 2; 6.2); whereas the *Apostolic Constitution* (*praef.*), Clement of Alexandria (*Strom.* 7.12, 74), and Justin Martyr (*Dial.* 110.4) speak of the Church as "The Lord's vine," apparently influenced by Isaiah and Psalm 79.

IGNATIUS OF ANTIOCH (*Trall.* 11.2) employed the tree with its branches in direct reference to the cross. This symbolism was related to the theological problem of membership in the Church and is developed by HIPPOLYTUS OF ROME following John's quotation of the *Logia* of Christ (*Bened. Isaac*), and also by Clement of Alexandria (*Quis dives* 37.6). ZENO OF VERONA explicitly refers to Isaiah (5.1–7) in his mystagogic catechesis for neophytes (*Tract* 2.28) preached during the Easter Vigil: "The Lord's vine was the former synagogue . . . but the Lord . . . planted another, our mother the Church." ASTERIUS THE SOPHIST wrote: "The divine and timeless vine sprung from the grave, bearing as fruits the newly baptized, like bunches of grapes on the altar'' (*Hom.* 14.1–2) to depict the full-fledged Paschal symbolism of the 4th century; he also employed the image used by Ignatius of Antioch: ''Christ the tree of life . . . has the Apostles for branches, the redeemed for fruit, words for leaves; baptism is the root, and the Father, the gardener'' (*Hom.* 1.5).

Tau Sign. The T, or Tau sign, made on the forehead, is said by St. Basil to be one of the most ancient of Christian symbols. The epitaph of ABERCIUS speaks of ''the glorious seal'' (*sphragis*) in connection with Baptism, and both Quodvultdeus (*De Symbolo* 1.1) and Augustine (*Conf.*) refer to this usage. Gregory Thaumaturgus used the sign of the cross ''to cleanse the pestilential atmosphere'' of a pagan temple (Gregory of Nyssa, *Vita Greg. Thaum; Patrologia Graeca,* ed., J. P. Migne, 161 v. (Paris 1857–66) 46:916). JOHN CHRYSOSTOM testified that the sign of the cross was used continually as ''a saving protection'' (*Hom. Phil.* 13.1).

Not only was the sign of the cross used as an exorcism, it also was tattooed on the foreheads of Christians (Mark the Deacon, *Vita Porphyrii Gazae*), and depicted both in the catacombs and on monuments, frescoes, bas-reliefs and mosaics, in the Greek and Latin form, respectively. While later writers used the T form in reference to the cross of the crucifixion, earlier sources connected the T sign with the Tau of Ezekiel, who speaks of the members of the Messianic community marked with the Hebrew Tau in the form of T or X (for cross sign) on their foreheads (Ez 9.4–6). In the Book of Revelation (7.3 and 14.1) the Tau sign signifies God the Father, and is related to the Name [of the Lord], which was a symbol used also in Acts (9.15); *Shepherd of Hermas* (*Sim.* 9.13.2–3); and the *DIDACHE*, where it means the Word of God. However, the Tau sign was early associated with the cross in the Epistle of BARNABAS (9.8), and in subsequent ages became the usual symbol for the crucifixion.

The Church as a Ship. Besides Christ's references to the Church as a temple or a flock, the early catechesis symbolized the Church as a ship, and this imagery reflects Old Testament and late Judaic thought that referred to a rough sea as a figure of eschatological trials. The incident of Christ's calming the waters for the 12 Apostles on the Lake of Tiberias was impressive and had antecedents in the story of Noah's ark. Justin Martyr indicated that the ship was not represented merely as a means of salvation but as the Church itself, which was the object saved: ''One cannot sail the seas,'' he says in describing the Cross of Christ, ''unless the trophy that is called the sail is properly set on the ship'' (*Apologia* 55.3). The archeological findings on ancient Judeo-Christian ossuaries in Palestine depict the ship with the transverse yard on the mast in the form of a cross.

Although the ship was used also on Greek, Roman, and Egyptian monuments and mausoleums as a symbol of hope in immortality, PHILO JUDAEUS had described the ark as an image of the soul sailing toward the life of blessedness, and Clement of Alexandria described ''the ship running before a favorable wind'' as one of the symbols on rings that Christians did not have to reject as idolatrous (*Paedag.* 3.11.59.2).

Justin Martyr described Noah's ark as a symbol of salvation in connection with ''Christ the firstborn of every creature [who] has become in a new sense the head of another race, of those whom he has brought to birth by water, faith, and the wood that holds the mystery of the Cross, just as Noah was saved in the wood of the Ark'' (*Contra Tryphonem* 138.1–2). Tertullian made the ship an explicit symbol of the Church (*De Bapt.* 12.7), an imagery that reflects the Judeo-Christian thought of the apocryphal Testaments. In his *De Idololatria* he says ''what was not [saved] in the ark, is not saved in the Church'' (24.4), and this theme leads to the aphorism ''Outside the Church, no salvation'' in the thought of ORIGEN and CYPRIAN, and in the early Roman theology of Church unity. Hippolytus changes the orientation and speaks of the local churches as ships (*Bened. Moysis*), with the Lord as the sheltered harbor.

Since in Hellenistic literature the ship symbolized the state, the two sources of the imagery were combined in its further development. But the original Christian usage came from Judaic sources. This symbol is depicted in the primitive area of the catacombs of Callistus at least four times, but it seems to have disappeared in the late 3d century. However, MINUCIUS FELIX stated explicitly that ''the ship is a reminder of the cross which can be seen in the mast and yard arm, particularly when running before the wind or in a storm'' (*Octav.* 29).

Living Water and the Fish. In the Gospel of John, Christ proclaimed himself to be a ''fount of living waters'' (7.37), evidently as He was standing in the temple during the libation connected with the Feast of Tabernacles. The allusion apparently is to Ezekiel (47.8–9) and Zechariah (14.8–10), who speak of the living water issuing from Jerusalem and flowing east and west while the nations go up to Jerusalem (14.16). Christ referred to the eschatological significance of this text, which symbolized the outpouring of God's life in the living waters beside the Temple. In the New Testament this idea is expanded in Baptism, which achieves the outpouring of the Spirit.

There is reference in Tertullian to the primordial waters of Genesis (1.2.20) that ''were commanded to bring forth living creatures'' (*De Bapt.* 3.4); and to the Tree of Life in the new paradise, fed by the river of living water as were the trees of the original Paradise by the four rivers. This imagery is notable in the Syrian catecheses and in the *Odes of Solomon,* and can be seen in the decoration of early BAPTISTERIES. The four rivers were identified with the four Gospels by Cyprian (*Epist.* 73.10), Hippolytus (*Comm. Dan.* 1.17), and Jerome (*Comm. Matt.,* Prolog.). Finally, this living water is recognized by Gregory of Elvira as the liquid that flowed from the side of Christ on the cross, guaranteeing the accomplishment of man's redemption (*Tract.* 15; *Suppl.* 1).

While the ordinary interpretation of the fish, which in Greek as ΙΧΘΥΣ is an acrostic for Ἰησοῦς Χριστὸς Θεοῦ Υἱὸς Σωτήρ (Jesus Christ, Son of God, Savior), in the older tradition, as expressed in the catacombs, the fish denotes the presence of living water and also the Christian enlivened in Baptism by the outpouring of eschatological water whose source is in Jerusalem. Evidence for this interpretation is supplied by a chain of texts or *testimonia* accredited to the authorship of Gregory of Nyssa.

The Plow and the Star. The text of Isaiah, "For the Law shall come from Sion and the Word of the Lord from Jerusalem . . . . They shall turn their swords into plowshares and their spears into sickles" (2.3–4) was quoted frequently by Justin Martyr (*Apol.* 39.1; *Dialogues* 110.3), Cyprian (*Test.* 2.18), and Origen (*Contra Cels.* 5.33). It is explained at length by Irenaeus, who speaks of "God's word as the law of liberty that changed the world . . . ." He states that the Lord made the plow and provided the sickle: this signifies the first seed time of man patterned in Adam, and the gathering of the harvest at the end of time, for the wood combined with iron in the plow is the materialized [for incarnate] Word, made one with the flesh (*Adv. Haer.* 4.34.4). He further comments on 2 Kings (6.5–7) wherein the Prophet Elisha brings an ax to the surface of the river by throwing in a piece of wood, and affirms that "the materialized *Logos* of God, lost by us through neglect, had to be retrieved through the Economy of the Wood [of the Cross]" (*ibid.* 5.17.4). This imagery is repeated by Tertullian (*Adv. Jud.* 13.19), Ambrose (*Myst.* 51), and Didymus the Blind; the last (*De Trin.* 2) specifies that the iron is sin, and the wood of the plow, the Cross of Christ. The cruciform character of the plow is developed as a theme by the later fathers; more recently its earlier usage has been discovered on the Judeo-Christian ossuaries in Palestine.

Justin Martyr testifies that in the *testimonia* concerning Christ, "He is called Wisdom, Day and Dawn" (*Dial.* 4), and later says: "He is called Wisdom by Solomon, Star by David, and Dawn by Zacharias" (*ibid.* 126.1). Justin is making reference to Numbers (24.17) and reflecting 2 Peter (1.19). There is also a relation between these designations and the quotation of Amos (5.25–26) in Stephen's discourse (Acts 7.42–43), and in Justin (*Dial.* 22.3–4), who commented on the coming of the Wise Men "from Arabia" by stating that it was a fulfillment of Balaam's prophecy (Nm 23.7). Origen likewise connected Balaam with the Magi's star (*Contra Cels.* 1.60; *Hom. Num.* 13.7) and gave evidence that the symbolism of Christ as the star was emphasized in the early Eastern Church as a corrective to Zoroastrian Magism. This may have an interesting connection with the infancy narrative in Matthew.

The Zodiac Christianized. Hippolytus of Rome wrote: "He [Christ] the Sun, once he had risen from the womb of the earth, showed the 12 Apostles to be as it were, 12 hours . . . . Once they were gathered together, the 12 Apostles like 12 months, proclaimed the perfect year, Christ . . . . Because the prophet [Is 61.2] refers to Christ as day, sun and year, the Apostles must be called hours and months" (*Bened. Moysis; Patrologia Graeca,* ed. J. P. Migne 27:171). This symbolism of the zodiac is common to the earliest Judeo-Christian imagery as witnessed by the apochryphal Clementine literature. It is reflected in Methodius of Olympus (*De Sanguisuga* 9.3), Asterius the Sophist (*Hom. in Ps.* 20.14, 15–16), Ambrose (*Exp. Luc.* 7.222), Zeno of Verona (*Tract.* 2.9.2), and Augustine (*Ennar.* Ps. 55.5). Clement of Alexandria testified to the heretical use made of it by the GNOSTICS (*Exc. Theod.* 25.2).

It is well known that, although the zodiac was a Hellenic device, it was also in use among the Jews of Palestine before the time of Christ as a decoration for the synagogues (Goodenough, 1.203, 248–251), and Philo Judaeus made the connection with the 12 Patriarchs (*Vita Mos.* 2.123–124) whereas Clement of Alexandria combined both Patriarchs and Apostles (*Strom.* 5.5.38.4–5). Thus a complicated series of symbols was created and used in the catacombs and funerary monuments. In these symbols Christ was compared to the sun, and depicted as such, for example, on the vault of the mausoleum (M, the family tomb of the Iulii) in the excavations under St. Peter's (*see* VATICAN). There Christ appears as the Helios; his head is surrounded by a radiant nimbus, and he is mounted on a chariot. The zodiac symbolism was further developed in the Middle Ages and the Renaissance.

Later Christian Literature

In both the monuments and the early and late patristic literature, Christian symbols were drawn from the Old and New Testaments and adapted to the cultural environment. These symbols included the anchor, the dove as symbol of the soul or the Holy Spirit, the Lamb and the Good Shepherd, the Monogram of Christ, the Wise Virgins, and almost innumerable other allusions that accompanied the allegorical and mystagogic interpretations of the Scriptures.

Personal Figures as Symbols. In the 3d century the symbol of a personal figure was widespread: the angler was the sign of the priestly office; the philosopher, of Christ as teacher. Daniel in the Lion's den, Jonah, the youths in the fiery furnace, Noah, and Susannah, were exemplifications of virtue. Jonah stood also for the death and resurrection of Christ (Sarcophagus of Aquileia); and the woman with a veil, for the Church (Aegedius sarcophagus, Perugia; wooden door of St. Sabina, Rome). In the 4th century the hand of God, the crown, and the cross gradually took on a multitude of significances; this development is particularly notable in regard to symbolic animals, such as the lamb, lion, dove, and stag. While in Roman symbolism the lion symbolized death (Gerona sarcophagus), in Christian symbolism he stood for St. Mark the Evangelist. Even the wolf had an ambiguous significance (Sarcophagus, Praetextatus catacomb, Rome: Art Gallery, Brescia), and the snake (Sarcophagus, Gerona; Pignatta sarcophagus, Ravenna) could be the tempter or the saving serpent of Moses (Jn 3.14).

Middle Ages and Renaissance. In the Carolingian period the idea of a symbol as an abbreviation for a fact or a hope was widespread. A reference to the Feast of Cana or the chalice placed beneath the cross, for example, stood for the Eucharist; the healing of the blind man, for Baptism. In the Middle Ages, symbolism developed in new areas of Christian thought. Individual saints were idealized as models of a particular virtue, e.g., as St. CRISPIN, model of industrious application. Animal symbolism proliferated; the lion signified everything about Christ from his birth and Resurrection to his mercy, power, and kindness, and served as well as the early Roman sign for death (Sarcophagus of Frederick II, Palermo); and the goat stood for the damned, the demons, and the impure. In the later Middle Ages and especially during the Renaissance, the union of the fables and myths of classical literature with Christian symbolism brought symbolism into a new and more complex stage.

Bibliography: J. DANIÉLOU, *Primitive Christian Synbols,* tr. D. ATTWATER (Baltimore 1964); *Théologie du judéo-christianisme* (Tournai 1958). E. TESTA, *Il simbolismo dei Giudeo-Cristiani* (Jerusalem 1962); *L'Osservatore Romano* (Rome 1849–) 224 (September 25, 1960) 3. B. BAGATTI, *ibid.* 182 (August 6, 1960) 4. E. R. GOODENOUGH, *Jewish Symbols in the Greco-Roman Period* (Bollingen Ser. 37; New York 1953–). R. B. WISCHNITZER, *The Messianic Theme in the Paintings of the Dura Synagogue* (Chicago 1948). P. A. UNDERWOOD, *Dumbarton Oaks Papers,* Harvard University 5 (Cambridge, MA 1950) 43–138, fountain of life. E. PETERSON, *Frühkirche, Judentum und Gnosis* (Rome 1959). H. RAHNER, ''Flumina de ventre Christi,'' *Biblica* 22 (1941) 269–332, 367–403; *Greek Myths and Christian Mystery,* tr. H. BATTERSHAW (New York 1963). J. CARCOPINO, *Études d'histoire chrétienne* (Paris 1953). J. LEGRAND *The Clergy Monthly* 23 (1959) 377–384, star. H. J. SCHOEPS, *Aus frühchristlicher Zeit* (Tübingen 1950). F. CUMONT, C. DAREMBERG and E. SAGLIO, *Dictionnaire des antiquités grecques et romaines d'après les textes et les monuments* (Paris 1877–1919) 5:1046–62, Zodiac. J. SEZNEC, *The Survival of the Pagan Gods,* tr. B. F. SESSIONS (Bollingen Ser. 38; New York 1953). F. PIPER, *Mythologie und Symbolik der christlichen Kunst,* 2 pts. (Weimar 1847–51) 2:276–310. L. RÉAU, *Iconographie de l'art chrétien,* 6 v. (Paris 1955–59) v.1–3. F. MAYR, et al., *Lexikon für Theologie und Kirche,* ed. J. HOFER and K. RAHNER, 10 v. (2d, new ed. Freiburg 1957–65); suppl., *Das ZweiteVatikanische Konzil: Dokumente und kommentare,* ed. H. S. BRECHTER et al., pt. 1 (1966) 9:1207–10. H. LECLERCQ, *Dictionnaire d'archéologie chrétienne et de liturgie,* ed. F. CABROL, H. LECLERCQ and H. I. MARROU, 15 v. (Paris 1907–53) 15.2:1778–1812. K. GALLING and K. WESSEL, *Die Religion in Geschichte und Gegenwart,* 7 v. (3d ed. Tübingen 1957–65) 6:543–548. T. KLAUSER, *Jahrbuch für Antike und Christentum* (Münster 1958–) 1 (1958) 20–51; 2 (1959) 115–145; 3 (1960) 112–133. W. M. BEDARD, *The Symbolism of the Baptismal Font in Early Christian Thought* (Cath. U. of Amer. Studies in Sacred Theology, 2d ser. no. 45; Washington 1951).

[F. X. MURPHY]

SYMBOLISM, THEOLOGICAL

This topic touches two vast areas of development in the history of theology. The first is typology, which involves the rich Christian symbolism growing out of the comparison of the New Testament with the Old. The second is sacramentalism: the study of the efficacious symbolism of the Christian rites themselves. Both of these developed out of the Pauline ''mysterion,'' which can be defined as the secret hidden in God from eternity and now revealed through Christ (Rom 16.25–26; Eph 3.1–6). In this definition the ''mysterion'' does not refer to God's invisible nature as such, but rather to the divine plan of salvation, hidden in God before the foundation of the world and then gradually manifested to the world, first in the Old Testament and subsequently at the fullness of time in Christ. Thus the Pauline ''mysterion'' is intimately connected with the economy of salvation. But it also contains the twofold idea of its hiddenness and of its visible manifestation in Christ and the Church.

Johannine Thought. This rich theological idea is found also in Johannine writings. Throughout the Fourth Gospel the figure of Moses and the events of Exodus stand in typological comparison with Christ and the spiritual events of His life (1.17, 45; 3.14; 6.31–32; 7.21–24). The manna in the desert is sign of the true bread from heaven given by the Father (6.31–32). Moses lifting up the serpent in the desert prefigures Jesus lifted up on the cross (3.14). The Revelation to John, describing the Christian liturgy as a heavenly cult centered around the Lamb, takes place in a heavenly temple while angels ascend and descend in constant communication between heaven and earth. In this imagery, taken over from Jewish apocalyptic literature, there is a connection between the heavenly and the earthly.

Epistle to the Hebrews. To explain this relationship, theologians turned to the dualism of sensible sign and spiritual reality, as witnessed by the use of typically Jewish symbolism in the Letter of Clement I to the Corinthians and in the Pseudo-Barnabas. The Epistle to the Hebrews is the earliest canonical document to make use of this dualism in an explicit way. The contrast between the heavenly and the earthly, the spiritual and the tangible, the perfect and the imperfect runs throughout the Epistle (see Cambier, 535–38). Although indirectly influenced by Greek thought, the dualism of the Epistle is not one that contrasts the concrete ''shadows'' of the sensible world with the abstract ''realities'' of the world of ideas. It is rather a dualism relating the Old Testament events and institutions to Christ and His unique salvation event. The former are sensible, imperfect''shadows'' of the latter. By His death and exaltation Christ, our high priest, entered once and for all into the heavenly holy of holies, the immediacy of God's presence. Christ then instituted a new, spiritual cult. The arrangements of the old dispensation were only an imperfect ''figure'' of this perfect heavenly cult. Thus the Epistle's dualism reflects Judeo-Christian thought and is very close to the method employed by PHILO JUDAEUS who had an evident influence on many later Greek and Latin Fathers.

The Greek Fathers. Much the same can be said of the Greek Fathers. ORIGEN, for example, whose thought was certainly influenced by Platonism, defined a sign as a visible thing that evokes the idea of another and invisible thing (*In epist. ad Rom.* 4.2; *Patrologia Graeca*, ed. J. P. Migne, 14:968). The examples that he gives to illustrate this definition indicate that his thought is much more deeply rooted in Scriptural typology: Jonah, coming out of the belly of the whale, is the sign of Christ's Resurrection. Circumcision, which God imposed on Abraham, is the sign of circumcision of the heart mentioned by Paul in Philippians 3.3. Origen's thought here is representative of the Alexandrian Fathers, whose speculations on the great Christian mysteries—Christ, the Church, the Christian—were cast in the framework of typological reflection on the economy of salvation.

The typology, having quickly become traditional among the Fathers, centers around the major Old Testament personages and events: Adam and paradise, Noah and the flood, Isaac and his sacrifice, Moses and the Exodus, Joshua and the crossing over into the Promised Land. Noe prefigures salvation in Christ. As the only just man spared from the flood's destruction, he became head of a remnant of purified humanity and thus pointed toward Christ, head of the community of the saved. The flood waters, cause of both destruction and salvation, foreshadowed Baptism's saving waters (Daniélou, *From Shadows to Reality* 69–103). Exodus is also a shadow of man's true liberation in Christ. Just as God miraculously delivered the Jews from Pharao's tyranny through Moses, so, also, through Christ the spiritual tyranny of Satan was shattered for the new people of God. In the day-to-day life of the Church, the Sacraments renew the *Mirabilia Dei* of the Exodus. In Baptism, the rite of purification and initiation, the reality foreshadowed by the Jews' wondrous passage through the Red Sea is witnessed. In the Eucharist the true manna of the desert is consumed (*ibid.* 153–217). The Jewish religious institutions also prefigured Christian mysteries. The Jerusalem Temple with God's presence looked ahead to the true spiritual Temple, which is either Christ Himself, the Christian community, or the individual Christian united to Christ.

In the Alexandrian writers, such as Clement, Origen, and Cyril, this typology develops very often into exaggerated allegory, while it is masterfully handled by Athanasius, Gregory of Nyssa, and John Chrysostom. But typology is not restricted to the Alexandrian school. It is found in Cyril of Jerusalem and Theodore of Mopsuestia, and, in the West, in such writers as Hilary, Ambrose, and Augustine (*ibid.* 1–7).

The Greek Fathers also made use of non-Biblical imagery for their sacramental theology. CLEMENT OF ALEXANDRIA, for example, is conscious of pagan mystery rites when he describes the Eucharist as the ''mysteries of the Logos'' (*Protrept.* 118; *Die griechischen christlichen Schriftsteller der ersten drei Jahrhunderte* 12.83). The Fathers describe Baptism by analogy with the seal (sphragis), an allusion to the baptismal rite of marking the forehead with the sign of the cross (see Daniélou, *The Bible and the Liturgy* 54–69). Clement of Alexandria informs us that Christians had several other ''seals'' (sphragides) or symbols, which today would be classified as sacramentals. He mentions the dove, the fish, the ship (*Paed.* 3.11; *Die griechischen christlichen Schriftsteller der ersten drei Jahrhunderte* 12:270). For further explanation of these symbols and others, such as the palm and crown, the vine and the tree of life, the living water and fish, see Daniélou, *Primitive Christian Symbols.*

Western Sacramental Theology. In the West the idea of the sacred military oath (sacramentum) was applied to Baptism, and exerted considerable influence on subsequent sacramental thought. Tertullian, Cyprian, Arnobius, and Optatus were especially responsible for this development (see Michel, 508–19). Furthermore, the controversy over DONATISM focused attention on the external rites themselves and forced the Church to elaborate her sacramental theory. The change of perspective from East to West can be seen in Saint AUGUSTINE. He borrowed his theory of signs from Origen: ''For a sign is a thing which, over and above the impression it makes on the senses, by itself causes something else to come into the mind'' (*De doctr. christ.* 2.1.1; *Patrologia Latina*, ed. J. P. Migne, 34: 35). But the way he illustrates this definition shows how he differs from Origen. The traces of an animal are the sign of its passage. Smoke is the sign of fire. The sound of the trumpet indicates the movement of an army. These examples are taken not from Bible history, but from natural symbolism. So, also, in applying this theory to the Sacraments, it is the natural religious symbolism of the rites that reveals the hidden meaning. ''The water of the Sacrament is visible, . . . it washes the body, but signifies what takes place in the soul'' (*In epist. Joannis ad Parthos* 6.11; *Patrologia Latina* 35:2026). Bread and wine ''are called Sacraments, because in them one thing is seen, another understood'' (*Sermo* 272; *Patrologia Latina* 38:1247). Here Augustine merely develops in an explicit way the implicit natural symbolism of the Sacraments. Therefore, in Augustinian thought the Sacrament is seen as a natural religious sign evoking the idea of a religious thing, of which it is the image.

Saint Thomas. As regards the dualism of sensible sign and spiritual reality, Saint Thomas provides a synthesis of sacramental theology. His theory begins with Augustine's definition of sign, which he interprets in such a way as to account for both typology and sacramentalism. The sign, precisely as sign and not as event, can signify past, present, and future. The Christian Sacrament, therefore, signifies: (1) the Passion of Christ, the past salvation event; (2) grace, the present spiritual reality in the soul; and (3) glory, the future eschatological state (*Summa theologiae* 3a, 60.3). The ''sacraments'' of the Old Testament merely prefigured those of the New without effecting what they symbolized, for they did not contain the reality, namely, Christ Himself or His priestly power.

Following the Augustinian tradition, the Council of Florence's *Decree for the Armenians* (1439) contains a short summary of Western sacramental doctrine spelling out the natural religious symbolism of the seven Sacraments. This document employs a dualism contrasting the natural with the supernatural. The birth, growth, and death of the natural living organism becomes an analogy for the supernatural life of the individual living in the Church. Thus Baptism symbolizes the Christian's spiritual birth; Confirmation, his spiritual fortification; the Eucharist, his spiritual nourishment; Penance, his spiritual healing; and Extreme Unction, the last healing of the soul, if not of the body, before his trip to heaven. Holy Orders and Matrimony are described more functionally: by Orders the Church is governed and multiplied spiritually; by Matrimony it is multiplied physically (H. Denzinger, *Enchiridion symbolorum*, ed. A. Schönmetzer, 1310–27).

Contemporary Theology. Western sacramental theology, by focusing its attention on the natural signs—water, bread, oil, baptizing, feasting, anointing—tended to interpret the meaning of the Sacraments more or less exclusively in terms of their natural significance. In modern theological investigation, however, the attempt to rediscover the full riches of Biblical and patristic symbolism indicates the growing awareness of the Church as a divine mystery in the Pauline sense. The Church, situated in the economy of salvation, is seen as the continuation of the Incarnation in and through the members of Christ's mystical body. As for the Sacraments, the analysis of the phenomenon of religious experience has shown that religious symbolism engages the whole person totally and existentially; the Sacraments are not merely ''signs'' to the intellect of an abstract theory, but rather a concrete means of personal encounter with a transcendent Deity. The Sacraments, then, are efficacious symbols that make the glorified Christ present to man here and now in a very human way.

See Also: EXEGESIS, BIBLICAL

Bibliography: J. CAMBIER, ''L'Épître aux Hébreux,'' A. ROBERT and A. FEUILLET, eds., *Introduction à la Bible (Tournai)*: v.2, *Nouveau Testament* (1959) 2:531–54. A. CODY, *Heavenly Sanctuary and Liturgy in the Epistle to the Hebrews* (St. Meinrad, Ind. 1961). J. DANIÉLOU, *The Bible and the Liturgy* (Notre Dame, Ind. 1956); *From Shadows to Reality,* tr. W. HIBBERD (Westminster, Md. 1960); *Primitive Christian Symbols,* tr. D. ATTWATER (Baltimore 1964). B. LEEMING, *Principles of Sacramental Theology* (new ed. Westminster, Md. 1960). A. MICHEL, *Dictionnaire de théologie catholique*, ed. A. VACANT et al., 15 v. (Paris 1903–50) 14.1:485–655. E. H. SCHILLEBEECKX, *Christ: The Sacrament of the Encounter with God* (New York 1963). A. VONIER, *A Key to the Doctrine of the Eucharist* (1925; reprint Westminster, Md. 1956). J. H. MILLER, *Signs of Transformation in Christ* (Englewood Cliffs, N.J. 1963). H. R. SCHLETTE, H. FRIES, ed., *Handbuch theologischer Grundbegriffe*, 2 v. (Munich 1962–63) 2:606–13.

[G. L. COULON]

SYMEON THE NEW THEOLOGIAN, MONK OF THE STUDION

Byzantine monk distinguished for his spiritual writings; b. Galatia (Paphlagonia), 949; d. March 12, 102. As a boy Symeon joined his uncle in the court circles of Constantinople to complete his education and achieve high office. Under the influence of a Studite monk, Symeon the Pious, however, he decided to become a monk. After a farewell visit to his ancestral home in Paphlagonia, he resigned his office and in 977 entered the monastery of Studion in Constantinople. His allegiance to his spiritual father, Symeon, resulted in a conflict with the abbot, who had him expelled, and he joined the monastery of St. Mamas in southwest Constantinople near the gate of

Xerocercos. He became a priest in 980 and head of St. Mamas when its abbot, Anthony, died. His vigorous discipline and penetrating though constructive criticism aroused opposition from some of his monks; and he was attacked by Stephen, the patriarch's *syncellus,* allegedly for his cult of his spiritual father, Symeon, who had died in 987, though rivalry between secular and monastic elements in the capital may have played a part. Symeon resigned his office as abbot in 1005 and was exiled by the patriarch in 1009. He retreated to the monastery of St. Marina, which he had restored, on the Asian shore of the Bosphorus, near Chrysopolis (Scutari), and attracted a large following, serving as confessor to the patrician families of the capital. Great indignation was felt at his exile, and evidently pressure was brought to bear upon the patriarch, who lifted the ban and offered Symeon an archbishopric. This Symeon refused, and though reconciliation was effected, he continued to live in St. Marina.

A wise abbot and a great spiritual leader, Symeon wrote extensively on cenobitic and eremitic monasticism reflecting his experience of both these ways of life. As his fame spread, he was called the Younger or the New Theologian, perhaps to distinguish him from the two earlier theologians, St. John the Evangelist and St. GREGORY OF NAZIANZUS. Symeon's works have been translated in part into modern Greek, Latin, and Russian; but it is only recently that the tangled MSS tradition has begun to be unraveled and that a definitive edition of some of his sermons has been put in process of publication. His writings consist mainly of sermons, a series of short rules called *capita,* or chapters, and letters; and the *Hymns of the Divine Loves* describe his spiritual experiences. A collection of his sermons contains the *catecheses,* or moral instructions, evidently preached to his monks at St. Mamas. Rich in personal touches as well as in vigorous criticism of current monastic conduct, these sermons appear to have been circulated in several editions during Symeon's lifetime. After his death, his disciple NICETAS STETHATOS, who wrote his life, also made a further edition of the *catecheses.* He seems to have been responsible for revising these sermons, incorporating material from Symeon's notes, but cutting out personal touches and passages open to misinterpretation to produce a version suitable for the general public as distinct from a particular monastic house.

Symeon's writings reveal a lifelong quest for knowledge of God and describe his own experiences as a foretaste of a personal union with the divine Being. For him the vision of the divine Light was something more than the presence of the eternal Light; it was a meeting with Christ Himself who spoke to him through the Holy Spirit. Symeon longed passionately for his monks to share this supreme experience, and he urged them to be aware that such miracles were as possible for them as they were for the Apostles in the days of the Incarnate Christ.

Feast: March 12 (Orthodox Church)

Bibliography: SYMEON THE NEW THEOLOGIAN *Catéchèse,* ed. B. KRIVOCHÉINE, tr. J. PARAMELLE, 3 v. (*Sources Chrétiennes* 96, 104; 1963–64), v.3; *Patrologia Graeca* v.120, Lat. tr. only of sermons and Hymns of the Divine Loves, Gr. and Lat. of *capita; Chapitres,* critical ed. by J. DARROUZÈS (*Sources Chrétiennes* 51; 1957); *Hymnen,* Ger. tr. by K. KIRCHHOFF (2nd ed. Munich 1951). Modern Gr. tr. of selected writings tr. by D. ZAGORAIOS (Venice 1790; 2nd ed. 1886). H. G. BECK, *Kirche und theologische Literatur im byzantinischen Reich* (Munich 1959). NICETAS STETHATOS, *Vie de Syméon le Nouveau,* ed. I. HAUSHERR, Fr. tr. by G. HORN (Orientalia Christiana 12; 1928). J. M. HUSSEY, *Church and Learning in the Byzantine Empire, 867–1185* (Oxford 1937). B. KRIVOCHÉINE, ''The Writings of St. Symeon the New Theologian,'' *Orientalia Christiana periodica* 20 (1954) 289–328.

[J. M. HUSSEY]

SYMMACHUS, POPE, ST.

Pontificate: Nov. 22, 498 to July 19, 514; b. Sardinia; d. Rome. The election that followed the death of Pope Anastasius II was disputed. The majority of the clergy, including those who had disapproved of the late pope's conciliatory policy toward Constantinople as well as those favoring the Ostrogothic king, THEODORIC THE GREAT, elected the Sardinian deacon and convert from paganism Symmachus at the Lateran. A minority of the clergy, including the philo-Byzantine party in the senate, elected the archpriest Laurentius at St. Mary Major. Both parties appealed to King Theodoric, which meant that a Gothic Arian decided who was to be the bishop of Catholic Rome. The king decided in favor of Symmachus. On his return from Ravenna, Pope Symmachus held a synod in Rome (March 1, 499), which forbade electioneering among the clergy during the lifetime of a pope and stipulated that a majority vote should prevail in an election. Laurentius ceded and was named bishop of Nocera. However, in the presence of Theodoric, his supporters accused Symmachus of having alienated ecclesiastical property contrary to the regulations of 483 with a view to ensuring his own election. They also claimed that he had sexual relations with certain women, and ordered the celebration of Easter on a date that differed from the usage of Alexandria, which was followed by all the churches.

Laurentian Schism. Summoned to Ravenna once more, Symmachus prepared to meet the king, but fled to Rome when he detected what he feared to be a trap. He took refuge in the church of Saint Paul's Outside the Walls, an action which some Roman clergy took as an admission of guilt and so withdrew Communion from him.

His flight angered Theodoric, who appointed Bishop Peter of Altinum as Roman *visitator* to administer the property of the Roman Church. Symmachus agreed to appear before a synod of Italian bishops that Theodoric summoned to judge the pope in Rome (501), but he did not concede that any synod had the right to judge the pope. While on the way to the Sessorian Palace, where the session was to be held, the supporters of Laurentius attacked the papal party in the streets, and some of the clergy were either killed or wounded. Symmachus returned to St. Peter's and refused to budge. The synod met (October 501) and decreed in its fourth session, known as the *Synodus palmaris*, that the pope could not be tried for the crimes of which he was accused and that his case must be left to the judgment of God. Since he was still the legitimate pope, the control of church property should be returned to him.

The decision displeased the Ostrogothic king, who sanctioned the return to Rome of the antipope Laurentius. For the next four years Rome was the scene of brawls and violence. The Laurentians gained possession of almost all of the churches, including the Lateran, but excluding St. Peter's, and the antipope's portrait was placed among those of the legitimate popes. Both sides launched into a war of pamphlets. The writer ENNODIUS, then a deacon in Milan, wrote an apology to show that the cause of the bishops of Rome could be judged by God alone. This theme was developed in a series of apocryphal works, composed for popular consumption and known as the Symmachan Forgeries. They were meant to provide a series of spurious historical precedents for the decrees of the synod of 501. Peace was restored through the intercession of Alexandrian deacon Dioscorus, who convinced Theodoric to have control of the churches and ecclesiastical property returned to Symmachus. The Laurentians gradually rallied to Symmachus.

Pope Symmachus defended himself against the charges of the Laurentians in a letter to the Emperor ANASTASIUS I, but he made no progress toward settling the ACACIAN SCHISM. A series of revolts against the emperor at Antioch and Constantinople itself persuaded the Byzantine ruler to attempt a reconciliation with Rome, and the pope was invited to preside over a general council at Heraclea to decide all the questions in dispute. However, Symmachus died before it arrived, and the imperial letter was received by his successor.

Symmachus maintained close relations with CAESARIUS OF ARLES, to whom the pope sent the pallium when he appointed him papal vicar for all of Gaul in place of his rival AVITUS, bishop of Vienne. Symmachus was responsible for many embellishments to St. Peter's; he converted the two round imperial mausolea nearby into chapels, constructed the earliest papal residence on the site of the present Vatican Palace, and erected lodgings for pilgrims. He was buried in the portico of the basilica.

The Symmachan Forgeries. These documents purported to be the Acts of the Synod of Sinuessa under Pope Marcellinus; the *Constitutum* of Pope Silvester I; the *Gesta* of Pope Liberius; and the Acts clearing Pope SIXTUS III of the accusation by Polychronius. Barbaric in style but expressing the doctrine on the papacy enunciated by GELASIUS I, the documents sought to supply precedents for the clearing of Pope Symmachus in similar actions performed by his predecessors. Their primary contention centers on the principle that no earthly power can sit in judgment over a pope. They were incorporated into the *Liber pontificalis* and achieved wide diffusion.

Feast: July 19.

Bibliography: Twenty-four letters are extant. *Patrologia Latina*, ed. J. P. MIGNE (Paris 1878–90) 62:49–80. A. THIEL, ed., *Epistolae romanorum pontificum* (Braunsberg 1868—) 1:639–738. *Monumenta Germaniae Historica: Auctores antiquissimi* (Berlin 1826—) 12:399–455. *Clavis Patrum latinorum*, ed. E. DEKKERS (Streenbruge 1961) 1678–82, critical eds. 1679–82, Apocrypha Symmachiana. *Liber pontificalis*, ed. L. DUCHESNE (Paris 1886–92) 1.44–46, 260–268; 3:87–90. G. SCHWAIGER, *Lexikon für Theologie und Kirche*, ed. J. HOFER and K. RAHNER (Freiburg 1957–65) 9:1217–19. H. LECLERCQ, *Dictionnaire d'archéologie chrétienne et de liturgie* (Paris 1907–53) 13.1:1213–15. H. FUHRMANN, ''Die Fälschungen im Mittelalter,'' *Historische Zeitschrift* 197 (1963) 529–554. W. ULLMANN, *The Growth of Papal Government in the Middle Ages* (New York 1962). R. VIELLIARD, *Recherches sur les origines de la Rome chrétienne* (Rome 1959). E. FERGUSON, ed., *Encyclopedia of Early Christianity* (New York 1997) 2:1098. H. JEDIN, *History of the Church* (New York 1980) 2:620–622. J. N. D. KELLY, *Oxford Dictionary of Popes* (New York 1986) 50–52. P. LEEWELLYN, ''The Roman Church during the Laurentian Schism: Priests and Senators,'' *Church History* 45 (1978) 417–4278. G. MELE and N. SPACCAPELO, eds., *Il Papato di San Simmaco (498–514) Studi e Ricerche di Cultura Religiosa*, n.s. 2 (Cagliari 2000). J. MOOREHEAD, ''The Laurentian Schism: East and West in the Roman Church,'' *Church History* 47 (1978) 125–136. J. RICHARDS, *Popes and Papacy the Early Middle Ages* (London 1979) 69–99. V. AIELO, ''Cassiodoro e la tradizione su Constantino,'' in *Cassiodoro. Dalla corte di Ravenna al Vivarium di Squillace. Atti Convegno internazionale di studi, Squillace, 25/27 ott. 1990* (1993) 131–57. R. MATHISEN, ''The 'Second council of Arles' and the Spirit of Compilation and Codification in Late Roman Gaul,'' *Journal of Early Christian Studies* 5 (1997) 511–54. CH. PIETRI, ''Le Sénat, le peuple chrétien et les partis du cirque à Rome sous le Pape Symmaque (498–514),'' in *Christiana Respublica. Éléments d'une enquête sur le christianisme antique* (Rome 1997) 771–87.

[J. CHAPIN/EDS.]

SYMMACHUS, QUINTUS AURELIUS

Roman statesman, orator, and champion of paganism; b. *c.* 345; d. *c.* 402. He was educated at Bordeaux, where he met and became a close friend of Ausonius. A man of marked ability as an administrator and as an orator, he was made prefect of the city of Rome in 384, and he attained the consulship in 391, although several years earlier he had supported the pagan usurper Maximus. As an enthusiastic adherent of paganism and an active participant in various pagan cults, he was regarded as the leader of the pagan party. He tried repeatedly to have the Altar of Victory restored to the Senate house, but was successfully opposed by Ambrose, the great bishop of Milan (*see* AMBROSE, ST.). Symmachus was a man of high character and, despite his support of paganism, was on friendly terms with many prominent Christians. His writings are valuable historical sources, but are composed in the highly rhetorical and bombastic style of his age.

Bibliography: *Q. Aurelii Symmachi quae supersunt,* ed. O. SEECK, *Monumenta Germaniae Historica Auctores antiquissimi,* (Berlin 1826–) 6.1. F. H. DUDDEN, *The Life and Times of St. Ambrose,* 2 vol. (Oxford 1935). O. SEECK, *Paulys Realenzyklopädie der klassischen Altertumswissenschaft,* ed. G. WISSOWA et al. (Stuttgart 1893–) 4.A1: 1146–58.

[M. R. P. MCGUIRE]

SYNAGOGUE

Local assembly of the Jews primarily for religious worship and their place of assembly for this purpose. The term synagogue is derived from the Greek συναγωγή and originally designated the assembly or community. In time it came to denote also the place where the community convened. Among modern Jews, reform congregations and some conservative ones call their synagogues "temples," whereas Yiddish-speaking Orthodox Jews employ the term *Schul* (school).

It is not possbile to pinpoint in time and place the origins of the synagogue. It is generally conjectured that its beginnings lie sometime in the period of the Babylonian Exile, during which time, it is known, the people came together in the homes of prophets or leaders of the Hebrew community probably to console one another in their common distress (Ez 8.6; 11.16; 14.1; 20.1; 33.1). In the postexilic period there appears to have been a broad development of the synagogue throughout Palestine and elsewhere where the Jews settled in sufficient numbers. Though in its primal origins the synagogue seems to have been chiefly a house of study, it became, with the passage of time, a house of prayer as well.

In Palestine the synagogue was usually given a prominent and convenient location within the town. The Jews of the DIASPORA were often constrained to build their synagogues outside the city limits, for the Romans were intolerant of alien places of worship within the precincts of their towns. Medieval Jewry built its synagogues within the ghetto, where in some instances (e.g., Rome) several synagogues stood side by side.

The ancient synagogues in Palestine were prevailingly constructed in the basilica form. In the Diaspora, by and large, no one style of synagogue architecture was preferred above the rest, but in each country and in each century that architectural mode was followed which prevailed generally. There is one notable instance of distinctive synagogue architecture. It was developed in Poland at a time when Jewish culture flourished in that country. The type of structure that emerged was eminently suited to the rites and uses of Jewish worship, for the requirements laid down by the Talmud were integrated into the basic design of the building.

As is known, a strict interpretation of Ex 20.4 rules out all carved and painted images of living beings for use anywhere, but especially in places of worship. However, from the decorations found in synagogues dating from different periods one must conclude that Jewish attitudes varied through the centuries as to what was allowable and appropriate for synagogue adornment. At one time, it seems, exception was taken to representations of men and animals. At another time such images were apparently acceptable as long as they were not in relief.

Originally, it appears, women did not go in any numbers to synagogue services, and so no special provisions were made for them in the ancient, Oriental synagogues; that is, women were permitted to worship in the same room with men. Among the Jews of the West it was more common for women to attend the synagogue. Though even in the West, in ancient times, no separation was made of men from women, eventually it became customary to set aside an area for women. This space was separated from the main hall by a grating. In recent times the separation has increasingly been made less of, so that in American reform congregations, for instance, no separation is observed between the sexes.

In antiquity the only required equipment for a synagogue was a chest to contain the sacred scrolls. This receptacle generally took the form of a portable wooden box and was sometimes spoken of as the "holy ark," an expression allusive of the ark of the convenant. In some places, it became the practice to cut out a niche for it in the east wall. At an early date a platform was introduced for reading the Torah. A lamp called the Ner Tumid (eternal light) was hung before the holy ark and was kept burning constantly out of reverence for the Torah.

Both Christ and his disciples maintained a constant contact with the synagogue. Luke recounts a visit by Christ at the outset of his public life to the synagogue in

His native Nazareth (Lk 4.16–28). Thereafter in the report of the ministry of Jesus found in the Gospels, there are frequent references to His attendance at the synagogue (e.g., Mt 9.35; Mk 1.39; Lk 4.44; Jn 6.59). The synagogue in the earliest days of Christianity served as a forum for proclaiming the Gospel. Both Stephen and Paul, in the beginning at least, pursued the practice of preaching Christ in the synagogue (e.g., Acts 6.9; 17.2).

Bibliography: *Encyclopedic Dictionary of the Bible,* translated and adapted by L. HARTMAN (New York, 1963) 2374–76. K. GALLING, *Die Religion in Geschichte und Gegenwart,* 7 v. (3d ed. Tübingen 1957–65) 6: (557–559). I. ELBOGEN, *Der jüdische Gottesdienst in seiner geschichtlichen Entwicklung* (Leipzig 1913). K. KOHLER, *The Origins of the Synagogue and the Church,* ed. H. G. ENELOW (New York 1929). M. I. ROSTOVTSEV, *Dura-Europos and Its Art* (Oxford 1938). E. SCHÜER, *A History of the Jewish People in the Time of Jesus Christ,* tr. J. MACPHERSON ET AL., 5 v. (Edinburgh 1897–98); new and abr. ed. N. N. GLATZER (New York 1961). E. L. SUKENIK, *Ancient Synagogues in Palestine and Greece* (London 1934). D. HOLISHER, *The Synagogue and Its People* (New York 1955).

[J. C. TURRO]

SYNAGOGUES, ANCIENT

After the Roman destruction of the Temple of Herod in Jerusalem (A.D. 70), the synagogue became the central religious building of ancient Judaism, both in the Holy Land and the Diaspora. Systematic archeological investigation of synagogues is a fairly recent development; previously, literary evidence (chiefly rabbinic, summarized by Krauss and Sonne) was considered normative, despite the fact that it said almost nothing about the Diaspora. Excavations have now proved that these earlier views were often parochial, incomplete, and on some matters (e.g., art in the synagogue) incorrect. In summarizing the more recent evidence, this article will be restricted to major and/or well-published buildings; for exhaustive lists of sites, see Saller and Goodenough.

Origins and Uses. The synagogue was two things at the same time: first, it was adjunct, alternative, and finally successor to the Jerusalem Temple; second, the common building of a specific community.

The earliest synagogues excavated thus far are at Masada and Herodium, palace-retreat-fortress complexes built by Herod the Great (ruled 37–4 B.C.); these finds and abundant literary evidence (e.g., the Gospels, Acts) indicate that there was a time when Judaism utilized Temple and synagogue side by side. Indeed, the synagogue built by Theodotus (*Corpus inscriptionum Judaicarum,* ed. J. B. Frey [Rome 1936–] 1404) was surely contemporary with Herod's Temple, and was also located in Jerusalem; later rabbinic tradition states that there were 480 synagogues in the city at that time. Nevertheless, there were great contrasts between the two institutions: the Temple with its sacrificial cult, ritual, and trained staff drawn from elite priestly families marked Jerusalem as the very heart of Judaism, a theological idea as much as a geographical location. Synagogues were democratic, devoted to laymen's prayer and study, the institution of a less centralized, worldwide religion. The literary evidence suggested that the synagogue originated during the Exile, after the destruction (587 B.C.) of the Temple of Solomon, when many Jews had been removed from the Holy Land; from that time on, most Jews would live in the Diaspora. After the Temple was rebuilt, it and the synagogue together were the architectural crystallization of the religion; in postbiblical Judaism, they and the home were the three focuses of worship, the emphasis of each supplementing that of the other two. With the destruction of Herod's Temple (A.D. 70), that side of the religious expression of Judaism represented by the Temple disappears; some of the most dramatic changes after the

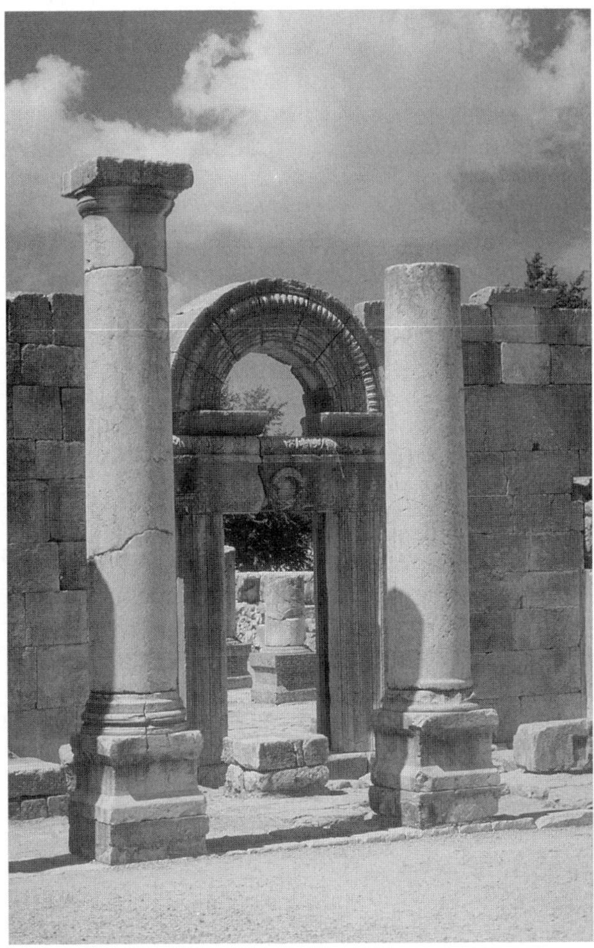

Ruins of ancient synagogue, 200 A.D., Bar Am, Israel. (©Richard T. Nowitz/CORBIS)

traumatic events of the First (A.D. 66–70) and Second (A.D. 132–135) Revolts issue from the fact that priest and clergy no longer balance rabbi and laity. The Judaism of the ancient synagogue is the result. (Discussion of the synagogue as a replacement for the Temple occurs in a later section of this article, ''Torah Shrine.'')

In a slightly later period, the relatively elaborate Christian forms of worship would lead to increasingly specialized religious buildings, e.g., the Byzantine churches of Constantinople; the simpler Jewish corporate worship (prayers, scripture reading, psalms) made no such demands. Something might be called a ''synagogue,'' literally ''place of assembly,'' *because* it was used for services; it may well have been built for and used for other worthy purposes. Structures built specifically as synagogues were also the locus for a number of community activities and events: the education of children and adults, civic meetings, and occasionally judicial proceedings. Community hospitality caused the synagogue or its side rooms to be used for common meals or as a shelter for travelers, e.g., the Theodotus synagogue (*Corpus inscriptionum Judaicarum* 1404) in Jerusalem; Er-Ramah (*ibid.* 979) and probably Khirbet Shema' in Galilee; and Dura, Stobi (*ibid.* 694), and Ostia in the Diaspora.

Diaspora Synagogues. Archeological and historical investigation indicate that the old distinction between ''Diaspora'' Judaism and Judaism in the Holy Land had been overdrawn; nevertheless, the following should be kept in mind when considering Diaspora synagogues: (1) they are the buildings of a minority faced with the problem of preserving its identity in a Gentile culture, thus they were often the only center of the Jewish community in a Diaspora town; this increased their importance, but also altered or expanded their functions. (2) The Jerusalem Temple was a great distance away; thus the tendency of the synagogue to take on ''Temple'' characteristics probably began earlier here than in the Holy Land. (3) These buildings in overall shape and specific feature borrow heavily from local architecture, e.g., Dura, Sardis, Ostia. (4) Local conditions sometimes made it advisable to screen the building and conceal its purpose, e.g., Dura, Priene, Ostia. (5) Rabbinic statements about synagogue architecture and usage are not concerned with, and thus are all but irrelevant to, the Diaspora west of the Holy Land, i.e., the bulk of the Roman Empire.

Dating and Architectural Styles. Sukenik, Goodenough, and Avi-Yonah all attempt to classify the excavated buildings architecturally, and in the Holy Land at least there are two clear types: (1) Examples of Sukenik's ''earlier'' type, Goodenough's ''Galilean'' type, and Avi-Yonah's ''early'' type all are simple basilicas with interior columnation (at the least, two rows of columns parallel to the long axis), the entrances (usually three doors) are in the wall closest to Jerusalem, and the building is without a fixed Torah shrine; examples are Capernaum, Beth Shearim, Baram, Chorazin. (2) Sukenik's ''new'' type, Goodenough's ''synagogues with mosaics,'' and Avi-Yonah's ''fifth-century synagogues'' have mosaic floors where the first type had flagstones; on the wall closest to Jerusalem is a permanent Torah shrine, often in a niche or apse, and usually opposite the main entrance; examples are Beth Alpha and Hammath Gadera. In the first type, the emphasis is on the exterior, particularly on the wall facing Jerusalem; customarily, this façade with its three entrance doors displayed the building's most elaborate and embellished architecture. In the second type, the emphasis is on the interior, with mosaic floor (often in complicated and colorful designs, e.g., the Beth Alpha zodiac) and decorated Torah shrine. Theologically, the most important difference is the presence in the second type of a permanent Torah shrine on the wall of orientation, the wall closest to Jerusalem, *opposite* the entrance. There are firm indications that the second type, with the fixed shrine, is generally later than the first; at Beth Shearim and Ein Gedi, and in the Diaspora at Sardis and Ostia, such shrines were added to buildings that originally lacked them, even though this was architecturally awkward.

Another architectural type is usually inserted between Sukenik's two: Goodenough's ''broadhouse type'' and Avi-Yonah's ''transitional type.'' In these, one of the *long* walls is the wall of orientation (hence broadhouse), closest to Jerusalem; the Torah shrine is on that wall, the entrances are often in one of the short walls; examples are Khirbet Shema', Susiya, and Eshtemoa. This type may represent attempts to deal with the change of building style and orientation caused by the introduction of the fixed Torah shrine.

Classification by architectural style was part of an attempt to date buildings, the excavations of which had produced minimal dating evidence; more recent finds suggest that dating on the basis of style be done only as a last resort, in the absence of stratigraphic evidence. In the Diaspora, building style may be determined more by local custom than by what Jews in the Holy Land were doing: the Dura synagogue was a broadhouse from its beginning in the late 2d century, before most if not all known examples of Sukenik's ''earlier type'' were built.

Certain interior furnishings were common to all types: permanent benches on two or more walls, portable lecterns, the seven-branched candlestick (menorah, both functional and symbolic), the bemah or speaking-platform (e.g., Khirbet Shema', Susiya, Beth Alpha), and on occasion special seating for the community's leaders, e.g., the ''seat of Moses'' (Mt 23.2) at Hammath Tiberias, Chorazin, Ein Gedi, and perhaps Capernaum, and the 70-place synthronon in the apse at Sardis.

Some buildings are designed in ways that would permit the separation of sexes during services: larger basilica-synagogues could have had a balcony or ''women's gallery'' (e.g., Chorazin, Capernaum). Of the broad-houses, Khirbet Shema' apparently had a balcony on its west wall, but none is possible at Eshtemoa since it lacks interior columns. In some buildings women could have been relegated to adjacent rooms, e.g., the forecourt at Ostia or Dura; at other sites, however, there is no obvious place where women could observe the services but be separate from the men.

Torah Shrine. Two important themes of postbiblical Judaism combined to produce the Torah shrine of the later synagogue: (1) the increasing importance of Scripture, and particularly the Torah (the Law, the Pentateuch); this begins while the Temple still stands and the sacrificial cult continues in Jerusalem, and reaches its climax in the Torah-centered rabbinic Judaism contemporary with the pre-Constantine Church; and (2) the tendency to replicate the Temple, by representing it in art and by suggesting it in synagogue architecture. One motivation may have been to display the Temple as a rival to pagan temples; another surely was to recall the glory of a splendid structure, central to earlier theology. In Jewish symbolism there occurs a shift in focus from the architecture of the temple to the architecture of the Torah shrine, or perhaps a merging of the two images, e.g., the Dura niche and frescoes, the Beth Alpha mosaic, the ''gold glasses'' (''Goodenough, index;'' see bibliography).

The Torah shrine thus indicates the increased importance of the Torah in the community; at the same time it heightens the impressiveness of the synagogue as successor to the Temple, in that it contributes to the general embellishment of the building and provides a permanent place for what is now the religion's most sacred ritual object, the Scroll of the Law. The increasing importance of the shrine is indicated by the fact that certain Jewish communities (Beth Shearim, Sardis, Ostia) felt compelled to add permanent shrines to synagogues that lacked them, even though it constituted a complete reversal of the direction of the building.

The shrine may take the form of a niche (e.g., Eshtemoa) or apse (e.g., Beth Alpha) or *aediculum* with rounded or gabled roof supported by columns (many representations, see ''Goodenough, index;''); the scrolls within are screened from sight by curtains or double doors.

Major Sites and Sources of Information. This discussion includes names of the major synagogues, their location, their description, and bibliographical material.

Beth Alpha. Beth Alpha is a 5th-century synagogue, just south of the Sea of Galilee, Israel. The building complex is 14 by 28 meters and consists of courtyard, forecourt, and main room (with apse in the south wall and mosaic floor). The north wall has the customary three entrance doors; the other three walls are provided with low benches. A bemah was a later addition, just northeast of the apse. The most important element of the building is the spectacular, three-panel main mosaic, dated by inscription to the 6th century: the first panel from the entrance depicts the biblical sacrifice of Isaac; the center section includes a zodiac; and the panel nearest the apse (i.e., the Torah shrine) displays a closed Torah shrine, two *menoroth* and other Jewish symbols. (See E. L. Sukenik, *The Ancient Synagogue of Beth Alpha* [Jerusalem, London 1932]; ''Goodenough, index;'' [see bibliography] and *Israel: Ancient Mosaics* [Paris 1960] pl. vi–xiv.)

Capernaum. Capernaum, from the 3d (or 4th?) century, is located in Galilee, northern Israel. The building complex is 28 by 32 meters with a synagogue, eastern enclosed court, and entrance platform common to both. The synagogue-basilica is 28 by 19 meters, with columns (to support a balcony?) on all but the south side, which has the usual three entrance doors. There are two-level benches on the east and west walls, and perhaps a ''seat of Moses'' (now in the southwest corner). A kind of cart, carved on one frieze-fragment, may represent the early, movable Torah shrine; it resembles a four-wheeled, columned building with rounded roof and one double door. Opposite the front of the synagogue is an octagon-shaped structure that tradition associates with the home of St. Peter (cf. Mt 8.14 and parallels); its use as a church is, in part, contemporary with the synagogue. (See B. Spair and D. Neeman, *Capernaum* [Tel Aviv 1967]; V. Corbo, S. Loffreda, and A. Spijkerman, *La Sinagoga di Cafarnao* [Jerusalem 1970].)

Dura-Europos. Dura-Europos, on the Euphrates River, Syria, is from the late 2d century A.D., renovated *c.* 244, and destroyed with the town *c.* 256. It is a broad-house, and measures 14 by 7 meters (interior, last phase) with a 13 by 10 meter forecourt; these could be reached only by passing through a nine-room dwelling complex controlled by the Jewish community. There are two-level benches on all four walls of the synagogue; and two entrances in the east wall, one in the center, a smaller one at the south end. There is a Torah niche in the center of the west wall. Spectacular tempera paintings decorate the niche and all four walls of the synagogue; they depict Old

Testament stories chiefly, but in Greco-Roman-Parthian style and idiosyncratic theological interpretation. (See C. H. Kraeling, *The Synagogue, Excavations at Dura-Europos, Final Report VIII, 1* [New Haven 1956]; Goodenough, v. 9–11; J. Gutmann, ed., *The Dura-Europos Synagogue: A Re-Evaluation [1932–1972]* [Missoula, Mont. 1973].)

Kirbet Shema'. This synagogue, from the 3d century, rebuilt in the 4th, is in Galilee, northern Israel (see illustration in gallery). It is a broadhouse, 18 by 9 meters (interior, including west stairway, frescoed room, and gallery). There is a detached ''house of study'' (7 by 7 meters) north of the northwest corner of the synagogue. There is one entrance in the north wall and one at the south end of the west wall. The west wall area is cut back into bedrock, which supports the west entrance's massive stairway and the gallery running the remaining length of the west wall; under the gallery is a small frescoed room, probably a study or scriptorium, and off this to the south (under the stairway) is a manmade storage cave or *genizah.* There is a mosaic floor and benches on some part of all walls. The focus of worship in the first phase was the *aediculum* or Torah shrine on the south wall (only fragments have been recovered); in the second phase it was a massive platform or bema. In second phase, the frescoed room may have functioned as the Torah shrine. The synagogue is the center of this small town (ancient Tekoa of Galilee?), and small buildings (chiefly private) are built against it.

Masada. Masada, on the Dead Sea in Israel, was built under Herod the Great (reigned 37–4 B.C.) and rebuilt between A.D. 66–73. The main room is 15 by 12 meters; its last phase is the product of Jewish guerillas who captured the entire Herodian palace-retreat-fortress complex from Roman troops and held it during the First Revolt. They removed the cross wall that had divided the Herodian building (which has not been proved to be a synagogue) and added a rough storage room in the north corner and four-level benches on the remainder of all walls. The storage room was used as a *genizah;* framents of Ezekiel and Deuteronomy were found buried beneath its floor. (See Y. Yadin, *Masada* [London 1966].)

Ostia. Ostia was in the port city of ancient Rome, Italy. It dates from the 4th century, but with an earlier synagogue beneath. The building complex is 37 by 23 meters: a synagogue plus kitchen and community (dining?) room. The synagogue is 25 by 13 meters and includes the forecourt with entrance off the street and three doors leading into the main room, an ''inner gateway'' or entrance portico with four marble columns (two inner, two outer) flanking the central door, and the main room. The west wall of the main room, opposite the triple entrance, was the original focus of worship; the wall is curved and has a bema six meters wide against it. Later a massive, freestanding Torah shrine was erected on the east wall (closest to Jerusalem), next to the ''inner gateway,'' blocking the southern entrance into the main hall. There is no evidence of benches or balcony. (See M. Floriani Squarciapino, ''The Synagogue at Ostia,'' *Archaeology* 16 [1963] 194–203.)

Sardis. Sardis, western Turkey, was from the 3d century, renovated in the 4th. The synagogue complex is 20 meters wide and includes a narrow, basilica-like main hall 60 meters long (with apse) and forecourt 22 meters long. The apse was a *synthronon,* with three levels of benches capable of seating more than 70 people; there is no evidence of other benches or of a balcony. A massive stone table (lectern?) stood before this apse. Opposite, on the east wall with its three entrances are two *aedicula,* one on each side of the center door; one was probably the Torah shrine, both are later than the apse. The floor is elaborate mosaic, the walls bore architectonic designs in cut marble, and the ceilings had painted decoration. The building is part of a large gymnasium-and-baths complex, a center of public life for all Sardis; rooms just west of the apse and shops just south of the synagogue (between it and a major thoroughfare) were at times owned by Jews. (See final publication by A. R. Seager, L. J. Majewski, D. G. Mitten, J. H. Kroll, and A. T. Kraabel in the series, *Archaeological Exploration of Sardis* [Cambridge, Mass. *c.* 1976].)

See Also: DIASPORA, JEWISH; JEWS, POST-BIBLICAL HISTORY OF THE.

Bibliography: M. AVI-YONAH, ''Ancient Synagogues'' *Ariel* (Spring 1973) 29–43; ''Synagogues: Architecture,'' *Encyclopedia Judaica.* G. FOERSTER, ''Les synagogues de Galilée,'' *Bible et Terre Sainte* (April 1971) 8–15. E. R. GOODENOUGH, *Jewish Symbols in the Greco-Roman Period,* 13 v. (Princeton 1953–68), ''Goodenough, index'' refers to the indispensable indexes in v. 13. H. KOHL and C. WATZINGER, *Antike Synagogen in Galiläa* (Leipzig 1916). S. KRAUSS, *Synagogale Altertümer* (Berlin, Vienna 1922), condensed as ''Synagoge,'' in *Paulys Realenzyklopädie der klassischen Altertumswissenschaft,* ed. G. WISSOWA et al. (Stuttgart 1893–). B. LIFSHITZ, *Donateurs et Fondateurs dans les Synagogues Juives* (Paris 1967), evidence from inscriptions. *Qadmoniot* 5.2 (18) 1972, preliminary articles on Susiya and Ein Gedi. S. J. SALLER, *Second Revised Catalogue of the Ancient Synagogues of the Holy Land* (Jerusalem 1972). I. SONNE, ''Synagogue,'' *The Interpreters' Dictionary of the Bible,* ed.G. A. BUTTRICK, 4 v. (Nashville 1962) 4.476–491. E. L. SUKENIK, *Ancient Synagogues in Palestine and Greece* (London 1934).

[A. T. KRAABEL]

SYNAXARY

A liturgical book in the Christian East containing a collection of abbreviated lives of the saints arranged by feast days in the ecclesiastical calendar for use in the *akoluthia*, or liturgical office, by monks or clerics. It usually offers information regarding the church or place where the saint or feast is held in special honor. The word is also frequently employed to signify a *Menologion*, or collection of saints' lives cited at length for spiritual reading. The most celebrated *Menologion* is attributed to Symeon Metaphrastes, who paraphrased material he found in various lives of the saints and arranged them in calendar order, although there is evidence of earlier such collections.

The small Synaxary is merely a calendar or listing of feast days arranged by months, following the Byzantine system, which runs from September 1 to August 31; the *Typikon*, on the other hand, is a species of perpetual *ordo*, or calendar, of stabilized feasts with rubrics for resolving problems arising from the coincidence of mobile and fixed feasts. The oldest example of the *Typikon* is that of St. SABAS, apparently originating in the 6th-century monastery that he founded in Palestine; it underwent considerable revisions in editions attributed to Sophronius of Jerusalem (d. 638), John Damascene (d. 749), and Nicholas of Constantinople (d. 925). It is to be distinguished from the monastic *Typica*, which were documents containing the rule, and frequently the foundation charter of a monastery.

The Synaxary of Constantinople is the most famous collection of liturgically oriented lives, and it witnesses to the official Byzantine cult of the saints. Spread throughout the Oriental churches, it has been preserved in innumerable manuscripts that pose an insoluble problem as to its time of origin. This Synaxary contains the feasts of Christ and the Blessed Virgin Mary; mobile feasts connected with Easter; the anniversaries of miraculous appearances of saints and angels; the patriarchs and prophets of the Old Testament; the apostles and disciples named in the New Testament; the martyrs of the early Church and of the Saracen, Bulgarian, and iconoclastic persecutions; and confessors of both Western and Eastern Churches, including the popes down to AGATHŌ (d. Jan. 10, 681). Most of the patriarchs of Constantinople, the emperors, empresses, and councils are mentioned; earthquakes and barbarian invasions are recalled, probably in connection with the services of thanksgiving rendered after deliverance from these dangers.

Modern research traces the existence of the Synaxary of Constantinople to at least the reign of Leo VI (886–911), but the largest number of versions are from the 10th and 11th centuries. Though frequently inconsistent in dates and biographical detail, they provide useful information regarding the churches and monasteries in which the feasts were kept. Similar synaxaries were used in the Slav, Syrian, Arab, Malabar, Armenian, Ethiopian, Copt, and Assyrian (Persian) Churches and provide a guide to hagiographical and liturgical material.

Bibliography: R. AIGRAIN, *L'Hagiographie* (Paris 1953). A. EHRHARD, *Überlieferung und Bestand der hagiographischen und homiletischen Literatur der griechischen Kirche*, 3 v. (*Texte und Untersuchungen zur Geschichte der altchristlichen Literatur*, 50–52; 1937–52). *Synaxarium ecclesiae Constantinopolitanae. Propylaeum ad Acta sanctorum novembris*, ed. H. DELEHAYE (Brussels 1902). H. DELEHAYE, ed., *Deux Typica byzantins* (Brussels 1921). N. NILLES, ed., *Kalendarium manuale utriusque ecclesiae*, 2 v. (Innsbruck 1896–97); ''Die Freilassung der alten slavischen liturgischen Bücher,'' *Zeitschrift für katholische Theologie* 29 (1905) 721–724. O. H. E. BURMESTER, ''. . .The Arabic Synaxarium of the Coptic Church,'' *Journal of Theological Studies* 39 (1938) 249–253. G. GRAF, *Geschichte der christlichen arabischen Literatur*, 5 v. (Vatican City 1944–53). P. PEETERS, ''Pour l'histoire du synaxaire arménien,'' *Analecta Bollandiana* 30 (1911) 5–26. S. DER NERSESSIAN, ''Le Synaxaire arménien,'' *ibid.* 68 (1950) 261–285.

[F. X. MURPHY/EDS.]

SYNDERESIS

The term synderesis (συντήρησις) refers to the natural or innate habit of the mind to know the first principles of the practical or moral order without recourse to a process of discursive reasoning. The notion was developed by Aristotle, who insisted that there must be a starting point for man's thought, and that the first truths that would serve as such could not be acquired, like other subsequent truths, discursively or demonstratively. Unwilling to accept SKEPTICISM or Plato's theory of innate ideas, Aristotle taught that the mind must have the potentiality to acquire fundamental truths with certitude and infallibility without having to reason to them. Though man does not possess such truths innately, he does possess an innate or natural habit for acquiring them as self-evident propositions, once he understands the terms involved. This teaching of Aristotle explaining man's knowledge of first principles in the speculative order was accepted by Saint Thomas Aquinas, and further developed to include explicitly the first principles of the practical order (*see* COGNITION SPECULATIVE-PRACTICAL; FIRST PRINCIPLES).

Historical Development. The term synderesis is derived from the Greek τηρέω used by Homer to mean ''guarding closely,'' and subsequently συντηρέω used by Aristotle in *De plantis* to mean ''preserving, keeping closely.'' The actual term συντήρησις seems to be of a Stoic origin and to lack any definite connection with συνείδησις, the similar word of Stoic philosophy, designating insight into simple matters of common knowledge. The latter term was used also by Chrysippus to describe the consciousness of harmony with oneself, which he regarded as a properly human expression of the fundamental impulse to self-preservation in all living things.

Scintilla Conscientiae. The term synderesis was introduced to the West by Saint JEROME as part of his interpretation of the four living creatures in the vision of Ezekiel (Ezekiel 1.10; *Patrologia Latina*, ed. J. P. Migne, 25:22). Jerome claims that most commentators use Plato's tripartite division of the soul (into the irascible, concupiscent, and rational parts) to interpret three of the creatures—the lion, the ox, and the man respectively. Over and above these there is also the eagle, which for Jerome represents what the Greeks call συντήρησις or "spark of conscience" (*scintilla conscientiae*). This spark was not lost by original sin, and even though we abandon ourselves to passion or appetite, it enables us to know we are doing wrong.

Saint Jerome's phrase, *scintilla conscientiae,* found greater vogue among medieval scholastics than the term synderesis. The first to note the above-mentioned text of Saint Jerome was PETER LOMBARD, but he did not speak of synderesis. The term itself was used by a Master Udo in what seems to be the first commentary on Lombard's *Sentences* (*c.* 1160–65), where he identified it with reason and held that it cannot sin or consent to evil. Apart from these, SIMON OF BISIGNANO identified synderesis with natural law; PETER OF POITIERS, with natural reason. The latter distinguished natural reason from deliberating reason on the basis that deliberating reason can consent to sin, while natural reason reacts against evil and inclines man to the good. A more extensive treatise was composed by STEPHEN LANGTON, who considered synderesis to be a natural tendency that protests against evil and inclines to the good; it itself is responsible for neither good nor evil, is superior to deliberating reason, and is concerned only with generalities.

Later Scholastic Views. The concept of synderesis as a simple habitual potency originated with ALEXANDER OF HALES in his *Summa Theologica.* His idea was taken up and developed by Saint BONAVENTURE, who placed the habit of synderesis in the WILL. Synderesis is to the will, he claimed, as judgment is to the reason. By nature man possesses a twofold source or aid to right living: conscience in the intellect to judge rightly, and synderesis in the will to dissuade from evil and stimulate to good. Thus, according to Bonaventure, synderesis is the original moral tendency of the will.

Saint ALBERT THE GREAT and Saint THOMAS AQUINAS both taught that synderesis belongs not to the will but to the INTELLECT. Albert, however, regarded it as the rational faculty endowed with the habit of first principles of the natural law, whereas Aquinas regarded it as an innate habit of practical reason (not a faculty itself), by which man comes to know immediately the first principles of the moral order.

The Oxford masters exploited Augustine's theory of ILLUMINATION in connection with synderesis. Most notable among these was ROBERT KILWARDBY, who held that synderesis is man's participation in God, the eternal light, present in and communicating Himself to the soul, there serving as the norm of man's judgments and the efficient cause of his moral life. It is also noteworthy that DUNS SCOTUS disagreed with Bonaventure and placed both conscience and synderesis in the practical reason.

Synderesis and Understanding. Some contemporary writers hold that Aquinas distinguishes two habits for grasping principles immediately: understanding for speculative principles, and synderesis for practical principles. Others hold that he allows but one habit of first principles. In this view, when the intellect grasps being as true, it apprehends the first rules of speculative thought, whereas when it grasps being as good, it knows the first rules of practical thought. Yet both sets of principles are known as true, and it is accidental to the functioning of the intellect that the latter are also known as good. This view thus identifies synderesis with UNDERSTANDING, stating in substance that a single intellectual habit, called understanding in the speculative order, is called synderesis when concerned with first principles in the practical or moral order.

As identified with, or similar to, the virtue of understanding, synderesis possesses this virtue's basic characteristics. Synderesis is therefore characterized, first of all, by the simplicity and immediacy of its operations. The principles attained by the intellect are so true and plain in meaning that they are accepted and used by all human beings, as soon as they are needed, even by a child.

Secondly, synderesis is natural, in a twofold way: first, in that it differs from a supernatural or infused habit, and secondly, in that its principles are obtained naturally, not through teaching or experimentation. The human intellect requires principles that are naturally known as a starting point for reasoned knowledge. Such first principles are not themselves natural or innate, but like all intellectual knowledge, have their origin in sense experience; yet man does have an innate or natural capacity to grasp their truth once he understands the concepts presupposed to their judgment. As a natural or innate habit, synderesis is possessed in equal degree by all men. Just as human nature is equally shared by all, so the principles attained by synderesis are self-evident to all. Nevertheless, one man may have greater insight into their meaning than another, if he has greater capacity of intellect; this in turn will depend upon the state of refinement of his internal and external sense powers (*see* SENSES).

Finally, synderesis is infallible. The human intellect cannot err regarding first and indemonstrable principles. A person whose intellect simply is not functioning, or is demented, or who has had physical injury to organs necessary for the exercise of his external and internal senses, will not of course come to know even these principles. But to speak otherwise of error with respect to such principles would be to remove the necessary basis for all ethical reasoning. Synderesis, then, is a natural capacity of man's mind, disposing him to grasp immediately and infallibly the truth of first principles in the moral order.

Relationship to Natural Law. The judgment forming a first principle must be so elementary that it will be seen as true as soon as the intellect understands the terms involved. Since the most general concept inducing man to action is that of the good, the first principle in the practical order must be: Good is to be done (with its necessary complement: Evil is to be avoided). This is therefore the basic principle for natural moral law. Following immediately from it, and thus known also by synderesis, are the simple or primary precepts of the natural law: A being must act according to its nature, a reasonable being must act reasonably, etc. The natural law prescribes those acts that are morally good for man, i.e., in accord with his natural inclinations: namely, in common with all living things, to maintain his life; in common with animals, to ensure continuation of his race by reproducing and caring properly for offspring; then, properly as human, to pursue truth, exercise freedom, and cultivate virtue. These are the basic natural inclinations of all men, at all times, everywhere. However, man's understanding of them increases with experience and with intellectual development. (*See* NATURAL LAW.)

Synderesis and Conscience. Synderesis is a habit, while CONSCIENCE is an act of judgment. Synderesis assures possession of the most general and universal knowledge of first principles of the moral order, whereas conscience is concerned with particular applications, i.e., with the practical reasoning that provides answers to particular moral problems.

Man explicitly or implicitly uses a kind of SYLLOGISM in his acts of CHOICE, and thus descends from universal principles or premises to particular moral conclusions. In this reasoning process synderesis provides the most universal moral principles, such as: Every evil is to be avoided. Reason supplies more specific and less universal precepts, adverting to the cause of a command or prohibition, such as: Adultery is evil, because it is against the law of God, or because it is unjust. Conscience then reaches the conclusion: Adultery should be, or should have been, avoided. (It may be noted that while synderesis is infallible, conscience can err in the process of reasoning.) This judgment of conscience then becomes a proximate principle for human action. Both synderesis and conscience, then, furnish norms for action: synderesis, by providing the most general and universal principles; conscience, by providing the immediate and particular reasoned judgment about a moral act.

See Also: HUMAN ACT

Bibliography: THOMAS AQUINAS, *Summa Theologiae* 1a, 79.12–13; 1a2ae, 94.1–2; *In 2 sent.* 24.2.3, 39.3.1; *De ver.* 16.1–3. R. EISLER, *Wörterbuch der philosophischen Begriffe*, 3 v. (4th ed. Berlin 1927–30) 4:199–200. O. LOTTIN, *Psychologie et morale aux 12e et 13e siècles,* 6 v. in 8 (Louvain 1942–60) 2:101–349. J. W. YEDLICKA, ''Synderesis as Remorse of Conscience,'' *The New Scholasticism* 37 (1963) 204–12. J. PÉTRIN, ''L'Habitus des principes spéculatifs et la syndérèse,'' *Revue de l'Université d'Ottawa* 18 (1948) section spéciale 208–16. J. DEBLIC, ''Syndérèse ou conscience?,'' *Revue d'ascétique et de mystique* 25 (1949) 146–57. J. ROHMER, *Dictionnaire de théologie catholique*, ed. A. VACANT et al., 15 v. (Paris 1903–50) 14.2:2992–96. O. RENZ, ''Die Synteresis nach dem Hl. Thomas von Aquin,'' *Beiträge zur Geschichte der Philosophie und Theologie des Mittelalters* 10.1–2 (1911).

[M. W. HOLLENBACH]

SYNERGISM

As a word, synergism may have a correct denotation: the interplay and concausality of God's GRACE and man's cooperation in the process of JUSTIFICATION and the working out of salvation. However, some proposals under the name of synergism reflect Semi-Pelagian doctrine.

In particular the term refers to P. MELANCHTHON's defense of the human will under grace, especially in connection with the question of conversion. As early as 1521, in his *Loci communes,* he avoided any discussion of determinism as such, although he stated clearly that since all things happen necessarily according to divine predestination, there is no freedom in man's will. Each new edition of *Loci* (there were 80 before his death) furnished more evidence that men are genuinely συνεργοί (1 Cor 3.9), that is, responsible agents to whom God entrusts the working out of His salvific design.

Sharing fully Luther's positive insight into the absolute gratuity of grace, Melanchthon nevertheless perceived the difficulties arising in the moral order from LUTHER's description of man as simultaneously sinful and just. The two reformers earnestly studied scriptural sources to solve the antinomy. When in December 1525 Luther's *De servo arbitrio* appeared in reply to Erasmus's *De libero arbitrio* of the preceding year, Melanchthon rejoiced that the controversy was bringing the crucial problem out into the open.

A humanist by attraction, Melanchthon never completely subscribed to Luther's teaching on the ineradicable depravity of human nature. On the contrary, using an empirical, psychological approach, he developed his own vital intuition of self-sanctification in the ethical sense. Steering clear of Pelagianism, in the 1535 *Loci* he showed from the dialogical character of the Law that God initiates not only man's justification, but also his sanctification: "You shall know that when we strive within ourselves, when aroused by the promise, we call God and resist our distrust and other vicious desires, that is the very way God desires to convert us."

To grasp Melanchthon's thought requires a study of the evolution of his appreciation of the three conjoined causes: "The Word, the Holy Spirit, and the will not wholly inactive in its own weakness." For him faith was a gift of the Holy Spirit demanding a dynamic reaction from man for its acceptance. "In conceiving faith there is a struggle within us," he explained in the 1532 *Commentary on Romans,* the struggle precisely between man's power to refuse and his power to receive God's Word. Against the growing number of his monergistic opponents, he held that conversion can take place only when a man, conscious of his personal responsibility, gives a meaningful "Yes," in answer to God's call to him individually. Melanchthon acknowledged the fact that after conversion man continues to bear within himself the wounds of sin, but once regenerated through faith in the Word he is "sweetly helped by the Holy Spirit" to bear witness to the new life given him.

Melanchthon always kept Luther informed of changes in his theological stance. Conversant as he was with Melanchthon's *Loci* of 1535 and 1544 and his 1537 *Examen ordinandorum,* Luther refused to reedit his own writings, saying: ". . . by the grace of God we have better methodical works, among which Philip's is the best." In the 20th century, scholars began to see, within the structure of Lutheran theology, the importance of Melanchthon's doctrine of synergism.

See Also: LUTHERANISM; FREE WILL AND GRACE; IMPUTATION OF JUSTICE AND MERIT.

Bibliography: J. PAQUIER, *Dictionnaire de théologie catholique*, ed. A. VACANT et al., (Paris 1903–50) 10.1:502–513. F. ZOEPFL, *Lexikon für Theologie und Kirche*, ed. J. HOFER and K. RAHNER (Freiberg 1957–65) 7:247–249. K. RAHNER, *ibid.* 9:1231. G. KAWERAU, *The New Schaff-Herzog Encyclopedia of Religious Knowledge*, ed. S. M. JACKSON (Grand Rapids, Mich 1951–54) 9:223–225. C. L. MANSCHRECK, *Melanchthon, The Quiet Reformer* (New York 1958).

[K. T. HARGROVE]

SYNESIUS OF CYRENE

Fourth-century philosopher and bishop of Ptolemais; b. Cyrene in Libya, Egypt, *c.* 370 or 375; d. Ptolemais, *c.* 414.

Life. Synesius studied at Alexandria under the philosopher Hypatia, visited Athens and Antioch, and settled in Cyrenaica as a well-to-do colonist, devoting time to hunting and literature. As an emissary to Constantinople (399–402), he obtained fiscal alleviations for the Pentapolis and exemption from curial duties for himself. He settled in Alexandria (403–404), where the Patriarch Theophilus blessed his marriage (*Epist.* 105). Upon the birth of a son, he returned to Cyrene to protect his family properties; but his villa was destroyed in 408 and he took refuge in Ptolemais, where in the summer of 410 the people chose him as bishop. Objecting that his love for his wife and his dedication to a more spacious life rendered him unfit, Synesius refused consecration; as a final argument he cited his Origenistic belief in the preexistence of souls, the eternity of the world, and his allegorical ideas concerning the Resurrection (*Epist.* 105 and 145). Theophilus of Alexandria, though opposed to Origenism (*see* ORIGEN AND ORIGENISM), consecrated him bishop (411) after Synesius had stipulated that he could not separate from his wife, and would accept only out of obedience to God, in the hope of finding "not a disavowal but a new advance in philosophy" (*Epist.* 11 and 96).

Synesius proved to be a conscientious bishop, zealous to maintain orthodoxy, which was menaced by the Eunomians, and courageous in excommunicating an unjust governor (*Epist.* 90), as well as in defending a friend of JOHN CHRYSOSTOM before Theophilus (*Epist.* 66). He found his pastoral duties to be oppressive, particularly when his three children died. He died before the massacre of Hypatia (415), to whom he had confided his tribulations in the last of his correspondence. It is probable that his brother Evoptius succeeded him as bishop for a prelate of that name represented the Pentapolis at the Council of EPHESUS in 431.

Synesius was a catechumen between 399 and 401, but his date of Baptism is unknown. In 404 he still indicated a greater interest in Greek wisdom than in Christian asceticism (*Dion Chrysos.* 9.13). Of an intelligence more subtle than vigorous, but honest and naturally religious, Synesius describes the effort required on the part of an intellectual living in the Hellenistic milieu of Alexandria upon becoming a Christian convert. This experience is revealed in the tracts he composed before becoming a bishop.

Writings. Writing in Greek, Synesius was admired by the Byzantines as a good example of an Atticist formed on classic culture. He is credited with ten hymns written before 408, though the last of them may not be authentic. While Hymns 1 and 3 reflect Jamblichus, the others celebrate the Trinity and the ''Son of the Virgin.'' Synesius wrote in Dorian in classic meters and boasts that he is the first to sing of Christ to the accompaniment of the zither. In the courageous discourse *On Royalty,* delivered before the Emperor Arcadius at Constantinople in 400, he traced the ideal portrait of a prince, and denounced the morals of the court, and decried the invasion of administrative offices and the army by barbarian officials.

His *Egyptian Recital* or *On Divine Providence* was written *c.* 402 and is a tract on the nature of reality under the cover of the myth of Osiris and Typho (symbolizing virtue and vice). It is neoplatonic in its notion concerning the final return of all things to their beginnings, but of definite Christian moral inspiration.

His *Dion Chrysostom* or *On the Way of Life,* written *c.* 404, is a self-justifying piece answering the philosophers who accused him of abandoning their literary interests. While he judges the Cynics with severity, he supplies one of the most pertinent criticisms of the Christian monks who despised culture and misconceived the idea of virtue, while granting that some of them achieved spiritual success. His tract *On Dreams* was also dedicated to Hypatia (*Epist.* 154) and maintains that dreams are divine revelations meant as inspirations. He wrote the essay *On Baldness* in answer to that of Dion Chrysostom *On Hair* (397), and a small piece *On the Gift,* which accompanied an astrolabe that he sent to Constantinople.

With two discourses or *Catastases* describing the barbarian invasion of the Pentapolis, there remain but two fragments of his homilies. His 156 letters written between 399 and 413 are addressed to some 40 correspondents. They are written with art and furnish precious descriptions of the period while revealing the author as an amiable character who, though dedicated to a gentle way of life, did not lack heroism when challenged by circumstances.

Bibliography: Works. *Patrologia Graeca,* ed. J. P. MIGNE, 161 v. (Paris 1857–66) 66:1021–1756. *Hymni et opuscula,* ed., N. TERZAGHI, 2 v. (Rome 1939–44); *Orationes,* ed., J. G. KRABINGER (*Opera omnia,* v.1, Landshut 1850); *Letters,* ed. and tr. A. FITZGERALD (London 1926); *Essays and Hymns,* ed. and tr. A. FITZGERALD, 2 v. (London 1930); *Oeuvres,* ed. and tr. H. DRUON (Paris 1878). R. HERCHER, ed., *Epistolographi Graeci* (Paris 1873) 638–739. Literature. J. QUASTEN, *Patrology,* 3 v. (Westminster, Md. 1950—) 3:106–114. C. LACOMBRADE, *Synésius de Cyrène, hellène et chrétien* (Paris 1951). J. C. PANDO, *The Life and Times of Synesius of Cyrene* (Catholic University of America, *Patristic Studies* 63; 1940). H. I. MARROU, *Revue des études grecques* 65 (1952): 474–484, conversion. H. VON CAMPENHAUSEN, *Paulys Realenzyklopädie der klassischen Altertumswissenwschaft,* ed. G. WISSOWA et al. 4.2A (1932): 1362–1365.

[P. CANIVET]

SYNOD OF BISHOPS

The Synod of Bishops is a permanent institution, established by Pope PAUL VI with the *motu proprio* entitled *Apostolica sollicitudo,* September 15, 1965, in response to the desire of the Fathers of the Second Vatican Council to keep alive the positive spirit engendered by the conciliar experience. The Second Vatican Council affirmed Paul VI's initiative and made explicit reference to *Apostolica sollicitudo* in *Christus Dominus,* the Decree on Bishops (no. 5).

Literally speaking, the word ''synod,'' derived from two Greek words *syn* meaning ''together'' and *hodos,* meaning ''road'' or ''way,'' signifies a ''walking together.'' The synod, generally speaking, represents the Catholic episcopate—pope and bishops—which is convoked by the pope to seek counsel in the governance of the universal Church. In this way, it is a particularly fruitful expression and instrument of the collegiality of bishops.

The ''synodal principle'' can be traced to the early days of the Church when Roman synods were called to examine serious problems. In the first millennium similar manifestations of the communion and collegiality of the episcopal college can be found in apostolic visits, pastoral letters, and synods of various types (metropolitan, regional and patriarchal). The Code of Canon Law adopts language from Paul VI's *motu proprio* in describing the administrative structure, membership, procedures, and authority of the Synod of Bishops, but changes some provisions found in *Apostolica sollicitudo* (*c.* 342–348).

The purpose of the Synod is ''to foster a closer unity between the Roman Pontiff and the bishops, to assist the Roman Pontiff with their counsel in safeguarding and increasing faith and morals and in preserving and strengthening ecclesiastical discipline, and to consider questions concerning the Church's activity in the world'' (*c.* 342). The Synod of Bishops, a standing (''permanent'') institution, meets in general assembly when convoked by the pope. Its membership consists of bishops elected to represent their episcopal conferences as determined by the special law of the synod (*ex electione*), other bishops designated by this law itself (*ex officio*) and bishops (*ex nominatione pontificia*) according to the norms of the special law. To this membership are added some priests—religious elected in accord with the norms of the same special law (*c.* 346). As an institution, the synod has a permanent general secretariat presided over by a gener-

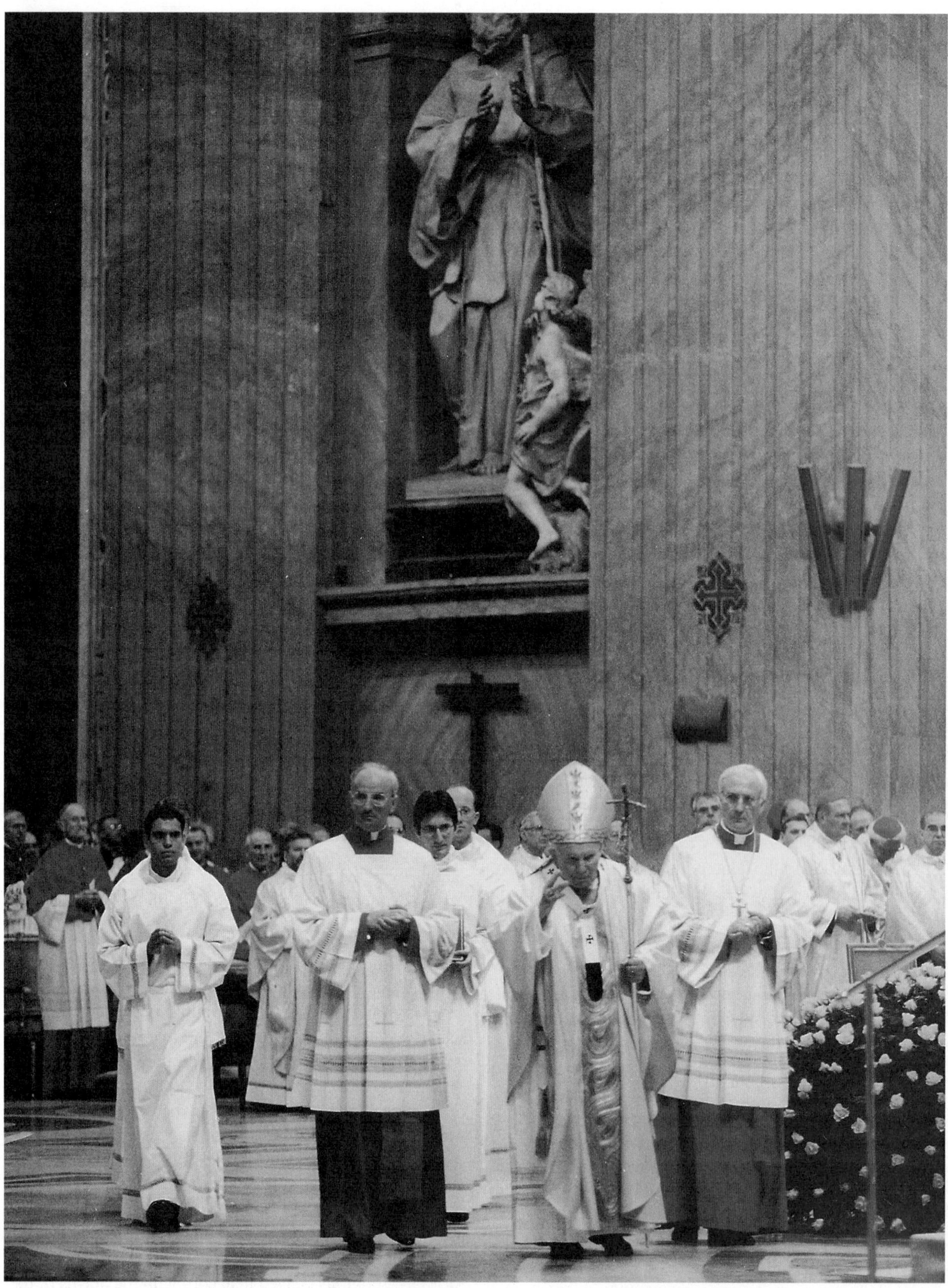

Pope John Paul II (center) opening the Synod of Bishops for Europe, 1999. (©Livio Anticoli/Liaison Agency)

Cardinals Paul Poupard (left) of France and Rosalio Jose Castillo Lara of Venezuela, Synod of Bishops, Vatican City, 1987. (AP/ Wide World)

al secretary appointed by the Roman Pontiff, who is assisted by a council made up of bishops, some of whom are elected in accord with the norm of its special law by previous general assembly of the Synod of Bishops and some of whom are appointed by the pope. The responsibilities of all members cease at the beginning of a new general session (*c.* 348). The synod is directly under the authority of the pope who calls the synod into session, ratifies the election of its members, determines the topics for discussion and the agenda, and presides over the proceedings either in person or through delegates. He alone has the power to conclude, transfer, suspend, or dissolve the synod (*c.* 344).

Similarly, the Code of Canons of the Eastern Churches states that the Roman Pontiff is assisted in exercising his office by the bishops who aid him in various ways, among these is the synod of bishops. Regarding membership, the participation in the Synod of Bishops of patriarchs and other hierarchs who preside over Churches *sui iuris* is regulated by special norms established by the Roman Pontiff (*c.* 46, § 2).

Canon law envisages three types of synods: in addition to general assemblies which meet in either ordinary or extraordinary sessions, there are ''special'' sessions (*c.* 345). As a general rule, the ordinary general assemblies since 1971 have met every three years. They address particular topics affecting the good of the Church worldwide, selected by the pope who through the general secretariat elicits input from individual episcopal conferences and bishops. A synod of bishops gathered in extraordinary general session deals with matters ''requiring a speedy solution.'' Special sessions convoke bishops to deal with regional issues; most bishops attending a special assembly are from that particular region (*c.* 346).

Once the pope settles on the theme of a synod, the general secretariat with the assistance of the council

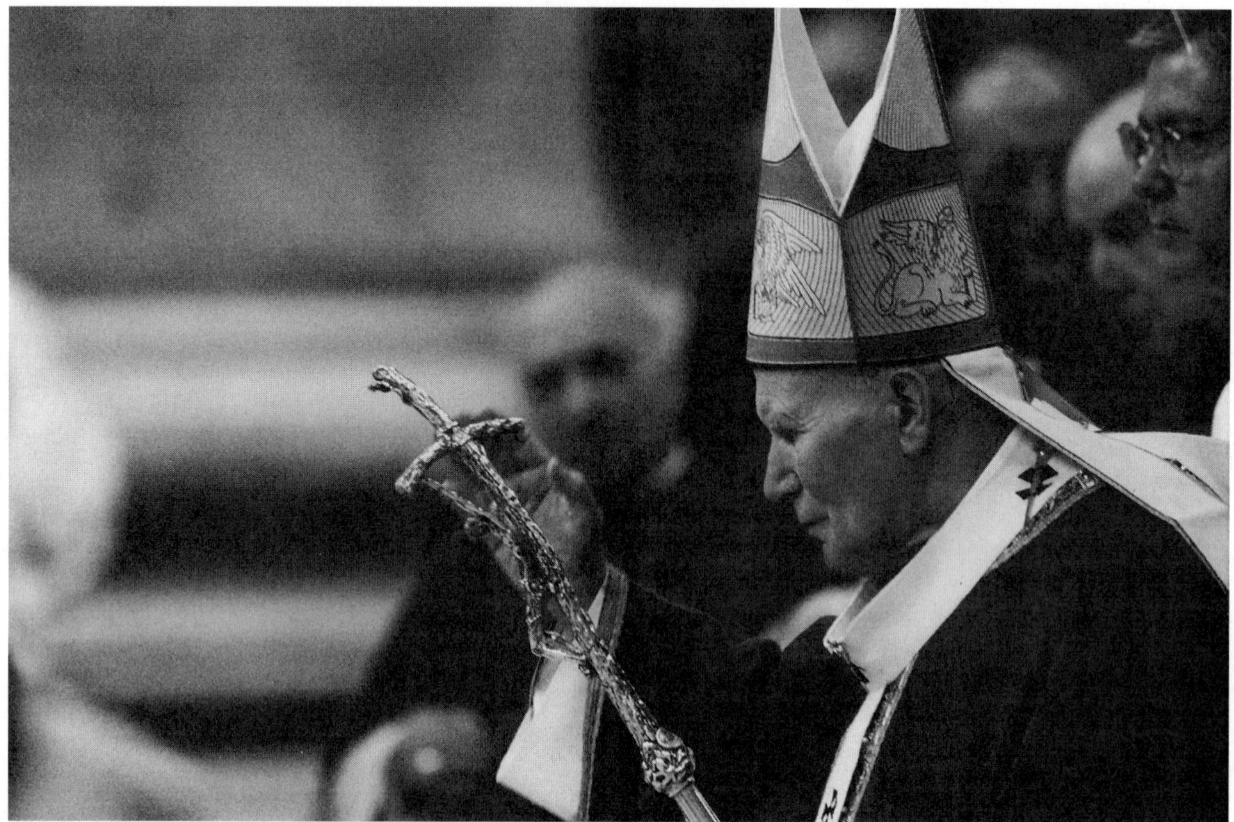

Pope John Paul II, Synod of American Bishops, 1997. (©Livio Anticoli/Liaison Agency)

members prepares the *lineamenta,* a broad ''outline'' of the topic, presented in such a way as to generate suggestions and observations on the local level. To provide guidance and a structure for formulating responses, a series of questions appears at the conclusion of the document. On the basis of the responses to the *lineamenta,* the general secretariat, assisted by this same council drafts the *instrumentum laboris* or ''working paper'' for submission to the Holy Father for his approval. This document becomes the point of reference for discussions in the synodal assembly. In the case of special assemblies, the Holy Father appoints a Pre-Synodal Council which collaborates with the general secretariat in preparing the above documentation as well as formulating a criteria for participation, for ultimate approval by the Holy Father, according to the foreseen categories, i.e., members *ex officio, ex electione, ex nominatione pontificia,* fraternal delegates, experts and observers.

The *Indictio,* that is, the Holy Father's official act of convocation, establishing the dates of the assembly, is communicated by the Secretary of State to the General Secretary, who in turn sees to contacting those concerned as well as rendering the information public. Technically speaking, the Holy Father is president of the general secretariat as well as president of each synodal assembly. Although present at plenary sessions of the synod, he customarily appoints presidents-delegate to oversee the proceedings in his name. He also appoints, the general *relator,* one or more special secretaries and other officials responsible for the day-to-day working of the synodal assembly, as well as specialists (*periti*) in various church and academic disciplines to assist the general relator and special secretaries, not to mention non-voting observers (*auditores*). Customarily, representatives from churches, church and ecclesial communities and other religions—depending on the character of each synodal assembly—have been invited to participate as fraternal delegates.

The working sessions of the synod consist of general congregations (*congregatio*) at which the synod fathers give their presentations (*interventiones*) and listen to those of others on some aspect of the synod topic as found in the *instrumentum laboris.* In this period, the fraternal delegates are also invited to speak. To further assist the synod fathers in their discussion, similar sessions (*auditiones*), depending on time, are also provided for the observers. The discussion period is followed by small groups (*circuli minores*) that focus attention on particular

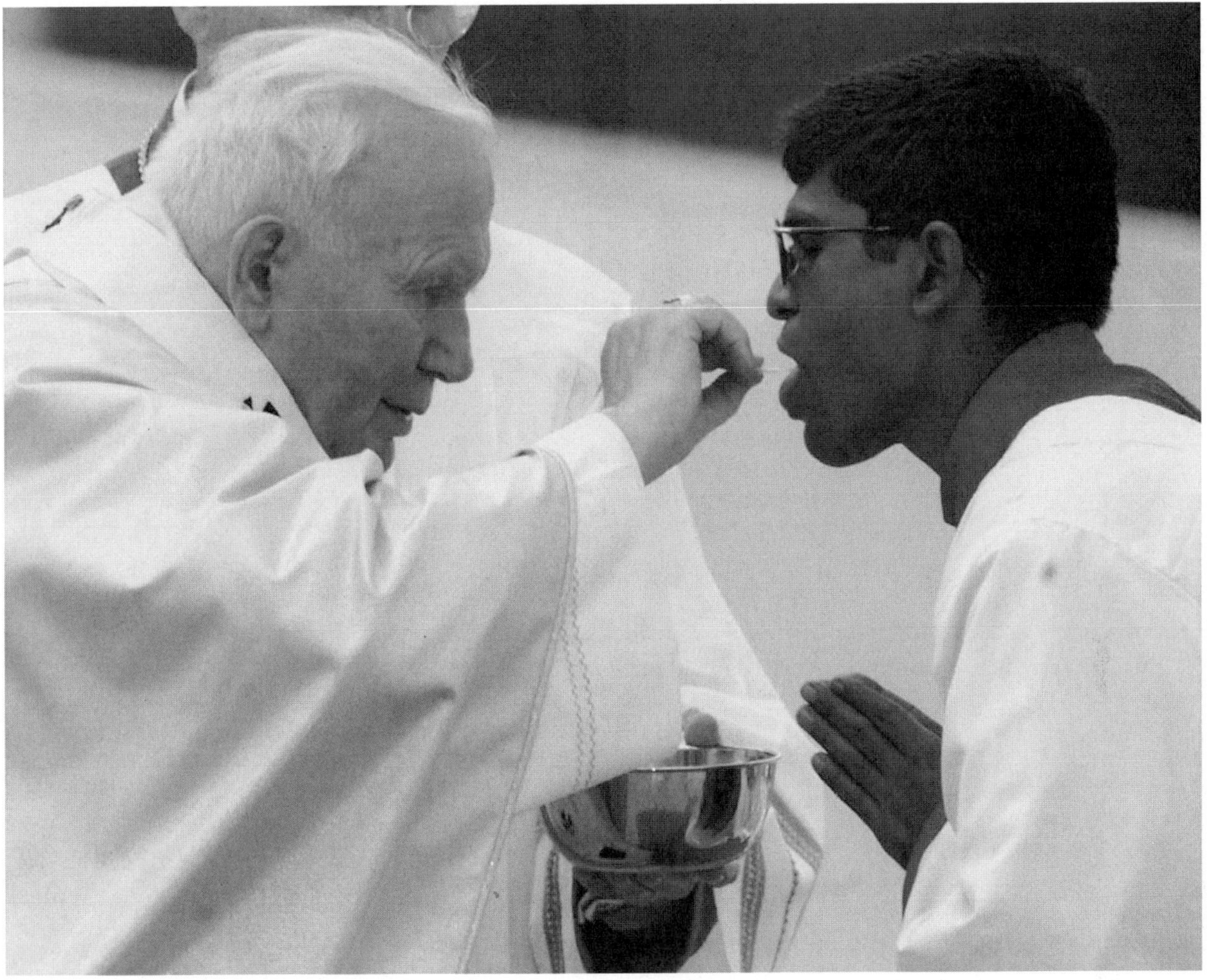

Pope John Paul II giving Holy Communion to a boy during a Holy Mass for the conclusion of the Special Assembly of the Asian Synod Bishops, at the Jawaharlal Nehru Stadium in Delhi, India, 1999. Photo by Kamal Kishore. (Reuters Newsmedia Inc./CORBIS)

points raised in the general congregations. Subsequently, the small groups make a report to the plenary session and then reconvene to formulate recommendations (*propositiones*) which, after an initial presentation in plenary session, are returned to the small groups for possible amendments. A final list of recommendations, compiled by the general relator and special secretary in collaboration with the relators of the small groups and experts, are then submitted to the vote of the synod fathers before they are finally submitted, with the results going to the Holy Father as the primary work of the synodal assembly. Popes Paul VI and JOHN PAUL II have used these recommendations, along with the entire synodal documentation, in drafting a post-synodal APOSTOLIC EXHORTATION (*exhortatio apostolica post-synodalis*), which has become the customary concluding document to a given synodal assembly. It has also become common practice for a synodal assembly, before adjourning, to issue a ''Message to the People of God'' (*nuntius*), as the first ''collegial'' fruit coming from the assembly, to offer encouragement to the Church on points related to the synod topic. Although the responsibilities of a synod assembly ceases at its conclusion, during each synod assembly the elected bishop-members usually form a council, which is composed of bishops chosen by the synod and those appointed by the Holy Father. This council, through the general secretariat, provides assistance to the Holy Father in analyzing the recommendations and drafting the text to the concluding document, as well as evaluating the follow-up of the synod assembly and attending to related matters.

The First Ordinary General Assembly of the Synod of Bishops (1967) considered a number of timely questions: the preservation and strengthening of the faith, the revision of the Code of Canon Law, and pastoral questions, including seminaries, mixed marriages, and the liturgy. Pope Paul VI convoked three more ordinary

Inauguration ceremony of the Synod of Bishops at St. Peter's Basilica, 1983. (Vittoriano Rastelli/CORBIS)

sessions to deal with the ministerial priesthood and justice in the world (1971), evangelization (1974) and catechesis (1977). Paul VI called the First Extraordinary General Assembly (1969) to examine issues of episcopal collegiality vis-à-vis papal primacy.

Bibliography: For the Latin text of *motu proprio* by POPE PAUL VI that is entitled *Apostolica sollicitudo,* see: *Acta Apostolicae Sedis* 57 (1965): 775–780. *Ordo Synodi Episcoporum celebrandae recognitus et auctus* (Vatican City 1971). J. A. CORIDEN, T. J. GREEN, and D. E. HEINTSCHEL, *The Code of Canon Law: A Text and Commentary* (New York 1985). J. P. SCHOTTE, *With the Church Towards the Third Millennium: The Second Vatican Council and the Synod of Bishops, Bishops' Conference of Malaysia and Singapore* (1986); ''The Synod of Bishops: A Permanent Yet Adaptable Church Institution,'' *Studia Canonica,* 26 (1992): 289–306; ''The Synod of Bishops: History, Work and Recent Experiences,'' in *The Bishop and His Ministry* (Vatican City 1998), 375–390.

[J. A. ABRUZZESE]

SYNOD OF BISHOPS (ASSEMBLIES)

In the first 35 years following *Apostolica sollicitudo* (1965), there were nine ordinary assemblies of the Synod of Bishops. Paul VI and John Paul II called one extraordinary assembly each. There were eight special assemblies in this period, though one of them was, technically, a particular assembly since it was convened before the 1983 Code of Canon Law.

Paul VI convened the first assembly of the synod of bishops in 1967. The topics reviewed included the revision of the Code of Canon Law, mixed marriages, seminaries, and the liturgy. Finally, the assembly addressed the functions of the synod and worked to better articulate its relationship to the Bishop of Rome and the magisterium.

Two years after the first ordinary assembly, the first extraordinary assembly was convened by Paul VI to explore collegial practices. It was decided that the synod

Lebanese bishops, at the Synod of Lebanese Bishops, Vatican, 1995. (©Livio Anticoli/Liaison Agency)

would be convened every three years and would consist of a general secretariat of 15 members. The latter move was to ensure consistency between assemblies.

The third meeting of the synod, the second ordinary assembly, was held in 1971. The goals of this meeting were less ambitious than those of its predecessors, but it did see the institution of the postsynodal apostolic exhortation. The practice of the bishops had been to draft a "Message to the People of God" as well as a list of propositions for the pope before adjourning. After the synod had met and discussed the topics of the ministerial priesthood and international injustice they forwarded their findings to Paul VI. Paul VI, as a fellow bishop and the convener of the assembly, wrote the postsynodal apostolic exhortation *Evangelica Testificatio.* It primarily addressed the renewal of religious life within the Church; the pope called religious to greater lives of prayer, emphasizing the interior life and the Eucharist.

The third ordinary assembly met in 1974 and primarily addressed evangelization. Marking the tenth anniversary of the closing of Vatican II, this assembly reflected upon the conciliar documents *Lumen gentium, Gaudium et spes,* and *Ad gentes.* In doing so, it hoped to focus the Church's evangelization efforts and articulate for the people of God not only the scope of its mission but the fundamental message of the mission, Jesus Christ. The apostolic exhortation that followed, *Evangelii nuntiandi,* defined evangelization as the "bringing of the good news into all the strata of humanity, and through its influence transforming humanity from within and making it new." The good news must be shared with all and must always reflect its message and He who revealed it.

The fourth ordinary assembly was the last convened by Paul VI, in 1977. He charged it to develop further the theme of catechesis. The pope recognized the Church's need better to understand religious education within the modern world. After the close of the assembly the propositions were forwarded to the pope, but he passed away without writing the apostolic exhortation. John Paul I had begun preparing the propositions for publication when he too died. The writing of the exhortation was left to John Paul II, who had participated in the assembly as the archbishop of Krakow. The exhortation, *Catechesi Tradendae,* asserted the centrality of Christ in the Church's instruction. Jesus Christ is the teacher and the subject taught. John Paul II presented a practical understanding of catechesis, asserting that catechists and pastors must be aware of age levels, contexts, catechetical methods,

Pope John Paul II (seated, left) leading bishops and cardinals at the Synod of Bishops 1990. (©Anatonello Nusca/Liaison Agency)

and nuances of the culture. He recognized the need for inculturation that not only respects the culture but maintains the content and validity of the faith. These would become important themes of future assemblies.

The fifth ordinary assembly of the synod of bishops was the first called by John Paul II, in 1980. The topic was the family in the modern world. The postsynodal apostolic exhortation, *Familiaris Consortio,* is a pastoral document that hopes to both encourage and guide the progress of the family in the modern world. John Paul II affirmed the rights of the family. The modern understanding of freedom, however, must be corrected in that it must be understood within the context of the entire community. The exhortation introduced the concept of the family as the domestic church. The ministry of the family is to society and the community of the church. Finally, this document spoke specifically of the role of women and their legitimacy in the social realm while affirming the importance of motherhood and domestic responsibilities.

Nineteen eighty-three marked the sixth ordinary assembly, which had as its theme "conversion and reconciliation." It dealt specifically with the issues of individual and general absolution as well as the role of catechesis and evangelization in the search for the conversion of the world. The pope's exhortation, *Reconciliatio et Paenitentia,* expanded upon the work of the bishops and addressed their concern more directly to the modern world. John Paul II first addressed the painful divisions of the world and asserted that at their root was an ignorance of both sin and redemption from sin. The Church's primary task, then, is to reconcile people with God, each other, and all of creation though catechesis and the sacraments.

John Paul II convened the second extraordinary assembly of the synod of bishops in 1985. The assembly was called to commemorate the twentieth anniversary of the Second Vatican Council and therefore concentrated upon knowledge and reception of the work of the council as well as further steps that could be taken to increase collegiality in the Church. Much of the discussion reflected the difficulties the Church was encountering. John Paul II did not promulgate an exhortation after this assembly but allowed, for the first time, the publication of the entire "Final Report" forwarded to him by the bishops.

Following the theme of COMMUNIO ecclesiology used by the second extraordinary assembly, the seventh ordinary assembly, which met in 1987, addressed the topic of the vocation and mission of the laity. The apos-

Pope John Paul II (center), seated with Cardinal Francisco R. Primatesta, Archbishop Jozef Tomko, and West German Cardinal Joseph Ratzinger (left to right), during a session of the 5th World Synod of Bishops, Vatican City, 1980. (Bettmann/CORBIS)

tolic exhortation, *Christifideles Laici,* primarily attended to the issue of the vocation of the laity to bring the gospel to the secular world. By nature of their baptism, the laity are permitted to perform certain ministerial roles in the Church. This document clarified these roles and their relation to the ordained. It explicitly affirmed the equality of women in dignity and nature.

The eighth ordinary assembly, which met in 1990, had as its theme ''Formation of Priests in the Circumstances of the Present Day.'' The role and function of the ministerial priesthood was affirmed, but greater clarification was needed as to the vocation of the priesthood and the appropriate means of training men for this vocation. The council and the exhortation that followed it, *Pastores dabo vobis,* asserted a twofold characterization of the priest as unique gift in the Church and as directed to the world in the building of the Kingdom of God.

The ninth ordinary assembly met in 1994 as the last general assembly of the second millennium. Since the bishops had recently dealt with the laity and ordained ministers, John Paul II chose as the theme ''Consecrated Life and Its Role in the Church and in the World.'' The bishops again wrestled with issues of inculturation, theology of charisms, and an ecclesiology of communion. Much of John Paul II's apostolic exhortation, *Vita Consecrata,* was meant to encourage those in consecrated life and remind them of their responsibility to evangelize the world through their witness and labor.

Distinct from the general (ordinary or extraordinary) assemblies of the synod of bishops, there has been one particular assembly and seven special assemblies. The particular assembly was for the Netherlands, convened in January 1980 to address pastoral divisions within the Dutch Church. The propositions were published not only to attempt to resolve some of the tensions but also to establish commissions that would continue the work thus begun.

After the fall of the Berlin Wall, the bishops of Europe recognized the need to address the great political, social, and religious shifts occurring on the continent. The resulting assembly, the first of the regional assemblies of the synod, convened in 1991 with only the propositions being published afterwards. The theme, ''We Are Witnesses of Christ Who Has Freed Us,'' demonstrates an emphasis on evangelization and celebration of the freedom experienced as a result of the fall of the Eastern Bloc.

Opening of the Synod of African Bishops, Vatican, 1994. (©Livio Anticoli/Liaison Agency)

Nineteen ninety-four marked the publication of John Paul II's TERTIO MILLENNIO ADVENIENTE. This apostolic letter called for several special assemblies of the synod of bishops, organized geographically, in preparation for the new millennium. Six special assemblies took place. The bishops of Africa met in 1994 to address the issues of inculturation and evangelization on the continent. The African context is unique to the rest of the Church, as John Paul II recognized in his apostolic exhortation *Ecclesia in Africa.* This document celebrated the gifts of African Christianity but also warned against the inappropriate mixing of culture and faith. Finally, it addressed several of the problems encountered by the Church in Africa including poverty, starvation, AIDS, and violence.

''Christ Is Our Hope: Renewed by His Spirit, in Solidarity, We Witness to His Love,'' was the theme of the 1995 special assembly for Lebanon. Lebanon held its own assembly because of the nation's great religious diversity and the peaceful relations that exist within it. Christians constitute a significant part of the population and live fruitfully and peacefully. It was believed Lebanon could stand as an example to the Church of the rest of the world. The apostolic exhortation written by John Paul II, ''A New Hope for Lebanon,'' celebrated the relations between the Roman Catholic Church, the Church of Antioch and other Patriarchal Churches, and Muslims. It also recognized the great strain the poverty of this nation was placing upon the family and social structure.

In 1997 the bishops of the Americas met with the chosen theme of ''Encounter with the Living Jesus Christ: The Way to Conversion, Communion, and Solidarity in America.'' Attending the meeting were bishops from the episcopal conferences of the United States, Canada, and Latin America. Again, evangelization played an important role in the meetings but the Latin American bishops continually raised the issues of social justice and social communication. In 1998 John Paul II returned to

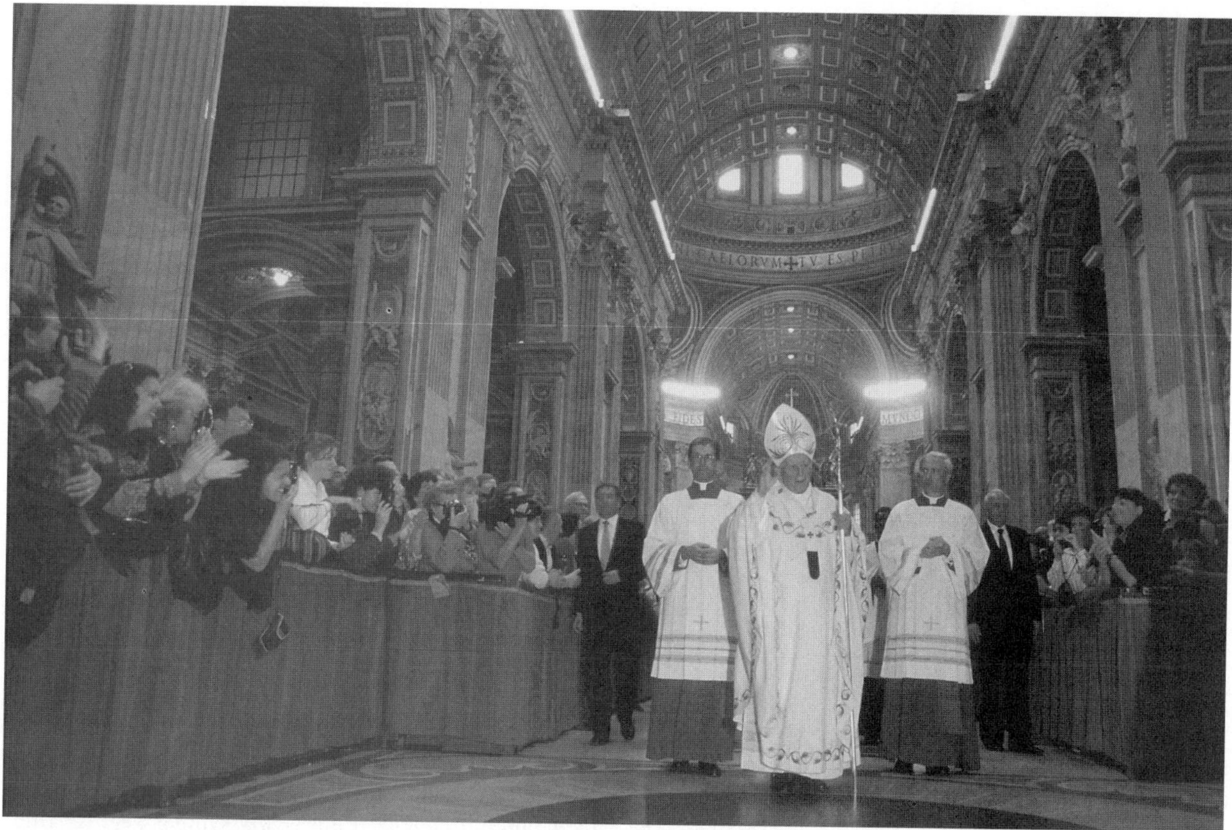

Pope John Paul II (center), Synod of Bishops, 1994. (©Livio Anticoli/ Liaison Agency)

America and promulgated the postsynodal apostolic exhortation *Ecclesia in America* in Mexico. The document located the Eucharist as the source of communion in America.

The next special assembly, which was convened in 1998, reflected upon the theme ''Jesus Christ the Savior and His Mission of Love and Service in Asia: 'That They May Have Life and Have It Abundantly.''' The Asian bishops reflected upon the uniqueness of the Church in Asia and all its difficulties. Four topics dominated their reflection: the poor, the laity and their relation to the church, interreligious dialogue, and INCULTURATION. The postsynodal apostolic exhortation, *Ecclesia in Asia,* witnessed again the important roles of evangelization and catechesis. This document not only echoed the Christological focus of the Church's message, but it also raised the pneumatological aspects that are effective and influential in Asian catechesis.

Nineteen ninety-eight witnessed a second special assembly, the meeting of the bishops of Oceania. The theme of this assembly was ''Jesus Christ and the Peoples of Oceania: Walking His Way, Telling His Truth, Living His Life.'' The bishops addressed six issues: inculturation, evangelization and catechesis, the laity, justice and peace, the Church as communion, and the Church's responsibility to react pastorally to those who suffer. Through these issues, the bishops also addressed the aboriginal people and their specific needs. As of the end of the Jubilee Year no exhortation had been promulgated by the Holy Father, but the ''Message to the People of God'' witnessed the great celebration of culture that accompanied the work of the bishops.

After the great political shifts that occurred in Europe during the 1990s, the need for a second special assembly was recognized. It convened in 1999 to reflect on the theme ''Jesus Christ, Alive in His Church, the Source of Hope for Europe.'' As this theme demonstrates, the Church in Europe had experienced a loss of hope and was still experiencing great division and strife. As the other continental assemblies had done, the European bishops reflected upon the Christological emphasis of the new evangelization, the Church as communion, and the role of the laity. The underlying hope of the bishops was to reenergize the faithful and re-present the message of Jesus Christ to a people who had been lured away from the Church and its message of hope. Ecumenism played a central role in the meetings as did recent political and social movements of the continent. Again, no apostolic exhortation was promulgated but the ''Message to the People of God'' was published in its entirety in the hopes of communicating hope to the European people.

In October of 2001 the Tenth General Assembly convened to discuss the revitalization of the bishops' ministry. The primary concerns of the assembly were the teaching functions of the episcopal office, shared church governance by bishops and Rome, and the relationships of the Vatican and episcopal conferences. Many bishops argued for the value of strong EPISCOPAL CONFERENCES in order to maintain authority and structure without sacrificing pastoral sensitivities which are more easily accessible to the local church. Again, the issues of social justice and world poverty played significant roles as the assembly reflected on the state of the Church in the modern world.

[B. M. DOYLE]

SYNODS, EARLY CHURCH

The words ''synod'' and ''council'' are interchangeable when they refer to the first centuries of the Church's history, although the ecumenical gatherings beginning with Nicaea in 325 are called councils, whereas gatherings of bishops from a province or region, as well as of the bishop and clergy of a diocese, are usually referred to as synods. The earliest recorded gathering of bishops to discuss doctrine and ecclesiastical policy was that of the Apostles and presbyters with SS. Paul and Barnabas in the so-called Council of Jerusalem in 54 (Acts 15:1–30).

There are indications in the letter of CLEMENT I OF ROME that the messengers sent to the Church in Corinth were to deal with a gathering of the presbyters or elders of the community, and St. IGNATIUS OF ANTIOCH spoke of the presbyters as the bishop's counsel. But the first recorded synodal gatherings of bishops took place in Asia Minor (*c.* 170) to deal with the heresy of MONTANISM and the exclusion of enthusiasts from the Church. Likewise *c.* 177, apparently in consequence of a synod in Gaul, Irenaeus of Lyons, while still a priest, was sent to Rome to deal with Pope ELEUTHERIUS regarding Montanism (Eusebius, *Ecclesiastical History* 5.16, 19).

Asia, Gaul, and Palestine. Consultations took place among the bishops of Asia, Palestine, and Gaul concerning the EASTER CONTROVERSY; and Pope VICTOR I (189–198) most probably held a synod in Rome that received an appeal for moderation from Irenaeus before the pope condemned the QUARTODECIMANS (*ibid.* 5.24). Yearly synods were held in Cappadocia under FIRMILIAN OF CAESAREA *c.* 250 and in other provinces of Asia to deal with the Modalist heresies of Beryllus of Bostra (*ibid.* 6.20), NOVATIAN, and PAUL OF SAMOSATA (*ibid.* 7.27–30).

A synod in Greece dealt with the canon of the Scriptures at the beginning of the 3d century (Tert., *De pud.* 10). In Alexandria in 231 or 232, as well as in Rome under Popes PONTIANUS (Eusebius, *Ecclesiastical History* 6.23) and Fabian (Ruf., *Apol.* 2.20), the orthodoxy of Origen was discussed in synods. In 220 Pope CALLISTUS I ruled that only a group of bishops could depose a bishop for cause, and this right seems to have been exercised thereafter in local synods.

The absolution of the *lapsi* and rebaptism were subjects of synods in Africa under Bishop Agrippinus and St. Cyprian and also in Rome under Popes Hippolytus and Callistus. Synods are recorded to have been held at Carthage, Rome, and Narbonne between 255 and 260 for the condemnation of the Novatians and their dealing with the *lapsi.* In Antioch, the Hypnopsychites, who believed in the Resurrection but not in the immortality of the soul, were condemned in synods between 244 and 249 (Eusebius, *Ecclesiastical History* 6.37). These instances of frequent gatherings of bishops in synod indicate that in the mid-3d century, in almost all the established provinces of the Church, frequent, if not yearly synods were the rule.

Representation and Decisions. The bishops, however, were not the representatives of the people of their dioceses, but rather the bearers of the episcopal charism or grace and came to a decision with the aid of the Holy Spirit, who was considered as presiding over their meeting in the same manner as at the gathering of the Apostles in Jerusalem with St. Paul (Acts 15). Bishops decided issues in the name of the Church and frequently acted as complainant and judge. Decisions were reached by unanimous acclamation, and anyone not in agreement was excluded from the Church's communion. Their regulations were recorded as the Church's canons or laws.

At Nicaea in 325 prescriptions for a bi-yearly holding of synods were agreed upon (canon 5), and provincial or regional synods were acknowledged as courts of first instance for complaints from bishops, and of second instance for those of the clergy. In the Synod of Sardica (342) canons 3 to 5 recognize the right of appeal to Rome by bishops deposed by their metropolitans or patriarchs (Athan., *Epist.* 69), and there is evidence of a yearly synod at Rome to handle such matters. By the time of Pope Leo I it was incumbent on the bishops of the *Vicarius Urbis* (including southern Italy, Sardinia, and Sicily) to attend.

Synodos Endemousa. In Constantinople the *Synodos endemousa,* or standing synod, was made up of bishops from the surrounding provinces living or visiting in the capital; they could be called into session by the patriarch and their decisions were recognized as part of the Church's law. After Nicaea the Arian, Donatist, and Christological problems made the holding of synods, often of conciliar proportions, frequent (*see* ARIANISM; DONATISM; CHRISTOLOGY, CONTROVERSIES ON [PATRISTIC]). The need to preserve integrity of faith and the observance of canonical and moral regulations as well as ecclesiastical unity occasioned the regular gathering of metropolitan, provincial, and regional synods throughout the *oikumene,* or universal territory of the Church.

In the provinces of East Syria, the bishops of the imperial province of Oriens were recognized as having the right to elect their patriarch in the Synod of Antioch (381), and in the Synod of Seleucia-Ctesiphon (510) the bishop of that city was recognized as the catholicos, or patriarch, of the Nestorian Church.

Bibliography: A. ADAM, *Die Religion in Geschichte und Gegenwart,* 7 v. (3d ed. Tübingen 1957–65) 3:1543–45. H. D. ALTENDORF, *ibid.* 1800–03. H. HESS, *The Canons of the Council of Sardica* (Oxford 1958). C. J. VON HEFELE, *Histoire des conciles d'après les documents originaux,* tr. and continued by H. LECLERCQ, 10 v. in 19 (Paris 1907–38) v. 1–3. P. JOANNOU, *Les Canons des synodes particuliers,* v. 1.2 of *Discipline générale antique (II e–IX e s.)* (Codificazione orientale, Ponti; Rome 1962) 492–550. J. GAUDEMET, *La Formation du droit séculier et du droit de l'église aux IVe et Vesiècles* (Paris 1957).

[P. JOANNOU]

SYNOPTIC GOSPELS

The Gospels of Matthew, Mark and Luke, which appear in that order in most early collections. J. J. Griesbach first used the term ''synoptic'' (from the Greek *sunopsomai,* ''to see together'') in his *Synopse* (1774). The work printed the three Gospels parallel to each other in order to show the agreements and disagreements. Thus it allowed the reader to observe the threefold *synoptic fact,* that virtually all the material in Mark appears in Matthew and/or Luke, that similarities in details and particularities of vocabulary and style exist in one or more of the Synoptic Gospels, and that the sequence of the pericopes are similar. The question of the literary relationship of the first three Gospels or, more specifically, the question of how the agreements and disagreements in the content and the order of their material are explained is called the Synoptic Problem.

Attempts to explain the Synoptics' similarities on the basis of dependence upon historical reminiscence (*Urevangelium* proposed by G. E. Lessing [1777] and J. G. Eichorn [1794], Fragment Hypothesis proposed by F. Schleiermacher [1817]), or, upon oral tradition (Oral Transmission Hypothesis proposed by J. G. von Herder [1796] and J. K. L. Gieseler [1818]) are usually rejected because of the detailed verbal agreement that points convincingly to the conclusion that the Synoptics are literarily dependent upon one another. The prevailing solution to the Synoptic Problem among most scholars, including Catholic, has been some variation of the Two Source Hypothesis.

Two Source Hypothesis. H. J. Holtzmann (1863) formally stated the Two Source Hypothesis proposing that an earlier form of Mark (Ger. *Urmarkus:* primitive or original Mark) and a no longer extant collection of Jesus' sayings (called Q from the German word *Quelle*) were used by Matthew and Luke independently of each other. The existence of doublets in Mark, such as the feeding of the five thousand together with the following passages in 6:30–7:37 and the feeding of the four thousand together with the subsequent verses in 8:1–26, and the absence in Luke (the ''great omission'') of passages corresponding to Mk 6:45–8:26 convinced some scholars that Mark used sources for his Gospel. Whether these sources constituted the *Urmarkus* that was abbreviated by Mark (H. J. Holtzmann) or whether various editors expanded the source (H. von Soden [1905], P. Wendland [1908]) is debated. Other scholars point to the ''minor agreements'' between Matthew and Luke, i.e., where the two Gospels agree with each other in their divergence from Mark, and the Markan passages omitted in Matthew and Luke as evidence for an *Urmarkus.* But the existence of an *Urmarkus* remains questionable. Today most would agree with R. Bultmann that an *Urmarkus* can scarcely be distinguished from the present text of Mark and that canonical Mark underlies Matthew and Luke.

There are two observations that periodically lead scholars to question the Two Source Hypothesis. First, Luke contains a large amount of special material and often disagrees with Mark in sections that they otherwise have in common. This can be particularly seen in the Passion Narrative. Some therefore contend that Luke used, besides Mark and Q, another narrative source or, at least, a different version of the Passion narrative than Mark (F. Rehkopf [1959], H. Schurmann [1968], J. B. Tyson [1976]). Others hold that Luke incorporated the Markan material into a proto-Luke (H. B. Streeter [1924], V. Taylor [1926]). H. B. Streeter proposed a Four Source (or Document) Hypothesis, a variation of the Two Source Hypothesis more widely accepted among British scholars, in which the material particular to Matthew and Luke is attributed to two ancient documents L and M. He suggested the existence of the proto-Luke, an earlier version of Luke compiled from Q and the Lucan L. Markan material was added to the Lucan sequence.

Second, the 4th-century historian Eusebius of Caesarea cites Papias, bishop of Hierapolis: "Now Matthew collected the oracles (*ta logia*) in Hebrew language, and each one interpreted them as he was able" (*Ecclesiastical History* III, 39, 15–16). From this statement some scholars conclude that an original apostolic Aramaic Gospel existed. They contend that the same sequence and common Old Testament citations in long passages of Matthew, Mark, and Luke, as well as the agreements between Matthew and Luke against Mark in the Markan material point to an Aramaic Matthew and its Greek translation behind the Synoptic Gospels (L. Vaganay [1954]). The hypothesis of an original Aramaic Matthew or of an oral Aramaic source for the Synoptic Gospels is not widely accepted. Most scholars contend that it is methodologically incorrect to explain the literary relationship of the Synoptic Gospels by appealing to Papias because he cannot give us more certain knowledge concerning the origin of the Synoptics than we can gain from the study of the texts themselves. Furthermore, it is likely that Papias's reference to *ta logia* refers to Matthew's Gospel (A. Wikenhauser [1972]).

The Q Document. Although in the past some Catholic scholars were reserved about the collection of Jesus' sayings and attempts to reconstruct this document were considered unsuccessful, in the latter part of the twentieth century research into the reconstruction, theology, and literary genre of Q led to advances beyond previous expectation. The literary evidence requires one to posit that Matthew and Luke used a Q document, which has its own theological view, rather than disconnected oral or written material. Today few would speak of Q as an amorphous layer ("stratum") of tradition (M. Dibelius [1935]). This document is not a "catechetical" supplement to the Gospels (B. H. Streeter) but contains a kerygma independent of the passion kerygma (H. Tödt [1969]).

The older reconstructions of A. von Harnack (1908), J. Schmid (1930), and T. W. Manson (1949) have been surpassed by the newer research of A. Polag (1979). It is generally accepted that Luke has preserved the sequence of the Q material, whereas Matthew has distributed it throughout his Gospel. Today many scholars contend that the Q document has undergone redaction and the Q material contains two types of sayings. First, prophetical sayings that announce the impending judgment of this generation (D. Lührmann [1969]) and contain the deuteronomistic understanding of history, i.e., the deuteronomistic tradition of the violent fate of the prophets who experienced Israel's impenitence in the form of hostility to them and their message (O. H. Steck [1967], A. Jacobson [1982]). Examples of this material are found in Lk 7:31–35; 11:19–20, 30, 31–32; 17:23–37. Second, there are sayings or community-directed "speeches" that are not formulated with outsiders in view. They are concerned with self-definition: attitude toward the world, discipleship, mission, and the prospect of persecution and death (J. Kloppenborg [1987]). Examples of such speeches are found in Lk 6:20–49; 9:57–60; 11:2–4, 9–13. The latter "speeches" are the earliest formative level of Q and they are framed as an *instruction* (J. Kloppenborg). The first group of sayings are a redactional addition and contain a polemic against "this generation." The positive Gentile response to preaching allows the deuteronomistic view of history to be transformed into an *Unheilszeichen* (Ger.: signs of disaster) for Israel. Although such passages as the story of the centurion of Capernaum in Lk 7:1–10 seem to indicate an openness to the Gentiles, it is disputed whither the saying source was used by a community engaged in Gentile mission (P. Meyer [1970], S. Schulz [1972]).

Research has not reached a consensus concerning the theology of Q, although there is general agreement concerning some aspects. Elements stand within the prophetic tradition and the community sees itself as successors to the persecuted prophets of the past (Lk 6:23). The deuteronomistic tradition provides the theological framework for the redaction of earlier material, which included apocalyptic parenesis (Lk 3:7–9, 16–17) and the imminent expectation of the Son of Man (Lk 17:24).

Source Criticism. The rise of redaction criticism led to the revival of source criticism and a reconsideration of the synoptic problem. In recent times a small but vocal minority have attacked the Two Source Hypothesis and supported J. J Griesbach's solution to the Synoptic Problem (W. R. Farmer [1976], B. Orchard [1976], H.-H. Stoldt [1980], C. S. Mann [1986]). Griesbach considered Mark to be written later than Luke and to be dependent on Matthew and Luke. This was similar to Augustine who gave priority to Matthew but held Mark was a summary of Matthew alone and Luke was dependent on Matthew and Mark. The most famous example used to support Griesbach's hypothesis is Mk 1:32 par.; Mark's wording, "that evening, at sunset" is said to originate from Mt 8:16, "that evening" and Lk 4:40, "when the sun was setting." The Griesbach hypothesis proposed by W. R. Farmer requires three instances of direct copying of Matthew by Luke and of Matthew and Luke by Mark. Thus, he explains the agreement between the two longer Synoptic Gospels by proposing that Luke used Matthew. The similarity in sequence between Matthew and Mark is explained by Mark's use of the Matthean outline except where it diverged from Matthew to follow Luke.

The main argument supporting the direct literary relationship between Matthew and Luke seems to be the "minor agreements" of Matthew and Luke. If one assumes that all minor agreements arose from a single cause, as Farmer appears to argue, then the advocates of the Griesbach hypothesis contend that the phenomenon becomes impressive. Nevertheless, at the risk of the atomization of the phenomena, many scholars would agree with B. H. Streeter that there are different reasons for these "minor agreements." Some may be attributed to the omission of unnecessary or unimportant Markan words or the correction of linguistically inadmissable words used by Mark. Others may be due to the influence of Q in sections where Mark and Q overlap. Certainly the minor agreements present a real problem for the Two Source Hypothesis, but it must be remembered that they constitute only a small percentage of the data on the total Synoptic Problem. Weighed against the evidence for Markan priority, they hardly warrant the abandonment of the Two Source Hypothesis. In the final analysis, the principal difficulties with the revival of the Griesbach hypothesis are that it fails to explain why Mark omitted so much of Matthew's material and to explain sufficiently the similar ordering of the material in Matthew and Mark. Since the sequence of material in Matthew, Mark, and Luke is the same only when Matthew and Luke agree with Mark, it would appear that K. Lachmann (1935) was correct when he held Mark to be the source used by Matthew and Luke.

Bibliography: R. A. EDWARDS, *A Theology of Eschatology, Prophecy, and Wisdom* (Philadelphia 1976). W. R. FARMER, *The Synoptic Problem: A Critical Analysis* (Dillsboro, N.C. 1976). J. A. FITZMYER, "The Priority of Mark and the 'Q' Source in Luke," *To Advance the Gospel: New Testament Studies* (New York 1981). I. Q. HAVENER, *The Sayings of Jesus* (*Good News Studies* 19; Wilmington 1987). A. JACOBSON, "Wisdom Christology in Q." Diss., Claremont Graduate School 1978); "The Literary Unity of Q," *Journal of Biblical Literature* 101 (1982) 365–89. J. S. KLOPPENBORG, *The Formation of Q: Trajectories in Ancient Wisdom Collections* (Philadelphia 1987). K. LACHMANN, "De ordine narrationum in evangeliis synopticis," *Theologische Studien und Kritiken* 8 (Zurich 1835) 570ff. D. LÜHRMANN, *Die Redaktion der Logienquelle (Wissenschaftliche Monographien zum Alten und Neuen Testament* 33; Neukirchen-Vluyn 1969). C. S. MANN, *Mark: A New Translation with Introduction and Commentary,* v. 27 (New York 1986). T. W. MANSON, *The Sayings of Jesus* (London 1949). P. MEYER, "The Gentile Mission in Q," *Journal of Biblical Literature* 89 (1970) 405–17. B. ORCHARD, *Matthew, Luke, and Mark* (Manchester 1976). A. POLAG, *Die Christologie der Logienquelle* (Neukirchen-Vluyn 1977); *Fragmenta Q. Textheft zur Logienquelle* (Neukirchen-Vluyn 1979). F. REHKOPF, *Die lukanische Sonderquelle: Ihr Umfang und Sprachgebrauch* (Tübingen 1959). J. SCHMID, *Matthäus und Lukas: Eine Untersuchung des Verhältnisses ihrer Evangelien* (Freiburg im Briesgau 1930). S. SCHULZ, *Q. Die Spruchquelle der Evangelisten* (Zürich 1972). H. SCHÜRMANN, "Protolukanische Spracheigentümlichkeiten?" *Traditionsgeschichtliche Untersuchungen zu den synoptischen Evangelien* (Düsseldorf 1968). O. H. STECK, *Israel und das gewaltsame Geschick der Propheten (Wissenschaftliche Monographien zum Alten und Neuen Testament* 23; Neukirchen-Vluyn 1967). H.-H. STOLDT, *History and Criticism of the Markan Hypothesis* (Macon 1980). B. H. STREETER, *The Four Gospels* (London 1924). V. TAYLOR, *Behind the Third Gospel: A Study of the Proto-Luke Hypothesis* (Oxford 1926). H. E. TÖDT, *Der Menschensohn in der synoptischen Überlieferung* (Gütersloh 1963). J. B. TYSON, "Sequential Parallelism in the Synoptic Gospels," *New Testament Studies* (1976–86) 276–308. L. VAGANAY, *Le Problème Synoptique* (Tournai 1954). A. VON HARNACK, *Beiträge zur Einleitung in das Neue Testament II: Sprüche und Reden Jesu* (Leipzig 1907).

[M. G. STEINHAUSER]

SYNTAGMA CANONUM ANTIOCHENUM

An important chronological collection of canons representing one of the main documentary sources of Byzantine law. It comprises, in addition to the canons of the Council of Antioch (341) referred to in the Council of Chalcedon (451), the enactments of the first Council of Constantinople (381) as well as the canons of the Council of Chalcedon. In the 6th century the provisions adopted by the Council of Ephesus (431), by the African council (419), and by the Council of Sardica (343) were added to this collection.

Subsequently, the second Council of Trullo, or *Quinisexta*, summoned by Emperor Justinian II in 692 mainly because of lack of disciplinary decrees in the second (553) and third Councils of Constantinople (680), formulated no dogmatic doctrine, but merely drew up 102 disciplinary canons as a supplement to the two previous general councils. It also included 85 canons of the Apostles and the canons of nine councils: Nicaea, which was given first place because of its preeminence, Ancyra, Neo-Caesarea, Gangra, Antioch, Laodicea, Constantinople, Ephesus, Chalcedon, Sardica, and several African canons from the 17th Council of Carthage (419). Decisions taken from the Fathers of the Church were also added, as well as the legal provisions of a council of Constantinople celebrated in 394 under Patriarch Nectarius.

The second ecumenical Council of Nicaea (787) added 22 canons (in the first of which it recognized the binding force of the canons of the Apostles) to the laws of the ecumenical Councils of Nicaea I, Constantinople, Ephesus, Chalcedon, Second of Trullo (*Quinisexta*); to the statutes approved by particular synods assembled for the purpose of promulgating the canons of said ecumenical councils; and to the canons of the Holy Fathers.

Bibliography: A. COUSSA, *Epitome praelectionum de iure ecclesiastico orientali*, 3 v. (Grottaferrata-Rome 1948–50; suppl. 1958).

[P. L. FRATTIN/EDS.]

SYNTHESIS

Synthesis, in Greek, Σύνθεσις from σύν and τίθημι, meaning a putting together or composition, is used for combinations of things, ideas, or words. ARISTOTLE uses it to characterize mechanical mixtures and chemical compounds, acts of the mind combining ideas in judgments, and the relation of subject and predicate in a proposition. EPICURUS uses it for the relations of atoms in a composite and the relation of sensations in composite notions. It is applied to propositions and to methods. In logical method it means either the combination of terms in propositions and systems, or the inferential procedure from principles to conclusions.

See Also: ANALYSIS AND SYNTHESIS; ATOMISM; METHODOLOGY (PHILOSOPHY).

[R. MCKEON]

SYON, ABBEY OF

The only medieval house of the BRIGITTINE SISTERS in England, at Isleworth, Middlesex. Urged on by Baron FitzHugh, King Henry V issued the foundation charter for this double MONASTERY in 1415 and in the following year provided a lavish endowment for it from the property of the Alien Priories. The community was enclosed in 1420 and throughout its existence enjoyed a reputation for enlightened and austere piety. Although strictly enclosed, the brethren, many of whom were university graduates, were influential as confessors, by their writings, and by preaching to pilgrims who came for the ''Pardon of Syon'' at Lammastide. The most prolific author was Richard WHITFORD, the Wretch of Syon, who composed many spiritual treatises, including a version of the Jesus Psalter. An attraction for the poor was the annual distribution of all surplus revenue on All Souls Day. Syon was one of the main centers of resistance to HENRY VIII's religious policy: St. Richard REYNOLDS was executed, and Thomas Brownel, a lay brother, died in prison. Of all the English monasteries only Syon never surrendered; and when the house was suppressed under PRAEMUNIRE in November 1539, many of the community continued to live the religious life in smaller groups. The abbey was reestablished during Queen Mary's reign, but in the time of Queen Elizabeth most of the nuns went abroad, and there the monastery maintained its existence, despite great hardships, until they returned to England in 1861. They are now at Marley, Devon.

Bibliography: *Catalogue of the Library of Syon Monastery, Isleworth,* ed. M. BATESON (Cambridge, England 1898). G. J. AUNGIER, comp., *The History and Antiquities of Syon Monastery . . .* (London 1840). J. R. FLETCHER, *The Story of the English Bridgettines of Syon Abbey* (Syon Abbey, South Brent, England 1933). D. KNOWLES, *The Religious Orders in England,* 3 v. (Cambridge, England 1948–60) v. 2, 3. D. KNOWLES and R. N. HADCOCK, *Medieval Religious Houses: England and Wales* (New York 1953).

[F. R. JOHNSTON]

SYRIA, THE CATHOLIC CHURCH IN

The Syrian Arab Republic is located in the Middle East, and is bordered on the north by Turkey, on the east by Iraq, on the south by Jordan, on the southwest by Israel and the Golan Heights, and on the west by Lebanon and the Mediterranean Sea. The region presents a series of belts of low and high lands running north-south; from west to east these are: a coastal plain, narrow, fertile and rich in small natural harbors; a mountain range, topped by Mt. Lebanon (10,132 feet), once heavily forested; a system of fertile valleys, formed by the Orontes River running north from near Baalbek and the Leontes River running south from there; a second, short range, less continuous, reaching 9,230 feet with Mt. Hermon; and an arid expanse of desert reaching to the Euphrates. Natural resources include oil, phosphates, crhomoe ore, iron ore, marble, gypsum and rock salt. Agricultural products consist of wheat, barley, cotton, beans, olives, sugar beets, dairy produce and livestock.

Its name, a shortened form of Assyria, Syria formerly denoted the regions of modern Syria, Lebanon, Israel and Jordan. The history of the region is largely that of its more powerful neighbors. At the crossroad of ancient civilizations, Syria never enjoyed lasting political unity of its own. By 2000 a shaky, backward economy and international rebuke over its aggressive posture in Lebanon diminished its ability to attract the investment needed for modernization.

Ancient History. For the Greeks, Syria (Συρία) was at first the Assyrian-Babylonian Empire (Herodotus 7.63) or its successor, the kingdom of the Seleucid Dynasty, but later only its western portion. For the Romans, the imperial province of Syria included Palestine. The Old Testament applies the term Aram (Heb. *ārām*) to the country north of Palestine: Ārām Naharaim (i.e., Aram of the Two Rivers) is northern Mesopotamia (Gn 24.10); Aram of Damascus (2 Sm 8.6) is central Syria around Damascus. In the New Testament, Syria is the region north of Palestine (Acts 15.23; Gal 1.21).

The first known settlers, who entered the region *c.* 2000 B.C., were AMORRITES in the east and Canaanites (*see* CANAAN AND CANAANITES) in the west (later, along the coast, known as PHOENICIANS to the Greeks). Seaports, such as UGARIT, BYBLOS, Sidon and Tyre were prosperous independent Canaanite centers in this early stage, though suffering recurring pressure from HITTITES, Babylonians and Egyptians. During the 12th century B.C., when Israelites and PHILISTINES occupied the region to the south of Syria proper, the restless ARAMAEANS invaded the interior and set up strong states especially around Hamath and Damascus. The latter, subjected once by David (2 Sm 8.5–8), was long the foe of the Israelites (2 Kgs *passim*). In the late 8th century B.C., Syria was subjugated by the Assyrians, a century later by the Babylonians under NEBUCHADNEZZAR, and in 539 B.C. by the Persians, and finally in 333 B.C. by Alexander the Great. After Alexander's death, Syria became a bone of contention between the kings of the Seleucid Dynasty and the Ptolemies, the former prevailing after 200 B.C. After being made a Roman province in 64 B.C., Syria suffered numerous invasions of the Parthians (*see* PERSIA) and was for a short time under the rule of PALMYRA. In A.D. 638 the Arabs wrested Syria from the Byzantine Empire and gradually imposed on it the language, culture and religion it retained into the modern era. Damascus, Aleppo and Baghdad shared supremacy in the Arab world for many centuries, being only slightly shaken by the Crusaders' short-lived hold during the 12th century.

The Modern Era. In 1516 the iron rule of the OTTOMAN TURKS isolated Syria from outside contacts. From this dark period the West, first through commercial and missionary expeditions, then by political interventions, awakened Syria. After World War I the Ottoman Empire was broken apart, and the region became a shared protectorate of France and Great Britain, characterized by restlessness and insurrections under the dual force of nationalism and Pan-Arabism. After World War II four independent states emerged: Syria proper in the north, LEBANON on the central coast, the State of ISRAEL and the Hashemite Kingdom of JORDAN in the south. In 1958 Syria joined EGYPT to form the United Arab Republic, but in 1961 it reestablished its complete independence. A military regime took power in 1963, followed by the dictatorship of Hafiz al Assad, who named himself president in February of 1971. A constitution based on Islamic law was promulgated on March 13, 1973. Al Assad died in June of 2000 and was succeeded by his son, Bashar al Assad.

During the Arab-Israeli War of 1967, Syria lost the Golan Heights region to Israeli forces. Considered a buffer zone by the Israeli government, the region continued to be contested into 2000, and became the focus of continuing political tensions between the two countries. In 1976 over 35,000 Syrian troops entered Lebanon, claiming a peacekeeping function, although their presence there, counteracted by the introduction of Israeli troops, remained hotly contested by both political and religious leaders, including Pope John Paul II and Maronite Patriarch Nasrallah Sfeir. In December of 1999 Israeli-Syrian peace talks resumed, and Israel withdrew its forces from Lebanon in May of 2000. By June of 2001 Syrian forces had also withdrawn from Beirut, although the situation in the Golan Heights had still to be resolved.

Capital: Damascus.
Size: 71,498 sq. miles.
Population: 16,305,660 in 2000; an additional 38,200 live in the Golan Heights.
Languages: Arabic; Kurdish, Armenian, Aramaic, and Circassian are spoken in various regions.
Religions: 815,270 Catholics (5%), 14,675,510 Sunni or other Muslims (90%), 326,120 Orthodox (2%), 488,760 practice other faiths.
Ecclesiastical organizations: Syria is represented by six churches. The Armenian Apostolic Church has an archeparchy in Aleppo and an eparchy in Kamichlié. The Chaldean Catholic Church has an eparchy in Aleppo. The Greek Melkite Catholic Church has a patriarchate in Antioch that oversees the archdiocese of Aleppo, with suffragans Bosrah and Hauran, Himş, and Damascus (the patriarchal eparchy). The Roman Catholic Church has an apostolic vicariate in Aleppo. The Maronite Church has archeparchies in Aleppo, with suffragan Latakia, and Damascus. The Syrian Catholic Church, with its patriarchate in Beirut, Lebanon, has metropolitans in Damascus and Ḫims and archeparchies in Aleppo, and Al Hassakah-Nisibi.

Under its constitution, the state granted freedom of religion, although proselytization by Christians was discouraged. While religion is required to be taught in Syrian schools, students could chose between Islam and Christianity. The small Jewish population of 100 had a separate primary school and was both denied government jobs and military service obligations. The Greek Orthodox Church was the largest Christian group in the country. Catholic churches included the Roman Catholic Church, the Armenian Apostolic Church, the Greek Melkite Church, the Maronite Church, the Syrian Catholic Church and the Chaldean Catholic Church. By 2000 there were 204 parishes tended by 174 diocesan and 74 religious priests in Syria, aided in their efforts by approximately 400 religious of the various Catholic churches.

Bibliography: F. M. ABEL, *Géographie de la Palestine,* 2 v. (Paris 1933–38) 1:1–17. H. R. FEDDEN, *Syria: A Historical Appreciation* (rev. ed. London 1955). P. K. HITTI, *Syria: A Short History* (New York 1959); *History of Syria, including Lebanon and Palestine* (2d ed. New York 1957). *Bilan du Monde* 2:820–827.

[M. TRECCO/EDS.]

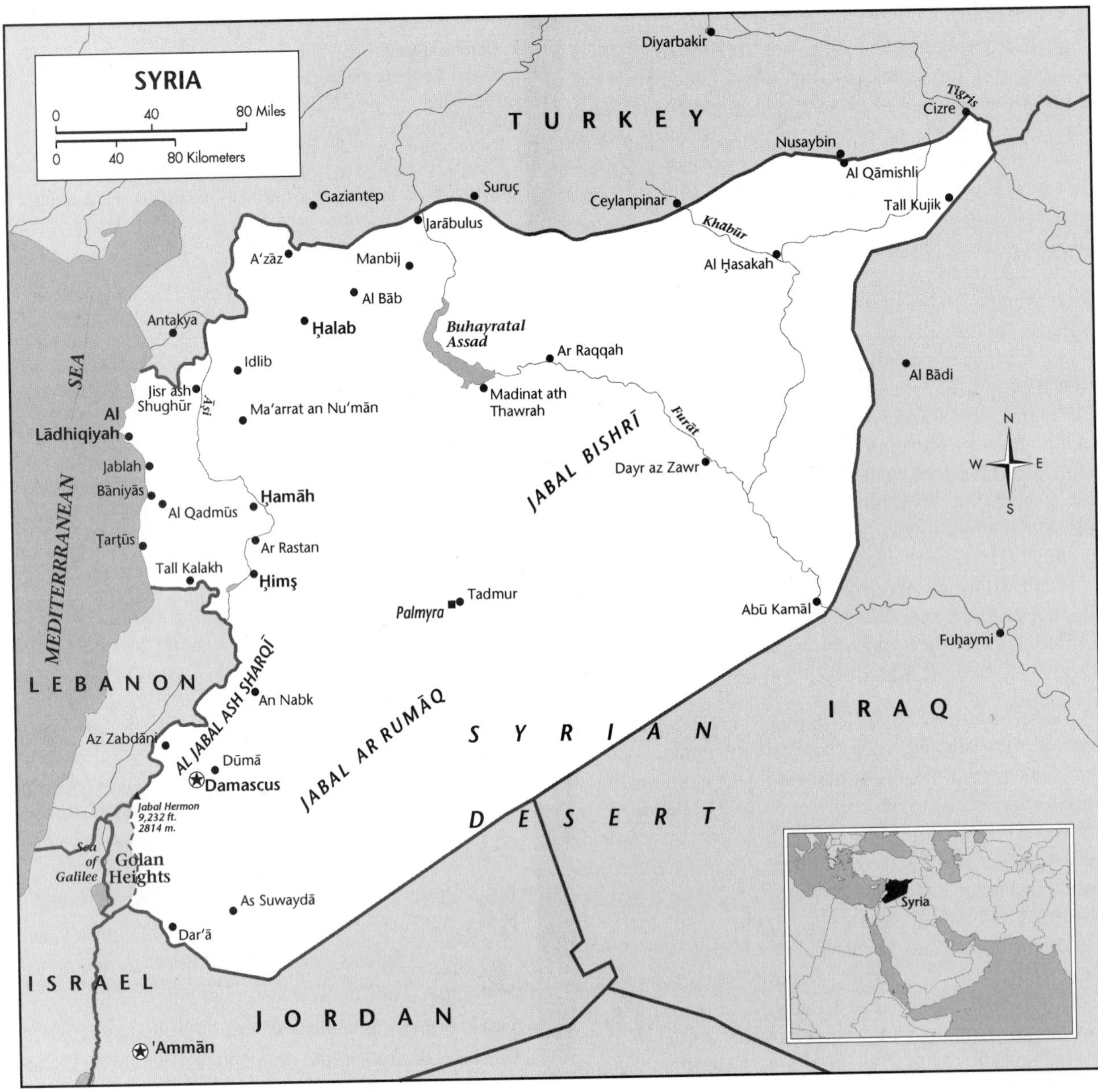

SYRIAC LANGUAGE AND LITERATURE

The intellectual and literary activity of Eastern Christendom today offers only a reduced picture of its past. Particularly those Christian communities in which the Syriac language was spoken experienced up to the end of the Middle Ages such an intense life that Syriac literature surpasses, from many angles, the other literatures of the Christian East (Armenian, Georgian, Arabic, Coptic, Ethiopian).

Aramaic and Syriac. Syriac emerged as an independent dialect of Aramaic in the early first century A.D. Since the 8th century B.C., ARAMAIC had been the Semitic language that served as the instrument of communication for the tribes of the Tigris and Euphrates basin. The earliest pagan inscriptions dates from the 1st century A.D. In spite of the competition offered by Greek under the Seleucids, it became the main vehicle of the Gospel in these vast regions. Around the year 150, if not sooner, northern Mesopotamia was reached by Christian evangelization. The eastern Aramaic dialect of Edessa (now Urfa in eastern Turkey), capital of the principality of Osrhoene, already possessed a literary character; as it developed, it became, under the name of Syriac, the liturgical and literary language of churches from the Mediterranean coast to Babylonia, and from the borders of Armenia to those of the Arabian peninsula. The oldest dated Syriac manuscript in our possession is from A.D. 411 (London, British Museum, Add. 12150); it is written in estrangelo, the basic uncial script from which derived the later western (serto) and eastern cursives. Maintained by usage in the schools of Edessa, Nisibis, and Seleucia-Ctesiphon, and by the tradition of monastic centers, the linguistic fixity of Syriac was only superficiall affected by the political upheavals and religious controversies that eventually divided the Syriac-speaking Churches. Thus we go without difficulty from the language of PHILOXENUS OF MABBUGH (d. *c.* 523) to that of BAR-HEBRAEUS (d. 1286). The possibilities of a linguistic evolution of Syriac, illustrated by the modern neo-Syriac dialects like Turoyo, were forestalled by the consequences of the Arab conquest. In the 9th century, Syriac began to be supplanted by Arabic in popular speech; its role was gradually reduced to merely that of a liturgical language and scholarly language.

Syriac Studies in the West. Of all the Eastern Christian literatures, Syriac is the best known, Western science having suspected as early as the Renaissance its importance for the textual criticism of the Bible. E. Renaudot (d. 1720) was, it has been said, "the first French scholar to realize the importance of the [Christian] oriental literatures" (Chabot). More than a century before him, however, Andreas Masius, a product of the Collegium Trilingue—the creation of which had been prompted by the genius of Erasmus, prince of humanists, at the University of Louvain—published in 1571 a Syriac grammar and lexicon; he had translated in 1569, from a manuscript since lost, the *De Paradiso* of Moses bar Kepha (d. 903), which remains our only source of information about this work. The *Bibliotheca Orientalis* (1719 to 1728) of J. S. Assemani revealed to the West the historical and doctrinal treasures of the Syriac manuscripts then recently acquired by the Vatican Library.

The real impetus toward Syriac studies, however, dates from the 19th century. It was stimulated in part by descriptive catalogues of the Syriac collections in European libraries. Notable among these is the catalogue in which W. Wright analyzed (1870 to 1872) the invaluable collection of the British Museum. Much of this collection comes from the same Syrian monastery in the Nitrian desert of Egypt that furnished Assemani with the most precious Syriac manuscripts for the Vatican Library. In 1934, J. B. Chabot estimated at 2,000 the number of Syriac manuscripts now in European depositories. They have furnished material for numerous text publications. The two principal collections of Eastern Christian texts, the *Corpus Scriptorum Christianorum Orientalium* of Louvain and Washington and the *Patrologia Orientalis* of Paris, which were started simultaneously in 1903, have given priority to Syriac texts. Among the some 260 volumes in the former, more than 110 concern Syriac literature. In 1922, the *Geschichte* of A. Baumstark provided Syriac studies with an incomparable working tool.

Evolution of Syriac Literature. Since every literature is a particular social phenomenon, Syriac literature cannot be paralleled either with the literatures of Greek and Roman antiquity or with modern literatures. Nor can its literary history be presented in the framework suitable to the others, since the material criterion of its content prevails over the formal one of evolution of literary types. A point of comparison would be better sought in Byzantine literature, the product of a similar medieval society whose thought patterns related in great measure to things religious and ecclesiastical, and in which scholarship was the prerogative of churchmen, especially monks. In inspiration and in content as well as in its authorship, Syriac literature is for the most part religious and churchly. Moreover, it depended closely, in its second period, on the Greek patristic and Byzantine literature.

Syriac literary productions before the 5th century reflect the distinct character of the Christian church in Syrian and Mesopotamian region. The Old Testament books were translated from Hebrew, and the Gospels took a specific form in the DIATESSARON of Tatian. There were a number of influential movements like that of Tatian, the Encratite (second half of 2d century), of the Gnostic Bar Daysan (d. 222), and of Mani (d. ca. 276). From the side of orthodoxy we should mention Aphrahat, called the Persian Sage (first half of the 4th century), and especially St. EPHREM (d. 373) whose literary productivity (Biblical commentaries, hymns for liturgical use, and homilies in verse form) and doctrinal authority have earned him the title of doctor of the Syrian churches.

The 5th century opens a second period, characterized by the growing influence of Byzantine Christianity, which steadily diminishes native Syrian peculiarities. Syriac poetry, however, was least influenced by the hellenization. The notable figures of this period are Jacob of Serug and Narsai. Of a cultural order, the hellenization of the Syriac-speaking churches is impeded neither by the confessional divisions intervening in the 5th and 6th centuries, nor by the diversity of political jurisdictions. Whether Monophysites or Diphysites, whether living in territories of Byzantine allegiance or in the Persian empire, writers in Syriac adopt as their principal role the translation of Greek works; they do so with a zeal witnessed by the rigid fidelity of their versions. The mass of what has been preserved in Syriac of Greek patristic texts gives the impression that few works escaped the translators' attention, and that the work of translating was pursued independently in numerous monastic centers. To give only a few examples, there are surviving fragments of at least five translations of the *Historia Lausiaca* of Palladius, four of the *Historia Monachorum in Aegypto,* two of several chapters from the *Historia Religiosa* of Theodoret of Cyr, two also of several works by Evagrius of Pontus, two again of the *Apophthegmata Patrum,* and of Pseudo-Dionysius the Areopagite.

Syriac literature remained copious until the beginning of the 14th century, at which time the decadence begun in the 10th century became an accomplished fact. The political event that most influenced conditions of literary productivity was the Arab invasion; in 636, Syria and Mesopotamia had fallen into the hands of Mohammed's followers. Arabic became progressively the idiom of the masses and was chosen as their literary medium even by Christian scholars, anxious to secure a Moslem audience. The last brilliance of ancient Syriac literature flares up in the Syrian Orthodox Bar-Hebraeus (d. 1286) and in the East Syrian 'ABDISHO BAR BERĪKĀ (d. 1318); both composed their works either in Arabic or in Syriac. A notable achievement of the Arab period was its systematic completion of the rendering of Greek works on medicine and philosophy into Syriac and then to Arabic (as witnessed by the work of Hunain ibn Ishaq, d. 873). In general, however, literary production seems to have fallen back on its illustrious past. This was the age of commentaries and compilations; these are precious to us for the sources they use, but originality of thought is at a minimum.

Subject Matter. A glance at the catalogues of Syriac manuscripts held in Western depositories informs us best on the content of the Syrian libraries from which these manuscripts came, and on the subjects covered by Syriac writers. The catalogue of the British Museum collection, the richest in Europe, analyzes 1,008 manuscripts. First are Biblical texts (numbers 1 to 167) and liturgical books of all kinds (numbers 168 to 526). The theological section (numbers 527 to 910) contains works of most of the Greek Fathers, writings of numerous Syrian authors, dogmatic catenae of polemic and antiheretical character, and canonical texts. History, hagiography included, takes up numbers 911 to 982. Last, under the title ''scientific literature,'' we find, in much smaller number (numbers 983 to 1,008) works on logic and rhetoric, grammar and lexicography, medicine, agriculture, alchemy, and natural history. Syrian ''science'' copied, as we can see, the subject matters of the Byzantine encyclopedia cursus; the only manuscript that Wright classified under natural history was the *Physiologus,* a history of animals comparable to the medieval bestiaries. The literature was thus of an almost exclusively religious and ecclesiastical character.

Historical Importance. In his *History of Asceticism in the Syrian Orient,* A. Vööbus traced from its origins the literary activity of the Syrian monasteries. Out of the huge mass of Syriac copies that came from their scriptoria, very few have reached us. To these few, whether now in Western libraries or still inaccessible in the East, history attaches an exceptional significance. Syriac-speaking churches adopted Christianity at a time very close to its origins, and they lived it in their own fashion for several centuries. They actively influenced their neighbors, the Armenian and Georgian churches, at the time of their birth. They took a preponderant part in the life of the universal Church in times critical to the development of its dogma and institutions. Finally, their geographic situation involved them in the politico-religious and cultural history of Byzantines, Persians, Arabs, and several populations of Central Asia. For these reasons, the general history of the Near East is tributary to the documentation afforded by Syriac literature. To patrology, to the history of dogmas, heresies, and spirituality, the Syriac translations of the Greek Fathers and writers bring indispensable assistance. They have kept for us precious works of which the Greek originals have long since been lost.

But even when we can still read the Greek originals, Syriac translations retain all their value. Done at a very early period and preserved often in very old manuscripts, they are often evidence of the condition of a Greek text anterior by centuries to that found in the oldest surviving Greek manuscripts of the same text. It is impossible to penetrate deeply into Greek patrology without consulting the Syriac tradition. Finally, regarding textual criticism of the New Testament, Syriac takes on a superlative importance. For this, one need only mention the Diatessaron of Tatian and the witnesses of the Old Syriac version, two creations of the earliest period of Syriac Christianity.

Although the monuments of Syriac literature have been exploited with perseverance by scholars of the last 100 years, they are far from having given all their wealth. By recording on microfilm in Sinai (1949 to 1950) the major part of the Syriac collection in the Monastery of St. Catherine, the Library of Congress in Washington has done an eminent favor to scientific research in this realm.

Bibliography: E. AYDIN, ''A Bird's Eye View of the Syriac Language and Literature,'' *Gouden Hoorn* 5 (1997). S. BROCK, ''An Introduction to Syriac Studies,'' in *Horizons in Semitic Studies,* ed. J. H. EATON (Birmingham 1980). R. DUVAL, *La Littérature syriaque* 3d ed. (Anciennes littératures chrétiennes 2; Paris 1907). A. BAUMSTARK, *Geschichte der syrischen Literatur* (Bonn 1922; reprint Berlin 1968). J. B. CHABOT, *Littérature syriaque* (Paris 1935). A. BAUMSTARK and A. RÜCKER, *Die syrische Literatur* (Handbuch der Orientalistik, ed. B. SPULER, v. 3.2–3; Leiden 1954). W. H. P. HATCH, *An Album of Dated Syriac Manuscripts* (Cambridge, Massachusetts 1946). T. NÖLDEKE, *Compendious Syriac Grammar* (Winnona Lake, Indiana: Eisenbrauns, 2001; reprint of the 1904 edition). A. VÖÖBUS, *History of Asceticism in the Syrian Orient* (Corpus scriptorum Christianorum orientalium 184, 197; 1958–60) v.1, 2.

[R. DRAGUET/EDS.]

SYRIAN CHRISTIANITY

Part I: Early History

The early 2nd-century bishop, IGNATIUS OF ANTIOCH, spoke of the "Church of Syria," indicating that from the beginning Christianity had quickly spread through this region. Early tradition connected the founding of the See of Antioch with Peter; and Saints Paul and Barnabas were sent on the mission to the Gentiles from Antioch. It appears that Christianity spread from Syria to Edessa and to Asia Minor.

Conquered by Pompey in 64 B.C., the territory (which included Palestine) was made a Roman province; and Septimius Severus divided it into two provinces: Coelesyria or *Syria maior* in the north with a temporary capital at Laodicea, and Syria Phoenice to the south with Beirut as capital. The city-state of PALMYRA declared itself independent under Zenobia in 267, but was reconquered by Aurelia (272) and destroyed in 273. Despite the prominence as trade and caravan centers of cities such as Antioch, Damascus, Laodicea, Apamea, Beirut, Edessa, Dura-Europos, and Heliopolis, the land remained an agricultural province under the Romans, and the country people preserved their native tongue and local organizations.

Spread of Christianity. In the cities Christianity was adapted to the Greco-Roman culture and ANTIOCH and Damascus became the two chief centers of religious activity and propaganda. There seems to have been a considerable Christianization of the country people as well, and in the 2d century the Jewish tradition of celebrating Easter on the 14 Nisan was still prevalent (QUARTODECIMANS). The epitaph of ABERCIUS testifies that there were Christian communities between Nisibis and the Euphrates in the 2d century, and bishops from Tyre and Ptolemais attended a synod in Palestine in 190. Antioch, with its outstanding early bishops, including Evodius, Ignatius, Heron, Babylas, Theophilus, and Serapion, took precedence, and in 264 and 268 two councils discussed the teachings of PAUL OF SAMOSATA, and finally condemned him for a dissolute life and for his use of the term *homoousios* in a modalistic sense. The theological school of Antioch was organized under LUCIAN OF ANTIOCH, to whom the Arians eventually appealed as their teacher, although his doctrines seem to have been developed in reaction to the heretical teaching of Paul of Samosata.

Antioch supplied EDESSA with its first bishop during the reign of Abgar IX (179–216), but the story of ADDAI AND MARI is apocryphal. It was from Edessa that Christianity spread into Mesopotamia. At least 22 bishops from Coelesyria attended the Council of NICAEA I in 325, including two *chorepiscopoi* or bishops working in the country regions.

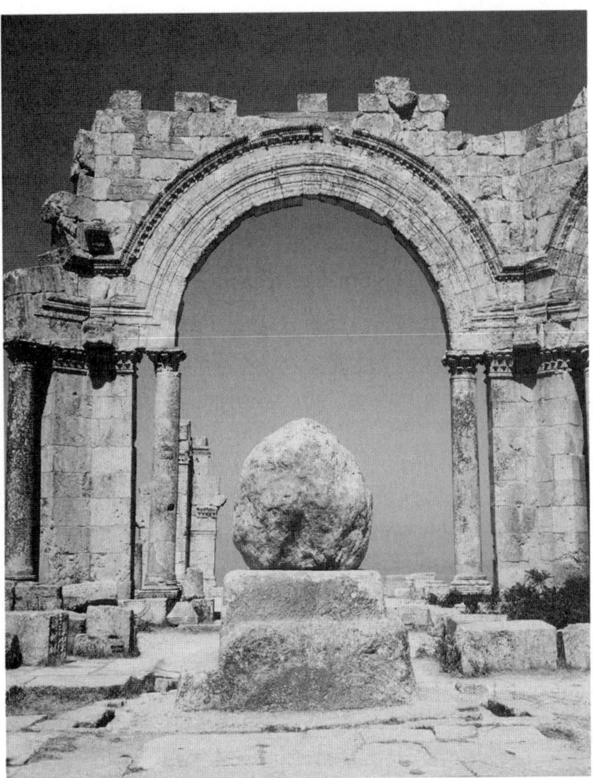

Ruins of church of Saint Simeon Monastery, Jebel Shaikh Barakat, Syria. (©John R. Jones/CORBIS)

Theological Writers. In the postapostolic age, important writings apparently had their origin in the region of Syria, and presented a Judaic Christianity different from that of Palestine and Asia Minor. They include in all probability: the Epistle of Pseudo-Barnabas, DIDACHE, the apocryphal Ascension of Isaias and the Apocryphon Joannis, and the Letters of Saint Ignatius of Antioch, which have points of contact with the Odes of Solomon and the Gospel of Truth. The heretic Menander lived in Syria at the end of the 1st century and spread GNOSTICISM through the West. Here also arose the Gospel of Peter, with the story of Christ's descent into Hades and His elevation over the angels, which became favorite themes in early Syrian theology. The Apocalypse of Peter and the Preaching of Peter, and perhaps the Didascalia, the PSEUDO-CLEMENTINE literature, the apostolic constitutions, and the *Epistolae ad Virgines* seem to be of Syrian origin. After 170, TATIAN lived in eastern Syria, and shortly later, BARDESANES also, who is generally considered to have been a heretic. Syrian theological activity is evident even in the earliest centuries, and a strong influence of the deacons is here apparent.

The greater writers came from the School of ANTIOCH, which produced Greek authors such as EUSTATHIUS OF ANTIOCH, DIODORE OF TARSUS, Saint JOHN CHRYSOS-

TOM, THEODORE OF MOPSUESTIA, THEODORET OF CYR, Polychronius, ISIDORE OF PELUSIUM, and NESTORIUS. Dionysius the Areopagite (*c.* 490–512) was possibly of Syrian origin (*see* PSEUDO-DIONYSIUS). Three Syrian bishops, ACACIUS OF BEROEA, SEVERIAN OF GABALA, and Antiochus of Ptolemais, were bitter opponents of John Chrysostom. The Syrian NEMESIUS, Bishop of Emesa, was an eclectic philosopher of the 5th century, and JOHN OF ANTIOCH, a chronicler of the early 7th century, who left historical fragments.

Bishoprics. In addition to Antioch and Damascus, Seleucia Pieria, Emesa, Sidon, Tyre, and Ptolemais were evangelized in postapostolic times; and Hierapolis (Mabbug) under Constantine I became the ecclesiastical metropolis of the *provincia* Euphratensis. Its bishop, Alexander, defended Nestorius at the Council of EPHESUS, and a later bishop, Stephen, was active at the Council of CHALCEDON. In the 4th century Beroea had an important group of Christians who were converts from paganism, and also some Judeo-Christians. Byblus had a bishopric after the age of Constantine with a flourishing Christianity, and Tripolis also had bishops by the 4th century. The same is true of Beirut, in whose famed law school Saints GREGORY THAUMATURGUS and GREGORY OF NAZIANZUS studied. Gerasa, which passed in 106 from the province of Syria to that of Arabia, had a bishop at the Council of Seleucia in 351. Damascus had its bishops at all the great councils before the Arab conquest, and Dura-Europos had a Christian church, erected about 232. Palmyra, the city where Baal was particularly worshiped, became an episcopal see in the Patriarchate of Antioch at an undetermined date. Laodicea is known to have had bishops from the 3d century. It had close contact with Alexandria, whence came its Bishop Eusebius in 260, and his successor Anatolius. Here the heretic Apollinaris became bishop about 360, and here in 481 a synod was held to adjudicate the case of Stephen, Bishop of Antioch. The Patriarchate of Antioch had already been acknowledged in the Council of Nicaea but developed its rights chiefly in the 4th and 5th centuries. It then embraced the churches of the political diocese of Oriens, with about 220 bishoprics.

Monasticism. In the 4th century the monastic life had a rapid spread in the desertlike region near Antioch. Syria and Palestine came immediately after Egypt in the spread of monasticism, and important archaeological remains, including columns of the STYLITES, testify to the flourishing monastic life here. Saint Hilarion of Gaza popularized the movement, which produced monks and hermits in the first half of the 4th century near Edessa. In Western Syria the mountains near Antioch and the desert of Chalcis (called the Syrian Thebaid) attracted hermits, and both Saint JEROME and Saint John Chrysostom spent some time among them.

Syrian Literature. An important national Christian literature developed in Syria during the 4th century, beginning with APHRAATES. He was followed by Saint EPHREM, who headed the school of Edessa. Other Syriac writers are Cyrillonas, Bali, Isaac of Antioch, and RABBULA. Heretical writers were Narses, PHILOXENUS OF MABBUGH, Jacob of Serugh, and STEPHEN BAR-SŪDHAILĒ. Among historical works the Chronicle of EDESSA, as well as a martyrology of the 4th century, and the works of Marutas and JOHN OF EPHESUS are of value.

Theological Disputes. In 430, Syrian theologians were generally opposed to the theology of Saint CYRIL OF ALEXANDRIA due to the differences between the Antiochean school and that from which Cyril sprang. The latter was opposed by Andrew of Samosata and Theodoret of Cyr. Bishop JOHN OF ANTIOCH and his Syrian suffragans refused to join Cyril at the Council of Ephesus, but both Cyril and John in 433 signed a profession of faith in which NESTORIANISM was condemned.

Syrian Monophysitism. After the Council of Chalcedon the region was divided between those who accepted the Chalcedonian faith and the Monophysites. The Monophysite monk Peter Fuller was enthroned four times and three times deposed as patriarch of Antioch between 463 or 464 and his death in 490, and the orthodox bishop Stephen was murdered here by a mob in 481.

In the countryside MONOPHYSITISM struck deep roots in the 5th century. One of the most active Monophysite bishops was the Syrian Philoxenus of Mabbugh. Syrian hatred of the Byzantine rule helps to explain the fanatical opposition to the Council of Chalcedon. The Syrian bishops, generally speaking, were too ready to change with every change in the imperial theological opinion, as appeared in their acceptance of the Encyclion of the Byzantine Emperor BASILISCUS in 475, and their reversal when the great majority signed the HENOTICON of Zeno a short time later.

Syrian Jacobites. SEVERUS OF ANTIOCH (512–18) taught a modified form of Monophysitism, and adherents of this heresy in Syria were called JACOBITES, from James (Jacob) Baradai, Bishop of Edessa, who consecrated many bishops and priests to carry on the Monophysite faith despite imperial opposition. Sergius of Antioch was a Monophysite (*floruit* 540). A good part of the Monophysite population of Syria accepted the monothelite heresy in the 7th century, when hatred for their Greek masters by the indigenous Syrians was marked. Christians who remained faithful to the Byzantine emperors, and in contact with Rome, were called Melkites, or the king's men.

The region suffered two earthquakes that in 526 and 528 took about 250,000 lives; and in 540 and 614 Persian invasions helped to alienate the Jacobites further from their Greek masters.

The Melkites were but a weak part of the population when Syria was invaded by the Arabs in 633. The latter took possession of Antioch in 638 and favored the Jacobites against the Melkites. The Melkite patriarchs of Antioch took refuge in Constantinople, and regained their see only in 742, but a number of the Syrians had already defected to Islam, while the remaining Monophysites held stubbornly to their opinions. Syrian Christians seem to have exerted an influence in Mozarabic Spain, where the Ummayad dynasty, based in Damascus, ruled from 755 to 1031.

Bibliography: G. DOWNEY, *A History of Antioch in Syria from Seleucus to the Arab Conquest* (Princeton 1961). H. JEDIN, *Handbuch der Kirchengeschichte*, 6 v. (Freiburg 1962–): v.1, K. BAUS, ed., *Von der Urgemeinde zur frühchristlichen Grosskirche*, with "Einleitung zur Kirchengeschichte" by H. JEDIN. J. DANIÉLOU and H. I. MARROU, *The First Six Hundred Years*, tr. V. CRONIN, v.1 *The Christian Centuries* (New York 1964–). A. FLICHE and V. MARTIN, eds., *Histoire de l'église depuis les origines jusqu'à nos jours* (Paris 1935–) v.1–5. L. DUCHESNE, *L'Église au VI*[e] *siècle* (Paris 1925). R. JANIN, *Les Églises Orientales et les Rites Orientaux* (Paris 1955). A. SANTOS HERNÁNDEZ, *Iglesias de Oriente* (Santander 1959).

[J. J. GAVIGAN/EDS.]

Part II: Syrian Orthodox Church (Oriental Orthodox)

Also known as the Jacobite Church, after the 6th century bishop Jacob Baradai of the anti-Chalcedonian faction which came to dominate in the Church.

Early History. The Syrian Church was entirely in union with the patriarch of Antioch until 431, when the first break occurred following the Council of Ephesus. The breach affected only a small portion of the population in the Eastern part of patriarchate. Certain bishops who supported NESTORIUS were exiled by order of the Byzantine Emperor or fled the imperial persecutions. They took refuge on the edge of the Roman Empire and Persia, where they were welcomed with open arms by the Sassanids.

Schism after Chalcedon. Of greater importance and scope was the schism that occurred within the Syrian Church in the mid-5th century when the Council of Chalcedon (451) formulated the doctrine of the two natures in Christ and anathematized those who refused to accept this doctrine. The Syrians were not the only ones to separate from the communion with the two Patriarchates of Rome and Constantinople which had upheld the council and sought the full adherence of its christological dogma. Egyptians, Ethiopians, Armenians, and Georgians followed the Syrians in resisting Chalcedon. The Greek-speaking populations in Syria and Egypt, however, remained loyal to the doctrine of the Council of Chalcedon. These loyal adherents were concentrated in Alexandria, in Antioch, and in the main cities of the Mediterranean coast in Syria where Greek language and culture had been firmly rooted.

This state of affairs points to the sad reality that the strife between pro-Chalcedonians and anti-Chalcedonians was a struggle between two rival linguistic and cultural traditions rather than between two diametrically opposite theological conceptions. Often, the dispute centered on semantics and accurate translation of dogmatic terminology from ecclesial Greek into the vernacular. The so-called MONOPHYSITISM of the anti-Chalcedonians actually differed considerably from that attributed to the Byzantine monk EUTYCHES, founder of monophysitism. The Syrians professed almost exactly the faith of Chalcedon, admitting in Christ Jesus "a single nature composed of the divinity and the humanity which remain without admixture and without confusion"; or again: "Christ is perfect God and perfect man."

Between 451 and 518, the Church of Antioch, despite its divisions concerning doctrine, remained united under the patriarch, who was sometimes a Chalcedonian but more often an anti-Chalcedonian. The accession of Emperor Justin I put an end to this confusion. Justin promised Pope Hormisdas that he would restore unity in the East on the basis of the Chalcedonian faith. Accordingly in July 518, the year of his accession to power, he convoked a synod at Constantinople composed of the bishops who resided in the capital and others who were passing through. The synod excommunicated and deposed more than 50 bishops and metropolitans who were anti-Chalcedonians or had monophysite tendencies. The measure was aimed especially at SEVERUS, Patriarch of Antioch since 512, a strong adversary of Chalcedon, whose influence had been felt far beyond the limits of his own patriarchate. Anticipating the execution of the imperial ordinance, Severus fled to Egypt.

The majority of the deposed bishops and their faithful adherents considered Severus the true patriarch of Antioch and regarded the Patriarch Paul, installed by Emperor Justin as Severus's successor, as a "Melkite," a collaborationist of imperial diplomacy and a mere politician. The anti-Chalcedonians claimed that Severus had been wrongfully and unjustly condemned and that he was a true Confessor who carried with him the apostolic succession.

The schism was definitive between the pro- and anti-Chalcedonian factions of the Syrian Church. None of the efforts of the Byzantine emperor Justin or his successors to patch up the schism met with any success. Thenceforth there were at the head of the ancient patriarchate of Antioch, two rival patriarchs who kept anathematizing one another. They governed two separate Churches, which although conserving for a time the same traditions, the same discipline, the same liturgy, came into contact only in efforts to tear one another apart. The Syrian Orthodox Church comprised about 75 percent of the population; while the Syrian Melkite Church embraced the Greek-speaking minority, and some isolated Syriac-speaking groups of monks and serfs living around the convent of Saint Maron in Syria Secunda who would later form the Maronite Church.

Arab Domination. The Arab invasion at the beginning of the 7th century, considerably reduced the size of the Syrian Orthodox Church, whose members' faith and piety had been diminished by the Christological controversies. They yielded to the pressure of invasions and bloody persecutions and embraced Islam in great numbers. Moreover, internal dissensions, the personal rivalries between bishops, the often scandalous intrigues, the shameful bargaining for accession to the patriarchal throne, the fact that the throne was simultaneously occupied by two or three patriarchs whose relative legitimacy was an insoluble riddle, all led to the defection of many of the faithful, often of the very best among them.

The periodic persecutions ordered by the Turks and culminating in those of 1916 to 1917 took a daily toll of the faithful of this Church. It was an important Christian body at the beginning of the 13th century when the barbarian hordes from Mongolia swept over Syria, leaving the land in ruins. After the passage of the barbarians, the Syrian Orthodox Church was only a remnant of its former self. The Turkish massacres during and after World War I further decimated a church that was caught in the middle of rival, maurading factions. Many Syrians fled the region, dispersing a close-knit community and diluting its presence in its ancient territoritories.

Historically, the Syrian Orthodox Patriarch resided in the ancient patriarchal see of Antioch until 1034. After wandering around the region, displaced by wars and intrigues, the patriarchal see was finally erected at Damascus in 1959. The Syrian Orthodox Patriarch is formally styled: ''Syrian Orthodox Patriarch of Antioch and All the East.''

Part III: Syrian Catholic Church (Eastern Catholic)

From the beginning of the 8th century sporadic movements can be detected in the Syrian Orthodox Church toward communion with Rome. In 709 George, Bishop of Myafarqin, made his profession of the Catholic faith. He was followed by Constantine, Bishop of Harran and his successor Leo.

At the beginning of the 11th century, Ignatius, Bishop of Malta; Moses of Hosn Zayed; Isaac of Arqa, secretary of the Patriarch John bar Abdun; and still others, too numerous to mention, also professed the Catholic faith. They were followed in the middle of the 11th century by Peter, Bishop of Aqra, Arun of Segestan (1166), and John of Mardin, called the ''Confessor.''

In 1237 Patriarch Ignatius Daud (Jacobite) and his Maphrian, John bar Maadani made profession of the Catholic faith; the Patriarch resigned his office and entered the Order of the Friars Preachers in Jerusalem.

In 1340 Benedict XII called for a provincial synod to be held in Cyprus, presided over by Bishop Elias. All the heads of the Christian communities took part without distinction of confession. At the conclusion of this synod, the Syrian Orthodox, Armenian, Georgian, and Assyrian bishops professed the Catholic faith and were followed by the whole of their flocks.

At the Council of FLORENCE (1437), the patriarch and many Syrian Orthodox bishops were reconciled with Rome. Among these were Behnam el-Hadly, one of the three patriarchs contending for the See of Antioch, and his emissary to Pope Eugene IV, Abdallah of Edessa.

After the Mongol invasion, the movement for return to unity with Rome gained new momentum. Syrian Catholics became more numerous. Some even claimed to have had, for a short period, a Catholic bishop as leader. Yet no Syrian Catholic hierarchy was constituted until the end of the 18th century. Bishops who came into communion with Rome, even when they had brought some of their faithful with them, could not keep their sees, nor could they remain under the jurisdiction of the Syrian Orthodox patriarch whose camp they had abandoned. Thus they were compelled to place themselves under the jurisdiction of one of the two Catholic hierarchies then in existence in the Near East: the Latin hierarchy in Jerusalem and Palestine, or the Maronite hierarchy on Mount Lebanon. Succeeding generations became Latins or Maronites—mostly the latter—and thus they lost the feeling for their Syrian origins.

Temporary Catholic Patriarchate. Many claim that a Syrian Catholic Church was constituted on the occasion of the accession of Andrew Akhidjan to the Patriarchate of Antioch, in 1662. But a Church *sui juris*, in order to be truly constituted as such, must have more than a patriarch assisted by one or two bishops; it must enjoy some degree of independence and have some chance of lasting for a reasonable length of time.

Andrew was a knowledgeable young cleric of the Syrian Orthodox Church from Aleppo. He made profession of the Catholic faith to a Carmelite who sent him in 1649 with a letter of recommendation to the Maronite Patriarch Joseph Aquri. Noting his great piety and thirst for knowledge, the Patriarch ordained him and sent him to the Maronite College in Rome, where he remained for three years.

In 1654 Andrew returned to Aleppo and worked zealously for the salvation of souls among the Syrian Orthodox. His zeal came to the attention of François Picquet, the French Consul, who requested the Syrian Orthodox patriarch to confer the episcopacy on his protégé Andrew. The Syrian Orthodox patriarch was evasive and Picquet turned to the Maronite patriarch who, after some hesitation, consecrated Andrew bishop on June 29, 1656. He was given the name Denis and instructed not to interfere among the Maronites of Aleppo.

Fearing the opposition of the Syrian Orthodox Church, Picquet had the Sultan issue an order of investiture to the effect that "Anyone not recognizing Andrew Akhidjan as Bishop will be considered an enemy of the Empire." The Holy See sent the young bishop its official recognition.

On the death of the Syrian Orthodox Patriarch, the leaders of the Syrian Catholic community of Aleppo thought the ideal moment had come to have their bishop raised to the patriarchal dignity. With the support of M. de Bonté, the French consul, and the intervention of the French ambassador to the Sultan, Mar Denis Akhidjan obtained the order of investiture, recognizing him as the only patriarch of the Syrians. The Holy See again gave its official recognition.

Mar Denis Akhidjan's reign was marked by many tribulations, but many bishops with a considerable portion of their flocks were united with Rome. The patriarch died July 24, 1677.

His successor was the Syrian Orthodox patriarch 'Abdulmassih, who wanted to regain Aleppo although a large number of the Syrians in Aleppo had become Catholic. He pretended union with Rome and anathematized the opponents of Chalcedon. But once safely in power and armed with an order of investiture, he showed himself a zealous partisan of the Jacobite party. The Catholics rejected him and chose as his successor his 37-year-old nephew, Gregory Peter Shahbadine. Five times the young patriarch got an order of investiture from the Sultan and took possession of the cathedral and its dependencies by military force. Five times he was expelled by his uncle or his uncle's successor who got an order of investiture postdating that of Gregory Peter. The Jacobites finally triumphed. Mar Ignatius Peter VI (Shahbadine) and his bishop were first imprisoned and later sent into exile at Adana. The bishop died in the prison of that city, Nov. 20, 1701, on the very day of their arrival; Patriarch Ignatius Peter VI died three months later.

Thus ended the brief period during which the Syrian Church had a Catholic patriarch. The Holy See tried to nominate even a patriarchal vicar to maintain the continuity of the patriarchate, but the court of Constantinople refused to give any nominee the investiture order. Without this official investiture, the Catholic prelates were entirely defenseless before the persecutions of the Jacobites.

The period had been difficult and painful for the Catholics, almost all of whom suffered repeated imprisonments, beatings, arrests, and severe fines to be paid either to the civil authorities or to the patriarch of the moment.

The Establishment of the Syrian Catholic Church. In the ensuing 70 years the Syrian Catholic Church, although deprived of leaders and church buildings, developed considerably, especially at Aleppo and in Syria. The time had come for it at last to take its rightful place, but it had to gain that place in a severe struggle.

On Feb. 23, 1766, the Syrian Orthodox patriarch consecrated the 35-year-old Michael Jarweh, a Catholic at heart, as bishop of Aleppo; the consecration took place at Mardin, the seat of the Syrian Orthodox Patriarchate since Michael the Great (1167–99). The Aleppan Catholics believed that the new bishop would be able to restore peace between the two rival communities. As a measure of prudence, Mar Michael Jarweh did not make his official profession of faith until Dec. 16, 1774, certain as he was that he and the Catholics would not have to suffer any persecutions as long as the patriarch still harbored any doubts about his private convictions.

Catholic Patriarchs. In July 1780 Patriarch Guewargis III died; the Jacobites convened to the patriarchal see to elect a successor. Under pressure from the leaders of the two assembled communities, Catholics and Jacobites, the bishops unanimously elected Michael Jarweh. The Catholic Jarweh refused to accept. The episcopal college insisted, promising that within a brief period of time all the bishops of the Syrian Orthodox Church would come into union with Rome. Mar Jarweh relented, left his diocese for Mardin, and on Jan. 22, 1782, received patriarchal consecration and enthronization to rule all the Syrians as Ignatius Michael III.

One need only leaf through the biography of Mar Ignatius Michael Jarweh to recognize the inanity of the promises of the bishop electors. Opposition set in almost at once. His reign was one of flights, exiles, imprisonment, and attacks. Twice the Sultan gave a document of investiture to one of Ignatius Michael's opponents, and the opponent hastened to dispossess Mar Michael of his churches, monasteries, and personal goods and chattels.

Finally, Mar Ignatius Michael took refuge in Lebanon among a predominantly Catholic population. He bought a two-room house that became the Patriarchal Seminary of Sharfet, which was to give the Syrian Church many priests and prelates. Mar Ignatius Michael died on Sept. 4, 1800, leaving behind him a young and vital Syrian Church.

The Patriarchate of his successor, Mar Ignatius Michael IV Daher, lasted eight years (1802–10) and was not distinguished. The patriarch resigned for personal reasons. During this brief patriarchate a great number of young Catholics flocked to Sharfet, which had become a spacious monastery; some came to follow the monastic rule and some to train for the diaconate and priesthood. Sharfet acquired a printing press and published liturgical books. The Syrian Church already had bishops governing the most important cities of the Near East—Aleppo, Mosul, Mardin, and Jerusalem—and several patriarchal vicars administering the other Catholic sees.

On Jan. 2, 1811, the college of bishops elected Mar G. Shem'un Zora to the patriarchal see. He accepted unwillingly, his most ardent desire being to live a monastic life. He soon resigned and retired to the monastery of Saint Ephrem in Lebanon.

He was succeeded in February 1820 by G. Peter Jarweh, nephew of the founder of the Syrian hierarchy; he took the name Peter Ignatius VII. He occupied the patriarchal see from 1820 to 1851 and saw the end of the fratricidal struggles between the Syrian Orthodox and Catholics. The Sultan Mahmoud, less venal than his predecessors, was disposed to accord the Syrian Catholics their independence from the Orthodox hierarchy. To obtain this independence, Mar Ignatius Peter VII had to send a bishop to Constantinople to represent him and take the necessary steps to get the decree. While he was looking for the person capable of pursuing the negotiations to a successful conclusion, Mar Antony Semhairy arrived at Sharfet.

Semhairy. Mar Antony Semhairy and Mar 'Issa were both auxiliaries in Mardin of the Syrian Orthodox Patriarch Ibn as-Sayar. In the absence of Ibn as-Sayar, who frequently resided at Diyarbekir, capital of the province, Mar Antony, who had been raised to the rank of maphrian, was discharging the functions of vicar-general. Meanwhile, one Holy Thursday, Mar 'Issa was summoned to assist his patriarch in the ceremony of the consecration of the Holy Chrism and, to his chagrin, noticed that the alleged annual ''miracle'' of the Holy Chrism, which was supposed to boil over its container during the procession, was a hoax. He would have liked to give vent to his indignation, at least to his colleague and friend, Mar Antony, but did not dare, since both were ardent Syrian Orthodox who considered the Catholics to be heretics.

However, Mar Antony, like a second Paul of Tarsus, was to find his Damascus Road in the archives of the patriarchate. He discovered, duly signed, dated, and sealed with the patriarchal seal, the professions of Catholic faith of four of the patriarchs who had been among the most savage persecutors of the Catholics; one of these professions was that of his own patriarch, Ibn as-Sayar. The discovery profoundly shocked Mar Antony, but he wanted to comprehend entirely before judging and went to Diyarbekir to see the patriarch, whom he entreated to give him a satisfactory explanation. The partiarch admitted frankly that the Syrian Orthodox Church was but a detached branch of the Catholic Church, adding that an open declaration of this would be inopportune.

Mar Antony was staggered to see that the pastors of his Church concealed a fundamental truth of which they were convinced, through fear of losing their rank, privileges, and above all considerable income, and that they were persecuting those whom they knew to be following the true path. He went back to Mardin and told Mar 'Issa in confidence of his conversation with the patriarch. Mar 'Issa in turn told Mar Antony about the hoax he had discovered. Both were determined to return to the Catholic Church but decided to say nothing until they had prepared the faithful of Mardin to follow them. They gave themselves over entirely to this task; and on April 17, 1827, they sought out the Catholic Armenian bishop of Mardin and made their profession of Catholic faith. They were followed by the entire Syrian Orthodox clergy of the city and by more than 150 families. Only two priests refused to follow. A few months later another Syrian Orthodox bishop, Mar Joseph Karrum, joined them in communion with Rome.

Independence. For two years, the two bishops administered the diocese without encountering excessively vigorous persecutions. Then Mar Antony decided to go to Sharfet to confer with Mar Ignatius Peter VII. Mar 'Issa remained in Mardin, where he was subjected to ignominy and physical torture by Patriarch Ibn as-Sayar. The French ambassador to the Sultan had to intervene to deliver him from almost certain death.

Mar Ignatius Peter VII, on being advised of Mar Antony's arrival, rushed to meet him, and informed him of the good dispositions of Sultan Mahmoud. He asked Mar Antony to represent him at the court of Constantinople and not to come back without the imperial decree legitimizing the independence of the Syrian Catholic Church from the Syrian Orthodox Church; Mar Antony was instructed also to bring along a document of investiture for himself as bishop of Mardin. Mar Antony set out at once, and a few months later he obtained the imperial decree in quadruplicate, sending one copy to Aleppo, one to Diyarbekir, the third to Mardin, and the fourth to Mosul, where they were duly registered with the civil authorities.

The Syrian Catholic Church, hierarchically constituted on Jan. 2, 1782, was constituted in civil law in the year 1247 of the Hegira (A.D. 1830); the civil constitution suppressed all authority that the Syrian Orthodox patriarchs might thenceforth claim over the persons and/or goods of the Catholics.

Now that he had nothing more to fear from his rival, Mar Ignatius Peter VII asked the Holy See for permission to transfer the patriarchal see from Sharfet to Aleppo. Permission was given, and he went to Aleppo on Nov. 28, 1830.

The Decree of 1830 opened the way to large-scale reunion of the the Syrian Orthodox Church with Rome. In Damascus, all but about 15 families entered the Roman communion. Their pastor, Mar J. Yaqub Haj Heliani, willingly followed them, and this community still has the archbishopric and the cathedral. The same was true of many other dioceses.

On Oct. 16, 1851, Mar Ignatius Peter VII Jarweh died after a patriarchate that had been most advantageous for the Syrian Catholic Church; he had received into communion with Rome one patriarch and eight bishops, all of whom had previously been Syrian Orthodox.

Growth and Development. The Synod of Syrian Bishops meeting in Sharfet on March 30, 1853, elected to the patriarchal see the man who had been the maphrian of the Jacobite Ibn as-Sayar before becoming the supporter of Mar Ignatius Peter Jarweh; this was Mar Antony Semhairy (1853–64).

Thanks to his skillful negotiations at the court of Constantinople, the Syrian Catholics lived in peace but they lacked churches, schools, priests; the debts they had contracted on all sides to pay the Princely Tribute, the large "gratuities," which had to be paid in order to get anything, were a heavy burden. The new patriarch undertook a tour in Europe, where he was greeted with fervor and sympathy by the peoples and courts. Gifts poured in, and churches and schools were built on a large scale. In his pastoral care for the Catholics, Mar Ignatius Antony did not forget the Syrian Orthodox and started missions that reached out to them.

His admiration for the Roman Church impelled him to some excesses. He wanted to introduce reforms into the very ancient Syrian liturgy to bring it into closer alignment with the liturgy of Rome. The respectful but firm representations of a simple priest, who became a great patriarch, George Shelhot, happily restrained the patriarch.

Mar Ignatius Antony Semhairy was succeeded by Mar Ignatius Philip 'Arkus (1866–74). Almost paralyzed and in frightful pain, he went to Rome with six of his bishops for Vatican Council I and then, feeling himself at the end of his strength, tendered his resignation, which Pius IX refused to accept. His great piety and prudence were needed to keep the peace within his own Church while schisms were erupting in many of the Catholic communities in the Near East: among the Melkites Catholics because of opposition to the adoption of the Gregorian calendar and among the Armenians and Chaldeans Catholics in protest against the encyclical *Reversurus.*

With the patriarchate of Mar Ignatius George Shelhot (1874–91), the Syrian Catholic Church entered on an era of unprecedented prosperity. Although at Mosul the Syrian Orthodox twice succeeded in plundering the Syrian Catholic churches, Archbishop Behnam Benni managed after a very bitter fight to get justice done and to recover the illustrious monastery of Mar-Behnam (5th century). With the zealous collaboration of one of his priests, Joseph David, he opened many schools, sent young deacons to study in Rome, and encouraged the sciences. His diocese became the most flourishing of the Syrian Catholic Church.

Elsewhere calm reigned, and the Syrian Catholic patriarch Mar Ignatius George Shelhot directed his solicitude toward organizing the Syrian Catholic Church and working assiduously for its growth. Thirteen churches were built in Syria, Cilicia, and Mesopotamia. A monastery was erected in Mardin for the Congregation of Saint Ephrem. A library was opened in Aleppo which collected a great number of ancient manuscripts. The finest work of his patriarchate was without doubt the Synod of Sharfet (1888) for which meticulous preparations were made by Monsignor Joseph David, now Archbishop of Damascus. Its decrees became the charter and canon law of the Syrian Catholic Church.

The liturgical books, carefully prepared and edited for the first time, included the Breviary, the *Fanqith,* and the *Liber Festivus.* The liturgical chants were reviewed and standardized.

The successor of Mar Ignatius George Shelhot, Mar Ignatius Behnam Benni (1893–97), initiated his patriarchate by a visit to Rome. He proposed that a synod of the Catholic Oriental patriarchs, presided over by the pope, be held in Rome. Leo XIII greeted this proposal favorably and the synod opened on Oct. 24, 1894. Besides the Oriental patriarchs, five cardinals were present, including the Cardinal Secretary of State, Rampolla, and Cardinal Ludokowsky, Prefect of the Congregation for the Propagation of the Faith. The fifth and last session was held on Nov. 8, 1896, and on December 6 the pope promulgated the encyclical *Orientalium Dignitas,* summarizing the proceedings of this extraordinary Synod.

The patriarchate of the Mar Ignatius Ephrem II Rahmani (1898–1929) is a landmark in the history of the Syrian Patriarchate of Antioch. Despite the many churches already built, he realized that many towns and villages, especially in Upper Mesopotamia, were without adequate facilities, and he undertook appropriate remedies. He was responsible for the church in Jerusalem, the diocese and church of Homs, the church and school in Hama, the Diocese of Mosul, the churches of Diyarbekir, Adana, Zahle, Katana, Yabrud, Sadad, Maskanat, Zeydal, Weyran-Shahr, Deireke, Mansuriet, Kalet-Mara, Kerboran, and two churches in Qaraqosh.

Turkish Massacre. All that had been built up with so much love, patience, and self-sacrifice was suddenly destroyed. Between 1915 and 1917, the Turks massacred in Upper Mesopotamia about 1,500,000 Christians, without distinction of confession: Armenian Oriental Orthodox, Armenian Catholics, Syrian Orthodox, Syrian Catholics, Assyrians, Chaldean Catholics, and Protestants. Many dioceses were wiped out, the clergy and faithful massacred, the churches pillaged and demolished. The famous city of Edessa had not a single Christian left. Mardin, Diyarbekir, and Nisibin, were scarcely in better state. In the city of Mardin alone, the Syrian lost 96,000, massacred together with their priests and deacons. The Syrian Catholics too were almost depleted. The Catholic bishop, Mar Gabriel Tappouni, was imprisoned.

The Syrian Catholic Patriarch Mar Ignatius Ephrem Rahmani in Beirut learned of these massacres through a note scrawled by the imprisoned bishop: ''I am making my 9th week of retreat and am constantly meditating on Matthew 2, 18'' (the massacre of the Holy Innocents). When peace returned, Mar Rahmani worked to save what could be saved. He was able to salvage something in the districts of Lebanon and Syria that were now under French mandate, but for the Church in Turkey, all was lost.

Mar Rahmani was a scholar known, respected, and admired by all devotees of Syriac studies in East and West alike. He published an impressive number of works, which are a continuing source of inspiration and are still being translated; he wrote in French, Latin, Syriac, and Arabic. His works include the *Testamentum Domini,* the four volumes of *Studia Syriaca,* and *The Oriental and Western Liturgies, Studied Separately and Compared.*

His successor, Mar Ignatius Gabriel Tappouni, elected by acclamation in 1929, first devoted himself to a judicious reorganization of the dioceses that had devastated by the Turkish massacres, and then endeavored to provide them, as well as the patriarchal see, with what they needed in order to be able to continue the missionary and evangelical work. He has been called the ''Cardinal Builder,'' since vast building campaigns have characterized the whole of his patriarchate. Mention should be made, among others, of the churches and rectories of Beirut, which since the end of World War I has become the official patriarchal seat of the Syrian Catholic Church.

Organization of the Syrian Catholic Church. The patriarch of the Syrian Catholic Church is formally styled: ''Patriarch of Antioch of the Syrians.'' The patriarchal seat is located in Bierut, Lebanon. All Syrian Catholic Patriarchs always add the name ''Ignatius'' at their enthronement, recalling the illustrious bishop of the ancient Syrian Church, Saint Ignatius of Antioch.

Bibliography: P. DE TARRAZI, *As-Salasil at-Tārāīẖiyat fī 'asāqifat al-abrašīyāt as-suryāniyat* (Beirut 1910). I. ARMALET, *Al-Qusarat fī nakabāt an-Nasārat* (Beirut 1910). D. E. NACCACHE, *'Ināyat ar-Rahmān fī hidāyat as-Suryān* (Beirut 1910). R. DUVAL, *La Littérature syriaque* (Les Anciennes littératures chrétiennes 2; 3d ed. Paris 1907). G. KHOURI-SARKIS, *L'Orient Syrien* 1 (1956) 3–30. W. DE VRIES, ''Dreihundert Jahre syrisch-katholische Hierarchie,'' *Ostkirchliche Studien* 5 (1956) 137–57; ''Antiochen und Seleucia-Ctesiphon: Patriarch und Katholikos,'' in *Mélanges Eugène Tisserant,* 7 v. (Studi e Testi 231–37; Rome 1964). R. ROBERSON, *The Eastern Christian Churches: A Brief Survey* (6th ed. Rome 1999).

[G. KHOURI-SARKIS/EDS.]

SYRIAN LITURGY

The Syrian liturgical rite is basically the ancient liturgical rite of the Antiochene Church of the 4th century. Greek was the liturgical language used especially in the Hellenized cities, but gradually it was changed to the vernacular Syriac. Today, Arabic is universally used, as the ancient Syriac tongue has fallen into general disuse. The two churches using the Syrian Liturgy today are the Syrian Orthodox Church and the Syrian Catholic Church.

Characteristics. There are a number of variable Anaphoras (Eucharistic prayers) in the ancient liturgical books. Historically there were 64 such anaphoras, but only a few are used, of which the Divine Liturgy of St. James is commonly used. According to the Liturgy of St. James, after the priest prays for the grace to celebrate worthily, he lights the candles and begins the *prothesis,* or ceremony of preparing the bread and wine. He then vests and returns to make a more solemn offering. Then he begins the Divine Liturgy proper, having rudimentary parts in common with the BYZANTINE LITURGY: the Trisagion, the scripture readings, usually from the Epistles of St. Paul, and the Gospels. A solemn entrance with the gifts (the "Great Entrance") is made, followed by an elaborate incense ritual, and climaxed by the recitation of the *Sedhro,* a long prayer in prose or verse begging forgiveness of sins. After the Creed is recited, the priest incenses the whole church and the people, washes his hands, and the Anaphora begins with the concelebrants' giving the kiss of peace by touching one another's hands. A prayer of inclination is followed by a long prayer of thanksgiving (the preface). After the words of consecration are solemnly chanted aloud by the priest and answered with an Amen by the people, the priest addresses the Anamnesis, not to God the Father (as is done in the Greek Liturgy of St. James) but to the Son. The Epiclesis is accomplished by the priest's fluttering his hands three times over the gifts and calling down the Holy Spirit upon them. The Anaphora concludes with the Great Intercession composed of six prayers commemorating the living, the dead, and the saints in heaven. The Communion is prefaced by the Lord's Prayer, a prayer of inclination, and the Elevation. A ritual characteristic of the Syrian Liturgy is the complicated but meaningful Fraction of the Body of Christ under the species of bread. The priest receives Communion with a spoon under both species. The faithful receive by means of a spoon or by intinction, i.e., the priest dips into the chalice a piece of consecrated bread held in his fingers and drops it into the mouth of the communicant. The Liturgy, like that of the Byzantine Liturgy, ends quickly with the prayer of thanksgiving and dismissal.

Church building. The church building is usually divided into three parts: the far east end containing the altar, the sanctuary; the middle section (*catastroma*), the choir; and finally, the nave. The altar is usually of wood or stone, quite similar to the altar of the West, about 6 feet long and 1½ feet wide. A baldachino surmounts the altar and a curtain hangs down from the baldachino in front of it. The top (*tablitho*) of the altar is of wood or stone with an inscription; this is consecrated with holy chrism by the bishop and is covered by embroidered cloths. There are also two side altars, used in the preparation of the *prothesis* and in vesting. The nave has sections for men toward the front; women are relegated to galleries or to the rear. Bells are not usually used because of Muslim prohibition; hence the pounding on wooden boards (the Byzantine *semandron*) is still used to summon the people to the Liturgy.

Vessels, vestments, and books. These are quite similar to those used in the Byzantine Liturgy: the paten, the chalice, the star, the spoon, the sponge (to cleanse the chalice), the veils (one for the paten, another for the chalice, and a larger one to cover both the paten and the chalice), the censer, and the *ripidia* (fans fixed on a staff with bells attached). The *deaconess* is a small finger-bowl of metal into which the wine and water are poured and mixed before being poured into the chalice; it is later used by the priest to wash his hands whenever he is about to touch the Holy Gifts. Cymbals are used at the Sanctus, Consecration, Epiclesis, Elevation, and blessing before the Communion of the laity. The altar bread is round and thick, made of leavened flour with salt added. It is supposed to be freshly baked for each day.

In the sanctuary the priest usually wears a special type of slipper called *m'sone.* Over the alb he wears the *uroro,* or large stole that fits around his neck and falls down in front almost to the ground. The girdle holds the stole and alb in place. Long, narrow cuffs hold in the broad sleeves of the priest's cassock. The *masnaphtho* is a hood of the same material as the outer garment worn by bishops and prelates such as the chorepiscopi. The *phaino* is like the Greek *phelonion* but divided up the front, looking more like a Latin cope with no hood. A small cross wrapped in silk is held in the right hand by bishops and used in giving blessings.

Syrians employ many books in celebrating the Liturgy. The first is the *Anafoura,* which contains the different Anaphoras or Canons. The *Evanghelion* contains the four Gospels arranged for liturgical reading, and the Epistles are found in the *Egartho dachlihe* (Epistles of the Apostles). The server follows the Liturgy by means of a small prayer book called the *Ktobo.*

Bibliography: R. JANIN, *Les Églises Orientales et les Rites Orientaux* (Paris 1955) 363–392. A. A. KING, *The Rites of Eastern Christendom,* 2 v. (London 1950) 61–210. D. ATTWATER, *The Christian Churches of the East,* 2 v. (rev. ed. Milwaukee, Wis. 1961–62) 1:147–157; 2:204–210. A. HÄNGGI and I. PAHL, *Prex Eucharistica* (Freibourg 1968).

[G. A. MALONEY/EDS.]

SYRO-MALABAR CHURCH

The official name in the *Annuario Pontificio* for the major Oriental Catholic group of indigenous Christians in India. This community along with other Oriental Christians in India was, according to an ancient unanimous tradition, founded by St. Thomas the Apostle. Hence the community was and still is known popularly as "St. Thomas Christians." "Malabar" was the name given probably by the Arabs to the southern part of the west coast of South India (from Ezhimala/Mt. de Eli to Kanyakumari/Cape Cimorin). The most ancient name of this locality was Kerala, and the Malayalam-speaking part of it forms the state of Kerala today. Another name is "Nazranis" (Nazarenes), which also probably originated from Arab sources. The early St. Thomas Christians used the East-Syrian (Persian) liturgy until the middle of the seventeenth century, when the group that gave allegiance to the Syrian (Jacobite) patriarch of Antioch began using the West Syrian liturgical tradition. It seems that Syrians ("Suriani" in Malayalam) came into use in order to distinguish them from the Latin rite Christians ("Latheen" in Malayalam) who emerged as a parallel Catholic community in Kerala from the sixteenth century onwards. The term "Syro-Malabar" was applied to this community by the Holy See toward the close of the nineteenth century, when it restored the Syro-Malabar hierarchy. The appellation "Syro-" is considered inappropriate by many within the community, and there are increasing calls for its removal.

The Syro-Malabar Church, together with the Syrian Orthodox (Jacobite), Marthoma, the Syro-Malankara, the Assyrian groups and even a section of the Church of South India, are considered to be the most ancient Christians of India. This combined community of Christians was one and undivided, but it began to split beginning in the middle of the seventeenth century. There are at present no fewer than eight groups of which two, the Syro-Malabar and the Syro-Malankara Churches, are in communion with Rome. The former follows the East-Syrian tradition in worship, the latter the West-Syrian tradition.

For further information on the various Catholic, Oriental Orthodox and Reformed communities of the St. Thomas Christians, *see* INDIA, CHRISTIANITY IN, under the heading "St. Thomas Christians." For further information on the Syro-Malankara Church, *see* SYRO-MALANKARA CHURCH.

EARLY HISTORY

East Syrian (Persian) connection. Both from oral tradition and extant fragmentary documents, it can be reasonably established that the Indian Church came into contact with the East Syrian (Persian) Church from early centuries. According to tradition, occasionally small colonies of East-Syrian Christians came to Kerala. The earliest of such colonies is said to have arrived in the fourth century. This event is attributed to the emergence of an endogamous group known as the "Knanaya community" (sometimes called the "Southists" or *Thekkumbhagar*), a small minority separate from the majority ("Northists," or *Vadakkumbhagar*). The Knanaya Christians trace their origin to the above-mentioned East-Syrian colony, which came under the leadership of a Knai Thomman, a merchant.

The Persian connection was beneficial to the Kerala Christians to a limited extent, especially for the fact that this connection opened the small Christian community to the larger Christian world. But many see this relationship as compromising the independence and local character of the community. It led to tighter controls, of the Church of Persia over the Kerala Christians. This adversely affected the spontaneous growth of the original community into a genuine Indian Church, with its Indian Christian patterns of thought, worship, and lifestyle. Not only were foreign bishops sent from Persia, but also the Kerala Christians were required to adopt Persian thought forms and formulas of faith, worship patterns, laws, church customs, and practices. It meant that the Kerala Christians had to lead a life not in one world but in two worlds at the same time: the geographical, political and socio-cultural environment of Kerala on the one hand, and on the other, the ecclesiastical world of Persia. This was somewhat an artificial and unnatural kind of life. The core elements of Christian life remained foreign, adapted only peripherally, that, too, in a country that possessed a rich culture, a rich philosophy, and a deep religious spirit comparable to—or even surpassing—the Greek culture, philosophy, and religious thought. It is this "artificial" and "unnatural" kind of life that some writers have characterized as "Hindu [Indian] in culture, Christian in religion and Syro-Oriental in worship."

Church life. Very early in their existence, the ancient Christians of Kerala developed a lifestyle. In Church matters, this lifestyle reflected to some extent the pattern of the Persian Christians. In the socio-cultural realm, it was similar to that of their Hindu neighbors. In the social setup of Kerala, they emerged as the peers of the higher classes, especially the *náyars.* The long experience they had acquired of the Hindu way of life and the good neighborly relations they maintained with their Hindu neighbors enabled them to acquire a more positive approach to Hinduism and "Hindu" practices. As a result of the Portuguese authorities' destruction of early writings, it is difficult to ascertain the extent of this integration in their world view, spiritual life, worship, and church structure. It appeared that the St. Thomas Christians led a privileged upperclass life with an amount of ecclesiastical and civil autonomy. The *yógam* (assembly of priests and lay people) at various levels was the administrative body that was responsible for exercising the functions related to this autonomy. It enjoyed ample power to administer Church affairs, mete out justice, and impose punishments.

Unique identity and theological vision. In addition to the institutions of the archdeacon and the yógam, the St. Thomas Christians possessed a unique theological vision that encompassed: (1) an implicit incarnational theology which pervaded their social and socio-ecclesiastical life and practice; (2) a lived theology of dialog with other faiths; and (3) a practiced theology of ecclesial autonomy and individuality as a particular Church. This individuality is expressed as ''Mar Thoma Margam'' (the ''Way of St. Thomas''), which many western writers called the ''Law of Thomas.'' This ''Margam'' is deemed distinct from the ''Margam'' established by St. Peter (Latin tradition) and other Apostles.

The East-Syrian prelates brought to Kerala their disciplinary codes of canons. Among the books condemned in the Synod of Diamper are such canonical texts as *Book of the Synods* (*Synodicon Orientale*) and the *Nomocanon* of Abdisho. Yet in the administration of Church affairs, these codes were practically ignored. What mattered for the archdeacon and his *yógam* was the ''Mar Thoma Margam,'' the traditions of the St. Thomas Christians, which functioned as their canon law. It was with the implementation of the decrees of the Synod of DIAMPER under the Latin bishops that a radical change took place: The Latin (western) canonical outlook came to prevail. This changed situation continued more or less, even after indigenous prelates were appointed for the Church in 1896. The code of canons for the Eastern Churches promulgated in 1990 is considered applicable to the Syro-Malabar Church too, although there are moves to include the ancient traditions of the community in the particular law that is being framed by the Syro-Malabar Synod.

Until the arrival of the Portuguese in India near the close of the sixteenth century, the Christians of St. Thomas enjoyed a privileged position in society and a significant amount of social and ecclesiastical autonomy. They led a life at the core of which was an identity consciousness, which, if not expressed in clear-cut formulas, was implicit in their attitude toward their traditions; their social, socio-religious, and religious customs and practices; and their theological outlook. It is this particular mode of life that came into conflict with the particular Christian vision and way of life of the Portuguese. The struggle began very early in the sixteenth century and led to a major crisis and schism in the mid-seventeenth century.

CONTACT WITH THE LATIN WEST

Early contacts. With the arrival of the Portuguese, the St. Thomas Christian community was thrust into the world of Latin or Western Christendom. This new world would, in the course of time, exert such a deep influence on them, whether they wanted it or not, that it became a difficult task to shed its traces. The first representatives of this world were cordially and even enthusiastically welcomed. Before long, the Portuguese posed a challenge to—even threatened— the particular identity, autonomy, and unity that the St. Thomas Christians had developed throughout many centuries. The new world did not only distort the identity, but shattered the unity and destroyed the autonomy of the Indian Church of St. Thomas.

Synod of Diamper. Attempts to bring the St. Thomas Christians under Portuguese *Padroado* (patronage) (*see* PATRONATO REAL) and to introduce Latin customs culminated in what is known as the Synod of Diamper, convoked in 1599 by Alexis de Meneses, archbishop of Goa, who was determined to bring the community once and for all under the *Padroado*. Historians and ecclesiologists have pointed out that the synod was invalid because it was summoned without proper authorization, it did not follow proper canonical form, and the decrees were obtained under duress. Nevertheless, its decrees became slowly the major part of the law of the St. Thomas Christians. The acts and decrees of the synod have become very significant in shedding light on pre-Diamper customs, practices, and the theological vision of the St. Thomas Christians.

Latinization. In the wake of the Synod of Diamper, Latin *Padroado* prelates were appointed to lead the Christians. The first *Padroado* bishop of the St. Thomas Christians, Francis Ros, S.J., returned his bishopric to its ancient location in Kodungalloor (Cranganore). He and subsequent prelates administered the church along Latin jurisdictional lines, implemented the synodal decrees, and enforced a program of latinization, resulting in stiff opposition from the St. Thomas Christians. This opposition culminated in a revolt in 1653, known as the ''Koonen (Bent) Cross Oath.'' Under the leadership of the archdeacon, a group of St. Thomas Christians swore that they would never live under the rule of the Jesuits, and insisted that they would not obey the Jesuit Archbishop Garcia of Goa. This schism marked the culmination of the storm that had been gathering on the horizon for over a century.

Crisis. The ensuing crisis was so serious that it demanded immediate and tactful handling, through the intervention of some agent other than the Portuguese. The Congregation for the Propagation of Faith dispatched Carmelite missionaries to India with full power to deal with the situation. The mission, under the leadership of Joseph Sebestiani, OCD, met with partial success. But as the Dutch wrested hegemony from the Portuguese, the foreign Carmelites were asked to leave Kerala. Before leaving in 1663, Sebestiani installed a local St. Thomas Christian priest, Alexander Parampil, as vicar apostolic of Malabar, a position Sebestiani had held from 1659. Except for one, all of the Carmelites left Kerala. Beginning in 1675, a few Carmelites were allowed in the area under a special arrangement with the Dutch. The initial goodwill that Sebestiani cultivated was destroyed when two recently arrived Carmelites pushed hard for an India-born Portuguese priest, Raphael Figueredo de Salgado, to be appointed coadjutor to Bishop Parampil. Chaos and strife ensued after Parampil's death in 1687. Finally in 1700 a foreign Carmelite, Angelo Francis, OCD, was appointed vicar apostolic. At the same time the Portugese Crown, which had earlier temporarily suspended the appointments of *Padroado* prelates, resumed the practice of appointing prelates to the See of Kodungalloor (Cranganore). *Padroado* archbishops or administrators governed Cranganore again in competition with the appointees of the Congregation for the Propagation of Faith. Thus the Catholic St. Thomas Christians came under a double regime—*Padroado* and *Propaganda*. This competition would continue until 1887, when the see was suppressed.

In any event, the new arrangement was highly unsatisfactory, and the St. Thomas Christians soon began complaining against the Carmelite prelates and missionaries, who were no better than their *Padroado* counterparts. In the eighteenth century, this dissatisfaction culminated in agitation for autonomous rule. An imminent revolt was averted only through timely negotiations, but it became increasingly clear to the St. Thomas Christians that only by regaining their autonomous status with an ecclesiastical head from their own community, could a satisfactory solution to their vexing problems found.

Frustrated by their failure to get one from among themselves appointed head of their Church, they turned to the East-Syrians or Chaldeans of Persia. The Chaldean Church was not immediately in position to intervene. But after four or five decades, when relations between the St. Thomas Christians and the Carmelite missionaries had further deteriorated, and when the Chaldean Church under the leadership of Patriarch Joseph VI managed to organize itself better, the interventions came, further complicating the situation. Against the explicit directive of Rome, the Chaldean patriarch sent to India Bishop Mar Rokos (1861), followed by Bishop Mar Millus (1974). The presence of these prelates caused schisms in the community. The first did not last long, but the second did, and the followers of Mellus eventually gave allegiance to the patriarch of the Assyrian Church of the East. This gave rise to the small Church, now called the Assyrian Church of India, which is not in communion with Rome.

Limited autonomy. This sorry state of affairs succeeded in convincing Rome that the community's aspirations required an impartial assessment and a suitable course of action. Pope Leo XIII's broad vision proved to be a decisive factor in the gradual process by which the St. Thomas Christians were granted the autonomy for which they had agitated for over three centuries. The separation of these Christians from the Latin jurisdiction and the creation in 1887 of two separate vicariates, Trissur and Kottayam, were the first milestones in the process. These two vicariates were subsequently divided into three in 1896 (Trissur, Ernakulam, Changanachery), and indigenous bishops were appointed from among the community. The Syro-Malabar hierarchy was established in 1923. Thus the Church of St. Thomas Christians was constituted an autonomous, self-ruled particular Church in communion with the See of Rome. It was made independent of any intermediary jurisdiction, whether Latin *Padroado/Propaganda* or Chaldean-Syrian. But what emerged was a hierarchy patterned after the Latin model, not the oriental model. Even the autonomy achieved was partial and limited. This situation would remain unchanged until Pope John Paul II elevated the Church to major archiepiscopal status.

Nevertheless, with the limited autonomy, the Church began to make tremendous progress. Already before 1923, the Kottayam Vicariate was created for the Knanaya (Southists) community. At the time of the establishment of Syro-Malabar hierarchy, Ernakulam was elevated to an archdiocese, and the other vicariates (Trissur, Kottayam, and Chenganacherry) became its suffragan dioceses. Later Ernakulam, Trissur, and Chenganacherry were divided into several dioceses, and Changanacherry was made a second archdiocese. New dioceses were created in the territories extended since 1954, to the north, south, and east, both in and outside Kerala. In 1962 the first mission territory (Chanda) was entrusted to this Church. Since then a few others were also established. (For a listing of the Syro-Malabar sees within and outside Kerala, *see* INDIA, CHRISTIANITY IN.)

The spiritual renewal of the Syro-Malabar Church that began in the nineteenth century gained strength and produced an unprecedented evangelical fervor. Thousands of these Christians now work as missionaries throughout India and abroad. Phenomenal progress has been made by the community in the fields of education and social welfare programs. Arts and science colleges, technical colleges and institutes, schools for various purposes, crèches, boarding houses, hostels, and homes for the aged run by Church institutions have multiplied manifold in the twentieth century. In addition, political involvement and the power of mass communications have rendered the St. Thomas Christians an influential community in the public life of Kerala.

Clerical training. Historically, clerical training was conducted usually in the parishes under the guidance of an elderly priest. However, a few centers arose where clerics from different parishes gathered around an erudite priest (''Malpan'' or teacher) for better training. These "seminaries" were known "malpanates." In 1541 the Franciscans started a seminary at Kodungalloor (Cranganore), but it soon lost its relevance because of its Latin orientation. In the last decades of the sixteenth century, the Jesuits started a seminary at Chennamangalam (Vaipicotta). It continued to function until the 1770s. The Carmelites started seminaries at Varapuzha (Verapoly) and Alangad. These were later amalgamated, and a common seminary began to function at Puthenpally. In 1932 this facility was transferred to Mangalapuzha (Aluva). This seminary functioned as a combined Oriental-Latin seminary until the year 1997, when it was bifurcated: Mangalapuzha for Oriental students and Carmelgiri for Latin students. In 1962, a seminary exclusively for the Orientals was established at Vadavadhur (Kottayam). Since then other seminaries for the Orientals have opened, or are in the planning stages, within and outside of Kerala.

TOWARD FULLNESS OF AUTONOMY

Elevation to major archiepiscopal status. Pope John Paul II's visit to Kerala in 1986 for the beatification of a son and a daughter of the Church, Blessed Kuriakose Elias Chavara and Blessed Alphonsa, became the impetus for the movement toward fuller autonomy and recognition of Syro-Malabar Church as a *sui juris* Oriental Church. The many petitions of the Syro-Malabar Church for full autonomy had started much earlier. Since the publication of the 1990 code of canons for the Oriental Churches, the autonomy process intensified. Perhaps the first sign of the process was in the erection in 1988 of the diocese of Kalyan in West India, mainly for the Syro-Malabar Christians settled down or working in and around Mumbai (Bombay). Following the visit of a special pontifical commission to Kerala in 1992, the Holy See elevated the Syro-Malabar Church to the rank of major archiepiscopal Church on Dec. 16, 1992, with Ernakulam (renamed Ernakulam-Angamaly) as the seat of the major archbishop; and the archbishop of Ernakulam, Antony Cardinal Padiyara, made the major archbishop. Archbishop Abraham Kattumana was appointed the first pontifical delegate to the Syro-Malabar Church.

Further developments. On March 13, 2001, the Holy See and the major archbishop of the Syro-Malabar Church announced the creation of a new diocese for the Syro-Malabar Church in the United States. Headquartered in Chicago, this new diocese is known as the Syro-Malabar St. Thomas Diocese, with Jacob Angadiath as its first bishop. This is a momentous event in the history of the Syro-Malabar Church, for it is the first Syro-Malabar diocese outside of India. It is also a sign of official recognition of the growing Syro-Malabar diaspora in North America.

Bibliography: L. BROWN, *The Indian Christians of St. Thomas* (Cambridge 1983). CHAI, *History of Christianity in India* (Bangalore 1984–89, 1998), v. 1 A. M. MUNDADAN, v. 2 J. THEKKEDATH, v. 3 E. R. HAMBYE. J. KOLLAPARAMBIL, *The Archdeacon of All India* (Rome 1972); *The Babylonian Origin of the Southists among the St. Thomas Christians* (Rome 1992). G. MENACHERY, ed., *The St. Thomas Christian Encyclopedia of India*, v. 2 (Trichur 1973). A. M. MUNDADAN, *Indian Christians: Search for Identity and Struggle for Autonomy* (Bangalore, 1984); *History and Beyond* (Aluva 1997); "Cultural Communications—Encounter of the St. Thomas Christians with the Hindus in Kerala," *Journal of Dharma* 24 (1999) 244–254. G. NEDUMGATT, *Laity and Church Temporalities* (Bangalore 2000). S. NEILL, *A History of Christianity in India*, 2 v. (Cambridge 1984–85). T. PALLIPURATHUKUNNEL, *The Double Regime* (Alwaye 1982). A. PAZHEPARAMBIL, *An Account of a Very Important Period of the History of the Catholic Syrians of Malabar* (Puthenpally 1920). H. C. PERUMALIL and E. R. HAMBYE, ed., *Christianity in India* (Alleppey 1972). P. J. PODIPARA, *The Individuality of the Malabar Church* (Alleppey 1972); *The Thomas Christians* (Bombay 1970). J. PERUMTHOTTAM, *A Period of Decline of the Mar Thoma Christians* (Kottayam 1994). J. A. PULIURUMPIL, *A Period of Jurisdictional Conflict in the Suriani Church of India (1800–1830)* (Kottayam 1994). A. THAZHATH, *The Juridiral Sources of the Syro-Malabar Church* (Kottayam 1987). F. THONIPPARA, *St. Thomas Christians of India: (1775–1787)* (Bangalore 1999). E. TISERANT, *Eastern Christianity in India* (Bombay 1957). C. VARICATT, *The Suriani Church of India (1877–1896)* (Kottayam 1995).

[A. M. MUNDADAN]

SYRO-MALABAR LITURGY

Beginnings. The Indian Church, which claims St. Thomas as its founder, might have started out with a very simple worship form that was congenial to the context in the 1st century. It is very difficult today, however, to discern any element of that worship form and structure. A few of the pre-Diamper manuscripts are extant but do not reveal much of the early Indian liturgy. The decrees and acts of the Synod of DIAMPER point unequivocally to the fact that the Indian Christians generally followed the East-Syrian (Chaldean) liturgical tradition in East Syriac language. The many missionary and other accounts on the lives and customs of the Indian Christians from the 16th century onwards confirm this picture. At the same time it is evident that a number of local observances connected with baptism, marriage, ceremonies for the dead, etc., were also in use. Many of the churches of Christians were built in the same architectural style as the Hindu temples. In the aftermath of the Synod of Diamper (1599), many churches began to be remodeled after the Portuguese style. A few adaptations in the pre-Diamper liturgy alluded to by one or two writers were the use of rice-bread and toddy or arrack for the Eucharist. A 16th-century eyewitness attested to the use (at least partial) of rice-bread. It is possible that in very few places the rice-bread or a mixture of rice and wheat bread was used, if not toddy or arrack. Not only the East-Syrian liturgy but also the local customs formed part of the heritage of the Christians, the "Mar Thoma Margam."

Latinization. With the arrival of the Portuguese in the 16th century, the liturgy was increasingly latinized. A few new elements were introduced into the text of the Eucharistic liturgy; the sacraments were patterned after the Latin models, although the divine office (liturgy of the hours) appeared to have continued untouched until the 19th century. All this was done due to lack of understanding on the part of Latin missionaries regarding Oriental practices and Indian customs. The acts and decrees of the Synod of Diamper became the norms for these changes. In the aftermath of Diamper, a latinized East-Syrian liturgical model remained in use for over three centuries. In the 19th century, the divine office was latinized.

Reversal of Latinization. Ever since the partial restoration of the autonomy of the SYRO-MALABAR CHURCH toward the end of the 19th century, differences of opinion have emerged on its identity and on the question of its liturgical reform. A small minority has persistently insisted on the complete restoration of the East-Syrian tradition with one or two exceptions, e.g., the use of leavened bread in the Eucharist and marriage of clergy. In the early years, they even wanted to reestablish the jurisdictional ties with the Chaldean Catholic patriarch, a position that was later abandoned. But the Syro-Malabar community as a whole, and the vicars apostolic in particular, were opposed to this minority view. After lying dormant for a while, the restorationists were invigorated by the support it received in Rome from 1930s onwards. In 1934 a papal commission was appointed for the revision of the Syro-Malabar Pontifical. Its work remained incomplete until the late 1950s. In 1954 Pius XII set up another commission for the restoration of the texts of Eucharistic liturgy, sacraments, and the divine office. A controversy arose in the wake of these actions of Rome, especially when the commission repeatedly ignored the suggestions of the Syro-Malabar bishops, who were opposed to restoration of texts without revision and adaptation. The Syro-Malabar community became divided: the majority supporting the position of the bishops and the minority supporting the Roman commissions. From the 1970s slowly a similar division emerged within the ranks of the bishops.

From a historical standpoint, the St. Thomas Christians had been following the East-Syrian (Chaldean) liturgical tradition. At the same time, being an autonomous Church founded in India by an apostle, it is also necessary to emphasize its Indian character. This concern for Indianization or indigenization was intensified especially in the new atmosphere created by Vatican II. This is no easy task. Under the rule of Latin prelates for about three centuries, not only their liturgy had been partially latinized, but a great deal of Latin law, practices, and customs influenced their life. The theological and spiritual outlook had been practically latinized and Westernized. The influence of the Latin West had and continues to influence the Oriental Churches in India, while the Oriental influence is only very feebly felt in the community.

Chaldeanization or Indianization? This particular predicament in which the Syro-Malabar Christians are placed, creates a grave problem leading to a sort of identity crisis. At the risk of overgeneralizing, the predicament has led to the rise of two opposing groups within the Syro-Malabar community. The first group, sometimes known as the Chaldeanization group, has remained a small minority within the Syro-Malabar community. It argues that only the Latin elements are foreign and as such they alone need be eliminated while the East-Syrian (Chaldean) elements are restored to their pristine state in the liturgy. Some members of this group have accepted the position that after the process of de-latinization is complete, then perhaps the question of indigenization or Indianization may be taken up. The second group, the Indianization group, has been able to gain the support of the majority of the Syro-Malabar Christians, especially the clergy and laity. This group asserts that both the Latin and the East Syrian (Chaldean) elements are foreign and both must be eliminated or retained as far as it is necessary for the emergence of a truly Oriental Indian Church.

Members of the Chaldeanization group have advanced arguments in support of their position as follows: The Syriac language, they allege, was known in Kerala even before the Christian era. This meant that the early culture of Kerala had much in common with the Persian culture. The insinuation attempted is that the St. Thomas Christians and the East-Syrian Christians shared a common culture and therefore the East-Syrian (Chaldean) customs and practices, especially the liturgy, belong to this common cultural context. They consider St. Thomas as the Apostle of both India and Persia, and the Christians of India might have shared the East-Syrian (Chaldean) liturgy and customs from the beginning.

Members of the Indianization group considers the Chaldeanization group's arguments and hypotheses as contestable half-truths and unsubstantiated conjectures that are weak and far-fetched. They counter with the following arguments: The Apostle St. Thomas preached the gospel in India and initiated a simple form of Christian praxis, which took root in the natural soil of India, "absorbing from its nourishing elements" and, if found good, even borrowing from elsewhere. They pointed out that the St. Thomas Christians, after having accepted the faith continued to live the same social-cultural life as their neighbors. They consecrated this life with its various aspects food, dress, ablutions, other hygienic practices, marriage customs, ceremonies connected with the dead, other family and social customs—with "the word and prayer" (cf. 1 Tm 4:5), made them acceptable to God with the Word they had received from the founder of their Church and the prayer he had taught them. This consecration would have gone on developing and produced, among other factors, an indigenous liturgy. This did not happen, they think, because of undue East-Syrian influence.

Restoration Process Continued. Despite the long-running disagreement between these two groups, the process of restoration based to a pristine East Syrian (Chaldean) liturgy under the Roman commissions continued. A Syro-Malabar Pontifical restored along East-Syrian lines was promulgated in 1958. After a few changes and alterations, the vernacular Malayalam translation of the portion for priestly ordination came into use. Many have pointed out that the two principal defects of this text were the absence of the Liturgy of the Word and of the Anointing. While this restored text is used in some dioceses, another text that has the Liturgy of the Word and the Anointing is used in other dioceses. Other parts of the Pontifical underwent some changes but were not promulgated except the text for episcopal ordination.

The restored text of the Eucharistic liturgy was approved in 1957 and came into use in 1962, part Syriac and part vernacular. The text was a great disappointment to the community as a whole. Revisions began soon until, finally in 1968, a more satisfactory vernacular text approved by all the bishops, was introduced *ad experimentium* with the consent of Rome. Despite a few dissenting voices, this text was in continuous use in all the dioceses until 1986.

Experiments. In the wake of the spirit of openness engendered by the Second Vatican Council, a few experimentations were introduced by some individual bishops and groups. Two or more forms of what is called Indian Liturgy were celebrated on an experimental basis in some places. A "short mass" text also came into use in restricted areas. In the absence of texts for sacraments, blessings and Holy Week in the Malayalam vernacular, experimental texts were published on individual initiatives. Vernacular texts for the recitation of the divine office were also made available. The pro-restoration Chaldeanization faction challenged these developments. At the instruction of Rome, the experimental texts were withdrawn after 1980.

Versus Populum* or *Versus Altare? Sometime in the late 1960s all the dioceses introduced the practice of the celebrant facing to the people (*versus populum*), fully or partially during Eucharistic celebration. In the late 1970s the pro-restoration diocese lobbied strongly for the practice of fully facing the altar (*versus altare*). Subsequently, the Synod of the Syro-Malabar Church adopted a compromise formula: *versus populum* during the pre-anaphora and part-communion prayers, but *versus altare* during the anaphora. As a result of stiff opposition from the vast number of clergy, religious, and laity, many bishops have had to waive the implementation of the synodal decision, allowing priests to face the people throughout the liturgy for the time being until an acceptable solution can be worked out.

Further Revisions. The 1968 text of the Eucharistic liturgy was an experimental text (*ad experimentum*). Rome began to insist on a final text. The Syro-Malabar Bishops' Conference (the Syro-Malabar Synod was established only in 1993, after the elevation of the Church to Major Archiepiscopal status) started work from 1980 onwards for a final text with the help of a Central Liturgy Committee. The text submitted in 1981 was rejected by Rome. Another text of the solemn form was sent to Rome with the note that the bishops had seen it ("visum"), implying that the Syro-Malabar Bishops' Conference had not approved it. On the basis of the visum, Rome approved it and Pope John Paul II used it for the beatifying ceremony of Bl. Chavara and Bl. Alphonsa during his visit to Kerala in 1986.

This 1986 text did not find favor with a significant majority of the faithful and clergy in most of the Syro-Malabar dioceses. What they wanted was a simple form of Eucharistic liturgy for ordinary use on Sundays. Disregarding the Roman directives, many parishes continued with the 1968 text. As a result of further communications between Rome and the Syro-Malabar bishops, the Congregation for the Oriental Churches issued its "Directives on the Order of Syro-Malabar Qurbana [Eucharist] in Solemn and Simple Forms." This was approved by the pope in 1988. Based on these "Directives" a new text was prepared, which Rome approved in 1989 and came into use in the same year. This text also did not satisfy the majority of the faithful and clergy. They acquiesced, however, for the time being, accepting the promise given by the prelates of further revision in the future.

Present Situation. On Dec. 16, 1992, the Syro-Malabar Church attained Major Archiepiscopal status. One of the restrictions imposed by Rome was on liturgical renewal, a reservation that was withdrawn only in 1998. Therefore, the whole process of revision and renewal rests with the Syro-Malabar Synod. Following Vatican II, the necessity of inculturating the liturgy to the pastoral needs of the local context has been emphasized by papal and dicastery documents. The Syro-Malabar bishops have acknowledged the importance of a liturgy that is truly pastoral and not a museum-piece or an exercise in archaism, and recognized the clamor of the faithful and clergy for such a liturgy. But no serious attempt has been made so far along these lines. The only positive measure is the introduction of Indian languages and forms of music. The experimental Eucharistic liturgies of the 1960s and 1970s have simply been dropped, at the instruction of the Congregation for the Oriental Churches. The tension between Chaldeanization and Indianization remains unresolved.

Bibliography: T. MANNURAMPARAMBIL, *The Anaphora and the Post-Anaphora of the Syro-Malabar Qurbana* (Kottayam 1984). A. M. MUNDADAN, *Sixteenth Century Traditions of St. Thomas Christians* (Bangalore 1970). A. NARIKULAM, "The Syro-Malabar Liturgical Reform," *Tanima* 1 (1993) 5–18. J. PARECATTIL, *Syro-Malabar Liturgy as I See It* (Ernakulam 1987). J. PODIPARA, *The Syrian Church of Malabar* (Chenganacherry 1938). R. F. TAFT, "The Syro-Malabar Liturgical Controversy," *Tanima* 4 (1996) 60–78. J. THALIATH, *The Synod of Diamper* (Rome 1958); *The Syro-Malabar Liturgy and Liturgical Renewal* (Alwaye 1980). E. TISSERANT, *Eastern Christianity in India* (Bombay 1957) 175–86. J. THOOMKUZHY, "Liturgy of the Syro-Malabar Church," *Tanima* 1 (1993) 79–105. J. VELLIAN, ed., *The Romanization Tendency* (Kottayam 1975).

[A. M. MUNDADAN]

SYRO-MALANKARA CHURCH

The Syro-Malankara Church with its ancient liturgical and theological patrimony adorns the Universal Church and is a witness to the diversity of the latter. The term "Syro" denotes the church's liturgical language as well as its family among the Oriental rites. The church uses the West Syrian Antiochene liturgy in its liturgical celebrations, translated into various Indian languages such as Malayalam, Tamil, and Hindi. *Malankara* is another ancient name for the modern Indian state of Kerala, the cradle of Christianity in India.

Early History

The Syro-Malankara Church traces its origin to the missionary endeavors of the apostle St. Thomas. According to ancient Eastern and Indian traditions, St. Thomas came to Kerala in A.D. 52, bringing the Gospel to Indian soil. The Indians who embraced the Gospel as a result of his preaching are known as the St. Thomas Christians. Evidence points to the arrival of Christians from Mesopotamia between the 4th and 9th centuries. Tradition also reveals that from as early as the 6th century the St. Thomas Christians received bishops from Mesopotamia. Since the bishops hailed from the Chaldean Church, the East Syrian rite attained prominence among the St. Thomas Christians and it was used in Kerala until the 17th century. As a result, the St. Thomas Christians became known also as Syrian Christians. The Church of the St. Thomas Christians was undivided until the arrival of the Portuguese in the 16th century. (*See* INDIA, CHRISTIANITY IN.)

Conflict with the Portuguese and Divisions. Initially, the Portuguese were received cordially by the indigenous St. Thomas Christians. The Portuguese set up their headquarters in Goa early in the 16th century, and the archbishop of Goa claimed jurisdiction over the whole of South India. The St. Thomas Christians' relationship with the Chaldean Church and their use of East Syrian liturgy created in the minds of the Portuguese suspicion of Nestorianism. The acceptance of indigenous customs, social practices, and cultural symbolism also aggravated the doubts of the Portuguese as to their orthodoxy. The Portuguese Archbishop Menezes of Goa convened a synod at Udayamperur (*see* DIAMPER, SYNOD OF) in June 1599 to correct alleged errors in the Church of the St. Thomas Christians. Although the liceity of the synod is in question, Archbishop Menezes coerced the indigenous delegates and their leader, Archdeacon George, into passing several decrees to latinize the St. Thomas Christians. Latin customs and usages were forcibly imposed while traditional customs and practices were proscribed. Since the last of the Chaldean bishops had died two years before the synod, the St. Thomas Christians were placed under the direct jurisdiction of the Portuguese archbishop of Goa. All this led to a situation of confrontation and the St. Thomas Christians lost their confidence in the Portuguese governance.

When Archdeacon George died in 1637, his nephew Thomas assumed leadership, and the spirit of confrontation escalated. This confrontation developed into a full-blown revolt in 1653 with the arrival in Cochin (Kochi) of a Chaldean bishop named Mar Ahatallah, carrying a letter from the pope. Thousands of Christians gathered in Cochin, demanding to see their bishop, but the Portuguese refused their request and sent him off to Goa. Rumors spread that the bishop was drowned. The angry faithful swore an oath never again to be under the Portuguese Episcopal leadership. Four months after this unfortunate incidence, the St. Thomas Christians declared their leader, Archdeacon Thomas, as their bishop, after 12 priests had laid their hands on his head.

The separated St. Thomas Christians, styled as *Puthenkoottukar* (i.e., people who have accepted a new loyalty), appealed for help to the Jacobite patriarch of Antioch, and in 1665 he sent a bishop to Kerala. Although this new prelate refused to consecrate Thomas as bishop, Thomas went ahead to assume Episcopal office and style himself as Mar Thoma I. The dissident faction was ruled by five successive separatist bishops without valid Episcopal ordination. In 1772 the Jacobite patriarch sent two bishops to Kerala, who consecrated Mar Thoma VI with the title Mar Dionysius I. The dissidents, who had held on to Catholic doctrines and practices, eventually accepted the Jacobite doctrines and practices. The Antiochean liturgy using West Syriac was introduced. The dissidents were begun to be called Jacobites and the faction called the Jacobite Church.

Attempts at Reunion. In the wake of the Dutch and the British conquests of India, various Protestant missions made successful inroads on the dissident faction. In addition, the Jacobite patriarch's demand for control not only over spiritual matters but also over temporal affairs led to an internal split. Many St. Thomas Christians longed for the pre-Portuguese unity of their Church. An attempt for reunion had been made in 1704 by Mar Thoma IV. He sent a petition to Rome with his signature and those of 12 of his leading clergymen, seeking communion with Rome. Rome did not respond to this petition. Mar Thoma made a further attempt for reunion. His petition to Rome in 1748 specifically prayed for the withdrawal of the Portuguese bishop and for permission to use leavened bread for the Holy Mass. He promised obedience to Rome and cooperation with the Latin Carmelites in Kerala. This effort, too, was fruitless, as a result of intense lobbying by the Portuguese.

The reunion of the Jacobite St. Thomas Christians was very nearly realized during the time of Mar Dionysius I. In 1778 he sent a long petition to Rome through Father Joseph Kariattil, who had dedicated himself to the reestablishment of unity among the St. Thomas Christians. At long last Rome's reaction was favorable. Father Kariattil was made a bishop in Rome and sent back to Kerala with proper authority to receive Dionysius I and his people into the Catholic communion. Unfortunately, Bishop Kariattil died under mysterious circumstances in Goa on his way back home. Hopes were kept alive when Dionysius I reunited with Rome in 1790 as a result of the efforts of Thachil Mathoo Tharakan, a Catholic layman. He even took up residence in the Catholic Church at Alleppy for about six months, hoping to receive the official mandate to rule his people. This was never realized, and Mar Dionysius, frustrated, returned to the midst of his Jacobite followers.

Mar Dionysius IV, who ruled the Jacobites from 1825 to 1853, also made a vigorous effort for reunion. He was disturbed by the Protestant influence among his people and disheartened by the demands of the Jacobite patriarch. His initial attempts at communion with Rome fizzled after he was told by the Latin archbishop of Kerala that he had to be content with a layman's status after reunion. To this list of reunion failures must be added that of Mar Dionysius V, who had been supported by Father Mani Nidhirikal. A successful large-scale reunion had to await the endeavors of Mar Ivanios in the 20th century.

Reunion Movement

Successful Reunion. Mar Ivanios was born in 1882 of an ancient Syrian family at Mavelikkara. He was brilliant and learned, the first Syrian priest to earn an M.A. degree from the University of Madras, and on him centered the hopes of his community. For four years he was principal of the high school of the Jacobite Church at Kottayam, and then he joined Serampore University (West Bengal) as professor of Syriac and economics. During his six-year teaching career there, Father P. T. Geevarghese (as he was then called) gathered around him a group of young men and inspired them to dedicate themselves to reform the moribund Jacobite Church. It was during this period, too, that he came under the influence of the High Church clergy and women religious of the Oxford Mission to Calcutta. When he left Serampore to start the Bethany Ashram (Order of the Imitation of Christ) and Convent in Kerala, he received guidance from them, especially from Mother Edith. The Bethany movement soon became a source of spiritual awakening in the Jacobite Church. Many parish churches served by the Bethany fathers sprang up in central Kerala.

In the early 20th century, the Jacobite Church in Kerala had split into two. The local metropolitan of the Malankara Church, Mar Geevarghese Vattasseril, who had resisted the Jacobite Patriarch Abdulla's demand for rights over Church properties, was excommunicated by the Jacobite patriarch in 1910. The metropolitan and his supporters, including Father Geevarghese, made contact with another patriarch, Abdul Messiah, from Antioch, and through him established a Catholicate in Kerala in 1912. The dispute between the patriarch and the metropolitan was taken to the court of law, and Geevarghese undertook a special study of the canons and ancient documents of the Jacobite Church to assist his party. This study showed him that the Jacobite documents and canons had conceded the primacy of the See of Rome. In 1925, at the age of 42, he was consecrated bishop with the name Mar Ivanios. The split in his own Church and its spiritual poverty strengthened his view that a solution to the problems of the Jacobites could be achieved in communion with the Church of Rome. Most Jacobite bishops shared his view, and with their concurrence Mar Ivanios started negotiations for communion.

In 1925 he wrote to the Catholic patriarch of Antioch at Beirut about reunion with the Catholic Church. As the reply from Beirut was long in coming, the Jacobite leaders counseled Mar Ivanios to negotiate directly with Rome. In November of 1926 he wrote to the Congregation for the Oriental Churches about reunion on two conditions, namely, the approval of the use of the Antiochene Liturgy (*see* ANTIOCHENE LITURGY) and the recognition of the Ordination (Orders) of the Catholicos party. The Roman Congregation requested a confidential report from Mr. Watts, an English Catholic, who was the Dewan of Travancore. In a meeting, Mr. Watts was impressed by the sincerity of Mar Ivanios and sent a favorable report to Rome. Rome's reply to Mar Ivanios, however, was noncommittal. Still Mar Ivanios continued his correspondence with the Holy See and with Archbishop Mooney (later cardinal of Detroit), the Apostolic Delegate in India. Meanwhile, the synod of the Catholicos party had raised Mar Ivanios to the position of metropolitan of Bethany, and his close associate, Father Jacob, to the episcopate with the title Mar Theophilus. Mar Ivanios was then at the height of his influence in his Church.

The synod of the Catholicos party had second thoughts on reunion, following their success in the court of law establishing their right to administer Church properties. They tried in various ways to undermine the influence of Mar Ivanios, whose face was set toward Rome. They asked him to turn over to them the management of the schools under him and sought control over his ashram and the Bethany churches. Opposition to Mar Ivanios slowly gathered force, and he was harassed by his own people. The synod decided to take legal action to evict Mar Ivanios from his ashram. He did not resist, but offered ''to leave everything and go away.'' In August of 1930 Mar Ivanios, with Mar Theophilus, 18 Bethany monks, and orphans who had decided to remain with him, left the ashram and settled in a small rented house near Tiruvalla.

Archbishop Mooney and Bishop Benziger of Quilon (within whose jurisdiction the Bethany Ashram stood) were impressed with the single-mindedness of Mar Ivanios, and they took up his cause with Rome. A few days after the self-exile of Mar Ivanios, the apostolic delegate communicated to him Rome's decision to receive him into the Catholic communion. Bishop Benziger was named to perform the ceremony. The historic event took place on Saturday, Sept. 20, 1930, in the chapel of the bishop's house, Quilon. Mar Ivanios and Mar Theophilus made their profession of faith and were received into communion with the Holy See. Members of a small representative group consisting of a priest (Father John), a deacon (Alexander), and a layman (K. G. Chacko) also entered into communion with Rome on the same historic occasion. On September 22 Mar Ivanios received into the Catholic Church the Bethany sisters and the monks of Bethany. A few days later he had the joy of receiving into the Church his own parents and two leading Rambans (monks) of the Catholicos party, Philippose Cheppad and Joseph Pulikottil. The historic document from the Oriental Congregation that authorized the communion also gave the assurance ''that the pure Syro-Antiochean rite shall be preserved, and that it will not thus be confused with the Syro-Malabars, whose rite is of Syro-Chaldaic origin, that Mar Ivanios and Mar Theophilus will be maintained in their respective office and jurisdiction and that they will depend immediately on the Holy See.'' Concerning the married clergy, the Oriental Congregation decided that no candidate shall be admitted in the future to Sacred Orders who does not promise to remain celibate.

Establishment of the Hierarchy and Growth. The effort initiated by Mar Ivanios was known as the Reunion Movement. Those who were separated from the communion with the See of Rome were by this time in different communions such as the Catholicos party (known from the early 20th century as Malankara Orthodox Church), the patriarch's party (known as the Syrian Orthodox Church or the Jacobite Church), Mar Thoma Church, Church Mission Society, and various other denominations. For all those who expected and desired unity among the churches, the Reunion Movement became the way to achieve their long cherished dream. Within a short time the Reunion Movement became for thousands of St. Thomas Christians the means for entering into communion with Rome.

Along with the work of reunion, the nascent Syro-Malankara Church engaged in the work of evangelization in Kerala and the neighboring states. The result was promising, especially in the civil districts of Kollam and Trivandrum in Kerala and Kanyakumari in Tamil Nadu.

In May of 1932 Mar Ivanios visited Rome and was warmly received by Pope Pius XI, who conferred on him the sacred pallium and sent him back as the archbishop of Trivandrum. The Syro-Malankara Hierarchy formally came into being with the Apostolic Constitution *Christo pastorum principi* of June 11, 1932. On March 11, 1933, Mar Ivanios dedicated his provisional Cathedral at Palayam, Trivandrum, and assumed office as the archbishop of the Metropolitan eparchy of Trivandrum and the head of the Syro-Malankara Church. The eparchy (diocese) of Tiruvalla was created in November of 1933 and Mar Theophilus was enthroned as its bishop. Two more Jacobite bishops, Archbishop Mar Severios in 1937 and Bishop Mar Dioscoros in 1939, sought communion with the Catholic Church. The latter had belonged to the patriarch's party (Syrian Orthodox or the Jacobite Church). On Jan. 29, 1953, Mar Ivanios consecrated Father Benedict of the Bethany congregation as his auxiliary and successor, who received the name Benedict Mar Gregorios. Mar Ivanios, the pioneer of the Reunion Movement, passed away on July 15, 1953. On Jan. 27, 1955, Mar Gregorios was appointed the metropolitan archbishop of Trivandrum. Archbishop Mar Severios, who was the administrator of the eparchy of Tiruvalla from 1938 onwards, assumed office as the bishop of the eparchy of Tiruvalla in 1950. Upon the demise of Mar Severios in 1955, Zacharias Mar Athanasios succeeded him. Mar Theophilus passed away on June 27, 1956.

Developments since Vatican II

The Reunion Movement made remarkable progress in every field under the able guidance of Mar Gregorios and Mar Athanasios. Both participated in the Second Vatican Council and Mar Gregorios was a permanent member of the Synod of Bishops of the Universal Church as the metropolitan of the Malankara Church. Mar Gregorios served the Kerala Catholic Bishops' Conference as president several times and also the Catholic Bishops' Conference of India from 1988 to 1990. Owing to his active involvement in every sphere of social life, the metropolitan eparchy of Trivandrum acquired a prestigious position. Mar Athanasios passed away on Sept. 28, 1977.

Paulos Mar Philexinos, the metropolitan of the Malabar Independent Church and a great Syriac scholar, came to the Catholic communion on Aug. 28, 1977. A priest and a few faithful also followed the path of Mar Philexinos and reunited with the Catholic Church. He was appointed titular bishop of Chayal and episcopal vicar of the metropolitan eparchy of Trivandrum.

The Syro-Malankara Church had another milestone in its growth when the eparchy of Bathery was created on Oct. 28, 1978, bifurcating the eparchy of Tiruvalla. On Dec. 28, 1978, Cyril Mar Baselios was consecrated bishop of Bathery and Isaac Mar Yoohanon the bishop of Tiruvalla. The Syro-Malankara Church had a great moment of joy when it celebrated the Golden Jubilee of its communion with Rome in December of 1980 at Kottayam. Cardinal Wadislaus Rubin visited the Syro-Malankara Church as the special delegate of Pope John Paul II. The occasion was graced with the priestly ordination of 20 young men and the religious profession of 22 young women; the joy of the Church was immense when it received a new bishop: Lawrence Mar Ephraem was consecrated the auxiliary of the metropolitan eparchy of Trivandrum.

The Syro-Malankara Church was honored with a visit from Pope John Paul II, who made a historic sojourn to St. Mary's Metropolitan Church, Pattom, Trivandrum, on Feb. 8, 1986. Upon the demise of Mar Yoohanon, Geevarghese Mar Timotheos was consecrated bishop of the eparchy of Tiruvalla on Aug. 6, 1987.

When Mar Gregorios passed away on Oct. 10, 1994, Cyril Mar Baselios, then bishop of Bathery, was appointed archbishop of Trivandrum and the metropolitan of the Syro-Malankara Church, and his *sunthroniso* (enthronement) took place on Dec. 14, 1995. As the metropolitan archbishop he received the sacred pallium from Pope John Paul II on Jan. 9, 1996. The time since then has been one of new vitality in ecclesial life. On Feb. 5, 1996, Geevarghese Mar Divannasios was consecrated as the bishop of the eparchy of Bathery. The Syro-Malankara Church was blessed with much growth, necessitating the erection of the new eparchy of Marthandom on Dec. 16, 1996. The eparchy of Marthandom was the fruit of the evangelizing work of the Syro-Malankara Church since the inception of the hierarchy. Lawrence Mar Ephraem, the auxiliary bishop of Marthandom, was appointed as the first bishop of the new eparchy. The formal inauguration of the eparchy and the *sunthroniso* of the bishop took place on Jan. 23, 1997.

On July 17, 1997, Thomas Mar Koorilos was consecrated as the auxiliary bishop of the eparchy of Tiruvalla. Bishop Lawrence Mar Ephraem died on April 8, 1997. Metropolitan Mar Philexinos passed away on Nov. 3, 1998. Yoohanon Mar Chrysostom was ordained bishop of the eparchy of Marthandom and he was enthroned on July 1, 1998. Joshua Mar Ignathios was ordained the auxiliary of the Metropolitan eparchy of Trivandrum on June 29, 1998.

The Malankara Church has undertaken pastoral work among its faithful outside its territorial limits, namely outside Kerala and India. It has centers in the Indian cities of New Delhi, Mumbai, Nasik, Pune, Calcutta, Bhopal, Bhilai, Surat, Bangalore, Mangalore, Chennai, and Hyderabad. A priest-coordinator is appointed to organize the pastoral work outside the state of Kerala. Priests and religious women are appointed to attend the pastoral needs of the faithful in the above places.

The Church also has centers of pastoral mission in the major cities of the United States, Canada, and Germany. To attend to the needs of the Malankara faithful in the diaspora, Isaac Mar Cleemis was appointed the apostolic visitor to the Malankara faithful in North America and Europe. His Episcopal Ordination took place on Aug. 15, 2001.

Faithful and Institutions. At the beginning of the 21st century, the Syro-Malankara Church has 381,178 faithful and 838 parishes and mission stations. It has 421 diocesan priests and 139 religious priests. The 9 prestigious university colleges reveal the Church's concern in the field of higher education. The Church operates 2 teachers' training schools, 6 technical institutes, 15 higher secondary schools, 53 high schools, 65 upper primary schools, 158 lower primary schools, 128 nursery schools, 11 orphanages, and 37 boarding schools. The Church's 16 hospitals and 10 homes for the aged take care of the sick and elderly. In addition the church has 7 printing presses, 4 bookstalls, and 8 publications. There are outreach programs for socially marginalized groups such as *dalits* and tribals, as well as programs for the theological formation of laity and religious.

A major seminary of its own for the promotion of the liturgical, spiritual, and theological traditions of the Church was a long-cherished dream of the Syro-Malankara Church. It was realized when a major seminary dedicated to Mary, Mother of God, was begun on June 29, 1983, at Pattom, Trivandrum. His Holiness Pope John Paul II, on the occasion of his historic visit to Trivandrum, blessed the foundation stone for the new seminary on Feb. 8, 1986. The seminary was shifted to Nalanchira, Trivandrum, when the first phase of the seminary building was completed in May 1989. The beginning of the theology course in 1992 marked the second phase in the growth of the seminary. The 30 students, who made up the first class of students, successfully completed their entire formation in the Malankara Seminary and were ordained priests in 1996.

St. Ephrem Ecumenical Research Institute (SEERI), in Kottayam, Kerala, is a center dedicated to in-depth study and research of Syriac language and literature and theological patrimony of the Eastern Churches. The national and international conferences organized by SEERI and the journal, *Harp,* published by SEERI, manifest its distinctive character and uniqueness.

Indigenous Religious Congregations. Most of the members of the Order of the Imitation of Christ and the Sisters of the Imitation of Christ entered into communion with the Holy See along with their founder, Mar Ivanios. Popularly known as Bethany Fathers and Bethany Sisters, members of both communities are engaged in ecumenical, missionary, and educational work. The Congregation of the Sisters of the Imitation was raised to pontifical status in 1956 and the Order of the Imitation of Christ received this status in 1966. There are 100 priests in the two provinces of the congregation. The Bethany Sisters have four provinces and there are 762 members.

In the early days of the Reunion Movement, Monsignor Joseph Kunzhinjalil founded the Congregation of the Daughters of Mary in 1938 to promote the work of reunion and evangelization. Started in the civil district of Kanyakumary in Tamil Nadu, the congregation carries out its ministries in all the eparchies of the Syro-Malankara Church and nine other dioceses in India. The congregation was raised to pontifical status in 1988 and at present they have two provinces and four regions. There are 759 members in the congregation.

The Franciscan Missionary Brothers have been doing apostolic work in the Syro-Malankara Church, especially in the metropolitan eparchy of Trivandrum, from 1936 onwards. They are principally involved in direct evangelization and faith formation and work for integral development of poor and young people.

The Kurisumala Ashram, founded in the eparchy of Tiruvalla in 1957, was an attempt to integrate the Eastern and Indian traditions of spirituality. The ashram was founded by Francis Mahieu, a Cistercian, and Bede Griffiths, a Benedictine. The Kurisumala Ashram serves as a center for spiritual and liturgical renewal and is known for its work in promoting unity among the various Christian denominations.

Bibliography: L. W. BROWN, *The Indian Christians of St. Thomas* (New Delhi, 1982). E. TISERANT, *Eastern Christianity in India,* tr. E. R. HAMBYE (Westminister, Md. 1957). M. GIBBONS, *Mar Ivanios* (Dublin 1962). PLACID, CMI, *The Thomas Christians and Their Syriac Treasures* (Alleppy 1974). C. MALANCHARUVIL, *The Syro-Malankara Church* (Alwaye 1973). I. THOTTUNKAL ed., *Emerging Trends in Malankara Catholic Theology—Vision and Contributions of Cyril Mar Baselios* (Rome 1995). M. IVANIOS, ''The Malabar Reunion,'' *Pax* 21 (1931) 1–15. E. R. HAMBYE, ''Syrian Jacobites in India,'' *Eastern Churches Quarterly* 11 (1955) 115–129. PLACID, CMI, ''The Efforts for Reunion in Malankara, South India,'' *Unitas* 5 (1953) 7–15, 89–98.

[C. A. ABRAHAM/J. PADIPURACKAL]

SYROPOULOS, SYLVESTER

Byzantine ecclesiastic and historian; b. Constantinople, end of the 14th century; d. after 1453. Syropoulos, probably the son of a deacon functionary of HAGIA SOPHIA, received a good education, became (*c.* 1430) Great Ecclesiarches and Dikaiophylax of St. Sophia. He accompanied the Patriarch Joseph II (1416–39) to Italy for the Council of FLORENCE, served as a member of various committees, and signed the decree of union; but on his return to Constantinople he became an active member of the antiunionist movement. He resigned his office to the unionist Patriarch Metrophanes, but seemingly retained the title. Several manuscripts in his hand date from this period. His name appears among the signatures of antiunionist manifestoes and documents preceding the fall of Constantinople (May 1453). Thereafter he is not heard of again, unless, under the name of Sophronius, he was the third patriarch of Constantinople after the capture, who reigned for one year and was deposed by the clergy.

Syropoulos is known almost exclusively for his *Memoirs,* edited in 1660, without the first section, by the Anglican Bp. Robert Chreyghton, with the title: *Vera historia unionis non verae,* an account of the Council of Florence with an introduction recording the preliminary negotiations. Syropoulos portrays himself as the most anti-Latin and antiunionist of the Greeks in Italy, who had been silenced in the private Greek meetings by the Emperor for his antiunionist influence; but was made to sign the decree of union. The *Memoirs* say extremely little of the public events of the Council; they are devoted almost entirely to backstage relations of Greeks with Greeks and, to a lesser degree, with the Latins. The *Memoirs* are in reality a thesis to prove that the union of the two churches achieved in Florence was the result of duress, and so no union at all. Syropoulos himself had signed the decree and had to explain why. As a historical document, the *Memoirs* are untrustworthy. Unquestionably they contain a vast number of facts, but one can never be sure one has the truth in its full context: at times their assertions can be disproved or called into doubt. Yet Syropoulos did not falsify facts deliberately. He wrote after 1444 from memory, but from a memory enmbittered by controversy and remorse, and by the hostility that the union had aroused in Constantinople.

Bibliography: W. GASS and P. MEYER, J. J. HERZOG and A. HAUCK, eds., *Realencyklopädie für protestantische Theologie,* 24 v. (3d ed. Leipzig 1896–1913) 19:306–308. M. JUGIE, *Échos d'Orient* 38 (1939) 70–71. H. G. BECK, *Kirche und theologische Literatur im byzantinischen Reich* (Munich 1959) 759–760. J. GILL "The Acta and the Memoirs of Syropoulos as History" *Orientalia Christiana periodica* 14 (1948) 303–355; *The Council of Florence* (Cambridge, Eng. 1959).

[J. GILL]

SZÁNTÓ, ISTVÁN (ARATOR)

Hungarian missionary, religious writer; b. Györ, 1541; d. Olmütz, 1612. After his early education in Vienna, the bishop of Györ sent him in 1560 to the German College in Rome, where he entered the Society of Jesus. As a result of his initiative, a Hungarian college under Jesuit direction was established in Rome and subsequently became amalgamated with the German college under the name of Collegium Germanicum-Hungaricum. In 1579 Gregory XIII sent Szántó together with other Jesuits to work for the Catholic reform in Erdély (Transylvania). Though successful in many respects, Szántó was unable to prevent the expulsion of the Jesuits from Transylvania and was forced to move to northern Hungary in 1600 and finally to Olmütz, Austria. Here he worked until his death on the Magyar translation of the Bible. Unfortunately, most of his manuscripts were lost. Szántó wrote the Hungarian part of the great dictionary of Calepino.

Bibliography: V. FRAKNÓI, "Egy magyar jezsuita a XVI században" *Katolikus Szemle* (Budapest 1888). J. SZINNYEI, *Magyar irók,* 14 v. (Budapest 1891–1914) v.1. A. STEINHUBER, *Geschichte des Collegium Germanicum-Hungaricum,* 2 v. (Freiburg 1906) v.1.

[G. C. PAIKERT]

T

TABB, JOHN BANISTER

Priest, poet; b. near Richmond, Va., March 22, 1845; d. Ellicott City, Md., Nov. 19, 1909. His father, Thomas Yelverton, a plantation owner in Amelia County, Va., married Marianna Bertrand Archer, a first cousin. Tabb was tutored at home, and enlisted in the Confederate Army at the outbreak of the Civil War. He was captured in June 1864, and sent to Point Lookout prison camp, where he formed a lasting friendship with the musician and poet, Sidney Lanier. After his release in February 1865, he went to Baltimore, hoping to become a concert pianist. Here he became a close friend of Alfred Curtis, an Episcopalian minister—later the Catholic bishop of Wilmington, Del.—whose religious practices turned his thoughts toward the Catholic Church, though he first thought of becoming an Episcopalian clergyman.

Tabb taught English (1870) at Racine College, an Episcopalian institution in Michigan. Called home because of his sister's illness, he stayed until he resolved his own religious crisis. He was baptized conditionally by Bp. James Gibbons in the Richmond Cathedral, Sept. 8, 1872. In November he was enrolled at St. Charles College, Catonsville, Md. He graduated in 1875, then taught at St. Peter's School in Richmond from 1875 to 1877 and at St. Charles' College from 1877 to 1881, where he also studied philosophy. He entered St. Mary's Seminary, Baltimore, in 1881, was ordained on Dec. 20, 1884, and returned to St. Charles. There he taught until blindness forced his retirement in 1907.

His first book, *Poems,* was privately printed in 1882. The poems written between 1882 and 1890 evidenced his critical renouncement of his earlier Victorian poetic style. Many of them were rejected by magazine editors, chiefly because their metaphysical and imagistic qualities were new and puzzling. After 1890 his poems found ready acceptance; *An Octave to Mary* (1893) was followed by *Poems* (1894), which won immediate acclaim and assured the success of his subsequent volumes. These include: *Lyrics* (1897), *Child Verse* (1899), *Two Lyrics* (1900), *Later Lyrics* (1902), *The Rosary in Rhyme* (1904), *Quips and Quiddities* (1907), and *Later Poems* (1910). His priestly character pervades his poetry; the New and Old Testaments, the liturgy, theology, and hagiography furnish the functional metaphors and symbols for his lyric and epigrammatic presentation of the world of nature and man.

Bibliography: F. E. LITZ, *Father Tabb: A Study of His Life and Works* (Baltimore 1923). J. B. TABB, *Letters—Grave and Gay, and Other Prose,* ed. F. E. LITZ (Washington 1950).

[F. E. LITZ]

TABENNISI

In the THEBAÏD, Upper Egypt, near Denderah on the right bank of the Nile, site of the first Pachomian monastery. From *c.* 318 PACHOMIUS gradually evolved a highly organized communal life in which over 1,000 monks prayed, worked, and ate together. The monastic compound was surrounded by a high wall within which were a church, kitchen, refectory, storehouse, garden, guest house, and many dwelling houses, with about 20 monks in each, grouped according to their work. The monks were tailors, smiths, carpenters, tanners, shoemakers, gardeners, copyists, camel drivers, and most commonly, weavers. Each house was governed by a *praepositus* to whom the monks owed strict obedience. The general duties of the compound were performed in weekly turns by the monks. Although Pachomius eventually made his second foundation Pbow, the motherhouse, the fame of Tabennisi was great enough to draw ATHANASIUS of Alexandria there on a visit in 330, and SOZOMEN reports that the Pachomian monks were called the Tabennesians.

Bibliography: SOZOMEN, *Historia Ecclesiastica,* 3:14 (*Patrologia Graeca,* ed. J. P. MIGNE, 67:1069–76). PALLADIUS OF HELENOPOLIS, *The Lausiac History,* ed. C. BUTLER (Cambridge, England 1898–1904) 1:235–241. H. LECLERCQ, *Dictionnaire d'archéologie chrétienne et de liturgie,* ed. F. CABROL, 15 v. (Paris 1907–53) 2.2:3047–3248, s.v. Cénobitisme. P. DE LABRIOLLE, "Les Débuts du monachisme," A. FLICHE and V. MARTIN, eds., *Histoire*

Decorative golden tabernacle, bread and wine holder, Novgrod, Russia. (©Dean Conger/CORBIS)

de l'église depuis les origines jusqu'à nos jours (Paris 1935–) 3:338–343; English tr. in J. R. PALANQUE et al., *The Church in the Roman Christian Empire,* tr. E. C. MESSENGER, 2 v. in 1 (New York 1953) 2:469–475. L. T. LEFORT, ''Les premiers monastères pacômiens,'' *Muséon* 52 (1939) 379–408.

[M. C. MCCARTHY]

TABERNACLE

An ornamented receptacle for liturgical vessels containing consecrated Bread reserved for the Communion of the sick, for communion services and for adoration.

Historically, the place and manner of the reservation of the Blessed Sacrament have differed at various periods and in different places. Sometimes it was reserved in the church, sometimes elsewhere (e.g., in the sacristy); in some churches, in a fixed mural ambry or in a ''Sacrament house,'' in others, in a movable vessel (casket, tower, pyx, or dove) placed near the altar or hanging above it. Only in the 16th century did a tabernacle placed on the main altar begin to be the normal manner of reservation, prescribed often by local law, and then by the general prescription of the Roman Ritual of 1614. Not until 1863, by decree of the Congregation of Rites, was the placement of the tabernacle on the principal altar made mandatory, all other ways of reservation forbidden.

Under the 1983 Code of Canon Law, there is to be only one tabernacle in a church or oratory (CIC 938 §1), which should be ''situated in some part of the church or oratory which is distinguished, conspicuous, beautifully decorated, and suitable for prayer'' (CIC 938 §2). The rationale for the placement of the tabernacle, if possible, in an area distinct from the place of Eucharistic celebration was first articulated in the Instruction on Eucharistic Worship (*Eucharisticum mysterium*) of the Congregation of Rites (*Acta Apostolicae Sedis* 59 [1967] 539–573, dated 25 May 1967): ''In the celebration of Mass the modes by which Christ is present in his Church become successively clearer: first he appears present in the very body of the faithful assembled in his name; then in his Word, when Scripture is read and explained; next, in the person of the minister; lastly, in a special manner under the eucharistic species [see *Sacrosanctum Concilium* 7]. From the viewpoint of sign, therefore, it is in better accord with the nature of liturgical celebration that the eucharistic presence of Christ not be at the altar where Mass is celebrated, since this presence is the result of the consecration and must appear to be such. . .'' (55). The tabernacle itself ''is to be immovable, made of solid and opaque material, and locked in such a way that the danger of profanation is avoided as much as possible'' (CIC 938 §3).

Bibliography: J. B. O'CONNELL, *Church Building and Furnishing* (Notre Dame, IN 1955). P. L. ANSON, *Churches: Their Plan and Furnishing* (Milwaukee 1948). H. E. COLLINS, *The Church Edifice and Its Appointments* (Westminster, Md. 1953). A. BUGNINI, ''Commentarium super decretum De Forma et Usu Tabernaculi, June 1, 1957,'' *Ephemerides litugicae* 71 (1957) 442–445. H. VON MEURERS, ''Altar und Tabernakel,'' *Litergisches Jahrbuch* 3 (1953) 10–28.

[J. B. O'CONNELL/F. R. MCMANUS/EDS.]

TABLET, THE

A Catholic weekly, founded in London in May 1840 by Frederick LUCAS, who two years earlier had converted from Quakerism. It was, at the start, a liberal paper: in a letter in the first issue the Irish politician Daniel O'CONNELL saw it as ''an organ to communicate to the public facts of importance to the religious liberty of all classes.'' Lucas's early moderation quickly turned to a zeal to combat all bigotry, as he saw it, against Catholicism. He also espoused the cause of Irish Home Rule, and moved, with his publication, to Dublin. After his death in 1855 the paper was purchased by John Wallis, again a convert, but, unlike Lucas, a Tory. He brought it back to London and changed the editorial stance to one more in sympathy with the Catholic establishment. Wallis sold the paper, then in financial difficulties, to Fr. Herbert Vaughan, an aristocratic cleric who had, on a visit to the United States, become persuaded of the importance of religious journalism. In 1872 Vaughan became bishop of Salford, and in 1892 archbishop of Westminster. He retained ownership, but handed over the editorship to a relative, John Snead-Cox. The editorial policy remained conservative, both theologically and politically; it also showed a great concern for education, an especial concern of Vaughan's. On his death he bequeathed *The Tablet* to the diocese of Westminster. Profits were to be divided between the upkeep of the cathedral and the foreign missionary society (the Mill Hill Fathers) Vaughan had founded. Snead-Cox retired in 1920, and was replaced briefly by his assistant James Milburn, who died in office in 1923. Cardinal Bourne's choice for editor, Ernest Oldmeadow, had been a Nonconformist minister in Canada, a wine merchant, and a novelist. He was a pugnacious convert, with a particular detestation of Anglicanism (and specifically of Lord Halifax and the Malines Conversations), in which he claimed to have been encouraged by the cardinal. Bourne's successor, Arthur Hinsley, was less aggressive. He also discovered that *The Tablet*, between the earlier division of profits and the fact that many of its potential readers had been alienated by its editor, was desperately short of funds. He sold it to a group of laymen led by Thomas Ferrier Burns, an editor with a wide circle of Catholic acquaintances. Among them was Douglas Woodruff, a leader-writer on *The Times*, who in April 1936 became *The Tablet*'s editor. The style immediately became much more political and international. It became, it was claimed, required reading in embassies around the world. It shared the right-wing attitudes of the greater part of the British establishment in the 1930s, in particular a sympathy with Franco. Woodruff was, on the other hand, unsympathetic to the Irish Free State. He attended the Second Vatican Council, and expressed himself as happy with the reforms. He achieved something of a coup when he received a letter for publication, defending Pius XII against the picture presented in Hochuth's play *The Representative*. It was written by Cardinal Montini when he was still archbishop, but reached the paper shortly after he had become pope. Tom Burns replaced Woodruff in 1967, and was immediately faced with the controversy over *Humanae vitae*, starting with the Majority Report of the commission on birth control, which he published. Burns remained a liberal Catholic, though conservative in politics. This particular stance, particularly his stand in favor of contraception, lost him many readers, and the paper came close to folding. Burns retired in 1982, at the end of the papal visit to Britain, and was replaced by John Wilkins, who had been an assistant on the paper from 1967 to 1972. Under Wilkins *The Tablet* retained a liberal outlook on things Catholic, but also, and for the first time since the death of Frederick Lucas, on politics likewise. The circulation has grown until it has far outstripped the sales of any period in its history.

Bibliography: M. J. WALSH, *The Tablet, 1840–1990, A Commemorative History* (London 1990).

[M. J. WALSH]

TABOR, MOUNT

A prominent landmark in southern Galilee. Rising on the northeast limit of the Plain of Esdraelon, Mt. Tabor (Heb., *har tābôr;* Gr., Ὄρος Θαβώρ or Ἰταβύριον; mod. Arabic, Jebel eṭ-Ṭōr) is located five and a half miles south-southeast of Nazareth, where the boundary lines of Issachar, Zebulon, and Nephthali met in former times. Although it rises only to 1,844 feet above sea level, its isolation from the surrounding hills and its steep sides give it an appearance impressive beyond its modest height (Jer 46.18).

Tabor has a long history of military significance. It was at Mt. Tabor that Barac assembled the 10,000 warriors from the northern tribes with which he defeated the forces of Sisara, the Canaanite leader (Jgs 4.12–15). The brothers of GIDEON were killed at Tabor by Zebah and Zalmunna (Jgs 8.18–19). In 218 B.C. Antiochus the Great conquered Tabor, as did Alexander Jannaeus in 100 B.C. In 57 B.C. Alexander, the son of Aristobolus, was defeated in battle at its foot by Gabinius, the commander of Pompey. In A.D. 67 Flavius JOSEPHUS organized a vain resistance on its plateau against Placidus, the lieutenant of Vespasian.

Topped by a plateau 1,239 yards long and 411 yards wide, Tabor has been likened to an altar inviting to worship [cf. Ps 88(89).13]. The reference in Hos 5.1 seems to indicate that in Israelite times there was a shrine to Yahweh there, and Dt 33.18–19 has been interpreted in the same way. Tabor's special interest for Christians lies in the fact that it has been traditionally identified with the mountain of the TRANSFIGURATION (Mk 9.1–7). This identification, however, is by no means certain; early tradition was not unanimous on the subject, although the identification was made as early as *c.* A.D. 150 in the *Gospel according to the Hebrews.*

Many churches have been built on Mt. Tabor in the course of the ages. The most impressive is the Basilica of the Transfiguration, completed in 1923.

Bibliography: *Encyclopedic Dictionary of the Bible*, tr. and adap. by L. HARTMAN (New York 1963) 2423–24. C. KOPP, *The Holy Places of the Gospels,* tr. R. WALLS (New York 1963) 242–247. B. MEISTERMANN, *Le Mont Thabor* (Paris 1900).

[P. HORVATH]

TABORGA, MIGUEL DE LOS SANTOS

Archbishop of Sucre, polemicist, and historiographer; b. Sucre, July 5, 1833; d. there, Sept. 4, 1905. With Crecente Errázuris of Santiago, Chile, and Federico González Suárez of Quito, he completes the trio of prelates who figure among the most eminent historiographers of Hispanic America. Taborga, of a noble Creole family, studied at the San Cristóbal seminary and was ordained before reaching the minimum age required by Canon Law. He was a priest in a modest town parish and was known for his religious zeal, his indefatigable activity, and his strong personality. In his political career, his aims were always the highest, his conduct exemplary. He was a delegate to various legislatures and twice a senator for Chuquisaca. A brilliant preacher, he was equally forceful in political assemblies. At the end of the 19th century when antireligious liberalism became very strong in the university, the courts, and the press, Taborga became the champion of Catholicism. In *El Cruzado,* a Christian weekly published in Sucre, he fought against unbelief and against the secularization of Bolivian society and government. His polished polemics gained him a wide reputation, and the Spanish Royal Academy made him a corresponding member. To historical research, Taborga devoted his best efforts. After carefully studying source materials, he arrived at exact dates and facts for Bolivian history, writing ten monographs on the subject. He intended to write a comprehensive history of the country based on documentary evidence, but he was unable to complete it. Among his most important works are: *Documentos para la historia de Bolivia, Aclaraciones sobre el 25 de Mayo, Crónicas de la catedral de Sucre,* and *Idea de una introducción a la historia de Bolivia.* From his unpublished studies, the publicist Luis Paz wrote *Estudios históricos de Monseñor Taborga* (Sucre 1913). In 1898 Taborga was named archbishop of Sucre, where he remained until his death.

[H. SANABRIA FERNÁNDEZ]

TABORITES

A radical group of HUSSITES, emerging *c.* 1415 from a rural movement in Bohemia. They were infected by CHILIASM and insisted on the reception of Holy Communion under both species. In order to defend their faith they formed the first brotherhood, or theocratic community, in Ústí. It was later transferred to Hradiště, which assumed the Biblical name of Tabor. John ŽIŽKA transformed it into a military unit. Under Nicholas of Pelhřimov, their first elected bishop, they became an autonomous ecclesiastical body, dissociated from the Church, in contrast to the moderate UTRAQUISTS. The Bible was the sole source of faith for the Taborites; the veneration of saints was abolished; and all holy days and sacramentals were eliminated. They destroyed churches, had a married clergy, and replaced Latin with Czech in the liturgy. Of the Sacraments only Baptism and Holy Eucharist were retained. They split into Moderates (called Orphans or Orebites after Žižka's death) and Radicals, led by Prokop the Bald, who opposed any reconciliation with the Church. The Radicals were defeated at the Battle of Lipany (1434) by the combined forces of Catholic and Utraquist lords, and were forced to comply with the *Compact.* They were condemned at the Diet of Prague (1444); their center was occupied by George of Poděbrad (1452)

Bibliography: H. KAMINSKY, ''Chiliasm and the Hussite Revolution,'' *Church History* (Philadelphia 1957) 26, 43–71; ''Hussite Radicalism and the Origins of Tabor,'' *Medievalia et humanistica* 10 (Boulder, CO 1956) 102–130. F. G. HEYMANN, ''The Hussite-Utraquist Church in the Fifteenth and Sixteenth Centuries,'' *Archiv für Reformationgeschichte* 52 (Gütersloh 1961) 1–16. P. DE VOOGHT, ''L'heresie des taborites sur l'Eucharistie, 1418–21,'' *Irenikon* 35 (1962) 340–350.

[L. NEMEC]

TACHÉ, ALEXANDRE ANTONIN

Second bishop and first archbishop of Saint Boniface, Manitoba, Canada; b. Fraserville, Quebec, Canada, July 23, 1823; d. St. Boniface, June 22, 1894. Taché was the son of Charles and Louise-Henriette (Boucher de la Broquerie) Taché. After his theological studies at the Grand Séminaire of Montreal, he joined the Oblates of Mary Immaculate and, while still a student, accompanied Pierre Aubert, first Oblate missionary in the West. Taché was ordained at Saint Boniface (Oct. 12, 1845), then went to Île-à-la-Crosse (1846), where he worked for the evangelization of the Cree and other native nations of the region: Chippewayans, Athabascans, and Caribou-Eaters. At 27 he was named coadjutor to Bp. Joseph N. Provencher of Saint Boniface and was consecrated titular bishop of Arath, Nov. 23, 1851, in Marseilles, France, by Bp. Charles J. de Mazenod, founder of the Oblates. When Provencher died (June 7, 1853), Taché succeeded to the see, but continued to visit his missions, traveling as far as Great Slave Lake, Northwest Territories, in 1855. In his see city he supervised the erection of a new cathedral (1861) following the loss by fire in December 1860 of his cathedral and his residence.

The transfer of the Northwest Territories to Canada and the disregard shown by the Canadian government for the rights of the local population brought serious troubles in 1869–70, culminating in an insurrection led by Louis RIEL. Taché was assisting at Vatican Council I, but returned in haste at the request of the Canadian government. He did much to calm spirits and obtain safeguards for the national and religious rights of the population. At the same time he played an important part in organizing the new province of Manitoba. He became an archbishop Sept. 22, 1871, with the bishop of St. Albert and the vicar apostolic of the North as suffragans.

He met the needs of an expanding Catholic population by providing new parishes or residential missions; these increased from nine in 1858 to 36 in 1888. He also founded a French Catholic newspaper for the defense of the rights of his flock, called the Provincial Council of Saint Boniface in 1889, and played an important part in the controversy over Catholic schools, suppressed by an unjust law in 1890 although guaranteed by the constitution of Manitoba.

He wrote many books and pamphlets about his Western missions, including *Vingt Années de Missions* (Montreal 1866) and *Esquisse du Nord-Quest* (Montreal 1869). He also wrote pamphlets about the amnesty—*L'Amnistie* (Montreal 1874) and *Encore l'amnistie* (St. Boniface 1875)—, the situation in the Northwest in 1885 (Quebec 1885), and the school question—*Denominational or Free Christian Schools in Manitoba* (Winnipeg 1877), *Les Écoles séparées de Manitoba* (St. Boniface 1890), *Un Page d'histoire des écoles de Manitoba* (Montreal 1894), and *Mémoire sur la question des écoles* (Montreal 1894).

Bibliography: J. P. A. BENOÎT, *Vie de Mgr Taché,* 2 v. (Montreal 1904). A. G. MORICE, *History of the Catholic Church in Western Canada: From Lake Superior to the Pacific, 1659–1895,* 2 v. (Toronto 1910); *Dictionnaire historique des Canadiens et Métis français de l'Ouest* (Quebec 1908). A. SAVAÈTE, *Vers l'abîme* v.7 (Paris 1910).

[A. CHAMPAGNE]

TACITUS

Cornelius Tacitus, one of the greatest of Roman historians and the first pagan author to record the crucifixion of Christ and, possibly, the persecution of the Christians; b. of a senatorial family, very probably in north Italy or south Gaul, *c.* A.D. 56; d. shortly after A.D. 115. In 88 he

Alexandre Antonin Taché.

was a praetor under the Emperor Domitian, and in 97 he was *consul suffectus.* He acquired fame as a prosecutor of Marius Priscus for mal-administration in Africa (100), and he served as pro-consul of the province of Asia under the Emperor Trajan in 112–113. His *Dialogus de oratoribus,* perhaps his earliest work, blames the changed political conditions for the decline of oratory. Its style is so different from that of his other works that its Tacitean authorship was often challenged in past centuries. His *De vita Iulii Agricolae,* a laudatory biography of his beloved father-in-law (d. 93) who established Roman rule in Britain on a solid foundation, reveals vividly the atmosphere of fear and terror at Rome under Domitian and the indelible impression left by the tyranny and savagery of that Emperor on the minds of men of senatorial rank. His monograph on the Germans, *De origine et situ Germanorum,* written in 98, is on the whole a reliable account based on good sources but tends to idealize too much in the direction of the ''noble savage'' tradition.

The major historical works of Tacitus are *Historiae* and *Annales.* The *Histories* covered the years 69 to 96. Only bks. 1 to 4⅓ are extant (the years 69–70). The *Annals* were a history of the years A.D. 14 to 68 or 69. Only bks. 1 to 6 and 11 ½ to 16 ½ have been preserved. Tacitus had copious sources at his disposal and used them critically and independently. But he is, primarily, a psychological historian who developed a somber outlook on life and tended to be inflexibly prejudiced in dealing with certain personalities, and, above all, in evaluating them. Even when he cannot condemn outright, a turn of phrase leaves an unanswered doubt in the mind of his readers. Rome and the affairs of Rome, rather than the administration of the empire as a whole, remained his chief center of interest. In his gloomy moralizing he was the heir of Sallust rather than of Livy. His style, especially in the *Histories* and *Annals,* is unique in Latin literature. It is characterized by lapidary brevity, contrast, variety of expression that approaches the extreme, deliberate avoidance of symmetry, aphorism, and irony. His hostile reference to the Christians (*Ann.* 15.44) is typical of his style and outlook: ''To suppress the rumor [that he had ordered the burning of Rome] Nero singled out the Christians as guilty, and punished them with refined cruelty—a class of men who were hated for their vices, and whom the masses called Christians. Christus, the founder of their name, had been sentenced to death by the procurator Pontius Pilate in the reign of Tiberius. The pernicious superstition was temporarily crushed, but it broke out again in Judaea, the home of the evil, and also in Rome itself, to which flow from every side all detestable and shameful practices to flourish there. Therefore, following the testimony of those who confessed, a large number of them were convicted not so much on the score of arson as on that of hatred of the human race. . . . Hence, in spite of a guilt which merited such novel and excessively severe forms of punishment, a feeling of pity arose because it was thought that they were being destroyed not in the interest of the public welfare but to serve the savagery of one individual.'' This passage reveals an attitude toward the Christians that is in striking contrast to that exhibited by his friend, PLINY THE YOUNGER.

See Also: NERO, ROMAN EMPEROR.

Bibliography: M. P. CHARLESWORTH, *The Oxford Classical Dictionary*, ed. M. CARY et al. (Oxford 1949) 876–878. J. W. and A. M. DUFF, *A Literary History of Rome in the Silver Age . . .* (2d ed. London 1960) 447–476, bibliog. 562–570. M. SCHANZ, C. HOSIUS, and G. KRÜGER, *Geschichte der römischen Literatur*, 4 v. in 5 (Munich 1914–35) 2:603–643. M. L. W. LAISTNER, *The Greater Roman Historians* (Berkeley 1947) 103–140. C. W. MENDELL, *Tacitus, the Man and His Work* (New Haven 1957). R. SYME, *Tacitus,* 2 v. (Oxford 1958). J. BEAUJEU, *L'Incendie de Rome en 64 et les Chrétiens* (Brussels 1960).

[W. R. F. TONGUE]

TADINI, ARCÁNGELO, BL.

Diocesan priest and founder of the Workers of the Holy House of Nazareth; b. Verolanuova near Brescia, Lombardy, Italy, Oct. 12, 1846; d. Botticino Sera, Brescia, May 20, 1912. Arcángelo was of an Italian noble family headed by Pietro Tadini who was a widower with seven children when he married his second wife, Antonia Gadola. She bore him four children, the youngest of whom was Arcángelo. Peitro, Arcangelo's father, was the communal secretary and a patriot during the struggle for Italian independence. He died in 1860.

A sickly child, Arcángelo studied locally until he entered secondary school at Lovere. He began his seminary studies in Brescia at age eighteen (1864). An accident during these years left him with a limp. He was ordained in 1870, and following recuperation from illness, he served as a parish priest and elementary school teacher in the mountain village of Lodrino in Voltrompia (1871–73), Santa Maria della Noce near Brescia (1873–85), and for a brief time at S. Nazzaro in Brescia. In 1885, he was transferred to Botticino Sera where he ministered for the rest of his life (1887–1912). There he proved himself a zealous pastor, who preached with a warmth and conviction that energized his parish to come alive with many activities including a choir, catechetical classes for all ages, and various confraternities.

Tadini gave flesh to the teachings of *RERUM NOVARUM* (Leo XIII, 1891) by promoting the sanctification of daily work. He established an agricultural cooperative (1893), built a textile mill with his own inheritance to provide work for the unemployed (1894), and acquired the adjacent villa to house the female workers. To ensure the continuance of his work, Father Tadini founded the *Suore Operaie della Santa Casa di Nazareth* in 1900. The sisters worked alongside those they sought to evangelize by their example. The order operates in Italy, England, Switzerland, Africa, and Latin America.

Tadini, the ''Apostle of the Working World,'' was buried in the cemetery of Botticino Sera. His cause for canonization was opened on Jan. 13, 1963. He was beatified by John Paul II, Oct. 3, 1999.

Feast: May 21.

Bibliography: L. FOSSATI, *Arcangelo Tadini e la sua opera sociale* (Brescia 1977). M. FRANCO and A COMUZZI, *Il prete sociale e le Operaie di Dio* (Brescia 1990). *L'Osservatore Romano,* daily edition (in Italian) (October 6, 1999): 2.

[K. I. RABENSTEIN]

TAGORE, RABINDRANATH

Bengali poet; b. Calcutta, India, May 7, 1861; d. there, Aug. 7, 1941. He was the 13th child of Maharshi Debēndranāth and grandson of Prince Dwārkanāth Tagore. He was educated at the Bengali Academy and St.

Xavier's College, Calcutta, where he early responded to the influence of Sanskrit literature, Vaishnava religious love poetry, and English romantic poetry. He visited England (1878), and attended lectures at London University. On returning to India (1880), he engaged in ceaseless literary work in Bengali. He married Mrinalini (1883); her death in 1902, coupled with other bereavements, led him to God and ushered in the great creative period of his life. During a visit to England (1912), he arranged for the publication of *Gitanjali,* a version of some of his Bengali songs (mainly of a devotional character); its great success and the award of the Nobel prize for Literature in 1913 facilitated the English publication of other volumes of poetry (e.g., *The Gardener, The Crescent Moon,* and *Fruit-Gathering*), plays (e.g., *Chitra, The Post Office,* and *The King of the Dark Chamber*), and novels (*The Home and the World* and *Gora*). After World War I, he traveled widely and lectured frequently; and founded the Visvabharati (University) at Shantiniketan as a center where an international community could live a life of creative harmony. Under the inspiration of Mahatma GANDHI, he wrote the play *Mukta-Dhāra* (1922) affirming the primacy of spiritual values in a world of advancing technology; and after witnessing the passion play at Oberammergau and prophetically seeing in Gandhi a possible martyr, he composed *The Child* (1931). He painted and continued writing almost to the very end of his life.

Rabindranath Tagore.

Tagore, a master of both verse and prose, was the greatest of modern Bengali writers, and one of the great literary figures of his time. He was preeminently the poet of love; nature, man, and God blended in his vision. He was no systematic thinker, but all he wrote or said carries the stamp of courage and integrity, as may be seen in a selection of his most significant work, *Towards Universal Man* (1961). To his admirers he was verily the "Gurudev," the great teacher.

Bibliography: *Collected Poems and Plays* (New York 1956); *The Religion of Man* (London 1931, Boston 1961); *Wings of Death,* tr. A. BOSE (London 1960); *A Tagore Reader,* ed. A. CHAKRAVARTY (New York 1961). K. R. KRIPALANI, *Rabindranath Tagore: A Biography* (New York 1962). D.W. ATKINSON, "Rabindranath Tagore: the Poet and the Absolute," *Studies in Religion/Sciences religieuses* 13 no. 2 (1984) 193–205. D.R. TUCK, "Rabindranath Tagore: Religion as a Constant Struggle for Balance in the Religion of Man," in *Religion in modern India* (New Delhi 1981) 247–276. J.H. WATSON, "Religious beliefs of Rabindranath Tagore" *Expository Times* 84 (1973) 373–377.

[K. R. SRINIVASA IYENGAR]

TAIGI, ANNA MARIA, BL.

Trinitarian tertiary and mystic; b. Siena, May 29, 1769; d. Rome, June 9, 1837. She was the daughter of a spendthrift apothecary, Giannetti, who went to Rome when she was six years old and later sent her to work as a maid in the house of a woman of doubtful morals. In 1790 she married Domenico Taigi, a man much older than herself, who was a valet at the Palazzo Chigi and encouraged her love of pretty clothes and amusements. We are told that one day a Servite priest who met her in the street heard an interior voice informing him that she would be entrusted to his direction and become a saint and that this prophecy was fulfilled when, after the birth of her first child, she went to the same priest for confession. From that time, she was favored with many extraordinary graces. The Blessed Virgin told her that it was her special vocation to show that holiness could be attained in every walk of life.

Added to her many penances undertaken voluntarily for the conversion of sinners and the needs of the church was the patient endurance of much affliction, including aridity and darkness of spirit. She served her hot-tempered husband as if he were Christ; she bore with her foolish mother, whom she nursed through a repulsive illness; and she brought up her own three boys and four girls in an overcrowded house, keeping the peace in a large family of very different temperaments. Despite these seemingly uncongenial surroundings, she was frequently in ecstasy and had prophetic gifts; she saw in front of her a ''mystic sun,'' a luminous globe surrounded by a crown of thorns in which she read the future and saw distant events, but she used this extraordinary gift only when charity demanded it. She was frequently consulted by Leo XII and Gregory XVI as well as by Napoleon's mother and his uncle, Cardinal Fesch. During the process of her beatification, her own husband and a daughter-in-law gave evidence of her outstanding virtue. She was beatified May 30, 1920.

Feast: June 9.

Bibliography: A. BESSIÈRES, *La Bienheureuse Anna-Maria Taïgi, mère de famille* 1769–1837 (Paris 1937); *Wife, Mother, and Mystic*, tr. S. RIGBY (Westminster MD 1952) C. SALOTTI, *La beata Anna Maria Taigi, secondo la storia e la critica* (Rome 1922).

[H. GRAEF]

TAINE, HIPPOLYTE

French philosopher, historian, critic of art and literature; b. Vouziers (Ardennes), Apr. 21, 1828; d. Paris, Mar. 5, 1893. After the death (1840) of his father, a lawyer, he went to Paris (1841) to study, entered the École normale supérieure (1848), where he excelled as a student yet failed his *agrégation* examination in philosophy because of his bold ideas. He spent a year at various teaching posts in the provinces, where his independence made him unpopular; and then he returned to Paris for further study. When his doctoral theses in psychology were not accepted, he prepared and defended at the Sorbonne theses on literature: *De personis platonicis* (in Latin), and *Essai sur les Fables de la Fontaine.* In 1855 he published *Voyage aux Pyrénées;* and in 1856, *Essai sur Tite-Live,* which was crowned by the French Academy. He published also numerous periodical articles, later collected in *Les Philosophes français du XIXe siècle* (1857) and in *Essais de critique et d'histoire* (1858). After completing in 1864 his four-volume *Histoire de la Littérature anglaise* (placed on the Index, June 11, 1866), he was appointed examiner at Saint-Cyr, and in 1864 he replaced Viollet-le-Duc as professor at the École des Beaux-Arts. Two decades of teaching there, plus visits to England, Belgium, Italy, Greece, and the Netherlands, prepared him for his works on the philosophy of art. His *Nouveaux essais de critique et d'histoire* appeared in 1865, and his humorous recollections of Parisian life, *Vie et opinions de Thomas Graindorge,* in 1867. *De l'Intelligence,* an important philosophical work, appeared in 1870. After the disappointments of the Franco-Prussian War, he went to England, taught at Oxford (May of 1871), and then retired for the remainder of his life to Menthon-Saint-Bernard in Savoy. During this period, he wrote *Notes sur l'Angleterre* (1872), the more important but incomplete *Les Origines de la France contemporaine* (6 v. 1875–93), and *Derniers essais de critique et d'histoire* (1894). He was elected to the French Academy in 1878. Although he did not return to religion, he asked to be buried after a Protestant service, thereby witnessing a sympathy for Christianity, which to him represented a great moral and social force. After his death appeared a four-volume edition of his correspondence, translated as *Life and Letters of H. Taine* (3 v. 1902–08), as well as a novel composed in 1861 under the influence of Stendhal, *Étienne Mayran* (1910).

Taine's writings are notable for their unity. As a philosopher, a historian, and a literary art critic, he was a leading proponent of SCIENTISM, applying to moral sciences the positive method of the natural sciences. In philosophy, as a disciple of CONDILLAC, HEGEL, COMTE, and Vacherot, he defined the conditions necessary for the development of the spirit. After attacking the spiritualism of COUSIN and Théodore Jouffroy, he exposed in his principal work, *De l'Intelligence,* a theory of knowledge that renewed Condillac's thesis on ''transformed sensation,'' asserting that from the confused mass of facts ''the constitutive properties of beings'' emerge, and permit us to eliminate the contingent and attain ''the eternal axiom.''

This experimental method he applied to literary or artistic criticism, which he studied like a chemist. To him spiritual phenomena ''are products like vitriol and sugar''; art and literature, normal functions of man. In every genius, he wrote, is discernible one ''master faculty'' that explains all others. But this dominant characteristic is influenced by geography, sun, climate, and above all by the three essential factors of race, environment, and moment. Taine explained the inequality of ''human plants'' born in identical circumstances by positing the application of a threefold principle: how important the ''master faculty'' is, how much good it does, and how well effects converge. In brief, he conceived aesthetics according to a rigorous determinism, but his innate clear-sightedness often permitted him to escape the logic of his system.

Taine's philosophical theories also inspired his historical study of the origins of contemporary France. Modern France he described as a plant, whose birth and growth must be known to be understood. In this great, sometimes controversial work, he insisted that the principal agent of the French Revolution was the classical spirit, which produced the excesses of Jacobinism, civil dissensions, and Napoleonic despotism. He held the revolution responsible for France's moral decline and its subsequent evils. He began this study with faith in POSITIVISM, but he completed it in disquiet, questioning the existence of any ideal regime and the ability of science to establish a modern constitution.

Taine's accounts of journeys revealed in him superior talents as an observer, creator, and portrait painter. His taut, richly colored style used violent, brutal images that moved readers; his pen accumulated materialist metaphors that seem to bring into being the spiritual world, and please by their clarity and life. Many of Taine's books, including his most famous ones, have been translated into English.

Bibliography: E. BOUTMY, *Taine, Schérer, Laboulaye* (Paris 1901). V. GIRAUD, *Essai sur Taine* (Paris 1901); *H. Taine* (Paris 1928). A. AULARD, *Taine, historien de la Révolution française* (Paris 1907). A. M. BARRÈS, *Taine et Renan* (Paris 1922). F. C. ROE, *Taine et l'Angleterre* (Paris 1923). A. CHEVRILLON, *Taine: Formation de sa pensée* (Paris 1932); *Portrait de Taine* (Paris 1958). S. J. KAHN, *Science and Esthetic Judgment: A Study in Taine's Critical Method* (New York 1953). G. MORRA, *Enciclopedia filosofica*, 4 v. (Venice-Rome 1957) 4:1070–73.

[J. DAOUST]

TAIWAN, THE CATHOLIC CHURCH IN

Capital: Taipei
Size: 13,807 sq. miles.
Population: 22,191,087 in 2000.
Languages: Mandarin Chinese (official), Taiwanese (Min), Hakka dialects.
Religions: More than 90% of the Taiwanese profess a mixture of Buddhism, Taoism and Confucian ancestor veneration. Christians comprise about 5% of the population. Approximately one-third of the Christian population are Catholics.
Metropolitan See: Taipei, with suffragans Hsinchu, Hwalien, Kaohsiung, Kiayi, Taichung, Tainan.

Located in East Asia on the Tropic of Cancer, off the southeastern coast of China and to the north of the Philippines, Taiwan is surrounded by the East China Sea, Philippine Sea, South China Sea and Taiwan Strait. More than three-fourths of the population are Hokkien and Hakka Chinese who migrated over the centuries, while some 14 percent are Mandarin-speaking nationalist Chinese who arrived in the aftermath of the 1949 communist victory in mainland China. About two percent are Malayo-Polynesian aboriginal, comprising some 70 tribes, the largest of which are the Ami, Atayal, and Paiwan.

Taiwan gained notoriety as a shelter and base for Chinese and Japanese pirates. In the 15th century Hakkas from central China emigrated to the island. Portuguese seafarers visited the island in 1590 and named it ''Ilha Formosa'' (Beautiful Island), but failed to leave any lasting imprint on the island. The Dutch established a settlement at An-p'ing (1624) in the southwest, while the Spaniards set up one at Chi-lung (1626) in the north. In 1646, the Dutch overran the Spaniards and gained control of the whole island. They, in turn, were expelled by the notorious Chinese-Japanese pirate Cheng Ch'eng-kung (Koxinga) in 1661, who used it as a base for launching attacks on the Manchurian Ch'ing dynasty. In 1683, the Ch'ing Dynasty captured Taiwan and made it part of Fujien (Fukien) province. The population of Taiwan swelled with an influx of mainland Hokkien Chinese fleeing famine in the Fujien (Fukien) province. In 1895, having lost the Sino-Japanese War, China ceded Taiwan and the Pescadores Islands to Japan under the Treaty of Shimonoseki. Taiwan remained a colony of Japan until the end of World War II, when it was returned to the Chinese Nationalist (Kuomintang) government. Following the fall of mainland China to communist hands in 1949, Taiwan received a huge wave of mainland nationalist emigrants and ordinary Chinese refugees. Taiwan became the seat of the nationalist government of China, with Taipei as its provisional capital.

History. The first Catholic missionaries, Bartólome Martínez and five Dominicans from Manila in 1626, and their successors, working in the north of the island, baptized about 4,500 aborigines but in 1642 were forced to leave when the Spanish garrison withdrew before the Dutch, who were holding the south of the island. Spanish Dominicans from the Philippines tried without success to restore their mission in 1673 and 1694 but could not return until 1859–60, when the Chinese, according to the Treaties of Tientsin, opened An-p'ing and other ports to foreign commerce and missionaries. Francisco Sainz, OP, opened a mission near Kaohsiung in the south, and new missions were opened in the north, including Tainan, the ancient capital. When the Japanese occupied Taiwan in 1895, after the Sino-Japanese War, the Taiwanese mission suffered from rebellions and Japanese reprisals.

Taiwan was part of the apostolic vicariate of Amoy until 1913, when it became an independent prefecture with its seat at Taipei. In 1938 there were 15 Dominican missionaries and 9,000 Catholics. In 1949 there was a great influx of foreign missionaries expelled by the Communists from the mainland, and two prefectures were established: Taipei in the north under the Chinese Congregation of the Disciples of the Lord, and Kaohsiung in the south under Dominicans. In 1950 Taichung was made a prefecture under the Maryknoll Fathers and Brothers, as were Chiayi (under Chinese secular clergy) and Hwalien (under the Paris Foreign Mission Society) in 1952, when Taipei became an archdiocese and metropolitan see. In 1961 Hsinchu, Tainan, and Kaohsiung be-

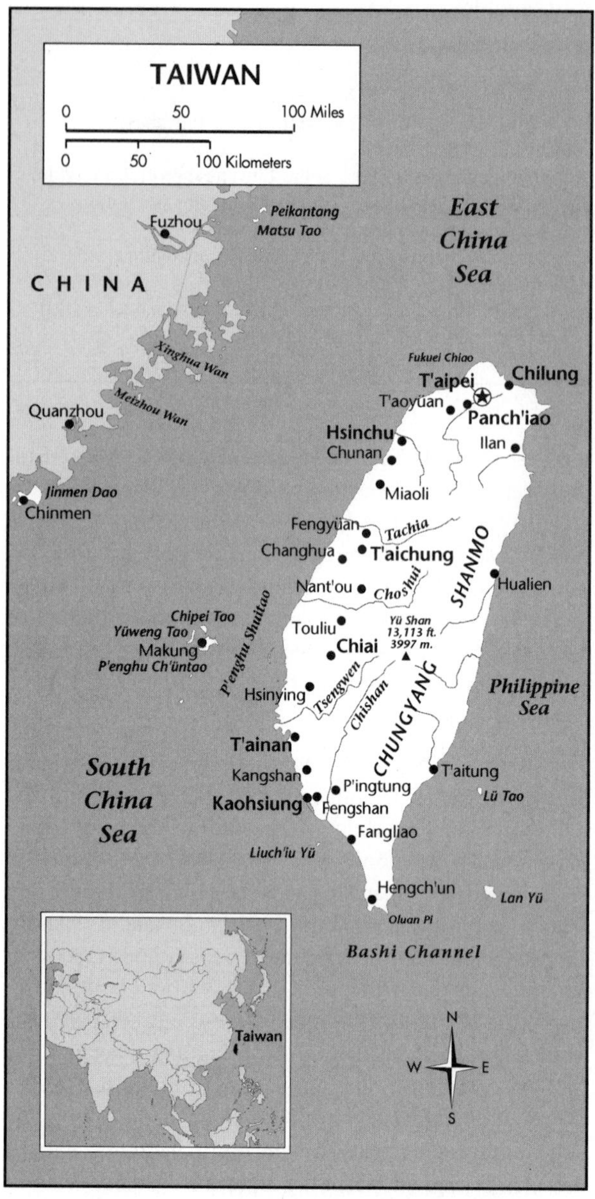

came dioceses with Chinese bishops. Taichung and Chiayi became dioceses in 1962, and Hwalien in 1963. The regional Chinese Bishops Conference was formally established in 1967.

The Church in Taiwan experienced a boom of conversions in the late 1950s and the 1960s. Since the 1970s, growth of the Church has become more qualitative than quantitative. In the wake of Vatican II, the laity has become more active in Church life. The first National Pastoral Workshop, held in 1969 in two sessions, first in Chinese in Tainan, and then in English in Taichung, sought to assess the new situation of the Taiwanese Church in the light of Vatican II, reflecting on the Church as a living community of the People of God. In 1971 the National Council for the Lay Apostolate was established. Each diocese has established its own Diocesan Council for the Lay Apostolate, which coordinates the various lay associations within the diocese. Most parishes have founded parish pastoral councils. The Fons Vitae Catechetical and Social Training Center, set up in 1962 in Taipei and transferred to Hsinchu in 1980, has trained more than 300 lay catechists from Taiwan, Hong Kong, Macau, Singapore, Malaysia, and Indonesia, and published more than a dozen catechetical and liturgical books in Chinese. Established in 1970 with its seat in Taipei, The Taiwan Pastoral Center has a two-year lay ministry course for men and women. Its monthly publication, *Witness Magazine,* responds to the signs of the times with the voice of Christian faith. The National Conference on ''Building the Local Church'' in 1976 added further momentum to the process of growth.

Originally founded as Fujen Catholic University of Peking, Oct. 1, 1925, and reopened in Taipei on Oct. 21, 1963, Fujen Catholic University remains a premier institution of higher learning in Taiwan. The Fujen Theological Faculty, a faculty with pontifical rights, was founded in 1929 in Shanghai for the education of Jesuit missionaries. Due to communist pressure it was transferred to Baguio, Philippines, in 1952. In 1967 it returned to Chinese soil in Taiwan, beside Fujen Catholic University, Taipei. In 1968 it opened its doors to non-Jesuit students. It publishes the theological quarterly *Collectanea Theologica Universitatis Fujen,* started in 1969, and a series of theological books, numbering some 37 volumes. The Fujen Theological Faculty also publishes various theological dictionaries, contributing to the process of developing a contextualized theology for the Taiwanese Church.

Since the death of President Chiang Kai Shek in 1975 and especially the abolition of martial law in 1987, Taiwan has entered a new phase of its history. To cope with the rapidly changing situation, the Catholic Church convoked a National Symposium on Evangelization, held at Fujen Catholic University from Feb. 8–13, 1988. The 230 delegates (among them a few representatives of Chinese overseas communities) drafted a declaration, which, among other practical directives, gave due attention to social realities: the movement for democratization, freedom, and modernization. While the declaration acknowledged the presence of Catholic leaders in the fields of education, economics, and social communications, it deplored the absence of Catholic leaders on the political platform.

The ''industrial miracle'' of Taiwan has created social problems characteristic of a rapidly changing industrial society. Statements of the Bishops Conference have repeatedly called upon Catholics to become a more visible and prophetic sign in modern Taiwan. The Commission for Social Development (with its sub-bureaus for justice and peace and for concern for migrant workers) has initiated programs to address the problems of migrant workers, rampant prostitution, wage inequality, corruption and environmental destruction. The Rerum Novarum Center for Social Studies and Action concentrates on the issue of capital-labor relations.

Ecumenical and interreligious dialogue. Much progress has been made more on the level of education and research, including the ecumenical Common Bible Translation Project; the research on economic development and quality of life in Taiwan (1978–1983) and its follow-up research on the quality of life in the bioregion of Taiwan (1990–1993); a Catholic-Buddhist workshop for priests and religious in 1992; and study seminars for high school teachers and university professors and employees (1993) and for thirty married couples, half Catholic and half Buddhist (1994). The Commission for Interreligious and Ecumenical Cooperation plays an active role in organizing these activities. Fujen Catholic University's Graduate School of Religious Studies (est. 1988) and Department of Religion (est. 1992) are also engaged in an ongoing dialogue and cooperation with other religions.

Bibliography: P. FERNANDES, *One Hundred Years of Dominican Apostolate in Formosa* (Quezon City 1959). H. K. TONG, *Christianity in Taiwan: A History* (Taipei 1961). M. K. CHANG, *A History of Christianity in Taiwan* (Tainan 1984). CHEUNG KA-HING, *Let Your Heart Be Bold* (Hong Kong 1989). CHINESE CATHOLIC BISHOPS CONFERENCE, *The Catholic Church in Taiwan Republic of China* (Taipei 1992). R. GAGNON, *The Chinese Family in Taiwan Today* (Taipei 1985). D. A. HUMPHREY, ed., *Sinicization. The Church as a Living Community. The Gospel of Christ in Modern China* (Taipei 1971). H. and F. SCHREIDER, ''Taiwan: The Watchful Dragon,'' *National Geographic* 135:1 (January 1969). SECRETARIAT OF THE CHINESE BISHOPS CONFERENCE, *Building Up the Chinese Local Church* (Taipei 1976).

[J. KRAHL/M. FANG/EDS.]

TAIZÉ, MUSIC OF

A corpus of chants specifically designed to enable the active participation of visitors at the ecumenical pilgrimage site in Taizé, France. The 232 musical pieces which originally comprised the Taizé corpus were composed by Jacques BERTHIER (1923–1994), in close collaboration with Brother Robert Giscard (1922–1993). From the beginning, one of the primary goals of the Taizé community has been to enable young people and all of their guests to participate in the worship that takes place at the great Church of Reconciliation three times a day.

Origin. The project of composing the Taizé chants began in 1974 when Brother Robert Giscard, who was responsible for leading the first ''Council of Youth'' realized the need to provide a form of sung prayer that could adequately promote the active participation of large, diverse gatherings of polyglot youth without sacrificing textual and musical excellence. Having worked with Jacques Berthier years earlier, he turned to Berthier for assistance. Berthier's background as a classically trained church musician made him eminently suitable for this project. Brother Robert worked directly with Berthier by compiling the texts and reacting to each of his compositional efforts, often guiding the composer through several revisions. Those involved in the music ministry, including the Brothers of Taizé and the Sisters of St. Andrew who serve as choir directors, participated with Berthier in the process of composing and reworking the music until it was determined to be accessible to large and varied groups of pilgrims.

Genres. The corpus of music, both published and unpublished, that Jacques Berthier composed for Taizé falls into one of four genres, with some special cases. These include ostinato responses and chorales, litanies, acclamations, and canons. Pieces from all four genres include basic harmonic support provided by keyboard and/or guitar. Some include verses performed by one or more cantors. Most also include options for instrumental verses written for a variety of melodic instruments. The assembly's part functions as the foundation of the performance, while the vocal and instrumental verses function as counter melodies.

Ostinato Response and Chorales. Berthier's idea to create the ostinato chant came out of his work with canons. Typically, an ostinato is a musical unit sung in continuous repetition and accompanied by other musical elements that are continually changing. The ostinato bass actually developed out of early seventeenth-century efforts to negotiate a reconciliation of the old counterpoint technique with the new monody. In the Taizé collections, the term ''ostinato'' describes a musical unit sung in continuous repetition by all. These ostinati are variously accompanied by solo vocal and instrumental parts. While Berthier did not create the ostinato form, his employment of it for liturgical song is unique, particularly because of the foundational role he assigns to the assembly. In the case of Berthier's music, the assembly, supported by the organ, is the principal music-maker, while the choir, instrumentalists, and soloists serve as the component of variation and embellishment. Berthier's ostinati fall into two categories: the short, designated as responses, and the long, designated as chorales. Examples of ostinato responses include *Confitemini Domino, In the Lord I'll Be Ever Thankful, Jesus Remember Me, Laudate Dominum, Nada Te Turbe, There is One Lord, Ubi Caritas, Surrexit Christus* and *Veni Sancte Spiritus*. Examples of ostinato chorales include *Bless the Lord My Soul* (Ps. 103), *O Lord Hear My Prayer*, and *Stay With Me*.

Litanies. In these pieces, invocations are sung between very short phrases that act as refrains. The invocations are performed by cantor and the refrain by the assembly. A typical example is *Eat This Bread*. Some of Berthier's litanies are designed to accommodate spontaneous verses. A simple harmonic accompaniment is written out which allows for a variety of possible texts. In this case, the final chord of the refrain is hummed by choir and assembly, while the cantors proclaim the texts in free improvisation over this sound. An example is *Alleluia No. 7*, in which the final D minor chord of the acclamation becomes the foundation for the cantor's improvisation of the verse.

Acclamations. This musical form entails a formula pronounced or sung by a group, expressing a common sentiment. Typically, they are brief but assertive, joyous, rhythmically strong, and melodically engaging. The two acclamations that Berthier frequently composed are the *Kyrie Eleison*, the *Alleluia* and *Amen*.

Canons. As a musical term, ''canon'' originally referred to a formula whereby a single melody, through strict (canonic) repetition in successive voices, created a polyphonic (many voiced) musical texture. The structure of the canon, sometimes also referred to as the round, employs a melodic theme based on a simple harmonic pattern. This versatile genre can be performed in a variety of ways, ranging from the simplest to the most complex. The options provide for variation in the use of voices, instruments, and dynamics. Some of Berthier's compositions include both principal and secondary canons. Examples include the *Gloria* (four voices), *Jubilate Servite* (two voices) and *Magnificat* (four voices).

Compositional and Performance Technique. Both in its conception and performance, Berthier's Taizé music is aleatory. The term, as it applies to Taizé, refers to the characteristic whereby the score provides for both numerous choices in the combination of individual parts and also a certain element of chance in the actual performance of the music. The element of chance may occur in the number of repetitions, the voice parts taken, the verses created, the time taken between the entrance of additional parts, the combination of instruments, and so on. This dimension of choice and chance comprises a defining characteristic of Taizé music. The result of this aleatory feature is a piece of music that is strikingly versatile, dynamic, and provisional. The instrumental parts are either accompaniments or solo parts. As accompaniments, the instrumental parts serve as harmonic support for the voices. As solos, the instrumental parts can be used in conjunction with the vocal music for which they are designed, or they may be arranged to form independent instrumental pieces.

Texts and Languages. The texts for Berthier's Taizé music are principally scriptural and liturgical. The majority of texts are direct scriptural quotations, while some are paraphrases with clear scriptural references. There are also several settings of liturgical texts, including texts of the Mass ordinary, and elements from the Good Friday liturgy and the Christmas liturgy. Additional texts have been composed by the brothers in order to provide verses, intercessory prayers, or invocations for the responses or litanies. The choice and arrangement of the texts was the work of Brother Robert or another one of the brothers. Concern to enable active participation and offer hospitality inspired efforts to ensure the accessibility of language. Over the span of almost 30 years, several solutions have been employed. In the early days of Taizé, before large groups of pilgrims joined the brothers, the prayer was conducted in French. In an initial attempt to respond to the international makeup of large groups of visitors, Latin was chosen as the language for the chants. Gradually, music was composed for specific living languages, and some music was set to more than one language. As a result, the music of Taizé has been set to about 20 different languages, including European languages, for example, English, French, German, Italian, Polish, Slovak, and Spanish, but also Asian languages, for example, Korean, Indian, and Japanese. However, the process does not simply involve literal translations of a text from one language into another. Berthier worked closely with native speakers to rewrite or adjust the music to a particular language.

New Compositions. Since the death of Jacques Berthier in 1994, new compositions have been added to the repertoire of the Taizé community. These have included chants composed by some of the brothers imitating Berthier's style and other pieces newly composed by Joseph Gelineau, SJ, and others. However, the music generally referred to as music from Taizé comprises the original chants that Berthier composed for Taizé.

Bibliography: J. BERTHIER, ''Jacques Berthier: Un serviteur de la musique liturgique,'' *Célébrer* 236 (January 1994) 3–16. M.-P. FAURE,''Jacques Berthier, a Friend of God,'' *Liturgy: Cistercians of the Strict Observance* 29 (1995) 93–86. J. M. KUBICKI, *Liturgical Music as Ritual Symbol: A Case Study of Jacques Berthier's Taizé Music* (Leuven 1999). J. L. GONZALEZ-BALADO, *The Story of Taizé* (London 1988). K. SPINK, *A Universal Heart: The Life and Vision of Brother Roger of Taizé* (London 1986).

[J. M. KUBICKI]

TALBOT, FRANCIS XAVIER

Author, editor; b. Philadelphia, Pa., Jan. 25, 1889; d. Washington, D.C., Dec. 3, 1953. He was the youngest of the seven children of Patrick Francis and Bridget (Peyton) Talbot. Graduating from St. Joseph's High School, Philadelphia, in 1906, he entered the Society of Jesus at St. Andrew-on-Hudson, Poughkeepsie, N.Y., the same year. His philosophical studies were made at Woodstock College, Woodstock, Md. (1910–13). He taught at Loyola School, New York City (1913–16) and at Boston College, Mass. (1917–18). He was ordained at Woodstock on June 29, 1921. In 1923 he was named literary editor of the national Catholic weekly review, *America,* and became editor in chief in 1936. He was president of Loyola College, Baltimore, Md. from 1947 to 1950. After a brief period as archivist at Georgetown University, Washington, D.C., he was appointed parish priest at St. Aloysius Church, Washington, D.C., in August 1950. He next engaged in retreat work at Manresa-on-the-Severn at Annapolis, Md. (1952–53). Shortly after returning to parish work at Holy Trinity Church in Georgetown, D.C., he died on the feast of his patronal saint.

Talbot's contribution to the cultural and intellectual life of U.S. Catholicism sprang particularly from his vision in guiding the beginnings of many organizations and activities that were destined to remain vigorous. Such were the Catholic Book Club (1928), the Catholic Poetry Society (1930), and the Spiritual Book Associates (1932). Under his editorship of *America,* the journal *Theological Studies* (now published at Woodstock College, Woodstock, Md.) was inaugurated. Talbot was active also in the organization of the Catholic Theatre Conference and of the Catholic Library Association, and from 1924 to 1936 was chaplain of and advisor to the National Motion Picture Bureau of the International Federation of Catholic Alumnae. His writings were: *Jesuit Education in Philadelphia* (1927), *Richard Henry Tierney* (1930), *Shining in Darkness* (1932), *Saint Among Savages* (1935), and *Saint Among the Hurons* (1949). He contributed frequently to the *Encyclopaedia Britannica* and to the *Britannica Yearbook.* He edited *The Eternal Babe* (1927), *The America Book of Verse* (1928), and *Fiction by Its Makers* (1928).

[H. C. GARDINER]

TALBOT, JAMES

Vicar Apostolic of the London District (1781–90); b. Shrewsbury House, Isleworth, Middlesex, 1726; d. Hammersmith, Jan. 26, 1790. Brother of the 14th earl of Shrewsbury, he was educated at Douay College and ordained there on Dec. 19, 1750. For several years he lectured in theology and philosophy until chosen to be coadjutor to Bishop Challoner of the London District, who consecrated him on Aug. 24, 1759. He was the last Catholic priest to be indicted in court for saying mass (1771). He embodied the spirit of penal times, and readjusted with difficulty to the relaxations effected by the First Relief Act of 1778. Gentle and unassuming, he spent his wealth generously in charitable works. He was buried in Hammersmith church, but in 1901 his body was transferred to the seminary of Old Hall, Ware.

Bibliography: E. H. BURTON, *The Life and Times of Bishop Challoner, 1691–1781,* 2 v. (London 1909). B. N. WARD, *The Dawn of the Catholic Revival in England, 1781–1803,* 2 v. (London 1909) v.1. J. KIRK, *Biographies of English Catholics in the Eighteenth Century,* ed. J. H. POLLEN and E. BURTON (New York 1909) 228.

[B. WHELAN]

TALBOT, JOHN, BL.

Lay martyr; b. at Thornton-le-Street (in the North Riding), Yorkshire, England; d. Aug. 9, 1600, hanged at Durham. He was arrested for being in the company of Bl. Thomas PALASER in the home of Bl. John NORTON, condemned for assisting a priest and refusing to attend the state church. He was beatified by Pope John Paul II on Nov. 22, 1987 with George Haydock and Companions.

Feast of the English Martyrs: May 4 (England).

See Also: ENGLAND, SCOTLAND, AND WALES, MARTYRS OF.

Bibliography: R. CHALLONER, *Memoirs of Missionary Priests,* ed. J. H. POLLEN (rev. ed. London 1924). J. H. POLLEN, *Acts of English Martyrs* (London 1891).

[K. I. RABENSTEIN]

TALBOT, MATT

Known as ''the saint in overalls,'' and regarded as a special example for reformed alcoholics; b. Dublin, Ireland, May 22, 1856; d. Dublin, June 7, 1925. He was the second of 12 children of the needy family of Charles Talbot and Elizabeth Bagnall. When 11, Matt received his only formal education, attending the Christian Brothers school for one year. He became a messenger of wine merchants, and fell into a habit of excessive drinking that lasted for 15 years. He worked for the Port of Dublin, for a building firm, and later for a lumberyard. Despite his drinking and smallness of stature, he was an effective worker. At 28, a seemingly hopeless alcoholic, he underwent a conversion, the beginning of which was occasioned by the failure of friends to treat him when his own money was gone. That day he took the pledge. Prior to this Matt had attended mass regularly but for some time had not received the sacraments. Upon his conversion he went to confession, and the next day received communion at early mass. Distrusting his ability to keep the pledge, he took it first for three months, then for a year, and finally for life. He began a life of prayer and penance that continued until his death. His severe penance never interfered with his work or his graciousness to others, nor did his poverty interfere with his personal cleanliness. He was accustomed to taking only 3 1/2 hours of sleep on two rough planks and a wooden pillow. He arose at 2 A.M., prayed, and then attended mass at 6 A.M. After work he visited a church, attended confraternity meetings, and gave himself to prayer and spiritual reading. He ate no meat for nine months of the year. His midday meal was a slice of dry bread and a cup of cold tea. A follower of St. Grignion de Montfort's ''True Devotion,'' he wore chains, which at death were found embedded in his flesh. Although Talbot lacked a formal education, he had singular gifts of prayer and understanding; the books he read were varied and scholarly. His kneeling figure on the church steps and in the church was a common sight, yet few really knew him. He died on Trinity Sunday, in the street, on his way to a second mass. He was buried as a Franciscan tertiary in Glasnevin Cemetery. The diocesan informative process for his beatification was opened in Dublin in 1931; the apostolic process began in 1947.

Bibliography: J. A. GLYNN, *Life of Matt Talbot* (2d ed. New York 1930), the basic work. J. BEEVERS, *Shining as Stars* (Westminster, Md. 1956). E. J. DOHERTY, *Matt Talbot* (Milwaukee 1953). M. PURCELL, *Matt Talbot and His Times* (Westminster, Md. 1955). F. SHEED, ''Matt Talbot,'' *The Irish Way,* ed. F. SHEED (New York 1932).

[P. J. KELLY]

TALBOT, PETER AND RICHARD

Sixth and eighth sons of Sir William Talbot, first Baronet of Carton, County Kildare, and Alison, daughter of John Netterville of Castletown, County Meath.

Peter. Archbishop of Dublin; b. 1620; d. 1680. Peter entered the Society of Jesus (1635) and was ordained in Rome, April 1648. He was dispatched on several important missions on behalf of the exiled King CHARLES II and simultaneously published extensively on religious matters. He resigned from the Jesuits in July of 1659 because of difficulties connected with a diplomatic mission to Ireland and England, but remained on good terms with the society. After the Restoration, he was created one of the Queen's almoners, but through the influence of James Butler, Duke of Ormonde, and Edward Hyde, Earl of Clarendon, he was soon deprived of the post.

In 1669 he was appointed archbishop of Dublin. At a national synod summoned by the primate, Bl. Oliver PLUNKETT, in June of 1670, a dispute arose considering the form of a declaration of allegiance for Catholics, and in 1672 there was further trouble concerning the primacy. In 1673 Talbot was compelled to leave Ireland because of persecution, but in 1675 he was allowed back to England, then in 1677, to Ireland.

In 1678 he was arrested in connection with the Titus Oates plot, although Ormonde was aware of the absurdity of the allegations. His petition for a priest, in April of 1679, was refused, but in June of 1680, when he appeared to be dying, Plunkett, who was confined in an adjoining cell, forced his way through the guards and administered the Last Sacraments.

Richard. Earl and titular Duke of Tyrconnell, Lord Lieutenant of Ireland; b. 1630; d. 1691. Richard was taken prisoner at Dungan Hill, Aug. 8, 1647, and again at the Rock of Drogheda, Sept. 11, 1649, but he escaped. He surrendered, probably under Kilkenny articles of May 1652, and went abroad. Returning to England in an attempt to assassinate Oliver Cromwell, he was captured, but escaped after interrogation by Cromwell. He served under Prince Louis Condé II and the Duke of York from 1655 to 1657. After the Restoration, he became spokesman for the Irish Catholics and thus came into conflict with Ormonde. As a result, he underwent two short imprisonments. He was arrested for supposed complicity in the ''Popish Plot'' (1678). After the death of Charles II, Talbot was appointed to command the army in Ireland, and was created Earl of Tyrconnell on June 20, 1685. On the King's instructions, he remodeled the army to include the Catholics. He was created Lord Lieutenant of Ireland, Feb. 11, 1687, and remained so until James II arrived in Ireland in March of 1689. James created him Duke of Tyrconnell. He fought at the Battle of the Boyne in 1690, and was left with plenary powers after the flight of James. He exerted himself vigorously for the continued resistance against the English in spite of difficulties with Patrick Sarsfield and Simon Luttrell. He was attainted by King William, May 11, 1691.

His first marriage was to Katherine, coheir of Mathew Boynton, Yorkshire, on April 3, 1669; after Katherine's death, he married Frances, widow of Sir George Hamilton and elder sister of Sarah, Duchess of Marlborough, on Nov. 2, 1681. He died of apoplexy Aug. 14, 1691, without issue, at Limerick.

See Also: IRISH CONFESSORS AND MARTYRS.

Bibliography: M. RONAN, *The Irish Martyrs of the Penal Laws* (London 1935). R. BAGWELL, *Ireland Under the Stuarts,* 3 v. (London 1909–16).

[J. G. BARRY]

TALEBEARING

The act of one who without necessity relates unfavorable things about another to certain persons. ''Unfavorable things'' includes not only statements that blacken a person's good name, but statements that can cause unnecessary harm or sorrow to one's neighbor. By ''good name'' is meant the esteem that others have for a person because of praiseworthy qualities. The talebearer relates unfavorable things to certain persons, namely, those who have a special relation to the one about whom he is talebearing. Thus, a child tells tales about his classmates to the teacher; another child tells tales about his brothers and sisters to his parents. The motives for talebearing are varied: dislike for another, envy, the desire of ingratiating oneself, mistaken notions about obligations to report on the actions of others, or a desire to sow discord or hard feelings between friends.

There is no doubt that talebearing is prevalent among children. Besides the various reasons given above, the child will have an added reason if he has been encouraged in this practice by his parents or teachers. A child who has received direct or indirect commendation from an adult for this type of action will be more inclined to continue the regrettable habit. The habit becomes more difficult to break as the child grows older. It is not correct, however, to think that talebearing is confined to children or to those who developed the habit as a child. Adults, both men and women, indulge in it.

The sinfulness of talebearing differs according to the various forms the act can take. Even if the unfavorable things reported are not harmful to the person's reputation, the act is still a violation of charity. If the unfavorable things are true and divulged without necessity and harm has been done to the person's good name, the action is comparable to detraction. If the unfavorable things are lies, and the person's good name has been blackened, the act is comparable to calumny. Relating unfavorable things in order to break up a good friendship or ''. . . to sow discord among brethren is hated by the Lord'' (Prv 6.19). However, not all revelations of unfavorable things about one's neighbor are sinful. The action is licit when there is a moral demand of equal or greater urgency. In other words, when the continued ignorance of the truth is causing harm, the unfavorable truth may be licitly revealed.

See Also: DETRACTION; CALUMNY; REPUTATION, MORAL RIGHT TO.

Bibliography: D. M. PRÜMMER, *Manuale theologiae moralis,* ed. E. M. MÜNCH, 3 v. (Freiburg-Barcelona 1955) 2:165–201. B. H. MERKELBACH, *Summa theologiae moralis,* 3 v. (Paris 1949) 2:423–432. THOMAS AQUINAS, *Summa Theologiae* 2a2ae, 73–74. H. DAVIS, *Moral and. Pastoral Theology* (New York 1958). K. B. MOORE, *The Moral Principles Governing the Sin of Detraction* . . . (Washington 1950).

[K. B. MOORE]

TALL BROTHERS

Four long-limbed Egyptian monks—Dioscorus, Ammonius, Eusebius, and Euthymius—pupils of Abbot Pambo, famed for their sanctity and scriptural knowledge. Although they were followers of Origen in exegesis, they rejected his unorthodox subordinationism and were exiled under the Arian VALENS (364–378). THEOPHILUS, Patriarch of Alexandria, later brought all four brothers to that city and ordained them priests. Dioscorus was even made bishop, but Ammonius escaped that dignity by severing an ear. Sickened by the avarice and other vices of Theophilus, they returned to the Nitrian desert, where they later gave hospitality to an old priest whom Theophilus had unjustly excommunicated. The furious patriarch thereupon excommunicated the Tall Brothers as Origenists (401). They fled first to Palestine and then to Constantinople. There they appealed to St. JOHN CHRYSOSTOM, who received them kindly, but withheld ecclesiastical fellowship pending their reconciliation with Theophilus. This came finally at the notorious Synod of the OAK (403).

Bibliography: C. BAUR, *John Chrysostom and His Time,* tr. M. GONZAGA, 2 v. (Westminster, Md. 1960–61) 2: 192–205. I. G. SMITH, ''Ammonius,'' *A Dictionary of Christian Biography,* ed. W. SMITH and H. WACE, 4 v. (London 1877–87) 1:102–103. E. VENABLES, ''Dioscorus,'' *ibid.,* 862. F. L. CROSS, *The Oxford Dictionary of the Christian Church* (London 1957) 1320. S. SCHIWIETZ, *Das morgendländische Mönchtum,* v. 1 (Mainz 1904) 332–337. H. RAHNER, ''Lange Brüder,'' *Lexikon für Theologie und Kirche,* ed. J. HOFER and K. RAHNER, 10 v. (2d, new ed. Freiburg 1957–65) 6:785.

[P. W. HARKINS]

TALLAGHT, ABBEY OF

Former Irish monastery, present-day site of a Dominican college, about five miles south of Dublin, Ireland. It was founded in 774 by the reformer, St. Maelruain, as a protest against the contemporary worldly spirit found in many Irish monasteries. The community was sworn to observe the primitive Irish monastic rule in all its strictness. Work was heavy; public and private prayer was constant; strict fasting was enforced. Unfortunately, three years after Maelruain's death (792), the Vikings appeared in Ireland, and Tallaght, being near the coast, was exposed to constant attacks. The reform movement as such collapsed though the monastery survived.

In 1111 it was included in the Diocese of Glendalough, and when Glendalough was united with the Archdiocese of Dublin (1214) Tallaght became an archiepiscopal manor. After the Reformation the Protestant archbishops resided there on occasion until 1650. In 1822 the property was sold to the government and the building was demolished. In 1842 the Dominican fathers erected a college there.

The *Félire Tamlachta Mael Ruain* or ''Martyrology of Tallaght'' (ed. R. I. Best and H. J. Lawler, London 1931), composed *c.* 800, contains a very full Roman calendar of saints and a corresponding calendar of Irish saints for each day of the year.

Bibliography: E. BALL, ''Descriptive Sketch of Clondalkin, Tallaght . . . ,'' *Journal of the Royal Society of Antiquaries of Ireland* 29 (1899) 93–108. E. J. GWYNN and W. J. PURTON, *The Monastery of Tallaght* (Proceedings of the Royal Irish Academy 29; Dublin 1911). E. J. GWYNN, ed., *The Rule of Tallaght* (Hermathena 44; Dublin 1927). J. F. KENNEY, *The Sources for the Early History of Ireland:* v.1, *Ecclesiastical* (New York 1929).

[J. RYAN]

TALLEYRAND-PÉRIGORD, CHARLES MAURICE DE

French statesman; b. Paris, Feb. 2, 1754; d. Paris, May 17, 1838. He was the second son of Charles Daniel and Alexandrine Eléonore de Damas d'Antigny. Since his family belonged to the highest aristocracy and his elder brother died during childhood, Charles Maurice should normally have pursued a career in the army or at court. But when in his fourth year an accident left him permanently disabled by a clubfoot, his parents decided on a clerical future for him. Charles Maurice studied for five years at the Seminary of Saint-Sulpice in Paris (1770–75) and was ordained on December 18, 1779, by his uncle, the archbishop of Reims, later cardinal. In 1780 he was appointed agent-general of the clergy, a most influential position involving political and financial activities.

Relation to the French Revolution. Although Talleyrand was already known as a freethinker and a Freemason, and as a man notorious for moral laxity, Louis XVI named him bishop of Autun in November of 1788. He was consecrated on January 16, 1789 and took possession of his see on March 15, but a few weeks later he was back in Versailles for the opening of the Estates-General, where he was one of the clergy's representatives. In this assemblage at the outbreak of the FRENCH REVOLUTION, he soon identified himself with the ''patriot'' majority led by his friends Mirabeau and Lafayette. He proposed in the Constituent Assembly the confiscation of Church property for the use of the nation. When the assembly decreed the CIVIL CONSTITUTION OF THE CLERGY, Talleyrand was one of the seven bishops who took the oath of allegiance to it demanded of the clergy. He also made possible the formation of the schismatic Constitutional Church by consecrating the first batch of newly elected bishops. This was his last act as a clergyman, for soon afterwards he adopted a secular status. When the revolution took a more radical turn, Talleyrand sought safety by going first to England, under the guise of a diplomatic mission (January of 1792) and from there to the United States (March of 1794). The fall of the ROBESPIERRE regime made possible his return to France in September of 1796. His friend Mme. de Staël persuaded the director, Vicomte de Barras, to appoint him minister of foreign affairs (July 18, 1797). While in this capacity, he had little more to do than to execute policies dictated by the Director Jean Reubell, but he used his position to amass himself a fortune through unscrupulous dealings.

Napoleonic Period. Talleyrand also recognized the potential value of friendship with Napoleon, whose ambitions he strove successfully to serve. He persuaded the government to let Bonaparte lead the French expedition in Egypt. Sensing the inevitable collapse of the Directory Régime, Talleyrand resigned his portfolio (July 20, 1799). When Bonaparte returned to France soon afterward, Talleyrand helped him prepare the Coup d'Etat of Brumaire. As a reward, the first consul named him minister of foreign affairs (November 22, 1799). Though Talleyrand had little influence over the main decisions of his imperious master, he was most useful in translating them into the forms of traditional diplomacy and cloaking usurpations and arbitrary acts in fine language. Occasionally, he was able to prevent misdeeds by delaying execution of orders long enough to give Napoleon time to reconsider. Though he was one of the most highly paid officials, he continued assiduously to acquire money from all his transactions, notably those by which the German states were reorganized after each phase of the wars. He also took advantage of the French CONCORDAT OF 1801, which he had helped frame, to wrest from Pope Pius VII his laicization (1802). Prodded by Bonaparte but without papal dispensation, he went through a civil marriage ceremony (1803) to his mistress Mrs. Grand, divorced wife of an official in the British East India Company.

When NAPOLEON I inaugurated the First Empire (1804), Talleyrand became grand-chamberlain, and in June of 1806, prince of Benevento. While serving the emperor well, he became increasingly uneasy with Napoleon's outsized undertakings. The emperor, on the other hand, became impatient with Talleyrand's counsels of moderation. After the Treaty of Tilsit (August of 1807)

Talleyrand was allowed to resign as minister, becoming vice-grand-elector ("the only vice he did not yet have," quipped Fouché). Napoleon still consulted him occasionally and had him accompany him to Erfurt for the famous interview with Czar ALEXANDER I in September of 1808. There Talleyrand startled the Russian autocrat with the revelation of the widening breach between Napoleon and French high officialdom. While Napoleon was critically involved in the conquest of Spain, Talleyrand plotted almost openly with his old rival Fouché, the minister of police. Napoleon, on his unexpected return in January of 1809, vented his wrath upon him. Thereafter, Talleyrand played no role in state affairs under Napoleon; he prepared quietly for his master's inevitable end.

Career, 1814 to 1838. When the victorious allies entered Paris on March 30, 1814, Talleyrand, who had been made by his fellow senators head of a provisional government, received Alexander I in his house and persuaded him that the only solution was to restore the Bourbon monarchy. As minister of foreign affairs for Louis XVIII, he negotiated with the allies the first Treaty of Paris (May of 1814) and took an outstanding part in the Congress of Vienna. After the Hundred Days, he returned with the king and was made president of the council (July 9, 1815), but he was soon compelled to resign (September 25). Throughout the Restoration period he remained aloof, though always hoping for a comeback. He secretly favored the Orléanist intrigue that finally brought Louis-Philippe to the throne. He served the new king as ambassador to London (1830–34), retiring finally from public service in November of 1834. On his deathbed he was reconciled with the Church.

Bibliography: *Mémoires,* ed. P. LÉON (Paris 1953—); *Memoirs of the Prince de Talleyrand,* tr. R. LEDOS DE BEAUFORT and A. HALL, 5 v. (New York 1891–92). G. LACOUR-GAYET, *Talleyrand.* 4 v. (Paris 1928–34). A. D. COOPER, *Talleyrand* (London 1932). L. MADELIN, *Talleyrand,* tr. R. FELTENSTEIN (New York 1948). C. BRINTON, *The Lives of Talleyrand* (New York 1936; pa. 1963).

[G. DE BERTIER DE SAUVIGNY]

Charles Maurice de Talleyrand-Périgord.

TALLIS, THOMAS

Outstanding composer of Catholic and Anglican liturgical music (also Tallys, Talys); b. Leicester, England, *c.* 1505; d. Greenwich, Nov. 23, 1585. Tallis, a lifelong Catholic, was probably organist at WALTHAM MONASTERY, Essex, for some time before its dissolution in 1540. At that time, of 70 laymen, Tallis received the highest gratuity for his services. In 1540 he became lay clerk at Canterbury and from *c.* 1542 until his death served as a gentleman of the chapel royal under Henry VIII, Edward VI, Mary, and Elizabeth I. In 1575, with William BYRD, he was given a monopoly on printing music and music paper in England. His Latin works comprise two Masses, two Magnificats, two Lamentations, Office hymns, and about 52 motets. His style varies from the florid to the simple homophonic idiom. Among his best-known works are the 6-voice antiphon *Gaude gloriosa,* the 40-voice *Spem in alium,* and the seven-voice *Miserere nostri* (with six voices in canon). His Office hymns are settings of even-numbered verses with the SARUM USE chant melody in the treble voice. Tallis was among the first to write liturgical music for English words; included in this category are some 18 anthems and Anglican service music, of which his "Short Service" (or "Dorian Service") is best known.

Bibliography: F. L. HARRISON, *Music in Medieval Britain* (New York 1958). G. REESE, *Music in the Renaissance* (rev. ed. New York 1959) 784–786. Y. ROKSETH, "The Instrumental Music of the Middle Ages and Early Sixteenth Century," *New Oxford History of Music,* ed. J. A. WESTRUP, 11 v. (New York 1957–) 3:458–464. P. DOE, "Thomas Tallis" in *The New Grove Dictionary of Music and Musicians,* ed. S. SADIE (New York 1980). M. HANSARD, *The Vocal Polyphonic Style of the Latin Church Music of Thomas Tallis (ca. 1505–1585)* (Ph.D. diss. University of Kentucky, 1971). J. R. MILSOM, *English Polyphonic Style in Transition: A Study of the Sacred Music of Thomas Tallis* (Ph.D. diss. Magdalen College, Oxford University, 1983). D. MORONEY, *"Under Fower sovereynes" Thomas Tallis and the Transformation of English Polyphony* (Ph.D. diss. University of California at Berkeley,

Thomas Tallis. (©Bettmann/CORBIS)

1980). K. MOYER, *The Anthems of Thomas Tallis* (Ph.D. diss. University of Rochester, 1980). D. M. RANDEL, ed., *The Harvard Biographical Dictionary of Music* (Cambridge 1996). N. SLONIMSKY, ed., *Baker's Biographical Dictionary of Musicians* (New York 1992).

[S. W. KENNEY]

TALMUD

The term ''Talmud'' (Heb. *talmûd,* teaching, learning, from the verb *lāmad,* to learn) designates the authoritative body of post-biblical Jewish laws and traditions, consisting essentially of two parts: an older nucleus, the MISHNAH, compiled toward the end of the 2d Christian century, and the commentaries on it, the GEMARAH, which has two forms—the Palestinian, compiled toward the end of the 4th century, and the Babylonian, compiled at the beginning of the 6th century. As a vast collection of various sayings of numerous RABBIS (Jewish teachers) over a period of at least six centuries, the Talmud is basically a recording in writing of traditional oral law. From the orthodox Jewish viewpoint, the ''oral law'' recorded in the Talmud is second only to the ''written law,'' the Sacred Scriptures; in theory it is considered almost on a par with the Scriptures, but in practice it is, in a certain sense, regarded as superior to it. Since the Jewish concept of oral law as found in the Talmud is so important, this article will first treat oral law before describing the origin and nature of the Talmud itself.

Beginning of oral law. Consideration will be given here to oral law before there was any written law, to oral law as a supplement of written law, and to the significance of the Babylonian Exile in the development of oral law.

Oral Law before Written Law. Modern biblical scholars have recognized that oral tradition is ordinarily to be presupposed before its various channels became stabilized in written documents. There were, for instance, from 800 to 1,300 years between the events of the patriarchal age and the written accounts of them in Genesis. Studies in the field of the ancient Near East show more and more conclusively that, despite the long pre-biblical period of predominantly oral transmission, much reliable historical material was preserved and transmitted to the authors of the documentary sources of the PENTATEUCH. This is true, not only of the historical, but also of the legal traditions, i.e., there was unwritten law based on custom before it was standardized and codified. For the time of the Patriarchs, the oral law corresponded more to legal concepts of the ancient Near East in the first half and middle of the 2d millennium B.C. than it did to the law that was later standardized in writing in the Pentateuch; for example, although in Lv 18.18 a man is forbidden to marry the sister of his wife while the latter is still alive, it is related in Gn 29.16–30 that Jacob married two sisters, Lia and Rachel. Marriage with two sisters was not considered illegal at that time in the ancient Near East [see M. Schorr, *Urkunden des altbabylonischen Zivil- und Prozessrechts* (Leipzig 1913) No. 4.5]. The way in which Abraham purchased the tomb of Machpelah (Gn 23.1–20) corresponds to the legal customs of the age of the Patriarchs, although there is nothing about this in the law set down later in the Pentateuch [see M. R. Lehmann, ''Abraham's Purchase of Machpelah and Hittite Law,'' *Bulletin of the American Schools of Oriental Research* 129 (1953) 15–18]. This passage, which belongs to the priestly document, the most recent Pentateuchal source, has obviously preserved a point of ancient legal custom.

Oral Law as a Supplement of Written Law. After the laws were stabilized in the Pentateuch, they were still supplemented by oral legal tradition. For example, it is presupposed in Ex 21.2 that there were regulations about the buying and selling of Hebrew slaves that obviously were contained only in the oral legal tradition. According to Dt 17.8–11, the highest court in Jerusalem gave decisions on questions that were not provided for in the written law. Examples of the existence of an oral legal tradition in addition to law fixed in writing can be found also in the Prophets and the other sacred writings. In Jer 17.21–22 the law forbidding the carrying of a load from one place to another on the Sabbath is more specific than the general Pentateuchal prohibition of work on the Sabbath. In Neh 10.32 the prohibition against transacting business on the Sabbath is expressed more clearly than in the Pentateuch. This type of supplementation and interpretation of the written law is referred to in Talmudic literature as *tôrâ šebbeʻal peh* (oral law) as distinct from *tôrâ šebiktāb* (written law).

Development of Oral Law in the Exile. After the Babylonian devastation of Judah and the deportation to Babylonia of the majority of its surviving inhabitants between 597 and 582 B.C., for people of the Jewish DIASPORA the law of God became the safeguard and the very condition of their existence. Therefore, from then on, they had an intensive concern for this law. The activity of the Pentateuchal PRIESTLY WRITERS and, in connection with this, the redaction of the whole Pentateuch were important results of this development; another was the formation of a special class of specialists in Scripture, the SCRIBES. Direct evidence of Jewish Scribes as a professional class, and indeed in Palestine itself, first appears at the beginning of the 2d century B.C. in Josephus *Ant.* 12.3.3 (for 198 B.C.) and Sir 39.1–11 (*c.* 180 B.C.), where they are said to be the preservers of tradition and the successors of the Prophets. Yet their profession surely went back to an earlier period. At first, in the Diaspora as well as in Palestine, the interpretation of the Law was reserved especially to men of priestly lineage; but in time the priestly element faded more and more into the background, and lay experts in Scripture came to the fore. Among the Pharisaic Scribes, priests ceased to play any role at all.

The Hebrew term for Scripture scholar is *sōpēr* (writer, scribe). The first to be mentioned with this title is EZRA; in Ezr 7.6 he is called "a Scribe skilled in the Law of Moses." Although his title, "Ezra the priest, the scribe of the law of the God of heaven" (Ezr 7.12, 21), in the Aramaic document of Ezr 7.12–26 refers primarily to his official rank in the bureaucracy of the Persian Empire, it was rightly understood by the Jews to mean an expert in Scripture, since an official had to be familiar with specifically Jewish laws as well as the laws of the Persian Empire.

The rise of professional Scribes was furthered also by the gradual formation of the OT canon in the postexilic period. The Scribes were, first of all, what their title signifies, professional copyists, occupied in producing faithful transcripts of the sacred text of the Scriptures. In *Kiddushin* 30a (unless otherwise specified, tracts cited here refer to the Babylonian Talmud), there is an allusion

Rabbi studying the Talmud. (©Bettmann/CORBIS)

to this function of the Scribes: "The ancients were called Scribes [*sōpe*rî*m*] because they used to count [*hāyû sōpe*rî*m*] the number of letters in the Law"; in typical Talmudic fashion this statement is based on a pun, *sōpēr,* meaning both writing and counting. With the function of copying was naturally joined that of interpreting the teachings and applying the traditional legal material to the new temporal circumstances.

The later houses of study and those of the synagogal service, the two centers of the developing oral tradition in Judaism, had their origins also in the Babylonian Exile. Jeremiah's letter to the exiles was addressed particularly to the elders, priests, and Prophets among them (Jer 29.1). Moreover, religious meetings of Ezekiel with the elders in Babylonia were referred to (Ez 8.1; 14.1; 20.1). Details are unfortunately lacking on the development from these hypothetical beginnings to the well-known rabbinical academies of Babylonia in the Christian Era. It is certain, however, that the study of law was cultivated by the Jews in Babylonia, nor is it by accident that the two most decisive figures of Judaism in the period of the Second Temple, Ezra and Hillel, came to Palestine from Babylonia.

Significance of oral law in Judaism. The concept of oral law belongs specifically to Pharisaism. It is true that other Jewish groups also (e.g., the Essenes of Qumran) were in possession of legal tradition derived from the OT that had been stabilized in writing since the 2d century B.C.; unequivocal and stricter interpretations of OT laws are found for instance in the Book of Jubilees and the Dead Sea Scrolls. While the latter, because of the proximate eschatological expectation of the priestly apocalyptic circle that sponsored them, contain extraordinarily severe laws, the Pharisaic legal interpretation is distinguished by much greater mildness. Thus, for example, in the Qumran-Essene Damascus Document (11.16.17) it is forbidden to use any instrument in saving a drowning man on the Sabbath, whereas in the Mishnah (*Yoma* 8.6) it is stated: ''Any danger to life supercedes the Sabbath laws.'' In contrast to the apocalytical groups, the Pharisaic understanding of the Law had a characteristic sense of what was within the realm of the possible [see K. Schubert, ''Die Jüdischen Religionsparteien im Zeitalter Jesu,'' *Der historische Jesus und der Christus unseres Glaubens* (Vienna 1962)].

Oral Law in Pharisaic Judaism. In the last pre-Christian centuries, oral tradition was of special importance because the Pharisees were of the opinion that after the death of the last three of the Minor Prophets, Haggai, Zechariah, and Malachi, the Holy Spirit, i.e., the gift of prophecy, had departed from Israel (*Tos. Soṭtah* 13.2; *Yoma* 9b; *Soṭtah* 48b; *Sanh.* 11a). According to the opinion of the rabbis, oral tradition was part of the heritage of prophecy as well. Thus, in the Mishnah (*Avoth* 1.1) it is stated: ''Moses received the Law on Sinai and handed it on to Joshua, Joshua to the elders, the elders to the prophets, and the prophets handed it on to men of the great Sanhedrin.'' The concept of oral tradition enabled the rabbinical scholars to establish a continuous link between Moses and themselves. For them, even their own interpretations and additions to the Law had already been given orally to Moses on Sinai (*Berakhot* 5a). According to a haggadic (*see* HAGGADAH) tradition, the only reason why the Mishnah had not been given to Moses in writing was so that it might not be translated into Greek and thus fall into the hands of the Gentiles. After the latter appropriated the written Law of Moses, God could recognize His chosen people only by their possession of the Mishnah, that is, the oral tradition incorporated in the Mishnah [*Pesikta rabbati 14b,* ed. M. Friedmann (Vienna 1880)]. Similarly, the well-known Palestinian teacher of the 3d century, Johanan bar Nappaḥa, said, ''The Holy One, praised be He, made the covenant with Israel solely for the sake of the orally handed-on word'' (Gittin 60b). For the rabbis, oral law was a necessary supplement to the written law and in their eyes of no less value than the latter. Certain precepts that the rabbis considered very old but for which no point of reference could be found in the Bible were given a special designation as ''Halakot [plural of HALAKAH] given to Moses on Sinai'' (Mishnah *Peah* 2.6; Mishnah *Eduyyot* 8.7; Mishnah *Yadayim* 4.3).

Prohibition against Writing New Religious Books. Closely connected with the idea of oral law was the so-called writing prohibition, regarding whose nature and continuance rabbinical tradition itself was not of one opinion. It probably meant no more than that the legal material was to be presented only orally, and originally it was only orally handed down, although there were not lacking defenders of the opinion that originally also the Haggadah would have fallen under the writing prohibition (*Temurot* 14b; *Gittin* 60b; for more details, see Strack, 9–16). Had the latter been the case, the full force of the writing prohibition would have been clearly directed against the various apocalyptical groups and their writings. The specifically Pharisaic character of the writing prohibition is evidenced by the fact that Sirach at the beginning of the 2d century B.C. and the authors of two Books of Maccabees wrote their works apparently without any scruples, but these works were not included in the Pharisaic canon. Likewise, Sirach's grandson, who translated his grandfather's work into Greek, either must not have known about a writing prohibition or else must have ignored it. Since the Book of Sirach did not stand in opposition to Pharisaism, which as such did not come into being until at least a generation after it was written, this book could still be cited on occasion by rabbinical scholars with as much reverence as the hagiographa (the last books in the Hebrew Bible) were cited (as, e.g., Sir 13.15 is quoted in *Baba Kamma* 92b). The collections of laws, however, that were drawn up independently of Pharisaism and in opposition to it, for example, those from the QUMRAN COMMUNITY, were undoubtedly rejected by the Pharisees [see K. Schubert, *The Dead Sea Community* (New York 1959)]. Opposition to the writing of religious works in general was typical of early Pharisaism. The literary products of the apocalyptical groups were called apocryphal (hidden) books, and the reading of them was strictly forbidden (Mishnah *Sanhedrin* 10.1). Pharisaism was thereby able to prevent Judaism from breaking up into numerous groups and to make its own doctrine that of normative Judaism after the destruction of the Temple in A.D. 70.

Toward the end of the 1st and the beginning of the 2d Christian century, when the legal material that had been handed down orally in Pharisaic circles became so vast that it had to be organized in writing, obviously no writing prohibition stood in the way. As the so-called Fasting Scroll shows, even in the period before the destruction of the Temple, there was a written list of certain feast days on which there was to be no fasting or mourning. It is suspected, however, that the Fasting Scroll originated among the ZEALOTS and not in Pharisaic circles [see M. Hengel, *Die Zeloten* (Leiden 1961) 19]. In any case, it was severely forbidden to draw the oral law from written sources.

Purpose of Oral Law. The concept of oral law was to make a permanent fixation of Judaism's external form of life impossible. Each generation was to adapt its particular life to the new circumstances in keeping with the Mosaic Law. Two examples may serve to show this: the modification of the Ketuba (marriage document) prescriptions by Simeon ben Shetaḥ and the prosbul of Hillel. By prescribing that the money a husband had to pay his wife in the event of a divorce or his death was fixed as a mortgage and surety on his estate, Simeon ben Shetaḥ succeeded both in limiting, in practice, the possibility of a divorce and in protecting a widow against her husband's heirs, who might be unwilling to pay her (*Ketubbot* 82b). In this, Simeon ben Shetaḥ reflected the finer moral sense of his time (the beginning of the 1st century B.C.). Hillel the Elder, a contemporary of Herod the Great, had to take account of the transition from a purely agrarian to a largely capitalistic economy. According to Dt 15.1–11, a creditor was obliged to remit a debt in the SABBATH YEAR; in fact, the creditor was to lend money even when the Sabbath year was near and thus had little prospect of recovering his loan. Despite the idealistic purpose of this precept, it was unrealistic in a time of more highly developed finance. The one who was really harmed by it was the poor man for whose good the law was meant but who now had little chance of getting a loan. Hillel's prosbul (πρὸς βουλῇ βουλευτῶν, at the council of the councilors) was to put an end to this situation. According to Hillel's enactment, the creditor could declare publicly in court that he would collect the debt, and in this way he was released from the duty of having to cancel it in the seventh year (Mishnah *Shebi'it* 10.3, 4; *Gittin* 36a).

Stabilization of oral law in the written Talmud. After the Romans destroyed the Temple of Jerusalem (A.D. 70), Pharisaic Judaism simply became normative Judaism. The other groups were eliminated by the new political circumstances. The members of these groups either were assimilated into Pharisaism or left the ranks of Judaism and joined Judeo-Christian or Gnostic groups. Under these circumstances, it became necessary for Pharisaism to collect, sift, and compile in writing the legal traditions that were scattered within its framework and had hitherto been handed down only by word of mouth. Halakah (moral teaching) and the interest awakened in it were now more in the foreground than ever before. The common bond of Judaism was secured through halakah, even though, as was the case with the Hekhalot mystics (who sought to ascend in spirit to the heavenly *hêkālōt* or palaces), themes and traditions were taken over from the apocalyptical groups that originally were in competition with Pharisaism (*see* GNOSTICISM, JEWISH). Thus it came about that, by the beginning of the 2d Christian century or even earlier, the legal material, which had already swollen in bulk, was organized and edited. This compilation bore the title *mishnâ rîshônâ,* or first mishnah (see e.g., in Mishnah *Sanhedrin* 3.4). Further Mishnah compilations were made in the course of the 2d century A.D. by Rabbi AKIBA BEN JOSEPH (on whose method, see *Avoth de Rabbi Natan*) and Rabbi Meir. However, the Mishnah that forms the basis of the Talmud is the compilation made by Rabbi JUDAH HA-NASI, who probably completed his work shortly after A.D. 200. Judah ben Samuel ha-levi (*Kusari* 3.67) dates its completion as 219–220. This date could be approximately correct, because Judah ha-Nasi probably died in 217 [see A. Guttmann, "The Patriarch Judah I: His Birth and His Death," *Hebrew Union College Annual* 25 (1954) 239–261].

The Mishnah. Medieval Jewish scholars were not in agreement whether the Mishnah of Judah ha-Nasi had been committed to writing by him. Despite denial by such an authority as RASHI (see his comments on *Shabbat* 13b and on *Eruvin* 62b), it is taken for granted that the Mishnah was recorded in writing by Judah ha-Nasi himself, to prevent this immense collection of legal material from being forgotten. Also that the teachers who are quoted in the Gemarah adhere very closely to the text of the Mishnah is evidence that it must have been available to them in writing, although in the rabbinical academies it continued to be handed down orally. In doubtful cases, however, a written text could be consulted (see K. Hruby, 116–117). In the generation following Judah ha-Nasi, his Mishnah received some additions. Such are the passages where he himself is quoted as holding a certain opinion or where teachers who were active after his time are quoted.

The Mishnah consists of six *s^e^dārîm,* or "orders," each of which contains several *massēkôt* (weavings), or tracts, and these in turn are divided into *p^e^rāqîm* (sections), or chapters. As divided in the printed editions, the whole Mishnah contains 63 tracts with a total of 525 chapters. The names of the orders and their contents are (1) *Zera'im* (seeds), containing 11 tracts, the first of which, BERAKHOT, deals with blessings and prayers. In this way reverence for God is given the primary position among the various laws. The other tracts deal principally with the religious laws connected with agriculture in Palestine. (2) *Mo'ed* (feast), containing 12 tracts that deal with religious FEASTS. (3) *Nashim* (women), containing 7 tracts that treat marital and family law. (4) *Neziqin* (damages), containing 10 tracts that deal with civil and criminal law. Included in this division of the Mishnah are the *Pirke Avoth* (chapters of the fathers), which summarizes the ethical doctrine of Pharisaic Judaism from a century before Christ to the time of Judah ha-Nasi. (5) *Kodashim* (sacred things), containing 11 tracts on the nature of the various sacrifices, on food regulations, and on the directions for the ritual slaughter (*šᵉḥîṭā*). (6) *Ṭohorot* (clean things), containing 12 tracts on the special laws for ritual purity.

The word ''Mishnah'' (repetition, study, from the verb *šānâ,* to repeat) signifies both the individual points of doctrine and the collection of these doctrines; the latter is now the usual meaning of the term. In its present form, the Mishnah consists of numerous *mišnāyôt,* Mishnah precepts. The Mishnah teachers are called Tannaim (literally repeaters, from the Aramaic root *tny* corresponding to the Hebrew root *šny*). There were altogether five generations of Tannaim.

Other Tannaitic Literature. Not all of the teachings of the Tannaim were incorporated into the official Mishnah of Judah ha-Nasi. Originally there were other collections of Tannaitic teachings, as can be seen, e.g., in *Yerushalmi* tractate *Horayot* 48c. In this passage there are mentioned, along with the Bible and the Mishnah, the Tosephta and ''large Mishnah collections, such as the *Mishnah rabba* of Rabbi Ḥiyya, the *Mishnah rabba* of Rabbi Hosha'yah, and the *Mishnah* of Bar Kappara.'' R. Ḥiyyah and Bar Kappara were students and friends of Judah ha-Nasi, and R. Hosha'yah was a student of the former two. These Mishnah compilations, therefore, were drawn up by men having scholarly connections with Judah ha-Nasi. Of the above-mentioned works, only the Tosephta has been preserved. The compilations of Tannaitic teachings outside the Mishnah of Judah ha-Nasi were regarded as Baraita (Aramaic for outside thing, i.e., excluded from the Mishnah), and therefore they were not passed on with the same care as the official Mishnah. In both Talmuds, however, Baraitot (plural of Baraita) are frequently quoted as authorities in order to give special weight to the arguments of the Amoraim in their controversies. Other Tannaitic material is contained in the Tannaitic Midrashim (*see* MIDRASHIC LITERATURE).

The Tosephta (addition, supplement) is a work in a class by itself; like the Mishnah, it contains six orders. In its presentation, the Tosephta is more diffuse than the Mishnah. [It has been edited by M. S. Zuckermandel (Pasewalk 1881) and S. Liebermann (New York 1955).] Although the Tosephta consists principally of Tannaitic teachings, it acquired also, as did the Mishnah, various additions in the early Amoraic period. As a kind of Tosephta to the Mishnah tract *Pirke Avoth* (Chapters of the Fathers) is the collection called the *Avoth de Rabbi Natan* (The Fathers according to Rabbi Nathan).

The Gemarah. The scholars who followed the Tannaim are called Amoraim (Hebrew plural of Aramaic *'ămōrā',* speaker, explainer). The Amoraim were limited to interpreting the Tannaim, and they could not explain away any Tannaitic doctrine as invalid. They therefore endeavored, by way of interpretation, to make the Tannaitic teachings fit their own ideas. If an Amora held a doctrinal opinion differing from that of his colleague, he endeavored to prove his point by quoting from the Mishnah or the Baraita. His colleague would then try on his part to propose an interpretation of the quotation that would neutralize the other's objection. In Palestine there were five, and in Babylonia, seven, generations of Amoraim who occupied themselves with the teachings handed down by the Tannaim. The disputes and teachings of the Amoraim are called Gemarah (completion). Whereas the Mishnah is in a late form of Hebrew (Mishnaic Hebrew), the Gemarah is mostly in Aramaic, a western dialect of it being used by the Palestinian Amoraim, an eastern one by the Babylonian Amoraim. The Mishnah and the Gemarah that rose in Palestine form what is inaccurately known as the Jerusalem (Heb. *yᵉrûšalmî*) Talmud; the Mishnah and the Gemarah that rose in Babylon is called the Babylonian (*bablî*) Talmud.

The most important rabbinical academies in Palestine were in Tiberias, Sephoris, Caesarea, and Lydda. The Palestinian Gemarah is much less extensive than the Babylonian. Therefore the Jerusalem Talmud was not regarded in Judaism as highly as the Babylonian, although it contains much old and important material. The shorter compass of the Palestinian Gemarah was a result, in part, of the political condition in Palestine. The 3d century was a century of soldier emperors, and, consequently, a period of inflation and impoverishment for wide sections of the Roman Empire. The decreasing standard of living in Palestine brought about a decline in halakic study. This, in turn, resulted in the increased importance of the Eastern Diaspora of the Jews, which, under the strong Sassanid rulers, enjoyed on the whole, despite a few reverses, a period of increasing prosperity.

The most important academies in Babylonia in the 3d century were in Sura, Nehardea, and Pumbedita; in these cities the greatest Jewish scholars of the century taught. Thus the reputation of these academies soon surpassed that of the Jewish schools in Palestine. This explains the passage in *Ketubbot* 111a: ''Rab Judah [bar Ezechiel] said in the name of [i.e., quoting] Samuel, As it is forbidden to go from Israel to Babylonia, so is it forbidden to go from Babylonia to other countries. . . . Rab Juda said [in his own name], 'If one lives in Babylonia, it is just as if he lived in Israel.''' In the 5th century, the persecutions of the Jews in the Sassanid Empire caused a serious crisis in the academic life of the rabbinical academies. Since it was feared that the merely oral presentation of the Amoraic teaching would be lost to memory, a compilation known as the Babylonian Gemarah, containing the teachings and elaborate discussion of the Babylonian Amoraim, was made in the 5th century. This editing of the Babylonian Talmud was due primarily to the efforts of Rab Ashi, an Amora of the sixth generation, who was head of the rabbinical academy of Mate Maḥseya, where he carried on his work under circumstances that were still politically favorable. In the following, last generation of the Amoraim and under the Saboraim (Hebrew plural of Aramaic *sābōrā',* ''thinker, opiner'') of the 6th century, the Babylonian Talmud received its final form.

Characteristics. The Mishnah itself, despite certain basic attempts at orderly arrangement, is not a digested corpus of law, but rather a collection of opinions by the various rabbis on questions that are more or less connected with the matters under discussion. The much larger Gemarahs are far more disorderly; one point leads to another on some extraneous matter that is then discussed at length, although it may have nothing at all to do with the main topic under discussion. About one third of the Babylonian Gemarah is not even on legal matters but contains digressions full of folklore, legends, history (usually of only little value), midrashic interpretations of biblical passages, moralizing sermons, etc. The style makes no pretense of being literary; short incomplete phrases abound. On the whole, the Talmud is like the notes and jottings made by students at rambling lectures or round-table discussions.

Later fate. Because of its obscurities and seeming inconsistencies, numerous commentaries on the Talmud were written throughout the centuries by rabbinical scholars. Official decisions on obscure points in the Talmud or adaptations of its teaching to changed conditions were given in the RESPONSA by the Geonim (plural of Gaon), the leaders of the Jewish community in the first post-Talmudic period (6th to 11th centuries). For practical use by ordinary Jews simplified summaries of Talmudic law were drawn up by various Jewish scholars, such as *Mishneh Torah* (repetition of the Law) by MAIMONIDES and the authoritative *Shulḥan Arukh* (set table) by Joseph CARO. Throughout the Middle Ages and, in certain parts of the world, even in recent times all aspects of Jewish life were regulated by the teachings of the Talmud; its influence on Judaism has been enormous.

Since non-Jews understood the important place that this work held for Jewish life, many of the outbreaks of anti-Semitism were accompanied by public burnings of the Talmud; e.g., 24 cartloads of Talmud MSS are said to have been burned in a Paris square on June 17, 1242. This is one of the chief reasons why only one complete MS of the Babylonian Talmud (the Munich Codex of 1369, Heb. MS no. 95) and only one complete MS of the Palestinian Talmud (the Leiden Codex) have been preserved, although several MSS of parts of the Talmud, especially the Babylonian, survive. The Babylonian Talmud was first printed by Daniel Bomberg (Venice 1520); several editions have since then been published. Although critical editions of particular portions of it have been issued, a critical edition of the whole Talmud is still badly needed. An English edition, *The Babylonian Talmud,* unabridged, with introductions, annotations, and index has been edited by I. Epstein (35 v. London 1938–52).

Bibliography: L. BLAU, *The Jewish Encyclopedia,* ed. J. SINGER (New York 1901–06) 12:1–37. H. REVEL and C. A. RUBENSTEIN, *Universal Jewish Encyclopedia* (New York 1939–44) 10:160–168. M. AVI-YONAH, *Geschichte der Juden im Zeitalter des Talmud* (Berlin 1962). W. BACHER, *Die Agada der Tannaiten,* 2 v. (Strassburg 1884–90); *Die Agada der palästinensischen Amoräer,* 3 v. (Strassburg 1892–99); *Die Agada der babylonischen Amoräer* (Strassburg 1878). E. L. BERKOVITS, *Was ist der Talmud?* (2d ed. Frankfurt a.M. 1962). L. FINKELSTEIN, ''The Transmission of the Early Rabbinical Tradition,'' *Hebrew Union Catalog Annual* 16 (1941) 115–135. S. FUNK, *Die Entstehung des Talmuds* (2d rev. ed. Leipzig 1910). N. GLATZER, *Untersuchungen zur Geschichtslehre der Tannaiten* (Berlin 1933); *Geschichte der talmudischen Zeit* (Berlin 1937). A. GUTTMANN, *Das redaktionelle und sachliche Verhältnis zwischen Mischna und Tosephta* (Breslau 1928); ''The Problem of the Anonymous Mishna,'' *Hebrew Union Catalog Annual* 16 (1941) 137–155. K. HRUBY, ''Die jüdische Liturgie zur Zeit Jesu,'' *Judaica* 18 (1962) 104–126. J. Z. LAUTERBACH, ''Midrash and Mishna,'' *Rabbinical Essays,* ed. J. Z. LAUTERBACH (Cincinnati, Ohio 1951) 163–256. M. MARGULIES, ed., *Entsiklopediyah le-hakhme ha-Talmud veha-geonim,* 2 v. (Tel Aviv 1960). G. F. MOORE, *Judaism in the First Centuries of the Christian Era: The Age of the Tannaim,* 3 v. (Cambridge, Mass. 1927–30). H. L. STRACK, *Einleitung in Talmud und Midraš* (5th rev. ed. Munich 1921). H. ALBECK, *Māvŏ leMišnâ* (Jerusalem 1959), introduction to the Mishna. M. E. ABRAMSKY, ''Ha-Tosephtâ biDephûs,'' *Kirjat Sepher* 29 (1953–54) 149–161, with complete bibliog.

[K. SCHUBERT]

TAMARON Y ROMERAL, PEDRO

16th bishop of Durango; b. Villa de la Guardia, Toledo, Spain, *c.* 1695; d. Bamoa, Sinaloa, Mexico, Dec. 21, 1768. In 1719 he went to America as a companion of Bishop Escalona, who had been named to the see of Caracas, and he completed his studies there at the University of Santa Rosa, receiving a doctorate in Canon Law. Subsequently he taught at the university. He remained in Caracas, holding a number of important ecclesiastical posts, until he was named bishop of Durango, New Spain, by Benedict XVI on December 21, 1758. He arrived in Durango in March 1759 and that autumn began his first general visitation of the diocese. He was more than 60 at the time, but his age did not handicap him; he inspected his vast diocese six times and as a result was referred to as the ''restless bishop.'' When Tamarón took possession of his bishopric, the cathedral was almost finished. Commenting that the lateral sides of the facade were built with ''notorious ugliness,'' he obtained the services of architect Pedro de Huertas to change them. Under his direction Huertas achieved a marvelous building, combining the baroque and churrigueresque styles of the period. Tamarón wrote a number of books, the most valuable being his description of his diocese, which he dedicated to the King of Spain, Charles III.

Bibliography: P. TAMARÓN Y ROMERAL, *Demostración del vastísimo obispado de la Nueva Vizcaya, 1765,* ed. V. ALESSIO ROBLES (Biblioteca histórica mexicana de obras inéditas 7; Mexico City 1937); *Bishop Tamarón's Visitation of New Mexico, 1760,* ed. E. B. ADAMS (Albuquerque 1954).

[I. GALLEGOS]

TAMBURINI, MICHELANGELO

14th general of the Society of Jesus; b. Modena, Sept. 27, 1648; d. Rome, Feb. 28, 1730. He taught scholastic philosophy at Bologna and theology at Mantua for 12 years. Such were his qualities of virtue, patience, and courage that he became successively rector of several colleges, provincial of the Venetian province, secretary general, and finally, in 1703, vicar-general. Upon the death of Thyrsus Gonzalez, he was elected general of his society on Jan. 3, 1706. His generalate saw the full flourishing of Jesuit missionary activity, such as the REDUCTIONS OF PARAGUAY, new missions in the Levant, and Constant Beschi's continuance of the traditions of ''Brahman Christianity'' initiated by Robert de NOBILI in India. But there were also unmistakable signs of the mounting opposition that would result in the society's suppression in 1773. The Jansenists especially, embittered by the suppression of PORT-ROYAL, in 1708 accused the Jesuits of failing to comply with the directions of Rome in adapting Christianity to non-European cultures. In 1710, when Clement XI condemned certain of the ceremonial customs that Jesuit missionaries had judged indifferent and had permitted to Indian and Chinese Christians, Tamburini went to the Vatican to make a formal declaration of fidelity of all Jesuits to the Holy See.

Bibliography: J. CRÉTINEAU-JOLY, *Histoire religieuse, politique et littéraire de la Compagnie de Jésus,* 6 v. (Paris 1844–46) v.2. L. KOCH, *Jesuiten-Lexikon: Die Gesellschraft Jesu einst und jetzt* (Paderborn 1934) 2:1725–26. C. SOMMERVOGEL, *Bibliotèque de la Compagnie de Jésus,* 11 v. (Brussels-Paris 1890–1932) 7:1827–30.

[J. H. CAMPANA]

TAMBURINI, TOMMASO

Jesuit moral theologian; b. Caltanisetta, Sicily, March 6, 1591; d. Palermo, Oct. 10, 1675. He entered the Society of Jesus on Sept. 21, 1606. After completing his studies he taught philosophy for four years, dogmatic theology for seven years, and moral theology for 17 years at the colleges of Messina and Palermo. His other offices included those of rector of several colleges (Palermo, Messina, Mont–Reale, and Caltanisetta), consultor and censor for the Sicilian Inquisition, and examiner for the episcopal curia of Palermo.

Tamburini's most notable works are the following: *Methodus expeditae confessionis* (5 v. Rome 1647), mainly a pastoral treatment of the Sacrament of Penance; *De Communione* (Palermo 1649), a treatise complementary to the preceding work and treating of the corporal and spiritual dispositions necessary for the reception of the Eucharist; *De Sacrificio Missae* (3 v. Palermo 1649). Because of the success of his *Methodus expeditae confessionis,* the Jesuit General, Vincent Caraffa, asked Tamburini to publish a summa of moral theology. The *Expeditae decalogi explicationes* (Venice 1654), and the *Expedita iuris divini . . . explicatio* (3 v. Palermo 1661) were written in response to this request. A large number of Tamburini's other writings were published to refute the charges of laxism leveled against him by Vincent BARON.

Tamburini was one of the most qualified casuists of the probabilist school during the 17th century. He reduced his exposition of moral doctrine to a minimum and gave solutions to thousands of cases. His writings are a copious compendium of information and opinions of authors. Because of their lucidity, brevity, and relative conciseness, Tamburini's works enjoyed a great success at the time they were written. Today their importance stems from their historical value, for they represent the trend of probabilism in the 17th century. His solutions to cases tended to take a less severe view, and in consequence of this he was often under attack. He claimed the validity of the probably probable opinion, which was sometimes confused with the tenuously probable opinion, and because of this he was sometimes classified as a laxist. D'Annibale and Prümmer acknowledged his learning and casuistic skill but said that he was too indulgent and should be read with caution. St. Alphonsus also pointed to the need for caution in reading his works, but considered him nevertheless a thorough theologian who solved questions by reducing them to their ultimate principles.

Bibliography: R. BROUILLARD, *Dictionnaire de théologie catholique,* ed. A. VACANT et al., 15 v. (Paris 1903–50; Tables générales 1951–) 15.1:34–38. C. SOMMERVOGEL et al, *Bibliothèque de la Compagnie de Jésus,* 11 v. (Brussels–Paris 1890–1932; v. 12

suppl. 1960) 7:1830–41. H. HURTER, *Nomenclator literarius theologiae catholicae,* 5 vol. in 6 (3d ed. Innsbruck 1903–13); v. 1 (4th ed. 1926) 4:279–281.

[G. V. KOHLS]

TAMETSI

Tametsi (Lat. ''although'') is the first word of the opening sentence of a decree concerning the juridical form of marriage enacted by the 24th session of the Council of Trent on Nov. 11, 1563 (*Concilium Tridentinum. Diariorum, actorum, epistularum, tractatuum nova collectio,* ed. Görres-Gesellschaft [Freiburg 1901–38] sess. 24 *de ref. matrim.,* c.1). In summary, the *Tametsi* decree stated:

> Although it is not to be doubted that clandestine marriages made with the free consent of the contracting parties are valid and true marriages, so long as the Church has not rendered them invalid; and consequently that those persons are justly to be condemned, as the Holy Synod doth condemn them with anathema who deny that such marriages are true and valid . . . nevertheless the holy Church of God has for reasons most just, at all times detested and prohibited such marriages . . . . Those who shall attempt to contract marriage otherwise than in the presence of the parish priest, or of some other priest by the permission of the said parish priest or of the Ordinary, and in the presence of two or three witnesses; the Holy Synod renders such wholly incapable of thus contracting and declares such contracts invalid and null, as by the present decree it invalidates and annuls them.''

Thus after much debate, a long-desired reform was accomplished. When the final vote was taken on the decree, 56 of the Council Fathers voted against it, 135 voted for it, and nine either cast no vote at all or simply deferred the matter to the judgment of the Holy See.

The Sacrament of Matrimony is unique in that it is administered not by a bishop or priest, but rather by the parties themselves who administer the Sacrament to each other. It was fear of a possible change in this doctrine that had caused the long debate on the *Tametsi* decree. Yet legislation as contained in the *Tametsi* decree had become increasingly necessary, mainly due to the often-condemned practice of clandestine (secret) marriages. The evil of such secret marriages consisted in the fact that often no proof was available that a marriage had indeed taken place, resulting in obvious legal and moral chaos. Hereditary rights were often endangered; shadows could be cast on the legitimacy of children; and conflicts between the internal and external forums could easily arise.

Tommaso Tamburini.

Various attempts to legislate against secret marriages had been made by local and provincial councils; e.g., Salzburg (1420), Magdeburg (1370), Padua (1351), Prague (1355), and Cologne (1280).

It is generally admitted, however, that historically clandestine or secret marriages were considered valid before the Council of Trent. The first universal law of the Church, which established a juridical form of marriage, was embodied in the decree *Tametsi* requiring for the validity of marriage the presence of the parish priest or of another priest authorized by the parish priest or by the ordinary and in the presence of two or three witnesses. Apart from the juridical form required for the validity of marriage, the *Tametsi* decree further prescribed that banns were to be published before a marriage was to take place. Moreover, a liturgical form for the celebration of marriage was determined. Newly married couples were exhorted to receive the priestly blessing in the church, to go to Confession, and to receive the Holy Eucharist. Finally provision was made for the recording of all marriages.

The *Tametsi* decree had several shortcomings as effective legislation. The weaknesses in the decree can here be only summarized: (1) Doubts continued—because of difficulties in determining a person's domicile—concerning the proper pastor before whom the marriage was to be contracted. (2) No exemption from the law was provided for baptized non-Catholics who consequently, if their marriages were to be valid, were to marry before a priest. (3) The most serious difficulty arose from the manner in which the new law was to be promulgated. The *Tametsi* decree stated: "This decree shall begin to take effect in every parish at the expiration of thirty days to be reckoned from the day of its first publication in that Church." The decree was actually never published in wide areas of the Church. Entire nations were left unaffected by it. In other nations the decree was published in some places while not in others; the result was again serious doubt concerning the validity or invalidity of many marriages. It was especially this last-mentioned weakness in the law that necessitated further legislation concerning the juridical form of marriage. The *NE TEMERE* decree of Aug. 2, 1907, attempted to settle the innumerable doubts resulting from the shortcomings of the *Tametsi* decree.

In summary, it can be said that in the decree *Tametsi* were contained all the means necessary for a successful reform in marriage law. However, further legislation had to be enacted to put the reform into universal effect.

Bibliography: E. FUS, *The Extraordinary Form of Marriage according to Canon 1098* (Catholic University of America Canon Law Studies 348; Washington 1954). J. CARBERRY, *The Juridical Form of Marriage* (Catholic University of America Canon Law Studies 84; Washington 1934). W. BOUDREAUX, *The "ab acatholicis nati" of Canon 1099.2* (Catholic University of America Canon Law Studies 227; Washington 1946). A. MARX, *The Declaration of Nullity of Marriage Contracted outside the Church* (Catholic University of America Canon Law Studies 182; Washington 1943).

[W. VAN OMMEREN]

TAMMUZ

God of springtime verdure in ancient Sumer and Babylonia. He became very popular in Syria and Phoenicia as *'ădōnî* (my lord) and in Hellenistic lands as Adonis. In Mesopotamian mythology he was the brother-consort of Ishtar, the goddess of fertility (J. B. Pritchard *Ancient Near Eastern Texts relating to the Old Testament* 84). According to the myth, Tammuz was killed every year by a wild boar but was rescued from the nether world by Ishtar, who brought him back to life and assured a new springtime. The natural cycle was thus symbolized by the myth. In ancient Egypt a similar myth was told of ISIS and Osiris. The 4th month of the year counting from the vernal equinox (June–July), when vegetation began to wither in the dry heat of summer, was called the month of Tammuz and was the occasion for a feast reenacting his descent to the nether regions. In pots filled with earth various herbs were planted and allowed to wither in the sun, symbolizing Tammuz's death. A wooden image of Tammuz, hidden in one of the pots, was then the object of a search by the women. When they found it, they buried it again or threw it, along with the pots, into a body of water amidst loud lamentation. Explicit reference to such a rite is found only once in the Bible (Ez 8.14), although the rite may be the background for the fast-growing plants of Is 17.10–11 that forebode an incurable blight.

Bibliography: *Encyclopedic Dictionary of the Bible,* translated and adapted by L. HARTMAN (New York, 1963) 2392–93. S. H. HOOKE, *Babylonian and Assyrian Religion* (New York 1953). A. MOORTGART, *Tammuz: Der Unsterblichkeitsglaube in der altorientalischen Bildkunst* (Berlin 1949). R. DE VAUX, "Sur quelques rapports entre Adonis et Osiris," *Revue Biblique* 42 (1933) 31–56.

[H. MUELLER]

TANCHELM

Medieval heretic, early critic of both the clergy and the sacramental system (especially the Eucharist) of the Church; d. Antwerp, Belgium, *c.* 1115. Historical sources give contradictory estimates of this man, whose activity centered in northern France and Flanders, especially Antwerp. One school described him as a gentle, humble, religious layman who, like many others of his day (*see* POVERTY MOVEMENT), was concerned about the spiritual life of his contemporaries, especially priests. Yet a letter by a Utrecht canon (*Monumenta Germaniae Scriptores* 16:42) to the archbishop of Cologne portrays Tanchelm as a fanatic. Obviously his preaching was capable of arousing excessive passions on all sides. The Life of NORBERT OF XANTEN (*Monumenta Germaniae Scriptores*12:690–691) says that a priest in "excessive zeal" cracked Tanchelm on the head and killed him. It was Tanchelm's rampant heresy that led the local bishop, Burchard of Cambrai, to invite Norbert of Xanten and the newly formed PREMONSTRATENSIANS to Antwerp in 1124. There Norbert's preaching and the new Premonstratensian foundation at St. Michael's, under the direction of Waltman of Antwerp, confuted Tanchelm's attack on priests and succeeded in renewing devotion to the Eucharist. A window in Antwerp cathedral recalls the Premonstratensian victory over Tanchelm.

Bibliography: C. J. KIRKFLEET, *History of Saint Norbert* (St. Louis 1916). É. AMANN, *Dictionnaire de théologie catholique,* ed. A. VACANT, 15 v. (Paris 1903–50; Tables générales 1951–) 15.1:38–40. A. HAUCK, *Kirchengeschichte Deutschlands,* 5 v. (9th ed. Berlin-Leipzig 1958) 4:95–97, 380. A. BORST, *Die Religion in Geschichte und Gegenwart,* 7 v. (3rd ed. Tübingen 1957–65) 6:610. J. PISTORIUS, *Lexikon für Theologie und Kirche,* ed. J. HOFER and K. RAHNER, 10 v. (2d, new ed. Freiburg 1957–65) 9:1287–88.

[L. L. RUMMEL]

TANCRED

Norman crusader; b. probably in the mid-1070s; d. Antioch, 1112. Tancred was a member of the Norman house of Hauteville, which had led the conquest of southern Italy and Sicily in the 11th century, and the nephew of Bohemund, Prince of Taranto and son of Robert Guiscard; he was born to Bohemund's half sister Emma and a Norman noble. Though without an inheritance, he possessed strong qualities of leadership, as contemporary sources reveal. In 1096 he joined his uncle in leading the Norman contingent from southern Italy on the First CRUSADE. Like Bohemund, he disliked and mistrusted the Byzantines and early embarked on a course to benefit himself at their expense. He took a leading role in the capture of ANTIOCH (June 3, 1098), which his uncle seized and held in his own name. Tancred also participated in the taking of Jerusalem and became Lord of Galilee (1099) and chief lieutenant to GODFREY OF BOUILLON, the Defender of the Holy Sepulcher. Tancred's ambition aimed at the throne of the Kingdom of JERUSALEM for himself and later for his uncle, Bohemund, but without success. The last part of his life was spent at Antioch (*see* CRUSADERS' STATES), where he ruled during the absence of Bohemund. Although captured by the Turks, he obtained his release and spent several years defending Antioch and his own domains in Cilicia.

Bibliography: RALPH OF CAEN, *Gesta Tancredi in expeditione Hierosolymitana* (*Recueil des historiens des croisades: Historiens occidentaux* 3; Paris 1866) 599–716. R. L. NICHOLSON, *Tancred* (Chicago 1940). S. RUNCIMAN, *A History of the Crusades*, 3 v. (Cambridge, England 1951–54) v.1.

[J. M. POWELL]

TANNER, ADAM

Jesuit theologian; b. Innsbruck, April 14, 1572; d. Unken, near Salzburg, May 25, 1632. Tanner, whom Mathias Scheeben singled out as the one great German theologian of the 17th century [*Handbuch der Dogmatik* v. 1 (Freiburg 1873) 452], entered the Society of Jesus in 1590. In Ingolstadt he studied under Gregory of Valencia and Jacobus Gretser. After ordination in 1597, he lectured on controversial and moral theology in Munich for five years. His *Relatio compendiaria* (Munich 1602) gave an account of the Catholic-Lutheran debates in Regensburg (Nov. 28 to Dec. 8, 1601). Tanner went to Regensburg as alternate speaker for the Catholic side. On the third day Gretser's sickness and lack of preparation forced his replacement by Tanner, who proceeded to turn the tide of argument. This success led to his appointment as professor in Ingolstadt (1603–18). In this period he defended Paul V against the Venetian government, wrote *Ketzerische Luthertum* (Ingolstadt 1608) against the Lutheran doctrine of justification, and compiled his controversial lectures in *Dioptra Fidei* (Ingolstadt 1617). A call to the University of Vienna (1618) interrupted Tanner's Ingolstadt teaching. In Vienna he began his magnum opus, *Theologia Scholastica,* but the Viennese libraries proved insufficient; and so, despite pressure from the Austrian emperor and the cardinal of Vienna, Tanner returned to Ingolstadt in the summer of 1619. After eight years his summa appeared in four volumes (v. 1, 2 Ingolstadt 1626; v. 3, 4 Ingolstadt 1627). Immediately after its publication Tanner was sent to Prague to serve as first Jesuit chancellor of the university. After 13 months doctors ordered him to return to the air of his native Tirol. In May 1631 he was back in Ingolstadt; but within a year illness and the advancing Swedish troops forced him to flee, and he died while en route to his native land.

Tanner's *Theologia Scholastica* follows the order of St. Thomas's *Summa Theologiae,* but is doctrinally dependent on Vasquez, Lessius, and especially Suárez. Noted for clarity and conciseness, he was careful to distinguish between dogma, the Molinist system, and his own opinions. Tanner's treatment of *scientia media* is a model of argumentation. To the question *an sit?* he responds with the classic Molinist texts (1 Samuel 23.10–12; Matthew 11.21) and with selected patristic citations. Tanner intimates his preference for congruous efficacious grace by arguing for *scientia media* from Augustine's words, ''cuius autem miseretur, sic eum [Deus] vocat, quomodo scit ei congruere, ut vocantem non respuat'' (*Ad Simplicianum* 1.2.13; PL 40:119). After adding four rational arguments for scientia media, Tanner turns to the question *quid sit?* and gives his original speculative explanation of the *medium-in-quo* of this knowledge. Whereas MOLINA had stressed the eminent perfection of divine knowing to the exclusion of any kind of object, Tanner postulates a quasi reflex grasp of the divine essence, specifically as the *ratio objectiva* for all possible universes of created being. Supposing *scientia media,* Tanner so explains providence, predestination, and reprobation as to stress God's loving choice more than the free decisions of men. He departs from Molina and Lessius to hold predestination before God's vision of final merit. God prevails by selecting perfectly adapted graces that are certain to produce consent in the elect; the reprobate are denied these congruous graces.

Some notable positions taken by Tanner were: in certain transactions interest can be licitly demanded; infidels (but not heretics) are mostly in invincible ignorance and should have full liberty of conscience; Mary was not excepted from original sin; the heavens are an incorruptible Aristotelian firmament. Tanner wrote forcefully against the irresponsible prosecution of witchcraft raging in southern Germany in his time. In his treatise on angels, he charged that many people were simply deluded on witchcraft; and, writing on justice, he excoriated the methods of torture, forced denunciation, and wholesale execution. This position left him open to suspicion of being in league with evil powers, but in condemning abuses he helped bring some moderation in the second half of the century.

Bibliography: J. GOETZ, *Dictionnaire de théologie catholique*, ed. A. VACANT et al., 15 v. (Paris 1903–50; Tables Générales 1951–) 15.1:40–47. W. LURZ, *Adam Tanner und die Gnadenstreitigkeiten des 17. Jahrhundert* (Breslau 1932). C. SOMMERVOGEL et al., *Bibliothèque de la Compagnie de Jésus*, 11 v. (Brussels-Paris 1890–1932; v.12, suppl. 1960) 7:1843–55. B. DUHR, *Die Stellung der Jesuiten bei den deutschen Hexenprozessen* (Cologne 1900).

[J. WICKS]

TANNER, EDMUND

Bishop of Cork and Cloyne, Ireland; b. *c.* 1526; d. Ossory, Ireland, June 4, 1579. It seems he was already a priest when at 39 he entered the Society of Jesus. He studied for a year in Rome, and in 1567 was sent with Father Rochfort to the University of Dillingen, where he took his D.D. Because of great illness he was forced to leave the Society. On Nov. 5, 1574, he was appointed bishop of Cork and Cloyne, and made commissary apostolic as well. This latter function gave him wide faculties in the Dioceses of Cashel and Dublin and in Dublin's suffragan sees in the absence of their own ordinaries. He set out from Rome in May 1575 to face a situation of extreme difficulty and danger; government correspondence is full of the reports of spies set to watch the priests. Tanner and his chaplain were arrested by Sir William Drury, President of Munster, and lodged in Clonmel jail, where Tanner was visited by a schismatic bishop, probably Patrick Walsh of Waterford and Lismore, whom Tanner reconciled to the Church. Released shortly afterward, ''he suffered great penury and want as well in prison as out of it'' and died exhausted by labor and ill-health.

Bibliography: E. HOGAN *Distinguished Irishmen of the Sixteenth and Seventeenth Centuries* (London 1894) 17–19, *passim.* W. P. BURKE, *History of Clonmel* (Waterford 1907) 36–37.

[J. J. MEAGHER]

TANQUEREY, ADOLPHE ALFRED

Sulpician theologian; b. Blainville, Normandy, May 1, 1854; d. Aix-en-Provence, Feb. 21, 1932. Tanquerey attended the College of Saint-Lô and studied for the priesthood at the diocesan seminary of Coutances (1873) and at Saint-Sulpice in Paris (1875). After graduate work at Rome (1876), he received his doctorate in theology in 1878. In the same year he was ordained and entered the Society of St. Sulpice. He was then assigned to the Sulpician novitiate, but this period was interrupted by his appointment to teach philosophy at Nantes from December 1878 to March 1879. After completing the novitiate he taught dogmatic theology in the seminary at Rodez (1879–87). In the summer of 1887 he went to St. Mary's Seminary, Baltimore, Md., where he taught dogmatic theology (1887–95) and canon law (1889–93). He played an important part in expanding the program of theological studies at St. Mary's. Recognizing the acute need for suitable textbooks in theology, he published his *Synopsis theologiae dogmaticae* (2 v., 1894) and in 1896 his *Synopsis theologiae dogmaticae fundamentalis.* From 1896 to 1902 he was professor of moral theology at St. Mary's and also served as its vice president.

His *Synopsis theologiae moralis* (2 v.) appeared in 1902. In the same year Tanquerey returned to Saint-Sulpice in Paris, where he taught moral theology until 1905, when the third volume of his work on moral theology was published. He left Paris in 1906 and retired to the Issy seminary, where from 1907 he acted as spiritual director for the English-speaking seminarians. In 1911 he published an abridged version of his work on dogmatic theology and two years later he did the same for his work on moral theology.

About 1915 he was named a consultor of the superior general, and from 1915 to 1926 he served as superior of the solitude, the Sulpician novitiate at Issy. These years were also devoted to a study of the spiritual life and the preparation of his *Précis de théologie ascetique et mystique* (1923). From 1921 to 1927 he published articles on spirituality and pedagogy in various French and English publications. In 1926 his *Dogme generateurs de la piété* was published and the same year marked the end of work as superior of the solitude. The next year he returned to the major seminary at Aix-en-Provence. From 1927 until his death he devoted himself to various works for the clergy and the publication of several booklets on spiritual topics. Tanquerey's textbooks have been widely used in seminaries in the U.S., France, and other countries. The various volumes of his theology have seen many editions, several of which were done by the author himself. The works were noted for their comprehensive treatments of the matter and for their emphasis on the practical application of the speculative truths. His treatise on ascetical theology, still recognized as a standard work, deals with the principles, nature, and means of the spiritual life and with the three classical ways. The book is comprehensive in scope and was written with the conviction that dogmatic truth is the foundation of ascetical theology and the source of true, balanced piety.

Bibliography: F. CIMETIER, *Dictionnaire de théologie catholique,* ed. A. VACANT et al., 15 v. (Paris 1903–50; Tables générales 1951–) 15.1:47–48.

[J. A. LAUBACHER]

TANSI, CYPRIAN MICHAEL IWENE, BL.

Baptized Michael; Trappist priest; b. Igboezunu near Aguleri, southwestern Nigeria, September 1903; d. Leicester, England, Jan. 20, 1964. Named Iwene (''sorrow will not kill you'') by his parents, Tabansi (d. 1904) and Ejikwevi (d. 1922). After his father's death, Iwene was raised by relatives who sent him (1909) to Saint Joseph's school where he was baptized Michael in 1912. Although an accident left him blind in his left eye, he completed school in 1919, and began teaching at his alma mater (1919–22), then at Holy Trinity Primary School in Onitsa (1922–24), and was appointed headmaster at Saint Joseph's in 1924. Michael entered the new seminary at Igbariam in 1925 and was ordained priest (Dec. 19, 1937) in Onitsha's cathedral, the second native priest of the diocese. During his years of active ministry he served in the parishes of Nnewi, Dunukofia (1939–45), Akpu (1945–49), and his hometown of Aguleri (1949–40). He catechized and baptized the future Cardinal Francis Arinze, who attended Tansi's funeral and concelebrated his beatification Mass.

Following a pilgrimage to Rome, Tansi joined (1950) the Trappists as an oblate at Mount Saint Bernard, Leicestershire, England and took the name Cyprian. Administrative problems delayed his entry into the novitiate until Dec. 8, 1953. He made his solemn profession Dec. 8, 1956. In the silence of the monastery, Father Cyprian wrote voluminously. As he gained a reputation for holiness, many came to the monastery to seek his prayers on their behalf. In 1963 his abbot announced that he had been appointed novice master for a monastery opening in Cameroon, but Father Cyprian died before he could undertake the assignment.

Tansi was initially buried in Leicestershire, but in 1988 his remains were exhumed and interred in the priests' cemetery near Onitsha's cathedral in Nigeria. Following his beatification they were translated to the parish church at Aguleri. The archdiocesan process for Tansi's beatification began in July of 1981; the decree of his heroic virtues was promulgated in 1995; a miracle was approved on June 25, 1996. He was beatified at Onitsha, Nigeria, by John Paul II, March 22, 1998.

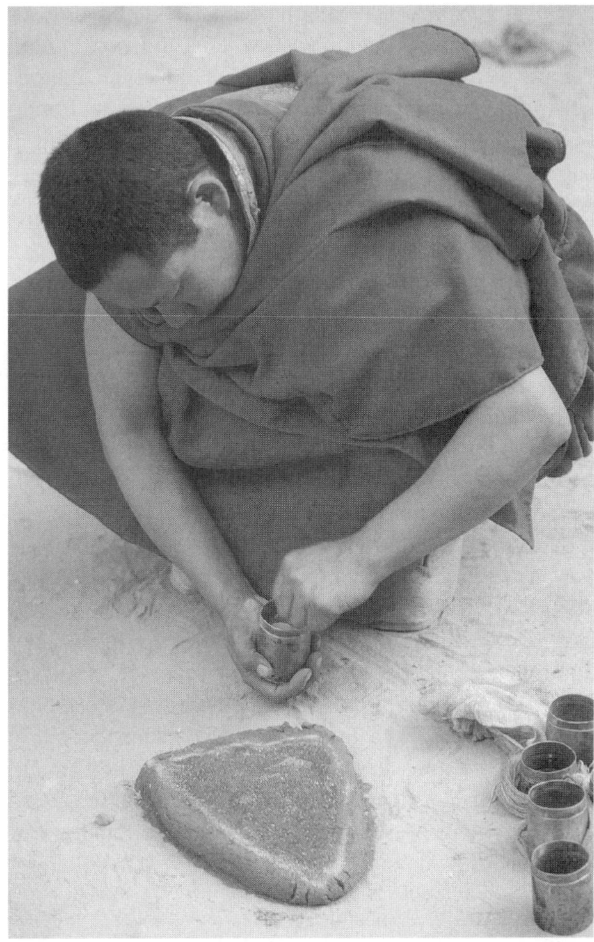

Lama meditates on charm during Tantric ritual, Hemis, Ladakh, South India. (©Charles & Josette Lenars/CORBIS)

Bibliography: A. E. ISICHEI, *Entirely for God: The Life of Michael Iwene Tansi* (London and Kalamazoo, Mich. 1980; Ibadan, Nigeria 1981). V. O. C. UMEGAKWE, *Fr. Tansi Solidarity Prayer Movement* (Onitsha, Nigeria 1989). E. E. NWOSU, *Pursuit of holiness* (Onitsha, Nigeria 1997).

[K. I. RABENSTEIN]

TANTRISM

The name of a religious movement that spread throughout India from about the 5th century A.D. It affected not only HINDUISM but also BUDDHISM and JAINISM. It was derived from the non-Vedic religion of the country and was connected especially with the worship of the Earth-Mother and her power (*shakti*). In contrast with the earlier Vedic religion, which was ascetic and confined to the higher castes, Tantrism was based on the development of the body and its powers and was open to all castes. Its method (*sādhana*) was the use of material things—*mantras* (sacred words), *mudrās* (symbolic gestures), and *maṇḍalas* (symbolic designs)—to acquire supernatural powers. Haṭha YOGA, with its aim of obtaining complete control of the body, was one of its typical products. In some forms of Tantrism great license was practiced, and sexual union was used as a method of obtaining supernatural power.

[B. GRIFFITHS]

TANUCCI, BERNARDO

Marchese, Neapolitan statesman who, in concert with other chief ministers of the Bourbon courts of Portugal, France, and Spain, worked tirelessly to oppose the papacy and to expel and suppress the Jesuits; b. Stia, Tuscany, Feb. 20, 1698; d. near Naples, April 29, 1783. Although born in poverty, Tanucci through generous patrons received a liberal education and completed law studies at the University of Pisa, where in 1725 he was assigned a chair of jurisprudence. Engaging in frequent controversies, he became known for vehemence and invective rather than for any notable erudition. Readiness to resort to drastic action, so evident in his later life, found early expression in the riots that he incited among the Pisans in his effort to prevail over a rival named Grandi, with whom he was quarreling over the Pandects of Justinian.

Minister of State. In 1734, when the future Charles III of Spain was marching through Tuscany to seize Naples, he heard of Tanucci's opposition to the right of asylum for criminals and to the claims of the Holy Roman Empire in Italy and persuaded Tanucci to accompany him. For nearly a quarter of a century, Tanucci served as Charles's adviser and chief minister for Neapolitan affairs; even after he had become king of Spain in 1759, Charles III sought Tanucci's advice.

As chief of the Council of Regents that was established to rule the Kingdom of Naples for Charles's young son Ferdinand, Tanucci controlled the royal household as well as the government; even after Ferdinand should have assumed the responsibilities of government, Tanucci kept him so steadily diverted by the pleasures of the chase and other frivolities that governmental responsibilities were left in his own hands.

Tanucci was especially careful that each dispute between the Church and the kingdom was resolved in favor of the State. The Concordat of 1741, instead of protecting the Church, was exploited by Tanucci to sanction and continue irregularities. He arbitrarily limited the number of religious and priestly vocations; he merged dioceses and prevented episcopal vacancies from being filled, so that diocesan revenues could be confiscated; and he abolished tithes and saw to it that wills that had been made in favor of the Church or its charitable organizations were altered or set aside so that money could be secured to balance deficits caused by Tanucci's unwise fiscal policies. Only (St.) Alphonsus LIGUORI'S indomitable persistence enabled him to found the Redemptorist Order, over Tanucci's opposition. The teaching authority of the Church was attacked, the general acceptance of Gallicanism was advocated, and the Church's efforts to prevent the spread of Jansenism were frustrated. For a time Tanucci had masked his hostility toward the Church and the Jesuits so effectively that the general of the order, Ignatius Visconti, declared him a special beneficiary of the spiritual works of the society.

Tanucci's energies were at times so concentrated on strengthening the State at the expense of the Church that the kingdom's external security was neglected. This negligence permitted an English fleet to slip into a position from which it forced Tanucci's government to sign a humiliating pledge of neutrality. Despite his preoccupation with the conflict with the Church, Tanucci always maintained some of his early interest in education, in jurisprudence, and in research. He directed the revision of the curriculum of the University of Naples, established a commission to revise the legal code, and began the excavations at Pompeii and Herculaneum.

Expulsion of the Jesuits. When Charles III, for reasons that had in large measure been suggested by Tanucci, but which the king said were to ''remain unrevealed in our royal bosom,'' expelled the Jesuits from Spain early in April of 1767, it was anticipated that Tanucci, despite his emphatic denials, would soon take similar action in the Kingdom of Naples. On November 3 of the same year, Tanucci struck with characteristic violence. Whereas the soldiers of Charles III had waited until dawn to knock at the doors of the Jesuit residences to gain admission, left the furniture intact, and allowed the fathers to take a change of clothing as they departed, Tanucci's men smashed the doors down at midnight, shattered the furniture, and hustled the fathers to the wharves with nothing but the clothing they were wearing.

Although Clement XIII could not deter Tanucci from expelling the Jesuits as Sebastião POMBAL, Gilbert CHOISEUL, and Pedro Aranda had done, he refused to yield to their insistence that the order be suppressed throughout the world. Just before the pope's death in 1769, Tanucci issued a pamphlet declaring that the pope was obliged to comply with the demands of the Catholic governments, and after the pope's death a special edition of the pamphlet was directed to each cardinal with the obvious intent of influencing the upcoming conclave.

For several years Tanucci had opposed Cardinal Ganganelli's prospective candidacy and even after the

Bourbon faction in the conclave had voted for the cardinal, Tanucci's disappointment was reflected in the coldness of the congratulations that reached Clement XIV from Naples. Between the election of Clement XIV in the spring of 1769 and the summer of 1773, Tanucci's bullying demands for the suppression of the Jesuits joined those of Joseé Moñino, who represented Charles III in Rome. Writing to Charles III just before the Brief of Suppression was issued in 1773, Tanucci expressed fear that he would not live until the Jesuits had been suppressed throughout the world, and with the evident purpose of averting this disappointment told another of the stories that was to impel Louis XV to call him "the most mischievous mendacious caviller that ever walked the earth." The story concerned someone caught while stalking King Ferdinand in Naples. According to Tanucci this would-be assassin was a Jesuit hireling from Terracina. After the death of Clement XIV, Tanucci wrote to Charles explaining that although the Jesuits really had not poisoned the pope, they had allowed him to believe he had been poisoned, and the antidotes taken under this misapprehension had killed him.

Tanucci continued to control the government of the Kingdom of Naples and to exchange advice with Charles until the marriage of King Ferdinand of Naples to Princess Marie Caroline of Austria. The new queen succeeded in aligning the government of Naples with that of Hapsburg Austria, rather than with Bourbon Spain, and Tanucci. after a determined struggle to prevent this realignment, was forced to resign in 1777. He withdrew to the countryside near Naples. where he died, friendless and alone, in 1783.

Bibliography: L. PASTOR, *The History of the Popes from the Close of the Middle Ages,* 40 v. (London–St. Louis 1938–61) v. 36–39. P. CALÀ-ULLOA, *Di Bernardo Tanucci e dei suoi tempi* (Naples 1875). C. LO SORDO, *Tanucci e la Reggenza al tempo di Ferdinando IV* (Bari 1912). H. M. ACTON, *The Bourbons of Naples (1734–1825)* (New York 1958). E. PONTIER, *Enciclopedia Italiana di scienzi, littere ed arti,* 36 v. (Rome 1929–39) 33:241.

[R. F. COPELAND]

TANZANIA, THE CATHOLIC CHURCH IN

Formerly the regions of Tanganika and Zanzibar, the United Republic of Tanzania is located on the east coast of Africa, and is bound on the north by Kenya, on the east by the Indian Ocean, on the south by Mozambique and Malawi, on the southwest by Zambia, on the west by the Democratic Republic of Congo, Burundi and Rwanda, and on the northeast by Uganda and Lake Victoria. Highlands in the north and south drop to a central plateau that descends further to coastal plains in the east. Mount Kilimanjaro, south of the border with Kenya, is the highest point on the African continent. The climate varies with the terrain, shifting from temperate in the higher elevations to tropical near the coast. Tanzania includes the Zanzibar island group, 22.5 miles east of the Tanzanian mainland in the Indian Ocean, which contains Zanzibar, Pemba and Mafia. Natural resources include hydropower, tin, phosphates, iron ore, coal, diamonds and other gems, gold and nickel; agricultural products consist of coffee, sisal, tea, cotton, ground nuts, tobacco, corn, wheat, fruits, vegetables and livestock. Cloves are produced on the island of Zanzibar.

Capital: Dar-es-Salaam.
Size: 362,800 sq. miles.
Population: 35,306,125 in 2000.
Languages: Kiswahili (Kiunguju), English, Arabic; many local languages are spoken regionally.
Religions: 9,532,655 Catholics (27%), 14,122,450 Muslims (40%), 3,530,510 Protestants (10%), 7,061,225 practice indigenous beliefs (20%), 1,059,285 without religious affiliation.

Both Tanganika and Zanzibar were governed as British mandates following World War I, having been British protectorates in the 19th century. Soon after Zanzibar gained its independence and proclaimed itself a republic on Jan. 12, 1964, it united with Tanganyika (independent in 1961) to form Tanzania under President Julius Nyerere. Mdugu Ali Hassan, who further stabilized the economy of the region, succeeded him. In 1992 multiple political parties were legalized and three years later the region held its first free democratic elections in two decades. The predominately Muslim population of Zanzibar included some 120 tribes, each with its distinctive dialect and customs, and by 2000 Islamic fundamentalism began to cause political discord on the island. In the late 1990s the mainland began to suffer economic stress due to the many refugees from Mozambique, Burundi and Rwanda that entered the country to avoid the violence in their respective countries.

History. Augustinian priests who accompanied Vasco da GAMA landed on the island of Zanzibar in 1499. The island remained Portuguese until the Arabs seized control and expelled all priests in 1698. Catholic missionary activity ceased from 1698 until 1860, when three priests and six sisters arrived. Zanzibar played an important role in the beginnings of the Church in East Africa because the first missionaries to Tanganyika and Kenya came from there. The HOLY GHOST FATHERS who arrived on Zanzibar in 1863 formed the first Catholic mission in Tanzania five years later, and were entrusted with the re-

Metropolitans	Suffragans
Arusha	Mbulu, Moshi, Same
Dar-es-Salaam	Dodoma, Mahenge, Morogoro, Tanga, Zanzibar
Mwanza	Bukoba, Geita, Musoma, Rulenge, Shinyanga
Songea	Iringa, Lindi, Mbeya, Mbinga, Mtwara, Njombe, Tunduru-Masasi
Tabora	Kahama, Kigoma, Mpanda, Singida, Sumbawanga

gion in 1872. By 2000 Zanzibar was almost totally Muslim, while on the mainland Muslim influences were in a minority and remained in the northern regions.

The islands belonged to the Vicariate Apostolic of Zanzibar, erected in 1906, and then to the diocese of Mombasa and Zanzibar, created in 1955, whose bishop resided in Mombasa, Kenya. In 1953 the hierarchy of Tanzania was established with two metropolitan sees. In 1965 the archbishop of Dar-es-Salaam was made the apostolic administrator of Zanzibar and Pemba, where the Precious Blood Sisters had charge of a government-owned home for the aged, tubercular patients and lepers, and ran a school in Zanzibar for children of all faiths.

By 2000 there were 769 parishes tended by 1,379 diocesan and 714 religious priests. Other religious included approximately 610 brothers and 6,700 sisters, many of whom operated the Church' nine primary and 172 secondary schools and cared for the large refugee populations to the north. While an active and vital Catholic Church worked to maintain friendly relations with Muslim leaders on both the mainland and the islands, an increase in Islamic fundamentalism and the imposition of Islamic law in certain regions caused increasing tensions between the two faiths by 2000. In April of 2000 a church was burned in a predominately Muslim region of Zanzibar, the second attempt on that property in three years. The constitution of April 25, 1977 (revised in October of 1984) respected freedom of religion and established Tanzania as a secular state. The government did grant the Church tax-exempt status, but discouraged proselytizing when offensive to other faiths.

Bibliography: *Le missioni cattoliche: Storia, geographia, statistica* (Rome 1950) 178–190. *Bilan du Monde* 2:827–833, 2:928–929. *Annuario Pontificio* has annual statistics on all dioceses.

[D. W. ROBINSON/EDS.]

TAPARELLI D'AZEGLIO, LUIGI

Jesuit philosopher and pioneer sociologist (baptized Prospero); b. Turin, Nov. 24, 1793; d. Rome, Sept. 20, 1862.

When he had completed his early studies in Siena and Turin, he was named by Napoleon to the military school of Saint-Cyr in Paris in 1809, but after six months there he obtained a dispensation to study for the priesthood. Upon the fall of Napoleon, Taparelli's father, Cesare, was made the ambassador of Victor Emmanuel I to the Holy See, and Cesare took his sons with him to Rome.

In 1814 the Society of Jesus was restored and Luigi entered the reopened novitiate of San Andrea. He was ordained in 1820 and became the first rector of the restored Roman College in 1824. He was made provincial of the Naples province in 1829, and in 1833 he was sent to Palermo where he taught philosophy for 15 years.

He became associated with *La Civiltà Cattolica* in 1849, and thus began his great series of writings on socio-economic problems. He labored to resuscitate St. Thomas's teachings on the natural law and apply them to the problems of the day. His chief work, *Saggio teoretico di diritto naturale appogiato sul fatto* (Palermo 1840–43, 5 v., subsequently reedited and translated many times), was, in a way, the beginning of modern political sociology. In it he developed the position that civil government originates in an extension of paternal power through the patriarchal head of groups of families. He alludes to a form of international organization, which he calls an ethnarchy, to which, he says, growing relationships between societies tend by the very nature of the societies. In his description of this higher and more comprehensive government, the natural outgrowth of lesser governments, many have seen an anticipation of the United Nations.

In addition to this work, a long series of articles and reviews in *La Civiltà Cattolica,* and monographs in political science, he produced *Esame critico degli ordini rappresentativi nella società moderna* (Rome 1854). Most notable of his series of articles in *La Civiltà Cattolica* is the one begun in 1856 on political economics, interrupted by his death, and republished in French by Jacquin: *Essai sur les principes philosophiques de l'éonomie politique* (Paris 1943).

Bibliography: M. CONNOLLY, ''A Pioneer Catholic Sociologist: Luigi Taparelli S. I., 1793–1862,'' *Irish Jesuit Directory and Year Book* 20 (1947) 167–176. A. PEREGO, ''L'imposta progressiva nel pensiero del P. L. Taparelli d'Azeglio,'' *La civiltà cattolica* 98.4 (1947) 136–144.

[W. J. FULCO]

TAPIA, GONZALO DE

Founder and first martyr of the Jesuit missions of North America; b. León, Spain, 1561; d. Tavoropa, Sinaloa, New Spain, July 10, 1594. At 16 he entered the novitiate of Villagarcía under the renowned master Baltasar ÁLVAREZ. After completing his studies, he volunteered for the missions and reached Mexico on Oct. 10, 1584. During the next year he taught metaphysics, learned Nahuatl, and was ordained. He then went west to Pátzcuaro, Michoacán, and began missionary excursions. In 1587 he went alone to the wild Chichimeca in Guanajuato. His humor, courage, and ready speech won them over, making possible the foundation of their town, San Luis de la Paz. He then wrote the General, Acquaviva, begging to be sent farther on. The Governor of Nueva Vizcaya, Rodrigo del Rio y Losa, a man of similar ideas, sensed that civilization would follow conversion. Viceregal permission was won, and the Provincial Díaz ordered him forward. With one companion, Martín Pérez, he rode 600 miles across the sierra to the Cahita people of northern Sinaloa and made his greatest conquest, some 10,000 conversions in three years. Two new companions, Santiago and Velasco, joined him in 1593, but the next year a medicine man, Nacabeda, plotted and executed Tapia's death. His mission formed the base for a broad advance.

It went on until it reached the present United States in Arizona and up through lower California. Tapia's heroic death brought hundreds to follow him and build his great memorial, the Christianity of northern New Spain.

Bibliography: W. E. SHIELS, *Gonzalo de Tapia (1561–1594) Founder of the First Permanent Jesuit Mission in North America* (New York 1934).

[W. E. SHIELS]

TAPPER, RUARD

Theologian; b. Enkhuysen, Belgium, Feb. 15, 1487; d. Brussels, March 2, 1559. He studied at the University of Louvain under the future pope ADRIAN VI. After his ordination, Tapper became dean of the faculty of arts at the university. In 1519, he was made a doctor in theology and taught in that faculty. He was named rector of the university in 1530. In 1537, he was appointed inquisitor general for all of the Low Countries. A man of great moderation but equal firmness, he announced that the policy of the INQUISITION would be ''to repress heresy, not by brute force, but by dint of sheer logic and teaching power.'' In 1545, he published a much-reprinted series of 59 dogmatic propositions for popular use. These formulated essential Catholic doctrine in a clear and precise way. They were especially commended by Pius IV in a brief issued in 1561. Tapper was called to assist at the Council of Trent in 1551 and had a notable part in the drafting of the doctrine on the Sacrament of Penance, considered in the 14th session. He returned to Louvain in 1552 and took part in the polemic against his former pupil Michael Baius (*see* BAIUS AND BAIANISM).

Bibliography: H. DE JONGH, *L'Ancienne faculté de théologie de Louvain au premier siècle de son existence, 1432–1540* (Louvain 1911). J. MERCIER, *Dictionnaire de théologie catholique,* ed. A. VACANT, 15 v. (Paris 1903–50; Tables générales 1951–) 15.1:52–54.

[C. R. MEYER]

TAPPOUNI, IGNATIUS GABRIEL

Cardinal, Catholic patriarch of Antioch of the Syrians; b. Mosul, Iraq, Nov. 3, 1879; d. Beirut, Lebanon, Jan. 29, 1968. He was baptized as Abdalahad Leo in an old Syrian Christian family, which in the late 18th century had entered the Syrian union with Rome. He spent ten years as a student in the Syro-Chaldean Seminary in his native city of Mosul and was ordained priest Nov. 9, 1902. His earliest years as a priest were spent in Mosul itself, first as teacher in the Syro-Chaldean Seminary and director of the Syrian Catholic school, then, after 1908, as secretary of the apostolic delegate to Mesopotamia, Jean Drure, O.C.D.

As Bishop. His growing reputation as a nonpartisan and capable administrator with a firm religious spirit led to his early episcopal nomination Sept. 12, 1912, as titular bishop of Danaba, but with an immediate change to the titular see of Batna because ''Danaba'' has an undignified quality in Arabic ears. He took the name Theophilus Gabriel at the time of his episcopal ordination Jan. 19, 1913, and began immediately to function as patriarchal vicar in Mardin, now in southeastern Turkey, which at that time was still officially the place of residence of the Syrian Catholic patriarch, although the reigning patriarch had taken up residence in Beirut.

Shortly after his arrival in Mardin, the difficulties of Christians in that part of the Ottoman Empire entered upon their gravest period; and on June 2, 1915, the Armenian Catholic Archbishop of Mardin, Ignatius Maloyan, faced with imminent imprisonment and eventually put to death, entrusted the administration of his see to Bishop Tappouni. In 1918 Tappouni himself was arrested by the Turkish authorities, accused of treason, court-martialed without regular trial, and imprisoned in Aleppo under threat of execution. The apostolic delegate in Istanbul succeeded in obtaining a stay of execution, and the Empress Zita of Austria, at the request of Pope Benedict XV, arranged for the Austrian ambassador to Turkey to intervene as well, so that the bishop was released October 7, as the English and French forces were occupying Syria. In the years immediately following, he was faced with the task of regrouping and rehabilitating the survivors of the massacres, a task which was not diminished when he was nominated Syrian archbishop of Aleppo, Feb. 24, 1921. Upon the death of the Patriarch Ignatius Ephrem II Rahmani the synod of bishops, on June 24, 1929, unanimously elected him as successor, and six days later he was enthroned in the cathedral in Beirut, with the name Ignatius Gabriel I. Pope Piux XI named him cardinal in the consistory of Dec. 16, 1935.

As Patriarch. His reign as patriarch saw the construction of the patriarchal residence in Beirut, a new seminary and summer residence at Sharfeh north of Beirut, and the beginning of a new cathedral in Beirut which he did not live to see finished. As the end of the French mandate in Syria and Lebanon approached he was active in the negotiations seeking to assure the rights of the Christian minorities in predominantly Muslim Syria. His liturgical concerns were reflected in the new edition of the West Syrian ferial office (1937) and pontifical (1950–52), and in the creation at the end of his reign of a commission for the revision of the Eucharistic liturgy. But it was with the quality of priestly formation in his Church that he was most interested, with a concern reflected in the attention he gave unceasingly to the development of the patriarchal seminary in Sharfeh. Always interested in the establishment of religious life in the Syrian Catholic Church, he had even as a young priest entertained the idea of establishing monastic life himself in the ancient monastery of Mar Behnam near Mosul, until he was dissuaded by the hierarchy. Although his community of Ephremite Sisters began to flourish before his death, his attempts as patriarch to establish a Syrian community of men never really succeeded.

His influence in Rome was perhaps greatest at the end of his life, when he served as one of the ten members, and the only Oriental member, of the council of presidents of Vatican Council II.

Bibliography: Archives of the Syrian Catholic Procuracy in Rome. *L'Osservatore Romano* (April 9, 1961) 6; (Jan. 31, 1968) 2.

[A. CODY]

TARASIUS, PATRIARCH OF CONSTANTINOPLE, ST.

Anti-iconoclast; b. Constantinople, *c.* 730; d. Constantinople, Feb. 18, 806 (feast, Feb. 25). A well-educated layman, and secretary to the Empress IRENE during her regency for her infant son, Tarasius was elected patriarch in December 784, by the priests and people of Constantinople at the insistence of the Empress. Consecrated on December 25, he sent a synodal letter to the pope announcing his election; to the letter he appended an orthodox profession of faith, particularly concerning veneration of images. Both Tarasius and Empress Irene then began preparations for an ecumenical council to condemn ICONOCLASM. Although he expressed his disapproval at the nomination of a layman as patriarch, Pope ADRIAN I recognized Tarasius, consented to the convocation of a council, and sent his legates. The first session of the Council, which assembled in Constantinople in 786, was disbanded by the rioting of iconoclastic-inspired imperial guards, and the following year it was reconvened at Nicaea under the presidency of Tarasius as the seventh ecumenical council. It condemned iconoclasm and defined the orthodox doctrine on the veneration of images.

Since the patriarch exercised leniency in dealing with bishops who had subscribed to iconoclasm, he was strongly criticized by the stricter faction within the Church and was forced by the monks to take strong action against simoniacal bishops. In 795 he was severely attacked for his failure to condemn the adulterous second marriage of Emperor Constantine VI, although after the deposition of the Emperor, Tarasius excommunicated the priest who had blessed the marriage.

Tarasius is credited with the composition of a refutation of the iconoclastic decisions of the Synod of 754 which was cited at the Third Council of Nicaea (787). His extant letters deal with the controversy over image worship. The sermon he preached on his installation as patriarch and another on the Presentation of Mary in the Temple are extant.

Bibliography: *Patrologia Graeca,* ed. J. P. MIGNE (Paris 1857–66) 98:1423–1500. J. D. MANSI, *Sacrorum Conciliorum nova et amplissima collectio,* (Florence-Venice 1757–98); reprinted and continued by L. PETIT and J. B. MARTIN (Paris 1889–1927; repr. Graz 1960–) 12:1119–28;13:208–356, 399–472. V. GRUMEL, *Les Regestes des actes du patriarcat de Constantinople* (Kadidoi-Bucharest 1932–) 12:350–373. É. AMANN, A. FLICHE and V. MARTIN, *Histoire de l'église depuis les origins jusqu'à nos jours* (Paris 1935–) 6:107–127. H. G. BECK, *Kirche und theologische Literatur im byzantinischen Reich* (Munich 1959) 489. G. OSTROGORSKY, *History of the Byzantine State,* tr. J. HUSSEY from 2d German ed. (Oxford 1956); American ed. by P. CHARANIS (New Brunswick, N. J. 1957) 158–163. IGNATIOS THE DEACON, *The Life of the Patriarch Tarasios,* trans. S. EFTHYMIADIS (Aldershot, Hampshire, U.K.; Brookfield, Vt. 1998).

[G. T. DENNIS]

TARDINI, DOMENICO

Prosecretary of state under PIUS XII, secretary of state under John XXIII; b. Rome, Feb. 29, 1888; d. Rome, July 30, 1961. After ordination (Sept. 20, 1912) Tardini became professor of sacramental theology and liturgy at the Roman Seminary and at the Propaganda College, *minutante* in the Congregation for Extraordinary Ecclesiastical Affairs (1921), and ecclesiastical assistant in the Italian Catholic Youth organization (November 1925). He became undersecretary in the above congregation (June 8, 1929), member of the Papal Congregation for Russia (1933), consultor of the Congregation for the Oriental Church (1934), substitute secretary of state and secretary of ciphering (1935), secretary for the Congregation for Extraordinary Ecclesiastical Affairs (1937), prosecretary of state (1952), and cardinal (Dec. 15, 1958).

Tardini was an upright and loyal character, somewhat rough externally, thorough and exact in comprehending and solving problems, and an outstanding statesman. Both his mind and glance were penetrating. In some instances, as in the Jewish question, he lacked dispassionate judgment. He was much interested in social problems and cooperated in an important fashion in John XXIII's encyclical *MATER ET MAGISTRA*. In other respects he was more conservative than John XXIII, but he acted as the Pope's right hand in the preparation of VATICAN COUNCIL II, a labor that exhausted his strength. Tardini founded the Casa Nazareth, a home in which he supplied board, lodging, and education for 60 orphan children until they were able to choose their calling. There he found recreation from his official duties.

Bibliography: W. SANDFUCHS, *Die Aussenminister der Päpste* (Munich 1962). C. F. CASULA, *Domenico Tardini, 1888–1961: l'azione della Santa Sede nella crisi fra le due guerre* (Rome 1988).

[R. LEIBER]

TARGUMS

Jewish Aramaic versions of the Old Testament. After explaining the origin and character of the Targums and their place in ancient Jewish liturgy, this article will treat the various Targums to the three main sections of the Hebrew Bible—the Pentateuch, the Prophets and the Writings. (A Targum is regarded as "related to" the book or books of the Bible of which it is a translation; hence the technical term, a Targum "to" the Pentateuch, etc.)

Origin and Character. The term "Targum" (plural, Targums or Targumim) comes from the Aramaic and post-Biblical Hebrew word *targûm,* meaning translation; in a limited sense used here it denotes specifically an Aramaic translation made by Jews of a book or books of the Hebrew OT. At some uncertain date after the Exile, but well before the Christian era, the majority of the Jews no longer understood Hebrew, since their vernacular in Babylonia and Palestine had become Aramaic. Because of the desire of having the people understand the doctrinal message of the Bible, particularly of the Pentateuch (Torah, Law), the custom was introduced of having the portions of the Law and the Prophets that were read in Hebrew in the SYNAGOGUES rendered into Aramaic in Aramaic-speaking communities. While the Jewish tradition (*Meg.* 3a) that traces the origin of Targums to the time of Ezra (based on Neh 8.8) is scarcely creditable, written Targums to some books (for example, the Targum to Job; see below), as well as oral translations of the Hebrew pericopes from the Law and the Prophets that were read in the synagogues, must have existed in New Testament times. Very probably there was also a Targum to the Psalms (cf, Mt 27.46; Mk 15.34).

Although the extant Targums differ greatly among themselves in language, nature and date of composition, they have certain common characteristics; thus, the anthropomorphisms and anthropopathisms of the Masoretic Text (MT) are generally avoided: God is said to act *ad extra* through his *memrā*' (word), a term used in this way only in Targumic literature: He guides Israel through [the shekinah (presence) of] His Glory; Israel sees not the Lord Himself but His Glory (*Tos. Meg.* 4.41; *Kidd.* 49a; confer, John 12.41; 1.14; etc.).

The Targums and the Synagogue Liturgy. In the Synagogue service before the time of Christ certain passages from the Pentateuch (Acts 15.21; 14.15) and the Prophets (Luke 4.16–21; Acts 13.14–15, 27) were read and, at least in Palestine, rendered into Aramaic [for details see G. F. Moore, *Judaism in the First Centuries of the Christian Era* (Cambridge, Mass. 1927–32) 1:296–307]. The rendering had to be given extempore, without the aid of written translations. Certain passages (for example, Gn 35.22; Ex 32.21–24; Nm 6.24–26) were read but not translated. Some current Aramaic translations (for example, of Lv 18.21; 22.28) were censured by the rabbis. It is probable that in early, even NT, times the OT was not read consecutively from service to service. The liturgical Targum may then have arisen only gradually, over a lengthy period. The Targum used for the common people would tend to be paraphrastic rather than literal, as is the case of the extant Palestinian Targum to the Pentateuch.

Targums to the Pentateuch. There are several Targums to the Pentateuch, the most important being the Babylonian, the Palestinian and the Samaritan Targums.

Babylonian Targum. This is the official Jewish Targum to the Books of Moses. It is customarily called the Onkelos Targum, although it is really an anonymous composition. The name of Onkelos, to whom it is ascribed in *bMeg.* 3a, is now generally considered to be merely a dialectic form of 'Ακύλας, i.e., Aquila, who is mentioned in the parallel passage of *jMeg.* 71c. Some scholars believe that Aquila's Greek version of the Hebrew OT was meant in both passages (See part 6 of this article). Onkelos is generally a literal translation that gives the correct halakic (*see* HALAKAH) understanding of nearly all the pertinent passages of the Pentateuch (not, however, of Lv 24.20). It is written in an Aramaic that imitates the Aramaic of the Bible. Although it was edited in Babylonia, probably between the second and the fifth centuries, to bring it into conformity with the Biblical text, the Mishnah and the Babylonian Talmud, Onkelos apparently originated in Palestine around the first Christian century. A comparison of certain passages of Onkelos with those of the Palestinian Targum indicates a relation between them (see W. Bacher, 60). Onkelos may actually be an early form of the Palestinian Targum later revised in Babylonia. Before its introduction from Babylonia *c.* A.D. 800, Onkelos was unknown to Palestinian Judaism, but it later replaced the older Palestinian Targum in Western Jewry. It was first printed at Bologna in 1482 and often later, for example, at Sabbioneta in 1557, and by A. Berliner with an excellent introduction (Leipzig 1882–84). A. Sperber published a new edition based on Yemenite manuscripts [*The Bible in Aramaic I* (Leiden 1959)]. In the West Onkelos was pointed with Tiberian (Western) vowels; the Yemenite manuscripts have a mixture of Eastern and Western vowel points. A. Díez Macho published Onkelos from manuscripts with Eastern vowel points for the Madrid POLYGLOT BIBLE [see *Vetus Testamentum,* 8 (1958) 113–133]. A Latin version of Onkelos is given in B. Walton's Polyglot Bible. An English translation (not always faithful) was published by J. W. Etheridge [*The Targums* . . . (2 v., London 1862–65)].

The Palestinian Targum. This is a paraphrastic translation of the Pentateuch that was current in Palestine and among Jews of Palestinian origin before it was replaced by the Onkelos Targum. Unlike Onkelos, the Palestinian Targum was never issued in an official edition, so that it is now known in several different forms. It has been preserved in the Codex Neofiti 1, in portions of Pseudo-Jonathan, in fragments from the Cairo Geniza, in the so-called Fragment Targum, in glosses (Tosefta) on Targum manuscripts and in rabbinic citations from the second to the 16th century.

The Codex Neofitì 1 of the Vatican Library, written at the beginning of the 15th century, was identified as a manuscript of the Palestinian Targum by A. Díez Macho between 1949 and 1956 [see *Vetus Testamentum,* 7 (1959) 222–245; *Christian News from Israel* (July 1962) 19–25]. It is a translation of the entire Pentateuch into good and relatively old Palestinian Aramaic. While the geographical data [see *Vetus Testamentum,* 7 (1959) 229] may point to the second Christian century as the date of composition, Codex Neofiti 1 itself appears to bear traces of later recension and to be in its present form a copy of a text that was made no earlier than the fifth century. The following passages show how the Mishnah with its Talmudic halakah compares with its Targumic renderings: confer, *Meg.* 4.9 with Leviticus 18.21; *Meg.* 4.10 with Genesis 35.22; Exodus ch. 32; Numbers 6.24–26; *jMeg.* 4.9.75c (*c.* A.D. 350) with Leviticus 22.28. Its translation of Genesis 6.2, 4 reproduces verbally the exegesis of R. Simeon ben Yohai (*c.* A.D. 150); confer, *Genesis Rabba* on Genesis 6.2, 4.

In the 14th century mention was made of a translation (*targûm*) of the Torah of which the author was said to be a certain Jonathan (ben Uzziel), a title due probably to a wrong solution of the abbreviation TJ as Targum of Jonathan instead of Targum of Jerusalem; hence the modern name of Pseudo-Jonathan. It is a translation that essentially represents the Palestinian Targum, but its text has been made to conform in many passages to that of Onkelos. It has some late references [for example, in Gn 21.21 (seventh century); Ex 26.9; Nm 24.24] and many paraphrases found in no other text of the Palestinian Targum. It has at least 12 antihalakic passages that are similar to the halakah of PHILO JUDAEUS and the Karaites. In many passages of halakah [see A. Marmorstein, *Zeitschrift für die alttestamentliche Wissenschaft,* 49 (1931) 234–235] and midrashic paraphrase, Pseudo-Jonathan is very old and probably pre-Christian. Some scholars, for example, P. E. Kahle [*Cairo Geniza* (2d ed. Oxford 1959) 203–204], would date its translation of Deuteronomy 33.11 to *c.* 130 B.C. The origin of Pseudo-Jonathan's composite text and the earlier history of its transmission are important, but unsolved, problems. It was first published at Venice in 1591; it was later uncritically edited from a manuscript of the British Museum by M. Ginsburger [*Pseudo-Jonathan* . . . (Berlin 1903)]; a new edition of the same manuscript is being prepared for the Madrid Polyglot.

The fragments of the Palestinian Targum from the Cairo GENIZA were published mainly by Kahle [*Masoreten des Westens* (Stuttgart 1930) 2:1–62; for other fragments see *Christian News* . . . 64], who dates the earliest manuscripts to the seventh and eighth centuries; J. L. Teicher, however, claims none is earlier than the mid-ninth century [*Vetus Testamentum,* (1951) 125–129; also see A. Díez Macho,*Vetus Testamentum,* 8 (1958) 116].

The so-called Fragment Targum, of which four manuscripts are known, translates only certain portions of the Pentateuch and is probably a collection of glosses on the Palestinian Targum taken from the manuscripts of Onkelos. It was published first at Venice in 1517; and later, in the Walton Polyglot (1654–57). A somewhat different type of text was published by M. Ginsburger [*Das Fragmententhargum* (Berlin 1899)] on the basis of Paris manuscript, 110.

The Samaritan Targum. This is a literal translation of the Samaritan Pentateuch into the Aramaic dialect of the SAMARITANS. Like the Palestinian Targum, its texts vary greatly among themselves. It was published first in the Paris Polyglot (1645), then in corrected form in the Walton Polyglot. It was edited by A. Brüll (1875) and from various manuscripts by H. Petermann and C. Vollers (1872–91). A new edition from recently discovered manuscripts [on which see *Estudios biblicos,* 18 (1959) 183–197] is in preparation. The PESHITTA of the Pentateuch is in some yet undetermined way related to the Palestinian Targum, on which it may be based to a certain extent.

Knowledge of the Palestinian Targum can be useful in NT exegesis. Despite some later editing, the extant texts of the Palestinian Targum appear to represent, in great part, the liturgical Targum of the NT period. It can have a bearing on NT exegesis because: (1) its Aramaic language is very close to that spoken in Palestine in Christ's day; (2) its free paraphrase represents many theological concepts then current among the ordinary Jews; (3) since it was connected with the synagogue, it would have been familiar to more people than would other Jewish writings of the period. Its value for NT exegesis is now becoming ever more appreciated; for a full list of examples and a view of earlier work, see A. Díez Macho, "Targum y Nuevo Testamento," *Mélange E. Tisserant,* v.1 (*Studi e Testi* 231; Vatican City 1964); M. McNamara, *The Palestinian Targum to the Pentateuch and the N.T.* (Rome 1966). Among the various forms of this Targum, that of Pseudo-Jonathan shows the closest relationship with the NT, particularly with the Apocalypse. For textual criticism all the Targums must be used with great caution (Eissfeldt, 945; Roberts, 211).

Targum to the Prophets. The Targum to the Former and the Latter Prophets (*see* PROPHETIC BOOKS OF THE OLD TESTAMENT) is written in Aramaic similar to that of Onkelos but with more extensive haggadah. It was edited in its present form in Babylonia, some time later than Onkelos, which it quotes; but it is of Palestinian origin and may contain some early, even pre-Christian paraphrase; confer, its Isaiah 65.5 with Revelation 20.14. The author of the Targum is unknown; the Jonathan (ben Uzziel) to whom it is ascribed in *Meg.* 3a is now taken to be a mere Hebraization of the name of Theodotion who translated the Bible into Greek. Some scholars believe that Theodotion's Greek translation is intended in *Meg.* 3a. In the Babylonian Talmud the Targum to Prophets is associated with the name of R. Jose of Pumbeditha (d. A.D. 333), although he is not its author. It was first printed in the RABBINICAL BIBLE of 1517, and often later, for example, by P. De Lagarde, *Prophetae Chaldaice* (Leipzig 1872) and A. Sperber, *The Bible in Aramaic,* v.2–3 (Leiden 1959–62). A new edition based on "Eastern" manuscripts will be published in the Madrid Polyglot. A Latin translation of it is given in the Walton Polyglot. Of a Palestinian Targum to the Prophets, which probably once existed, little is known.

Targums to the Writings. All these are written in Palestinian Aramaic and vary from one another in style and age. A written Targum to Job existed in the first Christian century (*Shabb.* 115a) and may be identical with that used at Qumran, extensive fragments of which (from *c.* 100 B.C.) have been found [see J. Van Der Ploeg, *Le Targum de Job de la grotte 11 de Qumran. . .* (Amsterdam 1962)]. The Qumran fragments differ from the traditionally known Targum to Job, which, with the Targum to the Psalms, forms a class apart, both in language and in the nature of its paraphrase. The Targum to the Psalms often agrees with Septuagint (LXX) against the MT, and at times it has conflated readings from both the LXX and the MT. It is probably an old work with later additions. From the paraphrase to Psalms 107 (108).12 some (for example, Bacher) date it before A.D. 476, but its language seems to be more recent (S. Bialoblocki). The Targum to Chronicles is similar in language to the Targum to Psalms and Job. Although it received its present form in the eighth or ninth century, it probably originated in the fourth century. The Targum to Proverbs, an extremely literal translation, is closely related to the Peshitta of the same book. Both were probably made from an old Jewish Syriac translation. The Targums to the Five Scrolls (i.e., Canticles, Ruth, Lamentations, Ecclesiastes and Esther) are, with the exception of the first Targum to Esther, very paraphrastic and recent compositions (from the eighth and ninth centuries) and possibly contain occasional older traditions (cf, the Targum to Lam 2.20 with Mt 23.35). A Targum to Esther existed as early as Tannaitic times (*Meg.* 2.1). There are three Targums to this book. The first is a literal translation; the second (*targûm šēnî*) and the third are similar to each other and are both paraphrastic. There is no known Targum to Daniel or to Ezra and Nehemiah. The Targum to the Writings (except to Chronicles) was first printed in 1517, and often later, for example, by P. de Lagarde, *Hagiographa Chaldaice* (Leipzig 1873). The Targum to Chronicles was first published by M. F. Beck (Augsburg 1680–83) and later from more complete manuscript by D. Wilkins (Amsterdam 1715).

Bibliography: E. MANGENOT, *Dictionnaire de la Bible,* ed., F. VIGOUROUX, 5 v. (Paris 1895–1912) 5.2:1995–2008. T. WALKER, *Dictionary of the Bible,* eds., J. HASTINGS and J. A. SELBIA, 5 v. (Edinburgh 1942–50) 4:678–683. S. BIALO-BLOCKI, *Encyclopaedia Judaica: Das Judentum in Geschichte und Gegenwart,* 10 v. (Berlin 1928–34), incomplete, 4:570–581. W. BACHER, *The Jewish Encyclopedia,* ed., J. SINGER, (New York 1901–06) 12:57–63. F. SCHÜHLEIN, *The Catholic Encyclopedia,* ed., C. G. HERBERMANN et al., 16 v. (New York 1907–14; suppl. 1922) 14:454–457. B. J. ROBERTS, *The Old Testament Text and Versions* (Cardiff 1951) 197–213. O. EISSFELDT, *Einleitung in das AT* (3d ed. Tübingen 1964) 944–947. P. E. KAHLE, *The Cairo Geniza* (2d ed. New York 1960) 191–208. P. CHURGIN, *Targum Jonathan to the Prophets* (Yale Oriental Series, Researches 14; New Haven 1907). R. H. MELAMED, "The Targum to Canticles according to Six Yemen MSS . . . ," *Jewish Quarterly Review,* 10 (1919–20) 377–410; 11 (1920–21) 1–20; 12 (1921–23) 57–117; repr. Philadelphia 1921. *The Aramaic Bible: The Targums,* 19 vols. ed., M. MCNAMARA, (Wilmington, Del. 1986–). *Estudios biblicos* (Madrid 1941–). *Vetus Testamentum* (Leiden 1951–). *Zeitschrift für die alttestamentliche Wissenschaft* (Giessen-Berlin 1881–).

[M. MCNAMARA]

TARPHON, RABBI

Dean of the Academy of Jabneh and Lydda and one of the more famous Tannaim (Jewish teachers of the first two Christian centuries). He lived in the second half of the first century and first quarter of the second century (d. *c.* 123). Born in a priestly family, he served as a youth in the Temple of Jerusalem. He studied in the Beth Shammai school, and also under GAMALIEL the Elder and JOHA-

NAN BEN ZAKKAI. But he was an independent halakist (*see* HALAKAH) and authored legal rulings on many subjects discussed in the TALMUD, in such fields as lost objects, payment of debts, damage caused by animals, relief for the poor, and special benedictions. Among his students were AKIBA BEN JOSEPH, who later became his colleague in teaching, and Judah ben Ilai, who became one of the teachers of JUDAH HA-NASI, the editor of the MISHNAH.

Tarphon, though a wealthy man and a leader in his community, was noted for his humility, charity, and piety. He was emphatic in his adherence to traditional religious principles. He valued labor and industriousness very highly and liked to picture the relationship of man toward God as similar to that of a laborer toward his master, e.g., ''The day is short, the labor vast, the toilers idle, the reward great, and the Master urgent'' (*PIRKE AVOTH* 1.15). His poetic expressions often reflected his loving memories of the temple; to express approval of what someone said, he would say, ''Like a knop and a blossom'' (*Bereshet Raba* 91.12; cf. Ex 25.31–36), i.e., ''You have spoken as beautifully as the adornments of the lampstand in the temple.'' He was affectionately called the ''father of all Israel.'' According to one version of a midrash, he was one of the famous Ten Martyrs of his era.

Bibliography: *The Jewish Encyclopedia* 12:56–57. *Universal Jewish Encyclopedia* 10:172–173. M. MARGULIES, ed., *Entsiklopediyah lehakhme ha-Talmud veha-geonim* 2 v. (Tel Aviv 1960).

[E. SUBAR]

TARSICIUS, ST.

Martyr. Tarsicius probably suffered martyrdom in the second half of the 3d century or the beginning of the 4th. The most ancient document concerning Tarsicius is a poem by Pope DAMASUS I (366–384) telling how the saint, while carrying the Blessed Sacrament, was attacked by a pagan mob. Rather than allow the Eucharist to be profaned, Tarsicius suffered death by stoning. He was buried in the cemetery of Pope Callistus on the Appian Way. In the 6th century the *Passio s. Stephani papae* erroneously indicated that Tarsicius had been Pope Stephen's acolyte. More probably the martyr was a deacon, for Pope Damasus compared him to the deacon protomartyr, St. STEPHEN, and deacons usually carried the Eucharist from the Pope's Mass to the presbyters of the principal Roman churches as a sign of unity. However, he may have been an acolyte or a layman commissioned to carry the Eucharist to Christian prisoners during persecution.

Feast: Aug. 15.

Bibliography: F. ROLFE, *Tarsicius, The Boy Martyr of Rome in the Diocletian Persecution, A.D. CCCXXX* (London 1972). A. BUTLER, *The Lives of the Saints*, rev. ed. H. THURSTON and D. ATTWATER, 4v. (New York 1956) 3:335. F. L. CROSS, *The Oxford Dictionary of the Christian Church* (London 1957) 1322.

[E. DAY]

Statue of composer Giuseppe Tartini, Pirano (Istria), Italy. (©FulvioRoiter/CORBIS)

TARTINI, GIUSEPPE

Violin virtuoso, teacher, and composer; b. Pirano (Istria), Italy, April 8, 1692; d. Padua, Feb. 26, 1770. After learning the rudiments of music in the town of his birth, he went to Padua (1709) to study at the university. His father desired him to enter the Friars Minors Conventual, but the youth gained his own wish to study law, while continuing his violin study. His secret marriage in 1713 to Elisabetta Premazona, a protégée of Cardinal Cornaro, met with strong disapproval, and Tartini fled to Assisi, where he stayed with the Franciscans for two years, composing and perfecting his violin technique. Following his reconciliation with the cardinal he returned to Padua, and from then on devoted himself to teaching, composing, and writing theoretical works such as *Trattato di musica secondo la vera scienza dell' armonia* (Padua 1754). In 1721 he was appointed violinist to the Cappella del Santo at Padua, and in 1728 he set up a violin school soon recognized throughout Europe for its excellence. In music history he stands out as a theorist and teacher rather than as a composer. His music follows the standard forms of the day: sonatas, trios, concerti, and church works, many of them still in MS.

Bibliography: E. HERON-ALLEN, *Grove's Dictionary of Music and Musicians*, ed. E. BLOM 9 v. (5th ed. London 1954) 8:312–315. A. CAPRI, *Giuseppe Tartini* (Milan 1945). P. BRAINARD, *Die Musik in Geschichte und Gegenwart*, ed. F. BLUME (Kassel-Basel 1949–). G. BEECHEY, "Giuseppe Tartini (1692–1770)," *The Consort* 48 (1992), 8–17. P. BRAINARD in in *The New Grove Dictionary of Music and Musicians,* ed. S. SADIE (New York 1980). M. DOUNIAS, *Die Violinkonzerte Giuseppe Tartinis: als Ausdruck einer Künstlerpersönlichkeit und einer Kulturepoche* (Zurich 1966). F. B. JOHNSON, "Tartini's *Trattato di musica secondo la vera scienza dell'armonio:* An Annotated Translation and Consideration of Its Historical Significance" (Ph.D. diss. Indiana University, 1985). A. PAVANELLO, "Il *Trillo del diavolo* di Giuseppe Tartini nell'edizione di Jean Baptiste Cartier," *Recercare* 11 (1999) 265–79. M. PINCHERLE, *Tartiniana* (Padova 1972).

[F. J. GUENTNER]

TASCHEREAU, ELZÉAR ALEXANDRE

First Canadian cardinal; b. Sainte Marie, Feb. 17, 1820; d. Quebec, Canada, April 12, 1898. The Taschereau family were members of the lesser nobility, who maintained their position in Canada after the English conquest and contributed many illustrious people to the military, the bench, and politics. Elzéar Alexandre was the sixth child of Jean Thomas and Marie (Panet) Taschereau. His father, one of the founding patriots of the newspaper *Le Canadien,* was removed and imprisoned by the English governor James Craig; his mother was the niece of Bp. Bernard Claude Panet of Quebec. At 16, after completing his classical studies in Quebec and making a trip to Rome, Taschereau entered the Grand Seminary; he was ordained Sept. 10, 1842. During the typhus epidemic of 1847 he volunteered for duty with the sick, contracted the disease, and nearly died. For many years he served as professor of various disciplines at the Seminary of Quebec and became its director and then superior. In 1852 he helped to found the University of Laval, Quebec, and he was its second rector (1860). He made several trips to Rome, earned a doctorate in canon law (1856), and was Abp. Charles François Baillargeon's theologian at Vatican Council I (1869–70). As vicar-general of the Archdiocese of Quebec from 1862, he became its administrator at the death of Baillargeon (1870), was named his successor, and was consecrated March 19, 1871.

During Taschereau's episcopacy he made many pastoral visits and was the leader and spokesman of the Canadian hierarchy. He convoked and presided at the Fifth, Sixth, and Seventh Provincial Councils of Quebec, and saved the College of Ste. Anne de la Pocatière from failure. He increased the number of religious in his diocese, adding the Redemptorists, the Clerks of St. Viator, the Religious of St. Vincent de Paul, the Marist Brothers, the Brothers of the Sacred Heart, and the Brothers of Charity. He actively favored the cause of beatification of Bp. F. de M. Laval and promoted devotion to the Holy Family. In 1886 Leo XIII chose him to be the first Canadian cardinal. The end of his life was clouded by a cerebral softening that affected his mental faculties. His works include *Remarques sur les mémoires de l'évêque de Trois-Rivières sur les difficultés religieuses en Canada* (Quebec 1882).

Bibliography: H. TÊTU, *Les Évêques de Québec* (Quebec 1889). P. G. ROY, *La Famille Taschereau* (Levis, Quebec 1901). O. E. MATHIEU in *L'Annuaire del'Université Laval, 1898–99* (Quebec 1898) 145–166, eulogy.

[H. PROVOST]

TATIAN

Christian apologist and theologian; b. Eastern Syria, *c.* A.D. 120; date and place of death unknown. He studied philosophy and became a pupil of JUSTIN MARTYR in Rome and a Christian convert. In 172 (Eusebius, *Hist. Eccl.* 4.29) he broke with the Roman church and returned to Mesopotamia, where he set up his own school. It was probably at this time that he composed his most important work, the *DIATESSARON*, a harmony of the four Gospels. He was a prolific writer, but his only complete surviving work is the *Oratio ad Graecos*, written in Greek, which is preserved in the Codex Arethas from which all other MSS derive. The date and occasion of the *Oratio* are obscure. A case has been made for its delivery as an inaugural lecture at the opening of Tatian's Syrian school, but the more current view is that it was written in the full fervor of conversion.

Tatian's conversion had been an intellectual one, arising from a search for truth, which had been met by his study of the Scriptures. These, he argues, are older and more divine than any Greek writings. He uses "Greek" as synonymous with "educated" and "barbarian" as implying the reverse. Christians are *ipso facto* "barbarian," because they make a clean break with culture. His work is full of virulent polemic against ancient and contemporary religious thought and practice, but has some value for its many references to mythology and ancient works of art. On the positive side, he expounds Christian monotheism, a doctrine of the Logos and creation, and theories about men, angels, and those fallen angels who lead men astray through polytheism.

The most striking feature of his theology is his emphasis on the transcendence of God. The Logos springs from God, yet Christ and sonship are not explicitly mentioned. The Spirit exists at two levels, a material spirit in men and animals and demons, and a divine spirit originally in man, but lost at the Fall. Nevertheless, knowledge can enable man to regain immortality. Matter was corrupted by sin, and so Tatian enjoins a strict asceticism. Irenaeus (Eusebius, *Hist. Eccl.* 4.29) even called Tatian the founder of the Encratites and criticized him for his affinity with Gnosticism—a view that is challenged by modern scholars.

Tatian had obviously read widely, and his thinking was greatly influenced by philosophical concepts; but there was much that he misunderstood or misrepresented. His style is turgid and often obscure. In fact, he typifies the education that he derided.

Bibliography: E. J. GOODSPEED, *Die ältesten Apologeten* (Leipzig 1914) 266–305. E. FASCHER, *Paulys Realencyklopädie der klassischen Altertumswissenschaft*, ed. G. WISSOWA et al. 4A.2 (1932) 2468–71. G. BARDY, *Dictionnaire de théologie catholique* 15.1:59–66. M. ELZE, *Tatian und seine Theologie* (Göttingen 1960). B. ALTANER, *Patrology*, tr. HILDA GRAEF 127–129. J. QUASTEN, *Patrology* 1:220–228.

[M. WHITTAKER]

TATWINE OF CANTERBURY, ST.

Ninth archbishop of Canterbury, also known as Tatwin, Tatuini, Tadwinus; d. July 30, 734. He was a Mercian who was a monk in the monastery of Bredon, Worcester, when consecrated archbishop of Canterbury in 731. The contemporary preeminence of the Mercian king probably explains the election of a Mercian to the Kentish See, but BEDE, who was finishing his *Ecclesiastical History* at the time, describes Tatwine as a religious and learned man. He was consecrated by the bishops of London, Lichfield, Rochester, and Winchester, the most distinguished, by and large, of the English episcopate. A little later he received the PALLIUM from the Pope. A letter of Pope Gregory III alleging that he went to Rome for it in person is not thought to be authentic. He was a man of some learning, and left a collection of riddles, a popular form of Anglo-Saxon intellectual exercise. His relics are enshrined in Canterbury Cathedral.

Feast: July 30.

Bibliography: BEDE, *Ecclesiastical History* 5.23. A. W. HADDAN and W. STUBBS, eds., *Councils and Ecclesiastical Documents Relating to Great Britain and Ireland,* 3 v. in 4 (Oxford 1869–78) 311–313. W. HUNT, *The Dictionary of National Biography from the Earliest Times to 1900,* 63 v. (London 1885–1900; suppl. 1901–) 19:383–390. M. MANITIUS, *Geschichte der lateinischen Literatur des Mittelalters,* 3 v. (Munich 1911–31) 1:203–206.

[E. JOHN]

TAULER, JOHANNES

Dominican preacher and mystic; b. Strasbourg, *c.* 1300; d. there, June 16, 1361. He entered the Dominican novitiate *c.* 1315 in his native city, where Meister ECKHART had been sent to teach in 1312. About ten years later Tauler, with HENRY SUSO, was at the Cologne *studium generale,* and it was during this period that they were greatly influenced by their teacher, Eckhart. We know that Eckhart was lecturing there in 1326, when he was formally accused of heresy. In the next year he died, and two years later, in John XXII's bull, *In agro dominico,* which condemned certain of Eckhart's propositions, we learn that on his deathbed he submitted himself and his doctrine to the Apostolic See.

Suso and Tauler never fully recovered from this tragic end to the career of one whom they had revered both as a man and a teacher. Their reactions were different, however. In Suso's writings, so similar in many ways to those of his English contemporary, Richard ROLLE, there is a constant element of lamentation, of railing against the world for the wrongs it has inflicted upon the chosen lovers of God. In sharp contrast, Tauler's tone is easy, gentle, equable; and though in places he gives his hearers to understand that part of Eckhart's misfortune was the incomprehension of those whom he had tried to teach—''He talked about eternity, but you took it as referring to time''—there is in Tauler no trace of bitterness or self-pity. In saying this, of course, one must allow for the difference in circumstances under which he and Suso composed their works. Suso's are set literary pieces, designed to reveal his private thoughts and written in times of great desolation.

The Preacher. Tauler, strictly speaking, wrote nothing. Apart from some writings long attributed to him but now universally rejected as spurious, he has survived only through his sermons, which seem to have been recorded, largely from recollection, by members of his audience, usually nuns of the Dominican houses of the Rhineland to which he ministered.

The style and the brevity of pulpit discourse suited him as an artist and as a theologian. Despite deficiencies in the surviving manuscripts, his power as a preacher is evident. He avoided rhetorical effect, making his points plainly, directly, and with a common sense and freedom from hyperbole that make him the antithesis of Eckhart as a writer. In Eckhart we are forced to recognize intellectualism gone astray, a carelessness, if not contempt, for the mental limitations of his public, a disregard of the harm he might be causing them. Tauler, however, preaching to his nuns, always has clearly in view their diversities of vocation. For us all, he insists with St. Thomas, that humility and simplicity are needful. The best possible exposition of the mystery of the Trinity is "more like a lie than the truth," and we must not be overawed by the subtleties of scholars who can do no more than "stammer something for the sake of Holy Church." Yet even so, he reminds us that we are called by God to employ all our faculties, such as they are, in the effort to reach Him. The road to God, he says, lies between knowing and unknowing.

Action and Contemplation. The rival claims upon the contemplative soul of activity and passivity presented acute difficulty in his time, when many had been seduced by the false passivity taught by such heretics as the "Brethren of the Free Spirit," whose doctrine in this matter seemed to be encouraged by Eckhart. But Tauler often speaks in praise of the active life, which, he reminds his nuns, some members of every religious community must lead. "When our Lord blamed Martha, it was not because she was working. What He blamed her for was her over-anxiety." Yet even so, those called to the contemplative life must find and use a true passivity. In a sermon on the Eucharist, he says that to receive its richest blessings we must be separated from the world and ourselves, we must cease from action and suffer God to act within us, and we must be one within ourselves with God. In such teaching on activity and passivity, he agrees with Ruysbroek that our lives must mirror the life of the Blessed Trinity, that we must go into God as the Persons enter into one another, and come out again from God, replenished and enriched by union with Him, to spend in the active life what in stillness and silence we have received. He praises such silence and stillness:

> Mary was enclosed; so too ought the handmaiden of God to keep herself apart . . . abstaining not only from those earthly activities that may seem of their nature to be harmful, but even from the merely sensory practices of virtues. She should very often be silent and at peace with herself, inwardly enclosed, hidden within the spirit, so that she may withdraw herself and escape from the senses and make for herself a place of silence and inward repose.

Suffering. To seek in distractions, however harmless, in pious colloquies, however edifying, or in consolations, an escape from the spirit's afflictions—dryness, grief, and desolation—is to turn aside from the road that God points to those who would follow and find Him. Such spiritual sufferings are often in Tauler's mind: in one place he says "What then remains to the man formed after God's image? A soul full of God and a body full of suffering." Elsewhere we read that when Christ in Heaven meets those who have suffered much for Him on earth, He will say "I am very pleased with you, because you helped Me to carry My Cross to Calvary." Yet such affective writing is entirely free from morbidity because Tauler's eyes are always fixed upon joys to be tasted in this life, joys not to be had without such sorrows, but which are ineffable:

> When, by this intolerable affliction, our Lord has prepared a soul thoroughly . . . He then comes and raises it up. . . . He unbinds our eyes and shows us the truth. The clear light of day dawns, and the soul is raised up out of all its afflictions. It is just as if God had raised us out of death into life. The Lord lifts us up, out of ourselves and up to Him, consoling us for all our miseries, healing all our wounds. We are drawn out of human activities into a divine life, out of all sorrow into a divine peace, in which man is so deified that everything which he is and does, God is and does in him.

Bibliography: J. TAULER, *Die Predigten Taulers,* ed. F. VETTER (Berlin 1910), standard ed. of the orig. medieval German; *Sermons de Tauler,* 3 v., tr. HUGUENY, et al. (Paris 1927–35), an excellent modern French trans. of the whole works, embodying much research; *Spiritual Conferences,* tr. and ed. E. COLLEDGE and M. JANE (St. Louis, 1961), an anthology in modern English, with intro.

[E. COLLEDGE]

TAUNTON, ETHELRED LUKE

Ecclesiastical writer, b. Rugeley, Staffordshire, England, Oct. 17, 1857; d. London, May 9, 1907. During his education at Downside School, he wished to become a Benedictine, but was prevented by delicate health. He studied music until he entered the Institute of St. Andrew at Barnet (1874), which he left to join the OBLATES OF ST. CHARLES at Bayswater (1880). After ordination (1883) he left the Oblates (1886) and served the mission at Stoke Newington in North London until physical injury partially paralyzed him and permanently incapacitated him from active work (1888). However he read widely, wrote numerous periodical articles and several books, translated some works, and founded the short-lived *St. Luke's Magazine* during his convalescence at Bruges, Belgium (1888–90). In church music and liturgy he was considered an authority, but a partisan tone, particularly evident in his historical writings, made him a controversial figure. Despite his professed objectivity, he was frequently charged with prejudice as well as inaccuracy. This was notably true of his best-known book, *The History of the Jesuits in England* (1901), and his article on the Jesuits in the 11th and subsequent editions of the *Encyclopaedia Britannica,* a revision of Littledale's hostile article in the ninth edition (1880).

Bibliography: *Downside Review* 26 (1907) 223–224. G. L. NORGATE, *The Dictionary of National Biography from the Earliest*

Times to 1900, 63 v. (London 1885–1900) 3:480. J. H. POLLEN, *Month* 97 (1901) 512–518; 98 (1901) 315–318; 117 (1911) 561–574, a critique of Taunton's writings.

[D. MILBURN]

TAUROBOLIUM

The *taurobolium,* a rite of uncertain origin often occurring in the cult of CYBELE, first appears in the 2d century A.D. The most detailed literary account is that by PRUDENTIUS (*Peristeph.* 10:1106–50), and many inscriptions bear witness to the rite. The recipient descended into a pit, over which a bull (*taurobolium* or goat (*kriobolium*) was sacrificed, drenching him in its blood. The rite is attested for many parts of the Roman Empire, especially in Gaul and in Rome itself, where it became part of the official cult, until the suppression of paganism under Theodosius the Great. It was performed both *pro salute imperatoris* or *imperii* and for individuals. Moreover, it became associated, especially in the 4th century, with the idea of rebirth, probably in connection with the belief—which may have come from Christianity—that blood washes away sin. It was sometimes repeated after 20 years, perhaps because the recipient was regarded as born anew in the first initiation (*see* RESURRECTION, GRECO-ORIENTAL) and therefore free from sin during his second infancy and youth of 20 years.

See Also: MYSTERY RELIGIONS, GRECO-ORIENTAL.

Bibliography: H. GRAILLOT, *Le Culte de Cybéle* (Paris 1912). G. WISSOWA, *Religion und Kultus der Römer* (2d ed. Munich 1912) 322–325. H. OPPERMANN, *Paulys Realenzyklopädie der klassischen Altertumswissenschaft,* ed. G. WISSOWA, et al. RE 5A. 1 (1934) 16–22. M. P. NILSSON, *Geschichte der griechischen Religion,* 2 v. (2d ed. Munich 1955–61) 2:624–627.

[H. S. LONG]

TAUSEN, HANS

Danish Church reformer; b. Birkende, Fyn Island, Denmark, 1494; d. Ribe, Denmark, Nov. 11, 1561. Of his peasant parents nothing is known beyond their names, Markvard (Marcus) and Catherina. Tausen entered the Order of St. John of Jerusalem and spent his youth in the priory in Antvorskov. Later he studied at the universities of Rostock (1516–19), Copenhagen (1521), Louvain (1522), and Wittenberg (1523–24), where he became acquainted with Martin Luther's ideas. He was transferred to the Johannite convent at Viborg (*c.* 1525), and there he started preaching LUTHERANISM and gathering the first Lutheran congregation of Denmark. Almost immediately after his expulsion from his convent, King Frederik I gave him a letter of protection (Oct. 23, 1526). During the next three years several Franciscan and Dominican priory churches were placed at the disposal of the Lutherans of Viborg. In 1529 the king appointed Tausen preacher of the church of St. Nicholas in Copenhagen. There he gathered a large Lutheran congregation and participated in the formulation of the 43 evangelical articles produced at the meeting of the Council of the Realm in July 1530. After the death of his patron, King Frederik I (1533), Tausen entered into a compromise with the bishop of Roskilde, Joachim Rønnow, that apparently ruined his reputation among Danish Lutherans. When the Catholic bishops were arrested and replaced by evangelical superintendents (1536), Tausen was passed over, and not until 1542 was he appointed bishop of Ribe. This post he held until his death. His place in the early history of Protestantism in Denmark has earned him the title ''The Danish Luther.''

Bibliography: P. RØN, *Sciagraphia Lutheri Danici* (Copenhagen 1757). *Dansk biografisk łeksikon* 23 (1944) 367–379. M. CHRISTENSEN, *Hans Tausen* (Copenhagen 1942). W. GÖBELL, *Die Religion in Geschichte und Gegenwart,* 7 v. (3rd ed. Tübingen 1957–65) 6:662.

[T. D. OLSEN]

TAVERNER, JOHN

Tudor organist and composer of Masses and motets; b. Tattershall?, England, *c.* 1495; d. Boston, Lincolnshire, Oct. 25, 1545. His name appears first in 1525 as clerk-fellow at the collegiate church of Tattershall near Lincoln, then as organist and choirmaster at Cardinal College, Oxford (1526–30). In 1528 he was imprisoned briefly for alleged heretical (Lutheran) leanings and released through Wolsey's intervention. From 1530 until his death he engaged in fanatical persecutions as paid agent of Thomas Cromwell in the destruction of monasteries. Taverner's music, probably all composed before 1530, comprises eight Masses, three Magnificats, 23 motets on liturgical texts, and some instrumental pieces. His style varied from a simple homophonic manner to the florid technique of his most inspired works, the Magnificats. The *cantus firmus* on the words *In nomine Domini* of the *Benedictus* of his Mass *Gloria Tibi Trinitas* was the thematic source for more than 100 instrumental pieces called *Innomine's,* by TYE and other English composers.

Bibliography: F. L. HARRISON, Music in Medieval Britain (New York 1958); ''English Polyphony *c.* 1470–1540,'' *New Oxford History of Music*, ed. J. A. WESTRUP, 11 v. (New York 1957–) 3:303–348. E. H. FELLOWES, *Grove's Dictionary of Music and Musicians*, ed. E. BLOM 9 v. (5th ed. London 1954) 8:323–324. G. REESE, *Music in the Renaissance* (rev. ed. New York 1959)

778–781. D. STEVENS, *Die Musik in Geschichte und Gegenwart*, ed. F. BLUME (Kassel-Basel 1949–) v.13. H. R. BENHAM, "The Music of John Taverner: A Study and Assessment" (Ph.D. diss. Southhampton, 1970). R. BOWERS and P. DOE, "John Taverner" in *The New Grove Dictionary of Music and Musicians, vol. 18,* ed. S. SADIE, (New York 1980) 598–602. C. HAND, *John Taverner: His Life and Music* (London 1978). D. S. JOSEPHSON, "John Taverner: A Documentary Study of His Life and Music" (Ph.D. diss. Columbia University, 1972); *John Taverner: Tudor Composer* (Ann Arbor 1979). D. M. RANDEL, ed., *The Harvard Biographical Dictionary of Music* (Cambridge 1996) 903–904. N. SLONIMSKY, ed., *Baker's Biographical Dictionary of Musicians, Eighth Edition* (New York 1992) 1856.

[S. W. KENNEY]

TAXATION AND MORAL OBLIGATION

A just tax, as distinguished from fees, licenses, assessments, etc., may be defined as a compulsory contribution to the government, imposed in the common interest for the purpose of defraying the expenses incurred in carrying out the public functions or imposed for the purpose of regulation, without reference to the special benefits conferred on the one making the payment. Theologians generally divide taxes into direct and indirect, but the division is not perfect. A direct tax is immediately imposed on the person himself, even though it may be imposed because of an individual's goods, trade, or business (in general all per capita taxes). An indirect tax is directly imposed on goods and affects the person only indirectly (customs, duties, sales tax).

General Catholic Doctrine. Scripture affirms the existence of a moral obligation to pay taxes. The three synoptic Gospels record as a saying of Christ with regard to paying the tribute to Caesar: "Render, therefore, to Caesar the things that are Caesar's, and to God the things that are God's" (Mt 22.21; cf. Mk 12.13–17; Lk 20.20–26). St. Paul in a discussion of civil authority as coming from God speaks of the duty of paying taxes: "For this is also why you pay tribute, for they are the ministers of God, serving unto this very end. Render to all men whatever is their due; tribute to whom tribute is due; taxes to whom taxes are due . . ." (Rom 13.6–7). The Fathers of the Church, especially in their comments upon St. Paul, teach the moral obligation of paying taxes. Pius XII merely reiterated the constant teaching of the Church in a letter of Oct. 2, 1956: "There can be no doubt concerning the duty of each citizen to bear a part of the public expense. But the state on its part, insofar as it is charged with protecting and promoting the common good of its citizens, is under an obligation to assess upon them only necessary levies, which are, furthermore, proportionate to their means" [original Fr. *Osservatore Romano,* Oct. 4, 1956; English *Pope Speaks,* 3 (1957) 327].

Moral Theology. There are four theories among Catholic moralists about the exact nature of the moral obligation of paying just taxes.

Penal Law Theory. According to this, there is no moral obligation to pay the tax but only to accept the penalty, if penalty is imposed for the failure to do so. Later theologians attribute the penal law theory to Angelo Carletti di Chivasso (d. 1495) and Martin ASPILCUETA (Doctor Navarrus; d. 1586). However, it is not at all clear that these theologians would have applied penal law theory to such taxation as exists at the present time. Two fundamental reasons account for the theory—the desire to save citizens from burdensome and unfair taxation and a somewhat voluntaristic concept of law. Among contemporary theologians there is a growing tendency to deny the existence of purely penal laws. In addition, Scripture and the repeated teaching in the Church appear to demand a moral obligation with regard to payment of the taxes themselves and not one that binds only regarding the acceptance of the penalty.

Commutative Justice Theory. The moral obligation of paying taxes stems from the virtue of commutative justice. This theory was originally based on a presumed contract or pact between the individual and the state. The tax is the price paid by the citizen for the services rendered to him and for him by the state. This theory rests, therefore, on what many theologians consider a misunderstanding of the relationship between the individual and society. Similarly, explanations proposed by some modern theologians and based on the right of eminent domain or the principle that the state incurs expenses in the name of all are not acceptable to most theologians.

Legal Justice Theory for Direct Taxes. Some theologians have taught that laws imposing indirect taxes are purely penal, whereas laws imposing direct taxes oblige from the virtue of legal justice. But the existence of purely penal laws is questionable; also, such a theory would be difficult to apply in practice because of the somewhat arbitrary distinction between direct and indirect taxes.

Legal Justice Theory for All Taxes. The more common opinion is that all just tax laws oblige in conscience from the virtue of legal justice. Legal justice, according to St. Thomas Aquinas, has the common good as its object. The individual member of society is bound to work and cooperate for the common good. Society needs tax revenue to provide for the common good. Consequently, the individual has an obligation in legal justice to pay just taxes. This theory has become more commonly held since greater attention has been paid to the relationship between the individual and society. Some speak of an obligation in social justice.

Government's Obligation. Distributive justice demands that the individual citizens be taxed according to their capabilities to support the common good. Tax legislation is unjust if it does not distribute the burden equally among the individual members of society. However, no human legislation can be perfect, and minor inequities do not render a tax law unjust.

Truly unjust tax laws do not oblige in conscience. In certain countries (especially under totalitarian or absolute political systems) tax laws might not be just. In some countries even today it is evident that the state knows of the existence of fraud and either levies correspondingly higher taxes to compensate for the fraud or simply accepts the existing situation. In such cases the conscientious Christian may defend himself against the unjust legislation.

Tax laws in the U.S., where income and corporation taxes are the most immediate concern for the majority, are generally just laws. However, some argue that the tax laws do not oblige in conscience for various reasons, for example, that much tax revenue is lost in graft, that tax revenues are frequently wasted, that taxes are levied for unreasonable purposes. However, the tax legislation of the U.S. appears to be a good example of a prudential ordering of reason (*ordinatio rationis*). The procedure of estimating the budget, the system of checks and balances among the branches of government, the fact of representative government, the opposition of political parties and the very popular political platform of lowering taxes if at all possible—all these elements indicate that tax legislation in the U.S. is basically reasonable and just.

Bibliography: M. T. CROWE, *The Moral Obligation of Paying Just Taxes* (CUA Studies in Sacred Theology 84; Washington 1944). P. LAND, ''Evading Taxes Can't Be Justified in Conscience,'' *Social Order* 5 (1955) 121–125; ''A Note on Tax Obligations,'' *ibid.* 276–277. C. CARDIJN and J. DELEPIERRE, *Frauder . . . ou payer ses impôts* (Brussels 1962). F. HAMM, *Zur Grundlegung und Geschichte der Steuermoral* (Trier 1908). A. JANSSEN, ''Le Devoir fiscal,'' *Ephemerides theologicae Lovanienses* 27 (Bruges 1951) 105–113. O. VON NELLBREUNING, *Staatslexikon,* ed. GÖRRES-GESELLSCHAFT, 8 v. (Freiburg 1957–63) 7:698–700. T. GOFFI, ''La coscienza morale del contribuente,'' *Divas Thomas* 59 (Piacenza 1956) 283–293. P. M. THÉAS, ''L'Obligation morale de l'impôt,'' *Documentation catholique* 56 (1959) 757–758. L. BABBINI, ''Le leggi fiscali obbligano in coscienza,'' *Palestra del clero* 39 (1960) 394–396. E. TRABUCCHI, ''A proposito di evasione fiscale,'' *La civiltà cattolica* 114 (Rome 1963) 1:119–130.

[C. E. CURRAN]

TAYLOR, FRANCES MARGARET

Foundress of the POOR SERVANTS OF THE MOTHER OF GOD; b. Stoke-Rockford, Lincolnshire, England, Jan. 20, 1832; d. London, June 9, 1900. She was the daughter of Henry Taylor, an Anglican minister. After his death (1842) the family moved to Bayswater, London, where it was influenced by the OXFORD MOVEMENT. At the age of 16 Fanny followed her elder sister, Emma, into Miss Sellon's Anglican sisterhood, but left after a few months. In 1853 she joined Florence Nightingale's Lady Volunteers and, after training at St. George's Hospital, set out for the Crimea (1854). While serving as nurse there in a hospital ward of Irish Catholic soldiers, she came in contact with Mother Mary Francis Bridgeman and the Sisters of Mercy. On April 14, 1855, she was received into the Catholic Church by Sydney Woollett, SJ, an army chaplain. In 1861 she entered the novitiate of the French Sisters of Charity, Rue de Bac, Paris, but her superiors and Cardinal MANNING urged her to return to London. There she founded the Poor Servants of the Mother of God (1869) and, as Mother Mary Magdalen, acted as superior general until her death. She was also active as a writer, as editor of the *Lamp,* and as a collaborator in the start of the periodicals the *Messenger of the Sacred Heart* and the *Month.*

Frances Margaret Taylor.

Bibliography: J. GILLOW, *A Literary and Biographical History or Bibliographical Dictionary of the English Catholics from*

1534 to the Present Time, 5 v. (London-New York 1885–1902; repr. New York 1961) 5:538–539, with list of her writings.

[M. GERALDINE]

TAYLOR, HUGH, BL.

Priest, martyr; b. *c.* 1560 at Durham, northeast England; hanged, drawn, and quartered Nov. 26, 1585 at York. He was ordained priest in 1584 at Rheims (or possibly Douai). On March 27, 1585, he was sent on the English Mission and immediately arrested together with Bl. Marmaduke BOWES. Taylor was the first martyr condemned under the recently enacted Statute 27 Eliz. c. 2. He was immediately executed. He was beatified by Pope John Paul II on Nov. 22, 1987, with George Haydock and Companions.

Feast of the English Martyrs: May 4 (England).

See Also: ENGLAND, SCOTLAND, AND WALES, MARTYRS OF.

Bibliography: R. CHALLONER, *Memoirs of Missionary Priests,* ed. J. H. POLLEN (rev. ed. London 1924). J. H. POLLEN, *Acts of English Martyrs* (London 1891). YEPES, *Historia Particular de la persecucion de Inglaterra* (Madrid, 1599). STAPLETON, *Post-Reformation Catholic Missions in Oxfordshire* (London, 1906).

[K. I. RABENSTEIN]

TAYLOR, JEREMY

Anglican bishop, polemicist, and author of theological and devotional works; b. Cambridge, England, 1613; d. Lisburn, Ireland, Aug. 13, 1667. He was educated at Cambridge University, elected a fellow of Caius College, and ordained in 1633. Two years later, through the favor of Abp. William LAUD, he was given a fellowship at All Souls College, Oxford, and a chaplaincy to King Charles I. He was a prominent preacher but was sometimes criticized as bookish and argumentative. He fell under a cloud of suspicion briefly because of his association with one of Queen Henrietta Maria's Franciscan chaplains, Christopher Davenport, but he disclaimed any leanings toward Catholicism. In a famous Gunpowder Plot sermon (Nov. 5, 1638) he equated recusancy and treason, insisted that Elizabeth's penal laws were mild, and said that the seal of confession was a cover for treason.

In 1638 Taylor was given a rectorship at Uppingham and later at Overstone; in 1644 he was with the Royalist army. He was captured, imprisoned, and released by the Roundheads in 1645, and after that episode retired into Wales to a private chaplaincy. He wrote extensively in Wales, but preached occasionally in London. He was imprisoned twice by the Commonwealth in 1655. He was a leading Royalist cleric and, with the Restoration in 1660, was nominated bishop of Down and Connor, and soon after, administrator of Dromore and vice chancellor of the University of Dublin. As a bishop in Ireland he was energetic in seeing that the law was used fully against both Catholics and Presbyterians, especially the clergy, and he wrote an abusive volume entitled *Dissuasive from Popery* (1664). He was not particularly happy as the bishop of areas in which there was so much religious contention, but he remained in residence and was a serious administrator.

His best-known theological work is *Liberty of Prophesying* (*Theologica eclectica*, 1646), and his best devotional works are *Rule and Exercise of Holy Living* (1650), which ran into dozens of printings, and *Holy Dying* (1651). His offensive polemics should be viewed with an eye to the politics of his day. Once suspect of "Roman leanings," men such as Taylor had to make it eminently clear to both Anglicans and Presbyterians that they were second to none in abhorring Catholicism. In his quieter works he advocated legal tolerance and careful justice for outlawed religious groups as "the way to win them." His devotional writings remain attractive in the style of his age, and his sermons, often argumentative and faintly rationalist, are in the classic literary mold.

Bibliography: *Whole Works*, ed. R. HEBER, 15 v. (London 1822), rev. ed. C. P. EDEN, 10 v. (London 1847–54). C. J. STRANKS, *The Life and Writings of Jeremy Taylor* (*Society for Promoting Christian Knowledge*; London 1952), a full-scale study with bibliog. of earlier studies. A. GORDON, *The Dictionary of National Biography from the Earliest Times to 1900* 19:422–429, bibliog. G. L. CROSS, *The Oxford Dictionary of the Christian Church* (London 1957) 1325.

[E. V. CLARK]

TAYLOR, MYRON CHARLES

Lawyer, industrialist, and diplomat who became the personal representative of presidents Franklin D. Roosevelt and Harry Truman to Pius XII during and immediately after World War II; b. Lyons, N.Y., Jan. 18, 1874; d. Locust Valley, N.Y., May 6, 1959. He was the son of William and Mary (Morgan) Taylor and received his LL.B. (1894) from Cornell University, Ithaca, New York. He served as chairman of the finance committee of the U.S. Steel Corporation (1927–34) and was chairman of the board of directors and chief executive office of that corporation (1932–38). Closely associated with the federal government, Taylor served in various capacities in the Hoover, Roosevelt, and Truman administrations. In 1929 he was on the executive committee of the President's National Business Survey Conference, and in 1931 he became a member of the President's Organization on Unemployment Relief. Subsequently (1933–35) he served as a member of the industrial board of the National Recovery Administration and was also the U.S. representative to the Evian Conference on Political Refugees. In 1939 when Taylor, an Episcopalian, was given the rank of ambassador and named personal representative of President Roosevelt to Pius XII, his main duties were to relay messages between Roosevelt and the pope and to harmonize the relief activities of the Vatican and the U.S. Taylor retained his Vatican post under Truman until 1950, when he resigned; his *Wartime Correspondence between President Roosevelt and Pope Pius XII* was published in 1947. For his various services to the U.S., Italy, and France during and after the war, Taylor received the Medal of Merit (U.S.); he was named Commander, Order of the Crown, Star of Solidarity (Italy), and Cross Commander, Legion of Honor (France). Because of his services to the Vatican, Taylor was made successively Knight, Order of Pius, first degree; Knight Grand Cross, SS. Mauritius and Lazarus; and Knight, Order of Malta.

[J. Q. FELLER]

TAYLOR, NATHANIEL WILLIAM

American Congregationalist theologian and founder of Yale Divinity School, who had a formative influence on the liberal orthodoxy of the New Haven tradition; b. New Milford, Conn., June 23, 1786; d. New Haven, Conn., March 10, 1858. The son of an apothecary and grandson of the local pastor, Taylor was prepared for Yale by a neighboring minister and entered the college in 1800; poor health delayed his graduation until 1807. He then studied theology under Timothy DWIGHT, acting for a time as his secretary. He was ordained in 1812 as pastor of the First Congregational Church, New Haven. He gave encouragement to a series of religious revivals beginning in 1815 and worked closely with Lyman BEECHER to promote the American Bible Society and various reform groups; at the same time he was engaged in controversy with UNITARIANS and Episcopalians (*see* EPISCOPAL CHURCH, U.S.). His departure from the theological tradition of Jonathan EDWARDS, evident in such sermons as "Salvation Free to the Willing" preached in 1819, was signalized in his 1828 "Concio ad Clerum" at New Haven. In this address he maintained that moral depravity is not sinfulness and that sin consists in "man's own act, consisting of a free choice of some object rather than God, as his chief good." He argued further that it was impossible for God to prevent sin while maintaining the moral system in which free agents are inalienably able to sin. This sermon involved him in a series of published debates with Bennett Tyler, Leonard Woods, and other spokesmen of the older New England tradition. His stress on the freedom of the will, particularly as interpreted by his disciples, was an underlying cause of the breakdown of the Congregational-Presbyterian Plan of Union, as well as a direct influence on the liberal theology of Horace BUSHNELL. In 1822 Taylor was instrumental in founding Yale Divinity School and became its first professor of didactic theology, a post he held, in addition to his pastoral charge, until his death. His classroom lectures were published posthumously as *Lectures on the Moral Government of God* (New York 1859).

Bibliography: S. E. MEAD, *Nathaniel William Taylor, 1786–1858: A Connecticut Liberal* (Chicago 1942). F. H. FOSTER, *A Genetic History of the New England Theology* (New York 1963). C. R. KELLER, *The Second Great Awakening in Connecticut* (New Haven 1942).

[R. K. MACMASTER]

TAYLOR, WILLIAM

LOLLARD; b. Worcestershire, England, date unknown; burned at Smithfield, March 2, 1423. A master of arts of Oxford by 1405, he was principal of St. Edmund Hall in 1405–06. About 1407, he was excommunicated for contumacy by Abp. Thomas ARUNDEL when he failed to answer a citation for Lollard opinions expressed in a sermon at St. Paul's Cross. Absolved by Abp. Henry CHICHELE in 1420, he was convicted of heresy in 1421 on the information of Thomas NETTER, and again in 1423, when he was degraded and executed by the state. Among the heresies of which he was accused, Taylor held that prayer should not be directed to Christ in respect of His humanity or to the saints.

Bibliography: *Fasciculi zizaniorum Magistri Johannis Wyclif cum tritico,* ed. W. W. SHIRLEY (*Rerum Britannicarum medii aevi scriptores,* 5; 1858) 412–413 gives Taylor's condemned beliefs. J. GAIRDNER, *Lollardy and the Reformation in England,* 4 v. (London 1908–13) 1:127–128. A. B. EMDEN, *A Biographical Register of the University of Oxford to A.D. 1500,* 3 vol. (Oxford 1957–59) 3:1852.

[F. D. BLACKLEY]

TE DEUM

A hymn of praise that was historically sung every Sunday at the end of MATINS since the 6th century during all times and seasons when the *Gloria* is used in the Mass and in extraliturgical ceremonies—e.g, after a consecration, ordination, or military victory, as well as at the conclusion of some medieval mystery plays.

Origin. The *Te Deum* is attributed in a dozen ancient Irish MSS to a "Bishop Nicet" whom G. Morin and A.

E. Burn have identified with NICETAS OF REMESIANA. Some scholars ascribe also the melody, as it has come down to us, to Nicetas, while others indicate that the first part bespeaks a pre-Gregorian source. Forty-eight other ancient MSS attribute the hymn to St. AMBROSE and St. AUGUSTINE, a source commonly accepted during the Middle Ages but now largely discredited. Only two MSS attribute it to St. HILARY OF POITERS; seven, to Bishop Sisebut; and two, to St. ABUNDIUS of Como. Another 49 MSS cite the hymn without mentioning the author's name or giving an anonymous source, as, e.g., "Hymn in Honor of the Holy Trinity" or simply "Hymn for Sunday." And Eric Werner in *The Sacred Bridge* has posited a close relation between the melody and that of a Yemenite *Shema* and a formula for chanting the *Torah.*

At present the following points are admitted by all critics: (1) The *Te Deum* was composed at the beginning of the 5th century. (2) It is of Latin composition and not a translation of a hymn written in Greek (as several German scholars have maintained since the 17th century); the Greek text of the *Te Deum* is actually a translation from the original made in the West in the 9th century. (3) Liturgical use of the *Te Deum,* first noticed in southeastern Gaul, at Milan, and in central Italy, leads one to seek the author in these regions. Among traditional assumptions regarding authorship Nicetas of Remesiana apparently best answers the demands of the critics.

The Melody. First of all, it should be noted that the solemn and simple tones that are found in the official Roman chant books are merely variants of the same melody. The Ambrosian melodic version is probably derived from the "Gregorian" version, but the melody transmitted in the notated Ambrosian MSS does not correspond to the primitive Ambrosian text that has been handed down to us in the oldest non-notated Milanese MSS. In fine, it is the version given in the *Antiphonale Monasticum* (1935), with its ancient stress on *si,* that most closely corresponds to the original melodic version. It seems difficult, however, to find the original melodic version of the *Te Deum,* since seven centuries separate the period of composition from that of the first notated evidence of its existence.

Musical Divisions of Chant Versions. From a musical as well as textual viewpoint the *Te Deum* consists of three parts: the first, from the beginning to the *Paraclitum Spiritum* (in praise of the Holy Trinity), is composed of a psalmody with two recitatives; the second part (in praise of Christ) uses the same recitative chords as the first, but here the cadence rests on the *mi,* avoiding, however, the passage of a semitone, whence there is a slight modal uncertainty, similar to that in the *Gloria XV* of the Vatican edition; the third part (*Salvum fac . . .*) is in fact an old series of verses with their responses, which one sometimes found attached to the Great Doxology, or the *Gloria in excelsis.* The first and last of these verses (Ps 27.9 and 30.2) are accorded the musical treatment of an antiphon, and the intervening verses are psalmodic in nature. The melodic substance is borrowed from the *Tu rex gloriae* theme. By the introduction of the semitone this part clarifies the modality; it finally ends in deuterus (Phrygian mode). According to a marginal rubric in an Ambrosian MS (Milan, Trivulz. A.14, 14th century) the *Te Deum* was sung *alta voce* from the verse *Per singulos dies.* In comparison with the rubrics for the *Gloria in excelsis* (in *sublimi voce* as opposed to *alta voce*) and with Berold's remarks (ed. Magistretti, 49), it must be concluded that the first part of the Ambrosian *Te Deum* was sung by children and the second part by men. This was customary elsewhere in the hymns and verses of the Office. The practice of alternating the verses between each side of the choir belongs to a more recent period.

Relation to Psalmody. The *Te Deum* is sung as a psalmody in the 2d mode (*Salvum fac . . . In te Domine speravi. . . .*) or as a psalmody in the 3d mode but with two reciting tones: a recitation on *do* in the first member (originally on *si*) and a recitation on *la* in the second member. This formula of two psalmodic tones is found in the famous *tonus peregrinus* from Sunday Vespers (Psalm 113, *In exitu*); it is unknown in the primitive Gregorian psalmody and probably comes from a Gallican (i.e., non-Roman) musical repertory.

Musical Analysis. The composition of the *Te Deum,* therefore, may be said to have been achieved in the simplest possible manner. Despite the length of the hymn, this simplicity does not become monotonous because of the variety of psalmodic tones in the various sections. Finally, the choice of the third tone gives the composition a brilliant and stirring character especially suited to a thanksgiving hymn. It should be noted that the triple *Sanctus* of the *Te Deum* is identical with the Trisagion in the Ambrosian Mass. The *Te Deum* has been most frequently rendered in polyphony. There are also numerous vernacular translations of this hymn.

Bibliography: A. E. BURN, ed., *Niceta of Remesiana* (Cambridge, Eng. 1905); *The Hymn Te Deum and its Author* (London 1926). P. CAGIN, *Te Deum ou Illatio?,* v.1 of *L'Euchologie latine* (Oxford 1906). M. FROST, *Journal of Theological Studeis* 34 (1933) 250–257; *ibid.* 39 (1938) 288–391; 43 (1942) 192–194. M. HUGLO et al., *Fonti e paleografia del canto ambrosiano* (Archivo Ambrosiano 8; Milan 1956) 64–65. J. A. JUNGMANN, *Zeitgeist für katholische Theologie* 61 (1937) 105–107. H. LECLERCQ, *Dictionnaire d'archéologie chrétienne et de liturgie,* ed. F. CABROL, H. LECLERCQ, and H. I. MARROU (Paris 1907–53) 15.2:2028–48. K. H. SCHLAGER and W. KIRSCH, *Die Musik in Geschichte und Gegenwart,* ed. F. BLUME (Kassel-Basel 1949–86). W. LIPPHARDT, *Zeitschrift für Kirchenmusik* 72 (1952) 219–222. G. MORIN, *Revue Bénédictine* 11

(1894) 49–77, 337–345. G. REESE, *Music in the Middle Ages* (New York 1940) 105. E. KÄHLER, *Studien zum T. D. und zur Geschichte des 24. Psalms in der alten Kirche* (Göttingen 1958).

[M. HUGLO]

TE LUCIS ANTE TERMINUM

Office hymn, in iambic dimeter, that was traditionally used daily in the office of COMPLINE. During the Middle Ages, it was sung in summer and on great feasts. In winter it was replaced by other hymns, e.g., the 9th-century composition *Christe, qui lux es et dies.* The hymn is clearly not the work of St. AMBROSE. Though the exact date of composition is unknown, it is at least of the 8th century, and is richly represented in medieval MSS. Mone cites it from an 8th-century MS at Darmstadt. Dreves and Blume cite it from one Irish MS of the 9th century, and in the British Museum it is found in three hymnaries of the English church, dating from the 11th century. Other 11th-century works that contain the hymn are a Mozarabic Breviary at Corpus Christi, Cambridge; a MS of St. Gall; and one MS at Durham. It is found in the Roman Breviary of Venice (1478) and in a slightly changed form in the edition published under Urban VIII in 1632. The present wording was substituted for earlier readings in these places: 1.3, *ut solita clementia;* 1.4, *sis praesul ad custodiam.* This latter reading is found in the *Grad. et Antiph. MS Nivernense* (Paris, BNL, nouv. acq. 1295, s.12). The original doxology (found in MS Rome S. Petri B. 79, fol. 49, 12–13) was: *Praesta Pater omnipotens/ per Iesum Christum Dominum/ Qui tecum in perpetuum/ regnat cum Sancto Spiritu.* The current doxology is that commonly used for hymns of this meter, and was employed in the first editions of the Breviary. Many English translations have been made.

Bibliography: J. JULIAN, ed., *A Dictionary of Hymnology* (New York 1957). *Analalecta hymnica* 51:42–43. J. SZÖVÉRFFY, *Die Annalen der lateinischen Hymnendichtung* (Berlin 1964–65) 1:95, 214.

[J. J. GAVIGAN]

TEACHERS, MINISTRY OF

Teaching within the framework of the Church has for many centuries been termed an apostolate or a vocation. In recent years, however, and with increasing frequency, teaching has been described as a ministry. This article considers whether teaching is indeed a genuine ministry or whether the term has been misapplied in an attempt to add dignity and support to today's teachers. The term's meaning and implications are also considered.

Basis in Scripture. The actions of Jesus Christ strongly support the concept of teaching as ministry, for Christ began his own ministry by teaching, trained his followers as they accompanied him on his trips of teaching and other service, then sent them out as ministers with the command to ''teach'' (Mt 28.20). Christ's major task, as that of most of the founders of the world's great religions, was teaching. This would seem to indicate that teaching is one of the most basic forms of religious ministry.

Bearing in mind that the root meaning of ''minister'' is ''servant'' or ''one who serves or cares for another,'' the words of Jesus support the basic concept of ministry: ''Anyone among you who aspires to greatness must serve the rest; whoever wants to rank first among you must serve the needs of all. The Son of Man has not come to be served but to serve. . .'' (Mk 10.43–45).

St. Paul refers to teaching as a specific form of service or ministry within the Church: ''It is he [Christ] who gave apostles, prophets, evangelists, pastors, and teachers in roles of service for the faithful to build up the body of Christ. . .'' (Eph 4.11–12); ''God has set up in the Church first apostles, second prophets, third teachers. . .'' (1 Cor 12.28). Although these passages basically confirm the concept of teaching as ministry, one other text should be noted. In his letter to the Romans, Paul seems to indicate some distinction between ministry and teaching: ''One's gift may be prophecy; its use should be in proportion to his faith. It may be the gift of ministry; it should be used for service. One who is a teacher should use his gift for teaching. . .'' (Rom 12.6–7).

The Concept through Church History. Teaching in the early Church usually occurred during informal gatherings, especially at the breaking of the bread. The teaching function belonged originally to disciples, then passed to those taught by the disciples. The role of teacher was not a formal office, but rather emerged from the practical needs of the community, much as the role of elder. In his extensive work, *Ministry to Word and Sacrament*, Bernard Cooke traces the concept: ''Early Christianity had possessed a somewhat distinct ministry of teaching, but this was very rapidly absorbed (along with prophecy) into the episcopal function. At the time of Nicaea there is certainly no explicit prohibition of teaching by others than the bishops. But it seems to be increasingly taken for granted that teaching of the faith should be done within episcopally directed circumstances, which practically means that it is to be done by clerics'' (Cooke 260). Through the years, views differed about whether the ministry of teaching belonged only to the clergy (e.g., Origen wanted to be ordained a presbyter so that he could teach, yet Clement taught with no apparent role in the official ecclesiastical structure).

Nevertheless, by the Middle Ages, the clerical role in education was dominant and the teaching ministry was identified with the priestly ministry. Although the humanist influence around 1500 secularized education, the Reformers in the following century returned the trend to a religious one. The end of the 18th century witnessed another movement away from church control, followed again by a reversal, a demand for education under religious auspices. The number of students to be taught at that time necessitated increasing the number of nonclerical teachers, usually through the service of religious orders. This movement to religious, coupled with the gradual increase of lay teachers since the 1950s, has reestablished a distinct ministry of teaching.

One of the most positive assessments of the teaching ministry appears in Henri Nouwen's *Creative Ministry*: ''The most universal and most appreciated role of the Christian ministry through the ages has been teaching. Wherever Christians went to be of service, they always considered teaching as one of the primary tasks because of their conviction that increasing insight in man and his world is the way to new freedom and new ways of life'' (Nouwen 3).

Teaching in Recent Church Documents. Just as the emphasis on a distinct ministry of teaching appears and disappears during the history of the Church, so too the use of the term in Church documents is somewhat irregular.

Documents of Vatican Council II. These clearly identify the formal teaching service with the clergy alone: ''As successors of the apostles, bishops receive from him the mission to teach all nations and to preach the gospel to every creature, so that all men may attain to salvation . . . . Now, that duty, which the Lord committed to the shepherds of his people, is a true service, and in sacred literature is significantly called *diakonia* or ministry'' (*Lumen gentium* 24).

The tone becomes a bit more open in the Declaration on Christian Education. First the Council stresses that teaching is a vocation as well as an occupation: ''Beautiful, therefore, and truly solemn is the vocation of all those who assist parents in fulfilling their task, and who represent human society as well, by undertaking the role of school teacher'' (*Gravissimum educationis* 5). Nevertheless, the document is very sparing with the concept of teaching as ministry. Only once, in a section on the Catholic school, is the phrase clearly stated: ''This holy Synod asserts that the ministry of such teachers is a true apostolate which our times make extremely serviceable and necessary, and which simultaneously renders an authentic service to society'' (*ibid.* 8).

U.S. Bishops' Statements. In 1972 the United States bishops issued *To Teach as Jesus Did*, a pastoral replete with references to teaching as ministry. The preface alone refers to education as ministry four times, and the pastoral itself habitually makes such statements as: ''. . .Catholic elementary and secondary schools are the best expression of the educational ministry to youth'' (*To Teach* 84); and ''religious education programs for Catholic students who do not attend Catholic schools are an essential part of the Church's total educational ministry. . .'' (*ibid.* 93).

The succeeding statement of the U.S. bishops in 1976, *Teach Them*, again freely uses the ministry concept: ''we affirm our debt to these dedicated ministers of education, sisters, brothers, priests and lay people, who teach by what they are'' (*Teach Them* 3). Moreover, the bishops in *Teach Them* clarify and broaden the list of participants in the ministry: ''There has been increased recognition that all share in the educational ministry, not just those specifically assigned to 'teach religion''' (*ibid.* 4). In fact, the document refers to other specific groups involved in the educational ministry: parents, teachers, administrators, pastors, and the community. (*ibid.* 6–8).

With this increasing use of the term in church documents, one could look for frequent references to the educational ministry in the 1977 statement from the Congregation for Catholic Education, *The Catholic School.* On the contrary, the document consistently avoids the term.

Recent church documents do not show a simple chronological development. The only pattern that seems to emerge is that Vatican sources tend to avoid references to teaching as ministry while the United States bishops freely use the term ministry to describe teaching and education.

Meaning and Implications. In the Church there is common agreement that whatever form ministry takes, it exists for the sake of the community as a whole (*see* MINISTRY [ECCLESIOLOGY]). For the teacher, this requires that the ministry be focused on others—the students, the school, and the broader community. For the educational minister, there can be no consideration of teaching as ''only a job.'' As Jean Vanier phrases it, the teaching minister finds that formal teaching is only the beginning, an entry point, ''a commitment to people, whatever may happen'' (Vanier 67).

Focus on the person is the reason that the ministry of teaching has never limited itself to the teaching of religion. Henri Nouwen explains: ''Education is not primarily ministry because of what is taught but because of the nature of the educational process itself. Perhaps we have paid too much attention to the content of teaching without realizing that the teaching relationship is the most important factor in the ministry of teaching'' (Nouwen 3–4).

Recent documents point out the necessity of the teachers' witnessing to their own faith in Christ, not only in word, but by their lives. For the educational minister three elements are essential: message, fellowship, and service (*see, To Teach* 14–32). The message cannot remain only verbal, but must overflow to one of Christian living and liturgy (cf. *Gravissimum educationis* 2, 4). Community, which is central to Christian education, is not only a concept to be taught, but also a reality to be lived—among faculty as well as students (*ibid.* 12). With so many unique resources, educational ministers in the Church must offer service to others and to each other by ways imitative of Jesus Christ: concern for the weak and poor; use of some time for reassuring and being available—rather than only for direct teaching; extended hours of service; ability to see talents and to build on them; respect for the right of others to make choices.

The distinct ministry of teaching—evident in the early Church and in recent documents of the United States bishops—does seem to be a genuine ministry with a scriptural basis. To emphasize this fact—for teachers themselves as well as for the broader community—a variety of commissioning ceremonies and recommitment services has been initiated on local as well as diocesan levels. Such recognition and supporrt can strengthen a continuin ministry of teaching in the Church.

Bibliography: CONGREGATION FOR CATHOLIC EDUCATION, *The Catholic School* (Washington, DC 1977). B. COOKE, *Ministry to Word and Sacrament* (Philadelphia 1976). NCCB, *To Teach as Jesus Did* (Washington, DC 1972); *Teach Them* (Washington, DC 1976). H. J. M. NOUWEN, *Creative Ministry* (New York 1971). J. VANIER, *Be Not Afraid* (New York 1975).

[C. J. RECK]

TEACHING AUTHORITY OF THE CHURCH (MAGISTERIUM)

The magisterium may be defined as the perennial, authentic, and infallible teaching office committed to the Apostles by Christ and now possessed and exercised by their legitimate successors, the college of bishops in union with the pope. This ministry of the Word must first be situated within its context: the mystery of the Church in the divine plan of SALVATION. One may then study the nature and functions of this teaching office (first in the APOSTLES and then in their successors); its subjects and their relationship to one another (the bishops, the pope, and others); the ways in which it can be exercised; its twofold object; and, finally, the assent owed to the magisterium.

It is God's sovereignly wise and free plan of salvation to communicate the riches of His divine life to men.

Unity in the Word. This plan, conceived from all eternity, was to be perfectly realized in and through His divine Son, the perfect paternal utterance and self-communication (*see* WORD, THE; LOGOS), who came in search of His own (Jn 1.11) to gather them to Himself and take them in Him to the Father. Just as all things were created one through the eternal Word, so it is through the Incarnate Word that the disunity caused by sin is destroyed (*see* INCARNATION), and the perfect community of the last times is brought into existence. In order to constitute this community, the Word sent by the Father revealed the mystery of the Father's love, and having accomplished His redemptive work, sent the Spirit of truth and love so that all who believe may be saved and come to the perfect knowledge of the truth (1 Tm 2.4). It is, therefore, through this divine action that the community of salvation comes into existence, the community of those who believing in Jesus, the author of man's salvation and God's perfect self-communication, possess this saving Word, not as a treasure to be hoarded, but as a precious gift received to be communicated to others. One sees here the twofold aspect of the mystery of the Church: first, as the community of the redeemed gathered together by God's saving Word, it is the *fruit* of the divine plan; second, as the efficacious sign or sacrament of God's saving will revealed in the Incarnate Word, it is the *instrument* through which God gathers all to Himself in perfect unity (1 Cor 15.28; Eph 1.22). In other words, the Church is the community called together and living by FAITH in the Word and sent to mediate this saving Word to all men. (*See* CHURCH, ARTICLES ON.)

Communal Faith. To understand this vocation of the Church it is necessary to grasp clearly the communal nature of faith. Men are saved by faith, i.e., by the personal and total commitment and surrender of the individual to the God who reveals Himself as infinite truth and love. But God reveals and hence communicates Himself in and through the historical Christ. Every man, therefore, must come into living personal contact with the Christ of history; and this takes place by coming into contact with and sharing in the faith of that community to which was communicated once and for all and perfectly God's revelation in Christ, and which was sent to mediate that saving Word to all men. (*See* REVELATION, THEOLOGY OF.)

It is in this context of the mystery of the Church that one must now seek to understand the authentic and infallible ministry of the Word, or magisterium. Since the revelation of God in Christ has been communicated to the whole Church, each and every member of the community has the responsibility to witness both by word and deed to this saving Word (*see* WITNESS TO THE FAITH), and the Holy Spirit vivifies and guides all the members, who through Baptism into Christ are essentially equal and form only one Body in Christ [Gal 3.28; Vatican II, *Lumen gentium* 32, 35, *Acta Apostolicae Sedis* 57 (1965) 38–39, 40–41; *see* MYSTICAL BODY OF CHRIST]. However, in order that this Body might be built up in faith and love and effectively carry out its mission to and in the world, Christ has given various gifts to various members, and among these gifts must be counted the stabile and authoritative ministry of the Word confided by Christ to the Apostles and their successors. This ministry is truly a ministry, or service, to and within the community for the faithful transmission and preservation of the revelation.

As Christ has been sent to reveal the Father, so He in His turn sends the Apostles to witness to the saving Word revealed to them. To these chosen and preordained witnesses He confides this mission, first during His public life (Mt 10.1–42; Lk 9.1–10) and then definitively after His Resurrection (Mt 28.18–20; Mk 16.15–18). They are sent not merely to bear witness to the truth, but to teach this truth with authority in the name of Christ (Mr 10.40; Lk 10.16). This authority given to them in virtue of their mission cannot be simply identified with the authority of the Word proclaimed. Entirely derived from Christ, whose ministers they are, and entirely relative to and in the service of the Word which they proclaim, it has been given to them to bring about obedience to faith among all the nations (Rom 1.5; *see* OFFICE, ECCLESIASTICAL).

In carrying out this authoritative ministry of the Word, the Apostles are conscious of the permanent assistance of Christ (Mt 28.20) and of the Holy Spirit (Jn 14.15–17, 26; 15.26–27; 16.12–14) and, hence, of the rectitude of the message that they preach. Sent by Christ to witness to Him even to the ends of the earth (Lk 24.48; Acts 1.8), they gather about them the community of those who, believing in the Word, are baptized into Christ Jesus. For just as Christ was sent by the Father, so they are sent by Him in view of this community and in order to constitute it. And it is to this community, united in faith and love around the teaching of the Apostles (Acts 2.42; 4.32–33; 5.12–13), that they communicate the revelation as a sacred deposit (1 Tm 6.20–21; 2 Tm 1.13–14).

This authoritative and infallible magisterium was committed to the Apostles as a college (Mt 28.18–20). To one of them, however, Simon Peter, as the rock upon which the Church would be built (Mt 16.18) and as the supreme pastor of the flock (Jn 21.15–17), is given the special commission of strengthening the faith of his brethren (Lk 22.32), and so of being the organ and center of unity in faith and love of the whole college [Vatican II, *Lumen gentium* 18–19, *Acta Apostolicae Sedis* 57 (1965) 21–23; *see* PRIMACY OF THE POPE].

The Church of all ages must remain apostolic (Eph 2.20). This APOSTOLICITY of the Church consists essentially in its fidelity to the teaching of the Apostles, the DEPOSIT OF FAITH, which, according to Catholic teaching, was fully constituted and closed with the death of the last Apostle (H. Denzinger, *Enchiridion symbolorum*, ed. A. Schönmetzer 3011, 3020, 3070, 3421), though its articulation in doctrine has developed over time. Thus the revelation committed to the Church by the preaching of the Apostles and to which it adheres by living faith becomes tradition, and it is within and through the Church that this apostolic doctrine is to be transmitted to all subsequent generations. [*See* TRADITION (IN THEOLOGY)]. The Church, the ''pillar and mainstay of truth'' (1 Tm 3.15), against which the gates of hell will not prevail (Mt 16.18), has always preserved and will always preserve uncontaminated this sacred deposit and, hence, always remain indefectible in its belief in and profession of the apostolic doctrine (*Enchiridion symbolorum* 1501). This INDEFECTIBILITY of the Church is the result of the unfailing action of the Holy Spirit, who animates and guides the Church in each of its members [Vatican II, *Lumen gentium* 12; *Acta Apostolicae Sedis* 57 (1965) 16–17]. However, He animates the Church according to its organic structure as constituted by Christ and so guides and assists in a special way those who succeed the Apostles in their office as authentic teachers (*see* SOUL OF THE CHURCH). It is, therefore, the Catholic belief that the proximate organ of the indefectibility of the Church is its living and perennial magisterium. If the essential apostolicity of the Church consists in its fidelity to the apostolic teaching, the efficacious sign or sacrament of this apostolicity consists in the apostolic succession of a body of teachers who authoritatively and infallibly guard the deposit and expose it. Just as the primitive Church was gathered around the Apostles and their teaching, so the Church of all generations remains steadfast in the teaching of the Apostles by faithfully adhering to the teaching of their successors, the guardians and interpreters of the faith of the Church contained objectively in its Scriptures and apostolic traditions (*Enchiridion symbolorum* 1501).

Traditional Faith about Magisterium. Vatican I taught that the authoritative teaching office confided by Christ to His Apostles was always to remain in the Church in the persons of their successors, not in order to promulgate new revelations, but to faithfully guard, defend, and expose the apostolic teaching (*Enchiridion symbolorum* 3011–12, 3018, 3020, 3050, 3070, 3074). It also taught that in the exercise of this office the teaching body of the Church is through the assistance of the Holy Spirit preserved from error, or infallible [*Enchiridion symbolorum* 3020, 3074; cf. Vatican II, *Lumen gentium* 25, *Acta Apostolicae Sedis* 57 (1965) 29–31; *see* INFALLIBILITY]. This conclusive teaching, already maintained by Trent (*Enchiridion symbolorum* 1501, 1507) against the reformers, who affirmed that the only apostolic authority in the Church is that of the Scriptures, is nothing else than a formal explicitation of the consciousness of the Church of being in infallible possession of the truth and at the same time hierarchically constituted according to the will of Christ. From the very beginning the leaders of the local Churches and, specifically, the monarchical bishops, who by the end of the 2d century were established everywhere and explicitly recognized as the successors of the Apostles, were acknowledged as having a special role to play in guarding and teaching the apostolic doctrine handed down in the Church. [*See* BISHOP (IN THE CHURCH).] The traditional teaching of all the Churches, witnessed to and taught authoritatively by the bishops in the apostolic succession, was affirmed to be the ultimate norm of faith, the doctrine to be believed. Among the early witnesses of this faith may be cited Ignatius of Antioch (Eph 3.2–4.1), Clement of Rome (1 Cor 42, 44), Hegisippus (in Eusebius, *Ecclesastical History* 4.22), Irenaeus (*Adversus haereses* 3.3.1–3), and Tertullian (*De praescrip. haer.* 20, 32, 36). These writers clearly affirm, especially in opposition to the esoteric teachings of the Gnostics and others who sought to justify their tenets by an appeal to a hidden doctrine or to the speculative teaching of schools, that only that doctrine is to be accepted which is in conformity with the teaching of the bishops, the authoritative witnesses and interpreters of the apostolic faith.

The bishops themselves were conscious of their responsibility and authority in guarding and expounding the faith, as is shown from the very early and frequent practice of convoking local synods to discuss and decide matters of FAITH and morals (e.g., in the middle of the 3d century the synods of Carthage, Antioch, and Rome against—the Novatian heresy; Elvira in Spain, *c.* 306; Arles in France, 314). There followed the great general councils of the Church, the first being that of Nicaea in 325, which were conscious of and claimed supreme authority to declare and define the doctrine to be believed by the whole Church (cf. *Enchiridion symbolorum* 126, 686, 1520, etc.). Although the Church progressed in its understanding of the role of the magisterium (especially with regard to the unique authority of the Roman pontiffs), there can be no doubt that it has always believed that its living and authoritative teaching office is an integral, necessary, and irreplaceable element in its on-going life.

Nature and Functions of Magisterium. In many respects the ministry of the Apostles was a unique and unrepeatable event in the life of the Church. They alone laid the foundation of the Church's faith and life once and for all; the task of their successors would be to guard and build upon this foundation. As Vatican I taught (*Enchiridion symbolorum* 3020, 3070), this traditional, continuing magisterium has a twofold function: to guard the deposit and infallibly to expose or declare it.

To Guard the Deposit. The primary function of the magisterium of the successors of the Apostles is guarding the deposit of faith. If their teaching is the norm or RULE OF FAITH for the members of the Church, it is in its turn ruled by the apostolic teaching. It is a ministry of the Word not directly revealed to them, as was the case with the Apostles, but of the Word fixed and determined forever by the ministry of the first and unique witnesses. This aspect of the magisterial office was most prominent during the first millennium of the Church's history, and hence the reference to the tradition, the doctrine, was always explicit and formal.

To Interpret and Define Infallibly. The mission of guarding the deposit and faithfully witnessing to it in every generation implies and demands the magisterial function of infallibly interpreting and defining the faith. Besides the authority of the revealed Word itself, the Church acknowledges the jurisdictional authority of its divinely appointed teachers to impose this Word for the belief of its members. (*See* GOVERNANCE, POWER OF.) The nature and extent of this authority has often been badly misunderstood not only by non-Catholics, but by Catholics themselves. The *scriptura sola* of the reformers was essentially an affirmation of the primacy and sufficiency of the WORD OF GOD, and they believed that the Catholic Church in affirming its authority to judge the meaning and interpretation of the Scriptures had subordinated the Word of God to the words of men. One may reply that the authority of the magisterium must be seen as essentially a relative authority. Entirely derived from the authoritative mission given by Christ to the Apostles, and for its efficacious exercise dependent upon the perpetual assistance of the Holy Spirit, it is relative to and bound by the authority of the revealed Word itself. When the bishops in council or the pope speaking EX CATHEDRA infallibly declare and define some doctrine, they are not inventing a new revelation but merely expressing in human words the Church's understanding of the Word once revealed. In its "human" pronouncements the Church does not pretend to judge the revealed Word itself; it only interprets it, though judging any interpretation of the Word contrary to its own. Infallibly guided by the Holy Spirit, it cannot teach any interpretation of the Word contrary to the Word since it is one and the same Spirit that revealed the Word, entrusted it to the Apostles, and now assists the Church in interpreting it. These authoritative interpretations must remain inadequate expressions of the faith of the Church and, hence, subject to completion; for, being human, they depend upon the present state of theological development and upon the greater or lesser fidelity of the pastors of the Church to the light and guidance of the

Spirit. Taking for granted this human weakness, both intellectual and even moral, one can see that the continual assistance of the Holy Spirit does not absolve the magisterium from a diligent study and meditation on the Word of God, in order that its teaching may be ever more perfectly faithful to, and express ever more adequately, the divine truth.

Stress on Definition. The defining function of the magisterium has been particularly stressed in the more recent history of the Church, especially in the context of various denials of the authority of the Church in matters of doctrine. Reflection upon this function has also resulted from the development of ECCLESIOLOGY since the Middle Ages with its emphasis on the juridical nature of the Church as a visible society instituted by Christ whose hierarchy has been endowed with power and authority. (*See* VISIBILITY OF THE CHURCH.) This consciousness of the juridical nature of the Church has grown apace with a more acute awareness of the way in which the Church grows in its explicit understanding of the revealed Word.

Among the Fathers, and even much later, little thought was given to the problem of the development of doctrine and, hence, also to the necessary role of the magisterium as the ultimate and final judge of the legitimacy of a particular development, of its conformity with the revealed truth. Even Trent was content to define that the faith, always preserved in the Church, was to be found objectively expressed in its Scriptures and apostolic traditions. But when greater consideration was given to the historical process, that the faith of the Church under the guidance of the Holy Spirit is a living faith constantly growing in its objective expression, it became imperative to insist upon the role of the magisterium to determine here and now what is to be believed. (*See* DOCTRINE, DEVELOPMENT OF.) The reference to the traditional doctrine was never denied or lost sight of, but more emphasis was placed on what the Church infallibly teaches today. Too much insistence upon the juridical function of defining, which certainly pertains to the magisterium, brought about the tendency to equate the teaching authority of the Church with the power of jurisdiction. This point of view overlooks the fact that the primary function of the teaching office is the pastoral function of witnessing to the traditional faith of the Church, and that this office is essentially a charismatic gift conferred by episcopal consecration, even though jurisdictional authority is required for its legitimate and efficacious exercise. Thus Vatican II teaches that "the episcopal consecration bestows, together with the function of sanctifying, the functions also of teaching and governing, though these functions of their very nature can be exercised only in hierarchical communion with the head and the members of the college" [*Lumen gentium* 21, *Acta Apostolicae Sedis* 57 (1965) 25; *see* DEFINITION, DOGMATIC].

Teaching Body's Essential Unity. The teaching office in the Church is possessed by many different persons and is exercised in various degrees and ways: individual bishops guiding and teaching their flocks, provincial and national synods, ecumenical councils, the pope defining some doctrine ex cathedra or writing an ENCYCLICAL letter to his fellow bishops. [*See* COUNCILS, GENERAL (ECUMENICAL), THEOLOGY OF.] Yet the teaching body is essentially one, just as the faith that it guards and interprets is one. Theologians are not in agreement in explaining the exact nature of the unity between the pope and the college (the bishops together with the pope, their head), both of which, as Vatican II teaches, are the subject of supreme and full power over the Church [see *Lumen gentium* 22; *Acta Apostolicae Sedis* 57 (1965) 25–27]. This unity, however, can be understood in the following way. The bishops in union with their head, the pope, form but one moral body, the episcopal college, and it is to this body that the mission has been given of proclaiming the gospel to every creature and of guarding and interpreting the faith of the universal Church.

It is in the context of this collegial mission and responsibility that one is to understand the special role of the Roman pontiff, who succeeds to the primatial office given by Christ to Peter. As the head of the college and the visible organ of its unity he possesses personally the full teaching authority of the college and, as such, has the special responsibility of strengthening the faith of his brethren and of acting as their spokesman as occasion demands. He is also by virtue of his primatial office the supreme judge in matters of faith and morals and, hence, infallible when defining solemnly some doctrine to be held by the universal Church (*Enchiridion symbolorum* 3065–75). As the ever-active head of the college he is distinct from it but never separated, and he teaches and defines not his own faith but that of the Church. Hence the pope must always remain in close communication and collaboration with his fellow bishops dispersed throughout the world, who with him guard and witness to that faith.

These bishops are ordinarily entrusted with the care of a particular portion of the flock and are authentic doctors and teachers in their own dioceses, teaching authoritatively in the name of Christ. As such they are the representatives of the college or universal magisterium in each local Church and so in the exercise of their office must always be mindful of their responsibility for the faith of the universal Church. They, too, must remain in close contact with the whole episcopate and especially with its head, to whose universal jurisdiction they are always subject [*Enchiridion symbolorum* 3060–61; cf. Vatican II, *Lumen gentium* 23, *Acta Apostolicae Sedis* 57 (1965) 27–29].

Ordinary Exercise of Teaching Office. As seen above, the first function of the magisterium is to guard the deposit of faith by witnessing to it while authoritatively teaching the faithful. This is the ordinary exercise of the magisterial office of each bishop in his diocese and of the pope for the universal Church. Each bishop is not personally infallible, but when the bishops, dispersed throughout the world yet morally united among themselves in union with the pope, teach some doctrine with moral unanimity and precisely as witnesses to the faith, this teaching is that of the whole college and hence infallible and must be believed by the universal Church [*Enchiridion symbolorum* 3011; Vatican II, *Lumen gentium* 25, *Acta Apostolicae Sedis* 57 (1965) 29–31]. Such teaching may be found expressed in different ways, e.g., in CREEDS or catechisms universally approved by the hierarchy, in the liturgical practice of the whole Church, or even in the tacit approval given to some doctrine universally taught by the theologians (cf. *Enchiridion symbolorum* 2879). However, one must be extremely cautious in determining concretely what is the ordinary and universal teaching of the college on a particular point. It is often extremely difficult, at times even impossible, to ascertain this moral unanimity. Catechisms are a case in point. Customarily in these catechisms no distinction is made between what pertains to the faith and what may be no more than a common teaching of a particular theological school or a generally accepted but not certainly revealed doctrine.

The ordinary exercise of the teaching office of the pope as supreme pastor is called universal because it is directed to the whole Church. It is an essential element of the ordinary and universal magisterium of the college but is not to be identified with it, and, hence, it is not necessarily infallible. It is, however, authoritative, and if the pope should make a definite pronouncement on some controverted subject, this could no longer be regarded as a matter of free debate among theologians (*Enchiridion symbolorum* 3885). Nevertheless, just because the pope should express his opinion or show his approval of something, it is not to be thought that he always wishes to close the debate. Because of the enhanced position of the Roman see consequent upon the ever clearer awareness of the pope's special role in guarding the faith and teaching the Church, recent popes from Pius IX have been able to exercise ever more effectively their magisterial office toward the universal Church, mostly through encyclical letters, addressed to their fellow bishops but intended for the instruction of all the faithful. A particular teaching contained in one of these letters may be infallible either because it reflects the general teaching of the universal episcopate or has become the traditional teaching of the Holy See. In the latter case, the Holy Spirit in His general guidance of the hierarchy and providence over the Church would see to it that the popes do not lead the whole Church into error.

Extraordinary Exercise of Teaching Authority. The function of defining the meaning of the deposit of revelation, i.e., of making a formal and definitive judgment on a precise point in matters of doctrine, is an extraordinary exercise of the teaching authority. It is called extraordinary because it is exercised in extraordinary circumstances and because the teaching office is primarily a ministry of witnessing to revelation rather than of defining in a juridical and solemn way its meaning. The bishops collegially exercise this extraordinary function in ecumenical councils, viz, assemblies of bishops that so represent the entire college that their decisions truly express the collegial consent of the entire episcopate. The definitive teachings of councils other than solemn definitions are an expression of the ordinary and universal teaching authority, and hence to that extent infallible witnesses to the faith of the Church. In interpreting conciliar definitions and teachings, one must clearly ascertain the intention of the bishops [e.g., see the explanations with regard to Vatican II's *Dogmatic Constitution on the Church, Lumen gentium, Acta Apostolicae Sedis* 57 (1965) 72–75]. Moreover, a clear distinction must always be made between what is positively taught or defined and the arguments and examples from Scripture or tradition that illustrate or confirm the doctrine defined or taught. The latter are not intended as infallible pronouncements, and it is within the competence of scholars to determine their historical or exegetical value.

The pope exercises this extraordinary function of the magisterium when he defines *ex cathedra* some point concerning faith and morals to be held by the universal Church. Such a solemn pronouncement is infallible and irreformable of itself and so does not need the subsequent juridical assent of the other bishops (*Enchiridion symbolorum* 3074; cf. Vatican II, *Lumen gentium* 25).

Participation of Others in Magisterium. In carrying out their mission, the bishops and the pope can and do associate with themselves others who may participate in some way in their authority.

Priests. The closest associates of the bishops in the exercise of their pastoral ministry of the Word, in guiding and teaching the faithful, are those who share with them the sacred office and power of the ministerial priesthood. Although priests do not possess the highest degree of the priesthood, and so are not members of the episcopal college, they are given the office and function of preaching and teaching as an integral part of their sacerdotal ministry [see Vatican II, *Lumen gentium* 28; *Acta Apostolicae Sedis* 57 (1965) 33–36]. And if they are faithful to their ministry, the Holy Spirit will not deny a special guidance and efficacy to their preaching. Those to whom a care of souls has been given have a special duty of faithfully witnessing to the faith of the Church, since in the ordinary course of events it is through their preaching that the faithful are instructed. Religious and laymen appointed by a competent authority to give religious instruction may be compared to the priest in so far as they are given a mandate to teach by those who possess the official magisterium in the Church. [*See* PREACHING, III (THEOLOGY OF).]

Roman Congregations. In the ordinary exercise of his pastoral office the pope associates with himself and delegates authority to the various Roman congregations. (*See* CURIA, ROMAN.) The Congregation for the Doctrine of the Faith especially can and does issue doctrinal decrees in the name of and with the authority of the pope, and these decrees are to be adhered to by the faithful (*Enchiridion symbolorum* 2880, 3408, 3503). They are usually concerned with settling a question as to whether or not a particular point of doctrine can be safely held or taught considering the state of dogmatic and theological development at the time. They are, therefore, subject to revision at a later date and are not meant to impede further investigation of the matter by Biblical scholars and theologians (*Enchiridion symbolorum* 3681, 3862–64).

Theologians. Theologians have a special role to play in the exposition and defense of the faith. They do not, however, pertain to the authoritative teaching body of the Church, even when they teach sacred doctrine in seminaries, etc., under the direct vigilance of and by virtue of a mandate from the pope or a competent bishop. Their role is to fulfill in a scientific way the requirement to come to an understanding of the faith. This requirement is imposed by the dynamism of faith itself on all believers; the competence of a theologian is particularly scientific. Generally speaking the doctrinal authority of a particular theologian will be in direct proportion to that competence together with his fidelity to the totality of the faith. Nevertheless, the teaching Church can and does give special approbation to the teachings and methods of certain individual theologians or schools, as in the case of scholastic theology in general (*Enchiridion symbolorum* 2676, 2814, 3883–84) and of the method and doctrine of St. Thomas (*Enchiridion symbolorum* 3135–40).

Like any other member of the community, theologians receive from the bishops, and owe allegiance to, the Church's credal formulations and official teachings. Yet they also have a vital role to play in doctrinal formulations, as well as in the further understanding and development (including revision) of doctrinal formulas. Though conflict and tensions are apt to persist between bishops and theologians, the ideal to be worked toward is one of mutual respect and cooperation, each seeking to safeguard the other's responsibility and competence.

Consultation. In the exercise of their teaching office the pope and bishops will also make use of and consult other competent and learned men when the need arises, for example, when there is question of ascertaining the relevance and import of a moral teaching of the Church in a concrete situation. Besides, they should also listen to and consult the faithful in general, remembering that the Holy Spirit animates and guides all the members of the Church and is wont to distribute His special gifts of understanding and light to those whom He wills without respect for persons. All believers share in some way in proclaiming and teaching the faith; all are in some way both teachers and taught. [See Vatican II, *Lumen gentium* 12, 37, *Acta Apostolicae Sedis* 57 (1965) 16–17, 42–43; *see* CHARISM.]

Object of Teaching Authority. The definition of Vatican I with regard to the infallibility of the pope affirms that the object of his infallible defining magisterium is coextensive to that with which Christ willed His Church to be endowed. This object is explicitly said to be "doctrine concerning faith and morals to be held by the universal Church" (*Enchiridion symbolorum* 3074). This technical expression (cf. equivalent, *Enchiridion symbolorum* 1507, 3007) embraces whatever concerns necessarily the truth of the religious relationship of men with God in Christ, or whatever pertains to the promotion of the Christian religion and the eternal salvation of men. In accord with the explanation given by the Relator of the Deputation of Faith at Vatican I, Bishop V. Gasser, theologians divide this general object into what are called the primary and secondary objects of the magisterium.

Primary Object. The former is the deposit of revelation: whatever has been revealed by God either explicitly or implicitly, promulgated by the Apostles, and preserved in the Scriptures and living tradition. It is clear from all that has been seen that the authentic teaching office in the Church is primarily and essentially a ministry. of the Word; and it is a DOGMA of faith that the teaching Church is infallible when defining the meaning of this revelation.

Secondary Object. Pertaining to the secondary object are other truths not revealed in themselves but so intimately connected with revelation that their profession and, eventually, their definition by the magisterium or the condemnation of errors that contradict them are necessary for the integral conservation of the deposit of faith. Following the teaching of recent popes and the fathers of

Vatican I, who vindicated the competence of the magisterium in these matters (*Enchiridion symbolorum* 2922, 3018, 3042, 3045), the *Dogmatic Constitution on the Church* of Vatican II declares: "This infallibility with which the divine Redeemer willed His Church to be endowed when it defines a doctrine of faith or morals is coextensive with the deposit of divine revelation, which must be religiously guarded and faithfully expounded" (*Lumen gentium* 25). Thus, although it is not a dogma of faith that the magisterium can infallibly define such truths, it is at least a magisterially taught THEOLOGICAL CONCLUSION (theologically certain) that flows from the nature of the Church and its magisterium as realities in history. For the Church does not guard inviolate and faithfully expose the deposit of faith in a vacuum or merely repeat in parrot fashion the Word of God; that Word must be made a living reality for the men of every generation, it must be defended against every sort of error, its relevance must be affirmed in concrete situations, and all this must be done by succeeding generations of living teachers. But these men could not carry out efficaciously this ever actual mission in history unless it lay within the scope of their teaching office to teach authoritatively and even to define infallibly the truth of certain facts or philosophical propositions so intimately linked with the revelation itself or its preservation by the Church that their denial would lead necessarily to the denial of that revelation proposed by the Church here and now.

The question of the secondary object was first explicitly posed when the followers of Cornelius JANSEN sought to evade the condemnation by Innocent X in 1653 of five propositions taken from Jansen's book, *AUGUSTINUS*, by affirming that the doctrine condemned was heretical but that Jansen had never taught it in his book. Alexander VII answered this subterfuge by declaring and defining that the condemned propositions had been taken from the book, and in the sense intended by the author, and demanded an internal assent under oath to this fact (2012, 2020). From that time on, the Church reflected more on the nature of the teaching office as a reality in history competent to teach authoritatively and infallibly whatever is intimately connected with the preservation and exposition of the deposit of revelation.

Extent of Secondary Object. Theologians differ in determining the precise extent of this object of the infallible magisterium. Most would include within this object the following: the fact that propositions opposed to the truths of the faith are contained or not contained in a certain book (the propositions of Jansen); that a council is legitimate and ecumenical or that a pope was legitimately elected (*see* DOGMATIC FACT); that a particular translation or version of the Scriptures is authentic (e.g., in the question of the Vulgate); the truth or falsity of philosophical truths intimately linked with the revelation itself or its acceptance (e.g., concerning the capacity of the mind to know truth); strictly theological conclusions from the revelation, sometimes called truths virtually revealed (e.g., necessity of jurisdiction to absolve validly; *see* REVELATION, VIRTUAL). In the practical sphere may be mentioned the solemn approbation of religious orders (that the rule approved is in accord with the evangelical life); laws promulgated for and binding on the universal Church (that they are in accord with the divine law and apt to promote the sanctity of the Church); the solemn canonization of saints. Of particular importance is the competence of the Church to interpret and apply the natural law, for its prescriptions are "necessary for salvation" to teach men about the natural law is part of the Church's prophetic office, "proclaiming to men what they truly are and reminding them of what they should be before God" [*Catechism of the Catholic Church* 2036].

Domain of Certitude. The whole problematic concerning the secondary object of the magisterium could perhaps be broadened. When the question of the competence in these matters of the magisterium is posed, it is usually in the context of the infallibility of the magisterium: can the pope or a council infallibly define the truth or falsity of a certain proposition? Yet infallibility is not the only category that can be opposed to falsity. Between it and ERROR there is the whole domain of sufficient CERTITUDE, guaranteed by the divine assistance that accompanies the exercise of spiritual authority without rendering it necessarily and absolutely infallible. The Catholic accepting in faith the competence of the divinely instituted pastoral ministry, can rest assured that these men do not seriously err in carrying out their ministry without demanding that in every instance they must be able to give an infallible and hence irrevocable definition. In insisting too much on the question of infallibility, one runs the risk of demeaning in the eyes of the faithful the ordinary pastoral function of the magisterium.

Assent Owed to Teaching of the Church. Whatever is proposed by the Church as a divinely revealed object of belief, either in a solemn decree or in its ordinary universal teaching, is, in the words of Vatican I, to be believed by "divine and Catholic faith" (*Enchiridion symbolorum* 3011). This is nothing more than a necessary conclusion that flows from what has been said about the authoritative and infallible ministry of the Word within the context of the Church as the community of faith possessed by and possessing indefectibly God's definitive and irrevocable Word. The assent given is one of divine faith, i.e., because of the authority of God revealing to the individual this truth. It is called Catholic because it is made within the context of the community of believers and through the mediation of those who have received the divinely assisted ministry of authoritatively witnessing to and eventually defining what is to be believed by the whole Church. Being a surrender in faith to the God who can neither deceive nor be deceived, the assent is irretractable and absolutely certain.

When the Church solemnly defines a dogmatic fact or truth not directly revealed but intimately connected with the revelation, one must also give an irrevocable and unconditional assent, at least because of the infallibility of the Church in defining such matters.

In all other cases when the Holy Father (directly or through the Roman congregations) or the bishops, in the exercise of their ordinary pastoral ministry toward the flock committed to their care, teach authoritatively, the assent owed on the part of the faithful to this teaching is a true internal assent, firm, though not necessarily definitive. Though this assent in its epistemological structure can be compared to that given in the ordinary course of affairs to men scientifically qualified in matters within their competence, it must be stressed that the motive of the assent is the religious motive of obedience due to those who have been given authority in the Church of God.

It also falls to the magisterium to warn the faithful of the dangers of certain opinions that, though not judged definitively to be *per se* erroneous, can lead to errors. ''The willingness to submit loyally to the teaching of the Magisterium on matters *per se not irreformable* must be the rule'' (*Instruction on the Ecclesial Vocation of the Theologian,* 24). The context in which alone this assent can be understood is that of the supernatural community of faith in which a stable and authoritative ministry of the Word has been established by Christ for the building up of the Body in truth and love. Since the Spirit guides and assists those to whom this ministry has been given, the faithful ordinarily can and should give an internal assent free from prudent fear of error (see Vatican Council II, *Lumen gentium* 25).

See Also: AUTHORITY, ECCLESIASTICAL; DOCTRINE; FREEDOM, INTELLECTUAL; REVELATION, FONTS OF; THINKING WITH THE CHURCH, RULES FOR.

Bibliography: J. V. BAINVEL, *De magisterio vivo et traditione* (Paris 1905). Y. M. J. CONGAR, *La Foi et la théologie* (Tournai 1962), especially 41–71, 157–168; *La Tradition et les traditions,* 2 v. (Paris 1960–63), v.1 *Essai historique,* especially 233–278, v.2 *Essai théologique; Jalons pour une théologie du laïcat* (3d ed. Paris 1964), English *Lay People in the Church,* tr. D. ATTWATER (Westminster, Maryland 1957) 258–308. Y. M. J. CONGAR and B. D. DUPUY, eds., *L'Épiscopat et l'église universelle* (Paris 1962). J. B. FRANZELIN *Tractatus de divina traditione et scriptura* (4th ed. Rome 1896). D. VAN DEN EYNDE, *Les Normes de l'enseignement chrétien dans la littérature patristique des trois premiers siècles* (Paris 1933). W. BARTZ, ''Le Magistère de l'église d'après Scheeben,'' *Recherches de science religieuse* 34 (1960) 309–327. G. DEJAIFVE., ''Revelation et l'église,'' *Nouvelle revue théologique* 85 (1963) 563–576. P. NAU, ''Le magistère pontifical ordinaire, lieu théologique,'' *Revue thomiste* 56 (1956) 389–412. R BROWN, ''Bishops and Theologians: 'Dispute' Surrounded by Fiction,'' *Origins* 7 (1978) 675–682. Y. CONGAR, ''Pour unc histoire sémantique du terme 'magisterium'''; ''Bref historique des formes du 'magistère' et de ses relations avec les docteurs.'' *Revue des sciences philosophiques et théologiques* 60 (1976) 85–112. A. L. DESCAMPS, ''Théologie et magistère,'' *Ephemerides theologicae Lovanienses* 56 (1976) 82–133. A. DULLES, ''What is Magisterium,'' *Origins* 6 (1976) 81—87. INTERNATIONAL THEOLOGICAL COMMISSION, *Theses on the Relationship between the Ecclesiastical Magisterium and Theology* (USCC Publication Office, Washington, D.C. 1977). R MCCORMICK and C. E. CURRAN, eds., *Dissent in the Church* (Readings in Moral Theology 6; New York 1988). F. A. SULLIVAN, *Magisterium: Teaching Authority in the Catholic Church* (New York 1983); *Creative Fidelity: Weighing and Interpreting the Documents of the Magisterium* (New York 1996). CONGREGATION FOR THE DOCTRINE OF THE FAITH, ''Instruction on the Ecclesial Vocation of the Theologian'' (May 24, 1990). R. R. GAILLARDETZ, *Teaching with Authority: A Theology of the Magisterium in the Church* (Collegeville, Minnesota 1997).

[J. R. LERCH/EDS.]

TEAM MINISTRY (CANON LAW)

The concept of team ministry is a direct outgrowth of Vatican II, which, among its many teachings on the nature of the Church, reshaped the pastoral office of the bishop, the model for all pastoral care, from its exclusive dependence on hierarchical activity to an office carried out in true collaboration with all the people of God. (See *Lumen gentium* 17, *Christus Dominus* 30, *Apostolicam actuositatem* 24.) This vision of collaboration was carried into the 1983 Code of Canon Law and given specific form. Thus, there are important theological and canonical principles behind the concept.

Because the parish is the primary arena for the exercise of pastoral care, parish is likewise the best place to look for models of team ministry. In the broad sense, team ministry is the spirit of collaboration which is intended to exist in any parish, even one with the traditional staffing model of a single pastor, through which all of the faithful understand and discharge their responsibilities as baptized persons for evangelization, catechesis and liturgical participation. The goal for any parish is that no individual is a passive recipient of pastoral care. (See canons 519, 528, 529, 759, 781.)

In a more narrow and highly specific sense, models for team ministry in parishes are found in canon 517 of the 1983 Code. This canon, an innovation in the law, provides for the staffing of parishes in ways which omit the traditional office of pastor and replace that single person with a group of persons or team. The canon distinguishes two basic possibilities: (1) the pastoral care of a parish (or multiple parishes) is entrusted to a group of priests *in solidum* (as equals) or (2) participation in the pastoral care of a parish is entrusted to one or more non-priests. In the first situation, according to canon 517, one of the priests of the team is named moderator of the group, directs its activities and represents the team before the bishop. However, despite this designation, all priests on the team bear the responsibilities ordinarily assigned to the pastor equally, while fulfilling them under the direction of the moderator (cc. 543, 544). The team must work out for itself how the various responsibilities which each member bears will be executed. The framers of the 1983 Code acknowledged that this arrangement, although not foreseen in the documents of Vatican II and clearly an exception, could be useful ''in certain circumstances.'' The canon, repeating that phrase, does not indicate what any of circumstances might be. Rather, implementation of this configuration of team ministry is left to the judgment of each diocesan bishop.

The second situation of team ministry, as stipulated in c. 517 § 2, is to be implemented only when there is a lack of priests. Under those circumstances, the diocesan bishop may entrust participation in pastoral care to ''a deacon, to another person who is not a priest, or to a community of persons.'' The word ''participate'' with reference to pastoral care is used designedly in the canon to distinguish between ''full'' pastoral care, which includes celebration of the sacraments, and the portion of pastoral care which can be made available by those who are not priests.

In this instance of team ministry, again, the parish does not have a pastor, but a priest is assigned to direct pastoral care. For such parishes, the team is composed of the priest-director and whatever persons have been entrusted with participation in pastoral care by the diocesan bishop. The team must work out for itself how its responsibilities will be carried out, how and when the priest-director will be available to the parish, whether there might be another priest to provide sacramental services, and what functions will be carried out by the non-priests. Establishment of this form of team ministry calls for careful preparation of the parish community both to accept an increased role of leadership from laity or deacons and a diminished role of presence, if not leadership, from the ordained. Official documents issued by the Holy See, especially ''Directory for Sunday Celebrations in the Absence of a Priest'' issued in 1988 have highlighted these concerns.

Bibliography: J. BEAL, et al. eds., *New Commentary on the Code of Canon Law* (Mahwah 2000). L. CHIAPPETTA, *Il Codice di Diritto Canonico: Commento giuridico-pastorale* (Naples 1988). J. RENKEN, ''Canonical Issues in the Pastoral Care of Parishes without Priests,'' *The Jurist* 47 (1987) 506–521. B. A. CUSACK and T. G. SULLIVAN, *Pastoral Care in Parishes without a Pastor: Applications of C. 517 § 2* (Washington, DC 1995).

[E. RINERE]

TECHNOLOGY, PHILOSOPHY OF

According to the authoritative bibliography of the philosophy of technology of C. Mitcham and R. Mackey, in the late 20th century there were at least seven separate and distinct meanings for the phrase ''philosophy of technology.'' It can mean (1) ethical and/or political critiques of technology, (2) religious critiques, (3) treatments of technology from the specialized perspectives of phenomenology or existentialism aimed at discerning the ''pure essence'' or the ''existential meaning'' of technology, (4) metaphysical analyses attempting to situate the phenomenon of technology in a larger speculative context other than the religious or phenomenological, (5) studies based on the techniques of linguistic analysis focusing on the meaning and uses of the term ''technology'' or related terms or of common statements in which the terms appear, (6) the commonsense ''philosophy'' of practicing engineers, applied scientists, and science managers (including the history and sociology thereof), and (7) what Mitcham and Mackey call ''comprehensive philosophies of technology,'' i.e., studies that combine two or more of the above approaches in an attempt to produce a philosophical synthesis of the meaning of technology as a phenomenon distinct, but not necessarily separable, from any other subject of philosophical inquiry.

Before selecting one of these meanings as a focus here, a further clarification is needed—namely, of the word ''technology'' itself. Jacques ELLUL, an internationally respected philosopher of technology, prefers the term ''technique'' and defines it so broadly that it includes any means-to-end rational organization of behavior, whether or not it uses or depends upon machines, computers, or scientific or technical knowledge of any sort. ''Technique'' in this broad sense Ellul takes to be the spirit or *Zeitgeist* of contemporary Western civilization. And he takes this ''spirit of technique'' to be an enslaving force from which he doubts that man will be able to free himself.

The difficulty with sweeping assertions of this sort is that they are almost impossible to deal with except as metaphor. Their acceptance or rejection depends not upon evidence but upon the persuasiveness of an image.

Consequently, one does not need to claim that he can give a perfectly objective definition of the term ''technology'' in order to reject Ellul's in favor of a more restrictive definition. What seems to be the common denominator in most treatments of technology is the association of the two terms ''science'' and ''technology.'' While some purists argue for a clear distinction between the two, both in the popular mind and in most broad-based treatments of technology there is an explicit assumption that modern technology is essentially related to science. Whether or not adequate distinctions can be made between pure science, applied science, and technology, or between a theoretically oriented science and a goal- or mission-oriented technology, the assumption is made here that in an adequate definition of technology one component must be its essential dependence on scientific knowledge.

A second common denominator in most treatments broad enough to be called philosophies of technology is the recognition that a definite social group is the carrier of technology—or at least of technological knowledge (where this is separated from the economic or political uses of technology). This carrier is generally referred to in the literature as the ''technical community'' and is usually taken to include a large number of scientists, nearly all engineers and technicians, and research managers in government or industry or specialized research institutes.

The term ''technology,'' then, can be taken to cover this scientific and technical community, including its inner structure and functions, its relationships to other social phenomena, its products, its particular values, and its implicit view of human nature. The term ''philosophy of technology'' will then mean a set of generalizations or a systematic treatment, in philosophical language, of one or another or all of the above aspects of this social phenomenon.

What validity there is in evaluations of technological society as a whole, or in assessments of the place of technology in the larger culture, is a questionable matter. Can such claims be meaningfully verified or falsified? It might be claimed by one or another critic or defender of technology that his view is objective, that he is simply reporting the facts as they are. As a counterclaim to this it would be too strong to say that all theories about technological society, like all large-scale social theories, must necessarily be moralistic or politically or ideologically biased in some way; it is enough to say that there is usually a direct correlation between an author's view of man in society—including his view of man in technological society—and his personal philosophy, his moral and political attitudes, and his concept of the nature of man. This means that for all practical purposes every proponent of a philosophy of technology is simply presenting his particular version of what a good technological society would be like or his view as to what is wrong with technological society as he sees it. Ideally, then, ''philosophy of technology'' ought to stand for an open forum in which various interpretations of technology and technological society are openly debated.

The range of interpretations of technology is broad. Only a limited sampling can be given here.

Marcuse, Skinner, and Mumford. One of the best-known critics of capitalist technology, or of its misuse in socialist countries, is the social philosopher Herbert Marcuse. His fundamental thesis—which has not varied greatly even when Marcuse has modified its expression in response to changing circumstances in the United States—is that technology is a tool in the hands of the ruling class helping to guarantee the enslavement of the masses by its totally alienating rational objectivity. According to Marcuse ''the prevailing forms of social control are technological''; they appear rational ''to such an extent that all contradiction seems irrational and all counteraction impossible.'' Marcuse feels that men in a technological society have reached an unprecedented level of alienation, an entirely objective alienation. The alienated individual ''is swallowed up by [his] alienated existence. There is only one dimension [the technological], and it is everywhere and in all forms'' (*One-Dimensional Man* 9, 11). Marcuse's analysis shows an obvious dependence on Marx, but he has also been influenced by Freud and betrays a stronger belief than Marx in a ''higher culture,'' which he sees as disappearing more each day in technological society.

Less pessimistic than Marcuse's is the popular philosophy of technology of B. F. Skinner. While Skinner also claims to have a place in his technological utopia for culture, his emphasis is primarily on technology. He argues for a wholesale and deliberate adoption of what he calls the ''technology of behavior,'' by which he means the adaptation of the techniques of laboratory conditioning to the purposes of social and political engineering. He feels that the process can remain democratic and is perfectly feasible; in fact he argues that it is necessary if mankind is to solve such social problems as overpopulation, war, and crime. The price for the elimination of these evils is to go ''beyond freedom and dignity,'' i.e., to consciously give up what Skinner takes to be the illusions of freedom and dignity. Man must admit that he is totally conditioned by his environment and make the best of it. Skinner often sounds optimistic about his technological utopia.

Another pessimistic philosophy of technology—one with an entirely different slant from that of Marcuse—is that of the historian and social commentator Lewis Mumford. Going back into history for his sources, Mumford claims that he has discovered a recurring ''myth of the machine'' in accord with which powerful rulers are willing to organize their subjects into vast machine-like organizations for the efficient attainment of their goals. The most striking analogy of this sort that Mumford uses is between the organization of manpower for the building of the pyramids and the organization of technical experts needed to get men to the Moon. Mumford's overall thesis is that such organization is usually turned toward the achievement of victory in war, and the other major image he uses to describe the dangers inherent in contemporary technology is the ''pentagon of power.'' Though his expression of the view is infinitely superior in style and erudition, Mumford thus has some affinity with critics of the so-called military-industrial complex.

Ellul, Marcel, Heidegger, and Dessauer. The last of these very general critiques of technological society as a whole to be taken up here can be lumped under the inexact but common heading of existentialism and phenomenology. Without intending to categorize him in any way that he would find reprehensible, one can say that Jacques Ellul probably fits best in this group of critics of technology. In any case much of the audience for his works in the United States has been among readers sympathetic with an existential anxiety about man's future in a technological world. Since Ellul's views have already been summarized briefly, it may be enough to relate them here to the thought of Gabriel MARCEL, the most outspoken critic of technological culture among those usually lumped under an existentialist label. Marcel, even in his most balanced essays, sees technological civilization as embodying what is worst in modern culture. Both he and Ellul share the view that only something such as divine grace can save modern man from the evil grip of technology.

Martin HEIDEGGER is another influential philosopher who is existentially pessimistic about technology. Heidegger's view of technology naturally borrows a great deal from his general philosophy of the ''concealment'' of Being in a multitude of beings. One path to the unconcealing of Being turns out to be an appropriate existential understanding of technology. Regrettably, in Heidegger's view, most technologists, technocrats, and ordinary users of the products of technology focus on technological products rather than on the meaning of Being that ought to infuse every aspect of existence. While this analysis might seem to lead to a hope that men in a technological society might come to realize that technology can be a path to Being, recognizing technology's internal self-limiting features when it is seen in this light, Heidegger is pessimistic about this ever happening.

On the other hand, the leading phenomenological philosopher of technology (though here the term ''phenomenology'' has more in common with Hegel than with those who are usually called phenomenologists today), Friedrich Dessauer, has a completely optimistic view of technology, seeing it as the transforming force in a totally new philosophy of culture appropriate to the contemporary world. Dessauer, who was little known in the United States until his work received a boost from Mitcham and Mackey, is a disciple of Kant who claims to have found in technology the means both to resurrect Kant and to move his critical philosophy onto a higher metaphysical ground. Briefly, Dessauer argues that technical invention, wherein the inventor finds himself drawn irresistibly toward a perfect solution to his technical problem (which is supposed to explain the discovery-like ''That's it!'' that often accompanies the solution of a technical problem), reveals the existence of a world of ''ideal forms'' that allows man to reach the knowledge of ''the thing in itself'' that Kant could never reach. Dessauer calls the knowledge of technology ''the fourth realm,'' beyond Kant's three realms of natural science, ethics, and aesthetics, and he sees it as the new foundation of a comprehensive metaphysics. This leaves philosophy of technology as the foundational discipline of an adequate contemporary philosophy and seems to leave the technologist aware of the meaning of his pursuit with an unlimited challenge for his God-like creative talents.

Futurology, and the Two Cultures. Aside from these very broad assessments of technological society, two other types of treatments of technology—''futurism'' or ''futurology'' and discussions of the so-called two-cultures controversy—while specialized are general enough in their implications to bear on philosophy of technology.

Futurology, in current usage, stands for science-based social planning for the future. Some of the best-known futurists include Bertrand de Jouvenel and his Futuribles group; Daniel Bell, the editor of the influential *Toward the Year 2000;* and Herman Kahn and Anthony Wiener, whose *The Year 2000: A Framework for Speculation on the Next 33 Years* achieved best-seller status in spite of its technical jargon and incomplete scenarios of the future. William Ewald has expressed the essence of what is distinctive about scientific futurology: ''We now [with the computer] have the capacity to study seriously the real-life multivariable complex interrelationships of the environment which the human mind could not possibly manage unaided'' (*Environment for Man: The Next Fifty Years,* 5). Employing computer-projected probabilities, the futurists believe that they can help mankind design an optimum environment for the future. They can do so because their probabilistic computer-based scenarios of the future—while they cannot predict the future absolutely any more than could earlier prophecies of the future—can make social engineering a scientific enterprise. If true, this would be a significant breakthrough, and ''technological man'' would turn out to have an awesome control of the future unshared by any previous culture. Not all, however, are agreed that the computer is so powerful, or that social engineering is any more palatable in this than in any other form.

The 1960s controversy triggered by C. P. Snow's *The Two Cultures* is also relevant to philosophy of technology. Although critics retorted that neither the scientific nor the humanistic community is unified enough to be called a culture, Snow seems to have put his finger on a real split in technological culture. In a world of high specialization, few scientists or engineers can lay claim to any greater degree of humanistic sophistication than an amateur interest in poetry or music or perhaps politics; nor can the average academic humanist usually claim that he even attempts to keep up with scientific knowledge. This split, whatever its explanation or prospects for healing, says something profound about technological society. A philosophy of technology, whether it attempts to explain or to solve the problem, must in some way come to grips with it.

It is in this context that some Catholic writers have turned to the thought of Pierre TEILHARD DE CHARDIN. His vision of the future convergence of science and religion has seemed to them to offer a way out for contemporary man. Others, however, see Teilhard de Chardin as distorting science and demeaning religion; they feel that a philosophical synthesis adequate for a scientific or technological age is yet to be discovered.

Finally, among these interpretations of technology, there seems to be no end to popularized ''philosophies of technology.'' The late 1960s and early 1970s in particular witnessed a flood of publications of this sort. Some of the most popular authors included Charles Reich, Theodore Roszak, Alvin Toffler, and, a little earlier, Marshall McLuhan. How many of their works will turn out to be ephemeral and how many will contribute to a serious philosophy of technology remains of course to be seen. No serious student of the history and philosophy of technology, however, can afford not to keep up with the popular literature. It reflects an aspect of technology—its acceptance in the popular mind—that must be included in some fashion in any comprehensive treatment of the issue. The same is also true of science fiction.

See Also: TECHNOLOGY, SOCIAL EFFECTS OF

Bibliography: C. MITCHAM and R. MACKEY, ''Bibliography: The Philosophy of Technology,'' *Technology and Culture* 14.2 (April 1973). C. MITCHAM and R. MACKEY, eds., *Philosophy and Technology: Readings in the Philosophic Problems of Technology* (New York 1972), excellent select bibliography. P. T. DURBIN, ''Technology and Values: A Philosopher's Perspective,'' *Technology and Culture* 13.4 (October 1972) 556–576. E. S. FERGUSON, *Bibliography of the History of Technology* (Cambridge, Mass. 1968). V. C. FERKISS, *Technological Man: The Myth and the Reality* (New York 1969), wide-ranging but unselective bibliography. E. G. MESTHENE, *Harvard University Program on Technology and Society, 1964–1972: A Final Review* (Cambridge, Mass. 1972); for a balanced critical evaluation of this, the best known of the academic programs relevant to philosophy of technology, see the review by G. BASALLA, ''Addressing a Central Problem,'' *Science* 180 (May 11, 1973) 582–584.

[P. T. DURBIN]

TECHNOLOGY, SOCIAL EFFECTS OF

A consistent, underlying theme of Vatican Council II is the importance of considering the specific qualities of culture and society shaping the contemporary world in its uniqueness. The Council directed its considerations to the concrete world of the 20th century, not to some abstract world without specific temporal definition. The concentration on this particular moment in space and time was to assure a proper understanding and embodiment of the reality of the Christian God who is appreciated as One who is immanent in transcendence, incarnate in divinity. The Lord is now present to and active in this world with all its uniqueness and particularities. The *Constitution on the Church in the Modern World* describes the present moment in human history as one profoundly unique in both social and cultural dimensions, so much so that one can speak of ''a new age in human history'' (*Gaudium et spes 54*). The range of change which brought about this new era is so pervasive that the Council admits that culture has taken a new form which in turn creates new ways of thinking and acting. To be a vital presence and force in this new context, the Church must understand this new situation and express its life in accordance with the dynamics of this new cultural setting.

Specific reference is made (ibid.) to the developments in modern technology because of its central influence on patterns of thought and action. Human thinking is more and more in the form of a ''technological mentality,'' a way of thinking that emphasizes analysis, planning, the use of specific techniques and, above all, the control of all the components in the situation. Besides the mindset which dominates a technological society, there are also the tangible results of that thinking in certain systems of operation and in the products created by research, planning, and production. From a religious point of view, the total range of technology deserves serious consideration and critical evaluation in terms of whether it enhances or detracts from the realization of the Kingdom of God on earth.

Impact of the Technological Mentality. This assessment takes on decided critical importance when the investigation concerns the effect of a particular aspect of technology on the human person. The technological mentality tends, for instance, to approach the human as object, number, an element of a process, a mere part of a material whole. If the human subject is reduced to the lesser proportions of object, if the sacred dignity of each person is judged worthwhile only to the extent that it contributes to some desired goal, then something God-given and essential is lost.

A further area of concern is the potential modification of the biological substratum of the human person through the rearrangement of the basic components of the living organism. Needed for this kind of assessment is an open and knowledgeable discussion between theologians, scientists, and informed citizens as to the ramifications of that kind of technological modification. In general, what is becoming clear with today's profound and rapid technological changes is that the possibilities for both good and evil are enhanced with the passage of time. TEILHARD DE CHARDIN pointed to this enhancement in his reflections on developments in science and technology. The harnessing of nuclear energy clearly gives evidence of the heightened ambivalence inherent in much of contemporary technology.

A more developed technology can be appreciated as incremental to the human ability to accomplish desires and plans effectively. The contemporary phenomenon of energy-consciousness brings to mind the dependence on energy sources outside ourselves that are needed in order to survive in the contemporary world. With more energy at their disposal, people can accomplish more, are more freed from a certain type of limitation. Their work can be done in more suitable surroundings. The products created can be mass-produced, thus making them potentially available to a greater number of users.

Perhaps in no other area has the impact of modern technology been more felt than in that of communication and travel. People have been brought closer together in a spatial sense which creates at least the possibility of a greater sense of community and an appreciation of the commonness of humanity throughout the earth. Of itself, technology does not create interpersonal closeness but it helps to create the conditions out of which real community can be established.

Yet the ambivalence of modern technology can be shown in referring to how technology makes people more self-sufficient, more able to accomplish their goals by themselves. They can travel alone in automobiles, be entertained in the privacy of their own dwellings by their own media center. Food can be prepared without outside assistance. It might be argued that modern technology has contributed to the ironic situation that people live in a time when community is facilitated by many inventions, yet persons feel quite alone and alienated from their sisters and brothers.

Impact of Technological Products. Much the same can be said about the products of technology. With a general expectation that all persons could benefit from possession of these products, many, in fact, do not. This raises questions of social justice, particularly with reference to the equitable distribution of goods and services. Part of the prophetic role of the Church is to alert its members and the world at large as to violations in the area of social justice. As life in the world becomes more dependent on the products of technology, sensitivity to availability and distributions becomes more a moral issue.

As humanity grows more dependent on and enamored of its technological might, it can tend to assume a practical autonomy from any other sources of energy outside itself and its tools. The need for God is eclipsed or considered meaningless because the areas of health, wealth, and happiness are now dominated by human creations, While this result is not at all mandated by an expanding technology, it must be admitted that many areas once of religious concern are now under the influence of a more effective technology.

Implied in the general cultural changes that accompany an ever-expansive technology is a requirement, therefore, that the proper range of religious interests be reexamined. Technological developments of the last century have given a new shape to the world, but it need not be said that the world is necessarily Godless. It can be argued that the extension of human ingenuity into ever more effective technologies is part of the God-given human capacity to further bring the world into the dynamics of life in the KINGDOM OF GOD. This can be particularly so when the results of technology are a more successful feeding of the hungry, sheltering of the homeless, or implanting of knowledge where ignorance formerly held sway. The perception brought forward in *Gaudium et spes* was that a careful distinction should be made between human progress and the realization of the Kingdom of God (30). Nevertheless, where human progress serves "to a better ordering of human society," the concerns of the Kingdom are being realized. The world is given to humanity by God as a trust. Like good stewards humans must respect the wished of the owner while at the same time using whatever resources there are to extend the love of God into the perfecting of the world for the enrichment of the human spirit and in the service of our common humanity.

Bibliography: I. G. BARBOUR. *Science and Secularity: The Ethics if Technology* (New York 1970). D. CALLAHAN. *The Tyranny of Survival* (New York 1973). I. GILKEY, *Religion and the Scientific Future* (New York 1970). B. MILLER. *Religion in a Technical Age* (Cambridge, Mass. 1978). G. VAHANIAN. *God and Utopia: The Church in a Technological Civilization* (New York 1977).

[D. M. THOMAS]

TECHO, NICOLÁS DEL

Missionary and historian of Paraguay; b. Lille, France, Nov. 28, 1611; d. in the Reduction of Apóstoles (Paraguay), Aug. 20, 1685. He entered the Society of Jesus on Jan. 10, 1630, and arrived in Buenos Aires at the end of 1640 as a member of the expedition of Father Díaz Taño. From 1645 until his death he served in the Guaraní missions, sometimes as general superior. The only exceptions occurred during 1671, when he was teacher of novices in Córdoba, and between 1677 and 1680 when he was rector at Asunción. He wrote the *Historia provinciae paraguariae Societaties Jesu* (Leija 1673) and *Decades virorum illustrium paraguariae Societatis Jesu* (Tyrnau 1759). This second work (only two copies are extant) includes 90 biographies of Jesuit missionaries in Paraguay. Of these Techo wrote 50; the rest were written by Nicolás Schmid from the notes of Ladislao Orosz.

Bibliography: E. CARDOZO, *Historiografía paraguaya* (Mexico City 1959–) 1:271–285.

[H. STORNI]

TEGERNSEE, ABBEY OF

Benedictine monastery in Southeast Bavaria, founded (746) in honor of the Savior by Counts Adalbert and Otkar of Warngau and Tegernsee. In the 9th century after an early period of prosperity, it was deprived of many of its possessions by Count Arnulf the Bad. The Magyar invasion of 907 completely destroyed it. It was restored in 979 by Otto II who invited Hartwich, a monk of ST. MAXIMIN of Trier, to become abbot. It soon became a flourishing center of monasticism, repopulating other abbeys that had been destroyed earlier in the century. Learning and the arts flourished, and to this period belongs the monk-poet Froumund (d. 1012). A glass works for fine stained glass was established at this time. During the 14th century the abbey suffered from wars in southern Germany and from the prodigality of several abbots; the practice of limiting admission to members of the nobility contributed to its decline. An apostolic visitation in 1426 decreed a thorough reform and forced the incumbent abbot to resign. Caspar Ayndorffer, at 25, the youngest member of the community, was then appointed abbot. During his long reign (1426–60) discipline was restored, and the customs of the Abbey of MELK were adopted as the basis of reform. From Tegernsee the reform gradually spread to other Bavarian monasteries and led to the formation in 1684 of the Bavarian Benedictine Union which comprised 19 monasteries under the abbot of Tegernsee who had the title of *Primas Bavariae.* The abbey flourished until it was suppressed in 1803. Its rich library of 60,000 volumes, 6,600 incunabula, and 2,000 MSS was transported to the National Library at Munich.

Bibliography: M. FUCHS, *Geschichte des ehemaligen Klosters Tegernsee* (Munich 1876). M. HARTIG, *Die Benediktinerabtei Tegernsee, 746–1803* (Munich 1946). *Studien und Mitteilungen aus dem Benediktiner und dem Cistercienser Orden* 60 (1946). V. REDLICH, *Lexikon für Theologie und Kirche,* ed. M. BUCHBERGER, 10 v. (Freiburg 1930–38) 9:1029–31.

[C. FALK]

TEILHARD DE CHARDIN, PIERRE

Paleontologist and proponent of a synthesis of the evolutionary perspective of modern science with the Christian world view; b. Sarcenat (Orcines, Puy de Dôme), France, May 1, 1881; d. New York City, Apr. 10, 1955. After preparation at the Jesuit College of Mongré, he entered the Society of Jesus (Province of Lyons) in 1899. He studied philosophy in Jersey, theology in Hastings, and was ordained in 1911. In 1912 he began work in paleontology at the Museum of Paris under the direction of M. Boule. Interrupted in his studies by service as a stretcher-bearer during World War I, he subsequently completed his doctoral thesis, *Les Mammifères de l'Éocèen inférieur français et leur gisements,* and successfully defended it at the Sorbonne in 1922.

Teilhard taught geology for a brief period at the Catholic Institute of Paris but soon left for China, where he resided from 1923 to 1946. There, as a consultant to the Geological Survey, he focused his attention on the stratigraphy and paleontology of northern China and Asia. In this role he collaborated in the excavations at Zhoukoudlanzhen near Beijing and in the discovery of *Sinanthropus.* He participated also in numerous scientific expeditions in Central Asia, India, and Burma. From 1946 until his death, at first in France, then in New York as a fellow of the Wenner-Gren Foundation for Anthropological Research, he gave himself to the elaboration of an anthropogenesis, a kind of new anthropology treating the genetic structure of humanity as a special biological unit of planetary scope. The foundation sent him to South Africa on two different occasions to organize expeditions to search out the origins of human life south of the Sahara desert. His correspondence [*Letters of a Traveller* (New York 1962)] is a basic source on his career and the evolution of his thought.

The evolutionary theme (the genesis of continents and of fauna), the thesis of increasing cephalization, and the ''law of the disappearance of evolutionary peduncles'' appear in the 170 or so articles and technical papers that Teilhard published between 1915 and 1945. His work was essentially in paleontology (Cenozoic mammals of Asia) and stratigraphy. Besides his interest in fauna and the evolution of organic collectivities (often interpreted in explicitly orthogenetic terms and without specific reference to Mendelian or neo-Darwinian theories of evolution), he added substantially to knowledge of sedimentary deposits and of stratigraphical correlations on the Asian continent. His studies in this area are most important to date the fossilized breccia at Zhoukoudianzhen and the fossil man of paleolithic China. But Teilhard's interest in man dominates all his research in these technical fields; it can be observed repeatedly in a series of general articles and essays published together in *La Vision du passé* (Paris 1957) and *L'Apparition de l'homme* (Paris 1956).

Teilhard's influence and the exceptional response his work has called forth from all quarters, as well as the controversy that it has engendered, are explained principally by his inquiry into the phenomenology of man, who in Teilhard's eyes constitutes the axis and arrowhead of the cosmic flow and the key for understanding of the universe [cf. *The Phenomenon of Man* (New York 1959); *Le Groupe zoologique humain* (Paris 1959)]. The central idea in *L'Avenir de l'homme* (Paris 1959) and *L'Energie humaine* (Paris 1962) is that the stuff of this world develops (cosmogenesis) according to a law of increasing complexity and consciousness until the appearance of man (anthropogenesis) and the noosphere, and then converges in a rhythm of hypersocialization toward an Omega point (Christogenesis). The fact that Teilhard places man at the structural center of all cosmic perspective leads him to situate Christianity in human history precisely as man himself is situated in nature, that is, as informing and consolidating man's axial and leading role and transforming all his human psychic energy.

From the scientific point of view, it is difficult to establish precisely the methodology employed by Teilhard and to accept as rigorously proven all of his conclusions. Moreover, the philosophical and theological implications of his system have sometimes aroused passionate discussion. This explains the *monitum* of the Holy Office on June 30, 1962, which warns against uncritical acceptance of his theories, although it does not question the value of his scientific work or the righteousness of his intentions and the sincerity or fervor of his spiritual life [for which see *The Divine Milieu* (New York 1960), a stirring expression of a spirituality both supremely original and profoundly traditional]. The *monitum* is neither a condemnation nor a listing in the Index, but a simple warning [*Acta Apostolicae Sedis* 54 (1962): 526, interpreted by G. Isaye, SJ, in *Nouvelle revue théologique* 84 (1962): 866–869]. Teilhard has been characterized as one of the great minds of the contemporary world, and eminent churchmen have invited scholars to continue to elaborate what Cardinal Feltin has called his marvelous and seductive ''global vision of the universe wherein matter and spirit, body and soul, nature and supernature, science and faith find their unity in Christ'' [*Documentation Catholique* 58 (1961): 1523].

Pierre Teilhard De Chardin. (Archive Photos)

Bibliography: Life. C. CUÉNOT, *P. Teilhard de Chardin: . . .*, tr. V. COLIMORE, ed. R. HAGUE (Baltimore 1965). Introd. C. TRESMONTANT, *Pierre Teilhard de Chardin: His Thought,* tr. S. ATTANASIO (Baltimore 1959). C. E. RAVEN, *Teilhard de Chardin: Scientist and Seer* (New York 1963). F. G. ELLIOTT, ''The World Vision of Teilhard de Chardin,'' *International Philosophical Quarterly* 1 (1961) 620–647. F. RUSSO, ''The Phenomenon of Man,'' *America* 103 (1960) 185–189. N. M. WILDIERS, *Pierre Teilhard de Chardin* (Paris 1961). Theology. H. DE LUBAC, *La Pensée religieuse du Père Teilhard de Chardin* (Paris 1962). G. CRESPY, *La Pensée théologique de Teilhard de Chardin* (Paris 1961). ''Systema Teilhard de Chardin ad theologicam trutinam revocatum,'' *Divinitas* 3 (1959) 219–364. C. D'ARMAGNAC, ''La Pensée du Père Teilhard de Chardin comme apologétique moderne,'' *Nouvelle revue théologique* 94 (1962) 598–621. Methodology. R. T. FRANCOEUR, ed., *The World of Teilhard* (Baltimore 1961). C. D'ARMAGNAC, ''Philosophie de la nature et méthode chez le Père Teilhard de Chardin,'' *Archives de philosophie* 20 (1957) 5–41. O. A. RABUT,

Bl. Kateri Tekakwitha. (©UPI/Corbis-Bettmann)

Teilhard de Chardin: A Critical Study (New York 1961). Philosophy. M. BARTHÉLEMY-MADAULE, *Bergson et Teilhard de Chardin* (Paris 1963). C. CUÉNOT, *Teilhard de Chardin* (Paris 1962), with biblio.

[E. L. BONÉ]

TEKAKWITHA, KATERI, BL.

First North American Indian to be declared blessed; b. ca. 1656, Ossernenon (Auriesville), NY; d. Apr. 17, 1680, Caughnawaga, Canada.

Kateri's mother was a Christian Algonquin, who was raised among the French at Three Rivers, taken captive by the Iroquois, and made the wife of a pagan chief of the Mohawk tribe. Of this marriage two children were born, Tekakwitha and her younger brother. At four years of age the girl was taken into the home of an uncle after she had lost her father, mother, and brother in a smallpox epidemic. The disease left her disfigured and with impaired eyesight.

In 1667 she had her first meeting with Christian missionaries, three of whom were given temporary lodging by her uncle. Although the girl was very favorably impressed by these Jesuit missionaries, shyness and fear of her uncle probably kept her from seeking instruction. In 1675, however, she met Rev. Jacques de Lamberville, who instructed her in the Christian faith and baptized her on Easter, Apr. 5, 1676, giving her the name of Kateri, or Katharine.

Katharine's conversion and her exemplary life stirred up so much opposition that the priest advised her to flee to the Christian native village on the St. Lawrence River, where she would be able to grow in virtue without external hindrance. After a trek of nearly 200 miles she arrived at Sault St. Louis, near Montreal, in October 1677; she received her first Holy Communion there on Christmas Day.

For the next three years, under the direction of Rev. Pierre Cholonec, and with the encouragement of an older Iroquois woman, Anastasia Tegonhatsihongo, she led a life of great austerity and charity. On Mar. 25, 1679, Katharine gave herself completely to Christ by a private vow of chastity—a most exceptional act for a native woman, whose maintenance depended upon getting a husband.

Her death at the age of 24 served as an inspiration to the Indian community and was followed by an extraordinary outburst of religious fervor among them. The three missionaries who knew her best, Jacques de Lamberville, Claude Chauchetière, and Pierre Cholonec, left a collection of biographical data, written during the 35 years following her death. This, together with other sources provided the documentation for her cause of beatification, which was introduced in Rome on July 11, 1932. The Tekakwitha League, located at Auriesville, publishes a quarterly and directs other activities to disseminate knowledge of her.

During the beatification ceremony (June 22, 1980), John Paul II praised Kateri as "the Iroquois maiden, who in 17th–century North America was the first to renew the marvels of the sanctity of SS. SCHOLASTICA, GERTRUDE, CATHERINE OF SIENA, Angela MERICI and ROSE OF LIMA. She preceded along the path of Love, her great spiritual sister, Thérèse of the Child Jesus." Her tomb at Caughnawaga is a pilgrimage site. Patron of Native Americans, ecology, and the environment.

Feast: April 17 (Canada); July 14 (U.S.A.)

Bibliography: *Katharine Tekakwitha, the Lily of the Mohawks: The Position of the S. Congregation of Rites on the Introduction of the Cause for Beatification . . .* (New York 1940). *Jesuit Relations and Allied Documents,* ed. R. G. THWAITES, 73 v. (Cleveland 1896–1901; New York 1959–). *Acta Apostolicae Sedis,* no. 73 (1981): 235–258. *L'Osservatore Romano,* English edition, no. 26 (1980): 10–11. H. BÉCHARD, *Kaia'tanóron Kateri Tekakwitha* (Québec 1992). M. C. BUEHRLE, *Kateri of the Mohawks* (Milwaukee 1954). M. R. and M. BUNSON, *Kateri Tekakwitha* (Huntington, IN 1993). L. FISHER, *Kateri Tekakwitha* (Boston 1996). É. LECOMPTE, *Glory of the Mohawks,* tr. F. RALSTON WERUM (Milwaukee 1944). U. DE URTASSUM, *La gracia triunfante en la vida de Catharina Tegakovita, india iroquesa* (Madrid 1994).

[J. D. L. LEONARD]

TELEOLOGICAL ETHICS

Teleological ethics (from *telos,* end or purpose; *logos,* discourse or study) is a method of ethical decision-making that determines the appropriateness of an action through an examination of the end or purpose of the act. In this context the act is understood to be a ''personal act,'' that is, a physical or mental activity in relation to the intention of the actor and the circumstances in which it is performed. By way of contrast, a deontological method (literally, science of duty) holds that the action contains ethical information that in itself determines a duty or obligation to act in a particular way regardless of the intention or circumstances.

Teleology is sometimes mistakenly equated with utilitarianism, which holds that an act is appropriate when it maximizes the welfare of oneself or of society, and is inapopropriate when it is destructive of the self or others. In other instances, teleological ethics is regarded as a kind of CONSEQUENTIALISM, suggesting that an act's consequences are the key to ethical or moral evaluation. Its defenders, however, insist that more is involved than simply the isolation of an act's utility or consequences.

Teleology is not simply a case of the end justifying the means, or ''all's well that ends well.'' All may not be well morally even when the consequences are what was legitimately desired, and all may be very well morally even when the consequences are far from what had been anticipated. The result in itself does not determine whether or not the activity is appropriate. The appropriateness of the act is determined by the presence or absence of proportionate reason in the decision to engage in or refrain from the act. The presence or absence of proportionate reason is central to the understanding of teleological ethics because it is that which distinguishes it from utilitarianism and consequentialism. It can be said, in fact, that utilitarianism and consequentialism are not methods of ethical decision-making in the true sense of the term. They seem better able to justify a past act because a knowledge of the result is necessary. The principles of teleogical ethics, on the other hand, allow one to determine the appropriateness of an act before it is performed.

See Also: MORAL THEOLOGY; PROPORTIONALITY, PRINCIPLE OF; DOUBLE EFFECT, PRINCIPLE OF.

Bibliography: P. KNAUER, SJ, ''The Hermeneutics of the Principle of Double Effect,'' *Readings in Moral Theology: Moral Norms and the Catholic Tradition,* C. CURRAN and R. A. MCCORMICK, SJ, eds. (New York 1979). R. A. MCCORMICK, SJ, ''Ambiguity in Moral Choice,'' *Doing Evil to Achieve Good: Moral Choice in Conflict Situations,* R. A. MCCORMICK and P. RAMSEY, eds. (Chicago 1978) 7–53. L. JANSSENS, ''Ontic Evil and Moral Evil,'' *Louvain Studies* 4 (1972) 115–156. T. O'CONNELL, *Principles for a Catholic Morality* (San Francisco 1978).

[J. F. TUOHEY]

TELESIO, BERNARDINO

Renaissance philosopher devoted to the study of nature; b. Cosenza, Calabria, Italy, 1509; d. there, October 1588. A sincere Catholic, Telesio enjoyed the esteem of several popes, especially Gregory XIII. He purported to interpret nature by following the lead of the senses and blamed the Aristotelians for indulging in idle speculation. Nature, he wrote in *De rerum natura*, must be studied in itself and its own principles, which are matter, heat, and cold. Matter is the passive and universal substratum of all physical change. It is not pure potency, as Aristotle taught, but something concrete and tangible. Heat is the source of life in plants and animals, and, together with cold, accounts for all natural events. The whole of nature is animated, and all beings are endowed with sensation in varying degrees (PANPSYCHISM).

Man is a composite of soul, body, and spirit. The spirit, which he has in common with all animals, is a very subtle material substance emanating from the warm element and generated with the body. The soul, or *mens*, informs both body and spirit, is created by God, and is immortal. Its operations transcend the sensible world and reach up to the divine.

Telesio, whom Francis BACON calls ''the first of the moderns,'' paved the way for the scientific method of Galileo GALILEI and set a trend in philosophy that was soon followed by Tommaso CAMPANELLA, Francis Bacon, and Thomas HOBBES. The weakness of his system, which is not free from contradictions, consists in its treating scientific problems with a philosophical method.

Bibliography: F. FLORENTINO, *Bernardino Telesio . . . ,* 2 v. (Florence 1872–74). N. C. VAN DEUSEN, *Telesio, the First of the Moderns* (New York 1932); ''The Place of Telesio in the History of Philosophy,'' *Philosophical Review* 44 (1935) 417–434. N. ABBAGNANO, *Bernardino Telesio* (Milan 1941). G. SOLERI, *Telesio* (Brescia 1945).

[B. M. BONANSEA]

TELESPHORUS, POPE, ST.

Pontificate 127 or 128 to 137 or 138. Telesphorus was the seventh successor to Peter (*see* CLEMENT I). Sources generally agree that he reigned for 11 years. Eusebius and Jerome begin his reign in 128. The *Liber pontificalis* makes him a Greek and, anachronistically, an anchorite. It also says that he fixed the Easter fast at seven weeks, a regulation more compatible with the seventh century than the second, and that he ordered the Gloria sung either at midnight Mass at Christmas or in daily Masses after Terce. The tradition that he was martyred under Hadrian is too well attested to be discredited. Irenaeus (*Adv. Haer.* 3.3) singles him out as the first Roman bishop so honored. Eusebius (*Historia Ecclesiastica* 4.5, 10; 5.6, 24) and the *Liber pontificalis* repeat the story. The legend that Telesphorus is buried in the Vatican is not borne out by modern excavations.

Feast: Jan. 5.

Bibliography: *Liber pontificalis*, ed. L. DUCHESNE (Paris 1886–92, 1958) 1:56–57, 129; 3:72. É. AMANN, *Dictionnaire de théologie catholique*, ed. A. VACANT et al., (Paris 1903–50) 15.1:82. E. CASPAR, *Geschichte de Papsttums von den Anfängen bis zur Höhe der Weltherrschaft* (Tübingen 1930–33) 1:21, 34, 48. J. N. D. KELLY, *Oxford Dictionary of Popes* (New York 1986). E. SAUSER, *Biographisch- Bibliographisches Kirchenlexikon* (Herzberg 1995). B. SODARO, *Santi e beati di Calabria* (Rosarno 1996).

[E. G. WELTIN]

TELESPHORUS OF COSENZA

Real or fictitious person, purported author of *De causis, statu, cognitione ac fine praesentis schismatis et tribulationum futurarum,* a book of prophecies concerning the Great Schism. It was composed between 1356 and 1365, with another writer's dedicatory epistle (1386) to Antonio Adornio, Doge of Genoa, then under French influence. The book claims to be written by a Telesphorus (Theophorus, Theolophorus) of Cosenza (in Calabria), a holy hermit priest; it recapitulates writings of Cyril of Constantinople, JOACHIM OF FIORE (of whom Telesphorus is said to have written a life), and other seers. The book is a FLORILEGIUM from popular medieval literature of the APOCALYPTIC MOVEMENT and is especially dependent on Joachim of Fiore and John of Roquetaillande. Without following a school, it shows the traits of this literature: ideal clerical poverty, salvation of Church and world by an ideal emperor and the *Pastor (Papa) Angelicus.* It predicts the schism's end in 1393; persecution by Frederick III; and election of the ''Angelic Pastor,'' after which the clergy embraces evangelical poverty, the pope ends the German electors' power to choose the emperor and crowns Charles of France as emperor, and a crusade restores all men to Christ. The interpretation of events favors French nationalism. Most authors hold that Telesphorus is a pseudonym; E. Donckel and P. Paschini deny this, asserting that he was a Franciscan hermit who entered the order of HIERONYMITES.

Bibliography: E. DONCKEL, ''Studien über die Prophezeiung des Fr. Telesforus von Cosenza,'' *Archivum Franciscanum historicum* 26 (1933) 29–104, 282–314, includes ed. of text. P. PASCHINI, *Enciclopaedia Italiana di scienzi, littere ed arti,* 36 v. (Rome 1929–39; suppl. 1938–) 33:437–438. F. FOBERTI, *Gioacchino da Fiore e il Gioacchinismo antico e moderno* (Padua 1942).

[A. CONDIT]

TELLO, ANTONIO

Franciscan chronicler; b. Spain, date unknown; d. Guadalajara, Jalisco, June 1653. From the province of Santiago de Galicia he went to that of Nueva Galicia, Jalisco, Mexico. In 1596 Tello and other Franciscans accompanied Gen. Sebastián Vizcaíno in his unsuccessful expedition to California. He returned to Jalisco and held the office of guardian at Zacoalco (1605), Amatlán (1620), Tecolotlán, and Cocula (1648). His valuable six-volume work, *Crónica miscelánea de la sancta provincia de Xalisco,* remained unedited for more than two centuries, but his manuscript was known and cited by historians of the 18th century. The original was lost and became an object of search for bibliophiles of the 19th century. Volume 1 was never found. A complete edition of all the extant volumes was in preparation in 1964, and parts had previously been published (v.2 Guadalajara 1891; v.3 Guadalajara 1942; v.4 with 27 chapters of v.5 Mexico City 1871). The original volumes 2 and 3 are in the John Carter Brown Library, Providence, R.I.; volumes 4, 5, and 6 (incomplete) are in the Public Library of Guadalajara, Jalisco. Tello anticipated bibliographers of the New World in introducing an alphabetical catalogue of Franciscan authors.

Bibliography: J. GARCÍA, ICAZBALCETA, *Obras,* 10 v. (Mexico City 1896–99), v.9, Biografías.

[E. GÓMEZ-TAGLE]

TEMBLEQUE, FRANCISCO DE

Franciscan who built the most magnificent aqueduct in colonial America; b. Tembleque, near Toledo, Spain, date unknown; d. Puebla, Mexico, 1589. He went to Mexico about 1540, and was sent to the town of Otumba. When he observed the terrible lack of water, he resolved to build an aqueduct, which was to be 34 kilometers long. He bored through the rock of the Tecajete hill and began a conduit about 30 kilometers long; the other four kilometers were formed of arches to cross three ravines, Amiltepec, Tepeyahualco, and another smaller one. In the Tepeyahualco he had to construct an aqueduct of 66 arches. The central arch had the incredible height of 38 meters (14 more than the central nave of the cathedral) and was 17 meters wide. It was necessary to make another arch in the middle of the high arch to reinforce it; it was also so high that the Oaxaca railroad later passed beneath it. The supporting pillars of the arches were 2.60 by 2.80 meters. They demonstrated great elegance and economy in the use of material, so that the aesthetic effect was extraordinary. The whole aqueduct was made of basalt, and it has been estimated that 10,000 square meters of stone were used. The centers of the arches were made of adobe, not wood. The construction took 17 years, from 1554 to 1571.

Bibliography: O. VALDÉS, *El padre Tembleque* (Mexico City 1945). M. ROMERO DE TERREROS Y VINENT, *Los acueductos de México en la historia y en el arte* (Mexico City 1949).

[F. DE LA MAZA]

TEMPERAMENT

In common usage, temperament means an innate leaning or predisposition toward characteristic modes of behavior, e.g., a natural leaning towards cheerfulness. Historically, the term has usually denoted a set of physical or physiological factors underlying and causing typical patterns of psychological response. It was supposed that the human body was made up of several components present in varying proportions; as one or another element assumed preponderance, it would affect not only the total physical ensemble, but—because of the dependence of mind on body—psychological dispositions as well. Temperament may be defined as an entitative HABIT by which several physiological or physical elements of human nature are variously proportioned among themselves, resulting in different characteristic psychological tendencies or leanings.

Classical Theory of Temperament. The notion of temperament is first proposed in the Hippocratic collections, a series of medico-philosophical treatises composed in the course of two or three hundred years at the height of the Greek classical period (*see* HIPPOCRATES). The famous physician Galen (*c.* A.D. 130–201) systematically proposed the theory in the form it was to keep, more or less unchanged, for the next 1,500 years. According to this systematization, four humors were present in the human body: blood, phlegm, black bile, and yellow bile. Every man has all these humors, but in varying proportions. An excess of blood makes one cheerful, unstable, quick, and sociable; it gives him a sanguine temperament. An excess of phlegm makes one torpid, weak, steady, and apathetic; he has a phlegmatic temperament. An excess of black bile makes one morose, misanthropic, and sad; it characterizes the melancholic temperament. And an excess of yellow bile makes one passionate, irascible, domineering, and tenacious; it produces the choleric temperament.

Medieval View. St. THOMAS AQUINAS accepted the four temperaments of classical theory and speculated about the roots of temperamental differences (*In lib. de memor.* 8.401, 403, 406; *Summa theologiae* 2a2ae, 156.1 ad 2). In the context of HYLOMORPHISM, he held that such differences would fundamentally affect the body, which is complex and can be variously disposed, and would then affect the soul, insofar as the soul is proportioned to the body as form to is matter (*Summa theologiae* 1a2ae, 46.5, 48.2 ad 1, 51.1, 63.1; *In 1 anim.* 2.22; *In 2 sent.* 32.2.3; *In 4 sent.* 44.2.1). Temperamental differences would make some men prone to chastity, others to lust; some to courage and irascibility, others to timidity and mildness; some would be temperamentally more scientific and prudent, others more affectionate and sociable; still others, morose and easily depressed. These differences, he held, were inheritable, and therefore innate.

Modern Variations. This classic division of the four temperaments, with some modifications by various authors, persisted in essentially the same form down to the 17th century. Advances in physiological science then led to the rejection of the theory of the four humors. In spite of this, however, the fourfold division of sanguine, choleric, melancholic, and phlegmatic continued to be employed as designations of psychological types in common parlance, literary usage, and even in scientific writing. I. Kant, W. Wundt, J. Herbart, O. Külpe, H. Ebbinghaus, and J. Spurzheim, among others, set themselves to the task of restating the classic theory. Thus Wilhelm Wundt (1832–1920), the father of experimental psychology, devised a system of interlocking temperamental characteristics, based on the traditional division. The sanguine man was emotionally quick and weak, affectively cheerful, oriented to the present, and active. The choleric man was emotionally quick and strong, affectively somber, oriented to the present, and active. The melancholic man was emotionally slow and strong, affectively somber, oriented to the past, and passive. The phlegmatic man was emotionally slow and weak, affectively cheerful, oriented to the past, and passive. For Wundt, these were simply psychological clusters of traits without a physiological basis or cause [*Grundzüge der physiologischen Psychologie,* 5th ed. (Leipzig 1902–03) 3:637–640].

Rostan and Sigaud. The theories of the French physician, L. L. Rostan [*Cours élémentaire d'hygiène,* (2nd ed.

Paris 1828)] were adopted and presented by C. Sigaud in correlation with various physical types. The classical sanguine type was associated with a face whose central parts were predominant and a physically well-developed thorax. The choleric type he associated with a rectangular face and thorax. The melancholic type had a triangular face with the apex pointed down and a long, lean thorax; while the phlegmatic had a triangular face with the base down and a predominance of abdomen. These types Sigaud called respectively: respiratory, muscular, cerebral, and digestive, according to the organic systems preeminent in each. He believed these differences were caused by environment—respiratory types developing in the mountains and sea coasts, muscular types in industrial towns, cerebral types in large cities, and digestive types in valleys (*La Forme humain,* Paris 1914).

See Also: HABIT.

[M. STOCK]

TEMPERANCE, VIRTUE OF

The virtue of moderation in desires and pleasures, especially those of the emotions (Gr. σωφροσύνη, Lat. *temperantia*).

Greeks and Early Christians. Ethical philosophers have always called for control over sensuous cravings, agreeing in this respect, though often with more pragmatism and less fanaticism, with a perennial ascetical and mystical tradition. Plato would have the charioteer mind curb passion, an ugly brute of a horse; Aristotle, to whom man was more compact of spirit and sense, would have the emotions tempered to serve the good life according to reason; and the Stoics give classical expression to the ideal of *temperies,* of the mind undisturbed by and even invulnerable to the fears and desires of the body.

The teachings of the philosophers lay ready at hand and were taken over by the Fathers, who, however, because of their faith were more urgent about spiritual regeneration and because of their pastoral office more emphatic about the vices. Saints Ambrose and Gregory the Great treated temperance as one of the cardinal or ''hinge'' virtues for Christian living. With them it came to mean more than a restrained comportment consonant with human dignity and was taken into the higher setting of grace; it moved out of the city of reason into the family of God; and its practice became less like the training required for an athlete or the purification of an initiate than a way of being conformed to Christ. The theme is less hygiene than mortification, and against the background of revealed salvation history the spirit was set against the flesh in a strife sharper and more dramatic than that considered by the philosophers. Nevertheless, practical lessons continued to be drawn from the Stoics in Christian ascetical literature.

St. Thomas Aquinas. St. Thomas Aquinas, whose treatment of temperance in the *Summa theologiae* is the *locus classicus* for moral theology, went to the Fathers and the Stoics when he was considering temperance as they did, as entering into the texture of all virtue. However, he brought out more clearly that it is not just repressive of the desire for pleasure, but rather a tempering in the original sense of mingling in due proportion, as in the making of steel or man's physical constitution. This recognition of its positive, as against its negative, function was made the more definite when he went on to consider it also as a special and limited sort of virtue, that is, not as being a general virtue, but as a particular kind of good ''having,'' a *habitus,* through a steady and effective bent to one type of right activity and consequent enrichment. As such he placed it in the emotions themselves; it is commanded, yet not elicited, by will power and consists in a finely modulated sensibility striking the note between immaturity and insensibility.

He shared neither the Stoic view of passions as sickness of soul nor the puritan suspicion of pleasure as guilty until proved innocent; sublimating and indeed extending the best Epicureanism, he saw the life of virtue spreading through the whole human organism, insofar as it can be suffused with intelligence and love, and therefore can be made gracious by the communication of divine life. The sensory perceptions and feelings man has generically in common with the animals are subsumed in the singleness of his substance under the seeing of meaning and the making of choices, and so become specifically human, *rationale per participationem.* Thus, and in accordance with the teaching of Aristotle, the ''concupiscible'' and the ''irascible,'' the seats of what are sometimes called the ''impulse emotions'' and the ''contending emotions,'' can be firmly disposed to their optimum by the virtues of temperance and courage respectively (*Summa theologiae* 1a2ae, 23, 24, 34, 59; *see* APPETITE).

Temperance as a Special Virtue. St. Thomas studied the concupiscible appetite at length (*ibid.* 25–39). Its interest is what is sensuously either agreeable or disagreeable; and, as the case may be, it begins with liking or disliking, goes on to seeking and expecting or avoiding or fearing, and ends with enjoying pleasure or suffering pain. In this way the pain-pleasure principle is paramount; and this St. Thomas was not squeamish about translating into the terms of unrarified experience. He referred to temperance as a special virtue to the pleasures of food, drink and sex arising from the sense of touch.

This localization has been criticized as being at once too narrow and too gross and as leading to the preoccupation of later authors with the palate (even in some cases, though mistakenly, with the digestion) and the genitals, and not without occasion for prurience. Temperance, it is urged, and particularly sexual temperance, is much more comprehensive and delicate. It should be observed first, however, that this was granted by St. Thomas when temperance was regarded as a general condition of all virtue; second, that his isolation of temperance to a special kind of activity was methodological; his ''virtue-morality'' no more than his ''faculty-psychology'' would break up the single acting substance into separate ''things''; third, that a given human situation can come under many headings of his classification (indeed courage rather than temperance seems more directly engaged in problems of human sentimentality that dispose one to look for an escape from the difficulties of real life rather than to search for pleasure); and last, that a possibly outmoded Aristotelian physiology may be overlooked when ''touch'' is taken according to a working psychology to stand for the most pervasive sensibility in the organism and the source of the most vehement feelings. He admitted that he was speaking in the most proper sense in assigning temperance to these special manifestations, and one happy effect is to see it in proportion, a necessary but not the greatest of the moral virtues.

Implications of St. Thomas's Teaching. That its implications are more far-reaching he made evident when he came to consider its parts. First its components, *integrales,* were described as *verecundia* and *honestas,* terms difficult to translate. The first implies a certain shyness and reserve, a distaste for indecency and smut, an instinctive modesty that does not of itself quite amount to virtue; the second is more positive and goes out with candor to what is noble, honorable and beautiful.

With the species, *partes subjectivae,* of temperance St. Thomas returned to its restricted consideration. They are *abstinentia,* which here means the restraint of greediness about food. Tobacco seems to be included, though the use of some drugs, in which pleasure seeking is not prominent, seems to be the concern of other virtues. Next, and with the same proviso, is sobriety in taking intoxicating drink. Third, there is chastity in matters of sex—here again total abstinence is not meant.

The associated virtues, *partes potentiales,* of temperance widen its field. They include *continentia,* the sound will that rides out the storm of passion, though St. Thomas was hesitant about describing it as a virtue since as such it does not pacify the disturbance. The names of others come from Andronicus and Macrobius: *humilitas,* which restrains pushfulness; *mansuetudo,* a mildness of temper and *clementia,* a gentleness and unwillingness to inflict pain, both of which regulate masochism, sadness and the ''punishing'' pleasures; *bona ordinatio,* a sense of occasion and of what is fitting; *ornatus,* a moderation in external apparel; *parcitas,* a self-containedness and spareness about superfluities; and *simplicitas,* a moderation and restraint about luxuries. As part of modesty St. Thomas characteristically added his own virtue of *studiositas,* or a lively interest in the surrounding world, noting its contrary vice of *curiositas,* a prying into what is not one's concern and an obsessive sexual prurience; also Aristotle's *eutrapelia,* a playfulness in fun and games. All these are closely interconnected and are placed in separate compartments in the *Summa theologiae* (2a2ae, 155–170) only by abstraction and for purposes of scientific study; they show how comprehensive is the complex and how versatile the virtue of temperance.

Bibliography: THOMAS AQUINAS, *Summa theologiae* 2a2ae, 141–170. A. MICHEL, *Dictionnaire de théologie catholique,* ed., A. VACANT et al., 15 v. (Paris 1903–50) 15.1:94–99. A. LAFÉTEUR, ''Temperance,'' *The Virtues and States of Life,* ed. A. M. HENRY, tr. R. J. OLSEN and J. PUTZ (Theology Library 4; Chicago 1957) 533–613. J. PIEPER, *Fortitude and Temperance,* tr. D. F. COOGAN (New York 1954).

[T. GILBY]

TEMPERANCE MOVEMENTS

Evidence of the use and abuse of alcoholic beverages can be found in the records of ancient civilizations. Pictorial records from Egypt show the effects of DRUNKENNESS; four laws in the Code of HAMMURABI relate to tavern keepers; and there are several passages in the Bible indicating alcohol and drinking in everyday life. In one of the earliest injunctions for abstinence, the Lord told Aaron that when he went to the meeting tent he and his sons were forbidden under pain of death and by perpetual ordinance throughout their generations from drinking any wine or strong drink (Lv 10.9). In the New Testament the angel told Elizabeth that the child she would bear (John the Baptist) would drink no wine or strong drink (Lk 1.15). Succeeding centuries saw the founding by St. Boniface in Germany and by St. Gilbert in England of monasteries that observed the rule of total abstinence. But such actions were exceptions to the general rule. On all levels of society alcohol in one form or another was an accepted part of life. The abuse of it was frowned upon (as was the abuse of anything else), but it was not a matter for long or widespread concern.

Beginnings. Modern temperance movements began in the era of the ENLIGHTENMENT. Motivated by humanitarianism, reform-minded men cast a quizzical glance over all aspects of life, defined the evils that affected society, pinpointed the sources of man's troubles, and set

Benjamin Rush, the earliest proponent of temperance in the United States.

about to make things right. Similar appraisals were made by the Quakers. In both cases there was a growing awareness of the relationship between drunkenness, poverty, and crime, and an interest in ways in which the causes of such problems could be eliminated.

England. In England the relationship between the availability of cheap alcohol and an increase in drunkenness was demonstrated graphically after the passage of an act of Parliament prohibiting the importation of spirits from foreign countries (1689). Up to that time beer, ale, wine, and Jamaica rum were popular. During the reign of William and Mary (1688–1702) the use of low-priced gin was introduced. The act of 1689, passed to aid agriculture, allowed any person to set up a distillery upon ten days notice and payment of a small fee. After 1702 no license was required. The result was a rapid increase in distilleries and in popular consumption of alcohol, mainly gin. Drinking clubs flourished. Soon the consumption of gin and the amount of public intoxication aroused the authorities, and the Gin Act of 1736 was passed. It required all who sold alcohol to get a yearly license and forbade the sale of mixed or unmixed liquor in less than two-gallon amounts. This amounted to a virtual prohibition. Popular indignation led to some riots and to widespread civil disobedience. The Gin Act was replaced in 1743 by the milder Tippling Act, which restricted the sale of alcohol to 20 shillings worth. Nevertheless, concern about the general lack of sobriety resulted in petitions to Parliament to do something about the situation. Its measures included stricter licensing arrangements and, during brief periods of crop shortages, prohibitions against the use of grain for spirits. No organized temperance movement existed, but William Hogarth's pictures of ''Gin Lane,'' ''Beer Street,'' and ''The Rake's Progress'' advertised the evils of intemperance. John Armstrong's *The Art of Preserving Health* (1744) urged moderation. A Scottish writer, James Burgh, published *A Warning to Dram-Drinkers* (1751). These men were the heralds of temperance societies that were established in Great Britain in the 1830s.

United States. Meanwhile, the cause of temperance made great progress in the United States. Its pioneer advocate was Dr. Benjamin Rush (1745–1813) of Philadelphia. As early as 1772 he published a work condemning the use of strong drink. A similar admonition was addressed to the Continental Army during the American Revolution. Rush's *Enquiry into the Effects of Spirituous Liquors on the Human Body and Mind* (1784) was widely reprinted and distributed for half a century; it challenged the common notion that alcohol was necessary or beneficial. Through his influence the Philadelphia College of Physicians went on record for the cause of temperance in 1787. He also acted as chairman of a committee of physicians to draft a memorial to the Pennsylvania legislature requesting a law to diminish the consumption of liquor. The physicians of Philadelphia presented a petition to the U.S. Congress in 1790 that sought to restrict traffic in liquor. It should be noted that Rush and his colleagues were not seeking to prohibit liquor but only to limit its excessive use.

As early as 1789, 36 of the leading men of Litchfield, Conn., formed a temporary association to discourage the use of spirituous liquors, agreeing not to use them during the coming season. The first American temperance society was founded in Moreau, N.Y., in 1808. Pledging themselves not to use liquor, its members worked to limit the use of spirits by the laboring classes. They hoped to win adherents by pamphlets and speeches, but they had little success. For most of the first three decades of the 19th century, temperance pledges were restricted principally to individuals, families, and parts of congregations. By 1810 only the Quakers and Methodists had recommended the disuse of ardent spirits. In 1811, through Rush's influence, the Presbyterians officially condemned the sin of drunkenness. The Protestant clergy, moreover, attempted to put their own house in order by eliminating the use of liquor at ordinations.

Organization in the United States. The man largely responsible for the real beginning of a nationwide movement was Lyman Beecher (1775–1863). Beecher was shocked by the drunkenness he observed during his student years at Yale. Later, while serving as pastor of the Presbyterian Church at East Hampton, Long Island, N.Y., he was outraged when a local liquor seller corrupted the Montauk tribespeople with drink. During this period Rush's pamphlet on the effects of drink made a deep impression on him. Between 1806 and 1809 he began to preach on the evils of intemperance. Similar sermons were preached in Connecticut Congregational churches by Ebenezer Porter at Washington and by Herman Humphrey at Fairfield. In 1811, a year after Beecher was transferred to Litchfield, the General Council of the Congregational Churches in Connecticut, aroused by the sermons of Porter and Humphrey, appointed a committee to see what could be done about the problem. When in 1812 the committee reported that it was unable to find a solution, Beecher promptly suggested that a new committee be appointed. This was done, and Beecher was made a member of it. To the amazement of his colleagues, he presented the following day a report that discussed the possibility of forming an organization to combat intemperance and the decline of public morals. His proposals gave pause to the more conservative clergymen; but in the end his report was adopted, printed, and distributed. Beecher urged that the pamphlets by Rush and Porter should also be circulated. In this way the cause was launched in Connecticut.

American Temperance Society. Following the War of 1812, the movement was given impetus by a wave of religious revivalism and a spirit of concern for the welfare of all classes of mankind. Justin Edwards, a Congregational clergyman at Andover, Mass., responded to Beecher's argument and began to preach temperance in 1815. Ten years later he published *A Well Conducted Farm* (1825), a description of a farm near Boston run on strict temperance principles. The work was widely distributed and presumably had great influence. Other tracts came from his pen. In 1826 Edwards joined with 15 others to found at Boston the American Society for the Promotion of Temperance. Edwards devoted a great deal of time to lecturing, organizing, and writing in behalf of the society. His temperance address at St. John's, New Brunswick, led to the establishment of the St. John's Temperance Society, which pioneered the cause in Canada.

The American Temperance Society sent lecturers around the country and used the approach of religious revivals. It employed paid campaign managers and used newspapers, pamphlets, and periodicals. Essay contests were conducted and the winning entries printed and circulated. The tempo of reform agitation was kept up by frequent local meetings, a large-scale annual meeting, and the publication of annual reports.

Susan B. Anthony, who espoused temperance in addition to women's causes.

Local Societies. Temperance societies sprang up throughout the land. In 1832 an overflow crowd attended a meeting held in the capitol in Washington, D.C., for the purpose of promoting temperance in the United States. Chaplains of the House and Senate participated, and the meeting was chaired by Secretary of War Lewis Cass, who later in the year issued an order that substituted coffee for the army's ration of spirits and prohibited sutlers from selling liquor to soldiers. Through the efforts of Sen. Theodore Frelinghuysen of New Jersey and Sen. Felix Grundy of Tennessee, a Congressional Temperance Society was formed in 1833. Cass was chosen as the first president. The example of Congress led to the establishment of temperance societies in the legislative bodies of various states.

Elsewhere in the country the cause gained ground. Women were encouraged to become active in temperance work. The tendency to make temperance a family concern also led to the establishment through Sunday schools of some children's temperance groups. The pledge was signed when the children were 12 or 14. By 1833 the American Temperance Society claimed that 4,000 local

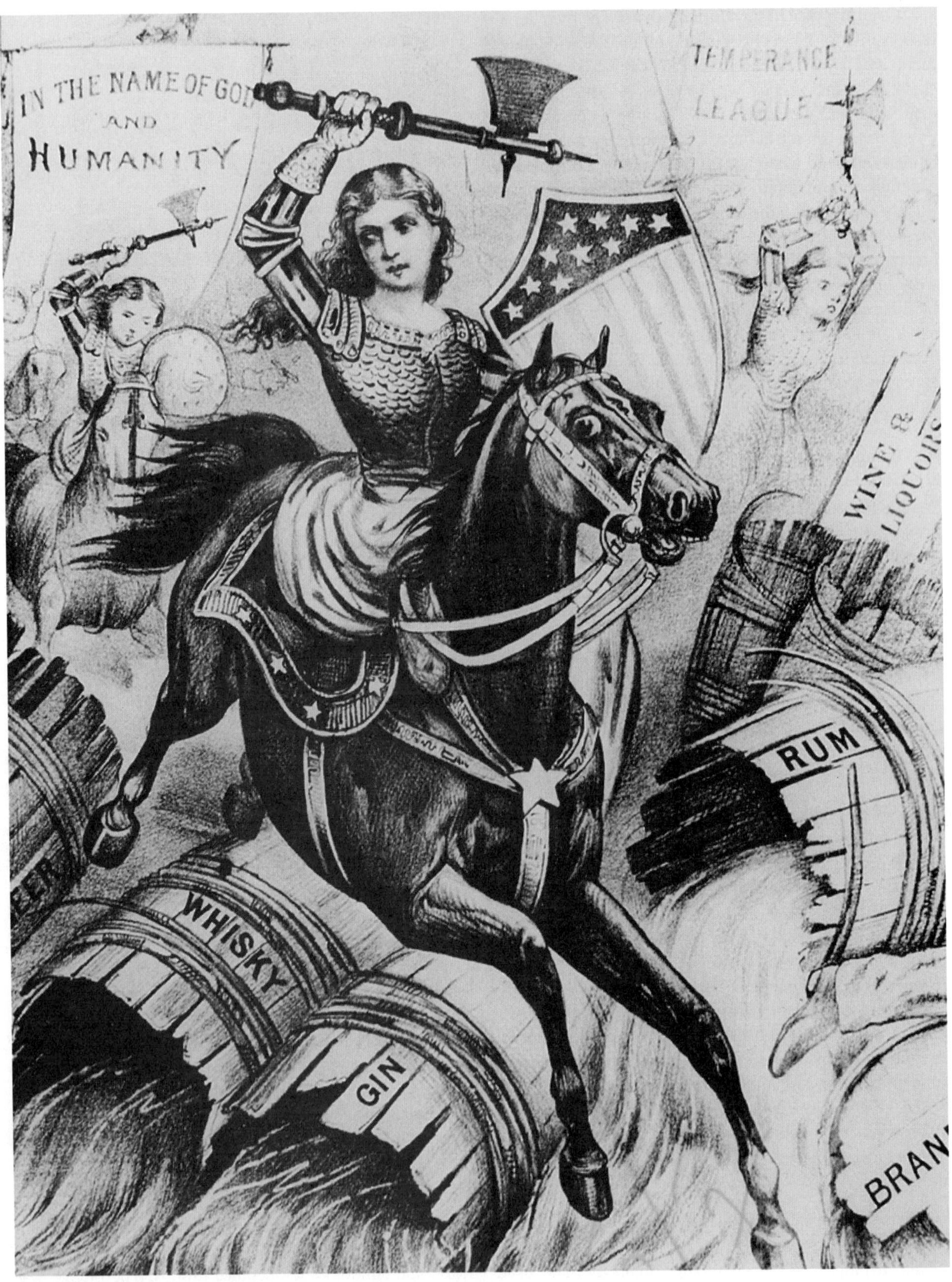

"Woman's Holy War," 1874, lithograph by Currier & Ives.

societies had been organized with a total membership of half a million. Groups that were affiliated with the American Temperance Society were in the minority; but since it was the largest organized group, the society wielded the greatest influence. The temperance agitation led to the opening of temperance hotels and to the adoption of a total abstinence rule by three newly built railroads.

American Temperance Union. This rapid growth soon produced some problems. In an effort to unite and coordinate the objectives of the various groups, the American Temperance Society held a convention in Philadelphia in 1833 that created the United States Temperance Union. A special committee was appointed to determine the ways and means of unifying the work of all societies. Nothing was done, however, until 1836, when the committee called for a convention of societies of the United States and Canada to meet at Saratoga Springs, N.Y., in August. Some 348 delegates from 19 states and from Canada assembled. In an effort to integrate the Canadian societies, a reorganization took place, and the name was changed to the American Temperance Union (ATU).

For some years dissension had been developing among the reformers about whether the goals of the organization were temperance or total abstinence. One group thought that the use of wine and malt beverages was not harmful. Also, in the case of wine, it was felt that a ban would conflict with sacramental uses and with certain scriptural passages. The total abstinence supporters felt that the pledge should ban the use of anything that could intoxicate, pointing out that wine and beer stimulated a craving for stronger drink. Under the leadership of Lyman Beecher, Justin Edwards, and Edward C. Delavan, the total abstinence group won the day; but an obscurely worded resolution was adopted in an effort to satisfy the losers.

This disagreement over goals was fought on various levels after the convention. All societies that affiliated with the reorganized ATU had to support a strongly worded pledge against the use of and traffic in intoxicating beverages. Societies that refused to take this pledge were considered inactive by the ATU. This decision split the movement and gradually led to a decline in membership and influence. The alienation of conservative members deprived the ATU of the financial support of prominent businessmen. There was dissension also about whether moral suasion or an organized effort for legal action was the best way to bring about reform. Another factor weakening the movement was the growing involvement of various temperance leaders in the crusade against slavery.

Washington Temperance Society. A great revival of total abstinence took place in 1840 as a result of activities of societies of reformed drunkards. Up to this time the reform impulse tended to treat drunkards as already lost and to concentrate on keeping persons from becoming such. A group of Baltimore drinkers who attended a temperance lecture in a spirit of fun were won over and decided to found their own organization. The Washington Temperance Society was the result. Using narrations of personal experience to create an emotional climate and parades, uniforms, and floats to build organizational morale, the Washington societies became popular and induced many persons to take the pledge. Women participated in the crusade through the Martha Washington Movement and through Ladies Benevolent Societies. By 1843 the Washingtonians claimed that 100,000 drunkards and a half million intemperate drinkers had signed their names to the temperance pledge.

Leaders of the older societies noted that few pledge signers joined the older temperance organizations, and few reformed drunkards seemed interested in religion. It seemed that at the conclusion of a Washington campaign either a new society was formed or an older one converted to the Washington model. They objected to the fact that Washington societies were opposed to legislative action to enforce temperance. On their part, the Washingtonians said that the older societies often criticized their principles and methods and refused to cooperate. Such dissension prevented unified action. Public confidence in the Washingtonians was impaired by the frequent relapse of pledge signers and by the lack of any centralized organization to give direction to the various units. Within ten years after its founding, the Washington movement as such virtually disappeared. Those members who were still faithful to their pledge gravitated to older societies or to fraternal orders.

Sons and Daughters of Temperance. Earlier, in 1842, a group of members of the Washington Society of New York, alarmed by the weakness of their parent group, had formed the Sons of Temperance. They had three goals: to prevent intemperance, to provide mutual assistance in case of sickness, and to elevate their characters. An initiation fee and the payment of weekly dues provided a fund for use in case of sickness. Soon the Sons of Temperance became a highly centralized and well-disciplined fraternal organization. Chapters were organized in other states. By 1850 the national organization reported a paid membership of more than 245,000 organized into 36 grand and 5,894 subordinate divisions. Two members of the New York Sons of Temperance helped to found the Daughters of Temperance, a mutual benefit association of women pledged to total abstinence. This movement also spread. In 1849 Susan B. Anthony gave her first address on temperance and women's rights before a Daughters of Temperance group in Canajoharie, N.Y.

Catholic Societies. Catholics, too, had become increasingly interested in the cause of temperance. As early as 1835 the Irish Temperance Society in Boston drew its membership from both Catholics and Protestants. Other independent Catholic groups were found elsewhere. Temperance societies were given encouragement and approval by the hierarchy at the Fourth Provincial Council in Baltimore (1840). The council recommended that societies be established in all parishes, and as a result many temperance and total abstinence groups were established by priests. Catholics in general tended to believe that the moderate use of alcohol was not wrong and that only the abuse of it resulted in the sin of intemperance (*see* TEMPERANCE, VIRTUE OF).

A more favorable attitude toward total abstinence was the result of the efforts of Theobald MATHEW, an Irish Capuchin. Beginning in 1838, Father Mathew had led an enormously popular movement for total abstinence in Ireland. News of his success encouraged priests and bishops in the United States, as well as Protestant temperance leaders. When the years of famine brought thousands of Irish to America, many of them carried with them their adherence to Father Mathew's pledge. Both Catholic and Protestant groups invited Mathew to visit the United States. Various problems postponed his visit until 1849, when he was entertained at the White House by President Zachary Taylor and made a successful tour of the country. When Mathew returned to Ireland in 1851, the New York *Herald,* a newspaper opposed to temperance, estimated that in his travels through 25 states the priest had given the pledge to almost half a million people, both Catholic and Protestant.

International Organization. The widespread interest in temperance, mainly in the United States and Europe, led to the first World's Temperance Convention in London in 1846. The American delegation included such prominent figures as Lyman Beecher, William Lloyd Garrison, and abolitionist and former slave Frederick Douglass.

Legislation. By mid-19th century nearly every state had some law licensing the sale of alcoholic beverages, but fees were low and regulations were lax. Urged on by reformers, various states experimented with firmer regulations and with local option. Massachusetts passed a law in 1838 that prohibited the selling of liquor in less than 15-gallon quantities. Many liquor dealers refused to obey the law, and their cases aroused a great deal of public interest. Finally, in 1840, the legislature repealed the law. Reliance was placed on local option laws that proved to be quite effective.

Under the leadership of Neal Dow, temperance advocates in Maine took advantage of the local enthusiasm for the Washington movement to build political support for the cause of prohibition. By 1846 they had sufficient support in the legislature to enact the first comprehensive state prohibition act. The enforcement of this measure depended on the way in which town selectmen granted licenses to sell alcohol for medicinal purposes, through which it was still possible to evade the law. This difficulty was overcome in 1851 by the passage of a law forbidding the manufacture or sale of intoxicating liquors in the state, authorizing the issuance of search warrants on the complaints of three citizens, and giving all fines collected to prosecuting officers.

News of the victory in Maine gave encouragement to temperance advocates both in the United States and abroad and led to a period of renewed activity. Between 1852 and 1855, 12 states and 1 territory passed prohibition laws. Prohibitionist forces narrowly missed enacting similar measures in two other states. But the victories were short-lived; some of these laws were declared unconstitutional, others repealed as a result of a change in public sentiment. By 1863 only six states still had prohibition statutes, and five of these subsequently repealed such laws.

Decline and Resurgence. Another landmark in the temperance crusade was the publication of Timothy Shay Arthur's *Ten Nights in a Barroom* (1850), which, widely read and dramatized, did much to maintain public interest in the cause. Nevertheless, the growing concern of Americans over the slavery question weakened the temperance movement. Several talented spokesmen found themselves more and more involved in the antislavery movement. Those who attempted to keep the slavery question out of temperance activities found themselves denounced by abolitionists as being friendly to slave owners and indifferent to the cause of the black American. The need to raise money to finance the Civil War led the government to impose an excise tax on liquor, and this action had a far-reaching effect—in later years prohibition proposals were weighed against the potential loss of revenue by federal and state authorities. One permanent achievement was the abolition of the spirit ration in the U.S. Navy (1862).

Origins of the Prohibition Party. Problems growing out of the war and reconstruction, discouragement about prohibition experiments, and the loss of financial support by various societies led to further decline in the public interest in temperance. Yet this same period saw the beginning of renewed activity by persistent reformers. In August 1865 temperance groups met at Saratoga Springs, N.Y., to reorganize and enlarge the work formerly carried on by the ATU. One result was the establishment of the National Temperance Society and Publication House, which soon became an important agency for research and education. The new group adopted a program aimed to make states dry and people total abstainers. One of the strongest general temperance societies in this period was the Independent Order of Good Templars, founded in 1851. Like many similar societies, it had concerned itself with moral suasion. In 1868, however, it called for the formation of a new political party. Since neither of the major political parties welcomed this revival of interest in temperance, a new Prohibition party was born in 1869. Three years later it ran its first candidate for the presidency, James Black of Pennsylvania.

Founding of the Woman's Christian Temperance Union and Anti-Saloon League. In Cleveland, Ohio, the National Women's Temperance Union was organized in 1874 and incorporated in 1883. Also in 1883 the World Woman's Christian Temperance Union was organized. At Oberlin, Ohio, a local temperance group organized the Ohio Anti-Saloon League in 1893; its aims were to preach the benefits of temperance and to close all saloons in Ohio. That same year an Anti-Saloon League was founded in the District of Columbia. In 1895 these two groups and 45 other local temperance organizations founded a national organization, the Anti-Saloon League of America.

Catholic Total Abstinence Movement. Catholic leaders also became more interested and active. The bishops believed that something had to be done about intemperance, that any new effort had to avoid the mistakes of the past, and that the effort had to be definitely Catholic and to depend first of all on spiritual means of improvement. These views were reflected in a decree of the Second Plenary Council of Baltimore (1866) that urged pastors to warn their people about the evils of drunkenness. Total abstinence pledges, the mutual encouragement of those who belonged to temperance societies, and frequent reception of the Sacraments were held out as means for overcoming the problem. Within the next few years interest in total abstinence revived, and many Catholic societies were formed. State organizations soon followed. A convention of Catholic temperance societies in Baltimore in 1872 led to the formation of the Catholic Total Abstinence Union of America (CTAUA). The CTAUA was moderate and nonprohibitionist, and it avoided politics. Publications sponsored by the CTAUA and by various Catholic groups and societies helped to keep temperance news before the public. Isaac T. HECKER, founder of the Paulist Fathers and editor of the *Catholic World,* was long active in the total abstinence movement. The most widely read paper was the *Catholic Total Abstinence News,* published in Philadelphia.

As a general rule, the CTAUA maintained its position on moral suasion, but it did lobby for high license fees. In the 1880s and 1890s, led by Abp. John IRELAND, the CTAUA became more interested in legislation and cooperated with nonsectarian pressure groups seeking dry goals. In 1895 Ireland was chosen as the second vice president of the Anti-Saloon League.

At the Third Plenary Council of Baltimore in 1884, Catholics who sold liquor were warned to consider the occasion of sin that surrounded their business and to choose, if they could, a more becoming way of making a living. Thirteen years later Bp. John A. Watterson of Columbus, Ohio, issued a notice barring saloon keepers from membership in Catholic societies of the diocese. This action was appealed to the apostolic delegate, Abp. Francesco SATOLLI, who upheld the bishop. Such zeal produced bad effects, for while the Catholic population as a whole became more temperate, it refused to become prohibitionist.

Movement for National Prohibition. Elsewhere in the nation the movement for prohibition gained ground, especially among women. It received national publicity as the result of the actions of Carry Nation, who with a hatchet or other weapons conducted a destructive campaign against Kansas saloons. Such flamboyant and illegal action did little to reassure conservative-minded persons about the wisdom of the temperance cause. To prevent complete suppression and to reach a compromise with the reformers many states enacted laws requiring a high license fee of saloon keepers and liquor dealers. It was thought that such laws would reduce the number of outlets for liquor and make them more respectable. Liquor dealers objected to the monopolistic tendencies inherent in the plan. Another compromise measure was making the retail sale of liquor a municipal or county monopoly. Experience with these substitutes convinced reformers that the best answer to the problem lay in national prohibition.

As the woman suffrage movement advanced, so did the cause of prohibition. Symptomatic of this new enthusiasm was the establishment of a Catholic Women's Auxiliary of the Anti-Saloon League in 1912. Similar auxiliaries sprang up elsewhere. World War I greatly increased the influence of women in American life. When a congressional investigation revealed that the antiprohibition and antifeminist German-American Alliance had also distributed pro-German propaganda, the goals of the reformers became patriotic goals. Persistence, patriotism, and the needs of war helped to push the 18th Amendment to the U.S. Constitution through the various state legislatures. The amendment, which prohibited the manufacture, transportation, and sale of alcoholic beverages, was adopted in 1919 and became effective the following year. Congress overrode President Woodrow Wilson's veto to pass the Volstead Act, which provided the necessary federal enforcement machinery.

One of the prominent Americans who did not share the popular enthusiasm for the amendment was Cardinal James GIBBONS, archbishop of Baltimore. Earlier in his career Gibbons had spoken for temperance, but he did not believe that total abstinence was essential for morality. He felt that local option was in keeping with the principle of self-government but that national prohibition was both unwise and unjust. While the amendment was being considered, he issued a statement condemning it as a product of fanaticism and as dangerous to personal and religious liberty.

A different view was taken by Father George Zurcher, of North Evans, N.Y., who in 1919 founded the Catholic Clergy Prohibition League of America. This league was instrumental in securing the passage of regulations governing sacramental wine that were incorporated into the Volstead Act. It also distributed thousands of copies of its official organ, *Catholics and Prohibition,* which proclaimed the benefits of prohibition and exposed the chicanery of wet Catholic politicians. In 1922 Zurcher made a trip to New Zealand, where he spoke in favor of prohibition.

The activities of American temperance societies in the 19th century had led to the formation of similar societies in Europe. These groups pursued goals ranging from temperance and total abolition to high license fees and prohibition. The Scandinavians, the Russians, and the Americans tried the national prohibition experiment, and all eventually repealed it.

Repeal. In the United States, the constitutionality of the adoption of the 18th Amendment was attacked in the courts. The amendment and the enforcement procedures contributed to the development of a widespread disrespect for law and authority and to the growth of the power and influence of organized crime. In 1932 Franklin D. Roosevelt ran for president on a Democratic party platform that called for the repeal of the prohibition amendment. Following his election, Congress in March 1933 passed the Beer and Wine Revenue Act to legalize beverages with an alcoholic content of 3.2 percent. Later in 1933 the 21st Amendment, which repealed the 18th, was adopted. The failure of the national experiment in prohibition tended to discredit the temperance leaders, including many Protestant clergymen who had endorsed it. The division of opinion in the Catholic Church over the relative merits of various aspects of the temperance crusade and the prohibition amendment helped Catholics to weather the reaction more easily.

Bibliography: S. D. BACON, ed., *Understanding Alcoholism* (*Annals of the American Academy of Political and Social Science* 315; 1958). J. BLAND, *Hibernian Crusade: The Story of the Catholic Total Abstinence Union of America* (Washington 1951). F. L. BYRNE, *Prophet of Prohibition: Neal Dow and His Crusade* (Madison 1961). *Standard Encyclopedia of the Alcohol Problem,* ed. E. H. CHERRINGTON et al., 6 v. (Westerville, Ohio 1925–30). M. CURTI, *The Growth of American Thought* (2d ed. New York 1951). J. R. GUSFIELD, *Symbolic Crusade: Status Politics and the American Temperance Movement* (Urbana, Ill. 1963). R. HOFSTADTER, *The Age of Reform* (New York 1955). J. A. KROUT, *The Origins of Prohibition* (New York 1925). A. SINCLAIR, *Prohibition: The Era of Excess* (Boston 1962).

[H. D. LANGLEY]

TEMPIER, ÉTIENNE

Tempier was born in Orléans, date unknown; and died Sept. 3, 1279. As chancellor of the University of Paris in 1263 and bishop of Paris in 1268, he influenced and checked the course of radical ARISTOTELIANISM and Latin AVERROISM at Paris. On Dec. 10, 1270, he condemned 13 philosophical errors associated with Averroism, and on March 7, 1277, following a request (Jan. 18, 1277) by Pope John XXI (Petrus Hispanus) to inquire into growing charges of heterodoxy, condemned 219 propositions taken from the writings of masters of the faculty of arts, among them SIGER OF BRABANT, and THOMAS AQUINAS (the statements from St. Thomas were removed from the list after his canonization in 1323). The condemnation was directed particularly against the reliance upon the pagan philosophers and the steady encroachment of philosophy upon theology.

Bibliography: L. THORNDIKE, *University Records and Life in the Middle Ages* (New York 1944). M. GRABMANN, *Lexikon für Theologie und Kirche*, ed. M. BUCHBERGER, 10 v. (Freiburg 1930–38) 9:1044. H. RASHDALL, *Universities of Europe in the Middle Ages,* ed. F. M. POWICKE and A. B. EMDEN, 3 v. (Oxford 1936). P. GLORIEUX, *Dictionnaire de théologie catholique*, ed. A. VACANT et al., 15 v. (Paris 1903–50; Tables Générales 1951–) 15.1:99–107. F. VAN STEENBERGHEN, *Aristotle in the West: The Origins of Latin Aristotelianism,* tr. L. JOHNSTON (Louvain 1955).

[P. KIBRE]

TEMPLARS

The Templars, officially the Poor Fellow-Soldiers of Christ and the Temple of Solomon (*Pauperes commilitones Christi templi Salomonici*), were one of the first of 12 religious MILITARY ORDERS of knighthood that came into being between 1100 and 1300. It was founded *c.* 1119 to protect and guide pilgrims in the Holy Land.

Foundation and Development. The foundation of the Templars was inspired by the religious military order of the Knights Hospitaller (*see* KNIGHTS OF MALTA), whose purpose was to aid pilgrims upon their arrival in the Holy Land. The Hospitallers ministered to exhausted pilgrims within the city of Jerusalem; travelers, however, were exposed to danger on the way to the city and needed guides and protectors. A group of knights (seven or nine) filled this need and formed the nucleus of the Templars. It is generally accepted that the Burgundian knight, Hugh des Payens, and a knight from northern France, Godfrey of Saint-Omer, were its founders. They organized a religious community, taking an oath to guard the public routes and, in the presence of Warmund, the Patriarch of Jerusalem, promised to observe the three monastic vows of poverty, chastity, and obedience. All pomp was eliminated, and no distinctive dress characterized the new order. An order such as the Templars was unusual and new to Christianity; the older communities were reluctant to live by the sword, but the Templars unhesitatingly combined religious and military life.

Baldwin II (d. 1131), King of Jerusalem, turned over to the knights a part of his palace, believed to be the Temple of Solomon, whence is derived their name. Because of their pronounced state of poverty, they became known as ''the poor brothers of the Temple.'' Gradually the Templars added to their original duties the obligation to fight all ''infidels'' threatening Christianity and to repel any force menacing Jerusalem or their religion.

As the fame of the order grew, partly through the propaganda writings of BERNARD OF CLAIRVAUX (*De laude novae militiae,* 1128), it began also to increase in size. Recruiting members from the nobility and waxing rich on gifts from grateful kings and princes, the Templars developed into an efficient military organization that adopted absolute secrecy to cover all internal activities. They became extremely influential—and their influence, together with their mounting prosperity, created enemies. Applicants ranged from lords who wished only to be considered part of the order to excommunicated knights who, after absolution by their bishop, joined in active participation hoping to expiate their sins. The latter group was responsible for the eventual privilege of the order whereby no member of the Temple could be excommunicated.

At the Council of Troyes (Jan. 13, 1128), at which Hugh appeared in person, the rule of the order, prepared by Bernard of Clairvaux, was considered and approved. The Templars were permitted to wear the white mantle of the CISTERCIANS, to which, in the pontificate of EUGENE III, the distinctive red cross was added. Heading the order was the Grand Master of the Temple of Jerusalem, assisted by a hierarchy of lesser officers. Though his power was not absolute, he had great authority over his subjects. Under certain specified circumstances, he was obligated to consult the general chapter, from which his authority was derived through a complicated election process. The first grand master was Hugh des Payens.

Before 1153 the order had been established in many kingdoms of Christendom: gifts of money and property were lavished upon it by royal families, and spiritual gifts and privileges were bestowed by the popes. Because the Templars were defenders of the Church, they were exempt from paying TITHES and, unless referred to by name, even from the effects of general papal decrees. At first only knights were admitted, and no specific length of service was required. Gradually the order began to admit members in three categories: knights, chaplains, and sergeants. The knights surrendered all of their property, joining for life. Originally they had the prerogative to leave at will; later, however, they could leave only to join another order with stricter rules. The chaplains were priests bound to the order for life, administering the Sacraments and serving the religious needs of the knights, owing obedience only to the grand master and to the pope himself. The sergeants were a group composed of wealthy bourgeois. Since the order formed an exempt ecclesiastical organization directly subject to the pope, frequent feuds resulted betweeen the Templars and the bishops in whose dioceses they had been established. Numerous papal decrees were issued on their behalf, and as long as the defense of the Holy Land was in question, attacks on the Templars were unsuccessful.

For more than 100 years the Templars remained powerful, influential, and wealthy. Their properties were scattered throughout Europe, and in consequence they competed with other religious military orders, such as the Hospitallers. Each order rivaled the other in its holdings and membership, and on occasion the orders engaged in actual skirmishes. But perhaps the seriousness of this competition has been exaggerated. The rivalry was actually productive, for the orders strove to outdo each other in magnificence and in other accomplishments in keeping with their rule.

The fall of JERUSALEM to the Muslims (October 1187) was a critical event in the history of the Templars. As each new CRUSADE, launched to recapture the city, failed, the crusading spirit waned and the military orders became largely anachronistic. After the Christians had been ousted from the Holy Land by 1291, the other religious military orders sought new goals: the Hospitallers transformed themselves into a maritime police force to combat Muslim piracy in the Mediterranean; the TEUTONIC KNIGHTS retired to the Baltic provinces of the empire to give their full attention to the heathen Slavs. The Templars, on the other hand, seemed about to become a standing international mercenary force at the disposal of anyone who had most to offer them. They thought of retiring to France, where they were particularly rich and powerful, centering their activity in Paris. There (and in London) the Temple became the depository of their wealth at which princes and commoners banked their private property. Even the royal funds of France were deposited there.

Trial and Suppression. In 1285 when PHILIP IV the Fair (1268–1314) ascended the French throne, the country was near bankruptcy. The king was constantly in need of money and land, and the Templars possessed both in great abundance. Their destruction would prove lucrative to Philip, and it would also give him an opportunity to strike indirectly at the papacy, with which he was in open conflict. He decided to humble the papacy vicariously; for if he attacked Boniface VIII directly, the pope could turn the religious military orders against the French throne.

Philip began his campaign by blaming the Templars for the loss of the Holy Land, accusing them of being more interested in banking and finance, and in their rich establishments, than in the Holy City. It seems probable that Philip was convinced that the Templars were plotting to establish a French enclave and that, consequently, they were dangerous.

For at least 40 years there had been rumors of heretical practices within the Temple, though there was no actual proof because of the complete secrecy of all rituals. This secrecy was especially strict with reference to initiation into the order; any revelation of those rites constituted grounds for expulsion. This reputation tended to bring together the enemies of the Templars and gave Philip the weapon he required. He devised false initiation rites for the order; and when these alleged rites were publicly revealed, the Templars of course denied them. The charges made by Philip claimed that the candidates had to undergo a ceremony involving sacrilegious and obscene practices. Feeling secure because of the protection of the Church and the falsity of the accusations, the Knights did nothing. By 1307, however, Philip had drawn up specific charges against the order and sent them to Pope CLEMENT V (1305–14), asking for an investigation. The pope promised one.

Regarding the pope's promise as consent, Philip then sent out orders to have all the Templars in France (*c.* 2,000) arrested on the same day, Oct. 13, 1307. The lands of the order were occupied by royal officers, and its property sequestrated. Public opinion in France was stirred up against the order by a vicious and skillful propaganda campaign, depicting the ''fighting arm of the Church'' as a rich, decadent organization, a malignant growth on the body of the Church and state alike.

Philip, however, was not satisfied to break the order only in France; he wanted to destroy the Templars throughout the Christian world. To do this he would have to prove to the pope that his charges were universally true. After a period of hesitation, the vacillating Clement (July 1308) approved a double inquest into the affairs of the Templars, one on the individual members, the other on the order itself. The former was to fall within the competence of the local ordinary with judgment rendered by provincial council; the latter was to await the decision of the general Council of Vienne. Philip, however, conducted his own inquest—without papal approval—using the services of the general inquisitor for France.

Extorting confessions under torture, the inquisitor ''demonstrated'' the guilt of the leading French Templars, mostly knights, including Grand Master JACQUES DE MOLAY. In England, Scotland, Ireland, Aragon, Castile, and Germany the Templars were found innocent on all counts; but in France and in areas under French influence, such as Provence, the Kingdom of Naples, and even the States of the Church, they were assessed guilty as charged. At length Clement brought the final decision to the floor of the Council, hoping that by satisfying Philip in regard to the Templars, he would be spared from undertaking the king's other demand: the canonical process leading to the condemnation of the memory of Boniface VIII. Early in December 1311, the Council voted overwhelmingly against the abolition of the Templars on grounds that the charges had not been proved. But in the bull *Vox in excelso* (*Conciliorum oecumenicorum decreta,* 312–319) of March 22, 1312, read in the second session on April 3, Clement suppressed the order by papal PROVISION, reserving the disposition of persons and property to the pope. Nevertheless, by order of the king, Jacques de Molay and the highest dignitaries of the order were burned at the stake (March 1314), repudiating their confession and asserting the complete innocence of the order.

The pope had no alternative but to dissolve the Templars. Yet Philip had not completely won. Since the order was condemned as heretical, its possessions still remained in the hands of the Church. It was finally agreed that they be turned over to the Knights Hospitaller. In Spain and Portugal, however, their property went to such military orders as the ORDER OF CHRIST and the KNIGHTS OF MONTESA. Philip did not accept the decision; he claimed that the Temple owed him money and presented a greatly exaggerated list of expenses incurred by the state. This enormous debt was settled by the Hospitallers.

The spectacular end of the Templars was, and remains, one of the most debated events of history. It is easy to understand that Philip the Fair, debt-ridden and desperate, would want to abolish an organization that represented a threat to his absolute power, especially if at the same time he could fill his coffers. It is likewise understandable that a weak and reluctant pope, who owed his election to King Philip, was forced to comply. It is clear also how public opinion could be turned against a prosperous and influential order that was accountable only to the pope, having an income four times that of the king of France. But it remains a mystery why the order, entrenched in the impenetrable Temple in Paris, submitted without resistance to the certainly inferior forces of the king.

Bibliography: H. FINKE, *Papsttum und Untergang des Templerordens,* 2 v. (Münster 1907). G. A. M. D' ALBON, ed., *Cartulaire général de l'Ordre du Temple,* 2 v. (Paris 1913–22). G. LIZERAND, *Clément V et Philippe le Bel* (Paris 1911); ed. and tr., *Le Dossier de l'affaire des Templiers* (Paris 1923). E. MŪLLER, *Das Konzil von Vienne,* 1311–1312 (Münster 1934). J. LECLERCQ, *Dictionnaire de théologie catholique,* ed. A. VACANT et al., 15 v. (Paris 1903–50; Tables générales 1951) 15.2:2973–79. *Conciliorum oecumenicorum decreta* (Bologna-Freiburg 1962) 312–336. E. SIMON, *The Piebald Standard* (London 1959). T. W. PARKER, *The Knights Templars in England* (Tucson 1963). G. BORDONOVE, *Les Templiers* (Paris 1963).

[G. GROSSCHMID]

TEMPLE, WILLIAM

Anglican archbishop of York (1929–42) and of Canterbury (1942–44), theologian and ecumenical leader; b. Exeter, Oct. 15, 1881; d. Canterbury, Oct. 26, 1944. The son of Frederick Temple, archbishop of Canterbury (1896–1902), he was educated at Rugby School and Balliol College, Oxford. His mild theological LIBERALISM assumed Value as ultimate, and religious formulas as tentative at best. An essay in *Foundations* (1912) proclaimed, ''The formula of Chalcedon is, in fact, a confession of the bankruptcy of Greek Patristic theology.'' *Mens Creatrix* (1917) attempted a philosophical basis for Christian theism. *Christus Veritas* (1924) is his most developed theory of the INCARNATION and is quite similar to the teachings of CHALCEDON, despite its neo-Nestorian flavor. His Gifford Lectures, published as *Nature, Man and God* (1934), explained his final position, styled dialectical realism. The ECUMENICAL MOVEMENT occupied him much. Many considered him an ideal chairman for such discussions; his keen, sympathetic mind often brought accord to seemingly deadlocked meetings. At the Conferences in Lausanne (1927), Jerusalem, and Edinburgh (1937) he greatly influenced the men who instituted the WORLD COUNCIL OF CHURCHES (1948). He was a man of broad interests, solid learning, and outstanding administrative ability. Until 1939 he believed that his ''Christo-centric metaphysics'' could make sense

Temple of Queen Hatshepsut, at Luxor, Egypt. (Archive Photos, Inc.)

out of the world as revealing God's intelligible Word; afterward he admitted that we can only believe that this chaotic world will be brought to sense in Christ some day, somehow, by God. He has been termed a ''Central Churchman.'' Some thought his idealistic ''finding some good in every thing'' a theological weakness, but it aided him to be what he predominantly was: a holy and intelligent Christian leader.

Bibliography: F. A. IREMONGER, *William Temple* (London 1948). J. FLETCHER, *William Temple: Twentieth-Century Christian* (New York 1963).

[D. J. BOWMAN]

TEMPLES

A temple is a place that reveals a sacred reality, is accepted as such by a community, and consequently is a cultic center. Although the word usually refers to a building and evokes the image of the religious monuments of great civilizations, the Latin root word *templum* denotes primarily a staked-off piece of land belonging to the people or to a deity. Greek τέμενος (from τέμνω, ''to cut off'') has the same connotation. The ancient Germanic peoples not only had temple buildings but held cairns in the open and certain forests as sacred also.

The Dwelling Place of the Divinity. As a rule, a temple is regarded as the dwelling place of a particular deity. Accordingly, the services of the priests are modeled on the tasks of servants at a royal palace; the temple is in the first place a god's residence, not, or only secondarily, the gathering place of a congregation. The idea of a god's dwelling place is widespread (Heb. *bēth'elohīm,* ''house of God''; Gr. ναός, ''sanctuary,'' derived from

Ruins of the Parthenon, atop the Acropolis, Athens, Greece. (©Susan D. Rock)

ναίω, to dwell, inhabit). In the temple as residence the deity is represented by an image or symbol in a special place that is architectonically secluded from the other areas either wholly or in part (exemplified respectively by Germanic and Hindu temples). In some (pastoral) cultures centers of cult are not fixed at any one site but are reestablished in various places in accordance with set precepts.

In the case of all types of sanctuary, even when due weight is given to the temple as the residence of a deity, the manifestation of the sacred in a particular place is the most universal and basic element in temple symbolism. As a rule, it is more important than the individual characteristics of a residing deity. Not one, but each, group of herdsmen in ancient Arcadia had its own holy place for Pan, and several authors (including Aristophanes and Plato) use the plural, *Panes.* Thus for his worshipers, the reality of Pan's sanctuary did not depend on the question of his singularity or plurality. A residing deity may change sex (as the Chinese divinity Kuan-yin, from female to male). Sacred places continue in spite of changes in characteristics that seem far-reaching to the observer. The preeminence of the sacred place is retained also in early BUDDHISM, where the most important holy centers are the places that were crucial in the Buddha's career. Once a place has been accepted as sacred it tends to keep its sacredness, even if the religion changes. This conservation is borne out by archeology: all pre-classical and classical civilizations show examples of temples built on the site of destroyed predecessors.

The temple as residence of a deity and the temple as sacred place are not mutually exclusive; as a rule the two ideas complement and support each other. Special mention should be made of some sacred buildings and religions that differ partly or wholly from this general rule. The occurrence of shifting sanctuaries has already been mentioned. The Buddhist *stūpa* is primarily a place for sacred relics. In Christianity many Protestant churches and meeting houses show only remote resemblance to temple symbolism. SYNAGOGUE and MOSQUE are principally houses of assembly and are therefore distinct from temples.

Orientation in Space. For religious man space is *not homogeneous* (G. van der Leeuw). The nonhomogeneity of space is not only an archaic, but a fundamental, human experience. All time is not measured in the same manner in man's experience, and neither is all space. In a chaotic space, of which no part seems different from another, man nevertheless *orients* himself toward certain reliable points. He finds that specific places are distinct from others and sacred as they form the only *real* or *really existing* space (M. Eliade). The basis of man's orientation in space is a hierophany, i.e., a manifestation of the sacred, which provides an absolutely reliable point. The dwelling place of man and the construction of temples are intrinsically related, as both presuppose an orientation symbolism in accordance with a particular hierophany. This suggests that the basic symbolism of sanctuaries is much older than the oldest sacred monuments known from history. The most primitive nomadic clans (as in Australia) do not pitch a camp at random but in a certain order, around a sacred center, usually indicated by a pole. A sacred pole or pillar almost universally symbolizes the communication with the other, sacred, world. Thus a fixed center in space is established that guarantees man's world (cosmos) as distinct from the surrounding chaos. This centrality is clearly marked in the symbolism of many sacred places and in the symbolic terminology of texts concerning temples in the whole ancient world (''middle of the world,'' ''navel of the earth.''

Orientation in Time. The temple, like the city in the ancient world, is a place where heaven, earth, and netherworld meet. However, this symbolic relationship is to be understood not only spatially but also in terms of time. Directly or indirectly each temple is related to the beginning of the world. In Egypt the elevation of temples was mythically identified with the primordial hill on which the creator god performed the first acts. Each Hindu temple has its *sthālapurāṇa,* the sacred account of the origin of the temple, which is always conceived in some way as having taken place in a mythical time, a time before our ''normal'' time. According to tradition the foundations of the temple of Jerusalem (likewise the foundations of the city of Babylon) were fixed on the primordial waters of chaos. Thus the sacred building represents not only an absolutely reliable point in space, but at the same time, temporally, the victory over chaos.

Cosmic Symbolism. Spatial (orientation) symbolism and mythical event are fused in the temple. The

Tibetan Buddhist Temple. (©Susan D. Rock)

mythical event is expressed not only in the establishment of the temple itself but also in the cult that is enacted. As a sacred place par excellence, as a place of communication with the other world, and above all as a structure in which the reality and the process of the world blend, the temple is in itself a cosmic image, *imago mundi.* The Inca Sun temple (Coricancha) had at its center an altar representing the whole cosmos with its emblems (sun, moon, atmosphere, heaven, earth, the main constellations). The surrounding garden presented a complete *imago mundi* in which all species of animals and plants were symbolized. Refined and detailed as such symbolism is, its beginnings can be seen in man's most archaic imagery, which summed up the cosmos in holy places of great simplicity consisting of three characteristic elements: a rock or mountain, water, and a tree, together forming a ''perfect landscape'' (the *paysage complet,* of J. Przyluski). At all stages of temple symbolism there is a close relation between the things in the immediate environment of man and in the universe in its sacred totality: an ambivalence that can be easily understood from the self-supporting nature of the home of the peasant in any agricultural civilization in its early days. The ambivalence is preserved both in the Latin word *mundus* and in the Greek word κόσμος.

Accordingly, temple, city, and the geography of state and world are interrelated. The earth is thought of as a square—the result of the projection of the four horizons—and the temple is so designed. All great civilizations continued the fundamental symbolism of orientation and the total cosmic imagery in their temples. The image of a cosmic mountain also occurs almost everywhere: Mount Meru in India and similar symbolisms in Mesopotamia, Palestine, and elsewhere. The Mesopotamian ziggurat is the most famous example of a temple representing the cosmic mountain, its seven levels corresponding to the seven planetary skies. (*See* MESOPOTAMIA, ANCIENT, 3.) Temples, then, are understood as replicas of this central cosmic mountain, which bears and preserves the universe. The Borobudur in Java is the most outstanding example in Buddhist art of a temple as such a cosmic mountain. The cosmic symbolism of the temple is in many cases crowned by the dome, which symbolizes the vault of heaven. The communication with the heavenly world is visible in the opening left in the dome. Thus the dome of the Roman Pantheon has in its center an *oculus* (''eye'').

As a Center of Speculation and Meditation. The holiness of a sanctuary should not be thought of in conde-

Pyramid of the Sun at Teotihuacan, Mexico. (Bettmann/ CORBIS)

scending fashion at any stage of man's history known to us. In spite of much superstition, the design and use of temples bear witness at all times to great subtlety of thought. High speculation on the temple as a replica of a transcendent model is not confined to the great classical civilizations. Among archaic root-crop cultivators, e.g., among the Kiwai of New Guinea, the temple is regarded as a reduplication of the realm of the dead, which is governed by the most important deity. Particularly in HINDUISM, JAINISM, and BUDDHISM, from the earliest times emphasis has been laid on the design of temples and their central objects of worship as instruments of meditation. The Buddha himself was at first not depicted at all. Instead, a symbol like the Bodhi tree at which he had reached his Enlightenment, or the Lord's feet, were represented as objects of worship.

Bibliography: G. VAN DER LEEUW, *Sacred and Profane Beauty: The Holy in Art,* tr. D. E. GREEN (New York 1963). S. KRAMRISCH, *The Hindu Temple,* 2 v. (Calcutta 1946). M. ELIADE, *Patterns in Comparative Religion,* tr. R. SHEED (New York 1958); *Cosmos and History* (New York 1954); *Le Symbolisme cosmique des monuments religieux* (Rome 1957). A. K. COOMARASWAMY, ''Symbolism of the Dome,'' *Indian Historical Quarterly* 14 (1938) 1–56. P. A. MEANS, *Ancient Civilizations of the Andes* (New York 1931). P. MUS, ''Bārābudur: Les Origines du stûpa et la transmigration. Essai d'archéologie religieuse comparée,'' *Bulletin d'École Française d'Extrême-Orient* 32 (1932) 269–439; 33 (1933) 577–980; 34 (1934) 175–400. W. ANDRAE, *Das Gotteshaus und die Urformen des Bauens im alten Orient* (Berlin 1930). R. HEINE-GELDERN, *Weltbild und Bauform in Südostasien* (Vienna 1930). W. BREDE KRISTENSEN, *Het leven uit den dood: Studiën over Egyptischen- en oud-Griekschen godsdienst* (Haarlem 1926). A. DE BUCK, *Eyyptische voorstellingen betreffende den oerheuvel* (Leiden 1922).

[K. W. BOLLE]

TEMPLES (IN THE BIBLE)

There was no specific word for temple in the Old Testament. God's abode was called simply His house (*bayit*) or palace (*hêkāl*), the same words that were used for a king's house or palace. A temple's plan even copied that of a royal palace.

Ancient Semitic Temples. In Syria and Palestine of the third millennium B.C., following the Assyrian pattern, a temple had a portal near the end of a long side of an oblong construction, from which the worshiper turned to approach the divine image at the farthest wall. In the second millennium the plan was modified to include a small, sometimes elevated room at the farthest end, in front of which stood a portico or vestibule, then came the temple's main hall; the portal had also been moved to the short side of the oblong, farthest from the innermost sanctuary. This three-roomed plan, with the vestibule moved from in front of the innermost room to just inside the portal, was the pattern for Israel's temples.

The daily service of the god also was patterned after royal custom: the image was dressed, food was placed before it, and an elaborate procession was held. All this ceremony demanded the erection of other buildings close to the god's palace: quarters for priests, storerooms, kitchens, etc.

The god, however, was not his statue, which was placed in the innermost room, although some simple folk may have believed he was; nor was he limited to one palace; he could have other temples in the same land or even in the same city. In fact, the powerful presence of the greatest gods, e.g., Assur, MARDUK, and BAAL, was thought to extend over the whole world. The Israelites adopted many of these ideas, purifying and adapting them to the Yahwistic religion, but retaining the basic notion that the Temple was Yahweh's abode on earth (1 Kgs 8.29).

Israelite Temples outside Jerusalem. The edifice at Shiloh, which substituted for the TENT OF MEETING as Yahweh's abode among His people and housed the ARK OF THE COVENANT, was the first of Yahweh's temples (1 Sm 1.7, 9; 3.3, 15; Jgs 18.31). It was the central sanctuary for the federation of the northern tribes (Jos 18.1; 19.51) during the later part of the period of the Judges. An annual pilgrimage feast was joyfully celebrated there (Jgs 21.19–21). Samuel's father came to it every year to worship Yahweh under the title SABAOTH, which probably

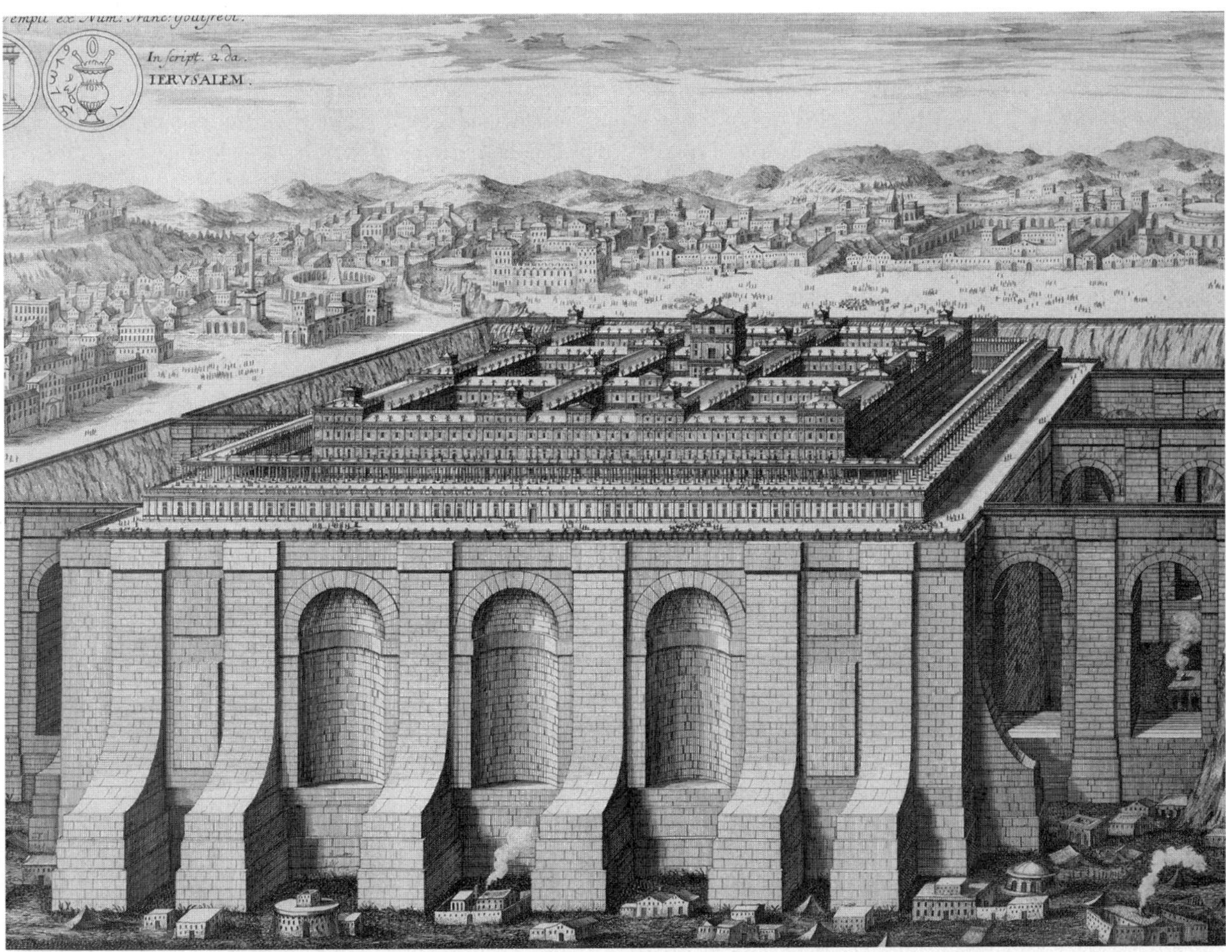

Temple of Solomon, engraving by Fischer von Erlach, c. 1721, Jerusalem. (Historical Picture Archive/CORBIS)

originated at Shiloh (1 Sm 1.3, 7). The Philistines apparently destroyed this temple (*c.* 1050 B.C.) after they defeated Israel and captured the ark at the battle of Aphec (1 Sm 4.10–11). About 50 years later, when King DAVID brought the ark to JERUSALEM, the city he himself had captured, he set up a tent for it there, thus making Jerusalem the central holy place for his kingdom, which included both the northern and southern federations of Israelite tribes.

Other Israelite temples were erected at traditional holy places, the most important of which were Yahweh's temples at Bethel and Dan, the chief sanctuaries for the Northern Kingdom. They were established at traditional holy places by Jeroboam I to attract his people away from the Jerusalem Temple (1 Kgs 12.27–30). At these royal sanctuaries Yahweh was worshiped as enthroned above a golden bull rather than above the ark of the covenant and the cherubim as He was in Jerusalem's Temple. The DEUTERONOMISTS who edited the books of Kings considered this worship to be illegitimate, however, and severely blamed the northern Kings for fostering it. The temple at Bethel continued to be a Yahwistic sanctuary even after the fall of the Northern Kingdom of Israel, until it was destroyed, along with other local sanctuaries, by Josia, King of Judah, in the great centralizing Deuteronomistic reform of the seventh century B.C.

Temples in Jerusalem. For more than 1,000 years (*c.* 950 B.C. to A.D. 70, except from 587 until 515 when the Temple was in ruins) Jerusalem's Temple was the most important sanctuary in Israel. Actually, there were three Temples, Solomon's, Zerubbabel's, and that begun by Herod the Great, *c.* 19 B.C.

Solomon's Temple. David proposed building a palace for Yahweh, but was forbidden to do so by an oracle (2 Sm 7.1–17). His son and successor SOLOMON was the actual builder; he contracted with Hiram, King of Tyre, for the timber and artisans and completed the structure in seven years, from the fourth to the 11th year of his reign (1 Kgs 5.3–6.1, 37–38). A later interpretation of the Biblical CHRONICLER, however, attributed much more of the preparation for the Temple's construction and services to David (1 Chr ch. 22–28).

The site chosen for Yahweh's palace (2 Chr 3.1) already had the essential requisites for a holy place: a divine intervention—the appearance of the ANGEL OF THE LORD to David; an act of salvation—the cessation of a plague; and the beginning of a cult to Yahweh—David's construction of an altar there and the first sacrifices (2 Sm 24.16–25).

The description of Solomon's Temple given in 1 Kgs 6.2–36; 7.15–51 was based on a document dating from the construction itself, but, because of its technical vocabulary and consequent scribal errors, it is open to diverse interpretations that cannot be checked by any known archeological evidence. The following summation, therefore, is in no way definitive.

The Temple was oblong, with a portal (probably facing the east) at one of its shorter sides. There were three interior sections, a vestibule (*'ûlām*), the main cultic room (*hêkāl*), and the innermost sanctuary, or back room (*d*[e]*bîr*), later called the Holy of Holies; the back room was the proper abode of Yahweh, housing also His throne, i.e., the ark of the covenant. The measurements given in the text are interior ones and do not give the thickness of the walls, but by projection one may conclude that the structure was about 115 feet long, 35 feet wide, and 50 feet high—not a very large public building according to modern standards and certainly not intended as a gathering place for the throngs that came up to Jerusalem for the great PILGRIMAGES. The building was carefully designed, however, and artistically decorated with wooden paneling and precious metals. A service annex, originally of one story, to which two other stories were later added, was built contiguous to the three nonportal sides of the main building and was used as a kind of sacristy and for the storage of supplies and treasures.

The *hêkāl* was the largest room and enclosed the altar of INCENSE, the table for the SHOWBREAD, and 10 lampstands; it was, then, the place where the priest performed cultic acts. It was separated from the Holy of Holies by a thin partition or a veil. The *d*[e]*bîr* was elevated above the level of the *hêkāl* by about seven feet and was entered by means of a stairway. Besides the ark, it contained the two large gilded wooden figures called the CHERUBIM, whose outstretched wings protected the ark and were thought to afford a throne for God, who, of course, was not represented by any figure.

Before the vestibule and separated from the Temple stood two bronze pillars about 27 feet high, the traditional STELES of Semitic cultic centers. Not much farther east from the pillars guarding the Temple's entrance stood the altar of sacrifices, made of bronze and open to the sky; on it animals were sacrificed to God. South of the altar stood the large bronze basin supported by 12 bronze figures of bulls. In the courtyard before the Temple were also ten pedestals on wheels, supporting smaller bronze basins, five each on either side of the Temple's entrance. These basins were used for purificatory purposes for both priests and victims.

The Temple was enclosed by walls forming the inner court, the southern wall being common with the inner court of the King's palace. The great court enclosed both the Temple and the royal palace. Later the inner court of the Temple was divided, or expanded, at the expense of the great court; and at one time, there was an upper and a lower court. It was here that the people congregated during the cultic services.

The Postexilic Temple of Zerubbabel. After the Exile of Israel, a more modest Temple was built according to the pattern and on the site of the former Temple (Ezra ch. 1; 3; 6). The rebuilding had been authorized by Cyrus in 538 B.C., but because of Samaritan opposition and the discouragement of many of the Jews, the work was not completed (515 B.C.) until the Prophets Haggai and Zechariah had encouraged Zerubbabel and Joshua to take up the task (Ezr 4.24–5.2; Hag 1.1–2.9; Zec 4.7–10). Although Zerubbabel's Temple was not as richly decorated and elaborate as Solomon's, it was probably the same in size and general plan and was of solid and careful construction (see the report of the Persian satrap of Trans-Euphrates in Ezr 5.8). In accord with the ideal altar of Ezechiel (Ez 43.13–17), the new altar of holocausts was the same size as Solomon's, but was made of stone rather than bronze. This Temple was plundered and desecrated in 169 B.C. by ANTIOCHUS IV EPIPHANES (1 Mc 1.21–26; 2 Mc 5.15–21). Judas Machabee replaced the sacred furniture and rededicated the Temple on a day in December that was henceforth celebrated as the Feast of the DEDICATION OF THE TEMPLE (1 Mc 4.36–59; 2 Mc 10.1-8; Jn 10.22).

Herod's Temple. In 20–19 B.C. Herod the Great undertook to reconstruct the Temple and its surrounding courts and buildings. The essential reconstruction was completed in about ten years, but work on the annexes and courts continued until well after Our Lord's public ministry. Like the Zerubbabel Temple, it had a Holy of Holies separated from the *hêkāl* by a veil, which was torn in two by Jesus' death (Mt 27.51). A lengthy description of Herod's Temple is given by Josephus (*Bell. Jud.* 5.5.1–6). The entire Temple area was destroyed by the Romans in A.D. 70, and its treasures and furnishings were carried off to Rome as trophies by Titus (Josephus, *Ant.* 15.11; *Bell. Jud.* 5.5).

Other Temples. Three other temples dedicated to Yahweh are known to have existed outside of Jerusalem in the postexilic period, but they were never recognized as legitimate by the officials in Jerusalem.

Samaritan Temple. The only certain thing known about this sanctuary on Mt. Garizim is that it was in existence when Antiochus IV Epiphanes dedicated it to Zeus in 167–166 B.C. The story of its foundation by a certain Manasses, recounted by Josephus in *Ant.* 11.7.2–8.4, is hardly credible and contradicts the account given in Neh 13.28. The temple was destroyed by John Hyrcanus in 129 B.C., but the text of Jn 4.20–21 indicates that there was still a cultic center on Mt. Garizim in Jesus' times.

Elephantine Temple. A Jewish military colony living at Elephantine in Egypt erected a sanctuary and an altar dedicated to Yaho (YAHWEH) during the sixth to the fifth century B.C. These mercenaries in the Persian army were completely ignorant of the Deuteronomic law that forbade the construction of any Yahwistic temple outside of Jerusalem. Their sanctuary was destroyed by the Egyptians in 410 B.C., but had been restored by 402. After the end of Persian rule in Egypt in the early fourth century B.C., the Elephantine colonists and their temple disappeared from history.

The Temple at Leontopolis. A certain Onias, the son of the high priest Onias III (2 Mc 4.33–34), built a temple and established a cult of Yahweh at Leontopolis in Egypt (*c.* 170 B.C.). It remained in existence until A.D. 73, when Vespasian ordered it to be destroyed to prevent any resurgence of Jewish nationalism.

Bibliography: *Encyclopedic Dictionary of the Bible*, tr. and adap. by L. HARTMAN (New York 1963) 2399–2400. H. LESÊTRE, *Dictionnaire de la Bible* 5.2: 2024–74. R. DE VAUX, *Lexikon für Theologie und Kirche*, ed. J. HOFER and K. RAHNER (Freiberg 1957–65) 9:1350–58. R. DE VAUX, *Ancient Israel, Its Life and Institutions,* tr. J. MCHUGH (New York 1961) 271–344. K. GALLING, *Die Religion in Geschichte und Gegenwart* (Tübingen 1957–65) 6:681–686. L. H. VINCENT and A. M. STÈVE, *Jérusalem de l'Ancien Testament,* 3 v. in 2 (Paris 1954–56) v.2.1.

[J. E. STEINMUELLER]

TEMPORAL VALUES, THEOLOGY OF

A theological orientation based on the acceptance of the temporal order as the relatively permanent and congenial condition for the fulfillment of the Christian vocation rather than as the condition of absolute transience and exile. In the history of Christian theology there have appeared two valid emphases regarding the relationship of the Christian to the world: the eschatological emphasis, characterized by a preoccupation with the eternal order and a relative indifference toward the temporal, and the incarnational emphasis, with its stress on the value of the temporal order itself because of its elevation by Christ's entrance into it.

Eschatological Emphasis. The doctrine of the New Testament regarding the relationship of man to the world was so dominated by the expectation of the PAROUSIA that it tended to draw attention away from a consideration of the Christian in the world and even from the immediate aftermath of the individual's death. In the apostolic and postapostolic period, the Christian community expected the Parousia imminently (Mk 13.30; Mt 24.3–51). Christ was to come again (Acts 1.11) so that His followers could save themselves from ''this perverse generation'' (Acts 2.40). They sold their goods and possessions and gave to the needy, spending their days in prayer and the breaking of Bread (Acts 2.42–47). God made the wisdom of the world foolish (1 Cor 1.20); Christ gave Himself for man's sins that He might deliver man from the wickedness of this present world (Gal 1.4); a condition of pure and undefiled religion before God the Father was to keep oneself unspotted from this world (Jas 1.27).

In the Didache [Syria(?) between 100 and 150] there was a heavy emphasis on the Parousia and its imminence (16.1; *Ancient Christian Writers,* ed. J. Quasten et al. [Westminster, MD 1946–] 6.24), but no mention of the beginnings of a structural hierarchy or a monarchical episcopate. It was typical of these writings of the Apostolic Fathers that they were eschatological in character and regarded the Second Coming of Christ as imminent. With the passing of the second generation of Christians and the failure of the Parousia to occur, thought was given to the fate of the Christian after death and before the ''last day.'' Chiliastic elements developed among the Greek Apologists (Justin, *Dial.* 5, 80; *Patrologia Graeca,* ed J. P. Migne [Paris 1857–66] 6:485–489, 664–668), as well as untraditional assertions that immortality is not natural to the soul, but is a reward for its having kept the commandments of God (Justin, *Dial.* 5, *Patrologia Graeca,* 6:485–489; Irenaeus, *Adv. haer.* 4.4.3, *Patrologia Graeca,* 7:982–983; Theophilus of Antioch, *Ad Autolycum* 2.27, *Patrologia Graeca,* 6:1094–95). The *Epistle to Diognetus* (5–6; *Patrologia Graeca,* 2:1173–76) goes beyond the anticipation of the Parousia to describe the task of Christians in the world.

The same current of thought can be found in later Fathers, with chiliasm appearing in the writings of some of the Alexandrians, in Palestine, among the Romans, in Tertullian, in Lactantius, and in other writers of the West, until it was dealt a death blow by the work of Origen. Coupled with a preoccupation with the last things was a disregard and even disdain for the world. Movements of Christians to segregate themselves from the world contributed to the rise of monasticism and to the separatism of cenobitism and the life of the stylites. Quite early the excess of utter disdain for the world resulted in heterodox doctrinal formulations, such as Montanism, and their convulsionary variations through the centuries.

Kept within orthodox limits, the emphasis on the last things is a salutary and necessary spiritual orientation; it helps Christians to avoid attachments that draw them away from God and from each other. In this sense, eschatology has benefited Christian spirituality and in part characterized its history.

Incarnational Emphasis. The origins of the incarnational emphasis in theology are vague, but it surely began to arise in the postapostolic period when the Parousia that was expected imminently failed to occur. With the interpretation of Christianity to the emperors by the Apologists and its remarkable expansion, especially at the time of Constantine, it was necessary for Christianity to reevaluate the role of temporal values. By the time of Augustine (see *The City of God*) much thought had gone into the formulation of a doctrine of man's relatively permanent place in the world as a Christian. With the rise of the papacy as an institution and the subsequent building up of a temporal empire, the culmination of its power being in the late 11th and early 12th centuries, when it was landlord of one-third of the tillable land of Europe, not to speak of Eastern holdings, there was articulated, at least implicitly, the doctrine of definite acceptance of and appreciation for worldly goods and temporal values. The impressive intellectual, artistic, economic, political, and religio-institutional structures of the flowering of the Middle Ages would have been neither possible nor desirable if the Christian's role in the world was absolutely transient and a form of exile. The Renaissance papacy indicated an overemphasis on the value of the temporal to the neglect of the eternal and contributed in large measure to the rupture of Christendom and the rise of Protestantism.

Tridentine and post-Tridentine theology, which followed so crucial an event as the Protestant Reformation, was preoccupied with reevaluations and reforms. More recently, in an atmosphere of comparative religious peace and ecumenical security, theologians have again turned to the question of the Christian and the world; and although there were to be found among prominent 20th–century theologians representatives of both emphases, the eschatological (J. DANIÉLOU and L. BOUYER) and the incarnational (G. Thils, Y. M. J. CONGAR, J. C. MURRAY, and P. TEILHARD DE CHARDIN), the incarnational seemed to have been predominant. It holds that the Christian should not withdraw from the world to save himself from it so much as to enter into the world to save it from itself. The dangers involved need not be feared exceedingly, since Christ became man in the world to elevate man, his institutions, and his culture. There are positive human values to be recognized and preserved, including those of labor (*Rerum novarum, Quadragesimo anno*), of education (*Divini illius magistri*), of marriage (*Casti connubii*), of the rights of individuals within the state (*Mit brennender Sorge*), of nations themselves and their social institutions (*Mater et magistra*), of international order (*Pacem in terris*), and throughout all of these, the value of religious liberty (*Dignitatis humanae, Gaudium et spes*).

A solid theology of temporal values is based on the INCARNATION; those who study it and promote it are motivated by the desire to *restore all things* in Christ (a theme of Pius X related to Irenaeus's RECAPITULATION of all in Christ). It is frequently conceptualized in the terms of recent anthropological, phenomenological, and technological advances. Its influences are being felt in a restudy of the relationships between grace and nature [K. Rahner, *Theological Investigations,* v.1, tr. C. Ernst (Baltimore 1961) 297–317], of the ecclesiology that emerged from Vatican II (especially with a view to expanding the role of the bishops and the laity in the life of the Church), of the structure of moral theology [B. Häring, *The Law of Christ,* v.1–2, tr. E. G. Kaiser (Westminster, Md. 1961)], and especially of the role of the Church in a pluralistic society [J. C. Murray, *We Hold These Truths* (New York 1960)] and its relationships with other Christian churches [Vatican II, *Decree on Ecumenism, Unitatis redintegratio; Acta Apostolicae Sedis* 57 (1965) 90–112].

See Also: ELEVATION OF MAN; ESCHATOLOGISM; ESCHATOLOGY (IN THEOLOGY); MAN, 3; SUPERNATURAL; SUPERNATURAL EXISTENTIAL.

Bibliography: Y. M. J. CONGAR, *Laity, Church, and World,* tr. D. ATTWATER (Baltimore 1960); *Lay People in the Church,* tr. D. ATTWATER (Westminster, Md. 1957). J. DANIÉLOU, *The Lord of History,* tr. N. ABERCROMBIE (Chicago 1958). H. DE LUBAC, *Catholicism,* tr. L. C. SHEPPARD (New York 1950; repr. 1958); *Surnaturel: Études historiques* (Paris 1946). L. HAMAIN, *Réalités terrestres et vie chrétienne,* 2 v. (Lille 1959). G. THILS, *Théologie des réalités terrestres,* 2 v. (Bruges 1946–49).

[J. P. WHALEN]

TEMPTATION

As here conceived, temptation is an inducement to sin. TEMPTING GOD is another sense of the term connoting the lack of trust that is contrary to the virtue of hope. For a treatment of temptation by God as a test of man's fidelity, *see* TEMPTATION (IN THE BIBLE).

Analysis. In every temptation man is confronted by a temporal good recognized as such and seen as conflicting with his eternal good. St. Thomas describes the attraction of a temporal good in terms of love. Instead of true love it is the inordinate love of self from which every sin arises: ''That man inordinately desires a temporal good proceeds from this that he inordinately loves himself. . . ''(*Summa Theologiae* 1a2ae, 77.4). Temptation, then, is an appeal to egoism in opposition to man's union by love with God, other persons, and himself.

Temptation is not sin, though the sorely tempted may think so; however, it does arise at times from past sinful indulgence. In itself it is essentially a situation of choice: a confrontation by evil toward which egoism inclines the subject, and a confrontation by the good. Temptation is a call to the Christian either to reaffirm his adherence to Christ or to commit his freedom to the values of Satan and the world. It is an occasion of authentic affirmation of the true self and of ratification of one's grafting onto Jesus by Baptism.

Sources. Satan is the arch-tempter of men, as Holy Writ teaches. Yet not every sin is to be ascribed to him as its source, except remotely by reason of his seduction of Adam, which effected CONCUPISCENCE in man. The DISCERNMENT of spirits in ascetical theology gives clues to Satan's activity. The world as temptation embraces other men or impersonal objects, either individually as proposing false values, or collectively as representing the cultural ethos insofar as this is foreign to Christ and His teaching.

In one sense temptation is man's continual lot. To escape all the allurements of evil would require flight from this life. In the proper sense, however, Satan and the world are sources of temptation only when their influence is consciously experienced and the subject responds by rejection or capitulation. This occurs when the external stimulus meets with an internal resonance in man's nature. The resonance is due to an elemental disharmony, a basic tension between sensibility and spirituality compounded with the wound in nature that is the consequence of original sin. In addition to this common nature, the heritage of all Adam's sons, there is the particular nature of each person fashioned by habitual patterns of response, basically oriented to love or to egoism, psychologically sound or unsound. Since external sources tempt only in conjunction with nature, all temptation is reducible to nature not as a principle of good but as moving toward egoism away from love.

Unique yet Common. Each temptation is a unique, singular experience. The same evil enticing the same person on two occasions does not add up to the same temptation. In reality the subject himself is not altogether the same. He is more experienced than before, more or less attentive, his social support greater or less. This does not mean that norms of conduct for temptation are worthless, but that they are no substitute for responsible personal judgment or the application of such norms to the unique situation.

Adam and Eve, detail of fresco by Masaccio, in the Brancacci Chapel of the Church of Santa Maria del Carmine, c. 1427, Florence. (©Vittoriano Rastelli/CORBIS)

The basis for the validity of these norms is the common elements that perdure through temptations. Men have common reactions to evil. Likewise the person is largely the same who experienced the earlier enticement. This is particularly so because of his habits and his basic orientation.

Good or bad habits affect the subject in that he brings to temptation a pattern of response, woven from his past decisions in the face of evil. These notably influence his present choice. The importance of forming good habits and undoing bad ones is thus elementary. Temptation is not solely a threat to present adherence to the moral ideal but it affects man's pattern of response to God's invitations.

More important still is the subject's basic orientation to the moral good and the person of Christ in the depths of his being, his fundamental posture of commitment to egoism or to the union of love with the Absolute Other. This adhesion to God in the spiritual depths of the person strongly influences all his moral decisions. By this general orientation all his subsequent choices are in part already made. This is the meaning of St. Thomas's demand that man order himself to his proper end upon reaching the use of reason (*Summa Theologiae* 1a2ae, 89.6).

Polarity. By opposing external and internal temptations, moralists do not mean that external temptations have no effect on the subject, whereas internal temptations do. The exterior temptation is one of which man is merely aware but by which he is not sensibly and effectively drawn. More accurately, temptation is characterized by an interior-exterior polarity: a given enticement is more or less interior or exterior, depending on the degree to which it engages the subject.

Temptations are also termed grave or light—grave when the subject is strongly inclined to choose a serious evil, and light if the evil is slight, or if it exerts little attraction. But many temptations are neither grave nor light. Experience of temptation is better expressed by a polarity of gravity-lightness, extending from grave through less grave, more or less light, to light enticements. This is important for the formulation of moral and ascetical directions for times of temptation.

Resistance. To resist temptation is a moral imperative, since temptation is a threat to the union of love with God. Moral theologians discuss the quality of resistance to be set up. In general, one must do what is required to keep from capitulating. This involves at least negative resistance, i.e., withholding consent though doing nothing more. But that such minimal effort does not suffice is clear from experience and from the Church's condemnation of the contrary teaching of QUIETISM (H. Denzinger, *Enchiridion symolorum,* ed. A. Schönmetzer 2217, 2237). Positive resistance, the use of some means, such as prayer or disapproval, is always advisable. Whether it is always a duty is disputed. It is a duty, generally speaking, when temptation is grave. Whether positive resistance need also be direct, that is by an act contrary to the temptation, e.g., humility when tempted to pride, cannot be generically stated. Sometimes, in fact, indirect means are to be preferred, e.g., diverting attention when tempted against faith or chastity.

Strategy. As an inducement moving the subject to egoism, temptation is best prevented by outgoing love. "Temptations are to be met by their contraries," says an old ascetic rule. This is true on three levels. At the deepest level, more intense commitment to the union of love (or recommitment if one has forsaken it) makes one basically stronger against evil. This includes growth in supernatural charity and sanctifying grace, or their recovery when lost. At the level of habitual response, the more vigorous the various virtues, concrete manifestations of love, and the more complete the freedom from vices and egoism, the more armed one is against evil. At the level of acts, to interpose an act of love is effectively to disarm temptation; such an act would be, e.g., service of others when tempted to prejudice.

Other generic defenses are prayer, by which actual grace is won, and the Sacraments, especially Penance with its sacramental graces, and the Eucharist, the Sacrament of love par excellence. Specific means are found in ascetic and pastoral-moral literature.

See Also: SIN, OCCASIONS OF; DEADLY SINS.

Bibliography: R. BROUILLARD, *Dictionnaire de théologie catholique,* ed. A. VACANT, 15 v. (Paris 1903–50; Tables générales 1951–) 15.1:116–127. A. KÖBERLE, *Die Religion in Geschichte und Gegenwart,* 7 v. (3d ed. Tübingen 1957–65) 6:1385–86. THOMAS AQUINAS, *Summa Theologiae* 1a2ae, 77.4–5; 79.1; 80.1–4. B. COOKE, "The Hour of Temptation," *Way* 2 (1962) 177–187. E. F. REGATILLO and M. ZALBA, *Theologiae moralis summa,* 3 v. (Biblioteca de Autores cristianos; Madrid 1952–54) 1:682–701. C. BAUMGARTNER, *Dictionnaire de spiritualité ascétique et mystique. Doctrine et histoire,* ed., M. VILLER et al. (Paris 1932) 2.1:1343–73. *Satan,* ed. BRUNO DE JÉSUS-MARIE, tr. M. CARROLL et al. (New York 1952). FRANCIS DE SALES, *Introduction to the Devout Life,* tr. M. DAY (Westminster, MD 1956) 206–218.

[R. H. SPRINGER]

TEMPTATION (IN THE BIBLE)

In the Bible the word temptation primarily denotes a trial in which man has a free choice of being faithful or unfaithful to God; only secondarily does it signify allurement or seduction to sin. After treating of the terminology and definition of temptation in the Bible, this article discusses the idea of temptation, first in the Old Testament, then in the New Testament.

Terminology. The Hebrew noun *massâ,* ordinarily translated as temptation, is derived from the verb *nāsâ,* meaning to try, prove, put to the test. The Hebrew verb *bāḥan,* originally meaning to assay (metals), is also used figuratively of God testing men. However, Hebrew does have several verbs with the specific meaning of seducing, or alluring into evil, such as *hit'â, hēsît* (from *sût*), and *niddaḥ* (nip'al of *ndḥ*). In classical Greek the verb πειράζω is used, first in the sense of "to attempt," and then in the meaning of "to try, to test," but not in the meaning of "to tempt" to evil; yet the latter connotation is common in the Greek of the Septuagint and the New Testament. The noun πειρασμός is an almost exclusively Biblical word, meaning not only trial or test, but also temptation (to evil).

Definition. Temptation in the Biblical sense is a situation in which one experiences a challenge to choose between fidelity and infidelity to one's obligations toward God. God "tempts," i.e., tests men's fidelity to Himself;

men by their fidelity or infidelity ''tempt,'' i.e., test Him to reward or punish them. Temptation presumes that God's word has been given and connotes the covenant relationship. Adherence to the covenant is fidelity (*ḥesed*), which entitles the faithful partner to a reward. God is never unfaithful to His own word. Man, however, by being seduced or deceived, trusts creatures, thereby testing God's patience. The evils that befall God's people appear as manifestations of His anger merited by infidelity.

Since the covenant, as an initiative of God's favor, became mutually effective only after being ratified (Ex 24.7–8; Jos 24.18; see also Mk 14.24; Mt 26.28; Lk 22.20), subsequent generations saw themselves obligated (tested) to fidelity in union with their forebears.

In the Old Testament. The concept of temptation is evident in the first pages of Genesis and recurs continually, although the word itself does not always occur. The account of the fall of man in Gn 2.4–3.24 describes the relationship of God and men as a mutual temptation or testing: God tests Adam and Eve's fidelity; Eve is deceived (Gn 3.13), thereby testing God's fidelity to His own threat (Gn 2.16–17), which He carries out (Gn 3.16–19). The propagation of the human race is described as coextensive with that of sin, which tempts or tests God's patience, resulting in the wiping out of humanity (except for NOAH and his family) by the flood (Gn 6.5–8.19). The patriarchal narratives (Gn 11.27–50.26) emphasize Abraham's justice, exemplified by belief in God's promise (Gn 15.6). The natural circumstance of advanced age rendered it unlikely that ABRAHAM and Sarah could beget children. Therefore God's promise of future posterity tested Abraham's faith. Abraham's belief, in return, obliged God to fulfill His promise, which He did. Abraham undergoes another temptation in being directed to sacrifice Isaac (Gn 22.2). His obedience merits a further promise (Gn 22.15–18).

In Early Israel. The Mosaic traditions of the EXODUS from Egypt and the desert journey of the Israelites constantly repeat the same theme, i.e., God's generosity while testing Israel's trust in His power to save, and Israel's incessant murmuring; the chosen people test God's patience, always demanding present necessities, instead of trusting God's providence. The ten plagues convinced Pharaoh of the power of Moses' God. The Israelites, however, test God's power to stall the pursuing Egyptians (Ex 14.10–12). The wondrous crossing of the Red Sea reduces them to silence, emphasizing their obligation to serve the God who has done this great sign (Ex 14.30–31). Immediately again, however, their murmuring and distrust lead God to provide water (Ex 15.24–25; 17.1–7), manna, and quails (Ex 16.1–5; Nm 11.1–9; 18.32). However, because Israel's murmurings test God's patience, catastrophes accompany these benefits. The incident of Ex 17.6–7 is so typical of the strained relations of God and His people during this period, that the names of the places at which these incidents occur (Massah, ''temptation,'' and Meribah, ''strife'') become bywords in later writings [Dt 33.8; Ps 94(95).8; 105(106).32].

The Sinai covenant (Ex 19.1–24.18, esp. 24.3–8) becomes the foundation of Israel's later obligations to God; Joshua renews it at Sichem after the invasion, making the covenant the foundation of Israelite life in the newly acquired land (Jos 24.1–28). The Deuteronomic history (Jos, Jgs, 1 and 2 Sam, 1 and 2 Kgs) stresses the constant tension existing between the covenant faith and the specious seductions of temporal security (Jgs 2.6–17). After describing the fall of the Northern Kingdom, the author explains the reason (2 Kgs 17.6–18): God's generosity has met with only ingratitude and infidelity; failing the test of faith in their purely spiritual God, the people of Israel have placed faith in the material idols of the Canaanites and in the seductive promises of foreign alliances, tempting God's patience to the breaking point. Exile results. The Southern Kingdom's history is radically the same (2 Kgs 17.19; 21.9).

In the Prophets. The pre-exilic prophets constantly accuse their contemporaries of infidelity to the covenant; Israel's calamities are punishments from God. In symbolic language they describe the testing and the infidelity (Jer 2.2; Is 5.2–7; Ez 16). They specify the sins which tempt God: idolatry (Jer 2.5; Hos 2.10–15; Am 2.4; Mi 1.7); wronging of the poor and weak (Am 3.9–10; Mi 2.1–2); reliance upon foreign alliances (Is 36.14–18; Jer 1.14–19); and infidelity of the leaders (Jer 5.13;30–31; Ez 13.10). The postexilic prophets also see infidelity as a testing of God's patience by both Israel (Hg 1.6–11; Mal ch. 2) and the gentiles (Ob 3; 10–14; Jl 14.1–8).

In the Psalms. Besides echoing many ideas of the Pentateuchal and prophetic traditions, the Psalms contain much individual piety. The psalmist often calls upon God to test or prove him [Ps 16(17).3; 25(26).2; 138(139).23]. The Hebrew verb in such passages is less frequently *nāsâ*, and more often *bāḥan* [Ps 7.10: 80(81).8]. The test here is radically the same, i.e., trust in the saving power of God over that of creatures [Ps 117(118).9; 145(146).3].

The sapiential writings equate doing the works of the Law with the practice of wisdom (Prv 10–22; Sir 1.23–24). The faithful must expect temptation (Sir 2.1–6; Wis 3.5–9); the seduced reject wisdom (Prv 10.17; 12.26; 28.10), fail the test, and merit doom (Prv 1.20–33). Job is the classic example of the man subjected to temptation. Here too God is ultimately the author of the temptation or trial; Satan works on Job only by God's permission (Jb

1.6–12; 2.1–7). Job, indignant at first (Jb 6.8–14), soon admits that it is man's lot to be tried by God (Jb 7.18–21). Hearing God's proclamation of His own divine transcendence (Jb 38–39; 40–41), Job submits (Jb 42.1–6), disclaiming any right to test God's dominion over creatures.

In the New Testament. According to New Testament concepts it is principally God alone who submits men to the supreme test, calling them to have faith in the saving power of Jesus' death and Resurrection (Mk 16.16; Lk 10.13–16). The Church is the society of those who respond, acceding to the test of faith. The Christian's life, however, is a constant struggle; he is beset by temptations to sin (Mt 18.6; Lk 17.1); furthermore, Satan constantly seeks to seduce him to reject Christ and continue in sin (Lk 22.3; Acts 5.3; 2 Cor 2.11).

In the Synoptic Gospels God unfolds His plan through Zachary, then through Joseph and Mary. All these are tested for their faith in God's power (Lk 1.20; 35–39; Mt 1.19). The Scribes and Pharisees often ''tempt,'' i.e., test, Jesus, seeking in His speech some infidelity to the Mosaic traditions (Mk 8.11; Lk 11.16). Jesus warns His followers against temptation, whereby they would follow creatures instead of God (Mt 6.13).

In the Pauline Epistles men are tempted by Satan to fail against Christian life (1 Cor 7.5; Gal 6.1). This tension is basic to spiritual growth (Rom 5.3; 2 Cor 6.4–10); temptations against Christian virtue come from within by the sinful desires of human nature (epitomized by σάρξ, the FLESH) and from without, by persons who strive to choke the Christian spirit from those who profess it. Christians, therefore, suffer in hope, enduring trials (θλίψεις) in fellowship with the sufferings and death of Jesus (1 Thes 3.7; Phil 3.10). In this struggle God gives grace sufficient to overcome sin (1 Cor 10.13; Gal 5.13–17). At the Last Judgment the Father will reward with eternal beatitude those who have been proved (δόκιμοι, 2 Cor 11.18; 2 Tm 2.15).

This state of temptation or trial, as characteristic of Christian life, is part of the message of St. John's Revelation. It symbolically portrays the state of the entire Church as subject to the insidious enmity of Satan (Rv 12.1–5; 20.7–10), who eventually will be vanquished. God will perform judgment (Rv 20.11–15), damning the unfaithful and bringing to His presence (Rv 22.3–5) those who by faith have withstood the temptation (3.10; see also 1 Jn 2.18–19; 2 Jn 8). The doctrine of the Catholic Epistles is similar (Jas 1.2–4, 13–18; 1 Pt 1.6–7; 4.1–6; 12).

Conclusion. Man constantly seeks salvation from earthly misery. Given God's supernatural revelation of Himself, first in the Old Covenant, later in Jesus, man must choose between creatures and God, placing hope in one or the other. Jesus as the suffering and resurrected Savior presents the supreme test; absolute faith in Him, exemplified by patient acceptance of trials and tribulations, overcomes temptation to sin, and makes the Christian live in confident hope of eternal union with God after bodily death.

See Also: TEMPTATIONS OF JESUS.

Bibliography: A. SOMMER, *Der Begriff der Versuchung im A.T. und Judentum* (Breslau 1935). J. H. KORN, Πειρασμός: *Die Versuchung des Gläubigen in der griechischen Bibel* in *Beiträge zu Wissenschaft vom Alen (und Neuen) Testament* (Leipzig–Stuttgart 1908–38) 4.20, 1937. A. HUMBERT, ''Essai d'une théologie du scandale dans les Synoptiques,'' *Biblica* 35 (1954) 1–28. *Encyclopedic Dictionary of the Bible,* tr. and adap. by L. HARTMAN (New York 1963), from A. VAN DEN BORN, *Bijbels Woordenboek* 2401–15.

[T. E. CRANE]

TEMPTATIONS OF JESUS

Immediately after the account of the BAPTISM OF THE LORD, the three Synoptic Gospels narrate the temptations of Jesus by the devil (Mt 4.1–11; Mk 1.12–13; Lk 4.1–13). These temptations are connected with the proclamation of the divine sonship and messianic dignity of Jesus (Mt 3.17). From the setting given this event, the Evangelists imply that the time is at the very beginning of our Lord's public life. The place, called ''the desert,'' is commonly understood to be the barren highland of Judea to the west of the Dead Sea and the lower Jordan. Tradition has identified the actual location with Jebel Qaranṭal, ''the Mountain of Forty Days,'' three miles northwest of Jericho.

Allusions to the Old Testament. The Evangelists see a link between the coming down of the Spirit during the baptism of Jesus and the impulse of the same Spirit, driving Christ into the desert. As at creation, the spirit of God brooded over the chaotic mass to bring forth order and life and light, so now the Holy Spirit impelled the Life and the Light of men to begin His work of bringing order out of the spiritual chaos of sin. The devil tempted the first Adam, to conquer him; now he is to tempt the second Adam and be conquered by Him. Another link is to be seen in the voice of God proclaiming Jesus to be His beloved Son, and the voice of the devil insinuating a doubt concerning the dignity of Jesus: ''if thou art the Son of God.''

Matthew and Luke point out that Jesus fasted for 40 days in the desert. The length of time recalls the 40 years of the Israelites in the desert (cf. Nm 14.26–35), where they were put to the test and failed [cf. Ps 94(95), 8–11]. As Moses fasted for 40 days on Mount Sinai to inaugu-

"Satan Tries to Tempt Christ in the Forest," c. Mid 17th Century. (©Historical Picture Archives/CORBIS)

rate the Old Covenant (Ex 34.28), so Christ, the new Moses, began His mission of establishing the New Covenant by His fast of 40 days.

Nature of the Temptations. Mark does not give any details on the temptations, but implies that they were continuous. Matthew and Luke recorded three individual attempts by the devil to turn Christ away from the will of His Father and from the accomplishment of His messianic mission. Whether the devil appeared externally cannot be determined; the Evangelists in narrating the temptations are concerned with their nature, not with the accidental features that might have accompanied them. So too, no conclusion can be drawn regarding the movements to Jerusalem or to a high mountain. This may simply be the literary device used by the Evangelists to describe the temptations. The same may be true of the temptations themselves. Biblical FORM CRITICISM of this event has led some scholars to see a midrashic style here (*see* MIDRASH). In view of this, Matthew and Luke would be paralleling the temptations of the old Israel with those of the new Israel, namely, Christ (cf. Mt 4.1–4 with Dt 8.3; Mt 4.5–7 with Dt 1.41–46; 6.16; Mt 4.8–10 with Dt 5.9; 6.13; 9.7–21).

In the recording of the three temptations, Matthew and Luke agree in all three, but the order of the second and third is changed. Luke, whose interest in Christ moving toward Jerusalem is manifest in his Gospel, puts in the last place the temptation in which the devil takes our Lord to the pinnacle of the temple. In the first temptation the devil seems to take his cue from the words of God concerning the sonship of Christ. If Christ is the Son of God, He should have the power to satisfy His hunger, as God had satisfied the hunger of the Israelites, God's sons in the Old Testament (Ex 4.22–23; Os 11.1). The answer (citing Dt 8.3) points out that God's sons are to live, not by bread, but by God's will. The next temptation (second in Matthew, third in Luke) is based on use of Scripture [Ps 90(91).11–12]: since God always protects the just man, He will certainly protect His Son, if He were to cast Himself from the pinnacle of the temple. The means to manifest the divine protection involved presumption, as our Lord points out (citing Dt 6.16). The last one (third in Matthew, second in Luke) is blunt and to the point. The devil assumes the role of God; all the kingdoms of the world are his to give at his price, devil worship. Christ's answer is preemptory and final: Begone, Satan! God alone is to be worshipped (Dt 6.13). The essence of Christ's temptations consisted in the devil's attempt to allure Him into accepting the popular but false idea of the Messiah as an earthly king who would bring world dominion to Israel.

Christ's victory was complete; yet as Luke remarks, the devil ''departed from him for a while.'' He would return, especially at the hour of darkness (Lk 22.53). Matthew and Mark note the presence of angels ministering to Him, a sign of His dignity as well as His victory.

Bibliography: J. M. VOSTÉ, *De baptismo, tentatione, et transfiguratione Jesu* (Rome 1934). H. J. VOGELS, ''Die Versuchungen Jesu,'' *Biblische Zeitschrift* 17 (1926) 238–255. A. KADIČ, ''Monumentum messianicum tentationum Christi,'' *Verbum Domini* 18 (1938) 93–96, 126–128, 151–160. P. DONCOEUR, ''La Tentation de Jésus au désert,'' *Études* 239 (Paris 1934) 5–17. H. P. HOUGHTON, ''On the Temptations of Christ and Zarathushtra,'' *Anglican Theological Review* 26 (1944) 166–175.

[G. H. GUYOT]

TEMPTING GOD

The attempt to put to the test or make trial of one or more of God's attributes, such as His knowledge, will, power, or wisdom. This testing of God can be made by word, deed, or omission. One can, for example, ask God to perform a miracle when, judging by the ordinary standards of prudence, it is not called for. It was to induce Christ to tempt God in this way that the devil suggested to Him that He cast Himself down from the pinnacle of the Temple in the expectation that God would preserve Him from harm (Mt 4.6). Similarly, it is tempting God for anyone to expect miraculous protection while neglecting the immediate and obvious ways of protecting oneself that divine providence has already provided. The expectation or hope, however, must be inordinate to amount to a tempting of God, for to ask of Him something within the ordinary course of divine providence or humbly to petition Him to grant even an extraordinary favor is not to tempt God but to honor Him by demonstrating trust in His omnipotence and mercy. The same can be said of the act of one who, moved by genuine divine inspiration, requests God to do something out of the ordinary but needed for a good purpose, as when, for example, certain saints asked God to perform miracles to help them in their apostolic work. Moreover, to be a tempting of God, a divine attribute must be put to the test, i.e., one must ask or expect God to do something. It is not tempting God to act imprudently or rashly with no expectation of God's intervention.

Theologians distinguish two kinds or degrees of tempting God. It is formal when one says or does something with the express or explicit intention of putting God on trial. In this case it makes no difference whether the testing proceeds from incredulity, as when one positively doubts the existence of a divine attribute, or whether it arises from presumption, as when one who firmly believes in the power of God exposes himself to danger of death to see whether God wants to save him. On the other hand, the tempting is virtual (implicit, interpretative) when one does not have the express intention of testing God but acts in such a way that a miracle or other extraordinary effect seems to be expected from Him.

Tempting God is condemned in the Scriptures (see Dt 6.16; Ps 77.18, 19.56; Mt 4.7). The formal or explicit tempting of God is a mortal sin, because it is an insult to God to question His attributes and to challenge Him to manifest them. It is a sin principally against the virtue of religion, which demands that due reverence and worship be given to God. It may also involve a sin against faith, e.g., when God is put to the test because some doctrine of faith is doubted. The virtual or implicit tempting of God may be a venial sin if God is recklessly tempted only in a slight matter or if there is not enough advertence to the intrinsic seriousness of the action.

Bibliography: THOMAS AQUINAS, *Summa Theologiae* 2a2ae, 97. R. BROUILLARD, *Dictionnaire de théologie catholique,* ed. A. VACANT, 15 v. (Paris 1903–50; Tables générales 1951–) 15.1:116–127. P. PALAZZINI, *Dictionary of Moral Theology,* 1211–12. D. M. PRÜMMER, *Manuale theologiae moralis* (Freiburg-Barcelona 1955) 2:526–528. H. DAVIS, *Moral and Pastoral Theology* (New York 1958) 2:31–32. L. G. FANFANI, *Manuale theorico-practicum theologiae moralis* 3 v. (Rome 1950–51) 3:110–112.

[P. CURRAN]

TEN THOUSAND MARTYRS, LEGEND OF

The Roman MARTYROLOGY commemorates two groups of 10,000 martyrs. The first is based upon the legendary account of 10,000 soldiers supposedly crucified on Mt. Ararat with their commander Acacius; they are commemorated on June 22. This legend is based on a document supposedly translated from a Greek source by the 9th–century Anastasius Bibliothecarius, although the martyrs are first mentioned as troops of the Emperor Hadrian in the 14th century by Bp. Peter of Equilio (d.

1371). According to the legend, these soldiers, while engaged in battle with rebels in the Euphrates region, were miraculously converted to Christ by the voice of an angel, and then won an outstanding victory for the emperor. But when they refused to sacrifice to the gods, they were crucified (*Acta Sanctorum* June 5:151). The historical improbabilities and inaccuracies of the tale indicate that it is apochryphal. Nevertheless, the martyrs were venerated in Denmark, Sweden, Poland, France, Spain, and Portugal. Churches in Vienne, Lisbon, and Coimbra, among others, claimed their relics.

The second group is commemorated on March 18 at Nicomedia and is probably the result of a great exaggeration of an authentic account of martyred soldiers mentioned in Eusebius (*Hist. Eccl. 8*) and Lactantius (*De Mortibus Persecut*).

Bibliography: F. MERSHMAN, *The Catholic Encyclopedia* (New York 1907–14; Suppl. 1922) 9:746. J. P. KIRSCH, *Lexikon für Theologie und Kirche* ed. M. BUCHBERGER 10:1049–50. F. L. CROSS, *The Oxford Dictionary of the Christian Church* (Oxford 1957) 1330–31.

[E. DAY]

''Martyrdom of the Ten Thousand,'' 1508 Renaissance style painting by Albrecht Dürer. (Francis G. Mayer/CORBIS)

TENCIN, PIERRE GUÉRIN DE

French statesman, cardinal, and anti-Jansenist; b. Grenoble, Aug. 22, 1680; d. Lyons, March 2, 1758. He was the son of the president of the Grenoble parliament, and brother of Claudina, the influential mistress of a famed salon. His early education under the Oratorians in Grenoble culminated in a doctorate from the Sorbonne. His career owed much to the speculator, John Law, to his sister, and to Cardinal Andre FLEURY. He became abbé of Vézelay in 1702, and archdeacon and vicar-general of Sens the next year. As Cardinal Armand Rohan's conclavist in 1721, he may have interceded with INNOCENT XIII to obtain the cardinalate for Abbé Guillaume DUBOIS. He served France as ambassador to the Holy See from 1721 to 1724 and from 1739 to 1742. Consecrated archbishop of Embrun, June 26, 1724, he convoked the Provincial Synod in 1727 that deposed his aged suffragan, Bishop Soanen of Senez, an appellant against *UNIGENITUS*. The deposition seriously weakened the Jansenists with whom Tencin engaged in a bitter pamphlet debate. As a reward Tencin received the cardinal's hat in 1739. He succeeded to the See of Lyons in 1740, and was appointed minister of state two years later. He remained on the Council until 1751, when he retired to his diocese.

Bibliography: J. CARREYRE, *Dictionnaire de théologie catholique,* ed. A. VACANT, 15 v. (Paris 1903–50; Tables générales 1951–) 15.1:115–116, is the best summary and locates Tencin's pastoral and diplomatic writings. For acts of synod of Embrun see: (Graz 1960–) 37:693–888. M. BOUTRY, *Une Créature du cardinal Dubois: Intrigues et missions du cardinal de Tencin* (Paris 1902).

[V. HEALY]

TENEBRAE

Latin for ''darkness.'' Historically, the traditional name given to the combined Offices of Matins and Lauds on the mornings of Holy Thursday, Good Friday and Holy Saturday. Historically, the service was thus designated because during the Middle Ages it was celebrated in complete darkness. Ancient characteristics of the Office may be seen in Tenebrae. There were no hymns, and the old system of readings was followed in the use of the Old and New Testaments (Epistles, not Gospels) and commentaries of the Fathers. According to the medieval practice, at the end of each psalm, one of the 15 candles was extinguished on the triangular candlestick placed before the altar. At the conclusion of Psalm 146, only one candle, at the top of the triangle, remained lighted. When *Benedictus* was sung, the six altar candles were extinguished one by one after every second verse; and when the antiphon *Traditor autem* was repeated after the canticle, the one lighted candle was taken from the triangle and hidden behind the altar, where it remained until the end of the service. Medieval liturgists seem to have introduced this custom, and thus their own allegorical interpretation probably accounts for the practice. The gradual extinguishing of all but the last candle was meant to point to the Apostles' desertion of Christ, and the last candle was supposed to depict Christ's burial (in its disappearance behind the altar) and resurrection (in its reappearance). The clatter at the end of Tenebrae originally had no significance; it was simply the din occasioned by the closing of the chant books at the end of every hour of Office when the abbot or superior gave the signal to leave. This came to be interpreted in Holy Week as representing the shaking of the earth at Christ's death.

The longest and most important chants were the responsories. In the first nocturn of Holy Thursday, it was the custom to follow each lesson (from the Lamentations of Jeremiah) with a responsory, but *Gloria Patri* was never sung. The first two responsories took the simple form Response-Versicle-Partial response; and the third, Response-Versicle-Partial response-Response, where the entire first section was repeated after the usual partial repeat. For the first nocturn the Lamentations of Jeremiah were read, while the lessons of the second and third nocturns were taken from St. Augustine and St. Paul, respectively. During the Middle Ages various chants were used for the Lamentations, at least one of them bearing strong resemblance to the cantillation of Yemenite Jews (*see* MUSIC, HEBREW). In more recent times the chant most generally drawn upon stems from the normal tone for the lessons, its main characteristics being a recitation tone (*tenor*) of *a,* and brief formulas for *flex, metrum* and full stop. A short melodic phrase is repeated for the Hebrew letter that begins each verse. On all 3 days the psalms are sung without *Gloria Patri,* and the antiphons are doubled. A significant feature of Lauds is the gradual extension of *Christus factus est,* with additions on Good Friday and Holy Saturday.

The most complete polyphonic setting of the Tenebrae text is that of VICTORIA, dedicated to the Holy Trinity (1585), and performed in the Sistine Chapel during Holy Week for more than 300 years. Victoria set the nine Lamentations for the first nocturn (but not its responsories), the remaining 18 responsories and other parts of the Holy Week liturgy. A set of 27 responsories by Ingegneri was formerly attributed to PALESTRINA and there are excellent settings also by CROCE and GESUALDO.

Bibliography: G. REESE, *Music in the Renaissance,* (rev. ed. New York 1959). R. M. STEVENSON, *Spanish Cathedral Music in the Golden Age* (Berkeley 1961).

[D. STEVENS/EDS.]

TENNESSEE, CATHOLIC CHURCH IN

A south central state bordered by Kentucky, Virginia, North Carolina, Georgia, Oklahoma, Mississippi, Arkansas and Missouri. Tennessee is regionally divided into eastern, western and central areas, with Nashville as its capital and Memphis as its largest city. The state comprises three dioceses: Nashville, Memphis and Knoxville, all suffragans of the Metropolitan See of Louisville, KY. Catholics comprise approximately 4% of the total state population.

History. Catholics came to Tennessee not too long after Europeans began to settle in North America, but they were few, and they left no enduring impressions. *The Final Report of the United States De Soto Commission,* prepared in behalf of the U.S. Government in 1939, concluded that Spaniard Hernando De Soto and his party entered what became Tennessee on June 1, 1540, during their exploration of much of the Southeast. Although the 1540 route cannot be determined with any certainty, the *Final Report* situates the Spanish in the area that was later to be Polk, Bradley, Hamilton, and Marion counties, the extreme southeastern corner of present-day Tennessee. Later, the Spanish moved into what is now Alabama before again entering Tennessee in its far southwestern corner. In this corner, near the site of present-day Memphis, they discovered what they called *El Rio del Santo Espiritu,* the "River of the Holy Spirit," now known as the Mississippi River. Accompanying De Soto were twelve priests. Presumably one of these priests celebrated Mass for the first time on Tennessee soil when the band was in southeastern Tennessee. They founded no missions, coming and going without leaving a trace in the region.

Over a century and a third passed before Catholics again were recorded as being in the Tennessee area. In 1673, the French expedition including Louis Joliet and the Jesuit, Père Jacques MARQUETTE, travelled southward on the river that they dedicated to the Immaculate Conception (the Mississippi). Marquette's journal recalls the group's pause at Chickasaw Bluffs, where Memphis later was located. He met natives of the area who told him that they had encountered other Europeans, and that these Europeans gave them what must have been rosaries and pictures of the saints. Once more, no missions or continuing Catholic presence was established.

Other French explorers, including priests, passed along the Mississippi River. The French founded Fort Prud'homme on the site of present-day Memphis in 1682. It later was called Fort Assumption, but it was not a missionary center. French fur traders from time to time were in Middle Tennessee at Salt Lick, a place on the Cumberland River where Nashville now stands. Generally, they too came and went, except Timothe De Monbreun, a

Catholic and one of the founders of the city. He built a permanent home where Nashville is today, and he lived there for many years. His son, William, was the first Caucasian born in what now is Middle Tennessee.

Nashville, at first ''Nashborough,'' was formed as a community on Dec. 25, 1780, when two groups, one coming overland, the other on the Cumberland River, arrived from North Carolina and Virginia. At least one Catholic, Hugh Rogan, who had fled British domination of Ireland, was in these expeditions. Rogan eventually settled in Sumner County, where he and his wife remained faithful Catholics.

The American Revolution eventually led to statehood for Tennessee on June 1, 1796, following a long and and bloody struggle. When Tennessee became the 16th state, it elected John Sevier as its first governor. Sevier was a great-grand-nephew of St. Francis XAVIER, although the new governor himself was born in North America and descended from the Huguenot branch of the saint's family. In 1799, Sevier offered Father Stephen Badin, whom he had met, enough land to settle 100 Catholic families, but Bishop John CARROLL declined the offer.

The first report of Catholics in any number in Tennessee came in a letter, dated 1800, from Father Badin to Archbishop John Carroll. It said that 100 Catholic families were in Hawkins County, in the northeastern corner of the state. The letter also noted that in the household of U.S. Senator William Blount, whose home still stands as a historical shrine in downtown Knoxville, there lived James Dardis, a Catholic Frenchman. While these Catholics had been found, and possibly there were others since Irish names appear in old records here and there, the Catholic population of Tennessee was tiny. But, it gradually grew, served by visiting priests. Father Badin was again in Knoxville in 1808 and preached four times in the State House. He returned in 1810 and spoke in the Court House about the Catholic belief in the Resurrection of Jesus.

The Catholic population of Nashville swelled when a sizeable group of Irish laborers came to the city to build a bridge across the Cumberland River. Their exact number is unknown, but they were large enough in size and determination to appeal to Bishop Benedict Joseph Flaget, S.S., in Bardstown, KY for a priest to serve them. The priest who came in 1820 was Father Robert Abell. He eventually built the first Catholic church in Tennessee, named in honor of the Holy Rosary, and situated about 100 yards from the site where the state capitol now stands, on land donated by the Grand Master of Nashville's Masons. In 1821, Bishop Flaget visited Nashville. Timothe De Monbreun received him. He also was entertained by Felix Grundy, later a U.S. senator and attorney general, and by a Presbyterian minister. Other Catholics in Tennessee seldom saw a priest, however, and the Church had no presence outside Nashville.

Diocese	**Year Created**
Knoxville	1985
Memphis	1971
Nashville	1837

On July 28, 1837, in response to an appeal by the American bishops, Pope GREGORY XVI founded three new dioceses in the United States: Dubuque, IA; Natchez, MS; and Nashville. The new See of Nashville received jurisdiction over the entire State of Tennessee. At the same time, GREGORY XVI named Father Richard Pius Miles, the Dominican provincial-general in America, as the first bishop. Ordained a bishop in Bardstown, KY, on Sept. 16, 1838, Miles was installed in Father Abell's little church in Nashville on the following October 15. He faced a daunting challenge. The Nashville cathedral was the only Catholic church in Tennessee, and the bishop himself was the only priest.

During the next 22 years, Bishop Miles met the challenge and finally created a Catholic presence, which in some instances still exists. Soon after arriving in Nashville, he began a tour of the state, looking for Catholics. He estimated that only 300 Catholics were among the population, enumerated in the 1830 U.S. Census at 682,000. On one trip to Jonesborough, in Washington County, in upper East Tennessee, he met the Aiken family. A son of this family, John F. Aiken, later entered the Jesuits in Maryland and was ordained a priest in 1844. He was the first Tennessean to be ordained. The bishop's first concern was to secure priests. He recruited priests from elsewhere in the United States, but he relied heavily on priests of his own order. At one time, most priests in Tennessee were Dominicans. These Dominicans founded the first parish in Memphis, St. Peter's, in 1840. Among the parishes founded by Miles, active parishes continue to exist in Chapel Hill, Chattanooga, Clarksville, Gallatin, McEwen, Memphis and Nashville.

In 1843, the State General Assembly finally and permanently fixed the capital in Nashville. Seated on the Cumberland River, and already incorporated for 63 years, Nashville was also the largest city in Tennessee. Wishing to make a mark in the city, as well as to serve its increasing numbers of Catholics, Bishop Miles dedicated a new cathedral on Oct. 31, 1844 in honor of the Seven Dolors of the Blessed Virgin Mary. It came to be known simply as "St. Mary's." Historians dispute as to who drew the plans, although most think it was Adolphus Heiman, a Prussian immigrant. In any case, the new cathedral, imposing in size for its time, and chaste and simple in its Grecian lines, instantly won the city's attention and admiration.

The Sisters of Charity of Nazareth, KY arrived in Nashville in 1841 and opened a school for girls, a hospital and an orphanage. These Sisters soon formed themselves as a new, independent congregation, the Sisters of Charity of Nashville. Into their number in 1852 came Julia Voorvoart, from a Nashville family, the first woman in Tennessee to profess vows as a nun. In 1851, Dominican Sisters from St. Catherine, KY, a community Miles had helped to found, along with other Dominican Sisters from St.Mary's Convent, Somerset, OH, arrived in Memphis. At the beginning of the new millennium, the Kentucky Dominican presence continues in Memphis.

Bishop Miles founded St. Joseph's Seminary and established a congregation of male religious, the Brothers of St. Patrick, though neither endeavor survived. When Miles first came to Tennessee, Catholics were more often a curiosity than the object of derision. Andrew Jackson even attended Mass in Nashville. Things changed somewhat with the development of the KNOW-NOTHING movement. When the Know-Nothings mounted a campaign for governor in 1854, the Catholics found for themselves a champion they had not expected, Andrew Johnson, former mayor of Greeneville and a congressman. In blistering language, he attacked the Know-Nothings' bigotry against Catholics. Johnson won. He went on to become a U.S. senator, military governor of Tennessee, vice president, president and finally a U.S. senator, again. He sent his children to Catholic schools, his daughter and daughter-in-law became Catholics, and he attended Mass regularly, giving generously to build the first Catholic church in Greeneville.

In 1850, Nashville was the scene of a convention of delegates from the 15 slave-holding states to discuss slavery. Tempers already were high. No action was taken, but clouds were gathering. Like most dioceses where slavery was considerable, the Diocese of Nashville paid virtually no attention to African Americans. However, old records show that slaves at times were baptized. Still, it must be assumed that Bishop Miles had no strong feelings against slavery. In fact, when the Civil War came at last, the diocese itself owned four slaves. Bishop Miles did not live to see the war. His health began to break as the 1850s ended. He asked the Holy See for a coadjutor, and on March 15, 1859, Pope PIUS IX named another Dominican, Father James Whelan, a native of Ireland, as the coadjutor bishop of Nashville. Whelan succeeded Miles when the elder bishop died on Feb. 20, 1860.

At about the same time, the Sisters of Charity of Nashville moved to Leavenworth, KS to form a new community. But, their absence was filled by more Dominican sisters from Ohio, who opened St. Cecilia Academy in Nashville. It was the only school the Federal authorities allowed to remain open during the wartime occupation of Nashville. Though long since in other buildings, the academy, the parent of Aquinas College, still exists, and the sisters formed their own congregation, the Dominican Sisters of St. Cecilia.

As events climaxed in the spring of 1861, Tennessee at first voted to remain in the Union. Later, Abraham Lincoln's call for troops to suppress the rebellion begun at Fort Sumter in the Charleston harbor turned the tables. Before formally receiving a request, the Confederate Congress admitted Tennessee to the Confederacy. In June 1861, the people voted overwhelmingly to secede, though the vote varied from region to region. In East Tennessee, secession failed, and some there even tried to form a new state, as occurred in the case of West Virginia when it was split from Virginia. But in Middle and West Tennessee, the vote to secede was heavy. The war was hard on Tennessee. More battles were fought on its soil than in any other state except Virginia. Thousands died. Many fought for the Union, though the majority fought for the Confederacy.

Among the dead was Father Emmeran Bliemel, a Confederate, once pastor of Assumption Church in Nashville, the only chaplain on either side to be killed in action. St. Mary's Cathedral was taken by the U.S. Army and used as a hospital and then a stable. Sts. Peter and Paul's Church in Chattanooga also was seized for military use. For reasons still unknown, Bishop Whelan resigned in 1863, before the war ended. Whether true or not, he had been thought to be a Union sympathizer, and in Nashville, where secession had carried seven to one, this made him very unpopular. When the war ended, men loyal to the Union, generally from East Tennessee, quickly took control of the state government. Under their direction, and with dispatch, they moved Tennessee back into the Union. Reconstruction, therefore, did not have all the earmarks it was to acquire elsewhere in the South, but it was still a difficult period.

Father Patrick Augustine FEEHAN, a native of Ireland who was then a pastor in St. Louis, was named the third bishop of Nashville in 1865. Bishop Feehan soon faced a much more insidious problem than a depressed, postwar economy. It was physical disease. Cholera struck Chattanooga, Memphis and Nashville, but it was yellow fever in Chattanooga and especially Memphis that were particularly devastating. By this time, Memphis had a considerable Catholic population with several churches and schools. Thousands died in the epidemics. The city suffered a mighty blow. But, Catholic nuns, many of whom died in caring for the stricken, won a respect for the Church that endured. For generations, the City of Memphis allowed Catholic nuns to ride its streetcars and buses free of charge, as a gesture of appreciation.

The loss of nuns and priests to these diseases was great, but Bishop Feehan found replacements. The diocese grew, in numbers and in institutional presence. In 1871, the Christian Brothers opened a school for boys in Memphis, which eventually became Christian Brothers University. Four years later, the Sisters of the Good Shepherd established a refuge for troubled girls in Memphis. The Sisters of Mercy also came, and they became a major source of teachers and, later, nurses in Tennessee's Catholic schools and hospitals. Despite reconstruction and the epidemics, the Church made strides.

The see of Nashville again fell vacant when on Sept. 10, 1880, Pope LEO XIII named Bishop Feehan the First Archbishop of Chicago. His replacement, Joseph Rademacher, a priest from the Diocese of Fort Wayne, IN, was appointed on April 3, 1883. Bishop Rademacher was in Nashville only ten years, returning to Fort Wayne in 1893 as its bishop. Still, the number of Catholic people and institutions grew during his tenure. Succeeding Bishop Rademacher was Father Thomas S. Byrne, a seminary rector in the Archdiocese of Cincinnati. Named on July 15, 1893, Bishop Byrne was to leave a deep mark on Tennessee Catholicity.

Byrne was an innovator. He had a vision, and he could press his vision through to reality. He encouraged Mother (Saint) Katharine DREXEL in founding facilities for African Americans in Jackson, Memphis, and Nashville. He invited Little Sisters of the Poor to open a home for the elderly in Nashville. He asked the Daughters of Charity to establish a Catholic hospital in Nashville. He formed mission centers in Harriman, Winchester and Johnson City. He built parishes and schools across the state. The Franciscan Sisters of Lafayette, IN opened St. Joseph's Hospital in Memphis in 1899. He mingled with the great and influential, making friends for the Church. He stressed native vocations, and the response was considerable. Four of his priests became bishops, including the future Samuel Cardinal Stritch. He always regarded as the crown of his tenure the Cathedral of the Incarnation, completed in 1914. Of strict Romanesque basilica style, the cathedral is one of the city's largest and most imposing churches. When he died in 1923, negotiations were in progress with the Jesuits to build a college and with the Brothers of Mary to open a high school in Nashville. Neither project developed, but high hopes were typical of the Byrne era.

Alphonse J. Smith, a priest of Indianapolis, was appointed the next ordinary on Dec. 24, 1923, by Pope PIUS XI. Bishop Smith suffered from two disadvantages, his poor health, and the Great Depression. Nevertheless under his leadership the Church of Tennessee grew. In 1929, he opened Father Ryan High School for boys in Nashville. The school was named in honor of Father Abram Ryan, the unofficial poet laureate of the South during and after the Civil War. In 1931, the Sisters of Mercy founded St. Mary's Hospital in Knoxville, and the Poor Clares established a monastery in Memphis. After only a relatively short time in office, Bishop Smith died suddenly on Dec. 16, 1935.

His successor, William L. Adrian, a priest of Davenport, IA, was to serve the diocese an unprecedented 30 years (1936–1966). Bishop Adrian founded a weekly diocesan newspaper, the *Tennessee Register*, and organized lay groups. In the years following World War II, he led the largest Catholic building campaign in Tennessee history, opening 65 churches, five secondary schools and 33 elementary schools across the state. At his behest, Sisters of Charity of Nazareth opened a hospital in Chattanooga, and the Sisters of Notre Dame of Cleveland, OH, founded St. Mary's Hospital in Humboldt. Over 100 priests, almost all of them native Tennesseans, were ordained.

Changing Times. By the time Pope PAUL VI accepted Bishop Adrian's resignation in 1966, the full impact of the 1954 U.S. Supreme Court decision, Brown v. Topeka Board of Education, that ended school desegregation had reverberated throughout Tennessee. It fell to Bishop Joseph A. Durick to deal with these momentous, and at times violent changes. Auxiliary bishop of Mobile-Birmingham, AL, Durick was named Bishop Adrian's coadjutor on Dec. 5, 1963. Not only did he help to implement the decisions of the second VATICAN COUNCIL and forcefully ended racial separation throughout the diocese, but he made himself, and the Church, the most obvious moral voices in an area still only minimally Catholic. Durick was able to undertake this role in great measure because of the strong institutional presence of the Church in the Tennessee cities, and because he took full advantage of a new day in communications, ecumenism, mobility, and outlook in America.

The Catholic Church in Tennessee reached a milestone on Jan. 6, 1971, when the Diocese of Memphis formally came into being. A new diocese for West Tennessee had been discussed for many years. Created by Pope Paul VI, the new diocese had a Virginia priest, Msgr. Carroll T. Dozier, as its first bishop. Bishop Dozier, who served until his retirement in 1978, in general continued the Durick policies, but in his own special style. He spoke against the Vietnam War and reiterated opposition to racism. As with Durick, admirers saw in him a prophet; others were less delighted.

Following the retirement of Bishop Dozier, Auxiliary Bishop (later Cardinal) J. Francis Stafford of Baltimore was appointed to Memphis by the Holy See. Although in Memphis for only a short time (1982–1986) before going to Denver as its archbishop, Stafford himself kept the spotlight on the Church's position on racism. JOHN PAUL II named Benedictine Daniel M. Buechlein, the rector of St. Meinrad Archabbey's seminary in Indiana to succeed Stafford in 1986. Like Stafford, Buechlein too did not stay long in Memphis, moving to Indianapolis as archbishop in 1992. Terry J. Stieb, S.V.D., an auxiliary bishop of St. Louis was appointed to Memphis in 1993.

In Nashville, Bishop Durick retired in March 1975, and Pope Paul VI appointed Msgr. James D. Niedergeses, a native of Lawrenceburg, TN, the ninth bishop of Nashville. Bishop Niedergeses attempted to steady the diocese after the turmoil of the preceding decade, and he built facilities to serve the growing Catholic population, especially in the small cities. This growth significantly contributed to Pope John Paul II's establishment on Sept. 8, 1988, of the new Diocese of Knoxville. A priest of the Diocese of Jefferson City, MO, and a native of County Clare, Ireland, Anthony J. O'Connell, was named its first bishop in 1988. Bishop O'Connell not only formed a diocesan structure, but his personality proved to be the adhesive holding together a vibrant Catholic community. When O'Connell was appointed bishop of Palm Beach in 1999, he was succeeded by Msgr. Joseph E. Kurtz of the Diocese of Allentown, and a native of Pennsylvania, as the second bishop of Knoxville.

In 1992, Pope John Paul II accepted the resignation of Bishop Niedergeses of Nashville, who had reached the retirement age, and Auxiliary Bishop Edward U. Kmiec of Trenton, and a native of New Jersey, became the tenth bishop of Nashville. Bishop Kmiec's achievements included the development of a long-range diocesan strategic plan, a development plan for the diocesan system, a reinstitution of the permanent diaconate and a program of nurturing vocations to the priesthood.

Post-World War II population growth in the state was significant and caused an increase in the Catholic population as well. Before 1980, 99% of the Catholics were white Americans. In the late 1970s, a significant number of Hispanics began to immigrate to Tennessee, and by the turn of the new century have constituted more than one-third of the state's total Catholic population. The Catholic demographic growth in Tennessee from 1970 to 2000 was greatest in the Nashville diocese, to a lesser degree in Knoxville, and mostly unchanged in Memphis. The number of Hispanic Catholics in the Nashville diocese alone in 2000 was reported as more than 50,000. African Americans comprise about 1% of the Catholic population. There is also a small but growing Vietnamese Catholic presence in the state.

Bibliography: V. F. O'DANIEL, *The Father of the Church in Tennessee, or the Life, Times and Character of the Right Reverend Richard Pius Miles, O.P.* (New York 1926). T. STRITCH, *The Catholic Church in Tennessee* (Nashville 1987). M. LOYOLA FOX, *A Return of Love* (Milwaukee 1966). R. MASSERANO, *The Nashville Dominicans* (Roslyn Heights, NY 1985). G. J. FLANIGEN, *Catholicity in Tennessee* (Nashville 1937). J. W. MCGRAW, *Between the Rivers: The Catholic Heritage of West Tennessee* (Memphis 1996). H. A. NORTON, *Religion in Tennessee: 1777–1945* (Knoxville 1981). M. D. GOHMAN, *Political Nativism in Tennessee* (Washington, DC 1938). A. B. MCGILL, *The Sisters of Charity of Nazareth, Kentucky* (New York 1917). D. A. QUINN, *Heroes and Heroines of Memphis* (Providence 1887). J. GILMORE, *Come North!* (New York 1951). O. F. CAMPION, *A History of the Diocese of Nashville*, unpublished thesis, 1962, in collection of the Tennessee State Library and Archives (Nashville, TN).

[O. F. CAMPION]

TENORIO, GONZALO

Franciscan theologian and missionary; b. Jaén, Peru, 1602; d. Spain, 1682? Tenorio, son of a noble family, was a professor of law at the University of San Marcos before entering the Franciscans on July 18, 1626. During his years in the order he taught most of the time, with the exception of the period from 1642 to 1647, when he worked in the Indian missions of Cerro de la Sal. While there he did some exploration of the rivers in an attempt to find a water route to link the missions of Peru and Quito. He became provincial of the Franciscan province of Peru in 1650, and in 1657 he was appointed by the Crown to survey and tax the lands of southern Peru. He was the author of a number of theological treatises (*Comentario a las sentencias, De auxiliis, Quaestiones scholasticae,* etc.). His major work, 16 manuscript volumes, which might be titled *Biblia virginea,* never received royal permission for publication because it was Scotistic. In it he centered the Bible and the Church about Mary; thus the work is important for the history of Mariology. However, he extended his concepts far beyond that. He saw a special providence unfolding in history through a chosen people, through Spain to the Creoles of the New World. He envisioned a future in which the pope would take refuge in Peru and govern the world from there. Tenorio stressed the superiority of the Creole learning and spirituality over that of the Europeans and exemplified the Creole pride on a theological level at the time when they were beginning to demand political equality with the peninsulares.

Bibliography: J. L. PHELAN, *The Millennial Kingdom of the Franciscans in the New World* (Berkeley 1956). A. EGUILUZ, ''Father Gonzalo Tenorio, O.F.M. and His Providentialist Eschatological Theories on the Spanish Indies,'' *Americas* 16 (1959–60) 329–356.

[A. EGUILUZ]

TENT OF MEETING

The center of worship, sign of God's presence, place for receiving oracles, and palladium during the desert journey of the Israelites. In the earlier ELOHIST source the tent is called *'ōhel mô'ēd* (tent of meeting), whereas the Priestly Code (P) source (*see* PRIESTLY WRITERS, PENTATEUCHAL) prefers *miškān* (dwelling), though the former term is found here also. The Elohist account pictures it as located outside the camp, as an oracle tent to which God descends from time to time to ''meet'' Moses, in order to communicate with him (Ex 33.7–11; Nm 11.24–30; 12.1–10); no further description of it is given in this source. The priestly account presents it as a large tent (45 by 15 feet) formed by stretching successive layers of fine linen, red-dyed rams' skins, and *taḥaš* skins (possibly fine treated leather) over an elaborate wooden frame; the ground plan was similar to that of the Temple Solomon would later erect [*see* TEMPLES (IN THE BIBLE)], with a larger ''Holy Place'' and a smaller ''HOLY OF HOLIES.'' Like the Temple, it housed the ARK OF THE COVENANT, and other cult objects (altar of incense, table for the SHOWBREAD, and golden lampstand) later placed in the Temple are found in it. It was located in the center of the camp and, like the Temple, was enclosed within an outer court (Ex 26.1–27.19; 36.1–38.40; Nm 2.1–34). Since the priestly description of the tent is so closely conformed to many details of the later Temple (except for the prefabricated construction and the dimensions—just half of those of the Temple), earlier critics had suggested that the tent never existed except as an imaginative and idealized form of the Temple retrojected into the ambit of the desert by priestly imagination. Today, however, there is evidence that some elements of the description are ancient (frame of acacia wood, red leather covering, etc.); portable tents housing the tribal idols were known among ancient Semitic nomads and were even one of the most important motifs of their religions. Yet undoubtedly the description has been somewhat accommodated to the later Temple. F. Cross has suggested that the immediate source utilized by the priestly writers was a description of the tent erected by David for the ark (2 Sm 6.17), which could very well have preserved elements of the desert tent while also manifesting Canaanite influence.

Little is known of the tent after the Israelites reached the Plains of Moab, where the last certain reference to it is found (Nm 25.6). Later references to it are found (e.g., Jos 18.1; 1 Sm 2.22; 2 Chr 1.3), but these seem to be late conjectures, for the structure that housed the ark at SILO was called a temple (Heb. *hêkāl*) and was, therefore, a substantial building (1 Sm 1.7; 3.3).

The theological and spiritual import of the tent is great, for it was the external manifestation of God's abiding presence in the midst of His people. This concept is developed in Jewish speculation on the SHEKINAH and finds its climax in the INCARNATION.

Bibliography: *Encyclopedic Dictionary of the Bible,* translated and adapted by L. HARTMAN (New York, 1963) 2413–14. R. DE-VAUX, *Ancient Israel, Its Life and Institutions,* tr. J. MCHUGH (New York 1961) 294–297. F. M. CROSS, JR., ''The Priestly Tabernacle,'' *The Biblical Archeologist* 10 (New Haven 1947) 45–68; *The Biblical Archeologist Reader,* ed. G. E. WRIGHT and D. N. FREEDMAN (Chicago 1961) 201–228. J. MORGENSTERN, *The Ark, the Ephod, and the Tent of Meeting* (Cincinnati 1945).

[J. E. STEINMUELLER/EDS.]

TEPL, MONASTERY OF

Premonstratensian abbey in the Archdiocese of Prague, founded by Bl. HROZNATA in 1193 and settled from STRAHOV. It survived the Hussite wars and the rebellion of monks under the influence of the Reformation in 1525. Abbots John Kurz (1555–59), John Meyskönig (1559–85), and Andreas Ebersbach (1598–1629) fostered monastic discipline and theological studies to combat insurrection and Lutheranism. It suffered seriously in the Thirty Years' War and in 1659 was burned down. During the Counter Reformation, Tepl had the pastoral care of all German districts in western Bohemia (about 50 parishes) and conducted the German *gymnasium* in Plzeň. It used the proceeds from its famous spa, Mariánské Lázně (Marienbad), built in the 19th century, to pay for its hospitals. The present cloister was built by Abbot Raymond II Wilfert (1688–1724); and the library, holding 600 MSS and 500 incunabula, by Abbot Gilbert Helmer (1900–44). The abbey, which had always been predominantly German, continued after 1918 under the Czechoslovak Republic. In 1938 its lands were annexed to the German Reich. After World War II it was suppressed, the community moving to Speinshart in Bavaria (restored by Tepl in 1921). Herman Tyl, a monk of Nová Ríše and a prisoner in Dachau (1940–45), was prevented from organizing a Czech community in 1950 and sentenced to 12 years in prison by a Communist court in 1957. The abbey is now a state museum. The Romanesque hall church with Gothic additions, restored in 18th-century baroque, is one of the oldest in Bohemia.

Bibliography: B. GRASSL, *Geschichte und Beschreibung des Stiftes Tepl* (Pilsen 1910). N. BACKMUND, *Monasticon Praemon-*

stratense, 3 v. (Straubing 1949–56). P. MÖHLER, *Lexikon für Theologie und Kirche,* ed. J. HOFER and K. RAHNER, 10 v. (2d, new ed. Freiburg 1957–65) 9:1365–66.

[L. NEMEC]

TER DOEST, ABBEY OF

Former Cistercian abbey in the town of Lissewege, seven miles northeast of Bruges, Belgium, near the canal connecting Bruges to the sea (Latin, *Thosanum*). Founded as a priory of SAINT-RIQUIER in 1106, it became a CISTERCIAN monastery on Jan. 1, 1176, as a daughter of the Abbey of LES DUNES. Under its first abbot, Hacket, and along with Dunes, Ter Doest began expansion of both its wool industry and its land holdings, which extended even to the islands in the estuary of the Lys and Schelde Rivers (*c.* 1240). The abbey church and conventual buildings were erected in 1244, but by 1309 the acute economic crisis forced the monks to sell some of the property. The decline continued until in 1559 Ter Doest was joined to the newly created Diocese of Bruges. Pillaged in 1571 by the Calvinists of Westkapelle and Ramskapelle and burned by them in 1578, the monastery was suppressed in 1624 and reunited to Dunes. Ter Doest was confiscated and sold at the time of the French Revolution but was bought back by the monks of Dunes and given to the Diocese of Tournai (today Bruges).

Bibliography: L. H. COTTINEAU, *Répertoire topobibliographique des abbayes et prieurés,* 2 v. (Mâcon 1935–39) 2:3134. M. A. DIMIER, *Dictionnaire d'histoire et de géographie ecclésiastiques,* ed. A. BAUDRILLART (Paris 1912–) 14:1039–44.

[M. J. STALLINGS]

TERESA MARGARET OF THE SACRED HEART, ST.

Discalced Carmelite nun and mystic; baptized Anna Maria Redi; b. Arezzo, Italy, July 15, 1747; d. Florence, March 7, 1770. She came of a Tuscan family of the lesser nobility. Her father, Ignatius, early recognized signs of spiritual genius in his child and tried to encourage her, without destroying her originality or disturbing her normal development. It was from him that she learned the devotion to the Sacred Heart that was later to play a major role in her spiritual synthesis.

Anna Maria entered the Discalced Carmelite convent in Florence on Sept. 1, 1764, and took the name Teresa Margaret of the Sacred Heart because of her devotion to the Sacred Heart and to SS. TERESA OF AVILA and MARGARET MARY ALACOQUE.

In the community Sister Teresa Margaret served as sacristan and infirmarian. Few suspected the intense working of grace in her soul. Our knowledge of her spirituality depends on the sworn testimony of her director, Ildephonse of St. Aloysius, OCD. Drawn to the hidden life, she sought to imitate not only the external phases of the hidden life of Christ, but also its expression in His intellectual and volitional life, so far as this was possible. The divine response to her desire was an aridity so intense that she was hidden from herself and had no suspicion of her high degree of sanctity.

St. Teresa Margaret was important as a herald of the Sacred Heart devotion, not only in Carmel, but in Tuscany and Italy as well, where Jansenism attempted to bring the devotion into disrepute. In her we have an example of a spirituality centered upon the Sacred Heart. Through this she reached lofty heights of Trinitarian contemplation.

She died at the age of 22, and her body has remained incorrupt. A portrait was made of her as she lay in death. She was canonized by Pius XI on March 19, 1934.

Feast: March 11.

Bibliography: STANISLAO DI SANTA TERESA, *St. Theresa Margaret of the Sacred Heart of Jesus,* tr. J. F. NEWCOMB (New York 1934). J. BARDI, *St. Theresa Margaret Redi,* tr. M. REPTON (Boston 1939). G. PAPASOGLI, *Santa Teresa Margherita Redi* (Milan 1958). GABRIELE DI SANTA MARIA MADDALENA, *La spiritualità di S. Teresa Margherita Redi del Cuor di Gesù* (Florence 1950); *From the Sacred Heart to the Trinity,* tr. S. V. RAMGE (Milwaukee, Wisc. 1965). TERESA MARGARET, *God Is Love; St. Teresa Margaret: Her Life* (Milwaukee, Wisc. 1964). *Ephemerides Carmeliticae* 10 (1959), special issue devoted to Teresa Margherita del Cuor di Gesù.

[S. V. RAMGE]

TERESA OF AVILA, ST.

Carmelite reformer and mystic; b. Avila, Spain, March 28, 1515; d. Alba, Oct. 4, 1582. Her family origins have been traced to Toledo and Olmedo. Her father, Alonso de Cepeda, was a son of a Toledan merchant, Juan Sánchez de Toledo and Inés de Cepeda, originally from Tordesillas. Juan transferred his business to Avila, where he succeeded in having his children marry into families of the nobility. In 1505 Alonso married Catalina del Peso, who bore him two children and died in 1507. Two years later Alonso married the 15–year–old Beatriz de Ahumada of whom Teresa was born.

Early Life. In 1528, when Teresa was 15, her mother died, leaving behind ten children. Teresa was the ''most beloved of them all.'' She was of medium height, large rather than small, and generally well proportioned. In her youth she had the reputation of being quite beautiful, and she retained her fine appearance until her last years

(María de S. José, *Libro de recreaciones,* 8). Her personality was extroverted, her manner affectionately buoyant, and she had the ability to adapt herself easily to all kinds of persons and circumstances. She was skillful in the use of the pen, in needlework, and in household duties. Her courage and enthusiasm were readily kindled, an early example of which trait occurred when at the age of seven she left home with her brother Rodrigo with the intention of going to Moorish territory to be beheaded for Christ, but they were frustrated by their uncle, who met the children as they were leaving the city and brought them home (Ephrem de la Madre de Dios, *Tiempo y Vida de Sta. Teresa,* 142–143). At about 12 the fervor of her piety waned somewhat. She began to take an interest in the development of her natural attractions and in books of chivalry. Her affections were directed especially to her cousins, the Mejias, children of her aunt Doña Elvira, and she gave some thought to marriage. Her father was disturbed by these fancies and opposed them. While she was in this crisis, her mother died. Afflicted and lonely, Teresa appealed to the Blessed Virgin to be her mother. Seeing his daughter's need of prudent guidance, her father entrusted her to the Augustinian nuns at Santa María de Gracia in 1531.

Vocation. The influence of Doña María de Brinceño, who was in charge of the lay students at the convent school, helped Teresa to recover her piety. She began to wonder whether she had a vocation to be a nun. Toward the end of 1532 she returned home to regain her health and stayed with her sister, who lived in Castellanos. Reading the letters of St. Jerome led her to the decision to enter a convent, but her father refused to give his consent. Her brother and confidant, Rodrigo, had just set sail for the war on the Río de la Plata. She decided to run away from home and persuaded another brother to flee with her in order that both might receive the religious habit. On Nov. 2, 1535, she entered the Carmelite Monastery of the Incarnation at Avila, where she had a friend, Juana Suárez; and her father resigned himself to this development. The following year she received the habit and began wholeheartedly to give herself to prayer and penance. Shortly after her profession she became seriously ill and failed to respond to medical treatment. As a last resort her father took her to Becedas, a small village, to seek the help of a woman healer famous throughout Castile, but Teresa's health did not improve. Leaving Becedas in the fall of 1538, she stayed in Hortigosa at the home of her uncle Pedro de Cepeda, who gave her the *Tercer Abecedario* of FRANCIS OF OSUNA to read. ''I did not know,'' she said, ''how to proceed in prayer or how to become recollected, and so I took much pleasure in it and decided to follow that path with all my strength'' (*Libro de la Vida,* the autobiography of St. Teresa 4.6).

Saint Teresa of Avila. (©Leonard de Selva/CORBIS)

Instead of regaining her health, Teresa grew even more ill, and her father brought her back to Avila in July 1539. On Aug. 15 she fell into a coma so profound that she was thought to be dead. After four days she revived, but she remained paralyzed in her legs for three years. After her cure, which she attributed to St. Joseph (*Libro de la Vida* 6.6–8), she entered a period of mediocrity in her spiritual life, but she did not at any time give up praying. Her trouble came of not understanding that the use of the imagination could be dispensed with and that her soul could give itself directly to contemplation. During this stage, which lasted 18 years, she had transitory mystical experiences. She was held back by a strong desire to be appreciated by others, but this finally left her in an experience of conversion in the presence of an image of ''the sorely wounded Christ'' (*Libro de la Vida* 9.2). This conversion dislodged the egoism that had hindered her spiritual development. Thus, at the age of 39, she began to enjoy a vivid experience of God's presence within her. However, the contrast between these favors and her conduct, which was more relaxed than was thought proper according to the ascetical standards of the time, caused some misunderstanding. Some of her friends, such as Francisco de Salcedo and Gaspar Daza, thought her favors were the work of the devil (*Libro de la Vida* 23.14). Diego de Cetina, SJ, brought her comfort by encouraging

Saint Teresa of Avila, Valladolid, Spain, 1625. (©CORBIS)

her to continue in mental prayer and to think upon the humanity of Christ. Francis BORGIA in 1555 heard her confession and told her that the spirit of God was working in her, that she should concentrate upon Christ's Passion and not resist the ecstatic experience that came to her in prayer. Nevertheless she had to endure the distrust even of her friends as the divine favors increased. When Pradanos left Avila in 1558 his place as Teresa's director was taken by Baltasar Álvarez, SJ, who, either from caution or with the intention of probing her spirit, caused her great distress by telling her that others were convinced that her raptures and visions were the work of the devil and that she should not communicate so often (*Libor de la Vida* 25.4). Another priest acting temporarily as her confessor, on hearing her report of a vision she had repeatedly had of Christ, told her it was clearly the devil and commanded her to make the sign of the cross and laugh at the vision (*Libro de la Vida* 29.5). But God did not fail to comfort her, and she received the favor of the transverberation (*Libro de la Vida* 29.13–14). In Aug. 1560 St. Peter of Alcántara counseled her: ''Keep on as you are doing, daughter; we all suffer such trials.''

Reformer. Her great work of reform began with herself. She made a vow always to follow the more perfect course, and resolved to keep the rule as perfectly as she could (*Libro de la Vida* 32.9). However, the atmosphere prevailing at the Incarnation monastery was less than favorable to the more perfect type of life to which Teresa aspired. A group assembled in her cell one September evening in 1560, taking their inspiration from the primitive tradition of Carmel and the discalced reform of St. Peter of Alcántara, proposed the foundation of a monastery of an eremitical type. At first her confessor, the provincial of the Carmelites, and other advisers encouraged her in the plan (*Tiempo y Vida de Sta. Teresa* 478–482); but when the proposal became known among the townsfolk, there was a great outcry against it. The provincial changed his mind, her confessor dissociated himself from the project, and her advisers ranged themselves with the opposition. Six months later, however, when there was a change of rectors at the Jesuit college, her confessor, Father Álvarez, gave his approval. Without delay Teresa had her sister Juana and her husband Juan de Ovalle buy a house in Avila and occupy it as though it were for themselves (*Libro de la Vida* 33.11). This stratagem was necessary to obviate difficulties with nuns at the Incarnation while the building was being adapted and made ready to serve as a convent. At Toledo, where she was sent by the Carmelite provincial at the importunate request of a wealthy and noble lady, she received a visit from St. Peter of Alcántara, who offered to act as mediator in obtaining from Rome the permissions needed for the foundation. While there she also received a visit from the holy Carmelite María de Yepes, who had just returned from Rome with permission to establish a reformed convent and who provided Teresa with a new light on the question of the type of poverty to be adopted by her own community. At Toledo she also completed in reluctant obedience to her confessor the first version of her *Vida.* She returned to Avila at the end of June 1562 (*Tiempo y Vida de Sta. Teresa* 506–507), and shortly thereafter the apostolic rescript, dated Feb. 7, 1562, for the foundation of the new convent arrived. The following Aug. 24 the new monastery dedicated to S. José was founded; Maestro Daza, the bishop's delegate, officiated at the ceremony. Four novices received the habit of the Discalced Carmelites. There was strong opposition among the townspeople and at the Incarnation. The prioress at the Incarnation summoned Teresa back to her monastery, where the Carmelite provincial Ángel de Salazar, indignant at her having put her new establishment under the jurisdiction of the bishop, rebuked her, but after hearing her account of things, was mollified and even promised to help quiet the popular disturbance and to give her permission to return to S. José when calm had been restored. On Aug. 25 the council at Avila met to discuss the matter of the new foundation, and on August 30 a great assembly of the leading townspeople gathered. The only one in the assembly to raise his voice against the popular indignation was Domingo BÁÑEZ, OP. A lawsuit followed in the royal court, but before the end of 1562 the founder, as Teresa of Jesus, was authorized by the provincial to return to the new convent. There followed the five most peaceful years of her life, during which she wrote the *Way of Perfection and the Meditations on the Canticle.*

Foundations. In April 1567 the Carmelite general, Giovanni Battista Rossi (Rubeo), made a visitation, approved Teresa's work, and commanded her to establish other convents with some of the nuns from the convent of the Incarnation at Avila. He also gave her permission to establish two houses for men who wished to adopt the reform. The extension of Teresa's work began with the foundation of a convent at Medina del Campo, Aug. 15, 1567. Then followed other foundations: at Malagon in 1568; at Valladolid (Río de Olinos) in 1568; at Toledo and at Pastrana in 1569; at Salamanca in 1570; and at Alba de Tormes in 1571. As she journeyed to Toledo in 1569 she passed through Duruelo, where John of the Cross and Anthony of Jesus had established the first convent of Discalced Brethren in November 1568, and in July 1569 she established the second monastery of Discalced Brethren in Pastrana.

These foundations were followed by an interval during which Teresa served as prioress at the Incarnation monastery in Avila, an office to which she was appointed by the apostolic visitator, Pedro Fernández, OP. This duty she was loath to assume, and she had much opposition to face on the part of the community. However, with the help of St. JOHN OF THE CROSS, who served as a confessor for the nuns, she was able to bring about a great improvement in the spiritual condition of the community. On Nov. 18, 1572, while receiving Communion from the hands of John of the Cross, she received the favor of the "spiritual marriage."

At the request of the Duchess of Alba she spent the first days of 1573 in Alba, and then went to Salamanca to put things in order at the foundation there. At the command of Jerome Ripalda, SJ, she started her *Book of the Foundations* the following August. On March 19, 1574, she established a foundation at Segovia, where the Pastrana nuns had been transferred because of conflicts with the Princess of Eboli. This marked the beginning of a second series of foundations. The next was made at Beas de Segura in February 1575. There Teresa met Jerome GRATIAN, apostolic visitator of the order in Andalucia, who ordered a foundation in Seville. The bishop objected, however, and Teresa sent Ana de S. Alberto to Caravaca to make a foundation there in her name on Jan. 1, 1576, and that of the Seville convent was delayed until June 3 of the same year.

Crisis between the Calced and Discalced. The entry of the Discalced Brethren into Andalusia was forbidden by Rossi, the general of the order, who opposed Teresa and Jerome Gratian in this matter. The general chapter at Piacenza in 1575 ordered the Discalced Brethren to withdraw from Andalusia, and Teresa herself was ordered to retire to a convent. The general put Jerome Tostado at the head of the Discalced Brethren. While the conflict raged between the Calced and Discalced Brethren, Teresa wrote the *Visitation of the Discalced Nuns,* a part of *The Foundations,* and her greatest book, *The Interior Castle.*

The nuncio Nicholas Ormaneto, a defender of the Discalced Brethren, died June 18, 1578, and his successor, Felipe Sega, was less favorably disposed toward them. John of the Cross was imprisoned in Toledo. Against Teresa's will the Discalced Brethren held a chapter in Almodovar on Oct. 9, 1578. The nuncio annulled the chapter and by a decree put the Discalced Brethren under the authority of the Calced provincials who subjected them to some harassment. The king intervened, and four were named to advise the nuncio, among them Pedro Fernández, OP. Ángel de Salazar was made vicar–general of the Discalced Brethren while negotiations were afoot for the separation of the Discalced from the Calced Brethren and the erection of a Discalced province.

Teresa then turned to visiting her convents and resumed the founding of new ones. On Feb. 25, 1580, she gave the habit to founders of the convent in Villanueva de la Jara. The brief *Pia consideratione,* dated June 22, 1580, ordered the erection of a distinct province for the Discalced. On March 3, 1581, the chapter of the Discalced was held in Alcalá, and Jerome Gratian, who was favored by Teresa, was elected the first provincial. Teresa's last foundations were at Palencia and Soria in 1581, at Burgos in 1582, and the most difficult of all, Granada (1582), was entrusted to the Venerable ANNE OF JESUS.

Teresa's body was interred in Alba. Paul V declared her a blessed April 24, 1614, and in 1617 the Spanish parliament proclaimed her the Patroness of Spain. Gregory XV canonized her in 1622 together with SS. Ignatius of Loyola, Francis Xavier, Isidore, and Philip Neri.

[O. STEGGINK]

Spiritual Doctrine. Among the writings of St. Teresa, three can be indicated as the depositories of her spiritual teaching: her autobiography, the *Way of Perfection,* and the *Interior Castle.* Readers must exercise some caution, however, and resist the temptation to hastily synthesize the doctrine in these books, because St. Teresa wrote from her personal experience at different stages of the spiritual life. For example, the doctrine of prayer found in the autobiography is not identical with that in the *Inte-*

rior Castle; more than a decade had elapsed between their composition, and Teresa had meanwhile attained a higher degree of spiritual maturity with its simultaneous expansion of experience.

The autobiography, written primarily as a manifestation of her spiritual state for her directors, was later enlarged in scope and in audience. Chapters 11 to 22 inclusive—a later addition—are devoted exclusively to the discussion of prayer, although additional comments and examples are scattered throughout the remaining 28 chapters. Teresa depicts different stages of the life of prayer in metaphorical terms taken from the manner of securing water to irrigate a garden. The ''first water'' is laboriously obtained from a well and carried in a bucket to the garden; this is in reference to beginners who, liberated from the more flagrant mortal sins, apply themselves to discursive prayer or meditation, although they experience fatigue and aridity from time to time. After speaking at length of meditation in its stricter meaning, Teresa made a brief reference to ''acquired'' contemplation before beginning her discussion of the ''second water.'' In this second stage, the gardener secures water through use of a windlass and bucket; here Teresa refers to the ''prayer of quiet,'' a gift of God through which the individual begins to have a passive experience of prayer. The third method of irrigation is the employment of water from a stream or river; the application made by Teresa is to the ''sleep of the faculties.'' Although Teresa considered this an important stage in the evolution of prayer when she wrote her autobiography, she later relegated it to a simple intensification of the ''prayer of quiet'' in the *Interior Castle.* The fourth method of irrigation is God–given: the rain; Teresa employs this metaphor to describe a state of union in prayer in which the soul is apparently passive.

Teresa addressed her *Way of Perfection* to her nuns, teaching them therein the major virtues that demand their solicitude, casting further light on the practice of prayer, and using the *Pater Noster* as a vehicle for teaching prayer at greater depth. This book is sometimes referred to as the apex of Teresa's ascetical doctrine.

The *Interior Castle* is the principal source of mature Teresian thought on the spiritual life in its integrity. Chief emphasis is laid on the life of prayer, but other elements (the apostolate, for example) are also treated. The interior castle is the soul, in the center of which dwells the Trinity. Growth in prayer enables the individual to enter into deeper intimacy with God—signified by a progressive journey through the apartments (or mansions) of the castle from the outermost to the luminous center. When a man has attained union with God in the degree permitted to him in this world, he is ''at the center'' of himself; in other words, he has integrity as a child of God and as a human being. Each of the apartments of the castle is distinguished by a different stage in the evolution of prayer, with its consequent effects upon every other phase of the life of the individual.

Bibliography: *The Collected Works of St. Teresa of Avila,* 3v. trans. K. KAVANAUGH and O. RODRIGUEZ (Washington, D.C.: v. 1, 2d rev. ed., 1987; v. 2, 1980; v. 3, 1985). *The Collected Letters of Saint Teresa of Avila,* v. 1, trans. K. KAVANAUGH (Washington, D.C. 2001). J. BILINKOFF, *The Avila of Saint Teresa: Religious Reform in a Sixteenth–Century City* (Ithaca, N.Y. 1989). J. CHORPENNING, *The Divine Romance: Teresa of Avila's Narrative Theology* (Chicago 1992). *Values and Ethics series 4,* E. MONTALVA and O. STEGGINK, *Tiempo y Vida de Santa Teresa,* 3 v. (Madrid 1968). H. HATZFELD, *Santa Teresa de Avila* (Twayne's World Authors Series 79; New York 1969). *Introduccion a la lectura de Santa Teresa,* ed. A. BARRIENTOS (Madrid 1978). M. LUTI, *Teresa of Avila–s Way: The Way of the Christian Mystics,* 13 (Collegeville, Minn. 1991). E. A. PEERS, *Handbook to the Life and Times of St. Teresa of Avila and St. John of the Cross* (Westminster, Md. 1964). C. SLADE, *St. Teresa of Avila: Author of a Heroic Life* (Berkeley, Calif. 1995). *Saint Teresa, Spiritual Adventure,* trans. C. O'MAHONEY (Burgos 1982). *Centenary of Saint Teresa,* Catholic University Symposium 15, 17 October 1982, ed. JOHN SULLIVAN (Carmelite Studies 3; Washington, D.C. 1984). A. WEBER, *Teresa of Avila and the Rhetoric of Femininity* (Princeton, N.J. 1990). R. WILLIAMS, *Saint Teresa* (London and New York 1991, repr. 2000).

[S. V. RAMGE]

TERESIAN INSTITUTE

An association of Catholic women founded in Spain by Rev. Peter Poveda in 1911; it subsequently spread throughout Western Europe, Mexico, South America, the Philippines, Japan, Formosa, Jordan, West Africa, and the Congo. In the U.S. the institute was established (1961) in Boston, MA, and Coral Gables, FL. Its members, known as Teresians, devote their lives to the apostolate of Christian education, teaching all age levels, irrespective of class or nationality. The aim of the institute is a harmonious blend of action and contemplation; every member must follow some course of study in order to obtain a university degree or other professional qualification. No habit or special uniform is worn by Teresians, whose patroness is St. Teresa of Avila.

[A. MANDIOLA]

TERILL, ANTHONY (BONVILLE)

Jesuit moral theologian; b. Canford (Dorsetshire), 1621; d. Liège, Oct. 11, 1676. His family name was Bonville, or Boville. Although his mother was a Catholic, his father was not, and Terill was brought up in heresy. At the age of 15 he was converted, whereupon he went to the English College of Saint-Omer, taking the name Terill in accordance with the practice, common among Catholics going abroad for study, of using an alias. After several years at St. Omer, Terill went to the English College at Rome to prepare for the priesthood. He was ordained March 6, 1647, and on June 20 of that year he entered the Jesuits. For some time after completing his novitiate he was penitentiary at Loreto and then he taught, successively, philosophy at Florence, philosophy and theology at Parma, and theology and mathematics at the English College at Liège where he was also director of studies and, for three years, rector.

In addition to several theological works, he wrote two books that earned him some distinction as a moral theologian. The first of these was *Fundamentum totius theologiae moralis seu tractatus de conscientia probabili* . . . (Liège 1668). Most moralists who discussed PROBABILISM did so as part of their treatment of broader topics. Terill was among the first to devote an entire book to the subject, which happened to interest him profoundly, perhaps because he himself was much tortured by scruples. In this book he devised an ingenious explanation of how a person, transgressing a law of which he is invincibly ignorant, does not in fact violate the law of God. Foreseeing in His *scientia media* of future free events that some individuals would be inculpably ignorant of the law or its applications, God incorporated those exceptions or departures from the general formula of the law into the law itself. This explanation, besides being open to all the objections against probabilism, outraged those to whom the concept of *scientia media* was unacceptable, and evoked a storm of protest. In reply to his critics Terill wrote his *Regula morum,* published posthumously at Liège in 1677, and directed especially against his chief adversaries, the Jesuit Miguel de ELIZALDE, and the Dominican DANIEL CONCINA.

Bibliography: *Bibliothèque de la Compagnie de Jésus* 7:1930–31, to be used cautiously because of errors in dates. *Nomenclator literarius theologiae catholicae* [3] 4:284–286. H. FOLEY, ed., *Records of the English Province of the Society of Jesus,* 7 v. (London 1877–82) 3.1:420–421; 6.1:352–353. R. BROUILLARD, *Dictionnaire de théologie catholique* 15.1:127–129.

[P. K. MEAGHER]

TERM (LOGIC)

A SIGN from which a simple PROPOSITION (oral, written, or mental) is made. It is the ultimate significant element into which a sentence or proposition may be resolved. The proposition ''man exists'' can be resolved into two concepts or terms, ''man'' and ''exists.'' This notion of term as being the ultimate element is indicated in Aristotle's use of ὅρος (*Anal. pr.* 24b 16) and St. Thomas's use of *terminus* (*In 1 perih.* 4.2); both have the primary meaning of limit or extreme and the secondary meaning of elementary part of a proposition.

Term is basically divided into mental, oral, and written term. All three types are signs; they signify something other than themselves. The concept or mental term is a sign of the thing; an oral or written term is immediately a sign of the concept, but principally a sign of the thing (*In 1 perih.* 2.5). Oral and written terms, inasmuch as they are both instrumental and conventional signs, are distinguished from the mental term, which is a formal and natural sign.

Moreover, terms are the primary components of a simple proposition, as ''man is just.'' (A compound proposition, as ''If man is just, he is pleasing to God,'' is primarily made up of simple propositions, and these in turn are composed of terms.)

A most important division of term, based on the manner of signifying, is that into univocal, equivocal, and analogous terms. A univocal term is one that signifies things divisively, according to their strictly common nature, or that signifies the things represented by one and the same concept; e.g., the word ''man'' signifies all men as identified in one and the same concept of human nature.

An equivocal term is one that signifies the things represented by several essentially different and unrelated concepts. In other words, an equivocal term signifies several things, not as they are united under a concept that has a certain unity—even a proportional unity—but as they differ, e.g., ''bark'' as signifying a canine sound and a tree's covering. The concept of the sound and the concept of the covering have nothing in common but the name; their content is completely different. *See* EQUIVOCATION (LOGIC).

An analogous term is one that signifies things represented by a concept that has a unity of proportion, e.g., ''healthy'' as referring to an animal and to a food, but not signifying the same thing in both. It is predicated of an animal because the organism possesses health; of a food, because it has a causal relation to the health that is formally found in the animal. *See* ANALOGY.

See Also: SUPPOSITION (LOGIC).

Bibliography: JOHN OF ST. THOMAS, *Cursus Philosophicus Thomisticus,* 3 v. (Turin 1930–37) 1:7–12, 85–112. J. MARITAIN, *Formal Logic,* tr. I. CHOQUETTE (New York 1946) 45–50. H. GRENIER, *Thomistic Philosophy,* tr. J. P. O'HANLEY, 3 v. (Charlottetown, Canada 1948–49) 1:29–38.

[J. F. PEIFER]

Fireworks illuminate the Giza pyramids during millennium celebrations, Egypt, 2000. (AP/WideWorld Photos)

TERTIO MILLENNIO ADVENIENTE

Pope John Paul II's apostolic letter, *As the Third Millennium Draws Near*, dated Nov. 10, 1994 outlines in great detail preparations to celebrate the Year of Jubilee at the beginning of the third millennium. The first of the five parts focuses on the person of Jesus Christ and explains the significance of the incarnation for salvation and redemption. Through the mediation of Christ, the Father sends the Holy Spirit, who enables humans to share the inmost life of God.

Part two situates the Year of JUBILEE in the history of salvation, recalling its origins and observance in the Old Testament, which included the emancipation of slaves, restoration of ancestral property, and the cancellation of debts. The foundations of this tradition were grounded in the theology of creation and divine providence, which holds that "the riches of creation were to be considered as a common good of the whole of humanity." Individuals who possessed goods as personal property "were really only stewards, ministers charged with working in the name of God." The jubilee year, meant to restore social justice, is a basis of the Church's social teaching that was reclaimed in the encyclical *RERUM NOVARUM*. A second important aspect of "this year of the Lord's favor" (Isaiah's description), is that it is a time "of remission of sins and of the punishments due them, a year of reconciliation between disputing parties, a year of manifold conversions and of sacramental and extrasacramental penance." In human terms, jubilees mark anniversaries in the lives of individuals and institutions, and the extraordinary jubilee that marks 2,000 years since the birth of Christ is significant "not only for Christians but indirectly for the whole of humanity, given the prominent role played by Christianity during these two [past] millennia." Jubilee speaks not merely of an inner joy but a jubilation that is manifested outwardly "for the coming of God is also an outward, visible, audible and tangible event."

Part three interprets many events of the past century, notably "the providential event" of the Second Vatican Council, as steps in the preparation for the celebration of the year of jubilee. The council drew much from the experiences of the immediate past, "especially from the intellectual legacy left by Pius XII," and the efforts of other popes. During the council, the Church examined its own identity, reaffirmed the universal call to holiness, made provision for the reform of the liturgy, gave impetus to renewal of church life at every level, and promoted the variety of Christian vocations from laity and religious to deacons, priests, and bishops. ''No council had ever spoken so clearly about Christian unity, about dialogue with non-Christian religions, about the specific meaning of the old covenant and of Israel, about the dignity of each person's conscience, about the principle of religious liberty, about the different cultural traditions within which the Church carries out her missionary mandate and about the means of social communication.'' The apostolic letter continues, ''the best preparation for the new millennium'' and, therefore, is a renewed commitment to the teachings and spirit of Vatican II. The series of synods, general and regional, national and diocesan, begun after the council have contributed to the preparation for the Year of Jubilee by promoting ''evangelization, or rather the new evangelization.'' The popes of the past century, each in his own way, prepared for the new millennium by his efforts ''to promote and defend the basic values of peace and justice in the face of contrary tendencies of our time.''

John Paul II states that the theme of the Great Jubilee as ''a new Advent'' is ''as it were a hermeneutical key to my pontificate.'' It is the key to understanding the importance he gives to his travels throughout the world, to visits with world leaders, and to his conversations with leaders of other churches. The Great Jubilee of the year 2000 builds on other jubilee years celebrated in the past century, notably the Marian Year and the Year of the Family.

The first three parts are prologue. The fourth and longest part of *Tertio millennio adveniente* outlines ''a specific program of initiatives for the immediate preparation of the Great Jubilee,'' the product of consultation with the College of Cardinals and proposals made by presidents of episcopal conferences. Initiatives during the first phase of the immediate preparation (1994–96) would be designed to raise the consciousness of the faithful as to the significance of the year of jubilee and the need for repentance, conversion, and renewal. ''The holy door of the Jubilee Year 2000 should be symbolically wider . . . because humanity, upon reaching this goal, will leave behind not just a century but a millennium.'' The Church cannot cross the threshold into a new millennium without encouraging her children to purify themselves, acknowledging their past errors, infidelities, and weaknesses. Among the sins that require repentance are those that have contributed to wound church unity in the past 1,000 years. The Great Jubilee demands fitting ecumenical initiatives so we can celebrate it, ''if not completely united, at least much closer to overcoming the divisions of the second millennium.'' Another ''painful chapter'' that the Church must review in a spirit of repentance ''is the acquiescence given, especially in certain centuries, to intolerance and even the use of violence in the service of truth.'' Above all, we must examine our conscience regarding the evils of the present day: religious indifference, confusion in the ethical sphere ''even about the fundamental values of respect for life and the family,'' erroneous theological views, and the crisis of obedience vis-à-vis the Church's magisterium. Must not Christians ask themselves about their acquiescence concerning the violation of human rights by totalitarian regimes? The examination of conscience must also consider the reception given to Vatican II. The witness of martyrs in our own century cannot be forgotten. In preparation for the year 2000, the Apostolic See would undertake to update the martyrologies for the universal Church. ''In particular, there is a need to foster the recognition of the heroic virtues of men and women who have lived their Christian vocation in marriage'' to encourage other Christian spouses. The cardinals and bishops emphasized the need for more regional synods in America, Oceania, and Asia, to address local problems of evangelization and other challenges.

The second phase in the preparations would take place over a span of three years (1997–99), each with its own focus and particular themes. The theme of year one is distinctly Christological, with a focus on ''Jesus Christ, the one savior of the world, yesterday, today and forever.'' It emphasizes baptism, the gift of faith, personal renewal, and solidarity with one's neighbor, especially the most needy. The theme of year two focuses on the Holy Spirit, the principle of God's self-communication in the order of grace, who makes present in the Church and in the soul of each individual the unique revelation of Christ. It calls for a renewed appreciation of the Sacraments, in particular Confirmation, the variety of charisms and ministries, and the new EVANGELIZATION. In view of the eschatological perspective of the KINGDOM OF GOD at the end of time, this year should be a time of revitalizing the theological virtue of hope. The final stage of preparation aims at broadening horizons so that believers will see things in the perspective of Christ's revelation of the Father in heaven. Because God is Father of all, year three is a time for special emphasis on interreligious dialogue, preeminently with Jews and Muslims. The third year of preparation highlights charity, recalling its twofold aspect, love of God and love of neighbor, as summing up the moral life of the believer. In each of the three years, different aspects of Mary's role in the story of salvation receive special attention.

The actual celebration of the Great Jubilee, the focus of the three years of preparation, is a separate phase. It will take place in the Holy Land, in Rome, and the local churches throughout the world. Its aim will be ''to give glory to the Trinity, from whom everything in the world and in history comes and to whom everything returns.'' The celebration will be ''intensely Eucharistic,'' culminating the International Eucharistic Congress in Rome. ''The ecumenical and universal character of the sacred jubilee can be fittingly reflected in a meeting of all Christians,'' but it must be carefully prepared in collaboration with Christians of other traditions and ''a grateful openness to those religions whose representatives might wish to acknowledge the joy shared by all the disciples of Christ.''

Part five concludes the apostolic letter with a reaffirmation, citing Vatican II and Pope John Paul II's own encyclicals, of the Church's missionary character. ''Indeed, missionary outreach is part of her very nature.'' It also says, ''the future of the world and the Church belongs to the younger generation'' who will reach maturity in the coming century. Beneath the changes in human history the Church maintains there are also many unchanging realities that ''have their ultimate foundation in Christ, who is the same yesterday and today and forever.''

Bibliography: For the text of *Tertio millennio adveniente,* see *Acta Apostolicae Sedis* 82 (1995) 5–41 (Latin); *Origins* 24, no. 24 (Nov. 24, 1994): 401–416 (English); *The Pope Speaks* 40 (1995) 85–113 (English).

[B. L. MARTHALER]

TERTULLIAN

Outstanding 3d-century theologian and ecclesiastical writer; b. probably at Carthage, *c.* 160; d. after 220. He was the son of a centurion in the service of the proconsul of Africa. Quintus Septimus Florens Tertullianus received an excellent education, chiefly in rhetoric and jurisprudence, and was professionally an advocate in the law courts of Rome. It is now generally agreed that he is to be identified with the jurist Tertullian, excerpts of whose writings are quoted in the Pandects.

Career and Character. Converted to Christianity (*c.* 195), Tertullian became an instructor of catechumens at CARTHAGE and in connection with this office began his literary career. As early as 206 his teaching began to reflect Montanist ideas, and *c.* 212 or 213 he broke with the Church and joined forces with MONTANISM in Africa, becoming the leader of a party subsequently known as Tertullianists. He was certainly married; whether he was a priest is still a matter of dispute.

According to St. JEROME (*De Viris illustribus* 53) he is said to have lived to an extreme old age: *''fertur vixisse usque ad decrepitam aetatem.''* There is no evidence that he returned to the Church before he died. The party that he founded continued in existence for some 200 years, the last remnant being reconciled to the Church by St. AUGUSTINE (*c.* 400).

The tragic course of Tertullian's life was determined, to a great extent, by the defects of his own character. Tertullian was an extremist. He tells that as a young man he ''drained the cup of lust to the dregs'' and that he had a passion for immoral plays and bloody spectacles in the arena; he was probably initiated into the mysteries of Mithra; and he confesses that he committed adultery frequently. It is not unreasonable to suppose that the exaggerated ascetism of his later views resulted, at least in part, from a reaction of disgust at the licentiousness of his earlier life.

Pierre DeLabriolle speaks of his ''mania'' for discipline; Matthew Arnold's sonnet on ''the stern Tertullian'' is well known; in Gibbon's famous indictment he is little better than a sadist; a 20th-century analyst, Bernhard Nisters, refers to schizoid features in Tertullian's temperament and suggests that his rigorism, his intolerance, his disputatious nonconformity, and his violent reaction to opposition approach paranoia. Such estimates are, in themselves, exaggerations. Tertullian's character was difficult, but it was not diseased. He was a man of ardent temperament, passionate, proud, and incapable of compromise with the truth as he saw it. It is true that he was impatient and irritable, but it is equally true that he was honest enough to admit this in the introduction to his beautiful treatise *De patientia.* Tertullian was a man of strong convictions and great moral earnestness. Through his excessive rigorism he adopted the extreme asceticism that warped his character and ruined his life. John Henry NEWMAN has written that impatience is the original sin of heretics; of no one can this be said with greater truth than of Tertullian.

Literary Genius. Tertullian was a literary genius, the greatest Christian writer in the West before St. Augustine and one of the greatest in the whole patristic period. The very characteristics that brought about his downfall contributed to the vigor and highly original quality of his prose. He illustrates perfectly the truth of Buffon's dictum that the style is the man. Tertullian knew the rules of the rhetoricians, and he could compose carefully according to these rules when it suited his purposes to do so. Yet he was too independent a character to be bound by conventional forms.

Tertullian was a writer of marvelous fertility and inventiveness, gifted with a felicity of expression rare among early Christian writers. He coined one epigram, one apothegm after another. He loved the PARADOX and the *reductio ad absurdum.* Puns and wordplay are scattered through all of his writings. He had a great power of invective and a genius for dispraise. Sarcasm was one of his favorite weapons. He almost always wrote like an angry man, and even his treatises on the Christian virtues are polemical. TACITUS he called a "first class chatterbox and a liar"; ARISTOTLE was the "wretched inventor of dialectics"; MARCION was "a rat from Pontus who gnaws away at the Gospels." Tags from his writings are known to everyone. "What has Athens to do with Jerusalem?" "The blood of Christians is seed." "It is certain because it is impossible." "Faith is patience with its lamp lit." "God is great when He is small." "Anima naturaliter Christiana." The list is endless.

Tertullian is the most quotable of all ancient Christian writers, and yet, though he is often quoted, he is seldom quoted at length. This is because he had a gift for the phrase rather than the paragraph and because most readers find it easier to appreciate his wit than to follow his arguments.

The difficulty of Tertullian's Latin is notorious, and there are references to it as early as LACTANTIUS and St. Jerome. Strangely conceived combinations of words and phrases, highly imaginative metaphors, cryptic allusions, multiple parentheses and antitheses, asyndeton, ellipsis (*"Quot verba, tot sententiae"* is the judgment of VINCENT OF LÉRINS), a unique vocabulary (there are almost a thousand neologisms in Tertullian), and above all an almost breathless brevity contribute to the obscurity of his style. He is, without doubt, the most difficult of all Latin prose writers, and yet so competent a critic as DeLabriolle has stated that after one acquires a taste for his pungent prose, all other Latin writers, including Tacitus, seem insipid; and Professor Wright considers him one of the five Latin writers who have done most to influence the developments of the language.

Writings. Thirty-one authentic treatises of Tertullian are extant. Five others attributed to him are spurious, and there are at least twelve that have been lost, including three of four written originally in Greek. The influence and popularity of these writings during the patristic period is attested by the frequency with which they are quoted—often without acknowledgment—by later Christian writers in the West.

Collections of his treatises were made at a very early date. St. Jerome relates that Cyprian "never passed a day without reading some portion of Tertullian's works"; and his daily request, "Da magistrum" (Give me the Master), suggests that he had in his possession a collection of Tertullian's writings. How many such collections remained after the condemnation of Tertullian's works by the so-called GELASIAN DECREE it is impossible to say.

The official opposition of the Church to the teaching of Tertullian is responsible, at least in part, for the defective text tradition of his works. The fact that in spite of this opposition at least six different collections of Tertullian's writings existed at the beginning of the Middle Ages reveals a liberalism that has not always been recognized as characteristic of this period. The works of Tertullian may be classified as (1) apologetical, (2) controversial, and (3) treatises on Christian discipline and ascetism.

Tertullian.

Apologetics. His *Apology* is one of the great classics of ancient Christian literature. It was written in A.D. 197, shortly after his conversion and well before Montanism became a serious influence in his life. The work is a passionate defense of the truth of Christianity. It was addressed to the provincial governors of the Roman Empire, and its proximate purpose was to prove the injustice of the persecutions directed against Christians. These persecutions arose from ignorance, misrepresentation, and fear. Tertullian's *Apology* argues brilliantly that the policy followed in the persecutions is inconsistent with the procedure regularly observed in criminal cases tried in Roman courts of justice. It shows that popular charges against the Christians of secret atrocities, sacrilege, and disloyalty are false; that Christian life and worship are blameless; and that Christianity, far from being a threat to the state, is actually one of the greatest sources of its strength because of the good moral lives that Christians lead and because Christianity supplies a sanction for the observance of law to which paganism can never rise.

Polemics. It has already been noted that Tertullian's writing is almost exclusively polemical. His apologetical treatises are concerned with the defense of Christianity against the attacks of paganism and infidelity. His controversial works, in the technical sense of the word controversial, defend Catholic truth against the attacks of heresy. The most important of these are the *De praescriptione hereticorum, Adversus Marcionem, Adversus Praxean,* and the *De anima;* of these, the *De praescriptione* (*c.* 200) is in a class by itself.

Praescriptio was a technical term in Roman law to describe a form of defense in which a litigant, in a statement prefixed to a brief (*praescribere*), took exception to some aspects of his opponent's case and thus attempted to have the case thrown out of court before it came to trial. The form of *praescriptio* with which Tertullian is here concerned is that of *longa possessio.* Heretics wish to establish the truth of their position from Scripture. The Church interposes a demurrer at once. Heretics have no right to argue from the Bible, because the Bible is the Church's book and has been the Church's book from the beginning. The content of revelation can be found nowhere except in churches founded by the Apostles, for the churches received the Gospel from the Apostles, either viva voce or in writing; the Apostles received it from Christ, and Christ, from God (*De praescr.* 21). Therefore no doctrine can be accepted that is contrary to the teaching of the apostolic churches.

Heretics who attempt to defend such doctrine by arguing from Scripture are wrong on two counts: first, because they are innovators—Catholic truth has been in possession from the beginning, and truth is always prior to error; second, because they are robbers—they are poaching on property that belongs to the Church alone.

Discipline and Asceticism. Tertullian's treatises on Christian discipline and asceticism, especially those that he wrote during the semi-Montanist and Montanist periods, are the least satisfactory of all his works. It is often said that Tertullian was a good logician but a poor casuist. This is a perspicacious appraisal, and it helps a great deal toward a more accurate, if not a more sympathetic, understanding of the man and his work. In the realm of abstract ideas, in apologetics, and in what is now called dogmatic or systematic theology, Tertullian is a model of good sense and objectivity. But when questions of conduct arise, for reasons that lie deep in the influences that had shaped his character, he seems to lose all sense of proportion, all appreciation of the force of an argument. His puritanical prejudices take over, and it is then that he abdicates reason in favor of emotion.

Tertullian's rigid moral code is most apparent in such treatises as the *De spectaculis* (*c.* 197–202), which forbids Christians to attend public amusements of all kinds—athletic events, the circus, the theater, gladiatorial combats—because of his belief that these amusements have their origin in IDOLATRY and are a source of immorality. The *De cultu feminarum* (*c.* 197–202) condemns the use of cosmetics, jewelry and other popular feminine adornments. Sin and death, it is stated, came into the world through a woman; therefore the only proper garb for a woman is the garb of penitence and mourning. The fanatic's preoccupation with details of legislation appears in the *De virginibus velandis* (before 207), which tells women to the inch how long their veils must be and what part of the head and neck they are to cover.

The evolution of Tertullian's teaching on marriage and remarriage affords a typical illustration of the gradual deterioration of his thought from Catholic orthodoxy to the harsh extremes of Montanist heresy. The beautiful treatise addressed to his wife, the *Ad uxorem* (*c.* 200), advises widows to remain unmarried, although it asserts that second marriage is no sin. In the *De exhortatione castitatis* (*c.* 204–212) his earlier counsel has become a strict command; and in the Montanist tract *De monogamia* (*c.* 217) he stigmatizes all second marriage as adultery, one of the capital sins that the Church may not absolve.

A similar evolution is to be found in his treatises on penitence. The Catholic work *De paenitentia* (*c.* 203) he places no restriction of any kind on the Church's power to forgive sins. The Montanist *De pudicitia* (after 212 or 213) introduces a distinction between remissible and irremissible sins, conceding a power to the bishop to forgive the former but restricting forgiveness of the latter to God alone.

Erudition and Doctrine. Although Tertullian, on occasion, attempted answers to metaphysical questions, his works, on the whole, reveal that his interests were scholarly rather than speculative. He may well have been one of the most learned men of his day. This was certainly the opinion of St. Jerome, a man of immense erudition himself; and Vincent of Lérins, after stating that Tertullian, of all Latin Christian writers, is *facile princeps,* challenges his readers to name anyone who was ''better versed in things human and divine.''

His knowledge of literature, both sacred and secular, was prodigious. He quoted from more than 100 different authors, and he was thoroughly familiar not only with the extensive heretical literature of the day but also with that of all the great philosophical systems of the Graeco-Roman world.

Theology. Almost all the crucial questions of theology are treated somewhere or other in his writings. It is impossible, in a brief synopsis, to do justice to the richness, variety, and permanent importance of his thought. In controversy with Hermogenes and Marcion, Gnosticism and paganism, he was concerned with the existence and the essence of God, His unity, His creative activity, and His divine providence. He writes of tradition and the rule of faith, ORIGINAL SIN and Redemption, GRACE and FREE WILL, the Church and the Sacraments (especially Baptism and the Eucharist), PRAYER and WORSHIP, the resurrection of the body and life everlasting. He is one of the earliest witnesses to the Church's doctrine on merit, satisfaction, and purgatory.

No one can know the history of the Sacrament of Penance in Christian antiquity unless he knows the treatises *De paenitentia* and *De pudicitia* of Tertullian. The closely reasoned arguments with which he defends the teaching authority of the Church in the *De praescriptione hereticorum* are of value for all time. He has a specialist's knowledge of the Bible, and he quotes it with an amazing facility and frequency. His works furnish invaluable source material for Scripture scholars interested in textual criticism, the history of the CANON, the origin of the Latin Bible, and early theories of exegesis.

In his teaching on the Trinity and the Incarnation, Tertullian made his most significant contributions to dogmatic theology. His language is remarkably precise for the early period at which he wrote. In the *Adversus Praxean,* particularly, his phrasing is so felicitous that some of the formulae found there have been taken over by the Church and are still regarded as definitive expressions of Catholic faith. As far as is known, the first use of the Latin word *trinitas* with reference to God is found in Tertullian's *Adversus Praxean* and *De pudicitia.* He was the first to use the term *persona* in a Trinitarian and Christological context, asserting that the Logos is distinct from the Father as person and not as substance and that the Holy Spirit is the "third person" in the Trinity (*Adv. Praxean* 12).

Tertullian states unequivocally that there are two natures, one human and one divine, which are joined in the one person, Jesus Christ (*Adv. Praxean* 27). He adds that the two natures remain distinct, in spite of their union; and he insists that they in no sense form a kind of *tertium quid,* "some composite essence formed out of two substances." Thus Tertullian refuted MONOPHYSITISM before it arose. His formula, *salva est proprietas utriusque substantiae* (*Adv. Praxean* 27) was borrowed by Leo the Great in his *Tome to Flavian,* and was eventually incorporated verbatim into the definition of the Council of Chalcedon. It may very well be that the Western Church was spared the ravages of the Christological controversies that divided the East because of its satisfaction with the Christology of Tertullian's *Adversus Praxean.*

Errors. In not a few areas of theology, Tertullian's views are, of course, completely unacceptable. Thus, for example, his teaching on the Trinity reveals a subordination of Son to Father that in the later crass form of ARIANISM the Church rejected as heretical. His views on the origin of the soul are infected by TRADUCIANISM, and his teaching on God and the angels makes it clear that he was unable to conceive noncorporeal substance. His MARIOLOGY contains much that is admirable, but it is defective in its denial of the perpetual virginity of Mary.

Tertullian's eschatology is chiliastic, and his preoccupation with what he conceived to be the proximity of the Parousia contributed, no doubt, to the formation of his views on the austere *Interimsethik* that he demanded of Christians. Although his distrust of human reason has sometimes been exaggerated, it must be admitted that he set up an opposition between faith and philosophy that is in striking contrast to the attitude of his Alexandrian contemporaries Clement and Origen.

The specifically Montanist errors that Tertullian espoused in later life were concerned, for the most part, with matters of discipline and asceticism. He insisted, for example, that flight during time of persecution was equivalent to APOSTASY, and he rejected the relatively mild legislation of the African Church on fasting in favor of the severe and frequent xerophagies demanded by the new prophecy. Outside the area of morals, his most dangerous Montanist errors lie in (1) his belief that the utterances of the Montanist prophets are the authentic word of God and (2) his defective ecclesiology.

As a Montanist, Tertullian held that there exists an internal "Church of the Spirit," which he contrasts with the external "Church of the bishops" (*De pudicitia* 21). He considered that all who possess the Spirit, whether they be priests or laymen, have powers that, in fact, are proper to the hierarchical order alone; and his principle that no one can communicate the Spirit except those who possess the Spirit, adumbrates DONATISM.

One can only regret that so great a talent as Tertullian's was dedicated to the defense of rigorism and heresy for so many of his most productive years and that, in spite of the magnificent contribution to the Church that his literary legacy represents, he cannot be recommended without reserve to Christian readers or honored with a place among the FATHERS OF THE CHURCH.

Bibliography: *Opera,* ed. E. DEKKERS et al. 2 v. (Corpus Christianorum. Series latina 1–2; Turnhout, Belg. 1954); ed. A. REIFFERSCHEID et al., 5 v. in *Corpus scriptorum ecclesiasticorum latinorum* 20 (1890), 47 (1906), 69 (1939), 70 (1942), 76 (1957). B. NISTERS, *Tertullian: Seine Persönlichkeit und sein Schicksal* (Münster 1950). H. HOPPE, *Syntax und Stil des Tertullian* (Leipzig 1903). R. BRAUN, *Deus christianorum: Recherches sur le vocabulaire doc-*

trinal de Tertullien (Paris 1962). A. D'ALÉS, *La Théologie de Tertullien* (2d ed. Paris 1905). R. E. ROBERTS, *The Theology of Tertullian* (London 1924). J. MORGAN, *The Importance of Tertullian in the Development of Christian Dogma* (London 1928). C. DE L. SHORTT, *The Influence of Philosophy on the Mind of Tertullian* (London 1933). J. QUASTEN, *Patrology*, 3 v. (Westminster, Md. 1950–) 2:246–340. O. BARDENHEWER, *Geschichte der altkirchlichen Literatur*, 5 v. (Freiburg 1913–32) 2:377–442. E. F. OSBORN, *Tertullian: First Theologian of the West* (Cambridge 1997).

[W. LE SAINT]

TESTAMENT (IN THE BIBLE)

In classical Latin the word *testamentum* denotes only the attested will by which a man designates what dispositions are to be made of his property after his death, and the English word ''testament,'' which is derived from it, should also etymologically be used only in this sense, as in the phrase, ''last will and testament.'' The corresponding term in classical Greek is διαθήκη. However, the Septuagint (LXX) translators used this Greek term consistently to render the Hebrew word *b*e*rît,* which never means ''last will.'' The meaning of *b*e*rît* is ''covenant, pact, agreement,'' for which the corresponding word in classical Greek is συνθήκη, the term used in Wis 12.21, as well as by Aquila, Symmachus, and Theodotion to translate *b*e*rît.* Perhaps the LXX translators felt that the connotation of a bilateral contract contained in the term συνθήκη was not in keeping with the fact that in the covenant made by Yahweh with Israel, Yahweh alone set the conditions. In any case, because the LXX translators gave this new meaning to διαθήκη, the corresponding Latin and English terms, *testamentum* and testament, also took on the meaning of ''covenant'' in Biblical language. For the significance of this term in the expressions Old Testament, New Testament, *see* COVENANT (IN THE BIBLE).

Although the New Testament, following the LXX usage, regularly employs the word διαθήκη in the sense of ''covenant'' (Lk 1.72; Acts 3.25; Rom 9.4; etc.) and even the phrase ἡ παλαιὰ διαθήκη, ''the Old Testament,'' in reference to the books written under the Old Covenant, there are two passages in the New Testament where the thought passes from this meaning of the term to the meaning that it has in classical Greek. In Gal 3.15–17 God's covenant with Abraham is compared to a man's last will and testament, with the emphasis on the definitive value of a will properly drawn up. This is clear from the verbs used by St. Paul—ratify, annul, alter—and from his introductory expression, ''I speak after the manner of men.'' In Heb 9.16–17 the point of comparison is the testator's death: just as a man's last will and testament becomes effective only when he dies, so Christ acts as mediator of the New Covenant between God and men only through His death whereby He expiates men's sins, because ''without the shedding of blood there is no forgiveness,'' i.e., legal pardon (v. 22). The effect of this redeeming efficacy of Christ's death is to allow ''those who are called'' to claim the promised inheritance.

Bibliography: L. G. DA FONSECA, ''Διαθήκη—foedus an testamentum?'' *Biblica* 8 (1927) 31–50, 161–181, 290–319, 418–441; 9 (1928) 26–40, 143–160. *Encyclopedic Dictionary of the Bible*, tr. and adap. by L. HARTMAN (New York 1963) 2414–15.

[A. YONICK]

TESTEM BENEVOLENTIAE

An apostolic letter of Pope LEO XIII to Cardinal Gibbons, Jan. 22, 1899. In this letter the pope, testifying to his esteem in the past for the Church and the people of the United States, indicates in a spirit of affection some matters that need correction. The Abbé Félix Klein's preface to the French translation of *The Life of Isaac Thomas Hecker* is cited by the pope as occasioning controversies concerning the manner of leading a Christian life; for in the preface of this translation it is advocated that the Church minimize certain points of the deposit of the faith and adapt itself to advanced civilization to make converts. Leo XIII cites Vatican Council I's teaching that the doctrine of faith is not proposed as a theory of philosophy but as a divine deposit to be faithfully guarded and infallibly declared; the Church must adhere in the same way to its doctrine at all times, and although adaptations may be made in the rule of Christian life to suit time, place, and national customs, these modifications may be made only by the Church, not by individuals in imitation of the prevailing false concept of civil liberty. The letter then attacks the argument that says that there is a wider field of action and thought in matters of religion because of the definition of papal infallibility; for Vatican Council I defined infallibility not to give license in matters of religion but to protect humanity from it. The consequences of the views expressed in the aforementioned preface are then treated; the need for external guidance in religion and the superiority of supernatural over natural virtue is stated. The distinction between active and passive virtues is rejected, since all virtue connotes action; the view that the vows of religion limit man's true liberty is rebutted, for they lead man to the fullness of real liberty. The pope attacks the view that methods of dealing with non-Catholics that have proved fruitful in the past should be abandoned. Appealing for unity in the Church, the letter closes with an approval of the term Americanism as applied to the characteristics that reflect honor on the American people.

Bibliography: An English translation may be found in J. T. ELLIS, ed. *Documents of American Catholic History. Vol*

2:1866–1966 (Wilmington, Del., 1987) 537–47. The entire issue of *U.S. Catholic Historian* 11:3 (summer 1993) is devoted to the Americanist Controversy. M. REHER, ''Leo XIII and Americanism,'' *Theological Studies* 34 (1973) 679–89. T.T. MCAVOY, *The Great Crisis in American Church History, 1895–1900* (Chicago 1957). D. KILLEN, ''Americanism revisited: John Spalding and *Testem Benevolentiae*,'' *Harvard Theological Review* 66 (1973) 413–454. W. L. PORTIER, ''Isaac Hecker and *Testem Benevolentiae*: a study in theological pluralism,'' in J. FARINA, ed., *Hecker Studies* (Ramsey, NJ, 1983) 11–48. G. P. FOGERTY, *The Vatican and the American Hierarchy from 1870 to 1965* (Wilmington 1985). D. J. O'BRIEN, *Isaac Hecker, American Catholic* (New York 1992).

[W. F. HOGAN]

TESTERA, JACOBO DE

Franciscan missionary; b. Bayonne, France, date unknown; d. Mexico, Aug. 8, 1543. Testera spent nearly 20 years as a Franciscan in Spain, principally in the area of Seville, before crossing over to the New World. In 1529 he came to New Spain with a group of missionaries led by Antonio de Ciudad Rodrigo. He began preaching there even before he had mastered any of the native languages, making use of paintings and interpreters to explain the doctrines of the faith. He was elected *custos* of the Custody of the Holy Gospel in 1533, becoming superior of all the Franciscans in Mexico. He visited the province of Michoacán and sent a large detachment of missionaries there. In 1534 he sent Toribio MOTOLINÍA to Guatemala with a group of friars while he himself went to Yucatán where he established a mission in the area of Champotón. His work was disrupted by the Spanish soldiers, who, in their quest for slaves to work in mines, stirred up the Indians against all things Spanish. He represented the Mexican Franciscans at the general chapter of the order in Mantua in 1541. While there he was appointed commissary general of the Franciscans in the New World. Returning to Mexico, he brought with him 150 friars for the missions.

[F. B. WARREN]

TESTIMONIA

In a broad sense the term ''testimonia'' is applied to the use of Old Testament texts in the New Testament to show that certain events of the Christian dispensation had been foreseen and foretold by the Prophets and inspired writers of Israel; in a narrower sense the term is used of written collections or anthologies of Old Testament texts for the use described and often called messianic proof-texts.

That such written collections existed and were used in the early centuries of the Christian Era is certain. St. Cyprian is credited with such a collection, and it is clear that he simply revised and expanded an earlier work; a leaf of another book of testimonies from the fourth century has also been found and is now in the John Rylands Library. The collecting of such Old Testament proof-texts to be applied to their own situation is also attested among the monks of the QUMRAN COMMUNITY.

Bibliography: J. R. HARRIS, *Testimonies I–II* (Cambridge, Eng. 1916–20). C. H. DODD, *According to the Scriptures* (New York 1953). A.M. HUNTER, *Paul and His Predecessors* (rev. ed. Philadelphia 1961) 58–64, 131–134.

[W. N. SCHUIT]

TETRARCH

Title of a petty ruler, derived from the Greek τετράρχης and denoting a ruler over the fourth part of a realm. Originally it was conferred by Philip of Macedonia upon the governors of the four districts of Macedonia, but by the beginning of the Christian Era it was used of any subordinate ruler in a given region without any indication of a fourfold political division of government. In the latter sense the title is given to Philip, Lysanias, and HEROD ANTIPAS (Lk 3.1–2, 19; 9.7; Mt 14.1; Acts 13.1). Philip and Antipas were members of the Herodian dynasty, but neither enjoyed the broad powers of Herod the Great. They had to be content with the lesser powers and title of tetrarchs.

Bibliography: *Encyclopedic Dictionary of the Bible,* translated and adapted by L. HARTMAN (New York, 1963) 2416.

[R. MERCURIO]

TETZEL, JOHANN

Preacher of indulgences at the time of Luther; b. Pirna near Meissen, 1465; d. Leipzig, Aug. 11, 1519. He studied at Leipzig and entered the Dominican Order there. He was prior at Glogau, and in 1509 was appointed inquisitor for Poland.

Tetzel is best known for his preaching of an indulgence that was the occasion—though not the cause—of Luther's rejection of the doctrine of indulgences. By 1517 Tetzel had already had much experience: he had preached indulgences in ten different cities from 1503 to 1510. In 1516 he was appointed subcommissioner in Meissen for the indulgence granted to those who contributed to the rebuilding of St. Peter's in Rome. In January 1517 he preached the indulgence in the territory of Albert of Brandenburg. His preaching of it at Jüterbog attracted the inhabitants of nearby Wittenberg, which was ruled by

Frederick the Wise (d. 1525), Elector of Saxony, where the indulgence could not be preached. Luther was already hostile to indulgences because of Frederick's traffic in them: 129,799 years' indulgence could be obtained by the faithful for venerating Frederick's collection of relics. He was further alienated by accounts of Tetzel's methods and attacked the whole system indiscriminately in his 95 theses.

Tetzel spent the remaining 22 months of his life defending his position. From Frankfurt on the Oder, he answered Luther with 122 theses (anti-theses) composed by K. WIMPINA (d. 1531). He also published in 1518 *Vorlegung,* a refutation of Luther's position.

In accordance with the polemical techniques of the period, Tetzel was grossly calumniated; accusations included charges of adultery, falsifying bulls, and the granting of absolutions without contrition and for future sins—all at a monetary price. Tetzel was orthodox in regard to indulgences for the living. In regard to those for the dead, however, he followed the teaching contained in the *Mainz Instruction* issued to preachers of indulgences. That is, he taught the then widespread, erroneous theological opinion that indulgences for the dead were gained independently of dispositions of contrition in the person seeking the indulgence, who also had the right to apply them absolutely to a specific soul in purgatory. Cajetan condemned this teaching at Rome. Exhausted by his labors and the cruel attacks upon his reputation, Tetzel died in the Dominican priory at Leipzig at the age of 54.

Bibliography: N. PAULUS, *Johann Tetzel der Ablassprediger* (Mainz 1899). *Historisches Jahrbuch der Görres-Gesellschaft* (1921) 80–86. H. C. GANSS, *The Catholic Encyclopedia*, ed. C. G. HERBERMANN et al., 16 v. (New York 1907–14; suppl. 1922) 14.2:539–541. J. BECKMANN, *Lexikon für Theologie und Kirche*, ed. M. BUCHBERGER, 10 v. (Freiburg 1930–38) 10:10. L. PASTOR, *The History of the Popes from the Close of the Middle Ages*, 40 v. (London-St. Louis 1938–61) 7:347–351, 354–358.

[C. M. AHERNE]

TEUTONIC KNIGHTS

The youngest of the three great religious MILITARY ORDERS (*Domus s. Mariae Theutonicorum in Jerusalem*).

Founding and Organization. The Teutonic Order emerged from a field hospital founded by merchants of Lübeck and Bremen in the camp of Acre in 1190. The company of hospitallers was approved in 1191 by CLEMENT III. On March 5, 1198, it was converted into a religious order of knighthood, and approved in 1199 by INNOCENT III. The order was given the rule of the Knights TEMPLARS; its first grand master (*magister generalis*) was the Rhenish knight Hermann Walpot of Bassenheim. HONORIUS III assured the Teutonic Knights a special status within the Church by issuing a total of 113 bulls defining their feudal relationship to the Roman Curia and forbidding the order to bind itself in vassalage to secular powers. Although there is only one recorded instance of the feudal investiture of a grand master (Gerard of Malberg, 1243), the Curia demanded a recognizance fee at the accession of each new grand master, even as late as the 14th century. The Curia also retained for itself the right to intervene in the internal affairs of the order while giving the knights the same exemption from episcopal authority as that enjoyed by the Templars. As early as 1207, the German king, Philip of Swabia, issued a protective patent for the Teutonic Knights, and in March 1226 Emperor FREDERICK II issued the Golden Bull of Rimini; in its composition the third Grand Master of the Teutonic Knights, HERMAN OF SALZA (1209–39), collaborated. It gave the grand master the same rights as a prince of the empire and permission to acquire the imperial feudal estates in Kulmerland on the Vistula River, promised him by Conrad of Masovia, and in the mission area of Prussia. Since the grand master could not enter into feudal relation with secular powers, he could not be incorporated into the imperial organization. In 1530, however, this did occur when the grand master was elevated to the rank of a prince of the empire, after two commanders of the order, the German master and the Livonian master, had become imperial princes.

At the head of the Teutonic Knights was the grand master, assisted by five grand commanders: the grand knight commander (in charge of the internal administration and deputy to the grand master); the marshal (for arms and supplies and for military affairs); the hospitaller (for medical services and the hospitals attached to each house of the order); the keeper of the wardrobe (for furnishings and victualing); and the treasurer (for finances). To these officials was added after 1309 the house commander of Marienburg. The Grand Assembly (chapter) included, in addition to these high dignitaries, the land commander of Livonia and the ''master in German and Italian lands'' (the German master), and also one or more land commanders. The order was composed of knights, usually of noble birth, priests, often from the middle class, servants, and, as early as the 13th century, sisters as well. In 1244, under the influence of Cardinal William of St. Sabina (formerly bishop of Modena), the rule of the order was redrafted, using that of the Templars as a basis. The priest brothers lived in the main according to the Rule of St. Dominic (*see* DOMINICANS), a fact that influenced the penal code of the Teutonic Knights. The common law that had developed in the order was recorded in its ''Laws'' and ''Customs.'' Attempts to change the statutes (the so-called Orseln Statutes) and to grant wider

Castle of the Order of Teutonic Knights, built 1287-1292 (destroyed 1945), Konigsberg (now Kaliningrad). (©Austrian Archives/ CORBIS)

rights to the grand master were unsuccessful. In the course of time, the status of the highest dignitaries and their relation to one another altered; as early as the 15th century the land master of Livonia and the German master were *de facto* equal in status with the grand master.

The seat of the grand master after the conquest of Acre (1191) was Montfort; after 1291, when Acre had been taken by the Saracens, the headquarters were located for a time in a house on the Grand Canal in Venice and, from 1309, at Marienburg. The Teutonic Knights early acquired estates in Palestine, Armenia, on Cyprus, in Apulia, and Sicily. The order's history in Germany can be traced from the end of 1198; in 1200 one of its houses was established at Halle an der Saale. The order received extensive endowments from imperial property and from that of the German princes in Thuringia, Hesse, Franconia, the Rhinelands, Swabia, the Netherlands, Westphalia, and Saxony, and in almost every imperial city, e.g., Nürnberg, Ulm, Strassburg, and Frankfurt. As early as the 13th century all the numerous holdings and rights of the Teutonic Knights were collected into 12 provinces (*Balleien*), headed by Land Commanders and subdivided into prebends whose chapters consisted usually of a small number of knights and priest brothers. They formed the reserve for the order in Palestine, Prussia, and Livonia. Outside Germany, provinces were established in Lombardy, in the duchy of Austria, in Bohemia, France, Spain (only temporarily), Apulia, and Sicily.

From the 13th to the 16th Century. In 1211 King Andrew II of Hungary called in the Teutonic Knights to aid him against the Cumans, a nomadic tribe of horsemen from the steppes; the king gave the knights holdings in the east border area and entrusted to them a portion of the frontier guard. But when the Teutonic Knights began to seek complete hegemony in this area (now eastern Transylvania around Klausenburg), they clashed with King

Andrew II and his son Bela IV and were expelled in 1226. In the same year the Grand Master Herman of Salza received an appeal for help from the Polish Duke Conrad of Masovia, whose country was threatened by the neighboring non-Catholic Prussians. Though he hesitated for a long time, Herman finally concluded the Treaty of Kruschwitz (June 1230) with Duke Conrad, whereby Kulmerland on the Vistula River was handed over to the Teutonic Knights with all lordly rights. In return, the Knights were to subdue the land of the Prussians. While the authenticity of this treaty has been disputed by Polish research, it is confirmed by German historians. In 1234 GREGORY IX guaranteed these acquisitions the protection of the Holy See. In the spring of 1231 the first Land Master of Prussia, Herman Balk, a Thuringian like Herman of Salza, began the conquest and subjugation of Prussia from the fortress of Nessau on the Vistula. The fortresses of Kulm, Thorn, and Marienwerder were erected in 1232; two years later, with the help of the citizens of Lübeck, the city of Elbing was founded. In 1243, the papal legate, William of St. Sabina, erected four dioceses: Pomesania with its see in Marienwerder (Kwidzyń), Kulm (Chełmno) with its see in Kulmsee (Chełmża), Ermland with its see in Heilsberg (Lidsbark Warmiński), and Samland with its see in Fischhausen.

The legal status of the subjugated Prussians was regulated in the Treaty of Christburg, Feb. 7, 1249, mediated by the papal legate James of Liège (later Pope URBAN IV). The Prussians declared that they preferred to be governed by Polish rather than German law, which had already been established on Dec. 28, 1233, by Herman of Salza for the cities of Kulm and Thorn (Charter of Kulm), but was later applied to rural settlements as well. In 1237 the Teutonic Knights inherited the holdings, rights, and obligations of the KNIGHTS OF THE SWORD (*Fratres militiae Christi*) when this order, founded in 1202 in Livonia, was incorporated into the Teutonic Knights, after lengthy negotiations in the Curia. Thereafter it became the policy of the order to establish an overland connection between the two areas by the acquisition of the Lithuanian Samogitia; its attempt ended in failure after a struggle of almost two centuries. In 1260 the Prussians rose against the rule of the Teutonic Order. By 1273 peace had been restored in the main, and in 1283 the remnant of the Prussian tribe of the Sudauen was settled in Samland, while the main portion emigrated to Lithuania. A large-scale colonization of the country by German settlers, mainly merchants and peasants, could now be initiated. Hundreds of German villages and numerous towns came into existence, protected by fortresses of the order and served by a rigidly centralized administration. At first the segregation of Prussians from Germans was strictly enforced; but this was relaxed as early as the 14th century, when the plague epidemic of 1356 left too few Germans for effective colonization. From the 14th century and in increasing numbers in the 15th, the order accepted both Lithuanian and Polish settlers (from Masovia, the ''Masurians'') into the eastern and southeastern areas of their jurisdiction.

The Teutonic Order was almost entirely occupied with the fight against Lithuania, which had been united with Poland (1385–86). Although the order succeeded in taking Pommerelia and the city of Danzig (Gdańsk) in the west (1309) and buying the Livonian districts of Harrien and Wirland and the city of Reval (Tallin) from Denmark (1346), it did not succeed in bringing Lithuania to her knees. On the contrary, the imprudence and ineptitude of the Grand Master Ulric of Jungingen led to the disastrous defeat at Tannenberg (Grunwald) on July 15, 1410. By the First Peace Treaty of Thorn (1411), the Teutonic Knights had to pay a large indemnity to Poland. The Treaty of Melnosee (1422) with Lithuania fixed the eastern border of the Prussian province of the order at a line where it remained until 1920. The overland link with Livonia, where the order was engaged in a bitter struggle with the archbishop and the city of Riga, was not secured. And so the Livonian master, left to his own devices, was compelled to maintain himself against the other Livonian princes—the archbishop of Riga and the bishops of Dorpat (Tartu) and Ösel-Wiek (Sarema)—and the cities of Riga and Reval, fighting domestically for his hegemony while at the same time trying to hold off the neighboring powers of Lithuania, Novgorod, and Moscow. Thus the Livonian master often had to pursue a policy that differed from that of the grand master of the knights.

Even in the Prussian region, where the order had but seldom granted large holdings to vassal knights, the commercial competition of the order's warehouses and agencies was regarded as an infringement on such thriving cities as Danzig, Elbing, and Königsberg, and the rule of the order was considered oppressive. The petty landed gentry, who had by now become stronger, attempted, in league with the cities, to achieve the right of codetermining the leadership of the order but encountered violent opposition. They banded together into the League of Lizards and rose against the heads of the order. In the Thirteen Years' War (1453–66) they sought and received the support of King Casimir IV of Poland. The order had to make concessions, and the Second Peace Treaty of Thorn (1466) involved the surrender by the order of Pommerelia, Danzig, Kulmerland, and West Prussia. The diocese of Ermland accepted Polish rule and the diocese of Kulm was incorporated into the archdiocese of Gniezno. Marienburg fell to the Poles and the administrative seat of the grand master was moved to the castle in Königsberg. Furthermore, the grand master was compelled to take an oath of homage to the Polish king. With an eye to improving the position of the order, the chapter in 1498 elected Duke Frederick of Saxony, and in 1511 Margrave ALBRECHT OF BRANDENBURG-ANSBACH, as grand master, so as to win support from the princes of the Empire. When this support was not forthcoming, Albrecht converted the Prussian province of the order into a secular duchy and placed it in vassalage to Poland. Since Albrecht converted to Lutheranism, the rank of grand master was transferred to the German master (1530). In Livonia, the Land Master Wolter of Plettenberg (1491–1535) rejected the summons of the estates of the realm to follow Albrecht's example. Only 25 years later, when Ivan IV of Moscow had attacked Livonia and the Reformation had penetrated the cities and the nobility, did the Land Master Gotthard Kettler decide to place a remnant of the order's Prussian province under Polish vassalage as the Duchy of Kurland and Semgallen (1561), while Reval and a part of Esthonia fell to Sweden, and Riga and Livonia to Poland.

From the 17th to the 20th Century. In the Catholic regions of the empire, the Teutonic Order continued to exist under the leadership of the German grand master, with headquarters in Mergentheim in Franconia; it survived also in some Protestant regions, e.g., in the Netherlands (Province of Utrecht, where it continued as a Protestant chivalric order) and in Hesse, where the office of land commander was filled regularly in turn by a Catholic, a Lutheran, and a Calvinist. In most areas, especially in Franconia, southern Württemberg, Baden, and the Austrian Hapsburg dominions, the order's holdings remained untouched and autonomous and the order itself to some extent enjoyed princely rights. In 1606 the rule of the order was revised. The knights fought in the wars with the Turks and even into the 18th century still preserved the idea of the old universal Empire. The richest and most powerful province was Franconia, whose land commanders had their residence, Ellingen Castle, enlarged into one of the most beautiful baroque castles of south Germany.

In 1805 the Teutonic Order was dissolved by Napoleon, and its richest possessions were allotted to the German princes. The Emperor Francis I of Austria restored to the order all its holdings in Austria and became its protector. The order's house in Vienna then became the seat of the grand master, who was henceforth to be an Austrian grand duke. In 1839, the knights received new statutes designed to limit their activity to charitable and pastoral undertakings. From 1840 the sisters of the order devoted themselves to nursing, and in 1845 two communities of priests were established at Lana in the Southern Tyrol and at Troppau in eastern Bohemia. In 1871, Pius IX approved new rules for the priests of the order. Upon the retirement of Grand Master Archduke Maximilian (1918), a priest was elected for the first time as grand master; the rule of Nov. 27, 1929, restored religious discipline within the order, which had declined during the 19th century as a result of the acceptance of secular knights. Up to 1939 there were four provinces—Austria, Troppau, Lana, and Laibach-Ljubljana in Yugoslavia. Troppau and Laibach were expropriated in 1945 together with all their holdings. In Austria the Teutonic Order was paralyzed during the National Socialist occupation. After 1945 it was able to resume its activity, and founded houses in Bavaria (Passau and Thann) and Hesse (Darmstadt and Sachenhausen near Frankfurt). The present headquarters of the order is in Vienna, where it has a fine church and extensive archives.

Bibliography: Sources. J. VOIGT, *Codex diplomaticus prussicus (1148–1404)*, 6 v. (Königsberg 1836–61). J. H. HENNES, *Codex diplomaticus ordinis S. Mariae Theutonicorum,* 2 v. (Mainz 1845–61). E. STREHLKE, *Tabulae ordinis Theutonici* (Berlin 1869). *Scriptores rerum Prussicarum* 5 v. (Leipzig 1861–74). *Livländische Reimchronik,* ed. L. MEYER (Paderborn 1876). M. TOEPPEN, *Akten der Ständetage Preussens unter der Herrschaft des D.O.,* 5 v. (Leipzig 1878–86). E. G. GRAF VON PETTENEGG, *Die Urkunden des Deutschordenszentralarchivs zu Wien,* v.1 (Prague-Leipzig 1887). *Liv-, Est- und Kurländisches Urkundenbuch nebst Regesten,* ed. F. G. V. BUNGE et al., 12 v. (Reval 1852–58; Riga 1881–1914). *Akten und Rezesse der livländischen Ständetage,* ed. O. STAVENHAGEN et al., 3 v. (Riga 1907–34). K. H. LAMPE, *Urkundenbuch der Deutschordensballei Thüringen,* v.1 (1140–1331) (Jena 1936). *Hessisches Urkundenbuch,* Abt. 1 *Urkundenbuch der Ballei Hessen,* ed. A. WYSS, 3 v. (Leipzig 1879–99). *Preussisches Urkundenbuch,* ed. F. PHILIPPI et al., 4 v. (Königsberg 1882–1944; Marburg 1958–63). *Die Staatsverträge des D.O. in Preussen im 15. Jahrhundert,* ed. E. WEISE, 2 v. (Königsberg 1939; Marburg 1955). *Regesta Ordinis S. Mariae Theutonicorum, 1198–1525,* ed. E. JOACHIM and W. HUBATSCH, 4 v. (Göttingen 1948–50). *Das grosse Ämterbuch des D.O.,* ed. W. ZIESEMER (Danzig 1921). *Das Marienburger Konventsbuch der Jahre 1399–1412,* ed. W. ZIESEMER (Danzig 1913). *Das Marienburger Tresslerbuch der Jahre 1399–1409,* ed. E. JOACHIM (Königsberg 1896). **Literature.** J. VOIGT, *Geschichte Preussens von den ältesten Zeiten bis zum Untergang der Herrschaft des D.O.,* 9 v. (Königsberg 1827–39); *Geschichte des Deutschen Ritter-Ordens in seinen 12 Balleien in Deutschland,* 2 v. (Berlin 1857–59). E. MASCHKE, *Der D.O. und die Preussen* (Berlin 1928). W. COHN, *Hermann von Salza* (Breslau 1930). E. E. STENGEL, *Hochmeister und Reich* (Weimar 1930). C. KROLLMANN, *Politische Geschichte des D.O. in Preussen* (Königsberg 1932). F. MILTHALER, *Die Grossgebietiger des Dt. Ritter-Ordens biss 1440* (Königsberg-Berlin 1940). R. TEN HAAF, *Deutschordensstaat und Deutschordensballeien* (Göttingen 1951). M. TUMLER, *Der D.O. im Werden, Wachsen und Wirken bis 1400* (Vienna 1954). W. HUBATSCH, ''Der D.O. und die Reichslehenschaft über Zypern,'' *Nachrichten von der Akademie der Wissenschaften in Göttingen* (1956) 245–306. B. SCHUMACHER, *Geschichte Ostund Westpreussens* (Königsberg 1937; 2d ed. Würzburg 1957). M. HELLMANN, ''Bemerkungen zur sozialgeschichtlichen Erforschung des D.O.,'' *Historisches Jahrbuch der Görres-Gesellschaft* 80 (1961) 126–142; ''Über die Grundlagen und die Entstehung des Ordensstaates in Preussen,'' *Nachrichten der Giessener Hochscludgesellschaft* 31 (1962) 108–126. H. PATZE, ''Der Frieden von Christburg vom Jahre 1249,'' *Jahrbuch für die Geschichte Mittelund Ostdeutschlands* 7 (Berlin 1958) 39–91. K. FORSTREUTER, *Die Gesch-*

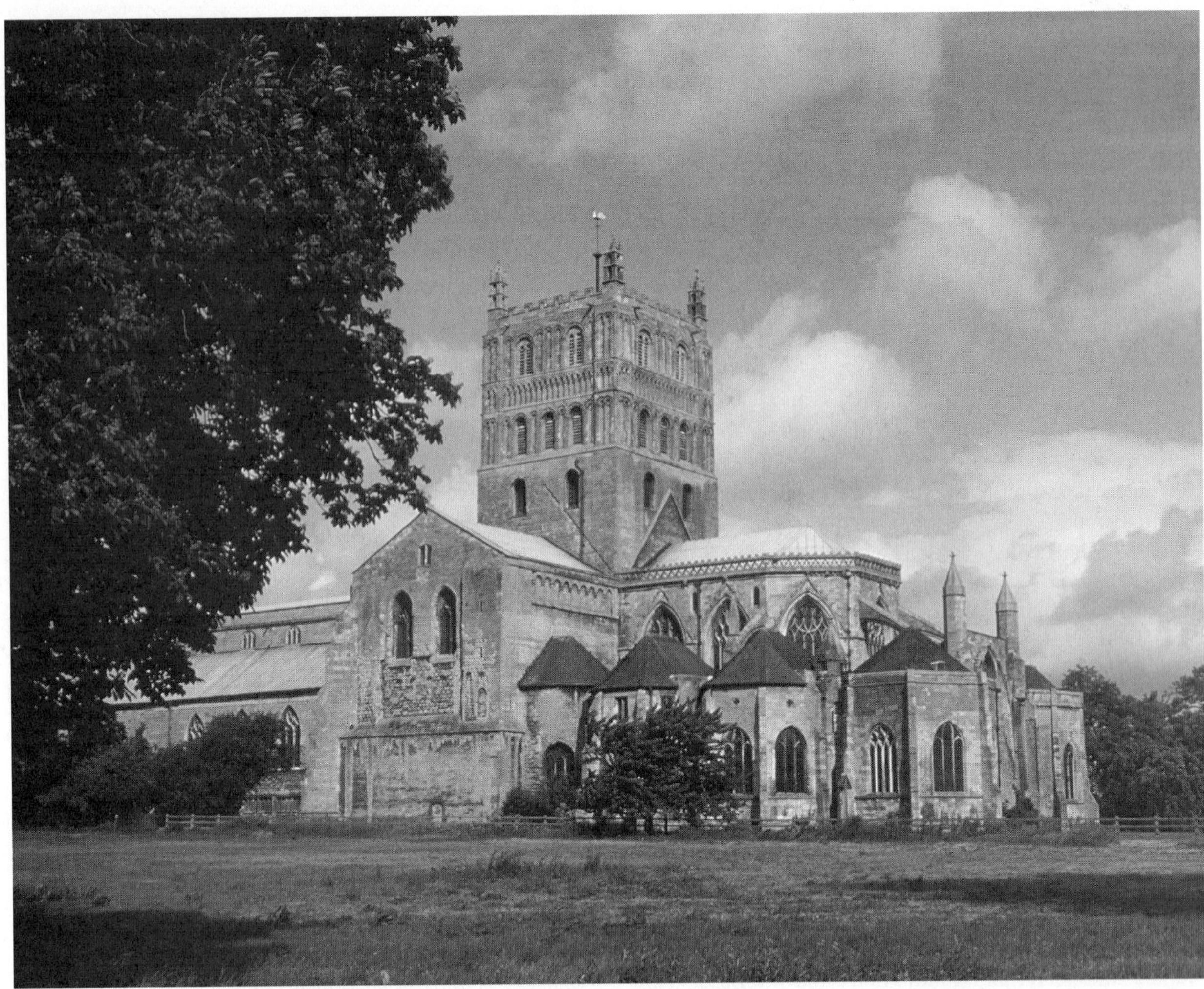

Abbey at Tewkesbury. (©Buddy Mays/CORBIS)

ichte der Generalprokuratoren von den Anfängen bis 1403 (Göttingen 1961). H. KOEPPEN, *Peter von Wormditt, 1403–1419* (Göttingen 1960). W. HUBATSCH, *Albrecht von Brandenburg-Ansbach* (Heidelberg 1960). H. FREIWALD, *Markgraf Albrecht von Ansbach-Kulmbach* (Kulmbach 1961). H. H. HOFMANN, ''Die Verfassung des D.O. am Ende des alten Reichs (1788),'' *Zeitschrift für bayrische Landesgeschichte* 27 (1963) 40–389. E. WEISE, ''Der Heidenkampf des D.O.,'' *Zeitschrift für Ostforschung* 12 (1963) 420–473, 622–672; 13 (1964) 401–420.

[M. HELLMANN]

TEWKESBURY, ABBEY OF

Former Benedictine monastery at Tewkesbury, Gloucestershire, England. There was a monastery on this site at the end of the 8th century. In 980 it became dependent on Cranborne Abbey (Dorset), which staffed it with a Benedictine prior and monks. It was reendowed (1107) by Robert Fitz-hamon, Lord of Gloucester and cousin to King William II, and the first Norman abbot of Cranborne, Gerald, subsequently transferred there with most of his community. The new abbey was consecrated in 1123. It is second only to WESTMINSTER in the number of great personages interred within its walls; e.g., the de Clares, Despensers, Beauchamps, and the Nevilles, who held the lordship of Tewkesbury, were buried in the abbey of which they had been generous patrons. The abbey had an insatiable appetite for the appropriation of churches, and its dependencies ultimately included Bristol, Cardiff, Cranborne, Deerhurst, Goldcliff, Llantwit Major, and an almshouse in Tewkesbury. During the episcopal visitations of 1279 and 1378 certain abuses came to light, and Henry Wakefield, Bishop of WORCESTER, found that the education of the younger monks was neglected and ordered the appointment of a competent teacher (1378). At its suppression in 1540 under King HENRY VIII, 36 monks were pensioned, and the last abbot, John Wakeman, was consecrated bishop of Gloucester,

1541. The abbey church is noted for its unique western arch and the great Norman tower.

Bibliography: *The Victoria History of the County of Gloucester,* ed. W. PAGE (London 1907–) v.2. M. R. JAMES, *Abbeys* (Garden City, NY 1926). D. KNOWLES, *The Religious Houses of Medieval England* (London 1940). D. KNOWLES, *The Monastic Order in England, 943–1216* (2d ed. Cambridge, England 1962).

[T. C. CROWLEY]

TEXAS, CATHOLIC CHURCH IN

After Alaska, Texas is the largest of the states. It embraces an area of 267,339 square miles divided into 254 counties. The boundaries, for the most part, are the natural ones: the Rio Grande on the west and south, the Gulf shore line and the Sabine River on the east, the Red River on much of the north. The Panhandle, separating Texas from Oklahoma and New Mexico, is delimited by straight lines established in conformity with various treaties and agreements. Texas can be divided roughly into four great natural regions stretching in irregular belts from north to south: the east Texas plains, an area of extensive timberlands and rich agricultural soil that supports cotton, corn, sugar cane, and dairy cattle; the Texas prairies, a fertile, grassy strip that is the most populous region of the state; the middle Texas province, which was the original cattle range of Texas; and the subhumid, arid western high plains. Almost 80 percent of the people live in urban areas. Houston is the largest city, and Austin is the capital. Other large metropolitan areas center on Dallas, San Antonio, El Paso, and Fort Worth.

In 2001 the state population was 20,851,820 with Catholics numbering 5,915,566, about 25 percent of the total. There were 15 dioceses, including the metropolitan see of San Antonio. San Antonio was established as a diocese in 1874 and made an archdiocese in 1926. The 14 suffragan sees as they stood in 2001 were Amarillo (est. 1926); Austin (1948); Beaumont (1966); Brownsville (1965); Corpus Christi (1912); Dallas (est.1890; redesignated Dallas-Fort Worth, 1953; returned to original designation, 1969); El Paso (1914), Fort Worth (1969); Galveston-Houston (Galveston, est. 1847; redesignated Galveston-Houston, 1959); Laredo (2000); Lubbock (1983); San Angelo (1961); Tyler (1986); and Victoria (1982).

Early Missions. The Apache, Comanche, and other native tribes inhabited the territory when the Spanish established their first settlement in 1682 near the site of present day El Paso. The Spanish occupation of the northernmost reaches of New Spain, including Texas, was accomplished largely by Franciscan missionaries. Between 1690 and 1794 they established a chain of 36 missions,

Archdiocese/Diocese	Year Created
Archdiocese of San Antonio	1926
Diocese of Amarillo	1926
Diocese of Austin	1948
Diocese of Beaumont	1966
Diocese of Brownsville	1965
Diocese of Corpus Christi	1912
Diocese of Dallas	1969
Diocese of El Paso	1969
Diocese of Fort Worth	1969
Diocese of Galveston-Houston	1959
Diocese of Lubbock	1983
Diocese of San Angelo	1961
Diocese of Tyler	1986
Diocese of Victoria in Texas	1982

clustered in three broad areas. In the years 1690 to 1693 and 1716 to 1719, the friars constructed a half-dozen missions in eastern Texas. They began with the establishment of Mission San Francisco de los Tejas in 1690 by Fray Damián Massanet. A second cluster was established in the vicinity of Matagorda Bay, inland from the Gulf of Mexico; and a third, centered around the mission San Antonio de Béxar, included the Mission San Antonio de Valero (the Alamo) built in 1718 by Fray Antonio de San Buenaventura y Olivares. Other missions in the last cluster were Mission San José y San Miguel de Aguayo constructed in 1720 and three established in 1731: La Purisima Conception, San Juan Capistrano, and San Francisco de la Espada.

For well over a century the missionaries, among whom Antonio MARGIL de Jésus was best known, labored on the frontier and at various places in the interior. The Spanish authorities had planned to convert each mission into a parish church and to turn the mission property over to self-reliant individuals who would be served by a parish priest while the padres moved into another frontier to begin the whole process anew. In theory the mission was dynamic, but in practice the results were largely ineffectual from the government's point of view. The mission system was gradually abandoned and secularization was completed by 1794, when the lands surrounding some of the missions were divided among friendly tribes. The social and political unrest attendant upon the gradual disintegration of Spanish sovereignty at the beginning of the 19th century gave rise to a prolonged period of political uncertainty. The remaining Spanish missionaries were expelled in 1820, departed, and secular priests were unavailable. A period of complete spiritual neglect set in, and there was no improvement under Mexican rule.

Although Texas was opened to foreigners, entry was restricted to Catholics. After 1825 Stephen F. Austin and

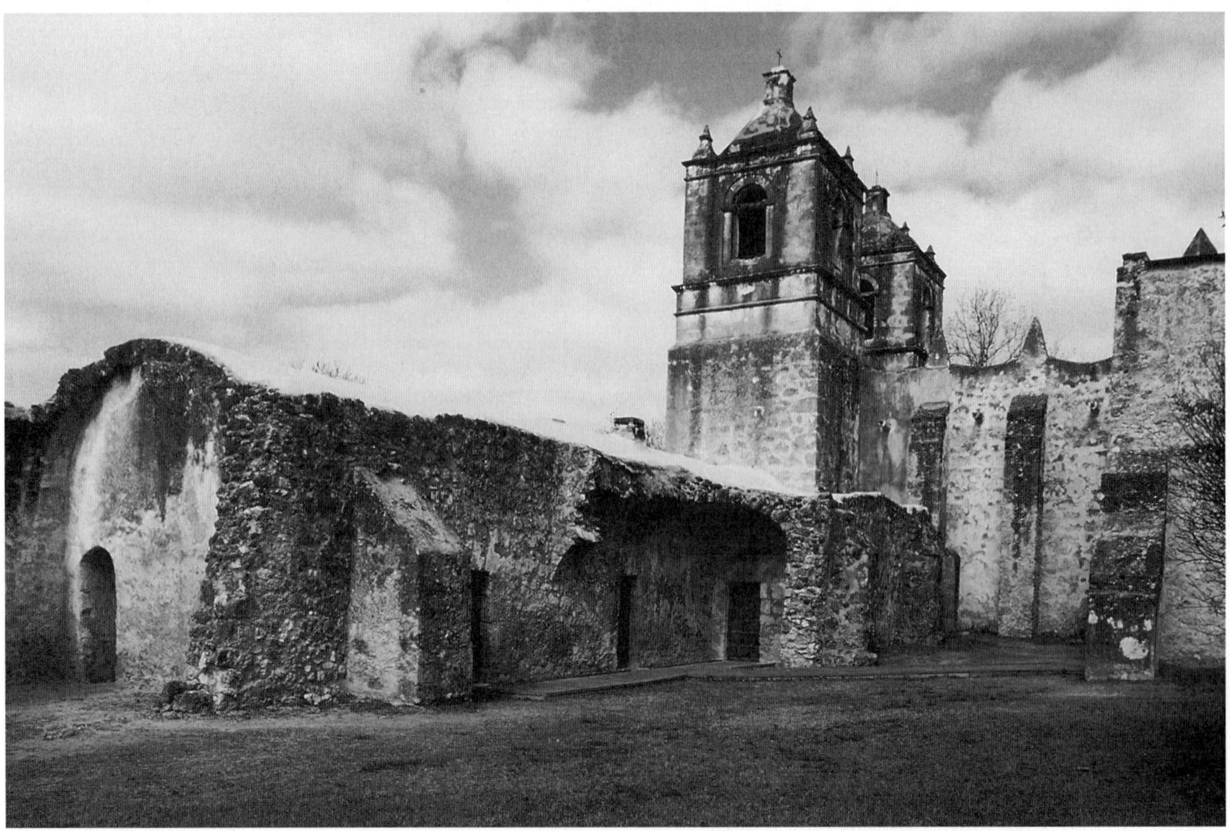

Exterior of Mission Concepcion, built between 1733 and 1755, San Antonio, Texas. (©Sandy Felsenthal/CORBIS)

other *empresarios* brought in numerous colonists from the United States who willingly accepted nominal membership in the Church. There were not enough priests, however, to serve the needs of practicing Catholics, let alone merely nominal ones.

Ninteenth-Century Developments. When Texas became an independent republic in 1836 and sought annexation to the United States, Texan Catholics technically remained under the spiritual jurisdiction of the bishop of Monterrey, Mexico. Bishop Anthony Blanc of New Orleans, La., recognizing that ecclesiastical jurisdictional difficulties would inhibit the revival of religion in the Republic of Texas, asked the Congregation for the Propagation of the Faith to study the problem. John TIMON, CM, who was sent to investigate in 1838, compiled a lengthy report on the basis of which the Holy See created a prefecture apostolic and assigned the Vincentians to the task of renewing religion. Timon was appointed prefect apostolic. In 1842 John M. Odin, CM, was consecrated bishop to head a separate vicariate apostolic, and in 1847 he was named bishop of the newly created diocese of Galveston.

With enlarged administrative powers Odin brought about a remarkable revival as old parishes were reoccupied and new ones begun to serve the immigrants who were settling in the eastern part of the state. In the 1830s Irish established Refugio and San Patricio de Hibernia. Germans populated New Braunfels (1844) and Fredericksburg (1848). Belgians, French, and Swiss settled west of San Antonio. In 1854 Polish immigrants founded Panna Maria (Virgin Mary) where Fr. Leopold Moczygemba, then a member of the Conventual Franciscans, dedicated the Church of the Immaculate Conception in 1856.

As the Church continued to flourish further administrative changes were necessitated. In 1874 a new diocese was established along the Rio Grande in SAN ANTONIO and Anthony Dominic Pellicer was named the first bishop (1874–80). In response to the needs of the Catholic population in north central Texas, the Dallas diocese was organized in 1890. The first bishop, Thomas F. Brennan (1891–92) resigned after a year and was succeeded by Bishop Edward Josesph Dunne (1893–10). In south Texas, where many people of Spanish descent lived and where the Oblates of Mary Immaculate served in a great number of parishes, the Diocese of Corpus Christi was erected in 1912. West Texas developed rapidly at the turn of the century, and the Diocese of EL PASO was created in 1914. At the time it included territory in southern New

Mexico. El Paso remained a suffragan see of the Archdiocese of Santa Fe until 1982.

Twentieth Century. As the 20th century advanced, the Church recognized the need for a general ecclesiastical reorganization to serve the greater needs of the state. On Aug. 3, 1926, PIUS XI raised San Antonio to an archdiocese and erected a new diocese in Amarillo. In 1948 the Diocese of Austin was organized in central Texas. Galveston, the oldest diocese in the state, was redesignated in 1959 as the diocese of Galveston-Houston, recognizing that Houston had become one of the populous cities in the country. Dallas began as a vicariate apostolic in 1874, was made a diocese in 1890; in 1953 it was redesignated as the Diocese of Dallas-Fort Worth, only to be redesignated as the Diocese of Dallas in 1969 when Fort Worth became a separate diocese. Meanwhile San Angelo, in west central Texas, was made an episcopal see in 1961. The Vicariate Apostolic established in 1874 in Beaumont and later subsumed into the diocese of Corpus Christi (1912), was made a diocese in 1966. As the Catholic population of Texas continued to grow, more new dioceses were created in the years after the second VATICAN COUNCIL: Victoria in 1982; Lubbock in 1983; Tyler in 1986, and Laredo in 2000. In 1964 the bishops established the Texas Catholic Conference to provide a forum in which the dioceses of the state can exchange information and coordinate their activities regarding government policy and legislation on social issues and other issues of concern to the Church.

In the wake of Vatican II, continued growth of the Catholic population, and social change, the Church experimented with new approaches to ministry. After the Vietnam War, communities of Asian Catholics necessitated the establishment of Vietnamese parishes in many places. Most dioceses established programs to prepare men for the permanent diaconate and nearly everyone had promoted the training of lay ministry. The laity took the lead in such movements as CHARISMATIC RENEWAL and MARRIAGE ENCOUNTER. The CURSILLO MOVEMENT, begun in Spain, had its American beginning in Texas. Laity and clergy alike made concerted efforts to maintain the best of the Hispanic heritage in Texas. In the 1970s advocacy groups like the Padres, an organization of Mexican-American priests and Las Hermanas, an organization made up chiefly of women religious, worked hard for the advancement of Hispanics. Their efforts and the efforts of similar groups led to the appointment of bishops with Hispanic ancestry. Bishop Patricio F. Flores, the first Mexican-American bishop in the nation, was appointed to the diocese of El Paso in 1978, to the archdiocese of San Antonio, the following year.

Education. In the belief that Catholic schools were necessary to put the Church on solid foundations, as early as 1847 Bishop Odin persuaded the Ursulines from New Orleans to start a school in Galveston. In 1851 another community of Ursulines was established in San Antonio. From these two solid establishments the Ursulines spread to various parts of Texas. Many other religious congregations of women joined them in the work of education, including the Congregation of the Incarnate Word, the Sisters of Divine Providence, the Sacred Heart Dominican Sisters, and the Sisters of the Holy Ghost and Mary Immaculate, who conducted schools for African Americans. In 1964 there were approximately 70 religious communities of women in Texas, most of them engaged in teaching. To take care of the education of boys in San Antonio, Odin secured the services of the Society of Mary, which furnished him with four teachers able to teach in English, Spanish, German, and French. The brothers opened St. Mary's Institute (1852), which developed into St. Mary's University, the largest Catholic college in the Southwest. In 2001 there were 235 elementary schools, 47 secondary schools, and eight colleges and universities under Catholic auspices in Texas.

In many parts of the state bilingual clergy and teachers were indispensible for those of Mexican descent, who form the largest minority in Texas. A special Catholic council was organized to provide for the religious, social, economic, educational, and cultural advancement of these Mexican-Americans. In 1945 this council was given status by the bishops of the Southwest when they formed their own bishops' committee for the Spanish speaking. Among its other tasks, the bishops' committee undertook the monitoring of the socioeconomic conditions of migrant workers, urging remedial legislation and providing educational opportunities for their children.

Bibliography: R. F. BAYARD, *Lone Star Vanguard: The Catholic Reoccupation of Texas, 1838–1848* (St. Louis 1945). C. E. CASTAÑEDA, *Our Catholic Heritage in Texas, 1519–1936,* 7v. (Austin 1936–58). B. DOYON, *The Cavalry of Christ on the Rio Grande, 1849–1883* (Milwaukee 1956). F. D. ALMARAZ, JR., ''The Legacy of Columbus: Spanish Mission Policy in Texas,'' *Journal of Texas Catholic History and Culture* 3 (1992) 17–36. P. FOLEY, ''Jean-Marie Odin, C.M., Missionary Bishop Extraordinaire of Texas,'' *Journal of Texas Catholic History and Culture* 1 (1990) 42–60. J. T. MOORE, *Through Fire and Flood: The Catholic Church in Frontier Texas, 1836–1900* (College Station 1992).C. E. NOLAN, ''Modest and Humble Crosses: A History of Catholic Parishes in South Central Region (1850–1984)'' in J. P. DOLAN, ed., *The American Catholic Parish,* v. 1. (New York 1987). M. C. MORKOVSKY, ''Challenges of Catholic Evangelization in Texas: The Response of Women Religious,'' *Journal of Texas Catholic History and Culture* 5 (1944) 65–90. R. E. WRIGHT, ''Pioneer Religious Congregations of Men in Texas Before 1990,'' *Journal of Texas Catholic History* 65–90.

[J. W. SCHMITZ/G. CARIE]

TEZZA, LUIGI, BL.

Camillus priest, founder of the Congregation of the Daughters of St. Camillus ; b. Nov. 1, 1841, Coneglione Veneto (Treviso), Italy; d. Sept. 26, 1923, Lima, Peru. Early in life Luigi's faith was nourished by that of his mother, Caterina Nedwiedt (d. 1880), who joined the Visitation nuns at Padua in 1858. His father, a doctor who worked untiringly until his death at age 36 (1850), gave direction to young Luigi's desire to serve God in his neighbor. He joined the CAMILLIANS on Oct. 29, 1856, at the novitiate in Verona. He was ordained priest May 21, 1864, and celebrated his first Mass at his mother's convent two days later.

He was assigned to the house at San Giuliano during the Battle of Custoza (June 1886) and when the Piedmontese troops entered the town on October 22. In 1886, the religious orders were suppressed. Tezza and two of his confreres accepted an invitation to join Bl. Daniele Comboni's African mission; however, permission was not granted.

He was appointed assistant master of novices in Rome (1869), then master of novices at Cuisery (France, 1870). In France he also served as superior and founder of four homes for the sick and aged until the religous orders were suppressed there (1880). He remained clandestinely for three months after the Camillians were expelled and was denounced several times, but managed to evade capture.

At the 1889 General Chapter, he was elected procurator general and retreated to the hospital at St. John Lateran, where he could serve the sick without molestation. Together with Bl. Giuditta (Giuseppina) VANNINI, whom he met on retreat (Dec. 17, 1891), Fr. Tezza founded a convent of young women dedicated to the service of the sick on Feb. 2, 1892.

In 1898, he returned to France and two years later he was sent to Lima as a visitator to settle a dispute that arose among the brothers there. The matter was settled within two months; however, the archbishop and apostolic vicar ordered him to remain in Lima until more brothers arrived. Obediently he remained there for another 23 years —until his death—working in the hospitals, serving as confessor to the archbishop, apostolic nuncio, priests, seminarians, and monks.

In 1948, his corpse was transferred to Buenos Aires, Argentina, where it rested in the chapel of the provincial house of the Daughters of St. Camillus until it was translated to the motherhouse chapel in Grottaferrata, Italy (December 1999). He was beatified by Pope John Paul II on Nov. 4, 2001.

Feast: Sept. 26.

Bibliography: L. MIGLIOLI, *Und er sagte ja: P. Luigi Tezza, Gründer der Töchter des Heiligen Kamillus* (Leutesdorf 1981). *I primi cinque capitoli generali dei Ministri degli infermi*, ed. P. SANNAZZARO (Rome 1979).

[K. I. RABENSTEIN]

THAILAND, SEVEN MARTYRS OF, BB.

Also known as Philip Siphong and Six Companions; d. December 1940 at Ban Songkhon on the banks of the Mekong River about 400 miles from Bangkok; beatified at Rome by John Paul II, Oct. 22, 1989.

A small village of rice farmers about 15 miles upstream from Mukdahan on the Mekong River was the home the first Thais to be raised to the altars of the Catholic Church. They were caught up in a persecution of Christians, particularly Catholics, that resulted in foreign missionaries being expelled from the country and religious pluralism actively suppressed by police who went from door to door. Two religious sisters and five catechists (one man and four women) were killed nearby for refusing to renounce their faith. Today a new church, displaying the glass-topped caskets of the martyrs, and a memorial site serve the 2,000 Catholics of the parish and a steady stream of pilgrims. The martyrs include:

Agatha Phutta, wife and mother; b. 1881; d. Dec. 26, 1940. She served the missionaries as cook prior to their banishment.

Agnes Phila, religious of the Servants of the Cross; b. 1909, Ban; d. Dec. 26, 1940. Sister Agnes, a teacher, was appointed superior of the Songkhon Catholic school in 1932. She encouraged the other women to remain steadfast and wrote a defense of the faith before her execution.

Cecilia Butsi, catechist; b. 1924; d. Dec. 26, 1940. She was martyred for publicly defending the faith in defiance of the police.

Lucy Khambang, religious of the Servants of the Cross; b. 1917, Viengkuk, Thailand; d. Dec. 26, 1940. She entered the congregation in 1931 and was sent to Songkhon in 1917.

Mary Phon, mission helper, catechist; b. 1926; d. Dec. 26, 1940 in the Songkhon cemetery.

Philip Siphong Onphitak, lay catechist, known as ''the man of oak''; b. Sept. 30, 1907, Nonseng, Thailand; d. Dec. 16, 1940, shot in the woods near the village (age 33). Blessed Philip and his wife Maria Thong had five children. While the priests were banished, he led the community, taught in the school, and served as the catechist. Despite the known danger of his actions, he followed behind the police to encourage the threatened faithful.

Viviane (Bibiana) Khampai, catechist; b. 1925; d. Dec. 26, 1940 in Songkhon cemetery.

Feast: Dec. 16.

Bibliography: *Acta Apostolicae Sedis* (Rome 1989) 1079.

[K. I. RABENSTEIN]

THAILAND, THE CATHOLIC CHURCH IN

Capital: Bangkok.
Size: 198,455 sq. miles.
Population: 61,230,874 in 2000; ethnic Thais comprise some three-fourths of the population. There is a small but economically significant ethnic Chinese community.
Religion: 95% of the Thai population are Buddhists, predominantly of the Theravada school. Muslims, who are found mainly in the southern region bordering Malaysia, account for about 4% of the population. The Christian community is very small, comprising less than 1% of the total population. Catholics account for about 0.5% of the total population.
Metropolitan Sees: Bangkok, with suffragans Chanthaburi, Chiang Mai, Nakhon Sawan, Ratchaburi, Surat Thani; Thare-Nongseng with suffragans Nakhon Ratchasima, Ubon Ratchathani, Udon Thani.

Located in Southeast Asia, bordered by Cambodia, Laos, Burma and Malaysia, Thailand was known as Siam until 1939. Modern-day Thailand, the ''Land of the Free'' has the distinction of being one of the few Asian countries that was never colonized by a European power. From the beginning, the region came under Mon (Burmese) and Khmer control. The emergence of the Sukhothai kingdom in 1238 marked the beginnings of a Thai kingdom independent of the Mon and Khmer empires. During this period, Theravada BUDDHISM took root and flowered among the Thai people. At the height of the Ayutthaya empire (1351–1767), Thai armies devastated the Khmer empire and sacked its famed capital, Angkor. Portuguese ships making their way northward after the conquest of Malacca in 1511 brought the first Europeans traders and missionaries to Ayutthaya, followed by the Dutch, English, Spanish and French, all of whom entered into diplomatic and trade relations with the Ayutthayan kings. In the years leading up to and ensuing from the collapse of the Ayutthaya empire, nationalistic sentiments resulted in the wholesale expulsions of Europeans.

Modern Thai history began with the ascent of General Chakri into power as King Rama I (1782–1809). Early in his reign, he transferred the royal capital to Bangkok. King Nang Klao, Rama III (1824–1851) initiated new trade relations with European powers, culminating in diplomatic treaties that were concluded between King Mongkut, Rama IV (1851–1868) and European governments. Setting out to refashion Siam into a modern nation on par with European nations, and wishing to fend off European attempts to colonize the land, King Mongkut initiated a series of social and economic reforms that were continued by his son, Chulalongkorn, King Rama V (1869–1910). Known as the Father of Modern Thailand, King Chulalongkorn is best remembered for his far-reaching reforms, including the abolition of slavery and the reform of administrative, educational, public welfare, legislative and judicial structures.

Siam's first encounter with Christianity took place in the 16th century with the arrival of Portuguese trading ships with Catholic chaplains on board. Missionary activity proper began with the arrival of two Portuguese Dominicans, Jeromino da Cruz and Sebastiao da Canto in Ayutthaya, the capital city in 1567. The Franciscans arrived in 1582, followed by the Jesuits in 1607. Until 1662, all missionaries in Siam were under the aegis of the Portuguese *Padroado.* On Aug. 22, 1662, three missionaries from the Paris Foreign Mission Society (Société Mission Étrangères de Paris, MEP), Msgr. Pierre Lambert de la Motte, Jean De Bourges, and M. Dedier arrived in Ayutthaya. They were welcomed by ten Portuguese priests and one Spanish priest serving a Christian community of about 2,000. Unlike the Dominicans, Franciscans and Jesuits, these three new arrivals were sent by the Congregation for the Propagation of the Faith (*Propaganda Fide*). Two years later, on Jan. 27, 1664, Msgr. François Pallu together with three MEP missionaries, M. Laneau, M. Haingues, M. Brindeau and a lay assistant De Chamesone-Folssy arrived in Siam. Their arrival corresponded with the long and prosperous period of King Narai the Great (1657-1688) who opened the country to foreigners and allowed missionaries to preach the Gospel. The decision of King Narai to ally with the French as a counterweight against the Dutch paved the way for the French MEP missionaries to operate in relative freedom.

In 1664, the MEP missionaries organized an assembly, the so-called the Synod of Ayutthaya. The 1664 synod approved the formation of a new apostolic congregation to be called Amateurs de la Croix de Jesus Christ, the erection of a seminary to train indigenous clergy, as well as the publication of Propaganda Fide's *Instructions to Vicar Apostolics* and *Instructions to Missionaries.* Implementing the decisions of the synod, Lambert de la

Motte opened a seminary for indigenous clergy, College General in Ayutthaya in 1665. Four years later, in 1669, he founded the first mission hospital in Ayutthaya. Besides Ayutthaya, missionaries preached the Gospel in Phitsanulok, Lopburi, Samkhok and Bangkok. In 1674, the church of the Immaculate Conception in Samsen district of Bangkok was built. While the Christian community was growing, it comprised mainly European traders, as well as Vietnamese, Chinese and Japanese nationals fleeing persecution in their homeland. After more than a century of missionary activity, there were only about 600 indigenous Siamese Catholics in 1674.

The 1688 revolution brought the anti-French Phra Phetraja in power. Phra Phetraja expelled many French missionaries, closed College General, and persecuted the local Christians. The persecution continued during the reign of King Taisra (1709–1733), who forbade missionaries to leave the capital or to use the Thai and Pali language in their teaching of religion. Sporadic persecutions continued through the fall of the Kingdom of Ayutthaya in 1767, into the reign of King Taksin (1768–1782), who ordered the expulsion of foreign missionaries.

With the advent of the Chakri dynasty in 1782, conditions for missionary activity improved gradually. Wishing to initiate new alliances and trading relations with European powers, King Rama I (1782–1809) welcomed missionaries to his capital. A. Launay recorded that there were about 2,500 Catholics in Siam in 1802, and about 3,000 in 1811. In 1827, Pope Leo XII granted ecclesiastical jurisdiction over Singapore to the Vicar Apostolic of Siam. In 1841, an outstanding missionary, Msgr. Jean-Baptiste Pallegoix was appointed Vicar Apostolic of Siam. Pallegoix, who was vicar apostolic from 1841 to 1862, had a brilliant mind and deep knowledge of the sciences, mathematics and languages. He acquired a profound knowledge of Siamese and Pali languages and was the author of the first ever Thai-Latin-French-English dictionary, the first such fundamental work for the Thai language While he was in residence at the Immaculate Conception church in the Samsen district of Bangkok, he learned Pali from Prince Mongkut (the future King Rama IV who ruled Thailand from 1851–68) who had entered the monkhood at the nearby Wat Rajathivas. In turn, Prince Mongkut took lessons in Latin, astronomy and mathematics from him.

The period from the 1860s to the beginning of the 20th century witnessed much growth, fueled by the arrival of Catholic refugees fleeing turmoil and persecution in China and Vietnam. In 1872, the Catholic community numbered some 10,000, with 20 foreign missionaries and 8 indigenous priests. By 1909, the number had grown to about 23,600 Catholics, with 59 seminarians, 44 foreign missionaries, 21 indigenous priests 17 religious men, 123 religious women, and 21 catechists. Much of the growth came about through the efforts of the indefatigable vicar apostolic, Msgr. Jean-Louis Vey (1875–1909). Thus far, missionary activities centered in central, eastern and western regions of Siam, with little activity in the northern region. Recognizing this deficiency, Msgr. Vey sent P. Prodhomme and P. Xavier Guego to begin a new northern mission on Jan. 2, 1881. Subsequent waves of missionaries worked their way northward into Laos. Recognizing the success of this mission, Pope Leo XIII erected the vicariate apostolic of Laos on May 4, 1899. His successor, Msgr. Perros (1909–1947) focused on the northwestern region, sending missionaries to Chiengmai, Chiengrai, and Lampang. Missionaries also advanced to Nakornratchasima. In addition to missionary activities, Msgr. Vey also established modern schools and hospitals. In 1885, with his encouragement, P. Colombet had founded Assumption College, the first Catholic college in Bangkok. In 1901, he invited the Brothers of St. Gabriel to Bangkok to take over the running of Assumption College. Similarly, Msgr. Vey founded the St. Louis Hospital and in 1898, he invited the Sisters of St. Paul de Chartres to take charge of it.

The period of the Second World War was a difficult time for Christians in Thailand. Anti-European ultranationalistic movements reacted strongly against the Catholic Church, viewing it as a French bastion in the country. The ultra-nationalists exerted extreme pressure on Thai Christians to renounce Christianity and embrace Buddhism, on the premise that to be a loyal Thai, one had to be Buddhist. Churches were burnt down or looted in many places. In Ban Songkhon, on the Mekong river (in the northeastern region of Thailand), seven Catholics who refused to renounce their faith were shot dead during December 1941. On Oct. 22, 1989, Pope John Paul II beatified these seven martyrs (*see* THAILAND, SEVEN MARTYRS OF, BB). A priest, Fr. Nicolas Bunkerd Kitbamrung died in prison on Jan. 12, 1944. Pope John Paul II beatified him on Mar. 5, 2000.

In the years following the conclusion of the Second Vatican Council, the Thai Church enthusiastically embraced the use of vernacular languages at Mass and explored opportunities to inculturate the Christian Gospel and the Church on Thai soil. The first step toward this end was made when Pope Paul VI, by the bull *Qui in fastigio,* formally established the local hierarchy on Dec. 18, 1965, creating the two ecclesiastical provinces of Bangkok and Thare Nongseng and appointing the first Thai archbishops. Another first occurred when Pope John Paul II made the second Archbishop of Bangkok, Michael Michai Kitbunchu a cardinal on Feb. 2, 1983. Subsequently, Pope John Paul II made the first ever papal visit to Thailand on May 10, 1984.

From its inception, the Thai Catholic Church has remained small in size. Nevertheless, it has played an important role in the Thai society. Its impact is felt especially in the field of education, social and public welfare. It has set up facilities to care for the huge number of AIDS victims from the 1980s onward. In 1975, the Catholic Office for Emergency Relief and Refugees (COERR) was created to minister to the social, pastoral and spiritual needs of refugees fleeing from Vietnam, Cambodia and Laos, and later from Burma. In remote mountain regions, missionaries continue to work with communities ravaged by poverty, lack of education and public health facilities, in a concerted effort to stem the problem of families selling their daughters into prostitution.

Worshipers inside a Thai Catholic Cathedral. (©Horace Bristol/ CORBIS)

Bibliography: J. GUENNOU, *Les Missions Étrangères* (Paris 1963–86). E.W. HUTCHINSON, *1688 Revolution in Siam: The Memoir of Father de Beze, S.J.* (Hong Kong 1968). A. LAUNAY, *Histoire de la mission de Siam,* 2 v. (Paris 1920–23). A. DA SILVA, *Documentacao para a Historia das Missoes do Padroado Portuges do Oriente* (Lisbon 1952).

[S. CHUMSRIPHAN]

THAÏS, ST.

Portrayed by legend as a Christian courtesan of Alexandria who was converted by the hermit Serapion and sealed in a cell of a woman's monastery to do penance. In other versions of the story either Paphnutius or Bessarion is credited with her conversion. After three years of rigorous confinement, Thaïs was released; she died within 15 days. Though two mummified bodies, identified as

Thaïs and Serapion, were discovered at Antinoë in Egypt at the beginning of the 20th century and were exhibited in the Musée Guimet at Paris, there is not enough evidence to substantiate the claim that these are the remains of the penitent courtesan and the hermit of the legend. In the earliest accounts the penitent is nameless. The story of Thaïs is a morality tale that enjoyed great diffusion in the Middle Ages.

Feast: Oct. 8.

Bibliography: H. LECLERCQ, *Dictionnaire d'archéologie chrétienne et de liturgie,* ed. F. CABROL, H. LECLERCQ, and H. I. MARROU, 15 v. (Paris 1907–53) 1.2:2339–40. A. BUTLER, *The Lives of the Saints*, rev. ed. H. THURSTON and D. ATTWATER, 4v. (New York 1956) 4:61–62.

[E. DAY]

THALHOFER, VALENTIN

Exegete and liturgist; b. Unterroth, near Ulm, Jan. 21, 1825; d. Eichstätt, Sept. 17, 1891. He was professor of scripture, pastoral theology, and liturgy, and head of the Georgianum, a seminary in Munich. His unshaken Catholic loyalty, scholarship, and gifts as a teacher marked him as a distinguished educator of priests. Through his two-volume *Handbuch der katholischen Liturgik* (Freiburg 1883–93), he awakened interest in genuine liturgical science in the 19th century. Without rejecting symbolic explanations, he gave precedence to historical method. Even today, the specifically theological sections of his work are of great interest.

Bibliography: A. SCHMID, *Valentin Thalhofer, Dompropst in Eichstätt: Lebensskizze* (Kempten 1892). *Allgemeine deutsche Biographie* (Leipzig 1875–1910) 37:646–648. L. EISENHOFER, *Lexikon für Theologie und Kirche,* ed. J. HOFER and K. RAHNER, 10 v. (2nd ed. Freiburg 1957–65) 10:19–20.

[B. NEUNHEUSER]

THANATOLOGY

The field called thanatology (the science or study of death) emerged quite suddenly at the end of the 1960s. There is little doubt that the most important contribution to this emergence was the book *On Death and Dying,* by Elisabeth Kübler-Ross. By the end of the 20th century the field of thanatology largely consisted of footnotes to Kübler-Ross's work. Thanatology principally attracts practitioners in psychology and counseling.

The other important contribution to the field's birth came from historians. Here the work of the maverick historian Philippe Ariés was particularly important. He amassed data on the shifting attitudes toward death throughout Western history. Many other historical studies of death in ancient and modern worlds contributed to thanatology. Most important in the United States were the detailed studies of death in Puritan society.

Thanatology has incorporated philosophical considerations regarding ethical issues in the care of the dying. It has tended to avoid a serious encounter with religion. Caregivers are cautioned not to push religion upon the dying. If dying people are religious, however, their beliefs are to be tolerated. This attitude of bare neutrality in most textbooks contrasts with Kübler-Ross herself who says that it was through caring for the dying that she became religious. To the extent that thanatology fits itself into the mold of a modern science, discussion of religious mystery or life beyond death is necessarily excluded.

There is no agreed upon division of thanatology. The five subheadings that follow can be found in many textbooks. Some authors consider one or more of these areas to be outside of thanatology. Others might cover all of these topics but divide the material into ten or a dozen subheadings.

Experience of Dying. One of the reasons for the rise of thanatology was the progress of medical technology. When this technology provides an extension of a full, human life, few people would argue with the word ''progress.'' Technology can also extend the act of dying almost interminably, a contribution that strikes most people as decidedly negative. In the ambiguous middle, technology can identify some fatal diseases and predict death months or years in the future. The disease of AIDS is the most dramatic but not the only instance of this long interim for death's preparation.

Those with knowledge of their immanent death often go through a long psychological journey as they prepare to die. Kübler-Ross, working with groups of seminarians in the 1960s, traced a chart of five stages through which most patients go. The author did not say that everyone must go through these five in proper sequence. However, as is almost inevitable with such ''stage theories,'' other people found Kübler-Ross's theory to be attractive for classifying people and for knowing what the next step on the road to dying should be.

Kübler-Ross gave these names to the steps she found in her dying patients: (1) denial; (2) anger; (3) bargaining; (4) depression; (5) acceptance. The categories are neither novel nor surprising; the terms are almost self-explanatory. The power of her book lies in the real-life case histories that illustrate each stage. From a quantitative viewpoint, the author gives much less space to ''bargaining'' than to the other four. There is no indication in the text, however, that this stage is any less important.

The author does say that the ''majority of our patients'' reach the fifth stage in the journey. This stage of ''acceptance'' is perhaps the one that needs clarification. Kübler-Ross has many times been accused of trying to romanticize or glorify death. If acceptance were to mean affirmation, then there might be grounds for the charge. But in *On Death and Dying,* death is not a kind of prize to reach and celebrate. ''Acceptance should not be mistaken for a happy stage,'' says the author. There can be elements of hope against hope and stubborn resistance to death even to the very end.

The difficulty in grasping her meaning of acceptance raises a larger question about the nature of stages and the image of sequence. Instead of there being five stages strung along an arrow, it would be more helpful to think of these stages as a dialectic of no or yes. The number five is less important than the fact of an odd number. A series of yes *or* no answers finally issues in a stage that says yes *and* no. That is, acceptance is not the acceptance of death so much as the final, simple recognition that the acceptance of living has always included the reality of dying. Only when one is close to death does it become unavoidably clear that yes and no belong together.

Care of the Dying. Here again a quite drastic change in medical technology is the urgent reason for discussion of ethical problems in the care of the dying. What kind of treatment should be used? Who should decide about its use? How long should treatment be continued when the case is evidently hopeless? Modern ethics and its recent subdivision ''medical ethics'' are not at all certain where to find answers. There is no authoritative text in this area. Discussion spills out into popular magazines and newspaper stories.

The underlying problem is that modern ethics was conceived as a flight from death. The founding fathers (Hobbes, Locke, and others) established ethics on the basis of the possession of ''rights.'' Each person is the owner of property starting with the closest property, his or her life. Other rights such as liberty or the pursuit of happiness are consequent upon the right to life. Nearly everyone in the modern world speaks this language, nowhere more so than in the United States.

The trouble arises when one tries to apply this language to the care of the dying. It simply does not fit. Ethicists consequently postulated a ''right to die,'' which, given the history of rights language, is an extraordinary contortion of language. The obsession of such groups as the Hemlock Society with a universal right to suicide is almost a parody of modern ethics. What gets lost in this discussion is the *care* of the dying, the responsibility of the human community to see that suicide not be a desirable good because the process of living and dying transpires within the love, care, and support of other people.

The original phrase in the discussion was ''the right to die with dignity.'' The emphasis should have been on the last two words of the phrase. Each person has a right to dignity even if he or she is dying. ''Dignity'' is perhaps one of the few categories that can form a bridge between ancient and modern ethics. Vatican documents bolster this assumption in their stress upon the dignity of the person. Each thing deserves to be treated and cared for in a manner proportionate to its dignity. Insects have a limited call on our care while domestic animals have a definite degree of care due to them. A human being, whatever its condition, deserves respect for its interior life and bodily integrity. The human being's capacity for self-direction should not be violated by other human beings or by human technology.

The Catholic Church has provided much of the practical guidance in this area. Modern secular society, lacking any consistent philosophy, turns to the courts for decisions when something must be done. But even at their wisest, judges are prepared to say only *who* decides; the moral issues of what and how go begging. The long, consistent tradition of Catholic moral thought has provided a firm basis for a number of documents in this area. As long ago as 1957, Pope Pius XII pointed out that there should be a limit to the means used to extend life. The Vatican document in 1980, ''Declaration of Euthanasia,'' went further in elaborating distinctions. The patient is at the center of the process with family as the first of expanding circles of decision makers. The document allows for a refusal of treatment ''that would only secure a precarious and burdensome prolongation of life.''

One of the most helpful developments in this area was the HOSPICE MOVEMENT. The word often refers to a place but it can also mean a way of treating people who are dying, especially in their homes. The modern hospital was established as a place to cure disease, not as a place for people awaiting death. Nonetheless, 80 percent of people in the United States die in hospitals, amid conditions that can be very alienating. The St. Christopher Hospice in London began a movement that spread rapidly in the United States after 1974. In the hospice setting, death is accepted as a reality and each person is cared for and helped to care for her or his own person. The emphasis on dignity means that there is little need for discussion of a right to die.

Near-Death Experiences. Modern technology has had its influence on this aspect of death although the experience itself has probably existed throughout history. What did not exist until recently were research-minded individuals who would search out, collect, and classify the data. The book that dominates this topic is Raymond Moody's *Life after Life.* Other people, including Kübler-

Ross, have, since Moody's book, added their own collection of data to the file.

''Near death'' is used to refer to the experience of seeming to have died and then of returning to consciousness. Until Moody's book appeared, individuals who had had this experience were generally reluctant to speak about it. With the assurance that others had a similar experience, many people responded to Moody's case studies by recounting their own. The discussion of near-death experiences become fairly common in the literature of the late 20th century.

In people who had died and then ''came back to life,'' Moody found remarkable similarity in their experiences. Perhaps the most surprising thing is that in nearly all cases the experience was so pleasant that coming back to life was somewhat disappointing. The great exception was the case of attempted suicides where the experience was generally unpleasant. People who have had one or more near-death experiences will usually say that death no longer holds much fear for them.

Moody's original study was based on about 150 cases, of which 50 were studies in detail. At the time, there was no language of the near-death experience so that there was no possibility of people using standard phrases or describing something they might have imagined happened to them although they were in fact remembering someone else's account. The people involved tended to think that no one else had had such an experience.

The isolation of the individual cases made all the more remarkable the similarity in the descriptions. With only slight variation in detail, the description was as follows: at the moment of dying the individuals passed through a tunnel and found themselves outside their bodies, which were often being worked upon by others. The individuals then recognized that they had bodies but of a different sort. Dead friends and relatives met them. And finally there was a great white light before which the individuals appeared. A review of life took place in a pleasant rather than fearful atmosphere. Then the limit was reached and earthly life drew the individuals back despite resistance on their parts. The cases in which someone did wish to come back involved people who felt that they still had responsibilities to fulfill, as was the case with one mother of three small children.

The description did not vary much across religious lines. Christians, however, tended to use a language of God and Christ for the powerful force at the center of the experience. What the descriptions do correlate with to a high degree is the *Tibetan Book of the Dead.* Moody's case descriptions could have been lifted directly from the first section of that book although none of the interviewees said they had read the book. It should perhaps be noted that in the *Tibetan Book of the Dead* the journey of the soul becomes unpleasant later on and that the journey of 49 days is somewhat depressing. The journey ends with reentry into the womb for another cycle of life. The near-death accounts do not prove anything about the reality or the nature of AFTERLIFE. But they provide an interesting challenge to our literalistic psychology in the West and they provide a comfort to some patients that the moment of death is one of peace and joy rather than terror and agony.

Bereavement. The phenomenon of bereavement is as old as death. All religious traditions have had a central place for rituals of bereavement (even a tradition such as Buddhism, which protests against wailing or animal sacrifice as disgraceful forms of bereavement). Bereavement has been studied as a universal experience although it is the highly dramatic instances of mass death that make bereavement easier to study. Thus, the Holocaust and Hiroshima have provided the basis for long-term studies of bereavement.

The classic study was Erich Lindemann's 1944 work based on the Coconut Grove fire in Boston. Lindemann uncovered the reality of denied grief and postponed grief. He also discovered what has since been amply confirmed, that the failure to find an outlet for grief does grave physical harm to the body. From a social angle the best study of the topic is Geoffrey Gorer's *Death, Grief, and Mourning,* which emphasizes the need for ritual and the contemporary absence of ritual for expressing grief. Gorer says that death is to the 20th century what sex was to the 19th; that is, one does not admit to it in public. Without traditional religions to supply ritual for the bereaved, the contemporary world is bewildered by what to do with grief.

One way that the phenomenon of grief is dealt with is by placing it into the larger study of a ''psychology of loss.'' Comparisons can undoubtedly be helpful. The losses of car keys, virginity, hair, a favorite sitting chair, and the life of one's spouse have some characteristics in common. Just as surely, they have differences; grief at the death of a loved person has characteristics all its own. Too casually lumping together grief with any kind of loss can be a way of avoiding the painful reality and distinctive character of death.

As all of the traditional religions have known, there are ''stages of bereavement.'' And at each stage of bereavement there should be social forms that have a degree of flexibility. The grieving individual cannot invent and should not have to invent the ritualized steps after death. Robert Kavanaugh has proposed seven stages of bereavement, which he names: shock, disorganization, volatile emotions, guilt, loss and loneliness, relief, and reestablishment. Kavanaugh has consciously modeled his description on Kübler-Ross's stages of dying. What might be simpler to say is that dying and bereavement are the same process experienced from different poles. The individual who grieves has to go through the same steps as the dying person.

What is most important is not the number seven but the odd number of stages. Bereavement is a dialectic of no to death followed by a yes to death. The yes that follows death requires a symbolic no to life. After some days or months of struggling with yes or no to life, the bereaved person is ready to say a yes that includes accepting death. The person who emerges from bereavement does not go back to life as before but to a life inclusive of death. The psychological wisdom embodied in religion is nowhere more apparent than in rituals surrounding bereavement.

Death Education. With death as a topic of intense concern, it could be expected that death education would not trail far behind. During the late 20th century courses were instituted in many colleges. The popularity of these courses was indicated by the flourishing textbook industry with titles such as *Deathing, The Last Dance,* and *Dying Dignified.* Many students took these courses in search of therapy; either someone close to them had died or else their own deaths pressed at the edge of consciousness. And in the wake of the September 11, 2001 tragedy in New York City, more students became aware of the threat of terrorism and its potential to end life randomly.

The case has been increasingly made that courses in death are necessary. Children should deal with death in high school, or even in elementary school. The comparison is often made to sex education and, indeed, sex and death have had a long, intimate relation. Neither sex nor death should be hidden, denied, or made into a disgusting subject matter. Attempting to shield children from any experience of death is one of the worst things adults can do to children. There is abundant evidence that children can handle death if the adult community does not go to pieces. Thus, a young child needs ''education'' in death but that should not be equated with courses in school. A few honest words in the classroom would help, but the child's education here, as with sex, is mainly in familial experiences.

Kavanaugh suggests the need for death courses to develop a ''folk language of death.'' As with sex, and perhaps even worse than with sex, young people lack a richly humane language to talk about death. The school's job is not to explain death but to demystify some aspects of it (for example, the funeral industry) and reduce the embarrassment surrounding death. The school could be a place for admitting in public that, in contrast to television and movie exploitation of the subject, real people suffer difficult deaths that cause painful sorrow. That kind of death education would reduce rather than increase young people's obsession with death. Robert Neal's *The Art of Dying* remains a model of healthy attitudes and practical exercises for college age and beyond. Neal allows religion into the discussion, which textbook makers are wary of doing.

The interest in high school courses has been spurred by the concern with teenage suicide. The rate of suicide among young people has risen dramatically since 1950. No one is sure of the cause and no one can guarantee a remedy. ''Suicidology'' is a whole field of its own these days, exemplified by the work of Edwin Shneidman. Much in the tradition of Durkheim's turn-of-the-century study of suicide, researchers assemble statistics on various groups and track down possible causes and conditions of suicide. That approach may be useful to the management of social agencies, but it is of doubtful use in the education of young people.

Teenage suicide requires some broader response than a school course directed at suicide prevention. There can be no more direct a challenge to the entire process of education than young people killing themselves. The most profound exploration of the subject in recent decades is James Hillman's *Suicide and the Soul.* Hillman analyzes suicide as a cry to die and be reborn, not a premature death but a delayed transformation. Instead of trying to prevent suicide, the friend or counselor has to help the person to find a different path to rebirth. Once again here, religion is unavoidable in discussing suicide. Unless religion can be admitted into the conversation, the genuine mystery of suicide is likely to remain an impenetrable problem.

Bibliography: P. ARIÈS, *The Hour of Our Death* (New York 1981). H. WASS, ed., *Death Education II: An Annotated Resource Guide* (New York 1986). G. GORER, *Death, Grief, and Mourning* (Garden City, NY 1965). J. HILLMAN, *Suicide and the Soul* (New York 1964). R. KAVANAUGH, *Facing Death* (New York 1972). E. KÜBLER-ROSS, *On Death and Dying* (New York 1969). E. LINDEMANN, ''Symptomatology and Management of Acute Grief,'' *American Journal of Psychiatry* 101 (1944) 141–148. R. MOODY, *Life after Life* (Atlanta, GA 1978). R. NEALE, *The Art of Dying* (New York 1973). E. SHNEIDMAN and N. FARBEROW, eds., *Clues to Suicide* (New York 1957).

[G. MORAN]

THANGMAR OF HILDESHEIM

Historian; b. of Saxon parentage, *c.* 950; d. Hildesheim, May 25, 1003–13. He first served as head of the cathedral school of Hildesheim, later as librarian and notary. Distinguished both as a scholar and as a statesman, he was the teacher of BERNWARD OF HILDESHEIM, Meinwerk of Paderborn, Ekkhard of Schleswig, BENNO OF MEISSEN, and Emperor HENRY II. As dean of the cathedral of Hildesheim under Bernward, he played a leading role in the dispute between his bishop and Abp. WILLIGIS OF MAINZ over rights to the Abbey of GANDERSHEIM. Over this issue he accompanied his ordinary to Rome (1001), appealing the case to SYLVESTER II and EMPEROR OTTO III; he also took part in the synods of Pölde, Frankfurt, and Todi. He is responsible for the oldest and most important parts of the *Vita Bernwardi* (*Monumenta Germaniae Scriptores* 4:754–782), for much of which he was an eyewitness and active participant. A plain and simple narrative with slight dependence on classical models, the *Vita* displays an affectionate yet factual regard for its subject; but it may be charged with partisanship in the discussion of the Gandersheim affair. Thangmar also fails to mention Bernward's early support of Ekkhard of Meissen against Henry II at the death of Otto III.

Bibliography: M. MANITIUS, *Geschichte der lateinischen Literatur des Mittelalters,* 3 v. (Munich 1911–31) 2:268–276. F. J. TSCHAN in *Medieval and Historiographical Essays . . . James W. Thompson,* ed. J. L. CATE and E. N. ANDERSON (Chicago 1938) 322–343; *St. Bernward of Hildesheim,* 3 v. (Notre Dame 1942–52). W. WATTENBACH, *Deutschlands Geschichtsquellen im Mittelalter. Deutsche Kaiserzeit,* ed. R. HOLTZMANN, v.1.1–4 (3d ed. Tübingen 1948; repr. of 2d ed. 1938–43) 1.1:58–62; 1.4:824. K. ALGERMISSEN, *Bernward und Godehard von Hildesheim* (Hildesheim 1960).

[O. J. BLUM]

THAYER, JOHN

Missionary; b. Boston, Mass., May 15, 1758; d. Limerick, Ireland, Feb. 17, 1815. He was the fourth of eight sons of Cornelius and Sarah (Plaisted) Thayer, who were members of the First Church (Unitarian), in Boston. After brief service as a tailor's apprentice, he attended Yale University, in New Haven, Connecticut, leaving in the third year but receiving an honorary A.B. in 1779. He served as chaplain for militia men on Governor's Island in Boston Harbor from 1780 to 1781. He next visited Europe, where Italian hospitality, contact with former Jesuits, and the canonization process of St. Benedict Joseph Labre all served to impress him with Catholicism, and he entered the Church in 1783. His published account of his conversion was widely read. A short stay at the English College in Rome, followed by three years of study at the Seminary of Saint-Sulpice in Paris, culminated in his ordination there on June 2, 1787.

In 1789 Thayer was sent to Boston, where Father Louis de Rousselet was stationed. There then began a period of dissension between the French and the Irish factions in Boston that ultimately led to court action. When Archbishop Carroll recognized Thayer as the pastor, the French stayed aloof from church, one parishioner going so far as to have a Protestant burial. Thayer's temperament was finally judged unsuitable for the Boston assignment, and in 1792 he departed for a mission in Virginia. After several years in New York, Albany, and Canada, he went to work in the Kentucky missions, where he championed the abolition of slavery long before social and civil conditions made it practical. In 1804, he left the United States, and after a year in London and another at La Trappe, France, he went to Ireland, spending some years in Dublin before moving to Limerick in 1811. Thayer's entire estate was willed to found an Ursuline convent and school in Boston.

Bibliography: J. THAYER, *An Account of the Conversion of the Reverend J. Thayer* (Baltimore 1788; London 1800; Dublin 1809). R. H. LORD et al., *History of the Archdiocese of Boston . . . 1604 to 1943,* 3 v. (Boston 1945).

[T. F. CASEY]

THEANDRIC ACTS OF CHRIST

The term—in Greek θεανδρικαὶ 'ενέργειαι, in Latin *operationes deiviriles,*—denotes the characteristic activity of the GOD-MAN, those acts or operations in which both the divine and the human natures cooperate. After a review of the origin and history of the term in the Monothelite controversy, its orthodox use and meaning will be explained.

Origin. The term theandric act (operation) was first used by PSEUDO-DIONYSIUS (*c.* 500), who said Christ ''did not perform divine acts as God nor human acts as man, but as the God-Man He manifested a kind of new *theandric operation*'' (*Epistola 4 ad Caium*). As used by him, the term favored the Monophysitic and Monothelitic theories of one nature and one will in Christ and was often misused (e.g., by Severus of Antioch).

Cyrus, Patriarch of Alexandria, won over to the formula by Sergius I, Patriarch of Constantinople, included it with his anathematisms at the time of the Act of Union (633) in his successful efforts to reconcile Egyptian Monophysites and Catholics: ''Christ performs human and divine acts by one theandric operation.'' In this sense Sergius had incorrectly understood the expression as synonymous with the formula of St. Leo I: ''Each nature performs . . . the functions proper to itself, yet in conjunction with the other nature'' (H. Denzinger, *Enchiridion symolorum,* ed. A. Schönmetzer 294). The chief opponent of Cyrus, Sergius, and the Monothelites was St. Sophronius, Patriarch of Jerusalem.

History. The history of the formula theandric or divine-human acts of Christ is in large part the history of MONOTHELITISM. In the controversy following Sophronius's opposition to Sergius over the question of whether to speak of two operations in the Word Incarnate or of only one, Sergius appealed to the pope, HONORIUS I. The pope's two evasive letters, imposing silence on the disputed question but failing to come to terms with the problem, would later bring upon him the castigations of the Third Council of Constantinople (*see* CONSTANTINOPLE III, COUNCIL OF) and Pope Leo II.

Understood in its Monothelitic sense of a double principle of activity but only one activity, the term theandric act was condemned (H. Denzinger, *Enchiridion symolorum,* ed. A. Schönmetzer 515) by Pope St. Martin I in the regional Council of the Lateran (649; *see* LATERAN COUNCILS), a condemnation later confirmed for the entire Church by Pope St. Agatho. Martin I permitted its use merely to designate the wondrous union in Christ of the two distinct operations. The final condemnation of Monothelitism came in Constantinople III (680–681), which defined two distinct wills and operations working together in perfect harmony and condemned by name the Monothelites Cyrus, Sergius, and his successors in the See of Constantinople, Pyrrhus, Paul, and Peter.

Orthodox Use. Besides the accepted usage recognized by Pope Martin I, St. Maximus Confessor, because of his admiration for Pseudo-Dionysius, also interpreted the term in an orthodox sense, not as a new divine-human action, but as the divine and human energies operating together to produce a single effect. St. JOHN DAMASCENE also used it correctly (*De fide orthodoxa* 3.19).

Explanation. Relative to the activity of the God-Man, the Church in condemning monergism and Monothelitism has defined that in Christ there are two distinct wills and two distinct modes of activity. For the will is a faculty proper to a nature, and every nature is a remote principle of activity proper to itself. In Christ, since there are two natures, there are also two wills and two modes of activity. The acting subject (*principium quod*) is but one, the Person of the Word, who wills and acts in both a divine and a human way.

Three types of operations or acts were distinguished in Christ in scholastic theology: purely divine, properly human, and so-called mixed acts. (1) Purely divine operations are operations of the WORD, both the internal processions (*see* PROCESSIONS, TRINITARIAN) and external creative activity (in common with the Father and the Holy Spirit), in which the human nature of Christ has no part whatever. These purely divine operations can in no way be called theandric acts. (2) Properly human operations are acts that, although they belong to the Divine Person of the Word as to their acting subject (*principium quod*), are elicited by the human nature only (*principium quo*). Such properly human operations are called theandric acts in a wide sense only. For, besides the natural and supernatural concursus required for human acts, the divinity enters into these acts only insofar as it is identified with the Person whose acts they are and from whom the acts receive an infinite moral value and dignity. (3) Mixed operations are acts in which the two natures, each exercising its own proper activity, join together in producing a single effect, the human being the instrument of the divine. These mixed operations are called strictly theandric acts. For in the complete activity we distinguish a human act and a divine act, joined in perfect harmony. When Christ performed a miracle, the divine nature provided the healing power, while the human nature lent its own proper activity as instrument by speaking, praying, touching. In this sense the divine nature as principal cause and the human nature as instrument united to produce a common action, that of healing miraculously. The human nature and the human will were not merely passive entities, but their full human activity was used by the divine will as an instrument in performing one theandric act.

Cardinal Louis BILLOT and others distinguished another category of theandric acts of Christ, the meritorious and satisfactory activity of Christ (see SATISFACTION OF CHRIST). Because His human acts are the acts of a Divine Person, they have an infinite value as merit and satisfaction. This type of theandric act really belongs to the second category above, but considered under the aspect of its unique value. The more usual distinction is based on the ontological constitution of the acts themselves.

See Also: HYPOSTATIC UNION; INCARNATION; JESUS CHRIST (IN THEOLOGY); JESUS CHRIST (IN THEOLOGY) (SPECIAL QUESTIONS), 3, 4, 7, 8; MONOPHYSITISM; PERICHORESIS, CHRISTOLOGICAL.

Bibliography: A. MICHEL, *Dictionnaire de théologie catholique,* ed. A. VACANT, 15 v. (Paris 1903–50; Tables générales 1951–) 15.1:205–217. M. JUGIE, *ibid.,* 10.2:2307–23. L. BILLOT, *De Verbo Incarnato* (7th ed. Rome 1927) thesis 31. P. GALTIER, *De Incarnatione ac Redemptione* (9th ed. Paris 1947) 136–141.

[C. J. MOELL]

THEATINES

(CR; Official Catholic Directory #1300); the Congregation of Regular Clerics (*Congregatio Clericorum Regularium*) was founded at Rome in 1524 by St. CAJETAN and his companions, Gian Pietro Caraffa (later Pope PAUL IV), Bonifacio de' Colli (d. 1558), and Paolo Ghisleri (1499–1557). Caraffa, first superior of the group, had been bishop of Chieti (*Theate,* in Latin), hence the name

Theatines. All these men had been previously members of the Oratory of Divine Love, an association of clerics and laymen who sought to promote the reform of Catholic life in the early 16th century.

Cajetan and his associates decided to lead the way in the reform of clerical life by forming a religious order dedicated to high standards of asceticism and apostolic work under the vows of chastity, obedience, and absolute poverty. They rejected all benefices and devoted themselves to the service of the faithful, especially the poor and the sick. Approved by Clement VII on June 24, 1524, the first Theatines made their solemn profession at St. Peter's tomb in September of the same year. The congregation was placed under the immediate jurisdiction and special protection of the Holy See. In addition to the works of the ministry, the Theatines concerned themselves also with liturgical reform and contributed to the revisions of the liturgical books later promulgated by Pius V.

After Cajetan's death in 1547 the congregation spread rapidly throughout Italy, so that in the 17th century there were over 50 monasteries located in the major cities. From there it spread to Spain, France, Germany, Austria, Poland, and Portugal. Beginning in 1626 the Theatines labored for over 70 years on the foreign missions in the Russian territories of Georgia, Mingrelia, Guria, and Imeretia. They went also to India where they evangelized many regions near Goa and opened a seminary for the native clergy. Meanwhile, in Rome, the Theatines collaborated in the founding of the Urban College, under the auspices of the Congregation for the Propagation of the Faith. Urban VIII asked them to staff and direct the college in 1641.

Amid the political upheavals of 19th-century Europe, and the suppression of religious communities, the congregation suffered great losses. Through the interest of Pius X, it was restored in Italy, Spain, U.S., Latin America, and Africa. Having been invited by Bp. Nicholas Matz of Denver, CO, the Theatines arrived in Durango, CO, on March 9, 1906, to take charge of that western parish and missions. From here their activities expanded to include additional parishes, schools, and social work.

The basic rule of Theatine life is taken from the common law of the Church and the example of the Apostolic Church. The constitutions were approved by Clement VIII on July 28, 1604. The generalate is in Rome; the U.S. provincialate is in Denver, CO.

Bibliography: P. H. HALLETT, *Catholic Reformer: A Life of St. Cajetan of Thiene* (Westminster, MD 1959). P. PASCHINI, *S. Gaetano Thiene, Gian Pietro Carafa e le origini dei Chierici Regolari Teatini* (Rome 1926).

[A. SAGRERA/EDS.]

THEBAID

An area of considerable size in Upper Egypt, named from the capital at Thebes, and in ancient times extending as far north as Memphis. Under Roman domination, the province extended only as far north as Antinoë and was divided into Upper and Lower Thebais. This region had many martyrs in the persecutions under both Septimius Severus in 202 and Diocletian in 303 (Eusebius, *Hist. Eccl.* 6.1).

In the third century the Thebaid proper was the birthplace of Christian monasticism which was influenced by the lives of Paul the hermit (*c.* 230–341), St. ANTHONY OF EGYPT, St. Palamon, SHENOUTE OF ATRIPE, DOROTHEUS of Thebes, and many other hermits. In the 4th century PACHOMIUS, a native of Esneh in the Thebaid, was inspired by its anchorites and gave it renown as the birthplace of cenobitic monasticism. Beginning in TABENNISI (*c.* 320) Pachomius founded nine monasteries for men: Pbow, where he established himself permanently; Schenesit, Temouschons, Thebion; farther north (near the modern Akhmim), Monchosis, Hermopolis, Armoutim; and farthest south, Phenoum, near Esneh. He also established two monasteries for women, one under his sister Mary at Athribis. Soon after his death the monk Bgoul established a monastery at Atripe for greater austerity. His nephew and successor, Shenoute of Atripe, is noted for excessive austerities. RUFINUS OF AQUILEIA, PALLADIUS, and Aetheria visited the monks of the Thebaid at the end of the fourth century; John CASSIAN probably did not carry out his intention of going there. ATHANASIUS OF ALEXANDRIA spent his third exile (356–362) with the monks of the Thebaid.

In 450 the area of Upper Egypt was divided into three ecclesiastical provinces: Thebais I, with metropolitan at Antinoë; Thebais II, with capital at Ptolemais Hermiu; and Arcadia, with OXYRHYNCHUS as metropolitan see. There were some 30 suffragan bishoprics in the area, and Palladius speaks of 1,200 monks and 12 convents for women (*c.* 400). The Thebaid had a strong influence on the development of the COPTIC rite and on the evolution of the Sahidic dialect, as well as on Coptic literature and art.

Bibliography: B. KÖTTING, *Lexicon für Theologie und Kirche*, ed. J. HOFER and K. RAHNER (Freiburg 1957–65) 10:13–14. H. JUNKER, *Oriens Christianus* 6 (1906) 319–411; 7 (1907) 136–253; 8 (1908) 2–109. H. LIETZMANN, *ibid.* NS 9 (1920) 1–19. A. M. KROPP, *ibid.* 3d ser. 7 (1932) 111–125. H. ROSWEYDE, ed., *Vitae Patrum*, 2 v. (Antwerp 1628; repr. *Patrologia Latina* 73–74). RUFINUS OF AQUILEA, *Historia monachorum*, PL 21:387–462. J. R. PALANQUE et al., *The Church in the Christian Roman Empire*, tr. E. C. MESSENGER, 2 v. in 1 (New York 1953) 2:421–512. F. VAN DER MEER and C. MOHRMANN, *Atlas of The Early Christian World*, ed. and tr. M. F. HEDLUND and H. H. ROWLEY (New York 1958) 17, 34.

[M. C. MCCARTHY]

THEBAN LEGION

St. Eucherius, bishop of Lyons (434–450), tells of the decimation of a legion of Christian soldiers, recruited at Thebes in Egypt, which took place because they refused to shed innocent Christian blood in a campaign waged near Lake Geneva in Switzerland. Other accounts say that the soldiers died because they refused to offer sacrifice. Whether the legion referred to is the *tertia Diocletiana Thebaeorum* or the *prima Maximiana Thebaeorum* is not known. A church built at Agaunum (St. Maurice-en-Valais) in the 4th century by Theodore, bishop of Octodurum (Martigny), established the fact of the martyrdom of St. Maurice, the *primicerius* of the legion, and his companions. As to how many troops actually perished, we have no certain knowledge. Eucherius himself added the names of Urso and Victor of Solothurn to the list of martyrs. In the 6th century Gregory of Tours claimed that 50 martyrs of Cologne were in the ranks of the Theban Legion. Because Agaunum was a popular pilgrimage spot, many places in western Europe boasted a representative among the Theban legionaries. Devotion to the legion was particularly strong in the region of the Rhine during the Middle Ages.

Bibliography: H. LECLERCQ, *Dictionnaire d'archéologie chrétienne et de liturgie,* ed. F. CABROL, H. LECLERCQ and H. I. MARROU, 15 v. (Paris 1907–53) 10.2:2699–2729. A. BUTLER, *The Lives of the Saints,* ed. H. THURSTON and D. ATTWATER, 4 v. (New York 1956) 3:619–621.

[E. DAY]

THÉBAUD, AUGUSTUS

First Jesuit president of Fordham University, author; b. Nantes, France, Nov. 20, 1807; d. New York City, Dec. 17, 1885. He studied for the priesthood in the local seminary, was ordained in 1832, and after three years in pastoral work at St. Clement's, Nantes, entered the Society of Jesus in Italy. After further studies in theology at Rome and in natural science at the Sorbonne in Paris, he was sent in 1839 to teach chemistry at St. Mary's College, Marion County, Kentucky. In 1846 the Jesuits withdrew from Kentucky to take charge of St. John's University (later Fordham University) in New York, where Thébaud served as president from 1846 to 1851, and from 1860 to 1863. Following his first term he taught chemistry at the university from 1851 to 1852, then served as pastor of St. Joseph's Church, Troy, NewYork, until 1860. In 1863 he returned to Troy where he remained for the next six years, leaving in 1869 for Canada. The following years were spent in pastoral work in Montreal, then in St. Joseph's Church, Hudson City, New York (1870–72), and finally (1874), at St. Francis Xavier's, New York City. He returned to Fordham shortly before his death, and he was buried there.

Thébaud was deeply concerned with immigration and sociological problems and at Troy he exerted a restraining influence in the Nativist agitation. He was a frequent contributor to *Catholic World,* and to *American Catholic Quarterly Review,* which published his essays ''Superior Instruction in Our Colleges'' (1882) and ''Freedom of Worship in the United States'' (1883). He was the author of *The Irish Race in the Past and the Present* (1873), *The Church and the Gentile World* (1878), *The Church and the Moral World* (1881), and two fictional works, *Louise Kirkbride: A Tale of New York* (1879) and *Twit Twats: A Christmas Allegorical Story of Birds* (1881).

Bibliography: Archives, New York Province of the Society of Jesus. T. J. CAMPBELL, ''Father Thébaud,'' in A. J. THÉBAUD *Forty Years in the United States of America,* ed. C. G. HERBERMANN (New York 1904). *Woodstock Letters, passim.*

[V. C. HOPKINS]

THECLA, ST.

Member of the Anglo-Saxon mission to Germany, also given as Tecla; b. England; d. *ca.* 790. She became a nun at WIMBORNE. At the request of St. BONIFACE, one of whose extant letters (No. 67) is addressed to her, she was sent by her abbess, Tetta, to work with LIOBA in Germany. At first she lived in the Abbey at Bischofsheim, over which Lioba, her relative, presided. Later, Boniface made her abbess of Ochsenfurt, and still later she succeeded Hadeloga(?), the foundress and abbess of Kitzingen. Thecla's name, however, does not appear in the extant list of abbesses of that house, but possibly it is she who is listed simply as ''Heilga,'' the saint. During her years in Germany, she worked diligently for the spread of Christian culture. Her relics were scattered during the Peasants' War in the 16th century.

Feast: Oct. 15.

Bibliography: *Acta Sanctorum* Oct. 7.1:59–64. J. B. STAMMINGER, *Franconia sacra* (Würzburg 1889–) 1:79–86. WILLIBALD OF MAINZ, *Vita quarta Bonifatii,* ed. W. LEVISON, *Monumenta Germaniae Historica* (Berlin 1826–), Scriptores rerum Germanicarum Ser. 6, 53:95. A. M. ZIMMERMANN, *Kalendarium Benedictinum: Die Heiligen und Seligen des Benediktinerorderns und seiner Zweige,* 4 v. (Metten 1933–38) 3:182–183. R. BAUERREISS, *Kirchengeschichte Bayerns* (2d ed. Munich 1958–) 1:56, 99. A. J. FESTUGIÈRE, tr., *Sainte Thècle, saints Côme et Damien, saints Cyr et Jean, saint Georges* (Paris 1971). S. MISSER, *El libro de Santa Tecla* (Barcelona 1977). G. DAGRON and M. DUPRÉ LA TOUR, trs. and eds., *Vie et miracles de sainte Thècle* (Brussels 1978). C. NAUERTH, *Thekla, ihre Bilder in der frühchristlichen Kunst* (Wiesbaden 1981). R. ALBRECHT, *Das Leben der heiligen Makrina auf dem Hintergrund der*

Thekla-Traditionen: Studien zu dem Ursprüngen des weiblichen Mönchtums im 4. Jahrhundert in Kleinasien (Göttingen 1986). M. MIGLIARINI, *Alle origini del Duomo: la basilica e il culto di santa Tecla* (Milan 1990). S. J. DAVIS, *The Cult of Saint Thecla* (Oxford 2001).

[L. MEAGHER]

THEFT

Theft was defined for English law by H. Bracton, who followed the definition of Roman law, as ''the fraudulent handling of another man's thing, without his agreement, and with the intention of stealing it.'' In present-day usage theft means the actual taking away of something belonging to another. Moral theology defines it as the secret taking away of another's property with the intention of keeping or disposing of it as one's own, against the reasonable will of its owner. Stealing, embezzling, cheating in buying and selling, the falsifying of weights and measures, and larceny come under the same condemnation as theft.

If theft is taken to mean the secret taking or keeping of what belongs to another it must be presupposed that a thing can belong to another, and that he can reasonably object to being deprived of it. The lawfulness of private ownership is taken by St. Thomas Aquinas as the point of departure for his treatise on theft (*Summa Theologiae* 2a2ae, 66). Only when he has established the truth that it is lawful for a man to possess a thing as his own does he ask whether theft, the secret taking of another man's property, is always a sin.

The word secret is introduced into the definition of theft to distinguish it from robbery, and the assigning of ''another man's thing'' as its object distinguishes it from other sins forbidden by the Decalogue. Whereas the Fifth Commandment forbids the taking of another's life, and the Sixth the taking of his wife, the Seventh forbids the taking of his property, his things.

There are circumstances in which what belongs to a man can be taken from him without injustice, and such taking must not be called theft. Theft is the unjust taking of what belongs to another. To signify this, the phrase ''against the owner's reasonable will'' is added to the definition. An individual's objection to having food belonging to him taken by a starving man to save himself from death would be unreasonable. In a case that occurs more often, a husband would not be reasonably unwilling that his wife should help herself to his money to meet the expenses of housekeeping or to provide moderate recreation for herself or their children. She might, by her surreptitious way of acting, offend against prudence, humility, or graciousness, but she would not be a thief. A thief is one who takes what belongs to another who has a strict right to withhold it from him and who reasonably maintains his right.

Gravity. Theologians are agreed that, generally speaking, theft is a mortal sin. That property rights should be respected is a matter of grave concern of any ordered society, whose very existence depends upon it. As St. Thomas puts it: ''If men were to rob one another habitually, human society would be undone. Therefore, theft, as being opposed to charity, is a mortal sin'' (*Summa Theologiae* 2a2ae,66.6). Theft, therefore, is not only an injustice but an offense against the common good, and against the friendship that keeps men united in the bond of peace.

Against this conclusion, it can be reasonably urged that it is absurd to call the theft of something of little value a mortal sin. It would seem altogether repugnant that for the theft of a pen or a pin a person should suffer eternal damnation. To this objection St. Thomas replied: ''Reason accounts as nothing that which is little; so that a man does not consider himself injured in very little matters; and the person who takes such things can presume that this is not against the will of the owner. For that reason, if a person takes very little things, he may be excused from mortal sin. Yet if his intention is to rob and injure his neighbor, there may be a mortal sin even in these very little things'' (*ibid.* ad 3).

All theologians agree with St. Thomas here that if a thief should set out with the intention of taking a sufficiently large sum of money by small installments he is guilty of grievous sin from the start, even before he actually steals anything. They find it difficult to determine precisely what amount is sufficiently large to make an act of theft, or the intention to commit such an act, a mortal sin.

This is too complicated a question to consider here in detail. It must suffice to say that the mathematical computation of what constitutes grave matter is not really possible in the form of a rule applicable to all cases. Often it will be less a question of whether a mortal sin has been committed—for as to that, much will depend upon the particular circumstances and the conscience of the thief—than a question of the gravity of the obligation to make restitution. If grave matter is involved, a confessor must insist that the penitent restore what he has taken, or at least have the intention of restoring it, as a condition for absolution.

Relative and Absolute Standard. There is a general consensus that the theft of a relatively small amount from a poor man may be a grievous sin, although the theft of a larger sum from a wealthy person might still be venial.

In all cases where it is meaningful, the so-called relative standard should be applied, i.e., the gravity of the matter depends upon the gravity of the injury actually suffered by the person who is wronged. To do a notable or serious injury to another is gravely sinful. In some cases, however, the relative standard is incapable of measuring the actual malice of an act of theft. Either the extent of the injury suffered by the one whose property is stolen is indeterminable, or the actual injury is slight, although the act is obviously, by reason of the amount stolen, a grievous violation of social order; for example, when a sum, fairly large by ordinary standards, is stolen from an extremely wealthy man, or a large corporation, or from the government. In these cases, according to the common teaching of theologians, the malice of the act is measured according to an absolute standard. By this standard that sum is grave that could not be regarded as trivial without damage to the general good of society.

Bibliography: THOMAS AQUINAS, *Summa theologiae* 2a2ae, 66. SISTER THERESE, ''Malice and Gravity of Injustice,'' *The Irish Ecclesiatical Record* 87 (Dublin 1957) 47–50. H. DAVIS, *Moral and Pastoral Theology* (New York 1958) 2:298–310.

[A. DOOLAN]

THEFT (IN THE BIBLE)

Theft is forbidden by the strongly negative precept of the Decalogue, ''You shall not steal'' (Ex 20.15; Dt 5.19; Lv 19.11). Some authors (R. Devaux, *Ancient Israel, Its Life and Institutions,* tr. J. MCHUGH 83) propose the possibility that it originally forbade the heinous crime of man-stealing, an evil so frequent, principally to supply the slave trade, that it incurred the death penalty (Ex 21.16; Dt 23.7; *see* Ez 27.13; Am 1.6; 1 Tm 1.10). Exodus 20.17 would have governed regard for property. The precept of Ex 20.15, however, is usually taken to be a prohibition of theft and that of v. 17 as dealing with the interior movements of the heart. The moral force of these precepts arises from God's command. Thus to steal is to dishonor God (Prv 30.9) and is one of the injustices that lead to God's destruction of the Temple (Jer 7.9). Even one who steals from want is under full penalty, though men excuse him (Prv 30.9; 6.30–31). The accomplice shares in the guilt of the thief (Lv 5.1).

The same moral condemnation appears in the New Testament. Theft is in the catalogue of sins that exclude from the kingdom of God (1 Cor 6.10) or for which a Christian should never be guilty (1 Pt 4.15). It is conduct that grieves the Holy Spirit of God (Eph 4.28, 30).

The juridic outlook on theft is more concerned with civil equity than criminal punishment, although the excessive retribution imposed is probably penal. To steal and slaughter an ox demands five in return; a sheep, four (Ex 21.37; 2 Sm 12.6). A stolen animal recovered alive demands twofold restitution (Ex 22.3). A thief caught stealing from a depositary makes twofold restitution (Ex 22.6); if he escapes, the depositary must swear his innocence before God (Ex 22.7, 10–11). Disputed ownership of stolen property is judged by God (either by ordeal, oracle, or swearing); the guilty one pays twofold (Ex 22.8).

These regulations are more humane than those of other Oriental laws that demanded exorbitant restitution and frequently death. The only permissible death for theft mentioned in the Code of the Alliance was the death of a housebreaker caught at night in the act of stealing; if he was killed after daylight, the householder was liable to blood vengeance (Ex 22.1–2; *see* Nm 35. 31–34). Even though theft was looked upon as so great an evil, in the New Testament Christ's Second Coming is likened to the coming of a thief in the night (1 Thes 5.2, 4; Rv 3.3; 16.15; See the metaphors in Jer 23.30 and abd 1.5).

Bibliography: H. CAZELLES, *Dictionnaire de la Bible,* suppl. ed. L. PIROT, et al. (Paris 1928–) 5:497–530. *Encyclopedic Dictionary of the Bible,* translated and adapted by L. HARTMAN (New York, 1963) 2431. J. GREENBERG, G. A. BUTTRICK, ed., *The Interpreters' Dictionary of the Bible,* 4 v. (Nashville 1962) 1:739–742. W. J. HARRELSON, *ibid.* 4:570–571.

[J. A. FALLON]

THEINER, AUGUSTIN

Historian, canonist; b. Wroclaw, Poland (Breslau), April 11, 1804; d. Civitavecchia, Italy, Aug. 8, 1874. Under the influence of his radically reform-minded brother Johann Anton, Theiner, a lawyer, left the Catholic Church. But his subsequent acquaintance with H. LAMENNAIS in Paris and with Cardinal K. A. von REISACH in Rome brought him to an inner conversion, and he eventually became an ORATORIAN in Rome. He tried hard to win recognition in Curia circles with his historical works, which were marked by a pronouncedly Romanophile viewpoint. He did in fact win the favor of Pope GREGORY XVI and of Pope PIUS IX, who in 1850 appointed him to the VATICAN ARCHIVES. With Pius IX's approval Theiner wrote *Geschichte des Pontifikats Clemens XIV* (Paris 1853). In this work on the pope who had suppressed the JESUITS, Theiner took a stand acutely hostile to the Society of Jesus. Despite sharp criticism of Theiner, Pius IX continued to support him and in 1855 appointed him prefect of the Vatican Archives. In preparing an edition of the *acta* of the Council of TRENT, Theiner committed a serious breach of official trust; despite the papal ban on the work's publication, Theiner kept transcripts of the *acta* of the council in his personal possession, and they were published after his death by J. J. Strossmayer and E. Voršak (Zagreb 1874) in an edition completely unsatisfactory from a scholarly point of view. Before this, during VATICAN COUNCIL I, Theiner informed Cardinal G. A. Hohenlohe (d. 1896) and other bishops of the opposition party about certain documents that related to the Council of Trent and that the Curia expressly wished to be kept secret. As a result Theiner was dismissed from the archives in 1870. Of his many historical works, only his editions of the sources and the three-volume continuation of BARONIUS (Rome 1856) are of any great value.

Bibliography: Works. *Geschichte der geistlichen Bildungsanstalten* (Mainz 1835), with autobiography; *Disquisitiones criticae in praecipuas canonum et decretalium collectiones* (Rome 1836); *Geschichte der Rückkehr der regierenden Häuser von Braunschweig und Sachsen in den Schoss der katholischen Kirche* (Einsiedeln 1843); *Vetera monumenta Hungariae,* 2 v. (Rome 1859–60), *Poloniae et Lithuaniae,* 4 v. (Rome 1860–64), *Slavorum meridionalium,* 2 v. (Rome 1863), *Hibernorum et Scotorum* (Rome 1864); *Die zwei allgemeinen Konzilien von Lyon und Konstanz und die weltliche Herrschaft des Heiligen Stuhles* (Freiburg 1862); *Histoire des deux concordats de la république française et de la république cisalpine conclus en 1801 et 1803,* 2 v. (Bar-le-Duc 1869). Literature. A. MAURI, ''A. Theiner,'' *Archivio-storico italiano* 21 (1875) 350–391. H. GISIGER, ''Theiner und die Jesuiten,'' in *Bilder aus der Geschichte der katholischen Reformbewegung* 1.5–6 (Strassburg 1875) 213–314. F. X. SEPPELT, *Lexikon für Theologie und Kirche,* ed. M. BUCHBERGER (Freiburg 1930–38) 10:27–28. É. AMANN, *Dictionnaire de théologie catholique,* ed. A. VACANT et al. (Paris 1903–50) 15.1:217–218.

[H. RUMPLER]

THEISM

Etymologically theism is indistinguishable from DEISM except that the former term is derived from the Greek word for God, θεός, while the latter comes from the Latin, *deus.* The term ''theism'' was first used by Ralph Cudworth in his *Intellectual System of the Universe,* in 1678. The terms ''theism'' and ''deism'' were employed indiscriminately until the 19th century, when it became customary to restrict deism to philosophical positions involving a denial of some part of the traditional Christian teaching concerning God's providence. Every form of deism includes at least the repudiation of divine revelation. It is on this point that deism and theism are distinguishable. While theism, like deism, is philosophically independent of revelation, the theist does not deny the possibility of divine revelation. While deism tends to regard God as totally outside the material universe, theism favors the notion of an immanent God. In general, theism is monotheistic; since its knowledge is attained by reason rather than revelation, however, theism is not trinitarian, nor does it include such essentially Christian doctrines as the INCARNATION or the REDEMPTION.

According to a popular but not precise use of the term, Christians such as SS. Augustine, Anselm, and Thomas Aquinas are referred to as theists, a form of reference that is justified inasmuch as these men, as well as other Christian theologians, have provided philosophical arguments for the existence and nature of God. Many of these arguments have been adopted by those who are theists in the stricter sense; that is, by men who, without taking a position against the possibility of revelation, limit themselves to knowledge attainable by experience and reason alone.

In contradistinction to PANTHEISM, theism does not regard God and the universe as identical. While God is thought to be immanent to a greater or lesser degree, depending upon the particular system of theism, He is also considered to be transcendent. That is, while God is operative ''in'' the universe, He is also to some extent beyond it. Finally, the God of theism is a personal God—omniscient, omnipotent, free, and infinitely perfect, a being worthy of unlimited worship. Certain modern philosophies that propose a god-in-process-of-becoming are, therefore, not theistic (*see* IMMANENCE; TRANSCENDENCE).

Early Forms of Theism. It is perhaps impossible to identify with exactitude the first theist in the history of Western philosophy. While there are intimations of theism in the philosophies of ANAXAGORAS and PYTHAGORAS, it is generally maintained that PLATO, in Book 10 of his *Laws,* provides definite beginnings of a ''natural theology'' that concludes to the existence of a supreme, intelligent, beneficent spirit (ψυχή). This spirit is the source and governor of all motion in the universe, and even, in some sense, the cause of the being and nature of things in the universe. This divine being, however, supreme among the various ''spirits'' in Plato's universe, might be inferior to the Ideas (εἴδη), which completely transcend the universe governed by God.

Plato's argument as found in the *Laws* was adopted, with significant changes, by Aristotle. Since Aristotle rejects Plato's transcendent Ideas, the first source of all motion, the ''prime mover,'' is for him absolutely supreme, and there is no question of dependence on the Ideas. In Aristotle's Eudoxian universe of concentric spheres, the outermost sphere, while communicating various movements to the inner spheres and ultimately to the earth, itself moves eternally and at an unchanging rate. Therefore, the unmoved mover of this outer sphere must be eternal and immutable; this immutability further entails that the prime mover eternally think one unchanging thought. Since only thought of himself is worthy of such a thinker, the prime mover is ''self-thinking thought'' or ''thinking about thinking'' (*Meta.* 1074b 15–35).

Here already is embodied much of what was to become theistic doctrine through the centuries. According to a widely accepted interpretation of Aristotle, however, he himself ought to be classified as a deist rather than a theist, for the Aristotelian prime mover is totally without cognizance of, or interest in, the happenings of the universe; he is completely transcendent. Whether or not this is an accurate interpretation of Aristotle, we can see here two problems that are most perplexing for the theist: (1) How can an unchanging God know a changing universe? (2) How can God be ''interested'' in the universe and yet be totally unaffected by it, as He must be if He is to be infinitely perfect, or—to use the Aristotelian terminology—''pure act''? These are questions, of course, for the Christian theologian as well as for the theist, and it was the genius of men such as St. THOMAS AQUINAS to suggest reasonable answers to them.

Neoplatonic Emanationism. With the advent of the Neoplatonists new theistic arguments were suggested and new problems raised. While opinion differs on whether the ''One'' of PLOTINUS is identically God, the fact that the One is absolutely supreme and the source of all the multiple beings of the universe by way of emanation would seem to justify this identification. The One, however, is so utterly transcendent that it cannot be called ''thought''; it cannot even be called ''being.'' It is above all thought, above all being. Nothing, in fact, can be predicated of the One. Moreover, nothing can be compared with the One; its eminence is absolute, not a matter of degree. This, too, poses a problem for both theist and theologian: how can one talk about God, or even name Him, without implying that He can be compared with creatures? The use of terms such as ''super-good'' and ''super-intelligent'' by PSEUDO-DIONYSIUS, as well as St. Thomas's theory of analogical predication, suggests means of meeting this difficulty.

Plotinus also questioned the way in which God is the cause of the universe. Assuming that the universe emanates from the One, is this emanation necessary, or a result of free choice? For Plotinus, it seems, no freedom is involved; since the One is above thought, no choice is possible (*see* EMANATIONISM). Later philosophers and theologians maintained that an absolutely perfect being ought to be free; yet they had difficulty explaining absolute freedom without ending in some form of divine arbitrariness. The history of theism includes those who, like Plotinus, have seen God as necessitated by His own nature and those who, like WILLIAM OF OCKHAM and R. DESCARTES, have made the Will of God supreme in such a way as to posit a divine capriciousness extending even to the fundamental laws of logic and morality. A third solution, putting into question the absolute supremacy of God, is that of G. W. von LEIBNIZ, who maintained that God, whose absolute goodness requires that He create the best possible world, is still determined by ''essences'' or ''possibles'' that are somehow independent of Him.

Evil and God's Existence. Another thorny problem facing the theist is that of EVIL in the universe. Granting an omnipotent, infinitely beneficent God, evil would seem to be impossible. Either God ''cannot'' prevent evil, the argument runs, and then He is not omnipotent; or He ''will not'' prevent evil, and then He is not infinitely beneficent. St. AUGUSTINE proposed one way out of this dilemma, namely, that evil in the universe serves to highlight the good, by way of contrast. Thus no evil is totally evil; it serves a purpose and is, on this account, reconcilable with an infinitely beneficent God. Leibniz, whose THEODICY was particularly concerned with the problem of evil, maintained that God creates as much good as is possible, but that all essences or possibles are not mutually compatible, or ''compossible.'' Therefore, if God chooses to actuate certain essences, other essences become incapable of actuation. Evil, then, has its source, not in God, but in essences. For St. Thomas and scholastics generally, evil is an absence of good, a ''nothing,'' and as such requires no cause.

These proposals, of course, are particularly intelligible when understood in relation to the doctrines of ORIGINAL SIN and Redemption. The theist, having no access to such mysteries, is left with a problem that is practically insoluble. Nor does this seem strange when one considers that even his most elementary problem, the problem of whether God exists, has been the source of so many difficulties. Indeed, a man as brilliant as Immanuel Kant was to reject as inconclusive all traditional proofs and to substitute one of his own, based on what he took to be the natural foundation of ethical conduct, the CATEGORICAL IMPERATIVE. Yet the Kantian argument—for which Kant himself never claimed scientific certitude—has few adherents today.

Another approach to a natural theology, this one based on modern science, is outlined by P. TEILHARD DE CHARDIN in his *Phenomenon of Man.* Here God is considered as an end toward which the universe is tending in its evolutionary process. While Teilhard's thesis is appealing in its timeliness, its emphasis on the dynamic, and its possibilities for a better understanding of the relation of the universe to God, it does not employ a logic sufficiently rigorous to compel assent.

In brief, the development of theism, from Plato to the present, can be regarded as a confirmation of St. Thomas's observation that it is extremely difficult for man, by reason alone, to arrive at a knowledge of God that is evidently true and not compounded with error (*Summa theologiae* 1a, 1.1).

Seal of Theobald of Canterbury from a charter, c. 1144.

See Also: GOD, PROOFS FOR THE EXISTENCE OF; RATIONALISM.

Bibliography: D. J. HAWKINS, *The Essentials of Theism* (New York 1949). J. J. MCLARNEY, *The Theism of Edgar Sheffield Brightman* (Washington 1936). P. A. BERTOCCI, *The Empirical Argument for God in Late British Thought* (Cambridge, Mass. 1938). G. SANTINELLO, *Enciclopedia filosofica,* 4 v. (Venice-Rome 1957) 4:1107–8. R. EISLER, *Wörterbuch der philosophischen Begriffe,* 3 v. (4th ed. Berlin 1927–30) 3:231. A. E. TAYLOR, *Encyclopedia of Religion and Ethics,* ed. J. HASTINGS, 13 v. (Edinburgh 1908–27) 12:261–287. F. SOLMSEN, *Plato's Theology* (Cornell Studies in Classical Philology 27; Ithaca 1942). B. P. BOWNE, *Studies in Theism* (New York 1879). S. HARRIS, *The Philosophical Basis of Theism* (New York 1883). F. W. NEWMAN, *Theism, Doctrinal and Practical* (London 1858).

[R. Z. LAUER]

THEOBALD OF CANTERBURY

Archbishop; d. April 18, 1161. Theobald, son of a knight, was born near the Abbey of Bec, in Normandy, where he became a monk probably *c.* 1115 and abbot in 1136. Bec had already provided two archbishops for Canterbury, Lanfranc and Anselm, which probably explains Theobald's election in 1138 despite his personal obscurity. He became papal legate in 1150, perhaps earlier. In the disturbed politics of the reign of King Stephen of England he attempted to maintain a neutral position. His main political ideal was the cooperation of church and state. ''When princes show due reverence to priests, and priests render faithful services to princes, then do kingdoms enjoy true peace. But if they clash, the vigour of the secular power will be impaired no less than the ecclesiastical.'' During Stephen's reigns, Theobald's first allegiance was, in practice, to the papacy. He attended Eugene III's council at Reims in 1148, though Stephen had forbidden it, and on papal orders he refused to crown the king's son, Eustace, in 1152. Under Henry II, however, he did not obey the pope unquestioningly. As papal judge-delegate, for instance, he refused to excommunicate Robert of Valoines because it was against the king's will. Although constantly worried by exclusion from Henry's inner counsels, Theobald recognized the king's right to decide which candidate to support in the papal schism resulting from the disputed election of ALEXANDER III in 1159. As metropolitan, Theobald accomplished much, though he was not an exciting personality. He is noted for the number of his surviving documents, for his policy of fostering the study of Canon Law, for his influence in several episcopal elections and for his talent for choosing subordinates. His household included the humanist JOHN OF SALISBURY and the Roman lawyer VACARIUS; it was a training ground for many of the leading ecclesiastics of the next generation, including Thomas BECKET. He was strongly opposed to monastic claims of exemption from the diocesan's authority.

Bibliography: Z. N. BROOKE, *The English Church and the Papacy* (Cambridge, Eng. 1931). JOHN OF SALISBURY, *Letters,* ed. and tr. W. J. MILLOR et al. (New York 1955). A. SALTMAN, *Theobald, Archbishop of Canterbury* (London 1956).

[H. MAYR-HARTING]

THEOBALD OF ÉTAMPES

Early Oxford master; b. Normandy, before 1070; d. after 1132. He was one of the earliest Oxford masters whose teaching and reputation helped to establish the schools there. Between 1085 and 1089 he studied in a school attached to Saint-Étienne, Caen, Normandy, and he later taught there. After declining an invitation to become chaplain to MARGARET, QUEEN OF SCOTLAND, he moved to Oxford between 1096 and 1102, probably at the request of Walter, provost of the chapel of St. George'sin-the-Castle. For at least 30 years he taught theology at Oxford and claimed to have lectured to 60 or 100 students. A secular clerk, he was probably a canon of St. George's.

Bibliography: *Epistolae, Patrologia Latina* 163:759–770. R. FOREVILLE, "L'école de Caen au XIe siècle et les origines normandes de l'université d'Oxford," *Études médiévales offertes à Augustin Fliche* (Paris 1952) 81–100. R. FOREVILLE and J. LECLERCQ, "Un débat sur le sacerdoce des moines au XIIe siècle," St Anselm 41 (1957) 8–118. A. B. EMDEN, *A Biographical Register of the University of Oxford to A.D. 1500* (Oxford 1957–59) 3:1754.

[M. M. CHIBNALL]

THEOBALD OF PROVINS, ST.

Camaldolese priest and hermit, Fr., Thibaut; b. Provins, Brie, France, 1017; d. Salarrigo, near Vicenza, June 30, 1066. Influenced by the asceticism of the monks of the desert, he left the world and sought solitude in the forest of Pettingen, Luxembourg. His growing reputation for sanctity forced him to retire to Italy, where he settled near Vicenza. He attracted so many disciples that the bishop of Vicenza ordained Theobald a priest the better to serve them. Before his death Theobald received the religious habit of the Camaldolese Order. Pope Alexander II canonized him in 1073. He is the patron saint of charcoal burners.

Feast: June 30, July 1.

Bibliography: J. MABILLON, *Acta sanctorum ordinis S. Benedicti*, 9 v. (Paris 1668–1701; 2d ed. Venice 1733–40) 9:163–188. *Acta Sanctorum* June 7:540–556. B. COLLINA, *Vita de S. Teobaldo, monaco et eremita Camoldolese,* ed. D. VALLE (Bologna 1752). A. ALLOU, *Vie de S. Thiebaut, prêtre et hermite, patron de la ville de Provins* (Meaux 1873). C. JAMOTTE, *Le Montaigue de saint Thibaut, ermite, prêtre, et religieux de l'ordre de Camuldule* (Namur 1898).

[D. S. BUCZEK]

THEOBALD OF VAUX-DE-CERNAY, ST.

Eldest son of Burkhard de Montmorency, ally of SIMON DE MONTFORT in the war against the ALBIGENSES; b. Marley near Paris, *ca.* 1200; d. Dec. 7, 1247. During the absence of his father, he went to the court of PHILIP II AUGUSTUS OF FRANCE, was knighted, and became renowned at tournaments. He joined the Cistercians at VAUX-DE-CERNAY (Versailles) in 1225, became prior under Abbot Richard, *ca.* 1230, and was elected abbot in 1235. Under his charge the community grew to 200, possessions were amplified, and a new dormitory and refectory were built. Through him the divorce between King LOUIS IX and Queen Margaret was averted. With the abbot of Châlis he wrote the Office for the feast of the Crown of Thorns.

Feast: July 8.

Bibliography: A. DUCHESNE, *Historiae Francorum scriptores,* 5 v. (Paris 1636–49) 5:406–407. *Bibliotheca hagiographica latina antiquae et mediae aetatis*, 2 v. (Brussels 1898–1901; suppl. 1911) 2:8029–30. L. MERLET and A. MOUTIÉ, eds., *Cartulaire de l'abbaye de Notre-Dame des Vaux-de-Cernay,* 3 v. (Paris 1857–58) v.2. L. MORIZE, *Étude archéologique sur l'abbaye de Notre-Dame des Vaux de Cernay* (Tours 1889). G. MÜLLER, *Cistercienser-Chronik* 15 (1903) 321–336.

[C. H. TALBOT]

THEOCENTRISM

The center of all natural and supernatural reality is God. All being basically, initially and ultimately, focuses around and in the transcendent God and finds in Him its *raison d'être.* Theocentrism (God-centeredness), an explicit recognition of this fact, is a characteristic of certain philosophies, religions, theologies (systematic and otherwise), and asceticisms.

In philosophy, theocentrism may ultimately be regarded as an answer to man's intellectual quest for a unified explanation of the orientation of his own being to the whole order of being. There is ultimately one, necessary, absolute Being, independent of and transcending any other. This absolute Being is reasoned to be the infinite, eternal, unparticipated Being, which accounts for the coming-to-be and continued existence of all contingent beings. Opposed to philosophical theocentrism is the ANTHROPOCENTRISM or cosmocentrism of humanism, rationalism, naturalism, secularism, and materialism. There is, however, a true philosophical anthropocentrism, compatible with true theocentrism, when the metaphysics of God and creature is not perverted into a metaphysics of God or creature.

Theocentrism is characteristic of all true religion and theology. In the OT and the theology of the OT theocentrism is evident. In the NT the divine plan is revealed as simultaneously theocentric and Christocentric. It is theocentric because it was conceived by God from all eternity, adapted and prepared by Him for its full realization, and tends finally to His glory. It has the character of Christocentrism because Christ, the man Jesus, the one mediator between God and men, is revealed as also somehow at the center of the plan. Before the Incarnation the course of history moves toward Christ, and after the Incarnation history derives its direction from Him.

Theocentrism is not necessarily opposed to anthropocentrism in various parts of theology as they strive for some intelligence of the mysteries. Views of sin, for instance, may, on the one hand, emphasize what man's sin does to man, or, on the other, what man's sin "does" to God. So also for theories of the Redemption: the Anselmian view is theocentric—God tolerates no disorder in His kingdom; the Thomistic view is anthropocentric—man has fallen and must be raised again. In this case, the reason for the nonopposition is that neither explanation pretends to be adequate.

True asceticism must also be theocentric. It necessarily focuses on man's way to God. In the light of dogma, it recognizes that this Way is Christ and thus is likewise Christocentric. Man seeks his own salvation, and thus it is also anthropocentric.

Bibliography: H. U. VON BALTHASAR, *Science, Religion and Christianity,* tr. H. GRAEF (Westminster, Md. 1958) 91–103. J. A. JUNGMANN, *Handing on the Faith,* tr. and rev. A. N. FUERST (New York 1959) 143–146, 170–171, 400–401. J. C. MURRAY, *The Problem of God Yesterday and Today* (The St. Thomas More Lectures 1; New Haven, Conn. 1964). K. RAHNER, *Theological Investigations,* tr. C. ERNST et al. (Baltimore 1961–) 1:79–148; *Lexikon für Theologie und Kirche,* ed. J. HOFER and K. RAHNER, 10 v. (2d, new ed. Freiburg 1957–65) 1:632–634.

[B. A. LAZOR]

THEOCRACY

A form of political government in which the deity directly rules the people. Since men are corporeal and need visible signs of God's rule, direct divine governance always has a human representative, usually a priesthood or a divinely chosen king. But theocracy as such is not necessarily opposed to popular rule nor to any other form of government, since the practical political arrangements can usually be presented as manifestations of a divine choice or a divine ratification of a human choice.

The word theocracy was first used by Josephus to describe government under Moses: "Our legislator. . . ordained our government to be what, by a strained expression, may be termed a theocracy, by ascribing the authority and power to God" (*C. Ap.* 2.16.165). Hebrews believed their government was by divine rule, whether under the original tribal form, the kingly form, or the high priesthood after the Exile until the Maccabees. The actual rulers or ruler, however, were held responsible directly to God; their deeds could not be arbitrary. They could, and at times did, deviate from the divine task as the examples of Saul and David show. The prophets witnessed such lapses in the name of an angry God and sought to correct them.

Theocracy as the rule of a priestly caste is often unsuccessful because of its vulnerability to military power, its lack of popular support, or its often implicit denial of a true human political task. The major historic examples of theocratic rule are ancient ISRAEL, TIBET, some Buddhist regimes of Japan and China, ISLAM, the Geneva of John CALVIN, Puritan New England, the PAPAL STATES, and Mormon Salt Lake City. Most of these quasi-priestly regimes have been quite small and short-lived. Usually, they have not been successful political entities in the eyes of their own and surrounding peoples.

Theocracy, however, has broader implications. All tribal and ancient peoples, including the Greeks and the Romans, believed that their cities and nations were under the protection of and dedicated to the gods. Both Peter and Paul in their letters held that civil authority was from God (1 Pt 2.13–14; Rom 13.1–7; Ti 3.1). Christian tradition, however, has always recognized that the things that were Caesar's were legitimately his and could not be taken from him (Mt 22.21–22). The distinction between the spiritual and the temporal received its classic form in the two-power theory of Pope GELASIUS I. A problem arose immediately, however. Who is to judge in the areas of conflict between the spiritual and the temporal? This became the major political issue of the Middle Ages. The temporal power and spiritual authority as combined in popes like GREGORY VII, INNOCENT III, and BONIFACE VIII were so great that many writers have called these regimes properly theocratic. Nevertheless, Christian political theory must preserve the autonomy of the temporal order. These popes were no exception to this rule, however far they may have gone in aggrandizing the legitimate rights of the temporal as against the spiritual in areas of conflict.

The further evolution of this problem came with James I of England and the so-called DIVINE RIGHT OF KINGS. This theory combined the spiritual and the temporal powers in one person, the temporal ruler. The king's rule comes directly from God, not from the people. Democratic theorists attacked this theocratic view, especially as stated in Robert Filmer's *Patriarchia,* by maintaining that God's authority came to the rulers because the people needed this authority and designated the rulers they chose. The subsequent history of theocratic ideas must be sought out in the history of ABSOLUTISM and in the SECULARIZATION of all human orders. Here, the absolute rule of social class, race, or nation comes to be the substitute for God's direct rule. This again serves to emphasize the practical importance of recognizing the limited autonomy of the public order.

Bibliography: R. DE VAUX, *Ancient Israel, Its Life and Institutions,* tr. J. MCHUGH (New York 1961) 65–209. L. GEINCOT, "La théocratie mediévale," *Revue Nouvelle* 29 (1959) 189–195. R. J. S. HOFFMAN, "Theocratic Heresy in Politics," *Thought* 24 (1949) 389–394. M. FAKHRY, "Theocratic Idea of the Islamic State," *International Affairs* 30 (1954) 450–462. J. C. BRAUER, "The Rule of the Saints in American Politics,'' *Church History* 27 (1958) 240–255.

[J. V. SCHALL]

THEODARD OF NARBONNE, ST.

Archbishop; b. Montauban, France, *ca.* 840; d, Montauban, May 1, 893. Apparently he was of noble origin, and he pursued his studies, both religious and secular, with such success he was chosen advocate at the synod of Toulouse that tried to settle a dispute between the Jews of Toulouse and Bishop Bernard. The presiding officer of the synod, Abp. Sigebod of Narbonne (873–885), afterward made Theodard his archdeacon, in which capacity he distinguished himself by piety and great charity toward the sick and the needy. Theodard succeeded Sigebod as archbishop in 885, was consecrated on August 15, and went to Rome to receive the pallium from Pope Stephen V in 886. At the synod of Villa Portus near Nîmes, 886–887, he resisted the metropolitan pretensions of the archbishop of Tarragona. Theodard did much to repair the damage that his archdiocese had suffered from the Saracens, and used the Church treasures to ransom Christian captives. He died and was buried in Montauban in the Benedictine Abbey of St. Martin, which became known as St. Theodard's.

Feast: May 1.

Bibliography: *Acta Sanctorum* (Antwerp 1643– ; Venice 1734– ; Paris 1863–) May 1:143–159. *Bibliotheca hagiographica latina antiquae et mediae aetatis*, 2 v. (Brussels 1898–1901; suppl. 1911) 2:8045. *Gallia Christiana*, v.1–13 (Paris 1715–85), v.14–16 (Paris 1856–65) 6:20–22. J. A. GUYARD, *Histoire de saint Théodard* (2d ed. Montauban, Fr. 1886). A. BUTLER, *The Lives of the Saints*, rev. ed. H. THURSTON and D. ATTWATER, 4v. (New York 1956) 2:210–211. J. UTTENWEILER, *Lexikon für Theologie und Kirche*, ed. M. BUCHBERGER, 10 v. (Freiburg 1930–38) 10:33–34.

[G. J. DONNELLY]

THEODICY

The term ''theodicy'' was coined by G. W. LEIBNIZ (from the Greek *theos*, ''God'' + *dike*, ''justice'') to describe his defense of God's goodness and omnipotence against arguments based on the multitude of evils in the world. Through the work of Leibniz and Christian Wolff the term came to encompass the general philosophical treatment of questions concerning God's existence and attributes. In the twentieth century, Thomists abandoned this use of the word, preferring to describe this branch of metaphysics as ''natural theology.'' Today, ''theodicy'' refers most commonly to the theological and philosophical response to the problem of EVIL.

The Problem of Evil. The formulation of the problem involves propositions something like the following: (1) since God is omnipotent, He could prevent the misery in humanity and in the natural world, and (2) since God is omnibenevolent, He would want to prevent such evil, yet (3) genuine evils—i.e., evils that are not merely good in disguise, serving instrumentally the good purposes of God's will—exist. Skeptics contend that fundamental Christian beliefs—God's omnipotence, omnibenevolence, and omniscience, etc.—are logically inconsistent with the existence of genuine evils (see Whitney, *Theodicy*). Theologians argue, in response, that belief in God assures us that He has morally justifiable and sufficient reasons for permitting evils, rather than creating a world in which there are fewer evils, or none at all (cf. Aquinas, *Summa Theologiae* 1a, 48; *SCG* II, c. 45; etc.). Recently, after decades of intense debate, skeptics generally have conceded that the attempt to establish a logical problem of evil has been unsuccessful, since no one has been able to demonstrate how there is logical inconsistency between the propositions. To establish inconsistency (see Rowe, *Philosophy of Religion*, ch. 6), an additional proposition would be required, one that must necessarily be true and, thus, incontestable. Theologians have been able to put forth an additional proposition, one that demonstrates on the contrary there is no logical inconsistency in the triad of propositions. Most theists have long held that God cannot do the logically impossible. Is it not, then, necessarily true that God cannot create a world inhabited by free creatures without the risk that such freedom will be used for evil? (see Plantinga, *Freedom*, etc.).

With the demise of the logical problem of evil, the focus has shifted to the so-called ''evidential problem of evil.'' Its proponents concede that human freedom cannot be structured by God in such a manner that freedom would be used only for good, and that freedom would not be genuine if God permitted its use only when He foresaw it would be used for good ends, while negating it if would be used for evil ends. They concede also that God may permit many of the evils caused by human free will as a means to bring about greater goods, not otherwise attainable. Yet the remaining problem is the sheer amount of evil, its horrendous nature in many cases, and its apparently gratuitous nature and unfair distribution. Skeptics contend that this presents strong evidence against belief in God, often citing Rowe's well-known example of a wounded fawn dying a lingering and painful death after being burned in a forest fire. In this suffering, there is apparently (or conceivably) no greater good not otherwise attainable. If we consider, moreover, the innumerable instances of such suffering, an even stronger evidential case can be made against belief in a God who could have disallowed such evils (cf. Rowe, *Philosophy*).

In response, theologians have argued that such apparently gratuitous evils, while troublesome, do not constitute decisive evidence against belief in a loving and powerful God. Some say that God has good reasons to permit these evils since, for example, His intervention with respect to the natural laws required for human life would negate their reliability and stability. Others argue that if God disallowed one case of gratuitous evil, then there would be no place for Him to stop until all such evils had been disallowed, thereby rendering free will and natural laws disingenuine. Still others resolve the issue theologically by denying that any evils are gratuitous, since all evils have some value from some perspective (see Whitney, ''Aesthetic Solution,'' and Whitney, *Theodicy* for other references). Theologians are intent not to reduce all evils to the disingenuine status of hidden goods, to merely instrumental means by which God achieves His preordained ends. The task is to present cogent arguments in support of this view in order to strengthen the theist's position that the evidential problem of evil is no more threatening to belief in God than was the logical problem.

Invalid Solutions. The Christian solution to the problem of evil must not deviate from the central doctrine of God—a God who is offended by sin, who is omnipotent, omniscient, and omnibenevolent—nor must it deny the genuine freedom and moral responsibility of the human will, nor the genuine reality of evil. Since both monistic and dualistic solutions deny one or more of these essential beliefs, they are unacceptable as resolutions to the problem of theodicy. MONISM reduces evil to illusion, to the product of human ignorance. There is an ever-present monistic tendency in Christianity, a tendency based on the belief that since God has created all things, all things must be goods and in accord with God's providential purposes. Evils are seen as goods in disguise, having no genuine reality in themselves. One must hold, however, that evils are not created nor desired by God, and that they are genuinely evil. That ''all things work together for good for those who love God'' (Rom 8:28) does not imply that evils are merely instrumental goods caused by God for His specific purposes. Rather, despite the evils caused by humanity's misuse of free will, God makes the best use of them. The Church acknowledges the dialectical tension between human freedom and responsibility for evil vis-à-vis God's providential plan, a dialectic found in Scripture (*see* EVIL) and throughout Church history. It resists any either/or denial of human free will or divine grace, the latter interpreted in terms of unilateral predestination (cf. Councils of Carthage in 415, Arles in 475, Orange in 529, Quiersy in 853, Valence in 855, Langres in 859, and Turro in 860). While God is acknowledged as the sole Creator and the entire creation is subject to His sovereignty, we must not be misled into interpreting evils, then, as other than genuine.

The Church must resist not only monism, but dualism. The Christian God alone is supremely sovereign, permitting or causing evils for morally sufficient reasons. Dualism in some forms postulates two competing divine forces, one good, the other evil. It solves the problem of evil by denying God's absolute sovereignty. The development of the doctrine of Satan in post-exilic Judaism has led to a constant threat of a dualist interpretation of Christianity. Another distinct form of dualism is the modified Gnostic dualism of Manicheism, which holds that there are two primal elements, God and matter, the latter regarded as unredeemably evil. Through gnosis, the knowledge rejected by Paul in 1 Timothy 6:20 and elsewhere, the human soul supposedly is freed from the darkness and evil of the material world and rejoins the spiritual world of goodness and light. Such a view makes evil a product of human ignorance, as does monism, rather than something ontologically genuine. It teaches that salvation is gained by human enlightenment, rather than by Christ's redemptive act, and thus is rejected by the Church.

Traditional Solution and Contemporary Challenges. The Augustinian solution, adapted and refined by St. Thomas Aquinas, has been the predominant Christian solution to the theodicy issue. Central to this multifaceted and complex solution is a ''contingency defense'' that purports to demonstrate how creatures are genuinely free and morally responsible for goods and evils (as secondary causes), despite divine preordained providential (primary, final) causation (cf. *SCG* I. 67; etc.). While God possesses necessary, infallible foreknowledge, this must not be understood to threaten or negate genuine contingency in creatures, since God is eternal, that is, beyond time. All events—future, past and present—are simultaneously present in God (cf. *Summa theologiae* 1a, 14; etc.). God's immutability, impassibility, aseity, and omnipotent control over creation likewise must not be understood to threaten our contingent acts and decisions. How this is the case has been a complex and difficult issue to comprehend, by friend and foe alike. Thomists hold that God ''premoves'' the human will to choose freely, while Molinists propose instead that God's will is concurrent with human choice, a view that includes *scientia media* (''middle knowledge''; see Whitney, *Theodicy*, chapter 3).

Luther denied St. Thomas' important distinction between God's ''permitting'' the sinful acts He foreknows without ''causing'' or ''willing'' them (see *Summa theologiae* 1a, 19, 22; and Luther, *Bondage*), and denied also the distinction between ''primary'' and ''secondary'' causation (see *SCG* III. 70; and Luther, *Bondage*), etc. In rejecting the very basis of traditional theodicy, the early Reformers were left without a free-will defense for moral evil. Their response was to deny free will altogether, and attribute all goods and evils to the predeterministic will of God. In Luther's translation of the Bible and in his teaching, he claimed that we are saved by grace *alone* (cf. Rom 1:17, Eph 2:8) since human free will was utterly destroyed at Adam's fall, rather than merely weakened as Augustine and the Church had taught. Thus, Luther affirmed God's "grace [alone] is sufficient" (2 Cor 12:9), implying there is no need for free will in us (see Sungenis, *Not By Faith Alone*, 600). Contemporary Protestants, however, have returned to a defense of human freedom by understanding of God's power as self-limited. This view, clearly contradictory to the traditional Augustinian-Thomistic theodicy, is perhaps best known in John Hick's influential "Irenaean theodicy" in which he argues that for God to create genuinely free human beings, He could not create the good (perfect) creatures portrayed in the traditional interpretation of the Genesis "myth," but created imperfect, morally neutral creatures who were at "an epistemic distance" from God and who found themselves in a less-than-perfect world.

A more substantial alternative to Augustinian-Thomistic theodicy, one that predates Hick's, was devised by Alfred North Whitehead (d. 1947) and Charles Hartshorne (d. 2000). It is based on a substantial metaphysics that implies a radical revision of God's attributes and the God-world relationship. Thomists and others have responded that neither Hick's theodicy nor the revised "neoclassical theism" of process theologians appreciates the subtleties of the Augustinian-Thomistic theodicy.

Bibliography: D. R. GRIFFIN, *God, Power and Evil* (Lanham, MD. 1990). C. HARTSHORNE, *Aquinas to Whitehead: Seven Centuries of Metaphysics of Religion* (Milwaukee 1976). J. HICK, *Evil and the God of Love* (New York 1966; rev. ed. 1978). M. LUTHER, *On the Bondage of the Will* (New York 1957). A. PLANTINGA, *God, Freedom and Evil* (New York 1974). W. ROWE, *Philosophy of Religion: An Introduction* (Bellmont, Calif. 1978). H. SCHWARZ, *Evil: A Historical and Theological Perspective,* tr. M. WORTHING (Minneapolis 1995). R. A. SUNGENIS, *Not By Faith Alone: The Biblical Evidence for the Catholic Doctrine of Justification* (Santa Barbara, Calif. 1997). B. WHITNEY, *Theodicy: An Annotated Bibliography on the Problem of Evil, 1960–1991* (New York 1993); "An Aesthetic Solution to the Problem of Evil," *International Journal for Philosophy of Religion* 35 (1994) 21–37.

[B. WHITNEY]

THEODORA

Name of both the wife and the daughter of Theophylactus, the first of the Counts of Tusculum.

Theodora the Elder, the wife of Consul Theophylactus, fl. *c.* 900 to 926; neither the place nor date of either her birth or death is known. In some documents she carries the title *vestaratrix.* According to the rather doubtful statement of LIUTPRAND OF CREMONA, her morals were extremely evil; EUGENIUS VULGARIUS, however, speaks of her as a pious and virtuous woman. More creditable, perhaps, is Caesar BARONIUS, who considers her influence pernicious. Besides being personally avaricious, she—together with her family—exercised undue influence on Pope SERGIUS III and Pope JOHN X, thus causing grave harm to the authority of the popes. Besides her namesake, she and Theophylactus had another daughter, MAROZIA.

Theodora the Younger, d. *c.* 950. She married the *consul* and *dux* John, of whom it is said that he was later consecrated bishop. According to prevailing opinion, Pope John XIII and Crescentius I (*see* CRESCENTII) were sons of her marriage with John. She played an important role in the partisan politics of the aristocracy of contemporary Rome.

Bibliography: H. K. MANN, *The Lives of the Popes in the Early Middle Ages from 590 to 1304,* 18 v. (London 1902–32) v.4. P. FEDELE, "Ricerche per la storia di Roma e del papato nel secolo X.," *Archivio della società romana di storia patria* 33 (1910) 177–247; 34 (1911) 75–115, 393–423. F. X. SEPPELT, *Geschichte der Päpste von den Anfängen bis zur Mitte des 20. Jh.* v.1, 2, 4, 5 (Leipzig 1931–41) v.2.

[W. M. PLÖCHL]

THEODORA, BYZANTINE EMPRESS (1)

Wife of Justinian I; b. Constantinople (Paphlagonia or Syria in later sources) *c.* 497; d. Constantinople, June 28, 548, perhaps of gangrene or cancer; buried in the Church of the Holy Apostles. The main source on her life, the *Anecdota* or *Secret History* of PROCOPIUS OF CAESAREA, is a hostile account, which tends to obscure historical truth. Allegedly the second of three daughters of Akakios, bearkeeper of the Green faction, she was at an early age sent by her widowed mother onto the stage, at the beginning as an aide to her elder sister Comito. Being an actress, she participated in obscene displays and was typically considered a prostitute by her contemporaries. She is said to have followed a certain governor of Pentapolis named Hecebolus to Libya. After he rejected her, she spent some time as an actress in Alexandria and the eastern provinces. Finally she returned to Constantinople, where she met JUSTINIAN and became his mistress. He conferred on her the title of a patrician, but the marriage became possible only after the death of the emperor Justin I's wife Euphemia, who opposed it, and the passage of a special law enabling former actresses to marry into

Theodora, Byzantine Empress (1), and her attendants, mosaic, circa 547 AD. (©Archivo Iconografico, S.A./CORBIS)

the highest rank of society. They married probably *c.* 524, and remained devoted to each other until the end. Justinian, who never remarried, commemorated her on various occasions after her death. After a victory in 559, he had his triumphal procession detour to the Holy Apostles, so candles could be lit before her tomb. The emperor also had her mentioned in an inscription on the church of St. Catherine's at Mt. Sinai. She had a daughter from an earlier liaison and two or three grandsons. The existence of an illegitimate son, whom she is said to have mistreated, is apocryphal.

Although Justinian had always been a supporter of Chalcedon, Theodora was a convinced Monophysite, perhaps as a result of her stay in Alexandria. The nature of their collaboration on ecclesiastical policy has been a matter of debate ever since Procopius. Justinian was sincerely interested in bridging the gap between the Chalcedonians and the Monophysites, and Theodora acted within the limits of imperial policy, aiming especially at the relaxation, although temporary (531–36), of the official persecution of the Monophysites, as well as at the philanthropic mitigation of its effects. With Justinian's knowledge, she kept many Monophysite monks and clergy loyal to the empire by sheltering them in her palace of Hormisdas. She was an intimate of SEVERUS OF ANTIOCH, and in 535 she briefly succeeded in having the originally Chalcedonian ANTHIMUS, who afterwards changed his views, appointed patriarch of Constantinople and the Monophysite Theodosius named patriarch of Alexandria. With Justinian's approval she even sent troops headed by Narses to Alexandria to support the election of Theodosius, who continued to enjoy her protection after he had moved to the capital. Subsequently, Theodora unsuccessfully attempted to have the anathemata of 536 against the Monophysite leaders revoked. To this end she worked for the appointment of the complaisant deacon VIGILIUS, the papal legate in Constantinople, as pope (537) in place of the suddenly deceased Agapitus. She also instructed Belisarius to remove Pope Silverius, who had been elected in the meantime. His imprisonment suited her religious agenda, but she probably believed that Silverius was guilty of treason as well. The extensive official conversion of pagans in Asia Minor was accomplished by her favorite, the Monophysite John of Ephesus. He is said to have agreed to work in the interests of the official Chalcedonian policy, but it is doubtful that the pagans were really converted. One case in which Theodora opposed the policy of Justinian was in their dispatch of separate Monophysite and Chalcedonian missionaries to Nubia, where the former prevailed in the end. Her response in 542 to an official request for bishops addressed to her by the Monophysite Ghassanid Arab allies of the empire also had lasting consequences. Justinian allowed the consecration of two bishops, including Jacob Baradaeus (Bar'Addai) as titular bishop of Edessa, who was subsequently instrumental in the establishment of a rival Monophysite ecclesiastical structure. It is no surprise, therefore, that she is praised by John of Ephesus and a pious version of her early life appears in later Syriac sources. Nonetheless, she is mentioned together with her husband in Orthodox establishments, such as the Monastery of St. Catherine on Mount Sinai. She naturally supported the emperor's edict (544) condemning as Nestorian the Three Chapters, that is certain writings of the deceased theologians Theodore of Mopsuestia, Ibas of Edessa, and Theodoret of Cyrrhus, but she died before its final approval by the Fifth Ecumenical Council.

Theodora was particularly active as a social worker, though in no systematic way. She founded the Convent of Repentance for the rehabilitation of former prostitutes, and she supported women who were abused, forced into prostitution, or suffered other injustice. Her name, mostly together with her husband's, was associated with various buildings and charitable foundations in the capital and elsewhere. Her only certain extant portrait is the wall mosaic in St Vitale, Ravenna, dedicated in 547/8 shortly before her death.

Bibliography: PROCOPIUS OF CAESAREA, *Historia quae dicitur arcana,* ed. J. HAURY and G. WIRTH (Leipzig 1963), tr. H. B. DEWING (Cambridge, Mass. 1935); G. A. WILLIAMSON (Harmondsworth 1966) (both with reprints). JOHN OF EPHESUS, *Lives of the Eastern Saints,* Syriac text ed. and tr. by E. W. BROOKS, *Patrologia Orientalis* 17/1, 18/4, 19/2 (1923–25; repr. 1974). C. DIEHL, *Théodora impératrice de Byzance* (Paris n.d. [before 1904]). E. STEIN, *Histoire du Bas-Empire II* (Paris, Brussels, Amsterdam 1949). B. RUBIN, *Das Zeitalter Justinians I* (Berlin 1960) 98–121. A. CAMERON, *Procopius and the Sixth Century* (London 1985; repr. 1996) 49–83. R. BROWNING, *Justinian and Theodora* (2d ed. London 1987). H.-G. BECK, *Kaiserin Theodora und Prokop* (Munich-Zurich 1986) 89–158. J. R. MARTINDALE, *The Prosopography of the Later Roman Empire III* (Cambridge 1992) 1240 f. J. A. S. EVANS, *The Age of Justinian* (London, New York 1996). L. GARLAND, *Byzantine Empresses* (London, New York 1999) 11–39. *The Cambridge Ancient History XIV. Late Antiquity. Empire and Successors* A.D. *425–600,* ed. A. CAMERON et al. (Cambridge 2000) esp. 64–82.

[T. ANTONOPOULOU]

THEODORA, BYZANTINE EMPRESS (2)

Reigned 842 to 855; wife of THEOPHILUS (reigned 829–842), mother of MICHAEL III (842–867), saint in the Orthodox Church; b. Paphlagonia, *c.* 810; d. Constantinople, 862. She was born of a wealthy family of partly Armenian origin. The future Emperor Theophilus chose Theodora as his wife at the traditional bride show presided over by his mother, Thecla, in spring 821. On becoming emperor in 829, Theophilus revived iconoclasm, but Theodora continued secretly to practice icon veneration. After the death of Theophilus she hesitated for a year before deciding to change the religious policy of her husband. On the advice of Manuel and the logothete, or prime minister, Theoctistus, appointed regents by Theophilus during the infancy of his son Michael III, and of the monk Methodius, who had lived at the court, Theodora convoked a local synod in 843. This deposed the iconoclastic patriarch of Constantinople, John the Grammarian; elected Methodius as his successor; and, after confirming the decisions of the Council of Nicaea II, condemned the iconoclastic heresy and its leaders. On Theodora's insistence the name of the Emperor Theophilus was not included in the list of condemned iconoclasts. The reestablishment of icon veneration was to be commemorated annually by the feast of Orthodoxy, celebrated on the first Sunday in Lent.

After the death of Methodius (847), fearing new complications from the rivalry between zealots who advocated the rigorous treatment of repentant iconclasts and liberal prelates who favored a moderate policy, Theodora appointed IGNATIUS patriarch of Constantinople without the convocation of a local council for the election.

Influenced by her ecclesiastical advisers she made vain efforts to force the PAULICIANS in Asia Minor, by persuasion and military expeditions, to abandon their heresy. In 855 Theodora constrained her son to marry the wife of her choice. Embittered by this, Michael III allied himself with his uncle Bardas, who had been ousted from the regency by Theoctistus. In a plot against the prime minister, Theoctistus was murdered, Bardas became regent, and Theodora was forced to abdicate when Michael III was proclaimed emperor. When Theodora with her supporters tried to reverse the situation, she was forced to enter a convent with her daughters. The Patriarch Ignatius refused to bless their monastic vestments and had to resign. Michael seems, however, to have become reconciled with his mother before his assassination by Basil. Because of her role in the restoration of icon veneration, Theodora was canonized by the Orthodox Church. Her vita was written by an unknown contemporary hagiographer.

Feast: Feb. 11.

Bibliography: V. E. REGEL, ed., *Analecta byzantinorussica* (St. Petersburg 1891) iii–xix, 1–19, *Vita. Acta Sanctae Sedis* Feb. 2:554–569. H. G. BECK, *Kirche und theologische Literatur im byzantinischen Reich* (Munich 1959) 562. J. B. BURY, *A History of the*

Eastern Roman Empire (London 1912) 81–82; 141 ff. F. DVORNIK, *The Photian Schism* (Cambridge, Eng. 1948). G. OSTROGORSKY, *History of the Byzantine State* (Oxford 1956; New Brunswick, NJ 1957) 190, 194–198, 221.

[F. DVORNIK]

THEODORE, ANTIPOPE

Pontificate: 687. Theodore was a Roman presbyter of Greek or Syrian origin who became involved in a contested election following the death of Pope John V (685-686). At this time there were two factions in Rome that often battled for the papacy: representatives of the local militia, and those of the Roman clergy. Theodore was the candidate of the militia; his rival was Peter, an archpriest supported by the clergy. Because of the dispute, Conon (686-687) was elected as a compromise candidate, and he served for a little less than a year. During that time Theodore was raised to the status of archpriest, and when Conon died, he was again involved in a contested election. Theodore was again the militia's candidate; he was elected pope and moved into the Lateran palace, as did his new rival, Paschal. From roughly October to December both men claimed to be pope, and as a result another compromise candidate, Sergius I (687–701), was elected and ratified by the exarch of Italy. Theodore accepted the new pope and nothing more is known of him. J. N. D. Kelly makes the point that since Theodore was never consecrated and stepped aside (unlike Paschal), it is probably incorrect to consider him an antipope, a view that G. Schwaiger appears to share.

Bibliography: L. DUCHESNE, ed. *Liber Pontificalis* (Paris 1886-92; repr. 1955–57) 1.368–72. P. JAFFÉ, *Regesta pontificum Romanorum* (Leipzig 1885-88; repr. Graz 1956) 1.243–4. J. RICHARDS, *The Popes and the Papacy in the Early Middle Ages, 476–752* (London 1979) 206–8, 266, 274. J. N. D. KELLY, *The Oxford Dictionary of Popes* (New York 1986) 81-82. G. SCHWAIGER, *Lexikon des Mittelalters* (Munich 1997) 8.630.

[P. M. SAVAGE]

THEODORE I, POPE

Pontificate: Oct. 12, 642, to May 14, 649; b. in Jerusalem of Greek ancestry. He came to the papal throne amid the political and ecclesiastical disorder consequent upon the promulgation of the *Ecthesis* by the Byzantine Emperor Heraclius. The *Ecthesis,* composed by SERGIUS I, Patriarch of Constantinople, and his successor, PYRRHUS I, affirmed the existence in Christ of only one will, proceeding from the Person of the Word Incarnate without prejudice to the integrity of either the divine or the human nature. Theodore condemned the document and insisted upon the canonical deposition of Pyrrhus. The exiled patriarch found refuge in Carthage where he defended MONOTHELITISM in a public dispute with MAXIMUS THE CONFESSOR, who proved that the doctrine of one will denied the integrity of the two natures in Christ and destroyed the doctrine of the Incarnation. Pyrrhus abjured his errors and made a public profession of faith at St. Peter's in Rome. Theodore reinstated the patriarch, but the latter, for political reasons, apostatized. Theodore convoked a synod at St. Peter's to pronounce against Pyrrhus the sentence of excommunication. The declaration was signed by the pope at the tomb of St. Peter, where Theodore is said to have dipped his pen in the Eucharistic Blood of Christ. In 647 Emperor CONSTANS II ordered the removal of the *Ecthesis* and promulgated the *TYPOS*, an edict forbidding discussion on the subject of one or two wills in Christ. Both documents were condemned by the Council of the Lateran in 649.

Bibliography: *Liber pontificalis*, ed. L. DUCHESNE 1:331–335. P. JAFFÉ, *Regesta pontificum romanorum ab condita ecclesia ad annum post Christum natum 1198*, ed. P. EWALD 1:228–230. J. D. MANSI, *Sacrorum Conciliorum nova et amplissima collectio* 10:991–998. THEOPHANES, *Chronographia,* ed. C. DE BOOR, 2 v. (Leipzig 1883–85). MAXIMUS CONFESSOR, *The Ascetic Life,* tr. P. SHERWOOD (Westminster, MD 1955). E. CASPAR, *Geschichte de Papsttums von den Anfängen bis zur Höhe der Weltherrschaft* 2:543–553. É. AMANN, *Dictionnaire de théologie catholique*, ed. A. VACANT et. al. 15.1:224–226. A. FLICHE and V. MARTIN, eds., *Histoire d'église depuis les origines jusqu'à nos jours* 5:160–166. R. BAUMER, *Marienlexicon,* (1994), s.v. "Teodor I." A. CHAVESSE, "L'Évangeéliaire romain de 645: un recueil. Sa composition (fançons et matériaux)," *Revue Bénédictine* 92 (1982), 33–75. G. KREUZER, *Biographisch–Bibliographisches Kirchenlexikon,* 14 (Herzberg 1997), s.v. "Theodor I, Papst." R. RIEDINGER, "Grammatiker–Gelehrsamkeit in den Akten der Lateran–Synode von 649," *Jahrbuch der Österreichischen Byzantinistik* 25 (Graz 1976) 57–61. C. SCHMIDT, *Lexikon der antiken christlichen Literatur* (Freiburg 1998) s.v. "Theodor von Rom." J. N. D. KELLY, *Oxford Dictionary of Popes* (New York 1986) 73.

[P. J. MULLINS]

THEODORE II, POPE

Pontificate: December 897 to December 897 or January 898; b. Rome; d. Rome. Despite his extremely short reign, Theodore is credited with two important accomplishments. Ignoring the "cadaveric" synod convened under Pope STEPHEN VI, Theodore held a synod that validated all ordinations by his predecessor Pope FORMOSUS, allowing clerics who had been degraded to resume their functions and ordering them to burn their forced resignations, which he returned to them. He formally vindicated Formosus's authority at this same synod. Secondly, he gave honorable burial at Saint Peter's to the corpse of Formosus, which had been cast up on the bank of the

Tiber and hastily buried by a monk. Seppelt thinks Theodore's courageous acts cost him his life.

Bibliography: *Liber pontificalis,* ed. L. DUSHESNE (Paris 1958) 1:331–335. L. JAFFÉ, *Regesta pontificum romanorum ab condita ecclesia ad annum post Christum natum 1198,* ed. S. LÖWENFELD 1:441. J. D. MANSI, *Sacrorum Conciliorum nova et amplissima collectio,* 31 v. (Florence-Venice 1757–98) 17:221–227. C. J. VON HEFELE, *Historie des conciles d'après les documents originaux,* tr. and continued by H. LECLERCQ (Paris 1907–38) 4:566. H. K. MANN, *The Lives of the Popes in the Early Middle Ages from 590 to 1304* (London 1902–32) 4:88–90. É. AMANN, *Dictionnaire de théologie catholique,* ed. A. VACANT (Paris 1903–50; Tables générales 1951–) 15.1:226. F. X. SEPPELT, *Geschichte der Päpste von den Anfängen bis zur Mitte des 20. Jh.* (Munich 1959) 2:342–343. E. PULSFORT, *Biographisch-Bibliographisches Kirchenlexikon,* 11 (Herzberg 1996). J. N. D. KELLY, *Oxford Dictionary of Popes* (New York 1986) 116.

[C. M. AHERNE]

THEODORE ASCIDAS

Sixth-century Origenist monk, archbishop of Caesarea in Cappadocia, and theological adviser to JUSTINIAN I; d. 558. Theodore first appears as a monk and perhaps abbot of the New Laura, near Tekoa in Palestine, which he represented at the synod of Constantinople against the Monophysites (536). In Constantinople, his fellow Origenist, LEONTIUS OF BYZANTIUM, introduced him to the court, and he became head of an Origenist party that defended the Christological formulas of the Council of CHALCEDON against the attack of the Monophysites by interpreting it in the light of the Christology of the Origenist EVAGRIUS PONTICUS. JUSTINIAN I made him archbishop of Caesarea in Cappadocia without the obligation of residence. When the second Origenistic controversy flared up in Palestine (*c.* 540), Theodore and the Origenist party unsuccessfully resisted the demand of the Patriarch of Constantinople MENNAS and the Roman deacon Pelagius, serving as papal legate, that Origen be condemned. However, by signing Justinian's edict against Origen in 543 Theodore maintained his position. He continued to support the Origenistic propaganda in Palestine until the second and final condemnation of the Origenists at the Council at CONSTANTINOPLE II in 553. He played a leading part in the events leading to the Council and in the preparation of the council's acts.

As early as 543, Theodore and Leontius had attacked Theodore of Mopsuestia as the spiritual father of the heretic NESTORIUS, almost certainly because they knew that many of the adversaries of Origen's teachings, including Pelagius, were in sympathy with the Mopsuestian Christology. In 544 Ascidas persuaded Justinian to issue an edict against the so-called THREE CHAPTERS and undertook to secure the support of the Eastern patriarchs. Pope VIGILIUS, who opposed the measure, was brought to Constantinople (547) and was persuaded to condemn the Three Chapters as the emperor wished (548). When Western bishops resisted and the pope was treated with violence, Vigilius excommunicated Theodore and his circle of Constantinopolitan prelates. In 553, before the council met, Vigilius accepted Theodore's retraction and apologies. During the council Ascidas served as one of Justinian's advisers and probably established its agenda. Nothing is known of him from the end of the council until his death five years later.

Bibliography: E. STEIN, *Histoire du Bas- Empire,* tr. J. R. PALANQUE (Paris 1949–59) v.2. L. DUCHESNE, *L'église au VIe siècle* (Paris 1925) 156–218. A. NAGL, ''Theodoros Askidas (50),'' *Paulys Realenzyklopädie der klassischen Altertumswissenschaft,* ed. G. WISSOWA et al. (Stuttgart 1893) 5A.2 (1934) 1890–93.

[D. B. EVANS]

THEODORE LECTOR

Church historian. Exact birth and death places and dates unknown. Theodore was a reader (*anagnōstēs*) of the Hagia Sophia Church of Constantinople in the first half of the sixth century. He wrote two significant ecclesiastical histories in Greek. The first, the *Historia tripartita,* written probably after 520 and completed by 530, recounted in four books the fortunes of the Church from the reign of Emperor Constantine I up to 439. It was a collection of extracts taken from the fifth-century Church histories of SOCRATES Scholasticus, SOZOMEN, and THEODORET OF CYR. Theodore selected those texts that in his opinion provided the most accurate source for particular events. His estimate of the relative value of each historian's account of different subjects is still useful. The *Historia tripartita* is also of service in establishing the textual history of the respective narratives of Socrates, Sozomen, and Theodoret. CASSIODORUS consulted this work in composing his own *Historia tripartita.* Unfortunately, only books one and two have been largely preserved, with the rest being preserved only in fragments.

Theodore wrote also a *Historia ecclesiastica* as a continuation of the *Historia tripartita.* It was divided into four books, and described the history of the Church from 439 up to the accession of Emperor JUSTIN I (518). Only a few fragments of this history, an important source for the obscure fifth century, have been preserved in such works as the *De imaginibus* of St. JOHN DAMASCENE, the Acts of the Council of Nicaea, the *Historia ecclesiastica* of Evagrius Scholasticus, and Pseudo-Codinus. Fragments of both the *Historia tripartita* and the *Historia ecclesiastica* owe their preservation to a lost epitome of Church history composed in the seventh or eighth century. Fragments of this epitome, which has not had a critical edition, are preserved in Cod. Paris. gr. 1555 a, Cod. Baroccianus 142, Paris. suppl. 1156, and Cod. Athous Vatopedi 286.

Bibliography: *Patrologia Graeca* 86.1:157–228. H. G. OPITZ, *Paulys Realenzyklopädie der klassischen Altertumswissenschaft,* ed. G. WISSOWA et al. (Stuttgart 1893) 5.2A (1934) 1869–81. É. AMANN, *Dictionnaire de théologie catholique,* ed. A. VACANT et al. (Paris 1903–50) 15.1:232–233. J. BIDEZ, *La Tradition manuscrite de Sozomène et la Tripartite de Théodore le Lecteur* (TU 32.2b; 1908).

[W. E. KAEGI, JR.]

THEODORE OF CANTERBURY, ST.

Greek archbishop of Canterbury, outstanding figure of the Church in ENGLAND; b. Tarsus, in Cilicia, *c.* 602; d. England, 690. During Theodore's early years Tarsus had been much troubled by Persian aggression; the city was taken by the Arabs in 660. Where Theodore received his earlier education is unknown, but at one time he studied in Athens. He was an accomplished Greek scholar and was also learned in philosophy and law. In 667 he was in Rome, already 65 years old, wearing the Eastern tonsure, and not yet ordained subdeacon. At this time the kings of Northumbria and Kent had sent an Englishman, Wighard, to Rome to be consecrated archbishop of Canterbury, but Wighard died in Rome. Pope VITALIAN asked Abbot HADRIAN OF CANTERBURY, an African, to accept the post. He refused but suggested Theodore of Tarsus. The pope consented, provided that Hadrian was willing to accompany Theodore to England. So Theodore was ordained subdeacon and, four months later, having been tonsured in Roman fashion, was consecrated archbishop by the pope. With Hadrian and BENEDICT BISCOP he started out for Britain on May 27, 668. They arrived there, after a difficult journey, exactly a year later. Theodore was now 67 years old, but he immediately set to work to remedy the confusion in which he found the English Church; many sees were vacant. He at once set out with Hadrian on an episcopal visitation, a long and toilsome journey of inspection, leaving Benedict Biscop in charge of SAINT AUGUSTINE's at Canterbury. Theodore made great progress, and in 637 called, at HERTFORD, the first gathering of the whole English Church at which he drew up nine canons dealing with faith and organization. He then set about attempting to divide up some of the greater dioceses and thus collided with WILFRID OF YORK, who in 678 appealed against his decision to the pope. In 680 Theodore held another synod at Hatfield; there a declaration of the orthodox faith of the English Church was drawn up. In 686 he made his peace with Wilfrid, the last recorded act of his long life. His school at CANTERBURY, where Greek and many other subjects were taught, became a great scholastic center. The PENITENTIAL attributed to him exercised much influence on the Western Church. His body was found incorrupt when translated in 1091 to the present cathedral of Canterbury.

Feast: Sept. 19.

Bibliography: BEDE, Ecclesiastical History 2.3; 4.1–3, 5, 6, 12, 17, 21, 23, 28; 5.8, 24. W. HUNT, *The Dictionary of National Biography From the Earliest Times to 1900* (London 1885–1900) 19:602–606. W. STUBBS, *A Dictionary of Christian Biography,* ed. W. SMITH and H. WACE (London 1877–87) 4: 926–932. G. F. BROWNE, *Theodore and Wilfrith* (New York 1897). F. M. STENTON, *Anglo-Saxon England* (2d ed. Oxford 1947). M. LAPIDGE, ed, *Archbishop Theodore: Commemorative Studies on His Life and Influence* (Cambridge; New York 1995).

[B. COLGRAVE]

THEODORE OF MOPSUESTIA

Bishop, leading exponent of the Antiochene School of exegesis and theology; b. Antioch, *c.* 350; d. Mopsuestia, 428. While studying rhetoric under the pagan sophist Libanius of Antioch, Theodore was persuaded by his fellow student John Chrysostom to enter the monastic school conducted by DIODORE, later bishop of Tarsus. When, after a first period of fervor, Theodore abandoned the monastery, an eloquent letter from Chrysostom (*Patrologia Graeca* 47:309–316) persuaded him to return. He continued his studies under Diodore's direction until 378; in 381 he was ordained a priest of the Church of Antioch and 11 years later was named bishop of Mopsuestia in Cilicia. There is good reason to believe that throughout his long episcopate he enjoyed an excellent reputation for eloquence, learning, and orthodoxy. He died in 428, the year in which another representative of the Antiochene School, NESTORIUS, became bishop of Constantinople.

During the decade following the condemnation of Nestorius by the Council of Ephesus (431), charges of heterodoxy were raised against Theodore's teaching by several prominent bishops, the most important of whom was CYRIL OF ALEXANDRIA, who wrote a work titled *Contra Diodorum et Theodorum,* only fragments of which are extant. Cyril accused Theodore of having taught the same ''impiety'' for which Nestorius had been condemned (*Patrologia Graeca* 77:340). However, at the Council of Chalcedon (451) the Fathers listened without protest to the letter of Ibas of Edessa that praised Theodore as a ''herald of truth and doctor of the Church'' (*Acta conciliorum oecumenicorum* 2.1:392). During the episcopate of Ibas many of Theodore's works were translated into Syriac, thus becoming the heritage of the Nestorian Church, which conferred on him the title ''the Interpreter'' in recognition of his merits as an exegete. At the Second Council of Constantinople, however, just 125 years after his death, his writings were the first of the THREE CHAPTERS to be condemned, and he himself was anathematized as heretical. This verdict prevailed until 1932, when the publication of a Syriac text of his *Catechetical Homilies* stimulated a fresh examination of the evidence. Some scholars now pronounce his authentic teaching thoroughly orthodox, while others still see in it the root error of NESTORIANISM.

Writings. Nestorian writers of the 13th and 14th centuries provide the best available lists of Theodore's works. The only complete work extant in Greek is his *Commentary on the Twelve Minor Prophets* (*Patrologia Graeca* 66:123–632). Of his other exegetical writings, we possess the greater part of his *Commentary on the Psalms,* fragments of his *Commentary on Genesis,* a Syriac version of his *Commentary on St. John's Gospel,* and a Latin version of much of his *Commentary on the Minor Epistles of St. Paul.* Greek catenae have yielded considerable fragments of his exegesis of the major Pauline Epistles, and of the Gospels of Matthew and John. Of his other works, the only complete texts are Syriac versions of his *Catechetical Homilies* and his *Controversy with the Macedonians.* Most of the extant fragments of his major theological works, *On the Incarnation* and *Against Apollinaris* (*Patrologia Graeca* 66:969–1002), were compiled by his adversaries. R. Devreesse and M. Richard have argued that these compilers so misrepresented Theodore's thought that their extracts are completely unreliable as a basis for a judgment on his doctrine. F. Sullivan's study of the evidence has led him to the conclusion that this verdict was not justified. Opinion among scholars on this question remains divided.

Exegesis. Theodore's exegesis is that of the Antiochene School, noted for its insistence on the literal sense, and its aversion for the allegorism characteristic of the Alexandrian School. Typical is his exegesis of the Psalms, which is based on these principles: David is the author of all the Psalms; each Psalm refers to a historical situation, to be determined in the light of the argument of the Psalm as a whole; this situation can be either in the life of David or future to him; in the latter case, David foresees the future event and speaks words appropriate to it. Of the 80 Psalms whose commentary we possess, he relates about 50 to events in the history of Israel from the time of Solomon to that of the Maccabees, and only three [2, 8, 44 (45)] to Christ. His *Commentary on the Minor Prophets* shows a similar insistence on the historical situation envisioned by each prophet. While Theodore saw in the Old Law a ''shadow'' of what was to come in the New, in only a few events of Israel's history did he recognize ''types'' of Christ or the Church. His commentaries on John and Paul show a sustained effort to follow and explain the argument of the Apostle, but his explanations often strongly reflect his own Antiochene theology.

Theology. The most distinctive elements of Theodore's theology are his Christology and his anthropology. Among his positive contributions to the development of Christology are his insistence on the human soul of Christ and on the significance of His free moral activity in the work of redemption. Rejecting the formula ''Word and flesh,'' he used the formula ''Word and assumed man,'' and insisted that these two ''natures'' constitute ''one Son'' and ''one Lord'' because they are united in one person (πρόσωπον). It hardly seems possible that Galtier was correct in affirming that Theodore understood this πρόσωπον to be the divine Person of the Word, since texts cited by friendly as well as by hostile sources show that this πρόσωπον is something brought about or effected by the union (*Patrologia Graeca* 66:981; *Patrologia Latina* 67:587, 753). A newly discovered fragment of Theodore's *Contra Eunomium* shows that in his view the πρόσωπον of Christ is not a ὑπόστασις (as is the πρόσωπον of Peter or Paul) but is a subject of honor and adoration [*Muséon* 71 (1958) 99–100]. The ineffable union that began in Mary's womb conferred on the assumed man a share in the honor, dominion, sonship, and adoration proper to the Word. Since the two natures are inseparably united, so also the adoration that we direct to the divine Word rightly includes the man in whom He dwells ''by good pleasure as in a son'' (*Patrologia Graeca* 66:976).

Fundamental to Theodore's anthropology is his doctrine of the ''two states'' of human existence: the present state of mortality and mutability, and the future state of immortality and immutability, of which the baptized already have a pledge, but which will be actually possessed only after the resurrection. It was God's design that we should first experience mortality, so that we would the more appreciate the blessings of immortality, but our present state is also the result of Adam's sin. Adam's disobedience, which God had foreseen, brought on the sentence of death that he transmitted, with his mortal nature, to his posterity. Theodore's explanation of Rom 5.19, ''By the disobedience of the one man the many were constituted sinners,'' is that the word ''sinners'' here means ''mortal and inclined to sin'' (*Patrologia Graeca* 66:800). While he held death and concupiscence to be effects of Adam's fall, it is very doubtful whether he taught that children are born in an inherited state of sin.

Bibliography: É. AMANN, *Dictionnaire de théologie catholique,* 15 v. ed. A. VACANT et al, (Paris 1903–50) 15:1:235–279. H. B. SWETE, *A Dictionary of Christian Biography,* ed. W. SMITH and H. WACE (London 1877–87) 4:934–948. W. DE VRIES, ''Der 'Nestorianismus' Theodors von Mopsuestia in seiner Sakramentenlehre,'' *Orientalia Christiana Analecta* 7 (1941) 91–148. R. DEVREESSE, *Essai sur Théodore de Mopsueste, Studi e Testi* 141 (Vatican Cty 1948). J. GROSS, ''Theodor von Mopsuestia: Ein Gegner der Erbsündenlehre,'' *Zeitschrift für Kirchengeschichte* 65 (1953–54) 1–15. F.A. SULLIVAN, *The Christology of Theodore of Mopsuestia* (Rome 1956). P. GALTIER, ''Théodore de Mopsueste: sa vraie pensée sur l'incarnation,'' *Recherches de science religieuse* 45 (1957) 161–186, 338–360. J. L. MCKENZIE, ''Annotations on the Christology of Theodore of Mopsuestia,'' *Theological Studies* 19 (1958) 345–373. L. ABRAMOWSKI, ''Zur Theologie des Theodors von Mopsuestia,'' *Zeitschrift für Kirchengeschichte* 72 (1961) 263–293. R. A. GREER, *Theodore of Mopsuestia, Exegete and Theologian* (London 1961). U. WICKERT, *Studien zu den Pauluskommentaren Theodors von Mopsuestia* (*Beihefte zur Zeitschrift für die Neutestamentliche Wissenschaft* 27, 1962). R.A. NORRIS, *Manhood and Christ: A Study in the Christology of Theodore of Mopsuestia* (Oxford 1963). J.E.M. DEWART, *The Theology of Grace of Theodore of Mopsuestia* (Washington, DC 1971). A. GRILLMEIER, *Christ in Christian Tradition* (London/Oxford 1975) 1:421–439. D. ZAHAROPOULOS, *Theodore of Mopsuestia on the Bible. A Study of His Old Testament Exegesis* (New York 1989). F.G. MCLEOD, ''Theodore of Mopsuestia Revisited,'' *Theological Studies* 61 (2000) 447–480.

[F. A. SULLIVAN]

THEODORE OF RHAITHU

Sixth-century monk and theological writer currently thought to be identical with Theodore, Bishop of Pharan, the Monergist proponent. Theodore, a monk and priest of a monastery at Rhaithu (*at-Tûr*), a port in southern Arabia, is considered the last of the Neo-Chalcedonian authors. He is credited with a *Proparaskeue*, or *Preparatio,* that attempts to harmonize Chalcedonian doctrine with the terminology of St. CYRIL OF ALEXANDRIA. Writing during a peaceful era (*c.* 580–620), Theodore intended to provide a theological indoctrination by exposing the errors of Manes, PAUL OF SAMOSATA, APOLLINARIS OF LAODICEA, THEODORE OF MOPSUESTIA, NESTORIUS, and EUTYCHES, and to demonstrate that the Church follows a secure path between heresies in its exposition of the doctrine of the Incarnation. He attacked more recent heretical movements particularly on the part of SEVERUS OF ANTIOCH and JULIAN OF HALICARNASSUS. In the MSS this treatise is connected with a philosophical tract that discusses the notions of essence, nature, hypostasis, and person and seems to be a compendium of the *Isogogues* of Porphyry and Aristotle's *Categories.* As the two parts are only loosely related, the authenticity of the second part has been challenged. A work on the Holy Trinity is also attributed to Theodore; but it is actually a section from the fifth book of the *Fabulae hereticorum* of Theodoret of Cyr.

J. Junglas considered Theodore the author of the *De Sectis,* which has been attributed also to LEONTIUS OF BYZANTIUM. F. Diekamp believed the *Preparatio* to be a commentary on the Dogmatic Tract of ANASTASIUS I, Patriarch of Antioch, and his hypothesis that the *Preparatio* was written between 580 and 620 has been supported by W. Elerts, who contends that Theodore is identical with the Monenergist Theodore, Bishop of Pharan, whose works are preserved only in fragments but to whom Maximus Homologethes attributes a tract on Essence, Nature, Hypothesis, and Person (*Patrologia Graeca* 91: 136).

Bibliography: *Patrologia Graeca* 91:1483–1504, *Preparatio,* pt.1. *Kirche und theologische Literatur im byzantinischen Reich* 382–383. F. DIEKAMP, *Analecta patristica* (Rome 1938) 173–222, *Preparatio,* pts. 1 and 2. W. ELERT, *Theologische Literaturzeitung* 76 (1951) 67–76, Theodor v. Pharan and Theodor v. Raithu. M. RICHARD, *Revue d'histoire ecclésiastique* 35 (1939) 712, Leontius of Byzantium; *Dictionnaire de théologie catholique* 15.1:282–284. V. GRUMEL, *Échos d'Orient* 27 (1928) 257–277, Monothelitism. É. AMANN, *Dictionnaire de théologie catholique* 15.1:279–282.

[F. CHIOVARO]

THEODORE OF SYKEON, ST.

Byzantine archimandrite, ascetic, and bishop of Anastasioupolis; b. Sykeon, Anatolia, mid-sixth century; d. April 22, 613. Theodore, the illegitimate son of Mary and Cosmas, an imperial messenger, was attracted to asceticism as a child and spent much time in fasting and reading the Scriptures at a neighboring shrine of St. George. Despite the opposition of his mother, he left home permanently at the age of 14. His ascetic labors so impressed Theodosius, bishop of Anastasioupolis, that he was appointed successively lector and subdeacon, and at 18 was a priest. After living some years in a suspended cage, he became archimandrite of the monastery of Sykeon. Reports of his miracles and pious works attracted many people. He reluctantly accepted election as bishop of Anastasioupolis and held that office for 11 years. Concern for his monastery and dislike of his administrative duties induced him to resign his bishopric and return to his monastery for the remainder of his life. His vita was written by a contemporary. His remains were translated to Constantinople.

Feast: April 22.

Bibliography: *Acta Sanctorum* April 3:32–61. A. BUTLER, *The Lives of the Saints*, rev. ed. H. THURSTON and D. ATTWATER, 4v. (New York 1956) 2:146–147. NICEPHORUS SCEUOPHYLAX, ''Encomium in S. Theodorum Siceotam,'' ed. C. KIRCH, B. DE GAIFFIER, *Analecta Bollandiana* 20 (1901) 249–272. E. GEŌRGIOS, *Vie de Théodore de Sykéôn* (Brussels 1970). J. O. ROSENQVIST, *Studien zur Syntax und Bemerkungen zum Text der Vita Theodori Syceotae* (Uppsala 1981). N. H. BAYNES and E. A. S. DAWES, trs., *Three Byzantine Saints* (Oxford 1948; repr. Crestwood, N.Y. 1996) 87–192.

[W. E. KAEGI, JR.]

St. Theodore the Studite, miniature in the 11th-century Menologion of Basil II.

THEODORE THE STUDITE, ST.

Byzantine monastic reformer and theologian; b. Constantinople,759; d. perhaps on the island of Prinkipo, 826. Theodore's family, particularly his mother, Theoctista, provided him with an excellent secular and religious education, and he entered the monastic life under the direction of his maternal uncle, Abbot Plato of Symbola, at Saccudium near Mt. Olympus in Bithynia. Ordained in 787 or 788, Theodore succeeded Plato as abbot in 794.

For his vigorous opposition to the adulterous second marriage of the Emperor Constantine VI and to the Patriarch Tarasius's toleration of it, Theodore was banished to Thessalonica in 796; but he was recalled a year later when the Empress IRENE deposed her son.

In 799 Theodore and his community moved to Constantinople and revived the dormant monastery of Studios. Continued conflict over Constantine's ''Moechian Affair'' led to Theodore's banishment again in 809 by the Emperor Nicephorus I. After this Emperor's death in 811, Theodore returned to his activities in the capital.

A resurgence under Leo V (813–820) of the controversy over ICONOCLASM resulted in a third period of exile for Theodore, a popular and eloquent defender of the veneration of images. Despite harsh treatment and virtual imprisonment, he continued to lead opposition to imperial policies by letters, which included appeals to Pope PASCHAL I. The Emperor Michael II was installed after Leo's assassination, but though pursuing a tolerant policy, he feared renewed agitation and refused to allow Theodore to settle permanently in Constantinople. Theodore died away from his monastery in semiexile, but his body was brought to Constantinople with that of his brother Joseph on the restoration of orthodoxy (Jan. 26, 844).

However impressive his courageous defense of Christian morality, orthodox doctrine, and ecclesiastical independence, Theodore's primary contributions were in the area of monastic regulation. By a prudent delegation of authority and duty, carefully outlined yet consonant with cenobitic asceticism, Theodore rendered his Studios community the model of Byzantine monasticism. Many of his regulations and exhortations were promulgated in two series of catecheses, or spiritual conferences, on the virtues and demands of communal religious life. The abbot delivered these talks to his monks.

In addition to the catecheses there survives a collection of 550 letters including many controversial tracts, as well as exhortatory and consolation pieces. He composed liturgical and penitential studies, several works of incisive anti-iconoclastic polemic (including 80 syllogisms that form a systematic theology of the veneration of images), spiritual orations, and verse pieces ranging from hymns to epigrams.

Feast: Nov. 11.

Bibliography: THEODORE THE STUDITE, *On the Holy Icons*; trans. C. P. ROTH (Crestwood, N.Y. 1981); *The Testament*, trans. N. P. CONSTAS, (Washington, D.C. 1991); *Theodori Studitae epistulae*, recensuit G. FATOUROS (Berolini; Novi Eboraci 1992, c1991). *Patrologia Graeca,* ed. J. P. MIGNE (Paris 1857–66) 99; 102:923–926. H. G. BECK, *Kirche und theologische Literatur im byzantinischen Reich* (Munich 1959) 491–495. É. AMANN, *Dictionnaire de théologie catholique,* ed. A. VACANT et al., (Paris 1903–50; Tables générales 1951–) 15.1:287–298. A. GARDNER, *Theodore of Studium* (London 1905). N. H. BAYNES AND H. ST. L. B. MOSS, eds., *Byzantium* (Oxford 1948) 136–165.

[R. J. SCHORK]

THEODORET OF CYR

Antiochean theologian, bishop, and controversial Church Father; b. Antioch, *c.* 393; d. before 466. His rich Christian family gave Theodoret a thorough education in classic culture, literature, and philosophy. Influenced by monastic asceticism, he became a lector at Antioch but decided only after the death of his parents to become a monk at Apamea. Consecrated bishop of Cyr in 423, he continued his ascetical practices while caring for his diocese and devoted himself successfully to the conversion of pagans, Jews, Arians, and Marcionites.

Career. At the start of the difficulties over NESTORIANISM, he became the champion of the Antiocheans, disputed the 12 anathemas of St. CYRIL OF ALEXANDRIA as tinged with APOLLINARIANISM, and refused to condemn Nestorius at the Council of EPHESUS in 431. He did accept the Act of Union between Cyril and JOHN OF ANTIOCH in 433, and he is credited with being responsible for both the creedal formula employed there and the acquiescence of his metropolitan, Alexander of Mabbugh. Faithful to his friends, Theodoret found himself in a difficult position when accused of Nestorian leanings. As an opponent of the Cyrillian theology he was condemned by the supporters of EUTYCHES and DIOSCORUS of Alexandria at the Robber Synod of Ephesus (449) and exiled by Theodosius II to his monastery at Apamea. On appeal to Pope LEO I, in which he acknowledged adherence to the Christology of Leo's *Tome to Flavian,* he was restored to his see by the Emperor Marcian and at CHALCEDON (451), after anathematizing Nestorius, was proclaimed an "orthodox father."

In the evolution of his doctrine, he contributed to the clarification of Christological teaching, but while he condemned "those who divide one unique Savior Jesus Christ in two, and those who say that the divinity of our Master and His humanity are one sole nature" (*Ep.* 119), he considered the peril of MONOPHYSITISM greater than that of NESTORIANISM (*Ep.* 144) and refused to accept the COMMUNICATION OF IDIOMS. He did affirm, however, that the Word had assumed a complete human nature and operations in order to guarantee man's salvation. His activities after 451 are unknown.

The Monophysite Bishop PHILOXENUS OF MABBUGH (d. *c.* 523) caused Theodoret's name to be removed from the DIPTYCHS at Cyr; and although the Nestorian Sergius II restored it, at the Council of CONSTANTINOPLE II in 553 Theodoret's writings against St. Cyril and the Council of Ephesus and his person were condemned as one of the THREE CHAPTERS. Among scholars there is still disagreement over the fundamental orthodoxy of his Christology.

Writings. In 450 Theodoret estimated that he had composed 35 works (*Ep.* 145; cf. *Ep.* 116). Although he spoke Syriac, he wrote in Greek in a rapid but correct style. Despite his inclination to erudition, he is less original in his profound thought than in his scholarly popularizations. Authoritative as an exegete, he takes a position midway between the historical literalness of THEODORE OF MOPSUESTIA and a purely spiritual exegesis, and he has left continuous commentaries on the Canticle of Canticles, the Psalms, Isaias, Daniel, and the Prophets. In his commentaries on the Epistles of St. Paul, he attempts to discover the author's purpose (*skopos*). After 453 he dealt with the Octateuch and Kings in *Quaestiones et Responsiones* but returned to commentary form for the *Book of Chronicles.*

Apologist. Theodoret mentions two books now lost, *Against the Persian Magicians* and *Against the Jews,* the latter connected with his polemical writings *Against the Greeks* (pagans). His *Graecorum affectionium curatio* (Cure of the Pagan Evils), composed before 423, resembles the traditional apologetic but is an original synthesis with contemporary, realistic application. Theodoret aims to cure minds of their prejudices and lead them from Hellenism to the Gospel with the aid of 350 citations of profane authors, which he found in part in the writings of CLEMENT OF ALEXANDRIA and EUSEBIUS OF CAESAREA, and in the florilegia. His ten *Discourses on Providence* were delivered in Antioch probably in 436.

Dogmatic Writings. Early in 431, at the request of John of Antioch, Theodoret wrote a *Refutation of the 12 Anathemas of Cyril of Alexandria,* which, although condemned in 553, seems to be preserved in the *Letter of Cyril to Evoptius* (*Acta conciliorum oecumenicorum* 1:6: 107–146). His *Pentalogos* (or five books against St. Cyril) is lost, except for Greek and Latin fragments, though it was described by PHOTIUS (Bibl. cod. 46). Two tracts, *On the Trinity* and *On the Incarnation of the Savior,* preserved under Cyril's name have been restored to Theodoret by A. EHRHARD and identified with his *De theologia S. Trinitatis et de oeconomia,* which was written against Apollinarianism before 430 and possibly revised in 432. His writings *Against the Arians, the Eunomians, Macedonians, Apollinaris and Marcionites* and his *Expositio rectae fidei,* preserved under the name of Justin Martyr, have been reclaimed for him by T. Lebon, while his *Quaestiones et Responsiones ad Orthodoxos* were restored by Papadopoulos-Kerameus in 1895. The book he mentions as *There Is but One Son after the Incarnation* (*Epp.* 16.109, 130) has been identified by E. Schwartz (*Acta conciliorum oecumenicorum* 1: 1: 6.3) and M. Richard (*Recherches des sciences religieuse* 14:34–61). Only fragments quoted at the Robber Synod of Ephesus in 449 remain of his *Defense of Diodore of Tarsus and Theodore of Mopsuestia,* written after 438; there is no trace of his *Liber Mysticius* or of his *De Virginitate.*

The *Eranistes* (Beggar), written *c.* 447, is a dialogue between a Monophysite (presumably the heretic Eutyches) and an orthodox champion; in it there are 238 citations from 88 different patristic works. It is most important for the explanation of his doctrinal views, and it caused great excitement among his opponents.

Historical Writings. Between 444 and 449 Theodoret composed his *Historia religiosa* (*philothea*), or lives of the monks of Syria, completed with a *Discourse on Charity.* In his *Church History,* written during his exile in 449, he continues the *Hist. Eccl.* of Eusebius from 323 to 428, utilizing a rich documentation culled from the same sources as those of SOCRATES THE HISTORIAN and SOZOMEN; but because of apologetical tendencies, he employs questionable historical opinions and critical views. Toward 453 Theodoret composed a *Haereticarum fabularum compendium,* a synopsis of all heresies down to Eutyches, describing in excellent brevity the variations of error with orthodox doctrine. ZACHARY THE RHETOR cites a *History of Chalcedon* as written by Theodoret, but there is no trace of it; and the *Libellus contra Nestorium ad Sporacium* is not his.

Sermons and Letters. Only fragments of his sermons have been preserved in the acts of contemporary councils and by Photius (Bibl. cod. 273). The panegyric *On the Nativity of St. John the Baptist* is not an authentic work. Of his correspondence, 232 letters have been preserved; they display deep personal interests despite their stylistic formality. Those written between 447 and 451 are doctrinal in subject matter, particularly his letter to Pope Leo I (*Ep.* 113); there are 36 of his letters inserted in conciliar acts.

It is now evident that Theodoret's doctrinal opinions developed in the course of controversy. The condemnation of his writings against Cyril and Ephesus as cited in extracts at Constantinople II was confirmed by Pope VIGILIUS *prout sonant*—as quoted—leaving his good faith unquestioned. In at least 12 letters to officials at Constantinople Theodoret himself protested against the calumny charging him with ''dividing the One Son of God into two Sons'' (*Epp.* 92–96, 99–101, 103, 104, 106, 107).

Bibliography: *Patrologia Graeca* v. 80–84. O. BARDENHEWER, *Geschichte der altkirchlichen Literatur* (Freiburg 1913–32) 4:219–247. J. QUASTEN, *Patrology* (Westminster Md. 1950) 3:536–554. B. ALTANER, *Patrology* (New York 1960) 295–297. E. VENABLES, *A Dictionary of Christian Biography*, ed. W. SMITH and H. WACE (London 1877–87) 4:904–919. H. G. OPITZ, *Paulys Realenzyklopädie der klassischen Altertumswissenschaft*, ed. G. WISSOWA et al. 5A:2 (1934) 1791–1801. G. BARDY, *Dictionnaire de théologie catholique*, A. VACANT et al., ed. 15 v. (Paris 1903–50) 15.1:299–325. Y. AZEMA, *Théodoret de Cyr d'après sa correspondance* (Paris 1952). P. CANIVET, *Histoire d'une entreprise apologétique au Ve siècle* (Paris 1958); ''Théodoret et le monachisme syrien . . . ,'' *Théologie de la vie monastique* (Paris 1961) 241–282. T. CAMELOT, *Das Konzil von Chalkedon: Geschichte und Gegenwart*, ed. A. GRILLMEIER and H. BACHT, (Wurzburg 1951–54) 1:232–242. I. ORTIZ DE URBINA, *ibid.* 400–409. M. RICHARD, *Revue des sciences philsophiques et théologiques* 24 (1935) 83–106; 25 (1936) 459–481; *Mélanges de science religieuse* 3 (1946) 147–156. E. HONIGMANN, *Patristic Studies* (*Studi e Testi* 173; 1953).

[P. CANIVET]

THEODORIC, ANTIPOPE

Pontificate: September 1100 to January 1101; he died in 1102. Theodoric (also Theoderic) was cardinal deacon of Santa Maria in Via Lata in 1084 and served as antipope Clement III's (1080; 1084–1100) legate in Germany. Clement made him cardinal bishop of Albano, and it is assumed that Theodoric hid Clement when the latter was forced to flee from the Castel Sant' Angelo in 1084. When Clement died, his Roman supporters met secretly in St. Peter's and elected Theodoric as his successor. He was consecrated that night, but he was only able to remain in the city for 105 days, until Paschal II (1099–1118) returned. Theodoric fled Rome, hoping for support from Henry IV (1056–1106), but the emperor was trying to reach an understanding with the legitimate pope. Thus Theodoric was arrested by Paschal's forces in January 1101 and became a monk in Holy Trinity monastery at La Cava near Salerno, which later was the place of confinement for antipopes Gregory VIII, 1118–21, and Innocent III, 1179–80. He died the following year and was buried in the monastery's cemetery.

Bibliography: L. DUCHESNE, ed. *Liber Pontificalis* (Paris 1886–92; repr. 1955–57) 2.298, 345. P. JAFFÉ, *Regesta pontificum*

Romanorum (Leipzig 1885–88; repr. Graz 1956) 1.772. P. KEHR, ''Zur Geschichte Wiberts von Ravenna (Clemens III),'' *Sitzungsberichte der Preussischen Akademie der Wissenschaften zu Berlin* (1921) 980–88. R. HÜLS, *Kardinäle, Klerus und Kirchen Roms, 1049–1130* (Tubingen 1977) 92–95.C. SERVATIUS, *Paschalis II* (Stuttgart 1979) 42ff, 70–72, 339. J. N. D. KELLY, *The Oxford Dictionary of Popes* (New York 1986) 161–62. G. TELLENBACH, *The Church in Western Europe from the Tenth to the Early Twelfth Century* (Cambridge 1993).

[P. M. SAVAGE]

THEODORIC BORGOGNONI OF LUCCA

Dominican bishop and pioneer in the practice of surgery; b. Lucca or Parma, 1205 or 1208; d. Bologna, 1298. He was the son of Hugh of Lucca, from whom he learned surgery and medicine, which he continued to practice all his life. Theodoric entered the Order of Preachers at Bologna in 1226, became a papal penitentiary, was consecrated bishop of Bitonto in 1262, and became bishop of Cervia in 1266. His most famous work is a treatise on surgery, *Chirurgia* (1266), which was translated into several vernaculars and went through five printed editions before being translated into English in 1955. Theodoric also wrote a veterinary treatise on horses, *Practica equorum,* of which early Spanish and French translations exist, and a work on falconry. Two lost treatises deal with the sublimation of arsenic and with mineral salts. The treatise on surgery was far in advance of its time and is a model of surgical practice. Theodoric strongly advocated aseptic surgery at a time when others taught that the formation of pus was necessary for healing. He strove for asepsis, careful hemostasis, elimination of dead tissue and foreign matter, the accurate reapproximation of the wound walls, and protection of the area. His methods were successfully applied by his pupil, Henry of Mondeville, the father of French surgery, but then fell into disuse for centuries. Theodoric also described the preparation and use of sponges to induce sleep before surgery, a prelude to anesthesia. He advised the use of mercurial ointments in the treatment of skin diseases, the sparing application of cautery, and progressive methods for treating fractures and dislocations.

Bibliography: *The Surgery of Theodoric,* tr. E. CAMPBELL and J. COLTON, 2 v. (New York 1955–60). *El libro de los caballos: tratado de albeitería del siglo XIII,* ed. G. SACHS (Madrid 1936). J. QUÉTIF and J. ÉCHARD, *Scriptores ordinis praedicatorum* (New York 1959) 1:355. G. SARTON, *Introduction to the History of Science* (Baltimore 1927–48) 2.2:654–656.

[W. A. WALLACE]

THEODORIC (DIETRICH) OF FREIBERG

German Dominican philosopher, theologian, and precursor of modern science, otherwise known as Theodoricus Teutonicus de Vriberg and Thierry de Fribourg; b. Freiberg in Saxony?, *c.* 1250; d. 1310 or shortly thereafter. An eclectic and independent thinker, Theodoric may be characterized as Neoplatonic and Augustinian in theology and as Aristotelian in philosophy; he was also an indefatigable researcher whose experimental and theoretical work on the rainbow was several centuries in advance of his time.

Life and Works. Theodoric was present at the University of Paris when HENRY OF GHENT disputed his first *quodlibet* in 1276. He was elected provincial of Germany by the general and provincial chapter of Strassburg in 1293, an office he held for three years. It is probable that he became a master in Paris in 1297. He is identified as ''Master Theodoric, Prior of Würzburg,'' in a document describing the work of a commission in which he took part at Koblenz in 1303. He was present at the general chapter of the order held in Toulouse in 1304, at which time the master general, Aymeric, asked him to put the result of his investigations on the rainbow into writing. The general chapter held at Piacenza in 1310 appointed him vicar provincial of Germany. In one of his last works he wrote that he had given up teaching for preaching, and he is noted as the first scholastic to preach in German (H. Denifle and F. Ehrle, *Archiv für Literatur- und Kirchengeschichte des Mittelalters,* 7 v. 2:421). He exerted considerable influence on the German mystics, particularly Berthold of Moosburg, Meister ECKHART, and Johannes TAULER.

Theodoric's writings were mainly in the form of *opuscula* on a variety of subjects in logic, psychology, metaphysics, theology, and natural science. In logic he dealt with the predicaments, the notion of quiddity, the nature of contraries, and the notions of more and less. His psychological treatises were concerned with the intellect and its object and with habits, while his metaphysical works dealt with essence and existence, accidents, and the heavenly bodies and their movers. In theology he was concerned with such subjects as the beatific vision, the knowledge of separated substances, the attributes of glorified bodies, and the Body of Christ after His death. His works in science include treatises on light, color, the rainbow, elements, compounds, and time.

E. Krebs has edited Theodoric's psychological writings; A. Maurer, his work on quiddity; F. Stegmüller, his works on time [*Archives d'histoire doctrinale et littéraire du moyen-âge* 13 (1940–42): 155–221] and on the predicaments [*ibid.* 24 (1957): 115–201]; and J. Würschmidt [*Beiträge zur Geschichte der Philosophie und Theologie des Mittelalters* 12.5–6 (1914): 33–204] and W. A. Wallace (*Methodology,* 305–376), most of his scientific treatises.

Teaching. Theodoric's work on the predicaments draws heavily from Aristotle's *Metaphysics* and Averroës's commentary on the same and is particularly concerned with the modes of causal origin by which the categories are constituted, for example, the intellect's causality in the formation of universals. His theory of knowledge, as expounded in the work on the intellect, is markedly influenced by the *LIBER DE CAUSIS* and by St. Augustine. Theodoric teaches that the agent intellect is unique in each man, that it is always in act, that it is what makes man be in God's image, and that it is a beatifying principle in the elect who see God in His essence.

Theodoric opposes St. THOMAS AQUINAS in denying the real distinction between essence and existence. Like the treatise on quiddity, that on essence and existence seems partially inspired by St. Thomas's *De ente et essentia.* Another metaphysical doctrine on which Theodoric sets himself in opposition to Thomas is his teaching on accidents, and particularly on whether it is possible for these to exist without a subject—which the German Dominican holds is absolutely impossible, both naturally and supernaturally. His view of the universe is Neoplatonic: it embraces God's unity, spiritual natures, souls, and bodies; interprets creation as a type of emanation; and conceives temporal development as a return to divine unity. Contrary to some authors, he was never a proponent of the metaphysics of light.

Theodoric's work in optics culminated in the first correct explanation of the primary and secondary rainbows in terms of the paths of light rays being reflected and refracted through spherical raindrops. His scientific methodology is a paradigm for the application of Aristotelian logic and dialectics to specific problems; it also anticipated the experimental methods of modern science. As a byproduct of this work, Theodoric elaborated a theory of light and color that attempts to explain such phenomena as the production of spectra and that links these to the structure of matter. He also worked out a theory of elements and compounds that accounts for the relations of the elements to primary matter. His analysis of gravitational motion allows for the fact that there might be a plurality of centers in the universe toward which matter gravitates. He also eliminated the generator as an efficient cause of falling motion, thereby anticipating later medieval developments in mechanics. His theory of the rainbow indirectly influenced the development of geometrical optics by Descartes and Newton.

See Also: SCIENCE (IN THE MIDDLE AGES).

Bibliography: E. KREBS, ''Meister Dietrich: Sein Leben, seine Werke, seine Wissenschaft,'' *Beiträge zur Geschichte der Philosophie und Theologie des Mittelalters* 5.5–6; (1905–06); ''Le Traité *De esse et essentia* de Thierry de Fribourg,'' *Revue néo-scolastique de philosophie* 18 (1911): 516–536. A. MAURER, ''The *De quidditatibus entium* of Dietrich of Freiberg and Its Criticisms of Thomistic Metaphysics,'' *Mediaeval Studies* 18 (1956): 173–203. W. A. WALLACE, *The Scientific Methodology of Theodoric of Freiberg* (Studia Friburgensia, new series 26; Fribourg 1959); ''Gravitational Motion according to Theodoric of Freiberg,'' *Thomist* 24 (1961): 327–352; ''Theodoric of Freiberg on the Structure of Matter,'' *Proceedings of the Tenth International Congress of History of Science, Ithaca, N.Y. 1962,* 2 v. (Paris 1964) 1:591–597. É. H. GILSON, *History of Christian Philosophy in the Middle Ages* (New York 1955) 433–437, 753–755.

[W. A. WALLACE]

THEODORIC THE GREAT

Ostrogothic king, ''the Amal'' (475–526) and ruler of Italy; b. *c.* 455; d. Aug. 30, 526, in Ravenna. While a hostage in Constantinople (462–471), he conceived an admiration for Greco-Roman culture, and this, together with his gifts of leadership and his barbarian power, made him the greatest of the first Germanic kings. As ruler of the Ostrogoths in Pannonia, he found himself in a struggle with Emperor Zeno and with Theodoric Strabo, a fellow Ostrogothic chieftain who died in 481. When Theodoric made peace with Zeno in 483, he received new lands and the titles Master of Troops and Patrician. In 488 Zeno commissioned him to occupy Italy and to drive out Odoacer, then dominating the peninsula. Theodoric won a decisive battle at the Adda River in 490, but only in 493 did he capture Ravenna and murder Odoacer.

As king of the Ostrogoths, in control of military power, he governed Italy as the emperor's viceroy and, with the support of the senatorial aristocracy, maintained the traditional Roman government. From Ravenna Theodoric governed wisely, restored prosperity, and encouraged arts and letters. Distrustful of the emperors in Constantinople, he strove to form a confederation of the western Germanic kingdoms. Matrimonial alliances with rulers of the Franks, Visigoths, Vandals, Burgundians, Heruls, and Thuringians contributed to this policy, but the rapid rise of Clovis upset his plan and led him to extend his own power into Provence and to assume control of the Visigothic monarchy.

Theodoric's religious policy was to preserve the separation of the Arian Ostrogoths and the Catholic Italo-Romans. CASSIODORUS considered this toleration a farsighted policy, but it may have sprung from expediency as much as from principle. Theodoric allowed the Church greater liberty than did most Germanic kings and was reluctant to intervene in Church matters. Invited by the

Catholics to mediate the dispute between Pope SYMMACHUS and the antipope Lawrence (498–506), Theodoric, himself an Arian, vacillated but then supported Symmachus. He protected Catholics from the efforts of Zeno and Anastasius to promote MONOPHYSITISM. The ACACIAN SCHISM (482–519) worked to his advantage, but he raised no obstacles when Pope Hormisdas carried on negotiations that ended it. After 523, Theodoric's program broke down as a result of the measures of the Emperor JUSTIN I against eastern Arians. Theodoric, with reason, saw in them an attempt to undermine his position in Italy. When certain prominent Romans endorsed Justin's measures, Theodoric suspected treason. In these circumstances he executed BOETHIUS and the senator Symmachus on political charges. Late in 525 Theodoric sent Pope John I to Constantinople to secure an amelioration of Justin's decrees, but John returned without all the desired concessions and died of natural causes soon after being imprisoned by Theodoric. Before his own death Theodoric procured the election of his own candidate, FELIX IV, as pope.

Bibliography: Decrees, edicts in *Monumenta Germaniae Historica: Auctores Antiquissimi* 12:393–455; *Monumenta Germaniae Historica: Leges* 5:145–179. A. NAGL, *Paulys Realenzyklopädie der klassischen Altertumswissenschaft,* ed. G. WISSOWA et al. (Stuttgart 1893) 5.2:1745–71.W. ENSSLIN, *Theoderich der Grosse* (2d ed. Munich 1959). E. STEIN, *Histoire du Bas-Empire,* tr. J. R. PALANQUE (Paris 1949–59) v.2.

[R. H. SCHMANDT]

THEODOSIUS, MONOPHYSITE PATRIARCH OF ALEXANDRIA

Reigned 535 to 566; d. June 19 or 22, 566. He succeeded Timotheus III (Feb. 10, 535) through the support of Empress THEODORA (1), who had Monophysitic leanings. Rejecting his election, the JULIANIST Monophysitic faction chose Gaian as rival patriarch. Theodosius, lacking popular support, fled Alexandria to take refuge in the Canopus Monastery until late May 535, when imperial troops drove the Julianists from Alexandria. After investigating the patriarchal election, the cubicularius Narses ruled that Theodosius was the legitimate Monophysite patriarch. Gaian was exiled, but the Gaianist controversy deprived Theodosius of wide local support. Byzantine Emperor JUSTINIAN I summoned him to Constantinople in November or December 536, but did not dare to depose him. At first Justinian treated Theodosius well, hoping to induce him to accept the Council of Chalcedon. Sent to enforced residence at Derkos for some time, Theodosius was ultimately recalled to Constantinople, where he spent the rest of his life in gentle captivity in the company of Monophysite clergy. Meanwhile, Justinian sent a series of Chalcedonian patriarchs to Alexandria in an unsuccessful endeavor to destroy Egyptian MONOPHYSITISM.

While in captivity Theodosius made important contributions to Monophysitism. After the death of SEVERUS OF ANTIOCH and the deposition of ANTHEMIUS of Constantinople (536), Theodosius exercised leadership over the Monophysites throughout the Byzantine Empire. Although he shrank from open struggle with Justinian, he favored and assisted James BARADAI and others in Monophysitic missionary activity and encouraged the formation of the Jacobite Church. Theodosius chose his own syncellus, Paul, as Monophysite patriarch of Antioch. After Justinian's death (565), Justin II gave Theodosius an audience and offered to permit him to return to Alexandria. Theodosius died soon after this meeting, and the imperial government buried him with honors at Constantinople.

Theodosius occupied himself during exile by writing treatises against the agnoete, tritheist, and condobaudite heresies. Among the extant works of this prolific writer are a letter to Severus of Antioch and one to Anthimus of Constantinople, fragments of a tome addressed to Empress Theodora, and other Coptic texts. In doctrine, he adhered to the Monophysitic views of Severus of Antioch.

Bibliography: *Patrologia Graeca,* ed. J. P. MIGNE (Paris 1858–66) 86.1:277–286. COSMAS INDICOPLEUSTES, *Christian Topography,* ed. E. O. WINSTEDT 314–315, works and fragments. E. A. T. W. BUDGE, ed. and tr., *Saint Michael the Archangel: Three Encomiums by Theodosius. . .* (London 1894). F. ROBINSON, tr., *Coptic Apocryphal Gospels* (Texts and Studies 4; Cambridge, Eng. 1896) 90–127. É. AMANN, *Dictionnaire de théologie catholique,* ed. A. VACANT et al. (Paris 1903–50) 15.1:325–328. L. DUCHESNE, *L'église au VIe siècle* 90–91, 101–108, 338–347. J. MASPERO, *Histoire des patriarches d'Alexandrie* 111–121.

[W. E. KAEGI, JR.]

THEODOSIUS II, BYZANTINE EMPEROR

Reigned 408 to 450; b. 401. He succeeded his father ARCADIUS while still a child (408), was inclined to intellectual pursuits rather than to politics or war and lived under the tutelage of regents and of strong personalities: the Praetorian Prefect Anthemius, his own sister the Empress PULCHERIA, and his minister Chrysaphius. In 421 he married Athenais Eudocia. The marriage of their daughter Licinia Eudoxia to her Western cousin VALENTINIAN III in 437 was an expression of the good relations between the two parts of the empire. Theodosius founded the University of Constantinople *c.* 425 and authorized

Bronze coin obverse (left) and reverse (right) of Byzantine Emperor Theodosius II, struck at Constantinople c. 420.

the Theodosian Code of 438, which codified Roman law from 312 to 437 and had particular importance in the West. He fortified Constantinople and defended the empire with partial success against the Huns and Germans.

Theodosius played an important role in the religious controversies concerned with NESTORIANISM and MONOPHYSITISM. In 431, he summoned the Council of EPHESUS, which condemned Nestorianism, supported its decisions with imperial decrees in 435 and in 448, and facilitated the reconciliation between CYRIL OF ALEXANDRIA and JOHN OF ANTIOCH in 433. Theodosius favored the Archimandrite EUTYCHES against Flavian, the Archbishop of Constantinople and in 449 convoked a council at Ephesus over which DIOSCORUS OF ALEXANDRIA presided, upholding its judgment despite the protests of Pope LEO I, who called it a ''Robber Synod'' (Latrocinium). The death of Theodosius brought his sister Pulcheria and her husband Marcian to the imperial throne and cleared the way for the condemnation of Monophysitism at the Council of Chalcedon.

Bibliography: E. STEIN, *Histoire du Bas-Empire,* tr. J. R. PALANQUE, 2 v. in 3 (Paris 1949–59). R. V. SELLERS, *The Council of Chalcedon* (London 1953). Codex Theodosianus, *The Theodosian Code and Novels,* ed. and tr. C. PHARR et al. (Princeton 1952).

[R. H. SCHMANDT]

THEODOSIUS I BORADIOTES, PATRIARCH OF CONSTANTINOPLE

Reigned 1179 to 1183. Theodosius was apparently an Armenian born in Antioch; he came to the patriarchal throne between February and July 30, 1179. At the end of the reign of Manuel I, he was drawn into the theological dispute occasioned by the emperor's eagerness to reword the form of the abjuration taken by converted Moslems. Manuel, already ill, yielded to Theodosius's persuasion and agreed to modify his original wording. On Manuel's death (1180) Theodosius lived through the troubled minority of Alexius II and saw the rise to power of Andronicus I. The patriarch appears to have protested against the violation of the rights of sanctuary by the rival political factions. Finally Theodosius incurred the hostility of Andronicus, who desired ecclesiastical sanction for the marriage of his illegitimate daughter Irene to Alexius, illegitimate son of Manuel I, despite decrees prohibiting such a union. Theodosius refused to accommodate the emperor and evidently had to abdicate, going to the monastery of Terebinthes. This occurred shortly before Sept. 3, 1183, when Andronicus became co-emperor; for in August, while Andronicus was still co-regent, Theodo-

Theodosius I, Roman Emperor, an engraving on a medallion. (Archive Photos)

sius had agreed to the expulsion of the dowager empress Mary from the imperial palace.

Bibliography: V. GRUMEL, *Les Regestes des actes du patriarchat de Constantinople* (Kadikoi-Bucharest 1932–47) v.1.3. V. GRUMEL, *Études byzantines* 1 259–260. M. I. GEDEON, Πατριαρχικοὶ πίνακες (Constantinople 1890).

[J. M. HUSSEY]

THEODOSIUS I, ROMAN EMPEROR

Reigned 379 to 395, ended the Arian dispute and established Catholicism as the religion of the empire. Called from his native Spain after the Roman defeat at Adrianople in 378, he became the general and then imperial colleague of the Emperor Gratian. Through arms and diplomacy, he ended the Visigothic threat by 382. As emperor, he governed the East, intervening in the West in 388 to prevent Maximus from displacing Valentinian II. After Valentinian's death in 392, Theodosius reigned alone, with his sons ARCADIUS and HONORIUS as Augusti. In 394 he defeated the pagan pretender Eugenius in Italy.

Shortly after his baptism in 380, Theodosius, totally unsympathetic to ARIANISM, ordered all Christians to profess the faith of the bishops of Rome and Alexandria, i.e., the NICENE CREED. He deposed the Arian bishop Demophilus of Constantinople and installed GREGORY OF NAZIANZUS. In 381 he forbade heretics to meet within cities and ordered all church buildings returned to Catholics. He then sought ecclesiastical support for his position, summoning in 381 the Council of CONSTANTINOPLE I, which finally abolished Arian claims. The acts of the council were ratified by Theodosius, who also published a decree establishing the orthodox Christian faith. Subsequently, Theodosius summoned the leaders of various heretical groups to colloquies, hoping to convert them. When his efforts failed, he promulgated laws in 383 and 384 renewing and strengthening measures against heretics.

Theodosius then outlawed paganism, proceeding by administrative measures as well as edicts. In 385 he renewed the prohibition of bloody sacrifices; in 391 he forbade all pagan ceremonies in Rome and extended the prohibition to Egypt; in 392, in the most comprehensive and precise terms, he outlawed every form of pagan worship, public and private, throughout the empire.

Although Theodosius acted according to the prevailing theory that the state enjoyed extensive prerogatives in regulating ecclesiastical affairs, his relations with St. AMBROSE of Milan show a willingness to recognize limitations. In 388 he accepted public humiliation at the hands of Ambrose and revoked an order for the Christians of Callinicum to restore Jewish property they had unjustly destroyed. Two years later, Ambrose apparently excommunicated Theodosius because of a massacre at Salonika. The Emperor resisted the bishop's claim to interfere, but finally accepted Ambrose's dictum that even in political matters the emperor was subject to the Church's moral judgments.

Bibliography: H. LECLERCQ, *Dictionnaire d'archéologie chrétienne et de liturgie*, ed. F. CABROL, H. LECLERCQ, and H. I. MARROU (Paris 1907–53) 15:2265–71. E. STEIN, *Histoire du Bas-Empire,* tr. J. R. PALANQUE, 2 v. in 3 (Paris 1949–59). N. Q. KING, *The Emperor Theodosius and the Establishment of Christianity* (Philadelphia 1960).

[R. H. SCHMANDT]

THEODOSIUS OF PALESTINE, ST.

Sixth-century monastic leader also called ''the Cenobiarch''; b. Mogarissus or Garissus in Cappadocia, *ca.* 423; d. Jan. 11, 529. Theodosius entered a monastery at Jerusalem and placed himself under the ascetic Longinus at the Tower of David. Desiring a more secluded life, he went to the monastery of the Cathisma of the Theotokos (between Jerusalem and Bethlehem). Through the favor of its founder, the pious lady Ikelia, he was given the administration of the monastery. Unwilling to be a hegoumenos, he fled to a grotto at Metopa. There he received many persons, including the influential official Acacius, who gave him the funds with which he built a hostel and a cenobium. His ascetic fame earned him election as archimandrite of the cenobite monks of Jerusalem. With the Patriarch of Jerusalem SABAS, he strongly opposed MONOPHYSITISM, and for this reason the Emperor ANASTASIUS I exiled Theodosius. On the death of Anastasius, Theodosius returned to his monastery for the rest of his life.

Feast: January 11.

Bibliography: CYRIL OF SCYTHOPOLIS, *Leben des Theodosios,* ed. E. SCHWARTZ 235241. THEODORE OF PETRA, *Vie de saint Théodosios,* tr. A.-J. FESTUGIÈRE (Paris 1963); *Der heilige Theodosios,* ed. H. USENER (Hildesheim 1975).

[W. E. KAEGI, JR.]

THEODOSIUS THE DEACON, COLLECTION OF

A collection of canonical and historical material pertaining to the Carthaginian synod of 419 (*see* CARTHAGE, COUNCILS OF), to the early Eastern councils, and to the personal history of St. ATHANASIUS. The collection itself is to be found solely in the Verona Chapter Library Codex LX (58), dating from about the year 700. Its contents were first published by S. Maffei in 1738. The unique interest of the collection is that it contains several important documents that are not found elsewhere. These are a letter to the bishops of the East from a Roman synod held in about 372, the canons of a synod at Carthage in 421, a paschal cycle, two letters from Athanasius to the Church at Alexandria, a letter from the Council of SARDICA, the *Historia Acephala,* and two letters relating to the MELETIAN SCHISM. Because of its large quantities of Carthaginian and Sardican material, C. H. Turner suggested that the collection grew up around the African jurisdictional dispute with Rome over Apiarius of Sicca, for upon this dispute the Sardican canons would have had bearing. E. Schwartz, W. Telfer, and H. Hess have modified this hypothesis, but it is generally agreed that the Sardican and other Eastern material in the collection represents an early fifth-century African inquiry into the nature of the Council of Sardica. The identity of the deacon Theodosius, whose subscription the MS collection bears, is unknown.

Bibliography: W. TELFER, "The Codex Verona LX (58)," *Harvard Theological Review* 36 (1943) 169–246. C. H. TURNER, "The Verona Manuscripts of Canons LX (58) and LIX (57)," *Guardian* (Dec. 11, 1958) 1921–22. H. HESS. *The Canons of the Council of Sardica, A.D. 343* 63–67. F. MAASSEN, *Geschichte der Quellen und der Literatur des canonischen Rechts im Abendlande bis dem Ausgang des Mittelalters* (Graz 1870; 1956) 546–551. E. SCHWARTZ, "Über die Sammlung des Cod. Veronensis LX," *Zeitschrift für die neutestamentliche Wissenschaft und die Kunde der älteren Kirche* 35 (1936) 1–23.

[H. HESS]

THEODOTUS

Gnostic disciple of VALENTINUS. No information about Theodotus survives, but portions of his writings were preserved by Clement of Alexandria in a sort of appendix to his *Stromata,* entitled *Excerpts from the works of Theodotus and the school called Oriental from the time of Valentinus.* According to Hippolytus, the Oriental school of Valentinians, as distinguished from the Italian school, held that the body of Christ belonged not to the psychic but to the pneumatic class, and this teaching is accepted in the *Excerpta ex Theodoto.* However, Theodotus cannot be identified with the Theodotus mentioned by Hippolytus (*Ref.* 7.3536). A date around A.D. 160–170 is often assigned to him. His teaching apparently was related to that of the Oriental Valentinian Marcus.

The *Excerpta* are an important source of our knowledge of Valentinianism but a difficult one to interpret because of their unsystematic arrangement and because they contain many of Clement's own ideas and comments. Excerpts 43 to 65 closely parallel Irenaeus' account of Valentinianism (*Adversus Haereses* 1.18) and probably use the same source. Typically Valentinian ideas such as the Pleroma, the Demiurge, and the pneumatic seeds are discussed in the *Excerpta.* Theodotus' personal contribution is concerned with the role of the angels and their baptism in the sacred Name.

See Also: GNOSTICISM.

Bibliography: THEODOTUS, *The Excerpta ex Theodoto,* ed. R. P. CASEY (Studies and Documents 1; London 1934); *Extraits de Thodote,* ed. F. SAGNARD. W. FOERSTER, *Von Valentin zu Herakleon, Zeitschrift für die neutestamentliche Wissenschaft und die Kunde der älteren Kirche,* Beiheft 7. 85–91. F. SAGNARD, *La Gnose valentinienne et le tmoignage de Saint Irne* 521–561.

[G. W. MACRAE]

THEODOTUS OF ANCYRA

Bishop of Ancyra and an early friend of NESTORIUS; d. *c.* 446. He exposed Nestorius's heretical teaching at the Council of EPHESUS; served as a member of the delegation sent to the Emperor THEODOSIUS II by the Council; and was excommunicated by the Antiochene bishops in their Synod of Tarsus for supporting CYRIL OF ALEXAN-

DRIA. Nothing further is known of his life. Four of his sermons are preserved in the acts of the Council of Ephesus: two homilies on the Nativity, a third against Nestorius, and a fourth on the feast of the lights that testifies to the celebration of the Purification at the beginning of the 5th century. He also wrote a commentary on the Symbol of Nicaea in which he maintains that Nestorius ideas were already condemned by that Council. A lost work of six books against Nestorius was cited at the Council of Nicaea III in 787. The authenticity of a homily on the Nativity and a sermon on the Theotokos has been challenged.

Bibliography: *Patrologia Graeca,* ed. J. P. MIGNE, 161 vol. (Paris 1857–66) 77:13071432. *Acta conciliorum oecumenicorum,* (Berlin 1914–) 1.1.2:7190. G. BARDENHEWER, *Geschichte der altkirchlichen Literatur,* 5 v. (Freiburg 1913–32) 4:197200. G. BARDY, *Dictionnaire de théologie catholique,* ed. A. VACANT et al., 15 v. (Paris 1903–50) 15.1: 328330.

[P. T. CAMELOT]

THEODULF OF ORLÉANS

A Visigoth, apparently of Spanish origin; an important figure at CHARLEMAGNE's court; and the most accomplished poet of his time; d. 821. He speaks of himself as ''exiled by immense misfortunes,'' probably referring to Moorish incursions in Spain. The classicism of his works and tastes indicates that he was educated in the classical tradition, which still survived in the schools of Spain.

Like the date of his birth, the date of his flight to the Franks is unknown. His first work for Charlemagne would seem to have been the *Libri Carolini,* begun in 790. He composed also epitaphs for Queen Fastrada (d. 794) and Adrian I. As bishop, later archbishop (800), of Orléans, he was intimate with the court circle, as his poems show. A tribute in verse to Charlemagne gives amusing portraits of ALCUIN, EINHARD, ANGILBERT, and other familiars of the court, as well as of the royal family. Except for PAULINUS OF AQUILEIA, he was the only foreigner honored with a bishopric; he ruled also the neighboring abbeys of Fleury, Micy, and Saint-Aignan. His church at Germigny-des-Prés is an important monument of Carolingian art and architecture.

In 798 he was sent as a *missus dominicus,* together with LEIDRADUS OF LYONS, through the southern, Visigothic regions of Charlemagne's realm. His verses *Ad iudices* describe this journey and contain enlightened recommendations for improving the judicial procedures of his day. This poem also furnishes evidence, in descriptions of gifts offered by litigants, for his interests as a connoisseur. Wall paintings with allegorical meanings decorated his refectory and were explained in verse. His artistic tastes are reflected also in the mosaics of Germigny and in the sumptuous Bibles produced in his scriptorium at Orléans, of which two exemplars survive. Theodulf's version of the Vulgate text, with its variant readings, is the most scholarly of the age. He produced also a work on the procession of the Holy Spirit and a treatise on Baptism. Two capitularies, directed to his clergy, show that Charlemagne's instructions regarding education were implemented in the See of Orléans.

The favor he enjoyed under Charlemagne was continued by Louis the Pious, but in 817 Theodulf was accused of complicity in the rebellion of Bernard of Italy, deprived of his benefices, and driven from his see. He died still protesting his innocence. With his interests in education, arts and letters, and classical as well as Christian authors, and his mastery of Latin meters, Theodulf is a fine example of medieval humanism and one of the brightest lights of the Carolingian renaissance.

Bibliography: *Opera omnia, Patrologia Latina* ed. J. P. MIGNE (Paris 1878–90) 105:187–380; *Carmina,* ed. E. DÜMMLER, *Monumenta Germaniae Historica: Poetae* 1:437–581. E. RZEHULKA, *Theodulf, Bischof von Orléans.* G. MONOD, ''Les moeurs judiciaires au VIIIe siècle d'après *la Paraenesis ad judices* de Théodulf,'' *Revue historique* 35 (1887) 1–20. C. CUISSARD, *Théodulfe, évêque d'Orléans* (Orléans 1892). H. PELTIER, *Dictionnaire de théologie catholique,* ed. A. VACANT et al. (Paris 1903–50) 15.1:330–334. S. T. COLLINS, ''Sur quelques vers de Thodulfe,'' *Revue Bénédictine* 60 214–218. P. M. ARCARI, ''Un goto critico delle legislazioni barbariche,'' *Archivio-storico italiano* 110 (1952) 3–37. A. FREEMAN, ''Theodulf of Orléans and the *Libri Carolini,*'' *Speculum* 32 663–705.

[A. FREEMAN]

THEŌDŪRUS ABŪ QURRA

Melkite bishop of Harran and first Christian writer to use Arabic (he also wrote in Syriac and in Greek); b. EDESSA, Syria, *c.* 750; d. *c.* 825. Theōdūrus is the Arabic form of Theodore. His Arabic surname Abū Qurra is of uncertain meaning. The many ways of writing his full name are the result of conventions or mistakes. Once regarded only as a witness to teaching on the hypostatic union, Theōdūrus now emerges as a striking figure in religious dialogue with the dissidents and non-Christians of his day. In the sixteenth and seventeenth centuries, his extant Greek works were printed with Latin translations, and efforts were made to reconstruct his biography. The printing of his Arabic works, begun in 1897, has been followed by the studies of G. Graf (since 1910) and I. Dick (since 1959). Sources for the life of Theōdūrus are his works and their titles, a generous paragraph in the writings of MICHAEL I, THE SYRIAN, some Arabic letters of Abū Rā'iṭa, and scattered references in Armenian and Georgian writings.

Life. Dick's reconstruction of Theōdūrus's life is attractive. In this, A.D. 813 is a known date; the other dates are more or less conjectural. Theōdūrus entered the LAURA (Monastery) of St. SABAS near Jerusalem, but it is not known at what age he went there or with what education and experience. Here he was nourished on the Scriptures and the writings of the Greek Fathers, especially St. JOHN DAMASCENE, who had died in this *laura* in 749. The Syriac and Arabic works of Theōdūrus belong to the period of his residence at St. Sabas and to the years immediately following, when he was bishop of Harran.

At that time Harran was no backwater. Its population included Chalcedonian and Jacobite Christians, Moslems, Jews, and pagan Sabaeans (*see* SABA). Theōdūrus engaged in discussion with all of them. It was at Harran that he wrote the ''Dialogue with the Prince of Edessa'' (his third treatise in *Patrologia Graeca* 97) and the ''Treatise on Image Worship'' (the third in C. Bacha's edition and the eighth in Graf's). Under circumstances no longer known, he was deposed by Theodoret, patriarch of Antioch (795–812), and some time after 801 he was back at St. Sabas.

His second stay at the *laura* seems to have been a time of intense asceticism and literary activity. About 813 Theōdūrus wrote his ''Letter to the Armenians'' and possibly a lost letter to Pope Leo III. Not long after this, about 815, he began a series of journeys. In support of the doctrine of the Council of CHALCEDON and the anti-Monothelite teaching of St. MAXIMUS THE CONFESSOR, he went to Alexandria and Armenia. At the court of the Armenian Prince Ashot Msaker, he developed his ''Explanation of Terms Used by the Philosophers,'' the longest of his Greek works. Ashot's initial reaction was favorable. But when Abū Rā'iṭa, the Jacobite metropolitan of Takrit, sent Nonnus, the archdeacon of Nisibis, to debate with Theōdūrus, things took an opposite turn. If the religious discussions before Caliph al-Ma'mūn and the Moslem prince are genuine, Theōdūrus carried his vigorous dialogue to Baghdad. Nothing more is known of his last years.

Works. Of the Greek works of Theōdūrus, 43 are published in *Patrologia Graeca* 97, all with the Greek text and Latin translation except the 18th (for which a reference is given to *Patrologia Graeca* 94, where this work with Latin translation appears among the works of St. John Damascene) and the 32d (for which there is only a Latin translation); most of these works are brief. Of his Arabic works, 14 are known: the first, unpublished, is J. Arendzen's Bonn thesis of 1897; the other 13 are ten published by Bacha (Beirut 1904), one by L. Cheiko [*al-Machriq* 15 (1912): 757–774, 825–842], two by Dick [*Muséon* 72 (1959): 53–67]. The first 12 have been translated into German by Graf. Of Theōdūrus's Syriac works, none have yet been found, although he himself says in the eighth work of Graf's translation (*Die arabischen Schriften,* 212; Bacha's ed., 60) that he composed 30 treatises in Syriac (so in the Arabic text; the German translation accidentally has *drei* instead of *dreizig*).

Theōdūrus's support for the Church's teaching authority and the primacy of Rome is striking. He maintains tradition against Monophysites and Monothelites. The treatments given to certain questions by Theōdūrus and the early MU'TAZILITES have resemblances that are beginning to be studied.

Bibliography: I. DICK, ''Un Continuateur arabe de saint Jean Damascène: Théodore Abuqurra, évêque melkite de Harran,'' *Proche Orient Chrétien* 12 (1962): 209–223, 319–332; 13 (1963): 114–129, with full bibliog. G. GRAF, *Die arabischen Schriften des Theodor Abû Qurra, Bishofs von Harrân* (*c.* 740–820) (Paderborn 1910); *Des Theodor Abû kurra Traktat über den Schöpfer und die wahre Religion* (Münster). G. GRAF, *Geschichte der christlichen arabischen Literatur,* 5 v. (Vatican City 1944–53) 2:7–26.

[J. A. DEVENNY]

THEOGNOSTOS

Ninth-century Byzantine archimandrite and exarch. As a supporter of the deposed patriarch IGNATIUS, Theognostos was sent to Rome to represent the patriarchs' interest; he remained there until 868, when he returned with a papal message for the emperor. Ignatius made him archimandrite of the Pege Monastery and skeuophylact of the Great Church. He made a second journey to Rome, after which nothing is known about him. He is generally credited with a Report to Pope NICHOLAS I on the ecclesiastical situation in Constantinople between 858 and 861; but this is actually the Letter of Appeal sent by Ignatius to the Pope, which Theognostos probably helped to compose. A panegyric on the saints and a short sermon of the *Koimsis* of the Mother of God have also been attributed to him.

Bibliography: *Patrologia Graeca,* ed. J. P. MIGNE, 161 vol. (Paris 1857–66) 105:849–856, Panegyric; 856–862, Report. M. JUGIE, ed. and tr., *Patrologia orientalis,* ed. R. GRAFFIN and F. NAU, (Paris 1903–) 16:456–462, ''Koimēsis''; *Dictionnaire de théologie catholique,* ed. A. VACANT et al., 15 v. (Paris 1903–50) 15.1:337–338; *Bessarione* 22 (1918), 162–174, life. H. G. BECK, *Kirche und theologische Literatur im byzantinischen Reich* (Munich 1959) 544.

[F. X. MURPHY]

THEOLEPTUS, METROPOLITAN OF PHILADELPHIA

Byzantine polemicist and spiritual writer; b. *c.* 1250; d. *c.* 1326. As opponent of the reunion of Rome and the Byzantine Church of 1274, he organized opposition in Bithynia against Emperor MICHAEL VIII's policies. He was a recently married deacon when, *c.* 1275, he left his wife and retired into solitude, probably to Mount Athos, and practiced the Hesychastic spirituality as taught by Nicephorus the Athonite. His writings link Nicephorus's 13th-century Hesychastic renaissance to the Palamite school of the 14th century. After the repudiation of the reunion with Rome, he was appointed archbishop of Philadelphia (1285) and became a central figure in the political and religious issues of the day. He wrote a trenchant treatise against the followers of JOHN XI BECCUS, and caused the dismissal of the patriarch of Constantinople, GREGORY II CYPRIUS, by his attacks on the latter's theory of the splendescent procession of the Holy Spirit through the Son.

Most of his works remain unedited, but in those works available, he shows himself as a safe spiritual guide wedded to the methods of HESYCHASM, rather than an original or technical theologian.

Bibliography: J. GOUILLARD, *Dictionnaire de théologie catholique,* ed. A. VACANT et al. (Paris 1903–50) 15.1:339–341, with list of works. S. SALAVILLE, ''Théolepte de Philadelphie,'' *Mélanges Joseph de Ghellinck,* 2 v. (Gembloux 1951) 2:877–887. A. EHRHARD in K. KRUMBACHER, *Geschichte der byzantinischen Literatur* (Munich 1897) 99. H. G. BECK, *Kirche und theologische Literatur im byzantinischen Reich* (Munich 1959) 693–694.

[G. A. MALONEY]

THEOLOGIA GERMANICA

The title given to an anonymous treatise written by a priest of the Teutonic Order at Sachsenhausen toward the end of the 14th century. The first printed edition was made under the direction of Martin Luther, who was influenced by it in the early phases of his career and who found its opposition to good works and its doctrine on individual religion favorable to his own convictions. The book enjoyed considerable favor among Protestants; it was paraphrased in Latin by S. Franck and later was much admired by the PIETISTS. Its English translation by Susanna Winkworth brought it some popularity in Great Britain. Among Catholics Luther's praise of the work caused it to be viewed with some suspicion. The work is not regarded as unorthodox, its few misleading expressions susceptible of pantheistic interpretation being of a kind not uncommon in mystical literature. The treatise's 54 chapters set forth an introduction to Christian perfection; it is in the Dionysian tradition as represented by Meister ECKHART and J. TAULER, and proposes poverty of spirit and abandonment to God as the means of transformation into the divine nature.

Bibliography: Text. Critical ed. F. PFEIFFER; Eng. tr. S. WINKWORTH, rev. J. BERNHART (New York 1949); Fr. *Le livre de la vie parfaite,* tr. J. PAQUIER. Literature. F. G. LISCO, *Die Heilslehre der Theologia deutsch* (Stuttgart 1857). M. WINDSTOSSER, *Étude sur la théologie germanique*. J. PAQUIER, *Un Mystique allemand au XIV siècle* (Paris 1922).

[P. K. MEAGHER]

THEOLOGICAL CONCLUSION

The expression theological conclusion is used to signify the conclusion of an argument one of the premises of which is from faith, the other from reason. Such is, for instance, the conclusion of the following argument: The same divine nature is common to all the Persons of the Holy Trinity truth from faith. Now, nature is the remote principle of operation truth from reason. Therefore operations are common to all the Persons of the Holy Trinity.

In order to have a real theological conclusion the consequence must follow from the premises by way of DEMONSTRATION; i.e., it must be the result of a deductive, not of an analytic, SYLLOGISM. But, in practice, it is hard to say when a syllogism is analytic and when it is deductive. Consequently it is hard to distinguish real from apparent theological conclusions. A case in which this difficulty created great confusion was that of the Immaculate Conception of Mary, a truth formally revealed, which, however, before the bull *Ineffabilis Deus,* was considered by many a theological conclusion, i.e., a virtually revealed truth.

The main objection against theological conclusions is that no syllogism built on premises belonging to two different levels of knowledge (one to the level of reason, the other to the level of faith) is correct, because it violates one of the fundamental rules of logic, the rule that prescribes that the middle term must keep the same meaning in the two premises. One may take as an example the following argument: The word proceeds from the intellect. But the Son is the WORD of the Father. Therefore the Word proceeds from the intellect of the Father. It is claimed, as regards this argument, that the conclusion is wrong, because the meaning of the middle term, word, is not the same in the major and in the minor premises: what one knows from reason about the word and the intellect is entirely different from what one knows from faith.

The answer to this objection is that the fact of a concepts belonging to two different levels of knowledge does not prevent it from having the same meaning, and, therefore, it does not prevent it from satisfying the rules of a syllogism: *terminus esto triplex* and *aut semel aut iterum medius generaliter esto.* To deny this with regard to faith and reason is to wreck the intelligibility of faith and to fall into the Averroistic theory of double truth, or into the Marcionistic theory of the unknown God. It must be said, however, that theological conclusions are legitimate only when the middle term expresses something pertaining to the essence of a thing and not to a peculiar historical circumstance. This point has been brought out with the utmost clarity by F. Marin-Sola in his *Évolution homogne du dogme catholique*, where he distinguishes between the essence considered in itself, i.e., in its metaphysical *ratio,* and the essence considered in the concrete, i.e., in its historical and physical realization. On the ground of this distinction he shows that one is allowed to apply to Christian realities only the predicates that belong to them essentially, otherwise the terms would be equivocal and the conclusion would not be valid. For instance, if it is revealed that God has become man in Jesus, one is authorized to conclude that He is endowed with reason and free will, but not that He is white or red. An important contribution to the understanding of theological conclusions has been given by (Y. M. J. Congar, who has shown that theological conclusions are not so much the result of speculative procedures as of the development of faith in its existential conditions, both human and supernatural (Y. M. J. Congar, *La Foi et la thologie* 113.)

Theological conclusions are strictly connected with revelation and, consequently, enter into the domain of the INFALLIBILITY of the Church. It is, however, disputed whether they enter into such a domain directly or indirectly, i.e., whether they are objects of ecclesiastical or of divine FAITH, and whether they are to be treated as dogma or not.

See Also: ANALOGY, THEOLOGICAL USE OF; ARGUMENTATION; DIALECTIC IN THEOLOGY; ERROR, THEOLOGICAL; METHODOLOGY (THEOLOGY); REASONING, THEOLOGICAL; REVELATION, VIRTUAL; THEOLOGY, ARTICLES ON.

Bibliography: Y. M. J. CONGAR, *Dictionnaire de théologie catholique,* ed. A. VACANT, 15 v. (Paris 1903–50; Tables générales 1951–) 15.1:341–502. S. SHNGEN, *Lexikon für Theologie und Kirche,* ed. J. HOFER and K. RAHNER, 10 v. (2d, new ed. Freiburg 1957–65); suppl., *Das ZweiteVatikanische Konzil: Dokumente und kommentare,* ed. H. S. BRECHTER et al., pt. 1 (1966) 6:453–454. J. F. BONNEFOY, *La Nature de la thologie selon saint Thomas d'Aquin* (Paris 1939) 6772. A. GARDEIL, *Le Donn rvl et la thologie* 162–186. P. WYSER, *Theologie als Wissenschaft: Ein Beitrag zur theologischen Erkenntnislehre* 112–120. *Sacrae Theolologiae Summa,* ed. Fathers of the Society of Jesus, Professors of the Theological Faculties in Spain (Madrid 1962) 1.3:698–737. E. DHANIS, ''Révélation explicite et implicite,'' *Gregorianum* 34 (1953) 187–237. M. R. GAGNEBET, Un Essai sur le probleme theologique, *Revue Thomiste* 45 (1939) 108–146. E. LANG, Die Gliederung und die Reichweite des Glaubens nach Thomas von Aquin und den Thomisten, *Divus Thomas* 20 (1942) 207–236, 335–346; 21 (1943) 79–97. A. M. LUBIK, ''De conclusionibus theologicis ad mentem M. Cani,'' *Antonianum* 36 (1961) 29–68. R. M. SCHULTES, ''De definibilitate conclusionum theologicarum,'' *La Ciencia tomista* 23 (1921) 305–333.

[G. B. MONDIN]

THEOLOGICAL TERMINOLOGY

''Terminology'' means the set of terms proper to a particular field of discourse; ''theological'' determines that field as the science, i.e., systematic knowledge, of the divine mysteries. This article supposes the validity of such a science (*see* THEOLOGY) and of meaningful discourse about God in general (*see* ANALOGY; ANALOGY, THEOLOGICAL USE OF; LOGICAL POSITIVISM), and deals only with the technical language of theologians, its history, and idea.

Historical. Already in Scripture we find a technical language, old words being drawn to new meanings. Thus John has two words for son, υἱός and τέκνον, by which he rigorously distinguishes Christ from those born of water and the Spirit. ''APOSTLE,'' by derivation, means simply ''sent,'' but receives a special if not fully defined sense in the New Testament. ''GOSPEL'' is good news, especially of victory, but becomes the good news of salvation in Jesus Christ. And so with a host of other terms.

The Fathers go beyond Scripture to develop their own technical terms, but meet violent oposition when they try to add these terms to the creeds. The classic example is the term consubstantial, HOMOOUSIOS (ὁμοούσιος), used by the First Council of NICAEA in 325 to define the perfect equality of Son and Father. The term is an innovation, and the Nicene Fathers know it. Eusebius of Caesarea writes his diocese at once to defend his assent to it. Athanasius says three separate times in his account of Nicaea that the subterfuges of their opponents forced the Fathers to use such terms, in order to reject Arian doctrine more distinctly and, in Newman's translation, ''to concentrate the sense of the Scriptures'' (*De decretis Nicaenae synodi* 19, 20, 32).

The Nicene Fathers, without intending to do so, set a precedent. Obliged to make an exception here, they are as opposed to further innovations as the Arians have been to this, and years later Athanasius dissuades the Churches from the use of ''HYPOSTASIS,'' urging the sufficiency of what Nicaea had written (*Tomus ad Antiochenos* 5, 6). But Gregory of Nazianzus says explicitly: ''It is permitted, for the sake of clarity, to coin new phrases'' (*Ora-*

tiones 39.12). The remark is casual, the application trivial, and opposition to new terms will continue long afterward, on the plea of fidelity to Ephesus, or Trent, or Vatican I, as the case may be. Still, a great principle has been uttered, and now a new mentality begins to appear among the Fathers. Augustine's writings are studded with Scripture, but he also forms terminology with such abandon as to be called the creator of theological language in the West. In the East John Damascene imports the terms of philosophy wholesale into theology and, eight centuries ahead of F. Suárez in this, prefaces his theological work with a lexicon of ''the best contributions of the Greek philosophers.''

The Middle Ages draw on Augustine and later on John Damascene for terms and procedures. Mention may be made of Alan of Lille's *Liber in distinctionibus dictionum theologicalium,* called by Y. Congar characteristic of the era (*Dictionnaire de théologie catholique*, ed. A. Vacant et al., 15 v. [Paris 1903–50] 15.1:370), but not really theological in our sense. In general, with the bitterness of Nicaea long past and the principle of the differentiation of language not yet explicit, medieval theologians are not vividly aware of the way their language differs from that of Scripture. Even Saint Thomas Aquinas adverts only briefly to the need for new terms (*Summa theologiae* 1a, 29.3 ad 1; cf. 2a2ae, 1.9 ad 1). The next real advance after patristic times occurs in our day with the emergence of the new sciences and the importing of their technical language into theology, e.g., such terms as consciousness, evolution, existentialist decision. More important still is the new historical sense grounding a grasp of differing thought patterns and language styles. There is still some demand for total rejection of theological terms in favor of Biblical terms, but the best exegesis makes free use of non-Biblical terms to explain Biblical categories; and P. Tillich rightly inveighs against expositions of Scripture that use the terms created by the work of philosophers and then denounce the work that so much enriched their language [*Biblical Religion and the Search for Ultimate Reality* (Chicago 1955) 7].

Systematic. The topic requires a general theory of language and its differentiations. If language is an expression of interiority (for Saint Thomas, outer word corresponding to inner), its varieties are best set forth in terms of internal operations. A basic scheme of such operations centers on INSIGHT, the act of understanding [*see* UNDERSTANDING (INTELLECTUS)] that has its agent object in the image and is formulated interiorly in the concept, which in turn is expressed exteriorly in language [B. Lonergan, ''The Concept of *Verbum* in the Writings of St. Thomas Aquinas,'' *Theological Studies* 7–10 (1946–49)]. The insight may be formulated in concepts or not formulated (the difference of science and art); the concept may be either descriptive or explanatory, according as it formulates the relations of things to the human subject (hot, rising and setting sun) or the relations of things to one another (temperature, solar system), with insight and language naturally corresponding in each case [B. Lonergan, *Insight* (New York 1957)]. The scheme gives three basic stages of ''language'' according as understanding is formulated or not, is formulated in descriptive or explanatory categories; and religious language follows the pattern.

The first stage, then, of religious language is that proper to symbolic religion: there is understanding of the God-man relationship; but it is not formulated, rites supplying for language, ways of living for doctrine. Second, as understanding is expressed in concepts and becomes articulate, language in the proper sense is added; if the interest is ''practical,'' categories used will relate the divine mysteries to the religious subject (*our* Father; He died for *me*) in what we may call the prophetic stage. Third, if the interest is ''theoretical,'' the categories will concern God in Himself (Father and Son as consubstantial) and the mysteries in relation to one another (the role of faith in justification), in what we may call the theological stage. The stages are not sharply differentiated in the concrete, where we find an infinite variety, but they are differentiated in source and idea and enable us to analyze the concrete, distinguish predominant elements, and locate the religious subject in his course of development. Thus the stage when symbolic action was a major means of expression leaves its traces in the early history of Israel (here P. Benoit's ''inspiration dramatique'' is relevant); later the ''word'' becomes increasingly important, a word to the people in their immediate needs; then, in Origen, theory is asserting its legitimacy. But in general, later stages do not replace earlier; they simply add meaning to them, and a full religious life makes harmonious use of all three.

Theological terminology derives, then, from the theological mentality and shares its characteristics. It is said, in contrast to Biblical language, to be abstract and philosophical, but the truth here must be assessed more accurately. ''Water'' and ''essence'' are both abstract, else they could not apply in different instances; but ''water'' abstracts only from relations to the senses of particular men, whereas ''essence'' abstracts from all such relations to consider the thing-in-itself (an explanatory category). Two fallacies must be avoided in calling theological terminology ''philosophical.'' First, it is not profane in contrast to sacred language; both ''water'' and ''essence'' have an original profane use and each has a sacred use in analogous application to the divine realities. Second, theology is not limited to philosophical categories; the accurate statement again is that it uses explanatory categories in contrast to descriptive, and of these some are philosophical while some are not.

It is from theological thinking too that this terminology derives its temptations: in the satisfaction of fixed technical phrases, to lose the sense of mystery (a tendency Dionysian negative theology might serve to counteract); and amid the familiar furniture of its esoteric world, to neglect the duty both of forging new terms in the language of contemporary thought (it is useful here to note that Latin was not naturally a scientific language, but was made such by the work of thinkers; cf. Chenu, 94) and of returning to the people with a message couched in their language (*see* KERYGMATIC THEOLOGY). The resources of the English language for supplying theological terminology have not yet been adequately tapped, at least by Catholic theologians. Finally, it is a simple corollary of the dependence of language on thought to say that it is meaning, not words, that matters most (cf. Athanasius, *Tomus ad Antiochenos* 5–6, and Gregory of Nazianzus, *op. cit.* 11).

See Also: DOGMATIC THEOLOGY; METHODOLOGY (THEOLOGY); THEOLOGY, HISTORY OF; THEOLOGY, INFLUENCE OF GREEK PHILOSOPHY ON

Bibliography: Historical. Y. M. J. CONGAR, *Dictionnaire de théologie catholique*, ed. A. VACANT et al., 15 v. (Paris 1903–50) 15.1:346–447. M. D. CHENU, *Introduction à l'étude de saint Thomas* (2d ed. Montreal 1954) ch. 3. B. LONERGAN, *De Deo Trino,* 2 v. (v.1 2d ed., v.2 3d ed. Rome 1964) 1:75–87; 2:47–53; and *passim.* Systematic. Scarcely anything is written precisely on this topic, but see *passim* works on speculative theology, demythologization, and the like. Works on theological language at present regularly consider only the general question of meaning in religious language. Cf. J. A. HUTCHISON, *Language and Faith* (Philadelphia 1963) chapter 9.

[F. E. CROWE]

THEOLOGY, ARTICLES ON

Theology, in its most fundamental sense, focuses on God, the Supreme Being, the Creator of the universe; for articles on this subject, see GOD, ARTICLES ON and TRINITY, HOLY, ARTICLES ON. In a broader sense, theology includes also discourse about things in relation to God, from the standpoint of knowledge gained by revelation and received in faith. The meaning of theology in any age will depend largely on how such terms as ''revelation'' and''faith'' are understood. Aside from the Church, the subject in the *Encyclopedia* that receives the greatest attention is theology.

The two major articles on Catholic theology are THEOLOGY and THEOLOGY, HISTORY OF. The subdivisions within theology that receive the most extended treatment are DOGMATIC THEOLOGY (see also DOGMATIC THEOLOGY, ARTICLES ON); MORAL THEOLOGY (see also MORAL THEOLOGY, HISTORY OF, in four articles); BIBLICAL THEOLOGY; and PATRISTIC THEOLOGY. Other areas of theology that receive separate attention include FOUNDATIONAL THEOLOGY; FUNDAMENTAL THEOLOGY; HISTORICAL THEOLOGY; LITURGICAL THEOLOGY; SACRAMENTAL THEOLOGY; SPIRITUAL THEOLOGY; and THEOLOGY, NATURAL.

Theological methodology is covered in a variety of articles: see, e.g., METHODOLOGY (THEOLOGY); THEOLOGICAL TERMINOLOGY; CONVENIENTIA, ARGUMENTUM EX; FIDES QUAERENS INTELLECTUM; LOCI THEOLOGICI; REASONING, THEOLOGICAL; THEOLOGICAL CONCLUSION; THEOLOGY AND PRAYER. For the dependence of theology on revelation, see REVELATION, THEOLOGY OF; REVELATION, FONTS OF; REVELATION, CONCEPT OF (IN THE BIBLE).There are also articles that deal with philosophical tools that are used in theology, e.g., HERMENEUTICS; THEOLOGY, INFLUENCE OF GREEK PHILOSOPHY ON; SCHOLASTIC TERMS AND AXIOMS; PRAXIS.

Different traditions of theology are treated under such headings as AUGUSTINIANISM, THEOLOGICAL SCHOOL OF; THOMISM; FRANCISCAN THEOLOGICAL TRADITION; etc. Most of the articles on individual theologians also contain treatments of their theology: the most extensive of these are AUGUSTINE, ST.; THOMAS AQUINAS, ST.; and BONAVENTURE, ST. There are many shorter articles dealing with different types of theology, Catholic and Protestant, e.g., APOPHATIC THEOLOGY; COVENANT THEOLOGY; DEATH OF GOD THEOLOGY; DIALECTICAL THEOLOGY; EXISTENTIAL THEOLOGY; FEMINIST THEOLOGY; KERYGMATIC THEOLOGY; LATINA THEOLOGY; LIBERATION THEOLOGY; MERCERSBURG THEOLOGY; MYSTERY THEOLOGY; NARRATIVE THEOLOGY; NEW HAVEN THEOLOGY; POLITICAL THEOLOGY; PROCESS THEOLOGY; RADICAL THEOLOGY; THEOLOGY OF HOPE; THOMISM, TRANSCENDENTAL; WOMANIST THEOLOGY.

Certain papal encyclicals are of interest in an examination of the structure of theology: see, e.g., *AETERNI PATRIS*; *HUMANI GENERIS*; *FIDES ET RATIO*.

Eastern theology is treated in BYZANTINE THEOLOGY; GREEK THEOLOGY; and RUSSIAN THEOLOGY, as well as in separate articles on Eastern theologians.

[G. F. LANAVE]

THEOLOGY

Discourse about God either from the point of view of what can be known about Him from the created world by the natural power of reason (natural theology) or from the point of view of a revelation given by God and received by man in FAITH (sacred theology).

The Word. Theology is the Greek word θεολογία, nowhere used in the Bible. In the sense of the rationale (λόγος) of the gods it was used by Plato (*Rep.* 379A) for demythologizing the Greek poets, but by Aristotle (*Meta.* 1026a) for the part of philosophy that explains the cosmos in terms of an unmoved mover. Applied also to the civic cult of pagan gods of Greece and Rome, the term was repugnant to early Christians. But as *gnosis* (biblical) had acquired more dangerous connotations, Origen turned to *theologia* to express the Christian *understanding* of God as distinguished from Christian faith. In the struggle with Arianism, this ''explanation of God'' (*theologia*) came to be used for Christian knowledge about the Persons of the Trinity (Athanasius, *Oratio 1 contra Arianos* 18; *Patrologia Graeca* 26:49) as distinct from what refers to God's plan of salvation through Christ (οἰκονομία; *see* ECONOMY, DIVINE). Pseudo-Dionysius used *theologia* for mysticism. The Western Fathers scarcely used the word. Augustine (*Civ.* 6.5) made critical use of the Stoa's threefold division into physical, mythic, and civic-cult theology (cf. also Tertullian, *Nationes* 2.1; *Patrologia Latina* 1:585–588) and regarded the (meta-)physical as true. But he used the name ''Christian doctrine'' for all Christian knowledge and understanding of God. After 1100 Abelard was the first to apply the term ''theology'' to methodical (dialectical) investigation of the whole Christian teaching (*Sic et Non*). The great theologians of the 13th century preferred such terms as ''sacred doctrine'' or ''erudition,'' ''Scripture,'' or the ''Sacred Page.'' Even St. Thomas Aquinas rarely used the word *theologia* and then restricted it to the scientific function within sacred teaching (*sacra doctrina*), a broader term he used for the subject of his *Summa theologiae.* It was chiefly St. Thomas who worked out the theory of theology as a science of revealed truth, carefully distinguishing it from PHILOSOPHY. Since then the term as used by Christians of their doctrine has meant the methodical elaboration of the truths of divine revelation by reason enlightened by faith; briefly, the science (in some sense) of Christian faith.

Theology of revelation. Theology in the Christian context may be described as ''faith seeking understanding'' (*see* FIDES QUAERENS INTELLECTUM). It is a branch of learning in which a Christian, using his reason enlightened by divine faith, seeks to understand the mysteries of God revealed in and through history (Eph 1.9). It involves a methodical investigation, presupposes Christian faith, and always proceeds in the light of this faith to its goal of understanding. What it tries to understand is God's revelation of Himself and of His love for man—that is, the mysteries hidden in God but revealed to men through His Spirit (1 Cor 2.7–16). These mysteries, it is true, so excel the created intellect that even after being revealed and accepted by faith, they remain veiled in obscurity. ''Nevertheless if reason enlightened by faith studies the mysteries in a serious, dedicated, and humble way, it does achieve . . . some understanding of them and a most profitable one'' (Vatican I in H. Denzinger, *Enchiridion symbolorum* 3016). It is this understanding that theology strives to attain—a knowledge that is not faith but an understanding of faith, a knowledge that is not infused but acquired with human effort, a knowledge that differs radically from philosophical knowledge about God because its object is revealed mystery and because it engages not reason alone but reason enlightened by faith. It is an understanding that although imperfect will continue to grow until faith is dissolved in the vision of God Himself. ''Let there be growth. . . and all possible progress in understanding, knowledge, and wisdom whether in single individuals or in the whole body, in each man as well as in the entire Church, according to the stage of their development'' (Vatican I quoting Vincent of Lerins in *ibid.* 3020).

Source: revelation heard in faith. Theology therefore has its external source in divine revelation and its internal source in reason enlightened by divine faith. In revelation God speaks to man, personally inviting him to share His own divine life. From His transcendent world, God has broken into history to bring man, set on the path of sin and destruction, the good news of His love. This love He manifested by mighty deeds to save His people: divine interventions into history, whose meaning He revealed through Moses and the Prophets. To enable His people to hear His revealing word, He communicated the first beginnings of divine life by putting faith into their hearts, calling them interiorly as well as by external words and actions to respond to His love. As His design was to give Himself and His divine life completely to men, He became one of them in the Person of His Son, so that a man could be God, live the life of God in the flesh, and give perfect human expression in being, thought, word, and action to the mystery of His complete self-gift to men. Moreover, this self-gift of God, given to His people from outside them, was expressed in human writing composed under His inspiration from within His people as its own record of faith.

This revelation, consisting of both divine intervention and revealing word heard in faith, includes not only the ontological gift of divinity itself to human nature but also the definitive expression of this gift in its human dimensions in the WORD Incarnate. Here perhaps one has the fundamental reason why there can be no new revelation. The definitive Word of the Father had been spoken, and there was nothing more for the Father to say. He had only to send His Spirit so that His Word of life would live and grow in the hearts of men. Christ's own humanly fashioned knowledge of what He saw in the Father was God's own translation of His mystery into human concepts and language. To this man who is the revelation of the Father the whole of the Old Testament points. To this man as revealer of the Father the APOSTLES give WITNESS. And this apostolic witness to divine life given in Christ and through Him to all men has been handed over to the Church to proclaim, protect, and interpret.

This progressive revelation of God's Word in history constitutes an experience of faith that formed the people of God. This experience was relived by faith, enriched by reflection, formulated in human concepts, and affirmed in judgments that God inspired His human authors to write down in sacred books. The Apostles and DISCIPLES themselves in reflecting on the fullness of revelation in Christ came to understand better and to formulate more clearly under the light of His Spirit the meaning of what they had seen and heard and believed. Later articulation and understanding of what this revelation contained continued always to be grounded in and to be interpreted by the faith of the Apostles. This faith lives on in the Church, which continues to repeat, interpret, and further transpose it into the language and cultures and developed understandings of all peoples, calling them to the Father by the Spirit (*see* ACCOMMODATION).

Tradition and magisterium. Although the revelation of God culminating in Christ was crystallized in writing under the inspiration of the Holy Spirit, the understanding that the apostolic community had of these writings was passed on to further generations in ways other than writing. These other ways are called tradition [*see* TRADITION (IN THEOLOGY)] and include the liturgy and customs of the Christian community by which the experience of faith—especially the paschal experience of the risen Lord—is passed on from the apostolic community to later ages. Although a good number of theologians think that at least some truths of revelation were passed on that are not contained in Scripture, others, such as J. Geiselmann, E. Ortigues, and G. Tavard, maintain that Scripture gives the content of tradition, whereas tradition provides the interpretation and mode of understanding according to which Scripture is received by postapostolic Christians. Thus tradition as a source of revelation for theology can never be separated from Scripture. Although distinct, they make up one authoritative source of revelation. And any progress in the understanding of revelation stems from both as they are united in the life of the Church.

Tradition represents the Church's continued possession and faithful transmission of the original experience of faith in God's Word, together with its progressive understanding and expression in the life of the Church. Tradition is a broader reality than the magisterium, or TEACHING AUTHORITY OF THE CHURCH for the magisterium is only a part of tradition. It is an active element within tradition that not only pushes tradition forward but gives it authentic, even infallible, expression. Tradition belongs to the whole Church, to laity as well as to hierarchy. The same is true of theology, which is the ferment within tradition where both laity and clergy reflect on the truths of revelation as they have been progressively understood in the Church in order to achieve under the guidance of the magisterium an understanding that is fuller, more accurate, and more suited to the current age. Thus Scripture handed down in the Church and therefore as interpreted by tradition (which includes the magisterium) is the source from which theology receives the revelation given men in Christ.

Theology, then, is nothing but the effort of God's people, committed in faith to their Lord, trying to understand in a reflective and orderly way what has been revealed to them in Him. It is the endeavor of the Church to understand itself ever more fully as the sacrament of God's Word in the world and to express this understanding for itself and for its members. Theology is not the whole life of the Church, but the Church could not live and grow without theology. But just as God's revelation was not given all at once in history, but gradually until it reached its fullness and completeness in the risen Lord, so too the assimilation by His people of that revelation has been a gradual process conditioned by history, even after the definitive revelation in Christ. Similarly the assimilation of this revelation in an individual is a historical process beginning with personal commitment to God in faith. The commitment grows as the individual listens in faith to the Word of God in the Church, continually asking and trying to answer from the sources what it means, how it is understood and to be understood better, how it is lived and to be lived better in his community. This process of growth in understanding reaches its culmination only when the Word of God is given immediately to men in the BEATIFIC VISION.

Theology as understanding the faith. Since Aristotle it has been customary to distinguish two operations of the human intellect; the first, called APPREHENSION, corresponds to the question "What is it?" or "Why is it?" It grasps the meaning or reason or cause of a thing or of a truth and strives to conceive and formulate a definition or hypothesis about it. The second operation, called JUDGMENT, corresponds to the question "Is it so?" It considers the evidence, evaluates it, and finally affirms on the basis of evidence that "it *is* so" or "it *is not* so." Only in this second operation is there found properly human knowledge, for only in this operation is existence affirmed. UNDERSTANDING in the first operation spontaneously tends toward judgment, and judgment invites to further understanding because man naturally desires to understand better what he already knows to exist or to be true.

Both apprehension and judgment are concerned with existing reality or being. Just as the being that is the proportioned object of man's intellect is one, although it is composed of structure (essence) and its actuality (act of existence), so the act of human knowledge is one but is composed of apprehension (understanding) and an act of judgment, by which the understanding is known to be true. And it is one and the same being that is understood by apprehension and affirmed to be by judgment.

Understanding: First Operation of Human Intellect. All understanding takes place in the first operation of the mind. In trying to understand the mysteries believed by faith, the question is not whether the mysteries are true (Christians believe that) but why or how they are true. One strives for INSIGHT to conceive ways of understanding it as well as possible. Each new insight into the mystery, however, brings up the question ''Is it a true insight?'' And this question is answered only in a judgment based on sufficient EVIDENCE. If true, then further questions arise in the first operation of the mind, ''How, why?'' It is in this continued cyclic process that understanding grows. Understanding itself is the fruit of the first operation of the mind. It can be more or less adequate or complete, but of itself it is neither true nor false. Understanding is true or false only when in the second operation one affirms on sufficient evidence that it is so or not so. The second operation does not produce understanding but only decides whether understanding is true or not. Theology, of course, wants understanding that is true.

The distinction and connection of these two operations in theology are explained by St. Thomas Aquinas as follows:

> [E]very activity is to be carried on in a manner consonant with its end. Theological discussion, however, can be ordered to a double end. Some discussions aim at resolving doubts as to whether a thing is so; and in this type of theological discussion, those authorities should be used who are accepted by those with whom one is discussing. But there is another type of discussion used by the masters in the schools that aims not at the removal of error but at the instruction of the listeners, that they may be led to an understanding of the truth in question; and in this type, one ought to employ reasons which penetrate to the roots of the truth and make known how the proposition is true; otherwise, if the master answers the question merely by appealing to authorities, the listener will be certain that the thing is so, but he will not have gained any knowledge or understanding, and will go away with nothing in his head. [*Quodl.* 4.9.3]

As will be seen, positive theology is concerned with the truth of understanding; speculative theology is concerned with understanding what is true. Even though God has revealed Himself to men in a way that surpasses any natural knowledge of God, since the mystery of God is never known in this life except through the mediacy of creatures, theological understanding will always be imperfect, analogical, and obscure. Because human understanding is conditioned by its history, lives in history, and grows in history, theological understanding too is historical, continually evolving and growing. Moreover, because human intelligence is dynamic and strives always to find some unity and order in what it knows, theological understanding will tend toward synthesis, even though any synthesis it achieves will itself be analogical, obscure, and evolving. But in spite of these limitations, such understanding is most fruitful and rewarding.

Conditions of Theological Understanding. Owing to the lack of proportion between man and God, theology can never arrive at intrinsic principles self-evident to men for understanding the mysteries—analytic principles that transcend the evolution of human understanding. Hence it does not have such principles or intrinsic reasons for demonstrating the truth of what it knows. Moreover, Jan. 8, 2002 it cannot conceive hypotheses that are clearly understood to be possible, since such hypotheses are also the product of human understanding of mysteries and so themselves are analogical and obscure.

Nevertheless, theology does attain TRUTH. First of all, the sources of revelation as handed on by the Church contain many certain truths from which as premises theology can determine with certainty the truthfulness of THEOLOGICAL CONCLUSIONS. Second, the more fully the implications of any theological conception or hypothesis agree with all that the theologian knows from faith (analogy of faith) or other sources of knowledge, the more certain he can be of the truth of his hypotheses.

Levels of Understanding. As with all human knowledge, theology can know the same object better and better, and this evolution in no way denies the identity of the object or truth that is known. Unlike the natural sciences, which are ever closer approximations to truth and are never closed until the last measurement is in, theology begins with absolutely certain truths of faith, and, as understanding develops, it constantly adheres to the same truths. This evolution occurs in one's very way of understanding. For example, in reading a foreign language a person may understand the meaning of each word in a sentence but still not understand the meaning of the sentence. Or he may have some understanding of the every individual sentence in a paragraph and still not understand the meaning of the whole paragraph. In each rereading of the paragraph he brings questions about what he does not understand. Eventually he can understand the whole paragraph as a unity, seeing in one act of understanding the whole and all its parts in relation to the whole. It is the same thing he is understanding from start to finish, but his way of understanding has been changing from understanding one thing by itself to understanding several things together and finally understanding all together.

The understanding of revelation likewise evolves from one way of understanding (e.g., catechetical understanding) to a more exact way of understanding the same truths (with careful exegesis) to a way of understanding many truths together (in biblical themes, for example) to ever more exact and comprehensive ways of understanding discovered in positive and speculative and historical theology. Thus, understanding the faith can be pursued on different levels: e.g., catechetical, humanistic, scientific. The term ''theology'' has generally been reserved for the scientific level, but with the development of ''college theology'' at mid-20th century, it has been applied widely to the humanistic level.

Scientific theology takes a reflectively critical stance toward its work. It is usually divided into positive and speculative theology. Exegesis [*see* EXEGESIS, BIBLICAL] as well as biblical, liturgical (*see* LITURGY, ARTICLES ON), conciliar, and KERYGMATIC THEOLOGY refer to parts of, or approaches used in, this twofold division.

Positive theology. The total task of positive theology is to discover and explain the relation between the contemporary dogmatic-theological context and its sources in revelation. Its functions are (1) to discover the truths of revelation in their original historical contexts (exegesis), (2) to discover and explain the development of revelation itself within the whole context of the Bible (BIBLICAL THEOLOGY), (3) to discover, determine, and explain the true development that has occurred in understanding these truths in history from the close of revelation to the present day, and (4) to further the true understanding of revelation thus far achieved in the contemporary dogmatic-theological context from further examination of its sources in history (3 and 4: DOGMATIC THEOLOGY).

Thus, positive theology includes exegesis, Biblical theology, and dogmatic theology. Its method basically is historical. It employs scientific exegesis as well as analysis and comparison of texts and contexts in search of reasons verifiable in history that may be used to determine, account for, and further develop the contemporary understanding of revelation. The exegete is concerned with explaining with all the resources at his disposal the explicit meanings of texts in particular authors (scriptural, liturgical, patristic, conciliar, etc.). His question is: ''What does this particular text or this particular book mean in its particular context?'' The biblical theologian is concerned with the genesis and dialectical development of revelation as it comes to be expressed in the succeeding authors and books of Scripture and finds its goal and full meaning in Christ. The dogmatic theologian is concerned with the genesis and dialectical development of this understanding of revelation gradually unfolding in different successive contexts in the Church up to the present. From his faith he may know the direction in which this understanding is evolving; but he cannot chart its course a priori, because development often results from conflicts of opinion and is determined by contingent factors, such as something's having been overlooked.

Context. Diversity of contexts is a vital consideration in positive theology. Context itself involves what is over and beyond the text itself. It denotes ''the remainder'' that is pertinent to any statement—a somewhat indeterminate group of other statements, outlooks, attitudes, ways of conceiving things, which qualify, explain, and complement the particular statement under consideration. The context in which the positive theologian lives and therefore the one out of which he works is the contemporary dogmatic-theological context; that is, what is currently taught and understood in the Church, what is taken for granted in the faith of the Church, what is taught and learned in schools of theology, what is set forth in contemporary scriptural, liturgical, patristic, and conciliar studies, including what is pertinent in contemporary philosophy and science for the understanding of dogmatic and theological statements (e.g., for understanding K. Rahner's SUPERNATURAL EXISTENTIAL). In regard to this context, the dogmatic theologian has two functions in positive theology: (1) the understanding of the connection between the contemporary theological knowledge and its sources in revelation and (2) the further development of the contemporary dogmatic-theological context.

The work of positive theology thus evidently concerns history, which is its laboratory. But it goes beyond the historical as event or datum for the theologian approaches Scripture and tradition in the light of his faith. He accepts the statements of Scripture and the witness of tradition in the Church not merely as historical facts or events but as statements of truth, as God's word in the Church, as something not to be contradicted.

Transcending Particular Context. Truth is transcendent. Because truth is an unconditioned affirmation of being, it is not relative to or dependent on any finite subject who knows it. It is neither confined to the subject nor dependent on his knowing it. The very same truth can be known by many, or known by one and believed on his authority by another. Moreover, truth is in a sense independent of the context in which it was first uttered. For although a statement is never without a context and its meaning can be determined only by the context in which it is uttered, still once the meaning in its original context is determined, the same meaning, the same truth, can be expressed in another context in which understanding of the realities involved is much more developed. For example, the truth enunciated by Christ at the Last Supper, "This is my body," is the same truth that is expressed in terms of a more developed understanding of reality in another age by the Council of Trent, when it said that the whole substance of the bread is changed into the substance of the body of Christ and that this change is properly called transubstantiation.

It is precisely this transcendence of truth that grounds the possibility of the development of doctrine—a transference, a transposition, that takes truths in the sense that they have in one context (in one mode of apprehension, one set of images or concepts) and expresses the same truths, the same meanings, in another context wherein understanding has undergone development. An important fundamental task of the dogmatic theologian is to show how the truths that have been defined by the Church, the dogmas believed in the contemporary context, have evolved from their original expression in revelation (Pius XII; cf. H. Denzinger, *Enchiridion symbolorum* 3886): for example, how the truth that one confesses in the Credo at Mass, that the Son of God is consubstantial with the Father (originally defined at Nicaea I), is the same truth that is expressed, but less clearly, in the Scriptures; how the truth about the Trinity that one professes each Sunday in the Preface of the Mass, "unity in essence, distinction in Persons, and equality in majesty," is contained in the DEPOSIT OF FAITH. In showing the relation between this contemporary expression of faith and its sources in revelation, the dogmatic theologian is elucidating in a meaningful way the content of the contemporary dogmatic-theological context.

Thematization. This process with which the dogmatic theologian is concerned is sometimes called the process of thematization. This means a transference from one type of apprehension and expression of truth to another type of apprehension and expression of the same truth. This process of itself neither changes the thing that is known nor does it make one's previous knowledge false, but it adds further knowledge, further clarification in a new mode of apprehension.

Thematization is a universal human phenomenon; it occurs in all the human sciences. Some obvious examples of this process are the doctor's examining his patient, the psychologist's examining his client, the judge's examining the accused. It is the same illness that the patient experiences and the doctor is investigating. The questions the doctor puts to the patient arise out of the context of the doctor's knowledge of medicine. As he listens to the patient describing his experience in the categories of common sense, the doctor interprets this description, translating and transposing it into the categories of medicine. The final result is that the doctor knows the illness of the patient better than the patient himself does. Evident here are two contexts: the experiential context of the patient expressed in the language of common sense, and the context of medical knowledge. The doctor must reconceive what is going on in the patient from the viewpoint of his own medical knowledge and translate this into the terms of his science. This example illustrates how one and the same reality and truths about the same reality can be transposed from one context and mode of apprehension to another. The positive dogmatic theologian studies this process as it is operative in the development of doctrine.

Contemporary Context: A Starting Point. Beginners normally start from the understanding of revelation that they have, usually from a simple statement of revealed truth as taught by the Church. Leading theologians today, such as K. Rahner and Y. M. J. Congar, are insistent on starting from the contemporary theological context. Rahner nearly always starts with an accurate, penetrating account of the current status of any doctrine he takes up for consideration. However, his concern usually is to develop further the contemporary context rather than to trace the genesis of its dogmas from their sources. Starting from the contemporary context in positive theology is recommended by Pius XII: "Together with the sources of positive theology God has given His Church a living teaching authority to make clear and explain what was left obscure in the deposit of faith and only present there implicitly . . . [Some mistakenly] use what is obscure to explain what is clear, as if the opposite procedure did not plainly recommend itself" (*ibid.* 3886).

Everyone starts with the understanding that he has, which is conditioned by the contemporary context. Insofar as the positive theologian is concerned with the contemporary context, he will return to the sources in order to understand better just where the turning points are in the process of development, and thus he may be saved from going down blind alleys. He then concentrates on these genetic moments to discover the elements of change in the apprehension and expression of the truth under consideration. After studying and comparing the differences (for example, the different modes of conceiving the divinity of the Son before Nicaea I), he then tries to account for these differences.

The Dialectical Element and True Development. The process he is studying is not one of pure development. For in the process there occur conflicts and oppositions, and here the dialectical element enters the process. For usually definitions of DOGMAS do not occur without condemnations of HERESIES; and these also form part of the history. Insofar as the theologian can find in the history itself the reason or norm for judging ''this is true development and that is false,'' he is accomplishing his task of showing how the formulas employed in the definition have their foundation in the original sources. The theologian knows, of course, from the infallible teaching of the Church that later developments that are defined as revealed are contained in the deposit of faith. But he cannot be content with authority. His task is to show *how* the doctrine is contained in the original sources, not just to agree with authority. And he fulfills this task only insofar as his study of history reveals reasons and norms for judging the true development. Insofar as the dialectical element, the conflict between position and counterposition, reveals an element of aberration in the counterposition, the theologian can provide from history itself an objective criterion of judgment by which he can pass from mere history to doctrine. A good example of this passage from history to doctrine is an essay of A. Grillmeier, SJ, ''Die theologische und sprachliche Vorbereitung der Christologischen Formel von Chalkedon,'' in *Das Konzil von Chalkedon* (Würzburg 1951) 1:1–242. Thus history provides the laboratory in which the theologian is able to give an account of the true development of doctrine, in which he can study how the human mind under the light of faith has struggled to give more exact expression to its increased understanding of the sources of revelation.

Reading the Text. An important caution for the positive theologian is not to read anything into the relevant historical text that is not there explicitly. He must examine each text in its own context to determine what its author explicitly intended to say. It seems he should not be concerned with what is implicit in the text for what is implicit for the interpreter may not have been implicit in the mind of the original author. Moreover, what is implied will come out in subsequent developments. Unless the theologian gets back to the thought as it was expressed prior to its development, how it was conceived before its explicitation or thematization, he can never account for the development. Thus, in achieving an understanding of how the contemporary context is reduced to its sources in revelation, the positive theologian can enrich and clarify contemporary understanding and formulation of revelation.

In attending carefully to what is said and to the context in which it is said, the dogmatic theologian, like the doctor or psychologist, will be bringing all the knowledge he has to bear on understanding what is said, reconceiving it in terms of contemporary theological knowledge, checking to see whether this interpretation takes into account all the evidence down to the least pertinent detail. If so, then he can conclude that the contemporary interpretation is correct and faithful to the sources, that this understanding is a true development of the understanding expressed in the sources.

Developing Contemporary Context. The second task of the dogmatic theologian is to develop further the contemporary theological context. His questions usually arise out of this context. That is, from inadequacies and obscurities that appear in it from his study of the sources or from contemporary scriptural, patristic, or conciliary studies or from confrontation with the contemporary human sciences. He knows that subsequent restatements of the truths contained in Scripture and tradition in terms of the developed understanding achieved by philosophy and science frequently fail to recapture the whole truth originally stated. In the course of controversy and development the new categories in which the original truth is reexpressed, especially if they are abstract, leave behind some of the richness of meaning contained in the original sources—for example, in the more primitive and picturesque images and metaphors of the biblical world. Thus there can be aspects of the truth that have been pushed to the periphery in theological and dogmatic development and perhaps forgotten (though never really lost). These aspects can be brought to light again and given their proper perspective in the contemporary context. In fact, by serious study of the sources the theologian will always find new light, because these sources are inexhaustible.

If he finds, with the help of contemporary biblical and other studies, certain elements or aspects of the truth that may not fit in well with the contemporary conception of the truth, even elements that have been overlooked in the course of theological development, then he will be led to reconsider this conception, to probe more deeply into the analogies that have been used, and even to go on to fashion new concepts to express the new insights that he has won. One can see this process at work, for example, in the writings of K. Rahner (e.g., on monogenism, on concupiscence, on death), in the works of B. Lonergan [e.g., on the consciousness of Christ: *De Verbo Incarnato* (2d ed. Rome 1964) 267–310], and in other contemporary theologians.

Thus, the positive theologian is concerned with *understanding* the truths of revelation as this understanding has developed and has been verified in history. In this process, he arrives at some understanding of the mysteries, at insights with their conceptualizations in which he understands many things and many truths not separately but together.

Speculative theology. Whereas positive theology is concerned with understanding the connection or relation between the present dogmatic-theological context and its origins in revelation, speculative theology is concerned with this context in relation to its goal of understanding, namely, a comprehensive understanding of the truths of revelation in an ordered synthesis. It pursues this goal (1) by comparing the mysteries with things, laws, and relationships that are naturally known and with which the mysteries have a certain similarity or proportion (*analogia*); (2) by comparing the mysteries among themselves in order to understand better their interrelationship, coherence, and order; and (3) by reflecting on the connection of the various mysteries and their implications with the supernatural end of man (cf. Vatican I in H. Denzinger, *Enchiridion symbolorum* 3016). The synthesis envisaged here is a comprehensive, scientific synthesis of revealed truths. It should be noted, however, that the theological syntheses, which are nothing but intelligible patterns of understanding, can be and have been achieved in categories other than those of scientific speculative theology.

Biblical Syntheses. For example, a biblical theologian can gather the events and truths of Scripture into an intelligible pattern by using biblical themes or categories; for example, as W. Eichrodt has done under the category of covenant for the OT or as S. Lyonnet has done for Pauline soteriology. Such syntheses can be very important and useful for understanding Scripture, and they help to put all its parts into perspective even, perhaps, for the exegete. Although a biblical synthesis in its very intention and organization goes beyond the expressed thought of any biblical author (and in this regard it is no longer biblical), it is still limited to the *type* of understanding possessed by the biblical writers.

It is a fact that the dynamism of the Christian mind manifested in history pushed beyond biblical categories to express more accurately and with fuller understanding the same truths that are expressed in the Bible. Even within the Bible, there is noticeable a movement that goes beyond mere description of concrete events and actions to more abstract expressions. This is true especially in the later sapiential books, where, for example, the description of God in action, image, symbol, and metaphor is transposed to a type of conceptualization that is more abstract and analogical; here, for example, God is called eternal, almighty, omniscient, etc. The thinking man, as he reads the Bible, comes face to face with questions that cannot be answered in the descriptive categories of the Bible; for example, the early Christological controversies could not be resolved within biblical categories but demanded clearer, more precise, and even more abstract expression of the mystery of Christ in such concepts as consubstantiality, Person, nature, and operation.

Humanistic Syntheses. Theological synthesis can also be achieved in contemporary humanistic categories, such as the whole Christ, the people of God, salvation history, and Christ the sacrament of encounter with God, and also possibly within the categories of phenomenology. Such syntheses are also important and useful, especially since they are made in terms more familiar and more readily understood by the contemporary educated man who is not a scientific speculative theologian. Moreover, such syntheses carry within them something of the power of concrete symbol and metaphor that are effective in moving men to religious response. This type of synthesis is of great importance in the *aggiornamento* of the Church, in keeping its KERYGMA continually up to date in a language that is meaningful to modern man. Humanistic syntheses, whether biblical or contemporary (and much of the biblical is still contemporary), are the work of intelligence, even specialized intelligence, operating in the concrete world of common sense. These syntheses are achieved in language that can be used in preaching the word of God. Thus they are kerygmatic in character rather than scientifically speculative.

Franciscan Synthesis. The synthesis achieved in the Augustinian tradition, especially by St. Bonaventure and the Franciscan school, might be described as affectively contemplative or mystical rather than scientifically speculative. At the root of the reaction in medieval AUGUSTINIANISM against the use of Aristotle in theology was the rejection of the role of any intrinsic ANALOGY in theology. For this school human reason was competent in regard to terrestrial things but not for spiritual and eternal realities. Science and philosophy could not enter internally into a theological elaboration of revealed truth; they were useful only as a propaedeutic for sharpening and training the mind or for providing extrinsic illustrations to explain the biblical images and symbols borrowed from the created world. There was no possibility for the human mind, even enlightened by faith, to ascend from creatures by an analogy of proportionality to some understanding of the divine mysteries; only the Scriptures and their interpretation by the Fathers and the holy men of God read and studied under the divine illumination given through the infused gifts of wisdom and understanding could manifest the true value and usefulness that creatures have. Whatever is true in philosophy is to be found in Scripture. Thus theology is a work of divine illumination rather than a work of reason enlightened by faith. In this tradition theology is primarily practical and affective rather than speculative; it is mystical in its mode rather than rational.

Scientific Speculative Synthesis. Each synthesis has its own special value in bringing to light the riches of revelation. If the theologian considers only those that are humanistic or phenomenological, he is neglecting a great deal of understanding of revelation in his work. Synthesis in scientific speculative theology means a systematic understanding of the truths of revelation achieved by defining as accurately as possible the (quasi) reasons of these truths and by comparing them with one another in order to understand them in an ordered unity coherent with but not measured by a reasoned conception of reality.

In this part of theology, reason enlightened by faith is used not to demonstrate the truths of revelation but to show how these truths fit coherently with or flow from a hypothesis that is postulated (St. Thomas Aquinas, *Summa theologiae* 1a, 32.1 ad 2). The goal or purpose of any synthesis is not certitude but understanding; and in scientific synthesis it is the understanding of what is already established with more or less certitude in positive theology but in a unified way that is consciously consistent with the nature and laws of being and the principles of its affirmation in truth.

The normal way of coming to this understanding is from the analogy of nature and from the internal coherence of the mysteries themselves. Without a naturally known term of comparison, the speculative theologian does not begin with his feet on the ground and, in applying the analogue to the mystery, can never find the point at which the analogy is transcended for analogy involves a twofold ignorance. One knows something that is similar and at the same time dissimilar; but he does not know either what the dissimilar element is or how significant it might be. The danger is in not paying enough attention to the dissimilar element, which can be recognized for what it is not by any appeal to a priori principles but by testing each point in the sources of revelation and by comparing it with the other mysteries. Whatever in the analogy or in the theory developed from analogy is not coherent with the understanding of revelation witnessed to in tradition becomes suspect.

Still it is only by locating a naturally known term of comparison, conceiving it adequately, and exploiting it fully, applying it exactly to all the data in the sources, that one can understand where the analogue is transcended—where the mystery is. Hence, although the validity of any understanding of mystery as it is achieved in speculative theology depends on the validity of the knowledge of nature that is used as an analogue and on the transcendent range of the human intellect, it depends principally on endurning contact with the sources of revelation that are the ultimate criterion of its truth. Thus, it is not surprising that the scientific synthesis in speculative theology that came into existence with the acceptance and use in theology of a philosophy of nature and a philosophy of being lost its vitality in the measure in which it lost contact with the sources of revelation.

Role of Analogy. From experience and reflective introspection, one learns that the proper and proportionate object of the human intellect is the intelligible in the sensible. However, as intellect, it is not limited in its range to this object, as is evidenced by the fact that man desires to know everything, not just material reality. And in pursuing a knowledge of things transcending its proper object, the human intellect proceeds by way of analogy with what it knows properly. Because effects are similar to their causes, the knowledge of the material world can be a stepping-stone to an analogical knowledge of its cause. Whereas the medium through which the philosopher pursues his knowledge of God is the material world of creation, the medium through which the theologian pursues his knowledge is the revelation God has given of Himself in history. Since God is simple and uncaused, there is no real order of reasons or causes in Him. But there can be an order in man's analogical knowledge insofar as one truth man believes or knows about God can be seen to be the reason in man's understanding of another truth that he believes or knows. Thus, the human mind can perceive in some fashion how the truths it believes or knows about God can be related to each other in man's understanding from the analogy of the order of causes that it knows in material creation.

Order in Understanding. For example, in one's study of God, when he discovers some analogous conception from which all else in his knowledge of God follows, he can understand this as nature or essence and construct an order in his analogical understanding of the attributes of God for essence in creatures is that from which the properties of being flow. Likewise, in the study of the Trinity one believes that there are in the one God two processions, three Persons, four relations, etc. Although in God Himself there is no priority whatever of substance over procession or relation or Person, nevertheless in one's analogical conception of these truths there is a priority such that the analogical conception of distinct Persons presupposes in human understanding a conception of opposed relations, which in turn presuppose intelligible emanations or processions.

Thus, by the hypothesis of intelligible emanations in God, the theologian can come to understand something of the implications of his own understanding of the Trinity and through this some understanding of the Trinity itself; that is, how the truths he believes can be understood in some way as a unity of truths, reflecting dimly the simple understanding that God has of Himself. A good illustration of this speculative procedure in regard to the Trinity is found in P. McShane, SJ, ''The Hypothesis of Intelligible Emanations in God,'' *Theological Studies* 23 (1962) 545–568; in regard to original sin and the order of grace, see the synthesis proposed by R. J. Pendergast, SJ, ''The Supernatural Existential, Human Generation, and Original Sin,'' *Downside Review* 82 (1964) 1–24; on the theory itself of speculative theology, see B. Lonergan, SJ, *De constitutione Christi* (3d ed. Rome 1961) 42–56.

The role of analogy is at the heart of scientific speculative theology. A hypothesis developed carefully on the basis of analogy can attain the status of theory if all the conclusions that can be drawn from the hypothesis agree with everything one believes or knows from other sources. Theory can sometimes even attain the status of truth, if in the judgment of wisdom made by the Church it is witnessed to as a true development of the understanding of revelation; for example, the basic theorem of the supernatural seems to be the object of this witness by the Church in Vatican Council I (H. Denzinger, *Enchiridion symbolorum* 3015–20).

Primary Synthetic Principle. Scientific syntheses in regard to the whole of revelation have rarely appeared in history and began only in the Middle Ages. Such syntheses stem from analogical conceptions or hypotheses that serve as primary principles for composing the truths of revelation into a pattern of unified understanding. For example, ''the whole Christ,'' conceived after the analogy of the human organism, was suggested as such a principle by Cassiodorus and developed to a certain extent by Robert of Melun, Robert Kilwardby, Odo Rigaldus, William of Melitona, Gabriel Biel, and Peter of Ailly; it has been taken up again in great detail by É. Mersch, ''L'Objet de la théologie et le *Christus totus,*'' *Recherches de science religieuse* 26 (1936) 129–157. The conception of all revealed truth in terms of ''things and signs'' suggested by Augustine was taken up by Peter Lombard. The conception of God as alpha and omega, principle and end, was the fundamental synthetic principle for Albert the Great and his disciple Ulric of Strassburg. St. Thomas Aquinas invented a term to express the fundamental analogical conception underlying his synthesis: God as revealable (*Deus in quantum revelabile*), a conception that is not at all the same as the later Thomistic conception, ''virtually revealed'' (*virtualiter revelatum*). Perhaps no on has explored the meaning of *revelabile* in St. Thomas better than É. Gilson in *Le Thomisme* (5th ed. Paris 1944) 8–41. [Cf. G. Van Ackeren, SJ, *Sacra doctrina: The Subject of the First Question of the* Summa theologiae *of St. Thomas Aquinas* (Rome 1952) 110–112.] Thomas's *revelabile* has never been seriously challenged, perhaps because relatively little attention has been paid to it. K. Rahner's outline of the dogmatic synthesis of theology [*Theological Investigations,* v. 1, tr. C. Ernst (Baltimore, Md. 1961) 19–37] is a thought-provoking attempt. It draws on M. HEIDEGGER's existentialism for its categories, and its basic theorem seems to be that all truths in theology can be understood in their unity only in terms of the humanity of the Word Incarnate, the revealer of the Father, and His personal encounter with men. Rahner's projected synthesis seems to be a kind of theological ANTHROPOLOGY, which has not been worked out as yet. Whether this conception is a further development of St. Thomas's *revelabile* remains to be investigated.

Living Contact with the Sources. In any case, the scientific speculative theologian must constantly remember that revelation was not given merely to satisfy man's mind but to enable him to live ever more fully the life of God given in Christ. This revelation has been given in concrete terms that engage the whole of man's being. Revelation is not a theory or a system, and the facts and truths of revelation do not fall easily into systematic order. Theories and systems, however, are unavoidable means by which the human mind extends its grasp upon reality, but they bear within themselves the limitations of an intellect that must use abstraction to progress in understanding. And something of the reality of the concrete existent is lost in the process, something of the richness and variety and depth of reality is compromised when put into systems that after all are constructs of the human mind; and hence any speculative synthesis that does not live within the sources of revelation is doomed to failure.

Just as man's life is not one type of activity but a composite of activities, more meaningful as they are distinguished and specialized and then unified in operation, so theology is not just one type of understanding (e.g., scientific) but a composite of various types of understanding that are distinguished and specialized but also unified in mutual interdependence in the accomplishment of its total task. Hence for the biblical scholar to say to the speculative theologian that he has no need of him is as harmful to theology as for the speculative theologian to take this attitude toward the exegete or biblical theologian [B. Lonergan, *Divinarum personarum conceptionem analogicam evolvit* (Rome 1957) 37–38].

Comparison of positive and speculative theology. In brief, then, positive theology discovers, analyzes, and determines as precisely as possible the content of revelation by investigating the analyses and consequent understanding that have been achieved and verified in history. Speculative theology, however, aims at achieving an ordered exposition of whatever understanding of the truths of revelation has been discovered and demonstrated (with varying degrees of certitude) in positive theology. Moreover, in its return to the sources, positive theology returns to the primitive, descriptive, and metaphorical way of understanding found in Scripture and moves to the more developed way of understanding achieved by insights verified in the witness of tradition. The movement of knowledge here is historical, moving from what is first known historically to the unknown, from what comes first in the acquisition of knowledge, from what is more obvious and manifest (*prius quoad nos*) to what is first in the order of being and intelligibility (*prius quoad se*).

For example, from the titles and description of Christ and His work in the Scriptures (descriptive understanding), positive theology finds in history the emergence of a new type of understanding of the constitution of Christ and His achievement in terms of Person, consubstantiality, natures, operations, acts, and effects, together with their mutual relations—an understanding confirmed by the witness of Christian tradition. These insights give a more accurate and deeper understanding of the unity, duality, and activity of Christ expressed in the witness of the Church and provide theological principles for understanding the teachings of Scripture in a unified, synthetic manner.

Speculative theology, however, follows a different order. It begins not with what is most manifest in the Scriptures but with what is deepest in the constitution of Christ Himself, the personal union of natures in the Word wherein everything in Christ and all that He does as related in Scripture finds its unity in being, its ontological order, and its explanation. Thus, whereas positive theology may be said to begin from Scripture, speculative theology ends in the Scripture. Enduring contact with the sources of revelation is the only way to assure that what is understood in synthesis is really the same truths that are contained in Scripture and tradition, and not theological speculations that have been divorced from their anchor in revealed truth.

Is theology practical? Because revelation is not merely a word about Someone but a word from Someone to someone heard in faith, a transforming salvific word, understanding the word involves understanding the response and transformation called forth and expected by the word. God Himself is not only the object moving the intellect through the external medium of revelation and the internal light of faith to some understanding of His mysteries in truth. He is also the supreme personal good that imperatively calls man's whole being to personal fulfillment in Him. By understanding this truth, the intellect inspires, illuminates, and directs the will toward total commitment to God in love. As the Word sent from the Father breathes forth love, so the Word sent into the mind of man breathes forth, as it were, the life of the Spirit. It is the Word of God that establishes the authentic Christian "can," "ought," and "may" in answer to the question "What must I do that I may enter eternal life?" Hence, theology, the understanding of the Word, must unfold the Christian imperative, the urgency of love (*caritas Christi urget nos*) to be incarnated in every human activity. It must lay out the pattern according to which the inner dynamic of the Christian commitment must work to assume mankind (individual, society, culture) into the current of God's salvific love—a work primarily achieved through participation in Christ's sacramental actions in the liturgy.

Practical theology (moral, ascetical, liturgical, practical), a poor term to describe what is meant, is concerned with the total response expected of man in hearing the word of salvation. It is not actually distinct from positive and speculative theology. In positive theology, faith uses historical reason to clarify the meaning as heard in the faith of the Church; in speculative theology, reason enlightened by faith endeavors to grasp a fuller understanding of this word and its expected response in the heart of man. Practical theology is that aspect of both positive and speculative theology that is directly concerned with man's response to God's revelation in full Christian living. Unfortunately, in the centuries following the Middle Ages it became separated from positive and speculative theology, and only since the 20th century has it been revitalized through a liturgical, kerygmatic, and pastoral renaissance.

The study of total Christian response to revelation as unfolded in individual, community, and liturgical action, if it remains on the level of principles and general applications, is referred to sometimes as speculatively practical theology. The existential engagement of this understanding of the word in directing human activity in one's personal life in community is called the practically practical aspect of theology—a work of prudence, according to St. Thomas, whose theory of scientific theology did not explicitly extend to the understanding of human action in its concrete individuality.

With the development of historical consciousness and the consequent specialization of intelligence with respect to concrete historical reality, modern theology demands not only a theology of SALVATION HISTORY (which of course is made up of concrete events and acts) but a theology of existential Christian living (which is actualized only in the concrete Christian response). Here one becomes concerned with theology as a rationally developed Christian WISDOM, which is not really possessed unless it manifests itself in wise Christian activity. A man may know what Christian wisdom requires of him in a concrete situation, but his wisdom breaks down unless he actually follows its direction. Practical theology therefore is an understanding of how the Incarnation of the Word is to be extended in space and time through individual and community action.

See Also: ANALOGY OF FAITH; ANALOGY, THEOLOGICAL USE OF; DOCTRINE, DEVELOPMENT OF; METHODOLOGY (THEOLOGY); MYSTERY (IN THEOLOGY); REASONING, THEOLOGICAL; REVELATION, THEOLOGY OF; SCHOLASTICISM; SYMBOL IN REVELATION; THEOLOGICAL TERMINOLOGY; THEOLOGY, ARTICLES ON; THEOLOGY, HISTORY OF; THEOLOGY, INFLUENCE OF GREEK PHILOSOPHY ON.

Bibliography: H. U. VON BALTHASAR, "What Should Theology Be Doing?" *Cross Currents* 4 (1954) 349–356; *Love Alone* (New York 1969); *The Glory of the Lord: A Theological Aesthetics,* v. 1, tr. E. LEIVA-MERIKAKIS, ed. J. FESSIO and J. RICHES (San Francisco; New York 1983). I. BARBOUR, *Myths, Models and Paradigms* (New York 1974). J. BEUMER, *Theologie als Glaubensverständnis* (Würzburg 1953); "Die Aufgabe der Vernunft in der Theologie des hl. Bonaventura," *Franziskanische Studien* 38 (1956) 129–149. D. BROWN, R. JAMES, and G. REEVES, *Process Philosophy and Christian Thought* (Indianapolis, Ind. 1971). D. CARROLL, "Hierarchia Veritatum," *Irish Theological Quarterly* 44 (1977) 125–133. M. D. CHENU, *La Théologie au XII e siècle* (Paris 1957); *La Théologie comme science au XIIIe siècle* (3d ed. Paris 1957). R. F. COLLINS, *Models of Theological Reflection* (Lanham, Md. 1984). C. COLOMBO, "La metodologia e la sistemazione teologica," in *Problemi e orientamenti di teologia dommatica* 1 (Milan 1957) 1–56. Y. M. J. CONGAR, *La Foi et la théologie* (Tournai 1962); *A History of Theology,* tr. and ed. H. GUTHRIE (Garden City, N.Y. 1968). Y. CONGAR et al., *Pluralisme et Oecuménisme en Recherches Théologiques* (Paris 1976). K. CONLEY, *A Theology of Wisdom* (Dubuque, Iowa 1963). I. U. DALFERTH, *Theology and Philosophy* (Oxford, Eng. and New York 1988). J. DANIÉLOU, "Unité et pluralité de la pensée chrétienne," *Études* 312 (1962) 3–16. C. DUMONT, "La Réflexion sur la méthode théologique," *Nouvelle revue théologique* 83 (1961) 1034–50; 84 (1962) 17–35. E. FARLEY, *Ecclesial Reflection: An Anatomy of Theological Method* (Philadelphia, Pa. 1983). F. S. FIORENZA and J. P. GALVIN, eds., *Systematic Theology: Roman Catholic Perspectives* (Minneapolis, Minn. 1991). P. FRANSEN, "Three Ways of Dogmatic Thought," *Heythrop Journal* 4 (1963) 3–24. H.-G. GADAMER, *Truth and Method,* tr. G. BARDEN and J. CUMMING (New York 1975). M. R. GAGNEBET, "La Nature de la théologie spéculative," *Revue thomiste* 44 (1938) 1–39, 213–255, 645–674. A. GARDEIL, *Le Donné révélé et la théologie* (Paris 1910). J. R. GEISELMANN, *Die lebendige Überlieferung als Norm des christlichen Glaubens* (Freiburg 1959). J. DE GHJELLINCK, *Le Mouvement théologique du XIIe siècle* (Bruges 1948). É. GILSON, *The Philosopher and Theology,* tr. C. GILSON (New York 1962). J. GILL, *I. Ramsey: To Speak Responsibility of God* (London 1976). C. GREFFRÉ, *A New Age in Theology* (New York 1974). M. GRABMANN, *Die theol. Erkenntnis- und Einleitungslehre des hl. Thomas von Aquin auf Grund seiner Schrift "In Boethium de Trinitate"* (Fribourg 1948—). C. JOURNET, *The Wisdom of the Faith,* tr. R. F. SMITH (Westminster, Md. 1952). A. GRILLMEIER, "Antikes und neuzeitliches Denken in Begegnung mit dem Christentum," *Scholastik* 34 (1959) 370–393. A. HAYEN, "La Théologie aux XIIe, XIIIe et XXe siècles," *Nouvelle revue théologique* 79 (1957) 1009–28; 80 (1958) 113–132. W. KASPER, *The Methods of Dogmatic Theology* (New York 1969). G. D. KAUFMAN, *An Essay on Theological Method* (Atlanta, Ga. 1995). N. LASH, "Decomposition or Rebirth: Recent Directions in Roman Catholic Theology," *Month* 240 (1979) 221–224, 269–274, 310–312, 341–344. B. J. F. LONERGAN, *Insight: A Study of Human Understanding* (New York 1957); "Theology and Understanding," *Gregorianum* 35 (1954) 630–48; *Method in Theology* (Toronto, Ont. 1994). A. MARC, *Raison philosophique et religion révélée* (Bruges 1955). F. MARÍN-SOLA, *L'Évolution homogène du dogme catholique,* 2 v. (2d ed. Fribourg 1924). E. L. MASCALL, *Words and Images: A Study in Theological Discourse* (New York 1957). É. MERSCH, *The Theology of the Mystical Body,* tr. C. VOLLERT (St. Louis, Mo. 1951). A. NYGREN, *Meaning and Method* (Philadelphia, Pa. 1972). W. PANNENBURG, "Hermeneutics and Universal History," *History and Hermeneutics* (New York 1967); *Theology and the Philosophy of Science* (Philadelphia, Pa. 1976); *An Introduction to Systematic Theology* (Grand Rapids, Mich. 1991). G. PHILIPS, "Deux tendances dans la théologie contemporaine," *ibid.* 85 (1963) 225–238. G. RABEAU, *Introduction à l'étude de la théologie* (Paris 1926). K. RAHNER, *Grundkurs des Glaubens: Einführung in den Begriff des Christentums* (Freiburg-im-Breisgau 1976), Eng. *Foundations of Christian Faith,* tr. W. V. DYCH (New York 1978); "Theology and Anthropology," *Theological Investigations* 9 (New York 1972), 28–45. J. RATZINGER, "Theologia perennis," *Wort und Wahrheit* 15 (1960) 179–188. ScCatt 78 (July–Oct. 1950). H. RONDET, *Do Dogmas Change?,* tr. M. PONTIFEX (New York 1961). E. SCHILLEBEECKX, *The Understanding of Faith* (New York 1974). T. SOIRON, *La Condition du théologien,* tr. Y. BECKER and J. R. HENNION (Paris 1953), adapted from *Heilige Theologie* (Regensburg 1935). G. SÖHNGEN, *Die Einheit in der Theologie* (Munich 1952); *Philosophische Einübung in die Theologie* (2d ed. Freiburg 1964). G. THILS, *Théologie des réalités terrestres,* 2 v. (Bruges 1946–49). T. TORRANCE, *Theological Science* (London 1969). D. TRACY, *Blessed Rage for Order* (New York 1974). G. F. VAN ACKEREN, "Reflections on the Relation between Philosophy and Theology," *Theological Studies* 14 (1953) 527–550. A. DE VILLALMONTE, *La teología kerigmítica* (Barcelona 1962). B. WELTE, *Die Wesensstruktur der Theologie als Wissenschaft* (Freiburg 1955). P. WYSER, *Theologie als Wissenschaft* (Leipzig 1938).

[G. F. VAN ACKEREN]

THEOLOGY, HISTORY OF

The history of the successive attempts at understanding the faith, varying with the variations of time and place. The message of the faith being summed up in the good news of man's SALVATION in Christ, two factors, besides the impact of external circumstances, mainly determine the variations in theology: the approach to the understanding of the mystery, or the method, positive or speculative; and the emphasis on one or other element in the KERYGMA, redemption or divinization, the juridical or the ontological. With attention to these two guiding principles, this article sketches the vicissitudes and the historical development in the understanding of the faith.

Theology in scripture. The burden of the inspired word of God in both Old and New Testaments is to convey the message of salvation. Being mediated by human authors, its expression implies an effort at understanding, or a theology. So a study of biblical theology investigates the meaning of the message as proposed at various stages by various authors.

The Old Testament message, in its progressive steps from patriarchal to monarchic and prophetic times, points to one fact: the coming of the Messiah, who is to usher in the kingdom of God. Therein lies the clue to Old Testament theology.

In the New Testament, which inaugurates the messianic times with the coming of Christ, the one theme of man's salvation in Christ, incarnate Son of God, is preached in varying theological settings. The Synoptic Gospel theology sums up the message in Christ, who by His life and passion, death, and resurrection initiates the spiritual messianic kingdom on earth and will complete it in His Second Coming at the end of time. It is mainly messianic theology, in close continuity with the Old Testament. Pauline theology, without breaking with the Old Testament, emphasizes in the mystery now revealed man's liberation from sin through the redemption of Christ, the risen Lord, and their incorporation into Him as members of His Body—a beginning only, to be fulfilled at Christ's return. It is emphatically soteriological and Christocentric. Johannine theology, while fully aware that Christ came to take away the sins of the world, exalts the divinity of Christ, Word Incarnate and Risen Lord; salvation means union with God in Christ, which is life eternal begun now and to be completed at the end of time. It is more mystical than redemptive.

These varying theologies implicit in Scripture, not denying but completing one another, herald the variations in the understanding of the faith (*see* BIBLICAL THEOLOGY).

Theology in the Fathers. Patristic theology covers a wide range. It proceeds from simple reflection on the theology of the New Testament through greater and greater syntheses, until finally it arrives at such all-embracing syntheses as, for example, that of St. Augustine, perhaps the greatest of the Fathers.

Beginnings. The early patristic texts, of the Apostolic Fathers (Didache, St. Clement, St. Ignatius of Antioch) hardly go beyond reflection on the theology of the Gospels: Christ is the Messiah, the risen Lord and Savior; they insist that faith and life must go hand in hand. With the apologists of the 2d century, particularly St. Justin (d. *c.* 165) and his vision of the Logos, reflection on the gospel message in the face of pagan objections to the Christian way of life prepares an apologetic approach in thinking out the message later to become a theology proper. Especially with St. Irenaeus (d. *c.* 202), sometimes called ''the first Christian theologian'' despite his opposition to speculation, the defense of the Christian message against heresies, particularly Gnosticism, develops into a synthetic view of the Christian mystery summed up in the RECAPITULATION of all things in Christ, who is revealer, redeemer, and author of man's divinization. Here too, reflection and practical spirituality go together.

Greek Fathers. It is in the school of ALEXANDRIA with Clement (d. between 211 and 216) and Origen (d. between 253 and 255) that systematic theology was born, with the adoption and Christianization of ''pagan'' philosophy as a means for the speculative understanding of the faith. Clement laid down the principle of theological speculation; Origen worked out a scholarly synthesis by his study of Scripture and speculative penetration of the mysteries through gnosis going beyond faith. Origen was, despite deficiencies in his pioneer attempt, the great initiator of Christian theology. Both Clement and Origen were typically Greek in their emphasis on the mystical and ontological side of the Christian mystery, on man's divinization rather than on his liberation from sin. Both united revelation and reason, Scripture and philosophy.

In the golden age of the Fathers, the elaboration of theology was stimulated mainly by the need to rectify misconceptions of the faith and to oppose Trinitarian and Christological errors. Part of the importance of the early general councils of the Church lay in their sanctioning concepts other than biblical for the clarification and expression of revealed truth. St. Athanasius (d. 373) defending the divinity of the Word (Incarnate) against the Arians, and the Cappadocians Basil (d. 379), Gregory of Nazianzus (d. between 389 and 390), and Gregory of Nyssa (d. *c.* 395) in their speculative penetration and exposition of the Trinitarian dogma, used to the full the resources of reason and of Platonic philosophy. So later, in the 5th century, did St. Cyril of Alexandria (d. 444) in his defense of the unity of the God-man against Nestorius and, in the 6th century, the opponents of Monophysitism. Without theorizing about theology and its method, they sought a correct technical expression of the faith in their meditation on the Scriptures. With all of them the stress was on the ontological side of man's salvation in Christ, on the Incarnation as the root of man's divinization more than on his Redemption from sin through Christ's passion, death, and resurrection. Their speculation kept close to life; it meant faith and morality, theology and mysticism all in one.

Alongside this speculative theology, which was approached by that of the theologian-poets of the Syrian school, such as St. Ephrem, the contemplative (d. 373), there was the KERYGMATIC THEOLOGY of preachers like

St. John Chrysostom (d. 407), both moralist and teacher, exegete and preacher; and the monastic tradition with its ascetical-mystical theology lived by more than thought out, harking back to both St. Paul and St. John; yet it too kept in the line of Johannine-Greek theology.

The last of the Greek Fathers, St. John Damascene (d. 749?), who faithfully summed up the tradition in a systematic, not to say scholastic manner, was "the first scholastic of the East," not merely because of his use of Aristotelian philosophy (Leontius of Byzantium, d. 542?, had preceded him in this) but also because of the less deliberately pastoral and more academic orientation of his theology.

Latin Fathers. In a vast literary output, the apologist Tertullian (d. after 220) had a decisive influence on subsequent theology by his expert, if not excessive, use of dialectics to defend Christian doctrine and life and by his juridical and anthropological approach to the Christian message. This approach was to mark Latin theology for Tertullian was, in a way, the founder of theology in the West. He explained Scripture more as a jurist than as a philosopher and was more concerned about the human than the divine side of man's salvation. St. Cyprian (d. 258) also proposed a theology more intent on the Christian life than on speculating about God: it centered around the Church, the Sacraments, and moral questions. Similarly, more man- than God-oriented was the theology of St. Ambrose (d. 397), his works being mainly scriptural and moral or ascetical. St. Jerome (d. 419 or 420) influenced theology by his scriptural writings more than by his polemical and doctrinal letters or treatises. As a man of positive science rather than as a theologian, he applied to biblical studies the resources of critical research.

The greatest among the Latin, if not among all, Fathers was St. Augustine (d. 430). His influence on the shaping of Christian theology was preponderant as regards both its method of uniting faith and reason and its content, the mystery of man's salvation. His formula *intellige ut credas, crede ut intelligas* well summed up his view and practice of theological contemplation. The formula supposed a first insight into the faith and faith in turn lighting up this understanding. For Augustine the whole man, head and heart, is taken up in the contemplation of the Christian mystery. The resources of reason must be used, and Augustine exploited to the full what (Neo-)Platonism had taught him; in this regard he was a speculative theologian. But the warmth of faith must transform an otherwise nominal understanding; thus he was also a mystical theologian. This was but natural for a man of genius at a time when no explicit distinction was made between the fields of nature and supernature, reason and faith. But his influence on Western theology was preponderant also because of the doctrines that were central in his vision of the Christian mystery. In his synthesis,the stress was on the redemptive aspect of man's salvation: the fall, redemption, grace of Christ. In this regard Augustine's theology was Pauline. But no less deep (and herein lay his greatness) was his insight into the divine mysteries, the Trinity and the divinization of man. He synthesized, one may say, both Pauline and Johannine theology. Besides, his theology, despite many speculative and apparently academic discussions, was pastoral and mystical. It was a theology for life, not for the school. Augustine was not a scholastic, though he became the great master of scholastic theologians.

For all his overwhelming influence, St. Augustine was not the only patristic authority for subsequent theology. St. Gregory the Great (d. 604) with his moral and pastoral treatises, St. Isidore of Seville (d. 636) with his encyclopedic works, St. Bede (d. 735) with his vast historical and exegetical output were authorities too, as was Boethius (d. 524), the translator of Aristotle. But their influence was restricted to one or another field; it did not determine the course of the history of theology as St. Augustine's theology did (*see* PATRISTIC THEOLOGY).

Transition, prescholastic theology: ninth to eleventh centuries. The end of the patristic age came with the break between Christian antiquity and the Middle Ages, marked by the fall of the Roman power and the conversion to Christianity of the barbarian nations. The break meant a new start in theology. The Fathers had been both theologians and witnesses to the ancient faith; their successors knew that faith through the legacy bequeathed to them by the Fathers.

The thread of the patristic tradition was picked up by the anonymous compilers of FLORILEGIA, anthologies from the Fathers. From these the new generation of theologians learned both the way of reading and explaining Scripture, or the *sacra pagina,* through the *catenae* of patristic comments, and of making use of the liberal arts, of reason. The term *sacra pagina,* which originally meant the Bible itself, came to mean those anthologies of patristic texts grouped according to the scriptural topics they were commenting on [see J. de Ghellinck, "Pagina et sacra pagina," *Mélanges Auguste Pelzer* (Louvain 1947) 23–59]. Hence the weight of the *auctoritates.* The Fathers were the *sancti doctores;* they had an authority that no scholastic teacher could claim. The "scholastic" method consisted in reading the text and commenting on it, i.e., in reading Scripture backed by comments of the Fathers; when Aristotle entered theology, the help of the new philosophy was added.

Carolingian Renaissance. With Alcuin (d. 804) and his work for the revival of the palace schools under Charlemagne, of the trivium (grammar, dialectic, rhetoric) and the quadrivium (arithmetic, geometry, music, astronomy) for both secular and clerical purposes, a slow revival of theology set in. The art of grammar was applied to the study of the message of Scripture and of the Fathers. Thanks to Aristotle's first entry in the West, with his *Categoriae* and *De interpretatione* as translated by Boethius, Alcuin became the main author of the CAROLINGIAN RENAISSANCE.

In the East, unaffected by the upheavals of the West, Byzantine theology continued to follow St. John Damascene. Contact with the West occasioned controversies, first about sacred images, then over the FILIOQUE, and later in the century more tragically around the person of Photius (d. *c.* 887). In the West itself the controversies over adoptionism (which held Christ Son of God both by nature and by adoption), over the predestinationism of Gottschalk (d. after 868), and over the Real Eucharistic Presence (Paschasius Radbertus, d. *c.* 860, opposed by Ratramnus, d. after 868) were signs of a theological revival. So was the work of John Scotus Eriugena (d. 870 or after), the translator of Pseudo-Dionysius, despite his apparent confusion between reason and faith.

Dialecticians and Antidialecticians. After the ''iron century,'' or the dark 10th century, the dawn of the 11th century saw the beginning of controversies around the use of DIALECTICS in the study and preaching of the faith. The antidialecticians, represented by St. Peter Damian (d. 1072), denied reason any place in Christian theology: the faith is given men to live by, not to discuss (the beginnings of MONASTIC THEOLOGY). Among the dialecticians, Lanfranc (d. 1089) defended a moderate use of dialectics in the study of Scripture, while an immoderate use of it led Berengarius of Tours (d. 1088) to deny the Real Eucharistic Presence. St. Anselm of Canterbury (d. 1109), the father of SCHOLASTICISM, sought understanding of the faith by reason applied to the faith, an *intellectus* intermediary between faith and vision. He constructed ''rational proofs'' for what he held from faith, e.g., the existence of God or even the Incarnation-Redemption. In fact, Anselm was not clear about the distinction and interaction between reason and faith.

The Byzantine East meanwhile (860–1050) was taken up with controversies around Photius; it was fertile mainly in homiletics and more still in hagiography. The mystical writings of Symeon the New Theologian (d. 1022) set the tone for later Byzantine mysticism.

Early scholastic theology: twelfth century. The progress of theology in the 12th century, preparatory to the golden age, was determined by two facts: the second entry of Aristotle, viz, of his entire *Organon,* making available in theology a theory of knowledge and demonstration; and the systematization of the patristic heritage in the *summae sententiarum.* The two influences combined prepared the balance between faith and reason, tradition and speculation.

Dialecticians and Antidialecticians. Of the two trends, localized roughly in the new urban schools and in the monastic centers respectively, the dialectic trend reached its acme in Peter Abelard (d. 1142). Dissatisfied with the moderation of his master, Anselm of Laon (d. 1117), in the use of dialectics in theology, Abelard rejected exaggerated reliance on the *auctoritates* in order to deal with the data of the faith by reason and personal reflection. He sought an understanding of the faith that did not rest content with words. His method *sic et non* lay in reconciling opposite authorities with a new view to systematic construction, which he achieved with the help of the ''second Aristotle.'' He was an important contributor to theological method. Later in the century, Gilbert de la Porrée (d. 1154) of the school of Chartres, more moderate in dialectics, initiated a theological methodology with its rules and principles. Alan of Lille (d. 1202) developed these rules and principles in his *Regulae de sacra theologia.* For all these theologians the starting point was the faith, Scripture and the Fathers. By investigating these data with the help of all the resources of reason, they developed the scholastic *quaestio:* first as part of the commentary on a text, gradually more loosely connected, and finally independent. Theology had then a twofold task: commentary on the text, or *lectio;* and disputation, or *quaestio.*

In opposition to the dialectic trend of scholastic theology, there existed the antidialectic trend of the monasteries. Its leader in the 12th century was St. Bernard (d. 1153), the passionate opponent of Abelard and of Gilbert. The founder of medieval Christocentric mysticism refused a merely academic use of dialectics in theology. He sought only the ''learning of the saints,'' often in a mystical or allegorical interpretation of Scripture. After him, however, monastic theology was less strongly antidialectical.

The school of St. Victor in Paris endeavored to effect a synthesis between the new philosophical trend and the traditional mystical approach. Hugh of St. Victor (d. 1141) was a man of tradition and a philosopher. In reaction to both St. Bernard and Abelard and in accordance with the Augustinian tradition concerning the use of the liberal arts in theology, enriched now with Aristotle's methodology, he restored the ''religious'' use of reason in the study of Scripture. He was clearly aware of the two orders of knowledge, reason and faith, human and divine learning. Richard of St. Victor (d. 1173) was both a remarkable theologian who improved the method, at once speculative and affective, and above all a mystic, the greatest theoretician of mysticism in the Middle Ages.

Summae Sententiarum. The new *summae,* successors to the *florilegia,* grouped the *auctoritates* according to a systematic plan. The most famous of them and the most influential on subsequent theology was that of Peter Lombard (d. 1160). His was preceded and followed by many others, such as the *summae* of Anselm of Laon and Robert Pullen (d. *c.* 1146), the anonymous *Sententiae divinitatis* and *Summa sententiarum.* Some of these may surpass Lombard's work in theological depth or originality; yet it was his four books of *Sententiae* that became the textbook in the schools because of their didactic qualities of clarity and completeness, their judicious choice of patristic texts, and their methodical orderliness. Lombard was moderate in tone and inspiration; while protesting against the abuse of dialectics in the sacred science, he still made good use of reason and strove to keep to the traditional line and orthodox doctrine. This harmonious systematization of traditional doctrine and a balance between authority and speculation made his *summa* the classic textbook (*see* SENTENCES AND SUMMAE).

During this period (1050–1200), Byzantine theology was concerned with the doctrine of the Holy Spirit. Niketas of Maroneia (d. *c.* 1145) attempted to compare the Greek *per filium* to the Latin filioque. There was a temporary revival of dialectics akin to Western early scholasticism with Michael (Constantine) Psellos (d. *c.* 1018) and John Italus (d. after 1082).

Golden age of scholastic theology: thirteenth century. Many complex factors shaped the golden age of scholastic theology. Two of these, largely external, were the rise of the universities (especially that of Paris, in which theology held the primary place among the three faculties, before arts and philosophy) and the foundation of the mendicant orders (Dominican and Franciscan, whose *studia generalia* were to play a leading intellectual role). The decisive factor in the development of theology was the third entry of Aristotle, when his metaphysics, psychology, and ethics—in addition to his natural sciences—became known in the West through the medium of Latin translations from the Greek or from the Arabic. The influence of the Aristotle was now no longer confined to a method of thought; it included a doctrine on man and the world, on many a point at variance with the Christian faith.

The reactions to the new philosophy were varied in the different schools of theology, but none of these could evade its influence. One reaction was mainly negative and defensive, in fidelity to the Augustinian tradition; such was the attitude of AUGUSTINIANISM, particularly that of the Franciscan school. Another attitude was one of uncritical acceptance of the new philosophy, even of its unchristian elements. This attitude sought an escape from theological censure in the unacceptable device of the double truth and came to be known as Latin AVERROISM. It was repudiated by the Church. A third reaction to the new Aristotle was acceptance of his philosophy in all that tallied with the Christian faith, eliminating or christening what was unacceptable and thus effecting a synthesis between Augustinianism and Aristotelianism. This was the achievement of the great Dominican school, with St. Albert the Great (d. 1280) for the sciences and St. Thomas Aquinas for philosophy. THOMISM, looked upon at first as an innovation (which it was) perhaps irreconcilable with true faith (which it was not), was to become the leading trend in Catholic theology.

St. Thomas Aquinas (1225–74). The principal significance of St. Thomas for the shaping of Catholic theology is his discovery of a philosophy of *being* that enables him to make a clear distinction between reason and faith, nature and supernature, philosophy and theology. This discovery, made possible for St. Thomas through Aristotle's philosophy, which offered a rational explanation of reality, is the heart of St. Thomas's insight and enables him to determine the nature and limits of speculative theology. Because reason leads to true knowledge of things within its orbit and can know the laws of being, philosophy offers an explanation of those things valid in itself. Theology remains faith seeking understanding, but reason also offers an answer to questions within its reach, questions about man and the world; it stops, however, before the mystery of God's grace, which was unknown by Aristotle. Here the gospel message alone and the authorities, the Fathers, transmitting the message within the Church are competent. Yet, even here reason and METAPHYSICS can help to understand, because the laws of being apply to all that is, not excluding the SUPERNATURAL. Even in the supernature, things are what they are because of their NATURE, not because of an arbitrary divine disposition. Thus a rational systematization of theology is truly possible, and that is what St. Thomas achieved. To his mind, theology is a speculative learning, seeking to know the reality of things whether natural or supernatural; it is not primarily practical or a teaching about what one ought to do to reach God. Because of this trust in reason, the intellect leads in theology, not the will or the heart. Yet for St. Thomas, as for the other great masters of his century, theology is inclusive, covering the entire effort at penetrating the supernatural reality: dogmatic, moral, spiritual, mystical, and canonical learning. His intellectualism differs from Augustinian contemplative theology and from Franciscan affective voluntarism; he keeps the balance between reason and faith because he knows both the value and the limits of reason. He thus realizes a synthesis of Augustinianism, Aristotelianism, and also, via Augustine and some newly discovered writings, such as those of Pseudo-Dionysius, Neoplatonism. St. Thomas further develops the existing practice of theology with his commentary on Holy Scripture, commentary on the *textus,* i.e., Peter Lombard's *Sententiae,* which includes speculative questions, more independent disputations, and, finally, the speculative synthesis of all of these in the *Summa theologiae.*

This trust in reason and in theology suffers, however, from one drawback: absence of a sense of historical development. St. Thomas's approach to texts and questions, as that of other scholastics of the time, is metaphysical, not historical (except in a minimum degree). Scholastic theology is intent on the metaphysics rather than the history of man's salvation. The drawback is not grave in a balanced genius who is a saint; it will lead to deviations in many an epigone.

St. Bonaventure (1221–74) and Duns Scotus (1270–1308). The Franciscan school, with and after its founder, Alexander of Hales (d. 1245), remained faithful to traditional Augustinianism. St. Bonaventure, though influenced by the new Aristotle, kept the Augustinian spirit in the mystical orientation of his doctrine, intent on seeking God by charity. Hence the primacy in his theology of the idea of the good, rather than of being, and the role of will and love, more than of intellect and knowledge, in the understanding of the faith. Love of God integrating in faith the light of reason leads to a mystical understanding of the faith. Philosophy, for the St. Bonaventure, in a way remains extrinsic to theology: creatures are hardly worth knowing in themselves or in their nature but only as images and mirrors of God; and it is Scripture that reveals their symbolic value. For all that, St. Bonaventure constructed his theology with the help of Aristotelian metaphysics. But his distrust in reason considered in itself weakened his systematization of the faith.

Bonaventure opened the way for the voluntarism of Duns Scotus, who laid at the basis of his theological system a thorough critique of man's knowledge of God, whether natural or supernatural. According to Scotus, metaphysics does not directly speak of God but only of creatures—of God solely in a confused way through the idea of being. Theology knows about God from what it derives *ex voluntate Dei revelantis.* The "necessary reasons" proposed in theology fail to give evidence of the necessity. God alone knows with evidence. God's will is the ultimate reason for what man believes. Holy Scripture or revelation is the basis of the connections between the data of the faith. For all its apparent reasoned construction, Scotus's theology cuts the main nerves, the organic connections, in his or any theological system—not man's insight into the nature of things revealed but God's will guarantees these connections. Thus Scotus makes explicit the latent voluntarism of St. Bonaventure. He prepares the way for NOMINALISM.

Other Theologians of the Great Century. Thomism at first met with opposition at the universities of Paris and Oxford, an offensive that died out only with the canonization of St. Thomas (1323). In the Dominican Order it gradually and definitely by the end of the century became the official doctrine of the order. Among its early defenders may be mentioned John (Quidort) of Paris (d. 1306) and Giles of Lessines (d. after 1304). William of Moerbeke (d. *c.* 1286), the translator of the Greek philosophers, became the initiator of 13th-century Neoplatonism. Among the secular theologians, traditional Augustinianism was represented by Gerard of Abbeville (d. 1272) and Henry of Ghent (d. 1293); a disciple of the latter, Godfrey of Fontaines (d. after 1306), gave up Augustinianism and inclined toward the Thomist school. Giles of Rome (d. 1316), general of the Augustinians, was also closer to Thomism, while yet maintaining on some points an Augustinianism akin to that of the Franciscan school. Throughout the great century, the danger or weakness inherent in speculative theology remained hidden under the balance between reason and tradition that the great masters maintained by contact with Scripture.

Byzantine theology during the years 1200 to 1330 was at first, after the erection of the Latin Empire of Constantinople (1204), taken up with anti-Latin polemics, particularly concerning the doctrine of purgatory. Toward the end of the century, while one section of Greek theologians advocated an anti-Latin interpretation of their tradition, others drew nearer to the Latin standpoint from the study of Greek patristics.

Decline and transition: fourteenth and fifteenth centuries. The 14th century, a century of crisis for Christianity, particularly since the Great Western Schism ended only in the Council of Constance (1414–18), saw the decline of speculative sciences and speculative theology. The various schools lived on but without great masters. Thomism had its defenders, such as Hervé of Nedellec (d. 1323), and its deserters, as Durandus of St. Pourçain (d. 1334). The Franciscan school had its Scotist sententiaries, among whom was Francis of Meyronnes (d. after 1328), *magister acutus abstractionum,* and its followers of St. Bonaventure, such as John of Erfurt (fl. 1300). In Giles of Rome's Augustinian school, Augustinus Triumphus (d. 1328) stood out with a *Summa de potestate ecclesiastica,* and also Gregory of Rimini (d. 1358), *doctor authenticus.* But the great novelty and the gravest sign of speculative decline was the rise of OCKHAMISM.

William of Ockham (d. *c.* 1349) united with a sincere faith in God and in His free and sovereign omnipotence a nominalist philosophy denying the realism of man's intellectual knowledge. One way only is open to men for knowledge of God and of His dispensation: revelation in Scripture; and the only answer man's reason can give as to the why of what is revealed is that God wills it. Religious experience makes up for the impotence of man's intellect to reach God. This nominalist theology was to spread swiftly and extensively; it would affect all theological schools.

The main topic of theology at this time of crisis for the Church was the Church (and State). James of Viterbo (d. 1307?) gave in his *De regimine christiano* the first treatise *De ecclesia.* The conciliar theories, exalting a general council above the pope, found defenders in Peter of Ailly (d. 1420) and Jean Gerson (d. 1429).

With the decline of speculative theology, the quest for God sought and found an outlet in mysticism. While the great masters of the 13th century were simultaneously speculative and mystical theologians, the 14th-century schools of spirituality developed apart from theology, some of them with a definite antispeculative slant. There was the great Dionysian school, steeped in the Neoplatonism of Pseudo-Dionysius, with the great German Dominican mystics: Meister Eckhart (d. 1327), Tauler (d. 1361), and Henry Suso (d. 1365); and the Flemish mystics, among whom the chief one was Bl. John Ruysbroeck (d. 1381). The school of Windesheim, initiated by Gerard Groote (d. 1384), deliberately antispeculative, gave the Church the *IMITATION OF CHRIST*. The Carthusian school had Ludolph of Saxony (d. 1378), with his most popular *Life of Christ,* and the great mystic, Denis the Carthusian (d. 1471), *doctor ecstaticus.* The school of Gerson sought to unite in a traditional spirituality both speculative and practical mysticism, the theory and the practice of the *experimentalis Dei perceptio.*

In Byzantine theology two facts were symptoms of a relative vitality. The first symptom is the Hesychast controversy, with Gregory Palamas (fl. 1350) and Nailos Kabasilos (d. 1361?) as chief representatives of an anti-intellectualist mysticism, which was opposed by Demetrios Kydones (d. 1397?), who took on the defense of Thomas Aquinas and translated into Greek his *Summa contra gentiles* and the *Summa theologiae* 1a2ae. The second symptom is the existence of the unionist and anti-unionist currents that were to lead, in the following century, to the attempt at reunion with Rome at the Council of Florence (1439–45), with Cardinal Bessarion (d. 1472) as the chief protagonist of reunion.

The 15th century brought the beginning of the Renaissance, which was the immediate preparation for the modern era. Its humanism, harking back to pre-Christian times, to classical Greek antiquity, initiated a restoration of the status of human reason to the point of exaggeration and tended to naturalism. Particularly in the Platonic academy of the Medicis it resuscitated Platonism; Marsilio Ficino (d. 1499) translated into Latin Plato, Plotinus, etc., and summed up their teaching in treatises of his own. The Aristotelians, refusing to acknowledge Plato's primacy, were divided between Averroists and Alexandrists over the question of the immortality of the soul. These heterodox deviations provoked sporadic but futile reactions from the decadent theology of the time and, early in the following century, a declaration of the Fifth Lateran Council (1513). A disaster was needed to awaken Catholic theology to the needs of the new times.

Renewal of theology at Trent and after: sixteenth and seventeenth centuries. The new spirit of modern times created by the Renaissance aroused new needs in theology as well; there was a desire for the renewal and adaptation of traditional teaching, an awakening of the sense of the historical in the study of Scripture and the Fathers, a shift from an objective to a subjective approach to the Christian message. Decadent scholastic theology seemed out of touch with reality, lost in dialectics, in oversubtle distinctions, in fixed and frozen notions, and in systems. The Renaissance and its humanism created in men such as Erasmus (d. 1536) an antischolastic, antispeculative, if not antidogmatic, spirit; while keeping the faith, Erasmus was averse to the whole of medieval theology, its spirit and form, method and conclusions.

Luther and the reformers met the new needs with a revolutionary reform of the Church's life and doctrine. Throwing overboard the scholasticism he knew, mainly nominalist, Luther went back to Holy Scripture, there to rediscover the message of salvation; distrustful of human reason in fallen man, he sought to substitute for scholastic theology a theology that is devout and based on Scripture. Taking shelter under the authority of St. Augustine, particularly for his teaching on grace and justification, Luther initiated a movement for reform of Christian doctrine and life that resulted in the disruption of Western Christianity.

Before the Council of Trent. The Catholic answer to the modern needs and to the Reformation as well came with the renewal of theology at Trent and after. Before the council, in the first half of the century, theology in many ancient schools continued to suffer from the preponderance of Ockhamism, after Gabriel Biel (d. 1495) and John Major (fl. 1540). The metaphysical-mystical reaction of Nicholas of Cusa (d. 1464) influenced, for example, the Augustinian General Giles of Viterbo (d. 1532) and turned him from Aristotelian scholasticism to

Platonism. In the Dominican schools a new vitality was awakening, helped by the substitution of St. Thomas's *Summa* as textbook for Lombard's *Sententiae.* This led to the great commentaries, such as those of Cajetan (d. 1534) and of Francesco de Vitoria (d.1546). Cajetan's commentaries on the *Summa* revealed his deep scholastic and Thomist learning, which combined subtlety of reasoning and nobility of thought with a serene power of synthesizing disputed questions. He also showed bold originality in proposing on many points new opinions of his own. A similar originality, if not eclecticism, in commenting on St. Thomas was shown by Vitoria, the pioneer theologian of Salamanca, who in his *relectiones theologicae* evolved his own method: the consideration of questions rather than particular sayings of the *Summa* and the treatment of these in ample developments. He thus initiated a new school of Thomistic thought.

Influence of the Counter Reformation. It was mainly, however, the Counter Reformation that led to a renewal of vigor in theology, which involved not merely a return to the great scholastics but also to the Scriptures and the Fathers. One new feature of this age was the rise of specializations, which eventually brought with it the fragmentation of theology. While the masters of the 13th century combined speculative, moral, and spiritual theology, scholastic theology now was divorced from mystical theology, which ever more, after the example given in the 14th and 15th centuries, tended to develop independently from speculative theology. The dissociation of moral from dogmatic, or scholastic, theology, begun in the second half of the 15th century, became the current practice in the last quarter of the 16th. A distinction was made between scholastic and positive theology, the latter meaning that branch of theology that investigates the data of revelation in Scripture and tradition, while scholastic theology was the speculative reflection on these data. Finally, by the middle of the 17th century, APOLOGETICS, considered the Christian demonstration that the Church's teaching truly represents revelation, grew into a separate treatise distinct from scholastic and positive theology.

The answer to the doctrinal novelties of the reformers was given in the controversial theology—a first step to a renewal of Catholic theology. Controversialists rose up not only in Germany with Johann Eck (d. 1543) and St. Peter Canisius (d. 1597), but also in England with St. John Fisher (d. 1535) and Cardinal Reginald Pole (d. 1558), in the Netherlands with Albert Pigge (d. 1542) and Ruard Tapper (d. 1559), in France with Jacques Davy Duperron (d. 1618) and St. Francis de Sales (d. 1622), and in Italy with the most famous of all, St. Robert Bellarmine (d. 1621). Bellarmine's method must be noted for its influence even on scholastic theology. For every disputed question (and he covered the whole field of the Protestant-Catholic differences) he constrasted the two doctrines, stated the teaching of the Church, and proved it using Scripture, decisions of Church authorities, patristic witness, practices of the Church, and agreement of theologians. He concluded by answering the difficulties. His whole approach was more positive than speculative.

The very nature of controversial theology, exposed to bias or one-sidedness, often prevented it from being great theology. The spirit of the Counter Reformation also printed its mark on scholastic theology and other branches of ecclesiastical learning; the impression has remained until the present day.

The century after the Council of Trent, until around 1660, was one of new greatness for Catholic theology. In exegesis great men like Alphonso Salmerón (d. 1585), Maldonatus (d. 1583), and Francisco de Toledo (d.1596) produced monumental works. Scholastic theology in the various schools knew scores of great men. In the Thomist school there were Domingo Báñez (d. 1604), the spokesman of the rigorous interpretation of Thomism; Bartolomé de Medina (d. 1580), the first to formulate the theory of probabilism; the two De Sotos of Salamanca, Domingo (d. 1560), theologian at the Council of Trent, and Pedro (d. 1563); and many others. Perhaps the most important for his influence on theological method was Melchior Cano (d. 1560), who in his *Loci theologici* laid the foundation for the modern classical method: proof from Scripture, from tradition, and from theological reason. John of St. Thomas (d. 1644), whose two *cursus* belong to the deepest and most enlightened expositions of Thomism, and Jean Gonet (d. 1681), with his *Clypeus theologiae thomisticae,* must also be mentioned. The Franciscan school gave great theologians to Trent, such as Andreas de Vega (d. 1560), and saw a revival of Scotism with Luke Wadding (d. 1657) and many others. Among the Jesuit theologians of the time a number were outstanding: Gregory of Valencia (d. 1603), Gabriel Vázquez (d. 1604), Didacus Ruiz (d. 1632), and, further, Juan de Ripalda (d. 1648), Juan de Lugo (d. 1660), and the Venerable Leonard Lessius (d. 1623). Overshadowing them all was the *doctor eximius,* Francisco Suárez (d. 1617), whose influence on later theology was almost universal. His system was an eclectic synthesis of Thomism and Scotism, his monumental work was marked by clarity and completeness more, perhaps, than by depth and originality (*see* SUAREZIANISM). It was mainly on the question of actual grace, *de auxiliis,* that the various schools proposed their own systems; particularly between the Dominican and the Jesuit theologians differences led to heated controversy (D. Báñez versus L. de Molina, d. 1600).

Spiritual and Moral Theology. For spiritual and mystical theology this was also a great century. In addition to the Benedictine mystics Cisneros (d. 1510) and Blosius (d. 1566) and the Dominicans Louis of Granada (d. 1588) and Vincent de Contenson (d. 1674), there was above all the Carmelite school with St. Teresa of Avila (d. 1582) and St. John of the Cross (d. 1591). Further, among the Franciscans there was St. Peter of Alcántara (d. 1562); among the Augustinians, Luis of León (d. 1591); among the secular clergy, Bl. John of Avila (d. 1569); among the Jesuits, Diego Alvarez de Paz (d. 1620) and Luis La Puente (d. 1624): the glorious century of Spanish mysticism. Lastly, there was the great French school: St. Francis de Sales, Cardinal Pierre de Bérulle (d. 1629), Charles de Condren (d. 1641), St. John Eudes (d. 1680), etc. In the field of moral theology one can only mention Tomás Sánchez (d. 1610) with his *De matrimonii sacramento,* Antonio Diana (d. 1663) with his 12 volumes of cases (some 30,000), and Vincent Baron, OP (d. 1674), with his *Summa theologiae moralis tripartita.*

Patristics, Hagiography. In the field of historical theology, pioneer work was done in patristics by Denis Petau (Petavius, d. 1652) and Louis Thomassin (d. 1695) for the immediate purpose of renewing dogmatic theology. Petau, who with good reason, De Ghellinck says, may be styled the "father of the history of dogma," showed notable understanding of the development of doctrine. Working in the same way to renew dogmatic theology were the members of the Benedictine MAURIST congregation, Jean Mabillon (d. 1707) being the most outstanding among them. Mention must also be made of the Bollandists (J. Bolland, d. 1665) and of their critical work in the field of the Church's hagiography.

Orthodox, Protestant, Anglican. In the East, Orthodox Greco-Russian theology gave way to Byzantine theology, its center shifting from Constantinople over Kiev to Moscow. In its defense against Protestant influences, Greek theology drew nearer to Catholic doctrines. Yet theologians like Georgios Koresios (d. *c.* 1646) opposed both Protestant and Catholic doctrines. In Russia, too, when Moscow became a patriarchate in 1589, polemics were aimed at both Protestants and Catholics. Peter Moghila (d. 1647) launched a renewal of Byzantine theology in Kiev that was linked with St. Thomas and Western scholasticism, under the influence of the Polish schools.

Protestant theology during its first century was centered in the symbols of faith written in the various confessions, particularly the Lutheran and Calvinist. Besides symbolic writings developing these creeds, this first age of Protestant orthodoxy developed its own scholastic theology in voluminous systematic works. This theology was based, doctrinally, on Scripture as the only source of the faith and, for its immediate orientation, on the *Loci* of P. Melanchthon (d. 1560), the basic dogmatic manual of Lutheranism.

Anglican theology, from its very beginnings after the establishment (1558 to 1563, the 39 Articles, 1576), showed the presence of the principles guiding its three main currents: the Protestant biblical principle of the Low Church (evangelicals), the Catholic sacramental principle of the High Church (ritualists, conservatives), and the critical rationalist principle of the Broad Church (liberals). Fluctuations and tensions between them led to the *via media* of the Caroline divines (i.e., under Charles I, 1625–44), who were to become the classic theologians of Anglo-Catholicism.

Decline of theology: late seventeenth and eighteenth centuries. The great century of Counter Reformation theology was followed by a decline marked by controversies over Jansenism, Gallicanism, and Febronianism, as well as the rationalist influence of the *Aufklärung* and the philosophers. A new development took place in the theology of the schools: the commentaries on the *Summa* of St. Thomas were replaced around 1680 by manuals that combined positive, scholastic, and controversial theology. This initiated modern dogmatic theology (not merely scholastic and speculative), which further developed Cano's method into that of the contemporary manuals: thesis, state of the question, positive proof from authority (Scripture, tradition, Church documents) and from theological reasoning, answers to objections, and corollaries (particularly for leading a Christian life). The tendencies of theology to build itself up into a system and to gather the theological sciences into pedagogical encyclopedias were additional indications of the new methods. These went together with the further development of specialization. Pastoral theology including homiletics and catechetics was born with a definitely utilitarian slant. Stress was laid on biblical and historical branches, and Church history became a separate discipline. Dogmatic theology itself tended to become a positive science, minimizing the scholastic speculative method and aiming at ascertaining the biblical-patristic foundations of the dogma, further opening out its speculative reflection to the new philosophies (of Leibniz, C. Wolff, Kant). Its unity was sought in the biblical idea of the kingdom of God. The introduction to dogma developed more and more as the *demonstratio christiana et catholica,* in reaction to the flood of rationalism in every field; due place in it was given to the teaching on the Church (apologetic treatise *De ecclesia*). All this was no doubt a sign of relative vitality and of reaction against the decline in theology; no great thinkers, however, had a decisive influence for a revival of ecclesiastical learning.

A few names need to be mentioned by way of example: C. Billuart (d. 1757) and V. Gotti (d. 1742) in the

Thomist school; C. Frassen (d. 1711) for Scotism; P. Antoine (d. 1743) and the *theologia wirceburgensis* of the Jesuits H. Kilber (d. 1783) and companions; H. Tournély (d. 1729) of the Sorbonne. For historical learning there was J. B. Mansi (d. 1769), the editor of the councils; the two Ballerinis, Pietro (d. 1769) and Girolamo (d. 1781), for critical editions of some Fathers; and L. Muratori (d. 1750) with his monumental editions and collections, e.g., *Antiquitatis italiae medii aevi.* For moral theology the most influential doctor was St. Alphonsus Liguori (d. 1787), who was also a great spiritual writer.

In spirituality the various schools, particularly those of religious orders, were less affected by the decline than theology itself. The French school, for example, had its saints and doctors: St. Vincent de Paul (d. 1660) and St. Margaret Mary Alacoque (d. 1690), Bossuet (d. 1704) and Fénelon (d. 1715) with their controversy about pure love, were so many signs of vitality. The 18th century too had its saints and spiritual doctors, e.g., St. Grignion de Montfort (d. 1716), St. Leonard of Port Maurice (d. 1751), and St. Paul of the Cross (d. 1775).

Orthodox theology during this time had its own polemics, e.g., concerning Baptism by washing, declared invalid in 1755 by the Patriarch Kyrillos of Constantinople. The monk of Athos, Nikodemos (d. 1809), wrote his famous *Philokalia.* Russia drifted further away from Greece. In the 18th century under the Czar Peter the Great, Russian theology was opened to Protestant, Anglican, and Gallican influences; there were both partisans and opponents of the new trends.

For Protestant theology the time of the *Aufklärung* ushered in coexistence of rationalism and pietism. The first trend rationalized the truths of Christian revelation, bringing them down to the level of a natural religion; it insisted on the merely relative truth of the facts of Christianity, i.e., on their being conditioned by the times. Pietism sought an inner and religious life either within one's own confession and church or in openness to other confessions. In Anglicanism the two trends, pietism and rationalism, coexisted as well. A theistic rationalism tending to unitarianism and advocating the rejection of the Athanasian Creed provoked an evangelical reaction.

Revival of theology: nineteenth and early twentieth centuries. After a gradually victorious reaction against the rationalism of philosophy and of the critical sciences, the 19th century brought a slow revival of theology. The revival included both a restoration of scholastic philosophy and theology and the development of positive historical theology. One decisive factor in this renewal was the work on the notion of dogmatic progress done by John Henry Newman (d. 1890) (*see* DOCTRINE, DEVELOPMENT OF). A particular feature was the lead given to the revival by ecclesiastical authorities, who not only warned theologians against deviations but also gave positive directives.

The beginnings of the renewal came with the rise of romantic theology in the school of Tübingen, whose founder, J. A. Möhler (d. 1838), united inner religiosity, deep dogmatic insight, and a critical-historical sense, e.g., in his famed *Symbolism.* Here was rediscovered a sense of the past, i.e., of the patristic tradition and the doctrines of medieval scholastics, and with the rediscovery theology regained a sense of history and of development. An attempt, moreover, was made to restore unity in the ecclesiastical sciences and to stress their vital import.

Under Popes Gregory XVI (1831–46) and Pius IX (1846–78), the Catholic answer to rationalism was given in solutions for the problems of the relations between faith and reason, supernature and nature. Various defective attempts at solutions, such as semirationalism (G. Hermes, d. 1831), which granted too much to reason, traditionalism (A. Bonnetty, d. 1879), and fideism (L. Bautain, d. 1867), which granted too little, or another deviation, ontologism (C. Ubaghs, d. 1875), were set aside by the popes, especially by Pius IX in the Syllabus of Errors (1864), and by Vatican Council I. A marked development of apologetics was one feature of the time. Another was the attempt to resolve questions regarding Church and State, along with the problem of individual liberty and its relation to authority—here also the popes intervened. Together with all this went the progress of positive theology, biblical exegesis, patrology, and history, as well as the application of the historical method to expound and prove dogma. The restoration of Thomism began in Italy with the encouragement of the popes and spread to the Roman College with L. Taparelli (d. 1862) as one of its chief promoters. The foundation of the *Civiltà cattolica* in 1850, blessed by the pope, initiated a movement of periodical literature that played an important role in the theological revival. The Marian movement found its crown in the definition of the Immaculate Conception by Pius IX (1854), while the positive teaching of Vatican Council I clarified the relation between faith and reason.

Pope Leo XIII (1878–1903) took doctrinal initiatives in many fields of ecclesiastical learning. He sanctioned and fostered the neoscholastic movement and in particular the revival of Thomism with the proclamation of St. Thomas as the ''common doctor.'' Neothomism meant not only a restoration of speculative theology but also the historical study of Thomism and scholasticism. Pope Leo's directives for the study of Holy Scripture and his opening of the Vatican archives for historical research were official encouragement for the ecclesiastical sciences. His social encyclical, *Rerum novarum,* marked the beginning of Catholic social doctrine. All these papal initiatives fanned the controversy in theology between progressivists and conservatives, particularly around the questions of revelation and criticism, revelation and dogma.

The Modernist crisis was the culminating conflict in the century of revival. Born of a desire to deal with the problems raised by biblical criticism and the historical study of Christian origins, the Modernist doctrines, influenced by a sort of agnostic philosophy, questioned the very nature of revelation and dogma. Their condemnation by St. Pius X (1907) saved Catholic doctrine, but it also encouraged a current of integralism, soon to be discouraged by Benedict XV. When the crisis was overcome, the revival again took its course more actively than before.

Prominent Theologians. Among the chief figures in the theological revival one may mention only a few. In Germany, after Möhler: J. Kuhn (d. 1887) and H. Klee (d. 1840); J. Kleutgen (d. 1883), the first great representative of neoscholasticism in Germany and an important theologian of Vatican I; H. Denzinger (d. 1883), famous for his *Enchiridion;* the greatest theologian of the century, M. Scheeben (d. 1888), who united speculative depth and positive learning with religious unction. For moral theology: A. Lehmkuhl (d. 1918) and H. Noldin (d. 1922); for Church history, C. Hefele (d. 1893), with his history of the councils, and F. Funk (d. 1907); for exegesis, R. Cornely (d. 1908), J. Knabenbauer (d. 1911), and F. von Hummelauer (d. 1914). In France: A. Vacant (d. 1901), founder of the *Dictionnaire de théologie catholique;* T. de Régnon (d. 1893), with his positive studies on the Trinity; A. Poulain (d. 1919), for mystical theology; for apologetics, A. Gratry (d. 1872), M. Blondel (d. 1949), L. de Grandmaison (d. 1927), who played an important role in the Modernist crisis, and A. Gardeil (d. 1931); in biblical exegesis, F. Vigouroux (d. 1915), founder of the *Dictionnaire de la Bible;* in Church history, L. Duchesne (d. 1922); in patristics, J. Migne (d. 1875), the editor of the two, Latin and Greek, patrologies. For Italy: C. Passaglia (d. 1887), theologian of the Immaculate Conception; J. Franzelin (d. 1886); for history, A. Theiner (d. 1874), work on the *acta* of Trent; H. Denifle (d. 1905) and his studies on Luther; G. de Rossi (d. 1894), the initiator of Christian archeology.

Orthodox, Protestant, Anglican. In the Greece of the 19th century, Orthodox theology was generally eclectic, influenced by Catholic, Protestant, and Russian theology. In Russia the study and translation of the Fathers was taken up; apologetics was anti-Western, in particular anti-Catholic. There were two great names: V. Solov'ev (d. 1900), the lay theologian of a *sophia*-theology, and A. Khomiakov (d. 1890), with his attempt at renewal of ecclesiology in the sobornost theory.

The Protestantism of the 19th century overcame the *Aufklärung.* With F. Schleiermacher (d. 1834), for whom religion meant awareness of one's dependence on the universe and its Creator God, religious experience became the theme in both orthodox or confessional-biblical, speculative or liberal, and eclectic theological currents. Exegesis and theology centered in the history of salvation. With A. Ritschl (d. 1889) the kingdom of God was considered as a moral value, and all Christian themes and church doctrines were treated historically; cf. A. Harnack (d. 1930) and his historicism in theology. The school of history of religions led to the rediscovery of the eschatological character of Jesus' message and of the numinous in religion. Liberalism and orthodox belief coexisted in Protestantism.

In Anglican theology the impact of the new critical-historical trends produced different reactions in the three churches. The latitudinarian manifesto, *Essays and Reviews* (1860), admitted Scripture inspiration only in a very broad sense and instituted a critique of miracles, later raising again the question of the Athanasian Creed. To this the Catholicizing High Church reacted, particularly in the Oxford Movement, stressing the Church's divine institution; it advocated not only ritualism but also study of Scripture and of Christian origins; cf. J. Lightfoot (d. 1889) and B. Westcott (d. 1901). Liberalism led by S. Coleridge (d. 1834) took a conservative stand.

Early twentieth century. When the Modernist crisis was over—or even before, with the establishment of the *École Biblique* of Jerusalem and the Biblical Institute in Rome—likewise with the return to normal after each of the two world wars, theology and ecclesiastical learning showed notable developments. Two great popes, Pius XI and Pius XII, took the lead.

Various movements for renewal in the life and apostolate of the Church, such as the liturgical and missionary movements, were incentives in the fields of theology. More directly decisive were the biblical and patristic movements and the return to the sources. Scholastic theology gained from the historical study of its masters, especially St. Thomas. Spiritual theology and studies in the history of spirituality knew a marked revival. A still restricted but growing ECUMENICAL MOVEMENT also profited theology. Finally, an important current studied and spread Catholic social doctrine. A decisive factor was the reorganization by Pius XI of ecclesiastical studies, a reorganization that sought a blend of traditional scholastic theology and the new positive sciences [the apostolic constitution *Deus scientiarum dominus,* May 24, 1931; *Acta Apostolicae Sedis* 23 (1931) 241–262].

One feature of the theological development was its international character. Biblical and patristic, liturgical and spiritual, historical and properly theological movements developed on an international scale. An increasing periodical literature in the various international languages was supported by international congresses ahd internationally organized research and publication efforts. Another feature was the multiplication of specializations, and with it the danger of the specialist's narrowing outlook. Two among the chief fields of development were MARIOLOGY and ECCLESIOLOGY.

Most marked in this research and activity, especially after World War II, was the desire for renewal and change both in method and in doctrine. Numerous studies took stock of ''present trends and problems in theology'' or reexamined theological method. The return to the Bible and the Fathers, from a desire of evangelical authenticity and an ecumenical spirit, brought a surge of interest in positive and a decline of interest in speculative theology. A danger consequent on this imbalance of the ''new theology'' and its overemphasis on the historical conditioning of the doctrine was ''dogmatic relativism,'' which Pius XII stigmatized in *Humani generis* (1950), although he upheld the need of theology to be in living contact with Scripture and the Fathers. Pius XII's personal magisterium, set forth in countless addresses and documents, was a stimulus for theology. The most crucial of his directives was his encyclical on biblical studies, *Divino afflante Spiritu* (1943), the charter that revolutionized Catholic exegesis and through it the whole of theology.

By the end of Pius XII's pontificate, the result of this movement for renewal in ecclesiastical learning was a slow emergence from a more or less unsettled state. Marked positive trends in theology were the biblical approach, greater contact with patristic tradition, and a definite orientation of doctrine to life (the divorce between theology and spirituality was definitely ended) and to pastoral action (liturgical and apostolic, social and missionary). Negative results were a decline in speculative theology, depreciation of scholasticism, not excluding Thomism, and a danger of shallowness and utilitarianism in doctrine. The balanced solution appeared to emerge from the study of the growth of doctrines as the key to their understanding; the historical perspective was recognized as being an essential requirement in theology. Consequent reflection on the data of revelation seen in their source and in their growth in the faith of the Church, in full awareness of the needs of the times, could prepare a renewed speculative theology.

Since Vatican II. Like faith, theology as a discipline entered a period of crisis in which negatively its own identity is called into question and positively it faces the challenge of creative renewal. The history of its recent past gives evidence of a radical metamorphosis in which metaphysical thinking (Neoscholasticism) has given way first to existential thinking (e.g. Bultmann and Rahner) and subsequently to historical thinking (e.g. Pannenberg and Metz). The approach to God has shifted from the objectivity of the cosmos, to an anthropocentric emphasis upon the immanence of thought and thence to radical historicality and *praxis*. The present altered status of the discipline can perhaps be schematically displayed in the following eleven considerations: (1) theology's scientific status; (2) theology and revelation; (3) theology and the Bible; (4) foundational theology; (5) the crisis of language; (6) theology as transcendental anthropology; (7) theology as method; (8) theology as hermeneutics; (9) theology as eschatology; (10) theology as process thinking; (11) additional characteristics.

(1) Scientific Status. Neoscholasticism transformed Thomas Aquinas's notion of theology as a subalternated science (*Summa theologiae* 1a, 1.3) into an exaggerated distinction between faith and reason, and it extenuated the Aristotelian notion of science (epistēmē) employed by Aquinas, in terms of Cartesian rationalism. This introduced a ruinous separation between the *fact* of God's revealing (acknowledged by faith and on the authority of the Church) and its *content* and meaning (appropriated by way of logically deducing conclusions from premises of faith). Theology became a science employing two distinct methodologies: the historical as ''positive theology,'' and the rational as ''speculative theology.'' In the first, it had two functions: to articulate the present teaching of the Church, and then to seek the foundations for such in Scripture and TRADITION. In speculative theology the function was to attempt a reasoned elaboration of such doctrine. In the modern era, these two elements were so dissociated that their complementarity was lost, with a resulting collapse of theology as a viable scientific enterprise in this sense. Among the factors in that demise were, preeminently: a growing awareness, since Kant, of the historicity of man and of all knowledge, which relativized the dogmatic and ecclesiastical character of the formulae of faith; a shift in the understanding of the revelation-event, which altered the notion of religious truth; and the transition from the intellectualism of classical culture to the empiricism of modern culture, in which rational certitude cedes to dialectical probability and priority is given to the experiential. In the face of this breakdown of an earlier structure, Rudolf Bultmann allowed a scientific function to exegesis alone and reduced theology to *kerygma*. More radically, Matthias Gatzenmeir (*Theologie als Wissenschaft*, 1974) claimed that its reliance upon an esoteric source of information (revelation), which appeals to authority and defies all rational

testing, gives theology an exclusively confessional character and denies it the criteria and the name of science. Serious theologians have countered by insisting that theology retains its claim to science, not on analogy with the natural sciences (*Naturwissenschaften*) but with the humane sciences (*Geisteswissenschaften*, in the sense of the word since W. Dilthey). It is rational and public discourse on the symbols of Christianity and as such interprets a depth dimension to common human experience, with its own critically employed criteria for both meaning and truth. It readily acknowledges its confessional character but maintains—in light of the principle generally recognized today, in reaction to the ideal of the Enlightenment, that all thought involves some commitment by way of a preunderstanding on the part of the investigator—that this does not mean it is without empirically verifiable grounding. Obviously, such grounding cannot be absolutized so as to limit theology to only the empirically verifiable. The truth it seeks to articulate is that proper to the human person, whose being is rooted in freedom and so is indigenously historical and linguistic.

(2) Theology and Revelation. The religious crisis that developed between the two World Wars precipitated a radical revision in the understanding of the nature of Christian belief and especially of divine revelation as its source. Revelation came to be looked upon not as God's imparting of truths about himself otherwise unattainable, but as the self-communication of a living God in present address to men. Faith response to this then appeared not as assent to propositions on the basis of authority (truth as *adaequatio*), but as existential encounter with the God who unveils himself to men (truth as *alētheia*). The locus of such an encounter is human consciousness, which is indigenously historical; thus, it involves both the a priori conditions of consciousness and the a posteriori conditions of historical occurrence. The linguisticality of man means the spontaneous articulation of this religious experience into language, of which the Bible is the privileged and normative instance. Originally, in the two thinkers most responsible for this revised understanding, the historical character of revelation was compromised. Karl Barth's ''Theology of the Word'' hypostatized that Word into God in his primal history with mankind (*Ursgeschichte*); Rudolf Bultmann reduced it to a divine summons to the existential decision of faith within human subjectivity (*kerygma*). A succeeding generation led by Ernst Käsemann recovered the relevance of history for faith by viewing history not as chronology or literal biography but as a record of intentions and life-commitments of the participants underlying the events. Present meaning is thus safeguarded from subjectivity in that it arises only out of tradition. More recent theories of revelation, inaugurated by Wolfhart Pannenberg and others, tend to move a step further in rejecting outright the distinction between fact and meaning (that is between *Historie*, as what the historian establishes by historical, critical method as actually having happened, and *Geschichte*, as the impact of past events upon present consciousness) that underlies the earlier position. Meaning, while distinct from event, is ingredient in events themselves; Revelation is not the Word of God somehow above history but is itself universal history. While appropriating both developments, Catholic theology at the same time has resisted the collapse into existential subjectivity, on the one hand, and the absolutizing of universal history on the other: the former by an emphasis on the concrete historical character of God's acts, the latter by an insistence upon the normative interpretation of such history both in the apostolic and the postapostolic Church. There is growing agreement, at any rate, on setting aside a priori concepts of general revelation in favor of an approach that begins with the Christ-event itself as a bearer of meaning on the basis of its concrete origin. Revelation is thus the opening up of possibilities for human existence (P. Ricoeur); its credibility is not so much rational as integrally human in kind (P. A. Liégé). The literary documents in which such experience issues are depositivized and not so much read for any ''objective'' truth they contain as (in a move beyond the Protestant principle of *sola scriptura* and the Catholic reliance upon Church magisterium) they are interpreted in a search for the meaning they bear for man today. Out of this arise theories of continuing development whose common note is an ever new thematization into language of a primal understanding that either transcends language or (more likely) at least cannot be exhausted in former language expressions. K. Rahner, for example, distinguishes between a ''transcendental revelation'' that is preconceptual and preverbal, and a ''categorical revelation'' that is the concrete thematization of the former in event and word. It is the texts themselves that in an objective way *communicate* truth not explicitly *stated* in words.

(3) Theology and the Bible. The recovery of the hermeneutical role clearly signals the end to the divorce between exegesis and theology. Earlier, exegesis had tended to assume an overly positivistic character, resistant to the schemas of theology that were becoming more and more rationalistic and ''speculative'' in the pejorative sense. Sacred Scripture is now viewed not as a deposit of truths but as a culturally and historically determined witness to the revelatory event. Exegesis, then, is not a neutral and naively objective historical study, because it demands a faith commitment and a preunderstanding on the part of the investigator. Faith is thus understood as not mere assent but as already initial interpretative understanding (E. Schillebeeckx); a gradual

awareness of its indispensible role in appropriating both the fact and the contents of revelation has led to a recovery of the primacy of Scripture and its function in theology as a *norma non normata.* As signs of this: any serious contention of a second autonomous source of revelation existing alongside Scripture has disappeared; later formulations of Christian truth appearing in post-biblical tradition are viewed as "the history of the effects of Scripture" (B. van Iersel). Noteworthy, too, is the emergence of biblical theology as a speculative act beyond, yet under the control of exegesis. None of this has meant the surrender by exegesis of its proper object and task—the recovery of the text in its original setting and the meaning it held for its author. But this function is put into the context of being a privileged moment in the larger hermeneutical task, which acknowledges that the text yields up its fullest meaning only in the perspective of an ongoing tradition.

(4) Foundational Theology. Theology is presently engaged in a critical reexamination of its own foundations in an attempt to provide itself with an epistemology, a method, and a set of categories for its interpretative work. This has meant the emergence of what is properly designated "foundational theology" to replace an earlier "fundamental theology," with a corresponding eschewing of prior procedures in the area of natural theology and apologetics, both concerned with seeking the rational grounds for, respectively, the existence of a Transcendent Cause and the credibility of revelation. Both remain legitimate pursuits but as conducted within the ambiance of revealed theology, i.e. the *point de départ* is the properly theological one of revelation understood as illumining the meaning of human existence. FOUNDATIONAL THEOLOGY, thus functioning analogously to philosophy in the latter's critical function, has thus become markedly anthropocentric and, in part, the believer's act of self-understanding. Foundational theology takes cognizance of the truth that knowledge of reality is available only on the basis of the structure of the particular being who questions it (Heidegger's *Dasein*) and takes historicity not as an accidental factor but as an essential constituent of human beingness. Further, all understanding is viewed as rooted in experience, the latter concept being broadened out to include "faith" as some sort of preunderstanding. Experience thus conditions both contact with the symbols of revelation and their interpretation. Exploration focuses on the relationship between the formulas of Christian faith and common human experience, even secular experience in its very secularity. In this way, theology retreats from being a science of God and man in the divine self-communicative act. Interest thus centers on the sacred texts as the language event emerging from tradition, and theology becomes hermeneutics. Contemporary theology is thereby rendered unavoidably pluralistic, resting on the two poles of religious pluralism and philosophical PLURALISM. The first means a climate of ecumenism not only in the sense of an irenic spirit but in the sense of theologians crossing confessional lines in doctrinal matters. The second is most obvious in the wide spectrum of epistemological options ranging from strict empiricism and linguistic analysis (Wittgenstein) to neoclassical metaphysics (Whitehead). The pluralism proper to theology is illustrated by David Tracy's discernment of five contemporary, viable "models": orthodox, liberal, neo-orthodox, radical, and revisionist (Tracy, *Blessed Rage for Order* 1975). Clearly discernible is a refusal of commitment to any one metaphysical system, a factor that gives rise to conceptual confusion, and not infrequently betrays an antimetaphysical bias, which undermines a traditional notion of theology as working under the sign of *logos.*

(5) Crisis of Language. At the bottom of theology's critical work lies the vexing problem of language. The "God is Dead" phenomenon of the 1960s graphically indicated that discussion had moved beyond the problem of believing in the reality of the Transcendent to the question as to whether it was possible to attach any meaning at all to speech that claimed to refer to what lay beyond the empirical order. The principle of empirical verification as employed in early Logical Positivism came to be qualified in attending to the distinctive consciousness from which religious language arose. This led to an understanding of how meaning is determined by the way language is used and so allowed a genuine cognitive character to the speech of believers. Also, the principle of verifiability has given way to that of falsifiability, in which theoretical refutability is seen as strengthening the case for belief (K. Popper). Nevertheless, the question of truth tends still to be bracketed as something dependent entirely upon faith-commitment and not susceptible of critical mediation—though Catholic theology remains sanguine about finding rational support for credibility. The modes of linguistic expression are multiple and varied, though all God-talk is recognized to be indirect, oblique, and relational. Emphasis falls heavily today on nonliteral modes of speech, divided basically into the mythical and the symbolic, both understood as vehicles of truth, though often truth not translatable into literal terms. Resource to literal (as opposed to figurative) language, however, is still deemed necessary as long as the literal retains its indirect, nonunivocal character; without this the truth function of myth and symbol seemingly becomes arbitrary. Theology as narration, employing story, autobiography, and self-ascriptive language is now regarded as indispensable to the discipline, though by itself it can offer no criteria for truth or falsity and stands in

need of conceptual language. The latter continues to be used primarily in the context of analogy, i.e. as concepts whose proper reference is to either realities of the cosmos (metaphysical analogy), or to subjective self-understanding (analogy in existential ontology), by means of which God is designated without being conceptually grasped. More frequently, concepts are used as hypothetical categories, as descriptive paradigms, and as disclosure models. Still, the necessity for an ontological undergirding of religious language continues to urge itself; metaphor and analogy are thus taken to be complementary in theological discourse. Much of the metaphysics deployed in theology is descriptive in kind, but of itself this raises the question of an interpretative metaphysics, of the move beyond language to being.

(6) Theology as Transcendental Anthropology. The dialectical theology of the Barth-Bultmannian axis sought to recoup the relevance of Christian faith by emphasizing respectively supernaturalism and existential decision, but in a way that radically reduced the significance of human nature on the one hand and history on the other. Attempts to surmount this, in a use of the transcendental philosophy of E. Husserl and M. Heidegger, led to a recasting of the discipline as theological anthropology, most notably in the work of Karl Rahner (*Theological Investigations*). The a priori (structure of human existence) and a posteriori (events of history) elements in religious encounter were thereby seen as illuminating each other. Scripture and church doctrine are shown to be the thematizations, in culturally determined images and concepts, of a prior awareness of God that is nonobjective and preconceptual, while still forming part of conscious existence. This latter ''prehension'' is not indigenous to man's nature but is an existential structure thereof, due entirely to grace and constituting a supernatural existential in which man stands open to the God of a possible revelation. The vigor of this revised ''theology of mediation'' continues to assert itself, although reservations have been expressed on its anthropomorphism, which runs the risk of measuring the mysteries of God by the meaning they bear for men. Hans Urs von Balthasar has strongly argued for the option of conceiving theology as aesthetics, in which God's concrete action in history, in its own splendor (*Herrlichkeit*), interprets itself to man in ways impossible to surmise from the latter's own existence.

(7) *Theology as Method.* Bernard Lonergan has employed the transcendental method differently, arguing that theology is less a discipline with its own nature than a method of thought. So transformed, it is isomorphic with the other humane sciences and rooted in the invariant structure of human consciousness as a dynamism of self-transcendence. Theology, on this view, comprises eight distinct but interrelated functional specialties: research, interpretation, history, dialectics, foundations, doctrines, systematics, and communications (Lonergan, *Method in Theology* 1972). What has precipitated this alteration is the transition from the classical culture of antiquity to the empirical culture of modernity. Here genuine objectivity lies not in naive realism but in the subjectivity of the believer as he structures his own world of meaning. Theology attends not to truths but to the acts of theologians striving to understand and respond to truth.

(8) Theology as Hermeneutics. In abandoning its former procedures and becoming an interpretation of the encounter with God, mediated through Christian symbols of the past, theology has been enormously influenced by the seminal work of Hans-Georg Gadamer and his insisting that language is the basis of all understanding. HERMENEUTICS is nothing more than a theory of the very process of understanding itself, as the uncovering of the hiddeness of things through the tradition of language. Understanding is neither naive objectivity on one hand, nor subjective behavior on the other, but a coordination of subject and object in which understanding ''belongs to the being of that which is understood'' (Gadamer, *Truth and Method* 1975, xix). Hermeneutics allows for the gradual emergence of meaning in the very process of reinterpretation that is tradition. The text possesses a life of its own wherein it meets the present interpreter and so ''can assert its truth against one's own foremeanings'' (*ibid.* 238). This dialogic ''fusing of the horizons'' is the merging of past and present in language; it enables one to hear *in the text* what was previously unheard. The past comes alive as the life of a community giving meaning to the present; historical events are known in an authentic way that unleases their meaning for the present.

(9) Theology as Eschatology. As hermeneutics, theology has developed from a hermeneutic of existence (in Bultmann's separation of meaning from event), to a hermeneutic of language (in the merging of fact and meaning in language-event by Gadamer and E. Fuchs), and, finally, to a hermeneutic of history (in which revelation occurs not merely in history but precisely as history: Pannenberg and Moltmann). In this latter stage, meaning is ingredient in events themselves insofar as they anticipate the end of history and so its final meaning. Revelation is here history itself in its universality (*Universalsgeschichte*), whose end has already appeared proleptically in the Resurrection of Jesus of Nazareth. This awareness of the end of history remains provisional because it is only anticipated in the destiny of Jesus; thus, theology moves beyond Hegel's absolutizing of history. At work here is an ideosyncratic reversal of time, in which the present comes to us not from the past but out of the future. This ontological priority of the future means that God lies not ''above'',

nor ''within'', but ''ahead''; his actions in history have the character of promise, to which the preeminent Christian response is hope, not faith. Thus, one views ''the world as history, history as the history of the end, faith as hope, and theology as eschatology'' [J. B. Metz: ''L'Église et le monde'' in *Théologie d'aujourd'hui et de demain* (1967) 140]. Of recent date, this use of universal history as hermeneutical key has tended to give way to a different emphasis on historical efficacy, in which *praxis* becomes at once a source and method for theology. Here the goal is not the interpretation of history from its end, but the transformation of a history still in the making, with concern centering upon the Church as mission (J. Moltmann, *The Church in the Power of the Spirit* 1977). The underlying methodology owes much to the ''critical theory of knowledge'' of the Frankfort School (J. Habermas and T. Adorno), which equates truth with intersubjective consensus achieved in unrestricted dialogue and societal action; recently it has received a Catholic adaptation (E. Schillebeeckx). Sometimes called POLITICAL THEOLOGY, its offspring is LIBERATION THEOLOGY, which advances Christianity as primarily committed to fostering liberation from political, racial, or sexual oppression.

(10) Theology as Process Thinking. The Anglo-Saxon, especially the American scene, has witnessed the rise of a distinct theological style committed to the primacy of change and becoming over being. Taking its inspiration from A. Whitehead's philosophy of actualism, becoming is understood not as history but as the foundational category of a neoclassical metaphysics. It delivers to theology the focal concept of a dipolar God, at once infinite and finite, eternal and temporal, engaged with the world in an endless process of creative becoming. The ultimate category is not God (who is one actual entity among others) but creativity, to which God and world are subordinate but which is not itself actual (*see* THEISM AND PROCESS THOUGHT). Obviously, this necessitates a radical reinterpretation of all the Christian mysteries; a Catholic parallel to it, in a limited respect, is to be found in Teilhard de Chardin's re-presentation of Christianity in terms of universal evolution.

Additional Characteristics. Its new ambiance has enabled theology to begin developing a suggestion made at Vatican Council II into a theory of the hierarchy of truths of Christian doctrine (*Unitatis redintegratio* 2). This represents an alternative to former concern with ''theological notes'' and both Y. Congar and C. Dumont urged it at the council as able to claim the authority of Aquinas. Order among the revealed truths is determined on the basis of proximity to the foundational truth who is Jesus the Christ. Basically, this allows differentiating primary truths (Trinity, Incarnation, redemption, etc.) from subordinate truths concerning the means of salvation (Church, Sacraments, apostolic succession, etc.). Another characteristic is the transfer of theology from the seminary to the university setting with the regaining of free inquiry. Also at work is an awareness of the need for dialogue with the nonbelieving world, in which theology attends to the genuine questions of contemporary mankind both within the believing community and outside it, including in the latter instance such questions as that of contemporary ATHEISM. Finally, mention should be made of attempts just getting under way to develop a genuine pastoral theology as a ''moment'' within theology proper, in which recourse would be had to the experience of Christians themselves and to the findings of the social sciences as rethought within a properly theological perspective.

See Also: THEOLOGY, ARTICLES ON; DOGMATIC THEOLOGY, ARTICLES ON; SPIRITUALITY (HISTORY OF); MORAL THEOLOGY, HISTORY OF (TO 700); MORAL THEOLOGY, HISTORY OF (700 TO VATICAN COUNCIL I); MORAL THEOLOGY, HISTORY OF (20TH CENTURY DEVELOPMENTS); MORAL THEOLOGY, HISTORY OF (CONTEMPORARY TRENDS); BYZANTINE THEOLOGY; RUSSIAN THEOLOGY; PROTESTANTISM; THEOLOGY, INFLUENCE OF GREEK PHILOSOPHY ON; DIALECTIC IN THEOLOGY; DIALECTICS IN THE MIDDLE AGES; BAROQUE THEOLOGY; EXPERIENCE THEOLOGY; EXISTENTIAL THEOLOGY.

Bibliography: F. CAYRÉ, *Manual of Patrology and History of Theology,* tr. H. HOWITT, 2 v. (Paris 1936–40). J. DE GHELLINCK, *Le Mouvement théologique du XIIe siècle* (2d ed. Bruges 1948). É. H. GILSON, *History of Christian Philosophy in the Middle Ages* (New York 1955). M. GRABMANN, *Die Geschichte der katholischen Theologie seit dem Ausgang der Väterzeit* (Freiburg 1933). A. GRILLMEIER and H. BACHT, *Das Konzil von Chalkedon: Geschichte und Gegenwart* (Würzburg 1951–54). A. VON HARNACK, *History of Dogma,* tr. N. BUCHANAN et al., ed. A. B. BRUCE, 7 v. (London 1896–99). E. HOCEDEZ, *Histoire de la théologie au XIXe siècle* (Brussels-Paris 1947–52). A. M. LANDGRAF, *Dogmengeschichte der Frühscholastick* (Regensburg 1952–56). A. M. LANDGRAF, *Einführung in die Geschichte der theologischen Literatur der Frühscholastik* (Regensburg 1948). J. LECLERCQ, *The Love of Learning and the Desire for God,* tr. C. MISRAHI (New York 1961). J. QUASTEN, *Patrology* (Westminster, Md. 1951—). M. J. SCHEEBEN, ''Zur Geschichte der Theologie,'' *Handbuch der katholischen Dogmatik,* v. 1 (Freiburg 1948), pars. 56–60, p. 447–491. P. HENRY, ''La Bible et la théologie,'' in *Guide to the Bible,* eds. A. ROBERT and A. TRICOT (Tournai–New York 1951–55; v. 1, rev. and enl. 1960) 1:964–998. P. DE LETTER, ''Trends and Fashions in Theology Today,'' *The Clergy Monthly* 23 (1959) 298–308. H. G. BECK, *Lexikon für Theologie und Kirche,* ed. J. HOFER and K. RAHNER (Freiburg 1957–65) 2:860–864. B. SCHULTZE, *ibid.* 7:1251–56. M. JUGIE, *Theologia dogmatica christianorum orientalium ab ecclesia catholica dissidentium* (Paris 1926–35) 1:392–640. H. U. VON BALTHASAR, *Love Alone* (New York 1969). I. BARBOUR, *Myths, Models and Paradigms* (New York 1974). D. BROWN, R. JAMES, and G. REEVES, *Process Philosophy and Christian Thought* (Indianapolis, Ind. 1971). D. CARROLL, ''Hierarchia Veritatum,'' *Irish Theo-*

logical Quarterly 44 (1977) 125–133. Y. CONGAR, *A History of Theology,* tr. and ed. H. GUTHRIE (Garden City, N.Y. 1968). Y. CONGAR et al., *Pluralisme et Oecuménisme en Recherches théologiques* (Paris 1976). H.-G. GADAMER, *Truth and Method,* tr. G. BARDEN and J. CUMMING (New York 1975). J. GILL, *I. Ramsey: To Speak Responsibility of God* (London 1976). W. KASPER, *The Methods of Dogmatic Theology* (New York 1969). B. LONERGAN, *Method in Theology* (New York 1972). A. NYGREN, *Meaning and Method* (Philadelphia, Pa. 1972). W. PANNENBURG, ''Hermeneutics and Universal History,'' *History and Hermeneutics* (New York 1967); *Theology and the Philosophy of Science* (Philadelphia, Pa. 1976). K. RAHNER, *Grundkurs des Glaubens: Einführung in den Begriff des Christentums* (Freiburg-im-Breisgau 1976). E. SCHILLEBEECKX, *The Understanding of Faith* (New York 1974). T. TORRANCE, *Theological Science* (London 1969). D. TRACY, *Blessed Rage for Order* (New York 1974). *History of Theology,* tr. M. J. O'CONNELL (Collegeville, Minn. 1996—).

[P. DE LETTER/W. J. HILL]

THEOLOGY, INFLUENCE OF GREEK PHILOSOPHY ON

The influence of Greek philosophy on Christian THEOLOGY has been complex and varied, decisive in shaping its mental cast. The Christian faith came to men in the gospel KERYGMA of salvation in Christ, a message proclaimed in the popular and concrete manner proper to the Semitic genius. Theology being the reflex and systematic expression of faith that seek understanding, Christian reflection on the history of man's salvation needed a philosophy. It so happened that it was the syncretic Middle Platonism and the Neoplatonism prevalent in the Hellenic world in the centuries that prepared and saw the birth and youth of Christianity that provided theologians with the phraseology and ideas for reflection on their faith. Christian theology might have looked different had it been born and had it grown up in another ideological and cultural, say a Hindu, milieu. Without entering into the historical details of the Greek influence, and at the inevitable risk of oversimplifying the historical facts, this article will outline its main positive and negative sides at the two historic junctures: (1) of the Biblical message and Hellenic philosophy in the early Christian centuries; (2) of Augustinianism and Aristotelianism in medieval scholasticism. In conclusion the article will briefly indicate the renewed influence of Greek philosophy in the contemporary renewal of theology.

Biblical Message and Hellenic Philosophy. The Christian message entered the Hellenic world as a great novelty. Not only was it proclaimed in the cast of the Hebrew mind, which is spontaneous and synthetic rather than reflex and analytic, bent on experience of the concrete rather than on abstraction and systematization; but the way in which it presented itself, viz, as a ''history'' of salvation rather than as a philosophy, jarred with the Greek mind, for which historical and concrete facts offered little interest—the Greeks had a science of history and of its cyclical returns, but no theology of history. Besides, the Biblical history of salvation carried a metaphysics in sharp contrast with the Hellenic vision of God, of man and the world.

Middle Platonism. The Middle Platonic world vision, predominantly Platonic with an alloy of Aristotelian and Stoic elements, presented one aspect appealing to the Christian mind: the opposition between the spiritual and the sensible, as of permanent values and fleeting things. But it saw God, the supreme spiritual reality, as the necessary cause of the cosmos either through emanation or through the work of a demiurge (world architect), often against the background of a dualistic pattern that placed an uncreated or eternal matter, the evil principle, in opposition to God. Man himself was to the Greek mind a duality of spirit and matter, a fallen soul imprisoned in a body, awaiting or striving for liberation from the body and return to God. (*See* PLATONISM.)

Into this ideological setting the Christian message of salvation entered: a God who out of love freely created the world and man and who after man's fall into sin promised and worked out his salvation; a Savior who came in the fullness of time and by His Passion, death and Resurrection redeemed God's people from sin and death, and now leads it to the ultimate fulfillment of history in a new world. Creationism, presupposed by salvation history, in which creation is the first act, eliminated from the concept of God all monistic idea of necessary creation. God is the supreme spirit, infinite, incomprehensible, immutable, almighty, in the sense of a transcendent free Creator, not fashioning the cosmos from an eternal, uncreated matter but making all things, men included, out of nothing at the beginning of time. Christened and purified from all monistic connections, the Hellenic idea of one God as infinite spirit served Christian theology to correct, if correction was needed, Biblical ANTHROPOMORPHISM.

Thus the idea of creation, unknown to the Greek, latent or implicit in the Bible, made explicit in early Christian teaching (note the opposition in the Nicene Creed between ''begotten'' and ''made''—Henry), may well be the cardinal innovation of Christian Greek theology. It vindicates the goodness of matter created by God and thereby sets dualism aside; it makes for the possibility of the otherwise unthinkable mystery of the INCARNATION—the Word could not assume what is evil. The idea of man himself becomes different both from the Biblical image of a living body and from the Greek concept of a soul imprisoned in the body: matter and spirit are seen as complementary principles of being. Resurrection becomes not just the revivifying of a once-living body but the reunion of man's natural components.

Neoplatonism. With its insistence on the One inaccessible Spirit—necessary cause of all degrees of being, matter not excluded—and on the return to the One as salvation of man's spirit, the NEOPLATONISM of PLOTINUS (3d century) made an even stronger appeal to Christian theologians, e.g., Saint Augustine, because of its thorough ''spiritual'' character and its firm and orderly structure. It needed christening by eliminating necessity from creation and removing the intermediary hypostases in the process of the descent of the multiple from the One. Its influence did not substantially modify Christian theology.

Selection. ''Orthodox Christian thought,'' thus, ''had *chosen* from Greek philosophy the elements that seemed to it to be serviceable, and it had rejected the metaphysical theses that to it seemed incompatible with its own principles and particular needs'' (Tresmontant, *Les Idées maîtresses* 15). Their *praeparatio evangelica* (Justin, Clement of Alexandria, Origen) was thus purified and completed.

Negative Side. In consequence of the Greek failure to integrate into its metaphysics TIME and history, there was also a negative side to the Greek influence on Christian theology. Greek thought, beguiled by the cyclic theory with its idea of history as the inexorable unfolding of a series of events, failed to perceive in time any real value or purpose. Early Greek theology, then, located the Redemption mainly in the fact of the Incarnation of the Word, while yet holding in faith the Passion, death, and Resurrection of Christ (see the creeds of the Nicaean and Constantinopolitan Councils). Influenced by the Greek ἀπάθεια, the early Fathers gave too little importance to the sufferings of Christ. For all that, in contrast with Hellenic philosophy, the Biblical metaphysics of time and history as an irreversible flow of unique, decisive, salvific events forced upon their theology a sense of the personal and existential.

Technical Concepts. This existential approach is apparent in the historic service that Christianized Greek philosophy rendered to the early councils by providing them with technical concepts needed to express the metaphysics of the two great mysteries of salvation history: Christ and the Trinity. The Biblical message spoke of God—Father, Son, and Holy Spirit—one God working out mankind's Redemption through the Son made man. It did not say in so many words that the Trinity is one God in three Persons or three Persons in one divine essence or nature; nor did it say that Jesus the Savior is a Divine Person in two natures, divine and human. Theologians, drawing from Greek philosophy the technical terms of nature, essence, and person, and adapting their meaning to the Christianized vision of God, the world and man, built up the reflexive expression of the Trinitarian and Christological mysteries. They often did so, in reaction to defective and unorthodox expressions, after long and harrowing discussions. Here Athanasius, the two Gregorys, and Basil played a decisive role. Thus one has the theology of the Son, or the WORD [LOGOS (λόγος)], and of the Spirit, consubstantial (ὁμοούσιος, originally a Gnostic term—Henry; *see* CONSUBSTANTIALITY; HOMOOUSIOS) with the Father, three HYPOSTASES (ὑποστάσεις; *see* SUBSISTENCE) or πρόσωπα in one divine nature (φύσις), or essence (οὐσία). One also has the unilinear pattern of the Trinitarian PROCESSIONS: from the Father, unborn principle, the Son proceeds by way of generation (γέννησις), and from the Father through the Son proceeds the Spirit (ἐκπορεύεται). Through the Incarnation the Son is consubstantial with men in their specific human nature, as He is consubstantial with the Father and the Spirit as God in the one divine nature, and with this difference: Christ is not a human person. Mary is THEOTOKOS (θεοτόκος), not merely χριστοτόκος, because Christ is one Divine Person.

The Greek councils did not go beyond the narrative of their creeds in the expression of the soteriological content of the Christian message. Its theological formulation comes mainly from Saint Augustine, who drew it from Scripture; it is not of Greek origin. Augustine insisted on the Fall and man's Redemption in Christ. Yet in metaphysics and theology he was a Platonist. He bequeathed to Christian theology a synthesis of Neoplatonism and reflex soteriology that, under the name of AUGUSTINIANISM, dominated Western thought for centuries.

Augustinianism and Aristotelianism. Meeting to blend in different proportions in the various schools of SCHOLASTICISM, particularly in THOMISM, Augustinianism and ARISTOTELIANISM each represented one trend of the Greek influence in theology. Augustine believed in the truth of a number of Neoplatonic ideas, and thanks to him the characteristic doctrines included in the ''Platonism of the Fathers'' passed on to early scholasticism: the opposition of two worlds, one intelligible and one sensible; God, Father of the universe and incomprehensible in His simplicity; the spirituality of the soul; a slighting of matter and the corporeal; a systematic view of the world with God as source and end; and, within this framework, all beings ordered according to the hierarchic degrees of being and simplicity. Yet, not its Platonism but its soteriology was the chief influence of Augustinianism on theology. Nor was Platonism here the chief Greek influence.

Wiith the arrival in the West of Aristotle's philosophy (in Latin translations from the Greek or the Arabic) and its adoption by scholasticism, another Greek influence on theology was added, mainly on that of the Latin West. The East, except for Saint John Damascene, ''the scholastic'' and Aristotelian of the East, remained in the Platonic current.

Aristotelianism's chief significance in theology was methodological, not merely for its use of Aristotle's logic and categories, but more especially for its acceptance of his rational vision of the world. This led, in Saint Thomas, to a definite distinction between faith and reason, natural and supernatural. A prerequisite to that acceptance was a Christianizing of Aristotle's metaphysics, of the two basic ideas: of God, the immobile mover of all things, only their moulder and not their creator; and of matter uncreated and eternal. The Christianizing was done by means of the great Christian corrective: creation out of nothing. Thus Christianized, Aristotle's metaphysics, built on the pairing of act and potency, or matter and form, as principles of being, covers the whole range of reality, from the pure act of God through the various degrees of beings composed of act and potency to the lowest degree of reality, that of pure potency, or prime matter. It gave a structured explanatory system of the entire order of nature, and it did so, in Saint Thomas's doctrine, without on any point contradicting the data of faith.

Even in the field of faith Aristotelian philosophy had a role to play. On the assumption that GRACE follows the pattern of nature, it applied the principles of reason to supernatural realities. Hence the attempt of Saint Thomas to extend hylomorphism, the metaphysics of act and potency, of the four causes (efficient and final, material and formal) to the field of supernature and grace: the mystery of God, of the Incarnation, of the life of grace, and of the sacramental economy of salvation. Scholasticism is ''theology under the regime of metaphysics'' (Congar), actually, of Christianized Aristotelian metaphysics. Such phrases express the deep-going influence of Greek philosophy in its Aristotelian form on Catholic theology.

Theologians Augustinian in orientation reacted against this intrusion of ''the Philosopher'' into theology, although they themselves had already accepted to varying extents his method and principles. Reason, they said, and they meant Aristotelian metaphysics, is competent in earthly things; it is not suitable for things spiritual and eternal—here only revelation is a safe guide. They found exaggerated Saint Thomas's trust in human reason with regard to the world of grace.

In fact, as subsequent developments and deviations were to prove, there is inherent in scholastic theology a danger of undue rationalization or conceptual systematization out of touch with reality. The Aristotelian theory of abstractive knowledge, which denies to human reason intellectual knowledge of the individual and the concrete, exposes a theology cast in its mould to the danger of drifting away from the specific object of Christian theology, viz, the gospel message about the history of salvation. Nor is the objection unfounded that the scholastic mind, following too closely Aristotelian principles, may lack a sense for the historical. But thanks, no doubt, to the persistent hold of the Augustinian tradition, soteriology and the soteriological meaning of Christ's Passion, death, and Resurrection always remained part and parcel of scholastic theology.

Renewed Greek Influence in Contemporary Theology. The reaction against scholasticism in contemporary theology—some have spoken of a ''crisis of Thomism''—provoked by and in turn fostering the renewal of Biblical and historical theology, may to all appearances tend to weaken the Greek influence as embodied and living in scholastic theology. But the present-day return to the sources, particularly to the Greek Fathers, includes a renewed Greek influence. Greek patristic theology differs in method a great deal from the scholastic; it is more pastoral and less academic, more spiritual and less speculative. Its revival may lead to an existential rather than essential, a more real rather than speculative approach to the history of salvation. This is one of the beneficent results of the patristic revival.

With regard to Catholic dialogue with non-Catholics or non-Christians, the awareness of the influence exercised by Greek philosophy in the shaping of Catholic theology should warn one of the possibility of expressing the gospel message of salvation in a theology built up under the influence of a different philosophy. Present-day theology is one way of expressing reflexively and systematically the riches of Christ. Under the influence of Chinese, Hindu, or African thought, future centuries may bring another.

See Also: DOGMATIC THEOLOGY, ARTICLES ON; GREEK PHILOSOPHY; GREEK PHILOSOPHY (RELIGIOUS ASPECTS); STOICISM; THEOLOGY, HISTORY OF; DIALECTIC IN THEOLOGY; THEOLOGICAL TERMINOLOGY

Bibliography: R. ARNOU, *Dictionnaire de théologie catholique*, ed. A. VACANT et al., 15 v. (Paris 1903–50) 12.2:2258–2392. Y. M. J. CONGAR, *ibid.* 15.1:341–502. P. HENRY, *Lexikon für Theologie und Kirche*, ed. J. HOFER and K. RAHNER, 10 v. (2d, new ed. Freiburg 1957–65) 5:215–22. A. H. ARMSTRONG and R. A. MARKUS, *Christian Faith and Greek Philosophy* (New York 1964). T. BOMAN, *Hebrew Thought Compared with Greek,* tr. J. L. MOREAU (Philadelphia 1960). J. DANIÉLOU, *Message évangélique et culture hellénistique aux IIe et IIIe siècles* (Tournai 1961). G. L. PRESTIGE, *God in Patristic Thought* (Society for Promoting Christian Knowledge; (London 1935; repr. 1959). 1935; repr. 1959). H. TARDIF, ''L'Unité du composé humain,'' in *L'Homme au regard de la foi,* ed. P. BARRAU et al. (Paris 1959) 45–95. C. TRESMONTANT,

A Study of Hebrew Thought, tr. M. F. GIBSON (New York 1960); *Les Idées maîtresses de la métaphysique chrétienne* (Paris 1962).

[P. DE LETTER]

THEOLOGY, NATURAL

The word ''theology'' is derived from the Greek *theos* and logos: ''discourse about God.'' Hence, it has come to mean ''knowledge about God'' or ''science of God.'' ''Natural theology'' or ''philosophical theology'' is the knowledge of God reached through human reason on its own resources; namely, through sense perception, understanding, and inference, which together yield evidence that is in principle accessible to all, independent of revelation. ''Sacred theology'' or ''revealed theology,'' by contrast, is knowledge of God based principally on what he is believed to have disclosed to us about himself through word and deed, which the theologian is believed to accept only through the supernatural help of grace. ''Theology'' without further qualification, then, normally refers to our best available knowledge of God, therefore to the discipline that uses philosophy but that is principally based on the testimony of God himself.

Many conclusions of natural theology are believed also to have been revealed, such as that a God exists and that there is only one God. Similarly, many arguments of natural theology are used within theology. The clearest difference between the two disciplines is that an argument from the authority of revelation is at best a plausible argument within natural theology. But in sacred theology revelation is the best evidence possible, and philosophical argument plays only an auxiliary role. Vatican Council I affirms that sacred theology involves an order of knowing that differs from that of natural reason in both principles and object (*Dei Filius* 4).

Vatican I and Thomas Aquinas. Vatican I follows Aquinas's account, which employs the logic and scientific method of Aristotle's *Analytics*. On this account, demonstrative or scientific knowledge consists in a conclusion affirming a predicate, P, of some subject, S, through a middle term, M, which, in the ideal case, is the cause of P's belonging to S. Humans (S) can be known to be the only animals capable of humor (P) when it is understood that they are alone capable of understanding and reason (M). The subsequent causal knowledge of SP can be laid out for logical accuracy in a syllogism in which the conclusion is seen to follow through major and minor premises, that is, through principles that respectively contain P and S. Each scientific conclusion must be inferred immediately or ultimately from principles that are *per se* known or that are evident in perception. ''Science'' in a more general sense refers to the ordered set of conclusions regarding a unified subject-genus, which conclusions are derived from axioms common to all sciences as well as from principles proper to the subject-genus. METAPHYSICS, the most general of the sciences, for example, proves properties of any being whatsoever, whether material or immaterial, through axioms true of all beings. One of its goals is to arrive through proof at the first efficient and final causes of all beings, and to infer from these grounds the nature of the highest beings.

Aquinas argues that theology too is a science in the Aristotelian sense: its subject-genus is God, and its first principles are the truths of revelation, summarized in the articles of the Christian Creeds (*Summa theologiae,* I.1–8). These principles, although mysteries to us, are per se known to God as part of his own self-understanding. Just as both biology and physics may look at the same thing through different principles, the latter through principles drawn partly from a prior science of mathematics, so theology and natural theology both draw conclusions about God. But theology relies on principles drawn from another, higher science, to which it is subalternated: namely, God's science of himself. As a result, the proper object of theology—God and things related to God considered precisely as revelabile—is different from that of natural theology. The central themes of Christian theology are the Trinity and Incarnation, which cannot be proved or completely understood through reason but which have their own inner logic and can be rationally examined given faith in revelation.

From the above, it may appear that natural theology like theology is a science in its own right. For practical purposes it is normally treated and taught as an independent discipline. Yet for Aquinas, natural theology is but a material part of the science of metaphysics. God is not a subject that can be studied directly as can an object of perception like a flower or a bear. Instead, God's very existence must be proved, and this is possible for Aquinas only by examining beings as effects that require a concurrent cause. God enters metaphysics not as its subject but as the cause of its subject, being in general. Furthermore, God's nature is known only negatively by ascribing to the first cause of being certain pure perfections of beings, such as goodness and wisdom, while denying systematically our imperfect ways of knowing these perfections. Still, natural theology like theology must examine not only God in himself, however indirectly, but also all other beings as related to God, their author and end.

The subsequent knowledge of a God, although indirect, can be certain and necessary, as Aristotle would want and as faith itself holds. According to VATICAN COUNCIL I, expressly citing Rom 1:20, by the light of natural reason it is possible to know with certainty, from created things, that God is the principle and end of all. For Aquinas, such knowledge also provides crucial preparation for the acceptance of faith, just as nature provides a foundation to be perfected by grace (*Summa Theologia,* I.2.2 ad 1). For him faith is not a mere blind leap into darkness. With the tradition he takes natural theology to establish, not the articles of the Creed, but its PREAMBLES, such as the existence of God and the end of human life. Nature and grace, reason and revelation have God as their author and so cannot truly contradict each other. Should the natural theology of the philosophers contradict revelation, insists Thomas, one may be sure that an error in reasoning has been committed.

History. The founder of natural theology in the West is often taken to be the fifth-century B.C. Ionian Presocratic thinker Xenophanes. He criticized the anthropomorphism of the Greek myths and affirmed one divine being as an unchanged, simple, and intelligent principle of natural events. Plato's critique of Homer and the poets in *Republic* 2 culminates the early Greek tradition, and Plato speaks there of a ''theologia'' that is needed as a corrective to mythologizing (379B). Although Aristotle uses the term *theologia* of the poets or ''theologians,'' he also calls his own First Philosophy or metaphysics ''theological science'' insofar as it treats the first principles and causes of things (*Metaphysics* E.1). Plato and Aristotle each offer proofs of the gods of their cosmologies and reflect upon the nature and attributes of first beings. In the fifth century A.D., Proclus's *Elements of Theology* systematizes the philosophical theology of Plotinus, the greatest pagan sage after Plato and Aristotle.

Natural theology has been practiced in various ways since the Greeks, under the inspiration of different philosophies, and with varying degrees of consciousness of and confidence in reason operating under its own principles. Only in stages did the project come to be seen as compatible with Christianity. Within Catholicism, complete fideism, such as Tertullian expressed, soon became no longer viable, but as harsh a critic of reason as Peter Damian is today a doctor of the Church. And outside of Catholicism, leading modern thinkers such as Karl Barth and Alvin Plantinga continue at times to question deeply the entire project of natural theology.

The Eastern and Western Church Fathers employed Platonic and Neoplatonic modes of thought, as did such subsequent thinkers as Boethius, Pseudo-Dionysius, John of Damascus, and John Scotus Erigena. Philosophy was not sharply distinguished from theology in the tradition of ''faith seeking reason'' that began with Augustine and that culminated with Anselm's great confidence in reason and his ONTOLOGICAL ARGUMENT. Simultaneously natural theology was pursued just as forcefully but with different degrees of orthodox approval within Judaism—from Philo to Maimonides—and within Islam, in the *kalam* tradition, as well as among the great Arabic thinkers al-Farabi, al-Ghazali, Avicenna, and Averroes. These traditions converged to produce Western Scholasticism's increased sense of the autonomy of natural reason in the thirteenth century, as in Albert the Great and Aquinas, followed by the critical reactions of Bonaventure, John Duns Scotus, and William Ockham. Natural theology continued to form an integral part of the great rationalist systems of Descartes, Spinoza, and Leibniz. But these inevitably evoked the radical critiques of Hume and Kant, questioning the very possibility of metaphysics as a science, critiques that continue to haunt natural theology today. In the last century, deep skepticism regarding even the legitimacy of religious language marked the ''philosophy of religion'' in its positivist origins. Yet postmodern critiques of a ''pure reason'' independent of community and affectivity have helped make room for renewed discussion of theism in both Continental and Anglo-American approaches.

Terminology. ''Natural theology'' in our current sense is not found prior to the sixteenth century. Augustine distinguishes ''natural'' from ''mythic'' and ''civic'' theology, describing the former as the fruit of philosophical argument (*City of God* 6.5). Yet his threefold division appears to be Stoic in origin, and for him as for the Stoics, ''natural theology'' affirms material deities. Ever since Augustine, then, one finds criticisms of ''natural theology'' as worldly and idolatrous, criticisms voiced by, among others, Aquinas and Suárez. Suárez, however, also speaks of ''natural theology'' as synonymous with metaphysics, proceeding under our ''natural light'' (*Metaphysical Disputations* 1). In Francis Bacon ''natural theology'' is first seen as a separate discipline from general metaphysics (*On the Dignity of the Sciences* 3.1.2–3), a distinction rendered widespread by Christian Wolff. Leibniz introduced the term ''theodicy,'' referring to a theological justification of God in the face of evil. Subsequently the term was often taken to be synonymous with natural theology. Finally, in the wake of Schleiermacher in nineteenth and early twentieth-century thought, ''natural theology'' takes on still a third sense, referring to an innate experience of the divine that is common to all humanity.

Bibliography: L. GERSON, *God and Greek Philosophy: Studies in the Early History of Natural Theology* (New York 1990). H. A. WOLFSON, *The Philosophy of the Church Fathers* (Cambridge, Mass. 1956). J. OWENS, ''Theodicy, Natural Theology and Metaphysics,'' *Modern Schoolman* 28 (1951) 126–137. H. DAVIDSON, *Proofs for Eternity, Creation, and the Existence of God in Medieval Islamic and Jewish Philosophy* (Oxford 1987). R. MCINERNY, *Being and Predication* (Washington 1986). L. ELDERS, *The Philosophical Theology of St. Thomas Aquinas* (New York 1990). J. WIPPEL,

Metaphysical Themes in Thomas Aquinas (Washington 1984). N. KRETZMANN, *The Metaphysics of Theism: Aquinas's Natural Theology in Summa Contra Gentiles* (Oxford 1997–1999). J. COLLINS, *God in Modern Philosophy* (Chicago 1959).

[D. B. TWETTEN]

THEOLOGY AND PRAYER

In ancient times the word theology did not mean exclusively a way of knowing about God but designated also a manner of praying. The Greek Fathers often used the word to describe the knowing and praying based on the ascetic life and leading to contemplation. This meaning was preserved also in the West during the greater part of the Middle Ages. For example, in the 11th century the name of the monastery of Tholey is explained as being derived from the fact that its monks spent themselves in the prayer of praise: ''. . . appellatur Theologium, quod theoricae vitae sit aptum, vel quod de Deo inibi frequens habeatur colloquium'' [*Acta Sanctorum* Sept. 5 (1866) 514]; ''. . . moderni Theologium dicunt . . . quod de Deo frequentius inibi a cohabitantibus versetur indisputabilis sermo'' [J. Mabillon, *Acta sanctorum ordinis S. Benedicti*, 9 v. (Venice 1733) 2:259].

THEOLOGY kept this meaning until the 12th century and even later: the word of God—*sermo de Deo, theologia*—not analyzed intellectually or discussed in school, but contemplated, loved, adored, proclaimed in praise and thanksgiving.

Principles. One must say, indeed, that theology is not merely PRAYER or a manner of praying. It is also knowledge, a way of knowing; it is a science, scientific knowledge. But for all that, it is an activity of the intellect which takes for granted and calls into play a certain interior experience, which is nothing else than FAITH. Living faith is vivified by CHARITY, it is conditioned by the acts and attitudes demanded by love, namely, consent and desire, and hence prayer. Desire for God is the psychological form love takes in the present life. Linked to faith and HOPE, it is the way in which man possesses in obscurity the indwelling God.

Because prayer is desire and seeking for God, the link between science and faith in theology is assured. Theology's object is God, an object apart from the theologian, which he can study, analyze, take apart metaphysically as it were, without having faith or, at least, living faith.

But the Christian who lives by faith must make a subject of this object, God. There must be a meeting of consciousness, exchange and dialogue. There must spring up an interpersonal attitude, be it only one of inquiry on the part of man. Need for God, desire for Him, LOVE: such is the action of faith-in-prayer, and it is the inquiry this inspires that theological knowledge answers. Living faith is necessarily a searching for God, a movement toward Him. Prayer expresses this aspiration, as well as the consent and welcome given to the gift already received. Prayer is an exercise of that faith whose substance constitutes the object of theological knowledge. So one really cannot separate faith from theological science or from prayer without destroying the integrity of either. Since prayer is the practice of faith, it serves as mediator between faith and theology. If there is to be not merely theological science but true theology in the full and traditional sense of the word, it must begin with prayer—with an *alloquium* as St. Anselm said—as its very principle. The theologian must begin with a prayer of supplication, and there must be prayer at the end: acceptance, thanksgiving, CONTEMPLATION. Between these two attitudes of prayer lies that activity of the intellect which consists in making more explicit the contents of faith, whose exercise is a concrete and personal relationship with God.

Application of Principles. One may say that there are three successive stages conditioning one another in the theologian's activity. The first is a blurred sort of faith, unorganized, conferring an initial intuition of the given revelation, and leading to the prayer of desire, of request. The second is theological reflection which develops the intuition, orders it, formulates it, allows it to move from confusion into clarity. This is the specific domain of theological study, but the search ought not to end there. One must turn back again in the other direction, proceeding from clarity to depth, from distinction to unity. Reflection should inspire new prayer, which is the third and final stage.

Such a religious attitude in the theologian depends upon his previous and habitual engagement. Generosity, watchfulness, love must characterize the whole life of the theologian. Only then will study be for him a spark touching off personal response to God, with prayer of utter consent, adoration, thanksgiving.

According to St. Thomas Aquinas (*Summa theologiae* 2a2ae, 188.6), the teaching of theology or *doctrina* is a work of the active life overflowing from the contemplative life. This is so, he says, first because the object of this teaching is God, to be known and made known; second, because the subject must be in a state of fervor of which the *doctrina* is an end result, the expression, the overflow. To illustrate this point in the words of Psalm 144(145).7: *Memoriam abundantiae suavitatis tuae eructabunt. . . . Memoria* is a certain ''remembrance of God'' which, according to Cassian, must be continuous. This delightful and overflowing remembrance is poured out in that *eructatio* which in Biblical language means love and enthusiasm. All of this, incidentally, is equally applicable to preaching.

What St. Thomas says of teaching theology is valid for those who are learning, and for identical reasons, viz, because of the object studied—God and His mysteries—and because of the dispositions required in the subject himself.

Normally speaking, then, classroom lectures and private reading should end in prayer, be prolonged in contemplation and in enjoyment of the truth.

To sum up, one may say that the problem consists in putting scientific study at the service of a theology which is not complete and does not even exist in its full and traditional sense if it is not founded on consecration to God, does not begin and end in prayer. The preparation of the heart and the *eructatio* or overflow of contemplation can be abbreviated into one word, fervor. This supernatural fervor, which should characterize the whole life of the theologian, is what gives to theology, not its clarity—that depends on the intellect—but its soundness and vigor.

Bibliography: J. LECLERCQ, *Études sur le vocabulaire monastique du moyen âge* (Studia anselmiana 48; Rome 1961) 70–79; *Theology and Prayer* (St. Meinrad, Ind. 1963); ''Théologie traditionelle et théologie monastique,'' Irénikon 37 (1964) 50–74.

[J. LECLERCQ]

THEOLOGY AND SOCIOLOGY

Concern for the connection between theology and sociology as methodologically distinct but related disciplines is relatively recent. It is rooted, however, in a much older question about the relation of religion and society. In that sense, the appropriate literature on theology and sociology would include such classic works, which predate the differentiation of academic disciplines, as Plato's *Republic*, Augustine's *City of God* and the writings of Montesquieu and de Tocqueville.

Historical Background. More precise methodological reflection on the relation between theology and sociology began in the Protestant theological world in 19th-century Germany as part of the discussion about the relation of faith and history, since sociology was primarily understood as a branch of history. Ernst Troeltsch is the major figure in this discussion. Troeltsch transformed theology by his attention to the institutional prerequisites and correlates of Christianity and the way Christian ideas become word-historical, shaping forces only by their elective affinity with ascendant carrier groups and the transmutation and exfoliation of these ideas through their contact with pregiven societal structures, groups, and culture. Troeltsch scholars in the U.S., e.g., H. Richard Niebuhr and James Luther Adams, continued his theoretical impulse. On a more practical level the disciplines were related by the use of sociology for pastoral planning in Protestant seminaries and church research agencies. For its part, the American Sociological Association, especially under the early leadership of Lester Ward and Albion Small, was much influenced by the social gospel movement.

Prior to 1960, Catholics did little methodological reflection on the relation between the two disciplines, although the American Catholic Sociological Association operated in its early years on the assumption that there was a specifically Catholic sociology. In Europe, church sociology, in the tradition of Gabriel Le Bras, was seen as a pretheoretical, ancillary, ''fact-finding'' discipline, useful for pastoral theology. In the aftermath of Vatican Council II, Catholic theologians began to dialogue with the proponents of sociology of knowledge and to inquire into new social action models to relate Church and society. Increasingly, dogma and theology are understood as strategic responses to pressing needs and claims of very particular times and places. Sociological analysis becomes an essential tool for hermeneutics in understanding the context and meaning of reactive dogmatic statements.

Evaluation of the Relationship. Many theologians now insist on social analysis as a necessary component in theological reflection. Sociology is essential for theology's task of ideology-critique and for delineating such key theological concepts as social sin, the Kingdom of God, liberation, and reading the signs of the times. Theologians turn to sociology to understand such processes as secularization and the privatization of religion. Sociology is no longer understood as a value-free purveyor of ''facts,'' in accord with a naive realism or positivism, but is seen to include a worldview, a special imagination, and a model of human understanding. Theology has shifted from an older hierarchical understanding of the division between the sciences with its notion of ''input'' disciplines to a new framework of interdisciplinary creative collaboration.

Bases of Relationship. Neither theology nor sociology is, strictly speaking, a unified discipline. Both are conflictive fields of competing theoretical and methodological positions, some of them simply contradictory. Every theology contains, implicitly, a sociology and a theory of the self. Theology must raise questions about the societal implications of God's law and Kingdom and the personality implications of sanctification and love. Every theological performance claim about this-worldly transformations of self and society is subject to empirical test. Every ecclesiology is also a theory about society. In the writings of some theologians, explicit theological motifs control the understanding of self and society. In others, secular theories of self and society determine theology. Thus, in choosing George Herbert Mead's understanding of self and society, H. Richard Niebuhr precludes certain theological options. Not every theology and sociology is compatible. It seems possible to draw up a taxonomy of the logical affinities between definite theological options and corresponding social theories.

On its part, sociology is not, in any simple sense, value-free. It includes hermeneutical presuppositions about the locus of the real, the flow of causality, and the power of value. Sociology sometimes slips from descriptive to prescriptive modes of analysis, since some vision of the future and the good society is operative in sociological and historical research.

Possible Responses of Theology to Sociology in Dialogue. (1) The relevance of sociology to theology may be rejected. This response is possible only for those who rigidly separate nature and grace, e.g., Karl Barth, or who maintain idealistic epistemological positions about the unbridgeable gap between fact and value. If religion is a social fact and society has a religious dimension, theology and sociology must be correlated.

(2) Selective elements from sociology can be added as ancillary motifs for theology. Selective borrowing is usually eclectic and runs the risk that data of sociology may be either distorted in the translation process or irrelevant to the theologian's questions.

(3) A reductionist position may be taken that destroys the autonomy of sociology by subjecting it to theology. Creative collaboration between disciplines demands making distinctions between them as autonomous modes of knowing.

(4) A dialogue would mean corroboration of conclusions reached and grounded on theological premises. This is mere illuminative exemplification by means of sociological evidence rather than true interdisciplinary collaboration.

(5) Sociological language can be translated into theological discourse and vice versa. Care must be exercised to respect the varying language games of the different disciplines.

(6) A reciprocal transformation of disciplines is possible by a two-way dialogue and mutual interpenetration and critical correlation of both modes of knowing. The Catholic theological bias, drawing upon assumptions of the ultimate unity of truth in God and the analogical unity of knowledge, would seem to favor the sixth strategy for relating the disciplines. Perhaps, however, there are some contradictions among and between the disciplines of knowledge which cannot be removed because they reflect the brokenness of society. Only when the cleavages in social life resulting from sin are overcome will science be one. In the meantime, Christians strive for the goal of unifying sociology and theology.

Bibliography: J. L. ADAMS, *On Being Human Religiously* (Boston 1976). G. BAUM, *Religion and Alienation* (New York 1975). R. N. BELLAH, *Beyond Belief* (New York 1970). J. A. COLEMAN, "Theology and Sociology," *Catholic Theological Society of America. Proceedings* 32 (1977) 55–71. H. R. NIEBUHR, *The Responsible Self* (New York 1963). E. TROELTSCH, *The Social Teaching of the Christian Churches*, tr. O. WYON (2 v., New York 1960). G. WINTER, *Elements for a Social Ethic* (New Work 1968). S. WOLIN, *Politics and Vision* (Boston 1960).

[J. A. COLEMAN]

THEOLOGY OF HOPE

"Theology of hope" is the name of a movement that gained international attention in 1964 with the publication of *Theologie der Hoffnung* by Jürgen Moltmann, a Reformed theologian who became a teacher at the University of Tübingen. Lutheran theologian Wolfhart Pannenberg and Roman Catholics Johannes Metz and Karl Rahner have since allied themselves with the movement.

Ernst Bloch, Philosophy of Hope. The name and movement were inspired by the philosophy of hope of the East German Marxist Ernst Bloch, especially in his three-volume *Das Prinzip Hoffnung* (1959). That work made Moltmann realize that hope in the future of history was a thoroughly biblical principle left undeveloped in Christian theology. He concluded that a theology based on that hope would remain faithful to the biblical message and yet speak meaningfully to modern man, since it shared with him his alienation from the past and his instinctive drive for meaning from the future. Moltmann sought to integrate three basic themes: the theology of ESCHATOLOGY of Karl Barth, Otto Weber, Hans-Joachim Iwand, Gerhard von Rad, and Ernst Käsemann, to which he had been introduced during his studies at the University of Göttingen (1948–57); the theology of the apostolate of J. C. Hoekendijk and especially of Arnold van Ruler (both of whom Moltmann studied, 1956–58), who made history meaningful in Christianity by combining with eschatology a social and political mission to the world as preparation for the KINGDOM OF GOD; and Bloch's philosophy of hope based on Hegel and Marx, which would serve largely as a philosophical and conceptual system of historical process useful for elucidating the biblical revelation.

Bloch, a Jew, was himself fundamentally inspired by the Judeo-Christian revelation transmitted to him through the theology of Thomas Münzer and Joachim of Fiore, which he interpreted in ''left-wing'' Aristotelian-Marxist categories. Bloch once summarized his whole philosophy as ''S is not yet P''; by this he meant that subject is not yet predicate, or being is not yet what it can be. He saw being as essentially dynamically oriented toward its essence or utopia, i.e., what it is capable of becoming when its potentialities reach fulfilment. This drive entails a dialectical process of history, now largely conducted by man, where the ''not-yet'' of the *futurum* is educed purely from the latencies and tendencies of creative matter. The present is the ''front-line'' between the unfinished past, transcended because it is not yet the ''kingdom of freedom,'' and the ''kingdom'' or the ''home of identity,'' where man and nature will be perfectly reconciled. History is the open-ended ''exodus'' of the ''not-yet'' of being-matter, striving to overcome the possibility of falling into Nothingness by realizing the All. The objectively real possibilities of the future reside in the ''core'' of matter yearning to be set free. It is this yearning that Bloch finds expressed in the data of man's fantasies and daydreams, in his basic hunger and love drives, in his literary, musical, and religious utopias. The ontological substratum pervading all these, however, is hope. Christianity has finally brought it to light as the human-eschatological messianic drive inherent in all reality. Bloch is grateful to Jesus and Christianity, he says, for turning the transcendent God into a vacuum and replacing Him with the human messiah and ultimately with the undiscovered hidden future realization of man and the world in ''eschatological brotherhood.'' Christ left behind a community of love to act as a steward of the messianic hope by serving as the building material and city of the future kingdom.

Jürgen Moltmann. In spite of Bloch's heavy influence, there remain a number of radically dissociating elements in Moltmann's thought. While Moltmann's theology of hope is essentially rooted in the perception that, from beginning to end, ''Christianity is eschatology, is hope'' (*Theology of Hope* 16), his systematic expression of the contents of this perception belies accommodation with Bloch and PROCESS THEOLOGY. Like Bloch, Moltmann speaks of the future as the ''mode of God's being.'' Unlike Bloch, Moltmann roots the nature of this future in the God who really exists ''ahead of us in the horizons of the future opened to us'' by his history of promise. Unlike Bloch, Moltmann speaks of the future as *adventus* (*parousia*) *Dei,* the arrival from ahead of us of ''the God of the coming kingdom,'' whose reality, glory, and divinity are made known from the experience of his future in its transforming effect upon the past and the present. History is not built upon utopian wish-fulfilment of what can emerge from the ''eternal process of the becoming and begetting of being,'' but is the continuing anticipation, in the past and the present, of the ''not-yet''—the radically ''new'' and transforming future ''which is neither in its reality nor in its potentiality already in existence'' (*Future of Hope* 10–15). Whereas *futurum* can never be completely new, *adventus* is full of the infinite possibilities possible only to God and thereby pointing always toward Him. It thus creates an ever-advancing ''front-line'' between the past that is ''obsolete and passing'' (the Old) and that which has never before been (the New).

Christian eschatology speaks of the future of God only from its reality-prolepsis in Christ's death and resurrection. In that event, God anticipated His future kingdom of *life out of death* and thereby created history as the time of hope. The glory of resurrection, however, shines forth in history from the crucified Christ and only there. The cross of Christ thus becomes the historical form of the resurrection and the kingdom of life with God becomes the future hope of the cross ''until he comes.'' Since Christ rose from the dead, his death on the cross marks God's final judgment upon all that contradicts the future of freedom. Christ's present reign takes place in the historical dialectic of the cross-resurrection event that already mediates to the godless and godforsaken world under the conditions of the present liberation from enslavement to sin and death.

The ''front-line'' of the future of new life occurs in history wherever the power and significance of the Christ event continue to be mediated to a dying world. This takes place in the proclamation of the Gospel, which, as Word-prolepsis of the eschatological hope of the kingdom to the poor, mediates hope itself. The sacrament of hope is further mediated to history in the creation of the Christian community of hope wherever, as the new People of God, it overcomes contradiction with the future kingdom it manifests. Hope is, finally, present wherever, as ''creative, battling, and loving obedience'' (*Future of Hope* 38) it transforms personal life and social, political, and cosmic orders in anticipation of the coming new world. Thus, in a mission of service to the world in the spirit of Christ's ''self-renouncing love,'' the Christian extends into the world the power of hope as the ontological force of the kingdom in history.

Hope is thus the power of faith that sets history in motion and gives it all its vitality. What is grounded in faith becomes effective through hope in the form of love of all reality in the service of its new birth. In its own way, Moltmann's theology of hope replaces a static metaphysics of being with a dynamic "metaphysics" of the Christ event, whose branches are visible in more recent developments in political and liberation theology.

Karl Rahner. Theology of hope finds expression in more recent writings of Karl Rahner, who endeavors to extract hope from its subordinate position to faith and love in traditional scholastic theology by seeing it as an enduring power of *dispossession of self* in radical self-commitment to the absolutely uncontrollable and utterly incalculable transcendence of the God of truth and love. This eschatological hope is that by which the individual knows that the promise of salvation, definitively offered to all in Christ's radical act of hope on the cross, is concretely conferred upon the individual as the promise of *his* salvation. On the basis of *Lumen gentium* 35, Rahner argues that this hope in the absolute future of God must express its self-dispossession outwardly in the "permanent transformation of the framework of secular life" (*Theological Investigations* 10, 256). In its continually revolutionary attitude toward petrified historical and social structures, Christian hope in practice obeys God's command to hope in his absolute future, sets out ever anew in an exodus toward that future, and sustains the future by making it real.

Vatican Council II gave official sanction to the "Eschatological Nature of the Pilgrim Church," the title of *Lumen gentium* ch. 7. The Church is seen as carrying on the mission of preparing for the "promised restoration" that has "already begun in Christ" and is "already anticipated in some real way" in the "imperfect holiness" of the Church (*Lumen gentium* 48). The "joys and hopes" of this age are the "joys and hopes . . . of the followers of Christ" (*Gaudium et spes* 1) until "there is a new heaven and a new earth" (*Lumen gentium* 48). The "children of promise" are obliged to express their hope in the glory to come "in their daily social and family life" by continually turning it toward God and wrestling it from the forces of evil (*ibid.* 35). In their service to the total human community in every temporal labor and joy, the faithful "consecrate the world itself to God" and "lead their brother men to that King whom to serve is to reign" (*ibid.* 34–36).

See Also: ESCHATOLOGY (IN THE BIBLE); PROGRESS; THEOLOGY AND HISTORY.

Bibliography: E. BLOCH, *Das Prinzip Hoffnung* (3 v. Frankfurt 1967); *Man on His Own,* tr. E. B. ASHTON (New York 1970); *A Philosophy of the Future,* tr. J. CUMMING (New York 1970). C. E. BRAATEN, *The Future of God* (New York 1969). W. H. CAPPS, *Time Invades the Cathedral* (Philadelphia 1970). M. D. MEEKS, *Origins of the Theology of Hope* (Philadelphia 1970); *Theology of the World,* tr. W. GLEN-DOEPEL (New World 1969). J. MOLTMANN, *Theology of Hope,* tr. J. W. LEITCH (New York 1967); *Religion, Revolution, and the Future,* tr. M. D MEEKS (New York 1969); "Theology as Eschatology," *The Future of Hope* ed. F. HERZOG, (New York 1970) 1–50; *Hope and Planning,* tr. M. CLARKSON (London 1971); *The Experiment of Hope,* tr. M. D. MEEKS (Philadelphia 1975). W. PANNENBERG, "The God of Hope," tr. G. H. KEHM, in *Basic Questions in Theology,* 2 (Philadelphia 1971) 234–249. K. RAHNER, *Theological Investigations,* 10, tr. D. BOURKE (New York 1973) 235–289. O. WEBER, *Grundlagen der Dogmatik,* 2 v. (Neukirchen/Moers 1955–62).

[M. R. TRIPOLE]

THEONAS OF ALEXANDRIA, ST.

Third-century bishop; d. Dec. 28, 300. Theonas succeeded Maximus in 282 as bishop of Alexandria (Eusebius, *Ecclesiastical History* 7.32.30–31) and constructed the church that St. Athanasius later rebuilt (*Apol. ad Const.* 15). He had Pierius as one of his priests and a certain Achillas as director of the catechetical school or Didaskaleion. During the uprising of Achilleus, who proclaimed himself emperor in 295, Alexandria was besieged for eight months by Diocletian's army, and the inhabitants suffered greatly. Theonas is credited with giving them aid and comfort. He is held in high esteem by the Copts and Ethiopians, and his name was added to the Roman Martyrology by ADO OF VIENNE. A letter to Lucian, prefect of Diocletian's chamberlains, ascribed to Theonas is a falsification, probably the work of Jerome VIGNIER (1606–61), which was accepted as authentic by Jean Luc d' Achéry (1672), but rejected by P. Batiffol and A. von Harnack.

Feast: December 28 (Copts); August 23 (Roman Martyrology).

Bibliography: *Acta Sanctorum Propylaeum* Dec. 355. B. EVETTS, ed. and tr. *History of the Patriarchs of the Coptic Church of Alexandria* (*Patrologia orientalis*, ed. R. GRAFFIN and F. NAU [Paris 1903–] 1.2, 1.4; 1907) 206–211. P. BATIFFOL, *Bulletin critique* 7 (1886) 155–160. A. HARNACK, *Texte und Untersuchungen zur Geschichte der altchristilichen Literatur* 24.3 (Berlin 1903) 93–117. H. LECLERCQ, *Dictionnaire d'archéologie chrétienne et de liturgie*, ed. F. CABROL, H. LECLERCQ, and H. I. MARROU, 15 v. (Paris 1907–53) 5.1:1218–20; 8.2:2773–75.

[H. CHIRAT]

THEOPHANES

The name of many Byzantine monks, scholars, and eccelsiastics.

Theophanes Graptos, saint and Byzantine poet; b. in the Moabite Mountains, Palestine, *c.* 775; d. probably Nicaea, 845. Theophanes became a monk at the Monastery of St. Saba near Jerusalem. As an anti-Iconoclast, he was

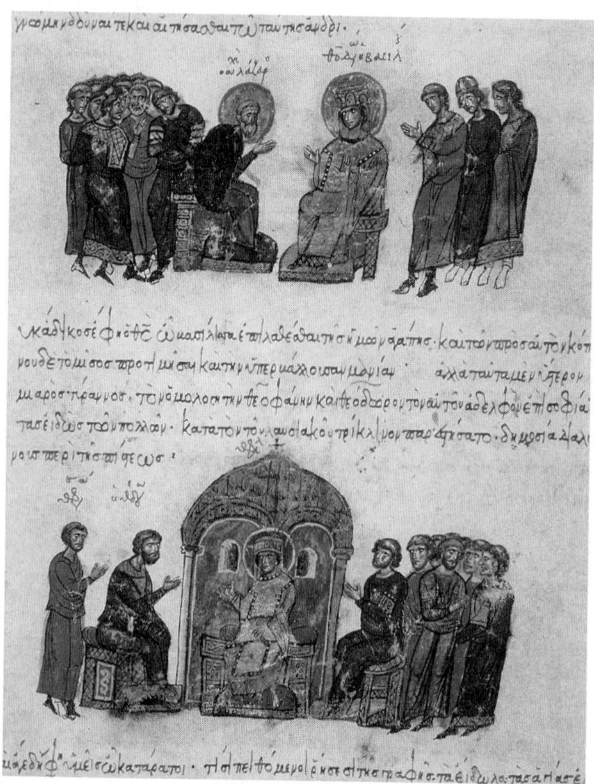

''Chronicles of John Skjlitzes: Persecution of the Monk Lazarus de Theophanes and his brother Theodoros,'' 14th century. (©Archivo Iconografico, S.A./CORBIS)

exiled with his brother Theodore Graptos by Emperor LEO V (813–29), and was sent into exile again during the reign of THEOPHILUS (829–42), who ordered 12 verses to be branded on his forehead. During the regency of Empress THEODORA he was appointed metropolitan of Nicaea. He wrote liturgical hymns of which 19 idiomela and 162 canons are authentic. Eustratiades attributes to him a greater number of anonymous canons and liturgical books. Most of his works are still in MS.

Theophanes, 9th century Byzantine monk, possibly the same as the priest and hegumen who wrote a notice enlarging the biography of Ignatius the Deacon with an account of the exile and death of Patriarch NICEPHORUS I and the translation of his relies. He is perhaps the author of a biography of St. Joseph the Hymnographer (d. 886) and of a canon or hymn honoring St. John, the pupil of Gregory Decapolites.

Theophanes Siciliotes, Sicilian Byzantine hymnographer, possibly of the 9th century, who wrote a canon or hymn in honor of St. Beryllus of Catania and is credited with four further canons in the liturgical books. A. Papadopulos-Kerameus considered him the biographer of St. Joseph the Hymnographer and the correspondent of the Patriarch Photius. The canon for St. John (April 18) should perhaps be attributed to the biographer of St. Joseph the Hymnographer (see above paragraph).

Theophanes III of Nicaea, Byzantine theologian and polemicist, metropolitan of Nicaea from 1366 to 1381; b. *c.* 1315?; d. Constantinople, *c.* 1381. First mentioned in 1366 as bishop of Nicaea, Theophanes was in the entourage of the Emperor John IV Cantacuzene in 1369 when the Emperor directed him to give the Latin patriarch of Constantinople an account of the Palamite controversy. Theophanes proved a faithful but discriminatory disciple of Palamas. He resided at Constantinople because Nicaea was occupied by the Turks after 1330; he served as a member of the permanent synod (*synodos endemousa*), and took part in the synod of 1370. Theophanes is the author of a large number of pastoral, polemic, liturgical, and theological works. Most of them are still in MS. He wrote a letter against the Jews and another against the Latins. Three of his pastoral letters to the clergy and laity of Nicaea have been published (*Patrologia Graeca,* 150:288–349), as has his ''Discourse on the Mother of God'' (ed. M. Jugie, Rome 1935). His treatise on ''The Eternity of the World'' is still in MS.

Theophanes of Medaia, metropolitan of Medaia in Thrace, 15th century antiunionist theologian; d. after 1474. A friend of the Byzantine Patriarch Gennadius II (George Scholarius) and a relative of Mark Eugenicus, he occupied various ecclesiastical positions, from the Great Teacher to Great Economo in the Byzantine Church. Between 1467 and 1470 he became metropolitan of Medaia. Theophanes was a sharp critic of ecclesiastical abuses and intrigues in the decades following the fall of Constantinople. He wrote theological and philosophical tracts in support of the antiunionist polemic of Gennadius and Marcus Eugenicus. One of these tracts deals with divine providence, another with the origin of the human soul. He exchanged letters with the philosopher Amirutzes about the problem of beatific vision.

Bibliography: Theophanes Graptos. H. G. BECK, *Kirche und theologische Literatur im byzantinischen Reich* (Munich 1959) 516–517. S. VAILHÉ, *Revue de l'Orient chrétien* 6 (1901) 313–332, 610–642. S. EUSTRATIADES, ΝΣιών 31 (1936) 5–10; 34 (1939). Theophanes (monk). A. EHRHARD, *Überlieferung und Bestand der hagiographischen und homiletischen Literatur der griechischen Kirche von den Anfängen bis zum Ende des 16. Jh.* (Leipzig-Berlin 1937-52) 1:427, 591. *Bibliotheca hagiographica Graeca,* ed. F. HALKIN (Brussels 1957) 1336–37. H. G. BECK, *Kirche und theologische Literatur im byzantinischen Reich* (Munich 1959) 561. Theophanes Siciliotes. A. PAPADOPULOS-KERAMEUS, *Byzantinische Zeitschrift* 9 (1900) 370–378. H. G. BECK, *Kirche und theologische Literatur im byzantinischen Reich* (Munich 1959) 602. C. EMEREAU, *Échos d'Orient* 25 (1926) 182–183. Theophanes III of Nicaea. *Patrologia Graeca,* ed. J. P. MIGNE (Paris 1858–66) 150:288–350. H. G. BECK, *Kirche und theologische Literatur im byzantinischen Reich* (Munich 1959) 746–747. P. AUBRON, *Recherches de science religieuse* 27 (1937) 257–274, Discourse. H. PINNA,

Ratio Incarnationis secundum Theophanem nicaenum (Cagliari 1949). S. SALAVILLE, *Revue des études byzantines* 11 (1953) 266–271. Theophanes of Medaia. E. STÉPHANOU, *Échos d'Orient* 31 (1932) 165–176, philosophical works. H. G. BECK, *Kirche und theologische Literatur im byzantinischen Reich* (Munich 1959) 773. S. and S. EUSTRATIADES, *Catalogue of the Greek Manuscripts in the Laura on Mt. Athos* (Cambridge, MA 1925) 412–434.

[E. EL-HAYEK]

THEOPHANES THE CONFESSOR, ST.

Byzantine chronicler; b. during the reign of Constantine V Copronymos, probably ca. 752; d. Samothrace, ca. 818. Theophanes, of noble origin, married the daughter of a Byzantine patrician, but shortly afterward, without consummating the marriage, retired to a monastery which he himself built on the shore of the Sea of Marmara between Cyzicus and the Kirmasti River. Ruins of this monastery still survive. His family later became related to the great Macedonian dynasty. As a monk, Theophanes ranked himself against the iconoclastic policy of Emperor LEO V the Armenian, was arrested, and finally exiled to the island of Samothrace where he died. He is included among the saints in both the Greek and Latin Churches.

Theophanes is the author of an important chronicle composed between 810 and 814 at the suggestion of the author's friend, George Syncellus; it covers the period from 284 to 813. The narrative, arranged in the form of annals, includes a number of chronological elements: the year since the creation of the world (according to the Alexandria era, which puts the creation of the world in 5493 before the Incarnation); the year since the Incarnation; the current year of the Byzantine, Persian, and Arab rulers; the current year of the bishop of Rome and the four patriarchates; and the number of the INDICTION cycle. It should be observed, however, that from the year of the creation 6102 (A.D. 609–610) to 6265 (A.D. 772–773), with the exception of the period of 6207 to 6218 (A.D. 714–715 to 725–726), Theophanes's dates fall one year behind the indiction. Theophanes derived his information from earlier historians and chroniclers, including perhaps a great world chronicle, which is no longer extant. His chronicle, along with that of NICEPHORUS I, Patriarch of Constantinople, constitutes the principal Byzantine historical source for the greater part of the 7th and 8th centuries. It was translated into Latin by ANASTASIUS, the papal librarian, in the 870s.

Feast: March 12.

Bibliography: *Theophanis chronographia,* ed. C. DE BOOR, 2 v. (Leipzig 1883–85). K. KRUMBACHER, *Geschichte der byzantinischen Literatur* (Munich 1890; 2d ed. 1897) 342–347. G. OSTROGORSKY, *History of the Byzantine State,* tr. J. HUSSEY from 2d German ed. (Oxford 1956); American ed. by P. CHARANIS (New Brunswick, N. J. 1957). M. E. COLONNA, *Gli storici bizantini dal sec. IV al sec. XV* (Naples 1956) 131–134. G. MORAVCSIK, *Byzantinoturcica,* 2 v. (2d ed. Berlin 1958) 1:531–537.

[P. CHARANIS]

THEOPHANY

Derived from the Greek (θεός, god; φαίνειν, to show forth, to be revealed), theophany means an appearance of God to man. Of similar meaning are hierophany and epiphany. Theophanies will be discussed here as they are found in the Old Testament and the New Testament.

In the Old Testament. The books of the Old Testament repeatedly assert that no man can see God (or see His angel, or speak with Him) and live (Ex 3.6b; 19.21; 33.20; Jgs 13.22). On the other hand, the Old Testament mentions various people who have, in fact, come into contact with God and survived the experience (Gn 32.30; Nm 12.5–8; Dt 4.33; 5.24; Jgs 6.22–23). Actually the very fabric of the Old Testament is woven of repeated self-revelations of God to Israel, often through theophanies.

The Pentateuch itself contains two basic types of theophany. One is primarily cultic and almost always involves an appearance of the GLORY OF GOD. Another is noncultic. The earliest tradition in the PENTATEUCH, the YAHWIST, recounts numerous outright encounters of Adam, Abraham, Hagar, Moses, etc., with the Lord in human form (Gn 3.8; 16.7–14; 18–19; 22.11–15; Dt 34.10). The theophanies are somewhat less direct in the ELOHIST tradition, which prefers to represent God as speaking from heaven (Gn 21.17) or appearing in dreams (Gn 20.3; 28.12). The DEUTERONOMIST tradition, which conceives of God as manifested primarily through His Law, omits almost all mention of theophanies except to remind that the Lord displayed no form at all when His voice was heard from the fire (Dt 4.15). The tradition of the PRIESTLY WRITERS is willing to admit that the Lord showed Himself to Abram (Gn 17.1) and Moses in ages past, but limits contemporary theophanies to dreams and visions and the sight of the glory.

One observes an increasing reluctance to portray God in direct converse with mankind. In later years editors tended to replace direct mention of Yahweh in such scenes with one of the various surrogates meant to take His role: His face (Dt 31.11), His angel (Ex 14.19), His spirit (Is 63.14), His word [Ps 32(33).6], etc.

Another type of theophany, harking back to the most primitive theological thought, considered natural phenomena such as lightning storms to be divine epiphanies [Hb 3.8–15; Jgs 5.4–5; Ps 28(29)].

In the prophetic literature, theophanies tend to take the form of inaugural visions, in which the Lord appears directly, usually surrounded by the mythological panoply of an Oriental monarch, and commissions the prophet to bear His message to the people (Is 6; Jer 1; Ez 1).

In its darker days Israel looked forward to a day of deliverance, the DAY OF THE LORD. Often this was anticipated as a worldwide theophany wherein the Lord would appear—again in Oriental majesty—to judge and destroy the nations that oppress His people, and to establish Jerusalem in prosperity and peace (Is 2.6–22; 10–11; 63.1–6).

In the New Testament. Theophanies are not frequent in the New Testament, for the very reason that Jesus Himself is the revelation of the Father par excellence (Jn 1.18; Heb 1.1–3). Few manifestations of His Divinity mark the Gospel accounts, and those for special reasons: at His conception and nativity, to indicate His true origins (Lk 2); at His baptism, the inaugural vision of His divine mission (Mk 1.9–11); at His transfiguration, to prepare His disciples for the climax of His mission (Lk 9.28–36); and as He commissioned the Apostles to preach the Gospel (Lk 24.36–49; Acts 9.1–9).

A second sort of theophany continues the eschatological tradition of the Old Testament, and looks to the future—not to any immediate salvation, but to the ultimate resolution of all creation in the PAROUSIA (Mt 24.29–31; 25.31–46; Rv 1.12–20; 21).

See Also: GLORY (IN THE BIBLE).

Bibliography: G. H. DAVIES, G. A. BUTTRICK, ed., *The Interpreters' Dictionary of the Bible,* 4 v. (Nashville 1962) 4:619–620. W. EICHRODT, *Theology of the Old Testament,* tr. J. A. BAKER (London 1961) v. 1. E. PAX, *Epiphaneia* (Munich 1955).

[J. T. BURTCHAELL]

THEOPHILANTHROPY

A religious cult established during the FRENCH REVOLUTION as a substitute for Catholic beliefs and practices. Jean Baptiste Chemin-Dupontès, who initiated it in his *Manuel de Théophilantropes* (1796), drew his inspiration chiefly from VOLTAIRE and ROUSSEAU. In April 1797, the theophilanthropists met in Paris at the Institute for Blind Workingmen of Valentin Haüy. Once they won the patronage of Révellière-Lépeaux, a member of the Directory, they shared with other cults the use of the Notre Dame cathedral and 17 other Parisian churches. GRÉGOIRE, leader of the Constitutional clergy, vigorously opposed this simultaneous possession of places of worship, and became theophilanthropy's chief critic. Except for curious crowds at the first few assemblies, the cult had little appeal to the masses, accustomed to the richer symbolism of the Catholic liturgy. It did attract a heterogeneous élite of scientists, politicians, and artists, including Jacques David. Theophilanthrophy never became a state religion, but it was used by the Directory as a counterweight to Catholic doctrine. By 1799 it was in complete decline. The CONCORDAT OF 1801 excluded the cult from the churches, and in March 1802, it was legally prohibited.

Theophilanthropy was a form of DEISM, founded on belief in the existence of God and the immortality of the soul. But its deity was a Voltairean ''God of reason''; and its concept of future life did not admit a resurrection of the body. Its morality consisted of a tolerance, which theoretically permitted no attack on other cults, and solidarity, which emphasized love of country and of the Republic. There were no other obligations and no sanctions. Whoever accepted these principles could be admitted to membership by a profession of faith in fraternity and in humanity. Presiding over religious services often was a functionary dressed in a white tunic, blue robe, and rose cincture, symbolizing the Republic's tricolor. Services lasted about an hour and a half, beginning with an invocation to the Father of Nature, followed by a silent examination of conscience, a discourse or reading from the Scriptures, the Koran, Zoroaster, Seneca, Voltaire, Fénelon, or, above all, Rousseau; and concluded with the singing of patriotic songs. Homage was frequently paid to great men who had honored humanity, such as Socrates, St. Vincent de Paul, Rousseau, or George Washington. There were also simple rites for baptisms, marriages, and funerals. The main purpose of theophilanthropy was the establishment of a religion completely free of dogma and all moral strictures other than the broadest generalities.

Bibliography: A. MATHIEZ, *La Théophilanthropie et le culte décadaire, 1796–1801* (Paris 1903). P. DE LA GORCE, *Histoire religieuse de la révolution française,* 5 v. (Paris 1909–23). A. LATREILLE, *L'église catholique et la révolution française,* 2 v. (Paris 1946–50). C. LEDRÉ, *L'église de France sous la révolution* (Paris 1949). J. LEFLON, *La crise révolutionnaire, 1789–1846* (Fliche-Martin 20; 1949). G. LEFEBVRE, *The French Revolution,* tr. E. M. EVANSON et al., 2 v. (New York 1961–64). J. BRUGERETTE, *Dictionnaire de théologie catholique,* ed. A. VACANT et al. (Paris 1903–50) 15:1:518–523.

[M. LAWLOR]

THEOPHILUS (RUGERUS)

Benedictine author of the *De diversis artibus;* fl. early 12th century. The results of modern research on the man and his work have been incorporated into the critical edition of the *De diversis artibus* by C. R. Dodwell (1961). On the basis of internal evidence, Theophilus was a German Benedictine monk and priest of the early 12th century. His name in religion was Rugerus or Rogerus, Theophilus having been assumed as a pseudonym. There is a strong probability that he should be identified with Roger of Helmarshausen, also a monk, who lived in the early 12th century and was a specialist in metal work. A comparison of the *De diversis artibus* with Eraclius, *De coloribus et artibus Romanorum* (11th or 12th century), and with the *Lumen animae,* a kind of encyclopedia of the arts (early 14th century), reveals its essential independence and superiority. In three books it covers a wide range of medieval arts and crafts and describes techniques with a businesslike detail that could come only from firsthand familiarity. But the work is unique in another respect, i.e., in that it presents a philosophy, or rather a theology, of art, especially in the preface to bk. 3. The artist's skill is considered a gift of God, and an inheritance of the abilities man enjoyed perfectly before the Fall and that he continues to retain. For Theophilus the artist serves the basic purpose of man, namely, to give glory to God. The skill of the artist is directed in a special way by each of the seven gifts of the Holy Spirit. Art in itself not only produces works of beauty, but constitutes an act of piety and worship. Through his adornment of a church the artist gives men cause to praise their Creator and proclaim Him wondrous in His works.

Bibliography: THEOPHILUS, *De diversis artibus,* ed. C. R. DODWELL (London and New York 1961), tr. from the Lat. with introd., nn, and bibliog.; *On Divers Arts: The Treatise of Theophilus,* ed. and tr. J. G. HAWTHORNE and C. S. SMITH (Chicago 1963), tr. from the medieval Lat. with introd. and nn; a new tr. without Latin text, but fuller bibliog. 16 plates and 27 figs. L. THORNDIKE, *A History of Magic and Experimental Science* 1:760–774. E. DE BRUYNE, *Études d'esthétique médiévale,* 3 v. (Bruges 1946) 2:413–417, his date for T., however, is too early.

[M. R. P. MCGUIRE]

THEOPHILUS, BYZANTINE EMPEROR

Reigned 829–842; d. Constantinople, Jan. 20, 842. Theophilus succeeded his father Michael II, bringing an energetic approach to all aspects of administration. With the support of patriarch John the Grammarian, he reinstituted Iconoclasm, forbidding all painted images. Non-conforming clergy and monks he exiled and imprisoned. The brothers Theodore and Theophanes achieved renown as *graptoi* (the inscribed) due to the iconoclastic verses Theophilus branded on their foreheads. Iconoclasm remained state policy until Theophilus' death, when the empress Theodora restored the veneration of images.

Theophilus' foreign policy was dominated by warfare against the Arabs in Asia Minor, Sicily, and southern Italy. In Asia Minor Theophilus won early victories against the caliph Ma'mun, and had some modest military success in 837, aided by generals Manuel and Theophobus. However, the caliph Mu'tasim defeated Theophilus at Dazimon (July 22, 838), captured Ancyra, then sacked Amorium (August 12, 838). The loss of Amorium, Theophilus' paternal city, was a humiliating blow. Only in 841, after Theophilus recaptured Germanicia and Melitene, did Mu'tasim sign a truce. Arab attacks on Sicily and southern Italy continued. Palermo was captured in 831 and Taranto was lost in 839. Theophilus' attempts to gain military aid from the Franks, and from the Spanish caliph, failed. Treaties signed in 840 and 841 between Frankish king Lothair and the Venetians guaranteed Venice's mainland security and confirmed all Venetian possessions. These treaties provided the basis for Venice's independence from Byzantium.

Theophilus strengthened the empire in several ways. He augmented the theme system by creating the new themes of Cherson, Paphlagonia, and Chaldia. He also added the three new *kleisourai* (military districts guarding mountain passes) of Charsianon, Cappadocia, and Seleukeia. Leo the Mathematician created a system of fire-signals across Asia Minor that conveyed to Constantinople messages about Arab incursions. For his Khazar allies, Theophilus also built the fortress of Sarkel on the lower Don River. He issued a new copper *follis* in large numbers. Indeed, sound fiscal policy provided him with the funds needed to launch a building program in Constantinople. The city's walls were refurbished and the palace adorned with new ceremonial halls that included the Triconch and Sigma. His throne he adorned with mechanized devices to impress visitors, including golden lions that roared. He built a new imperial palace in the Arab style at Bryas.

Theophilus gained a reputation as a colorful, charismatic personality, and as a lover of justice. The stories about him include that of his bride show, where he rejected the outspoken Kasia in favor of the modest Theodora, to whom he gave a golden apple. He received petitions from ordinary citizens against even the most powerful officials (he punished the empress' own brother Petronas for disobeying the law). So firm was his reputation as a lover of justice that in the 12th century satirical dialogue *Timarion* Theophilus is made a judge in hell. Modern scholarship views Theophilus' reign as an important part of the revival of the Byzantine state in the early ninth century.

Bibliography: W. TREADGOLD, *The Byzantine Revival, 780–842* (Stanford, CA 1988) 263–384; J. ROSSER, ''Theophilos (829–842),'' *Byzantiaka* 3 (1983) 37–56; J. B. BURY, *A History of* *the Eastern Roman Empire: From the Fall of Irene to the Accession of Basil I (A.D. 802–867)* (London, 1912) 120–153.

[J. ROSSER]

THEOPHILUS OF ALEXANDRIA

Patriarch 385 to 428, theologian, and ecclesiastical statesman. Theophilus, the uncle of Cyril of Alexandria, was evidently well educated although almost nothing is known of his background or early career. While still a priest or deacon he composed a table computing the dates of Easter and the paschal cycle for the years 380 to 479. As patriarch he engaged in a violent war on pagan survivals in Alexandria and, with the permission of Emperor THEODOSIUS I, destroyed (391) many pagan shrines, including the famous Sarapeum, the Mithraeum, and the Temple of Dionysius. He used the materials from these temples to construct a large number of new churches.

Evidently a follower of ORIGEN in his earlier years, Theophilus was challenged by a group of Egyptian monks on a statement in one of his pastoral letters concerning the incorporeity of God. He then changed his opinion in regard to the orthodoxy of Origen, siding with St. JEROME against Bp. JOHN OF JERUSALEM and RUFINUS OF AQUILEIA. In a synod at Alexandria (401) he condemned Origenism and began a persecution of the monks in the Nitrian Desert, four of whom, called the TALL BROTHERS, appealed for justification to JOHN CHRYSOSTOM in Constantinople. Theophilus used this development to organize a campaign against John, which ended at the Synod of the OAK near Chalcedon (403), in which John was deposed and exiled. Thereafter Theophilus seems to have played an important part in the politics of the Oriental Church and, at home, to have earned the title of ''Pharao.'' But this characterization depends on evidence supplied by his enemies and the friends of John Chrysostom. He was esteemed by Pope Leo I (*Epist.* 53, 63, 74) and Vigilius of Thapsus (*Contra Eutyches* 1.15), and was a friend of the abbots Orsiesi and Ammon, whom he considered his spiritual fathers. The *APOPHTHEGMATA PATRUM* (*Patrologia Graeca* 65:200) represents him as a reputable fosterer of monasticism.

Because Theophilus was considered suspect as the opponent of John Chrysostom, his works have been preserved only in part. Besides the *Paschal Canon,* he wrote many letters, among which were three letters addressed to Jerome regarding the Origenistic controversy and two to EPIPHANIUS OF SALAMIS. He was also in correspondence with John Chrysostom regarding the Tall Brothers, with Popes ANASTASIUS I and INNOCENT I, and with Bishops Flavian and Porphyrius of Antioch. Information regarding 26 of his paschal letters has been preserved; those for 401, 402, and 403 were translated into Latin by St. Jerome (*Epist.* 96, 98, 100); others are mentioned by contemporaries, and a few fragments have been found in Coptic.

Theophilus composed a violent pamphlet against John Chrysostom (Facundus of Hermiane, *Pro defensione trium capitulorum* 6.5), and Jerome translated it into Latin, preserving a fragment in his own *Epist.* 113. He also wrote against Origen (Theodoret, *Dialogues* 2), probably in his pastoral letters. Of his homilies six have been found and edited, while a number in Coptic and Ethiopic still await edition.

Many spurious works have been accredited to Theophilus, but recent scholarship indicates that he may be the author of the *De visione Isaiae VI.1–7,* edited by A. M. Amelli as a work of St. Jerome. Theophilus is commemorated as a saint in the Coptic Church on October 15; in the Syrian, on October 17.

Bibliography: *Patrologia Graeca,* ed. J. P. MIGNE (Paris 1857–66) 65:47–52. J. QUASTEN, *Patrology*, 3 v. (Westminster, Md. 1950–) 3:100–106. B. ALTANER, *Patrology*, tr. H. GRAEF from 5th German ed. (New York 1960). G. LAZZATI, *Teofilo d'Alessandria* (Milan 1935). W. BRIGHT, *A Dictionary of Christian Biography*, ed. W. SMITH and H. WACE, 4 v. (London 1877–87) 4:999–1008. J. FAIVRE, *Dictionnaire d'histoire et de géographie ecclésiastiques*, ed. A. BAUDRILLART et al. (Paris 1912–) 2:319–323. R. DELOBET and M. RICHARD, *Dictionnaire de théologie catholique*, ed. A. VACANT et al., 15 v. (Paris 1903–50; Tables Générales 1951–) 15.1:523–530. A. FAVALE, *Teofilo d'Alessandria* (Turin 1958). H. G. OPITZ, *Paulys Realenzyklopädie der klassischen Altertumswissenschaft*, ed. G. WISSOWA et al. 5A.2 (1934) 2149–65. M. RICHARD, *Muséon* 52 (1939) 33–50, writings. E. SCHWARTZ, *Christliche und jüdische Ostertafeln* (Berlin 1905). E. DRIOTON, *Revue d'Orient chrétien* 20 (1915–17) 92–100; 113–128, paschal letters. C. BAUR, *Revue Bénédictine* 23 (1906) 430–436; *John Chrysostom and His Time,* tr. M. GONZAGA, 2 v. (Westminster, Md. 1960–61). For the homilies see J. QUASTEN, *Patrology* 3:104–105.

[F. X. MURPHY]

THEOPHILUS OF ANTIOCH

Second-century bishop and Christian apologist (fl. 180); b. in the region of the Euphrates (*Ad Autol.* 2.24). Theophilus received an education in rhetoric and philosophy, became a Christian convert, and rose to be bishop of Antioch. He wrote tracts against MARCION and against Hermogenes, catechetical lectures (Eusebius, *Historia ecclesiastica* 4.24), commentaries on Proverbs and the Gospels (Jerome, *De viris illustribus* 25), a historical work (known only from his own references), and a harmony of the Gospels (Jerome, *Ep.* 121.6, 15). F. LOOFS attempted to identify portions of Irenaeus's *Adversus haereses* as extracts from the work against Marcion, but his thesis has met with little acceptance.

The only surviving work is an Apology, a treatise in three books addressed to Autolycus, which Eusebius called elementary. The archetype of this is the 11th-century Codex Marcianus 496, from which two other MSS are directly descended. The sole precise evidence for dating is a reference (3.27) to the death of Marcus Aurelius (March 17, 180). A mention of persecution (3.30) may refer to the Scillitan martyrs (July 17, 180). Of the three books, loosely linked by their address to Autolycus (of whom nothing is known), each could stand separately, for they include repetition of much polemic and ethical teaching. The first book is akin to a diatribe and in a conversational way counters anti-Christian objections. It treats of the nature of God, who is manifested in his works, of the immorality of the pagan gods, the absurdities of idolatry, and of the meaning of the name Christian. It uses homely examples to prove the possibility of resurrection.

The second book is theologically the most interesting. It contains a literal exegesis of Genesis; the author expounds a doctrine of Creation and then argues for the superiority of Genesis as a chronological record. In the third book, which is more disjointed, he again cites examples of the contradictions and immoral teachings of Greek poets, refutes false accusations against Christian morality by citing ethical precepts from the Old and New Testaments, and ends with a long chronological disquisition to support Christianity by the argument from antiquity.

Theophilus says that he was converted by a study of the Prophets (1.14). It seems as though he had been obliged to interpret Christianity with little guidance except from the Scriptures, and thus produced a strange amalgam of Hellenistic and Jewish thought. He is the first known writer to use the term Trinity (τριάς) of the Godhead, though he used it of God, Logos, and Wisdom (2.15). The Holy Spirit is the medium of revelation and as such is identified with Logos and Wisdom (2.10), and as the breath of God sustaining the whole of creation (1.7), like the Stoic *anima mundi.* The names of Jesus and Christ are never mentioned. The Logos is the Son, but Theophilus uses the Stoic term ἐνδιάθετος for God's intelligence immanent before Creation, distinct from the Logos uttered (i.e., προφορικός) to create (2.10), which also in the person of God spoke to Adam (2.22). The human soul is not created either mortal or immortal, but is capable of becoming either by the exercise of its free will.

Although Theophilus depended upon the Old Testament, he was the first writer who explicitly stated the inspiration of the New. For him the evangelists are Θεοφόρητοι, divinely inspired, on a par with the Prophets (2.22); the Gospels are a holy word; the Pauline Epistles, a divine word (3.13–14). Although he enjoyed a considerable popularity with later Christian writers, his pretentious style with its frigid rhetoric, his confused rationalism, the occasional ineptitude of his arguments, his failure to understand properly either the Christian faith or the Hellenistic philosophies that he attacks prevent his being considered a writer of the first rank. Historically, however, he is of importance for his development of the doctrine of the Logos.

Bibliography: THEOPHILUS OF ANTIOCH, *Trois livres,* tr. J. SENDER, ed. G. BARDY (*Sources Chrétiennes* 20; 1948). F. LOOFS, *Theophilus von Antioch* (*Texte und Untersuchengen zur Geschichte der altchristlichen Literatur* (Berlin 1882–) 46.2; 1930). R. M. GRANT, *Harvard Theological Review* (Cambridge, Mass. 1908–) 40 (1947) 227–256. B. ALTANER, *Patrology,* tr. H. GRAEF from 5th German ed. (New York 1960) 131–133. J. QUASTEN, *Patrology,* 3 v. (Westminster, Md. 1950–) 1:236–242.

[M. WHITTAKER]

THEOPHILUS OF CORTE, ST.

Friar Minor, ascetic, b. Biagio de'Signori Corte, Corsica, Oct. 30, 1676; d. Fucecchio, Tuscany, May 19, 1740. Biagio, although born of noble parents, entered the Corsican Franciscan Observants at Corte in 1693. After completing his studies at Rome and Naples, he was ordained in 1700, and at the urging of Thomas of Cori, his spiritual father, he embraced the austere life of the convent of retreat at Civitella. His life was spent in the retreat convent movement, first in the Roman Observant province at Civitella, where he passed intermittently almost 30 years, and then at Palombara. In both houses he held the offices of guardian, lector, confessor, and preacher. During the last decade of his life he founded two convents of retreat, at Zuani in his native Corsica, and at Fucecchio, Tuscany. Leo XIII beatified him on Sept. 24, 1895. Pius XI canonized him June 29, 1930.

Feast: May 19.

Bibliography: T. DOMENICHELLI, *Vita del B. Teofilo da Corte* (Florence 1896). ABBÉ ABEAU, *Vie du Bienheureux Théophile de Corté* (Paris 1896). C. MARIOTTI, *Il Ritiro di S. Francesco presso Civitella* (*Bellagra*) (Rome 1899). A. M. PAIOTTI, *S. Teofilo da Corte* (Rome 1930). D. DEVAS, *Month* 140 (1922) 28–37. A. BUTLER, *The Lives of the Saints,* rev. ed. H. THURSTON and D. ATTWATER, 4v. (New York 1956) 2:364–365 (1830).

[J. B. WUEST]

THEOPHYLACTUS

First of the TUSCULANI counts, lived toward the end of the 9th and the beginning of the 10th centuries; d.

probably 926. This important personality in the history of Rome is first mentioned by name in 901 in a Roman document of Emperor Louis III. He was the husband of THEODORA I and the father of MAROZIA and Theodora II. In various documents he is called *consul, vestararius,* etc. Aside from holding influential offices in the papal administration, he was the head of an aristocratic party that actively opposed the followers of Pope FORMOSUS. With his wife Theodora, he exercised a great influence on Pope SERGIUS III, an old friend. With the help of this pope he greatly increased his territorial possession. An extremely unscrupulous politician, he eventually acquired the countship of Tusculum.

Bibliography: O. BERTOLINI, *Roma di fonte a Bisanzio e ai Longobardi* (Bologna 1941). A. FLICHE and V. MARTIN, eds. *Histoire de l'église depuis les origines jusqu'à nos jours* (Paris 1935–) vol. 7.

[W. M. PLÖCHL]

THEOPHYLACTUS OF OCHRYDA

Archbishop of Ochryda (Ochrid, Yugoslavia), called the Bulgar, Byzantine prelate, scholar, and exegete; b. Euripus in Euboea, c. 1050; d. *c.* 1108. He studied philosophy at Constantinople under Michael Psellus, became the first teacher of rhetoric in the patriarchal school and tutor to CONSTANTINE VII PORPHYROGENITUS, son of Emperor Michael VII, and functioned as deacon in Hagia Sophia. About 1078, he was made bishop of Ochryda, at that time under the Bulgars. In letters to his friends in Constantinople he expresses a great longing to return and a suspicion that this post was an exile for him. He employed his native genius, joined with deep Biblical and patristic erudition, to produce commentaries on the four Gospels, the minor Prophets, the Acts of the Apostles, the Epistles of St. Paul, the canonical Epistles, and a compendium of the commentaries of St. JOHN CHRYSOSTOM on the Gospel of St. Luke. Only three of his sermons have been edited, along with two of his hagiographical writings, *History of the Fifteen Martyrs* and the *Life of St. Clement,* archbishop of Bulgaria. His letters display his theological interests and include the tract *Allocutio. . .de iis quorum Latini incusantur* (*Patrologia Graeca,* ed. J. P. Migne, 161 v. (Paris 1857–66) 126:221–249), written *c.* 1090, when Pope URBAN II and Emperor ALEXIUS I COMNENUS were considering a council for reunion. Theophylactus wrote in an irenic style against those who called certain Latin practices grave errors and cited as controverted practices three that have no dogmatic importance: clerical celibacy, fasting on Saturday, and the use of azyme or unleavened bread. At times he seems to reject the Catholic teaching on papal supremacy while yet allowing a Catholic interpretation of the primacy of Peter in the early Church. While he condoned the Latin doctrine of the FILIOQUE as a result of deficient theological vocabulary, he insisted on the teaching of PHOTIUS and Psellus that the eternal procession of the Holy Spirit comes from the Father alone (*see* PROCESSIONS, TRINITARIAN).

Bibliography: *Opera Omnia,* ed. J. F. B. DE RUBEIS, 4 v. (Venice 1754–63). M. JUGIE, *Theologia dogmatica christianorum orientalium ab ecclesia catholica dissidentium,* 5 v. (Paris 1926–35), v.1. M. JUGIE, *Échos d'Orient* 23 (1924) 5–8. H. G. BECK, *Kirche und theologische Literatur im byzantinischen Reich* (Munich 1959) 649–651. J. DRÄSEKE, ". . . Schrift gegen die Lateiner," *Byzantinische Zeitschrift* 10 (1901) 519–529. M. KUSSEFF, "St. Clement of Ochrida," *The Slavonic and East European Review* 27 (1948–49) 193–215. N. ADONTZ, *Byzantion* 11 (1936) 577–588. A. LEROY-MOLINGHEN, *ibid.* 589–592; 13 (1938) 253–262, letters to Gregory Taronitēs.

[G. A. MALONEY]

THEORY

Theory is a coherent set of hypothetical, conceptual, and pragmatic principles forming the general frame of reference for a field of inquiry. It is an association of ideas to coordinate any consideration of entities, facts, or other ideas. Basically, a theory is a set of concepts allowing a unified consideration of a number of phenomena, which, apparently diverse, can be considered to belong together. Theories can be general, special, and practical, covering various fields in which the pertinent concepts are not considered to be established truths. Scientific theory is sometimes defined as a set of formal relations from which can be deduced, by purely logical operations, a whole group of physical laws or generalizations of FACT.

[L. A. FOLEY]

THEOSOPHY

A modern gnostic movement begun in New York City (1875) by Helena Petrovna (Hahn) Blavatsky, Henry Steele Olcott, and William Q. Judge. At its inception, the stated purpose of the Theosophical Society was the study of Aryan and Eastern literature and the laws of nature, and the formation of a universal brotherhood. According to modern theosophists, theosophy is not a religion, but a philosophy of life uniting religion, philosophy, and science.

Doctrine. Theosophists deny fundamental Christian concepts regarding the nature of God and the soul; they teach the immanence of God in the world, understanding by this that there is no creation in the Christian sense and that God is not wholly external to creatures but a part of them. The evolution of the soul is a fundamental doctrine; for salvation comes by evolution, and the need for a vicarious atonement is denied. Evolution, in the theosophical sense, is a process of self-realization or manifestation carried on by the Cosmic Life by means of repeated incarnations. Its purpose is the perfecting of man and all creatures. All matter contains consciousness, which is evolving, not in a mechanical way but as a result of a divine plan guided by intelligence. It is conceived of as a twofold movement, involving descent into matter and ascent into spirit. The adept can speed up or direct his own course by recognizing nature's hidden laws through theosophy.

Mme. Blavatsky taught the septenary constitution of man, a reflection of the division of the universe into seven stages, or hierarchies. The first three are a "conscious crystallization of Spirit into Matter." In the fourth, Spirit turns upward again and begins to rid itself of the grossness of matter. The last three complete this process and Spirit emerges into Nirvana. The individual is composed of spirit, spiritual soul, human soul or mind, animal soul, vitality, astral body, and physical body; the first three are immortal, the others, mortal. Of these seven elements, clear distinctions are rarely possible, for they are "interblended around the monadic individuality to constitute the complete man," and are rarely perfectly balanced. Such exceptional cases were the Mahatmas or Masters of the theosophists. The astral body is defined, however, as the shadowy duplicate or idea of the physical body formed before birth, but equally mortal. Death involves a rebirth, liberating the human spirit from the physical body to enjoy the astral life, which will be, in turn, followed by forgetfulness and rebirth. The astral world is not the true heaven, but an emotional world, the true home of grosser men and animals. Heaven or the mental world is achieved only after repeated reincarnations; it is the true home of intelligence and the soul. Thus the four key doctrines of theosophy that are generally accepted are the divine origin of the soul in a pantheistic sense, evolution, reincarnation, and karma, which readjusts effects to causes for the achievement of absolute justice. The division of the movement into numerous sects has resulted from disagreement over succession to the prophetic mantle, rather than to major doctrinal differences.

Divisions. Helena Petrovna Hahn, born to a distinguished family in the Ukraine in 1831, was married to Gen. N. P. Blavatsky, but soon deserted him and left Russia. According to the *Memoirs* of her cousin, Count Witte, she spent some time in Cairo before arriving in New York in 1873. But her own contradictory statements make it impossible to construct a satisfactory account of her life in these years. In either version there is no possibility for the extended visit to Tibet, to which she later credited her revelations. Through a common interest in spiritualism, she became associated with Col. H. S. Olcott in the formation of occult groups, culminating in the 16-member Theosophical Society. In 1877 she published *Isis Unveiled,* a collection of material from Eastern thought, serpent worship, witchcraft, alchemy, and 19th-century science, which she ascribed to her Tibetan masters, but which was often taken verbatim from 50 standard works on occult subjects in Olcott's library.

In 1878 the theosophist leaders left Judge in charge of the sect in America and set out for India, purchasing land at Adyar, near Madras, for a center (1879) and winning important converts, among them A. P. Sinnett and A. O. Hume. In 1880 Olcott began missionary efforts in Ceylon, while Mme. Blavatsky began to edit the *Theosophist,* a periodical published under her direction at Madras (1879–88). Olcott succeeded her as editor (1888–1907). At the Adyar Temple, Mme. Blavatsky claimed that she had received direct written communications from two long-dead Tibetan Mahatmas. In 1885 investigation by the London Society for Psychical Research stamped the entire process as a deliberate fraud. However, this did little to dim Mme. Blavatsky's reputation on her arrival in England, where she published *The Secret Doctrine* (1888), which purports to be a portion of the Book of Dzyan, an otherwise unknown occult history of the earth. In her preface, she described it candidly as the "record of a people unknown to ethnology. . .written in a tongue unknown to philology" and stated that she was prepared to accept the charge that she had invented the whole.

With *The Secret Doctrine,* she began to lay greater stress on the occult and formed (1888) an Esoteric Section of the Theosophical Society in London for advanced study of the occult. Theosophy spread in England and Ireland among literary circles. The Irish Theosophical Society formed at Dublin by Charles Johnston in 1886 drew William Butler Yeats and others into its orbit, while the London Theosophists made an important convert in Annie (Wood) Besant in 1890. She was born in London of Irish ancestry in 1847, married an Anglican clergyman from whom she was later divorced, and had devoted herself since 1872 to advancing free thought, planned parenthood, labor unions, socialism, and other causes through the columns of the *National Reformer,* the *Pall Mall Gazette,* and other periodicals, as well as by the lecture platform. After Mme. Blavatsky's death (1891), Mrs. Besant became her successor as leader of the Theosophical Society. A division between the American theosophists developed in opposition to Mrs. Besant. In 1892 Judge was confirmed as president of the American section of the society, but an acrimonious controversy, involving more letters from the Mahatmas, allegedly forged by Judge, led to a permanent division in 1894–95, when he was elected for life as president of an independent Theosophical Society in America. At his death in 1896, Judge was succeeded by E. T. Hargrove, who published the *Theosophical Quarterly* at Chicago (1898–1935). A pro-Besant group, led by Alexander F. Fullerton and Kate Buffington Davis, formed the Theosophical Society of New York. Other divisions within the movement led to the founding of The Temple of the People (1899) at Syracuse, N.Y. (later transferred to Halcyon, Calif.); and to the formation of The Universal Brotherhood, under the leadership of Katherine A. Tingley and later of Gottfried de Purucker, which made its headquarters at Point Loma, Calif., until 1942. It was later established at Altadena, Calif., with James A. Long as its leader.

While the American theosophists divided on the question of the legitimate line of prophetic succession, the London and Adyar groups, under Olcott and Mrs. Besant, moved steadily in the direction of greater occultism. The influence of Charles W. Leadbeater, a former Anglican clergyman, became paramount. In 1895 Leadbeater published *The Astral Plane* and Mrs. Besant issued *The Self and Its Sheaths,* both devoted to occultism. In 1899 she moved permanently to Adyar, interesting herself in the establishment of the Central Hindu College, later affiliated to Allahabad University, and in Indian nationalism, as well as in the esoteric speculations revealed in *Esoteric Christianity* (1901) and *The Ancient Wisdom* (1899), which consider Christ as one of the incarnations of the Buddha. After a brief expulsion arising from charges of unnatural vice, Leadbeater was restored to the inner councils of the Theosophical Society in 1908, following Olcott's death and Mrs. Besant's rise to supreme power in the sect. Soon after he became convinced that the Christ was alive and would soon reappear. A Hindu youth, Jeddu Krishnamurti, was identified as the reincarnated Messiah. In 1911 the Order of the Star in the East was formed at a Congress of Theosophists held at Omnen, Holland, to prepare for the new avatar.

When four theosophists were ordained (1913–14) to the priesthood of the Old Catholic Church by Bp. Arnold Mathew, Leadbeater became interested in this development and was himself ordained (1916) bishop of the Old Catholic Church for Australasia. The aim of the LIBERAL CATHOLIC CHURCH, as this branch of theosophy was designated, was to prepare a church for Krishnamurti. Although shaken by a series of public scandals in 1919, it continued to exist. Opposition to the Krishnamurti movement centered in the German section of the society, led by Rudolf STEINER, who had founded (1912) the Anthroposophical Society (*see* ANTHROPOSOPHY). The following year Steiner's group was expelled by the Adyar Theosophists. The Order of the Star in the East was formally dissolved (1929) by Krishnamurti, who renounced all claims to divine origin or messianic mission. In a related move, Mrs. George Arundale was acknowledged by the Adyar group as ''World-Mother'' in 1928. On the death of Mrs. Besant (1933), leadership of the Adyar Temple passed to the Arundales. When George Arundale died (1945), C. Jinarajadrasi became spiritual leader. Subsequently a reaction to the excesses of the Besant-Leadbeater epoch led to an increased devotion to the memory of Mme. Blavatsky among British and American theosophists and to efforts to reunite the divided sect on the basis of commonly accepted dogmas.

Bibliography: *The Theosophical Movement 1875–1950* (Los Angeles 1951). E. A. GREENWALT, *The Point Loma Community* (Berkeley, Calif. 1955). C. P. RAMASWAMI AIJAR, *Annie Besant* (Delhi, India 1963). C. E. B. ROBERTS, *The Mysterious Madame* (New York 1931). G. L. WILLIAMS, *Priestess of the Occult* (New York 1946). G. H. WHYTE, *H. P. Blavatsky* (London 1909). J. SYMONDS, *Madame Blavatsky* (New York 1960). A. H. NETHERCOT, *The First Five Lives of Annie Besant* (Chicago 1960); *The Last Four Lives of Annie Besant* (Chicago 1963). T. M. FRANCIS, *Blavatsky, Besant and Co.* (St. Paul, Minn. 1939). F. P. SPINKS, *Theosophists Reunite!* (Boston 1958). C. J. RYAN, *What is Theosophy?* (Covina, Calif. 1944). L. W. ROGERS, *Elementary Theosophy* (Wheaton, Ill. 1950). I. S. COOPER, *Theosophy Simplified* (Wheaton, Ill. 1955). H. P. BLAVATSKY, *Key to Theosophy* (New York 1913). W. C. OHLENDORF, *An Outline of the Secret Doctrine* (Chicago 1941).

[R. K. MACMASTER]

THEOTOKOS

The fifth-century controversies over the union of the divinity and humanity of Christ had as one of their focal points the term Theotokos (θεοτόκος), ''God-bearer,'' ''Mother of God.'' Nestorius, a monk of Antioch who had become patriarch of Constantinople, insisted that, at most, the term Christotokos (χριστοτόκος), ''Christ-bearer,'' is proper in speaking of the Blessed Virgin. When challenged by St. CYRIL OF ALEXANDRIA, he replied:

> Whenever the Sacred Scriptures speak of Our Lord's activity, they never speak of the birth and suffering of the divinity, but of the humanity of Christ. That is why the most accurate way of speaking about the Holy Virgin is Christ-bearer, not God-bearer [Letter to Cyril 2.11; *Acta conciliorum oecumenicorum* (Berlin 1914–) 1.1.1.30–31; *Patrologia Latina*, ed. J. P. Migne, 48:820–821].

The title had been used as far back as the beginning of the fourth century. Alexander of Alexandria, an important figure at the Council of Nicaea I, had written: ''Our Lord Jesus Christ in very deed, and not merely in appearance, had a body from Mary, Mother of God [Theotokos].'' Gregory of Nazianzus considered the title part of the orthodox faith:

> If anyone denies that Saint Mary is God-bearer, he is far from God. If any one says that He passed through the Virgin as through a tube and was not formed in her in a divine and human way, divine because it was without intercourse with man, human because it took place like every other pregnancy, he is equally far from God [Letter 101; *Patrologia Graeca*, ed J. P. MIGNE, 37:177].

Eustathius of Antioch (fl. 326) and Gregory of Nyssa (d. 394) also used the term.

In the Council of EPHESUS (431) Nestorius was condemned and Cyril's Second Letter to Nestorius was read and approved as embodying the orthodox Catholic faith. In this letter Cyril writes: ''Thus they [the holy fathers] confidently called the Holy Virgin Theotokos . . .'' (H. Denzinger, *Enchiridion symbolorum*, ed. A. Schönmetzer 251). The Formula of Union (433) that interpreted the doctrine of Ephesus to the satisfaction of the Church of Antioch states: ''. . .we confess the Holy Virgin to be Theotokos'' (*Acta conciliorum oecumenicorum,* 1.1.4.17; *Patrologia Graeca,* 77:177). The Council of CHALCEDON also adopted the term in its definition on the HYPOSTATIC UNION: ''. . .for us and for our salvation born of Mary the Virgin Theotokos in His human nature. . .'' (*Enchiridion symbolorum*, 301, cf. 300). The use of this title by the Church was undoubtedly decisive for the growth in later centuries of Marian doctrine and devotion.

See Also: MOTHER OF GOD; MARIOLOGY; MARY, BLESSED VIRGIN, ARTICLES ON.

Bibliography: M. JUGIE, *Dictionnaire de théologie catholique*, ed. A. VACANT et al., (Paris 1903–50) 5.1:137–163. E. DUBLANCHY, *ibid.*, 9.2:2339–69. G. SÖLL, *Lexikon für Theologie und Kirche*, ed. J. HOFER and K. RAHNER (Freiberg 1957–65) 4:1126–27.

[J. M. CARMODY]

THEOTONIUS, ST.

Cofounder of SANTA CRUZ monastery in Coimbra; b. Ganfei, Galicia, Portugal, 1082; d. Coimbra, Portugal, Feb. 18, 1162. He received his early education at home. He became a canon and in 1112 prior of the cathedral chapter at Viseu. Two pilgrimages to the Holy Land influenced him to join with his former teacher, the Archdeacon Tello, in the foundation of a new monastery, Santa Cruz. There, by February 1132, the CANONS REGULAR were following the Rule of St. AUGUSTINE and the customs of Saint-Ruf. Theotonius, basically a contemplative, was named first prior of the community. He achieved a great reputation for sanctity, and this, with the favor of Portugal's first king, Afonso Henriques, made the monastery famous. Marvelous deeds before and after Theotonius's death led to his canonization on the following February 18 by the provincial council of Coimbra. This decision was confirmed by Pope Alexander III, *vive vocis oraculo.* The saint's relics were sent from his burial place at Santa Cruz throughout Portugal, where his feast day was celebrated with honor.

Feast: Feb. 18.

Bibliography: *Vita sancti Theotonii* in *Portugaliae monumenta historica, Scriptores* 1 (Lisbon 1856) 79–88. *Vida de S. Teotónio*, tr. and ed. M. H. DA ROCHA PEREIRA (Coimbra 1987). NICOLAO DE SANTA MARIA, *Chronica de Ordem dos Conegos Regrantes do Patriarcha S. Agostino,* 2 pt. (Lisbon 1668). E. A. O'MALLEY, *Tello and Theotonio: The Twelfth-Century Founders of the Monastery of Santa Cruz in Coimbra* (Washington 1954). *Santa Cruz de Coimbra, do século XI ao século XX: estudos no IX Centenário do Nascimento de S. Teotónio* (Coimbra 1984). A. BUTLER, *The Lives of the Saints*, rev. ed. H. THURSTON and D. ATTWATER, 4v. (New York 1956) 1:372.

[A. O'MALLEY]

THERAPEUTAE

A small Jewish religious community of men and women, originating and developing under the influence of the Hellenistic movement in Egypt toward the end of the 1st century B.C. Their Greek name, θεραπευταί, means devotees, persons wholly devoted to the service of God. The Alexandrian Jewish philosopher PHILO JUDAEUS is our sole authority for their existence and way of life. In his *De Vita Contemplativa* he tells us of their extraordinarily strict rule. They completely renounced the world, its treasures and pleasures; they handed over all their property to others; they practiced celibacy. In their Chartreuse-like retreat in the vicinity of Alexandria, these pre-Christian recluses lived in an encampment of individual huts. In their simple hovels they devoted themselves to contemplation, study, and fasting. In their emphasis on contemplation, to the exclusion of manual labor, they differed from the famous sect of the ESSENES in Palestine. At dawn and sunset they prayed; the remainder of the day was given to reflection on the Scriptures and their commentaries. They fasted six days of the week, taking their one simple meal after sunset. On the 7th day, they assembled for communal worship and a sermon on the Scriptures. Each 50th day was a solemn festival, closing with an all-night celebration with sacred music and dance.

Bibliography: PHILO JUDAEUS, *Philo about the Contemplative Life . . . Critically Edited, with a Defence of Its Genuineness,* ed. F. C. CONYBEARE (Oxford 1895). P. WENDLAND, *Die Therapeuten . . .* (Leipzig 1896). J. MOFFATT, and J. HASTINGS, eds., *Encyclopedia of Religion & Ethics,* 13 v. (Edinburgh 1908–27) 12:315–319.

[J. M. DOUGHERTY]

THÉRÈSE DE LISIEUX, ST.

French Carmelite nun celebrated for her autobiography; b. Alençon, France, Jan. 2, 1873; d. Lisieux, Sept. 30, 1897.

Early Life. Marie Françoise Thérèse Martin was the youngest of nine children born to Louis and Zelie (Guérin) Martin, two boys and two girls having died before her birth. Louis was a successful watchmaker and jeweler, while Zelie was a craftswoman. Their last child, Thérèse, was a sickly infant and had to be boarded with a wet nurse for the first year of her life. As she was a warm and affectionate child, deeply devoted to her family, her mother's death constituted a traumatic experience in her young life and plunged her into a state of sadness and sensitivity that she endured for eight years.

Thérèse, in her autobiography, divided her own early life into three distinct periods: the first was the happy and untrammeled period of her infancy before her mother died; the second, the eight years from 1877 to 1886, her "winter of trial," as she called it, a time of sensitivity and weariness and occasional religious scruples; the third was the period between 1886 and 1888, beginning with what she called her "conversion" and terminating with her entrance into the convent.

The family moved to Lisieux in 1881, and Thérèse was enrolled in the Benedictine Abbey school as a day student. She was a bright, retentive student, but shy and somewhat withdrawn, and consequently found school life unpleasant. In 1883 at the age of ten she contracted a strange illness during which she suffered a mixture of convulsions, hallucinations, and comas for three months. Finally, while earnestly imploring the help of the Blessed Virgin, she was instantaneously cured. Thérèse always believed her cure was miraculous and that the statue of Our Lady of Victories, before which she had been praying, actually smiled at her.

On Christmas 1886, Thérèse experienced her "conversion," an instant change which marked the inception of a new maturity and a more intense religious program. The actual occasion of this experience was simple. She had just returned from midnight Mass, and her father made a depreciatory remark about the festivities arranged for his youngest daughter. Ordinarily she would have been deeply hurt by the careless remark but, as she wrote: "Thérèse was different now, Jesus had changed her heart." Her sister Céline stated: "I was a witness to that sudden change, and I thought I was in a dream. That transformation was not limited only to a new self-possession but, at the same time, her soul could be seen to develop and grow in the practice of zeal and charity." From her earliest years Thérèse had been extraordinarily religious; in fact, she remarked near the end of her life that from the age of three she had never refused anything to the good God. She had been diligent at prayer and extremely conscientious in the practice of virtue. But the experience of Christmas 1886 marked a new stage in her religious development, as she acquired an intense interest in the apostolate, conceived a desire to suffer for God, and began to make immediate plans for entering the Carmelite convent in Lisieux.

A Carmelite. Her two older sisters, Pauline and Marie, had already entered the cloistered convent of the Discalced Carmelite nuns in Lisieux, and it was there that Thérèse wished to serve God. At one time she had wanted to become a foreign missionary but she finally concluded she could help in the conversion of even more souls by joining a contemplative order. She was only 14 when she made application to the Carmel, and while the nuns were willing to receive her, the Abbé Delatroette, ecclesiastical superior of the convent, felt she should wait until she was 21. Thérèse, accompanied by her father, visited Bishop Hugonin to petition her early admission to the Carmel. The bishop took the matter under advisement; and while waiting for his ultimately favorable reply, she and her father and her sister Céline embarked on a pilgrimage to Rome. During a general audience Thérèse was presented to Leo XIII, and despite the prohibition to speak she asked him to allow her entrance into Carmel at the age of 15. He gently assured her she would enter if it were God's will.

On April 9, 1888, at 15 she entered the Carmelite convent, spending the remaining nine-and-a-half years of her life in the red brick building on the Rue de Liverot. All was far from serene in the Carmelite convent of Lisieux during the years that Thérèse lived there, and the major part of the difficulties can be ascribed to her superior for most of her time in the convent, Mother Marie de Gonzague, a woman of mercurial temperament, jealously guarding her position of authority and allowing the convent to be split into two factions. Thérèse abstained from the inner politics of the convent and concentrated on her own life of prayer. She was intensely faithful to the rule of the order, quietly performing the duties assigned her; the full heroism of her life of fidelity and closeness to God was not even comprehended by most of the nuns in the convent until her memoirs were published posthumously.

In 1893 Thérèse was appointed acting mistress of novices, an office she held for the last four years of her life. During that time she articulated her ''Little Way,'' that attitude of approaching God that Benedict XV said ''contained the secret of sanctity for the entire world.'' There was nothing essentially new about her ''Little Way,'' but it was a fresh and vigorous restatement of basic Christian truths. Pius XI defined it by saying ''it consists in feeling and acting under the discipline of virtue as a child feels and acts by nature.'' Her ''Way,'' therefore, is not a single virtue or a slogan, but a whole attitude of soul, the basis of an entire relationship with God.

The first manifestations of a tubercular condition came some 18 months before her death, but she continued the monastic observances as well as she could for more than a year until she was finally placed in the convent infirmary. During her final illness she was often fatigued, racked with pain, and plunged into a bitter temptation against faith. Shortly before her death she said: ''I did not think it was possible to suffer so much.'' Her final words were: ''My God, I love You.''

Autobiography. One year after her death a form of her autobiography was published privately and mailed to a number of other Carmelite convents in lieu of the traditional obituary notice. There was an immediate demand for additional copies and a general printing was ordered. In the next 15 years it was translated in countries all over the world and more than a million copies were printed. Thérèse did not originally intend to compose an autobiography, and it was only in the last months of her life, when she realized she had a mission to teach others her ''Little Way,'' that she asked her sister to collect and edit her writings. The first section of the memoirs was written as a feast day present for her sister Pauline, the second as a short spiritual essay for her sister Marie, and the third for the prioress, Mother Gonzague. The document is epistolary in form and baroque in style, thus the language often appears coy and saccharine. Thérèse, writing in the full stream of the late Romantic movement, used the only language she knew, but she wrote with a complete honesty and candor that is the ultimate appeal of these amazingly successful memoirs.

Cult. Worldwide reaction to the young French nun was impressive. Pius XI called it a ''hurricane of glory.'' As Thérèse's autobiography gained popularity, letters began to inundate the Carmel of Lisieux and there were countless reports of favors, spiritual and material, granted through her intercession. The Holy See waived the usual 50 year waiting period, and allowed the investigations for beatification to be inaugurated. She was beatified in 1923 and canonized May 17, 1925, less than 28 years after her death. John Paul II declared her a doctor of the Church in 1997.

In the bull of canonization, Pius XI said that she fulfilled her vocation and achieved sanctity ''without going beyond the common order of things.'' This phrase is the key to understanding her message and popularity. Her life was simple, devoid of the drama and major conflict that characterize the lives of so many saints, but in the framework of that simple life she achieved sanctity.

Feast: Oct. 3.

Bibliography: THÉRÈSE OF LISIEUX, *St. Thérèse of Lisieux: Her Last Conversations*, trans. J. CLARKE (Washington, D.C. 1977); *Letters of St. Thérèse of Lisieux: General Correspondence 1 and 2*, trans. J. CLARKE (Washington, D.C. 1982 and 1988); *The Poetry of Saint Thérèse of Lisieux*, trans. D. KINNEY (Washington, D.C. 1995); *The Prayers of Saint Thérèse of Lisieux: The Act of Oblation*, trans. A. KANE (Washington, D.C. 1997); *Story of a Soul: The Autobiography of Saint Thérèse of Lisieux*, trans. J. CLARKE, 3d rev. ed. (Washington, D.C. 1996). P. AHERN, *Maurice & Thérèse: The Story of a Love* (New York 1998). P. DESCOUVEMENT, *Thérèse and Lisieux*, trans. S. SCIURBA and L. PAMBRUN (Toronto 1996). *Experiencing Saint Thérèse Today*, ed. J. SULLIVAN, *Carmelite Studies* 5 (Washington, D.C. 1990). G. GAUCHER, *The Story of a Life, St. Thérèse of Lisieux*, trans. A. M. BRENNAN (San Francisco 1987). J. GUITTON, *The Spiritual Genius of Saint Thérèse of Lisieux*, trans. F. LENG (Liguori, Mo. 1997). P. O'CONNOR, *Thérèse of Lisieux, A Biography* (Huntington, Ind. 1983). *Saint Thérèse of Lisieux: Her Life, Times, and Teaching*, ed. C. DE MEESTER (Washington, D.C. 1997).

[P. T. ROHRBACH]

THERESIA, BL.

Born *c.* 1178, daughter of Sancho I of Portugal; died Lorvão, June 17, 1250. Theresia's marriage, despite papal objections, to her cousin Alfonso IX of León (1191) was annulled *c.* 1196. She and her sister SANCIA, Cistercians, refused to surrender castles in Portugal to their brother Alfonso II (1211–23). In 1230 she renounced her daughters' rights to succeed Alfonso IX. She founded Cistercian cloisters at Lorvão, where she and Sancia are buried, and at Villabuena, where her daughters, also Cistercians, are buried. She and Sancia were beatified in 1705. She is discussed in the chronicles of Roger of Hoveden, Lucas of Tuý, and Rodrigo XIMENEZ.

Feast: June 17.

Bibliography: A. C. DE SOUSA, *História genealógica da casa real portugueza,* 12 v. (Lisbon 1735–48) 1:79–138; (new ed. Coimbra 1946–54) 1:49–87, unrevised. E. FLÓREZ, *Memorias de las reynas catholicas,* 2 v. (3d ed. Madrid 1790). P. B. GAMS, *Die Kirchengeschichte von Spanien,* 3 v. in 5 (Regensburg 1862–79; reprint Graz 1956) 3:61, 75. A. PIMENTA, *Idade-média* (Lisbon 1946).

John Joseph Therry.

J. GONZÁLEZ, *Alfonso IX,* 2 v. (Madrid 1944); *El Reino de Castilla en la epoca de Alfonso VIII,* 3 v. (Madrid 1960).

[E. P. COLBERT]

THERRY, JOHN JOSEPH

Pioneer priest in Australia; b. Cork, Ireland, 1790; d. Sydney, May 25, 1864. Having been educated at St. Patrick's College, Carlow, and ordained (1815), he volunteered for the Australian mission (1819) and was appointed one of the first official chaplains to the British convict colony in New South Wales. From 1820 to 1830 he struggled singlehandedly for religious liberty and equality of status for Catholics, against a colonial administration closely allied with the Anglican Church. A rugged, uncompromising character, he protested unremittingly to the authorities on behalf of his people and against the abuses of the convict system. He built the first Australian Catholic churches and schools. With the coming of Catholic Emancipation in England (1829), religious equality was soon achieved in New South Wales, but Father Therry had prepared the way and laid the foundations. With the arrival of the first bishop (1835), Therry became a parish priest outside Sydney (1835), later at Hobart in Tasmania, then at Melbourne (1846), and again in Sydney (1847). In 1858 he became an archpriest. He is buried in the crypt of St. Mary's Cathedral, which he founded.

Bibliography: E. M. O'BRIEN, *Life and Letters of Archpriest John Joseph Therry: The Foundation of Catholicism in Australia,* 2 v. (Sydney 1922).

[J. G. MURTAGH]

THESSALONIANS, EPISTLES TO THE

First Thessalonians. The New Testament canon includes two epistles of Paul to the Thessalonians. The order of the two in published editions of the New Testament is due to their respective lengths. The compilers of the New Testament codices placed the longer letters before their shorter counterparts. There is no textual evidence to support the theory of some scholars that 1 Thessalonians is a composite of fragments of Paul's earlier letters. Written before 2 Thessalonians, 1 Thessalonians is the oldest written document in the New Testament (*ca.* 50 A.D.). The letter was written shortly after the first visit of Paul, Silvanus, and Timothy to the Macedonian capital. Having heard good things about the life of the Thessalonians after their conversion to God (1.8–10) Paul wanted to return to Thessalonica but was prevented from doing so (2.17–18). In his stead he sent Timothy who returned with a glowing report, but also indicated that there was something missing in the faith of the community (3.5–6, 10). The first letter was written to compensate for this lack. Notwithstanding its theological content, the letter generally follows the accepted Hellenistic style of the personal letter, opening with the name of the author, those to whom it is written, and greetings (1.1), and closing with a series of greetings and a final farewell (5.26–28). The general outline of the letter is:

1.1 Epistolary Opening
1.2–2.12 First Thanksgiving
2.13–16 Second Thanksgiving
2.17–3.10 Timothy's Mission
3.11–13 First Wish Prayer
4.1–12 Exhortation on Sanctification and Love for Siblings
4.13–18 First Apocalyptic Period
5.1–11 Second Apocalyptic Period
5.12–22 Final Exhortations
5.23–24(25) Second Wish Prayer
5.26–28 Epistolary Closing

The issue that concerned Paul and that prompted him to write was the grief that the Thessalonians were experiencing as a result of the loss of some of their numbers through death, possibly as a result of violence against

Christians (2.14–15). Apparently they thought that the Parousia was to occur in the immediate future (4.15), but that had not happened. Paul responds (4.13–18) by citing an old credal formula (v. 14) and affirming his belief that as God had raised Jesus from the dead, so God will raise Christians from the dead so that they can enjoy life together with Jesus. Paul then uses images drawn from Jewish apocalyptic language and from the solemn entry of a king or conquering general into a city. Paul's short response is very important in the history of the development of Christian thought. Just 20 years after the death of Jesus, it 1) incorporates a pre-Pauline credal formula, 2) speaks of the life to come as ''life with Christ,'' and 3) uses apocalyptic language imaginatively to describe the possibility of the action of God.

The second apocalyptic period counterpoints the first by emphasizing that while awaiting God's future action Christians must continue to live a life of faith, love, and hope despite the difficulties of doing so (5.1–11).

The first thanksgiving period is unusually long for a Hellenistic letter. It's first part consists of a reminder of Paul's prayer of thanksgiving for the success of his preaching of the gospel among the Thessalonians (1.1–10). Their conversion and their life of faith, love, and hope were well known in the provinces of Macedonia and Achaia. The second part of the thanksgiving offers a fond reminiscence of Paul's visit to Thessalonica (2.1–12). The short second thanksgiving presents the synergy of God's action in the preaching of the gospel (2.13–16).

The first exhortation (4.1–2) encourages the Thessalonians to respond to the gift of the Holy Spirit by living holiness in marriage (reading 4.4 as ''to take a wife,'' RSV) and an expansive love for their fellow Christians (*Philadelphia*, sibling love). A series of parting instructions (5.12–22), to respect their leaders, help one another, and have a critical openness to the gift of prophecy, concludes the body of the letter whose wish prayers express Paul's profound concern for the present life (3.10–13) and future salvation (5.23–24) of his beloved brothers and sisters at Thessalonica.

Second Thessalonians. During the last quarter of the 20th century a majority of biblical scholars came to support the view that 2 Thessalonians is a pseudonymous composition. A substantial minority of biblical scholars continue to hold the traditional view that 2 Thessalonians was an actual letter written by the apostle Paul to a gathering of Christians at Thessalonica.

The view that the epistle was written in the name of Paul by one of his disciples gradually emerged during the course of two centuries of historical-critical scholarship. During this period some scholars held that 2 Thessalonians was a composite letter, woven together by scribes from fragments of Paul's early correspondence with the community. Many of these scholars held similar views about 1 Thessalonians. Close analysis of the structure of both letters brought new questions to light. The structure of 2 Thessalonians is:

1.1–2 Epistolary Opening
1.3–10 An Apocalyptic First Thanksgiving
1.11–12 First Prayer
2.1–12 Apocalyptic Period
2.13–15 Second Thanksgiving
2.16–17 A Wish Prayer
3.1–5 Request for Prayer and a Wish Prayer
3.6–15 Exhortation
3.16a Final Wish Prayer
3.16b–18 Signature and Final Greetings

This basic structure appears to follow almost slavishly the structure of 1 Thessalonians. A striking example of the similarity of the two structures is the presence of two thanksgiving periods in each text. This feature of 1 Thessalonians is quite unusual in Hellenistic correspondence. Consideration of this is one of the reasons that many scholars consider 2 Thessalonians to have been written on the basis of 1 Thessalonians rather than by the author of 1 Thessalonians.

Another reason to believe that 2 Thessalonians is pseudonymous derives from its use of apocalyptic language, especially in 2.1–12. The scenario of this passage is so different from the apocalyptic view of 1 Thess 4.13–18 that many scholars think that the two passages could not have come from the same author. 1 Thess 4.13–18 presents a view of the saving Lord, whose appearance (*Parousia*) is to be expected in the immediate future. 2 Thess 2.1–12 updates this view or responds to it by affirming that the Parousia will take place in some unknown future. Before the Parousia takes place, God's plan for human history must be realized.

The notion of a divine plan for history, with human history divided into neatly delineated periods, is a feature of apocalyptic thought. Thus, 2 Thessalonians affirms that before the Parousia there will be rebellion, perhaps the apostasy of some Christians, and a massive outbreak of evil, clearly the work of Satan (2.9). Then there will occur the appearance (*apokalypsis*) of ''The Lawless One.'' His conduct is described in images taken from Roman Emperor worship (2.4). Some kind of mysterious staying power is involved in the entire scenario (2.6–7). It is unclear whether this ''staying power'' refers to the perduring influence of evil forces, or to a power that restrains (stays) those forces. A tradition going back to the time of Tertullian interpreted this staying power of the Roman Empire and the Roman Emperor who restrained the effects of Satan's evil. Many scholars in the latter part of the 20th century interpreted this staying power in terms of the proclamation of the Gospel for which Paul was significantly responsible. Other scholars think of the staying power, not as the power to restrain, but as a power that maintains. These scholars interpret 2.6–7 of evil's power to sustain itself by means of those who are opposed to God.

The Lawless One is to be destroyed by the Lord Jesus at his coming (*Parousia*, 2.8). Rather than being salvific as in 1 Thess 4.14–17, his appearance is punitive. He is to destroy the Lawless One by the breath of his mouth. The epistle's first thanksgiving period (1.3–10) included a section written with apocalyptic imagery that described God's righteousness being realized in the revelation of his vengeance (1.7b–10). Together with his angels the Lord Jesus will be revealed in flaming fire. He will inflict vengeance on those who do not accept the gospel, banishing them from the divine presence and condemning them to eternal destruction. The christology that emerges from these two imaginative apocalyptic units centers on a future appearance of Jesus as Lord which presents him as the ultimate agent of divine vengeance.

The principal paraenetic unit is the exhortation of 3.6–15 which urges the members of the community, not so much to avoid idleness as to avoid unruliness so as to build up the community as a self-sustaining group of people (cf. 1 Thess 4.10b–12). Paul's ''signature'' (3.17) is truly unusual. It supposes that letters erroneously or falsely attributed to Paul were already in circulation. This would have been impossible were 2 Thessalonians to have been written by Paul just a few weeks after the sending of 1 Thessalonians.

[R. F. COLLINS]

THETFORD, PRIORY OF

The Cluniac foundation of St. Mary's, established directly under Cluny, 1103–04, by Roger Bigod with 13 monks from LEWES, inhabiting the former cathedral at Thetford, Norfolk, in the new Diocese of Norwich. The abbey moved to new buildings in 1114 and acquired the dependencies of Horkesley and Wangford. After a period of disorders (1240–48), it was revived by a discovery of relics, and its numbers increased to about 22. A new Lady Chapel was built. On two occasions (1237, 1300), the Bigod patrons disputed the abbot of Cluny's authority, and from 1376, the priory was denizen and almost independent. Its income in 1535 was £ 312. The Duke of Norfolk planned to convert it to a collegiate church, but it was suppressed in 1540. Lesser Thetford priories were held by Augustinian canons (Holy Sepulchre) and Benedictine nuns (St. George's).

Bibliography: T. MARTIN, *The History of the Town of Thetford* (London 1779), appendixes. G. R. C. DAVIS, *Medieval Cartularies of Great Britain: A Short Catalogue* (New York 1958) 110. *The Victoria History of the County of Norfolk,* ed. H. A. DOUBLEDAY and W. PAGE, 2 v. (Westminster, England 1901–06) 2:354–356, 363–369, 391–393. F. J. E. RABY, *The Cluniac Priory, Thetford, Norfolk: Official Guide* (London 1935).

[S. WOOD]

THÉVENET, CLAUDINE, ST.

Religious name: Marie Saint-Ignace; foundress of the Congregation of the Religious of Jesus and Mary; b. Lyons, France, March 30, 1774; d. Lyons, Feb. 3, 1837. Claudine's life, spent entirely in Lyons, was shaped by the French Revolution. From the age of nine until the outbreak of unrest, Claudine was entrusted to the Benedictines at Saint-Pierre Abbey for her education. Lyons was overrun by revolutionary troops May 29, 1793, leaving misery in its wake. Claudine witnessed her brothers—Louis-Antoine (age 20) and François-Marie (age 18)—executed while pardoning their executioner, and begging her to do the same (January 1794).

Wishing to alleviate some of the distress around her, Claudine became involved in acts of charity. In 1815, a young priest, Father Coindre, brought her two orphans he had found in the cold, whom she placed in the care of Marie Chirat. In the next several days, the Providence of the Sacred Heart was founded when five more children were taken into Chirat's home. On July 31, 1816, the small community became the Association of the Sacred Heart of Jesus and Thévenet was elected president. Two years later the sisters became the Religious of Jesus and Mary, a second Providence was opened, and Claudine left her mother's home (Oct. 5, 1818) to become Sister Marie Saint-Ignace.

The ''Providences'' were homes designed to provide education for young women, where they were taught household management, and to undertake the smallest chore with great care and love. As the congregation expanded, it established boarding schools, academies, and residences for poor girls and women involved in the literary profession. She was both beatified (Oct. 4, 1981) and canonized (March 21, 1993) by John Paul II.

Feast: Feb. 3.

Bibliography: G. PAPÁSOGLI, *Una vita, una missione. Claudine Thévenet* (Vatican City n.d.). *Acta Apostolicae Sedis* (1981) 952; (1993) 404–06. *L'Osservatore Romano*, Eng. ed. 41 (1981): 1, 12.

[K. I. RABENSTEIN]

ISBN 0-7876-4017-4